Directory of British Associations

& Associations in Ireland

Edition 18

CBD Research Ltd

15 Wickham Rd, Beckenham, Kent BR3 5JS, England
Tel: 020 8650 7745   Fax: 020 8650 0768
Email: cbd@cbdresearch.com www.cbdresearch.com

First Published	1965
Edition 18	2007
Copyright ©	2007 CBD Research Ltd
Published by	CBD Research Ltd
	15 Wickham Road, Beckenham, Kent, BR3 5JS, England

Telephone: 020 8650 7745   E-mail: cbd@cbdresearch.com
Fax: 020 8650 0768   Internet: www.cbdresearch.com
UK Registered Company No. 700855

ISBN	978-0-95545-141-6
Price	£215.00 US$430.00

No payment is either solicited or accepted for the inclusion of entries in this publication. Every possible precaution has been taken to ensure that the information it contains is accurate at the time of going to press and the publishers cannot accept any liability for errors or omissions however caused.

CBD Research Ltd

founder members of the Data Publishers Association (DPA) and the European Association of Directory Publishers, and are pledged to a strict code of professional practice designed to protect against fraudulent directory publishing and dubious selling methods.

Our membership of the DPA is your guarantee that this publication is comprehensive, authentic and reliable.

Printing and binding: Polestar Wheatons Ltd.

9005522577

The Directory of British Associations can't be right all the time.

We publish DBA every two years and contact every single body to verify their details, but every day, associations merge, or close, or change their names, or simply move.

And one day your letter comes back marked "Gone Away", or your e-mail bounces, or the "number you have dialled has not been recognised". Or perhaps the one association you really want to find isn't in DBA at all.

Infuriating isn't it? What do you do then?

You could search in other association directories, although none list as many British & Irish associations as DBA does. You could buy a directory that comes out annually, but that would simply work out to be more expensive in the long term. Or…

You could simply ask us!

Although we publish every two years, we update our data every day. Just contact us at CBD Research Ltd, by letter, phone, e-mail or fax, and you could have the information you need instantly – completely free of charge – whether you've bought the Directory of British Associations or not.

CBD Research Ltd is a small company, which means that whoever answers your call will at least understand your question, and may well be able to answer it. And if we don't immediately know the answer to your question, we'll work hard to track it down for you.

If it's not in DBA… Just ask CBD!

Tel: 020 8650 7745 Fax: 020 8650 0768

Email: cbd@cbdresearch.com

We welcome your enquiries.

Check on Internet that information is up to date.
(Aug 2011, ED)

CONTENTS

*NOTE: the explanations of abbreviations are repeated inside
the front and back covers.

© CBD Research Ltd · Beckenham · BR3 5JS · Tel 020 8650 7745 · Fax 020 8650 0768 · E-mail cbd@cbdresearch.com · www.cbdresearch.com

INTRODUCTION

1.   This book provides information on national associations, societies, institutes, and similar organisations – in all fields of activity – which have a voluntary membership. Regional and local organisations concerned with important industries and trades (e.g. Birmingham Metallurgical Association) are included, as are local chambers of commerce and county agricultural, archaeological, historical, natural history, and similar organisations which are the principal sources of information and contacts in their areas.

Particular attention has been given to the inclusion in DBA of national federations of local organisations and of 'controlling bodies' of various sports and interest which can usually provide a means of contact with local or specialised units. A complete listing of voluntary organisations in the British Isles, including all social, political, sports, young people's clubs and all specialised societies with major hobbies and interests would require a library of volumes the size of DBA.

Excluded are friendly societies, building societies, benevolent societies in aid of specific trades or professions, advice centres, trusts, and certain other categories; but a number of organisations strictly outside our definition of 'associations' are listed because the user of DBA might, from the wording of their names, expect to find them listed (e.g. British Business Awards Association) – such entries are marked § and generally contain an explanation of their status.

All entries are FREE, no payment is sought or accepted for entries in the Directory, nor are entries made conditional on the purchase of the book. The publishers reserve the right to edit information supplied, and to exclude any organisation considered to be outside the scope of the Directory, for any reason.

2. AREA

'British' in the title has been used in the sense of relating to the British Isles: England, Wales, Scotland, Northern Ireland, the Irish Republic, the Isle of Man and the Channel Islands. Some British organisations overseas (e.g. British Chamber of Commerce in Hong Kong) are also included.

3. BASIS OF COMPILATION

(a)   Questionnaires or revision documents were sent to all of the organisations listed and the courtesy of those who responded is acknowledged by the symbol ■ preceding their addresses. The abbreviation NR shows that the organisation failed to return our questionnaire, but that its validity has been checked by telephone or e-mail.

(b)   Entries for associations in the Republic of Ireland are distinguished by the letters IRL and are limited to name, abbreviation, date of formation and contact details. Most of them are included in DBA by courtesy of the Institute of Public Administration, Dublin, whose publication 'Administration Yearbook and Diary' contains extensive information about most associations and many other organisations in Ireland. Copies of the Yearbook are available from the Institute at Vergemount Hall, Clonskeagh, Dublin 6; telephone (from UK) 00 353 (1) 269 7011, fax 00 353 (1) 269 8644, e-mail information@ipa.ie.

(c)   Associations which we believe to exist, but for which we have not been able to find or validate the address, or from whose last known address our questionnaires have been returned marked 'Gone Away' are listed by name only, prefixed by two ** in the main directory. Any information regarding the existence and whereabouts of these organisations will be welcomed by the editors.

4. ARRANGEMENT AND ALPHABETISATION

DBA is arranged in four parts:

(a) The main directory, in the alphabetisation of which prepositions, articles and conjunctions are ignored, thus:

> Society of Antiquaries of London
> Society for Applied Philosophy
> Society of the Irish Motor Industry
> Society for the Promotion of New Music

(b) abbreviations index – an index to the initials, acronyms or other forms of abbreviation by which organisations are generally known.

(c) publications index – an index to the titles of publications notified by associations

(d) subject index – an index to the activities, professions, groups or interests served by associations

> SPECIAL NOTE

In the indexes names of associations are shortened to the words which govern their arrangement in the main directory, abbreviated as shown on page xiii and inside the back cover.

5. FORM OF ENTRY

Each entry in the main directory consists of:

Name of organisation – the full name as stated in Articles, Constitution or Rules

Abbreviation (in parentheses) by which the organisation is known

Date of formation (not necessarily the date of incorporation, which in many cases is later)

Validity indicator (see paragraph 3(a) above)

Address of headquarters, secretary or person to contact

Telephone number

Fax number

E-mail address

Website address

Letters (in parentheses) indicating whether the address is that of the organisation's permanent headquarters (hq), the honorary secretary's business or private address (hsb) or (hsp), registered office (regd off), official secretariat (asa) or other

Name of the organisation's secretary or other officer, with designation of office held

© CBD Research Ltd · Beckenham · BR3 5JS · Tel 020 8650 7745 · Fax 020 8650 0768 · E-mail cbd@cbdresearch.com · www.cbdresearch.com

Type of constitution (prefixed ▲)

Branches: number of branches in UK, number or location of branches elsewhere

Type of organisation and sphere of interest (prefixed ○): the symbol followed by a code letter (see
Abbreviations 1) indicate the type of organisation, a brief note amplifying or explaining the
purpose of the organisation may follow

Groups: details of specialist groups, sections, divisions, committees etc.

Activities (prefixed ●): a series of abbreviations – in a set order – indicating the types of activity
within the organisation, followed by notes of any special activities

Affiliations (prefixed <): especially international; in most cases this information is printed exactly
as received – often in the form of abbreviations or acronyms

Affiliations (prefixed >): bodies affiliated to the organisation

Membership data (prefixed M): indicating whether individuals (i), firms (f) or other organisations
(org) form the membership. "Firms" is used in the colloquial sense, to denote all forms of
commercial enterprise. Wherever received for publication, the number of members in each
category in the UK and overseas is shown (e.g. 250 i, 32 org UK/17 org o'seas) but in
many cases, a total has been received without analysis; thus 2,250 i, f & org = total
membership 2,250 made up of unspecified numbers of individuals, firms and other
organisations.

Publications (prefixed ¶): title, frequency (number of issues a year) and supply data. Titles such as
"Journal of the Society of Fireback Collectors" containing the whole name of the issuing
body are abbreviated to Jnl, Proceedings, etc. Other abbreviations used in this heading are
shown on page xi and inside front cover

Thus: Backfire – 4; ftm, £9.50 yr nm. NL – 12; ftm only

indicates that the society publishes a quarterly periodical called "Backfire" distributed free to
members and on sale to non-members at £9.50 per annum; and a free monthly newsletter
distributed to members only.

Previous names (prefixed ✕): if the name of the organisation has been changed within the last 5
years the former name or names and the date of the change are given. Names of
organisations which have been absorbed are also entered here

6. OTHER SOURCES

Users of DBA are reminded of standard sources for certain categories excluded from this
book. Advisory, consultative, executive and similar bodies, including Government agencies and
authorities, in Great Britain and Northern Ireland are listed, described and indexed in
COUNCILS, COMMITTEES AND BOARDS (CBD Research Ltd – see advert). Certain organisations
which used to appear in DBA have been transferred to our publication CENTRES, BUREAUX AND
RESEARCH INSTITUTES (see advert). Full details of building societies are given in the Building
Societies Yearbook (Charterhouse Communications) and of charitable organisations in the
Charities Digest (Waterlow Publishing). Friendly societies are to be found in the lists available
from the Registrar of Friendly Societies (Financial Services Authority).
A complete list of livery companies in the City of London is contained in the City of London
Directory (City Press Ltd, Colchester) and in Whitaker's Almanack. For full particulars of these

directories and many others that include local and specialised lists of associations, refer to CURRENT BRITISH DIRECTORIES (see advert).

Multi-national European associations (many of which are based in Great Britain) can be found in PAN-EUROPEAN ASSOCIATIONS (see advert).

For national associations in Europe we recommend our other publications: DIRECTORY OF EUROPEAN INDUSTRIAL & TRADE ASSOCIATIONS and DIRECTORY OF EUROPEAN PROFESSIONAL & LEARNED SOCIETIES (see adverts).

7. ENQUIRIES AND SUGGESTIONS

The greatest care is taken in the compilation of DBA and every effort is made to ensure the inclusion of all organisations which purchasers may reasonably expect to find listed; some associations have been omitted because the editors have doubts about their bona fides; certain others have been left out at the specific and reasonable request of their secretaries. The publishers have records of several thousand associations which, for various reasons, are not listed in DBA – these records are constantly under review and we are always glad to assist enquirers seeking to trace organisations not listed.

Secretaries of unlisted associations or of those marked "unverified and lost" are invited to use the questionnaire reproduced in this volume (or to write or telephone for another) so that their organisations can be recorded in readiness for the next edition.

8. ACKNOWLEDGEMENTS

We have benefited, as usual, from the helpful response of countless secretaries, and the advice of many users of the Directory who tell us of associations newly formed or recently defunct. Editors' names are not shown on the title page; the reason is simple: everyone in the 'CBD' team has been involved in all the tasks of mailing, verification, preparation of entries...
To all who have helped in any way we express our thanks.

ABBREVIATIONS: 1 – IN MAIN ALPHABETICAL DIRECTORY

Validity indicators:

■	entry based on questionnaire, or other document, returned by organisation
NR	No reply received for this edition
IRL	Irish entry - see introduction 3(b)
§	Organisation outside normal scope of DBA but included for convenience of users
**	Organisation unverified or lost

Address:

asa	official secretariat		hsp	honorary secretary's private address
hq	organisation's permanent headquarters		sb/p	secretary's business or private address
hsb	honorary secretary's business address		regd off	registered office

Name of secretary or chief executive, with designation of office held:

Chmn	Chairman	Sec	Secretary		Org Sec	Organising Secretary
Dir	Director	Gen Sec	General Secretary		Pres	President
Exec	Executive	Hon Sec	Honorary Secretary		Hon Treas	Honorary Treasurer
Mgr	Manager	Mem Sec	Membership Secretary		PRO	Public Relations Officer

▲   Type of constitution

Br   Branches

○   Type of organisation & sphere of interest: indicated by one or more of the following letters, with an amplification or explanation only where necessary; if an organisation's interests are obvious from its name, only the starred letter is given

*A	Art & Literature		*N	Co-ordinating bodies
*B	Breed Societies		*P	Professional
*C	Chambers of Commerce		*Q	Research Organisations
	Industry or Trade		*R	Religious Organisations
*D	Dance, Music & Theatre		*S	Sports
*E	Educational		*T	Trade
*F	Farming & Agriculture		*U	Trade Unions
*G	General Interest & Hobbies		*V	Veterinary & Animal Welfare
*H	Horticultural		*W	Welfare Organisations
*K	Campaigns & Pressure Groups		*X	International Friendship
*L	Learned, Scientific & Technical Socs		*Y	Youth Organisations
*M	Medical Interest		*Z	Political Organisations

Gp(s)   Groups

●   Activities:

Comp	Competitions		LG	Liaison with Government
Conf	Conference(s)		Lib	Library
Empl	Negotiations of pay & conditions of employment		Mtgs	Regular Meetings
ET	Education &/or training for professional or other qualifications		PL	Picture Library
Exam	Examinations for professional or other qualifications		Res	Scientific or other systematic research
Exhib	Exhibitions & Shows		SG	Study Groups
Expt	Export promotion		Stat	Collection of Statistics
Inf	Information service available		VE	Visits & Excursions

<   Affiliations to international & other organisations
>   Bodies affiliated to the organisation

M   Membership Data

     i=individuals   f=firms   org=organisations

¶   Publications

AR	Annual Report		m	members
ftm	free to members		NL	Newsletter
hbk	Handbook		nm	non-members
Jnl	Journal		Ybk	Year book
LM	List of members		yr	per annum

X   Former name or names of organisation if changed during past five years (preceded by date of change, if known)

ABBREVIATIONS 2 – IN INDEXES

Advy	Advisory	Gp	Group
Agricl	Agricultural	H'capped	Handicapped
Amal	Amalgamated	Hist	History
Amat	Amateur	Histl	Historical
Amer	American	Hortl	Horticultural
Archaeol	Archaeological	Inc	Incorporated
Assd	Associated	Ind	Industry
Assn	Association	Indep	Independent
Bd(s)	Board(s)	Indl	Industrial
Bldg	Building	Inf	Information
Brit	British	Inst	Institute
C'ee	Committee	Instn	Institution
Cent	Central	Intl	International
Cham	Chamber	Ir	Irish
Chart	Chartered	(IRL)	Republic of Ireland
Co	Company	Jt	Joint
Coll	College	Lond	London
Comm	Commerce	Manch	Manchester
Comml	Commercial	Mchts	Merchants
Conf	Conference	Med	Medical
Confedn	Confederation	Mfrg	Manufacturing
Consvn	Conservation	Mfrs	Manufacturers
Contrs	Contractors	Mgrs	Managers
Corpn	Corporation	Mgt	Management
Coun	Council	Mid	Midland
C'wealth	Commonwealth	Mult	Multiple
Dept	Department	N	North
Devt	Development	Nat	National
Distbn	Distribution	NI	Northern Ireland
Distbrs	Distributors	Nthn	Northern
E	East	Org	Organisation
Eastn	Eastern	Presvn	Preservation
Educ	Education	Profl	Professional
Educl	Educational	Pubr	Publisher
Emplr	Employer	R	Royal
Engg	Engineering	Res	Research
Engl	English	Rly	Railway
Engr	Engineer	S	South
Envt	Environment	Scot	Scottish
Envtl	Environmental	Soc	Society
Eqpt	Equipment	Sthn	Southern
Eur	European	Tr(s)	Trade(s)
Expt	Export	TV	Television
Fac	Faculty	U	Union
Fed	Federated	UK	United Kingdom
Fedn	Federation	Utd	United
GB	Great Britain	W	West
Gen	General	Whls	Wholesale
Gld	Guild	Wld	World
Govt	Government	Wstn	Western

A1 Motor Stores Ltd   (AIMS)   1983

NR A1 House / 3 Peckleton Business Park, PECKLETON COMMON, Leics, LE9 7RN.   (hq)
    01455 822000   fax 01455 824444
    email admin@a1motorstores.co.uk
    http://www.a1motorstores.co.uk
    Chief Exec: Derrick Lawton
▲ Company Limited by Guarantee
○ *T; voluntary group of independent automotive accessory & spare parts retailers. The association offers marketing & purchasing support
● Conf - Mtgs - ET - Exhib - Comp - Stat - Inf - Lib - VE - Empl - LG
M 115 f
¶ Newstime - 24; ftm only.

A T Society
    see **Ataxia-Telangiectasia Society**

AAA (Action against Allergy)   (AAA)   1978

■ PO Box 278, TWICKENHAM, Middx, TW1 4QQ.   (hq)
    020 8892 2711 + 4949   fax 020 8892 4950
    email aaa@actionagainstallergy.freeserve.co.uk
    http://www.actionagainstallergy.co.uk
    Exec Dir: Patricia Schooling
▲ Company Limited by Guarantee; Registered Charity
○ *G, *W; to provide support & information to those suffering any form of allergic illness & those who care for them
● Conf - Res - Inf - LG
M 1,000 i
¶ Allergy (NL) - 3; ftm, £15 yr nm.

Abbeyfield Society

§ 53 Victoria St (Room W1), ST ALBANS, Herts, AL1 3UW.
    01727 857536   fax 01727 846168
    email post@abbeyfield.com
    http://www.abbeyfield.com
    a non-membership charitable organisation providing care & support for the elderly

Aberdeen-Angus Cattle Society   1879

■ 6 King's Place, PERTH, PH2 8AD.
    01738 622477   fax 01738 636436
    email info@aberdeen-angus.co.uk
    http://www.aberdeen-angus.com
    Chief Exec: R McHattie
▲ Company Limited by Guarantee
○ *B
● Mtgs - Res - Exhib - Stat - Expt - Inf
M 1,100 i, f & org
¶ Aberdeen Angus Review - 1; ftm, £6 nm.
    Aberdeen-Angus Herdbook - 1; £30.   AR; free.

Aberdeen Fish Curers' & Merchants Association Ltd   (AFCMA)   1944

NR South Esplanade West, ABERDEEN, AB11 9AA.   (hq)
    01224 897744   fax 01224 871405
    Sec: Rhona Grant
▲ Company Limited by Guarantee
○ *T; to promote & protect the interests of fish merchants in Aberdeen & district
● Conf - Mtgs - ET - Inf - Empl
< Scottish Seafood Processors Fedn
M 60 f
¶ Ybk & Diary; free.
    LM - 1;   Information circulars - 52;   AR; all ftm only.

Aberdeen and Grampian Chamber of Commerce (Inc)   1877

■ Greenhole Place, BRIDGE OF DON, Aberdeenshire, AB23 8EU.   (hq)
    01224 343900   fax 01224 343943
    email info@agcc.co.uk   http://www.agcc.co.uk
    Chief Exec: Geoff Runcie
▲ Company Limited by Guarantee
○ *C
Gp UK West Africa Action Group; Aberdeen Freight Agents' Association; Business Gateway International Trade
● Conf - Mtgs - ET - Stat - Expt - Inf - VE - LG
< Scot Chams Comm; Brit Chams Comm
> Chambers of Commerce in: Moray, Cairngorms, Caithness, Sutherland, Inverness, Orkney, Western Isles
M 1,200 f
¶ Business Bulletin - 10; ftm, £30 yr nm.   AR; ftm.
    Scottish National Directory - 1; ftm, £50 nm.
    Members Listing (LM) - as required; £150.

Abertay Historical Society   1947

■ c/o Matthew Jarron, Museum Services, University of Dundee, DUNDEE, DD1 4HN.   (hsb)
    email museum@dundee.ac.uk
    Sec: Matthew Jarron
○ *L; to promote the study & discussion of local history in Dundee, Angus, Tayside & Fife
● Conf - Workshops - VE - Lectures
M i
¶ NL.
    Annual publication on specific aspects of the area.

Abortion Law Reform Association
    2003 merged with the National Abortion Campaign to form
    Abortion Rights

Abortion Rights   1936

NR 18 Ashwin St, LONDON, E8 3DL.   (hq)
    020 7923 9792
    Dir: Anne Quesney
▲ Un-incorporated Society
○ *K; to realise, in law & in practice, a woman's right to choose on abortion
● Conf - Res - Stat - Inf - Lobbying
< Pro-Choice Alliance
M i
¶ NL - 3; ftm.
× 2003 (Abortion Law Reform Association
        (National Abortion Campaign

Absorbent Hygiene Products Manufacturers Association   (AHPMA)   1995

■ 46 Bridge St, GODALMING, Surrey, GU7 1HL.   (hq)
    01483 418221
    Dir Gen: Tracy Stewart
▲ Company Limited by Guarantee
○ *T; to represent the non-competitive interests of UK companies involved in the manufacture of tampons, feminine hygiene products, disposable nappies & adult continence care products
● Mtgs
M 9 f

ACADEMI - Welsh National Literature Promotion Agency (ACADEMI) 1959
- ■ Mount Stuart House, Mount Stuart Square, CARDIFF, Glam, CF10 5FQ. (hq)
  029 2047 2266 fax 019 2049 2930
  email post@academi.org http://www.academi.org
  Chief Exec: Peter Finch
- ○ *L; to promote the literature of Wales & its authors
- ● Conf - Mtgs - ET - Comp - Lib
- M 516 i
- ¶ Taliesin (Jnl) - 4; £7 m, £3.50 each nm.
  New Welsh Review. A470 - 6; free.

Academy of Culinary Arts
- NR 53 Cavendish Rd, London, SW12 0BL.
  020 8673 6300 fax 020 8673 6543
  email info@academyofculinaryarts.org.uk
  http://www.academyofculinaryarts.org.uk
  Dir: Sara Jayne-Stanes
- ○ *P

Academy of Curative Hypnotherapists (ACH)
- NR Central Buildings, 15 Station Rd, Cheadle Hulme, STOCKPORT, Cheshire, SK8 5AE.
  0161-485 4009 fax 0161-485 4009
  email admin@ach.co.uk http://www.ach.co.uk
- ○ *M

Academy of Executives & Administrators (AEA) 2002
- ■ Warwick Corner, 42 Warwick Rd, KENILWORTH, Warks, CV8 1HE. (hsb)
  01926 855498 fax 01926 513100
  Pres: Prof H J Manners
- ○ *P
- ● ET - Exam
- < Academy of Multi-Skills, Inst of Mgt Specialists, Inst of Manufacturing, Profl Business & Technical Mgt
- ¶ Jnl - 2; ftm, £7 nm.

Academy of Experts 1987
- ■ 3 Grays Inn Square, LONDON, WC1R 5AH. (hq)
  020 7430 0333 fax 020 7430 0666
  email ara@atlas.co.uk
  http://www.academy-experts.org/
  Sec Gen: Nicola Cohen
- ○ *P; to promote a more effective use of experts in all professions & trades; to maintain & develop the excellence already achieved; to provide a cost efficient service to facilitate the quick resolution of disputes
- Gp Register of experts; Register of mediators
- ● Conf - Mtgs - ET - Exam - Exhib - SG - Inf - VE
- M [not for publication]
- ¶ The Expert (Jnl) - 4; ftm, £55 nm.
  NL - 12; Hbk; both ftm only.

Academy of Medical Sciences (AMS) 1998
- ■ 10 Carlton House Terrace, LONDON, SW1Y 5AH. (hq)
  020 7969 5288 fax 020 7969 5298
  email info@acmedsci.ac.uk
  http://www.acmedsci.ac.uk
  Chief Exec: Mrs Mary E Manning
- ▲ Company Limited by Guarantee; Registered Charity
- ○ *P; to promote advance in medical science & campaign to ensure these are converted as quickly as possible into healthcare benefits for society
- Gp specialist working groups created for specific studies & publications
- ● Conf - SG - LG
- M c 850 i
- ¶ Fellows' Directory - 1; ftm only. Review - 2 yrly.
  Miscellaneous Reports - see on website.

Academy of Multi-Skills (AMS) 1995
- ■ Academy House, Warwick Corner, 42 Warwick Rd, KENILWORTH, Warks, CV8 1HE. (hsb)
  01926 855498 fax 01926 513100
  Founder/Pres: Prof H J Manners
- ○ *P; to bring together 'those who have multi-skilled potential, those who wish to lift themselves to higher positions in life by perfecting & securing recognition for their skills...'
- ● ET - Exam
- M 3 org:
  Institute of Management Specialists
  Institute of Manufacturing
  Professional Business & Technical Management

Academy of Pharmaceutical Sciences (APSGB) 2001
- ■ 840 Melton Rd, Thurmaston, LEICESTER, LE4 8BN.
  0116-269 2299 fax 0116-264 0141
  email aps@associationhq.org.uk
  http://www.apsgb.org
  Sec: Robert Seager
- ▲ Company Limited by Guarantee
- ○ *L, *M, *Q
- ● ET - Res - SG
- M 310 i
- ¶ NL - 4; ftm only.

Academy for the Social Sciences (ACSS) 1982
- NR Berkshire House, 252-256 Kings Rd, READING, Berks, RG1 4HP. (hq)
  0118-953 3770
  http://www.the-academy.org.uk
  Exec Sec: Dr Caroline Bucklow
- ▲ Company Limited by Guarantee
- ○ *L, *N; the advancement of social science
- ● Conf - Mtgs - Res - SG - Inf - LG
- < UKCGE
- M 348 i, 43 org
- × 2002 Academy of Learned Societies for the Social Sciences

access CINEMA 1977
- IRL The Studio Building, Meeting House Sq, DUBLIN 2, Republic of Ireland.
  353 (1) 679 4420 fax 353 (1) 679 4166
  email info@accesscinema.ie
  Director: Maretta Dillon
- ○ *N

Accident Management Association (AMA) 2001
- ■ 105 St Peter's St, ST ALBANS, Herts, AL1 3EJ. (asa)
  01727 896086 fax 020 7689 6329
  email general@amassociation.co.uk
  http://www.amassociation.co.uk
  Sec: Paul Neale
- ▲ Company Limited by Guarantee
- ○ *T; for companies providing services to motorists involved in accidents that are not their fault - replacement vehicle hire, vehicle repair & legal insurance; supply of services to accident management companies - legal services & fleet car hire
- ● Mtgs - Inf - LG
- M 23 f
- ¶ Members' Bulletin - 12; AR - 1.

Account Planning Group (APG) 1978
- NR 16 Creighton Ave, LONDON, N10 1NU. (hq)
  020 8444 3692 fax 020 8883 9953
  email mail@apg.org.uk http://www.apg.org.uk
  Gen Sec: Steve Martin
- ▲ Un-incorporated Society
- ○ *P; to promote excellence in creative thinking in account planning & communications strategy in the advertising industry & business
- ● Conf - Mtgs - ET
- M 700 i, UK / 100 i, o'seas

Ace Credit Union Services   1999
- ■ 2 Chirton Wynd, Byker, NEWCASTLE upon TYNE, NE6 2PW. (hq)
  0191-224 4061   fax 0191-224 4061
  email rosalieperry@acecus.org   http://www.acecus.org
  Gen Mgr: Barbara S Hann
- ▲ Un-incorporated Society
- ○ *N; training & support for credit unions
- ● Conf - ET - Inf - LG - Provision of credit union stationery - Model rules for credit unions - Advice & support: computer specialist software, insurance, banking
- M 44 credit unions

ACFO Ltd   (ACFO)   1970
- ■ Rivendell House, Winton Rd, PETERSFIELD, Hants, GU32 3LL. (dir/mem/sp)
  01730 260162   fax 01730 263937
  Chmn: Tony Leigh,   Dir & Mem Sec: Stewart Whyte
- ▲ Company Limited by Guarantee
- Br 9 regions
- ○ *T; to represent all fleet operators to all levels of government, motor manufacturers, suppliers & insurance companies; to improve the professionalism of fleet managers
- Gp Motor cars & light vans up to 7.5 tonnes GVW; Fleet consultancy; Defect reporting
- ● Conf - Mtgs - LG
- M 12 i, 750 f
- ¶ Fleet Operator - 6;   NewsFax - 52; both ftm only.

ACG Ltd (Arts Centre Group)   (ACG)   1971
- ■ The Menier Chocolate Factory, 51-53 Southwark St, LONDON, SE1 1RU.   (hq)
  0845 458 1881
  email info@artscentregroup.org.uk
  http://www.artscentregroup.org.uk
  Sec: Susanne Scott
- ▲ Company Limited by Guarantee; Registered Charity
- ○ *A; to provide a network & support for Christians professionally involved in the arts, media & entertainment business
- Gp Actors, Dancers, Photographers, Architects, Graphics, Teachers, Writers, Musicians, Arts admin, Designers, Entertainers, Fashion & textiles, Media, Visual artists
- ● Mtgs - ET - Exhib - Comp
- M 500 i, 15 f, 20 org, UK / 30 i, 5 f, 10 org, o'seas
- ¶ E-info - 12; ftm only.

Acne Support Group   (ASG)   1992
- ■ PO Box 9, NEWQUAY, Cornwall, TR9 6WG.   (hq)
  0870 870 2263
  http://www.stopspots.org
  Chief Exec: Alison Dudley
- ▲ Registered Charity
- ○ *W; to provide information & support to anyone affected by acne or rosacea; to encourage research into causes & treatments
- ● Conf - ET
- < All Party Parliamentary Gp for Skin; Skin Care Campaign
- M 5,700 i, 15 f, UK / 100 i, o'seas
- ¶ Face Forward - 3; ftm.
  Publications list available (for six 2nd class stamps).

Action against Allergy
  see **AAA (Action against Allergy)**

Action with Communities in Rural England   (ACRE)   1987
- ■ Somerford Court, Somerford Rd, CIRENCESTER, Glos, GL7 1TW.   (hq)
  01285 653477   fax 01285 654537
  email acro@acre.org.uk   http://www.acre.org.uk
  Chief Exec: Sylvia Brown
- ▲ Company Limited by Guarantee; Registered Charity
- ○ *N, *W; to support sustainable rural community development
- ● Conf - Mtgs - ET - Res - Inf - Lib - LG
- M 38 rural community councils
- ¶ Publications list available on website:
  acre.org.uk/DOCUMENTS/publications_ACRE/publicationslist/pdf
- × 2003 Federation of Rural Community Councils (merged)

Action on Dementia
  see **Alzheimer Scotland - Action on Dementia**

Action for ME   1987
- ■ Canningford House (3rd floor), 38 Victoria St, BRISTOL, BS1 6BY.   (mail/address)
  0117-927 9551   fax 0117-927 9552
  email admin@afme.org.uk   http://www.afme.org.uk
- ▲ Registered Charity
- ○ *K; working to improve the lives of people with ME (Myalgic Encephalomyelitis), CFS (Chronic Fatigue Syndrome) & PVFS (Post Viral Fatigue Syndrome)
- ● Inf - Fundraising - Provision of services for people with ME - Campaigning
  lo-call 0845 123 2380
- M 8,000 i
- ¶ Interaction - 4; ftm only.
- × 2002 (September) Westcare UK (merged)

Action against Medical Accidents   (AvMA)   1982
- NR 44 High St, CROYDON, Surrey, CR0 1YB.   (hq)
  0845 123 2352   fax 020 8667 9065
  email admin@avma.org.uk   http://www.avma.org.uk
  Chief Exec: Peter Walsh
- ▲ Registered Charity
- ○ *K, *W; to offer advice & information to anyone who has been the victim of a medical accident; this can include referral to a specialist medical negligence solicitor
- ● Mtgs - Inf - Co-ordination of the Support Network
- M [not stated]
- × 2003 (December) Action for Victims of Medical Accidents

Action on Pre-Eclampsia   (APEC)   1991
- ■ 84-88 Pinner Rd, HARROW, Middx, HA1 4HZ.   (hq)
  020 8863 3271   fax 020 8424 0653
  email info@apec.org.uk   http://www.apec.org.uk
  Chief Exec: Mike Rich
- ▲ Company Limited by Guarantee; Registered Charity
- Br Australia, New Zealand
- ○ *W; to inform & educate parents & health professionals about pre-eclampsia; to support sufferers; to campaign for better care & promote research into all aspects of the condition
- ● Conf - ET - Inf
  Helpline: 020 8427 4217 (weekdays)
- < Australian Action on Pre-Eclampsia (AAPEC); Stichting Hellp Syndrom
- M 800 i, UK / 40 i, o'seas
- ¶ NL - 3;   AR - 1; both free.
  Information pack; ftm, £5 nm.

Action for Prisoners' Families   1990
■ Unit 21 Carlson Court, 116 Putney Bridge Rd, LONDON,
   SW15 2NQ.   (hq)
   020 8812 3600   fax 020 8871 0473
   email info@actionpf.org.uk
   http://www.prisonersfamilies.org.uk
   Dir: Lucy Gampell
▲ Company Limited by Guarantee; Registered Charity
Br 2
○ *K; to promote the development of a nationwide network of
   support groups for prisoners' families
Gp Family ties consultative
● Conf - Mtgs - ET - Res - Inf - LG
M 122 org
¶ NL - 4;   AR - 1.
   Danny's Mum - 1;   Tommy's Dad - 1; both £2 m, £3 nm.
   Finding Dad - 1; £3.50 m, £4.50 nm.
✕ 2002 Federation of Prisoners' Families Support Groups

**Action for the Proper Regulation of Private Hospitals
   (APROP)   1985**
■ PO Box 418, WEYBRIDGE, Surrey, KT13 0FJ.   (chmn/p)
   01932 849403
   Chmn: John J Lambie
▲ Un-incorporated Society
○ *K; to improve legislation & regulations to properly control
   private acute hospitals; to help those who have suffered the
   inadequacies of such hospitals
● Publicity - Lobbying - Liaison with Dept of Health - Advice to
   people affected by the inadequacies of private hospitals

Action on Rights for Children   (ARCH)
NR 62 Wallwood Road, LONDON, E11 1AZ.
   020 8558 9317
○ *K

Action for Sick Children   (ASC/NAWCH)   1961
■ c/o National Children's Bureau, 8 Wakley St, LONDON,
   EC1V 7QE.   (hq)
   0800 074 4519
▲ Registered Charity
○ *W; to raise awareness of the psychosocial & emotional needs
   of sick children at home & in hospital
● Conf - Mtgs - Res - Stat - Inf - Lib - LG - Parents advice service
   (free)
M 800 i, 150 f, UK / 10 i, o'seas
¶ Cascade (Jnl) - 4; ftm.
   Leaflets & other publications.

Action on Smoking & Health   (ASH)   1971
■ 102 Clifton St, LONDON, EC2A 4HW.   (hq)
   020 7739 5902   fax 020 7613 0531
   email enquiries@ash.org.uk   http://www.ash.org.uk
   Dir: Deborah Arnott
▲ Company Limited by Guarantee; Registered Charity
Br 14
○ *K; 'to work for a comprehensive societal response to tobacco
   aimed at achieving a sharp reduction & eventual elimination
   of the health problems caused by tobacco'
● ET - Stat - Inf - LG - Campaigning

Action for Victims of Medical Accidents
   since December 2003 **Action against Medical Accidents**

Acupuncture Society   (AS)   1992
■ 27 Cavendish Drive, EDGWARE, Middx, HA8 7NR.   (hsp)
   0773 466 8402
   email acupuncturesocietyuk@yahoo.co.uk
   http://www.acupuncturesociety.org.uk
   Chmn: Paul Robin
▲ Company Limited by Guarantee
○ *P; for professional acupuncturists & chinese herbal
   practitioners
Gp Acupuncture; Chinese herbal medicine
● Mtgs - ET - Exam - Res - SG - LG
< College of Chinese Medicine
M 50 i, UK / 10 i, o'seas

Additional Curates Society   (ACS)   1837
§ Gordon Browning House, 8 Spitfire Rd, BIRMINGHAM,
   B24 9PB.   (hq)
   0121-382 5533   fax 0121-382 6999
   email acsb@aol.com
   a Church of England charity

ADFAM   (ADFAM)   1986
§ Waterbridge House, 32-36 Loman St, LONDON, SE1 0EH.
   (hq)
   020 7928 8898   fax 020 7928 8923
   http://www.adfam.org.uk
   The national charity for the families & friends of drug users;
   provides a helpline offering confidential support &
   information; training for those wishing to set up drug-related
   family support projects.

Adhesive Tape Manufacturers' Association   (ATMA)   1950
■ Sussex House, 8-10 Homesdale Rd, BROMLEY, Kent,
   BR2 9LZ.   (asa)
   020 8464 0131   fax 020 8464 6018
   email tradeassn@craneandpartners.com
   Secs: Crane & Partners
   Assn Sec: Mrs Colleen Swan
▲ Un-incorporated Society
○ *T; to promote the sale of all types of pressure sensitive tape; to
   promote & undertake research into all forms of technical
   development in pressure sensitive adhesive tape
● Conf - Mtgs - LG
< Assn des Fabricants Européens de Rubans Auto-adhesifs
   (AFERA)
M 2 f
¶ LM - irreg; free.

ADI Federation
NR Kingsmith House, 63a Marshalls Rd, RAUNDS, Northants,
   NN9 6EY.   (hq)
   01933 461821
   email info@theadifederation.org.uk
○ *P; for approved driving instructors

**Adlerian Society (UK) & the Institute for Individual Psychology
   (ASIIP)   1952**
■ 73 South Ealing Rd, LONDON, W5 4QR.   (admin/p)
   020 8567 8360   fax 020 8567 8360
   email ann.hariades@virgin.net
   http://www.adleriansociety.co.uk
   Admin: Ann Rosemary Hariades
▲ Registered Charity
Br 5
○ *L; to promote the work & teachings of Alfred Adler (1870-
   1937), psychologist
● Conf - Mtgs - ET - Inf - Lib - Training counsellors in private
   practice - Parent education
< Intl Assn of Individual Psychology (IAIP); Brit Assn of Counselling
   & Psychotherapy (BASP); Parenting Educ & Support Forum
M 203 i, 1 org, UK / 12 i, Adlerian Soc of Latvia, o'seas
¶ NL - 4;   AER - 1; both ftm only.   Ybk - 1; £10.

Adoption UK   1971
NR   46 The Green, South Bar St, BANBURY, Oxon, OX16 9AB.
       (hq)
       01295 752240
       email admin@adoptionuk.org
       http://www.adoptionuk.org
       Dir: Jonathan Pearce
▲   Registered Charity
Br   coordinators in most counties
○   *W; self-help group for prospective & existing adoptive families
       giving information, advice & support through all stages of
       adoption
●   Conf - Mtgs - ET - Inf - Lib
<   Brit Assn for Adoption & Fostering; Nat Foster Care Assn;
       Natural Parents Support Gp; Nat Org for Counselling
       Adoptees & their Parents
M   3,500 i, adoption agencies
¶   Adoption Today - 6; ftm only.
       Publications list available.

**Adrenoleukodystrophy Support Trust   (ALD Family Support
       Trust)   1993**
■   4 Morley House, 320 Regent St, LONDON, W1B 3BB.   (hq)
       020 7631 3336   fax 020 7631 3336
       email info@aldfst.org.uk   http://www.aldfst.org.uk
       Founder/Coordinator: Attia G Attia
▲   Registered Charity
○   *G; to help & support sufferers & their families; a genetic
       disease carried by women but suffered by boys
●   Conf - Mtgs - Inf
<   Contact-a-Family; In Touch
M   95 families
¶   NL - 2.

Adrian Bell Society   1996
■   3 The Maltings, Church Close, COLTISHALL, Norfolk,
       NR12 7DZ.   (hsp)
       01603 737168
       Hon Sec: Moya Leighton
▲   Un-incorporated Society
○   *A; for those interested in the writing of Adrian Bell (1901-
       1980), who was born in London but lived & wrote mainly in
       Suffolk
●   Mtgs - Inf - VE
M   c 250 i, 2 org, UK / 3 i, o'seas
¶   Jnl - 2; ftm only.

ADSET   (ADSET)   1990
NR   Britannia House, 29 Station Rd, KETTERING, Northants,
       NN15 7HJ.   (hq)
       01536 410500   fax 01536 414274
       email info@adset.org.uk
       Gen Mgr: Hazel Edmunds
▲   Un-incorporated Society
○   *E, *T; organisations using or providing information on
       education, training guidance & the local economy; to ensure
       individuals have access to appropriate information for
       decision making about careers & lifetime learning
●   Conf - Inf - Lib - Seminars
<   ICG; NAEGA; NILTA
M   86 f, 3 org, UK / 1 f, o'seas
¶   Careers Software News - 3 (termly).   Opportunity - 1.
       Directory of Guidance Provision for Adults in the UK - 1.

Adult Education Officers' Association
IRL   Adult Education Centre, Main St, Blanchardstown, DUBLIN 15,
       Republic of Ireland.
       353 (1) 821 1518   fax 353 (1) 821 2702
       Hon Sec: Pat Higgins
○   *P
✕   2005 Adult Education Organisers' Assn

Adult Industry Trade Association   (AITA)   2003
NR   New Connaught Rooms, 61-65 Great Queen St, LONDON,
       WC2B 5DA.
       0191 527 3133
○   *T

Adult Residential Colleges Association   (ARCA)   1983
■   6 Bath Rd, FELIXSTOWE, Suffolk, IP11 7JW.   (hsp)
       fax 01394 271083
       email arcasec@aol.com   http://www.aredu.org.uk
       Hon Sec: Janet Dann
▲   Un-incorporated Society
Br   30
○   *E; to promote & disseminate knowledge of the opportunities
       for adult learning, in short-term residential situations, to
       central & local government, other institutions & the general
       public
●   Conf - ET - SG - Inf - Lib
M   32 colleges
¶   ARCA Short breaks - 1.   Leaflets.

Advantage   1978
NR   21 Provost St, LONDON, N1 7NH.   (hq)
       020 7324 3938
       http://www.advantage4travel.com
       Contact: Colin O'Neill
▲   Company Limited by Guarantee
○   *T; for independent travel agents
M   c 700 i, c 400 f
¶   Business Travel Jnl - 6;   Advantage News; both m only.
✕   2005 (May) National Association of Independent Travel Agents

Advertising Association   (AA)   1926
■   North Artillery House (7th floor), 11-19 Artillery Row,
       LONDON, SW1P 1RT.   (hq)
       020 7340 1100   fax 020 7222 1504
       email aa@adassoc.org.uk   http://www.adassoc.org.uk
       Dir-Gen: Peta Buscombe
○   *N, *T; to represent the common interests of all sides of the UK
       advertising business
●   Conf - Mtgs - Res - Stat - Inf - Lib - LG - Educational material
<   Intl Advertising Assn; Intl Cham Comm; Advertising Inf Gp
M   6 f, 24 org
¶   Quarterly Survey of Advertising Expenditure - 4; £590 yr m,
       £715 yr nm.
       Advertising Statistics Ybk - 1; £170 (2005).
       Long Term Advertising Expenditure Forecast - 1; £535 m,
       £995 nm.
       The European Advertising & Media Forecast; £730 yr m,
       £1,365 yr nm.
       The Marketing Pocket Book (2006); £34.95.   AR; free.
       List of constituent organisations on website.
       publications list available from the Information Centre or
       website.

Advertising Producers Association   (APA)   1978
NR   47 Beak St, LONDON, W1F 9SE.   (hq)
       020 7434 2651   fax 020 7434 9002
       Chief Exec: Stephen Davies
▲   Un-incorporated Society
○   *T; to represent the interests of commercial film production
       companies
●   Mtgs - ET - Inf
<   Comml Film Producers of Europe (CFP/E)
M   110 f

© CBD Research Ltd · Beckenham · BR3 5JS · Tel 020 8650 7745 · Fax 020 8650 0768 · E-mail cbd@cbdresearch.com · www.cbdresearch.com

Advice Services Alliance   (ASA)   1980
NR   New London Bridge House (12th floor), 25 London Bridge St,
     LONDON, SE1 9SG.   (hq)
     020 7378 6428   fax 020 7407 6822
     email admin@asauk.org.uk   http://www.asauk.org.uk
     Dir: Richard Jenner
▲   Company Limited by Guarantee
○   *N; brings together Citizens Advice Bureaux, Law Centres & a
     wide range of local & national independent advice agencies
●   Conf - Mtgs - ET - Res - Inf - LG
M   10 org:
     Advice UK
     Age Concern England
     Citizens Advice
     Citizens Advice Scotland
     Dial UK
     Law Centres Federation
     Scottish Association of Law Centres
     Shelter
     Shelter Cymru
     Youth Access
     16 associate members
¶   'We produce regular briefings for our members & occasional
     policy reports'

Advice UK   (Advice UK)   1979
NR   New London Bridge House (12th floor), 25 London Bridge St,
     LONDON, SE1 9SG.   (hq)
     020 7407 4070   fax 020 7407 4071
     email general@adviceuk.org.uk
     http://www.adviceuk.org.uk
     Chief Exec: Steve Johnson
▲   Company Limited by Guarantee; Registered Charity
○   *N; to promote the provision of independent advice centres
     across the UK; to provide services to support centres
     delivering independent advice to the public
●   ET - Inf - LG
M   940 f
¶   Network News (London only) - 6;   Membership News - 4;
     Jobsheet - 26; all ftm only.
     Note: Advice UK is the operating name of the Federation of
     Information & Advice Centres Ltd.

Advocates for Animals   (AFA)   1912
■   10 Queensferry St, EDINBURGH, EH2 4PG.   (hq)
     0131-225 6039   fax 0131-220 6377
     email info@advocatesforanimals.org.
     http://www.advocatesforanimals.org
     Dir: Ross Minett
▲   Company Limited by Guarantee
○   *K, *V; campaigns against all animal cruelty; promotes the
     protection of all animals through investigation, high profile
     campaigns, public education & political lobbying
●   Campaigning
M   2,000 i, UK / 1,000 i, o'seas
¶   Campaign Updates - 4; free.

AEMES (Ancient Egypt & Middle East Society)   (AEMES)   1987
■   2 Seathorne Crescent, SKEGNESS, Lincs, PE25 1RP.   (hsp)
     01754 765341
     email suek@beset.fsnet.co.uk   http://www.aemes.co.uk
     Hon Sec: Mrs Sue Kirk
▲   Un-incorporated Society
○   *G; the history, archaeology & cultures of the ancient Near East
●   Conf - Mtgs - ET - VE
M   89 i, UK / 2 i, o'seas
¶   AEMES Jnl - 2; ftm only.

The Aeroplane Collection Ltd   (TAC)   1972
■   7 Mayfield Avenue, Stretford, MANCHESTER, M32 9HL.   (hsp)
     0161-866 8255
     email aeroplanecol@aol.com
     Chmn: Edward Sherratt
▲   Company Limited by Guarantee; Registered Charity
○   *G; preservation, restoration & display of aircraft & associated
     artifacts
●   Mtgs - ET - Res
<   Brit Aviation Presvn Coun
M   24 i
¶   TAC NL - 12.

Aerosol Society   1986
NR   PO Box 34, Portishead, BRISTOL, BS20 7FE.   (hq)
     01275 849019   fax 01275 844877
○   *P; to promote: all scientific branches of aerosol research; the
     spread of information on an interdisciplinary basis; to make
     available a pool of expert knowledge; to assist in training; to
     encourage investment in aerosol research

Aethelflaed
NR   1a Auckland Rd, LONDON, SW11 1EW.
     020 7924 5868
     Hon Sec: Carole Madden
○   *L; research & scholarly activities relating to Alfred the Great's
     daughter Aethelflaed, the Lady of the Mercians; and to
     studies of manuscripts in Old English
●   Conf - Res
M   12 i

Aetherius Society   1955
■   757 Fulham Rd, LONDON, SW6 5UU.   (hq)
     020 7736 4187
     European HQ Sec: Dr Richard Lawrence
▲   Un-incorporated Society
Br   2; Australia, New Zealand, USA
○   *R; a metaphysical organisation dedicated to the service of
     mankind in numerous ways - mass healing, prayer &
     spiritual development

Afasic   (Afasic)   1968
NR   50-52 Great Sutton St (2nd floor), LONDON, EC1V 0DJ.   (hq)
     020 7490 9410   fax 020 7251 2834
     email info@afasic.org.uk   http://www.afasic.org.uk
     Chief Exec: Linda Lascelles
▲   Company Limited by Guarantee; Registered Charity
Br   50
○   *E, *W; to represent children & young adults with speech,
     language & communication impairments; to work for their
     inclusion in society; to support their parents & carers
●   Conf - ET - Res - Exhib - Inf - LG - Publications
     Helpline: 0845 355 5577
M   2,000 i, 65 org, UK / 20 i, o'seas
¶   Afasic News - 3; ftm only.   AR.
     Publications list available.

**African Studies Association of the United Kingdom   (ASAUK)
1963**
NR   c/o SOAS, University of London, Thornhaugh St, Russell Sq,
     LONDON, WC1H 0XG.   (hq)
     020 7898 4390   fax 020 7898 4389
     Hon Sec: Mrs Lindsay Allan
○   *L, *Q; advancement of African studies in the UK
●   Conf - Symposia - Inf
<   R African Soc
M   278 i, 6 libraries, UK / 304 i, 9 libraries, o'seas
¶   African Affairs (Jnl of Royal African Society) - 4; ftm.
     AR; free.

© CBD Research Ltd · Beckenham · BR3 5JS · Tel 020 8650 7745 · Fax 020 8650 0768 · E-mail cbd@cbdresearch.com · www.cbdresearch.com

Agents' Association (Great Britain) 1927
NR   54 Keyes House, Dolphin Sq, LONDON, SW1V 3NA.   (hq)
       020 7834 0515   fax 020 7821 0261
○   *P; to maintain the standard of ethics among members,
       performers & the entertainment industry in general
M   c 430 f

Agents & Organisers Association
       this is an internal Lib-Dem organisation

Aggregate Concrete Block Producers' Association
       incorporated in 1975 by the **British Concrete Masonry
       Association (incorporating the Aggregate Block Producers
       Association)**

Agricultural Economics Society (AES) 1926
■   The Mount Lodge, Church St, WHITCHURCH, Hants,
       RG28 7AR.   (admin/b)
       01256 892705   fax 01256 893090
       email aes@cingnet.org.uk   http://www.aes.ac.uk
       Hon Sec: Mr Wilfrid Legg
▲   Company Limited by Guarantee
○   *L; study & teaching of all disciplines relevant to agricultural
       economics as they apply to the agricultural, food & related
       industries & rural communities
●   Conf - Comp
<   Intl / Eur / Amer Assn[s] of Agricl Economics
M   300 i, 50 org, UK / 100 i, 600 org, o'seas
¶   Jnl of Agricultural Economics - 3; ftm, £250 yr nm.
       EuroChoices - 3; £12 m, £80 yr nm.

Agricultural Engineers' Association (AEA) 1875
■   Samuelson House, Paxton Rd, Orton Centre, PETERBOROUGH,
       Cambs, PE2 5LT.   (hq)
       01733 362925   fax 01733 370664
       email dg@aea.uk.com   http://www.aea.uk.com
       Dir Gen: J Vowles
▲   Company Limited by Guarantee
○   *F, *H, *T; for manufacturers of tractors & equipment used in
       agriculture, horticulture, forestry, professional turf & lawn &
       garden
Gp   Forestry; Grain & cereals; Lawn & garden; Livestock & grass;
       Professional turf; Root crops
       Councils, Overseas, Technical
●   Conf - Mtgs - ET - Exhib - Stat - Expt - Inf - LG
M   157 f, UK / 3 f, o'seas
¶   OPE Price Guide - 2; £30 (for 2 editions).   AR - 1.

Agricultural Industries Confederation (AIC) 2003
■   Confederation House, East of England Showground,
       PETERBOROUGH, Cambs, PE2 6XE.   (hq)
       01733 385230   fax 01733 385270
       email enquiries@agindustries.org.uk
       http://www.agindustries.org.uk
       Co Sec: Jeremy Smith
▲   Company Limited by Guarantee
○   *F, *T; to promote the benefits of modern, commercial,
       sustainable agriculture in the UK; to develop collaboration
       throughout the food chain
Gp   UK Association of the FIS
●   Conf - ET - Stat - LG
<   Intl Seed Fedn
M   300 f
¶   AIC Jnl - 4; ftm only.
✕   2003 (Fertiliser Manufacturers Association
            (UK Agricultural Supply Trade Association

Agricultural Law Association (ALA) 1975
NR   Kimblewick Cottage, Prince Albert Rd, WEST MERSEA, Essex,
       CO5 8AZ.   (hsp)
       01206 383521   fax 01206 385943
       email enquiries@ala.org.uk   http://www.ala.org.uk
       Consultant & Adviser: Geoff Whittaker
▲   Un-incorporated Society
○   *F, *P; 'to promote the study, knowledge & understanding of the
       law & practice relating to agriculture, the environment,
       farming, forestry & the rural community . . . in the United
       Kingdom of Great Britain & Northern Ireland & the European
       Union'
Gp   C'ees: European affairs, Land & property, Litigation & dispute
       resolution, Planning & environment, Taxation, Tenancies
●   Conf - Mtgs - ET - Res - LG
<   Comité Européen Droit de Rural (CEDR)
M   881 i, UK / 6 i, o'seas
¶   The Bulletin - 4; ftm only.

Agricultural Lime Association (ALA)
NR   Gillingham House, 38-44 Gillingham St, LONDON,
       SW1V 1HU.   (hq)
       020 7963 8000
○   *T; interests of the producers & promotion of lime products
       (burnt lime - calcium magnesium oxide) & hydrated lime
<   Quarry Products Assn
M   f

Agricultural Manpower Society (AMS) 1969
NR   c/o Farm Management Unit, School of Agriculture, Policy &
       Development, Earley Gate, University of Reading,
       Whiteknights Rd, PO Box 237, READING, Berks, RG6 6AR.
○   *F; the systematic study or applications of principles & practices
       in agriculture, which promote a satisfied & healthy workforce
M   i
¶   Jnl of Agricultural Manpower - 2.

Agricultural Science Association
IRL   Irish Farm Centre, Bluebell, DUBLIN 12, Republic of Ireland.
       353 (1) 460 3682   fax 353 (1) 456 5415
       email msasa@gofree.indigo.ie
       http://www.asaireland.ie
       Pres: James Fitzgerald
○   *F, *P

Aid for Children with Tracheostomies (ACT) 1983
■   Lammas Cottage, Stathe, BRIDGWATER, Somerset, TA7 0JL.
       (sp)
       01823 698398
       email support@actfortrachykids.com
       http://www.actfortrachykids.com
       Sec: Amanda Saunders
▲   Registered Charity
○   *W; a self-help group run by parents to give support & help to
       other parents with children with a tracheostomy; to promote
       knowledge nationally about the needs involved in the care of
       a child with a tracheostomy
●   Conf - Mtgs - Stat - Inf - Hire of medical equipment - Holiday
       caravan - Seminars for professionals in the medical field
<   Contact a Family
M   250 i
¶   NL - 4; ftm only.

Air-Britain (Historians) Ltd 1948

■ 74 High Ridge Rd, Apsley, HEMEL HEMPSTEAD, Herts, HP3 0AU.   (hsp)
 01442 267883
 http://www.air-britain.com
 Sec: Ronald A Webb
▲ Company Limited by Guarantee
Br 17; Holland & France
○ *G; for those interested in all aspects of current & historical aviation
Gp Specialists & groups cover the whole spectrum of aviation worldwide
● Res - Inf - Lib - PL - VE
< Amer Aviation Histl Soc
M 3,500 i, 10 f, UK / 120 i, 7 f, o'seas
¶ Subscription rates apply to (a) UK+NI+CI+BFPO, (b) Europe, (c) outside Europe:
 (1) News - 12; £43(a) £52(b) £58(c).
 (2) Aeromilitaria - 4; £25(a) £28(b) £31(c).
 (3) Archive - 4; £25(a) £28(b) £31(c).
  (1)+(2); £53(a) £62(b) £69(c).
  (2)+(3); £33(a) £38(b) £41(c).
  (1)+(3); £53(a) £62(b) £69(c).
  (1)+(2)+(3); £62(a) £72(b) £79(c).
  Membership only; £18(a) £20(b) £22(c).

Air Cleaner Manufacturers' Association   (ACMA)   2000

■ 2 Waltham Court, Milley Lane, Hare Hatch, READING, Berks, RG10 9TH.   (hq)
 0118-940 3416   fax 0118-940 6258
 email info@feta.co.uk   http://www.feta.co.uk
 Dir Gen: Cedric Sloan
○ *T; the manufacture or supply of quality equipment to remove tobacco products from public, work, recreational or entertainment areas
● Mtgs - Inf
< Heating & Ventilating Mfrs' Assn (HEVAC); Fedn Envtl Tr Assns (FETA)
M 7 f

Air Conditioning & Refrigeration Industry Board   (ACRIB)   1994

■ 76 Mill Lane, CARSHALTON, Surrey, SM5 2JR.   (hq)
 020 8647 7033   fax 020 8773 0165
 email acrib@acrib.org.uk
 Chief Exec: M J Horlick
▲ Company Limited by Guarantee
○ *N; for representative organisations with a direct interest in the provision or use of air conditioning, refrigeration & mechanical ventilation
Gp Working groups: Environment (incl energy efficiency); Education & training (incl implementation of NVQs); Food safety (incl de-regulation); Building regulations
M 3 org (Full members):
 Federation of Environmental Trade Associations
 Heating & Ventilating Contractors Association
 Institute of Refrigeration
 6 org (Associate members):
 Associated Air Conditioning & Refrigeration Contractors
 Association of Manufacturers of Domestic Electrical Appliances
 British Frozen Food Federation
 Cambridge Refrigeration Technology
 Chartered Institution of Building Services Engineers
 Cold Storage & Distribution Federation

Air League 1909

■ Broadway House, Tothill St, LONDON, SW1H 9NS.   (hq)
 020 7222 8463   fax 020 7222 8462
 email exec@airleague.co.uk
 http://www.airleague.co.uk
 Dir: Edward Cox
▲ Company Limited by Guarantee
○ *P; to promote the cause of British aviation
Gp The Air League Educational Trust (air education - awards flying scholarships & bursaries & engineering scholarships); Associate Parliamentary Aerospace Group
● Mtgs - ET - Comp - Inf - VE - LG
< Flight Safety Foundation
M 950 i, 115 f, 95 org, UK / 1 org, o'seas
¶ NL - 6; ftm only.

Air Safety Group   (ASG)   1964

■ 113 Arnison Avenue, HIGH WYCOMBE, Bucks, HP13 6BU.   (hsp)
 01494 522447
 email georgemaloney50@hotmail.com
 Hon Sec: George Maloney
▲ Un-incorporated Society
○ *K; 'a voluntary effort to promote greater safety for air travellers'
Gp Accident investigation; Certification requirements; Engineering; Medical; Operations
● Mtgs - Res - SG - Inf - LG
M 30 i

Air Transport Auxiliary Association   (ATA Assn)   1946

■ 40 Goldcrest Rd, CHIPPING SODBURY, S Glos, BS37 6XG.   (hsp)
 01454 319175   fax 01454 319175
 Hon Sec: Mrs M Viles
○ *G; for retired war-time ferry pilots
● Social gatherings only
< RAFA
M i
¶ NL - 1.

Aircraft Owners & Pilots Association   (AOPA)   1965

NR 50a Cambridge St, LONDON, SW1V 4QQ.   (hq)
 020 7834 5631   fax 020 7834 8623
 Admin Sec: Pam Stevenson
▲ Company Limited by Guarantee
○ *P, *T; 'to further the cause of pilots, instructors & flying training organisations; fighting for legislation etc to protect the rights of individuals in general aviation, keeping costs to a minimum'
● Conf - ET - Exhib - Inf
< Intl Coun of Aircraft Owner & Pilot Assns (IAOPA)
M 3,500 i, 150 f & org, UK / 100 i, o'seas
¶ Light Aviation - 4; ftm only.

Aircraft Owners & Pilots Association of Ireland   (AOPA Ireland)

IRL The Old Cottage, Rathdown Rd, GREYSTONES, Co Wicklow, Republic of Ireland.
 353 (87) 787 5000
 email platformfirst@eircom.net
 Hon Sec: Paul Chamberlain
○ *P, *T
< Intl Coun of Aircraft Owner & Pilot Assns (IAOPA)

© CBD Research Ltd · Beckenham · BR3 5JS · Tel 020 8650 7745 · Fax 020 8650 0768 · E-mail cbd@cbdresearch.com · www.cbdresearch.com

Aircraft Research Association Ltd   (ARA)   1952
- ■   Manton Lane, BEDFORD, Beds, MK41 7PF.   (hq)
      01234 350681   fax 01234 328584
      email ara.co.uk   http://www.ara.co.uk
      Chief Exec: B R Timmins
- ▲   Company Limited by Guarantee
- ○   *Q; aerodynamic wind-tunnel testing
- Gp   Research
- ●   Conf - Res - Inf - Lib
- <   AIRTO
- M   4 f
- ¶   Research Reports.

Aircrete Products Association
      to 2005-06 was the Autoclaved Aerated Concrete Products
      Association & is now a product association of the **British Precast
      Concrete Federation**

Aircrew Association   (ACA)   1975
- NR   11 Park Road, SOUTHPORT, Lancs, PR9 9JP.   (hsp)
      01704 549 454
      email secretary@aircrew.org.uk
      http://www.aircrew.org.uk
- ▲   Un-incorporated Society
- Br   90; 15 o'seas
- ○   *P; to foster comradeship amongst those who have been
      awarded an official flying badge, have qualified to operate
      military aircraft & are serving, or who have served, as
      military aircrew in the armed forces of nations allied to the
      UK & the Commonwealth
- ●   Conf - Mtgs - Inf - VE
- M   7,000 i, UK / 1,500 i, o'seas
- ¶   Intercom - 4; £2.50.

Aircrewman's Association   (ACA)   1977
- ■   18 Stathern Walk, Bestwood Park, NOTTINGHAM, NG5 6RR.
      (hsp)
      0115-849 9372
      http://www.aircrewman.org.uk
      Sec: Ian Williams
- ○   *P; membership is restricted to non-commissioned rating
      aircrew gaining flying wings whilst serving in the Royal Navy;
      all members fly, or have flown, in all types of naval
      helicopters; honorary membership is offered to widows of
      members, & associate membership to interested parties
- ●   Conf - Mtgs - Inf
- <   Fleet Air Arm; MOD (Navy) Assns
- M   380 i, UK / 30 i, o'seas
- ¶   T.A.C.A.N. (NL) - 2; ftm only.

Airport Operators Association   (AOA)   1934
- ■   3 Birdcage Walk, LONDON, SW1H 9JJ.   (hq)
      020 7222 2249   fax 020 7976 7405
      http://www.aoa.org.uk
      Chief Exec: Keith Jowett
- ▲   Company Limited by Guarantee
- ○   *T; the trade association that speaks for British airports -
      representing all of the nation's international hub & major
      regional airports as well as many of those serving
      community, business & leisure aviation
- Gp   Operations & safety; Environment & planning; Security;
      Government & industry affairs; General aviation; Finance
- ●   Conf - Mtgs - ET - Res - Inf - LG
- <   Airports Coun Intl (ACI)
- M   71 airports, 150 f (associates)
- ¶   Airport Operator (Jnl) - 5; free.

Airship Association   1971
- ■   The Light House, Barton Rd, KEINTON MANDEVILLE, Somerset,
      TA11 6EA.   (hsp)
      01458 223332   fax 01303 277650
      email secretary@airship-association.org
      http://www.airship-association.org
      Hon Sec: Martin Flanagan
- ▲   Company Limited by Guarantee
- ○   *G, *K, *L; a forum for those interested in the technology of
      airships
- ●   Conf - ET - Res - Exhib - Inf - LG
- M   336 i, UK / 313 i, o'seas
- ¶   Airship (Jnl) - 4; £15 m, £20 nm.
      Airships Today & Tomorrow, by Oliver Netherclift; £8.90.

**AIRTO Ltd: Association of Independent Research & Technology
Organisations   (AIRTO)   1986**
- ■   c/o CCFRA, Station Rd, CHIPPING CAMPDEN, Glos,
      GL55 6LD.   (hq)
      01386 842000
      Pres: Prof Richard Brook,
      Hon Sec: John Wilkinson
- ▲   Company Limited by Guarantee
- ○   N; to represent the contract research & knowledge transfer
      sector
- Gp   Finance & contracts; Marketing; Personnel; Secretaries; Health
      & safety; Testing & accreditation; Environment
- ●   Conf - Res - LG
- M   45 f
- ¶   AIRTO Review - 2;   Policy Papers - 2/3; both free.

Al-Anon Family Groups UK & Eire   (Al-Anon)   1960
- §   61 Great Dover St, LONDON, SE1 4YF.   (hq)
      020 7403 0888   fax 020 7378 9910
      email al-anonuk@aol.com   http://www.hexnet.co.uk/
      alanon
      Sec: Emily Sharman
- ▲   Registered Charity
- ○   *W; to provide understanding & support for families & friends
      of alcoholics, whether the alcoholic is still drinking or not

Al Bowlly Circle   1968
- ■   Memory Lane, PO Box 1939, LEIGH ON SEA, Essex,
      SS9 3UH.   (hsb)
      email ray@memorylane.org.uk
      http://www.memorylane.org.uk
      Sec: Ray Pallett
- ▲   Un-incorporated Society
- ○   *D, *G; to promote interest in the life & works of 1930s crooner
      Al Bowlly (1899-1941) & interest in the popular music of that
      time
- ●   Mtgs - Res - Inf - PL
- M   1,700 i, UK / 300 i, o'seas
- ¶   Memory Lane - 4; ftm, £4 nm UK (£5 o'seas).

Alan Rawsthorne Society
      since 2002 **Friends of Alan Rawsthorne**

**ALARM: the National Forum for Risk Management in the Public
Sector   (ALARM)**
- ■   Ladysmith House, High Street, SIDMOUTH, Devon,
      EX10 8LN.   (hq)
      01395 519083   fax 01395 517990
      email admin@alarm-uk.com
      http://www.alarm-uk.com
      Admin: Keith Southwell
- ▲   Company Limited by Guarantee
- ○   *P; 'to advise, encourage & represent public sector
      organisations in the development of risk management
      strategies to address the risks which might threaten the
      successful achievement of their objectives'
- ●   Conf - Mtgs - ET - Res - Exhib - Lib
- M   1,635 i, 117 f, UK / 13 i, o'seas

Albinism Fellowship   (AF)   1979
- ■   PO Box 77, BURNLEY, Lancs, BB11 5GN.   (mail/address)
  01282 771900
  email info@albinism.org.uk   http://www.albinism.org.uk
  Pres: Mike Sanderson
- ▲   Registered Charity
- ○   *W; to provide advice & support for people with Albinism, their
  family & those with a professional insterest in ALbinism
- ●   Conf - Mtgs
- M   350 i
- ¶   Albinism Life - 2.
  Real Lives; by Archie Roy & Robin Spinks (2005).
  (ISBN 0955 0344 0 X).

Alcohol Concern   1984
- ■   Waterbridge House, 32-36 Loman St, LONDON, SE1 0EE.
  (hq)
  020 7928 7377   fax 020 7928 4644
  email contact@alcoholconcern.org.uk
  http://www.alcoholconcern.org.uk
  Chief Exec: Srabani Sen
- ▲   Company Limited by Guarantee; Registered Charity
- ○   *K; to reduce the costs of alcohol abuse; to develop the range
  & quality of services available to problem drinkers & their
  families
- ●   Conf - Mtgs - ET - Stat - Inf - Lib
- M   c 1,000 i
- ¶   Straight Talk - 4;   Leaflets & Reports; prices on application.

Alcoholics Anonymous   (AA)   1947
- ■   PO Box 1, Stonebow House, Stonebow, YORK, YO1 7NJ.
  01904 644026   fax 01904 629091
  http://www.alcoholics-anonymous.org.uk
- ▲   Registered Charity
- Br   2,800; Worldwide
- ○   *K; 'primary purpose is to stay sober & help other alcoholics
  achieve sobriety'
- ●   Mtgs - Inf
- M   40-45,000 i, UK / c 1,750,000 i, o'seas
- ¶   AA News.
  List of publications.

Alcuin Club   1897
- ■   Ty Nant, 6 Parc Bach, TREFNANT, Denbighshire, LL16 4YE.
  (hsp)
  01745 730585
  email alcuinclub@waitrose.com
  http://www.alcuin.mcmail.com
  Mem Sec: J Ryding
- ▲   Registered Charity
- ○   *L; to promote study of Christian liturgy & worship - especially
  the Anglican Communion
- ●   Conf - Res - Inf - Lib
- M   370 i, 50 org, UK / 150 i, 50 org, o'seas
- ¶   Liturgical Studies - 2.
  Collections - 1; ftm, prices vary nm.   AR; ftm.

ALD Family Support Trust
alternative name for **Adrenoleukodystrophy Support Trust**

Alert against Euthanasia Co Ltd   (ALERT)   1991
- ■   27 Walpole St, LONDON, SW3 4QS.   (hsp)
  020 7730 2800   fax 020 7730 0818
  email alert@donoharm.org.uk
  http://www.donoharm.org.uk/alert
  Hon Sec: Mrs Chowdhary-Best
- ▲   Company Limited by Guarantee
- ○   *K; to defend vulnerable people's right to live; is against
  legalised euthanasia
- Gp   Carers
- ●   Conf - Mtgs - Res -Inf
- <   Care not Killing
- M   600 subscribers
- ¶   Various pamphlets; 3/4.
  [subscription to mailings £5 yr (£1 un-waged)]
- ×   ALERT - defending vulnerable people's right to live

Alexander Thomson Society   1991
- NR   Holmwood, 61-63 Netherlee Rd, GLASGOW, G44 3YU.
  (chmn/p)
  0141-637 2129
- ○   *A, *G; to promote knowledge & understanding of the life &
  work of the Glasgow architect Alexander (Greek) Thomson
  (1817-1875); to promote the protection of buildings &
  monuments created by him
- M   i & f
- ¶   NL - 3/4.

** Alexandra Palace Television Society
   Organisation lost: see Introduction paragraph 3

Alkan Society   1977
- ■   42 St Albans Hill, HEMEL HEMPSTEAD, Herts, HP3 9NG.   (hsp)
  01442 262895
  email secretary@alkansociety.org
  http://www.alkansociety.org
  Hon Sec: Nicholas King
- ▲   Un-incorporated Society
- ○   *D; to encourage the knowledge, understanding & appreciation
  of the life & works of the French pianist & composer C V
  Alkan (1813-1888)
- ●   Mtgs - Inf - Lib - 1-day lectures & recitals
- M   90 i, UK / 50 i, o'seas
- ¶   Bulletin - 3.   Discography & Library Catalogue - irreg;
  both ftm.

All British Martial Arts Council   (TABMAC)   1989
- NR   20 Hereson Rd, RAMSGATE, Kent, CT11 7DP.   (hq)
  01227 370055   fax 01227 370056
  Chief Exec: Joe Ellis
- Br   10; 3 o'seas
- ○   *N, *S; to act as governing body for member associations; to
  lay down minimum standards for teachers & instructors; to
  act as an advisory body to other authorities
- ●   Conf - Mtgs - ET - Exam - Res - SG - Stat - Inf - LG
- M   25 org, UK / 5 org, o'seas
- ¶   Safety Guidelines - 1; ftm.
  List of Approved Associations - 1; ftm.
  List of Approved Instructors - 1.
  Training & teaching manuals & videos; prices vary.

All England Netball Association Ltd   (AENA)   1926
- NR   9 Paynes Park, HITCHIN, Herts, SG5 1EH.   (hq)
  01462 442344
  Pres: Phyllis Avery
- ○   *S; to promote the game of netball in England for women of all
  ages
- M   c 52,000 i, 3,700 clubs
- ¶   Netball Magazine - 4.   Netball Rules.
  Note: the association is known as England Netball

All Year Round Chrysanthemum Growers' Association Ltd
since 2005 **UK Chrysanthemum Growers Association**

Allergy UK 1991
NR 3 White Oak Square, London Rd, SWANLEY, Kent, BR8 7AG.
    (hq)
    01322 619898   fax 01322 663480
    http://www.allergyuk.org
    Chief Exec: Mrs Muriel Simmons
▲ Registered Charity
○ *W; to provide information, support & advice for all people with
   allergies, their families & carers
● Conf - ET - Inf - National allergy masterclasses
< Brit Soc for Allergy & Clinical Immunology (BSACI)
M 6,000 i, 42 f, 135 org, UK / 35 i, 4 f, o'seas
¶ Publications list available.
   Note: Allergy UK is the operational name of the British Allergy
   Foundation.

Alliance for Better Food & Farming
   the alternative title of **Sustain: the Alliance for Better Food &
   Farming**

Alliance of Business Consultants
NR 40 Park Rd, Hampton Wick, Kingston upon Thames, Surrey,
    KT1 4AS.
    Chmn: David Peregrine-Jones
○ *P

Alliance against Counterfeiting & Piracy
   since 2005 **Alliance against Intellectual Property Theft**

Alliance for Health Professionals 1998
NR 14 Bedford Row, LONDON, WC1R 4ED.   (hq)
    020 7306 6683
    http://www.alliance.uk.com
    Coordinator: Lesley Mercer
▲ Un-incorporated Society
○ *N, *U; operating mainly in the health care sector
● Conf - Mtgs - ET - Empl - LG
M i in 7 org:
      British Dietetic Association
      British & Irish Orthoptic Society
      Chartered Society of Physiotherapy
      Community & District Nursing Association
      Federation of Clinical Scientists
      Society of Chiropodists & Podiatrists
      Society of Radiographers

Alliance of Independent Retailers (AIR) 1983
NR Adam House, Waterworks Rd, WORCESTER, WR1 3EZ.   (hq)
    01905 612733   fax 01905 21501
    email alliance@indretailer.co.uk
    http://www.indretailer.co.uk
    Sec: Len Griffin
▲ Un-incorporated Society
○ *T; to promote & protect independent retailers in the UK
Gp Alliance mailing services; Alliance design & graphics; Alliance
    national retail trade centre
● Exhib - Inf - LG
< Point of Purchase Advertising Inst (POPAI)
M 18,000 f
¶ The Independent Retailer - 12.
   The Hotelier - 12.
   Gardens & Gardening Retailer - 6.

Alliance against Intellectual Property Theft
NR 167 Wardour St, LONDON, W1F 8WL.
    020 7534 0595   fax 020 7534 0581
    email info@allianceagainstiptheft.co.uk
    Dir Gen: Susannah Winter
× 2005 Alliance against Counterfeiting & Piracy

Alliance of Literary Societies (ALS) 1973
NR 22 Belmont Grove, Bedhampton, HAVANT, Hants, PO9 3PU.
    (hsp)
    023 9247 5855   fax 0870 056 0330
    email rosemary@sndc.demon.co.uk
    http://www.sndc.demon.co.uk
    Hon Sec: Rosemary Culley,   Chmn: Nicholas Reed
▲ Un-incorporated Society
○ *N; to act as a liaison / spokesman for literary societies; to
   assist in any way with advice on anything concerning the
   societies; to promote interest in their work
● Conf - Mtgs - Res - Comp
> over 100 societies
M c 100 org UK / 3 org, o'seas
¶ NL - 2;   Open Book - 1; both ftm.

Alliance for Natural Health   (ANH)   2002
NR The Atrium, Curtis Rd, DORKING, Surrey, RH4 1XA.
    (asa/regd/office)
    01306 646600
    email info@alliance-natural-health.org
    http://www.alliance-natural-health.org
    Exec Dir: Dr Robert H J Verkerk
▲ Company Limited by Guarantee
○ *K, *W; to support the development of natural health care
   across Europe; to positively shape EU & international
   legislation affecting natural health
Gp Scientific; Legal
● Conf - Mtgs - ET - Res - Exhib - LG - Public appeals - Lobbying
   - Legal actions
< Inst for Complementary Medicine
M 800 i, 20 f, UK / 1,500 i, 20 f, o'seas
× 2002 (Feb-May) Free Choice for Supplements Alliance

Alliance of Occupational Pensioners
   merged in 2003 with the Confederation of Occupational Pensioner
   Associations to form the **Occupational Pensioners' Alliance**

Alliance of Private Sector Chiropody & Podiatry Practitioners
NR 3 Pendorlan Ave, COLWYN BAY, Conwy, LL29 8EA.
    01492 535795
    http://www.thealliancepsp.com
    Admin: Janet Taylor
○ *M, *P

Alliance of Registered Homeopaths   (ARH)
NR Millbrook, Millbrook Hill, NUTLEY, E Sussex, TN22 3PJ.
    08700 736339
    http://www.a-r-h.org
    Admin: Mrs Reid
○ *P

Alliance of Religions & Conservation   (ARC)   1995
NR The House, Kelston Park, BATH, BA1 9LE.
    01225 758004
    http://www.arcworld.org
    Sec Gen: Martin Palmer
▲ Company Limited by Guarantee
○ *K; to promote for the public benefit the protection and
   preservation of the natural environment throughout the
   world, in accordance with the religious teachings and beliefs
   which encourage respect for nature

Alliance of UK Virtual Assistants   (AUKVA)   2000
NR Walnut Trees, 4 Southwall Rd, DEAL, Kent, CT14 9QA.
    01304 389338
    Founders: Jo Johnston, Irene Boston, Di Chapman
▲ Un-incorporated Society
○ *P; to link, to clients, freelance workers with office skills, who
   will work from their own premises
Gp 21 covering different office skills
● Conf - ET - Inf - Mailing list - Support group
< Virtual Business Gp; A Virtual Solution; A Clayton's Secretary
M c 130 i

Alliance against Urban 4x4s   2004
- ■ c/o The Hub, 5 Torrens St (4th floor), LONDON, EC1V 1NQ. (hq)
    email info@stopurban4x4s.org.uk
    http://www.stopurban4x4s.org.uk
    Sec: Blake Ludwig
- ▲ a non-profit organisation
- ○ *K; a campaign for the increase of taxes & congestion charges on big 4-wheel drive vehicles & a ban on advertising in the mainstream media
- ● Mtgs - Res - LG - Lobbying - Promotion
- M [a non-membership body]
- ¶ [website only]

Allied Brewery Traders' Association
   since 2001-02 **Brewing, Food & Beverage Industry Suppliers Association**

Alopecia Patients Society
   see **Hairline International: the Alopecia Patients Society**

Alpine Club   (AC)   1857
- NR 55-56 Charlotte Rd, LONDON, EC2A 3QT.   (hq)
    020 7613 0755
    Hon Sec: Martin Scott
- ▲ Un-incorporated Society
- ○ *S; mountaineering in alpine & greater ranges (including ski mountaineering)
- ¶ Alpine Jnl.

Alpine Garden Society   (AGS)   1929
- ■ AGS Centre, Avon Bank, PERSHORE, Worcs, WR10 3JP.   (hq)
    01386 554790   fax 01386 554801
    email ags@alpinegardensociety.net
    http://www.alpinegardensociety.net
    Dir: Chris McGregor
- ▲ Registered Charity
- Br 60
- ○ *H; promotion of knowledge & cultivation of all plants suitable for rock gardens, frame or alpine house
- Gp Androsace; Frit
- ● Conf - Mtgs - ET - Comp - SG - Inf - Lib - PL - VE - Seed distribution scheme
- < R Horticl Soc
- M 11,500 i, 15 f, 5 org, UK / 2,500 i, 3 f, 3 org, o'seas
- ¶ Bulletin - 4;   NL - 4; both ftm.
    Gardens Open Directory - 1;   Show Hbk - 1; both free.
    Monographs & alpine titles.
    Publications list available on request.

Alternative Operators in the Communications Sector
   see **ALTO - Alternative Operators in the Communications Sector**

ALTO - Alternative Operators in the Communications Sector (ALTO)
- IRL 3 Lower Pembroke St, DUBLIN 2, Republic of Ireland.
    353 (086) 806 0022
    email info@alto.ie   http://www.alto.ie
    Chmn: Tom Hickey
- ○ *T
- × 2004 Association of Licensed Telecommunications Operators

Altrincham & Sale Chamber of Commerce   1909
- ■ 6B Old Market Place, ALTRINCHAM, Cheshire, WA14 4NP. (hq)
    0161-941 3250   fax 0161-941 1909
    email info@altrinchamchamber.co.uk
    http://www.altrinchamchamber.co.uk
    Chief Exec: John Pollard Smith
- ▲ Un-incorporated Society
- ○ *C; for the business community within South Trafford
- ● Mtgs - ET - Inf - LG & local & regional bodies - Advice service - Networking
- < Chams Comm NE; also local societies etc
- M 15 i, 405 f, 10 org
- ¶ Altruism - 6; ftm, £18 nm.   Diary (incl LM) - 1.
    Annual Accounts - 1.
- × 2004 (March) Greater Altrincham Chamber of Commerce, Trade & Industry
    2005 (September) Greater Altrincham Chamber of Commerce

Aluminium Alloy Manufacturing and Recycling Association   1958
- ■ Broadway House, Calthorpe Rd, Five Ways, BIRMINGHAM, B15 1TN.   (hq)
    0121-456 1103   fax 0870 138 9714
    email alfed@alfed.org.uk   http://www.alfed.org.uk
    Sec: Will Savage
- ○ *T; an independent organisation promoting the production of unwrought light alloys (aluminium) made in general from secondary light metals; the extension of the trade in products manufactured from the alloys
- ● Mtgs - Stat - Inf
- < a member association of the Aluminium Federation
- M 24 f

Aluminium Extruders Association   (AEA)
- ■ Broadway House, Calthorpe Rd, Five Ways, BIRMINGHAM, B15 1TN.
    0121-456 1103   fax 0870 138 9714
    email alfed@alfed.org.uk   http://www.alfed.org.uk
    Sec: Will Savage
- ○ *T
- < a member association of the Aluminium Federation
- M 11 f

Aluminium Federation Ltd   (ALFED)   1962
- ■ Broadway House, Calthorpe Rd, Five Ways, BIRMINGHAM, B15 1TN.   (hq)
    0121-456 1103   fax 0870 138 9714
    email alfed@alfed.org.uk   http://www.alfed.org.uk
    Sec Gen: Will Savage
- ○ *T; interests of those engaged in reduction, smelting, rolling, extrusion, drawing, casting, forging & flaking of aluminium & aluminium alloys
- ● Conf - Mtgs - ET - Exhib - Stat - Inf - Lib (technical enquiries & other queries) - LG
- < Eur Aluminium Assn
- M 200+ f
- ¶ AR.

Aluminium Finishing Association
- ■ Broadway House, Calthorpe Rd, Five Ways, BIRMINGHAM, B15 1TN.   (hq)
    0121-456 1103   fax 0870 138 9714
    email alfed@alfed.org.uk   http://www.alfed.org.uk
    Sec: T Siddle
- ○ *T; aluminium coatings & anodising
- < a member association of the Aluminium Federation
- M 28 f

Aluminium Packaging Recycling Association
   since 2002 **United Kingdom Aluminium Packaging Recycling Organisation**

© CBD Research Ltd · Beckenham · BR3 5JS · Tel 020 8650 7745 · Fax 020 8650 0768 · E-mail cbd@cbdresearch.com · www.cbdresearch.com

Aluminium Powder & Paste Association
- ■ Broadway House, Calthorpe Rd, Five Ways, BIRMINGHAM, B15 1TN. (hq)
  0121-456 1103   fax 0870 138 9714
  email alfed@alfed.org.uk   http://www.alfed.org.uk
  Sec: T Siddle
- ○ *T
- < a member association of the Aluminium Federation
- M f

Aluminium Primary Producers Association
- ■ Broadway House, Calthorpe Rd, Five Ways, BIRMINGHAM, B15 1TN. (hq)
  0121-456 1103   fax 0870 138 9714
  email alfed@alfed.org.uk   http://www.alfed.org.uk
  Sec: Will Savage
- ○ *T
- < a member association of the Aluminium Federation
- M f

Aluminium Rolled Products Manufacturers Association (ARPMA)
- ■ Broadway House, Calthorpe Rd, Five Ways, BIRMINGHAM, B15 1TN. (hq)
  0121-456 1103   fax 0870 138 9714
  email alfed@alfed.org.uk   http://www.alfed.org.uk
  Sec: Will Savage
- ○ *T
- ● Stat - Inf - Lib
- < a member association of the Aluminium Federation
- M 4 f
- ¶ Various booklets.

Aluminium Stockholders Association   (ASA)   1962
- ■ Broadway House, Calthorpe Rd, Five Ways, BIRMINGHAM, B15 1TN. (hq)
  0121-456 4938   fax 0121-456 4937
  email asa@alfed.org.uk
  Sec: Will Savage
- ▲ Un-incorporated Society
- ○ *T; representative body for UK aluminium, stainless steel & non-ferrous stockholders & distributors
- ● Conf - Mtgs - ET - Inf - VE
- < Aluminium Fedn
- M 19 f, 12 associates
- ¶ Review - 2;   NL - 6; free.

Alzheimer Scotland - Action on Dementia   1994
- ■ 22 Drumsheugh Gardens, EDINBURGH, EH3 7RN.   (hq)
  0131-243 1453   fax 0131-243 1450
  email alzheimer@alzscot.org   http://www.alzscot.org
  Chief Exec: Jim Jackson
- ▲ Company Limited by Guarantee
- ○ *K, *W; to be the national & local voice in Scotland, for people with dementia & their carers; to improve public policies & secure provision of high quality services; to provide high quality services
- ● Conf - ET - Res - Care service provision - Campaigning
  Helpline: 0808 808 3000
- < Alzheimer's Disease Intl; Alzheimer's Europe
- M 2,541 i, 35 f, 59 org
- ¶ Dementia in Scotland (NL) - 4; ftm, £1 nm.   AR; ftm.

Alzheimer's Society   (AS)   1979
- NR Gordon House, 10 Greencoat Place, LONDON, SW1P 1PH. (hq)
  020 7306 0606   fax 020 73606 0808
  email info@alzheimers.org.uk
  http://www.alzheimers.org.uk
  Dir: Neil Hunt
- ▲ Company Limited by Guarantee; Registered Charity
- Br c 200
- ○ *W; the leading care & research charity for people with dementia; to provide information, education & support for carers as well as day & home care
- ● Conf - Res - Inf - Lib
  Helpline: 0845 300 0336 (Mon-Fri 0830-1830); charged at local rates
- M c 24,000 i
- ¶ NL - 12.
  Publications list available.

Amalgamated Engineering & Electrical Union
  since 1 January 2002 **Amicus**

Amateur Athletic Association of England Ltd   (AAAofE)   1880
- NR Edgbaston House, 3 Duchess Pl, Edgbaston, BIRMINGHAM, B16 8NH.   (hq)
  0121-452 1500   fax 0121-455 9792
  http://www.englandathletics.org
  Hon Sec: Walter Nicholls
- ○ *S; governing body for athletics in England; to control, promote & provide athletic competitions, coaching & training
- M clubs

Amateur Boxing Association of England Ltd   (ABAE)   1880
- ■ Jubilee Stand, National Sports Centre, Crystal Palace, LONDON, SE19 2BB.   (hq)
  020 8778 0251   fax 020 8778 9324
  email hq@abae.org.uk   http://www.abae.co.uk
  Gen Sec: Paul King
- ▲ Company Limited by Guarantee
- Br 10 regions
- ○ *S; to further the sport of amateur boxing in England
- Gp Commissions: Coaching & performance, Development, Ethics, Medical, Referees & judges, Technical & rules
- ● Mtgs - ET - Exam - Comp - Inf
- < Intl Amat Boxing Assns (IABA); Eur Amat Boxing Assns (AEBA
- M 10,330 i, 638 clubs

Amateur Boxing Scotland   (ABS)   1908
- NR Strathdonan, High St, ELGIN, Morayshire, IV30 1AH.   (hsp/b)
  01343 544718   fax 01343 544718
  email donald@absboxing.fsnet.co.uk
  Admin: Donald Campbell
- ▲ Company Limited by Guarantee
- ○ *S; the governing body of amateur boxing in Scotland
- ● Sport
- < Amat Intl Boxing Assn (AIBA); Eur Amat Boxing Assn (EABA)
- × 2001 Scottish Amateur Boxing Association

Amateur Entomologists' Society   (AES)   1935
- ■ PO Box 8774, LONDON, SW7 5ZG.   (mail address)
  email enquiries@amentsoc.org   http://www.amentsoc.org
  Registrar: Nick Holford
- ▲ Registered Charity
- ○ *L; to promote the study of entomology (insects) particularly amongst amateurs & young people
- Gp AES Bug Club (for those aged 13 & under)
- ● Exhib - SG - Inf
- < R Entomological Soc London (RES)
- > R Entomological Soc London (RES)
- M 1,200 i, 20 org, UK / 100 i, 6 org, o'seas
- ¶ Bulletin - 6; free.
  Various handbooks & pamphlets.

Amateur Football Alliance (AFA) 1907
NR   55 Islington Park St, LONDON, N1 1QB.   (hq)
        020 7359 3493
○   *S; administration of Association Football clubs, referees &
        competitions (primarily in the Greater London area)

Amateur Jockeys Association of Great Britain Ltd   (AJA) 1996
■   Crews Hill House, Alfrick, WORCESTER, WR6 5HF.   (hq)
        01886 884488   fax 01886 884068
        email sph.oliver@btopenworld.com
        http://www.amateurjockeys.co.uk
        Chief Exec: Mrs Sarah Oliver
▲   Company Limited by Guarantee
○   *S; to protect & promote the role of amateur jockey
●   Mtgs - ET - Res - SG - Stat - Inf - LG
<   Fedn of Intl Gentlemen & Lady Amat Riders (FEGENTRI)
M   500 i
¶   NL - 3; free.
×   2001 (1 April) Amateur Jockeys Association of GB

Amateur Martial Association (AMA) 1972
■   66 Chaddesden Lane, DERBY, DE21 6LP.   (hq)
        01332 663086   fax 01332 280286
        email tom@amauk.co.uk
        http://www.amateurmartialassociations.co.uk
        Chief Exec: Tom Hibbert
▲   Un-incorporated Society
○   *S; martial arts
●   ET - Res - Comp

Amateur Motor Cycle Association Ltd   (AMCA) 1932
NR   28 Navigation Way, Mill Park, Hawkes Green Lane,
        CANNOCK, Staffs, WS11 2XT.   (hq)
        01543 466282
        Sec: Carol Davis
▲   Company Limited by Guarantee
○   *S; to promote motor cycle sporting events (off road)
●   Mtgs - Exhib - Comp - Inf - LG
<   Intl Motor Sport Band for Amateurs (IMBA); Motor Sports Org
        Land Access Rights Org (MOLARA)
M   5,000 i in 200 clubs

Amateur Rose Breeders Association (ARBA) 1975
NR   48 Shrewsbury Fields, SHIFNAL, Shropshire, TF11 8AN.   (hsp)
        01952 461333
        Hon Sec: Derrick Everitt
▲   Un-incorporated Society
○   *H; to protect & further the interests, knowledge & status of
        amateur rosebreeders by the best, honest means including a
        willingness by members to share their expertise & to
        cooperate with other organisations (amateur or professional),
        & a common interest in the rose
●   Mtgs - Res - Exhib - Comp - VE
<   R Nat Rose Soc (a specialist interest gp)
M   125 i, UK / 20 i, o'seas
¶   NL - 2/4.   ARBA Annual - 1.
        Specialist publications - irreg.

Amateur Rowing Association Ltd   (ARA) 1882
NR   The Priory, 6 Lower Mall, LONDON, W6 9DJ.   (hq)
        020 8237 6700
        Nat Mgr: Mrs Rosemary Napp
▲   Company Limited by Guarantee
○   *S; the governing body for the sport of rowing in England
●   Conf - Mtgs - ET - Exam - Exhib - Comp - Stat - Inf - Lib - LG
<   Fédn Intle des Socs d'Aviron (FISA)
M   c 17,000 i, 520 clubs
¶   Regatta Magazine - 10.
        British Rowing Almanack & Ybk - 1.

Amateur Swimming Association (ASA) 1869
■   Harold Fern House, Derby Sq, LOUGHBOROUGH, Leics,
        LE11 5AL.   (hq)
        01509 618700   fax 01509 618701
        email chiefexecutive@swimming.org
        Chief Exec: David Sparkes
Br   5 districts
○   *S; to promote the teaching & practice of swimming, diving,
        synchronised swimming & water polo; to stimulate public
        opinion in favour of provision of facilities for them; to enforce
        laws for the control of the four disciplines in England
Gp   Swimming; Diving; Water polo; Synchronised swimming;
        Education
●   Conf - Mtgs - ET - Exam - Comp
<   Fédn Intle de Natation Amateur (FINA); Ligue Eur de
        Natation (LEN)
M   194,443 i, 1,584 clubs, 30 org
¶   Hbk - 1; £6.   AR; free.

Amateur Swimming Federation of Great Britain Ltd
■   Harold Fern House, Derby Sq, LOUGHBOROUGH, Leics,
        LE11 5AL.   (hq)
        01509 618700   fax 01509 618701
        email chiefexecutive@swimming.org
        Chief Exec: David Sparkes
○   *N, *S; determination of policies for participation in world
        events
Gp   Swimming; Diving; Water polo; Synchronised swimming
●   Comp - Determination of policies for participation in world
        championships
<   Fédn Intle de Natation Amateur (FINA); Ligue Eur de Natation
        (LEN)
M   [not stated]
¶   AR - 1; ftm.

Amateur Yacht Research Society Ltd   (AYRS) 1955
■   BCM AYRS, LONDON, WC1N 3XX.   (hs)
        01727 862268
        Hon Sec: Sheila Fishwick
▲   Company Limited by Guarantee; Registered Charity
○   *G, *Q; to research into nautical science & maintain research &
        investigation into the design & construction of all kinds of
        nautical craft however propelled
Gp   England
●   Conf - Mtgs - Exhib
M   352 i, 29 org, UK / 281 i, 10 org, o'seas
¶   NL - 4; ftm.

Ambulance Service Association (ASA) 1994
■   Capital Tower (7th floor), 91 Waterloo Rd, LONDON,
        SE1 8RT.   (hq)
        020 7928 9620   fax 020 7928 9502
        email reception@asa.uk.net   http://www.asa.uk.net
        Chief Exec: Richard Diment
▲   Company Limited by Guarantee
○   *P; the promotion & management of efficient & economical
        ambulance services within the public sector
●   Conf - Mtgs - ET - Res - Exhib - Inf - Lib - LG
M   39 services
¶   Ambulance UK - 6; ftm, £20 yr nm.
        AR & Accounts - 1; ftm only.

Ambulance Service Institute (ASI) 1976
NR   23 Clifton St, BURY, Lancs, BL9 5DY.   (hsp)
        Nat Admin & Sec: Graham Sleight
▲   Company Limited by Guarantee; Registered Charity
Br   20; Hong Kong, Canada
○   *P; to promote, advance & encourage the education & training
        of ambulance service employees & to extend the training to
        the general public
●   Conf - Mtgs - ET - Exam - Comp - SG - LG
<   Inst of Ambulance Officers Australia (& N Zealand); Ambulance
        Service Assn
M   i
¶   NL - 4.

American Auto Club UK   (AAC UK)
NR   Beechwood, 235 Tile Cross Rd, Tile Cross, BIRMINGHAM,
       B33 0NA.
       0845 644 0345
       http://www.american-auto-club.co.uk
       Chief Exec: Richard Miller
○   *G

American Civil War Round Table (UK)   (ACWRT(UK))   1953
NR   50 Hinckley Close, HAREFIELD, Uxbridge, UB9 6AZ.   (msp)
       http://www.americancivilwar.org.uk
       Mem Sec: Mrs M Ward
▲   Un-incorporated Society
○   *L; serious & impartial study of the War Between The States
       1861-1865
●   Mtgs - SG - Inf - Lib - Historical research
<   Civil War Round Table Associates (USA)
M   c 170 i, UK / 10 i, o'seas
¶   Crossfire - 3; free.

**American Quarter Horse Association UK Ltd   (AQHA-UK)
1974**
NR   63 Laughton Rd, Lubenham, MARKET HARBOROUGH, Leics,
       LE16 9TE.
       0870 609 1654
▲   Registered Charity
○   *B; to promote, record & preserve the Quarter horse breed in
       the UK
●   ET - Exhib - Comp
<   Fedn of Eur Quarter Horses; American Quarter Horse Assn; Brit
       Horse Soc (BHS)
M   650 i
¶   Jnl - 4; ftm only.
       Stud Book Vols I-III.

American Saddlebred Association of GB   (ASA.GB)   1985
NR   Uplands, ALFRISTON, E Sussex, BN26 5XE.   (founder/pres/p)
       01323 870977   fax 01323 871375
       Founder/President: Cheryl R Lutring
▲   Un-incorporated Society
○   *B; to promote the breed in Great Britain
Gp   Display team
●   ET - Res - Exhib - Inf
M   100 i, UK / 25 i, o'seas
¶   The Rack-onteur (NL) - 4; ftm, postage nm.

Amicus   1851
NR   Hayes Court, West Common Rd, HAYES, Kent, BR2 7AU.   (hq)
       020 8462 7755   fax 020 8315 8234
       35 King St, LONDON, WC2E 8JG.
       020 7420 8900
       Gen Sec: Derek Simpson
○   *U; to provide quality employment representation & advice to
       our members on a collective & individual basis; to promote
       genuine partnership with employers in the workplace
●   Conf - Mtgs - ET - Res - Inf - Empl - LG
<   Intl Metal Workers Fedn; Eur Metal Workers Fedn; Public
       Service Intl; TUC; Labour Party
M   i
×   2002 (Amalgamated Engineering & Electrical Union (1
       January)
       2003 (Amicus-AEEU
       2004 (Amicus-MSF
           (Graphical, Paper & Media Union (merged)
           (Manufacturing Science & Finance Union (merged)
           (UNIFI (merged)

Amicus - CMA Section   1907
NR   CMA House, Ruscombe Business Park, Twyford, READING,
       Berks, RG10 9JD.   (hq)
       0118-934 2300   fax 0118-934 2087
       email amicus-cma.org.uk
Br   300
○   *P, *U; to represent managers & executives within the Post
       Office; an autonomous section of Amicus
Gp   Supervisors, Managers, Executives
●   Conf - Mtgs - ET - Res - Empl - LG
<   UNI
M   15,000 i, 1 f
¶   CMA News - 10; ftm, £20 nm.   AR - 1; ftm only.
×   2003 Communication Managers Association

Amusement & Gaming Industry Forum   (AGIF)   1985
NR   Alders House, 133 Aldersgate St, LONDON, EC1A 4JA.   (hq)
       020 7726 9826
▲   Un-incorporated Society
○   *T; to bring together the experience of users of amusement
       machines
●   Mtgs
M   12 f
×   1999 Coin Machine Users' Group

Anaesthetic Research Society   (ARS)   1958
NR   c/o Dr R P Mahajan, University Division of Anaesthesia &
       Intensive Care, Queen's Medical Centre, NOTTINGHAM,
       NG7 2UH.   (hsb)
       0115-823 1007
       Hon Sec: Dr R P Mahajan
▲   Registered Charity
○   *L; forum for discussion of current research in anaesthesia
●   Conf
M   650 i, UK / 75 i, o'seas
¶   Proceedings of Conferences - 3. (in British Jnl of Anaesthesia).

Anaphylaxis Campaign   1994
NR   PO Box 275, FARNBOROUGH, Hants, GU14 6SX.   (hq)
       01252 542029   fax 01252 377140
       http://www.anaphylaxis.org.uk/
       Dir: David Reading
▲   Registered Charity
Br   21 regions
○   *K; to offer support & guidance to those affected by potentially
       fatal food allergies; it is dedicated to raising awareness in the
       food industry; it is seeking to ensure that the medical
       profession at every level offers the best possible advice &
       treatment
●   Inf - LG
M   c 7,500 i
¶   Anaphylaxis Campaign (NL) - 4.

Anatomical Society of Great Britain & Ireland   1887
NR   Dept of Anatomy, National University of Ireland, CORK,
       Republic of Ireland.   (pres/b)
       353 (21) 4902246
       http://www.anatsoc.org.uk
       Pres: Prof John Fraher
▲   Registered Charity
○   *L, *Q; the promotion, study, development & advancement of
       research & education in the anatomical & related sciences
●   Conf - Mtgs - Res - Comp - Joint scientific meetings with Der
       Nederlandse Anatomen Vereniging
<   Eur Fedn for Experimental Morphology; Anatomische
       Gesellschaft
M   c 700 i
¶   Jnl of Anatomy - 8; ftm.   Ybk - 1.

Ancient Cattle of Wales
       see **Gwartheg Hynafol Cymru   (Ancient Cattle of Wales)**

Ancient Egypt & Middle East Society
       see **AEMES (Ancient Egypt & Middle East Society)**

© CBD Research Ltd · Beckenham · BR3 5JS · Tel 020 8650 7745 · Fax 020 8650 0768 · E-mail cbd@cbdresearch.com · www.cbdresearch.com

Ancient & Honourable Guild of Town Criers (AHGTC) 1978

■ 10 Weston Rd, GUILDFORD, Surrey, GU2 8AS. (hsp)
   01483 532796   fax 01483 833489
   email secretary@ahgtc.org.uk   http://www.ahgtc.org.uk
   Sec: D Peters
▲ Company Limited by Guarantee
Br Australia, Bahamas, Belgium, Canada, Germany, Netherlands,
   New Zealand, Poland, USA
○ *P; promotion & regulation of town-crying; preservation of
   ancient art of town-crying
● Conf - Mtgs - Comp - LG
> Gld of Eur Town Criers; Gld of Australian Town Criers
M c 120 i, UK / c 25 i, o'seas
¶ The Crier - 4; ftm only.

Ancient Monuments Society (AMS) 1924

■ St Ann's Vestry Hall, 2 Church Entry, LONDON, EC4V 5HB.
   (hq)
   020 7236 3934   fax 020 7329 3677
   email office@ancientmonumentssociety.org.uk
   http://www.ancientmonumentssociety.org.uk
   Chmn: Giles Quarme,   Sec: Matthew Saunders
▲ Registered Charity
○ *K; study & conservation of historic buildings of all types
Gp a working partnership with Friends of Friendless Churches
● Conf - Res - Inf - VE - Comments to local authorities on the
   demolition of listed buildings - Dissemination of methods &
   techniques of preservation - Advice to planning authorities on
   listed buildings
M 2,000 i, 200 libraries, UK / c 100 i, 50 libraries, o'seas
¶ Transactions - 1; ftm.   NL - 3.

Ancient Tree Forum

NR c/o Woodland Trust, Autumn Park, Dysart Rd, GRANTHAM,
   Lincs, NG31 6LL.
   01476 581135
   http://www.woodland-trust.org.uk/ancient-tree-forum
○ *K; conservation of ancient trees

Androgen Insensitivity Syndrome Support Group (AISSG)

○ *W
   Note: Address changes frequently - check website for contact

Angela Thirkell Society 1980

■ 54 Belmont Park, LONDON, SE13 5BN. (hsp)
   020 8244 9339
   email penny.aldred@ntlworld.com
   http://www.angelathirkellsociety.com
   Hon Sec: Mrs Penny Aldred
Br Eire, USA
○ *A, *G; to honour the memory of Angela Thirkell as a writer &
   to make her works available to new generations
● Mtgs - VE
< Alliance Literary Socs
M 150 i, UK / 500 i, o'seas
¶ Jnl - 1; ftm, £5 nm.

Anglers' Conservation Association (ACA) 1948

■ 6 Rainbow St, LEOMINSTER, Herefords, HR6 8DQ. (hq)
   01568 620447
   email admin@a-c-a.org   http://www.a-c-a.org
   Exec Dir: Mark Lloyd
▲ Un-incorporated Society
○ *G, *K, *S; a pollution fighting body set up in order to protect
   anglers' interest & fisheries in general, by pursuing any legal
   claim from members which arises from a pollution incident
● LG - Legal advice to members
M 8,000 i, 1,000 org
¶ AR - 1; ftm only.

Anglesey Agricultural Society 1886

■ Ty Glyn Williams, Anglesey Showground, Gwalchmai,
   HOLYHEAD, Anglesey, LL65 4RW. (hq)
   01407 720072
   Show Admin: Aled W Hughes
▲ Company Limited by Guarantee; Registered Charity
○ *F; to promote agriculture, horticulture & forestry
Gp Poultry; Rabbits; Goats; Pigs; Sheep; Dairy & beef cattle; Shire
   & heavy horses; Light horses; Show jumping; Cookery;
   Produce; Horticultural; Shearing; Dry stone walling
● Mtgs - ET - Exhib - Comp - Expt - Inf - LG
< Assn of Shows & Agricl Orgs
M 1,100 i
¶ Show Catalogue - 1.   AR - 1.
   Winter Show Catalogue - 1.
   Schedules of Events & Classes; - 1.

Anglesey Antiquarian Society & Field Club (AAS) 1911

■ 1 Fronheulog, Sling, TREGARTH, Caernarfonshire, LL57 4RD.
   (hsp)
   01248 752028
   http://www.hanesmon.btinternet.co.uk
   Hon Sec: S C G Caffell
▲ Registered Charity
○ *L; archaeology, natural science, art & literature of Anglesey
● Mtgs - Inf - Lib - VE
M 900 i, 118 org
¶ Transactions - 1; £6 m, £10 nm.   NL - 2; ftm.
   Studies in Anglesey History - irreg.

Angling Trades Association Ltd (ATA)

■ Federation House, STONELEIGH PARK, Warks, CV8 2RF. (hq)
   024 7641 4999   fax 024 7641 4990
   http://www.sportsandplay.com
   Chief Exec: David Pomfret
○ *T; to represent manufacturers, wholesalers & distributors; to
   defend angling
● Mtgs - Exhib - Stat - Expt - Inf - LG
< a group of the Fedn of Sports & Play Assns (FSPA)
M c 50 f

Anglo-Albanian Association (AAA) 1912

■ Strand Centre, Elm Park, LONDON, SW2 2EH.
   020 7582 6082
   email caroline@albaction.org
   Hon Sec: Caroline ffrench Blake
▲ Un-incorporated Society
○ *X; although not a charitable body it acts as an unofficial point
   of liaison for individuals involved in aid work in Albania &
   Kosova; it also provides information on developments in both
   countries with news of Anglo-Albanian events
● Social mtgs
M 190 i, UK / 9 i, o'seas

Anglo-Argentine Society 1948

■ 2 Belgrave Sq, LONDON, SW1X 8PJ. (hq)
   020 7235 9505   fax 020 7235 9505
   email mail@anglo-argentine.org.uk
   http://www.anglo-argentine.org.uk
   Chmn: Mrs H Van den Broucque,   Hon Sec: J Wilson
▲ Registered Charity
○ *X; to advance the education of the people of GB about
   Argentinian people, history, language, institutions & culture
   (& vice-versa)
● Conf - Mtgs - Exhib - Social gatherings
M i & f
¶ AR.

Anglo-Austrian Society   1954
NR   60 Brimmers Hill, Widmer End, HIGH WYCOMBE, Bucks,
       HP15 6NP.   (hq)
       01494 711116
       email info@angloaustrian.demon.co.uk
       http://www.angloaustrian.org.uk
       Sec: Peter Gieler
○   *X; promotion of friendship & understanding between peoples
       of GB & Austria
M   2,500 i

** Anglo Azeri Society
       Organisation lost: see Introduction paragraph 3

Anglo-Belgian Society   (ABS)   1918
■   5 Hartley Close, BICKLEY, Kent, BR1 2TP.   (hsp)
       020 8467 8442   fax 020 8467 8442
       Hon Sec: Patrick Bresnan
▲   Un-incorporated Society
Br   Belgium
○   *X; maintain & develop friendship between the British & Belgian
       peoples through cultural & social relations
●   Conf - Mtgs - VE - Cultural & social activities
M   480 i, 17 f, UK / 40 i, 5 f, o'seas
¶   LM - 5 yrly.   AR - 1.

Anglo-Brazilian Society   1943
NR   32 Green St, LONDON, W1K 7AU.   (hq)
       020 7493 8493
○   *X; to promote friendly relations between Brazil & the UK
●   Mtgs - VE - Concerts, social functions
M   c 400 i & f
¶   AR; free.

Anglo Catalan Society   (ACS)   1954
■   Dept of Hispanic Studies, University of Birmingham, Edgbaston,
       BIRMINGHAM, B15 2TT.   (hsb)
       0121-414 3820   fax 0121-414 3184
       email h.b.f.buffery@bham.ac.uk
       http://www.anglo-catalan.org
       Hon Sec: Dr Helena Buffery
▲   Un-incorporated Society
○   *L, *X; the promotion of Catalan language & culture, Catalan
       studies & Anglo-Catalan relations
●   Conf - Mtgs - ET - Res - Inf
<   Insitut Ramon Llull; Fundació Congrés de Cultura Catalana
>   NACS
M   200 i, 4 f, UK / 80 i, 5 f, o'seas
¶   NL - 2; free.   Annual Lecture - 1.
       Publications available at www.kent.ac.uk/acsop/

** Anglo Central American Society
       Organisation lost: see Introduction paragraph 3

Anglo-Chilean Society   1944
NR   12 Devonshire St, LONDON, W1G 7DS.   (hq)
○   *X

Anglo-Colombian Society   1960
NR   Flat 3h Grove End House, Grove End Rd, LONDON, NW8 9HP.
       020 7266 4116
       Sec: Myriam Martinez
○   *X; promotion of friendly relations between UK & Colombia
●   Mtgs - VE
M   c 200 i & f

Anglo-Danish Society   (A-DS)   1924
NR   6 Keats Ave, Littleover, DERBY, DE23 4ED.   (sp)
       01332 517160
       Sec: Mrs Margit Staehr
▲   Registered Charity
○   *X; to promote understanding between the two countries
●   Mtgs - VE - Award of scholarships to post-graduates for Danes
       to study in the UK & for British students to study in Denmark
       for a maximum of 6 months & worth £200 per month
<   Confedn of Scandinavian Socs of GB & Ireland (CoSCAN)
M   380 i, 40 f, UK / 10 i, Denmark
¶   News & Views Magazine - 4; ftm only.
       NL with visits & meetings programme - 4; ftm only.

Anglo-Ecuadorian Society
NR   81a Chester Square, LONDON, SW1P 9DP.
       Sec: Paulina Seabrook
▲   Un-incorporated Society
○   *X; to encourage & promote friendly relations between Ecuador
       & the UK; proceeds from cultural & social events provide
       funds for children-in-need charities in Ecuador
●   Mtgs - Annual dinner (Autumn) - Fiesta Latina (May in London)
M   [not stated]
¶   NL - 4; ftm only.

Anglo-German Family History Society   1987
NR   5 Oldbury Grove, BEACONSFIELD, Bucks, HP9 2AJ.   (hsp)
       01494 676812
       Hon Sec: Mrs Gwen Davis
▲   Un-incorporated Society
○   *G; family history for those wishing to research their German
       ancestors
●   Mtgs - Res - Inf - Lib - VE
<   Fedn of Family History Socs
M   1,500 i, UK / 150 i, o'seas
¶   Mitteilungsblatt - 4.

Anglo-Hellenic League   1913
■   The Hellenic Centre, 16-18 Paddington St, LONDON,
       W1U 5AS.   (hq)
       020 7486 9410
       email
       anglohellenic.league@virgin.net(09)hellenicbookservice.
       com/ahl.htm
       Chmn: Sir David Miers
       Admin: Dr Sophia B Economides
▲   Registered Charity
○   *X; to strengthen ties between GB & Greece; to spread
       information & encourage travel, social & cultural relations
       between the peoples of the two countries
●   Mtgs - VE - Administers the Runciman Literary Award, the Katie
       Lentakis Award (for students) & the Princess Marina Fund
       (awards for libraries)
M   360 i, 10 f, 2 org, UK / 50 i, o'seas
¶   The Anglo-Hellenic Review - 2; ftm, £6 (£7.50 o'seas) nm.
       AR.

Anglo-Indonesian Society   (AIS)   1956
NR   Church Cottage, Pedlinge, HYTHE, Kent, CT21 4JL.   (hsp)
       01303 260541   fax 01303 238058
       Chmn & Hon Sec: Christopher Scarlett
▲   Un-incorporated Society
○   *X; a non-political society fostering friendship & understanding
       between the people in Britain interested in Indonesia &
       people of Indonesian nationality resident in Britain; to
       encourage cultural, literary & social relations between the two
       countries
●   Mtgs - VE
M   250 i, 20 f
¶   NL - 26;   AR & Accounts - 1; both ftm only.

Anglo-Israel Association (AIA) 1949
NR   PO Box 47819, LONDON, NW11 7WD.   (hq)
　　　020 8458 1284
▲　Registered Charity
○　*X; to foster understanding between GB & Israel
●　Mtgs - Inf - Lecturers - Scholarships to Israel
M　i & f
¶　AR; ftm only.   Series of pamphlets.

** Anglo-Italian Society
　　　Organisation lost: see Introduction paragraph 3

Anglo-Jewish Association (AJA) 1871
■　107 Gloucester Place (suite 4), LONDON, W1U 6BY.   (hq)
　　　020 7486 5055
　　　email info@anglojewish.co.uk
　　　http://www.anglojewish.co.uk
　　　Pres: Michael Hilsenrath
▲　Registered Charity
○　*W; administration of charitable educational funds for Jewish
　　　students in financial need in higher education in the UK
●　Mtgs - ET - Arrangement of lectures
<　Conf on Jewish Material Claims
>　CCJO
M　500 i

Anglo-Jordanian Society (AJS) 1981
NR   PO Box 32663, LONDON, W14 9YZ.   (hsb)
　　　020 7603 8663
　　　email ajs@manara.com
　　　Hon Sec: Majed Najjar
▲　Registered Charity
○　*X
●　Mtgs - Exhib - Expt - VE
<　Jordan British Society
M　677 i, 39 f, UK / 53 i, o'seas
¶　Jordaniana - 3/4.

Anglo-Malagasy Society 1961
NR   1 Golding Crescent, STANFORD-le-HOPE, Essex, SS17 7AZ.
　　　(hsp)
　　　01375 677138
　　　Hon Sec: Stuart Edgill
○　*X; to further friendship between GB & Madagascar; to
　　　promote business with & visits to the Republic
●　Conf - Mtgs - Exhib
M　300 i, 20 f
¶　NL - 4.   AR; both ftm only.

** Anglo-Mongolian Society
　　　Organisation lost: see Introduction paragraph 3

Anglo-Netherlands Society 1920
NR   PO Box 68, Unilever House, LONDON, EC4P 4BQ.   (hq)
　　　020 7353 5729
○　*X; to promote friendship between British & Dutch subjects by
　　　organising events (in Britain) at which they can meet

Anglo-Norman Text Society (ANTS) 1938
■　c/o French Dept, Birkbeck College, Malet St, LONDON,
　　　WC1E 7HX.   (hsb)
　　　020 7631 6170 & 020 8239 9424
　　　email ishort@french.bbk.ac.uk
　　　Hon Sec: Prof Ian Short
▲　Registered Charity
○　*L; the publication of Anglo-Norman texts of literary, linguistic,
　　　historical & legal value & interest
●　Publication - Compilation of an Anglo-Norman Dictionary
M　74 i, 48 f, universities, UK / 114 i, 96 f, o'seas
¶　1 volume of Anglo-Norman text - 1.
　　　Prospectus (incl LM).   Occasional volumes.

Anglo-Norse Society 1918
■　25 Belgrave Sq, LONDON, SW1X 8QD.   (hq)
　　　020 7235 9529   fax 020 7235 9529
　　　email anglonorse@yahoo.co.uk
　　　Sec: Irene Garland
▲　Registered Charity
Br　Norway
○　*X; promotion of better understanding/knowledge of Norway in
　　　the UK
Gp　Bursaries for study of a 'Norwegian' subject
●　Mtgs - Selling books for language study, & Norwegian literature
M　c 400 i
¶　Anglo Norse Review - 2; ftm.

Anglo-Omani Society 1976
NR   29 Chipperfield Rd, BOVINGDON, Herts, HP3 0JN.
　　　01442 833589
　　　Sec: R R Owens
▲　Registered Charity; Un-incorporated Society
○　*X
●　Mtgs - VE - LG
M　600 i, 12 f

Anglo-Peruvian Society 1961
NR   PO Box 494, WEMBLEY, Middx, HA9 8ZB.   (hq)
　　　020 8908 1916
▲　Registered Charity
○　*X; to advance the education of the people of Great Britain
　　　about Peru, its people, history, language & literature,
　　　institutions, folklore & artistic & economic life
●　Conf - Mtgs - ET - Lectures - Concerts - Seminars - Fundraising
　　　- Cultural events
M　490 i, 14 f

Anglo-Polish Society 1832
NR   c/o The Polish Institute, 20 Princes Gate, LONDON,
　　　SW7 1PT.   (mail/address)
○　*X; to promote friendship & understanding between British &
　　　Polish people; to protect the interests of the Poles in Britain
M　i

Anglo-Portuguese Society 1938
NR   2 Belgrave Sq, LONDON, SW1X 8PJ.   (hq)
　　　020 7245 9738
　　　Sec: Miss Ann Waterfall
○　*X; the education of the people of the United Kingdom about
　　　Portugal, its people & its culture

Anglo-Spanish Society 1958
■　19 Consort Rise House, 203 Buckingham Palace Rd,
　　　LONDON, SW1W 9TB.   (hsp)
　　　020 7730 7438
　　　email anglospanish@clara.co.uk
　　　http://www.anglospanishsociety.org
　　　Hon Sec: Dorothy H McLean
▲　Registered Charity
○　*X; to promote friendship between the peoples of Britain &
　　　Spain through a knowledge of each other's customs,
　　　institutions, history & way of life
●　Mtgs - VE
M　300 i, 11 f, UK / 40 i, 1 f, o'seas
¶　Anglo-Spanish Quarterly Review - 4.

© CBD Research Ltd · Beckenham · BR3 5JS · Tel 020 8650 7745 · Fax 020 8650 0768 · E-mail cbd@cbdresearch.com · www.cbdresearch.com

Anglo-Swedish Society of Great Britain & Ireland   1919
NR   6a Oakfield St, LONDON, SW10 9JB.
       020 7352 0599   fax 020 7352 0599
       email info@angloswedishsociety.org.uk
       http://www.angloswedishsociety.org.uk
       Hon Sec: Kari Hedly
▲   Registered Charity
○   *X; to promote good relations & awareness between the
       peoples of GB & Sweden in the fields of culture, science, art,
       literature, music, history, economics & philosophy
●   VE - Scholarship scheme
M   283 i, 11 f
¶   NL - 3;   AR; both ftm only.

Anglo-Thai Society   1962
■   Southwood, 62a Dore Rd, SHEFFIELD, S Yorks, S17 3NE.   (hsp)
       0114-236 8129
       email info@anglothaisociety.org
       http://www.anglothaisociety.org
       Hon Sec: T J Knox
▲   Un-incorporated Society
○   *X
●   Mtgs
M   250 i, 10 f, UK / 20 i, o'seas

Anglo-Turkish Society   1953
■   c/o High Beeches, Boyneswood Rd, Four Marks, ALTON, Hants,
       GU34 5DY.   (hsp)
       01420 562506   http://www.anglo-turkish-society.co.uk
       Mem Sec: Mrs B A McKernan
▲   Company Limited by Guarantee; Registered Charity
○   *X; a social & cultural society
●   Lectures, social gatherings & outings
M   400 i, 2 f, UK / 10 i, o'seas

Anglo-Venezuelan Society   1976
NR   PO Box 930, ST ALBANS, Herts, AL1 9GE.   (mail/add)
       Sec: Valerie Lucien
▲   Un-incorporated Society
○   *X; to promote good relations between the UK & Venezuela
●   Conf - Mtgs - Lectures - Concerts - Annual dinner
M   90 i, 38 f, UK / 5 i, 1 f, o'seas

Animal Concern Ltd   1988
■   PO Box 5178, DUMBARTON, G82 5YJ.   (mail)
       01389 841639   fax 0870 706 0327
       email animals@jrobins.force9.co.uk
       http://www.animalconcern.org address
       Sec: John F Robins
▲   Company Limited by Guarantee
○   *K; for animal rights
●   ET - Inf - Lobbying
M   290 i, UK / 4 i, o'seas
¶   Animal Concern News - 2/3; free.

Animal Consultants & Trainers Association   (ACTA)   1989
NR   147 Coppermill Rd, WRAYSBURY, Middx, TW19 5NX.
       01753 683773
       http://www.acta4animals.com
       Sec: Jill Clark
○   *V; training & provision of animals for the film, television &
       advertising industries; provision of expert & professional
       advice; members must hold a valid licence under the
       Performing Animals (Regulation) Act 1925 & hold an
       adequate public liability insurance policy
M   30 i, 24 f, UK / 1 i, o'seas

Animal Health Distributors Association (UK) Ltd   (AHDA)   1985
NR   Gable Court, Parsons Hill, Hollesley, WOODBRIDGE, Suffolk,
       IP12 3RB.   (hq/sp)
       01394 410444
       Chief Exec: Dr Roger R Dawson
▲   Company Limited by Guarantee
○   *T; 'interests of distributors of animal health products -
       particularly those who distribute animal medicines to farmers
       (in order to try to prevent EU legislating members out of
       business)'
●   Conf - Mtgs - Exhib - LG
M   c 120 f
¶   NL - 12.   Animal Medicines Record Book.

Animal Medicines Training Regulatory Authority   (AMTRA)   1983
NR   8 Parsons Hill, Hollesley, WOODBRIDGE, Suffolk, IP12 3RB.
       (hsp)
       01394 411010
       Sec: Dr Roger R Dawson
▲   Company Limited by Guarantee
○   *N; independent regulatory body ensuring that the distribution
       of animal medicines in the UK is undertaken in a responsible
       manner by qualified persons
●   ET - Exam (for the staff of manufacturers) - LG - Register of
       those licensed to hold medicines & those qualified to
       distribute them
M   c 3,500 i
¶   AR;   Syllabus & examination course leaflet.

Animal & Plant Health Association   (APHA)
IRL   8 Woodbine Park, BLACKROCK, Co Dublin, Republic of
       Ireland.
       353 (1) 260 3050   fax 353 (1) 260 3021
       email info@apha.ie   http://www.apha.ie
       Dir: Brendan Barnes
○   *F, *T, *V; manufacturers & sole distributors of veterinary
       medicines & plant protection products/agrochemicals
M   c 30 f

Animal Transportation Association
       This organisation is closing its Redhill (Surrey) office & moving
       to Houston (Texas)

Animal Welfare Filming Federation   (AWFF)   1998
§   19 Greaves Rd, HIGH WYCOMBE, Bucks, HP13 7JU.   (hsp)
       0777 066 6088   fax 01494 441385
       email animalworld@bushinternet.com
       http://www.animalworld.org.uk
       Managing Dir: Carol Jones
       for those concerned with the welfare of animals used in film &
       TV

** Animal Welfare Science, Ethics & Law Veterinary Association
       Organisation lost: see Introduction paragraph 3

Anomalous Phenomena Research Agency   (APRA)
NR   c/o PO Box 135, DIDCOT, Oxon, OX11 9YA.
○   *G

Anorchidism Support Group   (ASG)
NR   PO Box 3025, ROMFORD, Essex, RM3 8GX.
       01708 372597
       email contact.asg@virgin.net
       Contact: Mrs Lorraine Bookless
○   *W; to support men & boys with anorchidism (congenital or
       acquired absence of the testes) & their families

Anthroposophical Medical Association   (AMA)
■   c/o St Luke's Medical Centre, 53 Cainscross Rd, STROUD,
     Glos, GL5 4EX.   (hq)
     01453 762151
     email medical.section@yahoo.co.uk
     Hon Sec: Dr Frank A Mulder
▲   Un-incorporated Society
○   *M; for doctors practising anthroposophical medicine in the UK
●   Conf - Mtgs - ET - Res - SG - Inf - LG
<   Intl Fedn of Anthroposophical Medical Assns (IVAA);
     Anthroposophical Health Professions Coun (AHPC)
M   60 i
¶   Anthroposophical Medical NL - 6;
     Worldwide NL - 6 (published in English in association with the
        medical section at the Goetheanum, Switzerland); both ftm.
     £30 yr for both publications, or £20 yr for 1, to nm.

Anthroposophical Society in Great Britain   (ASinGB)   1923
NR   Rudolf Steiner House, 35 Park Rd, LONDON, NW1 6XT.   (hq)
     020 7723 4400   fax 020 7724 4364
     Gen Sec: Nicholas C Thomas
▲   Registered Charity
Br   c 60 groups
○   *L; philosophy, art & education, based on the work of Rudolf
     Steiner - 'a union of human beings who desire to further the
     life of the soul, both in the individual & in society at large,
     based on a true knowledge of the spiritual world'
●   Conf - Res - Exhib - SG - Inf - Lib - 'Supports the many &
     varied activities developed on the basis of Rudolf Steiner's
     insights'
<   General Anthroposophical Soc (Switzerland)
¶   New View Magazine - 4.

Anti Common Market League   (ACML)   1961
■   28 Highdown, WORCESTER PARK, Surrey, KT4 7HZ.   (hsp)
     Mem Sec: Mrs J Phillips,   Chmn: Peter Dul
▲   Un-incorporated Society
○   *K; to campaign for British withdrawal from the European
     Union
●   Mtgs - Campaigning
<   Campaign for an Indep Britain (CIB); Anti Maastricht Alliance
     (AMA)
M   c 400 i, UK / c 50 i, o'seas
¶   Britain (NL) - 3/4; £10 yr.   Bound to Fail; £3.
     No Pound: No Independence by Brian Burkitt; £4.

Anti Copying in Design Ltd   (ACID)   1996
■   Adelaide House, London Bridge, LONDON, EC4R 9HA.   (hq)
     0845 644 3617   fax 0845 644 3618
     email help@acid.uk.com   http://www.acid.uk.com
     Chief Exec: Dids Macdonald
▲   a not-for-profit organisation
○   *K; for all designers & manufacturers; to fight copyright theft
Gp   Exhibitions & shows; Information service
●   Conf - Exhib - Inf

Anti Counterfeiting Group   (ACG)   1980
NR   PO Box 578, HIGH WYCOMBE, Bucks, HP11 1YD.   (hq)
     01494 449165   fax 01494 465052
     email admin@a-cg.com   http://www.a-cg.com
     Dir Gen: Ruth Orchard
▲   Company Limited by Guarantee
○   *T; to combat counterfeiting of branded products
Gp   Clothing & footwear; Watches; International; Public policy;
     Affiliates
●   Conf - Mtgs - ET - Res - Exhib - Comp - Stat - Inf - LG
<   Assn des Inds Marques (AIM); Alliance against Counterfeiting &
     Piracy (AACP)
M   130 f, UK / 44 f, o'seas
¶   NL - 5/6;   Enforcement Guides;
     Hbk;   AR - 1; all ftm only.

Anti-Graffiti Association
NR   Kemp House, 152-160 City Road, LONDON, EC1V 2NX.
     http://www.theaga.org.uk
○   *K, *T; 'to promote best practice in the management of graffiti,
     vandalism & related crime'

**Antiquarian Booksellers Association (International)   (ABA)
1906**
■   Sackville House, 40 Piccadilly, LONDON, W1J 0DR.   (hq)
     020 7439 3118   fax 020 7439 3119
     email admin@aba.org.uk   http://www.aba.org.uk
     Sec: John Critchley,   Pres: Robert Frew
▲   Company Limited by Guarantee (without a share capital)
○   *T; for dealers of rare books, manuscripts, maps, prints &
     ephemera in the British Isles
●   Lib - Books fairs - Benevolent fund
<   Intl League Antiquarian Booksellers
M   230 f, UK / 40 f, o'seas
¶   NL - 8;   AR - 1; both ftm only.
     LM (with geographical index & list of specialities); on request &
     on website.
     Book Fair Guide.

Antiquarian Horological Society   (AHS)   1953
NR   New House, High St, Ticehurst, WADHURST, E Sussex,
     TN5 7AL.   (hq)
     01580 200155
     Co Sec: Wendy Barr
▲   Registered Charity
○   *L; to foster & encourage the study of timepieces
Gp   Electrical horology; Turret clock
●   Conf - Mtgs - Res - Exhib - SG - Inf - Lib - VE
M   2,000 i, 100 f, 100 org
¶   Antiquarian Horology - 4.
     The Planetarium of Giovanni de Dondi by Baillie, Lloyd & Ward.
     Norfolk & Norwich Clocks & Clockmakers by Clifford &
     Yvonne Bird.
     Publications list available.

Antique Metalware Society   (AMS)   1991
■   PO Box 63, HONITON, Devon, EX14 1HP.   (mail/address)
     01404 42169   fax 01404 47623
     email amsmemsec@yahoo.co.uk
     http://www.basemetal.org
     Chmn: Anthony North
▲   Un-incorporated Society
○   *G; to study artifacts, mainly domestic, made of non-precious
     metals & their alloys, their manufacture & history
●   Mtgs - Res - VE
M   150 i, UK / 30 i, o'seas
¶   Jnl - 1;   Base Thoughts (NL) - 2; both ftm only
     Subscription £20 (single) £28 (joint).

Antiquities Dealers Association   (ADA)   1982
NR   Faustus Ancient Art & Jewellery, 41 Dover St, LONDON,
     W1S 4NS.   (hsb)
     020 7930 1864
     Sec: Mrs Susan Hadida
○   *T; for dealers, professionals & collectors of antiquities
Gp   Dealers; Collectors (associates)
●   ET - Exhib - Inf - LG - International fairs
<   Museums Association; Brit Art Market Fedn (BAMF)
M   61 i, UK / 38 i (dealers) o'seas, 35 i associates (collectors)
¶   LM.

AOHNP (UK)   (AOHNP)   1992

- ■ PO Box 11785, PETERHEAD, Aberdeenshire, AB42 5YG.
  (mail/address)
  0845 225 5937   fax 0845 255 5937
  email admin@aohnp.co.uk   http://www.aohnp.co.uk
  Admin: Linda Riseborough
- ▲ Un-incorporated Association
- ○ *P; to increase representation & raise the profile of
  occupational health nurses
- ● Conf - Mtgs - SG - LG (DoH, NMC) - Networking - Job
  introduction scheme
- M 350 i, UK / 6 i, o'seas
- ¶ OH Today (NL) - 6; ftm.
- × 2005-06 Association of Occupational Health Nurse
  Practitioners

Apostrophe Protection Society

- NR 23 Vauxhall Rd, BOSTON, Lincs, PE21 0JB.
  01205 350056
  http://www.apostrophe.fsnet.co.uk
  Founder: John Richards
- ○ *K; to preserve the correct usage of the apostrophe in written
  English

Applied Arts Scotland   (AAS)   1992

- ■ c/o Edinburgh College of Art, School of Design & Applied Arts,
  Hunter Building, Lauriston Place, EDINBURGH, EH3 9DF.
  (hq/pt-time)
  0131 221 6143
  email office@appliedartsscotland.org.uk
  Administrator: Clare Hillerby
- ▲ Registered Charity
- ○ *A; to support applied artists through providing business advice
  & services; to represent all crafts disciplines at every stage of
  development
- Gp Makers; Student makers; Organisations; Supporters (galleries &
  individuals)
- ● Conf - ET - Exhib - Comp - Expt - Inf
- M [not stated]
- ¶ The Bulletin - 12; £25 yr subscription.

Applied Vision Association
a group of the **College of Optometrists**

Approved Driving Instructors National Joint Council   (ADINJC)   1974

- NR 41 Edinburgh Rd, CAMBRIDGE, CB4 1QR.   (pres/p)
  Pres: Peter W Edwards
- ○ *N; a consortium of driving instructors associations representing
  the members in negotiations with official bodies likely to
  influence the sphere of their activities
- ● Conf - Mtgs - ET - SG - VE - LG
- M 6,500 i, 3 f
- ¶ Report of Annual Conference - 1; free.

Arab-British Chamber of Commerce   1975

- NR 43 Upper Grosvenor St, LONDON, W1K 2NJ.   (hq)
  020 7235 4363   fax 020 7245 6688
  Chief Exec & Sec-Gen: Dr Mohammad Smadi
- ○ *C; for trade & economic cooperation between the UK & Arab
  states
- M 400 i, UK / 22 countries o'seas

Arab Horse Society   1918

- NR Windsor House, Ramsbury, MARLBOROUGH, Wilts,
  SN8 2PE.   (hq)
  01672 521411   fax 01672 520880
  The Registrar
- ▲ Company Limited by Guarantee; Registered Charity
- Br 17 regional groups
- ○ *B, *S; breeding & importation of Arabian horses; encouraging
  the wider use of Arab blood in light horse breeding; welfare
  of horses; education of equestrian skills
- Gp C'ees: Stud Book; Registration activities; Marketing; Public
  relations
- ● Conf - Mtgs - ET - Comp - Lib - LG
- < Wld Arabian Horse Org (WAHO); Eur Conf of Arab Horse
  Orgs (ECAHO)
- M 3,013 i, UK / 171 i, o'seas
- ¶ Arab Horse Society News - 5.   NL - 3; ftm only.
  Ybk - 1 (December).
  Anglo Arab Stud Book.
  Directory of Pure Arabian Studs in GB & Ireland - 2 yrly.
  Arabian Type & Standard.   AR.

Arboricultural Association   (AA)   1964

- ■ Ampfield House, Ampfield, ROMSEY, Hants, SO51 9PA.   (hq)
  01794 368717   fax 01794 368978
  email admin@trees.org.uk   http://www.trees.org.uk
  Dir: Nick Eden
- ▲ Company Limited by Guarantee; Registered Charity
- Br 9
- ○ *H, *P; to promote excellence in tree care to government,
  professionals & society
- Gp Registered consultants; Approved contractors
- ● Conf - ET - Exhib - LG - Publishing information - Promotion of
  competent consultants & specialists
- M 1,600 i, 200 f, UK / 60 i, 25 f, o'seas
- ¶ Jnl - 4.   NL - 4.
  Directory of Approved Contractors; free.
  Directory of Registered Consultants; free.
  Guidance Note(s); all £12.50:
     1. Trees & Bats;
     3. Planting & Managing Amenity Woodlands;
     4. Amenity Valuation of Trees & Woodland;
  12 leaflets on maintenance of trees & hedges; £3 a set.
  publications list available.

ARCA Ltd - Asbestos Removal Contractors Association   (ARCA)   1980

- NR ARCA House, 237 Branston Rd, BURTON-upon-TRENT, Staffs,
  DE14 3BT.   (hq)
  01283 531126
  Chief Exec: Terry Jago
- ▲ Company Limited by Guarantee
- ○ *T; for licensed asbestos removal companies & UKAS
  accredited laboratories
- Gp Technical; Education
- ● ET - Inf - LG
- M c 200 f
- ¶ ARCA News - 4.

Archaeology Abroad   1972

- ■ 31-34 Gordon Sq, LONDON, WC1H 0PY.   (mail/address)
  020 8537 0849
  email arch.abroad@ucl.ac.uk   http://www.britarch.ac.uk/
  archabroad
  Hon Sec & Editor: Wendy Rix Morton
- ▲ Un-incorporated Society
- ○ *G; to list opportunities for volunteers & staff to work on
  archaeological excavations outside the UK
- ● Inf
- M 427 i, 90 f, UK / 100 i, 10 f, o'seas
- ¶ Archaeology Abroad - 2; £20-£24 i, £30-£34 instns.
  Factsheets; free for large sae, (general guidance & information
  for those interested in fieldwork in countries from which few
  entries are received).

Archaeology Cymru (AC) 1988
NR Dinas House, Wick Rd, Ewenny, BRIDGEND, Glam, CF35 5BL.
01656 766106
○ *L; 'to advance education in archaeology throughout the whole of Wales'
● Conf - Mtgs - ET - Res - Exhib - SG - Inf - VE
M c 200 i & org
¶ Jnl - 4; ftm, £3 nm.   Occasional reports.

Architectural & Archaeological Society for the County of Buckinghamshire 1847
■ County Museum, Church St, AYLESBURY, Bucks, HP20 2QP. (hq)
01296 678114 (Wed: 1000-1600 only)
Hon Sec: Maureen Brown
▲ Registered Charity
○ *L
Gp Natural history section
● Mtgs - Res - Lib - VE
< Coun Brit Archaeol
M 500 i, 14 org, UK / 6 i, o'seas
¶ Records of Buckinghamshire - 1; ftm, £16 nm.
NL - 2; ftm.

Architectural & Archaeological Society of Durham & Northumberland (AASDN) 1862
NR Broom Cottage, 29 Foundry Fields, CROOK, Co Durham, DL15 9JY. (hsp)
01388 762620
email belindaburke@aol.com
http://www.communigate.co.uk/ne/aasdn
Hon Sec: Belinda Burke
▲ Registered Charity
○ *L; to stimulate interest in all aspects of the archaeology & architecture of North East England
● Mtgs - VE
M 190 i
¶ Durham Archaeological Jnl - 1.

Architectural Association (Inc) (AA)
NR 34-36 Bedford Sq, LONDON, WC1B 3EG.
020 7887 4000
○ *P

Architectural Cladding Association
a product association of the **British Precast Concrete Federation**

Architectural Heritage Society of Scotland (AHSS) 1956
■ 33 Barony St, EDINBURGH, EH3 6NX. (hq)
0131-557 0019   fax 0131-557 0049
email headoffice@ahss.org.uk   http://www.ahss.org.uk
Dir: [vacant]
▲ Registered Charity
Br 7
○ *A, *G, *L; to promote the study, protection & conservation of Scotland's built heritage
● Conf - Mtgs - Inf - VE - LG - Representations on applications for listed building consent
< Soc Protection Ancient Bldgs; Georgian Gp; Victorian Soc; Nat Trust for Scotland; Scot Civic Trust; Twentieth Century Soc
M 1,400 i, 50 f, 40 org, UK / 10 i, o'seas
¶ Architectural Heritage Jnl - 1.
Magazine - 2.

Architectural & Specialist Door Manufacturers Association (ASDMA) 1989
■ 3 Coates Lane, HIGH WYCOMBE, Bucks, HP13 5EY.
01494 447370   fax 01494 462094
email info@asdma.com   http://www.asdma.com
(hsb)
Sec: Mrs L A Parry
○ *T; for specialists in timber doors & doorsets; to promote quality assured doors which meet all British & European standards of fire resistance & safety
Gp Full membership open to manufacturers, fabricators & suppliers of doorsets;
Associate membership open to companies providing associated components & services;
Sponsor membership open to providers of relevant testing &/or certification services
● Mtgs - Inf - LG
M 15 f (full), 11 f (associate), 1 sponsor
¶ The Facts on the Performance of Timber Doors & Doorsets.
LM - 2;   Leaflet on ASDMA - 1; both free.
Best Practice Guide to Timber Fire Doors (free download from website).

Architecture & Surveying Institute
in 2002 became a specialist group of the **Chartered Institute of Building**

Aristotelian Society 1870
NR Stewart House (room 281), Russell Square, LONDON, WC1E 6BT. (execsec/b)
020 7862 8685
email mail@aristoteliansociety.org.uk
http://www.aristoteliansociety.org.uk
Exec Sec: Rachel Carter
▲ Registered Charity
○ *L; to advance systematic study of philosophy
● Conf - Mtgs - Res
< Brit Philosophical Assn
M 500 i, UK / 150 i, o'seas
¶ Proceedings - 3 pts a yr (or 1 vol bound).
Supplementary volume - 1.
Various books.

Arkwright Society 1971
NR Cromford Mill, Mill Lane, CROMFORD, Derbys, DE4 3RQ. (hq)
01629 823256
Chmn: Bob Faithorn,   Sec: Dr Christopher Charlton
▲ Company Limited by Guarantee; Registered Charity
○ *L; the restoration of Sir Richard Arkwright's Cromford Mill; to preserve & promote conservation of buildings, monuments & machinery of industrial archaeological & historical interest
● Conf - Mtgs - ET - Res - Exhib - Inf - VE
< Regeneration through Heritage; Nat Coun Civic Trust Socs
M 250 i, 2 f
¶ NL - 4.   Cromford Venture Centre - 1.
Lecture Programmes - 2.   AR & Accounts - 1.
Cromford Venture Centre Prospectus - 1.

ARLIS UK & Ireland (the Art Libraries Society) (ARLIS) 1969
NR c/o Courtauld Institute of Art, Somerset House, The Strand, LONDON, WC2R 0RN.
http://www.arlis.org.uk
The Administrator
▲ Registered Charity
○ *A, *L; to promote art librarianship
● Conf - Mtgs - ET - SG - Stat - VE
< Library Assn; IFLA section of art libraries
M 100 i, 200 f, UK / 10 i, 80 f, o'seas
¶ Art Libraries Jnl - 4.   News-sheet - 6.
Directory - 1.

Armagh Field Naturalists Society
since 15 January 2003 **County Armagh Wildlife Society**

Arms & Armour Society   1950
NR   PO Box 10232, LONDON, SW19 2ZD.   (hsb)
       01323 844278
       Hon Sec: Anthony Dove
○   *L, *Q; the study of arms & armour from the earliest times to
       the present day; to conserve specimens of arms & armour for
       the future
●   Mtgs - Res - Inf - VE
M   i, f & org
¶   Jnl - 2 (Mar & Sep).   NL - 4.

Army Cadet Force Association   (ACFA)   1930
■   Holderness House, 51-61 Clifton St, LONDON, EC2A 4OW.
       (hq)
       020 7426 8377   fax 020 7426 8378
       email acfa@armycadets.com
       http://www.armycadets.com
       Gen Sec: Brig M Wharmby
▲   Company Limited by Guarantee; Registered Charity
Br   1,754
○   *Y; a voluntary youth organisation for 12-18 year old young
       men & women; to provide a challenging & stimulating
       environment & develop self respect & confidence through
       citizenship & service
●   Conf - Mtgs - ET - Exhib - Comp - Inf - LG
<   St John Ambulance; Heartstart; Duke of Edinburgh Award
>   Nat Coun Voluntary Youth Orgs
M   50,000 i, 80 f, 20 orgs
¶   Jnl - 4; ftm, £20 nm.   AR - 1; ftm only.

Army Parachute Association   (APA)   1963
NR   Airfield Camp, Netheravon, SALISBURY, Wilts, SP4 9SF.   (hq)
Br   Cyprus, Germany
○   *S; to run courses of basic sports parachuting for members of
       all three services
Gp   AFF (Accelerated Free Fall to gain competency in a quicker
       time); Tandem (the method of introducing non parachutists to
       sky diving with the minimum of instruction - approximately 3/
       4 hour)
●   ET - Res - Comp
<   Brit Parachute Assn

Army Records Society   1983
NR   c/o National Army Museum, Royal Hospital Rd, LONDON,
       SW3 4HT.   (mail/address)
       email ars@hall-mccartney.co.uk
       http://www.armyrecordssociety.org.uk
       Hon Sec: Dr William Philpott
▲   Registered Charity
○   *L; publication of original records concerning the history of the
       British Army
●   Res - Annual lecture
M   350 i, 30 org UK / 100 i, 30 org, o'seas
¶   Annual Volume - 1; ftm only.

Arnold Bennett Society   1955
■   4 Field End Close, Trentham, STOKE-on-TRENT, Staffs,
       ST4 8DA.   (hsp)
       01782 641337
       http://www.arnoldbennettsociety.org.uk
       Hon Sec: Carol Gorton
▲   Un-incorporated Society
○   *A; to promote the study & appreciation of the life, works &
       times of Arnold Bennett (1867-1931) & other provincial
       writers with particular reference to North Staffordshire
●   Mtgs
<   Alliance of Literary Societies
M   250 i, UK / 25 i, o'seas
¶   NL - 3; ftm, £1 nm.

Aromatherapy & Allied Practitioners Association
NR   PO Box 36248, LONDON, SE19 3YD.
       020 8653 9152   fax 020 8653 9152
       http://www.aromatherapyuk.net
○   *P

Aromatherapy Trade Council   (ATC)   1992
■   PO Box 387, IPSWICH, Suffolk, IP2 9AN.   (hq)
       01473 603630   fax 01473 603630
       email info@a-t-c.org.uk   http://www.a-t-c.org.uk
       Sec: Alan Harris,   Chmn: Geoff Lyth
▲   Company Limited by Guarantee
○   *T; to act as the authoritative body for the specialist
       aromatherapy essential oil industry & as the advertising code
       administrator for the appointed by the Medicines &
       Healthcare Products Regulatory Agency (Dept of Health); to
       offer advice on the responsible marketing of aromatherapy
●   Conf - Mtgs - Exhib - Expt - Inf - LG
<   Eur Fedn of Essential Oils (EFEO); Parliamentary Gp for
       Alternative & Complementary Medicine; Prince of Wales's
       Foundation for Integrated Health (FIH); Suffolk Cham Comm
M   56 f
¶   Guidelines on the Regulation, Labelling, Advertising &
       Promotion of Aromatherapy Products.
       General Information Booklet.   LM.

Arrhythmia Alliance   (A-A)
NR   PO Box 3697, STRATFORD upon AVON, Warks, CV37 8YL.
       01789 450787
       http://www.arrhythmiaalliance.org.uk
       Co-ordinator: Sarah Jacob

Art & Architecture   (A&A)   1972
NR   70 Cowcross St, LONDON, EC1M 6EJ.   (mail/address)
       Chmn: Graham Cooper
▲   Un-incorporated Society
○   *A, *K; promotes collaboration between artists, crafts people &
       architects in the interests of a better environment; campaigns
       for the Percent for Art scheme & for the employment of art &
       artists in architecture & construction; acts as a network for all
       concerned with public art
Gp   Public Art Forum
●   Conf - Mtgs - Res - Inf
M   500 i, 50 f, 50 org, UK / 50 i, o'seas
¶   Art & Architecture Jnl - 2.
       Art & Architecture NL - 2.

The Art Fund
       see the **National Art Collections Fund (The Art Fund)**

Art Libraries Society
       see **ARLIS UK & Ireland (the Art Libraries Society)**

Art Metalware Manufacturers' Association   (AMMA)   1965
■   10 Vyse St, BIRMINGHAM, B18 6LT.   (hq)
       0121-237 1149
○   *T
●   Mtgs - Inf
<   Brit Jewellery, Giftware & Finishing Fedn
M   6 f

Art Workers Guild   (AWG)   1884
NR   6 Queen Sq, LONDON, WC1N 3AT.   (hq)
       020 7713 0966
       Sec: Monica Grose-Hodge
○   *A; to advance education in all visual arts & crafts & to foster
       high standards of design & craftsmanship

Arthritic Association   (AA)   1942

■ 1 Upperton Gardens, EASTBOURNE, E Sussex, BN21 2AA.
01323 416550   fax 01323 639793
email info@arthriticassociation.org.uk
http://www.arthriticassociation.org.uk
Mgr: Bruce Hester

▲ Company Limited by Guarantee; Registered Charity
○ *M; to relieve symptoms of arthritis by natural methods
● Res - Inf
M 3,900 i, UK / 100 i, o'seas
¶ Rheumatic Review - Jnl.   Treating Arthritis Naturally.
A Balanced View: Practical Tips for a Healthy Diet.
Recipes Compiled for the Arthritic Association.
[subscription £6].

Arthritis Care   1947

■ 18 Stephenson Way, LONDON, NW1 2HD.   (hq)
020 7380 6500   fax 020 7380 6505
email helplines@arthritiscare.org.uk
http://www.arthritiscare.org.uk
Chief Exec: Neil Betteridge

▲ Company Limited by Guarantee; Registered Charity
Br 6
○ *W; a national voluntary organisation working with & for
people with arthritis
● ET - Publishing - Campaigning
Helplines: 020 7380 6555 (weekdays 1000-1600) &
Freephone 0808 800 4050 (weekdays 1200-1600)
M i
¶ Arthritis News - 6;   Information & advisory leaflets.
Publications list available.

Arthritis & Musculoskeletal Alliance   (ARMA)   1972

NR Bride House, 18-20 Bride Lane, LONDON, EC4Y 8EE.   (hq)
020 7842 0910   fax 020 7842 0901
Chief Exec: Sophie Edwards

▲ Registered Charity
○ *N; an umbrella organisation of professional & user groups
working together to ensure high quality services are
maintained for people with arthritis
● Mtgs
< EULAR; LMCA
M 23 org
✕ 2002 (May) British League against Rheumatism

**Arthritis & Rheumatism Natural Therapy Research Association
(ARNTRA)   1996**

■ Cracoe House Cottage, Cracoe, SKIPTON, N Yorks,
BD23 6LB.   (dir/p)
01756 730240   fax 01756 730240
Chief Exec: Dr Rex E Newnham

▲ Un-incorporated Society
○ *W; to research all natural methods for helping those with
arthritis & osteoporosis & to establish these methods so as to
help those who suffer
● Res - Inf
< Arthritis Assn of America
M 200 i, UK / 30 i, o'seas
¶ ARNTRA NL - 4; £15.   Here's Health; £12.
Beating Arthritis & Beating Osteoporosis; £6.
Note: is also called the Arthritis, Rheumatism & Osteoporosis
Natural Therapy Research Association

Arthrogryposis Group   (TAG)   1984

■ Beak Cottage, Dunley, STOURPORT-ON-SEVERN, Worcs,
DY13 0TZ.   (hq)
01299 825781
Chmn: Peter Lacey

▲ Registered Charity
○ *W; to offer support, contact & information for the families,
children & adults affected with arthrogryposis, & those
involved in their care
● Conf - Mtgs - Res - Inf - VE - Activity camps for young people
aged 10-15
M 800 i, 12 org, UK / 40 i, o'seas
¶ Tag Talk - 4; ftm.

Arthur Ransome Society Ltd   (TARS)   1990

NR Abbot Hall, Kirkland, KENDAL, Cumbria, LA9 5AL.
(regd/office)
01539 722464
▲ Company Limited by Guarantee
Br 5; Australia, Canada, Japan, New Zealand, USA
○ *A; to promote the works of Arthur Ransome (1884-1967) &
support research into his life & writings; to encourage
children in the reading of his books & to participate in
outdoor activities
● Conf - Mtgs - Res - Lib - VE
< Alliance of Literary Socs
M c 2,000 i, UK / c 500 i, o'seas
¶ Mixed Moss (Jnl) - 1;   Outlaw (junior magazine) - 2;
Signals (NL) - 3;   all ftm only.

**Artificial Insemination of Equines Trade Association   (AITA)
2006**

NR c/o Twemlows Hall, WHITCHURCH, Shropshire, SY13 2EZ.
01948 663239
○ *T; for all with an interest in equine AI

Arts & Business   1976

■ Nutmeg House, 60 Gainsford St, LONDON, SE1 2NY.   (hq)
020 7378 8143
http://www.aandb.org.uk
▲ Company Limited by Guarantee; Registered Charity
Br 13
○ *A, *T; to promote & encourage partnership between business
& the arts
Gp Development forum
● Conf - Mtgs - ET - Res - Stat - Inf - Lib - LG
< Coun for Business & the Arts in Canada; CEREC; Foundation
for Business in Support of the Arts (Hong Kong); Assn for
Corporate Support of the Arts (Japan)
M c 350 f, 700 org
¶ Re-creating Communities: business, the arts & regeneration.
AR (incl LM) - 1.

Arts Centre Group Ltd
see **ACG Ltd (Arts Centre Group)**

Arts Marketing Association   (AMA)   1993

NR 7A Clifton Court, CAMBRIDGE, CB1 7BN.   (hq)
01223 578078
Dir: Julie Aldridge
▲ Company Limited by Guarantee
○ *P; for those who have, or hope to have, a career in arts
marketing
Gp Freelancers
● Conf - Mtgs - ET - SG - Inf - Publications
M c 1,800 i
¶ Jnl of Arts Marketing - 4.   Ybk.   Books.

© CBD Research Ltd · Beckenham · BR3 5JS · Tel 020 8650 7745 · Fax 020 8650 0768 · E-mail cbd@cbdresearch.com · www.cbdresearch.com

ArtWatch UK
NR 15 Capel Rd, EAST BARNET, Herts, EN4 8JD.
020 8216 3492
Dir: Michael Daley
○ *A, *K; to preserve the integrity of works of art
M c 150 i
¶ NL - 4.

ASBCI - The Forum for Clothing & Textiles   (ASBCI)   1974
■ Unit 5, 25 Square Rd, HALIFAX, W Yorks, HX11 1QG.   (hq)
01422 354666   fax 01422 381184
email info@asbci.co.uk   http://www.asbci.co.uk
Nat Exec: Stephanie Ingham,
Vice-Chmn: Malcolm Ball, Diane Waterhouse
▲ Company Limited by Guarantee
○ *T; 'a recognised centre of excellence where companies at the
forefront of their specific sectors can discuss, share & develop
practices, processes & initiatives that will benefit their
organisations & the UK clothes & textile supply chain as a
whole'
Gp C'ees: Ball, Conference, Marketing, Student membership,
Technical
● Conf - Mtgs - ET - Comp - Inf - VG
< Soc of Dyers & Colourists (SDC); Textile Inst
> Soc of Dyers & Colourists; Textile Inst
M 10 i, 100+ f, UK / 2 f, o'seas
¶ Technical booklets available - details on website; £10 m,
£15 nm.
Conference Proceedings booklets; £30.
× 2005 Association of Suppliers to the British Clothing Industry

Asbestos Removal Contractors Association
see **ARCA Ltd - Asbestos Removal Contractors Association**

Ashford (Kent) Chamber of Commerce, Industry & Enterprise
since 2005 **Kent Invicta Chamber of Commerce**

**Ashmolean Natural History Society of Oxfordshire   (ANHSO)
1828**
NR 89 Merewood Avenue, Sandhills, OXFORD, OX3 8EQ.   (hsp)
01865 762951
Hon Sec: Linda Baldock
▲ Un-incorporated Society
○ *L; natural science
Gp Rare plants; Verges
● Mtgs - Comp - Lib - VE - Survey of rare plants
M 100 i
¶ Fritillary (Jnl) - 4; (produced in conjunction with the Berks,
Bucks & Oxon Naturalists' Trust).

**Aslib: The Association for Information Management   (aslib)
1924**
NR Holywell Centre, 1 Phipp St, LONDON, EC2A 4PS.   (hq)
020 7613 3031   fax 020 7613 5080
email aslib@aslib.com   http://www.aslib.com
Chief Exec: Roger N Bowes
▲ Registered Charity
○ *L, *P, *Q; to promote better management & provision of
information in information centres & libraries
Gp Information management; Knowledge management;
Librarianship
● ET - Res - Inf - Lib
< FID
M c 2,000 i, f & org
¶ Publications list available.

Asparagus Growers' Association   (AGA)
■ 133 Eastgate, LOUTH, Lincs, LN11 9QG.   (asa)
01507 602427   fax 01507 607165
email crop.association@pvga.co.uk
http://www.british-asparagus.co.uk
Sec: Mrs Jayne Dyas
○ *T; to provide technical, commercial & marketing information
for growers
● Conf - Mtgs - Res - Exhib - Stat - Inf - LG
M 120 f

Asphalt Industry Alliance   2000
NR 14a Eccleston St, LONDON, SW1W 9LT.   (hq)
020 7730 1100   fax 020 7730 2213
email asphalt@hmpr.co.uk
http://www.asphaltindustryalliance.com
▲ Un-incorporated Society
○ *T; to promote adequate funding of road maintenance
● Conf - Mtgs - Res - Stat - Inf - LG
M 2 org:
Quarry Products Association
Refined Bitumen Association
¶ Asphalt Now - 2;
Annual Local Authority Road Maintenance Survey - 1; both free.

Associated Chiropodists & Podiatrists Union   (ACPU)   1961
■ Anglesey House (Suite 21), Anglesey Rd, BURTON-on-TRENT,
Derbys, DE14 3NT.   (hq)
01283 741174
email admin@acpu.org.uk   http://www.acpu.org.uk
Gen Sec: David Elliott
Br 5
○ *P, *U
Gp Podiatrists
● Conf
M 415 i, UK / 20 i, o'seas
¶ ACPU Jnl - 4; ftm, £20 yr nm.
× 2002-03 Association of Chiropodists & Podiatrists

**Associated National Electrical Wholesalers Ltd   (ANEW Ltd)
1993**
■ Titmore Court (suite 3), Titmore Green, HITCHIN, Herts,
SG4 7JT.   (hq)
01438 750075
Chief Exec: Neal Wilcox
▲ Company Limited by Guarantee
○ *T; an alliance of electrical wholesalers
● Mtgs
< FEGIME Ltd
M 37 f
¶ LM - irreg; ftm only.

Associated Stress Consultants
A non-membership body which changed its name to BSY Ltd (a
distance learning college for alternative health &
complementary therapy) & as such is outside the scope of this
directory

Associated Train Crew Union   (ATCU)   2005
NR c/o 34 Lion Meadow, STEEPLE BUMPSTEAD, Essex, CB9 7BY.
0870 609 2229
email admin@atcu.org.uk   http://www.atcu.org.uk
Chmn of Formation C'ee: Steven Trumm
▲ Un-incorporated Society
Br 9
○ *U
Gp Crew section; Driver section
● Representation - Legal cover
M 50 i

Association for Accountancy & Business Affairs   (AABA)
NR PO Box 5874, Basildon, Essex, SS16 5FR.
○ *P

Association of Accounting Technicians   (AAT)   1980
NR   154 Clerkenwell Rd, LONDON, EC1R 5AD.
     020 7837 8600
     Chief Exec: Miss Jane Scott Paul
▲   Registered Charity
○   *E, *P; a vocational training body awarding NVs/SVQs levels 2,
     3 & 4 in accounting
●   Conf - ET - Exhib
M   22,000 i, UK / 3,000 i, o'seas
¶   Accounting Technicians Jnl - 12.   AR.

Association of Advertisers in Ireland Ltd   (AAI)   1951
IRL   Rock House, Main St, BLACKROCK, Co Dublin, Republic of
     Ireland.
     353 (1) 278 0499   fax 353 (1) 278 0488
     email info@aai.ie   http://www.aai.ie
     Hon Sec: Catherine Bent
○   *T

Association of Agricultural & Horticultural Colleges
IRL   Salesian Agricultural College, PALLASKENRY, Co Limerick,
     Republic of Ireland.
     353 (61) 393100   fax 353 (61) 393005
     Pres: Mike Pearson,   Sec: John McCarthy
○   *F

Association of Air Ambulance Charities   (AAAC)
NR   Unit 14, Wheelbarrow Park Estate, Pattenden Lane, MARDEN,
     Kent, TN12 9QJ.   (chmn/b)
     01622 833833
     Chmn: D Philpott
○   *N

Association of Airline Consolidators
     since 2002-3 **Association of ATOL Companies**

**Association of Alabaster Importers & Wholesalers   (AAI)
1977**
■   423 Upper Elmers End Rd, BECKENHAM, Kent, BR3 4DA.
     (hsp)
○   *T; interests of importers of unworked alabaster & articles made
     of alabaster
●   Mtgs - Inf - Lib - Stat - VE
M   4 f

Association of American Dancing   (AAD)   1936
■   Aspenshaw Hall, THORNSETT, High Peak, Derbys,
     SK22 1AU.   (hq)
     01663 744986
     Dir: Miss Anna Scott
▲   Un-incorporated Society
○   *D; an examining body promoting all forms of dance
     movement amongst professionals, teachers & the public
Gp   Modern art group (for younger people)
●   ET - Exam - Inf - Scholarships & awards
<   Coun for Dance Educ & Training
M   i (through examination qualification)
¶   Text books covering the five disciplines of dance within the
     syllabus.

**Association of Anaesthetists of Great Britain & Ireland
(AAGBI)   1932**
NR   21 Portland Place, LONDON, W1B 1PY.   (hq)
     020 7631 1650
▲   Company Limited by Guarantee
○   *L, *Q; to promote & support the speciality of anaesthesia
●   Conf - ET - Exhib - Inf - Lib - Seminars
<   R Coll Anaesthetists
M   c 5,200 i
¶   Publications list available.

Association of Applied Biologists   (AAB)   1904
■   Warwick HRI, Wellesbourne, WARWICK, CV35 9EF.   (hq)
     01789 472020   fax 01789 470234
     email carol.aab@warwick.ac.uk
     http://www.aab.org.uk
     Hon Gen Sec: A J Keys
▲   Registered Charity
○   *L, *Q; 'to promote the study & advancement of all branches of
     biology & in particular (but without prejudice to the generality
     of the foregoing) to foster the practice, growth &
     development of applied biology, incl the application of
     biological sciences for the production & preservation of food,
     fibre & other materials for the maintenance & improvement
     of the environment'
Gp   Applied micrology & bacteriology; Biological control;
     Entomology; Nematology; Pesticide application; Plant
     physiology & crop improvement; Post harvest biology;
     Virology; Weeds & agronomy
●   Conf - Mtgs - ET - Publication of scientific research
<   Assn of Learned & Profl Soc Publishers; Inst Biology
M   800 i, UK / 100 i, o'seas
¶   Annals of Applied Biology (Jnl) - 6.   NL - 3; ftm only.
     Tests of Agrochemicals & Cultivars - 1.
     Aspects of Applied Biology (proceedings of conferences) - irreg.
     Descriptions of Plant Viruses (CD-ROM) - irreg.

**Association of Archaeological Illustrators & Surveyors
(AAI&S)   1978**
■   c/o SHES, University of Reading, Whiteknights, PO Box 227,
     READING, Berks, RG6 6AB.   (mail/address)
     email info@aais.org.uk   http://www.aais.org.uk
     Hon Sec: Lesley Collett
○   *P; to set standards & promote best practice within the
     profession
●   Conf - Production of special technical reports on special
     material or technique
M   c 254 i, UK & o'seas
¶   Graphic Archaeology (Jnl) - 2.   AAI&S NL - 4.
     Technical Papers (1-13) - irreg.

Association of Art & Antique Dealers Ltd   (LAPADA)   1974
NR   535 Kings Rd, LONDON, SW10 0SZ.   (hq)
     020 7823 3511   fax 020 7823 3522
     email lapada@lapada.co.uk   http://www.lapada.co.uk
     Chief Exec: John Newgas
▲   Company Limited by Guarantee
○   *T; for professional art & antiques dealers
Gp   Antiques dealers; Art dealers; Specialist shippers; Art &
     antiques valuers & restorers
●   Conf - Stat - Expt - Inf - LG - Fairs
<   Confédn Intle des Négociants en Oeuvres d'Art (CINOA); other
     local associations
M   700 f, UK / 25 f, o'seas
¶   LAPADA Views (NL) - 2; ftm.   LM - 1; free.

Association of Art Historians   (AAH)   1974
■   70 Cowcross St, LONDON, EC1M 6EJ.   (hq)
     020 7490 3211   fax 020 7490 3277
     email admin@aah.org.uk   http://www.aah.org.uk
     Chmn: Colin Cruise
▲   Registered Charity
○   *P; to promote the study of art history & visual culture; to ensure
     a wider public recognition of the field. The national
     organisation for professional art historians & researchers
     (incuding academics, teachers, students & museum & gallery
     professionals)
Gp   Students; Museum & gallery professionals; University & college
     academics; School teachers; Independent freelance art
     historians
●   Conf - Mtgs - Res - Comp - VE - Empl - LG
<   Comité Intl d'Histoire de l'Art (CIHA); College Art Assn
     (CAA)(USA); Intl Assn of Art Critics (AICA)
M   c 1,200 i
¶   Art History (Jnl) - 5;   The Art Book (Jnl) - 4;
     Bulletin (NL) - 3; details on application.

© CBD Research Ltd · Beckenham · BR3 5JS · Tel 020 8650 7745 · Fax 020 8650 0768 · E-mail cbd@cbdresearch.com · www.cbdresearch.com

Association of Arts Fundraisers
NR   4 St Stephen's Rd, CHELTENHAM, Glos, GL51 3AA.
      01242 539579
      Admin: Hilary Jennings
○   *P

Association for Astronomy Education   (AAE)   1980
■   c/o Royal Astronomical Society, Burlington House, Piccadilly,
      LONDON, W1J 0BQ.   (mail/address)
      http://www.aae.org.uk
      Sec: Dr Anne Urquhart-Potts
▲   Registered Charity
○   *E; to promote & advance public education in the science of
      astronomy; to support the teaching of astronomy at all levels
      of education
●   Conf - Mtgs - ET
M   i & org
¶   Gnomon (NL) - 4; ftm.

Association of ATOL Companies   (AAC)   1995
NR   Beaumont House (1st floor), Lambton Rd, LONDON,
      SW20 0LW.   (secretariat)
      020 8288 1430   fax 020 8944 2993
      email secretariat@aac-uk.org   http://www.aac-uk.org
○   *T
●   Mtgs - LG
M   65 f
✕   2002-3 Association of Airline Consolidators

Association of Authorised Public Accountants Ltd   (AAPA)   1978
NR   10-11 Lincoln's Inn Fields, LONDON, WC2A 3BP.   (hq)
      020 7059 5921
      Contact: Tony Carlisle
▲   Company Limited by Guarantee
○   *P; 'a recognised Supervisory Body under the provisions of the
      Companies Act 1989.   No student membership or
      examinations are held as all members must already be fully
      qualified under the provisions of the Companies Act 1985
      section 389(1)(b) or section 389(2)'
●   Conf - LG
<   is part of the Association of Chartered Certified Accountants
M   c 600 f, UK / 200 f, o'seas
¶   Accounting Business (Jnl) - 10.   NL   LM.   AR.

Association of Authors' Agents   (AAA)   1974
■   c/o Johnson & Alcock Ltd, Clerkenwell House, 45-
      47 Clerkenwell Green, LONDON, EC1R 0HT.   (hsb)
      020 7251 0125
      email aaa@johnsonandalcock.co.uk
      http://www.agentsassoc.co.uk
      Sec: Anna Power,   Pres: Clare Alexander
▲   Un-incorporated Society
○   *T; to act as a forum for authors' agents
●   Mtgs
<   Amer Authors' Representatives (AAR)
M   80 f

Association of Auto Theft Investigators
      see **International Association of Auto Theft Investigators (UK
      branch)**

Association of Average Adjusters   (AAA)   1869
■   c/o The Baltic Exchange, St Mary Axe, LONDON, EC3A 8BH.
      (sb)
      020 7623 5501   fax 020 7369 1623
      email AAA@balticexchange.com
      http://www.Average-Adjusters.com
      Chmn: Nigel Rogers
▲   Un-incorporated Society
○   *P
●   ET - Exam
M   450 i
¶   AR; ftm.

Association of Bakery Ingredient Manufacturers   (ABIM)   1917
■   4a Torphichen St, EDINBURGH, EH3 8JQ.   (hq)
      0131-229 9415   fax 0131-229 9407
      email steven.birrell@sfdf.org.uk
      http://www.abim.org.uk
      Exec Sec: Steven Birrell
▲   Company Limited by Guarantee
○   *T; interests of manufacturers & suppliers of ingredients to the
      bakery trade
●   Mtgs - Inf
<   FEDIMA (EEC Assn of Suppliers of Raw Materials to the Baking
      Ind); Food & Drink Fedn; UK Baking Ind Consultative C'ee
      (UKBICC)
M   23 f

Association of Basic Science Teachers in Dentistry   (ABSTD)   1978
NR   c/o Genes & Proteins Lab, Institute of Comparative Medical
      Sciences, Level 5, University of Glasgow, Garscube Estate,
      GLASGOW, G61 1QH.   (hsb)
      0141 330 2539   fax 0141-330 2483
      email j.beeley@dental.gla.ac.uk
      http://www.leeds.ac.uk/dental/abstd.html
      Hon Sec: Dr Josie A Beeley
▲   Registered Charity
○   *E, *P; university lecturers concerned with education in dentistry
●   Conf - Mtgs
M   110 i
¶   NL - 2/3; free.

Association of Beekeeping Appliance Manufacturers   1960
NR   E H Thorne Ltd, Beehive Works, WRAGBY, Lincs, LN8 5LA.
      (hsb)
      01673 858555   fax 01673 857004
      Sec: Paul Smith
○   *T; to represent the trade at exhibitions, shows & in meetings
      with Defra & BBKA
●   Inf - LG
M   3 f

Association of Biomedical Andrologists   (ABA)
NR   Fertility Unit, Queen's Medical Centre, NOTTINGHAM,
      NG7 2UH.
      0114-226 8290
      http://www.aba.uk.net
○   *P

Association of Blind Piano Tuners   (ABPT)   1953
NR   31 Wyre Crescent, Lynwood, DARWEN, Lancs, BB3 0JG.   (hsp)
      01254 776148   fax 01254 773158
      email abpt@uk-piano.org   http://www.uk-piano.org/
      abpt
      Sec: Barrie Heaton
▲   Registered Charity
Br   4; 9 o'seas
○   *P; to give all possible assistance to blind piano tuners in
      carrying out their work
●   Conf - ET
M   80 i
¶   ABPT NL - 4 (on cassette).

Association of Block Paving Contractors
      see Interlay, the Association of Block Paving Contractors a product
      association of the **British Precast Concrete Federation**

Association for Boarding School Survivors
NR   145 Islingwood Rd, BRIGHTON, E Sussex, BN2 9SH.
      07791 045319
      http://www.abss.org.uk
○   *W

Association of Boat Safety Examiners   (ABSE)
- ■ 23 Keswick Drive, FRODSHAM, Cheshire, WA6 7LT.   (chmn/p)
  01928 732444   fax 01928 732444
  Chmn: Brian Hayes
- ▲ Un-incorporated Society
- ○ *P
- ● Mtgs - Inf - Lib
- M 132 i
- ¶ The Examiner - 4; ftm only.

Association of Bonded Sailing Companies
in September 2005 merged with the National Federation of Sea Schools & the Yacht Charter Association to form the **Marine Leisure Association**

Association of Bottled Beer Collectors
since 2003 **Association for British Brewery Collectables**

Association of Breast Surgery at BASO
a specialist group of **BASO ~ the Association for Cancer Surgery**

Association of Breastfeeding Mothers   (ABM)   1980
- ■ PO Box 207, BRIDGWATER, Somerset, TA6 7YT.   (mail/add)
  0870 401 7711
  email info@abm.me.uk   http://www.abm.me.uk
- ▲ Registered Charity
- ○ *W; to provide education in the techniques & benefits of breastfeeding; to train breastfeeding counsellors
- ● Conf - ET - Inf
- M 450 i, UK / 50 i, o'seas
- ¶ ABM Magazine - 3; ftm.
  Breastfeeding Leaflets.   AR.
  List of publications available.

Association of Brickwork Contractors Ltd   (ABC)   2004
- ■ Woodside House, Winkfield, WINDSOR, Berks, SL4 2DX.   (hq)
  01344 882607   fax 01344 890129
  email info@brickworkcontractors.info
  http://www.brickworkcontractors.info
  Chief Exec: Michael Driver
- ▲ Company Limited by Guarantee
- ○ *T; to promote quality brickwork by training of operatives & health & safety of site workers
- ● Mtgs - Inf - LG
- M 24 f, 10 associates
- ¶ [NL - 2; free. To come]

Association of British Bookmakers   2002
- NR Regency House, 1-4 Warwick St, LONDON, W1B 5LT.   (hq)
  020 7434 2111
- ▲ Company Limited by Guarantee
- ○ *T; for off course bookmakers
- Gp Racing security; Technical
- ● Conf - Mtgs - Res - Exhib - SG - Stat - Inf - Lib
- < Nat Sporting League
- M 148 f
- × 2002 (Betting Office Licensees Association
  (British Betting Office Association (merged)

Association for British Brewery Collectables   (ABBC)   1983
- ■ 28 Parklands, Kidsgrove, STOKE-ON-TRENT, Staffs, ST7 4US.   (ed/p)
  01782 761048
  email mike.breweriana@gmail.com
  http://www.abbclist.info
  Newsletter Editor: Mike Peterson
- ▲ Un-incorporated Society
- ○ *G; to promote the hobby of collecting brewery memorabilia
- ● Mtgs - Res - Inf
- M 150 i
- ¶ What's Bottling - 6; £7 m only.
- × 2003 Association of Bottled Beer Collectors

Association of British Certification Bodies   (ABCB)   1984
- NR Sanodver Centre, 129a Whitehorse Hill, CHISLEHURST, Kent, BR7 6DQ.   (hq)
  020 8295 1128   fax 020 8467 8091
  Chief Exec: Tim Inman
- ▲ Company Limited by Guarantee
- ○ *T; the UK's centre of excellence for product, quality management & environmental certification
- ● Mtgs - SG - Inf - LG
- < Intl Accreditation Forum (IAF); UK Accreditation Service (UKAS)
- M 22 f, UK / 3 f, o'seas
- ¶ NL - 4;   LM - up-dated;   AR - 1; all free.

Association of British Choral Directors   (ABCD)   1986
- ■ 15 Granville Way, SHERBORNE, Dorset, DT9 4AS.   (sp)
  01935 389482
  Gen Sec: Rachel Greaves
- ▲ Registered Charity
- Br 11; 1
- ○ *P; to promote the education, training & development of choral directors from all choral sectors; to encourage the composition of choral music
- ● Conf - Mtgs - ET - SG - Inf - VE - Workshops
- < Intl Fedn for Choral Music (IFCM); Inc Soc of Musicians; Music Educ Coun
- M 600 i, 50 f
- ¶ Mastersinger - 4; ftm.   Membership Annual - 1; m only.

Association of British Civilian Internees Far East Region (ABCIFER)   1994
- ■ c/o Guillaume & Sons, 2 St Martin's Ct, 37 Queens Rd, WEYBRIDGE, Surrey, KT13 9UQ.   (chmn/b)
  020 8398 1387   fax 01892 655888
  Chmn: R W Bridge, AFC
- ▲ Un-incorporated Society
- Br Australia, Canada, New Zealand, USA
- ○ *G, *K; to campaign for justice from the Japanese government in respect of losses & suffering endured during World War II at the hands of Japanese Imperial Forces; to maintain friendships formed during internment by the Japanese
- ● Mtgs - President's Memorial Library at the School of Oriental & African Studies
- M 480 i, UK / 380 i, o'seas
- ¶ Bamboo Wireless (NL) - 3; ftm only.

Association of British Climatologists   (ABC)   1974
- NR The Weather Facility, School of Geography, Earth & Environmental Sciences, University of Birmingham, BIRMINGHAM, B15 2TT.   (hsb)
  0121 414 5552   fax 0121 414 5528
  http://www.royal-met-soc.org.uk
- ▲ Registered Charity
- ○ *P; the study & development of climatology
- ● Conf - Mtgs - ET - VE
- < a specialist group of the R Meteorological Soc
- M 114 i, UK / 5 i, o'seas
- ¶ Climate News (NL) - 2; ftm only.

Association of British Climbing Walls   (ABC)   1994
- NR c/o Mile End Climbing Wall, Haverfield Rd, Bow, LONDON, E3 5BE.
  020 8980 0289
- ○ *P, *T

Association of British, Commonwealth & European Erotic Artists
see **Association of Erotic Artists**

© CBD Research Ltd · Beckenham · BR3 5JS · Tel 020 8650 7745 · Fax 020 8650 0768 · E-mail cbd@cbdresearch.com · www.cbdresearch.com

Association of British Concert Promoters   (ABCP)   1989
- ■ St David's Hall, The Hayes, CARDIFF, Glam, CF10 1SH.   (hsb)
  029 2087 8512   fax 029 2087 8517
  email s.king@cardiff.gov.uk
  Hon Sec: Susan King
- ○ *T; a forum for discussion between concert promoters
- ● Conf - Mtgs - SG - Inf
- M 38 f

Association of British Conifer Growers
  a group of the **Horticultural Trades Association**

Association of British Correspondence Colleges   (ABCC)   1956
- ■ PO Box 17926, LONDON, SW19 3WB.   (hq)
  020 8544 9559
  email info@homestudy.org.uk
  http://www.homestudy.org.uk
  Sec: Heather Owen
- ▲ Company Limited by Guarantee
- ○ *E, *P; to represent the major private correspondence colleges in the UK
- ● ET - Inf - LG - Advice on correspondence education in Britain
- M 21 f
- ¶ Learn at Home (leaflet) - 1; free.

Association of British Counties   (ABC)   1989
- ■ 28 Alfreda Rd, Whitchurch, CARDIFF, Glam, CF14 2EH.
  (chmn/p)
  029 2033 3728
  email peterboyce@ntlworld.com
  http://www.abcounties.co.uk
  Hon Sec: J M Bradford
- ▲ Un-incorporated Society
- ○ *K; to promote an awareness of the continuing existence of all the historic, traditional counties of Britain, as distinct from administrative counties
- Gp Campaign for True Identity; County of Middlesex Trust; Friends of Real Lancashire; Historic Counties Trust; Huntingdonshire Society; North Riding Society; Saddleworth White Rose Society; Staffordshire Society
- ● Mtgs - Inf
- < Historic Counties Trust
- M 1,000 i
- ¶ The Counties (Jnl) - 2; ftm only.
  Gazetteer - showing traditional counties & local government areas; on website: gazetteer.co.uk

Association of British Credit Unions Ltd   (ABCUL)   1979
- ■ Holyoake House, Hanover St, MANCHESTER, M60 0AS.   (hq)
  0161-832 3694   fax 0161-832 3706
  email info@abcul.org   http://www.abcul.coop
  Chief Exec: Mark Lyonette
- ▲ Industrial & Provident Society
- Br 3
- ○ *N; the principal trade association for credit unions in Britain with members in England, Scotland & Wales
- Gp 35 study groups
- ● Conf - Mtgs - ET - Res - SG - Inf - LG
- < Wld Coun of Credit Us (WOCCU); Co-operatives UK
- M 385 credit unions
- ¶ Credit Union News - 4;   AR - 1; both ftm.

Association of British Designer Silversmiths   (ABDS)   1996
- ■ PO Box 42034, LONDON, E5 9WG.
  0794 478 6011
  email info   http://www.theabds.co.uk   (admin)
  http://www.theabds.co.uk
  Chmn: Julie Chamberlain
- ○ *P, *T; to act as forum for silversmiths throughout the country; to promote the highest standards in design & craftsmanship
- Gp
  Full: full-time silversmith (by selection);
  Graduate: all graduates up to 3 years from leaving a course;
  Student; Friend - anyone interested in the field
- ● Mtgs - Exhib
- M 81 i, 12 f, 30 org
- ¶ NL - 4; ftm.

Association of British Dispensing Opticians   (ABDO)   1986
- ■ 199 Gloucester Terrace, LONDON, W2 6LD.   (hq)
  020 7298 5100   fax 020 7298 5111
  email general@abdo.org.uk   http://www.abdo.org.uk
  Gen Sec: Sir Anthony Garrett
- ▲ Company Limited by Guarantee
- ○ *P
- ● Conf - ET - Exam
- M 6,027 i, UK / 739 i, o'seas
- ¶ Dispensing Optics - 9.
  Bifocals without Tears (L E Swift).
  Practical Ophthalmic Lenses (M Jalie/Ray).
  Principles of Ophthalmic Lenses (M Jalie).
  Optics (A H Tunnicliffe & J G Hurst).
  Other publications available.

Association of British Drivers   (ABD)   1992
- ■ PO Box 2228, KENLEY, Surrey, CR8 5ZT.   (hsp)
  0800 358 9955   fax 0870 136 2370
  email enquiries@abd.org.uk   http://www.abd.org.uk
  Mem Sec: Susan Newby-Robson
- ▲ Company Limited by Guarantee
- ○ *G, *K; to provide an active, reasonable voice & lobby for the British driver
- ● Mtgs - Exhib
- < Amer Auto Enthusiast Club; Fiat Motor Club; Nat Assn of Street Clubs
- M 1,600 i, 3,775 affiliates, UK / 5 i, o'seas
- ¶ On the Road (NL) - 6; ftm, £2 nm.
  The Association of British Drivers is the operating name of Pro-Motor (a Company Limited by Guarantee).

Association of British Fire Trades Ltd
- NR Thames House, 29 Thames St, KINGSTON upon THAMES, Surrey, KT1 1PH.   (hq)
  020 8549 8839   fax 020 8547 1564
  email info@abft.org.uk
- ○ *T; to provide secretarial, accounting, computer, duplicating & other administration services to the 4 member organisations
- M 4 org:
  British Approvals for Fire Equipment
  British Fire Protection Systems Association
  Fire Extinguishing Trades Association
  Fire Fighting Vehicles Manufacturers Association

Association of British Healthcare Industries   (ABHI)   1988
- NR St George's House, 195-203 Waterloo Rd, LONDON, SE1 8WD.   (hq)
  020 7787 3060   fax 020 7787 3061
  email enquiries@abhi.org.uk   http://www.abhi.org.uk
  Dir Gen: John Wilkinson
- ▲ Company Limited by Guarantee
- ○ *T; for the medical technology industry - manufacturers & distributors of products ranging from plasters to pacemakers
- ● Mtgs - Expt - LG
- < Eucomed
- M 226 f, 5 trade assns
- ¶ Health-Care Focus - 6.   In Focus - 6.   Primed - 24.   AR.

Association of British Independent Oil Exploration Companies (BRINDEX) 1974

NR 55 Riddlesdown Rd, PURLEY, Surrey, CR8 1DJ. (admin/b)
     020 8668 3359
     email jackie@brindex.co.uk   http://www.brindex.co.uk
     Admin: Jackie Steers
○ *T; to develop & promote the British independent oil industry
Gp North Sea taxation
● Conf - Mtgs - SG
M 12 f

Association of British Insurers (ABI) 1985

■ 51 Gresham St, LONDON, EC2V 7HQ. (hq)
     020 7600 3333
     Dir-Gen: Stephen Haddrill
○ *T; for insurers authorised to transact any class of insurance
     business in the UK
● Mtgs - ET - Res - Stat - Inf
M 440 f
¶ Insurance Facts, Figures & Trends - 1.
     Insurance Trends - 4.   Insurance Ybk - 1.

Association of British Introduction Agencies (ABIA) 1981

■ 35 Market St (1st floor), TAMWORTH, Staffs, B79 7LR.
     (chmn/b)
     0845 345 2242   fax 01827 59514
     email enquiries@abia.org.uk   http://www.abia.org.uk
     Chmn: Lynda Davies
▲ Un-incorporated Society
○ *T; 'assisting consumer & agency with advice; monitoring
     industry & trying to get all agencies to a set minimum
     standard of service'
● Conf - Mtgs - ET - Stat - Inf - Lib - LG
M 32 f
¶ LM - (updated).   Code of practice.

Association of British Investigators (ABI) 1970

NR 27 Old Gloucester St, LONDON, WC1N 3XX. (hsb)
     0871 474 0006   fax 0871 474 0007
     email info@theabi.org.uk   http://www.theabi.org.uk
     Sec: Stuart Price
▲ Company Limited by Guarantee
Br 4
○ *P; for private investigators & process servers (many members
     are certified bailiffs)
● Conf - Mtgs - ET - Exam - Inf - LG
< Intle Kommission der Detektiv-Verbände (IKD)
M 369 i, UK / 61 i, o'seas
¶ Investigate - 4.   LM - 1.

Association of British & Irish Showcaves (ABIS)

■ c/o Peak Cavern, Peak Cavern Rd, Castleton, HOPE VALLEY,
     Derbys, S33 8WS.
     01433 620512
     http://www.visitcaves.com
     Chmn: John Harrison
○ *T; underground tourist attractions across the British Isles
M 12 f

Association of British Jazz Musicians (ABJM) 1987

■ c/o Jazz Services Ltd, 132 Southwark St (1st floor), LONDON,
     SE1 0SW. (hsb)
     020 7928 9089   fax 020 7401 6870
     email touring@jazzservices.org.uk
     http://www.jazzservices.org.uk
     Hon Sec: Chris Hodgkins
▲ Un-incorporated Society
○ *D; interests of jazz musicians in the UK
● Conf - Mtgs - Inf - LG
M i
¶ ABJM News - 4.

Association of British Kart Clubs (ABKC) 1990

■ Stoneycroft, Godsons Lane, Napton, SOUTHAM, Warks,
     CV47 8LX. (sp)
     01926 812177   fax 01926 812177
     email secretary@abkc.org.uk   http://www.abkc.org.uk
     Sec: Graham Smith
▲ Un-incorporated Society
○ *N, *S; provision of technical & procedural regulations for
     competition kart racing in the UK
● Conf - Mtgs - Comp - Stat - Inf - Organisation of national
     championships - Setting technical regulations for kart racing
< Motor Sports Assn
M 31 clubs
¶ ABKC News - 4; free.

Association of British Language Schools (ABLS) 1993

NR PO Box 182, POTTERS BAR, Herts, EN6 5ZG.
     01707 663311   fax 01707 663311
     email info@abls.co.uk   http://www.abls.co.uk
     Sec: Joanne Adcock
▲ Un-incorporated Society
○ *E, *P; accreditation body for establishments teaching English
     as a foreign language (TEFL)
● Conf - Mtgs - ET - Expt - Inf - LG - Lobbying embassies abroad
     - Networking for members
M c 30 f
¶ LM - 1; free.

Association of British Mining Equipment Companies (ABMEC) 1967

■ Unit 1 Thornes Office Park, Monckton Rd, WAKEFIELD, W Yorks,
     WF2 7AN. (hq)
     01924 360200   fax 01924 380553
     email deakin@abmec.org.uk
     http://www.abmec.org.uk
     Dir Gen: Philip Deakin
▲ Un-incorporated Society
○ *T; to promote the UK mining equipment manufacturers
● Conf - Mtgs - ET - Exhib - Expt - Inf - LG
M 33 f
¶ Buyers' Guide - 1. free.

Association of British Neurologists (ABN) 1933

■ Ormond House, 27 Boswell St, LONDON, WC1N 3JZ. (hq)
     020 7405 4060   fax 020 7405 4070
     email info@theabn.org   http://www.abn.org.uk
     Hon Sec: Dr David Bateman
▲ Registered Charity
○ *P; to promote education in, & the advancement of, the
     neurological sciences including the practice of neurology in
     the UK & Ireland
● Conf - ET - Res - Stat - LG
M 1,000 i

Association of British Offshore Industries (ABOI) 1983

NR 30 Great Guildford St (4th floor), LONDON, SE1 0HS. (hq)
     020 7928 9199
     Assn Dir: Ken Gibbons
○ *T; 'companies who develop specialist offshore systems &
     provide worldwide services & facilities for oil & gas
     exploration, production, transportation & conversion'
● Conf - Mtgs - Exhib - SG - Expt - LG
< Soc Maritime Inds
M f

Association of British Orchestras   (ABO)   1947

- ■ 20 Rupert St, LONDON, W1D 6DF.   (hq)
  020 7287 0333   fax 020 7287 0444
  email info@abo.org.uk   http://www.abo.org.uk
  Dir: Russell Jones
- ▲ Company Limited by Guarantee
- ○ *N, *T; to support, develop & advance the interests & activities of orchestras in the UK
- ● Conf - Mtgs - ET - Res - Stat - Inf - Lib - Empl - LG - Seminars - Public symposia
- < Intl Alliance of Orchestral Assns (IAOA); Performing Arts Employers Assns League Europe (PEARLE); American Symphony Orchestra League (ASOL); Inc Soc of Musicians (ISM); Nat Campaign for the Arts (NCA); Sound Sense
- M 11 i, 51 orchestras, 47 f, 21 associates
- ¶ ABO Update (email NL) - 12; ftm.
  A Sound Ear; A Wright Reid (2001); £10.
  Knowing the Score 2; A Lewis-Crosby & R Moon (2002); £20.
  Review of the Year.
  Publications list available.

Association of British Paediatric Nurses   (ABPN)   1937

- NR c/o Suzan Smallman, Child Health, Courtlands, Faculty of Health & Community Care, University of Central England, Westbourne Rd, Edgbaston, BIRMINGHAM, B15 3TN. (chmn/b)
  http://www.abpn.org.uk
  Chmn: Suzan Smallman
- ▲ Registered Charity
- Br 9
- ○ *P; discussion & improvement of standards & care given by paediatric nurses to sick children
- Gp Nurse teacher; Student
- ● Conf - Mtgs - Exhib - SG - LG - Awards & scholarships
- M 1,300 i, UK / 20 i, o'seas
- ¶ Jnl of Child Health Care - 4.   AR.
  Central Council Meetings - 4.
  Consultative Committee Members' Meeting - 4

Association of British Pewter Craftsmen   (ABPC)   1971

- ■ Unit 10 1st floor, Edmund Road Business Centre, SHEFFIELD, S Yorks, S2 4ED.   (asa)
  0114-252 7550   fax 0114-252 7555
  email enquiries@abpcltd.co.uk
  http://www.britishpewter.com
  Co Sec: Mrs C T Steele
- ▲ Company Limited by Guarantee
- ○ *T; the promotion of pewter
- ● Mtgs - Exhib - Inf
- < Worshipful Company of Pewterers
- M 35 f

Association of the British Pharmaceutical Industry   (ABPI)   1930

- NR 12 Whitehall, LONDON, SW1A 2DY.   (hq)
  020 7930 3477   fax 020 7747 1411
  http://www.abpi.org.uk
- ▲ Un-incorporated Society
- Br 3
- ○ *T
- ● Conf - Mtgs - ET - Exam - Stat - Inf - LG
- M [not stated]

Association of British Philatelic Societies Ltd   (ABPS)   1994

- NR PO Box 199, THETFORD, Norfolk, IP24 3WX.
  email abps.phil@elics.co.uk
  http://www.ukphilately.org.uk/abps
  Sec: M P Brindle
- ▲ Company Limited by Guarantee
- ○ *N; to promote philately in the UK; to represent philatelic societies
- ● Conf - Comp - SG - Inf
- < Fédn Intle de Philatélie; FEPA
- M c 400 org
- ¶ ABPS News (NL) - 4; ftm, £10 yr nm.
  National & Specialists Society Hbk - 1.
  ABPS Directory - 2 yrly; ftm, £15 nm.

Association of British Physiotherapists
  see **SMAE Fellowship (Association of British Physiotherapists)**

Association of British Picture Restorers
  since 2002 **British Association of Paintings Conservator-Restorers**

Association of British Primary Breeders & Exporters
  since 2001 **British Poultry Council**

Association of British Professional Conference Organisers   (ABPCO)   1981

- ■ Charles House (6th floor), 148-149 Great Charles St, BIRMINGHAM, B3 3HT.   (hq)
  0121-212 1400   fax 0121-212 3131
  email tony@abpco.org   http://www.abpco.org
  Sec: Tony Rogers (tony@abpco.org)
- ▲ Company Limited by Guarantee
- ○ *P
- ● Conf - Mtgs - ET - Exhib - Inf
- < Business Tourism Partnership
- M 72 i

Association of British Riding Schools   (ABRS)   1954

- ■ Queens Chambers, 38-40 Queen St, PENZANCE, Cornwall, TR18 4BH.   (hq)
  01736 369440   fax 01736 351390
  email office@abrs-info.org   http://www.abrs-info.org
  Chmn: Julian Marczak
- ▲ Company Limited by Guarantee
- ○ *P, *S; to raise the standards of riding instruction & horsemanship
- ● Conf - ET - Exam - Exhib - LG
- < Cent Coun for Physical Recreation (CCPR); Brit Equestrian Fedn (BEF); Lantra; Brit Equestrian Tr Assn (BETA); Nat Equine Forum
- M 450 i, 350 f, UK / 20 i, 16 f, o'seas
- ¶ NL - 3/4; ftm only.
  Locations leaflet - 1; free.

Association of British Roofing Felt Manufacturers
  has merged with the Flat Roofing Contractors Advisory Board to form the **Flat Roofing Alliance**; it is till in existence as a separate body & is administered by the Alliance

Association of British Sailmakers   (ABS)   1984

- NR 2 Orchard Rd, Lock's Heath, SOUTHAMPTON, Hants, SO31 6PR.   (hsp/b)
  01489 601517 (0900-1700)   fax 01489 601518
  Jt Secs: Mr L C & Mrs C A Olden
- ○ *T; to provide technical support for sailmakers
- ● Conf - Mtgs - ET - Res - Exhib - Expt - Inf - Lib

Association of British Salted Fish Curers & Exporters 1934

■ c/o Cawoods (Fish Curers) Ltd, Estate Rd No 6, South
  Humberside Industrial Estate, GRIMSBY, Lincs, DN31 2TG.
  (chmn/b)
  01472 342248   fax 01472 353100
  email cawoods@denholm-seafoods.co.uk
  Chmn: Richard J Turner
▲ Un-incorporated Society
○ *T; promotion of saltfish/bacalao
● Inf - LG
M 2 f

Association of British Science Writers (ABSW) 1947

NR Wellcome Wolfson Building, 165 Queen's Gate, LONDON,
   SW7 5HE.   (hsb)
   0870 770 3361
   Admin: Barbara Drillsma
○ *P; to encourage & improve science writing in the UK
● Mtgs - VE
< Eur U of Science Journalists' Assns (EUSJA)
M 900 i
¶ NL - 12; ftm only.

Association of British Scrabble Players (ABSP) 1986

■ 12 Northfield Terrace, EDINBURGH, EH8 7PX.   (hsp)
  0131-661 3869
  email amybyrne@nevik34.freeserve.co.uk
  http://www.absp.org.uk
  Hon Sec: Mrs Amy Byrne
○ *G; to promote matchplay scrabble tournaments
● Comp
< Wld Engl Speaking Scrabble Players Asn
M c 700 i
¶ The Last Word - 6; £15 yr m.

Association of British Tennis Officials (ABTO) 2000

NR Officiating Dept, The Lawn Tennis Association, The Queens
   Club, LONDON, W14 9EG.   (hq)
   020 7381 7044   fax 020 7381 7143
   Hon Sec: B L J Maddock,
   Officiating Mgr: W J Perkins
○ *P; to officiate at tennis events & apply & uphold rules &
   regulations in force; to promote advancement of high
   standards for tennis officials
Gp Referees; Umpires
● Mtgs - ET - Exam - Inf - Empl
< Lawn Tennis Assn
M 920 i, UK / 40 i, o'seas
¶ Officiating News (NL) - 4;   ABTO Members' Hbk - 1;
   ABTO Constitution & Procedures - 1;   AR - 1; all free.

Association of British Theatre Technicians (ABTT) 1961

NR 55 Farringdon Rd (4th floor), LONDON, EC1M 3JB.   (hq)
   020 7242 9200
▲ Registered Charity
Br 2
○ *A, *P; 'to act as a forum for theatre technicians & express their
   corporate view on matters affecting the industry; to collect &
   disseminate technical information; to advise on the planning
   of new theatres & the conversion of existing buildings'
Gp Archaeology; Safety; Training & education; IT; Technology;
   Theatre planning;
   Society of Theatre Designers
● Conf - Mtgs - ET - Res - Exhib - Inf - Lib - VE - LG
M 2,000 i
¶ ABTT Codes of Practice for the Theatre Industry:
   Model Standard Conditions + CD-ROM.
   Fibre Ropes / Wire Ropes.   Flying.
   A Modern Approach to Emergency Lighting in Theatres.
   Firearms & Ammunition.   Pyrotechnics & Smoke Effects.
   Guidance Notes on Exit Signs / Water.
   Various other publications: (cheques to Theatrical Trading Ltd)
   British Theatrical Patents by David Wilmore & Terence Rees.
   Guide to Fire Precautions in Existing Places of
   Entertainment.
   Theatres: Planning Guidance for Design & Adaptation by
   Roderick Ham.

Association of British Theological & Philosophical Libraries (ABTAPL) 1956

■ c/o Judith Shiel, John Rylands University Library of Manchester,
  2004 Oxford Rd, MANCHESTER, M13 9PP.   (hsb)
  0161-275 3751
  http://www.abtapl.org.uk
  Hon Sec: Judith B Shiel
○ *P; to promote bibliographical work & common interests
   among librarians specialising in theology, religious studies &
   philosophy
● Conf - ET - inf
< Bibliothèques Européenes de Théologie
M 97 i, 75 f, 5 org, UK / 29 i, 44 f, o'seas
¶ Bulletin - 3; ftm.

Association of British Tour Operators to France Ltd (ABTOF) 1993

NR PO Box 54, ROSS-ON-WYE, Herefords, HR9 5YQ.   (hq)
   01989 769140   fax 01989 769066
   email info@abtof.org.uk
   Chief Exec: Richard Brierly
▲ Company Limited by Guarantee
○ *T
Gp French & UK affiliate members who are suppliers of services to
   ABTOF members
● Conf - Mtgs - ET - Exhib - SG - Stat - Inf - VE - LG - PR Service
M 220 f, UK / 70 f, o'seas
¶ ABTOF News Update - 12; ftm only.

Association of British Transport & Engineering Museums (ABTEM)

NR c/o Tim Bryan, British Motor Heritage Trust Museum,
   Banbury Rd, GAYDON, Warks, CV35 0BJ.   (hsp)
   Hon Sec: Tim Bryan
▲ Un-incorporated Society
○ *N; to act as a clearing house for information for transport
   museums; to improve the standards of preservation &
   presentation of exhibits
● Mtgs (2 a yr) - VE
M c 20 i, c 50 org
¶ NL - 2; ftm only.

Association of British Travel Agents Ltd   (ABTA)   1950
NR   68-71 Newman St, LONDON, W1T 3AH.   (hq)
     020 7637 2444   fax 020 7637 0713
     email abta@abta.co.uk   http://www.abta.com
     Sec: Riccardo Nardi
▲   Company Limited by Guarantee
○   *T; interests of travel agents and tour operators in GB and
     Ireland; administration of codes of conduct; administration of
     tour operators bonds & their utilisation as public protection in
     the event of financial failure; administration of fund for
     compensation of holidaymakers in case of financial failure by
     retail travel agent
Gp   Airways; Railways; Roadways; Shipping; UK tourism;
     Technology; Insurance; Finance; Codes of conduct; ABTA
     National Training Board, Woking, Surrey
●   Conf - Mtgs - ET - Res - Inf - LG
<   Confedn of Brit Ind (CBI), Assn of Travel Agents & Tour
     Operators in the EU (ECTAA)
M   2,700 f
¶   ABTA Magazine - 12; ftm only.

Association of British Veterinary Acupuncture
     a group of the **British Small Animal Veterinary Association**

Association of British Wild Animal Keepers   (ABWAK)   1974
■   The Aviary, Leeds Castle, MAIDSTONE, Kent, ME17 1PL.   (hsb)
     http://www.abwak.co.uk
     Hon Sec: Laura Gardner
▲   Un-incorporated Society
○   *P, *V; captive husbandry of exotic animals in zoos & private
     collections
●   Conf
M   c 400 i
¶   RATEL (Jnl) - 4.
     Conference Proceedings - 1.   Ybk.

Association of Broadcasting Doctors   (ABD)   1988
NR   1 Lark Bank, Prickwillow, ELY, Cambs, CB7 4SW.   (hq)
     01353 688456
     email jackiepetts@aol.com
     http://www.broadcasting-doctors.org
     Dir: Jacqueline Petts
▲   Un-incorporated Society
○   *P; to represent practising clinicians who also broadcast on
     radio & TV; to improve the quality of medical broadcasting
     through training & advice
Gp   Dentists' media
●   Conf - Mtgs - ET - Inf - Lib - LG
<   GP Writers Assn
M   760 i
¶   NL - 12.

Association of Brokers & Yacht Agents   (ABYA)
■   The Glass Works, Penns Rd, PETERSFIELD, Hants, GU23 2EW.
     (hq)
     01730 710425   fax 01730 710423
     email info@ybdsa.co.uk   http://www.ybdsa.co.uk
     Chief Exec: Jane Gentry
▲   Company Limited by Guarantee
Br   Spain
○   *P; for yacht brokers, agents & dealers
●   Conf - Mtgs
M   85 i, UK / 15 f, o'seas
¶   NL - 4; ftm only.
     Note: Trades with the Yacht Designers & Surveyors Association
     as the Yacht Brokers, Designers & Surveyors Association
     (Holdings) Ltd

**Association of Building Cleaning Direct Service Providers
(ABCD)   1994**
■   PO Box 137, NORTHAMPTON, NN3 6AD.   (hsb)
     01604 678710   fax 01604 645988
     email information@abcdsp.org.uk
     http://www.abcdsp.org.uk
     Chmn: Ken Baker,   Sec: Patricia Wherton
▲   Un-incorporated Society
Br   3
○   *T; to support managers of direct service cleaning provision in
     local authorities throughout the UK
●   Conf - Mtgs - Res - Inf
<   Brit Cleaning Coun; Assn of Public Service Excellence; Brit Inst
     of Cleaning Science
M   46 f

**Association of Building Component Manufacturers Ltd
(ABCM)   1965**
■   Clark House, 3 Brassey Drive, AYLESFORD, Kent, ME20 7QL.
     (hq)
     01622 715577   fax 0870 054 3915
     email abcm@building-components.org
     http://www.building-components.org
     Dir: Peter B Caplin
▲   Company Limited by Guarantee
○   *T; to provide commercial & technical intelligence to members
Gp   Technical; Commercial c'ee
●   Conf - Mtgs - LG
<   BSI; Roofing Ind Alliance
M   24 f
¶   NL - 8; ftm only.

Association of Building Engineers   (ABE)   1925
■   Lutyens House, Billing Brook Rd, Weston Favell,
     NORTHAMPTON, NN3 8NW.   (hq)
     01604 404121   fax 01604 784220
     email building.engineers@abe.org.uk
     http://www.abe.org.uk
     Chief Exec: David R Gibson
▲   Company Limited by Guarantee
○   *P; to promote & advance the study & practice of the arts &
     sciences concerned with building technology, planning,
     design, construction, maintenance & repair of the built
     environment
Gp   Fire safety engineering; ABE Assess - home inspector training
●   Conf - ET - Exam - Inf - Lib - LG
<   Assn d'Experts Eur du Bâtiment et de la Construction (AEEBC);
     Construction Ind Coun
M   5,000 i, 200 f, UK / 400 i, o'seas
¶   Building Engineer - 12; ftm, £40 yr nm.
     AR; free.

Association of Building Hardware Manufacturers
     2005 merged with the Door & Shutter Manufacturers' Association to
     form the **Door & Hardware Federation**

Association of Burglary Insurance Surveyors Ltd
     since 2004 **Association of Insurance Surveyors**

Association of Burial Authorities Ltd (ABA) 1993
NR   Waterloo House, 155 Upper St, LONDON, N1 1RA.   (hq)
       020 7288 2522   fax 020 7288 2533
       Dir & Chmn: D S Weller,   Hon Sec: Deborah Powton
▲   Company Limited by Guarantee
○   *T; to promote & protect the interests of organisations engaged
       in the management & operation of burial grounds
●   Conf - Res - Comp - Inf - Lib - VE - LG - Advice on planning,
       designing & layout of burial grounds & extensions, & on
       acquisitions of burial grounds (incl churchyards, municipal &
       private cemeteries) - Legal advice
<   Fédn Intle des Assns Thanatologues FIAT/IFTA); Assn Significant
       Cemeteries Europe (ASCE); Eur Fedn of Funeral
       Services (EFFS); Coun Brit Funeral Services
M   8 i, 20 f, 280 local authorities
¶   ABA Info (NL) - 4.
       ABA Informatives - factsheets.   .
       Cemetery & Churchyard Regulations.
       Planning for Memorials.
       Planning for Memorials after Cremation.
       Guide to Funerals & Bereavement.
       ABA/ZM Guide to Safety in Burial Grounds.

Association of Business Administration (ABA) 1984
NR   PO Box 70, LONDON, E13 0UU.   [hq/hsb)
       020 8986 7539
       Dir: C Oham
○   *P; to professional training & examinations in business
       administration
●   ET - Exam - SG - Inf - Correspondence courses
M   i
¶   ABA Jnl (Business Administration News) - 3.
       Dictionary of Business Administration Terms.
       Membership Hbk.
×   2001 Association of Business Administration Studies

Association of Business-to-Business Agencies (ABBA) 1985
NR   c/o IAS Smarts, Queens Avenue, MACCLESFIELD, Cheshire,
       SK10 2BN.   (hq)
       01625 439874   fax 01625 434335
       email info@abba.co.uk   http://www.abba.co.uk
       Gen Sec: Olwyn Bloor
○   *P; to establish professional standards of service & competence;
       to encourage a strategic, business-focussed, integrated
       approach
M   15 f

Association of Business Executives (ABE) 1973
■   William House, 14 Worple Rd, LONDON, SW19 4DD.   (hq)
       020 8879 1973   fax 020 8946 7153
       email info@abeuk.com   http://www.abeuk.com
       Founder/Chmn: Lyndon Jones
▲   Company Limited by Guarantee
Br   11 countries
○   *P; examination board setting professional qualifications &
       advanced diplomas in business nominations, business
       information systems, travel, tourism & hospitality resource
       management
●   Conf - ET - Exam
M   4,000 i, UK / 18,000 i, o'seas
¶   Business Executives - 2; ftm, £20 nm.

Association of Business Managers & Administrators (ABMA) 1975
■   Wembley Point (18th floor), 1 Harrow Rd, WEMBLEY, Middx,
       HA9 6DE.   (hq)
       020 8733 7000   fax 020 8733 7033
       email info@abma.uk.com   http://www.abma.uk.com
       Senior Exec: Alan Hodson
▲   Company Limited by Guarantee
○   *T; a non-profit making, independent examinations board,
       recognised worldwide for providing a unique solution in
       terms of British qualifications; offers customised courses to
       suit the needs of both institutions & students as direct entry
       requirements for bachelor courses in the UK & USA
●   ET - Exam
M   c 12,000 i, 89 f, affiliated universities in UK & USA

Association of Business Psychologists (ABP) 2000
■   211-212 Piccadilly, LONDON, W1J 9HG.   (hsb)
       020 7917 1733
       email admin@theabp.org
       http://www.admin@theabp.org
       Gen Administrator: Richard Taylor
▲   Company Limited by Guarantee
○   *P; for practitioners in business psychology
●   Conf - Mtgs - ET - Res - Inf - LG
M   900 i, UK / 10 i, o'seas
¶   NL - 3 [email].

Association of Business Recovery Professionals (R3) 1990
NR   120 Aldersgate St (8th floor), LONDON, EC1A 4JQ.   (hq)
       020 7566 4200   fax 020 7566 4224
       http://www.r3.org.uk
▲   Company Limited by Guarantee
○   *P; for all those who deal with Britain's underperforming
       businesses & individuals in financial trouble
Gp   Insolvency practitioners; Turnaround specialists
●   Conf - Mtgs - ET - SG - Lib - LG
<   Insol Intl
M   3,400 i
¶   Recovery - 4; ftm only.

Association of Business Schools (ABS) 1992
NR   137 Euston Rd, LONDON, NW1 2AA.   (hq)
       020 7388 0007
       Chief Exec: Jonathan Slack
○   *P; to promote business & management education, training &
       development so as to improve the quality & effectiveness of
       the practice of management in the UK
●   Conf - Mtgs - Res - Inf - LG
M   100 f, 6 org
¶   The ABS Directory of Business Schools - 1.

Association of Button Merchants 1928
NR   Southernhay (suite 7), 207 Hook Rd, CHESSINGTON, Surrey,
       KT9 1HJ.   (asa)
       020 8391 2266   fax 020 8391 4466
       email abm@sleat.co.uk
       Sec: David M Hart
▲   Company Limited by Guarantee
○   *T; interests of button merchants in the UK
●   Mtgs - Inf
<   Brit Button Coun
M   15 f
¶   NL - irreg;   AR; both m only.

Association of C & C++ Users (ACCU) 1987

■ 6 King James Way, ROYSTON, Herts, SG8 7EF.   (sec/p)
   email secretary@accu.org
   Sec: Alan Bellingham
▲ Un-incorporated Society
Br Australia, Cuba, Germany, Russia, Spain, USA
○ *P, *G; for all interested in C & C++ computer programme & related languages
Gp Acorn C/C++ users; International Standards Devt Forum
● ET - Exhib - Inf - Representation at BSI for C & C++ standardisation
M 900 i, 40 f, UK / 100 i, 5 f, o'seas
¶ C Vu - 6; ftm only.   Hbk (incl LM) - 1; free.
   ISDF NL - 3; free to those qualifying.
   Overload - 6 free to C++ SIG.
   CAUGers - 6; free to Acorn SIG.

Association of Call Handling

NR 3 The Shrubberies (1st floor), George Lane, South Woodford, LONDON, E18 1BD.
   020 8989 0677

Association for Cancer Surgery
   see **BASO - the Association for Cancer Surgery**

Association of Cannibals' Equipment Suppliers (ACES) 2000

■ 15 Wickham Road, BECKENHAM, Kent, BR3 5JS.   (hq)
○ *T
Gp Headball
● Conf - Mtgs - Exhib - Expt - Lib - Stat - VE - LG
M f
¶ Eat You - 4; ftm only.
   Note: this is a control entry

Association of Canoe Trades (ACT) 1970

■ 929A Abbeydale Rd, SHEFFIELD, S Yorks, S7 2QD.   (hsb)
   0114-249 9563   fax 0871 871 6251
   email act@britishmarine.co.uk
   Chief Exec: Dean Maragh
▲ Un-incorporated Society
○ *T; the manufacture, retailing, design & safety of canoes, kayaks & their accessories
● Mtgs - ET - Res - Exhib - Stat - Expt - Inf - PL - LG
< Brit Marine Fedn
M 22 f

Association of Caravan & Camping Exempted Organisations (ACCEO) 1985

■ Unit 6a Top Barn Business Centre, Holt Heath, WORCESTER, WR6 6NH.   (hq)
   01905 621673
○ *N, *T; for camping & caravanning clubs holding meetings of not more than 5 days; site licences are not required if the site is under the supervision of an organisation holding the Dept of the Environment's Certificate of Exemption; ACCEO is one of 5 organisations permitted, in conjunction with member clubs, to hold meetings of up to 28 days
M i in c 200 clubs

Association of Cardiothoracic Anaesthetists (ACTA) 1985

NR Dept of Anaesthesia, St George's Hospital, Blackshaw Rd, LONDON, SW17 0QT.   (hsb)
   020 8725 3317   fax 020 8725 3135
   email jean-pierre.vanbesouw@stgeorges.nhs.uk
   http://www.acta.org.uk
   Hon Sec: Dr J P van Besouw
▲ Company Limited by Guarantee
○ *M, *P; promotion education, training, taching & research in the field of cardiothoracic anaesthesia & intensive care
● Conf - Mtgs - ET - Exam - Res - Stat - Inf
< Eur Assn of Cardiothoracic Anaesthesia
M 470 i
¶ ACTA News - 2; ftm only.

Association of Careers Advisers in Colleges offering Higher Education

dissolved

Association for Careers Education & Guidance (ACEG) 1969

■ 9 Lawrence Leys, Bloxham, BANBURY, Oxon, OX15 4NU.   (hsp)
   01295 720809   fax 01295 720809
   email aceg@freeuk.com   http://www.aceg.org.uk
   Sec: Alan Vincent
▲ Company Limited by Guarantee
○ *E, *P; to promote excellence & innovation in careers education & guidance for all young people
● Conf - ET - Res - Inf - LG
< Intl Assn Educl & Vocational Guidance; Fedn of Profl Assns in Guidance; Guidance Coun; Profl Assns Res Network
M 1,950 i
¶ Careers Education & Guidance (Jnl) - 5; ftm, £7.50 nm.
× 2006 (January) National Association of Careers & Guidance Teachers

Association of Catering Equipment Manufacturers & Importers
   an alternative name for the **Catering Equipment Suppliers Association**

Association of Cereal Food Manufacturers (ACFM) 1955

■ 6 Catherine St, LONDON, WC2B 5JJ.   (hq)
   020 7836 2460   fax 020 7836 0580
   Sec: Miss Joanne Moore
▲ Un-incorporated Society
○ *T; manufacturers of breakfast cereals
● Mtgs - Inf
< Eur Breakfast Cereal Assn (CEEREAL); Food & Drink Fedn
M 8 f

Association of Certified I.T. Professionals

NR Unit 3 Mill Road, STOKENCHURCH, Bucks, HP14 3BF.   (hq)
   0845 060 3456   fax 01494 483022
   Chief Exec: Garry Carter
▲ Company Limited by Guarantee
M 10,000 i
   no further information supplied

Association of Charitable Foundations (ACF) 1989

■ Central House (5th floor), 14 Upper Woburn Place, LONDON, WC1H 0AE.   (hq)
   020 7255 4499   fax 020 7255 4496
   email acf@acf.org.uk   http://www.acf.org.uk
   Chief Exec: David Emerson
▲ Company Limited by Guarantee; Registered Charity
○ *N; to promote & support the work of charitable grant-making trusts & foundations
Gp Alcohol & drugs; Arts; Children & young people; Disability; Education; Environment; Health; Housing; Individuals in need; International; Neighbourhood issues; Northern Ireland; Penal affairs; Race equality; Rural issues; Scotland; Strategic issues in the voluntary sector; Wales; Women's issues
● Conf - Mtgs - Inf - LG
M 300 org
¶ Trust & Foundation News - 4; ftm.   NL.   AR.
   A Guide to Giving (2nd ed); £20.
   Monitoring & Evaluation; a practical guide for grant-making trusts; £10.
   SORP Made Simple: a guidance for grant-making charities (2006).
   Why Rich People Give; £15.
   Various other publications.

Association for Charities   (AfC)   1999
NR   83 Priory Gardens, LONDON, N6 5QU.   (hsb/p)
    020 8348 9114
    Coordinator: Belinda McKenzie
▲   Un-incorporated Society
○   *K; to support & protect charities, trustees & beneficiaries
    affected by the actions of Charity Commission for England &
    Wales; to campaign for a fairer system of charity regulation
    & a more accountable Commission
●   Conf - Mtgs - Lib (video) - Public seminars
M   50 i, 30 charities
¶   New Help for Charities (2001): a leaflet.

Association of Charity Independent Examiners   (ACIE)   1999
■   Bentley Resource Centre, High St, Bentley, DONCASTER,
    S Yorks, DN5 0AA.   (asa)
    01302 828338   fax 01302 872973
    email info@acie.org.uk   http://www.acie.org.uk
    Dir: Fiona Gordon
▲   Registered Charity; Un-incorporated Society
○   *P; to promote the greater effectiveness of UK charities by
    providing support & encouraging professional standards for
    all persons acting as independent examiners of charity
    accounts
●   Conf - ET - Exam - Inf - LG
M   570 i
¶   Independent Examiner (NL) - 3; ftm, £40 yr nm.
    ACIE Hbk - 1; ftm, £10 nm.
    AR & Financial Statement - 1; free.

Association of Charity Officers   (ACO)   1946
■   Five Ways, 57-59 Hatfield Rd, POTTERS BAR, Herts,
    EN6 1HS.   (hq)
    01707 651777   fax 01707 660477
    email info@aco.uk.net
    Dir: Mrs Valerie J Barrow
    Chmn: Mike Carter
▲   Registered Charity
○   *N, *W; to promote efficiency & encourage liaison &
    cooperation between charities
Gp   Forums: Residential care - dealing with all matters relating to
    residential & nursing home care; Grant making - dealing
    with all matters relating to grant aid for individuals /
    benevolence & the interface with Social Security; special work
    on occupational benevolent funds; Under 5's group for very
    small charities
●   Mtgs - Res - LG
<   Age Concern; NCVO; HELPLINES for members
M   250 charities (giving non-contributory relief)
¶   NL - 4/5.   AR.
    Various other publications - irreg.

Association of Charity Shops   (ACS)   1999
■   Central House, Upper Woburn Place, LONDON, WC1H 0AE.
    (hq)
    020 7255 4470   fax 020 7255 4475
    email mail@charityshops.org.uk
    http://www.charityshops.org.uk
    Exec Sec: Lekha Klouda
▲   Company Limited by Guarantee
○   *N; to promote & support charities, that run shops as part of
    their fund-raising activities, by pooling expertise to enable
    them to run their shops as effectively as possible
●   Conf - Mtgs - ET - Res - Exhib - Stat - LG
<   Brit Retail Consortium
M   c 250 charities, c 30 associate m (commercial interests)
¶   Bulletin - 10;   AR - 1; both free.

**Association of Charter Trustee Towns & Charter Town Councils
(ACTCTC)   1975**
■   Barratts Court, Rectory Lane, Rock, KIDDERMINSTER, Worcs,
    DY14 9RR.   (hsb/hsp)
    01299 832797
    email charles@talbotkidder.demon.co.uk
    Hon Sec: Charles Ellis Talbot
▲   Un-incorporated Society
○   *N; to preserve & enhance the status & traditions of charter
    trustee cities, towns & charter town councils
●   Conf - Mtgs - Inf - LG
M   16 towns

Association of Chartered Certified Accountants   (ACCA)   1904
NR   29 Lincoln's Inn Fields, LONDON, WC2A 3EE.   (hq)
    020 7059 5700
○   *P;

**Association of Chief Archivists in Local Government   (ACALG)
1980**
NR   East Sussex Record Office, The Maltings, Castle Precincts,
    LEWES, E Sussex, BN7 1YT.   (hsb)
    01273 482349
    Hon Sec: Elizabeth Hughes
▲   Un-incorporated Society
○   *P; to represent the concerns of chief archivists in local
    government in England & Wales
●   Conf - Mtgs - ET - Res - Stat - Inf - LG
<   Intl Coun on Archives; Nat Coun on Archives; Local Govt Assn
M   92 i
×   1998-9 Association of County Archivists

Association of Chief Education Officers
    since 2002 **Confederation of Children's Services Managers**

**Association of Chief Estates Surveyors & Property Managers in
Local Government   (ACES)   1986**
■   23 Athol Rd, BRAMHALL, Cheshire, SK7 1BR.   (sb)
    0161-439 9589   fax 0161-440 7383
    email secretary@aces.org.uk   http://www.aces.org.uk
    Consultant Sec: T Foster
▲   Un-incorporated Society
Br   10
○   *P; to provide a forum for debate about public property;
    sharing of best practice in property asset management
Gp   Housing; Town centre management; Best value; PFI;
    Regeneration; Rural affairs; Compensation
●   Conf - Mtgs - Res - LG
<   Fedn of Property Socs
M   390 i
¶   The Terrier - 4; free,   Per Annum (Ybk) - 1; ftm only.

**Association of Chief Executives of Voluntary Organisations
(ACEVO)   1988**
■   1 New Oxford St, LONDON, WC1A 1NU.   (hq)
    0845 345 8481   fax 0845 345 8482
    email info@acevo.org.uk   http://www.acevo.org.uk
    Chief Exec: Stephen Bubb
▲   Company Limited by Guarantee
○   *P; for chief executives of voluntary organisations in England &
    Wales
●   Conf - Mtgs - ET - Res - Exhib - LG
M   1,500 i, 125 f, 40 org
¶   NoticeBoard (NL) - 9;   Hbk - 1;   Annual Review; all ftm only.
    Basic Guides to Good Practice [20 published]; £5 each.
    Replacing the State?; £12.50.
    Publications list available.
×   2000 (February) Association of Chief Executives of National
    Voluntary Organisations

© CBD Research Ltd · Beckenham · BR3 5JS · Tel 020 8650 7745 · Fax 020 8650 0768 · E-mail cbd@cbdresearch.com · www.cbdresearch.com

Association of Chief Officers of Scottish Voluntary Organisations
- ■ 20 Forth St, EDINBURGH, EH1 3LH.
  0131-550 3712
- ○ *P
  No further information supplied

Association of Chief Police Officers of England, Wales & Northern Ireland   (ACPO)   1948
- NR 25 Victoria St, LONDON, SW1H 0EX.   (hq)
- ○ *P
- Gp Specialist c'ees dealing with various aspects of policing
- M i

Association of Chief Police Officers (Scotland)   (ACPO(S))   1870
- ■ Police Headquarters, 173 Pitt St, GLASGOW, G2 4JS.   (hsb)
  0141-532 2052   fax 0141-532 2058
  email acpos.secretariat@strathclyde.pnn.police.uk
  http://www.scottish.police.uk/main.acpos
  Hon Sec: Sir William Rae
- ○ *N; to oversee the direction & development of the Scottish Police Service
- Gp Crime; Finance; General policing; Road policing; Information management; Personnel & training; Professional standards; Diversity; Criminal justice; Performance; Management
- ● Conf - Mtgs - Empl - LG
- M i
- ¶ AR - 1.

Association of Child Abuse Lawyers   (ACAL)
- NR Claremount House (suite 1), 22-24 Claremont Rd, SURBITON, Surrey, KT6 4QU.   (asa)
  020 8390 4701   fax 020 8399 1152
  Pres: Lee Moore
- ○ *P

Association for Child & Adolescent Mental Health   (ACAMH)   1956
- ■ St Saviour's House, 39-41 Union St, LONDON, SE1 1SD.   (hq)
  020 7403 7458   fax 020 7403 7081
  email acamh@acamh.org.uk
  http://www.acamh.org.uk
  Exec Dir: Ingrid King
- ▲ Registered Charity
- Br 2
- ○ *L; to further the study of the mental health of children, young people & their families, through the media of meetings & publications
- ● Mtgs - ET - Res - SG - Inf
- M 2,410 i, UK / 300 i, o'seas
- ¶ Jnl of Child Psychology & Psychiatry - 8.
  Child & Adolescent Mental Health - 4.
- ✕ 2006 (March) Association for Child Psychology & Psychiatry

Association for Child Psychology & Psychiatry   6
   since March 2006 **Association for Child & Adolescent Mental Health**

Association of Child Psychotherapists   (ACP)   1949
- NR 120 West Heath Rd, LONDON, NW3 7TU.   (hq)
  020 8458 1609   fax 020 8458 1482
  email acp@dial.pipex.com
  Sec: Angie Lee-Lazone
- ○ *P
- ● Mtgs - Lectures
- M 693 i

Association for Children with Hand or Arm Deficiency
   see **REACH: Association for Children with Hand or Arm Deficiency**

Association for Children with Heart Disorders
   since 2005 **Children's Heart Association**

Association of Children's Hospices
- ■ Canningford House (1st floor), BRISTOL, BS1 6BY.
  0117-989 7820
  http://www.childhospice.org.uk
  Chief Exec: Barbara Gelb
- ○ *M

Association for Children with Life-Threatening or Terminal Conditions & their Families   (ACT)   1993
- ■ Orchard House, Orchard Lane, BRISTOL, BS1 5DT.
  0117-922 1556 (admin)   fax 0117-930 4707
  email info@act.org.uk   http://www.act.org.uk
  Chief Exec Officer: Lizzie Chambers
- ▲ Company Limited by Guarantee
- ○ *K, *W; campaigns for the provision of locally coordinated palliative care services for terminally ill children; to provide information on services available to families caring for a child with a life-threatening or terminal condition
- Gp ACT Council (Chmn: John Overton),
  Children's palliative care (Chmn: Dr Chris Newman)
- ● Conf - Mtgs - ET - Inf - Lib - LG
  Helpline: 0845 108 2201
- < Inst of Child Health (Bristol)
- M [not stated]
- ¶ Act Now (NL); ftm, £2 each nm.
  Palliative Care for Young People 13-24 (2001); £10 nm.
  Guide to the Development of Children's Palliative Care Services (2003); £10.
  Publications list available.

Association of Christian Teachers   (ACT)   1971
- NR 94A London Rd, ST ALBANS, Herts, AL1 1NX.   (hq)
  01727 840298
  Chief Exec: Rupert Kaye
- ▲ Company Limited by Guarantee; Registered Charity
- Br 50
- ○ *E, *R; to support Christians employed in education
- ● Conf - ET - SG - Inf - Lib
- < Scripture U
- M 2,570 i, UK, / 50 i, o'seas
- ¶ Act Now - 3; ftm.
  Jnl of Education & Christian Belief.

Association for Church Editors
- NR 12 Grosvenor Rd, GLOUCESTER, GL2 0SB.
  01452 521062
  Sec: Lesley B Barrett

Association of Circulation Executives   (ACE)   1951
- NR 5 Willesborough Court, Willesborough Lees, ASHFORD, Kent, TN24 0SW.
  01233 662369
  Contact: Trevor Collier
- ▲ Un-incorporated Society
- ○ *P, *T; for senior executives responsible for circulation, marketing & distribution of newspapers, magazines, periodicals (national & regional); for the dissemination of information & promotion of goodwill between publishers (members) & the wholesalers & retailers who handle their publications
- ● Conf - Mtgs - ET - Exhib - SG
- M 420 i, UK / 6 i, o'seas
- ¶ Sisyphus (NL) - 4; free.

Association of Circus Proprietors of Great Britain   (ACP)   1932
- ■ PO Box 131, BLACKBURN, Lancs, BB1 9GA.   (hsp)
  01254 814789   fax 01254 814789
  email malcolmclay@talk21.com
  Sec: Malcolm S Clay
- ▲ Un-incorporated Society
- ○ *T; the conduct of the circus industry in GB; the welfare of animals in circuses
- ● Conf - Mtgs - Inf - LG
- M 20 f

Association of Civic Hosts
2006 merged with the **Association for Public Service Excellence**

Association of Civil Enforcement Agencies   (ACEA)   1996
■ Kensington House, 33 Imperial Square, CHELTENHAM, Glos,
    GL50 1QZ.   (regd/office)
    01242 241456   fax 01242 241421
    email dir-gen@acea.org.uk   http://www.acea.org.uk
    Dir Gen: Dr Steven Everson
▲ Company Limited by Guarantee
○ *P; to promote higher standards in the civil enforcement
    industry
● Mtgs - Res - Empl - LG
M 26 i, 31 f

Association of Classic Car Clubs
reported as dissolved

Association of Classic Trials Clubs Ltd   (ACTC)   1979
■ 6 Echells Close, BROMSGROVE, Worcs, B61 7EB.   (hsp)
    01527 878388
    email adrian@tpeake.screaming.net
    http://www.actc.org.uk
    Sec: Adrian Tucker-Peake
▲ Company Limited by Guarantee
Br 22
○ *K, *S; to promote grass-roots motorsport through national
    classic reliability trials championships for cars & motocycles
Gp Technical panel; Public relations; Rights of way; Championships
● Mtgs - Exhib - Comp - PL - LG
< R Automobile Club Motor Sports Assns Ltd; Byways &
    Bridleways Trust Coun
M c 3,000 i, 22 org
¶ Restart - 4.

Association for Clinical Biochemistry   (ACB)   1953
■ 130-132 Tooley St, LONDON, SE1 2TU.   (hq)
    020 7403 8001   fax 020 7403 8006
    email admin@acb.org.uk   http://www.acb.org.uk
    Chmn: Dr I D Watson;   Hon Sec: Dr G McCreanor
▲ Company Limited by Guarantee
○ *L; advancement of clinical biochemistry in the UK
Gp C'ees: Scientific, Education, Publications, Workforce advisory
● Conf - Mtgs - ET - Res - Exhib - Empl - LG
< Intl Fedn of Clinical Chemistry (IFCC)
M 1,835 i, 56 f, UK / 306 i, o'seas
¶ Annals of Clinical Biochemistry - 6; ftm, £136 yr nm.
✕ 2005 Association of Clinical Biochemists

Association of Clinical Biochemists in Ireland
IRL c/o Clinical Biochemistry Dept, St Vincent's University Hospital,
    Elm Park, DUBLIN 4, Republic of Ireland.   (sec)
    353 (1) 209 4789
    email r.reece@st_vincents.ie   http://www.acbi.ie b
    Hon Sec: Roland Reece
○ *P

Association of Clinical Cytogeneticists
a group of the **British Society for Human Genetics**

Association for Clinical Data Management   (ACDM)
■ 105 St Peter's Street, ST ALBANS, Herts, AL1 3EJ.   (hq)
    01727 896080
    http://www.acdm.org.uk
    Sec: Angela Ison
▲ Company Limited by Guarantee
○ *P; data management in the pharmaceutical industry
< Conf - Mtgs - ET - Exam - Exhib
M 1,438 i, UK / 259 i, o'seas

Association of Clinical Pathologists   (ACP)   1927
■ 189 Dyke Rd, HOVE, E Sussex, BN3 1TL.   (hq)
    01273 775700   fax 01273 773303
    email info@pathologists.org.uk
    http://www.pathologists.org.uk
    Gen Admin: Alison Martin
▲ Company Limited by Guarantee; Registered Charity
Br 12
○ *L, *P; the study & practice of clinical pathology
● Conf - Mtgs - ET
M 2,200 i, UK & o'seas
¶ ACP News - 3;   ACP Ybk - 1.

Association of Clinical Professors of Paediatrics   (ACPP)   1976
■ c/o Prof N J Bishop, Academic Unit of Child Health, Sheffield
    Children's NHS Trust, SHEFFIELD, S Yorks, S10 2TH.   (hsb)
    0114-271 9228   fax 0114-275 5364
    email n.j.bishop@sheffield.ac.uk
    Hon Sec: Prof N J Bishop
▲ Un-incorporated Society
○ *M, *P
● Mtgs - ET
< Fedn Clinical Professors
M 93 i

Association of Clinical Scientists
a group of the **Association of Respiratory Technology &
Physiology**

Association for Coaching   (AC)
NR 66 Church Rd, LONDON, W7 1LB.
    http://www.associationforcoaching.com
    Chmn: Katherine Tulpa
○ *P

Association of Coal Mine Methane Operators
■ Edwinstowe House, High St, EDWINSTOWE, Notts, NG21 9PR.
    01623 827927   fax 01623 827905
    email info@acmmo.org   http://www.acmmo.org
    Chmn: Dr Cameron Davies,   Co Sec: Steve Goalby
○ *T; extration of colal mine methane for generation of electricity.

Association for Cognitive Analytic Therapy   (ACAT)
■ South Wing (3rd floor), Division of Academic Psychiatry,
    St Thomas' Hospital, Lambeth Palace Rd, LONDON,
    SE1 7EH.
    020 7188 0692   fax 020 7928 0981
    email AofCAT@aol.com   http://www.acat.me.uk
    Admin: Jonathan Lopez-Real

Association of Collaborative Family Lawyers
a group of the **Law Society of Northern Ireland**

Association for College Management   (ACM)   1987
NR 35 The Point, MARKET HARBOROUGH, Leics, LE16 7QU.
    (admin)
    01858 461110   fax 01858 461366
    email administration@acm.uk.com
    http://www.acm.uk.com
    Chief Exec & Gen Sec: Peter Pendle
Br 110
○ *P, *U; a trade union for college managers (principals, vice-
    principals & other senior college managers)
Gp Many connected with vocational education & training
● Conf - Mtgs - ET - SG - Empl - LG
M 3,500 i, UK / 10 i, o'seas
¶ NL - 10;   Information & Briefing Sheet - irreg; both ftm only.

Association of College Registrars & Administrators
has merged with the **Association of Colleges**

Association of Colleges   (AoC)   1893
NR   Centre Point (5th floor), 103 New Oxford St, LONDON,
    WC1A 1DD.   (hq)
    020 7827 4600   fax 020 7827 4650
    Chief Exec: John Brennan
▲   Company Limited by Guarantee
○   *E, *N; 'leading body in the UK on further education'
●   Conf - Mtgs - ET - Expt - Inf - Empl - LG
M   c 500 colleges
✕   2000-02 Association of College Registrars & Administrators
    (merged)

Association of Coloproctology of Great Britain & Ireland   1990
■   c/o Royal College of Surgeons of England, 35-43 Lincoln's Inn
    Fields, LONDON, WC2A 3PE.   (hq)
    020 7973 0307   fax 020 7430 9235
    email acpgbi@asgbi.org.uk   http://www.acpgbi.org.uk
    Hon Sec: Nigel A Scott
▲   Registered Charity
○   *P; the advancement of the science & practice of
    coloproctology; to promote high standards in training &
    research
●   Conf - Mtgs - ET - Res - Exhib
M   1,213 i, UK / 149 i, o'seas
¶   Colorectal Disease - 9; prices vary (published by Blackwell
    Publishing).

Association of Commonwealth Universities   (ACU)   1913
NR   20-24 Tavistock Sq, LONDON, WC1H 9NF.   (hq)
    020 7380 6700
    Sec Gen: Prof Michael Gibbons
▲   Registered Charity
○   *E; a Commonwealth body, governed & financed by the
    membership throughout the Commonwealth which promotes
    contact & cooperation between universities
●   Mtgs - Exhib - Inf - Lib - Fellowships & scholarships
    administration - Appointments advertising service - Higher
    education management service
<   Intl Assn of Universities; UNESCO
M   100 university instns, UK / 380, o'seas
¶   Commonwealth Universities Ybk - 1.   Bulletin - 5.
    Awards series:
        for Postgraduate Study at Commonwealth Universities.
        for University Teachers & Research Workers.
        for First Degree Study at Commonwealth Universities.
        for University Administrators & Librarians.
    Who's Who of Vice-Chancellors, Presidents & Rectors of
    Commonwealth Universities (1996).
    LM - 1;   AR of the Council.

Association of Community & Comprehensive Schools   1982
IRL   10H Centrepoint Business Park, Oak Drive, DUBLIN 12,
    Republic of Ireland.
    353 (1) 460 1150   fax 353 (1) 460 1203
    email office@accs.ie   http://www.accs.ie
    Hon Sec: Jane Glanville
○   *E
M   92 schools

**Association for Community-based Maternity Care   (ACBMC)
1989**
NR   Newby End Farm, Newby, PENRITH, Cumbria, CA10 3EX.
    (admin/p)
    01931 714338
    email jennyatnewbyend@ukonline.co.uk
    Membership & Database Admin: Jenny Jones,
    Chmn: Richard Porter
▲   Un-incorporated Society
○   *P; to support & develop appropriate care, based in the
    community, for women during pregnancy, birth & the
    puerperium; to support those currently involved in promoting
    such care
●   Mtgs - ET - Inf

Association of Community Rail Partnerships   (ACoRP)   1999
■   Rail & River Centre, Canalside, Slaithwaite Civic Hall,
    15a New St, Slaithwaite, HUDDERSFIELD, W Yorks,
    HD7 5AB.   (hq)
    01484 847790   fax 01484 847877
    http://www.acorp.uk.com
    Sec: Philip Jenkinson
▲   Company Limited by Guarantee
○   *K; to encourage local communities to become actively involved
    with their local railway station/train service, predominantly in
    the rural sector
Gp   Station design; Rolling stock
●   Conf - Res - Exhib - SG - Inf - VE - LG
<   Community Transport Assn
>   Community Transport Assn; Heritage Rly Museums; Sustrans
M   8 i, 7 f, 49 org
¶   Train Times - 4; ftm, £70 nm (includes discounts at
    conferences, specialist advice & email NL).
    Research/consultancy Reports - 2/3; ftm.   AR.
✕   2004 Transport Research & Information Network (merged)

Association of Community Television Operators   (ACTO)   1989
NR   Institute of Local Television, 13 Bellevue Place, EDINBURGH,
    EH7 4BS.   (hq)
    0131-466 3021
    Co-ordinator: Dave Rushton
✕   2002-04 Association of Local Television Operators

Association for Commuter Transport   1997
NR   1 Vernon Mews, Vernon St, LONDON, W14 0RL.   (regd/off)
    020 7348 1987
○   *K; 'to drop the level of pollution caused by traffic; to reduce
    the use of cars for inappropriate journeys'

**Association of Company Registration Agents Ltd   (ACRA)
1978**
NR   20 Holywell Row, LONDON, EC2A 4XH.   (hsb)
    020 7377 0381   fax 020 7377 6646
    Hon Sec: M R Chettleburgh
▲   Company Limited by Guarantee
○   *P; 'to promote the interests of those using the facilities of the
    Companies Registration Office; to maintain a high standard
    among members'
●   LG
<   Law Services Assn
M   13 f

Association of Computer Cable Manufacturers   (ACCM)   1993
■   Kingsway House, Wrotham Rd, GRAVESEND, Kent,
    DA13 0AU.   (asa)
○   *T
●   Conf - Mtgs - LG - Lib
M   f

Association of Computer Engineers & Technicians
NR   Wellington House, East Rd, CAMBRIDGE, CB1 1BH.
    01223 451027   fax 01223 451100
    http://www.acet-uk.org
○   *P

Association of Computer Professionals   (ACP)   1984
■   Springbank House, The Drive, MARESFIELD, E Sussex,
    TN22 2HA.   (hq)
    01825 761410   fax 01825 760894
    email admin@acpexamboard.com
    http://www.acpexamboard.com
    Sec Gen: Mrs N Keats
○   *P; to provide high standards of efficiency throughout the
    industry; to prepare candidates, through examinations, for a
    successful career in computing
●   Exam (for: Certificate in computer programming; Diploma in
    computer design; Advanced diploma in computer studies)
M   i

Association of Concrete Industrial Flooring Contractors (ACIFC) 1994

■ Carthusian Court, 12 Carthusian St, LONDON, EC1M 6EZ. (asa)
0870 429 9176   fax 0870 429 9177
email acifc@hotmail.com   http://www.acifc.org.uk
Secretariat: S Doshi,   Chmn: David Harvey
▲ Un-incorporated Society
○ *T; interests of specialist contractors & the development of concrete floors
Gp Technical - all aspects of slab construction
● Conf - Mtgs - Inf - Liaison with technical & trade bodies
< ACIFC (France)
M 40 f, UK / 10 f, o'seas
¶ Technical publications, published through the Concrete Society:
Concrete Mix Design
Steel Fibre Reinforcement
Admixtures
Dry Shake Topping.

Association for Conferences & Events   (ACE)   1971

■ Riverside House, High St, HUNTINGDON, Cambs, PE29 3SG.   (hq)
01480 457595   fax 01480 412863
email ace@martex.co.uk   http://www.martex.co.uk/ace
Mem Mgr: John Thompson
▲ Company Limited by Guarantee
○ *N, *P, *T; information centre & forum for member organisations involved in the organising, marketing, accommodating & servicing of events
● ET - Inf - VE - LG
> Business Tourist Partnership (BTP)
M 150 f, UK / 2 f, o'seas
¶ NL - 12; ftm only.
Conference & Exhibition Fact Finder - 12; ftm, £36 nm.
ACE Ybk - Who's Who in the Meetings Industry - 1; ftm, £14.99 nm.
ACE Guide to a Career in Conferences (Hbk); ftm, £2.50 nm.
AR; ftm only.

Association for the Conservation of Energy   (ACE)   1981

■ Westgate House, Prebend St, LONDON, N1 8PT.   (hq)
020 7359 8000
Dir: Andrew Warren
▲ Company Limited by Guarantee
○ *K, *T; to encourage a positive national awareness of the benefits & need for energy conservation
● Res
< EUROACE
M 16 f
¶ The Fifth Fuel (NL) - 2; free.
Publications list available on website.

Association for Consultancy & Engineering   (ACE)   1913

NR 12 Caxton St, LONDON, SW1H 0QL.   (hq)
020 7222 6557   fax 020 7222 0750
email consult@acenet.co.uk   http://www.acenet.co.uk
Chief Exec: Nelson Ogunshakin
▲ Company Limited by Guarantee
○ *T
Gp Civil; Structural; Electrical; Mechanical; Chemical; Mining & metallurgy; Building services; Telecommunications; Gas; Marine & naval; Aeronautical; Production; Computer & control engineering; Civil engineering (incl road, rail, airports, docks & harbours)
● Conf - Exhib - SG - Stat - Expt - Inf - LG
< Fédn Intle des Ingénieurs Conseils; Eur Fedn of Consultancy Assns
M 750 f, UK / 10 f, o'seas
¶ Consult - 10; ftm only.
ACE Directory - 1; ftm, £35 nm.
Many other publications.
✕ 2004 Association of Consulting Engineers

Association of Consultant Approved Inspectors   (ACAI)   1996

NR c/o 14 Berkeley St, LONDON, W1J 8DX.
http://www.acai.org.uk
Hon Sec: Paul Timmins
▲ Un-incorporated Society
○ *P; to promote the role & development of private sector building control by approved inspectors instead of the use of local authorities in England & Wales.   Approved Inspectors are statutory appointees under Part II of the Building Act 1984, such appointees being made by the Secretary of State for Local Government & the Regions, or the Construction Industry Council
● Mtgs - SG - LG
M 14 i, 12 f, 7 affiliates
¶ LM.
✕ 2002-04 Association of Corporate Approved Inspectors

Association of Consultant Architects   (ACA)   1973

■ 98 Hayes Rd, BROMLEY, Kent, BR2 9AB.   (hq)
020 8325 1402   fax 020 8466 9079
email office@acarchitects.co.uk
http://www.acarchitects.co.uk
Sec Gen: Mrs Fiona Griffiths
▲ Company Limited by Guarantee
○ *T; for architects in private practice
Gp Planning advisory; Conservation; Small business
● Conf - Mtgs - Res - Exhib - Comp - SG - VE - LG
M 250 f
¶ NL - 4; ftm only.
ACA Specialist Services Directory - 1; ftm, £10 nm.
ACA Form of Building Agreement (Contract document); £7.87 m, £10.50 nm.

Association of Consulting Actuaries   (ACA)   1951

■ Warnford Court, 29 Throgmorton St, LONDON, EC2N 2AT. (hq)
020 7382 4594   fax 020 7374 6220
Hon Sec: Keith Barton
○ *P; to advise individuals, institutions, the government & corporate bodies on pensions, life & general insurance & other financial issues

Association of Consulting Engineers
since November 2004 **Association for Consultancy & Engineering**

Association of Consulting Engineers of Ireland

IRL 46 Merrion Sq, DUBLIN 2, Republic of Ireland.
353 (1) 642 5588   fax 353 (1) 642 5590
http://www.acei.ie
Exec Dir: Anne Potter
○ *P

Association of Consulting Scientists   1958

■ Sandown House, 8 St Clare Rd, COLCHESTER, Essex, CO3 3SZ.   (hsb)
http://www.consultingscientists.co.uk
Hon Sec: Dr D Simpson
▲ Company Limited by Guarantee
○ *P; to make known the services of consulting scientists; to promote scientific & technical research through contracts with member firms; to ascertain & make known the views of independent scientists on matters of wider interest
Gp Forensic & expert witness; Testing laboratories
● Conf - Mtgs - Res - Inf - LG
M 42 f
¶ NL - 4; free.
Directory of Members & Services - on website.

Association of Contact Lens Manufacturers Ltd   (ACLM)   1962
- ■ PO Box 735, DEVIZES, Wilts, SN10 3TQ.   (sec-gen/b)
   01380 860418   fax 01380 860863
   email info@aclm.org.uk   http://www.aclm.org.uk
   Sec Gen: Simon Rodwell
- ▲ Company Limited by Guarantee
- ○ *T; to promote the wearing of contact lenses
- Gp Technical working; Labelling; Ethics; EDI; PR; Packaging waste;
   Hygienic management
- ● Conf - Mtgs - ET - Exhib - Stat - LG - Regulatory [activities] in
   connection with CE marking
- < Eur Fedn Nat Assns Contact Lens Mfrs (Euromcontact);
   Eyecare UK (E-UK)
- M 3 i, 30 f
- ¶ ACLM Contact Lens Ybk - 1; £17.

Association for Contemporary Iberian Studies   (ACIS)   1968
- NR c/o Dr Mark Gant, Languages Dept, University of Chester,
   Parkgate Rd, CHESTER, Cheshire, CH1 4BJ.   (hsb)
   01244 513049   fax 01244 511311
   email m.gant@chester.ac.uk
   http://www.brighton.ac.uk/languages/acis
   Sec: Dr Mark Gant
- ○ *L; the study of social, economic & political affairs of the
   Iberian area, together with its languages
- ● Conf - ET - Res
- M 180 i, 30 f, UK / 20 i, o'seas
- ¶ International Jnl of Iberian Studies - 3.
   [see also: www.intellectbooks.com/journals/ijis.htm]

Association for Contemporary Jewellery   (ACJ)   1997
- NR PO Box 37807, LONDON, SE23 1XJ   (admin/p)
   020 8291 4201   fax 020 8291 4452
   email enquiries@acj.org.uk   http://www.acj.org.uk
   Admin: Sue Hyams,   Chmn: Susie Fortune
- ○ *G, *P, *T
- ● Conf - ET - Exhib - Inf - VE
- ¶ Findings - 4.

Association for Continence Advice   (ACA)   1981
- NR c/o Meeting Makers, Jordanhill Campus, 76 Southbrae Drive,
   GLASGOW, G13 1PP.   (hq)
   0141-434 1500   fax 0141-434 1519
- ▲ Company Limited by Guarantee; Registered Charity
- Br 14
- ○ *P; a multi-professional group open to all healthcare
   professionals interested in the promotion of continence &
   who have a concern for the better management of
   incontinence, treating those with bladder & bowel dysfunction
- ● Conf - Mtgs - ET - Exhib - SG - LG
- < The Continence Foundation; Incontact; Enuresis Resource & Inf
   Centre; Interstitial Cystitis Support Gp; PromoCon 2001
- M 692 i, 57 f, 6 org, UK / 39 i, 1 f, o'seas
- ¶ Continence (Jnl) - 4; ftm, subscription nm.
   The ACA Notes for Good Practice; ftm, subscription nm.
   The ACA Continence Promotion Pack - Nursing & Residential
   Homes.
   The ACA Abstract Service.

Association of Convenience Stores   (ACS)   1994
- NR Federation House, 17 Farnborough St, FARNBOROUGH,
   Hants, GU14 8AG.   (hq)
   01252 515001
   Chief Exec: James Lowman
- ▲ Company Limited by Guarantee
- ○ *T; to represent convenience stores across the UK; to foster the
   development of the whole of the professional convenience
   store sector, for the benefit of retailers, wholesalers &
   suppliers; to optimise the benefit to the sector of legislation
   emanating from UK & EU parliaments & by anticipating
   demand for information & training required by the sector
- Gp Association of News Retailing
- ● Conf - Mtgs - ET - Res - Exhib - Inf - VE - LG
- < Intl Fedn of Grocers' Assns
- M 31,000 stores
- ¶ ACS News - 12; ftm.

Association of Copyright Investigators   (ACI)   2000
- ■ 15 Wickham Rd, Beckenham, Kent, BR3 5JS.   (hq)
- ○ *P
- ● Mtgs - Stat - LG
- M i & f

Association of Corporate Approved Inspectors
   since 2002-04 **Association of Consultant Approved Inspectors**

Association of Corporate Treasurers   (ACT)   1979
- NR Ocean House, 10-12 Little Trinity Lane, LONDON,
   EC4V 2AA.   (hq)
   020 7213 9728
   Chief Exec: Richard Raeburn
- Br 16; Belgium, Eire, Hong Kong
- ○ *P; the management of financial risk, liquidity, corporate
   finance, the balance sheet
- ● Conf - Mtgs - ET - Exam - Res - Exhib - SG - Lib - LG
- M c 4,000 i
- ¶ The Treasurer - 12;   The Treasurers Hbk - 1; both ftm.

Association of Corporate Trustees   (TACT)   1974
- NR 3 Brackerne Close, Cooden, BEXHILL-on-SEA, E Sussex,
   TN39 3BT.   (hsb)
   01424 844144   fax 01424 844144
   Sec: W J Stephenson
- ▲ Un-incorporated Society
- ○ *P; to consider & act on items of mutual interest in the fields of
   law, taxation, investment & related technical & practical
   subjects
- Gp Pensions; Loan capital; Private trusts; Charities
- ● Mtgs - ET
- M 70 f, UK / 1 f, o'seas
- ¶ TACT Review - 2; free.

Association of Cost Engineers Ltd   (ACostE)   1962
- NR Lea House, Middlewich Rd, SANDBACH, Cheshire,
   CW11 1XL.   (hq)
   01270 764798
   Sec: Anne Fairless
- ▲ Company Limited by Guarantee
- Br 7; Hong Kong
- ○ *L, *P; 'to promote cost engineering as a recognised discipline
   of engineering technology'
- Gp Cost indices; Engineering; Planning
- ● Conf - ET - Stat - Lib
- < Intl Cost Engrs Coun; Engg Coun
- M 1,900 i, UK / 650 i, o'seas
- ¶ The Cost Engineer - 6.
   Cost Indices - 6; ftm only.   Ybk - 2; ftm only.

Association of Cost Management Consultants   (ACMC)   1999
NR   Blays House, Churchfield Rd, CHALFONT ST PETER, Bucks,
     SL9 9EW.   (hsb)
     01753 891313
     Hon Sec: Anthony Gibson
▲   Un-incorporated Society
Br   8
○   *P; cost management reduction in utilities &
     telecommunications
Gp   Utility consultants; Telecommunications consultants
●   Conf - Mtgs
M   6 i, 2 f

Association of Council Secretaries & Solicitors   (ACSeS)   1974
NR   4 Sutton Court Lawns, Sutton Poyntz, WEYMOUTH, Dorset,
     DT3 6LH.   (hq)
     01305 836328
○   *P; local government administration, law & management

Association for Counselling at Work
     a group of the **British Association for Counselling &
     Psychotherapy**

Association of Countryside Voluntary Wardens   (ACVW)   1967
NR   Cottage 1 / Ballinbreich Farm, Newburgh, CUPAR, Fife,
     KY14 6HJ.   (hsb)
     Sec: Jay Burkinshaw
▲   Un-incorporated Society
○   *P; to promote effective wardening by volunteers throughout the
     countryside
●   Conf - SG - LG
<   Coun of Nat Parks; LANTRA NTO
M   380 i
¶   NL - 2;   Newssheet - 2; both ftm only.

Association of County Chief Executives   (ACCE)   1974
■   Office of the Chief Executive, County Hall, TROWBRIDGE,
     Wilts, BA14 8JF.   (hsb)
     01225 713101   fax 01225 713092
     email jeanpotter@wiltshire.gov.uk
     Hon Sec: Dr K Robinson
▲   Un-incorporated Society
○   *P
●   Conf - Mtgs - LG
<   County section of the Society of Local Authority Chief Executives
M   38 i
¶   ACCE Members' Hbk; ftm.

Association of County Cricket Scorers   (ACCS)   1993
NR   190 Twentywell Lane, SHEFFIELD, S Yorks, S17 4QF.   (hsp)
     Hon Sec: Mike Snook
○   *P; to improve the standards of cricket scoring; 'to cooperate &
     cultivate good relations with all bodies associated with cricket
     for the betterment of the game'
●   AGM; Annual lunch
M   47 i
¶   The Scorer (NL) - 4; ftm only.

**Association of County Public Health Officers   (ASS CPHO)
1946**
NR   1 Cloatley Rd, Hankerton, MALMESBURY, Wilts, SN16 9LQ.
     (hsp)
     Hon Sec: N J Durnford
○   *P; collaboration with appropriate bodies for the advancement
     of public health
●   Mtgs - SG - Stat - Inf - VE
M   c 30 i

Association of Cricket Coaches
     has been replaced by the **England & Wales Cricket Board
     Coaches Association**

Association of Cricket Statisticians & Historians   (ACS)   1973
■   Archives Dept, Glamorgan Cricket, Sophia Gardens, CARDIFF,
     CF11 9XR.   (hsb)
     029 2041 9383
     email office@acscricket.org   http://www.acscricket.com
     Hon Sec: Andrew Hignell
▲   Un-incorporated Society
Br   Victoria (Australia)
○   *S; cricket history & statistics
●   Mtgs - Res - SG - Stat - Inf - Compilation of records of feats &
     matches worldwide
M   1,000 i, UK / 250 i, o'seas
¶   The Cricket Statistician - 4; ftm. 4.
     ACS International Cricket Ybk - 1.
     Various other annual publications.

Association of Cricket Umpires & Scorers   (ACU&S)   1953
■   PO Box 399, CAMBERLEY, Surrey, GU15 9JZ.   (hq)
     01276 27962   fax 01276 62277
     email admin@acus.org.uk   http://www.acus.org.uk
     Admin Mgr: Graham J Bullock
▲   Un-incorporated Society
Br   18; 25 o'seas affiliations
○   *S; all aspects of cricket umpiring & scoring; the application of
     cricket law; the standards of umpiring in general nationally &
     internationally
Gp   Umpiring; Scoring
●   Conf - Mtgs - ET - Exam
<   England & Wales Cricket Bd (ECB); Marylebone Cricket
     Club (MCC)
M   8,500 i, 120 f, 150 org, UK / 460 i, 20 f, 26 org, o'seas
¶   How's That! (Jnl) - 5; ftm only.
     Tom Smith's Cricket Umpiring & Scoring; £9.99.

**Association for Cultural Advancement through Visual Art
(ACAVA)   1983**
■   54 Blechynden St, LONDON, W10 6RJ.   (hq)
     020 8960 5015
     Artistic Dir: Duncan Smith
▲   Company Limited by Guarantee; Registered Charity
Br   6
○   *A; promotion of the visual arts by provision of facilities
     (including studios & galleries) & organisation of programmes
     for their production & access as well as education
●   ET - Exhib
M   300 i
¶   NL - 4; free.

Association for Cushing's Treatment & Help   (ACTH)   1993
■   54 Powney Rd, MAIDENHEAD, Berks, SL6 6EQ.
     (coordinator/p)
     01628 670389   fax 01628 415603
     email cushingsacth@btinternet.com
     http://www.cushingsacth.co.uk
     Coordinator: Mrs Elaine Eldridge
Br   Regional coordinators
○   *W; a self-help group of offering experience, help & advice to
     sufferers of Cushing's Sydrome (over production of
     cortocisterid hormones) & their carers
●   Mtgs (small & informal)
M   C 170 i
¶   Cushy (NL) - 3; ftm only.
     Directory of member contacts.
     Information booklet for newly diagnosed patients.
     Information booklet for post surgery.

Association of Cycle Traders (ACT) 1982
■ PO Box 5110, HOVE, E Sussex, BN52 9EB.   (hq)
  0870 428 8404   fax 0870 428 8403
  email act@cyclesource.co.uk
  http://www.act-bicycles.com
  Nat Sec: Anne Killick
▲ Company Limited by Guarantee
Br 30
○ *T; to promote the interests of the independent cycle trader
● Conf - Mtgs - ET - Exam - Exhib - Inf - LG - Operation of a
  national cycle technicians accreditation programme
< Eur Twowheel Retailers Assn; Bicycle Assn GB; Indep Retailers
  Consortium
M 30 i, 800 f
¶ The Independent - 4; ftm only.

** **Association of Dance & Freestyle Professionals**
  Organisation lost: see Introduction paragraph 3

**Association for Dance Movement Therapy UK Ltd   (ADMT
UK) 1982**
■ 32 Meadfoot Lane, TORQUAY, Devon, TQ1 2BW.   (mail)
  email queries@admt.org.uk
  http://www.admt.org.uk address
  Co Sec & Administrator: Andrew Clements
▲ Company Limited by Guarantee
○ *P; to promote mental & physical health by the use of dance
  movement therapy; to ensure that proper standards of
  professional competence & ethics are maintained
● Conf - Mtgs - ET - Inf - LG - Courses & accreditation of
  practitioners
< Eur Dance Movement Assn
M 200 i
¶ E-Motion (NL) - 4; ftm, £16 nm.   AR.

Association of Deer Management Groups (ADMG) 1992
NR Dalhousie Estates Office, BRECHIN, Angus, DD9 6SG.   (hsb)
  01356 624566   fax 01356 623725
  Sec: R M J Cooke
▲ Un-incorporated Society
○ *N; coordination & representation of deer management groups
  in Scotland; also representation of the Scottish wild venison
  industry
● Conf - Mtgs - ET - Res - Exhib - Stat - LG
M 36 groups
¶ NL - 2; free.

**Association of Denominational Historical Societies & Cognate
Libraries 1993**
■ Library, Religious Society of Friends, Friends House, Euston Rd,
  LONDON, NW1 2BP.   (sb)
  Sec: Heather Rowland,   Convener: Revd Martin Wellings
▲ Un-incorporated Society
○ *P, *R; to encourage research into the traditions of the various
  Christian denominations
● Conf - Mtgs - Res - Inf
M 21 soc & libraries
¶ NL - 1; ftm.

Association of Dental Anaesthetists
NR 21 Portland Place, LONDON, W1B 1PY.
  020 7631 8898   fax 020 7631 4352
  http://www.dentalanaesthesia.org.uk
  Pres: Dr Stuart Hargrave
○ *P

**Association of Dental Hospitals of the United Kingdom
(ADH) 1948**
NR Birmingham Dental Hospital, St Chad's Queensway,
  BIRMINGHAM, B4 6NN.
  0121-237 2722
  Chmn: Rick Roberts
Br 14
○ *N; for dental teaching hospitals
● Mtgs
M 28 i

Association of Dental Implantology (ADI) 1987
■ 98 South Worple Way, LONDON, SW14 8ND.   (hq)
  020 8487 5555   fax 020 8487 5566
  email office@adi.org.uk   http://www.adi.org.uk
  Hon Sec: Dr Vinod Soshi,   Chief Exec: Cherry Wilson
▲ Company Limited by Guarantee; Registered Charity
○ *P; to provide education in dental implantology to the public &
  the profession
Gp Dentists; Dental technicians; Hygienists; Nurses; Restorative
  consultants; Max-Fax surgeons
● Conf - Mtgs - ET - Res - Exhib - SG - Inf
M 1,500 i, 30 f, UK / 25 i, o'seas
¶ Dental Implant Summaries - 6;
  European Jnl for Dental Implantologists - 4; both ftm.

Association of Development Directors in Independent Schools
  since 2003 **Association for Marketing & Development in
  Independent Schools**

Association of Die Cutters & Converters of Adhesive Tapes
  since 2003-04 **Association of Distributors, Coaters &
  Converters of Adhesive Tapes**

**Association of Directors of Education in Scotland   (ADES)
1920**
NR Lochan House, Birse, ABOYNE, AB34 5FP.   (hsb)
  07817 611607
  email member@jstodter.freeserve.co.uk
  Sec Gen: John Stodter
○ *E, *P
● Conf - Mtgs - ET - Res - SG - Inf - Empl - LG
M ['not applicable']

Association of Directors of Public Health   (ADsPH)
NR c/o Faculty of Public Health, 4 St Andrews Place, LONDON,
  NW1 4LB.
○ *M, *P; maintenance of public health medicine
M i

Association of Directors of Social Services (ADSS) 1971
NR ADSS Business Unit, Local Government House, Smith Sq,
  LONDON, SW1P 3HZ.   (hsb)
  020 7072 7433
  Admin: Marinda Oosthuizen
▲ Registered Charity
Br 11
○ *P; promotion of a comprehensive social service for families,
  individuals & communities
● Conf - Mtgs - Res - Stat - Inf - LG
M 135 i
¶ ADSS News - 4/5.   AR - 1.   Hbk (incl LM).
  Directory of Contracting Officers.
  Abuse of Older People.   Towards Community Care.
  Training for the Caring Business.

Association of Directors of Social Work   (ADSW)   1969
- ■ Rosebery House (floor 1), 9 Haymarket Terrace, EDINBURGH, EH12 5XZ.   (hq)
  0131-474 9220   fax 0131-474 9292
  email sophie.mills@adsw.org.uk
  http://www.adsw.org.uk
  Sec: Jim Dean, Admin: Sophie Mills
- ○ *P; for senior social workers working in Scottish local government
- < Conf - Mtgs
- M 140 i

Association of Disabled Professionals   (ADP)   1971
- ■ BCM ADP, LONDON, WC1N 3XX.   (mail/address)
  01204 431638   fax 01204 431638
  email adp.admin@ntlworld.com
  http://www.adp.org.uk
  Chmn: Jane Hunt
- ▲ Registered Charity
- ○ *W; improvement of rehabilitation, education, training & employment opportunities of the disabled
- ● Conf - Res - Inf - LG
- M c 240 i, 3 f, UK / 3 i, o'seas
- ¶ Quarterly - 4.

Association of Distributors, Coaters & Converters of Adhesive Tapes   (ADCCAT)   2000
- NR PO Box 704, AYLESBURY, Bucks, HP22 9WQ.
  01296 747451
  http://www.adccat.com
- ○ *T; for companies and individuals involved in manufacture, supply & conversion of adhesive tapes
- ● Mtgs - Exhib - Expt
- M 40 f
- × 2003-04 Association of Die Cutters & Converters of Adhesive Tapes

Association of Dogs & Cats Homes   (ADCH)   1985
- NR c/o Battersea Dogs & Cats Home, Battersea Park Rd, LONDON, SW8 4AA.   (hsb)
  020 7627 9204   fax 020 7627 9200
  email adch@dogshome.org   http://www.adch.org.uk
  Sec: David Newall
- ○ *N; to provide a forum for people in dog & cat rescue organisations to discuss common issues
- ● Conf - Mtgs - VE
- M 42 org, UK / 3 org, o'seas
- ¶ Code of Practice - 4 yrly; ftm, 1st class stamp nm.

Association of Domestic Management   (ADM)   1948
- NR c/o Watson Associates, A6 Kingfisher House, Kingsway, Team Valley Trading Estate, GATESHEAD, Tyne & Wear, NE11 0JQ.
  07946 772620
  Business Mgr: Mrs Penny Harrison
- ▲ Company Limited by Guarantee
- Br 10
- ○ *P; for managers in the cleaning & support services, suppliers of goods for these services, & students & lecturers in colleges & universities
- Gp Cleaning
- ● Conf - Mtgs - ET - Exhib - SG - Inf - VE
- < Brit Cleaning Coun
- M c 300 i, c 50 f
- ¶ Excel (NL) - 4; ftm.   Annual Programme.
  Conference Report.   Guidance Booklets.   AR.
  Standards of Environmental Cleanliness in Hospitals.

Association of Drainage Authorities   (ADA)   1937
- NR 12 Cranes Drive, SURBITON, Surrey, KT5 8AL.   (hq)
  020 8399 7350
  Chief Exec: David Noble
- ○ *N; interests of drainage authorities (internal drainage boards)
- Gp Finance & administration; Publicity; Technical & environmental
- ● Conf - Mtgs - Exhib - Stat - Inf - VE - Demonstration of land drainage eqpt & products (3 yrly)
- M 225 members, 85 associate members
- ¶ ADA Gazette - 3; free.

Association of Drum Manufacturers
2004 merged with the Federation of Drum Reconditioners & the Rigid Intermediate Bulk Container Association to form the **Industrial Packaging Association**

Association of Ductwork Contractors & Allied Services   (ADCAS)
- NR PO Box 349, Thorney, PETERBOROUGH, Northants, PE6 0BF.
  fax 0870 240 1943
  Pres: Paul Roxburgh
- ○ *T

Association of Dunkirk Little Ships   (ADLS)   1966
- ■ 35 Finians Close, UXBRIDGE, Middx, UB10 9NW.   (hsp)
  01895 254193   fax 01895 813788
  email info@adls.org.uk   http://www.adls.org.uk
  Hon Sec: M Cormack
- ○ *G; to commemorate the Little Ships' rescue mission to Dunkirk in 1940, & to keep them afloat
- ● Mtgs:
  Afloat: Trip from Dover/Ramsgate to Dunkirk every 5 yrs - Annual commemorative cruise
  Ashore: AGM - Annual Fitting-out & Laying-up Supper
- M 130 privately owned boats (not people)
- ¶ NL - 2; ftm only, appropriate advertising accepted

Association for Education & Ageing   (AEA)   1985
- ■ 132 Dawes Rd, LONDON, SW6 7EF.   (hsp)
  020 7385 4641
  email carol@carolallen.wanadoo.co.uk
  http://www.aeaonline.org.uk/
  Hon Sec: Carol Allen
- ▲ Registered Charity
- Br 1
- ○ *E, *P; promotion of education in later life
- ● Conf - Mtgs - ET - Res
- M c 50 i, c 10 org
- ¶ AEA Digest (NL) - 4; ftm & to potential members only.
  Educational Gerontology (Jnl); £50 m, £200+ nm.

Association for Education & Guardianship of International Students   (AEGIS)   1994
- ■ 66 Humphreys Close, Randwick, STROUD, Glos, GL5 4NY.
  (chmn/p)
  01453 755160   fax 01453 755160
  email secretary@aegisuk.net   http://www.aegisuk.net
  Chmn: Paul Spencer Ellis
- ▲ Registered Charity
- ○ *W; to promote best & legal practice in all areas of guardianship in order to safeguard the welfare & happiness of overseas students at school in Britain
- ● Conf - Mtgs - ET
- M 14 f, 65 schools
- ¶ NL - 2;   LM - continuous; both free.
- × 2003 Association of Educational Guardians for International Students

Association for Education Welfare Management (AEWM) 1917

- 1 The Boundary, BRADFORD, W Yorks, BD8 0BQ.   (hsp)
  01924 305519   fax 01274 542295
  email jprice@wakefield.gov.uk
  Gen Sec: Jennifer A Price (01924 305519 (sb))
- ▲ Un-incorporated Society
- ○ *P; managers of education welfare & social work services; to help children & young people maximise their educational opportunities through regular attendance at school
- ● Conf - Mtgs - ET
- M 150 i

Association for the Education & Welfare of the Visually Handicapped
see **View: the Association for the Education & Welfare of the Visually Handicapped**

Association of Educational Guardians for International Students
since 2003 **Association for Education & Guardianship of International Students**

Association of Educational Psychologists (AEP) 1962

- 26 The Avenue, DURHAM, DH1 4ED.   (hsp)
  0191-384 9512   fax 0191-386 5287
  email sao@aep.org.uk,)(.aep.org.uk
  Gen Sec: Charles Ward
- ▲ Un-incorporated Society
- ○ *E, *P, *U; to promote educational psychology as a profession; to liaise with government, local authorities & others concerned with the development of children & young people
- ● Conf - Mtgs - ET - Res - Stat - Empl - LG
- < TUC; GFTU; IPSA; Nat Children's Bureau
- M 3,067 i
- ¶ Educational Psychology in Practice - 4; ftm, £67 i, £200 instns, £190 online, nm.

Association of Electoral Administrators (AEA)

- NR PO Box 201, South Eastern, LIVERPOOL, L16 5HH.   (hsb)
  0151-281 8246
  Nat Exec Officer: Gina Armstrong
- ○ *P; for the consistent & efficient administration of electoral registration & the conduct of elections
- Gp Election & electoral officers
- M i
- ¶ Arena (NL) - 4.

Association of Electrical Contractors, Ireland (AECI)

- IRL 16 Main St, BLACKROCK, Co Dublin, Republic of Ireland.
  353 (1) 288 6499   fax 353 (1) 288 5870
  Hon Sec: George Kennedy
- ○ *T
- M 360 f

Association of Electrical & Mechanical Trades (AEMT) 1945

- NR St Saviour's House, St Saviour's Place, YORK, N Yorks, YO1 7PJ.
  01904 674899
  Exec Sec: T Marks
- ▲ Company Limited by Guarantee
- ○ *T; interests of electrical motor apparatus repairers & manufacturers
- ● Conf - Mtgs - ET - Res - Exhib - VE - LG
- M 270 f, UK / 18 f, o'seas
- ¶ NL - 4; ftm only.   Hbk - 1; free.

Association of Electricity Producers (AEP) 1987

- 17 Waterloo Place (1st floor), LONDON, SW1Y 4AR.   (hq)
  020 7930 9390   fax 020 7930 9391
  email enquiries@aepuk.com   http://www.aepuk.com
  Chief Exec: David Porter
- ▲ Company Limited by Guarantee
- ○ *T; to promote & protect the interests of privately owned companies producing electricity
- Gp C'ees: Electricity & gas, Electricity trading, Environment, European, Health & safety, Renewable energy, Scottish
- ● Conf - Mtgs - Res - SG - Expt - Inf - Lib - VE - LG
- M 6 i, 97 f, 3 org

Association of Endoscopic Surgeons of Great Britain & Ireland
a group of the **Association of Surgeons of Great Britain & Ireland**

Association of English Singers & Speakers (AESS) 1913

- Melin-y-Grogue, Llanfair Waterdine, KNIGHTON, Powys, LD7 1TU.   (chmn/p)
  01547 510327   fax 01547 510327
  email graham.trew@virgin.net
  http://www.AofESS.org.uk
  Chmn: Graham Trew
- ▲ Registered Charity
- ○ *D, *P; to encourage the communication of English words in singing & speech, with clarity, understanding & imagination
- ● Mtgs - ET - Comp - Master classes - Concerts
- < Inc Soc of Musicians
- M 170 i
- ¶ NL - 3; ftm only.

Association for Environment Conscious Building (AECB) 1989

- PO Box 32, LLANDYSUL, Cardiganshire, SA44 5ZA.   (hq)
  0845 456 9773
  email info@aecb.net   http://www.aecb.net
  Sec: Peter Wilkinson
- ▲ Company Limited by Guarantee
- ○ *K, *T; to promote & encourage sustainable building within the construction industry
- Gp Energy efficiency; Tropical rain forests; Pollution; Native fauna & flora; Health & safety; Chemicals; Environment conscious housing
- ● Mtgs - ET - Res - Exhib - Inf - Lib - VE - LG
  GreenPro online [database listing products, all available in the UK; £11.75 subscription nm]
- M c 1,500 f & org
- ¶ Building for a Future - 4; prices vary m, £20 nm.

Association for Environmental Archaeology (AEA) 1979

- Palaeoecology Centre, School of Geography, Archaeology & Palaeoecology, Queen's University Belfast, BELFAST, BT7 1NN.   (memsec/b)
  028 9097 3978
  email membership@envarch.net   http://www.envarch.net
  Mem Officer: Dr N J Whitehouse
- ▲ Un-incorporated Society
- ○ *L, *Q; to study the human use of & effects on the environment in the past
- ● Conf - Mtgs - Res
- M c 400 i
- ¶ Environmental Archaeology: Jnl of Human Palaeoecology - 2; £38 m.

Association of Erotic Artists   (AEA)   2003

■ Flat 3 / 50 Britannia St, LONDON, WC1X 9JH.
  (co-founder/sp)
  020 7837 7049
  email admin@associationoferoticartists.co.uk
  http://www.associationoferoticartists.co.uk
  Co-Founders: Christopher J Ball,   Paul Woods
○ *A; to promote positive interest within the public & media with
  regard to the erotic arts; to generate debate & fight
  censorship of the production & display of erotic arts made by
  consenting adults
Gp Body painting/painters; Comic book artists; Dancers; Erotic art:
  galleries, collectors, publications; Film makers; Illustrators;
  Models (as muse); Multi-media artists; Musicians; Painters;
  Photographers; Pin-up artists; Poets; Printmakers; Sculptors;
  Videographers; Writers
● Mtgs - Res - Exhib - Comp - SG - Inf - VE - Awards
M 58 i, 3 f, UK / 9 i, o'seas
¶ [membership £35 i, £60 org]
  Note: membership is available by invitation, after submission of
  a panel of work which is viewed by all the members, & on its
  receiving a simple majority in favour
✕ Association of British, Commonwealth & European Erotic Artists

Association of European Trade Mark Owners
  **see MARQUES the Association of European Trade Mark
  Owners**

Association of Event Venues   (AEV)   2004

■ 119 High St, BERKHAMSTED, Herts, HP4 2DJ.   (hq)
  01442 873331   fax 01442 875551
  email info@aev.org.uk   http://www.aev.org.uk
  Sec: Trevor Foley
▲ Company Limited by Guarantee
○ *T; venues working in partnership with organisers & contractors
  to promote quality & value for exhibitors, thus raising the
  profile of exhibitions as a medium
● Conf - Mtgs - ET - Res - Inf - LG
M 24 f, UK / 15 f, o'seas
¶ Exhibition Standard - 6; ftm.

Association for Events Management Education   (AEME)   2004

NR UK Centre for Events Management, Leeds Metropolitan
  University, Calverley St, LEEDS, LS1 3HE.
  Contact: Glenn Bowdin
○ *P

Association of Exhibition Contractors   (AEC)   2003

■ 119 High St, BERKHAMSTED, Herts, HP4 2DJ.   (secretariat)
  01442 873331   fax 01442 875551
  email info@aec.gb.net   http://www.aec.gb.net
  Sec: Trevor Foley
▲ Company Limited by Guarantee
○ *T; for contractors working in partnership with organisers &
  venues to promote quality & value for exhibitors thus raising
  the profile of exhibitions as a medium
● Conf - Mtgs - ET - Res - Exhib - Inf - LG
< Events Ind Alliance (EIA)
M 73 f, UK / 1 f, o'seas
¶ Exhibition Standard - 6; ftm only.

Association of Exhibition Organisers Ltd   (AEO)   1921

■ 119 High St, BERKHAMSTED, Herts, HP4 2DJ.   (hq)
  01442 873331   fax 01442 875551
  email info@aeo.org.uk   http://www.aeo.org.uk
  Chief Exec: Trevor Foley
▲ Company Limited by Guarantee
○ *T; exhibition organisers working in partnership with contractors
  & venues to raise the profile of exhibitions as a medium
● Conf - Mtgs - ET - Res - Inf - LG
< Events Ind Alliance
M 184 f, UK / 20 f, o'seas
¶ Exhibition Standard - 6; ftm.

Association of External Verifiers

NR PO Box 97, New Ferry, WIRRAL, Cheshire, CH63 0QX.
  0151-343 0823
  http://www.ava.org.uk
○ *P

**Association for Families who have Adopted from Abroad
(AFAA)   1987**

■ 30 Bradgate, CUFFLEY, Herts, EN6 4RL.   (hsp)
  01707 872129   fax 01707 872129
  email information.afaa@ntlworld.com
  http://www.afaa.org.uk
  Gen Sec: Patricia Wordley
▲ Registered Charity
○ *W; to help adopted children to grow up happy & well
  adjusted, proud of their birth country and well integrated into
  their country of adoption
● Conf - Mtgs - ET - Inf - VE - LG
M 400 i, 20 org, UK / 6 i, o'seas
¶ NL - 2/3;   LM - 1;   AR - 1; all free.

**Association of Family History Societies of Wales   (AFHSW)
1981**

NR Peacehaven, Badgers Meadow, Pwllmeyric, CHEPSTOW,
  Monmouthshire, NP16 6UE.   (hsp)
  http://www.fhswales.info
  Sec: Geoff Riggs
▲ Un-incorporated Society
○ *G, *N; to coordinate the activities of Welsh family history
  societies
  Note: When writing to the Association, please enclose an SAE
  or 2 International Reply Coupons if a reply is required.

Association for Family Therapy   (AFT)   1976

NR Executive Suite, St James Court, Wilderspool Causeway,
  WARRINGTON, WA4 6PS.   (hq)
  01925 444414
  email s.kennedy@aft.org.uk   http://www.aft.org.uk
  Exec Officer: Sue Kennedy
▲ Company Limited by Guarantee
○ *N, *P; to promote & bring together professional disciplines
  involved in family therapy, training, research, family law &
  practice
M i & org
¶ Jnl of Family Therapy - 4; ftm.   NL - 4.

Association of Festival Organisers   (AFO)   1987

■ PO Box 296, MATLOCK, Derbys, DE4 3XU.   (hq)
  01629 827014   fax 01629 821874
  email info@folkarts-england.org
  http://www.folkarts-england.org
  Dir: Steve Heap
▲ Registered Charity
○ *D; to act as a channel of communication bewtween festivals &
  events in the folk, roots, traditional & acoustic music world,
  or community events
● Conf - Mtgs - ET - Res - Inf - LG
> Folk Arts England; Folk Arts Network; Shooting Roots Youth
  Project
M 4 i, 30 f, 150 org
¶ Folk Arts England News - 4; free.   LM - continuous.

**Association of Financial Controllers & Administrators   (AFCA)
1991**

■ Akhtar House, 2 Shepherd's Bush Rd, LONDON, W6 7PJ.   (hq)
  020 8749 7126   fax 020 8749 7127
  email icea@enta.net   http://www.icea.enta.net
  Chief Exec & Sec: Dr Sushil K das Gupta
▲ Company Limited by Guarantee
○ *P
● Conf - Mtgs - ET - Exam - Res - Exhib - SG - LG
M c 300 i, UK / c 500 i, o'seas
¶ Financial Controller - 2; ftm only.

Association of Fire Consultants
NR   20 Park St, PRINCES RISBOROUGH, Bucks, HP27 9AH.
　　　0870 011 4514

Association of First Division Civil Servants   (FDA)   1918
NR   2 Caxton St, LONDON, SW1H 0QH.   (hq)
　　　020 7343 1111   fax 020 7343 1105
　　　http://www.fda.org.uk
　　　Gen Sec: Jonathan Baume
○　 *U; the union of choice for senior managers & professionals in
　　　public service
●　 Conf - Mtgs - Res - Empl - LG
M　 12,000 i
¶　 Public Service Magazine - 6; ftm, £22.95 yr nm.
　　　trading as the First Division Association (FDA).

Association of Football Statisticians   (AFS)   1978
■　 18 St Philip Square, LONDON, SW8 3RS.   (regd/office)
　　　020 7720 5079
　　　email enquiries@11v11.com   http://www.11v11.co.uk
　　　Chief Exec: Mark Baker
○　 *S; research & publishing of football statistics from 1860
●　 Mtgs - Res - Stat - Inf - Lib
M　 1,100 i, UK / 400 i, o'seas
¶　 Magazine - 4.

Association of Foreign Banks   (AFB)   1947
■　 1 Bengal Court, LONDON, EC3V 9DD.   (hq)
　　　020 7283 8300
　　　http://www.foreignbanks.org.uk
　　　Managing Dir: John Treadwell
○　 *T; foreign banks operating in & out of the UK
●　 Mtgs - ET - SG - Inf
M　 f
×　 2002 (American Financial Services Association
　　　(Foreign Banks & Securities Houses Association

Association of Forensic Physicians
　　　2006 is winding down and transferring its assets to the Faculty
　　　of Forensic & Legal Medicine at the **Royal College of
　　　Physicians London**

**Association of Franchised Distributors of Electronic Components
Ltd   (AFDEC)   1970**
■　 The Manor House, High St, BUNTINGFORD, Herts,
　　　SG9 9AB.   (hq)
　　　01763 274748   fax 01763 273255
　　　email enquiries@afdec.org.uk   http://www.afdec.org.uk
　　　Sec: Jill Waite
○　 *T
M　 100 f

Association of Freelance Editors, Proofreaders & Indexers
IRL   11 Clonard Rd, Sandyford, DUBLIN 16, Republic of Ireland.
　　　353 (1) 295 2194   http://www.afepi.ie
　　　Contact: Brenda O'Hanlon
○　 *P; to act as a point of contact between members & publishers

Association of Freelance Journalists
　　　Ceased operating late 2005

Association for French Language Studies   (AFLS)   1981
NR   c/o Dr Emmanuelle Labeau, School of Languages & Social
　　　Sciences, Aston University, Aston Triangle, BIRMINGHAM,
　　　B4 7ET.   (sb)
　　　0121-204 3773
　　　http://www.afls.net
　　　Sec: Dr Emmanuelle Labeau
▲　 Registered Charity
○　 *L
●　 Conf - Mtgs - ET - Res - SG - Inf - LG - Workshops
M　 50 i, UK / 50 i, o'seas
¶　 Journal of French Language Studies - 3.
　　　Cahiers (NL) - 2.

Association of Friendly Societies   (AFS)   1995
NR   51 Gresham St, LONDON, EC2V 7HQ.   (hq)
　　　020 7216 7436   fax 020 7216 7373
　　　email info@afs.org.uk   http://www.afs.org.uk
▲　 Company Limited by Guarantee
○　 *T; for the Friendly Society movement
●　 Conf - Mtgs - ET - Exhib - Stat - Inf - LG
M　 57 friendly societies, 2 friendly society councils
¶　 Ybk - 1; ftm, £25 nm.   Friends for Life (leaflet); free.

Association of Friends of the Waterloo Committee   1972
NR   Hillcrest, 23A Wylde Green Rd, SUTTON COLDFIELD,
　　　B72 1HD.
　　　0121-240 9030
　　　Hon Sec: John S White
▲　 Registered Charity
○　 *L; to promote study & research into the events of the
　　　Napoleonic Wars, during 1789-1815, & the Battle of
　　　Waterloo & the campaigns of the Duke of Wellington
●　 Conf - Mtgs - Res - SG - Inf - VE
<　 Waterloo C'ee in Belgium; The Wellington Museum at Waterloo
M　 500+ i, 10 f, 15+ org, UK / 150+ i, o'seas
¶　 The Waterloo Jnl - 3; ftm only.

Association of Fundraising Consultants   (AFC)
■　 c/o Andrew Day, Suite 316, Linen Hall, 162-168 Regent St,
　　　LONDON, W1B 4JN.
　　　01582 762446   fax 01582 461489
　　　http://www.afc.org.uk
　　　Chmn: Andrew Day

Association of Garage Door Specialists   (AGDS)   1993
NR   PO Box 560, SOUTH PRESTON, Lancs, PR5 6FF.
　　　(mail/address)
　　　01772 334828
　　　http://www.agds.co.uk
　　　Chmn: Roy Chamberlain
▲　 Company Limited by Guarantee
○　 *T; to develop & maintain standards within the garage door
　　　industry in relation to products, installation & service
●　 Conf - Mtgs - ET
<　 Intl Door Assn
M　 80 f
¶　 Jnl - 3;   Update - 6; both ftm only.

Association of Gardens Trusts   (AGT)   1992
■　 70 Cowcross St, LONDON, EC1M 6EJ.   (hq)
　　　020 7251 2610   fax 020 7251 2610
　　　email agt@gardens-trusts.org.uk
　　　http://www.gardenstrusts.org.uk
　　　Admin: Kate Harwood
▲　 Registered Charity
○　 *N; a national organisation representing gardens trusts in
　　　counties of England & Wales, which are actively engaged in
　　　researching, documenting, protecting & caring for designed
　　　landscapes
●　 Conf - ET - Res - SG - Inf - Lib - LG
M　 34 county gardens trusts
¶　 NL - 2; ftm only.

Association of Gastroenterological Research Charities (AGRC) 1992

NR c/o CORE, 3 St Andrews Place, LONDON, NW1 4LB. (mail/add)
    The Chairman
○ *N; an umbrella organisation for charities which fund research into digestive disorders
    Note: this association is dormant

Association of Genealogists & Researchers in Archives (AGRA) 1968

NR 29 Badgers Close, HORSHAM, W Sussex, RH12 5RU. (sp)
    email agra@agra.org.uk   http://www.agra.org.uk
    Joint & Co Sec: David Young
▲ Company Limited by Guarantee
○ *P; to promote high standards of research amongst members
● Conf - Res
< Fedn of Family History Socs
M 100 i, 2 f
¶ NL - 2.   LM - 1.
✕ 2001 (July) Association of Genealogists & Record Agents

Association of Genetic Nurses & Counsellors
    a group of the **British Society for Human Genetics**

Association for Genito-Urinary Medicine
    2003 merged with the Medical Society for the Study of Venereal Diseases to form the **British Association for Sexual Health & HIV**

Association for Geographic Information (AGI) 1989

■ Morelands (Block C / 4th floor), 5-23 Old St, LONDON, EC1V 9HL. (hq)
    020 7253 5211   fax 020 7251 4505
    email info@agi.org.uk   http://www.agi.org.uk
    Chief Operating Officer: Angel Baker
▲ Company Limited by Guarantee
Br 3
○ *L, *P; to maximise the use of geographic information for the benefit of the citizen, good governance & commerce
Gp Address geography; Crime & disorder; Environment; European; Emergency planning; Health; Local government; Marine & coastal zone; Technical; Utilities; Public policy
● Conf - Mtgs - ET - Exhib - Inf - Lib
M 1,788 i, 322 f
¶ enewsletter - 26;   AR - 1; both free online.

Association of Geotechnical & Geoenvironmental Specialists (AGS) 1988

NR 83 Copers Cope Rd, BECKENHAM, Kent, BR3 1NR. (asa)
    020 8658 8212   fax 020 8663 0949
    email ags@ags.org.uk   http://www.ags.org.uk
    Admin: Dianne Jennings
▲ Company Limited by Guarantee
○ *T; site investigation, geotechnics, engineering geology & related disciplines of environmental engineering & contaminated land assessment & remediation
● Conf - Mtgs - LG
< Ground Forum
M 24 i, 85 f
¶ Geoenvironmental Site Assessment: guide to the model report.
    Electronic Transfer of Geotechnical Data from Ground Investigations; available as download from Internet.
    Collateral Warranties (2nd ed).
    Guide to Laboratory Testing.
    Guidelines for Combined Geoenvironmental & Geotechnical Investigation.

Association for Glycogen Storage Disease (UK) (AGSD(UK)) 1984

■ 9 Lindop Rd, Hale, ALTRINCHAM, Cheshire, WA15 9DZ. (pres/p)
    0161-980 7303
    email president@agsd.org.uk   http://www.agsd.org.uk
    Pres: Mrs Ann Phillips
▲ Registered Charity
Br 6 countries o'seas
○ *W; to provide support for all persons affected with some form of glycogen storage disease (which occurs when there is an absence or deficiency of the enzymes needed to produce or break down glycogen in the body).   It primarily affects the liver & muscles
Gp Project II - to establish centres for collating treatment of children & adults; Pompe's Research Fund; McArdles Clinic (Oswestry)
● Conf - ET - Res - Exhib - SG - Inf - Lib - VE
< Assn Glycogen Storage Disease (USA) & other countries o'seas
M 200 families, 100 professionals, libraries & health centres, UK / 8 i, o'seas
¶ NL - 2; ftm, £1.50 nm (incl all back numbers).
    Parent/Patient Hbk; £10.
    Special Reports & AR.   Workshop Reports; on website.

Association of Golf Club Secretaries (AGCS) 1933

■ 7A Beaconsfield Rd, WESTON-super-MARE, Somerset, BS23 1YE. (hq)
    01934 641166   fax 01934 644254
    email hq@agcs.org.uk   http://www.agcs.org.uk
    Nat Sec: Keith Lloyd
▲ Un-incorporated Society
Br 17 regions
○ *N, *P, *S; to provide support & help to secretaries, secretary/ managers & owners of golf clubs in the UK
Gp Institute of Golf Club Management
● Conf - Mtgs - ET - Exhib - Stat - Inf - Lib - Empl
M 2,500 i, UK / 50 i, o'seas
¶ Golf Club Management - 12; ftm, £5 each (£55 yr) nm.
    Members' Hbk - 1; ftm only.

Association of Golf Writers (AGW) 1938

■ 1 Pilgrim's Bungalow, Mulberry Hill, CHILHAM, Kent, CT4 8AH. (hsp)
    01227 732496   fax 01227 732496
    email andyfarrell@compuserve.com
    Hon Sec: Andy Farrell
▲ Un-incorporated Society
○ *P, *S; to liaise with governing bodies of golf for improved working conditions
● Liaison with golfing bodies
M 109 i, UK / 48 i, o'seas
¶ NL - 10; ftm only.   Members' Hbk - 1; free.

Association of Governing Bodies of Independent Schools 1941

■ Field House, Newton Tony, SALISBURY, Wilts, SP4 0HF. (hq)
    01980 629830
    email sec@agbis.org.uk   http://www.agbis.org.uk
    Sec: Shane Rutter-Jerome
▲ Registered Charity
○ *E; to support governing bodies of independent schools; to promote good school governance in the independent sector
● Conf - Mtgs - ET - Inf - LG
< Indep Schools Coun
M independent day & boarding schools
¶ NL - 2;   AR; both ftm.
✕ 2002 (Governing Bodies Association
        (Governing Bodies of Girls Schools' Association

Association of Government Veterinarians
    a group of the **British Veterinary Association**

© CBD Research Ltd · Beckenham · BR3 5JS · Tel 020 8650 7745 · Fax 020 8650 0768 · E-mail cbd@cbdresearch.com · www.cbdresearch.com

Association of Graduate Careers Advisory Services   (AGCAS) 1967
NR   Millennium House, 30 Junction Rd, SHEFFIELD, S Yorks,
    S11 8XB.   (hq)
    0114-251 5750
▲   Company Limited by Guarantee; Registered Charity
○   *E, *P; to support the work of careers services in higher
    education
Gp   C'ees: Training & development, Products & standards, Quality
    & accreditation;
    Board of Directors
●   Conf - ET - Exam - Res - LG
<   Higher Educ Careers Services Unit
M   1,050 i, 133 f, UK / 65 i, o'seas
¶   Phoenix (Jnl) - 4.

Association of Graduate Recruiters   (AGR)   1968
NR   The Innovation Centre, Warwick Technology Park, Gallows Hill,
    WARWICK, CV24 6UW.   (hq)
    01926 623236
    Chief Exec: Carl Gilleard
▲   Company Limited by Guarantee
○   *T; to provide a forum for the discussion of issues relevant to
    graduate recruitment
●   Conf - ET - Res - Exhib - Comp - SG - Stat - LG - Liaison with
    higher education establishments
M   600 f
¶   Janus (NL) - 4;   Code of Practice;
    Salaries & Vacancies Survey - 2; all ftm.
    AR.   Prospectus.

Association for Group & Individual Psychotherapy   (AGIP) 1974
NR   1 Fairbridge Rd, LONDON, N19 3EW.   (hq)
    020 7272 7013
▲   Registered Charity
○   *P; to promote education in psychotherapy; to make
    psychotherapy more widely available
M   i

Association of Guernsey Banks   (AGB)
■   c/o Kleinwort Benson (Channel Islands) Ltd, PO Box 44,
    ST PETER PORT, Guernsey, GY1 3BG.   (chmn/b)
    email stevehogg@hsbc.com
    Chmn: Jim Gilligan
▲   Un-incorporated Society
○   *T; to represent all licensed Guernsey banks
●   Mtgs - LG
M   48 f

Association of Guilds of Weavers, Spinners & Dyers   1955
NR   17 Shearer Rd, Fratton, PORTSMOUTH, PO1 5LL.   (hsp)
    email v.thorne@ntlworld.com   http://www.wsd.org.uk
    Correspondence Sec: Val Thorne
▲   Registered Charity
Br   102; 6 o'seas
○   *A, *G; to preserve & improve craftsmanship in handweaving,
    spinning & dyeing
●   Conf - Mtgs - ET - Exam - Exhib - SG - Inf
M   4,500 i, 102 org, UK / i, 9 org, o'seas
¶   The Jnl for Weavers, Spinners & Dyers - 4.

Association of H M Inspectors of Taxes
    since 2002 **Union of Senior Revenue Officials**

Association of Head Teachers in Scotland
    since March 2006 **Association of Headteachers & Deputies in
    Scotland**

Association of Heads of Foundation & Aided Schools
    2002 merged with the Foundation & Voluntary Aided Schools
    Association to become the **Foundation & Aided Schools National
    Association**

Association of Heads of Independent Schools   (AHIS)   1924
NR   St Mary's School, GERRARDS CROSS, Bucks, SL9 8JQ.
    (treas/b)
    01753 883370   fax 01753 890966
    Treas: Mrs Fanny Balcombe
○   *E; to further interests of education on independent lines

Association of Heads of Outdoor Education Centres   (AHOEC) 1963
NR   Woodlands Outdoor Education Centre, GLASBURY-on-WYE,
    Powys, HR3 5LP.   (chmn/b)
    01497 847272
    http://www.ahoec.org
    Chmn: Kevin Jackson
▲   Un-incorporated Society
○   *S; to encourage all-round personal development through
    residential experience & the use of the outdoors; to develop,
    establish & maintain safe practice in outdoor activities
●   Conf - Mtgs - ET
<   Engl Outdoor Coun
M   120 i, UK / 1 i, o'seas

Association of Headteachers & Deputies in Scotland   (AHDS) 1975
■   PO Box 18532, INVERURIE, Aberdeenshire, AB51 0WS.
    (mail/address)
    0845 260 7560
    email info@ahds.org.uk   http://www.ahds.org.uk
    Gen Sec: Greg Dempster
▲   Un-incorporated Society
○   *U; to represent the interests & perspectives of Scotland's
    headteachers & deputes from nursery, primary & special
    schools
Gp   Headteachers; Depute headteachers
●   Conf - Mtgs - ET - Empl - LG
<   Eur School Heads Assn
M   1,400 i
¶   Head to Head - 4; ftm only.
✕   2006 (March) Association of Head Teachers in Scotland

Association of Health Boards in Ireland
    has closed

Association of Healthcare Communicators   (AHC)   1997
■   PO Box 4277, DUNSTABLE, Beds, LU6 2WU.   (admin/p)
    01525 222155   fax 01525 222155
    email katherine.baldwin@virgin.net
    http://www.assochealth.org.uk
    Chmn: Lucy Betterton,   Admin: Kate Baldwin
Br   3
○   *P; for healthcare communications professionals working in, or
    mainly with, the NHS
●   Conf - ET - Res - Inf
M   388 i
¶   ARC News (NL) - 4; ftm only.
    Booklets:
        The Astoundingly Healthy Communications Crisis Guide;
        The Nitpicker's Guide to Communication;
        Pragmatics - the art of managing expectations;
        Managing the Messenger;
        The NHS Route Map;
        Diagnosis to Delivery; all £4 each.
        Caldicott: working with the media; £2.50.

Association of Healthcare Human Resource Management
    since 2005 **Healthcare People Management Association**

Association for Heritage Interpretation   (AHI)   1975
- ■ 18 Rose Crescent, PERTH, PH1 1NS.   (hq)
  01738 621996   fax 01738 621996
  email admin@heritage-interpretation.org.uk
  http://www.heritage-interpretation.org.uk
  Admin: Michael H Glen
- ▲ Registered Charity
- ○ *L; to encourage excellence in the presentation & management
  of our natural & cultural environments
- ● Conf - ET - Res - Inf - Lib - VE
- M 300 i, 250 f & org
- ¶ Jnl - 3;   NL - 6; both ftm only.

Association of Higher Civil & Public Servants
- IRL Fleming's Hall, 12 Fleming's Place, DUBLIN 4, Republic of
  Ireland.
  353 (1) 668 6077   fax 353 (1) 668 6380
  email info@ahcps.ie   http://www.ahcps.ie
  Gen Sec: Séan Ó Ríordáin
- ○ *P

**Association of History & Computing (UK Branch)   (AHC (UK))
1997**
- ■ c/o Derek Harding, Centre for Learning & Quality
  Enhancement, University of Teesside, MIDDLESBROUGH,
  Tees Valley, TS1 3BA.   (hsb)
  email derek.harding@tees.ac.uk   http://www.ahc.ac.uk
  Sec: Derek Harding
- ▲ Un-incorporated Society
- ○ *L; to promote the use of computers in historical research &
  training
- ● Conf - ET
- < Intl Assn of History & Computing
- M 100 i
- ¶ Publications available on website.

Association for the History of Glass   (AHG)   1977
- ■ c/o Society of Antiquaries, Burlington House, Piccadilly,
  LONDON, W1J 0BE.   (regd/office)
  http://www.historyofglass.org.uk
  Hon Sec: Justine Bailey
- ▲ Company Limited by Guarantee; Registered Charity
- ○ *L; to advance the education of the public in the historical,
  archaeological, aesthetic & technological study of glass, for
  all periods of history & all parts of the world; the problems of
  conservation & presentation
- ● Conf - Mtgs
- < Assn Intle pour l'Histoire du Verre
- M 180 + instns
- ¶ Glass News (NL) - 2; ftm, £5 nm.

Association of Home Information Packs Providers   (AHIPP)
- ■ 3 Savile Row, LONDON, W1S 3PB.
  0870 950 7739   fax 01858 545714
  http://www.hipassociation.co.uk
- ○ *T

Association of Hot Foil Printers   (AssHEP)   1991
- ■ 15 Hunt St, Atherton, MANCHESTER, M46 9JF.   (hq)
  0845 166 8395   fax 0845 166 8396
  email association@hotfoilprinting.org
  http://www.hotfoilprinting.org
  Sec: Paul Forshaw
- ▲ Un-incorporated Society
- ○ *T; to promote the benefits of hot foil printed products
- ● ET - Inf
- M [not available]
- ¶ Monthly Magazine - 12; £25 yr m only.
  Hot Foil Printing: a guide to the whole business; £25.
- × National Association of Hot Foil Printers

**Association for Humanistic Psychology in Britain   (AHP(B))
1968**
- NR BM Box 3582, LONDON, WC1N 3XX.   (mail/address)
  0845 707 8506
  email admin@ahpb.org.uk   http://www.ahpb.org.uk
- ▲ Registered Charity
- ○ *L; to encourage interest in humanistic psychology
- ● Conf - Mtgs - ET - SG - Inf
- M 1,000 i, 30 f
- ¶ Self & Society - 6.

Association of Illustrators   (AoI)   1973
- NR Back Building (2nd floor), 150 Curtain Rd, LONDON,
  EC2A 3AR.   (hq)
  020 7613 4328
  Chmn: Michael Bramman
- ▲ Company Limited by Guarantee
- ○ *P; to advance & protect illustrators' rights; to raise the profile
  of illustration & the standard of practice within the industry
- ● Conf - ET - Exhib - Comp - Inf - Empl
- < Soc of Illustrators (USA); Soc of Artists' Agents; Designers &
  Artists Copyright Agency
- M 1,100 i, 100 f, UK / c 35 i, o'seas
- ¶ Jnl - 6.   Advertising Directory.
  Survive - illustrators guide to a professional career.
  Rights - illustrators guide to professional practice.
  Trouble Shooting Guide.
  Publishing - editorial directories.

**Association for Improvements in the Maternity Services
(AIMS)   1960**
- ■ 5 Ann's Court, Grove Rd, SURBITON, Surrey, KT6 4BE.
  (chmn/p)
  0870 765 1433
  Chmn: Beverley Beech
- ▲ Un-incorporated Society
- ○ *K; a pressure group providing information to new parents on
  rights & choices in the maternity services; supports midwives
  as practitioners in their own right
- Gp VBAC (Vaginal birth after Caesarean Section) support; Home
  birth support
- ● Conf - Inf
- M 1,000 i
- ¶ AIMS Quarterly Jnl - 4.
  Wide range of books & leaflets.

** ** Association of Incorporated Managers & Administrators**
  Organisation lost: see Introduction paragraph 3

Association of Independent Advice Centres   (AIAC)   1995
- NR 1 Rushfield Avenue, BELFAST, BT7 3FP.   (hq)
  028 9064 5919
  Dir: Bob Strong
- ▲ Registered Charity
- ○ *N; umbrella group for advice centres
- ● Conf - Mtgs - ET - Res - Exhib - Stat - Inf - LG
- < Fedn of Indep Advice Centres
- M 4 i, 74 f, 8 org
- ¶ NL - 4;   AR - 1; both free.
  Note: is also known as Advice NI.

Association of Independent Care Advisers   (AICA)   1994
- ■ Orchard House, Albury, GUILDFORD, Surrey, GU5 9AG.   (hq)
  01483 203066   fax 01483 202535
  email info@aica.org.uk   http://www.aica.org.uk
  Chmn: Christopher Cain
- ▲ Un-incorporated Society
- ○ *P; to represent private organisations who offer independent
  advice to older people, their families & carers, to help find
  appropriate care at home or in residential care or nursing
  homes
- ● Conf - Mtgs - LG
- M 250 i, 12 f

© CBD Research Ltd · Beckenham · BR3 5JS · Tel 020 8650 7745 · Fax 020 8650 0768 · E-mail cbd@cbdresearch.com · www.cbdresearch.com

Association of Independent Clinical Research Contractors
ceased trading in March 2004 & was replaced by the **Clinical Contract Research Association**

Association of Independent Computer Specialists   (AICS) 1972

■ Honeyhill, Bismore, EASTCOMBE, Glos, GL6 7DG.   (hsp)
0701 070 1118   fax 0845 130 5812
email admin@aics.org.uk   http://www.aics.org.uk
Hon Sec: R K Brooks
▲ Company Limited by Guarantee
○ *T; the provision of specialist computer related services by individual practitioners & owner-directed firms
● Conf - Networking
M 40 i, 30 f
¶ NL - 4; ftm, £10 yr nm.

Association of Independent Construction Adjudicators   (AICA)

■ Carthusian Court, 12 Carthusian St, LONDON, EC1M 6EZ.
0870 429 6353   fax 0870 429 6352
email enquiries@aica-adjudication.co.uk
http://www.aica-adjudication.co.uk
Chmn: Peter Shiells
▲ Company Limited by Guarantee
○ *P; nomination body for appointment of adjudicators to resolve construction disputes
● Conf - Mtgs - ET - Inf
M 136 i

Association of Independent Crop Consultants   (AICC)   1980

■ Agriculture Place, Heath Farm, Heath Road East, PETERSFIELD, Hants, GU31 4HT.   (hq)
01730 710095   fax 01730 710096
http://www.aicc.org.uk
Chief Exec: Sarah Cowlrick
▲ Company Limited by Guarantee
○ *F, *P; for independent crop consultants
● Conf - Mtgs - ET - Inf - LG
M 180 i, 1 f
¶ NL - 4; ftm only.   LM - 1; free.

Association of Independent Financial Advisers   (AIFA)   1999

NR Austin Friars House, 2-6 Austin Friars, LONDON, EC2N 2HD.   (hq)
020 7628 1287
Dir Gen: Chris Cummings
▲ Company Limited by Guarantee
○ *P
● Conf - Mtgs - ET - Res - Stat - Inf - Lib - LG
M 13,364 i, 5,069 f, 1 org (CBI)

Association of Independent First Aid at Work Training Organisations

NR 185 Measham Rd, Moira, SWADLINCOTE, Derbyshire, DE12 6AJ.
01530 271144   fax 01530 271144
email aifawto@btconnect.com

Association of Independent Inventory Clerks   (AIIC)   1996

■ Willow House (Central Office), 16 Commonfields, West End, WOKING, Surrey, GU24 9HZ.
01276 855388   fax 01276 855388
email centraloffice@aiic.uk.com
http://www.aiic.uk.com
Hon Sec: Holly Doole
▲ Un-incorporated Society
○ *P
● ET - Inf
M 220 i
¶ The Declaration.

Association of Independent Libraries   1989

NR The Leeds Library, 18 Commercial St, LEEDS, W Yorks, LS1 6AL.   (chmn/b)
0113-245 3071
Chmn: Geoffrey Forster
○ *A; subscription libraries founded between c 1690 & 1841 before the creation of the public library service; to care for their historic collections & buildings; to supply the latest books, periodicals & a personal service to their members
M 28 libraries

Association of Independent Management & Maritime Services (AIMMS)   1991

■ Centre for Advanced Industry, Coble Dene, Royal Quays, NORTH SHIELDS, Tyne & Wear, NE29 6DE.   (hq (unmanned))
0191-236 4200   fax 0191-217 1887
email shipsexperts@aimms.co.uk
http://www.argonautics.co.uk
Hon Sec: Peter Wood,   Treas: Bryan Durose
▲ Un-incorporated Society
○ *P, *T; to provide management, industrial, project & technical consultants to the shipbuilding, conversion & repair, heavy engineering & ports industries worldwide
Gp Technology & management systems & design: (1) Shipbuilding (2) Shiprepair; Port design, development & operating systems; Engineering systems design & development; Facilities design for production incl: assistance with development & provision of technical experts
● Mtgs - ET - Res
< Argonautics Maritime Technologies (members of Northern Defence Industries Ltd (NDI)
M 3 i

Association of Independent Meat Suppliers   (AIMS)   2001

NR PO Box 125, NORTHALLERTON, N Yorks, DL6 2YG.
01609 761547   fax 01609 761548
○ *T; small & medium-sized abattoirs

Association of Independent Museums   (AIM)   1977

■ 75 Western Way, GOSPORT, Hants, PO12 2NF.   (admin/p)
023 9258 7751
email aimadmin@museums.org.uk
Administrator: Roger Hornsham
▲ Company Limited by Guarantee
○ *L, *N; to comnnect, support & represent independent museums (those not supported by government)
● Conf - Mtgs - ET - Stat - Inf - VE - LG
M 100 i, 100 f, 500 org
¶ AIM Bulletin - 5; free.

Association of Independent Music   (AIM)   1999

NR Lamb House, Church Street, LONDON, W4 2PD.   (hq)
020 8994 5599
Chief Exec: Alison Wenham
▲ Company Limited by Guarantee
○ *D, *T; independent record companies
● LG - Negotiating - Advising - Networking
< IMPALA
M 700 f
¶ AR; free.

Association of Independent Organ Advisers   (AIOA)

■ 47 Constable Rd, IPSWICH, Suffolk, IP4 2UZ.   (admin/p)
01473 219102
email admin@aioa.org.uk   http://www.aioa.org.uk
Admin: Timothy Lawford
○ *P; offer independent advice on new organs & restorations
● Mtgs - Inf - VE
M 11 i

Association of Independent Practitioners
a group of the **British Association for Counselling & Psychotherapy**

Association of Independent Psychotherapists
NR PO Box 1194, LONDON, N6 5PW.
     020 7700 1911
○   *P

Association of Independent Radio Stations
     since 2002 **IBI (Independent Broadcasters of Ireland)**

Association of Independent Research & Technology Organisations
     see **AIRTO Ltd: Association of Independent Research & Technology Organisations**

Association of Independent Specialist Medical Accountants (AISMA) 1995
NR 48 St Leonards Rd, BEXHILL-on-SEA, E Sussex, TN40 1JB.
     01424 730345   fax 01424 730330
     email aisma@honeybarrett.co.uk
     http://www.aisma.org.uk
     Sec: Liz Densley
▲   Un-incorporated Society
○   *P
●   Conf - Mtgs - Stat
M   62 f
¶   NL - 4; ftm only.
     Medical Practitioners' Financial Hbk - 3 yrly.

Association of Independent Tobacco Specialists (AITS) 1976
■   14 Wyndham Arcade, CARDIFF, Glam, CF10 1FJ.   (hsp)
     029 2066 4114
     Sec: Donald C Higgins
Br 103
○   *T; to keep the tobacconist in the high street
●   Conf - Mtgs - Exhib - SG - Inf - VE
M   73 i, 103 f
¶   NL - 12.   Tobacco Index - 1.
     National Tobacconists Trade Exhibition Catalogue.

Association of Independent Tour Operators (AITO) 1976
NR 133a St Margaret's Rd, TWICKENHAM, Middx, TW1 1RG.
     (hq)
     020 8744 9280   fax 020 8744 3187
     email info@aito.co.uk   http://www.aito.co.uk
     Chmn: Richard Hearn
○   *T; includes small & specialist tour operators
M   c 150 f

Association for Industrial Archaeology (AIA) 1973
NR AIA Liaison Officer, School of Archaeological Studies, Leicester
     University, LEICESTER, LE1 7RH.   (regd/office)
     0116-252 5337   fax 0116-252 5005
     Liaison Officer: James Gardiner
▲   Registered Charity
○   *L; to promote the study, preservation & presentation of Britain's
     industrial heritage; a national organisation for people who
     share an interest in Britain's industrial past
●   Conf - ET - Res - Inf - VE
M   900 i, 71 org
¶   Industrial Archaeology Review - 2;
     Industrial Archaeology News - 4; both ftm.

Association of Industrial Laser Users   (AILU) 1995
NR Oxford House, 100 Ock St, ABINGDON, Oxon, OX14 5DH.
     (hq)
     01235 539595
     Sec: Dr J M Green
▲   Company Limited by Guarantee
○   *T; to disseminate technical information about the use of high
     power lasers for materials processing (drilling, cutting,
     welding, marking); represent the interests of UK laser users
Gp Laser job shop
●   Conf - Mtgs - ET - Exhib - Stat - Inf
<   Eur Laser Applications Network (ELAN); Laser Inst of
     America (LIA)
M   50 i, 198 f, UK / 12 i, 12 f, o'seas
¶   The Industrial Laser User - 4; ftm only.

Association of Industrial Road Safety Officers   (AIRSO) 1965
■   68 The Boulevard, WORTHING, W Sussex, BN13 1LA.   (hsb)
     01903 506095   fax 01903 506095
     email airso@talk21.com   http://www.airso.org.uk
     Sec: Graham Feest
▲   Registered Charity
○   *P; to promote road safety within vehicle fleet undertakings;
     exchange of information on accident prevention schemes,
     driver training techniques & vehicle construction & usage
●   Conf - Mtgs - ET - LG
M   500 i, UK / 10 i, o'seas
¶   Directory of Members - 1; ftm only.

Association of Industrial Truck Trainers   (AITT) 1985
NR The Springboard Centre, Mantle Lane, COALVILLE, Leics,
     LE67 3DW.   (hsb)
     01530 277857   fax 01530 810231
     email sueaitt@aol.com   http://www.aitt.co.uk
     Sec: Mrs Susan Finney
▲   Un-incorporated Society
○   *P; research into methods of training, operation & maintenance
     of equipment
Gp Independent Training Scheme & Register Ltd (ITSSAR Ltd):
     provides standards & monitoring of training of fork lift truck
     operators & maintains a register of tutors, trainers &
     operators of fork lift trucks
●   Conf - Mtgs - ET - Exam - Res - Exhib - Inf - LG
<   Brit Indl Truck Assn (BITA)
M   i & f
¶   NL - 2;   LM - 1;   AR; all ftm only.

Association for Infant Mental Health UK   (AIMH UK)
NR Knowle Clinic, Broadfield Rd, BRISTOL, BS4 2UH.
     http://www.aimh.org.uk
     Hon Sec: Rosalind Bennet

Association for Information Management
     see **Aslib: the Association for Information Management**

Association of Information Officers in the Pharmaceutical Industry
     since 2005 **Pharmaceutical Information & Pharmacovigilance Association**

Association of Inland Navigation Authorities (AINA) 1996
■   Fearns Wharf, Neptune St, LEEDS, W Yorks, LS9 8PB.   (hq)
     0113-243 3125   fax 0113-245 8394
     email info@aina.org.uk   http://www.aina.org.uk
     Contact: The Executive Director
▲   Un-incorporated Society
○   *T; to develop, share & promote good practice in the
     management & use of the UK's inland waterways; to
     represent the views of owners & operators of the waterways
     to government & its agencies, local authorities, policy
     makers, funders & stakeholders
●   Conf - Mtgs - LG
M   30 org
¶   [Publications on website].

© CBD Research Ltd · Beckenham · BR3 5JS · Tel 020 8650 7745 · Fax 020 8650 0768 · E-mail cbd@cbdresearch.com · www.cbdresearch.com

Association of Inner Wheel Clubs in Great Britain & Ireland 1934
NR 51 Warwick Sq, LONDON, SW1V 2AT. (hq)
    020 7834 4600
    Sec/Admin: Ann Koh
Br 1,057
○ *W; 'friendship & service', membership is limited to the
    womenfolk of Rotarians
● Conf - Mtgs
< Intl Inner Wheel; Women's Nat Commission
M 29,500 i
¶ Inner Wheel - 3; m only.

Association of Installers of Unvented Hot Water Systems (Scotland & N Ireland)
    a group of the **Scottish & Northern Ireland Plumbing Employers' Federation**

Association for Institutional Multi-Manager Investing (AIMMI) 2002
■ Close TEAMS Ltd, Metropolitan House, 38-40 High St,
    CROYDON, Surrey, CR0 1YB. (chmn/b)
    020 8688 5999
    Chmn: Steve Delo
▲ Company Limited by Guarantee
○ *T; to promote (initially in the UK) multi-manager or manager-of-managers investing throughout the institutional pensions industry
● Conf - Mtgs - ET - Stat - LG - Res - Inf - Quality standards
M 4 f
× 2005 Association for Multi Manager Investing

Association for Instrumentation, Control, Automation & Laboratory Technology GAMBICA 1981
■ St George's House, 195-203 Waterloo Rd, LONDON,
    SE1 8WB. (hq)
    020 7642 8080   fax 020 7642 8096
    email assoc@gambica.org.uk
    http://www.gambica.org.uk
    Chief Exec: Geoff C Young
○ *T; 'for instrumentation, control, automation'
Gp Product areas: Industrial control & power electronics components & systems; Process measurement & control equipment & systems; Environmental analysis & monitoring equipment; Test & measurement equipment; Laboratory based analytical & measuring equipment; Laboratory technology
● Conf - Mtgs - ET - Exhib - Stat - Expt - Inf
M 150 f
¶ Product Guide - 1;   AR;   Brochure; all free.

Association of Insurance Intermediaries & Brokers
    2002 merged with the **British Insurance Brokers Association**

Association of Insurance & Risk Managers (AIRMIC) 1963
NR 6 Lloyd's Ave, LONDON, EC3N 3AX. (hq)
    020 7480 7610   fax 020 7702 3752
    Exec Dir: David Gamble
▲ Company Limited by Guarantee
○ *P; to provide a forum for the exchange of data & opinion concerning risk management in industry, commerce & local government
M i

Association of Insurance Surveyors Ltd (AIS)
NR Riverside House, 1-5 Como St, ROMFORD, Essex, RM2 7DN.
    (mail/address)
○ *P; research into methods of burglary protection; cooperation with security organisations
    No further information supplied
× 2004 Association of Burglary Insurance Surveyors

Association of Inter-Varsity Clubs (AIVC) 1946
NR c/o Manchester IVC, 94-96 Grosvenor St, MANCHESTER,
    M1 7HL. (forwarding/add)
    0870 321 0482
▲ Un-incorporated Society
Br 46; Bermuda
○ *N; coordinating body for member clubs; to provide cultural, social & sporting activities within the British Isles, for graduates & others of like interests
● Conf - Mtgs - ET - Inf - VE
M c 6,000 i, 46 clubs, UK / 20 i, 1 club, o'seas
¶ Newslines - 12;   LM - 2; both ftm only.
    (Each club publishes a monthly bulletin with a list of social events).

Association of Interchurch Families (AIF) 1968
■ Bastille Court, 2 Paris Garden, LONDON, SE1 8ND. (hq)
    020 7654 7251   fax 020 7654 7222
    email info@interchurchfamilies.org.uk
    http://www.interchurchfamilies.org.uk
    Exec Officer: Keith Lander
▲ Registered Charity
○ *E, *R; offers a support network for interchurch families (usually a Roman Catholic married to a Christian of another communion) & a voice for such families as they seek to contribute to the growing together of their churches
● Conf - Mtgs - Res - Inf - VE
< Interchurch Families Intl Network; (sister assns in Australia, Austria, Canada, France, Germany, Italy, N Zealand, N Ireland, Switzerland, USA)
M 940 i (mostly couples/families)
¶ Interchurch Families - 2.   AIF News - 3; ftm only.
    Issues, Reflections, News [internet bulletin]; 1/3; free.
    Annual Review - 1; free.

Association of Interior Specialists (AIS) 1998
■ Olton Bridge, 245 Warwick Rd, SOLIHULL, W Midlands,
    B92 7AH. (hq)
    0121-707 0077   fax 0121-706 1949
    email info@ais-interiors.org.uk
    http://www.ais-interiors.org.uk
    Chief Exec: Simon Forrester
▲ Company Limited by Guarantee
○ *T; to represent companies involved in the manufacture, supply & installation of all aspects of interior fit-outs & refurbishment; members operate in retail & commercial offices, the public sector, banks, hotels, hospitals, schools, factories etc
● Conf - Mtgs - ET - Res - Exhib - Stat - Inf - LG - website features an interactive directory search
< Nat Specialist Contrs Coun; Construction Products Assn
M 350 f, UK / 4 f, o'seas
¶ Interiors Focus - 2; ftm, free to specifiers nm.
    Interior Insight (NL) - 2; ftm only.
    LM - 2; ftm & specifiers.

Association of International Accountants Ltd (AIA) 1928
■ Staithes 3, The Watermark, Metro Riverside, NEWCASTLE UPON TYNE, NE11 9SN. (hq)
    0191-493 0277   fax 0191-493 0278
    email aia@aia.org.uk   http://www.aia.org.uk
    Chief Exec: Philip J J Turnbull
▲ Company Limited by Guarantee
Br 8; Caribbean, China, Hong Kong, Ireland, Malaysia, Singapore
○ *P; to offer a recognised professional accountancy qualification
● Conf - Mtgs - ET - Exam - Exhib - Comp - Expt - Inf - Lib
M i
¶ International Accountant - 4; ftm, £3 nm.
    The Professional Qualification for your Future (Prospectus); Student Guide;   Examinations & Reading List;   AR;   all ftm.
× 2003 (amalgamated) Institute of Company Accountants

Association for International Cancer Research (AICR) 1979

NR Madras House, South St, ST ANDREWS, Fife, KY16 9EH.   (hq)
01334 477910   fax 01334 478667
Chief Exec: Derek Napier
▲ Company Limited by Guarantee; Registered Charity
○ *Q; a charity which endeavours to support & fund basic (as opposed to clinical) research into the basic mechanisms which are involved in the development of those diseases commonly known as cancer
Gp Scientific advy c'ee (determines research direction)

Association of International Courier & Express Services (AICES) 1977

NR Global House, Poyle Rd, COLNBROOK, Berks, SL3 0AY.   (hq)
01753 680550
Sec Gen: Anne de Courcy
○ *T
● Mtgs - LG
M 46 f
¶ LM, AR; both free.

Association of International Marketing (AIM) 1983

NR PO Box 70, LONDON, E13 0UU.   (hq/hsb)
020 8986 7539
http://www.aim-org.com
Dir: C Oham
○ *P; promotion of international marketing
● ET - Exam - Res - Exhib - SG - Expt - Inf - Correspondence courses
M 85 i, 3 f, UK / 718 i, 5 f, o'seas
¶ International Marketing News (NL) - irreg via email.
Jnl of International Marketing - 4.
Dictionary of International Marketing.
A Guide to Marketing in Europe.
European Marketing Tips & Terms for the Single Market.
Other books available.

Association of International Savings Banks (in London)

closed in 2005

Association of Investment Trust Companies (AITC) 1932

NR 24 Chiswell St (9th floor), LONDON, EC1Y 4YY.   (hq)
020 7282 5555   fax 020 7282 5556
email info@aitc.co.uk   http://www.aitc.co.uk
Dir Gen: Daniel Godfrey
▲ Company Limited by Guarantee
○ *T; to work with member investment trust companies to add value to their shareholders over the long-term; to provide a coordinated response to any new developments in regulation or tax & initiate favourable legislative changes
● Conf - Mtgs - ET - Exhib - Stat - Inf - LG
Information line: 0800 085 8520
M 246 f
¶ Monthly Information Service - 12.
IT Hbk - 1.
Information packs & Factsheets.

Association of Irish Choirs 1980

IRL Drinan St, CORK, Co Cork, Republic of Ireland.
353 (21) 431 2296   fax 353 (21) 496 2457
email info@cnc.ie   http://www.cnc.ie
Chmn: Kevin O'Callaghan
○ *D; to promote choral music and singing in Ireland

Association of the Irish Dental Industry Ltd

IRL PO Box 59, DROGHEDA, Co Louth, Republic of Ireland.
353 (41) 983 8210   fax 353 (41) 983 8210
email aidi@iol.ie
Gen Sec: Anne Flaherty
○ *T

Association of Irish Humanists
since 2004 Humanist Assn of Ireland

Association of Irish Racecourses

IRL 63 Fitzwilliam Square, Dublin 2, Republic of Ireland
353 (1) 676 0911
email air@iol.ie   http://www.air.ie
Chief Exec: Paddy Walsh

Association of Jewish Ex-Servicemen & Women (AJEX) 1930

NR Shield House, Harmony Way, Victoria Rd, LONDON, NW4 2BZ.   (hq)
020 8202 2323   fax 020 8202 9900
email ajexuk@talk21.com   http://www.ajex.org.uk
Gen Sec: S J Weisser
▲ Registered Charity
Br 60
○ *W; to assist ex-service men & women & their dependents; to observe remembrance of the fallen; to combat religious & racial intolerance
Gp Public relations; Welfare & social services; Remembrance Jewish military museum
● Conf - Mtgs - Res - Exhib - SG - Inf - Lib & museum - VE
< Intl Congress of Jewish War Veterans
M c 5,000 i

Association of Jungian Analysts

NR Flat 3, 7 Eton Ave, LONDON, NW3 3EL.
○ *P

Association of Labour Providers (ALP) 2004

■ 29 Harley St, LONDON, W1G 9QR.   (mail/address)
020 7016 2786   fax 020 7637 0419
email info@labourproviders.org.uk
http://www.labourproviders.org.uk
Chmn: Mark Boleat
▲ Un-incorporated Society
○ *T; to represent the interests of, & provide services to, labour providers
● Res - LG
M 120 f
¶ NL - 12; ftm only.   AR - 1; free.

Association for Land Based Colleges
see Napaeo - the Association for Land Based Colleges

Association of Land Rover Clubs Ltd (ALRC) 1983

NR 1a Duncan Ave, HUNCOTE, Leics, LE9 3AN.   (regd/off)
email tonybirch@btopenworld.com
Hon Sec: Simone Birch
○ *G, *S; renovation & restoration of all Rover vehicles; Rover marque enthusiasts clubs
M org
× 2005 Association of Rover Clubs

Association of Landscape Contractors of Ireland (Northern Ireland) (ALCI) 1971

NR 22 Summerhill Park, BANGOR, Co Down, BT20 5QQ.   (hsp)
028 9127 2823   fax 028 9127 2823
http://www.alci.org.uk
Hon Sec: Debbie Eve
▲ Un-incorporated Society
○ *T; to represent the landscape industry in Northern Ireland
Gp Sportsground construction; Grounds maintenance; Tree surgery; General landscaping
● Conf - Mtgs - ET - Exhib - Comp - Inf - Lib - VE - LG
< Brit Assn Landscape Inds
M 10 i, 50 f, 4 org
¶ ALCI Directory - 2 yrly; free.

© CBD Research Ltd · Beckenham · BR3 5JS · Tel 020 8650 7745 · Fax 020 8650 0768 · E-mail cbd@cbdresearch.com · www.cbdresearch.com

Association for Language Learning   (ALL)   1990
- ■ 150 Railway Terrace, RUGBY, CV21 3HN.   (hq)
  01788 546443   fax 01788 544149
  email yvonneh@all-languages.org.uk
  http://www.all-languages.org.uk
  Office Mgr: Yvonne Hogben
- ▲ Registered Charity
- Br 21
- ○ *N, *P; 'the major professional organisation for language
  teachers in the UK; the teaching, learning & use of
  languages in education & society as a whole'
- Gp C'ees: Dutch, French, German, Italian, Russian, Spanish &
  Portuguese, Asian languages, Publications, Policy
- ● Conf - Mtgs - ET - Exhib - Inf - LG
- ¶ Language Learning Jnl - 2; £78 (£95 EU) (£107 o'seas).
  Language World (NL) - 4; free.
  Francophonie - 2; £60 (£72 EU) (£82 o'seas).
  Deutsch: Lehren und Lernen (the German Jnl) - 2; £60
    (£72 EU) (£82 o'seas).
  Vida Hispánica (the Spanish & Portuguese Jnl) - 2; £60 (£72 EU)
    (£82 o'seas).
  Tuttitalia (the Italian Jnl) - 2; £60 (£72 EU) (£82 o'seas).
  Russistika (the Russian Jnl) - 1; £32 (£37 EU) (£42 o'seas).
    All seven titles; £203 (£253 EU) (£300 o'seas).
  Onze Taal - 10; ftm only.

**** Association of Larger Local Councils**
  Organisation lost: see Introduction paragraph 3

Association for Latin Liturgy   (ALL)   1969
- ■ 47 Western Park Rd, LEICESTER, LE3 6HQ.   (hsp)
  0116-285 6158
  email enquiries@latin-liturgy.org.uk
  http://www.latin-liturgy.org
  Chmn: Bernard Marriott
- ▲ Registered Charity
- ○ *R; to promote understanding of the theological, pastoral &
  spiritual quality of the liturgy in Latin; to preserve the
  sacredness & dignity of the Roman rite; to secure, for the
  present & future generations, the Church's unique inheritance
  of liturgical music
- ● Mtgs - ET - Res - Inf - Liturgical celebrations - Talks by scholars
- < Latin Liturgy Assn (USA); Vereniging voor Latijnse
  Liturgie (Netherlands); Association pro Liturgia (France)
- M 340 i, UK / 30 i, o'seas
- ¶ NL - 3; ftm only.
  New Approach to Latin for the Mass; £12.
  New Latin-English Sunday Missal; £12 (paperback).
  Latin CD; £12.   A Voice for all Time; £6.
  Various musical publications.

Association for Latin Teaching   (ARLT)   1911
- ■ Cedarwood, West St, Childrey, WANTAGE, Oxon, OX12 9UL.
  (hsp)
  01235 751297
  email lindasoames@3b.co.uk   http://www.arlt.co.uk
  Hon Sec: Mrs Linda Soames
- ▲ Registered Charity
- ○ *E; to promote by discussion, cooperation & experiment, the
  teaching of classics in schools
- ● Conf - ET - Inf - Resources service to members
- < Jt Assn Classical Teachers (JACT)
- M 2,000 i
- ¶ The Jnl of Latin Teaching (published jointly with JACT) - 3;
  NL [by email] - 6; both ftm only.

Association of Law Costs Draftsmen   (ALCD)   1977
- ■ Church Cottage, Church Lane, Stuston, DISS, Norfolk,
  IP21 4AG.
  01379 741404   fax 01379 742702
  email enquiries@alcd.org.uk   http://www.alcd.org.uk
  Hon Sec: Joe Locke
- ▲ Voluntary Professional Association
- ○ *P; 'specialists in the law who operate by advising upon &
  applying laws & directions which relate to the evaluation &
  recovery of solicitors' fees'
  Members are based throughout England & Wales
- ● Conf - Mtgs - ET - Exam - Lib
- M 900 i, UK / 2 i, o'seas
- ¶ ALCD NL - 6; ftm only.

Association of Law Teachers   (ALT)   1965
- NR c/o Amanda Fancourt, UK Centre for Legal Education,
  University of Warwick, COVENTRY, CV4 7AL.   (hsb)
  024 7652 2394
  Hon Sec: Amanda Fancourt
- ▲ Un-incorporated Society
- ○ *E, *L; to study understanding & reform of the educational
  aspects of law & the teaching of law; to research into legal
  education systems & methods
- ● Conf - ET - Res - SG - LG
- < UK Assn for Eur Law
- M 800 i, UK / 50 i, o'seas
- ¶ The Law Teacher (Jnl) - 3.
  The Bulletin - 3.   LM - 1.

Association of Lawyers for Children   (ALC)   1993
- ■ PO Box 283, EAST MOLESEY, Surrey, KT8 0WH.   (hsp)
  020 8224 7071
  email admin@alc.org.uk   http://www.alc.org.uk
  Admin: Julia Higgins
- ○ *P; to promote justice for children & young people within the
  justice system; for lawyers involved in work relating to
  children
- ● Conf - Mtgs - ET - SG - LG
- M 1,200 i
- ¶ ALC NL - 4; ftm only.

Association of Lawyers & Legal Advisers   1995
- NR 40 Bowling Green Lane, LONDON, EC1R 0NE.
- ▲ Company Limited by Guarantee
- Br 2
- ○ *P; accreditation of persons or organisations who provide
  specialised legal services & advice & who are relied upon for
  legal information or opinions
  Note: The Association of Lawyers is a trading name owned &
  operated by the Association of Lawyers & Legal Advisers.

Association of Leading Visitor Attractions   (ALVA)   1990
- ■ 4 Westminster Palace Gardens, LONDON, SW1P 1RL.   (hq)
  020 7222 1728   fax 020 7222 1729
  email email@alva.org.uk   http://www.alva.org.uk
  Dir: Robin Broke
- ▲ Company Limited by Guarantee
- ○ *T; to represent the country's major visitor attractions on
  matters which concern the effectiveness of the tourism
  industry
- Gp Museums & galleries; Cathedrals; Heritage organisations;
  Large leisure attractions; Gardens & conservation sites
- ● Conf - Mtgs - ET - Stat - VE - LG
- M 29 org
- ¶ LM.   AR.

Association of Learned & Professional Society Publishers (ALPSP) 1972
- ■ South House, The Street, Clapham, WORTHING, W Sussex, BN13 3UU. (hsp)
  01903 871686 fax 01903 871457
  email sally.morris@alpsp.org http://www.alpsp.org
  Chief Exec: Sally Morris
- ▲ Company Limited by Guarantee
- Br Australia, N America, New Zealand
- ○ *N; to represent not-for-profit publishers & those who work with them
- Gp C'ees: Copyright, Professional development
- ● Conf - Mtgs - ET - Res - Exhib - Stat - Inf - VE - LG - Professional development
- < Intl Fedn of Scholarly Publishers
- M 216 f, UK / 124 f, o'seas
- ¶ Learned Publishing - 4; ftm (extra copies £60 yr), £75 (i), £145 (instns), £115/60 email only.
  ALPSP Alert - 12; ftm only.

Association of Learned Societies in/for the Social Sciences
  see **Academy for the Social Sciences**

Association for Learning Languages en Famille (ALLEF UK)
- NR 225 Carmel Rd, NORTH DARLINGTON, Co Durham, DL3 9TF.
  http://www.allef.org.uk
- ○ *X; arranges mutual exchanges between children in the UK, France & Germany

Association of Learning Providers
- NR Colenso House, 46 Bath Hill, Keynsham, BRISTOL, BS31 1HG. (hq)
  0117-986 5389
  Chief Exec: Graham Hoyle
- ▲ Company Limited by Guarantee
- ○ *E, *T; providers of work-based learning
- ● ET
- M c 800 f
- ✕ 2002 National Training Federation

Association for Learning Technology (ALT) 1993
- ■ Gipsy Lane, Headington, OXFORD, OX3 0BP. (hq)
  01865 484125 fax 01865 484165
  email alt@brookes.ac.uk http://www.alt.ac.uk
  Dir: Rhonda Riachi
- ▲ Registered Charity
- ○ *P; promotion of good practice in the use of learning technology in education & industry
- ● Conf - ET - Res - Inf
- M 426 i, 38 f, 104 universities, 52 colleges, UK / 38 i, o'seas
- ¶ Alt-J (Jnl) - 3; £10/£15.   Alt-N (NL) - 4; free.
  Conference Abstracts - 1; £5.   AR; free.

Association of Leasehold Enfranchisement Practitioners (ALEP) 2003
- ■ PO Box 1720, CROYDON, Surrey, CR9 4AY. (hsp)
  0870 720 2328 fax 0870 720 2320
  email info@alep.org.uk
  Hon Sec: Alex Greenslade
- ○ *P; to foster best practice & integrity & maintain professional standards in leasehold enfranchisement
- M 2 i, 1 f

Association of Leisure Industry Professionals (ALIP) 2001
- NR 2A The Drove Estate, Avis Way, NEWHAVEN, E Sussex, BN9 0EB. (hq)
  01273 612300 fax 01273 612812
  email info@alip.org.uk http://www.alip.org.uk
  Dir: Dr Michael Pinchbeck
- ▲ Un-incorporated Society
- ○ *P; tourism industry
- ● Conf - ET - SG - Inf
- > Intl Work Experience Program
- ¶ Lipservice (NL) - 4; ftm only.

Association of Library Equipment Suppliers (TALES) 1980
- ■ Forge Cottage, 3 Church End, Sandridge, ST ALBANS, Herts, AL4 9DL. (hsb)
  01727 837507
  email john@newtondavies.plus.com
  http://www.tales.org.uk
  Mem Sec/Hon Treas: John Newton-Davies
- ▲ Un-incorporated Society
- ○ *T; 'providing representation for suppliers into the library & information marketplace'
- Gp Shelving, furniture & associated equipment; Books, journals & other print material; Automation, ICT & security; Conservation, large print, AV & other media supply; Human resources & other professional services
- ● Mtgs - Exhib - Inf - LG
- < The British Library
- M 1 i, 46 f

Association of Licensed Aircraft Engineers (1981) (ALAE) 1981
- NR Bourn House, 8 Park St, BAGSHOT, Surrey, GU19 5AQ. (hq)
  01276 474888
  Chmn: Keith Rogers
- ▲ Un-incorporated Society
- ○ *U; for licensed aircraft maintenance engineers & flight engineers
- Gp Licensed aircraft maintenance engineers; Flight engineers; Aeronautical maintenance & certificate holders; Unlicensed engineers & aircraft engineers from HM Forces
- ● Empl - LG
- < Aircraft Engrs Intl
- M 1,680 i, UK / 100 i, o'seas
- ¶ Tech Log (NL) - 12; m only.

Association of Licensed Deep Sea Pilots
  see **Europilots - the Association of Licensed Deep Sea Pilots**

** **Association of Licensed Mortgage Advisors**
  Organisation lost: see Introduction paragraph 3

Association of Licensed Multiple Retailers (ALMR) 1992
- NR 9b Walpole Court, Ealing Studios, LONDON, W5 5ED. (hq)
  020 8579 2080 fax 020 8840 6217
  email info@almr.org.uk
  Admin: Niki Robinson
- ▲ Un-incorporated Society
- ○ *T; to promote members' interests; to be a positive influence for the future of licensed retailing
- Gp Corporate members: pub companies or other licensed retailers having at least 2 units
  Industry members: suppliers of foods & services to the licensed trade
- ● Conf - Mtgs - ET - Exhib - Comp - SG - Inf - LG
- < Jt Hospitality Ind Congress
- M 194 f
- ¶ The Pub Industry Hbk.

Association of Licensed Telecommunications Operators
  since 2004 **ALTO - Alternative Operators in the Communications Sector**

© CBD Research Ltd · Beckenham · BR3 5JS · Tel 020 8650 7745 · Fax 020 8650 0768 · E-mail cbd@cbdresearch.com · www.cbdresearch.com

Association of Light Touch Therapists (ALTT) 1988

- ■ 19B Bridge St, KIDWELLY, Carmarthenshire, SA17 4UU. (hsb)
  01554 891114
  email wedolighttouch@aol.com
  Sec: Geraldine V Jones
- ▲ Un-incorporated Society
- ○ *P; to assist in the establishment of light touch therapies within the normal health-care provision of the nation
- Gp Body mechanics; Biomobility; Bowen technique; Cranio-sacral therapy; Emotional freedom technique; Health kinesiology; Light touch healing; Lymph drainage; Metamorphic technique; Muscle release therapy; Orthobionomy; Polarity therapy; Pulsing; Rejuvanessence; Reflexology; Reharmonisation; Reiki; Spontaneous muscle release; Spinal touch therapy; Touch for health; Therapeutic touch
- ● Conf - Mtgs - Inf
- < Brit Complementary Medicine Assn (BCMA)
- M 73 i, UK / 1 i, o'seas
- ¶ NL - 4;   Register of Members - 1; both free.

Association of Lighthouse Keepers (ALK) 1988

- NR 9 Gwel Trencrom, HAYLE, Cornwall, TR27 6PJ. (msp)
  email info@alk.org.uk   http://www.alk.org.uk
  Mem Sec: Mike Millichamp
- ▲ Registered Charity
- Br Australia, Austria, Belgium, Canada, Germany, Italy, Netherlands, Norway, Sweden, Switzerland, USA
- ○ *G; to open a visitor centre to display the archive collection; to act as a source of reference for educational purposes on lighthouses & other navigational aids
- ● Mtgs - ET - Res - VE
- M 450 i, UK / 20 i, o'seas.
- ¶ Lamp (Jnl) - 4.

Association of Lighting Designers (ALD)

- NR PO Box 680, OXFORD, OX1 9DG. (sb)
  01707 891848   fax 01707 891848
  email office@ald.org.uk   http://www.ald.org.uk
  Admin Sec: Geoff Spain
- ▲ Un-incorporated Society
- ○ *P; for lighting designers in the entertainment field
- ● Conf - Mtgs - ET - Exhib - SG - Stat - Inf - Lib - VE - Empl
- M 486 i, 24 f, 29 org, UK / 45 i, 3 f, o'seas
- ¶ Focus (Jnl) - 6; ftm only.   Ybk - 1; ftm, £7.50 nm.

** Association of Lightweight Aggregate Manufacturers
Organisation lost: see Introduction paragraph 3

Association of Lightweight Campers
a group of the **Camping & Caravanning Club**

Association of Liner Producers
a group of **Horticultural Trades Association**

Association of Lipspeakers (ALS) 1992

- ■ 5 Furlong Close, Upper Tean, STOKE-on-TRENT, Staffs, ST10 4LB. (inf offr/p)
  01538 722482
  Inf Officer: Dilys Palin
- ▲ Un-incorporated Society
- Br regional gps
- ○ *P; for lipspeakers (providers of communication services for deaf & hard of hearing people who lipread)
- ● Conf - Mtgs - ET - Exhib - Inf - Workshops
- < R Nat Inst for Deaf People (RNID); Coun for the Advancement of Communication with Deaf People (CACDD); UK Coun on Deafness (UKCOD)
- M 115 i
- ¶ ALS News - 2.
  Leaflets: General, Legal, For Users, For Agencies.
  NOTE: please enclose SAE if an answer is required

Association of Livery Yard Owners & Operators
reported as no longer operating November 2006

Association of Lloyd's Members (ALM) 1983

- NR 100 Fenchurch St, LONDON, EC3M 5LG. (admin/dir)
  020 7488 0033   fax 020 7488 7555
  email mail@alm.ltd.uk
  http://www.association-lloyds-members.co.uk
  Snr Admin: Linda Evans
- ○ *P, *T; 'trade association for Names' - the underwriting members of Lloyd's of London (insurance market)
- M c 6,750 i, UK / c 2,250 i, o'seas
- ¶ ALM News (NL) - 6.
  Members' Agents' Profiles - 1.

Association of Load Restraint Equipment Manufacturers
is a section of the **Performance Textiles Association**

Association of Loading & Elevating Equipment Manufacturers (ALEM) 1973

- NR Orbital House, 85 Croydon Rd, CATERHAM, Surrey, CR3 6PD. (asa)
  01883 334494
  email alem@admin.co.uk   http://www.alem.org.uk
- ▲ Un-incorporated Society
- ○ *T; safety & good design of lift tables, dock levellers, platform lifts, tailboard lifts
- ● Mtgs - Exhib - SG - Inf - LG
- < Brit Materials Handling Fedn; Fédn Eur de la Manutention
- M 29 f
- ¶ LM & Product Guide; free.

** Association of Local Authority Business Consultants
Organisation lost: see Introduction paragraph 3

Association of Local Authority Chief Executives (ALACE) 1974

- ■ c/o Watford Borough Council, Town Hall, WATFORD, Herts, WD17 3EX. (hsb)
  01923 278186
  email alastair.robertson@watford.gov.uk
  http://www.alace.org.uk
  Hon Sec: Alastair Robertson
- Br 2
- ○ *U; to represent the chief executives of local authorities in England, Wales, Scotland & Northern Ireland. The Council of ALACE forms the 'staff side' of the Joint Negotiating Committee for Chief Executives (the body responsible for the salary & terms/conditions of employment & regulations which affect the role of the 'head of the paid service' together with issues such as reorganisation of local government)
- ● Mtgs - LG
- M 330 i
- ¶ NL - 4.

Association of Local Authority Risk Managers (ALARM)

- NR ALARM Office, Ladysmith House, High Street, SIDMOUTH, Devon, EX10 8LN.
  01395 519083   fax 01395 517990
  email admin@alarm-uk.com
  http://www.alarm-uk.com
- ○ *P
  Note: Also known as ALARM - The National Forum for Risk Management in the Public Sector

Association of Local Bus Company Managers (ALBUM) 1984

- NR c/o Blackpool Transport Services Ltd, Rugby Rd, BLACKPOOL, Lancs, FY1 5DD. (hsb)
  01253 473000
  Hon Sec: Stephen Burd
- ▲ Un-incorporated Society
- ○ *P, *T
- ● Conf - Mtgs - LG
- ¶ NL - irreg; ftm only.

Association of Local Government Archaeological Officers (ALGAO) 1996
- ■ Cornerstone, ALFORD, Aberdeenshire, AB33 8QH.
  01975 564071
  Contact: Caroline Ingle
- ▲ Un-incorporated Society
- ○ *P; to represent archaeologists working in local government throughout the UK
- Gp Maritime; Historic environment records; Historic buildings; Urban; European; Planning & legislation; Countryside
- ● Mtgs - ET - Res - Exhib - Stat - LG
- < Eur Assn Archaeologists
- M 115 local authorities

Association of Local Government Communications (LG Communications) 1971
- NR c/o Communications, New Forest District Council, Appletree Court, LYNDHURST, Hants, SO43 7PA. (v/chmn/b)
  023 8028 5142
  Vice-Chmn: David Atwill
- ▲ Un-incorporated Society
- ○ *P; to enhance the reputation of local government; to provide a united voice to public relations & communications functions in all UK principal local authorities
- ● Conf - Mtgs - Res - Comp - Stat - VE - LG
- M 158 local authorities
- ¶ NL - 12 (email based distribution); ftm only.

Association of Local History Tutors 1981
- NR 7 High St, Bishopstone, SWINDON, Wilts, SN6 8PH. (hsp)
  Hon Sec: Jane Golding
- ▲ Registered Charity
- ○ *P; to promote the teaching of local history to adults
- ● Conf
- M c 8 i
- ¶ Bulletin (NL) - 3.

Association of Local Television Operators
  since 2002-04 **Association of Community Television Operators**

Association of London Clubs
- ■ c/o The Farmers Club, 3 Whitehall Court, LONDON, SW1A 2EL. (hsb)
  020 7930 3751 fax 020 7839 7864
  Sec: Miss H J C McCulloch
- ○ *N
- ● Mtgs - Empl
- M 55 London clubs

Association of London Government (ALG) 1995
- NR 59½ Southwark St, LONDON, SE1 0AL. (hq)
  020 7934 9999
  Contact: Pauline McMahon
- ▲ Company Limited by Guarantee
- ○ *N; consultation with government & the European Union over matters relating to local authorities & the services provided by them
- Gp Equalities; Housing; Education; Environment; Employment; Social services; Health; Voluntary sector; Asylum seekers; Arts & leisure; Police; Local government; Crime; Training; Greater London Authority
- ● Conf - Mtgs - Res - Stat - Inf - LG
- M 33 London councils
- ¶ ALG London Government Directory - 1.
  ALG Directory of Funded Organisations - 1.
  ALG London Bulletin - 6.
  London Housing Magazine - 6.
  ALG Survey of Londoners - 1.
  Making Allowances Report - 1.

Association of Lorry Loader Manufacturers & Importers of Great Britain (ALLMI) 1978
- NR Second Floor Suite, 9 Avon Reach, Monkton Hill, CHIPPENHAM, Wilts, SN15 1EE. (hq)
  01249 659150 fax 01249 464675
  Sec: Mrs K R Howey
- ▲ Un-incorporated Society
- ○ *T; all members follow the code of practice & the BSI standards; is also concerned with: technical guidance & assistance, performance of products, reliability, safety & training
- Gp ALLMI Training Ltd - a separate company for training & examination
  Study gps: Technical sub-c'ee, Training sub-c'ee
- ● Mtgs - ET - Exam - Exhib - SG - Inf - LG
- M 50 f, UK / 1 f, o'seas
- ¶ ALLMI Code of Practice - as required.
  ALLMI Membership - 2.

Association for Low Countries Studies in Great Britain & Ireland (ALCS)
- NR Dept of Germanic Studies, University of Sheffield, SHEFFIELD, S Yorks, S10 2TN.
  0114-222 4396 fax 0114-222 2160
  email alcs@sheffield.ac.uk http://www.shef.ac.uk/alcs
  Sec: Dr Hugh Dunthorne, Pres: Prof Reinier Salverda
- ○ *L, *X; 'to promote the scholarly study of the Low Countries in the British Isles, to foster a greater public awareness & appreciation of this region, especially Dutch language & Dutch & Flemish culture, history & society, & to represent the interests of Low Countries Studies in higher education & at local & national level'
- ● Conf - Mtgs - ET - Res - Inf - LG - Postgraduate training days - Undergraduate days - Funding for projects in Low Countries studies - Co-ordination of lecture tours by scholars from the Low Countries
- < Intle Vereniging voor Neerlandistiek
- M 86 i, UK / 4 i, o'seas
- ¶ Dutch Crossing: a jnl of Low Countries studies - 2.
  LM - 2.
  Crossways - series of occasional books & collections of papers.

Association of Lurcher Clubs
- NR 171 Wash Lane, BURY, Lancs, BL9 7DP. (chmn/p)
  0161-764 0958
  Chmn: Alan Tyer
- ○ *B, *N; to promote the lurcher, a working farm dog

Association of Magisterial Officers
  2005 merged with the **Public & Commercial Services Union**

Association of Mainframe Operators & Network Administrators (AMONO) 1992
- ■ 1 Caryl House, Windlesham Grove, LONDON, SW19 6AH. (hsp)
- ○ *T; operation & maintenance of large computer systems
- M 879 i, 53 f, UK / 38 i, 4 f, o'seas

Association of Makers of Soft Tissue Papers
  since 2004 the Tissue group of the **Confederation of Paper Industries**

Association of Malt Product Manufacturers
  no longer functioning

Association for Management Education & Development (AMED) 1960

NR 12 Station Rd, St Ives, HUNTINGDON, Cambs, PE27 5BH. (hq)
01480 493253 fax 01480 493259
email amedoffice@amed.org.uk
http://www.amed.org.uk
Co-Chmn: David Shepherd, Helen Roome
▲ Company Limited by Guarantee; Registered Charity
○ *E, *P; a professional network for people in individual & organisational development (trainers, HR directors, management consultants & business school lecturers)
Gp Sustainable development; Leadership; Learning organisation
● Conf - Mtgs
< Eur Foundation for Mgt Devt
M 1,300 i, UK / 100 i, o'seas
¶ Organisation & People Jnl - 4; ftm, £50 nm, (£65 instns). AMED News - 10; ftm only.
Report & Accounts (Review) - 1.

Association of Management & Professional Staffs (AMPS) 1984

NR Citrine House, Borough Rd, WAKEFIELD, W Yorks, WF1 3AZ. (hq)
01924 371765
Exec Sec: Ian Waddell
○ *U; non-certificated, non-political managerial union for professional employees in science-based industries
< Amicus
M c 4,000 i

Association of Managerial Electrical Executives (AMEE) 1906

NR Hayes Court, West Common Rd, HAYES, Kent, BR2 7AU. (hq)
020 8462 7755
Sec: Anne Powter
○ *U

Association of Manufacturers of Domestic Appliances (AMDEA) 1969

■ 40-46 Lamb's Conduit St, LONDON, WC1N 3NW. (hq)
020 7405 0666 fax 020 7405 6609
email info@amdea.org.uk http://www.amdea.org.uk
Dir Gen: Peter Carver
▲ Company Limited by Guarantee
○ *T; interests of manufacturers of electric domestic appliances, and/or their components
● Mtgs - Exhib - Stat - LG
< Eur C'ee of Domestic Appliance Mfrs (CECED)
M 33 f

Association of Manufacturers of Power generating Systems (AMPS) 1977

■ Samuelson House, Paxton Rd, Orton Centre, PETERBOROUGH, Cambs, PE2 5LT. (hq)
01733 362925 fax 01733 370664
email dg@amps.org.uk http://www.amps.org.uk
Dir-Gen: J Vowles
▲ Company Limited by Guarantee
○ *T; for manufacturers & importers of generating systems, component & control systems
Gp Statistics; Technical
● Conf - Mtgs - Exhib - Stat - Expt - Inf - VE - LG
< Eur Generating Set Assn (EUROPGEN); Electrical Generating Systems Assn (EGSA)(USA)
M 57 f, UK / 3 f, o'seas
¶ Brochure (incl LM). Technical Guidelines.
AMPS Guide to ISO 8528 (BS 7698) Reciprocating Internal Combustion Engine driven Alternating Current Generating Sets:
Pt 1: Application rating & performance.
Pt 2: Specification for engines.
Pt 3: Specification for AC generators.
Pt 4: Control & switchgear.
Pt 5: Specification for generating sets.
Pt 6: Test methods.

Association for Marketing & Development in Independent Schools (AMDIS) 1993

■ 2 St Michael's St, MALTON, N Yorks, YO17 7LJ. (hq)
0700 062 3347
Admin: Victoria Gillingham
▲ Un-incorporated Society
○ *P; 'to promote good marketing practice in independent education'
● Conf - Mtgs - ET - Stat
< ADAPA (Australia)
M 360 schools
✕ 2003 Association of Development Directors in Independent Schools

Association for Marriage Enrichment (AME) 1979

NR 67 Between Streets, COBHAM, Surrey, KT11 1AA. (chmn/p)
01932 862090
http://www.ame-uk.org.uk
Jt Chmn: David & Judith Robinson
▲ Registered Charity
○ *W; aims to help couples (usually, but not necessarily married) acquire the necessary skills to strengthen their relationship & to improve communication
● Mtgs - ET - LG - Marriage support groups
M 400 i, UK / 10 i, o'seas
¶ NL - 3; ftm.

Association of Master Upholsterers & Soft Furnishers Ltd (AMU) 1947

NR Francis Vaughan House, 102a Commercial St, NEWPORT, Monmouthshire, NP20 1LU. (hq)
01633 215454
Chief Exec: Michael B Spencer
▲ Company Limited by Guarantee
Br 11
○ *T
< Fedn of Small Businesses
M c 550 f
¶ Upholsterer & Soft Furnisher - 12.
Note: incorporates the Chair Frame Manufacturers' Association.

Association of Masters of Harriers & Beagles 1891

NR Langley House, Winchcombe, CHELTENHAM, Glos, GL54 5AB.
01242 602564
email director@amhb.org.uk http://www.amhb.org.uk
Dir: Elizabeth Salmon
○ *F

Association of MBAs Ltd 1967

NR 25 Hosier Lane, LONDON, EC1A 9LQ. (hq)
020 7246 2686
Chief Exec: Jeanette Purcell; Co Sec: Pauline North
▲ Company Limited by Guarantee; Registered Charity
○ *E; for holders of the MBA degree; to promote management education in order to maximise its contribution to British industry
● Conf - Mtgs - ET - Res - Exhib - Stat - Inf - LG - Loan scheme - Accreditation of MBA courses
M 10,000 i, 70 f, 5 org, UK / 1000 i, o'seas
¶ Ambassador - 12. News - 4. Address Book - 1.
Guide to Business Schools - 1. AR.
Survey of MBA Salaries & Careers - 2 yrly.

Association of Meat Inspectors GB Ltd   (AMI)   1947
NR   9 Southfield Close, BRIDGWATER, Somerset, TA7 8HJ.   (chief
        exec/b)
        01278 684903   fax 01278 684903
        http://www.meatinspectors.co.uk
        Chief Exec: Pierce T Furlong
▲   Un-incorporated Society
Br   7
○   *P; meat inspection & hygiene in abattoirs, meat curing
        premises & cold stores; to promote research & publish the
        results; to promote high standards of meat inspection &
        hygiene
Gp   Technical, Legislative; Educational trust
●   Conf - Mtgs - ET - Res - Exhib - SG - Stat - Inf - Lib - PL - Empl -
        LG
M   c 1,200 i
¶   Meat Hygienist - 4; ftm only.

Association of Media Evaluation Companies   (AMEC)
■   55 Ramsden Rd, LONDON, SW12 8RA.   (hsp)
        020 8675 4442
        email jacquelinemilton@amecorg.com
        http://www.amecorg.com
        Admin: Jacqueline Milton
▲   Un-incorporated Society
○   *T; to represent the interest of media evaluation companies
●   Mtgs - Promotion of media evaluation
M   11 f, UK / 4 f, o'seas

Association of Media Practice Educators
        2006 merged with the Media, Communication & Cultural Studies
        Association to form **MeCCSA with AMPE**

**Association of Medical Advisers to British Orchestras
(AMABO)   1990**
■   Totara Park House (3rd floor), 34-36 Gray's Inn Rd, LONDON,
        WC1X 8HR.   (hq)
        020 7404 5888   fax 020 7404 3222
        email amabo@bapam.org.uk
        http://www.bapam.org.uk/amabo
        Sec: Dr Penny Wright
▲   Registered Charity
Br   19
○   *M, *P; for doctors attached to major British orchestras;
        research & training in performing arts medicine
●   Mtgs - ET - Res - SG
<   Brit Assn for Performing Arts Medicine
M   21 i

**Association of Medical Insurance Intermediaries   (AMII)
1998**
■   International House (suite 501), 223 Regent St, LONDON,
        W1B 2QD.   (hq)
        0870 112 0431   fax 0870 112 0451
        http://www.amii.org.uk
        Chmn: Stephen Walker,   Sec: Mike Izzard
○   *T; to offer specialist independent advice on health issues
●   Conf - Mtgs - ET - Exhib
M   c 98 f

Association of Medical Microbiologists   (AMM)   1983
■   c/o Dr S P Barrett, Dept of Medical Microbiology, Charing
        Cross Hospital, Fulham Palace Rd, LONDON, W6 8RF.
        (hsb)
        Hon Sec: Dr Stephen P Barrett
○   *L, *P; to further the science & practice of medical microbiology
●   Conf - Mtgs - ET - Inf - LG
M   510 i, UK / 15 i, o'seas
¶   Medical Microbiologists (Jnl) - 4; ftm only.

Association of Medical Research Charities   (AMRC)   1987
■   61 Gray's Inn Rd, LONDON, WC1X 8TL.   (hq)
        020 7269 8820   fax 020 7269 8821
        email info@amrc.org.uk   http://www.amrc.org.uk
        Chief Exec: Simon Denegri
▲   Company Limited by Guarantee; Registered Charity
○   *K, *M, *Q; to further medical interests in the UK generally & in
        particular the advancement of the effectiveness of those
        charities of which a principal activity is medical research
●   ET - LG
M   112 charities
¶   NL - 6/8; ftm only.   AR - 1; free.

**Association of Medical Secretaries, Practice Managers,
        Administrators & Receptionists   (AMSPAR)   1964**
NR   Tavistock House North, Tavistock Sq, LONDON, WC1H 9LN.
        (hq)
        020 7387 6005
        Chief Exec: Tom Brownlie
▲   Company Limited by Guarantee; Registered Charity
○   *P
●   Conf - Mtgs - ET - Exam - Inf
<   Eur Fedn of Med Secretary Assns
M   5,500 i, UK / 90 i, o'seas
¶   AMSPAR Magazine - 4.   NL - 4.
        Professional Guidelines.   Careers leaflets.

**Association of Member-Directed Pension Schemes   (AMPS)
1979**
NR   Barnett Waddingham, Chalfont Court, Hill Avenue,
        AMERSHAM, Bucks, HP6 5BB.   (hsb)
        01494 788100
        Hon Sec: Trevor Harvey
▲   Un-incorporated Society
○   *P
●   Conf - Mtgs - ET - Inf - LG
×   2005 (Association of Pensioneer Trustees
        (Sipp Provider Group

Association of Members of Boards of Visitors
        since 2003 **Association of Members of Independent
        Monitoring Boards**

**Association of Members of Independent Monitoring Boards
        (AMIMB)   1982**
NR   3 Forsham Cottages, Forsham Lane, Sutton Valence,
        MAIDSTONE, Kent, ME17 3WQ.   (chmn/p)
        Chmn: Mrs Angela Clay
▲   Registered Charity
○   *W; to educate, inform, advise & support members of
        independent monitoring boards of penal institutions in
        England & Wales; to educate & inform the public concerning
        the treatment of offenders
●   Conf - Mtgs - ET - SG - Inf - LG
<   Penal Affairs Consortium
M   400 i
¶   The Independent Monitor - 4; ftm only.
×   2003 Association of Members of Boards of Visitors

Association of Men of Kent & Kentish Men   (MKKM)   1897
NR   Cantium Lodge, Terrace Rd, MAIDSTONE, Kent, ME16 8HU.
        (hq)
        01622 758722
        Sec: Mrs T M Robinson
Br   19
○   *G, *K; to foster a sense of pride in the County of Kent; to
        protect the county's heritage & the beauty of the countryside
●   Conf - Mtgs - Inf - Lib - VE
M   3,000 i
¶   Kent - 3.

        © CBD Research Ltd · Beckenham · BR3 5JS · Tel 020 8650 7745 · Fax 020 8650 0768 · E-mail cbd@cbdresearch.com · www.cbdresearch.com

Association of Meter Operators   (AMO)   1996
NR   Gemserv, Centurion House (7th floor), 24 Monument St,
        LONDON, EC3R 8AJ.   (asa)
        020 7090 1000   fax 020 7090 1001
        http://www.meteroperators.org.uk
▲   Un-incorporated Society
○   *T; for meter operators in the UK electricity & gas markets
●   Mtgs - Inf (to members only)
M   14 f
¶   LM on website.

**Association of Miniature Engine Manufacturers   (AMEM)
1975**
■   423 Upper Elmers End Rd, BECKENHAM, Kent, BR3 3DA.
        (mail address)
○   *T; includes petrol, diesel & bio fuel, battery & solar powered
        units
●   Conf - Mtgs - SG - Inf - LG
¶   Mini-motion - 3/4; ftm only.

Association of Mining Analysts   (AMA)
NR   c/o Bankside plc, 1 Frederick's Place, LONDON, EC2R 8AE.
        (mail)
        07734 678584
        http://www.ama.org.uk add
        Sec: Paul Renken
▲   Un-incorporated Society
○   *P; for fund managers, bankers & analysts
●   Mtgs - VE
M   251 i, UK / 24 i, o'seas

Association of Model Agents   (AMA)   1974
■   122 Brompton Rd, LONDON, SW3 1JE.   (hq)
        020 7584 6466   fax 020 7581 2113
○   *T; to protect the reputation of models & model agents
●   Mtgs - Inf
M   22 f

**Association of Model Railway Societies in Scotland   (AMRSS)
1966**
NR   Model Rail Scotland, PO Box 19564, JOHNSTONE, PA6 7YP.
        (mail/address)
        0845 226 3061
▲   Un-incorporated Society
○   *G; to promote 'Modelrail Scotland', the national model
        railway exhibition held at the SECC Glasgow, on the last
        weekend in February
●   Exhib
M   34 clubs

Association of Mortgage Borrowers   1996
§   19 Widegate St, LONDON, E1 7HP.   (hq)
        0870 241 1940   fax 0870 241 3550
        http://www.associationmortgageborrowers.org
▲   Company Limited by Guarantee; Registered Charity
        A non-membership body which aims to relieve persons in need
        by the provision of independent & confidential advice &
        support for borrowers who are under the threat of
        repossession by lenders; to promote sensible actions by
        lenders & borrowers

Association of Motion Picture Sound   (AMPS)   1989
■   28 Knox St, LONDON, W1H 1FS.   (hq)
        020 7723 6727   fax 020 7723 6727
        email admin@amps.net   http://www.amps.net
        Hon Sec: Brian Hickin
▲   Un-incorporated Society
○   *P; to promote & encourage the science, technology & creative
        application of all aspects of motion picture sound recording
        & reproduction
Gp   Sound for film & television
●   Mtgs - Private film screenings
M   340 i, 35 f, UK / 23 i, 1 f, o'seas
¶   AMPS Jnl - 4.

**Association of Motor Racing Circuit Owners Ltd   (AMRCO)
1962**
NR   c/o BARC Ltd, Thruxton Circuit, ANDOVER, Hants, SP11 8PN.
        (sb)
        01264 882200   fax 01264 882233
        email amrco@barc.net
        http://www.motorsportsuk.co.uk
        Sec: Mrs A J Curley
▲   Company Limited by Guarantee
○   *T; to represent the interests of motor racing licensed circuit
        owners
●   Mtgs
M   17 f, UK / 1 f, o'seas

Association for Multi Manager Investing
        see **Association for Institutional Multi Manager Investing**

Association of Municipal Authorities of Ireland
IRL   c/o Tom Ryan, Rathnaleen, NENAGH, Co Tipperary, Republic of
        Ireland.
        353 (67) 42222
        email director@amai.ie
        Dir: Tom Ryan
○   *N

**Association of National Driver Improvement Scheme Providers
(ANDISP)   1998**
■   c/o Ian Powell (Herts County Council), County Hall, Pegs Lane,
        HERTFORD, SG13 8DN.   (hsb)
        01992 556817   fax 01992 556820
        email ian.powell@hertscc.gov.uk
        http://www.andisp.org.uk
        Hon Sec: Ian Powell
▲   Un-incorporated Society
○   *T; organisation & practice of driver improvement courses on
        behalf of police constabularies.   The association manages
        these courses on behalf of the Dept of Transport (DFT) &
        Association of Chief Police Officers (ACPO)
●   Mtgs - ET - LG
M   42 f & local authorities

Association of National Park Authorities   (ANPA)   1992
NR   126 Bute St, CARDIFF, Glam, CF10 5LE.   (hq)
        029 2049 9966
        http://www.nationalparks.gov.uk
        Co-ordinator: Cathryn Marcus
▲   Un-incorporated Society
○   *N; for the national park authorities of England & Wales
●   Conf - Mtgs - Res - Comp - SG - LG - Public relations of NPA's
        at national level
M   11 park authorities
¶   Annual Review - 1;   Technical papers - irreg.

**Association of National Tourist Office Representatives
(ANTOR)   1953**
■   PO Box 5017, HOVE, E Sussex, BN23 3ZD.   (mail/address)
        0870 241 9084
        email secretary@antor.com   http://www.antor.com
        Exec Sec: Peter Lilley
▲   Company Limited bu Guarantee
○   *T; 'the principal lobbying organisaton for the world's tourist
        offices'
●   Mtgs - Exhib - Inf - LG
M   60 overseas tourist offices represented in the UK
¶   LM - 1; free.

Association of Natural Burial Grounds (ANBG) 1994
NR   12a Blackstock Mews, Blackstock Rd, LONDON, N4 2BT.   (hq)
         0871 288 2098
         email nc@alberyfoundation.org
         http://www.naturaldeath.org.uk
         Acting Dir: Stephanie Wienrich
▲   Registered Charity
○   *K; 'to promote 'natural' burial, where trees or flowers are
         planted on the grave instead of having headstones'
●   Conf - ET - Res - Exhib - Stat - Inf - LG
<   Natural Death Centre
M   50 f
¶   The Natural Death Hbk - 3 yrly; £14.99.
         Living Will + Forms; £7.
✕   2002 Association of Nature Reserve Burial Grounds

Association of Natural Medicine (ANM) 1983
■   27 Braintree Rd, WITHAM, Essex, CM8 2DD.   (hq)
         01376 502762   fax 01376 502762
         email info@naturalmedicine.fsnet.co.uk
         http://www.associationnaturalmedicine.co.uk
         Chief Exec: Martin Duncombe
▲   Company Limited by Guarantee; Registered Charity
○   *P; training courses for professional practice of natural
         medicine & therapies
●   Mtgs - ET - Exam - Res - SG - Inf
<   Coun for Orgs Registering Homeopaths (CORH); Brit Massage
         Therapy Coun;Aromatherapy Orgs Coun; Parliamentary Gp
         for Integrated & Complementary Medicine
M   c 300 i
¶   Natural Medicine (Jnl) - 4.

Association of Nature Reserve Burial Grounds
         since 2002 **Association of Natural Burial Grounds**

**Association for Neuro-Linguistic Programming (UK) Ltd
         (ANLP) 1985**
NR   PO Box 3357, Wrotham Business Pk, BARNET, Herts,
         EN5 9NJ.   (admin/p)
         0870 444 0790
         Admin Mgr: C Coughlan,   Chmn: Carol Harris
▲   Company Limited by Guarantee; Registered Charity
○   *E
●   Conf - Mtgs - ET - SG - Inf
M   750 i, 40 f, UK / 50 i, o'seas
¶   Rapport (Jnl) - 4.   Information booklet - 1.
         Directory of Members.   AR; free.

Association of New Age Industries (ANAIS) 1995
■   c/o Honeybees, Milkhouse Water, PEWSEY, Wilts, SN9 5JX.
▲   Un-incorporated Society
○   *T
Gp   Water power; Wind power
M   i, f & org

Association of News Retailing
         a group of the **Association of Convenience Stores**

**Association of Newspaper & Magazine Wholesalers
         (ANMW) 1917**
NR   8-14 Vine Hill (3rd floor), LONDON, EC1R 5DX.   (hq)
         020 7520 0480
         email enquiries@anmw.co.uk
         Sec: Sofia Deus
▲   Un-incorporated Society
○   *T
●   Mtgs - ET - Inf - LG
M   29 f

Association of Noise Consultants (ANC) 1964
NR   105 St Peter's Street, ST ALBANS, Herts, AL1 3EJ.   (hq)
         01727 896092   fax 01727 896026
         http://www.association-of-noise-consultants.co.uk
         Secretariat: Kingston Smith
▲   Un-incorporated Society
○   *P; to improve the quality of professional services provided by
         noise & vibration consultants
●   Conf - Mtgs - Inf - LG
M   55 f

Association for Nonsmokers' Rights
         reported to us as being no longer in existence - we should
         appreciate confirmation

Association of North East Councils (ANEC) 1986
NR   The Guildhall, Quayside, NEWCASTLE UPON TYNE,
         NE1 3AF.   (hq)
         0191-261 7388   fax 0191-232 4558
         http://www.northeastcouncils.gov.uk
         Dir: Melanie Laws
▲   Un-incorporated Society
○   *N; an association of the local councils (county councils, district
         councils & metropolitan district councils) in the counties
         forming the North East Region of England - Durham,
         Northumberland, Tyne & Wear & Tees Valley; to promote the
         economic & social wellbeing of the people of the region.
         Is the Joint Directorate for the North East Assembly
●   Conf - Mtgs - Res - Stat - LG
M   24 local authorities
¶   NL - 6;   Corporate Plan - 1;
         State of the Region Profile Report - 2;
         State of the Region Fact Card - 2; all free.

Association of Northern Ireland Colleges (ANIC)
NR   Unit 3 The Sidings Office Park, Antrim Rd, LISBURN, Co Antrim,
         BT28 3AJ.
         028 9262 7512   fax 028 9262 7594
         http://www.anic.ac.uk
         Chief Exec: John D'Arcy

**Association of Northern Ireland Education & Library Boards
         (ANIELB) 1973**
■   Belfast Education & Library Board, 40 Academy St, BELFAST,
         BT1 2NQ.   (hsb)
         028 9056 4030   fax 018 9043 3861
         email johnm@belb.co.uk
         Pres: Rev Gary Haire,   Hon Sec: John McCullough
▲   Un-incorporated Society
○   *E, *N; to seek to achieve the highest standards in education &
         library services fro all the people of Northern Ireland
●   Conf - Mtgs
M   202 i

**Association of Northumberland Local History Societies
         (ANLHS) 1966**
■   c/o The Black Gate, Castle Garth, NEWCASTLE UPON TYNE,
         NE1 1RQ.   (hq)
         Contact: Hon Sec
▲   Registered Charity
○   *L; to bring together all interested in the history & traditions of
         the historical County of Northumberland
Gp   Projects (incl research)
●   Conf - Mtgs - Res - Exhib - SG - Inf - VE
<   Brit Assn for Local History; Historical Assn
M   93 i, 54 org, UK / 3 i, o'seas
¶   Tyne & Tweed (Jnl) - 1; £2.50 yr m, £3 yr nm.   AR; free.

Association of Nursery Training Colleges Ltd (ANTC) 1934
■   Chiltern College, 16 Peppard Rd, Caversham, READING,
         Berks, RG4 8JZ.   (regd/off)
▲   Registered Charity
○   *E; promotion of nursery nurse training
●   Mtgs - ET - LG

Association of Nurses in Substance Abuse **(ANSA)** **1983**
NR 37 Star St, Ware, Herts, SG12 7AA.
0870 241 3503 fax 01920 462730

Association of Nursing Religious & Co-Workers **(ANRCW)** **1952**
■ 4 Park St, PEMBROKE DOCK, Pembrokeshire, SA72 6JG.
(pres/p)
01646 682837
Pres: Catherine P Lehane
▲ Registered Charity
○ *P
● Conf - Mtgs - ET
< Conf of Religious (COR); Nat Board of Catholic
Women (NBCW); CAFOD
M 75 i
✕ 2005 Association of Nursing Religious

Association of Occupational Health Nurse Practitioners
since 2005-06 **AOHNP (UK)**

Association of Occupational Therapists of Ireland **(AOTI)**
IRL 29 Gardiner Place, DUBLIN 1, Republic of Ireland.
353 (1) 878 0247
email aoti@eircom.net http://www.aoti.ie
Chmn: Yvonne Finn-Orde
○ *P

Association of Occupational Therapists in Mental Health
is a specialist section of the **British Association of Occupational Therapists**

Association of Old Vehicle Clubs in Northern Ireland **(AOVC)** **1973**
■ 38 Ballymaconnell Rd, BANGOR, Co Down, BT20 5PS. (hsb)
028 9146 7886 fax 028 9146 3211
email secretary@aovc.co.uk http://www.aovc.co.uk
Dir & Co Sec: Trevor Mitchell
▲ Company Limited by Guarantee
○ *G; the restoration & use of all types of historic vehicles in
Northern Ireland
Gp Car clubs; Vintage clubs
● Mtgs - Exhib - VE
< Fedn of Brit Historic Vehicle Clubs
M i, 28 clubs
¶ Ybk - 1; free to affiliated clubs.

Association of On-Track Labour Suppliers
since 2006 (January) see **Rail Industry Contractors Association**

Association for One Parent Families
see **Gingerbread (an Association for One Parent Families) Ltd**

Association of Online Publishers **(AOP)** **2002**
NR Queen's House, 28 Kingsway, LONDON, WC2B 6JR. (hq)
020 7400 7510 fax 020 7404 4167
email alex.white@ukaop.org.uk
http://www.ukaop.org.uk
Head: Alexandra White
▲ Company Limited by Guarantee
○ *T; for interactive (online) publishers from all sectors of media,
whether from newspaper, magazine or broadcasting
industries, or solely online. The primary purpose of AOP is to
raise standards & revenue across all sectors of online
publishing, & to raise the credibility & profile of the industry
● Conf - Mtgs - ET - Res - Comp - SG - Stat - Inf - LG - Annual
Awards
< Periodical Publishers Assn (PPA)
M 12 f
¶ e-mail NL - 26; free

Association of Operating Department Practitioners **(AODP)** **1945**
NR PO Box 1304, WILMSLOW, Cheshire, SK9 5WW. (hq)
0870 746 0984 fax 0870 746 0985
Br 21
○ *P; those qualified in operating department practice; to protect
patients by self regulation & maintaining & improving
standards of practice & education in theatre practice
Gp C'ees: Education, Patient care & management; Register of
qualified members
● Conf - ET - Exhib - SG - Stat
< Assn of Surgical Technologists (AST)(USA); Australasian Soc of
Anaesthetic Technicians (ASAT)
M 5,000 i, UK / 45 i, o'seas
¶ Technic - 12; Code of Conduct; both ftm only.
Curriculum Framework for Operating Department
Practice; £12.

Association of Optometrists **(AOP)** **1946**
■ 61 Southwark St, LONDON, SE1 0HL. (hq)
020 7261 9661
Chief Exec: Bob Hughes
▲ Company Limited by Guarantee
○ *P; to represent the interests of optometrists
Gp Hospital optometrists
● Conf - Mtgs - ET - Inf - Empl - LG - Professional indemnity
insurance - Provision of representation of individual members
in legal & disciplinary cases
< Eur Coun of Optometry & Optics; Jt Optical C'ee on the EU
M 11,000 i, UK / 100 i, o'seas
¶ OT (Optometry Today/OpticsToday) - 26; Blink (NL) - 4; both
ftm.

Association of Optometrists: Ireland
IRL 18 Greenmount House, Harold's Cross Rd, DUBLIN 6W,
Republic of Ireland.
353 (1) 453 8850 fax 353 (1) 453 8867
email info@optometrists.ie
Sec: Peter Coleman
○ *P

Association of Paediatric Anaesthetists (Great Britain & Ireland) **(APAGBI)** **1973**
■ c/o Dr K Wilkinson, Dept of Anaesthesia, Norfolk & Norwich
University Hospital, Colney Lane, NORWICH, NR4 7UY.
(hsb)
01603 287086
Hon Sec: Dr Kathleen Wilkinson
▲ Un-incorporated Society
○ *L, *P; education & research in paediatric anaesthesia
Gp Clinical trials; Guidelines; Peer review
● Conf - ET - Res - SG - LG - Liaison with medical royal colleges
< Fedn of Eur Assns in Paediatric Anaesthesia; Assn of
Anaesthetists
M 450 i, UK / 180 i, o'seas
¶ NL - 12; free.

Association for Palliative Medicine of Great Britain & Ireland **(APM)** **1985**
NR Bellis House, 11 Westwood Rd, SOUTHAMPTON, Hants,
SO17 1DL. (hq)
023 8067 2888
Chmn: Dr Andrew Hoy, Admin Sec: Mrs Sheila Richards
▲ Registered Charity
○ *P
● Conf - Mtgs - ET - Res - SG
< Eur Assn for Palliative Care
M 500 i, UK / 10 i, o'seas
¶ NL - 2; ftm only.

Association of Parallel Importers
no longer operating

Association of Past Rotarians   1960
- ■ 6 Vivian Park, SWANAGE, Dorset, BH19 1PJ.   (hsp)
  Hon Sec: Eric J Dymond
- ▲ Un-incorporated Society
- ○ *G; a fellowship of member clubs of former Rotarians
- ● Conf - Mtgs - VE
- M 18 i, 34 clubs (686 i)
- ¶ Proclaim - 4;   AR; both free.
  Pioneers & Pathfinders (1948) [&] Forty Years On (2000) by
  W R Braide, (histories of the Past Rotarian movement).

**Association for Pastoral Care in Mental Health   (APCMH)
1986**
- ■ c/o Marylebone Parish Church, Marylebone Rd, LONDON,
  NW1 5LT.   (postal/address)
  020 7383 0167   fax 020 8395 9022
  email john.rawson@blueyonder.co.uk
  http://www.pastoral.org.uk
  Co Sec: John Vallat
- ▲ Registered Charity
- Br 4
- ○ *W; to support & facilitate groups who wish to seek advice on
  setting up projects for people with mental health problems -
  mainly in the churches
- ● Conf - Mtgs - ET - Drop in centres - Befriending schemes -
  Awareness raising conferences
  Helpline: 01483 538936
- < Gld of Health; Nat Schizophrenia Fellowship
- M 200 i, 20 org
- ¶ NL - 6; ftm only.

Association for Pastoral & Spiritual Care & Counselling
a group of the **British Association for Counselling &
Psychotherapy**

Association for Payment Clearing Services   (APACS)   1985
- NR Mercury House, Triton Court, 14 Finsbury Sq, LONDON,
  EC2A 1LQ.   (hq)
  020 7711 6200
  Chief Exec: Paul Smee
- ○ *T; to oversee & coordinate the operation, planning &
  development of money transmission & payment clearing
  services in the UK
- Gp Operational clearing companies; Plastic card policy
- ● Res - Stat - Inf
- M 30 f
- ¶ AR.   Hbk.   LM.
  Note: has taken over the functions of the Credit Card Research
  Group

Association of Pension Lawyers   (APL)   1984
- ■ PMI House (room 10), 4-10 Artillery Lane, LONDON,
  E1 7LS.   (mail) add
  Hon Sec: Kris Weber
- ○ *P; to promote awareness of the importance of the role of law
  in the provision of pensions; to afford opportunities for
  discussion & consideration of matters of interest as well as
  education
- Gp Education & seminars; International; Investment; Leigislative &
  parliamentary; Litigation Investment
- ● Conf - Mtgs - LG
- M c 950 i
- ¶ Pension Lawyer - 4.

Association of Pensioneer Trustees
2005 merged with the Sipp Provider Group to form the **Association
of Member-Directed Pension Schemes**

Association for People with Lower Limb Abnormalities
see **STEPS: the Association for People with Lower Limb
Abnormalities**

Association for Perioperative Practice   (NATN)   1964
- ■ Daisy Ayris House, 6 Grove Park Court, HARROGATE, N Yorks,
  HG1 4DP.   (hq)
  01423 508079   fax 01423 531613
  email hq@afpp.org.uk   http://www.afpp.org.uk
  Chief Exec: John Brunt
- ▲ Company Limited by Guarantee; Registered Charity
- Br 15
- ○ *P; for those working in & around operating theatres
- ● Conf - Mtgs - ET - Res - Exhib - SG - Inf - Lib - VE
- M 8,500 i, 10 f, UK / 250 i, o'seas
- ¶ Jnl of Perioperative Practice - 12; ftm, £60 yr nm.
- × 2004-05 National Association of Theatre Nurses

Association of Personal Injury Lawyers   (APIL)   1989
- ■ 11 Castle Quay, NOTTINGHAM, NG7 1FW.   (hq)
  0115-958 0585   fax 0115-958 0885
  email mail@apil.com   http://www.apilonline.com
  Sec: Frances Swaine,   Chief Exec: Denise Kitchener
- ▲ Company Limited by Guarantee
- ○ *P; to promote full & prompt compensation for all types of
  personal injury; to promote wider redress for personal injury
  in the legal system; to campaign for improvements in
  personal injury law for the public good
- Gp Special interest: Procedure, Brain injury, Child abuse, Child
  injury, Clinical negligence, Costs & funding, Damages,
  Environment, International, Military, Multi party actions,
  Occupational health, Product liability, Spinal cord injury,
  Transport
- ● Conf - Mtgs - ET - Exam - Res - Exhib - Stat - Inf - LG
- M 5,213 i, UK / 62 i, o'seas + 150 f
- ¶ Jnl - 4.
  Focus (NL) - 6; Agenda - 12; both ftm only.
  Rehab Directory - 1; ftm, £20 nm.
  Membership Directory - 1; ftm, £100 nm.   AR; free.

Association of Personal Trainers
dissolved

Association of Pet Behaviour Counsellors   (APBC)   1989
- NR PO Box 46, WORCESTER, WR8 9YS.   (mail)
  01386 751151   fax 01386 750743
  http://www.apbc.org.uk address
- ○ *P; for practising pet behaviour therapists who work exclusively
  on referral from veterinary practitioners, to treat behaviour
  problems in dogs & cats primarily, but also horses, rabbits,
  parrots & occasional exotic species
- M practices

Association of Pet Dog Trainers   (APDT)   1995
- ■ PO Box 17, KEMPSFORD, Glos, GL7 4WZ.   (hq)
  01285 810811
  email apdtoffice@aol.com   http://www.apdt.co.uk
  Chmn: Mary Burnside
- ▲ Un-incorporated Society
- Br Belgium, Italy, Netherlands, Spain
- ○ *P; to promote the practice of good dog training amongst
  veterinary surgeons & the public
- ● Mtgs - ET - Exam - SG - Inf - Lib - Workshops - Forum
- M 400 i
- ¶ NL - 3;   LM; both ftm.

Association for Petroleum & Explosives Administration (APEA) 1958
■ PO Box 106, SAFFRON WALDEN, Essex, CB11 3XT.   (hq)
  01799 502929   fax 01799 541816
  email admin@apea.org.uk   http://www.apea.org.uk
  Business Mgr: Jane Mardell
▲ Company Limited by Guarantee
○ *P; to represent all sides of the petroleum industry (incl:
  national & local government, oil companies, equipment
  manufacturers & suppliers, service & installation
  organisations & training establishments)
● Conf - Mtgs - ET - Exhib - Inf - VE - LG - Publication
M 630 i, 321 f, UK / 32 i, 24 f, o'seas
¶ Guidance for the Design, Construction & Maintenance of Petrol
  Filling Stations - 1; £30 m, £90 nm.

Association of Pharmacy Technicians   1952
NR 1 Mabledon Place (4th floor), LONDON, WC1H 9AJ.
  020 7551 1551
○ *P; dispensing prescriptions for doctors at doctors' surgeries

Association of Photographers Ltd   1968
■ 81 Leonard St, LONDON, EC2A 4QS.   (hq)
  020 7739 6669
  Chief Exec: Gwen Thomas
▲ Company Limited by Guarantee
Br 3
○ *P, *T; for professional photographers working in fashion,
  advertising & editorial fields
● Conf - Mtgs - ET - Exhib - Comp - Inf - Lib - Copyright advice
  service
< Pyramide Europe; Brit Photographers Liaison C'ee; Pyramide
  GB
M 1,000 i, 10 f, 18 org, UK / 21 i, o'seas
¶ Image - 12;   The Annual Awards - 1;
  Business Info Beyond the Lens; all ftm.

Association for Physical Education   (APE) 1899
■ Building 25, London Rd, READING, Berks, RG1 5AQ.   (hq)
  0118-378 6240
  email enquiries@afpe.org.uk   http://www.afpe.org.uk
  Sec: John Matthews
▲ Company Limited by Guarantee; Registered Charity
Br 2
○ *E, *P; to promote & maintain high standards & safe practice in
  all aspects of physical education
● Conf - Mtgs - ET - Res - SG
< Intl Coun of Sport Science & Physical Educ (ICSSPE); Eur
  Physical Educ Assn EUPEA)
M 2,000 i, 50 f, UK / 50 i, 10 f, o'seas
¶ Physical Education Matters - 4;
  Physical Education & Sports Pedagogy - 3;
  Members Ybk - 1; all ftm.
✕ 2006 (British Association of Advisers & Lecturers in Physical
  Education
  2006 (March) (Physical Education Association

Association of Physical & Natural Therapists   (APNT)
■ 27 Old Gloucester St, LONDON, WC1N 3XX.
  0845 345 2345
  email info@apnt.org
  Gen Sec: Sally Reynolds
○ *P

Association of Pioneer Motor Cyclists   (APMC) 1928
■ Heather Bank, May Close, Liphook Rd, Headley, BORDON,
  Hants, GU35 8LR.   (hsp)
  01428 712666
  Hon Sec: Mrs J McBeath
Br Counties; Belgium, Holland, USA
○ *G; for all who contributed to the establishment of the sport,
  pastime & industry of motorcycling. 'Companion'
  membership available to those having held a licence for 40+
  years, 'Pioneer' membership for those licensed for 50+ years
● Mtgs - Comp - VE - Social activities
M 550 i, UK / 20 i, o'seas
¶ NL - 4;   Rules & register of members - 2; ftm only.

Association of Planning Supervisors
  since 2004 **Association for Project Safety**

Association of Play Industries   (API)
■ Federation House, STONELEIGH PARK, Warks, CV8 2RF.   (hq)
  024 7641 4999   fax 024 7641 4990
  http://www.api-play.org
  Co Sec: Deborah Holt
▲ Company Limited by Guarantee
○ *T; manufacturers & suppliers of play equipment & impact
  absorbing surfaces (incl inflatable structures)
● Mtgs - Exhib - Inf - LG
< a group of the Fedn of Sports & Play Assns (FSPA)
M c 60 f

Association of Pleasure Craft Operators   1954
■ Unit 1 The Boatyard, High St, WEEDON, Northants,
  NN7 4QD.   (hq)
  01327 340174   fax 01327 340174
  email apco@britishmarine.co.uk
  Sec: Samantha Clarke
▲ Un-incorporated Society
○ *T; interests of members who are all in business connected with
  inland waterways in the UK
Gp Sections: Hotel boat, Passenger boat
● Conf - Mtgs - ET - Stat - Inf - LG
< Brit Marine Fedn
M 130 f
¶ NL - 4; ftm.   LM - 1; free.
  Members Directory -1; free.

Association of Plumbing & Heating Contractors   (APHC) 1925
■ 14 Ensign House, Ensign Business Centre, Westwood Way,
  COVENTRY, Warks, CV4 8JA.   (hq)
  024 7647 2503   fax 024 7647 0942
  email info@aphc.co.uk   http://www.aphc.co.uk
  Chief Exec: Clive Dickin
▲ Company Limited by Guarantee
○ *T; for employers in the plumbing & heating industry in England
  & Wales
● Conf - Mtgs - ET - Exam - Exhib - Empl - LG
M 1,200 f
¶ Hot & Cold - 6; free.

Association of Police Authorities   (APA) 1997
NR 15 Greycoat Place, LONDON, SW1P 1BN.
  020 7664 3096
○ *N

Association of Police & Court Interpreters
■ PO Box 321, ASHTEAD, Surrey, KT21 9AA.
  Chmn: Ellen Parladorio
○ *P

**Association of Police & Public Security Suppliers   (APPSS)
1993**
■   Marlborough House, Headley Rd, Grayshott, HINDHEAD,
Surrey, GU2 6LG.   (hq)
01428 602627   fax 01428 602628
email inform@appss.org.uk   http://www.appss.org.uk
Dir: Peter May
▲   Company Limited by Guarantee
○   *T; to support the UK public security industry;   to promote UK
products to police, prisons and other public security agencies
worldwide
Gp   UK security export focus group
●   Conf - Res - Expt - Inf - Lib - VE - LG
<   a division of the Defence Mfrs Assn
M   250 f
¶   Public Security - 4; free.
Directory of Police & Public Security Suppliers - 1.

Association of Policy Market Makers   (APMM)   1992
NR   PO Box 37996, LONDON, SW4 7JA.   (hq)
0845 833 0088   fax 0845 833 0089
email enquiries@apmm.org   http://www.apmm.org
▲   Company Limited by Guarantee
○   *T; 'to promote the business of policy market makers in the
acquisition & disposal of traded (second-hand) endowment
policies'
●   Mtgs - Stat - Inf - LG
M   f [not given]
¶   AR - 1; ftm only.

Association of Port Health Authorities   (APHA)   1899
NR   2-02 Suffolk Enterprise Centre, Felaw Maltings, Felaw St,
IPSWICH, Suffolk, IP2 8SJ.   (hq)
01473 407040
Exec Sec: Peter Rotheram
▲   Company Limited by Guarantee
○   *T; health control of ships & aircraft & the people & cargo
landed from them on arrival in the UK
Gp   C'ees: Imported food; Environmental health & hygiene; Airport
liaison
●   Conf - Mtgs - Inf - LG
M   80 port health & local authorities
¶   Port Health Lookout (NL) - 12;
Port Health Hbk - 1;   AR; all free.

Association for Postnatal Illness   (APNI)   1979
NR   145 Dawes Rd, LONDON, SW6 7EB.   (hq)
020 7386 0868   fax 020 7386 8885
email info@apni.org   http://www.apni.org
Hon Sec: Mrs Diane Nehmé
▲   Registered Charity
○   *W; to offer advice & support to women suffering from
postnatal depression; support is offered by volunteers who
are all ex-sufferers
●   Inf
M   4,455 i
¶   Puerperal Psychosis;   Post Natal Depression;   Baby Blues &
Post Natal Depression; all free.

Association of Practising Accountants   (APA)   1987
■   105 St Peter's St, ST ALBANS, Herts, AL1 3EJ.   (hq)
01727 896000   fax 01727 8960262
email ksamle@kingstonsmith.co.uk
http://www.kingstonsmith.co.uk
Chmn: Michael J Snyder
▲   Un-incorporated Society
○   *P; for medium sized firms of chartered accountants
●   Mtgs - Inf
M   16 f
¶   Becoming a Chartered Accountant - training with a medium
sized firm.
Medium sized firms of Chartered Accountants - the vital link
between businesses & the City.
Research document: challenge & opportunity for medium sized
accountancy firms; ftm, £70 nm.

Association of Primary Care Groups & Trusts
since 2006 **NHS Trusts Association**

Association of Printing Machinery Importers   (APMI)   1959
■   65 Hazlewell Rd, LONDON, SW15 6UT.   (hq)
020 8780 2966   fax 020 8780 2864
Sec: Andrew Hamilton
▲   Un-incorporated Society
○   *T; for importers of printing machinery, equipment & allied
products
●   Conf - Mtgs - ET - Exhib - Stat
M   39 f
¶   m only.

**Association of Private Client Investment Managers &
Stockbrokers   (APCIMS)   1990**
■   114 Middlesex St, LONDON, E1 7JH.   (hq)
020 7247 7080   fax 020 7377 0939
email info@apcims.co.uk   http://www.apcims.co.uk
Chief Exec: Mrs Angela Knight
▲   Company Limited by Guarantee
○   *T; for firms who advise & deal for private investors
Gp   UK & European financial regulation; Corporate governance;
Clearing & settlement; Indices
●   Conf - Mtgs - Res - Stat - Inf - LG
<   [APCIMS now incorporates the Eur Assn of Securities
Dealers (EASD)]
M   200 f, UK / 20 f, o'seas
¶   APCIMS Update - 12;   Q Review - 4;   LM - 1;
AR - 1; all free.

Association of Private Crematoria & Cemeteries   (APCC)   1944
NR   129 Bloomsbury Lane, Timperley, ALTRINCHAM, Cheshire,
WA15 6NS.   (sp)
0161-291 8547
Sec: Andrew P Helsby
▲   Un-incorporated Society
○   *T; interests of proprietary cemeteries & crematoria
●   Mtgs - Stat - Inf - LG
<   Fedn Brit Cremation Authorities; Cremation Soc; Inst of Burial &
Cremation Administration
M   15 crematoria, 7 cemeteries
Note: incorporates the Cemeteries Association.

Association of Private Market Operators   (APMO)   1990
■   4 Worrygoose Lane, Whiston, ROTHERHAM, S60 4AD.   (sb)
01709 700072   fax 01709 703648
Gen Sec: David J Glasby
▲   Company Limited by Guarantee
○   *T; interests of private market operators in the UK; to foster
professionalism in the UK retail markets
●   Mtgs - Inf - LG
<   Brit Chams Comm
M   20 f
¶   Hbk - 2/3 yrly; free.

**Association of Private Pet Cemeteries & Crematoria   (APPCC)
1993**
NR   Paws to Rest, Nunclose, Armathwaite, CARLISLE, CA4 9TJ.
01697 472232   fax 01697 472260
email contact@appcc.org.uk   http://www.appcc.org.uk
Chmn: N J Ricketts
▲   Company Limited by Guarantee
○   *T; to provide a post death pet care service; to educate pet
owners, vets & others in the pet world, to the advantages of
giving pet animals a decent, dignified departure
●   Conf - Mtgs - Res - LG - Keeping abreast of the deluge of EU
legislation which threatens the livelihood of members
Helpline 01252 844478
<   Coun of Brit Funeral Services
M   41 f
¶   Chairman's Update - irreg; free.

Association of Private Railway Wagon Owners   (APRO)

NR   Homelea - Westland Green, Little Hadham, WARE, Herts,
        SG11 2AG.   (hsp)
        01279 843487
        email geoffrey.pratt@btconnect.com
        Sec Gen: Geoffrey Pratt
○   *T

Association of Professional Ambulance Personnel   (APAP)   1981

NR   6 The Old Brewery, The Charlton Estate, SHEPTON MALLET,
        Somerset, BA4 5QE.   (hq)
        0870 167 0999
        Finance Officer: Graham Sleight
Br   49
○   *U; for ambulance services personnel
●   Conf - Mtgs - ET - Exhib - Inf - Empl - LG
M   3,000 i
¶   Ambulance Assessment - 6; ftm, postage nm.

Association of Professional Astrologers   (APA)   1990

NR   8 Queen Close, HENLEY-on-THAMES, Oxon, RG9 1BP.
        (chmn/p)
        0800 074 6113
        Sec: Sharon Knight,   Chmn: Maureen Randall
○   *P; to provide a forum for professional discussion of astrology
        on all levels; to promote astrology as a serious subject,
        counter the star-sign image of the astrologer & take active
        steps to correct misinterpretation in the press
M   69 i, UK / 5 i, o'seas
¶   NL - 4;   Consultants list - updated;
        Minutes of AGM & all meetings; all free.

Association of Professional Foresters of Great Britain
        2002 merged with the Timber Growers Association to form the
        Association of Timber Growers & Forestry Professionals

Association of Professional Genealogists in Ireland   (APGI)   1987

IRL   30 Harlech Crescent, Clonskeagh, DUBLIN 14, Republic of
        Ireland.   (hsb)   http://www.apgi.ie
        Hon Sec: Mary Beglan
○   *G; the promotion of genealogical research by members using
        records for the whole of Ireland
M   i (NI), i (Republic of Ireland)
¶   LM - 1; free.

Association of Professional Landscapers
        a specialist group of the **Horticultural Trades Association**

Association of Professional Music Therapists   (APMT)   1976

NR   61 Church Hill Rd, EAST BARNET, Herts, EN4 8SY.   (hq)
        020 8440 4153   fax 020 8440 4153
        email apmtoffice@aol.com   http://www.apmt.org.uk
        Admin: Louise Karena
▲   Un-incorporated Society
○   *P
Gp   Courses liaison; Jobs; Grading; Parliamentary; Employment
●   Conf - Mtgs - Res - SG - Inf - Clearing house for jobs - Register
        of members
<   Brit Soc for Music Therapy (BSMT); Links with overseas
        associations
M   540 i, UK / 25 i, o'seas

Association of Professional Opinion Poll Organisations
        has closed

Association of Professional Political Consultants   (APPC)   1994

NR   c/o Connect Public Affairs, Millbank Tower (3rd floor), Millbank,
        LONDON, SW1P 4QP.   (sb)
        020 7222 3533
        Sec: Mary Shearer
▲   Company Limited by Guarantee
○   *P; the representative & regulatory body for political consultants
        (professional Lobbyists)
●   Mtgs - ET - Self-regulation, regular compliance checks
M   25 f
¶   Register of Members' Interests; on request.

Association of Professional Recording Services Ltd   (APRS)   1947

■   PO Box 22, TOTNES, Devon, TQ9 7YZ.   (hq)
        01803 868600   fax 01803 868444
        email info@aprs.co.uk   http://www.aprs.co.uk
        Chief Exec: Peter Filleul
▲   Company Limited by Guarantee
○   *T; for all commercially involved in professional sound
        recording & associated fields
Gp   Sound recording studios & post-production facilities;
        Manufacturers & distributors; Consultancies, education &
        hire; Mastering & music services; Individuals - freelance &
        industry professionals; Students
●   ET - Expt - Inf - LG
M   250 i, 200 f, 8 educational org, UK / 10 i, o'seas
¶   NL.   LM.   Hbk.   AR; all ftm.

Association of Professional Sales Agents (Sports & Leisure Industries)   (APSA)

■   Federation House, STONELEIGH PARK, Warks, CV8 2RF.   (hq)
        024 7641 4999   fax 024 7641 4990
        email apsa@sportsandplay.com
        http://www.sportsandplay.com
        Assn Mgr: Mrs Jane Montgomery
▲   Company Limited by Guarantee
○   *T
●   Mtgs - Exhib - Inf
<   a group of the Fedn of Sports & Play Assns (FSPA)
M   55 i
✕   2002-03 Association of Professional Sports Agents

Association of Professional Sports Agents
        since 2003-04 **Association of Professional Sales Agents
        (Sports & Leisure Industries)**

Association of Professional Staffs in Colleges of Education & Humanities   (APSCEH)

IRL   c/o Irish Federation of University Teachers, 11 Merrion Sq,
        DUBLIN 2, Republic of Ireland.
        353 (1) 661 0910   fax 353 (1) 661 0909
        email ifut@eircom.net   http://www.ifut.ie
○   *E, *P
✕   2002 Association of Professional Staffs in Colleges of Education
        (APSCE)

** Association of Professional Sugaring
        Organisation lost: seeing Introduction paragraph 3

Association of Professional Tourist Guides   (APTG)   1987

NR   Amicus-MSF Centre, 33-37 Moreland St, LONDON,
        EC1V 8HA.   (hq)
        020 7505 3073   fax 020 7505 0026
        email aptg@aptg.org.uk
        http://www.touristguides.org.uk
        Admin: Annie Simpson,   Chmn: Robina Brown
○   *P; for London registered blue badge tourist guides
●   Conf - SG - VE - Walking tours - Tours with private car & guide
        - General sightseeing tours
<   ICOMOS; Wld Fedn of Tourist Guides Assns; Fedn of Eur
        Tourist Guides Assns
        is part of Amicus U
M   465 i
¶   Tourist Guides' Directory - 1.

Association of Professional Videomakers   (APV)   1994

NR   7 Nether Grove, Shenley Brook End, MILTON KEYNES, Bucks,
        MK5 7BQ.   (hq)
        01908 522145   fax 01908 524699
        http://www.apv.org.uk
        Sec: Jan Parry
▲   Company Limited by Guarantee
○   *P, *T; to provide help & support to the small independent video
        provider in the wedding & event video industry
●   Conf - Mtgs - ET - Exhib - Comp
M   500 i, UK / 10 i, o'seas
¶   Videoprofessional - 6; ftm, £2 nm.

**Association of Professionals in Education & Children's Trusts
(ASPECT)   1919**

NR   Woolley Hall, Woolley, WAKEFIELD, W Yorks, WF4 2JR.   (hq)
        01226 383428   fax 01226 383427
        email info@aspect.org.uk   http://www.aspect.org.uk
        Gen Sec: John Chowcat
○   *P, *U
Gp   Sub-groups: Assessment; Design & technology; Early years;
        GNVQ; Religious education
●   Conf - Mtgs - ET - Res - SG - Inf - Lib - Empl - LG - Business
        register - Optional professional indemnity insurance - Policy
        statements
M   c 4,000 i
¶   Information Bulletin - 6;   Briefing - 6; both ftm only.
        AR; free.
×   2005 (November) National Association of Educational
        Inspectors, Advisors & Consultants

**Association for Professionals in Services for Adolescents
(APSA)   1969**

■   The Mount Lodge, Church St, WHITCHURCH, Hants,
        RG28 7AR.   (admin/office)
        01256 892705   fax 01256 893090
        email apsa@cingnet.org.uk   http://www.apsa-web.info
        Admin: Mrs C Ingram,   Chmn: Neil Hemstock
▲   Registered Charity
○   *P, to promote the study, understanding & care of adolescents;
        to generate new thinking about problems of adolescent care,
        both residential & community-based
●   Conf - ET
<   Young Minds; Nat Children's Bureau
M   360 i, UK / 25 i, o'seas
¶   The Jnl of Adolescence - 6; ftm, £220 nm.
        APSA Rapport - 4; ftm, £16 nm.

Association for Project Management   (APM)   1972

■   150 West Wycombe Rd, HIGH WYCOMBE, Bucks, HP12 3AE.
        (hq)
        0845 458 1944   fax 01494 528937
        email infgo@apm.org.uk   http://www.apm.org.uk
        Hon Sec: David Roper,   Co Sec: John Salisbury
▲   Company Limited by Guarantee; Registered Charity
Br   12; Hong Kong
○   *P; run by project managers for project managers
Gp   Contracts & procurement; Earned value; Governance of project
        management; Programme management; Programme
        management; Project & programme excellence; People;
        Value management; Women in project management
●   Conf - Mtgs - ET - Exam - Res - Exhib - Comp - Stat - Inf - LG
<   Intl Project Mgt Assn (IPMA); Engg Coun UK
M   13,630 i, 355 f, UK / 673 i, 8 f, o'seas
¶   Project (Jnl) - 10.   Network (NL) - 10; Ybk - 1;   AR - 1;
        all ftm only.
        International Jnl of Project Management - 8; £35 m, 217 nm.

Association for Project Safety   (APS)   1995

■   16 Rutland Sq, EDINBURGH, EH1 2BB.   (hq)
        0131-221 9959   fax 0131-221 0061
        email info@aps.org.uk   http://www.aps.org.uk
        Chief Exec: Brian B Law
▲   Company Limited by Guarantee
Br   15
○   *P; to provide support, guidance & development to those
        working as planning supervisors (under the CDM regulations)
        across the construction industries
Gp   Planning supervision; Construction (Design & Management)
        Regulations 1994; Construction health & safety
●   Conf - ET - Inf - LG
<   Construction Ind Coun (CIC)
M   4,094 i, 921 f, UK / 20 i, o'seas
¶   NL - 5.   Practice Notes - 5.   AR; ftm.
        Planning Supervisor's Guide; £75 m.
        Health & Safety Plan 2004; £75 m. £140 nm.
        Form of Appointment 2004; £7.70 m (pack of 5; £35.25).
×   2004 Association of Planning Supervisors

Association for Promoting Retreats   (APR)   1913

■   The Central Hall, 256 Bermondsey St, LONDON, SE1 3UJ.
        (hq)
        020 7357 7736   fax 020 7357 7724
        email apr@retreats.org.uk
        Admin: Paddy Lane
▲   Registered Charity
○   *R; promoting retreats; to provide a national network of those
        able to advise on the subject
●   Conf - ET - Exhib - Inf
M   1,700 i, 300 org
¶   Retreats - 1.

Association for the Promotion of Preconceptual Care
    see **Foresight, the Association for the Promotion of
    Preconceptual Care**

**Association for the Promotion of Quality in TESOL Education
(QuiTE)**

■   c/o Institute of Education, University of London, 20 Bedford
        Way, LONDON, WC1H 0AL.   (chmn/b)
        http://www.quality-tesol-ed.org.uk
        Chmn: John Norrish
○   *E; for teacher educators, course providers & all working in
        areas relating to the training, education & development of
        teachers of English to speakers of other languages
●   Seminars

Association of Property Unit Trusts
    since 2005 **Association of Real Estate Funds**

Association for the Protection of Rural Scotland   1926
NR   Gladstone's Land (3rd floor), 483 Lawnmarket, EDINBURGH,
        EH1 2NT.   (hq)
        0131-225 7012 & 7013   fax 0131-225 6592
        Dir: Charles Strang
▲   Charitable Company; Limited by Guarantee
○   *G; to improve, protect & preserve the rural scenery &
        amenities of country districts, towns & villages in Scotland for
        the benefit of the public
●   Conf - Mtgs - Res - Exhib - Comp - Inf - Lib - VE - Annual
        award for buildings in a rural setting
M   675 i, 11 f, 133 org
¶   NL - 3.   AR - 1.
        trading as ruralScotland

**Association for Psychoanalytic Psychotherapy in the NHS
        (APP)   1981**
■   5 Windsor Rd, LONDON, N3 3SN.   (hq)
        020 8349 9873   fax 020 8343 3197
        email joycepiper@compuserve.co
        http://www.app-nhs.org.uk
        Chmn: Dr R Doctor
▲   Registered Charity
○   *M; to promote psychoanalytic psychotherapy in the NHS
Gp   Adult psychiatry; Child & adolescent; Group section; Nursing;
        Older adults; Primary care
●   Conf - Mtgs - Res
<   Eur Fedn for Psychoanalytic Psychotherapy (EFPP); Brit
        Psychoanalytic Coun; Assn Child Psychotherapists (ACP)
M   800 i, UK / 20 i, o'seas
¶   Psychoanalytic Psychotherapy (Jnl) - 4; ftm, £71 yr nm.
        APP NL - 2.   AR.

Association for Psychological Therapies   (APT)
NR   1 Saxby St, LEICESTER, LE2 0ND.   (mail/address)
        0116-255 5963
○   *P
<   Mtgs

Association of Psychosexual Nursing   1998
NR   PO Box 2762, LONDON, W1A 5HQ.
○   *M

Association of Public Analysts   (APA)   1953
NR   Burlington House, Piccadilly, LONDON, W1J 0BG.   (regd/off)
○   *P; to coordinate the activities of public analysts in the provision
        of scientific advice to local authorities on matters concerning
        food, water, animal feeds, consumer safety & the
        environment

Association of Public Analysts of Scotland   (APAS)   1897
■   c/o Analytical & Scientific Services, 4 Marine Esplanade,
        EDINBURGH, EH6 7LV.   (hsb)
        0131-555 7980   fax 0131-555 7987
        Hon Sec: Dr Andrew Mackie
▲   Un-incorporated Society
○   *P; analysis of food, waters, environmental materials, consumer
        products, & agricultural products for public protection;
        interpretation of public protection legislation
Gp   Sub-gps: Chemistry, Microbiology, Quality & IT
●   Mtgs - ET - LG
<   Assn Public Analysts
M   9 i

Association of Public Health Observatories   2000
NR   Alcuin Research & Resource Centre, University of York,
        Heslington, YORK, N Yorks, YO10 5DD.
        01904 724493   fax 01904 724588
○   *P

Association for Public Service Excellence   (APSE)   1981
NR   Washbrook House (2nd floor), Lancastrian Office Centre,
        32 Talbot Rd, Old Trafford, MANCHESTER, M32 0FP.   (hq)
        0161-772 1810   fax 0161-772 1811
        email enquiries@apse.org.uk   http://www.apse.org.uk
        Chief Exec: Paul O'Brien
▲   Un-incorporated Society
Br   2
○   *N, *T; the networking organisation which consults, develops,
        promotes & advises on best practice in the delivery of local
        authority services
Gp   Advisory groups for local authority service areas; Performance
        networks; Best value consultancy: Life long learning
●   Conf - Mtgs - ET - Res - Exhib - SG - Stat - Inf - Lib - LG
M   3 f, 244 local authorities
¶   Direct News - 6;   Briefing Notes - 1; both ftm only.
        AR (incl LM) - 1; ftm.   Publications - 2; at cost.
×   2006 (merged) Association of Civic Hosts

Association of Publishing Agencies   (APA)   1993
NR   Queen's House, 55-56 Lincoln's Inn Fields, LONDON,
        WC2A 3LJ.   (hq)
        020 7404 4166   fax 020 7404 4167
        email info@apa.co.uk   http://www.apa.co.uk
        Chief Exec: Patrick Fuller
○   *T; to promote the customer magazine publishing industry; to
        promote awareness of the effectiveness of such magazines as
        a marketing tool
●   Mtgs - Res - Inf - Marketing - Awards
<   Periodical Publishers Assn (PPA)
M   29 f, UK / 5 f, o'seas
¶   NL - 4;   A Guide to Customer Publishing - 1;
        Case Studies - 2; all free.
        The Case for Customer Magazines;   Info Pack;
        Membership pack; all on request.

Association for Punjab Studies (UK)   (APS (UK))   1994
NR   34 Armorial Road, Styvechale, COVENTRY, Warks, CV3 6GJ.
        (hsp)
        024 7641 1464
        Hon Sec: S S Thandi
▲   Company Limited by Guarantee
○   *L; promotion of punjab studies in the UK
●   Conf - ET - Res - SG
M   6 i, 25 org
¶   International Journal of Punjab Studies - 2.

**Association of Qualified Curative Hypnotherapists   (AQCH)
        1985**
NR   PO Box 6148, THATCHAM, Berks, RG19 9BR.   (admin)
        0121-693 1223
        email info@aqch.org   http://www.aqch.org
        Hon Sec: Maureen Simmonds
▲   Registered Charity
○   *P; to improve the understanding & practice of hypnotherapy &
        to enhance its recognition as a means of curing
●   Conf - Mtgs - ET - Exam - Res - Exhib - Inf
M   80 i, UK / 1 i, o'seas
¶   Hypnotherapy Jnl - 2; ftm, £1.50 nm.
        LM - updated continuously; free.

Association for Qualitative Research   (AQR)   1980
■   Davey House (suite 14), 31 St Neots Road, Eaton Ford,
        ST NEOTS, Cambs, PE19 3BA.   (hq)
        01480 407227   fax 01480 211267
        email info@aqr.org.uk   http://www.aqr.org.uk
        Sec: Rose Molloy
▲   Company Limited by Guarantee
○   *P, *T; for qualitative research
●   Conf - ET
M   1,100 i, UK / 75 i, o'seas
¶   In Brief (Jnl) - 6; ftm, subject to availability nm.
        Directory - 1; free.

Association for Quality in Health & Social Care
    since 2002 the Health & Social Care group of the **Institute of Quality Assurance**

Association of Racing Kart Schools Ltd   (ARKS)   1994
■ Stoneycroft, Godsons Lane, Napton, SOUTHAM, Warks,
    CV47 8LX.   (sp)
    01926 812177   fax 01926 812177
    email secretary@arks.co.uk   http://www.arks.co.uk
    Sec: Graham Smith
▲ Company Limited by Guarantee
Br 13; Dubai
○ *T
● Conf - ET - Exam - Stat - Inf
< Motor Activities Training Coun (MATC)
M 13 f, UK / 1 f, o;seas

Association for Radiation Research   (ARR)   1958
NR c/o Dr Tracy Robson, Reader in Molecular Pharmacology,
    Experimental Therapeutics, School of Pharmacy,
    Queen's University Belfast, Medical Biology Centre,
    97 Lisburn Rd, BELFAST, BT9 7BL.
    028 9097 2360   fax 028 9024 7794
    http://www.graylab.ac.uk/usr/arr/home.html
    Hon Sec: Dr Tracy Robson
○ *L; promotion of learning & education in the field of radiation
    research
M i
¶ NL - 2;   Hbk.

Association of Radical Midwives   (ARM)   1976
■ 16 Wytham St, OXFORD, OX1 4SU.   (sp)
    01865 248159
    email sarahmontagu@postmaster.co.uk
    Admin Sec: Sarah Montagu
▲ Registered Charity
Br 50 local contacts
○ *K, *P; to preserve & increase the choices in childbirth for
    women; to restore & strengthen the role of midwife
● Conf - Mtgs - LG
< Intl Confedn of Midwives; Eur Midwives Liaison C'ee
M 1,200 i, 140 orgs & colleges, UK / 80 i, o'seas
¶ Midwifery Matters - 4; ftm, £2 each nm.

Association of Railway Training Providers   (ARTP)   1997
■ 22 Headfort Place, LONDON, SW1X 7RY.   (asa)
    020 7201 0778   fax 020 7235 5777
    email info@artp.co.uk   http://www.artp.co.uk
    Secretariat: Peter Loosley
▲ Company Limited by Guarantee
○ *T; for training providers competence assessors to the railway
    industry
Gp Audit protocols (Achilles); Communications; Competence
    management; Rule book / standards / documentation; Track
    safety assessment; Track safety plans
● Conf - Mtgs - ET - Res - Wxhib - Inf
< Rly Ind Assn
M 100 f
¶ E-NL - 4; ftm only.

Association for Rational Emotive Behaviour Therapy
NR Englewood, Farningham Hill Rd, FARNINGHAM, Kent,
    DA4 0JR.
    01376 572777
    http://www.arebt.org

Association for Real Change   (ARC)   1976
■ ARC House, Marsden St, CHESTERFIELD, Derbys, S40 1JY.
    (hq)
    01246 555043   fax 01246 555045
    email contact.us@arcuk.org.uk
    http://www.arcuk.org.uk
    Chief Exec: James Churchill
▲ Company Limited by Guarantee; Registered Charity
Br 22
○ *T, *W; to support providers of services for people with a
    learning disability
● Conf - Mtgs - ET - Inf - Lib - LG
< Eur Assn for Service Providers for Persons with a
    Disability (EASPD); Nat Coun for Voluntary Orgs (NCVO);
    Assn Chief Execs of Voluntary Orgs (ACEVO); Brit Inst of
    Learning Disabilities (BILD); Indep Care Orgs
    Network (IVCON)
M 433 f
¶ My Money MAtters; £15 m, £25 nm.
    From Your Place to Mine; £17.50 m, £35 nm.
    Challenged by Complexity; £20 m, £40 nm.
    Telling it Like it is (CD-ROM); £25 m, £50 nm.
    Services for All (manual & video); £45 m, £85 nm.
× 2003 Association for Residential Care

Association of Real Estate Funds   (AREF)   1970
NR 60 London Wall, LONDON, EC2M 2TQ.   (hq)
    0772 034 3792
    http://www.aref.org.uk
    Chief Operating Officer: Rachel McIsaac
○ *T; to develop the interests of property unit trusts
● Conf - Mtgs - Stat
M 56 f
¶ Ybk - 1; free.
× 2005 Association of Property Unit Trusts

*Association of Recognised English Language Services / Federation of English
    Language Course Organisations Ltd*
    since 12 May 2004 **English UK**

Association of Reflexologists   (AoR)   1984
NR 5 Fore St, TAUNTON, Somerset, TA1 1HX.   (hq)
    0870 567 3320   fax 01823 336646
    email info@aor.org.uk   http://www.aor.org.uk
    Chief Exec: Simon Duncan
▲ Un-incorporated Society
Br 3
○ *P; to promote the knowledge & understanding of reflexology;
    to provide a network of practitioners to which the public can
    refer with confidence
Gp AoR: Accredited schools council, Examination board, Sales
● Conf - Mtgs - ET - Res - Exhib - Inf
< Intl Coun of Reflexologists; Reflexology in Europe Network;
    Reflexology Forum
M 6,674 i, UK / 171 i, o'seas
¶ Reflexions (Jnl) - 4.
    Register of Practitioners - 4.
    Examination Database Book - 2 yrly.
    Curriculum for AoR Accredited Courses - 1.
    Research Reports - 1.   Leaflets.

Association of Regional City Editors   1969
■ 1 Fern Dene, Ealing, LONDON, W13 8AN.   (hsp)
    020 8997 6868
    Hon Sec: John Heffernan
○ *P; interests of those concerned with economic & financial news
    (incl London-based wire service correspondents, & radio)
M 22 i

Association of Registrars of Scotland   (AROS)   1865
- ■ Area/Registration Office, Municipal Buildings, College St, DUMBARTON, G82 1NR.   (hsb)
  01389 738350   fax 01389 738352
  email tony.gallagher@west-dunbarton.gov.uk
  Hon Sec: A (Tony) P P Gallagher
- ▲ Un-incorporated Society
- ○ *P; to promote the registration service in Scotland on behalf of registrars & the legislation which may affect them
- ● Conf - Mtgs - ET - Exam
- M 250 i
- ¶ Informant (NL) - 2; ftm only.

Association of Registration & Celebratory Services   (ARCS) 1962
- NR Banbury Register Office, Bodicote House, Bodicote, BANBURY, Oxon, OX15 4AA.   (sb)
  01295 267312
  Sec: Jill Brand
- ○ *P
- M 800 i
- ✕ 2004 (Conference of Supervisory Registrars
  (Institute of Population Registration
  (Society of Registration Officers

Association for Rehabilitation of Communication & Oral Skills (ARCOS)   1992
- NR Whitbourne Lodge, 137 Church St, MALVERN, Worcs, WR14 2AN.   (hq)
  01684 576795   fax 01684 576895
  email arcos@globalnet.co.uk   http://www.arcos.org.uk
  Dir: Kay Coombes
- ▲ Registered Charity
- ○ *W; provision of specialist help for children & adults with voice, speech, language, eating (swallowing) problems, & for their families & those working with them
- ● ET - Lib
- ¶ AR - 1.

Association of Relocation Agents
   since 2005-06 **Association of Relocation Professionals**

Association of Relocation Profesionals   (ARP)   1986
- ■ PO Box 189, DISS, Norfolk, IP22 1PE.   (hq)
  0870 073 7475   fax 0870 071 8719
  email info@relocationagents.com
  http://www.relocationagents.com
  Chief Exec: Tad Zurlinden
- ▲ Company Limited by Guarantee
- ○ *P; to promote the services & benefits of using relocation agents
- ● Conf - Mtgs - ET - Res - Exhib - Stat - Inf - LG
- < US Employee Relocation Coun; Eur Relocation Assn; CBI; Relocation Network (Australia)
- M 140 f, UK / 15 f, o'seas
- ¶ Directory of Members - 1; free.
  Guide to the United Kingdom - 2 yrly; £5 m, £9.95 nm.
  Guide to Homesearch (for those starting a business) - 1; ftm, £75 nm.
- ✕ 2005-06 Association of Reloction Agents

Association of Research Centres in the Social Sciences (ARCISS)   1997
- NR c/o Gill Clisham, NIESR, 2 Dean Trench St, Smith Square, LONDON, SW1P 3HE.   (hsb)
  020 7222 7665
  http://www.arciss.ac.uk
  Hon Sec: Gill Clisham
- ▲ Registered Charity
- ○ *Q; promotion, management & dissemination of independent social science research
- ● Conf - Res
- M c 45 non-profit independent university-based centres

Association for Research in the Voluntary & Community Sector (ARVAC)   1978
- NR 2d Aberdeen Studios, 22-24 Highbury Grove, LONDON, N5 2EA.   (hq)
  020 7704 2315
  http://www.arvac.org.uk
  Dir: Lesley Symes
- ▲ Company Limited by Guarantee; Registered Charity
- ○ *P, *N; to promote effective community action through research; to help community groups carry out their own research
- ● Conf - Inf - Training workshops
- M 200 i, 150 org
- ¶ ARVAC Bulletin - 4; £30 i, £75 org.

Association of Researchers in Medicine & Science Ltd   (ARMS) 1979
- NR c/o Dunhill Research Laboratories, Guy's Hospital (5th floor TGH), LONDON, SE1 9RT.   (hsb)
  http://www.hop.man.ac.uk/arms/arms.html
  Hon Sec: Dr Tony Marinaki
- ▲ Company Limited by Guarantee
- ○ *P; the interests of scientists engaged in research in medical & allied fields; to promote public awareness of that research
- ● ET - Inf - LG
- M i
- ¶ NL - 3/4 monthly.   AR; free.
  Career Prospects for Research Workers in the Biological & Medical Sciences;
  Academic Research in the UK: its organisation & effectiveness;
  Survey of Post-doctoral Researchers;
  Survey of Contract Researchers;   all free.

Association of Resettlement & Employment Advisors   (AREA) 1981
- ■ The Old Magazine, Fort Fareham Business Park, Newgate Lane, FAREHAM, Hants, PO14 1AH.   (hsb)
  01329 284562
  Hon Sec: Jeffrey T Murphy
- ○ *P; for companies providing a UK-wide resettlement & employment advice service for members of the armed forces & the public
- ● Mtgs - Res
- M f & org

Association for Residential Care
   since 2003 **Association for Real Change**

Association of Residential Letting Agents   (ARLA)   1981
- ■ Maple House, 53-55 Woodside Rd, AMERSHAM, Bucks, HP6 6AA.   (hq)
  0845 345 5752   fax 01494 431530
  email info@arla.co.uk   http://www.arla.co.uk
  Chief Exec: Adrian Turner
- ▲ Company Limited by Guarantee
- ○ *T
- ● Conf - Mtgs - ET - Exam - Exhib - LG
- M 1,000 i, 1,700 f
- ¶ Agreement (NL) - 6; ftm, £54 nm.

Association of Residential Managing Agents Ltd   (ARMA) 1991
- ■ 178 Battersea Park Rd, LONDON, SW11 4ND.   (hq)
  020 7978 2607   fax 020 7498 6153
  email info@arma.org.uk   http://www.arma.org.uk
  Contact: The Executive Secretary
- ▲ Company Limited by Guarantee
- ○ *P; members focus exclusively on matters relating to block management of leasehold property (at least 50% of the flats are lessee-owned properties)
- ● Conf - Mtgs - ET - LG
- M 200+ f
- ¶ [publications available to nm are on website]

Association of Respiratory Technology & Physiology (ARTP) 1972

■ Sovereign House (Suite 4), 22 Gate Lane, Sutton Coldfield, BIRMINGHAM, B73 5TT.   (hq)
0121-354 8200
Admin: Mrs Jackie Hutchinson
▲ Registered Charity
○ *P
Gp Education; Manufacturers liaison
● Conf - Mtgs - ET - Exam - Res - Inf - Empl - LG
< Brit Thoracic Soc; Assn of Clinical Scientists; Registration Coun for Clinical Physiology
M 530 i, 25 f (affiliated), UK / 5 i, 5 f (affiliated), o'seas
¶ Inspire - 3; ftm only.

Association of Retired & Persons over 50
has been replaced by **Heyday**

Association of Retirement Housing Managers (ARHM) 1991

NR Southbank House, Black Prince Rd, LONDON, SE1 7SJ.   (hq)
020 7463 0660
▲ Company Limited by Guarantee
○ *P; to represent managers of private sheltered housing
● Conf - Mtgs - ET - LG
M 45 f
¶ NL - 6;   AR; both ftm.   Code of Practice.

Association of Risk Management

NR 7 Rutherford Court, Stafford Technology Park, STAFFORD, ST18 0GP.   (hq)
0845 166 2030
○ *T

Association of Rivers Trusts 2004

■ Bradford Lodge, Blisland, BODMIN, Cornwall, PL30 4LF.   (hq)
01208 851369   fax 01208 851376
email arlin@associationofriverstrusts.org.uk
http://www.associationofriverstrusts.org.uk
Dir: Arlin Rickard,   Sec: Alan Hawken
▲ Company Limited by Guarantee; Registered Charity
○ *K; to improve the rivers of England & Wales; to advance the education of the public in the management of water & environmental protection, conservation, rehabilitation & improvement, & the understanding of rivers & their basins, fauna & flora
● Conf - ET - Res - LG
M 6 i, 6 org
¶ E-newsletters; free.

Association for Road Traffic Safety & Management   (ARTSM) 1933

NR Epic House (Office 8), 128 Fulwell Rd, TEDDINGTON, Middx, TW11 0RQ.   (hq)
020 8977 6952
http://www.artsm.org.uk
Gen Sec & Admin: Phil Crickmay
▲ Un-incorporated Society
○ *T; interests of makers & suppliers of road traffic signs, portable traffic signals, variable message signs, vehicle & pedestrian detectors, sign luminaires, fittings, fixings & components, sign design software & related products & services
Gp Technical; Portable traffic signals; Variable message signs
● Mtgs - ET - Exhib - Inf - VE - LG - Liaison with BSI, CEN, CENELEC & the EC
< BSI
M 1 i, 49 f
¶ NL - 9; ftm only.   ARTSM Brochure - 2 yrly; free.

Association for Roman Archaeology (ARA) 1966

NR 75 York Rd, SWINDON, Wilts, SN1 2JU.   (hsp)
01793 534008   fax 01793 534008
Dir: Bryn Walters
▲ Company Limited by Guarantee
○ *K, *L; free access to Roman archaeology events & venues
● Conf - Mtgs - Inf - VE
< Coun Brit Archaeology (CBA)
M 2,500 i
¶ ARA News Bulletin - 2.

Association of Rooflight Manufacturers
since 2002-04 **National Association of Rooflight Manufacturers**

Association of Rover Clubs Ltd
since 2005 **Association of Land Rover Clubs**

Association of Royal Navy Officers (ARNO) 1925

■ 70 Porchester Terrace, LONDON, W2 3TP.   (hq)
020 7402 5231
▲ Registered Charity
○ *W; to give general & financial assistance to members, their widows & families (membership is open to serving & retired officers of the RN, RM, WRNS, QARNNS & their Reserves)
● Inf - VE
< Officers' Assn
M 8,500 i, UK / 300 i, o'seas
¶ Ybk - 1; ftm only.

Association of Safety Fencing Contractors
see **Fencing Contractors' Association**

Association of Salmon Fishery Boards (ASFB) 1932

■ 5a Lennox St, EDINBURGH, EH4 1QB.   (hsb)
0131-343 2433   fax 0131-332 2556
Dir: Andrew Wallace
▲ Un-incorporated Society
○ *F, *N; to protect, preserve & develop salmon fisheries in Scotland; to coordinate the work of district salmon fishery boards
● Mtgs - LG
M 44 district salmon fishery boards

Association for Sandwich Education & Training (ASET) 1982

NR 3 Westbrook Court, Sharrow Vale Rd, SHEFFIELD, S Yorks, S11 8YZ.   (hq)
0114-221 2902   fax 0114-221 2903
email aset@aset.demon.co.uk
http://www.asetonline.org
Admin: Keith Fildes
▲ Company Limited by Guarantee; Registered Charity
○ *E; to develop, promote & implement the concept of higher education courses that integrate periods of relevant work in an employing organisation
● Conf - Mtgs - Res - Exhib - Comp - Stat - LG
M 47 i, 110 f & universities, UK / 2 i, 2 f, o'seas
¶ ASET Directory of Sandwich Courses - 1.

Association of School & College Leaders (ASCL) 1975

NR 130 Regent Rd, LEICESTER, LE1 7PG.   (hq)
0116-299 1122   fax 0116-299 1123
email johndunford@ascl.org.uk
Gen Sec: Dr John Dunford
Br c150
○ *E, *P; for leaders of schools & colleges
● Conf - Mtgs - ET - Res - Exhib - Empl - LG - Legal support - Provision of professional publications
M 9,100 i
× 2006 Secondary Heads Association

Association for Science Education   (ASE)   1963
- ■ College Lane, HATFIELD, Herts, AL10 9AA.   (hq)
  01707 283000
  http://www.ase.org.uk
  Chief Exec: Dr Derek Bell
- ▲ Registered Charity
- ○ *E; improvement of the teaching of science in schools
- ● Conf - Mtgs - ET - Res - Exhib - SG - Stat - Inf
- M 18,000 i
- ¶ School Science Review - 4;   Education in Science - 5.
  Primary Science Review - 5;   all ftm.

Association for the Scientific Study of Anomalous Phenomena (ASSAP)   1981
- ■ PO Box 230, PLYMOUTH, Devon, PL1 2ZR.   (hsb)
  email enquiries@assap.org   http://www.assap.org
  Hon Sec: Maurice Townsend
- ▲ Company Limited by Guarantee; Registered Charity
- ○ *G, *Q; to obtain & store information & to encourage research & investigation on all aspects of the paranormal & observed phenomena for which, as yet, there is no generally accepted explanation; to educate & promote an informed public attitude
- Gp Altered states of consciousness; Dowsing; Hauntings; Leylines; Mental mediumship; Metal-bending; Physical mediumship; Poltergeists; Regressive hypnosis & survival of bodily death; UFOs; Fortean events; Earth mysteries
- ● Conf - Mtgs - Lib
- M 350 i
- ¶ Anomaly (Jnl) - 2.   ASSAP News (NL) - 12.

Association of Scintigraphers   1994
- ■ Beau Lodge, Kelsey Lane, BECKENHAM, Kent, BR3 3NF.   (hsp)
- ▲ Un-incorporated Society
- ○ *P; veterinary radiology
- ● Conf - Mtgs - ET - LG
- M i

Association of Scotland's Colleges   (ASC)
- NR Argyll Court, The Castle Business Park, STIRLING, FK9 4TY.   (hq)
  01786 892100
  Co Sec: Shena Mitchell
- ▲ Registered Charity
- ○ *E; furthering the interests in the further education field in Scotland
- ● ET - SG - Stat - Expt - Inf - LG
- M org
- ¶ AR & Accounts - 1.
- × 2006 Association of Scottish Colleges

Association in Scotland to Research into Astronautics Ltd (ASTRA)   1953
- ■ Flat 65 - Dalriada Block, 56 Blythswood Court, Anderston, GLASGOW, G2 7PE.   (treas/p)
  0141-221 7658
  email astra@dlunan.freeserve.co.uk
  http://www.astra.org.uk
  Treas: Duncan Lunan
- ▲ Company Limited by Guarantee
- Br 2
- ○ *L; all aspects of space research & related subjects; to stimulate public interest
- Gp Waverider aerodynamic study programme; Aidrie public observatory; Exhibitions; Publications; Amateur rocketry
- ● Conf - Mtgs - ET - Res - Exhib - PL - VE - Amateur astronomy & rocketry
- < Scot Astronomers Gp; Fedn of Astronomical Socs; Scot Coun for Voluntary Orgs
- M 65 i, UK / 5 i, o'seas
- ¶ Spacereport - 4;   ASGARD - irreg; both ftm only.

Association of Scotland's Self-Caterers   (ASSC)   1978
- ■ PO Box 23, TAYNUILT, Argyll, PA35 1WX.   (hsb)
  01866 822122
  Sec: Jenifer Moffat
- ▲ Un-incorporated Society
- ○ *T; representation, services & marketing for owners of holiday properties; 'the only trade association to represent the self-catering industry in Scotland'
- ● Conf - Mtgs - Res - Inf - LG
- < Fedn of Nat Self-Catering Assns (FONSCA); Scot Tourism Forum (STF)
- M 560 f
- ¶ The Standard (NL) - 2.

Association of Scottish Colleges
  since 2006 **Association of Scotland's Colleges**

Association of Scottish Community Councils   (ASCC)   1993
- ■ 28 Bank St, BRECHIN, Angus, DD9 6AX.   (hq)
  01356 623330   fax 01356 623330
  email secretary@ascc.org.uk   http://www.ascc.org.uk
  Sec: Douglas Murray
- ▲ Un-incorporated Society
- ○ *N; to provide advice & information to Community Councils in Scotland; to promote their role, effectiveness & status through liaison with local & national governments
- ● Conf - Mtgs - Res - SG - Stat - Inf - Lib - LG
- M 625 community councils
- ¶ ASCC NL - 4; ftm.

Association of Scottish Genealogists & Researchers in Archives (ASGRA)   1981
- NR 93 Colinton Rd, EDINBURGH, EH10 5DF.   (hsp)
  http://www.asgra.co.uk
  Hon Sec: Hazel Weir
- ▲ Un-incorporated Society
- ○ *G; genealogical & family history research in Scotland
- ● Res
- < Scot Assn of Family History Socs
- M 25 i
- × 2005 Association of Scottish Genealogists & Record Agents

Association for Scottish Literary Studies   (ASLS)   1970
- ■ Dept of Scottish History, 9 University Gardens, GLASGOW, G12 8QH.   (hq)
  0141-330 5309   fax 0141-330 5309
  email asls@asls.org.uk   http://www.asls.org.uk
  Gen Mgr: Duncan Jones
- ▲ Registered Charity
- ○ *A, *L; to promote the study, teaching & writing of Scottish language & literature
- ● Conf - Comp
- < Scot Arts Coun
- M 343 i, 91 f, UK / 121 i, 55 f, o'seas
- ¶ Scottish Studies Review (Jnl) - 2;   Scotlit - 2;
  Scottish Language (Jnl) - 1; all ftm only.
  New Writing Scotland (Anthology) - 1; ftm, £6.95 nm.
  Scotnotes (study guides); £3.60 m, £4.50 nm.
  ScotLit (NM); ftm.
  Annual Volume (book); ftm, £25 nm.

Association of Scottish Philatelic Societies   (ASPS)   1924
- ■ 44 Rennie St, FALKIRK, Stirlingshire, FK1 5AL.   (hsp)
  01324 415558
  email scottishphilately.co.uk
  http://www.scottishphilately.co.uk
  Hon Sec: Alan Watson
- ▲ Un-incorporated Society
- ○ *N; to promote philately & allied areas within Scotland
- ● Conf - Exhib - Comp
- < Assn of Brit Philatelic Socs
- M 41 societies
- ¶ Scottish Philately (NL) -6; ftm, postage nm.

Association of Scottish Police Superintendents   (ASPS)   1924
NR   Strathclyde Police HQ, 173 Pitt St, GLASGOW, G2 4JS.   (asa)
     0141-221 5796
     Pres: Chief Supt Tom Buchan
Br   8
○   *P
●   Conf - Mtgs - Res - Stat - Inf - Empl - LG
<   Intl Assn Chiefs Police (IACP)
M   200 i
¶   NL - 4;   AR; both free.

Association of Scottish Schools of Architecture   (ASSA)   1983
NR   Scott Sutherland School of Architecture & the Built Environment,
     The Robert Gordon University, Schoolhill, ABERDEEN,
     AB10 1FR.   (chmn/b)
     01224 263700
     Hon Chmn: David McClean
▲   Un-incorporated Society
○   *N; to maintain & improve the education provision for
     architecture in Scotland; to foster areas of collaboration
     between the schools
Gp   Professional practice; Environmental design
●   Mtgs - ET - Exhib - Comp - SG
<   R Incorporation of Architects in Scotland
M   80 staff, 1,500 students, 6 schools

Association of Scottish Shellfish Growers   (ASSG)   1983
NR   Mountview, ARDVASAR, Isle of Skye, IV45 8RU.   (chmn/p)
     01471 844324
     email douglasmcleod@aol.com
     Chmn: D A McLeod
▲   Company Limited by Guarantee
○   *T; interests of Scottish shellfish farmers
Gp   Mussels; Scallops; Oysters
●   Conf - Mtgs - ET - Res - Exhib - Inf - LG
<   Shellfish Assn of GB
M   200 f, 25 org
¶   The Grower - 4; ftm, £2 nm.   Ybk - 1; £5 m.

Association of Scottish Visitor Attractions   (ASVA)   1989
NR   Argyll's Lodging, Castle Wynd, STIRLING, FK8 1EG.   (hq)
     01786 475152   fax 01786 474288
     email info@asva.co.uk   http://www.asva.co.uk
     Devt Mgr: Eva McDiarmid
▲   Company Limited by Guarantee
○   *T; concerned with the improvements at, & marketing of, visitor
     attractions in Scotland
Gp   covering each of the first 9 activities below
●   Conf - Mtgs - ET - Exhib - SG - Stat - Inf - VE - LG -
     Consultancy
M   500 org
¶   Scotland's Finest Visitor Attractions - 1.

Association of Scottish Yacht Charterers   (ASYC)   1980
NR   7 Torinturk by Tarbert, ARGYLL, PA29 6YE.   (sp)
     01880 820012
     Sec: Robert Fleck
▲   Un-incorporated Society
○   *T; represents sailing school, yacht & motor cruiser charter
     companies in Scotland
●   Conf - Mtgs - Exhib - Inf - LG
<   Sail Scotland Ltd
M   18 f
¶   LM - irreg; free.

**Association of Sea Fisheries Committees of England & Wales
(ASFCEW)   1919**
■   6 Ashmeadow Rd, Arnside, CARNFORTH, Lancs, LA5 0AE.
     (hsp)
     01524 761616
     Chief Exec: Peter Winterbottom
○   *N; regulation & development of inshore fisheries (within
     territorial limits)
●   Mtgs
M   15 sea fisheries' committees

Association of Sea Training Organisations   (ASTO)   1971
NR   Unit 10 North Meadow, Royal Clarence Yard, GOSPORT,
     Hants, PO12 1PB.   (hq)
     023 9250 3222
     http://www.asto.org.uk
○   *Y; to further personal development of young people & adults
     by seamanship training under sail
●   Mtgs - ET - Exhib - Comp - Inf
M   18 org
¶   Sail to Adventure - 1; free.

Association of Sealant Applicators Ltd   (ASA)   1986
NR   15 Knightswick Rd, CANVEY ISLAND, Essex, SS8 9PA.   (asa)
     01268 696878   fax 01268 511247
     email arichardson@rowlandhall.co.uk
     http://www.associationofsealantapplicators.org
     Sec: A E Richardson
▲   Company Limited by Guarantee
○   *T; for sealant applicators & manufacturers
●   Mtgs - ET
<   Nat Specialist Contrs Coun
M   51 f

Association of Second Home Owners
NR   PO Box 17, YORK, YO41 4WS.
     email paul@associationofsecondhomeowners.co.uk
     Contact: Paul Rouse
○   *G

Association of Secondary Teachers, Ireland   (ASTI)   1909
IRL   ASTI House, Winetavern St, DUBLIN 8, Republic of Ireland.
     353 (1) 604 0160   fax 353 (1) 671 9287
     email info@asti.ie   http://www.asti.ie
     Gen Sec: John White
○   *E, *P

Association of Security Consultants   (ASC)   1990
■   PO Box 22, HAMPTON, Middx, TW12 2XE.   (sb)
     07071 224865   fax 020 8979 5323
     email info@securityconsultants.org.uk
     http://www.securityconsultants.org.uk
     Sec: Maurice Parsons
▲   Company Limited by Guarantee
○   *P; for independent security consultants having no allegiance to
     specific suppliers of goods or services; to stay in the forefront
     of work on security methods, technology & applications; to
     contribute to the development of national & international
     standards
●   Conf - Mtgs - ET - Exhib - LG
<   Jt Security Ind Coun
M   59 i
¶   NL.   Consultancy Resources Directory - 1; free.
     Your Introduction to the ASC - 1; free.

**Association of Senior Children's & Education Librarians
(ASCEL)   1995**
■   c/o Lesley Sim, West Sussex County Council Library Service,
     Tower St, CHICHESTER, W Sussex, PO19 1QJ.   (chmn/b)
     01243 382557
     email lesley.sim@westsussex.gov.uk
     http://www.ascel.org.uk
     Chmn: Lesley Sim
○   *A, *E, *N, P; to stimulate developments & respond to initiatives
     to ensure that quality services for children & young people
     through public libraries & education services are offered for
     all
●   Conf - ET - LG
M   240 i
¶   ASCEL NL - 3;   LM - 1.

Association of Separated & Divorced Catholics   (ASDC)   1981
- ■ c/o 250 Chapel St, SALFORD, M3 5LL.   (hq)
     http://www.asdcengland.org.uk
- ▲ Registered Charity
- Br 19
- ○ *W; to provide mutual help and spiritual support to those who
     have experienced the pain of marriage failure
- ● Conf - Mtgs
     Helpline: 0113-264 0638
- M c 200 i
- ¶ New Vision - 6; £6 yr.

Association of Service Providers   (ASP)   1985
- ■ Edgcott House, Lawn Hill, Edgcott, AYLESBURY, Bucks,
     HP18 0QW.   (sb)
     01296 770458   fax 01296 770423
     email bc@aspfm.cc
     Sec: Brian Copsey
- ○ *T; the agency for radio licensing outside of the UK
- ● Inf - LG
- M i & f
- ¶ NL - irreg.

Association of Sewing Machine Distributors   (ASMD)   1992
- ■ Sheaf House, Holland Fen, LINCOLN, LN4 4QH.   (asa)
     01205 280094
     Sec: Mike Houldershaw
- ▲ Un-incorporated Society
- ○ *T; importers & suppliers of domestic sewing machines &
     overlockers
- ● Mtgs - Stat - LG
- M 6 f

Association for Shared Parenting   1993
- NR PO Box 2000, DUDLEY, W Midlands, DY1 1YZ.
     01789 751157 (helpline message only)   (mail/address)
     Hon Sec: Jim Rowan
- ▲ Registered Charity
- Br 5
- ○ *K; to promote the right of children to continue to receive love
     & nurture from both their parents after separation or divorce
- ● Conf - Mtgs - ET - Advice & support sessions open to the public
     - Telephone helpline - Child contact centre (where children
     can meet the parent they no longer live with)
- M 100 i

**Association of Show & Agricultural Organisations   (ASAO)
1923**
- NR Oakley Farm, Merstham, REDHILL, Surrey, RH1 3QN.   (sp)
     01737 645857   fax 01737 645121
     email info@asao.co.uk   http://www.asao.co.uk
     Sec: Paul J Hooper
- ▲ Company Limited by Guarantee; Registered Charity
- ○ *F; to promote improvement of agriculture, kindred shows &
     allied industries
- ● Conf - Mtgs - ST - LG
- M 189 org
- ¶ Annual list of shows & sales - 1.

**Association of Small Historic Towns & Villages of the United
Kingdom   (ASHTAV)   1988**
- ■ 2 Warwick Court, Abbey Rd, GREAT MALVERN, Worcs,
     WR14 3HU.   (sp)
     01684 566543   fax 0870 136 0926
     email mail@ashtav.org.uk   http://www.ashtav.org.uk
     Hon Sec: Dan Wild
     Vice-Chmn: Ed Grimsdale
- ▲ Registered Charity
- ○ *K, *N; uniting amenity societies & groups, parish & town
     councils in small historic towns & villages in a common effort
     for the preservation, protection & where appropriate,
     sensitive adaptation of their features of historic & public
     interest; to encourage high standards of architecture &
     planning; to stimulate the public interest & care for the
     beauty, character & fabric of small historic towns & villages in
     the context of an understanding of the social & economic
     changes which affect them
- ● Conf - Mtgs - ET - Res - SG - Inf - VE
- < Coun for the Protection of Rural England
- M 35 i, 2 f, 85 amenity org & parish / town councils
- ¶ ASHTAV News - 4; ftm.

Association of Social Alarms Providers
      since 2005 **Telecare Services Association**

**Association of Social Anthropologists of the UK & the
Commonwealth   (ASA)   1946**
- ■ c/o RAI, 50 Fitzroy St, LONDON, W1T 5BT.   (hq)
     020 7387 0455
     email admin@theasa.org
     Hon Sec: Dr Simone Abram
- ▲ Un-incorporated Society
- ○ *L; to promote the study & teaching of social anthropology
- ● Conf - ET
- < Academy of the Learned Socs in the Social Sciences (ALSISS)
- M 452 i, UK / 134 i, o'seas
- ¶ Annals - 1;   LM - 2-yearly; both ftm, £50 together nm.

**Association of Solicitor Notaries in Greater London   (ASN)
1996**
- NR 15 William Mews, LONDON, SW1X 9HF.   (asa)
     020 7235 7216   fax 020 8681 8183
     Dir: Hans J Hartwig
- ○ *P; representation of notaries in the Greater London region who
     are also qualified solicitors &/or foreign lawyers
- ● Conf - Mtgs - ET - Res - SG - LG - Devt of 'best standards' for
     international documentation & translations
- M 30 i
- ¶ Membership Register - 1; ftm.

**Association of Solicitors & Investment Managers   (ASIM)
1993**
- NR Riverside House, River Lawn Rd, TONBRIDGE, Kent, TN9 1EP.
     (hq)
     01732 783548   fax 01732 362626
     email admin@asim.org.uk
     Sec: Elaine Reilly
- ▲ Company Limited by Guarantee
- ○ *P, *T; to encourage the wider provision of portfolio investment
     services by solicitor's firms
- ● Conf - Mtgs - ET - Stat - VE - LG
- M 51 f
- ¶ NL - 4.   LM - 1.   AR.
- × 2004 Association of Solicitor Investment Managers

Association of South East Asian Studies in the UK   (ASEASUK)
NR   Centre for South East Asian Studies, SOAS/University of
London, Thornhaugh St, Russell Square, LONDON,
WC1H 0XG.
Contact: Dr Justin Watkins
○   *L; 'to facilitate cooperation & coordination between individual
scholars & institutions in the development of South East Asian
studies & research programmes... the circulation of
professional information amongst scholars with South East
Asian interests & the projection of South East Asia as an
important field of study within the UK generally'
●   Conf
<   Coordinating Coun of Area Studies Assns (CCASA)
M   180 i, UK / 20 i, o'seas
¶   Aseasuk News - 2; ftm only.

Association of Speakers Clubs   (ASC)   1972
■   36 Pemberton Rd, Winstenley, WIGAN, Lancs, WN3 6DA.
(nat/sp)
email natsec@tiscali.co.uk   http://www.the-asc.org.uk
Nat Sec: Mrs Gwyneth Millard
▲   Un-incorporated Society
Br   141
○   *G; promotion of the art of public speaking, chairmanship &
the proper conduct of meetings
●   Conf - Mtgs - ET - Comp - SG
M   2,000 i, 141 clubs
¶   The Speaker - 3.

Association for Specialist Fire Protection   (ASFP)   1975
■   99 West St, FARNHAM, Surrey, GU9 7EN.   (asa)
01252 739142   fax 01252 739140
email info@associationhouse.org.uk
http://www.asfp.org.uk
Sec: John G Fairley
▲   Company Limited by Guarantee
○   *T; all questions affecting the fire protection of structural
steelwork & buildings
Gp   Fire testing & standards; Spray applied materials; Health &
safety; Contracting conditions; Intumescent materials;
European harmonisation; Assessment of fire tests; BSI
representation; Technical matters
●   Conf - Mtgs - ET - Res - Exhib - Inf
<   Eur Assn for Structural Fire Protection; BSI
M   54 f, UK / 4 f, o'seas
¶   Fire Protection for Structural Steel in Buildings, 2nd ed; £30.
Supplement to 2nd ed; £5.
Ybk & Directory of Members - 1; free.
Other publications & guidance notes; list available.
×   Association of Specialist Fire Protection Contractors &
Manufacturers Ltd.

**Association of Specialist Technical Organisations for Space
(ASTOS)   1988**
NR   c/o Mr J Barrington-Brown, Nohmia Ltd, 79 Larksway,
BISHOPS STORTFORD, Herts, CM23 4DG.   (chmn/b)
01279 505047
Chmn: James Barrington-Brown
▲   Company Limited by Guarantee
○   *T; aims to promote & support the interests of UK small &
medium enterprises in the space industry
●   Mtgs - Res - Inf - VE - LG - Guest Speaker programme
M   20 f

Association of Specialist Underpinning Contractors
since 2003 **ASUCplus - Subsidence Repair Techniques &
Engineered Foundation Solutions**

**Association of Speech & Language Therapists in Independent
Practice   (ASLTIP)**
NR   WSS, Coleheath Bottom, Speen, PRINCES RISBOROUGH,
Bucks, HP27 0SZ.
01494 488306
○   *P

Association of Speedway Referees
NR   1 Stephen Crescent, Bolton Lane, BRADFORD, W Yorks,
BD2 4BH.
Sec: D Dowling

Association for Spina Bifida & Hydrocephalus   (ASBAH)   1966
NR   42 Park Rd, PETERBOROUGH, Cambs, PE1 2UQ.   (hq)
01733 555988   fax 01733 555985
email info@asbah.org   http://www.asbah.org
Exec Dir: Andrew Russell
▲   Registered Charity
Br   5 regional
○   *W; provides information & advice to people with spina bifida
&/or hydrocephalus & their carers.   Team of area advisers
is backed by specialist advisers in education, continence,
hydrocephalus etc
●   LG - Study days
<   Nat Coun for Voluntary Orgs (NCVO); Assn Med Res Charities;
R Assn for Disability & Rehabilitation (RADAR); Disabled Living
Foundation; Neurological Alliance
M   14,000 i
¶   Link (Jnl) - 6.
AR.   Various booklets (list available).

**Association for Spinal Injury Research, Rehabilitation &
Reintegration   (ASPIRE)   1983**
■   Aspire National Training Centre, Wood Lane, STANMORE,
Middx, HA7 4AP.   (hq)
020 8954 5759
email info@aspire.org.uk   http://www.aspire.org.uk
Chief Exec: Brian Carlin
▲   Registered Charity
○   *Q; support of research to improve quality of life for spinal
cord injured; support of an integrated sports & rehabilitation
centre for able-bodied & disabled people
●   ET - Res - Sporting events - Support of housing for patients
leaving spinal units - Human needs fund for buying
equipment for spinally injured people
M   [not given]
¶   Aspirations! (NL) - 2; free.

Association of Sports Historians
has ceased trading

Association of Stainless Fastener Distributors   (ASFAD)   1988
■   c/o Stainless Threaded Fasteners Ltd, Baldray Park,
Mount Pleasant, BILSTON, Staffs, WV14 7NH.   (hq)
01902 490490   fax 01902 496583
http://www.asfad.org
Sec: Keith Harrison
▲   Company Limited by Guarantee
○   *T; interests of stainless steel fastener distributors
●   Mtgs - ET - Exhib
<   Eur Fastener Distbrs Assn
M   13 f
¶   LM; ftm only.

Association for Standards & Practices in Electronic Trade - EAN UK Ltd
since 2005 **GS1 (UK) Ltd**

Association of State Veterinary Officers
has changed its name to the Associaton of Government Veterinarians
& isa group of the **British Veterinary Association**

Association of Stillwater Game Fishery Managers (ASGFM) 1983
NR   Packington Fisheries, Meriden, COVENTRY, Warks, CV7 7HR.
       (hq)
       01676 522754
       Sec: Mrs Penny Wigley
○   *T; for owners &/or managers of stillwater fishery businesses
●   Conf - Mtgs - ET - Exhib - LG
<   Country Landowners Assn
M   100 i & f
¶   Newsline - 2/3; ftm only.

Association of Street Lighting Electrical Contractors (ASLEC) 1952
NR   Bowden House, 1 Church St, HENFIELD, W Sussex, BN5 9NS.
       (hq)
       01273 491145   fax 01273 491147
       email info@bowden-house.co.uk
       http://www.streetlighting.uk.com
       Dir: Vasos J Siantonas
▲   Registered Charity
○   *T; contractors operating in the highway electrical industry, in
       particular street lighting
●   Conf - Mtgs - ET
M   41 f

Association of Stress Therapists (AST) 1991
■   14 Sycamore Close, MARGATE, Kent, CT9 4NL.   (founder/p)
       01843 291255
       email ssnashfold@hotmail.com
       Founder: Nita M Yeoman,
       Business Admin: Sandra L Snashfold
▲   Un-incorporated Society
○   *M, *P; to establish a network of therapists to alleviate the
       physical & mental symptoms caused by stress
●   ET - Exam - SG
<   Brit Complementary Medicine Assn (BCMA); Crystal Healing
       Fedn (CHF)
M   50 i, UK / 3 i, o'seas
¶   NL; ftm.

Association for Student Residential Accommodation (ASRA) 1997
■   Residences Property Manager, University of the Arts, Furzedown
       Hall, 5 Spalding Rd, LONDON, SW17 9BB.   (chmn/b)
       020 8672 0131   fax 020 8767 6433
       email chair@asra.ac.uk   http://www.asra.ac.uk
       Chmn: Terence Treadwell
▲   Un-incorporated Society
Br   6
○   *P; concerned with student housing whether institutionally
       owned, managed or private sector
●   Conf - Mtgs - ET - LG
<   Assn for College & University Housing Officers (ACUHOI)
M   500+ f
¶   NL (website); m only.

Association for Studies in the Conservation of Historic Buildings (ASCHB) 1968
■   Institute of Archaeology, 31-34 Gordon Sq, LONDON,
       WC1H 0PY.   (mail/address)
       email michelle.barber@turntown.co.uk
       Contact: The Secretary
▲   Registered Charity
Br   4
○   *L; to provide a forum to foster & enhance studies in the
       conservation of historic buildings
●   Conf - Mtgs - VE
<   ICCROM; ICOMOS UK; COTAC; UKSCS
M   450 i, c 20 universities etc, UK / 70 i, o'seas
¶   Transactions - 1; ftm, on request nm.   NL - 4; free.

Association of Studio & Production Equipment Companies Ltd (ASPEC) 1993
NR   17 Ember Farm Way, EAST MOLESEY, Surrey, KT8 0BH.   (sb)
       email contact@aspec-uk.com   http://www.aspec-uk.com
▲   Company Limited by Guarantee
○   *T; to represent the interests of all film facility companies
       providing their services to the film & television production
       industry
Gp   Lighting; Studio; Camera
●   Mtgs - ET - Empl
<   Production Eqpt Rental Assn (PERA) (USA)
M   25 f

Association for the Study of Ethnicity & Nationalism (ASEN) 1990
NR   London School of Economics, Houghton St, LONDON,
       WC2A 2AE.   (hq)
       020 7955 6807   fax 020 7955 6218
       email asen@lse.ac.uk   http://www.lse.ac.uk/asen
       Chief Exec: Mitchell Young
▲   Un-incorporated Society
○   *Q; an academic association fostering research into the areas
       of ethnicity & nationalism
●   Conf - Res - SG
<   London School of Economics
M   180 i, 3 university research centres, UK / 120 i, o'seas
¶   Nations & Nationalism (Jnl) - 4.
       Studies in Ethnicity & Nationalism [SEN] - 2.

Association for the Study of German Politics (ASGP) 1974
NR   c/o Dr Charles Lees - Dept of Politics, University of Sheffield,
       Elmfield, Northumberland Rd, SHEFFIELD, S10 2TU.   (hsb)
       0114-222 1702   fax 0114-273 9769
       email c.s.j.lees@sheffield.ac.uk
       http://www.bham.ac.uk/asgp/
       Sec: Dr Charles Lees,   Chmn: Prof Emil Kirchner
▲   Registered Charity
○   *L; to promote the study & teaching of German politics &
       society in the widest possible context
●   Conf - Mtgs - ET - Res - Comp - Inf - VE
<   German Studies Assn
>   German Studies Assn
¶   German Politics - 4.   ASGP NL - 2.   Books.

Association for the Study of Medical Education (ASME) 1957
■   12 Queen St, EDINBURGH, EH2 1JE.   (hq)
       0131-225 9111
       Chief Exec: Prof Frank Smith
▲   Registered Charity
○   *E, *P, *Q; to bring together doctors, behavioural scientists &
       educationalists with interests & responsibilities in medical
       education
Gp   Research c'ee
●   Conf - Mtgs - ET - Res - Exhib - Inf
M   c 850 i, UK / c 350 i, o'seas, 90 corporate
¶   Bulletin - 6;   AR - 1; both free.
       Booklets; prices vary.
       List of publications available.

Association for the Study of Modern & Contemporary France (ASMCF) 1979
■ Park Bldg - King Henry I St, University of Portsmouth, PORTSMOUTH, Hants, PO1 2DZ.   (hsb)
     023 9284 8484
     email secretary@asmcf.org   http://www.asmcf.org
     Hon Sec: Emmanuel Godin
▲ Registered Charity
Br Oxford, S Wales & W of England
○ *L; to promote research & scholarship into all aspects of modern French history, politics, society & culture, as well as relations between France & other countries, including those in the French-speaking world
● Conf - Mtgs - ET - Res - SG
M [not stated]
¶ Modern & Contemporary France - 4; ftm, £78 nm.
     Annual Conference Proceedings.

Association for the Study of Modern Italy   (ASMI)   1982
NR c/o Dr P Filippucci, New Hall, CAMBRIDGE, CB3 0DF. (mail/address)
     email pf107@cam.ac.uk   http://www.staffs.ac.uk/asmi
     Sec: Dr Paola Filippucci
▲ Registered Charity
○ *L; the study of modern & contemporary Italian history, society, politics, culture & economy in the period between 1780 & the present
● Conf - Comp
M 61 i, UK / 2 i, o'seas
¶ Jnl of Modern Italy - 2.

Association for the Study of Obesity   (ASO)   1967
NR 20 Brook Meadow Close, WOODFORD GREEN, Essex, IG8 9NR.   (hsb)
     020 8503 2042   fax 020 8503 2042
     email chris@aso.ndo.co.uk   http://www.aso.org.uk
     Admin Officer: Christine Hawkins
▲ Registered Charity
○ *L, *Q; study of causes, treatment & prevention of human obesity
● Conf - Res - Stat - Inf
< Intl Assn for the Study of Obesity; Eur Assn for the Study of Obesity
M 490 i, UK / 24 i, o'seas

Association for the Study & Preservation of Roman Mosaics (ASPROM) 1978
NR 38 Oaklea, Ash Vale, ALDERSHOT, Hants, GU12 5HP   (hsp)
     01252 316018
     Hon Sec: Steve Cosh
▲ Registered Charity
○ *G, *L; study & preservation of Roman mosaics, principally from Britain
● Conf - Mtgs - Res - Lib
< Assn Intle pour l'Étude de la Mosaïque Antique (AIEMA)
M 220 i & f
¶ Mosaic (Jnl) - 1;   ASPROM NL - 2; both ftm only.

Association for the Study of Primary Education (ASPE) 1987
NR The Swallow Barn, Brandon Court, Station Rd, LONG MARSTON, Herts, HP23 4RA.   (hsb)
     email mary@swallowbarn.fsnet.co.uk
     http://www.aspe.org.uk
     Hon Sec: Mary Woodcock
▲ Registered Charity
○ *P; dedicated to the belief that good primary school practice should be based on best scholarship & research evidence available
● Conf - Mtgs - Res - SG
< Brit Educl Res Assn (BERA)
M 135 i
¶ Education 3-13 (Jnl) - 3.

Association of Subscription Agents & Intermediaries   (ASA) 1934
■ 10 Lime Avenue, HIGH WYCOMBE, Bucks, HP11 1DP.   (sp)
     01494 534778
     Sec: Rollo Turner
▲ Un-incorporated Society
○ *T; interests of periodical subscription agents & intermediaries worldwide
● Conf - Mtgs - Discussion groups
M 4 f, UK / 36 f, o'seas
¶ NL - irreg; ftm.   LM - irreg; free.
     The Work of Subscription Agents - irreg; free.

Association of Supervisors of Midwives   (ASM)   1912
■ 31 Cotmer Rd, Oulton Broad, LOWESTOFT, Suffolk, NR33 9PN.   (hsp)
     01502 564805
     email elayne.guest@jpaget.nhs.uk
     Hon Sec: Mrs Elayne Guest,   Pres: Sandra Arthur
▲ Un-incorporated Society
○ *P; to promote a high standard of supervision of midwives in the practice & teaching of midwifery
● Conf - Mtgs
< Intl Confedn of Midwives
M 350 i

Association of Suppliers to the British Clothing Industry
     since 2005 **ASBCI - the Forum for Clothing & Textiles**

Association of Suppliers to the Furniture Industry   (ASFI) 1978
■ The Counting House, Mill Rd, Cromford, MATLOCK, Derbys, DE4 3RQ.   (hq)
     01629 827039   fax 01629 826997
     email info@asfi.co.uk   http://www.asfi.co.uk
     Gen Mgr: Graham Holdsworth
▲ Company Limited by Guarantee
○ *T; to promote component suppliers to the furniture industry
● Conf - Mtgs - Res - Exhib - Expt - Inf - LG
M 176 f, UK / 5 f, o'seas
¶ Trade Talk (NL) - 4; ftm.
     Members Directory & Product Guide - 2 yrly.
     Export Directory & Product Guide - 2 yrly.

Association for Supported Employment
     in 2006 merged with the National Association of Supported Employment to form the **British Association for Supported Employment**

Association of Surgeons of Great Britain & Ireland   (ASGBI) 1920
NR at the Royal College of Surgeons, 35-43 Lincoln's Inn Fields, LONDON, WC2A 3PE.   (hq)
     020 7973 0300
▲ Company Limited by Guarantee; Registered Charity
○ *P; advancement of science & art of surgery - general surgery to include GI, vascular, endocrine, breast, transplant, endoscopic
Gp Association of Coloproctology GB&I; Association of Endoscopic Surgeons GB&I; Association of Surgeons in Training; Association of Upper Gastro Intestinal Surgeons; British Association of Endocrine Surgeons; Vascular Surgical Society
● Conf - ET - Exhib - LG
M i
¶ LM - 1; ftm only.

© CBD Research Ltd · Beckenham · BR3 5JS · Tel 020 8650 7745 · Fax 020 8650 0768 · E-mail cbd@cbdresearch.com · www.cbdresearch.com

Association of Surgeons in Training   (ASiT)   1976
NR   c/o Royal College of Surgeons, 35-43 Lincoln's Inn Fields,
       LONDON, WC2A 3PN.   (hq)
       020 7973 0300   fax 020 7430 9235
       email asit@asgbi.org.uk   http://www.asit.org
▲   Registered Charity
○   *M, *P; surgical training
●   Conf - Mtgs - ET
M   768 i
¶   Ybk; ftm.

Association for Survey Computing   1971
■   PO Box 60, CHESHAM, Bucks, HP5 3QH.
       01494 793033   fax 01494 793033
       email admin@asc.org.uk   http://www.asc.org.uk
       Admin: Diana Elder
○   *T; market research & government surveys
●   Conf
M   450 i & f
¶   Survey Computing - NL.

Association of Systematic Kinesiology   (ASK)   1988
■   47 Sedlescombe Road South, St LEONARDS on SEA, E Sussex,
       TN38 0TB.   (hq)
       0845 020 0383
       http://www.systematic-kinesiology.co.uk
       Chief Exec: Mrs Marie Cheshire
▲   Registered Charity
○   *M, *P; applied systematic kinesiology (muscle testing) enables
       holistic functional analysis of nutritional sensitivities/needs &
       structural imbalances; helps resolve emotional problems
●   Mtgs - ET - Exam - Exhib
M   160 i

Association of Tank & Cistern Manufacturers   (ATCM)   1965
■   22 Grange Park, St Arvans, CHEPSTOW, Monmouthshire,
       NP16 6EA.   (hsp)
       01291 623634   fax 01291 623634
       email imce@atcmtanks.org.uk
       http://www.atcmtanks.org.uk
       Chmn & Sec: Ian McCrone
○   *T; for manufacturers of vessels for storing drinking water,
       waste water & other liquids (incl domestic heating oil &
       chemicals); to promote good practice in the manufacture of
       tank & cistern products
Gp   Thermoplastics tanks & cisterns; GRP tanks & cisterns; Plastic oil
       tanks; Plastic chemical tanks; Steel tanks & cisterns
●   Mtgs - Inf
<   Inst of Plumbing (as industrial associate)
M   11 f
¶   ATCM News Update - 12; free.

Association of Taxation Technicians   (ATT)   1989
■   12 Upper Belgrave St, LONDON, SW1X 8BB.   (hq)
       020 7235 2544   fax 020 7235 4571
       email info@att.org.uk   http://www.att.org.uk
       Sec: Andrew R Pickering
▲   Company Limited by Guarantee; Registered Charity
Br   27; Europe, Hong Kong, Singapore
○   *P; to provide an appropriate qualification for individuals
       working in taxation on a day-to-day basis
●   Conf - Mtgs - ET - Exam - Lib
<   Chart Inst of Taxation
M   5,406 i
¶   Tax Adviser - 12.   LM - 2 yrly.
       Annotated Finance Act - 1.
       Tax Advisers Practice Hbk.   AR.
       Professional Rules & Practice Guidelines.
       Note: the association is sponsored by the Chartered Institute of
       Taxation

Association of Teachers & Lecturers   (ATL)   1884
NR   7 Northumberland St, LONDON, WC2N 5RD.   (hq)
       020 7930 6441
       http://www.atl.org.uk
       Gen Sec: Mary Bousted
○   *P, *U; to promote & protect the interests of education
       professionals from early years through further education, in
       England, Wales, Northern Ireland & the Channel Islands
●   Conf - Mtgs - Res - Exhib - Inf - LG
<   Trade Union Congress
M   150,000 i
¶   Jnls;   NLs; all ftm.
       Publications list available.

Association of Teachers of Lipreading to Adults   (ATLA)   1976
■   Westwood Park, London Rd, Little Horkesley, COLCHESTER,
       Essex, CO6 4BS.   (mail/address)
       email atla@lipreading.org.uk
       http://www.lipreading.org.uk
       Chmn: Bert Smale,   Sec: Mary Baynton
▲   Registered Charity
○   *P; to maintain & develop standards of lipreading teaching to
       adults; to promote understanding of the needs of adults with
       any level of acquired hearing loss
Gp   Deaf; Deafened; Hard of hearing
●   Conf - Mtgs - ET - Exhib - LG
<   UK Coun on Deafness (UKCOD)
M   300+ i, 4 org, UK / 6+ i, o'seas
¶   Catchword - 2;   NL - 2; both ftm only.

Association of Teachers of Mathematics   (ATM)   1952
NR   Unit 7 Prime Industrial Park, Shaftesbury St, DERBY,
       DE23 8YB.   (hq)
       01332 346599
       Hon Sec: Cheryl Periton
▲   Company Limited by Guarantee; Registered Charity
Br   17
○   *E, *P; to support the teaching & learning of mathematics
       teaching by encouraging increased understanding &
       enjoyment of maths, understanding how people learn maths,
       the exploration of new ideas & practices
Gp   Working gps: All-ability teaching & learning, Early childhood
       maths, Flash, Small software, Teaching & learning undergrad
       maths, KS/1/2, Overseas links learning undergraduate
       maths; Teaching & learning enquiry; Small software
●   Conf - ET - SG
M   2,900 i, 760 instns, UK / 650 i, 510 instns, o'seas
¶   Mathematics Teaching & NL - 4; with Micromath - 3.
       Publications list available.

Association of Teachers of Singing   (AOTOS)   1975
■   Weir House, 108 Newton Rd, BURTON-UPON-TRENT, Staffs,
       DE15 0TT.   (hsp/b)
       01283 542198
       email coralgould7@aol.com   http://www.aotos.co.uk
       Hon Sec: Coral Gould
▲   Registered Charity
○   *E, *P; to promote the understanding of aspects of the teaching
       of singing
●   Conf - ET (teacher training course) - Inf
<   Eur Voice Teachers Assn; Inc Soc Musicians
>   Voice Care Network
M   400 i, 8 f, UK / 75 i, o'seas
¶   Voice - 2; ftm, £4 nm.

Association for Teaching Psychology (ATP) 1971

- ■ c/o The British Psychological Society, 48 Princess Road East, LEICESTER, LE1 7TR. (mail)
  http://www.theatp.org address
  Chief Exec: Tim Cornford
- ○ *E, *L, *P; to further the study & teaching of psychology
- ● Conf - Mtgs - ET - Exam - LG
- < Brit Psychological Soc
- M 38,485 i, UK / 3,705 i, o'seas
- ¶ Psychology Teaching (Jnl) - 1; ftm, £5 nm.
  ATP NL - 3; ftm only.
  Various other publications.

Association for the Teaching of the Social Sciences (ATSS) 1965

- ■ Old Hall Lane, MANCHESTER, M13 0XT. (regd/office)
  0116-248 9375
  email atss@btconnect.com   http://www.atss.org.uk
  Chmn: Andy Pilkington
- ▲ Company Limited by Guarantee; Registered Charity
- ○ *P; dissemination of good teaching practices in the field of social science
- ● Conf - ET - LG
- < Brit Sociological Assn (BSA)
- > General Teaching Coun
- M c 500 i
- ¶ Social Science Teacher (Jnl) - 3; ftm only.

Association of Technical Lighting & Access Specialists (ATLAS) 1946

- ■ 4c St Mary's Place, The Lace Market, NOTTINGHAM, NG1 1PH. (hq)
  0115-955 8818   fax 0115-941 2238
  email info@atlas-1.org.uk   http://www.atlas-1.org.uk
  Sec: R Wollerton
- ○ *T; interests of steeplejacks & firms involved in the erection & maintenance of lightning conductors
- Gp Chimney steeplejacks; Lightning conductor engineers; Training
- ● Mtgs - ET - Inf - Empl
- M 59 f
- ¶ LM - 1; free.   Codes of Practice.
- ✕ 2003 (November) National Federation of Master Steeplejacks & Lightning Conductor Engineers

Association of Technology Staffing Companies (ATSCO) 1999

- ■ 109 Regent House, 291 Kirkdale, LONDON, SE26 4QD. (hq)
  020 8676 9888   fax 020 8676 9933
  email info@atsco.org   http://www.atsco.org
  Chief Exec: Ann Swain
- ▲ Company Limited by Guarantee
- ○ *T; IT, telecomms & professional level engineering; to inform on industry changes & knowledge
- ● Conf - Mtgs - Res - Stat - Inf - LG - Industry awards
- M 80 f, 2 org, UK / 2 f, o'seas
- ¶ NL - 4;   LM - 12;   Ybk - 1;   AR - 1; all ftm only.

Association of Thallophyte Treatment Plants (ATTP) 1997

- ■ 1 Caryl House, Windlesham Close, LONDON, SW19 6AH. (sb)
- ○ *T;
- ● Conf - Mtgs - LG - VE
- M 6 f

Association of Therapeutic Communities (ATC) 1972

- NR Barns Centre, Church Lane, Toddington, CHELTENHAM, Glos, GL54 5DQ. (mail/add)
  01242 620077   fax 01242 620077
  email post@therapeuticcommunities.org
  http://www.therapeuticcommunities.org
  Chmn: Dr Rex Haigh
- ▲ Registered Charity
- ○ *W; to further implementation of the therapeutic community approach & ideology in the psychiatric hospital & social services for the psychiatric patient & appropriate related fields
- ● Conf - ET - Res
- M 87 i, 49 f, UK / 37 i, 3 f, o'seas
- ¶ Therapeutic Communities Jnl - 4.
  NL - 4.

Association for Therapeutic Healers (ATH) 1983

- NR 23 Chiswick Court, Moss Lane, PINNER, Middx, HA5 3AP. (hsp)
  07074 222284
  email enquiries@ath.org.uk   http://www.ath.org.uk
  Sec: Helen Spark
- ▲ Un-incorporated Society
- ○ *P; for professional healers who combine healing with other therapies; to promote health, well-being & self wisdom
- ● Mtgs - Clinic (at above address) - Professional liability service for members
- < Confedn of Healing Orgs; UK Healers
- M 70 i, UK / 2 i, o'seas
- ¶ NL - 3.

Association for Therapeutic Philosophy (ATP) 1983

- ■ 33 Marlborough Rd, SWINDON, Wilts, SN3 1PH. (hq)
  01793 538586   fax 01793 538586
  Sec: Dr Andreas Sofroniou
- ▲ Un-incorporated Society
- Br 2
- ○ *P
- Gp Therapeutic philosophy; Psychotherapy; Hypnotherapy; Development of people, management & systems; Political philosophy
- ● Conf - Mtgs - ET - Exam - Res - SG - Stat - Inf - Lib - VE - LG
- > Assn for Psychological Counselling & Training (USA)
- M 270 i, 2 f, 3 org, UK / 130 i, 2 f, o'seas
- ¶ Books:
  Therapeutic Philosophy for the Individual & the State.
  Philosophic Counselling for the People & their Governments.
  A Town Called Morphou (a collection of poems).
  Business Information Systems.
  Joyful Parenting (bringing up children).
  Publications list available.

Association of Therapy Lecturers (ATL) 1963

- ■ 18 Shakespeare Business Centre, Hathaway Close, EASTLEIGH, Hants, SO50 4SR. (hq)
  0870 420 2022   fax 023 8062 4398
  email info@fht.org.uk   http://www.fht.org.uk
  Chief Exec: Mrs Jacqueline Palmer
- ▲ Company Limited by Guarantee
- ○ *P; to promote & maintain the highest standard of professionalism within the following industries: beauty, holistic & sports therapies therapy
- ● Conf - Mtgs - ET - Exhib - Comp - Inf - LG
- < is part of the Fedn of Holistic Therapists
- M [not stated]
- ¶ International Therapist - 6; ftm only.

Association of Timber Growers & Forestry Professionals (ATGFP) 2002
NR   5 Dublin Street Lane South, EDINBURGH, EH1 3PX.   (hq)
    0131-538 7111
    Chmn: John Firn
▲   Company Limited by Guarantee
○   *T; 'for all those involved in woodlands whether for business or
    pleasure'
●   Conf - Mtgs - ET - Inf - VE - LG
M   1,742 i, 106 f, 19 org
¶   Timber Grower - 4.   Bulletin (NL) - 4.
    Hbk - 2 yrly.   AR.
    Note: trading as Forestry & Timber Association; preparing to
    amalgamate with the **Confederation of Forest Industries**
×   2002 (Association of Professional Foresters
    (Timber Growers Association

Association of Tourism Teachers & Trainers
    a specialist section of the **Tourism Society**

Association of Town Centre Management (ATCM) 1991
NR   1 Queen Anne's Gate, LONDON, SW1H 9BT.   (hq)
    020 7222 0120
▲   Company Limited by Guarantee
○   *T; to promote the long term survival of the town centre as a
    place to live, work, shop & find entertainment
M   f

Association of Town Clerks of Ireland
IRL   c/o Town Clerk, A/a/ras Chaiseal Mumhan, Friar St, CASHEL,
    Co Tipperary, Republic of Ireland.
    353 (62) 64700   fax 353 (62) 64797
    email seamus.maher@casheltc.ie
    Hon Sec: Seamus Maher
○   *P

Association of Train Operating Companies (ATOC) 1994
NR   40 Bernard St (3rd floor), LONDON, WC1N 1BY.   (hq)
    020 7841 8000
    Customer Services Mgr: Tony Ewers
○   *T; for the passenger rail industry
●   Conf - Mtgs - Res - Inf - LG
M   27 f
¶   [In-house only]

Association of Translation Companies (ATC) 1976
■   Greener House (5th floor), 66-68 Haymarket, LONDON,
    SW1Y 4RF.   (hq)
    020 7930 2200   fax 020 7451 7051
    email info@atc.org.uk   http://www.atc.org.uk
    Gen Sec: Geoffrey A R Bowden
▲   Company Limited by Guarantee
○   *T; to encourage use of professionally produced translations by
    industry, commerce, public sector organisations &
    government depts
●   Conf - Mtgs - ET - Stat - Inf - LG
<   Eur U of Assns of Translation Companies
M   137 f, UK / 19 f, o'seas
¶   Communicate - 4; free.

Association of Transport Co-ordinating Officers   (ATCO)   1974
■   c/o Group Manager, Integrated Transport Unit - Environment
    Dept, Somerset County Council, County Hall, TAUNTON,
    Somerset, TA1 4XE.   (hsb)
    01823 358176   fax 01823 356868
    email mapedlar@somerset.gov.uk
    http://www.atco.org.uk
    Hon Sec: Mark Pedlar
▲   Un-incorporated Society
Br   8
○   *P; to secure nationwide a better transport service for
    passengers
Gp   Sub-c'ees: Performing management; Best value; Bus;
    Community health & social transport; Education transport;
    Information & ticketing; Rail
●   Conf - Mtgs - ET - Res - Exhib - Stat - LG
<   Assn County Councils; Convention Scot Local Authorities;
    County Surveyors Soc
M   600 i
¶   ATCO News - 4;   Membership Directory - 1; both ftm only.

Association of Transport Photographers & Historians   (ATPH) 1996
■   14 Gannon Rd, WORTHING, W Sussex, BN11 2DT.   (hsp)
    01903 235167
    email info@transportphotos.com
    http://www.transportphotos.com
    Hon Sec: Robert Jenner Hobbs
○   *G; to encourage the preservation of original images of
    transport, travel & trade & the study of the sociological,
    economic or environmental effects of transportation through
    photographs; to promote awareness of the need to preserve
    images
Gp   Aviation; Maritime; Railway; Road transport
●   PL - Support organisation for the National Archive of Transport,
    Travel & Trade
<   Assn Brit Transport & Engg Museums; Transport Trust
M   256 i, UK / 4 i, o'seas
¶   PhotoNews:
    Aviation Section - 10;
    Road Section - 9; both free.
    Bespoke Catalogues & Listings - irreg; ftm, £5 nm.

Association of Tutors (AoT) 1958
■   Sunnycroft, 63 King Edward Rd, NORTHAMPTON, NN1 5LY.
    (hsp)
    01604 624171   fax 01604 624718
    http://www.tutor.co.uk
    Hon Sec: Dr D J Cornelius
▲   Un-incorporated Society
○   *E; *P; for independent private tutors; the Association is
    registered with the Criminal Records Bureau & has stringent
    vetting procedures
●   Conf - Mtgs - Inf
M   i
¶   NL - 2;   LM - 1; both ftm only.
    Information Leaflets; free.

Association of UK Media Librarians (AUKML) 1986
■   PO Box 14254, LONDON, SE1 9WL.   (mail)
    email chair@aukml.org.uk
    http://www.aukml.org.uk address
    Chmn: Katharine Schöpflin
▲   Un-incorporated Society
○   *P; for librarians & information specialists in the media industry
●   Conf - Mtgs - ET - VE
M   [70 i, UK / 30 i, o'seas
¶   Deadline (NL) - 4; ftm only.

Association of Unit Trusts & Investment Funds
    2002 merged with the Fund Managers Association to become the
    Investment Management Association

Association of United Kingdom Oil Independents   (AUKOI) 1976

NR   Cutlers Cottage, Carbrooke Lane, Shipdham, THETFORD,
     Norfolk, IP25 7RP.   (hsb)
     01362 820739   fax 01362 820124
     email secretariat@aukoi.co.uk
     Sec: M I Annesley
▲   Un-incorporated Society
○   *T; to represent & protect within the UK & the EEC the common
     interests of independent oil importers &/or distributors
Gp   Oil: distribution, importation, wholesaling, retailing
●   Mtgs - LG - Liaison in EU
<   Union Pétrolière Européenne Indépendant (UPEI)
M   11 f

Association of University Administrators   (AUA)   1993

■   The University of Manchester, Oxford Rd, MANCHESTER,
     M13 9PL.   (hq)
     0161-275 2063
     Exec Sec: Lynn Rawlinson
▲   Registered Charity
Br   180
○   *E, *P; for all with administrative & managerial responsibilities
     in higher education incl the Republic of Ireland
Gp   Equal opportunities working gp; Quality assurance network;
     Corporate planning forum; S/NVQ national support & focus
●   Conf - Mtgs - ET - Exhib - SG - VE - LG
M   4,000 i, UK / 52 i, o'seas
¶   Perspectives (Jnl) - 4; ftm, £120 nm.
     Newslink (NL) - 4;   AR - 1; both ftm only.

Association for University & College Counselling
     a group of the **British Association for Counselling &
     Psychotherapy**

**Association of University Radiation Protection Officers
(AURPO)   1961**

NR   Occupational Health & Safety Unit, University of Wales Bangor,
     Penbre, College Rd, BANGOR, Gwynedd, LL57 2DB.   (hsb)
     01248 382779   fax 01248 383259
     email d.hague@bangor.ac.uk   http://www.aurpo.org
     Sec: Tony Richards
▲   Un-incorporated Society
○   *P; radiation protection from ionizing & non-ionizing radiations
●   Conf - Mtgs - ET - Res - LG
<   Intl Radiation Protection Assn
M   208 i, 13 f, UK / 3 i, o'seas
¶   NL - 4; ftm only.

Association of University Research & Industry Links   (AURIL) 1994

NR   c/o Queen's University, Lanyon North, University Rd, BELFAST,
     BT7 1NN.   (hq)
     028 9097 2589   fax 028 9097 2570
     email auril@qub.ac.uk
     10 Fleet Place (3rd floor), Limeburner Lane, LONDON,
     EC4M 7SB.   (regd office)
     Exec Dir: Dr Philip Graham
▲   Company Limited by Guarantee
○   *N, *P; to support universities in the UK & Eire in the
     development of mutually beneficial partnerships with industry
     & other sectors, in the field of research, technology &
     knowledge transfer, consultancy & related activities
Gp   Research; Medical research; Consultancy; Intellectual property;
     Costing & pricing
●   Conf - Mtgs - ET - Res - SG - Stat - Inf - LG
<   loose affiliations to CBI & ICARG
M   100 higher instns (UK & Eire), 50 associates (f, govt depts &
     agencies)
¶   LM - 2; ftm only.
     Research Partnerships between Industry & Universities: a guide
     to better practice, 1997; £15. (AURIL & CBI).

Association of University Teachers   (AUT)   1919

■   Egmont House, 25-31 Tavistock Place, LONDON,
     WC1H 9UT.   (hq)
     020 7670 9700
     Gen Sec: Sally Hunt
Br   Birmingham, Edinburgh, Manchester, Portsmouth
○   *E, *P, *U; concerned with pay & conditions of university
     professional staff; higher education policy
Gp   Staff groups: Library, Computer, Administrative, Research
●   Conf - Mtgs - ET - Res - Stat - Empl - LG
<   Trade Union Congress
M   42, 500 i
¶   AUTlook (Jnl) [incl Equalise] - 3;   AUT Update (NL) - 8;   Hbk
     - 1;   all ftm only.
     Note: amalgamated on 1 June 2006 with NATFHE - the
     University & College Lecturers' Union to form the University &
     College Union.
     A transitional year will exist until full operational unity is
     achieved in June 2007.

Association of University Teachers (Scotland)
     a section of the Association of University Teachers (which is in the
     process of amalgamating with NATFHE - the University & College
     Lecturers' Union) to form the **University & College Union**

**Association of Unpasteurised Milk Producers & Consumers
(AUMPC)   1989**

NR   Hardwick Estate Office, WHITCHURCH, Oxon, RG8 7RE.
     (hsb)
     0118-984 2955
     Founders: Sir Julian Rose,   Marwood Yeatman
▲   Un-incorporated Society
○   *F, *K, *T; for producers & consumers of unpasteurised milk; to
     keep small producers in business & allow consumers
     freedom of choice
●   Inf - LG
¶   The Case for Untreated Milk.
     Note: The association was first formed in 1989 to fight the
     attempt by the previous government to ban the sale of
     unpasteurised milk. It has been re-activated, to mobilise
     public opinion again, to fight another move by the current
     government to ban the milk.

Association of Upper Gastro Intestinal Surgeons
     a group of the **Association of Surgeons of Great Britain &
     Ireland**

Association of Users of Research Agencies   (AURA)   1965

NR   51 Dalkeith Rd, HARPENDEN, Herts, AL5 5PP.   (admin/p)
     01582 620331
     http://www.aura.org.uk
     Admin: Peter Goudge
▲   Company Limited by Guarantee
○   *P; forum for clientside researchers to exchange information
Gp   General Insurance Market Research Association; Advertising;
     Database marketing; International research
●   Mtgs - Res - Networking
M   240 i, UK / 135 i, o'seas

Association of Valuers of Licensed Property   (AVLP)   1894

■   c/o Fleurets, Wellesley House, 96 East St, SUDBURY, Suffolk,
     CO10 2TP.   (hsb)
     01787 378050   fax 01787 880292
     email bob.whittle@fleurets.com
     Hon Sec: R Whittle
○   *P; for auctioneers, surveyors & valuers whose sole or main
     business is concerned with the sale & valuation of hotels,
     public houses & licensed property generally
M   c 120 i

Association of Vehicle Recovery Operators Ltd   (AVRO)   1977
- ■ 1 Bath St, RUGBY, Warks, CV21 3JF.   (hq)
  01788 572850   fax 01788 572850
  email info@avrouk.com   http://www.avrouk.com
  Chief Exec: Gary Satchwell
- ▲ Company Limited by Guarantee
- ○ *T
- Gp AVRO show; Finance; Insurance; Legal; Magazine, Directory,
  Website; Membership; Motoring organisations; Police
  schemes; Standards & safety
- ● Mtgs - Inf - LG
- < Intl Fedn Recovery Services
- M 500 f
- ¶ Recovery Operator Magazine - 6; ftm, £2.40 nm.
  Members NL - 6; ftm only.   AR; free.
  Members Directory - 1; ftm, £15 nm.

Association of Veterinarians in Industry
  a group of the **British Veterinary Association**

Association of Veterinary Anaesthetists
  a group of the **British Small Animal Veterinary Association**

Association of Veterinary Clinical Pharmacology & Therapeutics
  a group of the **British Small Animal Veterinary Association**

Association of Veterinary Soft Tissue Surgery
  a group of the **British Small Animal Veterinary Association**

Association of Veterinary Students
  a group of the **British Veterinary Association**

Association of Veterinary Teachers & Research Workers
  a specialist division of the **British Veterinary Association**

**Association of Visitors to Immigration Detainees   (AVID)
1997**
- ■ PO Box 7, OXTED, Surrey, RH8 0YT.   (mail/address)
  01883 717275   fax 01883 717275
  email coordinator@aviddetention.org.uk
  http://www.aviddetention.org.uk
  Chmn: Eike Müller,   Coordinator: Helen Ireland
- ▲ Registered Charity
- ○ *N, *W; an umbrella organisation supporting visiting groups,
  individual visitors & immigration detainees held in removal,
  reception & holding centres by the Immigration Service; to
  advocate for improved conditions in detention
- ● Conf - ET - Res - Stat - Inf - LG
- M 350 i, 25 gps
- ¶ Hbk - ftm, £5 nm.   AR.

Association for Vocational Colleges International
  has ceased all activities

Association of Volunteer Managers   2007
- ○ *P; for those coordinating or administering volunteers
- M potentially 200,000 i
  to be launched June 2007

Association of Welding Distributors   (AWD)   1973
- ■ Enterprise House, Stafford Park 1, TELFORD, Shropshire,
  TF3 3BD.   (hq)
  01952 290036   fax 01952 290037
  email info@awd.org.uk   http://www.awd.org.uk
  Dir: Leslie (Mike) Vacher
- ▲ Un-incorporated Society
- ○ *T; for the welding supply industry - distributors, manufacturers,
  wholesalers & importers with a UK operational base
- ● Conf - Mtgs - ET - Exhib - Stat - Inf - Lib - VE - LG (through
  METCOM)
- < Mechanical & Metal Trades Confedn (METCOM)
- M 161 f
- ¶ NL - 12; m only.
  AWD Business Bulletin - 4; free.

**Association of Wellhead Equipment Manufacturers
(AWHEM)   1961**
- NR PO Box 197, ABERDEEN, AB9 6EE.   (mail) address
- ▲ Un-incorporated Society
- ○ *T; repair & manufacture of well control equipment used within
  the Continental shelf

Association of Wheelchair Children
- NR 6 Woodman Parade, North Woolwich, LONDON, E16 2LL.
  (hq)
  0870 121 0050
- ▲ Registered Charity
  no further information supplied

**Association of Wholesale Electrical Bulk Buyers Ltd   (AWEBB)
1975**
- NR AWEBB House, 2 Kensington Works, Hallamfields Rd,
  ILKESTON, Derbys, DE7 4BR.   (hq)
  0115-944 3334
  Chief Exec: John Horton
- ○ *T
- M 59 f

Association of Wine Educators
- ■ Scots Firs, 70 Joiners Lane, CHALFONT St PETER, Bucks,
  SL9 0AU.
  01494 589201
  Admin: Andrea Warren
- ○ *P

** **Association for Women in Science & Engineering**
  Organisation lost: see Introduction paragraph 3

Association of Woodwind Teachers
  is temporarily in abeyance

Association of Workers for Children with Emotional & Behavioural Difficulties
  since February 2003 **Sebda - the Social, Emotional &
  Behavioural Difficulties Association**

**Association of X-ray Equipment Manufacturers   (AXrEM)
1974**
- ■ St George's House, 195-203 Waterloo Rd, LONDON,
  SE1 8WB.   (hq)
  020 7642 8083   fax 020 7642 8096
  email axrem@gambica.org.uk
  Dir: Peter J Lawson
- ▲ Un-incorporated Society
- ○ *T; medical X-ray diagnostic & radiotherapy equipment
- ● Mtgs - Stat - LG
- < Eur Coordination C'ee of the Radiological & Electromedical
  Ind (COCIR)
- M 7 f

Association of Young Medical Scientists
  a group of the **Medical Research Society**

Association of Young People with ME   (AYME)   1996
■   PO Box 5766, MILTON KEYNES, MK10 1AQ.   (hq)
      email info@ayme.org.uk   http://www.ayme.org.uk
      Chair of Trustees: Jill Moss
▲   Company Limited by Guarantee; Registered Charity
○   *M, *W, *Y; 'cheerful support, friendship & information to
      children & young people aged 0 to 25 with ME. Free
      membership to eligible applicants living in the UK'
●   Conf - Inf - Lib - Peer support
      Helpline: 0845 123 2389
M   2,000 i
¶   NL - 6.
      Books:
          Somebody Help ME; £14.95.   Three Villains?; £6.50.
          My Daughter & ME; £7.50.
      Videos:
          ME Is Not Fatigue!; £8.50.   Letting Go; £4.
          What Do You Know About ME?; £11.
      Numerous other publications for sufferers, schools & doctors.
×   Association of Youth with ME

Assurance Medical Society   (AMS)   1893
■   Lettsom House, 11 Chandos St, LONDON, W1G 9EB.   (hq)
      020 7636 6308
      Exec Sec: Col Richard Kinsella-Bevan
○   *L; life assurance medicine
●   Mtgs
<   Intl Congress Life Assurance Medicine
M   450 i, 70 f
¶   Transactions - 2; ftm only.

ASTA BEAB Certification Services   (ASTA BEAB)   1938
NR   1 Station View, GUILDFORD, Surrey, GU1 4JY.   (hq)
      01483 455466
○   *T
M   f
×   2004 (ASTA Certification Services
          (British Electrotechnical Approvals Board

Asthma Society of Ireland
IRL   26 Mountjoy Square, DUBLIN 1, Republic of Ireland.
      353 (1) 878 8511   fax 353 (1) 878 8128
      email office@asthmasociety
      http://www.asthmasociety.ie
      Chmn: Angela Edghill
○   *W

Asthma UK   1990
NR   Summit House, 70 Wilson St, LONDON, EC2A 2DB.   (hq)
      020 7786 4900   fax 020 7256 6075
      http://www.asthma.org.uk
      Scotland: 4 Queen St, EDINBURGH, EH2 1JE.
          0131-226 2544.   fax 0131-226 2401.
      Chief Exec: Donna Covey
▲   Registered Charity
Br   45
○   *K, *W; to research into asthma & related allergy; to give
      information & advice for people with asthma, their relatives,
      carers & health professionals
●   Conf - ET - Res - Inf - PL - LG - Asthma
          helpline: 0845 7010203
<   Assn Medical Res Charities
M   20,000 i
¶   Asthma News - 4;   A for Asthma - 4;   AR; all free.
      Factsheets & pamphlets.
×   2004 National Asthma Campaign

Astrological Association of Great Britain   (AA)   1958
NR   Unit 168 Lee Valley Technopark, Tottenham Hale, LONDON,
      N17 9LN.   (hq)
      0845 125 9153   fax 0845 125 9145
      email office@astrologicalassociation.com
      http://www.astrologicalassociation.com
      Chmn: Wendy Stacey
▲   Un-incorporated Society
○   *G; for people interested in western & Vedic astrology
●   Conf - Inf - Lib - VE
M   1,200 i, UK / 500 i, o'seas
¶   Astrological Jnl - 6.
      Transit Magazine - 6.
      Correlation (research jnl) - 2.
      Cosmos & Culture - 4.
      Astrology & Medicine NL - 3.

Astrological Lodge of London   (ALL)   1915
■   50 Gloucester Place, LONDON, W1U 8HQ.   (mail/address)
○   *P; the study of astrology in all its branches
●   Mtgs - ET - Comp - SG - Lib
M   400 i, UK / 90 i, o'seas
¶   Astrology - 4.

Astronomical Society of Edinburgh   (ASE)   1924
NR   105/19 Causewayside, EDINBURGH, EH9 1QG.   (hq)
          0131-556 4365
      Sec: Graham Rule
▲   Registered Charity
○   *L; to promote interest in astronomy in Edinburgh
●   Mtgs - ET - Exhib - SG - Lib - PL
<   Fedn of Astronomical Socs; Brit Astronomical Assn
M   120 i
¶   Jnl - 2; ftm.   Bulletin - 12;   AR; both free.

**ASUCplus - Subsidence Repair Techniques & Engineered
Foundation Solutions   (ASUCplus)   1991**
■   99 West St, FARNHAM, Surrey, GU9 7EN.   (asa)
      01252 739142   fax 01252 739140
      email asuc@associationhouse.org.uk
      http://www.asuc.org.uk
      Sec: John Fairley
○   *T; 'specialists in subsidence repair techniques & engineered
      foundation solutions, including new build foundations &
      basement development'
●   Conf - Mtgs - ET - Exhib
M   20 f
×   2003 Association of Specialist Underpinning Contractors

Ataxia-Telangiectasia Society   (A-T Society)   (ATS)   1989
NR   c/o IACR - Rothamsted, HARPENDEN, Herts, AL5 2JQ.   (hq)
      01582 760733   fax 01582 760162
      email ATCharity@aol.com   http://www.atsociety.org.uk
      Hon Sec: Mrs Maureen Poupard
▲   Registered Charity
○   *M, *W; the relief of suffering caused by A-T through supporting
      medical research & fundraising; providing information for
      families & professionals; support for families & sufferers
●   Mtgs - Res - Inf
<   Eur Org for Rare Disorders; Assn Med Res Charities; Genetic
      Interest Gp; Contact a Family
M   95 i, UK / 5 i, o'seas
¶   A-T Society NL - 2; free.
      Ataxia-Telangiectasia [guides for/to]: Therapies; Parents;
      Teachers.

© CBD Research Ltd · Beckenham · BR3 5JS · Tel 020 8650 7745 · Fax 020 8650 0768 · E-mail cbd@cbdresearch.com · www.cbdresearch.com

Ataxia UK   (ATAXIA)   1964
■   Winchester House, Kennington Pk, Cranmer Rd, LONDON,
      SW9 6EJ.   (hq)
      020 7582 1444   fax 020 7582 9444
      email office@ataxia.org.uk   http://www.ataxia.org.uk
      Chief Exec: Alastair MacDougall
▲   Registered Charity
Br 8
○   *W; to provide advice, support & information to sufferers & their
      families; to finance research into Friedreich's, cerebellar &
      other ataxias; to offer information for health-care & social
      service professionals
●   Conf - Inf
      Helpline: 020 7820 3900
<   Neurological Alliance; Genetic Interest Gp
M   1,854 i, f & org, UK / 51 i, f & org, o'seas
¶   The Ataxia - 4;   AR - 1; both ftm only.
      Freidreichs Ataxia / Cerebellar (leaflets); free.
✕   2002 Friedreich's Ataxia Group

Athletics Association of Wales
      since 2005 **Welsh Athletics**

Atlantic Council of the United Kingdom
NR Winchester House, 80 Back Church Lane, LONDON, E1 1LT.
      (hq)
      020 7481 4576
      http://www.atlantic-council.org.uk
      Dir: Alan L Williams
▲   Registered Charity
○   *K; 'to explain, in simple & lucid terms to schools, universities &
      public opinion generally, the implications of the momentous
      changes that have taken place in Europe since the end of the
      Cold War'
<   Atlantic Treaty Assn (ATA)
M   400 i

Attend   (Attend)   1949
NR 11-13 Cavendish Square, LONDON, W1G 0AN.   (hq)
      0845 450 0285
      email info@hc-friends.org.uk
      Chief Exec: David Wood
▲   Registered Charity
○   *N, *W; to promote & strengthen the work of member charities
      by provision of services
●   Conf - ET - Comp - Inf - LG - Specialist advice & support to
      member leagues - Grants - Insurance & savings schemes -
      Local support networks
M   c 800 leagues
¶   Hospital & Community Friend - 4.
      AR.   Training publications.
✕   2005 National Association of Hospital & Community Friends

Aubrac Cattle Society of the UK Ltd   1990
■   Gore Farm, Ashmore, SALISBURY, Wilts, SP5 5AR.   (hsp)
      01747 811157   fax 01747 811157
      Sec: Mrs Jennifer Biles,   Pres: Sir John Eliot Gardiner
○   *B; promotion, registration & import of registered Aubrac beef
      cattle
M   2 i

Audio Engineering Society (British Section)   (AES)   1970
■   PO Box 645, SLOUGH, Berks, SL1 8BJ.   (hq)
      01628 663725   fax 0870 7626137
      email uk@aes.org   http://www.aes.org
      Sec: Mrs Heather Lane
○   *L, *P
M   i & f
¶   Jnl - 10.

Audio Visual Association
      is a specialist group within the **British Institute of Professional
      Photography**

Audio Visual Federation
IRL Confederation House, 84-86 Lower Baggot St, DUBLIN 2,
      Republic of Ireland.
○   *P
<   IBEC

Audiobook Publishing Association   (APA)   1994
■   18 Green Lanes, HATFIELD, Herts, AL10 9JT.   (hsp)
      07971 280788
      email charlotte.mccandlish@ntlworld.com
      http://www.theapa.net
      Admin: Charlotte McCandlish
○   *P
●   Mtgs - Comp - Stat - Inf - Social events
M   c200 i, c100 f
¶   APA Resources Directory - 1; ftm.
✕   2004 Spoken Word Publishing Association

Australia & New Zealand Chamber of Commerce
      since 2006 **Australian Business**

Australian Business   1910
■   Dudley House, 34-35 Southampton St, LONDON,
      WC2E 7HE.   (hq)
      0870 890 0720   fax 0870 890 0721
      email enquiries@australianbusiness.co.uk
      http://www.australianbusiness.co.uk
      Dir: Melissa Brown
▲   Non-profit organisation
○   *C; to promote & facilitate bilateral trade between Australia/
      New Zealand & the UK
Gp UK, Australia/New Zealand Business
●   Inf - Lib - Events & functions relevant to business involving
      Australasia & the UK
<   Australian Brit Cham Comm
M   500 i, 2300 f, 3,000 org UK / 10 i, 10 f, 1,000 org, o'seas
¶   Up & Under Updates - 6; ftm.
✕   2006 Australia & New Zealand Chamber of Commerce

Austro-British Chamber   (ABC)   1963
NR Dominikanerbastei 4, A-1011 VIENNA, Austria.
      43 (1) 890 70 00   fax 43 (1) 890 70 00 15
○   *C;
✕   2004 British Trade Council in Austria

Authors' Licensing & Collecting Society   (ALCS)   1977
NR Marlborough Court, 14-18 Holborn, LONDON, EC1N 2LE.
      (hq)
      020 7395 0600
      Chief Exec: Owen Atkinson
▲   Company Limited by Guarantee
○   *T; the British rights management society for all writers; to
      distribute fees to writers whose work has been copied,
      broadcast or recorded
●   Inf
<   Intl Confedn of Socs for Authors & Composers (CISAC); Intl
      Forum for Reprographic Rights (IFRRO); Soc of Authors;
      Writers Gld of GB
M   15,000 i, UK / 1,000 i, o'seas
¶   ALCS News - 3; ftm only.
      Information leaflet; on request.

Autism Independent UK (Society for the Autistically Handicapped) (SFTAH) 1987
NR 199-203 Blandford Avenue, KETTERING, Northants, NN16 9AT. (hq)
   01536 523274   fax 01536 523274
   email autism@autismuk.com
   http://www.autismuk.com
   Dir: Keith Lovett
▲ Registered Charity
○ *W; to promote the understanding & awareness of autism; to provide support for families and carers; training for professionals
● Conf - ET - Res - Lib - LG - Provision of low-cost holiday facilities for autistic children & their families
< TEACCH (USA)
M 209 i, 850 org, UK / 20 i, o'seas
¶ Autism News - 4. AR.

Auto-Cycle Union Ltd (ACU) 1903
NR ACU House, Wood St, RUGBY, Warks, CV21 2YX. (hq)
   01788 566400 fax 01788 573585
   email admin@acu.org.uk
   http://www.motorcyclinggb.com
   Gen Sec: Gary Thompson
▲ Company Limited by Guarantee
○ *S; governing body of British motorcycle sport & leisure
● Conf - Mtgs - ET - Exhib - Comp - Inf
< Fédn Intle Motocyclisme (FIM)
M 29,415 i, 650 clubs
¶ Motorcycling GB - 4. ACU Hbk - 1.

Auto Locksmiths Association (ALA) 1997
NR c/o Brian Meynell (Attend A Lock), The Gate House, Yoxford, SAXMUNDHAM, Suffolk, IP17 3LG. (sb)
   Sec: Brian Meynell
○ *T; to enhance & develop the auto locksmith industry
● Conf - Mtgs - ET - Res - Exhib - Inf - Lib - VE - LG
M 50 i
¶ NL - 6; ftm only.

Autoclaved Aerated Concrete Products Association
   has changed name to Aircrete Products Association & as such is a product association of the **British Precast Concrete Federation**

Autograph Club of Great Britain (ACOGB) 1998
NR 47 Webb Crescent, Dawley, TELFORD, Shropshire, TF4 3DS. (hsp)
   01952 410332
   email gregson@blueyonder.co.uk
   http://www.acogb.co.uk
   Chmn: Robert Gregson
▲ Un-incorporated Society
○ *G; to keep autograph collectors in touch with each other; to raise money for charities
● Mtgs - Exhib - Inf
< Dr Who Autograph Club; The Star Directory
M c 200 i
¶ [website only].

Automated Material Handling Systems Association Ltd (AMHSA) 1986
NR PO Box 7113, LEICESTER, LE7 9XX. (hq)
   0116-259 8518
▲ Company Limited by Guarantee
○ *T; to promote the use of automated material handling & unit load conveyor systems in the UK
Gp System Integrator; Conveyor
● Mtgs - ET - Stat - LG - Participation in work on UK & European Standards
< Fédn Eur Manutention (FEM) Section IX; Brit Materials Handling Fedn
M 22 f
¶ GN 101: Availability tests for automated material handling systems.
   GN 103: Planning, management & implementation of... systems.
   AMHSA 88 (contract conditions): General Conditions for the Supply of Automated Material Handling Systems.

Automatic Door Suppliers Association (ADSA) 1985
NR 411 Limpsfield Rd, The Green, WARLINGHAM, Surrey, CR6 9HA. (hq)
   01883 624961
   Dir: G F Elliott
○ *T; safety standards for automatic door installations
● Mtgs - Exam - Stat - Inf - LG
M 13 f

Automatic Identification Manufacturers & Suppliers Association (AIM) UK 1984
NR The Old Vicarage, All Souls Rd, HALIFAX, W Yorks, HX3 6DR. (hq)
   01422 368368
   Chief Exec: Ian G Smith
○ *T; for automatic data capture industry - bar codes, radio frequency identification & communication, optical character recognition, magnetic strip cards, voice recognition

Automatic Vending Association (AVA) 1929
NR 1 Villiers Court, 40 Upper Mulgrave Rd, CHEAM, Surrey, SM2 7AJ. (hq)
   020 8661 1112 fax 020 8661 2224
   email info@ava-vending.org
   http://www.ava-vending.org
   Dir: Janette Gledhill
▲ Company Limited by Guarantee
Br 5
○ *T; for the automatic refreshment industry
Gp Coinage; Commodities; Technical
● Conf - Mtgs - Res - Exhib - Stat - Inf - Lib - LG - Preparation of technical standards - Sales promotion & publicity
< Eur Vending Assn; Brit Retail Consortium; CBI
M 29 i, 264 f, UK / 6 f, o'seas
¶ VENDinform - 6. LM - 1. Census - 1.
   Explaining Vending; Vending Quality Standards.
× Automatic Vending Association of Britain

Automobile Association (AA) 1905
NR Carr Ellison House, William Armstrong Drive, NEWCASTLE-UPON-TYNE, NE4 7YA. (hq)
   0870 600 0371
   email customer.services@theaa.com
   http://www.theaa.com
▲ Un-incorporated Society
○ *G
● Insurance services - Motoring services - Publishing
M c 12,000,000 i
¶ AR.

© CBD Research Ltd · Beckenham · BR3 5JS · Tel 020 8650 7745 · Fax 020 8650 0768 · E-mail cbd@cbdresearch.com · www.cbdresearch.com

Automotive Aftermarket Association (AAA) 1974
NR   Roydsdale House, Roydsdale Way, Euroway Trading Estate,
       BRADFORD, W Yorks, BD4 6SE.   (hq)
       01274 654600
Br   550
○   *T; to protect the automotive aftermarket industry (distribution of
       parts, supplies to garages & truck fleets); to enhance its
       trading environment & business conditions
M   700 f
¶   Motor Factor - 12.   Members Hbk - 1.   LM; on-line.

Automotive Distribution Federation (ADF) 1930
■   68-70 Coleshill Rd, Hodge Hill, BIRMINGHAM, B36 8AB.   (hq)
       0870 458 2300   fax 0870 458 2205
       email admin@adf.org.uk   http://www.adf.org.uk
       Chief Exec: Brian Spratt
▲   Company Limited by Guarantee
○   *T; interests of manufacturers, importers & wholesale
       distributors of vehicle components operating in the
       independent automotive aftermarket (the section of the motor
       trade independent of the vehicle manufacturers & their
       dealers)
Gp   Commercial vehicle section (specialists in components for
       trucks & buses);
       Bodyshop supply section (specialists in supplying the body
       repair industry)
●   Conf - Mtgs - ET - Exhib - Comp - SG - Stat - Expt - Inf - Lib -
       LG - Provision of business services (insurance, pensions,
       credit management & information, stationery)
<   Intl Fedn of Automotive Aftermarket Parts &
       Wholesalers (FIGIEFA); Eur Liaison C'ee for Automotive Parts
       Wholesalers (CLEDIPA)
M   320 f
¶   Eyes & Ears - 6; ftm, £2 each nm.   AR - 1; ftm only.

Automotive Glazing Executive [UK] Ltd
       closed down 2005

Automotive Manufacturers' Racing Association (AMRA) 1952
NR   The Nook 27 Top Side, Grenoside, SHEFFIELD, S Yorks,
       S35 8RD.   (hsp)
       0114-246 4878   fax 0114-246 4858
       email info@amrauk.com   http://www.amrauk.com
       Coordinator: Stuart Barnes
▲   Company Limited by Guarantee
○   *T; to raise standards & efficiency of service to competitors
       throughout motor sport
●   Conf - Mtgs - ET - Exhib - Expt - LG
M   4 i, 112 f, 3 org
¶   AMRA News - irreg.

Aviation Environment Federation (AEF) 1975
NR   Broken Wharf House, 2 Broken Wharf, LONDON, EC4V 3DT.
       (hq)
       020 7248 2223   fax 020 7329 8160
       email info@aef.org.uk   http://www.aef.org.uk
       Chief Exec: Tim Johnson
▲   Company Limited by Guarantee
○   *K; 'the principal UK environmental association concerned
       specifically with the environmental & amenity aspects of
       aviation'
●   Conf - ET - Res - SG - Stat - Inf - Lib - LG
<   Intl Coalition for Sustainable Aviation (ICSA); Eur Fedn for
       Transport & Envt (T&E)
M   50 i, 15 f, 84 org, UK / 1 org, o'seas
¶   Flying Green (NL) - 6.
       Members Briefing - 3.   AR.

Aviation Insurance Offices Association
       is dormant

Aviation Society (TAS) 1973
NR   The Airport Tour Centre, MANCHESTER AIRPORT, M90 1SZ.
       (hq)
       0161-489 2443   fax 0161-436 3030
       email admin@tasmanchester.com
       http://www.tasmanchester.com
       Chmn: Peter Hampson
▲   Un-incorporated Society
○   *G; all aspects of aviation for enthusiasts
Gp   Civil & military; Aviation; Manchester airport
●   Mtgs - Res - Exhib - Comp - SG - Stat - Inf - VE - Coach tours &
       flights to airports in the UK & o'seas
M   2,000 i
¶   Winged Words (NL) - 12; ftm.

Avicultural Society (AS) 1894
■   Arcadia, The Mounts, East Allington, TOTNES, Devon,
       TQ9 7QJ.   (hsb)
       Sec: Paul Boulden
▲   Un-incorporated Society
○   *L; study of British & foreign birds in freedom & captivity
●   VE
<   Nat Coun Aviculture
M   200 i, 10 instns, UK / 50 i, 66 instns, o'seas
¶   The Avicultural Magazine - 4.

Ayrshire Agricultural Association (AAA) 1836
NR   Oswald Hall, Auchincruive, AYR, KA6 5HW.   (hsp)
       0845 201 1460   fax 01292 525939
       email lorrainem@ayrcountyshow.co.uk
       Hon Sec: Mrs Lorraine Murdoch
▲   Registered Charity
○   *F; to promote agriculture in Ayrshire
●   Exhib
<   Assn of Agricl Shows
M   2,110 i
¶   NL - 1.   Schedule of Livestock - 1.
       Catalogue & Show Guide - 1.

Ayrshire Cattle Society of Great Britain & Ireland 1887
NR   17 Barns St, AYR, Ayrshire, KA7 1XB.   (hq)
       01292 267123
       Gen Mgr: Mrs Janet McComiskey
▲   Registered Charity
○   *B; to promote & register Ayrshire dairy cows
●   Conf - Mtgs - Promotion of breed - Register cattle
M   1,100 i, UK / 30 i, o'seas
¶   Ayrshire Jnl - 2.
       Ayrshire Dairyman (NL) - 2.   AR.

Ayrshire Chamber of Commerce & Industry   (ACCI)   1992
NR Glasgow Prestwick International Airport (suite 1005),
        PRESTWICK, Ayrshire, KA9 2PL.   (hq)
        01292 678666
        Chief Exec: Bob Leitch
▲ Company Limited by Guarantee
○ *C
Gp Lunchtime seminars; Membership data; Publications;
        Conferences; Export documentation
● Conf - Mtgs - ET - Res - Expt - Inf - LG
< Scot Chams Comm
M c 400 f
¶ Your Business - 6.

Ayurvedic Medical Association UK   1995
NR 59 Dulverton Rd, SELSDON, Surrey, CR2 8PJ.   (hsp)
        020 8682 3876   fax 020 8333 7904
        email dr-nsmoorthy@hotmail.com
        Gen Sec: Dr N Sathiya Moorthy
▲ Company Limited by Guarantee
Br 3; India, Sri Lanka
○ *M, *P; to promote the Ayurvedic medical system (which aims to
        boost the immune system in order to return the body to true
        health)
Gp Qualified Ayurvedic physicians from India, Sri Lanka & Pakistan
● Conf - Mtgs - ET - Exam - Res - Exhib - SG - Inf - Lib
< Inst of Complementary Medicine
M 60 i, UK / 25 i, o'seas
¶ [to come].

© CBD Research Ltd · Beckenham · BR3 5JS · Tel 020 8650 7745 · Fax 020 8650 0768 · E-mail cbd@cbdresearch.com · www.cbdresearch.com

Baby Equipment Hirers Association (BEHA) 2000
- ■ 8 Anselm Rd, HATCH END, Middx, HA5 4LJ.
  020 8621 4378
  http://www.beha.co.uk
  Contact: Juliette Morrison
- ○ *T; to supply members with insurance & equipment through buyers
- ● Conf - Res
- M 10 i
- ¶ BEHA News - 6;   AR; both ftm only.

Baby Life Support Systems
  see **BLISS - National Charity for the Newborn**

Baby Milk Action   1979
- ■ 23 St Andrew's St, CAMBRIDGE, CB2 3AX.   (hq)
  01223 464420   fax 01223 464417
  email info@babymilkaction.org
  http://www.babymilkaction.org
  Office Mgr: Alison Mortlake
- ▲ Company Limited by Guarantee
- ○ *K; 'to save infant lives & to end the avoidable suffering caused by inappropriate infant feeding by working within a global network (IBFAN); to strengthen independent, transparent & effective controls on the marketing of the baby feeding industry worldwide; the Independent Baby Food Action Network is a coalition of more than 200 citizen & health worker groups in more than 100 countries working for better child health & nutrition through the promotion of breastfeeding & the elimination of irresponsible marketing of infant foods, bottles & teats
- ● Conf - ET - Exhib - LG
- < Intl Baby Food Action Network (IBFAN)
- M 2,000 i
- ¶ Update NL - 2; ftm, £15 nm.

Baby Products Association (BPA) 1945
- NR 2 Carrera House, Merlin Court, Gatehouse Close, AYLESBURY, Bucks, HP19 8DP.   (hq)
  0845 456 9570
- ○ *T; nursery furniture & bedding, safety goods (stair gates & barriers etc) car seats & restraints, wheeled goods (prams & pushchairs etc)
- ● Conf - Mtgs - ET - Exhib - Inf - Lib
- < BSI; CEN
- M 80 f, UK / 10 f, o'seas
- ¶ Official Catalogue Baby & Child International Fair.

BackCare
  is the abbreviated name of the **National Backpain Association**

Backpackers Club (BPC) 1972
- NR 11 Morton Avenue, Clay Cross, CHESTERFIELD, Derbys, S45 9PX.   (hsp)
  01246 251509
  http://www.backpackersclub.co.uk
  Sec: Alan J Crowe
- ▲ Un-incorporated Society
- Br County groups; Canada, Holland
- ○ *G; lightweight camping travelling on foot, by bicycle, canoe or ski
- ● Mtgs - Inf - Lib - Informal weekends
- M 1,150 i, UK / 24 i, o'seas
- ¶ Backpack (Jnl) - 4; ftm only.

Badge Collectors Circle (BCC) 1980
- ■ 57 Middleton Place, LOUGHBOROUGH, Leics, LE11 2BY.   (sp)
  01509 569270
  email f.setchfield@ntlworld.com
  Editor: Frank Setchfield
- ○ *G; collecting non-military, enamel & tin lapel badges as a hobby
- Gp Badges: Button, Enamel
- ● Mtgs - Res - SG - Inf - Swapping badges
- M 450 i, 2 f, UK / 6 i, o'seas
- ¶ The Badger (NL) - 6; £15 yr (£2.50 each).

Badger Face Welsh Mountain Sheep Society (Cymdeithas Defaid Torddu Cymreig Torwen) (BFWMSS) 1976
- ■ Stall House, VOWCHURCH, Herefords, HR2 0QD.   (hsp)
  01981 550685
  email lucy.levinge@fwi.co.uk
  http://www.badgerfacesheep.co.uk
  Gen Sec: Miss L K Levinge
- ▲ Un-incorporated Society
- ○ *B
- ● Mtgs - Exhib - Comp
- M 250 i, UK / 2 i, o'seas
- ¶ NL - 4; ftm only.   Flockbook - 1; ftm, £5 nm.

Badger Trust
  the working name of **National Federation of Badger Groups**

Badminton Association of England (BA of E) 1893
- NR National Badminton Centre, Bradwell Rd, Loughton Lodge, MILTON KEYNES, Bucks, MK8 9LA.   (hq)
  01908 268400
  http://www.baofe.co.uk
  Chief Exec: Stephen Baddeley
- ▲ Company Limited by Guarantee
- Br 41 assns
- ○ *S; the governing body for the game of Badminton in England, the Channel Islands and the Isle of Man
- Gp Badminton Umpires Association; English Schools' Badminton Association; Regional coaching scheme
- ● Conf - Mtgs - ET - Exam - Exhib - Comp - Stat - Inf - VE - LG
- < Intl Badminton Fedn; Eur Badminton U
- M 45,000 i, 2,000 clubs
- ¶ Badminton Magazine - 4.   Coaches Register - 4.
  ESBA Post - 10.   Ybk.   AR & Accounts.
  Note: trading as BADMINTON England.

Badminton Umpires Association
  a group of the **Badminton Association of England**

Bagpipe Society   1985
- ■ 11 Queens Place, OTLEY, W Yorks, LS21 3HY.   (mem/sp)
  email bagpipes@snozz.com
  http://www.bagpipesociety.org.uk
  Mem Sec: Michael Ross
- ▲ Un-incorporated Society
- ○ *D; to promote the playing & music of bagpipes, including English, Scottish, French, Spanish & Balkan bagpipes
- ● Workshops
- M 250 i, UK / 100 i, o'seas
- ¶ Chanter - 4; ftm, £3 on request nm.

Bakers', Food & Allied Workers' Union   (BFAWU)   1849
NR   Stanborough House, Great North Rd, Stanborough,
        WELWYN GARDEN CITY, Herts, AL8 7TA.   (hq)
        01707 260150
        Gen Sec: Joe Marino
Br   235; Ireland
○   *U
Gp   Health & safety; National Information Technology Centre
        (Preston)
●   Conf - Mtgs - ET - Res - Exhib - Stat - Inf - Lib - PL - VE - Empl -
        LG
<   Intl U for Food Workers; Eur C'ee of Food Workers
M   29,325 i, UK / 1,025 i, o'seas
¶   Food Worker - 6.

Balint Society   1969
■   Tollgate Medical Centre, 220 Tollgate Rd, LONDON, E6 5JS.
        (hsb)
        020 7473 9399   fax 020 7473 9388
        email david.watt@gp-f84093.nhs.uk
        http://www.balint.co.uk
        Hon Sec: Dr David E Watt
▲   Registered Charity
○   *L; an organisation of general practitioners seeking to promote
        the study of the healer-patient relationship, particularly in
        general practice, as first investigated by the psychoanalyst
        Dr Michael Balint
●   Conf - Mtgs - ET - Res - Comp - SG
<   Intl Balint Fedn
>   Assn Psychosexual Nursing
M   140 i, UK / 50 i, o'seas
¶   Jnl - 1; ftm, £8 nm.

Ball & Roller Bearing Manufacturers Association   (BRBMA)
■   Heathcote House, 136 Hagley Rd, BIRMINGHAM, B16 9PN.
        (asa)
        0121-454 4141   fax 0121-454 4949
        email info@brbma.org   http://www.brbma.org
        Sec: Victor Lyttle
▲   Un-incorporated Society
○   *T
Gp   Standards
●   Conf - Mtgs - Stat - Standards
<   Fedn of European Bearing Mfrs Assn (FEBMA)
M   6 f

Ballroom Dancers Federation   (BDF)   1956
NR   12 Warren Lodge Drive, KINGSWOOD, Surrey, KT20 6QN.
        (sp)
        Sec: David Sycamore
▲   Un-incorporated Society
○   *D; competitive ballroom & Latin American dancing

Ballymena Borough Chamber of Commerce & Industry
NR   4 Wellington Court, Wellington St, BALLYMENA, BT43 6EQ.
        (hq)
        Pres: William McKean
○   *C
×   2006 Ballymena Chamber of Commerce & Industry

Baltic Air Charter Association   (BACA)   1949
■   c/o The Baltic Exchange, St Mary Axe, LONDON, EC3A 8BH.
        (hsb)
        020 7623 5501   fax 020 7369 1623
        http://www.baca.org.uk
        Chmn: Stephen F Wells
▲   Un-incorporated Society
○   *T; chartering, sale, purchase & lease of aircraft
●   Conf - Mtgs - Inf
M   86 f, UK / 14 f, o'seas
¶   LM - 1;   AR; both ftm only.   Diaries - 1; £7.50.

Balwen Welsh Mountain Sheep Society   1985
NR   Ty-deri, Llanethrine, ABERGAVENNY, Gwent, NP7 8PY.   (hsp)
        01873 821224
        Sec: Chris Lewis
○   *B
●   Mtgs - Exhib - Comp
<   Nat Sheep Assn
M   150 i

Bamboo Society
        since 2005-06 **British Bamboo Society**

Banana Group
        ceased trading 2005

Banbury & District Chamber of Commerce   1947
■   Mercia House, 51 The Green, South Bar Street, BANBURY,
        Oxon, OX16 9AB.   (hq)
        01295 201140   fax 01295 201142
        email bcoc@banburychamber.com
        http://www.banburychamber.com
        Sec: Simon Smith
▲   Company Limited by Guarantee
○   *C; business interests of Banbury & the surrounding area
Gp   Business & professional; Industrial; Retail
●   Mtgs
M   3 i, 150 f, 1 org
¶   NL - 6.   AR.

Bankruptcy Association   1983
■   4 Johnson Close, Abraham Heights, LANCASTER, LA1 5EU.
        (hq)
        01524 64305   fax 01524 389717
        email bankruptcyassociation@gbandi.freeserve.co.uk
        http://www.theba.org.uk
        Chief Exec: John McQueen
▲   Un-incorporated Society
○   *K, *W; to provide help & advice to bankrupts & debtors; to
        campaign for reform of insolvency legislation
●   Mtgs - Res - Inf - LG
M   c 1,500 i
¶   NL - 3; free.
        Bankruptcy Explained.
        List of books available.
×   2002-03 Bankruptcy Association of Great Britain & Ireland

Bantock Society
        this society is inactive at present (2006)

Baptist Historical Society   1908
NR   PO Box 44, 129 Broadway, DIDCOT, Oxon, OX11 8RT.
        (regd/office)
        01235 517700
        email stephen.bhs@dial.pipex.com
        Sec: Rev S L Copson
▲   Registered Charity
○   *L, *Q; study of Baptist history in the UK
●   Conf - Mtgs - Res - Inf - Lib
M   600 including 150 libraries, churches & colleges
¶   Baptist Quarterly - 4.

Baptist Union of Great Britain   (BU)   1812
NR PO Box 44, 129 Broadway, DIDCOT, Oxon, OX11 8RT.   (hq)
   01235 517700   fax 01235 517715
   http://www.baptist.org.uk
   Gen Sec: Rev Jonathan Edwards
○ *R
Gp Theological; Sociological; Current affairs; Christian education;
   Women; Young people; Trusts & property; Pensions; Christian
   ministry
● Conf - Mtgs - Exhib - SG - Stat - Inf - Lib - VE
< Baptist Wld Alliance; Free Church Federal Coun; Conf of Eur
   Churches; Eur Baptist Fedn; Coun of Churches for Britain &
   Ireland; Churches Together in England
M c 140,000 i in 2,000 churches, 6 theological colleges
¶ Baptist Times - 52.
   Baptist Union Directory - 1.   AR - 1.

Bar Association for Commerce, Finance & Industry   (BACFI)
1965
NR PO Box 3663, BRACKNELL, Berks, RG12 2FH.   (mail)
   01344 868752 address
   Sec: Lesley Whitlow
○ *L, *P; to represent the interests of members of The Bar who are
   employed in commerce, finance & industry
M i
× 2004 Employed & Non-Practising Bar Association (merged)

Bar Association for Local Government & the Public Service
(BALGPS)   1945
NR Chief Legal Officer, Birmingham City Council, Ingleby House,
   11-14 Cannon St, BIRMINGHAM, B2 5EN.   (chmn/treas/b)
   0121-303 9991
   email chairman@balgps.org.uk
   http://www.balgps.org.uk
   Chmn/Treas: M F N Ahmad
▲ Un-incorporated Society
○ *P; professional rights of barristers in local government & the
   public sector
● Conf - ET - Inf - LG - Representation on Bar Council
M c 110 i
¶ NL;   Careers for Barristers in Local Government, 1998;
   Barristers in Local Government - facts, 1998; all free.
   Implications of the Human Rights Act 1998 for UK Local
   Government (1999); ftm.

Bar Entertainment & Dance Association   (BEDA)
NR 5 Waterloo Rd, Stockport, Cheshire, SK1 3BD.
   0161-429 0012

Barbirolli Society   1972
NR 2 Cedar Close, UTTOXETER, Staffs, ST14 7NP.   (chmn)
   01889 564562   fax 01889 564562 p
   Hon Chmn: Miss R P Pickering
▲ Registered Charity
○ *D; to advance knowledge, understanding & appreciation of
   music in general & of the work of Sir John Barbirolli in
   particular
M 400 i, UK / 50 i, o'seas
¶ Jnl - 2;   NL - irreg; both ftm only.

Barema   (BAREMA)   1977
■ The Stables, Sugworth Lane, RADLEY, Oxon, OX14 2HX.   (hq)
   01865 736393   fax 01865 736393
   email barema@btinternet.com
   http://www.barema.org.uk
   Chmn: M F Freeman,   Sec: Harrie Cooke
▲ Company Limited by Guarantee
○ *T: to promote the interests of suppliers to the NHS/private
   sector for anaesthetic & respiratory products
● Mtgs - Inf - LG
< Eur Med Device Tr Assn (EUROM VI); Assn of Brit Health Care
   Inds (ABHI)
M 31 f
¶ Barema Hbk - updated; ftm, £10 nm.
× 2003-04 British Anaesthetic & Respiratory Equipment
   Manufacturers' Association

Barge Association
   see correct title **Dutch Barge Association**

Barking & Dagenham Chamber of Commerce   1995
NR Roycraft House (ground floor), 15 Linton Rd, BARKING, Essex,
   IG11 8HE.   (hq)
   020 8591 6966
   Admin: John Tame
▲ Company Limited by Guarantee
○ *C
● Mtgs - ET - Inf - VE - LG
< London Cham Comm & Ind
M 180 f
¶ NL - 12;   Ybk - 1; both free.

Barn Owl Conservation Network
   a group of the **Hawk & Owl Trust**

Barnsley Chamber of Commerce & Industry   (BCCI)   1882
NR Barnsley Business & Innovation Centre, Innovation Way,
   Wilthorpe, BARNSLEY, S Yorks, S75 1JL.   (hq)
   01226 217770
   http://www.barnsleychamber.co.uk
   Chief Exec: R J Nunns
▲ Company Limited by Guarantee
○ *C
Gp Business club; Export club; Law & order forum; Education
   forum; Town centre forum
● Conf - Mtgs - ET - Exhib - SG - Stat - Expt - Inf - LG
< Brit Chams Comm (BCC)
M c 900 f
¶ The Review - 12; ftm only.   LM - 1; ftm.

BaseballSoftballUK   (BSUK)   1890
■ Ariel House (5th floor), 74A Charlotte St, LONDON,
   W1T 4QJ.   (hq)
   020 7453 7055   fax 020 7453 7007
   email info@baseballsoftballuk.com
   http://www.baseballsoftballuk.com
   Chief Operations Dir: John Boyd
▲ Un-incorporated Society
○ *S; to promote the games of Baseball & Softball in Britain
Gp Scorers; Umpires; Coaching; Old Timers; Players
● Conf - Mtgs - ET - Comp - Stat - Inf - PL
< Brit Olympic Assn (BOA); Intl Baseball Assn (IBA); Confedn of
   Eur Amat Baseball; CCPR
M c 1,500 i, 50 teams (baseball); c 3,000 i, 240 teams (softball)
¶ Baseball & Softball Bulletins - 12;
   Information booklets; all free.
× 2002 (British Baseball Federation
        (British Softball Federation

Basement Development Group
   has been formalised as the Basement Information Centre,
   which is outside the scope of this Directory.

Basketball Association of Wales (BAW) 1956
NR c/o 30 Eileen Place, Treherbert, CARDIFF, CF42 5BU. (hsp)
Sec: Will Jones
○ *S; governing body for basketball in Wales

Basketball Ireland
is the marketing name of the **Irish Basketball Association**

Basketball Scotland
is the marketing name of the **Scottish Basketball Association**

Basketmaker's Association (BA) 1975
■ Glenwayth, Hervines Rd, AMERSHAM, Bucks, HP6 5HS. (hsp)
0845 201 1936
email rae@glenwayth.wanadoo.co.uk
http://www.basketassoc.org
Hon Sec: Rae Gillott
○ *T; to promote the design, practice & teaching of basket
making, chair seating & allied crafts
● ET - Exam - Exhib - Inf - PL
M 800 i, UK / 100 i, o'seas
¶ NL - 4; ftm, £20 nm.

Basketware Importers Association
this organisation has been reported to us as no longer in
existence - confirmation would be appreciated

Basking Shark Society 1995
■ Cronk Mooar, Curragh Rd, ST JOHN'S, Isle of Man,
IM4 3LN. (hq)
01624 801207
email kenwatterson@iom.com
http://www.isle-of-man.com/interests/shark/index.htm
▲ Registered Charity
○ *G, *K; research into & preservation of basking sharks
● ET - Res
¶ NL - 2.   Basking Shark & Whale Report - 1.

**BASO ~ the Association for Cancer Surgery (BASO-ACS)
1973**
■ at the Royal College of Surgeons, 35-43 Lincoln's Inn Fields,
LONDON, WC2A 3PE. (hq)
020 7405 5612   fax 020 7404 6574
email lucydavies@baso.org.uk   http://www.baso.org.uk
Hon Sec: Andrew Baildam
▲ Registered Charity
○ *P; to advance the practice of surgical oncology for surgeons
involved with cancer
Gp Association of Breast Surgery at BASO; British Stomach Cancer
Gp
● Conf - Mtgs - ET
M 740 i, UK / 20 i, o'seas
¶ European Jnl of Surgical Oncology - 6; ftm.
Note: this organisation deals with enquiries from professional
members ONLY & does not answer queries from the general
public.
✕ 2003 British Association of Surgical Oncology

BASP UK Ltd 1978
■ 20 Lorn Drive, GLENCOE, Argyllshire, PH49 4HR. (hsp)
01855 811443
email skipatrol@basp.org.uk   http://www.basp.org.uk
Sec: Fiona Gunn
▲ Company Limited by Guarantee
○ *P; ski patrol & rescue; exchange of knowledge & information
internationally with other patrollers
Gp First aid training in the outdoors; Training & grading of ski
patrollers
● ET - Stat
< Fédn Intl Patrouilles de Ski (FIPS); Brit Assn of Snowsport
Instructors (BASI)
M 125 i, UK / 5 i, o'seas
¶ NL - 4.   BASP Outdoor First Aid & Safety Manual; £10.
✕ 2004 British Association of Ski Patrollers

Bat Conservation Trust (BCT) 1990
NR 15 Cloisters House, 8 Battersea Park Rd, LONDON,
SW8 4BG. (hq)
020 7627 2629
email enquiries@bats.org.uk   http://www.bats.org.uk
Chief Exec: Amy Coyte
▲ Company Limited by Guarantee; Registered Charity
○ *K; the conservation of bats & their habitats; to stop further
declines in populations & aid the recovery of threatened
species
● Conf - ET - Res - Exhib
M c 4,000 i in 90 gps
¶ Bat News - 4;   Young Batworker - 4;
Bat Monitoring Post - 4; all ftm.
Books & educational leaflets.

Bates Association for Vision Education (BAVE) 1989
NR 11 Crest Rd, LONDON, NW2 7LT. (hsp)
020 8452 3473
http://www.seeing.org
Hon Sec: Nora Mathews
▲ Un-incorporated Society
○ *P; to advance the knowledge & practice of the methods of
visual re-education developed by the late William H Bates
● Conf - ET - Inf
< Inst Complementary Medicine
M 27 i, UK / 3 i, o'seas
¶ Vision Education News (NL) - 4.

Bath Chamber of Commerce Inc 1902
■ Trimbridge House, Trim St, BATH, Somerset, BA1 1PB. (hq)
01225 460655
▲ Company Limited by Guarantee
○ *C
< is part of Business West the trading name of the Bristol
Chamber of Commerce & Industry
M i, f & org

Bathroom Manufacturers' Association (BMA) 2001
NR Federation House, Station Rd, STOKE-ON-TRENT, Staffs,
ST4 2RT. (hq)
01782 747123
Sec: Yvonne Orgill
▲ Un-incorporated Society
○ *T; interests of bathroom manufacturers trading in the UK
● Conf - Mtgs - Stat - Expt - Inf - LG
< Builders' Merchants Fedn (BMF); Construction Products
Assn (CPA); Inst of Plumbing (IoP); Assn of Plumbing &
Heating Contrs (APHC)
M 17 f, 1 org
¶ Factsheets - 1;   LM - irreg; both ftm only.

Batten Disease Family Association (BDFA) 1998
■ c/o Heather House, Heather Drive, TADLEY, Hants,
RG26 4QR. (mail/address)
0791 406 0742
http://www.bdfa-uk.org.uk
Sec: Debbie Jordan
▲ Registered Charity
○ *M, *W; to promote the welfare of persons affected by all tupes
of neuronal ceroid lipofuscinosis (Batten disease); to advance
the education of the medical profession & general public on
the disease & its implications for the family
● Conf - ET - Res - Direct family liaison
< Batten Disease Support & Res Assn (BDSRA) [in Australia, New
Zealand, USA]
M c 160 i, associates
¶ NL - 2; ftm.

Battery Vehicle Society   (BVS)   1973
- ■ Coasters Cottage, Hermitage, DORCHESTER, DT2 7BB.
  (chmn/p)
  01963 210449
  http://www.bvs.org.uk
  Chmn: Alan Ward,   Sec: John Lilly
- ▲ Un-incorporated Society
- Br 3
- ○ *K; the exchange of information on battery-powered vehicles
- ● Mtgs - Exhib - Comp - Inf - Lib - VE
  01874 730320 (for road vehicle coordinator & competitions)
- < Transport Trust
- M 361 i, UK / 20 i, o'seas
- ¶ Battery Vehicle Review - 6; ftm, £12 yr nm (subscription).

Battle of Britain Historical Society
- NR Greenfields, Gunthorpe, MELTON CONSTABLE, Norfolk, NR24 2NS.
  01263 861476
  email billatBOBHS@aol.com
  http://www.battleofbritain.net
  Chief Exec: Bill Bond
- ▲ Registered Charity
- ○ *L; 'education of the young regarding the Battle of Britain'
- ● Conf - Mtgs - ET
- M c 1,500 i
- ¶ Scramble (NL) - 6.
  Battle of Britain Remembered - 1.

Battlefields Trust   1993
- ■ Meadow Cottage, 33 High Green, Brooke, NORWICH, Norfolk, NR15 1HR.   (regd/office)
  01508 558145   fax 01508 558145
  email battlefieldtrust@aol.com
  http://www.battlefieldstrust.com
  Mem Sec: Michael Rayner
- ▲ Company Limited by Guarantee; Registered Charity
- ○ *K; preservation, interpretation & presentation of battlefields worldwide
- ● Conf - ET - Res - Inf - VE
- M 380 i, 5 f, 15 org, UK / 10 i, o'seas
- ¶ NL - 4; ftm only.

Bead Society of Great Britain   (BSGB)   1989
- ■ 1 Casburn Lane, Burwell, CAMBRIDGE, CB5 0ED.   (hsp)
  01638 742024   fax 01638 742024
  email carole.morris2@ntlworld.com
  http://www.beadsociety.freeserve.co.uk
  Hon Sec: Dr Carole Morris
- ▲ Un-incorporated Society
- ○ *G; for all interested, either privately or professionally, in beads ancient & modern, of all shapes, sizes, materials & colours, their techniques of manufacture & their application
- ● Mtgs - Exhib - Workshops - Annual fair
- M 1,050 i, UK / 50 i, o'seas
- ¶ NL - 5; ftm only.

BEAMA: British Electrotechnical & Allied Manufacturers' Associations   (BEAMA)   1905
- ■ Westminster Tower, 3 Albert Embankment, LONDON, SE1 7SL.   (hq)
  020 7793 3000   fax 020 7793 3003
  Chief Exec: David Dossett
- ○ *N, *T; the national grouping of trade associations serving the electrical, electronic & allied manufacturing industries in Britain
- Gp BEAMA Installation (BINST) (Dir: Dr Howard Porter)
  for manufacturers of electrical installation & cable management equipment
  BEAMA Energy (BENERGY) (Dir: Dr Howard Porter)
  BEAMA Metering & Communications Association (BEMCA)
  Domestic Water Treatment Association (DWTA)
  European Association of Copper Clad Laminate Manufacturers (ELAM)
  Control Manufacturers Association incorporating the Domestic Heating Controls Group (TACMA)
  Electric Heating & Ventilation Association (TEHVA)
  Thermostatic Mixing Valves Association (TMVA)
  BEAMA Power (BPOWER) (Dir: Nigel Grant)
  BEAMA Power Ltd
  BEAMA Capacitor Manufacturers' Association (BCMA)
  Rotating Electrical Machines Association (REMA)
  Welding Manufacturers' Association
- ● Conf - Exhib - Stat - LG
- M [see groups above]
- ¶ BEAMA Bulletin - 4; ftm only.   AR; free.

BEAMA Capacitor Manufacturers' Association
  as part of BEAMA Power Ltd, is a group of **BEAMA**

BEAMA Energy
  is a group of **BEAMA**

BEAMA Installation
  a group of **BEAMA**

BEAMA Metering & Communications Association
  a part of BEAMA Energy a group of **BEAMA**

BEAMA Power
  a group of **BEAMA**

Bean Curd & Tofu Canners & Preservers Group   1976
- ■ 32 Coombe End, CROWBOROUGH, E Sussex, TN6 1NH.
  (mail) address
- ○ *T
- Gp Freeze drying
- ● Conf - Mtgs - Stat - LG
- M 17 f
- ¶ AR; ftm only.

Beat - beating eating disorders
  the working title of the **Eating Disorders Association**

Beatrix Potter Society   1980
- NR The Lodge, Salisbury Avenue, HARPENDEN, Herts, AL5 2PS.
  (admin/p)
  01582 769755
  Mem Sec: Jenny Akester
- ▲ Registered Charity
- ○ *L; to promote the study & appreciation of the life & works of Beatrix Potter (1866-1943) author, artist, diarist, farmer & conservationist
- ● Conf - Mtgs - VE
- M c 750 i
- ¶ NL - 4.   LM - 1.   Books.
  Studies (papers presented at conferences) - 2 yrly.

Beaumont Society   (BS)   1966
- 27 Old Gloucester St, LONDON, WC1N 3XX.   (mail)
  01582 412220
  email enquiries@beaumontsociety.org.uk
  http://www.beaumontsociety.org.uk address
  Pres: Janett Scott
○ *W; self-help group for those that cross-dress, or who are
  transsexual; support for partners & families
Gp Transvestite; Transsexual
● Conf - Mtgs - ET - Res - Lib - VE
< Beaumont Trust
M 852 i, UK / 22 i, o'seas
¶ Beaumont Magazine - 4; ftm.

Beckford Society   1995
- The Timber Cottage, Crockerton, WARMINSTER, Wilts,
  BA12 8AX.   (hsp)
  01985 213195
  email sidney.blackmore@btinternet.com
  Hon Sec: Sidney Blackmore
▲ Un-incorporated Society
○ *A; to promote interest in the life & work of William Beckford,
  writer & art collector (1760-1844)
● Conf - Mtgs - SG - VE
M 151 i, 5 f, UK / 101 i, o'seas
¶ The Beckford Jnl - 1; ftm, £10 nm.   NL - 2; ftm only.

Bedfordshire, Cambridgeshire, Northamptonshire & Peterborough Wildlife
Trust
  since 2003-04 the **Wildlife Trust for Bedfordshire,**
  Cambridgeshire, Northamptonshire & Peterborough

Bedfordshire Historical Record Society   (BHRS)   1912
- 48 St Augustine's Rd, BEDFORD, MK40 2ND.   (hsp)
  01234 309548
  email rsmart@ntlworld.com
  Hon Sec: Dr Richard Smart
▲ Company Limited by Guarantee; Registered Charity
○ *L; the publication of sources & monographs relating to the
  history of Bedfordshire
● Res
M 150 i, 50 org, UK / 50 i, 50 org, o'seas
¶ Vauxhall Motors & the Luton Economy 1900-2002 - 1; £12 m,
  £25 nm.

Bee Farmers Association of the United Kingdom   (BFA)
NR 8 Olivers Close, West Totton, SOUTHAMPTON, Hants,
  SO40 8FH.   (hsp/b)
  023 8090 7850
  Gen Sec: John Howat
○ *P, *T
● Conf - Mtgs - Exhib - Stat - Inf - VE - LG
< NFU
M c 300 i
¶ Bulletin - 8;   Products Directory - 1;   LM - 1; all ftm only.

Bee Improvement & Bee Breeders Association   (BIBBA)   1964
NR 26 Coldharbour Lane, Hildenborough, TONBRIDGE, Kent,
  TN11 8JT.   (sec/p)
  01732 833984
  Sec: John Hendrie
▲ Registered Charity
○ *B, *G; conservation, restoration, study, selection &
  improvement of our native honeybees of GB & Ireland
● Conf - Mtgs - Exhib
M 350 i, UK / 20 i, o'seas
¶ Bee Improvement - 4.

Beef Shorthorn Cattle Society   1936
NR 4th Street, Stoneleigh Park, KENILWORTH, Warks, CV8 2LG.
  (hq)
  024 7669 6549   fax 024 7669 6729
  email shorthorn@shorthorn.co.uk
  http://www.shorthorn.co.uk
  Sec: Frank Milnes
▲ Registered Charity
○ *B
● Conf - Mtgs - Res - Exhib - Comp - SG - Stat - Expt - Inf - PL -
  VE - Empl
M 330 i, UK / 30 i, o'seas
¶ Shorthorn Jnl - 1.   Coates Herd Book - 1.

Behçet's Syndrome Society   1983
- 3 Church Close, Lambourn, HUNGERFORD, Berks,
  RG17 8PU.   (chief/exec/p)
  01488 71116
  http://www.behcets.org.uk
  Chief Exec: Mrs Georgina Seaman
▲ Registered Charity
○ *M, *W; a charity providing a contact support network,
  information & financial aid for sufferers of the disease (a
  vasculitic disorder with orogenital ulceration, uveitis &
  arthritis)
● Conf - Res - Inf
< Longterm Medical Conditions Alliance (LMCA); UK Rare
  Diseases Assn
M 1,650 i, UK / 70 i, o'seas
¶ NL - 2;   Leaflets; free.

Belgian-Luxembourg Chamber of Commerce in Great Britain
(BLCC)
- Riverside House, 27-29 Vauxhall Grove, LONDON, SW8 1SY.
  0870 246 1610   fax 0870 429 2148
  email info@blcc.co.uk   http://www.blcc.co.uk
  Chief Exec: Michel Van Hoonacker
▲ Company Limited by Guarantee
○ *C; to help Belgian & Luxembourg companies exporting to the
  UK, & British companies wishing to do business with Belgian
  & Luxembourg exporters
● Conf - Mtgs - ET - Res - Exhib - Comp - SG - Expt - Inf - VE -
  Empl - LG
< Coun of Foreign Chams Comm; Belgian Fedn of Chams
  Comm
M 12 i, 68 f, UK / 49 f, o'seas
¶ BELUX (NL) - 3; ftm.

Belted Galloway Cattle Society   1922
NR Parklea, TONGLAND, Kirkcudbrightshire, DG6 4ND.   (hsp)
  Sec: Myrna Corrie
○ *B
● Mtgs - Exhib - Expt
< Nat Beef Assn
M 380 i, UK / 50 i, o'seas
¶ Belted Galloway News - 1.

Beltex Sheep Society   1989
- Lawns Farm, Orrell, WIGAN, Lancs, WN5 8UH.   (hq)
  01695 627626   fax 01695 627626
  email beltexsheep@aol.com   http://www.beltex.co.uk
  Sec: Miss Helen Ashton
▲ Company Limited by Guarantee
○ *B
● Mtgs - ET - Res
< Nat Sheep Assn
M 400 i
¶ Ybk - 1; free.

Benesh Institute of Choreology
  see **Royal Academy of Dance incorporating the Benesh**
  Institute

© CBD Research Ltd · Beckenham · BR3 5JS · Tel 020 8650 7745 · Fax 020 8650 0768 · E-mail cbd@cbdresearch.com · www.cbdresearch.com

Bereavement Care
see **Cruse - Bereavement Care**

Berkshire Archaeological Society   1871
NR   19 Challenor Close, WOKINGHAM, Berks, RG40 4UJ.   (hsp)
       0118-973 2882
       Hon Sec: Andrew Hutt
▲   Registered Charity
○   *L, *Q

Berkshire Archaeology Research Group   (BARG)   1958
■   20 Rances Lane, WOKINGHAM, Berks, RG40 2LH.   (chmn/p)
       0118-978 2161
       email GCJohnson@oakingham.freeserve.co.uk
       http://www.berkshire-archaeology.info
       Chmn: G C Johnson
▲   Un-incorporated Society
○   *L; to provide an opportunity for people to partake in the
       practical investigation, understanding & publication of
       archaeology in Berkshire
Gp   Archive research; Excavation; Fieldworking; Geophysical
       surveying; Hedgerow dating; Post-excavation analysis; Site
       monitoring
●   Mtgs - ET - Res - Exhib - Inf - Lib - VE
M   65 i, UK / 1 i, o'seas
¶   In the Field (NL) - 4.
×   2002 Berkshire Field Research Group

Berkshire Field Research Group
       since 2002 **Berkshire Archaeology Research Group**

Berlioz Society   1952
NR   12 Elm Way, LONDON, N11 3NP.   (hsp)
       020 8361 6771
       email elgarbrown@aol.com
       Sec: Adrian Brown
▲   Un-incorporated Society
○   *D; to bring together & provide a focal point for all enthusiasts
       of the music & writing of Hector Berlioz
●   Mtgs - Lib
M   46 i, UK / 66 i, 20 libraries, o'seas
¶   The Bulletin - 3;   NL - 4; both ftm only.

Berwickshire Agricultural Association   1885
■   The Cottage, Nabdean Farm, PAXTON, Berwickshire,
       TD15 1SZ.   (hsb)
       01289 386412   fax 01289 386852
       email dunsshow@btopenworld.com
       Sec: Natalie Cormack
▲   Registered Charity
○   *F; to promote the interests of agriculture primarily through the
       organisation of the Berwickshire County Show
●   Exhib - Comp
M   250 i, 75 f
¶   Show Schedule & Catalogue.   AR.

Berwickshire Naturalists' Club   (BNC)   1831
■   c/o The Borough Museum, The Barracks, BERWICK-UPON-
       TWEED, TD15 1DQ.   (hq)
       01289 330933
▲   Registered Charity
○   *L; all matters connected with the natural history & antiquities of
       Berwickshire & North Northumberland
●   Mtgs - Res - Exhib - Stat - Inf - Lib - VE
<   Coun Brit Archaeology
M   360 i, 39 org
¶   History of the Berwickshire Naturalists' Club - 1; ftm, £10 nm.

BESO (British Executive Service Overseas)
       in April 2005 merged with **Voluntary Service Overseas**

Betjeman Society   1988
■   6 St Anne's Rd, SHREWSBURY, Shropshire, SY3 6AU.   (hsp)
       01743 350372
       email colin@colin-wright.freeserve.co.uk
       Hon Sec: Colin Wright
▲   Un-incorporated Society
Br   7
○   *A; 'to advance the education of the public in the works of Sir
       John Betjeman by promoting the knowledge, appreciation &
       study of his life & works'
●   Mtgs - ET - Res - Exhib - VE
M   878 i, 4 f, UK / 17 i, 2 f, o'seas
¶   The Betjemanian (Jnl) - 1.

Better Brickwork Alliance   (BBA)   1999
■   c/o BDA, Woodside House, Winkfield, WINDSOR, Berks,
       SL4 2DX.   (hsb)
       01344 885651   fax 01344 890129
       email brick@brick.org.uk
       Sec: Michael Driver
▲   Un-incorporated Society
○   *N, *T; an alliance of organisations interested in the
       development of all aspects of masonry, with special interest
       in the training / recruitment of craftspeople
●   Mtgs - ET
M   15 f

Betting Office Licensees Association
       November 2002 merged with the British Betting Office Association to
       become the **Association of British Bookmakers**

Beverage Council of Ireland
IRL   Unit 19a Naas Road Business Park, DUBLIN 12, Republic of
       Ireland.
       353 (1) 460 0811   fax 353 (1) 460 0814
       email bci@esatlink.com
       Dir: Bernard J Murphy
○   *T

Beverage Service Association
NR   Hartfield House, 40-44 High St, NORTHWOOD, Middx,
       HA6 1UJ.
       01923 848392
       Exec Dir: Dr Jim Devlin
○   *T

Bewick Society   1985
■   c/o Natural History Society of Northumbria, The Hancock
       Museum, NEWCASTLE UPON TYNE, NE2 4PT.   (hsb)
       http://www.bewicksociety.org
       Hon Sec: Dr David Gardner-Medwin
▲   Un-incorporated Society
○   *L; to study the life & work of Thomas Bewick (naturalist &
       wood engraver, 1753-1828); to encourage wood engraving
●   Mtgs - VE
M   140 i, UK / 10 i, o'seas
¶   Cherryburn Times - 2; ftm only.

BFM Ltd (British Furniture Manufacturers)   (BFM)   1943
NR   30 Harcourt St, LONDON, W1H 4HT.   (hq)
       020 7724 0851   fax 020 7706 1924
       email info@bfm.org.uk   http://www.bfm.org.uk
       Managing Director: Roger Mason
▲   Company Limited by Guarantee
○   *T; the manufacture, sale & export of furniture
●   ET - Res - Exhib - Stat - Expt - Inf - Empl - LG
M   378 f
¶   Export Directory - 1;   UK Directory of Members - 1; both free.

Biblical Creation Society   (BCS)   1976
NR   PO Box 22, RUGBY, Warks, CV22 7SY.   (mail)
         01788 810633
         http://www.biblicalcreation.org.uk address
         Sec: Dr David J Tyler
▲   Registered Charity (Scotland)
○   *L, *R; a Christian society that advances & defends biblical
         teaching on creation; to think through issues related to
         origins from a biblical & scientific standpoint; to challenge
         Christians who have accepted the evolutionary theory
●   Mtgs - ET - Lectures
M   c 500 i
¶   Origins (Jnl) - 2.
         The Creation Manifesto (a systematic overview of the...
         implications of the Genesis account of the Creation).

Bibliographical Society   1892
■   c/o Institute of English Studies, University of London,
         Senate House, Malet St, LONDON, WC1E 7HU.   (hsb)
         020 7862 8679
         email admin@bibsoc.org.uk   http://www.bibsoc.org.uk
         Sec: Margaret Ford
▲   Registered Charity
○   *L; promotion of study & research of historical, analytical,
         descriptive & textual bibliography; the history of the book
         (printing, publishing, collecting & bookbinding)
●   Mtgs - Res - Lib - Awards grants to support bibliographical
         research
M   400 i, 100 f, UK / 400 i, 100 f, o'seas
¶   The Library - 4; £33 m.   AR; ftm.
         Monographs - irreg; prices vary.

Bicycle Association of Great Britain Ltd   1973
■   Starley House, Eaton Rd, COVENTRY, Warks, CV1 2FH.   (hq)
         024 7655 3838
         email office@ba-gb.com
         Sec: Mrs Patricia Morris
○   *T
Gp   Mfrs: Bicycles, components & accessories; Concessionaires
         (bicycles); Ancillary members
●   Mtgs - Exhib - Stat - LG
<   Comité de Liaison des Fabricants de Pièces et Equipements de
         Deux-Roues (COLIPED)
M   50 f
¶   AR.   LM.

Bingo Association   (BAGB)   1998
NR   Lexham House, 75 High Street North, DUNSTABLE, Beds,
         LU6 1JF.   (hq)
         01582 860921
         email info@bingo-association.co.uk
         http://www.bingo-association.co.uk
         Chief Exec: Paul Talboys
▲   Un-incorporated Society
○   *T; to promote & develop the interests of the licensed bingo
         industry; to represent members' interests in contact with third
         parties
●   Conf - Mtgs - Res - Stat - Inf - LG
M   125 f

Biochemical Society   1911
■   Eagle House (3rd floor), 16 Procter St, LONDON,
         WC1V 6NX.   (hq)
         020 7280 4110   fax 020 7280 4170
         email genadim@biochemistry.org
         http://www.biochemistry.org
         Chief Exec: Dr Chris Kirk
▲   Registered Charity
Br   2
○   *L; to advance the science of biochemistry in the context of
         cellular & molecular life sciences as a seamless continuum
Gp   Theme panels: Genes, Molecular structure, Bioenergetics &
         metabolism, Cell biology, Biotechnology & bioinformatics,
         Development & disease & disease
●   Conf - Mtgs - ET - Res - Exhib - Stat - Inf
<   Fedn Eur Biochemical Socs; Intl U Biochemistry
M   6,000 i
¶   Biochemical Jnl - 24.   Clinical Science - 12.
         Transactions - 6.   Symposia - 1.
         Biotechnology & Applied Biochemistry - 6.
         Essays in Biochemistry - 2.

Biodynamic Agricultural Association   (BDAA)   1928
■   Painswick Inn Project, Gloucester St, STROUD, Glos,
         GL5 1QG.   (hq)
         01453 759501   fax 01453 759501
         email office@biodynamic.org.uk
         http://www.biodynamic.org.uk
         Exec Dir: Bernard Jarman
▲   Registered Charity
○   *F, *H, *Q; to support, promote & develop biodynamic farming,
         gardening & forestry; part of a worldwide movement inspired
         by the insights of Rudolf Steiner (1861-1925) Austrian
         philosopher, scientist & social reformer
Gp   Training; Demeter (organic certification UK6) scheme;
         Biodynamic seed gp
●   Conf - ET - Exhib - Inf - Lib - LG - Training apprenticeships -
         Res & devt of seeds suited to organic & biodynamic systems
<   Intl Fedn of Organic Agricl Movements (IFOAM);
         Anthroposophical Soc (GB); GM Freeze; Sustain; Agricl Dept
         of the School of Spiritual Science
M   800 i, UK / 50 i, o'seas
¶   Star & Furrow - 2; £4.50.   Newssheet - 4; free.

BioIndustry Association   (BIA)   1985
NR   14-15 Belgrave Sq, LONDON, SW1X 8PS.   (hq)
         020 7565 7190
         Chief Exec: Aisling Burnand
Br   BIA Scotland
○   *T; to promote the commercial interests of companies actively
         involved in biotechnology in the UK; interests include:
         biotechnology, genetic engineering, monoclonal antibodies,
         fermentation, pharmaceuticals, recombinant DNA; all
         aspects of industrial biotechnology
M   f & org
×   2001 Scottish Biomedical Association (merged & is now BIA
         Scotland & acts as the Scottish branch)

Biological Recording in Scotland   (BRISC)
■   140 Pitcorthie Drive, DUNFERMLINE, Fife, KY11 8BJ.
         (mem/sp)
         http://www.brisc.org.uk
         Mem Sec: Duncan Davidson
▲   Registered Charity
○   *P; to promote best practise in biological recording methods; to
         provide liaison between local records centres
●   Conf - ET - Inf
M   100 i, 30 f
¶   Recorder News - 4.

Biology Curators Group
         merged in 2003 with the Natural Sciences Conservation Group to
         form the **Natural Sciences Collections Association**

© CBD Research Ltd · Beckenham · BR3 5JS · Tel 020 8650 7745 · Fax 020 8650 0768 · E-mail cbd@cbdresearch.com · www.cbdresearch.com

Biosciences Federation (BSF) 2002

■ PO Box 502, CAMBRIDGE, CB1 0AL. (sb)
      01223 4001811   fax 01223 246858
      email info@bsf.ac.uk   http://www.bsf.ac.uk
      Chief Exec: Dr Richard Dyer
▲ Registered Charity
○ *L; to promote the advancement of the biosciences; to influence
      policy & strategy in biology-based research & in school &
      university teaching
Gp Animal science; European Liaison; Science policy; Education
      C'ee
● Conf - Inf - LG
M 40 i
¶ NL - 4;   Science Policy Report - 12;   E.U.News - 12.
   Science Policy Priorities 2005-2009.
   Building on Success.   Enthusing the Next Generation.
   [all online at:
      www.bsf.ac.uk/elg/default.htm   &
      www.bsf.ac.uk/newsletters.htm.]

Birdcare Standards Association

NR Market Link, 30 St George's Square, WORCESTER, WR1 1HX.
      01905 726575
      email enquiries@birdcare.org.uk
      Sec: Steve Paddock
○ *T
M 10 f

Birmingham Chamber of Commerce & Industry (BCCI) 1813

NR 75 Harborne Rd, Edgbaston, BIRMINGHAM, B15 3DH. (hq)
      0121-607 0809   fax 0121-455 8670
      email info@birminghamchamber.org.uk
      http://www.birmingham-chamber.com
      Chief Exec: Sue Battle
▲ Company Limited by Guarantee
Br 2
○ *C
● Conf - Mtgs - ET - Expt - Inf - LG
M 4,000 f

Birmingham Metallurgical Association (B MET A) 1903

NR c/o School of Metallurgy & Materials, University of Birmingham,
      Edgbaston, BIRMINGHAM, B15 2TT. (hsb)
      Hon Sec: Prof Rex Harris
▲ Company Limited by Guarantee
○ *L; to promote the science & application of engineering
      materials
● Conf - Mtgs - ET - Comp - VE
< Inst of Materials (IOM)
M c 120 i
¶ AR & Accounts; ftm only.

Birmingham & Midland Institute (BMI) 1854

■ 9 Margaret St, BIRMINGHAM, B3 3BS. (hq)
      0121-236 3591   fax 0121-212 4577
      email admin@bmi.org.uk   http://www.bmi.org.uk
      Admin & Gen Sec: Philip A Fisher
▲ Registered Charity
○ *A, *L; the diffusion & advancement of science, art & literature
Gp Birmingham & Midland Society for Genealogy & History;
      Society for the History of Astronomy
● Conf - Mtgs - ET - Res - SG - Lib
< Assn of Indep Libs
M 300 i
¶ BMI Insight - 1; ftm, £3.50 nm.   AR; free.

Birmingham & Midland Society for Genealogy & History
      is a group of the **Birmingham & Midland Institute**

Birmingham Natural History Society (BNHS) 1858

■ 23 Crosbie Rd, Harborne, BIRMINGHAM, B17 9BG. (hsp)
      0121-427 1010
      http://www.freespace.virgin.net/clare.h/bnhs.htm
      Hon Sec: Dr Peter Jarvis
▲ Registered Charity
○ *L; all aspects of natural history
Gp Entomology; Mycology [with the Warwickshire Fungus Survey -
      http://freespace.virgin.net/william.moodie/wfs.htm]
● Mtgs - Res - Inf - Lib - Supervision of Edgbaston Nature
      Reserve (SSSI)
M 120 i, 4 org
¶ Proceedings - 2 yrly; ftm, £5 nm.   NL - 3; ftm.
   Programmes - 2; ftm.

Birmingham Transport Historical Group (BTHG) 1963

■ 21 The Oaklands, DROITWICH SPA, Worcs, WR9 8AD. (hsp)
      01905 778243
      Hon Sec: Peter Jaques
▲ Un-incorporated Society
○ *G; research into public passenger transport in Birmingham &
      the West Midlands from its commencement to the present
      day
● Mtgs - Res - Inf
M 21 i, 1 org
¶ A Comprehensive History - vol 1.   Various booklets.

Birmingham & Warwickshire Archaeological Society (BWAS) 1870

NR c/o Birmingham & Midland Institute, Margaret St,
      BIRMINGHAM, B3 3BS. (hq)
      http://www.bwas.org.uk
      Hon Sec: Miss S Middleton
▲ Registered Charity
○ *L; study of archaeology in Birmingham, Warwickshire & West
      Midlands
Gp Field
● Mtgs - VE - Field study - Publishing
< Birmingham & Midland Inst
M c 150 i, c 75 org
¶ Transactions - 1; price varies nm.   NL;   AR; all ftm only.

Birth Trauma Association 2004

NR PO Box 671, IPSWICH, Suffolk, IP1 9AT.
      http://www.birthtraumaassociation.org.uk
○ *W

Birthmark Support Group 1998

NR PO Box 327, WEST MALLING, Knet, ME19 6WW.
      (mail/address)
      http://www.birthmarksupportgroup.org.uk
      Amanda Smith
▲ Registered Charity
○ *G; to provide information & advice to people affected by
      birthmarks
● Mtgs - Inf
M [not stated]
¶ NL - 2; free.

Biscuit, Cake, Chocolate & Confectionery Alliance
      since January 2004 **Biscuit, Cake, Chocolate & Confectionery**
      Association

Biscuit, Cake, Chocolate & Confectionery Association (BCCCA) 1901
- ■ 6 Catherine St, LONDON, WC2B 5JJ.   (hq)
     020 7420 7200   fax 020 7420 7201
     email office@bccca.org.uk   http://www.bccca.org.uk
     Dir-Gen: P A Hawley
- ▲ Company Limited by Guarantee
- ○ *T; to promote the interests of manufacturers of biscuits, cakes, chocolate & confectionery
- Gp C'ees: Commercial, Communications, Cocoa research, Technical & regulatory, Technology conference;
     Sub-c'ees: Microbiology & hygiene, Residues & contaminants
- ● Conf - Mtgs - Res - Stat - Inf - LG
- < EU Assn for Mfrs of Biscuits, Chocolate & Confectionery (CAOBISCO); Food & Drink Fedn
- M 100 f, UK / 5 f, o'seas
- ¶ Fortnightly Summary - 26; ftm only.   Annual Review - 1; free.
- × 2004 (January) Biscuit, Cake, Chocolate & Confectionery Alliance

BKSTS - the Moving Image Society (BKSTS) 1933
- NR Pinewood Studios, IVER HEATH, Bucks, SL0 0NH.   (hq)
     01753 656656
- ▲ Company Limited by Guarantee
- Br 5; 1 o'seas
- ○ *L; to support those who creatively or technologically are involved in providing moving images & associated sound
- M 1,450 i, 90 f, 10 org, UK / 250 i, 10 f, 3 org, o'seas
- ¶ Image Technology - 12.   Cinema Technology - 4.
     Members Directory - 1.

Black & Asian Studies Association (BASA) 1991
- ■ c/o ICS, 28 Russell Sq, LONDON, WC1B 5DS.   (hsb)
     http://www.blackandasianstudies.org.uk
     Sec: Caz Bressey
- ▲ Un-incorporated Society
- ○ *L; to encourage research & publish the history of Black peoples in the UK
- Gp Education c'ee; Archives working party
- ● Conf - Res - Exhib - LG
- M 180 i, UK / 15 i, o'seas
- ¶ BASA NL - 3.

Black Country Chamber (BCCBL) 2001
- ■ Dudley Court South, Waterfront East, BRIERLEY HILL, W Midlands, DY5 1XN.   (hq)
     0845 113 1234   fax 01384 360560
     email info@bccbl.com
     Chief Exec: John Reader
- ▲ Company Limited by Guarantee
- Br 3
- ○ *C
- ● Mtgs - Expt - Inf - Lib - VE - LG
- M 3,380 f
- ¶ Prosper - 4.   Chamber Directory - 1; ftm, £90 nm.
- × 2001 Dudley Chamber of Industry & Commerce

Black Country Society (BCS) 1967
- ■ PO Box 71, KINGSWINFORD, W Midlands, DY6 9YN.   (hsb)
     http://www.blackcountrysociety.co.uk
     Hon Sec: Judith Watkin
- ▲ Un-incorporated Society
- Br 5
- ○ *G; to promote interest in the past, present & future of the Black Country
- Gp Indl Archaeology Branch
- ● Mtgs - Res - Exhib - Inf - VE
- < Civic Trust; Assn Indl Archaeology; Family Hist Soc
- M c 2,200 i, f & org, UK / 32 i, o'seas
- ¶ The Blackcountryman - 4; ftm, £2.75 each nm.
     Wordsley (in the Britain in old photographs series, in conjunction with Sutton Publishing).
     Publications list available.

Black Simmental Society 1997
- ■ Grove Farm, Felbrigg, NORWICH, NR11 8PL.   (hsb)
     01263 512028
     Sec: Brian Filby
- ○ *B; British Black Simmental cattle

Black Welsh Mountain Sheep Breeders' Association 1798
- ■ Lake Villa, Bradworthy, HOLSWORTHY, Devon, EX22 7SQ.
     01409 241579   fax 01409 241579
     email blackwelsh@lakevilla.co.uk
     Sec: Lesley Lewin
- ▲ Company Limited by Guarantee; Registered Charity
- ○ *B
- ● Mtgs - ET - Exhib - Comp - SG - Stat - Inf - LG
- < Nat Sheep Assn
- M 250 i, UK / 15 i, o'seas
- ¶ NL - 2/3; ftm only.   LM - 1; free.
     Ybk (Flock Book); ftm, £5 nm.

Blackface Sheep Breeders' Association 1920
- NR Brae View, Drumharvie, CRIEFF, Perthshire, PH7 3PG.
     01764 683746
     Sec: Aileen McFadzean
- ○ *B; incl matters relevant to hill & upland farming
- ● Mtgs - Exhib - Inf
- < Nat Sheep Assn
- M 1,600 i
- ¶ Jnl - 1; free.

Blair Bell Research Society (BBRS) 1986
- NR Dept of Obstetrics & Gynaecology, University College London, 86-96 Chenies Mews, LONDON, WC1E 6HX.   (hsb)
     020 7679 6051   fax 020 7388 7429
     email d.peebles@ucl.ac.uk
     Sec: Dr Donald Peebles
- ▲ Registered Charity
- ○ *P, *Q; clinical & basic science research in obstetrics & gynaecology
- ● Conf - Mtgs - Res
- M i
- ¶ Abstracts (of papers presented at meetings) are published in the British Jnl of Obstetrics & Gynaecology.

Blake Society at St James's 1986
- ■ St James's Church, 197 Piccadilly, LONDON, W1J 9LL.
     (mail/address)
     020 7495 5654
     email secretary@blakesociety.org.uk
     http://www.blakesociety.org.uk
     Hon Sec: Dr Keri Davies
- ▲ Registered Charity
- ○ *A; to celebrate the life work of William Blake (1757-1827) poet, printer, visionary
- Gp 250th anniversary celebration
- ● Conf - Mtgs - VE
- M 300 i, UK / 40 i, o'seas
- ¶ Blake Jnl - 1; ftm.

BLC, Leather Technology Centre Ltd (BLC) 1984
- NR Leather Trade House, King's Park Rd, Moulton Park, NORTHAMPTON, NN3 6JD.   (hq)
     01604 679999
- ▲ Limited Company
- ○ *Q, *T; servicing leather manufacturing & related industries
- Gp Divns: Commercial, Research
- ● Conf - Mtgs - ET - Res - Exhib - SG - Stat - Expt - Inf - Lib
- < a subsidiary of BLC Research
- M f & org
- ¶ BLC Monthly Jnl - 12;   NL - 12; both ftm only.
     Laboratory Reports.   Information Documents.   AR.

© CBD Research Ltd · Beckenham · BR3 5JS · Tel 020 8650 7745 · Fax 020 8650 0768 · E-mail cbd@cbdresearch.com · www.cbdresearch.com

BLISS - National Charity for the Newborn (BLISS) 1979
NR 68 South Lambeth Rd (1st floor), LONDON, SW8 1RL. (hq)
      0870 770 0337   fax 0870 770 0338
      email information@bliss.org.uk   http://www.bliss.org.uk
      Chief Exec: Rob Williams
▲ Company Limited by Guarantee; Registered Charity
Br 40
○ *K, *W; to campaign for improved neonatal services; to support
      nurse training; to support families
Gp Befriending service for parents of babies born with problems
● Conf - Mtgs - ET - Exhib - SG - Stat - Inf - Lib - PL - Provision of
      specialist equipment - Funds research
M 1,000 i
¶ Newborn News - 4; free.   AR - 1.
      prefers to be known as BLISS - the premature baby charity
✕ 1999 Baby Life Support Systems

Blood Pressure Association 2000
■ 60 Cranmer Terrace, LONDON, SW17 0QS.
      020 8772 4994   fax 020 8772 4999
      http://www.bpassoc.org.uk
      Exec Dir: Nickie Roberts
▲ Registered Charity
○ *M, *W; for people whose lives are affected by their blood
      pressure

Blue Albion Cattle Society
NR Cronkstone Grange, Hurdlow, BUXTON, Derbys, SK17 9QL.
      01298 832246
      Sec: Tonia Fox
○ *B

Blue Badge Network (BBN) 1991
NR 198 Wolverhampton St, DUDLEY, W Midlands, DY1 1DZ. (hq)
      01384 257001
      http://www.bluebadgenetwork.org
      Chmn: Mrs Mary Grace
▲ Registered Charity
Br 44
○ *W; 'to help disabled people integrate more effectively with
      people in the community at large'
● Exhib - Inf - LG - Advocacy
M c 10,500 i
¶ Blue Badge Network NL - 4; ftm.

Bluebell Railway Preservation Society (BRPS) 1960
NR Sheffield Park Station, UCKFIELD, E Sussex, TN22 3QL. (hq)
      01825 720800   fax 01825 720804
      Hon Sec: Gavin Bennett
▲ Un-incorporated Society
○ *G; railway preservation & running 'The Bluebell Line' (part of
      the Lewes & E Grinstead Railway)
● Conf - Mtgs - ET - Exhib - Lib - VE
< Heritage Rly Assn
M c 10,000 i
¶ Bluebell News - 4; ftm, £2 nm.

**Bluefaced Leicester Sheep Breeders Association (BLSBA)
1962**
NR Formiston Farm, Casphairn, CASTLE DOUGLAS,
      Dumfriesshire, DG7 3TE. (hq)
      01556 505484   fax 01556 505484
      email info@blueleicester.co.uk
      http://www.blueleicester.co.uk
      Sec: Jean Gibbon
▲ Registered Charity
○ *B
● Mtgs - Exhib - Inf - VE
M c 1,400 i
¶ Looking Ahead - 1; November News - 1; both ftm.
      Flock Book - 1; ftm.

BMF Sailmakers Association
  a group of the **British Marine Federation**

Boarding Schools Association (BSA) 1966
■ Grosvenor Gardens House, 35-37 Grosvenor Gdns,
      LONDON, SW1W 0BS. (hq)
      020 7798 1580   fax 020 7798 1581
      email bsa@boarding.org.uk
      http://www.boarding.org.uk
      Nat Dir: Adrian Underwood
▲ Company Limited by Guarantee
○ *E; to promote the qualities of boarding education; to
      encourage the highest standards of welfare in boarding
      schools
● Conf - Mtgs - ET - Res - Inf - LG
M 500 schools, UK / 50 schools, o'seas
¶ Good Practice in Boarding Schools: a resource handbook for
      all those working in boarding.
      The Guide to Accredited Independent Boarding Schools in the
      UK.
      Choosing a Boarding School: a guide for parents.
      Briefing Paper(s) 1-17.
      Other publications available.

Boat Jumble Association (BJA) 1987
NR Compass Marine, Compass Cottage, DARTMOUTH, Devon,
      TQ6 0JN. (sb/p)
      01803 835915
      Sec: Tim Mear
▲ Un-incorporated Society
○ *G, *T; organisation & regulation of boat jumbles
Gp Stallholders; Event organisers
● Exhib
M 1,350 i, 650 f
¶ Boat Jumble Fixtures List - 1.

Boat Retailers & Brokers Association
  a group of the **British Marine Federation**

Body Control Pilates Association 1997
NR 6 Langley St, Covent Garden, LONDON, WC2H 9JA.
      020 7379 3734   fax 020 7379 7551
      http://www.bodycontrol.co.uk
      Dir: Lynne Robinson
○ *S; exercise similar to the Alexander technique
      Note: send sae for details

**Boiler & Radiator Manufacturers Association Ltd (BARMA)
1941**
NR Mirren Court (One), 119 Renfrew Rd, PAISLEY, Renfrewshire,
      PA3 4EA. (hq)
      0141-847 1265
      email barma@metcom.org.uk
      London office: 235-237 Vauxhall Bridge Rd, LONDON,
      SW1V 1EJ.
      020 7233 7011   fax 020 7828 0667.
      Sec: Fiona Cruickshanks
▲ Company Limited by Guarantee
○ *T
Gp Commercial boiler; Technical c'ee
● Mtgs - Stat - LG
< Eur Heating Ind (EHI); Eur Radiator Assn (EURORAD)
M 8 f
¶ LM; free.

Bonded Warehousekeepers' Association (BWA) 1885
NR PO Box 29089, DUNFERMLINE, Fife, KY11 9WB. (hsb)
      07736 633162
      Hon Sec: Ian M Gray
▲ Un-incorporated Society
○ *T; (incl implementation of UK & EC legislation as it effects HM
      Customs & Excise & related documentation issues)
Gp Health & safety; HM Customs & Excise
● Conf - Mtgs - ET - Inf - VE - LG
< Scotch Whisky Assn; Road Haulage Assn; Freight Transport
      Assn; Wine & Spirit Assn; Gin & Vodka Assn
M 65 i, 45 f
¶ NL - 4.   LM - 1.   Minutes of meetings.

Bone Research Society (BRS) 1950
- ■ c/o Dr T R Arnett, Dept of Anatomy & Developmental Biology, University College London, Gower St, LONDON, WC1E 6BT.   (pres/b)
  020 7679 3309
  email t.arnett@ucl.ac.uk   http://www.brsoc.org.uk
  Sec: Dr Tim Arnett
- ▲ Registered Charity
- ○ *L, *Q; to advance basic & clinical research into the calcified tissues
- ● Conf - Mtgs - ET - Res - Inf - PL - LG
- < Intl Osteoporosis Foundation; Brit Endocrine Socs
- M 211 i, UK / 20 i, o'seas
- ¶ NL (on website) - 3; free.
  Meeting abstracts published in Jnl of Bone & Mineral Research - 1.
- × 2005 Bone & Tooth Society

Bone & Tooth Society
   since 2005 **Bone Research Society**

** Book Packagers Association
   Organisation lost: see Introduction paragraph 3

Bookmark Society 1991
- NR 53 Victoria Rd, Horwich, Bolton, Lancs, BL6 5ND.
  01204 692458   (hsp)
  Hon Sec: Joe Stephenson
- ○ *G; collecting & research into bookmarks
- ● Mtgs - Res - Inf - VE
- M i
- ¶ Bookmark - 4; ftm.
  Note: please enclose an SAE with any enquiries requiring a reply.

Bookplate Society 1983
- ■ 11 Nella Rd, LONDON, W6 9PB.   (hsp)
  020 7385 3099
  email geoffreyvevers@tiscali.co.uk
  http://www.bookplatesociety.org
  Hon Sec: Geoffrey Vevers
- ▲ Registered Charity
- ○ *A, *G; to promote the study & collecting of bookplates; to publish material & arrange exhibitions
- ● Mtgs - Res - Exhib - VE
- < Fédn Intle des Sociétés d'Amateurs d'Exlibris
- M 250 i
- ¶ The Bookplate Jnl - 2; ftm.
  NL - 2; ftm only.   Book - 2 yrly; ftm, prices vary nm.
  [subscription £30 (UK), (£34, $60, 50, RoW)]

Booksellers Association of the United Kingdom & Ireland (BA) 1895
- ■ Minster House, 272 Vauxhall Bridge Rd, LONDON, SW1V 1BA.   (hq)
  020 7802 0802   fax 020 7802 0803
  email mail@booksellers.org.uk
  http://www.booksellers.org.uk
  Chief Exec: T E Godfray
- ▲ Company Limited by Guarantee
- Br 15
- ○ *T
- Gp Academic bookselling; Children's bookselling; Christian bookselling; Internet bookselling; Library supply; School supply; Small business forum
- ● Conf - Mtgs - Exhib - Stat - Inf - LG
- M 1,282 f, UK / 165 i, o'seas
- ¶ Bookselling Essentials - 4/5;   AR; both free.
  Directory of Booksellers - 1; ftm, £34 nm.
  Directory of Book Publishers - 1; £58.75 m, £76.38 nm.
  The Complete Guide to Starting & Running a Bookshop; £28.

Booktrust 2004
- § Book House, 45 East Hill, LONDON, SW18 2QZ.   (hq)
  020 8516 2977   fax 020 8516 2978
  email query@booktrust.org.uk
  http://www.booktrust.org.uk
  Chief Exec: Chris Meade
  an independent charity that promotes books & reading

Boot & Shoe Manufacturers' Association (BASMA) 1882
- NR 24-25 Bloomsbury Sq, LONDON, WC1A 2PL.   (hq)
  020 7612 7757
  Chief Exec: Michael Gilbert
- ▲ Company Limited by Guarantee
- ○ *T; to provide credit management services (including debt recovery, credit reporting & credit insurance) to the footwear manufacturing sector in the UK & overseas
- ● Inf - Credit management
- M c 380 f
- ¶ BASMA News - 4; free.

Border Union Agricultural Society 1813
- NR Showground Office, Springwood Park, KELSO, Scottish Borders, TD5 8LS.   (hq)
  01573 224188
- ▲ Registered Charity
- ○ *F; organisation of events & competitions; to promote interest in agriculture
- Gp Agricultural show; Ram sales; Championship dog show
- ● Exhib - Comp
- < Assn of Show & Agricl Orgs
- M c 1,200 i
- ¶ Border Union Show Catalogue - 1.   Prize List - 1.
  Canine Section Catalogue - 1.
  Kelso Ram Sales Catalogue - 1.

BOSS Federation
   see **British Office Supplies & Services Federation**

Boston Chamber of Commerce & Industry (BCC) 1930
- NR Boston Business Centre, Norfolk St, BOSTON, Lincs, PE21 9HH.   (hq)
  01205 358800
- ▲ Company Limited by Guarantee
- ○ *C
- ● Mtgs - ET - Expt - Inf - Lib - LG - Networking
- < Brit Chams Comm
- M 240 f

Botanical Society of the British Isles (BSBI) 1836
- ■ c/o Dept of Botany, Natural History Museum, Cromwell Rd, LONDON, SW7 5BD.
  020 7942 5002 (answerphone)
  http://www.bsbi.org.uk
  Hon Gen Sec: D Pearman
- ▲ Registered Charity
- ○ *L; study of flowering plants, cryptogams & charophyta of the British Isles & of the problems of their conservation
- Gp Records; Meetings; Publications; Science & research; Training & education
- ● Conf - Mtgs - Res - Exhib - SG - Inf - Surveys
- M 2,800 i, 60 libraries, UK / 150 i, o'seas
- ¶ BSBI News - 3; ftm only.
  Watsonia - 2;   Abstracts - 1; both ftm, prices on application nm.
  (to Mr R G Ellis, 41 Marlborough Rd, Roath, CARDIFF, CF23 5BU)

Botanical Society of Scotland (BSS) 1836
- ■ c/o Royal Botanic Garden Edinburgh, 20A Inverleith Row, EDINBURGH, EH3 5LR. (hsb)
  http://www.botsocscot.org.uk
  Hon Sec: Dr M P Cochrane
- ▲ Registered Charity
- ○ *L; all branches of botanical science
- Gp Cryptogamic; Alpine plants; Conservation
- ● Conf - Mtgs - Exhib - Conf - VE
- M 300 i, 1 school, UK / 17 i, o'seas
- ¶ Botanical Jnl of Scotland - 2; ftm, £18.75 each nm (UK).
  BSS News - 2; ftm only.

Bottled Water Cooler Association
  since 2005 **British Water Cooler Association**

Bournemouth Chamber of Trade & Commerce (bctc) 1916
- ■ Top Table House, 15 Alum Chine Rd, Westbourne, BOURNEMOUTH, Dorset, BH4 8DT. (hq)
  01202 540870   fax 01202 751997
  email info@bournemouthchamber.org.uk
  http://www.bournemouthchamber.org.uk
  Chief Exec: Peter J Goodson
- ▲ Un-incorporated Society
- ○ *C
- Gp C'ees: Local government affairs; Executive
- ● Mtgs - Inf - VE - LG
- < Dorset Cham Comm & Ind
- M 2 i, 350 f
- ¶ [emails to members]

Bowls Group
  since 2006 **Sports Manufacturers & Retailers Trade Association**

Box Culvert Association
  a product association of the **British Precast Concrete Federation**

Boys' Brigade (BB) 1883
- ■ Felden Lodge, Felden Lane, HEMEL HEMPSTEAD, Herts, HP3 0BL. (hq)
  01442 231681   fax 01442 235391
  email enquiries@boys-brigade.org.uk
  http://www.boys-brigade.org.uk
  Brigade Sec & Chief Exec: Steven Dickinson
- ▲ Company Limited by Guarantee; Registered Charity
- Br 1,650; 70 o'seas
- ○ *Y; Christian youth work with boys & young people aged 4-18
- < Global Fellowship of Christian Youth
- M 75,000 i, UK / 600,000 i, o'seas
- ¶ The Boys' Brigade Gazette - 4.

Boys' & Girls' Clubs of Northern Ireland (NIABC) 1940
- NR 22 Stockmans Way, Musgrave Park Industrial Estate, BELFAST, BT19 7JU. (hq)
  028 9066 3321
  email office@boysandgirlsclubs-ni.org.uk
  http://www.boysandgirlsclubs-ni.org.uk
  Chief Exec: Paul Curran
- ▲ Registered Charity; Un-incorporated Society
- ○ *N, *Y; the headquarters for youth clubs in Northern Ireland
- ● Conf - Mtgs - ET - Res - Comp - Events: International youth soccer, International (4 nations) youth boxing competitions
- < Nat Assn Clubs for Young People; Boys' & Girls' Clubs Scotland (& Wales)
- M 3,000 clubs

Boys' & Girls' Clubs of Scotland (BGCS) 1928
- ■ 88 Giles St, EDINBURGH, EH6 6BZ. (hq)
  0131-555 1729   fax 0131-555 5921
  email secretary@bgcs.co.uk   http://www.bgcs.co.uk
  Chief Officer: Tom Leishman
- ▲ Company Limited by Guarantee
- Br 5 local federations
- ○ *Y; to create & offer opportunities to young people
- ● Mtgs - Comp - SG - Lib - LG
- < Eur Fedn of Youth Service Orgs (EFYSO); Clubs for Young People (CYP)
- M 15,000 i

Bradford Chamber of Commerce & Industry (BCofC) 1851
- ■ Devere House, Vicar Lane, Little Germany, BRADFORD, W Yorks, BD1 5AH. (hq)
  01274 772777   fax 01274 771081
  email info@bradfordchamber.co.uk
  http://www.bradfordchamber.co.uk
  Chief Exec: Sandy Needham
- ▲ Company Limited by Guarantee
- ○ *C
- ● Conf - Mtgs - ET - Res - Exhib - Stat - Expt - Inf - Lib - VE - LG
- < Brit Chams Comm
- M 1,000 f
- ¶ Business Plus - 6; ftm, £2.50 nm.   M Dir - 1; ftm, £125 nm.

Braid Society 1993
- ■ Thyrnegate, The Street, Gasthorpe, DISS, Norfolk, IP22 2TL. (hsp)
  01953 681779
  email inkles@tiscali.co.uk   http://www.braidsociety.org
  Hon Sec: Anne Dixon
- ▲ Un-incorporated Society
- ○ *G; education & practice in the art & craft of making constructed or embellished braids & narrow bands
- ● Mtgs - Exhib - Comp - SG - VE
- M 138 i, UK / 32 i, o'seas
- ¶ Strands (Jnl) - 1; ftm, £3.75 nm.
  NL - 4;   LM - 1;   Booklist - 2 yrly;
  Suppliers' List - 2 yrly;   all ftm only.
  Tutors' List - 1; free.

Brain Injury Association
  see **HEADWAY - the Brain Injury Association**

Brain Tumour UK 1997
- ■ PO Box 94, WHITEHAVEN, Cumbria, CA28 7WZ. (hq)
  0845 450 0386   fax 0845 450 0386
  email info@braintumouruk.org.uk
  http://www.braintumouruk.org.uk
  Inf & Support Services Mgr: Jane Stephens
- ▲ Registered Charity
- ○ *M; all aspects of brain tumours, their treatment & effects of treatment
- ● Conf - Res
- < NCVO; Assn of Chief Execs for Voluntary Orgs
- M 2,800 i
- ¶ [Magazine - 4; free. 'to come']
- X 2004 United Kingdom Brain Tumour Society

Brainwave, the Irish Epilepsy Association 1967
- IRL 249 Crumlin Rd, DUBLIN 12, Republic of Ireland.
  353 (1) 455 7500   fax 353 (1) 455 7013
  email info@epilepsy.ie
  Chief Exec: Mike Glynn
- ○ *W

Branch Line Society (BLS) 1955

■ 73 Norfolk Park Avenue, SHEFFIELD, S Yorks, S2 2RB. (hsp)
　0114-275 2303　fax 0114-275 2303
　email BLS.Sales@tesco.net
　http://www.branchline.org.uk
　Hon Gen Sec: N J Hill
▲ Un-incorporated Society
○ *G; study of branch & minor railway lines, principally in the British Isles, but also throughout the world
● Mtgs (annual) - Inf - VE
M 1,000 i, 4 org, UK / 20 i, o'seas
¶ Branch Line News - 24;　AR; both ftm only.

Brassica Growers Association

■ 133 Eastgate, LOUTH, Lincs, LN11 9QG.　(hq)
　01507 602427　fax 01507 607165
　email crop.association@pvga.co.uk
　Co Sec: Mrs Jayne Dyas
▲ Company Limited by Guarantee
○ *T; marketing information, research & development
Gp British Sprout Growers Association
● Conf - Mtgs
M 25 f

Brazilian Chamber of Commerce in Great Britain

NR 32 Green St, LONDON, W1K 7AT.
　020 7399 9281　fax 020 7499 0186
　email pavlova@brazilianchamber.org.uk
　http://www.brazilianchamber.org.uk
　Chmn: Sir Peter Heap
▲ Company Limited by Guarantee
○ *C; bilateral trade between Brazil & the UK
Gp Brazilian exporters to the UK; British investors in Brazil
● Conf - Mtgs - Expt - Inf - LG
M i, f & org
¶ Brazil Business Brief - 3; ftm only.

Breast Implant Information Society (BIIS) 1998

■ Highway Farm, Horsley Rd, Downside, COBHAM, Surrey, KT11 3JZ.　(founder/p)
　0704 147 1225　fax 0704 147 1225
　email info@biis.org　http://www.biis.org
　Founder: Maxine Heasman
▲ Company Limited by Guarantee; Registered Charity
○ *G; to provide comprehensive information & advice &/or guidance to women who have, or are considering, breast implant surgery
● ET - Res - Stat - Inf - Lib - LG
　Helpline: 0704 147 1255 (weekdays 1800-2000 hours, not Bank Holidays)
M c 350 i, UK / 20 i, o'seas
¶ B-Plus - 1; m only.
　The Ultimate Cleavage: a complete practical guide to cosmetic breast enlargement surgery.

Brecknock Hill Cheviot Sheep Society

NR 13 Lion St, BRECON, Brecknockshire, LD3 7HY.
　01874 622488
　Contact: Peter Francis
○ *B

Brecknockshire Agricultural Society (Brecon County Show) 1755

■ Parclands House, RAGLAN, Monmouthshire, NP15 2BX.　(hq)
　01291 691134
　Admin: Vicki Spencer
▲ Registered Charity
○ *F; interests of farming & breed societies
● Mtgs - ET - Exhib - Comp - Brecknock Show
M 500 i, 15 f, 10 org
¶ LM;　AR.

Brewer's Licensed Retailers Association of Scotland
　since 2002 **Scottish Beer & Pub Association**

Brewers' Association of Scotland
　since 2002 **Scottish Beer & Pub Assn**

Brewers & Licensed Retailers Association
　since 25 October 2001 **British Beer & Pub Association**

Brewery History Society 1972

■ Manor Side East, Mill Lane, Byfleet, WEST BYFLEET, Surrey, KT14 7RS.　(chmn/p)
　01932 341084
　email chairman@breweryhistory.com
　http://www.breweryhistory.com
　Chmn: Jeff Sechiari
○ *L; research into the history of the British brewing & related industries
● Conf - Mtgs - Res - Exhib - Lib - PL - VE
> Engl Heritage; Assn for Indl Archaeology
M 400 i, 50 f, 10 org, UK / 10 i, 1 f, 5 org, o'seas
¶ Jnl - 4; ftm, £15 nm.　NL - 4.

Brewing, Food & Beverage Industry Suppliers Association (BFBi) 1907

■ PO Box 4563, WOLVERHAMPTON, W Midlands, WV1 9BX.　(hq)
　01902 795742　fax 01902 795744
　email info@bfbi.org.uk　http://www.bfbi.org.uk
　Chief Exec: Ruth Evans
▲ Un-incorporated Society
Br 5
○ *T; companies supplying raw materials, engineering components, process control & consultancy to the brewing, food & beverage industries
● Conf - Mtgs - ET - Res - Exhib - SG - Inf - VE - LG
M 156 i, 350 f, UK / 8 f, o'seas
¶ Directory - 1; ftm, £95 nm.
✕ 2000-02 Allied Brewery Traders' Association

Briar Pipe Trade Association (BPTA)

NR Cadogan, 20 Vanguard Way, Shoeburyness, SOUTHEND-on-SEA, Essex, SS3 9RA.
▲ Company Limited by Guarantee
○ *T; manufacturers & wholesalers of briar pipes
● Mtgs - Exhib
M 9 f

Brick Development Association Ltd (BDA) 1954

■ Woodside House, Winkfield, WINDSOR, Berks, SL4 2DX.　(hq)
　01344 885651　fax 01344 890129
　email brick@brick.org.uk
　Chief Exec: Michael Driver
▲ Company Limited by Guarantee
○ *T; interests of clay brick industry
● Mtgs - ET - Exhib - Comp - Stat - Inf - Lectures - Symposia
< Fédn Européenne des Fabricants de Tuiles et de Briques; Construction Products Assn; Brit Ceramic Res Ltd; Brit Ceramic Fedn
M 24 f (representing 95% of UK clay & calcium silicate & 100% of Republic of Ireland clay & brickmaking interests)
¶ Brick Bulletin - 2; £10 yr.　Technical literature.

Bridge Deck Waterproofing Association (BWA) 1990

NR 4 Meadows Business Park, Blackwater, CAMBERLEY, Surrey, GU17 9AB.　(hsb)
　01276 608700　fax 01276 608701
　Sec: Colin Cleverly
▲ Company Limited by Guarantee
○ *T; for those concerned with the waterproofing of bridges (highway, railway & waterway)
Gp Sheet application; Spray application
● Mtgs - LG - Representation of members in relation to codes & specifications
M 10 i, 10 f
¶ Members Directory - 1; ftm.

© CBD Research Ltd · Beckenham · BR3 5JS · Tel 020 8650 7745 · Fax 020 8650 0768 · E-mail cbd@cbdresearch.com · www.cbdresearch.com

Bristol Chamber of Commerce & Industry   1823

NR   Leigh Court Business Centre, Abbots Leigh, BRISTOL,
       BS8 3RA.   (hq)
       01275 373373
       email info@businesswest.co.uk
       http://www.businesswest.co.uk
       Jt Managing Dirs: John Savage, Phil Smith
▲   Company Limited by Guarantee
○   *C
Gp   Information services; Export services
●   Expt - Inf - Lib
<   Business Link West; Euro Info Centre Network; Brit Chams
       Comm
M   2,500 f
¶   Business Update - 10; ftm only.
       Members Directory - 1; ftm, £62.50 nm
       Note: uses the trading name of Business West

Bristol & Gloucestershire Archaeological Society   (BGAS)   1876

■   Stonewatch, Oakridge Lynch, STROUD, Glos, GL6 7NR.   (hsp)
       01285 760460
       http://www.bgas.org.uk
       Hon Gen Sec: John Loosley
▲   Registered Charity
○   *L; to promote the study of the history, archaeology &
       antiquities of Bristol & Gloucestershire; to encourage
       conservation
Gp   Sections: Bristol, Gloucester
●   Mtgs - Lib - VE - Publications of historical records of
       Gloucestershire
M   700 i, 70 org, UK / 10 i, 60 org, o'seas
¶   NL - 2; ftm only.   Transactions - 1; ftm, £12 nm.
       Record Series - 1; £12 m, £30 nm.

Bristol Industrial Archaeological Society   (BIAS)   1967

NR   c/o Museum of Bath at Work, Camden Works, Julian Rd, BATH,
       BA1 2RH.   (mail)
       01225 318348   fax 01225 318348 address
       Chmn: Stuart Burroughs
○   *L; research into industrial archaeology of the Bristol region
<   Assn for Indl Archaeol
M   i, f & org

Bristol Steamship Owners' Association   (BSSO)   1907

NR   2 Downleaze, PORTISHEAD, N Somerset, BS20 8BJ.   (hsp)
       01275 842110   fax 01275 849386
       email bsso@virgin.net
       Hon Sec: J A White
○   *T; to defend the interests of shipping; to take note of all bills
       brought into parliament affecting British maritime commerce
●   Mtgs
<   Cham Shipping (London)
M   c 40 i & f

Bristol & Western Engineering Manufacturers' Association Ltd
       since 2003 **British Engineering Manufacturers' Association Ltd**

Britain-Australia Society   (B-AS)   1937

NR   Swire House, 59 Buckingham Gate, LONDON, SW1E 6AJ.
       (hq)
       020 7630 1075   fax 020 7828 2260
       email britaus@britain-australia.org.uk
       http://www.britain-australia.org.uk
       Nat Dir: Kim Hemmingway
▲   Un-incorporated Society
Br   10
○   *X
●   Mtgs - VE
M   1,200 i, 30 f
¶   Brit Oz Bulletin - 3; ftm only.

Britain in Europe Campaign

       ceased activities August 2005

Britain & Ireland Association of Aquatic Science Libraries & Information Centres   (BIASLIC)   1969

■   c/o Information & Library Services, Centre for Environment
       Fisheries & Aquaculture Science, Pakefield Rd, LOWESTOFT,
       Suffolk, NR33 0HT.   (hsb)
       01502 524210   fax 01502 524525
       email s.l.carter@cefas.co.uk
       Sec: Sarah Carter,   Chmn: I McCulloch
▲   Un-incorporated Society
○   *P; to bring together librarians & information workers in marine
       biology, oceanography, fisheries, aquatic ecology, freshwater
       scientific & technological research
●   Mtgs
M   i
¶   Serial Holdings of the UK Marine & Freshwater Sciences
       Libraries - irreg.
       Directory of Library & Information Facilities - irreg; free.

Britain-Nepal Chamber of Commerce   (BNCC)   1995

NR   12A Kensington Palace Gardens, PO Box BNCC, LONDON,
       W8 4QU.   (asa)
       01483 304150   fax 01483 428668
       email bncc@nepal-trade.org.uk
       http://www.nepal-trade.org.uk
       Sec: Kevin Hastings-Rose
▲   Un-incorporated Society
○   *C; to promote 2-way trade between the UK & the Kingdom of
       Nepal
●   Mtgs - Expt - Inf
M   f

Britain Nepal Society   (BNS)   1960

■   2 West Rd, GUILDFORD, Surrey, GU1 2AU.   (hsb)
       01483 569719   fax 01483 306380
       email neilweir@btinternet.com
       Hon Sec: Neil Weir
▲   Un-incorporated Society
○   *X; to promote good relations between the peoples of the UK &
       Nepal; & in particular between UK citizens with an interest in
       Nepal & Nepalese citizens resident in the UK
●   Mtgs - VE
>   Britain Nepal Cham Comm; R Nepalese Embassy in UK; Britain
       Nepal Otology Service
M   450 i, 20 f, UK / 50 i, o'seas
¶   BNS Jnl - 1; ftm only.
       Note: also at the same address is the British Nepal Otology
       Service - a charity dedicated to the prevention & treatment of
       deafness in Nepal.

Britain-Nigeria Association   (BNA)   1961

NR   2 Vincent St, LONDON, SW1P 4LD.   (hq)
       020 7828 5588   fax 020 7828 5251
       http://www.britain-nigeria.fsnet.co.uk
       Hon Sec: J Rivett
▲   Un-incorporated Society
○   *X
●   Mtgs - LG - Social gatherings & receptions
<   Nigeria-Britain Assn, Nigeria
M   c 850 i & f
¶   BNA NL - 3; ftm only.

Britain Nigeria Business Council   1978

NR   2 Vincent St, LONDON, SW1P 4LD.   (hq)
       020 7828 9661   fax 020 7828 9779
       email bnbc-uk@btconnect.com
       Exec Sec: Brian Watkins
▲   Company Limited by Guarantee
Br   Nigeria
○   *C; to promote trade between the UK & Nigeria
●   Conf - Mtgs - Exhib - Expt - Inf - LG
M   c 80 f
¶   NL - 12;   AR; both ftm only.

Britain-Tanzania Society (BTS) 1975
NR   3 Lowther Rd, LONDON, SW13 9NX.   (hsp)
         020 8563 1456
         http://www.btsociety.org
         Hon Exec Sec: Judy Tice
▲   Un-incorporated Society
Br   2; Tanzania
○   *X; to increase mutual knowledge, understanding & respect
         between the peoples of the two countries
●   Conf - Mtgs - Exhib - Inf - VE - LG
<   BOND
M   750 i, UK / 100 i, o'seas, & 20 org
¶   Tanzanian Affairs - 3; ftm, £7.50 nm.
         NL;   AR; ftm only.

Britain-Zimbabwe Society (BZS) 1981
NR   1 Castle View, Sydney Wharf, BATH, BA2 4EG.   (sp)
         email diana.jeater@uwe.ac.uk
         Chmn: Diana Jeater
○   *X; to foster friendship & understanding between the peoples of
         Zimbabwe & Britain; to encourage open discussion about
         Zimbabwean affairs; to inform the British & Zimbabwe public
         about Zimbabwean culture & economy
¶   Britain-Zimbabwe Review - 6.
         Dayschool Report - 1.

Britcham Shanghai
         the abbreviated title of **British Chamber of Commerce Shanghai**

British Abrasives Federation (BAF) 1968
■   Toad Hall, Hinton Rd, HURST, Berks, RG10 0BS.   (hsp)
         0845 612 1380   fax 0845 612 1380
         email info@thebaf.org.uk   http://www.thebaf.org.uk
         Sec: Stuart Lane
▲   Un-incorporated Society
○   *N, *T; the setting of industrial standards & the establishment of
         appropriate regulations for the manufacture of abrasive
         products
Gp   Abrasives product groups: Coated, Bonded, Super; Grains
         (silicon carbide, aluminium oxide, industrial diamonds)
●   Conf - Mtgs - ET - Stat - Inf
M   23 f

British Academy 1902
■   10 Carlton House Terrace, LONDON, SW1Y 5AH.   (hq)
         020 7969 5200   fax 020 7969 5300
         email secretary@britac.ac.uk   http://www.britac.ac.uk
         Sec: P W H Brown
▲   Registered Charity
○   *L; the Uk's national academy for the provision of the
         humanities & social sciences. Scholars are elected for
         distinction in their area of study
Gp   Classical antiquity; Theology & religious studies; African &
         oriental studies; Linguistics & philology; Early modern
         languages & literature; Modern languages, literature & other
         media; Archaeology; Medieval studies: history & literature;
         Early modern history to c1800; Modern history from c1800;
         History of art & music; Philosophy; Law; Economics &
         economic history; Social anthropology & geography;
         Sociology, demography & social statistics; Political studies:
         political theory, government & international relations;
         Psychology
●   Conf - Mtgs - Res - Comp - LG - Awards to support
         fundamental research - Symposia
M   c 800 i
¶   Proceedings;   Review (monographs) - irreg; ftm, prices
         vary nm.
         Directory - 1; ftm only.   AR - 1; free.
×   2005-06 British Academy for the Promotion of Historial,
         Philosophical & Philological Studies

British Academy of Audiology (BAA) 1985
NR   PO Box 346, PETERBOROUGH, Northants, PE6 7ES.   (hq)
         01733 253976
         http://www.baaudiology.org
         Pres: Jonathan Parsons
▲   Company Limited by Guarantee
○   *P; the professional body for audiologists in the UK
●   Conf - ET - Exam - Exhib - Inf - LG
×   2004 (British Association of Audiological Scientists
               (British Association of Audiologists
               (British Society of Hearing Therapists

British Academy of Composers + Songwriters (BAC+S) 1999
■   British Music House, 26 Berners St, LONDON, W1T 3LR.   (hq)
         020 7636 2929   fax 020 7636 2212
         email info@britishacademy.com
         http://www.britishacademy.com
         Chief Exec: Chris Green
▲   Company Limited by Guarantee
○   *P; the interests of composers & songwriters across all genres
●   Mtgs - Comp - Inf - LG - Administration of the Ivor Novello &
         the Gold Badge Awards
<   Creators' Rights Assn; Brit Music Rights; MCPS; PRS
M   2,500 i
¶   The Works - 2;   Four Four - 4; both ftm only.

British Academy of Dramatic Combat (BADC) 1969
NR   3 Castle View, HELMSLEY, N Yorks, YO62 5AU.
         email enquiries@badc.co.uk
         Sec: Dr Ian G Stapleton
○   *D, *P; to improve standard of stage & screen fighting in Britain
●   Mtgs - Res - Inf
M   50 i, UK / 10 i, o'seas
¶   The Fight Director - 3; ftm.

British Academy of Film & Television Arts (BAFTA) 1963
■   195 Piccadilly, LONDON, W1J 9LN.   (hq)
         020 7292 5800   fax 020 7292 5868
         email reception@bafta.org.   http://www.bafta.org
         Chief Exec: Amanda Berry
▲   Registered Charity
○   *A; to support, develop & promote the art forms of the moving
         image
Gp   Film; Games; Television
●   Awards - Events - Archive
M   c 5,000 i, UK / 1,500 i, o'seas

British Academy of Forensic Sciences (BAFS) 1959
NR   Anaesthetic Unit, The Royal London Hospital, Whitechapel,
         LONDON, E1 1BB.   (hsb)
         020 7377 7135
         Hon Sec: Dr P J Flynn
○   *L; to encourage the study, improve the practice & advance the
         knowledge of legal medicine & forensic science
M   i
¶   Medicine, Science & the Law (Jnl) - 4.

British Accounting Association (BAA) 1984
NR   Sheffield University Management School, 9 Mappin St,
         SHEFFIELD, S Yorks, S1 4DT.   (admin/b)
         0114-222 3462
         Admin: Kathryn Hewitt
▲   Registered Charity
○   *E; *Q; advancement of education & encouragement of
         research in accounting
M   i

British Acoustic Neuroma Association   (BANA)   1992
NR   Oak House, Ransom Wood Business Park, Southwell Road
        West, MANSFIELD, Notts, NG21 0HJ.   (hq)
        01623 632143
        Chmn: Eric Dawes
▲   Registered Charity
Br   19
○   *W; for people with acoustic neuromas (brain tumours), their
        families & interested medical personnel
●   Conf - Mtgs - Res - Inf - Lib
M   c 650 i

British Activity Holiday Association   (BAHA)   1986
■   58 Station Approach, South Ruislip, RUISLIP, Middx, HA4 6SA.
        (sp)
        020 8842 1292   fax 020 8842 1121
        http://www.baha.org.uk
        Contact: Roger Southcott
▲   Company Limited by Guarantee
○   *T; for operators in the holiday activity sector
Gp   School groups; Unaccompanied children; Adults; Families
●   Conf - Mtgs - ET - Inf
<   Nat Coun for Outdoor Educ; Skills Active
M   26 f
¶   Guide - 2; free.

British Actors' Equity Association   (Equity)   1936
NR   Guild House, Upper St Martin's Lane, LONDON,
        WC2H 9EG.   (hq)
        020 7379 6000
        email info@equity.org.uk   http://www.equity.org.uk
        Gen Sec: Christine Payne
▲   Un-incorporated Society
Br   27
○   *U; for performers, stage managers, choreographers, directors,
        stunt arrangers & professional broadcasters in theatre,
        television, radio, film & variety
Gp   Departments: Theatre & variety, Film, Radio & TV
●   Conf - Mtgs - Empl
<   Intl Fedn of Actors; TUC; STUC; Nat Campaign for the Arts
M   c 37,500 i
¶   Equity Jnl - 4.   AR.

British Acupuncture Council   (BAcC)   1995
■   63 Jeddo Rd, LONDON, W12 9HQ.   (hq)
        020 8735 0400   fax 020 8735 0404
        email info@acupuncture.org.uk
        http://www.acupuncture.org.uk
○   *P; to represent acupuncturists; to maintain standards of
        education, methods & practice in the acupuncture profession
        in the UK
Gp   Finance; Code of Practice, ethics & disciplinary procedures;
        Education; Conference; Admissions; Research; Safe practice;
        PR & marketing; Regulation
●   Mtgs - ET - Res - Inf - LG
<   Wld Fedn of Acupuncture Socs; Brit Acupuncture Accreditation
        Bd
M   2,600 i
¶   LM - 1.   AR.
        List of Local Practitioner Members - daily.

British Adhesives & Sealants Association   (BASA)   1983
■   5 Alderson Rd, WORKSOP, Notts, S80 1UZ.   (sb)
        01909 480888   fax 01909 473834
        email secretary@basaonline.org
        http://www.basaonline.org
        Sec: John Murdoch
▲   Un-incorporated Society
○   *T; interests of British manufacturers of sealants & adhesives
●   Conf - ET - SG - Stat - Inf - LG
<   Assn of Eur Adhesives Mfrs (FEICA); Alliance of Ind Assns
M   82 f
¶   BASA Bulletin - 3; ftm only.   AR; free.
        BASA Members Hbk - 1; ftm, £40 nm.
        Manuals:
            Guide to Reach; free.
            Manual of Sealant Practice; ftm, POA nm.

British Aerobatic Association   (BAeA)   1974
NR   Mayfield House, Wrens Warren, Chuck Hatch, HARTFIELD,
        E Sussex, TN7 4WW.   (hq)
        01892 771310
        email info@aerobatics.org.uk
        http://www.aerobatics.org.uk
        Co Sec: David Cowden
▲   Company Limited by Guarantee
○   *S; for all interested in aerobatic flying
●   ET - Comp - Arranging contests
<   R Aero Club
M   200 i, 5 f, UK / 10 i, o'seas
¶   Aerobatics News Review - 6; ftm only.

British Aerobiology Federation   (BAF)   1990
■   c/o National Pollen & Aerobiology Research Unit, University of
        Worcester, WORCESTER, WR2 6AJ.   (hsb)
        01905 855200   fax 01905 855234
        email j.emberlin@worc.ac.uk
        http://www.pollenuk.co.uk
        Pres: Prof J Emberlin
▲   Registered Charity
○   *P; aerobiology, pollen counts, pollen spores, hayfever, asthma
●   Conf - Mtgs - ET
<   Intl Assn for Aerobiology
M   15 i, 30 f
¶   NL - 2; ftm only.

British Aerophilatelic Federation   (BAeF)   1985
NR   97 Albany Park Avenue, Enfield Highway, LONDON,
        EN3 5NX.   (mem/sp)
        020 8292 8206
        email cze416@tiscali.co.uk
        http://www.britishairmailsociety.co.uk
        Mem Sec: Martin C A Czech
▲   Un-incorporated Society
○   *G; to encourage & contribute to the advancement & study of
        all material relating to the carriage of mail by air
●   Conf - Mtgs - Res - Exhib - Comp - SG - Lib - VE
<   Assn of Brit Philatelic Socs
M   280 i, UK / 50 i, o'seas
¶   Airmail News - 4; free.

British Aerosol Manufacturers Association   (BAMA)   1961
NR   Kings Buildings, Smith Sq, LONDON, SW1P 3JJ.   (hq)
        020 7828 5111
        Communications Mgr: Caroline Fuller
▲   Company Limited by Guarantee
○   *T; to promote & protect the aerosol industry & its products
●   Mtgs - Stat - Inf - LG
<   Chemical Inds Assn
M   c 75 f
¶   Volatile Substance Abuse - be aware.
        BAMA Code of Practice.
        BAMA Electrostatic Guidelines.
        BAMA Guide to Safety in the Laboratory.
        Aerosol Product Recall Guide.
        Other similar publications.

British African Business Association   (BABA)
NR   2 Vincent St, LONDON, SW1P 4LD.
           020 7828 5544   fax 020 7828 5251
           http://www.waba.co.uk
○   *N
●   Mtgs - Expt - LG
M   3 org:
           Eastern Africa Association
           Southern Africa Business Association
           West Africa Committee

British Agencies for Adoption & Fostering
      since 2002 **British Association for Adoption & Fostering**

British Aggregates Association   (BAA)   1999
NR   PO Box 99, LANARK, ML11 8WA.   (mail/address)
           01206 274057   fax 01555 664111
           email baa@cloburn.co.uk
           http://www.british-aggregates.com
           Dir: Robert Durward,   Sec: Peter Huxtable
           Exec Officer: Richard Bird
▲   Company Limited by Guarantee
○   *T; to represent the independent, privately owned SME quarry
           operator in consultation with government, EU regulators,
           officials & politicians
●   Conf - Mtgs - ET - Inf - LG
<   Confedn of Brit Ind (CBI); Construction Product Assn (CPA);
           Mineral Ind Res Org (MIRO)
M   52 f (indep), 24 associates

**British Agricultural & Garden Machinery Association
(BAGMA)   1917**
NR   Salamander Quay West (entrance B/1st floor), Park Lane,
           HAREFIELD, Middx, UB9 6NZ.   (hq)
           0870 205 2834   fax 0870 205 2824
           email info@bagma.com   http://www.bagma.com
           Dir Gen: Ian Jones
▲   Un-incorporated Society
○   *F, *H, *T; farming & agriculture
●   Mtgs - ET - Inf - Empl - LG
<   Brit Hardware Fedn
M   c 900 f
¶   BAGMA Bulletin - 6; free.

British Agricultural History Society   (BAHS)   1952
■   Dept of Humanities, Arts & Languages, London Metropolitan
           University, 166-220 Holloway Rd, LONDON, N7 8DB.   (hsb)
           020 7133 2781
           Hon Sec: Dr John Broad
▲   Registered Charity
○   *L; to encourage the study of all aspects of the history of the
           countryside
●   Conf - Mtgs - Res
M   c 500 i, 450 f, UK & o'seas
¶   Agricultural History Review - 2.
           Rural History Today - 2.

British Air Boat Association   (BABA)   1989
           Chief Exec: Ron Davis
▲   Un-incorporated Society
○   *S; for the safe use of airboats & advancement of their design
●   ET - Comp
M   50 i
¶   BABA News - 1; free.
           is now run from the Turkish Republic of Northern Cyprus.

British Air Line Pilots Association   (BALPA)   1937
NR   81 New Rd, Harlington, HAYES, Middx, UB3 5BG.   (hq)
           020 8476 4000
           email balpa@balpa.org   http://www.balpa.org
           Gen Sec: Jim McAusnan
▲   Un-incorporated Society
○   *U; the representation of British commercial airline pilots &
           flight engineers to their employers & aviation authorities
●   Mtgs - SG - Empl - LG
<   Intl Fedn of Airline Pilots Assns; Eur Cockpit Assn
M   9,000 i, UK / 300 i, o'seas
¶   The Log - 6.

British Air Transport Association   (BATA)   1976
NR   Artillery House, 11-19 Artillery Row, LONDON, SW1P 1RT.
           (hq)
           020 7222 9494
           Sec Gen: Roger Wiltshire
▲   Un-incorporated Society
Br   1
○   *T; to encourage the safe, healthy & economic development of
           UK civil aviation
Gp   Aviation security; UK operators technical; Flight operations
           liaison;
           Operational charges c'ee
●   Mtgs - LG
M   13 f

British Airgun Shooters' Association   (BASA)
NR   3 The Courtyard, Denmark St, WOKINGHAM, Berks,
           RG40 2AZ.
           0118-977 1677
           Sec: Nigel Allen
○   *G
M   c 4,500 i

**British Airport Services & Equipment Association   (BASEA)
1988**
NR   Homelife House, 26-32 Oxford Rd, BOURNEMOUTH, Dorset,
           BH8 8EZ.   (hq)
           01202 299088
▲   Un-incorporated Society
○   *T; to promote the British suppliers to the airport industry & their
           products in the UK & overseas; to serve as a bureau for
           purchasers of airport equipment & services worldwide; to
           offer members a wide range of marketing support services
●   Mtgs - Res - Exhib - Stat - Expt - Inf - Lib - VE - LG
M   89 i, 87 f, 2 org (Airport Owners Assn & Jt Security Ind Coun)
¶   Directory of Members - 1; free.

British Allergy Foundation
      see **Allergy UK**

British Alliance of Healing Associations   (BAHA)   1977
■   7 Ashcombe Drive, EDENBRIDGE, Kent, TN8 6JY.   (hsp)
           01732 862478
           Chmn: Ken Baker
▲   Registered Charity
○   *N; an umbrella organisation for independent healing groups
           & centres throughout the UK; to promote spiritual healing &
           healer training
●   Conf - Mtgs - ET - Res - Exhib - Inf
<   Eur Confedn of Healing Orgs; Confedn of Healing
           Orgs (CHO); UK Healers
M   15,000 i in 60 orgs
¶   Alliance Review - 2.

British Alpaca Society   (BAS)
NR   c/o Grassroots Systems Ltd, PO Box 251, EXETER, Devon,
       EX2 8WX.
       01382 437788   fax 01392 270421
○   *B
●   Mtgs
M   i
¶   Alpaca - 4; ftm £1 nm.

**British Amateur Gymnastics Association (British Gymnastics)
(BAGA)   1888**
NR   Ford Hall, Lilleshall National Sports Centre, NEWPORT,
       Shropshire, TF10 9NB.   (hq)
       01952 820330
▲   Company Limited by Guarantee
○   *S; governing body for gymnastics in GB
●   Conf - ET - Exam - Comp - Inf - Lib - PL - LG
M   c 103,000 i
¶   Gymnast Magazine - 6; ftm only.

British Amateur Rugby League Association   (BARLA)   1973
NR   4 New North Parade, HUDDERSFIELD, W Yorks, HD1 5JP.   (hq)
       01484 544131   fax 01484 519985
       email info@barla.org.uk   http://www.barla.org.uk
       Sec: Nigel Hollingworth
▲   Un-incorporated Society
○   *S; the governing body of amateur Rugby League football in
       Great Britain
●   Conf - Mtgs - ET - Exam - Res - Exhib - Comp - Stat - Inf - PL -
       VE - LG
<   BARLA is the amateur section of the Rugby Football League
M   1,400 teams, 900 youth & junior sides
¶   BARLA Bulletin - 6.   Hbk - 1.

British Amateur Weight Lifters Association
       since 2002 **British Weight Lifters Association**

British Ambulance Association
NR   PO Box 100, PAIGNTON, Devon, TQ3 1YE.
       01803 843966
       email info@baa999.com
○   *T; for private ambulance providers

British Ambulance Society   (BAS)   1977
■   21 Victoria Rd, HORLEY, Surrey, RH6 9BN.   (sp)
       Chmn: Roger Leonard,   Gen Sec: Graham Andrews
▲   Un-incorporated Society
○   *G; compilation & storage of ambulance history: vehicles,
       uniforms, badges, equipment & photographs & any other
       artifacts concerning ambulance manufacture, services etc
Gp   National ambulance register (preserved vehicles); Modelling
●   Mtgs - ET - Res - Exhib - SG - Inf - Lib - PL - VE - Staging the
       annual National Ambulance Show
<   Coun Vehicle Soc (UK); Profl Car Soc (America); Fire Service
       Presvn Gp
M   c 300 i, f & org
¶   Ambulance World (Jnl) - 3.   Ambulance Scene (NL) - 5.

British American Business Council   (BABC)   1954
■   235 Montgomery Street (suite 907), SAN FRANCISCO CA
       94104, USA.   (hq)
       1 (415) 296 8645   fax 1 (415) 296 9649
       email info@baccsf.org   http://www.baccsf.org
       Exec Dir: Mostyn T Lloyd
▲   Company Limited by Guarantee
○   *C; to provide a forum for information, networking &
       identification of business opportunities, trade & investment in
       Northern California & the UK pursuing
●   Conf - Mtgs - Expt - Inf - Lib - LG
<   Brit Amer Business Coun
M   85 i, 165 f, o'seas
¶   Membership Directory - 1; ftm only.
✕   2005-6 British American Chamber of Commerce Northern
       California

British-American Business Inc   (BABi)   1920
■   75 Brook St, LONDON, W1K 4AD.   (hq)
       020 7467 7400   fax 020 7493 2394
       http://www.babinc.org
       Chief Exec Officer: Richard Fursland
▲   Company Limited by Guarantee
○   *C; to promote the growth & development of trade between
       British & American companies in both Britain & USA
●   Conf - Mtgs - Stat - Expt - Inf - Lib - LG
<   Eur Coun of Amer Chams Comm; Brit-Amer Cham Comm
M   700 f
¶   Network London - 4;   Network New York - 4; both free.
       British American Business, the UK Hbk - 1; ftm; £60 nm.
       American British Business - 1; ftm, £60 nm.
       Membership Directory - 1; ftm only.

British American Chamber of Commerce Northern California
       since 2005-06 **British American Business Council**

British American Football Association   (BAFA)   1987
NR   West House, Hedley-on-the-Hill, STOCKSFIELD,
       Northumberland, NE43 7SW.   (chmn/p)
       01661 843179
       Chmn: Gary Marshall
▲   Company Limited by Guarantee
○   *S; to act as the governing body for amateur American football
       in GB
M   c 4,500 i

**British Amusement Catering Trades Association   (BACTA)
1974**
NR   Alders House, 133 Aldersgate St, LONDON, EC1A 4JA.   (hq)
       020 7726 9826
       Chief Exec: Leslie Macleod-Miller
Br   10
○   *T; to represent the pay-to-play leisure machine industry
       including manufacturers, suppliers & amusement centre
       owners
Gp   Seaside amusement arcades; Inland amusement centres;
       Manufacturers, importers, distributors of amusement
       machines; Operators of amusement machines
●   Conf - Mtgs - ET - Exhib - SG - Stat - Expt - Inf - Lib - VE - LG
<   Fedn of Coin Machine Trade Assns of Europe (EUROMAT);
       Music Users' Coun of Europe; Nat Amusements Coun; Music
       Users' Coun
M   1,205 i, 800 f, UK / 10 i, 8 f, o'seas
¶   NL - 10 ftm only.   AR; free.
       Hbk (LM) - 1; ftm.

British Anaesthetic & Respiratory Equipment Manufacturers Association
       see **Barema**

British Andrology Society   (BAS)   1975
NR   Academic Unit of Reproductive & Developmental Medicine,
       University of Sheffield, Level 4, Jessop Wing, Tree Root Walk,
       SHEFFIELD, S Yorks, S10 2SF.   (hsb)
       0114-226 8195
       Sec: Dr Alizera Fazeli
○   *Q; promotion of research & professional training in male
       infertility & reproduction research
M   i

British Angora Goat Society   1981
NR   5 The Langlands, HAMPTON LUCY, Warks, CV35 8BN.   (hq)
       01789 841930
       email secretary@angoragoat.fsnet.co.uk
       http://www.britishangoragoats.org.uk
       Sec: Mrs E Graham
○   *B
M   i & groups
¶   NL - 3.   Ybk - 1.

British Antique Dealers' Association   (BADA)   1918
■   20 Rutland Gate, LONDON, SW7 1BD.   (hq)
      020 7589 4128   fax 020 7581 9083
      email info@bada.org   http://www.bada.org
      Sec Gen: Mrs Elaine J Dean
▲   Company Limited by Guarantee
○   *T; for the leading antique dealers in the UK - the association
      was incorporated in 1951
●   ET - Exhib - Stat - Inf - LG
<   Confédn Intle des Négociants en Oeuvres d'Art (CINOA)
M   400 f
¶   LM - 2; free.

**British Antique Furniture Restorers Association   (BAFRA)
1979**
NR   The Old Rectory, Warmwell, DORCHESTER, Dorset,
      DT2 8HQ.   (hq)
      01305 854822   fax 01305 854822
      email headoffice@bafra.org.uk
      http://www.bafra.org.uk
      Sec: Annette Blume,   Chmn: Michael Barrington
▲   Un-incorporated Society
○   *P; to promote study & research in furniture conservation &
      restoration; to maintain high professional standards among
      members
Gp   Full & associate members; Student section;
      Specialist full members - Lacquer & japanning, Gilding &
      carving, Metalwork
●   Conf - Mtgs - ET - Exam - Res - Exhib - Comp - Inf - VE
<   the 9 UK colleges running HND & degree &/or diploma
      courses in furniture conservation &/or restoration
M   c 100 i
¶   BAFRA Jnl - 3.
      BAFRA Conservation/Restoration Guide - 1.

British Aphasiology Society   (BAS)   1987
NR   Speech & Language Therapy Dept, Adults in the Community,
      Newcastle General Hospital, Westgate Rd,
      NEWCASTLE upon TYNE, NE4 6BE.   (hsb)
      0191-256 3463
      Hon Sec: Frauke Buerk
▲   Un-incorporated Society
○   *L; to foster the study of aphasia (language disorder following
      brain injury); to promote professional & scientific work on
      aphasia
●   Conf - Inf - Student essay & project prizes
<   R Coll of Speech & Language Therapists
M   500 i, UK / 20 i, o'seas
¶   NL - 4; ftm only.   Conference Proceedings.
      Where to begin in Aphasia Research.

British Appaloosa Society   (BApS)   1976
NR   Crook Farm, Roadhead, CARLISLE, Cumbria, CA6 6PJ.
      01697 748347
      http://www.appaloosa.org.uk
      Chmn: Brian Entwistle,
      Sec: Suzanne Entwistle
▲   Registered Charity
○   *B; to provide a registry for Appaloosa horses; to preserve &
      improve the breed
●   Conf - Mtgs - Comp - Expt
<   Brit Horse Soc
M   750 i
¶   NL - 4; ftm only.   Register of Horses - 1.
      Stallion Directory - 2.

British Apparel & Textile Confederation   (BATC)   1992
■   5 Portland Place, LONDON, W1B 1PW.   (hq)
      020 7636 7788   fax 020 7636 7515
      email batc@dial.pipex.com
      Dir Gen: John Wilson
▲   Company Limited by Guarantee
○   *T; representation of the apparel & textile industry in the UK to
      government, the press & others
●   Mtgs - Stat - Inf - LG
<   Eur Apparel & Textile Org (EURATEX)
M   7 f, 2 org, 13 trade org

British Approvals for Fire Equipment   (BAFE)   1984
NR   29 Thames St, KINGSTON upon THAMES, Surrey, KT1 1PH.
      (hq)
      020 8541 1950   fax 020 8547 1564
      email bafe@abft.org.uk   http://www.bafe.org.uk
▲   Company Limited by Guarantee
○   *P; registration & certification of providers of active fire
      protection equipment & services
●   Mtgs - LG - Certification & registration
M   c 100 f, UK / 4 f, o'seas
¶   BAFE Brochure;   BAFE Supplement;
      BAFE List of Approved Registered Organisations; all free.

British Arachnological Society   1963
NR   100 Hayling Avenue, Little Paxton, ST NEOTS, Cambs,
      PE19 6HQ.   (hsp)
      01480 471064
      Hon Sec: Ian Dawson
▲   Registered Charity
○   *L, *Q; distribution, behaviour, taxonomy etc of spiders
      (araneae), harvestmen (opilionidae), & pseudoscorpions
      (pseudoscorpionidae)
●   Conf - Mtgs - ET - Res - SG - Stat - Inf - Lib - PL
M   c 300 i, 20 libraries & universities, UK / 275 i, 100 libraries &
      universities, o'seas
¶   Bulletin - 3.   NL - 3.   Hbk.

British Archaeological Association   (BAA)   1843
NR   18 Stanley Rd, OXFORD, OX4 1QZ.
      01865 724378
      http://www.britarch.ac.uk/baa   (hsb)   (hsp)
      Hon Sec: John McNeill
○   *L; study of archaeology & the preservation of national
      antiquities

British Argentine Chamber of Commerce   (BACC)   1995
NR   65 Brook St, LONDON, W1K 4AH.   (hq)
      020 7495 8730
      http://www.britargcham.co.uk
      Chmn: Peter Edbrooke
▲   Company Limited by Guarantee
○   *C; trade & investment promotion
●   Conf - Exhib - Stat - Expt - VE - LG
¶   Bulletin.

British Arm Wrestling Federation
NR   24 Oakmere Close, Oakdale, BLACKBURN, Lancs, BB2 4TN.
      (pres/p)
      07801 819812
      Pres: Neil Pickup
○   *S

British Art Market Federation
NR   10 Bury St, LONDON, SW1Y 6AA.   (hq)
      020 7389 2148
      Chmn: Anthony Browne
▲   Un-incorporated Society
○   *T
M   30 i, 14 org

© CBD Research Ltd · Beckenham · BR3 5JS · Tel 020 8650 7745 · Fax 020 8650 0768 · E-mail cbd@cbdresearch.com · www.cbdresearch.com

British Art Medal Society (BAMS) 1982
- ◼ c/o Dept of Coins & Medals, British Museum, LONDON,
    WC1B 3DG.   (hsb)
    020 7323 8260   fax 020 7323 8171
    Sec: Philip Attwood
- ○ *A; study of the history of the medal
- ● Conf - Mtgs - Exhib - Comp
- M c 370 i, f & org
- ¶ The Medal - 2

British Artist Blacksmiths Association (BABA) 1978
- ◼ Anwick Forge, 62 Main Rd, ANWICK, Lincs, NG34 9SU.   (hsb)
    01526 830303
    email babasecretary@baba.org.uk
    http://www.baba.org.uk
    Hon Sec: Tim Mackereth
- ▲ Un-incorporated Society
- ○ *P, *T; to encourage a greater awareness of the blacksmiths' art
    amongst architects, interior designers & the general public
- ● Conf - Mtgs - ET - Exhib - Comp - SG - Inf - PL
- M 638 i, UK / 30 i, o'seas
- ¶ Artist Blacksmith - 4;
    Members' Address Book - 1; both ftm only.

British Arts Festivals Association (BAFA) 1970
- NR 28 Charing Cross Rd (2nd floor), LONDON, WC2H 0DD.
    (hq)
    020 7240 4532
    email info@artsfestivals.co.uk
    Admin: Kim Hart
- ▲ Registered Charity; Un-incorporated Society
- ○ *A, *N; the meeting point of arts festivals in the UK. It aims to
    strengthen the arts festivals; to raise their profit & status; to
    provide a centre for information
- ● Conf - Mtgs - ET - Res - Inf
- < Eur Festivals Assn
- M c 100 festivals
- ¶ Arts Festivals Calendar & Directory - 1; free.

British Association of Academic Phoneticians (BAAP) 1982
- ◼ Dept of English Language, The University, GLASGOW,
    G12 8QQ.   (archivist)
    0141-330 4596   fax 0141-330 3531
    email m.macmahon@englang.arts.gla.ac.uk b
    Hon Sec & Archivist: Prof M K C MacMahon
- ▲ Un-incorporated Society
- ○ *P; for people with a teaching or research post in phonetics in
    an institute of higher education in the UK or the Republic of
    Ireland
- ● Conf
- M 150 i, UK / c 50 i, o'seas
    Note: The Convenorship changes every 2 years.

British Association for Accident & Emergency Medicine
    since 2004-05 **British Association for Emergency Medicine**

British Association for Adoption & Fostering (BAAF) 1980
- NR Saffron House, 6-10 Kirby St, LONDON, EC1N 8TS.   (hq)
    020 7421 2600
    email mail@baaf.org.uk   http://www.baaf.org.uk
    Dir: Felicity Collier
- ▲ Registered Charity
- Br 6
- ○ *N, *W; to promote the interests of children separated from
    their parents
- ● Conf - Mtgs - ET - Inf - Lib - LG (Dept of Health)
- M 1,250 i, 210 agencies, 80 associate members
- ¶ Adoption & Fostering (Jnl) - 4.
    Adoption & Fostering News - 8.
    List of Agency Members.   Legal Member Directory.
    Medical Member Directory.
    Be My Parent Newspaper - 6.
    Focus on Fives NL - 26.   AR - 1.
- ✕ 2002 British Agencies for Adoption & Fostering

**British Association for the Advancement of Science (The BA)
1831**
- NR Wellcome Wolfson Building, 165 Queen's Gate, LONDON,
    SW7 5HE.   (hq)
    020 7019 4930   fax 020 7019 4923
    email help@the-ba.net   http://www.the-ba.net
    Chief Exec: Dr Roland Jackson
- ▲ Registered Charity
- ○ *L; 'to connect science with people, making science itself & the
    ways in which it is applied accessible to all'
- Gp 16 sections covering the main areas of science, social science,
    engineering, mathematics & medicine
- ● Conf - Mtgs
- M 3,000 i, 100 f, 200 org, UK / 100 i, o'seas
- ¶ Science & Public Affairs.

British Association of Advisers & Lecturers in Physical Education
    in 2006 merged with the Physical Education Association to form the
    Association for Physical Education

**British Association of Aesthetic Plastic Surgeons (BAAPS)
1985**
- ◼ at the Royal College of Surgeons, 35-43 Lincoln's Inn Fields,
    LONDON, WC2A 3PE.   (hq)
    020 7405 2234 (advice line)   fax 020 7242 4922
    email secretariat@baaps.org.uk
    http://www.baaps.org.uk
    Pres: Adam Searle
- ▲ Company Limited by Guarantee; Registered Charity
- ○ *P; teaching & research of aesthetic plastic surgery
- ● Conf - Mtgs - ET - Res - Exhib - Stat - Inf - PL
- < Intl Soc of Aesthetic Plastic Surgeons (ISAPS); Brit Assn of Plastic
    Surgeons (BAPS); Intl Confedn of Plastic & Reconstructive
    Surgery
- M 170 i, UK / 5 i, o'seas
- ¶ Factsheets on Aesthetic Surgery.
    Syllabus for Surgeons.   LM; all free.

**British Association of American Square Dance Clubs
(BAASDC) 1953**
- ◼ 87 Brabazon Rd, HESTON, Middx, TW5 9LL.   (hsp)
    Sec: Mrs Patricia Clare Woodcock
- ▲ Un-incorporated Society
- Br 230
- ○ *D; promotion of modern American square dancing for fun &
    friendship
- Gp Square Dance Clubs; Round Dance Clubs
- ● Mtgs
- M c 5,000 i
- ¶ Let's Square Dance - 10.

British Association for American Studies (BAAS) 1955
- ◼ Dept of Humanities, Fylde Building, University of Central
    Lancashire, PRESTON, Lancs, PR1 2HE.   (hsb)
    01772 893039   fax 01772 892970
    email heidimacpherson@baas.ac.uk
    http://www.baas.ac.uk
    Sec: Dr Heidi Macpherson
- ▲ Registered Charity
- Br 2
- ○ *L; to promote serious study of the United States of America
- ● Conf - Mtgs - ET - Res
- < Eur Assn for Amer Studies; Amer Studies Assn; Canadian Assn
    for Amer Studies; Ir Assn for Amer Studies
- M 500 i, UK / 30 i, o'seas
- ¶ Jnl of American Studies - 3.   NL - 2.
    American Studies (book series) - 3.

British Association of Anger Management (BAAM) 2001
NR Mill Place Farm House, Mill Place Farm, Kingscote,
  EAST GRINSTEAD, E Sussex, RH19 4LG. (hq)
  0845 130 0286 fax 01883 650183
  email info@angermanage.co.uk
  http://www.angermanage.co.uk
▲ Un-incorporated Society
○ *G, *P; all issues concerning anger, conflict & stress
  management for people, education, organisations &
  government bodies; training for those wishing to move into
  anger management
● Conf - ET - Inf - Programmes in anger management & conflict
  management - One-to-one therapy
< The Association follows the codes of the British Association for
  Counselling & Psychotherapy & the UK Council for
  Psychotherapy
M 1,200 i, 40 f, 20 org
¶ NL - 4.

British Association for Applied Linguistics (BAAL) 1967
■ PO Box 6688, LONDON, SE15 3WB. (asa)
  020 7639 0090 fax 020 7635 6014
  email admin@baal.org.uk http://www.baal.org.uk
  Chmn: Prof Ron Carter
▲ Registered Charity
○ *L; to promote the study of language in use; to foster
  interdisciplinary collaboration; to provide a common forum
  for those engaged in the theoretical study of language & for
  those whose interest is in the practical applications of such
  work
● Conf - Mtgs - ET - Res
< Assn Intl de Linguistique Appliquée (AILA)
M 737 i, 20 f, UK / 201 i, o'seas
¶ NL - 3; LM - 1; Annual Proceedings - 1; all ftm only.
  Publications of the International Association:
  AILA News - 2/3; AILA Review - 1; both ftm.

British Association of Art Therapists Ltd (BAAT) 1991
■ 24-27 White Lion St, LONDON, N1 9PD. (hq)
  020 7686 4216 fax 020 7837 7945
  email info@baat.org http://www.baat.org
  Chief Exec: Val Hvet
▲ Company Limited by Guarantee
○ *U; to promote art therapy in hospitals, clinics & special
  schools; to support therapists
Gp Art therapy &: Autism & spectrum disorder, Education,
  Forensics, Learning disabilities, Neurology, Older people
● Conf - Mtgs - ET - SG - Inf - Empl - LG
M i & org
¶ Inscape - International Jnl of Art Therapy - 2; ftm, £25 nm.
  Newsbriefing Magazine (NL) - 4;
  Newsbulletin (jobs & news) - 12; both ftm only.

British Association of Audiological Physicians (BAAP) 1977
NR c/o Dr Ewa Raglan, St George's Hospital, Blackshaw Rd,
  LONDON, SW17 0QT. (hsb)
  020 8725 1988
  Hon Sec: Dr Ewa Raglan
○ *M, *P; for consultant & trainee physicians & paediatricians
  practising audio-vestibular medicine
Gp Audit & evidence-based medicine gp; Education subc'ee
● Conf - Mtgs - ET - Res - SG - Stat - Inf - Hallpike symposia
< Brit Soc Audiology; Nat Coun Profls in Audiology
M 100 i UK, 3 i o'seas

British Association of Audiologists
  2004 merged with the British Association of Audiological Scientists &
  the British Society of Hearing Therapists to form the **British
  Academy of Audiology**

British Association of Aviation Consultants (BAAC) 1972
NR c/o Transport Research Laboratory, Crowthorne House,
  Nine Mile Ride, WOKINGHAM, RG40 3GA. (hq)
  01344 770424 fax 01344 770618
  email committee@baac.org.uk http://www.baac.org.uk
  Co Sec: Peter Mackenzie-Williams
▲ Company Limited by Guarantee
Br Australia, New Zealand
○ *P, *T; to ensure that all services provided by its registered
  Aviation Consultants are subjected to definite standards of
  professional competence with the interests of the customer
  paramount
● Consultancy services - Training - Personnel selection - Social
  events
< Academy of Experts; Farnborough Aerospace Consortium
M c 80 i
¶ NL - 2/3; ftm only. Register (LM) - 1; free.

British Association of Balloon Operators (BABO) 1993
NR St Francis Chambers, 23 High St, PEWSEY, Wilts, SN9 5AF.
  (hsb)
  01672 564536
  email secretary@babo.org.uk http://www.babo.org.uk
  Hon Sec: Sandra Hossack
▲ Company Limited by Guarantee
○ *T; to represent UK Balloon Air Operators Certificate holders
  (passenger carrying hot air balloons)
● Mtgs - ET - Inf
< Brit Balloon & Airship Club
M c 70 f
¶ NL - 12; ftm only.

British Association of Barbershop Singers (BABS) 1974
■ Druids Lea, Upper Stanton Drew, BRISTOL, BS39 4EG. (hsp)
  01275 332778 fax 01275 332778
  email babs@crbennett.co.uk
  http://www.singbarbershop.com
  Dir of Admin & Co Sec: C Bennett
▲ Company Limited by Guarantee; Registered Charity
Br 50+
○ *D; to encourage barbershop singing in the UK
Gp Guild of Judges; Directorate of music services (education)
● Conf - ET - Comp - Inf
< Barbershop Harmony Soc (USA)
M 1,800 i
¶ Harmony Express - 6; ftm. AR - 1.

**British Association of Beauty Therapy & Cosmetology Ltd
(BABTAC) 1977**
NR Meteor Court, Barnett Way, Barnwood, GLOUCESTER,
  GL4 3GG. (hq)
  0845 065 9000
  email enquiries@babtac.com http://www.babtac.com
○ *P

© CBD Research Ltd · Beckenham · BR3 5JS · Tel 020 8650 7745 · Fax 020 8650 0768 · E-mail cbd@cbdresearch.com · www.cbdresearch.com

British Association for Behavioural & Cognitive Psychotherapies (BABCP) 1972
NR   19 The Globe Centre, St James Square, ACCRINGTON, Lancs,
        BB5 ORE.   (hq)
        01254 875277   fax 01254 239114
        email babcp@babcp.com   http://www.babcp.com
        Admin: Jennifer Riggs
▲   Registered Charity
Br   12
○   *K; to advance the theory & practice of the psychotherapies; in
        particular the application of experimental methodology &
        learning techniques to the assessment & modification of
        behaviour in a wide variety of settings
●   Conf - Mtgs - ET - SG - Inf - Accreditation & registration of
        psychotherapists
<   Eur Assn for Behaviour & Cognitive Therapy (EABCT); Ir Assn for
        Behaviour & Cognitive Therapies (IABCP); UK Coun
        Psychotherapy (UKCP)
M   6,000 i
¶   Behavioural & Cognitive Psychotherapy - 4.
        BABCP News - 4.
        Directory of Accredited Behavioural / Cognitive & REBT
        Psychotherapists - 1.

British Association for Biofuels & Oils
        merged in 2006 with **Renewable Energy Associaton**

British Association for Canadian Studies (BACS) 1975
■   21 George Sq, EDINBURGH, EH8 9LD.   (hq)
        0131-662 1117   fax 020 7117 1875
        email info@canadian-studies.net
        http://www.canadian-studies.net
        Admin Sec: Jodie Robson
▲   Registered Charity
○   *L; to foster teaching & research about Canada; to locate
        sources for the study of Canada
Gp   Library & resources; History; Canadian business & economic
        studies; Canada/UK Architecture Group; Social policy;
        Groupe des Recherches et Etudes sur le Canada français;
        Literature; Aboriginal studies
●   Conf - Mtgs - Res - SG - Inf
<   Intl Coun for Canadian Studies
M   300 i, 40 f, UK / 80 i, 120 f, o'seas
¶   British Jnl of Canadian Studies - 2;   NL - 3; both ftm only.

British Association for Cancer Research (BACR) 1960
■   c/o Institute of Cancer Research, 15 Cotswold Rd, SUTTON,
        Surrey, SM2 5NG.   (hq)
        020 8722 4208
        email bacr@icr.ac.uk   http://www.bacr.org.uk
        Hon Sec: Dr Sue Bailey
▲   Registered Charity
○   *P, *Q; clinical & basic researchers interested in cancer
●   Conf - Mtgs - ET
M   1,589 i

British Association for Cemeteries in South Asia (BACSA) 1977
■   135 Burntwood Lane, LONDON, SW17 0AJ.   (hsp)
        email rosieljai@clara.co.uk
        Hon Sec: Dr Rosie Llewellyn-Jones
▲   Registered Charity
Br   India
○   *K; preservation of historical cemeteries; conversion of those
        dilapidated beyond repair to social use; recording &
        publishing information relating to Europeans in Asia
●   Mtgs - Res - Exhib - SG - Inf - VE - Collecting monumental
        inscriptions from UK churches, or churchyards, with
        references to S Asia
<   Fedn Family History Socs; Indian Nat Trust of Art & Cultural
        Heritage (INTACH); Assn for Presvn of Histl Cemeteries in
        India (APHCI)
M   c 1,900 i, f & org
¶   Chowkidar (Jnl) - 2.
        Publications list available.

British Association for Central & Eastern Europe   (BACEE) 1967
NR   10 Westminster Palace Gardens, Artillery Row, LONDON,
        SW1P 1RL.   (hq)
        020 7976 0766   fax 020 7976 8831
        email bacee@bacee.org.uk   http://www.bacee.org.uk
        Dir: Nicholas Jarrold
▲   Company Limited by Guarantee
○   *X; a closer understanding between the people of the UK & the
        peoples of Albania, Bosnia & Herzegovina, Bulgaria, the
        Czech & Slovak Republics, Croatia, Estonia, Hungary, Latvia,
        Lithuania, Macedonia, Romania, Poland, Serbia,
        Montenegro, Moldova, Slovenia, Belarus, Ukraine & Turkey
        through closer cultural, social & other contacts
●   Conf - VE
M   c 250 i
¶   NL - 2; ftm only.

British Association for Chemical Specialities (BACS) 1977
NR   Simpson House, Windsor Court, Clarence Drive, HARROGATE,
        N Yorks, HG1 2PE.   (hq)
        01423 700249   fax 01423 520297
        email enquiries@bacsnet.org   http://www.bacsnet.org
        Co Sec: John Reid
▲   Company Limited by Guarantee
○   *T; manufacturers & formulators of speciality chemicals &
        intermediates (incl maintenance products for consumer &
        industrial use), disinfectants & industrial biocides (incl water
        treatment chemicals & services) & speciality surfactants
Gp   Biocides forum; Speciality surfactants; Water treatment;
        Formulated products
●   Conf - Mtgs - ET - Exam - Stat - LG
<   Assn de la Savonnerie, de la Détergence et des Produits
        d'Entretien (AISE); Confedn Brit Ind; Brit Business Bureau
M   160 f
¶   AR - 1; free.   LM; ftm, £45nm.

British Association for Chinese Studies (BACS) 1976
NR   c/o Areas Office, University of Essex, COLCHESTER, Essex,
        CO4 3SQ.
        01206 872543
        http://www.bacsuk.org.uk
        Hon Sec: Carol Rennie
        Admin Sec: Lynn Baird (admin@bacsuk.org.uk)
▲   Registered Charity
○   *L; to promote & support Chinese studies in the UK
●   Conf - Mtgs - Inf - VE - LG
<   Eur Assn of Chinese Studies; Coordinating Coun Area Studies
        Assns; Jt E Asian Studies Conf/C'ee
M   c 200 i & org
¶   Bulletin - 1; ftm only.

British Association of Clinical Anatomists (BACA) 1977
■   School of Medicine, Health Policy & Practice, University of East
        Anglia, NORWICH, NR4 7TJ.   (hsb)
        01603 591104
        email d.heylings@uea.ac.uk
        Hon Sec: Dr David Heylings
▲   Registered Charity
○   *E, *M, *P
●   Mtgs - Res
<   Amer Assn of Clinical Anatomists (AACA); Australian & New
        Zealand Assn of Clinical Anatomists (ANZACA)
>   Amer Assn of Clinical Anatomists (AACA); Australian & New
        Zealand Assn of Clinical Anatomists (ANZACA)
M   171 i, UK / 69 i, o'seas
¶   Clinical Anatomy - 8.

British Association of Colliery Management, Technical Energy Administrative Management (BACM-TEAM) 1947
- ■ 17 South Parade, DONCASTER, S Yorks, DN1 2DR.   (hq)
  01302 815551
  Gen Sec: P M Carragher
- Br 7
- ○ *U; for energy management, technical & administrative management employees
- ● Lib - Empl - LG
- < EC Steel & Coal; Fédn Eur des Cadres de l'Energie et de la Recherche; Trades U Congress
- M 4,065 i, c 30 f, UK / 5 i, o'seas
- ¶ Focus NL - 4;   AR - 1; both ftm only.

British Association of Communicators in Business Ltd (BACB)
- ■ Oak House (GA2), Woodlands Business Park, Linford Wood, MILTON KEYNES, Bucks, MK14 6EY.   (hq)
  01908 313755   fax 01908 313661
  email enquiries@cib.co.uk   http://www.cib.co.uk
- ▲ Company Limited by Guarantee
- ○ *P; 'aims to be the market leader for those involved in corporate media management & practice by providing professional, authoritative, dynamic, supportive & innovative services'
- ● Conf - Mtgs - ET - Exhib - Comp - SG - Lib
- < Fedn Eur Indl Editors Assns (FEIEA)
- M 1,050i, UK / 30 i, o'seas
- ¶ Communicators - 10; ftm.

British Association for Community Child Health
  a group of the **Royal College of Paediatrics & Child Health**

British Association of Community Doctors in Audiology (BACDA) 1985
- ■ c/o 23 Stokesay Rd, SALE, Cheshire, M33 6QN.   (sb)
  0161-962 8915   fax 0161-291 9398
  email bacda@boltblue.com
  Sec: Pam Williams
- ▲ Registered Charity
- ○ *M, *P; the study of audiology & the prevention, diagnosis & management of hearing impairment in children; the promotion of standards in training, & of regular exchange of views between medical staff & professional colleagues
- Gp Research group; Training group
- ● Conf - Mtgs - ET
- M c 270 f
- ¶ Audiens - 2; ftm only.

British Association of Conference Destinations (BACD) 1969
- ■ Charles House (6th floor), 148-149 Great Charles St, BIRMINGHAM, B3 3HT.   (hq)
  0121-212 1400   fax 0121-212 3131
  email info@bacd.org.uk   http://www.bacd.org.uk
  Chief Exec: Tony Rogers (mobile 078 8759 6727)
- ▲ Company Limited by Guarantee
- ○ *N; to support, promote & represent British conference destinations
- ● Conf - Mtgs - ET - Exhib - Inf - Lib - LG
- < Intl Congress & Convention Assn; Business Tourism Partnership
- M 75 f (& 100 affiliates)
- ¶ British Conference Destinations Directory - 1; ftm, £15 nm. (free to bona fide event organisers).
  LM - updated; ftm, £50 nm.
  Database of Event & Conference Organisers - updated; scale of rental charges available.

British Association of Cosmetic Doctors
- NR 30b Wimpole St, LONDON, W1U 2RW.
  0800 328 3613
  email info@cosmeticdoctors.co.uk
  http://www.cosmeticdoctors.co.uk

** **British Association of Cosmetic Surgeons**
  Organisation lost: see Introduction paragraph 3

British Association for Counselling & Psychotherapy (BACP) 1977
- ■ 35-37 Albert St, RUGBY, Warks, CV21 2SG.   (hq)
  0870 443 5252   fax 0870 443 5161
  email bacp.co.uk   http://www.bacp.co.uk
  Chief Exec: Laurel Clarke
- ▲ Company Limited by Guarantee; Registered Charity
- ○ *P; to lead the effort to make counselling & psychotherapy widely recognised as a profession whose purpose & activity is understood by the general public; to be the professional body for counselling & psychotherapy
- Gp Association of Independent Practitioners (AIP); Association for Counselling at Work; Association for Pastoral & Spiritual Care & Counselling (APSCC); Association for University & College Counselling; Counselling Children & Young People (CCYP); Faculty of Healthcare Counsellors & Psychotherapists Ltd (FHCP)
- ● Conf - Mtgs - ET - Res - Exhib - Inf - Lib - LG
- M 24,500 i, 1,000 f, UK / 326 i, 12 f, o'seas
- ¶ Therapy Today - 10; ftm, £69 nm.
  Counselling & Psychotherapy Research (CPR) - 4; ftm, £54 nm.
  Healthcare Counselling & Psychotherapy Jnl - 4; ftm, £30 nm.
  Counselling at Work (Jnl of the Assn for Counselling at Work) - 4; free to ACW members, £30 nm.
  AUCC (Jnl of the Assn for University & College Counselling) - 4; free to AUCC members, £30 nm.

British Association of Crystal Growth (BACG) 1969
- ■ c/o Dr G Steele, AstraZeneca R&D, Charnwood, LOUGHBOROUGH, Leics, LE11 5RH.   (hsb)
  01509 644695
  Hon Sec: Dr G Steele
- ▲ Registered Charity
- ○ *L; to encourage discussion of the theory & practice of crystal growth in industry, government laboratories & universities in the UK including all types of inorganic & organic crystalline materials including metals, ceramics, polymers & electronic device materials
- Gp Semiconductor materials; Biological / chemical materials; Optical materials; Oxide materials
- ● Conf - Mtgs - ET - Exhib - Comp
- < Intl Org Crystal Growth (IOCG)
- M 400 i, UK / 50 i, o'seas
- ¶ NL - 2; ftm only.

British Association for Day Surgery (BADS) 1989
- NR 35-43 Lincoln's Inn Fields, LONDON, WC2A 3PN.   (hq)
  020 7973 0308   fax 020 7973 0314
  email bads@bads.co.uk   http://www.bads.co.uk
  Admin: Mrs V Hall   Hon Sec: Douglas McWhinnie
- ▲ Registered Charity
- ○ *P; to promote good practice in day surgery
- ● Conf - Mtgs - ET - Res - Exhib - VE - LG
- < Intl Assn of Ambulatory Surgery
- M c 750 i
- ¶ Jnl of One-Day Surgery - 4.

British Association of Dental Nurses (BADN) 1940
- NR Hillhouse International Business Centre (Room 200), THORNTON CLEVELEYS, Lancs, FY5 4QD.   (hq)
  01253 338360   fax 01253 338360
  email admin@badn.org.uk   http://www.badn.org.uk
  Chief Exec: Pamela Swain
- Br local gps
- ○ *P; the only professional association representing the interests of dental nurses
- Gp National gps: Teaching (for those involved in training / education of dental nurses; Armed forces (for dental nurses working in or for the armed forces); Special care (for dental nurses working with patients with special needs); Orthodontic (for dental nurses working in ortho conscious sedation / anaesthesia) [in process of formation]
- ● Conf - Mtgs - Inf - Lib - Empl
- M c 5,600 i
- ¶ British Dental Nurses' Jnl - 4; ftm.

British Association of Dental Therapists (BADT) 1961
- ■ 24 Boundary St, BRYNMAWR, Gwent, NP23 4EX. (sp)
  email secretary@badt.org.uk http://www.badt.org.uk
  Sec: Kate Oakes
- Br c 8
- ○ *P
- ● Conf - Mtgs - ET - Inf - LG
- M 300 i
- ¶ Contact Point (NL) - 4.

British Association of Dermatologists (BAD) 1921
- ■ 4 Fitzroy Sq, LONDON, W1T 5HQ. (hq)
  020 7383 0266 fax 020 7388 5263
  email admin@bad.org.uk http://www.bad.org.uk
  Hon Sec: Dr J C Sterling
- ▲ Registered Charity
- ○ *P; study & teaching of dermatology (diseases of the skin)
- Gp British Contact Dermatitis Group; British Dermatological
  Nursing Group; British Society for Paediatric Dermatology;
  British Society for Dermatopathology; British Society for
  Investigative Dermatology; British Photodermatology Gp;
  British Society for Dermatological Surgery
- ● Conf - Mtgs - ET - Res - Exhib - SG
- M 741 i, UK / 202 i, o'seas
- ¶ British Jnl of Dermatology - 12; ftm, £446 yr nm.
  NL - 4; Hbk - 1; both ftm only.

British Association of Domiciliary Care
    since 2004 **Ceretas**

British Association of Dramatherapists (BADth) 1976
- NR 41 Broomhouse Lane, LONDON, SW6 3DP. (sp)
  020 7731 0160
  Sec: Gillian Eckley
- ○ *P; the development of dramatherapy in this country & abroad

British Association for Early Childhood Education (Early Education) 1923
- ■ 136 Cavell St, LONDON, E1 2JA. (hq)
  020 7539 5400 fax 020 7539 5409
  email office@early-education.org.uk
  http://www.early-education.org.uk
  Operations Mgr: Jenny Rabin
- ▲ Company Limited by Guarantee; Registered Charity
- Br 52
- ○ *E, *K, *W; to promote the right of all children to education of
  the highest quality; to provide a multi-disciplinary network of
  support & advice for everyone concerned with the care &
  education of children from birth to eight
- ● Conf - Mtgs - ET - Res - Exhib - Inf
- M 6,000 i, UK / 25 i, o'seas
- ¶ Early Education (Jnl) - 3; NL - 3; AR - 1; all ftm only.

British Association of Electrolysists Ltd
    2004 merged with the Institute of Electrolysis to form the **British Institute & Association of Electrolysis**

British Association for Emergency Medicine (BAEM) 1967
- ■ at the Royal College of Surgeons, 35-43 Lincoln's Inn Fields,
  LONDON, WC2A 3PE. (hq)
  020 7831 9405 fax 020 7405 0318
  email baem@emergencymedicine.uk.net
  http://www.emergencymed.org.uk
  Hon Sec: Mrs Alison Gammon
- ▲ Registered Charity
- ○ *L, *P; to promote the speciality of accident & emergency
  medicine
- ● Conf - Mtgs - ET - Res - Inf - Lib - LG
- < Intl Fedn of Emergency Medicine
- M 1,449 i, UK / 86 i, o'seas
- ¶ Emergency Medicine Jnl - 6; free to full m, £50 to other m.
- X 2004-05 British Association for Accident & Emergency Medicine

British Association of Endocrine Surgeons (BAES) 1980
- NR ASGBI, at the Royal College of Surgeons, 35-43 Lincoln's Inn
  Fields, LONDON, WC2A 3PE. (asa)
  020 7304 4771
- ▲ Registered Charity
- ○ *P; to advance standards of practice in surgical endocrinology;
  to promote research
- < Assn Surgeons GB & I
- M i

British Association of European Pharmaceutical Distributors (BAEPD) 1984
- ■ 4 Connaught Rd, Chingford, LONDON, E4 7DL. (sb)
  020 8529 3646
  Sec: Catherine Evans
- ▲ Company Limited by Guarantee
- ○ *T; the importation of licensed pharmaceutical products from
  within the EU
- M 20 i, 6 f, UK / 1 i, 1 f, o'seas

British Association for Fair Trade Shops (BAFTS) 1996
- NR Unit 7 / 8-13 New Inn St, LONDON, EC2A 3PY. (hq)
  0779 605 0045
  email info@bafts.org.uk http://www.bafts.org.uk
  Contact: Chris Davis
- ▲ Company Limited by Guarantee
- ○ *K, *T; to develop fair trade retailing; to raise profile of fair
  trade shops; to campaign on fair trade issues
- ● Conf - Inf
- < Intl Fedn for Alternative Trade (IFAT); Network of Eur Wld Shops
  (NEWS)
- M c 80 org
- ¶ NL; AR; both ftm only.

British Association of Fastener Distributors (BAFD)
- ■ Heathcote House, 136 Hagley Rd, BIRMINGHAM, B16 9PN.
  (hq)
  0780 103 0543 fax 0709 231 0932
  email mike@bafd.org.uk http://www.bafd.org
  Sec: M J H Philpots
- ▲ Un-incorporated Society
- ○ *T; interests of all fastener distributors
- ● Conf - Mtgs - ET - Exhib - Stat - Lib
- < Eur Fastener Distributors Assn
- M 75 f
- ¶ News from BAFD - 2; LM - 1; both ftm.

British Association of Feed Supplement & Additives Manufacturers (BAFSAM) 1968
- NR 238 Chester Rd, Hartford, NORTHWICH, Cheshire,
  CW8 1LW. (hsb)
  01606 783314 fax 01606 783314
  email hwebafsam@onetel.com
  Sec-Gen: H W Evans
- ▲ Company Limited by Guarantee
- ○ *T
- ● Mtgs - Consultees to FSA, DEFRA, VMD in all legislative matters
  in relation to animal nutrition
- < Eur Fedn of Mfrs of Animal Feed Additives (FEFANA)
- M 20 f

**British Association of Flower Essence Producers   (BAFEP)
2000**
- ■ PO Box 100, Exminster, EXETER, Devon, EX6 8YT.   (hsp)
01392 832005   fax 01392 832005
email info@bafep.com   http://www.bafep.com
Hon Sec: Sue Lilly
- ▲ Un-incorporated Society
- ○ *T; for producers of flower & all types of essences meeting
manufacturing standards in the UK
- ● Inf - LG
- M 57 f, UK / 2 f, o'seas
- ¶ The Bioneer (NL) - 4; ftm only.
Guidelines Hbk; free.
Note: formed by practitional members of the British Flower &
Vibrational Essences Association to fight the political issues
that have arisen

British Association in Forensic Medicine   (BAFM)   1951
- ■ Wales Institute of Forensic Medicine, Cardiff University College
of Medicine, Heath Park, CARDIFF, CF14 4XN.   (hsb)
029 2074 4830
http://www.bafm.org
Hon Sec: Dr A M Davidson
- ▲ Un-incorporated Society
- ○ *P; to advance the study & practice of forensic pathology; to act
as a negotiating & advisory body when required
- ● Conf
- M 135 i, UK / 35 i, o'seas

**British Association of Former United Nations Civil Servants
(BAFUNCS)   1977**
- NR c/o UN Association, 3 Whitehall Court, LONDON,
SW1A 2EL.   (mail/address)
01435 872647
email bafuncs@globalnet.co.uk
http://www.bafuncs.imo.org/home.htm
Hon Sec: Sheila Cooper
- ▲ Un-incorporated Society
- Br 10 regions
- ○ *W; comradeship, fellowship and associated social activities
- ● Mtgs - VE
- < Fedn of Assns of Former UN Civil Servants (FAFICS)
- M 769 i, UK /c 76 i, o'seas
- ¶ NL - 2;   LM; both ftm.

British Association of Friends of Museums   (BAFM)   1973
- ■ The Shrubbery, 14 Church St, WHITCHURCH, Hants,
RG28 7AB.   (hq)
01256 893231
email secretary@bafm.org.uk   http://www.bafm.org.uk
Sec: Deborah Woodland
- ▲ Registered Charity
- Br 330
- ○ *A, *N; 'the only national independent organisation for friends,
volunteers & supporters of museums, galleries, archives,
libraries, historic house gardens & parks, churches & other
institutions preserving the UK's cultural heritage'
- ● Conf - Mtgs - SG - Inf - Lib - VE - LG
Central source of inf: 'about Friends for Friends'
- < Wld Fedn of Friends of Museums
- M 97 i, 30 museums etc, 330 Friends gps (representing
200,000 i)
- ¶ NL - 3.   Hbk for Friends.   Information Sheets 1-15 - irreg.
Charter & Hbk for Volunteer Managers & Administrators.

**British Association of Golf Course Constructors   (BAGCC)
1981**
- ■ The Dormy House, Cooden Beach Golf Club, BEXHILL-on-SEA,
E Sussex, TN39 4TR.   (hq)
01424 842380   fax 01424 843375
email mightyspyder@aol.com
Chief Exec: David White
- ▲ Un-incorporated Society
- ○ *T; golf course construction, remodelling & renovation
- Gp Golf course constructors (full members); Suppliers (associate
members)
- ● Conf - Mtgs - Exhib - Inf
- M 15 f (constructors), 32 associates (supply)
- ¶ Folder of brochures of BAGCC members; free.

British Association of Green Crop Driers Ltd   (BAGCD)   1950
- ■ Silverwood, Stone St, Westenhanger, HYTHE, Kent,
CT21 4HT.   (asa)
01303 267317   fax 01303 267317
email info@bagcd.org   http://www.bagcd.org
Sec: Roger H Earl
- ▲ Company Limited by Guarantee
- ○ *T; to promote use of dried green crops for animal feed
- ● Conf - Mtgs - Inf - VE - LG
- < Commission Intersyndicale des Déshydrateurs Européens
- M [not stated]

British Association of the Hard of Hearing
an alternative title of **Hearing Concern**

**British Association of Head & Neck Oncologists   (BAHNO)
1968**
- NR Dept of Maxillofacial Surgery, Sunderland Royal Hospital,
Kayll Rd, SUNDERLAND, SR4 7TP.   (hsb)
0191-569 9132
Hon Sec: Ian Martin
- ▲ Registered Charity
- ○ *P; to advance the understanding & treatment of head & neck
cancer. Members are surgeons, oncologists, pathologists &
other interested medical staff involved in the care &
management of patients with head & neck cancer
- ● Conf - Mtgs - Res - SG
- M c 450 i, UK / 50 i, o'seas
- ¶ Abstracts of meetings incl in Clinical Oncology - 1.

**British Association of Health Services in Higher Education
(BAHSHE)   1947**
- ■ 35 Hazelwood Rd, Bush Hill Park, ENFIELD, Middx, EN1 1JG.
(hq)
020 8482 2412   fax 010 8482 2412
email s.furmston@middx.ac.uk
http://www.bahshe.demon.co.uk
Admin Officer: Sandra Furmston
- ▲ Registered Charity
- ○ *W; health of students studying in universities & colleges in UK
- ● Conf

British Association of Homoeopathic Manufacturers   (BAHM)
- NR 65 Church St, Langham, OAKHAM, Leics, LE15 7JE.
(secretariat)
01572 771115   fax 01572 724627
Sec: Penny Viner
- ▲ Un-incorporated Society
- ○ *T; to advance the knowledge & practice of homoeopathy; to
maintain standards, research, quality control & development
of homoeopathic medicines
- < Homoeopathic Devt Foundation
- M 6 f
NOTE: is active only in a crisis; eg with a change of the
licensing law

** **British Association of Homoeopathic Pharmacists**
Organisation lost: see Introduction paragraph 3

© CBD Research Ltd · Beckenham · BR3 5JS · Tel 020 8650 7745 · Fax 020 8650 0768 · E-mail cbd@cbdresearch.com · www.cbdresearch.com

British Association of Homoeopathic Veterinary Surgeons (BAHVS) 1981
NR Alternative Veterinary Medicine Centre, Chinham House, STANFORD-IN-THE-VALE, Oxon, SN7 8NQ. (hsp/b)
01367 718115
http://www.bahvs.com
Hon Sec: Christopher E I Day
○ *L, *P, *V; to promote veterinary homoeopathy amongst the veterinary profession
● Conf - ET - Res (clinical only) - SG - Inf
< Intl Assn for Veterinary Homoeopathy
M c 140 i
¶ NL - 2; ftm only.

British Association of Hospitality Accountants (BAHA) 1969
NR Merley House Business Centre (suite 6), Merley House Lane, WIMBORNE, Dorset, BH21 3AA. (hq)
01202 889430   fax 01202 887969
Admin: Philippa Graham
○ *P; interests of financial managers in the hotel, catering & leisure industry
● Conf - Mtgs - ET - Exam - Advice
< Chart Inst Mgt Accountants (CIMA) - for BAHA's training programme
M 550 i, UK / 150 i, o'seas
¶ BAHA Times (NL) - 10;   AR - 1; both ftm only.
✕ 1998 British Association of Hotel Accountants

British Association of Hotel Representatives (BAHREP)
NR 127 New House Park, ST ALBANS, Herts, AL1 1UT. (hsb)
01727 812722
Sec: Diana Hall
▲ Un-incorporated Society
○ *P
● Mtgs - ET - Exhib - Inf - LG
M 60 i, 60 f

British Association for Human Identification (BAHID) 2001
■ 2 Market Square, STONEHAVEN, Aberdeenshire, AB39 2BT. (asa)
01569 760022
email info@bahid.org   http://www.bahid.org
Treas: Mr Black
▲ Un-incorporated Society
○ *P; to bring together forensic practitioners & academics involved in the field of human identification & address common problems & develop research & communication
Gp Forensic: Anthropology, Archaeology, Entomology, Pathology, Podiatry, Radiology;
Facial analysis; Molecular genetics; Police; Anatomy
● Conf - ET - Res - Current information on up-dated website
M c 300 i, UK / c 60 i, o'seas
¶ [Textbook on Human ID; in preparation]

British Association for Immediate Care (BASICS) 1977
NR Turret House, Turret Lane, IPSWICH, Suffolk, IP4 1DL. (hq)
0870 165 4999   fax 0870 165 4949
email admin@basics.org.uk   http://www.basics.org.uk
Hon Sec: Dr Peter Holder
▲ Registered Charity
○ *W; to promote & improve all aspects of immediate care (provision of skilled medical help at the site of accidents & other emergencies)
● Conf - Mtgs - ET - Exam - Res - Exhib - SG - Stat - Inf - Lib
M c 1,300 i
¶ NL - 3;   AR - 1; both ftm only.   Monographs.

British Association for Information & Library Education & Research (BAILER) 1962
■ c/o Prof J Feather, Dept of Information Science, Loughborough University, LOUGHBOROUGH, Leics, LE11 3TU. (chmn/b)
01509 223050
email j.p.feather@lboro.ac.uk   http://www.bailer.ac.uk
Chmn: Prof John Feather,   Sec: William Foster
○ *E, *P; information & library studies education & research in the UK
Gp Information policy; Information management; Records management
● Conf - Mtgs - ET - Res
M 220 i
¶ Directory of Courses in Library & Information Studies in the UK - 1; free.

British Association for Irish Studies (BAIS) 1985
NR Geography Dept, University of Manchester, Oxford Rd, MANCHESTER, M13 9PL. (hq)
0161-275 3623
Chmn: Mervyn Busteed
▲ Registered Charity
○ *E; promotion & support for Irish studies in the UK
Gp Conference & cultural; Irish language; Publications; Education
● Conf - ET - LG - Organisation of public lectures
M c 300 i & f, UK / 30 i, o'seas
¶ Irish Studies Review - 3.   NL - 4.

British Association of Japanese Studies (BAJS) 1974
NR BAJS Secretariat, University of Essex, COLCHESTER, Essex, CO4 3SQ.
01206 872543   fax 01206 873408
Exec Sec: Mrs Lynn Baird
○ *L
¶ NL -3;   Japan Forum - 3.

British Association of Journalists
■ 89 Fleet St, LONDON, EC4Y 1DH.
020 7353 3003   fax 020 7353 2310
Gen Sec: Steve Turner
○ *P, *U; raising the status & rewards of journalists: seeks to protect & improve fees for freelance members & pay, condition & pensions for staff members
M 960 i, UK / 25 i, o'seas
¶ BAJ News (NL) - 4.

British Association of Korean Studies (BAKS) 1983
■ c/o Dr J Grayson, School of East Asian Studies, University of Sheffield, SHEFFIELD, S Yorks, S10 2TN.
http://www.dur.ac.uk/BAKS
Pres; Dr J Grayson
▲ Un-incorporated Society
○ *L, *X; to promote, in the UK, the study & understanding of Korea
● Conf
< UK Area Studies Assn
M 59 i, UK / 8 i, o'seas
¶ Papers - 1-2 yrly; prices vary.

British Association of Landscape Industries (BALI) 1972
■ Landscape House, STONELEIGH PARK, Warks, CV8 2LG. (hq)
0870 770 4971   fax 0870 779 4972
email contact@bali.org.uk   http://www.bali.org.uk
Chief Exec Officer: Sandra Loton-Jones
▲ Company Limited by Guarantee
Br 9
○ *T; to represent UK firms undertaking landscaping, both interior & exterior, & a wide range of associated suppliers
Gp Affiliates; Designers; Domestic; Grounds; Interiors; Maintenance; Students
● Mtgs - ET - Exhib - Comp - Inf - VE - LG - Annual awards ceremony
< Eur Landscape Contrs Assn (ELCA)
> Assn of Landscape Contrs Ireland (Northern & Southern) (ALCI)
M 54 i, 687 f, UK / 9 f, o'seas
¶ Landscape News - 4.   Business News - 4; Awards Brochure - 1; all ftm only.
Who's Who Directory - 1; ftm, £40 nm.

British Association of Leisure Parks, Piers & Attractions (BALPPA) 1936
NR BALPPA House, 57-61 Newington Causeway, LONDON, SE1 6BD. (hq)
020 7403 4455
Chmn: David Cam
▲ Company Limited by Guarantee
○ *T; for British private sector leisure parks, piers, attractions & suppliers to the industry
Gp Catering & retail; Coin machine operators; Engineers; Trade associations supplying goods & services
● Conf - Mtgs - ET - Exhib - SG - Expt - VE - LG
< EUROPARKS
M 247 f, UK / 33 f, o'seas

British Association for Literacy in Development (BALID)
■ 14 Dufferin St, LONDON, EC1Y 8PD. (hq)
020 7426 5849   fax 020 7251 1314
email balid@education-action.org
http://www.balid.org.uk
Sec: Juliet McCaffery
▲ Un-incorporated Society
○ *E, *K, to promote literacy & numeracy for adults as an integral part of human development; to increase awareness of the relationship between literacy & numeracy & economic development & social change
● Conf - Mtgs - Res
< UNESCO; Universities of: Pennsylvania, Brighton, London, East Anglia & Sussex
> Education Action Intl; Nat Res & Devt Centre; Nottingham University
M [not stated]
¶ Reports [on website].

British Association for Local History (BALH) 1982
■ PO Box 6549, Somersal Herbert, ASHBOURNE, Derbys, DE6 5WH. (hq)
01283 585947
http://www.balh.co.uk
Business Mgr: A Jones
▲ Registered Charity; Un-incorporated Society
○ *L; to promote the advancement of public education through the study of local history
● Conf - SG - Inf - VE
M c 2,300 i
¶ The Local Historian - 4.   Local History News - 4.

British Association for Lung Research (BALR) 1982
NR c/o Dr N K Harrison, Respiratory Unit, Morriston Hospital, SWANSEA, SA6 6NL. (hsb)
01792 7032131   fax 01792 703845
Chmn: Dr Kim Harrison
▲ Registered Charity
○ *P
● Conf - Mtgs
M c 350 i
¶ NL - 3; ftm only.   LM.

British Association of Medical Hypnosis 2001
NR 28 Old Brompton Rd (suite 296), LONDON, SW7 3SS.
020 8998 4436
http://www.rnp@medicalhypnotherapy.co.uk
Organising Sec: Dr Rumi Peynovska
○ *P
¶ European Journal of Clinical Hypnosis.

British Association of Medical Managers (BAMM) 1992
NR Petersgate House (3rd floor), 64 St Petersgate, STOCKPORT, Cheshire, SK1 1HE. (hq)
0161-474 1141
Chief Exec: Dr Jenny Simpson
▲ Company Limited by Guarantee
○ *P; for clinicians in management who are part of the medical profession
Gp Medical; Clinical governance
● Conf - Mtgs - ET - Res
M i

British Association of Mountain Guides (BMG) 1975
■ Siabod Cottage, CAPEL CURIG, Conwy, LL24 0ES. (regd/office)
01690 720386   fax 01690 720248
email guiding@bmg.org.uk   http://www.bmg.org.uk
Hon Sec: Alun Richardson
▲ Company Limited by Guarantee
○ *P, *S; professional mountaineering services, mountain guiding, rock climbing, ice climbing, alpine guiding, ski mountaineering
● Mtgs - ET - Exam
< Intl Fedn of Mountain Guide Assns (IFMGA)
M 133 i, UK / 43 i, o'seas
¶ NL - 3;   AR; both ftm.
Members' Directory; free (also available on website).

British Association of Nature Conservationists (BANC) 1997
NR Denton Wood Farm. Bedford rd, NORTHAMPTON, NN7 2EA. (memsec/b)
email banc@dentonwood.co.uk   http://www.banc.org.uk
Mem Sec: Karen Cropper
▲ Company Limited by Guarantee, Registered Charity
○ *K; to advance nature conservation in the UK; to act as a network for conservationists & people who care about the natural world
M i & org
¶ Ecos: a review of conservation - 3; ftm.

British Association of Numismatic Societies (BANS) 1953
■ c/o General Services, 42 Campbell Rd, LONDON, E3 4DT. (hsp)
020 8980 5672
email bans@mernicks.com
http://www.coinclubs.freeserve.co.uk
Hon Sec: Philip Mernick
▲ Un-incorporated Society
Br 60
○ *N; to promote & coordinate interest & research by local & regional societies
● Conf - Res - SG - Inf - PL - VE
M c 2,000 i
¶ Doris Stockwell Memorial Papers - irreg; price varies.

© CBD Research Ltd · Beckenham · BR3 5JS · Tel 020 8650 7745 · Fax 020 8650 0768 · E-mail cbd@cbdresearch.com · www.cbdresearch.com

British Association of Nursery & Pram Retailers
ceased trading 2005

British Association for Nutritional Therapy   (BANT)   1997
NR   27 Old Gloucester St, LONDON, WC1N 3XX.   (mail)
0870 606 1284   fax 0870 606 1284
email theadministrator@bant.org.uk
http://www.bant.org.uk address
Sec: Susan McGinty
▲   Company Limited by Guarantee
○   *P; the application of nutrition science in the promotion of
optimum health & peak performance, disease prevention &
patient care
●   Conf - ET
M   c 1,500 i
¶   The BANT Membership NL - 4.
✕   2002 British Association of Nutritional Therapists

**British Association of Occupational Therapists Ltd   (BAOT/
COT)   1932**
■   106-114 Borough High St, LONDON, SE1 1LB.   (hq)
020 7357 6480   fax 020 7450 2299
http://www.cot.org.uk
Sec: Julia Scott
▲   Company Limited by Guarantee; Registered Charity
○   *P, *U; for all occupational therapy staff & students in the UK
Gp   College of Occupational Therapists; Association of
Occupational Therapists in Mental Health; Housing; HIV/
AIDS oncology, palliative care & education; Neurology; Rapid
intervention; Paediatric; Rheumatology; Work practice &
productivity; Working with people with learning disabilities;
Independent practice, Older people, Trauma & orthopaedics
●   Conf - Mtgs - ET - Comp - Res - Exhib - SG - Lib - Empl - LG
<   Wld Fedn of Occupational Therapists (WFOT); Coun of
Occupational Therapists for the Eur Countries (COTEC)
M   27,000 i, UK / 500 i, o'seas
¶   British Journal of Occupational Therapy - 12; ftm, £153 nm.
Occupational Therapy News - 12; ftm.   AR; free.
Publications list on website.

British Association for Open Learning
2003 merged with the Forum for Technology in Training to form the
British Learning Association

**British Association of Oral & Maxillofacial Surgeons
(BAOMS)   1962**
NR   at the Royal College of Surgeons, 35-43 Lincoln's Inn Fields,
LONDON, WC2A 3PN.   (hq)
020 7405 8074   fax 020 7430 9997
○   *L, *P
●   Conf - Mtgs - ET - Res - SG
M   797 i, UK / 303 i, o'seas
¶   British Journal of Oral & Maxillofacial Surgery - 6; ftm.

**British Association of Otorhinolaryngologists - Head & Neck
Surgeons   (ENT.UK (BAO-HNS))   1943**
■   at the Royal College of Surgeons, 35-43 Lincoln's Inn Fields,
LONDON, WC2A 3PE.   (hq)
020 7404 8373   fax 020 7404 4200
email admin@entuk.org   http://www.entuk.org
Hon Sec: Chris A Milford,
Admin Mgr: Barbara Komoniewska
▲   Registered Charity
○   *L, *M, *P; to promote education research & audit & works to
achieve the highest standards of medical & surgical practice
in otology, laryngology, rhinology & head & neck surgery
●   Conf - Mtgs - ET - Exhib - Inf - LG
>   Brit Otology, Hearing & Balance Gp
M   1,179 i, UK / 50 i, o'seas
¶   NL - 6;   AR;   LM & Constitution - irreg; all ftm only.
Note: in Autumn 2003 adopted the working name of ENT.UK

British Association of Paediatric Surgeons   (BAPS)   1954
NR   Royal College of Surgeons of England, 35/43 Lincoln's Inn
Fields, LONDON, WC2A 3PN.   (hq)
020 7312 6638
Secs: Kate Billington & Wendy Rees
○   *P
●   Conf - Mtgs - Exhib - Inf
M   140 i, UK / 460 i, o'seas
¶   Jnl of Paediatric Surgery - 6;   NL - 4;   LM - 1; all ftm.

**British Association of Paintings Conservator-Restorers
(BAPCR)   1943**
■   PO Box 258, Blofield, NORWICH, Norfolk, NR13 4WY.   (sb)
01603 858129   fax 0870 478 1490
email secretary@bapcr.org.uk   http://www.bapcr.org.uk
Sec: Lucy Jane Tetlow
▲   Un-incorporated Society
○   *A, *P; conservation & restoration of paintings
●   Conf - Mtgs - ET - Exam - VE
<   Intl Inst for Consvn (IIC); Scot Soc for Consvn &
Restoration (SSCR); Inst of Paper Consvn (IPC)
M   400 i, UK / 30 i, o'seas
¶   The Picture Restorer (Jnl) - 2; ftm, £3.50 each nm.
Conference preprints.
✕   2002 Association of British Picture Restorers

British Association of Paper Historians   (BAPH)   1989
■   27 North End, Longhaughton, ALNWICK, Northumberland,
NE66 3JG.   (memsec/p)
01665 577988
http://www.baph.org.uk
Littlefield, Christmas Common, WATLINGTON, Oxon,
OX45 5HR.   (chmn/p)
Hon Chmn: P R Crockett
▲   Un-incorporated Society
○   *L; to promote all aspects of the study of paper & papermaking
history
●   Conf - Mtgs - VE
M   170 i, 37 f, UK / 40 i, 18 f, o'seas
¶   The Quarterly (Jnl) - 4.   LM - 1.
BAPH News (NL) - 4.   Conference Report - 1.

**British Association for Performing Arts Medicine   (BAPAM)
1984**
■   Totara Park House (4th floor), 34-36 Gray's Inn Rd, LONDON,
WC1X 8HR.   (hq)
020 7404 5888   fax 020 7404 3222
email admin@bapam.org.uk
http://www.bapam.org.uk
Chief Exec: Naomi Wayne
▲   Registered Charity
○   *K, *P; to ensure the highest standards of medical care for
those involved in the performing arts; to monitor the
incidence of performing arts injuries & to record the way in
which they are treated
●   Conf - ET - Res
M   350 i, 5 f, UK / 5 i, o'seas
¶   Jnl - 2;   NL - 4; both ftm only.

British Association of Perinatal Medicine   (BAPM)   1976
■   50 Hallam St, LONDON, W1W 6DE.   (hq)
020 7307 5627   fax 020 7307 5601
email bapm@rcpch.ac.uk   http://www.bapm.org
Hon Sec: Dr Andrew Lyon
▲   Registered Charity
○   *M, *P; to improve the standards of perinatal care (from the
seventh month of pregnancy to the first week of the baby's
life)
●   Conf - ET - Res - Exhib - SG - Inf - LG
<   R Coll Paediatrics & Child Health; R Coll Obstetricians &
Gynaecologists
M   800 i, UK / 50 i, o'seas
¶   BAPM News - 4; ftm only.   AR - 1; ftm, [online; nm].

British Association of Pharmaceutical Physicians   (BrAPP)
NR   Royal Station Court, Station Rd, Twyford, READING, Berks,
      RG10 9NF.
      0118-934 1943
      Assn Mgr: Elizabeth Langley
○   *P
¶   Jnl - 6.

**British Association of Pharmaceutical Wholesalers   (BAPW)
1966**
■   90 Long Acre, LONDON, WC2E 9RA.   (hq)
      020 7031 0590   fax 020 7031 0591
      email mail@bapw.net   http://www.bapw.net
      Sec: Sarah Ewen
▲   Company Limited by Guarantee
○   *T; to secure the safest & most cost effective distribution of a
      comprehensive range of healthcare products & related
      services; to advance efficient healthcare management
●   Conf - SG - Inf - LG
<   Intl Fedn of Pharmaceutical Wholesalers; Groupement Intl de la
      Réparation Pharmaceutique des Pays de la CE; Assn of the
      Brit Pharmaceutical Ind
M   11 f (full), 43 f (associate), 3 f (affiliate)

British Association for Physical Training   (BAPT)   1919
NR   14 Moorside Close, WEYMOUTH, Dorset, DT4 7RQ.
      (jt/chmn/p)
      01305 784637
      Jt Chmn: Gordon Knowles
○   *P; promotion of physical education
M   i
¶   Bulletin - 3; ftm only.

**British Association of Picture Libraries & Agencies   (BAPLA)
1975**
NR   18 Vine Hill, LONDON, EC1R 5DZ.   (hq)
      020 7713 1780
      Chief Exec: Linda Royles
▲   Company Limited by Guarantee
○   *T, *P; issues relevant to the picture library industry: copyright
      laws & rights, technology, standards, digital imagery,
      archiving
Gp   Collective management; Copyright; Technology - digital images
●   Conf - Mtgs - ET - Res - Exhib - SG - PL - VE - LG
M   4 i, 450 f, UK / 2 f, o'seas
¶   Lightbox - 4.   Weekly NL - 52.
      BAPLA Directory of Picture Libraries & Agencies - 1.

**British Association of Plastic, Reconstructive & Aesthetic
Surgeons   (BAPRAS)   1946**
■   at the Royal College of Surgeons, 35-43 Lincoln's Inn Fields,
      LONDON, WC2A 3PE.   (hq)
      020 7831 5161   fax 020 7831 4041
      email secretariat@bapras.co.uk
      http://www.bapras.co.uk
      Hon Sec: J H E Laing
▲   Company Limited by Guarantee, Registered Charity
○   *L, *M, *P, *Q; promotion & development of plastic surgery; to
      advance education in the field
Gp   Breast special interest; Head & neck; Overseas service of
      training
●   Conf - Mtgs - ET - Res
<   Brit Assn of Aesthetic Plastic Surgeons (BAAPS)
M   570 i, UK / 160 i, o'seas
¶   Jnl of Plastic, Reconstructive & Aesthetic Surgery - 12; ftm.
×   2006 British Association of Plastic Surgeons

British Association of Play Therapists   (BAPT)   1992
NR   1 Beacon Mews, South Rd, WEYBRIDGE, Surrey, KT13 9DZ.
      (admin/asst/p)
      01932 828638
      email info@bapt.uk.com   http://www.bapt.uk.com
      Chmn: Judy Gray
○   *P; to promote & develop standards of training in play therapy
●   Conf - Mtgs - Res - SG - Inf
M   c 350 i
¶   NL - 4; ftm only.   Jnl for Play Therapy - 1.
      What is Play Therapy? (leaflet for parents & carers).
      What is Play Therapy? (booklet for children).
      A Guide to Play Therapy.

British Association of Pool Table Operators   (BAPTO)   1975
NR   176 High St, London Colney, St Albans, Herts, AL2 1JY.
      01727 854986
      Sec: Tom Gilvarry
▲   Company Limited by Guarantee
○   *T; to promote the game of pool
●   Conf - Mtgs - ET - Exam - Comp - Stat - Inf
M   c 50 f

British Association for Print & Communication   (BAPC)   1979
NR   Concorde House, 56 Station Rd, LONDON, N3 2SA.   (hq)
      020 8349 3009   fax 020 8224 9090
      http://www.bapc.co.uk
      Dir: Tony Honnor
○   *T; representing the high street copyshops & printers - dealing
      with all aspects of training, specialising in 'quickprint'
      operations
M   i & f
¶   The Quickprinter - 6; free.
×   1999-2000 British Association of Printers & Copycentres Ltd

British Association of Prosthetists & Orthotists   (BAPO)   1994
NR   Sir James Clark Building, Abbeymill Business Centre, PAISLEY,
      Renfrewshire, PA1 1TJ.   (hq)
      0141-561 7217   fax 0141-561 7218
      email admin@bapo.com   http://www.bapo.org
      Exec Profl Officer: Ken Andrews
      Chmn: Steven Lindsay
▲   Un-incorporated Society
○   *M, *P; prosthetics: health care involved in fitting artificial limbs
      (prostheses)
      Orthotics: health care in fitting orthoses (braces, splints, & other
      devices applied externally to the human body)
●   Conf - Mtgs - ET - Exhib - SG - Inf - LG
<   Health Profls Coun
M   900 i, UK / 40 i, o'seas
¶   List of publications available on request.

British Association for Psychological Type   (BAPT)   1989
NR   17 Royal Crescent, CHELTENHAM, Glos, GL50 3DA.   (sp)
      01242 282990
      email office@bapt.org.uk   http://www.bapt.org.uk
      Sec: Bill Davies
▲   Registered Charity
○   *L; Jungian psychological type theory
      no further information supplied

British Association for Psychopharmacology   (BAP)   1974
NR   36 Cambridge Place, Hills Rd, CAMBRIDGE, CB2 1NS.   (hq)
      01223 358395   fax 01223 321268
      email susan@bap.org.uk   http://www.bap.org.uk
      Exec Officer: Mrs Susan Chandler (01223 358428)
▲   Registered Charity
○   *L; to advance education & research in the science of
      psychopharmacology both clinical & experimental
●   Conf - Mtgs - ET
M   850 i, UK / 150 i, o'seas
¶   Jnl of Psychopharmacology - 4.   NL - 4; ftm.

British Association of Psychotherapists (BAP) 1951

■ 37 Mapesbury Rd, LONDON, NW2 4HJ. (hq)
020 8452 9823   fax 020 8452 0310
email mail@bap-psychotherapy.org
http://www.bap-psychotherapy.org
Chief Exec: Mrs Elise Ormerod
Publicity Officer: Dr Tim Fox
▲ Registered Charity
○ *E, *P; a training organisation for adult, child & adolescent psychoanalytic & Jungian analytic psychotherapy; to offer assessment & where appropriate, treatment for people seeking individual psychotherapy.
The BAP aims to provide information to the public & to the caring professions, to make psychotherapy more widely available; to maintain standards in training & clinical practice & professional conduct
Gp Jungian analytic; Psychoanalytic (adult); Psychoanalytic (child & adolescent)
● Conf - Mtgs - ET - Res - SG - Lib - Assessment for, & provision of, psychotherapy
< Assn Child Psychotherapists (ACP); Brit Confedn of Psychotherapists (BCP); Intl Assn of Analytical Psychology (IAAP)
M 500 i, UK / 12 i, o'seas
¶ Jnl - 2; ftm, £27 i, £55 instns, nm.

British Association of Public Safety Communications Officers (BAPCO) 1994

NR P O Box 374, LINCOLN, LN1 1FY.
01522 575542
Chief Exec: Ken Mott
M c 1,500 i

British Association for the Purebred Spanish Horse (BAPSH) 1982

NR 28a St John's St, DEVIZES, Wilts, SN10 1NN. (hsp)
01380 720326
Sec: Maria Ward-Jones
○ *B
● Exhib
< Jefatura de Cria Caballar; FICCE
M c 400 i
¶ Pura Raza Española - 4; ftm.

British Association of Record Dealers (BARD) 1988

NR Colonnade House (1st floor), 2 Westover Rd, BOURNEMOUTH, Dorset, BH1 2BY. (hq)
01202 292063
email admin@bardltd.org.uk
Dir Gen: Kim Bayley
▲ Company Limited by Guarantee
○ *T; interests of retailers selling recorded music, videos & computer games
Gp Marketing; Operations; Information technology
● Conf - Mtgs - Stat - LG
< Nat Assn of Recorded Merchandisers (USA)
M 174 i
¶ NL - 4;   Bulletin - 12; both ftm only.

British Association of Remote Sensing Companies (BARSC) 1985

NR c/o Vega Group PLC, 2 Falcon Way, Shire Park, WELWYN GARDEN CITY, Herts, AL7 1TW. (hsb)
01707 391999
http://www.barsc.org.uk
Exec Sec: Gareth Davies
▲ Un-incorporated Society
○ *T; companies undertaking activities directly connected with remote sensing (the collection of information about physical objects & the environment from remote platforms - aircraft & satellites)
Gp Applications working gp - focus on commercial opportunities to exploit earth observation data
● Conf - Mtgs - Exhib - Expt - LG - Liaison European agencies
M 18 f

British Association of Removers (BAR) (BAR) 1900

NR Tangent House, 62 Exchange Rd, WATFORD, Herts, WD18 0TG. (hq)
01923 699480   fax 01923 699481
email info@bar.co.uk   http://www.bar.co.uk
Gen Sec: Robert D Syers
▲ Company Limited by Guarantee
○ *T; for the professional moving industry; to maintain standards for the benefit of members & their customers
Gp National & European domestic moves; Overseas; Commercial
● Conf - Mtgs - ET - Exam - Exhib - Comp - SG - Inf - VE - LG
< Fedn Eur Moving Assns (FEDEMAC); Fedn Intl Movers (FIDI)
M 650 f, UK / 250 f, o'seas
¶ Removals & Storage - 12.

British Association Representing Breeders
since 2006 **British Association of Rose Breeders**

British Association for Research Quality Assurance (BARQA) 1977

NR 3 Wherry Lane, IPSWICH, Suffolk, IP4 1LG. (hq)
01473 221411
Assn Mgr: David Weller
▲ Company Limited by Guarantee
○ *P; to evaluate & appraise the quality assurance aspects of regulations, guidelines & principles, both national & international, related to studies conducted on chemicals, biologicals & devices which affect humans, animals & the environment known as good laboratory practice (GLP), good clinical practice (GCP) & good manufacturing practice (GMP)
Gp C'ees: Meetings; Education & training; Good clinical practice; Good manufacturing practice; Animal health; Field studies; Computing; Good laboratory practice; Publications
● Conf - Mtgs - ET - Exam - Comp - SG - Inf
< Eur Quality Assurance Soc (EQAS); US Soc of Quality Assurance (SQA); Japan Soc of Quality Assurance (JSQA)
M 1,100 i, UK / 500 i, o'seas
¶ Quasar Magazine - 4;   AR - 1; Members' Directory - 1;   all ftm only.

British Association Rose Breeders (BARB) 1973

■ 17 The Wren Centre, Westbourne Rd, EMSWORTH, Hants, PO10 7SU. (hq)
01243 389532   fax 01243 389509
email info@barbuk.org.uk
Pres: Colin Dickson,   Gen Mgr: Ian Kennedy
▲ Un-incorporated Society
○ *H, *T; to encourage, improve & extend the introduction & growing of roses & other ornamental plants under Plant-Breeders' Rights
Gp Plant breeders; Roses, Rose growers
● Mtgs - Exhib - Stat - Inf - Rose trials - International liaison
M 32 i, 23 f
¶ Ybk (listing protected plants available through BARB) - 1; free.
✕ 2006 British Association Representing Breeders

British Association of Rose Growers
see **British Rose Growers Association**

British Association of Seating Equipment Suppliers (BASES)

■ Federation House, STONELEIGH PARK, Warks, CV8 2RF. (hq)
024 7641 4999   fax 024 7641 4990
email bases@sportsandplay.com
http://www.sportsandplay.com
▲ Company Limited by Guarantee
○ *T; manufacturers & suppliers of various types of audience seating
● Mtgs - Inf - LG
< a group of the Fedn of Sports & Play Assns (FSPA)
M 5 f

British Association of Seed Analysts (BASA) 1925

NR   Confederation House, East of England Showground,
      PETERBOROUGH, PE2 6XE. (hq)
      01733 385271 fax 01733 385270
      email paul.rooke@agindustries.org.uk
      Sec: Paul Rooke
○   *T; advancement of seed testing & seed testing stations
●   Conf - Mtgs - Inf - VE
<   UK Agricl Supply Tr Assn
M   80 i
¶   e-newsletters

British Association for Service to the Elderly (BASE) 1974

■   119 Hassell St, NEWCASTLE-UNDER-LYNE, Staffs, ST5 1AX.
      (hq)
      01782 661033 fax 01782 661033
      http://www.base.org.uk
▲   Registered Charity
Br 4
○   *W; to provide education & training for all those working with
      older people, vulnerable adults & their carers in health &
      social care
●   ET
M 720 i, 100 f
¶   Quality in Agency - 4; £55 m.

**British Association of Settlements & Social Action Centres
(BASSAC) 1920**

NR   33 Corsham St, LONDON, N1 6DR. (hq)
      0845 241 0375
      Contact: Carole McQueen
▲   Company Limited by Guarantee; Registered Charity
○   *W; 'is a national organisation of multi-purpose urban centres
      committed to helping local communities to bring about social
      change'
M c100 centres
¶   Monthly ENews - 10; ftm.   BASSAC Directory - 1.

British Association for Sexual Health & HIV (BASHH) 1922

■   c/o Royal Society of Medicine, 1 Wimpole St, LONDON,
      W1G 0AE. (hq)
      020 7290 2968 fax 020 7290 2989
      email bashh@rsm.ac.uk http://www.bashh.org
      Gen Sec: Dr Keith Radcliffe
▲   Registered Charity
○   *L, *M; to promote the study of the art & science of diagnosing
      & treating sexually transmitted infections, including HIV &
      other sexual health problems
Gp British Co-operative Clinical Group; Genito-Urinary Physicians
      Colposcopy Group
      Special interest: Adolescence, Bacterial, Herpes simplex virus,
      HIV, HPV, Sexual dysfunction
●   Conf - Mtgs - ET - Res - Lib - LG
M 900 i, UK / 72 i, o'seas
¶   Guidelines - irreg; AR; both free.
×   2003 (Association for Genito-Urinary Medicine
      (Medical Society for the Study of Venereal Diseases

**British Association for Sexual & Relationship Therapy
(BASRT) 1972**

■   PO Box 13686, LONDON, SW20 9ZH. (mail)
      020 8543 2707 fax 020 8543 2707
      email info@basrt.org.uk
      http://www.basrt.org.uk address
      Chief Exec Officer: Corinna Furse
▲   Company Limited by Guarantee
○   *P; for clinicians & therapists who treat sexual & relationship
      problems
●   Conf - ET - Res - Approves training courses in sex therapy -
      Provides list of local therapists
M 680 i, UK / 40 i, o'seas
¶   Sexual & Relationship Therapy - 3; ftm.

British Association for Shooting & Conservation (BASC) 1908

■   Marford Mill, Rossett, WREXHAM, Denbighshire, LL12 0HL.
      (hq)
      01244 573000 fax 01244 573001
      email enq@basc.org.uk http://www.basc.org.uk
      Chief Exec: John Swift
Br 7
○   *S; national representative body for country shooting; to
      promote responsible gun ownership coupled with practical
      conservation & wildlife management
Gp Gamekeeping; Wildfowling
●   ET - Res - Inf - LG - Public relations - Member services
<   Fedn of Eur Hunting Assns (FACE); Brit Shooting Sports
      Coun (BSSC)
M 123,000 i, 1,600 org
¶   Shooting & Conservation (Jnl) - 6; ftm.
      The Custodian (for Gamekeepers) - 6.

British Association of Show Caves
      see correct title **Association of British & Irish Show Caves**

British Association of Ski Patrollers
      since 2004 **BASP UK Ltd**

British Association of Skin Camouflage (BASC) 1986

■   PO Box 202, MACCLESFIELD, Cheshire, SK11 6FP. (asa)
      01625 871129
      email basc9@hotmail.com
      http://www.skin-camouflage.net
      Chmn: Liz Hawkins
○   *P; to promote, support & further the remedial technique of skin
      camouflage, for the relief of those who need to be restored
      to confidence in a normal appearance, by means of
      prescribable camouflage creams
●   Conf - Mtgs - ET - Inf
M c 60 i, UK
¶   NL - 4; free.

**British Association for Slavonic & East European Studies
(BASEES) 1953**

NR   Dept of Russian, School of Slavonic & East European Studies,
      UCL, Senate House, Malet St, LONDON, WC1E 7HJ.
      (infoffr/b)
      020 7862 8950
      Inf Officer: Dr Philip Bullock
▲   Registered Charity
○   *L; study of language & literature, history, politics, economics &
      society of the former USSR & Eastern Europe
M c 650 i
¶   NL - 3; ftm only.

British Association of Snowsport Instructors (BASI) 1913

NR   Glenmore, AVIEMORE, Inverness-shire, PH22 1QU. (hq)
      01479 861717 fax 01479 861718
      email basi@basi.org.uk http://www.basi.org.uk
      Chief Exec: Peter Kuwall
▲   Company Limited by Guarantee
○   *P, *S; the UK authority for training & grading professional
      snowsport instructors
Gp Skiing: Alpine, Nordic, Telemark, Adaptive (disabled);
      Snowboarding
●   ET - Exam
M c 4,000 i
¶   BASI News (Jnl) - 2;   BASI Manual - 1;
      BASI Alpine Manual - 2 yrly; all ftm only.

British Association of Social Workers   (BASW)   1970
- ■   16 Kent St, BIRMINGHAM, B5 6RD.   (hq)
  0121-622 3911   fax 0121-622 4860
  email membership@basw.co.uk
  http://www.basw.co.uk
  Dir: Ian H Johnston
- ▲   Registered Charity
- Br   4
- ○   *P; to promote an active involvement of members who share a commitment to good social work practice & uphold the code of ethics of the association
- ●   Conf - Mtgs - ET - Exhib - SG - Policy reports - Professional publications
- <   Intl Fedn of Social Work
- M   9,836 i
- ¶   British Jnl of Social Work - 8.   Practice (Jnl) - 4.
  Professional Social Work - 12; ftm, corporate subscription only nm.

British Association of Spinal Surgeons
a specialist society of the **British Orthopaedic Association**

British Association of Sport & Exercise Medicine   (BASEM)   1952
- NR   15 Hawthorne Ave, Norton, DONCASTER, S Yorks, DN6 9HR.   (hsp)
  01302 709342
  email basemcentral@basem.co.uk
  Mgr: Kathy Jones
- ▲   Company Limited by Guarantee; Registered Charity
- Br   9 regions in England; Scotland, Wales
- ○   *S; for sports orientated consultants & dental surgeons, GP's, chartered physiotherapists, educationalists, osteopaths, podiatrists (sports medics & paramedics), veterinary surgeons, chiropodists, pure & applied scientists
- ●   Conf - ET
- <   Intl Fedn of Sports Medicine; Eur Fedn of Sports Medicine
- M   1,000 i, UK / 100 i, o'seas
- ¶   British Jnl of Sports Medicine - 6.

British Association of Sport & Exercise Sciences   (BASES)   1985
- ■   BASES - Leeds Metropolitan University, Carnegie Faculty of Sport & Education, Fairfax Hall, Headingley Campus Beckett Park, LEEDS, LS6 3QS.   (hq)
  0113-283 6162   fax 0113-283 6162
  email info@bases.org.uk   http://www.bases.org.uk
  Chmn: Prof Craig Mahoney
  Hon Sec: Prof Edward Winter
- ▲   Company Limited by Guarantee
- ○   *P, *S; to promote excellence in sport & exercise sciences through evidence-based practice
- Gp   Psychology; Physiology; Bio-mechanics; Interdisciplinary
- ●   Conf - Mtgs - ET - Res - Exhib - Stat
- M   3,300 i
- ¶   The Sport & Exercise Scientist - 4; m only [various rates].

British Association for Sport & Law
- NR   c/o Pridie Brewster, 29-39 London Rd (1st floor), TWICKENHAM, Middx, TW1 3SZ.   (asa)
  020 8892 3100
  Contact: John Auber
- ○   *P

British Association of State English Language Teaching
since 12 May 2004 **English UK**

British Association of Steel Bands   (BAS)   1995
- ■   20 Queensbury Road, WEMBLEY, Middx, HA0 1LR.   (hsp)
  07956 546724
  email debi@panpodium.com
  http://www.panpodium.com
  Hon Sec: Debi Gardner
- ▲   Company Limited by Guarantee
- ○   *D
- ●   Conf - Mtgs - ET - Comp - Acts as booking agency
- M   10 i, 43 org, UK / 2 org, o'seas
- ¶   Panpodium (Jnl) - 2; ftm, £3 yr nm.

British Association for the Study of Community Dentistry   (BASCD)   1974
- ■   c/o N M Thomas, Rotherham Primary Care Trust, Oak House, Moorhead Way, Bramley, ROTHERHAM, S Yorks, S66 1YY.   (hsb)
  01709 302170   fax 01709 302175
  email nigel.thomas@rotherhampct.nhs.uk
  Hon Sec: Nigel Thomas
- ○   *L, *M; study, research & teaching of all aspects of dentistry in the community
- Gp   Community clinical practice; Education; Epidemiology
- ●   Conf - ET - Res
- <   Eur Assn Dental Public Health
- M   500 i
- ¶   Community Dental Health - 4; £50 m, £88 nm (EU).

British Association for the Study of Headache   (BASH)   1992
- ■   The Princess Margaret Migraine Clinic, Charing Cross Hospital (room 12/L20), Fulham Palace Rd, LONDON, W6 8RF.   (regd/office)
  fax 020 8846 1183
  http://www.bash.org.uk
  Hon Sec: Dr Fayyal Ahmed
- ▲   Company Limited by Guarantee; Registered Charity
- ○   *M; to relieve persons suffering from headache by the advancement of scientific study into that condition
- Gp   Management guidelines writing c'ee;
  Working gps: Organisation of headache services; Education
- ●   Conf - ET - Res - LG
- <   Intl Headache Soc; Eur Headache Fedn

British Association for the Study & Prevention of Child Abuse & Neglect   (BASPCAN)   1975
- NR   17 Priory St, YORK, YO1 6ET.   (hq)
  01904 613605   fax 01904 642239
  email baspcan@baspcan.org.uk
  http://www.baspcan.org.uk
  Hon Chmn: David Spicer
  Nat Office Admin: Judy Sanderson
- ▲   Registered Charity
- Br   10
- ○   *P
- ●   Conf - ET - Res - SG - Inf - LG
- <   Intl Soc for the Study & Prevention of Child Abuse & Neglect
- M   1,590 i, 50 f, UK / 38 i, 3 f, o'seas
- ¶   Child Abuse Review - 6; ftm, (on sale nm).
  BASPCAN News - 4; ftm.

British Association for the Study of Religions   (BASR)   1954
- NR   Dept of Religious Studies, Arts Faculty, The Open University, Walton Hall, MILTON KEYNES, Bucks, MK7 6AA.   (hsb)
  01908 654033   fax 01908 653750
  email g.harvey@open.ac.uk
  http://www.basr.open.ac.uk
  Hon Sec: Dr Graham Harvey
- ▲   Registered Charity
- ○   *L; to promote the academic study of religions
- ●   Conf
- <   Intl Assn for the History of Religions; Eur Assn for the Study of Religions
- M   200 i, UK / 10 i, o'seas
- ¶   Bulletin - 3; ftm only.

British Association for Supported Employment (BASE) 1991
■ c/o 24 Ribchester Drive, BURY, Lancs, BL9 9JT. (hq)
  01752 306664
  email admin@base-uk.org http://www.base-uk.org
  Chmn: Huw Davies
▲ Company Limited by Guarantee; Registered Charity
○ *K; promotion & development of supported employment in
  order to enable people with a disability to be able to succeed
  in employment
Gp Supported business interest group
● Conf - Mtgs - Exhib - Inf - LG
< Eur U of Supported Employment
M 220 org
✕ 2006 (Association for Supported Employment
    (National Association of Supported Employment

British Association for Surgery of the Knee
    a specialist society of the **British Orthopaedic Association**

British Association of Surgical Oncology
    since 2003 **BASO ~ the Association for Cancer Surgery**

**British Association of Symphonic Bands & Wind Ensembles
(BASBWE) 1981**
NR 118 Woodside Rd, Beaumont Park, HUDDERSFIELD, W Yorks,
   HD4 5JW. (chmn/p)
   Chmn: Simeon Yates
▲ Un-incorporated Society
○ *D; to support wind band music in the UK by helping the
  formation of new bands
M i, f & org
¶ Winds - 4; ftm. LM - 1; ftm only.
  Leaflets Series - 1; ftm.

British Association of Teachers of Conservative Dentistry
NR University of Dundee Dental School, Park Place, DUNDEE,
   DD1 4HN.
   01382 635984
   Sec: Dr D Ricketts
○ *P

British Association of Teachers of Dancing (BATD) 1892
■ 23 Marywood Sq, GLASGOW, G41 2BP. (hq)
  0141-423 4029 fax 0141-423 0677
  email enquiries@batd.co.uk http://www.batd.co.uk
  Gen Sec: Mrs Katrina Allan
▲ Registered Friendly Society
Br 8; Canada, USA.
○ *D, *P; all forms of dancing
● Conf - Mtgs - ET - Exam - Exhib - Comp - Stat - Inf - VE
< Stage Dance Council Intl; Brit Dance Council; Scot Official Bd
  of Highland Dancing; Cent Coun Physical Recreation (CCPR)
M 2,000 i, UK / 1,500 i, o'seas
¶ Conference Guide - 1; Conference Report - 1;
  December Bulletin - 1; all ftm only.

British Association of Teachers of the Deaf (BATOD) 1976
■ 175 Dashwood Ave, HIGH WYCOMBE, Bucks, HP12 3DB.
  01494 464190 fax 01494 464190
  email secretary@batod.org.uk
  Sec: Paul A Simpson
▲ Un-incorporated Society
Br 7 regions
○ *P; to promote the interests of all hearing impaired children &
  young people; to safeguard the interests of their teachers
Gp Audiology; Education & research; Teacher training for teachers
  of the deaf; Pre-school; GCSE; Transition & post-16;
  Conference; Publications
● Conf - Mtgs - ET - Res - Exhib - Stat - Inf - LG
M 1,750 i, UK / c 25 i, o'seas
¶ Deafness & Education (Jnl) - 4; ftm, £50 yr nm.
  Association Magazine - 5; ftm only.

British Association for Tissue Banking (BATB)
NR Red Lion Court, LONDON, EC4H 3EF.
○ *M

British Association of Toy Retailers
    since 2004 **Toy Retailers Association**

British Association of Urological Surgeons (BAUS) 1945
NR Royal College of Surgeons, 35-43 Lincoln's Inn Fields,
   LONDON, WC2A 3PN. (hq)
   020 7869 6950
▲ Registered Charity
○ *P; to promote high standards in practice of urology
● Conf - Mtgs - ET - Exhib
M 900 i, UK / 300 i, o'seas
¶ Members Hbk - 1; ftm only.

British Association for Vedic Astrology
NR 74 Saxon Way, ROMSEY, Hants, SO51 5RH.
   http://www.bava.org
   Sec: Geoffrey Pearce

British Association of Veterinary Emergency Care
    a group of the **British Small Animal Veterinary Association**

British Association of Veterinary Ophthalmologists
    a group of the **British Small Animal Veterinary Association**

British Association of Women Entrepreneurs (BAWE) 1953
■ 112 John Player Building, STIRLING, FK7 7RP. (pres/b)
  01786 446044
  http://www.bawe-uk.org
  Nat Pres: Tatjana Hine
▲ Company Limited by Guarantee
Br 4; 50
○ *P; to bring together all women who are qualified to be called
  'Heads of Business', whether they operate alone, with co-
  directors, or with members of their families; to confine
  activities to economic matters; to explore & advise on the
  means by which the rights & duties of women in business,
  industry & domestic spheres may be reconciled & improved
● Conf - Mtgs - ET - Exhib - Comp - SG - Expt - Inf - VE - Empl -
  LG
< Les Femmes Chefs d'Entreprises Mondiales (FCEM); Amer
  Cham Comm; CBI; IoD; London Cham Comm
M 150 i
¶ BAWE National NL - 4; BAWE West NL - 4; FCEM News
  International - 4; all ftm only.

British Astrological & Psychic Society (BAPS) 1976
■ BAPS - PO Box 5687, Springfield, MILTON KEYNES, Bucks,
  MK6 3WZ. (mail/address)
  0906 470 0827
  email info@baps.ws http://www.baps.ws
  Sec& Co Sec: Mrs Eve Bingham
▲ Company Limited by Guarantee
Br 3
○ *G, *P; astrology & all esoteric/psychic disciplines - tarot, runes,
  palmistry, astrology, numerology, psy cards, crystal
  divination, psychic perception, mediumship, clairvoyance,
  aura readings etc
Gp BAPS School of: Astrology (1995) / Palmistry, runes, tarot
  (1996) / Numerology (correspondence courses)
● ET - Exhib - Workshops
M 257 i, 100 vetted counsellors, UK / 10 i, o'seas
¶ Mercury (Jnl) - 4; ftm, £3.50 each nm.
  National Register of Consultants; ftm, cover price nm.

British Astronomical Association   (BAA)   1890

NR   Burlington House, Piccadilly, LONDON, W1J 0DU.   (hq)
      http://www.britastro.org
▲   Company Limited by Guarantee; Registered Charity
Br   Australia (New South Wales)
○   *L; organisation of observers in the work of astronomical
      observation, encouragement of popular interests in
      astronomy
Gp   Solar; Lunar; Mercury & Venus; Mars; Asteroids & remote
      planets; Jupiter; Saturn; Comet; Variable star; Meteor;
      Aurora; Deep sky; Computing; Instruments & imaging
●   Mtgs - ET - Res - Exhib - Comp - SG - Inf - Lib - VE
M   c 3,500 i, c 100 org
¶   Jnl - 6.   Hbk - 1.

British Audio Dealers Association   (BADA)   1982

■   248 Lee High Rd, LONDON, SE13 5PL.   (hq)
      020 8150 6741   fax 020 8318 0909
      email info@bada.co.uk   http://www.bada.co.uk
      Operations & Marketing Mgr: Phil Hansen
▲   Company Limited by Guarantee
○   *T; to promote, raise & monitor the standards of retail practice
      in the UK Hi Fi industry
●   Mtgs - ET - Stat
M   75 f

British Autogenic Society   (BAS)   1984

NR   c/o Royal London Homeopathic Hospital, Gt Ormond Street,
      LONDON, WC1N 3HR.   (hq)
      020 7391 8908
      email admin@autogenic-therapy.org.uk
      http://www.autogenic-therapy.org.uk
      Sec: Mrs Jane Bird,   Chmn: Mrs Sonia Saunders
▲   Company Limited by Guarantee; Registered Charity
○   *P; 'the professional & regulatory body for autogenic therapists
      & psychotherapists in the UK; sets training standards, runs
      training courses & provides information for the public.
      Autogenic therapy is self-help for mind & body. Therapists
      teach easy mental exercises over 8-10 weeks; allows switch-
      off of stress response, helps many problems & also helps
      realise potential in many areas'
●   Mtgs - ET - SG
<   Intl C'ee for Autogenic Therapy (ICAT); Eur Assn for
      Psychotherapy (EAP)
M   94 i, UK / 12 i, o'seas
¶   NL - 2; ftm only.

**British Automatic Fire Sprinkler Association Ltd   (BAFSA)
1974**

■   Richmond House, Broad St, ELY, Cambs, CB7 4AH.   (hq)
      01353 659187   fax 01353 666619
      email info@bafsa.org.uk   http://www.bafsa.org.uk
      Sec Gen: Stewart Kidd
▲   Company Limited by Guarantee
○   *T; to promote the use of automatic sprinkler & other systems
      using water as a means of controlling & extinguishing fires in
      all types of premises
Gp   Technical; Contractual; Marketing & promotion
●   Conf - Exhib - LG
<   Fire Ind Confedn; Fire Ind Coun (Trade Enterprises) Ltd;
M   96 f, 3 org
¶   LM & affiliates;   Sprinkler Systems: the facts; both free.
      Sprinklers for Safety; ftm, £25 nm.
      Sprinklers in:
         Schools; Heritage Buildings; Retail Premises; Warehouses.
      Sprinkler Facts (CD-ROM).   Domestic Sprinkler Systems.
      Joint Code of Practice for Sprinklers in Schools; £5.

British Automatic Sprinkler Association Ltd
   since 2005 **British Automatic Fire Sprinkler Association**

British Automation & Robot Association Ltd   (BARA)   1976

NR   International Manufacturing Centre, University of Warwick,
      COVENTRY, Warks, CV4 7AL.   (hq)
      024 7657 3742   fax 024 7657 3743
      email info@bara.org.uk   http://www.bara.org.uk
      Chmn: Ken Young,   Admin: Kathryn Miele
▲   Company Limited by Guarantee
○   *T; the development & application of automation in British
      industry
Gp   Advanced; Education; Safety; Suppliers; Systems integrators;
      Users
●   Mtgs - ET - Res - Exhib - Stat - Inf - LG
<   Intl Fedn of Robotics (IFR)
M   3,000 i, 50 f
¶   AR; both free.

British Automobile Racing Club   (BARC)   1912

NR   Thruxton Circuit, ANDOVER, Hants, SP11 8PN.   (hq)
      01264 882200
      Chief Exec: Dennis Carter
▲   Company Limited by Guarantee
Br   7; Canada
○   *S; organisation of circuit motor racing, hill climbs & sprints
●   Mtgs - Social events
M   4,500 i, UK / 1,500 i, o'seas
¶   Startline - 6; ftm.

British Aviation Enthusiasts Society   (BAES)   2001

■   28a Frogmore Lane, Lovedean, WATERLOOVILLE, Hants,
      PO8 9QL.   (hsp)
      023 9242 1903   fax 023 9242 1903
      email mail@baes.org.uk   http://www.baes.org.uk
      Sec: Deryn Hawkins
▲   Un-incorporated Society
○   *G; to visit aviation facilities worldwide (airports, airfields, air
      forces, museum collections); to experience, photograph &
      record details of aircraft & historic aviation buildings
●   Mtgs - VE (an experienced tour escort is provided)
M   180 i, UK / 23 i, o'seas
¶   NL - 4; ftm only.

British Aviation Preservation Council   (BAPC)   1967

NR   19 Acton Place, High Heaton, NEWCASTLE upon TYNE,
      NE7 7RL.   (chmn/p)
      email secretarybapc@btconnect.com
      Chmn: Steve Hague, Sec: Brian Dixon
▲   Un-incorporated Society
○   *N; coordinating body for all aviation museums & collections
      working for the advancement of aviation preservation &
      promotion of aviation heritage
Gp   National Aviation Heritage Registers; Stopping the Rot
      conferences
●   Conf - Mtgs - ET - Res - Inf
<   Eur Aviation Presvn Coun
M   135 org, UK / 10 org, o'seas
¶   Update (NL) - 4; ftm only.

British Badge Collectors Association

■   PO Box 1362, LICHFIELD, Staffs, WS13 7YD.
○   *G
M   i
      no further information supplied

British Ballet Organization Ltd   (BBO)   1930

NR   Woolborough House, 39 Lonsdale Rd, Barnes, LONDON,
　　　SW13 9JP.   (hq)
　　　020 8748 1241
　　　Dir: John Travis
▲　Company Limited by Guarantee
Br　Australia, New Zealand
○　*D, *G; ballet, tap, jazz & modern dancing examinations; ballet
　　　& tap teaching qualifications
●　Conf - Mtgs - ET - Exam - Lib
<　Regd by Coun for Dance Education & Training (UK) (CDET)
M　c 300 teachers, UK / 135 teachers, o'seas
¶　The Dancer - 1.

British Balloon & Airship Club   (BBAC)   1965

NR　c/o Cameron Balloons, St John St, Bedminster, BRISTOL,
　　　BS3 4NH.   (pro/b)
　　　0117-953 1231　fax 0117-966 1168 (shared)
　　　email information@bbac.org　http://www.bbac.org
　　　PRO: Hannah Cameron,　Chmn: Crispin Williams
▲　Company Limited by Guarantee
Br　regional clubs
○　*S; to promote all aspects of lighter than air flight, including hot
　　　airballooning, gas ballooning & aurship flying; to serve
　　　sporting & commercial interests equally
Gp　Clubs: Regional in UK, Competitions
●　Conf - Mtgs - ET - Exam - Comp - Inf - LG
　　　BBAC carries delegated authority from the CAA for
　　　airworthiness & pilot training
<　UK Civil Aviation Authority
>　British Balloon Museum & Library
M　c 2,300 i, 20 f, UK / 100 i, o'seas
¶　Aerostat - 6.

British Bamboo Society   1982

■　The Tote House, Catterick Racecourse, RICHMOND, N Yorks,
　　　DL10 7PE.   (hsp)
　　　01208 812892
　　　email secretary@bamboo-society.org.uk
　　　http://www.bamboo-society.org.uk
　　　Sec: Greville Worthington
▲　Un-incorporated Society
○　*H; to study the distribution of bamboo plants & seeds grown in
　　　the UK
●　Mtgs - ET - VE
<　Eur Bamboo Soc
M　163 i, 6 org, UK / 4 i, o'seas
¶　NL - 4; ftm only.

British Bankers' Association   (BBA)   1919

■　Pinners Hall, 105-108 Old Broad St, LONDON, EC2N 1EX.
　　　(hq)
　　　020 7216 8800　fax 020 7216 8811
　　　http://www.bba.org.uk
　　　Chief Exec: Angela Knight
○　*T; for banks carrying out business in the UK
Gp　Press Office (020 7216 8989)
●　Conf - Stat - LG
M　300 f
¶　NL; ftm.

British Banking History Society   (BHSS)   1980

■　71 Mile Lane, Cheylesmore, COVENTRY, Warks, CV3 5GB.
　　　(hsp)
　　　024 7650 3245
　　　email info@banking-history.co.uk
　　　http://www.banking-history.co.uk
　　　Hon Sec: John Purser
▲　Un-incorporated Society
○　*G; to encourage & popularise the collection of cheques,
　　　banknotes & memorabilia relating to banking; to promote
　　　the study of the history of banking
●　Mtgs - Res - Inf
M　110 i, 10 f, UK / 30 i, o'seas
¶　Counterfoil - 4; subscription only.
×　2003-04 British Cheque Collectors Society

British Baseball Federation
　　　2002 merged with British Softball Federation to become
　　　BaseballSoftballUK

British Basketball Federation   2005

■　PO Box 3971, SHEFFIELD, S Yorks, S9 3TW.
　　　email info@british-basketball.co.uk
○　*S

British Battery Manufacturers Association   (BBMA)   1986

NR　3 London Wall Buildings, London Wall, LONDON,
　　　EC2M 5SY.   (hq)
　　　020 7826 2690　fax 020 7826 2601
　　　email info@bbma.co.uk　http://www.bbma.co.uk
　　　Gen Sec: Jonathan Roberts
▲　Company Limited by Guarantee
○　*T; manufacturers of primary (non-rechargeable) & secondary
　　　(re-chargeable) portable consumer batteries - NOT
　　　automotive lead-acid
●　Mtgs - Stat - Inf - LG
<　Eur Portable Battery Assn (EPBA)
M　7 f
¶　LM.
　　　Guidelines on: Battery Safety; Battery Compartment; Battery
　　　Insertion; Battery Ingestion.
　　　The Future for Dead Batteries: disposal & recycling of portable
　　　batteries.

British Bavarian Warmblood Association
　　　ceased trading September 2005

British Bazadaise Cattle Society   1989

NR　Western Green, Spa Lane, AYLSHAM, Norfolk, NR11 6UE.
　　　(hsp)
　　　01263 733508
　　　Hon Sec: Mrs C Matthews
▲　Company Limited by Guarantee; Registered Charity
○　*B
M　44 i

British Bedding & Pot Plant Association   (BBPA)   1980

NR　PO Box 475, HUNTINGDON, Cambs, PE28 3YP.   (hq)
　　　08702 416526
　　　Sec: Dawn Smith
○　*H, *T; 'to represent bedding & pot plant growers in aspects of
　　　promotion, political & technical issues relating to their
　　　business'
●　Conf - Mtgs - ET - Res - Exhib - SG - Stat - Inf - PL - VE - Empl -
　　　LG - Social events
<　Nat Farmers U
M　180+ i, 100 f, 25 org
¶　NL - 12;　News & Views - 4; both ftm only.

British Bee-Keepers' Association (BBKA) 1874

■ National Beekeeping Centre, NAC, Stoneleigh Park,
  KENILWORTH, Warks, CV8 2LG.   (hq)
  024 7669 6679
  Gen Sec: Martin Tovey
▲ Registered Charity
Br 61
○ *G, *T; to further the craft of keeping bees
Gp Appliance trade; Bee health; Bee disease; Insurance; Research;
  Education; Bee breeding; Protection against spray &
  pesticides
● Conf - ET - Exam - Res - Exhib - LG
< Cent Assn of Beekeepers; Bee Improvement & Bee Breeders
  Assn; Assn of Beekeeping Appliance Mfrs
M 9,824 i, 5 org
¶ BBKA News - 5; ftm.

British Beer & Pub Association 1904

■ Market Towers, 1 Nine Elms Lane, LONDON, SW8 5NQ.   (hq)
  020 7627 9191   fax 020 7627 9123
  email enquiries@beerandpub.com
  http://www.beerandpub.com
  Chief Exec: Robert Hayward
▲ Company Limited by Guarantee
○ *T; to represent the beer & pub industry when dealing with
  government & government bodies in the UK & EU; to
  enhance the reputation of the brewing & pub sector
● Conf - Mtgs - ET - Res - Comp - Stat - Expt - LG
< Hotels, Restaurants & Cafés in Europe (HOTREC); The Brewers
  of Europe (BoE); Confedn of Brit Ind (CBI)
M 72 f
¶ Digest - 11; ftm only.
  Statistical Hbk - 1; £27.75 m, £47.50 nm.   AR; ftm.
  Publications list available from: Brewing Publications Ltd, at
  above address.
✕ 2001 (25 October) Brewers & Licensed Retailers Association

British Beermat Collectors' Society (BBCS) 1960

■ 69 Dunnington Avenue, KIDDERMINSTER, Worcs, DY10 2YT.
  (hsp)
  http://www.britishbeermats.org.uk
  Hon Sec: Tony Matthews
▲ Un-incorporated Society
○ *G; to encourage the hobby of beer mat collecting (tegestology)
● Mtgs
M 260 i, UK / 41 i, o'seas
¶ Beermat NL - 12; ftm only.

British Belgian Blue Cattle Society (BBBCS) 1982

NR Fell View, Blencarn, PENRITH, Cumbria, CA10 1TX.   (hq)
  01768 88775
  Sec: John Fleming
▲ Company Limited by Guarantee
Br 14 countries o'seas
○ *B
● Mtgs - ET - Res - Exhib - Comp - Expt - Inf - LG
M 600 i
¶ Herd Book - 1; free.

British Berrichon du Cher Sheep Society 1986

■ Woodston Manor, Lindridge, TENBURY WELLS, Worcs,
  WR15 8JG.   (sp)
  01584 881657
  Sec: Emma Hillhouse
▲ Company Limited by Guarantee
○ *B
● Exhib - Inf
< Nat Sheep Assn
M 150 i, UK / 2 i, Republic of Ireland
¶ NL - 4;   Magazine - 1;   Flock Book - 1;   all free.

British Betting Office Association
  November 2002 merged with the Betting Office Licensees Association
  to form the **Association of British Bookmakers**

British Big Cat Society (BBCS) 2001

NR Dartmoor Wildlife Park, Sparkwell, PLYMOUTH, Devon,
  PL7 5DG.
  01752 837645
  email info@britishbigcats.com
  http://www.britishbigcats.org
  Contact: Danny Bamping
○ *G, *V; to actively seek evidence of big cats in the UK
M c 500 i

British Binders & Finishers Association
  since 2004-05 BPIF Finishers, a special interest group of the **British
  Printing Industries Federation**

British BioGen
  2005 merged with the Renewable Power Association to form the
  Renewable Energy Association

British Biomagnetic Association (BBA)

NR The Williams Clinic, 31 St Marychurch Rd, TORQUAY, Devon,
  TQ1 3JF.   (hq)
  01803 293346
  Exec Vice-Chmn: Graham Gardener
▲ Un-incorporated Society
○ *E, *M; post graduate training & research in the use of magnet
  application to acupuncture points for the correction of
  skeletal mis-alignments

British Biophysical Society (BBS) 1966

NR c/o Dr R M Cooke, GlaxoSmithKline, New Frontiers Science
  Park, Third Avenue, HARLOW, Essex, CM19 5AW.   (hq)
  01279 627981
  Hon Sec: Dr R M Cooke
▲ Registered Charity
○ *L; advancement of science of biophysics - 'the study of the
  functioning & structure of living organisms viewed from a
  physical standpoint, & the application of physical & physio-
  chemical techniques to biological problems'

British Bird Council (BBC) 1970

NR 1159 Bristol Rd South (1st floor), Northfield, BIRMINGHAM,
  B31 2SL.   (hq)
  0121-476 5999
  http://www.britishbirdcouncil.com
▲ Un-incorporated Society
○ *G; to encourage the keeping, breeding & exhibiting of British
  birds in captivity
● Mtgs - Exhib - LG - a DEFRA supplier of rings
< Nat Coun of Aviculture
M 1,500 i, 20 org, UK / 12 i, o'seas

British Bison Association (BBA) 1991

■ Bush Farm, West Knoyle, WARMINSTER, Wilts, BA12 6AE.
  (hsp)
  01747 830263   fax 01747 830263
  email info@bisonfarm.co.uk
  http://www.bisonfarm.co.uk
  Hon Sec: Lord Seaford
▲ Un-incorporated Society
○ *B; to promote the interests of bison & bison farmers
● Mtgs - Exhib - Inf - LG
< Nat Bison Assn (USA)
M 40 i, UK / 4 i, o'seas
¶ NL - 2;   Bison Hbk; £20 nm.   AR.

British Bleu du Maine Sheep Society   1982
■ Long Wood Farm, Trostrey, USK, Monmouthshire, NP15 1LA.
(sp)
01291 673816
Breed Sec: Mrs Jane Smith
▲ Registered Charity
○ *B
● Mtgs - Res - Exhib - SG
M 250 i, 10 f
¶ NL - 4;   Flock Book - 1; ftm only.
Breeder's Directory [LM] - 2/3 years; free.

British Blind & Shutter Association   (BBSA) 1919
NR 42 Heath St, TAMWORTH, Staffs, B79 7JH.   (hq)
01827 52337
Sec: A D Skelding
▲ Company Limited by Guarantee
○ *T; represents leading UK manufacturers of interior & exterior
window blinds, security shutters & grilles
● Mtgs - Exhib - ET - Inf - VE
M 350 f, UK / 8 f, o'seas
¶ Blinds & Shutters - 4.

British Blonde Society   2002
NR 4th Street, National Agricultural Centre, Stoneleigh Park,
KENILWORTH, Warks, CV8 2LG.   (hq)
024 7641 9058
email secretary@britishblondesociety.co.uk
http://www.britishblondesociety.co.uk
Admin: Lynn Snell,   Sue Steiner
▲ Company Limited by Guarantee; Registered Charity
Br 9
○ *B
● Mtgs - Exhib - Comp - SG - Expt - Inf - VE - Recording of
pedigree cattle
< Fédn Intle des Eleveurs de la Race Blonde d'Aquitaine (FIEBRA);
Nat Cattle Assn (NCA)
M c 600 i
¶ Blonde (Jnl) - 1;   NL - 4; both free.

British Blood Transfusion Society   (BBTS) 1983
NR Greenheys, Manchester Science Park, Pencroft Way,
MANCHESTER, M15 6JJ.   (hq)
0161-232 7999   fax 0161-232 7979
email bbts@bbts.org.uk   http://www.bbts.org.uk
Hon Sec: Dr Sheila MacLennan
▲ Registered Charity
○ *M, *P; for those engaged in transfusion medicine & transfusion
science in hospitals & blood centres
● Conf - Mtgs - ET - Exam - Res - SG
M 1,400 i & f, UK / 300 i, o'seas
¶ Transfusion Medicine (Jnl) - 6.
NL - 4; ftm only.

British Bluegrass Music Association   (BBMA) 1989
NR 10 Mansel St, Gowerton, SWANSEA, SA4 3BU.   (hsp)
email keysell@lycos.co.uk   http://www.bbma.net
Hon Sec: Roland Emmanuel
▲ Un-incorporated Society
○ *D; promotion of Bluegrass music & associated traditions in UK
● Mtgs - Inf - Organising tours - Producing CDs - Sponsoring
events - Teaching / tuition - Publicising concerts & tours
< Intl Bluegrass Music Assn
M c 600 i, UK / c 20 i, o'seas
¶ British Bluegrass News - 4; ftm, £2 yr nm.

British Bob Skeleton Association
NR Dept of Sport Development & Recreation, University of Bath,
CLAVERTON DOWN, BA2 7AY.
01225 323696
http://www.bobskeleton.org.uk
Contact: Phil Searle
○ *S

British Bobsleigh Association Ltd   (BBA) 1956
NR 4-10 Bartelot Rd, HORSHAM, W Sussex, RH12 1DQ.   (hq)
01403 221844   fax 01403 219079
http://www.bobteamgb.org
Admin: Jane Clark
▲ Company Limited by Guarantee
○ *S; to promote British bobsleighing; to attain world prominence
in championships
M i
¶ The British Bobsleigh Annual - 1; ftm.

British Body Piercing Association   (BBPA)
NR 11/12 St John's Square, GLASTONBURY, Somerset, BA6 9LJ.
01458 831666
http://www.bbpa.org.uk
○ *P

British Bodyboarding Club   (BBC) 1993
NR International Surf Centre, Fistral Beach, NEWQUAY, Cornwall,
TR7 1HY.   (hsb)
Hon Sec: Steve Berriman
○ *S; a form of surfing
M i

British Boomerang Society   (BBS) 1980
■ 36 Fox Dene, GODALMING, Surrey, GU7 1YG.   (chmn/p)
01483 417236
email mckennaslade@britishlibrary.net
http://www.boomerangs.org.uk
Chmn: Sean McKenna-Slade
▲ Un-incorporated Society
○ *S; to promote boomerang throwing as a sport; to provide
designs of boomerangs & the materials to make
boomerangs from; to research the history of boomerangs &
the physics of their flight
● Mtgs - Res - Comp - Talks on various aspects of boomerangs
< Intl Fedn of Boomerang Assns
M 50 i, 3 f, UK / 5 i, c 20 org, o'seas
¶ BBS Jnl - 4; ftm only.

British Bottlers' Institute   (BBI) 1953
■ PO Box 374, SOUTHAMPTON, Hants, SO31 4WZ.   (hsp)
0776 100 5276   fax 023 8056 1646
email secretary@bbi.org.uk   http://www.bbi.org.uk
Gen Sec: John Yates
▲ Un-incorporated Society
○ *T; a forum for those concerned with the bottling, canning &
packaging of beverages, food & other products, enabling
them to share their experience & problems
● Conf - Mtgs - Exhib - Comp - VE
M 40 i, 70 f, UK / 2 i, 2 f, o'seas

British Box & Packaging Association
since 2003-04 **British Packaging Association**

British Branded Hosiery Group
no longer exists.

British Brands Group   (BBG)
■ 8 Henrietta Place, LONDON, W1G 0NB.   (hq)
0702 093 4252
email info@britishbrandsgroup.org.uk
http://www.britishbrandsgroup.org.uk
Dir: John Noble
▲ Company Limited by Guarantee
○ *K, *N; 'to represent brand manufacturers with a mission to
create a deeper understanding of brands & their benefits; to
help create an environment of fair competition'
● Mtgs - ET - Res - Exhib - Inf - PL - VE - LG
< AIM (Brussels)
M 25 f
¶ NL - 4.

© CBD Research Ltd · Beckenham · BR3 5JS · Tel 020 8650 7745 · Fax 020 8650 0768 · E-mail cbd@cbdresearch.com · www.cbdresearch.com

British Brick Society (BBS) 1972
■ 19 Woodcroft Rd, STANMORE, Middx, HA7 3PT.   (hsp)
   email mikesheila67@hotmail.com
   http://www.britishbricksoc.free-online.co.uk
   Hon Sec: Mike Oliver
▲ Un-incorporated Society
○ *G, *L; to study & record all aspects of the archaeology &
   history of brick, brickmaking & brick building
● Inf - VE - Coordinating records of brickmaking sites &
   manufacturers' names in the British Isles
< Brit Archaeological Assn (Brick section)
M c 300 i, c 20 f, UK / c 20 i, o'seas
¶ BBS Information (NL) - 3; ftm, back issue prices on
   application nm.

British Bridalwear Association   (BBA)
NR 11 Boldmere Road, SUTTON COLDFIELD, West Midlands,
   B73 5UY.
   0121-321 3121
   http://www.bbabridalwear.com
○ *P, *T;

British Brush Manufacturers Association   (BBMA)   1908
■ Brooke House, 4 The Lakes, Bedford Rd, NORTHAMPTON,
   NN4 7YD.   (hq)
   01604 622023   fax 01604 631252
   email bbma@brookehouse.co.uk
   http://www.bhhma.co.uk
   Sec: A G Johnson
○ *T
Gp Brushes: Artists, Household, Pet, Clothes, Industrial, Personal;
   Brush machinery; Brush raw materials; Paint applicators
● Conf - Mtgs - Exhib - Expt - Inf - Empl - LG
< Eur Brush Fedn (FEIBP); CBI
M 32 f
¶ NL - 12;   Membership Directory - 1; ftm, £75 nm.
   Note: incorporated within the British Hardware & Housewares
   Manufacturers' Association 1 January 1995 as a sub-product
   sector

British Bryological Society   (BBS)   1896
NR Ivy House, Wheelock St, MIDDLEWICH, Cheshire,
   CW10 9AB.   (hsb)
   Hon Sec: M A Walton
▲ Registered Charity
○ *L, *Q; study & conservation of mosses & liverworts, especially
   those in the British Isles
Gp Reading circle; Tropical bryology
● Conf - Mtgs - ET - Res - Exhib - SG - Stat - Inf - Lib - VE
< N Western Naturalist U
M 382 i, UK / 215 i, o'seas
¶ Jnl of Bryology - 4; ftm.
   Bulletin - 2; ftm.

British Buddhist Association   (BBA)   1974
■ 11 Biddulph Rd, LONDON, W9 1JA.   (hq)
   020 7286 5575
   Dir: A Haviland-Nye
▲ Registered Charity
○ *R
● Conf - Mtgs - ET (courses & weekends) - SG - VE - Courses for
   teachers of religious education in schools
M 'confidential'

British Bulgarian Chamber of Commerce   (BBCC)   1993
■ PO Box 123, BROMLEY, Kent, BR1 4ZX.   (hq)
   020 8464 5007   fax 020 8464 5007
   email info@bbcc.bg   http://www.bbcc.bg
   Exec Dir: Mrs Christine Booth
▲ Company Limited by Guarantee
Br Bulgaria
○ *C; promotion of business between Britain & Bulgaria
● Conf - Mtgs - Expt - Inf - LG - Business missions
M 100 f, UK / 40 f, o'seas
¶ NL - 52 [email only]; ftm only.

British Bulgarian Friendship Society   (BBFS)   1952
■ 22 Modena Rd, HOVE, E Sussex, BN3 5QG.   (hsb)
   01273 726433   fax 01273 726433
   email bbfs@care4free.net   http://www.bbfs.org.uk
   Hon Sec: K Barker
▲ Un-incorporated Society
○ *X; to promote friendship between British & Bulgarian peoples
● Mtgs - Exhib - Inf - Lib - VE
M c 300 i,
¶ NL - 3/4; ftm.

British Burn Association   (BBA)   1967
■ Burn Centre (Acute Block), Wythenshawe Hospital, Southmoor
   Rd, Wythenshawe, MANCHESTER, M23 9LT.   (hsb)
   0161-291 6323   fax 0161-291 6323
   email bba@smuht.nwest.nhs.uk
   Hon Sec/Treas: J Edwards
▲ Registered Charity
○ *P; to promote burn prevention, treatment, care & rehabilitation
● Conf - Mtgs - Exhib
< Intl Soc for Burn Injuries
M c 400 i

British Business Angels Association   (BBAA)   2005
NR New City Court, 20 St Thomas Street, LONDON, SE1 9RS.
   020 7089 2305   fax 020 7089 2301
   http://www.bbaa.org.uk
   Sec: Liz Carrington
○ *T

British Business Awards Association   1993
§ The Stables, Highfield Park, CREATON, Northants, NN6 8NT.
   01604 505480
   Chief Exec: David Wright
   a trading company organising business awards, principally for
   regional newspapers

**British Business and General Aviation Association   (BBGA)
1975**
■ 19 Church St, Brill, AYLESBURY, Bucks, HP18 9RT.   (hq)
   01844 238020   fax 01844 238087
   email info@bbga.aero   http://www.bbga.aero
   Chief Exec: Mark Wilson
▲ Company Limited by Guarantee
○ *T; to represent companies operating & trading in the industry -
   including manufacturers, business aviation operators,
   organisations in repair & overhaul, training & aircraft &
   helicopter sales, also spares stockists & supporting
   organisations in finance, insurance & publishing
Gp Sales & support; Air transport; Engineering; Flying training;
   Airport working
● Conf - Mtgs - Res - Exhib - SG - Stat - Inf - LG
M 160 f
¶ BBGA Industry Directory - 18 months; free.
× 2004 (Business Aircraft Users' Association
        (General Aviation Manufacturers & Traders Association

British Butterfly Conservation Society Ltd
   since 29 November 2003 **Butterfly Conservation**

British Button Society   (BBS)   1976
■ 32 Chichester Rd, TONBRIDGE, Kent, TN9 2TL.   (hsp)
   01732 364309
   http://www.britishbuttonsociety.org
   Hon Sec: Mrs A Clark
▲ Un-incorporated Society
○ *G; the collection & preservation of antique & modern buttons
● Mtgs - Res - Lib - VE - Publication of articles on, & photographs
   of, buttons
M 300 i, 10 f, UK / 50 i, o'seas
¶ Button Lines - 4; ftm only.

British Cables Association   (BCA)   1965
NR   8 Twinoaks, COBHAM, Surrey, KT11 2QP.   (hq)
    01372 844126   fax 01372 844126
    email admin@bcauk.org   http://www.bcauk.org
    Sec-Gen: P M A Smeeth
▲   Un-incorporated Society
○   *T; manufacturers of metallic & optical fibre cables & wires for
    transmission & distribution of electric power for
    communications (telephones, electronic data control &
    broadcasting)
Gp   Covered Conductors Association; Data & control cables;
    General wiring cables; Mains cables; Supertension cables;
    Telephone cables
●   Conf - Mtgs - Res - SG - Stat - Expt - LG
<   Eur Confedn Assns Mfrs Insulated Wires & Cables
    (EUROPACABLE); CBI; BEAMA
M   16 f

British Cactus & Succulent Society   (BCSS)   1945
■   49 Chestnut Glen, HORNCHURCH, Essex, RM12 4HL.   (hsp)
    01708 447778   fax 01444 454061
    email bcss@cactus-mall.com   http://www.bcss.org.uk
    Hon Sec: E A Harris
▲   Registered Charity
Br   94; Republic of Ireland
○   *H; study & conservation of cacti & succulent plants
Gp   Robins
●   Conf - Mtgs - Res - Exhib - Comp - LG
<   Cactus & Succulent Soc of America, German Cactus &
    Succulent Soc; Succulent Soc S Australia; R Horticl Soc
M   3,500 i, UK / 500 i, o'seas
¶   Cactus World (Jnl) - 4; £15 m (£20 or 38 o'seas).
    Bradleya (Ybk) - 1; £16 m, (£20 o'seas)

British Calcium Carbonates Federation   (BCCF)   1943
■   Omya UK Ltd, Omya House, Stephensons Way, Wyvern
    Business Park, Chaddesden, DERBY, DE21 6LY.   (hsb)
    01332 887435
    Sec: Mike Nocivelli
▲   Un-incorporated Society
○   *T; to foster & develop the manufacture & sale of calcium
    carbonates
●   Mtgs - Stat - Inf
M   5 f
¶   LM; ftm only.

British Camargue Horse Society   (BCHS)   1991
■   The Cottage - Valley Rd, Wickham Market, WOODBRIDGE,
    Suffolk, IP13 0ND.   (hq)
    01728 746916
    http://www.valleyfarmonline.co.uk
    Sec: Sarah Ling
○   *B; to promote the Camargue horse & educate children
●   ET - VE
M   40 i

British Camelids Association   (BCA)   1987
■   Puckpitts Farm, Tredington, SHIPSTON-on-STOUR, Warks,
    CV36 4NH.   (hsp)
    01608 661893
    email camelids@btinternet.com
    http://www.britishcamelids.co.uk
    Sec: Jane Brown
▲   Company Limited by Guarantee; Registered Charity
○   *B; breeding & farming of Camelids - Vicunas, Lamas, Alpacas,
    Guanacoes
Gp   Lama Glama; Lama Pacos (Alpacas); Lama Guanacos;
    Vicugna Vicugna (Vicunas); Bactrian & dromedary camels
●   Conf - Res - Exhib - Comp - Inf - VE - LG
<   Fedn of Eur S Amer Camelid Assns (FESACA); Brit Veterinary
    Camelid Soc
M   558 i, 18 f, UK / 28 i, 2 f, o'seas
¶   The Camelids Chronicle - 4.
    LM - 2.   Gala Sales List - up-dated.
    British Camelids Hbk - updated annually.
    Welfare Guidelines.   Welcome to the Camelid Family.
    Note: is the trading name of British Camelids Ltd.
×   2005 British Camelids Owners & Breeders Association

British Canadian Chamber of Trade & Commerce   1951
■   PO Box 1358, Station K, TORONTO, Ontario, Canada,
    M4P 3J4.   (hq)
    1 (416) 502 0847   fax 1 (416) 502 9319
    Contact: The National Secretary
○   *C; to foster bi-lateral trade between Britain & Canada
M   i & f

British Candlemakers Federation   1995
■   c/o Tallow Chandlers Hall, 4 Dowgate Hill, LONDON,
    EC4R 2SH.
    020 7248 4726
▲   Un-incorporated Society
○   *T; to ensure that the skills & arts of candlemaking in Britain are
    continued along with modern methods & future development
●   Mtgs - Exhib - Stat
<   Eur Candlemakers Fedn
M   33 f, UK / 1 f, o'seas

British Canoe Union   (BCU)   1936
■   Adbolton Lane, West Bridgford, NOTTINGHAM, NG2 5AS.
    (hq)
    0115-982 1100   fax 0115-982 1797
    email info@bcu.org.uk   http://www.bcu.org.uk
    Chief Exec: Paul Owen
▲   Company Limited by Guarantee
Br   10 regions
○   *S; the national body governing the sport of canoeing
Gp   Sprint racing; Marathon; Slalom; Canoe sailing; Wild water
    racing; Surf; Canoe polo; Sea canoeing; Freestyle;
    Coaching; Lifeguards; Touring
●   ET - Exhib - Comp - SG - Stat - Inf - Lib - VE
<   Intl Canoe Fedn; Eur Canoe Assn; Brit Olympic Assn; C'wealth
    Games Coun for England; Cent Coun for Physical
    Recreation (CCPR)
M   21,430 i, 420 org
¶   Canoe Focus - 6; ftm, £2 each nm.
    Canoeing Hbk - 1; £15.95.

British Caravanners Club
    a group of the **Camping & Caravanning Club Ltd**

© CBD Research Ltd · Beckenham · BR3 5JS · Tel 020 8650 7745 · Fax 020 8650 0768 · E-mail cbd@cbdresearch.com · www.cbdresearch.com

British Cardiac Patients Association   (Zipper Club)   (BCPA)   1982
- ■ Unit D1, 2 Station Rd, SWAVESEY, Cambs, CB4 5QJ.   (hq)
    01954 202022   fax 01954 202022
    email admin@bcpa.co.uk   http://www.bcpa.co.uk
    Chmn: Keith Jackson
- ▲ Registered Charity
- Br 20
- ○ *W; to offer practical advice, support & reassurance to all heart
    patients & families, particularly those awaiting or who have
    undergone investigations, procedures or heart surgery
- ● Mtgs
- M 4,000 i, UK / 20 i, o'seas
- ¶ Zipper News - 6; ftm, £1.00 each nm.

British Cardiac Society
    since 2006 **British Cardiovascular Society**

British Cardiovascular Society   (BCS)   1922
- NR 9 Fitzroy Sq, LONDON, W1T 5HW.   (hq)
    020 7383 3887
    Admin Dir: Finola McNicholl
- ○ *L; advancement of knowledge of diseases of the heart &
    circulation
- M i
- ✕ 2006 (April) British Cardiac Society

British Carillon Society   (BCS)   1976
- ■ 19 Mathias House, Mathias Close, EPSOM, Surrey,
    KT18 7RX.   (hsp)
    01372 728568
    Hon Sec: John Knox
- ▲ Un-incorporated Society
- ○ *D; to promote the art of the carillon in the British Isles (a
    musical instrument of 23 or more cast bronze bells played
    from a baton keyboard & pedal-board); to propagate music
    for the same
- Gp B.C.S. Music Publications
- ● Mts - Exhib - Lib - VE
- < Wld Carillon Fedn
- M 2 org, 1 f, UK / 19 i, 1 f, 1 org, o'seas
- ¶ NL - 3.
    Music Albums (anthologies) for Carillon of 2 or 3 octaves; irreg.

British Carpet Manufacturers' Association Ltd
    amalgamated in 2001 with the **Carpet Foundation**

British Cartographic Society   (BCS)   1963
- ■ c/o Royal Geographical Society, 1 Kensington Gore, LONDON,
    SW7 2AR.   (mail/address)
    01823 665775   fax 01823 665775
    email admin@cartography.org.uk
    http://www.cartography.org.uk
    Hon Sec: Dr Tim Rideout
- ▲ Registered Charity
- ○ *E, *L, *P, *Q; to promote & represent the cartographic
    profession, including surveying
- Gp Map Curators Gp; Historical Military Mapping Gp; Design Gp
- ● Conf - ET - Exhib - SG - Lib - VE
- < Intl Cartographic Assn (ICA); Intl Map Trade Assn (IMTA);
    Geoforum: assn for Geographic Inf (AGI)
- M 559 i, 39 f, UK / 63 i, o'seas
- ¶ The Cartographic Jnl - 3; ftm, £61 i UK+EU ($102 USA),
    £152 instns UK+EU ($266 USA).
    Maplines (NL) - 3; ftm only.
    Cartographiti (NL) - 3; ftm, £10 UK (£15 airmail).
    Maps & Surveys (NL) - 2; ftm, £10 UK (£15 airmail).

British Carton Association
    since 2005 BPIF Cartons, a special interest group of the **British
    Printing Industries Federation**

British Casino Association Ltd   (BCA)   1973
- ■ 38 Grosvenor Gardens, LONDON, SW1W 0EB.   (hq)
    020 7730 1055
    Dir Gen: David Beeton
- ▲ Company Limited by Guarantee
- ○ *T; representing the interests of the casino industry in GB
- ● Conf - Mtgs - Inf - LG
- M 117 f (casinos)
- ¶ NL - irreg; ftm only.

British Cattle Breeders' Club   (BCBC)   1947
- ■ Lake Villa, Bradworthy, HOLWORTHY, Devon, EX22 7SQ.
    01409 241579   fax 01409 241579
    email lesley.lewin@cattlebreeders.org.uk
    http://www.cattlebreeders.org.uk
    Sec: Mrs Lesley Lewin
- ▲ Company Limited by Guarantee; Registered Charity
- ○ *B; improvements in sphere of cattle breeding; dissemination of
    information & new ideas
- ● Conf - Publication of proceedings
- M 238 i
- ¶ Digest - 1; ftm, £25 nm.   NL - irreg; ftm only.

British Cattle Veterinary Association
    a group of the **British Veterinary Association**

British Cave Rescue Council   (BCRC)   1967
- ■ Pearl Hill, Dent, SEDBURGH, Cumbria, LA10 5TG.   (hsp)
    01539 625412; 0780 302 8830 (mobile)
    email secretary@caverescue.org.uk
    http://www.caverescue.org.uk
    Hon Sec: Pete Allwright
- ▲ Un-incorporated Society
- ○ *G, *W; representation & coordination of voluntary cave rescue
    throughout the UK
- ● Conf - Mtgs - ET - Stat - Inf - LG
- < UK Search & Rescue (UKSAR); Mountain Rescue England &
    Wales; Brit Caving Assn
- > Mountain Rescue England & Wales
- M 16 member teams
- ¶ Information & Briefing CD; ftm only.
    Incident Report - 1 [on website, donation appreciated].

British Cave Research Association   (BCRA)   1973
- ■ The Old Methodist Chapel, Great Hucklow, BUXTON, Derbys,
    SK17 8RG.   (hq)
    01298 873810
    email enquiries@bcra.org.uk   http://www.bcra.org.uk
    Chmn: Steve Whitlock
- ▲ Registered Charity
- ○ *L; all aspects of sciences & technology associated with caves,
    caving & karst: geology, hydrology, archaeology, biology,
    surveying, photography, cave exploration, etc
- Gp Cave radio & electronics; Cave surveying; Hydrology;
    Speleohistory; Explosives users
- ● Conf - Mtgs - ET - Res - SG - Lib
- < U Intl de Speleologie (UIS); Brit Caving Assn (BCA)
- M 500 i, 10 f, 100 org, UK / 100 i, 2 f, 10 org, o'seas
- ¶ Cave & Karst Science - 3;   Speleology - 4;
    Prices for both on application.

British Caving Association   (BCA)   2004
- ■ Old Methodist Chapel, Great Hucklow, BUXTON, Derbys, SK17 8RG.
  01298 873810   fax 01298 873801
  email enquiries@british-caving.org.uk
  http://www.british-caving.org.uk
  Insurance Mgr: Nick Williams
- ▲ Un-incorporated Society
- ○ *N, *S; to act as the governing body of the sport in the UK; to act as the umbrella organisation on behalf of 9 constituent bodies in respect of Sports Council aid
- Gp British Cave Rescue Council; British Cave Research Association; National Association of Mining History Organisations; William Pengelly Cave Studies Trust Ltd & 5 regional Caving Councils (Southern, Northern, Cambrian, Derbyshire, Devon & Cornwall)
- ● Mtgs - ET - Inf - LG
- < Intl Speleological U (UIS)
- M 4,000 i, 10 f, 250 org, UK / 500 i, 10 org, o'seas
- ¶ NL;   Hbk;   Speleology; all ftm only.
- × 2004 (1 January) National Caving Association

British Cement Association   (BCA)   1935
- NR 4 Meadows Business Park, Blackwater, CAMBERLEY, Surrey, GU17 9AB.   (hq)
  01276 608700   fax 01276 608701
  email library@bca.org.uk   http://www.bca.org.uk
  Chief Exec: Mike Gilbert
- ○ *Q, T; to research into: concrete, the greater & better use of concrete, the British Portland Cement industry
- Gp Centre for Concrete Information; Cement Industry Suppliers' Forum
- ● Conf - ET - Res - Exhib - Inf - Lib - PL - LG - Production of technical publications - Development of standards
- < Cembureau; Concrete Industry Alliance
- M 4 f
- ¶ Concrete Quarterly (Jnl) - 4.   Industry Update - 4.
  Concrete Current Awareness - 12.

British Ceramic Confederation   (BCC)   1986
- ■ Federation House, Station Rd, STOKE-ON-TRENT, Staffs, ST4 2SA.   (hq)
  01782 744631   fax 01782 744102
  email bcc@ceramfed.co.uk
  Dir: K C Farrell
- ▲ Un-incorporated Society
- ○ *T
- Gp Gift & tableware; Sanitaryware; Tiles; Bricks; Roofing tiles; Pipes & land drains; Industrial ceramics; Refractories; Material supplies; Plant & machinery
- ● Conf - Mtgs - Comp - SG - Stat - Expt - Inf - VE - Empl - LG
- < Cerame Unie; CBI
- M 120 f
- ¶ Bulletin - 6;   Briefing Documents - irreg; both ftm only.

British Ceramic Gift & Tableware Manufacturers' Association (BCGTMA)
- ■ Federation House, Station Rd, STOKE-ON-TRENT, Staffs, ST4 2SA.   (hq)
  01782 744631   fax 01782 744102
  email bcc@ceramfed.co.uk
  Sec: C P Hall
- ▲ Un-incorporated Society
- ○ *T
- ● Mtgs - SG - Stat - Expt - Inf - LG
- < Brit Ceramic Confedn (BCC); Fédn Eur des Inds de Porcelaine et de Faïence de Table et d'Ornementation (FEPF)
- M 26 f

British Ceramic Plant & Machinery Manufacturers Association
has closed

British Ceramic Research Ltd / CERAM   1948
- NR Queens Rd, Penkhull, STOKE-ON-TRENT, Staffs, ST4 7LQ.   (hq)
- ▲ Company Limited by Guarantee
- ○ *Q; research, development, consultancy, testing, environmental & information services, materials & materials processing development, technology transfer
- M f

British Cervical Spine Society
a specialist society of the **British Orthopaedic Association**

British Chamber of Business in Southern Africa   (SABRITA)   1965
- NR PO Box 66, 2121 Parklands, JOHANNESBURG, South Africa.   (hq)
  27 (11) 786 9436   fax 27 (11) 786 0388
  email info@britishchamber.co.za
  CEO: Sandra Van Lingen
- ○ *C; promotion of trade & investment between UK & South Africa
- < SABA (UK)
- M i, f & org

British Chamber of Commerce in the Argentine Republic
see **Cámara de Comercio Argentino Britanica**

British Chamber of Commerce for Belgium   (BCCB)   1898
- NR Boulevard Saint-Michel 47, 1040 BRUXELLES, Belgium.   (hq)
  32 (02) 540 9030   fax 32 (02) 512 8263
  http://www.britcham.be
- ▲ Company Limited by Guarantee
- ○ *C; to encourage business contacts between Belgium & the UK; to help members achieve their business objectives
- Gp C'ees: Business development, EU, ICT
- ● Conf - Mtgs - Exhib - Lib - VE - LG (EU institutions)
- M 5 i, 5 f, UK / 290 f, Belgium
- ¶ BCC NL - 10.   Trade & Membership Directory - 1.

British Chamber of Commerce in China - Beijing   (BCCC)   1993
- NR The British Centre, China Life Tower (Room 1001), No 16 Chaoyangmenwai Avenue, BEIJING 100020, CHINA.   (hq)
  86 (10) 8525 1111   fax 86 (10) 8525 1100
  email information@pek.britcham.org
  http://www.britcham.org
  Exec Dir: Christopher Baron
- ○ *C
- ¶ British Business in China (Jnl) - 4.

British Chamber of Commerce in the Czech Republic
- NR Pobezní 3, 186 00 PRAGUE 8, Czech Republic.
  420 2 2483 5161   fax 420 2 2483 5862
  http://www.britishchamber.cz
  Exec Dir: Renata Scharfova
- ○ *C

British Chamber of Commerce in Germany e.V.   (BCCG)   1960
- ■ Franzoesischestrasse 48, D-10117 BERLIN, Germany.   (hq)
  49 (30) 20 67 080   fax 49 (30) 20 67 08 29
  email info@bccg.de   http://www.bccg.de
  Exec Dir: Andreas Meyer-Schwickerath
- ▲ Eingetragener Verein
- Br London; 8 in Germany
- ○ *C; to further British-German trade, business contacts & cooperation
- M 900 i, f & org, UK & Germany
- ¶ NL - 3-4; E-NL - 52; both ftm.
  LM - 1; Ybk; both ftm, 200 nm.

British Chamber of Commerce in Hong Kong   1987

NR   Emperor Group Centre (room 1201), 288 Hennessy Rd,
       WAN CHAI, Hong Kong.   (hq)
       (852) 2824 2211
       email info@britcham.com
       Exec Dir: Christopher Hammerbeck
▲   Company Limited by Guarantee
○   *C
●   Conf - Mtgs - ET - Inf - VE - LG
M   450 f
¶   British Business in China (LM) - 1.
       The British Directory (LM) - 1.

British Chamber of Commerce in Hungary   (BCCH)   1991

NR   Bank U 6 11/7, H-1054 BUDAPEST, Hungary.   (hq)
       36 (1) 302 5200   fax 36 (1) 302 3069
       email bcch@bcch.com   http://www.bcch.com
       Exec Dir: Valéria Abelovszky
○   *C; the enhancement of trade between the UK & Hungary
Gp   Interest: Legal, SME, Social
●   Conf - Mtgs - Res - Exhib - Inf - Lib - VE - Empl - LG - Seminars
¶   BCCH Business News (NL) - 6.
       BCCH Trade & Membership Directory - 1.

British Chamber of Commerce & Industry in Brazil   (BCCIB)   1916

NR   Rua Ferreira de Araújo, 741-1° andar Pinheiros, São Paulo SP,
       SÃO PAULO SP 05428-002, Brazil.   (hq)
       55 (11) 3819 0265
       http://www.britcham.com.br
       Exec Dir: Philip Hamer
▲   Registered Charity
Br   Rio de Janeiro
○   *C; to encourage the growth of trade & commercial
       relationships between Great Britain & Brazil
Gp   Legal; Tax; Foreign trade; Foreign investment; Events; Seminar
●   Conf - Mtgs - ET - Expt - Inf - Lib
<   Eurochambres; Brit Cham Comm in Latin-America; London
       Cham Comm & Ind
M   2 f, UK / 5 f, o'seas
¶   Britain Brasil - 6.   Doing Business in Brazil - 1.   Ybk - 1.

British Chamber of Commerce for Italy, Inc   (BCCI)   1904

■   via Dante 12, I-20121 MILANO, Italy.   (hq)
       39 (02) 877 798   fax 39 (02) 8646 1855
       email bcci@britchamitaly.com
       http://www.britchamitaly.com
       Chief Exec: Morfa Downs
▲   Incorporated Society
Br   London: 020 7222 7040
○   *C
Gp   Commercial services; English language consultancy service;
       Business examinations; Events (seminars, cultural events);
       English courses in UK
●   Conf - Mtgs - ET - Exam - Res - Inf - Debt & VAT recovery -
       Company searches
<   Maintains ties with Dept of Trade & Ind (GB); Coun of Brit
       Chams Comm in Continental Europe
M   i, f, UNIONESTERE, COBCOE
¶   Britaly (NL online) - 12;   Focus on Italy - 1;
       Speak to the World - 1; all free.
       Trade Directory - 2 yrly; ftm, 25.

British Chamber of Commerce in Japan   (BCCJ)   1948

■   3F Kenkyusha Eigo Centre Building, 1-2 Kagurazaka, Shinjuku-
       ku, TOKYO 162-0825, Japan.   (hq)
       81 (3) 3267 1901   fax 81 (3) 3267 1903
       email info@bccjapan.com   http://www.bccjapan.com
       Chief Exec: Ian de Stains
○   *C; to promote Anglo-Japanese commercial relations
Gp   C'ees: Membership, Finance, Technology; Property forum;
       British Industry Centre
●   Conf - Mtgs - Stat - Expt - Inf - LG
<   Britain in Asia Pacific

British Chamber of Commerce in Korea   1981

NR   Regus Business Centre (20th floor), Korea First Bank Bldg, 100
       Gongpyong-dong, Jongro-gu, SEOUL 110 702.   (hq)
       82 (2) 720 9406
       Dir Gen: Ms Jeongmi Seo
○   *C
●   Mtgs - Stat - Inf
M   c 200 f
¶   NL - 12; free.

British Chamber of Commerce in Latvia   (BCCL)   1996

■   Kr Valdemara 21-605, LV-1010 RIGA, Latvia.   (hq)
       371 703 5216   fax 371 703 5518
       email info@bccl.lv   http://www.bccl.lv
       Exec Dir: Juris Benkis
▲   Un-incorporated Society
○   *C; promoting trade & partnership in British-Latvian business
●   Conf - Mtgs - Expt - Inf - VE - LG
<   Foreign Investors' Coun in Latvia
M   17 i, 99 f, 3 org
¶   British Latvian Trade (Jnl) - 6; free.

British Chamber of Commerce for Luxembourg   (BCC)   1992

■   6 rue Antoine de Saint Exupéry, L-1432 LUXEMBOURG.   (hq)
       00 352 (-) 465466   fax 00 352 (-) 220384
       email mail@bcc.lu   http://www.bcc.lu
       Mgr: Sophie Kerschen
○   *C
●   Conf - Mtgs - LG
¶   LM - 2 yrly; free.

British Chamber of Commerce for Morocco   (BCCM)   1923

■   65 rue Hassan Seghir, 20000 CASABLANCA, Morocco.   (hq)
       212 (22) 44 88 60/61/65   fax 212 (22) 44 88 68
       email britcham@casanet.net.ma
       http://www.bccm.co.ma
       Pres: Barry Marsh
○   *C; to promote bi-lateral trade between the UK & Morocco
●   Conf - Mtgs - Exhib - Expt - Inf - Lib - VE
<   Moroccan Brit Business Coun (MBBC); Assn des Chambres de
       Commerce et d'Industrie Européenne au Maroc (ACCIEM)
M   10 f, UK / 400 f, Morocco
¶   Business Link - 4;   Annual Review - 1; both ftm only.

British Chamber of Commerce in Poland
       since 2000-01 **British Polish Chamber of Commerce**

British Chamber of Commerce Shanghai   (Britcham Shanghai)   1995

NR   1703 Westgate Tower, 1038 Nanjing Road West, SHANGHAI
       200041, People's Republic of China.   (hq)
       86 (21) 6218 5022   fax 86 (21) 6218 5066
       email admin@sha.britcham.org
       http://www.britcham.org
       Exec Dir: Ian Crawford
○   *C; to promote & deepen the relationship between China & the
       UK; to support the increasing number of business interests in
       Shanghai & the East China region; to act as a central source
       of information, including a contract data-base, on issues
       facing foreign companies operating in China
●   Conf - Mtgs - Inf - LG
M   86 i, 535 f
¶   The Beat - 12; free.
       British Business in China Directory.

British Chamber of Commerce Singapore

■   138 Cecil St, 11-01 Cecil Court, SINGAPORE 069538.   (hq)
       00 (65) 6222 3552   fax 00 (65) 6222 3556
       email info@britcham.org.sg
       http://www.britcham.org.sg
       Chief Exec Officer: Ray Bigger
○   *C
●   Conf - Mtgs - Inf

British Chamber of Commerce in the Slovak Republic
NR Sedlárska 5, 811 01 BRATISLAVA, SLOVAK REPUBLIC.
     421 (2) 5292 0371   fax 421 (2) 5292 0371
     http://www.britcham.sk
     Exec Dir: Lívia Eperjesiová
○   *C

British Chamber of Commerce in Spain   (Cámara de Comercio Britanica en España) 1908
NR C/ Bruc, 21 1° 4a, 08010 BARCELONA, Spain.
     34 933 173 220
     http://www.britishchamberspain.com
     Dir: Sarah Jane Stone
○   *C

British Chamber of Commerce in Taipei   (BCCT)
■ 207 Dun Hwa N Rd (8th floor), TAIPEI 10595, Taiwan.   (hq)
     00 (02) 2547 1199   fax 00 (02) 2547 2378
     http://www.bcctaipei.com
     Chmn: Paul Burke,   Exec Dir: Lee Ting
▲   Company Limited by Guarantee
○   *C; to promote & develop trade & investment between Britain & Taiwan; to provide members in both countries with a forum to express their views on commercial & trade related issues affecting the two countries
●   Mtgs - Res - Inf - VE - LG
<   Britain in Asia Pacific (BIAP)
M   10 i, 100 f, (Taiwan)
¶   Effective Business in Taiwan - 1; ftm, £30 nm.
     LM - 1; ftm, £120 nm.

British Chamber of Commerce Thailand   (BCCT) 1946
NR 208 Wireless Rd (7th floor), Lumphini, Pathumwan, BANGKOK 10330, Thailand.   (hq)
     66 (2) 651 5350-3   fax 66 (2) 651 5354
     email greg@bccthai.com   http://www.bccthai.com
     Exec Dir: Greg Watkins
○   *C
●   Conf - Mtgs - ET - Exam - Exhib - SG - Stat - Expt - Inf - Lib - VE - LG
M   c 620 f
¶   The Brief - 6;   The Digest - 12;
     Annual Hbk: Partners in Progress;
     Monthly Industry Sector Reports;
     Annual Expatriate Cost of Living Survey (online);
     Annual Compensation & Benefits Survey (online);
     LM (online);   all ftm only.

British Chamber of Commerce of Turkey (Association)   (BCCT)
NR Mešrutiyet Caddesi 18, Aslihan Kat 6, Tepebaši/Beyoğlu, TR-80050 ISTANBUL, Turkey.   (hq)
     90 (212) 249 06 58   fax 90 (212) 252 55 51
     email buscenter@bcct.org.tr   http://www.bcct.org.tr
     Sec Gen: Mr İlter Koral
○   *C; to promote Anglo-Turkish trade
●   Conf - Mtgs - Exhib - Expt - Inf - Lib - VE
<   Assn Brit Cham Comm
M   51 i, UK / 410 i, Turkey – under Turkish law, only individuals can be members
¶   Trade Journal [in English] - 4; ftm.
     Trade Journal [in Turkish] - 6; ftm.
     Trade Fairs & Exhibitions in Turkey - 1; free.
     Hints to Businessmen: Turkey - 1; ftm.

British Chambers of Commerce   (BCC) 1890
NR 65 Petty France, LONDON, SW1H 9EU.   (hq)
     020 7654 5800   fax 020 7654 5819
     email info@britishchambers.org.uk
▲   Company Limited by Guarantee
Br 58
○   *C; business representation, international, national & local
Gp Trade & Professional Alliance (26 member associations)
●   Conf - Mtgs - ET - Exam - Res - Exhib - Comp - SG - Stat - Expt - Inf - VE - LG
<   Eurochambres
M   130,000 i, f & org
¶   Quarterly Economic Survey - 4.   Small Firms Survey - 8.
     Member Directory - 1.   Trade Mission Hbk - 1.
     Various Policy Position Papers - irreg.
✕   2002 British Chambers of Commerce Executives (merged)

British Chambers of Commerce Executives
    merged in 2002 with the **British Chambers of Commerce**

British Charolais Cattle Society Ltd   1962
■ Avenue M, Stoneleigh Park, KENILWORTH, Warks, CV8 2RG. (hq)
     024 7669 7222   fax 024 7669 0270
     email charolais@charolais.co.uk
     http://www.charolais.co.uk
     Sec: David Benson
▲   Company Limited by Guarantee; Registered Charity
○   *B
●   Conf - Mtgs - Exhib - Comp - Expt - Inf - VE - Empl - LG
M   3,000 i, UK / 100 i, o'seas
¶   Charolais News - 3; free.

British Charollais Sheep Society Ltd   (BCSS) 1977
NR Crogham Farm, Youngmans Rd, WYMONDHAM, Norfolk, NR18 0RR.   (hq)
     01953 603335   fax 01953 607626
     Jt Secs: Jonathan & Carroll Barber
○   *B
Gp Trials: Ram, Halfbred ewe, Crossbred lamb; Charollais lamb marketing org
●   Conf - Mtgs - ET - Res - Exhib - SG - Stat - Expt - Inf - VE
<   UPRA Mouton Charollais (France); Nat Sheep Assn
M   1,100 i
¶   Flock Book - 1.   LM.   NL - 3.   AR.

British Chauffeurs Guild
NR 13 Stonecot Hill, SUTTON, Surrey, SM3 9HB.
     020 8544 9777   fax 020 8544 1177
○   *P

British Cheerleading Association   (BCA) 1984
NR 102 White Horse Rd, WINDSOR, Berks, SL4 4PH.   (chmn)
     01753 867713
     email bob@cheerleading.org.uk
     Chmn: Bob Kiralfy
▲   Un-incorporated Society
○   *G; to act as the governing body for cheerleading in Britain
●   Mtgs - ET - Exam - Exhib - Comp - Stat - Inf - PL - VE - Parades & shows
<   Intl Teachers Assn; Wld Cheerleading Assn; CCPR
M   c 11,500 i in 310 clubs
¶   Cheerleader - 4.   News Update - 12.

British Chelonia Group   (BCG) 1976
NR PO Box 1176, CHIPPENHAM, Wilts, SN15 1XB.   (mail)
     http://www.britishcheloniagroup.org.uk address
     Gen Sec: Diana Scott
▲   Registered Charity
○   *G, *L; the study, conservation & welfare of tortoises, terrapins & turtles worldwide
●   Conf - Mtgs - ET - Exhib - Inf - Lib - LG - Annual symposia
M   1,600 i
¶   Testudo (Jnl) - 1.   NL - 6.

© CBD Research Ltd · Beckenham · BR3 5JS · Tel 020 8650 7745 · Fax 020 8650 0768 · E-mail cbd@cbdresearch.com · www.cbdresearch.com

British Chemical Distributors & Traders Association Ltd (BCDTA) 1923
■ Lyme Building, Westmere Drive, Crewe Business Park, CREWE, Cheshire, CW1 6ZD.   (hq)
   01270 258200   fax 01270 258444
   email bcdta@bcdta.org.uk   http://www.bcdta.org.uk
   Dir: Peter J Newport
▲ Company Limited by Guarantee
○ *T; interests of chemical distributors, traders & manufacturers
● Conf - Mtgs - ET - Exhib - Inf - LG - Technical support, advice & industry training
< Fédn Européenne du Commerce Chimique (FECC); Confedn of Brit Ind Tr Assn Forum (CBI TAF); S Cheshire Cham Comm
M 120 f
¶ Outlook (NL) - 3.   AR.
   Where to Buy Directory - 1; ftm, £60 nm (£70 o'seas).

British Chemical Engineering Contractors Association (BCECA) 1966
NR 1 Regent St, LONDON, SW1Y 4NR.   (hq)
   020 7839 6514
   Dir: Peter Fagiano
▲ Un-incorporated Society
○ *T; interests of the principal companies in the UK which provide engineering, procurement, construction & project management services to the process industries
M 22 f

British Cheque Cashers Association   (BCCA) 1994
■ PO Box 3414, CHESTER, Cheshire, CH1 9BF.   (hq)
   01244 505904   fax 01244 505909
   email info@bcca.co.uk   http://www.bcca.co.uk
   Chief Exec: Geoff Holland
▲ Company Limited by Share
○ *T; for companies in the UK offering third party cheque encashment services & pay day advances (consumer credit)
● Conf - Mtgs - ET - Res - Inf - LG - Liaison with orgs in the finance sector
< Fedn of Eur Cheque Cashers; Tr Assn Forum; Confedn Brit Ind (CBI)
M 350 f
¶ NL - 4;   Members' Extra - 4;   Confidential Extra - 4;   Money Laundering Guidelines - irreg;   AR - 1; all ftm only.
   Code of Practice; free.

British Cheque Collectors Society
   since 2003-04 **British Banking History Society**

British Chess Federation
   since 2005 **English Chess Federation**

British Chicken Association Ltd
   since 2001 **British Poultry Council**

British Chilean Chamber of Commerce   (BCCC) 1989
■ 12 Devonshire St, LONDON, W1G 7DS.   (hq)
   020 7323 3053   fax 020 7580 5901
   email info@bcc.org.uk   http://www.bccc.org.uk
   Gen Mgr: Merilyn K Potter
▲ Conmpany Limited by Guarantee
○ *C; to promote bi-lateral trade between Chile & the UK
Gp Mining; Extractive industries; Exhibitions
● Conf - Exhib - Inf - LG
< Santiago Cham Comm; Chilean Brit Cham Comm
M 68 f
¶ Chile News (NL) - 6.

British Chilean Chamber of Commerce [Santiago]
   see **Cámara Chileno Britanica de Comercio (British Chilean Chamber of Commerce)**

British Chiropody & Podiatry Association   (BChA) 1959
NR 149 Bath Rd, MAIDENHEAD, Berks, SL6 4LA.   (pres/b)
   01628 632440
   Hon Pres: Michael J Batt,   Chmn: M G Paynton
▲ Un-incorporated Society
○ *P; for fully trained chiropodists & podiatrists
● Conf - Mtgs - Exhib - SG - Inf - VE - Empl - LG
M 10,000 i, UK / 1,000 i, o'seas
¶ Jnl - 4; ftm.   Footnotes - 4; ftm.

British Chiropractic Association   (BCA) 1925
■ 59 Castle St, READING, Berks, RG1 7SN.   (hq)
   0118-950 5950   fax 0118-958 8946
   email enquiries@chiropractic-uk.co.uk
   http://www.chiropractic-uk.co.uk
   Exec Dir: Susan Wakefield
▲ Company Limited by Guarantee
○ *P; the registration body for chiropractors; an independent branch of medicine which specialises in mechanical disorders of the joints (particularly those of the spine) & their effect on the nervous system
● Conf - Mtgs - ET - Res - Exhib - Stat - Inf - LG
< Eur Chiropractic U; Wld Fedn of Chiropractic
M 1,073 i, UK / 36 i, o'seas
¶ Contact (NL) - 4;   In Touch - 12; both ftm only.

British Christmas Tree Growers Association   (BCTGA) 1980
■ 13 Wolrige Rd, EDINBURGH, Midlothian, EH16 6HX.   (hq)
   0131-664 1100   fax 0131-664 2669
   http://www.christmastree.org.uk
   Sec: Roger Hay
▲ Un-incorporated Society
○ *T; to provide marketing assistance & technical advice to growers of live Christmas trees
● Conf - Mtgs - Stat - Inf
< Timber Growers Assn; Christmas Tree Growers Assn of Western Europe; Amer Nat Christmas Tree Assn
M 300 i, 50 f, 1 org, UK / 1 i, o'seas
¶ NL - 2; ftm.   LM.   AR; ftm.

British Civil Engineering Test Equipment Manufacturers Association   (CTMA) 1968
■ 28 Wing Rd, Linslade, LEIGHTON BUZZARD, Beds, LU7 2NJ.   (chmn)
   01525 854819   fax 01525 854819
   email jtc@jtconsult.co.uk b
   Chmn: John Turner
▲ Un-incorporated Society
○ *T; for manufacturers & suppliers of test equipment for the construction industry (civil engineering & building)
● Mtgs - BSI Standards Development (Test Methods) C'ees
M 8 f

British Classification Society   (BCS) 1986
NR c/o Dr J Padmore, University of Sheffield Management School, 9 Mappin St, SHEFFIELD, S Yorks, S1 4DT.   (sb)
   0114 222 3439   fax 0114-222 3348
   email j.padmore@sheffield.ac.uk
   http://www.shef.ac.uk/bcs
   Sec: Dr Jo Padmoreler
▲ Un-incorporated Society
○ *L; to encourage the cooperation & exchange of views & information among those interested in the principles & practice of classification in any discipline where they are used
● Conf - Mtgs - Res - Stat
< Intl Fedn of Classification Socs (ICFS)
M c 50 i

British Cleaning Council (BCC Ltd)   (BCC)   1982
- ■ PO Box 1328, KIDDERMINSTER, Worcs, DY11 5ZJ.   (hsb)
  01562 851129   fax 01562 851129
  email info@britishcleaningcouncil.org
  http://www.britishcleaningcouncil.org
  Co Sec / Treas: John A Stinton
- ▲ Company Limited by Guarantee
- ○ *N, *T; interests of the cleaning industry in general
- ● Conf - Mtgs - ET - Exhib - LG - Voice of Industry - Council of
  Associations
- M 18 org
- ¶ The Voice - 4; free.

British Clematis Society   1991
- NR 12 Oakway Drive, FRIMLEY, Surrey, GU16 8LF.   (sp)
  01276 28630
  http://www.britishclematis.org.uk
  Sec: William Davies
- ▲ Registered Charity
- ○ *H; to promote the cultivation & preservation of clematis
- ● Mtgs - Exhib - Inf - Slide library - VE - Seed exchange - Plant
  sales
- < R Horticl Soc
- M c 1,000 i
- ¶ The Clematis (Jnl) - 1.

British Clothing Industry Association   (BCIA)   1981
- NR 5 Portland Place, LONDON, W1B 1PW.   (hq)
  020 7636 7788   fax 020 7636 7515
  email bcia@dial.pipex.com
  Dir: John R Wilson,   Asst Dir: Elizabeth P Fox
- ○ *T; to encourage, promote, develop & protect the clothing
  industry of the UK
- Gp Sectors: Shirt, Workwear, Women's & girls' outerwear, Men's &
  boys' outerwear, Foundation & swimwear; Tailoring
  Guild of British Tie Makers; Knitting Industries Federation
- ● Mtgs - Stat - Inf - Empl - LG
- < Intl Apparel Fedn; CBI; Apparel, Knitting & Textiles Alliance; Brit
  Apparel & Textile Confedn
- M f (membership covers 70% of UK production)
- ¶ News Sheet - 12;   Fact Card - 1;   AR; all ftm.

**British Coalition of Heritable Disorders of Connective Tissue
1990**
- ■ Rochester House, 5 Aldershot Rd, FLEET, Hants, GU51 3NG.
  Founder/Coordinator: Mrs Diane L Rust
- ○ *M, *W; to promote contact & cooperation between voluntary
  organisations working with connective tissue disorder
- M Independent support groups representing patients with
  rheumatological & orthopaedic symptoms
- ¶ Leaflet.

British Coatings Federation Ltd   (BCF)   1993
- NR James House, Bridge St, LEATHERHEAD, Surrey, KT22 7EP.
  (hq)
  01372 360660
  Chief Exec: Mrs M T McMillan
- ▲ Company Limited by Guarantee
- ○ *T; interests of UK manufacturers of paints & industrial coatings
  & printing inks
- Gp Wallcoverings Sector Council
- M 160 f, UK / 6 f, o'seas
- × 2005 Wallcoverings Manufacturers' Association of GB (merged)

British Coffee Association   2001
- ■ PO Box 5, CHIPPING NORTON, Oxon, OX7 5UD.   (hq)
  01608 644995   fax 01608 644996
  http://www.britishcoffeeassociation.org
  Communications Mgr: Zoë Wheeldon
- ▲ Un-incorporated Society
- ○ *T
- ● Mtgs - Inf
- < Assn EEC Soluble Coffee Mfrs (AFCASOLE); Food & Drink Fedn
- M 2 f

British Colombian Chamber of Commerce
   see **Cámara de Comercio Colombo-Británica**

British & Colombian Chamber of Commerce   (B&CCC)   1996
- ■ Canning House, 2 Belgrave Square, LONDON, SW1X 8PJ.
  (hq)
  020 7235 2106   fax 020 7235 0933
  email director@britishandcolombianchamber.com
  http://www.britishcolombianchamber.com
  Chmn: Alexander Kennedy,   Exec Dir: Tania Hoxos
- ▲ Company Limited by Guarantee
- Br Colombia
- ○ *C; to promote commercial links between Colombia & the
  United Kingdom
- ● Conf - Mtgs - ET - Expt - Inf - VE - LG
- M 20 i, 60 f, UK / 15 f, o'seas
- ¶ Colombian Correspondent (NL) - 52; ftm, £30 nm.

British Colostomy Association
   has closed

British Colour Makers Association   (BCMA)   1932
- NR Linden House, Shore Rd, Garelochead, HELENSBURGH,
  Argyll & Bute, G84 0EL.   (sp)
  01436 810722
  email secretary@bcma.org.uk   http://www.bcma.org.uk
  Sec: P D Johnson
- ▲ Un-incorporated Society
- ○ *T; the manufacturing & marketing of pigments
- Gp Standing technical c'ee
- ● Mtgs - ET - SG - Inf - LG
- < Eurocolour; ETAD; Colour Pigment Mfrs of America; Alliance of
  Ind Assns (AIA)
- M 11 f

British Coloured Sheep Breeders Association   1985
- NR Daren Uchaf, Cwmyoy, ABERGAVENNY, Monmouthshire,
  NP7 7NR.   (sp)
  01873 890712
  Sec: Sarah Stacey
- ○ *B; to promote coloured sheep & use of their fleece & by -
  products
- ● Inf - Demonstrations
- M 120 i
- ¶ Coloured Sheep News - 4.

British Combustion Equipment Manufacturers Association
   since May 2004 **ICom Energy Association**

British Comedy Society   (BSC)   1991
- ■ 37 Langbourne Ave, LONDON, N6 6PS.   (regd/office)
  020 8347 0115   fax 020 8347 0115
  email johngatenby@yahoo.com
  Treas: John Gatenby
- ▲ Company Limited by Guarantee
- ○ *G; to preserve & foster the tradition of British Comedy
- ● Plaque unveilings - Charity fundraising - Celebrity luncheons -
  Pinewood Studio Hall of Fame - Elstree Wall of Fame
- M 150 i
- ¶ NL - irreg.

British Commercial Boatbuilders Association
   a group of the **British Marine Federation**

British Commercial Glasshouse Manufacturers Association
   association is dormant

British Committee for Standards in Haematology
   a group of the **British Society for Haematology**

British Compact Collectors' Society (BCCS) 1994
■ PO Box 131, WOKING, Surrey, GU24 9YR. (hsp)
　 http://www.compactcollectors.co.uk
　 Pres: Juliette Edwards
○ *G; for collectors of ladies' powder compacts & related vintage
　 glamour items
● Conf - Res - Exhib
M c 400 i
¶ Face Facts - 3; ftm only.
　 Note: Please enclose sae on initial contact

British Comparative Literature Association (BCLA) 1975
NR Dept of French, University of Manchester, Oxford Rd,
　 MANCHESTER, M13 9PL. (hsb)
　 Sec: Mrs Penny Brown
○ *A; to promote the scholarly study of literature without
　 confinement to national or linguistic boundaries
● Conf - Mtgs - Comp
< Intl Comparative Literature Assn
M 150 i
¶ New Comparison - 2; ftm.
　 Comparative Criticism - 3.

British Complementary Medicine Association (BCMA) 1992
■ PO Box 5122, BOURNEMOUTH, Dorset, BH8 0WG. (hq)
　 0845 345 5977
　 email info@bcma.co.uk　 http://www.bcma.co.uk
　 Admin: Tracy Smith
▲ Un-incorporated Society
○ *M, *P; complementary medicine & healthcare; to make
　 available public efficacious & safe complementary medicine
Gp Professional organisations; Practitioners register
● Mtgs - ET - Res - Exhib - SG - Inf - LG - Maintaining the register
　 of practitioners
< Indep Care Org Coun
M 20,000 i, 40 assns, 30 colleges/schools
¶ NL;　 AR; both ftm only.

British Compressed Air Society (BCAS) 1930
■ 33-34 Devonshire St, LONDON, W1G 6PY. (hq)
　 020 7935 2464　 fax 020 7935 3307
　 email enquiries@britishcompressedairsociety.co.uk
　 http://www.britishcompressedairsociety.co.uk
　 Exec Dir & Co Sec: C P Dee
▲ Company Limited by Guarantee
○ *T; manufacturers & distributors of compressed air products &
　 services in the UK; to represent members to UK government
　 & European institutions; to provide a forum for the
　 manufacturers & the broad distribution, supply & installation
　 interests in the compressed air, vacuum & pneumatics
　 industry
Gp Industrial process compressors; Portable compressors &
　 contractors tools; Industrial tools; Pneumatic control & air
　 treatment; Service industries equipment;
　 C'ees: Air treatment & pneumatic control, Compressor &
　 vacuum, Distributors, Tools
● Mtgs - ET - Stat - Inf - LG
< Eur C'ee of Mfrs of Compressors, Vacuum Pumps & Pneumatic
　 Tools PNEUROP
M 5 i, 105 f, UK / 7 f, o'seas
¶ NL - 12; ftm [email].
　 Air treatment & general services:
　　 Installation Guide.　 Pipe Joint Guide.
　　 Compressed Air Condensate.
　　 Air Treatment Contamination & Purity Classes &
　　　 Measurement Methods.　 AR - 1; free.

British Compressed Gases Association (BCGA) 1971
■ 6 St Mary's St, WALLINGFORD, Oxon, OX10 0EL. (hq)
　 01491 825533　 fax 01491 826689
　 http://www.bcga.co.uk
　 Dir: Doug Thornton
▲ Company Limited by Guarantee
○ *T; interests of companies engaged in the manufacture,
　 distribution & safe use of gases, cylinders & equipment
● Conf - Mtgs - Exhib - Inf - LG - Representation on BSI, CEN &
　 ISO C'ees - Advice on use & application of gases
< Eur Indl Gases Assn (EIGA); Engg Eqpt & Materials Users Assn;
　 CBI; BSI; Tr Assn Forum; Instn Mechanical Engrs
M 57 i, 3 associate memebrs
¶ Codes of Practice & Guidance Notes;　 Technical Reports;
　 Leaflets - all 3-yrly; prices vary.

British Computer Association of the Blind
NR 58-72 John Bright St, BIRMINGHAM, B1 1BN.
　 0845 430 8627
　 http://www.bcab.org.uk
　 Chmn: Derek Naysmith
○ *G; visually impaired computer professionals & users

British Computer Society (BCS) 1957
NR North Star House (Block D 1st floor), North Star Avenue,
　 SWINDON, Wilts, SN2 1FA. (hq)
　 01793 417417
　 Chief Exec: David Clarke
▲ Registered Charity
○ *P; 'the authoritative voice of those seeking excellence in
　 computing; a national source of advice to government &
　 industry on all issues affected by computing; maintaining
　 both technical & ethical standards in the profession'
M　 i

** **British Concrete Masonry Association (inc the Aggregate
　　 Concrete Block Producers' Association)**
　 Organisation lost: see Introduction paragraph 3

British Concrete Pumping Group
　 a special interest group of the **Construction Plant-hire
　 Association**

British Confectioners Association (BCA) 1905
NR c/o Mr T Cutress, Unit 4 Home Farm Business Centre,
　 BRIGHTON, E Sussex, BN1 9HU. (hsb)
　 01273 601404
　 Hon Sec: Tim Cutress
▲ Un-incorporated Society
○ *T; to promote craftsmanship & good training in the flour
　 confectionery trade (not sugar confectionery sweets)
● Mtgs - ET - Exhib - Comp - SG - VE
M　 i
¶ LM - 1; ftm only.

British Confederation of Psychotherapists
　 since 2005-06 **British Psychoanalytic Council**

British Connemara Pony Society (BCPS) 1947
■ 2 East Green, Bowsden, BERWICK upon TWEED,
　 Northumberland, TD15 2TJ. (sb)
　 01289 388800
　 email secretary@britishconnemaras.co.uk
　 http://www.britishconnemaras.co.uk
　 Sec: Mrs S Mansell
○ *B
< Connemara Pony Breeders Soc (Republic of Ireland)
✕ 2003-04 English Connemara Pony Society

British Constructional Steelwork Association Ltd   (BCSA)   1906
- ■   4 Whitehall Court, LONDON, SW1A 2ES.   (hq)
      020 7839 8566
      Chief Exec: Dr Derek Tordoff
- ▲   Company Limited by Guarantee
- ○   *T; fabricators of constructional steelwork & suppliers of
      components & services to the steel construction industry
- Gp Steel construction certification scheme; Register of Qualified
      Steelwork Contractors Scheme
- ●   Conf - Mtgs - ET - Res - Comp - SG - Stat - Expt - Inf - VE - LG
- <   Eur Convention for Constructional Steelwork (ECCS)
- M   150 f
- ¶   Directory for Specifiers & Buyers - 1;
      Steel Construction News [incl LM] - 3;
      New Steel Construction [incl LM] - 6;   Annual Review; all free.
      Various technical publications: list available.

British Contact Dermatitis Group
    a group of the **British Association of Dermatologists**

British Contact Lens Association   (BCLA)
- NR Walmar House, 288-292 Regent St, LONDON, W1B 3AL.
      020 7580 6661   fax 020 7580 6669
      http://www.bcla.org.uk
      Sec-Gen: Vivien Freeman
- ▲   Registered Charity
- ○   *T
- Gp Overseas; Optometric; Dispensing; Technical; Medical; Student
      membership
- ●   Conf - Mtgs - ET
- M   1,800 i
- ¶   Jnl.

British Contract Furnishing Association Ltd   (BCFA)   1970
- ■   Project House, 25 West Wycombe Rd, HIGH WYCOMBE, Bucks,
      HP11 2LQ.   (hq)
      01494 896790   fax 01494 896799
      email enquiries@bcfa.org.uk   http://www.thebcfa.com
      Contact: Trudy Pearce
- ▲   Company Limited by Guarantee
- ○   *T
- ●   Mtgs - ET - Exhib - Stat - Inf
- M   300 f
- ¶   UK Contract Furnishing Directory - 1; ftm, £85 nm.

British Contract Manufacturers & Packers Association   (BCMPA)
- NR St Mary's Court, The Broadway, OLD AMERSHAM, Bucks,
      HP7 0UT.
      01494 582013   fax 01494 778147
      email info@bcmpa.org.uk   http://www.bcmpa.org.uk
      Chief Exec: Rodney Steel

British Cooperative Clinical Group
    a specialist group of the **British Association for Sexual Health &**
    HIV

British Correspondence Chess Society   (BCCS)   1962
- NR 3 Badgers Close, WOKING, Surrey, GU21 3JF.   (hsp)
      01483 714635
      email ukchess@aol.com
      Sec: Alon W A Risdon
- ▲   Un-incorporated Society
- ○   *G; to encourage the playing of chess by correspondence; to
      foster chess playing generally
- Gp Under 21 championships; End-game tourneys
- ●   Conf - ET - Stat - Lib - Annotation service - Correspondence
      course - Grading list - Overseas matches
- <   Brit Postal Chess Fedn
- M   625 i
- ¶   Correspondence Chess - 6.

British Costume Association   (BCA)   1986
- NR PO Box 136, ASHINGTON, Northumberland, NE62 5ZX.
      (chmn/p)
      0845 230 515
      http://www.incostume.co.uk
      Chmn: Peter Denton
- ▲   Un-incorporated Society
- ○   *T; costume & fancy dress suppliers
- ●   ET - Exhib - Inf - LG
- M   300 f
- ¶   In Costume - 4; ftm.

British Cotton Growing Association Ltd
- §   12 Princes Parade, LIVERPOOL, Merseyside, L3 1BG.
      0151-242 7500
      A wholly owned subsidiary of Cargill plc

BRITISH COUNCIL ...
    For details of British Councils, other than those below, see the
    companion volume **'Councils, Committees & Boards'**

British Council for Offices   (BCO)   1990
- NR 38 Lombard St, LONDON, EC3V 9BS.   (hq)
      020 7283 4588   fax 020 7626 2223
      email mail@bco.org.uk   http://www.bco.org.uk
      Chief Exec: Richard Kauntze
- ▲   Company Limited by Guarantee
- ○   *N, *T; to research, develop & communicate best practice in all
      aspects of the office sector; to provide a forum for discussion
      & debate of relevant issues; members are organisations
      involved in creating, acquiring & occupying office space
- ●   Conf - Mtgs - Res - Awards programme
- M   c 1,000 i & f
- ¶   Publications list available.

British Council of Shopping Centres   (BCSC)   1983
- NR 1 Queen Anne's Gate, LONDON, SW1H 9BT.   (hq & regd
      office)
      020 7222 1122
      Head of Secretariat: Michael D Taplin
- ▲   Company Limited by Guarantee
- ○   *T; for those engaged in the development, design &
      management of shopping centres & the retailing & other
      functions therein
- Gp Centre management; Security; Government affairs; Technical;
      Finance & investment; Awards
- ●   Conf - Mtgs - ET - Res - Exhib - SG - Inf - VE - LG
- <   Intl Coun of Shopping Centres
- M   700 i, 400 f, UK / 30 i, 20 f, o'seas
- ¶   Beyond the Horizon (Jnl) - 2;   Annual Review - 1;
      Checkout (technical NL) - 4; all free.
      Ybk of members - 1; ftm only.

British Country Music Association   (BCMA)   1969
- ■   PO Box 240, HARROW, Middx, HA3 7PH.   (mail)
      01273 559750   fax 01273 559750
      email theBCMA@yahoo.com   http://www.cmib.co.uk/
      bcma address
- ○   *A; promotion of country music in GB
- ●   Comp - Inf - VE
- M   3,000 i, UK / 80 i, o'seas
- ¶   Bulletin - 6;   Ybk - 1; both ftm only.

British Crossbow Society   (BCS)   1964
- NR 24 Ivy Rd, POYNTON, Cheshire, SK12 1BE.   (hsp)
      01625 877900
      Hon Sec: Graeme Peatfield
- ▲   Un-incorporated Society
- ○   *S; to promote competitive amateur crossbow shooting at
      national & club level in the British Isles
- ●   Mtgs - ET - Comp - Inf - Lib - VE - LG
- <   Eur Community of Historic Armed Glds (EGS)
- M   c 70 i
- ¶   NL - 4; ftm.

British Crown Green Bowling Association (BCGBA) 1907
NR   94 Fishers Lane, Pensby, WIRRAL, Merseyside, CH61 8SB.
         (chief/exec/p)
         0151-648 5740
         Chief Exec: John Crowther
○   *S; the governing body of crown green bowling
●   Comp
M   180,000 i, 3,500 clubs
¶   Hbk - 1.

British Cryoengineering Society
         2006 reverted to its previous title **British Cryogenics Council**

British Cryogenics Council (BCC) 1997
NR   PO Box 41, LEATHERHEAD, Surrey, KT22 9YY.   (hsp)
         01372 376544   fax 01372 376544
         http://www.bctyo.org
         Hon Sec: P Cook
▲   Registered Charity
○   *P; to promote knowledge & interest in cryogenics (low
         temperature science & technology); to foster development &
         application of cryogenics for public benefit
●   Conf - Mtgs - ET
M   70 i
¶   Low Temperature News - 4; ftm only.
✕   2006 British Cryoengineering Society

British Crystallographic Association (BCA) 1982
NR   Northern Networking Ltd, 1 Tennant Avenue, College Milton
         South, East Kilbride, GLASGOW, G74 5NA.   (asa)
         01355 244966   fax 01355 249959
         email bca@glasconf.demon.co.uk
         http://www.bca.cryst.bbk.ac.uk/bca/index.html
         Contact: Elaine Fulton
▲   Registered Charity
○   *L; for those interested in study & research into crystallography
         - of biological structures, chemical, industrial & physical
         applications
Gp   Biological structure; Chemical crystallography; Industrial;
         Physical crystallography
●   Conf - Mtgs - ET - Awarding bursaries for students
<   Intl U of Crystallography (IUCr)
M   c 875 i
¶   Crystallography News - 4.

British Culinary Federation
NR   PO Box 10532, ALCESTER, Warks, B50 4ZY.
         01789 491218   fax 01789 491218
         http://www.britishculinaryfederation.co.uk
         Admin: Jayne Mottram
○   *P
✕   2005 (Chefs & Cooks Circle
                (Midlands Association of Chefs

British Cutlery & Silverware Association   (BCSA)
■   Unit 10 1st floor, Edmund Road Business Centre, SHEFFIELD,
         S Yorks, S2 4ED.   (hq)
         0114-252 7550   fax 0114-252 7555
         Chief Exec: Mrs C T Steele
○   *T; promotion of cutlery & silverware
●   Conf - Mtgs - Inf
M   f

British Cycling Federation (BCF) 1959
NR   National Cycling Centre, Stuart St, MANCHESTER,
         M11 4DQ.   (hq)
         0870 871 2000
         email info@britishcycling.org.uk
         Chief Exec: Peter King
▲   Un-incorporated Society
○   *S; to act as the governing body of UK cycle sport
Gp   British Cycle Speedway Commission; British Schools Cycling
         Association; Women's Cycle Racing Association
●   Conf - Mtgs - ET - Exam - Res - Exhib - Comp - Inf - VE - LG
<   U Cycliste Intle (UCI); U Eur de Cyclisme (UEC)
M   19,000 i, 1,000 clubs

British Dam Society (BDS) 1950
NR   Institution of Civil Engineers, 1-7 Great George St, LONDON,
         SW1P 3AA.   (hq)
         020 7665 2234
         email bds@ice.org.uk
         Sec: Tim Fuller,   Chmn: Dr Andy Hughes
▲   Registered Charity
○   *P; to stimulate interest & encourage improvements in the
         design, construction, maintenance, operation & safety of
         dams & reservoirs
●   Conf - Mtgs - ET - Res - Exhib - Comp - Inf - LG
<   Intl Commission Large Dams (ICOLD)
M   i & f
¶   Dams & Reservoirs (NL) - 4.

British Damage Management Association   (BDMA) 1999
■   Willow Business Centre, Connect House, 21 Willow Lane,
         MITCHAM, Surrey, CR4 4NA.   (hq)
         0700 0843 2362   fax 0700 0236 2329
         email info@bdma.org.uk   http://www.bdma.org.uk
         Chmn: Bob Spencer
▲   Company Limited by Guarantee
○   *T
Gp   Damage management; Fire & flood restoration
●   Conf - Mtgs - Exam
M   1,110 i, 600 f
¶   Recovery - 4; free.

British Darts Organisation Ltd   (BDO) 1973
■   2 Pages Lane, Muswell Hill, LONDON, N10 1PS.   (hq)
         020 8883 5544
         Hon Sec: O A Croft
▲   Company Limited by Guarantee
Br   66; 44 countries
○   *S; promoting the sport of darts
●   Comp
<   Wld Darts Fedn
M   25,000 i in 63 member counties, 60 affiliated darts boards
¶   Ybk.

British Deaf Association (BDA) 1890
■   69 Wilson St, LONDON, EC2A 2BB.   (hq)
         020 7588 3520   fax 020 7588 3527
         email tony@signcommunity.org.uk
         http://www.signcommunity.org.uk
         Chief Exec: Doug Alker
▲   Registered Charity
Br   4
○   *W; a democratic, membership-led body campaigning on
         behalf of deaf sign language users in the UK; to increase
         deaf people's access to lifestyles that most hearing people
         take for granted
●   Conf - ET - Inf
         Textphone: 0800 652 2965;
         Videophone: 020 7496 9539
M   3,500 i, UK / 15-20 i, o'seas
¶   Sign Matters; £25 yr (annual sub).

British Deaf Sports Council (BDSC) 1930
- ■ 49 Fonnerau Rd, IPSWICH, IP1 3JN.   (hq)
   fax 01268 510621
   Sec: Mike Webster
- ▲ Company Limited by Guarantee; Registered Charity
- Br 115
- ○ *S; national governing body for sport for deaf people locally, regionally, nationally (England, Scotland, Wales) & internationally
- ● Mtgs - Comp
- < Comité Intl de Sport de Sourds (CISS); Eur Deaf Sports Org EDSO)
- M 3,000 i, 115 clubs

British Decorators Association
   2002 merged with the Painting & Decorating Federation to form the
   Painting & Decorating Association

British Decoy Wildfowl Carvers Association (BDWCA) 1990
- ■ 26 Shendish Edge, HEMEL HEMPSTEAD, Herts, HP3 9SZ. (hsp)
   01442 247610
   http://www.bdwca.org.uk
   Sec: Janet Nash
- ▲ Un-incorporated Society
- Br 8
- ○ *A; for decoy (bird) & wildfowl carvers & collectors
- ● Mtgs - ET - Res - Exhib - Comp - SG - Inf - VE
- M 174 i, 4 f, UK / 8 i, o'seas
- ¶ NL - 4; free.

British Deer Farmers Association (BDFA) 1978
- NR The Counting House, Mill Rd, CROMFORD, Derbyshire, DE4 3RQ. (sp)
   01629 827037
   Jt Secs: Felicia Knowles,   Claire Parkinson
- ▲ Un-incorporated Society
- ○ *F, *T; to promote deer farming & the interests of deer farmers & venison producers
- ● Conf - ET - Inf - VE - LG
- M f
- ¶ Deer Farming (Jnl) - 4.   Deer News (NL) - 6.

British Deer Society (BDS) 1963
- ■ The Walled Garden, Burgate Manor, FORDINGBRIDGE, Hants, SP6 1EF. (hq)
   01425 655434   fax 01425 655433
   email h.q@bds.org.uk   http://www.bds.org.uk
   Gen Mgr: Sarah Stride
- ▲ Company Limited by Guarantee; Registered Charity
- ○ *L, *V; to promote & conserve the 6 species of wild deer within the UK
- ● Mtgs - ET - Res - Exhib - Comp - Stat - Inf - VE - LG
- M c 6,000 i, UK & o'seas
- ¶ Deer (Jnl) - 4; ftm, £5 nm.   Annual Review; ftm, postage nm.

** British Dendrobatid Group
   Organisation lost: see Introduction paragraph 3

British Dental Association (BDA) 1880
- ■ 64 Wimpole St, LONDON, W1G 8YS. (hq)
   020 7935 0875   fax 020 7487 5232
   email enquiries@bda.org   http://www.bda.org
   Sec: Peter Ward
- ▲ Company Limited by Guarantee
- Br 21
- ○ *P, *U; to represent dentists in the UK
- Gp Dental services: Community, Hospital; University dental teachers & research workers; Armed forces dentists
- ● Conf - Mtgs - SG - Stat - Inf - Lib - Empl - LG
- < Fédn Dentaire Intl; C'wealth Dental Assn
- M 20,500 i, UK / 600 i, o'seas
- ¶ British Dental Jnl - 24.   BDA News (NL) - 12.
   Hbk - 1;   AR.

British Dental Hygienists Association (BDHA) 1949
- NR Mobbs Miller House, Ardington Rd, NORTHAMPTON, NN1 5LP. (admin/b)
   0870 243 0752
   Admin: Mrs Ann Craddock
- ○ *L, *P; study & practice of oral hygiene
- M i

British Dental Practice Managers Association (BDPMA) 1993
- ■ Osprey House, Primett Rd, STEVENAGE, Herts, SG1 3EE. (hq)
   0870 840 0381   fax 0870 840 0382
   email info@bdpma.org.uk   http://www.bdpma.org.uk
   Chmn: Miss Bridget M Crump
- ▲ Un-incorporated Society
- Br 7
- ○ *P; to promote a payscale & job description; to offer job opportunities
- ● Conf - Mtgs - ET - Res - Exhib - Inf - Empl
- M 460 i
- ¶ Networking (NL) - 4; ftm only.

British Dental Trade Association (BDTA) 1923
- ■ Mineral Lane, CHESHAM, Bucks, HP5 1NL. (hq)
   01494 782873   fax 01494 786659
   email admin@bdta.org.uk   http://www.bdta.org.uk
   Exec Dir: A H Reed
- ▲ Company Limited by Guarantee
- ○ *T; to promote the dental industry & trade
- Gp Manufacturers; Importers/Exporters; Dental dealers; Financial services; Computer services; Wholesalers; Publishers
- ● Conf - ET - Exam - Exhib - Stat - Inf - LG
- < Fedn of the Eur Dental Ind (FIDE); Assn of Dental Dealers in Europe (ADDE); Assn Brit Health Care Inds (ABHCI)
- M 99 f, UK / 3 f, o'seas
- ¶ The Dental Trader (Jnl) - 4;   NL;   LM;
   Exhibition Catalogue - 1;   AR; all ftm.

British Dermatological Nursing Group
   a group of the **British Association of Dermatologists**

British Design & Art Direction
   since 2003-04 **D&AD**

British Dietetic Association (BDA) 1936
- ■ Charles House (5th floor), 148-9 Great Charles St, Queensway, BIRMINGHAM, B3 3HT. (hq)
   0121-200 8080
   email info@bda.uk.com   http://www.bda.uk.com
   Chief Exec: Andy Burman
- ▲ Company Limited by Guarantee; Registered Charity
- ○ *P; for qualified dieticians; to advance the science & practice of dietetics & associated subjects
- Gp Renal dialysis; Paediatric; Mental health; Parenteral & enteral nutrition; Metabolic & research; Nutrition advice for the elderly; Community nutrition; National dietetic managers; Diabetes management & education; Dieticians in HIV/AIDS.
- ● Conf - Mtgs - ET - Res - Empl
- M 7,500 i, UK / 180 i, o'seas
- ¶ Jnl of Human Nutrition & Dietetics - 6;
   Dietetics Today (NL) - 12;   all ftm.   AR - 1.

British Disc Golf Association (BDGA)
- ■ 50 Spring Lane, KENILWORTH, Warks, CV8 2HD. (dir/p)
   01926 864136
   email secretary@bdga.org.uk   http://www.bdga.org.uk
   Nat Dir: Derek Robins
- ▲ Un-incorporated Society
- ○ *S; the national governing body for the sport of disc golf; to be responsible for coordination of competitive disc golf; to promote disc golf
- ● Comp - Inf
- < Wld Flying Disc Fedn; Profl Disc Golf Assn
- M 80 i
- ¶ In Flight Magazine - 4; ftm only.

British Display Society Ltd   (BDS)   1943
- ■   146 Welling Way, WELLING, Kent, DA16 2RS.   (hsb)
    020 8856 2030   fax 020 8856 9394
    http://www.britishdisplaysociety.co.uk
    Sec: Pat Simpson
- ▲   Registered Charity
- ○   *P; for visual merchandising, display, point-of-sale, exhibition
    design & training
- ●   ET - Exam - Comp
- M   [not disclosed]
- ¶   BDS NL - 11; free.   AR; ftm only.

British Disposable Products Association
    since 2003-04 **Foodservice Packaging Association**

British Doll Artists Association
    officially closed 16 October 2005

British Doll Collectors' Club
    closed due to retirement

British Domesticated Ostrich Association   (BDOA)   1992
- ■   33 Eden Grange, Little Corby, CARLISLE, Cumbria,
    CA4 8QW.   (asa)
    01228 562532   fax 01228 562187
    email craig@bdoa.info   http://www.ostrich.org.uk
    Sec: F C Culley
- ▲   Un-incorporated Society
- ○   *B, *F; promotion of ostrich farming in the UK
- M   140 i, 113 f, UK / 20 i, 13 f, o'seas
- ¶   NL - 4; ftm, £10 nm.

British Double Reed Society   (BDRS)   1988
- ■   Beech Cottage, Tilthams Green, GODALMING, Surrey,
    GU7 3BT.   (hsp)
    01483 417649
    Hon Sec: Jefferey Cox
- ▲   Registered Charity
- ○   *D; for practitioners & enthusiasts of the bassoon, oboe & other
    double reed instruments; to improve the standards of
    teaching; to encourage research into design & to encourage
    the writing of new music
- ●   Conf
- <   Intl Double Reed Soc (IDRS)
- M   c 1,000, UK & o'seas
- ¶   Double Reed News (Jnl) - 4; ftm, £3.95 nm.

British Doula Association   (BDA)   1998
- ■   49 Harrington Gdns, LONDON, SW7 4JU.   (hsb)
    020 7244 6053   fax 020 7244 9035
    email info@britishdoulas.co.uk
    http://www.britishdoulas.co.uk
    Sec: Mrs Jean Birtles
- ▲   Un-incorporated Society
- ○   *W; to promote Doula care for pregnant, birthing & postpartum
    mothers; care is that traditionally offered by mothers or
    experienced sisters & concentrates on helping the mother
    rather than caring only for the child
- ●   Conf
- M   150 i, UK / 20 i, o'seas
- ¶   Doula News - 1.

British Dovecote Society
    no longer exists

British Dragon Boat Racing Association   (BDA)   1987
- ■   13 The Prebend, Northend, ROYAL LEAMINGTON SPA, Warks,
    CV47 2TR.   (hsp)
    01295 770734
    Co Sec: David A Cogswell
- ▲   Company Limited by Guarantee
- ○   *S; governing body for Chinese Dragon Boat racing in the UK
- ●   Conf - Mtgs - Comp
- <   Intl Dragon Boat Fedn (IDBF); Eur Dragon Boat Fedn (EDBF);
    C'wealth Dragon Boat Fedn (CDBF)
- M   800 i, 35 clubs, UK / 50 i, o'seas
- ¶   Dragon Line NL - 12; ftm only.

British Dragonfly Society   (BDS)   1983
- ■   23 Bowker Way, Whittlesey, PETERBOROUGH, Northants,
    PE7 1PY.   (hsp)
    01733 204286
    email bdssecretary@dragonflysoc.org.uk
    http://www.dragonflysoc.org.uk
    Hon Sec: Henry Curry
- ▲   Registered Charity
- ○   *L; to promote & encourage the study & conservation of
    dragonflies & their natural habitats
- Gp   Dragonfly Conservation
- ●   Mtgs - ET - Inf - Lib - PL - VE - LG
- <   Soc Intle Odontologica; Wld Dragonfly Assn
- M   1,400 i, 15 f, UK / 75 i, o'seas
- ¶   Jnl - 2;   Dragonfly News - 2; both ftm only.

British Dressage
    a discipline member of the **British Equestrian Federation**

British Dried Flowers Association   (BDFA)   1988
- NR   Stonedge, Manor Rd, Staverton, DAVENTRY, Northants,
    NN11 6JD.   (chmn/b)
    01327 702565   fax 01327 702565
    http://www.flowergrowers.co.uk
    Sec: Vernon Hurst
- ▲   Un-incorporated Society
- ○   *H, *T; for producers & suppliers of British dried flowers &
    grasses
- ●   ET - Exhib - Inf - VE
- M   10 f
- ¶   Members' Directory; free.

British Drilling Association Ltd   (BDA)   1975
- NR   Wayside, London End, Upper Boddington, DAVENTRY,
    Northants, NN11 6DP.   (hsb)
    01327 264622   fax 01327 264623
    email office@britishdrillingassociation.co.uk
    Nat Sec: B J Stringer
- ▲   Company Limited by Guarantee
- ○   *T; to group together companies engaged in all aspects of
    ground drilling
- ●   Conf - Mtgs - ET - Exhib - SG - Stat - Inf
- M   600 i, 130 f
- ¶   BDA NL - 6.   LM - 1.

British Driving Society   (BDS)   1957
- NR   83 New Rd, Helmingham, STOWMARKET, Suffolk, IP14 6EA.
    (hsp)
    01473 892001   fax 01473 892005
    email email@britishdrivingsociety.co.uk
    http://www.britishdrivingsociety.co.uk
    Co Sec: Mrs T K Styles
- ▲   Company Limited by Guarantee
- ○   *S; to encourage & assist those interested in the driving of
    horses & ponies
- Gp   Carriage Foundation
- ●   Conf - Mtgs - ET - Exam - Exhib - Comp - Inf - VE
- M   75 driving clubs
- ¶   NL - 4.   Ybk.

British Durum Association   1955
NR   c/o Heywards, Remo House (6th floor), 310-312 Regent St,
     LONDON, W1B 3BS.   (asa)
     020 7299 8150
     Contact: Asgar Kudrati
○   *T; for those concerned with durum wheat (used in the
     manufacture of pasta)
M   f

British Dyslexia Association   (BDA)   1972
NR   98 London Rd, READING, Berks, RG1 5AU.   (hq)
     0118-966 2677
○   *N; to represent all with dyslexia; to work towards early
     identification & appropriate remediation, teacher training &
     support
●   Helpline: 0118-966 8271
M   i

British Earth Sheltering Association   (BESA)   1983
■   4 Station Rd, Coelbren, NEATH, Glam, SA10 9PL.   (hsp)
     01639 701481
     email besa@caerllan.co.uk   http://www.besa-uk.org
     Hon Sec: David Woods
▲   Un-incorporated Society
○   *P; to promote the development of earth sheltered building
     design in the UK for the environmental & energy saving
     benefits to be accrued
●   Mtgs - Inf - Lib
M   150 i, 10 f, 5 org, UK / 15 i, o'seas
¶   NL - 4; ftm, £2.50 nm.

British Ecological Society   (BES)   1913
NR   26 Blades Court, Deodar Rd, LONDON, SW15 2NU.   (hq)
     020 8871 9797   fax 020 8871 9779
     Exec Sec: Dr Hazel J Norman
▲   Registered Charity
○   *L; promotion of the study of ecology through research
M   i

British Edible Pulse Association   (BEPA)   1935
■   c/o Stuart Cree, Ebbage Seeds, The Stable Yard, Ryston Hall,
     DOWNHAM MARKET, Norfolk, PE38 0AA.   (mail/address)
     01366 387877   fax 01366 384285
     email stuartcree@ebbageseeds.co.uk
     http://www.bepa.co.uk
     Pres: John Mantin
▲   Registered Charity
○   *T; 'to promote the uses of edible pulses from the farmer to the
     housewife'
●   Conf - Mtgs - Exhib - Comp - Stat - Expt - Inf - LG
M   48 f
¶   Monthly Member Report - 12; free.

British Educational Distributors & Contractors Group
     a group of the **British Educational Suppliers Association**

British Educational Furniture Manufacturers Group
     a group of the **British Educational Suppliers Association**

**British Educational Leadership, Management & Administration
Society   (BELMAS)   1971**
■   c/o Sheffield Hallam University, Collegiate Crescent,
     SHEFFIELD, S Yorks, S10 2BP.   (hq)
     0114-225 2328   fax 0114-225 5649
     email info@belmas.org.uk   http://www.belmas.org.uk
     Hon Sec: Nigel Bennett
▲   Registered Charity
○   *E; development of practice, teaching, training & research in
     educational administration
Gp   Teachers of education management; Research in education
     management
●   Conf - Mtgs - Res
<   Eur Forum on Educ Admin (EFEA); C'wealth Coun for Educl
     Admin & Mgt (CCEAM)
M   c 550 i, c 50 org UK / c 30 i, o'seas
¶   Education Management & Administration - 4.
     Management in Education - 5.
     Books on related subjects.

British Educational Research Association   (BERA)   1974
■   3 The Stables - Hall Farm Yard, Main St, KIRKLINGTON, Notts,
     NG22 8NN.   (hq)
     01636 819090   fax 01636 819090
     email admin@bera.ac.uk   http://www.bera.ac.uk
     Academic Sec: Prof Martin Lawn
▲   Registered Charity
○   *E, *L, *Q; to further the communication of education research
     findings to all interested in the theory & practice of education,
     both within the educational system & in the community at
     large
●   Conf - Mtgs - ET - Res
<   Eur Educl Res Assn; ALSISS
M   1,775 i, UK / 284 i, o'seas
¶   British Educational Research Jnl - 6; ftm.
     Research Intelligence (NL) - 4; ftm, £25 yr nm.
     BERA Occasional Publications - irreg.

British Educational Suppliers Association   (BESA)   1933
■   20 Beaufort Court, Admirals Way, LONDON, E14 9XL.   (hq)
     020 7537 4997   fax 020 7537 4846
     email besa@besa.org.uk   http://www.besa.org.uk
     Dir Gen: D J S Savage
▲   Company Limited by Guarantee
○   *T; for the British educational supply industry; to represent
     manufacturers & distributors of educational equipment,
     materials, consumables, books, furniture, technology, ICT
     hardware & software related services in the UK & to
     international markets
Gp   Educational Software Publishers Association (ESPA); British
     Educational Furniture Manufacturers Group (BEFMG);
     Engineering Training Equipment Manufacturers
     Association (ETEMA); British Educational Distributors &
     Contractors Group (BEDCG)
●   Conf - Mtgs - Res - Expt - Inf - LG
M   260 f
¶   BESAbook - 1; free.   ICT in State Schools - 1; ftm, £350 nm.
     UK Schools Survey on Budget & Resource Provision - 1; ftm,
     £350 nm.

British Educational Travel Association   (BETA)   2003
■   PO Box 182, CARSHALTON, Surrey, SM5 2XW.   (hq)
     01795 420710   fax 01795 424367
     email nfo@betauk.com   http://www.betauk.com
     Exec Dir: Emma English
▲   Company Limited by Guarantee
○   *T; to promote youth, student & educational travel to, from &
     within the UK
●   Conf - Mtgs - ET - Res - Exhib - SG - Stat - Inf - VE - LG
<   Intl Student Travel Confedn; Fedn of Intl Youth Travel Orgs;
     English UK
M   120 f, UK / 20 f, o'seas
¶   NL - free.

British Egg Association   (BEA)   1961
NR   89 Charterhouse St (2nd floor), LONDON, EC1M 6HR.   (hq)
        020 7608 3760   fax 020 7608 3860
        email Louisa.Platt@britisheggindustrycouncil.com
        http://www.britegg.co.uk
        Sec: Louisa Platt
▲   Company Limited by Guarantee
○   *F, *T
●   Mtgs - ET - Res - Stat - Inf - VE - LG
<   Eur U of Whlsrs with Eggs, Egg Products, Poultry &
        Game (EUWEP); Brit Egg Ind Coun
M   26 i, 30 f
¶   Quarterly Report;   LM;   AR; all ftm only.

British Egg Products Association   (BEPA)   1971
NR   89 Charterhouse St (2nd floor), LONDON, EC1M 6HR.   (hq)
        020 7608 3760   fax 020 7608 3860
        email Louisa.Platt@britisheggindustrycouncil.com
        http://www.britegg.co.uk
        Sec: Louisa Platt
▲   Company Limited by Guarantee
○   *T; to maintain & improve the high quality of egg products
●   Mtgs - Res - Stat - Inf - LG
<   Intl Egg Commission (IEC); Brit Egg Ind Coun (BEIC)
M   10 f
¶   Import & Export Statistics - 10;
        Breaking & Production - 10; both ftm only.

British Elastic Rope Sports Association   (BERSA)   1989
NR   33A Canal St, OXFORD, OX2 6BQ.   (hq)
        01865 311179   fax 01865 426007
        email info@bersa.org
        Chmn: David Boston
▲   Company Limited by Guarantee
Br   10; Eire, Greece, Spain
○   *S; promotion & safety regulation of bungee jumping & other
        elastic rope sport
●   Mtgs - Exam - Res - Comp - Stat - Inf - Lib - PL - LG
<   RoSPA; Brit Standards Inst
M   i, f & org
¶   Code of Safe Practice.
        Guidelines for Local Safety Officers.

British Elbow & Shoulder Society
    a specialist society of the **British Orthopaedic Association**

British Electrical & Allied Manufacturers Association Ltd
    see **BEAMA: British Electrotechnical & Allied Manufacturers'
    Associations**

British Electroless Nickel Society
    a division of the Metal Finishing Association which is a group of the
    Surface Engineering Association

British Electrophoresis Society
    since 2004 **British Society for Proteome Research**

British Electrotechnical Approvals Board
    merged in 2004 with ASTA Certification Services to become **ASTA
    BEAB Certification Services**

British Endodontic Society   (BES)   1963
NR   PO Box 707, GERRARDS CROSS, Bucks, SL9 0DR.   (admin/p)
        01494 581542   fax 01494 581542
        Hon Sec: Annabel Thomas
▲   Registered Charity
○   *L; to promote and advance the study of all endodontic
        procedures; to improve dental services to the public
●   Conf - Mtgs - ET - Res - SG - LG
<   Amer Assn Endodontics; Eur Soc Endodontology
M   760 i, UK / 40 i, o'seas
¶   International Endodontic Jnl - 6; ftm, £60 yr nm.

British Endurance Riding Association
    since 2002 **Endurance GB**

**British Energy Association of the World Energy Council
    (BEAWec)   1924**
■   12 St Hildas Close, College Gardens, LONDON, SW17 7UL.
        (mem/sp)
        020 8768 9744   fax 020 8767 9744
        email BEAwec@aol.com   http://www.worldenergy.org
        Mem Sec: Di Hammet
▲   Registered Charity; Un-incorporated Society
○   *N; to promote the sustainable supply & use of energy for the
        greatest benefit of all people
●   Conf - Mtgs - SG - Inf - LG
<   Utd Nations (cat 3); Wld Coal Inst; Wld Nuclear Assn; Wld
        Renewable Energy Congress
>   Energy Inst; Westminster Energy Policy Forum
M   13 i, 23 f. 11 org
¶   BEA Chronicle - 1; free (by e-mail).

**British Engineering Manufacturers' Association Ltd   (BEMA)
    1936**
NR   BEMA House / Unit 1 Millers Court, Windmill Rd, Kenn,
        CLEVEDON, N Somerset, BS21 6UL.   (hq)
        0870 998 0268   fax 0870 998 0269
        email enquiries@bema.co.uk   http://www.bema.co.uk
        Dir: J M Whitlow
▲   Company Limited by Guarantee
○   *T; for engineering companies operating nationally
●   Mtgs - ET - Exhib - Expt - Inf - Lib - VE - LG
M   150 f
¶   Handbook - 12; ftm, on request nm.
×   2003 Bristol & Western Engineering Manufacturers' Association

British Engineers' Cutting Tools Association
    In February 2004 merged with the British Hardmetal Association to
    form the **British Hardmetal & Engineers' Cutting Tools
    Association**

British Engraved Stationery Association
    is a special interest group of the **British Printing Industries
    Federation**

**British Entomological & Natural History Society   (BENHS)
    1872**
NR   The Pelham-Clinton Building, Dinton Pastures Country Park,
        Davis St, Hurst, READING, Berks, RG10 0TH.   (hq)
▲   Registered Charity
○   *L; study of natural history, particularly entomology & insect
        conservation; principally in the British Isles but extends into
        Europe as a whole
M   i

British Epigraphy Society   1996
NR   19 Purcell Rd, Marston, OXFORD, OX3 0EZ.
        SecL Dr Peter Haarer
○   *L; the study of Greek, Roman & other inscriptions, texts &
        historical documents.

British Epilepsy Association   (BEA)   1950
NR   New Anstey House, Gate Way Drive, Yeadon, LEEDS, W Yorks,
    LS19 7XY.   (hq)
    0113-210 8800
    email epilepsy@epilepsy.org.uk
    Chief Exec: Philip Lee
▲   Registered Charity
Br   140
○   *W; to provide care in the community for those with epilepsy
●   Conf - Mtgs - ET - Res - Exhib - Stat - Inf - LG
    Helpline: freephone 0808 800 5050 (Mon-Thurs 0900-1630,
    Fri 0900-1600)
M   21,000 i
¶   Epilepsy Today - 4.   AR.
    Various publications.
    Note: the working title of this body is Epilepsy Action.

British Equestrian Federation   (BEF)   1972
■   Stoneleigh Park, KENILWORTH, Warks, CV8 2RH.   (hq)
    024 7669 8871   fax 024 7669 6484
    http://www.bef.co.uk
    Chmn: Hugh Thomas
▲   Company Limited by Guarantee
○   *N, *S; acts as the international secretariat on behalf of
    member disciplines & represents their interests in all matters
    concerned with the Fédération Equestre Internationale (FEI)
Gp   Discipline members: Association of British Riding Schools;
    British Dressage; British Equestrian Trade Association; British
    Equestrian Vaulting Association; British Eventing Association;
    British Horse Driving Trials Association; British Reining; British
    Show Jumping Association; Endurance GB; Riding for the
    Disabled; Scottish Equestrian Association
●   Mtgs - Comp - SG - Stat - Inf - LG
<   Fédn Equestre Intle; a member of the Brit Horse Ind Confedn
M   6 org (discipline members),
    affiliates: British Horse Society, Pony Club

British Equestrian Trade Association   (BETA)   1979
■   East Wing, Stockeld Park, WETHERBY, W Yorks, LS22 4AW.
    (hsb)
    01937 587062   fax 01937 582728
    email info@beta-uk.org   http://www.beta-uk.org
    Chief Exec: Claire Williams
▲   Company Limited by Guarantee
○   *T; to promote the British equestrian industry from retailers to
    manufacturers, associated services & dealers; to promote
    riding as a sport
Gp   Feed merchants; Mobile retailers; Saddlers; Pharmaceutical,
    Equestrian organisations; Dealers; Safety equipment
●   Mtgs - ET - Exam - Res - Exhib - Stat - Expt - Inf - LG -
    Administration of VAT second hand scheme for horses &
    ponies on behalf of HM Customs & Excise - BETA Body
    Protector Standard
<   Brit Equestrian Fedn; Brit Horse Soc; Countryside Alliance; Soc
    of Master Saddlers; Horse & Pony Taxation C'ee
M   700 f, 5 org, UK / 5 org, o'seas
¶   Equestrian Trade News - 12; free to retailers
    (£59 manufacturers).
    British Equestrian Directory - 1; £9.95 m.
    Trade Suppliers Directory - 1; £16 m.
    What to Wear - 2 yrly; £5.50.

British Equestrian Vaulting Association
    a discipline member of the **British Equestrian Federation**

British Equine Veterinary Association
    a group of the **British Veterinary Association**

British Essence Manufacturers' Association   (BEMA)   1917
■   PO Box 172, CRANLEIGH, Surrey, GU6 8WU.   (hq)
    01483 275411   fax 01483 275411
    email secretariat@bemaorg.org
    http://www.bemaorg.org
    Sec: Julie Young
▲   Un-incorporated Society
○   *T; interests of makers of essences & flavours for food & drink
●   Mtgs - Inf
<   Intl Org Flavour Ind (IOFI); Eur Flavours & Fragrances
    Assn (EFFA); Food & Drink Fedn
M   68 f, UK / 2 f, o'seas

British Essential Oils Association Ltd   (BEOA)   1978
■   15 Exeter Mansions, Exeter Rd, LONDON, NW2 3UG.   (hsp)
    020 8450 3713
    Sec: Malcolm Irvine
▲   Company Limited by Guarantee
○   *T
Gp   Technical c'ee
●   Conf - Mtgs - ET - Res - SG - Inf - Lib - LG
<   Eur Flavour & Fragrance Org (EFFA)
M   53 f, UK / 3 f, o'seas
¶   NL - 3; free.   Hbk & LM - 1; ftm only.

British & European Geranium Society   (BEGS)   1970
NR   8 Roses Close, Wollaston, WELLINGBOROUGH, Northants,
    NN29 7ST.   (hsp)
▲   Un-incorporated Society
Br   11
○   *H; to promote interest in the cultivation & hybridisation of
    pelargoniums & geraniums by amateurs & professionals
●   Conf - Mtgs - ET - Exhib - Comp - SG - Stat - VE - Lectures -
    Advisory panel for information

British European Potato Association
    closed 2005 due to lack of members

British Eventing
    a discipline member of the **British Equestrian Federation**

British Executive Service Overseas
    since 2003-04 **BESO (British Executive Service Overseas)**

British Exhibition Contractors' Association   (BECA)   1913
■   BECA House, Uplands Business Park, Blackhorse Lane,
    LONDON, E17 5QJ.   (hq)
    020 8523 5262   fax 020 8523 5024
    email info@beca.org.uk   http://www.beca.org.uk
    Dir: Lynn Felton
▲   Un-incorporated Society
○   *T; for UK based companies active within the worldwide
    exhibition industry; 'the main emphasis is on employment
    relations'
Gp   Council of management; Electrical; Environmental; Health &
    safety; Training
●   Mtgs - ET - Exhib - Inf - Empl - LG
M   230 f
¶   Members News - 12; ftm only.

British Exporters Association   (BExA)   1940
■   Broadway House, Tothill St, LONDON, SW1H 9NQ.   (hq)
    020 7222 5419   fax 020 7799 2468
    email bexamail@aol.com   http://www.bexa.co.uk
    Dir: H W Bailey
▲   Un-incorporated Society
○   *T; to lobby on behalf of members on export, export credit
    insurance & trade finance issues
●   Mtgs - VE - LG
M   70 f
¶   AR.

British Falconers' Club (BFC) 1924
NR   Westfield, Meeting Hill, Worstead, NORTH WALSHAM, Norfolk,
        NR28 9LS.   (hsb)
        http://www.britishfalconersclub.co.uk
        Sec: Jackie Morris
▲   Un-incorporated Society
Br   9 regions
○   *G; the promotion of practical falconry in the British Isles; to
        promote the captive breeding of birds of prey
●   Mtgs - Lib
<   Intl Assn for Falconry & Consvn of Birds of Prey (IAF); Fedn of
        Field Sports Assns of the EEC (FACE); Countryside Alliance
M   956 i, UK / 89 i, o'seas
¶   Falconer (Jnl) - 1; ftm.   NL - 2; ftm.

British False Memory Society (BFMS) 1993
■   Newtown, BRADFORD-ON-AVON, Wilts, BA15 1NF.
        fax 01225 862251
        Dir: Madeline Greenhalgh
▲   Registered Charity
○   *K; a support group for accused parents
●   Conf - Mtgs - Res - Stat - Inf - Lib
        Helpline: 01225 868682

British Fantasy Society (BFS) 1971
■   201 Reddish Rd, STOCKPORT, Cheshire, SK5 7HR.   (sp)
        0161-476 5368
        http://www.britishfantasysociety.org.uk
        Sec: Robert Parkinson
▲   Un-incorporated Society
○   *A, *G; to promote interest in the fields of horror & fantasy
        literature & art
●   Conf - Mtgs
M   350 i, UK / 50 i, o'seas
¶   Prism NL - 6; ftm, £2 nm.   Dark Horizons - 2; £3 m.

British Federation of Audio Ltd (BFA) 1994
NR   PO Box 365, FARNHAM, Surrey, GU10 2BD.   (hq)
        01428 714616
        Sec: C I C Cowan,   Chmn: S N Harris
▲   Company Limited by Guarantee
○   *T; to promote the use of domestic audio equipment & the
        interests of the UK audio manufacturers & the British high
        fidelity audio industry
Gp   BTI sponsorship to overseas exhibitions
●   Mtgs - Exhib - Stat - LG
<   Intellect
M   c 45 f
×   2001 (August) British Federation of Audio

British Federation of Brass Bands (BFBB) 1997
NR   Unit 12 Maple Estate, Stocks Lane, BARNSLEY, S Yorks, S75
        2BL.   (hq)
        01226 771015   fax 01226 732630
        http://www.bfbb.co.uk
        Gen Sec: Carol Tattersfield
▲   Registered Charity
○   *D; promotion of amateur music making, specifically brass
        bands
●   Conf - Mtgs - ET - Res - Comp - SG - Inf - Lib - VE - LG
<   Eur Brass Band Assn
M   c 500 org
¶   Directory of Brass Bands - 1; £5.

British Federation of Care Home Proprietors
        ceased trading

British Federation of Festivals for Music, Dance & Speech
        since 2002 **British & International Federation of Festivals for
        Music, Dance & Speech**

British Federation of Film Societies (BFFS) 1945
NR   Unit 315 The Workstation, 15 Paternoster Row, SHEFFIELD,
        S Yorks, S1 2BX.   (hq)
        0845 603 7278
        email info@bffs.org.uk
        Chief Exec: David Phillips
○   *A, *N; a national body which promotes voluntary film
        exhibition & represents the interests of film societies
●   Technical & legal advice
M   171 societies

British Federation for Historical Swordplay (BFHS) 1998
NR   213 Queenspark Rd, BRIGHTON, E Sussex, BN2 2ZA.   (dir/p)
        01273 685664
        http://www.bfhs.org
        Pres: Andrew Feest
▲   Un-incorporated Society
Br   16
○   *G, *N; for individual groups & societies studying & practising
        fencing & European martial arts
●   Conf - Mtgs - ET -Exam - Res - Inf
M   16 org

**British Federation of Sand & Land Yacht Clubs   (British
        Landsailing) 1962**
■   y Bwythyn, Druidston Cross, BROAD HAVEN, Pembrokeshire,
        SA62 3ND.   (hsp)
        01437 781458   fax 01437 767151
        email secretary@bfslyc.org.uk
        http://www.britishlandsailing.co.uk
        Sec: Andy Parr
▲   Un-incorporated Society
Br   18
○   *S; to regulate, administer & promote land yachting in the UK
Gp   Landsailing; Landyachting; Sandyachting; Parakarting; Kite
        buggying
●   Mtgs - ET - Res - Comp - Inf - LG
<   Fedn Intl of Sand & Land Yachting
M   800 i, 18 org
¶   Land Sailor (Jnl) - 4; ftm.

**British Federation against Sexually Transmitted Diseases
        (BFSTD) 1948**
■   c/o Dept of GU Medicine, St Mary's Hospital, Milton Rd,
        PORTSMOUTH, Hants, PO3 6AD.   (hsb)
        023 9286 6790   fax 023 9286 6769
        email jean.tobin@porthosp.nhs.uk
        Hon Sec: Dr Jean M Tobin
▲   Registered Charity
○   *L, *M; issues relating to sexually transmitted infections
        including HIV/AIDS
Gp   representatives from main UK organisations working in the field
        of sexual & reproductive health
●   Mtgs - ET - Inf - LG
<   EUROPAP
M   21 org
¶   AR; free.

British Federation of Women Graduates (BFWG) 1907
■   4 Mandeville Courtyard, 142 Battersea Park Rd, LONDON,
        SW11 4NB.   (hq/regd)
        020 7498 8037   fax 020 7498 5213
        email bfwg@bfwg.demon.co.uk
        http://www.bfwg.org.uk office
        Exec Sec: Mrs A B Stein
▲   Company Limited by Guarantee; Registered Educational
        Charity
Br   35
○   *E, *P, *X
●   Conf - Mtgs - Comp - SG - Stat - Lib - VE - LG
<   Intl Fedn of University Women (Geneva)
M   180,000 i, UK & o'seas
¶   NL;   LM;   AR; all ftm.

British Federation of Young Choirs   (youngchoirs)   1983
- ■ PO Box 7877, LOUGHBOROUGH, Leics, LE11 2WW.
  (admin/p)
  01509 211664   fax 01509 211664
  email admin@youngchoirs.net
  http://www.youngchoirs.net
  Chief Exec: Malcolm Goldring,   Admin: Mrs Eleri Bristow
- ▲ Company Limited by Guarantee; Registered Charity
- ○ *D, *Y; creating opportunities for young people to discover the joy of choral singing
- ● Conf - Mtgs - ET - Res - Comp - Inf - VE - Events
- < Eur Fedn of Young Choirs
- M not given
  youngchoirs.net
- ¶ AR - 1; free.

British Fencing Association   1902
- NR 1 Barons Gate, 33-35 Rothschild Rd, LONDON, W4 5HT.   (hq)
  020 8742 3032
  Gen Sec: Gillian Kenneally
- ▲ Company Limited by Guarantee
- ○ *S; governing body for the sport of fencing in the UK
- M i & clubs

British Fertility Society   (BFS)   1974
- ■ 22 Apex Court, Woodlands, Bradley Stoke, BRISTOL,
  BS32 4NQ.   (asa)
  01454 642217
  http://www.britishfertilitysociety.org.uk
- ▲ Company Limited by Guarantee
- ○ *M; to promote the knowledge & study of fertility & infertility
- Gp Doctors; Scientists; Counsellors; Nurses
- ● Conf - Mtgs - ET
- < Intl Fedn of Fertility Socs
- M 760 i, 12 f
- ¶ Human Fertility (Jnl) - 3.   NL - 3.

British FIB (Flying Inflatable Boat) Association   (FIBA)   2004
  Chief Exec: Ron Davis
- ▲ Un-incorporated Society
- ○ *S; the promotion of organised, safe operation of microlight flying boats
- M 35 i, 1 f, UK / 11 i, o;seas
- ¶ NL - 4.
  is run from the Turkish Republic of Northern Cyprus.

British Film Institute   (BFI)   1933
- NR 21 Stephen St, LONDON, W1T 1LN.   (hq)
  020 7255 1444   fax 020 7436 7950
  http://www.bfi.org.uk
- ▲ Registered Charity
- ○ *A, *Q; development of the art of the film & television; to promote public appreciation of it as an art form & record
- M i, f & org

British Fire Consortium   (BFC)   1982
- NR 47 Poplar Avenue, HOVE, E Sussex, BN3 8PT.   (hsb)
  01273 275501
  email secretariat@tbfc.co.uk
  Gen Sec: Roger Chamberlain
- ▲ Company Limited by Guarantee
- ○ *T; for nationally based independent fire protection companies
- Gp Fire: Extinguisher mfrs, Extinguisher suppliers, Protection service companies, Alarms
  Training; Consultants; Signs; Intumescent materials; Health & safety
- ● Conf - Mtgs - ET - Exam - Res - Exhib - Lib
- < BSI
- M 150 f
- ¶ NL - 4; ftm only.

British Fire Protection Systems Association Ltd   (BFPSA)   1966
- NR Thames House, 29 Thames St, KINGSTON upon THAMES,
  Surrey, KT1 1PH.   (hsb)
  020 8549 5855   fax 020 8547 1564
  email bfpsa@abft.org.uk   http://www.bfpsa.org.uk
- ▲ Company Limited by Guarantee
- ○ *T; equipment for the detection & extinguishing of fire for the protection of industry & the public
- Gp Fire detection & alarms; Fire extinguishing systems
- ● Mtgs - Res - SG - Inf - Representation on the Office of Deputy Prime Minister Fire Alarms Consultative C'ee
- < EURALARM; BSI; FIC; EUROFEU
- M 120 f
- ¶ LM;   AR.
  Fighting Fires with Foam [CD-ROM].
  Guidance for Power Supplies for use in Fire Detection Systems.
  Code(s) of Practice for:
    The Design, Installation & Servicing of Voice Alarm Systems Associated with Fire Detection Systems.
    Category 1 Aspirating Detection Systems.

British Fire Services Association   (BFSA)   1950
- NR 8 Clover House, Boston Rd, SLEAFORD, Lincs, NG34 7HD.
  (hq)
  01526 830255
  Gen Sec: Derrick Crouch
- ▲ Registered Charity
- ○ *T; for fire fighters
- M i, f & org

British Fireworks Association
- NR c/o Cosmic Fireworks Ltd, Fauld Industrial Estate, BURTON on
  TRENT, Staffs, DE13 9HS.
  01283 520771   fax 01283 520351
  http://www.b-f-a.org
  Chmn: John Woodhead
- M 16 f

British Flat Roofing Council
  This body is dormant

British Florist Association   (BFA)   1979
- NR 68 First Avenue, Mortlake, LONDON, SW14 8SR.   (asa)
  0870 240 3208
  email maurice@mlionel.freeserve.co.uk
  Co Sec/Treas: Maurice Evans
- ▲ Company Limited by Guarantee
- ○ *N, *T; umbrella organisation for other florists' associations
- ● Conf - ET - Exhib - Comp - LG
- < Fédn Europeénne Unions Professionelles de Fleuristes
- > Interflora
- M 5 i, 300 f
- ¶ Floristry News (NL) - 4; free.

British Flower Bulbs Association   1945
- NR Springfield Gardens, Camelgate, SPALDING, Lincs,
  PE12 6ET.   (hq)
  01775 724843   fax 01775 711209
  Sec: David Norton
- ▲ Un-incorporated Society
- ○ *T; all connected in the sale & distribution of flower bulbs, corms etc in the UK
- ● Mtgs - Inf
- M 40 f
- × 2006 Bulb Distributors' Association

British Flower & Vibrational Essences Association   (BFVEA) 1997

■ BM BFVEA, LONDON, WC1N 3XX.   (mail/address)
   0775 722 3199
   email info@bfvea   http://www.bfvea.com
   Chmn: David Corre
▲ Un-incorporated Society
○ *T; to stimulate interest in flower & vibrational essences
● Conf - ET - Res - Training & validation for practitioners
< Brit Assn of Flower Essence Producers
M 110 i, UK / 11 i, o'seas, 11 lay members of the public
¶ Essence - 4; ftm, £15 yr nm.

British Flue & Chimney Manufacturers' Association   (BFCMA) 1977

■ 2 Waltham Court, Milley Lane, Hare Hatch, READING, Berks,
   RG10 9TH.   (hq)
   0118-940 3416   fax 0118-940 6258
   email info@feta.co.uk   http://www.feta.co.uk/
   Dir Gen: C Sloan
○ *T; natural draught flues & chimneys
● Mtgs - SG - Representation on standards c'ees
< Fedn Envtl Tr Assns (FETA)
M 15 f

British Fluid Power Association (incorporating AHEM)   (BFPA) 1959

■ Cheriton House, Cromwell Park, CHIPPING NORTON, Oxon,
   OX7 5SR.   (hq)
   01608 647900   fax 01608 647919
   http://www.bfpa.co.uk
   Chief Exec: Ian Morris
▲ Company Limited by Guarantee
○ *T; engineering, hydraulic & pneumatic fluid power equipment
   systems
Gp Commercial & promotions; Component performance;
   Connectors; Contamination control; Control components;
   Cylinders; Education & training; Electrohydraulic control
   systems; Fluids; Market forecasting & statistics; Pneumatic
   equipment; Quality assurance; Research; Seals
● Conf - Mtgs - ET - Exhib - SG - Stat - Expt - Inf - Lib
< Comité Eur des Transmissions Oléohydraulique et
   Pneumatique (CETOP); CBI; BSI; METCOM
M 100 f
¶ NL - 10; ftm only.   Directory - irreg;   Product list - 1;
   LM;   AR; all free.
   Publications lists BFPA/CETOP.

British Fluid Power Distributors' Association   (BFPDA)   1989

■ Cheriton House, Cromwell Park, CHIPPING NORTON, Oxon,
   OX7 5SR.   (hq)
   01608 647000   fax 01608 647919
   http://www.bfpa.co.uk
   Chief Exec: Ian Morris
▲ Company Limited by Guarantee
○ *T; for British distributors of oil-hydraulic & pneumatic
   equipment
● Conf - Mtgs - ET - Exhib - SG - Stat - Expt - Inf - Lib
< Brit Fluid Power Assn
M 100 f
¶ NL - 4; ftm only.   Directory - irreg;   Product list;   LM;
   AR; all free.
   Publications lists BFPA.

British Fluoridation Society   1969

NR c/o Sheila Jones, (Ward 4) Booth Hall Children's Hospital,
   Charlestown Rd, MANCHESTER, Lancs, M4 7AA.   (hq)
   0161-220 5223   fax 0161-220 5223
   http://www.bfsweb.org
   Inf & Res Officer: Sheila Jones
▲ Company Limited by Guarantee
○ *K; 'to promote fluoridation of the public water supplies for the
   benefit of dental health'
● Conf - ET - Res - Inf - Lib - LG
¶ Briefings on various aspects of fluoridation & dental health
   statistics - irreg.

British Flute Society   (BFS)   1983

NR 41 Devon Avenue, TWICKENHAM, Middx, TW2 6PN.   (hsp)
   020 8241 7572
   Hon Sec: Julie Wright
▲ Registered Charity
○ *D; furtherance & enjoyment of playing the flute
Gp Junior Section
● Mtgs - ET - Comp - SG - Inf - Concerts - Flute Festivals
M c 1,800 i
¶ Pan - 4.

British Flyball Association   (BFA)   1993

NR PO Box 109, PETERSFIELD, Hants, GU32 1XZ.   (sp)
   01753 620110
   email bfa@flyball.org.uk
   Sec: Penny Charlton
▲ Un-incorporated Society
○ *G, *S; to promote flyball - a team sport for dogs & dog owners
● Conf - ET - Exam - Exhib - Comp - Internet information
< Australian / Dutch / North American / South African [Assns];
   Belgian Flyball Fedn
M c 1,000 i
¶ Flyball Record - 4.

British Food Importers & Distributors Association   (BFIDA) 1997

■ Crescent House, 34 Eastbury Way, SWINDON, Wilts,
   SN25 2EN.   (asa)
   01793 7273878   fax 01793 7264869
   email foodimporters@aol.com
   Sec: Walter J Anzer
○ *T; to represent the interests of food importers in the UK
● LG
< FRUCOM
M 22 f

British Foosball Association

NR BCM 1731, LONDON, WC1N 3XX.
   http://www.britfoos.com
   Sec: Jude Fitzgerald
○ *S; table football

British Footwear Association   (BFA)   1996

■ 3 Burystead Place, WELLINGBOROUGH, Northants,
   NN8 1AH.   (hq)
   01933 229005   fax 01933 225009
   email inf@britfoot.com   http://www.britfoot.com
   Chief Exec: Niall Campbell
▲ Company Limited by Guarantee
Br 2
○ *T; to promote & protect the interests of the UK footwear
   industry
● Conf - Mtgs - Stat - Expt - Empl - LG
< Eur Footwear Mfrs Confedn (CEC)
M 96 f
¶ BFA NL - 12; free.
× 2003 (April) Northamptonshire Footwear Manufacturers'
   Association (merged)

British Fragrance Association 1941
- ■ PO Box 173, CRANLEIGH, Surrey, GU6 8WU.
  - 01483 275411   fax 01483 275411
  - email secretariat@bfaorg.org   http://www.bfaorg.org
  - Sec: Julie Young
- ▲ Un-incorporated Society
- ○ *T; for makers of fragrances for cosmetics, toiletries & perfumes
- ● Mtgs - Distribution of code of practice
- < Intl Fragrance Assn (IFRA); Eur Flavours & Fragrances Assn (EFFA)
- M 41 f, UK / 2 f, o'seas
- ¶ Report - 2; AR; both ftm.

British Franchise Association Ltd   (BFA)   1977
- ■ Thames View, Newtown Rd, HENLEY-ON-THAMES, Oxon, RG9 1HG.   (hq)
  - 01491 578050   fax 01491 573517
  - email mailroom@british-franchise.org.uk
  - http://www.british-franchise.org.uk
  - Dir-Gen: Brian Smart
- ▲ Company Limited by Guarantee
- ○ *T; promoting ethical franchising, voluntary self-regulatory body for franchisors, providing advice to potential franchisees / franchisors, education in franchising, lobbying on behalf of franchise community
- ● Conf - Mtgs - ET - Res - Exhib - Stat - Inf - LG
- < Wld Franchise Coun; Eur Franchise Assn
- M 250 f
- ¶ Members Newsline (NL) - 12; ftm only.
  - Franchise Link - 2; ftm, part of infopacks for nm.
  - Franchisee Guide.   Franchisor Guide.

British Free Range Egg Producers Association   (BFREPA)   1991
- ■ 25-26 Norton Enterprise Park, Whittle Rd, Churchfields, SALISBURY, Wilts, SP2 7YU.   (hsb)
  - 01722 410775   fax 01722 410775
  - email admin@bfrepa.co.uk   http://www.bfrepa.co.uk
  - Chmn: Tom Vesey
- ▲ Un-incorporated Society
- ○ *F, *T
- ● Conf - Mtgs - ET - Res - Exhib - Stat - Inf - PL - VE - LG
- < Brit Egg Assn; Nat Farmers U
- M 271 i, 41 f
- ¶ The Ranger - 12; ftm, £35 (+VAT) yr nm.

British Freediving Association   (BFA)
- NR 2 Buckingham St (top floor flat), BRIGHTON, E Sussex, BN1 3LT.   (chmn/p)
  - http://www.britishfreediving.org
  - Chmn: Emma Farrell
- ○ *S; parachuting

British Friction Materials Council   (BFMC)   1957
- ■ Brazennose House, Lincoln Sq, MANCHESTER, M2 5BL.   (asa)
  - 0161-834 5777
  - Contact: June Jenkins
- ○ *T
- M 4 f
  - no further information supplied

British Friesland Sheep Society   1980
- ■ Weir Park Farm, Waterwell Lane, Christow, EXETER, Devon, EX6 7PB.   (hsp)
  - 01647 252549
  - Hon Sec: Peter Baber
- ▲ Company Limited by Guarantee
- ○ *B; to promote the use of British Friesland sheep as a supreme dairy animal & as a crossing sire to produce profitable cross-bred ewes for prime lamb production
- ● Mtgs (AGM)
- < Nat Sheep Assn
- M 48 i
- ¶ NL - irreg.   Hbk;   LM - updated.

British Frozen Food Federation   (BFFF)   1951
- NR Springfield House (3rd floor), Springfield Rd, GRANTHAM, Lincs, NG31 7BG.   (hq)
  - 01476 515300
  - Contact: Emma Holberry
- ○ *T
- M f

British Fruit Juice Association   (BFJA)   1947
- ■ Shoelands House, Seale, FARNHAM, Surrey, GU10 1HL.   (hq)
  - 01483 811433   fax 01483 813733
  - email clive@clivewebster.co.uk
  - Sec: Clive Webster
- ▲ Un-incorporated Society
- ○ *T; advice to members & others on fruit juice production, importation, packaging & other relevant topics
- ● Conf - ET - Inf
- M 54 f, UK / 4 f, o'seas
- × 2002 British Fruit Juice Importers Association

British Fuchsia Society   (BFS)   1938
- ■ PO Box 178, EVESHAM, Worcs, WR11 3WY.   (hsp)
  - 01386 45158
  - http://www.thebfs.org.uk
  - Hon Sec: Geoffrey Oke
- ▲ Registered Charity
- ○ *H; to further interest in the cultivation & understanding of Fuchsias
- Gp Special Interest: Hybridising, Species, Pre-1914 cultivars; Show organisation & exhibiting; Photography; Fuchsia (collecting fuschsia memorabilia)
- ● Conf - ET - Exam - Exhib - Comp - Inf
- < Fuchsia Res Intl; Eurofuchsia; R Horticl Soc
- > Fuchsia Res Intl
- M 3,800 i, 280 org, UK / 325 i, 20 org, o'seas
- ¶ Spring [& Autumn] Bulletin(s) - 1; ftm, £3 nm.
  - Annual publication - 1; ftm, £4 nm.

British Fur Trade Association Inc   (BFTA)   1964
- ■ Brookstone House, 6 Elthorne Rd, LONDON, N19 4AG.   (hq)
  - 020 7281 9299   fax 020 7281 1374
  - email info@britishfur.co.uk   http://www.britishfur.co.uk
  - Contact: The Executive Officer
- ▲ Company Limited by Guarantee
- ○ *T
- ● Mtgs - Exhib - Comp - Expt - Inf - Empl
- M 50 f

British Furniture Confederation
- NR c/o 30 Harcourt St, LONDON, W1H 4AA.   (hq)
  - 020 7724 0851   fax 020 7706 1924
  - http://www.britishfurnitureconfederation.org.uk
  - Chmn: Martin Jourdan

British Furniture Manufacturers
  see BFM Ltd (British Furniture Manufacturers)

British Gear Association   (BGA)   1986
- ■ Suite 43 Imex Business Park, Shobnall Rd, BURTON-upon-TRENT, Staffs, DE14 2AU.   (hq)
  01283 515521   fax 01283 515841
  email admin@bga.org.uk   http://www.bga.org.uk
  Technical Exec: Andrew Harry
- ▲ Company Limited by Guarantee
- ○ *E, *Q, *T; to promote technical, economic, educational, training & research activities in the interest of the mechanical power transmission sector
- Gp C'ees: Technical, Education & training; Marketing; Research Foundation
- ● Conf - Mtgs - ET - Res - Exhib - SG - Stat - Expt - Inf - Lib - VE - LG
- < Eur C'ee of Assns of Mfrs of Gears & Transmission Parts (EUROTRANS); Mechanical & Metal Trs Confedn (METCOM)
- M 6 i, 82 f, 8 org
- ¶ BGA NL - 4; free.
  Technical Bulletin - 12;   Technical Literature Survey - 12;
  AR - 1; all ftm only.
  Buyers Guide - 2 yrly; ftm, £10 nm.

British Gelbvieh Cattle Society   1972
- NR Castlefield, Graig Llwyn Rd, Lisvane, CARDIFF, CF14 0RP.
  (hsp)
  Hon Sec: Mandy Hawkins
- ▲ Registered Charity
- ○ *B
- ● Conf - Exhib - Comp - VE - Shows
- M c 20 i
- ¶ NL - 4;   AR - 1; both ftm.   LM - 1; free.

British Generic Manufacturers' Association   (BGMA)   1989
- NR 3 London Wall Buildings, London Wall, LONDON, EC2M 5SY.   (hq)
  020 7826 2600   fax 020 7826 2601
  email info@britishgenerics.co.uk
  http://www.britishgenerics.co.uk
  Sec: Alex Harris
- ▲ Company Limited by Guarantee
- ○ *T; for UK manufacturers & suppliers of generic medicines; to promote the industry
- ● Mtgs - LG
- < Eur Generic Medicines Assn (EGA)
- M 14 f

British Geomembrane Association   (BGA)   1999
- ■ c/o Environmental Lining Systems Ltd, Westland Square, LEEDS, W Yorks, LS11 5SS.   (hsb)
  0113-277 5635   fax 0113-277 5454
  email derek@environmentallinings.co.uk
  http://www.bga.uk.net
  Sec: W D Mitchell
- ▲ Un-incorporated Society
- ○ *T
- ● Conf- Mtgs - ET - Exam
- M 1 i, 20 f

British Geomorphological Research Group
a group of the **Geological Society**

British Geophysical Association
a group of the **Geological Society**

British Geotechnical Association   (BGA)   1949
- NR c/o Institution of Civil Engineers, 1-7 Great George St, LONDON, SW1P 3AA.   (hq)
- ▲ Registered Charity
- ○ *P; promotion of cooperation among engineers & scientists for the advancement of knowledge in the fields of soil & rock mechanics & engineering geology & their application to engineering
- M i
- × 2000 (June) British Geotechnical Society

British Geriatrics Society   (BGS)   1947
- NR Marjory Warren House, 31 St Johns Sq, LONDON, EC1M 4DN.   (hq)
  020 7608 1369   fax 020 7608 1041
  email info@bgs.org.uk   http://www.bgs.org.uk
  Hon Sec: Dr David Beaumont
- ▲ Registered Charity
- ○ *P; to improve standards of health; to put the case for a well-funded health & community care service for elderly people
- Gp Bladder & bowel; Cardiovascular; Cerebral ageing & mental health; Diabetes; Drugs & prescribing; Falls & bone health; Gastroenterology & nutrition; Health services research; Medical ethics; New technology in elderly care; Parkinson's disease; Primary & continuing care; Respiratory
- ● Conf - Mtgs - ET - Res
- < Intl Assn of Gerontology
- M c 2,000 i, UK / 500 i, o'seas
- ¶ Age & Ageing (Jnl) - 6; ftm.

British-German Association   (BGA)   1951
- NR 34 Belgrave Sq, LONDON, SW1X 8QD.   (hq)
  020 7235 1922   fax 020 7235 1902
  email info@britishgermanassociation.org
  http://www.britishgermanassociation.org
  Exec Sec: Martina Schmidt
- ▲ Company Limited by Guarantee; Registered Charity
- ○ *X; promotion of understanding between British & German peoples, their culture & history
- ● Conf - Mtgs - Annual Nutcracker Ball
- < Deutsch-Englische Gesellschaft (Berlin)
- M c 700 i
- ¶ British-German Review - 4; ftm.

British-German Jurists' Association   (BGJA)   1970
- NR 14 New St, LONDON, EC2M 4HE.   (chmn/b)
  020 7972 9727   fax 020 7972 9721
  http://www.bgja.org.uk
  Hon Chmn: Dr Sybille Steiner,
  Hon Sec: Peter Stevens
- ○ *P
- ● Conf - Mtgs
- < Deutsch-Britische Juristenvereinigung eV (Hamburg)
- M 350 i
- ¶ NL.

British Gladiolus Society   (BGS)   1926
- ■ 197 Aston Clinton Rd, AYLESBURY, Bucks, HP22 5AD.   (hsp)
  01296 6303607
  email duckglads@aol.com   http://www.britglads.com
  Hon Sec: Susan Fawcett
- ▲ Un-incorporated Society
- ○ *H; the cultivation, breeding & exhibition of all types of gladiolus
- Gp 3 test grounds for cultivars supplied for trial from UK & o'seas, in Midlands, North of England & Scotland
- ● Conf - Mtgs - Res - Exhib - Stat - Inf - Lib - PL - Regional annual show
- < N Amer Gladiolus Coun (NAGC)
- M 275 i, 55 affiliated socs, UK / 22 i, o'seas
- ¶ NL - 3.   Ybk.

British Glass Manufacturers' Confederation   (British Glass) 1988
- 9 Churchill Way, SHEFFIELD, S Yorks, S35 2PY.   (hq)
  0114-290 1850
  email info@britglass.co.uk   http://www.britglass.org.uk
  Dir Gen: David Workman,   Inf Officer: Theresa Green
- ▲ Company Limited by Guarantee
- ○ *T; to represent the interests of members to government at EU, national & local level; to provide technical & consultancy services to members & non members
- Gp Glass Technology Services (the technical arm of British Glass offering specialist services in consultancy, project management, environmental monitoring & all types of glass analysis)
- ● Conf - Mtgs - ET - Res - Stat - Inf - Lib - LG
- < FGUE; CPIV; EDGA; EDG; CBI; CETUE; CEN; Packaging Fedn
- M 95 f, UK / 2 f, o'seas
- ¶ NL - 2;   Legislative Update;   Digest of Information - 4; Various NL;   AR - 1; all ftm.

British Gliding Association Ltd   (BGA)   1929
- Kimberley House, 47 Vaughan Way, LEICESTER, LE1 4SE.   (hq)
  0116-253 1051   fax 0116-251 5939
  email bgs@gliding.co.uk   http://www.gliding.co.uk
  Chief Exec: Peter Stratten
- ▲ Company Limited by Guarantee
- ○ *S; promotion of every aspect of gliding & soaring
- M c 11,000 i

British Glove Association   (BGA)   1998
- Sussex House, 8-10 Homesdale Rd, BROMLEY, Kent, BR2 9LZ.   (asa)
  020 8464 0131   fax 020 8464 6018
  email tradeassn@craneandpartners.com
  http://www.gloveassociation.org
  Sec: Mrs Colleen Swan
- ○ *T; to promote glove sales; to encourage designers; to bring together manufacturers & retailers
- M 30 f

British Go Association   (BGA)   1953
- 10 Stacey Ave, Wolverton, MILTON KEYNES, Bucks, MK12 5DL.
  01908 653327 (0900-1700) & 01908 315342   (hsp)
  email bga@britgo.org   http://www.britgo.org
  Sec: Fred Holroyd
- ▲ Un-incorporated Society
- Br 68 clubs
- ○ *G, *S; to promote the playing of the ancient oriental board game of Go
- ● Conf Mtgs - ET - Comp - SG
- < Intl Go Fedn; Eur Go Fedn
- M c 600 i, UK; 50 i, o'seas
- ¶ British Go Jnl - 4; ftm, £3.50 nm.
  BGA NL - 6; ftm only.

British Goat Society   (BGS)   1879
- 34-36 Fore St, Bovey Tracey, NEWTON ABBOT, Devon, TQ13 9AD.   (hq)
  01626 833168
  Sec: Ms Susan Knowles
- ▲ Registered Charity
- ○ *B; to increase supply & consumption of goats milk; to improve the various breeds of goats; to safeguard against cruelty; production of cashmere & cashgora fibre, hides & leather
- Gp Working party on the composition & utilisation of goats milk; Caprine & Ovine Breeding Services Ltd (artificial insemination)
- ● Conf - Mtgs - ET - Res - Exhib - SG - Stat - Expt - Inf - Sales of products allied to goat keeping & dairy work, production of butter, cheeses & yoghurt
- < Breed Societies: Saanen, Brit Saanen, Toggenburg, Brit Toggenburg, Anglo-Nubian, Brit Alpine, Golden Guernsey; Harness Goat Soc; Regional Goat Socs
- M 3,000 i, 15 f, 100 org, UK / 50 i, o'seas
- ¶ Jnl - 11.   Ybk.   Herdbook - 1.   AR.

British Goldpanning Association   1988
- NR 2 Spout Cottages, The Spout, ELLESMERE, Shropshire, SY12 0NE.   (sp)
  01691 623954
  http://www.british-goldpanning-association.com
  Sec: Barbara Copley
- ○ *G; for British goldpanners
- < Wld Goldpanning Assn
- M c 45 i

British Golf Industry Association   (BGIA)   1919
- Federation House, STONELEIGH PARK, Warks, CV8 2RF.   (hq)
  024 7641 7141   fax 024 7641 4990
  email bgia@sportsandplay.com
  http://www.bgia.org.uk
  Sec: Mrs Jacqui Baldwin
- ▲ Company Limited by Guarantee
- ○ *T; manufacturers & distributors of golf equipment
- ● Conf - Mtgs - Res - Stat - Expt - Inf - LG
- < Eur Golf Ind Assn; Fedn of Sports & Play Assns (FSPA)
- M 70 f
  Note: A new European Golf Industry Association was formed in 2003
- × 2002 European Golf Industry Association

British Goose Producers Association
  since 2001 **British Poultry Council**

British Gotland Sheep Society   (BGSS)   1990
- Whitehall Farm, Luppitt, HONITON, Devon, EX14 4TR.   (hsp)
  01404 42141
  http://www.gotlandsheep.com
  davidbarlo@aol.com   (chmn)
  Sec: Mrs Lyn Barlow
- ▲ Un-incorporated Society
- ○ *B
- ● Mtgs - ET - Exhib - LG - Promotion & breed registration of British Gotland Sheep
- < Nat Sheep Assn
- M 26 i
- ¶ NL - 4;   Flock Book - 1; both ftm only.
  Breed Hbk - 2 yrly; ftm, £2 nm.

British Grassland Society   (BGS)   1945
- NR Dept of Agriculture (PO Box 237), University of Reading, READING, Berks, RG6 6AR.   (hq)
  0118-931 8189   fax 0118-966 6941
  email office@britishgrassland.com
  http://www.britishgrassland.com
  Chief Exec: Jessica Buss
- ▲ Registered Charity
- ○ *A, *L; grass & forage production, study & research
- ● Conf - Mtgs - Exhib - Comp - Inf - Lib
- < Foundation of Science & Technology; Inst of Biology
- M c 850 i
- ¶ Grass & Forage Science - 4.
  Grass Farmer - 3.
  Publications list available.

British Grooms Association   (BGA)   2007
- Lucy Katan
- ○ *P
  to be formed April 2007

British Group of Altimeter Specialists
  a group of the **Challenger Society for Marine Science**

© CBD Research Ltd · Beckenham · BR3 5JS · Tel 020 8650 7745 · Fax 020 8650 0768 · E-mail cbd@cbdresearch.com · www.cbdresearch.com

British Guild of Beer Writers   1988

- ■ Lee Farm, WINSFORD, Somerset, TA24 9HX.   (hsp)
  01643 851469
  Hon Sec: Adrian Tierney-Jones
- ▲ Un-incorporated Society
- ○ *P; to improve the standards of beer writing; to extend public knowledge of beers & brewing
- ● Conf - Mtgs - Res - Comp - Inf
- < Intl Fedn of Beer Writers
- M 132 i, 21 f, UK / 10 i, o'seas
- ¶ BGBW NL - 10; ftm.

British Guild of Travel Writers   (BGTW)   1960

- NR 51B Askew Crescent, LONDON, W12 9DN.   (hsb)
  020 8749 1128
- ○ *P; for specialist travel writers, broadcasters, producers, editors & photographers
- ● Mtgs - Res - Inf - VE
- < all members are also members of Eur Fedn of Tourism Journalists (FEDAJT)
- M 220 i
- ¶ Globe Trotter - 12; ftm only.

British Gymnastics
  see **British Amateur Gymnastics Association**

British Haiku Society   (BHS)   1990

- ■ 38 Wayside Ave, HORNCHURCH, Essex, RM12 4LL.   (hsp)
  01708 475774
  http://www.britishhaikusociety.org
  Gen Sec: Doreen King
- ▲ Registered Charity
- ○ *A; to promote the appreciation of writing of haiku, senryu, haibun, runku (Japanese poetry & prose)
- ● Conf - Mtgs - Comp - SG - Inf - Lib - VE
- M c 500 i, c 50 org, UK / c 500 i, c 50 org, o'seas
- ¶ Blithe Spirit (Jnl) - 4; ftm.

British Hamster Association   (BHA)

- ■ PO Box 825, SHEFFIELD, S Yorks, S17 3RU.   (mail/address)
  01373 300766
  email hamsters@somershire.freeserve.co.uk
  42 Stonebridge Drive, FROME, Somerset, BA11 2TN.
  01373 300766   (hsp)
  Sec: Mrs Wendy Barry
- ▲ Un-incorporated Society
- ○ *B; to encourage high standards of management & care of all species of hamster
- ● Mtgs - ET - Exhib - Comp - Inf - Maintains a breeders' register
- M 600 i, UK / 10 i, o'seas
- ¶ [NL] - 4; 95p.
  Information leaflets on various types of hamster.

British Hand Knitting Confederation   (BHKC)   1990

- ■ c/o NWTEC, Lloyds Bank Chambers, 43 Hustlergate, BRADFORD, W Yorks, BD1 1PH.
  Contact: R Peter Ackroyd
- ○ *K, *T; to create a desire to knit
- ● Mtgs - ET - Res - Exhib
- M 9 f (manufacturers & distributors of knitting yarns)
- ¶ LM.

British Handball Association
  see **England Handball Association**

British Hang Gliding & Paragliding Association   (BHPA)   1974

- ■ The Old Schoolroom, Loughborough Rd, LEICESTER, LE4 5PJ.   (hq)
  0116-261 1322   fax 0116-261 1323
  email office@bhpa.co.uk   http://www.bhpa.co.uk
- ▲ Company Limited by Guarantee
- Br 120
- ○ *S; control & development of the sport of hang gliding & paragliding
- Gp Over land towed ascent; Self launched (unassisted) flight
- ● Conf - ET - Exhib - Comp - Stat
- < R Aero Club; CCPR; Fédn Aéronautique Intle
- M 8,000 i, 120 clubs
- ¶ Skywings (Jnl) - 12; ftm, £2.50 nm.

British Hanoverian Horse Society   1992

- NR Ecton Field Plantation, Ecton Lane, SYWELL, Northants, NN6 0BP.
  01604 492750
  http://www.hanoverian-gb.org.uk
  Sec: John Shenfield
- ○ *B
  No further information supplied

British Hardmetal Association
  merged in February 2004 with British Engineers' Cutting Tools Association to form the **British Hardmetal & Engineers' Cutting Tool Association**

British Hardmetal & Engineers' Cutting Tool Association   (BHECTA)   2004

- ■ c/o Institute of Spring Technology, Henry St, SHEFFIELD, S Yorks, S3 7EQ.   (MTA/hq)
  0114-278 9143   fax 0114-275 5573
  email info@britishtools.com
  http://www.britishtools.com
  Dir Gen (MTA): Andrew Manly
- ▲ Un-incorporated Society
- ○ *T; to act as the national organisation representing the interests of manufacturers within the hardmetal & cutting tool industry
- Gp Research & development (hardmetal)
- ● Conf - Mtgs - Res - Exhib - Stat - Expt - Inf - VE - LG - Standardisation with ISO & BDI - Cooperation with other countries re standards & technical barriers to trade
- < World Cutting Tool Conf; Eur Cutting Tool Assn
- M 30 f
  Note: in April 2006 was incorporated into the Manufacturing Technologies Association
- × 2004 (British Engineers' Cutting Tools Association (British Hardmetal Association

British Hardware Federation   (BHF)   1899

- NR 225 Bristol Rd, Edgbaston, BIRMINGHAM, B5 7UB.   (hq)
  0121-446 6688   fax 0121-446 5215
  email information@bhfgroup.co.uk
  Managing Dir: Jonathan Swift
- Br 37
- ○ *T; retailers of hardware, ironmongery, housewares, garden products, DIY, tools & building supplies
- Gp Cookshop & Housewares Association; Hardware & Garden Retail Association; National Association of Tool Dealers; Pet Product Retail Association
  Builders' Supplies Divn
- ● Conf - Mtgs - ET - Res - Exhib - SG - Stat - Inf - Lib - VE - Empl - LG - Business services for retailers
- < Intl Fedn Ironmongers; Assn Brit Chams Comm; Brit Retail Consortium
- M 4,463 f
- ¶ Hardware Today - 12.
  Hbk & LM - 1.

British Hardware & Housewares Manufacturers' Association (BHHMA) 1958
- Brooke House, 4 The Lakes, Bedford Rd, NORTHAMPTON, NN4 7YD. (hq)
  01604 622023   fax 01604 631252
  email bhhma@brookehouse.co.uk
  http://www.bhhma.com
  Chief Exec: Allen G J Johnson
▲ Company Limited by Guarantee
○ *T
Gp Housewares; Cookware; Hardware; DIY; Brush
● Conf - Mtgs - Exhib - Stat - Expt - Inf - LG
< Intl Housewares Assn (USA); Fedn of Eur DIY Mfrs (FEDIYMA)
M 300 f, 10 affiliate org
¶ NL - 12; free.   Membership Directory - 1; ftm, £75 nm.

British Harness Racing Club (BHRC) 1963
- Burlington Crescent, GOOLE, E Yorks, DN14 5EG. (regd/office)
  01405 766877   fax 01405 766878
  email harnessgb@aol.com   http://www.bhrc.org.uk
  Sec: Miss Geraldine Berry
▲ Company Limited by Guarantee
○ *S; governing body for harness racing in GB
● Mtgs - Comp - Inf - Race meetings - Issuing of licences
< Wld Trotting Assn
M 1,500 i (licence holders)
¶ Calendar - 6; £12.   Fixtures List (Jan).
  Record Book - 1; £14.

British Hat Guild (BHG) 1978
NR 4 The Laurels, 65 Palmerston Rd, BUCKHURST HILL, Essex, IG9 5NT.
  email info@britishhatguild.co.uk
  http://www.britishhatguild.co.uk
▲ Un-incorporated Society
○ *T; to encourage & promote hat making & millinery in the UK
● ET - Exhib - Receptions
M 25 i, 25 f

British Hawking Association (BHA) 1967
NR 43 Amherst Crescent, HOVE, E Sussex, BN3 7EP. (chmn/p)
  0870 755 0211
  Chmn: Jose Souto
▲ Un-incorporated Society
Br 6
○ *G
● Mtgs - ET - Apprenticeship scheme - campaign to licence raptor keepers in the UK
< 3 Spanish falconry clubs
M 'Unable to disclose due to constitution'
¶ Yarak Jnl - 1;   Yarak NL - 4; both ftm.

British Hay & Straw Merchants' Association (BHSMA) 1917
NR Top Farm, Coppingford, HUNTINGDON, Cambs, PE17 5XX. (hsb)
  01487 830980   fax 01487 830980
  Ivy Lodge, Braceborough, STAMFORD, Lincs, PE9 4NT.
  01778 561113   fax 01778 561114   (treas/p).
  Sec: Mrs Jane Lawman,   Treas: Mike North
○ *T; interests of members incl new uses of straw
Gp Technical
● Mtgs - SG - Inf - VE - Arbitration service - Legal advice
M 50 f

British Health Care Association (BHCA) 1931
NR 26-28 Headlands, KETTERING, Northants, NN15 7HP.   (hq)
  01536 519960   fax 01536 519379
  email cbell@bhca.org.uk   http://www.bhca.org.uk
  Chief Exec: Carolyn Bell
▲ Un-incorporated Society
○ *W; to encourage the extension of hospital contributory schemes; to assist in the establishing of new schemes; to encourage voluntary effort for the benefit of hospital patients, others in need & medical charities, including research
● Conf - Mtgs - SG - Stat - Inf - Lib - LG
M 30 f
¶ NL - 4; ftm only.   AR (incl LM) - 1; free.
  Caring for the Nation's Health (brochure) - 1; free.

British Health Professionals in Rheumatology (BHPR) 1985
- Bride House, 18-20 Bride Lane, LONDON, EC4Y 8EE.   (hq)
  020 7842 0900   fax 020 7842 0901
  email bhpr@rheumatology.org.uk
  http://www.rheumatology.org.uk
  Chief Exec: Samantha Peters
▲ Registered Charity
○ *P; to encourage & emphasise the multi-disciplinary approach to the management of people with rheumatic diseases; to provide a forum for health professionals to exchange knowledge, skills & experience
● Conf - Mtgs - ET - Res - Annual clinical prize - Annual Spring meeting
< Brit Soc for Rheumatology (BSR); Arthritis & Musculoskeletal Alliance (ARMA)
M 600 i, UK / 3 i, o'seas
¶ BHPR NL - 2;   BHPR Hbk - 2 yrly, both ftm only.

British Healthcare Business Intelligence Association (BHBIA)
NR 105 St Peter's St, St Albans, Herts, AL1 3EJ.
  01727 896085   fax 01727 896026
  email admin@bhbia.org.uk   http://www.bhbia.org.uk
○ *P

British Healthcare Trades Association (BHTA) 1917
NR New Loom House, 101 Backchurch Lane, LONDON, E1 1LU. (hq)
  020 7702 2141
  email bhta@bhta.com   http://www.bhta.com
  Dir Gen: Ray Hodgkinson
▲ Company Limited by Guarantee
○ *T; to represent companies providing healthcare & assistive technology products & services
Gp Beds & support services; Dispensing appliance contractors; First aid medical equipment; Health & safety training organisations; Infection control; Mobility access & stairlifts; Mobility vehicles (manufacturers, distributors); Orthotics; Postural control; Prosthetics; Rehabilitation products; Seating & positioning; Stoma & continence; Visual impairment products & services
● Conf - Mtgs - ET - Stat - Inf - LG
M 350 f
¶ Friday Morning at BHTA (NL) - 52;   Bulletin; both ftm only.

British Heather Growers
  a specialist group of the **Horticultural Trades Association**

British Hedgehog Preservation Society (BHPS) 1982
- ■ Hedgehog House, Dhustone, LUDLOW, Shropshire, SY8 3PL. (hq)
  01584 890801   fax 01584 891313
  email bhps@dhustone.fsbusiness.co.uk
  http://www.britishhedgehogs.org.uk
  Chief Exec: Fay Vass
- ▲ Registered Charity
- ○ *K, *V; to encourage & give advice to the public on the care of hedgehogs, particularly when injured, sick, orphaned or in any other danger; to fund research into behavioural habits in order to assist their survival; to encourage the younger generation to value and respect our natural wildlife & to foster their interest in hedgehogs
- ● Conf - ET - Res - Exhib - Inf - Lib
- M 11,000 i, UK & o'seas
- ¶ NL - 2; ftm, 60p nm.   Catalogue - 1; free.

British Helicopter Advisory Board Ltd (BHAB) 1969
- NR Fairoaks Airport, Graham Suite West Entrance, CHOBHAM, Surrey, GU24 8HX.   (hq)
  01276 856100   fax 01276 856126
  email info@bhab.org   http://www.bhab.org
  Chief Exec: Peter Norton
- ○ *T; 'to promote the use of helicopters in the UK; to help helicopter operations to be conducted safely & responsibly'
- Gp Onshore operations; Offshore operations; Heliport & environmental matters; Technical matters
- ● Mtgs - Inf - Lib - LG
- < Eur Helicopter Assn (EHA)
- M i, f & org
- ¶ The Rotorhead - 4; ftm only.   Leaflets.
  BHAB Information Hbk - 1; ftm.

British Hellenic Chamber of Commerce (BHCC) 1945
- ■ 25 Vas Sophias Avenue, GR-106 74 ATHENS, Greece.   (hq)
  30 (210) 72 10 361   fax 30 (210) 72 12 119
  email info@bhcc.gr   http://www.bhcc.gr
  Jt Pres: Harilaos Goritsas & Irene Watson
- ▲ Un-incorporated Society
- ○ *C; to serve the business world in Greece & Britain
- ● Conf - Mtgs - Exhib - Inf - Social events
- M 2 i, 21 f, UK / 85 i, 307 f, o'seas
- ¶ BH Magazine - 4; free.
  Business Directory of Members - 1; ftm, £50 nm.

British Herb Trade Association (BHTA) 1976
- ■ 133 Eastgate, LOUTH, Lincs, LN11 9QG.   (hq)
  01507 602427   fax 01507 600689
  email tim.mudge@pvga.co.uk   http://www.bhta.org.uk
  Chmn: M H Prestwich
- ▲ Un-incorporated Society
- ○ *T; for herb growers, processors & retailers in the UK
- ● Conf - Mtgs - Res - LG
- < Nat Farmers U
- M 80 f
- ¶ Herbnews - 4; ftm only.

British Herbal Medicine Association (BHMA) 1964
- NR 1 Wickham Rd, Boscombe, BOURNEMOUTH, BH7 6JX.
  01202 433691
  Sec: Mrs Diana Foreman
- ▲ Company Limited by Guarantee
- ○ *K, *T; to advance & protect the status of herbal medicine & the right to choose herbal remedies; to foster research into phytotherapy; to continue to revise & publish the British Herbal Pharmacopoeia
- Gp Advertising; Scientific; Database; Pharmacopoeia; Code of advertising practice
- ● Conf - Mtgs - Res - Inf
- < Nat Inst of Med Herbalists; Natural Medicine Gp
- M c 300 i, f & org
- ¶ BHMA Post - 4.
  The British Herbal Pharmacopoeia; 1996.
  British Herbal Compendium, Vol 1 & 2.
  A Guide to Traditional Herbal Medicines.

British Herpetological Society (BHS) 1948
- NR c/o Zoological Society of London, Regent's Park, LONDON, NW1 4RY.   (hsp)
  020 8452 9578   fax 020 8452 9547
  Sec: Trevor Rose
- ▲ Registered Charity
- ○ *L; to promote the study, protection, captive breeding, research & conservation of amphibians & reptiles
- Gp Captive breeding; Conservation
- ● Mtgs - Res - Inf - Lib
- M c 450 i, UK / 350 i, o'seas
- ¶ Jnl - 4;   Natterjack (NL) - 3;   Bulletin - 4.

British Hip Society
  a specialist society of the **British Orthopaedic Association**

British Hire Cruiser Federation
  a group of the **British Marine Federation**

British Historical Games Society (BHGS) 1996
- ■ 8 West Hill Avenue, EPSOM, Surrey, KT19 8LE.
  01372 812132   fax 01372 817038
  email bhgs@slitherine.co.uk   http://www.bhgs.co.uk
  Chmn: J D McNeil
- ▲ Un-incorporated Society
- ○ *G; to organise & run table top wargaming with miniature figurines on a tournament basis; to liaise with other national bodies to organise tournaments internationally
- ● Exhib - Comp
- < Intl Wargames Fedn
- M 500 i

British HIV Association (BHIVA)
- ■ c/o Mediscript Ltd, Unit 1 Mountview Court, 310 Friern Barnet Lane, LONDON, N20 0LD.   (hq)
  020 8369 5380; 020 8446 8898   fax 020 8446 9194
  email bhiva@bhiva.org   http://www.bhiva.org
  Hon Sec: Dr Jane Anderson
- ▲ Registered Charity
- ○ *M; for the relief of sickness, protection & preservation of health through the development & promotion of good practice in the treatment of HIV & related illnesses; to act as a national advisory body to the profession & other organisations on all aspects of HIV care
- ● Conf - ET - Res - Promotion of graduate & continuing medical education within HIV care
- < Intl Aids Soc
- M 566 i, UK / 8 i, o'seas
- ¶ HIV Medicine - 4.

British Holiday & Home Parks Association   (BH&HPA)   1952
- ■ 6 Pullman Court, Great Western Rd, GLOUCESTER, GL1 3ND.   (hq)
  01452 526911   fax 01452 508508
  email enquiries@bhhpa.org.uk
  http://www.ukparks.com
  Dir-Gen: Mrs Ros Pritchard
- Br 22
- ○ *T; for owners of caravan holiday parks, touring parks, mobile home parks, chalets & all types of self-service holiday accommodation
- ● Conf - Mtgs - ET - Exhib - SG - PL - LG
- < Eur Fedn of Camping/Caravanning Orgs
- M 2,500 i, 3,000 f
- ¶ Jnl - 6;   Ybk - 1;   NL - irreg; all ftm only.

British Holistic Medical Association   (BHMA)   1983
- NR PO Box 371, BRIDGWATER, Somerset, TA6 9BG.   (hq)
  01278 722000
  Admin: Diana Brown
- ▲ Registered Charity
- ○ *L; education of doctors & medical students to the principles & practice of holistic medicine & dissemination of information to the public
- ● Conf - Mtgs - ET - Inf - Lib
- M c 600 i
- ¶ Jnl of Holistic Healthcare - 4.   LM.
  Tapes for Health.

British Homoeopathic Association   (BHA)   1902
- ■ Hahnemann House, 29 Park Street West, LUTON, Beds, LU1 3BE.   (hq)
  0870 444 3950   fax 0870 444 3960
  email info@trusthomeopathy.org
  http://www.trusthomeopathy.org
  Chief Exec: Sally Penrose
- ▲ Registered Charity
- ○ *P, *Q; to provide an information service to the public; to campaign for more homeopathy in the NHS; to fund research & training in homeopathy
- Gp Supporters' scheme - Friends of the BHA
- ● Inf - LG - Provides list of homeopathic doctors, dentists, pharmacists, vets & podiatrists
- M 3,000 i
- ¶ Health & Homeopathy - 4.

British Homoeopathic Dental Association
- ■ Hahnemann House, 29 Park Street West, LUTON, Beds, LU1 3BE.
  0870 444 3950   fax 0870 444 3960
  email phil@tooth1.freeserve.co.uk
  Contact: Philip Wander
- ○ *P

British Horn Society   (BHS)   1980
- NR The Cottage, Ramsdell Rd, Monk Sherborne, TADLEY, Hants, RG26 5HS.   (chmn/p)
  01256 855066
  Chmn: Michael Thompson
- ▲ Registered Charity
- ○ *D; promotion & knowledge of the art, craft & fun of horn & horn playing - the French Horn & Wagner Tuba
- ● ET - Music festivals - Regional horn days - Lectures & seminars for teachers of the horn
- < Nat Fedn of Music Socs; Voluntary Arts Network
- M 660 i
- ¶ The Horn Player (Jnl) - 3; ftm only.

British Horological Federation   (BHF)   1935
- NR Upton Hall, Upton, NEWARK, Notts, NG23 5TE.   (hq)
  01636 813795
  Sec Gen: W M Geoffrey Evans
- ▲ Company Limited by Guarantee
- ○ *T; for the watch & clock industry
- ● Mtgs - Exhib - Expt - Inf - LG
- M 50 f, UK / 1 org, o'seas
- ¶ Horological Jnl - 12; ftm.

British Horological Institute   (BHI)   1858
- NR Upton Hall, Upton, NEWARK, Notts, NG23 5TE.   (hq)
  01636 813795   fax 01636 812258
  email clocks@bhi.co.uk   http://www.bhi.co.uk
  The Secretary
- ▲ Company Limited by Guarantee
- Br 20; 6 area representatives o'seas
- ○ *P; promotion of the art & science of horology to cover both the professional & the amateur member
- ● Conf - Mtgs - ET - Exam - Exhib - Inf - Lib - LG
- M c 3,000 i, UK / 500 i, o'seas
- ¶ Horological Journal - 12; ftm only.

British Horse Driving Trials Association
is a discipline member of the **British Equestrian Federation**

British Horse Society   (BHS)   1947
- NR Stoneleigh Deer Park, KENILWORTH, Warks, CV8 2XZ.
  0870 120 2244 & 01926 707700
  fax 01926 707800   (hq)
  email enquiry@bhs.org.uk   http://www.bhs.org.uk
  Chief Exec: Graham Cory
- ▲ Registered Charity
- ○ *B, *V; to promote the welfare, care & use of the horse & pony; to encourage horsemanship & the improvement of horse management & breeding
- Gp Access & rights of way; Welfare; Riding & road safety; Training & education; Riding clubs
- ● Conf - ET - Exam - Exhib - Comp - Inf - LG
- M c 100,000 (with those in affiliated riding clubs)
- ¶ British Horse - 6;   Ybk - 1; both ftm only.   AR; free.

British Horseball Association   (BHA)   1991
- ■ Arkenfield Stables, Lowdham Rd, Gunthorpe, NOTTINGHAM, NG14 7ER.   (hsp)
  0115-966 4574
  email mary.pettifor@lstrillium.com
  http://www.horseball.org.uk
  Intl Sec: Mary Pettifor
- ▲ Company Limited by Guarantee
- Br 10
- ○ *S; to promote & regulate the sport of horseball
- ● Mtgs - ET - Exam - Comp
- < Fedn Intl Horseball (FIHB)
- M 200 i, 10 org, UK / 7,000 i, o'seas
- ¶ BHA NL - 4; free (on website).   BHA Ybk - 1; ftm, £2.50 nm.

British Hospitality Association   (BHA)   1910
- NR Queen's House, 55-56 Lincoln's Inn Fields, LONDON, WC2A 3BH.   (hq)
  020 7404 7744   fax 020 7404 7799
  email bha@bha.org.uk   http://www.bha-online.org.uk
  Chief Exec: Bob Cotton
- ▲ Company Limited by Guarantee
- ○ *T; to be 'the effective voice of the national hotel & food service industry'
- ● Conf - Mtgs - ET - Stat - Inf - LG
- < Intl Hotel & Restaurants Assn (IH&RA); Eur Hotel, Restaurant & Catering Assn (HOTREC); Eur Fedn of Contract Caterers (FERCO)
- M 25,000 f
- ¶ Hospitality Matters (Jnl) 3-6; ftm, £30 yr nm.
  Contract Catering Survey - 1; ftm, £35 nm.
  Trends & Statistics - 1; ftm, £195 nm.

© CBD Research Ltd · Beckenham · BR3 5JS · Tel 020 8650 7745 · Fax 020 8650 0768 · E-mail cbd@cbdresearch.com · www.cbdresearch.com

British Hosta & Hemerocallis Society (BHHS) 1980
■   Cherry Trees, 37 St John's Rd, STANSTED, Essex, CM24 8JS.
    (hsp)
    01279 813887
    email dave.loynds@tesco.net
    http://www.hostahem.org.uk
    Hon Gen Sec: D Loynds
▲   Registered Charity
○   *H; to promote the breeding & growing of hosta & hemerocallis
Gp Hosta; Hemerocallis
●   Mtgs - Res - Exhib - SG - Inf - Lib - VE - Lectures
<   R Horticl Soc; Hardy Plant Soc
M   350 i, 18 f, UK / 26 i, 8 f, 2 org, o'seas
¶   British Hosta & Hemerocallis Society Bulletin - 1; ftm, £5 nm.
    NL - 3; ftm, 75p nm.

British Housewives League (BHL) 1945
■   Birchfield House, Mounton Rd, CHEPSTOW, Monmouthshire,
    NP16 5BS.   (hsp)
    01291 621748   fax 01291 621748
    Hon Sec: Mrs Lynn Riley
▲   Un-incorporated Society
○   *K; to provide housewives with an effective non-party political
    voice in all matters concerning the welfare of themselves &
    their families; mainly pro-British independence, family &
    farming matters
Gp Medical ethics; Nutrition
●   Conf - Mtgs - Res - Inf - LG
M   i
¶   The Lantern (Jnl) - 4; £15 m (includes free entry to Lantern
    lectures), £10 nm.

British Humanist Association (BHA) 1963
■   1 Gower St, LONDON, WC1E 6HD.   (hq)
    020 7079 3580   fax 020 7079 3588
    email info@humanism.org.uk
    http://www.humanism.org.uk
    Exec Dir: Hanne Stinson
▲   Company Limited by Guarantee; Registered Charity
Br 50
○   *K; 'to promote humanism & campaign against religious
    privilege & discrimination on grounds of religion or belief'
Gp Education
●   Conf - Mtgs - ET - Res - Inf - Lib
<   Intl Humanist & Ethical U
M   4,000 i, UK / 50 i, o'seas
¶   BHA News - 6.
    Books on non-religious ceremonies:
        Funerals without God; £4.50.
        New Arrivals; £4.
        Sharing the Future; £5.
    Booklets & leaflets on humanism & ethical issues.

British Hydrological Society (BHS) 1983
NR c/o Institution of Civil Engineers, 1-7 Great George St,
    LONDON, SW1P 3AA.   (hq)
    020 7665 2234   fax 020 7799 1325
    email bhs@ice.org.uk   http://www.hydrology.org.uk
    Sec: Tim Fuller,   Hon Sec: Dr Tim Jolley
▲   Registered Charity
Br 6
○   *L; to promote interest & scholarships in both scientific &
    applied aspects of hydrology
●   Conf - Mtgs - VE - LG
<   Instn of Civil Engrs; Inst of Hydrology
M   736 i, UK / 68 i, o'seas
¶   Circulation (NL) - 4.

British Hydropower Association (BHA) 1975
■   12 Riverside Park, Station Rd, WIMBORNE, Dorset,
    BH21 1QU.   (hq)
    01202 886622   fax 01202 886609
    email info@british-hydro.org
    http://www.british-hydro.org
    Chief Exec: David Williams
▲   Company Limited by Guarantee
○   *G, *K; to represent the interests of the UK Hydropower industry
    & its associated stakeholders
Gp Exporters
●   Conf - Mtgs - ET - Res - Exhib - Stat - Expt - Inf - VE - LG
<   Intl Hydropower Assn; Eur Small Hydro Assn (ESHA); Scot
    Renewables Forum
M   20 i, 80 f, 5 org
¶   NL - 4.

British Hyperlipidaemia Association
    merged in 2002 with the Family Heart Association to form **Heart UK**

British Hypertension Society (BHS) 1981
■   Hampton Medical Conferences Ltd, 113-119 High St,
    HAMPTON HILL, Middx, TW12 1NJ.   (meetingssec/b)
    020 8979 8300   fax 020 8979 6700
    email hmc@hamptonmedical.com
    http://www.bhsoc.org
    BHS Information Service, c/o Jackie Howarth:
        Clinical Sciences Bldg (Level 5), Leicester Royal Infirmary,
        PO Box 65, LEICESTER, LE2 7LX.   0771 746 7973.
        email bhs@le.ac.uk
    Meetings Sec: Mrs Gerry McCarthy
    Pres: Prof Morris Brown
▲   Registered Charity
○   *L, *M, *P; the pathophysiology, epidemiology, detection,
    investigation & treatment of arterial hypertension & related
    vascular diseases
●   Conf - ET - Res - Inf - LG
>   Nurses' Hypertension Assn
M   226 i, UK / 20 i, o'seas

British Hypnotherapy Association (BHA) 1958
■   67 Upper Berkeley St, LONDON, W1H 7QX.   (hq)
    020 7723 4443
    email bha@thewordsmith.co.uk
    http://www.british-hypnotherapy-association.org
    Hon Sec: Mrs Alison Wookey
▲   Un-incorporated Society
○   *P; for psychotherapists using hypnotherapy (when appropriate)
    in the treatment of nervous disorders, relationship difficulties,
    emotional problems
●   Mtgs - ET - Exam - Res - SG - Inf - Lib - LG - Provision of
    speakers for seminars & lectures
M   368 i, UK / 16 i, o'seas
¶   Publications list available.
    [Publication prices range from £1 to £20].

British Icelandic Sheep Breeders Group 1994
NR Cefn MAen Isa, SARON, Denbighshire, LL16 4TH.   (HSP)
    01745 550515
    Hon Sec: Jill Tyler
▲   Un-incorporated Society
○   *B
●   Mtgs - Exhib - Inf - LG
<   Nat Sheep Assn
M   24 farms
¶   Flock Book - 1.

British Île de France Sheep Society
- 6 Fort Rd, Kilroot, CARRICKFERGUS, BT38 9BS.   (hsp)
  028 9336 6225
  Sec: Edward Adamson
- ▲ Un-incorporated Society
- ○ *B
- ● Mtgs - Exhib - Comp - VE
- < Nat Sheep Assn
- M 50 i

British Imaging & Photographic Association
on 10 January 2002 merged with the British Photographic Enterprise Group, the British Photographic & Imaging Association, the Imaging Products Group & the Photographic Waste Management Association to form the **Photo Imaging Council**

British In-situ Concrete Paving Association
since 2000-2002 **Britpave**

British In Vitro Diagnostics Association Ltd   (BIVDA Ltd) 1992
- NR 1 Queen Anne's Gate, LONDON, SW1H 9BT.   (hq)
  020 7957 4633   fax 020 7957 4644
  email enquiries@bivda.co.uk   http://www.bivda.co.uk
  Dir Gen: Doris-Ann Williams
- ▲ Company Limited by Guarantee
- ○ *T; for companies with major involvement & interest in the IVD industry (In Vitro Diagnostics - products used in vitro for the examination of body fluids & tissue to aid clinical diagnosis)
- Gp Working parties: Regulatory affairs, Procurement, Point of care testing, Export, Market audit, Genetic testing, Operations, Public relations;
  Campaigns: Osteoporosis, Diabetes, Microbiology;
  EQA (External Quality Assurance) Forum
- ● Mtgs - ET - Exhib - Stat - Expt - Inf - LG
- < Eur Diagnostic Mfrs Assn (EDMA)
- M 112 f
- ¶ NL - 10;   LM - 1; both ftm only.
  Diagnostics Review - 4;   Annual Review - 1; both free.

British Incoming Tour Operators Association
since November 2004 **UKinbound**

British Independent Fruit Growers Association   (BIFGA)
- Aylsham, Broad Oak, Brenchley, TONBRIDGE, Kent, TN12 7NN.   (contact/p)
  01892 722080
  Contact: Mrs Perry
- ○ *T

British Independent Motor Trade Association   (BIMTA)   1998
- NR 14B Chapel Place (1st floor), TUNBRIDGE WELLS, Kent, TN1 1YG.   (hq)
  01892 515425   fax 01892 515495
  email queries@bimta.org   http://www.bimta.org
  Gen Sec: Richard Moore
- ▲ Un-incorporated Society
- ○ *T; for all sectors of the independent motor trade
- Gp Importers of European & Japanese vehicles; Parts suppliers & servicing agents; Professional PR & lobbying
- ● Conf - Mtgs - Inf - LG
- < Eur Assn of Indep Vehicle Traders (EAIVT); Eur Parallel Import Coalition (EPIC)
- M c 140 fUK / 4 f, o'seas
- ¶ LM; free for sae.

British Independent Plastic Extruders Association   (BIPEA) 1981
- c/o 89 Cornwall St, BIRMINGHAM, B3 3BY.   (asa)
  0121-236 1866   fax 0121-233 1116
  Sec: G C Saunders
- ▲ Company Limited by Guarantee
- ○ *T; manufacturers of extrusions in nearly all plastic materials, incl finishing & fabrication operations
- ● Mtgs
- < Brit Plastics Fedn - Vinyls Gp
- M 10 f
- ¶ Brochure incl LM; free.

British Indoor Cricket Association   (BICA)   1997
- 11a Harmon Rd, SUTTON COLDFIELD, W Midlands, BB72 1AH.   (hq)
  email bica@bica.co.uk   http://www.bica.co.uk
  Chmn: Bob Manca
- ▲ Company Limited by Guarantee
- ○ *S
- ● Comp - Inf
- M [not stated]

British Industrial Ceramic Manufacturers Association
merged in June 2002 with the Refractories Association of Great Britain to form **British Refractories & Industrial Ceramics**

British Industrial Furnace Construction Association   (BIFCA) 1946
- McLaren Building (6th floor), 35 Dale End, BIRMINGHAM, B4 7LN.   (hq)
  0121-200 2100   fax 0121-200 1306
  email enquiry@bifca.org.uk   http://www.bifca.org.uk
  Sec: David B Corns
- ▲ Company Limited by Guarantee
- ○ *T; to represent the interests of leading manufacturers of industrial furnaces & component suppliers
- ● Mtgs - Exhib - LG - Seminars - Tech course
- < METCOM; Eur C'ee Indl Furnace & Heating Eqpt Mfrs (CECOF)
- M 17 f

British Industrial Truck Association Ltd   (BITA)   1942
- 5-7 High St, Sunninghill, ASCOT, Berks, SL5 9NQ.   (hq)
  01344 623800   fax 01244 291197
  http://www.bita.org.uk
  Sec Gen: James Clark
- ○ *T; industrial fork lift trucks industry
- Gp Major mfrs; Smaller mfrs; Suppliers; Importers; Finance houses
- ● Conf - Mtgs - ET - Exhib - SG - Inf - LG
- M c 70 f
- ¶ LM & their products; free.   AR; ftm.
  Operators Safety Code for Powered Industrial Trucks.
  List of publications available.

British Industry Offset Group
a group of the **Defence Manufacturers Association**

British Infection Society   1974
- NR c/o Dr M Wiselka, Dept of Infection & Tropical Medicine, Leicester Royal Infirmary, Infirmary Square, LEICESTER, LE1 5WW.   (hsb)
  0116-258 6952   fax 0116-258 5067
  Hon Treas: Dr M Wiselka
- ▲ Registered Charity
- ○ *V, *P, *Q; to relieve sickness by the study of all aspects of infection; to promote the wide dissemination of relevant knowledge
- ● Conf - Mtgs - ET - Res
- < Fedn of Infection Socs
- M c 600 i, UK / 100 i, o'seas
- ¶ Jnl of Infection - 6.

British Infertility Counselling Association   (BICA)   1988
NR   69 Division St, SHEFFIELD, S Yorks, S1 4GE.   (mail/address)
       01744 750660
       email info@bica.net   http://www.bica.net
       Chmn: Mollie Graneek
▲   Registered Charity
○   *P, *W; to promote highest standards of counselling for those
       considering, or undergoing, fertility investigations & treatment
●   Conf - Mtgs - ET - SG - Inf - LG
M   c 170 i
¶   Jnl of Infertility Counselling - 3; ftm.

British Inline Skater Hockey Association   (BiSHA)   1984
NR   17 Queen's Rd, BRIXHAM, Devon, TQ5 8BG.   (hq)
       01803 850644
▲   Company Limited by Guarantee
Br   12; Denmark, France, Germany, Holland, Switzerland
○   *S; governing body for (roller) skater hockey in Britain (formerly
       known as street hockey)

British Institute of Agricultural Consultants   (BIAC)   1957
NR   The Estate Office, Torry Hill, Milstead, SITTINGBOURNE, Kent,
       ME9 0SP.   (hq)
       01795 830100   fax 01795 830243
       email info@biac.co.uk   http://www.biac.co.uk
       Chief Exec: C Anthony Hyde
Br   1
○   *F, *H, *P; independent qualified specialists in agriculture,
       horticulture, forestry & related sciences which have
       application in the countryside; members work in the UK &
       overseas
Gp   International; Expert opinion; Business management; Livestock;
       Engineering; Environment; Rural planning
●   Conf - Mtgs - ET - Exhib
<   Brit Consultants Bureau
M   c 300 i
¶   NL - 12;   LM - 1; both free.

British Institute for Allergy & Environmental Therapy   1987
■   Ffynnonwen, Llangwyryfon, ABERYSTWYTH, Ceredigion,
       SY23 4EY.   (hq)
       01974 241376   fax 01974 241795
       email allery@onetel.com   http://www.allergy.org.uk
       Dir: Donald M Harrison
▲   Un-incorporated Society
○   *M, *P; 'to offer courses in the diagnosis & treatment of food,
       chemical & environmental allergy for health professionals; to
       maintain a register of therapists working in this field & is
       concerned with the development of techniques & the
       dissemination of information to & from health professionals
       & the media'
●   SG - Inf
M   308 i, UK / 6 i, o'seas

British Institute of Architectural Technologists
       since 2005 **Chartered Institute of Architectural Technologists**

British Institute & Association of Electrolysis Ltd   1956
NR   40 Parkfield Rd, ICKENHAM, Middx, UB10 8LW.   (sb)
       0870 128 0477
       email sec@electrolysis.co.uk
       Sec: Nicky Wilsher
▲   Company Limited by Guarantee
○   *P
Gp   some members offer specialised treatment of broken veins,
       removal of warts, moles & skin tags
●   Conf - Mtgs - ET - Exam - Exhib - Comp - Inf
M   c 320 i
¶   The BIAE Probe - 6;   AR; both ftm only.
       LM - up-dated; free.
×   2004 (British Association of Electrolysists
       (Institute of Electrolysis

British Institute of Cleaning Science   (BICS)   1960
NR   9 Premier Court, Boarden Close, Moulton Park,
       NORTHAMPTON, NN3 6LF.   (hq)
       01604 678710
       Chief Exec: Keith Aldis
○   *P; training, education, qualification & certification for the
       cleaning industry
●   ET
M   i & f

British Institute of Embalmers   (BIE)   1927
■   21c Station Rd, Knowle, SOLIHULL, W Midlands, B93 0HL.
       (hq)
       01564 778991   fax 01564 770812
       email info@bioe.co.uk   http://www.bioe.co.uk
       Admin Sec: I Grainger
○   *P; to encourage & promote the practice of embalming
M   i
¶   The Embalmer - 4; ftm.

British Institute of Energy Economics   (BIEE)   1976
NR   37 Woodville Gardens, LONDON, W5 2LL.   (hq)
       020 8997 3707
       Sec: Peter Craig
▲   Registered Charity
○   *L, *P; the study & exchange of information about energy
       economics

British Institute of Facilities Management Ltd   (BIFM)   1993
NR   67 High St, SAFFRON WALDEN, Essex, CB10 1AA.   (hq)
       01799 508606
       Sec: Philip Margesson,   Chief Exec: Ian Fielder
▲   Company Limited by Guarantee
Br   10
○   *P; to promote & develop the science & understanding of
       facilities management (planning & designing office premises,
       buying office equipment & furniture); the institute provides a
       national qualification & continuing professional development
       (CPD) through presentations, meetings & visits
Gp   C'ees: Communications, Executive, Health & safety,
       Membership, Professional development, Research
       Special interest groups: Building services, Information
       management
●   Conf - Mtgs - ET - Exam - Res - Exhib - Inf - Lib - VE - LG
<   EURO FM
M   c 10,000 i, 375 fK / 117 i, o'seas
¶   FM World - 26; ftm only.

British Institute of Funeral Directors   (BIFD)   1981
■   Norwood, 41 Bridge St, TRANENT, E Lothian, EH33 1AH.   (sp)
       0131-554 1113   fax 0131-554 7662
       email enquiries@bifd.org.uk   http://www.bifd.org.uk
       Chief Exec: John M G Payne
▲   Un-incorporated Society
○   *P; a professional organisation for individual qualified funeral
       directors
●   Conf - Mtgs - ET - Exhib - LG - Diploma in funeral directing
<   Coun of Brit Funeral Services
M   1,657 i, UK / 10 i, o'seas
¶   Jnl - 4; ftm, £12.50 yr nm.
       LM - 1;   Membership Hbk - 1; both ftm only

British Institute of Graphologists   (BIG)   1983
■   PO Box 3060, GERRARDS CROSS, Bucks, SL9 9XP.   (admin/p)
       01753 891241   fax 01753 886412
       email laine.quigley@britishgraphology.org
       http://www.britishgraphology.org
       Chmn: John Beck,   Admin: Mrs Gill Beale
▲   Registered Charity
○   *P; to promote the use of graphology as a scientific tool in
       understanding the behavioural patterns & potential of people
Gp   Counselling; Recruitment; Team building
●   Conf - Mtgs - ET - Exam - Res - SG
M   109 i, UK / 30 i, o'seas
¶   The Graphologist - 4; ftm, £4 nm.

British Institute of Innkeeping (BII) 1981

NR   Wessex House, 80 Park St, CAMBERLEY, Surrey, GU15 3PT.
(hq)
01276 684449
Chief Exec: John McNamara
▲   Company Limited by Guarantee; Registered Charity
○   *P; the education & training of persons concerned with the day-
to-day running of premises having a Justice's full licence for
the sale of intoxicating liquor
●   Conf - Mtgs - ET - Exam - Res - Exhib - Comp - SG - LG
M   c 17,500 i
¶   biiBUSINESS - 10.   AR.

**British Institute of International & Comparative Law   (BIICL)
1958**

NR   Charles Clore House, 17 Russell Sq, LONDON, WC1B 5DR.
(hq)
020 7862 5151
Dir: Prof Gillian Triggs
▲   Registered Charity
○   *L, *Q; an established independent centre with unique focus on
linking academics & legal practitioners in the understanding
& development of international law including the law of
Human Rights, the Commonwealth & the European Union.
Our mission is to understand & influence the development of
law as this applies to an increasingly international
community.
This mission is fulfilled by serving as: a research organisation;
the publisher of academic volumes; a training & advice
centre
●   Conf - Mtgs - ET - Res - SG - Lib - LG
M   c 2,500 i. UK / 1,250 i, o'seas
¶   International & Comparative Law Quarterly - 4.
Bulletin of International Legal Developments - 26.
Academic volumes.

British Institute of Learning Disabilities   (BILD)   1972

NR   Campion House, Green St, KIDDERMINSTER, Worcs,
DY10 1JL.   (hq)
01562 723010   fax 01562 723029
email enquiries@bild.org.uk   http://www.bild.org.uk
Chief Exec: Keith Smith
▲   Registered Charity
○   *W; to contribute towards quality lifestyles for people with
learning disabilities
Gp   People with learning disabilities; People with profound &
multiple disabilities
●   Conf - ET - Res - Inf - Lib - Publishing
<   University of Birmingham
M   c 1,300 i, f & org
¶   British Jnl of Learning Disabilities - 4;
Learning Disability Bulletin - 4;
Journal of Applied Research in Intellectual Disabilities - 4;
Current Awareness Service - 12; all ftm.

British Institute of Musculoskeletal Medicine   (BIMM)   1992

NR   34 The Avenue, WATFORD, Herts, WD17 4AH.   (hsp)
01923 220999   fax 01923 249037
email info@bimm.org.uk   http://www.bimm.org.uk
Chief Exec: Deena Harris
▲   Registered Charity
○   *E, *M, *P; dissemination of knowledge & increase of expertise
in musculoskeletal medicine within the medical profession
●   Conf - Mtgs - ET - Res
<   Brit League against Rheumatism (BLAR); Intl Fedn Manual
Medicine (FIMM)
M   300 i, UK / 60 i, o'seas
¶   Jnl of Orthopaedic Medicine - 4; ftm.

British Institute of Non-Destructive Testing   (BInstNDT)   1954

NR   1 Spencer Parade, NORTHAMPTON, NN1 5AA.   (hq)
01604 630124
email info@bindt.org   http://www.bindt.org
Sec: Matthew E Gallagher
▲   Company Limited by Guarantee; Registered Charity
Br   12
○   *L; 'to promote the advancement of the science & practice of
non-destructive testing & all other associated materials
testing disciplines'
Gp   Aerospace; Research; Condition monitoring
●   Conf - Mtgs - ET - Exam - Exhib - Inf
<   Intl C'ee for NDT (ICNDT); Eur Fedn for Non-destructive
Testing EFNDT); Engg Coun (EC)
M   c 2,000 i
¶   Insight (non-destructive testing & condition monitoring) - 12.
News Link - 12.   NDT News - 12.   NDT Ybk.

British Institute of Occupational Hygienists
2002 merged with the **British Occupational Hygiene Society**

British Institute of Organ Studies   (BIOS)   1976

■   39 Church St, Haslingfield, CAMBRIDGE, CB3 7JE.   (hsp)
01223 872190   fax 01223 872190
http://www.bios.org.uk
Hon Sec: Mrs José Hopkins
▲   Registered Charity
○   *L; promotion of scholarly research into the history of organs
(particularly British organs); preservation & conservation of
historic organs; information sources & materials
Gp   Brit Organ Archive; National Pipe Organ Register; Historic
organs certificate scheme
●   Conf - Mtgs - Res - SG - VE - LG
M   671 i
¶   Jnl - 1;   Reporter - 4; both ftm.

British Institute of Persian Studies   (BIPS)   1961

NR   c/o The British Academy, 10 Carlton House Terrace, LONDON,
SW1Y 5AH.   (hq)
020 7969 5203
Hon Sec: Dr Vesta Sarkhosh Curtis
▲   Registered Charity
○   *L; promotion of Iranian studies incl language, history, art
history & archaeology
●   Conf - Mtgs - Res
M   i
¶   Iran (Jnl) - 1.
Occasional Monographs.

British Institute of Professional Dog Trainers   (BIPDT)   1974

■   Bowstone Gate, Disley, STOCKPORT, Cheshire, SK12 2AW.
(regd/off)
01663 762772   fax 01663 762772
http://www.bipdt.net & http://www.bipdt.org.uk
Co Sec: Tom Buckley
▲   Company Limited by Guarantee
○   *P; 'to compile a register of bona fide persons suitably qualified
as trainers of working dogs, courses & examinations'
Gp   Security
●   ET - Exam - Inf - Seminars
M   600 i, 20 f, 30 org, UK / 40 i, o'seas
¶   Training & Education Jnl - 3.

© CBD Research Ltd · Beckenham · BR3 5JS · Tel 020 8650 7745 · Fax 020 8650 0768 · E-mail cbd@cbdresearch.com · www.cbdresearch.com

British Institute of Professional Photography   (BIPP)   1901
■   Fox Talbot House, 2 Amwell End, WARE, Herts, SG12 9HN.
      (hq)
      01920 464011   fax 01920 487056
      email info@bipp.com   http://www.bipp.com
      Exec Officer: M Berry
▲   Company Limited by Guarantee
○   *P
Gp Advertising; Architectural; Audio Visual Association; Cine;
      Commercial/Industrial; Education; Medical; Photo-science;
      Portraiture; Theatre; Wedding
●   Conf - Mtgs - ET - Exam - Exhib - Comp - SG - Inf - LG
<   Wld Coun Profl Photographers; Fedn Eur Photographers; Profl
      Photographers of America; Brit Copyright Coun; BSI; Photo
      Imaging Coun
M   3,673 i, UK / 260 i, o'seas
¶   The Photographer - 12; ftm, £4,25 nm.   AR; ftm only.

British Institute of Radiology   (BIR)   1897
NR 36 Portland Place, LONDON, W1B 1AT.   (hq)
      020 7307 1400
      Gen Sec: Dr Tim Hogan
▲   Registered Charity
Br 4
○   *L; an independent forum to bring together all the professions
      in radiology; to share medical & scientific knowledge to
      detect & treat disease
Gp Scientific c'ees
●   Conf - Mtgs - ET - Exhib - Inf - Lib
<   Intl Soc of Radiology; Intl Soc for Radiation Protection; Eur Assn
      of Radiology; Rontgen Soc of N America
M   1,400 i, 50 f, UK / 250 i, o'seas
¶   British Jnl of Radiology - 12.   Imaging - 4.

British Institute of Securities Laws   (BISL)   1977
NR c/o Dr B A K Rider, Jesus College, CAMBRIDGE, CB5 8BL.
○   *L; to promote the study of securities regulation & company
      law; to facilitate research & establish a reference facility
●   Conf - Res - SG - Inf - Lib
M   i

British Institute of Traffic Education Research
      folded 2004

British Institute of Verbatim Reporters   (BIVR)   1887
■   73 Alicia Gardens, Kenton, HARROW, Middx, HA3 8JD.
      (regd/office)
      email sec@bivr.org   http://www.bivr.org.uk
      Sec: Mary Sorene
▲   Company Limited by Guarantee
○   *P; promotion of more efficient practice of the art of machine &
      pen shorthand in connection with legal & other proceedings
M   179 i
¶   NL - 3; free.

British Insurance Brokers' Association   (BIBA)   1977
■   BIBA House, 14 Bevis Marks, LONDON, EC3A 7NT.   (hq)
      0844 770 0266   fax 020 7626 9676
      email enquiries@biba.org.uk   http://www.biba.org.uk
      Chief Exec: Eric Galbraith
▲   Company Limited by Guarantee
○   *T; representing insurance brokers & independent
      intermediaries
●   Conf - Mtgs - ET - Inf - LG
M   2,100 f
¶   The Broker (Jnl) - 4;
      BIBA Membership Directory - 1; both ftm only.
×   2002 Association of Insurance Intermediaries &
      Brokers (merged)

British Insurance Law Association   (BILA)   1964
NR 17 Russell Square, LONDON, WC1B 5DR.   (hq)
      020 7862 5864
      Secretariat: Sue Rogers
▲   Un-incorporated Society
○   *P; to consider & discuss matters of general interest arising out
      of the law, (both statutory & common, including tax law &
      regulations & current revenue practice) in so far as it affects
      any branch of insurance
●   Conf - Mtgs - Res - SG
<   Assn Intle de Droit d'Assurance (AIDA)
M   c 200 i, 290 f
¶   Jnl - 3; ftm.

British Interactive Media Association   (BIMA)   1984
■   Briarlea House, Southend Rd, BILLERICAY, Essex, CM11 2PR.
      (hsp)
      01277 658107   fax 0870 051 7842
      email info@bima.co.uk   http://www.bima.co.uk
      Principal Admin: Janice Cable
○   *T; to promote the use of interactive media in commerce &
      industry
●   Conf - Mtgs - ET - Exhib - Comp - SG - Expt - Inf - LG - BIMA
      Awards
M   i & f
¶   E-Newsletter - 12; m only.

British Interior Design Association   (BIDA)   1966
NR 3/18 Chelsea Harbour Design Centre, Lots Rd, LONDON,
      SW10 0XE.   (hq)
      020 7349 0800   fax 020 7349 0500
      email enquiries@bida.org
      Sec: Karin Velzario
▲   Company Limited by Guarantee
○   *P, *T; to support the interior decorator/designer member & the
      corporate member
●   Mtgs - ET - Exhib - PL - VE
<   Intl Fedn of Interior Architects (IFI)
M   c 1,100 i & f
¶   Review - 4; ftm, £117.50 nm.
      Directory of Members & Associates - 1; ftm.
×   2002 (Interior Designers & Decorators Association Ltd
            (International Interior Design Association (UK chapter)

British Interior Textiles Association   (BITA)   1987
NR 5 Portland Place, LONDON, W1B 1PW.   (hq)
      020 7636 7788   fax 020 7636 7515
      email bita@dial.pipex.com
      http://www.interiortextiles.co.uk
      Sec: Adam Mansell
○   *T
●   Mtgs - Exhib - Comp - Stat - Expt - LG
<   Brit Apparel & Textile Confedn
M   f

British Interlingua Society   (BIS)   1955
NR 14 Ventnor Court, Wostenholm Rd, SHEFFIELD, S Yorks,
      S7 1LB.   (hsp)
      0114-258 2931
      Sec: B C Sexton
▲   Un-incorporated Society
○   *K; to inform as many people as possible, mainly in GB, of the
      existence & character of the international auxiliary language
      'Interlingua'; to promote & coordinate its use
●   Mtgs - ET - Comp - Inf - Publications - Agent for overseas
      books on Interlingua
<   U Mundial pro Interlingua
M   c 20 i
¶   Lingua e Vita - 3.   Contacto - 3.

British & International Federation of Festivals for Music, Dance & Speech   1921
- ■ Festivals House, 198 Park Lane, MACCLESFIELD, Cheshire, SK11 6UD.   (hq)
  0870 774 4290
  Chief Exec: Liz Whitehead
- ▲ Company Limited by Guarantee
- Br 327; Europe, Australia, Bermuda, Canada, Sri Lanka, Zambia, Zimbabwe
- ○ *G; headquarters of the amateur competitive festival movement
- ● Conf - Mtgs - ET - Comp - Inf
- M 600 i, 313 f, UK / 6 f, o'seas
- ¶ NL - 4; m only.   Ybk - 1.
- × 2002 British Federation of Festivals for Music, Dance & Speech

British International Freight Association   (BIFA)   1944
- ■ Redfern House, Browells Lane, FELTHAM, Middx, TW13 7EP.
  (hq)
  020 8844 2266   fax 020 8890 5546
  email bifa@bifa.org   http://www.bifa.org
  Dir Gen: Colin Beaumont
- ▲ Company Limited by Guarantee
- ○ *T; for the international transport sector
- Gp Freight forwarders; Logistics services supplies; Supply chain management; International traders; General sales agents; Transit shed operators; Export packers
- ● Conf - Mtgs - ET - Exhib - LG - Political lobbying - Promotion & advice
- < Intl Fedn of Freight Forwarders Assns (FIATA); Intl Air Transport Assn (IATA); Eur Org for Forwarding & Logistics (CLECAT)
- M 1,203 f
- ¶ Bifalink (NL) - 12; ftm.   AR - 1; both ftm.
  Freight Services Directory - 1; ftm, £95 nm.
  in 2004 the individual members of BIFA became the Freight Forwarding Forum of the **Chartered Institute of Logistics & Transport**

British & International Golf Greenkeepers' Association   (BIGGA)   1987
- NR BIGGA House, Aldwark, Alne, YORK, YO61 1UF.   (hq)
  01347 833800
  Chief Exec Dir: John Pemberton
- ▲ Un-incorporated Society
- ○ *P; to represent golf greenkeepers throughout the UK
- Gp Sales & marketing; Membership service; Education & training; Administration & Finance
- ● Conf - Mtgs - ET - Exam - Exhib - Comp - Stat - Lib - PL
- < Fedn of Eur Golf Greenkeepers Assns (FEGGA)
- M c 7,000 i
- ¶ Greenkeeper International - 12.   .

British International Studies Association   (BISA)   1975
- NR Dept of Politics & International Studies, University of Birmingham, BIRMINGHAM, B15 2TT.   (hsb)
  0121-414 2979   fax 0121-414 3496
  Sec: Dr Donna Lee
- ▲ Registered Charity
- ○ *P; to promote the study of international relations & related subjects through teaching, research & facilitating contact between scholars
- M c 900 i
- ¶ Review of International Studies.   NL.

British Internet Publishers Alliance   (BIPA)   1997
- ■ 49 Park Town, OXFORD, OX2 6SL.   (hsb)
  01865 310732
  http://www.bipa.co.uk
  Hon Sec: Angela Mills Wade
- ▲ Un-incorporated Society
- ○ *T
- ● Mtgs - ET - Res - Inf - LG
- < Digital Content Forum
- M 8 f, 2 org

British Interplanetary Society   (BIS)   1933
- NR 27-29 South Lambeth Rd, LONDON, SW8 1SZ.   (hq)
  020 7735 3160
  Exec Sec: Suszann Parry
- ○ *L; promotion of the science, engineering & technology of astronautics
- M i
- ¶ Jnl of BIS - 12.
  Spaceflight - 12.   Space Chronicle - 2.

British Investment Casting Trade Association
  2001 merged with British Foundry Association & British Metal Casting Association to become **Cast Metals Federation**

British Iris Society   (BIS)   1922
- NR 40 Willow Park, Otford, SEVENOAKS, Kent, TN14 5NF.   (hsp)
  01959 523017
  Hon Sec: Mrs H Towers
- ▲ Registered Charity
- Br 3
- ○ *H; irises & their cultivation; registration & trials for new cultivars
- Gp Remontant; Species; Siberian; Spuria & Japanese; Crocus
- ● Conf - Mtgs - Exhib - Comp - SG - Inf - Lib - PL (& slides)
- < R Horticl Soc; American / NZ / S African / Australian Iris Soc(s)
- M c 650 iUK / 247 i, o'seas
- ¶ The Iris Ybk - 1.   NL - 3.
  Various booklets on specific irises & their cultivation.

British & Irish Association of Law Librarians   (BIALL)   1969
- NR The Boots Library, Nottingham Trent University, Goldsmith St, NOTTINGHAM, NG1 5LS.   (hq)
  0115-848 2893
  Hon Sec: Angela Donaldson
- ▲ Un-incorporated Society
- ○ *P; to promote the better administration & exploitation of law libraries & legal information units; to encourage bibliographical study & research in law & librarianship, & cooperation with other organisations & societies
- Gp Marketing; Academic; Law libraries
- ● Conf - Mtgs - ET - Exhib - Inf
- < Amer Assn of Law Libs (AALL); Canadian Assn of Law Libs (CALL)
- M c 610 i, 160 instns
- ¶ Legal Information Management - 4.   NL - 4; ftm only.

British & Irish Association of Zoos & Aquariums   (BIAZA)   1966
- NR Regent's Park, LONDON, NW1 4RY.   (hq)
  020 7449 6351   fax 020 7449 6359
  http://www.biaza.org.uk
  Dir: Dr Miranda Stevenson,   Admin: Gwen Manning
- ▲ Registered Charity
- ○ *P, *V; to represent the zoo community in Britain & Ireland; to maintain the world's biodiversity, the welfare of animals in zoos & the advancement of scientific knowledge
- ● Conf - Mtgs - ET - Inf - LG
- < Wld Assn Zoos & Aquaria (WAZA); Wld Consvn U (IUCN); Eur Assn Zoos & Aquaria (EAZA)
- > Wld Assn of Zoos & Aquariums (WAZA); Eur Assn of Zoos & Aquaria (EAZA)
- M 66 i, 69 zoos
- ¶ Zoo Federation News - 3;   LM; both ftm only.
- × Federation of Zoological Gardens of Great Britain & Ireland

British & Irish Basketball Federation
  since 2004 **Great Britain Basketball**

© CBD Research Ltd · Beckenham · BR3 5JS · Tel 020 8650 7745 · Fax 020 8650 0768 · E-mail cbd@cbdresearch.com · www.cbdresearch.com

British & Irish Legal Education Technology Association (BILETA) 1986
NR c/o Dana Ciocan, UK Centre for Legal Education, University of Warwick, COVENTRY, Warks, CV4 7AL.   (hq)
  024 7652 3117   fax 024 7652 3290
  Secretariat: Dana Ciocan
○ *P; promoting technology in legal education & improving contacts between academics & practising professionals in UK & Ireland
● Conf - Mtgs - ET - SG
M i

British & Irish Ombudsman Association (BIOA) 1993
■ PO Box 308, TWICKENHAM, Middx, TW1 9BE.
  020 8894 9272
  email secretary@biao.org.uk   http://www.bioa.org.uk
  (hq)
  Sec: IAn Pattison
○ *P; the role of ombudsmen in both public & private sectors
● Conf - Mtgs - SG - Inf - LG
M 112 i, 45 org, UK / 11 i, 6 org, o'seas
¶ NL - 3/4;   Reports of Conferences - 2 yrly; both ftm only. Directory of Ombudsmen - up-dated; on Internet.

British & Irish Orthoptic Society (BIOS) 1937
■ Tavistock House North, Tavistock Sq, LONDON, WC1H 9HX.
  (hq)
  020 7387 7992   fax 020 7383 2584
  email bos@orthoptics.org.uk
  http://www.orthoptics.org.uk
  Hon Sec: Mrs June Carpenter
  Exec Officer: Mrs Denise Malone
▲ Company Limited by Guarantee; Registered Charity
Br 6
○ *M, *P, *U; to encourage, study & improve practice of orthoptics
Gp Glaucoma; Low vision; Special learning difficulties; Stroke & rehabilitation
● Conf - Mtgs - ET - Stat - Inf - Empl - LG
< Intl Orthoptic Assn (IOA); Orthoptistes de la Communauté Européenne (OCE)
M 1,450 i, UK / 72 i, o'seas
¶ British Orthoptic Jnl; ftm, £50 nm.
  Parallel Vision - 12; ftm only.
✕ 2004 (January) British Orthoptic Society

British & Irish Spa & Hot Tub Association
  is part of **Swimming Pool & Allied Trades Association**

British Isles Backgammon Association (BIBA) 1989
NR 2 Redbourne Drive, LINCOLN, LN2 2HG.   (hq)
  01522 888676   fax (telephone first)
  Dir: Michael Crane
▲ Un-incorporated Society
○ *S; to promote the game of backgammon
● Conf - Mtgs - ET - Comp - Stat - Inf
M 1,200 i, clubs
¶ Bibafax (NL) - 6; free.

British Isles Baton Twirling Association (BIBTA)
NR 208 Horninglow Rd, Firth Park, SHEFFIELD, S Yorks, S5 6SG.
  (hq)
  0114-220 4010
  Sec: D Lucas
▲ Registered Charity
○ *G
● Mtgs - ET - Exhib - Comp - Inf - VE
✕ 2002 British Isles Majorette Association

British Isles Bowls Council (BIBC) 1903
■ 23 Leysland Avenue, Countesthorpe, LEICESTER, LE8 5XX.
  (hsp)
  0116-277 3234
  email michaelswatland@btinternet.com
  http://www.britishislesbowls.com
  Hon Sec: Michael W G Swatland
▲ Un-incorporated Society
○ *S; the game of flat green bowls
● Comp - Organisation of British Isles championships; & the Senior & Junior International series
< World Bowls Ltd
> English / Scottish / Irish / Welsh / Jersey / Guernsey Bowling Assns
M 265,000 i

British Isles Indoor Bowls Council (BIIBC)
NR 16 Hendre Avenue, Ogmore Vale, BRIDGEND, Glam, CF32 7HD.   (hsp)
  01656 841361   fax 01656 849160
  email briandaviesbowls@btinternet.com
  http://www.biibc.org.uk
  Hon Sec & Treas: Brian Davies
▲ Un-incorporated Society
Br 5
○ *S; to promote the game of indoor bowls & to be responsible for the promotion of all British Isles run championships
● Mtgs - Comp - Inf
< Wld Indoor Bowls Coun
> English / Welsh / Scot / Guernsey Indoor Bowling Assn[s]; Assn of Irish Indoor Bowls; Brit Wheelchair Bowling Assn
M 13,781 i, 6 f, 435 org

British Isles Majorette Association
  since 2002 **British Isles Baton Twirling Association**

British-Israel Chamber of Commerce (B-ICC) 1950
NR 1 Belvedere Rd, LEEDS, W Yorks, LS17 8BU.   (hq)
  0113-393 0200
▲ Company Limited by Guarantee
○ *C; to provide bi-lateral trade & investment between Britain & Israel
M f

British Italian Society (BIS) 1941
■ c/o The Venice in Peril Fund, Hurlingham Studios (Unit 4), Ranelagh Gardens, LONDON, SW6 3PA.   (mail/address)
  020 7924 6883
  email info@british-italian.org
  http://www.british-italian.org
  Hon Dir: Mrs susan Kikoler,   Treas: Mrs Gillian Wettern
▲ Registered Charity
○ *X; to increase knowledge & understanding in the UK of Italian culture in terms of history, institutions, way of life, language & contribution to civilisation; to promote the traditional friendship between UK & Italy
● Mtgs - Exhib - Inf - VE - Archive
< Associazione Cultivale Italia-Inghilterra (Sardinia); St Peter's Italian Church (London)
M 445 i, 9 f, 1 org, UK / 17 i, 1 org, o'seas
¶ Rivista - 3/4; free.

British Jazz Society (BJS) 1964
■ 10 Southfield Gardens, TWICKENHAM, Middx, TW1 4SZ.   (hq)
  020 8891 3809   fax 020 8892 4283
  email jb@johnboddyagency.co.uk
  Hon Sec: John G Boddy
▲ Un-incorporated Society
○ *D
● Res - Inf - Festival consultation service
M c 800 i

British Jewellers' Association   (BJA)   1887
■   10 Vyse St, BIRMINGHAM, B18 6LT.   (hq)
      0121-237 1110   fax 0121-237 1113
      http://www.bja.org.uk
○   *T; representing manufacturing jewellers, silversmiths, fashion
      jewellers, & dealers in bullion, precious stones, & horology
<   Brit Jewellery, Giftware & Finishing Fedn
M   f

British Jewellery, Giftware & Finishing Federation Ltd   (BJGF)   1970
■   10 Vyse St, BIRMINGHAM, B18 6LT.   (hq)
      0121-236 2657   fax 0121-236 3921
      http://www.bjgf.org.uk
      CEO: Krys Zalewska
▲   Company Limited by Guarantee
○   *N, *T; to support 6 trade associations in the jewellery, giftware,
      leathergoods & metal finishing industries
Gp   Giftware; Jewellery; Surface engineering; Travel goods &
      accessories
●   Conf - Mtgs - Exhib - SG - Expt - Inf - Lib - LG available
<   Art Metalware Mfrs' Assn (AMMA); Brit Jewellers' Assn (BJA); Brit
      Travelgoods & Accessories Assn (BTAA); Giftware Assn (GA);
      JewelleryDistributors' Assn (JDA); Surface Engg Assn (SEA)
M   1,800 f, UK / 50 f, o'seas, 721 others
¶   Export News - 4.
×   2004 British Jewellery & Giftware Federation

British Jigsaw Puzzle Library   (BJPL)   1933
■   Clarendon, Parsonage Rd, HERNE BAY, Kent, CT6 5TA.   (hsp)
      01227 742222
      http://www.britishjigsawpuzzlelibrary.co.uk
      Owner: Dave Cooper
○   *G; lending library of wooden jigsaws operated on a postal
      basis to private individuals who join by subscription;
      (personal callers by appointment only)
●   Lib
M   c 350 i, UK / 10 i, o'seas

British Judo Association Ltd   (BJA)   1948
NR   Loughborough Technology Park (suite B), Epinal Way,
      LOUGHBOROUGH, Leics, LE11 3GE.   (hq)
      01509 631670   fax 01509 631680
▲   Company Limited by Guarantee
○   *S; the governing body to control, foster & develop the practice
      & spirit of judo
●   Conf - Mtgs - ET - Exam - Res - Comp - Stat - Inf
<   Intl Judo Fedn; Eur Judo U; Brit Olympic Assn; Sports Coun;
      Central Coun for Physical Recreation (CCPR)
M   30,000 i
¶   British Judo (club NL) - 6.   AR; both ftm only.
      List of Clubs per Area; on request.

British Junior Chamber
      in 2005 became Junior Chamber International & is no longer a
      British body

British Kerry Cattle Society
NR   Windle Hill Farm, Sutton on the Hill, ASHBOURNE, Derbys,
      DE6 5JH.   (hsp)
      01283 732377
      Hon Sec: Mrs Joan Lennard
▲   Registered Charity
○   *B
●   Inf
M   c 40 i
¶   NL - irreg.

British Kidney Patient Association   (BKPA)   1975
NR   Oakhanger Place, BORDON, Hants, GU35 9JZ.   (hq)
      01420 472021
      Pres: Mrs Elizabeth Ward
▲   Company Limited by Guarantee; Registered Charity
○   *W; benefit & welfare of kidney patients & their families; to
      lobby for more & improved facilities & increased government
      funding so that all patients may benefit from improvements
      in technology & pharmaceutical achievements
●   Inf
M   i
¶   Silver Lining Appeal Brochure - 1; free.

British Kite Surfing Association
NR   PO Box 7871, EAST LEAKE, Leics, LE12 6WL.
      01509 856500
      email info@kitesurfing.org   http://www.kitesurfing.org
      Sec: Mark Ward
○   *S

British Knitting & Clothing Export Council
      during 2003-04 adopted its promotional name as the official title
      UK Fashion Exports

British Kodály Academy   (BKA)   1981
■   13 Midmoor Rd, LONDON, SW19 4JD.   (h/treas/p)
      020 8971 2062   fax 020 8946 6528
      email BKAhelp@aol.com
      http://www.britishkodalyacademy.org
      Hon Treas: Celia Cviić,   Hon Sec: Judy Hildesley
▲   Registered Charity
○   *E; a music education charity, using the voice as the main
      instrument; to improve British music education through
      courses for anyone wanting to develop their own, or others,
      musical skills, using Kodály's principles
Gp   Courses: Certificate in early years music education; Certificate
      in primary education; Intermediate & advanced diplomas in
      Kodály's musicianship; Elementary & foundation courses,
      early years & SEN
●   Conf - ET - Exam - Res - Exhib - Inf - Lib
<   Intl Kodály Soc (IKS)
M   210 i
¶   NL - 3; ftm.
      How Can I Keep from Singing (songbook for ages 8-11);
      £11 m, £13.50 nm.

British Korfball Association   (BKA)   1946
■   PO Box 179, MAIDSTONE, Kent, ME14 1LU.   (hsp)
      0781 400 4135
      email bka@korfball.co.uk   http://www.korfball.co.uk
      12A Penwith Rd, Earlsfield, LONDON, SW18 4QF.
      Hon Gen Sec: Jackie Hoare
▲   Un-incorporated Society
○   *S; governing body of the sport of Korfball in the UK
Gp   Area associations; Competitions; Exams
●   Mtgs - ET - Exam - Comp
<   Intl Korfball Fedn (IKF)
M   1,900 i, 60 org
¶   Korfball - 3; ftm, £1.50 each nm.

British Kune Kune Pig Society   (BKKPS)   1993
NR   1 Hilliers Farm Cottages, Upper Wyke, ST MARY BOURNE,
      Hants, SP11 6EE.   (hsp)
      Sec: Hannah Smith
▲   Un-incorporated Society
○   *B
●   Mtgs - ET - Expt - Inf - PL
<   New Zealand Kune Kune Pig Soc
M   c 300 i

British Laboratory Animals Veterinary Association
      has changed name to Laboratory Animals Veterinary Association & is
      a group of the **British Veterinary Association**

British Lace Federation   (BLF)   1914
NR   c/o David Marshall, Lemans, 29 Arboretum St, NOTTINGHAM,
      NG1 4JA.   (asa)
      0115-978 7291
      Contact: David Marshall
○   *T; all aspects of lace manufacture
M   f

British Ladder Manufacturers Association   (BLMA)   1947
■   PO Box 183, LEEDS, W Yorks, LS11 1AG.   (hsb)
      0845 260 1048   fax 0845 260 1049
      Sec: Cameron Clow
○   *T; for manufacturers of access equipment in the UK
●   Conf - Mtgs - LG
M   37 f
¶   Leaning Ladder & Stepladder User Guide.

British Laminate Fabricators Association
NR   PO Box 8841, NOTTINGHAM, NG11 1AJ.
      0115-921 3889   fax 0115-921 3889
      http://www.blfa.co.uk
      Contact: Christopher D Thomas
○   *T

British Land Speedsail Association   (BLSA)   1989
NR   103 Mead Vale, Worle, WEST-SUPER-MARE, N Somerset,
      BS22 8XE.   (chmn/p)
      01934 511780
      Chmn: Chris Moore
○   *S; 'to promote speedsailing in the UK; to organise racing
      events, & offer insurance & training to people wishing to
      partake in the sport; a speedsail is a cross between a
      skateboard & a windsurf board'
Gp   Land sailing; Para karting; Sand yachting
●   Comp
<   Intl Fedn Sand & Land Yachts; Brit Fedn Sand & Land Yacht
      Clubs
M   20 i

British Landsailing
      the short title for the **British Federation of Sand & Land Yacht
      Clubs**

British Lawn Mower Racing Association   (BLMRA)   1973
■   Hunt Cottage, Wisborough Green, BILLINGSHURST, W Sussex,
      RH14 0HN.   (hsp)
      01403 700220   fax 01403 700037
      http://www.racemower.com
      Pres & Hon Sec: Jim Gavin
▲   Company Limited by Guarantee
○   *G; organisation of lawn mower races
●   Mtgs - ET - Comp - Inf - VE - Film shows
<   R Automobile Club
M   c 300 i, UK & o'seas
¶   Cuttings (NL) - 12; ftm.

British Leafy Salad Association
■   133 Eastgate, LOUTH, Lincs, LN11 9QG.   (asa)
      01507 602427   fax 01507 607165
      email crop.association@pvga.co.uk
      Sec: Mrs Jayne Dyas
○   *T; to provide technical, commercial & marketing information
      for growers of all lettuces
●   Conf - Mtgs - Res - Exhib - Stat - Inf - LG
M   120 f

British League against Rheumatism
      since May 2002 **Arthritis & Musculoskeletal Alliance**

British Learning Association   (BLA)   1990
■   Pixmore Centre (suite 12), Pixmore Ave, LETCHWORTH
      GARDEN CITY, Herts, SG6 1JG.   (hq)
      01462 485588   fax 01462 485633
      http://www.british-learning.com
      Gen Mgr: Brian Merison
▲   Company Limited by Guarantee; Registered Charity
○   *E; a dynamic community, within global reach, committed to
      innovation, best practice & excellence in innovative & well
      established techniques & technologies for learning
●   Conf - Mtgs - Res - Exhib - Inf - LG
M   314 i & org (a network of 600 i)
¶   Connect (Jnl) - 4;
      Learning Blitz (NL) [online] - 26; both ftm only.
×   2003 (British Association for Open Learning
            (Forum for Training & Technology

British Leavers Lace Manufacturers' Association
      in process of folding

British Lebanese Association
NR   1 Hyde Park Gate, LONDON, SW7 5EW.
      020 7370 2572
      Dir: Lenia Tannous
○   *X

British Legal Association   (BLA)   1964
■   Metropole Chambers, Salubrious Passage, SWANSEA, Glam,
      SA1 3RT.   (hq)
      01792 648096
      Contact: Liz McGlynn
○   *P; to look after the interests of solicitors in general
M   1,700 i

British Legion
      see **Royal British Legion**

British Lichen Society   (BLS)   1958
NR   c/o Botany Dept, Natural History Museum, Cromwell Rd,
      LONDON, SW7 5BD.   (hsb)
      020 7942 5250
      Sec: Dr S La Greca
▲   Registered Charity
○   *L; to promote the study of lichens
●   Mtgs - ET - Res - Exhib - Inf - Lib
M   c 600 i, 160 institutions
¶   The Lichenologist - 6.   Bulletin - 2.

British Limb Reconstruction Society
      a specialist society of the **British Orthopaedic Association**

British Limbless Ex-Service Men's Association (BLESMA) 1932

■ Frankland Moore House 185-187 High Rd, Chadwell Heath, ROMFORD, Essex, RM6 6NA. (hq)
020 8590 1124 fax 020 8599 2932
email headquarters@blesma.org
http://www.blesma.org
Gen Sec: J W Church
▲ Company Limited by Guarantee; Registered Charity
Br 36
○ *W; to promote the welfare of all those, of either sex, who have lost limb(s) or eye(s), or the use of limb(s) or sight, after or as a result of service in any branch of HM Forces (incl their needy dependents)
Gp Amputee counselling; Residential homes
● Conf - Mtgs - Res - Inf - VE - LG - Counselling service for amputees - Welfare visiting service - Residential homes - Grants
< Wld Veterans Fedn; Intl Soc of Prosthetics & Orthotics; Confedn of British Service & Ex-service Orgs; NCVO; RADAR
M 4,720 i, UK / 95 i, o'seas
¶ BLESMAG - 3; ftm, £1 each nm.
Out on a Limb [history of association] (1982); £2 m, £5 nm.
Making the Best of Amputation (2003); ftm, 20p + postage nm.
Driving after Amputation (1991); postage.
Amputees Guide; £1. AR; free.

British Lime Association (BLA) 1989

NR Gillingham House, 38-44 Gillingham St, LONDON, SW1V 1HU. (hq)
020 7963 8000
○ *T; interests of the producers of lime products: burnt lime (calcium/magnesium oxide) & hydrated lime
● Conf - Mtgs - ET - Exhib - Stat
M 6 f

British Limousin Cattle Society Ltd (BLCS) 1970

■ National Agricultural Centre, Stoneleigh Park, KENILWORTH, Warks, CV8 2RA. (hq)
024 7669 6500
Chief Exec: Iain Kerr
▲ Registered Charity
○ *B; pedigree beef cattle society
● Mtgs - Expt - VE
< Intl Limousin Coun; Eurolim; Nat Beef Assn
M 2,500 i, 10 f, 10 org
¶ News Magazine - 3. Studbook - 1. AR.
Herdbook - 1. Sire & Dam Summary - 1.

British Livestock Genetics Consortium Ltd

NR Narracombe, Ilsington, NEWTON ABBOT, Devon, TQ13 9RD.
01364 661506
Contact: Rob Wills
○ *T; the development & maintenance of profitable long-term business generated by exports of British livestock & genetics; to create a positive, favourable image in international markets & promote Britain as a supplier of high quality animals & germplasm

British Llama Society (BLS) 2006

■ Puckpitts Farm, Tredington, SHIPSTON-ON-STOUR, Warks, CV36 4NH
email secretary@britishllamasociety.org
Chmn: Paul Rose
○ *B

British Locksmiths Association 1991

NR 1 Trafalgar House, Thames Industrial Park, EAST TILBURY, Essex, RM18 8RH.
01375 488030
○ *P

British Long-Bow Society

The society has asked not to be listed in this directory:
'This Society is NOT concerned with modern Target archery.
Please contact the **Grand National Archery Society'**

British Long Distance Swimming Association (BLDSA) 1956

■ 16 Elmwood Rd, Barnton, NORTHWICH, Cheshire, CW8 4NB. (hsp)
01606 75298
email m6a6u9k8ice-fer1@tiscali.co.uk
http://www.bldsa.org.uk
Hon Sec: Maurice Ferguson
▲ Un-incorporated Society
○ *S; to further & promote the sport of open water, long distance (below 25km) & marathon (25km & above) swimming
● Mtgs - ET - Exam - Comp - Stat
M c 450 i, c 20 org
¶ Hbk - 1.

British Longevity Society

this Society is being re-structured & is at present inactive

British Lop Pig Society (BLPS) 1920

■ 9 Bluebell Close, BIGGLESWADE, Beds, SG18 8SL. (hsp)
01767 315926 fax 01767 315926
Hon Secs: Guy & Melany Kiddy
▲ Un-incorporated Society
○ *B
● Mtgs
< Rare Breeds Survival Trust
M c 40 i
¶ Herd Book - 1; £3.

British Lubricants Federation Ltd
since 1 January 2005 **United Kingdom Lubricants Association Ltd**

British Luggage & Leathergoods Association
see **British Travelgoods & Accessories Association**

British Lymphology Society (BLS) 1985

NR PO Box 196, SHOREHAM, Kent, TN13 9BF. (hq)
01959 525524
Admin: Tracy Hirst-Marsden
▲ Registered Charity
○ *P; for health care professionals & other interested parties involved in the management of lymphoedema; to raise awareness of oedema amongst all health professionals
● Conf - Mtgs - ET - Res
< Lymphoedema Support Network; Leg Ulcer Forum; MLD UK
M 500 i, 8 corporate
¶ NL - 3. Constitution. Business Plan.
✕ British Lymphology Interest Group

British Machine Vision Association & Society for Pattern Recognition (BMVA) 1990

■ c/o Dr Andrew Fitzgibbon, Microsoft Research Ltd, 7 J J Thomson Avenue, CAMBRIDGE, CB3 0FB. (hsb)
01223 479899
http://www.bmva.ac.uk
Hon Sec: Dr Andrew Fitzgibbon
▲ Company Limited by Guarantee; Registered Charity
Br 3
○ *L; to promote knowledge & application of machine vision & pattern recognition
Gp Computer vision, image analysis; Machine vision education & training
● Conf - Mtgs - ET - Res - Exhib - SG - Stat - Inf - PL - VE - LG
< Intl Assn for Pattern Recognition (IAPR); Mammographic Image Analysis Soc
M c 400 i, UK / c 50 i, o'seas
¶ BMVA News - 4; free.
Proceedings of the British Machine Vision Conference - 1; free to delegates, £25 (sales).

British Magical Society (BMS) 1905
NR 20 Nortune Close, Kings Norton, BIRMINGHAM, B38 8AJ.
    (hsp)
    0121-451 3944
    Hon Sec: Paul Cadley
▲ Un-incorporated Society
○ *G, *P; the furtherance of the art of magic
Gp Junior section (ages 10-16)
● Mtgs - Comp - Lib
M 107 i, UK / 4 i, o'seas
¶ BMS News - 6; ftm only.

British Malaysian Society (BMS) 1983
NR Asia House, 63 New Cavendish St, LONDON, W1G 7LP.
    (asa)
    020 7307 5454
▲ Un-incorporated Society
○ *X; bi-lateral friendship society
● Conf - Mtgs - ET - Expt - Inf (all in relation to Malaysia)
< The Malaysian - British Society
M c 50 i, 150 f

British Malignant Hyperthermia Association (BMHA) 1983
    Sec: Mrs Alison Winks
▲ Registered Charity
    To raise funds for research into the inherited & potentially fatal
    condition of malignant hyperthermia (progressive raising of
    body temperature during general anaesthesia); to link
    affected people; to inform medical people of the problem

British Manual Lymph Drainage Association (BMLDA) 2000
NR PO Box 309, SUTTON, Surrey, SM1 9DE. (hsp)
    020 8133 5686
    Contact: Nina Pearson
▲ Company Limited by Guarantee
Br Regional
○ *M, *P; to advance education & knowledge & develop the
    standards of practice of therapists in the treatment of manual
    lymph drainage; membership is open to those who have
    qualified
● Conf - Mtgs - ET - Exam - Res - Exhib - Inf
< Inst of Complementary Medicine; Brit Lymphology Soc
M c 50 i & f
¶ Networks (NL) - 6; ftm only.

British Marine Aggregate Producers' Association (BMAPA) 1993
NR Gillingham House, 38-44 Gillingham St, LONDON,
    SW1V 1HU. (hq)
    020 7963 8000
○ *T; interests of the producers of marine aggregates (those
    dredged from the sea bed)
< Quarry Products Association
M f

British Marine Electronics Association
    a group of the **British Marine Federation**

British Marine Equipment Association (BMEA) 1966
■ 30 Great Guildford St (4th floor), LONDON, SE1 0HS. (hq)
    020 7928 9199   fax 020 7928 6599
    email bmea@maritimeindustries.org
    http://www.maritimeindustries.org
    Dir: John S Southerden
▲ Company Limited by Guarantee
○ *T; 'representing the interests of suppliers of marine equipment
    & associated services for every type of merchant vessel, from
    low tonnage work-boats through every class of cargo-
    carrying ship, including container carriers & tankers,
    specialist ships, passenger-car ferries, Ro-Ro's, up to the
    largest cruise liners'
● Conf - Mtgs - Exhib - Expt - Inf - LG - Trade missions
> Soc of Maritime Inds
M 200 f
¶ Directory 2005-2006 - 1.

British Marine Equipment Council
    since 2001 **Society of Maritime Industries**

British Marine Federation (BMF) 1913
NR Marine House, Thorpe Lea Rd, EGHAM, Surrey, TW20 8BF.
    (hq)
    01784 473377
    Chief Exec: John Clarke
▲ Company Limited by Guarantee
○ *T; for the leisure marine industry
Gp Regional marine industries associations:
    Anglian, Southern, Kent & Sussex, Scottish; North Wales;
    Midland Boating Industries Association; Wessex Marine
    Business Association; Boating Industry South West; Thames
    Boating Trades Association; South Wales Boating Industry
    Association
    Group associations:
    Association of Canoe Trades (ACT); Association of Pleasure
    Craft Operators (APCO); BMF Sailmakers Association; Boat
    Retailers & Brokers Association (BRBA); British Commercial
    Boatbuilders Association (BCBA); British Hire Cruiser
    Federation (BHCF); British Marine Electronics
    Association (BMEA); British Sailing; British Small Boatbuilders
    Association (BSBA); Broads Hire Boat Federation (BHBF);
    Canal Boatbuilders Association (CBA); Insurance Financial &
    Legal Services Association (ILFSA); Leisure Boat Builders
    Association (LBBA); Marine Engine & Equipment
    Manufacturers Association (MEEMA); Marine Leisure
    Associaton (MLA); Marine Trades Association (MTA);
    Superyacht UK; Thames Hire Cruiser Association (THCA);
    Yacht Harbour Association (TYHA)
● Conf - Mtgs - ET - Res - Exhib - Stat - Expt - Inf - Lib - PL - Empl
    - LG
M c 1,500 f
¶ BM News - 12; ftm only.
    Membership Hbk & Classified Buyers' Guide - 1; ftm.
    Industry Statistics - 1; ftm.
    Publications list available.
✕ January 2002 British Marine Industries Federation

British Marine Federation Scotland 1920
NR Westgate, Toward, DUNOON, Argyllshire, PA23 7UA. (hsp)
    01369 870251   fax 01369 870251
    Sec: Michael B Balmforth
▲ Un-incorporated Society
○ *T; to service & further the interests of the marine leisure &
    small commercial boating industry in Scotland
● Conf - Mtgs - ET - Expt - Inf - VE
< Intl Congress of Marine Inds Assns (ICOMIA); Brit Marine
    Fedn (BMF)
M c 60 f
    Note: is a branch of the British Marine Federation
✕ 2002-03 British Marine Industries Association Scotland

British Marine Finfish Association   (BMFA)   1987
NR   15 Shielhill Park, STANLEY, Perthshire, PH1 4QT.   (hsp)
    01738 8281706
    Sec/Admin: Richard Slaski
▲   Company Limited by Guarantee
○   *T; to investigate marketing & technical issues concerning the
    farming of Atlantic halibut in Britain; to provide
    representation for farmers of other marine fish eg cod, turbot
    & lemon sole
Gp   Hatchery operators; Ongrowers; Feed companies
●   Conf - Res - LG
M   22 f
¶   Jnl - 4; ftm only.

British Marine Industries Association Scotland
    since 2002-03 **British Marine Federation Scotland**

British Marine Life Study Society   (BMLSS)   1990
■   Glaucus House, 14 Corbyn Crescent, SHOREHAM-BY-SEA,
    W Sussex, BN43 6PQ.   (hsb)
    01273 465433
    email glaucus@hotmail.com   http://www.glaucus.org.uk
    Chief Exec: Andy Horton
▲   Un-incorporated Society
○   *G, *L; the study of the wildlife & ecology of the marine
    environment of the British Isles; for the layman, amateur &
    professional naturalist
Gp   Aquariology (aquaria); Scuba diving; Rockpooling (seashore
    study); Marine biology; Biological recording
●   Exhib - SG - Inf - Lib - PL
<   Inst of Biology; Nat Fedn of Biological Recording
M   349 i
¶   Glaucus (Jnl) - irreg; m only.
    Shorewatch (NL) - irreg.
    Torpedo (electronic NL) - 12.

British Maritime Law Association   (BMLA)   1908
■   Beaufort House, 15 St Botolph St, LONDON, EC3A 7EE.   (asa)
    020 7247 6555   fax 020 7247 5091
    email adt@richardsbutler.com   http://www.bmla.org.uk
    Sec & Treas: Andrew Taylor
▲   Un-incorporated Society
○   *P; to coordinate the contributions of members, who operate
    within the shipping & support industries, to national &
    international shipping related legislation
●   Conf - Mtgs - ET - Res - SG - Inf - Lib - LG
<   Comité Maritime Intl (CMI)
M   260 i, 52 f
¶   AR & Accounts; ftm.

British Market Research Association
    2006 incorporated into the **Market Research Society**

British Masonry Society   (BMS)   1986
■   Shermanbury, Church Rd, WHYTELEAFE, Surrey, CR3 0AR.
    (hsp)
    020 8660 3633   fax 020 8668 6983
    Hon Sec: Dr K Fisher
▲   Registered Charity
○   *L; the science & technology of masonry materials, their
    interaction & the finished structure; covers all forms of
    masonry, mortar & ancillary components
●   Conf - Mtgs - ET
M   200 i, 23 f, UK / 100 i, 1 f, o'seas
¶   Masonry International (Jnl) - 3; £53 m, £64 nm.
    Proceedings - irreg.   AR; free.

British Matchbox, Label & Booklet Society   (BML&BS)   1945
■   122 High St, MELBOURN, Cambs, SG8 6AL.   (hsp)
    01763 260399
    email secretary@phillumeny.com
    http://www.phillumeny.com
    Hon Sec: Arthur Alderton
▲   Un-incorporated Society
○   *G; for collectors of match-boxes, labels, bookmatch covers,
    containers, strikers & associated ephemera
●   Mtgs - Res - Exhib - Inf - Lib
M   480 i, UK / 110 i, o'seas
¶   Match Label News (Jnl) - 6; ftm, £3.50 nm.

British Materials Handling Federation   (BMHF)   1964
■   McLaren Building (6th floor), 35 Dale End, BIRMINGHAM,
    B4 7LN.   (hq)
    0121-200 2100   fax 0121-200 1306
    email enquiry@bmhf.org.uk   http://www.bmhf.org.uk
    Sec: David B Corns
▲   Company Limited by Guarantee
○   *N; 'constitutes the British national c'ee of FEM & is the UK's
    voice in Europe on materials handling matters'
●   Mtgs - Exhib - Stat - Inf - LG - Intl Handling & Storage
    Exhibition (3 yrly)
<   Fédération Européenne de la Manutention
M   5 associations:
    Association of Loading & Elevating Equipment Manufacturers
    Automated Material Handling Systems Association
    British Industrial Truck Association
    International Powered Access Federation
    Storage Equipment Manufacturers' Association
¶   Ybk & Dir - 1; ftm.

British Measurement & Testing Association   (BMTA)   1990
■   East Malling Enterprise Centre, New Rd, EAST MALLING, Kent,
    ME19 6BJ.   (hq)
    0845 644 4603   fax 01732 897453
    email enquiries@bmta.co.uk   http://www.bmta.co.uk
    Sec: Peter Russell
▲   Company Limited by Guarantee
○   *T; interests of the measurement & testing laboratory
    community to government, UK Accreditation Service, BSI &
    other official bodies & UK laboratories in Europe through
    EUROLAB
Gp   Accredited laboratories
●   Conf - Mtgs - Exhib - Inf - LG
<   EUROLAS
M   5 i, 75 f
¶   Electronic NL - 4; free.

British Meat Federation
    2003 merged with the British Meat Manufacturers' Association to
    form the **British Meat Processors Association**

British Meat Manufacturers' Association
    2003 merged with the British Meat Federation to form the **British
    Meat Processors Association**

British Meat Processors Association   (BMPA)   2003
NR   12 Cock Lane, LONDON, EC1A 9BU.   (hq)
    020 7329 0776   fax 020 7329 0653
    email info@bmpa.uk.com   http://www.bmpa.uk.com
    Dir: Maurice McCartney
▲   Company Limited by Guarantee
○   *T; slaughtering, processing, manufacturing, wholesale
    distribution & packaging sectors of the meat industry
●   Conf - Mtgs - Inf - LG
M   f
×   2003 (British Meat Federation
    (British Meat Manufacturers' Association

British Medical Acupuncture Society (BMAS) 1980
■ BMAS House, 3 Winnington Court, NORTHWICH, Cheshire, CW8 1AQ. (hq)
01606 786782 fax 01606 786783
email admin@medical-acupuncture.org.uk
http://www.medical-acupuncture.org.uk
Gen Mgr: Jane Llewellyn
▲ Registered Charity
Br London: 020 7713 9437
○ *L; training for doctors, dentists, vets & registered health professionals in medical acupuncture
● Conf - Mtgs - ET - Exam - Res - SG - LG
< Intl Coun of Med Acupuncture & Related Techniques (ICMART)
> Acupuncture Assn of Chart Physiotherapists (AACP); Brit Academy of Wstn Acupuncture (BAWA)
M 2,100 i, UK / 120 i, o'seas
¶ Acupuncture in Medicine - 4; ftm, £11 each nm.

British Medical Association (BMA) 1832
■ BMA House, Tavistock Square, LONDON, WC1H 9JP. (hq)
020 7387 4499
http://www.bma.org.uk
Chief Exec/Sec: Tony Bourne
▲ Company Limited by Guarantee
Br Offices in the 3 national capitals, a regional network
○ *E, *P, *U; to promote the medical & allied sciences, to maintain the honour & interests of the medical profession; to promote the achievement of high quality health care
Gp C'ees on: Equal opportunities, Medical ethics, Medical education, Science, International affairs
Practice c'ees: Central consultants & specialists, General practitioners, Junior doctors, Medical academic staff, Medical students, Public health medicine & community health, Staff & associate specialists
● Conf - Mtgs - ET - Res - Stat - Inf - Lib - Empl - LG
M 115,512 i, 19.053 students, UK / 3.060 i, o'seas
¶ British Medical Jnl. Specialist Jnls. AR.
Branch of Practice Committees ARs.
Various other reports on health & health policy.

British Medical Laser Association (BMLA) 1983
■ Photobiology Unit, University of Dundee, Ninewells Hospital & Medical School, DUNDEE, DD1 9SY. (hq)
01382 636722 fax 01382 646047
email h.moseley@dundee.ac.uk
http://www.bmla.co.uk
Pres: Dr Harry Moseley
▲ Registered Charity
○ *L, *M, *P; medical uses of lasers & associated technology
● Conf - Mtgs - ET - LG
< Eur Laser Assn
M 100 i, UK / 20 i, o'seas
¶ Lasers in Medical Science (Jnl) - 4; ftm.

British Medical Ultrasound Society (BMUS) 1984
NR 36 Portland Place, LONDON, W1B 1LS. (hq)
020 7636 3714 fax 020 7323 2175
email secretariat@bmus.org http://www.bmus.org
Gen Sec: Mrs Ann Tailor
▲ Company Limited by Guarantee
○ *L; the advancement of the science & technology of ultrasonics as applied in medicine; the maintenance of the highest standards
● Conf - Mtgs - ET - Exhib - Comp - SG - Lib
< Eur Fedn Socs for Ultrasound in Medicine & Biology
M c 2,500 i
¶ Jnl of Ultrasound - 4.

British Menopause Society (BMS) 1989
NR 4-6 Eton Place, MARLOW, Bucks, SL7 2QA. (hq)
01628 890199
▲ Company Limited by Guarantee; Registered Charity
○ *L; the advancement of knowledge, interest & study of all matters connected with the menopause; to promote high standards of training for those involved in advising women
● Conf - Mtgs - ET - Res
< Intl Menopause Soc; Eur Menopause & Andropose Soc
M 1,500 i
¶ Jnl - 4.

British Menswear Guild Ltd (BMG) 1959
○ leathergoods & umbrellas; to promote & increase export worldwide

British Metal Casting Association
2001 merged with British Foundry Association & British Investment Casting Trade Association to become **Cast Metals Federation**

British Metallurgical Plant Constructors' Association (BMPCA) 1963
■ UK Steel / EEF, Broadway House, Tothill St, London, SW1H 9NQ. (hq)
07785 255218 fax 020 7222 3531
email enquiries@bmpca.org.uk
Dir: R W Welburn
○ *T; the design & manufacture of systems, plant & equipment for the metals industry worldwide
● Mtgs - Exhib - Stat - Expt - Inf - VE - LG
< EEF; UK Steel
M 30 f
¶ List of Member Companies & Product Range; free.

British Metals Federation
2001 merged with the British Secondary Metals Association to form the **British Metals Recycling Association**

British Metals Recycling Association (BMRA) 1919
■ 16 High St, Brampton, HUNTINGDON, Cambs, PE28 4TU. (hq)
01480 455249 fax 01480 453680
email admin@recyclemetals.org
http://www.recyclemetals.org
Dir Gen: Lindsay Millington
▲ Company Limited by Guarantee
○ *T; to represent metal recyclers
Gp Exporters; Shredders division
● Conf - Mtgs - ET - Exhib - SG - Stat - Expt - Inf - LG
< Bureau Intl de la Récupération (BIR); Eur Ferrous Recovery & Recycling Fedn (EFR); Freight Transport Assn (FTA); CBI
M 350 f, UK / 30 f, o'seas
¶ Recycling Health & Safety Manual - 4; ftm only.
✕ 2001 (British Metals Federation (British Secondary Metals Association

British Mexican Society (BMS) 1942
NR Cameo House, 11 Bear St, Leicester Square, LONDON, WC2H 7AS.
0870 922 0679
▲ Registered Charity
○ *X
M i & f

British Microcirculation Society   (BMS)   1963
NR   Microvascular Research Laboratory, Dept of Physiology,
     Preclinical Veterinary School, University of Bristol,
     Southwell St, BRISTOL, BS2 8EJ.   (hsb)
     0117-928 9818
     Hon Sec: Dr David Bates
▲   Registered Charity
○   *L; study of microvascular structure, function & disease &
     related vascular phenomena
●   Conf - Mtgs
M   c 250 i

British Microlight Aircraft Association   (BMAA)   1979
■   Bull Ring, Deddington, BANBURY, Oxon, OX15 0TT.   (hq)
     01869 338888   fax 01869 337116
     email general@bmaa.org   http://www.bmaa.org
▲   Company Limited by Guarantee
Br   100; France, Gambia, Portugal, Spain
○   *S; to foster & safeguard the interests of microlight flying in the
     UK
Gp   Flying schools (training of students up to PPL(A) microlights
     standard)
●   ET - Exam - Exhib - Comp - Inf
<   Fédn Aéronautique Intle; R Aero Club of GB
M   4,300 i, 100 clubs & schools
¶   Microlight Flying - 6; ftm only.

British Milksheep Society   1983
■   St Kenelms, Broad Lane, Tanworth in Arden, SOLIHULL,
     W Midlands, B94 5HX.   (sp)
     01564 742398
     Sec: W J Hopkins
▲   Un-incorporated Society
Br   France, Hungary
○   *B; registration, promotion & export of British milksheep
●   Mtgs - Exhib - Expt
<   Nat Sheep Assn
M   26 i, 4 f, UK / 1 i, 2 f, o'seas

British Miniature Horse Society   (BMHS)   1992
NR   Zeals House, Lower Zeals, WARMINSTER, Wilts, BA12 6LG.
     (hsb)
     01747 861619
     email mail@bmhs.co.uk
     Chmn: Wendy Edgar
○   *B
●   Comp
<   Brit Central Prefix Registry; Brit Horse Soc
M   400 i, UK / 200 i, o'seas

British Model Flying Association   (BMFA)   1922
■   Chacksfield House, 31 St Andrews Rd, LEICESTER, LE2 8RE.
     (hq)
     0116-244 0028   fax 0116-244 0645
     email admin@bmfa.org   http://www.bmfa.org
     Chief Exec: David Phipps
▲   Company Limited by Guarantee
○   *G, *S; the promotion, protection, organisation &
     encouragement of model aircraft building, flying &
     development in all its aspects in the UK
Gp   Control line; Free flight; Gas turbines; Indoor; Model rocketry;
     Radio control power (fixed wing & rotary wing); Radio control
     silent flight (thermal, slope soaring, electric)
●   Conf - Mtgs - ET - Exam - Res - Exhib - Comp - Stat - Inf - VE -
     LG
<   Fédn Aéronautique Intle (FAI); R Aero Club (RAC); Cent Coun of
     Physical Recreation (CCPR)
M   37,000 i, 740 clubs
¶   BMFA News - 6; ftm, £1.50 nm.   AR - 1; ftm only.
     Members Hbk - 3 yrly; ftm, £3 nm.
     Note: BMFA is the trading name of the Society of Model
     Aeronautical Engineers Ltd

British Model Soldier Society   (BMSS)   1935
■   12 Savay Lane, Denham Green, DENHAM, Bucks, UB9 5NH.
     (hsp)
     01895 832757   fax 01895 832757
     Hon Sec: Julie Newman
▲   Un-incorporated Society
Br   22
○   *E, *G, *Q; to promote research & scholarship in all aspects of
     military history, weaponry, uniforms etc, through the media of
     military models & the portraying of historical events
Gp   American civil war; Artillery; Military bands; Britain's figures;
     Conversions; Indian army; Military aircraft; Military vehicles;
     Yeomanry
●   Mtgs - ET - Res - Exhib - Comp - SG - Inf
M   425 i, UK / 50 i, o'seas
¶   Bulletin - 4;   Bulletin Extra - 4;   Hbk - irreg; all ftm only.

British Morgan Horse Society   (BMHS)   1975
■   Boundary Farm, Nethercote, RUGBY, Warks, CV27 8AS.   (hq)
     01788 890111   fax 01788 890111
     email admin@morganhorse.org.uk
     http://www.morganhorse.org.uk
     Exec Officer: Dawn Sharif
○   *B; to promote the Morgan horse in Britain
●   Conf - Exhib - Comp - Inf
<   Amer Morgan Horse Assn (AMHA)
M   85 i (adult), 33 i (youth)
¶   NL - 6.
     European Morgan Horse Magazine - 1.

British Moroccan Society   (BMS)   1976
■   35 Westminster Bridge Rd, LONDON, SE1 7JB.   (v-chmn/b)
     0778 237 3937   fax 020 7401 6883
     http://www.bmsociety.com
     Hon Sec: Lady Slynn of Hadley
▲   Un-incorporated Society
○   *X; to foster links between the Kingdoms of Great Britain &
     Morocco through commercial, cultural & social contacts; to
     promote events to raise money for Moroccan charitable
     institutions
●   Mtgs - VE - Social events - Dinner (November) to raise money
     for the most needy in Morocco
M   400 i, UK / 2 i, o'seas
¶   NL - 8; free.

British Motor Cycle Racing Club Ltd   (BEMSEE)   1909
NR   Lydden Circuit, Wootton, CANTERBURY, Kent, CT4 6RX.   (hq)
     01304 831714   fax 01304 831715
     Chief Exec: David Stewart
▲   Company Limited by Guarantee; Registered Charity
○   *S; organising motor cycle racing
●   Comp
<   Auto-Cycle U; Assn of Motor Racing Circuit Owners (AMRCO);
     Motorcycle Racing Org (MRO)
M   3,000 i

British Motor Racing Marshals Club
since 2002 **British Motorsport Marshals Club**

British Motorcyclists' Federation   (BMF)   1960
■   Jack Wiley House, 25 Warren Park Way, Enderby, LEICESTER, LE19 4SA.   (hq)
    0116-284 5380
    Press & PR Mgr: Jeff Stone
    Chief Exec Officer: Simon Wilkinson-Blake
▲   Company Limited by Guarantee
○   *K, *S; to pursue, protect & promote the interests of motorcyclists
●   Mtgs - ET - Res - Exhib - SG - Stat - Inf - VE - LG - Attendance at exhibitions & rallies - Legal & insurance advice - European lobbying - Preservation of green lanes
<   Eur Motorcyclists U (EMU); CCPR; RAC; Motorcycle Inds Assn (MCIA); Nat Motorcycle Coun (NMC); Fedn Eur Motorcyclists (FEM)
M   25,000 i, 115,000 i (affiliates), 100 f, 330 clubs, UK / 40 i, o'seas
¶   Motorcycle Rider - 6.

British Motorsport Marshals Club   (BMMC)   1957
■   58 Alfred Rd, BUCKHURST HILL, Essex, IG9 6DP.   (hsp)
    020 8502 9304
    email info@bmmc.org.uk   http://www.marshals.co.uk
    Hon Sec: Chris N Stoddart
▲   Company Limited by Guarantee
Br 7
○   *S; to bring together, train & organise marshals for all types of motor sport events
●   Mtgs - ET - Exhib - Comp
<   RAC Motor Sport Assn (RACMSA)
>   Brit Rally Marshals Club
M   1,500 i
¶   Trackside - 4; ftm, £2 nm.
×   2002 British Motor Racing Marshals Club

British Mountaineering Council   (BMC)   1944
NR 177-179 Burton Rd, MANCHESTER, M20 2BB.   (hq)
    0870 010 4878
    email office@thebmc.co.uk
    Chief Exec: Dave Turnbull
▲   Company Limited by Guarantee
○   *S; to help, protect & promote the interests of British climbers, hill walkers & mountaineers
M   i & clubs

British Mule Society   (BMS)   1978
■   2 Boscombe Rd, SWINDON, Wilts, SN25 3EY.   (hsp)
    01793 615478
    email anndyer57@aol.com
    http://www.britishmulesociety.org.uk
    Hon Sec: Mrs Ann Hunter
▲   Company Limited by Guarantee; Registered Charity
○   *B; to encourage the breeding of good quality mules
●   Conf - Mtgs - ET - Res - Exhib - Comp - Stat - Inf - Lib - VE
<   Brit Driving Soc; Amer Donkey & Mule Soc
M   150 i, 2 org, UK / 19 i, 5 org, o'seas
¶   The Mule - 4; ftm only.

British Museum Friends   (BMS)   1968
NR c/o The British Museum, Great Russell St, LONDON, WC1B 3BR.   (hq)
    020 7323 8605; 8195   fax 020 7323 8985
    email friends@thebritishmuseum.ac.uk
    Chmn: Prof Barry Cunliffe
    Head of Friends: Carolyn Young
▲   Registered Charity
Br Canada, USA
○   *G; to support the British Museum
●   Mtgs - ET - Res - Exhib - Inf - VE
M   c 12,000 i
¶   British Museum Magazine - 3.

British Music Hall Society   (BMHS)   1963
■   Meander, 361 Watford Rd, Chiswell Green, ST ALBANS, AL2 3DB.   (hsb)
    01727 768878
    http://www.music-hall-society.com
    Hon Sec: Mrs Daphne Masterton
○   *D; to preserve the history of music hall & variety; to recall the artistes who were part of the scene; to support the entertainers of the present
●   Conf - Mtgs - Res - Exhib - SG - Inf - VE - 5 shows a year at the Concert Artistes Association, 20 Bedford St, London, WC2E 9HP
M   900 i, UK / 50 i, o'seas
¶   The Call Boy - 4; ftm, £3 each nm.

British Music Rights   1996
NR British Music House, 26 Berners St, LONDON, W1T 3LR.   (hq)
    020 7306 4446   fax 020 7306 4449
    email britishmusic@bmr.org   http://www.bmr.org
    Dir Gen: Frances Lowe
○   *N, *P, *T; an umbrella organisation representing the interests of composers, songwriters & music publishers

British Music Society   (BMS)   1978
■   7 Tudor Gardens, UPMINSTER, Essex, RM14 3DE.   (mem)
    01708 224795
    http://www.musicweb-international.com/BMS sec p
    Hon Membership Sec: Stephen C Trowell
▲   Registered Charity
○   *D; to promote the music of neglected British composers who do not have a society, or trust, to champion their cause
●   Mtgs - Res - Exhib - Comp - Inf - Lib - VE - Concert promotion - Recordings - Publications
M   475 i, 5 f, 14 org, UK / 95 i, 3 org, o'seas
¶   Jnl - 1; ftm, £5 nm.   NL - 4; ftm only.

British Music Writers' Council
    a group of the **Musicians' Union**

British Mycological Society   (BMS)   1896
NR Joseph Banks Building (room 7), Royal Botanic Gardens - Kew, RICHMOND, Surrey, TW9 3AB.
    020 8332 5720   fax 020 8332 5768
    email info@britmycolsoc.org.uk
▲   Registered Charity
○   *L, *Q; to promote all aspects of mycology (fungi, ecology, molecular biology, biodiversity, conservation, pathogens, biocontrol, systematics, physiology, secondary metabolites)
M   c 2,000 i

British Narrow Fabrics Association   (BNFA)
■   12 Beaumanor Rd, LEICESTER, LE4 5QA.
    0116-266 3332   fax 0116-266 3335
    email directorate@knitfed.co.uk
    Sec: John Harrison
▲   Un-incorporated Society
○   *T; to promote the narrow fabrics industry in the UK - is a non-profit making organisation
●   Mtgs - ET (of technical textiles technicians) - Inf - Empl
<   Knitting Inds Fedn
M   f
¶   NL - 12;   AR - 1; both ftm only.

British National Carnation Society   (BNCS)   1948
NR Linfield, Duncote, TOWCESTER, Northants, NN12 8AH.   (hsp)
    01327 351594   fax dianthusinduncote@tiscali.co.uk
    Hon Sec: Mrs B M Linnell
▲   Un-incorporated Society
○   *H; cultivation, breeding & exhibition of the Dianthus family of carnations & pinks
●   Competitive shows & displays
<   R Horticl Soc
M   c 370 i
¶   NL - 2; ftm only.   Carnation Ybk - 1; ftm.

British National Martial Arts Associations (BNMAA) 1992
- ■ International House (suite 501), 223 Regent St, LONDON, W1B 2QD. (hq)
  0871 990 3203   fax 0871 990 3204
  email info@bnma.co.uk   http://www.bnma.co.uk
  Chief Exec Officer: Paul Griffin,   Sec: Iris Balding
- ▲ Un-incorporated Society
- Br 4; Malta, Spain, USA
- ○ *N, *S; the safe development of traditional & freestyle martial arts
- Gp Competitions - the S factor (skill no contact); Training provider - Mastarr; Grade register - official grade
- ● Conf - Mtgs - ET - Exam - Res - Exhib - Comp - SG - Stat - Expt - Inf - PL - VE - LG
- < Wld Black Belt; Sports Coach; Mastarr; Chart Inst of Envtl Health; Office of Fair Trading; Sports Devt Initiative
- > Wld Black Belt; Profl Unification of Martial Arts (PUMA)
- M 270,000 i, 1,040 f, 5 org, UK / 200,000 i, 150 f, 2 org, o'seas
- ¶ NL - 12;ftm only.   Online magazine - updated; free.

British National Temperance League (BNTL Freeway) (BNTL) 1834
- ■ Unit 31A / M1 Commerce Park, Markham Lane, Duckmanton, CHESTERFIELD, Derbys, S44 5HS. (hq)
  01246 240500
  email bntl@btconnect.com   http://www.bntl.org
  Chief Exec & Co Sec: Mrs Barbara Briggs
- ▲ Company Limited by Guarantee; Registered Charity
- ○ *E, *K, *Y; an initiative of the League that offers children & young people the options to not drink alcohol, or take illegal drugs, solvents or other addictive substances, through educational resources & training
- ● ET
- M 35 i, 1,000 i (associates)
- ¶ Freeway (NL) - 4.   AR - 1; both free.
  Note: uses the abbreviated title of BNTL Freeway

British Natural Hygiene Society (BNHS) 1956
- ■ Shalimar 14 The Weavers, Farndon Rd, NEWARK-ON-TRENT, Notts, NG24 4RY. (hsp)
  01636 682941
  Pres & Hon Sec: Dr K R Sidhwa
- ▲ Un-incorporated Society
- ○ *K; to propagate the message of natural healthy living in accordance with natural law
- Gp Nutrition; Diet; Fasting for health
- ● Conf - Inf
- < Intl Assn of Profl Natural Hygienists; Amer Natural Hygiene Soc
- M c 400 i
- ¶ The Hygienist - 4.

British Naturalists' Association (BNA) 1905
- NR PO Box 5682, CORBY, Northants, NN17 2ZW.
  01536 262977
  http://www.bna-naturalists.org
- ▲ Company Limited by Guarantee; Registered Charity
- Br 9
- ○ *K; the education of the public in natural history areas & sanctuaries
- ● Conf - Mtgs - Exhib - Comp - Inf
- M magazine distribution to i & org
- ¶ Country-Side - 2.   British Naturalist - 2.   AR.

British Naturopathic Association (BNA) 1992
- ■ Goswell House, 2 Goswell Rd, STREET, Somerset, BA16 0JG. (hsb)
  0870 745 6984
  Sec: M W F Szewiel
- ▲ Company Limited by Guarantee
- ○ *P; for qualified & registered naturopaths
- ● Conf - Mtgs - Res - Inf
- M 310 i, UK / 19 i, o'seas
- ¶ British Naturopathic Jnl - 4.

British Naval Equipment Association (BNEA) 1973
- ■ 30 Great Guildford St (4th floor), LONDON, SE1 0HS. (hq)
  020 7928 9199   fax 020 7928 6599
  email bnea@maritimeindustries.org
  http://www.maritimeindustries.org
  Assn Dir: Christopher S McHugh
- ○ *T; 'dedicated to the needs of companies in the British naval industrial sector which build, refit & modernise warships, supply operations & weapons systems & other equipment; also dedicated to the needs of the companies providing related services in design, consultancy & finance'
- ● Conf - Mtgs - ET - Exhib - SG - Expt - LG
- < Soc Maritime Inds
- M f

British Neuropathological Society (BNS) 1950
- NR c/o Dr D Hilton, Dept of Histopathology, Derriford Hospital, Derriford Rd, PLYMOUTH, Devon, PL6 8DH. (hsb)
  01752 763599   fax 01752 763590
  Hon Sec: Dr David Hilton
- ▲ Registered Charity
- ○ *L; to promote research, education & clinical practice relating to neuropathy (study of brain, nerve & muscle disorders)
- ● Conf - Mtgs - ET - Res
- < Intl Soc Neuropathology
- M c 200 i
- ¶ Neuropathology & Applied Neurobiology - 10.

British Neuropsychiatry Association (BNPA) 1987
- NR St Aidan, Ealing Green, LONDON, W5 5EN. (admin/p)
  020 8840 9266   fax 020 8840 9266
  email admin@bnpa.org.uk   http://www.bnpa.org.uk
  Admin: Jackie Ashmenall,   Hon Sec: Dr Hugh Rickards
- ○ *M, *P; to provide a forum for cross-disciplinary discussion among psychiatrists, neurologists, neuropsychologists & workers in the related sciences, as well as qualified persons with an interest in brain function in relation to behaviour
- ● Mtgs
- M c 400 i

British Neuropsychological Society
- NR c/o Dr Georgina Jackson, University of Nottingham, Division of Psychiatry & Behavioural Sciences, A Floor / Queen's Medical Centre, NOTTINGHAM, NG7 2UH. (sb)
  0115-970 9119
  http://www.psychology.nottingham.ac.uk/bns/
  Sec: Dr Georgina Jackson
- ○ *M

British Neuroscience Association (BNA) 1965
- ■ The Sherrington Buildings, Ashton St, LIVERPOOL, L69 3GE.
  0151-794 4943
  Admin: Samantha Potts
- ▲ Registered Charity
- ○ *L, *P; to promote an understanding of the structure, function & development of the nervous system in health & disease
- ● Conf - Mtgs - ET - Res
- < Intl Brain Res Org (IBRO); Fedn of Eur Neuroscience Socs (FENS)
- M c 1,900 i, 9 f, UK / c 1,000 i, o'seas
- ¶ BNA NL - 4; free.
  National Meeting Book of Abstracts - 2 yrly; ftm.

© CBD Research Ltd · Beckenham · BR3 5JS · Tel 020 8650 7745 · Fax 020 8650 0768 · E-mail cbd@cbdresearch.com · www.cbdresearch.com

British/New Zealand Trade Council (Incorporated)   (BNZTC) 1917
- ■ PO Box 37162, Parnell, AUCKLAND, New Zealand.   (hq)
  64 (9) 522 0526
  http://www.bnztc.co.nz
  Exec Dir: Colin Wilson
- ▲ Registered Charity
- Br 2 o'seas
- ○ *C; to promote, foster & protect interests of British trade, commerce, industry & investment in New Zealand; & reciprocal trade between the two countries
- ● Mtgs - Res - Exhib - Stat - Expt - Inf - VE
- < Australia & New Zealand Cham Comm UK
- M 5 f, 16 trade assns & chams comm, UK / 1 i, 110 f, o'seas
- ¶ NL - 6;   LM - 1; AR - 1; all ftm only.

British Non-Ferrous Metals Federation   (BNFMF)
- ■ c/o Copper Development Association, 1 Brunel Court, Corner Hall, HEMEL HEMPSTEAD, Herts, HP3 9XX.   (hq)
  01442 275705   fax 01442 275716
  email mail@copperdev.co.uk
  Exec Sec: Carol Godfrey
- ▲ Un-incorporated Society
- ○ *T; fabricators of copper & copper-based alloy wire, tube, sheet & strip, & rods & profiles
- ● Mtgs
- M 14 f
- ¶ LM.

British North American Research Association   (BNARA)
- NR Warnford Court, 29 Throgmorton St, LONDON, EC2N 2AT. (hq)
  email bnara@underlinegroup.com
  Chmn: Sir Paul Judge
- ▲ Registered Charity
- Br Canada; USA
- ○ *X; promotion of Anglo-North American trade, commercial & political relations
- ● Conf - Mtgs - ET - Res - SG
- M 45 i, UK / 30 i, o'seas

British Nuclear Energy Society   (BNES)   1962
- NR 1-7 Great George St, LONDON, SW1P 3AA.   (hq)
  020 7665 2241   fax 020 7799 1325
  http://www.bnes.com
  Sec: Mark Askew
- ▲ Registered Charity
- Br 5
- ○ *L; the application of nuclear energy & ancillary objects
- Gp Decommissioning & waste
- ● Conf - Mtgs - Inf
- < Eur Nuclear Soc; Inst Civil Engrs
- M 1,000 i, UK / 100 i, o'seas
- ¶ Nuclear Energy - 6.

British Nuclear Industry Forum
  since June 2003 **Nuclear Industry Association**

British Nuclear Medicine Society   (BNMS)   1969
- NR Regent House, 291 Kirkdale, LONDON, SE26 4QD.   (hq)
  020 8676 7864   fax 020 8676 8417
  email suehatchard@bnms.org.uk
  http://www.bnms.org.uk
  Pres: John Frank,   Sec: Mrs Susan Hatchard
- ▲ Registered Charity
- ○ *P; to advance the science & public education in nuclear medicine
- ● Conf - ET - Exhib
- M c 700 i
- ¶ Nuclear Medicine Communications - 12.

British Number Plate Manufacturers Association   (BNMA)
- NR PO Box 23, BLACKPOOL, Lancs, FY4 3DA.   (chmn/b)
  01253 345287   fax 01253 344595
  email tmc@bestplate.com
  Chmn: Tony McNamee
- ▲ Un-incorporated Society
- ○ *T
- ● Mtgs - Res - LG
- M 9 f

British Numismatic Society   (BNS)   1903
- ■ c/o Warburg Institute, Woburn Sq, LONDON, WC1H 0AB. (hsb)
  01223 332915
  email secretary@britnumsoc.org
  http://www.britnumsoc.org
  Hon Sec: Dr Elina Screen
- ▲ Registered Charity
- ○ *L; promotion of numismatic science with regard to the coins, tokens & medals of Great Britain, our Empire & Commonwealth, & the English speaking world
- ● Mtgs - Inf - Lib
- < Brit Assn of Numismatics Socs
- M 393 i, 50 org, UK / 112 i, 62 org, o'seas
- ¶ British Numismatic Jnl - 1; ftm only.
  Specialist numismatic publications; at cost m.

British Numismatic Trade Association Ltd   (BNTA)   1973
- ■ PO Box 2, RYE, E Sussex, TN31 7WE.   (hq)
  01797 229988   fax 01797 229988
  email bnta@lineone.net   http://www.bnta.net
  Gen Sec: Mrs R Cooke
- ▲ Company Limited by Guarantee
- ○ *T; to ensure a high standard of ethical conduct within the numismatic trade
- ● Coin fairs
- < Fedn of Eur Numismatic Trade Assns (FENAP)
- M 73 i & f

British Nutrition Foundation   (BNF)   1967
- ■ High Holborn House, 52-54 High Holborn, LONDON, WC1V 6RQ.   (hq)
  020 7404 6504   fax 020 7404 6747
  email postbox@nutrition.org.uk
  http://www.nutrition.org.uk
  Sec: P D Leigh
- ▲ Company Limited by Guarantee; Registered Charity
- ○ *L; to provide unbiased information; to encourage education; to foster research concerned with human nutrition
- Gp School education; Publishing
- ● Conf - Mtgs - ET - Inf
- M 42 f
- ¶ BNF Bulletin - 4; £67 yr.   AR - 1; £10.

British Oat & Barley Millers' Association   (BOBMA)   1978
- ■ 6 Catherine St, LONDON, WC2B 5JJ.   (hq)
  020 7420 7109   fax 020 7836 0580
  email grace.foyle@fdf.org.uk
  Exec: Grace Foyle
- ▲ Un-incorporated Society
- ○ *T; interests of UK millers of oat & barley for human consumption
- ● Mtgs
- < Eur Breakfast Cereal Assn (CEEREAL); Food & Drink Fedn (FDF)
- M 8 f

British Obesity Surgery Patient Association
- NR PO Box 704, Waterrow, TAUNTON, Somerset, TA4 2Z0.
  0845 602 0406
  http://www.bospa.org
- ○ *G, *K

British Obesity Surgery Society   (BOSS)   2000
- ■ c/o Prof J N Baxter, Dept Surgery, Morriston Hospital, SWANSEA, SA6 6NL.   (asa)
  01792 703573   fax 01792 703574
  email j.n.baxter@swan.ac.uk
  Hon Pres: Prof J N Baxter
- ▲ Un-incorporated Society
- ○ *L, *P; to promote awareness of obesity surgery; to advise on training & accreditation
- ● Conf - ET
- < Intl Fedn for the Surgery of Obesity (IFSO); Assn for the Study of Obesity (ASO); Assn of Upper GI Surgeons (AUGIS)
- M 70 i
- ¶ NL - 2/3; free.

British Occupational Hygiene Society   (BOHS)   1953
- NR 5-6 Melbourne Business Court, Millennium Way, Pride Park, DERBY, DE24 8LZ.   (hq)
  01332 298101
  email admin@bohs.org
  Hon Sec: Heather Jackson
- ▲ Company Limited by Guarantee; Registered Charity
- Br 8 regions
- ○ *L; to promote the good practice of occupational hygiene; to prevent workplace conditions affecting the health & wellbeing of workers
- Gp Technology; Standards; Chemical hazard & risk; Environmental; Management; Microbiology; NHS; Offshore; Radiation; Sampling & analytical methods
- ● Conf - Mtgs - ET - Res - SG
- < Intl Occupational Hygiene Assn
- M c 1,200 i
- ¶ Annals of Occupational Hygiene - 8.   NL - 4. Abstracts of Conference Papers - 1.   AR.
- ✕ 2002-04 (merged) British Institute of Occupational Hygienists

British Off-Road Driving Association   (BORDA)   1995
- NR Leisure House, Salisbury Rd, ANDOVER, Hants, SP11 7DN. (hq)
  01484 852800
  Mem Sec: David Heaton
- ▲ Un-incorporated Society
- ○ *T; to encourage best practice in the organisation of events among member operators; to develop technical guidance for off-road driving
- ● Conf - Mtgs
- < Motor Activities Trg Coun; LARA
- M 45 f
- ¶ BORDA Code(s) of practice - 1; ftm only: Health & Safety;   Environment;   Corporate Events; Recreational Off-road Driving; Advanced Off-road Driving.

British Office Supplies & Services Federation   (BOSS Federation)   1987
- NR 12 Corporation St, HIGH WYCOMBE, Bucks, HP13 6TQ.   (hq)
  0845 450 1565
  http://www.bossfederation.co.uk
  Chief Exec: Keith Davies
- ▲ Company Limited by Guarantee
- Br 13
- ○ *T; to represent manufacturers, importers, wholesalers, distributors, mail order, resellers, retailers, dealers, superstores & commercial contract dealers
- Gp Domestic Manufacturing Stationers' Association; Letter File Manufacturers' Association; Office Products & Stationery Association; Rubber Stamp Manufacturers' Guild
- ● Conf - Mtgs - ET - Exam - Exhib - Comp - SG - Stat - Expt - Inf - LG
- < Eur Stationery & Office Products Trade Assn
- M f

British Oil Spill Control Association
   since 2004 **UK Spill Association**

British Olive Oil Buyer's Association   (BOOBA)
- ■ Kingsway House, Wrotham Rd, Meopham, GRAVESEND, Kent, DA13 0AU.   (asa)
- ○ *T
- ● Conf - Mtgs - Stat - LG
- M 7 f

British Olympic Association   (BOA)   1905
- ■ 1 Wandsworth Plain, LONDON, SW18 1EH.   (hq)
  020 8871 2677   fax 020 8871 9104
  http://www.olympics.org.uk
  Chief Exec: Simon Clegg
- ○ *S; to provide services to elite sport in the UK; to promote the Olympic movement in the UK; to prepare & manage the Great Britain Olympic team for the games
- ● Conf - ET - Res - Inf - Lib - LG
- < Intl Olympic C'ee
- M 2,289 i
- ¶ Cutting Edge (NL) - 4;   Inside Track (NL) - 4.   AR - 1.

British Oncological Association   (BOA)   1985
- NR Royal Marsden Hospital, Downs Rd, SUTTON, Surrey, SM2 5PT.
  020 7352 8171 ext 3063   (sb)
  Sec: Romayne McMahon
- ▲ Registered Charity
- ○ *L, *P, *Q; for clinicians & scientists working in oncology specialities
- ● Conf - Mtgs - ET - Comp
- M c 400 i
- ¶ BOA News - 4; ftm only.

British Oncology Data Managers Association   (BODMA) 1987
- NR PO Box 87, BANBRIDGE, Co Down, BT32 3YT.   (asa)
  028 9753 3758   fax 028 9753 3758
  email bodma@pfhconsulting.com
  http://www.bodma.com
  Chmn: Kevin Fishwick
- Br 4 regional groups
- ○ *P; to promote oncology data management & trial coordination within the UK
- ● Mtgs - ET - Res - SG - Stat - Inf
- < Eur Org for Res & Treatment of Cancer (EORTC Gp on Data Management)
- M c 380 i
- ¶ NL - 4; ftm only.

British Onion Producers' Association
- ■ 133 Eastgate, LOUTH, Lincs, LN11 9QG.
  01507 602427   fax 01507 607165
  email crop-association@pvgn.co.uk
  http://www.onions.org.uk
- ○ *F, *T

British Orchid Council   (BOC)   1971
- ■ 30 Idoria Rd, Perton, WOLVERHAMPTON, W Midlands, WV6 7NQ.   (hsp)
  Hon Sec: John Spires
- ▲ Registered Charity
- ○ *H; to provide a single forum for amateur & commercial orchid growers & orchid scientists; to broaden the knowledge of orchids; to promote & encourage excellence in their culture
- Gp Trainee judges scheme; Lecturers panel; Slide library
- ● Conf - Exhib - SG - Inf - PL
- < Eur Orchid Coun; Intl Orchid Commission
- M 16 f, 48 org
- ¶ A Grower's & Buyer's Guide - 1; ftm, 30p nm.

© CBD Research Ltd · Beckenham · BR3 5JS · Tel 020 8650 7745 · Fax 020 8650 0768 · E-mail cbd@cbdresearch.com · www.cbdresearch.com

British Orchid Growers Association (BOGA) 1949

■   c/o Plested Orchids, 38 Florence Rd, College Town,
      SANDHURST, Berks, GU47 0QD.   (hsb)
      01276 32947   fax 01276 32947
      email plestedorchids@aol.com
      http://www.bogo.org.uk
      Hon Sec: Mrs Janet Plested
○   *H, *T; 'for orchid growers & sundries traders to promote &
      maintain the highest standards of our trade'
●   Conf - Mtgs - Exhib - Inf - LG re CITES (Convention for
      International Trade of Endangered Species)
<   Brit Orchid Coun
M   17 f
¶   Grower's & Buyer's Guide (LM) - 1; ftm, 50p or 2 1st class
      stamps nm.

British Organ Archive
      a group of the **British Institute of Organ Studies**

British Organ Donor Society (BODY) 1984

§   Balsham, CAMBRIDGE, CB1 6DL.   (chmn)
      01223 893636
      email body@argonet.co.uk   http://www.argonet.co.uk/
      body p
▲   Registered Charity
      A non-membership, self-help group offering emotional support
      for donor, recipient & waiting recipient families

British Organisation of Non-Parents
      Disbanded 2004

British Oriental Rug Dealers Association (BORDA) 1993

NR   c/o RuGallery Ltd, 42 Verulam Rd, ST ALBANS, Herts,
      AL3 4DQ.   (hsb)
      01727 841046
      Sec: Richard H Mathias
▲   Un-incorporated Society
○   *T
Gp Exhibitions; Information
●   Mtgs - Inf - PL
M   20 f

British Orienteering Federation Ltd (BOF) 1967

■   Riversdale, Dale Road North, Darley Dale, MATLOCK, Derbys,
      DE4 2HX.   (hq)
      01629 734042   fax 01629 733769
      email bof@britishorienteering.org.uk
      http://www.britishorienteering.org.uk
      Chief Exec: Mike Hamilton
▲   Company Limited by Guarantee
○   *S; national governing body for the sport of orienteering
Gp Federated regional & home national associations & affiliated
      clubs
●   Conf - Mtgs - ET - Comp - LG
<   Intl Orienteering Fedn (IOF)
M   8,500 i, 140 clubs
¶   Focus Magazine (NL) - 4;   Fixtures List - 4; both ftm only.
      Leaflets & posters.

British Origami Society (BOS) 1967

■   2a The Chestnuts, COUNTESTHORPE, Leics, LE8 5TL.
      (mem/sp)
      Mem Sec: Mrs P A Groom
▲   Registered Charity
○   *A; the development of Origami (folding paper) & related
      techniques of manipulation of paper as a form of art,
      education, therapy & recreation
●   Conf - Mtgs - ET - Exhib
<   Origami associations worldwide
M   350 i, UK / 350 i, o'seas
¶   British Origami - 6; ftm only.

British Ornithologists' Club (BOC) 1892

NR   c/o British Ornithologists' Union, Dept of Zoology, University of
      Oxford, South Parks Rd, OXFORD, OX1 3PS.   (mail) address
○   *L; to promote scientific discussion & facilitate publication &
      dissemination of scientific information connected with
      ornithology; to maintain a special interest in avian
      systematics, taxonomy & distribution
M   i

British Ornithologists' Union (BOU) 1858

NR   Dept of Zoology, University of Oxford, South Parks Rd,
      OXFORD, OX1 3PS.   (hq)
      01865 281842
      Admin: Steve P Dudley
▲   Registered Charity
○   *L; advancement of the science of ornithology
●   Conf - Mtgs - Res - Comp - Inf - Lib - LG
M   c 1,000 i, UK / c 1,000 i, o'seas
¶   Ibis (Jnl) - 4.

British Orthodontic Society (BOS) 1994

NR   12 Bridewell Place, LONDON, EC4V 6AP.   (hq)
      020 7353 8680   fax 020 7353 8682
      Sec: Ann Wright
▲   Company Limited by Guarantee; Registered Charity
○   *P; a branch of dentistry concerned with developmental
      abnormalities of the teeth & face
Gp Consultant orthodontists; Community; Practitioners; Specialist
      practitioners; Training grades; University teachers
●   Conf - Mtgs - Res - LG
<   Orthodontic Technicians Assn
M   1,600 i, UK / 160 i, o'seas
¶   British Jnl of Orthodontics - 4.   BOS NL - 4.

British Orthopaedic Association (BOA) 1918

NR   at the Royal College of Surgeons, 35-43 Lincoln's Inn Fields,
      LONDON, WC2A 3PN.   (hq)
      020 7405 6507   fax 020 7831 2676
      http://www.boa.ac.uk
      Chief Exec: D C Adams,   Hon Sec: Robin Allen
▲   Company Limited by Guarantee; Registered Charity
○   *P; science, art & practice of orthopaedic surgery
Gp Specialist societies: British Association of Spinal Surgeons;
      British Association for Surgery of the Knee; British Cervical
      Spine Society; British Elbow & Shoulder Society; British Hip
      Society; British Limb Reconstruction Society; British
      Orthopaedic Foot Surgery Society; British Orthopaedic
      Oncology Society; British Orthopaedic Research Society;
      British Orthopaedic Specialists Association; British
      Orthopaedic Sports Trauma Association; British Orthopaedic
      Trainees Association; British Scoliosis Society; British Society
      for Children's Orthopaedic Surgery; British Trauma Society;
      Rheumatoid Arthritis Surgical Society; Society for Back Pain
      Research
●   Conf - ET - Exhib - Stat - Inf - LG
<   World Orthopaedic Concern
M   c 3,600 i
¶   Jnl of Bone & Joint Surgery - 16.
      British Orthopaedic News - 2.
      Hbk & LM - 1; ftm only.   AR - 1; free.

British Orthopaedic Foot Surgery Society (BOFSS) 1978

■   British Orthopaedic Association, 35-43 Lincoln's Inn Fields,
      LONDON, WC2A 3PN.   (hq)
      020 7405 6507
      Hon Sec: Dishan Singh
▲   Company Limited by Guarantee
○   *L, *Q; study & promotion of orthopaedic surgery of feet &
      ankles; research on ankle & foot problems
●   Conf - Mtgs - ET
<   Eur Fedn of Foot & Ankle Socs (EFFAS); Collège Intl du Pied
      (CIP)
M   120 i
¶   Proceedings in supplement to Jnl of Bone & Joint Surgery
      (British Orthopaedic Association) - 1.

British Orthopaedic Oncology Society
a specialist society of the **British Orthopaedic Association**

British Orthopaedic Research Society
a specialist society of the **British Orthopaedic Association**

British Orthopaedic Specialists Association
a specialist society of the **British Orthopaedic Association**

British Orthopaedic Sports Trauma Association
a specialist society of the **British Orthopaedic Association**

British Orthopaedic Trainees Association
a specialist society of the **British Orthopaedic Association**

British Orthoptic Society
since January 2004 **British & Irish Orthoptic Society**

British Osteopathic Association   (BOA)   1998
NR 3 Park Terrace, Manor Rd, LUTON, Beds, LU1 3HN.   (hq)
01582 488455   fax 01582 481533
email boa@osteopathy.org   http://www.osteopathy.org
Chief Exec: Michael Watson
▲ Company Limited by Guarantee
○ *M, *P; to provide independent representation, care & support
for osteopaths
● Conf - Res - Inf
M c 2,600 i
¶ Osteopathy Today - 12.

British Othello Federation   (BOF)   1984
■ 1 Beaconsfield Terrace, Victoria Rd, CAMBRIDGE, CB4 3BP.
(chmn/p)
01223 336197   fax 01223 333992
email ag24@gen.cam.ac.uk
http://www.britishothello.org.uk
Chmn: Aubrey de Grey
○ *S; to promote the playing & understanding of the game of
Othello - a board game of pure skill sometimes known as
'Reversi'
● Comp
< US Othello Assn; Fédn Française d'Othello; Japan Othello
Assn
M 50 i, UK / 50 i, o'seas
¶ NL - 2; ftm, £3 nm.

British Outdoor Professionals Association   (BOPA)   1993
■ PO Box 9, LLANDRIDNOD WELLS, Powys, LD1 6WJ.   (hq)
07071 225853   fax 07071 225853
email bopa@outdoor-sport.u-net.com
Gen Sec: Chris Charters
○ *P; to encourage professionalism in providing the best training
in outdoor activities (incl abseiling, archery, ballooning,
caving, gliding, golf, horse-riding, orienteering, sailing etc)
● ET - Database providing activities available, instructors & their
qualifications - Workshops & seminars
M 1,200 i (associate membership for trainees)
¶ NL - 12; free.

British Packaging Association   (BPA)   1908
NR 24 Grange St, KILMARNOCK, E Ayrshire, KA1 2AR.   (hq)
01563 570518   fax 01563 572728
email nac@natpack.org.uk
http://www.boxpackaging.org.uk
Sec: Susan Hunter
▲ Un-incorporated Society
○ *T; (members are mainly small to medium sized owner-run
boxmakers)
● Conf - Mtgs - Comp - Inf - Empl
< CITPA
M 70 f, UK / 3 f, o'seas
✕ 2003-2004 British Box & Packaging Association

British Paediatric Cardiac Association
a group of the **Royal College of Paediatrics & Child Health**

British Paediatric Neurology Association
a group of the **Royal College of Paediatrics & Child Health**

British Paediatric Pathology Association
a group of the **Royal College of Paediatrics & Child Health**

British Paediatric Respiratory Society
a group of the **Royal College of Paediatrics & Child Health**

British Pain Society (the British Chapter of IASP)   1968
NR Churchill House (3rd floor), 35 Red Square, LONDON,
WC1R 4SG.   (hq)
Hon Sec: Dr Cathy Stannard
▲ Registered Charity
Br 14 regional
○ *P; to relieve the suffering of pain by promotion of education,
research & training; to increase professional & public
awareness of the prevalence of pain & the facilities available
for its management
Gp (deal with specific aspects of pain - acute, in children, etc)
● Conf - ET - Res - Exhib - Inf - LG
< Intl Assn for the Study of Pain (IASP)
M 1,387 i, 5 f
¶ NL; ftm only.   Information for Patients; free.
Desirable Criteria for Pain Management Programmes.

British Palomino Society   (BPS)
■ Penrhiwllan, LLANDYSUL, Cardiganshire, SA44 5NZ.   (hq)
01239 851387   fax 01239 851040
email britpal@lineone.net
http://www.britishpalominosociety.co.uk
Hon Sec: Mrs Peter Howell
▲ Company Limited by Guarantee
○ *B
● Annual show
M i
¶ Palomino - 3; ftm, £3 nm.

British Parachute Association   (BPA)   1962
■ 5 Wharf Way, Glen Parva, LEICESTER, LE2 9TF.   (hq)
0116-278 5271   fax 0116-247 7662
email skydive@bpa.org.uk   http://www.bpa.org.uk
Chmn: Chris Allen
▲ Company Limited by Guarantee
Br 23; Cyprus, Germany
○ *S; governing body of sport parachuting in the UK
Gp Safety & training; Development; Competitions (international &
national)
● Mtgs - ET - Exam - Exhib - Comp
< Fédn Aéronautique Intle; Sports Coun; CCPR; R Aero Club; UK
Sport
M 4,500 i, 25,000 i (students)
¶ Skydive, the British Mag - 6; ftm, £22 nm.

British Paralympic Association   (BPA)   1989
■ 40 Bernard St, LONDON, WC1N 1ST.   (hq)
020 7211 5222   fax 020 7211 5233
email info@paralympics.org.uk
http://www.paralympics.org.uk
Chief Exec: Philip Lane
▲ Registered Charity
○ *S; to support & manage British Paralympic team
● Mtgs - Comp - Organisation of teams for the winter & summer
Paralympic Games
< Intl Paralympic C'ee
M 78 org

British Parking Association (BPA) 1970
■ Stuart House, 41-43 Perrymount Rd, HAYWARDS HEATH,
   W Sussex, RH16 3BN.   (hq)
   01444 447300   fax 01444 454105
   email info@britishparking.co.uk
   http://www.britishparking.co.uk
   Managing Dir: Keith Banbury
▲ Company Limited by Guarantee
○ *T; to promote the advancement of knowledge & standards in
   the management, planning, design, improvement, regulation
   & maintenance of all types of parking facilities on & off-street
● Conf - Mtgs - ET - Exhib - Inf - Lib - LG
M c 600 i, f & local authorities
¶ Parking News (Jnl) - 10; ftm only.

British Parthenais Cattle Society 1988
■ Eastcote Hall Farm, Barston Lane, Hampton in Arden,
   SOLIHULL, W Midlands, B92 0HR.   (hsp)
   01675 446081
   Chmn & Hon Sec: Mrs Rose Cookes
▲ Company Limited by Guarantee
○ *B; to promote the Parthenais breed for pedigree & beef
   production
● Agricultural shows - Beef events
< Nat Beef Assn
M 30 i, UK / 1 i, o'seas
¶ NL - 5/6;   Promotional leaflets; both free.

British Patton Historical Society
   since 2000-02 **Patton Historical Society**

British Peanut Council (BPC) 1967
■ c/o 20 St Dunstan's Hill, LONDON, EC3R 8NQ.   (hq)
   020 7283 2707
   Sec: Stuart Logan
▲ Company Limited by Guarantee
○ *T; to protect & promote the interests of the British peanut
   industry
Gp Manufacturers; Packers; Importers & distributors; Traders
● Mtgs - Inf - LG
M 34 f, 1 org, UK / 5 f, o'seas
¶ BPC NL - 4; ftm only.   BPC Hbk - 1.

British Pelargonium & Geranium Society (BPGS) 1951
■ Lyneham, Hullbrook Lane, Shamley Green, GUILDFORD,
   Surrey, GU5 0UQ.   (hsp)
   01483 892163
   email john.morbey@bpgs.org.uk
   Hon Sec: Mrs Gwen Ward
▲ Registered Charity
○ *H; the conservation & study of pelargoniums & geraniums; to
   provide information, techniques & data for members
Gp Geraniaceae
● Conf - Mtgs - Exhib - Comp - Inf - LG
< Intl Geranium Soc of Amer; R Horticl Soc
M 400 i, 50 org, UK / 20 i, o'seas
¶ Pelargonium News (Jnl) - 3; ftm, £1 nm.
   Pelargonium News (Ybk) - 1; ftm, £1 nm.

** **British Pensioners & Trade Unions Action Association   (British
   Pensioners)**
   Organisation lost: see Introduction paragraph 3

British Percheron Horse Society (BPHS) 1919
NR Three Bears Cottage, Burston Rd, DISS, Norfolk, IP22 5UF.
   (hsp)
   01379 740554
   email secretary@percheron.org.uk
   http://www.percheron.org.uk
▲ Company Limited by Guarantee
○ *B
● Mtgs - Res - VE - Progress Days - Open Days - Marathons -
   Trials
M c 270 i
¶ NL - 4; ftm only.   Studbook, Vol XIV.

British-Peruvian Chamber of Commerce (BPCC) 1988
NR Torre Parque Mar (piso 22), Av José Larco 1301, LIMA 18, Peru.
   511 617 3090   fax 511 617 3095
   email bpcc@bpcc.org.pe   http://www.bpcc.org.pe
   Pres: Roger Alderson
▲ Registered Charity
○ *C
● Conf - Mtgs - ET - Comp - Expt - Inf - Lib - LG
< Assn Binational Chams Comm of Peru (ACCB)
M i & f
¶ Opportunities (Jnl) - 6; free.

British Pest Control Association (BPCA) 1942
■ 1 Gleneagles House, Vernongate, DERBY, DE1 1UP.   (hq)
   0870 609 2687   fax 01332 295904
   email enquiry@bpca.org.uk   http://www.bpca.org.uk
   Exec Dir: R J Strand
▲ Company Limited by Guarantee
○ *T; for servicing companies & others engaged in the control of
   food, hygiene or nuisance pests, or having a close interest in
   industrial pest control; it includes control of pests in food
   storage & preparation areas in domestic premises, factories,
   hospitals, hotels, restaurants, shops & transport; BPCA also
   represents manufacturers & distributors of the pesticides &
   equipment used by the servicing companies & responsible &
   safe use of pesticides in the interests of the general public
● Mtgs - ET - Exam - Exhib - Inf - LG
M 22 i, 229 f, UK / 38 f, o'seas
¶ Professional Pest Controller (Jnl) - 4; free.
   Membership Directory - 1; free.   AR.

British Pétanque Association
   closed in 2004; has been replaced by the **British Pétanque
   Federation**

British Pétanque Federation 1974
NR 19 St Andrews Crescent, CARDIFF, CF10 3DB.   (hq)
   029 2022 1300
   http://www.britishpetanque.org
○ *S; to promote the game of pétanque (the French game of
   boules)

British Pharmacological Society (BPS) 1931
■ 16 Angel Gate, City Rd, LONDON, EC1V 2SG.   (hq)
   020 7239 0171   fax 020 7417 0114
   email ml@bps.ac.uk   http://www.bps.ac.uk
   Exec Officer: Sarah-Jane Stagg
▲ Company Limited by Guarantee; Registered Charity
○ *L; to promote & advance the science of pharmacology
Gp Clinical pharmacology; Pharmacology
● Conf - Mtgs - ET - Exam - Res - Exhib
< Intl U of Pharmacology; Fedn of Eur Pharmacological Socs; Eur
   Assn for Clinical Pharmacology & Therapeutics
M 1,700 i, UK / 8060i, o'seas
¶ British Jnl of Pharmacology - 12; £103 m.
   British Jnl of Clinical Pharmacology - 12; £55 m.
   PA2 (NL) - 4; ftm only.   AR; free.

British Phonographic Industry Ltd   (BPI)   1973
NR   Riverside Building, County Hall, Westminster Bridge Rd,
      LONDON, SE1 7JA.   (hq)
      020 7803 1300   fax 020 7803 1310
      email general@bpi.co.uk   http://www.bpi.co.uk
      Exec Chmn: Peter Jamieson
▲   Company Limited by Guarantee
○   *T; for British record companies
●   Mtgs - Res - Stat - Inf - Lib - LG
<   Intl Fedn of the Phonographic Ind (IFPI)
M   c 370 f
¶   BPI Statistical Hbk - 1.   LM - website.

British Photodermatology Group   (BPG)   1988
■   c/o Mr David Taylor (Clinical Scientist), Gloucester Royal
      Hospital, Great Western Rd, GLOUCESTER, GL1 3NN.   (sb)
      0845 422 5976   fax 0845 422 6489
      email david.taylor@glos.nhs.uk   http://www.BPG.org.uk
      Hon Sec: David Taylor
○   *L, *N, *Q; the study & effects of optical radiations, in health &
      disease, on human skin
●   Conf - Mtgs - ET - Res - Inf
<   Brit Assn of Dermatologists; Photomedicine Soc (USA)
M   c 110 i, UK / c 10 i, o'seas

British Photographic Enterprise Group
      on 10 January 2002 merged with the British Imaging & Photographic
      Association, the British Photographic & Imaging Association, the
      Imaging Products Group & the Photographic Waste Management
      Association to form the **Photo Imaging Council**

British Photographic & Imaging Association
      on 10 January 2002 merged with the British Imaging & Photographic
      Association, the British Photographic Enterprise Group, the Imaging
      Products Group & the Photographic Waste Management Association
      to become the **Photo Imaging Council**

British Photovoltaic Association
      on 1 April 2006 merged with the **Renewable Energy Associaton**

British Phycological Society   1952
■   c/o Dr Jackie Parry, Dept of Biological Sciences, Lancaster
      University, LANCASTER, LA1 4YQ.   (hsb)
      01524 593489
      Hon Sec: Dr Jackie Parry
▲   Registered Charity
○   *L; study of algae
●   Conf - Res - SG - VE
<   Biosciences Fedn
M   613 i, UK & o'seas
¶   European Jnl of Phycology - 4.   NL - 3.

British Piemontese Cattle Society Ltd   1988
■   33 Eden Grange, Little Corby, CARLISLE, Cumbria, CA4 8QW.
      01228 562946   fax 01228 562187
      email craig@piemontese.info
      http://www.piemontese.org.uk
      Sec: F C Culley
▲   Company Limited by Guarantee; Registered Charity
○   *B
M   70 i, 6 f, UK / 3 i, o'seas
¶   NL - 4; ftm.

British Pig Association   (BPA)   1884
NR   Trumpington Mews, 40b High St, Trumpington, CAMBRIDGE,
      CB2 2LS.   (hq)
      01223 845100
      email bpa@britishpigs.org.uk
      Chmn: R Overend
▲   Company Limited by Guarantee; Registered Charity
○   *B, *V; to represent the pig industry
●   Conf - Mtgs - Inf - LG - Recording of pedigrees
<   Eur Pig Selection & Production Assn; Rare Breeds Survival Trust
M   i, f & org
¶   Herd Book - 1.

British Pig Executive   (BPEX)
NR   statutory body - part of meat and livestock commissionbased at
      Milton Keynes -   home BSAS!

British Plant Gall Society   (BPGS)   1986
NR   2 The Dene, NETTLEHAM, Lincs, LN2 2LS.   (hsp)
      01522 875939
      http://www.britishgalls.org.uk
      Hon Sec: Graeme Clayton
○   *L; to encourage & co-ordinate the study of cecidology (plant
      galls), with particular reference to the British Isles
Gp   Checklist; Insect & invertebrate; Recording
●   Conf - Mtgs - PL
M   147 i
¶   Cecidology (Jnl) - 2.   NL.   Occasional papers.

British Plastics Federation   (BPF)   1933
NR   6 Bath Place, Rivington St, LONDON, EC2A 3JE.   (hq)
      020 7457 5000   fax 020 7457 5045
      email bpf@bpf.co.uk
      Dir Gen: Peter Davis
○   *T; for all sectors of the plastics industry; to carry out
      commercial studies & provide commercial trade &
      information services
●   Plastics & Rubber Advisory Service: 0906 190 8070
M   f

**British Plumbing Fittings Manufacturers' Association
(BPFMA)   1988**
■   c/o Copper Development Association, 1 Brunel Court, Corner
      Hall, HEMEL HEMPSTEAD, Herts, HP3 9XX.   (hq)
      01442 275705   fax 01442 275716
      email mail@copperdev.co.uk
      Contact: Mrs A Vessey
▲   Un-incorporated Society
○   *T; UK manufacturers of copper & copper alloy 'in-line'
      plumbing fittings
●   Mtgs
M   3 f
¶   LM; free.

British Polarological Research Society   (BPRS)   1970
■   6 Beechvale, Hillview Rd, WOKING, Surrey, GU22 7NS.   (hq)
      Pres & Res Dir: Emeritus Research Prof W J Parker
▲   Un-incorporated Society
○   *L, *Q; 'scientific & statistical operational research studies of
      polarological phenomena; development of polarological
      operational-research theory & sciences for forecasting,
      optimisation, problem solving & decision making in non-
      orthodox OR scenarios in all disciplines'
Gp   Medical OR polarology; Environmental OR polarology
●   Mtgs - SG - Inf - Research into: polarological fog dispersal,
      CO-poisoning, p-prevention (by chimneying of gas-heater
      wall-vents), cardiovascular p-therapy instrumentation,
      hospital 'bed-blocker' p-rehabilitation; Water aid (drinking
      water p-production)
<   Brit Polarographic Res Inst; Nat Inst of Polarology;
      Polarographic Soc; UK Instn of Polarological Sciences
M   i (Post-doctoral research fellows, polarological OR intelligence
      officers & scientists)
¶   (Research papers are published in journals).

British Polio Fellowship (BPF)   1939
NR   Unit A (ground floor), Eagle Office Centre, The Runway,
    SOUTH RUISLIP, Middx, HA4 6SE.   (hq)
    0800 018 0586
    email info@britishpolio.org.uk
    Chief Exec: Graham Ball
▲   Registered Charity
Br   52
○   *W; welfare of people in the UK & Ireland who are disabled by
    poliomyelitis
●   Inf
M   c 9,000 i
¶   Bulletin - 6; free.

British-Polish Chamber of Commerce   (BPCC)
■   240 King St, LONDON, W6 0RF.   (hq)
    020 8563 0044   fax 020 8563 0026
    email manageruk@bpcc.org.pl   http://www.bpcc.org.pl
    London Mgr: Anna Maria McKeever
Br   3
○   *C; to develop British business links with Poland
●   Conf - Res - Expt - Inf
<   the British office of BPCC in Warsaw
M   2 i, 30 f, UK / 10 i, 350 f, o'seas
¶   Contact - 6; free.   Membership Directory - 1; ftm, £45 nm.

British-Polish Chamber of Commerce   (BPCC)
NR   Ul Fabryczna 16-22, PL-00-446 WARSAW, Poland.   (hq)
    48 (22) 320 01 00   fax 48 (22) 621 19 37
    Exec Dir: Barbara Stachowiak
▲   Company Limited by Guarantee
Br   London
○   *C
Gp   C'ees: Banking, Energy, Environment, Human resources &
    management training, Privatisation, Tax
●   Conf - Mtgs - ET - Res - Inf - Lib - LG
<   Confedn Brit Chams Comm Continental Europe (COBCOE);
    Assn Brit Chams Comm
M   5 i, 24 f, UK / 16 i, 301 f, Poland
¶   Contact (NL) - 6.
    Membership Directory - 1.
×   2001 British Chamber of Commerce in Poland

British Polyolefin Textiles Association   (BPTA)   1971
■   c/o Scott & Fyfe Ltd, Nelson St, TAYPORT, Fife, DD6 9DQ.
    (hsb)
    01382 553502   fax 01382 552170
    Sec: Thomas Hill
○   *T; interests of UK producers of polyolefin tapes, yarns, fibres &
    fabrics
●   Mtgs - Stat - Inf - LG
M   5 f

British Porphyria Association   (BPA)   1998
■   14 Mollison Rise, GRAVESEND, Kent, DA12 4QJ.
    (regd/address)
    01474 369231
    email helpline@porphyria.org.uk
    http://www.porphyria.org.uk
    Chmn: John Chamberlayne,   Admin: Karen Harris
▲   Registered Charity
○   *W; to encourage research & improve understanding of
    Porphyria; to offer help & advice to sufferers & their families
Gp   Porphyria interest group (of consultants & physicians dealing
    with the condition; Orphan Europe (a pharmaceutical
    company)
●   Mtgs - ET - Res - Inf
<   Eur Porphyria Initiative; Amer (& Canadian) Porphyria Assn(s)
>   Porphyria Interest Gp
M   c 300 families
¶   NL - 2.
    Patients booklets & drugs list.

British Ports Association   (BPA)   1992
NR   Africa House, 64-78 Kingsway, LONDON, WC2B 6AH.   (hq)
    020 7242 1200   fax 020 7430 7474
    email info@britishports.org.uk
    http://www.britishports.org.uk
    Dir: David Whitehead,   Sec: David Bishop
▲   Un-incorporated Society
○   *T; to represent the interests of member ports in the UK &
    Europe
●   Conf - Mtgs
M   110 f & org
¶   Monthly Update - 12; m only.

**British-Portuguese Chamber of Commerce (Câmara de Comércio
Luso-Britânica) (BPCC)   1911**
■   Rua da Estrela 8, P-1200-669 LISBOA, Portugal.   (hq)
    351 (21) 394 2020   fax 351 (21) 394 2029
    email bpcc@bpcc.pt   http://www.bilateral.biz
    Chief Exec: Chris Barton
▲   Un-incorporated Society
○   *C; to promote Anglo-Portuguese trade relations; to provide
    services for members
●   Conf - Mtgs - ET - Expt - Inf - Lib - VE
<   Coun of Brit Cham Comm in Continental Europe
M   29 f, UK / 16 i, 742 f, Portugal
¶   Members Directory - 1; ftm, £25 nm.   AR; free.

British Postmark Society   (BPS)   1958
■   12 Dunavon Park, STRATHAVEN, Lanarks, ML10 6LP.   (hsp)
    01357 522430
    email johlen@stracml10.freeserve.co.uk
    Hon Sec: John A Strachan
▲   Registered Charity
○   *G; 'to promote & to co-ordinate the study & collection of
    British postal markings, particularly of the 20th century &
    subsequently, & the means & & methods by which they are
    applied; to publish & disseminate the results of such study for
    the education of the public'
Gp   Printed Postage Impression Study Circle
●   Mtgs - Res - Comp - SG - Lib - Yearly auction - Yearly sale -
    Circulating exchange packets
M   218 i, UK / 14 i, o'seas
¶   Quarterly Bulletin; ftm, £10 yr nm.
    PPI News & Junk Mail (NL) - 2/3; ftm.
    LM - 2/3 yrly;   Library List - 2/3 yrly; both ftm only.

British Potato Trades Association   (NASPM)   1940
NR   Britannia House, Bentwaters Park, Rendlesham,
    WOODBRIDGE, Suffolk, IP12 2TW.   (regd/off)
    01394 460075
    http://www.bpta.org.uk
    Jt Secs: C D Fradd, Hugh Edmond
▲   Un-incorporated Society
○   *T
●   Mtgs - ET - SG - Inf - VE - LG
<   Brit Eur Potato Assn; Jt Potato Trade Coun; Nat Inst Agricl
    Botany
×   2006 (National Association of Seed Potato Merchants
    (Scottish Potato Trades Association

British Poultry Breeders & Hatcheries Association Ltd
since 2001 **British Poultry Council**

British Poultry Council   (BPC)   2002
■ Europoint House, 5 Lavington St, LONDON, SE1 0NZ.   (hq)
    020 7202 4760   fax 020 7928 6366
    email bpc@poultry.uk.com   http://www.poultry.uk.com
    Chief Exec: Peter Bradnock
▲ Company Limited by Guarantee
○ *T; to promote the interest of the British poultry meat production
    (all species - chicken, turkeys, ducks & geese are
    represented)
● LG
< avec (Association of Poultry Processors & Poultry Import &
    Export Trade in the EU)
M 95% of the sector
× 2001 (Association of British Primary Breeders & Exporters
        (BCA (Co-operative & Export) Ltd
        (British Chicken Association Ltd
        (British Goose Producers Association
        (British Poultry Breeders & Hatcheries Association
        (British Poultry Meat Federation
        (British Turkey Federation Ltd
        (Duck Producers Association Ltd
        (Hen Packers Association

British Poultry Meat Federation Ltd
    since 2001 **British Poultry Council**

British Precast Concrete Federation Ltd   (BPCF)   1964
■ 60 Charles St, LEICESTER, LE1 1FB.   (hq)
    0116-253 6161   fax 0116-251 4568
    email info@britishprecast.org
    http://www.britishprecast.org.uk
    Sec: David J Zanker
▲ Company Limited by Guarantee
○ *T; promoting the interests of the precast concrete industry;
    provision of central services; (is structured on product
    associations)
Gp 17 product associations:
    Aircrete Products Association
    Architectural Cladding Association
    Box Culvert Association
    Concrete Block Association
    Concrete Pipeline Systems Association
    Concrete Sleeper Manufacturers' Association
    Concrete Tile Manufacturers Association
    Construction Packed Products Association
    Interlay, the Association of Block Paving Contractors
    Interpave, the Precast Concrete Paving & Kerb Association
    Modern Masonry Alliance
    Precast Flooring Federation
    Prestressed Concrete Association
    Sectional Chamber Association
    Structural Precast Association
    Traditional Housing Bureau
    Tunnel Lining Manufacturers Association
● Mtgs - Inf - Empl - LG
< Bureau Intl du Beton Manufacture
M 106 f, UK / 5 f, o'seas

British Precision Pilots Association   (BPPA)   1975
NR Hill Farm, Yoxford, SAXMUNDHAM, Suffolk, IP17 3HU.
    01728 668354
    Chmn: R J D Blois
○ *P; aerial orienteering by navigation without radio aid;
    representing GB in international competitions
● Comp
M c 30 i

British Pressure Gauge Manufacturers Association
    since 2003-04 **Pressure Gauge & Dial Thermometer
    Association**

British Printing Industries Federation   (BPIF)   1900
NR Farringdon Point, 29-35 Farringdon Rd, LONDON,
    EC1M 3JF.   (hq)
    0870 240 4085
    Chief Exec: Michael Johnson
▲ Company Limited by Guarantee
○ *T; to encourage efficiency & profitability in the printing industry
Gp Sections: Inplant printers, Young managing printers, Book
    production, Business information;
    Gps: Cartons (Pro Carton), Digital, Direct marketing special
    products, Finishers; Heidelberg users, Magazine & media
    production, Promotional finishers
    British Binders & Finishers Association; British Carton
    Association; British Engraved Stationery Association; British
    Roll Label Association; Pressure Sensitive Manufacturers
    Association
● Conf - Mtgs - ET - Exhib - SG - Stat - Inf - VE - Empl - LG
M f
¶ AR; ftm only.   List of publications; free.

British Printing Society   (BPS)   1944
■ 54 Hereward Way, Deeping St James, PETERBOROUGH,
    Northants, PE6 8QB.   (hsp)
    email enquiries@bpsnet.org.uk
    Sec: Martin D Adkins
▲ Un-incorporated Society
Br 20; Germany, Italy, Japan, N Zealand, South Africa, Spain,
    USA
○ *G; to unite full-time, part-time & hobby printers in friendly
    association; to improve the standards of craftsmanship of its
    members; to encourage printing as a hobby
Gp Publishing; Blockmaking; Letterpress; Bookbinding
● Conf - Mtgs - Exhib - Inf - Lib - VE
M 500 i, UK / 30 i, o'seas
¶ Small Printer - 12.   Small Printing - 1.
    Basic Letterpress for Beginners (Jubilee issue).
    1: History of Printing Ink.
    2: Glossary of Printing Terms.
    3: Index to ISPA News & Small Printer (Pt 1) 1954-82.
    4: The Adana Collection: a history of the Adana Company &
        its machines.

British Professional Toastmasters Authority   1995
■ 12 Little Bornes, Dulwich, LONDON, SE21 8SE.   (chmn/b)
    020 8670 5585   fax 020 8670 0055
    http://www.ivorspencer.com
    Chmn & Chief Exec: Ivor Spencer
○ *P; to monitor all aspects of the profession & to provide
    comprehensive advice (for which there is a charge) to
    companies regarding the profession
● Conf - Exam
< Gld of Intl Profl Toastmasters
M 20 affiliated toastmasters

British Promotional Merchandise Association   (BPMA)   1965
NR Bank Chambers, 15 High Rd, BYFLEET, Surrey, KT14 7QH.
    (hq)
    01932 355660   fax 01932 355662
    email enquiries@bpma.co.uk   http://www.bpma.co.uk
    Sec: Colin Levine
▲ Company Limited by Guarantee
○ *T; companies supplying merchandise & services for
    promotions, incentives, motivation schemes & related
    activities
● ET - Exhib - Inf - LG
M c 750 i
¶ Promotions Buyer - 6; free.   BPMA Ybk.

© CBD Research Ltd · Beckenham · BR3 5JS · Tel 020 8650 7745 · Fax 020 8650 0768 · E-mail cbd@cbdresearch.com · www.cbdresearch.com

British Property Federation (BPF) 1974

NR 1 Warwick Row (7th floor), LONDON, SW1E 5ER.   (hq)
    020 7828 0111   fax 020 7834 3442
    email info@bpf.org.uk   http://www.bpf.org.uk
    Chief Exec: Liz Peace,   Co Sec: Alice McMahon
▲ Company Limited by Guarantee
○ *T; to represent the views of the property industry, both
    commercial & residential
Gp Ad hoc working parties & standing c'ees on different aspects of
    Taxation, Planning, the Environment
● Conf - Mtgs - Res - Inf - LG
< Eur Property Fedn
M 430 i, f & org
¶ AR; free.

British Psychoanalytic Council (BPC) 1993

■ West Hill House, 6 Swains Lane, LONDON, N6 6QS.   (hq)
    020 7267 3626   fax 020 7267 4772
    email mail@psychoanalytic-council.org
    http://www.psychoanalytic-council.org
    Admin: Carol Grower
▲ Company Limited by Guarantee
○ *N; an association of organisations that are training institutions
    & professional associations of psychotherapists, analytical
    psychologists, psychoanalytic psychotherapists & child
    psychotherapists
● Conf - Mtgs - ET - Res
< the BCP sends a delegate to the Eur Fedn of Psychoanalytic
    Psychotherapists (EFPP)
M 1,400 i, 11 org
¶ Register of Psychotherapists - 1; ftm, £35 nm.
    Brochures:
       Finding a Therapist;
       Psychoanalytic Psychotherapy; both free.
✕ 2005-06 British Confederation of Psychotherapists

British Psychoanalytical Society 1913

NR Byron House, 112A Shirland Rd, LONDON, W9 2EQ.
    020 7563 5000   fax 020 7563 5001
    http://www.psychoanalysis.org.uk
    Hon Sec: M Mercer
▲ Registered Charity
○ *L, *P; promotion & dissemination of the theory & practice of
    Freudian psychoanalysis
● Conf - Mtgs - ET - Inf - Lib - VE
< Intl Psychoanalytical Assn; Eur Psychoanalytical Fedn
M 352 i, UK / 97 i, o'seas
¶ International Jnl of Psychoanalysis - 6.

British Psychodrama Association (BPA) 1984

NR Flat 1/1, 105 Hyndland Rd, GLASGOW, G12 9JD.   (hq)
    0141-339 0141
    Sec: James Scanlan
▲ Company Limited by Guarantee
○ *L, *P; to promote & encourage the use of psychodrama
● Conf - ET - Res - Lib - Accreditation & registration of training
    organisations
< Fedn of Eur Psychodrama Training Orgs; UK Coun for
    Psychotherapy (UKCP)
M i & org
¶ The British Jnl of Psychodrama & Sociodrama - 2.
    Tele (NL) - 2.

British Psychological Society (BPS) 1901

■ 48 Princess Road East, LEICESTER, LE1 7DR.   (hq)
    0116-254 9568   fax 0116-247 0787
    email mail@bps.org.uk   http://www.bps.org.uk
    Chief Exec: Tim Cornford
▲ Registered Charity
Br 7
○ *L, *P; advancement of knowledge of psychology both pure &
    applied
Gp Sections: Cognitive, Consciousness, Developmental, Education,
    History & philosophy, Lesbian & gay, Mathematical, Statistical
    & computing, Psychobiology, Psychotherapy, Social, Sports &
    exercise, Transpersonal, Women
    Divisions: Clinical, Counselling, Educational, Forensic, Health,
    Neuropsychology, Occupational, Teachers & researchers;
    Special groups: Social services
● Conf - Mtgs - ET - Exam - LG
< Eur Fedn of Psychological Assns
M 38, 485 i, UK / 3,705 i, o'seas
¶ The Psychologist - 12; ftm, £66 yr nm.
    British Jnl of Psychology - 4; £17 m.
    British Jnl of Clinical Psychology - 4.
    British Jnl of Developmental Psychology - 4.
    British Jnl of Educational Psychology - 4.
    British Jnl of Health Psychology - 4.
    British Jnl of Mathematical & Statistical Psychology - 2.
    Jnl of Occupational & Organisational Psychology - 4.
    Psychology & Psychotherapy - 4.
    Legal & Criminological Psychotherapy - 2.

British Pteridological Society (BPS) 1891

■ c/o Dept of Botany, Natural History Museum, Cromwell Rd,
    LONDON, SW7 5BD.   (mail/address)
    020 8850 3218   fax 010 8850 3218
    email secretary@ebps.org.uk   http://www.ebps.org.uk
    Gen Sec: Dr Yvonne C Golding
▲ Registered Society
○ *H, *L, *Q; study, growing & conservation of ferns & other
    pteridophytes
Gp Tree-ferns
● Conf - Mtgs - ET - SG - Inf - VE - Spore & plant exchange
< Nat Coun Consvn Plants & Gardens; Plantlife; R Horticl Society
M 478 i, UK / 248 i, o'seas
¶ Fern Gazette - 1;   Pteridologist - 1;   Bulletin - 1; all ftm only.
    Special publications series - irreg.

British Pugwash Group 1959

■ Ground floor flat, 63A Great Russell St, LONDON,
    WC1B 3BJ.   (hq)
    020 7405 6661
    email pugwash@mac.com   http://www.pugwash.org/uk
    Exec Sec: Sally Milne
    Chmn: Prof R Hinde,   Sec: Prof C R Hill
▲ Un-incorporated Society
○ *L; social implications of development of science & technology,
    especially in military area (international relations, nuclear
    weapons, peace research, science policy); education &
    dissemination of information
● Conf - Mtgs - ET - Res
< Pugwash Conferences on Science & World Affairs
M 240 i, UK / 10 i, o'seas
¶ Pugwash NL - 2.   BPG Reports - irreg;   Occasional Reports.

British Pump Manufacturers' Association   (BPMA)   1941
■   McLaren Building (6th floor), 35 Dale End, BIRMINGHAM,
     B4 7LN.   (hq)
     0121-200 1299
     email admin@bpma.org.uk   http://www.bpma.org.uk
     Dir: Brian Huxley
○   *T; liquid pumps
Gp C'ees: Marketing/commercial; Marketing data; Small firms;
     Technical; Training
●   Conf - Mtgs - ET - Res - Expt - Inf - LG
<   C'ee Eur Pump Assns (EUROPUMP); Mechanical & Metal Trs
     Confedn (METCOM)
M   c 80 f
¶   Pumps from Britain - 2 yrly.

British Puppet & Model Theatre Guild   (BPMTG)   1925
■   65 Kingsley Ave, LONDON, W13 0EH.   (chmn/p)
     020 8997 8236   fax 020 8997 8236
     email peter@peterpuppet.co.uk
     http://www.puppetguild.org.uk
     Hon Chmn: Peter Charlton
○   *D; to advocate the use of puppets & model theatres; to
     encourage the art & practice of puppetry
●   Mtgs - Inf - Shows
M   c 270 i & org
¶   Puppet Master - 1;   NL - 12; both ftm.

**British Pyrotechnists' Association (incorporating the Firework
Makers' Guild)   (BPA(FMG))   1980**
NR 8 Aragon Place, Kimbolton, HUNTINGDON, Cambs,
     PE28 0JD.   (asa/hsb)
     01480 861975   fax 01480 861108
     Sec: Tom Smith
○   *T; a non-commercial organisation promoting the safe
     manufacture, handling & use of pyrotechnics
M   37 f

British Quality Foundation   (BQF)   1993
NR 32-34 Great Peter St, LONDON, SW1P 2QX.   (hq)
     020 7654 5000
     Chief Exec: Joe Goasdoué
▲   Company Limited by Guarantee
Br 8 regional groups
○   *T; 'total quality management & business excellence'
Gp Automotive; Construction; Education & training; Engineering,
     projects & operations; Financial services; Food & drink;
     Founder members; Health; IT & telecommunications;
     Insurance; Local authorities; Printing, paper, packaging &
     media; Social care; T Q professionals; Tourism & hospitality
●   Conf - Mtgs - ET - Res - SG - Inf - Lib
<   Eur Foundation for Quality Mgt
M   c 1, 000 f
¶   UK Excellence - 6.

British Quilt Study Group
     is a group of the **Quilters' Guild of the British Isles**

** **British Quiz Association**
     Organisation lost: see Introduction paragraph 3

British Rabbit Council   (BRC)   1918
■   Purefoy House, 7 Kirkgate, NEWARK, Notts, NG24 1AD.   (hq)
     01636 676042   fax 01636 611683
     email info@thebrc.org   http://www.thebrc.org
     Sec: Mrs Jo Jalland,   Hon Treas: J F Fletcher
▲   Un-incorporated Society
○   *B; to protect, further & coordinate the interests of all British
     rabbit breeders; to promote education & research of a
     scientific or practical nature
●   ET - Res - Exhib - Comp - Lib
M   3,500 i, 250 clubs & org
¶   Fur & Feather (inc Rabbits).

British Racing & Sports Car Club   (BRSCC)   1946
NR Homesdale Business Centre, Platt Industrial Estate,
     Maidstone Rd, BOROUGH GREEN, Kent, TN15 8JL.   (hq)
     01732 780100
     Exec Dir: Drew Furlong
Br 6
○   *S; organisation of motor racing
M   c 2,500 i
¶   British Racing News - 12; ftm only.

British Radio Car Association   (BRCA)   1972
■   Park View, Uffculme, CULLOMPTON, Devon, EX15 3DN.
     (mem/sp)
     01884 840158   fax 01884 840158
     email membership@brca.org   http://www.brca.org
     Mem Sec: Jacquie Rowcliffe
○   *G; to organise all aspects of radio controlled model car racing
     in Britain
●   Organising races
<   RAC
M   9,500 i, 230 clubs
¶   Circuit Chatter (NL) - 4;   BRCA Hbk - 1; both ftm only.

British Rally Marshals Club
     see **British Motorsport Marshals Club**

British Ready Mixed Concrete Association   (BRMCA)   2005
■   Riverside House, 4 Meadows Business Park, Station Approach -
     Blackwater, CAMBERLEY, Surrey, GU17 9AB.   (hq)
     01276 606800   fax 01276 606801
     http://www.brmca.org
○   *T; re-launched with new branding the BRMCA represents the
     interests of ready-mixed concrete producers within the
     Quarry Products Association; to promote building systems
     using ready-mixed concrete; its remit covers generic
     technical, environmental & health & safety issues
<   Quarry Products Assn
M   f

British Record Society Ltd   1888
NR Richmond Herald, College of Arms, Queen Victoria St,
     LONDON, EC4V 4BT.   (hsb)
     Hon Sec: P L Dickinson
○   *L
●   Compilation & publication of indexes to historical records,
     particularly testamentary records

British Recording Media Association
     wound up 2006

British Records Association   (BRA)   1932
NR c/o Finsbury Library, 245 St John Street, LONDON,
     EC1V 4NB.   (hq)
     020 7833 0428   fax 020 7833 0416
     email britrecassoc@hotmail.com
     Hon Sec: Elizabeth Hughes,   Admin: Jean Harper
▲   Registered Charity
○   *L; to encourage & assist the preservation, care, study &
     publication of records; acts as a clearing-house & rescue
     body for historic documents
Gp Records preservation
●   Conf - Inf
M   551 i, 416 f (incl museums, galleries, libraries, universities)
¶   Archives Jnl - 2.   Archives & the User - irreg.

British Recovered Paper Association
     since 2004 the Recovered Paper group of the **Confederation of
     Paper Industries**

British Red Cross Society (BRCS) 1870
- ■ 44 Moorfields, LONDON, EC2Y 9AL.   (hq)
  020 7877 7000   fax 020 7562 2000
  email information@redcross.org.uk
  http://www.redcross.org.uk
  Chief Exec: Sir Nicholas Young
- ▲ Registered Charity
- Br 70; 8 o'seas
- ○ *W; an officially recognised organisation for humanitarian aid;
  disaster preparedness & response; refugees & asylum
  seekers; overseas development; first aid training & health
  activities; supporting statutory authorities in UK; community
  services, education / youth & schools
- ● Conf - Mtgs - ET - Res - Exhib - SG - Stat - Inf - Lib - PL - LG
- < Intl Red Cross; Red Crescent Movement
- M 40,000 i
- ¶ Lifeline (Jnl).   Information pack.
  Annual Review.   Trustees' Report & Accounts.

British Reed Growers' Association (BRGA) 1967
- ■ c/o Brown & Co, Old Bank of England Court, Queen St,
  NORWICH, Norfolk, NR2 4TA.
  01603 629871   fax 01603 760756
  email ilonsdale@brown-co.com
  http://www.mhp-ltd.co.uk (associate's site)   (hsb)
  Sec: I D Lonsdale,   Chmn: R Buxton
- ▲ Un-incorporated Society
- ○ *T; promotion of reed & sedge growing; coordination of supply
  to thatchers, monitoring supply & demand; promotion of
  research into improved production
- ● Mtgs - Res - Stat - Inf - LG
- M 16 i, 5 f, 15 org
- ¶ Reedbed Management for Commercial & Wildlife
  Interests; £14.95 (published by RSPB).
  Norfolk Reed Roofing Today;   Buying & Selling Reed;
  Reedbed Management for Bitterns;
  New Wetland Harvests - New Life for the Broads Fens; all free.

British Reflexology Association (BRA) 1985
- ■ Monks Orchard, Whitbourne, WORCESTER, WR6 5RB.   (hq)
  01886 821207   fax 01886 822017
  email bra@britreflex.co.uk   http://www.britreflex.co.uk
  Chmn: Miss Nicola Hall
- ▲ Company Limited by Guarantee
- ○ *P; to promote the practice of reflexology
- ● Conf - Mtgs - Res - Inf
- < Reflexology in Europe Network (RIEN)
- M 700 i
- ¶ Footprints (NL) - 4; £10 yr (UK) (£13 Europe).

British Refractories & Industrial Ceramics (BRIC) 1918
- NR Federation House, Station Rd, STOKE-ON-TRENT, Staffs,
  ST4 2SA.   (hq)
  01782 744631   fax 01782 744102
  email bcc@ceramfed.co.uk   http://www.ceramfed.co.uk
  Sec: A McRae
- ○ *T
- ● Conf - Mtgs - ET - Stat - Inf
- < Eur Refractories Fedn; Brit Ceramic Confedn
- M 35 f
- × 2002 (British Industrial Ceramic Manufacturers Association
  (Refractories Association of Great Britain

British Refrigeration Association (BRA) 1940
- ■ 2 Waltham Court, Milley Lane, Hare Hatch, READING, Berks,
  RG10 9TH.   (hq)
  0118-940 3416   fax 0118-940 6258
  email info@feta.co.uk   http://www.feta.co.uk/
  Dir Gen: C Sloan
- ○ *T; the interests of the refrigeration & air conditioning plant &
  equipment industry
- Gp Refrigeration machinery & air conditioning machinery; Cabinet
  & cold store; Contractors; Components; Education &
  training; Statistics; Users & specifiers; Refrigeration
  monitoring controls
- ● Conf - Mtgs - ET - Exhib - SG - Stat - Inf - Lib - VE - Empl
- < Fedn Envtl Tr Assns (FETA)
- M 127 f
- ¶ NL - 4; ftm.   LM - 1;   AR; both free.

British Register of Complementary Practitioners (ICM-BRCP) 1989
- NR PO Box 194, LONDON, SE16 7QE.   (hq)
  020 7237 5165
  Chief Exec: Michael Endacott
- ▲ Registered Charity
- ○ *P; to provide a register for referral of practitioners
  professionally trained, subject where appropriate to clinical
  supervision - insured for professional indemnity & public
  liability - governed by a code of practice & ethics
- Gp Divisions: Aromatherapy, Chinese medicine, Colour therapy,
  Counselling, Energy medicine, Healer counselling,
  Homoeopathy, Hypnotherapy, Massage, Nutrition,
  Osteopathy, Reflexology
- ● Registration
- M i

British Reining
  a discipline member of the **British Equestrian Federation**

British Resorts & Destinations Association (BRADA) 1921
- ■ Crown Buildings, 9-11 Eastbank St, SOUTHPORT, Merseyside,
  PR8 1DL.   (hsb)
  0151-934 2286   fax 0151-934 2287
  email bresorts@sefton.u-net.com
  http://www.britishresorts.co.uk
  Hon Sec: Mr G Haywood   Dir: Peter Hampson
- ○ *T; interests of UK inland & seaside resorts & tourist regions
- ● Conf - Mtgs
- M 60 local authorities, 8 tourist boards
- ¶ AR; m only.
- × 2006 (1 April) British Resorts Association

British Retail Consortium (BRC) 1992
- NR 21 Dartmouth St (2nd floor), LONDON, SW1H 9BP.   (hq)
  020 7854 8900   fax 020 7854 8901
  email info@brc.org.uk   http://www.brc.org.uk
  Dir Gen: Dr kevin Hawkins
- ▲ Company Limited by Guarantee
- Br 2; Belgium
- ○ *T; 'represents over 90% of the retail industry'
- < EUROCOMMERCE (retail, wholesale & international trade
  representation to the European Community)
- M f

British Retinitis Pigmentosa Society   (BRPS)   1975
- ■ PO Box 350, BUCKINGHAM, MK18 1GZ.
  01280 821334   fax 01280 815900   (hsp)
  email info@brps.org.uk   http://www.brps.org.uk
  Hon Sec/Trustee: Mrs L M Cantor
- ▲ Registered Charity
- Br 30 & o'seas
- ○ *W; to raise funds for scientific research; to provide treatments leading to a cure for RP
- ● Res - Inf - Provision of a welfare & guidance service to members
  Helpline: 0845 123 2354
- < Retina Intl; Assn Med Res Charities (AMRC); Genetic Interest Gp (GIG)
- M 2,800 i, UK / 300 i, o'seas
- ¶ NL - 4.   List of booklets & information sheets; on request.

British Rig Owners' Association   (BROA)   1983
- ■ Carthusian Court, 12 Carthusian St, LONDON, EC1M 6EZ. (hq)
  020 7417 2827   fax 020 7726 2080
  email edmund.brookes@broa.org
  Gen Mgr: E J N Brookes
- ○ *T; promote & protect the interests of British oil rig owners & managers
- ● Mtgs - SG - Inf - LG
- M 9 f

British Rigid Urethane Foam Manufacturers' Association Ltd (BRUFMA)   1967
- NR Portland Tower (2nd floor), Portland St, MANCHESTER, M1 3LF.   (hq)
  0161-236 7575
- ▲ Company Limited by Guarantee
- ○ *T; interests of manufacturers, raw materials & chemicals suppliers & machinery manufacturers of rigid urethane foam
- Gp Technical; Building applications; Environmental health & safety
- ● Conf - Mtgs - LG
- < Fedn of Eur Rigid Polyurethane Foam Assns (BING); Brit Plastics Fedn
- M 18 f
- ¶ LM - on change of details.   AR.
  Information Documents - irreg.

British Rootzone & Top Dressing Manufacturers Association (BRTMA)   2000
- ■ Federation House, STONELEIGH PARK, Warks, CV8 2RF.   (hq)
  024 7641 4999   fax 024 7641 4990
  email brtma@sportsandplay.com
  http://www.brtma.com
  Sec: Jacqui Baldwin
- ▲ Un-incorporated Society
- ○ *T; 'manufacture of quality construction mixes & top dressings'
- ● Mtgs - ET - Res - Stat - Inf
- < a group of the Fedn of Sports & Play Assns (FSPA)
- M 11 f
- ¶ Ybk - 1; free.

British Rope Skipping Association   (BRSA)
- NR 56 Toms Town Lane, STUDLEY, Warks, B80 7QP.
  01527 450962
  http://www.brsa.org.uk
  Contact: Richard McGhee
- ○ *G, *S

British Rose Growers Association   (BRGA)   1965
- ■ Horticulture House, 19 High St, THEALE, Berks, RG7 5AH. (hq)
  0118-930 3132   fax 0118-930 4989
  email info@the-hta.org.uk   http://www.the-hta.org.uk
  Sec: Mrs A Smith
- ▲ Company Limited by Guarantee
- ○ *H, *T; to promote & further the business of commercial rose-growers in the UK
- ● Mtgs - ET - Res - Stat - Inf - Lib - PL - VE - LG
- < Horticultural Trades Assn
- M 70 f
- ¶ NL - 4; ftm.
  Also known as the British Association of Rose Growers.

British Rouge de l'Ouest Sheep Society
- ■ Brockhole Farm, Morebath, TIVERTON, Devon, EX16 9BZ.
  0845 600 1503
  Sec: John Wescott
- ▲ Company Limited by Guarantee; Registered Charity
- ○ *B
- < Nat Sheep Assn
- M c 120 i

British Rubber Manufacturers' Association Ltd   (BRMA)   1968
- NR 6 Bath Place, Rivington St, LONDON, EC2A 3JE.   (hq)
  020 7457 5040   fax 020 7972 9008
  email mail@brma.co.uk   http://www.brma.co.uk
  Dir: A J Dorken,   Admin: Christine Joyce
- ▲ Company Limited by Guarantee
- ○ *T; to promote & protect the interests of the rubber manufacturing industry in the UK
- Gp Tyre management c'ee (TNC); General rubber goods (GRG)
- ● Conf - Mtgs - ET - Stat - Inf - LG
- < Eur Rubber Assn (BLIC); Tyre Ind Coun (TIC)
- M 61 f

British Saddleback Pig Breeders Club   1995
- ■ Dryft Cottage, Station Rd, South Cerney, CIRENCESTER, Glos, GL7 5UB.   (hsp)
  01285 869666   fax 01285 860229
  email mail@saddlebacks.org.uk
  http://www.saddlebacks.org.uk
  Hon Sec: Richard Lutwyche
- ▲ Un-incorporated Society
- ○ *B
- ● Mtgs - Comp - Workshops
- M 120 i, 5 f, UK / 2 i, o'seas
- ¶ NL.

British Safety Industry Federation   (BSIF)   1994
- NR Unit 3 St Asaph Business Park, ST ASAPH, Denbighs, LL17 0LJ.   (asa)
  01745 585600   fax 01745 585800
  email nfo@bsif.co.uk   http://www.bsif.co.uk
  Press Officer: Simon Wray
- ▲ Company Limited by Guarantee
- ○ *T
- Gp BSIF Assns: Personal Safety Mfrs; Occupational health & safety eqpt mfrs; Test & certification; Consultant & training; Distribution
- ● Conf - Mtgs - ET - Res - Exhib - Stat - Expt - Inf - LG
- M 150 f
- ¶ Health & Safety Europe - 12; subscription.

British Sailing
    a group of the **British Marine Federation**

British Sandwich Association (BSA) 1990

■ Archway House, Moor St, CHEPSTOW, Monmouthshire,
  NP16 5DB. (hq)
  01291 636338   fax 01291 630402
  email admin@sandwich.org.uk
  http://www.sandwich.org.uk
  Dir: Jim Winship
○ *T; to raise standards in the UK sandwich industry
● Conf - Mtgs - Res - Comp - Inf - VE - LG
M 1,450 i & f, UK / 87 i & f, o'seas
¶ Sandwich & Snack News - 8; ftm, £55 yr nm.

British Sausage Appreciation Society (BSAS) 1992

■ PO Box 44 Winterhill House, Snowdon Drive, MILTON KEYNES,
  Bucks, MK6 1AX. (hq)
  01908 844194   fax 01908 671722
  email theresa_bignall.mlc.org.uk
  http://www.meatmatters.com
  Sec: Alison Cook
▲ Un-incorporated Society
○ *G; to promote interest in British sausage eating & the range of
  sausages available in Britain
● ET - Comp - Inf - Promotional roadshow
M 7,396 i
¶ The Missing Link - 1.
  No further information supplied

British Science Fiction Association Ltd (BSFA) 1958

NR 39 Glyn Ave, NEW BARNET, Herts, EN4 9PJ. (msp)
  http://www.bsfa.co.uk
  Mem Sec: Peter Wilkinson
▲ Company Limited by Guarantee
○ *A, *G; promotion of science fiction & related genre in all
  media
Gp Orbiter: postal writers' workshops
● Inf - Publishing
M 550 i, UK / 50 i, o'seas
¶ Vector (Jnl) - 6;   Matrix (NL) - 6;
  Focus (Writers' Jnl) - 2; all ftm.

British Scoliosis Society
  a specialist society of the **British Orthopaedic Association**

British Scooter Sport Organisation (BSSO) 1969

■ 219 Elmers End Rd, BECKENHAM, Kent, BR3 4EL. (sp)
  020 8658 4378   fax 020 8249 3510
  email sylvia.caldecutt@ntlworld.com
  http://www.scooterracing.org.uk
  Gen Sec: Sylvia Caldecutt
○ *S; to promote scooter road racing
Gp Road racing: Scooter cross (off road, on grass)
● Mtgs - Comp
< Auto-Cycle U
> Lambretta Club of GB; Vespa Club of GB
M 100 i, 500 org
¶ NL - 12; ftm only.

British Secondary Metals Association
  2001 merged with the British Metals Federation to become the
  British Metals Recycling Association

British Security Industry Association Ltd (BSIA) 1967

■ Security House, Barbourne Rd, WORCESTER, WR1 1RS. (hq)
  01905 21464   fax 01905 613625
  email info@bsia.co.uk   http://www.bsia.co.uk
  Chief Exec: David Dickinson
▲ Company Limited by Guarantee
○ *T; to represent the security sector; members have to adhere to
  British Standards & codes of practice
Gp Security Manufacturers' Export Council
  Cash & property marking; Closed circuit television; Information
  destruction; Manned security; Physical security; Security
  systems; Transport; Transport (cash handling)
● Conf - Mtgs - Res - Exhib - Comp - Stat - Expt - Inf - LG -
  Formation of technical standards & codes of practice
< Eurosafe; Euralarm; CoESS
M 450 f, UK / 10 f, o'seas
¶ Spectrum (NL) - 2;   Security Direct (directory) - 1; both free.
  LM - 6; free (& on website).
  Publications list on website.
× 2001 Nationwide Association for Information Destruction
  (merged)

British Sedimentological Research Group
  a group of the **Geological Society**

British Sheep Dairying Association (BSDA) 1983

NR The Estate Office, Terry Hill, Milstead, SITTINGBOURNE, Kent,
  ME9 0SP. (hsp)
  email bsda@btopenworld.com
  http://www.sheepdairying.com
○ *T; to sponsor the improvement of dairy sheep in the UK; to
  promote the marketing of sheep milk
Gp Sheep milk marketing; Milk products
● Conf - Comp - SG - Expt - Inf - VE - LG
< Schweiz Milchschafzucht-Genossenschaft; N Amer Sheep
  Dairying Soc
M c 300 i
¶ Sheep Dairy News (Jnl) - 3; ftm.

British Shell Collectors Club (BSCC) 1972

NR 38 Redlands Rd, READING, Berks, RG1 5HD. (hsp)
  0118-987 4294
  email tom@tmwalker.co.uk
  http://www.britishshellclub.org.uk
  Hon Sec: Tom Walker
○ *G, *L; to promote the study of all aspects of shells, both land &
  marine, British & foreign, & of the molluscs which produce
  them
● Exhib - Comp
M c 230 i
¶ Pallidula (NL) - 2; ftm only.

British Shippers Council
  a group of the **Freight Transport Association**

British Shogi Federation (BSF)

NR 29 Lavender Close, CORBY, Northants, NN18 8NX. (hsp)
  Sec/Treas: Stuart Patterson
Br 3
○ *S; the play & study of Shogi (Japanese chess) & its variants
● Comp - British Shogi championship
< Fedn of Eur Shogi Assns (FESA); Nihon Shogi Renmai
  (Japanese Shogi Assn)
M c 60 i

British Shooting Sports Council   (BSSC)   1978
NR   PO Box 53608, LONDON, SE24 9YN.   (hsp/b)
     020 7095 8181
     http://www.bssc.org.uk
     Sec: David Penn
▲   Un-incorporated Society
○   *S; to promote & safeguard the lawful use of firearms & air
     weapons for sporting & recreational purposes in the United
     Kingdom
●   Mtgs - Res - Inf
<   Wld Forum on the Future of Sports Shooting Activities (WFSA)
M   13 org
¶   AR; ftm, £5 nm (free from website).

British Shops & Stores Association   (bssa)   1989
■   Middleton House, 2 Main Rd, Middleton Cheney, BANBURY,
     Oxon, OX17 2TN.   (hq)
     01295 712277   fax 01295 711665
     email info@british-shops.co.uk
     http://www.british-shops.co.uk
     Chief Exec: John Dean
▲   Company Limited by Shares
○   *T; a non-food trade association for independent small retail
     businesses
●   Conf - Mtgs - ET - LG
M   5,500 f
¶   Retail Review - 12;   Wages Survey - 1; £50 m, £150 nm.

British Shorinji Kempo Federation   (BSKF)   1974
NR   2 Cavendish Court, Sylvester Rd, WEMBLEY, Middx,
     HA0 3AE.   (hsp)
     020 8902 7471
     Gen Sec: Yasue Kadowaki
▲   Un-incorporated Society
○   *S; Shorinji Kempo (a Japanese martial art incorporating
     punching, kicking & blocking techniques with releases, pins &
     throws, combined with meditation, therapeutic massage &
     basic philosophy)

**British Show Hack, Cob & Riding Horse Association
(BSHC&RHA)   1936**
NR   2 High St, HITCHIN, Herts, SG5 1BH.   (hq)
     01462 437770   fax 01462 437776
     http://www.showhackandcob.org.uk
     Sec: Tracy Hullat
▲   Company Limited by Guarantee
○   *S; to promote the showing & breeding of the ridden hack, cob
     & riding horse; to promote equine welfare
●   Conf - Mtgs - ET - Comp
M   c 1,500 i
¶   NL - 4.

British Show Jumping Association
     is a discipline member of the **British Equestrian Federation**

British Show Pony Society   (BSPS)   1949
■   124 Green End Rd, Sawtry, HUNTINGDON, Cambs,
     PE28 5XS.   (hq)
     01487 831376   fax 01487 832779
     Chief Exec/Sec: Mrs P J Hall
▲   Un-incorporated Society
○   *S; to promote & encourage the showing of children's ponies
     via classes & competitions for show ponies, show hunter
     ponies, working hunter ponies, & mountain & moorland, for
     riders between the ages of 3 and 25 & ponies up to 15.2hh
●   Mtgs
M   4,601 i, 20 f
¶   News Review - 10; £20.   Ybk - 1; £20.   Rule Book; free.

British Sign & Graphics Association Ltd   (BSGA)   1977
NR   5 Orton Enterprise Centre, Bakewell Rd, Orton Southgate,
     PETERBOROUGH, Cambs, PE2 6XU.   (hq)
     01733 230033   fax 01733 230993
     email info@co.uk   http://www.bsga.co.uk
     Dir: Peter W Tipton
▲   Company Limited by Guarantee
Br   2
○   *T; interests of sign manufacturers & traders in the UK
Gp   Sign manufacture - illuminated & non-illuminated; Sign writing;
     Publicity items - banners, buntings, flags, plaques etc
●   Conf - Mtgs - Exhib - Comp - Inf
<   Eur Fedn of Illustrated Signs; Outdoor Advertising Coun
M   240 f, UK / 14 f, o'seas
¶   Signs Jnl - 10; ftm.   LM - irreg.
     News Update - 6;   AR; both ftm only.

British Simmental Cattle Society Ltd   (BSCS)   1971
■   NAC, Stoneleigh Park, KENILWORTH, Warks, CV8 2LG.   (hq)
     024 7669 6513   fax 024 7669 6724
     email information@britishsimmental.co.uk
     http://www.britishsimmental.co.uk
▲   Registered Charity
○   *B
M   1,400 i, UK / 200 i, o'seas
¶   Review - 1; ftm, £12 nm.

British Sjogren's Syndrome Association   (BSSA)   1987
■   PO Box 10867, BIRMINGHAM, B16 0ZW.   (hq)
     0121-455 6532
     email kate@bssa.uk.net   http://www.bssa.uk.net
     Office Mgr: Kate Endacott
▲   Company Limited by Guarantee; Registered Charity
Br   15 regional groups
○   *W; to provide information on Sjogren's Syndrome (an auto-
     immune disorder in which the body's immune system turns
     against itself, destroying the mucous-secreting glands as
     though they were foreign bodies); to spread information on
     alleviation of the symptoms; to support medical research
●   Mtgs - Res - Inf
M   c 2,500 i, UK & o'seas
¶   Sjogren's Today - 4; ftm, £2.50 per back issue nm.
     New Sjogren's Hbk (3rd ed 2005); £17.50 m, £18.50 nm.
     Advisory Guide for Patients & Doctors; ftm, £2.50 nm
     (£3.50 o'seas).

British Skewbald & Piebald Association   (BSPA)   1989
NR   PO Box 67, ELY, Cambs, CB7 4FY.
     01354 638226
     Sec: Mrs ALice Neaves
▲   Un-incorporated Society
○   *B
●   Mtgs - Comp - Inf - Registration - Stallion licensing - Shows
<   Brit Horse Database; Brit Cent Prefix Register
M   c 1,800 i, f & org
¶   NL - 3;   Hbk; both ftm only.
     Stallion List - 1; on application.

British Ski Club for the Disabled   (BSCD)   1974
NR   17 Silk Mill Rd, Resbourn, St ALBANS, Herts, AL3 7GE.
     (v/chmn/p)
     01582 793518
     Contact: Elizabeth Philpott
▲   Registered Charity
○   *S; to enable disabled people to ski on artificial slopes in the
     UK; to provide holidays on snow;   to train people as guides
Gp   Artificial slopes
●   ET
<   Central Coun for Physical Recreation; Brit Winter Sports
     Commission; Ski Club of GB; English Ski Coun
M   c 600 i, 25 affiliated members
¶   NL - 3/4; ftm only.
     Leaflet giving list of artificial slopes.

British Ski & Snowboard Federation
  trades as **Snowsport GB**

British Slate Association
  an affiliate of the **Stone Federation**

British Sleep Society (BSS) 1989
■ PO Box 247, Colne, HUNTINGDON, Cambs, PE28 3UZ. (hq)
    fax 01480 840618
    email bssoffice@btopenworld.com
    http://www.sleeping.org.uk
    Hon Sec: Paul Reading
▲ Registered Charity
○ *L, *Q; to promote knowledge & research in sleep & its
    disorders & treatment
● Conf - Mtgs - ET - Res - SG
< Wld Fedn of Sleep Res Socs; Eur Sleep Res Soc
M 500 i, 10 f, UK / 30 i, o'seas
¶ NL - 2; ftm, £5 nm.   Conference Papers Abstracts - 1.

British Slot Car Racing Association (BSCRA) 1964
■ 48 Wiltshire Gardens, Bransgore, CHRISTCHURCH, Dorset,
    BH23 8BJ. (hsp)
    01425 672060
    email info@bscra.co.uk   http://www.bscra.co.uk
    Hon Sec: C M Frost
▲ Un-incorporated Society
Br 64; 13 countries o'seas
○ *G, *S; controlling body for slot car racing in the UK; the cars
    are controlled by a guide running in a slot in the track, (NOT
    radio-controlled)
● Conf - Mtgs - Exhib - Comp - Inf - Promotion of national &
    international championships
< Intl Slot Racing Assn (ISRA)
M 300 i, 64 org, UK / 13 org, o'seas
¶ Slot Car Racing News - 6; ftm, £20 yr nm.
    Members Handbook - 2 yrly; ftm, £3 nm.
    [subscription,£20 yr].

British Small Animal Veterinary Association (BSAVA) 1956
NR Woodrow House, 1 Telford Way, Waterwells Business Park,
    QUEDGELEY, Glos, GL2 2AB. (hq)
    01452 726700   fax 01452 726701
    email admin@bsava.com   http://www.bsava.com
    Hon Sec: Grant Petrie
▲ Registered Charity
Br 13 regions; 1
○ *P; to foster & promote high scientific & educational standards
    in small animal medicine & surgery
Gp Association of British Veterinary Acupuncture; Association of
    Veterinary Anaesthetists; Association of Veterinary Clinical
    Pharmacology & Therapeutics; Association of Veterinary Soft
    Tissue Surgery; British Association of Veterinary Emergency
    Care; British Association of Veterinary Ophthalmologists;
    British Veterinary Dental Association; British Veterinary
    Dermatology Study Group; British Veterinary Neurology Study
    Group; Veterinary Orthopaedic Association; Companion
    Animal Behaviour Therapy Study Group; Veterinary
    Cardiovascular Society; European Society for Feline Medicine
● Conf - Mtgs - ET - Res - Exhib - SG - Stat - Inf - LG
< Wld Small Animal Veterinary Assn (WSAVA); Fedn of Eur
    Companion Animal Veterinary Assns (FECAVA); Brit
    Veterinary Assn (BVA)
M c 5,600 i
¶ Jnl of Small Animal Practice - 12; ftm.
    Manuals & CD-ROMs:
        Practice Resource Manual.
        Client Information leaflets.

British Small Boatbuilders Association
  a group of the **British Marine Federation**

British Snoring & Sleep Apnoea Association (BSSAA) 1991
§ Castle Court, 41 London Rd, REIGATE, Surrey, RH2 9RJ. (hq)
    01737 245638   fax 0870 052 9212
    email info@britishsnoring.co.uk
    http://www.britishsnoring.co.uk
    Dir: Mrs Marianne Davey
▲ Company Limited by Guarantee
    a non-membership body offering help & advice on snoring &
    sleep apnoea

British Snowboard Association
  no longer exists

British Society of Aesthetics (BSA) 1963
NR c/o Kathleen Stock, Dept of Philosophy / Arts B, University of
    Sussex, Falmer, BRIGHTON, E Sussex, BN1 9QN. (hsb)
    email kathleen@british-aesthetics.org
    http://www.british-aesthetics.org
    Hon Sec: Kathleen Stock
▲ Company Limited by Guarantee; Registered Charity
○ *A, *L; to promote study, research & discussion of the fine arts
    & related types of experience from a philosophical,
    sociological, historical, critical & educational standpoint
● Conf
< Intl Assn of Aesthetics; Amer Soc for Aesthetics
M 170 i
¶ British Jnl of Aesthetics - 4.   NL - 2.

British Society for Allergy & Clinical Immunology (BSACI) 1947
■ 17 Doughty St, LONDON, WC1N 2PL.
    020 7404 0278   fax 020 7404 0280
    email info@bsaci.org   http://www.bsaci.org
    Co Sec: Mrs Fiona Rayner
▲ Registered Charity
○ *L; to advance & encourage the study of allergy & clinical
    immunology & their recognition as specialised branches of
    medicine
Gp Occupational allergy; ENT allergy; Ophthalmology; Primary
    Health Care; Gastroenterology; Paediatrics; Anaphylaxis;
    Dermatology
● Conf - Mtgs - Res
< Intl Union Immunological Socs; Intl Assn Allergy & Clinical
    Immunology; Eur Academy Allergology & Clinical
    Immunology; Allergy UK; Brit Soc Immunology
M 400 i, UK / 80 i, o'seas
¶ Clinical & Experimental Allergy (Jnl) - 12;
    Allergy Update (NL)- 3;   both ftm only.
    UK Allergy Clinic Database available on website.

British Society for Allergy, Environmental & Nutritional Medicine
  since 2005 **British Society for Ecological Medicine**

British Society of Animal Science (BSAS) 1943
■ PO Box 3, PENICUIK, Midlothian, EH26 0RZ. (hq)
    0131-445 4508   fax 0131-535 3120
    email bsas@sac.ac.uk   http://www.bsas.org.uk
    Chief Exec: Mike Steele
▲ Registered Charity
○ *E, *L; an educational charity for those interested in animal
    production, animal products & related sciences
● Conf - Mtgs - ET - Res - SG - LG
< Eur Assn Animal Production; Biosciences Fedn; Genesis
    Faraday; Assn of Learned & Profl Soc Publishers
M 600 i, UK / 200 i, o'seas
¶ Animal Science - 6.   BSAS Annual Proceedings; ftm, £50 nm.

British Society for Antimicrobial Chemotherapy   (BSAC)   1972
NR   11 The Wharf, 16 Bridge St, BIRMINGHAM, B1 2JS.   (hq)
    0121-633 0410
    Exec Officer: Miss Tracey Guest
▲   Registered Charity
○   *L, *Q; to facilitate the acquisition & dissemination of
    knowledge in the field of antimicrobial chemotherapy
Gp   Microbiology; Mycology; Virology
●   ET
<   Intl Soc of Chemotherapy; Fedn of Infection Socs
M   c 625 i, UK / 175 i, o'seas
¶   Jnl of Antimicrobial Chemotherapy - 12.

British Society of Audiology   (BSA)   1967
■   80 Brighton Rd, READING, Berks, RG6 1PS.   (hq)
    0118-966 0622   fax 0118-935 1915
    email bsa@thebsa.rog.uk   http://www.thebsa.org.uk
    Admin Sec: Jan Deevey,   Hon Sec: Andrew Reid
▲   Registered Charity
○   *P; for professionals working in hearing & balance
Gp   Hearing
    Interest groups: Auditory process, Balance, Paediatric
●   Conf - Mtgs - ET - SG - Inf
M   1,169 i, 24 f, UK / 226 i, o'seas
¶   International Jnl of Audiology - 12.
    BSA News - 3.

British Society for Cell Biology   (BSCB)   1959
NR   Dept of Biological Science, Firth Court, University of Sheffield,
    SHEFFIELD, S10 2TN.   (hsb)
    0114-222 4635
    Hon Sec: Prof Elizabeth Smythe
○   *L; cell biology including: cell membranes, cell secretions,
    cytoskeleton, nuclei, growth factors, cell differentiation, cell
    matrix & cell motility etc

British Society for Children's Orthopaedic Surgery
    a specialist society of the **British Orthopaedic Association**

British Society of Cinematographers Ltd   (BSC)   1949
■   PO Box 2587, GERRARDS CROSS, Bucks, SL9 7WZ.   (regd)
    01753 888052   fax 01753 891486
    email bscine@btconnect.com
    http://www.BSCine.com office
    Sec Treas: Mrs Frances K Russell
▲   Company Limited by Guarantee
○   *P; motion picture cinematography
Gp   Full members: Directors of photography;
    Honorary members: Retired DoPs & camera operators;
    Associate members: Top [film] camera operators;
    Patron members: Companies closely associated with motion
    picture photography
●   Mtgs - ET - Exhib - Awards
<   Eur Fedn of Cinematographers (IMAGO); Cine Guilds of Great
    Britain (CGGB)
M   260 i, UK / 41 i, o'seas
¶   BSC NL - 4; ftm only.
    British Cinematographer Magazine - 6; £16.80 yr
    (£3.50 each).

British Society for Clinical Cytology   (BSCC)   1962
NR   12 Coldbath Square, LONDON, EC1R 5HL.   (hsb)
    020 7278 60907
▲   Registered Charity
○   *L, *P; promotion of the growth & practice of cytopathology
<   Eur Fedn Cytology Socs
M   i

British Society of Clinical Hypnosis   (BSCH)   1987
■   125 Queensgate, BRIDLINGTON, E Yorks, YO16 7JQ.   (hq)
    01262 403103
    email sec@bsch.org.uk   http://www.bsch.org.uk
    Sec: Tom Connelly
▲   Un-incorporated Society
Br   2
○   *P; to maintain a register of properly trained therapists; to set &
    maintain the standard for hypnotherapy in the UK
●   Inf - Liaison between the public & the body of therapists
M   1,435 i

British Society of Clinical Neurophysiology   (BSCN)   1942
■   c/o Dr Robin Kennett, Radcliffe Infirmary, OXFORD,
    OX2 6HE.   (contact/b)
    01865 224589   fax 01865 228541
    email bscn@secretariat.freeserve.co.uk
    http://www.bscn.org
    Sec: Dr Robin Kennett
▲   Registered Charity
○   *M, *P; 'education & scientific advancement in the field of
    electrodiagnostic medicine & physiological investigation of
    the human nervous system'
Gp   Electroencephalography; Infra-operative monitoring
●   Conf - Mtgs - ET
<   Intl Fedn for Clinical Neurophysiology (IFCN)
M   c 400 i
¶   Abstracts of presentations to society scientific meetings - 3;
    NL - 1; both free.

British Society of Comedy Writers   (BSCW)   1999
■   61 Parry Rd, WOLVERHAMPTON, W Midlands, WV11 2PS.
    (pres/p)
    01902 722729
    email info@bscw.co.uk   http://www.bscw.co.uk
    Pres: Kenneth Rock
Br   5
○   *P; to develop & promote the work of comedy writers & the art
    of comedy writing
Gp   Situation comedy; Sketch shows; Soap operas; quiz shows;
    Speeches; Corporate videos; Radio; Stage; Films;
    Publications
●   Conf - Mtgs
M   c 100 i
¶   NL - 4; ftm only.

British Society of Criminology   (BSC)
■   c/o Law School (Room DH021), University of East London,
    High St, Stratford, LONDON, E15 2JB.   (hq)
    020 8223 2902   fax 020 8223 7869
    email crimsoc@aol.com   http://www.britsoccrim.org
    Pres: Prof Tim Newburn
▲   Company Limited by Guarantee, Registered Charity
Br   7
○   *L, *P; promotion of criminological knowledge
●   Conf - Mtgs - ET - Comp - Inf - LG
M   850 i, UK / 80 i, o'seas
¶   NL - 4; ftm only.

**British Society of Dental & Maxillofacial Radiology   (BSDMFR)
1958**
■   School of Dentistry, University of Manchester, Higher
    Cambridge St, MANCHESTER, M15 6FH.   (s/b)
    0161-275 6742   fax 0161-275 6840
    email vivian.e.rushton@manchester.ac.uk
    Sec: Dr Vivian Rushton
▲   Registered Charity
○   *L; to promote study & research into all aspects of dental &
    maxillofacial radiology & radiography
●   Conf - Mtgs - Comp - SG - LG
M   110 i, UK / 20 i, o'seas
¶   NL - 2; ftm only.

British Society for Dental Research   (BSDR)   1950
NR   c/o Prof Tim Watson, Depts of Biomaterials & Conservative
       Dentistry, King's College London Dental Institute,
       Guy's Hospital, London Bridge, LONDON, SE1 9RT.   (hsb)
       020 7188 1582
       Hon Sec: Prof Tim Watson
▲   Registered Charity
Br   2
○   *L, *Q; to advance research & increase knowledge for the
       improvement of oral health worldwide
Gp   Mineralised tissue research; Oral biology; Oral microbiology &
       immunology; Dental materials; Implant research;
       Behavioural sciences & health services
●   Conf - Res - Exhib - SG - LG
<   Intl Assn of Dental Res (USA)
M   898 i, 3 org, UK / 14 i, o'seas
¶   Jnl of Dental Research - 12.   NL - 1.

British Society for Dermatological Surgery
       a group of the **British Association of Dermatologists**

British Society for Dermatopathology
       a group of the **British Association of Dermatologists**

British Society for Developmental Biology   (BSDB)   1964
■   Centre for Regenerative Medicine, Developmental Biology
       Programme, Dept of Biology & Biochemistry, University of
       Bath, BATH, BA2 7AY.   (hsb)
       01225 383828   fax 01225 386779
       email r.n.kelsh@bath.ac.uk
         http://www.bms.ed.ac.uk/services/webspace/bsdb/
       welcome.htm
       Sec: Dr Robert Kelsh
▲   Registered Charity
○   *L; research in developmental biology (concerned with the
       mechanisms of embryonic development, growth &
       regeneration in animals & plants)
●   Conf - ET - Res
<   Eur Developmental Biology Org; Biological Sciences Fedn;
       Company of Biologists
M   c 900 i, UK / c 300 i, o'seas
¶   NL - 2; ftm only.

British Society for Disability & Oral Health   (BSDH)   1976
NR   138 Woodstock Rd, OXFORD, OX2 7NG.   (hsb)
       http://www.bsdh.org.uk
       Hon Sec: Pauline Watt-Smith
▲   Registered Charity
○   *P; to improve, preserve & protect the oral health of peoples of
       all ages with disabilities
●   Conf - Inf
<   Intl Assn for Disability & Oral Health
M   549 i
¶   Proceedings - 1.
       Guidelines for standards of dental care for people with
       disabilities.

British Society of Dowsers   (BSD)   1933
■   2 St Ann's Rd, MALVERN, Worcs, WR14 4RG.   (hq)
       01684 576969   fax 01684 576969
       email info@britishdowsers.org
       http://www.britishdowsers.org
       Dir: John Moss
▲   Company Limited by Guarantee; Registered Charity
○   *L; to promote a greater understanding of dowsing & its use in
       all its forms
Gp   Dowsing research; Earth energies; Health & healing; Water
       divining
●   Conf - Mtgs - ET - Res - Exhib - SG - Lib - VE - LG
M   1,200 i, UK / 200 i, o'seas
¶   Dowsing Today (Jnl) - 4; ftm, £6 nm.

British Society for Ecological Medicine   (BSEM)   1981
NR   PO Box 7, KNIGHTON, Powys, LD7 1WT.   (hq)
       01547 550378
       Contact: Mrs Sue Price
▲   Registered Charity
○   *P; to promote the study of allergy, environmental & nutritional
       medicine
●   Conf - Mtgs - Res - LG
M   140 i, UK / 20 i, o'seas
×   2005 British Society for Allergy, Environmental & Nutritional
       Medicine

British Society of Enamellers   (BSOE)   1985
NR   74 Easedale Drive, SOUTHPORT, Lancs, PR8 3TS.   (hsp)
       Hon Sec: Ruth Ball
▲   Un-incorporated Society
○   *P; to promote excellence in British enamelling & professional
       enamellers worldwide
●   Conf - ET - Exhib - Lib - PL
<   societies in: Australia, France, Germany, Holland, Spain, USA
M   49 i, 51 i (associates)
¶   NL - 4; ftm only.

**British Society of Experimental & Clinical Hypnosis   (BSECH)
1977**
■   Hollybank House, Lees Rd, Mossley, ASHTON-under-LYME,
       Lancs, OL5 0PL.   (hsp)
       01457 839363   fax 01457 839363
       email honsec@bsech.com   http://www.bsech.com
       Hon Sec: Dr Ann Williamson
▲   Company Limited by Guarantee; Registered Charity
○   *L; to promote the study, teaching & use of hypnosis in the field
       of medicine, dentistry & psychology
Gp   Health professionals
●   Conf - Mtgs - ET - Res
<   Intl Soc of Hypnosis (ISH); Eur Soc of Hypnosis (ESH)
M   223 i
¶   Contemporary Hypnosis - 4; £39 m, £91 nm.

British Society of Flavourists   (BSF)   1960
■   1 Wansford Close, BRENTFORD, Essex, CM14 4PU.   (hsp)
       01277 224587
       email christogoddard@aol.com   http://www.bsf.org.uk
       Sec: Christopher A Goddard
▲   Un-incorporated Society
○   *L, *P, *Q; the technology & application of flavours
●   Conf - Mtgs - ET - Exhib - VE
<   American Flavour Soc; Brit Soc Perfumers
M   c 500 i, UK / c 150 i, o'seas
¶   News & Views - 4;   LM;   AR; all ftm.

British Society of Gastroenterology   (BSG)   1937
■   3 St Andrews Place, LONDON, NW1 4LB.   (hq)
       020 7387 3534   fax 020 7487 3734
       email bsg@mailbox.ucc.ac.uk   http://www.bsg.org.uk
       Hon Sec: Dr J de Caestecker
▲   Registered Charity
○   *L; advancement of gastroenterology (incl endoscopy,
       pathology, radiology, basic science, liver disease, colorectal
       disease)
Gp   Pathology; Radiology; Basic science; Endoscopy; Pancreas;
       Paediatrics; Oesophagus; Surgery; Liver; Small bowel;
       Nutrition
●   Conf - ET - Exhib
M   1,500 i, UK / 300 i, o'seas
¶   Gut - 12; ftm, £260 nm.

British Society for General Dental Surgery   (BSGDS)   1981
■ c/o Centre for Excellence in Dentistry, 10 Priory Queensway, BIRMINGHAM, B4 6BS.   (hsb)
0121-236 2277   fax 0121-236 3149
email birmingham@jameshull.co.uk
http://www.bsgds.com
Hon Sec: Roy Dixon
▲ Registered Charity
○ *P; quality of care in general dental practice; training of dentists in primary care
● Conf - ET - Res
M 359 i, UK / 15 i, o'seas
¶ NL - 4; free.

British Society of Gerontology   (BSG)   1973
NR European Institute of Health & Medical Sciences, Duke of Kent Building, University of Surrey, GUILDFORD, Surrey, GU2 7TE.   (hsb)
01483 682542
http://www.britishgerontology.org
Hon Sec: Dr Ingrid Eyers
▲ Registered Charity
○ *L, *Q; to promote research & study of human ageing & later life
● Conf - Mtgs - Res
< Intl Assn of Gerontology (Eur Region); Academy of Learned Socs for the Social Sciences
M 441 i, 19 org, UK / 34 i, o'seas
¶ Generations Review - 4; ftm.   Ageing & Society - 6; £29 m. Directory of Members' Research - 2 yrly; ftm only.

British Society of Graphoanalysts   1985
■ Stone Edge, Dunkerton, BATH, Somerset, BA2 8AS. (pres&sp/b)
01761 437809
Contact: Lawrence Warner
○ *G, *P; personality assessment through handwriting analysis; examination of questioned documents
Gp Personality assessment; Questioned document examiners
● Mtgs - ET - Exam - Res - SG
M 52 i
¶ NL - 4; ftm only.

British Society of Gynaecological Endoscopy   (BSGE)   1989
■ Castle Hill Hospital, COTTINGHAM, E Yorks, HU16 5JQ. (hsb)
01482 875875   fax 01482 624051
Sec: Kevin Phillips
▲ Registered Charity
○ *M, *P, *Q; to promote endoscopic gynaecological surgery & research; to coordinate training & teaching programmes; to advise on safety in diagnostic & operative hysteroscopy & laparoscopic surgery
Gp Gynaecologists; Laparoscopic surgeons
● Conf - Mtgs - ET - Res - SG
< Eur Soc of Gynaecological Endoscopy; Amer Assn of Gynaecological Laparoscopists
M c 450 i

British Society of Habromaniacs
NR 81 Park View, Collins Rd, LONDON, N5 2UD.
○ *G; 'for mutual appreciation of morbid gaiety'
● Exhib - Mtgs - PL - VE
M ['confidential']
¶ Happy Talk (NL) - irreg.

British Society for Haematology   (BSH)   1960
■ 100 White Lion St, LONDON, N1 9PF.   (hq)
020 8643 7305   fax 020 8770 0933
email info@b-s-h.org.uk   http://www.b-s-h.org.uk
Sec: Dr J K M Duguid
▲ Company Limited by Guarantee; Registered Charity
○ *L; to advance the practice & study of haematology
Gp Brit C'ee for Standards in Haematology (BCSH); Sub-c'ees: Paediatric (PHF); Clinical science (CSHF)
● Conf - Mtgs - ET - Res - Exhib
< Intl Soc for Haematology; Intl Coun for Standardisation in Haematology
M 993 i, 28 f, UK / 113 i, o'seas
¶ British Jnl of Haematology - 16; (price on application). [www.bloodmed.com]
BSH Bulletin - 3; ftm only.
Guidelines Documents - irreg; ftm only. (Published in haematology jnls). [www.bcshguidelines.com].

British Society of Hearing Aid Audiologists Ltd   (BSHAA)   1954
■ 9 Lukins Drive, GREAT DUNMOW, Essex, CM6 1XQ.   (sp)
01371 876623   fax 01371 876623
email secretary@bshaa.com   http://www.bshaa.com
Sec: Jill Humphreys,
Pres: K Finch
▲ Company Limited by Guarantee
○ *P; to represent the interests of the private hearing aid dispenser; to provide ongoing education
● Conf - Mtgs - ET - Exhib
M 950 i, UK / 50 i, o'seas
¶ BSHAA News - 4; ftm.

British Society of Hearing Therapists
2004 merged with the British Association of Audiological Scientists & the British Association of Audiologists to form the **British Academy of Audiology**

British Society for the History of Mathematics   (BSHM)   1971
NR School of Computing & Mathematical Sciences, University of Greenwich, Maritime Greenwich Campus, Old Royal Naval College, Park Row, Greenwich, LONDON, SE10 9LS.   (hsb)
http://www.bshm.org
Hon Sec: Tony Mann
▲ Registered Charity
○ *L; to provide a forum for all interested in the history & development of mathematics & related disciplines
● Conf - Mtgs - SG - VE
M 282 i, 3 org, UK / 142 i, o'seas
¶ NL - 2/3;   AR - 1; both ftm only.

British Society for the History of Medicine   (BSHM)   1965
NR New Barn, 39a Grange Rd, BROADSTAIRS, Kent, CT10 3ER.
email ann.ferguson@doctors.org.uk
Sec: Ann Ferguson
▲ Un-incorporated Society
Br 17
○ *N; to foster interest & research in the history of medicine & bring together various smaller societies
● Conf - Mtgs
< Intl Soc for the History of Medicine
M 24 org
¶ NL - 1; free.

© CBD Research Ltd · Beckenham · BR3 5JS · Tel 020 8650 7745 · Fax 020 8650 0768 · E-mail cbd@cbdresearch.com · www.cbdresearch.com

British Society for the History of Pharmacy   (BSHP)   1967
■ 840 Melton Rd, Thurmaston, LEICESTER, LE4 8BN.
    (mail/address)
    0116-264 0083   fax 0116-264 0141
    email bshp@associationhq.org.uk
    http://www.bshp.org
    Hon Sec: Peter G Homan
▲ Registered Charity
○ *L; to act as a focus for the development of all areas of the
    history of pharmacy, from the works of the ancient
    apothecary to today's ever changing role of the community,
    hospital, wholesale or industrial chemist
● Conf - Mtgs - Res - VE
< Intl Soc for the History of Pharmacy; R Pharmaceutical
    Soc of GB
M 250 i, 4 org, UK / 24 i, 4 org, o'seas
¶ The Pharmaceutical Historian (NL) - 4; ftm, £1.50 each nm.

British Society for the History of Philosophy   (BSHP)   1984
■ Dept of Philosophy, Faculty of Arts, Open University,
    MILTON KEYNES, Bucks, MK7 6AA.   (sb)
    01908 659137
    http://www.open.ac.uk/arts/bshp/bshp.htm
    Sec: Dr Cristina Chimisso
▲ Registered Charity
○ *P; to promote & foster all aspects of the study of the history of
    philosophy
● Conf - Mtgs
M 100 i
¶ British Jnl for the History of Philosophy - 4.

British Society for the History of Science   (BSHS)   1947
■ 5 Woodcote Green, FLEET, Hants, GU51 4EY.   (hsb)
    01252 641135
    Exec Sec: Philip Crane
▲ Registered Charity
○ *L; to further the study of history & philosophy of science
Gp Education (to promote the wider use of the history of science in
    the teaching of both science & history in schools)
● Conf - Mtgs - Publication
M 850 i
¶ British Jnl for the History of Science - 4.   NL - 3.
    List of theses in history of science in British universities in
        progress, or recently catalogued.
    Guide to History of Science Courses in Britain.

British Society for Human Genetics   (BSHG)   1996
■ Clinical Genetics Unit, Birmingham Women's Hospital,
    Edgbaston, BIRMINGHAM, B15 2TF.   (hq)
    0121-627 2634   fax 0121-623 6971
    email bshg@bshg.org.uk   http://www.bshg.org.uk
    Gen Sec: Dr Graham Taylor
▲ Registered Charity
○ *P; to advance the science of human genetics; to promote
    research relating to health & disease; to promote public
    awareness of human genetics
Gp Association of Genetic Nurses & Counsellors; Clinical Genetics
    Society; Association of Clinical Cytogeneticists; Clinical
    Molecular Genetics Society;Cancer Genetics Group
● Conf - Mtgs - ET - Res - SG - Inf - LG
< Intl Fedn of Human Genetics Socs
M i
¶ BSHG NL - 3.

British Society of Hypnotherapists (1950)   (BSH)   1950
■ 37 Orbain Rd, LONDON, SW6 7JZ.   (hsp/b)
    020 7385 1166   fax 020 7385 1166
    email syhyp@onetel.net   http://www.hypnotism.org.uk
    Hon Sec: S C Young
▲ Un-incorporated Society
○ *P; the practice of hypnotherapy in dealing with nervous &
    psychosomatic conditions, phobias & unwanted habits;
    dissemination of information to the public
● Conf - Inf
< Hypnotherapy Training Inst of Britain
M [not stated]
¶ Minutes of Meetings; ftm only.

British Society for Immunology   (BSI)   1956
NR Triangle House, Broomhill Rd, LONDON, SW18 4HX.   (hq)
    020 8875 2400
    Gen Sec: Prof Adrian Hayday
▲ Registered Charity
Br 18
○ *P; to advance the science of immunology
Gp Autoimmunity; Biochemistry; Cellular signalling; Clinical
    immunology; Comparative & veterinary immunology;
    Developmental immunology; Histocompatibility &
    immunogenetics; Infection & immunity; Lymphocyte
    Immunosenescence & differentiation; Mucosal;
    Neuroimmunology; Nutritional immunology; Parasitology;
    Reproductive immunology; Tumour immunology; Vaccines
● Conf - Mtgs - ET - Exhib - Inf - LG
< Intl U Immunological Socs; Eur Fedn Immunological Socs;
    UK Life Sciences C'ee
M c 3,500 i, UK / 500 i, o'seas
¶ Immunology - 12.   Immunology News - 6.
    Clinical & Experimental Immunology - 12.
    Directory - 1; ftm only.   AR - 1; ftm.

British Society for Investigative Dermatology
    a group of the **British Association of Dermatologists**

British Society of Magazine Editors   (BSME)   1960
■ c/o Gill Branston Associates, 137 Hale Lane, EDGWARE,
    Middx, HA8 9QP.   (hq/admin)
    020 8906 4664   fax 020 8959 2137
    email admin@gillbranston.com   http://www.bsme.com
    Admin: Gill Branston
○ *P; for magazine editors in the UK
    no further information supplied

British Society of Master Glass Painters   (BSMGP)   1921
■ PO Box 15, MINEHEAD, Somerset, TA24 8ZX.   (regd)
    01643 862807
    email secretary@bsmgp.org.uk
    http://www.bsmgp.org.uk office
    Hon Sec: Chris Wyard
▲ Company Limited by Guarantee
○ *P; to promote contemporary stained glass & the appreciation
    & scholarly study of historic glass
● Conf - Mtgs - ET - Res - Exhib - Inf - Lib - VE
M c 600 (incl 50 instns, libraries etc)
¶ The Jnl of Stained Glass - 1.
    Stained Glass (NL) - 4; ftm.

British Society of Medical & Dental Hypnosis (BSMDH) 1953

■ 28 Dale Park Gardens, Cookridge, LEEDS, W Yorks,
LS16 7PT. (hsp)
0700 056 0309 fax 0700 056 0309
email natoffice@bsmdh.com http://www.bsmdh.com
Nat Sec: Angela Morris
▲ Registered Charity
Br 5
○ *L; to promote the study, training & research in the principles &
practice of hypnosis by doctors, dentists & other
paramedicals approved by the society
● Conf - Mtgs - ET - Exam - Res - Inf
< Intl Soc of Hypnosis (ISH); Eur Soc of Hypnosis
M 269 i
¶ NL - 3; free.
NOTE: all communications needing a reply should have a
stamped addressed envelope enclosed.

British Society for Medical Mycology (BSMM) 1965

■ Mycology Reference Centre, Dept of Microbiology, Leeds
General Infirmary, LEEDS, W Yorks, LS1 3EX. (hsb)
0113-392 2835
email richard.hobson@leedsth.nhs.uk
http://www.bsmm.org
Hon Sec: Dr Richard Hobson
▲ Registered Charity
○ *P; to advance research into fungal infections in humans &
animals, the pathogenesis & virulence of fungal infections,
diagnosis & treatment, agents & mechanics of resistance
Gp Diploma working party; Standards of care working party
● Conf - ET - Grant funding (travel grants)
< Intl Soc for Human & Animal Mycology; Biosciences Fedn; Inst
Biology
M 212 i, UK / 75 i, o'seas
¶ BSNN News (NL) - 2; LM; both ftm only.

British Society for Mercury Free Dentistry (BSMFD) 1984

NR Holistic Dental Centre, 5 Hart House - The Hart, FARNHAM,
Surrey, GU9 7HA. (hq)
01252 820004
Contact: Dr Gareth Rhidian
▲ Registered Charity
○ *P; the investigation of potential side-effects of dental materials,
particularly mercury; to identify patients affected
● Conf - Mtgs - ET - Res - SG - Inf

British Society for Middle Eastern Studies (BRISMES) 1973

■ Institute for Middle Eastern & Islamic Studies, University of
Durham, Elvet Hill Rd, DURHAM, DH1 3TU. (admin)
0191-334 5179 fax 0191-334 5661
email a.l.haysey@durham.ac.uk
http://www.brismes.ac.uk
Admin: Louise Haysey
▲ Registered Charity
○ *L; to promote the study of the Middle Eastern region, its
culture, languages, literature, history & politics
● Conf - ET
< Middle East Studies Assn of America (MESA); Eur Assn of
Middle Eastern Studies (EURAMES)
M 400 i, 2 f, 18 org, UK / 200 i, o'seas
¶ British Jnl of Middle Eastern Studies - 2; ftm, £64 nm.
Business NL - 3; ftm, £20 nm

British Society of Miniaturists (BSM) 1895

NR Briargate, 2 The Brambles, ILKLEY, W Yorks, LS29 9DH.
(hsp/b)
01943 609075
email britpaint@aol.com http://www.britpaint.com
Dir: Margaret Simpson
○ *A; to promote excellence in the art of miniature painting; to
promote the sale of miniature paintings
● Exhib - Comp - Inf - Free entry to view exhibitions
< Intl Gld Artists; Brit Watercolour Soc; Brit Soc of Painters (in oil,
pastel & acrylic)
M 40 i, 4 org, UK / 10 i, o'seas
¶ Exhibition Catalogues - 2; £1.

British Society for Music Therapy (BSMT) 1958

■ 61 Church Hill Rd, EAST BARNET, Herts, EN4 8SY. (hq)
020 8441 6226 fax 020 8441 4118
email info@bsmt.org http://www.bsmt.org
▲ Registered Charity
○ *D; to promote the use of music therapy in the treatment,
education, rehabilitation & training of children & adults
suffering from physical, emotional or mental handicap
● Conf - Mtgs - ET - Res - Exhib - Inf
M 600 i, 50 f, UK / 50 i, 150 f, o'seas
¶ British Jnl of Music Therapy - 2.
BSMT Bulletin - 3.

British Society of Neuroradiologists (BSNR) 1970

NR c/o Dr John Straiton, Dept of Neuroradiologists, Leeds General
Infirmary, Belmont Grove, LEEDS, W Yorks, LS2 9NS. (sb)
0113-392 3683 fax 0113-392 5196
email john@bsnr.co.uk http://www.bsnr.co.uk
Sec: Dr John Straiton
▲ Un-incorporated Society
○ *P; all matters relating to neuroradiology
● Conf - LG
< Wld Fedn of Neuroradiological Socs
M 190 i, UK / 10 i, o'seas

British Society for Oral & Maxillofacial Pathology (BSOP) 1967

■ Diagnostic Services / Level 6, Medical & Dental School,
University of Leeds, LEEDS, W Yorks, LS2 9LU. (hsb)
0113-343 6115 fax 0113-343 6264
email a.s.high@leeds.ac.uk
Hon Sec: Dr Alec S High
▲ Un-incorporated Society
○ *L, *M, *P; to promote & encourage the study & practice of
head & neck histopathology; to facilitate communication
between pathologists with an interest in head, neck, oral &
dental disease
Gp Council; Members; Overseas members; Teachers
● Conf - ET - Res
M 110 i, UK / 20 i, o'seas

British Society for Oral Medicine (BSOM) 1976

NR Prof Lewis, Head of Oral Surgery, Medicine & Pathology, Dental
School, Wales College of Medicine, Heath Park, CARDIFF,
CF14 4XN. (pres/b)
029 2074 2541
Pres: Prof M A O Lewis
○ *L; oral soft tissue disease
● Conf - ET - Comp - Inf - Devt of higher training programmes
M c 180 i
¶ NL - 1; free.

British Society of Paediatric Dentistry
NR 32 Balmoral Close, CHIPPENHAM, Wilts, SN14 0UT.
    Hon Sec: Sarah Dewhurst
▲ Registered Charity
Br 13
○ *P; dental care of children
Gp Consultants; Teachers
● Conf - Mtgs - ET - Res - LG
< Intl Assn of Paediatric Dentistry
M c 800 i
¶ Intl Jnl of Paediatric Dentistry - 4.

British Society for Paediatric Dermatology
    a group of the **British Association of Dermatologists** & of the
    Royal College of Paediatrics & Child Health

British Society of Paediatric Endocrinology & Diabetes
    a group of the **Royal College of Paediatrics & Child Health**

British Society for Paediatric Gastroenterology & Nutrition
    a group of the **Royal College of Paediatrics & Child Health**

British Society for Paediatric Neurology
    a group of the **Royal College of Paediatrics & Child Health**

British Society of Painters (in Oil, Pastels & Acrylic)
NR Briargate, 2 The Brambles, ILKLEY, W Yorks, LS29 9DH.   (dir)
    01943 609075
    email britpaint@aol.com   http://www.britpaint.com b/p
    Dir: Margaret Simpson
○ *A; to promote excellence in the field of painting
● Exhib - Comp - Free entry to exhibitions
M 50 i, UK / 3 i, o'seas
¶ Catalogue; £1.

British Society for Parasitology   (BSP)   1962
NR 27 Village Rd, Cockayne Hatley, SANDY, Beds, SG19 2EE.
    (asa)
    01767 621878
    Secretariat: Cathy Fuller
▲ Registered Charity
Br 2
○ *L; to advance the study of parasitology; to promote wider
    dissemination of advances in the subject
M i

British Society of Perfumers   (BSP)   1963
NR 15 Underwood Close, CANTERBURY, Kent, CT4 7BS.   (gen-sp)
    http://www.bsp.org.uk
    Gen Sec: Roger Duprey
▲ Un-incorporated Society
○ *P; the art, craft & science of creative perfumery
● Mtgs - Occasional workshops
< La Société Technique des Parfumeurs de France
M c 200 i
¶ NL; m only.

British Society of Periodontology   (BSP)   1949
NR 44 Pool Rd, Hartley Wintney, HOOK, Hants, RG27 8RD.
    (admin/p)
    01252 843598
    Sec: Mrs A Hallowes
▲ Registered Charity
○ *P; to promote the art & science of dentistry & in particular the
    art & science of periodontology
Gp Teachers; General practitioners
● Conf - Mtgs - ET - Comp - LG
M c 700 i, UK / 125 i, o'seas
¶ The Jnl of Clinical Periodontology - 12; ftm.

British Society for the Philosophy of Science   (BSPS)   1959
NR c/o Dr J Ladyman, Dept of Philosophy, University of Bristol, 9
    Woodland Rd, BRISTOL, BS8 1TB.   (hsb)
    Hon Sec: Dr James Ladyman
▲ Registered Charity
○ *L; to study the logic, methods & the philosophy of science, as
    well as those of the various special sciences, incl the social
    sciences
● Conf - Mtgs - Res - Inf
M i
¶ British Jnl for the Philosophy of Science - 4.

British Society of Plant Breeders Ltd   (BSPB Ltd)   1960
■ Woolpack Chambers, Market St, ELY, Cambs, CB7 4ND.   (hq)
    01353 653200
    Chief Exec: Dr Penny Maplestone
▲ Company Limited by Guarantee
○ *T; licensing and collection of royalties on plant varieties
● LG
< Intl Seed Fedn; Eur Seed Assn
M 50 f, UK / 1 i, 2 f, o'seas

British Society for Plant Pathology   (BSPP)   1981
NR 1 St Fillans Grove, ABERDOUR, Fife, KY3 0XG.   (hsp)
    01383 860695
    email secretary@bspp.org.uk   http://www.bspp.org.uk
    Sec: Bill Rennie
▲ Company Limited by Guarantee; Registered Charity
○ *L; advancement of plant pathology (study & control of plant
    disease)
● Conf - ET - Res - LG
< Intl Society for Plant Pathology (ISPP); Eur Foundation for Plant
    Pathology (EFPP)
M c 600 i
¶ Plant Pathology (Jnl) - 6.   Molecular Plant Pathology - 6.
    NL - 3.   New Disease Reports - continuous; online.

British Society for Population Studies   (BSPS)   1974
■ PS 201, London School of Economics, Houghton St, LONDON,
    WC2A 2AE.   (hq)
    020 7955 7666   fax 020 79556831
    email pic@lse.ac.uk   http://www.bsps.org.uk
    Sec/Admin: Anne Shepherd
▲ Registered Charity
○ *L, *P; to further the study of biological, economic, historical,
    medical, social & other disciplines connected with human
    populations; to contribute to public awareness of these
    problems; to provide facilities for study & research
● Conf - Mtgs - Inf
M 250 i, 10 f, UK / 50 i, o'seas
¶ BSPS News - 4; free.

British Society for Proteome Research   (BSPR)   1984
■ Conway Institute for Biomolecular & Biomedical Research,
    University College Dublin, Belfield, DUBLIN 4, Republic of
    Ireland.   (hsb)
    353 (1) 716 2807
    email gerard.cagney@acd.ie   http://www.bspr.org
    Hon Sec: Prof Stephen Pennington
▲ Registered Charity
○ *L; to promote the study of proteomics - the study of proteins as
    a system group
● Conf - ET - Res - Exhib - SG - Inf - LG
< Biosciences Fedn
M 165 i
¶ NL - 2/3; ftm only.
✕ 2004 British Electrophoresis Society

British Society of Psychosomatic Obstetrics, Gynaecology & Andrology (BSPOGA) 1988
■ 11 Hagholm Rd, Cleghorn, LANARK, ML11 7SG.   (treas/p)
   01698 366349   fax 01698 366347
   email treasurer@bspoga.org   http://www.bspoga.org
   Exec Treas: Dr Ian C Allen,
   Chmn: Kevan Wylie
▲ Registered Charity
○ *L, *M; to promote & increase knowledge & research into
   psychological problems related to all aspects of reproductive
   medicine incl pre & post menopause
● Conf - ET
< Intl Soc of Psychosomatic Obstetrics & Gynaecology
M 100 i
¶ NL - 2.

British Society of Rehabilitation Medicine (BSRM) 1984
NR c/o Royal College of Physicians, 11 St Andrews Place,
   LONDON, NW1 4LE.   (mail/address)
   01992 638865
   Exec Sec: Sandy Weatherhead
▲ Registered Charity
○ *M, *P; to promote the development, understanding &
   management of acute & chronic disabling diseases & injuries
● Conf - Mtgs - ET - LG - Publications
< Intl Fedn of Physical Medicine & Rehabilitation
M 350 i, UK / 10 i, o'seas
¶ NL - 2.   Clinical Rehabilitation - 8.

British Society for Research on Ageing (BSRA) 1947
NR c/o Dr Sian Henson,
   Dept of Immunology & Molecular Pathology,
   University College London, 46 Cleveland St,
   LONDON, W1T 4JF.   (hsb)
   Hon Sec: Dr Sian Henson
▲ Registered Charity
○ *L, *Q; promotion of teaching & research on the biology of
   ageing
< International Association of Gerontology
M 370 i
¶ Lifespan - 2; ftm only.

British Society for Restorative Dentistry (BSRD) 1968
■ Restorative Dentistry (Room 6,24), Leeds Dental Institute,
   Worsley Building, University of Leeds, LEEDS, LS2 9LU.
   (admin/s)
   0113-343 7829   fax 0113-343 6165
   http://www.bsrd.org
   Hon Sec: Prof Paul A Brunton
   Admin Sec: Hilary Griffiths
▲ Registered Charity
○ *M, *P; to promote study & high standards of restorative
   dentistry
● Conf - ET
< Brit Prosthodontic Conference
M 704 i
¶ European Jnl of Prosthodontics & Restorative Dentistry - 4; ftm,
   £60 nm.
   NL - 1; ftm only.

British Society of Rheology (BSR) 1940
NR c/o Prof Tim Phillips, Cardiff School of Mathematics, Cardiff
   University, Senghennydd Rd, CARDIFF, CF24 4AG.   (hsb)
   029 2087 4194
   Hon Sec: Prof Tim N Phillips
▲ Registered Charity
○ *L, *Q; to promote science & disseminate knowledge in pure &
   applied rheology - defined as the science of the flow &
   deformation of matter.   Rheology finds application in
   engineering, materials processing, physics, chemistry,
   applied maths & biological / medical systems
● Conf - Lib - Awards - Student sponsorships
< Intl C'ee of Rheology; Eur Soc of Rheology
M 400 i, UK / 200 i, o'seas
¶ Bulletin - 3.   Rheology Abstracts.

British Society for Rheumatology (BSR) 1984
■ Bride House, 18 Bride Lane, LONDON, EC4Y 8EE.   (hq)
   020 7842 0900   fax 020 7842 0901
   email bsr@rheumatology.org.uk
   http://www.rheumatology.org.uk
   Chief Exec: Samantha Peters
▲ Registered Charity
○ *L, *P; to advance the knowledge & practice in the field of
   rheumatology; to work for high standards of care for patients
   with rheumatic disorders
● Conf - Mtgs - ET - Res - Stat - Lib
< Arthritis & Musculoskeletal Alliance (ARMA); Brit Health Profls in
   Rheumatology (BHPR)
M 950 i, UK / 450 i, o'seas
¶ Rheumatology (Jnl) - 12; ftm, prices vary nm.
   BSR News - 3;   Hbk - 2 yrly;   AR; all ftm only.

British Society of Scientific Glassblowers (BSSG) 1960
■ Glendale, Sinclair St, THURSO, Caithness, KW14 7AQ.   (hq)
   01847 895637   fax 01847 802971
   email ian.pearson@ukaea.org.k(9>bssg.co.uk
   Chmn: Ian Pearson
▲ Un-incorporated Society
○ *P
● Conf - Mtgs - Exam - Comp - Inf - Lib
< Amer Soc Scientific Glassblowers; Soc Glass Technology; Glass
   Mfrs Confedn
M 200 i, 5 f, UK / 40 i, 1 f, o'seas
¶ Jnl - 4; £5 m, £6 nm.

British Society for Sexual Medicine (BSSM) 1997
NR Holly Cottage, Fisherwick, LICHFIELD, Staffs, WS14 9JL.
   01543 432757   fax 01543 433303
   http://www.bssm.org.uk
   Sec: Mrs Sally Hackett
○ *M; 'for the purpose of promoting research & exchange of
   knowledge of impotence & other aspects of sexual function &
   dysfunction'

British Society of Soil Science (BSSS) 1947
NR Macaulay Institute, Craigiebuckler, ABERDEEN, AB15 8QH.
   (secretariat)
   01224 498200
   Admin: Dr J H Gauld
▲ Un-incorporated Society
○ *L; to promote the study of soils & increase awareness of the
   importance of soils in many aspects of life
● Conf - ET - Exhib
< Intl Soc of Soil Science
M 750 i, UK / 250 i, o'seas
¶ European Jnl of Soil Science.
   Soil Use & Management - 4.

British Society of Sports History
NR Dingle Barn, Bradley, FRODSHAM, Cheshire, WA6 7EP.
   Contact: Dr Richard W Cox
○ *G, *P; to stimulate, promote & coordinate interest in the
   historical study of sport, physical education, recreation &
   leisure; to encourage & assist in the preservation &
   cataloguing of historical records
● Conf - Mtgs - Courses - Tours
< Brit Assn of Advisers & Lecturers in Physical Educ
M i & org

© CBD Research Ltd · Beckenham · BR3 5JS · Tel 020 8650 7745 · Fax 020 8650 0768 · E-mail cbd@cbdresearch.com · www.cbdresearch.com

British Society for Strain Measurement   (BSSM)   1964
NR   7 Tythe Close, FLITWICK, Beds, MK45 1LE.   (hq)
        01525 712779
        email bianagale@bssm.org   http://www.bssm.org
        Admin: Biana Gale
▲   Company Limited by Guarantee
Br   11
○   *L; engineering strain measurement & associated measurement
Gp   C'ees: Technical, Centrification
●   Conf - Mtgs - ET - Exam - Res - Exhib - Comp - SG - Inf
<   Soc of Experimental Mechanics (USA)
M   100 i, 100 f, UK / 20 i, o'seas
¶   Strain (Jnl) - 4; ftm, £50 yr nm.

**British Society for the Study of Prosthetic Dentistry   (BSSPD)
1953**
NR   Restorative Dentistry / School of Dental Sciences, Newcastle
        University, Framlington Place, NEWCSTLE UPON TYNE,
        NE2 4BW.   (hsb)
        0191-222 8198
        Acting Sec: Dr Janice Ellis
▲   Registered Charity
○   *L; the study & development of prosthetic dentistry (the artificial
        replacement of teeth)
M   c 500 i
¶   NL - 2;   Proceedings of the Annual Conference - 1; ftm.

British Society for the Study of Religions   (BASR)   1954
■   The Open University - Faculty of Arts, Dept of Religious Studies,
        Walton Hall, MILTON KEYNES, MK7 6AA.   (hsb)
        01908 654033
        Sec: Dr Graham Harvey
▲   Registered Charity
○   *L; to promote the study of world religions
●   Conf
<   Intl Assn for the History of Religions; Eur Assn for the Study of
        Religions
M   230 i, UK / 7 i, o'seas
¶   BASR Bulletin - 3; ftm only.

British Society for the Study of Vulval Diseases
NR   c/o Dr D Mandal, Dept of GU Medicine, Kendrick Wing,
        Warrington Hospital, Lovely Lane, WARRINGTON, Cheshire,
        WA5 1QG.   (hsb)
        01925 662476   fax 01925 275217
        http://www.bssvd.org
        Sec: Dr D Mandal
○   *M

British Society for Surgery of the Hand   (BSSH)   1968
■   at the Royal College of Surgeons, 35-43 Lincoln's Inn Fields,
        LONDON, WC2A 3PE.   (hq)
        020 7831 5162   fax 020 7831 4041
        email secretariat@bssh.ac.uk   http://www.bssh.ac.uk
        Hon Sec: R Savage
▲   Company Limited by Guarantee, Registered Charity
○   *M, *P; to promote & direct development of hand surgery; to
        foster & co-ordinate education, study & research
●   Conf - Mtgs - ET - Res
<   Intl Fedn of Socs for the Surgery of the Hand
M   520 i, UK / 150 i, o'seas
¶   Jnl of Hand Surgery (European volume) - 6; ftm only.

British Society of Toxicological Pathologists   (BSTP)   1985
NR   PO Box 222, HARROGATE, N Yorks, HG2 9XL.   (admin)
        email bstpsecretariat@aol.com   http://www.bstp.org.uk
        Secretariat
▲   Registered Charity
○   *P; to advance education in toxicological pathology for the
        public benefit
●   Conf - Mtgs - ET
M   105 i, UK / 67 i, o'seas
¶   BSTP NL - 1; ftm only.

** British Society of Underwater Photographers
        Organisation lost: see Introduction paragraph 3

British Sociological Association   (BSA)   1951
■   Palatine House (Bailey suite), Belmont Business Park, DURHAM,
        DH1 1TW.   (hq)
        0191-383 0839   fax 0191-383 0782
        email enquiries@britsoc.org.uk
        http://www.britsoc.co.uk
        Chief Exec: Judith Mudd
▲   Company Limited by Guarantee; Registered Charity
○   *P; promotion of interest in sociology & advancement of its
        study & application in the UK
Gp   over 30 specialist study groups
●   Conf - Mtgs - ET - Res - Exhib - Comp - SG - Stat - Inf - LG
<   Intl Sociological Assn; Foundation for Science & Technology;
        Standing Conf of Arts & Social Sciences; Amer/ Australian /
        Indian Sociological Assn(s); Canadian Sociological &
        Anthropological Assn
M   2,127 i, UK / 180 i, o'seas
¶   Sociology (Jnl) - 6; ftm, £59 yr nm.
        Work, Employment & Society (Jnl) - 4; ftm, £58 yr nm.
        [1st copy to m, free; 2nd copy, £35].
        Network (NL) - 3;   AR; both ftm only.

British Soft Drinks Association   (BSDA)   1987
■   20-22 Stukeley St, LONDON, WC2B 5LR.   (hq)
        020 7430 0356   fax 020 7831 6014
        email bsda@britishsoftdrinks.com
        http://www.britishsoftdrinks.com
        Dir Gen: Jill Ardagh
▲   Company Limited by Guarantee
○   *T; for all manufacturers of soft drinks, fruit juices & bottled
        waters
Gp   Various specialist c'ees
●   Conf - ET - Inf - PL - LG
<   UNESDA; EFBW; AIJN
M   47 f, 47 f (associates)
¶   Publications list available.

British Softball Federation
        2002 merged with British Baseball Federation to become
        BaseballSoftballUK

**British Soluble Coffee Packers & Importers Association
(BSCPIA)   1994**
■   Crescent House, 34 Eastbury Way, SWINDON, Wilts,
        SN25 2EN.   (sb)
        01793 723387   fax 01793 726486
        email bscpia@aol.com
        Sec: Walter J Anzer
▲   Company Limited by Guarantee
○   *T; to represent the needs of the soluble coffee packers &
        importers on an international basis supplying the British & EU
        markets
●   LG
M   10 f
¶   Code of Practice for the Soluble Coffee Industry in the UK; ftm,
        £5 nm.

British Sound Recording Association   (BSRA)   1958
■   11 Shernfold, Kents Hill, MILTON KEYNES, Bucks, MK7 6HR.
        (hsp)
        01908 679424
        email mcl@mclstudios.co.uk
        http://www.soundhunters.com/bsra/
        Hon Sec: Martyn Lycett
○   *G; all aspects of amateur sound recording, including video
Gp   Video recording
●   Conf - Mtgs - Comp - VE
<   Fédn Intle des Chasseurs de Sons (Intl Fedn Soundhunters)
M   65 i, 2 f, 4 org
¶   Recording News - 4;
        Sound Track Audio Magazine - 4; both ftm only.
×   2002 Federation of British Tape Recordists

British Spas Federation
    since 2004 **Spa Business Association**

British Speedway Promoters Association   (BSPA)   1965
NR   ACU House, Wood St, RUGBY, Warks, CV21 2YX.   (hq)
          01788 560648   fax 01788 546785
          email office@bspa.fsbusiness.co.uk
          Contact: Mrs Angela Price
○   *S; organisation of British speedway racing
M   25 f

British Sporting Rifle Club
    'we wish to discontinue this entry'

British Spotted Pony Society   (BSpPS)   1946
■   Heiffers Farm, Rackenford, TIVERTON, Devon, EX16 8EW.
          (hsp)
          01884 881258   fax 01757 288087
          Chmn & Sec: Miss M C Pollard
▲   Company Limited by Guarantee; Registered Charity
○   *B
●   Mtgs - Exhib - Comp - Inf - PL - LG - Breed show
M   i
¶   NL - 2; ftm.

British Sprouts Growers Association
    is a group of the **Brassica Growers Association**

British Stainless Steel Association   (BSSA)   1992
■   Broomgrove, 59 Clarkehouse Rd, SHEFFIELD, S Yorks,
          S10 2LE.   (hq)
          0114-267 1260   fax 0114-266 1252
          email enquiry@bssa.org.uk   http://www.bssa.org.uk
          Dir: Nigel Ward
▲   Un-incorporated Society
○   *T; to promote & develop the use of stainless steel in all regions
          of the UK
Gp   Industry forum; Rebar; Architecture & building construction;
          Finishing section
●   Conf - Mtgs - ET - Exhib - Stat - Inf - LG
<   Intl Stainless Steel Forum; Euro-Inox
>   Nickel Inst
M   100 f
¶   Stainless Steel Industry (Jnl) - 6; £84 m (UK & Europe),
          £105 nm (UK & Europe).
          NL - 6.

British Stammering Association   (BSA)   1978
■   15 Old Ford Rd, LONDON, E2 9PJ.   (hq)
          020 8983 1003
          email mail@stammering.org   http://www.stammering.org
          Chief Exec Officer: Norbert Lieckfeldt
▲   Registered Charity
○   *W; to promote awareness of stammering; to offer support for
          all whose lives are affected by stammering; to identify &
          promote effective therapies; to initiate & support research
          into stammering
Gp   Helping stammering pupils project
●   Conf - ET - Inf - Lib - Counselling & information service on
          speech therapy
          Counselling & information service on speech therapy provision
          & self-help groups for the whole of the UK
          Helpline: 0845 603 2001
<   Intl Fluency Assn; Intl Stuttering Assn
M   1,600 i
¶   Speaking Out - 4; ftm only.

British Standards Institution
    see **BSI**

British Standards Society   (BSS)   1960
NR   c/o BSI, 389 Chiswick High Rd, LONDON, W4 4AL.   (hq)
Br   6 regions; 1 o'seas
○   *K; to promote techniques & benefits of standardisation; to help
          standards users in their understanding & use of standards
Gp   Building; Electronics; Health & environment; Consumer
          products & services; IT; Management systems; Public services
●   Conf - Mtgs - ET - Inf - Lib
<   Intl Fedn of Standards Users
M   500 i, UK / 50 i, o'seas
¶   NL - 4;   Hbk - 1;   Meetings Programme - 1; all ftm only.
          Note: is a part of BSI

British Starch Industry Association   (BSIA)   1989
■   6 Catherine St, LONDON, WC2B 5JJ.   (hq)
          020 7836 2460   fax 020 7836 0580
          email bob.price@fdf.org.uk
          Sec: R D Price
▲   Un-incorporated Society
○   *T
●   Mtgs - LG
<   Eur Starch Assn; Food & Drink Fedn
M   6 f

British Stickmakers Guild   (BSG)   1984
■   Ebbisham, 19 Woodmancote Rd, WORTHING, W Sussex,
          BN14 7HT.   (hsp)
          01903 205015
          http://www.thebsg.org.uk
          Hon Sec: Charles Hutcheon
▲   Un-incorporated Society
○   *G; for all interested in the history, making, collection,
          stickdressing & uses of walking sticks, canes & crooks
●   Exhib - Comp
M   1,940 i, UK / 41 i, o'seas
¶   The Stickmaker - 4.

British Stock Car Drivers Association   (BSCDA)   1956
NR   PO Box 662, HALIFAX, W Yorks, HX3 0WZ.   (hsp)
          Hon Sec: Barry Tempest
▲   Un-incorporated Society
○   *P
●   Mtgs - Comp
M   i
¶   NL - 12; ftm only.

British Stomach Cancer Group
    a specialist group of **BASO ~ the Association for Cancer
    Surgery**

British Structural Waterproofing Association   1992
NR   Westcott House, Catlins Lane, PINNER, Middx, HA5 2EZ.
          020 8866 8339   fax 020 8868 9971
M   c 100 f

British Sub-Aqua Club   (BS-AC)   1953
NR   Telford's Quay, South Pier Rd, ELLESMERE PORT, South Wirral,
          CH65 4FL.   (hq)
          0151-350 6200
          Operations Mgr: Mary Tetley
▲   Company Limited by Guarantee
Br   c 1,000; c 400 o'seas
○   *L, *S; the governing body for the sport of sub-aqua in the UK
●   Conf - Exhib - Inf
M   45,000 i
¶   Publications list available.

British Sugar Beet Seed Producers Association (BSBSPA) 1936
- ■ c/o BSPB, Woolpack Chambers, Market St, ELY, Cambs, CB7 4ND. (hsb)
  01353 653200
  Sec: Dr Penny Maplestone
- ▲ Un-incorporated Society
- ○ *T; interests of sugar beet seed producers & breeders in the UK
- ● Mtgs - LG
- < Brit Soc of Plant Breeders
- M 12 f

British Sugarcraft Guild (BSG) 1983
- ■ Wellington House, Messeter Place, LONDON, SE9 5DP. (hq)
  020 8859 6943   fax 020 8859 6117
  Nat Sec: N Fuller
- ▲ Un-incorporated Society
- Br 225; Japan
- ○ *G; to promote & stimulate interest in sugarcraft as an art form
- ● Conf - Mtgs - ET - Exam - Res - Exhib - Comp - SG - Expt - Inf
- M 6,700 i, UK / 1,500 i, o'seas
- ¶ The British Sugarcraft News - 4; ftm only.

British Sundial Society (BSS) 1989
- ■ 4 New Wokingham Rd, CROWTHORNE, Berks, RG45 7NR. (hsp)
  01344 772303
  email douglas.bateman@btinternet.com
  http://www.sundialsoc.org.uk
  Hon Sec: Douglas Bateman
- ▲ Registered Charity
- ○ *G, *L; to promote the science of gnomonics & knowledge of all types of sundial; research & advice on the restoration & preservation of old sundials in the British Isles & the construction of new ones
- Gp Restoration; Education; Recording; Mass dials
- ● Conf - Mtgs - ET - Res - SG - Inf - Lib - PL - VE - Cataloguing the dials which still exist in the British Isles
- < N Amer Sundial Soc; R Astronomical Soc
- M 400 i, 12 f, 25 org, UK / 150 i, o'seas
- ¶ The Bulletin (Jnl) - 4; ftm, £6.50 nm.
  Make a Sundial (book for schools); £7.
  Sets of Slides for lectures (6 sets); £5.50 each.
  Listing of Dials in UK - 3 yrly; m only.
  Sundial Makers.

British Surface Treatment Suppliers Association
is a group of the **Surface Engineering Association**

British Surfing Association (BSA) 1966
- NR International Surfing Centre, Fistral Beach, NEWQUAY, Cornwall, TR7 1HY. (hq)
  01637 876474   fax 01637 878608
  email info@britsurf.co.uk   http://www.britsurf.co.uk
  Admin: Karen Walton
- ▲ Company Limited by Guarantee
- ○ *S; the national governing body for surfing
- Gp Boarding: Long, Body, Short, Knee
- ● Mtgs - ET - Exam - Comp - Stat - Inf - LG
- < Intl Surfing Assn
- > Surfing Assns: English, Welsh, Scottish, Channel Islands
- M c 10,000 i & org
- ¶ Groundswell (NL) - 12.

British Suzuki Institute (BSI) 1980
- NR Charles House (4th floor), 375 Kensington High Street, LONDON, W14 8QH. (hq)
  020 7471 6780   fax 020 7471 6778
  email bsi@suzukimusic.force9.co.uk
  http://www.britishsuzuki.com
  Chief Exec Officer: Landa Melrose
- ▲ Registered Charity
- ○ *D; to advance education in the Suzuki method of teaching for violin, cello, flute, piano & recorder
- Gp Music education
- ● Conf - Mtgs - ET - Exam - Inf - Teacher training - Concerts
- < Eur Suzuki Assn
- M 2,000 i, UK / 100 i, o'seas
- ¶ Ability - 4; ftm, £3 nm.

British Swedish Chamber of Commerce in Sweden (BSCC) 1954
- NR Jakobs Torg 3 (4th floor), Box 16050, SE-10321 STOCKHOLM, Sweden. (hq)
  46 (8) 506 12617
  Sec gen: Martin DWorén
- ▲ Company Limited by Guarantee
- ○ *C
- M c 120 f

British-Swiss Chamber of Commerce (BSCC) 1920
- NR 12 York Gate, LONDON, NW1 4QS. (hq)
  020 7544 4850
  UK Mgr: Wendy Crammond
- Br Switzerland (hq)
- ● Mtgs - ET - SG - Inf - VE - LG
- < Coun of Brit Chams Comm in Continental Europe (COBCOE)
- M 154 f, UK / 489 f, o'seas
- ¶ Membership Directory - 1.

British-Swiss Chamber of Commerce [Switzerland] (BSCC) 1920
- NR 155 Freiestrasse, CH-8032 ZÜRICH, Switzerland. (hq)
  41 (1) 422 3131
  Mgr: Vicki Guntern
- Br 8 regional chapters
- ○ *C; to support the development of Anglo Swiss business relations; to assist individual entrepreneurs & businesses in advancing their own commercial interests
- Gp Legal/tax chapter; Education & training dept (learning English in UK & CH)
- ● Conf - Mtgs - ET - SG - Expt - Inf - Lib
- < Coun of Brit Chams Comm in Continental Europe (COBCOE)
- M c 700 f
- ¶ BSCC NL - 4.
  British Parent Companies with Swiss Subsidiaries.

British Tarantula Society (BTS) 1984
- ■ 3 Shepham Lane, POLEGATE, E Sussex, BN26 6LZ. (hsp)
  Hon Sec: Angela Hale
- ▲ Un-incorporated Society
- ○ *B, *G; to educate & provide information on captive husbandry of theraphosid spiders & associated fauna (scorpions etc)
- Gp Captive breeding directory
- ● Mtgs - Res - Exhib - SG - Inf - Lib
- M c 700 i
- ¶ Jnl - 4.

British Tattoo Artists Federation   (BTAF)   1975
- ■   389 Cowley Rd, OXFORD, OX4 2BS.   (hq)
     01865 715253   fax 01865 775610
     email btaf@tattoo.co.uk   http://www.tattoo.co.uk
     Sec: Lionel Titchener
- ○   *P; to improve & encourage high standards of hygiene in
     professional tattoo studios   & neck
- Gp Tattoo history museum, archives & library
- ●   LG
- <   Tattoo Club of GB
- M   500 i
- ¶   Tattoo International - 6.
     Note: is part of the Tattoo Club of Great Britain

British Technical Council of the Motor & Petroleum Industries
     since 1 July 2005 **BTC Testing Advisory Group**

British Technion Society   (BTS)   1951
- NR   62 Grosvenor St, LONDON, W1K 3JF.   (hq)
     020 7495 6824
     Sec: Suzanne Posner
- ▲   Registered Charity
- Br   7
- ○   *K; to promote the Technion (Israel Institute of Technology); to
     ensure research, by introducing active partners; to fundraise
     for various projects
- Gp London & provincial c'ees
- ●   Conf - Mtgs - VE
- <   Technion Socs in America / Canada / Israel & other countries
- M   c 900 i
- ¶   NL - irreg;   AR.

British Television Distributors Association
     no longer exists: members were invited to join the **Producers
     Alliance for Cinema & Television** as part of its Rights
     Exploitation membership category

British Temperance Society   (BTS)   1950
- ■   Stanborough Park, Garston, WATFORD, Herts, WD25 9JZ.
     (hq)
     01923 672251   fax 01923 893212
     Hon Exec Dir: Richard J B Willis
- ▲   Un-incorporated Society
- Br   2
- ○   *E, *W; to create a philosophy of total abstinence
- Gp Breathe Free: Plan to Stop Smoking (non-profit making project
     to help individuals to stop smoking)
- ●   Conf - Mtgs - ET - Exhib - SG - Inf - Film library
- <   Intl Temperance Assn
- M   17,000 i
- ¶   Leaflet.

British Tennis Coaches Association   (BTCA)
- NR   c/o Wolverhampton Lawn Tennis & Squash Club, Neville Lodge,
     Newbridge Crescent, WOLVERHAMPTON, WV6 0LH.
     01902 758500
     Admin: Amanda Yates
- ○   *P, *S
- ¶   Coachline - 6.

British Tenpin Bowling Association   (BTBA)   1961
- NR   114 Balfour Rd, ILFORD, Essex, IG1 4JD.   (hq)
     020 8478 1745
     Contact: Mrs Bernice Bass
- ○   *S; to act as the governing body for tenpin bowling in the UK;
     to promote the sport
- M   c 30,000 i

British Tensional Strapping Association   (BTSA)   1950
- NR   PO Box 94, SELBY, N Yorks, YO8 5YJ.   (hq)
     01757 708555
     Sec: Graham Cooper
- ▲   Un-incorporated Society
- ○   *T; strapping equipment & materials
- ●   Mtgs - SG - Stat
- M   7 f
- ¶   An Introduction to Tensional Strapping.
     Health & Safety guides:
        Steel strapping.   Non-metallic strapping.
        Strapping machines.
     Hazard Data Sheets.

British Texel Sheep Society Ltd   (BTSS)   1972
- ■   4th Avenue NAC, Stoneleigh Park, KENILWORTH, Warks,
     CV8 2LG.   (hq)
     024 7669 6629   fax 024 7669 6472
     email office@texel.co.uk   http://www.texel.co.uk
     Chief Exec & Co Sec: Steven J McLean
- ▲   Company Limited by Guarantee; Registered Charity
- ○   *B
- ●   Exhib - Comp - Expt - Inf
- <   Nat Sheep Assn
- M   2,500 i, 1 f, 19 breeders' clubs
- ¶   Jnl - 1;   Texel Bulletin - 4; both free.

British Textile Machinery Association   (BTMA)   1940
- ■   Mount Pleasant, Glazebrook Lane, Glazebrook,
     WARRINGTON, Lancs, WA3 5BN.   (hq)
     0161-775 5710   fax 0161-775 5485
     email btma@btma.org.uk   http://www.btma.org.uk
     Dir: Alan Little
- ▲   Company Limited by Guarantee
- ○   *T
- Gp Sub-c'ees: Exhibitions, Technical, Executive
- ●   Mtgs - Exhib - Stat - Expt - Inf - LG
- <   Eur C'ee Textile Machinery Mfrs (CEMATEX)
- M   100 f
- ¶   Monthly Circular - 12;   Export Financing & Insurance;
     Outfitter conditions;   AR; all ftm only.
     BTMA Directory - 1; free.

British Textile Technology Group   (BTTG)   1988
- NR   Wira House, West Park Ring Rd, LEEDS, W Yorks, LS16 6QL.
     (hq)
     0113-259 1999
     Chmn: William Laidlaw
- ▲   Company Limited by Guarantee
- Br   4
- ○   *Q; a centre of excellence in textile & materials related testing,
     investigation & evaluation
- Gp Spinning & nonwovens; Shirley technologies; Certification;
     Wiratec; CASE (Coatings, adhesives, sealant & encapsulate
     testing); Fire technology services; BCTC (British Carpet
     Technical Centre)
- ●   Conf - ET - Res - Inf - Exhib
- M   143 f, UK / 19 f, o'seas
- ¶   Independent - 4.

British Theatre Dance Association   (BTDA)   1973
- ■   Garden St, LEICESTER, LE1 3UA.   (hq)
     0845 166 2179   fax 0845 166 2189
     Gen Sec: Helen Mence
- ▲   Company Limited by Guarantee
- ○   *P; to provide dance syllabi for teachers throughout the UK &
     overseas
- ●   Mtgs - ET - Exam - Comp
- M   1,800 i, UK / 100 i, o'seas
- ¶   Danceworld - 2.

British Throwsters Association
NR   5 Portland Place, LONDON, W1B 1PW.   (hq)
        020 7636 7788   fax 020 7636 7515
        email bta@dial.pipex.com
        Dir: Adam Mansell
○   *P; promotion & protection of the UK texturising & throwsting
        industry (both stages in yarn preparation)
●   Mtgs - LG
<   Brit Apparel & Textile Confedn

British Tinnitus Association   (BTA)   1979
■   Unit 5 Acorn Business Park, Woodseats Close, SHEFFIELD,
        S Yorks, S8 0TB.   (hq)
        0114-250 9922 freephone: 0800 018 0527   fax 0114-
        258 2279
        email info@tinnitus.org.uk   http://www.tinnitus.org.uk
        Operations Mgr: Mrs Val Rose
▲   Company Limited by Guarantee; Registered Charity
Br   80 self-help groups
○   *M, *W; to support people with information & advice; to fund
        tinnitus research projects in order to find a cure; to promote
        awareness & understanding of the condition
●   Conf - Mtgs - ET - Res - Pen pal register
M   c 10,000 i, UK / c 300 i, o'seas
¶   Quiet (Jnl) - 4.
        Leaflets;   Audio cassette relaxation tapes.

British Titanic Society   (BTS)   1986
NR   PO Box 401, Hope Carr Way, LEIGH, Lancs, WN7 3WW.
        Sec: Steve Rigby
▲   Un-incorporated Society
○   *G; to research & preserve the memory of RMS Titanic & her
        passengers & crew
●   Conf - Res - Exhib - Comp - SG - VE
M   1,000 i, UK / 200 i, o'seas
¶   Atlantic Daily Bulletin (NL) - 4.

British Toilet Association   (BTA)   1999
■   Lane End, Edward Road, WINCHESTER, Hants, SO23 9RB.
        01962 850277   fax 01962 870220   (dir/p)
        email enquiries@britloos.co.uk
        http://www.britloos.co.uk
        Dir: Richard Chisnell
○   *K; pressure group campaigning for more & better public
        lavatories
●   Conf - Mtgs - Res - Stat - Inf - Lib - LG - Awards: Loo of the
        Year & Attendant of the Year
M   i, f, org
¶   NL - 3/4; free.

British Tomato Growers Association   (TGA)   1997
■   Pollards Nursery, Lake Lane, BARNHAM, W Sussex, PO22 0AD.
        01243 554859   fax 01243 554645
        email tga@britishtomatoes.co.uk
        http://www.britishtomatoes.co.uk
        Sec: Mrs Julie Woolley
▲   Company Limited by Guarantee
○   *H, *T; represents British growers; marketing information,
        research & development
●   Conf - Mtgs - ET - Res - Exhib - LG
M   45 f

British Toxicology Society   (BTS)   1979
NR   PO Box 249, MACCLESFIELD, Cheshire, SK11 6FT.   (hq)
        01625 267881
        email secretariat@thebts.org
        Sec: PAul Whitehead,   Meetings Sec: Dr E Martin
▲   Registered Charity
○   *L; to advance the science & education of toxicology & the
        safety of chemicals for people & the environment
Gp   Biotechnology; Human toxicology; Immunotoxicology;
        Neurotoxicology; Occupational toxicology; Regulatory
        toxicology; Safety pharmacology
●   Conf - Mtgs - Specialist working parties on scientific topics
<   Intl U of Toxicology; Fedn of Eur Socs of Toxicology; Biological
        Coun
M   800 i, UK / 130 i, o'seas

British Toy & Hobby Association Ltd   (BTHA)   1944
■   80 Camberwell Rd, LONDON, SE5 0EG.   (hq)
        020 7701 7271   fax 020 7708 2437
        email admin@btha.co.uk   http://www.btha.co.uk
        Dir Gen & Sec: David L Hawtin
○   *T
●   Mtgs - Res - Exhib - Stat - Expt - Inf
M   180 i & f
¶   Buyers Guide - 1; ftm, £15 nm.
        NTC leaflets; free.

British Toy Importers Association   (BTIA)   1950
■   Somers, Mounts Hill, BENENDEN, Kent, TN17 4ET.   (asa)
        01580 240819   fax 01580 241109
        Sec: Alan Milne
▲   Un-incorporated Society
○   *T
●   Conf - Mtgs - Exhib - LG - Lobbying European Commission -
        Advice on toy safety
M   c 2 i, 100 f, UK / 1 f, o'seas
¶   LM - updated.
        Advice on toy safety & importing quality procedures - updated
        on law or regulations change.

British Toymakers Guild   (BTG)   1955
NR   PO Box 240, UCKFIELD, E Sussex, TN22 9AS.   (hq)
        01225 442440
        email info@toymakersguild.co.uk
        http://www.toymakersguild.co.uk
        Mgr: Robert Nathan
▲   Un-incorporated Society
○   *T; to promote excellence in toy design & manufacture
Gp   Craft toy making
●   Mtgs - Exhib - Stat - Inf - LG
M   35 i, 140 f
¶   The Toymaker - 4.   Directory - 1.

British Trade Council in Austria
        since 2004 **Austro-British Chamber**

British Transplantation Society   (BTS)   1971
NR   Triangle House, Broomhill Rd, LONDON, SW18 4HX.   (hsb)
        020 8875 2430   fax 020 8875 2434
        Sec: J Forsythe
▲   Company Limited by Guarantee; Registered Charity
○   *L; to advance the study of the biological & clinical problems of
        tissue & organ donation; to facilitate contact between persons
        interested in transplantation; to make new knowledge
        available for the general good of the community
Gp   Clinical trials; Standards; Training
●   Mtgs - ET - Res
M   c 650 i
¶   NL - 2.

British Transport Officers' Guild   (BTOG)   1944
NR   Hayes Court, West Common Rd, HAYES, Kent, BR2 7AU.   (hq)
▲   Un-incorporated Society
Br   14
○   *U; a section of Amicus-AEEU
M   i

British Trauma Society
   a specialist society of the **British Orthopaedic Association**

British Travel Health Association   (BTHA)   1999
NR   PO Box 336, SALE, M33 3UU.   (hq)
      0870 042 3640
      Hon Sec: Dr George Kassianos
○   *K, *M; to promote a multi-disciplinary approach to travel
      health; to increase public awareness of travel health hazards
●   Conf - Mtgs - ET - Res - SG - Inf
M   c 530 i
¶   Jnl - 2;   Travelwise - 4; both ftm only.

British Travelgoods & Accessories Association   (BTAA)   1918
■   10 Vyse St, BIRMINGHAM, B18 6LT.   (hq)
      0121-237 1107
      http://www.btaa.org.uk
      Sec: Diana Fiveash
▲   Company Limited by Guarantee
○   *T; representing manufacturers, distributors & importers of
      luggage, handbags & small leathergoods
●   Conf - Mtgs - Exhib - Expt - Inf - LG
<   Brit Jewellery, Giftware & Finishing Fedn
M   90 f
¶   Buyer's Guide - amended as necessary.
×   2005-06 British Luggage & Leathergoods Association

British Triathlon Association Ltd   (BTA)   1984
NR   PO Box 25, LOUGHBOROUGH, Leics, LE11 3WX.   (hq)
      01509 226161
▲   Company Limited by Guarantee
Br   11 regions
○   *S; to govern, administer & develop the sport of triathlon by
      providing opportunities for athletes of all ages & abilities to
      compete at the highest level
Gp   Tri-stars aged 8-13; Youths 14-16; Juniors 17-20; all others are
      sectioned in 5 year age bands
●   Mtgs - ET - Exam - Res - Exhib - Comp - Inf - LG - School visits
      - Talks
<   Intl Triathlon U (ITU); Eur Triathlon U (ETU); Brit Olympic Assn
M   7,000 i, 300 affiliated clubs
¶   Trinews (NL) - 6.   Triathlon/Duathlon Hbk - 1.
      Young Triathletes File - 1.

British Trolleybus Society   (BTS)   1961
■   2 Josephine Court, Southcote Rd, READING, Berks,
      RG30 2DG.   (hsp)
      0118-958 3974
      Hon Sec: A J Barton
▲   Registered Charity
○   *G; to study the history & development of the trolley bus &
      trolley bus networks
●   Mtgs - VE
M   320 i, UK / 10 i, o'seas
¶   Trolleybus - 12.   Bus Fare - 12.   Wheels - 12.

British Trombone Society   (BTS)   1983
NR   91 High St, EDGWARE, Herts, HA8 7DB.   (hsb)
      024 7671 1900
      Sec: Steven Greenall
▲   Un-incorporated Society
○   *D; to promote the trombone & trombone-related issues in the
      UK
●   Conf - Exhib - Comp - Inf - Commissioning of compositions
<   Intl Trombone Assn
M   700 i, UK / 100 i, o'seas
¶   The Trombonist - 3.

British Trout Association Ltd   (BTA)   1982
■   The Rural Centre, West Mains, INGLISTON, Midlothian,
      EH8 8NZ.   (hq)
      0131-472 4080   fax 0131-472 4083
      email mail@britishtrout.co.uk
      http://www.britishtrout.co.uk
      Chief Exec: David Bassett
▲   Company Limited by Guarantee
○   *T; to represent the UK trout aquaculture industry; research
      relating to trout health & welfare
Gp   Quality Trout UK; Quality Assurance Scheme (QTUK); British
      Trout Farmers Restocking Association
●   Conf - Mtgs - Res - Stat - Inf - VE - LG - Marketing - PR -
      Technical advice - QA scheme
<   Fedn of Eur Aquaculture Producers (FEAP); Fedn of Scot
      Aquaculture Producers (FSAP)
M   100 f
¶   NL - 4;   AR - 1; both ftm.
      Code of Practice;   QTUK Standards;   Technical Briefing
      Notes; all ftm only.

British Trout Farmers' Restocking Association
   a group of the **British Trout Association**

British Truck Racing Association   (BTRA)   1985
NR   50 Barrow Grove, SITTINGBOURNE, Kent, ME10 1LA.   (treas)
      01795 420440
      Treas: Kate Read
▲   Un-incorporated Society
○   *S; to further interest in motoring & motor sport with trucks
●   Mtgs - Comp - SG - Inf
M   137 i, 14 f, UK / 14 i, 2 f, o'seas
¶   NL - 10; ftm only.

British Trust for Conservation Volunteers   (BTCV)   1959
NR   Sedum House, Mallard Way, Potteric Carr, DONCASTER,
      S Yorks, DN4 8DB.   (hq)
      01302 388888
      email information@btcv.org.uk   http://www.btcv.org
      Chief Exec: Tom Flood
▲   Registered Charity
Br   150
○   *K; to ensure that the potential for voluntary action for the
      environment is fully realised; to ensure that people of the
      world value their environment & take practical action to
      improve it
●   Conf - Mtgs - Exhib - PL - VE - Working holidays - Community
      group affiliation scheme
<   Environment Trainers Network (ETN); New Opportunities Fund
M   130,000 i, 1,358 i in BTCV Supporters' Club, UK /
      1,950 associated BTWC groups
¶   Conserver - 4.
      Conservation Holidays - 2.   Strategic Plan - 1.
      Environments for All (Annual Review) - 1.
      Environments for all (Base Review) - 1.
      Facts & Figures - 1;   Reports & Accounts - 1; all ftm.

British Trust for Ornithology   (BTO)   1933
NR   The Nunnery, THETFORD, Norfolk, IP24 2PU.   (hq)
    01842 750050   fax 01842 750030
    email general@bto.org   http://www.bto.org
    Dir: Prof J J D Greenwood,   Sec: Gareth W Phillips
▲   Company Limited by Guarantee; Registered Charity
Br   BTO Scotland, Stirling
○   *L; 'to promote & encourage wider understanding, appreciation
    & conservation of birds through scientific studies... by
    members, other birdwatchers & staff'
Gp   Habitats research: Coastal & wetlands, Terrestrial
    Populations research: Ringing, Censuses, Nest records
    Membership & development; Administration
●   Conf - Mtgs - ET - Res - SG - Stat - Inf - Lib - LG - Research &
    monitoring consultancy
M   9,000 i, 300 org, UK / 500 i, 20 org, o'seas
¶   Bird Table - 4.
    Bird Study - 3.   BTO News (NL) - 6.
    Ringing Migration - 2.   AR,

British Tugowners Association   (BTA)   1934
■   Carthusian Court, 12 Carthusian St, LONDON, EC1M 6EZ.
    (hq)
    020 7417 2875   fax 020 7600 1534
    email info@britishtug.org.   http://www.britishtug.org
    Sec: David Asprey
▲   Un-incorporated Society
○   *T; 'members own/operate tugs for shiptowage services in ports
    of the UK, coastal & ocean towage & salvage'
●   Conf - Mtgs - ET - Stat - Inf - LG
<   Eur Tugowners Assn
M   18 f, UK / 1 f, o'seas

British Tunnelling Society   (BTS)   1971
NR   c/o Institution of Civil Engineers, 1-7 Great George St,
    LONDON, SW1P 3AA.   (hq)
▲   Registered Charity
○   *L, *Q; to develop the art, science & techniques of tunnelling
●   Conf - Mtgs - Comp - Inf
<   Intl Tunnelling Assn
M   780 i, 40 f, UK / 165 i, o'seas
¶   Tunnels & Tunnelling International - 12.
    NL - 3.   AR.

British Turf & Landscape Irrigation Association   (BTLIA)   1978
NR   41 Pennine Way, Great Eccleston, PRESTON, Lancs, PR3 0YS.
    (sp)
    01995 670675   fax 01995 670675
    email info@btlia.org.uk   http://www.btlia.org.uk
    Sec: Martyn T Jones
▲   Company Limited by Guarantee
○   *T; to promote the proper & responsible installation of turf &
    landscape irrigation schemes; to provide eductional
    opportunities to fulfil these criteria
Gp   Irrigation: Equipment manufacturers, Consultants, Installation
    contractors
●   Conf - Mtgs - ET - Exam - Exhib - Inf
<   Irrigation Assn (USA); Eur Irrigation Assn; UK Irrigation Assn
M   c 50 f
¶   LM - 1; ftm, on request nm.

British Turkey Federation Ltd
    since 2001 **British Poultry Council**

British Turned-Parts Manufacturers Association   (BTMA)   1920
■   Pear Tree Cottage, Snitterfield Lane, Norton Lindsey, WARWICK,
    CV35 8JQ.   (dir/p)
    01789 730877   fax 01789 730899
    email iangold@btma.org   http://www.btma.org
    Dir: Ian Gold
○   *T: for precision turned parts & machined component
    manufacturers
●   Conf - Mtgs - ET - Exhib - SG - Stat - Inf - VE - LG
M   75 f
¶   BTMA Buyer's Guide (LM) - 1; free.

British UFO Research Association   (BUFORA)   1963
■   BM BUFORA, LONDON, WC1N 3XX.   (hsp)
    email enquiries@bufora.org.uk
    http://www.bufora.org.uk
    Hon Sec: Mrs Judith M Jaafar
▲   Company Limited by Guarantee
¶   [all publications on website].
    originally named the British Unidentified Flying Object Research
    Association; this is now a non-membership organisation
    researching unidentified flying phenomena throughout the
    UK; disseminating & collating evidence & cooperates with
    others doing similar research throughout the world.

British Union for the Abolition of Vivisection   (BUAV)   1898
■   16a Crane Grove, LONDON, N7 8NN.   (hq)
    020 7700 4888   fax 020 7700 0252
    email info@buav.org   http://www.buav.org
    Acting Chief Exec: Lindsey Lavender
▲   Company Limited by Guarantee
○   *K; campaigning to end all animal experiments
●   Conf - Res - Exhib - Comp - Stat - Inf - Lib - PL - LG - Lobbying
    UK/EU legislation - Undercover investigations
<   Intl Coun for Animal Protection in OECD Programmes; Eur
    Coalition to End Animal Experiments
¶   BUAV Action (NL) - 3 (email - 6);   BUAV Update (NL) - 4; AR -
    1; all free.

British Universities Film & Video Council   (BUFVC)   1948
NR   77 Wells St, LONDON, W1T 3QJ.   (hq)
    020 7393 1500
    Dir: Murray Weston
▲   Registered Charity
○   *E; to foster the production, study & use of film & related audio-
    visual media (incl TV, video & computer-based multi media)
    for higher education & research
M   c 220 universities, insts etc
×   2004 (April) Learning on Screen (merged)

British Universities Industrial Relations Association   (BUIRA)   1950
NR   c/o Bristol Business School, University of the West of England,
    Frenchay Campus, Coldharbour Lane, BRISTOL,
    BS16 1QY.   (hsb)
    0117-344 3469
    Contact: Kylie Dursley
○   *P; the academic study of industrial relations & allied areas in
    Britain & internationally
●   Conf - Res - SG - Specialist bibliographies research register
<   Intl Indl Relations Assn; Academy of Learned Socs for the Social
    Sciences
M   i

British Universities Sports Association (BUSA) 1994
NR 20-24 Kings Bench St, LONDON, SE1 0QX. (hq)
    020 7633 5080 fax 020 3268 2120
    http://www.busa.org.uk
    Chief Exec: Ian Randall
▲ Registered Charity
○ *S, *K; organisation & promotion of sport to students in higher
    education through organisation of championships
    representing fixtures & British teams for international events
● Conf - Mtgs - ET - Comp - Sporting championships
    Fixtures & results: www.busaresults.org.uk
M 150 universities
¶ Hbk - 1; AR - 1; both free.

British Urban Regeneration Association (BURA) 1990
■ 63-66 Hatton Garden, LONDON, EC1N 8LE. (hq)
    020 7539 4030 fax 020 7404 9614
    email info@bura.org.uk http://www.bura.org.uk
    Chief Exec: Jon Ladd
▲ Company Limited by Guarantee
○ *K, *P; to provide a forum for the exchange of ideas on
    regeneration issues; to identify examples of best practice
Gp Steering & development forum
● Conf - Mtgs - Res - Exhib - SG - Inf - VE - LG - Award schemes
M 1,500 i, 550 f, UK / 50 i, 10 f, o'seas
¶ Urban Regeneration - a handbook; £18.99.
    Learning from Experience; £10.
    Guide to Best Practice in Sport & Regeneration; £10.
    Breaking old Ground - a guide to contaminated land; £10.

British Urethane Foam Contractors Association Ltd (BUFCA) 1980
NR PO Box 12, HASLEMERE, Surrey, GU27 3AH. (hq)
    01428 654011 fax 01428 651401
    Co Sec: Mrs Eve Skidmore
▲ Company Limited by Guarantee
○ *T; contractors & suppliers in the sprayed urethane foam
    industry for thermal insulation of buildings & plant
Gp Health & safety; Fire hazards; Coatings; Foam specification
● Conf - Mtgs - Exhib - SG - Stat - Inf
M f
¶ NL; Technical Bulletin; Technical Guidelines; all ftm only.

British-Uruguayan Chamber of Commerce
    see **Cámara Comercio Uruguayo-Británica (British-Uruguayan Chamber of Commerce)**

British Uruguayan Society 1945
NR 222 Brooklands Rd, WEYBRIDGE, Surrey, KT13 0RJ. (sp)
    01932 847455
    Sec: Jill Quaife
▲ Registered Charity
○ *X; to advance the knowledge of Britons about Uruguay &
    Uruguayans about the UK
● Mtgs - Exhib - Comp - SG - Inf - Lib (at Hispanic Council,
    Canning House) - VE
M c 250 i, UK / c 30 i, o'seas
¶ El Hornero - 2.
    Tales of Uruguay (members' reminiscences of Uruguay) 1988.
    A History of the Society 1945-1985.

British Used Printing Machinery Suppliers Association (BUPMSA) 1993
NR 20 Spencer Bridge Rd, NORTHAMPTON, NN5 5EZ.
    01604 756100 fax 01604 750910
○ *T
● Mtgs - Exhib

British Vacuum Council (BVC) 1965
NR 76 Portland Place, LONDON, W1B 1NT. (hq)
    020 7470 4800 fax 020 7470 4848
    Sec: P Main
▲ Registered Charity
○ *L; to promote & advance the understanding & teaching of
    vacuum science, technology & its applications
● Sponsorship of conferences & training courses organised by its
    affiliated bodies
< Intl U of Vacuum Science, Technique & its Applications
M 2 org:
    Institute of Physics
    Royal Society of Chemistry
¶ Vacuum Technology, Applications & Ion Physics - 12.

British Valve & Actuator Association Ltd (BVAA) 1939
■ 9 Manor Park, BANBURY, Oxon, OX16 3TB. (hq)
    01295 221270 fax 01295 268965
    email enquiry@bvaa.org.uk http://www.bvaa.org.uk
    Dir: Rob Bartlett
▲ Company Limited by Guarantee
○ *T; to represent interests of British manufacturers, distributors &
    repairers of industrial valves & actuators
Gp Technical; Marketing; Actuator; Executive; Manufacturing &
    quality; Training
● Conf - Mtgs - ET - Exhib - Stat - Expt - Inf - VE
< CBI Trade Assn Forum
M 75 f (annual)
¶ NL - 4; Buyers Guide - 3 yrly; AR; all free.
    Valve Users Manual (Technical Handbook); £10.
✕ 2002-03 British Valve & Actuator Manufacturers' Association

British Vehicle Rental & Leasing Association Ltd (BVRLA) 1967
NR River Lodge, Badminton Court, AMERSHAM, Bucks,
    HP7 0DD. (hq)
    01494 434747 fax 01494 434499
    email info@bvrla.co.uk http://www.bvrla.co.uk
    Dir Gen: John Lewis
▲ Company Limited by Guarantee
○ *T; to represent the interests of operators of daily rental,
    leasing, contract hire & fleet management for cars, minibuses
    & light & heavy commercial vehicles
Gp Vehicle rental; Vehicle leasing & contract hire
● Conf - Mtgs - ET - Exam - Exhib - SG - Stat - Inf - VE - LG
< Eur Car & Truck Rental Assn (ECATRA)
M c 800 f
¶ BVRLA News (NL) - 12; BVLRA Directory - 1; both ftm only.
    Fair Wear & Tear Guides; prices vary.
    Various other publications - list available.

British Vehicle Salvage Federation (BVSF) 1998
■ Bates Business Centre, Church Rd, Harold Wood, ROMFORD,
    Essex, RM3 0JF. (hq)
    01708 381046 fax 01708 340485
    email email@bvsf.org.uk http://www.bvsf.org.uk
    Chmn & Sec Gen: Alan W Greenouff
▲ Un-Incorporated Society
○ *T; representative body for the UK vehicle salvage industry
Gp Management c'ee
● Conf - Mtgs - LG
< Assn of Brit Insurers; Motor Repair Res Centre (Thatcham)
M 98 f
¶ Vehicle Salvage Professional - 4; free. AR.

British Vendeen Sheep Society   1984
■ Darkes House, Conderton, TEWKESBURY, Glos, GL20 7PP.
　(hsp)
　01386 725229
　email info@vendeen.co.uk
　Sec: Andrew John
▲ Registered Charity
○ *B; the promotion & improvement of British Vendeen sheep
Gp Sire reference scheme
● Comp - Inf
M 80 i
¶ Flock Book - 1; £10.

British Venture Capital Association
　see **BVCA (British Venture Capital Association)**

British Veterinary Association   (BVA)   1881
NR 7 Mansfield St, LONDON, W1G 9NQ.   (hq)
　020 7636 6541
　email bvahq@bva.co.uk   http://www.bva.co.uk
　Co Sec: Henrietta Alderman
▲ Company Limited by Guarantee
Br Scottish, Welsh, Northern Ireland & territorial divns
○ *P, *V; standards of animal health; veterinary surgeons' working
　practices; profl standards of quality of service; relations with
　external bodies; policy development; service provision
Gp Association of Government Veterinarians; Association of
　Veterinarians in Industry; Association of Veterinary Students;
　Association of Veterinary Teachers & Research Workers;
　British Cattle Veterinary Association; British Equine Veterinary
　Association; British Small Animal Veterinary Association;
　British Veterinary Hospitals Association; British Veterinary
　Poultry Association; British Veterinary Zoological Society; Fish
　Veterinary Society; Goat Veterinary Society; Laboratory
　Animals Veterinary Association; Pig Veterinary Society; Royal
　Army Veterinary Corps Division; Sheep Veterinary Society;
　Society of Greyhound Veterinarians; Society of Practising
　Veterinary Surgeons; Society for the Study of Animal
　Breeding; Veterinary Deer Society; Veterinary Public Health
　Association
● Conf - Mtgs - ET - SG - Inf - Empl - LG
< Fedn of Veterinarians in Europe; Commonwealth Veterinary
　Assn; Wld Veterinary Assn
M c 10,000 i UK & o'seas
¶ The Veterinary Record - 52.   In Practice - 10.
　Off the Record - 12;   Ybk.   Annual Review.
　Other publications.

British Veterinary Camelid Society   (BVCS)   1994
■ Foxes Grove, Punnetts Town, HEATHFIELD, E Sussex,
　TN21 9PE.   (hsp)
　01435 864422
　email secretary@camelidvets.org
　http://www.camelidvets.org
　Sec: Janet Nuttall
▲ Un-incorporated Society
○ *V; to stimulate knowledge of diseases & management of South
　American camelids (alpaca, llama, guanaco & vicuña); to
　promote interest in these fascinating animals with respect to
　their management, breeding, feeding, health & disease
● Conf - Mtgs - ET - Inf - LG
M c 110 i, f & org
¶ Proceedings of Conference - 1.

British Veterinary Dental Association
　a group of the **British Small Animal Veterinary Association**

British Veterinary Dermatology Study Group
　a group of the **British Small Animal Veterinary Association**

British Veterinary Hospitals Association   (BVHA)   1960
■ c/o Station Bungalow, Main Rd, STOCKSFIELD,
　Northumberland, NE43 7HJ.   (office/manager/p)
　0796 690 1619   fax 0781 391 5954
　email office@bvha.org.uk   http://www.bvha.org.uk
　Office Manager: Christine Shield,
　Hon Sec: Chris Trickey
▲ Un-incorporated Society
○ *P, *V; to promote the highest standards of excellence in animal
　treatment through the design, construction & equipping of
　veterinary hospitals
● Conf - ET - Exhib - Comp - Inf - VE
< a division of the Brit Veterinary Assn
M 108 i, 116 f
¶ Bulletin - 4; ftm only.

British Veterinary Neurology Study Group
　a group of the **British Small Animal Veterinary Association**

British Veterinary Nursing Association Ltd   (BVNA)   1965
■ 11 Shenval House, South Rd, HARLOW, Essex, CM20 2BD.
　(hq)
　01279 450567   fax 01279 420866
　email bvna@bvnaofficeplus.com
　http://www.bvna.org.uk
▲ Company Limited by Guarantee
○ *P, *V; for veterinary nurses
● Conf - ET - Exam - Exhib - Inf
< Intl Veterinary Nurses & Technicians Assn (IVNTA)
M 4,020 i, UK / 59 i, o'seas
¶ Veterinary Nursing Jnl - 12; free.

British Veterinary Orthopaedic Association
　a group of the **British Small Animal Veterinary Association**

British Veterinary Poultry Association
　a group of the **British Veterinary Association**

British Veterinary Zoological Society
　a group of the **British Veterinary Association**

British Video Association   (BVA)   1980
NR 167 Great Portland St, LONDON, W1W 5PE.   (hq)
　020 7436 0041   fax 020 7436 0043
　http://www.bva.org.uk
　Dir Gen: Mrs Lavinia Carey
▲ Company Limited by Guarantee
○ *T; to represent copyright-owning producers & distributors of
　pre-recorded VHS & DVD video
● Conf - Mtgs - Res - Exhib - Stat - Inf - LG
M c 40 f
¶ NL - 12.   LM - 12.   Ybk - 1.

British Vintage Wireless Society   (BVWS)   1976
NR c/o Vintage Wireless & Television Museum, 23 Rosendale Rd,
　LONDON, SE21 8DS.   (hq)
　020 8670 3667
　http://www.bvws.org.uk
　Sec: Graham Terry,   Chmn: Mike Barker
▲ Un-incorporated Society
○ *G; the history & preservation of vintage wireless & television
　equipment
● Mtgs - Res - Exhib - Comp - Inf - Lib - PL
M 1,400 i, 55 org, UK / 200 i, 16 org, o'seas
¶ Bulletin (incorporating 405 Alive) - 4; ftm only.

British Violin Making Association   (BVMA)   1995
- ■   7 Widcombe Parade, BATH, BA2 4JT.
  01225 337734
  email secretary@bvms.org.uk   http://www.bvma.org.uk
  Sec: Corrie Schrijver
- ▲   Un-incorporated Society
- ○   *P, *T; to raise the standards & skills of violin & bow makers & restorers; to encourage dissemination of information amongst them
- ●   Conf - ET - Exhib - Comp
- M   479 i, 20 org
- ¶   [Jnl] - 4

British Voice Association   (BVA)   1991
- ■   Institute of Laryngology & Otology, 330 Gray's Inn Rd, LONDON, WC1X 8EE.   (hq)
  020 7713 0064   fax 020 7915 1388
  email bva@dircon.co.uk
  http://www.british-voice-association.com
  Co Sec: Kristine Carroll-Porczynski
- ▲   Company Limited by Guarantee
- ○   *P; for all professionals interested in the human voice
- Gp   Laryngology; Singing; Speech therapy; Phonetics; Voice teaching; Singing teaching
- ●   Conf - Mtgs - ET - Res - Comp - Inf - Professional standards in related medical groups
- <   Intl Assn of Logopedics & Phoniatrics
- M   448 i, UK / 35 i, o'seas
- ¶   Logopedics, Phoniatrics & Vocology - 4;
  NL - 3;   LM - 1; all ftm only.

British Volleyball Federation   (BVF)   1981
- NR   Loughborough Technology Centre(suite B), Epinal Way, LOUGHBOROUGH, Leics, LE11 3GE.   (hsb)
  01509 631699   fax 01509 631689
  email general@eng-volleyball.demon.co.uk
  Sec: Toomas Ojasoo
- ▲   Un-incorporated Society
- ○   *N, *S; umbrella organisation to coordinate activities of the English, Northern Ireland, Scottish & Welsh Volleyball Associations
- Gp   Volleyball Association(s): English / Northern Ireland / Scottish / Welsh;
  Great Britain National Volleyball Teams
- M   4 org

British Walking Federation   (BWF)   1983
- ■   Sheaf House, Holland Fen, LINCOLN, LN4 4QH.   (asa)
  01205 280094
  email marketing@bwf-ivv.org.uk
  http://www.bwf-ivv.org.uk
  Marketing & Publicity: Mike Houldershaw
- ▲   Un-incorporated Society
- ○   *G, *S; walking for health
- ●   Conf - Mtgs - LG - Monitoring of non-competitive walks
- <   Intl Fedn of Popular Sports (IVV)
- M   clubs
- ¶   Footprint - 6.

British Warm Air Hand Drier Association   (BWAHDA)   1981
- NR   Technology House, Oakfield Industrial Estate, Eynsham, OXFORD, OX8 1TH.   (regd/office)
  01865 882330
  Sec: Graham Davis
- ▲   Company Limited by Guarantee
- ○   *T; promotion of warm air hand driers
- ●   Mtgs - Inf - LG
- M   5 f, UK / 1 f, o'seas

British Warm-Blood Society   (BWBS)   1977
- ■   Lower Tredenham, Lanivet, BODMIN, Cornwall, PL30 5HL.   (hsp)
  01208 832940   fax 01208 831956
  http://www.bwbs.co.uk
  Contact: Mrs S Wason
- ▲   Company Limited by Guarantee
- ○   *B; the controlled breeding of warm-blood horses, particularly Hanoverians, Holsteins & Dutch, Swedish & Danish Warm-Bloods, Trakehners & cross breeds
- ●   2-yearly show with mare & stallion gradings - Registering & passporting horses
- <   Brit Horse Soc; Nat Stallion Approval Scheme
- M   400 i
- ¶   BWBS News - 2.

British Watch & Clock Makers Guild   (BWCMG)   1907
- ■   PO Box 2368, ROMFORD, Essex, RM1 2YZ.   (hsp)
  01708 750616   fax 01708 750616
  http://www.bwcmg.org
  Hon Sec: P Craddock
- ▲   Company Limited by Guarantee
- ○   *P, *T; for those professionally engaged in the manufacture, restoration or repair of watches & clocks
- ●   Inf
- M   1,000 i, UK / 15 i, o'seas
- ¶   NL - 2; ftm only.

British Water   1993
- ■   1 Queen Anne's Gate, LONDON, SW1H 9BT.   (hq)
  020 7957 4554   fax 020 7957 4565
  email info@britishwater.co.uk
  http://www.britishwater.co.uk
  Chief Exec: David Neil-Gallacher
- ▲   Company Limited by Guarantee
- ○   *N, *T; to represent the collective interests of the industry in relation to government, trade promotion, industry standards, legislative & regulatory affairs. Membership includes civil & process contractors, management, engineering & IT consultants, equipment manufacturers & suppliers, law firms, financial institutions & specialist research & training organisations
- Gp   Market gps: Industrial, Municipal;
  Technical forum & technical focus gps; International forum & manufacturers' & equipment suppliers' gp;
  Overseas (Americas, Asia-Pacific, Africa, Europe, Middle East)
- ●   Conf - Mtgs - ET - Exhib - Expt - Inf - LG
- <   Intl Water Assn (IWA); Aqua Europa; Mechanical & Metal Trs Confedn (METCOM)
- M   175 f
- ¶   Codes of Practice; prices vary.   AR; both free.

British Water Cooler Association   (BWCA)   1991
- NR   Hartfield House, 40-44 High St, NORTHWOOD, Middx, HA6 1UJ.   (asa)
  01923 825355
  email info@bwca.org.uk
  Sec Gen: Phillipa Clow
- ○   *T; all aspects of chain of supply from water source to satisfaction & health of consumers.
- ●   Mtgs - ET - Res - SG - Stat - Inf - LG
- M   f
- ¶   Handbooks.
- ✕   2005 Bottled Water Cooler Association

© CBD Research Ltd · Beckenham · BR3 5JS · Tel 020 8650 7745 · Fax 020 8650 0768 · E-mail cbd@cbdresearch.com · www.cbdresearch.com

British Water Ski Federation Ltd   (BWSF)   1951
NR   The Tower, Thorpe Rd, CHERTSEY, Surrey, KT16 8PH.   (hq)
      01932 570885   fax 01932 566719
      email info@bwsf.co.uk   http://www.britishwaterski.co.uk
      Exec Officer: Gavin Kelly
▲   Company Limited by Guarantee
Br   2
○   *S; the governing body for waterskiing in the UK
●   ET - Exam - Comp - Inf
<   Intl Water Ski Fedn (IWSF)
M   c 11,000 i, 150 clubs
¶   British Water Ski & Wakeboard - 5; free.

British Waterbed Association   (BWA)   1984
■   Manchester Waterbeds, 7a Victoria Lane, Whitefield,
      MANCHESTER, M45 6BL.   (sb)
      0870 603 0202   fax 0870 603 0202
      Sec: Michael Hand
▲   Un-incorporated Society
Br   35; Belgium, Denmark, Holland
○   *T; to promote quality waterbed products; to advance sleep
      research; to increase consumer awareness & advise
      waterbed users
Gp   Manufacturers, Wholesalers, Retailers
●   Exhib - Annual trade show
<   Speciality Sleep Assn (USA)
M   35 f, UK / 4 f, o'seas
¶   Waterbeds - the facts.   Fact & Fiction.
      Backaches & Waterbeds.   Arthritis & Waterbeds.
      Waterbed Owners Manual.

British Watercolour Society   (BWS)   1985
NR   Briargate, 2 The Brambles, ILKLEY, W Yorks, LS29 9DH.   (hq)
      01943 609075
      email britpaint@aol.com   http://www.britpaint.com
      Dir: Leslie Simpson
○   *A; to promote excellence in the field of watercolours, both in
      the UK & internationally
M   i
¶   Catalogue - 2.

British Waterfowl Association   (BWA)   1887
■   PO Box 163, OXTED, Surrey, RH8 0WP.   (mail/add)
      01892 740212
      email info@waterfowl.org.uk
      http://www.waterfowl.org.uk
      Sec/Treas: Mrs Sue Schubert
▲   Registered Charity
○   *B, *G; to promote the conservation, education & preservation
      of wildfowl & domestic waterfowl; to assist breeders
●   Mtgs - Exhib - Inf - LG - Open days
<   Nat Coun for Aviculture
>   Call Duck Assn; Indian Runner Duck Assn
M   750 i, 6 f, UK / 30 i, o'seas
¶   Waterfowl (Spring & Summer) - 3; ftm; ftm, £3.5 nm.
      The Breeders Directory - 1.   Ybk - 1.

British Web Design & Marketing Association   (BWDMA)
NR   PO Box 3227, LONDON, NW9 9LX.
      020 8204 2474
○   *T

British Weight Lifters Association   (BWLA)   1904
NR   Lilleshall National Sports Centre, NEWPORT, Shropshire,
      TF10 9AT.   (hq)
      01952 604201
      Admin: Lorraine Fleming
▲   Company Limited by Guarantee
○   *S; promotes & controls all aspects of weight lifting, power
      lifting & weight training
M   i & clubs
¶   The British Weightlifter - 6.
×   2002 British Amateur Weight Lifters Association

British Weights & Measures Association   (BWMA)   1995
NR   11 Greensleeves Avenue, BROADSTONE, Dorset, BH18 8BJ.
      (hsb)
      Pres: Vivian Thornton Linacre,   Dir: John Gardner
▲   Un-incorporated Society
○   *K; preservation & promotion of imperial weights & measures;
      to oppose compulsory metrication & the repeal of EEC/EU
      directives as enforced by UK government
Gp   Technical research; Historical & cultural; Educational;
      International
●   Conf - Mtgs - ET - Res - LG - Political representation
M   [not given]
¶   The Yardstick - 4; ftm.

British Western Dance Association   (BWDA2000)   1989
NR   13 Coltsfoot Drive, WATERLOOVILLE, Hants, PO7 8DF.   (hq)
      023 9226 6205   fax 023 9226 6205
      email bwda.2000@ntlworld.com
      http://www.bwda2000.com
▲   Un-incorporated Society
○   *D, *K; to promote Country Western Line & Partner dancing
●   Mtgs - ET - Exam - Inf
M   400 i, UK / 6 i, o'seas
¶   The Western Dancer Magazine - 6; ftm only.

British Westerners Association   (BWA)   1973
NR   6 Renoir Close, Blackdam, BASINGSTOKE, Hants,
      RG21 3EW.   (chmn/p)
      01256 331337
      Chmn: Mark Gaden
▲   Un-incorporated Society
○   *G; for anyone interested in all aspects of the American West
●   Conf - Mtgs - Res - Exhib - Comp - Inf - VE
<   Westerners Intl (USA)
M   1,200 i, 30 f, 40 org, UK / 20 i, o'seas
¶   Round-Up - 4; ftm.

British Wheel of Yoga   (BWY)   1965
NR   25 Jermyn St, SLEAFORD, Lincs, NG34 7RU.   (hq)
      01529 306851
▲   Registered Charity
Br   11
○   *G; to further the practice & teaching of yoga
●   Conf - Mtgs - ET - Exam - Exhib - SG - Inf
<   Eur U of Fedns of Yoga
M   c 8,500 i
¶   Spectrum - 4;   Yoga the World Over - 4; both ftm only.

British Wheelchair Bowls Association   (BWBA)   1984
NR   Kerria, Station Rd, EAST PRESTON, W Sussex, BN16 3AJ.
      (chmn/b)
      Chmn: Ian Blackmore
▲   Registered Charity
○   *S
●   ET - Comp - Inf
<   Brit Wheelchair Sports Foundation, Brit Isles Indoor Bowls Assn,
      Brit Paralympic Assn, English Bowling Assn, English Indoor
      Bowls Assn
M   150 i, 20 bowls clubs
¶   The Shot - 4; ftm only.

British Wheelchair Sports Foundation
      since 2004-05 **Wheelpower: British Wheelchair Sport**

British Whippet Racing Association   (BWRA)   1967
NR   25 Prior Deans Cescent, Leigh Park, HAVANT, Hants,
         PO9 3AR.   (sp)
         023 9248 6578
         Sec: Mrs D Hopkins
▲   Un-incorporated Society
Br   8
○   *S; to promote & control all issues to do with non-pedigree
         whippet racing, breeding, registering & welfare
●   Race mtgs
M   c300 i, 23 clubs
¶   [pages in Whippet News - 12].

British White Cattle Society   (BWCS)   1918
NR   Southfield Rd, Woodbastwick, NORWICH, Norfolk,
         NR13 6AL.   (breed/sec/p)
         01603 722288
         Breed Sec: Angela Hamilton
▲   Un-incorporated Society
○   *B
●   Mtgs - Expt - Inf - Lib (archive) - VE
<   Nat Cattle Assn; Rare Breeds Survival Trust
M   291 i
¶   Ybk (incl Herdbook) - 1; ftm.
         NL - 4; ftm.   Leaflet.

British Wild Boar Association   (BWBA)   1989
■   64 Linden Gardens, LONDON, W4 2EW.   (hsp)
         020 8994 4010   fax 020 8630 9666
         Sec: John Hammond
▲   Un-incorporated Society
○   *B, *F; to promote the commercial development, welfare &
         understanding of husbanded wild boar in Britain
●   Conf - Mtgs - Res - Exhib - Stat - Inf - PL - LG
M   33 i, 27 f, UK / 2 org, o'seas
¶   Various publications; m only.

British Wind Energy Association   (BWEA)   1979
■   1 Aztec Row, Berners Rd, LONDON, N1 0PN.   (hq)
         020 7689 1960   fax 020 7689 1969
         email info@bwea.com   http://www.bwea.com
         Chief Exec: Marcus Rand
▲   Company Limited by Guarantee
○   *T; to represent companies in the UK wind & marine
         renewables industries
Gp   Wind energy development; Onshore & offshore; Small scale
         wind systems; Wave & tidal stream; Associated services from
         manufacturing through planning & consultancy
●   Conf - ET - Res - Exhib - Stat - PL - LG
<   Eur Wind Energy Assn (EWEA); Scot Renewables Forum (SRF)
M   320 f
¶   Real Power (Jnl) - 4;   Annual Review - 1.
         Specialist topic conference & seminar briefing sheets.

British Women Pilots Association   (BWPA)   1955
■   Brooklands Museum, Brooklands Rd, WEYBRIDGE, Surrey,
         KT13 0QN.   (mail/address)
         http://www.bwpa.co.uk
         Hon Sec: Lucy Rodger,   Chmn: Tricia Nelmes
▲   Un-incorporated Society
○   *G, *P; to encourage & help women who have an interest in
         aviation, either as a private pilot or commercially
●   Mtgs - ET - Comp - VE - LG
<   Fedn of Eur Women Pilots; R Aero Club; Aircraft Owners &
         Pilots Assn; Air League
M   c 300 i
¶   NL - 5;   Annual Gazette - 1; both free.
         Careers book - irreg; ftm.

British Women's Tennis Association
         has closed

**British Wood Preserving & Damp-proofing Association
   (BWPDA)   1930**
■   1 Gleneagles House, Vernongate, DERBY, DE1 1UP.   (hq)
         01332 225100   fax 01332 225101
         email info@bwpda.co.uk   http://www.bwpda.co.uk
         Dir: Dr C R Coggins
▲   Company Limited By Guarantee
○   *L; serving the property care & wood protection industry;
         remedial treatment, pre-treatment, fire proofing
Gp   Divisions: Property Care Association, Wood Protection
         Association, Structural Waterproofing Gp
●   Conf - Mtgs - ET - Exam - Inf - Lib to public
M   47 i, 286 f, 13 org, UK / 11 i, 37 f, 40 org, o'seas
¶   Property Care Magazine - 3;   Property Care NL - 10;
         Wood Protection NL - 4;   Members Directory - 1; all free.

British Wood Pulp Association   (BWPA)   1896
■   48 Park Rd, Limpsfield, OXTED, Surrey, RH8 0AW.   (hsp)
         01883 722875   fax 02883 722975
         email bwpasec@aol.com   http://www.woodpulp.org.uk
         Sec: Christopher J Mills
▲   Un-incorporated Society
○   *T; to further the interest of the pulp selling industries to the UK
●   Mtgs - Stat
<   Europulp
M   50 i, 30 f
¶   AR.

British Wood Turners Association   (BWTA)   1946
■   12 Elan Close, WYMONDHAM, Norfolk, NR18 9LW.   (hsp)
         01953 600927
         http://www.britishwoodturners.co.uk
         Hon Sec: Roger Pugh
▲   Un-incorporated Society
○   *T; to promote British wood turners & their production
         capabilities
●   Mtgs - LG
<   Brit Woodworking Fedn
>   Brit Woodworking Fedn
M   35 f
¶   Members Directory - 2/3 yrly.

British Woodcarvers Association   (BWA)   1987
■   25 Summerfield Drive, Nottage, PORTHCAWL, Glam,
         CF36 3PB.   (hsp)
         01656 786937   fax 01656 786937
         email johnb@sullivanjb.freeserve.co.uk
         http://www.bwa-woodcarving.fsnet.co.uk
         Nat Sec: John Sullivan
▲   Un-incorporated Society
Br   Australia, Canada, France, Netherlands, Russia, S Africa, USA
○   *A, *P
Gp   Chainsaw; Lovespoons; Netsuke; Sticks (walking)
●   Conf - Mtgs - ET - Exhib - Comp - Inf - VE
M   c 600 i, UK / c 20 i, o'seas
¶   Woodcarver Gazette; ftm only.

British Woodworking Federation   (BWF)   1976
NR   55 Tufton St, LONDON, SW1P 3QL.   (hq)
         0870 458 6939
         http://www.bwf.org.uk
         Dir: Richard Lambert
○   *T; joinery & woodworking incl timber frame construction &
         timber engineering, architectural & general joinery, windows,
         doors & kitchen furniture
M   i, f & org

British Wrestling Association   (BWA)   2001

NR   12 Westwood Lane, CHESTERFIELD, Derbys, S43 1PA.
            (admin/p)
            01246 236443
            Admin: Yvonne Ball
▲   Company Limited by Guarantee
○   *S; to develop Olympic free-style wrestling in the UK
●   Comp - Sporting activities
<   Fédn Intle des Lottes Associées (Switzerland)
M   c 2,500 i, 40 clubs
¶   Takedown - 4.

British Youth Band Association   (BYBA)   1974

■   19 The Maltings, CAMBOURNE, Cambs, CB3 6FR.   (chmn/p)
            01954 715173
            Chmn: T Patrick; Sec: Mrs P Ingram
▲   Registered Charity
Br   regions
○   *D, *G; to raise the profile of bands nationally; to encourage
            the playing of all forms of wind & percussion instruments
●   Mtgs - ET - Comp - Marching bands
M   1,500 i

British Zen Aiki Association   (BZA)   1994

NR   57 Bittacy Rise, Mill Hill, LONDON, NW7 2HH.   (hsp)
            Hon Sec: Larry Marks
▲   Un-incorporated Society
Br   3
○   *R, *S; to promote study & interest in the twin philosophies of
            traditional (Original) Northern Zen Buddhism & the works of
            the late Morihei Ueshiba o Sensei.   Zen (Northern
            tradition): enlightenment is a gradual & natural process -
            Taijiquan: emphasis on use of non-aggressive neutralisation
            of negative energy
M   i

British Zeolite Association   (BZA)   1977

■   c/o Dr M Stockenhuber, Catalysis & Nanoscience
            Laboratory,Nottingham Trent University, Clifton Lane,
            NOTTINGHAM, NG11 8NS. NOTTINGHAM NG11 8NS.
            (sec/b)
            0115-848 6694   fax 0115-848 6694
            email michael.stockenhuber@ntu.ac.uk
            http://www.bza.org
            Sec: Dr Michael Stockenhuber
▲   Registered Charity
○   *L; the study & research into the technology & applications in
            the fields of chemistry, geology, chemical engineering & other
            branches of science & engineering of zeolites (aluminosilicate
            minerals)
●   Conf - Mtgs - ET
<   Intl Zeolite Assn; Fedn of Eur Zeolite Assns
M   117 i, UK / 88 i, o'seas
¶   Template - 1; free.

**Britpave (British In-situ Concrete Paving Association)
(Britpave)   1991**

NR   Riverside House, 4 Meadows Business Park, Station Approach,
            Blackwater, CAMBERLEY, Surrey, GU17 9AB.   (hq)
            01276 33160
            email djones@britpave.org.uk
            http://www.britpave.org.uk
            Dir & Co Sec: D P Jones
▲   Company Limited by Guarantee
○   *T; the authoritative voice of the in-situ concrete paving industry
Gp   Airfields; Environment; Rail; Roads; Specialist applications
●   Conf - Mtgs - ET - Res - Exhib - VE - LG
M   50 f, UK / 2 f, o'seas
¶   NL - 3; free.   Technical Guidance Sheets - 12; ftm only.
            Videos & CD-ROMs.

Brittle Bone Society   (BBS)   1972

■   30 Guthrie St, DUNDEE, DD1 5BS.   (hq)
            0800 028 2459   fax 01382 206771
            email bbs@brittlebone.org   http://www.brittlebone.org
            Chief Exec: Raymond Lawrie
▲   Registered Charity
Br   6
○   *K; to promote research into the causes, inheritance &
            treatment of osteogenesis imperfecta & similar disorders; to
            provide advice, encouragement & practical help for patients
            & their families
●   Conf - Mtgs - Inf
M   1,000 i, UK / 300 i, o'seas
¶   NL - 4; free.   Factsheets.

**Broadcasting Entertainment Cinematograph & Theatre Union
(BECTU)   1991**

NR   373-377 Clapham Rd, LONDON, SW9 9BT.   (hq)
            020 7346 0900   fax 020 7346 0901
            email rbolton@bectu.org.uk   http://www.bectu.org.uk
            Gen Sec: Roger Bolton
▲   Un-incorporated Society
Br   300; Channel Islands, Ireland, Isle of Man
○   *U; for workers (not performers) in broadcasting, film, theatre &
            other areas of the entertainment & media industry
●   Conf - Mtgs - Inf - Empl - LG
<   Media Entertainment Intl; Fedn of Entertainment Us; TUC;
            STUC; Labour Party
M   c 27,000 i
¶   Stage Screen & Radio (Jnl) - 10.
            Directories of Members (freelance) - irreg; prices vary.
            AR - 1; ftm.

Broadland Owners Association

▲   Un-incorporated Society
            wound up 2005

Broads Hire Boat Federation
            a group of the **British Marine Federation**

Brontë Society   1893

■   Brontë Parsonage Museum, Haworth, KEIGHLEY, W Yorks,
            BD22 8DR.   (hq)
            01535 642323   fax 01535 647131
            http://www.bronte.info
            Hon Council Sec: Lyn C Glading
            Mem Sec: Hedley Hickling
▲   Registered Charity
Br   1; 7 countries
○   *L; preservation of the history, home & literature of the Brontë
            family
●   Conf - Mtgs - ET - Res - Exhib - SG - Inf - Lib - VE
M   2,000 i, UK / 900 i, o'seas
¶   Transactions - 2;   Gazette - 2; both ftm.

Brooklands Society Ltd   1967

■   Culverden, Azalea Drive, HASLEMERE, Surrey, GU27 1JR.
            (hsp)
            01428 645724   fax 01428 645724
            http://www.brooklands.org.uk
            Hon Sec: Len Battyll
▲   Company Limited by Guarantee
○   *G; to perpetuate the story, history & preservation of the
            Brooklands Motor course & site
●   Disseminating Brooklands motor course history
<   Fedn Brit Historic Vehicle Clubs; Motor Sports Assn
M   1,150 i
¶   Gazette - 4; with NL - 4; £25 (joint subn).

Brown Swiss Cattle Society (UK)   1973
- ■ Shawcroft Farm, Wootton, ASHBOURNE, Derbys, DE6 2GW. (asa)
  01335 324009
  http://www.brownswissuk.co.uk
  Sec: Angus Dalton
- ▲ Registered Charity
- ○ *B; Brown Swiss dairy cattle
- ● Mtgs - SG - VE - Open farm days
- M 110 i, 5 f, UK / 5 i, 1 f, o'seas
- ¶ Swiss Chimes Jnl - 4; ftm only.

Browning Society   1970
- NR 84 Addison Gardens, LONDON, W14 0DR.   (hsp)
  020 7602 3094
  Hon Sec: Dr Pamela Neville-Sington
- ▲ Registered Charity
- ○ *A; to promote appreciation of the poetry of Robert & Elizabeth Barrett Browning
- ● Mtgs
- < Browning Institute Inc (New York)
- M 40 i, UK / 20 i, o'seas
- ¶ Browning Society Notes - irreg; ftm.

BSES Expeditions   (BSES)   1932
- NR at the Royal Geographical Society, 1 Kensington Gore, LONDON, SW7 2AR.   (hq)
  020 7591 3141
  Exec Dir: William Taunton-Bornet
- ▲ Company Limited by Guarantee; Registered Charity
- ○ *E; to foster the spirit of exploration & self-reliance in young people, through expeditions with a scientific purpose
- M c 4,000 i, 120 schools
- ¶ NL - 3; ftm.   AR; ftm.

BSI   1901
- NR 389 Chiswick High Rd, LONDON, W4 4AL.   (hq)
  020 8996 9000
  Chmn: Stevan Breeze
- ▲ Royal Charter
- Br 4
- ○ *G, *T; the development & promulgation of standards
- ● Expt - Inf - Lib - Testing, certification & inspection services delivered on a global basis through facilities in 86 countries
- < Intl Org for Standardization (ISO)
- M 18,500 f
- ¶ Business Standards - 6.   Update Standards - 12.

BSRIA Ltd   (BSRIA)   1955
- NR Old Bracknell Lane West, BRACKNELL, Berks, RG12 7AH.   (hq)
  01344 465600
  Dir: Andrew Eastwell
- ○ *T, *Q; 'provision of collaborative research programmes; supply of information & expertise'
- Gp Information centre; Market intelligence centre; Building energy management systems; Test; Instrument Hire; Ventilation & air movement; Energy utilisation; Quality; Systems design; Operations & management
- ● Mtgs - ET - Res - SG - Inf - Lib
- M c 1,000 f
- ¶ 'too numerous'.

BTC Testing & Advisory Group   (BTC)   1963
- ■ Lynk House, 17 Peckleton Lane, DESFORD, Leics, LE9 9JU. (regd/address)
  01455 821921   fax 01455 821921
  email btc@cadena.org.uk   http://www.btctag.org
  Co Sec: Mrs Lyn Dearling
- ▲ Company Limited by Guarantee
- ○ *Q; for technical & procedural consultation between organisations conducting vehicle &/or engine dynamometer based testing & research
- Gp Engine coolants; Laboratory managers; Technician training; Vehicle & engine emissions
- ● Mtgs - ET - Res - SG - VE - Training for technicians engaged in testing activities in motor, petroleum & chemical industries
- M 60 i, 20 f
- × 2005 (1 July) British Technical Council of the Motor & Petroleum Industries

Bucks County Agricultural Association   (Bucks County Show)   1840
- ■ The Old Barn, Wingbury Courtyard, Business Village, Leighton Rd, WINGRAVE, Bucks, HP22 4LW.   (hq)
  01296 680400   fax 01296 680445
  email alison@buckscountyshow.co.uk
  http://www.buckscountyshow.co.uk
  Sec: Mrs Alison Baylis
- ▲ Company Limited by Guarantee, Registered Charity
- ○ *F, *H; agricultural county show promoting agriculture, farming & country life
- ● Comp - County show
- < Brit Show Jumping Assn; Nat Show Pony Soc; all: horse breed socs, cattle socs & sheep socs
- M 800 i

Buddhist Society   1924
- ■ 58 Eccleston Sq, LONDON, SW1V 1PH.   (hq)
  020 7834 5858   fax 020 7976 5238
  email info@thebuddhistsociety
  http://www.thebuddhistsociety.org
  Registrar: Louise Marchant
- ▲ Registered Charity
- ○ *R; to publish & make known the principles of Buddhism; to encourage the study & practice of Buddhism
- Gp Pure Hand; Theravada; Tibetan; Zen
- ● Mtgs - ET - SG - Inf - Lib - Lectures - Summer schools
- < Wld Fellowship of Buddhists
- M 2,000 i, UK / 500 i, o'seas
- ¶ The Middle Way (Jnl) - 4; ftm, £4.50 each nm.
  The Buddhist Directory; 2004-06; £12 m, £14 nm. [subscription; £18].

Budgerigar Society   (BS)   1925
- NR Spring Gardens, NORTHAMPTON, NN1 1DR.   (hq)
  01604 624549   fax 01604 627108
  http://www.budgerigarsociety.com
  Gen Sec & Treas: Dave Whittaker
- ○ *B, *G; to promote the breeding & development of the budgerigar in all parts of the world
- ● Promotion of annual world championship Budgerigar Show (held at Doncaster in November)
- < Wld Budgerigar Org; Soc for the Protection of Aviculture
- > [Budgerigar organisations in GB & worldwide]
- M 3,500 i, UK / 160 i, o'seas
- ¶ The Budgerigar - 6; ftm only.

Buglife

NR 170A Park Road, PETERBOROUGH, Cambs, PE1 2UF.
    01733 201210
    email info@buglife.org.uk   http://www.buglife.org.uk
○ *G; conservation of inverterbrates

Builders' Conference 1935

■ Unilink House, 21 Lewis Rd, SUTTON, Surrey, SM1 4BR. (hq)
    020 8770 0111
    Chief Exec: Mike Butler
○ *T; to provide pre & post tender information to the construction industry
● Conf - Mtgs - ET - Stat - Inf
M 350 f
¶ List of Contractors - 1; ftm.   AR; ftm only.

Builders Merchants Federation (BMF) 1901

■ 15 Soho Sq, LONDON, W1D 3HL. (hq)
    0870 901 3380
    Dir: J H Hawksley
○ *T
● Mtgs - ET - Inf - LG
< Eur Assn Nat Builders' Merchants Assns (UFEMAT); Eur Fedn Heating & Sanitary Wholesalers (FEST)
M 300 f (with 3,000 outlets)
¶ Internal NL - 12;   LM - 1;   Ybk - 1; all ftm only.

Building Controls Industry Association
    is a member association of the **Federation of Environmental Trade Associations**

Building Cost Information Service (BCIS) 1962

NR 12 Great George St, LONDON, SW1P 3AD. (hq)
    020 7695 1500   fax 020 7695 1501
    email bcis@bcis.co.uk   http://www.bcis.co.uk
    Gen Mgr: Andrew Thompson
▲ Company Limited by Guarantee
○ *T; to publish information services relating to cost of construction & occupancy & maintenance of buildings
Gp Building Maintenance Information (BMI)
● Conf - ET - Res - Stat - Inf
< is a trading division of RBS Ltd (Royal Institution of Chartered Surveyors Building Services Ltd)
M 2,000 f, UK / 50 f, o'seas
¶ BCIS Bulletin (online) - constant; £355-£1,315.
    BMI Bulletin - 12; £365 m, £465 nm.
    Review of Building Prices - constant; £225-£765.
    Rebuilding Cost Guides for Houses & Flats - 1; £65.
    Guide to Daywork Rates - 1; £37.50.
    BMI Price Book - 1; £75.
✕ 2004 (January) Building Maintenance Information

Building Maintenance Information
    since 2004 is part of the **Building Cost Information Services of the Royal Institution of Chartered Surveyors**

Building Materials Federation

IRL Confederation House, 84-86 Lower Baggot St, DUBLIN 2, Republic of Ireland.
    353 (1) 605 1621   fax 353 (1) 638 1621
    email paul.kelly@ibec.ie   http://www.ibec.ie/bmf
    Dir: Paul Kelly
○ *T
< IBEC

Building Societies Association (BSA) 1869

■ 3 Savile Row, LONDON, W1S 3PB. (hq)
    020 7437 0655   fax 020 7734 6826
    http://www.bsa.org.uk
    Dir Gen: Adrian Coles
▲ Un-incorporated Society
○ *T
● Conf - Mtgs - Res - Stat - Inf - Lib - LG
M 63 f
¶ Building Society News - 12.   AR.   Ybk.

Building Societies Members Association (BSMA) 1982

NR 6 Bramley Court, Marden, TONBRIDGE, Kent, TN12 9QN.
    (hsp)
    01622 831904
    Hon Sec: Mrs Edith M Davis
▲ Un-incorporated Society
○ *K; 'our field of interest is the maintenance of the principles of mutuality in building societies; we campaign against them in converting to PLCs;. . . to advocate that building societies' rules are framed to allow & encourage the maximum participation by members in their societies' affairs. . .'
● Mtgs
M 200 i
¶ BSMA NL - 4; free.

Buildings Energy Efficiency Federation (BEEF) 1997

NR Westgate House, Prebend St, LONDON, N1 8PT. (chmn/b)
    020 7359 8000
    Chmn: Andrew Warren
▲ Un-incorporated Society
○ *N, *T; to act as a coordination body for the energy efficiency industry & for liaison purposes between the industry & the Energy Efficiency Office; to stimulate the market for products & processes used in buildings (predominantly domestic)
● Mtgs - LG
M 17 org

Bulb Distributors' Association
    2006 **British Flower Bulbs Association**

Bumblebee Conservation Trust (BBCT)

NR School of Biological & Environmental Sciences, University of Stirling, STIRLING, FK9 4LA.
    http://www.bumblebeeconservationtrust.co.uk
    Dir: Prof David Goulson

Burney Society 1990

■ 36 Henty Gardens, CHICHESTER, W Sussex, PO19 3DL. (hsp)
    01243 532231
    email tregeardavid@hotmail.com
    http://www.dawsoncollege.qc.ca/text/burney/purpose.htm
    Hon Secs: David & Janet Tregear
▲ Un-incorporated Society
○ *A, *G; life & times of Fanny Burney (Madame D'Arblay)
● Conf
M 75 i, UK / 90 i, o'seas
¶ Burney Letter - 2; ftm, £5 nm.   Burney Jnl - 1; ftm, £10 nm.

Burns Federation
    see full title **Robert Burns World Federation Ltd**

Burton & District Chamber of Commerce & Industry   1936
- Gretton House, Waterside Court, Third Avenue, Centrum 100, BURTON-upon-TRENT, Staffs, DE14 2WQ.   (hq)
  01283 563761   fax 01283 510753
  email services@burtonchamber.co.uk
  http://www.sstaffschamber.co.uk
  Mgr: Chris Towe
- ▲ Company Limited by Guarantee
- ○ *C
- ● Conf - Mtgs - ET - Expt - Inf - Advice & assistance for small & medium businesses - Lobbying local authorities & national government representation
- < Brit Cham Comm & Ind
- M 400 f
  Note: is a division of Southern Staffordshire Chamber of Commerce & Industry
- ✕ Burton upon Trent & District Chamber of Commerce & Industry

Bury St Edmunds Chamber of Commerce & Industry   1938
- 90 Guildhall St (2nd floor), BURY ST EDMUNDS, Suffolk, IP33 1PR.   (hq)
  01284 700800
  http://www.burystedmundschamber.co.uk
  Sec: Robert Bourne
- ▲ Company Limited by Guarantee
- ○ *C
- ● Mtgs - Inf - VE - Lobbying
- M 200 f
- ¶ NL - 12; free.

Bus Users UK   (BUUK)   1985
- PO Box 320, PORTSMOUTH, Hants, PO5 3SD.   (hq)
  023 9281 4493   fax 023 9286 3080
  email enquiries@bususers.org   http://www.bususers.org
  Chmn: Gavin Booth,   Pres: Dr Caroline Cahm
- Br 18
- ○ *K; to campaign for better services for bus users; to increase the influence of bus users in public transport issues; to improve communication between bus users & providers
- ● Conf - Mtgs - Comp - Bus appeals body
- < Transport 2000; Pedestrians' Assn
- M 725 i, 110 f, 82 org
- ¶ Bus User (NL) - 4; £10 yr m, £1 each nm.
  Welcome Aboard: good practice - 2; free (send sae).
- ✕ 2005 National Federation of Bus Users

Business & Accounting Software Developers Association
since 2003-04 **Business Application Software Developers Association Ltd**

Business Aircraft Users Association Ltd
2004 merged with the General Aviation Manufacturers' & Traders' Association to form the **British Business & General Aviation Association**

Business Application Software Developers Association (BASDA)   1993
- Temple Stow, Longbottom Lane, Seer Green, BEACONSFIELD, Bucks, HP9 2UL.   (chmn/b)
  01494 677699   fax 01494 681894
  email info@basda.org   http://www.basda.org
  Chief Exec: Dennis Keeling
- ▲ Company Limited by Guarantee
- ○ *T; to bring together people & organisations with an interest in the accreditation, development & marketing of business & accounting software products
- Gp EMU - the introduction of the Eurp; VAT-specification; eCommerce-business-to-business (eBIS); VAT-specification
- ● Conf - Mtgs - Exhib - SG - Stat - Inf - LG
- ¶ BASDA News (NL) - 3. ftm only.
  eBusiness Booklet;   IFRS White Paper;
  Sarbanes Oxley White Paper;
  Selecting a Business System & Selecting a Reseller - 1; all free.
- ✕ 2003-04 Business & Accounting Software Developers Association

Business Archives Council   (BAC)   1934
- c/o Lloyds TSB Group Archives, 25 Gresham St, LONDON, EC2V 7HN.   (hq)
  020 7860 5945
  email karen.sampson@lloydstsb.co.uk
  Hon Sec: Karen Sampson
- ▲ Registered Charity
- ○ *L; promoting the efficient management, preservation & use of business records
- M i, f & org
- ¶ Jnl - 2;   NL - 4;   Ybk - 1; all ftm.

Business Centre Association   (bca)   1988
- ECC London City, 3 Bunhill Row, LONDON, EC1Y 8YZ.   (hq)
  020 7847 4018   fax 020 7847 4081
  email info@bca.uk.com   http://www.bca.uk.com
  Exec Dir: Jennifer Brooke
- ▲ Company Limited by Guarantee
- ○ *T; for owners & operators of business centres & managed workspaces
- ● Conf (& exhibition showcase) - Inf - LG - Annual industry awards gala dinner
- M 700+ business centres / managed workspaces
- ¶ bca News (NL) - 4; ftm only.

Business Continuity Institute   (BCI)   1994
- NR 10 Southview Park, Marsack St, CAVERSHAM, Berks, RG4 5AF.   (hq)
  0870 603 8783   http://www.thebci.org
  Membership Services Dir: Lorraine Darke
- ▲ Company Limited by Guarantee
- Br Australia, Canada, New Zealand, S Africa, USA
- ○ *P; promotion of the art & science of business continuity management
- ● Conf - ET - Res - SG - Stat - Inf - LG - Certification scheme for business continuity practitioners, managers & consultants
- M c 3,000 i
- ¶ Continuity - 4.

Business English UK
a group of **English UK**

Business Management Association   1981
- 23 Castalia Square, LONDON, E14 3NG.   (hq)
  020 7544 1416   fax 020 7544 1499
  http://www.businessmanagement.org.uk
- ○ *P; with specific reference to small business to improve the performance of business management at every level in terms of management skills, education & planning
  no further information supplied

Business & Professional Women UK Ltd   (BPW UK Ltd)   1938
- PO Box 214, 24 Knifesmithgate, CHESTERFIELD, Derbys, S40 1XW.   (hq)
  01246 211988   fax 01246 211983
  email hq@bpwuk.co.uk   http://www.bpwuk.co.uk
  Office Mgr: Susan Tonge
- ▲ Company Limited by Guarantee
- Br 45
- ○ *K, *P; 'for all working women to discuss, develop, network, influence & participate in issues affecting women'
- Gp Carers; Computers; Finance; Lawyers; Health; Property; Science; Training; Criminal justice; Marketing & media; Women in business
- ● Conf - Mtgs - ET - LG
- < Intl Fedn Business & Profl Women; Eur Fedn of Business & Profl Women
- ¶ BPW News - 4;   Annual Review; both ftm only.

© CBD Research Ltd · Beckenham · BR3 5JS · Tel 020 8650 7745 · Fax 020 8650 0768 · E-mail cbd@cbdresearch.com · www.cbdresearch.com

Business Services Association Ltd   (BSA)   1993
NR   Warnford Court, 29 Throgmorton St, LONDON, EC2N 2AT.
    (hq)
    020 7786 6300   fax 020 7786 6309
    email norman.rose@bsa-org.com
    http://www.bsa-org.com
    Dir-Gen: Norman H Rose
▲   Company Limited by Guarantee
○   *T; representing major companies which provide outsourced
    services in the public & private sectors
●   Res - LG
<   Confedn Brit Ind
M   19 f (employing 600,000 i)
¶   Publications to m only.

Business Software Alliance   (BSA)   1988
NR   79 Knightsbridge, LONDON, SW1X 7RB.   (European hq)
    020 7245 0304   fax 020 7245 0310
    email europe@bsa.org
Br   Singapore, USA
○   *K, *T; to eradicate software piracy
Gp   Computer software publishers
●   Mtgs - ET - Res - Stat - Inf - LG
M   f

Business Tourism Scotland   (BTS)   2000
NR   c/o Meeting Makers Ltd, Crawford Building, 76 Southbrae
    Drive, GLASGOW, G13 1PP.
▲   Un-incorporated Society
○   *T

Business Volunteer Mentors Association
    is run by the **National Federation of Enterprise Agencies**

Business West
    is the trading name of **Bristol Chamber of Commerce & Industry**

Butterfly Conservation   1968
■   Manor Yard, East Lulworth, WAREHAM, Dorset, BH20 5QP.
    (hq)
    0870 774 4309   fax 0870 770 6150
    email info@butterfly-conservation.org.
    http://www.butterfly-conservation.org
    Chief Exec: Dr Martin Warren
▲   Company Limited by Guarantee
Br   32
○   *B, *L; conservation of British wild butterflies, moths & their
    habitats; to research into their life needs; to set up reserves
    for the rarer species
●   Conf - Mtgs - ET - Res - Exhib - Inf - PL
>   Butterfly Consvn Europe
M   12,000 i
¶   Butterfly - 3; ftm only.
×   2003 (29 November) British Butterfly Conservation Society Ltd

Buttonhook Society   1979
NR   PO Box 1089, MAIDSTONE, Kent, ME14 9BA.   (hq)
    01622 752949
    email buttonhooksociety@tiscali.co.uk
    http://www.thebuttonhooksociety.com
    Mem Sec: Angela Walmsley
▲   Un-incorporated Society
Br   USA
○   *G; to encourage the research into, collection & preservation of
    buttonhooks & ancillary articles; to build up archives on the
    50,000 known buttonhooks researched
●   Conf - Mtgs - Res - Exhib - Stat - Inf - Lib - Provision of
    speakers
M   c 230 i, UK / 140 i, o'seas
¶   The Boutonneur (NL) - 6.   Compendium of Buttonhooks - 1.
    A Part Work Encyclopaedia (pts 1-98).

BVCA (British Venture Capital Association)   (BVCA)   1983
■   Tower 3, 3 Clements Inn, LONDON, WC2A 2AZ.   (hq)
    020 7025 2950   fax 020 7025 2951
    email bvca@bvca.co.uk   http://www.bvca.co.uk
    Chief Exec: Peter Linthwaite
▲   Company Limited by Guarantee
○   *T; 'the public face of the industry providing services to its
    members, investors & entrepreneurs, as well as government
    & media'
●   Conf - Mtgs - ET - Res - Exhib - Stat - Expt - Inf - LG
M   180 f, 175 f (associate)
¶   Directory (LM) - 1; ftm, £10 nm.
    A Guide to Private Equity; free.
    Report of Investment Activity - 1; ftm, £50 nm.

Byron Society   1971
NR   6 Gertrude St, LONDON, SW10 0JN.   (hq/dir)
    020 7352 5112 p
    Hon Dir: Mrs Elma Dangerfield
▲   Registered Charity
Br   2; 36
○   *A; to promote research into the life & work of the English poet
    Lord Byron (1788-1824)
M   i
¶   The Byron Jnl - 1.

Caernarvonshire Historical Society   (Cymdeithas Hanes Sir Caernarfon) (CHS) 1939
NR County Offices, Shirehall St, CAERNARFON, Caernarfonshire, LL55 1SH. (hsb)
01286 679088   fax 01286 679637
Hon Sec: Ann Rhydderch
▲ Registered Charity
○ *L; to collect & preserve the history relating to the county of Caernarfon
● Mtgs - VE
M 460 i, 10 org, UK / 20 i, o'seas
¶ Transactions (Jnl) - 1.

Café Society   1992
■ Archway House, Moor St, CHEPSTOW, Monmouthshire, NP16 5DB. (hq)
01291 636338   fax 01291 630402
email enq@cafesociety.org.uk
Sec: Jim Winship
▲ Company Limited by Guarantee
○ *T; to promote quality standards in the coffee market in the UK
● Conf - Mtgs - ET - Inf - LG - Promotion - Awards dinner
M 14 i, 68 f
¶ Café Culture Magazine - 4; ftm, £25 yr nm.

Cairngorms Chamber of Commerce
■ PO Box 15, KINGUSSIE, Inverness-shire, PH20 1WF.
01479 812373
○ *C
no further information supplied

Caithness Agricultural Society   (CAS)   1830
■ Katana, Sibmister Rd, Murkle, THURSO, Caithness, KW14 8SP. (sp)
01847 851654
http://www.caithnessshow.co.uk
Sec: Kathleen Mackey
▲ Registered Charity
○ *F;
● Mtgs - Comp - Agricultural show
< Clydesdale Horse Soc; Highland Pony Soc; Shetland Pony Stud-Book Soc
M c 490 i

Caithness Paperweight Collectors Club   (CPCC)   1976
NR Caithness Glass Ltd, INVERALMOND, Perthshire, PH1 3TZ. (hq)
01738 637373   fax 01738 492300
http://www.caithnessglass.co.uk
Mgr: Caroline Clark
○ *G; for collectors of paperweights in traditional, contemporary, limited & open editions
M c 6,500 i

Caithness & Sutherland Chamber of Commerce
NR Bryn Tyrion, Castlegreen Rd, THURSO, Caithness, KW14 7DN. (sp)
Sec: George Bruce
○ *C
✕ Caithness Chamber of Commerce

Caledonian Railway Association   (CRA)   1983
NR 12 Greenacres View, MOTHERWELL, N Lanarkshire, ML1 3BG. (hsp)
01698 261858
Org Sec: David Coddington
▲ Un-incorporated Society
Br 2
○ *G; to study the former Caledonian Railway Company
● Mtgs - Res - Exhib - Inf - Lib - VE
M 310 i, 12 f, 7 org, UK / 16 i, o'seas
¶ The True Line (Jnl) - 4; ftm, £5 nm.   LM - 1; £3 m only.

Call Centre Association
since 2005 **Customer Contact Association**

Call Centre Management Association (UK) Ltd   (CCMAUK) 1995
■ International House, 174 Three Bridges Rd, CRAWLEY, W Sussex, RH10 1LE. (asa)
01293 538400   fax 01293 521313
email admin@ccma.org.uk   http://www.ccma.org.uk
Sec: Roy Bailey
○ *P
● Mtgs - ET
M 350 i, UK / 20 i, o'seas
¶ NL
✕ 2001 (September) Call Centre Management Association

Calligraphy & Lettering Arts Society   1994
■ 54 Boileau Rd, LONDON, SW13 9BL.
020 8741 7886
email info@clas.co.uk   http://www.clas.co.uk
Admin: Sue Cavendish
○ *A
M 1,500 i

Camanachd Association   1893
NR Queen Anne House, High St, FORT WILLIAM, Inverness-shire, PH33 6DG. (hq)
01397 703903   fax 01397 703903
email enquiries@shinty.com   http://www.shinty.com
Chief Exec Officer: Richard Tulloch
▲ Un-incorporated Society
○ *S; to foster & develop the Scottish national game of shinty
Gp Coaching; Youth development; Development
● Conf - Mtgs - Comp
< Sportscotland
> Glasgow Celtic Soc; MacAulay Assn; Camanachd Referees' Assn
M 3,100 i, 51 org
¶ Camanachd Association Annual - 1.

Cámara Chileno-Británica de Comercio (British Chilean Chamber of Commerce) 1917
NR El Bosque Norte 0125, Las Condes, SANTIAGO, Chile. (hq)
56 (2) 370 4175   fax 56 (2) 370 4164
Gen Mgr: Andrew Robshaw
○ *C
● Mtgs - Comp - Expt - Inf - Lib
M 24 i, 130 f (in Chile)
¶ NL - 12; ftm.   Economic Report - 4; ftm.
Directory of Members; ftm, £10.

Cámara de Comercio Argentino-Británica (CCAB) 1914
- ■ Avenida Corrientes 457 / Piso 10, (C1043AAE) BUENOS AIRES, Argentina. (hq)
54 (11) 4394 2762   fax 54 (11) 4326 3860
email info@ccab.com.ar   http://www.ccab.com.ar
Chief Exec: Monica Mesz
- ▲ Registered Charity
- ○ *C; to promote general trade & commerce between the UK & Argentina
- Gp Lawyers; Executive education; HHRR & IT
- ● Conf - Mtgs - ET - Exhib - Expt - Inf - LG
- M 140 f, Argentina
- ¶ NL - 26; ftm only.

Cámara de Comercio Británica AC (British Chamber of Commerce in Mexico) 1921
- NR Rio de la Plata 30, Col Cuauhtémoc, 06500 MEXICO DF, Mexico. (hq)
52 (5) 256 09 01   fax 52 (5) 211 54 51
email britcham@infoabc.com
Dir Gen: Teresa de Lay
- ○ *C; to promote trade & investment between the UK & Mexico

Cámara de Comercio Britanica en España
   see **British Chamber of Commerce in Spain**

Cámara de Comercio Colombo-Británica (British Colombian Chamber of Commerce) (CCCB) 1981
- NR Calle 95 No 13-55, Oficina 409, BOGOTÁ, Colombia. (hq)
57 (1) 621 2401   fax 57 (1) 621 2421
http://www.colombobritanica.com
Exec Dir: Patricia Tovar
- ○ *C; to promote commerce & investment between Colombia & GB
- ● Conf - Mtgs - Exhib - Expt - Inf - Lib - VE - LG
- ¶ NL - 6; ftm.

Câmara de Comércio Luso-Británica
   see **British-Portuguese Chamber of Commerce**

Cámara de Comercio Peruano-Británica
   see **British-Peruvian Chamber of Commerce**

Cámara de Comercio Uruguayo-Británica (British-Uruguayan Chamber of Commerce) 1969
- NR Av Lib Brig Gral Lavalleja 1641, P2 Of 201, 11100-MONTEVIDEO, Uruguay. (hq)
598 (2) 908 0349   fax 598 (2) 900 0936
email camurbri@netgate.com.uy
http://www.camurbri.com.uy
Sec: Nota Cardenas
- ○ *C; to promote Anglo-Uruguayan commercial relations

Cámara Venezolana Británica de Comercio (CVBC) 1951
- NR Multicentro Empresarial del Este, Edif Miranda Nucleo B (piso 9), Oficina B-91, Apartado 60102, CARACAS, Venezuela. (hq)
58 (2) 267 3112   fax 58 (2) 257 9366
http://www.britcham.com.ve
Gen Mgr: Helen Wadham
- ○ *C; to improve commercial relations between UK & Venezuela
- Gp Commercial dept; Events dept; Young executive section (to help develop business & English language skills in both a business & social environment)
- ● Conf - Mtgs - Res - Comp - Expt - Inf - Lib - VE - Overseas missions
- M 2 i, 22 f, UK / 55 i, 107 f, o'seas, 20 i (young execs section)
- ¶ Directory - 1.

Cambrian Archaeological Association (Cymdeithas Hynafiaethau Cymru) 1846
- NR Halfway House, Pont y Pandy, BANGOR, Gwynedd, LL57 3DG. (contact/p)
01248 364865
Contact: Peter Llewellyn
- ▲ Registered Charity
- ○ *L; to examine, preserve & illustrate the ancient monuments & remains of the history, language, manners, customs, arts & industries of Wales & the Marches
- Gp Research; Meetings
- ● Conf - Mtgs - Res - Comp - Lib - VE - LG
- < Coun for Brit Archaeology (CBA)
- M 600 i, 140 org, UK / 30 i, 30 org, o'seas
- ¶ Archaeologia Cambrensis - 1.   LM - 2 yrly.

Cambrian Railways Society
- ▦ Oswald Rd, OSWESTRY, Shropshire, SY11 1RB. (hq)
01691 671749
email information@cambrian-railways-soc.co.uk
http://www.cambrian-railways-soc.co.uk
Sec: A M Hignett
- ▲ Company Listed by Guarantee, Registered Charity
- ○ *G; to acquire, preserve & restore any & all of the Cambrian Railways Company's infrastructure, buildings, lines & artifacts
- ● Mtgs - ET - Res - Exhib - Inf - VE
- M 488 i, UK / 5 i, o'seas
- ¶ Cambrian Line Magazine - 4; ftm, £1 nm.

Cambridge Antiquarian Society (CAS) 1840
- ▦ 21 High St, West Wickham, CAMBRIDGE, CB1 6RY. (hsb)
http://www.camantsoc.org
Hon Sec: Janet Morris
- ▲ Registered Charity
- ○ *L; archaeology & history of the city & county of Cambridge
- ● Conf - Mtgs - ET - Inf - Lib - VE - LG (local)
- < Coun Brit Archaeology
- M 465 i, 52 affiliated socs, 85 subscribing org
- ¶ Proceedings - 1; ftm, £14.50 nm.   The Conduit - 1; ftm only.

Cambridge Bibliographical Society 1949
- ▦ University Library, West Rd, CAMBRIDGE, CB3 9DR. (hsb)
01223 333000   fax 01223 333160
email nas1000@cam.ac.uk
Hon Sec: N Smith
- ▲ Registered Charity
- ○ *L; to promote the study of bibliographical & palaeographical research
- ● Mtgs - VE
- M 150 i, 10 f, 50 org, UK / 45 i, 15 f, 120 org, o'seas
- ¶ Transactions - 1; £12.   Monographs - irreg; price varies.

Cambridge & District Chamber of Commerce & Industry
   see **Cambridgeshire Chambers of Commerce**

Cambridge Paperweight Circle
   since 2003-04 **Paperweight Collectors Circle**

Cambridge Philosophical Society (CPS) 1819
- NR Bene't St, CAMBRIDGE, CB2 3PY. (hq)
01223 334743
email philosoc@hermes.cam.ac.uk
http://www.cam.ac.uk/societies/cps
Exec Sec: Mrs B Larner
- ▲ Registered Charity
- ○ *L; promotion of scientific enquiry
- ● Conf - Mtgs - Participation in upkeep & management of Scientific Periodicals Library of the University of Cambridge
- M 1,900 i
- ¶ Mathematical Proceedings [articles on original research] - 6. Biological Reviews [long reviews on the state of research in a particular field of Biology - NOT book reviews] - 4.

Cambridge Refrigeration Technology   **(CRT)**   **1945**
- ■   140 Newmarket Rd, CAMBRIDGE, CB5 8HE.   (hq)
  01223 365101   fax 01223 461522
  email crt@crtech.demon.co.uk   http://www.crtech.co.uk
- ▲   Company Limited by Guarantee
- ○   *Q; research, development, testing, consultancy & information services relating to all types of refrigerated transport & storage
- Gp   Refrigerated Transport Information Society
- ●   Conf - ET - Res - Exhib - Inf - Lib - PL
- <   Intl Inst Refrigeration (IIR); Amer Soc Heating, Refrigerating & Air-Conditioning Engrs Inc (ASHRAE); Assn Indep Res & Technology Orgs (AIRTO); BSRIA; Inst Refrigeration; Brit Refrigeration Assn
- M   5 i, 10 f, 10 org, UK / 6 i, 30 f, 2 org, o'seas
- ¶   NL - 4; ftm only.
  The Transport of Perishable Foodstuffs; £6.50.
  Cargo Companion (3 vol); ftm, £155 nm.

Cambridge Sheep Society   **1978**
- ■   Pharm House, Neston Rd, Willaston, NESTON, Cheshire, CH64 2TL.   (hsp)
  0151-327 5699
  Hon Sec: D Alan R Davies
- ▲   Company Limited by Guarantee
- ○   *B
- ●   Mtgs - ET - Res - Exhib - Stat
- <   Nat Sheep Assn
- M   20 i
- ¶   LM - 1; free.   AR; ftm only.

Cambridge Society for the Application of Research   **(CSAR)** **1956**
- NR   c/o Cambridge Enterprise, 10 Trumpington St, CAMBRIDGE, CB2 1QA.   (organising)
  01223 333543   fax 01223 332988
  email bt224@cam.ac.uk   http://www.csar.org.uk s
  Contact: Dr R Jennings
- ▲   Un-incorporated Society
- ○   *L; to bring together & promote cooperation within & between the University of Cambridge & industry of all kinds with a view to the expeditious use of resources & research
- ●   Mtgs - VE
- M   150 i, 35 f, 10 university depts

Cambridge Society of Musicians
    ceased operation 28 February 2006

Cambridgeshire Chambers of Commerce   **(CCC)**   **1918**
- NR   Endeavour House, Vision Park, Histon, CAMBRIDGE, CB4 9ZR.   (hq)
  01223 237414
  http://www.cambridgeshirechamber.co.uk
  Chief Exec: John Bridge
- ▲   Company Limited by Guarantee
- Br   Ely, Fenland, Huntingdonshire, Peterborough
- ○   *C
- Gp   Technology; Retail; Professional; Policy
- ●   Conf - Mtgs - ET - Exhib - Stat - Expt - Inf - Lib - Export documentation - Advice skills training
- <   Brit Chams Comm
- M   f
- ×   2003 (Cambridge & District Chamber of Commerce & Industry (Greater Peterborough Chamber of Commerce & Industry

Cambridgeshire Local History Society   **(CLHS)**   **1951**
- NR   5 Sleaford Close, Basham, CAMBRIDGE, CB1 6DP.   (hsp)
  01223 892430
  Hon Sec: Andrew Westwood-Bate
- ▲   Company Limited by Guarantee; Registered Charity
- ○   *L; to encourage the study of local history & impart information on it
- Gp   Photographic recording
- ●   Conf - Mtgs - Res - Exhib - VE
- <   Cambridge Antiquarian Soc
- M   160 i, 10 org
- ¶   Review - 1.

Cambridgeshire Records Society   **(CRS)**   **1972**
- NR   c/o County Record Office, Box No RES1009, Shire Hall, CAMBRIDGE, CB3 0AP.   (hsb)
  01223 364706
  Hon Sec: Mrs Francesca Ashburner
- ▲   Un-incorporated Society
- ○   *L; to publish documentary sources relating to the history of Cambridgeshire & neighbouring areas
- M   c 100 i, UK / c 20 i, o'seas
- ¶   Source material - 1.

Camera Club   **1885**
- NR   16 Bowden St, LONDON, SE11 4DS.   (hq)
  020 7587 1809
  http://www.thecameraclub.co.uk
  The Hon Secretary
- ▲   Un-incorporated Society
- ○   *G; to foster the art & science of photography by provision of affordable, high quality darkrooms & studio, exhibition gallery & courses
- ●   Mtgs - ET - Exhib - SG - Inf - Lib
- M   320 i, 10 f, UK / 4 i, o'seas
- ¶   Club News - 12; free.

Campaign for Angling
    a campaign of the **Countryside Alliance**

Campaign against Arms Trade   **(CAAT)**   **1974**
- ■   11 Goodwin St, LONDON, N4 3HQ.   (hq)
  020 7281 0297   fax 020 7281 4369
  email enquiries@caat.org.uk   http://www.caat.org.uk
  Coordinator: Ann Feltham
- ▲   Un-incorporated Society
- ○   *K; information & campaigning about the arms trade
- ●   Mtgs - Res - Exhib - Inf - Lib - Day schools
- M   3,500 i, 300 org, UK / 200 i, o'seas - as supporters
- ¶   NL - 6; ftm, £1 nm.

Campaign against Censorship   **(CAC)**   **1968**
- ■   25 Middleton Close, FAREHAM, Hants, PO14 1QN.   (hsp)
  01329 284471
  Hon Sec: Mrs Mary M Hayward
- ▲   Un-incorporated Society
- ○   *K; to uphold freedom of speech & publication; to oppose censorship in all fields
- ●   Inf - Lobbying
- <   Liberty
- ¶   Uncensored - irreg; ftm.

Campaign for Community Banking Services   1997
■   50 Roundwood Park, HARPENDEN, Herts, AL5 3AF.   (dir/p)
     01582 764760   fax 01582 764760
     http://www.communitybanking.org.uk
     Hon Dir: Derek P G French
▲   Un-incorporated Society
○   *K; 'to promote the continued existence of convenient access to
     banking services within communities in order to sustain local
     commercial activity; to combat financial & social exclusion &
     assist the vulnerable, disabled & elderly'
●   Res - Stat - Inf - LG - Lobbying financial service providers -
     Publicity
M   27 org

Campaign for Courtesy (Polite Society)   1986
■   16 Grice Rd, Hartshill, STOKE-ON-TRENT, Staffs, ST4 7PJ.
     (hsp)
     01782 614407   fax 01782 614407
     Contact: Rev Ian Gregory
▲   Registered Charity
○   *K; to encourage courtesy & good manners in all ages & walks
     of life; to engender respect for other people & good
     behaviour generally
●   Conf - ET - Res - National Day of Courtesy (Friday May 26 or
     the Friday prior to the May Bank Holiday)
M   10,000 i & f, 52 org
¶   NL - 2; ftm, 20p each nm.
     [subscription £15].

Campaign for Dark Skies   (CFDS)   1990
NR   c/o Burlington House, Piccadilly, LONDON, W1J 0DU.   (hq)
     email info@dark-skies.org
     Coordinator: Bob Mizon
Br   118 local officers
○   *K; a scientific (astronomical) pressure group set up to counter
     the increasing threat to the visibility of the night sky from
     waste upward artificial light
     Note: this is a campaign of the British Astronomical
     Association.

Campaign for the Defence of the Traditional Cathedral Choir
     since 2006 **Campaign for the Traditional Cathedral Choir**

Campaign against Drinking & Driving   (CADD)   1986
NR   PO Box 62, BRIGHOUSE, W Yorks, HD6 3YY.   (hq)
     0845 123 5543
     http://www.cadd.org.uk
     Mgr: Carole Whittingham
▲   Company Limited by Guarantee; Registered Charity
○   *K, *W; to support victims & families of those killed & injured by
     drunk & irresponsible drivers; to work for a reduction of
     deaths & injuries on the road
●   Conf - Inf - LG
<   Eur Fedn Victim Families (Geneva); Eurocare (Brussels); BRAKE;
     Parliamentary Advy C'ee on Transport (PACTS)(London)
M   c 600 i & f
¶   NL - 4.

Campaign for an English Parliament
NR   Box 125 / 61 Great Underbank, STOCKPORT, Cheshire,
     SK1 1LE.
     07071 220234
○   *K

Campaign against Euro-federalism   (CAEF)   1991
NR   PO Box 46295, LONDON, W5 2UG.
     email caef@caef.org.uk   http://www.caef.org.uk
▲   Un-incorporated Society
○   *K; the campaign is based on the rights of states to self-
     determination & national democracy.   The campaign
     opposes: Britain's membership of the European Union,
     joining the single currency, the EU constitution & charter of
     fundamental rights including a common foreign policy &
     European army
●   Conf - Public mtgs
<   Intl Alliance of Euro-critical Movements & Orgs (TEAM);
     Campaign for an Indep Britain; Anti Maastricht Alliance
M   [not stated]
¶   The Democrat - 12.
     Democratic Broadsheet - irreg.
     Various pamphlets & leaflets.

Campaign for Freedom of Information   (CFOI/CFI)   1984
§   16 Baldwins Gardens (suite 102), LONDON, EC1N 7RJ.   (hq)
     020 7831 7477   fax 020 7831 7461
     email admin@cfoi.demon.co.uk   http://www.cfoi.org.uk
     Dir: Maurice Frankel
▲   Company Limited by Guarantee
     campaigns against unnecessary official secrecy & for a freedom
     of information act; to press for more disclosure in the private
     sector, if the information is of public interest.
     The campaign publishes briefings & other publications - list
     available.

Campaign for Freedom from Piped Music   (Pipedown)   1992
■   1 The Row, High St, Berwick St James, SALISBURY, Hants,
     SP3 4TP.   (mail address)
     01722 790622
     email newpipedown@btinternet.com
     http://www.pipedown.info
     Hon Sec: Nigel Rodgers
▲   Un-incorporated Society
Br   Germany (associated)
○   *K; 'to campaign for the freedom in public spaces (shops,
     hospitals, doctors' surgeries, rail/bus stations, airports, trains,
     buses) from piped music (muzak), meaning music (of any
     sort) relayed nonstop around a room, building etc'
●   Conf - Mtgs - Stat - Inf - LG - Co-ordinated letter writing
     campaigns - Lobbying Parliament for a bill - Handing out
     protest cards - Peaceful demonstrations - Listing muzak-free
     places
M   1,800 i, UK / 50 i, o'seas
¶   Newsletter - 4; ftm, £2 nm.

Campaign for Homosexual Equality   (CHE)   1969
NR   PO Box 342, LONDON, WC1X 0DU.   (mail)
     07702 326151   fax 020 8743 6252
     email valerie.buxton@virgin.net address
     Sec: Barry Cutler
▲   Un-incorporated Society
○   *K; 'promotion of equality in law & society for lesbians, gays &
     bisexuals'
●   ET - Inf
M   150 i & affiliates
¶   Publications list available.

Campaign against Hysterectomy & Unnecessary Operations on Women   (CAH)   1995
- ■ PO Box 300, WOKING, Surrey, GU22 0YE.   (mail/add)
  email sandra.simkin@ntlworld.com
  Dir: Sandra Simkin
- ▲ Un-incorporated Society
- Br 4
- ○ *K; to campaign, on behalf of all women, for an Act of Parliament - 'Women's Medical Protection Act' - to protect women for all time against unnecessary surgery; to raise women's awareness of their right to choose what happens to their bodies; to provide women with information which will enable them to challenge ignorant decisions; to research into the consequences of unnecessary surgery
- Gp Information; Informed consent; Legal
- ● Conf - Res - Inf
- < Rights of Women
- M i
- ¶ Bulletin - 4; ftm only.
  The Case against Hysterectomy.

Campaign for an Independent Britain   (CIB)   1989
- NR 81 Ashmole St, LONDON, SW8 1NF.   (sb)
  020 8340 0314   fax 020 7582 7021
  email info@cibhq.co.uk   http://www.cibhq.co.uk
  Hon Sec: Sir Robin Williams
- ▲ Un-incorporated Society
- Br 20
- ○ *K; to halt the drive to political, economic & monetary union in the EC; to regain for Britain the rights, freedoms & powers of an independent nation
- ● Conf - Mtgs - ET - Res - Stat - Inf
- < Anti-Common Market League; Campaign against Euro Federalism; Cheaper Food League; Labour Euro-Safeguards Campaign; Conservatives against a Federal Europe
- M 3,000 i
- ¶ Independence - 4.   Leaflets.
  Common Fisheries Policy - End or Mend?
  There is an Alternative.   A Price not worth Paying.
  From Rome to Maastricht - a reappraisal of Britain's membership of the EC.

Campaign for Independent Food
  a campaign under the title Honest Food - the Campaign for Independent Food run by the **Countryside Alliance**

Campaign for Industry   (CFI)   1987
- ■ 6 Southgate Green, BURY ST EDMUNDS, Suffolk, IP33 2BL.
  (hq)
  01284 754123   fax 01284 704121
  email robertcorfe@tiscali.co.uk
  Chmn: Robert Corfe
- ▲ Un-incorporated Society
- ○ *K; 'to promote British-based manufacturing by working for changes to financial institutions for the more effective financing of industrial investment; to work for a better political environment for the productive sector; to promote a pro-industrial ethos in society through education'
- ● Conf - Mtgs - SG - Stat - Inf
- M 1 f, org
- ¶ NL.   Pamphlets.

Campaign for Learning   1997
- ■ 19 Buckingham Street (basement), LONDON, WC2N 6EF.
  (hq)
  020 7930 1111   fax 020 7930 1551
  http://www.campaign-for-learning.org.uk
  Chief Exec: Susie Parsons
- ▲ Company Limited by Guarantee; Registered Charity
- Br 3
- ○ *K; an independent voluntary organisation working for an inclusive society in which learning is valued, understood, freely available & accessible to everyone as of right; to stimulate learning that will sustain people for life
- Gp Family learning; Workplace learning; Learning to learn in schools
- ● Conf - ET - Res - Inf - LG - Learning at Work day - Family Learning week
- ¶ Learning to Live (NL) - 4; [email].

Campaign for National Community Service   (CNCS)   1976
- ■ Flag House, 7 Ridgeway Rd, HERNE BAY, Kent, CT6 7LL.
  (chmn/p)
  Chmn: G R Wanstall
- ▲ Un-incorporated Society
- ○ *K; 'to promote a new form of national community service to afford a disciplined service for the young to meet their needs & the needs of the community as a whole'
- ● ET
- M 1,000's of supporters

Campaign for Nuclear Disarmament   (CND)   1958
- NR 162 Holloway Rd, LONDON, N7 8DQ.   (hq)
  020 7700 2393   fax 020 7700 2357
  email enquiries@cnduk.org   http://www.cnduk.org
  Chmn: Kate Hudson
- ▲ Un-incorporated Society
- Br 12
- ○ *K; works for international peace & disarmament & a world in which the vast resources now devoted to militarism are dedicated to the real needs of the human community
- Gp Scottish; Welsh; Irish; Youth; Student; Trade union; Labour; Christian
- ● Mtgs - Inf - Campaigns - Lobbying
- M 30,000 i, 600 org
- ¶ CND Today - 1.   Campaign - 3.
  Lobby - irreg.
  Annual Review; ftm only.

Campaign for Philosophical Freedom   (CPF)   1985
- NR 12a Westover Rise, BRISTOL, BS9 3LU.   (hsp)
  http://www.cfpf.org.uk
  Hon Sec: Michael Roll
- ○ *K; to obtain a balance on all media & educational outlets; to disestablish the Church & make the second House of Parliament an elected chamber; to give a secular balance to all religious affairs departments; to challenge orthodox scientific thinking
- ● Res - Inf
- M 20,000 i, UK / 500 i, o'seas
- ¶ Censored in Great Britain: the scientific proof of survival after death;
  Uncomfortable Historical Facts that we are never taught at School about the theocracy of Great Britain;
  The Mode of Future Existence by Sir Oliver Lodge;
  all free, please send sae.

Campaign against Political Correctness
- NR Trevose House, Orsett St, LONDON, SE11 5PN.
  07092 040916   fax 07092 040916
  email info@capc.co.uk   http://www.capc.co.uk
  Co-founders: Laura & John Midgley
- ○ *K

Campaign for Press & Broadcasting Freedom   (CPBF)   1979
NR   23 Orford Rd (2nd floor), LONDON, E17 9NL.   (hq)
        020 8521 5932
        email freepress@cpbf.org.uk   http://www.cpbf.org.uk
        Nat Sec: Jonathan Hardy
Br   2
○   *K; to campaign for diverse, democratic & representative
        media; to carry out research & generate debate on
        alternative forms of media free from state control or business
        domination
Gp   Media manifesto for General Election
●   Conf - Mtgs - ET - Res - Exhib - SG - Stat - Inf - LG
M   1,500 i, 50 org, UK / 50 i, o'seas
¶   Free Press - 6.

Campaign to Protect Rural England   (CPRE)   1926
NR   128 Southwark St, LONDON, SE1 0SW.   (hq)
        020 7981 2800   fax 020 7981 2899
        email info@cpre.org.uk   http://www.cpre.org.uk
        Dir: Shaun Spiers
▲   Company Limited by Guarantee; Registered Charity
Br   43
○   *G, *K; 'to promote the beauty, tranquillity & diversity of rural
        England by encouraging the sustainable use of land & other
        natural resources in town & country; to promote positive
        solutions for the long term future of the countryside & to
        ensure change values its natural & built environment'
●   Mtgs - Res - Lib - PL - LG
M   43,000 i
¶   CPRE Voice - 3;   AR; both ftm only.
        publications list available.
✕   2003 (June 18) Council for the Protection of Rural England

**Campaign for the Protection of Rural Wales   (Ymgyrch Diogelu
Cymru Wledig)   (YDCW)   (CPRW)   1928**
■   Tŷ Gwyn, 31 High St, WELSHPOOL, Powys, SY21 7YD.   (hq)
        01938 552525   fax 01938 552741
        email info@cprwmail.org.uk   http://www.cprw.org.uk
        Dir: Peter Ogden
▲   Registered Charity
Br   17
○   *G; to protect & improve the rural scenery & amenities in Wales
●   Inf - Lib
¶   Rural Wales / Cymru Wledig - 3; ftm.

Campaign for Qualified Politicians
        since 2003 **Cognition: the Campaign for Qualified Politicians**

Campaign for Real Ale Ltd   (CAMRA)   1971
■   230 Hatfield Rd, ST ALBANS, Herts, AL1 4LW.   (hq)
        01727 867201   fax 01727 867670
        email camra@camra.org.uk   http://www.camra.org.uk
        Chief Exec: Mike Benner
▲   Company Limited by Guarantee
Br   200
○   *K; to promote quality, choice & value for money; to support
        the public house as a focus for community life; to maintain
        consumer rights & increase the appreciation of traditional
        beers & ciders
●   Conf - Mtgs - Res - Exhib - Comp - Stat - Lib - VE - LG
<   Eur Beer Consumers U (EBCU); Sustain; Nat Coun for Voluntary
        Orgs (NCVO)
M   79,000 i, UK / 1,000 i, o'seas
¶   What's Brewing - 12; ftm only.
        Good Beer Guide - 1; £10 m, £13.99 nm.
        Good Bottled Beer Guide - 1; £7.99 m, £9.99 nm.
        CAMRA's Good Cider Guide - 2/3 yrly; £8.99 m, £10.99 nm.
        Good Beer Guide to Germany; £10.99 m, £12.99 nm.

Campaign for Real Education   (CRE)   1987
■   12 Pembroke Sq, LONDON, W8 6PA.   (hsp)
        020 7937 2122   fax 020 7938 1638
        email cred@cre.org.uk   http://www.cre.org.uk
        18 Westlands Grove, Stockton Lane, YORK, YO31 1EF.
        01904 424134   (chmn/p).
        Hon Sec: Dr Vera Dalley,   Chmn: Nick Seaton
○   *E, *K; an association of parents, teachers & academics which
        campaigns for higher standards in state schools & colleges;
        to support individuals & groups with similar interests; to
        promote educational research & the dissemination of
        information
M   c 3,000 i, UK / c 30 i, o'seas

Campaign for Real Milk   (CAMILK)   1998
■   1 Stoodley Barn, Holne, ASHBURTON, Devon, TQ13 7RY.
        (hsp)
        01364 631212
        email richard@copur.fsbusiness.co.uk
        Co-founder: Richard Copur
▲   Un-incorporated Society
○   *K; to promote raw un-pasteurised milk
●   Inf
<   Weston Price Foundation (www.realmilk.com) (USA)

**Campaign for the Restoration of the National Anthem & Flag
(CRNAF)   1985**
NR   Flag House, 7 Ridgeway Rd, HERNE BAY, Kent, CT6 7LL.
        (chmn/p)
        Chmn: G R Wanstall
○   *K; to promote & restore the British national anthem & flag to
        life in general at public performances & on public buildings

Campaign for Science & Engineering in the UK   (CASE)   1986
NR   29-30 Tavistock Square, LONDON, WC1H 9QU.   (hq)
        020 7679 4995
        Dir: Dr Peter Cotgreave
▲   Un-incorporated Society
○   *K; to communicate to the public, parliament & the government
        a proper appreciation of the economic & cultural benefits of
        scientific & technological research & development, with the
        consequent importance to the nation of adequate funding of
        research by government & industry
●   Conf - Mtgs - Stat - Pressure group activities
M   i, f & org
✕   2005 Save British Science Society

Campaign for Shooting
        a campaign of the **Countryside Alliance**

Campaign for a Smoke-Free Environment
        see **CLEANAIR - Campaign for a Smoke-Free Environment**

Campaign against Stage Hypnosis   (CASH)   1994
■   62 Station Rd, Hesketh Bank, PRESTON, Lancs, PR4 6SP.
        (hsp/b)
        01772 813052
        Jt Secs: Connell Harper,   Nora Harper
○   *K; to inform the public of the abuse & dangers of stage
        hypnosis
●   Inf - LG
M   [not stated]

Campaign for State Education   (CASE)   1961

NR   98 Erlanger Rd, LONDON, SE14 5TH.   (exec/sp)
        020 8944 8206   fax 020 8944 8206
        email case@casenet.org.uk   http://www.casenet.org.uk
        Exec Sec: Margaret Tulloch
▲   Un-incorporated Society
○   *E, *K; to campaign for the right of all children to the best
        possible education via a locally accountable & democratic
        education system; comprehensive education; a partnership
        between home, school & the community
●   Conf - Mtgs - Inf - Lobbying
M   1,000 i
¶   Parents & Schools - 5; ftm, £20 for 3 issues nm.

Campaign for the Traditional Cathedral Choir   (CFTCC)   1996

NR   Clifton Lodge, 8 Mattock Lane, LONDON, W5 5BG.   (asa)
        020 8579 3662
        http://www.ctcc.org.uk
        Hon Sec: David Blumlein
▲   Un-incorporated Society
○   *K; to champion the ancient tradition of the all-male choir in
        cathedrals, chapels royal, collegiate churches, university
        chapels & similar ecclesiastical foundations; to encourage
        parish churches which maintain, or seek to establish, all-
        male voice choirs
●   Mtgs - Res - Campaigning
M   i
¶   Bulletin - 2; ftm, £2 nm.   NL - 2; ftm only.
✕   2006 Campaign for the Defence of the Traditional Cathedral
        Choir

Campden & Chorleywood Food Research Association
(CCFRA)   1919

■   Station Rd, CHIPPING CAMPDEN, Glos, GL55 6LD.   (hq)
        01386 842000
        Co Sec: J Wilkinson
▲   Company Limited by Guarantee
○   *Q; research & services for the food & allied industries (food
        packaging, machinery, manufacturers, distributors, retailers
        & growers, drink, cereals processing)
●   Conf - Mtgs - ET - Res - Exhib - SG - Stat - Inf - Lib - LG
M   800 f, UK / 200 f, o'seas
¶   Campden & Chorleywood NL - 12; free.
        Research Reports;   Guidelines;   Specifications;   Reviews;
        Symposium Proceedings - all irreg; prices vary.

Camping & Caravanning Club Ltd   1901

■   Greenfields House, Westwood Way, COVENTRY, CV4 8JH.
        (hq)
        024 7669 4995   fax 024 7685 6788
        http://www.campingandcaravanningclub.co.uk
        Dir Gen: David J R Welsford
▲   Company Limited by Guarantee
○   *G; 'the promotion & servicing of the pastime of mobile
        recreational camping & caravanning'
Gp   Association of Lightweight Campers; British Caravanners Club;
        Canoe-Camping Club; Motor-Caravan section; Folk dance &
        song; Trailer-Tent; Youth Camping Club; Photographic;
        Boating
●   Inf
<   Fédn Intl de Camping et de Caravanning (FICC)
M   c 400,000 i
¶   Camping & Caravanning Magazine - 12;
        Your Place in the Country (site guide) - 1;
        Your Big Sites Book (site guide) - 2 yrly; all ftm only.
        Carefree Camping & Caravanning Guide to Europe - 1.

Can Makers   1981

NR   30-34 New Bridge St, LONDON, EC4V 6BJ.   (hq)
        020 7072 4083
        email canmakers@gciuk.com
        http://www.canmakers.co.uk
        Contact: Dave Knowles
○   *T; promotion of beverage cans & can recycling
●   Conf - Res - Stat - Inf (on beverage cans, beer & soft drinks
        market)
<   Metal Packaging Mfrs Assn
M   f
¶   Can Makers Report - 2 yrly; free.

Canada/UK Architecture Group
        is a group of the **British Association for Canadian Studies**

Canada-United Kingdom Chamber of Commerce   1921

■   38 Grosvenor St, LONDON, W1K 4DP.   (hq)
        020 7258 6576   fax 020 7258 6594
        email info@canada-uk.org   http://www.canada-uk.org
        Exec Dir: Nigel Bacon
▲   Company Limited by Guarantee
○   *C; promotion of trade & investment between Canada & the
        UK in both directions
●   Conf - Mtg - Res - Inf
<   Canadian High Commission; Coun of Foreign Chams Comm
M   c 200 i, f & org
¶   NL - 6;   Membership Book - 1; both ftm only.

Canal Boatbuilders Association   (CBA)

■   Unit 1 The Boatyard, High St, WEEDON, Northants,
        NN7 4QQ.   (hq)
        01327 340174   fax 01327 340174
        email cba@britishmarine.co.uk
        Sec: Samantha Clarke
▲   Un-incorporated Society
○   *T; for those in business connected with the inland waterways
        building or supply of narrowboats
●   Conf - Mtgs - ET - Stat - Inf - LG
<   Brit Marine Fedn
M   98 f
¶   How to Buy a Boat - 1; free.

Canal Card Collectors Circle   (CCCC)   1978

■   18 Kilpatrick Way, Yeading, HAYES, Middx, UB4 9SX.   (hsp)
        020 8841 3788
        email ianjwilson4@uwclub.net
        http://www.gongoozler.org
        Hon Sec/Treas & Mem Sec: Ian J Wilson
        mobile: 0788 518 9765
▲   Un-incorporated Society
○   *G; the collection of post cards of canals & inland navigations
●   Mtg (Annual in June) - VE
<   Inland Waterways Assn
>   Shardlow Heritage Centre
M   55 i, 1 org, UK / 3 i, o'seas
¶   Gongoozler - 4; ftm, 50p nm.

Cancer Genetics Group
        a group of the **British Society for Human Genetics**

Canine & Feline Behaviour Association   (CFBA)

■   Applewood House, Ringshall Rd, Dagnall, BERKHAMSTED,
        Herts, HP4 1RN
        0870 062 4449
        email mail@cfba.co.uk

Canoe Association of Northern Ireland   (CANI)

NR   Unit 2 River's Edge, 13-15 Ravenhill Rd, BELFAST, BT6 8DN.
        0870 240 5065
        http://www.cani.org.uk
        Admin: David Bell
○   *S
●   Mtgs - Comp

Canoe-Camping Club
    a group of the **Camping & Caravanning Club**

Canterbury Chamber of Commerce
    a branch of **Kent Invicta Chamber of Commerce**

Canterbury & York Society   1904
NR   Borthwick Institute, University of York, Heslington, YORK,
     N Yorks, YO10 5DD.   (hsb)
     email cf13@york.ac.uk   http://www.ihrinfo.ac.uk/
     cantyork/
     Hon Sec: Dr C Fonge
▲   Registered Charity
○   *L; publication of the records of the medieval English church
●   Publishing
M   101 i, 141 libraries
¶   Annual Volume; prices vary (c £15 i, c £20 instns).

Capel: the Chapels Heritage Society   (CAPEL)   1986
■   61 Brookhurst Avenue, BROMBOROUGH, Wirral,
     CH63 0HS.   (hsp)
     01513 343635
     email peter.mason18@btopenworld.com
     http://www.rcahmw.org.uk/capel/
     Hon Sec: Dr Peter Mason
▲   Registered Charity
○   *G, *L, *R; the study & preservation of the non-conformist
     heritage in Wales, with particular regard to chapel buildings
     & their records
●   Conf - Mtgs - Exhib - Inf - VE
M   c 300 i
¶   Capel NL - 2; ftm, £1 nm.

Captive Animal Protection Society   (CAPS)   1957
NR   PO Box 4186, MANCHESTER, Lancs, M60 3ZA.   (hq)
     0845 330 3911
     email info@captiveanimals.org
     http://www.captiveanimals.org
▲   Company Limited by Guarantee
Br   4
○   *K; to expose the abuse of captive animals, mainly in zoos &
     circuses; to abolish all such institutions
●   Mtgs - ET - Res - Exhib - Stat - Expt - Inf - Lib - PL - LG
M   i
¶   Release - 2; free.

Car Park Appreciation Society   (CPAS)   2005
■   1 Rowborough Close, Astwood Bank, REDDITCH, Worcs,
     B96 6DQ.   (hsp)
     01527 894088   fax 01527 522545
     email kevin@beresfordB96.freeserve.co.uk
     Sec/Pres: Kevin Beresford
▲   Un-incorporated Society
○   *G; to collect photographs & interesting data on car parks
     throughout Britain & the Irish Republic
●   Mtgs - VE
<   AA Insurance
M   2 i
¶   Car Parks of GB Calendar - 1; £8.
     Get Carter Calendar (the Gateshead car park) - 1; £6 m,
     £8 nm.
✕   nncs014

Car Rental Council of Ireland
IRL   5 Upper Pembroke St, DUBLIN 2, Republic of Ireland.
     353 (1) 676 1690   fax 353 (1) 661 9213
     email predmond@simi.ie
     http://www.carrentalcouncil.ie
     Chief Exec: Paul Redmond
○   *T

Caravan Club Ltd   1907
NR   East Grinstead House, EAST GRINSTEAD, W Sussex,
     RH19 1UA.   (hq)
     01342 326944   fax 01342 410258
     http://www.caravanclub.co.uk
     Dir Gen: Trevor Watson
○   *G; for touring caravanners; providing sites, travel &
     information services
<   Fédn Intle de Camping et Caravanning (FICC); Alliance of Intl
     Tourism (AIT); Fédn Intle Automobile (FIA); Soc of Motor Mfrs
     & Traders (SMMT)
M   323,000 i, UK / 1,000 i, o'seas
¶   Caravan Club Magazine - 12;
     Sites Directory & Map - 2 yrly;
        Site Supplement - 2 yrly (alt yrs to above); all ftm.
     Caravanning Europe [year] 2 vol - 1; £8.50 per vol m,
        (£9.99 nm).

Carbon Monoxide & Gas Safety Society   (COGasSafety)
   1995
§   Station Building, The Parade, CLAYGATE, Surrey, KT10 0PE.
     01372 466135   fax 01372 468965
     email office@co-gassafety.co.uk
     http://www.co-gassafety.co.uk
     a registered charity & non-membership body campaigning to
     reduce gas related accidents worldwide, from carbon
     monoxide & other gas dangers; to support gas related
     accident victims.

** Carbon Monoxide Support
     Organisation lost: see Introduction paragraph 3

Cardiff Chamber of Commerce, Trade & Industry   1866
NR   St David's House East (floor 2/suite 1), Wood St, CARDIFF,
     Glam, CF10 1ES.   (hq)
     029 2034 8280   fax 029 2037 7653
     email enquiries@cardiffchamber.co.uk
     http://www.cardiffchamber.co.uk
     Chief Exec: Mrs Helen Conway
▲   Company Limited by Guarantee
○   *C
Gp   Export documentation; Business & export information;
     Networking events; Courses & seminars
●   Conf - Mtgs - ET - Res - Exhib - Stat - Expt - Inf - Lib - LG
<   ABCC
M   1,300 f
¶   Welsh Business - 12; ftm, £2 each nm.   NL.   LM.

Cardiff Naturalists' Society   (CNS)   1867
NR   36 Rowan Way, Lisvane, CARDIFF, CF14 0TD.   (hsp)
     Sec: Mike Dean
▲   Un-incorporated Society
○   *E, *L; to promote the study of the natural sciences & the
     conservation of the natural environment, with special
     reference to the counties of Glamorgan
●   Mtgs - Res - SG - Lib - VE - Field meetings
M   275 i
¶   NL - 4; free.

Cardiomyopathy Association   (CMA)   1989
- ■ 40 The Metro Centre, Tolpits Lane, WATFORD, Herts,
WD18 9SB.   (hq)
01923 249977   fax 01923 249987
email info@cardiomyopathy.org
http://www.cardiomyopathy.org
Chmn: Peter McBride
- ▲ Registered Charity
- Br 1
- ○ *K, *W; to provide counselling & support for sufferers &
families; to provide accurate & up-to-date information about
cardiomyopathy (a heart muscle disease) to patients, family
members, doctors & medical staff
- ● Conf - Mtgs - ET - Inf
- < Children's Heart Fedn; GIG; Heart Transplant Families
Together; NVCO
- M 900 i, 5 org, UK / 21 i, o'seas
- ¶ NL - 2;   AR; both ftm.

Care of Collections Forum
in 2005 merged with the Institute of Paper Conservation,
Photographic Materials Conservation Group & the United Kingdom
Institute for Conservation of Historic & Artistic Works to form the
Institute of Conservation

Care not Killing Alliance   2006
- ■ PO Box 56322, LONDON, SE1 8XW.   (mail/address)
020 7633 0770   fax 020 7681 1924
email info@carenotkilling.org.uk
http://www.carenotkilling.org.uk
Chmn: Brian Iddon
- ▲ Un-incorporated Society
- ○ *K; a UK alliance of individuals & organisations bringing
together groups concerned with human rights, healthcare,
palliative care, as well as faith based organisations, with the
aim of 1) promoting more & better palliative care;
2) opposing euthanasia & assisted suicide; 3) influencing the
balance of public opinion
- ● ET - Res - Inf - LG - Campaigning
- M 200+ i, 30+ orgs

Care Leavers Association   (CLA)
- NR St Thomas Centre, Ardwick Green North, MANCHESTER,
Lancs, M12 6FZ.   (hq)
0161-275 9500
email info@careleavers.org   http://www.careleavers.org
Sec: Jim Goddard
- ▲ Company Limited by Guarantee
- ○ *K, *W; 'to protect, promote & strengthen rights for care
leavers; to challenge negative public perceptions of care
leavers & children in care; to ensure care leavers receive the
support services they require'
- ● Conf - Mtgs - ET - Res - Inf - LG
- M 50 i, 2 org, UK / 1 i, o'seas
- ¶ The Grapevine (NL) - 4; free.

Care Management Group
a group of the **Chartered Management Institute**

Career Development Group   1895
- NR c/o CILIP, 7 Ridgmount St, LONDON, WC1E 7AE.   (hsb)
0785 579 0716
http://www.careerdevelopmentgroup.org.uk
Hon Sec: Lorna Robertson
- ▲ Registered Charity
- Br 15 regional gps
- ○ *P
- ● Conf - Mtgs - ET - Res - Exhib
- < Library Assn
- M 5,000 i
- ¶ Impact - 10; £34 yr m (£39 o'seas, £98 USA).

Careers Writers' Association   (CWA)   1978
- ■ 113 Greenway Lane, FAKENHAM, Norfolk, NR21 8EL.
(devt/offr)
01328 855215
email ann@ann50.freeserve.co.uk
http://www.careerswriters.co.uk
Devt Officer: Ann Mason
- ▲ Un-incorporated Society
- ○ *P; to promote the values of accuracy, clarity, impartiality,
creativity & integrity in written & other forms of careers
information
- ● Mtgs - ET
- M 28 i
- ¶ Booklet - 1.

Carers Association
- IRL 6 John's Quay, KILKENNY, Republic of Ireland.
353 (56) 772 1424   fax 353 (56) 775 3531
email ceo@carersireland.com
http://www.carersireland.com
Chmn: Frank Goodwin
- ○ *W

Carers UK   1965
- ■ Ruth Pitter House, 20-25 Glasshouse Yard, LONDON,
EC1A 4JT.   (hq)
020 7490 8818   fax 020 7490 8824
email info@carersuk.org   http://www.carersuk.org
Chief Exec: Imelda Redmond
- ▲ Company Limited by Guarantee; Registered Charity
- Br 80
- ○ *W; to campaign for the rights of carers & to advise carers
about their rights & entitlements to support
- ● ET - Inf - LG
Helpline: 0808 808 7777 (Wed & Thurs 1000-1200 + 1400-
1600)
- M 10,000 i, 569 f
- ¶ Caring (Jnl) - 4; m only.
Publications list.

Caribbean-British Business Council   (CBBC)   1974
- ■ 2 Belgrave Sq, LONDON, SW1X 8PJ.   (hq)
020 7235 9484   fax 020 7823 1370
email admin@cb-bc.org
http://www.caribbean-council.org
Exec Dir: David Jessop
- ▲ Un-incorporated Society
- Br Brussels
- ○ *T; to promote & support trade & investment between Britain &
the Caribbean
- ● Conf - Mtgs - Exhib - Expt - Inf - LG
- M 8 i, 87 f, 3 org, UK / 3 f, o'seas
- ¶ Caribbean Briefing - 52; ftm, £210 yr nm.
Caribbean Airline News - 6;   The Week in Europe;
Weekly NL - 52; all ftm only.

Caring for Carers
see **Crossroads: Caring for Carers**

Carlyle Society   1929
- ■ c/o Prof Ian Campbell, University of Edinburgh, David Hume
Tower, George Sq, EDINBURGH, EH8 9JX.   (pres/b)
0131-650 4284   fax 0131-650 6898
email ian.campbell@ed.ac.uk
Pres: Prof Ian Campbell
- ○ *A, *L; the study & encouragement of knowledge & information
on the life & writing of the Carlyles - Thomas (1795-1881) &
Jane (1801-1866)

© CBD Research Ltd · Beckenham · BR3 5JS · Tel 020 8650 7745 · Fax 020 8650 0768 · E-mail cbd@cbdresearch.com · www.cbdresearch.com

Carnival Band Secretaries League   (CBSL)   1936
- ■ 15 Brendon Way, LONG EATON, Notts, NG10 4JS.   (hsp)
  0115-972 5285   fax 01332 573266
  email info@cbsl.org.uk   http://www.cbsl.org.uk
  Hon Sec: Bert Cook
- ▲ Un-incorporated Society
- ○ *D; to promote the use of carnival marching showbands & the holding of band contests & arena displays at carnivals etc
- Gp Competitions (3-6 bands); Exhibitions (1-6 bands)
- ● Exhib - Comp - Massed band displays - Cabaret
- M [not stated]

Carnival Guild
> see **National Carnival Guild - the National Federation of Carnival Associations**

Carnivorous Plant Society   (CPS)   1978
- NR Whornes Cottage, 43 Rochester Rd, Cuxton, ROCHESTER, Kent, ME2 1AD.   (treas/p)
  Treas: Mrs Felicity-Ann Foreman
- ▲ Registered Charity
- ○ *H; to bring together all interested in carnivorous plants, whether beginners or experts
- ● Mtgs - Exhib - SG - Inf - Lib - PL - VE - Seed bank
- < R Horticl Soc
- M 500 i, UK / 100 i, 6 org, o'seas
- ¶ Jnl - 1;   NL - 4;   Guide to Carnivorous Plants; all ftm only.

Carp Society   1983
- NR Horseshoe Lake, Burford Rd, LECHLADE, Glos, GL7 3QQ.   (hq)
  01367 253959   fax 01367 252450
  email info@thecarpsociety.com
  Commercial Mgr: David Mannall
- ○ *G; for those interested in fishing for carp
- ● Conf - Exhib
- M c 3,500 i
- ¶ Various.

Carpet Foundation   2001
- ■ MCF Complex, 60 New Rd, KIDDERMINSTER, Worcs, DY10 1AQ.   (hq)
  01562 755568   fax 01562 865405
  email info@carpetfoundation.com
  http://www.carpetfoundation.com
  Chief Exec: Mike H Hardiman
- ▲ Company Limited by Guarantee
- ○ *T; British carpet industry; Registered Specialists (qualified independent retailers) & manufacturers
- ● Mtgs - Res - Stat - Inf - LG - Promoting public awareness of the benefits of carpet through the Quality Mark & media campaigns
- M 14 mfrs, 1,244 retailers, 5 associates
- ¶ NL - 4; ftm.
- ✕ 2001 British Carpet Manufacturers' Association (amalgamated)

Cartoonists' Club of Great Britain   (CCGB)   1960
- ■ 7 Gambetta St, LONDON, SW8 3TS.   (hsp/b)
  020 7720 1884
  email jedstone@tunamoon.demon.co.uk
  http://www.ccgb.org.uk
  Hon Sec: Jed Stone
- ▲ Un-incorporated Society
- ○ *P, *G; to champion the art & craft of the cartoon; to provide contact between members
- ● Conf - Mtgs - Exhib - Comp - PL - VE
- < Fedn Eur Cartoonist Orgs (FECO)
- M 200 i, UK / 10 i, o'seas
- ¶ The Jester (NL) - 12; ftm only.
  LM - 1; ftm, free on request nm.

Cartophilic Society of Great Britain Ltd   1938
- ■ 6 Oxford Gardens, Chiswick, LONDON, W4 3BW.   (hsp)
  http://www.csgb.co.uk
  Hon Sec: Mike Walker
- ▲ Company Limited by Guarantee
- Br 12
- ○ *G; 'propagating, enhancing & preserving the hobby of cigarette & trade card collecting'
- ● Conf - Mtgs - Res - Inf - Lib
- M 900 i, UK / 100 i, o'seas
- ¶ Cartophilic Notes & News - 6.

Casino Operators' Association
- NR PO Box 55, Thornecombe, CHARD, Somerset, TA20 4YT.
  01297 678312   fax 01297 678785
  http://www.casinos-coa.co.uk
  Gen Sec: Brian Lemon
- ○ *T

Caspari Foundation for Educational Therapy & Therapeutic Teaching   2000
- ■ Caspari House, 1 Noel Rd, LONDON, N1 8HQ.   (hq)
  020 7704 1977   fax 020 7704 1783
  email casparihouse@btconnect.com
  http://www.caspari.org.uk
  Contact: Sister Bernadette Hunston
- ▲ Registered Charity
- ○ *E; to develop theory & practice of educational therapy as a treatment for those with learning difficulties; to promote the psychological insight of teachers in general into the emotional factors in learning & failing to learn
- ● Conf - Mtgs - ET - Inf - Lib - LG - Educational therapy - Lectures
- < Nat Children's Bureau
- M 80 i, 30 f, UK / 10 i, 5 f, o'seas, school services in corporate membership
- ¶ Educational Therapy & Therapeutic Teaching - 1; ftm, £10 nm.

Caspian Breed Society   (CBS(UK))   1999
- ■ Sparrow Farm, Lanhill, CHIPPENHAM, Wilts, SN14 6LX.   (hsp)
  01249 782246   fax 0871 251 3199
  email uk.caspian.society@virgin.net
  http://www.caspianbreedsociety.co.uk/
  Sec: Ronald J Scott
- ▲ Company Limited by Guarantee
- ○ *B; the promotion & preservation of the Caspian horse, an ancient breed from 3,000 BC
- Gp Horse breeding; Miniature horse
- ● Mtgs - Exhib - Breed show - Agricultural show promotion
- < Brit Horse Soc; Brit Assn of Equine Socs; Central Prefix Register
- M 52 i, UK / 14 i, o'seas
- ¶ CBS News (NL) - 6;   AR - 1; both free.

Caspian Horse Society   (CHS)   1987
- ■ Eglentyne, 6 Nuns Walk, VIRGINIA WATER, Surrey, GU25 4RT.   (hsp)
  01344 843325
  email rlharris@talk21.com
  http://www.caspianhorsesociety.org.uk
  Sec: Dr Rosemary Harris
- ▲ Company Limited by Guarantee; Registered Charity
- ○ *B
- ● Conf - Mtgs - Comp - Expt - LG
- < Intl Caspian Soc; Brit Horse Soc (Breeds C'ee); Central Prefix Register; Nat Equine Forum
- M 95 i
- ¶ The Caspian (Jnl) - 4; ftm.

Cast Iron Drainage Development Association   (CIDDA)
- NR c/o Wyatt International Ltd, Wyatt House, 72 Francis Rd, Edgbaston, BIRMINGHAM, B16 8SP.
  0121-454 8181
  Contact: Caren Carbutt
- ○ *T

Cast Metals Federation   (CMF)   2001

- ■ National Metalforming Centre, 47 Birmingham Rd, WEST BROMWICH, W Midlands, B70 6PY.   (hq)
  0121-601 6390   fax 0121-601 6391
  email admin@cmfed.co.uk
  http://www.castmetalsfederation.com
  Chief Exec: John Parker
- ▲ Company Limited by Guarantee
- ○ *T; for the UK metal casting industry
- Gp Sections: Costs, Raw materials, Health & safety;
  Gps: Iron castings, brass & bronze; Investment castings; Light metals; Steel; Suppliers; Zinc
- ● Conf - Mtgs - Inf - LG
- < C'ee of Assns of Eur Foundries (CAEF); METCOM
- M c 200 f

Castlemilk Moorit Sheep Society   1973

- ■ Creacombemoor Cottage, Rackenford, TIVERTON, Devon, EX16 8EW.   (hsp)
  01884 881222   fax 01884 881222
  email ewenique@eclipse.co.uk
  Hon Sec: John Sanders
- ○ *B; conservation & promotion of Britain's rarest sheep breed
- ● Mtgs - Exhib - Livestock shows - Workshops
- < Rare Breeds Survival Trust
- M 60 i
- ¶ NL - 3; ftm only.

Castor Manufacturers' (UK) Association

disbanded January 2005

Casualties Union   (CU)   1942

- ■ PO Box 1942, LONDON, E17 6YU.   (hsp)
  0870 078 0590   fax 0870 078 0590
  email hq@casualtiesunion.org.uk
  http://www.casualtiesunion.org.uk
  Hon Gen Sec: Caroline Thomas
- ▲ Registered Charity
- Br 40; 7 o'seas
- ○ *W; to supply trained casualties for the training of first aid, nursing & rescue
- Gp Make-up; Acting; Staging
- ● Conf - Mtgs - ET - Exam - Res - Comp - SG
- M 440 i, UK / 20 i, o'seas
- ¶ Casualty Simulation - 4; ftm only.

Catenian Association   1908

- NR Copthall House (2nd floor), Station Sq, COVENTRY, Warks, CV1 2FY.   (hq)
  024 7622 4533
  http://www.thecatenianassociation.org
  Admin: Mrs Jai Milward
- ▲ Company Limited by Guarantee; Registered Charity
- Br 255; Australia, Eire, Hong Kong, Malta, S Africa, Zambia, Zimbabwe
- ○ *R; Catholic business & professional men
- Gp Benevolent & children's fund; Bursary fund
- ● Conf - Mtgs - VE
- M 9,500 i, UK / 1,000 i, o'seas
- ¶ Catena - 12.

Catering Equipment Distributors Association of Great Britain   (CEDA)   1972

- NR PO Box 194, BINGLEY, W Yorks, BD16 2XW.   (hsb)
  01274 826056   fax 01274 777260
  email secretary@ceda.co.uk   http://www.ceda.co.uk
  Sec: J A North
- ▲ Un-incorporated Society
- ○ *T; design, supply, installation & after-sales service of commercial kitchens & all catering equipment
- Gp CEDACARE (a catering equipment service initiative)
- ● Conf - Mtgs - ET - Exhib - Stat - Inf - LG
- M 80 f
- ¶ CEDA News - 4; free.

Catering Equipment Supplier's Association   (CESA)   1938

- NR Carlyle House, 235-237 Vauxhall Bridge Rd, LONDON, SW1V 1EJ.   (hq)
  020 7233 7724   fax 020 7828 0667
  email enquiries@cesa.org.uk   http://www.cesa.org.uk
- ▲ Un-incorporated Society
- Br 2
- ○ *T; to promote cooperation between those engaged in the food service equipment industry
- Gp Statistics; Exports; Technical
- ● Conf - Mtgs - Exhib - Stat - Expt - Inf - Lib - Empl - LG
- < Eur Fedn of Catering Eqpt Mfrs (EFCEM); Confedn of Brit Ind (CBI); Mechanical & Engg Tr Confedn (METCOM)
- M 104 f
- ¶ NL - 6.   LM - 1.   Autocad Symbol Library 1.
  Technical Guide - 1.   Buyers' Guide - 1.
  Note: is also known as the Association of Catering Equipment Manufacturers & Importers
- × 2003-04 Catering Utensils Association

** Catering Managers Association of Great Britain & the Channel Islands

Organisation lost: see Introduction paragraph 3

Catering Utensils Association
since 2003-04 **Catering Equipment Supplier's Association**

Cathedral Architects' Association   (CAA)   1948

- ■ 46A St Mary's St, ELY, Cambs, CB7 4EY.   (hsb)
  01353 660660   fax 01353 660661
  Hon Sec: Anthony Felton King
- ▲ Un-incorporated Society
- ○ *P; sharing information on technical, aesthetic & ecclesiastical problems associated with cathedrals or churches of similar status
- ● Conf - VE - LG
- < Eur Cathedrals Assn
- M 45 i (34 honorary), UK / 8 i, o'seas
- ¶ Conference Notes & Proceedings - 1-2 yrly; ftm only.

Cathedral & Church Shops Association   (CCSA)

- ■ The West Cloister, Wells Cathedral, WELLS, Somerset, BA5 2PA.   (hsb)
  01749 672773 ext234   fax 01749 832209
  email ccsa.sec@btinternet.com   http://www.ccsa.org.uk
  Hon Sec: Mrs Elizabeth Stafford
- ▲ Un-incorporated Society
- ○ *T; 'to extend the ministry of the church through the sale of Christian books & cards; by providing a presence in a church or cathedral; by making a 'bridge' into the worship building'
- ● Conf - Mtgs - ET - Exhib
- M cathedrals & churches

Cathedral Organists' Association   (COA)   1946

- ■ 19 The Close, SALISBURY, Wilts, SP1 2EB.   (hsb)
  Hon Sec: Prof J Harper
- ▲ Un-incorporated Society
- ○ *P; interests & training of cathedral & collegiate church organists in the UK
- ● Conf - Mtgs - ET - SG - VE - Empl - Liaison with the Church of England
- M 127 i

CATHOLIC...

for Catholic organisations, other than those listed below, please refer to the **Catholic Directory** published by Gabriel Communications.

© CBD Research Ltd · Beckenham · BR3 5JS · Tel 020 8650 7745 · Fax 020 8650 0768 · E-mail cbd@cbdresearch.com · www.cbdresearch.com

Catholic Archives Society   1979
- ■ Innyngs House, Hatfield Park, HATFIELD, Herts, AL9 5PL.   (hsp)
  Hon Sec: Margaret Harcourt Williams,
  Chmn: Barbara Jeffery
- ▲ Un-incorporated Society
- ○ *L; to promote the care & preservation of archives of dioceses, religious orders, & other institutions of the Catholic Church in the UK & Ireland
- ● Conf (May)
- M 200-250 i
- ¶ Catholic Archives - 1; ftm, £5 nm.   Bulletin - 1/2; ftm only.
  Directory - 3 yrly; ftm, £3 nm.   Occasional other publications.

Catholic Family History Society   (CFHS)   1983
- NR 14 Sydney Rd, ILFORD, Essex, IG6 2ED.   (memsec/p)
  Mem Sec: Mrs K M Black
- ▲ Registered Charity
- Br 4
- ○ *G; to encourage research into the history of Catholic families in England, Wales & Scotland from the 16th to the 19th centuries
- ● Conf - Mtgs
- < Fedn of Family History Socs
- M 650 i, UK / 35 i, o'seas
- ¶ Catholic Ancestor (Jnl) - 3; ftm, £2 nm.   NL - 1; ftm only.
  Publication - irreg; ftm, price varies nm.

Catholic Record Society   (CRS)   1905
- NR 12 Melbourne Place, WOLSINGHAM, Co Durham, DL13 3EH.   (hsp)
  01388 527747
  Hon Sec: Dr L Gooch
- ○ *L; publication of original documents & occasional monographs relating to the English Catholics from the Reformation to the end of the 19th century (but NOT genealogical)
- ● Conf - Regular publishing programme
- M 350 i, 350 org
- ¶ Recusant History - 2.   Records & Monograph.

Catholic Truth Society
    see **Incorporated Catholic Truth Society**

Catholic Union of Great Britain   (CU)   1870
- ■ St Maximilian Kolbe House, 63 Jeddo Rd, LONDON, W12 9EE.   (hsb)
  020 8749 1321   fax 020 8735 0816
  email phiggs@cathunion.fsnet.co.uk
  http://www.catholicunion.org
  Sec: Peter H Higgs
- ▲ Un-incorporated Society
- ○ *R; non-political association of Roman Catholic laity to watch over Catholic interests, especially in matters arising from government action, proposed legislation or activities of local or other public bodies
- ● Inf - LG
- < Catenian Assn; Nat Coun Lay Assns
- M 1,700 i
- ¶ NL - 4; free.   AR; ftm only.

Cats Protection   (CP)   1927
- NR Chelwood Gate, HAYWARDS HEATH, Sussex, RH17 7TT.   (hq)
  0870 209 9099   fax 0870 770 8649
  email cpl@cats.org.uk   http://www.cats.org.uk
  Chief Exec: Helen Ralston
- ▲ Registered Charity
- Br 250 with 23 shelters
- ○ *V; to rescue stray & unwanted cats & kittens to rehabilitate & re-home them; to encourage the neutering of all cats & kittens; to inform the public on their care
- ● Conf - ET - Res - Exhib - Comp - Stat - Assistance with neutering
  Helpline: 01403 221919
- M 79,000 i
- ¶ The Cat - 6; ftm.
  Leaflets on cat care.

Cement Admixtures Association Ltd   (CAA)   1963
- ■ 38a Tilehouse Green Lane, KNOWLE, W Midlands, B93 9EY.
  (sp)
  01564 776362   fax 01564 776362
  http://www.admixtures.org.uk
- ▲ Company Limited by Guarantee
- ○ *T; to encourage responsible use of admixtures in concrete, mortar & cement mixes
- < Eur Fedn of Cement Admixture Assns (EFCA)
- M 12 f

Cementitious Slag Makers Association   (CSMA)   1985
- NR Maybrook House, Godstone Rd, CATERHAM, Surrey, CR3 6RE.   (hq)
  01883 331071   fax 01883 331072
  Dir Gen: Dr D D Higgins
- ▲ Un-incorporated Society
- ○ *T; to promote the use of ground granulated blast furnace slag (a cementitious material widely used in concrete)
- ● Conf - Res
- M 4 f

Cemeteries Association
    is incorporated in the **Association of Private Crematoria & Cemeteries**

Central Association of Agricultural Valuers   (CAAV)   1910
- NR Market Chambers, 35 Market Place, COLEFORD, Glos, GL16 8BD.   (hq)
  01594 832979   fax 01594 810701
  email enquire@caav.org.uk   http://www.caav.org.uk
  Sec & Adviser: Jeremy Moody
- ▲ Company Limited by Guarantee
- Br 27
- ○ *P; representation & qualification of agricultural valuers
- ● Conf - Mtgs - ET - Exam - Stat - LG
- M 2,100 i
- ¶ NL - 4;   Hbk - 1;   AR; all ftm only.
  LM; on website.
  Tenanted Farm Survey - 1; £10.
  Costings of Agricultural Operations - 1; ftm, £20 nm.
  Other professional publications.

Central Council for British Naturism   (CCBN)   1964
- NR 30-32 Wycliffe Rd, NORTHAMPTON, NN1 5JF.   (hq)
  01604 620361   fax 01604 230176
  email headoffice@british-naturism.org.uk
  http://www.british-naturism.org.uk
  Gen Sec: Tracey Major
- ○ *G; promotion of physical, moral & mental wellbeing through indoor & outdoor recreation without clothes, either individually or socially in private grounds, premises or on official beaches
- ● Mtgs
- < Intl Naturist Fedn
- M c 25,000 i
- ¶ Brit Naturism Magazine - 4; ftm only.
  Note: trades as British Naturism

Central Council of Church Bell Ringers 1890
- ■ The Cottage, School Hill, Warnham, HORSHAM, W Sussex, RH12 3QN. (hsp)
  01403 269743
  http://www.cccbr.org.uk
  Hon Sec: I H Oram
- ▲ Registered Charity
- ○ *G, *R; the ringing of bells for Christian worship, their maintenance & standards of change ringing
- Gp Education; Towers & belfries; Restoration funds; Redundant bells; Records; Peal compositions; Publications; Public relations
- ● Conf - ET - Res - Exhib - Stat - Inf - Lib
- M 27 i, 61 org, UK / 6 org, o'seas
- ¶ The Ringing World - 52; £1.60.

Central Dredging Association   (CDA)
- NR Institution of Civil Engineers, 1-7 Great George St, LONDON, SW1P 3AA. (hq)
  020 7665 2239
  http://www.dredging.org
  Sec: Janice Leung
- ○ *P
- < the British section of Ceda-Delft (Dutch parent body)

Central Organisation for Maritime Pastimes & Support Services (COMPASS) 1990
- ■ 178 Woodfield Park, Cool Oak Lane, LONDON, NW9 7ND. (hq)
  020 8205 4492   fax 020 8200 6792
  Sec: Cmdr Gerald F Beck
- ▲ Registered Charity
- ○ *G; to promote character development of girls & boys through adventure & education using the practice of seafaring & seamanship
- M c 3,000 i

Central & West Lancashire Chamber of Commerce & Industry
  since 2004 **North & Western Lancashire Chamber of Commerce**

CENTRE ...
  see **'Centres, Bureaux & Research Institutes'** (Introduction 6)

CERAM
  see **British Ceramic Research Ltd**

Ceramic & Allied Trades Union
  since 2006 **Unity**

Cereal Ingredients Manufacturers' Association   (CIMA) 1986
- NR 6 Catherine St, LONDON, WC2B 5JJ. (hq)
  020 7836 2460   fax 020 7836 0580
- ▲ Un-incorporated Society
- ○ *T
- ● Mtgs
- < Food & Drink Fedn
- M 6 f

Ceredigion Antiquarian Society (Cymdeithas Hynafiaethwyr Ceredigion)
  since 2003-03 **Cymdeithas Hanes Ceredigion Historical Society**

Ceredigion Historical Society
  see **Cyndeithas Hanes Ceredigion Historical Society**

Ceretas   (BADCO) 1988
- ■ 88 Kingsway, Holborn, LONDON, WC2B 6AA. (hsp)
  020 7841 1060   fax 020 7841 1001
  email info@ceretas.org.uk   http://www.ceretas.org.uk
  Chief Exec: Mary Bryce
- ▲ Company Limited by Guarantee
- ○ *P; *W; for people who work in home care
- ● Conf - Mtgs - ET - Workshops - Seminars
- M 600 i, 50 f
- ¶ NL - 4; ftm.
  Good Practice Guidelines; £5 each or £60 for complete pack.
    Handling Service Users' Finances & Valuables.
    Caring for Staff.   Dementia.   Elder Abuse.
    Food Hygiene.   Managing Absence.   Medication.
    Personal & Professional Boundaries;   Personal Safety.
    Safe Hygiene Practice.   Staff Support, Supervision & Appraisal.
- × 2004 (November) British Association for Domiciliary Care

Certificated Bailiffs' Association
  since 2003 **Enforcement Services Association**

Chair Frame Manufacturers' Association   (CFMA) 1940
- NR Francis Vaughan House, 102a Commercial St, NEWPORT, Monmouthshire, NP20 1LU. (hq)
  01633 215454
  Chief Exec: Michael Bennett Spencer
- ▲ Company Limited by Guarantee
- ○ *T; interests of manufacturers of upholstery frames & associated components
- ● Conf - Mtgs - Exhib - Inf - Lib - VE - LG
- < Fedn of Small Businesses
- M 18 f
- ¶ Upholsterer & Soft Furnisher - 12.
  Note: This association is incorporated into the Association of Master Upholsterers.

Challenger Society for Marine Science 1903
- NR 251/20 Southampton Oceanography Centre, Empress Dock, SOUTHAMPTON, Hants, SO14 3ZH. (execsec/b)
  023 8059 6149   fax 023 8059 6149
  email jxj@soc.soton.ac.uk
  Exec Sec: Jennifer Jones
- ▲ Registered Charity
- ○ *L; to advance the study of marine science through research & education; to encourage a wider interest in the study of the seas & an awareness of their proper management
- Gp British Group of Altimeter Specialists; Ocean modelling; Marine chemistry discussion group; Ocean colour special interest group
- ● Conf
- < Eur Fedn of Marine Science & Technology Socs (EFMS)
- M 500 i, 6 f, UK / 50 i, o'seas
- ¶ Ocean Challenge (Jnl) - 3.

Chamber Business
- ▲ Company Limited by Guarantee
  since 2006 **(The) Chamber [Luton]**

Chamber Business Connections [Oldham]
  2004 merged with Manchester Chamber of Commerce & Industry to form the **Greater Manchester Chamber of Commerce**

Chamber of Commerce of Greenock
  see **Chamber of Commerce & Manufacturers of Greenock**

Chamber of Commerce Herefordshire & Worcestershire
  see registered title **Herefordshire & Worcestershire Chamber of Commerce Training & Enterprise**

Chamber of Commerce & Manufactures of Greenock   (Greenock Chamber of Commerce)   1813
- ■ The Business Store, 75-81 Cathcart St, GREENOCK, Renfrewshire, PA15 1DE.   (hq)
  01475 715555   fax 01475 715566
  email hugh.bunten@greenock-chamber.org.uk
  http://www.greenock-chamber.org.uk
  Exec Admin: Hugh Bunten
- ▲ Un-incorporated Society
- ○ *C; to promote local business, both home & export trade
- ● Mtgs - ET - Inf - LG - Networking events
- < Brit & Scot Chams Comm
- M 150 f
- ¶ Bulletin - 4;   AR.

Chamber of Commerce North West Ltd
- NR International Business Centre, Delta Crescent, Westbrook, WARRINGTON, Lancs, WA5 7WQ.
  01945 715166
  Contact: The Director
- ○ *C
- M 19 chambers in the North West

The Chamber [Luton]   1998
- NR Business Competitiveness Centre, Kimpton Rd, LUTON, Beds, LU2 0SX.   (hq)
  0845 357 0357   fax 01582 522409
  email info@chamber-business.com
  http://www.chamber-business.com
  Chief Exec: Richard Lacy
- ▲ Company Limited by Guarantee
- Br 3
- ○ *C
- ● Conf - Mtgs - ET - Res - Exhib - Stat - Expt - Inf - Lib - LG
- M 1,350 f
- ¶ Focus (Jnl) - 10.
- × 2006 Chamber Business

Chamber of Shipping Ltd   1975
- ■ Carthusian Court, 12 Carthusian St, LONDON, EC1M 6EZ.
  020 7417 2800   fax 020 7726 2080
  email stewart.conacher@british-shipping.org
  http://www.british-shipping.org/
  Sec: Stewart Conacher,   Asst Co Sec: Tim Springett
- ▲ Company Limited by Shares
- ○ *T; to protect & promote the interests of the British owners & managers of merchant ships
- ● Mtgs - Stat - LG
- < Intl Cham of Shipping; Intl Shipping Fedn; EC Shipowners' Assn
- M 120 f
- ¶ AR; ftm.
- × 2003-04 Short Sea Committee now part of the Chamber

Chambers of Commerce of Ireland
    since 2006 **Chambers Ireland**

Chambers Ireland   (CCI)   1923
- IRL 17 Merrion Sq, DUBLIN 2, Republic of Ireland.   (hq)
  353 (1) 661 2888   fax 353 (1) 661 2811
  email info@chambersireland.ie
  http://www.chambers.ie
  Chief Exec: John Dunne
- ○ *C
- × 2006 Chambers of Commerce of Ireland

Chambre de Commerce Française de Grande-Bretagne (CCFGB)   1883
- NR 21 Dartmouth St, LONDON, SW1H 9BP.   (hq)
  020 7304 4040   fax 020 7304 7034
  email mail@ccfgb.co.uk   http://www.ccfgb.co.uk
  Managing Dir & Co Sec: Stéphane Bossavit
- ▲ Company Limited by Guarantee
- Br 2; France
- ○ *C; business development between France & Britain
- Gp Public relations; Business consultancy; Finance & administration
- ● Conf - Mtgs - ET - Exam - Res - Exhib - Comp - SG - Stat - Expt - Inf - VE
- < U des Chambres de Commerce et de l'Industrie Françaises à l'Etranger; Franco-Scottish Business Club
- M 531 f, UK / 70 f, o'seas
- ¶ Info (Jnl) - 6; ftm, £45 yr nm.
  The Franco-British Trade Directory - 1; ftm, £100 nm.
  The List of French Investments in the UK - 1:
    (book) £85 m, £120 nm.   (CD) £450 m, £700 nm.
  A range of practical & professional guides to daily & business life in Britain & France; ftm, £5-£30 nm.

Champagne Agents' Association   1908
- NR c/o D G Sills, 71 Lincoln's Inn Fields, LONDON, WC2A 3JF.
  Sec: D G Sills
- ○ *T
- M f

Channel Chamber of Commerce
- NR Shearway Business Park, Shearway Rd, FOLKESTONE, Kent, CT19 4RH.
  01303 270022
  Chief Exec: Peter Hobbs
- ○ *C

Channel Crossing Association   2001
- NR 103 Station Rd, Lydd, ROMNEY MARSH, Kent, TN29 9LJ.   (hsp/b)
  01797 329479
  email channelcrossings@aol.com
  http://www.channelcrossingassociation.com
  Sec: Andy King
- ▲ Company Limited by Guarantee
- ○ *S; to promote, organise & support Channel crossings by unorthodox craft & assisted Channel swims; to record & ratify successful attempts
- M i

Channel Swimming Association Ltd   (CSA)   1927
- ■ Little Gables, Woodhill Rd, SANDON, Essex, CM2 7SK.   (hsp/b)
  01245 473581   fax 01245 473581
  email swimsecretary@btinternet.com
  http://www.channelswimmingassociation.com
  Hon Sec: Mrs Alison Read
- ▲ Company Limited by Guarantee
- ○ *S; the governing body for English Channel swimming
- ● Inf - LG - Observing Channel swim attempts during Summer - Annual dinner
- M 100 i, UK / 100 i, o'seas
- ¶ NL - 3.   Info pack - 1;   Hbk; both price on application.

Chapels Heritage Society
    see **Capel: the Chapels Heritage Society**

Chapels Society 1988

- ■ 1 Newcastle Ave, BEESTON, Notts, NG9 1BT. (hsp)
  0115-922 4930
  email rphillips@beeston12.freeserve.co.uk
  http://www.britarch.ac.uk/chapelsoc
  Hon Sec: Robin Phillips
- ▲ Registered Charity
- ○ *K, *L; to foster the understanding, study & preservation of nonconformist (ie non-Anglican) places of worship & related buildings in the UK (includes Roman Catholic, Orthodox & Jewish)
- ● VE - LG
- < Capel: the Chapels Heritage Soc; Coun for Brit Archaeology; Heritage Link
- M 267 i, 2 f, 24 org, UK / 4 i, 1 org, o'seas
- ¶ NL - 2; ftm.   LM; ftm.   AR; on website.
  Occasional publications.

Charcot-Marie-Tooth United Kingdom
  see **CMT United Kingdom**

Charcuterie Guild

- ■ PO Box 1525, GILLINGHAM, Dorset, SP8 4WA.   (hq)
  01747 822290   fax 01747 822289
  Chmn: Robert Farrand
  trains staff involved in charcuterie retailing to NVQ standard

Charities Property Association   (CPA)   1976

- ■ 1 Millbank, LONDON, SW1P 3JZ.   (hq)
  020 7222 1265   fax 020 7222 1250
  email info@charity-property.org
  http://www.charity-property.org
  Chmn: The Lord Cameron of Dillington
- ▲ Un-incorporated Association
- ○ *K; to monitor legislation, or changes in policy of public bodies, that may affect the property investments of charities
- ● Conf - Mtgs - Inf - LG
- M 100 charities
- ¶ NL - 4.

Charities' Tax Reform Group   (CTRG)   1980

- ■ 1 Millbank, LONDON, SW1P 3JZ.   (hq)
  020 7222 1265   fax 020 7222 1250
  email info@ctrg.org.uk   http://www.ctrg.org.uk
  Chmn: Mike Parkinson
- ▲ Un-incorporated Society
- ○ *K; to campaign to relieve the tax burden on charities, particularly VAT
- ● Conf - Mtgs - Res - Inf - LG
- < Eur Charities' C'ee on VAT [ECCVAT]
- M 350 charities

Charity Christmas Card Council   (4C)   1966

- NR 49 Cross St, LONDON, N1 4LY.   (hq)
  0845 230 0046   fax 0845 230 0048
  email 4c@charitycards.org   http://www.charitycards.org
  Chief Exec: Neville C Bass
- ▲ Company Limited by Guarantee
- ○ *K; to raise funds for member charities by the design, publishing & marketing of charity Christmas cards to the corporate sector & abroad
- Gp Depts: Design & publishing, Marketing
- ● Conf - Exhib - Stat - Design & publishing
- M 96 charities
- ¶ Executive Range Catalogue - 1;   AR; both free.

Charity Finance Directors' Group   (CFDG)   1988

- NR Downstream Building (3rd floor), 1 London Bridge, LONDON, SE1 9BG.   (hq)
  0845 345 3192   fax 0845 345 3193
  email info@cfdg.org.uk   http://www.cfdg.org.uk
  Dir: Shirley Scott
- ▲ Company Limited by Guarantee; Registered Charity
- ○ *T; to assist in improving financial standards in the charity sector; to provide an additional focal point within the charity world to which others can refer for an informed view
- ● Conf - Mtgs - ET - LG
- M 900 i, 850 org
- ¶ Charity Finance Ybk - 1; ftm.

Charity Law Association   1992

- NR c/o Russell Cooke, 2 Putney Hill, Putney, LONDON, SW15 6AB.   (sb)
  020 8394 6486
  email shivas@russell-cooke.co.uk
  http://www.charitylawassociation.org.uk
  Hon Sec: Shivaji Shiva
- ○ *P; 'to advance the understanding of charity law; to act as a forum for charity law specialists to consult & be consulted in the field'
- Gp Working parties: Responding to consultative documents; Examining areas of charity law in need of development
- ● Mtgs - Joint project with NCVO & Liverpool University on the development of new legal structure for charities
- M 600 f (solicitors, barristers, accountants, charities)

Charles Close Society for the Study of Ordnance Survey Maps   1980

- ■ c/o The Map Library, British Library, 96 Euston Rd, LONDON, NW1 2DB.   (mail)
  http://www.charlesclosesociety.org.uk address
  Hon Sec: Rob C Wheeler
- ▲ Registered Charity
- ○ *L; to promote interest in, & research into, the maps, plans & other activities of the Ordnance Surveys of Great Britain & Ireland.
  The Society is named after Col Sir Charles Close, Director of the Ordnance Survey 1911-1922
- ● Mtgs - Res - Exhib - SG - Inf - VE
- M 477 i, 6 f, 14 org, UK / 10 i, o'seas
- ¶ Sheetlines (Jnl/NL) - 3; ftm.
  Publications mainly on the 1 inch Ordnance Survey maps.

Charles Lamb Society   1935

- NR BM Elia, LONDON, WC1N 3XX.   (mail/address)
  http://www.users.ox.ac.uk/~scat1492/clsoc.htm
- ○ *L; to study the life, works & times of Charles Lamb (Elia) & his circle; to stimulate the Elian spirit of friendliness & humour

Charles Rennie Mackintosh Society   (CRM Soc)   1973

- ■ Queens Cross, 870 Garscube Rd, GLASGOW, G20 7EL.   (hq)
  0141-946 6600   fax 0141-945 2321
  email info@crmsociety.com   http://www.crmsociety.com
  Chief Exec: Stuart Robertson
- ▲ Registered Charity
- Br 3
- ○ *G, *L; the conservation & improvement of the buildings & artifacts designed by Mackintosh & his contemporaries; the society's address is that of the only church designed by Mackintosh to be built
- ● Res - Exhib - Inf - Lib - VE - Mackintosh tour organisers
- < l'Assn Charles Rennie Mackintosh en Rousillon
- M 1,010 i, 281 f, 19 org, UK / 207 i, o'seas
- ¶ Jnl - 2; ftm, £6 nm.

© CBD Research Ltd · Beckenham · BR3 5JS · Tel 020 8650 7745 · Fax 020 8650 0768 · E-mail cbd@cbdresearch.com · www.cbdresearch.com

Charles Williams Society   1976
- ■ 35 Broomfield, Stacey Bushes, MILTON KEYNES, MK12 6HA. (hsp)
  01908 316779
  email charles_wms_soc@yahoo.co.uk
  http://www.geocities.com/charles_wms_soc
  Hon Sec: Dr R L Sturch
- ▲ Registered Charity
- ○ *A; research into, & encouragement of the study of, the life & work of the author, lay theologian & poet Charles Williams (1886-1945)
- ● Conf - Mtgs - SG - Lib
- < Alliance of Literary Socs
- M 92 i, UK / 37 i, 3 org, o'seas
- ¶ Charles Williams Quarterly - 4.

Charlotte M Yonge Fellowship   (CMYF)   1995
- ■ 8 Anchorage Terrace, DURHAM, DH1 3DL. (hsp)
  0191-384 7857
  email c.e.schultze@durham.ac.uk
  http://www.cmyf.org.uk
  Mem Sec: Dr Clemence E Schultze
- ▲ Un-incorporated Society
- Br USA
- ○ *A; to provide a forum for all who enjoy reading the work of Charlotte M Yonge; to offer opportunities to learn more about her life & writings
- ● Conf - Mtgs - Res
- < Alliance of Literary Socs
- M 160 i, UK / 30 i, o'seas
- ¶ Review - 2; ftm.   Jnl - 1; £9.

Charmoise Hill Sheep Society
- NR Garnwen Penuwch, TREGARON, Ceredigion, SY25 6RA. (chmn/p)
  01974 821628
  http://www.charmoisesheep.co.uk
  Chmn: Peter Jones
- ○ *B
- < Nat Sheep Assn
  Note: also known as the Charmoise Sheep Society

Chart & Nautical Instrument Trade Association   (CNITA)   1918
- NR Dalmore House, 310 St Vincent Street, GLASGOW, G2 5QR.
  0141-228 8000   fax 0141-228 8310
  email cnita@biggartbaillie.co.uk
  Secs: Biggart Baillie
- ○ *T; suppliers of equipment & information to national & merchant navies
- Gp Admiralty chart agents; Magnetic compass mfrs; Magnetic compass adjusters; Nautical publishers; Nautical instrument mfrs & stockists
- ● Conf - Mtgs - Exam
- < Brit Standards Instn
- M 9 i, 14 f, UK / 19 f, o'seas
- ¶ LM - 1; ftm.

Charter 88   1988
- NR 6 Cynthia St, LONDON, N1 9JF. (hq)
  0845 450 7210   fax 020 8880 6089
  email info@charter88.org.uk
  http://www.charter88.org.uk
  Dir: Peter Facey
- ▲ Company Limited by Guarantee
- ○ *K; political pressure group campaigning for a modern & fair democracy through a democratic parliament, a freedom of information act, a bill of rights, decentralisation of power, a proportional voting system & a written constitution
- ● Conf - Mtgs - Res - Inf - LG
- M 83,000 i
- ¶ Citizen - 4; ftm in 1st year.
  Publications list available.

Chartered Institute of Arbitrators   (CIArb)   1915
- ■ International Arbitration & Mediation Centre, 12 Bloomsbury Sq, LONDON, WC1A 2LP. (hq)
  020 7421 7444   fax 020 7404 4023
  email info@arbitrators.org   http://www.arbitrators.org
  Dir Gen: Michael Forbes-Smith
- ▲ Registered Charity
- Br 13; 18
- ○ *P; promote & facilitate the determination of disputes by arbitration & alternate forms of dispute resolution
- M i
- ¶ Arbitration (Jnl) - 4; ftm.
  NL - 4;   LM - 1; both ftm.   AR - 1; free.

Chartered Institute of Architectural Technologists   (CIAT)   1965
- ■ 397 City Rd, LONDON, EC1V 1NH. (hq)
  020 7278 2206   fax 020 7837 3194
  email info@ciat.org.uk   http://www.ciat.org.uk
  Chief Exec: Mrs Francesca Berriman
- ▲ Company Limited by Guarantee
- Br 15; Republic of Ireland, Hong Kong
- ○ *P; qualifying body for professionals in architectural technology
- ● Conf - Mtgs - ET - Res - Exhib - Comp - Inf - LG
- M 6,500 i, UK / 500 i, o'seas
- ¶ Architectural Technology (Jnl) - 6; ftm, £2 nm.
  Directory of Practices - 1;   Membership Booklet - 1;
  The Architectural Technology Careers Hbk - 1;   AR - 1;
  all free.
- × 2005 British Institute of Architectural Technologists

Chartered Institute of Bankers in Scotland   1875
- NR Drumsheugh House, 38b Drumsheugh Gardens, EDINBURGH, EH3 7SW. (hq)
  0131-473 7777   fax 0131-473 7788
  email info@ciobs.org.uk   http://www.ciobs.org.uk
  Chief Exec: Prof C W Munn
- ○ *L, *P
- M 12,500 i

Chartered Institute of Building   (CIOB)   1834
- NR Englemere, Kings Ride, ASCOT, Berks, SL5 7TB. (hq)
  01344 630700   fax 01344 630777
  email reception@ciob.org.uk   http://www.ciob.org.uk
  Chief Exec: Chris Blythe
- ▲ Registered Charity
- Br 8; Australia, China, Hong Kong, Malaysia, South Africa
- ○ *P; promotion of the science & practice of building
- Gp Architecture & Surveying Institute; Association of Building Conservation Management; FM Society
- ● Mtgs - ET - Exam - Res - Exhib - Comp - Inf - Lib - LG
- < Architects & Surveyors Inst (ASI)
- M 33,500 i, 470 f, UK / 7,650 i, o'seas
- ¶ Construction Manager - 10; ftm, £50 nm.   AR; free.
  Construction Information Quarterly - 4; £38 (£44 o'seas) m, £88 nm.
  Contact (NL) - 6; ftm only.
  Construction Information Quarterly (Jnl) - 4;
- × 2002 Architecture & Surveying Institute (merged).

Chartered Institute of Environmental Health   (CIEH)   1883
- NR Chadwick Court, 15 Hatfields, LONDON, SE1 8DJ. (hq)
  020 7928 6006
  Admin Mgr: Elaine Sample
- ▲ Registered Charity
- ○ *P; the promotion of environmental health & dissemination of knowledge about environmental issues

Chartered Institute of Housing   (CIoH)   1965
NR   Octavia House, Westwood Way, COVENTRY, Warks, CV4 8JP.
         (hq)
         024 7685 1700   fax 024 7669 5110
         email customer.services@cih.org   http://www.cih.org
         Chief Exec: David Butler
▲   Registered Charity
Br   12; Hong Kong
○   *P; to promote the provision & management of good quality
         housing for all through education & continuing professional
         development
●   Conf - Mtgs - ET - Exam - SG - LG
M   c 10,500 i, UK / c 1,000 i, o'seas
¶   Housing - 12; ftm.

Chartered Institute of Journalists   (IOJ)   1890
NR   2 Dock Offices, Surrey Quays Rd, LONDON, SE16 2XU.   (hq)
         020 7252 1187   fax 020 7232 2302
         Gen Sec: Dominic Cooper
▲   Un-incorporated Society
○   *P; for all journalists - freelance, national & provincial
         newspaper, press & public relations, international,
         parliamentary & broadcasting
M   i
¶   The Jnl - 6; ftm only.

Chartered Institute of Library & Information Professionals
      see **CILIP: Chartered Institute of Library & Information
      Professionals**

Chartered Institute of Linguists   (IoL)   1910
■   48 Southwark St, LONDON, SE1 1UN.   (hq)
         020 7940 3100   fax 020 7940 3101
         email info@iol.org.uk   http://www.iol.org.uk
         Chief Exec: John Hammond
▲   Company Limited by Guarantee
○   *P
●   ET - Exam - Interpreting - Translating - Production
M   5,000 i, UK / 1,500 i, o'seas
¶   The Linguist - 6; ftm, £39 yr nm.
×   2005-06 Institute of Linguists

Chartered Institute of Logistics & Transport   (CILT(UK))   1990
NR   Logistics & Transport Centre, Earlstrees Court, Earlstrees Rd,
         CORBY, Northants, NN17 4AX.   (hq)
         01536 740100
▲   Company Limited by Guarantee; Registered Charity
Br   31; 1 o'seas
○   *P; to promote & develop the concept of logistics & transport
Gp   Resources Faculty:
         Customs & international trade, Environment, Logistics
            directors forum, Logistics research network, Logistics
            safety forum
      Supply-Chain Faculty:
         Defence, Manufacturing logistics, Northern Ireland,
            Procurement & outsourcing, Supply chain inventory
            management
      Technology Faculty:
         IT, RFID (radio frequency identification), Warehousing &
            materials handling
      Transport
         Aviation, Bus, E-travel, Freight forwarding, Freight
            transport, Passenger transport, Road capacity & charging,
            Strategic rail, Transport planning
●   Conf - Mtgs - ET - Exam - Res - Exhib - Inf - Lib - VE - LG
<   Eur Logistics Assn (ELA)
M   21,450 i, 284 f, UK / 1,767 i, o'seas
¶   Logistics & Transport Focus - 10.
      SIG NL.   Regional Diary - 10. Ybk.
      Note: in 2004 the individual members of the British
            International Freight Association became the CILT(UK) Freight
            Forwarding Forum
×   2004 Institute of Logistics & Transport

Chartered Institute of Logistics & Transport in Ireland
IRL   1 Fitzwilliam Place, DUBLIN 2, Republic of Ireland.
         353 (1) 676 3188   fax 353 (1) 676 4099
         email info@cilt.ie   http://www.cilt.ie
         Hon Sec: Patrick Casey
○   *P
×   2002 Chartered Institute of Transport in Ireland (merged)

Chartered Institute of Loss Adjusters   (CILA)   1942
NR   Peninsular House, 36 Monument St, LONDON, EC3R 8LJ.
         (hq)
         020 7337 9960
         http://www.cila.co.uk
         Exec Dir: Graham Cave
▲   Un-incorporated Society
Br   Australia
○   *P
●   Conf - ET - Exam - SG - Lib
M   2,600 i, UK / 400 i, o'seas
¶   Jnl;   NL;   AR;   Books & Technical Bulletins - all irreg;
         prices vary.

**Chartered Institute of Management Accountants   (CIMA)
1919**
NR   26 Chapter St, LONDON, SW1P 4NP.   (hq)
         020 8849 2251
         http://www.cimaglobal.com
○   *P; to promote the science of management accountancy across
         all sectors of the economy
M   137,000 i

Chartered Institute of Marketing   (CIM)   1911
NR   Moor Hall, Cookham, MAIDENHEAD, Berks, SL6 9QH.   (hq)
         01628 427500   fax 01628 427499
         email info@cim.co.uk   http://www.cim.co.uk
         Inf Services Mgr: Dawn A Southgate
▲   Registered Charity
Br   37; Australia, Ghana, Hong Kong, Kenya, Malaysia, Poland,
         Singapore
○   *P; 'the world's largest professional services body, which aims
         to provide marketers with best practice marketing knowledge
         & support to create long-term value for businesses'
      Areas of interest:
         Marketing, Sales, Direct marketing, CRM, Database
            marketing, sponsorship, Branding, Product marketing,
            Distribution, Market research, Marketing education,
            Marketing training
Gp   Groups:
         Construction industry; Financial services; Food, drink &
            agriculture; Medical marketing; National marketing group
            for learning & business support; Professional sales; Travel
         CIM Technology International; Hotel Marketing Association;
            Hotel Marketing Association Northern England
●   Conf - Mtgs - ET - Exam - Res - Exhib - Stat - Inf - Lib
<   World Marketing Assn (WMA); Eur Marketing Coun (EMC)
>   CAM Foundation
M   39,175 i, 75 f, org, UK / 16,035 i, o'seas
¶   the marketer - 10.
×   2004 (incorporated) Institute of Professional Sales

Chartered Institute of Patent Attorneys   (CIPA)   1882
NR   95 Chancery Lane (3rd floor), LONDON, WC2A 1DT.   (hq)
         020 7405 9450
         email mail@cipa.org.uk   http://www.cipa.org.uk
         Sec: Mr M C Ralph
▲   Incorporated by Royal Charter
○   *P; protection of industrial property - patents, trade marks,
         designs, copyright
●   Conf - Mtgs - ET - Exam - Inf
M   2,800 i, UK / 220 i, o'seas
¶   CIPA (Jnl) - 12.   LM.
      Register of Patent Agents - 1.
      CIPA Directory of Patent Agents.
×   2006 Chartered Institute of Patent Agents

© CBD Research Ltd · Beckenham · BR3 5JS · Tel 020 8650 7745 · Fax 020 8650 0768 · E-mail cbd@cbdresearch.com · www.cbdresearch.com

Chartered Institute of Personnel & Development (CIPD) 1913
■ 151 The Broadway, LONDON, SW19 1JQ. (hq)
  020 8612 6200 fax 020 8612 6201
  email cipd@cipd.co.uk http://www.cipd.co.uk
  Chief Exec: Geoff Armstrong
Br 48; Ireland
○ *P; promotion of the art & science of the management &
  development of people for the public benefit
● Conf - Mtgs - ET - Exam - Res - Exhib - Inf - Lib - LG
< Intl Fedn of Training & Devt Orgs; Wld [& Eur] Fedn of
  Personnel Mgt Assns; Eur Training & Devt Fedn
M 119,784 i, 5,046 f, UK / 4,000 i, o'seas
¶ People Management - 12. AR.

Chartered Institute of Public Finance & Accountancy
  see **CIPFA (the Chartered Institute of Public Finance &
  Accountancy)**

Chartered Institute of Public Relations (CIPR) 1948
■ Public Relations Centre, 32 St James's Square, LONDON,
  SW1Y 4JR. (hq)
  020 7766 3333 fax 020 7766 3344
  email info@cipr.co.uk http://www.cipr.co.uk
  Dir Gen: Colin Farrington
▲ Un-incorporated Society
Br 13 regional
○ *P; to represent the PR industry
Gp Construction & property; Corporate & financial; Education &
  skills; Government affairs; Health & medical; Internal
  comunications; International PR; Marketing &
  communications; Motor industry; Science, engineering &
  technology; Voluntary sector; Women in PR
● Conf - ET - Exam - Res - Exhib - Lib
< Global Alliance for PR & Communication Mgt; Confédn Eur de
  Relations Publiques (CERP)
M 7,800 i, UK / 377 i, o'seas
¶ Profile (Jnl) - 6; ftm, £55 yr nm.
  Annual Review; ftm, free online nm.
✕ 2005 Institute of Public Relations

Chartered Institute of Purchasing & Supply (CIPS) 1931
NR Easton House, Easton on the Hill, STAMFORD, Lincs,
  PE9 3NZ. (hq)
  01780 756777 fax 01780 751610
  email info@cips.org http://www.cips.org
  Chief Exec: Ken James
▲ Registered Charity
○ *L, *P; raising standards in purchasing & supply chain
  management
M i
  No further information supplied

Chartered Institute of Taxation 1930
NR 12 Upper Belgrave St, LONDON, SW1X 8BB. (hq)
  020 7235 9381 fax 020 7235 2562
  http://www.tax.org.uk
  Sec Gen: Robert Dommett
▲ Registered Charity
Br 6
○ *P
● Conf - Mtgs - ET - Exam - Res - Lib
< Confédn Fiscale Eur
M 11,000 i, UK & o'seas
¶ Tax Adviser - 12; LM - 1; AR;
  Annotated Taxing Statutes - as enacted; all ftm.

Chartered Institute of Transport in Ireland
  2002 merged with Institute of Logistics [IRL] to become **Chartered
  Institute of Logistics & Transport in Ireland**

**Chartered Institution of Building Services Engineers (CIBSE)
1897**
NR 222 Balham High Rd, LONDON, SW12 9BS. (hq)
  020 8675 5211 fax 020 8675 5449
  http://www.cibse.org
  Chief Exec: Julian Amey
▲ Registered Charity
Br 19; Australia, New Zealand, Republic of Ireland
○ *P; the art, science & practice of engineering services
  associated with the built environment (incl heating,
  ventilating, air conditioning, lighting, public health, internal
  transportation, electrical services)
Gp Lighting; Electrical services; Thermal storage; Lifts; Information
  technology; Public health; Building Services Heritage
● Conf - Mtgs - Res - ET - Exam - Exhib - Stat - Inf - LG
< Fedn Heating & Air Conditioning Assns (REHVA); Commission
  Intle de l'Eclairage
M 12,000 i, UK / 3,000 i, o'seas
¶ Building Services Jnl - 12.
  Lighting Research & Technology - 4.
  Building Services Engineering Research & Technology - 4.
  AR. Publications list available.

Chartered Institution of Wastes Management (CIWM) 1898
■ 9 Saxon Court, St Peter's Gardens, NORTHAMPTON,
  NN1 1SX. (hq)
  01604 620426 fax 01604 621339
  email ciwm@ciwm.co.uk http://www.ciwm.co.uk
  Chief Exec: Steve Lee
▲ Company incorporated by Royal Charter; Registered Charity
Br 10
○ *L, *P; promotion of scientific, technical & practical aspects of
  wastes management
Gp Waste collection; Street cleansing; Treatment & disposal;
  Reclamation; Recycling; Regulation
● Conf - Mtgs - ET - Exhib - Inf - Lib - VE - LG
< Eur C'ee Waste Mgt Org; WHO; Inst of Solid Wastes
  Assn (ISWA); Waste Mgt Ind Training & Advy Bd (WAMITAB);
  Soc for the Envt
M 6,123 i, 346 f, UK / 390 i, 8 f, o'seas
¶ Wastes Management (Jnl) - 12, ftm, £84 yr nm.
  News On-line (NL on Web page) - 52; AR; both free.
  CIWM Register of Consultants - 1; ftm, £15 nm.
  Technical publications, Codes of practice, Advice notes.
  Note: The Institution administers a Registered Environmental
  Body - CIWM(EB)
✕ 2002 Institute of Wastes Management

**Chartered Institution of Water & Environmental Management
(CIWEM) 1895**
■ 15 John St, LONDON, WC1N 2EB. (hq)
  020 7831 3110 fax 020 7405 4967
  email admin@ciwem.org http://www.ciwem.org
  Exec Dir: Nick Reeves
▲ Registered Charity; Incorporated by Royal Charter
Br 14 in UK; Hong Kong; Republic of Ireland
○ *P; to advance the science & practice of water & environmental
  management
Gp Environment; Rivers & coastal; Scientific
● Conf - Mtgs - ET - Exam - Exhib - SG - Inf - VE
< Eur Water Assn (EWA); Water Envt Fedn (WEF)
M 9,900 i, UK / 1,300 i, o'seas
¶ Jnl - 4; ftm, £165 yr nm.
  Water & Environment Manager - 10; ftm, £98 yr nm.
  Manuals & handbooks - list available.

Chartered Insurance Institute (CII) 1912
NR 42-48 High Rd, LONDON, E18 2JP. (hq)
  020 8989 8464 fax 020 8530 3052
○ *P

Chartered Management Institute (CMI) 1992
- ■ 2 Savoy Court, Strand, LONDON, WC2R 0EZ.　(hq)
  01536 204222　fax 01536 201651
  email membership@managers.co.uk
  http://www.managers.co.uk
  Chief Exec: Mary Chapman,　Inst Sec: Valerie Hamill
- ▲ Company Limited by Guarantee; Registered Charity
- Br 90; Hong Kong, Malaysia, Singapore, Sri Lanka
- ○ *P; to promote the art & science of management
- Gp Care Management Group (CMG); Institute of Management
  Consultancy (IMC); Police Professional Network; Women in
  Management (WiM)
- ● ET - Res - Inf - Lib - LG
- < Eur Foundation for Mgt Devt; Conseil Eur du Comité Intl de
  l'Org Scientifique (CECIOS)
- M 65,000 i, 300 f, UK / 5,500 i, o'seas
- ¶ Professional Manager - 6; ftm, £3.60 nm.　AR; free.
- ✕ 2002 Institute of Management

Chartered Society of Designers (CSD) 1930
- ■ 1 Cedar Court, Royal Oak Yard, Bermondsey St, LONDON,
  SE1 3AG.　(hq)
  020 7357 8088　fax 020 7407 9878
  email info@csd.org.uk　http://www.csd.org.uk
  Chief Exec: Frank Peters
- ▲ Registered Charity
- Br Regional Gps; Hong Kong
- ○ *P
- Gp Design: Exhibition, Fashion, Graphic, Interactive, Interior,
  Product, Textile
  Design education; Design management
- ● Mtgs - ET - Res - Comp - SG - Expt - Inf - LG
- < Design Assn
- > Design Assn
- M 3,000 i, UK / 250 i, o'seas
- ¶ The Designer - 4; ftm, £5 nm.
  Various professional publications - list available.

Chartered Society of Physiotherapy (CSP) 1894
- NR 14 Bedford Row, LONDON, WC1R 4ED.　(hq)
  020 7306 6666　fax 020 7306 6611
  http://www.csp.org.uk
  Chief Exec: Philip Gray
- ▲ Un-incorporated Society
- Br 78
- ○ *E, *P, *U
- ● Conf - ET - Res - Inf - Empl - LG - Professional advice -
  Disciplinary matters re rules of conduct
- < Wld Confedn Physical Therapy; TUC; Alliance Health Profls
- M 40,000 i
- ¶ Physiotherapy - 12.　Frontline - 26.　AR.

Chatham House
　see registered title **Royal Institute of International Affairs**

Chefs & Cooks Circle
　2005 merged with the Midlands Association of Chefs to form the
　British Culinary Federation

Chelmsford Chamber of Commerce (Mid Essex)
　is a branch office of the **Essex Chambers of Commerce**

Chemical Hazards Communication Society (CHCS) 1994
- ◨ PO Box 222, LYMINGTON, Hants, SO42 7GY.　(chmn)
  0700 079 0337　fax 0700 079 0338
  email chcs@chcs.org.uk　http://www.chcs.org.uk & sp
  Chmn & Mem Sec: Desmond Waight
- ▲ Un-incorporated Society
- ○ *P; to promote awareness of chemical hazards & improvements
  in their identification & communication; to provide a forum
  for sharing experiences, views & information; to promote the
  need for specific training & aim toward setting of competency
  standards
- ● Conf - Mtgs - Exhib - SG
- M 400 i, UK / 20 i, o'seas
- ¶ NL - 3/4;　LM - 1; both ftm only.

Chemical & Industrial Consultants Association (CICA) 1988
- NR 12 Oughton Close, YARM, Cleveland, TS15 9SZ　(hsp)
  01642 783639　fax 01642 783639
  email secretary@chemical-consultants.co.uk
  http://www.chemical-consultants.co.uk
  Sec: Dr Jim Bickerton
- ▲ Un-incorporated Society
- ○ *L, *T; independent consultancy practices advising on the
  applications of chemistry to all sectors of industry
- ● Mtgs - Res - Exhib - Inf
- M 42 i
- ¶ LM; on website.

Chemical Industries Association Ltd (CIA) 1966
- NR Kings Buildings, Smith Sq, LONDON, SW1P 3JJ.　(hq)
  020 7834 3399　fax 020 7834 8586
  Dir Gen: Stephen Elliott
- ○ *T; promotion of cooperation within chemical industry of the
  UK; negotiation with government & other bodies; problems
  in the economic, social, commercial, labour & technical fields
  affecting interests of members
- Gp Nat Sulphuric Acid Assn
- M c 180 f

Chemical Recycling Association (CRA) 1998
- ■ 62 Lower St, STANSTED, Essex, CM24 8LR.　(hsp)
  01279 814035　fax 01279 814035
  email chemrecycass@aol.com
  Hon Sec: Roger Creswell
- ○ *T; to promote, protect, represent & otherwise assist the
  members engaged in the recovery, recycling &/or re-use of
  contaminated chemicals, including secondary fuels
- ● Mtgs - Stat - Inf - LG
- M 5 f
- ¶ NL - 4; ftm only.

Chemists' Defence Association (CDA)
- NR 38-42 St Peters Street, ST ALBANS, Herts, AL1 3NP.　(hq)
  01727 832161　fax 01727 840858
  email npa@npa.co.uk　http://www.npa.co.uk
  Sec: R J C Maw
- ▲ Company limited by shares
- ○ *T; provision of legal advice & representation & professional
  indemnity
- M c 10,500 f
- ¶ AR.
  Note: CDA is a wholly-owned subsidiary of the National
  Pharmacy Association

Cherished Number Dealers Association
　is a group of the **Retail Motor Industry Federation**

Yn Cheshaght Ghailckagh (the Manx Gaelic Society)   1899

- ■ 16 Hilary Rd, DOUGLAS, Isle of Man, IM2 3EG.   (hsp)
  01624 623821
  email bstowell@mcb.net
  http://www.homepages.enterprise.net/kelly
  Hon Sec: Dr T Brian Stowell
- ▲ Company Limited by Guarantee
- Br 102; Isle of Man
- ○ *K, *L; preservation & revival of Manx Gaelic
- ● Conf - Mtgs - ET - Inf - LG - Publishing books
- M 140 i, UK (incl 102 i, Isle of Man) / 13 i, o'seas
- ¶ Dhooraght (NL) - ftm only.

Cheshire Agricultural Society   (CAS)   1838

- ■ The Tabley Estate Office, Chester Rd, Tabley, KNUTSFORD,
  Cheshire, WA1 0HF.   (hq)
  01565 722050   fax 01565 732830
  email info@cheshirecountyshow.org.uk
  http://www.cheshirecountyshow.org.uk
  Exec Dir: Nigel Evans
- ▲ Registered Charity
- ○ *F, *H; to encourage agricultural enterprise; to improve the
  breeding, rearing & health of livestock
- ● Exhib - Comp
- < Assn Show & Agricl Orgs
- M 1,300 i
- ¶ Schedule of Classes - 1; free.   AR; ftm only.
  Show Catalogue of Entries - 1; £3.
  Programme of Events - 1; £2.

Chess Scotland   1884

- NR PO Box 67, 15 Hope St, GLASGOW, G2 6AQ.   (hq)
  0141-221 6464
  Gen Sec: Sam Collins
- ▲ Registered Charity
- ○ *S; promotion & organisation of chess in Scotland
- Gp Scottish Chess & Draughts Association of the Deaf; Scottish
  Correspondence Chess Association; Scottish Junior Chess
  Association; Scottish National Chess League; Scottish
  Universities Chess Assn
- ● Conf - Mtgs - ET - Exam - Exhib - Comp - SG - Stat
- M i & clubs
- ¶ Scottish Chess - 6.
- × 2001 Scottish Chess Association

Chester Archaeological Society   (CAS)   1849

- NR Netherleigh House, Eaton Rd, CHESTER, CH4 7EW.   (hsb)
  01244 327750
  http://www.chesterarchaeolsoc.org.uk
  Hon Sec: Anthony Holliday
- ▲ Registered Charity
- ○ *L; study of archaeology, history & architecture of Chester,
  Cheshire & N Wales
- Gp Fieldwork
- ● Conf - Mtgs - ET - Res - Exhib - Lib - VE
- < Coun of Brit Archaeology
- M 350 i, 40 org, UK / 5 i, 5 org, o'seas
- ¶ Jnl - 1/2 yrly, ftm, £8 nm.
  The Antiquary (NL) - 2; free.

Chester, Ellesmere Port & North Wales Chamber of Commerce   1920

- NR 3 Grosvenor Court, Foregate St, CHESTER, CH1 1HG.   (hq)
  01244 405930   fax 01244 405935
  http://www.cepnwchamber.org.uk
  Chief Exec: Stephen Welch
- ▲ Company Limited by Guarantee
- ○ *C
- Gp Transport; Environment; Economic; Exporting
- ● Mtgs - Expt - Inf - Lib - LG
- < Brit Chams Comm
- M 950 f
- ¶ In Business - 12; ftm.

Chesterfield Canal Trust Ltd   (CCT)   1998

- NR 18 Barncliffe Crescent, Lodge Moor, SHEFFIELD, S Yorks,
  S10 4DA.   (hsp)
  0114-229 6355
  Hon Sec: Martin Broomfield
- ▲ Company Limited by Guarantee; Registered Charity
- ○ *G; to make the Chesterfield canal fully navigational
- ● Mtgs - Res - Exhib - SG - VE - LG - Campaigning - Physical
  restoration work
- < Inland Waterways Assn
- M i, f & org
- ¶ The Cuckoo (Jnl) - 4; ftm, £1 nm.
  Relevant information on the canal & associated activities.

Chesterton Society   (GKCSoc)   1964

- ■ 11 Lawrence Leys, Bloxham, BANBURY, Oxon, OX15 4NU.
  (hsp)
  01295 720869; 0776 671 1984 (mobile)
  fax 01295 720869
  email rmcallum@onetel.com
  Hon Sec: Rev Deacon Robert Hughes
- ▲ Registered Charity
- ○ *A; to promote interest & study of the works of G K Chesterton
  (1874-1936), critic, novelist & poet
- ● Lib
- M 250 i, UK / 50 i, o'seas
- ¶ G K Quarterly - 4; £2.

Chetham Society for the Publication of Remains Historical & Literary Connected with the Palatinate Counties of Lancaster & Chester   1843

- NR 77 Wellington St, PRESTON, Lancs, PR1 8TQ.   (hsp)
  01772 827835
  Hon Sec: Dr Alan Crosby
- ○ *L; to publish documents & monographs on the history of
  Lancashire & Cheshire
- ● Annual Mtg - Publication of records & monographs
- < Brit Records Assn
- M c 150 i, 100 universities & libraries, UK / 100 universities &
  libraries, o'seas
- ¶ Monograph / Record - c 1.

Cheviot Sheep Society   1891

- NR Holm Cottage, LANGHOLM, Dumfries & Galloway,
  DG13 0JP.   (sp)
  01387 380222
  email info@cheviotsheep.org
  http://www.cheviotsheep.org
  Sec: Mrs Isobel J McVittie
- ▲ Registered Charity
- ○ *B
- ● Mtgs
- < Nat Sheep Assn
- M 118 i
- ¶ Flock Book 1.   AR.
  Breed Leaflet - 2 yrly.

Chichester Chamber of Commerce & Industry

- NR 3 Chapel St, CHICHESTER, W Sussex, PO19 1BU.
  01243 531765
- ○ *C

Chief & Assistant Chief Fire Officers' Association
in 2004 changed name to **Chief Fire Officers' Association**

Chief Building Surveyors Society   1975
NR   Property Division, Endeavour House, 8 Russell Rd, IPSWICH,
        Suffolk, IP1 2BX.   (sb)
        01473 265252
        Sec: Bill Smith
○   *P; to share knowledge & experience & promote awareness of
        property maintenance & management within local
        government
●   Mtgs - Stat - LG
<   Fedn Property Socs
M   c 80 i

Chief Cultural & Leisure Officers Association   (CLOA)   1976
NR   Mallan House, Bridge End, HEXHAM, Northumberland,
        NE46 4DQ.   (hq)
        01434 606155
        http://www.cloa.org.uk
        Policy Officer: Peter Cooke,
        Admin: Mo Bascombe
▲   Un-incorporated Society
○   *P; interest of arts, sports & recreation management; to
        represent chief leisure officers in England & Wales
M   320 i & local authorities
×   2003 Chief Leisure Officers Assn

Chief Fire Officers' Association   (CFOA)   1974
■   9-11 Pebble Close, Amington, TAMWORTH, Staffs, B77 4RD.
        (hq)
        01827 302300   fax 01827 302399
        email info@cfoa.org.uk
        Gen Mgr: Steve Currey
▲   Company Limited by Guarantee
○   *P; 'to reduce the loss of life, personal injury & damage to
        property & the environment by improving the quality of
        firefighting, rescue, fire protection & fire prevention in the UK'
Gp   Policy c'ees: Appliances, equipment & uniform;
        Communications & computing; Fire safety; Operations;
        Personnel & training; Health & safety
●   Conf - Mtgs - ET - Res - Exhib - Comp - Inf - LG - Serving on
        standards groups (BSI, CEN & ISO)
<   Metrochiefs
M   186 i
×   2004 Chief & Assistant Chief Fire Officers' Association

Chief Fire Officers Association Ireland
IRL   c/o Fire Station, NENAGH, Co Tipperary, Republic of Ireland.
        353 (67) 31771
        email dcarroll@northtippcoco.ie
        Hon Sec: David Carroll
○   *P
M   i

Chief Leisure Officers Association
        since 2003 **Chief Cultural & Leisure Officers Association**

CHILD
        in 2003 merged with Issue (the National Fertility Association) to form
        Infertility Network UK

Child Growth Foundation   (CGF)   1977
■   2 Mayfield Ave, LONDON, W4 1PW.   (chmn/p)
        020 8995 0257   fax 020 8995 9075
        email cgflondon@aol.com
        http://www.heightmatters.org.uk
        Chmn: Tam Fry
▲   Registered Charity
○   *W; to seek regular growth assessment for every UK child; to
        ensure that every growth-related abnormality is immediately
        referred to an endocrine specialist for care of treatment
●   Conf - Res
M   1,100 i, UK / 25 i, o'seas
¶   NL - 2; ftm only.
        Publications list available.

Children 1st   1884
■   83 Whitehouse Loan, EDINBURGH, EH19 1AT.   (hq)
        0131-446 2300   fax 0131-446 2339
        email info@children1st.org.uk
        http://www.children1st.org.uk
        Chief Exec: Margaret McKay
Br   37
○   *K, *W, *Y; to give every child in Scotland a safe & secure
        childhood; to support families under stress; to protect
        children from harm & neglect; to protect their rights &
        interests; to help them recover from abuse

Children's Books History Society   (CBHS)   1969
NR   26 St Bernard's Close, BUCKFAST, S Devon, TQ11 0EP.   (sp)
        01364 643568
        email cbhs@abcgarrett.demon.co.uk
        Chmn: Mrs Pat Garrett
○   *G; to promote an appreciation of children's books; to study
        their history, bibliography & literary content
●   Conf - Mtgs - Exhib - VE - Biennial Harvey Darton Award
<   Library Assn; Osborne Collection (Toronto, Canada)
M   Libraries & Universities
¶   NL - 3; ftm, £4 nm.   Occasional papers - 1; ftm, £4 nm.

Children's Chronic Arthritis Association   (CCAA)   1990
■   Amber Gate, City Walls Rd, WORCESTER, WR1 2AH.   (hq)
        01905 745595   fax 01905 745703
        email info@ccaa.org.uk   http://www.ccaa.org.uk
        Gen Sec: Mrs Caroline Cox
▲   Registered Charity
○   *M, *W; to provide help & information for children with arthritis,
        their families & professionals involved in their care; to raise
        awareness of arthritis of childhood in the community
●   Conf - Mtgs - ET - Inf - Annual support weekend for children
        with arthritis & their families
M   2,000 i
¶   Joint Report (NL) - 2.
        Chat;   Chat 2;   Chat for Teachers; free on joining.

Children's Heart Association   (CHA)   1973
NR   26 Elizabeth Drive, Helmshore, ROSSENDALE, Lancs, BB4 4JB.
        01706 221988
        http://www.heartchild.info
▲   Registered Charity
Br   7 in Scotland
○   *W; to give support & understanding in everyday care & welfare
        to parents & families of children with heart disorders; to raise
        money for research into congenital heart disorders; to
        improve facilities & maintain improvements in hospitals
●   Mtgs - Inf - Family, teenage & young adult weekends - Fund
        raising
<   Heart Care
M   families
¶   Heart Beat - 2; free.
        Information pack; free for parents of a heart child.
×   2005 Association for Children with Heart Disorders

Children in Hospital Ireland
IRL   Carmichael Centre, Coleraine House, Coleraine St, DUBLIN 7,
        Republic of Ireland.
        353 (1) 878 0448   fax 353 (1) 873 5283
        email info@childreninhospital.ie
        Chief Exec: Mary O'Connor
○   *W

Children Law UK   1974
NR   15 The Aberdeen Centre, 24 Highbury Grove, LONDON,
N5 2EA.   (hq)
020 7704 9919   fax 020 7354 1205
email info@childrenlawuk.org
http://www.childrenlawuk.org
Chief Exec: Glyn Farrow
▲   Registered Charity
○   *P; to improve the operation of legal processes for the benefit
of children
●   Conf - ET - Res - SG - VE
<   Intl Assn of Youth & Family Judges & Magistrates
M   c 300 i

**Children Living with Inherited Metabolic Diseases   (Climb)
1981**
■   Climb Building, 176 Nantwich Rd, CREWE, Cheshire,
CW2 6BG.   (hq)
0800 770 0325   fax 0870 770 0327
email info@climb.org.uk   http://www.climb.org.uk
Exec Dir: Steven Hannigan
▲   Company Limited by Guarantee; Registered Charity
Br   5
○   *W; to further research into metabolic diseases; to support
families of children suffering from such diseases (1,300
known diseases)
Gp   support 700 (of potential 1,300) metabolic diseases
●   Conf - ET - Res (fund) - Inf - LG
Helpline: 0800 652 3181
<   Eur Org for Rare Diseases (EURODIS); Contact a Family (CAF);
Genetic Interest Gp
M   857 i, 52 org, UK / 64 i, 7 org, o'seas
¶   Climb (Jnl) - 3; ftm, £3.50 each nm.   AR.

Children's Rights Alliance for England   (CRAE)
NR   94 White Lion St, LONDON, N1 9PF.
020 7278 8222   fax 020 7278 9552
email info@crae.org.uk   http://www.crae.org.uk
Nat Coordinator: Carolyne Willow
○   *W

Children in Scotland   1983
NR   Princes House, 5 Shandwick Place, EDINBURGH, EH2 4RG.
(hq)
0131-228 8484   fax 0131-228 8585
email info@childreninscotland.org.uk
http://www.childreninscotland.org.uk
Chief Exec: Bronwen Cohen
Br   Glasgow, Inverness
○   *N, *W; Scotland's national agency for voluntary, statutory &
professional organisations & individuals working with
Scotland's children & their families
●   Conf - Mtgs - Res - SG - Stat - Inf - LG
<   Nat Children's Bureau; Children in Wales
M   78 i, 450 org
¶   NL;   AR; both ftm.   Factsheets.
List of publications on aspects of child & family policy.

Children's Services Research Group   (CSRG)   1984
■   c/o EMIE Service at NFER, The Mere, Upton Park, SLOUGH,
Berks, SL1 2DQ.   (hsb)
01753 523156   fax 01753 531458
http://www.csrg.org.uk
Chmn: John Wiseman,   Sec: Valerie Gee
▲   Un-incorporated Society
○   *E, *P; to provide a forum for discussion of current & emerging
educational issues & developments in children's services
●   Conf - Mtgs
M   i
×   2006 (7 July) Local Education Authorities Research Group

Chilled Ceilings Association   (CCA)   1996
■   2 Waltham Court, Milley Lane, Hare Hatch, READING, Berks,
RG10 9TH.   (hq)
0118-940 3416   fax 0118-940 6258
email info@feta.co.uk   http://www.feta.co.uk/
Dir Gen: C Sloan
○   *T; to promote the use of chilled beams & chilled ceilings &
encourage best practice in their development & application
●   Mtgs
<   Heating, Ventilating & Air Conditioning Mfrs' Assn (HEVAC);
Fedn Envtl Trade Assns (FETA)
M   11 f
¶   Chilled Ceilings (leaflet); free.

Chilled Food Association Ltd   (CFA)   1989
■   PO Box 6434, KETTERING, Northants, NN15 5XT.   (hsb)
01536 514365   fax 01536 515395
email cfa@chilledfood.org   http://www.chilledfood.org
Sec Gen: Miss Kaarin Goodburn
▲   Company Limited by Guarantee
○   *T; to represent the interests & promote the standards of the UK
chilled food industry
Gp   C'ees: Executive, Technical
Specialist working gps (transient)
●   Mtgs - ET - Res - SG -LG
<   Eur Chilled Food Fedn (ECFF); Food & Drink Fedn (FDF)
>   North West Food Alliance
M   27 f, UK / 1 f, o'seas
¶   Best Practice Guidelines for the Production of Chilled Foods -
irreg; £80 m, £100 nm.
Handwash (training poster) - irreg; £10 m, £25 nm.
Water Quality Management - irreg; £40, £55 nm.
Regulatory Guidance - irreg.

Chillingham Wild Cattle Association Ltd   1939
■   Warden's Cottage, Chillingham, ALNWICK, Northumberland,
NE66 5NP.   (regd/office)
01668 215250
http://www.chillingham-wildcattle.org.uk
Mem Sec/Treas: Mrs A Widdows,   Vice-Chmn: James Joicey
▲   Company Limited by Guarantee; Registered Charity
○   *B; a registered charity set up to ensure the survival of the
Chillingham wild cattle in their own environment at
Chillingham Park, Northumberland
●   VE - Open to visitors
M   390 i, UK / 30 i, o'seas
¶   NL - 4;   AR - 1; both ftm, sae nm.
History leaflet - 1; £1.

China-Britain Business Council   (CBBC)   1991
NR   1 Warwick Row, LONDON, SW1E 5ER.   (hq)
020 7802 2000   fax 020 7802 2029
email enquiries@cbbc.org   http://www.cbbc.org
Chief Exec: Peter Nightingale
Br   2; China
○   *T; to promote British business in China through seminars,
missions to & from China & offices in China (Beijing,
Shanghai, Qingdao, Shenzhen, Wuhan & Chengdu)
●   Conf - Mtgs - Expt - Inf - Lib - LG
<   Euro-China Business Assn
M   250 f
¶   China-Britain Trade Review - 12.

China, Glass & Giftware Retailers' Association
has closed

China Society 1906
- ■ 16 Bridge St, CHRISTCHURCH, Dorset, BH23 1EB.   (chmn)
    01202 482717 & sp
    Chmn & Sec: Dr James Cantlie
- ▲ Un-incorporated Society
- ○ *L; 'to encourage interest on any aspect of China, past or present'
- ● Mtgs - Lectures (at the Society of Antiquaries, London)
- M 100 i, 5 f, UK / 5 i, o'seas
- ¶ NL - 4; ftm;   Booklets - 1.

Chinese Takeaway Association (UK) (CTAUK) 1993
- ■ 40 Gerrard St, LONDON, W1D 5QE.   (mail)
    07748 884 3876
    email chinesetauk@hotmail.com add
    Chmn: Thomas Chan
- ▲ Company Limited by Guarantee
- ○ *T; Chinese takeaways in the UK
- ● ET - Inf - LG
- M c 400 f

Chippendale Society 1963
- NR c/o Temple Newsam House, LEEDS, W Yorks, LS15 0AE.   (hsb)
    0113-264 7321
    Hon Curator: James Lomax
- ▲ Registered Charity
- ○ *A, *L; to promote appreciation of the work of Thomas Chippendale (1718-1790) & the art of woodcarving
- ● Mtgs - Exhib - Inf - VE to country houses - Lectures
- M 400 i, 3 f, 2 org
- ¶ NL - 3/4; ftm.   Occasional publications.

Chiropractic Patients' Association (CPA) 1965
- ■ 8 Centre One, Lysander Way, Old Sarum Park, SALISBURY, Wilts, SP4 6BU.   (hq)
    01722 415027   fax 01722 415028
    email c.p.a@dial.pipex.com
    http://www.chiropatients.com
    Sec: Nastasya Blissett
- ▲ Registered Charity
- ○ *K, *W; to support chiropractic; to advance knowledge & increase awareness of chiropractic treatment
- ● Mtgs
- < Eur Fedn of Pro-Chiropractic Assns
- M 923 i
- ¶ Back Chat (NL) - 3; ftm only.

Chocolate Society 1987
- NR Bar Lane, BOROUGHBRIDGE, N Yorks, YO51 9LS.   (hq)
    0845 230 8899   fax 01423 322253
    email info@chocolate.co.uk
    http://www.chocolate.co.uk
    Chmn: Alan Porter
- ▲ Company Limited by Guarantee
- Br 3
- ○ *G; to promote awareness of & make available fine chocolate
- ● ET - Exhib - Inf
- M 5,000 i, UK / 500 i, o'seas
- ¶ NL.

Choice in Personal Safety (CIPS) 1983
- ■ Mount House, Urra, Chop Gate, MIDDLESBROUGH, TS9 7HZ.   (chmn/p)
    01642 778302
    http://www.users.aol.com/forgood/seatbelt/
    Chmn: Don Furness
- ▲ Un-incorporated Society
- ○ *G, *K; campaigning to repeal the seatbelt compulsion legislation, which our research has shown to be actuallly inimical to personal safety & is thereby a malign interference with freedom of choice
- ● Mtgs - LG
- < Soc for Individual Freedom; Assn of Brit Drivers
- M 40 i, UK / 3 i, o'seas
- ¶ Minutes of Meetings - 5; free.

Choir Schools Association (CSA) 1919
- NR Wolvesey, College St, WINCHESTER, Hants, SO23 9ND.   (pt/time/hq)
    01962 890530   fax 01962 869978
    http://www.choirschools.org.uk
    Admin: Mrs Susan Rees
- ▲ Registered Charity
- ○ *A, *E
- Gp Bursary trust (to ensure that no child is denied a choristership on financial grounds)
- ● Conf - Mtgs
- M 44 schools, UK / 4 schools, o'seas
- ¶ Choir Schools Today - 1; ftm.

Chopin Society (London)
have stated that they do not wish to be included since people can find their details from other sources

Christian Booksellers Association
this organisation has closed its UK office & is now located in ColoradoSprings, USA

Christian Education (CEM) 2001
- ■ 1020 Bristol Rd, Selly Oak, BIRMINGHAM, W Midlands, B29 6LB.   (hq)
    0121-472 4242   fax 0121-472 7575
    email enquiries@christianeducation.org.uk
    http://www.christianeducation.org.uk
    Gen Sec: Peter Fishpool
- ▲ Company Limited by Guarantee
- Br 25
- ○ *P; 'to promote Christian concerns in education generally & religious education in schools particularly'
- Gp Study & research
- ● Conf - ET - Res - Exhib - Comp - LG
- M 4,500 i, 6,500 associated schools
- ¶ Publications list available.

Christian Endeavour Union of Great Britain & Ireland (CE) 1896
- NR Wellesbourne House, Walton Rd, WELLESBOURNE, Warks, CV35 9JB.   (hq)
    01789 470439   fax 01789 470439
    Hon Sec: K F Rankin
- ▲ Company Limited by Guarantee; Registered Charity
- ○ *R; interdenominational spiritual fellowship & action

Christian Evidence Society (CES) 1870
- ■ 5 Vicarage Lane, CHELMSFORD, Essex, CM2 8HY.   (hsp)
    01245 478038
    http://www.christianevidenceociety.org.uk
    Admin: Canon Harry Marsh
- ▲ Company Limited by Guarantee; Registered Charity
- ○ *R; 'the proclamation, defence & study of the Christian Faith'
- ¶ Booklets; details available on website.
    Note: The Christian Evidence Society does not provide grants.

Christian Social Order (CSO) 1965
- ■ 157 Vicarage Rd, LONDON, E10 5DU.   (hq)
    020 8539 3876   fax 020 8539 3876
    email social-owner@smartgroups.com
    http://www.smartgroups.com/vault/social
    Sec: Ronald King
- ▲ Un-incorporated Society
- ○ *K, *R; to oppose organised naturalism by promoting a Christian social order
- Gp Pugin Gild
- ● Mtgs - Res - SG - Stat - Inf - Lib - PL
- M [not given]
- ¶ The Keys of Peter - 6; £5 (£6 o'seas).

© CBD Research Ltd · Beckenham · BR3 5JS · Tel 020 8650 7745 · Fax 020 8650 0768 · E-mail cbd@cbdresearch.com · www.cbdresearch.com

Chromatographic Society

NR c/o Meeting Makers, Jordanhill Campus, 76 South Brae Drive, GLASGOW, G13 1PP. (hq)
   0141-434 1500   fax 0141-434 1519
   http://www.chromsoc.com
   Sec: Maria McHugh
▲ Registered Charity
○ *L, *Q; to promote & disseminate knowledge on chromatography & separation techniques - gas, liquid, thin-layer & column liquid chromatography & capillary electrophoresis, supercritical fluids & HPLC
● Conf - Mtgs
M i
¶ Chromatography Abstracts - 10.   Bulletin - 3/4.

Church of England Record Society   1991

■ c/o 13 Tarleton Gardens, LONDON, SE23 3XN.   (exec/sb)
   020 8699 0820
   http://www.coers.org
   Exec Sec: Miss Melanie Barber
▲ Registered Charity
○ *L; to promote interest & knowledge of the Church of England, from the 16th century onwards, by the publication of primary sources of information
● Mtgs - Publication (1 vol a year)
M c 450 i & org
¶ Annual Volume - 1.

Church Lads' & Church Girls' Brigade   (CL&CGB)   1891

■ 2 Barnsley Rd, Wath-upon-Dearne, ROTHERHAM, S Yorks, S63 6PY.   (hq)
   01709 876535   fax 01709 878089
   email brigadesecretary@clcgb.org.uk
   http://www.clcgb.org.uk
   Brigade Sec: A Millward
▲ Company Limited by Guarantee; Registered Charity
○ *R; 'a uniformed voluntary organisation which, through a wide range of recreational, cultural & spiritual activities, seeks to equip young people & children for life & encourages them to be faithful members of the Church of England'
● Mtgs - ET - Comp - VE
< Nat Coun of Voluntary Orgs; Nat Coun of Volunteer Youth Services
M 5,000 i
¶ NL - 3;   AR; both ftm only.

Church Monuments Society   (CMS)   1979

■ c/o Society of Antiquaries, Burlington House, Piccadilly, LONDON, W1J 0BE.   (mail/address)
   01837 851483   fax 01837 851483
   email churchmonuments@aol.com
   http://www.churchmonumentssociety.org
   Contact: The Hon Sec
▲ Registered Charity
○ *L; to promote the study & conservation of all church monuments both in the UK & abroad
● Conf - Mtgs - SG - Inf - VE
M 398 i, 5 f, 43 org, UK / 18 i, 1 f, 25 org, o'seas
¶ Church Monuments (Jnl) - 1; ftm, £15 nm.
   NL - 2; ftm, £1.50 nm.

Churchill Society London   1990

■ 18 Grove Lane, IPSWICH, Suffolk, IP4 1NR.
   01473 413533
   email secretary@churchill-society-london.org.uk
   http://www.churchill-society-london.org.uk
   Chmn: Mrs Pamela Timms,   Gen Sec: Mrs Judith O'Hanlon
○ *G; the education of young people about the causes & consequences of war, about Churchill, & the encouragement of all the fine arts & crafts
● Conf - Mtgs - ET - Exhib - Comp - SG - Inf - Lib
¶ All publications are listed on the society's website.

Cigarette Packet Collectors' Club of Great Britain   1980

■ Talisker, Vines Cross Rd, Horam, HEATHFIELD, E Sussex, TN21 0HF.   (hsp)
   01435 812453
   email bkr@horehamroad.wanadoo.co.uk
   http://www.cigarettepacket.com
   Hon Sec: Barry Russell
▲ Un-incorporated Society
○ *G; preservation of, & research into, the history of cigarette packets, tins & boxes; the collection of ephemera connected with the tobacco trade - packets of cigarette rolling papers (Rizla), tobacco trade price lists etc
● Mtgs - Lib - Auctions (qtrly)
M 215 i, UK / 35 i, o'seas
¶ The Cigarette Packet - 4; ftm; £14 (25 EU) ($30 USA).
   Auction lists - 4; ftm.
      [subscription £14].

CILIP: Chartered Institute of Library & Information Professionals   (CILIP)   1877

■ 7 Ridgmount St, LONDON, WC1E 7AE.   (hq)
   020 7255 0500   fax 020 7255 0501
   email info@cilip.org.uk   http://www.cilip.org.uk/
   Chief Exec: Bob McKee
▲ Registered Charity
Br 12
○ *P; for librarians & information managers
Gp Divns: Scottish Library Association, Welsh Library Association
   Special interest: Professional development; Subject interests; Employment sectors
   Online User Group
● Conf - Mtgs - ET - Exam - Inf - Empl - LG
M 22,830 i, 461 f, UK / 999 i, 178 f, o'seas
¶ Update (Jnl) - 12.
   Gazette (NL) - 12.
× 2002 (Institute of Information Scientists (Library Association

Ciné Guilds of Great Britain   (CGGB)   1988

■ 72 Pembroke Rd, LONDON, W8 8NX.   (sp)
   020 7602 8319   fax 020 7602 8319
   email cineguildsgb@btinternet.com
   Sec: Sally Fisher
▲ Un-incorporated Society
○ *P; maintaining levels of excellence in UK film-making crafts
● Mtgs - ET - Res - LG
M 2,500 i in 7 guilds

Cinema Advertising Association Ltd   (CAA)   1953

NR 12 Golden Sq, LONDON, W1F 9JE.   (hq)
   020 7534 6363   fax 020 7534 6464
   Pres: Debbie Chalet,   Sec: Terry Lince
▲ Company Limited by Guarantee
Br Ireland
○ *T; for cinema advertising contractors in the UK & Eire
Gp CAVIAR - Cinema & Video Industry Audience Research
● Mtgs - Res - Stat - Inf
< Screen Advertising Wld Assn
M 2 f
¶ CAA Cinema Check - 2; ftm.
   Master List of Cinemas - irreg; ftm.
   Cinema & Video Industry Audience Research - 1.
   UK Advertising Admissions Monitor - 12; ftm.
   Coverage & Frequency Guide - 1; ftm.

Cinema Exhibitors Association (CEA) 1912
NR 22 Golden Sq, LONDON, W1F 9JW. (hq)
    020 7734 9551
    Chief Exec: John Wilkinson
▲ Un-incorporated Society
Br 6
○ *T; interests of cinema exhibitors
Gp Independent cinemas; Specialist exhibition
● Conf - Mtgs - ET - Stat - Inf - VE - LG - Liaison with production
    & distribution in UK & overseas
< U Intle Cinémas; Media-Salles
M c 180 f, UK / 5 f, o'seas
¶ NL - 6;   Guidance notes on operations;   AR; all free.

Cinema Organ Society (COS) 1952
NR Dolby House, Barrington Gate, Holbeach, SPALDING, Lincs,
    PE12 7DA. (memsec/p)
    http://www.cinema-organs.org.uk
    Mem Sec: David Shepherd
○ *G; for those interested in the cinema (theatre) organ for
    entertainment
M i

Cinema Theatre Association (CTA) 1967
■ 44 Harrowdene Gardens, TEDDINGTON, Middx, TW11 0DJ.
    (hsp)
    020 8977 2608
    Hon Sec: Adam Unger
▲ Company Limited by Guarantee; Registered Charity
Br 2
○ *D, *G, *K; promotes serious interest in all aspects of cinema
    buildings (architecture, lighting, film projection & stage
    facilities); promotes their study in terms of the history of
    entertainment, social & architectural history; campaigns for
    the preservation & continued use of cinemas for their original
    purpose
● Mtgs - Res - Inf - Lib - PL - VE - Lectures, talks & shows -
    Archive available for public research
M 1,500 i
¶ Picture House - 1; ftm, £4.50 nm.
    CTA Bulletin - 6; ftm, £2 nm.

**CIPFA (Chartered Institute of Public Finance & Accountancy)
(CIPFA) 1885**
NR 3 Robert St, LONDON, WC2N 6RL. (hq)
    020 7543 5600   fax 020 7543 5700
    http://www.cipfa.org.uk
▲ Registered Charity
○ *P; professional accountancy body for public services (both
    public & private sectors) providing education & training in
    accountancy & financial management; to set & monitor
    professional standards
M i

Circle of State Librarians
    since 2005 the **Network of Government Library & Information
    Scientists**

Circle of Wine Writers (CWW) 1960
■ Scots Firs, 70 Joiners Lane, CHALFONT St PETER, Bucks,
    SL9 0AU. (admin/p)
    01494 589201   fax 01494 589201
    email administrator@winewriters.org
    http://www.winewriters.org
    Admin: Andrea Warren
▲ Un-incorporated Society
○ *P; to improve the standard of writing, broadcasting & lecturing
    about wines & spirits; to promote wines & spirits of good
    quality & to comment adversely on faulty products & dubious
    practices; the Circle is open to all currently being published,
    including photographers
● Mtgs - ET - Comp - VE - Wine tastings
M 195 i, UK / 83 i, o'seas
¶ Circle Update - 5.   LM (email only) - 12 ftm, £95 nm.
    [subscription £60].

Circular Chess Society (CCS) 1996
NR 11 North Parade, LINCOLN, LN1 1LB. (sp)
    01522 887666
    Pres: David Reynolds
▲ Un-incorporated Society
○ *G; to promote the game of circular chess to persons of all
    standards of play
● Mtgs - Comp - Stat - Inf
M i
¶ NL - 4.   LM - 4.

Circus Friends Association of Great Britain (CFA) 1934
■ The Kremlin - 172 Hebble Lane, Wheatley, HALIFAX, W Yorks,
    HX3 5JN. (mem/sec/p)
    01422 341062
    email cirkshop@btinternet.com
    http://www.circusfriends.co.uk
    Mem Sec: Sue Roylance
▲ Un-incorporated Society
○ *G; to support traditional circus as a popular entertainment &
    valuable part of British culture
● Mtgs - ET - Res - Exhib - Comp - Inf - Lib - VE - Video archive -
    Rallies
M 700 i, UK / 150 i, o'seas
¶ King Pole - 5; £25 yr.

Circus Society 1983
NR 6 Sherwood Court, 372 London Rd, Langley, SLOUGH, Berks,
    SL3 7HX. (pres)
    01753 547081 p
    Pres: R Bartlett
▲ Un-incorporated Society
Br 9 areas
○ *P, *T; promotion of circus & circus artistes; to oppose anti-
    circus activities by various animal rights groups & local
    authorities
Gp Circus: proprietors, artistes, artistes agents, friends &
    supporters, clowns, staff
● Inf
M 100 i
¶ Circus News - 4; £2 m, £2.75 nm.
    Note: any request for information should be accompanied by
    an sae.

Citizens Advice
    the name by which the **National Association of Citizens Advice
    Bureaux** is now more commonly known

Citizens Advice Bureaux (NACAB) 1939
■ Myddelton House, 115-123 Pentonville Rd, LONDON,
    N1 9LZ. (hq)
    020 7833 2181   fax 020 7833 4371
    http://www.citizensadvice.org.uk + adviceguide.org.uk
    Chief Exec: David Harker
▲ Registered Charity
Br 17
○ *K, *N, *W; provision of free, confidential & impartial advice &
    information on all subjects; social policy campaigning;
    lobbying
● Conf - Mtgs - ET - Res - EXhib - Stat - Inf - Empl - LG
M 475 bureaux
¶ Mid Month NL - 12; m only.   Hbk; £6 m, £12 nm.   AR.
    Social Policy Reports - irreg.
✕ 2003 National Association of Citizens Advice Bureaux

© CBD Research Ltd · Beckenham · BR3 5JS · Tel 020 8650 7745 · Fax 020 8650 0768 · E-mail cbd@cbdresearch.com · www.cbdresearch.com

Citizens Advice Scotland   (CAS)   c 1940
NR   Spectrum House, 2 Powderhall Rd, EDINBURGH, EH7 4GB.
        (hq)
        0131-550 1000   fax 0131-550 1001
        email info@cas.org.uk   http://www.cas.org.uk
        Contact: Jackie Cummings
▲   Company Limited by Guarantee
○   *N, *W; supporting Scottish Citizens Advice Bureaux; provision
        of free, confidential & impartial information, guidance,
        counselling & support to all individuals
Gp   Legal; Fundraising; Executive advice; Homelessness project;
        Social policy; Information writing
●   Conf - Mtgs - ET - Res - Exhib - Stat - Inf - Lib - LG
M   70 org (Scotland)
¶   newsCASt - 4;   Scottish Citizen - 4;   AR & accounts; all free.

City Information Group   (CiG)   2002
■   PO Box 13297, LONDON, SW19 8GH.
        020 8543 7339   fax 020 8543 7639
        email admin@cityinformation.org.uk
        http://www.cityinformation.org.uk
        Chmn & Trustee: Mandy Sullivan
▲   Company Limited by Guarantee; Registered Charity
○   *P; to promote, develop & advance the professional practice of
        collecting, collating & evaluating financial & business
        information
●   Mtgs - ET
M   500 i
¶   CIGLET (NL) - 4; ftm [past editions on website; free].
        Ybk - free.
        Note: was a special interest group of the Institute of Information
        Scientists

City Property Association   (CPA)   1904
NR   1 Warwick Row (7th floor), LONDON, SW1E 5ER.   (hq)
        020 7630 1782   fax 020 7630 8344
▲   Un-incorporated Society
○   *T; interests of owners of property in the City of London
●   Mtgs - Inf - LG
<   Brit Property Fedn Ltd
M   125 f
¶   NL.   AR (incl LM).

City of Sheffield & District Chamber of Trade
        merged in 2004 with **Sheffield Chamber of Commerce &
        Industry**

Civil Court Users Association   (CCUA)
NR   Orchard Court, WELLESBOURNE, Warks, CV35 9GA.   (hq)
        01789 472195   fax 01789 472196
        http://www.ccua.org.uk
        Admin: Clare Green
○   *K; to liaise with debt collection companies & the Lord
        Chancellor's office; to encourage the updating of laws to
        benefit both debt collectors & debtors
●   LG
M   c 150 f

Civil Engineering Contractors' Association   (CECA)   1996
NR   55 Tufton St, LONDON, SW1P 3QL.
        020 7227 4620   fax 020 7227 4621
        http://www.ceca.co.uk
        Dir: Rosemary Beales
○   *T
        no further information supplied

Clarice Cliff Collectors Club   (CCCC)   1982
■   PO Box 2706, ECCLESHALL, Staffs, ST21 6WY.   (hsb)
        email information@claricecliff.com
        http://www.claricecliff.com
        Hon Sec: Leonard Griffin
▲   Un-incorporated Society
○   *G; for collectors of ceramics designed by Clarice Cliff between
        1927-1964
Gp   Wensites: (1) public, (2) members only
●   Conf - Mtgs - Res - Exhib - SG - PL - VE
M   [confidential]
¶   NL - 4; ftm only.   NL [email] - 4; £25 yr.

Clarinet Heritage Society   (CHS)   1945
■   47 Hambalt Rd, LONDON, SW4 9EQ.   (hsp/b)
        020 8675 3877
        email chs@chello.se
        Hon Sec: Stephen Bennett
▲   Un-incorporated Society
Br   USA
○   *D, *K; to encourage the literature, repertoire, research, study &
        playing of clarinet music
Gp   Research (music, history, evolution & development); Recording
        & music publishing; Commissions; Teaching & study; Public
        relations & promotion
●   ET - Res - SG - Expt - Inf - Lib
M   500 i, UK / 400 i, Library of Congress, o'seas
¶   Sheet music, records, cassettes & CDs; £12-£15.

**Clarinet & Saxophone Society of Great Britain   (CASS GB)
1976**
NR   8 Garden Close, HAMPTON, Middx, TW12 3EG.   (msp)
        020 8487 3937
        email membership@clarinetandsaxophone.co.uk
        Mem Sec: Miss Susan Moss
▲   Company Limited by Guarantee
○   *D, *Q; all aspects of the music for, & playing of, clarinet &
        saxophone
●   Conf - ET - Comp - Inf - Lib
M   1,500 i, 12 f, 8 org, UK / 75 i, 2 f, 1 org, o'seas
¶   Clarinet & Saxophone - 4;   Library Catalogues;
        Resources Hbk;   LM - 1; all ftm only.

Clarsach Society
        see **Comunn na Clàrsaich**

Classic Rally Association
NR   PO Box 633, NEWPORT, Monmouthshire, NP20 5ZX.   (hq)
        01633 263366
        http://www.classicrally.org.uk
        Dir: Jeremy Dixon
○   *S; for competitors in classic (car) rallies
M   c 2,500 i

Classical Association   (CA)   1904
■   Senate House, Malet St, LONDON, WC1E 7HU.   (hq)
        020 7862 8706   fax 020 7255 2297
        email office@classicalassociation.org
        http://www.classicalassociation.org
        Hon Sec: Dr D Cairns,   Admin: Miss Clare L Roberts
▲   Registered Charity
○   *E, *L; promotion of awareness of & education in, the Classics
        & the ancient world
●   Conf - Publishing
<   Jt Assn of Classical Teachers
M   3,875 i, 70 f, UK / 700 i, 170 f, o'seas
¶   Classical Review (Jnl) - 2; £31 m, £88 nm.
        Classical Quarterly - 2; £29 m, £81 nm.
        Greece & Rome - 2; £25 m, £69 nm.

Clay Pigeon Shooting Association Ltd   (CPSA)   1928
- ■ Edmonton House, Bisley Camp, Brookwood, WOKING, Surrey, GU24 0NP.   (hq)
  01483 485400   fax 01483 485410
  email info@cpsa.co.uk   http://www.cpsa.co.uk
  Chief Exec Officer: Phil Boakes
- ▲ Company Limited by Guarantee
- ○ *S; national governing body for the sport of clay target shooting in England
- ● Mtgs - ET - Exam - Exhib - Comp - Inf - LG
- < Intl Clay Target Shooting Coun (ICTSC); Intl Shooting U (UIT); C'wealth Shooting Fedn (CSF); Fédn Intle de Tir aux Armes Sportives de Chasse; Brit Shooting Sports Coun
- M 26,065 i, 170 f, 380 clubs, UK / 2,000 i, 30 org, o'seas
- ¶ Pull! - 10; ftm, £2 nm.

Clay Pipe Development Association Ltd   (CPDA)   1965
- NR Tree Tops, Bellingdon, CHESHAM, Bucks, HP5 2XL.   (hq)
  01494 791456   fax 01494 792378
  email cpda@aol.com   http://www.cpda.co.uk
  Sec & Consultant: L W Richardson
- ▲ Company Limited by Guarantee
- ○ *T; to foster the design, manufacture & sale of vitrified clay sewer & drain pipes & fittings, ducts for services & related products through research, representation, technical literature & direct advice
- ● ET - Res - Inf - LG
- < Eur Clay Pipe Fedn (FEUGRES)
- M 15 f
- ¶ Technical publications on clay pipes, relevant standards, design & construction of drains & sewers; list available.

Clay Roof Tile Council   (CRTC)
- NR Federation House, Station Rd, STOKE-ON-TRENT, Staffs, ST4 2SA.   (hq)
  01782 744631   fax 01782 744102
  email bcc@ceramfed.co.uk   http://www.clayroof.co.uk
  Sec: A McRae
- ▲ Un-incorporated Society
- ○ *T
- ● Mtgs - Exhib - Inf
- < Brit Ceramic Confedn
- M 7 f
- ¶ Promotional matter.

CLÉ: the Irish Book Publishers' Association   (CL)É   1970
- IRL 25 Denzille Lane, DUBLIN 2, Republic of Ireland.
  353 (1) 639 4868
  email info@publishingireland.com
  http://www.publishingireland.com
  Admin: Jolly Ronan
- ○ *T
- < Fedn Eur Pubrs; Intl Pubrs Assn

CLEANAIR - Campaign for a Smoke-Free Environment (CLEANAIR)   1972
- NR 33 Stillness Rd, LONDON, SE23 1NG.   (dir/p/b)
  020 8690 4649
  http://www.ezme.com/cleanair/
  Hon Dir: Biman Mullick
- ○ *K; to restore the basic human right to breathe clean air, free from unnecessary & avoidable pollution created by smoke from tobacco & other substances; to implement policies on 'smoking at work & in public places'
- M c 1,200 i
- ¶ Posters.   Various publications (sae for list).

Cleaning & Hygiene Suppliers' Association Ltd   (CHSA)   1979
- ■ PO Box 770, MARLOW, Bucks, SL7 2SH.   (sb)
  01628 478273   fax 01628 478286
  email secretary@chsa.co.uk   http://www.chsa.co.uk
  Gen Sec: Graham G Fletcher
- ▲ Company Limited by Guarantee
- ○ *T; to represent manufacturers & distributors / suppliers to the cleaning industry
- ● Mtgs - Res - Stat - Inf
- < Intl Sanitary Supply Assn; Brit Cleaning Coun
- M 200 f
- ¶ AR; free.

Cleaning & Support Services Association   (CSSA)   1967
- NR Warnford Court, 29 Throgmorton St, LONDON, EC2N 2AT.   (hq)
  020 7920 9632   fax 020 7256 9630
  http://www.cleaningindustry.org
  Dir Gen: Andrew Large
- ▲ Company Limited by Guarantee
- ○ *T
- Gp Membership; Marketing; Employment; Standards
- ● Conf - Mtgs - Exhib - Comp - SG - Stat - Inf - LG
- < Wld Fedn of Bldg Services Contrs (WFBSC); Eur Fedn of Cleaning Inds (EFCI)
- M 250 f, UK / 6 f, o'seas
- ¶ The Supporter (NL) - 12;   LM - 1; both ftm only.
  Code of Practice;   Membership Benefits;
  How to Profit from Contracting out;
  It Makes Sense to Choose a Member of the CSSA; all free.

Cleft Lip & Palate Association   (CLAPA)   1979
- NR Green Man Tower (1st floor), 332 Goswell Rd, LONDON, EC1V 7LQ.   (hq)
  020 7833 4883
  http://www.clapa.com
  Chief Exec: Gareth Davies
- ▲ Registered Charity
- Br 40
- ○ *W; to provide advice & support to the parents of cleft lip &/or palate children & subsequently to the children themselves; to encourage research into craniofacial abnormalities
- ● Mtgs - ET - Res - Inf - VE - Holds stocks of feeding equipment
- < Contact-a-Family
- M [not stated]
- ¶ Clapanews & AR - 1; ftm only.
  Publication list available on receipt of SAE.

Cleveland Agricultural & Horticultural Society   1974
- ■ Stewart Park, The Grove, Marton, MIDDLESBROUGH, TS7 8AR.
  01642 312231   fax 01642 300276
  Sec: Mrs M Dale
- ○ *F, *H; to hold the annual Cleveland Show on 4th Saturday in July
- M 75 i

Cleveland Bay Horse Society   (CBHS)   1884
- NR York Livestock Centre, Murton, YORK, YO19 5GF.   (hq)
  01904 489731   fax 01904 489782
  http://www.clevelandbay.com
  Hon Sec: J F Stephenson
- ▲ Registered Charity
- ○ *B; preservation & promotion of Britain's only clean legged native breed of horse
- < sister socs in Australia & North America
- M c 250 i, 1 f, UK / c 50 i, o'seas
- ¶ NL - 3/4; ftm only.   Magazine - 1; ftm, £5 nm.
  Stud Book - 3 yrly; £15-£25.

Clinical Contract Research Association   (CCRA)   1988
NR   PO Box 1055, OADBY, Leics, LE2 4XZ.   (admin/b)
     0116-271 9727   fax 0116-271 3155
     Dir of Operations: S N Dilks
Br   15; Belgium, Netherlands
○   *T; clinical research organisations
●   Conf - ET
M   15 f, UK / 2 f, o'seas
✕   2004 (replaced) Association of Independent Clinical Research
     Contractors

Clinical Dental Technicians Association   (CDTA)   1949
NR   12 Upper St North, NEW ASH GREEN, Kent, DA3 8JR.   (hq)
     01474 879430   fax 01474 872086
     email cdta@btinternet.com   http://www.cdta.org.uk
     Chief Exec: Christopher James Allen
▲   Un-incorporated Society
Br   4
○   *T; to establish a class of denturists recruited, trained &
     qualified from amongst experienced dental technicians to
     supply dentures directly to the public
●   Conf - Mtgs - ET - Exam - Exhib - SG - Inf - LG
<   Intl Fedn of Denturists; Denturist Assn Canada
M   140 i
¶   NL - 4; free.

Clinical Genetics Society
     is a group of **British Society for Human Genetics**

Clinical Molecular Genetics Society
     a group of the **British Society for Human Genetics**

Cloth Insignia Research & Collectors Society
     see **Military Heraldry Society (the Cloth Insignia Research &
     Collectors Society)**

Cloth Merchants Association   1934
■   c/o H Lesser & Sons (London) Ltd, Unit, A 43-53 Markfield Rd,
     LONDON, N15 4QA.   (sb)
     020 8275 6400   fax 020 8275 6401
     Sec: David Lesser
▲   Company Limited by Guarantee
○   *T
●   Conf - Mtgs - Exhib - Expt - Inf - LG
M   10 f

Clothing Interest Group
     a group of the **Defence Manufacturers Association**

Club Cricket Conference   (CCC)   1915
NR   38 Hampton Rd, TWICKENHAM, Middx, TW2 5QB.   (hq)
     020 8336 0586   fax 0870 143 2824
     email ccc@club-cricket.com
     http://www.club-cricket.com
     Hon Operations Mgr: Simon Dyson
○   *N, *S; 'wide ranging representational, advisory, procurement,
     legal & other support services for over 1,500 recreational
     cricket clubs & league members throughout the south /
     south-east / Home Counties of England & Wales'
●   Overseas tours
<   Eur Cricket Coun; E&W Cricket Bd; League Cricket Conf
>   Assn Cricket Umpires & Scorers (ACUS); Nat Playing Fields
     Assn (NPFA)
M   312 i, 6 f, 1,500 clubs & leagues, UK / 1 f, o'seas
¶   Extra Cover (Jnl) - 4.
     CCC Ybk - 1.

Clun Forest Sheep Breeders' Society Ltd   1925
NR   Guifron Bank, Beguildy, KNIGHTON, Powys, LD7 1UD.   (hsb)
     01547 510342
     Sec: Diana Lavers
▲   Registered Charity
○   *B
M   180 i, UK / 2 i, o'seas
¶   Flock Book - 1; ftm.   Hbk - 3/4 yrly; free.

Clydesdale Horse Society   (CHS)   1870
NR   Kinclune, Kingoldrum, KIRRIEMUIR, Angus, DD8 5HX.   (hsp)
     01575 570900
     email secy@clydesdalehorse.co.uk
     http://www.clydesdalehorse.co.uk
     Sec: Marguerite Osborne
▲   Registered Charity
○   *B
●   Mtgs
M   700 i, UK / 50 i, o'seas
¶   NL - 4.   Stud Book - 1.

CMT United Kingdom   1986
■   PO Box 5089, CHRISTCHURCH, Dorset, BH23 7ZX.   (hsp)
     0870 774 4314
     email secretary@cmt.org.uk   http://www.cmt.org.uk
     Sec: Mrs Karen Butcher
▲   Company Limited by Guarantee; Registered Charity
Br   10
○   *W; to offer support, advice & information to people affected by
     the common (though little known) neuro-muscular condition
     called Charcot-Marie-Tooth disease
●   Conf - Inf
<   Genetic Interest Gp; Neurological Alliance
M   1,200 i, UK / c 100 i, o'seas
¶   Comment (NL) - 4; £10.50 m only.   AR - 1; ftm.
✕   2001 (April) CMT International UK

Co-Dependents Anonymous   (CoDA)   1989
■   PO Box 2365, BRISTOL, BS6 9XJ.   (mail/address)
     0700 026 3645
     email coda_uk@hotmail.com   http://www.coda-uk.org
▲   Un-incorporated Society
Br   52
○   *W; is an informal fellowship (based on Alcoholics Anonymous)
     of men & women whose common problem is a difficulty in
     maintaining functional relationships, with themselves &
     others as a result of co-dependency in their lives. The
     organisation uses the Twelve Steps & Traditions, as used by
     the AA, as a central part of its suggested programme of
     recovery from co-dependency & for building healthy
     relationships in a safe & confidential environment
●   Mtgs
M   i
¶   NL - 6;   Meeting List; both free.
     Information Leaflets & Step Leaflets.

Co-operatives UK Ltd   1869
NR   Holyoake House, Hanover St, MANCHESTER, M60 0AS.   (hq)
     0161-246 2900   fax 0161-831 7684
     email enquiries@cooperatives-uk.coop
     http://www.cooperatives-uk.coop
     Chief Exec: Dame Pauline Green
▲   An Industrial & Provident Society
Br   3
○   *T, *Z; national representational, promotional & advisory body
     for consumer co-operatives in the UK
●   Conf - ET - Exhib - Stat - Inf - LG - Legal registration of co-
     operatives & other social enterprises & charities
<   Intl Co-op Alliance
M   50 i, 450 f, 100 org
¶   Co-operatives - 3;   AR; both free.
     Co-operatives UK Briefing - 12; ftm only.
✕   2001 (Co-operative Union
     (Industrial Common Ownership Movement

Coach & Bus First Aid Association (CABFAA) 1930
NR 11 Chertsey Rd, WINDLESHAM, Surrey, GU20 6EN. (hsp)
        07721 457735
        Hon Sec: David Crew,   Pres: Joe Mackie
▲ Un-incorporated Society
Br 80
○ *W; first aid advice to the coach & bus industry
Gp Voluntary first aid training
● ET - Comp - Inf - LG - Keeping members aware of current
        legislation
< Bus & Coach Coun
M 2,000 i, 80 f
¶ CABFAA NL - 4; free.

Coach Operators Federation (COF) 1955
■ Oakwood, Radway, SIDMOUTH, Devon, EX10 8TW.
        0776 884 6138   fax 01395 513508
        http://www.cofed.net
        Sec: Ted Reece
▲ Un-incorporated Society
○ *T
● Mtgs - VE - Empl - LG
M 5 i, 42 f, UK / 1 i, o'seas

Coach Tourism Council (CTC) 1989
NR PO Box 750, OLNEY, Beds, MK46 5WZ. (hq)
        0870 850 2839
        email info@coachtourismcouncil.co.uk
        http://www.coachtourismcouncil.co.uk
        Chief Exec: Graham Beacom
▲ Un-incorporated Society
○ *T; promotion of travel & tourism by coach
● Conf - Mtgs - ET - Res - Exhib - VE
< Confedn of Passenger Transport; Visit Britain / London /
        England; Tourism Alliance
M 400 f, UK / 23 f, o'seas
¶ NL - 6; ftm only.   Ybk - 1; ftm, £40 nm.

** Coaching Club
        Organisation lost: see Introduction paragraph 3

**Coal Merchants Association of Scotland Ltd   (CMAS Ltd)
1913**
■ PO Box 9224, KILMACOLM, Renfrewshire, PA13 4YP.
        (mail/address)
        01505 874389   fax 01505 874389
        email norrie.johnstone@btinternet.com
        Sec: Norman Johnstone
▲ Company Limited by Guarantee
○ *T
● Mtgs - SG
< Solid Fuel Assn; Coal Merchants Fedn (GB) Ltd
M 130 i
¶ AR.

Coal Merchants Federation (Great Britain) Ltd   (CMF) 1934
■ 7 Swanwick Court, ALFRETON, Derbys, DE55 7AS. (hq)
        01773 835400   fax 01773 834351
        email cmf@solidfuel.co.uk
        http://www.coalmerchants.co.uk
        Gen Sec: Mrs J Heginbotham
▲ Company Limited by Guarantee
Br 13
○ *T
● Mtgs - ET - Res - Stat - Inf - LG
< Solid Fuel Assn
M 850 f
¶ Coal Trader - 4; free.

Coalition for Medical Progress (CMP) 2003
NR Waterloo Business Centre, 117 Waterloo Rd, LONDON,
        SE1 8UL. (hq)
        020 7921 0080
        email info@medicalprogress.org
        http://www.medicalprogress.org
        Dir: Jo Tanner
▲ Un-incorporated Society
○ *Q, *T; communications & public relations concerning the
        advancement of medicine via research
● Conf - ET - Inf
M 14 f, 16 org
¶ Publicity / Explanatory booklets.

Coble & Keelboat Society (CKS) 1987
■ 20 The Green, SALTBURN-BY-THE-SEA, Cleveland,
        TS12 1NF. (hsp)
        01287 623661
        http://www.coble-keelboatsociety.org
        Hon Gen Sec: A Edgar Readman
▲ Un-incorporated Society
○ *G; preservation of traditional working boats of the North East
        coast of England
Gp Preservers; Historians; Researchers
● Mtgs - Inf
< Sailing Smack Assn; 40+ Fishing Boat Assn; Bridlington Sailing
        Coble Presvn Soc; Sunderland Marine Sports Club; W Wales
        Maritime Heritage Soc
M 180 i, 400 org, 1 assn, UK / 6 i, o'seas
¶ The Coble & Keelboat Society (Jnl) - 2; ftm, 50p nm.
        Coblegram (NL) - 4; ftm only.

Cockatiel Society
        a member body of the **Society for the Protection of Aviculture**

Cockburn Association - The Edinburgh Civic Trust   1875
NR 55 High St, Trunks Close, EDINBURGH, EH1 1SR. (hq)
        0131-557 8686   fax 0131-557 9387
        Dir: David McDonald
○ *K; protection of the beauty of Edinburgh by the
        encouragement of enlightened planning & the preservation
        of good buildings of all ages
M c 1,200 i

Cocoa Association of London Ltd
        since 2003 **Federation of Cocoa Commerce**

Coeliac Society of Ireland
IRL 4 North Brunswick St, DUBLIN 7, Republic of Ireland
        353 (1) 872 1471   fax 353 (1) 873 5737
        email coeliac@iol.ie   http://www.coeliac.ie
        Sec: Mary Thowig-Murray
○ *W

Coeliac UK 1968
NR Suites A-D Octagon Court, HIGH WYCOMBE, Bucks,
        HP11 2HS. (hq)
        01494 437278   fax 01494 474349
        email admin@coeliac.co.uk   http://www.coeliac.co.uk
        Chief Exec: Sarah Sleet
○ *W; to support the health, welfare & rights of coeliacs & those
        with dermatitis herpetiformis (DH); to promote & commission
        research into causes, alleviation, treatment, care & cure of
        these conditions; to educate the public & those in the
        appropriate sectors of health, government, commerce &
        industry
M 50,000 i
¶ Crossed Grain Magazine - 3.
        Food & Drinks Directory of the United Kingdom - 1.
        Publications list available.
✕ 2001 (July) Coeliac Society

Coffee Trade Federation   (CTF)   1949
NR   Blackfriars Foundry, 156 Blackfriars Rd, LONDON, SE1 8EN.
    (hq)
    020 7328 5222   fax 020 7328 5444
    email secretariat@coffeetradefederation.org.uk
    http://www.coffeetradefederation.org.uk
    Sec: Chris Rogers
▲   Company Limited by Guarantee
○   *T; interests of importers, dealers, brokers & roasters
●   Mtgs - Inf - Arbitration
<   C'ee Eur Coffee Assn; Eur Fedn of Assns of Coffee Roasters
M   c 60 f

**Cognition: the Campaign for Qualified Politicians
(Cognition)   1998**
■   96 Broomfield Rd, SWANSCOMBE, Kent, DA10 0LT.   (asa)
○   *K; 'we believe that a new political qualification, covering
    business & financial studies, national & international current
    affairs & general knowledge, should become compulsory for
    all those wishing to stand for Parliament - such a
    qualification only being obtainable through involvement in
    the foregoing'
●   Mtgs - Stat - Lib
M   i, f & org

Coir Association   1956
■   1 Gate Lodge Way, Noak Bridge, LAINDON, Essex,
    SS15 4AR.   (asa)
    01268 532797   fax 01268 272549
    email coirassociation@tiscali.co.uk
    Sec: David G Sunderland
○   *T; coir & allied products
●   Mtgs
M   4 f, UK / 8 f, o'seas
¶   LM - 1;   Panel of arbitrators;   AR; all ftm.

Coke Oven Managers Association   (COMA)   1915
NR   c/o Universal Contractors Ltd, Strata Industrial
    Estate,Rotherham Rd - Dinnington, SHEFFIELD, S25 3RG.
    (hsb)
    01909 518778   fax 01909 518838
    email stratag@aol.com
    Hon Gen Sec: R G Sargent
▲   Un-incorporated Society
Br   3 sections UK; 1 o'seas
○   *P; the science & technology of coal carbonisation, the recovery
    & chemical processing of by-products & peripheral
    technologies
Gp   Editorial c'ee
●   Conf - Mtgs - Stat - Inf
M   i & f
¶   Bulletin - 2; ftm.   COMA Ybk (incl LM); ftm.
    Technical publications; prices vary.

Cold Rolled Sections Association   (CRSA)   1946
NR   The National Metalforming Centre, 47 Birmingham Rd,
    WEST BROMWICH, W Midlands, B70 6PY.   (sb)
    0121-601 6350   fax 0121-601 6373
    http://www.crsauk.com
○   *T; to sponsor research & promote use of cold rolled sections
●   Mtgs - Res - Inf

Cold Storage & Distribution Federation   (CSDF)   1911
■   Downmill Rd, BRACKNELL, Berks, RG12 1GH.   (hq)
    01344 869533   fax 01344 869527
    email info@csdF.org.uk   http://www.csdf.org.uk
    Chief Exec: John Hutchings
▲   Company Limited by Guarantee
○   *T; represents & covers all aspects of temperature-controlled
    storage & distribution in the UK; it includes both frozen &
    chilled sectors
●   Conf - Inf - LG
M   150 f
¶   NL - 4; free.   Information Broadsheet - 12; ftm only.
    Guide/Directory - 2 yrly; ftm, £35 nm.
    RFIC Fire Prevention Guide; ftm, £43 nm.
    RFIC Storage & Handling of Frozen Foods; ftm, £12 nm.
    RFIC Guidance on the Assessment of Fire Risk; ftm, £17 nm.
    CSDF Material Handling Safety Guide; ftm, £50 nm.
    CSDF Fire Risk Minimisation Guidance; ftm, £75 nm.
    CSDF Business Continuity Guide; ftm, £50 nm.

Cold War Research Group
    is a group of **Subterranea Britannica**

College of Emergency Medicine   (CEM)   1993
■   Churchill House, 35 Red Lion Square, LONDON,
    WC1R 4SG.   (hq)
    020 7405 7071   fax 020 7405 0318
    email cem@emergencymedicine.uk.net
    http://www.emergencymed.org.uk/cem
    Registrar: Dr Ruth Brown
▲   Company Limited by Guarantee; Registered Charity
○   *E, *M; the college has responsibility for the training &
    academic standards of the speciality of emergency medicine
●   Conf - ET - Exam - Res - LG
M   1,700 i, UK / 200 i, o'seas
×   2005-06 Faculty of Accident & Emergency Medicine

College of Occupational Therapists
    part of the **British Association of Occupational Therapists**

College of Optometrists   (BCO)   1980
NR   41-42 Craven St, LONDON, WC2N 5NG.   (hq)
    020 7839 6000   fax 020 7839 6800
    email optometry@college-optometrists.com
    Chief Exec: Bryony Pawinska
▲   Registered Charity
○   *P; 'awards the sole registrable qualification in optometry in the
    UK'
Gp   Applied Vision Association
●   Conf - Mtgs - ET - Exam - Res - Inf - Lib - Museum
<   Wld Coun of Optometry
M   c 6,500 i
¶   Ophthalmic & Physiological Optics - 4; ftm.
    NL; m only.   AR.

College of Piping   1944
NR   16-24 Otago St, GLASGOW, G12 8JH.   (hq)
    0141-334 3587   fax 0141-587 6068
    Principal: Robert Wallace
▲   Registered Charity
Br   1; Canada, Japan, USA
○   *D, *E; the teaching of the Highland Bagpipe; dissemination of
    information on piping
●   Conf - Mtgs - ET - Exam - Res - Comp - Inf - Lib
M   200 i, UK / 100 i, o'seas
¶   The Piping Times - 12.

College of Teachers 1849
NR 57 Gordon Square, LONDON, WC1H 0NU. (hq)
    020 7947 9536 fax 020 7947 9536
    email info@cot.ac.uk http://www.cot.ac.uk
    Chief Exec & Registrar: Prof Ray Page
▲ Registered Charity
○ *E, *P; to promote sound learning & advance the interests of
    education
Gp Primary education; Secondary education; F/HE
● Conf - Mtgs - ET - Exam
M 2,000 i, 100 schools, 20 org, UK / 200 i, 2 f, 12 org, o'seas
¶ Education Today (Jnl) - 4; ftm, from £110 yr nm.
    NL - 4; ftm only (incl AR).

Colloquium for Scottish Medieval & Renaissance Studies 1958
■ 101 Sibsey St, LANCASTER, LA1 5DQ. (hsp)
    email ross@tjellicoe.fsnet.co.uk.uk
    Hon Sec: Dr Ross Trench-Jellicoe
▲ Scottish Charity
○ *L; to further the study of the medieval & renaissance history of
    Scotland; to enable scholars with an interest to meet &
    exchange information; to make representation to
    government, academic & voluntary bodies
● Conf - SG - LG - Organisation of teams of scholars to publish
    books of use to students & scholars in the subject area
M 230 i, UK / 218 i, o'seas

Colour Group (Great Britain) (CGGB) 1940
■ c/o Applied Vision Research Centre, The City University,
    LONDON, EC1V 7DD. (mail/address)
    email colourgroupgb@city.ac.uk
    http://www.colour.org.uk
    Hon Sec: Prof Lindsay MacDonald
▲ Registered Charity
○ *L; to encourage the study of colour in all its aspects; to
    promote education of the public in the field of colour; to
    further research into the uses of colour in art & science
● Conf - Mtgs - ET - Res - Exhib - Comp - Inf - Travel awards for
    students of colour - Mtgs are at the above address
< Assn Intle de la Couleur (AIC); Commission Intle de
    l'Eclairage (CIE); Intl Soc of Colour Couns (ISCC)
M 162 i, 14 f, UK / 19 i, o'seas
¶ NL - 12; ftm only.

Coloured Horse & Pony Society (CHAPS(UK)) 1983
NR 1 McLaren Cottages, Abertysswg, Rhymney, TREDEGAR, Gwent,
    NP22 5BH. (hsp)
    01685 845045 fax 01685 845045
    email admin@chapsuk.datanet.co.uk
    http://www.chapsuk.com
    Sec: Miss Lorraine Amor
▲ Company Limited by Guarantee
○ *B
● Shows - Issuing passports to horses - Studbook - Performance
    award scheme
< Brit Horse Soc; Central Prefix Register
M 1,200 i, UK / 12 i, o'seas
¶ A World of Colour - 3.

Combined Cadet Force Association (CCFA) 1952
■ Holderness House, 51-61 Clifton St, LONDON EC2A 4OW.
    (hq)
    020 77426 8377 fax 020 7426 8378
    email acfa@armycadets.com
    http://www.armycadets.com
    Sec: Brig M Wharmby
▲ Company Limited by Guarantee; Registered Charity
Br 280
○ *Y; a national youth organisation working in schools to develop
    leadership, citizenship & self belief; for young men & women
    aged 13-18
● Comp - Mtgs - ET - Comp - Stat - Inf - LG
M 50,000 i
¶ Ybk - 1; AR - 1; both free.

Combined Edible Nut Trade Association (CENTA) 1970
■ 62 Wilson St, LONDON, EC2A 2BU. (asa)
    020 7782 0007 fax 020 7782 0939
    email treenuts@compuserve.com
    Sec: D G Sunderland
○ *T
Gp Almonds; Brazil nuts; Cashews; Hazelnuts; Pistachios; Walnuts
M 27 f, UK / 17 f, o'seas

Combined Heat & Power Association (CHPA) 1968
NR 35-37 Grosvenor Gardens, LONDON, SW1W 0BS. (hq)
    020 7828 4077 fax 020 7828 0310
    email info@chpa.co.uk http://www.chpa.co.uk
    Dir: Phillip Piddington
▲ Company Limited by Guarantee
○ *T; to promote energy efficiency & environmental improvement
    through the provision of integrated energy services & the
    wider use of combined heat, power & community heating
● Conf - Mtgs - Inf - Lib - LG
M 15 i, 100 f
¶ CHPA Ybk; £35.
    Publications list available.

Combustion Engineering Association (CEA) 1932
NR 1a Clarke St, Ely Bridge, CARDIFF, Glam, CF5 5AL. (hq)
    029 2040 0670 fax 029 2055 5542
    http://www.cea.org.uk
    Dir: David Arnold
▲ Registered Charity
○ *L, *Q; to further the cause of combustion engineering
Gp Steam users; Combustion fuels & emissions
● Conf - Mtgs - ET - Res - SG - Inf - LG
M 40 i, 50 f, UK / 3 i, o'seas
¶ CEA NL - 4; Steam Users Group NL - 4; both ftm only.

Comics Creators Guild (CCG) 1977
NR 22 St James' Mansions, West End Lane, LONDON,
    NW6 2AA. (mail) address
    Sec: Ben Counter
▲ Un-incorporated Society
○ *P; for those working in the comic strip or graphic narrative
    medium; to promote this medium as an art form

Commemorative Collectors Society (CCS) 1972
■ Lumless House, Gainsborough Rd, WINTHORPE, Newark,
    Notts, NG24 2NR. (hsp)
    01636 671377
    Hon Sec: Steven N Jackson
▲ Un-incorporated Society
○ *A, *G; to research, publish & offer advice & information to
    members & manufacturers, on the design & issuing of all
    'popular' commemorative items made from glass, ceramics,
    metal, wovens, paper & all printed materials etc
● Mtgs - ET - Res - Exhib - Stat - Inf - Lib - LG
M 3,619 i, 36 f, UK / 1,391 i, 22 f, o'seas
¶ Jnl - 4; ftm. Review - irreg.

Commemoratives Museum Trust (CMT) 2003
■ Lumless House, 77 Gainsborough Rd, Winthorpe, NEWARK,
    Notts, NG24 2NR. (hq)
    01636 671377
    Chief Exec: Steven N Jackson
▲ Registered Charity
○ *A; to maintain & display a collection of commemorative items
    for information of private collectors, designers & historians
● ET - Res - Exhib - Inf
M 489 i, UK / 218 i, o'seas

Comment on Reproductive Ethics (CORE)
NR PO Box 4593, LONDON, SW3 6XE.
    020 7581 2623 fax 020 7581 3868
    http://www.corethics.org

© CBD Research Ltd · Beckenham · BR3 5JS · Tel 020 8650 7745 · Fax 020 8650 0768 · E-mail cbd@cbdresearch.com · www.cbdresearch.com

Commercial Bar Association   (COMBAR)
NR   3 Verulam Buildings, LONDON, WC1R 5NT.
     020 7404 2022   fax 020 7404 2088
○   *P
M   598 i

Commercial Boat Operators Association   (CBOA)   1989
NR   1 Plumstead Avenue, Bradwell Common, MILTON KEYNES,
     Bucks, MK13 8AE.   (hsp)
     01908 236261
     Gen Sec: Tony Boston
▲   Un-incorporated Society
○   *T; the maintenance & furtherance of cargo carrying by inland
     waterway
●   Mtgs - ET - Inf - LG - Trade furtherance
M   130 i, 20 f
¶   NL - 4; ftm only.
✕   1999 Commercial Narrowboat Operators Association

Commercial Coarse Fisheries Association
     since 2005-06 **Professional Coarse Fisheries Association**

Commercial Farmers Group   1998
■   Church House, Horkstow, BARTON UPON HUMBER, Lincs,
     DN18 6BG.
     01652 618329   fax 01652 618447
     email henry@horkstow.freeserve.co.uk
     Chmn: H R Fell
▲   Un-incorporated Society
○   *F; 'agricultural politics'
●   Mtgs - LG - Media relations
M   17 i

Commercial Horticultural Association   (CHA)   1978
■   Stoneleigh Park, KENILWORTH, Warks, CV8 2LG.   (asa)
     024 7669 0330   fax 024 7669 0334
     email info@cha-hort.com   http://www.cha-hort.com
     Hon Sec: Dr Chris Wood,   Expt Promoter: Peter Grimbly
▲   Un-incorporated Society
○   *T; for manufacturers & suppliers of equipment, products &
     services to the commercial horticultural industry worldwide
●   Conf - Exhib - Expt - Lib - LG
M   120 f
¶   NL - 5; ftm only.
     Buyers' Guide: association details, members & what they
     provide - 1; free (also on website).

Commercial Radio Companies Association   (CRCA)   1973
NR   77 Shaftesbury Ave, LONDON, W1D 5DU.   (hq)
     020 7306 2603   fax 020 7470 0062
     email info@crca.co.uk   http://www.crca.co.uk
     Chmn: Lord John Eatwell
▲   Company Limited by Guarantee
○   *T; for commercial radio, representing UK commercial radio to
     government, the Regulator & the media
●   Conf - Mtgs - Res - LG - Negotiation with copyright bodies
<   Assn Eur des Radios
M   255 f
¶   Bulletin - 26; ftm only.   LM - updated; free.

Commercial Trailer Association   (CTA)   1980
NR   Forbes House, Halkin St, LONDON, SW1X 7DS.   (hq)
     020 7235 7000
     Sec: Robin Dickeson
▲   Un-incorporated Society
○   *T; interests of manufacturers of heavy trailers
Gp   Council; Technical c'ee
●   Mtgs - Exhib - Stat - Expt - Inf
<   Eur Trailer Constructors C'ee (CLCCR); Soc of Motor Mfrs &
     Traders (SMMT)
M   10 f
¶   LM;   AR; both ftm only.

Commissioning Specialists Association   (CSA)   1990
■   14 West St, HORSHAM, W Sussex, RH12 1PB.   (hq)
     01403 754133   fax 01403 754134
     email office@csa.org.uk   http://www.csa.org.uk
     Sec: Julie Parker
▲   Un-incorporated Society
○   *T; for commissioning specialists within the construction industry
Gp   Commissioning for: Heating & ventilation, Air conditioning,
     Refrigeration
●   ET - Inf
M   208 i, 54 f, UK / 20 i, 4 f, o'seas
¶   Index (NL) - 4.   LM.   Guidance Notes.
     Commissioning Engineers Compendium; £12.50 m, £16 nm.
     Technical Memoranda; £7.50 m, £10 nm.

COMMITTEE . . .
     For details of official & non-official committees, other than the
     following, see the companion volume **'Councils, Committees &**
     Boards'

Committee on the Administration of Justice   (CAJ)   1981
■   45-47 Donegall St, BELFAST, BT1 2BR.   (hq)
     028 9096 1122   fax 028 9024 6706
     email info@caj.org.uk   http://www.caj.org.uk
     Dir: Maggie Beirne
▲   Company Limited by Guarantee
○   *G, *K; works for a just & peaceful society in Northern Ireland
     where the human rights of all are protected
●   Conf - ET - Res - Inf - Lib - Campaigning, lobbying & advising
<   Intl Fedn for Human Rights
M   180 i, 40 org, UK / 120 i, o'seas
¶   AR - 1.
     Publications list available.

Committee of Registered Clubs Associations   (CORCA)   1983
■   253-254 Upper St, LONDON, N1 1RY.   (hq)
     020 7226 0221   fax 020 7354 1847
     Sec: Kevin Smyth
○   *N; 'for separate club organisations who meet regularly for
     mutual benefit'
●   Mtgs - Stat - Empl - LG
M   8,000,000 i, 6 org
¶   CORCA-NJIC Wages Booklet - 1; 20p m, £2 nm.
     All Parliamentary Party Progress Report - 1; £2.

**Commons, Open Spaces & Footpaths Preservation Society
(Open Spaces Society)   1865**
■   25a Bell St, HENLEY-ON-THAMES, Oxon, RG9 2BA.   (hq)
     01491 573535   fax 01491 573051
     email hq@oss.org.uk   http://www.oss.org.uk
     Gen Sec: Miss Kate Ashbrook
▲   Registered Charity
○   *K; to create & conserve common land, village greens, open
     spaces & rights of public access, in town & country, in
     England & Wales
●   Inf
M   2,460 i, local & national org, amenity groups, etc
¶   Open Space (Jnl) - 3; ftm only.
     Our Common Land (book); £14 m, £25 nm.
     Various other leaflets & publications.
     Note: the registered title of this organisation is Commons,
     Open Spaces & Footpaths Preservation Society; it is now
     better known under the title of Open Spaces Society

Commonwealth Games Federation
     A holding organisation with most of the activity carried out by
     individual country associations

Communication Managers Association
     in 2003 became **AMICUS CMA Section**

Communication Workers Union   (CWU)   1995
NR   150 The Broadway, LONDON, SW19 1RX.   (hq)
     020 8971 7200   fax 020 8971 7300
     http://www.cwu.org
     Gen Sec: Billy Hayes
○   *U; for people working in the postal & telecommunications
     industries
●   Conf - ET - Res - Stat - Lib - Empl - LG
<   U Network Intl; Labour Party; Trades U Congress
M   300,000 i
¶   Voice - 10; ftm.

Communications Management Association   (CMA)   1958
■   Ranmore House, The Crescent, LEATHERHEAD, Surrey,
     KT22 8DY.   (hq)
     01372 361234   fax 01372 810810
     email cma@thecma.com   http://www.thecma.com
     Chief Exec: Glenn Powell
▲   Company Limited by Guarantee; Registered Charity
Br   3
○   *P; to represent companies who are significant users of
     communications systems & professional individuals who have
     responsibility, or manage,these systems in commerce,
     industry or public sector
Gp   Billing & information management; Business continuity; Contact
     centres; Mobility; Network services; Regulation; Risk &
     security
●   Conf - Mtgs - ET - Res - LG
<   Intl Telecoms User Gp (INTUG)
M   1,500 i, 120 f
¶
     Newsline (feature articles) - 6;
     Roundup (news of high importance) - 6;
       both are ftm and by email only.

Community   1917
■   Swinton House, 324 Gray's Inn Rd, LONDON, WC1X 8DD.
     (hq)
     020 7239 1200   fax 020 7278 8378
     email info@community-tu.org
     http://www.community-tu.org
     Gen Sec: M Leahy
Br   480
○   *U; covering all aspects of the steel, metals, knitwear, apparel,
     footwear industries & blind & disabled workers
●   Conf - Mtgs - ET - Res - Stat - Inf - Empl - LG
×   2004 (Iron & Steel Trades Confederation
         (National Union of Knitwear, Footwear & Apparel
           Trades

Community Composting Network
■   67 Alexandra Rd, SHEFFIELD, S Yorks, S2 3EE.
     0114-258 0483
     http://www.communitycompost.org.uk
○   *H, *K, *N; promotes community composting at a national level
     & through local groups
●   Conf - Inf - Lib - LG
M   230 org
¶   The Growing Heap - 4.   Guide to Community Composting.

Community Development Finance Association   (cdfa)   2001
■   Hatton Square Business Centre (Room 101), 16-16a Baldwins
     Gardens, LONDON, EC1N 7RJ.
     020 7430 0222
     email info@cdfa.org.uk   http://www.cdfa.org.uk
     Chief Exec: Bernie Morgan
▲   Company Limited by Guarantee
○   *T; for community development finance institutions -
     sustainable, independent financial institutions that provide
     capital & support to enable individuals to develop & create
     wealth in disadvantaged communities or under-served
     markets
●   Conf - Mtgs - ET - LG
M   5 i, 104 f
¶   Inside Out (survey of sector) - 1; £15, £15 +postage nm.
     Enterprise Communities (wealth beyond welfare); free.
     Money-go-Round: recycling finances, realising capital.
     Community Investment Relief Guide; £10 m, £12.50 nm.
     Guide to Building a CDFI;£200 m, £200 +postage nm.

Community & District Nursing Association UK   (CDNA)   1971
NR   Walpole House, 18-22 Bond St, Ealing, LONDON, W5 5AA.
     (hq)
     020 8231 0180   fax 020 8231 0187
     http://www.cdna-online.org.uk
     Dir: Anne Duffy
Br   40
○   *P, *U
●   Conf - Mtgs - ET - Exhib - SG - Empl - LG
M   5,090 i
¶   Nursing Care - 4; ftm, £1.20 nm.   Nurse Prescribing; £3.
     Key Issues in District Nursing 1, 2 & 3; £4.   AR.
     Innovations in Primary Health Care Nursing; £5.

Community Foundation Network   1991
■   Arena House, 66-68 Pentonville Rd, LONDON, N1 9HS.   (hq)
     020 7713 9326   fax 020 7713 9327
     email network@communityfoundations.org.uk
     http://www.communityfoundations.org.uk
     Dir: Stephen Hammersley
▲   Company Limited by Guarantee; Registered Charity
○   *N; 'a support organisation for community trusts & foundations
     & those wishing to establish them in the UK'
●   Conf - Mtgs - Res - Stat - Inf - Lib - VE - LG
M   56 trusts / foundations
¶   NL - 4; ftm.
     Giving Shares & Securities: information pack for financial
       advisers; ftm.
     A Guide to European Funding; ftm.
     Community Foundations & Community Needs Assessment; ftm.
     Tackling Multiple Disadvantage; ftm.
     Changing the Future; ftm.
       Publications list available.

Community Hospitals Association   (CHA)   1969
NR   Meadow Brow, Broadway, ILMINSTER, Somerset, TA19 9RG.
     (hsb)
     01460 55951   fax 01460 53207
     Chief Exec: Mrs Barbara Moore
▲   Un-incorporated Society
○   *K, *M; promotion of community hospitals
●   Conf - Res - Stat - Inf - VE - LG
<   Assn for GP Maternity Care; Scot Assn of GP Community
     Hospitals
M   25 i, 10 org, 250 hospitals
¶   NL - 4; ftm.

Community Matters
   see **National Federation of Community Organisations**

© CBD Research Ltd · Beckenham · BR3 5JS · Tel 020 8650 7745 · Fax 020 8650 0768 · E-mail cbd@cbdresearch.com · www.cbdresearch.com

Community Media Association (CMA) 1983
- ■ 15 Paternoster Row, SHEFFIELD, S Yorks, S1 2BX.   (hq)
  0114-279 5219   fax 0114-279 8976
  email cma@commedia.org.uk
  http://www.commedia.org.uk
  Dir: Diane Reid
- ▲ Company Limited by Guarantee
- ○ *K, *N; to represent community media in the UK to
  government, regulators & industry
- ● Conf - Lib - LG
- < Wld Assn of Community Radio Broadcasters (AMARC)
- M 200 i, 300 f, UK / 10 i, 10 f, o'seas
- ¶ Airflash (Jnl) - 4; ftm only (subscription £5-£60).

Community Psychiatric Nurses' Association
  since 2003 (April) **Mental Health Nurses Association**

Community Self Build Scotland   (CSBS)
- ■ The Wright Centre, 1 Lonmay Rd, GLASGOW, G33 4EL.   (hq)
  0141-773 6214   fax 0141-773 6234
  http://www.selfbuild-scotland.org.uk
  Admin: Allison Dempster
- ▲ Company Limited by Guarantee
- ○ *G; to provide information on self-build; to work with
  individuals, housing associations & district councils to provide
  & give training on self-build schemes
- ● ET - Inf
- < SCVO
- ¶ NL - 4; free.

Community Service Volunteers   (CSV)   1962
- ■ 237 Pentonville Rd, LONDON, N1 9NJ.   (hq)
  020 7278 6601   fax 020 7833 0149
  email information@csv.org.uk   http://www.csv.org.uk
  Chief Exec: Elisabeth Hoodless
- ▲ Company Limited by Guarantee; Registered Charity
- Br 120
- ○ *W; to create opportunities for people to take an active part in
  the life of their community through volunteering, training &
  community action;Please note that CSV is NOT able to offer
  sponsorship or grants
- Gp Retired & senior volunteers programme; Full-time volunteering,
  social care up to 12 months; Employee volunteering; Social
  action broadcasting; Education consultancy; Vocational
  training
- ● Conf - ET - Res - Exhib - Inf
- M 190,000 i (per year)

Community Transport Association UK   (CTA)   1982
- ■ Highbank, Halton St, HYDE, Cheshire, SK14 2NY.
  0870 774 3586   fax 0870 774 3581
  email ctauk@communitytransport.com
  http://www.ctauk.org
  Chief Exec: Keith Halstead
- ▲ Company Limited by Guarantee; Registered Charity
- Br 7
- ○ *W; any form of non-profit transport provision for people with
  mobility problems
- Gp Dial-a-Ride; Rural transport; Community car scheme; Training
- ● Conf - Mtgs - ET - Exhib - Inf - Lib - PL - LG - Vehicle purchase
  scheme - Issue of minibus permits
- < NCVO
- M 1,250 org, UK / 10 org, o'seas
- ¶ Community Transport - 6; ftm, £21 nm.   AR; free.
  Publications list available.

** **Community & Youth Work Association**
  Organisation lost: see Introduction paragraph 3

Community & Youth Workers Union   (CYWU)   1971
- NR 302 The Argent Centre, 60 Frederick St, Hockley,
  BIRMINGHAM, B1 3HS.   (hq/nat)
  0121-244 3344   fax 0121-244 3345
  http://www.cywu.org.uk office
  Gen Sec: Doug Nicholls
- ○ *U; trade union for full & part-time youth, community & play
  workers in the statutory or voluntary sector
- ¶ Rapport - 6.

Companion Animal Behaviour Therapy Study Group
  a group of the **British Small Animal Veterinary Association**

Company Chemists Association Ltd   (CCA)   1898
- NR Regus House, Fairbourne Drive, Atterbury, MILTON KEYNES,
  MK10 9RG.   (hq)
  01908 487532   fax 01908 487870
  http://www.thecca.org.uk
  Contact: Michael Keen
- ○ *T; for all corporations engaged in the business of retail
  pharmacy
- ● Mtgs - LG
- M 8 f

Company of Goldsmiths of Dublin   1637
- IRL Assay Office, Dublin Castle, DUBLIN 2, Republic of Ireland.
  353 (1) 475 1286; 478 0323   fax 353 (1) 478 3838
  email hallmark@assay.ie
  Hon Sec: Douglas Bennett
- ○ Controls & conducts the Assay Office

Compassionate Friends   (TCF)   1969
- ■ 53 North St, BRISTOL, BS3 1EN.   (hq)
  0845 120 3785   fax 0845 120 3786
  email info@tcf.org.uk   http://www.tcf.org.uk
  Chmn: Diana Youdale
- ▲ Company Limited by Guarantee; Registered Charity
- Br Australia, Europe, New Zealand, USA
- ○ *W; to offer support & friendship to bereaved parents & their
  families through 250 local contacts
- Gp Childless parents; POMC - parents of murdered children;
  Shadow of suicide; SIBBS - support in bereavement for
  brothers & sisters
- ● Mtgs - Inf - Lib - Annual weekend gathering - Personal &
  telephone support
  Helpline: 0845 123 2304
- M 10,000 families, 100 f, 100 org, UK / 50 families, o'seas
- ¶ TCF NL - 4; £30 m only.

Complementary Medical Association   (CMA)   1995
- NR 67 Eagle Heights, The Falcons, Bramlands Close, LONDON,
  SW11 2LJ.   (hq)
  0845 129 8435
  http://www.the-cma.org.uk
  Pres: Jayney Goddard
- ▲ Un-incorporated Society
- Br 2; Bulgaria, Georgia, India, Nepal, Portugal, S Africa
- ○ *P; a register of complementary medical practitioners & training
  organisations
- ● Conf - ET - Exam - Res - Exhib - Comp - SG - Inf - VE - LG -
  Educational programmes to PhD level
- M 15,000 i (worldwide), 10 f, 3 org, UK / 3 f, o'seas
- ¶ With Our Complements - 4.

Component Obsolescence Group (COG) 1997
■ PO Box 314, HARPENDEN, Herts, AL5 4XL. (asa)
   01582 762934   fax 01582 461928
   email info@cog.org.uk   http://www.cog.org.uk
   Chief Exec: Michael Trenchard
▲ Company Limited by Guarantee
○ *G; to provide a forum for industry professionals concerned
   with obsolescence of electronic, mechanical & software
   components in industries where equipment life is long
Gp Website maintenance; Standardisation & guidance
● Conf - Mtgs - ET - Exhib - Inf - LG
M 135 f, UK / 40 f, o'seas

Composites Processing Association Ltd (CPA) 1989
■ Sarum Lodge, St Anne's Court, Talygarn, PONTYCLUN, Glam,
   CF72 9HH. (hq)
   01443 228867   fax 01443 239083
   email info@composites-proc-assoc.co.uk
   http://www.composites-proc-assoc.co.uk
   Sec: Ken L Forsdyke
▲ Company Limited by Guarantee
○ *T; representing companies involved in the production of
   composite components or materials, the supply of raw
   materials, machinery or services ancillary to that industry
Gp Phenolic composites
● Conf - Mtgs - Res - Exhib - Stat - Inf - Lib - VE - LG
M 90 f
¶ CPA News - 4; free.
   Note: The registered name is 'The Composites Processing
   Association Ltd'

Composting Association (CA) 1995
■ Avon House, Tithe Barn Rd, WELLINGBOROUGH, Northants,
   NN8 1DH. (hq)
   0870 160 3270   fax 0870 160 3280
   email info@compost.org.uk
   http://www.compost.org.uk
   Chief Exec: Dr Jane Gilbert
▲ Company Limited by Guarantee
○ *Q; to promote the sustainable management of biodegradable
   resources & the use of biological treatment techniques
● Conf - ET - Res - Exhib - Inf - Lib - LG
M 150 i, 500 f, 50 org
¶ Composting News (Jnl) - 4; ftm only.
   Technical Manuals:
   A Guide to Anerobic Digestion + a Directory of
   Suppliers; £25 m, £50 nm.
   A Guide to In-Vessel Composting + a Directory of Suppliers;
   £45 m, £65 nm.
   Health & Safety at Composting Sites - a guide for managers;
   £45 m, £65 nm.
   Standardised Protocol for the Sampling & Enumeration of
   Airborne Microorganisms at Composting Facilities (1999); £5
   m, £25 nm.
   Hazard Analysis & Critical Control Point for
   Composting; £35 m, £55 nm.

Composting Association of Ireland (CR/Ea/)
IRL PO Box 310, NAAS, Co Kildare, Republic of Ireland.
   email info@compostireland.ie
   http://www.compostireland.ie
   Chmn: Fiacra Quinn
○ *T

Compulsory Annuity Purchase Protest Alliance (CAPPA) 1999
NR 85 Oldfield Rd, SHEFFIELD, S Yorks, S6 6DU. (hsp)
   0114-234 0630   fax 0114-234 0630
   email cappa@firework.uk.com
   http://www.cappa.org.uk
   Sec: Tony Davies
▲ Un-incorporated Society
○ *K; to seek reform of Finance Acts which compel private
   pension fund holders to buy an annuity at age 75
● Mtgs - ET - Inf - LG
M 1,500 i, UK / 15 i, o'seas
¶ NL - 2/3; free.

Computer Conservation Society (CCS) 1988
NR 25 Comet Close, Ashvale, ALDERSHOT, Hants, GU12 5SG.
   (hsp)
   Sec: Kevin Murrell
▲ Un-incorporated Society
Br 2
○ *G; conservation & restoration of historic computers; collection
   of archive material in history of computing, including
   hardware, software, publications & reminiscences
Gp Working parties: Elliott 803; Elliott 401; Ferranti Pegasus; DEC;
   S100 BUS; Turing bombe
● Mtgs - Working parties to restore historic computers
< Parent Org: Brit Computer Soc, Science Museum South
   Kensington, Museum of Science & Ind in Manchester
M c 700 i, 1 f, UK / c 25 i, o'seas
¶ Computer Resurrection (Jnl) - 3/4; ftm.

Computer & Peripherals Equipment Trade Association
(COMPETA) 1976
NR 10 Edenham Close, Lower Earley, READING, Berks,
   RG6 3TH. (asa)
   0118-926 1187   fax 0118-926 2224
   email bnoyce@intersystem.co.uk
   Sec: Mrs Barbara Noyce
○ *T; interests of companies in the UK involved in the
   manufacture, distribution or use of computer peripherals
● Mtgs
M 25 f

Computing Services & Software Association
   2002 merged with FEI - Federation of the Electronics Industry to form
   Intellect

Computing Suppliers Federation
   has closed

Comunn na Clàrsaich   (the Clarsach Society) 1931
■ 22 Durham Road South, EDINBURGH, EH15 3PD. (admin)
   0131-669 8972
   email clarsachs@blueyonder.co.uk
   http://www.clarsachsociety.co.uk p
   Admin: Alistair Cockburn
▲ Registered Charity
Br 11
○ *D; to encourage the playing of the clarsach (Celtic harp); to
   preserve its place in the national life of Scotland, particularly
   among Gaelic speaking people
Gp Wire strung harp
● ET - Comp - Inf - Harp hire service to members - Organisation
   of the Edinburgh Harp Festival
< An Comunn Gaidhealach
M 900 i, UK / 50 i, o'seas
¶ Branch newsletters - irreg; ftm only.
   Folios of Music (detailed catalogue on request).
   AR (incl list of harp makers).
   Diary of Events - 2; free to branches.

An Comunn Gaidhealach [The Highland Association]   1891

- ■ 109 Church St, INVERNESS, Highland, IV1 1EY.   (hq)
     01463 231226   fax 01463 715557
     http://www.ancomunn.co.uk
- ○ *L; promotion of the Gaelic language, literature, arts & music
- M c 2,500 i

Concert Artistes' Association   (CAA)   1897

- ■ 20 Bedford St, LONDON, WC2E 9HP.   (hq)
     020 7836 3172   fax 020 7836 3172
     email office@the caa.org   http://www.thecaa.org
     Sec: Barbara Daniels,   Pres: Bill Pertwee
- ○ *A, *D; for all those interested in the entertainment profession
     with particular reference to concerts, cabarets, radio,
     television & West End productions
     The association has its own West End club - the Club for Acts &
     Actors
- Gp General committee & several sub-committees; Trustees of the
     benevolent fund
- ● Mtgs - ET - Exam - Exhib - Comp - SG - VE - Rehearsals, shows
     - Theatrical productions
- < Catholic Stage Gld
- M 998 i, 1 guild, UK / 50 i, o'seas
- ¶ NL - 3;   Chairman's Report -1;   LM - 2 yrly; all ftm only.
     But - What do you do in the Winter? (book by Larry Parker); £8.

Concert Promoters Association   (CPA)   1986

- NR 6 St Mark's Rd, HENLEY-on-THAMES, Oxon, RG9 1LJ.   (sp)
     01491 575060   fax 01491 414082
     email carolesmith.cpa@virgin.net
     Sec: Carole Smith
- ▲ Company Limited by Guarantee
- ○ *T; the interests of promoters of contemporary music concerts/
     tours in the UK
- ● Mtgs - LG
- < Music Users' Coun of Europe; Music Users' Coun; Nat Music
     Coun
- M [not given]

Conchological Society of Great Britain & Ireland   (CSGBI)
1876

- ■ 447B Wokingham Rd, Earley, READING, Berks, RG6 7EL.
     (hsp)
     Hon Sec: Rosemary Hill
- ▲ Registered Charity
- ○ *L; to promote the study of the mollusca in all its aspects;
     actively engaged in biographical distribution of marine &
     non-marine molluscs
- ● Conf - Mtgs - Res - Stat
- < Brit Trust Consvn Volunteers; Coun Nature
- M 280 i, 20 org, UK / 100 i, 20 org, o'seas
- ¶ Journal of Conchology - 2; ftm, £40 nm.
     Mollusc World - 3; ftm, £3 nm.
     Other occasional publications.

Concrete Advisory Service
     is part of the **Concrete Society**

Concrete Block Association
     a product association of the **British Precast Concrete Federation**

Concrete Bridge Development Group   (CBDG)   1992

- NR 4 Meadows Business Park, Blackwater, CAMBERLEY, Surrey,
     GU17 9AB.   (hq)
     01276 608700   fax 01276 608701
     Co Sec: Colin Cleverly
- ▲ Company Limited by Guarantee
- ○ *T; to enhance the design, construction & management of
     concrete bridges
- Gp New techniques; Durable post tensioned bridges; Design &
     detailing guide; Whole life costing; Assessment; Foundation
     & substructures; Testing systems for existing bridges;
     Aesthetics; Technical publications
- ● Conf - Mtgs - ET - Exhib - Comp - SG - Inf - VE
- < Brit Cement Assn; Instn of Civil Engrs; Instn of Highways &
     Transportation
- M 100 f, 8 org, UK / 4 f, o'seas
- ¶ NL - 6.
     LM - 6.   Hbk (Directory) - 1.
     Ready Mixed Concrete in Bridge Constructures.
     Whole Life Costing - concrete bridges.
     Integral Bridges.
     Durable Post Tensioned Bridges; £25 m, £35 nm.
     Concrete Bridges; ftm, £1 nm.
     Concrete Substructures for Bridges; ftm, £1 nm.

Concrete Manufacturers' Association of Ireland

- IRL Confederation House, 84-86 Lower Baggot St, DUBLIN 2,
     Republic of Ireland.
- ○ *T
     incorporated in the **Construction Industry Federation**

Concrete Pipeline Systems Association
     until 2003 was named Concrete Pipe Association and is a product
     association of the **British Precast Concrete Federation**

Concrete Repair Association   (CRA)   1988

- ■ 99 West St, FARNHAM, Surrey, GU9 7EN.   (asa)
     01252 739145   fax 01252 739140
     email cra@associationhouse.org.uk
     http://www.concreterepair.org.uk
     Sec: John G Fairley
- ▲ Company Limited by Guarantee
- ○ *T; to promote the practice of concrete repair
- ● Conf - Mtgs - ET - Exhib - Inf - Seminars - Quality assurance &
     control system implementation
- M 38 f
- ¶ LM - 3; free.
     Standard Method of Measurement; £5 m, £10 nm.
     Application & Measurement of Protective Coatings; free.
     Route to a Successful Concrete Repair; £2.50 m, £5 nm.

Concrete Sleeper Manufacturers' Association
     a product association of the **British Precast Concrete Federation**

Concrete Society   1966

- NR Riverside House, 4 Meadows Business Park, Station Approach,
     Blackwater, CAMBERLEY, Surrey, GU17 9AB.   (hq)
     01276 607140
     email enquiries@concrete.org.uk
     http://www.concrete.org.uk
- ▲ Company Limited by Guarantee
- Br 20
- ○ *L, *T; to bring together all who are interested in concrete to
     exchange information, to encourage innovation, to promote
     excellence in design, construction, appearance &
     performance
- Gp Materials; Design; Construction
- ● Conf - Mtgs - ET - Res - Inf - Lib - PL - LG - Annual awards -
     Advisory service
- < Fédn Intle du Beton; Eur Concrete Soc Network
- M 1,000 i, 500 f
- ¶ Concrete (Jnl) - 10.
     Concrete Engineers International Jnl - 4.

Concrete Structures Group
    see **Construct: Concrete Structures Group**

Concrete Tile Manufacturers' Association
    is a product group of the **British Precast Concrete Federation**

Confederation of Aerial Industries Ltd   (CAI)   1978
NR   Fulton House Business Centre, Fulton Rd, WEMBLEY PARK,
        Middx, HA9 0TF.   (hq)
        020 8902 8998   fax 020 8903 8719
        email office@cai.org.uk   http://www.cai.org.uk
        Sec: Mrs Beverley K Allgood
▲   Company Limited by Guarantee
○   *T; for the aerial & satellite industry
●   ET - Exam - Exhib - LG
M   c 750 f
¶   Feedback - 4;   LM - 1;   Ybk - 1; Codes of practice; all free.

Confederation of British Industry   (CBI)   1965
NR   103 New Oxford St, LONDON, WC1A 1DU.   (hq)
        020 7379 7400
        Dir Gen: Digby Jones
○   *T; employers organisation promoting the prosperity of British
        industry

Confederation of British Metalforming
■   National Metalforming Centre, 47 Birmingham Rd, WEST
        BROMWICH, W Midlands, B70 6PY.   (hq)
        0121-601 6350   fax 0121-601 6373
        email info@britishmetalforming.com
        http://www.britishmetalforming.com
        Dir Gen: John Houseman
○   *T
●   Conf - Mtgs - Inf
M   300 f

Confederation of the British Security Industry   (CBSI)   2005
■   Unit 4 Beaufort, Parklands, GUILDFORD, Surrey, GU2 9JX.
        (asa)
        0870 754 0726   fax 0870 754 0727
        email info@the-cbsi.org.uk   http://www.the-cbsi.org.uk
        Dir: Nicholas O'Connor,   Chmn: Richard Childs
○   *T; to assist the security industry to develop an on-going
        strategy for the future
Gp   Security: Manned, Retail & leisure, Trainers, IT &
        telecommunications, Defence & homeland, Systems;
        Academic qualifications
●   Conf - Mtgs - ET - Res - SG - Stat - Expt - Inf - Lib - Empl - LG
<   Fedn Employed Door Supervisors; Nat Training Inspectorate for
        Profl Dog Users
M   50 i, 40 f, 10 org
¶   Risk Management Round-up (e-jnl) - 1; free via website.
        Note: The Confederation is run by BCBSI Ltd, whose sole
        objective is to operate the Confederation

**Confederation of British Service & Ex-Service Organisations
(COBSEO)**
NR   c/o GVAMP, The Baird Medical Centre, Gassiott House,
        St Thomas' Hospital, Lambeth Palace Rd, LONDON,
        SE1 7EH.
        020 8348 9811   fax 020 8341 3521
        email rose.wrac@virgin.net   http://www.cobseo.org.uk
○   *N, *W

Confederation of British Wool Textiles Ltd   (CBWT)   1979
■   Merrydale House, Roysdale Way, BRADFORD, W Yorks,
        BD4 6SB.   (hq)
        01274 652207   fax 01274 652218
        email info@cbwt.co.uk
        Dir Gen: John Lambert
▲   Company Limited by Guarantee
○   *T; representation of interests of the UK wool textile industry
●   Conf - Mtgs - ET - Stat - Empl - LG
<   Intl Wool Textile Org; Interlaine; Brit Apparel & Textiles Confedn
M   170 f

Confederation of Burial Authorities
        since 2004-05 **Institute of Cemetery & Crematorium
        Management**

**Confederation of Children's Services Managers   (ConfEd)
1970**
NR   Humanities Building (3rd floor), University of Manchester,
        Oxford Rd, MANCHESTER, M13 9PL.   (hq)
        0161-275 8810   fax 0161-275 8811
        Sec: Sarah Caton
○   *P
●   Conf - Mtgs - Res - LG - Representation to government & other
        bodies on educational matters
M   950 i
×   2002 (Association of Chief Education Officers
            (Society of Education Officers
        2005 (Confederation of Education Service Managers

Confederation of Co-operative Housing   1993
■   Fairgate House, 205 Kings Rd, Tyseley, BIRMINGHAM,
        W Midlands, B11 2AA.
        0121-449 9588
        http://www.cch.coop
        Chmn: Nic Bliss
▲   Company Limited by Guarantee
○   *N; for all housing co-operatives & tenant controlled housings
        bodies

Confederation of Construction Specialists   (CCS)   1983
■   1 Walpole House, 2 Pickford St, ALDERSHOT, Hants,
        GU11 1TZ.   (hq)
        01252 312122   fax 01252 343081
        email infoconstructionspecialists.org
        http://www.constructionspecialists.org
        Group Dir: A R Gibbs
▲   Un-incorporated Society
○   *N, *T; central representative body for specialist building & civil
        engineering firms
●   Conf - Mtgs - ET - Res - SG - Stat - Inf - Lib - LG - Advisory &
        consultancy service - Commercial intelligence service
<   Construction Specialists Gp
M   f & affiliated trade assns
¶   NL - 10; ftm.
        Performance Bond; £10.   Certificate of vesting; £10.
        Standard forms of contract & sub-contract; £5-£10.

Confederation of Dental Employers   (CODE)   1978
■   5a Stanhope Square, HOLSWORTHY, Devon, EX22 6AP.   (hq)
        01409 254354   fax 01409 254364
        email info@codeuk.com   http://www.codeuk.com
        Chief Exec: Dr Paul Mendlesohn
▲   Incorporated Society
○   *P; to represent the interests of practice owners in the UK
●   Conf - ET - Res - Exhib - Inf - LG - Management services -
        Helpline
M   450 i, 8 f
¶   Dentistry Opportunities - 4; ftm.

Confederation of Education Service Managers
        since 2005 **Confederation of Children's Services Managers**

Confederation of English Fly Fishers   (CEFF)   1974
NR   1 Bridge Terrace, BEDLINGTON, Northumberland, NE22 7JT.
       (hsp)
       01670 823839   fax 01670 823598
       email peter@pgassoc.freeserve.co.uk
       Hon Sec: Peter Godfrey
○   *G; to foster all aspects of fly fishing; to promote the sport
       including respect for the environment
M   c 5,000 i

Confederation of Forest Industries   (CONFOR)
NR   5 Dublin Street Lane South, EDINBURGH, EH1 3PX.
       0131-524 8080
       http://www.confor.org.uk
○   *T

Confederation of Healing Organisations   (CHO)   1981
NR   27 Montefiore Court, LONDON, N16 5TY.   (hsp)
       020 8800 3569
       email michaeldibden@virgin.net
       Sec: Michael Dibden
▲   Registered Charity
○   *K, *N; to establish healing as a recognised therapy in the NHS
       & private medicine; to conduct controlled trials by medical
       scientists
●   Conf - Mtgs - ET - Res - Inf - Lib
M   12,000 i in 16 org

**Confederation of Long Distance Racing Pigeon Unions of Great
Britain & Ireland**
NR   20 Gorsey Lane, Banks, SOUTHPORT, PR9 8EH.   (hq)
       01704 232164
       Hon Sec: Brian Newsome
○   *N, *S

Confederation of Occupational Pensioners Associations
       merged in 2003 with the Alliance of Occupational Pensioners to form
       the **Occupational Pensioners' Alliance**

Confederation of Paper Industries Ltd   (CPI)   1999
■   Papermakers' House, Rivenhall Rd, Westlea, SWINDON, Wilts,
       SN5 7BD.   (hq)
       01793 889600
       http://www.paper.org.uk
       Dir-Gen: Dr M Oldman
▲   Company Limited by Guarantee
○   *N; the authoritative & effective voice of the UK's paper-related
       industries
Gp   Corrugated packaging manufacturers; Papermaking;
       Recovered paper; Tissue makers
●   Conf - Mtgs - ET - Stat - Inf - Empl - LG
<   Confedn of Eur Paper Inds (CEPI); Fédn Eur des Fabricants de
       Carton Ondulé (FEFCO); Eur Recovered Paper Assn (ERPA)
M   100 f
¶   CPI News - 26;   Daily Data - daily;   MP's NL - 4;
       statistics (various); all ftm only.
       Annual Review - 1; free.

Confederation of Passenger Transport UK   (CPT)   1974
NR   Imperial House, 15-19 Kingsway, LONDON, WC2B 6UN.
       (hq)
       020 7240 3131   fax 020 7240 6565
       email cpt@cpt-uk.org   http://www.cpt-uk.org
       Dir Gen: Brian Nimick
▲   Company Limited by Guarantee
○   *T; representing bus & coach operators
●   Conf - Mtgs - ET - Res - Exhib - SG - Stat - Inf - PL - LG
M   1,200 f
¶   Newsline (NL) - 10;   Annual review;
       Bulletins - irreg;   Hbk - 1; all ftm.

Confederation of Roofing Contractors Ltd   (CRC)   1985
■   72 Church Rd, Brightlingsea, COLCHESTER, Essex, CO7 0JF.
       (hq)
       01206 306600   fax 01206 306200
       email enquiries@corc.co.uk   http://www.corc.co.uk
       Chief Exec: Allan Buchan
▲   Company Limited by Guarantee
Br   4
○   *T; 'the main consumer protection organisation in the roofing
       industry'
●   ET - Inf - Lib - LG
M   625 i, 625 f
¶   The Roofing Trades Jnl - 6; free.

Confederation of Scottish Counselling Agencies
       since 2002 **COSCA (Counselling & Psychotherapy in Scotland)**

**Confederation of Shipbuilding & Engineering Unions   (CSEU)
1890**
NR   140-142 Walworth Rd, LONDON, SE17 1JW.   (hq)
       020 7703 2215   fax 020 7252 7397
       Gen Sec: J Wall
▲   Un-incorporated Society
Br   36
○   *U
●   Empl
M   8 unions
¶   AR; ftm.

**Confederation of Tourism, Hotel & Catering Management
(CTHCM)**
NR   118-120 Great Titchfield St, LONDON, W1W 6SS.   (hq)
       020 7612 0170   fax 020 7612 0171
       http://www.cthcm.com
       Admin Mgr: Sue Davie
○   *E; through its council (comprising individuals from
       educational, professional & commercial backgrounds) the
       confederation aims to set & maintain standards of education
       through approval of teaching facilities & the provision of
       course syllabuses & examinations, which reflect the constantly
       changing requirements of industry in the UK & overseas
●   ET - Exam
M   (in 4 grades according to age &/or previous experience or
       qualifications)

Confederation of Trades & Commerce   1999
NR   Marlborough House, 159 High St, WEALDSTONE, Middx,
       HA3 5DX.
       020 8427 8934   fax 020 8426 0523
○   *P; 'to support, protect & enhance the businesses of its
       members'

Confederation of Transcribed Information Services (COTIS) 1986
- ■ Project Office, 67 High St, TARPORLEY, Cheshire, CW6 0DP. (admin)
  01829 733351   fax 01829 732408
  email administrator@cotis.org.uk
  http://www.cotis.org.uk
  Admin: Mrs S Jones
- ▲ Registered Charity
- ○ *N; to improve the provision & quality of information provided in formats other than normal print
- ● Mtgs - Inf - Workshops
- M 12 i, 63 f, UK / 1 f, o'seas
- ¶ On Track (NL) - 3;   Basic Principles; both ftm, £1 nm.
  Guidelines; £5 each, (10% discount m):
    1: General Recording Technique;
    2: General Presentation;
    3: Reading Skills;
    4: Publicity;
    5: Computer;
    6: Recording Illustrations;
    7: Labelling & Packaging;
    8: How to Create a DIY Studio;
  Tapes; £8 each, (10% discount m):
    Technical Hints;
    Reading Masterclass;
    Describing Illustrations.
- ✕ 2000-2002 Confederation of Tape Information Services

Confederation of UK Coal Producers (COALPRO) 1991
- ■ Confederation House, Thornes Office Park, Denby Dale Rd, WAKEFIELD, W Yorks, WF2 7AN.   (hq)
  01924 200802   fax 01924 200796
  email db@coalpro.co.uk   http://www.coalpro.co.uk
  Dir Gen: David Brewer,   Gen Mgr: Mrs A Fellows
- ▲ Company Limited by Guarantee
- ○ *T; represents the majority of UK companies engaged in coal extraction
- Gp Marketing & Development; Safety & Health; Opencast Mining; British Standards; Deep Mining
- ● Conf - Mtgs - Exhib - Stat - Inf - Lib - PL - LG - Liaison with European Commission - Liaison with associate organisations worldwide
- < Euriscoal, Brussels; CHPA, UK; CBI
- M 21 f
- ¶ LM - 1.   Mines Database.
  Technical Information - 12.   AR.   NL - 12.

Conference of Drama Schools (CDS) 1969
- ■ PO Box 34252, LONDON, NW5 1XJ.   (hsp)
  020 7692 0032   fax 020 7692 0032
  email info@cds.drama.ac.uk   http://www.drama.ac.uk
  Exec Sec: Saul Hyman
- ▲ Company Limited by Guarantee
- ○ *P; to provide a voice for drama trainers; to give advice to prospective students
- ● Conf - Mtgs - ET - Res - Comp - Inf
- < Nat Coun for Drama Training
- M 21 f
- ¶ Official Guide to Vocational Courses for Drama & Technical Theatre - 1; free.

Conference of Heads of Irish Universities
   since 2005 **Irish Universities Association**

Conference Interpreters Group (CIG) 1979
- NR 10 Barley Mow Passage, LONDON, W4 4PH.   (hq)
  020 8995 0801   fax 020 8742 1066
  email ciglondon@aol.com
  http://www.cig-interpreters.com
  Sec: Andrew Brock
- ▲ Company Limited by Guarantee
- ○ *P; cooperative grouping of simultaneous interpreters
- M 22 i
  No further information supplied.

Conference of Professional Dance Schools
   a group of the **Council for Dance Education & Training (UK)**

Conflict Research Society (CRS) 1963
- ■ c/o Prof Jim Bryant, Sheffield Hallam University, City Campus, SHEFFIELD, S Yorks, S1 1WB.   (chmn/b)
  0114-225 5555
  http://www.conflictresearchsociety.org.uk
  Chmn: Prof Jim Bryant
- ▲ Registered Charity
- ○ *L, *Q; to promote research into, & the extension of knowledge about, conflict processes at all levels
- M c 80 i
- ¶ Jnl of the Conflict Research Society - 1; ftm, £10 nm (£15 o'seas).

Confraternity of Saint James (CSJ) 1983
- ■ 27 Blackfriars Rd, LONDON, SE1 8NY.
  020 7928 9988   fax 020 7928 2844
  email office@csj.org.uk   http://www.csj.org.uk
  Sec: Marion Marples
- ▲ Registered Charity
- ○ *G; a nondenominational organisation for all interested in the pilgrimage to Santiago de Compostela; to promote research into the history of the pilgrimage in Britain; to identify & safeguard works of art connected with St James & the pilgrimage
- Gp Research working party
- ● Conf - Mtgs - Res - Exhib - SG - Inf - Lib - PL - VE - Concerts
- < European Assn Friends Road to St James; Graduate Centre Mediaeval Studies (Reading University)
- M 2,500 i, 15 org, UK / 300 i, 3 org, o'seas
- ¶ Bulletin - 4; ftm, £2.50 nm.
  Pilgrim Guides & other publications: list on application.

Congenital CMV Association 1986
- NR 128 Northfields Lane, BRIXHAM, Devon, TQ5 8RH.   (hq)
  http://www.mysite.freeserve.com/CMVsupport
  Contact: Keri Dudley,
  Organiser (inf & family matching): Mrs Fay Courtney
- ○ *W; the welfare & support of families with congenital cytomegalovirus (of the herpes virus group); to support research
- ● Res (support for)
- < In Touch; Contact a Family
- M c 32 i
- ¶ Information leaflets on Congenital CMV; free.

Congregational Union of Ireland 1829
- NR 1 Bradford Heights, CARRICKFERGUS, Co Antrim, BT38 9EB.   (hsp)
  Hon Sec: Sidney Johnston
- ▲ Company Limited by Guarantee
- ○ *R
- M i & churches

CONNECT 1972
- NR 30 St George's Rd, LONDON, SW19 4BD.   (hq)
  020 8971 6000   fax 020 8971 6002
  email union@connectuk.org   http://www.connectuk.org
  Gen Sec: Adrian Askew
- ○ *U; working for managers & professionals in the communications sector

Connemara Pony Breeders Society
- IRL The Showgrounds, Hospital Rd, CLIFDEN, Co Galway, Republic of Ireland.
  353 (95) 21863   fax 353 (95) 21005
  email enquiries@cpbs.ie
  Sec: Niamh Philbin
- ○ *B

© CBD Research Ltd · Beckenham · BR3 5JS · Tel 020 8650 7745 · Fax 020 8650 0768 · E-mail cbd@cbdresearch.com · www.cbdresearch.com

Conservatoires UK   (CBC)
NR   Leeds College of Music, 3 Quarry Hill, LEEDS, N Yorks,
        LS2 7PD.   (hsb)
        0113-222 3426
        Hon Sec: David Hoult
○   *D, *E; music education & training
●   Conf - Mtgs - SG - LG
<   Assn of Eur Conservatoires
M   7 conservatoires
×   2003 Federation of British Conservatoires

**Consortium of Lesbian, Gay & Bisexual Transgendered Voluntary
    & Community Organisations   (LGBT Consortium)**
■   Unit J414 Tower Bridge Business Complex, 100 Clements Rd,
        LONDON, SE16 4DG.   (hq)
        020 7064 8383   fax 020 7064 8283
        email jstewart@lgbtconsortium.org
        http://www.lgbtconsortium.org.uk
        Chief Exec: Mark Redman
▲   Company Limited by Guarantee; Registered Charity
○   *N
Gp   Lesbian; Gay; Bisexual; Transgendered
●   Conf - Res - Inf - Lib
M   c 400 i in 300 org

Consortium of Research Libraries in the British Isles
        see **CURL: Consortium of Research Libraries in the British
        Isles**

Consortium of University Research Libraries
        since 2004 **CURL: Consortium of Research Libraries**

Constitutional Monarchy Association
        is part of the **Monarchist League**

Construct: Concrete Structures Group Ltd   (Construct)   1993
NR   4 Meadows Business Park, Blackwater, CAMBERLEY, Surrey,
        GU17 9AB.   (hq)
        01276 38444
        Exec Sec: Colin Cleverly
▲   Company Limited by Guarantee
○   *T; to widen & strengthen the market for concrete by enhancing
        & increasing productivity & competitiveness
Gp   Reference panels to show finishes to BS 8110; Hybrid concrete
        structures; Tolerances; Training
●   Conf - Mtgs - ET - Exhib - SG - VE - LG
<   Amer Soc of Concrete Construction; Brit Cement Assn
M   c 70 f & org
¶   NL - 4.   In-situ Concrete Frames.
        Guide to Contractor Detailing of Reinforcement in Concrete.

Construction Confederation   (CC)   1817
NR   55 Tufton St, LONDON, SW1P 3QL.   (hq)
        0870 898 9090   fax 0870 898 9095
        email enquiries@thecc.org.uk   http://www.thecc.org.uk
        Chief Exec: Stephen Ratcliffe
▲   Un-incorporated Society
○   *N, *T; 'the predominant representative organisation for the UK
        construction industry'
Gp   5 contractor orgs:
        Civil Engineering Contractors Association (CECA)
        Major Contractors Group (MCG)
        National Contractors Federation (NCF)
        National Federation of Builders (NFB)
        Scottish Building
        British Woodworking Federation (BWF)
●   Conf - Mtgs - ET - Res - Exhib - SG - Stat - Inf - Empl - LG
M   5,000 f
¶   Construction Trends Survey - 4; £200 yr.

Construction Employers Federation Ltd   (CEF)   1945
NR   143 Malone Rd, BELFAST, BT9 6SU.   (hq)
        028 9087 7143   fax 028 9087 7155
        email mail@cefni.co.uk   http://www.cefni.co.uk
        Dir: W A Doran
▲   Company Limited by Guarantee
○   *T
Gp   Private housing; Public authority housing; General contracting;
        Export; Civil engineering
●   Conf - Mtgs - ET - Exhib - Stat - Expt - Inf - VE - Empl - LG
M   500 f
¶   Bulletin - 12;   AR; both ftm.

Construction Equipment Association   (CEA)   1942
NR   Orbital House, 85 Croydon Rd, CATERHAM, Surrey,
        CR3 6PD.   (asa)
        01883 334499
        email cea@admin.co.uk   http://www.coneq.org.uk
        Secs: Administration Services Ltd
▲   Un-incorporated Society
○   *T; to serve construction equipment manufacturers, their
        component & accessory suppliers & service providers
●   Conf - Mtgs - Exhib - Stat - Expt - Inf - VE - LG
<   C'ee for Eur Construction Eqpt (CECE); Fédn Eur de la
        Manutention (FEM)
M   100 f
¶   Newsline - 4; ftm.

Construction Fixings Association   (CFA)   1977
■   c/o Institute of Spring Technology, Henry St, SHEFFIELD, S Yorks,
        S3 7EQ.   (hq)
        0114-278 9143   fax 0114-275 5573
        email info@britishtools.com
        http://www.fixingscfa.co.uk
        Assn Dir: J R Markham
○   *T; manufacturers of construction fixings
●   Mtgs - Res - Inf
<   Comité Eur de l'Outillage (CEO); Fedn Brit Hand Tool Mfrs
M   6 f
¶   Guidance Notes on the Correct Selection & Application of
        Fixings (a series of 10) - download from website; free.

Construction History Society   1981
NR   c/o Library & Information Services Manager, The Chartered
        Institute of Building, Englemere, Kings Ride, ASCOT, Berks,
        SL5 8TB.   (hsb)
        01344 630741   fax 01344 630764
        email michael.tutton@virgin.net
        http://www.constructionhistory.co.uk
        Hon Sec: Michael Tutton
▲   Registered Charity
○   *L; to focus attention on the problems of historical information
        about the construction process becoming lost by default; to
        undertake a survey to establish the records available & their
        accessibility
●   Conf - Mtgs - Lib
M   300 i
¶   Construction History Jnl - 1.

Construction Hoist Interest Group
        a special interest group of the **Construction Plant-hire
        Association**

Construction Industry Computing Association (CICA) 1973
NR National Computing Centre, Oxford House, Oxford Rd,
    MANCHESTER, M1 7ED. (hq)
    0161-242 2262
    email postmaster@cica.org.uk   http://www.cica.org.uk
▲ Company Limited by Guarantee
○ *T; to promote the use of computers in the construction industry
    by advising all concerned
● Conf - Mtgs - ET - Exhib - Comp - SG - Inf - Lib - VE -
    Evaluation of software - Consultancy - Feasibility studies -
    Market research
< Intl Fedn Nat Construction Computer Users Gps
M 380 f, UK / 46 f, o'seas
¶ CICA Bulletin - 4; ftm only.
    Evaluation reports;   Survey reports; prices vary.
    Publication list available.

Construction Industry Council (CIC) 1987
NR 26 Store St, LONDON, WC1E 7BT. (hq)
    020 7399 7400   fax 020 7399 7425
    email cic@cic.org.uk   http://www.cic.org.uk
    Chief Exec: Graham Watts
▲ Company Limited by Guarantee
○ *N, *T; to represent organisations in the built environment & to
    provide a forum for discussion, particularly for professional
    bodies
● Conf - Mtgs - Res - Inf - LG
M 34 full, 15 associate, 17 affiliate
¶ AR.   Publications list available on website.

Construction Industry Federation
IRL Construction House, Canal Rd, DUBLIN 6, Republic of Ireland.
    353 (1) 406 6000   fax 353 (1) 496 6953
    email cif@cif.ie   http://www.cif.ie
    Dir Gen: Liam B Kelleher   Sec: Eugene P O'Neill
Br 13
○ *T
M c 3,000

Construction Industry Information Group (CIIG) 1962
NR 26 Store St, LONDON, WC1E 7BT. (mail)
    http://www.ciig.org.uk address
○ *N, *P; to promote good practice in libraries & information
    services within the construction industry
Gp Freelance librarians
● Conf - VE
M 180 i
¶ NL - 12;   Review - irreg;   LM - 1; all ftm only.

**Construction Industry Research & Information Association
(CIRIA) 1960**
NR Classic House, 174-180 Old St, LONDON, EC1V 9BP. (hq)
    020 7549 3300   fax 020 7253 0523
    email enquiries@ciria.org   http://www.ciria.org
    Chief Exec: Tim Broyd
▲ Company Limited by Guarantee
○ *Q; 'best practice research into issues relating to construction &
    the environment'
Gp Construction Ind Envt Forum (CIEF); Construction Productivity
    Network (CPN)
● Conf - Mtgs - ET - Res
M 70 f, 500 subscribers
¶ Publications list available.

Construction Industry Trading Electronically (CITE) 1999
NR 20 Hardwick Drive, HALESOWEN, W Midlands, B62 8TF. (hq)
    0870 112 3639
    email info@cite.org.uk   http://www.cite.org.uk
    Admin Mgr: Carole Christensen
▲ Company Limited by Guarantee
○ *T; 'to make electronic information exchange happen within the
    construction industry by promoting awareness, encouraging
    collaboration, providing industry representation & developing
    exchange standards'
Gp EDMS (Electronic Data Management Systems) & project
    collaboration; Legal & security issues; Project information
    exchange; Tendering & valuation project; Trading & product
    data project
● Conf - Mtgs - ET - Exhib - SG - Inf - LG - Promoting awareness
    & best practice with DTI
M 5 i, 193 f, 4 org, UK / 11 f, o'seas
¶ Insight (NL) - 4;   Electronic Hbk - 2; both ftm only.

Construction Packed Products Association
    a product association of the **British Precast Concrete Federation**

Construction Plant-hire Association (CPA) 1941
■ 27-28 Newbury St, Barbican, LONDON, EC1A 7HU. (hq)
    020 7796 3366   fax 020 7796 3399
    email enquiries@cpa.uk.net   http://www.cpa.uk.net
    Chief Exec: Colin Wood
▲ Un-incorporated Society
○ *T; to represent the interests of plant hirers nationally
Gp Rail Plant Association; British Concrete Pumping Group
    Special Interest Groups: Crane, Construction hoist, Powered
    access, Shoring technology, Tower crane
● Conf - Mtgs - Stat - Inf - LG
< Intl Powered Access Fedn; Construction Confedn; Freight
    Transport Assn
> Intl Powered Access Fedn
M 1,410 f
¶ The Bulletin - 4; free.   Plant Finder - 1; ftm, £30 nm.

Construction Products Association (CPA) 2000
NR 26 Store St, LONDON, WC1E 7BT. (hq)
    020 7323 3770   fax 020 7323 0307
    email enquiries@constprod.org.uk
    http://www.constprod.org.uk
    Chief Exec: Michael Ankers
▲ Company Limited by Guarantee
○ *N, *T; to represent the UK's manufacturers & suppliers of
    products to the construction industry
Gp Construction products manufacturers & distributors
● Conf - Mtgs - Exhib - SG - Stat - Inf - PL - LG
< Coun of Eur Producers of Materials for Construction; CBI
M 22 f, 40 trade assns, 7 associates, 7 affiliates
¶ Construction Industry Forecasts - 2.
    Construction Markets Trends - 12.
    Construction Products Trade Survey - 4.
    Construction Products Briefing - 6.
    Weekly Notes - 52.   AR.

Construction Specialists Group
■ 1 Walpole House, 2 Pickford St, ALDERSHOT, Hants,
    GU11 1TZ.
    01252 312122   fax 01252 343081
    email constructiongroup@btconnect.com
    This group includes the long standing Confederation of
    Construction Specialists & 2 organisations formed in 2001 -
    the Institute of Construction Specialists & the Construction
    Specialists Academy.
    The Confederation represents the interests of specialist
    construction companies;
    the Institute serves the interests of construction staff, & offers
    professional qualifications for management; the Academy
    'provides contractual training needs of Institute candidates &
    general training needs of companies'.

Constructors Liaison Group
  see **Specialist Engineering Contractors Association**

Consumer Credit Association (United Kingdom) (CCA) 1978
NR   Queens House, Queens Rd, CHESTER, CH1 3BQ.   (hq)
        01244 312044   fax 01244 318035
        email cca@ccauk.org   http://www.ccauk.org
        Dir: John Lamidey
▲   Un-incorporated Society
○   *T; 'main representative trade association for the home credit
        industry'
●   Conf - Mtgs - ET - SG - Inf - VE - LG - Provide regulated credit
        agreements & other documentation
<   Consumer Credit Assn (Republic of Ireland)
M   500 f
¶   CCA News - 4; ftm, £7.50 nm.   LM - 1; ftm only.   AR; free.
        Distributors of PSI Report.

Consumer Credit Trade Association (CCTA) 1891
■   The Wave (suite 4), 1 View Croft Rd, SHIPLEY, W Yorks,
        BD17 7DU.   (hq)
        0845 257 1166
        email info@ccta.co.uk   http://www.ccta.co.uk
        Dir Gen: R Keith Mather
▲   Company Limited by Guarantee
○   *T; to support businesses involved in consumer credit
●   Conf - Mtgs - ET - Res - Inf - LG
<   Eur Fedn of Finance House Assns (EUROFINAS)
M   20 i, 450 f
¶   Consumer Credit - 6; £24 m, £39 yr nm.
        Information leaflet - 6.

Consumer Electronics Distributors Association
IRL   Confederation House, 84-86 Lower Baggot St, DUBLIN 2,
        Republic of Ireland.
        353 (1) 605 1582   fax 353 (1) 638 1582
        email ceda@ibec.ie
        Dir: Tommy McCabe
○   *P
<   IBEC

Consumer Health Information Consortium
  merged in 2005 with the **Patient Information Forum**

Consumer Protection Association (CPA)
■   CPA House - 11 North Bridge St, SHEFFORD, Beds,
        SG17 5DQ.   (hq)
        01462 850062   fax 01462 817161
        email helpline@thecpa.co.uk   http://www.thecpa.co.uk
▲   Company Limited by Guarantee
○   *T; consumer protection; insurance backed guarantees

Consumers' Association (CA) 1957
NR   2 Marylebone Rd, LONDON, NW1 4DF.   (hq)
        020 7770 7000   fax 020 7770 7600
        email editor@which.co.uk   http://www.which.net
        Dir: Peter Vicary Smith,   Co Sec: Andrew Reading
▲   Registered Charity
○   *K, *Q; independent research & testing of consumer products &
        services; results published by CA's trading subsidiary Which?
        Ltd; campaigning on behalf of consumers
●   Res - Inf - Comparative testing of consumer goods & services
<   Consumers Us Intl; Bureau Européen des Unions de
        Consommateurs (BEUC)
M   982,000 i
¶   Which? - 12.   Holiday Which? - 4.
        Gardening Which? - 10.
        Health Which? - 6.   Consumer Policy Review - 10.

Consumers Association of Ireland Ltd 1966
IRL   43-44 Chelmsford Rd, Ranelagh, DUBLIN 6, Republic of
        Ireland.
        353 (1) 497 8600
        email cai@consumerassociation.ie
        http://www.consumerassociation.ie
        Chief Exec: Dermott Jewell
○   *K

Consumers for Health Choice 1995
NR   Southbank House, Black Prince Rd, LONDON, SE1 7SJ.
        020 7463 0690
        http://www.healthchoice.org.uk
○   *K; for the right of consumers to have ready access to a wide
        range of natural health products, including vitamin & mineral
        supplements and health remedies.
M   i & f

Contact the Elderly 1965
■   15 Henrietta St, LONDON, WC2E 8QG.   (hq)
        020 7240 0630   fax 020 7379 5781
        email info@contact-the-elderly.org.uk
        http://www.contact-the-elderly.org.uk
        Dir: Roderick Simell
▲   Registered Charity
Br   280
○   *W; to alleviate the loneliness & isolation of frail elderly people
        in their 70s, 80s & beyond
●   Mtgs - Provision of social support through regular monthly
        meetings
M   4,500 i
¶   Contact News (NL) - 1/2; free.   AR - 1.

**Container Handling Equipment Manufacturers' Association
(CHEM) 1969**
NR   Hinchley, The Highlands, Painswick, STROUD, Glos, GL6 6SL.
        01452 814812   fax 01452 814812
        Technical Sec: David H Buxton
▲   Un-incorporated Society
○   *T; 'vehicles & equipment for the collection, transportation &
        handling of dry waste: to create standards for the interface of
        equipment with containers & to promote safe operations; to
        participate in the drafting of standards for equipment used in
        the collection & transportation of dry waste'
Gp   Technical c'ees for refuse collection vehicles (RCVs) of all types;
        skip loaders, hook loaders, static compactors
●   Mtgs - LG (DTI & Dept of Transport) - Liaison with standards
        institutes BSI & CEN
M   26 f

Contemporary Art Society (CAS) 1910
■   Bloomsbury House, 74-77 Great Russell St, LONDON,
        WC1B 3DA.   (hq)
        020 7612 0730   fax 020 7631 4230
        email cas@contempart.org.uk
        http://www.contempart.org.uk
        Dir: Gill Hedley
▲   Company Limited by Guarantee; Registered Charity
○   *A; to acquire works of art by living artists for gift to public art
        galleries & museums; to promote collecting by individuals &
        companies
●   Exhib - VE
M   700 i, 96 org, UK / 100 i, o'seas
¶   NL - 2;   Events NL - 2;   AR - 1.

Contemporary Art Society for Wales (CASW) 1937
NR   6 Le Sor Hill, Peterstone-Super-Ely, CARDIFF, Glam, CF5 6LW.
        (hsp)
        Hon Sec: Jean Williams
▲   Registered Charity
○   *A; the purchase of contemporary art for free distribution to
        public galleries & museums throughout Wales
●   Conf - Mtgs - Exhib - Comp - VE - Purchase of art works
M   500 i, 18 f, 21 org
¶   AR; ftm.   Exhibition catalogues - irreg; £3-£5.

Contemporary Glass Society (CGS) 1997

NR c/o Broadfield House Glass Museum, Compton Drive,
KINGSWINFORD, W Midlands, DY6 9NS. (mail/address)
01603 507737   fax 01603 507737
email admin@cgs.org.uk   http://www.cgs.org.uk
Admin: Pam Reekie
▲ Un-incorporated Society
○ *A; 'to encourage excellence in glass as a creative medium; to
develop a greater public awareness & appreciation of
contemporary glass world wide; for all those involved with
glass in an artistic, technological, manufacturing &
supportive capacity'
Gp Glass makers
● Conf - Mtgs - ET - Exhib
M 305 i, 15 f, UK / 10 i, o'seas
¶ Glass Network (NL) - 4; ftm only.

Contract Flooring Association Ltd (CFA) 1973

■ 4c St Mary's Place, The Lace Market, NOTTINGHAM,
NG1 1PH. (hq)
0115-941 1126   fax 0115-941 2238
email info@cfa.org.uk   http://www.cfa.org.uk
Dir: Richard Wollerton   Office Mgr: Mrs H E Tidmarsh
○ *T; to further the progress of flooring technology by education
of all concerned
Gp Contractors; Manufacturers; Distributors & consultants:
Adhesives, Carpets, Rubber, Vinyl, Cork, Linoleum, Raised
modular, Resin
● Conf - Mtgs - ET - Res - Exhib - Inf - Lib - Empl
< Nat Specialist Contrs Coun (NSCC)
M 500 f, UK / 5 f, o'seas
¶ The Contract Flooring Jnl - 10; ftm, £30 yr nm.

Contract Heat Treatment Association
is a group of the Surface Engineering Association

Contractors Mechanical Plant Engineers (CMPE) 1957

NR c/o EA-Direct Ltd, 128 Arkleston Rd, PAISLEY, PA1 3TZ.
0870 720 2502   fax 0870 762 7332
http://www.cmpe.org
Nat Sec: Wendy Pitches
▲ Un-incorporated Society
Br 15
○ *L; all aspects of mechanical plant used in the construction &
building industries
● Conf - Mtgs - ET
M [not stated]

Control Manufacturers Association
a part of BEAMA Energy is a group of BEAMA

Convention of Scottish Local Authorities (COSLA) 1975

NR 9 Haymarket Terrace, EDINBURGH, EH12 5XZ. (hq)
0131-474 9200   fax 0131-474 9292
email enquiries@cosla.gov.uk   http://www.cosla.gov.uk
Chief Exec: Rory Mair
○ *N; the association for local authorities in Scotland
Gp Local government
● Conf - Mtgs - ET - Res - Inf - Empl
M 32 councils in Scotland
¶ Publications list on application.

Cookery & Food Association
**see Craft Guild of Chefs (incorporating the Cookery & Food
Association)**

Cookshop & Housewares Association
a group of the British Hardware Federation

Copper Development Association (CDA) 1933

■ 1 Brunel Court, Corner Hall, HEMEL HEMPSTEAD, Herts,
HP3 9XX. (hq)
01442 275700   fax 01442 275716
email mail@copperdev.co.uk   http://www.cda.org.uk
Dir & Co Sec: Angela Vassey
▲ Company Limited by Guarantee
○ *T; promotion of the correct use of copper & copper alloys
Gp Brass advisory service; Copper Club; Copper in architecture;
Power quality partnership; UK Copper Board
● Conf - Exhib - Comp - Inf - PL
< Intl Copper Assn; Eur Copper Inst
M 8 f, UK / 2 f, o'seas

Coracle Society 1990

■ 19 Watling St, Leintwardine, CRAVEN ARMS, Shropshire,
SY7 0LW. (chmn/p)
email webmaster@coracle-fishing.net
http://www.coracle-fishing.net
5 Cedar Close, TEIGNMOUTH, Devon,
TQ14 8VZ. (mem/s)
Chmn: Peter Faulkner,   Mem Sec: Brian Pearce
▲ Un-incorporated Society
○ *G, *L; to promote the knowledge of coracles & allied craft,
their making, use & study; to support the continuance of
coracle fishing; to encourage the craft of coracle building
● ET (courses) - Exhib - Comp - VE - Demonstrations - Seaboat
construction - Use of hides as 'skin'
M 120 i, UK / 10 i, o'seas
¶ NL - 1; ftm only.

Cork Chamber of Commerce 1820

IRL Fitzgerald House, Summerhill North, CORK, Republic of
Ireland.
353 (21) 450 9044   fax 353 (21) 450 8568
email info@corkchamber.ie   http://www.corkchamber.ie
Chief Exec: Michael Geary
○ *C

Cork Industry Federation (CIF) 1966

■ 13 Felton Lea, SIDCUP, Kent, DA14 6BA. (hsp)
020 8302 4801   fax 020 8302 4801
http://www.cork-products.co.uk
Hon Sec: Mrs Joy Bell
○ *N, *T; the umbrella organisation for all aspects of cork in the
UK; decorative cork for floors & walls; industrial &
construction materials (cork based); cork closures for wine &
drinks industry
● Mtgs - Res
< Confédn Européenne du Liège
M 16 f
¶ LM.

Cornish Chamber of Mines & Minerals (CCMM) 1917

■ Old Mine Offices, Wheal Jane, Baldhu, TRURO, Cornwall,
TR3 6EE. (regd/office/hsb)
01872 560200   fax 01872 562000
Sec: B J Ballard
▲ Company Limited by Guarantee
○ *T; to promote & protect mining (incl china clay & stone) in
Cornwall & Devon
Gp Legislation
● Mtgs
< CBI
M 15 i, 6 f, 2 org
¶ AR; ftm.

Cornish Language Board
see Kesva an Taves Kernewek (Cornish Language Board)

© CBD Research Ltd · Beckenham · BR3 5JS · Tel 020 8650 7745 · Fax 020 8650 0768 · E-mail cbd@cbdresearch.com · www.cbdresearch.com

Cornish Language Council (Cussel an Tavas Kernuack)   1988
NR   25 Hurland Rd, TRURO, Cornwall, TR1 2BU.   (hsp)
     01872 262667
     Sec: Mina Dresser
▲   Un-incorporated Society
Br   support group in Australia
○   *G, *K; to promote the Cornish language & research its past
●   Mtgs - ET - Res - Exhib - SG - Inf - VE
M   12 i (committee)
¶   An Garack - 4.
     Publications covering all grades of study.

** **Cornish Mining Development Association**
     Organisation lost: see Introduction paragraph 3

Cornish Pasty Association   (CPA)
■   Cornwall Taste of the West, 7 The Courtyard, Trewolland Farm,
     LISKEARD, Cornwall, PL14 3NL.
     01579 349363
     Mgr: Angela Coombs
○   *T; Cornish pasty manufacturers & bakers
M   54 f
     no further information supplied

Cornwall Archaeological Society   (CAS)   1961
NR   Roaring Stile, Lanarth, St Keverne, HELSTON, Cornwall,
     TR12 6RQ.   (hsp)
     http://www.cornisharchaeology.co.uk
     Pres: Tony Blackman (2007-)
▲   Registered Charity
○   *E, *L
Gp   Cornwall branch of Young Archaeologists' Club
●   Conf - Mtgs - ET - Res - SG - VE - Lectures
M   600 i
¶   Jnl - 1.

Cornwall Chamber of Commerce & Industry   (CCCI)   1988
NR   West Cornwall Enterprise Centre, Cardrew, REDRUTH,
     Cornwall, TR15 1SS.   (hq)
     01209 216006   fax 01209 765164
     email chamber@ccci.org.uk   http://www.ccci.org.uk
     Dir of Operations: Lyn Morris
▲   Company Limited by Guarantee
○   *C; to support Cornish industry
Gp   Export; Training courses; Information provision
●   Conf - Mtgs - ET - Expt - Inf - Lib - LG
<   Brit Chams Comm
M   160 f
¶   NL - 4; free.

**Coronary Artery Disease Research Association   (CORDA)
1975**
■   Chelsea Square, LONDON, SW3 6NP.   (hq)
     020 7349 8686   fax 020 7349 9414
     email corda@rbht.nhs.uk   http://www.corda.org.uk
     Exec Dir & Sec: Jennifer Jenks
▲   Company Limited by Guarantee; Registered Charity
○   *Q; to support high quality clinical research into the prevention
     of heart attacks & strokes through non-invasive techniques
●   Res

Coroners' Society of England & Wales   1846
NR   The Court House, Bewdley Rd, STOURPORT-ON-SEVERN,
     Worcs, DY13 8XE.   (hsp)
     http://www.coroner.org.uk
     Hon Sec: Victor Round
▲   Un-incorporated Society
○   *P
●   Conf - Mtgs - Empl - LG
¶   Annual Report & Directory; m only.

Corporate Event Association
     2005 merged with the Incentive Travel & Meetings Association to form
     Eventia

Corporate Responsibility Coalition
NR   26-28 Underwoood Street, LONDON, N1 7JQ.
     020 7566 1665   fax 020 7490 0881

**Corporation of Insurance, Financial & Mortgage Advisers Ltd
(CIFMA)   1968**
NR   5 Ollersett Lane, NEW MILLS, High Peak, Derbys, SK22 4JE.
     (hq)
     01663 746742
     Gen Sec: George Rogers
▲   Company Limited by Guarantee
○   *P, *T; for all practitioners in the insurance, mortgage &
     healthcare industry
●   Conf - Res - Inf - LG
M   c 700 i, c 300 f
¶   News & Views - irreg.   NL - 6.

Corps of Drums Society   1977
NR   103 Clare Lane, East Malling, MAIDSTONE, Kent, ME19 6JB.
     (hsp)
     email info@corpsofdrums   http://www.corpsofdrums.com
○   *D; to promote & preserve the tradition of drum & fife/flute
     music; to research & record the history of corps of drums

Corrosion Prevention Association   1992
■   99 West St, FARNHAM, Surrey, GU9 7EN.
     01252 739144   fax 01252 739140
     email cpa@associationhouse.org.uk
     http://www.corrosionprevention.org.uk
     Sec: John Fairley
▲   Company Limited by Guarantee
○   *P
●   Seminars - Workshops
M   27 f
¶   Brochure;   LM (with areas of expertise);
     Special Feature Supplement;   all free.
     Reinforced Concrete: History, Properties & Durability; £5.
     Cathodic Protection of Reinforced Concrete: Status Report; £35.

Corrugated Packaging Association
     since 2004 the Corrugated Packaging group of the **Confederation
     of Paper Industries**

**COSCA (Counselling & Psychotherapy in Scotland)   (COSCA)
1990**
■   18 Viewfield St, STIRLING, FK8 1UA.   (hq)
     01786 475140
     email info@cosca.org.uk   http://www.cosca.org.uk
     Chief Exec: Brian Magee
▲   Company Limited by Guarantee; Registered Charity
○   *N, *W; to coordinate & promote development of training &
     good practice in counselling in Scotland; to encourage
     communication & cooperation between agencies &
     individuals engaged in similar activities
Gp   Gps who perform counselling services; Gps whose work
     includes some counselling skills
●   Conf - Mtgs - ET - LG
<   Eur Assn for Counselling
M   org
¶   Counselling in Scotland - 4; ftm, subscription nm.
×   2002 Confederation of Scottish Counselling Agencies

Cosmetic, Toiletry & Perfumery Association Ltd   (CTPA)   1945
- ■ Josaron House, 5-7 John Princes St, LONDON, W1G 0JN.
     (hq)
     020 7491 8891   fax 020 7493 8061
     email info@ctpa.org.uk   http://www.ctpa.org.uk
     Co Sec: D A Hunter
- ▲ Company Limited by Guarantee
- ○ *T; representing cosmetic, toiletry & perfumery manufacturers,
     raw materials suppliers & contract services in the UK -
     technical & legislative advice ONLY given to member
     companies
- Gp Technical: Environment, Legal, Oral care, Packaging, Perfumery
     Scientific: Analytical, Cosmetic colourants, Cosmetic
     ingredients, Environmental legislation, Toxicology, Talc,
     (+c10 others)
- ● Conf - Mtgs - Expt - LG
- < Eur Cosmetic Tr Assn (COLIPA); CBI
- M 140 f
- ¶ NL - 12; ftm only.   What is CTPA?;   AR; both free.
     Publications list available.

Costume Society   1965
- ■ c/o Moore Stephens, St Paul's House, 8 Warwick Lane,
     LONDON, EC4P 4BN.   (asa)
     http://www.costumesociety.org.uk
     Hon Sec: K I Stewart
     Chmn: Valerie Cumming
- ▲ Registered Charity
- ○ *L; to promote the study of costume & its history; to help in the
     preservation of significant examples of historical &
     contemporary dress
- Gp Sub-c'ees: Programme, Symposium
- ● Conf - Mtgs - ET - SG - VE
- M 1,000 i, 100 libraries, UK / 300 i, o'seas
- ¶ Costume (Jnl) - 1; £24.   NL - 2; ftm only.

Costume Society of Scotland   (CSS)   1965
- ■ 72 Dundas St, EDINBURGH, EH3 6QZ.   (hsp)
     0131 556 9300
     email cossocscotland@hotmail.com
     Hon Sec: Alison Rosie
- ▲ Un-incorporated Society
- ○ *G, *L; to promote interest in, & study of, costume
- ● Mtgs - Exhib - VE
- < Costume Soc; Canadian Costume Museum & Archives of BC;
     Northern Soc of Costume & Textiles; Textile Soc; Cymdeithas
     Gwisgoedd a Thecstilau Cymru
- M 67 i, 6 museums etc, UK / 3 i, o'seas
- ¶ Bulletin - 1; ftm only.

Cot Death Research & Support
     see **Foundation for the Study of Infant Deaths - Cot Death
     Research & Support**

Cot Death Society
     in 2004 activities were absorbed by the **Foundation for the Study
     of Infant Deaths - Cot Death Research & Support**

Cotswold Sheep Society   1891
- ■ 2 Upper Longwood, Eaton Constantine, SHREWSBURY,
     Shropshire, SY5 6SB.   (hsb)
     01952 740731
     email info@cotswoldsheep.org
     http://www.cotswoldsheep.org
     Hon Sec: Davina Stanhope
- ▲ Registered Charity
- ○ *B; conservation of the rare breed
- ● Mtgs - Exhib - Stat - Inf - Breeder workshops
- M 170 i, 8 org, UK / 5 i, o'seas
- ¶ NL - 4; ftm.   AR.
     Flock Book (incl LM) - 1; ftm, £3.50 nm.

Cottage Garden Society   (CGS)   1982
- NR Brandon, Main Rd, Betley, CREWE, Cheshire, CW3 9BH.
     (admin/p)
     01270 820940
     Admin: Clive Lane
- ▲ Un-incorporated Society
- Br 20
- ○ *H; to promote interest in cottage gardens & cottage garden
     plants
- ● Mtgs - Exhib - Garden visits
- M 8,500 i, UK / 500 i, o'seas
- ¶ The Cottage Gardener - 4.

COUNCIL ...
     For details of official & non-official councils, other than those
     listed below, see our companion volume **Councils,
     Committees & Boards** (note in introduction paragraph 6)

Council of Academic & Professional Publishers
     a group of the **Publishers Association**

**Council for the Advancement of Arab-British Understanding
(CAABU)   1967**
- ■ 1 Gough Square, LONDON, EC4A 3DE.   (hq)
     020 7832 1310   fax 020 7832 1329
     email caabu@caabu.org   http://www.caabu.org
     Dir & Chief Exec: Chris Doyle
- ▲ Company Limited by Guarantee
- ○ *X; 'Arab-British relations, Israel-Palestine, Iraq, War on Terror'
- Gp Education section (gives talks to schools); Parliamentary;
     Membership
- ● Conf - Mtgs - ET - Res - Exhib - Inf - LG
- ¶ Jnl - 6; £12 yr m, £20 yr nm.
     AR - 1; both free.

Council for Aluminium in Building   (CAB)   1995
- ■ Bank House, Bond's Mill, STONEHOUSE, Glos, GL10 3RF.
     (hq)
     01453 828851   fax 01453 828861
     http://www.c-a-b.org.uk
     Dir: Justin Ratcliffe
- ▲ Company Limited by Guarantee
- ○ *T; to represent all companies who use aluminium products in,
     or supply to, the construction industry
- Gp Fabricators & installers; System companies; Specialist suppliers;
     General suppliers
- ● Conf - Mtgs - ET - Inf - LG
- < Construction Products Assn
- M 10,000 i, 100 f
- ¶ NL.   LM - updated.
     Technical publications; £10 m, £20 nm.

Council of British Archaeology   (CBA)   1944
- ■ St Mary's House, 66 Bootham, YORK, YO30 7BZ.   (hq)
     01904 671417   fax 01904 671384
     email info@britarch.ac.uk   http://www.britarch.ac.uk
     Dir: Dr Mike Heyworth
- ▲ Company Limited by Guarantee; Registered Charity
- Br 13
- ○ *G, *L, *N; to advance the study & care of Britain's historic
     environment; to improve public awareness of Britain's past
- Gp Research & conservation; Education; Publication; Industrial
     archaeology panel; Young archaeologists' club
- ● Conf - Mtgs - ET - Res - Exhib - Comp - Inf - Lib - VE - LG
- < Eur Forum of Heritage Assns
- M 6,000 i, 505 org, UK / 300 i, o'seas
- ¶ British Archaeology - 6; ftm, £25 yr nm.
     British & Irish Archaeological Bibliography - 2; free.
     Publications catalogue available.

Council of Cricket Societies   (CofCS)   1969

NR   2 Jodrell Rd, WHALEY BRIDGE, High Peak, Derbys,
        SK23 7AN.   (hsp)
        01663 732866
        Hon Sec: Bob Wood
Br   25; Australia, New Zealand, South Africa, Zimbabwe
○   *S; to maintain interest in cricket during the 'off-season' period
●   Mtgs - Inviting speakers to address societies
M   c 3,000 i, UK / 1,000 i, o'seas
¶   NL - 1; ftm only.   NL of individual socs - irreg; free.

Council for Dance Education & Training (UK)   (CDET)   1978

■   Old Brewer's Yard, 17-19 Neal St, Covent Garden, LONDON,
        WC2H 9UY.   (hq)
        020 7240 5703   fax 020 7249 2547
        email info@cdet.org.uk   http://www.cdet.org.uk
        Dir: Serena Williams
▲   Company Limited by Guarantee; Registered Charity
○   *D; 'to advance the education of all persons & principally
        children, young people & students, in the art, practice &
        appreciation of the cultural significance of dance; to promote
        high standards in dance education & training'
Gp   Teaching society c'ee; Negotiation Board; Conference of
        Professional Dance Schools
●   Conf - Mtgs - ET - Res - Stat - Inf - LG - Accreditation &
        assessment service
M   20 i, 30 org
¶   UK Directory of Registered Dance Teachers - 1; ftm.
        Information sheets on dance education & training.
        AR - 1; ftm only.

Council of Docked Breeds   (CDB)   1991

NR   Marsburg, Whitehall Lane, THORPE le SOKEN, Essex,
        CO16 0AE.   (hsp/b)
        0700 078 1262
        email info@cdb.org   http://www.cdb.org
        Sec: Mrs Ginette Elliott
▲   Un-incorporated Society
○   *B, *V; to maintain the freedom of dog breeders to choose the
        docking option; to support the interests of owners & breeders
        (of traditional docked dog breeds) to government, the
        veterinary profession, the media & other interested parties
●   Inf - LG
<   is the UK branch of the Fedn of Field Sports Assns of the
        EU (FACE UK)
M   15,000 i, 500 socs
¶   Action pack sent on initial joining.

Council of Gas Detection & Environmental Monitoring (COGDEM)   1975

■   Unit 11 Theobald Business Park, Knowle Piece, Wilbury Way,
        HITCHIN, Herts, SG4 0TY.   (hq)
        01462 434322   fax 01462 434488
        email cogdem@aol.com   http://www.cogdem.org.uk
        Admin: Leigh Greenham
▲   Company Limited by Guarantee
○   *T; to safeguard the standards of, & expand the market for, gas
        detection, gas analysis & environmental monitoring
        equipment & services
Gp   Sub-groups: Carbon monoxide, Industrial
●   Mtgs - ET - Exam - Exhib - SG - Stat - Inf - Lib - LG
M   33 f, 2 org, UK / 2 f, o'seas

Council for Hospitality Management Education   (CHME)   1979

■   c/o Centre for International Hospitality Management Research,
        Faculty of Organisation Management, Sheffield Hallam
        University, Howard St, SHEFFIELD, S1 1WB.   (chmn/b)
        0114-225 2948   fax 0114-225 3343
        email s.ball:shu.ac.uk   http://www.chme.co.uk
        Chmn: Prof Stephen Ball
▲   Un-incorporated Society
○   *E; to enhance the professional development & status of
        hospitality management education
Gp   Industrial tutors; Learning teaching & assessment; Placement
        Advisers for Tourism & Hospitality (PATH); Research
●   Conf - Mtgs - ET - Res - Comp - Inf - LG - Lobbying
<   Coun of Australian University Tourism & Hospitality
        Educ (CAUTHE); Nordic Tourism Res Assn (NOTRA)
M   1i, 28 universities & colleges, UK / 3 i, o'seas
¶   A Review of Hospitality Management Education in the UK - 1;
        ftm, £25 nm.
        AR - 1; free.

Council for Independent Archaeology   1989

■   9 Nassington Rd, LONDON, NW3 2TX.   (chmn/p)
        020 7435 7517   fax 020 7916 2405
        email cia@archaeology.co.uk
        http://www.independents.org.uk
        Chmn: Andrew Selkirk,   Hon Sec: Anthony Clifford
▲   Registered Charity; Un-incorporated Society
○   *L; the promotion of archaeology independent of government,
        especially amateur archaeology
●   Conf - Mtgs - ET - Res - Inf - VE - LG
M   200 i, UK / 20 i, o'seas
¶   NL - 4; ftm only.

Council for Independent Education   (CIFE)   1973

NR   75 Foxbourne Rd, LONDON, SW17 8EN.   (hsp)
        020 8767 8666   fax 020 8767 9444
        email enquiries@cife.org.uk   http://www.cife.org.uk
        Hon Sec: Dr Norma R Ball
▲   Un-incorporated Society
○   *E, *P; for academic sixth form & tutorial colleges in the UK
●   Conf - Mtgs - ET - Exam - Comp - Inf - LG - Provider of first
        attempt & retake GCSE & A+A/S level courses
<   Brit Accreditation Coun
M   27 colleges
¶   LM & Guide to Courses - 1; free.
✕   2006 Council for Independent Further Education

Council for Independent Further Education
   since 2006 **Council for Independent Education**

Council of Mortgage Lenders   (CML)   1989

■   3 Savile Row, LONDON, W1S 3PB.   (hq)
        020 7437 0075
        http://www.cml.org.uk
▲   Un-incorporated Society
○   *T; interests of the UK residential mortgage market
●   Conf - Mtgs - ET - Res - Stat - Inf - Lib - LG
M   151 f
¶   [all on website]

Council of Organisations Registering Homeopaths   (CORH)   1999

■   11 Wingle Tye Rd, BURGESS HILL, W Sussex, RH15 9HR.
        (admin/p)
        01444 239494   fax 01444 236848
        email admin@corh.org.uk   http://www.corh.org.uk
        Admin: Peter Mitchell
▲   Un-incorporated Society
○   *P; to establish a single voluntary, self-regulating UK register of
        professional homeopaths
Gp   Working: Accreditation, CPD, Ethics, Registration
●   Conf - SG - Inf
M   12 org
¶   CORH News;   Consultation Document - irreg; both free on
        website.

Council for the Protection of Rural England
since June 18 2003 **Campaign to Protect Rural England**

Council for Registered Gas Installers (CORGI) 1991
■ 1 Elmwood, Chineham Park, Crockford Lane, BASINGSTOKE,
Hants, RG24 8WG. (hq)
0870 401 2200   fax 0870 401 2600
email enquiries@corgi-group.com
http://www.corgi-gas-safety.com
Chief Exec: Mike Thompson,   Co Sec: Philippa Caine
▲ Company Limited by Guarantee
○ *T; the national watchdog for gas safety
● Inf - LG - Inspection of registered businesses - Dealing with
customer complaints regarding gas safety - Gas safety
publicity - Nationally accredited certification scheme for
individual gas fitting operatives
M 52,000 f
¶ Gas Installer Magazine - 11; ftm.
AR; free.

**Council for the Registration of Schools Teaching Dyslexic Pupils
(CReSTeD) 1993**
■ Greygarth, Littleworth, Winchcombe, CHELTENHAM, Glos,
GL54 5BT. (regd/office)
01242 604852   fax 01242 604852
email admin@crested.org.uk
http://www.crested.org.uk
Admin: Christine Hancock
▲ Registered Charity
○ *W; to register schools & other educational institutions
providing facilities for & care of dyslexic pupils (those with
learning difficulties)
● Mtgs - Inf
< Brit Dyslexia Assn; Dyslexia Inst
M 85 schools
¶ Register of Schools that help Dyslexic Children - 2; free.

Council for Responsible Nutrition
NR 67 Upshire Rd, WALTHAM ABBEY, Essex, EN9 3NZ.
020 8807 4247
email info@crn-uk.org
Exec Sec: Julie Hayward
○ *T; for dietary supplement companies; manufacturers of
vitamins, minerals & micronutrients

Council for Scottish Archaeology (CSA) 1944
NR c/o National Museums of Scotland, Chambers St, EDINBURGH,
EH1 1JF. (hq)
0131-247 4119   fax 0131-247 4126
http://www.britarch.ac.uk/csa
Dir: Eila McQueen
▲ Registered Charity
○ *E, *G, *N; to secure Scotland's past for the future by
promoting public education & appreciation of Scotland's
archaeology

Counselling 1998
■ 62 Douglas Towers, Radwell Drive, BRADFORD, W Yorks,
BD5 0QR. (hsp)
email info@counselling.ltd.uk
http://www.counselling.ltd.uk
Sec: Dean Greenhough
▲ Company Limited by Guarantee; Registered Charity
○ *W; to provide free counselling to those on low income
throughout the UK; to maintain a website of counselling
colleges & counselling related matters
● ET - Exam - Res - Stat - Inf
M 2,500 i, c 250 f
¶ Counselling NL - 12;   LM (website);   AR - 1; all free.

Counselling & Psychotherapy in Scotland
since 2002 **COSCA (Counselling & Psychotherapy in Scotland)**

Country Doctors Association (CDA) 1998
NR 114 Burford Way, HITCHIN, Herts, SG5 2XP. (chmn/p)
01462 434515
http://www.countrydoctor.co.uk
Chmn: Dr David Roberts
▲ Un-incorporated Society
○ *M; education & welfare & promotion of country doctors & their
staff
Gp Dispensing by doctors; Rural welfare; Rural diseases; Zoonoses
● ET - Res - Stat
M i & f
¶ www.countrydoctor.co.uk; daily updates (no password
required).

Country Gentlemen's Association Ltd (CGA) 1903
§ Chalke House, Station Rd, Codford, WARMINSTER, Wilts,
BA12 0JX. (hq)
01985 850706   fax 01985 850378
email enquiries@thecga.co.uk
http://www.thecga.co.uk
Chmn: Colin Ingleby-Mackenzie
○ to provide goods by mail order & insurance & professional
services to members

Country Houses Association Ltd
has closed

Country Land & Business Association (CLA) 1907
NR 16 Belgrave Sq, LONDON, SW1X 8PQ. (hq)
020 7235 0511   fax 020 7235 4696
email mail@cla.org.uk   http://www.cla.org.uk
Pres: David Fursdon
▲ Un-incorporated Society
Br 20
○ *P; the national association of owners of rural land &
businesses in England & Wales
Gp Advice: Agriculture & land use; Water; Legal; Tax
● Conf - Mtgs - Stat - Inf - VE - LG
< Eur Landowners Org
M 40,000 i
¶ Country Landowner - 12; ftm.

Countryside Alliance 1997
■ The Old Town Hall, 367 Kennington Rd, LONDON,
SE11 4PT. (hq)
020 7840 9200   fax 020 7793 8484
email info@countryside-alliance.org
http://www.countryside-alliance.org
Pres: Baroness Ann Mallalieu
▲ Un-incorporated Society
○ *K; to champion & campaign for country sports, the countryside
& the rural way of life
Gp Specialist campaigns for: Angling, Coursing, Falconry,
Fisheries, Hunting, Rural issues, Shooting
Honest Food - the Campaign for Independent Food
● ET - Res - Stat - Inf - VE - LG
< Fedn Eur Field Sports Gps (FACE)
M 80,000 i, 1,500 f, 320,000 org
¶ Country Sports - 4; ftm.

Countryside Ireland 1970
IRL 100 Ballygall Road East, Glasnevin, DUBLIN 11, Republic of
Ireland.
353 (1) 834 8279
email secretary@countrysideireland.com
Hon Sec: Philip E de N Lawton
○ *S
× 2002 (June) Irish Field & Country Sports Society

Countryside Management Association   (CMA)   1966
- ■   Writtle College, Lordship Rd, Writtle, CHELMSFORD, Essex, CM1 3RR.   (hq)
  01245 424116   fax 01245 420456
  http://www.countrysidemanagement.org.uk
  Admin: Mike Anderson
- ○   *P; to promote professional & sustainable management of the countryside & urban greenspace
- ●   Conf - Mtgs - ET - LG
- M   i
- ¶   Ranger - 4; ftm, £5 nm.

Countrywide Holidays Association
  the activities of the CHA have been transferred to the Countryside UK Trust, which is outside the scope of this Directory

County Antrim Agricultural Association (Ballymena Show) (CAAA)   1898
- ■   The Showgrounds, Warden St, BALLYMENA, Co Antrim, BT43 7DR.   (hq)
  028 2565 2666   fax 028 2565 2666
  email ballymena.showoffice@virgin.net
  Sec: Mrs Jane Lamont
- ▲   Registered Charity
- ○   *F; to encourage the breeding of all classes of farm stock; the cultivation of farm crops & products; to encourage cottage industries, agricultural & horticultural education
- ●   Exhib - Comp
- <   Assn Show & Agricl Orgs; NI Shows' Assn
- M   450 i

County Armagh Wildlife Society   (CAWS)   1952
- ■   Drumherriff Lodge, 37 Old Orchard Rd, LOUGHALL, Co Armagh, BT61 8JD.   (hsp)
  028 3889 1317
  http://www.armaghwild.mysite.wanadoo-members.co.uk/index.jhtml
  Hon Sec: Dr J S Faulkner
- ▲   Un-incorporated Society
- ○   *L; the study of the natural history, botany, zoology & geology of County Armagh & Ireland
- Gp   Butterfly & moth recording on behalf of Ulster Wildlife Trust in local nature reserve
- ●   Mtgs - Stat - Lib - VE
- M   c 80 i, 1 org
- ¶   AR; ftm.   LM.
- ×   2001 (15 January) Armagh Field Naturalists Society

County Education Officers of Two Tier Authorities
- ■   c/o Graham Badman, Kent County Council, Sessions House, County Hall, MAIDSTONE, Kent, ME14 1XQ.
  01622 696550
- ○   *E

County Surveyors Society   (CSS)   1885
- ■   Environmental Services Dept, Wiltshire County Hall, TROWBRIDGE, Wilts, BA14 8JD.   (hsb)
  01225 756556   fax 01225 713985
  email css@wiltshire.gov.uk   http://www.cssnet.org.uk
  Hon Sec: George Batten
- ▲   Un-incorporated Society
- Br   3
- ○   *P
- Gp   C'ees: Engineering, Finance, Strategic planning & regeneration, Transport & environment, Waste
- ●   Conf - Mtgs - ET - Res - SG - Stat - LG
- M   116 i, 221 honorary members, 43 special honorary members
- ¶   A wide variety of technical reports.
- ×   2002 CSS (County Surveyors Society)

Coventry & District Archaeological Society   (CADAS)   1965
- NR   86 Potters Green Rd, Potters Green, COVENTRY, Warks, CV2 2AN.   (hsp)
  Hon Sec: Angela Warner
- ▲   Un-incorporated Society
- ○   *L; to promote archaeology in the Coventry area; to care for Coventry heritage

Coventry & Warwickshire Chamber of Commerce   1997
- NR   Oak Tree Court, Binley Business Park, Harry Weston Rd, COVENTRY, Warks, CV3 2UN.   (hq)
  024 7665 4321   fax 024 7645 0242
  email info@cw-chamber.co.uk
  http://www.cw-chamber.co.uk
  Chief Exec: Louise Bennett
- ▲   Company Limited by Guarantee
- Br   Rugby, Coventry & South, Mid & Northern Warwickshire
- ○   *C
- Gp   Retail; Engineering & manufacturing; Professional & commercial; Building & construction; Transport; Hotel & leisure
- ●   Conf - Mtgs - ET - Exams - Res - Exhib - Stat - Expt - Inf - Lib - LG
- <   BCC
- M   2,300 f
- ¶   Enterprise Newspaper - 12;   Update - 12; both ftm.
  AR - 1; free.
- ×   2001 (6 April) Coventry & Warwickshire Chamber of Commerce, Training & Enterprise

Covered Conductors Association
  a group of the **British Cables Association**

CP Sport England & Wales
- NR   Unit 5 Heathcoat Building, Nottingham Science & Technology Park, NOTTINGHAM, NG7 2QJ.   (hq)
  0115-925 7027   fax 0115-922 4666
  http://www.cpsport.org
- ○   *S; for sportspeople with cerebral palsy

Craft Brewing Association   (1995)
- NR   49 Belper Rd, DERBY, DE1 3EP.
  01332 347601
  email enquiries@craftbrewing.org.uk
  http://www.craftbrewing.org.uk
  Coordinator: James McCrorie
- ○   *P, *T; to uphold the tradition of private brewing to the highest standards
- M   400 i & f

Craft Guild of Chefs (incorporating the Cookery & Food Association)   (CFA)   1885
- NR   1 Victoria Parade, by 331 Sandycombe Rd, RICHMOND, Surrey, TW9 3NB.   (hq)
  020 8948 3870   fax 020 8948 3944
- ○   *P; to promote the art & science of cookery, supervisory & management skills
- M   i

Craft Guild of Traditional Bowyers & Fletchers (CGTBF) 1988
■ Yew Corner, 29 Batley Court, OLDLAND, South Glos,
BS30 8YZ. (clerk/p)
0117 932 3276 fax 0117 932 3276
email guildclerk@btinternet.com
http://www.bowyersandfletchersguild.org
Clerk; Mrs V M Soar
▲ Un-incorporated Society
○ *P; a forum for all involved in the manufacture of quality,
traditional archery equipment; to maintain & improve the
standard of bow & arrow making
Gp Bowyers; Fletchers; Arrowsmiths; Stringmakers
● Conf - ET (incl apprentices) - Exam (for apprentices &
established craftsmen before membership)
M 35 i, UK / 10 i, o'seas
¶ News Booklet - 2; Bulletin - irreg; both ftm only.

Craft Potters' Association of Great Britain (CPA) 1957
NR 25 Fouberts Place, LONDON, W1F 7QF. (hq)
020 7437 6781
email cpa@ceramicreview.com
Sec: Tony Ainsworth
▲ Company Limited by Guarantee; Registered Charity
○ *A; promotion of high quality, hand-made ceramics,
particularly work of original design & individual character
made by members
● Conf - Mtgs - Exhib - VE
M 150 fellows, 600 associates, 200 professional, UK /
50 associates, o'seas
¶ Ceramic Review - 6.
CPA News - 6. Potters - 2 yrly.

Crane Interest Group
a special interest group of the **Construction Plant-hire
Association**

Cranio Facial Support Group
since 2003 **Headlines, the Cranio Facial Support Group**

Craniofacial Society of Great Britain 2001
NR c/o Faculty of Dental Surgery, 35-43 Lincoln's Inn Fields,
LONDON, WC2A 3PE. (hsb)
020 7869 6802
email honsec@cfsgb.org.uk http://www.cfsgb.org.uk
Admin: Natalia Ford
▲ Company Limited by Guarantee; Registered Charity
○ *M, *P; for those concerned with cleft lip & palate & other
craniofacial anomalies
Gp Plastic surgeons; Orthodontists; Speech therapists; Maxillofacial
surgeons; Nurses
● Conf - Mtgs - ET - Res
M 300 i, UK / 20 i, o'seas

Craniosacral Therapy Association of the UK (CSTA) 1990
■ Monomark House, 27 Old Gloucester St, LONDON,
WC1N 3XX. (mail/address)
0700 078 4735
email secretary@craniosacral.co.uk
http://www.craniosacral.co.uk
Sec: Roger R James
▲ Un-incorporated Society
○ *P; to disseminate information about craniosacral therapy; to
regulate training organisations
● Conf - Mtgs - ET - Res - Inf - Maintain a register of qualified
members
M 450 i, 5 org
¶ The Fulcrum - 3; ftm, £18.50 yr nm.

Creator's Rights Alliance (CRA) 2000
NR British Music House, 26 Berners Street, LONDON, W1P 3DB.
(hq)
020 7436 7296
Chmn: David Ferguson
▲ Un-incorporated Society
○ *N; an alliance of the major organisations representing
copyright creators & content providers throughout the media,
particularly television, radio & the press
● Conf - Mtgs - Inf - LG
M 14 orgs
¶ Between a Rock & a Hard Place (the problems facing freelance
creators in the media market place).
Creators Have Rights (Video).

Credit Protection Association plc (CPA) 1914
■ CPA House, 350 King St, LONDON, W6 0RX. (hq)
020 8846 0000 fax 020 8741 7459
email info@cpa.co.uk http://www.cpa.co.uk
Hon Sec: E P T Roney
Chmn & Managing Dir: David S Baber
Br Bolton, Bristol, Birmingham, Doncaster, Newmarket, Falkirk
○ *T; for credit management services & debt recovery
● Inf
< Amer Collectors Assn (USA); Credit Services Assn (UK)
M 2,800 f
¶ The Flow - irreg; free.

Credit Services Association (CSA) 1902
■ Wingrove House (2nd floor east), Ponteland Rd, NEWCASTLE
UPON TYNE, NE5 3AJ. (hq)
0191-286 5656 fax 0191-286 0900
email info@csa-uk.com http://www.csa-uk.com
Exec Dir: Kurt Obermaier
○ *T
Gp Debt buyers & sellers
● Conf - Mtgs - ET - Exhib - LG - City & Guilds diploma course
for the debt collection industry
< Fedn Eur Nat Collection Assns (FENCA)
M 260 f, UK / 30 f, o'seas
¶ NL - 6; AR - 1; both ftm.

Cremation Society of Great Britain 1874
■ 16-16a Albion Place (2nd floor), MAIDSTONE, Kent,
ME14 5DZ. (hq)
01622 688292/3
email info@cremation.org.uk
http://www.cremation.org.uk
Sec: R N Arber
▲ Registered Charity
○ *L; promotion of cremation; supply of technical & other
information on every aspect of cremation & crematorium
administration
● Conf - Stat - Inf - Lib - LG
< Intl Cremation Fedn
M i
¶ Pharos International (Jnl) - 4; £28.
Directory of British Crematoria - 1; £21 (inserts)(£25 with
binder).
British Crematoria in Public Profile; £4.13.
Directory of Pet Crematoria; £2.50.
May Catholics choose Cremation?; 35p.
AR & Accounts - 1; ftm only.
Other prices on application.

Cricket & Hockey Association
since 2006 **Sports Manufacturers & Retailers Trade
Association**

© CBD Research Ltd · Beckenham · BR3 5JS · Tel 020 8650 7745 · Fax 020 8650 0768 · E-mail cbd@cbdresearch.com · www.cbdresearch.com

Cricket Memorabilia Society (CMS) 1987
- ■ [communication by email only] (hsp)
  email cms87@btinternet.com   http://www.cms.cricket.org
  Hon Sec: Steve Cashmore
- ▲ Un-incorporated Society
- ○ *G; the preservation of cricket memorabilia
- ● Mtgs - Res - Exhib - Inf - Valuations
- M 850 i
- ¶ Jnl - 4; free.
  Directory of Collectors Interests - 2 yrly; ftm only.

Cricket Scotland 1908
- NR National Cricket Academy, Ravelston, EDINBURGH,
  EH4 3NT. (hq)
  0131-313 7420
- ▲ Un-incorporated Society
- ○ *S; governing body of cricket in Scotland
- ● Conf - Mtgs - ET - Exam - Comp - Stat - Inf - Lib
- < Intl Cricket Coun
- M 650 i, 72 life members, 168 clubs
- ¶ Scottish Cricket - 1.   NL - 2.
- ✕ 2004 Scottish Cricket Union

Cricket Society 1945
- ■ PO Box 6024, LEIGHTON BUZZARD, Beds, LU7 2ZS. (hsp)
  01525 370204
  email davidwood@cricketsociety.com
  http://www.cricketsociety.com
  Hon Sec: David Wood
- ▲ Un-incorporated Society
- Br 3
- ○ *S; to encourage a love of cricket in all its spheres - for all ages
  & interests - playing, watching, reading or listening
- ● Mtgs - Lib
- M 1,900 i, UK / 100 i, o'seas
- ¶ Jnl - 2; ftm, £3 nm.   News Bulletin - 8; ftm only.

Crime Concern 1988
- NR Beaver House, 147-150 Victoria Rd, SWINDON, Wilts,
  SN1 3BU. (hq)
  01793 863500   fax 01793 514654
  email info@crimeconcern.org.uk
  http://www.crimeconcern.org.uk
  Chief Exec: Roger Howard
- ▲ Registered Charity
- ○ *K; to specialise in issues involving youth crime - criminality,
  high crime neighbourhoods, business & town centre crime, &
  rural crime, as well as hospital, passenger, school & women's
  safety
- ● Conf - ET - Res - Exhib - Comp - Inf - Lib - LG
- < Eur Forum for Urban Security; Intl Centre for the Prevention of
  Crime
- M 25 f
- ¶ Crime Concern Annual Review; free.
  Various other publications.

Crime Reporters Association (CRA) 1945
- NR c/o John Steele, Daily Telegraph, 1 Canada Square (12th
  Floor), LONDON, E14 5DT. (hsb)
  Gen Sec: John Steele
- ○ *P; to represent crime reporters of the responsible media, in
  consultations with Home Office & police organisations

Crime Writers Association (CWA) 1953
- ■ PO Box 273, BOREHAMWOOD, Herts, WD6 2XA. (hsb)
  email info@thecwa.co.uk   http://www.thecwa.co.uk
  Sec: Liz Evans
- ▲ Company Limited by Guarantee
- ○ *P; for all involved in crime writing (authors, publishers, agents,
  booksellers)
- ● Conf - Mtgs - Comp - Inf - Administration of: CWA Cartier
  Diamond Dagger, Gold Dagger, New Blood Dagger, Ian
  Fleming Steel Dagger, Duncan Lawrie Dagger (International
  Dagger) - Ellis Peters Award - Debut Dagger
- < Mystery Writers of America
- M 400 i, UK / 100 i, o'seas
- ¶ Red Herrings - 12;   LM - 1; both ftm only.

Crimean War Research Society 1983
- ■ 4 Castle Estate, RIPPONDEN, W Yorks, HX6 4JY. (hsp)
  01422 823529
  http://www.crimeanwar.org/
  Hon Sec: David Cliff
- ▲ Un-incorporated Society
- ○ *L, *G; to encourage research into all aspects of the Crimean
  War, 1853-1856
- ● Conf - Mtgs - Res - Exhib - SG - Inf - Lib
- M 250 i, UK / 100 i, o'seas
- ¶ The War Correspondent (Jnl) - 4; £15 UK (£20 o'seas) m only.

Criminal Bar Association of England & Wales (CBA) 1969
- NR 289 High Holborn (2nd floor), LONDON, WC1V 7HZ. (hq)
  020 7242 1289   fax 020 7242 1107
  email jbradley@barcouncil.org.uk
  http://www.criminalbar.com
  Admin: Julian Bradley
- ▲ Un-incorporated Society
- ○ *P; practising members of the Bar of England & Wales
- ● Conf - Mtgs - ET - Res - SG - Inf - Lib - Empl - LG
- M c 3,000 i
- ¶ NL - 4; free.   Brochure.

Criminal Justice Association
is no longer active.

Criminal Law Solicitors' Association 1990
- NR New England House (Suite 2 Level 6), New England St,
  BRIGHTON, E Sussex, BN1 4GH. (hq)
  01273 676725
  Admin: Sue Johnson
- ▲ Un-incorporated Society
- ○ *P
- Gp Training divn
- ● Conf - Mtgs - ET - Res - Exhib - SG - Inf - LG
- M 1,200 i
- ¶ Membership & agency list - 1; £15 m, £21 nm.

Critics' Circle 1913
- ■ c/o Catherine Cooper Events, 69 Marylebone Lane, LONDON,
  W1U 2PH. (admin/b)
  020 7224 1410
  http://www.criticscircle.org.uk
  Admin: Catherine Cooper,   Hon Sec: Charles Hedges
- ○ *P; critics of the performing arts

Crohn's in Childhood Research Association   1978
■ Parkgate House, 356 West Barnes Lane, MOTSPUR PARK,
   Surrey, KT3 6NB.   (hq)
   020 8949 6209   fax 020 8942 2044
   email support@cicra.org   http://www.cicra.org
   Chmn Bd of Trustees: Mrs Margaret Lee
▲ Registered Charity
○ *K, *W; to create wider awareness & understanding of Crohn's
   disease & ulcerative colitis, particularly as it affects children &
   young adults; to raise funds to support medical research
   aimed at finding more effective treatments & eventual cure
Gp Children & youth; Health
● Conf - Mtgs - Res
M 3,000 i
¶ The Insider - 4.

Cromwell Association   1935
■ c/o Dr Peter Gaunt - Dept of History, University of Chester,
   Parkgate Rd, CHESTER, CH1 4BJ.   (chmn/b)
   01244 347341   fax 01244 373379
   email pgaunt@chester.ac.uk
   http://www.olivercromwell.org
   Chmn: Dr Peter Gaunt,   Hon Sec: Dr Judith Hutchinson
▲ Un-incorporated Society
○ *L; to commemorate Oliver Cromwell (1599-1658); to
   stimulate interest in Cromwell & the general history of the
   British Isles & dependent territories from the birth of
   Cromwell to the Restoration; to encourage scholarly study of
   the period
● Conf - ET - Comp - Lib
M c 600 i, 6 libraries, UK / c 30 i, 1 library, o'seas
¶ Cromwelliana - 1; ftm, £7.50 nm.   NL - 2; ftm only.

Crop Protection Association   (CPA)   1928
■ 18-20 Cully Court, Orton Southgate, PETERBOROUGH,
   Cambs, PE2 6XS.   (hq)
   01733 367219   fax 01733 367212
   http://www.cropprotection.org.uk
   Chief Exec: Peter Sanguinetti
▲ Company Limited by Guarantee
○ *T; the responsible & safe manufacture & use of agrochemicals
   with due regard for the interests of the community & the
   environment
● Mtgs - Exam - Exhib - Stat - Inf
< Eur Crop Protection Assn (ECPA)
M 40 f
¶ Annual Review;   Hbk; both free.
   Publications & other resources.

Croquet Association   (CA)   1897
■ Cheltenham Croquet Club, Old Bath Rd, CHELTENHAM, Glos,
   GL53 7DF.   (hq)
   01242 242318
   Sec: Klim Seabright
▲ Un-incorporated Society
Br 9
○ *S; the governing body for the game of croquet
● Conf - ET - Exam - Res - Comp - Stat - Inf - LG
M 1,600 i, 120 clubs, UK / 60 i, 20 clubs, o'seas
¶ The Croquet Gazette - 6.

Crossroads: Caring for Carers   1974
■ Information & Communications Dept, 49 Charles St (3rd floor),
   CARDIFF, CF10 2GD.
   0845 450 0350   fax 029 2022 2311
   email communications@crossroads.org.uk
   http://www.crossroads.org.uk
   10 Regent Place, RUGBY, Warks, CV21 2PN.   (regd/office).
   Chief Exec: Anne Roberts
▲ Company Limited by Guarantee; Registered Charity
Br 200 (England & Wales)
○ *W; to provide practical support for carers; to supply trained
   support workers to relieve carers for essential breaks
M i
× 2002-03 Caring for Carers (Crossroads Association)

Crossword Club   1978
■ Coombe Farm, Awbridge, ROMSEY, Hants, SO51 0HN.   (hsb)
   01794 524346   fax 01794 514988
   email bh@thecrosswordclub.co.uk
   http://www.thecrosswordclub.co.uk
   Sec: Brian Head
▲ Registered Business Name
○ *G; promotion of the art of the crossword - especially the
   setting & solving of puzzles of a high level of construction &
   difficulty
   NOTE: 'we do not offer non-members free advice on selling
   crosswords'
M c 700 i, 2 f, UK / c 50 i, 2 org, o'seas
¶ Crossword - 12; ftm only.   Hbk - irreg; free.
   Crossword Club Guide to Playfair; £1.25.

** Crown Imperial
   Organisation lost: see Introduction paragraph 3

Croydon Chamber of Commerce & Industry   1891
■ Commerce House, 1 Wandle Rd, CROYDON, Surrey,
   CR9 1HY.   (hq)
   020 8680 2165   fax 020 8688 4587
   email info@croydonchamber.org.uk
   http://www.croydonchamber.org.uk
   Chief Exec: Hardeep Kalsi
▲ Company Limited by Guarantee
○ *C
● Conf - Mtgs - ET - Exhib - Expt - Inf - LG - Workshps - Seminars
< Brit Chams Comm (BCC); London Cham Comm Ind (LCCI)
M c 950 i, f & org
¶ Business South - 10; ftm, £1.50 nm.
   Directory of Members - 1;   AR; both ftm only.

**Croydon Natural History & Scientific Society Ltd   (CNHSS)
1870**
■ 96A Brighton Rd, SOUTH CROYDON, Surrey, CR2 6AD.   (hq)
   020 8688 4539
   http://www.greig51.freeserve.co.uk/cnhss
   Pres: Arnold H Shaw,   Hon Sec: Brian Lancaster
▲ Company Limited by Guarantee; Registered Charity
○ *L; covering NE Surrey, NW Kent & southern London boroughs
Gp Archaeology; Botany & mycology; Entomology; Geology;
   Industrial studies; Local history; Meteorology; Ornithology
● Conf - Mtgs - Res - Exhib - SG - Inf - Lib - VE - Museums
   The library may be visited by appointment only, contact Paul W
   Sowan 020 8681 6293
< Botanical Soc of the Brit Isles; Brit Assn for Local History; Coun
   for Brit Archaeology; Geologists' Assn
M 411 i, 21 org
¶ Proceedings - irreg;   Bulletin - 2; ftm, prices vary nm.
   Croydon Church Townscape; £4.50.
   The River Wandle: Distribution of its Flora;   The
   Nonconformist Experience in Croydon; both £1.
   From Palace to Washhouse: A Study of the Old Palace,
   Croydon, from 1780 to 1887; £3.50.
   The Archbishop's town: the making of mediaeval
   Croydon; £2.95.
   Many other publications on Croydon & its history.

Cruising Association   (CA)   1908
NR CA House, 1 Northey St, Lime House Basin, LONDON,
   E14 8BT.   (hq)
   020 7537 2828   fax 020 7537 2266
   email office@cruising.org.uk
   http://www.cruising.org.uk
   Gen Mgr: Ian Barker
○ *S; an amateur organisation encouraging cruising in yachts &
   boats; protection of the interests of yachtsmen

© CBD Research Ltd · Beckenham · BR3 5JS · Tel 020 8650 7745 · Fax 020 8650 0768 · E-mail cbd@cbdresearch.com · www.cbdresearch.com

Crusaders   1906

NR   Kestin House, 45 Crescent Rd, LUTON, Beds, LU2 0AH.   (hq)
     01582 589850   fax 01582 721702
     Exec Dir: Matt Summerfield
▲   Registered Charity
○   *R, *Y; committed to sharing the Christian gospel with young
     people through interdenominational youth groups, overseas
     projects & holidays
●   Conf - ET - Exhib - Comp - SG - Inf
<   Nat Youth Org; Evangelical Alliance
M   20,000 i

Cruse - Bereavement Care   (CRUSE)   1959

NR   Cruse House, 126 Sheen Rd, RICHMOND, Surrey, TW9 1UR.
     (hq)
     020 8939 9530   fax 020 8940 7638
     email info@crusebereavementcare.org.uk
     Exec Dir: Anne Viney
▲   Company Limited by Guarantee; Registered Charity
Br   180
○   *W; offers help to people bereaved by death, in any way,
     whatever their age, nationality or belief; also free counselling
     service, advice on practical matters & opportunities for
     contact with others through support groups
●   Conf - Mtgs - ET - Res - Stat - Inf - Lib - Counselling services -
     Training in bereavement counselling & to external
     organisations in bereavement awareness
     Helpline: 0870 167 1677
<   Intl Fedn Widows & Widowers Orgs; NCVO
M   6,000 i
¶   Publications list available.

Crystal & Healing Federation   (CHF)   1997

NR   6 Buer Rd, LONDON, SW6 4LA.   (hsp)
     020 7736 0283   fax 020 7736 0283
     email vhflondon@aol.com
     http://www.crystalandhealing.com
     Hon Sec: Henriette Maasdijk,
     Chief Exec: Lettie Vantol
○   *P; practitioners in crystal healing, vibration healing & Bach
     flower remedies
●   Mtgs - ET - Exam - Res - Exhib - SG
<   Brit Crystal Healers (BCH)
M   112 i, UK / 7 i, o'seas
¶   NL - 4; ftm, £10 yr nm.
     Crystals & Healing for Everyone [book].

Crystal Palace Foundation   (CPF)   1979

■   Crystal Palace Museum, Anerley Hill, LONDON, SE19 2BA.
     (hq)
     0788 933 8812   fax 0870 133 7920
     email crystalpalacefoundation@hotmail.com
     http://www.crystalpalacefoundation.org.uk
     Sec: David Britton,   Chmn: Melvyn Harrison
▲   Registered Charity
○   *G; to support the Crystal Palace Museum
●   ET - Res - Exhib - SG - Inf - Lib - PL - VE - Promotes education
     & research - Publishing work concerned with Crystal Palace
<   Assn Indep Museums (AIM); Brit Assn Friends of Museums;
     Urban Parks Forum (UPF)
M   700 i, 10 org, UK / 50 i, o'seas
¶   Crystal Palace Foundation News - 4; ftm only.
     New Crystal Palace Matters - 4; ftm, £1 nm.

CTC - the UK's national cyclists' organisation
     see **Cyclists' Touring Club**

Cue Sports Association
     since 2006 **Sports Manufacturers & Retailers Trade
     Association**

Cued Speech Association   (CSA)   1980

■   9 Jawbone Hill, DARTMOUTH, Devon, TQ6 9RW.   (hq)
     01803 832786   fax 01803 835311
     email info@cuedspeech.co.uk
     http://www.cuedspeech.co.uk
     Chief Exec: Anne Worsfold
▲   Company Limited by Guarantee; Registered Charity
○   *W; to provide information & training in cued speech - a simple
     sound-based system comprising eight handshapes, used in
     four positions near the mouth, in conjunction with the lip
     patterns of normal speech so as to make all the sounds of
     the English language clearly understandable to deaf children
     & adults
●   ET - Exam - Exhib - Inf - Provision of information about training
     in cued speech
<   UK Coun on Deafness
M   70 i
¶   NL - 4;   AR - 1; both free.
     Booklet; £2.   Information sheets; free.
     Video (information); £5.   Video (instruction); £10.
×   2000 National Centre for Cued Speech

Cumann na Scribheann nGaedhilge
     see **Irish Texts Society (Cumann na Scribheann nGaedhilge)**

Cumberland Agricultural Society   1836

■   Warcarr, Greenhead, BRAMPTON, Cumbria, CA8 7HY.   (sp/b)
     01697 747397   fax 01697 747397
     email cumberland.show@virgin.net
     http://www.cumberlandshow.co.uk
     Sec: Donella Rozario
▲   Un-incorprated Society with charitable status
○   *F
●   Mtgs - Exhib (Cumberland Agricultural Show) - Comp - Inf
M   c 1,000 i
¶   Catalogue - 1; £2.50.   Schedule - 1; free.

**Cumberland & Westmorland Antiquarian & Archaeological
     Society   (CWAAS)   1866**

NR   Brantbeck, Windy Hall Rd, BOWNESS-on-WINDERMERE,
     Cumbria, LA23 3HX.   (hsp)
     01539 563919
     email eajones@skynow.net   http://www.cwaas.org.uk
     Hon Sec: E A Jones
▲   Registered Charity
○   *L; the study of the archaeology, history, genealogy, customs &
     traditions of the old counties of Cumberland, Westmorland &
     Lancashire north of the sands
Gp   C'ees: Parish registers; Industrial archaeology; Regional;
     Research
●   Mtgs - Res - Inf - Lib - VE
<   Coun of Brit Archaeology
M   c 850 i, c 120 org
¶   Transactions - 1; ftm, £15 nm.   NL - 3; ftm only.
     Research series, Record series & Extra series - all irreg;
     prices vary.

Cumbria Chamber of Commerce   (CCC)   1999

NR   James Street, CARLISLE, Cumbria, CA2 5DA.   (hq)
     01228 534120   fax 01228 515602
     email contact@cumbriachamberofcommerce.co.uk
     http://www.cumbriachamberofcommerce.co.uk
     Chief Exec: Rob Johnston
▲   Un-incorporated Society
Br   Kendal
○   *C; support & services for the Cumbrian business community
●   Expt - Inf - Lib - LG
<   Brit Cham Comm
M   f & org
¶   Business Networking - 6.

Curia Baronis   1985
NR   Woodbury Manor, Woodbury Close, CANVEY ISLAND, Essex,
    SS8 9PP.   (dir/p)
    01268 697815
    Dir: R Woodbury
○   *G; for barons & lords of the manor; keeps members informed
    of current legislation & events relating to feudal times
Gp   Stewardship service; Register of feudal titles; Research dept
●   Conf - Res - Inf - Lib - Registration
M   [private]
¶   Publications - 4.

**CURL: Consortium of Research Libraries in the British Isles
(CURL)   1985**
■   The Old Gymnasium, University of Birmingham, Edgbaston,
    BIRMINGHAM, W Midlands, B15 2TT.   (hq)
    0121-415 8108   fax 0121-415 8109
    http://www.curl.ac.uk
    Exec Dir: Robin Green
▲   Company Limited by Guarantee; Registered Charity
○   *P; to increase the ability of research libraries to share
    resources for the benefit of the local, national & international
    research community
●   Res - Lib
<   Ligue des Bibliothéques Européennes de Recherche (LIBER);
    Digital Presvn Coalition; Counting Online use of Networked
    Electronic Resources (COUNTER)
M   29 research libraries
¶   AR - 1.
✕   2004 Consortium of University Research LIbraries

Curwen Institute   1972
■   5 Bigbury Close, Stivichell, COVENTRY, Warks, CV3 5AJ.
    (dir/p)
    024 7641 3010   fax 024 7641 3010
    email admin@johncurwensociety.org.uk
    http://www.johncurwensociety.org.uk
    Dir: John Dowding
○   *E; to develop & extend the teaching of music in schools by
    means of a modern version of John Curwen's Tonic Sol-fa
    system
    The Institute is funded by the John Curwen Society.

Cussel an Tavas Kernuack
    see **Cornish Language Council (Cussel an Tavas Kernuack)**

**Custom Electronic Design & Installation Association   (CEDIA
UK)**
NR   Unit 2 Phoenix Park, ST NEOTS, Cambs, PE19 8EP.
    01480 213744   fax 01480 213469
    email info@cedia.co.uk   http://www.cedia.co.uk

Customer Contact Association   (CCA)   1996
■   20 Newton Place, GLASGOW, G3 7PY.   (hq)
    0141-564 9010   fax 0141-564 9011
    email cca@cca.org.uk   http://www.cca.org.uk
    Chief Exec: Colin Mackay
▲   Company Limited by Guarantee
○   *T; development & promotion of customer contact
Gp   Industry council; Standards council
●   Conf - Mtgs - ET - Res - Exhib - Inf - LG
M   c 800 f UK, 20 f o'seas
✕   2005 Call Centre Association

Cutlery & Allied Trades Research Association   (CATRA)   1952
■   Henry St, SHEFFIELD, S Yorks, S3 7EQ.   (hq)
    0114-276 9736   fax 0114-272 2151
    email info@catra.org   http://www.catra.org
    Dir of Research: R C Hamby
▲   Company Limited by Guarantee
○   *Q; research & technology organisation, specialising in all
    aspects of domestic & industrial tools, blades, knives, cutters,
    surgical instruments, razors & shaving systems, kitchen
    gadgets & cookware
Gp   Cutting technology; Shaving; Blade manufacturing technology
●   Res - Inf - Testing & product evaluation - Commercial
    consultancy
M   15 f
¶   [numerous publications].

Cutting Edge
■   186 Bawtry Rd, Wickersley, ROTHERHAM, S Yorks, S66 1AG.
    (hsb)
    01709 543335
    Sec: Robin Healy
○   *T
●   Conf - Mtgs - Exhib
M   60 f
¶   Cutting Edge Magazine - 4.
✕   2003 Federation of Shoe Repair Suppliers

Cyclamen Society   1977
NR   14 Lower Minley Cottages, Minley Rd, BLACKWATER, Surrey,
    GU17 9UD.   (hsp)
    Hon Sec: Martyn Denney
▲   Registered Charity
○   *H; the study of the cyclamen species
●   Conf - Res - Exhib - Comp - Inf - Lib - VE - Seed distribution
M   1,200 i, UK / 200 i, o'seas
¶   Cyclamen Jnl - 2; ftm, c £2 nm.

Cycle Engineers' Institute   (CEI)   1896
■   28 King St, SANDWICH, Kent, CT13 9BT.   (sp/b)
    01304 617161   fax 01304 617161
    Sec: Arthur H Lock
▲   Un-incorporated Society
○   *L; for the highest standards of design & manufacture of
    custom-built & made to measure bicycles
Gp   Designing; Building; Engineering methods
●   Conf - Res - Inf
<   League Intl (cycle racing); Eur Inst of Cycle Engg
M   c 50 i, UK / 10 i, o'seas
¶   Proceedings - 6;   LM - 1;   Rules - irreg; all ftm only.

Cyclical Vomiting Syndrome Association UK
■   77 Wilbury Hills Road, LETCHWORTH, Herts, SG6 4LD.   (hsp)
    0151-342 1660
    email info@cvsa.org.uk   http://www.cvsa.org.uk
    Chmn of Trustees: Dr Robin Dover
▲   Registered Charity
○   *W; 'cyclical vomiting syndrome: promotion of education,
    research, & offering support to sufferers & their families'
●   Mtgs - ET - Inf
M   300 i, UK / 20+ f, o'seas
¶   Bi-Annual NL - 2; ftm.

© CBD Research Ltd · Beckenham · BR3 5JS · Tel 020 8650 7745 · Fax 020 8650 0768 · E-mail cbd@cbdresearch.com · www.cbdresearch.com

Cycling Time Trials   (CTT)   1937
- ■ 77 Arlington Drive, Pennington, LEIGH, Lancs, WN7 3QP.   (hq)
  01942 603976   fax 01942 262326
  email phil.heaton@cyclingtimetrials.org.uk
  http://www.ctt.org.uk
  Nat Sec: Phil Heaton
- ▲ Company Limited by Guarantee
- Br 2
- ○ *S; governing body for road cycle time trials in England & Wales
- ● Conf - Mtgs - ET - Comp
- M 1,062 clubs
- ¶ Hbk - 1; £6.   AR.
- ✕ 2002 Road Time Trials Council

Cyclists' Touring Club   (CTC)   1878
- NR Parklands, Railton Rd, GUILDFORD, Surrey, GU2 9JX.   (hq)
  0870 873 0060   fax 0870 873 0064
  Dir: Kevin Mayne
- ○ *K, *S; provision of services to cyclists; campaigning for cyclists' rights
  Note: The club is known as CTC - the national cyclists' organisation

Cymdeithas Amaethyddol Frenhinol Cymru Cyf
  see **Royal Welsh Agricultural Society Ltd (Cymdeithas Amaethyddol Frenhinol Cymru Cyf)**

Cymdeithas Cymru-Ariannin   1939
- ■ Rhos Helyg, 23 Maesyrefail, Penrhyn-coch, ABERYSTWYTH, Ceredigion, SY23 3HE.   (hsp)
  01970 828017
  email rhoshelyg@btinternet.com
  Sec: Ceris Gruffudd
- ▲ Registered Charity
- ○ *X; to form a link between Wales & the Welsh community in Chubut, Argentina; to organise & sponsor exchange visits for Welsh teachers, students & ministers of religion, & any Argentinian student wishing to go to Wales to expand their educational horizon
- ● Mtgs - Exhib - Inf - Annual celebration to mark the landing of the first Welsh settlers in Chubut - Sponsorship of annual literary competition (in the Welsh lanugauge) at the National Eisteddfod of Wales
- < Wales Intl
- M 231 i, 1 org, UK / 6 i, o'seas
- ¶ AR; free.

Cymdeithas Ddawns Werin Cymru (Welsh Folk Dance Society (WFDS))   (CDdWC)   1949
- NR Bryn Gwiog Cottage, Rhosesmor Rd, Hendre, MOLD, Clwyd, CH7 5QP.   (puboffr/p)
  07971 683929
  Publicity Officer: Angharad James
- ▲ Registered Charity
- Br 27; Australia, New Zealand, USA
- ○ *D; promoting Welsh folk dancing & music through the medium of Welsh language & English
- ● Conf - Mtgs - ET - Exam - Res - Exhib - Comp - SG - Inf - Lib - VE - Dancing displays - Publishing dance notations, records & tapes
- < Welsh Amat Music Fedn (WAMF)
- M 196 i, 67 families, 29 groups, UK / 21 i, o'seas
- ¶ Ddawns (Jnl) - 1.   NL - 1.   Hbk.   AR (incl LM).
  Dance notations, records & tapes.

Cymdeithas Ddrama Cymru
  see **Drama Association of Wales (Cymdeithas Ddrama Cymru)**

Cymdeithas Defaid Llanwenog Sheep Society   1957
- ■ Nantygwyn, Llanfair Rd, LAMPETER, Ceredigion, SA48 8YJ.   (hsb)
  01570 423135
  email llanwenogsheep@hotmail.com
  http://www.llanwenog-sheep.co.uk
  Sec: Miss Meinir Green
- ○ *B
- ● Conf - Mtgs - Exhib - Comp - Lib - VE
- < Nat Sheep Assn
- M 170 i
- ¶ Ybk;   NL;   LM;   AR; all ftm only.

Cymdeithas Defaid Torddu Cymreig Torwen
  see **Badger Face Welsh Mountain Sheep Society (Cyndeithas Defaid Torddu Cymreig)**

Cymdeithas Hanes Ceredigion Historical Society   1909
- ■ Penygeulan, Abermagwr, ABERYSTWYTH, Ceredigion, SY23 4AR.   (hsb)
  01974 261222
  email nonbaskerville@onetel.com
  Hon Sec: Mrs Eirionedd A Baskerville
- ▲ Registered Charity
- ○ *L; local history, antiquities & folklore of Ceredigion
- Gp Archaeological
- ● Mtgs - VE
- M 500+ i
- ¶ Ceredigion (Jnl) - 1.
  County History, 3 vol; in course of publication.
- ✕ 2002-03 Ceredigion Antiquarian Society

Cymdeithas Hanes Sir Caernarfon
  see **Caernarvonshire Historical Society (Cymdeithas Hanes Sir Caernarfon)**

Cymdeithas Hanes Sir Ddinbych - Denbighshire Historical Society   1950
- NR 1 Green Park, WREXHAM, Denbighshire, LL13 7YE.   (hsp)
  01978 353363
  Hon Sec: David Jones
- ▲ Registered Charity
- ○ *L; study of the history of the old county of Denbighshire, including family history, folklore & archaeology
- ● Mtgs - VE
- M c 410 i & org
- ¶ Transactions - 1.

Cymdeithas Hynafiaethau Cymru
  see **Cambrian Archaeological Association (Cymdeithas Hynafiaethau Cymru)**

Cymdeithas yr Iaith Gymraeg   (Welsh Language Society)   1962
- NR Penroc, Marine Terrace, ABERYSTWYTH, Ceredigion, SY23 2AZ.   (hq)
  01970 624501   fax 01970 627122
  email swyddfa@cymdeithas.org
  Contact: Dafydd Morgan Lewis
- ○ *K, *Z; 'a socialist organisation to ensure the future of the Welsh language'
- ● Conf - Mtgs - ET - SG - Inf - VE
- M [not given]

Cymdeithas Melinau Cymru
  see **Welsh Mills Society (Cymdeithas Melinau Cymru)**

Cymmrodorion Society
  see **Honourable Society of Cymmrodorion**

Cyngor Gweithredu Gwirfoddol Cymru
   see **Wales Council for Voluntary Action (Cyngor Gweithredu Gwirfoddol Cymru)**

Cystic Fibrosis Trust 1964
NR 11 London Rd, BROMLEY, Kent, BR1 1BY. (hq)
    020 8464 7211 fax 020 8313 0472
    http://www.cftrust.org.uk
    Chief Exec: Rosie Barnes
▲ Registered Charity
Br 97
○ *Q, *W; to fund hospital & university research into improved detection & treatment of cystic fibrosis; to provide a comprehensive support & advice network for people with cystic fibrosis & their families
● Conf - Mtgs - ET - Res - Exhib - Helpline 0845 859 1000
< Intl Cystic Fibrosis (Mucoviscidosis) Assn (ICF(M)A)
M 16,000 i
¶ CF Today;   CF Talk; both free.   Annual Review.
    Books, information leaflets, videos - list available.

Cystitis & Overactive Bladder Foundation   (COB Foundation) 1994
■ 76 High St, STONY STRATFORD, Bucks, MK11 1AH. (hq)
    01908 569169 fax 01908 565665
    email info@cobfoundation.org
    http://www.cobfoundation.org
    Devt Mgr: Edward Zawisza
▲ Registered Charity
Br 35
○ *W; support for sufferers & their families; information dissemination to the medical profession on causes & treatments of, & research into, all forms of cystitis & overactive bladder
● Mtgs - Stat - Inf
< Interstitial Cystitis Assn of America
M 2,000 i
¶ A Wee Ray of Hope (NL) - 4.
✕ 2003 Interstitial Cystitis Support Group

D&AD (D&AD) 1962
NR 9 Graphite Sq, Vauxhall Walk, LONDON, SE11 5EE. (hq)
020 7840 1120 fax 020 7840 0840
email info@dandad.co.uk http://www.dandad.org
Chief Exec: Michael Hockney
▲ Registered Charity
○ *A, *P; to work on behalf of the design & advertising industries;
to set standards of creative excellence & educate & inspire
the next creative generation; to promote good design &
advertising to the business area
● Conf - ET - Exhib - Annual Congress
< Art Directors Club of Europe (ADCE)
M 1,900 i, UK / 400 i, o'seas
¶ D&AD Annual & DVD Showreel - 1; ftm, £150 nm.
D&AD Student Annual - 1; ftm, £10 nm.
The Copy Book. The Art Directors Book.
The Commercials Book. The Product Book.
The Graphics book.
× 2003-04 British Design & Art Direction

D H Lawrence Society 1974
■ 24 Briarwood Ave, NOTTINGHAM, NG3 6JQ. (hsp)
0115-950 3008
Hon Sec: Ron Faulks
▲ Registered Charity
○ *A; promotion of interest in the life & work of D H Lawrence
(1885-1930) novelist, poet & essayist
● Conf - Mtgs - Inf - Lib - VE
< Assn of Literary Socs; societies in Australia, France, Italy, Japan,
USA
M 126 i, UK / 75 i, o'seas
¶ Jnl - 1; ftm, £7 nm. NL - 2; ftm, £2 nm.

Dad's Army Appreciation Society (DAAS) 1993
■ 29 Brockley Rd, Leonard Stanley, STONEHOUSE, Glos, GL10
3NB. (hsp)
email info@dadsarmy.co.uk http://www.dadsarmy.co.uk
Hon Sec (members): Tony Pritchard,
Hon Sec (articles): Paul Carpenter
▲ Un-incorporated Society
○ *G; to promote & research the television series & share with
like-minded people rare footage, photographs & information
Gp Rare videos & photographs; Filming locations; Archives
● Mtgs - Exhib - Inf - PL
M 1,540 i, UK / 51 i, o'seas
¶ NL [Permission to Speak Sir!] - 4; £8; UK m only.Dad's Army
Companion (all the facts about the programme); £12 m,
£14 nm.

Daffodil Society 1898
NR 105 Derby Rd, Bramcote, NOTTINGHAM, NG9 3GZ. (hsp)
0115-925 5498
Hon Sec: Mrs Terry Braithwaite
▲ Registered Charity
○ *H; cultivation & exhibition of the genus narcissus
● Exhib - Regional meetings
< R Horticl Soc
M 670 i, 220 org, UK / 123 i, o'seas
¶ Jnl - 1; NL - 1; ftm only.

Dairy Executives Association
IRL 33 Kildare St, DUBLIN 2, Republic of Ireland.
353 (1) 676 1989 fax 353 (1) 676 7162
email dairyexe@indigo.ie
Gen Sec: Michael B McCann
○ *P; executives & managers in the dairy industry & agribusiness

Dairy Industry Association
in 2004 became **Dairy UK**

Dairy UK 1933
NR 93 Baker St, LONDON, W1U 6QQ. (hq)
020 7486 7244 fax 020 7847 4734
Atholl House, 4 Torphichen St, EDINBURGH, EH3 6JQ.
0131-229 1401
8 Ranfurly Ave, BANGOR, Co Down, BT20 3SN.
028 9147 1300
Director General: Jim Begg
○ *T; body dealing with matters relating to manufacture &
distribution of milk & milk products, & relating to wages &
conditions of employees in the industry
M f & org
× 2002 Dairy Industry Federation
2004 Dairy Industry Association2005 (Northern Ireland Dairy
Association
(Scottish Dairy Association

Daisy Network Premature Menopause Support Group 1995
NR PO Box 183, ROSSENDALE, Lancs, BB4 6WZ. (mail/address)
http://www.daisynetwork.org.uk
▲ Registered Charity
○ *W; to link sufferers & provide help, advice & support
● Inf
< Infertility Network UK
M 200 i, 20 f, 10 org, UK / 3 i, 5 f, 2 org, o'seas
¶ Update - 4; ftm only.

Dalcroze Society UK (Inc) 1926
■ 100 Elborough St, LONDON, SW18 5DL. (admin/p)
020 8870 1986 fax 020 8870 1986
Admin: Jane Rivers
▲ Registered Charity
○ *D; musical education through movement
● ET - Exam
< Institut Jaques Dalcroze (Geneva)
M 150 i, UK / i, o'seas
¶ NL - 2; ftm. Publications list available.

Dales Pony Society (DALES PS) 1916
■ Greystones, Glebe Ave, Great Longstone, BAKEWELL, Derbys,
DE45 1TY. (hsb)
01629 640439 fax 01629 640439
email dalespony@dalespony.fsnet.co.uk
http://www.dalespony.org
Hon Sec: Mrs J C Ashby
○ *B
● Conf - Comp - Inf
< Nat Pony Soc; Ponies Assn
M 700 i
¶ NL - 2; ftm.

Dalesbred Sheep Breeders Association Ltd 1930
NR Gib Hey Cottage, Chipping, PRESTON, Lancs, PR3 2WU. (hsb)
01995 61570
Sec: John Whitaker
○ *B
M c 120 i

Dance UK Ltd   1982
- ■ Battersea Arts Centre, Lavender Hill, LONDON, SW11 5TN. (hq)
  020 7228 4990   fax 020 7223 0074
  email info@danceuk.org   http://www.danceuk.org
  Dir: Caroline Miller
- ▲ Company Limited by Guarantee; Registered Charity
- ○ *D, *W; 'the lead organisation for the dance profession; we work to create a diverse, dynamic & healthy future for dance & to build a stronger sense of a UK-wide dance community'
- Gp National Choreographers Forum; Communication & advocacy; Healthier dance practice; Professional development; Support & development of African dance
- ● Conf - Mtgs - ET - Res - Stat - Inf
- M 800 i, 130 f, UK / 50 i, 10 f, o'seas
- ¶ Dance UK News (Jnl) - 4.   Your Body Your Risk.
  Look Before You Leap.
  Choreography as Work.
  Dance Teaching Essentials.
  18 information sheets.   Poster series.
  Warm Up Cool Down Posters.

Dancesport Scotland
- NR 93 Hillfoot Drive, Bearsden, GLASGOW, G61 3QG.   (hsp)
  0141-563 2001
  Exec Admin: Mrs Margo Fraser
- ○ *S
- × 2006 Scottish Dancesport

Danish-UK Chamber of Commerce   (DUCC)   1989
- NR 55 Sloane St, LONDON, SW1X 9SR.   (hq)
  020 7259 6795   fax 020 7823 1200
  email info@ducc.co.uk   http://www.ducc.co.uk
  Chief Exec: Martin Mortensen
- ▲ Company Limited by Guarantee
- ○ *C; to promote & assist the Anglo-Danish business community in both UK & Denmark
- Gp Managing Directors Network; Young Professionals Network (YPN); The Junior Chamber
- ● Mtgs
- M 150 i, 250 f
- ¶ Trade Directory - 1; free.

Daresbury Lewis Carroll Society   1970
- ■ Clatterwick House, Little Leigh, NORTHWICH, Cheshire, CW8 4RJ.
  01606 891303 & 781731 (evgs)   (hsb)
  Hon Sec: Kenneth N Oultram
- ○ *L; to honour & promote the work of C L Dodgson (Lewis Carroll)

Dartmoor Pony Society   (DPS)   1946
- NR Swn yr Afon, Thornhill Rd, Cwmgwili, LLANELLI, SA14 6PT. (hsp)
  01269 844303
  http://www.dartmoorponysociety.com
  Hon Sec: Mrs Viv Brown
- ▲ Company Limited by Guarantee
- ○ *B
- ● Conf - Res - Exhib - Comp - Expt - Inf - Compilation of history of breed
- < Nat Pony Soc
- M 550 i, UK / 100 i, o'seas
- ¶ NL - 4.   Dartmoor Diary.

Dartmoor Preservation Association   (DPA)   1883
- ■ Old Duchy Hotel, Princetown, YELVERTON, Devon, PL20 6QF.   (pt/time)
  01822 890646
  email info@dartmoorpreservation.com
  http://www.dartmoorpreservation.com hq
  Chief Exec: Jonathan Cardale
- ▲ Registered Charity
- ○ *G, *K; protection, preservation & enhancement in the public interest of landscape, antiquities, flora & fauna, natural beauty & scientific interest of Dartmoor; preservation of Dartmoor Commons
- ● Mtgs - ET - Res - Exhib
- < Coun Protection Rural England (CPRE); Coun Nat Parks (CNP); Open Spaces Soc (OSS)
- M 2,400 i, UK / 30 i, o'seas
- ¶ Dartmoor Matters (NL) - 3; free.

Dartmoor Sheep Breeders Association   (DSBA)   1909
- ■ The Old Rectory, Clannaborough, CREDITON, Devon, EX17 6DA.   (hsp)
  01363 85205
  email greyface.dart@care4free.net
  http://www.greyface-dartmoor.org.uk
  Sec: Wilson Mitchell
- ▲ Registered Charity
- ○ *B; for breeders of Greyface Dartmoor sheep
- ● Inf
- M 190 i, 10 f, 3 org (rare breed parks or societies)
- ¶ Flock Book - 1.

Darts Association
since 2006 **Sports Manufacturers & Retailers Trade Association**

Data Federation
a special interest group of the **Federation against Copyright Theft**

Data Publishers Association   (DPA)   1970
- ■ Queens House, 28 Kingsway, LONDON, WC2B 6JR.   (hq)
  020 7405 0836   fax 020 7404 4167
  email christine@dpa.org.uk   http://www.dpa.org.uk
  Sec: Christine Scott
- ▲ Company Limited by Guarantee
- ○ *T; to represent data & directory publishers in the UK; to promote the interests of the industry both in print & electronic media
- ● Conf - Mtgs - Stat - LG
- < Eur Assn of Directory & Database Pubrs (EADP); Advertising Assn; Periodical Pubrs Assn; Digital Content Forum
- > Periodical Pubrs Assn
- M 80 f
- ¶ News in Brief - 12;   Members' Hbk - 1; both ftm, on request nm.
  AR; free.
- × 2005 Directory & Database Publishers Association

David Hume Institute   1985
- NR 25 Buccleugh Place, EDINBURGH, EH8 9LN.   (hq)
  0131-667 9609   fax 0131-667 9609
  http://www.davidhumeinstitute.com
  Dir: Jeremy Peat
- ○ *L, *Q; to promote discourse & research on economic & legal aspects of public policy questions

David Jones Society   1996
- 22 Gower Rd, Sketty, SWANSEA, SA2 9BY.   (dir/p)
  01792 206144   fax 01792 470385
  email anne.price-owen@sihe.ac.uk
  http://www.sihe.ac.uk/davidjones
  Dir: Anne Price-Owen
- ▲ Un-incorporated Society
- ○ *A; to promote interest in the life & works of the painter-poet David Jones (1895-1974) & his sense of unity within the world & its people
- Gp Visual artists; Poets; Literary criticism
- ● Conf - Mtgs - Res - Exhib - PL - VE - Poetry readings - Seminars
- M 150 i, 20 f, UK / 50 i, 6 f, o'seas
- ¶ The David Jones Jnl - 1; £7.50 m, £10 nm.

Dawn Duellists' Society   (DDS)   1994
- GF1, 15 Halmyre St, EDINBURGH, EH6 8QA.   (hsp)
  0131-538 0745
  http://www.dawnduellists.co.uk
  Sec: Paul Macdonald
- ▲ Un-incorporated Society
- ○ *S; revival of historically accurate swordplay from c1300-1900; to research teaching & practice of duelling techniques
- ● Mtgs - ET - Res - Demonstrations
- M 20 i, UK / 3 i, o'seas
- ¶ Information leaflets.

De Vere Society   1989
- Brookmans Old Farm, Iwerne Minster, BLANDFORD, Dorset, DT11 8NG.   (hsp)
  01747 811020   fax 01747 811020
  email malim@btinternet.com
  http://www.deveresociety.co.uk
  Hon Sec: R C W Malim
- ▲ Registered Charity
- ○ *A, *L, *Q; Shakespeare authorship question with 2 propositions:
  a) that William Shakespeare (1564-1616) did not write any (or any significant part) of the works now attributed to him
  b) that Edward de Vere, 17th Earl of Oxford (1550-1604) is substantially the best candidate for (or plays a major role in) such authorship
- ● Conf - Mtgs - ET - Res - Exhib - Inf - Lib - VE
- < Shakespeare Oxford Soc (USA)
- M 150 i, UK / 60 i, o'seas
- ¶ NL - 3/4; ftm only.   Occasional study papers - irreg.
  Great Oxford Collection of Newsletter Essays 1996-2004; £12 m, £14 nm.

Deaf Blind UK   1928
- NR National Centre for Deafblindness, John & Lucille van Geest Place, Cygnet Rd, Hampton, PETERBOROUGH, Cambs, PE7 8FD.   (hq)
  01733 358100 (voice & minicom)   fax 01733 358356
  email info@deafblind.org.uk
  http://www.deafblind.org.uk
  Chief Exec: Jeff Skipp
- ▲ Registered Charity
- ○ *W; to further the interests of deafblind people by offering the full range of support services, education & training
- ● Conf - ET - Exhib - Stat - Inf - VE
- < Brit Assn Disabled People
- M 3,520 i
- ¶ Open Hand Magazine - 4.   Snippets (NL) - 52.
  Both publications are available in Braille, Moon, large print, tape or disk format.
  Annual Review; free.

Deaf Broadcasting Council   (DBC)   1980
- NR c/o 50 Clevedon Rd, LONDON, SE20 7QQ.   (chmn/p)
  fax 020 8676 0534
  email pennybes@aol.com
  Chmn: Penny Beschizza
- ▲ Registered Charity
- ○ *K; to ensure that that deaf people have access to TV & video & that the access is of suitable quality
- ● LG
- < UK Coun on Deafness; Telecommunications Action Gp; Coun for the Advancement of Communication with Deaf People
- M 350 i, 13 org
- ¶ Mailshot - 2.

Deaf Education through Listening & Talking   (DELTA)   1980
- The Con Powell Centre, 3 Swan Court, Cygnet Park, PETERBOROUGH, PE7 8FD.   (hq)
  0845 108 1437   fax 01733 569322
  email enquiries@deafeducation.org.uk
  http://www.deafeducation.org.uk
  Chief Exec: Dr Keith Gladstone
- ▲ Company Limited by Guarantee; Registered Charity
- ○ *W; a support group of teachers & parents of deaf & hearing-impaired children, providing information, advice & support to guide parents in helping their children develop normal speech & live independently in a hearing society
- Gp Deaf children & families; Professionals who support them
- ● Conf - Mtgs - ET - Res - Exhib - Stat - Inf
- < Alexander Graham Bell Assn Deaf & Hard of Hearing; Brit Academy Audiology; Brit Assn Educ Audiologists; Brit Cochlear Implant Users Assn; Elizabeth Foundation; Ewing Foundation
- M 258 i
- ¶ Chat - 4;   Good Practice Guide; both ftm.
  Parents Guide 1; £10.   Parents Guide; £15.

** Debendox Action Group
  Organisation lost: see Introduction paragraph 3

Defence Manufacturers Association   (DMA)   1976
- Marlborough House, Headley Rd, Grayshott, HINDHEAD, Surrey, GU2 6LG.   (hq)
  01428 607788
  email enquiries@the-dma.org.uk
  http://www.the-dma.org.uk
  Dir Gen: Maj Gen Alan G Sharman
  Co Sec: Elaine A Luck
- ▲ Company Limited by Guarantee
- ○ *T; to represent the interests of the British defence industry
- Gp British Industry Offset Group (BiOG)
  Clothing Interest Gp (CLING)
  DMA Marketing Committee
  Exclusive Economic Zone (EEZ)
  Export Group for Aerospace & Defence (EGAD)
  Industrial Participation Forum
  Maritime Interest Group (MIG)
  NBC UK;   Section 5
  UK Simulation & Training Action Group (UKSTAG)
- ● Conf - Exhib - Expt - Inf - Lib - VE - LG
- < Eur Defence Inds Gp; Nat Defence Ind Coun; Defence Ind Coun; CBI
- M 440 f
- ¶ Register of Members Products & Services - 1.
  Worldwide Directory on Defence & Security Prime Contractors - 2 yrly.
  Export Opportunities Alerting Service NL - 52.
  DMA Annual Review; free.

Delius Society   1962

■ 21 Woodlands Drive, Brooklands, SALE, Cheshire, M33 3PQ.
  (hsp)
  0161-282 3654
  http://www.delius.org.uk
  Hon Sec: Ann Dixon
▲ Registered Charity
Br 3; 2 USA
○ *D; to develop a wider understanding & appreciation of Delius
  & his music; to encourage the performance, recording &
  publishing of his works
● Mtgs - Res - VE
< Delius Trust
M 380 i, 9 f, UK / 111 i, 17 f, o'seas
¶ Jnl - 2; ftm, £2-£3 nm.   NL - 2; ftm only.

Delphinium Society   1928

▥ 2 The Grove, Ickenham, UXBRIDGE, Middx, UB10 8QH.
  (promotionsec/p)
  01895 464694   fax 0870 052 9321
  email promotions@delphinium.demon.co.uk
  http://www.delphinium.demon.co.uk
  Promotions Sec: Dr Roger D Beauchamp
▲ Registered Charity
Br 3
○ *H; the study of delphiniums in all their aspects - botanical,
  horticultural, genetic, physiological & general interest for
  non-specialists; investigation of species & their ecology; is
  also a forum for the more scientifically minded
Gp Species & Breeders Communications Forum
● ET - Exhib - Comp - Inf - VE
< R Horticl Soc Jt Delphinium C'ee
M c 600 i, c 20 affiliates, UK / c 150 i, o'seas
¶ Autumn Bulletin - 1 (Oct).   Delphiniums (Ybk) - 1.
  The Delphinium Garden; published on the 75th anniversary.

Democracy Movement

NR 449 Great West Rd, HOUNSLOW, Middx, TW5 0BU.   (hq)
  020 8570 5681   fax 020 8570 5213
  email mail@democracymovement.org.uk
  http://www.democracymovement.org.uk
Br 160
○ *K; a non-party campaign to keep the pound & stop the EU
  superstate
M c 320,000 i

Denbighshire & Flintshire Agricultural Society Ltd   1839

NR 1 Cross St, HOLYWELL, Flintshire, CH8 7LP.   (hq)
  01352 712131   fax 01352 712098
  email denbandflintshow@ukonline.co.uk
  Sec: Mrs Linda Brooks-Roberts
▲ Company Limited by Guarantee; Registered Charity
○ *F, *H; the encouragement of agriculture & horticulture by
  education, scientific research, experimental work & the
  holding of shows
Gp Horses; Cattle; Sheep; Poultry; Bantams; Pigeons; Rabbits;
  Eggs; Horticulture; Floral art; Honey; WI; Merched y Wawr;
  Vintage machinery & cars; Classic cars & motorcycles
● Mtgs - Comp - VE - Show
< Assn of Show & Agricl Orgs; Various breed socs
M 1,200 i, 20 f
¶ Show Day Catalogue - 1.
  Show Schedule - 1.   AR.

Denbighshire Historical Society
  see **Cymdeithas Hanes Sir Ddinbych - Denbighshire**
  Historical Society

Dental Laboratories Association Ltd   (DLA)   1961

▦ 44-46 Wollaton Rd, Beeston, NOTTINGHAM, NG9 2NR.   (hq)
  0115-925 4888   fax 0115-925 4800
  http://www.dla.org.uk
  Chief Exec: Richard Daniels
▲ Company Limited by Guarantee
Br 16
○ *T; interests of proprietors of dental laboratories; to represent
  views of dental technology to professional bodies &
  government
Gp Education; Materials & technical standards; Business
  development
● Conf - Mtgs - ET - Res - Exhib - SG - Stat - Inf - Empl
< Fédn Eur des Patrons Prosthétistes Dentaires (FEPPD); Brit
  Dental Health Foundation (BDHF)
M c 1,000 i
¶ Dental Laboratory (Jnl) - 12; ftm, £28 yr nm.
  DLA Directory - 1; ftm, £20 nm.   Year Planner - 1; free.

Dental Practitioners Association   (DPA)   1954

▦ 61 Harley St, LONDON, W1G 8QU.   (hq)
  020 7636 1072   fax 020 7636 1086
  email info@uk-dentistry.org   http://www.uk-dentistry.org
  Chief Exec: Derek Watson
▲ Un-incorporated Society
○ *P, *U; the promotion of the welfare & interests of general
  dental practitioners, especially those working in high street
  practice
● Conf - Mtgs - Stat - Inf - Empl - LG
< Eur U of Dentists (EUD)
M 3,000 i, UK / 3 f, o'seas
¶ General Dental Practitioner - 6; ftm only.
× 2005 General Dental Practitioners Association

Dental System Suppliers Association   (DSSA)   1990

NR c/o Geoff Emery, Elopak House, Rutherford Close, STEVENAGE,
  Herts, SG1 2EF.   (chmn/b)
  01483 245000
  Chmn: Geoff Emery
▲ Un-incorporated Society
○ *P, *T; promotion of & setting standards for management
  computer systems for dental surgeries
Gp Dental surgeons; Suppliers of computer systems for dental
  surgeons & allied trades
● Exhib - Inf - LG
M 5 f, 3 associates
¶ LM - updated; free.

Dental Technicians Association

NR PO Box 6520, NORTHAMPTON, NN3 9ZX.
  0870 243 0753
○ *P

Depression Alliance   (DA)   1979

NR 212 Spitfire Studios, 63-71 Collier St, LONDON, N1 9BE.   (hq)
  0845 123 2320
  email information@depressionalliance.org
  http://www.depressionalliance.org
  Sec: Paul Lanham
▲ Company Limited by Guarantee; Registered Charity
Br 3
○ *W; information & understanding for anyone affected by
  depression
● Inf - Co-ordination of self-help groups, correspondence
  schemes & e-mail group
M 2,500 i, UK & o'seas
¶ Various Booklets & Leaflets.

Derby Porcelain International Society (DPIS) 1984
- ■ PO Box 6997, COLESHILL, Warks, B46 2LF.   (hsp)
  01675 481293
  email a.varnam@farming.co.uk
  Hon Sec: Anthony Varnam
- ▲ Registered Charity
- ○ *G, *L; the history & research of Derbyshire ceramics from 1748 to date
- ● Res - SG - VE
- M 230 i, UK / 22 i, o'seas
- ¶ DPIS NL - 2; ftm, £2 nm.   DPIS Jnl - 2yrly; ftm, £15 nm.

Derbyshire Agricultural & Horticultural Society Ltd   (DAHS) 1860
- ■ 5 Willow Park Way, Western Rd, Aston on Trent, DERBY, DE72 2DF.   (hsp)
  01332 793068   fax 01332 793068
  email anne.james@talk21.com
  http://www.derbyshirecountyshow.org.uk
  Gen Sec: Mrs Anne James,
  Chmn: Edward Hicklin
- ▲ Registered Charity
- ○ *F, *H; farming & agriculture, horticulture & staging the Derbyshire County Show
- < Assn of Show & Agricl Orgs
- M 592 i
- ¶ Show Catalogue - 1; price varies.

Derbyshire Archaeological Society (DAS) 1878
- NR 2 The Watermeadows, SWARKESTONE, Derbys, DE73 1JA. (hsp)
  01332 704148
  email barbarafoster@talk21.com
  http://www.derbyshireas.org.uk
  Hon Sec: Barbara Foster
- ▲ Registered Charity
- ○ *L; to promote the study of archaeology & history of Derbyshire
- Gp Archaeological research; Architecture; Industrial archaeology; Local history; Vernacular architecture (Derbyshire Buildings Record)
- ● Mtgs - ET - Res - Lib - VE - LG (local)
- < Coun for Brit Archaeology; Assn for Indl Archaeology; Newcomen Soc
- M 502 i, 60 org
- ¶ Derbyshire Archaeological Jnl - 1; ftm, varies nm.
  Derbyshire Miscellany - 2; £4 m, £5 nm.
  Gazeteers of Industrial Archaeology - irreg.
  [subscription, £15].

Derbyshire Chamber & Business Link   2003
- NR Commerce Centre, Canal Wharf, CHESTERFIELD, Derbys, S41 7NA.
  0845 601 0138   fax 01246 233228
  http://www.derbyshirechamber.com
  Chief Exec: George Cowcher
- ○ *C
- × 2003 (North Derbyshire Chamber of Commerce & Industry (South Derbyshire Chamber of Commerce & Industry

Derbyshire Gritstone Sheepbreeders Society (DGSS) 1906
- NR 5 Bridge Close, Waterfoot, ROSSENDALE, Lancs, BB4 9SN. (hsp)
  01706 228520
  Hon Sec: Mrs S Coppack
- ▲ Registered Charity
- ○ *B
- ● Mtgs - Society show & sale at Clitheroe
- < Nat Sheep Assn
- M 160 i
- ¶ NL - 1;   Booklet; both ftm only.

Derbyshire Record Society (DRS) 1977
- ■ 57 New Rd, Wingerworth, CHESTERFIELD, Derbys, S42 6UJ. (treas/p)
  01246 231024
  email neapen@aol.com
  http://www.merton.dircon.co.uk/drshome.htm
  Hon Treas: D G Edwards,   Hon Sec: Philip Riden
- ▲ Registered Charity
- ○ *L; publication of historical records relating to Derbyshire
- ● Res
- M 300 i, 15 org, UK / 15 i, o'seas
- ¶ NL - 2; ftm only.

Derry Chamber of Commerce
  see **Londonderry Chamber of Commerce**

Design & Artists Copyright Society Ltd   (DACS) 1983
- ■ 33 Great Sutton St, LONDON, EC1V 0DX.   (hq)
  020 7336 8811   fax 020 7336 8822
  email info@dacs.org.uk   http://www.dacs.org.uk
  Chief Exec: Joanna Cave
- ▲ Company Limited by Guarantee
- ○ *A, *T; the copyright & collecting society for the visual arts in the UK; to administer & protect the rights of visual creators; membership is open to all artists & photographers
- Gp Artists copyright
- ● ET - Inf - LG - Collecting society
- < Eur Visual Artists (EVA); IFRRO; CISAC; Brit Copyright Coun
- M i
- ¶ AR - 1; free.

Design Association (DA) 2001
- ■ 1 Cedar Court, Royal Oak Yard, Bermondsey St, LONDON, SE1 3AG.   (hq)
  020 7357 8282   fax 020 7407 9878
  email info@design-association.org
  Chief Exec: Frank Peters
- ▲ Company Limited by Guarantee
- ○ *T; accreditation of design businesses
- ● ET - Stat - Expt
- < Chart Soc of Designers
- M f
- ¶ Various professional publications & practice documents.

Design Business Association (DBA) 1986
- NR 35-39 Old St, LONDON, EC1V 9HX.   (hq)
  020 7251 9229   fax 020 7251 9221
  email deborah.dawton@dba.org.uk
  http://www.dba.org.uk
  Chief Exec: Deborah Dawton
- ▲ Company Limited by Guarantee
- ○ *T; 'to demonstrate the contribution that design makes to society & to promote professional excellence in bringing together creativity & commerce'
- ● Conf - Mtgs - ET - Res - Exhib - Comp - Expt - Inf - LG
- M 200 f, UK / 2 f, o'seas

Design History Society (DHS) 1977
- ■ MoDA - Middlesex University, Cat Hill, BARNET, Herts, EN4 8HT.   (hsp)
  email z.hendon@mdx.ac.uk
  http://www.designhistorysociety.org
  Hon Sec: Zoe Hendon
- ▲ Registered Charity
- ○ *A; to promote the study of & research into, design history; to disseminate & publish the useful results; to exchange information with other bodies & individuals concerned with design history
- ● Conf - Mtgs - ET - Exhib - SG - Inf - VE
- M 200 i, 100 libraries & colleges, UK / 30 i, o'seas
- ¶ Jnl of Design History - 4;   NL - 4; both ftm.

Design & Industries Association   (DIA)   1917
NR   Studio 303 Custard Factory, Gibb St, BIRMINGHAM, B9 4AA.
        0121-772 4242
        Nat Chmn: Kevin White
▲   Registered Charity
Br   4
○   *P; to provide a forum for those engaged in education, design
        & industry with the common aim of raising the standards of
        design & the public awareness of the value of good design
●   Mtgs - ET - Comp - VE - LG - Bi-annual design auction -
        Lectures - Awards
<   Design Unity
M   200 i
¶   NL - 3;   Ybk - 1; both ftm.

Design & Technology Association   (DATA)   1989
NR   16 Wellesbourne House, Walton Rd, WELLESBOURNE, Warks,
        CV35 9JB.   (hq)
        01789 470007   fax 01789 841955
        email data@data.org.uk   http://www.data.org.uk
        Chief Exec: Richard Green
▲   Company Limited by Guarantee; Registered Charity
○   *E, *P; for all those involved in design & technology education
        & associated subject areas; to promote the advancement of
        education & in particular, but not exclusively, to support,
        encourage, promote, develop & maintain design &
        technological education in all its branches
Gp   Advisory groups: Primary, Secondary, Initial teacher education,
        Special educational needs
●   Conf - Mtgs - ET - Res - Exhib - Stat - Inf (members only) - Lib -
        LG
M   5,423 i, 54 f, UK / 118 i, o'seas
¶   DATA News - 3;   DATA Jnl - 3;   MODUS - 6; all ftm only.
        Designing Magazine - 3; £18 m, £21 nm.

Despatch Association   (DA)   1985
NR   Lamb's End House, 36 Church Rd, KING'S LYNN, Norfolk,
        PE34 3DG.   (hq)
        01553 813479   fax 01553 813479
        email phil@despatch.co.uk   http://www.despatch.co.uk
        Chief Exec: Phillip Stone
▲   Un-incorporated Society
○   *T; to represent the despatch & courier industry
●   Res - Inf - LG
<   Eur Express Assn
M   250 f
¶   Despatches Magazine - 6; ftm, £1.10 nm.
        Despatches Magazine - online; ftm.

Dessert & Cake Mixes Association
        is an association within the **Food Processers' Association**

Deutsche-Britische Industrie- und Handelskammer
        the German title of the **German-British Chamber of Industry &
        Commerce**

Development Education Association   (DEA)   1993
NR   River House (1st floor), 143-145 Farringdon Rd, LONDON,
        EC1R 3AB.   (hq)
        020 7812 1282   fax 020 7812 1272
        email dea@dea.org.uk   http://www.dea.org.uk
        Dir: Dr Douglas Bourn
▲   Company Limited by Guarantee; Registered Charity
○   *E, *N; an umbrella body working to support & promote
        greater awareness & understanding of global & international
        development issues in the UK; member organisations work
        within schools & education, youth organisations, community
        groups etc to bring a global perspective to learning at all
        ages
●   Conf - Mtgs - ET - Res - Inf - Lib - LG
M   45 centres, 230 org
¶   Development Education (Jnl) - 3.
        DEA Bulletin - 10;   Schools News (NL) - 2;
        Global Youth Work (NL) - 2;   AR;
        Worldlywise (adult education) (NL) - 2; all ftm only.

Development Studies Association   (DSA)   1978
■   PO Box 108, BIDEFORD, Devon, EX39 6ZQ.   (admin/b)
        01288 331360
        email admin@devstud.org.uk   http://www.devstud.org.uk
        Exec Dir: Frances Hill
▲   Registered Charity
○   *G, *K; to connect & promote the development research
        community in the UK & Ireland
Gp   DSA Scotland
        Study groups: Ageing & development; Agriculture & rural
        development; Bridging research & policy, Conflict & human
        security, Corporate social responsibility, Design &
        development, Development ethics, Development
        management, Disasters & development, Economics, finance
        & trade, Environment, resources & sustainable development,
        European development policy, History & development, HIV/
        AIDS, Information technology & development, Livestock,
        Media & development, Multi-dimensional poverty, NGOs in
        development, Public engagement in development, Research
        students, Tourism & development, Urban policy, Women in
        development
●   Conf - Mtgs - ET - SG - Inf - LG
<   Brit O'seas NGOs for Devt; Devt Educ Assn; Eur Assn Devt
        Training Insts
M   1,000 i, 80 f, UK / 250 i, o'seas
¶   Jnl of International Development - 8; £52 yr m, £340 yr nm.

Development Trusts Association   (DTA)   1992
NR   33 Corsham St, LONDON, N1 6DR.   (hq)
        0845 458 8336   fax 0845 458 8337
        email info@dta.org.uk   http://www.dta.org.uk
        Dir: Steve Wyler
▲   Company Limited by Guarantee; Registered Charity
○   *N; to support existing development trusts & the creation of new
        ones
Gp   Forums: Coalfields, Coastal, Rural
●   Conf - Inf - VE - LG
<   Brit Urban Regeneration Assn; Indl Common Ownership
        Movement; Neighbourhood Initiatives Foundation
M   295 trusts, 140 associate m (local authorities, government
        agencies, businesses)
¶   Networker (NL) - 4; ftm.
        Other publications.

Development Trusts Association Scotland
NR   54 Manor Place, EDINBURGH, EH3 7EH.
        0131 220 2456   fax 0131 220 3777
○   *K

Devon Archaeological Society   (DAS)   1929
■   Royal Albert Memorial Museum, Queen St, EXETER, Devon,
        EX4 3RX.   (hsb)
▲   Registered Charity
○   *L, *Q; archaeological promotion & conservation within Devon
●   Conf - Mtgs - ET - Res - Exhib - SG - Inf - Lib - VE
M   940 i, 52 org, UK / 20 i, o'seas
¶   Proceedings - 1; ftm, £18 nm.   NL - 3; ftm only.
        Devon Archaeology - 1; ftm, from £1.50 nm (as available).

Devon Cattle Breeders' Society   (DCBS)   1884
■   Wisteria Cottage, Iddesleigh, WINKLEIGH, Devon,
        EX19 8BG.   (sp)
        01837 810942   fax 01837 810942
        http://www.redrubydevon.co.uk
        Sec: Andrew Lane
▲   Company Limited by Guarantee; Registered Charity
○   *B; to further the breeding of the Devon (Red Ruby) breed of
        cattle
●   Mtgs - Comp - Stat - Expt - Inf - Lib
<   Devon Cattle Breeder Socs in: Australia, New Zealand, Brazil &
        USA
M   c 400 i
¶   NL - 4;   AR; both ftm only.
        Davy's Devon Herd Book - 1.

© CBD Research Ltd · Beckenham · BR3 5JS · Tel 020 8650 7745 · Fax 020 8650 0768 · E-mail cbd@cbdresearch.com · www.cbdresearch.com

Devon Closewool Sheepbreeders Society   1923
■   c/o Holtom & Thomas, The Elms Office, Bishops Tawton,
    BARNSTAPLE, Devon, EX32 0EJ.   (sp)
    01271 326900
    Sec: R F Y Smith
▲   Un-incorporated Society
○   *B
●   Comp
<   Nat Sheepbreeders Assn
M   65 i, 2 f
¶   Flock Book - 1; ftm, £2 nm.

Devon & Cornwall Longwool Flock Book Association   1977
NR Pelkham View, Kentisbeare, CULLOMPTON, Devon, EX15 2EY.
    01884 266201
    Sec: M J Britton
▲   Registered Charity
○   *B; breeding of pedigree longwool sheep; production of good
    lustre wool
●   Mtgs - Comp
M   60 i
¶   Flock Book - 1.

Devon & Cornwall Record Society   (DCRS)   1904
■   c/o Devon & Exeter Institution, 7 Cathedral Close, EXETER,
    Devon, EX1 1EZ.   (hsb)
    01392 274727
    http://www.cs.ncl.ac.uk/genuki/DEV/DCRS
    Admin: Mrs E Franceschini
▲   Registered Charity
○   *L; publication of local records, promotion of local historical
    studies & genealogical research
●   Res - Lib - Collection of transcripts of parish registers & other
    source material
M   500 i, 50 org, UK / 15 i, 40 org, o'seas, (org are libraries &
    institutions)
¶   Publications list available.

Devon County Agricultural Association   (DCAA)   1872
NR Westpoint, Clyst St Mary, EXETER, Devon, EX5 1DJ.   (hq)
    01392 446000   fax 01392 444808
    http://www.devoncountyshow.co.uk
    Co Sec: M Hosking
▲   Registered Charity
○   *F; promotion of agriculture, forestry, horticulture & commerce
    in Devon
●   Agricultural shows, exhibitions & events
M   2,212 i, f & org
¶   Devon County Show Catalogue - 1.   DCAA Ybk; ftm only.
    Devon County Show Programme - 1.

Dexter Cattle Society   1892
NR RASE Offices (1st floor), STONELEIGH PARK, Warks,
    CV8 2LZ.   (hsb)
    024 7669 2300   fax 024 7669 2400
    Sec: Mrs Yvonne Froehlich
▲   Registered Charity
○   *B; to promote the development of the breed & its market
●   Mtgs - Res - Exhib - Stat - Expt - Inf - VE - LG - Registration
    database for Dexter cattle
<   Nat Cattle Breeders' Assn
M   1,023 i, UK / 60 i, o'seas
¶   The Dexter Bulletin - 3; ftm.   Herd Book - 1.

Diabetes Federation of Ireland
IRL 76 Lower Gardiner St, DUBLIN 1, Republic of Ireland.
    353 (1) 836 3022   fax 353 (1) 836 5182
    email info@diabetes.ie   http://www.diabetes.ie
    Hon Chmn: Dr Tony O'Sullivan
○   *W

Diabetes UK   1934
■   10 Parkway, LONDON, NW1 7AA.   (hq)
    020 7424 1000   fax 020 7424 1001
    email info@diabetes.org.uk
    http://www.diabetes.org.uk
    Chief Exec: Douglas Smallwood
▲   Registered Charity
Br 6
○   *W; to fund research into diabetes; to raise awareness of the
    seriousness of the condition; to provide information to people
    with diabetes, their families, healthcare professionals & the
    general public
Gp Healthcare professionals
●   Conf - ET - Res - Exhib - Stat - Inf - Lib - PL - VE - LG
<   Intl Diabetes Fedn (IDF)
M   180,000 i
¶   Balance - 6; ftm, £2.95 nm.
    Diabetic Medicine - 12.
    Diabetes Update (for healthcare professionals) - 4; ftm.

Dickens Fellowship   1902
■   48 Doughty St, LONDON, WC1N 2LX.   (hq)
    020 7405 2127   fax 020 7831 5175
    email dickensfellowship@btinternet.co.uk
    http://www.dickensfellowship.org
    Jt Hon Gen Secs: Mrs Thelma Grove, Dr Tony Williams
Br 15; 32 o'seas
○   *L; literary society for lovers of the works of Charles Dickens;
    preservation of buildings & objects associated with him

Diecasting Society   (DCS)   1966
■   Broadway House, Calthorpe Rd, Five Ways, BIRMINGHAM,
    B15 1TN.   (hq)
    0121-456 6103   fax 0870 138 9714
    email dcs@alfed.org.uk
    Sec: Will Savage
▲   Company Limited by Guarantee; Registered Charity
Br 3
○   *P; to advance the study of diecasting, the technology &
    methods, to promote research & disseminate the results
●   Conf - Mtgs - ET - Exhib - SG - Inf - Lib - VE
M   153 i, 90 f, UK / 5 i, o'seas
¶   NL - 3; ftm only.
    Conference Proceedings - 2 yrly; £20.

Digital Content Forum   (DCF)   2000
NR 167 Wardour St, LONDON, W1F 8WL.   (hq)
    020 7534 0589
    http://www.dcf.org.uk
    Chmn: Paul Jackson
○   *N
M   28 org

Dignity in Dying   1935
■   13 Prince of Wales Terrace, LONDON, W8 5PG.   (hq)
    020 7937 7770   fax 020 7376 2648
    email info@dignityindying.org.uk
    http://www.dignityindying.org.uk
    Chief Exec: Deborah Annetts
▲   Un-incorporated Society
○   *K; to make it legal for a competent adult, who is suffering
    unbearably from an incurable illness, to receive medical help
    to die at their own considered & persistent request.
    The VES distributes forms for living wills in order to refuse
    unwanted life-prolonging treatment & advises on their usage
    (which is legally enforceable)
●   LG
M   15,000 i
¶   NL - 4; ftm only.   Living Wills; £15.
×   2006 Voluntary Euthanasia Society

Dinosaur Society UK   1993
NR   c/o Prof Richard Moody, 21 Victoria Rd, SURBITON, Surrey,
        KT6 4JZ.
        email enquiries@dinosaursociety.com
        http://www.dinosaursociety.com
        Chmn: Prof Richard Moody
▲   Registered Charity
○   *K; to raise the awareness & to advance the education of the
        general public in the scientific aspects of the dinosaurs,
        palaeontology & earth science generally; to support the work
        of people engaged in forwarding the science of
        palaeontology
●   Conf - Exhib - Comp - VE
M   550 i
¶   Quarterly Review (Jnl).   DinoMite (children's NL) - 6.

Diplomatic Service Families Association
NR   Foreign & Commonwealth Office, Old Admiralty Building
        (Room 1/95), LONDON, SW1A 2PA.
        020 7008 0283
        email dsfa.genofficefco@gtnet.gov.uk
        Chmn: Tina Attwood
○   *W

Dipterists Forum   1993
NR   c/o BENHS, The Pelham-Clinton Building, Dinton Pastures
        Country Park, Hurst, READING, RG10 0TH.
○   *P, *G

Direct Marketing Association (UK) Ltd   (DMA)   1992
NR   DMA House, 70 Margaret St, LONDON, W1W 8SS.   (hq)
        020 7291 3300
        Chief Exec: Colin Lloyd
▲   Company Limited by Guarantee
Br   3
○   *T; 'to raise the stature of the direct marketing industry, giving
        the consumer trust & confidence in direct marketing'
●   Conf - Mtgs - Res - Exhib - Stat - Expt - Inf - Lib - LG
M   680 f, UK / 40 f, o'seas

Direct Selling Association Ltd   (DSA)   1965
■   29 Floral St, LONDON, WC2E 9DP.   (hq)
        020 7497 1234   fax 020 7497 3144
        http://www.dsa.org.uk
        Dir: Richard M Berry
▲   Company Limited by Guarantee
○   *T; to represent companies who use independent salespeople to
        sell their products, by party plan or person to person, &
        whose marketing plans are legal & who have agreed to
        abide by the DSA codes of practice
●   Conf - Mtgs - Res - Stat - Inf - Lib - LG
<   Wld Fedn of Direct Selling Assns (USA); Fedn of Eur Direct
        Selling Assns (FEDSA)
M   63 f, 24 associates (suppliers of services)
¶   Shopping at Home: consumer guide including the DSA Code of
        Practice;
        A People Business: guide to earnings opportunities in direct
        selling;
        Report - Independent Code Administration - 1; all free.
        Direct Selling, Consumer Goods in the UK (survey) - 1; ftm,
        £25 nm.
        Direct Selling: from door to door to network marketing; £17.99.

Directors Guild of Great Britain   (DGGB)   1983
NR   4 Windmill St, LONDON, W1T 2HZ.   (hq)
        020 7580 9131   fax 020 7580 9132
        Gen Sec: Piers Haggard
○   *P, *U; represents the interests of directors in all media: theatre,
        film, TV, ballet, opera, commercials, videos etc
Gp   Recorded media: Film, Television, Video, Radio
        Live media: Theatre, Opera, Dance
●   Conf - Mtgs - Res - Inf - Empl - LG - Events - Networking -
        Masterclasses
<   Fedn of Eur Film Directors (FERA), Informal Eur Theatre Meeting
        (IETM), Nat Campaign for the Arts (NCA)
M   1,000 i, 50 f, 22 org, UK / 20 i, o'seas
¶   Direct (NL) - 4.   LM - 2 yrly.
        Rates Cards (Schedule of rates of pay) - 1.
        Contract Guide - 1.
        Monitoring Report on Theatre Directors.

Directory & Database Publishers Association
        since 2005 **Data Publishers Association**

Disability Alliance   1974
■   Universal House, 88-94 Wentworth St, LONDON, E1 7SA.
        (hq)
        020 7247 8776 (1000-1600 hrs)   fax 020 7247 8765
        email office.da@dial.pipex.com
        http://www.disabilityalliance.org
        Chief Exec: Lorna Reith,   Sec: Michael Odedairo
▲   Company Limited by Guarantee; Registered Charity
○   *K, *W; to break the link between poverty & disability by
        providing information to disabled people about their
        entitlements; to campaign for improvements to the social
        security system & for increases in benefits
Gp   Tribunal support unit
●   ET - Inf - LG
M   350 org
¶   Disability Rights Bulletin - 3; £3.75 each.
        Disability Rights Hbk - 1; £14 (£9.60 for individuals on any
        social security benefit).
        Publications list available.

Disability Federation of Ireland   (DFI)
IRL   Fumbally Court, Fumbally Lane, DUBLIN 8, Republic of Ireland.
        353 (1) 454 7978   fax 353 (1) 454 7981
        email info@disability-federation.ie
        Chief Exec: John Dolan
○   *N, *W

Disability Sport England
        2005 became Disability Sport Events, the events division of the
        English Federation of Disability Sport

Disabled Drivers' Association
        2005-06 merged with Disabled Drivers Motor Club to form **Mobilise
        Organisation**

Disabled Drivers' Motor Club Ltd
        2005-6 merged with Disabled Drivers Association to form **Mobilise
        Organisation**

Disabled Motorists Federation   (DMF)   1955
- ■ Chester-le-Street CVS & Volunteer Centre, Clarence Terrace, CHESTER-LE-STREET, Co Durham, DH3 3DQ.   (hq)
  0191-416 3172   fax 0191-416 3172
  email jkillick2214@compuserve.com
  145 Knoulbery Rd, Blackfell, WASHINGTON, Tyne & Wear, NE37 1JN. (hsp)
      email jkillick2214@compuserve.com.   (hsp)
  Hon Sec: J E Killick
- ▲ Registered Charity
- Br 11 affiliated clubs; Russia
- ○ *W; to provide motoring information to the disabled & their carers on all matters of disabled travel; to run social clubs & to negotiate with national bodies on all matters connected with disabled travel, not specialising in motoring
- ● Mtgs - Inf - LG
- M c 2,000 i, 11 affiliated clubs
- ¶ The Way Ahead - 4; ftm, £1.25 nm.
  Publications list available.

Disablement Income Group Scotland   (DIG Scotland)   1966
- NR 5 Quayside St, EDINBURGH, EH6 6EJ.   (hq)
  0131-555 2811   fax 0131-554 7076
  email info@digscotland.co.uk
  Chmn: Mike Coveney,   Co Sec: Frank Cochrane
- ▲ Company Limited by Guarantee
- ○ *W; free welfare benefits information & advice service for disabled people & carers throughout Scotland
- ● Talks to disability & carers' groups - Training for professionals - Advice clinics at hospital & cancer care centres
- M 2,900 i, 15 org
- ¶ NL - 4; m only.
  AR & Chairman's Report.

Discrimination Law Association   (DLA)   1995
- ■ PO Box 6715, RUSHDEN, Northants, NN10 9WL.
  (mail/address)
  01933 228742   fax 01933 228742
  email info@discrimination-law.org.uk
  http://www.discrimination-law.org.uk
  Hon Sec: Melanie Crufts
- ▲ Company Limited by Guarantee
- ○ *K, *P; to promote & improve services to victims of discrimination; to expand teaching & disseminate information & views on discrimination law; to secure improvements in discrimination law & practice
- ● Conf - Mtgs - ET - Inf
- M 233 i, 41 f, 133 org
- ¶ Discrimination Law Briefings - 4; ftm, c£20 each nm.
  Directory of Members - 2; free.
  Directory of Trainers - 2; free.
  NL - 4; ftm.   AR; ftm, £1 nm.

Dispensing Doctors Association Ltd   (DDA)   1997
- NR Low Hagg Farm, Starfitts Lane, KIRKBYMOORSIDE, N Yorks, YO62 7JF. (hsb)
  01751 430835   fax 01751 430836
  email ddalimited@aol.com
  http://www.dispensingdoctor.org
  Chief Exec: Dr David Baker
  Sec: Jeff Lee
- ▲ Company Limited by Guarantee
- ○ *P; for doctors providing pharmaceutical services in rural areas
- Gp Financial; Publicity
- ● Conf - ET - Inf - LG
- M c 2,400 i, 25 f
- ¶ Jnl - 4.

District Auditors Society
- NR c/o Sue Exton / Audit Commission, Millbank Tower (1st floor), Millbank, LONDON, SW1P 4HQ.   (pres/b)
  020 7828 1212
  Pres: Sue Exton
- ○ *P
- < Mtgs
- M i

District Courts Association   (DCA)   1980
- NR Civic Centre, MOTHERWELL, Lanarks, ML1 1TW.   (hsb)
  01698 302273   fax 01698 302339
  email handsp@northlan.gov.uk
  http://www.district-courts.org.uk
  Hon Sec: Phyllis M Hands
- ▲ Un-incorporated Society
- ○ *N, *P; consultation, discussion & dissemination of information for District Courts in Scotland; training of Justices of the Peace in Scotland
- ● Conf - Mtgs - ET - SG - Stat - LG
- < C'wealth Magistrates & Justices Assn; Magistrates Assn
- M 30 local auths
- ¶ DCA NL - 2; ftm only.

District Surveyors Association Ltd   (DSABRO)   1991
- ■ 137 Lupus St, LONDON, SW1V 3HE.   (hq)
  020 7641 8737   fax 020 7641 8739
  email info@labc-services.co.uk   http://www.labc.co.uk
  Sec & Chief Exec: Paul Everall
- ▲ Company Limited by Guarantee
- ○ *P; to promote & support local authority building control in the public sector
- ● Mtgs - LG
- M [not stated]
  Note: Trades as LABC.
- × (District Surveyors Association
  (District Surveyors Ltd (trading as LABC Services)

Doctor E F Schumacher Society   (Schumacher UK)   1978
- ■ The Create Centre, Smeaton Rd, BRISTOL, BS1 6XN.   (hq)
  0117-903 1081   fax 0117-903 1081
  email admin@schumacher.org.uk
  http://www.schumacher.org.uk
  Dir: Richard St George
- ▲ Company Limited by Guarantee
- Br 3; Germany, India, Ireland, USA
- ○ *G; to promote the philosophy of Dr E F Schumacher; to promote human scale sustainable development in the UK & abroad
- Gp Schumacher book service
- ● Conf - ET - Res - Inf - VE - Presentation of annual Schumacher award
- < Members of the Schumacher Circle:
  Centre for Alternative Technology; Intermediate Technology; New Economics Foundation; Soil Association
- > Schumacher College
- M 500 i, 5 f, 5 org, UK / 50 i, o'seas
- ¶ Schumacher NL - 2; ftm, £2 nm.
  Schumacher Briefings - 2/3; ftm, £6-£8 nm.

Doctor Richard Bright Society
- NR c/o Dr Richard Bright Renal Unit, Southmead Hospital, BRISTOL, BS11 5NR.   (mail) address
  Hon Sec: Diana Berry (0117-973 1937)
- ○ *G
- M c 30-40 i

** Doctors & Lawyers for Responsible Medicine
  Organisation lost: see Introduction paragraph 3

Dogs Trust   1891
- ■   17 Wakley St, LONDON, EC1V 7RQ.   (hq)
       020 7837 0006   fax 020 7833 2701
       email info@dogstrust.org.uk
       http://www.dogstrust.org.uk
       Chief Exec: Clarissa Baldwin
- ▲   Registered Charity
- Br   15
- ○   *V; 'working towards the day when all dogs can enjoy a happy
       life, free from the threat of unnecessary destruction'
- ●   Conf - Mtgs - ET - Res - Exhib - Comp - Stat - Expt - Inf - PL
- M   15,825 i, 826 f, 262,775 supporters, UK / 96 i, 808
       supporters, o'seas
- ¶   NL - 3; free.   AR; ftm only.
       Educational literature.
- ×   2003 National Canine Defence League

Doll Club of Great Britain
- NR   c/o 16 Clifton Gardens, Warwick Avenue, LONDON,
       W9 1DT.   (mail) address
       Hon Sec: Mrs Margaret Towner
- ▲   Un-incorporated Society
- ○   *G; the study & appreciation of dolls, dolls houses & other
       nursery bygones of the past
- ●   Mtgs - Comp - SG - VE
- M   150 i, UK / 20 i, o'seas
- ¶   Plangon - 4; ftm only.

Dolmetsch Historical Dance Society   (DHDS)   1970
- ■   17 Well Lane, Stock, INGATESTONE, Essex, CM4 9LT.   (hsp)
       01277 840473   fax 01277 840473
       email secretary@dhds.org.uk   http://www.dhds.org.uk
       Hon Sec: Mrs Jo Saunders
- ▲   Registered Charity
- ○   *A, *D, *G, *L, *Q; conducting & promoting original research
       into & practice of dance, from the 14th-19th centuries &
       allied subjects of music, literature, art, costume & social
       history
- ●   Conf - Mtgs - Res - Inf
- M   93 i, UK / 16 i, o'seas
- ¶   Historical Dance (Jnl) - 2/3 yrly; ftm, £8 nm.
       NL - 3; ftm only.   Teaching Resource Packs.
       Summer School Booklets & CDs (dance instructions & music) -
       1; prices vary.
       Conference Proceedings - 2 yrly; prices vary.

Domestic Appliance Service Association   (DASA)   1978
- ■   145-157 St John St, LONDON, EC1V 4PY.   (asa)
       0870 224 0343   fax 0870 224 0358
       email dasa@dasanet.org.uk
       http://www.dasanet.org.uk
       Chmn: W Russell
- ▲   Un-incorporated Society
- ○   *T; repair & servicing of domestic appliances
- ●   Mtgs - ET - Exhib - LG
- <   Brit Quality Foundation; Electrical & Electronics Servicing
       Training Coun;Trade Assn Forum
- M   100 i, 30 f
- ¶   Orbit (NL) - 6; ftm only.   LM [website].

Domestic Fowl Trust   1974
- NR   Honeybourne Pastures, Honeybourne, EVESHAM, Worcs,
       WR11 5QG.   (hq)
       01386 833083   fax 01386 833364
       email dlf@domesticfowltrust.co.uk
       http://www.domesticfowltrust.co.uk
       Chief Exec: Mrs Bernie Landshoff
- ○   *B; conservation of the domestic fowl & rare breeds of farm
       animals; marketing of poultry housing & equipment, hybrid &
       traditional breeds of poultry, books & gifts
- ●   ET
- M   350 i, UK / 30 i, o'seas

Domestic Heating Controls Group
   incorporated with the Control Manufacturers Association which is part
   of BEAMA Energy, a group of **BEAMA**

Domestic Manufacturing Stationers Association
   is a group of the **British Office Supplies & Services Federation**

Domestic Water Treatment Association
   as part of BEAMA Energy is a group of**BEAMA**D17[S102UA]
   (06)Malcolm Dutton/0114-263 2431D17[S102UA]   (06)Malcolm
   Dutton/0114-263 2431

Doncaster Chamber of Commerce   (DCCE)   1941
- NR   ICON / First Point, Balby Carr Bank, DONCASTER, S Yorks,
       DN4 5JQ.   (hq)
       01302 341000   fax 01302 328382
       http://www.doncaster-chamber.co.uk
       Chief Exec: Neville Dearden
- ▲   Company Limited by Guarantee
- ○   *C
- ●   Conf - Mtgs - ET - Res - Exhib - Comp - Stat - Expt - Inf - Lib -
       VE - Empl - LG
- <   Brit Chams Comm
- M   1,000 f
- ¶   Chamber News - 6;   Chamber Link - 6; both free.

Donizetti Society   1973
- NR   146 Bordesley Rd, MORDEN, Surrey, SM4 5LT.   (hsp)
       020 8648 9364
       Hon Sec: J P Clayton
- ○   *D; to promote interest in the works of Gaetano Donizetti
       (1797-1848) & the music of his period
- M   i

Donkey Breed Society   (DBS)   1967
- NR   The Hermitage, Pootings, EDENBRIDGE, Kent, TN8 6SD.   (hsb)
       01732 864414   fax 01732 864414
       email carol@morse.freeserve.co.uk
       http://www.donkeybreedsociety.co.uk
       Sec: Carol Morse
- ○   *B; to encourage the use, appreciation, well being & protection
       of the donkey
- Gp   Championship show; Shows & judges; Driving; Studbook;
       Welfare; Juniors
- ●   Conf - ET - Comp - SG - Inf
- <   Brit Horse Soc
- M   c 1,000 i
- ¶   Magazine - 1.   NL - 4.

Donor Watch   1995
- ■   Turner House, 153 Cromwell Road, LONDON, SW5 0TQ.
       (hsp)
       020 7373 5560   fax 020 7373 5560
       email selbywhittingham@hotmail.com
       Sec-Gen: Dr Selby Whittingham
- ▲   Un-incorporated Society
- ○   *L; campaigning in support of fidelity to the conditions on
       which money, or objects, are given or bequeathed for the
       benefit of the public
- ●   Campaigning
- M   [not stated]
- ¶   NL - 2/3; ftm only.

Door & Hardware Federation   (DHF)   1970
- NR   42 Heath St, TAMWORTH, Staffs, B79 7JH.   (hq)
       01827 52337
       Sec: M P Skelding
- ▲   Company Limited by Guarantee
- ○   *T
- ●   Conf - Mtgs - Stat - Inf
- ×   2005 (Association of Building Hardware Manufacturers
       (Door & Shutter Manufacturers' Association

© CBD Research Ltd · Beckenham · BR3 5JS · Tel 020 8650 7745 · Fax 020 8650 0768 · E-mail cbd@cbdresearch.com · www.cbdresearch.com

Door & Shutter Manufacturers Association
    2005 merged with the Association of Building Hardware
    Manufacturers to form the **Door & Hardware Federation**

Dorchester Agricultural Society   (DAS) 1841
■   Agriculture House, Acland Rd, DORCHESTER, Dorset,
    DT1 1EF. (hq)
    01305 264249   fax 01305 251643
    email info@dorsetcountyshow.co.uk
    http://www.dorsetcountyshow.co.uk
    Sec: Samantha E Mackenzie-Green
▲   Company Limited by Guarantee; Registered Charity
○   *F
●   Comp
M   1,500 i, 20 f

Dorothy L Sayers Society   1976
■   Rose Cottage, Malthouse Lane, HURSTPIERPOINT, W Sussex,
    BN6 9JY. (chmn/p)
    01273 833444   fax 01273 835988
    email jasmine@sayers.org.uk
    http://www.sayers.org.uk/
    Chmn: Christopher J Dean
▲   Registered Charity
○   *A; study of the life & works of Dorothy L Sayers;
    encouragement & advice on production & research of her
    works
●   Conf - Res - SG - Inf
M   260 i, UK / 255 i, o'seas
¶   DLS Bulletin - 6; ftm.   Sidelights on Sayers - 2; £3.
    Annual Proceedings - 1; £3.

Dorset Chamber of Commerce & Industry   (DCCI) 1949
NR Chamber House, Acorn Office Park, Link Rd, Tower Park,
    POOLE, Dorset, BH12 4NZ. (hq)
    01202 714800
    Chief Exec: Peter Scott
▲   Company Limited by Guarantee
○   *C
    Note: is known as Dorset Business.

Dorset Down Sheep Breeders' Association   (DDSBA) 1906
NR c/o Glasper's Land Agency Ltd, Coombe View Farm,
    Branscombe, SEATON, Devon, EX12 3BT.
    01297 680218   fax 01297 680594
    Breed Sec: Trevor Glasper
▲   Company Limited by Guarantee; Registered Charity
○   *B
●   Mtgs - Exhib - Comp - Stat - Expt - Inf - VE
<   Nat Sheep Assn
M   54 i, UK / 1 i, o'seas
¶   NL - 2; m only.   Breed Flock Book - 1; ftm, £5 nm.

Dorset Horn & Poll Dorset Sheep Breeders' Association (DHSBA) 1891
■   Agriculture House, Acland Rd, DORCHESTER, Dorset,
    DT1 1EF. (hq)
    01305 262126   fax 01305 262126
    email mail@dorsetsheep.org
    http://www.dorsetsheep.org
    Breed Sec: Mrs M Cowley
▲   Registered Charity
○   *B
●   Mtgs - Comp - Expt - Inf - Breed show & sales
M   300 i
¶   Flock Book - 1; ftm, £20 nm.

Dorset Natural History & Archaeological Society   (DNH&AS) 1875
■   66 High West St, DORCHESTER, Dorset, DT1 1XA. (hq)
    01305 262735
    email dorsetcountymuseum@dor-mus.demon.co.uk
    http://www.dorsetcountymuseum.org
    Dir: Judy Lindsay
▲   Registered Charity
○   *A, *L; archaeology, local history, natural history & geology, art
    & literature (including Thomas Hardy) of Dorset
Gp Natural history; Archaeology; Geology; Junior members
●   Conf - Mtgs - ET - Res - Exhib - Comp - SG - Inf - Lib - PL - VE
    - Conservation
M   1,900 i, 100 org
¶   Proceedings - 1.   AR.
    Archaeological Monographs.   Dorset Series.

Dorset Record Society
    is a sub-committee of the **Dorset Natural History &**
    Archaeological Society

Double Harness Scurry Driving
    since 2005 **Scurry Driving Association**

Dover & District Chamber of Commerce & Industry
NR White Cliffs Business Centre, Enterprise Zone - Whitfield,
    DOVER, Kent, CT16 3EH.
    01304 824955   fax 01304 822354
    Mgr: Julia Chambers
○   *C

Down's Syndrome Association   (DSA) 1970
NR Langdon Down Centre, 2A Langdon Park, TEDDINGTON,
    Middx, TW11 9PS. (hq)
    0845 230 0372   fax 020 8682 4012
    email info@downs-syndrome.org.uk
    http://www.downs-syndrome.org.uk
    Chief Exec: Carol Boys
▲   Company Limited by Guarantee; Registered Charity
○   *W; to help people with Down's syndrome to live full &
    rewarding lives; to provide information, counselling &
    support as well as being a resource to interested
    professionals
Gp Parent self-help
●   Conf - ET - Res - Inf - Lib - PL - LG
M   7,500 i, 1,800 f & org
¶   Jnl - 3; ftm only.   AR - 1; free on request.
    A wide range of information literature & other materials; largely
    ftm, prices on request nm.

Down's Syndrome Scotland   1982
■   158-160 Balgreen Rd, EDINBURGH, EH11 3AU. (hq)
    0131-313 4225   fax 0131-313 4285
    email info@dsscotland.org.uk
    http://www.dsscotland.org.uk
    Dir: Karen Watchman
▲   Registered Charity
Br 10
○   *W; a national support group giving information & support to
    people with Down's Syndrome & their families in Scotland
●   Conf - ET - Inf - Lib - Local group activities
M   1,200 i, 500 professionals
¶   Publications list available; 50p - £5.
×   2001 (Sep) Scottish Down's Syndrome Association

Dozenal Society of Great Britain   (DSGB)   1960
- ■ 32 Lansdowne Crescent, CARLISLE, Cumbria, CA3 9EW.   (gsp)
    01228 596834
    http://www.dozenalsociety.org.uk
    Gen Sec: Shaun Ferguson
- ▲ Un-incorporated Society
- ○ *K; 'following the introduction of place-value arithmetic it was recognised calculations to a divisible scale of twelve numerals would not only simplify the operations but allow a precise representation of the basic ratios required to define the physical world or manage our material affairs. The Society affirms this view with the object of unifying scientific & social practices'
- Gp Arithmetic & mathematics; Historical metrology; Metrication
- ● Res - Inf - Lib - Publishing - Cooperation with the British Weights & Measures Association providing technical information & informed criticism of attempts to impose decimal-metric methods in areas where they are inappropriate
- < Dozenal Soc of America (NY); Brit Weights & Measures Assn
- M 200 i, UK / 15 i, o'seas
- ¶ The Dozenal Jnl - 1.
    T.G.M. a coherent dozenal metrology.
    Booklets & reprints of salient articles.

Dracula Society   1973
- ■ PO Box 30848, LONDON, W12 0GY.   (mail)
    http://www.thedraculasociety.org.uk address
    Chmn & Treas: Julia Kruk
- ○ *G; 'Since it is named after the most evocative title in the entire genre, the Society naturally devotes a good deal of its attention to the book & its author, Bram Stoker. However vampires, werewolves, mummies & all the other monsters spawned by the Gothic genre fall within its field of interest, which also embraces stage & screen, adaptations & the sources of inspiration in myth & folklore'
- ● Mtgs - VE
- < The Vampire Empire (NY)
- M c 90 i, UK / c 20 i, o'seas
- ¶ Voices from the Vaults (NL) - 4; ftm only.

Dragonfly Conservation Group
    a group of the **British Dragonfly Society**

Drake Exploration Society   (DES)   1996
- ■ 7 Rosewood Ave, BURNHAM-ON-SEA, Somerset, TA8 1HD. (hsp)
    01278 783519
    email sfdsociety@aol.com   http://www.chantec.co.uk/drakesociety/
    Founder: Michael Turner
- ▲ Un-incorporated Society
- ○ *G; to perpetuate the memory of Sir Francis Drake through research, fieldwork, lectures & publications
- ● Mtgs - Res - Exhib - SG - Inf - Lib - PL - VE - Illustrated lectures & fieldwork
- < Drake Navigator's Guild (USA)
- M 26 i, 2 f, 3 org, UK / 6 i, o'seas
- ¶ The Drake Broadside - 1; ftm, £12 nm.

Drama Association of Wales   (Cymdeithas Ddrama Cymru) (DAW)   1973
- ■ The Old Library, Singleton Rd, Splott, CARDIFF, Glam, CF24 2ET.   (hq)
    029 2045 2200   fax 029 2045 2277
    email aled.daw@virgin.net
    Admin: Gary Thomas
- ▲ Registered Charity
- ○ *A; to promote amateur theatre in Wales & worldwide; to encourage new writing
- ● Mtgs - ET - Res - Comp - SG - Inf - Lib (world's largest collection of playscripts) - LG - Publishing
- < Intl Amat Theatre Assn; Cent Coun for Amat Theatre; Nat Assn Youth Theatre; Wales Assn for the Performing Arts
- M 221 i, 16 f, 267 org, UK / 11 i, 1 f, 6 org, o'seas
- ¶ Dawn (NL) - 4; ftm.

Drama League of Ireland
- IRL Carmichael House, North Brunswick St, DUBLIN 7, Republic of Ireland.
    353 (1) 872 5550
    email dli@eircom.net   http://www.dli.ie
    Sec: Marianne Gibney
- ○ *D; to promote amateur drama & theatre in Ireland

Draught Proofing Advisory Association Ltd   (DPAA)   1980
- NR PO Box 12, HASLEMERE, Surrey, GU27 3AH.   (hq)
    01428 654011   fax 01428 651401
    Dir: Gillian Allder
- ▲ Company Limited by Guarantee
- ○ *T; representing the draught proofing industry
- ● Mtgs - Inf - LG
- M f
- ¶ NL; m only.   LM.

Dress & Textile Specialists   (GCTSM)
- NR c/o Curator of Domestic Collections, Museum of Welsh Life, St Fagans, CARDIFF, CF5 6XB.   (hsb)
    029 2057 3420
    Hon Sec: Christine Stevens
- ▲ Un-incorporated Society
- ○ *P; to support museum professionals working with costume & textile collections
- ● Conf - Mtgs - ET
- < Museums Assn
- M 88 i, 44 f
- ¶ NL - 2; ftm only.
- × 2003 Group for Costume & Textile Staff in Museums

Driffield Agricultural Society
- NR The Showground, Kellythorpe, DRIFFIELD, E Yorks, YO25 9DN.
    01377 2574943
    email office@driffieldshow.co.uk
- ○ *F, *H
- ● Show
- M i & f

Drilling & Sawing Association Ltd   (DSA)   1984
- ■ North Mill (suite 5.O), Bridgefoot, BELPER, Derbys, DE56 1YD.   (asa)
    01773 820000   fax 01773 821284
    email dsa@drillandsaw.org.uk
    http://www.drillandsaw.org.uk
    Sec: Hugh C Wylde
- ▲ Company Limited by Guarantee
- ○ *T; concrete drilling & sawing industry
- Gp Specialist drilling & sawing contractors; Suppliers of drilling & sawing equipment
- ● Mtgs - ET - Exhib - Inf - VE
- < Intl Assn of Concrete Drillers & Sawers
- M 100 f, UK / 5 org, o'seas
- ¶ Concrete Cutter (Jnl) - 2.   LM.   Brochure.

© CBD Research Ltd · Beckenham · BR3 5JS · Tel 020 8650 7745 · Fax 020 8650 0768 · E-mail cbd@cbdresearch.com · www.cbdresearch.com

Drinking Fountain Association
  see **Metropolitan Drinking Fountain & Cattle Trough Association**

Drinks Industry Group of Ireland
IRL   Anglesea House, Anglesea Rd, Ballsbridge, DUBLIN 4, Republic
        of Ireland.
        353 (1) 668 0215   fax 353 (1) 668 0448
        Hon Sec: Donal O'Keeffe
○   *T

Driving Instructors Association   (DIA)   1978
NR   Safety House, Beddington Farm Rd, CROYDON, Surrey,
        CR0 4XZ.   (hq)
        0845 345 5151   fax 020 8655 5565
        Sec: Tina Tutton
▲   Registered Charity
○   *P; to raise the standard of driver education & improve road
        safety by means of professional training
Gp   Holders of Diploma in Driving Instruction; Specialist LGV & PCV
        instructors
●   Conf - Mtgs - ET - Exam - Res - Exhib - Comp - SG - Stat - Inf -
        Lib - VE
<   Soc of Motor Mfrs & Traders; Parliamentary Advy Coun for
        Traffic Safety; Intl Assn for Driver Education (IVV)
M   10,000 i, UK / 180 i, o'seas
¶   Driving Magazine - 6.
        Driving Instructor - 6.

Drogheda Chamber of Commerce
IRL   Chamber Buildings, 10 Dublin Rd, DROGHEDA, Co Louth,
        Republic of Ireland.
        353 (41) 983 3544
        email enquiries@droghedachamber.com
        http://www.droghedachamber.com
        Pres: Graham O'Rourke
○   *C

Drum Corps of the United Kingdom   1980
NR   Croft House, Garden St, SHEFFIELD, S Yorks, S1 4BJ.
        0114-249 1922
        Sec: Jill Boyington
○   *D
M   c 1,500 i

Dry Stone Walling Association of Great Britain   (DSWA)   1968
■   Westmorland County Showground, Lane Farm, Crooklands,
        MILNTHORPE, Cumbria, LA7 7NH.   (mail)
        01539 567953
        http://www.dswa.org.uk address
▲   Registered Charity
Br   19
○   *G; to foster an interest in dry stone walling & dyking; to ensure
        that the best craftsmanship of the past is preserved
●   Mtgs - ET - Exam - Comp - Inf (send sae) - LG
M   1,200 i, 15 f, UK / 10 i, o'seas
¶   Waller & Dyker (Jnl) - 3; ftm, £2.50 nm.
        Register of Certificated Wallers/Dykers; free with sae.
        Building & Repairing Dry Stone Walls; £1.50.
        In There Somewhere; £5.   [all plus p&p].

Dublin Chamber of Commerce   1783
IRL   7 Clare St, DUBLIN 2, Republic of Ireland.
        353 (1) 644 7200   fax 353 (1) 676 6043
        email info@dublinchamber.ie
        http://www.dublinchamber.ie
        Chief Exec: Gina Quin
○   *C

Duchenne Family Support Group   (DFSG)   1987
■   6 Laburnum Rd, SANDY, Beds, SG19 1HQ.   (hsp)
        0870 241 1857   fax 0870 241 1857
        email info@dfsg.org.uk   http://www.dfsg.org.uk
        Hon Sec: Mrs Ann Patterson
▲   Registered Charity
○   *W; is run by families for families affected by Duchenne
        muscular dystrophy (a severely disabling & life-limiting
        muscle wasting condition)
●   Conf - Mtgs - Inf - VE - National support network of parents,
        their families & professionals - National helpline
M   2,000 i, 230 org, UK / 40 i, 10 org, o'seas
¶   Duchenne News - 4; free.

Dugdale Society   1920
■   The Shakespeare Centre, STRATFORD-upon-AVON, Warks,
        CV37 6QW.   (hq/hsb)
        01789 204016   fax 01789 296083
        email records@shakespeare.org.uk
        http://www.shakespeare.org.uk/dugdale
        Chmn: Prof C C Dyer,   Hon Sec: Mrs Cathy Millwood
▲   Registered Charity
○   *L; publication of original documents on history of
        Warwickshire (named after Sir William Dugdale, antiquary
        1605-1680)
●   Res
M   250 i, 70 org, UK / 50 org, o'seas
¶   Volumes & Occasional Papers - irreg; ftm, varies nm.
        AR.

Dumfries & Galloway Chamber of Commerce   1987
■   16 Buccleuch St, DUMFRIES, DG1 2AH.   (hq)
        01387 270866
        email dgcc@btconnect.com   http://www.dgcc.org.uk
        Admin: Sue Taylor
▲   Company Limited by Guarantee
○   *C
●   Mtgs - Inf - Seminars
<   Scot Chams Comm; Glasgow Cham Comm
M   2,400 i, 90 f
×   2001 Dumfries & Galloway Chamber of Trade & Commerce

**Dumfriesshire & Galloway Natural History & Antiquarian
Society   (DGNHAS)   1862**
■   5 Arthur's Place, LOCKERBIE, Dumfriesshire, DG11 2EB.   (hsp)
        http://www.users.quista.net/dgnhas
        The Honorary Secretary
▲   Registered Charity
○   *L
●   Mtgs - VE
M   300 i, 50 org, UK / 50 i, o'seas
¶   Transactions - 1.

Dun Horse & Pony Society   (DHAPS)   1999
NR   4 Elderfield Rd, Kings Norton, BIRMINGHAM, W Midlands,
        B30 3PE.   (chmn/p)
        0121-451 3479
        http://www.dhaps-online.co.uk
        Chmn: Andrew Ward
◔   *B; for those interested in dun horses & ponies (Palomino
        coloured, but with black mane & tail); to promote dun horses
        in all spheres of the horse industry
●   Comp - Horse show sponsorship
M   100 i
¶   The Dun Thing - 4;   The Dun Thing Update - 2/3;   DHAPS
        Hbk - 1; all ftm only.

Dundalk Chamber of Commerce
IRL Hagan House, Ramparts Rd, DUNDALK, Co Louth, Republic of
      Ireland.
      353 (42) 933 6343   fax 353 (420 933 2085
      email info@dundalk.ie   http://www.dundalk.ie
      Chief Exec: Bill Tosh
○   *C

Dundee & Tayside Chamber of Commerce & Industry   1835
NR   Chamber of Commerce Buildings, Panmure St, DUNDEE, Fife,
      DD1 1ED.   (hq)
      01382 228545   fax 01382 228441
      email admin@dundeechamber.co.uk
      http://www.dundeechamber.co.uk
      Chief Exec: Mervyn Rolfe
○   *C
●   Mtgs - Exhib - Expt - Inf - LG (local) - Business support
<   Brit Chams Comm; Assn Scot Chams Comm
M   750 f
¶   The Business - 6;   Annual Diary.

Durham County Agricultural Society   (DCAS)   1841
■   PO Box 58, CHESTER le STREET, Co Durham, DH3 3GB.   (hsp)
      0191-534 6482
      Sec: Mrs C M Duke
○   *F, *H; to organise the Durham County Show

Durham County Local History Society   (DCLHS)   1964
NR   21 St Mary's Grove, Tudhoe, SPENNYMOOR, Co Durham,
      DL16 6LR.   (hsp)
      01388 816209
      email johnbanham@tiscali.co.uk
      http://www.durhamweb.org.uk/dclhs
      Sec: Dr J D Banham
▲   Registered Charity
○   *L; to encourage & promote interest in the study of the history
      of County Durham, and of the North East in general
<   Brit Assn for Local History
M   220 i, 32 org, UK / 2 i, 8 org, o'seas
¶   Bulletin - 2.   NL - 4.
      Documentary Series; prices vary.
      Occasional Papers (including):
         Durham Biographies (edited by Batho) vol 1-3.
         The Durham Crown Lordships (Reid).
         Durham City and its MPs (Heesom).

Durham Wildlife Trust   (DWT)   1971
■   Rainton Meadows, Chilton Moor, HOUGHTON-le-SPRING,
      Tyne & Wear, DH4 6PU.   (hq)
      0191-584 3112   fax 0191-584 3934
      email info@durhamwt.co.uk
      http://www.wildlifetrust.org.uk/durham
      Chief Exec: Richard Wood
▲   Company Limited by Guarantee; Registered Charity
○   *K; protection of wild life & natural beauty of Durham County &
      Tyne & Wear south of the Tyne; management of the Trust's
      nature reserves
Gp   10 local groups; 26 nature reserves; 3 visitor centres
●   Conf - Mtgs - ET - Exhib - SG - Inf - VE
<   R Soc of Wildlife Trusts (UK Office)
M   8,500 i, 55 f
¶   Durham Wildlife - 3; tm, £1.50 nm.

Dutch Barge Association   (DBA)   1992
■   3 Norfolk Court, Norfolk Rd, RICKMANSWORTH, Herts,
      WD3 1LT.   (regd/off)
      07000 BARGES (227437)   fax 01932 765734
      email info@barges.org   http://www.barges.org
      Hon Sec: Les Gibson
▲   Company Limited by Guarantee
○   *G; support group for barge owners
Gp   Continental cruising; Sailing barge; Thames
●   Mtgs - ET - Inf - Liaison with navigation authorities, trade assns
      & other clubs - Arrangement of member discounts for goods
      & services
M   700 i & f, UK / 400 i & f, o'seas
¶   Blue Flag - 4; ftm.   Barge Buyers' Hbk.

Dvořák Society for Czech & Slovak Music   1974
NR   Church House, Lyonshall, KINGTON, Herefords, HR5 3HR.
      (sp)
      http://www.dvorak-society.org
      Hon Sec: Don Preddy
▲   Registered Charity
○   *D; 'to educate the public in the arts & sciences & in particular,
      the music of the Czech Republic & Slovakia'
●   Mtgs - ET - Res - Exhib - Inf - Lib - VE
<   Le Mouvement Janáček (France), Dvořák Soc (Czech Republic),
      Janáček Soc (Switzerland), Czech Music Socs (Czech Republic
      & USA), Martinů Soc (Czech Republic), Slovak Music
      Foundation, Czech Music Foundation, Smetana Soc (Czech
      Republic), František Kmoch Czech Bands Soc (UK)
M   400 i, 7 f, 2 org, UK / 140 i, 9 f, 5 org, o'seas
¶   Czech Music - 1.
      NL - 4/5.   Ybk.

Dylan Thomas Society of Great Britain   1977
■   Fernhill / 24 Chapel St, Mumbles, SWANSEA, Glam,
      SA3 4NH.   (chmn)
      01792 363785 p
      Chmn: Mrs Cecily Hughes
Br   Australia, Canada
○   *G; to foster & stimulate interest in the work of Dylan Thomas &
      the literature of Anglo-Welsh writers
●   Mtgs - VE
M   240 i, UK / 20 i, o'seas
¶   NL - 2; ftm, £1 nm.
      2003 commemorative publication: I Sang In My Chains, Essays
      & Poems in Tribute to Dylan Thomas; £10.

Dyslexia Association of Ireland   1972
IRL 1 Suffolk St, DUBLIN 2, Republic of Ireland.
      353 (1) 679 0276   fax 353 (1) 679 0273
      email info@dyslexia.ie   http://www.dyslexia.ie
      Dir: Ann Hughes
○   *K, *W

Dyslexia Institute   (DI)   1974
■   Park House, Wick Rd, EGHAM, Surrey, TW20 0HH.   (hq)
      01784 222300   fax 01784 222333
      email info@dyslexia-inst.org.uk
      http://www.dyslexia-inst.org.uk
      Exec Dir: Mrs S Cramer
▲   Company Limited by Guarantee; Registered Charity
Br   27 dyslexia institutes
○   *E, *W; assessment of children & adults; teaching of dyslexic
      children & adults; teacher training
Gp   Assessment; Teaching
●   Conf - ET - Exhib - Comp - Inf - LG - Fund raising
<   Brit Dyslexia Assn
M   'friends'
¶   As We See It (NL) - 1; free.   Leaflets.
×   2005 (July) Hornsby Dyslexia Charity (merged)

© CBD Research Ltd · Beckenham · BR3 5JS · Tel 020 8650 7745 · Fax 020 8650 0768 · E-mail cbd@cbdresearch.com · www.cbdresearch.com

Dyslexia Scotland   1968
- ■ Stirling Business Centre, Wellgreen, STIRLING, FK8 2DZ.   (hq)
   01786 446650   fax 01786 471235
   email info@dyslexiascotland.org.uk
   http://www.dyslexiascotland.org.uk
   Chief Exec: Fiona Hird
- ▲ Company Limited by Guarantee; Registered Charity (Scotland)
- Br 13 (Scotland)
- ○ *K, *W; 'to enable & encourage dyslexic people, regardless of their age & abilities, to reach their potential in education, employment & life'
- ● Conf - Mtgs - ET - Stat - Inf - Lib - LG
   Resource centre of books, teaching materials, computer software, audio & visual aids
- M 700 i, 20 f
- × 2004 Scottish Dyslexia Association

Dyspraxia Foundation   1987
- NR 8 West Alley, HITCHIN, Herts, SG5 1EG.   (hq)
   01462 455016   fax 01462 455052
   email dyspraxia@dyspraxiafoundation.org.uk
   http://www.dyspraxiafoundation.org.uk
   Admin: Mrs Eleanor Howes
- ▲ Registered Charity
- Br 2
- ○ *W; to support parents & professionals caring for children with dyspraxia ('clumsy child syndrome')
- Gp Adults with dyspraxia
   Helpline: 01462 454986 (Mon-Fri 1000-1400)
- ● Conf - Mtgs - Res - Exhib - Stat - Inf - LG
- M c 2,000 i
- ¶ Praxis Makes Perfect.   Information pack. other publications available.

Dystonia Society   (TDS)   1983
- ■ Camelford House (1st floor), 89 Albert Embankment, LONDON, SE1 7TP.   (hq)
   0845 458 6211   fax 0845 458 6311
   email info@dystonia.org.uk
   http://www.dystonia.org.uk
   Chief Exec: Philip Eckstein
- ▲ Registered Charity
- Br 24
- ○ *M, *W; to raise awareness of dystonia, a neurological movement disorder; to support those affected by dystonia & provide information
- Gp Young Dystonia - support group for families
- ● Conf - Mtgs - Inf
- < Eur Dystonia Fedn; Neurological Alliance
- M 3,000 i, UK / 115 i, o'seas
- ¶ NL - 4; free.

Dystrophic Epidermolysis Bullosa Research Association (DEBRA)   1978
- NR 13 Wellington Business Park, Duke's Ride, CROWTHORNE, Berks, RG45 6LS.   (hq)
   01344 771961   fax 01344 762661
   email debra@debra.org.uk   http://www.debra.org.uk
   Dir: John Dart
- Br 16 o'seas
- ○ *W; to help all people with Epidermolysis Bullosa (blistering of the skin) & their families; to fund research
- ● Conf - Res - SG - Inf
- < DEBRA Intl; DEBRA Europe
- ¶ NL - 4;   AR; both free.

E F Benson Society   1984
- ■ The Old Coach House, High St, RYE, E Sussex, TN31 7JF. (hsp)
  01797 223114
  Sec: Allan V Downend
- ▲ Un-incorporated Society
- ○ *A; furtherance of the knowledge & appreciation of the Benson family & particularly E F Benson (the author) & his works
- ● Mtgs - Exhib - VE - Walks
- M 200 i, UK / 30 i, o'seas
- ¶ Dodo (Jnl) - 1; ftm, £3 nm.   NL - 4; ftm only.

EAN Ireland
   since 2005 **GS1 Ireland**

EAN UK Ltd
   since 2005 **GS1 UK**

Early Dance Circle   (EDC)   1984
- ■ Hunters Moon, Orcheston, SALISBURY, Wilts, SP3 4RP.   (sp)
  01980 620339   fax 01980 620339
  email dianacruic@aol.com
  http://www.earlydancecircle.co.uk
  Chmn: Diana Cruickshank
- ▲ Un-incorporated Society
- ○ *D; to promote & foster the knowledge, understanding & appreciation of dance & its context in European society up to the beginning of the 20th century
- ● Conf - Mtgs - ET - Res - SG - Inf - Advisory service
- < Nat Early Music Assn (NEMA); Nat Resource Centre for Historical Dance (NRCHD)
- M 166 i
- ¶ NL - 4; ftm only.
  Publications list available.

Early Education
   the working title of **British Association for Early Childhood Education**

Early English Text Society   (EETS)   1864
- ■ c/o Prof V A Gillespie, Lady Margaret Hall, OXFORD, OX2 6QA.   (exec)
  01865 284066
  http://www.eets.org.uk sec b
  Exec Sec: Prof V A Gillespie
- ▲ Un-incorporated Society
- ○ *L; printing of English texts earlier than 1558
- M i, f & org
- ¶ 1 or 2 books a yr.

Earth Science Teachers Association   (ESTA)   1968
- NR c/o Low Row, Hesket Newmarket, WIGTON, Cumbria, CA7 8JU.   (hsp)
  01697 478353
  email susan.lowrow@virgin.net   http://www.esta-uk.org
  Hon Sec: Mrs Susan Beale
- ▲ Registered Charity
- Br 3
- ○ *E, *P; to further the teaching of earth science & geology at all levels
- Gp Primary; Secondary; Teacher Education; Higher Education; Fieldwork
- ● Conf - SG - Stat - Inf
- M 740 i, UK / 60 i, o'seas
- ¶ Teaching Earth Sciences (Jnl) - 4; ftm only.

East of England Agricultural Society   1797
- ■ East of England Showground, PETERBOROUGH, Cambs, PE2 6XE.   (hq)
  01733 234451   fax 01733 370038
  email info@eastofengland.org.uk
  http://www.eastofengland.org.uk
  Chief Exec: Andrew Mercer
- ○ *F
- ● Conf - Exhib - Comp - SG - Inf - E of England Show
- M c 8,000 i
- ¶ NL.   Show Catalogue.

East Hampshire Chamber of Commerce & Industry   (EHCCI)
- NR The Regional Business Centre, Harts Farm Way, HAVANT, Hants, PO9 1HR.
  023 9244 9449
  Sec: Andrew Gordon
- ○ *C

East Herts Archaeological Society   (EHAS)   1898
- NR 11 St Leonards Close, Bengeo, HERTFORD, SG14 3LL.   (hsp)
  Hon Sec: Mrs G Pollard
- ▲ Registered Charity
- ○ *L; to promote interest in, & preservation of, archaeology in the county, old buildings & local history
- Gp Old buildings survey
- ● Exhib - Inf - Lib - VE
- < Coun Brit Archaeology; Hertfordshire Archaeol Trust
- M 130 i
- ¶ Hertfordshire Archaeology - irreg; ftm, £15 nm.
  NL.   AR.
  A Century of Archaeology in East Herts; £9.95 (£4.95 paperback).

East Kent Chamber Ltd
   see **Thanet & East Kent Chamber Ltd**

East Kilbride Chamber of Commerce
   in 2003 amalgamated with the Clyde Vale, Hamilton & Clydesdale, and Motherwell & District Chambers of Commerce and the Cambuslang & Rutherglen Business Group to become **Lanarkshire Chamber of Commerce**

East Lancashire Chamber of Commerce & Industry   (ELCCI) 1991
- ■ Red Rose Court, Clayton Business Park, ACCRINGTON, Lancs, BB5 5JR.   (hq)
  01254 356400   fax 01254 388900
  email info@chamberelancs.co.uk
  http://www.chamberelancs.co.uk
  Chief Exec: Michael Damms,   Co Sec: Valerie Miles
- ▲ Company Limited by Guarantee
- ○ *C; business support
- Gp Business support; International trade; Supply train; ICT; Training
- ● Conf - Mtgs - ET - Res - Exhib - Stat - Expt - Inf - LG
- < Brit Chams Comm
- M 1,000 f
- ¶ Lancashire Business View - 6.

© CBD Research Ltd · Beckenham · BR3 5JS · Tel 020 8650 7745 · Fax 020 8650 0768 · E-mail cbd@cbdresearch.com · www.cbdresearch.com

East Lothian Antiquarian & Field Naturalists' Society (ELAFNS)   1924
- ■ 13 Stories Park, EAST LINTON, E Lothian, EH40 3BN.   (hsp)
  01620 860812
  email amc@eleutheria.madasafish.com
  http://www.el4.org.uk
  Sec: Allison Cosgrove
- ▲ Registered Charity
- ○ *L; antiquities, archaeology & natural history of the district
- ● Mtgs - Exhib - VE
- M 264 i, 11 org, UK / 1 org, o'seas
- ¶ Transactions (incl LM) - 3 yrly; ftm.   AR - 1; free.

Eastbourne & District Chamber of Commerce Ltd   (EDCC Ltd) 1892
- NR 7 Hyde Gardens, EASTBOURNE, E Sussex, BN21 4PN.   (hq)
  01323 641144   fax 01323 730454
  email info@eastbournechamber.co.uk
  http://www.eastbournechamber.co.uk
  Co Sec: Mrs Christine Purkess
- ▲ Company Limited by Guarantee
- ○ *C
- ● Conf - Mtgs - ET - Exhib - Inf - LG
- M 600+ f
- ¶ NL - 12;   Directory - 1;   both ftm only.

Eastern Africa Association   (EAA)   1964
- ■ 2 Vincent St, LONDON, SW1P 4LD.   (hq)
  020 7828 5511   fax 020 7828 5251
  email jcsmall@eaa-lon.co.uk
  http://www.eaa-lon.co.uk
  Chief Exec: John C Small
- ▲ Company Limited by Guarantee
- Br Kenya, Uganda
- ○ *T; to facilitate the participation of firms & companies from other countries in the economic development of Kenya, Eritrea, Ethiopia, Madagascar, Mauritius, Rwanda, Seychelles, Tanzani & Uganda
- ● Conf - Mtgs - Inf - LG
- < Brit African Business Assn
- M 30 i, 245 f, UK & o'seas
- ¶ The East African NL - 8; ftm only.

Eating Disorders Association   (EDA)   1989
- ■ Wensum House, 103 Prince of Wales Rd, NORWICH, Norfolk, NR1 1DW.   (hq)
  0870 770 3256 (admin only)   fax 01603 664915
  email info@edauk.com   http://www.edauk.com
  Chief Exec: Mrs Susan Ringwood
  Media & Inf Mgr: Steve Bloomfield
- ▲ Company Limited by Guarantee; Registered Charity
- Br UK-wide network of local help groups
- ○ *M, *W; to provide help & support for people affected by eating disorders, especially anorexia & bulimia nervosa; to provide training & help for professionals
- ● Conf - ET - Service specifications guidelines for treatment
  Helpline: 0845 634 1414 (Mon-Fri 1030-2030)
  Youthline (up to age 18): 0845 634 7650 (Mon-Fri 1600-2030)
  Recorded Information Service: 0906 302 0012 (Calls cost 50p per minute)
- M i
- ¶ Signpost (Jnl) - 4; ftm.   Lists of treatment by area.
  European Eating Disorders Review (professional jnl).
  Note: uses the working name of Beat - beating eating disorders.

ECB Coaches Association
  see **England & Wales Cricket Board Coaches Association**

Ecclesiastical History Society   (EHS)   1962
- NR 32 Highfield Ave, Great Sankey, WARRINGTON, Cheshire, WA5 2TW.   (hsb)
  email stella@ravenna123.freeserve.co.uk
  http://www.ehsoc.org.uk
  Hon Sec: Dr Stella Fletcher
- ▲ Registered Charity
- ○ *L; study of ecclesiastical history & maintenance of relations between British historians & scholars abroad
- ● Conf - Res
- < Commission Intle d'Histoire Ecclésiastique Comparée (CIHEC)
- M 700 i, 35 colleges & Libraries, UK / 200 i, o'seas
- ¶ Studies in Church History - 1.

Ecclesiological Society   1839
- NR 38 Rosebery Ave, NEW MALDEN, Surrey, KT3 4LS.   (hsp)
  http://www.ecclsoc.org
  Chmn: Trevor Cooper
- ▲ Registered Charity
- ○ *A, *L; the study of the arts, architecture & liturgy of the Christian church
- ● Conf - Mtgs - Inf - Lib - PL - VE
- M 800 i, 20 org, UK / 20 i, o'seas
- ¶ Ecclesiology Today - 3; ftm.
  Monographs & publications - irreg; prices vary.

Eckhart Society   1987
- ■ Summa - 22 Tippings Lane, Woodley, READING, Berks, RG5 4RX.   (hsp)
  0118-969 0118
  email ashleyyoung@aysumma.demon.co.uk
  http://www.eckhartsociety.org
  Hon Sec & co-Chmn: Ashley Young
  co-Chmn: Rev Richard Woods (rjwoods@cs.com)
- ▲ Registered Charity
- Br River Forest (USA) [co-Chmn]
- ○ *G, *R; to promote understanding & appreciation of the writings of Meister Eckhart (1260-1327, a Dominican preacher) & their importance for Christian thought & practice; to facilitate scholarly research into Eckhart's life & works; to promote the study of Eckhart's teaching as a contribution to religious dialogue
- ● Conf - SG
- M 200 i, UK / 130 i, o'seas
- ¶ The Eckhart Review - 1; ftm, £8.50 nm.
  Tapes from annual conference - 1; £7.25 each.
  CDs from annual conference - 1; £8.50 each.
  Publications list available.
  [subscription £18.50].

Economic History Society   1927
- NR Dept of Economic & Social History, University of Glasgow, Lilybank House, Bute Gardens, GLASGOW, G12 8RT.   (hq)
  0141-330 4662   fax 0141-330 4889
  email ehsocsec@arts.gla.ac.uk   http://www.ehs.org.uk
  Hon Sec: Prof P S Fearon,   Pres: Prof N F R Crafts
- ▲ Registered Charity
- ○ *L; to promote the study of economic & social history; to publish & sponsor publications
- Gp Urban; Financial; Transport
- ● Conf - Mtgs - ET - Res - Inf
- < Intl Historical Congress; Intl Economic History Assn
- M 1,500 i, libraries & colleges
- ¶ Economic History Review - 4; ftm only.   NL - 4.   AR.

Economic Research Council   (ERC)   1943

- ■ 7 St James's Sq, LONDON, SW1Y 4JU.   (mail)
    020 7439 0271
    http://www.ercouncil.org address
    Hon Secs: James Y Bourlet,   Dan Lewis
- ▲ Registered Charity
- ○ *L; to promote education in the science of economics with
    particular reference to monetary practice
- ● Mtgs - Res - Comp - SG - Dinners with talks
- M c 400 i, c 20 f, UK / c 30 i, o'seas
- ¶ Britain & Overseas - 4; £20.   Occasional Research Papers.

Economic & Social History Society of Ireland   1967

- IRL c/o Dept of Modern History, Trinity College, DUBLIN 2, Republic
    of Ireland.
    353 (1) 608 1020   fax 353 (1) 608 2291
    email niall.ociosain@nuigalway.ie
    Sec: Dr Niall O Ciosáin
- ○ *L, *P

Economic & Social Research Institute   (ESRI)   1960

- IRL 4 Burlington Rd, DUBLIN 4, Republic of Ireland.
    353 (1) 667 1525   fax 353 (1) 668 6231
    email admin@esri.ie   http://www.esri.ie
    Dir: Brendan J Whelan
- ○ *L

Economics & Business Education Association   (EBEA)   1946

- ■ The Forum, 277 London Rd, BURGESS HILL, W Sussex,
    RH15 9QU.   (hq)
    01444 240150   fax 01444 240101
    email office@ebea.org.uk   http://www.ebea.org.uk
    Chief Exec: Duncan Collimore,
    Sec: Ian Wilson
- ▲ Registered Charity
- ○ *E, *L; supporting teachers / lecturers in the fields of
    economics, business studies & enterprise
- Gp Business studies; Economics; Enterprise
- ● Conf - Mtgs - ET - Inf - LG
- < Assn Eur Economics Educators
- M 1,400 i, 200 org, UK / 50 i, 100 org, o'seas [schools, colleges
    & universities]
- ¶ Teaching Business & Economics (Jnl) - 3.
    Beeline (NL) - 6.

Ectodermal Dysplasia Society   (EDS)   1984

- ■ 108 Charlton Lane, CHELTENHAM, Glos, GL53 9EA.
    01242 261332
    email diana@ectodermaldysplasia.org
    http://www.ectodermaldysplasia.org
    Sec: Diana Perry,   Chmn: David Wyatt
- ▲ Registered Charity
- ○ *M, *W; to promote the health of people affected by ectodermal
    dysplasia & any related condition, & to support their families
    & carers; 'ectodermal dysplasias are heritable conditions in
    which there are abnormalities of two or more ectodermal
    structures such as the hair, teeth, nails, sweat glands, cranial-
    facial structure, digits & other parts of the body'
- ● Conf - Mtgs - Res - Inf
- M 332 i, UK / 79 i, o'seas
- ¶ NL - 4; ftm.

Edinburgh Bibliographical Society   (EBS)   1890

- ■ c/o National Library of Scotland, George IV Bridge,
    EDINBURGH, EH1 1EW.   (treas/b)
    0131-623 3893
    Treas: Dr S Marshall,   Sec: Dr Warren MacDougall
- ▲ Registered Charity
- ○ *L; study of books & manuscripts, particularly those of Scottish
    interest
- ● Mtgs (at above address) - VE
- M c 200 i & org
- ¶ Transactions - irreg; ftm only (£10 i, £15 org).

Edinburgh Chamber of Commerce   1785

- ■ Capital House, 2 Festival Sq, EDINBURGH, EH3 9SU.   (hq)
    0131-221 2999   fax 0131-221 2998
    email info@edinburghchamber.co.uk
    http://www.edinburghchamber.co.uk
    Chief Exec: Ron Hewitt
- ○ *C
- Gp Business training; Membership
- ● Conf - Mtgs - ET - Expt
- M 1,400 f
- × 2001 Edinburgh Chamber of Commerce & Enterprise
    2002 Management Association of South-East Scotland
    (merged)

Edinburgh Civic Trust
    see **Cockburn Association - the Edinburgh Civic Trust**

Edinburgh Geological Society   1834

- NR c/o British Geological Survey, West Mains Rd, EDINBURGH,
    EH9 3LA.   (mail)
    0131-667 1000   fax 0131-668 2683 add
- ○ *L; to stimulate public interest in geology; advancement of
    geological knowledge

Edinburgh Highland Reel & Strathspey Society   1881

- NR The Hazel Hall, St Ninian's Episcopal Church, 39 Comely Bank
    Rd, EDINBURGH, EH4 1AF.
    0131-343 1923
    Sec: Nicola Foy
- ○ *D
- M c 50 i
    no further information supplied.

Edinburgh Mathematical Society   (EMS)   1883

- ■ School of Mathematics, University of Edinburgh, JCMB,
    King's Buildings, Mayfield Rd, EDINBURGH, EH9 3JZ.   (hsb)
    0131-650 5040
    email edmathsoc@ed.ac.uk   http://www.maths.ed.ac.uk/
    edmathsoc/
    Hon Secs: Prof T H Lenagan,   Dr A D Gilbert
- ▲ Registered Charity
- ○ *L; advancement of mathematics, especially in Scotland
- ● Conf - Mtgs - Res - Lib
- < Eur Mathematical Soc
- M 360 i, UK / 60 i, o'seas
- ¶ Proceedings - 3; £22 yr m, £145 yr nm.

Edinburgh Sir Walter Scott Club   1894

- ■ 16/7 Albert Terrace, EDINBURGH, EH10 5EA.   (hsp)
    0131-447 6133
    email murfra@btinternet.com
    Hon Sec: Fraser Elgin
- ▲ Un-incorporated Society
- ○ *A; to keep alive & cherish the memory of Sir Walter Scott
- ● Mtgs
- M 380 i, UK / 40 i, o'seas
- ¶ Bulletin - 1; £7.50.

Edith Nesbit Society   1996

- ■ 21 Churchfields, WEST MALLING, Kent, ME19 6RJ.   (chmn/p)
    email mccarthy804@aol.com
    http://www.the-railway-children.co.uk
    Chmn: Mrs Margaret McCarthy
- ▲ Un-incorporated Society
- ○ *A; to promote interest in the life & works of author Edith Nesbit
    (1858-1924) & her friends
- Gp Archives
- ● Mtgs - Res - Exhib - SG - VE
- M 81 i, 2 org, UK / 3 i, o'seas
- ¶ NL - 4; ftm only.

Education Law Association   (ELAS)
NR   33 College Rd, READING, Berks, RG6 1QE.   (sp)
       0118-966 9866
       http://www.educationlawassociation.org.uk
       Sec: Catherine Croft
○   *P
M   c 320 i

Education Otherwise   (EO)   1977
■   PO Box 325, KINGS LYNN, Norfolk, PE34 3XW.   (mail)
       0870 730 0074
       email enquiries@education-otherwise.org.
       http://www.education-otherwise.org address
       Co Sec: Pam Bellinger
▲   Company Limited by Guarantee; Registered Charity
Br   local groups
○   *E, *K; self-help organisation offering support, advice &
       information to families practising, or contemplating, home-
       based education as an alternative to schooling.
       We take our name from the Education Act which states that
       parents are responsible for their children's education, 'either
       by regular attendance at school or otherwise'
●   Conf - Mtgs - Exhib - Comp - Inf - VE - Liaison with LEA's
M   4,500 families
¶   NL - 6;   Hbk - 1;   Contact List - 1;
       School is Not Compulsory; all ftm only.
       Publications list available [see website].

Educational Centres Association   (ECA)   1920
■   21 Ebbisham Drive, NORWICH, Norfolk, NR4 6HQ.
       (chmn/p)
       0870 161 0302   fax 01603 469292
       email info@e-c-a.ac.uk
       Chmn: Bernard Godding
▲   Registered Charity
○   *E; promotion of lifelong learning
●   Conf - Mtgs - Inf - LG
<   Eur Assn Educ Adults; Community Sector Coalition; engage;
       Nat Inst Adult Continuing Educ
>   engage; Nat Inst Adult Continuing Educ
M   i, f & org
¶   NL - 3;   AR; both ftm.

Educational Institute of Scotland   (EIS)   1847
■   46 Moray Place, EDINBURGH, EH3 6BH.   (hq)
       0131-225 6244   fax 0131-220 3151
       email enquiries@eis.org.uk   http://www.eis.org.uk
       Gen Sec: Ronald A Smith
▲   Un-incorporated Society
Br   38
○   *E, *U; promotion of sound learning & the interests & welfare of
       teachers
●   Conf - Mtgs - ET - Empl
<   Education Intl; Eur Trade U C'ee on Educ; TUC; STUC
M   57,068 i
¶   Scottish Educational Jnl - 6; ftm, £12 yr nm.
×   2003 Scottish Further & Higher Education Association (merged)

Educational Publishers Council
       a group of the **Publishers Association**

Educational Software Publishers Association
       a group of the **British Educational Suppliers Association**

Edward Thomas Fellowship   1980
■   1 Carfax, Undercliff Drive, ST LAWRENCE, Isle of Wight,
       PO38 1XG.   (hsp)
       01983 853366
       Hon Sec: Colin G Thornton
▲   Un-incorporated Society
○   *L; to perpetuate the memory of the writer Edward Thomas & to
       preserve the countryside known to him; to further interest in
       his life & work
●   Conf - Mtgs - Res - VE
<   Alliance of Literary Socs
M   450 i, 2 colleges, 1 museum, UK / 25 i, 1 library, o'seas
¶   NL - 2; ftm, £2 nm.

EEF, the manufacturers' organisation   (EEF)   1896
NR   Broadway House, Tothill St, LONDON, SW1H 9NQ.   (hq)
       020 7222 7777   fax 020 7222 2782
       http://www.eef.org.uk
       Dir-Gen: Martin Temple
○   *T; to represent employers in the engineering industry
M   f
×   2003 Engineering Employers' Federation
       2002 (Stainless Steel Wire Industry Association
            (UK Steel Association

Egg Crafters Guild of Great Britain   1979
■   The Studio, 7 Hylton Terrace, NORTH SHIELDS, Tyne & Wear,
       NE29 0EE.   (hq)
       0191-258 3648   fax 0191-258 3648
       Chief Exec: Joan Cutts
▲   Un-incorporated Society
Br   30; 10 o'seas
○   *A, *G; to encourage the craft of egg decoration
●   Conf - Mtgs - ET - Exhib - SG
M   1,500 i, UK / 500 i, o'seas
¶   The Egg Crafter (NL) - 4; ftm.

Egypt Exploration Society   (EES)   1882
■   3 Doughty Mews, LONDON, WC1N 2PG.   (hq)
       020 7242 1880   fax 020 7404 6118
       email contact@ees.ac.uk   http://www.ees.ac.uk
       Sec: Dr Patricia A Spencer
▲   Company Limited by Guarantee; Registered Charity
Br   London, Manchester
○   *L; promotion of the study of the history & archaeology of
       ancient Egypt
●   Conf - Mtgs - Res - Lib - PL - VE - Archaeological excavations
M   2,608 i, 281 libraries
¶   Jnl of Egyptian Archaeology - 1; £40 m, £50 nm.
       Egyptian Archaeology - 2; £4.95.   AR; ftm.

Egyptian British Chamber of Commerce   (EBCC)   1981
■   PO Box 4AG, 299 Oxford St, LONDON, W1A 4AG.   (hq)
       020 7499 3100   fax 020 7499 1070
       email info@theebcc.com
       Sec-Gen: T Sherif
▲   Company Limited by Guarantee
○   *C; to promote commercial, industrial & tourist relations
       between Egypt & the UK
●   Conf - Mtgs - Exhib - Stat - Expt - Inf - Lib - LG
¶   Egyptian-British Trade - 4; free.
       Bulletin - trade opportunities - 26; ftm only.

**** Eighteen Nineties Society (incorporating the Francis Thompson
       Society)**
       Organisation lost: see Introduction paragraph 3

EIS Association (EISA) 1990
NR Tylers Croft, Hitchen Hatch Lane, SEVENOAKS, Kent,
TN13 3AY. (hsp)
01732 465828 fax 01732 462657
email eisa@dialstart.net http://www.eisa.org.uk
Chief Exec: Peter A Woodrow
▲ Company Limited by Guarantee
○ *T; an association of companies & firms which are involved in
the promotion of the Enterprise Investment Scheme (a
government scheme to promote investment) for the benefit of
small & medium sized companies
Gp Tax committee; EISA Council
● Inf - LG
M 30 f
¶ LM; [website].

Ekbom Support Group (ESG) 1988
■ 18 Rodbridge Drive, THORPE BAY, Essex, SS1 3DF. (hsp)
01702 582002
email gill@ekbom-88.demon.co.uk
http://www.ekbom.org.uk
Coordinator: Mrs Eileen Gill
▲ Un-incorporated Society
○ *W; to support sufferers from Ekbom Syndrome (also known as
Restless Legs Syndrome); to educate the medical profession;
works with RLS UK a committee of professionals - doctors,
consultants etc in the UK
● Conf - Mtgs - Res - SG - Inf - Penfriend service
M c 200 i. UK / 4 i, o'seas
¶ NL - 2; free.
Note: please enclose an SAE when writing to the ESG.

eLearning Network (eLN) 1989
■ 34 Albury Ride, CHESHUNT, Herts, EN8 8XF. (hsb)
01992 634244 fax 01992 634248
email info@elearningnetwork.org
http://www.elearningnetwork.org
Chmn: Vaughan Waller
▲ Un-incorporated Society
○ *G; to provide leadership in the application of technologies to
learning; to provide an independent perspective on the issues
● Conf - Mtgs - ET - Res - Inf
M 15 i, 84 f, 10 org

Electoral Reform Society Ltd (ERS) 1884
■ 6 Chancel St, LONDON, SE1 0UU. (hq)
020 7928 1622 fax 020 7401 7789
email ers@reform.demon.co.uk
http://www.electoral-reform.org.uk
Sec: Dr Ken Ritchie
▲ Company Limited by Guarantee
○ *K; to campaign for the introduction of the single transferable
vote for all UK public elections & elections within common
interest bodies; to provide election monitoring & voter
education for emerging democracies internationally
Gp Subsidiaries: Electoral Reform Ballot Services Ltd, Electoral
Reform International Services Ltd; McDougall Trust
(educational charity)
● Conf - Mtgs - ET - Res - Exhib - SG - Stat - Inf - Lib - VE - LG -
Votes At 16 Campaign
< UNESCO; CVD (USA); NLGN; NCVO; Make Votes Count
M 2,300 i, 2 f, 6 org, UK / 40 i, 2 org, o'seas
¶ Representation: jnl of democracy & electoral systems - 4; ftm,
£25 yr nm.
ERS News - 4; AR; both free.

Electric Boat Association (EBA) 1980
■ 150 Wayside Green, Woodcote, READING, Berks, RG8 0QJ.
(sp)
01491 681449 fax 01491 681945
email eboat@mail.com
http://www.electric-boat-association.org.uk
Hon Sec: Mrs B Penniall
▲ Un-incorporated Society
○ *T; to promote the technology & use of electrically-propelled
boats worldwide
Gp User group (boat owners)
● Conf - Res - Exhib - Comp - SG - Stat - Expt - Inf - LG
M c 300 i, 50 f
¶ Electric Boat News - 4; ftm, on application nm.

Electric Guitar Appreciation Society (TEGAS)
NR 65 Stapleton Lane, Barwell, LEICESTER, LE9 8HE.
01455 457928
http://www.tegas.co.uk
Founder / Pres: John Williams
○ *G, *D

Electric Heating & Ventilation Association
s a part of BEAMA Energy is a group of **BEAMA**

Electric Railway Society (ERS) 1946
■ 17 Catherine Drive, SUTTON COLDFIELD, W Midlands,
B73 6AX. (hsp)
0121-354 8332
email iwfrew@tiscali.co.uk
Hon Sec: Dr Iain D O Frew
▲ Un-incorporated Society
Br 2
○ *G; to study the history, development & practice of electric
railways incl rapid transit metro lines; to evaluate their
effectiveness in public transport in major cities throughout the
world
● Mtgs - Exhib - SG - PL - VE
< Rly Soc Sthn Africa; Asociacíon Uruguaya Amigos Riel; Pacific
Railroad Soc; Scot Intl Tramway Assn; Australian Electric
Traction Assn
M 271 i, 7 f, 4 org, UK / 105 i, 2 f, 3 org, o'seas
¶ The Electric Railway - 6; ftm, £13.00 nm.
[subscription £13.50].

Electric Security Fencing Federation
see **Fencing Contractors Association**

Electric Steel Makers' Guild (ESMG) 1956
■ 193 Fitzwilliam St, Swinton, MEXBOROUGH, S Yorks,
S64 8RW. (hsp)
01709 584135
Assistant Sec: John Kitchen
○ *T; improving steelmaking in electric arc furnaces (commercial
quantities only)
● Conf - Mtgs
M 51 i, UK / 3 i, o'seas

Electric Trace Heating Industry Council (ETHIC) 1988
■ Spinney Cottage, Barlow Fold, Romiley, STOCKPORT,
SK6 4LQ. (sp/b)
0161-430 8493
Sec: J W Young
▲ Un-incorporated Society
○ *T; the correct use of approved quality equipment;
establishment & upholding of industry specifications,
standards & codes of practice; communication between
manufacturers, designers & installers of electric trace heating
equipment & the specifiers & users of the equipment
● Mtgs - ET - Preparation of International Standards
< Energy Ind Coun; Electricity Assn; Brit Nat C'ee for Electroheat;
BSI
M 7 f

Electrical Contractors' Association (ECA) 1901
NR 34 Palace Court, LONDON, W2 4HY.   (hq)
   020 7313 4800   fax 020 7221 7344
   email electricalcontractors@eca.org.uk
   http://www.eca.co.uk
   Dir: David Pollock
▲ Company Limited by Guarantee
Br 64
○ *T; the association guarantees work of member firms in the UK
   & Eire (but not Scotland) & that the job will be completed at
   the original price if a member firm should run into difficulties
Gp Control systems & new technology (covering interests in control
   systems & instrumentation); Security systems
● Conf - Mtgs - ET - Inf - Empl
< Intl Assn of Electrical Contrs
M 2,300 f
¶ Electrical Contractor - 12.   LM.

Electrical Distributors Association (EDA) 1914
■ Union House, Eridge Rd, ROYAL TUNBRIDGE WELLS, Kent,
   TN4 8HF.   (hq)
   01892 619990   fax 01892 619991
   email info@eda.org.uk   http://www.eda.org.uk
   Dir: Nigel Ellis
▲ Company Limited by Guarantee
○ *T
● Mtgs - ET - Stat
< Eur U of Electrical Whlsrs (EUEW)
M 30 f
¶ Ybk - 1; ftm, £59.50 nm.

Electrical & Electronic Retailers Association of Ireland
IRL Marina House, Clarence St, DÚN LAOGHAIRE, Co Dublin,
   Republic of Ireland.
   353 (1) 663 8700   fax 353 (1) 663 8704
   Pres: John Kilkelly
○ *T

Electrical & Engineering Staff Association (EESA) 1971
NR Hayes Court, West Common Rd, HAYES, Kent, BR2 7AU.   (hq)
   020 8462 7755   fax 020 8315 8234
   http://www.eesa.org.uk
   Nat Sec: Michael Murdoch
Br 120
○ *U
● Conf - Mtgs - ET - Res - Empl - LG
M 40,000 i
¶ FPA Journal - 4;   Union News - 4; both ftm only.

Electrical Industries Federation of Ireland (EIFI) 1934
IRL Unit H12, Centrepoint Business Park, Oak Rd, DUBLIN 12,
   Republic of Ireland.
   353 (1) 429 0088   fax 353 (1) 429 0090
   email eifi@etci.ie
   Hon Sec: Jimmy Whan
○ *T

Electrical Insulation Association (EIA) 1911
■ PO Box 2462, STAFFORD, ST16 9AE.   (hq)
   01785 661306
   email jeremy.wheeler@ferret.co.uk   http://www.eiauk.org
   Sec: Dr Jeremy C G Wheeler
▲ Un-incorporated Society
○ *T; laminates, mouldings, castings; liquid finishes, varnishes,
   insulators, bushings for power engineering applications;
   papers, cloths, fibres & film
Gp C'ees: Technical, Commercial; Organisers of the INSUCON
   Conference
● Conf - Mtgs - ET - VE - Seminars
M 19 f

Electricity Arbitration Association (EAA) 1990
■ 5 Meadow Rd, Great Gransden, SANDY, Beds, SG19 3BD.
   (hq)
   01767 677043   fax 01767 677043
   Sec: Donald H J Lester
○ *T; to provide dispute resolution services for the UK electricity
   industry
M f

Electro-Technical Council of Ireland (ETCI)
IRL Unit H12, Centrepoint Business Park, Oak Rd, DUBLIN 12,
   Republic of Ireland.
   353 (1) 429 0088   fax 353 (1) 429 0090
   email admin@etci.ie   http://www.etci.ie
   Chmn: J Egan
○ *T

Electro-physiological Technologists' Association (EPTA) 1949
NR c/o Neurophysiology Dept, Charing Cross Hospital, Fulham
   Palace Rd, LONDON, W6 8RF.   (chmn/b)
   Chmn: Evadne Cookman
▲ Company Limited by Guarantee
○ *P; to promote a high standard of training & education in the
   field of neurophysiology
● Conf - Mtgs - Exam - Exhib - SG - Empl
M 800 i
¶ Jnl of Electro-physiology & Technology - 4.

Elgar Society 1951
■ 29 Van Diemens Close, CHINNOR, Oxon, OX39 4QE.   (hsp)
   01844 354096
   email elgar@music.com   http://www.elgar.org
   Hon Sec: Wendy Hillary
▲ Registered Charity
Br 10; Canada
○ *A; to promote the study, performance & appreciation of the
   works of Sir Edward Elgar & research into his life & music
Gp Elgar Enterprises (trading company)
● Conf - Mtgs - ET - SG - Inf - VE - Awards to young composers -
   Sponsorship of CDs & concerts - Grants for the hire of
   orchestral parts
M 1,700 i, UK / 50 i, o'seas
¶ The Elgar Jnl - 3;   The Elgar News - 3; both ftm only.

Ellesmere Port Chamber of Commerce

Elsie Jeanette Oxenham Appreciation Society (EJO Society) 1989
■ 32 Tadfield Rd, ROMSEY, Hants, SO51 5AJ.   (memsec/p)
   01794 517149
   email abbey@bufobooks.demon.co.uk
   http://www.bufobooks.demon.co.uk/abbeylnk.htm
   Mem Sec/Treas: Ruth Allen,   Editor: Fiona Dyer
▲ Un-incorporated Society
Br Canada & USA, Australia & New Zealand
○ *A; to provide a postal meeting point for all who are interested
   in the work & collect the books of Elsie J Oxenham (1880-
   1960); to investigate the settings used for the books & the
   folk dances which form the backdrop to many of her titles
● Inf - Lib - VE - Web pages with discussion board
< Alliance of Literary Socs
M 470 i, 2 org, UK / 64 i, o'seas
¶ The Abbey Chronicle (Jnl) - 3; ftm only, £2-£3 back issues.
   LM (suppt to Jnl) - 1; ftm only.

EM Gauge Society Ltd   (EMGS)   1955
NR   41 Enstone Rd, Ickenham, UXBRIDGE, Middx, UB10 8EZ.
       (hsp)
       http://www.emgs.org
       Sec: Graham Vicary
▲   Company Limited by Guarantee
Br   12; Australia, Canada, Ireland, New Zealand, USA
○   *G; for modellers in 4mm fine scale modelling; promotes &
       provides the specialist support needed for modellers in the
       EM & 18.83mm gauges for whatever prototype or period
       modelled
●   Mtgs - Res - Exhib
<   Chiltern Model Rly Assn (CMRS)
M   2,400 i, UK / 200 i, o'seas
¶   EMGS NL - 5;   EMGS Manual - up-dated; both ftm only.
       Trade price list - 1; ftm (from D J Fairhurst, 4 Meadway,
       Freezywater, Enfield, Middx, EN3 6NU).

Embroiderers' Guild   1906
NR   Apartment 41 Hampton Court Palace, EAST MOLESEY, Surrey,
       KT8 9AU.   (hq)
       020 8943 1229   fax 020 8977 9882
       email administrator@embroiderersguild.org
       http://www.embroiderersguild.org
       Dir: Michael Spender
▲   Registered Charity
Br   210
○   *A; to promote an understanding of embroidery history, design
       & technique ensuring the long-term future of this craft
Gp   Young embroiderers (aged 5-18)
●   Mtgs - ET - Res - Exhib - Comp - SG - Inf - Lib - PL - VE
M   c 13,000 i
¶   Embroidery - 6.   NL - 2.
       Stitch with the Embroiderers' Guild - 6.
       The Workbook.   Ybk.
       Various other publications.

EMC Industry Association   (EMCIA)   2002
■   c/o Nutwood UK Ltd, Eddystone Court, De Lank Lane,
       St Breward, BODMIN, Cornwall, PL30 4NQ.   (asa)
       01208 851530   fax 01208 850871
       email emcia@emcia.org   http://www.emcia.org
       Sec: Alan Hutley
▲   Un-incorporated Society
○   *P, *T; for EMC (electromagnetic compatibility) product & service
       providers; EMC is defined as 'the ability of an equipment or
       system to function satisfactorily in its electromagnetic
       environment without introducing intolerable electromagnetic
       disturbances to anything in that environment'
●   Conf - Mtgs - Exhib - Expt - Inf - LG
M   35 i, 35 f

Emergency Planning Society   (EPS)   1993
■   The Media Centre, Culverhouse Cross, CARDIFF, CF5 6XS.
       (hq)
       0845 600 9587   fax 029 2059 0396
       email accounts@the-eps.org   http://www.the-eps.org
       Chief Exec: Debbie Spargo
▲   Company Limited by Guarantee
Br   14
○   *P; to promote emergency planning & management in the UK
       (all functions relating to the preparation for the assessment of
       a response to emergencies for the benefit of people, property
       & the environment)
Gp   Society issues; Professional issues
●   Conf - Mtgs - ET - Exhib - SG - Inf - LG
<   Soc of Indl Emergency Services Officers (SIESO)
M   2,000 i
¶   Blue Print Magazine - 4; ftm only.

**Emergency Response & Rescue Vessel Association   (ERRVA)
1979**
NR   PO Box 1385, CALNE, Wilts, SN11 8YZ.   (chmn/b)
       01249 816618
       http://www.errva.org.uk
       Chmn: John Wilson
▲   Company Limited by Guarantee
○   *N, *T; to foster the effective use of standby ships.   Standby
       ships are specially equipped ships stationed at offshore
       installations to rescue people from the sea; to assist in the
       evacuation of installations in emergencies; to warn off ships
       which present a collision hazard
●   ET - Liaison with other industry bodies - To conduct trials & tests
       on any relevant equipment

Emergency Social Services Association   (ESSA)   1997
■   PO Box 473, GUILDFORD, Surrey, GU4 7ZL.   (hsb)
       01483 517898   fax 01483 517895
       http://www.essauk.com
       Hon Sec: Terri Goodwin,   Treas: Sylvia Watkins
○   *P; to promote high standards in (& the significance of) out-of-
       hours social work
●   Conf - Mtgs
M   c 100 authorities
¶   ESSA News (NL) - 3; ftm only.

Employed & Non-Practising Bar Association
       in 2003 merged with the **Bar Association for Commerce,
       Finance & Industry**

Employers Forum on Age   (EFA)   1996
NR   Downstream Bldg (3rd floor), 1 London Bridge, LONDON,
       SE1 9BG.   (hq)
       0845 456 2495   fax 020 7785 6536
       email efa@efa.org.uk   http://www.efa.org.uk
       Dir: Samantha Mercer
▲   Registered Charity
○   *N; to support member organisations in achieving an age-
       diverse workforce
●   Conf - Mtgs - ET - Res - Stat - Inf
M   160 f, UK / 1 f, o'seas
¶   Newsline (NL) - 4; free.
       Research reports; ftm, prices vary nm.
       Demographic factsheets; ftm only.

Employers Forum on Disability
§   Nutmeg House, 60 Gainsford St, LONDON, SE1 2NY.
       020 7403 3020   fax 020 7403 0404
       email efd@employers-forum.co.uk
       http://www.employers-forum.co.uk
       Chief Exec: Susan Scott-Parker
○   *N

Employment Lawyers Association   (ELA)   1992
NR   PO Box 353, UXBRIDGE, Middx, UB10 0UN.
       01895 256972   fax 01895 256972
○   *P

Employment & Planning Law Association
       a group of the **Law Society of Northern Ireland**

© CBD Research Ltd · Beckenham · BR3 5JS · Tel 020 8650 7745 · Fax 020 8650 0768 · E-mail cbd@cbdresearch.com · www.cbdresearch.com

ENABLE (ENABLE) 1954

NR 7 Buchanan St (6th floor), GLASGOW, G1 3HL. (hq)
0141-226 4541 fax 0141-204 4398
email enable@enable.org.uk
http://www.enable.org.uk
Chief Exec: Norman Dunning
▲ Registered Charity; Un-incorporated Society
Br 57
○ *W; to support people with learning difficulties & their families in Scotland; to achieve equal opportunities & better services
Gp ACE - national advisory committee of people with learning disabilities
● Conf - Mtgs - Inf - Lib - LG
< Inclusion Intl; Inclusion Europe; Disability Agenda Scotland; Learning Disability Alliance Scotland
M c 4,000 i
¶ Newslink (NL) - 4. AR.

ENCAMS (ENCAMS)

NR Elizabeth House, The Pier, WIGAN, Lancs, WN3 4EX. (hq)
01942 612621 fax 01942 824778
http://www.encams.org
Chief Exec: Alan Woods
○ *K; long-term improvement of local environments - the durability of buildings & the quality of life for those who live in them

Encephalitis Society 1994

■ 7b Saville St, MALTON, N Yorks, YO17 7LL. (hq)
01653 699599 fax 01653 604369
email mail@encephalitis.info
http://www.encephalitis.info
Resource Centre Mgr: Elaine Dowall
▲ Company Limited by Guarantee; Registered Charity
○ *M, *W; to provide support, everyday advice & general information to families & carers of children or adults with encephalitis; to raise public awareness & gather more information to aid research into encephalitis. Contact between families in similar situations is encouraged so mutual experiences can be shared
● Conf - Mtgs - ET - Res - Inf
< Eur Org for Rare Disorders (EURORDIS); Children's Acquired Brain Injury Interest Gp (CABIIG); Contact-a-Family; Long-term Medical Conditions Alliance (LMCA); Neurological Alliance; Rare Disorders Alliance; R Assn for Disability & Rehabilitation (RADAR); UK Acquired Brain Injury Forum (UKABIF)
M 800 i
¶ NL - 3; Annual Review; free.
Note: Encephalitis Society is the operating name of the Encephalitis Support Group

Encephalitis Support Group
operates as the **Encephalitis Society**

Endurance GB (EGB) 2001

■ National Agricultural Centre, Stoneleigh Park, KENILWORTH, Warks, CV8 2RP. (hq)
024 7669 8863 fax 024 7641 8429
email enquiries@endurancegb.co.uk
http://www.endurancegb.co.uk
Chmn: Wendy Dunham
▲ Company Limited by Guarantee
Br 22
○ *S; to promote & enhance the sport of endurance (competitive long distance) riding in the UK ... for all levels of rider
● Conf - Mtgs - ET - Exhib - Comp
< Brit Equestrian Fedn
M 2,200 i, UK / 100 i, o'seas
¶ Magazine - 4; ftm;
Branch Group NL - 12; AR - 1; all ftm only.
× 2002 (British Endurance Riding Association
(Endurance Horse & Pony Society

Energy Industries Council (EIC) 1943

■ 45 Notting Hill Gate, LONDON, W11 3LQ. (hq)
020 7221 2043 fax 020 7221 8813
email info@eic-uk.com
Chief Exec: Mike Gregory
▲ Company Limited by Guarantee
○ *T; manufacturers, contractors & financial institutions serving the oil, petrochemical, natural gas, coal, power & process industries
● Conf - Mtgs - Exhib - Expt - Inf - VE
< Fedn of Eur Petroleum & Gas Eqpt Mfrs
M 362 f
¶ NL - 17; m only.
Catalogue of British Suppliers - 2 yrly; ftm, £45 nm.
Technical publications, specification & datasheets.

Energy Institute (EI) 2003

NR 61 New Cavendish St, LONDON, W1G 7AR. (hq)
020 7467 7100 fax 020 7255 1472
email info@energyinst.org.uk
http://www.energyinst.org.uk
Chief Exec: Louise Kingham
▲ Registered Charity
Br 13
○ *L, *Q; 'promotion of the safe, environmentally responsible & efficient supply & use of energy in all its forms & applications'
Gp Discussion group; Information for Energy Group (IFEG)
● Conf - Mtgs - ET - Res - Exhib - Comp - SG - Stat - Inf - Lib - VE - LG
M 12,000 i, 400 f, UK & o'seas
¶ Petroleum Review - 12; ftm, £190 (UK), £220 (o'seas) nm.
Energy World - 10; ftm, £115 (UK), £135 (o'seas) nm.
Codes of Safe Practice. Recommended Practices.
AR; free via website.
× 2003 (Institute of Energy
(Institute of Petroleum

Energy Intensive Users Group

NR Broadway House, Tothill St, London, SW1H 9NQ. (hq)
020 7654 1536 fax 020 7222 2782
Dir: Jeremy Nicholson
○ *K; campaigning for secure industrial energy supplies at internationally competitive prices
< Intl Fedn Indl Energy Consumers
M 11 f & org

Energy Networks Association

NR 18 Stanhope Place, LONDON, W2 2HH.
020 7706 5100
Co Sec: Andy Banks
○ *T; UK gas & electricity transmission & distribution licence holders
Note: is one of the three associations formed by the closing of the Electricity Association

Energy Retail Association

NR 17 Waterloo Place (4th floor), LONDON, SW1Y 4AR.
020 7930 9175
Head of Communications: Russell Hamblin-Boone
○ *T
Note: was formed on the closing of the Electricity Association

Energy Systems Trade Association (ESTA) 1982

NR PO Box 77, BENFLEET, Essex, SS7 5EX. (hq)
07041 492049 fax 07041 492050
Exec Dir: Alan Aldridge
▲ Company Limited by Guarantee
○ *T; to promote the efficient use of energy in industry, commerce & the public sector
M c 100 f
¶ Energy Efficiency Ybk (incl LM) - 1; free.

Enforcement Services Association   1906
NR   Park House, 10 Park St, BRISTOL, BS1 5HX.   (accom)
      0117-907 4771   fax 0117-915 4521
      email enquiries@ensas.org.uk
      http://www.ensas.org.uk address
      Exec Dir: Vernon Phillips
▲   Un-incorporated Society
○   *P
●   Mtgs - ET - Exam - Res - Inf - LG
M   58 i, 30 f
¶   NL;   Ybk - 1; both free.
✕   2003 Certificated Bailiffs Association

engage: National Association of Gallery Education   1988
NR   108 Old Brompton Rd (basement), LONDON, SW7 3RA.   (hq)
      020 7244 0110   fax 020 7373 7223
      email info@engage.org   http://www.engage.org
      Dir: Jane Sillis
▲   Registered Charity
○   *A, *E, *G, *P; to promote greater understanding & enjoyment
      of the visual arts by engaging with the public, artists, galleries
      & educators
M   i, f & org
¶   engage review - 2; ftm.
      engagements - 4; ftm only.

Engineering Construction Industry Association   (ECIA)   1994
NR   Broadway House, Tothill St, LONDON, SW1H 9NQ.   (hq)
      020 7799 2000   fax 020 7233 1930
      http://www.ecia.co.uk
      Managing Dir: Michael Hockney
▲   Un-incorporated Society
Br   8 regions
○   *T
●   Mtgs - ET - Stat - Inf - Empl - LG
<   CBI; Engg Emplrs Fedn; Eur Construction Inst
M   c 300 f (employing 65,000 i)
¶   Data Bank Estimating Norms.
      Safety Manual for Mechanical Plant Construction, 2 vol, loose-
      leaf.
      ECIA Directory of Member Companies.
      Safety Booklet.   AR.
        publications list available.

Engineering Employers' Federation
      since 2003 **EEF, the manufacturers' organisation**

**Engineering Equipment & Materials Users Association
      (EEMUA)   1949**
■   10-12 Lovat Lane, LONDON, EC3R 8DN.   (hq)
      020 7621 0011   fax 020 7621 0022
      email info@eemua.org   http://www.eemua.org
      Exec Dir: C Tayler
▲   Company Limited by Guarantee
○   *L; for companies that use engineering equipment & materials
      in the construction, operation & management of chemical &
      petrochemical process plants, offshore rigs, power
      generation, storage & distribution & transport systems &
      similar industrial & production assets
Gp   Electrical; Mechanical (pressure equipment, storage tanks,
      piping & valve systems, rotating machinery); Materials
      technology; Inspection; Instruments & control
●   Mtgs - ET - SG - Inf - LG
>   Eur C'ee User Inspectorates
M   17 f, UK / 2 f, o'seas
¶   c 60 technical guides & handbooks.
      Free price list available.

Engineering Industries Association   (EIA)   1940
NR   62 Bayswater Rd, LONDON, W2 3PS.   (hq)
      020 7298 6455   fax 020 7298 6456
      email head.office@eia.co.uk   http://www.eia.co.uk
      Pres: Sir Ronald Halstead
▲   Company Limited by Guarantee
Br   3 regions
○   *T; representation & promotion of the interests of the
      engineering manufacturing sector in UK, European & global
      markets
●   Conf - Mtgs - Exhib - Expt - Inf - VE - LG
M   400 f
¶   NL - 12;   Trade Leads - 12;   Buyers' Guide - 1; all ftm.

Engineering Integrity Society   (EIS)   1985
■   5 Wentworth Ave, SHEFFIELD, S Yorks, S11 9QX.   (regd/off)
      0114-262 1155   fax 0114-262 1120
      email cpinder@e-i-s.org.uk   http://www.e-i-s.org.uk
      Chmn: Dr Peter Blackmore
▲   Registered Charity
○   *P; 'to advance the education of persons working in the field of
      engineering by providing a forum for the interchange of
      ideas & information on integrity of engineering practice'
Gp   Durability & fatigue; Noise, vibration & harshness; Simulation,
      test & measurement
●   Conf - Mtgs - ET - Exhib
M   100 i, 37 f, UK / 26 i, o'seas
¶   Engineering Integrity (Jnl) - 2; ftm, £50 yr nm.
      EIS News (NL) - 2; free.

Engineering & Machinery Alliance   (EAMA)   2001
NR   62 Bayswater Rd, LONDON, W2 3PS.   (hq)
      020 7298 6450   fax 020 7298 6434
      email eama@mta.org.uk
      Sec: Rupert Hodges
▲   Un-incorporated Society
○   *N, *T; for the engineering, production machinery, components
      & tooling manufacturing sectors in the UK
●   LG
M   6 associations:
      British Automation & Robot Association
      British Turned Part Manufacturers Association
      Gauge & Tool Makers Association
      Manufacturing Technologies Association
      Picon Ltd
      Processing & Packaging Machinery Association

Engineering Teaching & Equipment Manufacturers' Association
      a group of the **British Educational Suppliers Association**

Engineers for Disaster Relief
      see **RedR - Engineers for Disaster Relief**

Engineers Hand Tools Association
      a group of the **Federation of British Hand Tool Manufacturers**

Engineers Ireland
      is the operating name of the **Institution of Engineers of Ireland**

England Basketball   (EBBA)   1936
NR   c/o EIS Sheffield, Coleridge Rd, SHEFFIELD, S Yorks, S9 5DA.
      (hq)
      0870 774 4225
      Chief Exec: Keith Mair
▲   Company Limited by Guarantee
○   *S; to govern & promote the game of basketball
M   30,000 i, 1,000 clubs
¶   Zone Press - 6.   Competitions Hbk - 1.   AR.
      Note: Also known as the English Basketball Association.

England Handball Association   (EHA)   1968
NR   40 Newchurch Rd, RAWTENSTALL, Lancs, BB4 7QX.   (hq)
        01706 229354   fax 01706 229354
        http://www.englandhandball.com
        Chief Exec: Stephen Neilson
▲   Company Limited by Guarantee
○   *S; national governing body for the sport
<   Intl Handball Fedn; Eur Handball Fedn; C'wealth Handball
        Assn; Brit Olympic Assn; Cent Coun of Physical Educ
M   i, schools & org
¶   NL - 4; ftm.   Hbk - 1;   AR.
        Note: Registered as the British Handball Association.

England Hockey
NR   The National Hockey Stadium, Silbury Boulevard, MILTON
        KEYNES, Bucks, MK9 1HA.   (hq)
        01908 544644
        Exec Chmn: Philip Kimberley
▲   Un-incorporated Society
○   *S; governing body for hockey in England (men, women &
        mixed)
M   i, clubs & schools
×   has replaced the English Hockey Association

England Netball
        see **All England Netball Association**

England Squash
        see **Squash Rackets Association (England Squash)**

**England & Wales Cricket Board Coaches Association   (ECB
        Coaches Association)   (ECB CA)   2002**
NR   Warwickshire Cricket Ground, Edgbaston, BIRMINGHAM,
        B5 7QX.   (hq)
        0121-440 4332   fax 0121-440 7605
        email coaches.association@ecb.co.uk
        http://www.ecbca.co.uk
        Communications Officer: Chris Dirkin
▲   Company Limited by Guarantee
○   *S; ongoing education, development & support of cricket
        coaches at all levels in UK, Europe & overseas
●   Conf - Mtgs - ET - Exhib - Inf - LG
M   9,599 i
¶   Hitting the Seam (NL) - 2.   Ybk.
        Performance Hbk - 1.   AR.
        Note: has replaced the Association of Cricket Coaches.

þa Engliscan Gesiþas   (the English Companions)   1966
■   67 Seaburn Rd, Toton, BEESTON, Notts, NG9 6HN.   (hsp)
        0115-972 4615
        http://www.tha-engliscan-gesithas.org.uk
        Hon Sec: Mrs Beryl Bickerstaffe
▲   Company Limited by Guarantee
Br   16; Australia, Canada, New Zealand, Republic of Ireland, USA
○   *G; to encourage interest in the history & other aspects of Old
        English or the Anglo-Saxon period, its language, culture &
        traditions
Gp   Living history; Local shire (scir) gps; Old English
        correspondence course
●   Mtgs - ET - Res - Exhib - Comp - SG - Lib - VE - Lectures
M   544 i, UK / 42 i, o'seas
¶   Wiþowinde (Bindweed) (Jnl) - 3;
        Hrafnes Wisprung (Raven's Whisper) (NL) - 3; both ftm only.

English Amateur Dancesport Association
        (Organisation lost: see paragraph 3)

English Apples & Pears Ltd   (EAP)   1990
■   Bradbourne House, East Malling, WEST MALLING, Kent,
        ME19 6DZ.   (hq)
        01732 529781   fax 01732 529783
        Chief Exec: Adrian Barlow
▲   Company Limited by Guarantee
○   *H, *K, *T; 'to further the interests of shareholder members who
        are top fruit (apples & pears) growers in UK'
●   Inf - PL
M   280 i

English Association   1906
NR   University of Leicester, University Rd, LEICESTER, LE1 7RH.
        (hq)
        0116-252 3982   fax 0116-252 2301
        email engassoc@le.ac.uk   http://www.le.ac.uk/
        engassoc
        Sec: Helen Lucas
▲   Company Limited by Guarantee; Registered Charity
Br   Australia, South Africa
○   *L; promotion of knowledge & appreciation of English
        language & literature
Gp   Graduate students
●   Conf
M   i & org
¶   NL - 3.   English 4-11 - 3.
        The Use of English - 3.
        Year's Work in English Studies - 1.
        Essays & Studies - 1.
        Year's Work in Critical & Cultural Theory - 1.

English Association of American Bond & Shareholders
NR   Broomfield Business Centre, 80-82 Broomfield Rd,
        CHELMSFORD, Essex, CM1 1SS.   (hq)
        01245 259911
        Sec: Navin Khattar
○   *G

**English Association of Self Catering Operators   (EASCO)
        1985**
■   PO Box 567, HAYES, Middx, UB3 9EW.   (hsp)
        020 7078 7329   fax 0870 136 6638
        email info@englishselfcatering.co.uk
        http://www.englishselfcatering.co.uk
        Chief Exec: Martin Sach
▲   Un-incorporated Society
○   *T; to represent owners of self-catering accommodation
        businesses
●   Mtgs - Res - Inf - LG
<   Fedn of Nat Self Catering Assns; Tourism Alliance
M   25 i, 15 f

English Baseball Association
■   Beau Lodge, Kelsey Lane, BECKENHAM, Kent, BR3 3NF
○   *S
M   34 org

English Basketball Association
        see **England Basketball**

English Boccia Association   (EBA)   1999
NR   5 Heathcoat Bldg, Nottingham Science & Technology Park,
        University Boulevard, NOTTINGHAM, NG7 2QJ.   (hq)
        0115-925 7027
        http://www.cpsport.org
        Contact: Bob Feeney
○   *S; to develop quality opportunities for players of all disabilities
        to participate in the sport of Boccia under the regulations of
        the International Boccia Commission (Boccia is a game akin
        to indoor bowls)
●   ET - Res - Inf - Lib - Referee courses - Level 1 training courses
<   Intl Boccia Commission
M   i & org

English Bowling Association   (EBA)   1903
- ■ Lyndhurst Rd, WORTHING, W Sussex, BN11 2AZ.   (hq)
  01903 820222   fax 01903 820444
  http://www.bowlsengland.com
  Chief Exec: Tony Allcock
- ▲ Un-incorporated Society
- ○ *S; governing body of men's outdoor bowls in England
- Gp Greens maintenance; Coaching
- ● Comp - Inf
- < Brit Isles Bowling Coun; Wld Bowls Bd
- M c 130,000 i, 2,500 clubs
- ¶ Jnl - 12; ftm.   NL - 3;   AR; both free.

English Bridge Union   (EBU)   1936
- NR Broadfields, Bicester Rd, AYLESBURY, Bucks, HP19 8AZ.   (hq)
  01296 317200   fax 01296 317220
  email postmaster@ebu.co.uk   http://www.ebu.co.uk
  Gen Mgr & Co Sec: Barry Capal
- ▲ Un-incorporated Society
- ○ *S; governing body for the game of duplicate contract bridge
- Gp Bridge for All (learn & play programme)
- ● Conf - Mtgs - ET - Comp - SG - Stat - Inf - Lib
- < Wld Bridge Fedn; Eur Bridge League
- M 30,000 i, 1,100 clubs
- ¶ English Bridge - 6.   Club NL - 6.   County NL - 4.   .
  Really Easy. . . (7 titles).

English Chess Federation   (BCF)   1904
- NR The Watch Oak, Chain Lane, BATTLE, E Sussex, TN33 0YD.
  (hq)
  01424 775222   fax 01424 775904
  email office@englishchess.org.uk
  http://www.englishchess.org.uk
  Admin: Cynthia Gurney
- ▲ Un-incorporated Society
- ○ *S; the governing body for chess in England
- ● ET - Comp - Inf
- < Fédn Intl des Echecs
- > County assns
- M 1,600 i
- ¶ Chess Moves (NL) - 6.   Ybk.
- ✕ 2005 British Chess Federation

English Civil War Society Ltd   (ECWS)   1980
- NR Flat 11 The Stables, Milton Park, PETERBOROUGH, Cambs,
  PE6 7AF.   (sb)
  01733 380177   fax 01733 380072
  http://www.english-civil-war-society.org
  Co Sec: George Bowyer
- ▲ Company Limited by Shares
- ○ *G; to further interest in 17th century English history; to
  organise & perform re-enactments of the English Civil War
- Gp The King's Army; The Roundhead Assn; Friends of the English
  Civil War Soc (supporting gp)
- ● Mtgs - Res - SG
- < Nat Coun for Voluntary Orgs
- M c 3,000 i
- ¶ King's Army NL - 6;   Roundhead Association NL; both ftm
  only.
  Friends of the ECWS NL - 4.

English Clergy Association   (ECA)   1938
- ■ The Old School, Norton Hawkfield, BRISTOL, BS39 4HB.
  (chmn/p)
  01275 830017
  email masding@breathe.co.uk
  http://www.clergyassoc.co.uk
  Chmn: Rev J W Masding
- ▲ Registered Charity; Un-incorporated Society
- ○ *P, *R; a professional organisation for the clergy of the Church
  of England, & lay members supportive of the traditional
  place of the clergy
- ● Conf - Mtgs - Nominations for Clergy Holiday Grants -
  Monitoring the processes of legislation & other changes
- M 'no reliable figures available'
- ¶ Parson & Parish - 2; ftm, £6 yr nm.

English Community Care Association   (ECCA)   2004
- NR 145 Cannon St, LONDON, EC4N 5BQ.   (hq)
  020 7220 9595   fax 020 7220 9596
  email info@ecca.org.uk   http://www.ecca.org.uk
  Chief Exec: Martin Green
- ▲ Company Limited by Guarantee; Registered Charity
- ○ *T; representative body for providers of continuing care homes
  registered under the 1984 Registered Homes Act; seeks to
  protect & promote high standards of treatment & care in the
  independent sector
- Gp Medical & rehabilitation units; Nursing homes; Residential
  homes
- ● Conf - Mtgs - Res - Stat - Inf
- M Care homes
- ¶ Bulletin;   AR;   both ftm.
- ✕ 2004 Independent Healthcare Association

English Companions
  see **Engliscan Gesíþas (the English Companions)**

English Connemara Pony Society
  since 2003-04 **British Connemara Pony Society**

English Cross Country Association   (ECCA)   1883
- ■ 22 Denham Drive, BASINGSTOKE, Hants, RG22 6LR.   (hsp)
  01256 328401   fax 01256 328401
  Sec: I S Byett
- ○ *S; to encourage & support cross-country running for men &
  women & organise national championships
- M clubs

English Curling Association   (ECA)   1971
- NR 14 Donnelly Drive, BEDFORD, Beds, MK41 9TU.   (sp)
  email development@englishcurling.co.uk
  http://www.englishcurling.co.uk
- ▲ Un-incorporated Society
- Br 3
- ○ *S; the sport of curling in England
- ● Mtgs - Comp - VE
- < Wld Curling Fedn; Eur Curling Fedn
- M c 130 i (England)
- ¶ Ybk - 1.

English Draughts Association   (EDA)   1897
- ■ 54 Mayfield Rd, RYDE, Isle of Wight, PO33 3PR.   (chmn/p)
  01983 565484
  email iancaws@msn.com   http://www.home.clara.net/
  davey
  Chmn: Ian H Caws
- ▲ Un-incorporated Society
- ○ *G, *S; to promote the game of draughts (checkers)
- ● Conf - Mtgs - Comp
- < Fédn Mondiale du Jeu de Dames; World Checkers/Draughts
  Fedn
- > County draughts assns
- M 200 i, UK / 35 i, o'seas
- ¶ English Draughts Jnl - 4; ftm, (50p back issues, nm).

English Federation of Disability Sport
NR   Manchester Metropolitan University, Alsager Campus,
       Hassall Rd, Alsager, STOKE on TRENT, Staffs, ST7 2HL.
       0161-247 5294
       http://www.efds.co.uk
       Chief Exec: Colin Chaytors
○   *S
✕   2005 Disability Sport England (merged)

English Folk Dance & Song Society   (EFDSS)   1932
■   Cecil Sharp House, 2 Regent's Park Rd, LONDON,
       NW1 7AY.   (hq)
       020 7485 2206   fax 020 7284 0534
       email info@efdss.org   http://www.efdss.org
       Chief Officer: Hazel Miller
▲   Company Limited by Guarantee; Registered Charity
○   *D, *G; 'putting English traditions into the hearts & minds of the
       people of England'
●   ET - Res - Inf - Lib - PL
M   3,500 i, 562 affiliates, UK & o'seas
¶   EDS (English Dance & Song) - 4; ftm, £2.50 nm.
       Folk Music Jnl - 1; ftm, £7.50 nm.
       Members' Quarterly; ftm only.

English Goat Breeders Association   (EGBA)   1978
■   Heathgate Farm, Gills Lane, Rooksbridge, AXBRIDGE,
       Somerset, BS26 2TZ.   (hsp)
       01934 750602
       http://www.egba.org.uk
       Hon Sec: Mrs J A Parry
▲   Registered Charity
○   *B; preservation & promotion of English goats
●   Mtgs - Exhib - Inf - LG
<   Brit Goat Soc
M   c 90 i
¶   Jem - 6; ftm, 75p nm.

English Goethe Society   (EGS)   1886
NR   c/o Dept of German, Kings College, Strand, LONDON,
       WC2R 2LS.   (hsb)
       020 7848 2131   fax 020 7848 2089
       email matthew.bell@kcl.ac.uk   http://www.sas.ac.uk/
       igs/hpegs.htm
       Hon Sec & Treas: Dr Matthew Bell
▲   Registered Charity
○   *L; to promote the work & thought of Goethe, as well as other
       18th century German writers & some later writers, notably
       Thomas Mann
●   Conf - Mtgs - ET - Res - Comp
<   Goether-Gesellschaft (Weimar)
M   150 i, UK / 20 i, o'seas
¶   Publications of the English Goethe Society - 1; ftm, £20 nm.

English Golf Union   (EGU)   1924
NR   National Golf Centre, The Broadway, WOODHALL SPA, Lincs,
       LN10 6PU.   (hq)
       01526 354500   fax 01526 354020
       email info@englishgolfunion.org
       http://www.englishgolfunion.org
       Sec: Paul Baxter
▲   Un-incorporated Society
○   *S; to promote, administer & encourage amateur golf in
       England; to maintain a uniform system of handicapping
Gp   Championships; Coaching; Golf services; Golf development;
       Junior golf
●   Mtgs - ET - Exhib - Comp - Inf - LG
<   Eur Golf Assn; Cent Coun of Physical Recreation
M   730,000 i, 1,900 clubs
¶   English Golf - 6.   Chipping In - 4.

English Guernsey Cattle Society   (EGCS)   1884
NR   Scotsbridge House, Scots Hill, RICKMANSWORTH, Herts,
       WD3 3BB.   (hq)
       01923 695204   fax 01923 695215
       email egcs@guernseycattle.org.uk
       http://www.guernseycattle.com
       Admin: Mrs K Jenkins
▲   Company Limited by Guarantee; Registered Charity
○   *B
●   Conf - Mtgs - SG
M   280 i, UK / 20 i, o'seas
¶   Guernsey Breeders NL - 3; ftm.

English Heritage
       a Statutory Body giving grants for the upkeep & repair of listed
       buildings - for full information see our companion volume
       'Councils, Committees & Boards' (Introduction paragraph 6).

English Historic Towns Forum   (EHTF)   1987
NR   PO Box 22, BRISTOL, BS16 1RZ.   (hq)
       0117-975 0459   fax 0117-975 0460
       email ehtf@uwe.ac.uk   http://www.ehtf.org
       Director: Chris Winter
▲   Un-incorporated Society
○   *K; to establish & encourage contact between local authorities
       having responsibility for the management of historic towns &
       cities, & between these authorities & other public, private &
       voluntary sector agencies
Gp   Built environment; Retail; Tourism; Transport
●   Conf - Mtgs - ET - Res - Exhib - SG - Inf - VE - LG
<   Eur Assn of Historic Towns & Regions (EAHTR)
M   i, f & org
¶   NL - 4;   AR; both free.
       Membership Directory - 1; ftm only.
       Publications list available on request.

English Hockey Association
       suspended operations in 2002; replaced in 2003 by **England
       Hockey**

English Indoor Bowling Association   (EIBA)   1971
■   David Cornwell House, Bowling Green, Leicester Rd, MELTON
       MOWBRAY, Leics, LE13 0FA.
       01664 481900   fax 01664 482888
       email enquiries@eiba.co.uk   http://www.eiba.co.uk
       Sec: S Rodwell
○   *S; indoor bowls (men only)
M   340 org
¶   Woods & Jack (NL) - 5.   Ybk; £3 m.

English Lacrosse Association   (ELA)   1996
■   26 Wood St, MANCHESTER, M3 3EF.   (hq)
       0161 834 4582
       email info@englishlacrosse.co.uk
       Chief Exec: David Shuttleworth
▲   Company Limited by Guarantee
○   *S; the governing body for men's & women's lacrosse in Britain
M   c 4,000 i, c 100 org

English Place-Name Society   (EPNS)   1923
■   Institute for Name-Studies, School of English Studies, University
       Park, NOTTINGHAM, NG7 2RD.   (hq)
       0115-951 5919   fax 0115-951 5924
       email name-studies@nottingham.ac.uk
       http://www.nottingham.ac.uk/english/
       Hon Dir: Prof Richard Coates,   Hon Sec: Prof Turville-Petre
▲   Registered Charity
○   *L; to survey the place-names & field-names of England, county
       by county, & publish the results of the survey
●   Annual Meeting - Res - Inf - Lib
M   625 i
¶   The Place Names of [county] - 1; £35 m (£40 o'seas),
       £40 nm (£45 o'seas).
       Jnl - 1; ftm, £12 nm.   AR.

English Playing-Card Society   (EPCS)   1984
- PO Box 29, NORTH WALSHAM, Norfolk, NR28 9NQ.   (hsp)
   01692 650496   fax 0870 127 2448
   email secretary@epcs.org   http://www.wopc.co.uk/epcs
   Sec: John Sings
▲ Un-incorporated Society
○ *G; to provide information for collectors & researchers of
   English playing cards & children's card games
● Mtgs - Res - SG - Inf
< Ephemera Soc
M 130 i
¶ NL (incl LM) - 3; £20 m.

English Poetry & Song Society   (EPSS)   1983
- 76 Lower Oldfield Park, BATH, Somerset, BA2 3HP.   (hsp)
   01225 313531   fax 01225 313531
   email menistral@yahoo.co.uk
   Chief Exec: Richard Carder
○ *D; the promotion of English art song by performance,
   publication & recording
● Mtgs - Res - Comp - Lib
< Nat Fedn of Music Socs
M 50 i, UK / 2 i, o'seas
¶ NL & Song List - 2; £12 m.

English Pool Association   (EPA)   1979
- 88 Crescent Rd, Hadley, TELFORD, Shropshire, TF1 4JX.   (sp)
   01952 641682
   email ivor.edwards22@blueyonder.co.uk
   http://www.epa.org.uk
   Gen Sec: Ivor Edwards
Br 46
○ *S; to organise, administer the game of pool in England
Gp English Pool Referees Association
● Mtgs - Exhib - Comp - LG - selection of national teams -
   organisation of fixtures & inter-league events
< Wld Eight Ball Pool Fedn; Eur Eight Ball Pool Fedn
M 18,000 i
¶ Hbk - 1; ftm; £5 nm.

English Pool Referees Association
   a group of the **English Pool Association**

English Racketball   1998
- 50 Tredegar Rd, Wilmington, DARTFORD, Kent, DA2 7AZ.
   (hsp/b)
   01322 272200   fax 01322 289295
   email idw@kentsra.co.uk
   Hon Sec: Ian D W Wright
○ *S
< is part of England Squash

English School [sport] Association
   no school sports associations are included in this directory - see
   controlling body for the sport concerned

English Ski Council
   trades as **Snowsport England**

English Speaking Union of the Commonwealth   (ESU)   1918
NR Dartmouth House, 37 Charles St, LONDON, W1J 5ED.   (hq)
   020 7529 1550   fax 020 7495 6108
   email esu@esu.org   http://www.esu.org
   Dir Gen: Mrs Valerie Mitchell
▲ Registered Charity
Br 40; 38 o'seas
○ *X; 'to promote international understanding & human
   achievement through the widening use of the English
   language throughout the world'
● Conf - Mtgs - ET - Exhib - Comp - Inf - Lib - VE - Public
   speaking & debates - Youth exchange & work experience
   schemes - Cultural & literary events
< English Speaking U (USA)
M 5,193 i, 57 f, UK / 449 i, o'seas
¶ Concord (Jnl) - 2;   ESU NL - 10; both ftm.

English Sports Association for People with Learning Disability
   in 2005 integrated with **MENCAP**

English Table Tennis Association   (ETTA)   1926
- Queensbury House, Havelock Rd, HASTINGS, E Sussex,
   TN34 1HF.   (hq)
   01424 722525   fax 01424 422103
   email admin@ettahq.freeserve.co.uk
   http://www.etta.co.uk
   Gen Sec: R H Sinclair,   Chief Exec: Richard Yule
▲ Company Limited by Guarantee
○ *S; governing body for the sport in England
● Conf - Organisation of national championships
< Intl Table Tennis Fedn; Eur Table Tennis U
M 40,000 i, 4,500 clubs
¶ Table Tennis News - 8; £2.75.

English Tiddlywinks Association   (ETwA)   1958
- c/o Dr P J Barrie, Chemical Engineering Dept, University of
   Cambridge, Pembroke St, CAMBRIDGE, CB2 3RA.   (hsb)
   01223 331864   fax 01223 334796
   email pjb10@cam.ac.uk   http://www.etwa.org
   Chmn: Dr P J Barrie,   Sec: P Moss
▲ Un-incorporated Society
○ *S; to promote the game of tiddlywinks throughout the UK
Gp Societies & clubs: New London, Oxford, Cambridge, St
   Andrews, York Universities
● Mtgs - Comp - Inf
< Intl Fedn Tiddlywinks Assns
M 80 i, UK / 5 i, o'seas
¶ Winking World - 2; ftm, £3 nm.   NL - 6; free.

English UK   2004
- 56 Buckingham Gate, LONDON, SW1E 6AG.   (hq)
   020 7802 9200   fax 020 7802 9201
   email info@englishuk.com   http://www.englishuk.com
   Chief Exec: Tony Millns
▲ Registered Charity
○ *E, *P; British Council accredited English language teaching
   providers
Gp Business English UK; Work Experience UK
● Conf - ET - Res - Exhib - Inf - LG
< Eur Fedn of Nat Assns for Teaching Mother Tongues to Foreign
   Students (ELITE); Assn of Language Teaching Orgs (ALTO)
M 330 f
¶ English UK News - 4;   English in the UK - 1; both free.
✕ 2004 (Association of Recognised English Language Services
   (British Association of State English Language Teaching

English Volleyball Association   (EVA)   1971
NR   Suite B Loughborough Technology Centre, Epinal Way,
       LOUGHBOROUGH, Leics, LE11 3GE.   (hq)
       01509 631699   fax 01509 631689
       email general@eng-volleyball.demon.co.uk
       Chief Exec: Toomas Ojasoo
○   *S; to promote the game of volleyball in England, both for men
       & women; to develop the game in schools
M   c 18,000 i
       Note: is known as Volleyball England.

English Westerners Society   (EWS)   1954
NR   130 The Keep, KINGSTON-upon-THAMES, Surrey, KT2 5UE.
       (hsp)
       email kgalvin.bas@gtnet.gov.uk
       http://www.english-westerners-society.org.uk
       Hon Sec: Kevin Galvin
▲   Un-incorporated Society
○   *G; study of the history of the American West, incl ethnological
       & cultural background
●   Res
<   Westerners Intl (USA)
M   145 i, UK / 55 i, o'seas
¶   Tally Sheet - 1; ftm only.
       Brand Book - 1; ftm, £4.50 - £7.50 nm.
       Special publications - irreg; ftm, £5 - £15 nm.

English Wine Producers   (EWP)   1992
■   PO Box 5729, MARKET HARBOROUGH, Leics, LE16 8WX.
       01536 772264   fax 01536 772263
       email info@englishwineproducers.com
       http://www.englishwineproducers.com
       Contact: Julia Trustram Eve
○   *T
<   UK Vineyards Assn
M   c 20 i

English Wine Society
       no longer exists

English Women's Bowling Association   (EWBA)   1931
■   Victoria Park Bowling Green, Archery Rd, ROYAL LEAMINGTON
       SPA, Warks, CV31 3PT.   (hq)
       01926 430686   fax 01926 430686
       email office@englishwomensbowling.net
       http://www.englishwomensbowling.net
       Chief Exec: Pauline A Biddlecombe
Br   1950 clubs
○   *S; to encourage the sport of flat green bowls for ladies
       outdoors in England
Gp   Youth development scheme; Child protection panel
●   Mtgs - Comp - VE - LG
<   Wld Bowls Ltd; Intl Women's Bowling Coun; Eur Bowls U; Brit
       Isles Womens Bowling Coun
M   46,000 i, 35 counties
¶   NL - 1; ftm.   Ybk - 1; £4 m.

English Women's Indoor Bowling Association   (EWIBA)   1951
■   3 Moulton Business Park, Scirocco Close, Moulton Park,
       NORTHAMPTON, NN3 6AP.   (hq)
       01604 494163   fax 01604 494434
       email ewiba@btinternet.com   http://www.ewiba.com
       Nat Sec: Mrs Tricia Thomas
▲   Un-incorporated Society
○   *S; to promote & foster the game of flat green indoor bowls for
       women in England
●   ET - Comp
<   Wld Indoor Bowls Coun; Brit Isles Women's Indoor Bowls Coun
M   49,069 i, 323 clubs
¶   Ybk (incl list of clubs); £2.50.

Enid Blyton Society   1995
NR   93 Milford Hill, SALISBURY, Wilts, SP1 2QL.
       01722 331937
       http://www.enidblytonsociety.co.uk

Entertainment & Leisure Software Publishers Association Ltd
       (ELSPA)   1989
NR   167 Wardour St, LONDON, W1F 8WL.   (hq)
       020 7534 0580   fax 020 7534 0581
       email roger.bennett@elspa.com   http://www.elspa.com
       Dir Gen: Roger Bennett
▲   Company Limited by Guarantee
○   *T; for interactive consumer software publishers, including
       computer & video games
Gp   Publishers; Developers; Distributors; Duplicators; Suppliers;
       Hardware Mfrs; Trade & Consumer Media; Legal
●   Conf - ET - Res - Exhib - Stat - Expt - Inf - LG - Anti piracy
       (crime unit) - Accreditation (duplicators)
<   Video Standards Couns: VUD (Germany); SELL (France); ISF-E
M   120 f, 4 org
¶   The Britsoft Book

Entertainment Software Retailers Association
       ceased operations 1 April 2004

Envelope Makers' & Manufacturing Stationers' Association
       (EMMSA)   1940
NR   Church View, 7A Church Lane, Arrington, ROYSTON, Herts,
       SG8 0BD.   (hsp)
       01223 208665   fax 01223 208665
       email emmsauk@aol.com   http://www.envelope.org
       Dir: M J Dellar
▲   Un-incorporated Society
○   *T
●   Conf - ET - Stat - Inf - LG
<   Eur Envelope Makers Assn (FEPE); CBI
M   c 50 f
¶   AR - 1; ftm.

Environmental Communicators' Organisation   (ECO)   1972
■   8 Hooks Cross, Watton-at-Stone, HERTFORD, SG14 3RY.
       (chmn)
       01920 830527   fax 01480 830538 p
       Chmn: Alan Massam,   Hon Sec: Barbara Jefferies
▲   Un-incorporated Society
○   *K; promotion of conservationist ideas among professional
       journalists & broadcasters
●   Res - Inf - PR support for green orgs
<   Brit Naturalists Assn
M   300 i
¶   NL - irreg.

Environmental Health Officers' Association   1949
IRL   39A Main St, BRAY, Co Wicklow, Republic of Ireland.
       353 (1) 276 1211   fax 353 (1) 276 4665
       http://www.ehoa.ie
       Hon Sec: Sheila Ryan
○   *P

Environmental Industries Commission Ltd   (EIC)   1995
■   45 Weymouth St, LONDON, W1G 8ND.   (hq)
       020 7935 1675   fax 020 7486 3455
       email info@eic-uk.co.uk   http://www.eic-uk.co.uk
       Chief Exec: Adrian Wilkes
○   *N, *T; to represent the UK's environmental technology sector
●   Conf - Mtgs - Res - Exhib - Expt - Inf - Lib - LG
M   295 f, UK / 5 f, o'seas
¶   Envirotech News EU - 4;   Envirotech News UK - 12;
       both ftm, £135 nm.

Environmental Industries Federation Ltd　(EIF)　1998
■　Unit 32 Owners, High St, Newburn, NEWCASTLE UPON TYNE,
　　NE15 8LN.　(hq)
　　0191-229 1824　fax 0191-229 1825
　　email info@eif.org.uk　　http://www.eif.org.uk
　　Sector Devt Mgr: Joanne Bennison
▲　Company Limited by Guarantee
○　T; to provide a voice for, & promote the interests of, northern
　　businesses involved in the environmental sector
●　Conf - Mtgs - ET - Stat - Expt - Inf - Lib - LG
M　70 f
¶　Ecobrief - 4; free.

Environmental Investigation Agency　(EIA)　1984
NR　62-63 Upper St, LONDON, N1 0NY.　(hq)
　　020 7354 7960　fax 020 7354 7961
　　email info@eia-international.org
　　http://www.eia-international.org
　　Chmn: Allan Thornton
▲　Company Limited by Guarantee
Br　USA
○　*K; 'an independent, non-profit organisation fighting to protect
　　endangered wildlife & the natural world. Working closely with
　　governments, enforcement agencies & other organisations,
　　EIA develops effective long-term solutions to environmental
　　problems'
●　Res - Lib - PL - LG - Undercover investigations
M　10,000 i
¶　NL - 2.　Various publications.

Environmental Noise Barrier Association
　　see **Fencing Contractors Association**

Environmental Services Association　(ESA)　1969
■　154 Buckingham Palace Rd, LONDON, SW1W 9TR.　(hq)
　　020 7824 8882　fax 020 7824 8753
　　email info@esauk.org　　http://www.esauk.org
　　Chief Exec: Dirk Hazell
▲　Company Limited by Guarantee
○　*T; for the waste management industry (including collection,
　　treatment, disposal, recovery, recycling, & use of waste in the
　　commercial & industrial sectors), specialist equipment
　　manufacturers, & consultants
Gp　Plant & equipment mfrs; Consultants; Overseas; Affiliates
●　Conf - Mtgs - ET - Res - Exhib - SG - Expt - Inf - Lib - VE - LG -
　　Annual lunch & AGM
<　Fedn Waste Mgt & Envtl Services (FEAD); Confedn of Brit Ind
　　(CBI); UN GlobalCompact
M　250 f
¶　Guidelines; ftm, prices vary nm.　AR; free.
×　2001 Energy from Waste Association (merged)

**Environmental & Technical Association for the Paper Sack
　Industry　(ETAPS)**
NR　24 Grange St, KILMARNOCK, E Ayrshire, KA1 2AR.　(hq)
　　01563 570518　fax 01563 572728
　　email npc@natpack.org.uk
　　http://www.papersacks.org.uk
　　Sec: Allan Glen
▲　Un-incorporated Society
○　*T; for paper sack producing companies
●　Mtgs - Exhib - Inf
M　6 f, UK / 2 f, o'seas

Environmental Transport Association
　　see **ETA Services**

Ephemera Society　(Ephsoc)　1975
■　PO Box 112, NORTHWOOD, Middx, HA6 2WT.
　　01923 829079　fax 01923 825207
　　Admin: Valerie Jackson-Harris
▲　Un-incorporated Society
Br　1; Australia, Austria, Canada, USA
○　*G; the conservation, study & presentation of printed &
　　handwritten ephemera (the minor transient documents of
　　everyday life)
●　Mtgs - Inf - VE - Bazaars
<　Foundation for Ephemera Studies
M　700 i, f & org
¶　The Ephemerist - 4;　Members' Hbk - updated; both ftm only.

Epilepsy Action
　　see **British Epilepsy Association**

Epilepsy Action Scotland　(EAS)　1954
NR　48 Govan Rd, GLASGOW, G51 1JL.　(hq)
　　0141-427 4911　fax 0141-419 1709
　　email enquiries@epilepsyscotland.org.uk
　　http://www.epilepsyscotland.org.uk
　　Chief Exec: Susan Douglas-Scott
▲　Company Limited by Guarantee; Registered Charity
Br　10
○　*W; to provide information, support & advice for people with
　　epilepsy, their families, carers & professionals involved in
　　their care
●　Conf - Mtgs - ET - Exam - Res - Exhib - Inf - LG
<　Intl Bureau for Epilepsy; Mobility Intl; Jt Epilepsy Coun (UK &
　　Ireland)
M　601 i, 12 f, 10 org
¶　Epilepsy News (NL) - 2.　AR.
　　Factsheets.
　　Note: this organisation trades as Epilepsy Scotland
×　2001 Epilepsy Association of Scotland

Epiphytic Plant Study Group　(EPSG)　1968
NR　31 Ribble Drive, Barrow-upon-Soar, LOUGHBOROUGH, Leics,
　　LE12 8LJ.　(hsp)
　　01509 413541
　　email john@jhorobin.freeserve.co.uk
　　http://www.epiphytes.co.uk
　　Sec: John F Horobin
▲　Un-incorporated Society
○　*H; to foster an interest in epiphytic plants; to circulate
　　information about such plants that would not otherwise be
　　readily available
M　175 i, UK & o'seas
¶　Epiphytes (Jnl) - 4.

Eppynt Hill & Beulah Speckled Face Sheep Society
NR　The Firs, 63 Garth Rd, BUILTH WELLS, Brecknockshire,
　　LD2 3NH.
　　01982 553726
　　Sec: D J Jones
○　*B

Equestrian Federation of Ireland
IRL　Kildare Paddocks, KILL, Co Kildare, Republic of Ireland.
　　353 (45) 886 678　fax 353 (45) 878 430
　　email efi@horsesport.ie　　http://www.horsesport.ie
　　Sec Gen: Daniel Butler
○　*B, *T

Equine Behaviour Forum (EBF) 1978
- ■ Grove Cottage, Brinkley, NEWMARKET, Suffolk, CB8 0SF. (hsp)
  01638 507502
  email f.l.burton@udcf.glasgow.ac.uk
  http://www.gla.ac.uk/external/ebf/
  Sec: Mrs Olwen Way,   Chmn: Francis Burton
- ▲ Un-incorporated Society
- ○ *L; to exchange information on the behaviour of horses in all situations
- ● Lib (advice)
- M c 300 i, UK / c 50 i, o'seas
- ¶ Equine Behaviour - 4.

Equine Shiatsu Association
- NR Hill Farm House, Mill Rd, Stanford, BIGGLESWADE, Beds, SG18 9JH.
  01462 811933
  http://www.equineshiatsuassociation.com
- ○ *V

Equine Sports Massage Association (ESMA)
- NR Haycroft Barn, Lower Wick, DURSLEY, Glos, GL11 6DD.
  01453 511814
  http://www.equinemassageassociation.co.uk
- ○ *V

Ergonomics Society (ES) 1949
- ■ Elms Court, Elms Grove, LOUGHBOROUGH, Leics, LE11 1RG. (hq)
  01509 234904   fax 01509 235666
  email ergsoc@ergonomics.org.uk
  http://www.ergonomics.org.uk
  Hon Sec: David O'Neill
- ▲ Company Limited by Guarantee; Registered Charity
- ○ *L; promotes ergonomics & the work of ergonomists, whose anatomical, physiological & psychological knowledge can help solve problems that arise between people, their working environment & the things they use
- Gp Professional affairs board; Regional & special interest groups
- ● Conf - Mtgs - Exhib - Inf - VE - LG
  Providing ergonomics information to young people through www.ergonomics4schools.com
- < Intl Ergonomics Assn
- M 1,100 i, 59 f, UK / 300 i, o'seas
- ¶ The Ergonomist NL - 12; ftm only.
  Comsultancy Register.
  Applied Ergonomics - 6; £80 m.
  Behaviour & Information Technology - 6; £50 m, £192 nm.
  Ergonomics - 15; £50 m, £805 nm.
  Ergonomics in design - 4; £29 m.
  International Jnl of Injury Control & Safety Promotion - 4; £51.50 m, £60 nm.
  Jnl of Sports Sciences - 12; £60.
  Theoretical Issues in Ergonomics - 6; £50 m, £166 nm.
  Work & Stress - 4; £50 m, £13 nm.

Eriskay Pony Society
- NR Southfield Farmhouse, Cousland, DALKEITH, Midlothian, EH22 2NX.
  0131-663 3485
  http://www.eriskayponies.com
  Chmn: Fiona Misselbrook
- ○ *B
- M c 130 i

ERoSH, the National Consortium for Sheltered Housing (ERoSH)
- ■ PO Box 2616, CHIPPENHAM, Glos, SN15 1WZ. (hq)
  01249 654249   fax 01249 654249
  email info@shelteredhousing.org
  http://www.shelteredhousing.org
  Hon Sec: Linda Milton
- ○ *W
- ● Conf - ET - Comp - Inf

Esperanto-Asocio de Skotlando
  see **Scottish Esperanto Association**

Esperanto Association of Britain (Esperanto-Asocio de Britio) (EAB) 1904
- ■ Esperanto House, Station Rd, Barlaston, STOKE-on-TRENT, Staffs, ST12 9DE. (hq)
  0845 230 1887   fax 01782 372229
  email eab@esperanto-gb.org
  http://www.esperanto-gb.org
  Hon Sec: Geoffrey Sutton
- ▲ Registered Charity
- ○ K; to advance the education of the public in the international language Esperanto in the furtherance of international communication without discrimination & of the natural right of all people & peoples, their languages & cultures to be treated equally
- ● Conf - ET - Exam - Res - SG - Inf - Lib - LG
- < Universala Esperanto-Asocio (UEA)
- M 460 i
- ¶ La Brita Esperantisto (Jnl) - 2; ftm, £2.40 nm.
  EAB Update (NL) - 4; ftm only.

Essex Agricultural Society 1858
- NR c/o Writtle Agricultural College, Lordship Lane, Writtle, CHELMSFORD, Essex, CM1 3RR. (hq)
  01245 424113
  Sec: Mike Hall
- ▲ Company Limited by Guarantee; Registered Charity
- ○ *F; to promote & advance agriculture for the benefit of the public through education & publicity; sponsorship of the County Farms competition & County Ploughing Championship (not the Essex Show)
- ● ET - Exhib - Comp - Ploughing match - Farms competition
- M 350 i
- ¶ NL - 4;   AR; both free.

Essex Archaeological & Historical Congress (EAHC) 1964
- ■ Roseleigh, Epping Rd, EPPING, Essex, CM16 5HW. (hsp)
  01992 813725
  email pmd2@ukonline.co.uk
  http://www.essexhistory.net/essexcongress.htm
  Hon Sec: Mrs Pauline Dalton
- ▲ Registered Charity
- ○ *L; to advance the education of the public in archaeology, history & conservation in Essex
- ● Conf - Mtgs - Res - Exhib - Inf
- < Brit Assn for Local History (BALH); Coun Brit Archaeology
- M 95 org
- ¶ Essex Jnl - 2; £10 yr (£5 each).   NL - 3;   AR; both ftm.

Essex Chambers of Commerce (ECCI) 1997
- ■ 8-9 St Peter's Court, COLCHESTER, Essex, CO1 1WD. (hq)
  01206 765277   fax 01206 578073
  email info@essexchambers.co.uk
  http://www.essexchambers.co.uk
  County Exec: John Clayton
- ▲ Company Limited by Guarantee
- Br Chelmsford (Mid Essex), Westcliff-on-Sea (S Essex)
  10 affiliated chambers within the county
- ○ *C, *N
- ● Conf - Mtgs - ET - Exam - Res - Exhib - Comp - Expt - Inf - Lib - VE - LG
- < Brit Chams Comm
- M 2,500 f including affiliated chambers
- ¶ Business Plus - 12; ftm & enquirers.
  Essex Chambers Directory (incl LM/firms) - 1; ftm, £30 nm.

Essex Society for Archaeology & History   (ESAH)   1852
NR   2 Landview Gardens, ONGAR, Essex, CM5 9EQ.   (hsp)
       Hon Sec: Michael Leach
▲   Registered Charity
○   *L
●   Conf - Lib - VE
<   Coun Brit Archaeology; Inst Histl Res
M   300 i
¶   Essex Archaeology & History - 1; ftm.
     Essex Archaeology & History News - 3; ftm.

Essex Wildlife Trust Ltd   (EWT)   1959
■   Abbotts Hall Farm, Gt Wigborough, COLCHESTER, Essex,
     CO5 7RZ.   (hq)
     01621 862960   fax 01621 862990
     email admin@essexwt.org.uk
     http://www.essexwt.org.uk
     Sec: Valerie M Crookes
▲   Company Limited by Guarantee; Registered Charity
○   *G; nature conservation
●   ET - VE
<   The Wildlife Trusts
M   17,500 i, 470 f, UK / 9 i, o'seas
¶   Essex Wildlife - 3; free.

Est à Laine Merino Sheep Society
     has closed

Estuarine & Coastal Sciences Association   (ECSA)   1971
NR   c/o Dr Michael Elliott, Dept of Biological Sciences, University of
       Hull, HULL, HU6 7RX.   (pres/b)
       01482 465503   fax 01482 465458
       http://www.ecsa-coast.org
       Pres: Dr Michael Elliott
▲   Registered Charity
○   *L, *P, *Q; to promote knowledge & understanding of estuaries
     & brackish waters in order to prevent environmental
     deterioration; to encourage resource management for the
     public benefit
M   i & f

ETA Services Ltd   (ETA)   1990
NR   68 High St, WEYBRIDGE, Surrey, KT13 8BL.   (hq)
       01932 828882   fax 01932 829015
       email eta@eta.co.uk   http://www.eta.co.uk
       Dir: Andrew Davis
▲   Company Limited by Guarantee
○   *K; 'for an environmentally sustainable transport policy for
     Britain; to provide an innovative range of quality &
     competitive services directly to those on the move
     (Breakdown)'
Gp   Insurance - travel, motor, house & home, cycle; Road rescue;
       Vehicle inspection; Carbon neutral products; Membership
●   Conf - Mtgs - Res - Inf - LG
<   Carplus; Slower Speed Initiative
M   18,000 i, 500 f
¶   Going Green - 4.   Car Buyer's Guide - 1.
     also known as the Environmental Transport Association

Ethical Trading Initiative   (ETI)   1998
■   Cromwell House (2nd floor), 14 Fulwood Place, LONDON,
     WC1V 6HZ.   (hq)
     020 7404 1463   fax 020 7831 7852
     email eti@eti.org.uk   http://www.ethicaltrade.org
     Dir: Dan Rees
▲   Company Limited by Guarantee
○   *K; an alliance of companies, NGOs & trade unions committed
     to working together to identify & promote good practice in
     the implementation of codes of labour practice
●   Conf - Mtgs - ET - Res - Inf - LG
M   c 50 orgs
¶   Various occasional publications.

Eton Fives Association   (EFA)   1930
■   3 Bourchier Close, SEVENOAKS, Kent, TN13 1PD.   (hsp)
     01732 458775
     email efa@etonfives.co.uk   http://www.etonfives.co.uk
     Hon Sec: Mike Fenn
▲   Company Limited by Guarantee
○   *S; to promote & encourage the playing of Eton Fives both at
     school & adult level
●   Comp - Inf
M   550 i, 70 org, UK / 25 i, 8 org, o'seas
¶   NL - 1.   AR - 1; both ftm only.

EURISOL-UK Ltd (UK Mineral Wool Association)   (EURISOL-UK)   1985
■   PO Box 35084, LONDON, NW1 4XE.   (hq)
     020 7935 8532   fax 020 7935 8532
     email info@eurisol.com   http://www.eurisol.com
     Sec Gen: C Dunn-Meynell
▲   Company Limited by Guarantee
○   *T; interests of manufacturers of glass wool & rock wool; to
     promote the usage of mineral wool products for thermal &
     acoustic insulation & fire protection in building, industry &
     commerce
●   Mtgs - Exhib - LG
M   4 f
¶   Technical publications & general guidance notes for home
     insulation.

European Association of Copper Clad Laminate Manufacturers
     as a part of BEAMA Energy is a group of **BEAMA**

European Association of Securities Dealers
     in April 2001 was incorporated by the **Association of Private
     Client Investment Managers & Stockbrokers**

European Atlantic Group   (EAG)   1954
■   6 Gertrude St, LONDON, SW10 0JN.   (hq)
     020 7352 1226   fax 020 7352 1226
     email info@eag.org.uk   http://www.eag.org.uk
     Pres: Baroness Hooper,
     Dirs: Elma Dangerfield, Justin Glass
▲   Registered Charity
○   *K; to promote closer relations between the European & Atlantic
     countries by providing a regular forum in Britain for informed
     discussion of their problems & possibilities for better
     economic & political cooperation with each other & the rest
     of the world
●   Mtgs - SG - Inf - Lib - overseas delegations
M   100 i (council & committee), 900 i, 100 f
¶   European-Atlantic Jnl - 1; ftm.

The European Atlantic Movement   (TEAM)   1958
NR   Cloverdown, Green Hill, HIGH WYCOMBE, Bucks,
       HP13 5QH.   (chmn/p)
       Chmn: Laurence Smy
▲   Registered Charity
○   *K; 'to encourage research & disseminate information about
     the European & Atlantic communities & their institutions.'
●   Conf - SG - VE
<   Atlantic Coun
M   95 i, 25 schools, UK / 35 i, o'seas
¶   Publications list available.

European Catering Association (Great Britain) (ECA) 1937
- ■ Bourne House, Horsell Park, WOKING, Surrey, GU21 4LY. (hq)
    01483 765111   fax 01483 751991
    email admin@ecagb.co.uk   http://www.ecagb.co.uk
    Admin: Vic Laws
- ▲ Company Limited by Guarantee
- Br 8
- ○ *P; provision of catering services - comprising managers, executives, contract caterers, etc
- ● Conf - Mtgs - ET - Exhib - Comp - Inf - Lib - VE - Book service
- < Eur Catering Assn
- M 200 i, 30 f

European Information Association (EIA) 1991
- NR Central Library, St Peter's Sq, MANCHESTER, M2 5PD.   (hq)
    0161-228 3691   fax 0161-236 6547
    email eia@libraries.manchester.gov.uk
    http://www.eia.org.uk
    Hon Sec: Angela Stogia
- ▲ Registered Charity
- Br 7
- ○ *P; to develop, coordinate & improve access to European Union information
- ● Conf - Mtgs - ET - Exhib - Inf - Liaison with European Union institutions
- M 40 i, 100 f, 200 org, UK / 10 i, 40 f, 100 org, o'seas
- ¶ Focus - 12;   LM - 1;   AR; all ftm only.
    Publications on various subjects linked to European information.

European Liquid Roofing Association
    since 2005-06 **European Liquid Waterproofing Association**

European Liquid Waterproofing Association (ELWA) 1979
- ■ Fields House, Gower Rd, HAYWARDS HEATH, W Sussex, RH16 4PL.   (hq)
    01444 417458   fax 01444 415616
    email info@elwassociation.org.uk
    http://www.elwassociation.org.uk
    Co Sec: William A Jenkins
- ▲ Company Limited by Guarantee
- ○ *T; for manufacturers of liquid applied waterproofing systems
- Gp Roofing; Car park decks; Balconies & walkways; Bridge decks
- ● Mtgs - ET - Inf - Drafting industry standards & technical guidance notes
- M 21 f
- ¶ LM.
- × 2005-06 European Liquid Roofing Association

European Movement of the United Kingdom Ltd 1948
- ■ 7 Graphite Sq, LONDON, SE11 5EE.   (hq)
    020 7820 9965   fax 020 7735 2515
    email info@euromove.org.uk
    http://www.euromove.org.uk
    Dir: David Stephen,
    Chmn: Lord Haskins
- ▲ Company Limited by Guarantee
- Br 50
- ○ *K; to campaign for support for, & understanding of, the European Union & other European institutions
- ● Conf - Mtgs - SG - Inf
- M 2,500 i

Europilots - the Association of Licensed Deep Sea Pilots
- NR 2 Dormy Avenue, Mannamead, PLYMOUTH, Devon, PL3 5BY.
    01752 262845
    http://www.europilots.org.uk
- ○ *P

Evacuees Reunion Association (ERA) 1996
- NR The Mill Business Centre, Mill Hill, GRINGLEY-ON-THE-HILL, Notts, DN10 4RA.   (hq)
    01777 816166
    email era@evacuees.org.uk   http://www.evacuees.org.uk
    Chief Exec: James Roffey
- ▲ Registered Charity
- ○ *W; to relieve the physical & mental suffering of former evacuees of the Second World War; to advance the education of the public on the subject of child evacuation during the War
- ● Conf - Mtgs - ET - Res - Exhib - SG - Inf - VE
- M 3,500 i, UK / 100 i, o'seas
- ¶ The Evacuee - 12; ftm, 50p nm.

Evaluation International (EI) 1963
- ■ East Malling Enterprise Centre, New Rd, EAST MALLING, Kent, ME19 6BJ.   (hsb)
    0845 644 4603   fax 01732 897453
    email info@evaluation-international.com
    http://www.evaluation-international.com
    Mgr: Peter Russell,   Sec: Dr Derek Cornish
- ▲ Company Limited by Guarantee
- ○ *T; to commission independent evaluations of instruments, for measurement & control, on behalf of member companies who are instrument users
- Gp Technical panel
- ● Conf - Mtgs - Res - Exhib - Stat - Inf - Lib - LG - Preparation of instrumentation guides
- < Intl Instrument Users' Assn; WIB (Netherlands); EXERCA (France)
- M 10 f, UK / 75 f, o'seas
- ¶ Electronic NL - 6; free.
    Instrument Evaluation Reports - 20; ftm only.
    Instrument Selection Guides - 20; ftm, £50-£200 each nm.

Evangelical Alliance UK (EAUK) 1846
- NR 186 Kennington Park Rd, LONDON, SE11 4BT.   (hq)
    020 7207 2100   fax 020 7207 2150
    email info@eauk.org   http://www.eauk.org
    Gen Dir: Rev Joel Edwards
- ▲ Registered Charity
- Br England, Wales, Northern Ireland
- ○ *N, *R; providing a voice for evangelical Christians to government, the media & society
- Gp Alliance commission on unity & truth among evangelicals; Reaching older people; Stewardship forum; Evangelical coalition on drugs;
    Networks: Care for pastors, Disability; EA youth & children
- ● Conf - Inf - LG
- < Wld Evangelical Fellowship; Eur Evangelical Alliance
- M 38,000 i, 6,000 churches, 725 org
- ¶ idea (Jnl) - 6;
    Leaders-digest.com - 6 (online); both ftm only.

Event Services Association (TESA) 1991
- ■ Archway House, Moor St, CHEPSTOW, Monmouthshire, NP16 5DB.   (hq)
    01291 636338   fax 01291 630402
    email info@tesa.org.uk   http://www.tesa.org.uk
    Dir: Jim Winship
- ○ *T
- Gp Security; Mobile units; Fireworks; Electrics; Event organisers & venues
- ● Mtgs - Inf - LG
- M 20 i, 180 f, UK / 4 f, o'seas
- ¶ Event Organiser - 6; ftm, £48 nm.

Eventia

NR 26-28 Station Rd, REDHILL, Surrey, RH1 1PD.   (hq)
     01737 779928   fax 01737 779749
     http://www.eventia.org.uk
▲ Company Limited by Guarantee
○ *T; for organisations providing business solutions through the
     use of events
● Conf - Mtgs - ET - Exhib - LG - Annual awards ceremony &
     dinner
✕ 2005 (Corporate Events Association
         (Incentive Travel & Meetings Association

Events Industry Alliance   (EIA)   2006

■ 119 High St, BERKHAMSTED, Herts, HP4 2DJ.   (hq)
     01442 873331   fax 01442 875551
     email info@eventsindustryalliance.com
     http://www.eventsindustryalliance.com
     Sec: Trevor Foley
▲ Company Limited by Guarantee
○ *N, *T; a marketing alliance for trade organisations within the
     exhibition industry; works with contractors, organisers &
     venues to raise the profile of exhibitions as a medium
● Conf - Mtgs - ET - Res - Inf - LG
M 281 f, UK / 26 f, o'seas
¶ Exhibition Standard - 5; ftm.

Events Sector Industry Training Organisation   (ESITO)   1995

NR 15 Osborne Gardens, THORNTON HEATH, Surrey, CR7 8PA.
     (dir/p)
     020 8771 1290   fax 020 8771 1290
     email peterw@rightrack.co.uk
     Dir: Peter Worger
▲ Company Limited by Guarantee
○ *N; forum for training & development in the events sector:
     which comprises conferences, meetings, exhibitions, outdoor
     events, events services, incentive & business travel & venues.
     Also acts as the coordinating body for pursuing these issues
     & the development of occupational standards & NVQs with
     government departments, educational bodies, NTOs & other
     organisations
● ET - Exam - SG - Inf - LG
< Business Tourism Partnership (BTP); Association for Conferences
     & Events (ACE)
M 6 org, UK / 3 org, o'seas
¶ AR; ftm.

Excellence Ireland Quality Association   (EIQA)   1969

IRL 9 Appian Way, Ranelagh, DUBLIN 6, Republic of Ireland.
     353 (1) 660 4100   fax 353 (1) 660 4280
     email info@eiqa.com   http://www.eiqa.com
     Man Dir: Paul O'Grady
○ *L, *P
✕ 2004 Excellence Ireland

Exclusive Economic Zone
     a group of the **Defence Manufacturers Association**

Executives' Association of Great Britain Ltd   (EAGB)   1929

NR 5 Factory Yard, Wycombe End, BEACONSFIELD, Bucks,
     HP9 1NA.   (hq)
     01494 675940   fax 01494 677846
     email info@eagb.co.uk   http://www.eagb.co.uk
     Dir of Operations: David Britton
Br 4; Canada, South Africa, USA
○ *P; business contacts & opportunities for networking
● Conf - Mtgs
< Intl Coordinators' Conf of Executives Assns
M 250 f, UK / 5,000 f, o'seas
¶ Bulletin - 12;   NL - 4;   Ybk - 1; all ftm only.

Exeter Chamber of Commerce (1992) Ltd   1992

■ 6 Sunhill Lane, Topsham, EXETER, Devon, EX3 0BR.
     (admin/office)
     01392 879595   fax 01392 877939
     email enqiries@exeterchamber.co.uk
     http://www.exeterchamber.co.uk
     Hon Sec: Michael Martin
▲ Company Limited by Guarantee
○ *C
● Mtgs - Inf
M 350 f
¶ LM - 1;   AR - 1; both ftm.

Exhibition Study Group   (ESG0)   1980

■ 2 Crescent Rd, NEW BARNET, Herts, EN4 9RF.   (hsp)
     020 8440 3574
     Hon Sec: Don Knight
▲ Un-incorporated Society
○ *G; collectors of memorabilia of national & international
     exhibitions & world fairs (souvenirs, books, commemorative
     china, postcards etc).
● Conf - Res - Exhib - SG - Book publishing
M 100 i, UK / 5 i, o'seas
¶ Jnl - 4.

Exhibition Venues Association   (EVA)   1997

■ 15 Keeble Court, Fairmeadows, NORTH SEATON,
     Northumberland, NE63 9SF.   (hq)
     01670 523568   fax 01670 818801
     email info@exhibitionvenues.co.uk
     http://www.exhibitionvenues.co.uk
     Exec Sec: Robin Anderson
▲ Company Limited by Guarantee
○ *T
M 20 f
¶ The UK Exhibition Facts - 1; £235.

Exmoor Horn Sheep Breeders Society   1906

■ School Farm, East Down, BARNSTAPLE, Devon, EX31 4LX.
     (hsp)
     01271 850298   fax 01271 883625
     email exmoorhornbreeders@yahoo.co.uk
     Sec: Allison Bulled
○ *B; to further the breeding of Exmoor sheep & their crosses
● Mtgs - Exhib - Inf - VE
< Nat Sheep Assn
M 175 i
¶ NL - 4;   Flock Book - 1; £2.

Exmoor Pony Society   1921

■ Woodmans, Brithem Bottom, CULLOMPTON, Devon,
     EX15 1NB.   (hsp)
     01884 839930
     email secretary@exmoorponysociety.org.uk
     Sec: Sue McGeever
▲ Company Limited by Guarantee; Registered Charity
○ *B
● Comp - Inf
M 600 i, UK / 25 i, o'seas
¶ NL - 1; ftm only.

Exmouth Chamber of Trade & Commerce   1896

NR c/o The Tourist Information Bureau, Alexandra Terrace,
     EXMOUTH, Devon, EX8 1NZ.   (hq)
     01395 275133
     Sec: Simon Wood
▲ Un-incorporated Society
○ *C
M c 150 i & f
¶ NL - 4; ftm.

Experimental Psychology Society   (EPS)   1946
- ■ Dept of Psychology, University of York, Heslington, YORK, YO10 5DD.   (hsb)
  01904 434362   fax 01904 433181
  email g.altmann@psych.york.ac.uk
  http://www.eps.ac.uk
  Hon Sec: Prof G Altmann
- ▲ Registered Charity
- ○ *P; for the furtherance of scientific enquiry within the field of psychology & cognate subjects
- ● Mtgs - Res - Inf
- M c 600 i
- ¶ Quarterly Jnl of Experimental Psychology:
  Section A: Human Experimental Psychology - 4;
  Section B: Comparative & Physiological Psychology - 4;
  [Joint subscription available.]

Expert Witness Institute   (EWI)   1996
- NR 7 Warwick Court (1st floor), LONDON, WC1R 5DJ.   (hq)
  0870 366 6367
  email info@ewi.org.uk   http://www.ewi.org.uk
- ▲ Company Limited by Guarantee
- ○ *P; the support of the proper administration of justice & the early resolution of disputes through fair & unbiased expert evidence; to encourage the use by lawyers of experts
- ● Conf - Mtgs - ET - Inf - LG - Helpline
- M c 1,200 i & org
- ¶ NL - 3/4; ftm only.

Explosives Industry Group   (EIG)
- NR Centrepoint, 103 New Oxford St, London, WC1A 1DU.
  020 7395 8063   fax 020 7497 2597
  email info@eig.org.uk   http://www.eig.org.uk
  Sec: Brig Charles Smith
- ○ *T

Export Group for Aerospace & Defence
  a group of the **Defence Manufacturers Association**

Extruded Sealants Association
- NR 18 Furness Avenue, Simonstone, BURNLEY, Lancs, BB12 7SU.
  (sp)
  01282 771260
  Sec: Paul Liles
- ○ *T
- M f
- ✕ 2003 Hot Extruded Sealants Association

Fabian Society   1884
NR   11 Dartmouth St, LONDON, SW1H 9BN.   (hq)
    020 7227 4900   fax 020 7976 7153
    email info@fabian-society.org.uk
    http://www.fabian-society.org.uk
    Gen Sec: Sunder Katwala
▲   Un-incorporated Society
Br   1 o'seas
○   *Q; social & political research
Gp   Social policy; Philosophy; Women; Race; Housing; Youth;
    International
●   Conf - Mtgs - Res - SG
<   Labour Party
M   5,700 i worldwide & local org
¶   Fabian Review - 6; ftm.   AR - 1; free.
    Pamphlets - 6; ftm.   Discussion Paper - 6.

Fabricated Access Cover Trade Association   1995
NR   42 Heath St, TAMWORTH, Staffs, B79 7JH.
    01827 52337
    Sec: Michael Skelding
○   *T; for manufacturers of manhole covers etc
M   6 i
    No further information supplied.

Facilities Management Association   (FMA)   1995
NR   Charter House, 13-15 Carteret St, LONDON, SW1H 9DJ.
    (hq)
    0796 042 8146
    email info@fmassociation.org.uk
    http://www.fmassociation.org.uk
    Exec Sec: Mary Taffler
▲   Company Limited by Guarantee
○   *T; for organisations / companies engaged in the provision of
    facility management services to clients
●   Conf - Mtgs - ET - LG
<   Intl Facilities Mgt Assns; Trade Assn Forum at CBI
M   30 f

Factoring Services Group
    since 2005 **Group Auto Union UK & Ireland Ltd**

Factors & Discounters Association   (FDA)   1996
■   Boston House (2nd floor), The Little Green, RICHMOND-
    UPON-THAMES, Surrey, TW9 1QE.   (hq)
    020 8332 9955   fax 020 8332 2585
    http://www.factors.org.uk
    Chief Exec: Kate Sharp
▲   Company Limited by Guarantee; Registered Charity
○   *P; an association of British & Irish companies in business to
    business financial services
●   Conf - Mtgs - ET - Exam - Stat - Inf - LG
M   42 f
¶   NL - 4; ftm & limited associated companies

Faculty of Accident & Emergency Medicine
    has become the**College of Emergency Medicine**

Faculty of Actuaries in Scotland   1856
NR   18 Dublin St, EDINBURGH, EH1 3PP.   (hq)
    0131-240 1300   fax 0131-240 1313
    email faculty@actuaries.org.uk
    http://www.actuaries.org.uk
    Sec: Richard Maconachie
○   *P; for the actuarial profession, life assurance, pensions &
    general insurance, investment
●   Mtgs - ET - Exam - Res - SG - Stat - Lib
<   Intl Actuarial Assn
M   c 2,000 fellows & students, UK & o'seas
¶   British Actuarial Jnl.   Members Hbk.

Faculty of Advocates   1682
NR   Advocates' Library, Parliament House, EDINBURGH, EH1 1RF.
    (hq)
    0131-226 5071   fax 0131-225 3642
    http://www.advocates.org.uk
    Clerk of the Faculty: Andrew Stewart
○   *P; the practice of Scots law in all its aspects
●   Mtgs - Exam - Inf - Lib
<   IBA; CCBE; ILA; UIA; BIALL; SCOLCAP; SCOLAG; SEPLIS
M   734 i
¶   Regulations to Intrants;   A Career in Advocacy; both free.

Faculty of Astrological Studies   1948
NR   BM Box 7470, LONDON, WC1N 3XX.   (pres/b)
    07000 790143   fax 07000 790143
    http://www.astrology.org.uk
    Pres: Clare Martin
○   *P; study of basic natal astrology
M   c 2,000 i

Faculty of Building   (FB)   1946
NR   35 Hayworth Rd, Sandiacre, NOTTINGHAM, NG10 5LL.   (hq)
    0115-949 0641   fax 0115-949 1664
    Sec: David R Winson
▲   Company Limited by Guarantee
Br   17; Hong Kong, Ireland
○   *L, *P; a multidisciplinary learned society for the built
    environment; to promote & improve communication &
    understanding between professionals involved within the
    construction industry
●   Conf - Mtgs - Comp - Inf - VE - LG
M   3,500 i, UK / 150 i, o'seas
¶   Jnl (incl NL) - 6;   Beaver (NL) - 6; both ftm only.
    Register - 2 yrly;   Technical papers - irreg; both ftm.

Faculty of Church Music   1956
■   27 Sutton Park, Blunsdon, SWINDON, Wilts, SN26 7BB.   (hsp)
    020 8675 0180
    Hon Gen Sec: Rev G Gleed,   Asst Hon Sec: M N Gretason
▲   Un-incorporated Soc
○   *D, *P; to raise the standard of church music, both practical &
    theoretical
●   Exam
M   i
¶   NL - 2; ftm.

Faculty of Dental Surgery   1947
NR   Royal College of Surgeons of England, 35-43 Lincoln's Inn
    Fields, LONDON, WC2A 3PE.   (hq)
    020 7869 6810
○   *E, *L; advancement of science & art of dentistry

Faculty of Family Planning & Reproductive Healthcare of the RCOG   (FFPRHC)   1993
■   27 Sussex Place, LONDON, NW1 4RG.   (hq)
    020 7724 5534
    email mail@ffprhc.org.uk   http://www.ffprhc.org.uk
    Co Sec: Corin Jones
▲   Company Limited by Guarantee; Registered Charity
○   *P; to maintain & develop standards of care & training of all
    providers of family planning & reproductive health care; to
    advance knowledge in the discipline & encourage research;
    to give academic status to the discipline
●   Conf - ET - Exam - Res - Inf (m only) - Essay competition for
    medical undergraduates
<   R Coll of Obstetricians & Gynaecologists
M   11,000 i, UK / 300 i, o'seas
¶   Journal of Family Planning & Reproductive Healthcare - 4;
    President's NL - 4;   AR;
    Recommendations for Clinical Practice - 1/2; all ftm.

Faculty of General Dental Practitioners (UK)
NR The Royal College of Surgeons of England, 35-43 Lincoln's Inn
     Fields, LONDON, WC2A 3PN.
     020 7312 6754
○   *M, *P

Faculty of Healthcare Counsellors & Psychotherapists
     a group of the **British Association for Counselling &
     Psychotherapy**

Faculty of Homeopathy   1950
■   Hahnemann House, 29 Park Street West, LUTON, Beds,
     LU1 3BE.   (hq)
     0870 444 3955   fax 0870 444 3960
     email info@trusthomeopathy.org
     http://www.trusthomeopathy.org
     Chief Exec: Sally Penrose
▲   Un-incorporated Society
Br 20
○   *L, *M, *P; to promote the academic & scientific development of
     homeopathy; the Faculty regulates the education, training &
     practice of homeopathy by doctors, veterinary surgeons,
     dentists, nurses, midwives, pharmacists & other statutorily
     regulated healthcare professionals
●   Conf - Mtgs - ET - Exam - Res - Exhib - SG - Inf - Lib - LG
<   Liga Medicorum Homoeopathica Internationalis (LIGA); Eur
     C'ee for Homeopathy
M   800 i, UK / 300 i, o'seas
¶   Homoeopathy Jnl - 4;   Simile (LM) - 4;
     Membership Directory - 18 months; all ftm only.

Faculty of Occupational Medicine   (FOM RCP)   1978
■   6 St Andrews Place, Regent's Park, LONDON, NW1 4LB.   (hq)
     020 7317 5890   fax 020 7317 5899
     email fom@facoccmed.ac.uk
     http://www.facoccmed.ac.uk
     Chief EXec: Nichola Wilkins
▲   Registered Charity
○   *L, *P; to promote high standards in the training & practice of
     occupational medicine
●   Conf - Mtgs - ET - Exam - Exhib - LG
<   EU of Med Specialities/section of Occupational Medicine; R
     Coll of Physicians of London
M   1,700 i
¶   NL;   eletters;   Periodicals;   AR - 1.
     Guidance on Ethics for Occupational Physicians; £25 nm.
     Guidance on Alcohol & Drug Misuse in the Workplace; £26
     nm.

** **Faculty of Personal Community & Welfare Accounting**
     Organisation lost: see Introduction paragraph 3

**Faculty of Pharmaceutical Medicine of the Royal College of
     Physicians of the United Kingdom   (FacPharmMed)
     1989**
NR 1 St Andrew's Place, LONDON, NW1 4LB.   (hq)
     020 7224 0343   fax 020 7224 5381
     http://www.fpm.org.uk
     Registrar: Dr Jane Barrett
▲   Registered Charity
○   *L, *P; the setting, maintenance & improvement of standards in
     pharmaceutical medicine
●   Conf - Mtgs - Exam
M   768 i, UK / 563 i, o'seas

Faculty of Public Health   1972
NR 4 St Andrew's Place, LONDON, NW1 4LB.   (hq)
     020 7935 0243   fax 020 7224 6973
     http://www.fph.org.uk
     Chief Exec: Paul Scourfield
○   *M, *N; is a joint faculty of the Royal Colleges of Physicians in
     the UK & shares in their efforts for the advancement of
     medical knowledge & care in the field of public health &
     medicine (the prevention of disease & the prolonging of life)
×   2003 Faculty of Public Health Medicine

Faculty of Royal Designers for Industry   1936
NR 8 John Adam St, LONDON, WC2N 6EZ.   (hq)
     020 7930 5115   fax 020 7839 5805
     email melanie.andrews@rsa.org.uk
○   *P; 'the distinction of Royal Designer for Industry (RDI) was
     established by the Royal Society of Arts in 1936, to be
     conferred on persons who have achieved sustained
     excellence in aesthetic & efficient design for industry. Persons
     holding the distinction are members of the Faculty'

Faculty of Taxation Consultants & Advisers   (FTCA)   1997
■   Oakdene House, Kenton, EXETER, Devon, EX6 8NN.   (sp)
     01626 891222   fax 01626 891555
     email admin@fta.uk.com   http://www.fta.uk.com
     Managing Dir & Sec: P T Harmsworth
▲   Company Limited by Guarantee
○   *P; to offer suuport to tax advisers
●   ET - Exam - Inf - LG
M   720 ii
¶   NL - 12; ftm only.

Fair Organ Preservation Society   (FOPS)   1958
■   47 Bitteswell Rd, LUTTERWORTH, Leics, LE17 4EN.   (hsp)
     01455 553356
     email honsec@fops.org
     Hon Sec: Ian Rogers
▲   Un-incorporated Society
Br 1; Australia, USA
○   *D, *G; promotion & encouragement of all forms of interest in,
     & the preservation of, fair organs & mechanical musical
     instruments
●   Conf - Mtgs - Res - Stat - Inf - VE - Register of organs available
     for events, nationwide
     Archives held within the National Fairground Archive at the
     University of Sheffield, (email: fairground@sheffield.ac.uk)
M   650 i, UK / 85 i, o'seas
¶   The Key Frame - 4; ftm only.
     On Display (128 pages 205 photos).

Fair Play for Children Association   (FPFC)   1972
■   35 Lyon St, BOGNOR REGIS, W Sussex, PO21 1BW.   (hsp)
     0845 330 7635
     email fairplay@arunet.co.uk   http://www.arunet.co.uk/
     fairplay/
     Hon Sec: Jan Cosgrove
▲   Company Limited by Guarantee; Registered Charity
○   *K; a campaign for more, safer & better play facilities &
     services for children. The FPFC Charitable Trust (same
     address) provides information on training in play & safety for
     children
●   Conf - ET - Inf - LG
¶   Playaction - 4; ftm, £4 nm.
     Playaction Guides - irreg; ftm, 3 1st class stamps+SAE nm.

Fairground Association of Great Britain   (FAGB)   1976
NR 5 Crooks Lane, STUDLEY, Warks, B80 7QX.   (ed/p)
     Editor: Graham Downie
▲   Un-incorporated Society
○   *G; to record, study & publish history & current information on
     the British fairground industry

Fairground Society   1962

- ■ c/o 66 Carolgate, RETFORD, Notts, DN22 6EF.   (chmn/b)
     01777 702872
     PO Box 549, Tweedale, TELFORD, TF7 5WA.   (mem/s)
     Chmn: Jack Schofield,   Sec: Claire D Booth
     Mem Sec: S Harris
- ▲ Un-incorporated Society
- ○ *G; to promote interest in the British fairground heritage &
     history of fairs
- ● Mtgs - Exhib - Inf - VE - Archive
- M c 800 i
- ¶ The Platform - 4; ftm.

Fairy Ring   1999

- NR Harmony Country Lodge, Limestone Rd, Burniston,
     SCARBOROUGH, N Yorks, YO13 0DG.   (hq)
     01723 870276   fax 01723 870276
     email sue@fairyring.co.uk   http://www.fairyring.co.uk
     Pres: Susan Hewitt
- ▲ Un-incorporated Society
- ○ *G; 'the aim of the fairy ring is to further the knowledge, love &
     respect of fairies & angels'
- ● Mtgs - Inf
- M 1,100 i, UK / 25 i, o'seas
- ¶ Fairy Tales (Jnl) - 4; m only.

Falkland Islands Association   1976

- ■ c/o Falkland House, 14 Broadway, LONDON, SW1H 0BH.
     (hq)
     0845 260 4884
     http://www.fiassociation.com
     Treas & Mem Sec: E C J Clapp
- ▲ Un-incorporated Society
- Br 2
- ○ *K, *W; 'to support the wish of the people of the Falkland
     Islands to decide their own future for themselves without
     being subjected to pressure direct, or indirect, from any
     quarter'
- M c 850 i & f, UK / c 120 i & f, o'seas
- ¶ NL - 2.

Falklands Conservation   1979

- NR 1 Princes Avenue, LONDON, N3 2DA.   (hq)
     020 8343 0831   fax 020 8343 0831
     http://www.falklandsconservation.com
     UK Sec: Ann Brown
- ▲ Registered Charity
- Br Falkland Islands
- ○ *Q; research & study of the flora & fauna of the Falkland
     Islands; to protect & preserve the sites of scientific importance
     & outstanding natural beauty in the islands & surrounding
     seas
- ● ET - Res - Exhib - Inf - LG
- < Intl U for the Consvn of Nature (IUCN); Birdlife Intl
- M c 600 i & f
- ¶ NL - 12;   AR.

Fall Arrest Safety Equipment Training   (FASET)   2000

- ■ Carthusian Court, 122 Carthusian St, LONDON, EC1M 6EZ.
     020 7397 8128   fax 020 7397 8121
     email enquiries@faset.org.uk   http://www.faset.org.uk
     Sec: Stephen Kennefick
- ▲ Company Limited by Guarantee
- ○ *T; a trade association & training body for the safety net rigging
     & fall arrest industry
- ● Mtgs - ET - Stat - LG
- < Nat Access & Scaffolding Confedn (NASC)
- M 32 f
- ¶ [publications on website].

Falsely Accused Carers & Teachers   (FACT)   2000

- ■ PO Box 3074, CARDIFF, CF3 3WZ.   (hsp)
     029 2077 7499
     email info@factuk.org   http://www.factuk.org
     Hon Sec: Michael Barnes
- Br 10
- ○ *K; 'we support carers & teachers (& their families) who have
     been falsely accused or wrongly convicted of child abuse; we
     also campaign for justice, lobby for change in the criminal
     justice system, & seek to raise awareness of issues relating to
     false allegations of abuse'
- ● Conf - Mtgs - Inf - LG - Prison support - Lobbying
- M 500 i, UK / 100 i, o'seas
- ¶ FACTion - 12; ftm only.

Families Anonymous   (FA)   1980

- ■ Doddington & Rollo Community Association, Charlotte Despard
     Ave, LONDON, SW11 5HD.   (hq)
     0845 120 0660   fax 020 7498 1990
     email office@famanon.org.uk
     http://www.famanon.org.uk
- ▲ Un-incorporated Society
- Br 66; 23 countries
- ○ *W; to support families & friends of drug abusers by weekly
     meetings
- ● Mtgs (totally confidential)
- M c 750 i
- ¶ The FA NL - 4; 50p.   Publications list available.

Families Need Fathers   (FNF)   1974

- ■ 134 Curtain Rd, LONDON, EC2A 3AR.   (hq)
     0870 760 7111   fax 020 7739 3410
     email fnf@fnf.org.uk   http://www.fnf.org.uk
     Chief Executive Officer: Geoff Fielding,   Sec: Ian Julian
- ▲ Company Limited by Guarantee; Registered Charity
- Br 29
- ○ *K; to provide support, advice & information on children's
     issues to parents, following separation / divorce
- ● Conf - Mtgs - ET - Res - Inf - LG
- M 2,750 i, UK / 30 i, o'seas
- ¶ McKenzie Magazine (Jnl) - 6; ftm, £25 nm.

Family Education Trust (Family & Youth Concern)

- ■ Jubilee House 19-21 High St, Whitton, TWICKENHAM, Middx,
     TW2 7LB.   (hq)
     020 8894 2525   fax 020 8894 3535
     email fyc@ukfamily.org.uk
     http://www.famyouth.org.uk
     Dir: Norman Wells
- ▲ Company Limited by Guarantee; Registered Charity
- Br 3; Republic of Ireland
- ○ *W; to advance the education of the public in matters of family
     welfare; to stimulate & promote research into the social,
     medical, economic & psychological consequences of family
     breakdown
- Gp Educational material
- ● Conf - Mtgs - Res - SG - Stat - Inf - Lib - PL
- < Nat Coun of Women
- ¶ Family Bulletin - 4; ftm, £10 nm.
     Educational Modules;   Books;   Booklets;
     Videos; prices vary.

Family Farmers' Association   (FFA)   1979

- ■ Osborne Newton, Aveton Gifford, KINGSBRIDGE, Devon,
     TQ7 4PE.   (chmn b/p)
     01548 852794   fax 01548 852794
     Chmn: Mrs Pippa Woods
- ▲ Un-incorporated Society
- ○ *F, *K; to represent the family farmer; to prevent the decline of
     rural areas; to make farming more accessible to new
     entrants
- ● LG
- M 250 i
- ¶ NL - 4; ftm.

© CBD Research Ltd · Beckenham · BR3 5JS · Tel 020 8650 7745 · Fax 020 8650 0768 · E-mail cbd@cbdresearch.com · www.cbdresearch.com

Family Heart Association
    merged in 2002 with the British Hyperlipidaemia Association to form
    Heart UK

Family Holiday Association   (FHA)
§   16 Mortimer St, LONDON, W1T 3JL.
     020 7436 3304
     a charity specialising in the provision of grants for deprived
         families under pressure so that they can have a one-week
         holiday as a family

Family Law Association of Scotland   (FLA)   1989
■   123½ Crown St, ABERDEEN, AB11 6HP.   (hsb)
     01224 593100   fax 01224 593200
     email anne@mcintoshmctaggart.com
     http://www.mcintoshmctaggart.com
     Sec: Anne G McTaggart (of McIntoshMcTaggart)
▲   Un-incorporated Society
○   *P; for solicitors involved in family law
●   Conf - Mtgs - ET - Inf
M   300 i

Family Law Bar Association   (FLBA)   1947
NR   2-3 Cursitor St (2nd floor), LONDON, EC4A 1NE.   (hsb)
     020 7242 1289
     http://www.flba.co.uk
     Admin: Carol Harris
▲   Un-incorporated Society
○   *P; for members of the Bar practising in the field of family law
         & cases involving children
M   c 1,300 i

Family Matters Institute   (FMI)   1988
NR   The Park, MOGGERHANGER, Beds, MK44 3RW.   (hq)
     01767 641002
     email family@familymatters.org.uk
     http://www.familymatters.org.uk
     Chief Exec: Matt Buttery
▲   Registered Charity
○   *R, *W; exists to mobilise church faith & community groups into
         action to strengthen & support marriage & family life
●   Conf - ET - Res - Exhib - Inf - LG - Parent support & advice on
         household finances

Family Mediation Scotland   (FMS)   1987
■   18 York Place, Edinburgh, EH1 3EP.   (hq)
     0845 119 2020   fax 0845 119 6089
     Chmn: Hugh Donald,   Dir: Mike Reid
▲   Company Limited by Guarantee
○   *N, *W; a coordinating body for 13 affiliated family mediation
         services operating throughout Scotland
     Family mediation is a voluntary process which enables
         separating or divorced parents to negotiate their own
         mutually acceptable resolutions to disputes relating to the
         continued parenting of their children
●   Conf - Mtgs - ET - Res - Stat - Inf - Lib - LG
<   Nat Family Mediation
M   13 org
¶   NL - 2.   AR.
     Various guidance leaflets & training videos.

Family Mediators' Association   (FMA)   1988
■   Grove House, Grove Rd, BRISTOL, BS6 6UN.   (hq)
     0117-946 7062   fax 0117-946 7181
     email info@fmassoc.co.uk   http://www.fmassoc.co.uk
     Chmn: Linda Glees
▲   Registered Charity
○   *P; to provide assistance through mediation for adults &
         children who are affected by family breakdown
Gp   Family mediators; Family mediator professional consultants;
         Family mediation training faculty
●   Conf - Mtgs - ET - Res
     Helpline: 0808 200 0033
<   UK Coll of Family Mediators
>   ADR [alternative dispute resolution] Gp
M   250 i
¶   NL - 4;   LM; both free.

Family Planning Association
    since 2005-6 **fpa**

Family Rights Group   (FRG)   1974
■   The Print House, 18 Ashwin St, LONDON, E8 3DL.   (hq)
     020 7923 2628   fax 020 7923 2683
     http://www.frg.org.uk
     Chief Exec: Cathy Ashley
▲   Company Limited by Guarantee; Registered Charity
○   *W; to promote policies which fully involve families in decisions
         about their own children; to advise parents & relations whose
         children are known to social services; to promote good
         practice by social workers & solicitors working with families
●   Conf - ET - Res - LG
     Advice line: 0800 731 1696 (Mon-Fri 1000-1200 + 1330-
     1530)
¶   Family Matters - 2;   Conference NL - 3;   AR; all ftm.

Family Welfare Association   (FWA)   1869
§   501-505 Kingsland Rd, LONDON, E8 4AU.   (hq)
     020 7254 6251   fax 020 7249 5443
     email fwa.headoffice@fwa.org.uk
     Chief Exec: Helen Dent
     A registered charity & non-membership body providing social
         work & social care services to families & individuals; it
         administers trusts for grants to people in desperate need &
         offers educational grant advice.

Family & Youth Concern
    since 2005-06 **Family Education Trust (Family & Youth
    Concern)**

Fan Manufacturers' Association   (FMA)   1979
■   2 Waltham Court, Milley Lane, Hare Hatch, READING, Berks,
     RG10 9TH.   (hq)
     0118-940 3416   fax 0118-940 6258
     email info@feta.co.uk   http://www.feta.co.uk/
     Dir Gen: C Sloan
○   *T; interests of fan manufacturers, irrespective of the final
         application of their products. The association covers fans &
         similar air moving devices of any type & size & for any
         application, including: heating, ventilating, air conditioning,
         industrial processing, fume & dust removal, pneumatic
         conveying, combustion, heat transfer, drying, mines & tunnel
         ventilation, power generation or any other purpose involving
         movement & control of air or other gases as defined in
         Eurovent Terminology Document ref 1/1 paragraph 2 &
         within the scope of British Standard 848/1979
Gp   Technical & Economic committees
●   Mtgs - ET - Res - Exhib - Stat - Expt - Inf
<   HEVAC; BSI; Fedn Envtl Tr Assns (FETA)
M   30 f

Fanderson: the official Gerry Anderson Appreciation Society 1981
- ■ PO Box 12, BRADFORD, W Yorks, BD10 0YE. (mail)
  http://www.fanderson.org.uk address
  Sec: Nick Williams
- ▲ Un-incorporated Society
- ○ *G; to promote the appreciation & preservation of Gerry Anderson productions - Thunderbirds & UFO & other TV series
- ● Conf - ET - Res - Exhib - Comp - Inf - PL
- M 1,000 i, UK / 400 i, o'seas
- ¶ FAB - 4; ftm only.

Farm 2002
- NR PO Box 51336, LONDON, N1 9XS.
  email info@farm.org.uk   http://www.farm.org.uk
- ○ *A; *K; 'fighting for a viable future for independent & family farms'

Farm Machinery Preservation Society Ltd (FMPS) 1968
- ■ 6 Lordship Rd, WRITTLE, Essex, CM1 3EH. (chmn/p)
  01245 420168
  Chmn: H W Preston
- ▲ Company Limited by Guarantee
- ○ *G, *K; to promote interest in & knowledge of vintage agriculture & horticulture machinery
- ● Mtgs - Exhib - VE
- < Fedn of Brit Historic Vehicle Clubs
- M 330 i
- ¶ NL - 4; free.

Farm Retail Association
in 2004 merged with the National Association of Farmers' Markets to form the **National Farmers' Retail & Markets Association**

Farm Tractor & Machinery Trade Association
- IRL c/o Irish Farm Centre, Bluebell, DUBLIN 12, Republic of Ireland.
  353 (1) 450 9954   fax 353 (1) 450 4420
  email info@ftmta.ie   http://www.ftmta.ie
  Chief Exec: Michael Moroney
- ○ *F, *T; farm & garden machinery industry

Farmers for Action (FFA) 2000
- NR Old Llanshien Farm, Llangovan, MONMOUTH, NP25 4BU.
  01291 690224
  email secretary@farmersforaction.org
  http://www.farmersforaction.org
- ○ *F, *K; to secure a sustainable level of income for farmers & growers

Farmers Club 1842
- ■ 3 Whitehall Court, LONDON, SW1A 2EL. (hq)
  020 7930 3751   fax 020 7839 7864
  http://www.thefarmersclub.com
  Chief Exec: Gp Capt G P Carson
- ○ *F; social club for those interested in agriculture; furthers knowledge of agriculture by educational activities
- ● Mtgs - Inf
- M 5,700 i
- ¶ Jnl - 6; ftm, £20 yr nm.

Farmers' Union of Wales (FUW) 1955
- NR Llys Amaeth, Plas Gogerddan, ABERYSTWYTH, Ceredigion, SY23 3BT. (hq)
  01970 820820   fax 01970 820821
  http://www.fuw.org.uk
- ▲ Un-incorporated Society
- Br 12
- ○ *F; to represent the interests of Welsh agriculture & rural Wales
- Gp Milk; Beef; Sheep; Tourism; Environment; Hill farming; Rural economy
- ● Conf - Mtgs - Exhib - SG - PL
- M 12,000 i
- ¶ Welsh Farmer (Y Tir) - 12; ftm.

Farming & Wildlife Advisory Group (FWAG) 1962
- NR National Agricultural Centre, Stoneleigh Park, KENILWORTH, Warks, CV8 2RX. (hq)
  024 7669 6699   fax 024 7669 6760
  email info@fwag.org.uk   http://www.fwag.org.uk
  Chief Exec & Sec: James Money-Kyrle
- ▲ Company Limited by Guarantee; Registered Charity
- Br 55
- ○ *F; provision of environmental & conservation advice & technical support to farmers & land managers throughout England, Scotland, Wales & Northern Ireland
- ● Conf - Mtgs - Res - Exhib - Comp - SG - Stat - Inf - VE - LG
- M i, c 17 f
- ¶ AR.   Booklets.

Farms for Schools (FFS)
- ■ Unit 4c Topland Farm, Cragg Rd, MYTHOLMROYD, W Yorks, HX7 5RW. (hq)
  01422 882708   fax 01422 885533
  email amanda-marsden@farmsforschools.org.uk
  http://www.farmsforschools.org.uk
  Chief Exec: Gary Richardson
- ▲ Registered Charity
- ○ *E, *F; 'to ensure that school trips to farms are safe, enjoyable & educationally worthwhile'
- ● Conf - Mtgs - ET - Inf
- < an initiative of the Nat Farmers' U
- M 140 farms
- ¶ NL - 4; free.

Farnborough Air Sciences Trust (FAST) 1990
- NR Trenchard House, 85 Farnborough Rd, FARNBOROUGH, Hants, GU14 6TF. (hq)
  01252 375050
  Chmn of Trustees: Dr G F Rowlands
- ▲ Registered Charity
- ○ *K; to establish an air sciences centre & museum detailing research done at the Royal Aircraft Establishment 1918-1990
- Gp Aeronautical research; Museums
- ● Mtgs - ET - Res - Inf - Lib - PL - LG
- M 700+ i, 5 f
- ¶ Fast News - 4; ftm, £2.50 nm.

Fast Legal Advisory Group
a group of the **Federation against Software Theft**

Fastener & Engineering Research Association
- NR National Metalforming Centre, 47 Birmingham Road, WEST BROMWICH, W Midlands, B70 6PY.
  0121 601 6350
  Gen Sec: J M Fletcher
- ○ *P

Fawcett Society   1866

NR   1-3 Berry St, LONDON, EC1V 0AA.   (hq)
       020 7253 2598   fax 020 7253 2599
       http://www.fawcettsociety.org.uk
       Dir: Dr Katherine Rake
▲   Company Limited by Guarantee
Br   local gps
○   *K; campaign for equality of women
●   Conf - Res - LG
M   2,000 i, 100 org
¶   Towards Equality - 4.
       Campaign reports.   AR.

Federation of Active Retirement Associations   (FARA)

IRL   Shamrock Chambers, 1-2 Eustace St, DUBLIN 2, Republic of
        Ireland.
        353 (1) 679 2142   fax 353 (1) 679 2142
        email fara@eircom.net   http://www.fara.ie
        Pres: Eithne Carey
○   *W

Federation of Aerospace Enterprises in Ireland   (FAEI)

IRL   Confederation House, 84-86 Lower Baggot St, DUBLIN 2,
        Republic of Ireland.
        353 (1) 605 1562   fax 353 (1) 638 1562
        email info@faei.ie   http://www.faei.ie
        Dir: Paul Kelly
○   *P
<   IBEC

Federation of Aerospace Support Services   (FASS)   2000

■   Charter House, White Gates, Clyst Rd, Topsham, EXETER,
        Devon, EX3 0DB.   (hsp/b)
        01392 875809   fax 01392 875809
        email jc@fass.org.uk   http://www.fass.org.uk
        Chief Exec: Jon Cousens
▲   Company Limited by Guarantee
○   *T; the supply of temporary workers to the aircraft maintenance
        industry
●   Mtgs - ET - LG
M   16 f, UK / 1 f, o'seas
¶   FASS Information - 1; free.

Federation of Artistic & Creative Therapy

§   Ground Floor, 29 Old St, LONDON, EC1V 9HL.
        020 7490 4140
        email fact1@btopenworld.com
        FACT runs hourly sessions for people with learning difficulties &
        disabilities who are supported by workers from a professional
        body. It also offers an outreach service, currently running
        sensory sessions in schools

Federation of Artistic Roller Skating

NR   10 The Broadway, THATCHAM, Berks, RG19 3JA.
        01635 877322   fax 01635 877323
        http://www.fars.co.uk
        Pres: Mike Ward
○   *S

**Federation of Associations for Country Sports in Europe
(FACE(UK))   1977**

NR   c/o Countryside Alliance, 367 Kennington Rd, LONDON,
        SE11 4PT.   (hsb)
        020 7840 9200   fax 020 7793 8899
        Sec: Col T P B Hoggarth
▲   Un-incorporated Society
○   *K; to support, maintain & promote the rights of all field
        sportsmen in the UK; it assists authorities by providing expert
        advice & information & monitors subsequent proposals &
        decisions
        This is the UK branch, the FACE hq is in Brussels
●   Mtgs - Inf - LG - Political lobbying in Europe
<   FACE-Europe
M   19 org
¶   Brochure.

Federation of Astronomical Societies   (FAS)   1974

■   10 Dovedale Rd, Perry Common, Erdington, BIRMINGHAM,
        B23 5BG.   (hsp)
        email secretary@fedastro.org.uk
        http://www.fedastro.org.uk
        Sec: Samuel George
▲   Un-incorporated Society
Br   Gibraltar
○   *N; to help & advise local astronomical societies
●   Inf - Conventions
<   Assn for Astronomy Educ
M   170 org
¶   FAS NL - 4; ftm only.   Hbk - 1; ftm, £4 nm.
        Astrocalendar - 1.

**Federation of Authorised Energy Rating Organisations
(FAERO)   1999**

■   c/o Elmhurst Energy Systems, Elmhurst Farm, Bow Lane,
        Withybrook, COVENTRY, Warks, CV7 9LQ.   (asa)
        01788 833386   fax 01788 832690
        email faero@elmhurstenergy.co.uk
        http://www.faero.org.uk
        Sec: Stephen J O'Hara
Br   3
○   *P; 'to promote the use of authorised SAP energy ratings in all
        areas of the domestic housing market'
●   ET - Res - LG
M   3 f

**Federation of Automatic Transmission Engineers   (FATE)
1978**

■   c/o Mrs Pamela Crummay, J P Automatics, Units 4a & 4b
        Peartree Industrial Estate, UPPER LANGFORD, N Somerset,
        BS40 5DJ.   (mail)
        07885 228595
        http://www.fedauto.co.uk address
○   *T; for rebuilders of automatic transmissions
●   Conf - Mtgs - ET - Res - Exhib - Expt - Inf - Lib
M   c 50 f

Federation of Bakers   (FOB)   1942

■ 6 Catherine St, LONDON, WC2B 5JW.   (hq)
    020 7420 7190   fax 020 7379 0542
    email info@bakersfederation.org.uk
    http://www.bakersfederation.org.uk
    Dir: Gordon Polson
▲ Un-incorporated Society
○ *T; representation of the UK's leading bakeries; a £2 billion
    industry producing 80% of the nation's bread
● Conf - Mtgs - ET - Stat - Inf - LG
< Assn Intle de la Boulangerie Industrielle (AIBI); Food & Drink
    Fedn; CBI
M 56 f
¶ LM;   AR.
    Information Sheets 1-21 (on various aspects of bread & bread-
    making).
    Health & Safety publications:
      Breathe Easy: a training video; £46.86.
      Federation Safety Memoranda; £75 (the set).
      Safety Information Notes; ftm.
      publications list available.

Federation of Bloodstock Agents (GB) Ltd   (FBA)   1978

NR 9 Paddocks Drive, NEWMARKET, Suffolk, CB8 9BE.   (hsb)
    01638 561116   fax 01638 560332
    http://www.bloodstock-agencies.com
    Sec: Andrew Mead
▲ Company Limited by Guarantee
○ *T; to represent bloodstock agents in Great Britain
● Mtgs - Liaison with horseracing industry through British
    Horseracing Board
M 45 f
¶ LM & Hbk - 1; free.

**Fédération Britannique des Alliances Françaises   (FBAF)
1905**

NR 1 Dorset Sq, LONDON, NW1 6PU.   (hq)
    020 7223 6439
    http://www.alliancefrancaise.org.uk
▲ Registered Charity
Br 60; 1,300
○ *X; to widen access to French language & culture by offering
    French classes & social & cultural events about France
● Conf - Mtgs - ET - Exam - Comp - Inf
< Alliance Française
M 8,000 i, 60 org, UK / 130,000 i, 1,300 org, o'seas
¶ Cultural Programmes - 1;   Language Class Brochures - 1;
    both free.

Federation of British Aquatic Societies   (FBAS)   1938

NR 44 Weekes Rd, RYDE, Isle of Wight, PO33 2TL.   (chmn/p)
    01983 613575
    http://www.fbas.co.uk
    Chmn: Les Pearce
▲ Un-incorporated Society
○ *N; all aspects of fishkeeping, breeding, & showing

Federation of British Artists   (FBA)   1961

■ 17 Carlton House Terrace, LONDON, SW1Y 5BD.   (hq)
    020 7930 6844   fax 020 7839 7830
    http://www.mallgalleries.org.uk
    Co Sec: John Sayers
▲ Company Limited by Guarantee; Registered Charity
○ *A; to provide exhibition facilities for member societies
● Conf - Mtgs - Exhib - Comp - SG - Commissions bureau
M 9 org:
      Hesketh Hubbard Art Society
      New English Art Club
      Pastel Society
      Royal Institute of Oil Painters
      Royal Institute of Painters in Water Colours
      Royal Society of British Artists
      Royal Society of Marine Artists
      Royal Society of Portrait Painters
      Society of Wildlife Artists
¶ NL.   Catalogues of each society's exhibitions.

Federation of British Bonsai Societies   (FOBBS)   1962

■ 32 Giles Close, Hedge End, SOUTHAMPTON, Hants,
    SO30 2TH.   (sp)
    01489 789962
    email paul@eslinger.com   http://www.fobbsbonsai.co.uk
    Hon Sec: Paul Eslinger
▲ Company Limited by Guarantee
○ *H, *N; to educate & promote the ancient art of bonsai
    (training of miniature trees in pots)
Gp Friends of the National Bonsai Collection
● ET - Exhib - Comp - Inf - PL
< Eur Bonsai Assn; R Horticl Soc
M 45 org
¶ NL (in Bonsai Europe published in the Netherlands) - 6.

Federation of British Conservatoires
    since 2003 has become **Conservatoires UK**

Federation of British Cremation Authorities   (FBCA)   1924

■ 41 Salisbury Rd, CARSHALTON, Surrey, SM5 3HA.   (sb)
    020 8669 4521
    Sec: D McCallum
○ *T; practice of cremation & administration & operation of
    crematoria
● Conf - Mtgs - Res - ET - Exhib - Stat - Inf
M 18 f, 183 org (mainly local authorities)
¶ Resurgam - 4; ftm.   Code of practice.
    Technical leaflets & booklets.   AR.

Federation of British Electrotechnical & Allied Manufacturers' Associations
    see **BEAMA: British Electrotechnical & Allied Manufacturers'
    Associations**

** Federation of British Engineers' Tool Manufacturers
    Organisation lost: see Introduction paragraph 3

Federation of British Fire Organisations   (FOBFO)   1963

NR London Rd, MORETON-in-MARSH, Glos, GL56 0RH.   (asa)
    01608 812500
    Contact: Jonathan O'Neill
▲ Un-incorporated Society
○ *N, *T; to promote the services of constituent member
    organisations, both nationally & internationally in the fight
    against fire
Gp Intl Technical Committee for the Prevention & Extinction of
    Fire (CITF); Fire equipment trade
    Conferencing administration carried out by Fire FOBFO Ltd
● Conf - Mtgs - Exhib - SG - LG
< Comité Technique Intl de Prévention et d'Extinction du
    Feu (CITF)
M 18 f & org including Institution of Fire Safety
¶ [Three magazines produced by constituent orgs].

Federation of British Hand Tool Manufacturers (FBHTM) 1944

- ■ c/o Institute of Spring Technology, Henry St, SHEFFIELD, S Yorks, S3 7EQ. (hq)
  0114-278 9143 fax 0114-275 5573
  email info@britishtools.com
  http://www.britishtools.com
  Assn Dir: J R Markham
- ○ *T; interests of manufacturers of hand tools
- Gp Construction Fixings Association; Engineers' Hand Tools Association; Horticultural & Contractors Tools Association; Powder Actuated Systems Association (dormant); Woodworkers, Builders & Miscellaneous Tools Association
- ● Conf - Mtgs - Exhib - Stat - Expt - Inf - LG - Standardisation with BSI & ISO
- < Comité Eur de l'Outillage (CEO);
- > Construction Fixings Assn; Engrs' Hand Tools Assn; Horticl & Contractors' Tools Assn; Powder Actuated Systems Assn
- M 30 f

Federation of British Historic Vehicle Clubs (FBHVC) 1988

- ■ Kernshill, Shute St, Stogumber, TAUNTON, Somerset, TA4 3TU. (sp/b)
  01984 656995 fax 01984 656762
  email admin@fbhvc.co.uk http://www.fbhvc.co.uk
  Sec: Jim Whyman
- ▲ Company Limited by Guarantee
- ○ *G, *K; to present the view of the UK historic vehicle movement to government. The aim is 'to uphold the freedom to continue the use without unreasonable, or legal, administrative restrictions of all mechanically propelled road vehicles & to encourage laws & procedures which facilitate their use, preservation, documentation & display'
- ● Conf - Inf - LG - Monitoring proposed legislation - Campaigning
- > Classic British Quality Charter
- M 1,000 i, 200 f, c 350 org
- ¶ NL - 6; ftm, £11 yr nm.

Federation of British Port Wholesale Fish Merchants Associations 1928

- ■ Wharncliffe Rd, Fish Docks, GRIMSBY, Lincs, DN31 3QJ. (s/b)
  01472 350022 fax 01472 240775
  email ce@grimsbyfma.com
  Sec: Steve Norton
- ▲ Company Limited by Guarantee
- ○ *N; a federation of fish merchants associations collective lobbying on behalf of the seafood industry
- ● Inf - LG
- > Grimsby (& Hull) Fish Merchants Assn(s)
- M 7,200 f

Federation of British Tape Recordists
    since 2002 **British Sound Recording Association**

Federation of Building Specialist Contractors (FBSC) 1970

- NR Unit 9 Lakeside Industrial Estate, STANTON HARCOURT, Oxon, OX29 5SL. (hq)
  01865 883508
  Dir: M Fitchett
- ▲ Un-incorporated Society
- ○ *T; for specialist sub-contractors in the building industry
- M f

Federation of Chefs Scotland (FCS) 1994

- ■ 2 Helenslee Court, Kirktonhill, DUMBARTON, G82 4HT. (hsb/p)
  01698 232603 fax 01698 232600
  email nthomson@motherwell.co.uk
  http://www.scottishchefs.com
  Sec: Neil Thomson
- ▲ Un-incorporated Society
- ○ *P; promoting excellence in the art of professional cookery
- ● Conf - Mtgs - ET - Exhib - Comp
- < Wld Assn Cooks Socs (WACS)
- M 200 i, 4 f

Federation of Children's Book Groups (FCBG) 1968

- ■ 2 Bridge Wood View, Horsforth, LEEDS, W Yorks, LS18 5PE. (hq)
  0113-258 8910
  email info@fcbg.org.uk http://www.fcbg.org.uk
  Hon Secs: Sinead & Martin Kromer
- ▲ Registered Charity
- Br 40
- ○ *A; 'to bring children & good books together; to foster a love of books & reading in children'
- ● Conf - Mtgs - Exhib - Comp - Inf - Children's Book Award
- M 110 i, 125 f (libraries, schools, publishers etc), 40 groups, UK / 3 i, o'seas
- ¶ NL - 3; 50p m only.
  Booklists; ftm, 15p nm.

Federation of City Farms & Community Gardens (FCFCG) 1980

- NR The GreenHouse, Hereford St, Bedminster, BRISTOL, BS3 4NA. (hq)
  0117-923 1800 fax 0117-923 1900
  email admin@farmgarden.org.uk
  http://www.farmgarden.org.uk
  Dir: Jeremy Iles
- ▲ Company Limited by Guarantee; Registered Charity
- ○ *F, *H, *V; supports, promotes & represents city farms, community gardens & similar organisations across the UK
- ● Conf - Exhib - Inf - Lib - LG
- < Eur Fedn City Farms; CEE; NCVO; Soil Assn; Thrive; Nat Soc of Allotment & Leisure Gardens; HDRA; Greenspace
- M 300 org
- ¶ Growing Places (Members NL) - 4; ftm only.
  Public NL - 2; AR; both free.

Federation of Clothing Designers & Executives (FCDE) 1943

- NR 36 Convent Close, HITCHIN, Herts, SG5 1QN. (hsp)
  01462 457872
  Hon Gen Sec: A Cannon Jones
- ▲ Un-incorporated Society
- Br 3
- ○ *T; technical federation for the garment industry (working & independent members) covering manufacture, IT, retail, design technology, & utilities
- ● Conf - Mtgs - VE - Social
- M 130 i, London College of Fashion, UK / 10 i, o'seas

Federation of Cocoa Commerce (FCC) 1929

- NR Cannon Bridge House, 1 Cousin Lane, LONDON, EC4R 3XX. (hq)
  020 7379 2884 fax 020 7379 2389
  email fcca@liffe.com http://www.cocoafederation.com
  Chief Exec: P M Sigley
- ▲ Company Limited by Guarantee
- ○ *T; to promote, protect & regulate the cocoa trade
- ● Conf - Mtgs - ET - Res - SG - Inf - Arbitration system for settlement of disputes without resort to the courts
- < Intl Cocoa Trade Fedn (ICTF); Eur Community Cocoa Trade Org (ECCTO)
- M c 100 f
- ¶ News Reports - ftm daily via email. Contract Book.
- ✗ 2002 Cocoa Association of London

Federation of Commercial Audio Visual Libraries Ltd
        see **FOCAL - Federation of Commercial Audio Visual Libraries Ltd**

Federation of Commodity Associations   (FCA)   1943
■   GAFTA House - 6 Chapel Place, Rivington St, LONDON,
        EC2A 3SH.   (hq)
        020 7814 9666   fax 020 7814 8383
        Sec: Mrs Pamela Kirby Johnson
▲   Company Limited by Guarantee
○   *N, *T; to protect the interests of European commodity
        associations
Gp   C'ees: Legal & arbitration; Shipping; Taxation
●   Mtgs - ET - SG - Expt - Inf
<   Intl Cham of Comm; Freight Transport Assn
M   c 100 f & org
¶   Book of Rules & Regulations (incl LM); m only.

Federation of Communication Services   (FCS)   1981
NR   Burnhill Business Centre, Providence House, Burrell Row,
        BECKENHAM, Kent, BR3 1AT.   (hq)
        020 8249 6363   fax 0870 120 5927
        email fcs@fcs.org.uk   http://www.fcs.org.uk
        Chief Exec: Mrs Jacqui Brooks
▲   Company Limited by Guarantee
○   *T; to represent the views of the mobile & telecommunications
        industry
Gp   Mobile phone mfrs; Mobile phone service providers & resellers;
        Communications equipment installers; Independent dealers,
        retailers, & distributors; Private mobile radio; Common base
        station operators
●   Conf - Mtgs - Exhib - Inf - LG - Industry promotion - PR -
        Lobbying
<   Mobile Gateway Operators Assn; Onsite Paging Assn; Mobile
        Radio Training Trust; Assn of Communications Services
        Providers; Fixed Service Providers Assn
M   2 i, 150 f, 2 org
¶   FCS Bulletin - 5/6; ftm only.

**Federation for Community Development Learning   (FCDL)
1977**
■   Furnival House (4th floor), 48 Furnival Gate, SHEFFIELD,
        S Yorks, S1 4QP.
        0114-273 9391   fax 0114-276 2377
        email info@fcdl.org.uk   http://www.fcdl.org.uk
        Head of Agency: Janice Marks
▲   Company Limited by Guarantee; Registered Charity
○   *E; to support the development of communities through the
        advancement & promotion of community development
        learning at local, regional & national levels; to create
        relevant opportunities for good quality training &
        qualifications
Gp   Support for Ubuntu - the national training network for Black
        Minority Ethnic practitioners who share an interest in
        promoting & developing community development from Black
        perspectives
●   Conf - Mtgs - ET - Res - Inf - Lib
M   43 i, 133 f
¶   Federation News (NL) - 4; ftm only.
        Resource Packs for the Community Development
            Programme; £54 m, £60 nm.
        Get Accredited (guidance pack); £9 m, £10 nm.
        [see website for other publications].
×   2003 (1 April) Federation of Community Work Training Groups

Federation against Copyright Theft   (FACT)   1982
NR   Unit 7 Victory Business Centre, Worton Rd, ISLEWORTH, Middx,
        TW7 6DB.   (hq)
        020 8568 6646   fax 020 8560 6364
        email bc@fact-uk.org.uk   http://www.fact-uk.org.uk
        Dir Gen: Brian Conlon
▲   Company Limited by Guarantee
○   *N; copyright protection of motion pictures
Gp   Data Federation
<   Motion Picture Assn
M   20 f

Federation of Crafts & Commerce   (FCC)   1983
■   Federation House, 4 The Briars, Waterberry Drive,
        WATERLOOVILLE, Hants, PO7 7YH.   (hq)
        023 9223 7010   fax 023 9223 2120
        Gen Sec: David Pinnock
▲   Company Limited by Guarantee
○   *T; provision of management services for small & medium sized
        businesses
Gp   Credit management; Debt recovery; Advisory services; Status
        checks etc
●   Inf - Status enquiry - Debt recovery - Legal advisory services &
        many other similar services
M   10,000 i & f
¶   FCC News (NL) - 4; ftm.

Federation of Dredging Contractors   1950
NR   c/o Alliotts, 9 Kingsway, LONDON, WC2B 6XF.   (asa)
        020 7240 9971   fax 020 7240 9692
        Sec: N Armstrong
○   *T; to further the interests of the UK dredging industry
M   3 f

Federation of Drug & Alcohol Professionals
        is the trade name of **National Association of Alcohol & Drug
        Abuse Counsellors**

Federation of Drum Reconditioners
        2004 merged with the Association of Drum Manufacturers & the Rigid
        Intermediate Bulk Container Association to form the **Industrial
        Packaging Association**

Federation of the Electronics Industry
        in 2002 merged with the Computing Services & Software Association
        to form **Intellect**

Federation of Employed Door Supervisors & Security
NR   PO Box 57007, LONDON, EC1N 1TN.
        0870 756 5555   fax 020 7253 2172
        http://www.fedforum.com
○   *U

Federation of Engine Re-Manufacturers   (FER)   1937
NR   59 Mewstone Ave, Wembury, PLYMOUTH, Devon, PL9 0JT.
        (sb)
        01752 863681   fax 01752 863682
        http://www.fer.co.uk
        Sec: Brian Ludford
○   *T; for engine reconditioners & their suppliers; to discourage
        unscrupulous traders
●   Mtgs - ET - Exhib - Comp - VE - LG
M   165 f, UK / 2 f, o'seas
¶   Jnl.

Federation of Engineering Design Companies Ltd   (FEDC) 1956
NR   PO Box 700, RAYLEIGH, Essex, SS6 7AT.   (hq)
    01268 772996   fax 01268 772996
    http://www.fedc.org.uk
    Gen Sec: Grace Thomas
▲   Company Limited by Guarantee
○   *T; 'interests of companies engaged in or contributing to the
    fields of engineering design, technical recruitment, technical
    publications, information services & associated professions at
    government & trade union level'
●   Conf - Mtgs - ET - Stat - Expt - Empl - LG
M   29 f

Federation of English Language Course Organisations Ltd
    was the second title of the Association of Recognised English
    Language Services, which on 12 May 2004 amalgamated with the
    British Association for State English Language Teaching to become
    English UK

Federation of Entertainment Unions   (FEU)   1990
■   1 Highfield, Twyford, WINCHESTER, Hants, SO21 1QR.   (sp)
    01962 713134   fax 01962 713134
    email harris.s@btconnect.com
    Sec: Steve Harris
○   *U, *N
Gp   Committees: European; Training & equal opportunities; Film &
    electronic media
●   Mtgs - LG
M   170,000 i in 7 org

Federation of Environmental Trade Associations   (FETA)   1977
■   2 Waltham Court, Milley Lane, Hare Hatch, READING, Berks,
    RG10 9TH.   (hq)
    0118-940 3416   fax 0118-940 6258
    email info@feta.co.uk   http://www.feta.co.uk/
    Dir Gen: C Sloan
○   *N, *T; 'common action concerning environmental control in
    buildings'
M   11 assns:
    Air Cleaner Manufacturers' Association
    British Flue & Chimney Manufacturers' Association
    British Refrigeration Association
    Building Controls Industry Association
    Chilled Ceilings Association
    Fan Manufacturers' Association
    Heat Pump Association
    Heating, Ventilating & Air Conditioning Manufacturers'
      Association
    Hose Manufacturers & Suppliers Association
    Residential Ventilation Association
    Smoke Control Association

** Federation of Ethical Stage Hypnotists
    Organisation lost: see Introduction paragraph 3

Federation of Family History Societies   (FFHS)   1974
■   PO Box 2425, COVENTRY, Warks, CV5 6YX.   (admin/b)
    07041 492032
    email info@ffhs.org.uk   http://www.ffhs.org.uk
    Admin: Maggie Loughran
▲   Company Limited by Guarantee; Registered Charity
○   *G, *L, *N; to bring together societies with a common interest in
    genealogy, heraldry & allied subjects
●   Conf - ET
M   163 org, UK / 54 org, o'seas
¶   Family History News & Digest - 2; ftm.
    List of specialised publications.

Federation of Garden & Leisure Equipment Exporters Ltd
    see **GARDENEX: the Federation of Garden & Leisure
    Manufacturers Ltd**

Federation for Healthcare Science   2002
NR   12 Coldbath Sq, LONDON, EC1R 5HL.
    020 7833 5807
    http://www.fedhcs.net
○   *P

Federation of Heating Spare Stockists
NR   PO Box 249, Heacham, KING'S LYNN, Norfolk, PE31 7XD.
    (sp)
    01485 572219   fax 01485 570885
    email enquiries@heat-spares.co.uk
    http://www.heat-spares.co.uk
○   *T
M   f

Federation of Holistic Therapists   (FHT)   1962
■   18 Shakespeare Business Centre, Hathaway Close, EASTLEIGH,
    Hants, SO50 4SR.   (hq)
    0870 420 2022   fax 023 8062 2499
    email info@fht.org.uk   http://www.fht.org.uk
    Chief Exec: Mrs Jacqueline Palmer
▲   Company Limited by Guarantee
○   *P; to promote & maintain the highest standards of
    professionalism in holistic therapies (aromatherapy,
    reflexology, massage) & health & fitness therapies & beaty
    therapies
Gp   International Federation of Health & Beauty Therapists;
    International Council of Holistic Therapists; International
    Council of Health Fitness & Sports Therapists; Association of
    Therapy Lecturers; Profl Assn of Clinical Therapists; Health &
    Beauty Emplrs Fedn
●   Conf - ET
M   21,000 i
¶   The International Therapist - 6; ftm only.
    Note: The FHT has formed the Professional Association of
    Clinical Therapists (PACT), to represent the interests of all our
    clinical therapists & to givethem a choice as to their current
    or future employment. PACT is recognised by the bodies
    currently working towards formalised recognition

Federation of Image Consultants Ltd   (TFIC)   1988
NR   13 Dunstable Rd, Studham, DUNSTABLE, Beds, LU6 2QG.
    (regd/off)
    07010 701018
    Pres: Frances Bodington
▲   Company Limited by Guarantee
Br   New Zealand
○   *P; personal presentation, appearance & image development
    for men, women, business clients & corporations
●   Conf - Mtgs - Exam - Exhib - Inf
<   Assn of Image Consultants Intl (AICI)(USA)
M   200 i, UK / 6 i, o'seas
¶   TFIC News - 2.   Image Update - 2.

Federation of Independent Detectorists   (FID)   1982
NR   44 Heol Dulais, Birchgrove, SWANSEA, W Glam, SA7 9LT.
    (hsp)
    01792 814615   fax 01792 814615
    Hon Sec: Colin Hanson
▲   Un-incorporated Society
Br   2
○   *G; for those interested in recreational metal detecting
Gp   Emergency call out for veterinary tranquilliser dart recovery
●   Conf - Exhib - Comp - Inf - LG - Insurance - Advice line - Free
    recovery service (metal items)
M   5,000 i, UK / 750 i, o'seas
¶   NL - 4; ftm only.

Federation of Independent Mines of Great Britain   (FIM) 1948

■ 14 Moorland Avenue, BARNSLEY, S Yorks, S70 6PQ.   (hsp)
01226 244437
email d7l7b7@gmail.com
Hon Sec: Douglas Bulmer
▲ Un-incorporated Society
○ *T; to represent the interests of coal producers & associated industry
● Mtgs - ET - Exam - Stat - Expt - Inf - LG - Advice on legal matters (common, employment & mining law)
\> Coal Pro, Wakefield
M 12 f, 2 museums

Federation of Independent Practitioner Organisations   (FIPO)

NR 14 Queen Anne's Gate, LONDON, SW1H 9AA.
020 7222 0975
email info@fipo.org   http://www.fipo.org
○ *M, *N; to represent medical professional organisations in Britain that have private practice committees

Federation of Information & Advice Centres
since July 2003 operating as **Advice UK**

** Federation of Internet Traders

Organisation lost: see Introduction paragraph 3

Federation of Irish Beekeepers' Associations   (FIBKA)

IRL Ballinakill, ENFIELD, Co Meath, Republic of Ireland.
353 (46) 954 1433
email mgglee@eircom.net
http://www.irishbeekeeping.ie
Hon Sec: Michael Gleeson
○ *F

Federation of Irish Societies   (FIS)   1971

NR 95 White Lion St, LONDON, N1 9PF.   (hq)
020 7833 1226   fax 020 7833 3214
○ *X; to promote the interests of the Irish community in GB through welfare, cultural & youth activities

Federation of Jewellery Manufacturers of Ireland

IRL Marina House, Clarence St, DÚN LAOGHAIRE, Republic of Ireland.
353 (1) 663 8700   fax 353 (1) 663 8704
Chmn: Joe Harbourne
Sec: Ida Kiernan
○ *T

Federation of Licensed Victuallers Associations   (FLVA)   1992

■ 126 Bradford Rd, BRIGHOUSE, W Yorks, HD6 4AU.   (hq)
01484 710534   fax 01484 718647
email admin@flva.fsbusiness.co.uk
http://www.flva.co.uk
Chief Exec: W A Payne
○ *T; to offer help & advice to members with any problems arising from the day-to-day running of their business, whether as tenants, free traders or lessees
● Conf - Mtgs - Exhib - Inf - VE - LG
\< UK & Ireland Licensed Trade Assn
M 700 i, 9 f
¶ NL - 4; free.   Publicans Guide to the Health & Safety Act.
Guidance Notes; both ftm only:
Food Safety;
General Food Hygiene Regulations.

Federation of Manufacturing Opticians   (FMO)   1917

■ 199 Gloucester Terrace, LONDON, W2 6LD.   (hq)
020 7298 5123   fax 020 7298 5120
email info@fmo.co.uk   http://www.fmo.co.uk
Contact: the Hon Sec
▲ Company Limited by Guarantee
○ *N, *T; a federation for the ophthalmic optical manufacturing & distributing industry consisting of 4 trade associations each concerned with a separate branch of the industry
Gp Optra Exhibitions UK; Optical Equipment Manufacturers' & Suppliers' Association; Optical Frame Importers' & Manufacturers' Association; Ophthalmic Lens Manufacturers' & Distributors' Association
● Conf - Mtgs - Exhib
\< EUROM
M 152 f, UK / 1 f, o'seas
¶ In-Focus (NL) - 3;   AR (incl LM) - 1; both ftm only.

Federation of Master Builders   (FMB)   1941

■ Gordon Fisher House, 14-15 Great James St, LONDON, WC1N 3DP.   (hq)
020 7242 7583   fax 020 7405 0854
email central@fmb.org.uk
http://www.findabuilder.co.uk
Dir Gen: Ian P Davis
▲ Company Limited by Guarantee
Br 11
○ *T; for the construction industry
● Conf - Mtgs - ET - Exhib - Inf - Lib - VE - Empl - LG
\< Eur Bldrs Fedn
M 13,000 f
¶ Masterbuilder - 12; ftm, £3.50 each nm.

Federation of Multiple Sclerosis Therapy Centres
in June 2002 became the National Multiple Sclerosis Therapy Centres, which in 2003 changed name to **Multiple Sclerosis Therapy Centres**

Federation of Museums & Art Galleries in Wales

NR Abergavenny Museum & Castle, Castle St, ABRGAVENNY, Gwent, NP7 5EE.   (hsb)
01873 854282   fax 01873 736004
http://www.welshmuseumsfederation.org.uk
Hon Sec: Rachael Rogers
▲ Un-incorporated Society
○ *P; to encourage the highest professional standards within the museum profession in Wales
● Mtgs - ET
\< Museums Assn
M 30 i, 20 f
¶ Y Mag - 2; ftm.

Federation of Music Services

NR 7 Courthouse St, Otley, LEEDS, LS21 3AN.
01943 463311
Chief Exec: Colin Brackley Jones
○ *D; 'to advance the education of the public in the art of music'
● Conf - Mtgs - ET - Stat - Inf - LG
M 130+ org

Federation of National Self Catering Associations   (FoNSCA)   1996

■ l/o EASCO, PO Box 567, HAYES, Middx, UB3 9EW.   (v-chmn/b)
020 7078 7329
email ce@englishselfcatering.co.uk
Vice-Chmn: Martin Sach
○ *T; furthering the interests of self catering holiday accommodation providers; promoting the use of self catering accommodation & maintaining standards within the sector
● Mtgs - Inf - LG
M 4 org, UK / 1 org, o'seas

Federation of Oils, Seeds & Fats Associations Ltd (FOSFA) 1970

- ■ 20 St Dunstan's Hill, LONDON, EC3R 8NQ. (hq)
  020 7283 5511
  Chief Exec: Stuart Logan
- ▲ Company Limited by Guarantee
- ○ *N, *T
- Gp Oils & fats; Oilseeds & HPS groundnuts
- ● Mtgs - ET - Res - Inf - LG
- < African Groundnut Coun (AGC); Amer Oil Chemists
  Soc (AOCS); AOAC Intl; Argentine Oil Ind Chamber (CIARA);
  Deutscher Verband des Grosshandels mit Ölen, Fetten und
  Ölrohstoffen eV (GROFOR); Eur Oleochemicals & Allied
  Products Gp (APAG); Intl Assn of Seed Crushers (IASC);
  Fishmeal & Fish Oil Org (IFFO); Intl Margarine Assn
  Countries Europe (IMACE); Malayan Edible Oil Mfrs
  Assn (MEOMA); Nat Inst Oilseed Products (NIOP); Nat
  Renderers Assn (NRA); Netherlands Oils, Fats & Oilseeds Tr
  Assn (NOFOTA); Palm Oil Refiners Assn Malaysia (PORAM);
  Seed Crushers & Oil Processors Assn (SCOPA)
- M 800 f
- ¶ NL - 4. FOSFA International Manual. Contracts.
  Rules of Arbitration. Codes of Practice.

Federation of Ophthalmic & Dispensing Opticians (FODO) 1985

- NR 199 Gloucester Terrace, LONDON, W2 6LD. (hq)
  020 7298 5151
  Chief Exec & Gen Sec: Robert G Hughes
- ▲ Company Limited by Guarantee
- ○ *T; representation of optical employers & businesses including
  both dispensing & ophthalmic practices; 'FODO represents
  all of the high street companies & most of the large groups'
- Gp FODO educational charity
- ● Mtgs - SG - Stat - Empl - LG
- < Eur Coun of Optometry & Optics
- M 140 f
- ¶ Optics at a Glance - 1; Vouchers at a Glance - 1;
  Opticians in Business - 12;
  Hbk (inc AR & accounts) - 1; all free.

Federation of Overseas Property Developers, Agents & Consultants (FOPDAC) 1973

- NR Suite 2, 17 Alpine Rd, HOVE, E Sussex, BN3 5HG. (asa)
  0870 350 1223 fax 0870 350 1233
  email info@fopdac.com http://www.fopdac.com
- ▲ Un-incorporated Society
- ○ *T; to seek to protect the interests of those who have decided to
  purchase an overseas property
- ● Mtgs - ET - Exhib - Stat - Inf - Awards to best property journalist
  etc
- < Confédn Eur de l'Immobilier
- M 62 f, UK / 19 f, o'seas
- ¶ LM. Brochure.

Federation of Petroleum Suppliers Ltd (FPS) 1979

- ■ 3 Slaters Court, Princess St, KNUTSFORD, Cheshire,
  WA16 6BW. (hq)
  01565 631313 fax 01565 631314
  email info@fpsonline.co.uk http://www.fpsonline.co.uk
  Chief Exec: Susan Hancock
- ▲ Company Limited by Guarantee
- Br 9; Republic of Ireland
- ○ *T; interests of oil distribution industry
- ● Conf - Mtgs - Comp - ET - Exhib - Stat - Inf - LG
- M 3 i, 230 f, UK / 30 f, o'seas
- ¶ Publication - 4; ftm, single complimentary copies only nm.

Federation of Piling Specialists (FPS) 1964

- NR 83 Copers Cope Rd, BECKENHAM, Kent, BR3 1NR. (asa)
  020 8663 0947 fax 020 8663 0949
  email fps@fps.org.uk http://www.fps.org.uk
  Sec: Dianne Jennings
- ▲ Company Limited by Guarantee
- ○ *T; specialist subcontractors carrying out all aspects of
  foundation construction & design
- ● Mtgs
- < Eur Fedn of Foundation Contrs; Nat Specialist Contrs Coun;
  Ground Forum
- M 18 f
- ¶ LM. AR; m only.

Federation of Plastering & Drywall Contractors (FPDC)

- ■ The Building Centre, 26 Store St, LONDON, WC1E 7BT. (hq)
  020 7580 3545 fax 020 7580 3288
  email admin@fpdc.org http://www.fpdc.org
  Dir: Emma Tomlin
- ▲ Un-incorporated Association
- ○ *T
- ● Conf - Mtgs - ET - Comp - LG
- < Nat Specialist Contrs Coun
- M c 230 f
- ¶ Spec Finish - 4; AR - 1; both free.
- ✕ 2005-06 Scottish Plastering & Drylining Association (merged)

Federation of Prisoners' Families Support Groups
since 2002 **Action for Prisoners' Families**

Federation of Private Residents' Associations (FPRA) 1971

- ■ 59 Mile End Rd, COLCHESTER, Essex, CO4 5BU. (hq)
  0871 200 3324; 01206 855888 fax 020 8989 3153
  email info@fpra.org.uk http://www.fpra.org.uk
  Chief Exec: Robert Levene
- ▲ Company Limited by Guarantee
- ○ *K; advice to members on leasehold & freehold management
  issues
- ● Mtgs - Inf - LG
- M 500 org
- ¶ NL - 4; ftm only.
  Information pack (advice on forming a residents'
  association); £10.

Federation of Railway Clubs

- NR 24 Robin Goodfellow Lane, March, Cambs, PE15 8JA. (hsp)
  01354 654287 fax 01354 654287
  Sec: Terry Stevens
- ○ *K

Federation of Recorded Music Societies (FRMS) 1936

- ■ 2 Fulmar Place, Meir Park, STOKE-ON-TRENT, Staffs,
  ST3 7QF. (regd)
  01782 399291 office
  Hon Sec: Tony Baines
- ▲ Company Limited by Guarantee
- Br 230 affiliated societies
- ○ *D, *N; to promote the development & extension of societies or
  organisations using recorded music as part of their activities
- ● Conf - Mtgs
- M 12,000 i, UK / 80 i, o'seas
- ¶ Bulletin - 2; £1.75.

Federation of the Retail Licensed Trade Northern Ireland (FRLTNI) 1872

NR   91 University St, BELFAST, BT7 1HP.   (hq)
        028 9032 7578   fax 028 9032 7578
        email enquiries@ulsterpubs.com
        http://www.ulsterpubs.com
        Chief Exec: Nicola Carruthers
▲   Un-incorporated Society
○   *T; promotion of the licensed trade; advice & information for members
●   Conf - Mtgs - ET - Res - Inf - LG
<   UK & Ireland Licensed Trade Assn
M   1,200 i
¶   Federation section within Catering & Licensing Review - 12; ftm.

Federation of Rural Community Councils
        merged in 2003 with **Action with Communities in Rural England**

** **Federation of Scottish Skateboarders**
        Organisation lost: see Introduction paragraph 3

Federation of Scottish Theatre Ltd   (FST)

NR   c/o Theatre Workshop, 34 Hamilton Place, EDINBURGH, EH3 5AX.   (hq)
        0131-220 6393   fax 0131-220 6373
        email fst@scottishtheatre.org
        Dir: Lizzi Nicoll
▲   Company Limited by Guarantee
○   *N, *P; to act as the voice of theatre in Scotland; to work with unions, the Scottish Arts Council, local authorities & other organisations to further interests & development of the theatre industry in Scotland
●   Conf - Mtgs - Res - Inf - Empl - LG
M   50 f

Federation of Services for Unmarried Parents & their Children
        since 2005 **National Federation of Services for Unmarried Parents & their Children**

Federation of Shoe Repair Suppliers
        since 2003 **Cutting Edge**

Federation of Sidecar Clubs   (FOSC)   1958

NR   97 Mandeville Rd, HERTFORD, SG13 8JL.   (mem/sp)
        Mem Sec: Steve Wood
○   *N, *G; sidecars & motorcycle combinations
●   Conf - Mtgs - Exhib - Stat - Inf - Lib - Rallies
M   c 400 i
¶   Outlook.

Federation of Small Businesses   (FSB)   1974

■   Press & Parliamentary Office, 2 Catherine Place, LONDON, SW1E 6HF.   (hq)
        020 7592 8100   fax 020 7828 5919
▲   Company Limited by Guarantee
Br   200; Belgium
○   *K, *T; lobby organisation for small businesses
●   Conf - Mtgs - Stat - Inf - Lib - LG
<   Eur Alliance for Small Businesses (ESBA)
M   195,000 f
¶   First Voice - 6.

Federation against Software Theft   (FAST)   1984

NR   York House, 18 York Rd, MAIDENHEAD, Berks, SL6 1SF.   (hq)
        01628 622121
        http://www.fast.org.uk
        Chief Exec: Geoffrey Webster
▲   Company Limited by Guarantee
○   *T; protecting the interests of member companies from copyright infringement; to counter software piracy & increase public awareness of the damage to investment & innovation from unauthorised copying - to promote the legal use of software
Gp   Fast Legal Advisory Group (FLAG); Data Federation
●   Conf - ET - Inf - LG
<   Computing Services & Software Assn (CSSA); Business Software Alliance (BSA); Software Publishers Association (SPA)(USA)
M   C 2,700 F
¶   Fast (NL) - 2;   Industry Bulletin - 3/4; both ftm.
        Corporate Bulletin - 3/4; ftm.
        Information/Audit Pack;   Industry Membership Brochure.

Federation of Specialist Restaurants   (FSR)   2006

■   PO Box 416, SURBITON, Surrey, KT1 9BJ.   (hq)
        020 8397 7517   fax 020 8397 4593
        email groveint@aol.com   http://www.menu2menu.com
        Sec: Colleen Grove
▲   Un-incorporated Society
○   *T; to publicise & further the interests of UK restaurants offering a specialist cuisine
●   Res - Stat - Inf - PL
M   200 f
¶   Publications on website only.

Federation of Sports & Play Associations   (FSPA)   1919

■   Federation House, STONELEIGH PARK, Warks, CV8 2RF.   (hq)
        024 7641 4999   fax 024 7641 4990
        email admin@sportsandplay.com
        http://www.sportsandplay.com

        Head of Membership & Communications: Jane Montgomery
▲   Company Limited by Guarantee
○   *N, *S, *T; to represent the sports goods & play industries
Gp   Specialist:
        Angling Trades Association Ltd
        Association of Play Industries
        Association of Professional Sales Agents (Sports & Leisure Industries)
        British Association of Seating Equipment Suppliers
        British Golf Industry Association
        British Rootzone & Top Dressing Manufacturers Association
        European Golf Industry Association
        Golf Consultants Association
        Inflatable Play Manufacturers Association
        Play Providers Association
        Professional Anglers Association
        Professional Darts Players Association
        Sports & Fitness Equipment Association
        Sports & Play Construction Association
        General:
        Register of Play Inspectors International Ltd
●   Conf - Mtgs - ET - Exam - Res - Exhib - Stat - Expt - Inf - Lib - LG
<   Wld Fedn of the Sporting Goods Ind (WFSGI); Fedn of the Eur Sporting Goods Ind
>   Profl Darts Corporation (PDC)
M   991 f
¶   Sportslife - 4; ftm, £1.75 each nm.
        Membership Directory - 1; free.

Federation of Stadium Communities (FSC) 1992
NR   Haywood House, 160 Moorland Rd, Burslem, STOKE-on-
       TRENT, Staffs, ST6 1EB.   (hq)
       01782 790606   fax 01782 790303
       http://www.stadiumcommunities.org.uk
       Chief Exec: Judy Crabb
▲   Company Limited by Guarantee
○   *K; to improve the quality of life of those communities that exist
       in the shadow of sports stadia; to encourage & assist the
       formation of constructive partnerships between sports clubs,
       local communities, local authorities & other interested parties
●   Conf - Mtgs - ET - Res - Inf - LG - Advocacy - Representation -
       Consultancy
M   245 community groups
¶   The Shadow NL - 4;   AR; both free.

Federation of Street Traders Unions
NR   Unit 1 Balmoral Trading Estate, River Rd, BARKING, Essex,
       IG11 0EG.   (hq)
       020 8591 1004
       Hon Sec: Wally Watson
○   *T

Federation of Swiss Societies in the UK (FOSSUK) 1949
NR   Swiss Embassy, 16-18 Montagu Place, LONDON, W1H 2BQ.
       020 7616 6000   fax 020 7724 7001
▲   Un-incorporated Society
○   *X
Gp   Unione Trichese; City Swiss Club; Swiss Rifle Assn
●   Mtgs - LG
<   Org of the Swiss Abroad (Berne)
M   30 org
¶   Swiss Review (Jnl) - 6;   Regional News (supplement) - 4;
       both ftm & Swiss people registered abroad.

Federation of Synagogues 1887
NR   65 Watford Way, LONDON, NW4 3AQ.   (hq)
       020 8202 2263   fax 020 8203 0610
       Chief Exec: Gordon Coleman
▲   Registered Charity
○   *R; to provide services to Orthodox rabbis; to assist
       congregations in erection, reconstruction or redecoration of
       synagogues; to assist in maintenance of Orthodox religious
       instruction.   Is also a burial society providing an orthodox
       Jewish funeral to its members & others of the Jewish faith
M   9,000 i

Federation of Tax Advisers (FTA) 1997
NR   Oakdene House, Kenton, EXETER, Devon, EX6 8NN.
       01626 891222
       http://www.fta.uk.com
○   *P

Federation of Technological Industries (FTI) 2003
NR   Tuscan House (ground floor), Beck Court, Cardiff Gate Business
       Park, CARDIFF, CF23 8RP.
       0870 850 6120   fax 0870 850 6121
       http://www.fti.org.uk
       Chmn & Sec: Fred Howarth
○   *K; traders of mobile phones & computer chips

Federation of Tour Operators (FTO) 1969
■   14-16 Sussex Rd, HAYWARDS HEATH, W Sussex, RH16 4EA.
       (hq)
       01444 457900   fax 01444 457901
       email general@fto.co.uk   http://www.fto.co.uk
       Dir Gen: Andrew Cooper
▲   Company Limited by Guarantee
○   *T; co-ordination of industry activity in the areas of crisis
       management, health & safety & responsible tourism;
       representation of tour operating sector, demonstration of
       benefits to consumers
●   Mtgs - Res - Stat - LG
<   Intl Fedn Tour Operators
M   10 f

** Federation for Ulster Local Studies Ltd
       Organisation lost: see Introduction paragraph 3

Federation of Water Fitness Professionals
■   Harold Fern House, Derby Square, LOUGHBOROUGH, Leics,
       LE11 5AL.   (hq)
       01509 618746
       email istc@swimming.org.uk
       http://www.swimming.org.uk
       Admin: Jane Nickerson
○   *P, *S

Federation of Wholesale Distributors (FWD) 1918
NR   9 Gildredge Rd, EASTBOURNE, E Sussex, BN21 4RB.   (hq)
       01323 724952   fax 01323 732820
       Dir Gen: John Murphy
▲   Un-incorporated Society
○   *T; interests of food & drink wholesalers in the UK
Gp   Food & drink wholesalers; Catering & institutional suppliers
●   Conf - ET - Empl - LG
M   c 550 f
¶   Pro Wholesaler - 12; ftm only.   Ybk; ftm, £8.95 nm.
       Committee & section reports.

Federation of Window Cleaners (FWC) 1947
■   Summerfield House, Harrogate Rd, Reddish, STOCKPORT,
       Cheshire, SK5 6HQ.   (hq)
       0161-432 8754   fax 0161-947 9033
       email info@fwcuk.oerg   http://www.fwcuk.org
       Gen Sec: Mrs Beryl A Murray
○   *T; an employers' trade association for self-employed window
       cleaners
●   Conf - ET - Exhib - Comp
M   1,800 i,
¶   Window Talk (Jnl) - 4; ftm only.
×   2006 (1 January) National Federation of Master Window &
       General Cleaners

**Federation of Women's Institutes of Northern Ireland (WI)
1932**
■   Federation House, 209-211 Upper Lisburn Rd, BELFAST,
       BT10 0LL.   (hq)
       028 9030 1506 & 028 9060 1781   fax 028 9043 1127
       email wini@btconnect.com
       Gen Sec: Mrs Irene A Sproule
▲   Registered Charity
Br   190 (NI)
○   *W; 'confidence building: encouraging women to reach their
       potential, giving opportunities to meet other women, learn
       new skills & provide new opportunities'
●   Conf - Mtgs - Exhib - Comp
<   Associated Countrywomen of the Wld (ACWW)
M   7,000+ i
¶   Ulster Countrywoman - 10; 85p.

Federation of Worker Writers & Community Publishers (FWWCP) 1976

NR Burslem School of Art, Queen St, STOKE-on-TRENT, Staffs, ST6 3EJ. (hq)
    01782 822327
    Coordinator: Tim Diggles
▲ Company Limited by Guarantee
○ *A, *N; to make writing & publishing more accessible
● Conf - ET - Res - Inf
M org

Federation of Zoological Gardens of Great Britain & Ireland (Zoo Federation)
    since 2004 **British & Irish Association of Zoos & Aquariums**

FEI - Federation of the Electronics Industry
    2002 merged with the Computing Services & Software Association to form **Intellect**

Fèisean nan Gàidheal 1991

NR Meall House, Portree, ISLE of SKYE, IV51 9BZ. (hq)
    01478 613355 fax 01478 613399
    email fios@feisean.org http://www.feisean.org
    Dir: Arthur Cormack
▲ Company Limited by Guarantee
○ *A, *D; the promotion of Gaelic arts tuition with emphasis on young people
< Traditional Music & Song Assn of Scotland
M c 35 i & org
¶ Faileas (NL) - 4; Tutors Directory - 2 yrly; both free.

Fell Pony Society (FPS) 1898

■ Ion House, Great Asby, APPLEBY, Cumbria, CA16 6HD. (hsp)
    01768 353100 fax 01768 353100
    http://www.fellponysociety.org
    Sec: Elizabeth Parkin
▲ Company Limited by Guarantee
Br Germany, Netherlands
○ *B
● Mtgs - Exhib - Comp - Inf
< Brit Assn Equine Socs; Nat Pony Soc; Brit Horse Soc; Brit Central Prefix Register
M 1,020 i, UK / 80 i, o'seas
¶ Stud Book - 1; price varies.

Fell Runners Association (FRA) 1970

NR 8 Leygate View, NEW MILLS, High Peak, Derbys, SK22 3EF.
    (sp)
    01663 746476
    http://www.fellrunners.org.uk
    Sec: Alan Brentnall
▲ Un-incorporated Society
○ *S; the governing body of fell-running in England; to encourage & promote fell-running; to provide services to competitors; to establish regulations for the the conduct of clubs, competitors & race organisers
● Organisation of fell-running activities
< UK Athletics; Wld Mountain Running Assn
M c 4,500 i & org
¶ The Fell Runner - 3;
    Hbk & Fixtures Calendar - 1; both ftm only.

Fellowship of Cycling Old-Timers (FCOT) 1965

NR 5 Avocet Close, South Oulton Broad, LOWESTOFT, Suffolk.
    (sp)
    01502 563262
    http://www.fcot.co.uk
    Gen Sec: Sian Charlton
▲ Un-incorporated Society
○ *G; for cyclists of age 50 & up who wish to stay cycling or return to it; to keep in touch with old cycling friends
● Mtgs
M 1,160 i, UK / 60 i, o'seas
¶ Fellowship News - 4; ftm, £2 nm.

Fellowship of Depressives Anonymous (FDA) 1973

■ c/o Self-Help Nottingham, Ormiston House, 32-36 Pelham St, NOTTINGHAM, NG1 2EG. (hsb)
    0870 774 4320
    email fdainfo@hotmail.co.uk
    http://www.depressionanon.co.uk
    Hon Sec: Peter Fryer
▲ Registered Charity
○ *W; support & encouragement for people with depression, & for their relatives & friends
● Pen/phonefriend scheme
M 400 i
¶ NL - 6; ftm, £1.50 each nm.   AR; free.
    Leaflets/Factsheets; ftm, 50p nm.
    Book List; all free.

Fellowship of Independent Evangelical Churches (FIEC) 1922

■ 39 The Point, Rockingham Rd, MARKET HARBOROUGH, Leics, LE16 7QU. (hq)
    01858 434540 fax 01858 411550
    email admin@fiec.co.uk http://www.fiec.org.uk
    Gen Sec: Richard J Underwood
▲ Registered Charity; Un-incorporated Society
Br 475
○ *R; establish & strengthen independent evangelical churches & uphold & proclaim the Christian Gospel
Gp Prepared for service - a training course for Christian ministry; Pastors' Association - supporting, equipping & setting standards for ministers & their churches
● Conf - Mtgs - ET - Inf
< Brit Evangelical Coun
M 23,000 i, 475 churches, UK / 100 i, o'seas
¶ Together - 2; ftm only.   Churches Hbk - 3 yrly; £10.
    FIEC Directory - 2 yrly; £5 m, £8 nm.

Fellowship of Makers & Researchers of Historical Instruments (FoMRHI) 1975

NR c/o Lewis Jones, London Metropolitan University, 41 Commercial Rd, LONDON, E1 1LA. (hsb)
    020 7320 1841 fax 020 7320 1830
    email ljones@lgu.ac.uk
    Hon Sec: Lewis Jones
○ *L; to promote authenticity in the making, restoration & use of historical musical instruments
● Conf - Res - SG - Inf
M 700 i, UK & o'seas
¶ FoMRHI Quarterly - 4; ftm only.   LM - 1 (updates - 4).
    Note: Information is only given to persons writing theses if they are members.

Fellowship of Postgraduate Medicine (FPM) 1919

■ 12 Chandos St, LONDON, W1G 9DR. (hq)
    020 7636 6334 fax 020 7436 2535
    email admin@fpm-uk.org
    Chief Exec: Dr Gordon C Cook
▲ Registered Charity
○ *E, *P; promotion of postgraduate medical education (NOT personal assistance)
M c 60 i
¶ Postgraduate Medical Jnl - 12.

Fellowship of the White Boar
    see **Richard III Society - Fellowship of the White Boar**

Fencing Contractors' Association   (FCA)   1942
■   Hillside Grange, Warren Rd, TRELLECH, Monmouthshire,
     NP25 4PQ.   (hq)
     0700 056 0722   fax 01600 860888
     email info@fencingcontractors.org
     http://www.fencingcontractors.org
     Chief Exec: Wendy A Baker
▲   Un-incorporated Society
○   *T; contracting, supplying & manufacturing for fencing & safety
     barriers
Gp Incorporating:
     Association of Safety Fencing Contractors
     Electric Security Fencing Federation
     Environmental Noise Barrier Associaton
     Gate Automation & Access Barrier Association
●   Conf - Mtgs - Inf - Empl - LG
M   230 f
¶   NL - 4; ftm only.   LM; free.

Feng Shui Society   (FSS)   1993
NR 377 Edgware Rd, LONDON, W2 1BT.   (asa)
     07050 289200
     email info@fengshuisociety.org.uk
     http://www.fengshuisociety.org.uk
     Chmn: Raymond Catchpole
▲   Un-incorporated Society
Br 12
○   *G, *P; 'the only independent, not for profit professional body
     regulating regulating the professional practice of feng shui in
     the UK'
●   Conf - Mtgs - ET - Exam - Res - Exhib - SG - Inf - Lib - PL - VE -
     LG
M   400 i, UK / 100 i, o'seas
¶   Feng Shui News; ftm only.

FeRFA: the Resin Flooring Association   (FeRFA)   1969
■   99 West St, FARNHAM, Surrey, GU9 7EN.   (hq)
     01252 739149   fax 01252 739140
     email Ferfa@associationhouse.org.uk
     http://www.ferfa.org.uk
     Hon Sec: J G Fairley
▲   Company Limited by Guarantee
○   *T; UK manufacturers, contractors & associated companies
     involved in industrial resin systems
Gp Working parties: 1992 liaison, Industrial flooring, Test methods,
     Publicity & promotions
●   Conf - Mtgs - Exhib - Comp - LG
M   68 f
¶   Resin Flooring Industry Hbk.

Fertiliser Manufacturers Association
     2003 merged with the UK Agricultural Supply Trade Association to
     form the **Agricultural Industries Confederation**

Fertility Care Scotland (Natural Family Planning)   1976
■   196 Clyde St, GLASGOW, G1 4JY.   (hq)
     0141-221 0858
     email info@fertilitycare.org.uk
     http://www.fertilitycare.org.uk
     Contact: Office Administrator
▲   Registered Charity
Br 12
○   *M, *W; to promote the Billings ovulation method of natural
     family planning
Gp Educational presentations & resourcing; Teaching Billings
     ovulation method; Fertility/infertility awareness; Natural
     family planning tuition
●   Mtgs - ET - Exam - Inf
<   Wld Org Ovulation Method Billings (WOOMB)
M   70 i

Ffederasiwn Cerddoriaeth Amatur Cymru
     see **Welsh Amateur Music Federation   (Ffederasiwn
     Cerddoriaeth Amatur Cymru)**

Ffestiniog Railway Society Ltd   (FRSL)   1954
NR PO Box 1832, WARRINGTON, Cheshire, WA4 2FR.   (hq)
     fax 0870 052 0091
     email ffestiniograilway.org.uk   http://www.festrail.co.uk
     Registrar & Sec: Roger Schofield
▲   Company Limited by Guarantee; Registered Charity
Br 20
○   *G; conservation of the Ffestiniog Railway
●   Conf - Mtgs - ET - Voluntary work
<   Heritage Rly Assn
M   5,300 i, UK / 200 i, o'seas
¶   Ffestiniog Railway Magazine - 4; ftm.

**Fibre Bonded Carpet Manufacturers' Association   (FBCMA)
1968**
NR Tower House, 269 Walmersley Rd, BURY, Lancs, BL9 6NX.
     (asa)
     0161-761 5231   fax 0161-761 3001
     Sec & Treas: C A Nuttall
▲   Un-incorporated Society
○   *T; for manufacturers of fibre-bonded carpets
●   Conf - Mtgs - Res - Inf - LG
<   Intl Standards Org; Comité Eur de Normalisation; BSI
M   9 f

Fibre Cement Manufacturers' Association Ltd   (FCMA)   1984
■   ATSS House Station Rd East, STOWMARKET, Suffolk,
     IP14 1RQ.   (hq)
     01449 676053   fax 01449 770028
     email fcma@ghyllhouse.co.uk   http://www.fcma.co.uk
     Sec-Gen: Tony Hutchinson
▲   Company Limited by Guarantee
○   *T; fibre cement building products, their technical development
     & safe utility
Gp Technical; Health & safety
●   Res - Inf - LG
M   2 f

Fibreoptic Industry Association   (FIA)   1990
■   The Manor House, High St, BUNTINGFORD, Herts,
     SG9 9AB.   (hq)
     01763 273039   fax 01763 273255
     email jane@fiasec.demon.co.uk
     http://www.fia-online.co.uk
     Co Sec: Jane Morrison
▲   Company Limited by Guarantee
○   *T; to facilitate the development & professionalism of the UK's
     fibre optic industry; to represent end users of fibre optics,
     installers, distributors, training providers, consultants &
     component manufacturers
●   Mtgs - ET - SG - Inf
M   5 i, 210 f, UK / 5 i, o'seas
¶   NL - 6;   Members' Guide to Products & Services (2000);
     both free.
     Technical publications; ftm (website password); prices vary nm.

Fibromyalgia Association UK   (FMA UK)   1994
NR PO Box 206, STOURBRIDGE, W Midlands, DY9 8YL.   (hq)
     0870 220 1232   fax 0870 752 5118
     email fmauk@hotmail.com
     http://www.fibromyalgia-associationuk.org
▲   Registered Charity
Br 65
○   *W; support & information for sufferers, their families, carers &
     medical professionals
●   Conf - Mtgs - ET - Res - Inf - Lib - LG
<   Intl Fibromyalgia Exchange (IFME); Nat Fibromyalgia Assn
     (USA)
M   8,000 i, 65 org, UK / 100 i, o'seas
¶   Family Magazine - 12.   Leaflets.

Field Studies Council   (FSC)   1943

■ Preston Montford, Montford Bridge, SHREWSBURY, Shropshire, SY4 1HW.   (hq)
01743 852100   fax 01743 852101
email fsc.headoffice@field-studies-council.org
http://www.field-studies-council.org
Chief Exec: A D Thomas,   Sec & Treas: C J Bayliss
▲ Company Limited by Guarantee; Registered Charity
Br 17
○ *E, *L; promotion of environmental understanding for all environmental & special course operators
● ET - Res - SG - VE
M 4,000 i, UK / 250 i, o'seas
¶ Field Studies Magazine - 2; ftm only.   AR; free.
Catalogue of publications; on request.

Fife Agricultural Association   (FAA)

■ Chesterhill, Boarhills, ST ANDREWS, Fife, KY16 8PP.   (hsp)
01334 880518
Sec: Louise Roger
▲ Registered Charity
○ *F
● Exhib
M 600 i

Fife Chamber of Commerce & Enterprise Ltd   1988

NR Wemyssfield House, Wemyssfield, KIRKCALDY, Fife, KY1 1XN.
(hq)
01592 201932   fax 01592 641187
email chiefexecutive@fifechamber.co.uk
http://www.fifechamber.co.uk
Chief Exec: Alan Russell
▲ Un-incorporated Society
Br 2
○ *C
Gp Export development
● Conf - Mtgs - ET - Expt - Inf - Lib - VE - LG
< Brit Chams Comm
M 350 f
¶ Chamber News - 12; free.   AR; free.
Membership Directory - 1; ftm.

Fifteen-0-Nine (1509) Society
no longer active

Film Distributors' Association   (FDA)   1915

■ 22 Golden Sq, LONDON, W1F 9JW.   (hq)
020 7437 4383   fax 020 7734 0912
http://www.launchingfilms.com
Chief Exec & Sec: Mark Batey
▲ Company Limited by Guarantee
○ *T
● Mtgs - Inf - LG - Liaison with all industry & other bodies where distributor interests are concerned
< Intl Fedn Film Distributor Assns (FIAD)
M 13 f

Film Makers Ireland
since 2003 **Screen Producers Ireland**

Film & Video Institute
the shorter name for **Institute of Amateur Cinematographers**

Filtration Society   1964

■ 5 Henry Dane Way, Newbold Coleorton, COALVILLE, Leics, LE67 8PP.   (hsp)
01530 223124   fax 01530 223124
email r.j.wakeman@lineone.net   http://www.filtsoc.com
Sec: Prof Richard Wakeman
▲ Registered Charity
Br 8 o'seas
○ *L; filtration, separation & related processes; design, manufacture & use of filtration equipment & processes
● Conf - Mtgs - ET - Res - Exhib - Lib - VE
M 400 i, UK / 870 i, o'seas
¶ Jnl - 4.

Finance Industry Standards Association

NR 8 Parrys Court, Northgate, SLEAFORD, Lincs, NG34 7BN.
01529 305698   fax 01529 308755
Gen Sec: J Harper
○ *T; an advisory body representing lenders & brokers
M c 270 i & f

Finance & Leasing Association   (FLA)   1992

■ 15-19 Imperial House, Kingsway, LONDON, WC2B 6UN.
(hq)
020 7836 6511   fax 020 7420 9600
Dir Gen: Martin Hall
▲ Company Limited by Guarantee
○ *T; to represent companies providing consumer credit, business finance & leasing & motor finance
Gp Divns: Asset finance & leasing, Consumer finance, Motor finance
● Conf - Mtgs - ET - Exam - Stat - LG
< Eur Fedn of Finance House Assns (EUROFINAS); Eur Fedn Eqpt Leasing Co Assns (LEASEUROPE)
M 100 f, 56 associates
¶ Annual Survey of Business Finance.
Code of Practice.   AR; free.
Early Settlement Rebate (leaflet).

Financial Services Ireland   1968

IRL Confederation House, 84-86 Lower Baggot St, DUBLIN 2, Republic of Ireland.
353 (1) 605 1586   fax 353 (1) 638 1586
email fsi@ibec.ie   http://www.fsi.ie
Dir: Aileen O'Donoghue
○ *T
< IBEC
× 2002 Financial Services Industry Assn

Fine Art Trade Guild   (FATG)   1910

■ 16-18 Empress Place, LONDON, SW6 1TT.   (hq)
020 7381 6616   fax 020 7381 2596
email info@fineart.co.uk   http://www.fineart.co.uk
Managing Dir: Christrose Sumner
▲ Company Limited by Guarantee
○ *T; for the picture trade & fine art publishing
Gp Art galleries; Suppliers to the fine arts; Picture framers; Picture restorers; Fine art printers; Artists
● Conf - Mtgs - ET - Exam - Exhib - Comp - Expt - Inf - Lib - LG
M 48 i, 1,520 f, UK / 2 i, 87 f, o'seas
¶ Art Business Today (Jnl) - 5; ftm, £24 yr nm.
The Directory - 1; ftm, £50.50 nm.   LM (on disk); £141 m only.
The Artist's Guide to Selling Work; ftm, £9.99 nm.

Fingerprint Society   1974
- ■ Warwickshire Police, SSU, High St, SOUTHAM, Warks, CV47 0HB.   (sb)
  01926 415834
  email kathryn.smith@warwickshire.pnn.police.uk
  http://www.fpsociety.org.uk
  Sec: Kathryn Smith
- ○ *P; to advance the study & application of fingerprints & to facilitate the co-operation among persons interested in this field of personal identification
- ● Conf - Mtgs - ET
- M c 400 i, UK / c 200 i, o'seas
- ¶ Fingerprint Whorld - 4; ftm only.

Finnish-British Chamber of Commerce   2001
- NR 5 Arlington St, LONDON, SW1A 1RA.   (hq)
  020 7647 4496   fax 020 7408 4426
  email admin@fbcc.co.uk   http://www.fbcc.co.uk
  Gen Mgr: Mrs Hely Abbondati
- ▲ Company Limited by Guarantee
- ○ *C; to promote & develop trade & other economic relations between Finland & Great Britain; to retain direct contacts with & express the views of members to both the Finnish & British governments
- ● Mtgs - Expt - Inf - VE - Junior Chamber of Commerce
- M f

Fire Brigade Society   (FBS)   1963
- ◼ 4 Burway Meadow, ALREWAS, Staffs, DE13 7EB.   (gsp)
  http://www.thefirebrigadesociety.com
  Gen Sec: Steve Dodge
- Br 14; worldwide
- ○ *G; 'for people who have an interest in all matters 'fire & rescue''
- ● Mtgs - Lib - VE
- M 800 i, 12 orgs, UK / 100 i, o'seas
- ¶ Fire Cover - 4; ftm only.

Fire Brigades' Union   (FBU)   1918
- ◼ 68 Coombe Rd, KINGSTON-upon-THAMES, Surrey, KT2 7AE. (hq)
  020 8541 1765   fax 020 8546 5187
  Gen Sec: M Wrack
- ○ *U; for all uniformed fire service personnel
- M c 56,000 i

Fire Extinguishing Trades Association   (FETA)   1916
- NR Thames House, 29 Thames St, KINGSTON-upon-THAMES, Surrey, KT1 1PH.   (hq)
  020 8549 8839   fax 020 8547 1564
  email feta@abft.org.uk   http://www.feta.org.uk
- ▲ Company Limited by Guarantee
- ○ *T; mfrs & specialist distributors of fire extinguishers of all types, incl portable fire fighting eqpt & fittings
- Gp Mfrs: Fire extinguisher, Fittings & hose; Servicing companies
- ● Conf - Mtgs - ET - Exam - Exhib - Inf - LG - Standards
- < Eur C'ee Mfrs Fire Protection & Safety Eqpt & Fire Fighting Vehicles (Europe); Fire Ind Coun; Fire Protection Assn; BSI
- M 85 f, UK / 5 f, o'seas
- ¶ LM; free.
  Guide to the servicing of portable fire extinguishers.

Fire Fighting Vehicles Manufacturers' Association   (FFVMA) 1970
- NR 25 Westfield Rd, GUILDFORD, Surrey, GU1 1RR.   (sec/b)
  01483 506678
  http://www.ffvma.org.uk
  Sec: Christine Tollman
- ▲ Un-incorporated Society
- ○ *T; interests of manufacturers of fire appliances & pumps
- Gp Executive c'ee; Technical; Council
- ● Mtgs - Res - Exhib - Stat - Expt - Inf
- < Eur C'ee Mfrs Fire Protection & Safety Eqpt; Fedn of Brit Fire Orgs
- M 9 f
- ¶ LM;   AR; both ftm only.

Fire Industry Confederation   (FIC)   1988
- NR Thames House, 29 Thames St, KINGSTON-upon-THAMES, Surrey, KT1 1PH.   (hq)
  020 8549 8839   fax 020 8547 1564
  email fic@abft.org.uk   http://www.the-fic.org.uk
- ○ *N; to deal, on behalf of members, with matters beyond the scope of any one association
- ● Mtgs - LG
- < Eur C'ee Mfrs Fire Protection & Safety Eqpt & Fire Fighting Vehicles (EUROFEU)
- M 4 org

Fire Mark Circle   (FMC)   1934
- ◼ 8 Seymour Rd, LONDON, N8 0BE.   (hsp)
  020 8341 1846
  email trevorpetch@aol.com
  http://www.firemarkcircle.com
  Hon Sec: Trevor Petch
- ▲ Un-incorporated Society
- ○ *G; for persons interested in the origin & history of fire insurance companies, their fire marks, fire brigades & all that pertains to the past of fire insurance
- ● Conf - Mtgs - Res - Inf - Lib - Valuation of collections
- < Fire Mark Circle of America
- M 200 i, UK / 2 i, o'seas
- ¶ FMC News - 2;
  Membership List, Rarity Guide, both 2 yrly; all ftm.

Fire Officers Association   (FOA)   1994
- ◼ London Rd, MORETON in the MARSH, Glos, GL56 0RH.   (hq)
  01608 652023   fax foa@fireofficers.org.uk
  http://www.fireofficers.org.uk
  Gen Sec: Graham Setterfield
- ○ *U; the efficiency & status of the fire service; to maintain the conditions of service of its employees
- ● LG
- M 2,500 i
- ¶ Magazine - 4; ftm only.

Fire Protection Association   (FPA)   1946
- NR London Rd, MORETON-in-MARSH, Glos, GL56 0RH.   (hq)
  01608 812500   fax 01608 812501
  email fpa@thefpa.co.uk   http://www.thefpa.co.uk
  Managing Dir: Jonathan O'Neill
- ▲ Company Limited by Guarantee
- ○ *L, *P; the UK's national fire safety organisation, providing authoritative advice, information & training on all aspects of fire safety
- ● ET - Res - Exhib - Stat - Inf - Lib - LG
- < Confedn of Fire Protection Assns - Europe (CFPA-Europe)
- M 3,500 i, UK / 1,500 f, o'seas
- ¶ Fire Prevention (Jnl) - 12.
  Fire Protection Ybk.   Handbooks - 1.
  Technical publications & CDs on aspects of fire fighting; catalogue available.

Fire & Rescue Suppliers Association   (FIRESA)
NR   Thames House, 29 Thames St, KINGSTON upon THAMES,
    Surrey, KT1 1PH.
    020 8549 8839
    http://www.firesa.org.uk
○   *T

Fire Resistant Glazing Group
    a group of the **Glass & Glazing Federation**

Fire Service Preservation Group   (FSPG)   1968
■   50 Old Slade Lane, IVER, Bucks, SL0 9DR.   (hsp)
    01753 652207
    email admin@firespg.freeserve.co.uk
    http://www.firespg.freeserve.co.uk
    Treas: Andrew Scott
▲   Un-incorporated Society
Br   12
○   *G; for those interested in the history of the fire service, the
    preservation of fire engines & associated equipment.
    Appliances owned by the group & its members date from
    1730 to 1987
●   Mtgs
<   Fedn Brit Historic Vehicles Clubs
M   c 600 units, UK / 6 units, o'seas
¶   Off the Run - 12; ftm only.

Fire Sprinkler Association Ltd   1998
NR   Park Court, Brimpton, Nr READING, Berks, RG7 4ST.   (hq)
    0118-971 2322   fax 0118-971 3015
    email info@firesprinklers.info
    http://www.firesprinklers.info
    CEO: Sir George Pigot
▲   Company Limited by Guarantee
○   *T; 'the reduction of fire casualties by the wider use of life safety
    fire sprinklers'
Gp   Fire brigades forum, Sprinkler mfrs, Technical c'ee
●   Conf - Mtgs - ET - Exam - Exhib - Stat - Inf - LG
<   Intl Fire Sprinkler Assn; Eur Fire Sprinkler Assn
M   96 f
¶   RSA NL - 4; free.
×   2002-03 Residential Sprinkler Association

Firework Makers Guild
    see **British Pyrotechnists' Association**

First Division Association
    the trading name of the **Association of First Division Civil
    Servants**

Fish Veterinary Society
    a group of the **British Veterinary Association**

Fishermen's Association Ltd   1995
NR   11 Burns Road, ABERDEEN, AB15 4NT.   (sb)
    01224 313473   fax 01224 310385
    email roddy@mccollassociates.com
    Secs: Roddy McColl (McColl & Associates Ltd)
Br   8
○   *T; a trade protection association for the fishing industry
●   Conf - Mtgs - ET - Inf - LG
<   Shellfish Assn of GB
>   NI Fish Producers Org; Scot Ship Chandlers' Assn; S Devon &
    Channel Shellfish Fishermen's Assn
M   100 i, 260 f
¶   FAL NL - 2.   FAL Ybk & Diary - 1.

Fishing Co-operatives (UK) Ltd
    in November 2001 became **Marineco**

Fitness Industry Association   (FIA)   1991
NR   61 Southwark St (4th floor), LONDON, SE1 0HL.   (hq)
    020 7202 4700   fax 020 7202 4701
    email info@fia.org.uk   http://www.fia.org.uk
    Exec Dir: Nigel Wallace,   Hon Pres: Lord Paddy Ashdown
▲   Company Limited by Guarantee
○   *T; for the health & fitness industry
Gp   Educational establishments; Operators; Sports centres;
    Suppliers; Students; Individuals
●   Conf - Mtgs - ET - Res - Exhib - Comp - SG - Stat - Expt - Inf -
    Lib - VE - Empl - LG
<   Intl Health, Racquet & Sportsclubs Assn
M   1,600 clubs
¶   Leisure Management - 12;   Health Club Management - 12;
    Leisure Opportunities - 24;   CBI - 12;
    On Track Magazine - 4;   all ftm.

Fitness League   1930
NR   6 Station Parade, SUNNINGDALE, Berks, SL5 0EP.   (hq)
    01344 874787
    Office Mgr: Terri Adams
▲   Registered Charity
Br   370; Canada, Ireland, Netherlands, New Zealand, S Africa,
    Zimbabwe
○   *G; the provision of exercise & movement to music classes for
    all ages & abilities
Gp   Classes: Children's, Teenagers', Men's
●   Exercise classes - Teacher training
<   Cent Coun for Physical Recreation
M   c 14,000 i
¶   History of the League.

Fitness Northern Ireland   1953
NR   The Robinson Centre, Montgomery Rd, BELFAST, BT6 9HS.
    (hq)
    028 9070 4080
    Chmn: Eileen Boyd
▲   Company Limited by Guarantee
○   *G; exercise for women & men of all ages
M   [not stated]

Fitness Products Association
    since 2006 **Sports Manufacturers & Retailers Trade
    Association**

Fitness Scotland
    merged in 2004 with **Scottish Gymnastics Association**

**Fjord Horse National Stud Book Association of Great Britain
(FNSA)   1984**
NR   Cilyblaidd Manor, Pencarreg, LLANYBYDDER, Carmarthenshire,
    SA40 9QL.   (hsp/b)
    0870 415 5541   fax 01570 480012
    email info@fjord-horse.co.uk
    http://www.fjord-horse.co.uk
    Sec: L D Moran
○   *B; to promote, preserve & certify the fjord horse in GB in
    accordance with the Mother Stud Book in Norway
●   Mtgs - Res - Exhib - Stat - Inf
<   Fjordhesteavlen i Danmark
M   106 i, UK / 24 i, o'seas
¶   Jnl - 1.
×   Fjord Horse Society of GB

© CBD Research Ltd · Beckenham · BR3 5JS · Tel 020 8650 7745 · Fax 020 8650 0768 · E-mail cbd@cbdresearch.com · www.cbdresearch.com

Flag Institute   1971

■   44 Middleton Rd, Acomb, YORK, YO24 3AS.   (mem/sec/p)
    01904 339985
    email dir@flaginstitute.org   http://www.flaginstitute.org
    Contact: Michael Faul
▲   Un-incorporated Society
○   *L; research & publication of information of all types on flags of
    all countries, periods & kinds - the technical term is
    vexillology
●   Mtgs - Res - Inf - Lib
<   Fédn Intle des Assns Véxillologiques
M   c 500 i, f & org
¶   Flagmaster - 4; ftm.

Flat Glass Council   (FGC)   1977

NR   44-48 Borough High St, LONDON, SE1 1XB.   (hq)
     0845 257 7950   fax 0870 042 4266
     email lcavender@ggf.org.uk   http://www.ggf.org.uk
     Nat Sec: Mrs L Cavender
▲   Company Limited by Guarantee
○   *N; formal liaison with the UK & EEC flat glass manufacturers
    on behalf of glaziers, merchants & flat glass processors
●   Mtgs - ET - Stat - Inf - Empl
M   200 f
¶   Code of Practice: Window Installation Safety.
    Note: The FGC is the employers' organisation in the Glass and
       Glazing Federation. The Council forms, with the three trade
       unions concerned (GMBU, AMICUS-AEEU & GPMU) the
       National Joint Council for the Flat Glass Industry
    Negotiations are manifest in the NLA & Manual of Training

Flat Glass Manufacturers' Association
    see **United Kingdom Flat Glass Manufacturers' Association**

Flat Roofing Alliance   (FRA)   1997

■   Fields House, Gower Rd, HAYWARDS HEATH, W Sussex,
    RH16 4PL.   (hq)
    01444 440027   fax 01444 415616
    Dir/Co Sec: William A Jenkins
▲   Company Limited by Guarantee
○   *T; to promote & extend the use of approved bituminous flat
    roofing & felt based products; to promote approved
    contractors
●   Mtgs - Inf - Empl - LG
<   Nat Roofing Contrs Assn (USA); Nat Specialist Contrs Coun
M   100 f (on completion of a one-year assessment period)
¶   LM; free.   Roofing Hbk.
    Householders Guide to Flat Roofing; free.
    Note: although the Association of British Roofing Felt
       Manufacturers merged to form the Alliance it has not been
       closed & is administered from this address.

Fleece Washers & Dyers Association   (FWA)   1935

■   423 Upper Elmers End Rd, BECKENHAM, Kent, BR3 3DA.
    (mail) address
○   *T
●   Mtgs - Inf - Lib
M   4 f

Fleet Safety Forum
    a group of **Brake**

Flexible Packaging Association   (FPA)   1962

■   4 The Street, Shipton Moyne, TETBURY, Glos, GL8 8PN.   (hq)
    01666 880406
    Dir & Sec: M I H Unwin
○   *T; interests of the UK flexible packaging industry
M   f

Flintshire Historical Society   (FHS)   1911

■   69 Pen-y-Maes Ave, RHYL, Denbighshire, LL18 4ED.   (hsp)
    01745 332220
    Hon Sec: Mrs N P Parker
▲   Registered Charity
○   *L; archaeology & history of Flintshire
●   Mtgs - VE
<   Coun of Brit Archaeology
M   382 i, 34 org, UK / 4 i, 12 org, o'seas
¶   Jnl; £7.50 m, £21 nm.

Floatation Tank Association UK / Eire   (FTA)   1988

NR   7 Clapham Common South Side, LONDON, SW4 7AA.
     (contact/b)
     020 7627 4962   fax 020 7627 3381
     http://www.floatationtankassociation.net
     Communications: Ron Kemeny
▲   Un-incorporated Society
Br   USA
○   *G; to promote & disseminate information on floatation (a
    method of deep relaxation & stress management) & on
    accredited public float centres
●   Stat - Inf
M   25 f

Flood Protection Association

NR   10 Cavalry Ride, NORWICH, Norfolk, NR3 1UA.
     0870 242 2340
     Chmn: Ron Whitehead
○   *T

Flower Import Trade Association

■   68 First Avenue, Mortlake, LONDON, SW14 8SR.
    020 8939 6473   fax 020 8878 9983
○   *T
    no further information supplied

Flowers & Plants Association Ltd   (F&PA)   1984

■   266-270 Flower Market, New Covent Garden Market,
    LONDON, SW8 5NB.   (hq)
    020 7738 8044   fax 020 7738 8083
    email info@flowers.org.uk   http://www.flowers.org.uk
    Chief Exec: Veronica Richardson
▲   Company Limited by Guarantee
○   *T; to promote commercially grown cut flowers & houseplants;
    to work on behalf of the horticulture industry
●   ET - Res - Exhib - Comp - Stat - Inf - PL
<   Links with equivalent orgs worldwide
M   c 200 f, UK & o'seas
¶   NL - 4; ftm only.
    Leaflets & Factsheets - irreg; ftm, (nm please send sae).

Flydressers Guild   1967

■   Woryem, Blackgate Lane, HENFIELD, E Sussex, BN5 9HA.
    (hsp)
    01273 493473
    email woryem@globalnet.co.uk   http://www.the-fdg.org
    Chmn: A Middleton
▲   Un-incorporated Society
○   *G, *T; 'teaching the art of tying artificial flies for fishing'
●   Mtgs - ET - Exhib - Comp
M   2,200 i, UK / 200 i, o'seas
¶   The Flydresser - 4; ftm, £3 nm.

Flying Farmers Association   (FFA)   1974
■   Moor Farm, West Heslerton, MALTON, N Yorks, YO17 8RU. (hsb)
01944 738281   fax 01944 738240
http://www.ffa.org.uk
Hon Sec: Paul A Stephens
▲   Company Limited by Guarantee
○   *P; to safeguard members' special interests as aircraft, or airstrip, owners by representation on the General Aviation Safety Council
●   Mtgs - Inf - VE - LG (Civil Aviation Authority) - Insurance
M   c 370 i
¶   NL;   LM;   Map of Members' Airstrips; all m only.

FM Society
is a specialist group of the **Chartered Institute of Building**

FOCAL International Ltd - Federation of Commercial Audiovisual Libraries Ltd   (FOCAL)   1985
■   Pentax House, South Hill Ave, SOUTH HARROW, Middx, HA2 0DU.   (hq)
020 8423 5853   fax 020 8933 4826
email info@focalint.org   http://www.focalint.org
Gen Mgr: Julie Lewis
Comml Mgr: Anne Johnson
▲   Company Limited by Guarantee
○   *T; for audio-visual libraries, researchers, producers & facility houses, promoting the use of library footage, stills & sound in programming, advertising, corporate videos, multi media projects etc.
●   Conf - Mtgs - ET - Res - Stat - Inf - Informing users of footage where to go for footage & advice - Helping to find film researchers
M   100 i, 100 f, UK / 25 i, 75 org, o'seas
¶   Archive Zones - 4; ftm, £50 yr nm.
LM - 1; ftm, £25 nm.

Folio Society
§   44 Eagle St, LONDON, WC1R 4FS.
020 7400 4200   fax 020 7400 4242
email enquiries@foliosoc.co.uk
http://www.foliosoc.co.uk
a book club which publishes 'editions of the world's great literature in a format worthy of the contents, at a price within the reach of everyman'

Folk Music Society of Ireland   1971
IRL   63 Merrion Sq, DUBLIN 2, Republic of Ireland.
353 (1) 661 9699
Chmn: Dr Seóirse Bodley
○   *D

FolkArts England
NR   PO Box 296, MATLOCK, Derbys, DE4 3XU.
01629 827014   fax 01629 821874
email info@folkarts-england.org
○   *G; music: folk, acoustic, roots & traditional

Folklore of Ireland Society   1926
IRL   Roinn Bhéaloideas Éireann, An Coláiste Ollscoile, DUBLIN 4, Republic of Ireland.
353 (1) 716 8216   fax 353 (1) 716 1144

Folklore Society   1878
■   c/o The Warburg Institute, Woburn Sq, LONDON, WC1H 0AB.   (hq)
020 7862 8564   fax 020 7862 8565
Sec: Dr Juliette Wood
○   *L; systematic comparative study of oral traditions & cultures
●   Conf - Mtgs - Res - Exhib - Inf - Lib
M   c 500 i, c 600 org
¶   Folklore - 3.   FLS News - 3; ftm.
New Books in Folklore - 2.   Current Folklore - 2.

Followers of Rupert   1983
■   29 Mill Rd, LEWES, E Sussex, BN7 2RU.   (hsp)
01273 480339   fax 01273 480339
http://www.see.ed.ac.uk/~afm/followers/
Hon Sec: John Beck
▲   Un-incorporated Society
Br   5
○   *A, *G; for all interested in the literature concerning Rupert Bear, his artists & storytellers
●   Mtgs - Res - Comp - Inf - Lib (members only) - PL
M   1,250 i, UK / 100 i, o'seas
¶   Nutwood (NL) - 4; ftm, £18 yr nm.

Folly Fellowship   1988
NR   7 Inches Yard, Market St, NEWBURY, Berks, RG14 5DP. (chmn/b)
01635 42864
Chmn: Michael Cousins
▲   Registered Charity
Br   6; Netherlands
○   *G; preservation, protection, promotion, conservation of follies, grottoes & garden buildings
●   Conf - Mtgs - ET - Res - Exhib - Comp - Inf - Lib - PL - VE
<   Fountain Soc
M   c 850 i, f & org, UK / c 250 i, f & org, o'seas
¶   Follies - 4.

Food Additives & Ingredients Association   (FAIA)   1977
■   10 Whitchurch Close, MAIDSTONE, Kent, ME16 8UR.   (exec sec/p)
01622 682119   fax 01622 682119
email rbr1@btconnect.com   http://www.faia.org.uk
Exec Sec: Richard Ratcliffe
○   *T; 'to encourage a positive attitude [to food additives], through clear understanding of food additives & ingredients among identified key audiences including manufacturers, retailers, health professionals, regulatory authorities & consumers'
●   Mtgs - Inf (members only) - LG
<   Fedn Eur Food Additives & Food Enzymes Inds (ELC)
M   25 f

Food from Britain Fast Track   (FFB)
NR   Manning House (4th floor), 22 Carlisle Place, LONDON, SW1P 1JA.   (hq)
020 7233 5111   fax 020 7233 9516
email info@foodfrombritain.com
http://www.foodfrombritain.com
Chief Exec: David McNair
Br   11 o'seas offices
○   *T; the membership arm of Food from Britain (export agency)
●   Conf - Res - Exhib - Stat - Expt - Inf
M   c 120 f
No further information supplied.

Food & Chemical Allergy Association   1976
§   27 Ferringham Lane, Ferring, WORTHING, W Sussex, BN12 5NB.   (hs/chmn/p)
Chmn & Sec: Mrs Ellen Rothera,   Treas: Mrs B Rogers
Advice & practical help to anyone suffering from any form of allergy or allergy-based illness. A booklet is available: 'Understanding Allergies'; £2 with A5 sae

Food Development Association
■   c/o Dewberry Boyes, Apex House, London Rd, Northfleet, GRAVESEND, Kent, DA11 9JA.
0870 746 6396   fax 0870 746 5196
http://www.fooddev.co.uk
no further information supplied

Food & Drink Federation   (FDF)   1973

■ 6 Catherine St, LONDON, WC2B 5JJ.   (hq)
  020 7836 2460   fax 020 7836 0580
  http://www.fdf.org.uk & www.foodanddrink.org.uk
  Dir Gen: Melanie Leech
▲ Company Limited by Guarantee
○ *M, *T; to represent, promote & further the interests of the UK
  food manufacturing industry with government, EEC
  institutions & other decision making bodies
● Conf - Mtgs - SG - Stat - Lib
< Confédn des Inds Agro-Alimentaires; CBI
M 150 f, 12 trade associations

Food & Drink Industry Ireland   1968

IRL Confederation House, 84-86 Lower Baggot St, DUBLIN 2,
  Republic of Ireland.
  353 (1) 605 1500   fax 353 (1) 638 1500
○ *T
< IBEC

Food Poverty Network
  is a group of **Sustain: the Alliance for Better Food & Farming**

Food Processors' Association   (FPA)   2001

NR 6 Catherine St, LONDON, WC2B 5JJ.   (hq)
  020 7420 7113   fax 020 7836 0580
  http://www.fdf.org.uk
○ *N, *T; to represent members' common interests & issues,
  particularly contaminants, labelling & the environment
M acts as an umbrella association for:
  Dessert & Cake Mixes Association
  Pickles & Sauces Association
  Soup, Gravy & Produce Processors' Association
  UK Sweet Spreads Association

Foodservice Consultants Society International (UK)   (FCSI (UK))

■ Bourne House, Horsell Park, WOKING, Surrey, GU21 4LY.
  01483 761122   fax 01483 750991
  email admin@fcsi.org.uk   http://www.fcsi.org.uk
  Chmn: Richard Wedgbury
▲ Un-incorporated Society
○ *P; 'to promote professionalism in foodservice & hospitality
  consulting while returning maximum benefits to all members'
● Conf - Mtgs - ET - Exam - Exhib - Comp - VE
M 136 i

Foodservice Packaging Association   (FPA)   1969

■ The Old Rectory, Bletchingdon, KIDLINGTON, Oxon, OX5
  3DH.   (hq)
  01869 351139   fax 01869 350231
  email admin@foodservicepackaging.org.uk
  Contact: Martin Kersh
▲ Un-incorporated Society
○ *T; to promote both the concept & the marketing of disposables
  manufactured in the UK for use in industry, public service &
  the home
Gp Technical c'ees
● Mtgs - Exhib - Inf
M 60 f
¶ NL - 3/4;
  Booklets on: Drinking vessels, Napkins, Plates & bowls;
  Serviettes; Straws; all free.
× 2003-04 British Disposable Products Association

Football Association of Ireland   (FAI)

IRL 80 Merrion Sq, DUBLIN 2, Republic of Ireland.
  353 (1) 703 7500   fax 353 (1) 661 0931
  http://www.fai.ie
  Chief Exec: John Delaney
○ *S

Football Association Ltd   (FA)   1863

NR 25 Soho Sq, LONDON, W1D 4FA.   (hq)
  020 7745 4545   fax 020 7745 5545
  email info@thefa.com   http://www.thefa.com
  Chief Exec: Brian Barwick
▲ Company Limited by Guarantee
○ *S; the governing body for English football; to promote, control,
  organise & administer Association Football in England
● Conf - Exam - Comp - Stat - PL - LG
< U des Assns Eur de Football (UEFA); Fédn Intle de Football
  Assns (FIFA)
> County Football Assns; Football Clubs
M 30 org
¶ The FA Ybk - 1. The FA Hbk - 1.
  The FA Annual Review; free.

Football Association of Wales Ltd   (FA of Wales)   1876

NR 11/12 Neptune Court, Vanguard Way, CARDIFF, CF24 5PJ.
  (hq)
  029 2043 5830   fax 029 2049 6953
  email dcollins@faw.co.uk   http://www.faw.org.uk
  Sec Gen: David Collins
○ *S; administration of Association Football in Wales

Football League Ltd   1888

■ Edward VII Quay, Navigation Way, PRESTON, Lancs, PR2 2YF.
  (hq)
  0870 442 0 1888   fax 0870 442 1188
  email fl@football-league.co.uk
  http://www.football-league.co.uk
  Chmn: Sir Brian Mawhinney
▲ Company Limited by Guarantee
Br 2
○ *S
M 72 clubs
¶ NL - weekly during season.   Hbk - 1; ftm, £13.50 nm.
  Fixture Booklet - 1; ftm, £4.50 nm.

Football Supporters' Federation   (FSF)   2002

NR The Fans' Stadium - Kingsmeadow, Jack Goodchild Way,
  422A Kingston Rd, KINGSTON upon THAMES, Surrey,
  KT1 3PB.   (sb)
  http://www.fsf.org.uk
  Sec: Mike Williamson
▲ Un-incorporated Society
Br England national; Welsh national
○ *S; representing to the Government & football authorities the
  views & concerns of football supporters at all levels of the
  game; information interchange between member clubs on
  best practice & crisis management
Gp Insurance scheme offered for personal accident & late
  cancellation of matches
● Conf - Mtgs - Res - Exhib - LG
> Nat Assn of Disabled Supporters; The Football Programme
  Directory
M 110,000 in 120 supporters clubs UK / 75 i, o'seas
¶ FSF News - 4.   .
  FSF Members NL - 4.
× 2002 (Football Supporters Association
  (National Federation of Football Supporters' Clubs

Football Writers' Association

NR c/o Paul Hetherington, Daily Star, The Northern & Shell Building,
  10 Lower Thames St, LONDON, EC3R 6EN.
  http://www.footballwriters.co.uk
  Chmn: Paul Hetherington
○ *P

Forecourt Equipment Federation   (FEF)   1969
■ PO Box 35084, LONDON, NW1 4XE.   (asa)
    020 7935 8532   fax 020 7935 8532
    email office@fef.org.uk   http://www.fef.org.uk
    Sec: C Dunn-Meynell
○ *T; includes liaising with government depts on safety, weights &
    measures legislation & regulation
● Mtgs - Res - Inf - LG
M 9 f, 2 associate

Foreign Banks & Securities Houses Association
    December 2002 merged with the American Financial Services
    Association to become the **Association of Foreign Banks**.

Foreign Bird Association
    a member body of the **Society for the Protection of Aviculture**

Foreign Bird League
    a member body of the **Society for the Protection of Aviculture**

Foreign Press Association in London   (FPA)   1888
NR 11 Carlton House Terrace, LONDON, SW1Y 5AJ.   (hq)
    020 7930 0445   fax 020 7925 0469
    email secretariat@foreign-press.org.uk
    http://www.foreign-press.org.uk
    Dir: Gerry McCrudden
○ *P; to assist correspondents in their work by arranging press
    conferences, tours, functions etc
● Mtgs - Inf
M 210 i, UK / 500 i, o'seas
¶ LM - 1; ftm, £50 nm.

Forensic Science Society   (FSSoc)   1959
NR Clarke House, 18a Mount Parade, HARROGATE, N Yorks,
    HG1 1BX.   (hq)
    01423 506068   fax 01423 566391
    email president@forensic-science-society.co.uk
    http://www.forensic-science-society.co.uk
    Hon Sec: Shirley Marshall
▲ Registered Charity
○ *L; to advance the study, application & standing of forensic
    science
● Conf - Mtgs - ET - Exam - Inf
< California Assn of Criminalists
M 1,750 i, 83 f, UK / 405 i, 13 f, o'seas
¶ Science & Justice - 4;   Interfaces - 4; ftm.

**Foresight, the Association for the Promotion of Preconceptual
Care   1978**
■ 178 Hawthorn Rd, BOGNOR REGIS, W Sussex, PO21 2UY.
    (hq)
    01243 868001   fax 01243 868180
    http://www.foresight-preconception.org.uk
    Founder & Dir: Mrs Belinda Barnes,   Sec: Julia Martin
▲ Registered Charity
Br 32; 12 o'seas
○ *W; promotion &/or execution of preconceptual care to
    overcome infertility, miscarriage, perinatal death, prematurity,
    low birth weight, malformation &/or compromised health in
    mother or baby
● Conf - Mtgs - ET - Res - Exhib - SG - Stat - Inf - Lib - LG
M c 2,500 i, UK / c 250 i, o'seas
¶ NL - 3; ftm only.

Forestry Contracting Association Ltd   (FCA)   1992
NR PO Box 11443, ELLON, AB41 7WX.   (hq)
    0870 042 7999
    email members@fcauk.com   http://www.fcauk.com
    Nat Chmn: Brendan Burns
▲ Company Limited by Guarantee
○ *T; covers all parts of the forestry industry
Gp Arboriculture; British horse loggers; Charcoal & coppice;
    Timber haulage
● Conf - Mtgs - ET - Res - Exhib - Inf
M 967 i, 382 f
¶ FCA News - 6; ftm only.

Forestry & Timber Association
    the trading name of the **Association of Timber Growers &
    Forestry Professionals**

Forestry Trade Group
    a group of the **Horticultural Trades Association**

Fork Lift Truck Association   (FLTA)   1972
■ Manor Farm Buildings, Lasham, ALTON, Hants, GU34 5SL.
    (hq)
    01256 381441   fax 01256 381735
    email mail@fork-truck.org.uk
    http://www.fork-truck.org.uk
    Chief Exec: David Ellison
▲ Company Limited by Guarantee
Br 280; Eire, France, Germany
○ *T; to promote the industry for customers, dealers,
    manufacturers & suppliers; to raise standards of education,
    training & health & safety; to provide advice & guidance on
    operational & related matters
● Mtgs - ET - Exhib - Stat - Inf
M 170 f, UK / 5 f (Europe)
¶ Uplift (NL) - 4; ftm.   Directory - 1; £25 m, £75 nm.
    Health & Safety Manual.   Risk Assessment Manual.
    Personnel Manual.
    Safety booklets; £2.20 m, £3.30 nm.
✕ 2001 Fork Truck Association.

Fork Truck Association
    since November 2001 **Fork Lift Truck Association**

Formula Air Racing Association   (FARA)   1972
■ c/o Chadwick International, 137 High Holborn, LONDON,
    WC1V 6PW.   (hsb)
    020 7269 0920   fax 020 7269 0929
    email chadwick@chadwick-international.com
    Contact: Andrew Chadwick
▲ Company Limited by Guarantee
○ *S; promotion & management of formula air racing in the UK
● Comp - LG - Races in UK & Europe
< FGédn Aeronautique Intle (PAKIS); R Aero Club, London
M 6 i

**Fort Cumberland & Portsmouth Militaria Society   (FC&PMS)
1964**
NR 5 Herne Rd, Cosham, PORTSMOUTH, Hants, PO6 3PB.   (hsp)
    023 9242 3649
    Sec: Allan Dickenson
▲ Registered Charity
○ *G; preservation of historical buildings; popularising local
    military history; maintaining Fort Cumberland Guard: display
    group re-enacting drill of 1830-40 & 1860 Royal Marines
    incl musket & cannon firing & drum corps drill
Gp Fort Cumberland Guard
● Mtgs - ET - Res - Exhib - Inf - Lib - PL - VE
< UK Fortifications Club
M 40 i, 2 f

Fortress Study Group   (FSG)   1975
■   6 Lanark Place, LONDON, W9 1BS.   (hsp)
020 7286 5512
Hon Sec: W H Clements
▲   Registered Charity
○   *G, *L; the study of fortification since the introduction of artillery
●   Conf - Res - SG - Inf - Lib
<   Intl Burgen Institut; Intl Fortress Coun
M   c 750 i, 50 f
¶   Fort (Jnl) - 1;   Casemate (NL) - 3; both ftm only.

Forty Plus (40+) Fishing Boat Association   1995
■   Hillcrest, 63 Birch Hill Crescent, ONCHAN, Isle of Man,
IM3 3DA.   (founder/p)
01624 627568
email mike@mcb.net   http://www.homepages.mcb.net/
40fba
20 Briavels Grove, Ashley Hill, BRISTOL, BS6 5JJ.
0797 124 4943.
Co-Founders: Michael Craine,   Mike Smylie
○   *G; to encourage research into the historical & social elements
of fishing boats; to represent their owners; to encourage
liaison between boat owners, museums, heritage centres,
trusts, businesses & other organisations in the promotion of
the importance of our islands' fishing boat heritage
●   Res - Exhib - Stat - Inf - PL - LG - Compiling register of all boats
over 40 years old
M   520 i, 50 f, 20 org, UK / 10 i, o'seas
¶   Fishing Boats (NL) - 3; £10 m, £15 nm.

Forum for Clothing & Textiles
the alternative title for **ASBCI - the Forum for Clothing & Textiles**

Forum of Private Business   (FPB)   1977
NR   Ruskin Chambers, Drury Lane, KNUTSFORD, Cheshire,
WA16 6HA.   (hq)
01565 634467   fax 0870 241 9570
email info@fpb.co.uk   http://www.fpb.co.uk
Chief Exec: Nick Goulding
▲   Company Limited by Guarantee
Br   2
○   *K; to support private businesses; to influence laws & policies
that affect private businesses
Gp   Members information service;
FPB: Insurance, Telecoms, Legal protection, Payline, Grant
search, Streamline, Rates appeal
●   Res - SG - Stat - Inf - Empl - LG
<   Eur Assn of Small & Medium-sized Enterprises (UEAPME)
M   600,000 i, 25,000 f
¶   eNewsletter - 52.   Referendum - 4.   Eurolink - 12.
Action Report:
England & Wales - 2.   Scotland - 2.
Quarterly Survey of Private Businesses - 4.
Bank Survey - 2 yrly.

Fostering Network   1974
NR   87 Blackfriars Rd, LONDON, SE1 8HA.   (hq)
020 7620 6400   fax 020 7620 6401
email info@fostering.net   http://www.fostering.net
Chief Exec: Robert Tapsfield
▲   Registered Charity
Br   46 local groups
○   *W; to improve the quality of service given to children in care;
to bring together representatives of organisations &
authorities concerned with fostering
Gp   Assessment of foster carers; Relatives & friends as foster carers
●   Conf - Mtgs - ET - Res - SG - Stat - Inf - Lib - LG - Advice &
mediation service
M   21,500 i, 213 local authorities, 145 org
¶   Foster Care - 4.   AR.
Publication & resources catalogue available.
×   2001 National Foster Care Association

**Foundation & Aided Schools National Association   (FASNA)
1992**
■   11 The Orchard, Blackheath, LONDON, SE3 0QS.   (hsp)
020 8318 0872
email fasna@fasna.org.UK   http://www.fasna.org.uk
Gen Sec: George Phipson
▲   Company Limited by Guarantee; Registered Charity
○   *E, *P; to provide educational & professional support for
headteachers & governors of foundation & voluntary aided
schools
●   Conf - ET
M   800 schools
¶   NL - 3; ftm only.
×   2002 (Association of Heads of Foundation & Aided Schools
(Foundation & Voluntary Aided Schools' Association

**Foundation for the Study of Infant Deaths - Cot Death Research &
Support   (FSID)   1971**
NR   Artillery House, 11-19 Artillery Row, LONDON, SW1P 1RT.
(hq)
020 7222 8001   fax 020 7222 8002
email fsid@sids.org.uk   http://www.sids.org.uk/fsid/
Sec-Gen: Joyce Epstein
Br   140
○   *Q, *W; to raise funds for research into the causes & prevention
of cot death; to support bereaved parents; to disseminate
information about cot death & infant care
●   Conf - Mtgs - ET - Res - SG - Stat - Inf - Lib - LG
Helpline (24 hour) 020 7233 2090
M   12,000 i on mailing list
¶   NL - 2.   AR.
Various information books & leaflets.
×   2004 Cot Death Society (absorbed)

Foundation & Voluntary Aided Schools' Association
2002 merged with the Association of Heads of Foundation & Aided
Schools to form the **Foundation & Aided Schools National
Association**

Foundry Equipment & Supplies Association Ltd   (FESA)   1925
■   15 Walters Rd, OLDBURY, W Midlands, B68 0QA.   (hsb)
0121-601 6976   fax 0121-423 4582
email secretary@fesa.org.uk   http://www.fesa.org.uk
Sec: Andrew Turner
▲   Company Limited by Guarantee
○   *T
●   Conf - Exhib - Expt
<   Comité Européen des Matériels et Produits pour la
Fonderie (CEMAFON)
M   28 f
¶   Foundry Trade Jnl - 10; ftm, £174 nm (£380 o'seas, $380
USA).
Foundry Ybk - 1; ftm, £149 nm (+p&p).

** **Fountain Society**
Organisation lost: see Introduction paragraph 3

4children
NR   City Reach, 5 Greenwich View Place, LONDON, E14 9NN.
(hq)
020 7512 2112   fax 020 7512 2010
email info@4children.org.uk
http://www.4children.org.uk
Dir: Anne Longfield
▲   Registered Charity
○   *W; to promote & campaign for the provision of out of school
care for school age children
●   Conf - ET - Res - Inf - LG
<   Intl Play Assn; NCVO
M   c 1,000 org
×   2004 Kids' Club Network

fpa (FPA) 1930
- 2-12 Pentonville Rd, LONDON, N1 9FP. (hq)
  020 7837 5432   fax 020 7837 3042
  http://www.fpa.org.uk
  Chief Exec: Anne Weyman
- ▲ Registered Charity
- Br 6
- ○ *W; to improve the sexual health & reproductive rights of all
  people throughout the UK
- ● ET - Res - Inf - Lib - LG - Sexual Health Direct
  SHD Helpline: 0845 310 1334 (Mon-Fri 0900-1800)
- < Intl Planned Parenthood Fedn
- M 1,000 i
- ¶ Publications catalogue available.
- × 2005-06 Family Planning Association

Fragile X Society   1990
- NR Rood End House, 6 Stortford Road, GREAT DUNMOW, Essex,
  CM6 1DA. (nat/contact/p)
  01371 875100
  http://www.fragilex.org.uk
  National Contact: Lynne Zwink
- ▲ Registered Charity
- ○ *W; to provide mutual understanding & support for families
  with members carrying the 'fragile' X chromosome; to assist
  in research
- ● Conf - Mtgs - Res - Inf
- < Contact a Family; Soc for the Study of Behavioural Phenotypes
- M c 1,000 i families
- ¶ NL - 4.   AR.   Books, Papers & Leaflets.

Francis Bacon Society Inc   1886
- ■ Flat 1 Lee House, 75A Effra Rd, LONDON, SW19 8PS. (hsp)
  http://www.baconsocietyinc.org
  Hon Sec: Gerald Salway
- ▲ Company Limited by Guarantee; Registered Charity
- ○ *L; to promote the study of the works of Francis Bacon, (Baron
  Verulam of Verulam) 1561-1626, as a philosopher,
  statesman & poet; to examine evidence of his authorship of
  the plays ascribed to Shakespeare; to investigate his
  connection with other works of the Elizabethan period
- ● Mtgs - Res - Lib
- M 90 i, UK / 50 i, o'seas
- ¶ Baconiana (Jnl) - irreg; ftm, on application nm.

Francis Brett Young Society   (FBY Soc)   1979
- ■ 92 Gower Road, HALESOWEN, W Midlands, B62 9BT. (hsp)
  0121-422 8969
  http://www.fbysociety.co.uk
  Hon Sec: Mrs J Hadley
- ▲ Registered Charity
- ○ *A; to collate research done on the life & work of Francis Brett
  Young; to promote his works, & the work of promising writers
  born in Halesowen
- ● Mtgs - ET - Res - Inf - VE - Speakers on Brett Young provided on
  request
- < Alliance Literary Socs
- M 189 i, 8 org, 6 org, UK / 10 i, o'seas
- ¶ Jnl - 2; ftm.

**Franco-British Chamber of Commerce & Industry   (FBCCI)
1872**
- ■ 31 rue Boissy d'Anglas, F-75008 PARIS, France.
  33 (1) 53 30 81 30   fax 33 (1) 53 30 81 35
  email information@francobritishchamber.com
  http://www.francobritishchamber.com
  Catherine Le Yaouanc
- ○ *C; 'to assist companies to promote & develop their activities
  from both sides of the channel'
- ● Conf - Mtgs - ET - Exam - Res - Expt - Inf - Lib - LG
- < Coun Brit Chams Comm Continental Europe (COBCOE)
- M 750 f
- ¶ NL - 3; ftm only.

Franco-British Society   1944
- ■ 2 Dovedale Studios, 465 Battersea Park Rd, LONDON,
  SW11 4LR. (hq)
  020 7924 3511   fax 020 7924 3511
  email execsec@francobritishsociety.org.uk
  http://www.francobritishsociety.org.uk
  Chmn: The Rt Hon The Baroness Shepherd of Northwold
- ▲ Company Limited by Guarantee; Registered Charity
- ○ *X; an educational charity for the encouragement of British
  understanding of French artistic, scientific, social & economic
  achievements, through travel, personal contacts & meetings
- M i

Franco-Scottish Society of Scotland   1895
- ■ 2 Huntly Drive, Bearsden, GLASGOW, G61 3LD. (sp)
  0141-942 6756
  Gen Sec: Mrs Anne Marker
- ▲ Registered Charity
- Br 7; Canada, France
- ○ *X; promotion of knowledge of all matters of Franco-Scottish
  interest & of Franco-Scottish friendship & understanding
  through cultural, educational & social activities & personal
  contacts
- ● Conf - Mtgs - Res - Exhib - Lib - VE - Annual award:
  Lansdowne Prize - Each of the branches organises its own
  programme
- < Assn Franco-Ecossaise (France); Franco-Scottish Soc (Canada)
- M c 300 i, UK / c 200 i, o'seas
- ¶ Bulletin - 1; ftm.

František Kmoch Czech Bands Society
  since 1 January 2003 **Kmoch European Bands Society**

Free Choice for Supplements Alliance
  since 2002 **Alliance for Natural Health**

Free Trade League   (FTL)   1905
- ■ 1 Fern Dene, LONDON, W13 8AN. (hsp)
  020 8997 6868
  email john.hefferman@virgin.net
  Hon Sec: John Hefferman
- ▲ Un-incorporated Society
- ○ *K; 'to promote the economic & political case for unilateral UK
  trade policy of dismantling protection'
- ● Mtgs -VE
- M i, f & org
- ¶ The Free Trader - 1.

Freedom Association Ltd   (TFA)   1975
- ■ PO Box 2820, BRIDGNORTH, Shropshire, WV16 6YR. (hq)
  01746 861267   fax 01746 861267
  email mail@tfa.net   http://www.tfa.net
  Organising Sec: Mrs Vicki Stevens
- ▲ Company Limited by Guarantee
- ○ *K, 'a political pressure group campaigning for individual
  freedom & national independence'
- ● Conf - Mtgs - Political lobbying
- M 4,000 i, UK / 1,000 i, o'seas
- ¶ Freedom Today (Jnl) - 6; ftm, £3 nm.

**Freedom Organisation for the Right to Enjoy Smoking Tobacco
(FOREST)   1981**
- NR 33 Margaret St (6th floor), LONDON, W13 0JD. (hq)
  07071 766537   fax 020 7630 6226
  email forest@forest-on-smoking.org.uk
  http://www.forest-on-smoking.org.uk
  Dir: Simon Clark
- ▲ Company Limited by Guarantee
- ○ *K; to promote equal rights for smokers
- ● Res - Inf - LG - Media lobbying
- M i, uk & o'seas
- ¶ Burning Issues - 4; free.
  Various research papers & information sheets.

Freelance Hair & Beauty Federation Ltd   (FHBF Ltd)   1993
■ The Business Centre, Kimpton Rd, LUTON, Beds, LU2 0LB.
   (hq)
   01582 431783
   email enquiries@fhbf.org.uk   http://www.fhbf.org.uk
   Dir: Sheila Abrahams
○ *T
● Conf - ET - Inf
M not disclosed
¶ Highlights (NL) - 4; ftm only.

Freemen of England & Wales   (FEW)   1964
NR Richmond House, Beech Close, Oversley Green, ALCESTER,
   Warks, B49 6PP.   (hsp)
   01789 762574
   Hon Sec: R E Leek
▲ Registered Charity
○ *N; interests of the freemen of the cities & boroughs of England
   & Wales; to advance the knowledge of the history & legal
   custom of the boroughs & the legal institution of freedom
Gp Freemen's Guilds; Groups of freemen of towns & cities in
   England & Wales
● Mtgs - ET - Res - LG
M 7,000 i, 44 guilds
¶ Freemen of England & Wales (NL) - 3; ftm only.

Freemen & Guilds of the City of Chester
NR The Guildhall, Watergate St, CHESTER, Cheshire, CH1 2LA.
   (hq)
   01244 320431
▲ Un-incorporated Society
○ *N; founded in the 14th century the guild upholds & promotes
   the history of the individual craft companies; to support the
   Lord Mayor & Chester Council by participating in their civic &
   cultural duties
< Freemen of England & Wales
M i
¶ The Deva Pentice - 1.   Guildhall.

Freight Transport Association   (FTA)   1889
■ Hermes House, St John's Rd, ROYAL TUNBRIDGE WELLS, Kent,
   TN4 9UZ.   (hq)
   01892 526171   fax 01892 534989
   email enquiries@fta.co.uk   http://www.fta.co.uk
   Chief Exec: Richard Turner
▲ Company Limited by Guarantee
Br 5; Brussels (Belgium)
○ *T; interests of companies in the transport industry
Gp British Shippers Council; Utilities Group
● Conf - Mtgs - ET - Res - Exhib - Stat - Inf - VE - LG - Support
   services
< Intl Road Transport U (IRU)
M 12,000 f
¶ Freight - 12; ftm, £25 yr nm.   Ybk - 1; ftm, £34 nm.
   International Manual - 1; ftm, £60 nm.

French Chamber of Commerce in Great Britain
   see **Chambre de Commerce Française de Grande-Bretagne**

Fresh Produce Consortium (UK)   (FPC)   1993
■ Minerva House, Minerva Business Park, Lynch Wood,
   PETERBOROUGH, Cambs, PE2 6FT.   (hq)
   01733 237117   fax 01733 237118
   email info@freshproduce.org.uk
   http://www.freshproduce.org.uk
   Chief Exec: Nigel R Jenney
▲ Company Limited by Guarantee
○ *T; to develop the competitive performance of the produce &
   floral industries of the UK
Gp Divisions: Importers, Wholesale, Floral, Technical, Business
   services, Retail, Freshfel, Growers & potato packers
● Conf - Mtgs - ET - Res - Exhib - VE - LG - Promotion of
   consumption of fresh produce through education in schools
   & the wider community
< Freshfel Europe; Produce Marketing Assn (USA)
M 1,000 f
¶ Hbk - 1.

Freshwater Biological Association   (FBA)   1929
NR The Ferry House, Far Sawrey, AMBLESIDE, Cumbria,
   LA22 0LP.   (hq)
   01539 442468   fax 01539 446914
   email info@fba.org.uk   http://www.fba.org.uk
▲ Company Limited by Guarantee; Registered Charity
Br 1
○ *L, *Q; to investigate the biology of animals & plants found in
   fresh & brackish waters
● Conf - ET - Res - Inf - Lib
M c 1,800 i, corporate & students
¶ Freshwater Forum (Jnl) - 1.   NL - 2.
   Special Publications - irreg.
   Publications list available.

Friedreich's Ataxia Group
   since 2002 **Ataxia UK**

Friends of Alan Rawsthorne   1989
■ The Alpines, Main St, Hemingbrough, SELBY, N Yorks,
   YO8 6QF.   (sp)
   01757 630256
   email erato2@onetel.com
   http://www.musicweb-international.com/rawsth/
   index.htm
   Sec: John M Belcher
▲ Un-incorporated Society
○ *D; promotion of music by Alan Rawsthorne, British composer
   1905-1971
● Mtgs - Inf - Lib - Concerts
M 70 i, 5 org
¶ The Creel (Jnl) - 1.   The Sprat (NL) - irreg.
× 2003 Alan Rawsthorne Society

Friends of Alfred Williams   1969
NR 27 Belgrave St, Swindon, Wilts, SN1 3HR.   (hsp)
   01793 349575
   Hon Sec: Chris Bowles
○ *A; to further public interest in the life & works of Alfred
   Williams - poet, author & collector of folk songs

Friends of Arthur Machen   1986
NR Stable Cottage, Priestbank Rd, Kildwick, KEIGHLEY, N Yorks,
   BD20 9BH.   (hsp)
   Hon Sec: Mark Valentine
▲ Company Limited by Guarantee; Registered Charity
○ *A; to honour the life & work of writer Arthur Machen (1863-
   1947); to support research students, publishers, writers etc
   interested in Machen's work
Gp Green Round Press (publishing imprint)
M i, libraries & universities
¶ Faunus (Jnl) - 1; ftm.   Machenalia (NL) - 2; free.

Friends of Blue   (FOB)   1973
- ■ PO Box 122, DIDCOT DO, Oxon, OX11 0YN.   (hsp)
  01235 816266
  Sec: Arthur C Roberts
- ▲ Un-incorporated Society
- ○ *G; to promote study & interest of English blue & white transfer printed ceramics of 18th & 19th centuries
- ● Res
- M 407 i, UK / 53 i, o'seas
- ¶ Bulletin - 4; ftm only.
  True Blue (1998); £9.50 m, £11.50 nm.

Friends of Cathedral Music   (FCM)   1956
- ■ 27 Old Gloucester St, LONDON, WC1N 3XX.   (hq)
  email info@fcm.org.uk   http://www.fcm.org.uk
  Hon Sec: Roger Bishton
- ▲ Registered Charity
- ○ *D, *R; to safeguard the heritage of cathedral music; to increase public knowledge & appreciation of cathedral music; to encourage high standards in choral & organ music
- ● Mtgs - Exhib - Inf - Awards of grants to cathedral authorities to assist in maintaining choral services
- M 2,700 i, 30 org, UK / 300 i, o'seas
- ¶ Cathedral Music Singing in Cathedrals: a listing of choral services in the UK - 2; ftm, £3.50 nm.

Friends of Classics   (FoC)
- NR 51 Achilles Rd, LONDON, NW6 1DZ.
  020 7431 5088   fax 020 7431 5129
  http://www.friends-classic.demon.co.uk
  Exec Sec: Jeannie Cohen
- ○ *G

Friends of Coleridge   1986
- ■ 11 Castle St, NETHER STOWEY, Somerset, TA5 1LN.   (hsp)
  01278 733338
  http://www.friendsofcoleridge.com
  87 Richmond Rd, Montpelier, BRISTOL, BS6 5EP.
     0117-942 6366.   (conf organiser)
  Hon Sec: Mrs Shirley M Watters
  Conf Org: Graham Davidson
- ▲ Registered Charity
- Br Canada, USA (Mems worldwide)
- ○ *A, *L; to promote the work of Samuel Taylor Coleridge (1772-1834); to support Coleridge Cottage with the National Trust
- ● Conf - Mtgs - SG - VE
- M 250 i, 3 org, UK / 65 i, 2 org, o'seas
- ¶ The Coleridge Bulletin - 2; ftm.
  Conference brochure - 2 yrly (even yrs); free.

Friends of Dr Watson   (FDW)   1996
- NR 13 Crofton Avenue, ORPINGTON, Kent, BR6 8DU.   (mem/sec)
  Mem Sec: R J Ellis
- Br Belgium
- ○ *G; to promote interest in the life, times & work of Dr John H Watson MD (from the Sherlock Holmes stories by Arthur Conan Doyle) & the society of the period; to study the medical aspects of Conan Doyle's work
- ● Res - Comp - Inf - VE - Annual dinner - Maiwand luncheon - Dr Watson Day
- < Franco-Midland Hardware Co (an international Sherlock Holmes study group)
- M 33 i, 2 f, UK / 19 i, 1 f, o'seas
- ¶ The Formulary (Jnl) - 2; £4 (US$8) m, £6 (US$12) nm.
  Watson's Wanderings; £4 (US$8) m, £6 (US$12) nm.
  Watson's Wanderings Again; £4 (US$8) m, £6 (US$12) nm.
  The London Practice; £4 (US$8) m, £6 (US$12) nm.
  The Maiwand Luncheon Monograph;   Watson's Weapons;
  The Maiwand Dispatch No 1;   From Netley to Maiwand;
     all £5 m (US$10); £7 nm (US$14).
  5th Birthday Annual; ftm, £5 nm (US$10).   AR; free.

Friends of the Dymock Poets   (FDP)   1993
- ■ Burgage House, 19 The Southend, LEDBURY, Herefords, HR8 2EY.   (hsp)
  01531 634796
  email cateluck2003@yahoo.com
  http://www.dymockpoets.co.uk
  Hon Sec: Catharine Luck
- ○ *A; to foster an interest in the group of poets associated with the Dymock area in Gloucestershire before the First World War (Lascelles Abercrombie, Rupert Brooke, John Drinkwater, Robert Frost, Wilfrid Gibson & Edward Thomas)
- ● Conf - Mtgs
- < Alliance of Literary Socs
- M 325 i, UK / 25 i, o'seas
- ¶ NL - irreg;   Dymock Poets & Friends - 1; both ftm only.

Friends of the Earth   (FOE)   1971
- ■ 26-28 Underwood St, LONDON, N1 7JQ.   (hq)
  020 7490 1555   fax 020 7490 0881
  email info@foe.co.uk   http://www.foe.co.uk
  Exec Dir: Tony Juniper
- ▲ Company Limited by Guarantee; Registered Charity
- Br 12
- ○ *K; environmental issues
- ● ET - Res - Stat - Inf - PL
- < Friends of the Earth Intl
- M c 100,000 i
- ¶ Earth Matters - 3; ftm only.
  Publications list available.

Friends of Friendless Churches   1957
- ■ St Ann's Vestry Hall, 2 Church Entry, LONDON, EC4V 5HB. (hsb)
  020 7236 3934   fax 020 7329 3677
  email office@ancientmonumentssociety.org.uk
  http://www.friendsoffriendlesschurches.org.uk
  Chmn: Roger Evans,   Hon Dir: Matthew Saunders
- ▲ Registered Charity
- ○ *K; the ownership of 38 disused but architecturally important places of worship
- ● Inf
- < Ancient Monuments Soc (working partnership)
- M 2,000 i
- ¶ AR;   Appeals.

Friends Historical Society   (FHS)   1903
- NR c/o The Quakers Library, 173-177 Euston Rd, LONDON, NW1 2BJ.   (hsb)
  http://www.quaker.org.uk
  Clerk, Treas & Mem Sec: Brian Hawkins
- ▲ Un-incorporated Society
- ○ *L; history of the Quakers
- ● Conf - Mtgs
- ¶ Jnl - 1; ftm, £6 nm.   NL - 2; ftm only.
  Meeting Houses in Britain (1999); David Butler.

Friends of the Lake District   (FLD)   1934
- NR Murley Moss, Oxenholme Rd, KENDAL, Cumbria, LA9 7SS. (hq)
  01539 720788   fax 01539 730355
  Exec Dir: Andrew Forsyth
- ▲ Registered Charity
- ○ *K; protect & cherish the landscape & natural beauty of the Lake District & Cumbria
- ● Conf - Mtgs - Exhib - Inf - VE - Joint action with other societies for protection of the environment
- < CPRE; Nat Trust; Ramblers' Assn; Coun Nat Parks
- M c 6,700 i & org
- ¶ NL - 2;   Conserving Lakeland - 2; both ftm only.

© CBD Research Ltd · Beckenham · BR3 5JS · Tel 020 8650 7745 · Fax 020 8650 0768 · E-mail cbd@cbdresearch.com · www.cbdresearch.com

Friends of Medieval Dublin   (FMD)   1975

IRL   c/o Medieval History Dept, Trinity College, DUBLIN 2, Republic
    of Ireland.
    353 (1) 608 1801   fax 353 (1) 608 3995
    Hon Sec: Stuart Kinsella
○   *L

Friends of Mendelssohn   (F of M)   1995

■   35 Northcourt Avenue, READING, Berks, RG2 7HE.   (hq)
    0118-987 1479
    Founder & Dir: Mrs Pam Gulliver
▲   Un-incorporated Society
○   *D; to promote the music of Felix Mendelssohn & his
    contemporaries; to campaign for higher standards in
    performances & recordings of such work
Gp   Team Mendelssohn (sporting events for charity)
●   Mtgs - Res - SG - Inf - Lib - VE
M   20 i

Friends of the National Bonsai Collection
    is part of the **Federation of British Bonsai Societies**

Friends of the National Collections of Ireland

IRL   Ivy House, ATHBOY, Co Meath, Republic of Ireland.
    353 (46) 943 2114
    Hon Sec: Jennifer Waldron-Lynch
○   *A

Friends of the National Libraries   (FNL)   1931

■   c/o Dept of Manuscripts, The British Library, 96 Euston Rd,
    LONDON, NW1 2DB.   (hsb)
    020 7412 7559
    http://www.friendsofnationallibraries.org.uk
    Hon Sec: Michael Borrie
▲   Registered Charity
○   *G; to promote the acquisition by national libraries of printed
    books, manuscripts & records of historical, literary, artistic,
    architectural, musical or suchlike interest by grants for
    purchases, channelling benefactions & legacies & public
    appeals
●   Mtgs - VE
M   c 700 i, 100 f
¶   AR.

Friends of the Pianola Institute   (FPI)   1985

■   The Granary, Wharf Rd, Fenny Compton, SOUTHAM, Warks,
    CV47 2FE.   (chmn/p)
    01295 770103   fax 01295 770301
    email mike@pianola.org   http://www.pianola.org
    Chmn: Mike J Davies
▲   Un-incorporated Society
○   *D; for supporters of the Institute, which exists to promote
    pianolas & music for pianolas
Gp   Pianola roll production
●   Mtgs - Res - Concerts - Roll & record production
M   65 i, UK / 15 i, o'seas
¶   Jnl - 1; ftm, £10 nm.   NL - 4; ftm only.

Friends of Real Lancashire   (FoRL)   1992

■   1 Belvidere Park, GREAT CROSBY, Lancs, L23 0SP.   (chmn/p)
    0151-928 2770
    email csd@forl.co.uk   http://www.forl.co.uk
    Chmn: C S Dawson
○   *G; to promote the true identity of the ancient & geographical
    county of Lancashire
●   Inf - LG
<   Assn of Brit Counties
M   660 i, 13 f, 8 org
¶   The Lancastrian - 1; ftm, £150 nm.   NL - 3; free (sae nm).

Friends of St Bride Library   (FSBL)

■   c/o St Bride Library, Bride Lane, Fleet St, LONDON,
    EC4Y 8EE.   (hq)
    020 7353 4660   fax 020 7583 7073
    email friends@stbride.org   http://www.stbride.org
    Hon Sec: Stephen Lubell,   Chmn: Robert Banham
▲   Registered Charity (as pt of the St Bride Foundation)
○   *G, *K; to promote, support, improve, & raise money to
    safeguard the future of the St Bride Library (contains
    collections on printing & allied subjects - paper, binding,
    design, typography, typefaces, calligraphy, illustration &
    printmaking)
●   Conf - Mtgs - Exhib - Lectures
<   St Bride Foundation
M   c 2,000 i
¶   The Ravilious Notebook; Caroline Archer & Robert Harling.
    The Nymph and the Grot; James Mosley.
    Typefounders London A-Z; Justin Howes & Nigel Roche.
×   2004 (April) Friends of St Bride Printing Library

Friends of War Memorials
    see **War Memorials Trust**

Friesian Horse Association of Great Britain & Ireland   (FHAGBI)   1995

■   Harbours Hill Farm, Hanbury Rd, STOKE PRIOR, Worcs,
    B60 4AG.   (hsp)
    01527 821276
    email jcca2000@aol.com   http://www.fhagbi.co.uk
    Hon Sec: Liz Spurdens
▲   Company Limited by Guarantee
○   *B
●   Annual inspections - Social events
<   Het Friesch Paarden-Stamboek (Netherlands)
M   100 i

Frozen & Chilled Potato Processors' Association   (FCPPA)   1972

NR   6 Catherine St, LONDON, WC2B 5JJ.   (hq)
    020 7836 2460   fax 020 7836 0580
▲   Un-incorporated Society
○   *T; to raise the standard & quality of raw materials; to
    exchange ideas & information
●   Mtgs - Res - Stat - Inf - LG
<   Food & Drink Fedn (FDF); Potato Processors' Assn (PPA)
M   10 f

Fund Managers Association
    2002 merged with the Association of Unit Trusts & Investment Funds
    to form the **Investment Management Association**

Fund for the Replacement of Animals in Medical Experiments   (FRAME)   1969

■   Russell & Burch House, 96-98 North Sherwood St,
    NOTTINGHAM, NG1 4EE.   (hq)
    0115-958 4740   fax 0115-950 3570
    email frame@frame.org.uk   http://www.frame.org.uk
    Chmn of the Trustees: Prof Michael Balls
▲   Registered Charity
○   *K; to promote, research & develop the use of alternative
    methods in medical & related research, which reduce or
    replace the use of laboratory animals
●   Conf - ET - Res - Inf
M   500 i, 50 f org, UK / 5 f, o'seas
¶   ATLA Jnl - 6; £126 yr.   AR - 1; ftm.
    Frame News - 3 (with) Friends of Frame - 3; £15.

Funeral Furnishing Manufacturers Association   (FFMA)   1939
- ■ 15 Riverside Drive, SOLIHULL, W Midlands, B91 3HH.   (sb)
     0121-705 5133
     email burtonnr@aol.com
     Sec: N R Burton
- ▲ Un-incorporated Society
- ○ *T; 'to promote the provision of coffins & other services to
     funeral directors; legal, technical & environmental issues are
     also under constant discussion'
- ● Conf - Mtgs - Exhib - LG
- M 38 f

Funeral Standards Council
     has become the Funeral Planning Authority; for further details
     see the companion volume 'Councils, Committees & Boards'
     (Introduction paragraph 6)

Furniture History Society   (FHS)   1964
- ■ 1 Mercedes Cottages, St John's Rd, HAYWARDS HEATH,
     W Sussex, RH16 4EH.   (msp)
     01444 413845   fax 01444 413845
     email furniturehistorysociety@hotmail.com
     http://www.furniturehistorysociety.com
     Mem Sec: Dr Brian Austen
- ▲ Registered Charity
- ○ *L; the study of the history of furniture & furnishings on a
     worldwide basis
- ● Conf - Mtgs - ET - Res - SG - VE
- M 1,200 i, 30 f, 80 org, UK / 300 i, 30 f, 70 org, o'seas
- ¶ Furniture History - 1;   NL - 4;   AR; all ftm.

Furniture Industry Research Association   (FIRA)   1949
- ■ Maxwell Rd, STEVENAGE, Herts, SG1 2EW.   (hq)
     01438 777700   fax 01438 777800
     email info@fira.co.uk   http://www.askfira.co.uk
     Managing Dir: Hayden Davies
- ▲ Company Limited by Guarantee
- ○ *Q; furniture & related products
- ● Conf - Mtgs - Res - Stat - Inf - LG - Testing - Consultancy
- < EURIFI
- M 550 f, UK & o'seas
- ¶ NL - 4; free.   Ybk; ftm only.

Further Education Research Association   (FERA)   1973
- NR External Affairs Office, University of Worcester, Henwick Grove,
     WORCESTER, WR2 6AJ.   (chmn/b)
     01905 855145   fax 01905 855132
     email g.elliott@worc.ac.uk   http://www.fera.uk.net
     Chmn: Prof Geoffrey Elliott
- ▲ Un-incorporated Society
- ○ *E, *L, *Q; research within & about further education (post 16)
- ● Conf - Mtgs - ET - Res - Inf
- M 100+ i
- ¶ Research in Post-Compulsory Education - 3; ftm, £36 each nm.

Futon Association of Britain   (FAB)   1994
- NR 24 Beauchamp Rd, LONDON, SW11 1PQ.
     020 7223 7212   fax 020 7223 7212
     http://www.futonsonline.co.uk
- ▲ Un-incorporated Society
- ○ *T; promotion & education on all matters concerning futon
     furniture
- ● ET - Stat - Inf - Lib
- < Futon Assn Intl (FAI)
- M 20 i, 15 f

Futures & Options Association   (FOA)   1993
- NR 36-38 Botolph Lane (2nd floor), LONDON, EC3R 8DE.   (hq)
     020 7929 0081   fax 020 7621 0223
     Chief Exec: A M Belchambers
- ○ *T; for the derivatives industry; to monitor & respond to
     regulatory & tax changes; to heighten industry & product
     awareness
- M f
- ¶ NL - 8; ftm only.   AR; free.

Gaelic Athletic Association 1884
IRL   Croke Park, DUBLIN 3, Republic of Ireland.
     353 (1) 836 3222   fax 353 (1) 836 6420
     email info@gaa.ie   http://www.gaa.ie
○   *S; promotion of Gaelic football, hurling, handball and
     rounders

Gallipoli Association 1969
■   Earleydene Orchard, Earleydene, ASCOT, Berks, SL5 9JY.
     (hsp)
     01344 626523
     http://www.gallipoli-association.org
     Hon Sec: J C Watson Smith
▲   Un-incorporated Society
○   *G; to keep alive the memory of the Gallipoli campaign of
     1915; for those interested in the campaign
●   Mtgs - VE - 2 lunches a year - Tour to Dardanelles
M   c 1,000 i, UK & o'seas
¶   The Gallipolian - 3; ftm.

Galloway Cattle Society of Great Britain & Ireland 1877
■   15 New Market St, CASTLE DOUGLAS, Kirkcudbrightshire,
     DG7 1HY.   (hq)
     01556 502753   fax 01556 502753
     email info@gallowaycattlesociety.co.uk
     http://www.gallowaycattlesociety.co.uk
     Sec: Dorothy J Goldie
▲   Registered Charity
○   *B; to promote & keep pure Galloway cattle
Gp   Farmers; Small holding-farms; Farmers' markets
●   Exhib
M   500 i, UK / 150 i, o'seas
¶   Jnl - 1; free.   Herd Book - 1; £10.

Galpin Society 1946
■   37 Townsend Drive, ST ALBANS, Herts, AL3 5RF.   (chmn/p)
     http://www.galpinsociety.org
     Chmn of Trustees: Graham Wells
▲   Registered Charity
○   *L, *Q; the study of the history, construction, development & use
     of musical instruments
●   Conf - Mtgs - Res
M   400 i, UK / 600 i, o'seas, c 300 universities & libraries
     worldwide
¶   Jnl - 1; ftm.   NL - 3; ftm only.

Galton Institute 1907
■   19 Northfields Prospect, Northfields, LONDON, SW18 1PE.
     (hq)
     020 8874 7257
     email betty.nixon@talk21.com
     Gen Sec: Betty Nixon
▲   Company Limited by Guarantee; Registered Charity
○   *L, *Q; to study the effects of hereditary & environmental
     factors on inborn human qualities; to promote a responsible
     attitude to parenthood; Population problems
●   Conf - ET - Res
<   Inst Biology
M   300 i, UK / 100 i, o'seas
¶   NL - 4; m only.
     Proceedings of Conference (book) - 1; ftm, £5 nm.

Galvanizers Association (GA) 1949
■   56 Victoria Rd, Wrens Court, SUTTON COLDFIELD,
     W Midlands, B72 1SY.   (hq)
     0121-355 8838   fax 0121-355 8727
     email ga@hdg.org.uk   http://www.galvanizing.org.uk
     Gen Mgr: David M Baron
▲   Company Limited by Guarantee
○   *T; to provide technical & marketing services for the hot dip
     galvanizing industry in the UK & Ireland
●   Conf - Mtgs - ET - Res - Exhib - Stat - Inf - Lib - VE
M   37 f, UK / 48 f, o'seas
¶   Hot Dip Galvanizing (Jnl) - 4; free (1st 10 copies ftm).
     Brochure: Engineers' & Architects' Guide to Hot Dip
     Galvanising (2001); £1.50 m, £5 nm.

Galway Chamber of Commerce & Industry
IRL   Commerce House, Merchants Rd, GALWAY, Republic of
     Ireland.
     353 (91) 563536   fax 353 (91) 561963
     email info@galwaychamber.com
     http://www.galwaychamber.com
     Chief Exec: Michael Coyle
○   *C

GAMBICA Association Ltd
     see **Association for Instrumentation, Control, Automation &
     Laboratory Technology (GAMBICA)**

Game Conservancy Trust / Game Conservancy Ltd (GCT / GCL) 1980
NR   Burgate Manor, FORDINGBRIDGE, Hants, SP6 1EF.   (hq)
     01425 652381   fax 01425 655848
     email info@gct.org.uk   http://www.gct.org.uk
     Chief Exec: Teresa Dent
▲   Registered Charity
Br   50; Germany, USA
○   *Q; research & advice into conservation & habitat of all game
     species.   Associated research in agriculture, arable insects,
     songbirds & pesticides/herbicides
M   i, f & org
¶   Jnl - 2.   Trade Directory - 1.   AR.

Game Farmers Association (GFA) 1918
■   Colnbrook, Withington, CHELTENHAM, Glos, GL54 4BW.
     (sec&treas/p)
     01242 890372   fax 01242 890372
     email jimatgfa@aol.com
     Sec & Treas: E J Day
▲   Un-incorporated Society
○   *F
●   Mtgs - ET - Seminars
<   in close co-operation with the Nat Gamekeepers Assn
M   179 i, 29 f, UK / 3 f, o'seas
¶   Game Farming NL - 4; ftm only.

Garage Equipment Association   (GEA)   1945

- ■ 2-3 Church Walk, DAVENTRY, Northants, NN11 4BL.   (hq)
  01327 312616   fax 01327 312606
  email name@gea.co.uk   http://www.gea.co.uk
  Chief Exec: Dave Garratt
- ▲ Company Limited by Guarantee
- ○ *T; represents the interests of all sectors of the garage equipment industry; manufacturing, servicing, installation, selling & distribution of garage equipment & provision of training
- Gp Manufacturers; Distributors; Service; MOT liaison; Code of Practice; Exhibitions
- ● Mtgs - Exhib - Stat - LG
- < Eur Garage Eqpt Assn (EGEA)
- M 115 f
- ¶ The World of Emissions (on emission testing).

Garage Watch Ltd   2001

- NR 43 Broadway, SHIFNAL, Shropshire, TF11 8BB.   (hq)
  01952 463273
  email admin@garagewatch.org
  http://www.garagewatch.org
  CEO: Mark Bradshaw
- ▲ Company Limited by Guarantee
- ○ *K, *T; for independent petroleum retailers
- ● Exhib - Inf - LG
- < Fedn of Petroleum Suppliers; Assn of Convenience Stores
- M 1,500 f
- ¶ Garage Watch NL - 6; free.

Garden Centre Association Ltd   (GCA)   1979

- ■ 19 High St, Theale, READING, Berks, RG7 5AH.   (hq)
  0118-932 3360   fax 0118-930 8915
  email info@gca.org.uk   http://www.gca.org.uk
  Admin: Gillie Westwood
- ▲ Company Limited by Guarantee
- ○ *T
- ● Conf - Comp - SG - Inf
- < Intl Garden Centre Assn
- M 160 f, 183 associate f
- ¶ GCA Ybk - 1; ftm, £45 nm.   LM; ftm, £50 nm.

Garden History Society   (GHS)   1965

- NR 70 Cowcross St, LONDON, EC1M 6EJ.
  020 7608 2409   fax 020 7490 2974
  email enquiries@gardenhistorysociety.org
  http://www.gardenhistorysociety.org
  Chmn: Dr Colin Treen
- ▲ Registered Charity
- ○ *H, *L; to promote study into the history of gardening & horticulture in all aspects; to protect historic gardens
- Gp Conservation
- ● Conf - Mtgs - Res - Exhib - Stat - Inf - VE - Advising on restoration & preservation of historic gardens
- < ICOMOS; Civic Trust; CPRE; Brit Assn for Local History
- M 1,800 i, UK / c 250 i, o'seas, also university & civic libraries
- ¶ Garden History (Jnl) - 2.   NL - 3.

Garden & Landscape Designers Association   (GLDA)

- IRL 73 Deerpark Rd, MOUNT MERRION, Co Dublin, Republic of Ireland.
  353 (1) 278 1824   fax 353 (1) 283 5724
  email info@glda.ie   http://www.glda.ie
  Hon Sec: Lisa Murphy
- ○ *G, *P

Garden Organic
the working title of the **Henry Doubleday Research Association**

Garden Writers Guild   (GWG)   1991

- ■ at the Institute of Horticulture, 14-15 Belgrave Sq, LONDON, SW1X 8PS.   (hq)
  020 7245 6943   fax 020 7245 6943
  email gwg@horticulture.org.uk
  http://www.gardenwriters.co.uk
  Admin: Kiersty Darnell
- ▲ Un-incorporated Society
- ○ *P; to raise the quality of garden writing & broadcasting; to help members to improve communications between members & liaison between writers, photographers, broadcasters, publishers & the horticultural industry
- ● Mtgs - Annual awards for garden writing, broadcasting & photography
- M 400 i, UK / 10 i, o'seas
- ¶ GWG News - 6; ftm only.
  Garden Writers' Guild Ybk (incl LM) - 1; ftm, £50 nm.

GARDENEX: the Federation of Garden & Leisure Manufacturers Ltd   (GARDENEX)   1961

- NR The White House, High St, BRASTED, Kent, TN16 1JE.   (hq)
  01959 565995   fax 01959 565885
  email info@gardenex.com   http://www.gardenex.com
  Chief Exec: Amanda Sizer Barrett
- ▲ Company Limited by Guarantee
- ○ *T; to promote the export of British manufactured products, services, plants etc in international markets
- M f

Gardening for the Disabled Trust & Garden Club   1973

- NR Hayes Farm House, Hayes Lane, PEASMARSH, E Sussex, TN31 6XR.   (hsp)
  Hon Sec: Julia Sebline
- ○ *G, *H; a charity to encourage disabled people of all ages to enjoy gardening as a creative hobby
- ● Planning & building special gardens
- M i & org
- ¶ NL - 4.
- × 2002-04 Gardens for the Disabled Trust & Garden Club

Gas Forum   1994

- NR Gemserv, Centurion House (7th Floor), 24 Monument St, LONDON, EC3R 8AJ.   (hq)
  020 7090 1000
- ▲ Company Limited by Guarantee
- ○ *T; for companies shipping gas through the national gas pipeline system & those supplying gas to industrial, commercial & domestic customers
- Gp Legal affairs standing c'ee
  Work Gps: Technical & safety, Domestic code of practice, Industrial & commercial code of practice, VAT, Independent gas transporters, European, Transco price control review, Suppliers, Major incidents & gas supply emergencies, Suppliers metering forum, Security of supply, Engineering sub work, Gas industry governance, Standards of service
- ● Conf - Mtgs - Res - LG
- M 20 f

** Gascon Cattle Society

Organisation lost: see Introduction paragraph 3

Gaskell Society   1985

NR   Far Yew Tree House, Chestnut Rd, Tabley, KNUTSFORD,
       Cheshire, WA16 0HN.   (hsp)
       01565 634668
       email joanleach@aol.com
       http://www.gaskellsociety.users.btopenworld.com
       Sec: Mrs Joan Leach
▲   Registered Charity
Br   2; Japan
○   *A; to promote interest in Mrs Elizabeth Cleghorn Gaskell's life
       & writings
●   Conf - Mtgs - SG
<   Alliance of Literary Socs
M   500 i, UK / 120 i, o'seas
¶   Jnl - 1.   NL - 2.

Gasket Cutters' Association   (GCA)   1993

NR   105 St Peter's St, ST ALBANS, Herts, AL1 3EJ.   (asa)
       01727 896084   fax 01727 896026
       email info@gcassociation.co.uk
▲   Un-incorporated Society
○   *T; interests of companies cutting gaskets & associated
       conversion processes
●   Conf - Mtgs - SG - Inf - LG
M   30 f
¶   The Informer - 4; ftm only.

Gate Automation & Access Barrier Association
       see **Fencing Contractors Association**

Gaucher's Association   1991

■   3 Bull Pitch, DURSLEY, Glos, GL11 4NG.   (hq)
       01463 549231   fax 01463 549231
       email ga@gaucher.org.uk   http://www.gaucher.org.uk
       Exec Sec: Tanya Collin-Histed
▲   Company Limited by Guarantee; Registered Charity
○   *M, *W; information & support group for people with
       Gaucher's disease (abnormal storage of lipids) & their
       families
●   Conf - Mtgs - Res - Inf - LG
M   494 i, 454 f, UK / 30 i, 272 f, o'seas
¶   Gauchers News - 2; free.

Gauge & Tool Makers Association   (GTMA)   1942

■   3 Forge House, Summerleys Rd, PRINCES RISBOROUGH,
       Bucks, HP27 9DT.   (hq)
       01844 274222   fax 01844 274227
       email gtma@gtma.co.uk   http://www.gtma.co.uk
▲   Un-incorporated Society
○   *T
Gp   Metrology; Mould & die; Special purpose machinery; Press tool;
       Tool & workholding eqpt
●   Conf - Mtgs - ET - Exhib - Stat - Expt - Inf - Lib - VE
<   Intl Special Tooling Assn
M   320 f
¶   GTMA Directory of Gauging & Toolmaking Products &
       Services - 1; ftm.

GB Wheelchair Rugby Association   (GBWRA)   1998

NR   8 Oak Close, FELIXSTOWE, Suffolk, IP11 2LS.
       Sec: D Hilton
○   *S

GEM Motoring Assist
       the trading name of the **Guild of Experienced Motorists**

**Gemmological Association & Gem Testing Laboratory of Great
Britain   (GEM-A)   1925**

NR   27 Greville St, LONDON, EC1N 8SU.   (hq)
       020 7404 3334
       Dir: R R Harding
▲   Company Limited by Guarantee
○   *L, *P; for gemmologists
●   Conf - Mtgs - ET - Exam - Res - Testing & grading of gemstones
       - Supply of instruments & books - Conducts gem & diamond
       grading courses - Laboratory service for members
<   Commission Intle de Bijouterie, Joaillerie et Orfevrerie (CIBJO);
       Canadian Gemmological Assn; Gem & Mineral Soc S Africa;
       Singapore Gemmologist Soc
M   1,600 i, 100 f, 2 org, UK / 1,900 i, o'seas
¶   Journal of Gemmology - 4;
       Gem & Jewellery News - 4; (jt publication with Society of
       Jewellery History);   AR - 1; all ftm only.

Gender Trust   (GEMS)   1990

■   PO Box 3192, BRIGHTON, E Sussex, BN1 3WR.   (hq)
       0700 079 0347
       email info@gendertrust.org.uk
       http://www.gendertrust.org.uk
       Trust Admin: Rosemary Turner
▲   Registered Charity
Br   12
○   *W; information & support for transsexual people, their families
       & partners
Gp   Gender; Transsexual
●   Conf - ET - Inf - Telephone service
M   450 i, 2 f, 20 org, UK / 6 i, o'seas
¶   Membership magazine - 4; £29 yr m only.
       Employers Guide;   Sex Reassignment Surgery;
       Standards of Care;   all £2.50.
       Gender Trust Guide; £6 m, £8 nm.

General Aviation Manufacturers & Traders Association Ltd
       2004 merged with the Business Aircraft Users' Association to form the
       British Business & General Aviation Association

General Council of County Councils

IRL   Fitzmaurice Place, PORTLAOISE, Co Laois, Republic of Ireland.
       353 (57) 867 1288   fax 353 (57) 866 2977
       email info@gccc.ie   http://www.councillors.ie
       Dir: Liam Kenny
○   *N

General Council for Massage Therapy   (GCMT)   2002

■   Whiteway House, Blundells Lane, Rainhill, PRESCOT,
       Merseyside, L35 6NB.   (hsb)
       0870 850 4452
       email gcmt@btconnect.com   http://www.gcmt.org.uk
       Sec: Wendy Kavanagh
▲   Un-incorporated Society
○   *N, *P; for the self-regulation of massage therapy in the UK; to
       bring together organisations engaged in representing, or
       teaching, massage therapy, for the protection of the public
●   Mtgs - ET - Res - SG - If - LG
>   CTHA; LCSP; MTI; MTIGB; PACT; SMTO
M   670 i, 6 org

General Council & Register of Consultant Herbalists
       trading name of the **International Register of Consultant
       Herbalists & Homoeopaths**

General Council & Register of Naturopaths   (GCRN)   1967
■ Goswell House, 2 Goswell Rd, STREET, Somerset, BA16 0JG. (hsb)
  0870 745 6984
  Sec: M W F Szewiel
▲ Company Limited by Guarantee
○ *L, *P; to register suitably qualified naturopathic practitioners; to set minimum standards for the training of practitioners for the benefit of the public
● Conf - ET - LG
M 310 i, UK / 19 i, o'seas
¶ Register of Practitioners Members - 1.

General Dental Practitioners Association
  since 2005 **Dental Practitioners Association**

General Federation of Trade Unions   (GFTU)   1899
NR Central House, Upper Woburn Place, LONDON, WC1H 0HY. (hq)
  020 7387 2578   fax 020 7383 0820
  email gftuhq@gftu.org.uk   http://www.gftu.org.uk
  Gen Sec: Michael Bradley
▲ Un-incorporated Society
○ *N; a federation of unions providing benefits & services to affiliates
● Conf - Mtgs - ET - Res - Stat - Inf - Lib - LG
M 35 unions
¶ Federation Jnl - 2/3;   Federation News - 2/3;
  Report - 2 yrly; all free.

General Insurance Market Research Association
  is a special interest group of the **Association of Users of Research Agencies**

General Insurance Standards Council
  the responsibilities of the Council have been taken over by the Financial Services Authority; for further details see the companion volume **Councils, Commitees & Boards**

Genetic Interest Group   (GIG)   1990
NR 4D Leroy House, 436 Essex Rd, LONDON, N1 3QP.   (hq)
  020 7704 3141   fax 020 7359 1447
  email mail@gig.org.uk   http://www.gig.org.uk
  Dir: Alastair Kent
▲ Registered Charity
○ *M; to improve services for all people with genetic disorders; to increase understanding & knowledge of human genetics
● Conf - Mtgs - ET - Inf - LG
< Eur Alliance of Genetic Support Groups
M 120 org
¶ GIG Today (NL) - 4;   AR; both free.

Genetics Society   1919
■ Roslin Biocentre, Wallace Building, ROSLIN, Midlothian, EH25 9PP.   (hq)
  0131-200 6391   fax 0131-200 6394
  email mail@genetics.org.uk
  http://www.genetics.org.uk
  Exec Officer: Jayne Richards
▲ Registered Charity
○ *L; Gene structure, function & regulation; Cell & development genetics; Evolutionary, ecological & population genetics; Genomics; Applied & quantitative genetics; Corporate genetics & biotechnology
● Conf - Mtgs - Inf
< Intl Genetics Fedn (IGF); Fedn Eur Genetics Socs (FEGS); Inst Biology (IoB); BioSciences Fedn (BSF)
M 2,000 i, UK / 300 i, o'seas
¶ Heredity - 12; £28 m, £138 nm.
  Genes & Development - 24; £128 m.

Genito-Urinary Physicians Colposcopy Group
  a special interest group of the **British Association for Sexual Health & HIV**

Geographical Association   (GA)   1893
■ 160 Solly St, SHEFFIELD, S Yorks, S1 4BF.   (hq)
  0114-296 0088   fax 0114-296 7176
  email ga@geography.org.uk
  http://www.geography.org.uk &
  www.geographyshop.org.uk
  Chief Exec: Dr David Lambert
▲ Registered Charity; Un-incorporated Society
Br 33
○ *E, *L, *P; to further the study & teaching of geography at all levels
Gp Section c'ees: Primary & middle school, Secondary education, Post-16;
  Phase c'ees: Early years & primary, Secondary, Post-16 & HE
  Working gps: Field studies, Environmental & sustainable development education, Independent schools, Information & communications technology, Geography advisers & inspectors network, Assessment & examinations, Intl c'ee
● Conf - Mtgs - ET - Res - Exhib - Comp - SG - Inf - VE - LG
< Coun for Brit Geography
M 4,000 i, 4,000 schools, colleges & universities
¶ Geography - 3;   Primary Geographer - 3;
  Teaching Geography - 3; prices on request.
  NL - 3; ftm.   AR; free.   Publications list available.

Geographical Society of Ireland   1934
IRL c/o Dept of Geography, University College Dublin, Belfield, DUBLIN 4, Republic of Ireland.
  353 (1) 716 8179   fax 353 (1) 269 5597
  Sec: Dr Niamh Moore
○ *L

Geological Society   1807
■ Burlington House, Piccadilly, LONDON, W1J 0BG.   (hq)
  020 7434 9944
  Exec Sec: Edmund Nickless
○ *L; furtherance of all aspects of geological science
Gp C'ees: Conservation, Stratigraphy;
  Gps: Borehole research; British geomorphological research; British Geophysical Association; British sedimentological research; Coal geology; Earth systems science; Engineering; Environment; Environmental & industrial geophysics; Geochemistry; Geological curators; Geological information; Geological remote sensing; Geoscience information; History of geology; Hydrogeological; Joint Association of Geoscientists for International Development; Joint Association for Quaternary Research; Joint C'ee for Palaeontology; Marine studies; Metamorphic studies; Mineral deposits studies; Petroleum; Quaternary Research Association; Tectonic studies; Volcanic & magmatic studies

Geologists' Association   (GA)   1858
NR Burlington House, Piccadilly, LONDON, W1J 0DU.   (hq)
  020 7434 9298
  Exec Sec: Mrs Sarah Stafford
▲ Registered Charity
Br 18 local groups
○ *G, *L; to promote awareness of our geological heritage; to promote interest in & the study of geology & its allied sciences, at all levels
● Mtgs - Lib - VE
< Rockwatch (children's club)
M 2,200 i, UK / 100 i, o'seas
¶ Proceedings - 4.   G.A. Magazine - 4.   Circular - 4.
  Geological guide books.

George Borrow Society   1991
■ 1 Holywell Close, Meads, EASTBOURNE, E Sussex,
      BN20 7RX.   (chmn/p)
      01323 737209   fax 01323 737209
      email adaskyns@yahoo.co.uk
      http://www.clough5.fsnet.co.uk
      Hon Sec: Andrew Dakyns
▲ Un-incorporated Society
○ *A; to promote the knowledge of the life & works of the English
      author George Borrow (1803-81), best known for his novels
      'Lavengro', 'The Romany Rye', 'The Bible in Spain' & 'Wild
      Wales'
● Conf - Mtgs - Res - Annual memorial lecture
< Alliance of Literary Socs; Centre of East Anglian Studies, UEA,
      Norwich; Friends of Brompton Cemetery
M 128 i, 11 libraries, UK / 33 i, 2 orgs, o'seas
¶ George Borrow Bulletin - 2; ftm, £4 nm.

George Eliot Fellowship   1930
■ 71 Stepping Stones Rd, COVENTRY, Warks, CV5 8JT.   (hsp)
      024 7659 2231
      Hon Sec: Mrs K M Adams
▲ Registered Charity
Br Japan, USA
○ *A; to honour George Eliot & to promote interest in her life &
      writings; to encourage collection of her books & manuscripts
      & other ephemera connected with her
● Mtgs - Res - Comp - SG - Inf - VE
< Alliance Literary Socs
M 357 i, 6 org, UK / 243 i, 1 org, o'seas
¶ George Eliot Review - 4; ftm, £10 nm.   NL - 4; ftm only.
      Those of Us Who Loved Her: the men in George Eliot's
      life; £7.50 m.
      Pitkin Guide to George Eliot; £3.50.

George Formby Society   (GFS)   1961
NR 42 Ullswater Ave, DEWSBURY, W Yorks, WF12 7PW.
      (contact/p)
      Contact: Peter Pollard
▲ Un-incorporated Society
○ *G; to perpetuate the music & memory of George Formby, MBE
● Conf - Mtgs
M c 850 i
¶ Vellum - 4; ftm only.

George MacDonald Society   1981
NR 10 Appian Court, Parnell Rd, LONDON, E3 2RS.   (regd/add)
      http://www.george-macdonald.com
      Sec: Roger Bardet
▲ Registered Charity
○ *A; to promote public interest & knowledge in the life & works
      of George MacDonald (1824-1905), author
● Conf - Mtgs - Res - Exhib - Inf - Lib - VE
M 74 i, 16 org, UK / 78 i, org, o'seas
¶ North Wind - 1.   Orts (NL).

Georgian Group   1937
NR 6 Fitzroy Sq, LONDON, W1T 5DX.   (hq)
      0871 750 2936
      Sec: Robert Bargery
▲ Registered Charity; Un-incorporated Society
○ *G; preservation & appreciation of buildings of the Georgian
      period (18th century) & those in the classical style
● Conf - VE
M 2,600 i, 100 f
¶ Jnl - 1.   NL - 3.   AR.

German-British Chamber of Industry & Commerce   1971
NR 16 Buckingham Gate, LONDON, SW1E 6LB.   (hq)
      020 7976 4100   fax 020 7976 4101
      email mail@ahk-london.co.uk
      http://www.ahk-london.co.uk
      Dir-Gen: Ulrich Hoppe
      Contact: Thesy Lobitzer (020 7976 4112)
▲ Company Limited by Guarantee
○ *C; promotion of trade & investment between Germany & the
      United Kingdom
Gp Business: Information, Partner search, Promotion;
      Legal; Marketing services; Trade Fairs; Green Dot; VAT refund
● Conf - Res - Exhib - Expt - Inf
< Assn of German Chams of Ind & Comm (Germany)
M 640 f, 60 org (chambers of commerce), UK / 140 f, 60 org,
      o'seas
¶ Publication details on request.
      Note: the German title is - Deutsch-Britische Industrie- und
      Handelskammer.
✕ 2003-04 German-British Chamber of Industry & Commerce in
      the UK

German History Society   1979
NR c/o Dr Mark Hewitson, German Dept, University College
      London, Gower St, LONDON, WC1E 6BT.   (hsb)
      Sec: Dr Mark Hewitson
▲ Un-incorporated Society
○ *L; academic research on German history
● Conf - Res
M c 200 i, UK / c 50 i, o'seas
¶ German History - 4.

German Railway Society   (GRS)   1980
■ Shalimar - 10 Beechwood Rd, MIRFIELD, W Yorks, WF14 9JX.
      (hsp)
      01924 495929
      Sec: P Dransfield
▲ Un-incorporated Society
Br 6 groups
○ *G; for enthusiasts & modellers of German & Austrian railways
● Mtgs - Exhib - Lib
M c 800 i
¶ Merkur - 4; ftm only.

Gestalt Association UK   (GAUK)
NR PO Box 53803, LONDON, SE27 9XW.
○ *P

Giftware Association   (The GA)   1947
■ 10 Vyse St, BIRMINGHAM, B18 6LT.   (hq)
      0121-237 1104   fax 0121-237 1106
      http://www.ga-uk.org
      Chief Exec: Isabel Martinson
○ *T; promotion & provision of supporting business services to
      British manufacturers, importers & distributors of giftware
Gp Gift Retailers' Guild
● Conf - Res - Comp - Expt - Inf - LG
< Brit Jewellery, Giftware & Finishing Fedn
M 500 f
¶ Newsline - 4.

Giftware Retailers Guild
      a group of the **Giftware Association**

Gilbert & Sullivan Society (G&SS) 1924
■ 12 Ostlers View, BILLLINGSHURST, W Sussex, RH14 9LU. (hsp)
Hon Sec: Stuart Box
▲ Registered Charity
Br 11; Australia, Canada, Israel, South Africa, USA
○ *D; to inform, educate & entertain all who are interested in the
    works of Gilbert & Sullivan & the Savoy operas
Gp Music; Theatre; Opera; Appreciation Society
● Conf - Mtgs - ET - Res - Inf - Lib
< Nat Fedn Music Socs
M 1,000 i, UK / 500 i, o'seas
¶ Gilbert & Sullivan News - 3; ftm, (or £2 each),
    £8 yr nm (£12 o'seas).

Gilt-Edged Market Makers' Association (GEMMA) 1986
NR 5 The North Colonnade, Canary Wharf, LONDON, E14 4BB
    (chmn/b)
    020 7623 2323
    Chmn: Euan Harkness
○ *T; Stock Exchange firms dealing in government securities

GIMA (1999) Ltd (GIMA) 1977
NR 225 Bristol Rd, Edgbaston, BIRMINGHAM, B5 7UB. (hq)
    0121-446 5213   fax 0121-446 5215
    email info@gima.org.uk
    Dir: Peter Marsh,   Sec: Maisie Slater
○ *T; represent manufacturers of garden products
● Conf - Mtgs - ET - Res - SG - Stat
M 140 f
¶ NL;   LM; both m only.   AR; ftm.

Gin & Vodka Association of Great Britain (GVA) 1991
■ Cross Keys House, Queen St, SALISBURY, Wilts, SP1 1EY. (hq)
    01722 415892   fax 01722 415840
    email gva@ginvodka.org.uk   http://www.ginvodka.org
    Dir Gen: Edwin Atkinson
▲ Company Limited by Guarantee
○ *T; to protect & promote the interests of the gin & vodka trades
    generally both at home & abroad; to prevent any
    malpractices or abuses that might arise in connection with
    the production, importation or sale of gin or vodka
● Stat - Inf - LG
< Confédn Eur des Producteurs de Spiritueux (Brussels)
M 29 f
¶ NL - 4;   AR; both ftm.

Gingerbread (an Association for One Parent Families) Ltd 1970
■ 307 Borough High St, LONDON, SE1 1JH. (hq)
    020 7403 9500   fax 020 7403 9533
    email office@gingerbread.org.uk
    http://www.gingerbread.org.uk
    Chief Exec: Gwen Vaughan
▲ Registered Charity
Br 2
○ *W; to give support & help to lone parent families
● Mtgs
M 11,000 i
¶ NL - 4;   e-newsletter - 12; both ftm only.   AR.

Girlguiding UK 1910
■ 17-19 Buckingham Palace Rd, LONDON, SW1W 0PT.   (hq)
    020 7834 6242   fax 020 7828 8317
    email chq@girlguiding.org.uk
    http://www.girlguiding.org.uk
    Chief Exec: Denise King
▲ Registered Charity
Br 7
○ *Y; to help girls & young women to develop emotionally,
    mentally, physically & spiritually so that they can make a
    positive contribution to the community & the wider world
Gp Rainbow Guides (5-7 yrs) (in Ulster (4-7)); Brownie Guides (7-
    10 yrs); Guide (10-14 yrs); Ranger Guides; Young leaders;
    Adult leaders
● Mtgs - ET
< Wld Assn Girl Guides & Girl Scouts
M 600,000 i
¶ Guiding - 12; ftm (16+yrs only); £2 nm.   AR - 1.
    Note: registered as the Guide Association.
✕ 2002 Guide Association

Girls' Brigade England & Wales 1893
■ PO Box 196, 129 Broadway, DIDCOT, Oxon, OX11 8XN.   (hq)
    01235 510425   fax 01235 510429
    http://www.girlsbrigadeew.org.uk
    Nat Dir: Miss Ruth E Gilson
▲ Registered Charity
Br 966; 55 o'seas
○ *R, *Y; acts as the National Council for England & Wales with
    regard to the spiritual & personal development of girls &
    young women
● Conf - Mtgs - ET - Exhib - Comp - Stat - VE
< Girls' Brigade Intl Coun
M 31,782 i, 996 f, UK / 55 f, o'seas
¶ The View - 6.   AR.

Girls' Schools Association (GSA) 1973
■ 130 Regent Rd, LEICESTER, LE1 7PG.   (hq)
    0116-254 1619   fax 0116-255 3792
    email office@gsa.uk.com   http://www.gsa.uk.com
    Gen Sec: Sheila Cooper
▲ Company Limited by Guarantee
○ *E, *P; policy & administration of independent girls' schools
● Conf - Mtgs - ET - Res - Exhib - Inf - VE - LG
M c 212 schools; c 88 associates & o'seas

Girls' Venture Corps Air Cadets (GVCAC) 1964
■ Phoenix House, 3 Handley Sq, Doncaster Sheffield Airport,
    DONCASTER, S Yorks, DN9 3GH.   (hq)
    01302 775019   fax 01302 775020
    email gvcachq@btopenworld.com
    http://www.gvcac.org.uk
    Co Sec: Mrs B Layne
▲ Company Limited by Guarantee; Registered Charity
Br 30
○ *W, *Y; uniformed youth organisation for girls aged 11-20
    years of age who are interested in sport, community service,
    aviation, the Duke of Edinburgh Award Scheme, millennium
    volunteers, camps
● Conf - Mtgs - ET - Exam - Comp - VE
< Air Training Corps; Army Cadet Force; WARMA
M 600 i
¶ Circuit - 2; free.

Glamorgan History Society 1957
NR 87 Gabalfa Rd, Sketty, SWANSEA, Glam, SA2 8ND.   (hsb)
    Sec: Paul Reynolds
○ *L; promote the study of the history of Glamorgan
M i & org

Glasgow Agricultural Society   (GAS)   1898
■ The Faulds, Kilmany, CUPAR, Fife, KY15 4PT.   (sp)
   01382 330710   fax 01382 330710
   Sec: Miss Mardy Whiteford
○ *B, *F, *G; to promote & encourage the breeding & showing of
   horses & ponies; to organise the national stallion show
   annually (for in-hand Clydesdales, Highlands, Shetlands &
   mountain & moorland horses & ponies); farrier competitions
< Nat Pony Soc; Highland Pony Soc; Clydesdale Horse Soc;
   Shetland Pony Studbook Soc
M 394 i

Glasgow Archaeological Society   (GAS)   1856
■ c/o Dept of Archaeology, University of Glasgow, GLASGOW,
   G12 8QQ.   (hsp)
   Mem Sec: S Hunter
▲ Registered Charity
○ *L; promotion of & interest in archaeology, particularly in
   Glasgow & West of Scotland
● Conf - Mtgs - Res - Exhib - Inf - VE
< Coun Brit Archaeology
M 325 i, 2 f, 5 org, UK / 20 i, o'seas
¶ Scottish Archaeological Jnl - 2; ftm, £18 nm.
   Bulletin - 2; ftm, £5 nm.

Glasgow Chamber of Commerce   1783
NR 30 George Square, GLASGOW, G2 1EQ.   (hq)
   0141-204 2121   fax 0141-221 2336
   email chamber@glasgowchamber.org
   http://www.glasgowchamber.org
   Chief Exec: Dr L Sawyers
○ *C; interests of the business community of Glasgow & West of
   Scotland
● Mtgs - Stat - Expt - Inf - LG
< Assn Brit Chams Comm; Assn Scot Chams Comm
M 1,550 f
¶ The Journal - 6.   Hbk.
   Scottish Chambers of Commerce Directory - 1; ftm only.

Glasgow Mathematical Association   (GMA)   1927
NR Mathematics Dept, University of Glasgow, University Gardens,
   GLASGOW, G12 8QW.   (treas/b)
   Hon Treas: Dr F H Goldman
▲ Un-incorporated Society
○ *L; to stimulate study & teaching of mathematics at all levels; to
   provide a forum for professional mathematicians, especially
   teachers, to exchange ideas
● Mtgs - Annual lecture for pupils aged 16+
< Mathematical Assn; American / Australian / Indian
   Mathematical Assn(s)
M 45 i, UK / 1 i, o'seas

Glasgow Natural History Society   1851
NR c/o Zoology Museum, Graham Kerr Building, University of
   Glasgow, GLASGOW, G12 8QQ.
   http://www.glasgownaturalhistory.org.uk
▲ Registered Charity
○ *L

Glass Association   1983
NR Bradfield House Glass Museum, Compton Drive,
   KINGSWINFORD, W Midlands, DY6 9NS.
○ *G, *P.

The Glass Circle   1937
■ 66 Corringham Rd, LONDON, NW11 7BX.   (hsp)
   020 8455 7348   fax 0870 167 1903
   email secretary@glasscircle.org
   http://www.glasscircle.org
   Hon Sec: Marianne Scheer
▲ Un-incorporated Society
○ *G; to promote the study, understanding, appreciation & history
   of artistic & collected glass
● Conf - Mtgs - Exhib - Lib - VE
M 405 i, 4 f, 6 org, UK / 70 i, 4 org, o'seas
¶ Glass Circle New - 4; ftm, £5 nm.
   Glass Circle Jnl - 2; ftm, £20 nm.

Glass & Glazing Federation   (GGF)   1977
■ 44-48 Borough High St, LONDON, SE1 1XB.   (hq)
   0870 042 4255
   Chief Exec: Nigel D Rees
▲ Company Limited by Guarantee
○ *T; interests of companies engaged in glazing (glass & plastics),
   including solar control, leaded & stained glass, shopfronts,
   patent glazing, double glazing, merchanting, laminating,
   toughening, bending, conservatories manufacturing of sealed
   units, mirrors, compounds, all flat glass processing, external
   relations with government & all other relevant bodies
Gp Fire resistant glazing
● Conf - Mtgs - ET - Res - Comp - Inf - LG
M f
¶ Glazing Manual (containing technical data sheets);
   Consumer Literature;   Codes of Practice;   AR; all ftm.

** ** Glenn Miller Society**
   Organisation lost: see Introduction paragraph 3

Global Commons Institute   (GCI)   1991
NR 37 Ravenswood Rd, LONDON, E17 9LY.   (hq)
   020 8520 4742
   Exec Dir: Aubrey Meyer
○ *K: 'GCI is concerned with global warming & climate change;
   our focus is the promotion of 'Contraction & Convergence'
   (C&C). C&C is a global greenhouse gas emissions
   management framework based on the principles of
   precaution & equity. These principles make possible an
   effective overall response to global climate change'

Glosa Education Organisation   (GEO)   1987
■ PO Box 18, RICHMOND, Surrey, TW9 2GE.   (hsp)
   020 8288 0257
   http://www.glosa.org
   Hon Sec: Sabine Asenkerschbaumer,
   Mem Sec: Wendy Ashby
▲ Registered Charity
Br 5 o'seas
○ *E, *X, to promote the international language Glosa; to put
   speakers & penfriends in touch with each other; to provide
   teaching materials & establish study centres worldwide
● Mtgs - ET - Inf - Penfriends service
M 180 i, 6 org, UK / 150 i, 10 org, o'seas
¶ Plu Glosa Nota - 4; £6.50 yr.
   Dictionaries & textbooks; £1 - £10.95.

Gloster Convention
   a member body of the **Society for the Protection of Aviculture**

Gloucester Cattle Society   1972
NR The Old School House, Hasfield, GLOUCESTER, GL19 4LJ.
   01452 780993
   Sec: Gill Heaven
▲ Un-incorporated Society
○ *B; recording, support & development of the breed of
   Gloucester cattle
● Inf
< Rare Breeds Survival Trust
M 140 i

Gloucestershire Chamber of Commerce & Industry 1902

■ Chargrove House, Main Rd, Shurdington, CHELTENHAM, Glos, GL51 5GA. (hq)
01242 864164
email john.cripps@gloscci.org   http://www.gloscci.org
Managing Dir: John Cripps
Br 2
○ *C
Gp Retail; Industrial; Business club
< Bristol Cham Comm & Ind
M 500 i & f

Gloucestershire Old Spot Pig Breeders' Club   (GOSPBC) 1992

NR 2 St John's Rd, STANSTED, Essex, CM24 8JP.   (hsp)
07768 368053
http://www.oldspots.com
Sec: Carol Knights
▲ Un-incorporated Society
○ *B
● ET - Expt - Inf - VE
M 300 i, UK / 10 i, o'seas
¶ Spot Press (NL) - 4.

Gloucestershire Society for Industrial Archaeology   (GSIA) 1964

■ Oak House, Hamshill, Coaley, DURSLEY, Glos, GL11 5EH. (hsp)
01453 860595
email ray.wilson@freeuk.net   http://www.gsia.org.uk
Hon Sec: Dr R Wilson
▲ Registered Charity
Br 2
○ *L; to stimulate interest in, to record, to study & where appropriate to preserve, items of industrial archaeology especially in the county of Gloucestershire
● Conf - Mtgs - Res - Exhib - SG - Inf - PL - VE
< Assn Industrial Archaeology
M 215 i, 1 f, 7 org, UK / 1 i, o'seas
¶ Jnl - 1; ftm, £8 nm.   NL - 4; free.

Glued Laminated Timber Association   (GLULAM/GLTA) 1988

■ Chiltern House, Stocking Lane, HIGH WYCOMBE, Bucks, HP14 4ND.   (hq)
01494 565180   fax 01494 565487
Sec: Mrs P M Presland
○ *T; an independent trade association of manufacturers, distributors & suppliers of glulam
● Promotion of glued laminated timber - Publication of technical information
M f

Go Outdoors - Outdoor Industries Association   1961

NR Morritt House, 58 Station Approach, South Ruislip, RUISLIP, Middx, HA4 6SA.   (hq)
020 8842 1111   fax 020 8842 0090
email info@go-outdoors.org.uk
http://www.go-outdoors.org.uk
Dir: Roger Southcott
▲ Un-incorporated Society
○ *T; to promote interests of retailers & manufacturers in the outdoor leisure & camping trades
● Mtgs - Res - Exhib - Comp - Stat - Expt - Inf - LG
M 360 f & org
¶ Go Outdoors Bulletin - 4.   LM - 1.
Exhibition Catalogue - 1.

Goat Veterinary Society
a group of the **British Veterinary Association**

Golden Guernsey Goat Society   1986

NR Gelli Isaf, Rhydcymerau, LLANDIELO, Carmarthenshire, SA19 7PY.
01558 685060
email gellisaf@hotmail.com
http://www.goldenguernseygoat.org.uk
Sec: Mrs Carole Lovell
○ *B

Goldfish Club   1942

■ 24 Bridgewater Drive, Great Glen, LEICESTER, LE8 9DX.   (hsp)
0116-259 2105
email richardshepherd@dsl.pipex.com
Hon Sec: Richard W M Shepherd
▲ Un-incorporated Society
Br Australia, Canada, Cyprus, N Zealand, USA
○ *G; to maintain comradeship arising from 'coming down in the drink'; to maintain close contact with military aviation to improve chances of others' survival; to foster ideas & suggestions to improve survival equipment
● VE - Annual Re-union dinner
M 400 i, UK / 85 i, o'seas
¶ The Goldfish Club (NL) - 4; ftm only.

Golf Club of Great Britain   (GCGB)   1986

NR 3 Sage Yard, Douglas Rd, SURBITON, Surrey, KT6 7TS.   (hq)
020 8390 3113
Sec: Kate Brown
○ *S; to promote golfing activities for members & their guests
M 3,200 i, 50 org, UK / 1,000 i, 3 org, o'seas
¶ NL - 4.   Directory of Friendly Golf Clubs.

Golf Consultants Association   (GCA)   1999

■ Federation House, STONELEIGH PARK, Warks, CV8 2RF.
024 7641 4999   fax 024 7641 4990
email gca@sportsandplay.com
http://www.golfconsultants.org
Sec: Jacqui Baldwin
▲ Un-incorporated Society
○ *P, S; to provide a point of reference for those requiring independent professional golf consultancy services world-wide
● Conf - Mtgs
< a group of the Fedn of Sports & Play Assns (FSPA)
M 12 i

Golfing Union of Ireland   1891

IRL Carton House, MAYNOOTH, Co Kildare, Republic of Ireland.
353 (1) 505 4000   fax 353 (1) 505 4001
email 09>gui.ie
Gen Sec: Seamus Smith
○ *S

Good Gardeners' Association   (GGA)   1960

■ 4 Lisle Place, WOTTON-under-EDGE, Glos, GL12 7AZ.   (hsb)
01453 520322
email info@goodgardeners.org.uk
http://www.goodgardeners.org.uk
Hon Sec: Matt Adams
▲ Registered Charity
○ *H; a membership based charity for people who want to grow & eat nutritious food; to promote the concept of 'moving beyond organic'; no dig gardening & the use of compost
● Conf - ET - Res
M 300 i, 5 f, 10 org, UK / 5 i, o'seas
¶ NL - 4; ftm only.

© CBD Research Ltd · Beckenham · BR3 5JS · Tel 020 8650 7745 · Fax 020 8650 0768 · E-mail cbd@cbdresearch.com · www.cbdresearch.com

Goon Show Preservation Society (GSPS) 1972
- 114 Fountains Rd, IPSWICH, Suffolk, IP2 9TW. (sp)
  01473 422730   fax 01473 438179
  http://www.thegoonshow.org.uk
  Sec: Tina Hammond
Br 6; Australia, Canada, Germany, Japan, S Africa, USA
○ *; to ensure that as many Goon Show recordings & other related information / recordings / articles as possible are archived; to meet like-minded people
Gp Archive recordings: Audio, video & print
● Conf - Mtgs - Res - Writing & performing 21st century Goon Shows
< Goon Appreciation Socs: Perth & Victoria (Australia)
M 456 i, UK / 92 i, o'seas
¶ GSPS NL - 4; £11 m only.

Gooseberry Society 1980
- Mayfair, 14 Staddon Gdns, TORQUAY, Devon, TQ2 8BB. (hq)
  01803 324663
  Founder: The Hon Anthony de Freston
○ *H; to promote & protect the gooseberry (grossularia uva crispa) & other rare fruits & the breeding of new varieties
● ET - Res - Exhib - Comp - Stat - Inf - Lib - PL
M (honorary only)

Governing Bodies Association
  in 2002 merged with the Governing Bodies of Girls' Schools Association to become the **Association of Governing Bodies of Independent Schools**

Governing Bodies of Girls Schools Association
  in 2002 merged with the Governing Bodies Association to become the **Association of Governing Bodies of Independent Schools**

Governing Council of the Cat Fancy (GCCF) 1910
- 4-6 Penel Orlieu, BRIDGWATER, Somerset, TA6 3PG. (hq)
  01278 427575
  Office Mgr: Miss Jackie Beeson
○ *V
● Registration of pedigree cats - Licensing of cat shows for pedigree cats
M 143 cat clubs

Gower Society 1947
- The Orchard, Perriswood, Penmaen, SWANSEA, Glam, SA3 2HN. (hsp)
  01792 371665
  Hon Sec: Mrs Ruth Ridge
▲ Registered Charity
○ *L; promotion of knowledge of the history & conservation of the physical aspects of the Lordship of Gower
Gp Planning search; Publication; Footpaths; Working party; Programmes
● Conf - Mtgs - ET - Inf - VE - LG - Archives - Weekly excursions - Clearing footpaths
< Nat Trust; Campaign Protection Rural Wales; Ramblers' Assn
M 1,700 i
¶ Jnl - 1; ftm, £5.95 nm.   Guide to Gower; £4.95.
  Gower Walks; £3.   Butterflies of Gower; £2.50.
  Gower Way (leaflet); 75p.
  Vernacular Gower; £8.50 (hardback) £4.50 (paperback).

Grain & Feed Trade Association Ltd (GAFTA) 1971
- GAFTA House, 6 Chapel Place, Rivington St, LONDON, EC2A 3SH. (hq)
  020 7814 9666   fax 020 7814 8383
  email post@gafta.com   http://www.gafta.com
  Dir-Gen: Mrs Pamela Kirby Johnson
○ *T; to promote international trade in grains, animal feeding-stuffs, pulses & rice
Gp Shippers; Brokers; Crushers; Dealers & manufacturers; Grain, protein, feeding stuffs & marine & animal products; Pulses
● Conf - Mtgs - ET - Res - Exhib - SG - Stat - Inf - Arbitration - Contracts
M c 900 f in 80 countries
¶ NL - 6; ftm, £2 nm.   Forms of Contract.
  Hbk - 1;   AR - 1; both ftm.

Grainger Society
  see **Percy Grainger Society**

Grand Lodge of Antient Free & Accepted Masons of Scotland (The Grand Lodge of Scotland) 1736
- Freemason's Hall, 96 George St, EDINBURGH, EH2 3DH. (hq)
  0131-225 5304   fax 0131-225 3953
  email gladmin@grandlodgescotland.org
  http://www.grandlodgescotland.com
  Grand Sec: David M Begg
Br 658
○ *N; freemasonry
● Mtgs - Lib - VE
< Scot Museums Coun
M 26,000 i, UK / 12,000 o'seas
¶ Ybk - 1; £10.

Grand National Archery Society (GNAS) 1861
- Lilleshall National Sports Centre, NEWPORT, Shropshire, TF10 9AT. (hq)
  01952 677888   fax 01952 606019
  email enquiries@gnas.org   http://www.gnas.org
  Chief Exec: David Sherratt
▲ Company Limited by Guarantee
Br clubs
○ *S; national governing body for the sport of archery in all its forms; to act as the contact office for all clubs in the UK
Gp Clubs: Target, Field, Popinjay, Flight, Clout, Recurve, Compound
  Bow types: Olympic, Compound, Long bow, Cross bow
● Conf - Mtgs - Exhib - Comp
< Fédn Intle de Tir à l'Arc (FITA); Brit Olympic Assn (BOA); Brit Paralympic Assn
M 25,000+ i, 1,100 clubs
¶ Archery UK - 4; ftm, £4.25 nm.

Grand Priory of the Most Venerable Order of the Hospital of St John of Jerusalem 1888
NR The Chancery, St John's Gate, St John's Lane, Clerkenwell, LONDON, EC1M 4DA. (hq) & museum
  The St John Ambulance - offers first aid training for industry, commerce & & general public; also responsible for Public first aid duties; Ophthalmic Hospital in Jerusalem (eye hospital); Care of the elderly; Community care

Grandparents Action Group (GAG) 2001
NR 7 Hilda Hook Close, Madeley, TELFORD, Shropshire, TF7 4HU. (hq)
  01952 582621   fax 01952 582621
  Chmn: Mrs Pamela Wilson,   Sec: Mrs Denise Matekie
○ *G, *K; to help grandparents maintain & protect the relationship between grandchildren & grandparents when contact is an issue
● Conf - Res - Stat - Inf - LG
M 208 i

Grandparents' Association   1986

NR   Moot House, The Stow, HARLOW, Essex, CM20 3AG.   (hq)
    01279 428040   fax 01279 428040
    email info@grandparents-association.org.uk
    http://www.grandparents-association.org.uk
    Dir: Mrs Lynn Chesterman
▲   Registered Charity
○   *K, *W; to work with all grandparents for the best interests of
    children; we particularly support those who are denied
    contact with their grandchildren, who are raising their
    grandchildren or who have childcare responsibilities
Gp   Support groups in some areas; Information; Hearings
●   Conf - Mtgs - ET - Support groups
    Helpline: 01279 428040
<   Children's Rights Alliance for England; Nat Coun for Voluntary
    Child Care Organisations; Nat Coun for Voluntary
    Organisations
M   950 i, 40 org, UK / 10 i, o'seas
¶   Grandparent Times (NL) - 3;   AR; both free.
    Specialist publications:
      Relative Values... Missing out on Contact?
      Relative Values... The Best Interests of the Child?
      Residence Order Allowance Survey.
      Jettison the Jargon.
      Looking After Your Grandchildren.
×   Grandparents Federation

Grantham Chamber of Commerce   1961

■   Springfield House Business & Conference Centre, Springfield
    Rd, GRANTHAM, Lincs, NG31 7BG.
    01476 568970   fax 01476 575758
    Sec & Chief Exec: Mrs J S P Smith
▲   Company Limited by Guarantee
○   *C
●   Expt - Inf - Lib
<   Brit Chams Comm
M   20 f

Graphical, Paper & Media Union
    in 2004 became an autonomous industrial sector within **Amicus**

Great Britain Basketball   (GBB)   1970

■   Southampton Solent University, East Park Terrace,
    SOUTHAMPTON, Hants, SO14 0YN.
    023 8031 9058   fax 023 8031 9940
    email trevor.pountain@solent.ac.uk
    Sec: Trevor Pountain
▲   Un-incorporated Society
○   *N, *S; deals with all matters concerning British basketball; to
    represent basketball on the national Olympic Committee
●   Mtgs
<   Brit Olympic Assn
>   Brit Basketball League; Brit Universities Sports Assn; Gt Britain
    Wheelchair Basketball Assn
M   3 org
×   2004 British & Irish Basketball Federation

Great Britain Diving Federation   (GBDF)   1993

NR   42 Kennelwood Crescent, New Addington, CROYDON, Surrey,
    CR0 0DQ.   (chief/exec/p)
    01689 847910
    email johnw@skline.freeserve.co.uk
    http://www.diving-gbdf.com
    Chief Exec: John Whitby
▲   Un-incorporated Society
○   *S
●   Conf - ET - Comp - Inf
<   Cent Coun for Physical Recreation (CCPR); Scot Amat
    Swimming Assn (SASA)
M   850 i

Great Britain Luge Association

NR   61 West Malvern Rd, MALVERN, Worcs, WR14 4NF.
    Sec Gen: Mark Armstrong
○   *S; luge racing

Great Britain Postcard Club   (GBPCC)   1961

■   34 Harper House, St James Crescent, LONDON, SW9 7LW.
    (hsp)
    020 7771 9404
    email drenebrennan@yahoo.co.uk
    Chief Exec: Drene Brennan
▲   Un-incorporated Society
○   *G, *X; postcard collecting; world friendship
●   Conf - Res - Comp
<   Clubs in USA: Disney, Duneland, Metropolitan, San Francisco;
    Sunshine; Tuscan; Webfoot
M   200 i, UK / 100 i, o'seas
¶   Postcard World - 6; £10 yr m.

Great Britain Racquetball Federation   (GBRF)   1984

NR   78 Suffolk Drive, WOODBRIDGE, Suffolk, IP12 2TP.   (hsp)
    01394 461069
    Pres: Alan Aburrow-Newman
    Sec: Jan Aburrow-Newman
▲   Un-incorporated Society
○   *S; to promote the game of racquetball
●   Mtgs - Comp
<   Eur Racquetball Fedn (ERF); Intl Racquetball Fedn (IAF)
M   1,500 i
¶   European Racquetball NL - 4.

Great Britain Target Shooting Federation   (GBTSF)   1988

■   1 The Cedars, GREAT WAKERING, Essex, SS3 0AQ.   (hsp)
    01702 219395
    Hon Sec: Keith Murray
▲   Un-incorporated Society
○   *N, *S; a coordinating body for services & international events
    undertaken by target shooting associations
M   4 org & 4 national bodies (England, Scotland, Wales & N
    Ireland)

Great North of Scotland Railway Association   (GNSRA)   1964

■   19 Seafield Terrace, PORTSOY, Banffshire, AB45 2QB.   (hsp)
    Hon Sec: G Boardman
▲   Un-incorporated Society
○   *G; study, acquisition & preservation of documents, illustrations
    & information relating to the railway
Gp   Specialist groups according to the research on hand
●   Mtgs - Res - Exhib - Inf - VE
M   315 i, 5 org, UK / 3 i, o'seas
¶   Great North Review - 4; (Index every 5 yrs); LM - 1; all ftm.

Great Northern Railway Society   (GNR Society)   1981

■   57 North Rd, GLOSSOP, Derbys, SK13 7AU.   (hsp)
    01457 852851
    http://www.gnrs.150m.com
    Hon Sec: Peter Hall
▲   Un-incorporated Society
○   *G; historical research & study of the former Great Northern
    Railway & its joint lines from inception to present day
●   Mtgs - Res - Exhib - SG - Inf - PL
M   c 300 i, UK / 5 i, o'seas
¶   GN News (Jnl) - 6; ftm only.
    Booklets with information on coaches, wagons etc; prices vary.

Great Western Society Ltd (GWS) 1961
■ DIDCOT, Oxon, OX11 7NJ. (hq)
　01235 817200　fax 01235 510621
　email didrlyc@globalnet.co.uk
　http://www.didcotrailwaycentre.org.uk
　Sec: F Cooper
▲ Company Limited by Guarantee; Registered Charity
Br 8
○ *G; study of history, equipment & operation of the former Great
　Western Railway; preservation of items of interest -
　locomotives, rolling stock, buildings, etc
● Conf - Mtgs - ET - Res - Exhib - SG - Inf - VE
< Assn of Independent Museums; Heritage Railways; Assn of Brit
　Transport & Engineering Museums; Transport Trust
M 4,520 i, UK / 120 i, o'seas
¶ Great Western Echo - 4; ftm, £1 nm.
　NL - 7;　AR; both ftm only.

Greater Altrincham Chamber of Commerce, Trade & Industry
　since September 2005 **Altrincham & Sale Chamber of**
　Commerce

Greater London Industrial Archaeology Society (GLIAS)
1968
■ 14 Eversleigh Rd, NEW BARNET, Herts, EN5 1NE.　(hsp)
　020 8440 3654
　email secretary@glias.org.uk
　Hon Sec: Brian Strong
▲ Company Limited by Guarantee; Registered Charity
○ *L; informing the public of London's industrial history, & the
　preparation of photographic & documentary records of
　industrial monuments in Greater London
Gp Recording
● Res - SG - Inf - VE - Lectures - Walks
< Assn Indl Archaeology (AIA)
M c 600 i, c 50 org
¶ London's Industrial Archaeology (Jnl) - irreg; ftm.
　NL - 6; free.

Greater Manchester Chamber of Commerce 1820
NR Churchgate, 56 Oxford St, MANCHESTER, M60 7HJ.　(hq)
　0161-236 3210　fax 0161-236 4160
▲ Company Limited by Guarantee
○ *C; promotion of trade & industry & provision of specialist
　information & representation for NW England
M f
✕ 2004 (Chamber Business Connections [Oldham]
　(Manchester Chamber of Commerce & Industry

Greater Peterborough Chamber of Commerce & Industry
　the Peterborough office of the **Cambridgeshire Chambers of**
　Commerce

Greek Institute 1969
■ 34 Bush Hill Rd, LONDON, N21 2DS.　(hsp)
　020 8360 7968　fax 020 8360 7968
　email info@greekinstitute.co.uk
　http://www.greekinstitute.co.uk
　Dir: Dr Kypros Tofallis
Br 20
○ *L; to promote modern Greek studies in UK
● Mtgs - Exam - Res - ET - Comp - Inf - VE
M 20 i, f
¶ Greek Institute Review - 4; ftm.

Green Alliance Trust 1978
■ 36 Buckingham Palace Rd, LONDON, SW1W 0RE.　(hq)
　020 7233 7433　fax 020 7233 9033
　email ga@green-alliance.org.uk
　http://www.green-alliance.org.uk
　Dir: Guy Thompson
▲ Registered Charity
○ *K; to promote sustainable development by ensuring that the
　environment is at the heart of decision-making
Gp Environment
● Conf - Mtgs - Res - Inf - LG
< Eur Envt Bureau
M 450 i, 100 f, 30 org, UK
¶ Parliamentary NL - 26.
　Inside Track - 4.　AR.

Green Lane Association (GLASS) 1995
NR PO Box 918, PETERBOROUGH, Cambs, PE1 9DX.
　email glass@glass-uk.org　http://www.glass-uk.org
　Chmn: D Codrai
▲ Un-incorporated Society
Br 12
○ *G, *K; to promote & protect vehicular rights of way &
　unsurfaced highways
● Mtgs - ET - Res - Exhib - SG - LG
< Brit Trust for Consvn Volunteers (BTCV); Land Access &
　Recreation Assn (LARA)
M 520 i, 20 org
¶ Green Lanes - 4;　Northern Bulletin - 4;
　Southern Bulletin - 4; all ftm only.

Greenock Chamber of Commerce
　see under full name **Chamber of Commerce & Manufacturers of**
　Greenock

GreenSpace
NR Caversham Court, Church Rd, Caversham, READING, Berks,
　RG4 7AD.
　0118-946 9060　fax 0118-946 9061
○ *F

Greenwich, Bexley & Lewisham Chamber of Commerce 2005
■ 46 Greenwich Church St, LONDON, SE10 9BL.　(hq)
　020 8293 3456　fax 020 8293 9168
　Sec: Clive Barker
▲ Company Limited by Guarantee
○ *C
● Conf - Mtgs - ET - Inf - LG
M 750 f
¶ Masthead - 12; free.
✕ 2004 Lewisham Chamber of Commerce (merger)

Greeting Card Association (GCA) 1919
■ United House, North Rd, LONDON, N7 9DP.　(hq)
　020 7619 0396　fax 020 7607 6411
　email gca@max-publishing.co.uk
　http://www.greetingcardassociation.org.uk
　Admin: Sharon Little
▲ Company Limited by Guarantee
○ *T; to promote, protect & celebrate the greeting card industry
● Mtgs - ET - Inf - LG
M 320 f
¶ Progressive Greetings - 12; £50 yr.

Grieg Society of Great Britain 1992
- ■ c/o The Royal Norwegian Embassy, 25 Belgrave Sq, LONDON, SW1X 8QD. (mail)
  01634 714434 fax 01634 714434 address
  Chmn: Beryl Foster, Mem Sec: Audrey Banker
- ▲ Un-incorporated Society
- ○ *A; to promote interest & encourage appreciation of the music of Edvard Hagerup Grieg (1843-1907) & other Norwegian composers
- ● Conf - Mtgs - Res - Exhib - Inf - Lib - Recitals & concerts
- < Intl Grieg Soc (Bergen, Norway);
  Grieg Soc(s) in: Oslo (Norway), Moscow (Russia), Münster & Leipzig (Germany), Tokyo (Japan), Groningen (Netherlands), New York (USA), Tokyo (Japan)
- M 100 i, UK / 8 i, o'seas
- ¶ The Grieg Companion (Jnl) - 1; ftm, £3 nm.
  NL - 3; ftm only.

Ground Forum 1992
- NR 83 Copers Cope Rd, BECKENHAM, Kent, BR3 1NR. (asa)
  020 8663 0947 fax 020 8663 0949
  email gforum@ground-forum.org.uk
  http://www.ground-forum.org.uk
  Hon Sec: Dianne Jennings
- ▲ Un-incorporated Society
- ○ *T; all aspects of geotechnical engineering (site investigation, foundation construction, tunnelling, ground improvement & remediation, geoenvironmentalism)
- ● Mtgs - LG
- < Construction Ind Coun (CIC)
- M 9 org

Ground Limestone Producers Association
- IRL Confederation House, 84-86 Lower Baggot St, DUBLIN 2, Republic of Ireland.
- ○ *T
- < IBEC

Group-Analytic Society (London) (GAS) 1952
- NR 102 Belsize Lane, LONDON, NW3 5BB. (hq)
  020 7435 6611
- ▲ Registered Charity
- ○ *P; promotion & development of group analysis as a treatment, prophylaxis & science

Group Auto Union UK & Ireland Ltd 1974
- NR Roydsdale House, Roydsdale Way, Euroway Trading Estate, BRADFORD, W Yorks, BD4 6SE. (hq)
  01274 654600 fax 01274 654610
  http://www.gau.co.uk
- Br 550
- ○ *T; a specialist business group for independent motor factors
- M 550 f (motor factors), 120 f (mfrs as supplier partners)
- ¶ Motor Factor - 12. Hbk - 1.
- × 2005 Factoring Services Group

Group for Costume & Textile Staff in Museums
  since 2003 **Dress & Textile Specialists**

Group for Education in Museums (GEM) 1948
- NR Primrose House, 193 Gillingham Rd, GILLINGHAM, Kent, ME7 4EP. (hq)
  01634 312409
- ▲ Un-incorporated Society
- Br 8
- ○ *E; to promote educational work in museums & related institutions; to foster the highest standards in museum education
- M i

Group Travel Organisers Association (GTOA) 1992
- ■ Beechcroft, Weston under Lizard, SHIFNAL, Shropshire, TF11 8JT. (hsp)
  01952 860269 fax 0792 585 0269
  email mltebbutt@lineone.net http://www.gtoa.co.uk
  Hon Sec: Michael Tebbutt
- ▲ Un-incorporated Society
- Br 5
- ○ *T; for group travel organisers & travel trade suppliers
- ● Conf - Mtgs - SG - VE - LG
- M 213 i, 370 org, UK / 2 f, o'seas
- ¶ GTOA News - 4; Hbk - 3 yrly; AGM Report - 1;
  NL (to the 5 branches) - 4; all ftm.

Growing Media Association
- NR Horticulture House, 19 High St, Theale, READING, Berks, RG7 5AH. (hq)
  0118-930 3132
  http://www.growingmedia.co.uk
  Chief Execs: Tim Briercliffe & Innes Mathieson
- ▲ Un-incorporated Society
- ○ *T; the development, production, marketing & sale of growing media & soil improvers in the UK & Ireland
- ● Mtgs - Inf - LG
- M 24 f
- ¶ NL - 4; ftm only.
- × 2002 Peat Producers Association

GS1 Ireland
- IRL Confederation House, 84-86 Lower Baggot St, DUBLIN 2, Republic of Ireland.
  353 (1) 605 1539 fax 353 (1) 662 5863
  email info@gs1ie.ie http://www.gs1ie.org
  Dir: Jim Bracken
- ○ *T; the article number industry
- < IBEC
- × 2005 EAN Ireland

GS1 UK 1976
- ■ 10 Maltravers St, LONDON, WC2R 3BX. (hq)
  020 7655 9000
  email info@gs1uk.org http://www.gs1uk.org
  Chief Exec: Steve Coussins
- ▲ Company Limited by Guarantee
- ○ *T; dedicated to the development of global data standards for the supply chain
- ● Conf - Mtgs - ET - Res
- < GS1
- M 17,000 f
- ¶ GSQ - 4; ftm.
  e-Highlights (email NL) - 4; ftm only.
- × 2005(February) Association for Standards & Practices in Electronic Trade - EAN UK Ltd

Guernsey Chamber of Commerce 1808
- NR 16 Glategny Esplanade (suite 3), ST PETER PORT, Guernsey, Channel Islands, GY1 1WN. (hq)
  01481 727483 fax 01481 710755
  email director@chamber.guernsey.net
  http://www.chamber.guernsey.net
  Dir: Mike Collins
- ▲ Company Limited by Guarantee
- ○ *C; to link together the members of the business community so that they can speak with an authoritative voice on matters concerning the trade, industry & commerce in the Isle of Guernsey
- ● Mtgs - Inf - LG
- < Brit Chams Comm
- M c 600 f (Guernsey)
- ¶ Contact - 12; ftm (extra copies £2.50), £2.50 nm.

© CBD Research Ltd · Beckenham · BR3 5JS · Tel 020 8650 7745 · Fax 020 8650 0768 · E-mail cbd@cbdresearch.com · www.cbdresearch.com

Guernsey Growers Association (GGA) 1894

- ■ Landes du Marche, VALE, Guernsey, Channel Islands, GY6 8DE. (hq)
  01481 253713   fax 01481 254015
  Sec: Mrs V Mechem
- ○ *F; the farming & growing of crops under glass & in the open
- ● Conf - Mtgs - Exhib - Comp - Stat - Inf - VE
- M 250 i & f (mainly local growers)
- ¶ NL.   Ybk.   AR.

Guide Association
the registered title of **Girlguiding UK**

Guide Dogs for the Blind Association (GDBA) 1934

- NR Hillfields, Burghfield, READING, Berks, RG7 3YG.   (hq)
  0118-983 5555
  http://www.gdba.org.uk
  Chief Exec: Bridget Wall
- ▲ Registered Charity
- ○ *W; to enhance the mobility, independence & quality of life of sight impaired people by providing guide dogs & other services
- ● ET - Res - PL - Rehabilitation services to past, present & potential guide dog owners
- M i

Guild of Agricultural Journalists 1946

- ■ Isfield Cottage, Church Rd, CROWBOROUGH, E Sussex, TN6 1BN.   (hsp/b)
  01892 611618
  Hon Gen Sec: Don Gomery
- ▲ Registered Charity
- ○ *P
- ● Conf - Mtgs - ET - Comp - VE - LG
- < Intl Fedn Agricl Journalists (IFAJ)
- M 600 i, UK / 13 i, o'seas
- ¶ NL - 4.   AR.   Ybk.

Guild of Air Pilots & Air Navigators of London (GAPAN) 1929

- ■ Cobham House, 9 Warwick Court, Gray's Inn, LONDON, WC1R 5DJ.   (hq)
  020 7404 4032
  Clerk: Paul J Tacon
- ▲ Livery Company - un-incorporated association
- Br Australia, Hong Kong, N Zealand
- ○ *E, *P; a livery company of the City of London; achievement of air safety through the highest standards for pilots & navigators
- Gp C'ees: Technical & air safety, Education & training, Trophies & awards;
  Benevolent Fund Board of Management [for airmen & their dependents]
- ● Conf - Mtgs - ET - Res - SG - VE - LG
- M 1,700 i, UK / 500 i, o'seas
- ¶ Guild News (Jnl) - 6; ftm only.

Guild of Air Traffic Control Officers (GATCO) 1954

- NR Central Admin Facility, 4 St Mary's Rd, Bingham, NOTTINGHAM, NG13 8DW.   (hq)
  01949 876405
  http://www.gatco.org
  Pres: Richard Dawson
- ▲ Un-incorporated Society
- Br 5
- ○ *P
- Gp C'ees: Technical; Professional
- ● Conf - Mtgs - Exhib - SG - Inf - LG
- < Intl Fedn of Air Traffic Control Assns (IFATCA); Flight Safety C'ee; Gen Aviation Safety Coun; Parliamentary Advy Coun on Transport Safety (PACTS)
- M 2,250 i, 29 f, UK / 150 i, 3 f, o'seas
- ¶ Transmit (Jnl) - 4.   LM - 8.   AR.

Guild of Antique Dealers & Restorers (GADAR) 1989

- NR 2 Willow Cottages, Hereford Rd, SHREWSBURY, Shropshire, SY3 7QL.   (hq)
  01743 271852
  http://www.gadar.co.uk
  Sec: Maureen Edmondson
- ▲ Un-incorporated Society
- ○ *T; to facilitate & offer advice on: repairs & restoration to all antiques, & valuations for insurance & probate
- ● Res - Comp - Stat
- M 150 i, UK / 10 i, o'seas
- ¶ NL - 4; ftm only.

Guild of Architectural Ironmongers (GAI) 1961

- ■ 8 Stepney Green, LONDON, E1 3JU.   (hq)
  020 7790 3431   fax 020 7790 8517
  email info@gai.org.uk   http://www.gai.org.uk
  Dir: Peter Spill
- ▲ Company Limited by Guarantee
- ○ *T; the best possible materials & service for use in each project
- ● Conf - Mtgs - ET - Exam - Exhib - Comp - SG - Stat - Inf - VE
- < Door & Hardware Inst (USA)
- M 175 full members (distributors), 80 associates (manufacturers)
- ¶ Architectural Ironmongery Jnl - 4; ftm, £10 nm.
  LM - 2 yrly; ftm, £9.50 nm.
  Training Manuals from £5 each.

Guild of Aviation Artists (GAvA) 1971

- NR Trenchard House, 85 Farnborough Rd, FARNBOROUGH, Hants, GU14 6TF.   (hq)
  01252 513123
- ○ *A, *P; encouragement of Aviation Art in all its forms
- ● Conf - Mtgs - ET - Exhib - Comp - SG - Inf - PL - VE
- < R Aero Club
- M i

Guild of Bricklayers 1932

- ■ 83 Windsor Rd, Ashton-in-Makerfield, WIGAN, Lancs, WN4 9ET.   (treas/p)
  01942 724927
  email barry@walton120.freeserve.co.uk
  http://www.guild-of-bricklayers.org.uk
  Nat Treas: Barry Walton
- ▲ Registered Charity
- ○ *T
- ● Conf - Mtgs - ET - Comp
- M 500 i, 5 colleges
- ¶ Jnl - 1;   NL - 1; both free.

Guild of British Camera Technicians (GBCT) 1978

- ■ c/o Panavision, Metropolitan Centre, Bristol Rd, GREENFORD, Middx, UB6 8GD.   (hq)
  020 8813 1999   fax 020 8813 2111
  email admin@gbct.org   http://www.gbct.org
  Co Sec & Office Mgr: Christine Henwood
- ○ *P; for professionally recognised camera technicians with the film, TV & video industry
- ● Conf - ET - Exhib
- M 500 i, UK / 50 i, o'seas
- ¶ GBCT TECHS Magazine - 6; ftm, £12 yr.

Guild of British Coach Operators (1985)

- ■ PO Box 5657, SOUTHEND on SEA, Essex, SS1 3WT.   (hq)
  email admin@coach-tours.co.uk
  http://www.coach-tours.co.uk
  Admin: Richard Delahoy
- ▲ Company Limited by Guarantee
- ○ *T; to increase public recognition of the role that coaches play in tourism & public transport; to establish working relationships with organisations & bodies involved in transport
- < Intl Motor Coach Gp (USA)
- M 21 f

Guild of British Découpeurs   (GBD)   1999

- Chimneys, 18 Pembridge Close, CHARLTON KINGS, Glos, GL52 6XY.   (sp)
  01242 235302
  Sec: Mrs Madeleine Smith
- ○ *A, *G; to provide information & education in the art & authentic techniques of découpage (the art of applying decorative paper cut-outs to surfaces)
- ● Mtgs - ET - Inf - PL
- M 35 i, UK / 290 i, o'seas
- ¶ Shortcuts - 2; ftm only.

Guild of British Film & Television Editors   (GBFE)   1966

- 72 Pembroke Rd, LONDON, W8 6NX.   (hsp)
  020 7602 8319   fax 020 7602 8319
  Sec: Sally Fisher
- ○ *P
- ● Conf - Res - Exhib - Inf - VE - Film shows
- < BECTU
- M 91 i, UK / 8 i, o'seas
- ¶ NL - irreg.
- ✕ 2005-06 Guild of British Film Editors

Guild of British Tie Makers
a group of the **British Clothing Industry Association**

Guild of Builders & Contractors   (GBC)   1994

- NR Crest House, 102-104 Church Rd, TEDDINGTON, Middx, TW11 8PY.   (hq)
  020 8977 1105
  Exec Dir: E A Goddard
- ▲ Company Limited by Guarantee
- ○ *T; for individuals & firms who are actively engaged in the building industry, who are experienced & knowledgeable & trade with integrity
- ● Mtgs - Stat - Inf - VE - LG
- M 1,500 i, 750 f
- ¶ NL - 3;   Technical Information Reports - 4; both ftm only.

Guild of Business Travel Agents
since 2005 **Guild of Travel Management Companies**

Guild of Catholic Doctors - Guild of St Luke, Sts Cosmas & Damian   1923

- Hospital of St John & St Elizabeth, 60 Grove End Rd, LONDON, NW8 9NH.   (hq)
  020 7266 4246   fax 020 7806 4001
  http://www.catholicdoctors.org.uk
- ▲ Registered Charity
- Br 29
- ○ *P; professional support in medical ethics; informed opinion about implications of developments in medicine & social policy
- Gp C'ees: Medical ethics, Standing parliamentary
- ● Conf - Mtgs - SG - Inf - LG
- < Intl Fedn of Catholic Doctors (FIAMC); Eur Fedn of Catholic Doctors (FEAMC); Eur Doctors U
- M 1,000 i, UK / 10 i, o'seas
- ¶ Catholic Medical Quarterly - 4.

Guild of Church Braillists   (GCB)   1911

- c/o 8 St Raphael's Court, Avenue Rd, ST ALBANS, Herts, AL1 3EH.   (hsp)
  01727 864076
  Chmn: Mrs Margaret Chambers
- ▲ Registered Charity
- ○ *P, *R; to advance the Christian religion in particular by transcribing Christian literature from print into braille: a) to supply at the request of individuals or groups, b) to increase the number of Christian books in the National Library for the Blind
- ● Mtgs - ET
- < Nat Library for the Blind; R Nat Inst for the Blind
- M c 45 i (blind proof readers, Braille consultants, transcribers)
- ¶ AR inc LM; free.

Guild of Church Musicians   (GCM)   1888

- St Katharine Cree, 86 Leadenhall St, LONDON, EC3A 3DH.   (hsb/regd/office)
  01883 743168
  http://www.churchmusicians.org
  Gen Sec: John Ewington
- ▲ Registered Charity
- Br Australia
- ○ *L; to promote the highest standards in church music & liturgy
- ● Conf - Mtgs - ET - Exam (for Archbishop's certificate in church music & in public worship; Fellowship of Guild of Church Musicians)
- < University of Newcastle (NSW)
- M 720 i, UK / 80 i, o'seas
- ¶ Laudate - 3; ftm;   Ybk - 1; both ftm.

Guild of Cleaners & Launderers   (GCL)   1949

- 1 Wellfield Rd, Offerton, STOCKPORT, Cheshire, SK2 6AS.   (hsb)
  0845 600 1838   fax 0161-483 4655
  email enquiries@gcl.org.uk   http://www.gcl.org.uk
  Gen Sec: Mrs Sandra Pearce
- ▲ Registered Charity
- Br 9
- ○ *P; examining body of the textile care industry & joint awarding body with SVQs/NVQs
- Gp Laundry & dry cleaning
- ● Conf - Mtgs - Exam - Inf - Lib
- M 450 i, UK / 25 i, o'seas
- ¶ NL - 6.   Retail Sales Garment Cleaning.
  Textiles for Launderers & Drycleaners.
  The After Care of Silk.   Stain Removal Guide.
  Other publications.

Guild of Curative Hypnotherapists   (GCH)   1992

- NR Healing Touch, 4 Bath Rd, WORCESTER, WR5 3EJ.   (hq)
  01905 640598
  Pres: John R Freeman Cartwright
- ▲ Un-incorporated Society
- ○ *P; promotion & protection of hypnotherapy
- ● Mtgs - ET - Exam - Inf - LG
- < Inst Complementary Medicines
- M 15 i
- ¶ NL - irreg; ftm only.

Guild of Drama Adjudicators   (GODA)   1947

- 25 The Drive, Bengeo, HERTFORD, Herts, SG14 3DE.   (hsp)
  01992 581993
  email crossley@bengeo25.freeserve.co.uk
  http://www.amdram.co.uk/goda
  Hon Sec: Mrs Joan Crossley
- ▲ Registered Charity
- ○ *P; to supply qualified adjudicators to all organisations promoting amateur drama
- ● Conf - Mtgs - ET - Inf - Adjudication at drama festivals
- M 125 i
- ¶ News & Views - 3; ftm only.   Asides - 1; free.
  A Directory of Drama Adjudicators - 1; free.

© CBD Research Ltd · Beckenham · BR3 5JS · Tel 020 8650 7745 · Fax 020 8650 0768 · E-mail cbd@cbdresearch.com · www.cbdresearch.com

Guild of Enamellers (GE) 1978
NR c/o 24 Coltsgate Hill, RIPON, N Yorks, HG4 2AB. (memsec/p)
▲ Un-incorporated Society
Br 7
○ *A; to promote the craft of enamelling on metal; to exert a
  progressive influence on standards of workmanship & design
● Conf - Mtgs - Exam - Exhib - Comp - Inf - Lib - VE
M 182 i, UK / 5 i, o'seas
¶ Jnl - 4; ftm only.

Guild of Erotic Artists 2002
■ Beaumont Hall Studios, Beaumont Hall Lane, Redburn Rd,
  ST ALBANS, Herts, AL3 6RN. (hq)
  01582 791661 fax 01582 793332
  http://www.theguildoferoticartists.com
  Sec: Colin Ballard
○ *A
Gp Artists; Models; Photographers; Sculptors & bodycasters;
  Corporate; Patrons
● Mtgs - ET - Exhib - SG - Inf - PL - Demonstrations of artists'
  skills including photography, sketching, bodycasting, shibari,
  life model drawing, body painting etc
M 160 i, 5 f, UK / 6 i, o'seas
¶ Jade - 6; ftm, £35 nm.

Guild of Experienced Motorists (GEM) 1932
NR Station Rd, FOREST ROW, E Sussex, RH18 5EN. (hq)
  01342 825676 fax 01342 824847
  email dw@roadsafety.org.uk
  http://www.roadsafety.org.uk
  Chief Exec: David Williams
○ *G; motoring & road safety
● ET - Inf - LG
M 65,000 i, UK / 1,000 i, o'seas
¶ Good Motoring Magazine - 4; free.
  Note: since January 2004, trading as GEM Motoring Assist.

Guild of Fine Food Retailers (GFFR) 1995
■ PO Box 1525, GILLINGHAM, Dorset, SP8 4WA. (hq)
  01747 822290 fax 01747 822289
  email obfarrand@finefoodworld.co.uk
  http://www.finefoodworld.co.uk
  Nat Dir: Bob Farrand
▲ Company Limited by Guarantee
○ *T; to champion the cause of speciality food retailers &
  producers
Gp UK Cheese Guild; Charcuterie Guild
● ET - Res - Exhib - Comp - LG - Cheese training to NVQ
  standard - Charcuterie training - Great Taste & World
  Cheese Awards
< UK Cheese Gld
M 1,100 f
¶ Fine Food Digest - 9; ftm, £25 yr (UK).
  Artisan - 6; ftm, £20 nm. Good Cheese - 1; ftm, £2.50 nm.

Guild of Food Writers (GFW) 1984
■ 9 Colman House, High St, LONDON, SE20 7EX. (admin/p)
  020 8659 0422
  email admin@gfw.co.uk http://www.gfw.co.uk
  Admin: Jonathan Woods
▲ Un-incorporated Society
○ *P; to contribute to the growth of public interest in, & knowledge
  of, the subject of food; to campaign for improvements in the
  quality of food
● Conf - Mtgs - ET - Comp - VE - LG
M 360 i
¶ LM - 1; ftm, £190 nm.

Guild of Freemen of the City of London 1908
■ PO Box 1202, KINGSTON UPON THAMES, Surrey, KT2 7XB.
  (mail)
  020 8541 1435 fax 020 8541 1455
  email clerk@guild-freemen-london.co.uk address
  Clerk: Brig M I Keun
▲ Company Limited by Guarantee; Registered Charity
○ *G, *W; within the City of London: to support traditions &
  institutions, to promote fellowship & good citizenship, to help
  the needy & underprivileged & to support & promote
  education & training
● ET - VE - Charity work & benevolence
< Hon Company of Freemen of the City of London of N America
M 3,000 i, UK / 200 i, o'seas
¶ The Freeman (Jnl) - 1; ftm, £7.50 nm.   AR; ftm only.

Guild of Glass Engravers 1975
■ 87 Nether St, LONDON, N12 7NP. (hq)
  020 8446 4050
  http://www.gge.org.uk
  Sec: Mrs Christine Reyland
▲ Registered Charity
Br 9
○ *A, *G, *P; to promote the highest quality of creative design &
  craftsmanship among glass engravers & advance the
  education of the public in the art of glass engraving & other
  forms of surface decoration on glass
● Conf - Mtgs - ET - Exhib - Assessments
M 380 i, UK / 53 i, o'seas
¶ NL - 4; ftm only.

Guild of Health Ltd 1904
NR c/o St Marylebone Parish Church, 17 Marylebone Rd,
  LONDON, NW1 5LT. (mail/address)
  020 7563 1389
  email gohealth@freeuk.com   http://www.gohealth.org.uk
  Chmn: Mrs Pamela Freeman
▲ Company Limited by Guarantee; Registered Charity
Br 25; Canada
○ *W; to bring together Christian people (clergy, laity, health care
  professionals) with a concern for healing, wholeness &
  'finding God in all things'
● Conf - Mtgs - Prayer & meditation - Workshops - Retreats -
  Seminars - Literature
< Retreat Assn
M 350 i, 2 org, UK / 11 i, o'seas
¶ Way of Life (Jnl) - 4; ftm, £8 yr nm.   AR - 1; ftm only.

Guild of Health Writers 1994
■ Dale Lodge, 88 Wensleydale Rd, HAMPTON, Middx,
  TW12 2LX. (chmn/p)
  020 8941 2977 fax 020 8941 2977
  email admin@healthwriters.com
  http://www.healthwriters.com
  Chmn: Caroline White
○ *P; for journalists dedicated to providing accurate, broad-based
  information about health & related subjects to the public
Gp Ageing; Children's health; Complementary medicine; Fitness;
  General medicine; Health & education; Medical ethics;
  Mental health; Mind body medicine; Preventative medicine;
  Psychology & psychotherapy; Relationships; Women's health
● Mtgs - ET - Comp
M c 230 i
¶ Health Writer - 4; ftm only.

Guild of Healthcare Pharmacists
  is an autonomous professional body within **Amicus**

Guild of International Butler Administrators & Personal Assistants 1981

■ 12 Little Bornes, Dulwich, LONDON, SE21 8SE. (dir/b)
  020 8670 5585
  http://www.ivorspencer.com
  Pres & Dir: Ivor Spencer
▲ Un-incorporated Society
Br USA, Hong Kong
○ *P; to promote the British butler worldwide; to encourage the highest standards among British trained butlers throughout the world
● Mtgs - ET - Exam - Comp - Expt - Inf - VE - Empl - Speakers bureau - Placement service
< Toastmasters for Royal Occasions; Gld Intl Profl Toastmasters
M 60 i, UK / 75 i, o'seas
¶ NL - 2; ftm only.

Guild of International Professional Toastmasters 1990

■ 12 Little Bornes, Dulwich, LONDON, SE21 8SE. (pres/b)
  020 8670 5585
  http://www.ivorspencer.com
  Pres & Chmn: Ivor Spencer
▲ Un-incorporated Society
○ *P; to organise banquets worldwide & to advise companies & embassies on protocol on these occasions; to lecture on the art of after-dinner speaking; to train toastmasters & butlers
● Conf - ET - International award for Best After-Dinner Speaker of the Year
< Toastmasters for Royal Occasions
M 20 i

Guild of Letting & Management   (GLM Ltd) 1997

NR Unit 6 Pardix House, Cadmore Lane, CHESHUNT, Herts, EN8 9LQ.
  01992 420022   fax 01992 625628
  Chmn & Dir: Frank Ciraolo
▲ Company Limited by Guarantee
Br 3
○ *P; for property management letting agents
● Conf - Mtgs - ET - Exam - Res - SG - Stat - Inf - Lib - LG
M 350 i, 350 f
¶ Guild News - 6.   Guild Letting Companion (manual) - 1.

Guild of Macebearers 1950

■ 54 Winifred Rd, COULSDON, Surrey, CR5 3JE. (sb)
  020 8668 5997   fax 020 8407 3062
  http://www.civicprotocol.com
  Guild Clerk: Peter Townsend
▲ Un-incorporated Society
○ *P; to uphold & preserve the customs of the civic & corporate life of the country & Commonwealth & the dignity of the office of mayor; to offer advice on such matters
● Conf - ET - Inf
M 260 i, UK / 1 i, o'seas
¶ The Mace-Bearer - 3;   LM - 1; both ftm only.
  The Manual of the Mace; £10 m only.

Guild of Master Craftsmen   (GMC) 1974

■ 166 High St, LEWES, E Sussex, BN7 1XU. (hq)
  01273 478449   fax 01273 478606
  email theguild@thegmcgroup.com
  http://www.guildmc.com
  Jt Secs: Jennifer & Jonathan Phillips
▲ Company Limited by Guarantee
○ *A, *P, *T; for skilled craftspeople & professionals
● Inf - Legal advice - Debt collection - Assistance to members in finding work - Promotional material Insurance & financial services - Discounts on business expenses
M 20,000 i
¶ All journals below are supplied at a discount to members:
  Woodturning.   Woodcarving.   New Woodworking.
  The Router.   Furniture & Cabinetmaking.
  Outdoor Photography.   Black & White Photography.
  Knitting.   Machine Knitting News.
  The Dolls' House Magazine.   Organic Life.

Guild of Motoring Writers 1944

NR 30 The Cravens, SMALLFIELD, Surrey, RH6 9QS.   (secretariat)
  01342 843294
  Contact: The General Secretary
▲ Company Limited by Guarantee
○ *P; to improve the standard of motoring journalism; to encourage motoring, motor sport & road safety
● Mtgs - ET - Comp
M i

Guild of Musicians & Singers 1993

NR 4 Cranbrook Terrace, CRANLEIGH, Surrey, GU6 7ES.   (sp)
  http://www.musiciansandsingers.org.uk
  Sec-Gen: Michael Newman-Horwell
○ *L, *P; for professional & amateur musicians; to promote a high standard of musical performance
● Mtgs - Concerts - Lectures & talks
M c 200 i
¶ NL - 2.

Guild of Nurses & Midwives (UK)

  has disbanded

Guild of One-Name Studies   (GOONS) 1979

■ 14 Charterhouse Buildings (Box G), Goswell Rd, LONDON, EC1M 7BA.   (mail)
  0800 011 2182
  email guild@one-name.org
  http://www.one-name.org address
  Sec: Mrs Kirsty Gray
▲ Registered Charity
○ *L; study of surnames & family history
● Conf - Mtgs - Lib - e-Lib - Registration of one-name studies
M 2,000 i
¶ Jnl of One-Name Studies - 1; ftm, £2 nm.
  Register of One-Name Studies - 1; ftm, £2 nm.

Guild of Pastoral Psychology   (GPP) 1937

NR 13 Ascot Lodge, Greville Place, LONDON, NW6 5JD.
▲ Registered Charity
○ *P; for all those interested in the relation between religion & depth psychology; especially that of C G Jung & his followers
● Conf - Mtgs - SG - Lib
M 500 i, 30 org, UK / 30 i, o'seas
¶ Pamphlets - 5;   List of groups - 1; both ftm only.
  Printed lectures - 3/4.   Cassette recordings;   AR.

Guild of Photographers UK   (GP) 1988

■ Moorlinch, BRIDGWATER, Somerset, TA7 9DD.   (hq)
  0870 240 9242
  Dir: Joan Roberts
▲ Un-incorporated Society
○ *P; training & qualifying photographers in the skills of wedding & portrait photography
● ET - Exam - Comp - Inf
< Wedding & Portrait Photographers Intl (USA)
M 300 i, UK / 4 i, o'seas

Guild of Polyglots 1987

■ 191 Westcombe Hill, LONDON, SE3 7DR.   (mail) address
▲ Un-incorporated Society
○ *G; for people interested in speaking languages other than their native tongue
● Mtgs - ET - Exam - SG - Lib - VE
M 77 i, 2 f
¶ NL; ftm only.

© CBD Research Ltd · Beckenham · BR3 5JS · Tel 020 8650 7745 · Fax 020 8650 0768 · E-mail cbd@cbdresearch.com · www.cbdresearch.com

Guild of Professional Beauty Therapists Ltd   (GPBT)   1994
■   320 Burton Rd, DERBY, DE23 6AF.   (hq)
     0870 000 4242   fax 0870 000 4247
     email info@beautyguild.com
     http://www.beautyguild.com
     Managing Dir: Paul Archer
▲   Limited Company
○   *P; to represent the interests of professional beauty therapists &
     salon owners
●   ET - Res - Exhib - Comp - Stat - Inf - LG
M   6,000 i
¶   Guild Gazette - 6;   Beautyguild Bulletin (email NL) - 26.

Guild of Professional Estate Agents   (GPEA)   1993
NR   121 Park Lane, LONDON, W1K 7AG.   (hq)
     020 7629 4141   fax 020 7629 2329
     email theguild@property-platform.com
     http://www.property-platform.com
     Man Dir: Malcolm Lindley
▲   Company Limited by Guarantee
○   *T; for independent estate agencies
●   Marketing
M   400 f
¶   The Property Magazine - 12.

Guild of Professional Teachers of Dancing   (GPTD)   1973
■   43 Telfer Rd, Radford, COVENTRY, CV6 3DG.   (hsp)
     024 7659 7907
     Gen Sec: Terry Perkins
Br   4
○   *U; an independent trade union representing teachers of
     dancing, movement to music & dramatic arts
Gp   Teachers of dance & movement to music; Ballroom; Stage;
     Aerobics; Keep fit; Irish dance; Indian dance; Western line
     dancing; Dramatic arts
●   Conf - Mtgs - ET - Exhib - Comp - Inf - Empl - LG
M   1,200 i, UK / 10 i, o'seas
¶   Tempo - 4; ftm only.

Guild of Professional Toastmasters   1963
■   32 Shearman Rd, Blackheath, LONDON, SE3 9TN.   (hsp)
     020 8852 4621
     email rgrosse@guild-of-toastmasters.co.uk
     http://www.guild-of-toastmasters.co.uk
     Hon Sec: Robert Grosse
▲   Un-incorporated Society
○   *; for toastmasters, masters of ceremonies & compères
Gp   Profl Toastmasters' Academy
●   Conf - Mtgs - ET - Exam
M   25 i

Guild of Professional Videographers   (GPV)   1991
■   11 Telfer Rd, Radford, COVENTRY, Warks, CV6 3DG.   (hq)
     024 7627 2548   fax 024 7627 2548
     email mail@professionalvideographers.co.uk
     http://www.professionalvideographers.co.uk
     Sec: Mrs Ann Middleton
▲   Company Limited by Guarantee
○   *P; to assist members with legal problems; advise on training;
     advise on grants available to small/medium business
●   Mtgs - ET - Exam - Inf
M   140 i, 10 f, UK / 25 i, 3 f, o'seas
¶   [all communications to members is sent by email].

Guild of Professional Wedding Services
NR   18 Bond St, BRISTOL, BS1 3LU.
     0117-945 1821
     Gen Sec: Elaine Robinson
Br   3

Guild for the Promotion of Welsh Music
     since 2003 **Welsh Music Guild**

Guild of Psychotherapists   1974
■   47 Nelson Sq, Blackfriars Rd, LONDON, SE1 0QA.   (hq)
     020 7401 3260   fax 020 7401 3472
     email info@guildofpsychotherapists.org.uk
     http://www.guildofpsychotherapists.org.uk
     Hon Sec: Tania Glynn
▲   Registered Charity
○   *P; training in psychoanalytic psychotherapy
●   Conf - Mtgs - ET - SG - Lib - Low-cost clinic for Southwark,
     Lambeth & Lewisham
<   UK Coun for Psychotherapy (UKCP)
M   260 i

Guild of Q Butchers   (Q butchers)   1997
■   PO Box 26139, DUNFERMLINE, Fife, KY12 7WJ.   (hq)
     01383 432622   fax 01383 432626
     email qbutcher@rossmuir.co.uk
     http://www.guildofqbutchers.co.uk
     Contact: Chief Exec
▲   Company Limited by Guarantee
○   *T; for progressive independent meat retailers (members'
     premises are subject to independent inspection by EFSIS)
Gp   Specialists: Sausage, Cooked meat, Deli, B-B-Q, Meal
●   Mtgs - Comp - Promotion
M   300 f
¶   Q News - 4; ftm only.

Guild of Railway Artists   1979
■   45 Dickins Rd, WARWICK, CV34 5NS.   (admin)
     01926 499246
     http://www.railart.co.uk p
     Chief Exec: F P Hodges
▲   Un-incorporated Society
○   *A; to forge a link between artists depicting railway subjects
●   Mtgs - Exhib - Inf
<   Assn of Rly Presvn Socs
M   158 i, UK / 6 i, 1 org
¶   Wheel & Palette - 4; ftm.

Guild of Registered Tourist Guides   1950
■   The Guild House, 52D Borough High St, LONDON,
     SE1 1XN.   (hq)
     020 7403 1115   fax 020 7378 1705
     email guild@blue-badge.org.uk
     http://www.blue-badge.org.uk
     Gen Mgr: Mehmet Ahmet
▲   Un-incorporated Society
○   *P; the national professional association of Blue Badge Guides
●   Conf - Mtgs - ET - Exam - Exhib - SG - Inf - Lib - VE - Empl -
     LG
<   Wld Fedn of Tourist Guides Assns; Fédn Eur des Guides
     Touristiques
M   800 i, 40 f, 39 org, UK / 10 i, 2 f, o'seas
¶   Guide Post - 12; free.   Guild Directory - 1; ftm, £23.50 nm.
     National Guide's Guide - 1; ftm, £8.90 nm.
     London Guide's Guide - 1; ftm, £5.90 nm.

Guild of Shareholders
NR   PO Box 192, UPMINSTER, Essex, RM14 3WB.   (admin/office)
     01708 855113
     Contact: Mrs Ford
▲   Company Limited by Guarantee
○   *K; to enable shareholders to influence the way their
     companies are run
M   i
¶   Jnl - 4; ftm.

Guild of Straw Craftsmen   1989
NR   82 Manor Rise, Chasetown, BURNTWOOD, Staffs, WS7 4TS.
    (pres/p)
    01543 676826
    email peteshelleystraw@yahoo.com
    http://www.strawcraftsmen.co.uk
    Pres: Pete Shelley
▲   Un-incorporated Society
○   *G; to promote straw craft in all its many facets; to bring straw
    artists & workers together to develop the craft
●   Conf - Mtgs - ET - Exam - Res - Exhib - Comp - SG - Inf - Lib -
    PL - VE
M   100 i, UK / 40 i, o'seas
¶   Guild News (NL) - 2; ftm, £1.50 nm.

Guild of Stunt & Action Coordinators   (SCAG)   1986
■   72 Pembroke Rd, LONDON, W8 6NX.   (hsb)
    020 7602 8319   fax 020 7602 8319
    email stunts.uk@btinternet.com
    Sec: Sally Fisher
▲   Un-incorporated Society
○   *P; film stunt coordinators
●   Mtgs - ET - LG
M   25 i

Guild of Taxidermists   (GOT)   1976
■   Glasgow Museums Resource Centre, 200 Woodhead Rd, South
    Nitshill, GLASGOW, G53 7NN.   (hsb)
    0141-276 9445   fax 0141-276 9305
    Hon Sec: Duncan A Ferguson,   Chmn: James Dickinson
○   *P; to raise standards & awareness of taxidermy in the UK
●   Conf - Mtgs - ET - Exam - Exhib
<   Eur Taxidermy Fedn
M   190 i, UK / 10 i, o'seas
¶   Jnl - 1; ftm, £5 nm.

Guild of Television Cameramen   1972
NR   1 Churchill Rd, Whitchurch, TAVISTOCK, Devon, PL19 9BU.
    (admin/p)
    01822 614405   fax 01822 615785
    http://www.gtc.org.uk
    Admin Officer: Sheila Lewis
○   *P; improve the art & craft of television cameramen for
    broadcast television
M   c 1,200 i

Guild of Theatre Prompters
■   191 Westcombe Hill, LONDON, SE3 7DB.
○   *P
M   i

Guild of Travel Management Companies   (GTMC)   1967
NR   Queens House, 180-182 Tottenham Court Rd, LONDON,
    W1T 7PD.   (hq)
    020 7637 1091   fax 020 7580 6593
    Chief Exec: Philip Carlisle
▲   Company Limited by Guarantee
○   *T; to speak for business travellers & the agents who act for
    them
Gp Working parties: Air, Hotel, Surface transport, European,
    Technology
●   Conf - Mtgs - ET - Exam - SG - Stat - LG
<   Gld Eur Business Travel Agents
M   40 f
×   2005 Guild of Business Travel Agents

Guild of Travel & Tourism   1995
■   Suite 193 Temple Chambers, 3-7 Temple Avenue, LONDON,
    EC4Y 0DB.   (hq)
    020 7583 6333   fax 01895 834028
    email nigel.bishop@traveltourismguild.com
    http://www.traveltourismguild.com
    Chief Exec: Nigel Bishop
▲   Company Limited by Guarantee
○   *P; 'to promote the interests & needs of people within the travel
    industry & those organisations involved in transport, travel &
    tourism'
Gp Travel industry trade assn
●   Mtgs - Seminars
M   i, f
¶   The Travel Business (NL) - 4; free.

Guillain Barré Syndrome Support Group   (GBS)   1985
■   Lincolnshire County Council Offices, Eastgate, SLEAFORD,
    Lincs, NG34 7EB.   (hq)
    01529 304615   fax 01529 304615
    email admin@gbs.org.uk   http://www.gbs.org.uk
    Sec: Mrs Anne Bennett
▲   Registered Charity
Br Ireland, Scotland
○   *W; to support sufferers of the disease & their families; to
    promote research & treatment
Gp GBS &: pregnancy, children, diabetes
●   Conf - Mtgs - Res - Inf - Fund raising
<   Guillain Barré Syndrome Foundation Intl
M   2,000 i
¶   Reaching Out (Jnl) - 3; £18 (£7.50 concessions).
    A Quick Guide to Guillain Barré Syndrome;
       Other guides on the syndrome; all free.

Gulf Veterans Association   (GVA)   1994
■   MEA House (4th floor), Ellison Place, NEWCASTLE upon TYNE,
    NE1 8XS.   (hq)
    0191-230 1065   fax 0191-260 2558
    email larry@gvanewcastle.freeserve.co.uk
    http://www.gulfveteransassociation.co.uk
    Chmn: Larry Cammock
▲   Un-incorporated Society
○   *K; to support & act for all members & their families whether
    they were Army, Navy, RAF or civilians, who fought in the
    Gulf War & service personnel who have served in that area
    since
Gp Service pensions; Crisis advocate
●   Res - Inf - LG
<   Nat Vietnam & Gulf War Veterans Coalition; Nat Gulf War
    Resource Centre
M   2,000 i, UK / 500 i, o'seas

Gun Trade Association Ltd   (GTA)   1896
■   PO Box 43, TEWKESBURY, Glos, GL20 5ZE.   (hq)
    01684 291868   fax 01684 291864
    email enquiries@guntradeassociation.com
    http://www.guntradeassociation.com
    Dir: John Batley
▲   Company Limited by Guarantee
○   *T; interests of the sporting firearms, ammunition, accessories
    industry & those providing related services; liaison with proof
    authorities, police & other government agencies
Gp Joint Venture C'ee - organises British Pavilion at overseas trade
    fairs
●   Conf - Mtgs - ET - Res - Exhib - Stat - Expt - Inf - LG
<   Brit Shooting Sports Coun; Standing Conf on Countryside
    Sports; Eur Inst for Hunting & Sporting Guns; Wld Forum on
    the Future of Sport Shooting Activities
M   550 i & f, UK / 10 f (associates), o'seas
¶   NL - 6; ftm only.

Gwartheg Hynafol Cymru (Ancient Cattle of Wales) (GHC/ ACW) 1981
- ■ Croesheddig Newydd, Pentre'r Bryn, LLANDYSUL, Ceredigion, SA44 6NB. (hsp)
    01545 560255
    email xheddig@tiscally.co.uk
    Hon Secs: Sian & Gareth loan
- ▲ Un-incorporated Society
- ○ *B; the breeding of Welsh cattle of colours other than black
- M 30 i
- ¶ NL - irreg; free.

Gwent Wildlife Trust (GWT) 1963
- ■ Seddon House, Dingestow Court, MONMOUTH, NP25 4DY. (hq)
    01600 740358   fax 01600 740299
    email gwentwildlife@cix.co.uk
    http://www.wildlifetrust.org.uk/gwent
    Chief Exec: Julian Branscombe
- ▲ Registered Charity
- ○ *L
- Gp Education; Reserves; Conservation; Membership; Local groups; Volunteers
- ● ET - Inf - VE
- M 5,600 i, 10 f, 20 org, UK / 3 i, o'seas
- ¶ Local News - 3;   Supplement in Natural World - 3;   Annual Review;   all free.

Gypsum Products Development Association (GPDA) 1956
- ■ PO Box 35084, LONDON, NW1 4XE.   (asa)
    020 7935 8532   fax 020 7935 8532
    email office@gpda.com   http://www.gpda.com
    Sec: C Dunn-Meynell
- ○ *T
- ● Mtgs - Inf
- < Eurogypsum
- M 4 f

Gypsy Cob Society
- NR Chywoon Farm, Church Brough, KIRKBY STEPHEN, Cumbria, CA17 4EJ.
    01768 341319
    email info@gypsycobsociety.org
- ○ *B

H G Wells Society (HGWS) 1960
- ■ Flat 3 / 27b Church Rd, LONDON, NW4 4EB.   (hsp)
  http://www.hgwellsusa.50megs.com
  Hon Gen Sec: Mark Egerton
- ▲ Un-incorporated Society
- ○ *A, *L; to promote an interest in, & appreciation of the life,
  work & thought of Herbert George Wells (1866-1946)
- ● Conf - Lib
- < Alliance of Literary Socs
- M 100 i, UK / 100 i, o'seas
- ¶ The Wellsian (Jnl) - 1.
  NL - 2; both ftm only.

** Hackney Chamber of Commerce
Organisation lost: see Introduction paragraph 3

Hackney Horse Society 1883
- ■ Fallowfields, Little London, Heytesbury, WARMINSTER, Wilts,
  BA12 0ES.   (hq)
  01985 840717   fax 01985 840616
  email admin@hackney-horse.org.uk
  http://www.hackney-horse.org.uk
  Sec: Mrs Dawn Hicketts
- ▲ Registered Charity
- ○ *B; improvement of breeding of Hackney horses & ponies;
  harness & driving horses
- ● Exhib - Comp
- M 650 i, 28 org, UK / 50 i, o'seas
- ¶ Hackney Stud Book - 5 yrly; £30.   Ybk - 1; £12.

Haemochromatosis Society 1990
- NR Hollybush House, Hadley Green Rd, BARNET, Herts, EN5 5PR.
  020 8449 1363
  Dir: Mrs Janet Fernau
- ▲ Company Limited by Guarantee; Registered Charity
- ○ *W; to provide support, awareness & information for families
  affected by this iron overload genetic disorder & to the
  medical profession
- ● Res (support) - Inf - Support for members
- < Brit Liver Trust; Genetic Interest Gp; Contact-a-Family
- M c 600 i
- ¶ NL - 4;   Treatment card;   Leaflet; all free.

Haemophilia Society United Kingdom 1950
- ■ Petersham House, 57A Hatton Garden, LONDON,
  EC1N 8JG.   (hq)
  020 7831 1020   fax 020 7405 4824
  email info@haemophilia.org.uk
  http://www.haemophilia.org.uk
  Chief Exec: Margaret Unwin
- ▲ Registered Charity
- Br 17 groups
- ○ *W; the national patient organisation for people with
  haemophilia & related bleeding disorders, including von
  Willebrand's, in the UK; to ensure that people with these
  disorders receive the best quality of care & support
- ● Conf - Mtgs - Inf
  Helpline: 0800 018 6068 (Mon-Fri 1000-1600)
- > Wld Fedn of Hemophilia; Eur Haemophila Consortium
- M 4,000 i, UK / 122 i, o'seas
- ¶ Haemophilia Quarterly - 4;
  HQtoo! (NL for young people) - 4;   AR- 1; free.
  Publications list available.

Haflinger Society of Great Britain (HSGB) 1970
- ■ 11 Northumberland Place, RICHMOND, Surrey, TW10 6TS.
  (hsp)
  020 8948 6599
  http://www.haflingersgb.com
  Sec: Carolyn Hallett
- ▲ Registered Charity
- ○ *B; to promote the breeding of the Haflinger horse & publish
  the pedigrees of those in Great Britain
- ● Mtgs - Comp - Inf - Young stock inspections - Breed Show
- < Wld Haflinger Fedn
- M c 400 i
- ¶ Focus on Haflingers (NL) - 4; ftm only.

Hairdressing & Beauty Suppliers Association Ltd (HBSA) 1926
- NR Greenleaf House, 128 Darkes Lane, POTTERS BAR, Herts,
  EN6 1AE.   (hq)
  01707 649499   fax 01707 649497
  http://www.hbsa.uk.com
  Chief Exec: David Macklin
- ▲ Company Limited by Guarantee
- ○ *T; for manufacturers & suppliers of professional hair & beauty
  products
- Gp Wig makers' section
- ● Conf - Mtgs - ET - Exhib
- M 120 f
- ¶ HBSA News - 6; ftm only.

Hairline International: the Alopecia Patients Society 1995
- NR Lyons Court, 1668 High Street, KNOWLE, W Midlands,
  B93 0LY.   (hq)
  01564 775281
  Dir & Founder: Elizabeth Steel
- ▲ Un-incorporated Society
- ○ *K, *W; an international support network for patients with
  alopecia, offering independent & un-biased support &
  information on all aspects of hair loss, its causes & treatment
- Gp Trichotillomania (compulsive hair-pulling); Chemotherapy (hair
  loss caused by medical treatment)
- ● Conf - Mtgs - ET - Res - SG - Stat - Inf - Campaigns
- M i
- ¶ The Hair Loss Cure by Elizabeth Steel.

Hakluyt Society 1846
- NR c/o The Map Library, The British Library, 96 Euston Rd,
  LONDON, NW1 2DB.   (mail)
  01428 641850
  email office@hakluyt.com
  http://www.hakluyt.com address
  Admin: Richard Bateman
- ▲ Registered Charity
- ○ *L; 'to advance education by the publication of records of
  voyages, travels, naval expeditions & other geographical
  material & to promote public knowledge of these matters'
- ● Mtgs
- < American Friends of the Hakluyt Soc
- M 810 i, 350 org, UK / 1,454 i, o'seas
- ¶ Volumes - 2/3.   NL - 1.   AR.   LM.
  Text of Annual Lecture.
  Publications list available.

© CBD Research Ltd · Beckenham · BR3 5JS · Tel 020 8650 7745 · Fax 020 8650 0768 · E-mail cbd@cbdresearch.com · www.cbdresearch.com

Hallé Concerts Society   (The Hall)é   1858
- NR   Bridgewater Hall, Lower Mosley St, MANCHESTER, M1 5HA.
  (hq)
  0161-237 7000
  Chief Exec: John Summers
- ▲   Registered Charity
- ○   *D; promotion of Hallé concerts & management of the Hallé orchestra
- ●   Symphony concerts & recitals
- <   Assn of Brit Orchestras
- M   i & f
- ¶   Prospectuses: Season, Proms, Opus One - 1; free.
  Ybk; ftm.   AR.

Halliwick Association of Swimming Therapy   1952
- ■   c/o ADKC Centre, Whitstable House, Silchester Rd, LONDON, W10 6SB.   (chmn/b)
  020 8968 7609   fax 020 8968 7609
  Sec: Eric Dilley
- ▲   Registered Charity
- Br   22; 2 o'seas
- ○   *S, *W; to teach swimming to people with disabilities using the 'Halliwick' method; to provide training for volunteers & professionals in the basic methods of 'Halliwick'; to organise galas at club, regional & national level
- ●   Mtgs - ET (training courses) - Exam - Res - Comp
- <   Intl Halliwick Assn (IHA)
- M   i & org
- ¶   Swimming for People with Disabilities (hbk).
  Rainbow Series: Instructors & Students Guides.
  Leaflets.   Videos.

Halon Users National Consortium Ltd   (HUNC)   1993
- NR   PO Box 111, PETERSFIELD, Hants, GU31 4PL.   (hq)
  01730 264040
  Co Sec: Brian Dale
- ▲   Company Limited by Guarantee
- ○   *T; to provide information & brokerage house for refrigerants & halons (also used in fire control/fighting)
- Gp   Refrigerant Users Gp
- ●   Conf - Mtgs - Inf - Lib - LG
- M   c 180 f
- ¶   NL - 4.

Hamilton & Clydesdale Chamber of Commerce
in 2003 amalgamated with the Clyde Vale, East Kilbride and Motherwell & District Chambers of Commerce and the Cambuslang & Rutherglen Business Group to become **Lanarkshire Chamber of Commerce**

Hammer Circle   1952
- NR   10 Pershore Close, BEDFORD, MK41 8NS.   (hsp)
  Hon Sec: Darren Kerr
- ○   *S; support & promotion of British hammer throwing
- ●   ET - Stat - Lib
- <   Midland Counties Athletic Assn; Amateur Athletic Assn
- M   200 i, UK / 3 i, o'seas
- ¶   AR; ftm.

Hamper Industry Trade Association Ltd   (HITA)   1984
- ■   7 Aston Hall Drive, North Ferriby, HULL, E Yorks, HU14 3EB.
  (hsp)
  01482 631410   fax 01482 631446
  email neil@europaths.karoo.co.uk
  http://www.hitauk.co.uk
  Hon Sec: Neil M Henderson-Begg
- ▲   Company Limited by Guarantee
- ○   *T; suppliers of Christmas hampers & gifts for sale to the public
- ●   Mtgs - LG - Arbitration between members - Policing the code of practice
- M   5 f
- ¶   Be Sure (leaflet);   Code of practice; both free.

Hampshire Down Sheep Breeders Association   (HDSBA)   1889
- ■   Rickyard Cottage, Denner Hill, GREAT MISSENDEN, Bucks, HP16 0HZ.   (hsp/b)
  01494 488388   fax 01494 488388
  email richard.dhill@virgin.net
  http://www.hampshiredownsociety.org.uk
  Sec: Richard J Davis
- ▲   Company Limited by Guarantee; Registered Charity
- Br   4
- ○   *B
- ●   Mtgs - Res - Exhib - Inf
- <   Nat Sheep Assn
- M   140 i, 20 f, UK / 40 i, 4 org, o'seas
- ¶   NL - 6; ftm only.   Flock Book - 1; ftm, £10 nm.

Hampshire Field Club & Archaeological Society   (HFC)   1885
- ■   17 Castle Malwood Lodge, Minstead, LYNDHURST, Hants, SO43 7HB.   (pres/p)
  http://www.fieldclub.hants.org.uk
  Pres: Peter Roberts
- ▲   Registered Charity
- ○   *L, *Q; archaeology, history & natural history of Hampshire
- Gp   Archaeology; Landscape; Local history; Historic buildings; New Forest
- ●   Conf - Mtgs - ET - Res - Lib - VE
- M   577 i, 79 org
- ¶   NL - 2.   Monographs - ad hoc.   Hampshire Studies - 1.

Handbag Liners & Repairers Association   (HLRA)   1972
- ■   76c The Avenue, BECKENHAM, Kent, BR3 2ES.   (mail) address
- ○   *T
- ●   Mtgs - Exhib
- M   13 f

Handbell Ringers of Great Britain   (HRGB)   1967
- NR   87 The Woodfields, Sanderstead, SOUTH CROYDON, Surrey, CR2 0HJ.   (hsp)
  020 8651 2663   fax 020 8651 2663
  email info@hrgb.org.uk   http://www.hrgb.org.uk
  Hon Sec: Mrs Sandra Winter
- ▲   Registered Charity
- Br   8 regions
- ○   *D; to encourage & develop the art of handbell tune ringing (as distinct from change ringing); also hand-chime & belleplate ringers
- ●   Concerts, rallies, workshops & seminars
- <   Making Music (the Nat Fedn of Music Socs)
- M   3,500 i
- ¶   Reverberations - 2;   Regional NLs - irreg; both ftm only.

Handcycling Association   (HCAUK)   1999
- NR   4 Monty Place, Fenton, STOKE ON TRENT, Staffs, ST4 3RQ.
  (chmn/p)
  01782 593647
  http://www.handcycling.org.uk
  Chmn: Marcus Asbury
- ○   *S
- M   120 i

Handley Page Association   (HPA)   1979
- ■   16 Guernsey Drive, FLEET, Hants, GU51 2TG.   (hsp)
  01252 626996
  Hon Sec: A H Fraser-Mitchell
- ▲   Un-incorporated Society
- ○   *G, *L, *Q; to keep alive the memories of the Handley Page companies, their founder & their aircraft; to encourage new ideas & development in aeronautics & promote their application in the spirit of Sir Frederick Handley Page
- ●   Mtgs - Comp - Inf - PL - VE
- M   400 i, 1 f, 2 org, UK / 20 i, o'seas
- ¶   NL - 6; ftm.   LM; £1 m.   Video; £13 m only.

Hansard Society for Parliamentary Government   1944
NR   40-43 Chancery Lane, LONDON, WC2A 1JA.   (hq)
        020 7438 1222
        Chief Exec: Clare Ettinghausen
▲   Registered Charity
Br   Scotland
○   *L, *Z; to promote knowledge & interest in parliamentary
        democracy & government
●   Conf - ET - Res - SG - LG
M   356 i
¶   The Challenge for Parliament: Making Government
        Accountable.
     Elections in the Age of the Internet: Lessons from the US.
     2001: Cyberspace Odyssey;   Race & Political Recruitment.
     Parliament, the City & Financial Regulation.
     The Internet in the UK Election.

Hardware & Garden Retail Association
     a group of the **British Hardware Federation**

Hardy Plant Society   (HPS)   1957
■   Little Orchard, Great Comberton, PERSHORE, Worcs,
        WR10 3DP.   (hq)
        01386 710317   fax 01386 710117
        email admin@hardy-plant.org.uk
        http://www.hardy-plant.org.uk
        Admin: Mrs Pam Adams,
        Hon Sec: Mrs Anita McAree
▲   Registered Charity
Br   45
○   *H; cultivation of hardy herbaceous plants (excluding rock
        plants)
Gp   Half hardy; Hardy geranium; Pulmonaria; Peony; Variegated
        plants; Correspondents
●   Conf - Mtgs - Exhib - SG - PL - VE
M   11,000 i, 10 org, UK / 500 i, 2 org, o'seas
¶   The Hardy Plant (Jnl) - 2;   NL - 3;   Seed distribution list - 1;
        all ftm only.

Harleian Society   1869
■   College of Arms, Queen Victoria St, LONDON, EC4V 4BT.
        (hsb)
        020 7236 7728   fax 020 7248 6448
        http://www.harleian.co.uk
        Hon Sec: T H S Duke
▲   Registered Charity
○   *L; transcribing, printing & publishing heraldic visitations of
        counties, parish registers or any manuscripts relating to
        family history, genealogy or heraldry
M   210 i & org, UK / 105 i & org, o'seas
¶   Publications - irreg (c 1); free to subscribers, £25 (i),
        £30 (instns), £35 nm.

Harness Goat Society   (HGS)   1986
NR   Overbrook, Cutwell, TETBURY, Glos, GL8 8EB.   (chmn/p)
        01666 503563
        Chmn: Mrs J Bamford
▲   Un-incorporated Society
○   *V; the driving of goats & their welfare
●   Mtgs - Exhib
<   Brit Goat Soc
M   80 i, UK / 10 i, o'seas
¶   Harness Goat Society - 4; ftm.

Harry Roy Appreciation Society   (HRAS)   1972
NR   6 Cambridge Gardens, Winchmore Hill, LONDON,
        N21 2AT.   (hsp)
        020 8360 3547
        Hon Sec: Keith R Farbridge
▲   Un-incorporated Society
○   *G; for all appreciative of the Harry Roy Dance Band (1930's &
        1940's)
●   Mtgs - Inf
M   i
¶   The Bugle Call Rag - 3; free.

Harveian Society of Edinburgh   1782
NR   c/o Prof Dr Kelvin Palmer, Dept of Gastroenterology, Western
        General Hospital, EDINBURGH, EH24 2XU.   (sb)
        0131-537 1000
        Sec: Dr Kelvin Palmer
○   *L

Harveian Society of London   1831
■   Lettsom House, 11 Chandos St, LONDON, W1G 9EB.   (hq)
        020 7580 1043
        Exec Sec: Col Richard Kinsella-Bevan
○   *L; advancement of medical science
●   Mtgs - VE
M   i

Hastings & St Leonards Chamber of Commerce
     see **Ten Sixty Six Enterprise**

Hat Pin Society of Great Britain   1980
■   PO Box 625, HULL, E Yorks, HU5 3WJ.   (mail)
        http://www.hatpinsociety.org.uk address
        Chmn: Valerie Pugh
▲   Un-incorporated Society
○   *G; collecting hat pins & hat pin holders
●   Mtgs
<   Amer Hatpin Soc
M   196 i, UK / 34 i, o'seas
¶   NL - 4; ftm only.

Havergal Brian Society   (HBS)   1974
■   5 Eastbury Rd, WATFORD, Herts, WD19 4PT.   (hsp)
        01923 224607   fax 01923 250506
        email hbs@havergal.demon.co.uk
        http://www.havergalbrian.org
        Sec: Dr Alan Marshall
▲   Registered Charity
○   *D; promote knowledge & appreciation of the works of William
        Havergal Brian (1876-1972) English composer & writer on
        music
●   Publication of Brian's music, studies of Brian's work & his own
        writing on music - Concerts - Recordings
M   167 i, 2 org, UK / 47 i, o'seas
¶   NL - 6; ftm, 50p nm.
     Havergal Brian's Gothic Symphony - two studies; £10.
     The Complete Music for Solo Piano; £11.
     Havergal Brian on Music, Vol 1: British Music; £17.95 m,
        £19.95 nm, (paperback £8.50 m, £9.50 nm) (in association
        with Toccata Press).

Hawick Archaeological Society   (HAS)   1856
NR   Orrock House, Stirches Rd, HAWICK, Roxburghshire,
        TD9 7HF.   (hsp)
        01450 375546
        Hon Sec: I W Landles
▲   Un-incorporated Society
○   *L, *Q; antiquities & natural history of Hawick & district
M   i

Hawk & Owl Trust   (HOT)   1969
NR   PO Box 100, TAUNTON, Somerset, TA4 2WX.   (asa)
        0870 990 3889
        Dir: Linda Bennett
▲   Company Limited by Guarantee; Registered Charity
○   *K, *V; conservation & protection of all birds of prey, including
        owls in the wild & their habitats
Gp   Barn Owl Conservation Network
●   Conf - Mtgs - ET - Res - Exhib - SG - Stat - Inf - PL - LG
<   Birdlife Intl
M   6,000 i, 3 f, 40 org, UK / 98 i, 20 org, o'seas
¶   Peregrine (NL) - 2.   Adopt a Box (NL) - 2.
     Various publications.

Haydn Society of Great Britain   1979
NR   2 Aldcliffe Mews, LANCASTER, LA1 5BT.   (dir)
     01524 61553   fax 01524 61553
     email d.mccaldin@lancaster.ac.uk
     http://www.haydnsocietyofgb.netfirms.com p
     Dir: Prof Denis McCaldin
▲   Un-incorporated Society
○   *A; to promote a wider knowledge & understanding of the
     music of Joseph Haydn
●   Conf - Res - Exhib - Inf - Lib - VE
<   Burgenland Haydn Festival (Eisenstadt, Austria)
M   240 i, 1 f, 10 org, UK / 10 i, 1 org, o'seas
¶   NL - 1; ftm, £1.50 nm.
     Programmes for Haydn Society promotions (concerts); 50p.

HDRA - the Organic Organisation
     see under the registered title **Henry Doubleday Research**
     Association

Headlines, the Craniofacial Support Group   1993
NR   128 Beesmoor Rd, Frampton Cotterell, BRISTOL, BS36 2JP.
     01454 850557
     Admin: Gil Ruff
○   *W
✕   Cranio Facial Support Group

Headmasters' & Headmistresses' Conference   1869
NR   12 The Point, Rockingham Rd, MARKET HARBOROUGH, Leics,
     LE16 7QU.   (sb)
     01858 469059
     Sec: G S Lucas
○   *P; for headmasters & headmistresses of independent schools
●   Conf - Mtgs - ET - Stat - Inf - LG
<   Indep Schools Coun; Secondary Heads Assn
M   250 i, UK / 80 i, o'seas

Headteachers' Association of Scotland   (HAS)   1936
NR   University of Strathclyde, Jordanhill Campus, Southbrae Drive,
     GLASGOW, G13 1PP.   (hq)
     0141-950 3298   fax 0141-950 3434
     email head.teacher@strath.ac.uk
     Gen Sec: Bill McGregor
▲   Un-incorporated Society
○   *E, *P; professional support & representation for members
     relating to secondary school education in Scotland
●   Conf - Mtgs - ET - SG - Stat - Empl - LG
<   Secondary Heads Assn
M   500 i
¶   Scottish Headlines - 3;   Scottish Bylines - 6; both free.

HEADWAY - the Brain Injury Association   (HEADWAY)   1979
■   4 King Edward Court, King Edward St, NOTTINGHAM,
     NG1 1EW.   (hq)
     0115-924 0800   fax 0115-958 4446
     email enquiries@headway.org.uk
     http://www.headway.org.uk
     Chief Exec: Peter McCabe
▲   Company Limited by Guarantee; Registered Charity
Br   110
○   *K, *M, *W; to provide information, support & services to
     people with acquired brain injuries, their families, carers &
     related professionals
●   Conf - Mtgs - ET - Inf - VE
<   Eur Brain Injury Soc; Brain Injured & Families Eur Confedn (BIF)
M   800 i, 11 f, UK / 40 org, o'seas
¶   Headway News - 4; ftm, 75p each nm.
     Noticeboard (NL) - 6; ftm only.
     Publications on varying aspects of head injury; list available.

Health & Beauty Employers Federation   (HBEF)   1969
■   18 Shakespeare Business Centre, Hathaway Close, EASTLEIGH,
     Hants, SO50 4SR.   (hq)
     0870 420 2022
     email info@fht.org.uk   http://www.fht.org.uk
     Exec Sec: Mrs Jacqueline M Palmer
○   *T; representing owners & managers of health & beauty therapy
     establishments incl: saunas, health hotels, beauty clinics etc
●   Conf - Exhib - Inf
<   part of the Fedn of Holistic Therapists
M   [not stated]

Health Care Supplies Association   1960
■   41-47 Hartfield Rd, LONDON, SW19 3RG.   (exec/dir/b)
     020 8545 7131   fax 020 8545 7120
     email john.smith@swlha.nhs.uk
     http://www.healthcaresupplies.org.uk
     Exec Dir: John Smith
▲   Un-incorporated Society
Br   12
○   *P; to promote the work of health care supplies staff at all levels
●   Conf - Mtgs - ET - Exhib - LG - Seminars - Annual awards
<   Chart Inst of Purchasing & Supply
M   720 i
¶   Official Procurement Guide - 1; ftm, £50 nm.

** Health Care Tutors' Association
     Organisation lost: see Introduction paragraph 3

Health Food Institute   (IHFR)   1979
NR   Gothic House, Barker Gate, NOTTINGHAM, NG1 1JU.   (hsb)
     0115-941 4188
     Hon Sec: Peter Campbell-McBride
▲   Company Limited by Guarantee
○   *P; to increase knowledge & education in nutritional & health
     matters; to promote & maintain standards in nutrition &
     health food retailing
●   Conf - Mtgs - ET - Exam - Res - Exhib - Stat - Inf - LG
M   200 i
¶   Jnl - 1.
✕   2002 Institute of Health Food Retailing

Health Food Manufacturers' Association   (HFMA)   1965
■   63 Hampton Court Way, THAMES DITTON, Surrey, KT7 0LT.
     (hq)
     020 8398 4066
     http://www.hfma.co.uk
     Dir: David Adams
▲   Un-incorporated Society
○   *T; interests of manufacturers of health foods & allied products
Gp   Food supplements; Herbal; Health foods
●   Conf - Mtgs - SG - Expt - Inf - LG
<   Intl Alliance of Dietary/Food Supplement Assns (IADSA); Eur
     Fedn of Health Product Mfrs Assn (EHPM)
M   c 150 f
¶   NL;   LM; both ftm only.

**Health & Medical Public Relations Association   (HAMPRA)
1991**
■   Upper Beechwood, Guestling Thorn, HASTINGS, E Sussex,
     TN35 4LU.   (hq)
     01424 812847
     Pres: Lord Walton of Detchant,   Chmn: Philip Paul
○   *P; to improve communications in respect of public relations
     work on behalf of corporate interests concerned with medical
     treatment & healthcare
●   Mtgs
M   [confidential]

Health & Safety Sign Association   (HSSA)   1994
NR PO Box 377, REDHILL, Surrey, RH1 2RZ.   (mail/add)
      Sec: Charles Hardway
○   *T; for manufacturers of safety & other statutory signs
●   LG
M   f

Healthcare Financial Management Association   (HFMA)   1950
■   Albert House (suite 32), 111 Victoria St, BRISTOL, BS1 6AX.
      (hq)
      0117-929 4789   fax 0117-929 4844
      http://www.hfma.org.uk
      Chief Exec: Mark Knight
▲   Registered Charity
Br 14
○   *P; for accountants engaged in healthcare financial
      management in the UK
●   Conf - Mtgs - ET - Res - Exhib - Inf
<   Eur Healthcare Mgt Assn; HFMA (USA)
M   4,000 i
¶   Healthcare Finance - 10; ftm.   Ybk - 1.   AR - 1.

Healthcare People Management Association   1974
NR Gothic House, 3 The Green, RICHMOND, TW9 1PL.
      (admin/b)
      020 8334 4530
      http://www.hpma.org.uk
      Admin: Hannah Barnett
▲   Un-incorporated Society
○   *P; to bring together healthcare professionals to enable them to
      develop, influence & promote high quality human resource
      management in the NHS
●   Conf - Mtgs - Comp - Empl - LG
M   288 i, 320 f
¶   Network - 4; free.
×   2005 Association of Healthcare Human Resource Management

Healthcare Supplies Association
      see **Health Care Supplies Association**

HealthWatch   1988
NR Box BM HealthWatch, LONDON, WC1N 3XX.   (B)
      020 8789 7813 Monomarks
      Press & Inf Officer: Michael E Allen
▲   Registered Charity
○   *K; to provide reliable information about health matters,
      especially treatments, whether orthodox or alternative
●   Mtgs - Inf
M   141 i
¶   NL - 4.

Hearing Concern   1947
■   95 Gray's Inn Rd, LONDON, WC1X 8TX.   (hq)
      020 7440 9871   fax 020 7440 9872
      email info@hearingconcern.org.uk
      http://www.hearingconcern.org.uk
      Chief Exec: Damian Barry
▲   Charity Limited by Guarantee; Registered Charity
Br 3
○   *W; to improve the quality of life for people who are deaf or
      hard of hearing; is a volunteer-led organisation
Gp Hearing advisory service; Broadcasting c'ee; Resource centres
●   ET - Exhib - Inf - VE
<   Intl Fedn of the Hard of Hearing; UK Coun on Deafness; Nat
      Coun for Voluntary Orgs
M   1,671 i, 34 f, 90 org, UK / 5 org, o'seas
¶   AR - 1; free.
×   2003 British Association of the Hard of Hearing (incorporated)

Heart of England Fine Foods   (HEFF)   1998
■   PO Box 1, MUCH WENLOCK, Shropshire, TF13 6WH.   (hq)
      01746 785185   fax 01746 785186
      email office@heff.co.uk   http://www.heff.co.uk
      Chief Exec: Karen Davies
▲   Private Limited Company
○   *T; organisation for the promotion of West Midlands food &
      drink
●   Conf - Mtgs - Inf
M   236 f

Heart Line Association   1980
■   Community Link / Health House, Knoll Rd, CAMBERLEY, Surrey,
      GU15 3HH.   (hq)
      01276 707636   fax 01276 707642
      Office Mgr: Pamela Lawrence
▲   Registered Charity
Br 20
○   *W; support for families with children who have heart
      conditions
●   Support groups
M   1,400 i
¶   NL - 4; free.   Heart Children: a practical handbook; £6.

Heart UK   1986
■   7 North Rd, MAIDENHEAD, Berks, SL6 1PE.   (hq)
      01628 628638
      Chief Exec: Michael Livingston
▲   Company Limited by Guarantee; Registered Charity
○   *K, *W; support & information for people at high risk of
      premature coronary heart disease, especially families with
      inherited (genetic) blood cholesterol or triglyceride problems
Gp Diet & Lifestyle help-line, dieticians & other health professionals
      respond to members' enquiries by phone & post
●   Conf - ET - Res - SG - Stat - Inf - LG - Publications - Lectures -
      Professional training
<   Nat Heart Forum; Genetic Interest Gp; Parliamentary Food &
      Health Forum; Long Term Medical Conditions Alliance
M   c 1,500 i
¶   Digest - 6; ftm, £2.50 nm.
×   2002 (British Hyperlipidaemia Association
      (Family Heart Association

Heat Pump Association   (HPA)   1994
■   2 Waltham Court, Milley Lane, Hare Hatch, READING, Berks,
      RG10 9TH.   (hq)
      0118-940 3416   fax 0118-940 6258
      email info@feta.co.uk   http://www.feta.co.uk/
      Dir Gen: C Sloan
○   *T; promotes the benefits & proper use of heat pumps & heat
      pump technology by increasing the awareness of heat pumps
      as a means of using energy efficiently, cost effectively & with
      the minimum impact on the environment
●   Mtgs - Comp - Inf
<   Fedn of Envtl Tr Assns (FETA)
M   10 full members, 1 associate

Heat Transfer & Fluid Flow Service   (HTFS)   1968
NR c/o Aspen Tech Ltd, C1 Reading International Business Park,
      Basingstoke Rd, READING, Berks, RG2 6DT.   (hq)
      0118 922 6405   fax 0118 922 6401
      email htfs@aspentech.com   http://www.htfs.com
      Dir: T Ralston
▲   Company Limited by Guarantee
Br National Engineering Laboratory, E Kilbride
○   *Q; heat exchange design & associated fluid flow equipment
Gp Heat exchangers: Shell & tube, Air-cooled, Cryogenic, Plate fin;
      Condensers; Boilers; Furnaces; Refrigeration & air
      conditioning plant; Fired heaters
●   Conf - Mtgs - Res - Software
M   40 f, UK / 100 f, o'seas
¶   NL;   AR; both ftm.

© CBD Research Ltd · Beckenham · BR3 5JS · Tel 020 8650 7745 · Fax 020 8650 0768 · E-mail cbd@cbdresearch.com · www.cbdresearch.com

Heather Society   1963

■ Denbeigh, All Saints Rd, Creeting St Mary, IPSWICH, Suffolk, IP6 8PJ.   (admin)
  01449 711220   fax 01449 711220
  email heathers@zetnet.co.uk
  http://www.heathersociety.org.uk p
  Admin: Mrs A Small,   Hon Sec: J Julian
▲ Registered Charity
Br 13; USA
○ *H; study, research & development of heather varieties
Gp Technical c'ee responsible for trials at Harlow Car, Harrogate & RHS Garden, Wisley; also for compiling the International Register of Heather Names
● Conf - Res - ET - Exhib - Comp - Inf - PL (slides only) - VE
< R Horticl Soc; Nederlandse Heidevereniging Ericultura; Gesellschaft der Heidefreunde; N Amer Heather Soc
M 1,500 i, 125 f, 15 university libraries, UK / 100 i, 12 f, 15 university libraries, o'seas
¶ News Bulletin - 3.   Ybk; ftm only.

Heating Oil Buyers Association   (HOBA)   1998

■ Unit 27 / 15 Ladyloan Place, GLASGOW, G15 8LB.   (hq)
  0141-944 4999   fax 0141-944 4812
  email enquiries@oilbuyers.co.uk
  http://www.oilbuyers.co.uk
  Co Sec: Kirsty Thomson
▲ Company Limited by Guarantee
○ *T; to assist kerosene buyers to save money on kerosene purchases
● Inf
M [not stated]

Heating, Ventilating & Air Conditioning Manufacturers' Association Ltd   (HEVAC)   1962

■ 2 Waltham Court, Milley Lane, Hare Hatch, READING, Berks, RG10 9TH.   (hq)
  0118-940 3416   fax 0118-940 6258
  email info@feta.co.uk   http://www.feta.co.uk/
  Dir Gen: C Sloan
○ *T; interests of heating, ventilating & air conditioning equipment manufacturers
Gp Air conditioning; Air curtains; Air distribution; Fan coils; Filters; House ventilation; Humidity; Noise & vibration control
● Mtgs - ET - Exhib - Comp - SG - Stat - Expt - Inf
< Fedn of Envtl Trade Assns (FETA)
M 122 f
¶ NL - 12; ftm only.

Heating & Ventilating Contractors' Association   (HVCA)   1904

■ Esca House, 34 Palace Court, LONDON, W2 4JG.   (hq)
  020 7313 4900   fax 020 7727 9268
  email contact@hvca.org.uk   http://www.hvea.org.uk
  Chief Exec: Robert Higgs
Br 9 in 11 regions
○ *T; refrigeration & air unit conditioning, home heating, duct work, ventilation, service & facilities
Gp Central services; Commercial & legal; Communications & public affairs; Education & training; Employment affairs; Finance; Membership services; Publications; Specialist group services; Technical & safety
  Building Engineering Services Competence Accreditation Ltd (BESCA), 0800 652 5533 info@besca.org.uk
M f
¶ HVCA Newslink (NL).

Heavy Transport Association   (HTA)   1983

NR Century House, High St, TATTENHALL, Cheshire, CH3 9PX.   (hsb)
  01829 771774
  Sec: John Bradley Dyne
▲ Un-incorporated Society
○ *T; to promote the interests of the heavy haulage industry
Gp Working Groups: LG, Private escorting, STGO review
● Mtgs - LG
< Eur Assn of Heavy Haulage Transport & Mobile Cranes (ESTA)
M 83 f, UK / 2 f, o'seas
¶ Heavy Talk - 1; free.   Hbk - 2 yrly; ftm, priced nm.

Hebe Society   1985

■ 20 Beech Farm Drive, MACCLESFIELD, Cheshire, SK10 2ER.   (hsp)
  01625 611062
  1 Woodpecker Drive, HAILSHAM, E Sussex, BN27 3EZ.   (mem/sec/p)
  01323 840517   fax 01323 840517
  email lhaywood@btinternet.com
  http://www.hebesoc.vispa.com
  Hon Sec: Tony Hayter,   Treas: V Haywood
▲ Registered Charity
○ *H; a specialist plant society encouraging the cultivation & conservation of Hebe, Parahebe & all other New Zealand native plants
● Exhib
< New Zealand Alpine Garden Soc; R Horticl Soc
M 263 i, 22 f, libraries & arboreta, UK / 21 i, o'seas
¶ Hebe News (NL) - 4; ftm, £2 nm (with Index & Author index). Bibliography of books on hebes & other plants; ftm (incl in new members' starter pack).

Hebridean Sheep Society   1986

■ Gibshiel, Tarset, HEXHAM, Northumberland, NE48 1RR.   (hsp)
  01434 240435
  email info@hebrideansheep.org.uk
  http://www.hebrideansheep.org.uk
  Hon Sec: Jane Wilson
○ *B
● ET - Exhib - Comp - Stat - Inf
< Nat Sheep Assn
M 300 i, UK / 2 i, o'seas
¶ The Black Sheep (Ybk) - 1;   NL - 4; both ftm only.

Hedgeline   1998

NR 1 Applebees Meadow, HINCKLEY, Leics, LE10 0FL.   (admin/p)
  0870 240 0627
  http://www.hedgeline.org
  Admin: Max Ayriss
▲ Un-incorporated Society
Br Regional & local
○ *K; for the legislative control of hedge nuisance
● Political lobbying
M c 3,700 i
¶ Hedgeline - irreg; free.

Hellenic Society
  see **Society for the Promotion of Hellenic Studies (Hellenic Society)**

Help International Plant Protein Organisation (HIPPO) 1999
- ■ The Old Vicarage, Llangynog, CARMARTHEN, Carmarthenshire, SA33 5BS.   (hq)
  01267 241547
  email hippocharity@aol.com
  Dir: Neville Heath Fowler
- ▲ Registered Charity
- ○ *K; 'Third World' aid designed to encourage use of vegetable protein foods for direct human consumption instead of livestock products, for reasons of efficiency, ecology, health & animal welfare
- ● Mtgs - Inf
- M 120 i, UK / 10 i, o'seas
- ¶ Hippo News (NL) - irreg; free.

Hen Packers Association
  since 2001 **British Poultry Council**

Henkeepers' Association 2006
- ■ Church Lane, Troston, BURY St EDMUNDS, Suffolk, IP31 1EX.   (hsp)
  01359 268322
  email info@henkeepersassociation.co.uk
  http://www.henkeepersassociation.co.uk
  Sec: Francine Raymond
- ▲ Company Limited by Guarantee
- ○ *G; to inform & support henkeepers who keep small flocks in their garden for pleasure
- ● Inf
- M 60 i

Henry Bradshaw Society (HBS) 1890
- NR 5a Green Place, OXFORD, OX1 4RF.   (hsb)
  email peter.jackson14@btinternet.com
  http://www.uea.ac.uk/~q506/hbs/
  Hon Sec: Peter Jackson
- ▲ Registered Charity
- ○ *L; editing of liturgical texts from manuscripts or rare printed books
- ● Res - Inf
- < Laurentins Petri Sällskapet (Stockholm); Alcuin Club; Societas Liturgica
- M 45 i, 70 org, UK / 65 i, 100 org, o'seas
- ¶ Edition series; Subsidia series - irreg; prices vary.
  AR; ftm only.

Henry Doubleday Research Association (HDRA) 1958
- NR Garden Organic, Ryton-on-Dunsmore, COVENTRY, Warks, CV8 3LG.   (hq)
  024 7630 3517   fax 024 7663 9229
  email enquiry@hdra.org.uk   http://www.hdra.org.uk
  Chief Exec: Dr Susan Kay-Williams
- ▲ Company Limited by Guarantee; Registered Charity
- Br 60
- ○ *F, *H, *Q; to research & promote organic horticulture & food
- ● Conf - ET - Res - Inf - Lib - VE
- M 30,000 i, UK / 700 i, o'seas
- ¶ NL - 4;   AR; both ftm.   Books & pamphlets; prices vary.
  Mail order catalogue - 1; free.
  Note: is also known as HDRA - the Organic Organisation

Henry Williamson Society (HWS) 1980
- ■ 7 Monmouth Rd, DORCHESTER, Dorset, DT1 2DE.   (hsp)
  01305 264092
  http://www.henrywilliamson.co.uk
  Farm Cottage, Scotch Meadows, ALLENHEADS, Northumberland, NE47 9JQ.
  Sec: Sue Cumming,   Chmn: Andrew Sanders
- ▲ Registered Charity
- ○ *L; to encourage interest & a deeper understanding of the life & work of the 20th century English writer Henry Williamson (1895-1977)
- ● Mtgs - Comp - SG - VE
- M 525 i, 5 libraries, UK / 21 i, o'seas
- ¶ Jnl - 1;   NL - 1; both ftm, (subn £12).

Henty Society 1977
- ■ 205 Ickneild Way, LETCHWORTH, Herts, SG6 4TT.
  .   (hsp)
  Hon Sec: David Walmsley
- ▲ Un-incorporated Society
- ○ *A; to further study the life & work of George Alfred Henty (1832-1902) Victorian writer & war correspondent
- Gp Biographical research; Biographical study; Publications of rare work
- ● Conf - Res - Exhib - SG - Inf
- < Alliance Literary Socs
- M 90 i, UK / 55 i, o'seas
- ¶ Bulletin - 2;   Literary Supplements - occasional.
  Bibliographical Research (for UK, Canadian & American editions) - 1; all ftm only.

Heraldry Society 1950
- ■ PO Box 772, GUILDFORD, Surrey, GU3 3ZX.   (hq)
  01483 237373
  email secretary@theheraldrysociety.com
  Sec: Melvyn Jeremiah
- ▲ Company Limited by Guarantee; Registered Charity
- ○ *L; heraldry, armory, chivalry & genealogy
- ● Conf - Exam - Exhib - Lib - VE
- M 900 worldwide
- ¶ The Heraldry Gazette - 4; ftm only.
  Coat of Arms - 2.

Heraldry Society of Scotland 1977
- ■ 25 Craigentinny Crescent, EDINBURGH, EH7 6QA.   (treas/p)
  0131-552 2232
  http://www.heraldry-scotland.co.uk
  Treas: Stuart G Emerson
- ▲ Registered Charity
- ○ *L; to encourage the study & practice of heraldry in Scotland, taking into account its European & international context
- ● Conf - Mtgs - Res - Inf - Lib - VE
- < Heraldry Soc (London)
- M c 300 i, UK / c 100 i, o'seas
- ¶ The Double Tressure (Jnl) - 1; ftm.
  Tak Teut (NL) - 1/2;   LM - irreg; both m only.
  Special publications - irreg.

Herb Society 1927
- ■ Sulgrave Manor, Sulgrave, BANBURY, Oxon, OX17 2SD.   (hq)
  01295 768899   fax 01295 768069
  email info@herbsociety.org.uk
  http://www.herbsociety.org.uk
  Chief Exec: Roger Tabor,   Sec: Nicolette Westwood
- ▲ Company Limited by Guarantee; Registered Charity
- ○ *G, *H; promotion of knowledge & use of herbs
- ● Conf - Mtgs - ET - Exhib - Comp - Inf - Lib - VE
- < R Horticl Soc; Henry Doubleday Res Assn
- M 1,750 i, UK / 258 i, o'seas
- ¶ Herbs - 4; £20 yr m.

Herb Trust 1985
- ■ Mayfair, 14 Staddon Gdns, TORQUAY, Devon, TQ2 8BB.   (founder/p)
  01803 324663
  Founder: The Hon Anthony de Freston
- ○ *H; to research & protect the cultivation & conservation of herbs for medicinal, culinary, perfumery & food uses
- ● Res - Inf
- M 'pending'
- ¶ The Herb Trust.

© CBD Research Ltd · Beckenham · BR3 5JS · Tel 020 8650 7745 · Fax 020 8650 0768 · E-mail cbd@cbdresearch.com · www.cbdresearch.com

Herbert Howells Society   1987
NR   32 Barleycroft Rd, WELWYN GARDEN CITY, Herts, AL8 6JU.
    (hsp)
    01707 335315
    email andrew.millinger@virgin.net
    Hon Sec: Andrew Millinger
▲   Un-incorporated Society
Br USA
○   *D; to commemorate the life & work of Herbert Howells (1892-
    1983); to encourage the performance, recording &
    publication of his music
●   Inf - Working with publishers, recording companies & concert
    promoters
M   200 i, 2 f, UK / 30 i, o'seas
¶   NL - 1; ftm.

Herdwick Sheep Breeders' Association   (HSBA)   1916
■   c/o The Old Stables, Redhills, PENRITH, Cumbria, CA11 0DT.
    (hsp)
    01768 869533
    http://www.herdwick-sheep.com
    Sec: G F Brown
○   *B
<   Nat Sheep Assn
M   150 i
¶   Flock Book - 2 yrly.

Hereford Cattle Society   1878
■   Hereford House, 3 Offa St, HEREFORD, HR1 2LL.   (hq)
    01432 272057   fax 01432 377529
    email postroom@herefordcattle.org
    http://www.herefordcattle.org
    Sec: D E Prothero
▲   Company Limited by Guarantee; Registered Charity
○   *B
●   Conf - Exhib - Expt
<   21 other Hereford Cattle Societies throughout the world
M   850 i, UK / 860 i, o'seas
¶   Jnl - 1; ftm, £5 nm.

Herefordshire & Worcestershire Chamber of Commerce   1839
■   Severn House, Prescott Drive, Warndon Business Park,
    WORCESTER, WR4 9NE.   (hq)
    0800 104010
    Chief Exec: Christine Jones
○   *C
●   Conf - Mtgs - ET - Res - Stat - Expt - Inf - Lib - LG - Business
    advice - Seminars - Training & Enterprise Council (TEC)
    services
<   Brit Chams Comm
M   c 2,700 f
¶   New Direction (Jnl) - 6.
    Note: uses title of Chamber of Commerce Herefordshire &
    Worcestershire

Heritage Afloat   (HA)   1994
■   9 Strode St, EGHAM, Surrey, TW20 9BT.   (mem/sp)
    http://www.heritageafloat.org.uk
    Mem Sec: Bernard Hales,
    Publicity Officer: Hannah Cunliffe
○   *K, *G; preservation, history & interest in old & historic vessels
●   Mtgs - Inf - LG
M   57 i, 28 f, UK / 1 i, o'seas
¶   NL; free.

Heritage Building Contractors Group
    an affiliate group of the **Stone Federation**

**** **Heritage Protection Society**
    Organisation lost: see Introduction paragraph 3

Heritage Railway Association   (HRA)   1996
■   7 Robert Close, POTTERS BAR, Herts, EN6 2DH.   (press offr/p)
    01707 643568
    http://www.heritagerailways.com
    Press Officer: John Crane
▲   Company Limited by Guarantee
○   *N, *T; for the heritage railway movement - heritage railways &
    railway centres
●   Conf - Mtgs - ET - Exhib - Comp - Inf - LG
<   Eur Fedn of Museum & Tourist Rlys (FEDECRAIL)
M   55 f (railways)
¶   Jnl - 3;   Information Papers - irreg; both ftm.
    Sidelines (NL) - 6;   AR.   Guidelines - irreg.

Herpes Viruses Association - SPHERE   (HVA-SPHERE)   1983
■   41 North Rd, LONDON, N7 9DP.   (hq)
    0845 123 2305
    http://www.herpes.org.uk
    Dir: Marian Nicholson
▲   Registered Charity
○   *W; to supply information, advice & counselling to people with
    herpes simplex (cold sores, whitlow & genital sores)
Gp Shingles Support Society (provides information of self-help
    therapies & drugs to patients with PHN, & their GPs)
●   Conf - Mtgs - Res - Stat - Inf - Lib - Counselling & advice to
    people with herpes viruses - Provision of correct information
    to the media
<   Skin Care Campaign; All Party Parliamentary Gp on Skin; Brit
    Assn for Sexual Health & HIV (BASHH)
M   1,000 i, 12 f, 20 clinics, UK / 30 i, o'seas
¶   Sphere (NL) - 4; ftm.
    Herpes Simplex - A Guide; £1 m, 30p in bulk nm.

Herring Buyers Association Ltd   (HBA)   1976
NR   36 Springfield Terrace, South Queensferry, EDINBURGH,
    EH30 9HF.   (hq)
    0131-331 1222
    Mgr: E Leedham
○   *T; for buyers of pelagic fish (herring, mackerel, sprats,
    pilchards)

Hertfordshire Agricultural Society   1801
■   The Showground, Dunstable Rd, REDBOURN, Herts, AL3 7PT.
    (hq)
    01582 792626   fax 01582 794027
    email office@hertsshow.com
    http://www.hertsshow.com
    Sec: Mike Harman
▲   Company Limited by Guarantee; Registered Charity
○   *F, *H; to promote a better understanding of farming,
    agriculture & the country way of life in Hertfordshire
●   Exhib (Organising the County Agricultural Show)
<   Brit Show Jumping Assn; other breed societies
M   300 i
¶   NL - 2;   AR - 1; both ftm only.
    Show Catalogue - 1; £3.   Show Schedule - 1; free.

Hertfordshire Chamber of Commerce & Industry   1971
NR   45 Grosvenor Rd, ST ALBANS, Herts, AL1 3AW.   (hq)
    01727 813680
    Chief Exec: Tim Hutchings
▲   Company Limited by Guarantee
○   *C

Hesketh Hubbard Art Society
    a member organisation of the **Federation of British Artists**

Heyday 2006
- ■ 169 Euston Rd, LONDON, NW1 2AE. (hq)
  020 8675 7666   fax 020 7388 4617
  email signup@heyday.org.uk
  http://www.heyday.org.uk
  Dir: Ailsa Ogilvie
- ▲ Registered Charity
- ○ *K; 'a membership organisation promoting modern retirement'
- ● Conf - Mtgs - ET - Res - Exhib - Comp - SG - Stat - Inf - Lib - VE - Empl - LG
- ¶ Heyday Magazine - 6.
  Note: has replaced the Association of Retired & Persons over 50

High Sheriffs Association of England & Wales
  is the trading name of the **Shrievalty Association**

Higher Education Liaison Officers' Association (HELOA) 1990
- ■ HELOA Office, University of Essex, Wivenhoe Park, COLCHESTER, Essex, CO4 3SQ. (hq)
  01206 873423   fax 0871 661 5779
  email heloa@essex.ac.uk   http://www.heloa.ac.uk
  Hon Sec: John Wright
- ▲ Un-incorporated Society
- Br 9 regional groups
- ○ *P; to provide information & assistance to students, parents & careers advisers on entry to higher education in the UK; to advise government & other organisations on needs & attitudes of students & their parents to higher education
- ● Conf - ET - LG
- M 535 i, 134 f

Highland Association
  see **Comunn Gaidhealach**

Highland Cattle Society (HCS) 1884
- NR 59 Drumlanrig St, THORNHILL, Dumfriesshire, DG3 5LY. (hq)
  01848 331866   fax 01848 331183
  email info@highlandcattlesociety.com
  http://www.highlandcattlesociety.com
  Office Mgr: Susan Campbell
- ▲ Un-incorporated Society
- ○ *B
- Gp Local groups throughout the UK
- ● Conf - Mtgs - ET - Exhib - Comp - Inf - LG
- < Highland Cattle Socs: Australia, Canada, Denmark, Finland, France, Germany, Netherlands, New Zealand, Norway, Sweden, Switzerland, USA
- M 883 i, UK / 189 i, o'seas
- ¶ Highland Breeders Jnl - 1.   NL - 4.
  AR; ftm only.

Highland Pony Society (HPS) 1923
- ■ Grosvenor House, Shore Rd, PERTH, PH2 8BD. (hq)
  01738 451861   fax 01738 451861
  http://www.highlandponysociety.com
  Sec: Mrs Susie Robertson
- ▲ Company Limited by Guarantee; Registered Charity
- ○ *B; to keep the purity of the breed; to promote breeding for use in farm work, forestry, riding or driving & for sporting & show purposes
- ● Conf - Mtgs - ET - Res - Comp - Expt - Inf - VE
- < Nat Pony Soc
- M 1,500 i, UK / 100 i, o'seas
- ¶ Stud Book - 1.

Highland Railway Society
- ■ Ringmarsh Cottage, Horsington Marsh, TEMPLECOMBE, Somerset, BA8 0EL. (h/treas/p)
  01963 370697   fax 01963 370697
  http://www.hrsoc.org.uk
  Treas: J Roake
- ▲ Un-incorporated Society
- ○ *G; study & recording of all aspects of the Highland Railway Company
- ● Mtgs - Lib - PL
- M 280 i, 10 org, UK / 15 i, o'seas
- ¶ Highland Railway Jnl - 4; ftm only.

Highlands & Islands Sheep Health Association Ltd (HISHA) 1988
- ■ Drummondhill, Stratherrick Rd, INVERNESS, Highland, IV2 4JY. (hq)
  01463 713687   fax 01463 713687
  email info@hisha.org.uk   http://www.hisha.org.uk
  Sec: Eleanor A Fraser
- ▲ Company Limited by Guarantee
- ○ *B, *F; to create awareness of the dangers & financial implications of enzootic abortion of ewes (EAE)
- Gp Highland Mule Breeders Association
- ● Mtgs - Inf - Promotion of the availability of the EAE-free stock of members
- < Scot Agricl Org Soc (SAOS)
- M 280 i, 1 org
- ¶ HISHA NL - 3/4;   AR - 1;
  List of Accredited Flocks - 1; all ftm only.

Highway Electrical Manufacturers & Suppliers Association (HEMSA) 1998
- NR Bowden House, 1 Church St, HENFIELD, W Sussex, BN5 9NS.
  01273 491146   fax 01273 491147
  email info@bowden-house.co.uk
  http://www.streetlighting.uk.com
  Dir: Vasos Siantonas
- ○ *T; for manufacturers & suppliers to the street lighting industry
- ● Conf - Mtgs - Exhib
- M 29 f

Hill Radnor Flock Book Society (HRFBS) 1949
- ■ c/o Montague Harris & Co, 16 Ship St, BRECON, Brecknockshire, LD3 9AD. (hsb)
  01874 623200
  Sec: John A Lewis
- ▲ Un-incorporated Society
- ○ *B; to keep the rare breed alive
- ● Mtgs - Annual show & sale
- < Nat Sheep Assn
- M 45 i
- ¶ Flock Book - 1.

Hilliard Society of Miniaturists 1982
- ■ Priory Lodge, 7 Priory Rd, WELLS, Somerset, BA5 1SR. (hq)
  01749 674472
  email hilliardsociety@aol.com
  http://www.art-in-miniature.org
  Exec Sec: Pamela Taylor
- ▲ Un-incorporated Society
- ○ *A; to promote & inform on contemporary & modern miniature paintings
- ● Exhib - VE
- M c 250 i
- ¶ NL - 2; ftm, £2 nm.

Hinckley & District Knitting Industry Association
  has now closed.

© CBD Research Ltd · Beckenham · BR3 5JS · Tel 020 8650 7745 · Fax 020 8650 0768 · E-mail cbd@cbdresearch.com · www.cbdresearch.com

Hispanic & Luso-Brazilian Council   1943

■ Canning House, 2 Belgrave Sq, LONDON, SW1X 8PJ.   (hq)
020 7235 2303   fax 020 7235 3587
email enquiries@canninghouse.com
http://www.canninghouse.com
Dir Gen: Barry Hamilton,   Chmn: Peter Garratts

▲ Registered Charity

○ *E, *X; promotion of closer relations between the UK & the
Hispanic & Luso-Brazilian countries

Gp Units: Corporate (Monica Caro), Trade & business serices;
Culture & education (Miss Larissa Litchfield), Library &
information ((Alan Biggings) information

● Conf - ET - Exhib - Expt - Inf - Lib - LG

M i, f & schools

¶ British Bulletin of Publications on Latin America, Spain &
Portugal - 2; ftm.
NL - 4; ftm, £15 nm.   Cultural Programme - 4; ftm.
AR - 1; ftm.   Information Leaflets on Special Events.
Note: is also known as Canning House.

Historic Aircraft Association   (HAA)   1979

NR 17 Ravensdale Ave, ROYAL LEAMINGTON SPA, Warks,
CV32 6NQ.   (hsp)
Sec: Stuart Powney

○ *G, *K; to further the preservation of historic aircraft in a flying
condition (which involves the provision of a flight safety
service to the public, the authorities, owners & display
organisers)

Gp Register of Pilots

● Mtgs - ET - Inf

< R Aero Club (RAC); Aircraft Owners & Pilots Assn (AOPA)

M 170 i, UK / 10 i, o'seas

Historic Artillery   (HA)   1987

■ 23 Viewside Close, Corfe Mullen, WIMBORNE, Dorset,
BH21 3ST.   (hsp)
01202 690224
email richardbarton@caving5.freeserve.co.uk
Sec: Richard Barton

▲ Un-incorporated Society

○ *G; research into the science of artillery in history; promotion of
historical re-enactment for educational purposes

Gp Field research; Workshop; Research into siege weapons &
techniques; Computer database; Artillery Association GB

● Res - SG - Inf - VE - Re-enactment

< Siege Warfare in the Midlands; Coalhouse Fort Project

M 20 i, 2 org

Historic Canoe & Kayak Association   (HCKA)   1989

■ 48 Russell Way, HIGHAM FERRERS, Northants, NN10 8EJ.
(hsp)
01933 314672   fax 01933 314672
Hon Sec: J F Pearton

▲ Un-incorporated Society

○ *G; to promote an interest in historic canoes & kayaks

● Res - Inf - Displaying historic craft

> R Marines Museum

M i

¶ Paddles Past (Jnl) _ 4; ftm.   LM - 1.
[subscription £13].

Historic Caravan Club   (HCC)   1993

■ 29 Linnet Close, Lodgefield Park, HALESOWEN, W Midlands,
B62 8TW.   (hsp)
0121-561 5742
email bbissechcc@aol.com   http://www.hcclub.co.uk
Hon Sec: Barbara Bissell

▲ Un-incorporated Society

Br 9 area coordinators

○ *G; to encourage the rescue, restoration, display & use of
trailer caravans up to 1960, including horse-drawn ancestors
of the touring caravan

● Mtgs - Res - Exhib - Inf - Provision of displays at vintage rallies

< Fedn of Brit Historic Vehicle Clubs; Assn of Caravan &
Camping Exempted Orgs

M 210 i, UK / 3 i, 4 org, o'seas

¶ Wanderer (NL) - 8;   LM - 1;   Register of Member's
Caravans - 1; all ftm only.
Membership Hbk - free on joining.
Historic Caravan Scene (Jnl) - irreg; ftm, £2.25 each nm.

Historic Commercial Vehicle Society   (HCVS)   1957

■ Iden Grange, Cranbrook Rd, STAPLEHURST, Kent, TN12 0ET.
(hsp)
01580 892929   fax 01580 893227
email hcvs@btinternet.com   http://www.hcvs.co.uk
Snr Exec Officer & Vice-Pres: Michael J Banfield

▲ Company Limited by Guarantee; Registered Charity

Br 11

○ *G; to promote the study & preservation of historic commercial
vehicles over 20 years old

● Mtgs - Inf - Lib - LG

< Intl Historic Vehicle Org (IHVO)

M 3,500 i, UK / 60 i, o'seas

¶ Historic Commercial News - 9; ftm, £2.50 nm.   AR.

Historic Houses Association   (HHA)   1973

■ 2 Chester St, LONDON, SW1X 7BB.   (hq)
020 7259 5688
email info@hha.org.uk   http://www.hha.org.uk
Dir Gen: Nick Way

○ *K, *N; an association of owners & guardians of historic
houses, parks, gardens & places of interest (& their
associated contents) of Great Britain; formed to promote &
safeguard their legitimate interests so far as they are
consistent with the interests of the nation

● Conf - Mtgs - Res - Exhib - Inf - Cooperation with art galleries
& museums - Seminars

< U Historic Houses

M 1,500 i, 20,000 friends

¶ Historic House - 4.   Jnl; ftm.
Technical papers & guidelines.

Historic Society of Lancashire & Cheshire   (HSLC)   1848

■ Flat 4 / 3 Bramhall Rd, Waterloo, LIVERPOOL, L22 3XA.   (hsb)
0151-920 8213
email roger@bram4.freeserve.co.uk
http://www.hslc.org.uk
Hon Sec: Roger Hull

▲ Registered Charity

○ *L; to promote the study of any aspect of the history of
Lancashire & Cheshire

● Mtgs - Lib

M 269 i, 149 org; UK & o'seas

¶ Transactions - 1.

Historical Association   (HA)   1906

NR   59a Kennington Park Rd, LONDON, SE11 4JH.   (hq)
    020 7735 3901   fax 020 7582 4989
    email enquiry@history.org.uk   http://www.history.org.uk
    Chief Exec: Madeline Stiles
▲   Company Limited by Guarantee; Registered Charity
Br   59
○   *E, *P; 'to bring together people who share an interest in, &
    love for, the past'; to promote the study & teaching of history
    at all levels
●   Conf - Mtgs - ET - VE
M   5,300 i, 500 f, 2,000 schools, UK / 400 i, o'seas
¶   The Historian - 4.   History - 4.
    Teaching History - 4.   Primary History - 3.
    Annual Bulletin of Historical Literature.
    Pamphlets.   AR.

Historical Breechloading Smallarms Association   (HBSA)   1973

NR   PO Box 288, TADWORTH, Surrey, KT20 6WD.   (hq)
    020 7381 7212
    Hon Sec: Jonathan Lewis
○   *G; study of the development of breechloading smallarms &
    ammunition

Historical Diving Society   (HDS)   1990

NR   Little Gatton Lodge, 25 Gatton Rd, REIGATE, Surrey,
    RH2 0HB.   (hsp)
    01737 249961   fax 01384 896079
    email info@thehds.com   http://www.thehds.com
    Hon Sec: Michael Fardell
▲   Registered Charity
Br   Australia, Canada, Denmark, Germany, Italy, S Africa, USA
○   *G; to provide a forum for all interested in the history of
    underwater descent, including all aspects of diving
    (commercial, amateur, naval, military, experimental &
    scientific)
Gp   Sections: Bibliophile, Film; Working historical equipment
●   Conf - Mtgs - Exhib - Lib
<   Assn Brit Transport & Engg Museums; Diving Histl Soc Australia;
    Historical Diving Socs / Canada / Denmark / Italy / Norway
    / S Africa / USA
M   i, f & org
¶   Historical Diving Times (NL) - 3; ftm, £5 nm.
    Membership Register - 1; ftm only.

Historical Metallurgy Society Ltd   (HMS)   1962

NR   22 Easterfield Drive, Southgate, SWANSEA, Glam, SA3 2DB.
    (hsp)
    01792 233223   fax [by arrangement]
    http://www.hist-met.org
    Hon Gen Sec: Peter Hutchison
▲   Company Limited by Guarantee; Registered Charity
○   *L; study, research & preservation of the historical &
    archaeological evidence of the extraction, smelting &
    working of metals & the manufacture of metal objects
●   Conf
<   Inst Materials
M   340 i, 31 org, UK / 170 i, 42 org, o'seas
¶   Historical Metallurgy (Jnl) - 2.   NL - 3.

Historical Military Mapping Group
    a group of the **British Cartographic Society**

Historical Model Railway Society   (HMRS)   1950

■   Midland Railway (Butterley), Butterley Station, RIPLEY, Derbys,
    DE5 3QZ.   (hq)
    01773 745959
    email studycentremanager@hmrs.org.uk
    http://www.hmrs.org.uk
    Chmn: T Johnson
▲   Registered Charity
○   *G; for the study & recording of information relating to all the
    railways of the British Isles; public education on matters
    concerning these railways; construction, operation,
    preservation & public exhibition of models depicting them.
    (Nothing to do with toys)
●   Mtgs - ET - Res - Exhib - Comp - SG - Inf - Lib - PL - VE
M   1,900 i, UK & o'seas
¶   HMRS Jnl - 4;   HMRS News - 6; both ftm.
    North Eastern Record:
        Volume 1: Infrastructure;
        Volume 2: Rolling Stock;
        Volume 3: Locomotives;
    The Locomotives of the Stockton & Darlington Railway;
    British Railways Mark 1 Coaches;
        [all above; £24.95.]
    Private Owner Wagons from the Ince Waggon & Ironworks Co;
    Oil on the Rails;
    Brunel's Cornish Viaducts;
        [all above; £19.95.]
    Locomotives of the Hull & Barnsley Railway; £5.95.
    GWR Iron Minks; £4.50.
    British Railway Brakevans & Ballast Ploughs; £12.95.
    Modelling Historic Architecture; £8.95.
    William Bradshaw - a Leicestershire railway
        photographer; £11.95.
    [Special discounts are available to members]

History of Anaesthesia Society   (HAS)

■   49 Howey Lane, FRODSHAM, Cheshire, WA6 6DD.   (hsp)
    01928 731888
    email gasflo@btinternet.com
    http://www.histansoc.org.uk
    Hon Sec: Dr Ann M Florence
▲   Un-incorporated Society
○   *L; to promote interest & study in the world-wide history of
    anaesthesia
●   Mtgs
<   contact with other specialist anaesthetic societies
M   350 i, UK / 84 i, o'seas
¶   Proceedings - 2/3; ftm, £4 nm.

History Curriculum Association   (HCA)   1990

NR   Windover, Punnetts Town, HEATHFIELD, E Sussex, TN21 9DS.
    (dir/p)
    01435 830109
    Dir: Chris McGovern
▲   Un-incorporated Society
○   *G, *K; to restore the history curriculum within the UK education
    system
●   Res - SG - Inf - LG
<   Granted a statutory right to be consulted on the National
    Curriculum
M   supporters

History of Education Society (UK)   (HES(UK))   1967

NR   27 Burgh Wood, BANSTEAD, Surrey, SM7 1EW.   (hsb)
    http://www.historyofeducation.org.uk
    Sec: Dr S Spencer
▲   Registered Charity
○   *L; study of & research into the history of education
●   Conf - Mtgs
<   Intl Standing Conf for the History of Education
M   156 i, 85 libraries
¶   History of Education - 6; £45 m, £498 nm.
    History of Education Researcher - 2; ftm only.

© CBD Research Ltd · Beckenham · BR3 5JS · Tel 020 8650 7745 · Fax 020 8650 0768 · E-mail cbd@cbdresearch.com · www.cbdresearch.com

Hitchin Chamber of Commerce & Industry (HCCI)
- ■ c/o 27 Churchyard, HITCHIN, Herts, SG5 1HP. (chmn/b)
  01462 453335
  Chmn: Mrs Catherine Chamberlain
- ▲ Un-incorporated Society
- ○ *C
- ● Mtgs - ET - LG
- M [not stated]
- ✕ Hitchin & District Chamber of Commerce.

HL7 UK Ltd 2000
- NR PO Box 7230, HOOK, Hants, RG27 9WX.
  0870 011 2866   fax 0870 011 2867
  http://www.hl7.org.uk
- ○ *P, *T; to support the development, promotion & implementation of HL healthcare standards, in order to meet the needs of healthcare organisations, professionals & healthcare software suppliers in the UK

Holiday Centres Association (HCA) 1935
- ■ 58 Popham Close, College Mews, TIVERTON, Devon, EX16 4DG. (hq)
  01884 243820   fax 01884 243820
  email holidaycentres@aol.com
  http://www.holidaycentres.co.uk
  Chief Exec: David Howell
- ▲ Company Limited by Guarantee
- ○ *T; interests of holiday centres
- ● Conf - Mtgs - Res - Stat - Inf - LG
- < Music Users Coun of Europe; Tourism Alliance
- M 53 f
- ¶ NL - 2; ftm only.   LM - 1; free.

Holistic Healers Association 1998
- ■ 79-81 Bowman St, GLASGOW, G42 8LF.
  0141-423 5952
  Contact: K Lawrence
- ○ *P
- M 900 i
  no further information supplied

Hollyhock Society, England, Scotland, Wales 1991
- ■ Ground floor flat, 5 Clarence Rd, CHELTENHAM, Glos, GL52 2AY.
  01242 261459
  Pres & Hon Sec: Mrs Patricia A Meyrick
- ○ *H; study & protection of hollyhocks
- ● Exhib - VE
- M 9 i
  Note: also includes the Hollyhock Painting Society.

Holstein UK 1909
- NR Scotsbridge House, Scotts Hill, RICKMANSWORTH, Herts, WD3 3BB. (hq)
  01923 695200
  Admin: Jacky Palmer
- ○ *B
- M c 10,000 i
- ✕ 2002 Holstein UK & Ireland

Home Beer & Wine Manufacturers Association (HBWMA) 1986
- NR Mulberry House, Main St, SIBFORD FERRIS, Oxon, OX15 5RE. (asa)
  01295 780242
  Admin: Miss Linda Lane
- ○ *T; to represent manufacturers, wholesalers & retailers; to increase public awareness of the benefits of home beer & winemaking
- Gp Way forward group; Exhibition group
- ● Mtgs - Exhib - LG
- M 23 f, UK / 2 f, o'seas

Home Builders Federation (HBF) 1947
- NR Byron House, 7-9 St James's St, LONDON, SW1A 1DW. (hq)
  020 7960 1600   fax 020 7960 1601
  http://www.hbf.co.uk
  Chief Exec: Robert Ashmead
  Head of Media Relations: Pierre Williams
- ▲ Un-incorporated Society
- Br 8
- ○ *T; to ensure a favourable economic, political & planning climate in the UK in which private housebuilders can operate
- Gp Planning; Political; Technical; Public relations; Taxation; Europe
- ● Conf - Mtgs - ET - Stat - LG
- < Intl Housing Assn; Eur U Developers & Housebuilders
- M 800 f
- ¶ House Builder Magazine - 10;   NL - 4; both ftm.
- ✕ 2005 (April) House Builders Federation

Home Business Alliance (HBA) 1984
- NR 14 Werrington Business Centre, Papyrus Rd, PETERBOROUGH, Cambs, PE4 5BH. (hq)
  0871 474 1015   fax 0871 474 1016
  email info@homebusiness.org.uk
  http://www.homebusiness.org.uk
  Chmn: Leonard Tondel,   Sec: Marion Owen
- ○ *T; 'production & exchange of information on successful business methods for business owners & home businesses - to expand existing businesses & set up new ones'
- M i
- ¶ The Boss (NL).

Home Decoration Retailers' Association (HDRA) 1955
- NR 225 Bristol Rd, Edgbaston, BIRMINGHAM, B5 7UB. (hq)
  0121-446 6688
  Co Sec: Diana Truman
- ▲ Company Limited by Guarantee
- ○ *T; to promote the independent home decor specialist retailer
- ● Mtgs - Inf - Lib
- M 750 f
- ¶ Home Decor & Furnishings - 6.   NL - 4.
  The Gold Decor Directory - 1.

Home Education Advisory Service (HEAS) 1995
- ■ PO Box 98, WELWYN GARDEN CITY, Herts, AL8 6AN. (mail)
  01707 371854   fax 01707 371854
  email enquiries@heas.org.uk
  http://www.heas.org.uk address
  Sec: Mrs Brenda Holliday
- ▲ Company Limited by Guarantee; Registered Charity
- ○ *E; advice & information on education at home instead of school
- ● Conf - ET - Inf - Lib - Subscribers' advice line
- M [not stated]
- ¶ HEAS Bulletin - 4; ftm only.
  HEAS Introductory Information Pack; £2.50.
  HEAS Resources Book;   Home Education Hbk; both £8.50.
  Information leaflets:
    Special Education Needs; £1.50.
    Examinations;   Dyslexia; both £1.
  Home Education Overseas; £1.50.

Home Laundering Consultative Council (HLCC) 1966
- NR 5 Portland Place, LONDON, W1B 1PW. (hq)
  020 7636 7788   fax 020 7636 7515
  Sec: A Mansell
- ○ *T; promotion & administration of a uniform system of care-labelling, both nationally & internationally
- ● Mtgs - Inf
- < GINETEX
- M 70 f, c 70 trade assns & educational bodies with an interest in care-labelling
- ¶ LM;   AR.   Other publications.

Homeless Link   2001
- ■ 10-13 Rushworth St, LONDON, SE1 0RB.   (hq)
  020 7960 3010   fax 020 7960 3011
  email info@homelesslink.org.uk
  http://www.homeless.org.uk
  Chief Exec: Jenny Edwards
- ▲ Company Limited by Guarantee; Registered Charity
- ○ *K, *N; relief of poverty, sickness & need caused by, or resulting in, a condition of homelessness
- ● Conf - Mtgs - ET - Res - Exhib - LG
- M not stated]
- ¶ Connect - 4; ftm, £40 yr nm.
  Members Mailing - 12; ftm only.   AR - 1; free.
  Various books & guides; listed on website.

Homeopathic Medical Association   (HMA)   1985
- ■ 6 Livingstone Rd, GRAVESEND, Kent, DA12 5DZ.   (hq)
  01474 560336   fax 01474 327431
  email info@the-hma.org   http://www.the-hma.org
  Coun Sec: Mrs Parm Randhawa
- ▲ Company Limited by Guarantee
- ○ *M, *P; 'members must have passed a qualifying examination at a college approved by the Council &/or proved their worthiness to practise the art & science of Homoeopathy. . . members are bound by a strict code of ethics & practice & obliged to carry professional indemnity insurance'
- ● Conf
- M i
- ¶ Homeopathy International (Jnl) - 4; £25.
- ✕ 2001 United Kingdom Homeopathic Medical Association

Homes for Scotland
- ■ Forsyth House, 93 George St, EDINBURGH, EH2 3ES.   (hq)
  0131-243 2595   fax 0131-243 2596
  email info@homesforscotland.com
  http://www.homesforscotland.com
  Exec Dir: Bruce Black
- ▲ Company Limited by Guarantee
- Br 1
- ○ *T; to promote the long-term interests of the Scottish home building industry; to create awareness of the economic, social & environmental significance of home builders; interests include planning, water & drainage, design, environmental quality
- Gp Housing planning
- ● Mtgs - Inf - LG
- M 160 f
- ¶ NL - 12; ftm only.
- ✕ SHBA Ltd (Homes for Scotland)

Homestay Providers Association
  has closed

Honest Food - the Campaign for Independent Food
  a campaign run by the **Countryside Alliance**

Honey Association   (HA)   1940
- ■ Crescent House, 34 Eastbury Way, SWINDON, Wilts, SN25 2EN.   (hsb)
  01793 727387   fax 01793 726486
  email honeyassociation@aol.com
  http://www.honeyassociation.com
  Sec: Walter J Anzer
- ▲ Company Limited by Guarantee
- ○ *T; interests of British honey importers & packers
- ● Mtgs - PR - Technical services
- < Eur Fedn Honey Packers & Distributors (FEEDM)
- M 16 f

Hong Kong Association   1961
- ■ Swire House, 59 Buckingham Gate, LONDON, SW1E 6AJ.   (hq)
  020 7963 9447   fax 020 7828 6331
  email info@hkas.org.uk   http://www.hkas.org.uk
  Exec Dir: Capt Robert Guy
- ▲ Company Limited by Guarantee
- ○ *T, *X; to nurture the business & commercial relationship between the Hong Kong SAR & the UK
- ● Mtgs - LG
- < Hong Kong Soc
- M 100 f

Honorable Society of King's Inns   1200
- IRL Henrietta St, DUBLIN 1, Republic of Ireland.
  353 (1) 874 4840   fax 353 (1) 872 6048
  email info@kingsinns.ie   http://www.kingsinns.ie
  Senior Bencher: Colm Condon
- ○ *P

Honourable Society of Cymmrodorion   1751
- ■ 30 Eastcastle St, LONDON, W1W 8DJ.   (hsb)
  020 7631 0502
  email aelodau1751we@yahoo.co.uk
  http://www.cymmrodorion1751.org
  Hon Sec: John Samuel
- ▲ Registered Charity
- ○ *L; encouragement of the literature, arts & sciences of Wales
- ● Mtgs - Res - Lib
- M c 800 i, c 80 org, UK / 30 i, 40 org, o'seas
- ¶ Transactions - 1; £25.

The Honourable The Irish Society   1613
- ■ Salters Hall, 4 Fore St, LONDON, EC2Y 5DE.   (hq)
  020 7786 9876
  54 Castleroe Rd, COLERAINE, Co Londonderry, BT51 3RL.
  028 7034 4796   fax 028 7035 6527 (Irish office)
  Sec: C J H Fisher
  Note: is a charitable trust

Hop Merchants Association   (HMA)   1917
- ■ Charles Faram & Co Ltd, Monkfield Lane, Newland, MALVERN, Worcs, WR13 5BB.   (pres/b)
  01905 830734
  Chmn: Paul Corbett
- ▲ Un-incorporated Society
- ○ *T; to promote the interests of members trading in hops grown in England
  no further information supplied

Hopkins Society   1990
- NR 41 North Drive, RHYL, Flintshire, LL18 4SW.   (memsec/p)
  Mem Sec: Imelda Jones
- ▲ Un-incorporated Society
- ○ *A; for those interested in the work & life of Gerard Manley Hopkins, English poet & priest
- M i

Horatian Society   1934
- ■ c/o John S C Eidinow, Merton College, OXFORD, OX1 4JD.   (mail/add)
  Hon Sec & Treas: J S C Eidinow
- ▲ Un-incorporated Society
- ○ *A; 'the poet Horace & his works'
- ● Annual dinner
- M 200 i
- ¶ AR (incl LM); ftm only.

Horse Rangers Association   (HRA)   1954
NR   c/o The Royal Mews, Hampton Court Palace, EAST MOLESEY,
        Surrey, KT8 9BW.   (hq)
        020 8979 4196   fax 020 8941 3310
        Chief Exec: Mrs Cynthia Piper
▲   Registered Charity
Br   7
○   *Y; 'voluntary uniformed youth movement with horses
        incorporating able-bodied & special needs riders from 8
        years old'
●   Mtgs - ET - Inf - VE
<   Brit Horse Soc; Riding for the Disabled Assn
M   i

**Horserace Writers & Photographers Association   (HWPA)
1927**
■   65 Penwood Heights, Penwood, Highclere, NEWBURY, Berks,
        RG20 9EZ.   (pres/p)
        01635 253150
        email glester7@hotmail.com   http://www.hwpa.co.uk
        Pres: Geoff Lester
▲   Un-incorporated Society
Br   3
○   *P; to represent the interests of all racing media (TV, radio,
        newspapers, photographers) within the racing industry
●   Derby awards lunch (London, 1st Monday in December)
<   Nat Turf Writers Assn (USA)
M   303 i
¶   NL - 4/5.   Derby Awards brochure - 1.

Horseracing Sponsors Association   (HSA)   1993
NR   Stirling Way, BOREHAM WOOD, Herts, WD6 2AZ.   (hq)
        020 8207 4114
        Chief Exec: Nigel Payne
▲   Company Limited by Guarantee
○   *T; to provide practical help & advice for race sponsors; to work
        with racecourses to attract new sponsors; to represent
        sponsors within the industry
●   Conf - Mtgs - Comp - Inf - VE
M   50 f, 30 racecourses
¶   Brandwagon (NL) - 2/3.

Horticultural Association of Retail Traders Ltd   (HART)   1994
NR   Team House (suite 7), Braybon Business Park, Victoria Estate,
        BURGESS HILL, W Sussex, RH15 9ND.   (hq)
        01444 462040
        Chief Exec: Eimert de Graaff
▲   Company Limited by Guarantee
○   *T; to protect & maintain the profitability & viability of
        independent garden centres
Gp   Marketing; Buying; IT
●   Conf - Mtgs - Exhib - Inf - VE
<   SESACO
M   c 300 f

Horticultural & Contractors Tools Association
   a group of the **Federation of British Hand Tool Manufacturers**

Horticultural Exhibitors' Association   (HEA)   1946
NR   30 Sea Rd, Milford-on-Sea, LYMINGTON, Hants, SO41 0PG.
        (hsp)
        Hon Sec: Mrs Fiona Whittles
○   *T; interests of horticultural producers & suppliers who exhibit at
        horticultural & agricultural shows
●   Mtgs
M   154 f, 66 org
¶   NL - 4;   HEA Ybk - 1; both ftm only.

Horticultural Research Association
   since 2003-04 **Horticulture Research International Association**

Horticultural Trades Association   (HTA)   1899
■   Horticulture House, 19 High St, Theale, READING, RG7 5AH.
        (hq)
        0118-930 3132
        Dir Gen: David Gwyther
▲   Company Limited by Guarantee
○   *H, *T; to represent the UK garden industry; to promote the
        profitable growth of its retail & grower members
Gp   Association of British Conifer Growers; Association of
        Professional Landscapers (APL); Association of Liner
        Producers (ALP); British Heather Growers (BHG); British Rose
        Growers Association (BRGA); Forestry Trade Group
●   Conf - Mtgs - ET - Exam - Res - Exhib - Stat - Inf - Lib - VE - LG
M   3,000 f
¶   HTA News - 12; ftm, £2 nm.   AR; free.

Horticulture Research International Association   (HRIA)   1994
NR   c/o Warwick HRI, Wellesbourne, WARWICK, CV35 9EF.
        (hq/hsb)
        024 7657 4455
        Contact: Ruth Ashfield
○   *H, *Q; to provide a forum for members to keep in touch with
        the latest research developments in horticulture (in particular
        at Horticulture Research International); to enable research
        staff to meet growers & others in the industry for discussions
×   2003-04 Horticultural Research Association

Hose Manufacturers' & Suppliers' Association   (HMSA)   1999
■   2 Waltham Court, Milley Lane, Hare Hatch, READING, Berks,
        RG10 9TH.   (hq)
        0118-940 3416   fax 0118-940 6258
        email info@feta.co.uk   http://www.feta.co.uk
        Dir Gen: Cedric Sloan
○   *T; the manufacture or supply of quality flexible hoses to the
        heating, ventilating & air conditioning industry
●   Mtgs - Inf
<   Heating & Ventilating Mfrs' Assn (HEVAC); Fedn Envtl Tr
        Assns (FETA)
M   6 f

Hospital Broadcasting Association
   trading name of **National Association of Hospital Broadcasting
Organisations**

Hospital Caterers Association   (HCA)   1948
■   University Hospital of North Staffs, City General Site,
        Newcastle Rd, STOKE-on-TRENT, Staffs, ST4 6QG.   (hsb)
        01782 552790   fax 01782 553350
        email sandra.roberts@uhns.nhs.uk
        http://www.hospitalcaterers.org
        Hon Sec: Mrs Sandra Roberts
Br   17
○   *P; to promote & improve the standards of catering in hospitals
        & healthcare; in Great Britain, Northern Ireland & elsewhere;
        to ensure the education & training of persons engaged in
        healthcare catering services & the improvement of their
        professional interests & status
●   Conf - Mtgs - ET - Exhib - Comp - Inf - Lib - LG
<   Healthcare Catering Intl
M   700+ i
¶   Hospital Caterer (Jnl) - 6.   Hospital Caterer Ybk - 1.
     Hygiene Good Practice Guide.
     Food Service Standards at Ward Level: good practice guide.

Hospital Consultants & Specialists Association   (HCSA)   1948
- ■ 1 Kingsclere Rd, Overton, BASINGSTOKE, Hants, RG25 3JA. (hq)
  01256 771777
  Head of Admin: Steve George
- ▲ Un-incorporated Society
- ○ *P, *U; to promote, protect & advance the interests of consultants in their relationship with hospital authorities & the progress of medical practice in the NHS
- ● Conf - Mtgs - SG - Stat - Inf - Empl
- < TUC
- M 3,000 i
- ¶ HCSA News.

Hospital & Medical Care Association   (HMCA)   1978
- NR Scriven Park, Ripley Rd, KNARESBOROUGH, N Yorks, HG5 9DF.   (hq)
  01423 866985
  Sec: Ian Cooke
- ○ *T
  to provide benefits for members (by making arrangements on their behalf) with duly authorised insurers; to act as advisers on the making of insurance provision on all types of insurance.

Hospital Saving Association   (HSA)   1922
- § Hambleden House, ANDOVER, Hants, SP10 1LQ.
  01264 353211   fax 01264 333650
  http://www.hsa.co.uk
  Sickness insurance, charitable activities, grants to hospitals, scholarships for nurses

Hospital Scientists Association   (HSA(NI))   1972
- NR Royal Hospitals Trust, Kelvin Laboratories, Bacteriology Dept, Grosvenor Rd, BELFAST, BT12 6BA.   (hsb)
  028 9024 0503   fax 028 9031 1416
  Hon Sec: Dr Hugh O'Neill
- ○ *P; to represent clinical scientists in the NHS in Northern Ireland on all professional matters
- Gp liaison with government through c'ees & information service providers
- ● Mtgs - SG - Inf - LG
- M 52 i

Hot Extruded Sealants Association
  since 2003 **Extruded Sealants Association**

Hotel Booking Agents Association   (HBAA)   1997
- NR 122 Bath Rd, CHELTENHAM, GL53 7JX.   (asa)
  0845 603 3349
  email secretary@hbaa.org.uk   http://www.hbaa.org.uk
  Chmn: Bob Dixon
- ▲ Company Limited by Guarantee
- ○ *T; to represent the hotel & conference agency community
- Gp Hotel booking agents; Charter parties; Charter signees
- ● Conf - Mtgs - ET - Exhib
- M 57 agencies, 40 charter partners, 79 charter signees
- ¶ Code of Working Practice.

Hotel & Catering International Management Association   (HCIMA)   1971
- NR Trinity Court, 34 West St, SUTTON, Surrey, SM1 1SH.   (hq)
  020 8661 4900
  Chief Exec: Col Philippe Rossiter
- ▲ Registered Charity
- ○ *P; to promote & maintain the highest professional & ethical standards for management, education & training in the international hotel & catering industry
- Gp Working gps: Technical advisory, Environmental, Quality assurance
- ● Conf - Mtgs - ET - Exam - Res - Exhib - Comp - Stat - Inf - Lib - LG
- M 20,000 i, UK / 3,000 i, o'seas, 20 patrons, 22 business affiliates
- ¶ Hospitality - 10.   Hospitality Ybk.
  Corporate brochure - up-dated.   AR.

Hound Trailing Association   (HTA)   1906
- ■ Ash Cottage, Blencow, PENRITH, Cumbria, CA11 0DB. (hsp/b)
  01768 483686
  email hta.margaret@btopenworld.com
  Sec: Margaret Baxter
- ▲ Company Limited by Guarantee
- ○ *S; hound racing following aniseed scent; a traditional Cumbrian sport (not a blood-sport)
- ● Mtgs - Comp
- M c 1,000 i
- ¶ Ybk; £2.50.   AR; free.

House Builders Federation
  since 2005 **Home Builders Federation**

Houses, Castles & Gardens of Ireland
- IRL 16A Woodlands Park, BLACKROCK, Co Dublin, Republic of Ireland.
  353 (1) 288 9114
  email info@castlesgardensireland.com
  Chmn: Frieda O'Connell,   Sec: Collette Scullion
- ○ *G

Housing Institute of Ireland   1989
- IRL c/o 50 Merrion Sq, DUBLIN 2, Republic of Ireland.
  353 (1) 661 8334   fax 353 (1) 661 0320
  Co-ordinator: Sally Blair
- ○ *P

Housing Management Contractors Association
  a group of the **Public Contractors Association**

Housman Society   1973
- ■ 80 New Rd, BROMSGROVE, Worcs, B60 2LA.   (chmn/p)
  01527 874136
  email info@housman-society.co.uk
  Chmn: J C Page
- ▲ Registered Charity
- Br 1; Japan, USA
- ○ *L; to foster interest in & promote knowledge of A[lfred] E[dward] Housman (1865-1959), his sister Clemence & brother Laurence
- ● Mtgs - Res - Exhib - Inf - Lib - VE - Publications
- < Alliance of Literary Socs
- M 300 i, UK / 40 i, o'seas
- ¶ Housman Jnl - 1; ftm, £6 nm.   NL - 2; free.
  Unkind to Unicorns.   Housman's Places.
  A Westerly Wanderer.   Three Bromsgrove Poets.
  Soldier I Wish You Well.
  (subscription; £10).

Hover Club
  since 2002-03 **Hovercraft Club of Great Britain Ltd**

Hovercraft Club of Great Britain Ltd   (HCGB)   1966
- ■ PO Box 328, BOLTON, Lancs, BL6 4RR.   (inf/pubns/office)
  01204 841248
  email info@hovercraft.org.uk
  http://www.hovercraft.org.uk
  Chmn: Peter Kemp
  Vice-Chmn: Chris Barlow
- ▲ Company Limited by Guarantee
- ○ *G, *S; construction & development of light sports hovercraft;
  including regulation of design & construction safety
- Gp Competitions; Cruising & coastal events; Specialist publications
- ● Mtgs - Comp - Lib/Archive - National hovercraft series racing -
  Cruising events (river & coastal) - Coastal racing
- < Wld Hovercraft Fedn; Eur Hovercraft Fedn
- > Hovercraft Museum
- M 700 i, 10 f, 5 org, UK / 30 i, 2 f, o'seas
- ¶ Light Hovercraft - 12; ftm, £2 nm.   AR - 1; free.
  Inland Racing Competition Regulation - 1; ftm; £4 nm.
  Racing Construction Regulation - 1; ftm; £4 nm.
  Cruising Construction Regulations - 1; £4.
  Coastal Racing Construction Regulations - 1; £4.
  Guide to Making Model Hovercraft - irreg; £4.
  Hovercraft Construction Guide - irreg; £17.
- × 2002-03 Hover Club

Hovercraft Museum Trust   (HMT)   1986
- ■ HMS Daedalus, Chark Lane, LEE-on-the-SOLENT, Hants,
  PO13 9NY.   (hq)
  023 9255 2090   fax 023 9255 2090
  email warwick@hovercraft-museum.org
  http://www.hovercraft-museum.org
  Mgr: W Jacobs
- ▲ Registered Charity
- ○ *L, *Q; to promote the hovercraft educational museum trust
- ● Conf - Mtgs - ET - Res - Exhib - Comp - Stat - Expt - Inf - Lib -
  PL - VE - LG Lectures - Open days - Restoration
- < Brit Aviation Presvn Coun
- M 400 i, 50 f
- ¶ Hovercraft Museum NL - 4; £20.
- × 2004-06 Hovercraft Society & Hovercraft Museum Trust

Hovercraft Society
    the society has closed - see **Hovercraft Museum Trust**

Howard League for Penal Reform   1921
- NR 1 Ardleigh Rd, LONDON, N1 4HS.   (hq)
  020 7249 7373
  Dir: Frances Crook
- ▲ Company Limited by Guarantee; Registered Charity
- ○ *K; advancement of constructive penal & social policies
- ● Conf - Mtgs - ET - Res - VE - LG
- < John Howard Soc of: Canada / S Australia / British Columbia
- M 3,000 i, 50 f, 50 org, UK / 300 i, 10 f, 10 org, o'seas
- ¶ HLM: Howard League Magazine - 4.
  Missing the Grade: Education for Children in Prison.
  Suicide & Self Harm Prevention (4 reports).
  Children in Prison (10 reports).

HR Society Ltd   1970
- NR Bridge House, Church Rd, BURNHAM ON CROUCH, Essex,
  CM0 8BZ.   (hq)
  01621 781035   fax 01621 782327
  email hrsoc@netcomuk.co.uk
  http://www.hrsociety.co.uk
  Sec: Mrs Sheila Nutt
- ▲ Company Limited by Guarantee; Registered Charity
- ○ *L; to promote the study & advancement of education in the
  field of manpower policy (human resources) management,
  planning & utilisation
- Gp Financial services special interest
- ● Conf - Mtgs - ET - Res - SG - Inf
- M 63 i, 22 f
- ¶ Manpower News - irreg; ftm only.   AR - 1; free.
  Spotlight (NL) - 4; ftm & free to Health Service.
- × 2002 Manpower Society

Huguenot Society of Great Britain & Ireland   1885
- ■ Huguenot Library, University College, Gower St, LONDON,
  WC1E 6BT.   (college/library)
  020 7679 5199
  email library@ucl.ac.uk
  http://www.huguenotsociety.org.uk
  Hon Sec: Barbara Julien
- ▲ Registered Charity
- ○ *L; collection & publication of information on the history &
  genealogy of the Huguenots, particularly those who took
  refuge in the British Isles; their influence on the culture,
  politics & economy of Britain & Ireland
- Gp Irish section (Dublin)
- ● Conf - Mtgs - Res - Inf - Lib - VE
- M 1,086 i, 107 libraries, UK / 245 i, o'seas
- ¶ Proceedings - 1;; ftm, £8 nm.   NL - 2; ftm only.
  Quarto Series - irreg; £5-£11 m, £12-£24 nm.
    CD Roms of some of the above; £17.50 m, £19.99 nm.
      As a set: £125 m, £150 nm.
  Microfiches of Quarto Series 1-47; £4 (each) m, £5 (each) nm.
  New series - irreg; £10-£15 m, £15-£15 nm.

**Hull & Humber Chamber of Commerce, Industry & Shipping
1837**
- NR 34-38 Beverley Rd, HULL, HU3 1YE.   (hq)
  01482 324976   fax 01482 213962
  email info@hull-humber-chamber.co.uk
  http://www.hull-humber-chamber.co.uk
  Chief Exec: Ian Kelly
- ▲ Company Limited by Guarantee
- Br Offices in Bridlington, Goole, Grimsby, Hull, Scunthorpe
- ○ *C
- ● Mtgs - ET - Exhib - Expt - Inf - VE - LG
- < Brit Chams Comm
- M 1,600 f, 5 org
- ¶ Business Intelligence - 10;   Ybk; both ftm.

Human Genetics Alert   (HGA)
- ■ c/o 22B St Kilda's Rd, LONDON, N16 5BZ.   (hsp)
  020 7502 7516   fax 020 7502 7516
  email info@hgalert.org   http://www.hgalert.org
  Sec: David King
- ▲ Company Limited by Guarantee
- ○ *K; a watch-dog group for human genetics
- ● Inf
- M 30 i
- ¶ Human Genetics NL - 6.
- × 2001 (February) Campaign against Human Genetic
  Engineering

Human Rights Society   (HRS)   1969
- ■ Mariners Hard, Cley, HOLT, Norfolk, NR25 7RX.   (hsb)
  01263 740990
  Sec: Mrs J J Murray
- ▲ Un-incorporated Society
- ○ *K, *M; to oppose the legalisation of voluntary euthanasia
- ● ET - Inf (on hospices & pain relief in terminal illness)
- M c 2,500 i
- ¶ NL - 1; m only.
  Publications list available; sae please.

Humane Slaughter Association   (HSA)   1911
- NR The Old School, Brewhouse Hill, WHEATHAMPSTEAD, Herts,
  AL4 8AN.   (hq)
  01582 831919   fax 01582 831414
  email info@hsa.org.uk   http://www.hsa.org.uk
  Sec: Donald Davidson
- ▲ Registered Charity
- ○ *V; promotion of humane methods of slaughter; introduction of
  reforms in cattle markets; welfare of animals in transit
- ● ET - Res - Exhib - Inf - Lib - LG
- M 605 i, 30 f, UK / 20 i, o'seas
- ¶ AR.   NL; both ftm.
  Numerous educational booklets, technical notes, videos.

Humanist Association of Ireland   1993
IRL   47 Sugarloaf Crescent, BRAY, Co Wicklow, Republic of Ireland.
      353 (1) 286 9870   http://www.irish-humanists.org
      Pres: Justin Keating
○   *K
×   2004 Association of Irish Humanists

Humanist Society of Scotland   (HSS)   1989
NR   272 Bath St, GLASGOW, G2 4JR.   (hq)
     0870 874 9002
     Hon Sec: Ron McLaren
▲   Registered Charity (Scotland)
○   *G; 'to promote in Scotland the principles & practice of
     humanism defined as the moral, intellectual & social
     development of individuals & the community free from
     theistic, religious & dogmatic beliefs & dogmas'
Gp   Register of officiants for humanistic funerals & other ceremonies
●   Conf - ET - Inf - School visits - Conduct of funerals etc
<   Intl Humanist & Ethical U (IHEU)
M   c 450 i
¶   Humanism Scotland - 4.

Humanities Association   (HA)   1984
■   11 Lloyd St, RYTON, Tyne & Wear, NE40 4DJ.   (hsp)
    0191-413 2262   fax 0191-413 2262
    email peter@j-walsh.freeserve.co.uk
    http://www.hums.org.uk
    Mem Sec: Peter Walsh
○   *P; development of humanities learning
●   Conf - Mtgs - Exhib - LG
<   Devt Educ Assn
M   130 i, UK / 5 i, o'seas
¶   Humanities Too;   Humanities Now; both available on website.

Hundred (100) Group
■   c/o Philip Broadley, Prudential plc, Laurence Pountney Hill,
    LONDON, EC4R 0HH.   (chmn/b)
    Chmn: Philip Broadley
○   *P; finance directors
M   i
    no further information supplied

Hunter Archaeological Society   1912
■   34 Elwood Rd, SHEFFIELD, S Yorks, S17 4RH.   (hsp)
    0114-236 1850
    Hon Sec: Paul Caldwell
▲   Registered Charity
○   *L; to study & preserve the archaeology & history of S Yorkshire
    & N Derbyshire
●   Mtgs - VE - Excavations - Field work
M   250 i
¶   Transactions - biennial; ftm.

Hunterian Society   1819
■   c/o Betty Smallwood, Lettsom House, Chandos St, Cavendish
    Sq, LONDON, W1G 9EB.   (hsb)
    http://www.hunteriansociety.org.uk
    Hon Sec: Neil Weir
▲   Registered Charity
○   *L; the cultivation & promotion of the science & practice of
    medicine
    The society was formed to commemorate the surgeon &
    anatomist John Hunter
●   Mtgs
M   490 i
¶   Transactions - 1.

Hunting Association of Ireland
IRL   7-8 Upper Mount St, DUBLIN 2, Republic of Ireland.
      353 (1) 639 4651
      email hunting@hai.ie
      Contact: Gavin Duffy
○   *S

Huntingdonshire Local History Society   1959
■   3 The Lanes, Houghton, HUNTINGDON, Cambs, PE28 2BW.
    (hsp)
    01480 463007
    Hon Sec: Mrs Mary Hopper
▲   Registered Charity
Br   1
○   *L; to promote the advancement of public education through
    the study of local history in the former County of
    Huntingdonshire (now part of Cambridgeshire)
●   Mtgs - Res - Exhib - SG - VE
<   Cambridge Antiquarian Soc
M   c 200 i
¶   NL - 2;   AR.
    Records of Huntingdon - 1; (special Oliver Cromwell edition
    available).

Huntington's Disease Association   (HDA)   1971
NR   Down Stream Building, 1 London Bridge, LONDON,
     SE1 1BG.   (hq)
     020 7022 1950   fax 020 7022 1953
     email info@hda.org.uk   http://www.hda.org.uk
     Chmn: Sue Watkin
▲   Registered Charity
Br   12 regional
○   *W; to provide help & support to sufferers of the disease; to
    promote research
●   Conf - Mtgs - ET - Res - Inf - LG - Family counselling service -
    Support groups - Films - Speakers available
<   Intl Huntington's Disease Assn
M   400 i
¶   NL - 2;   AR;   Factsheets; all free.
    Case Notes for Professionals; £8.50.
    Physicians Guide to the Management of Huntington's
    Disease; £5.75.
    Publications list available.

Hurdy-Gurdy Society   (HGS)   1982
■   47 Tudor Gardens, STONY STRATFORD, Bucks, MK11 1HX.
    (hsp)
    01908 565339
    email michaelpmuskett@beeb.net
    Hon Sec: Michael Muskett
▲   Un-incorporated Society
Br   80
○   *D, *G; to further the knowledge of the hurdy-gurdy, its history,
    construction, playing techniques & repertoire
●   ET - Res - Inf - Regional playing days
M   80 i, 1 f, UK / 6 i, 2 f, o'seas
¶   Jnl - 4.   LM - 1.

Hurlingham Polo Association   (HPA)   1874
■   Manor Farm, Little Coxwell, FARINGDON, Oxon, SN7 7LW.
    (hq)
    01367 242828   fax 01367 242829
    email enquiries@hpa-polo.co.uk
    http://www.hpa-polo.co.uk
    Chief Exec: David Woodd
Br   affiliated clubs in British Isles & Commonwealth
○   *S; to act as the governing body for polo in the UK
●   Inf
<   Fedn of Intl Polo
M   2,000 i, 50 org, UK / 28 org, o'seas
¶   HPA Ybk (Blue Book) - 1; ftm, £10 nm.
    HPA Arena Ybk - 1; ftm, £10 nm.

© CBD Research Ltd · Beckenham · BR3 5JS · Tel 020 8650 7745 · Fax 020 8650 0768 · E-mail cbd@cbdresearch.com · www.cbdresearch.com

Hydrographic Society UK   2004
- PO Box 103, PLYMOUTH, Devon, PL4 7YP.   (hq)
  01752 223512   fax 01752 223512
  email helen@ths.org.uk   http://www.ths.org.uk
  Mgr & Co Sec: Helen Atkinson
- ▲ Company Limited by Guarantee; Registered Charity
- Br 5; Ireland, Middle East, International
- ○ *L; to promote the development & understanding of
  hydrography & hydrographic learning; to facilitate the
  exchange of ideas & practices
- ● Conf - Mtgs - Exhib - Inf - Publications
- < Intl Fedn of Hydrographic Socs; UK GeoForum
- M c 475 i, c 60 f, UK / c 110 i, c 30 f, o'seas
- ¶ Soundings - 4; free. - 4; ftm, £70 yr nm.
  Conference/Seminar Proceedings - irreg; £5.
  Proceedings of seminars & symposia; & Special
  Publications; £3.50. £50.
  Publications list available; free.
  Note: in 2004 the Hydrographic Society was incorporated as
  the Hydrographic Society UK.
  in 2005 the Hydrographic Society restructured & became the
  International Federation of Hydrographical Societies (& as
  such is outside the scope of this directory).
- ✕ 2004 Hydrographic Society

Hymn Society of Great Britain & Ireland   1936
- 99 Barton Rd, Scotforth, LANCASTER, LA1 4EN.   (hsp)
  01524 66740   fax 01524 66740
  email robcanham@haystacks.fsnet.co.uk
  http://www.hymnsocietygbi.org.uk
  Hon Sec: Rev Robert A Canham
- ▲ Registered Charity
- ○ *A, *L; to promote the use of hymns in Christian worship;
  research into hymnody
- Gp Art & literature; Educational; General interest & hobbies;
  Learned, scientific & technical societies; Research
  organisations; Religious organisations
- ● Conf - Res - SG - Inf
- < Hymn Soc in the USA & Canada
- M 369 i, 54 libraries, UK / 72 i, o'seas
- ¶ Bulletin - 4; ftm, £2.50 nm.   NL - 4; free.
  Festival of Hymns (booklet) - 1; ftm, £2.50 nm.
  Occasional Papers - irreg; ftm, £2.50 nm.   AR - 1; free.

Hyperactive Children's Support Group   (HACSG)   1977
- 71 Whyke Lane, CHICHESTER, W Sussex, PO19 7PD.   (hsp/b)
  01243 539966   fax 0243 539966
  email hyperactive@hacsg.org.uk
  http://www.hacsg.org.uk
  Dir & Founder: Mrs Sally Bunday
- ▲ Registered Charity
- Br London
- ○ *K; to support,advise & provide information for parents, carers
  & professionals interested in ADHD/hyperactivity & autistic
  spectrum disorders; to promote research & disseminate
  information on the rule of diet & nutrition
- ● Conf - ET - Inf
- < Foresight; Autism Unravelled; FAB-Food & Behaviour Res;
  Sustain; Food Cmsn; Brain Bio-Centre
- M 450 i, 50 f, 10 org, UK / 12 i, o'seas
- ¶ Jnl - 3; £15 m, £2 each nm.
  ADHD / Hyperactive Children: A Guide for Parents; ftm, £6 nm.
  Introductory pack; free.

Hypermobility Syndrome Association   (HMSA)   1992
- PO Box 1122, Nailsea, BRISTOL, Somerset, BS48 2YZ.   (hsp)
  email info@hypermobility.org
  http://www.hypermobility.org
  Sec: Cathy Elliott
- ▲ Registered Charity
- ○ *W; to provide information & support for those affected by the
  inheritable syndrome; to promote knowledge &
  understanding within the medical profession & general public
- < Brit Coalition Heritable Disorders (Connective Tissue)
- M 400 i, UK / 60 i, o'seas

Hypnotherapy Register
   see**National Council for Hypnotherapy (including the
   Hypnotherapy Register)**

Hysterectomy Association   1998
- 60 Redwood House, Charlton Down, DORCHESTER, Dorset,
  DT2 9JH.   (hq)
  0871 781 1141
  email info@hysterectomy-association.org.uk
  http://www.hysterectomy-association.org.uk
  Dir: Linda Parkinson-Hardman
- ▲ Un-incorporated Society
- ○ *M, *W; to provide impartial, clear & timely information &
  support to women who have, or who are thinking of having,
  a hysterectomy
- ● ET - Res - Inf
- < Nat Coun for Voluntary Orgs; Brit Assn for Counselling &
  Therapy
- M 1,000 i, UK / 500 i, o'seas
- ¶ The Pocket Guide to Hysterectomy; £7.
  101 Handy Hints for a Happy Hysterectomy; £7.

ia: the Ileostomy & Internal Pouch Support Group   (ia)   1956
- ■ 1-5 Mill Rd, BALLYCLARE, Co Antrim, BT39 9DR.   (nat/sec/p)
  028 9334 4043   fax 028 9332 4606
  email info@the-ia.org.uk   http://www.the-ia.org.uk
  Nat Sec: Mrs Anne Demick
- ▲ Registered Charity
- Br 55
- ○ *W; to help people return to full & active lives following surgery for the removal of the colon; to promote research into the causes of inflammatory bowel diseases (ulcerative colitis & Crohn's disease)
- Gp Internal pouch; Trained visitors; Welfare
- ● Conf - Mtgs - Res - Exhib - Inf - VE - LG
  Helpline: 0800 018 4724
- < Intl Ostomy Assn (IOA); Eur Ostomy Assn (EOA)
- M 10,000 i, 25 f
- ¶ ia Jnl - 4; ftm.   The Ostomy Book; £10.
  The ia Journal, omnibus edition [Hbk]; £3.75.
  Leaflets on various aspects of ileostomy; free.

IBI (Independent Broadcasters of Ireland)
- IRL c/o Limerick Live 95FM, Richmond Court, Dock Rd, LIMERICK, Republic of Ireland.
  353 (61) 400195
  Chmn: David Tighe
- ○ *T
- × 2002 (June) Association of Independent Radio Stations

IBS Network   1991
- ■ Unit 5 / 53 Mowbray St, SHEFFIELD, S Yorks, S3 8EN.   (hq)
  0114-272 3253
  email info@ibsnetwork.org.uk
  http://www.ibsnetwork.org.uk
  Sec: P J Nunn
- ▲ Company Limited by Guarantee; Registered Charity
- ○ *K, *M, *W; a self-help organisation for people with irritable bowel syndrome
- Gp Local self-help; Befriender/penpal scheme; Media list; Reviewer list
- ● Conf - ET - Res - Exhib - Comp - Inf
- < Nat Coun Voluntary Orgs (NCVO); Long-term Medical Conditions Alliance (LMCA); Patients Forum
- M 3,000 i, 10 f, 18 org, UK / 50 i, o'seas
- ¶ Gut Reaction - 4; ftm only.   Factsheets; ftm, £1 each nm.
  [back copies of Gut Reaction; £2.50 m, £5 nm].

ICC United Kingdom
  see **International Chamber of Commerce - UK National Committee**

Ice Cream Alliance Ltd   (ICA)   1945
- ■ 3 Melbourne Court, Pride Park, DERBY, DE24 8LZ.   (hq)
  01332 203333   fax 01332 203420
  email info@ice-cream.org   http://www.ice-cream.org
  Chief Exec: Mark Gossage
- ▲ Company Limited by Guarantee
- Br 10
- ○ *T; to protect, inform & represent the UK ice cream industry
- ● Conf - Mtgs - Res - Exhib - Comp - Inf - Lib - PL - VE - LG
- M 800 i, f, 1 org, UK / 100 i, f & org, o'seas
- ¶ Ice Cream - 11; £110 m.

Ice Cream Federation
  a group of the **Food & Drink Federation**

Ice Hockey Players Association   (IHPA(BGB))   1993
- ■ 25 Caxton Ave, Coombelands, ADDLESTONE, Surrey, KT15 1LJ.   (execdir/p)
  01932 843660   fax 01932 844401
  email ihpa.gb@virgin.netM   http://www.ihpa.co.uk
  Exec Dir: Mrs Joanne Collins
- ▲ Un-incorporated Society
- ○ *P, *S, *U; for professional ice-hockey players
- ● ET - Empl - LG
- < Intl Ice Hockey Players Assn (IIHPA); Inst of Profl Sport (IPS); Central Coun for Physical Recreation (CCPR)
- M 600 i, UK / 50 i, o'seas
- ¶ NL - 4; free.

Ice Hockey UK   (IHUK)   1991
- NR Berkeley House, 18-24 High St, EDGWARE, Middx, HA8 7RP. (hq)
  020 8732 4505   fax 020 8952 9515
  http://www.icehockeyuk.co.uk
- ▲ Company Limited by Guarantee
- ○ *S; national governing body for the sport of ice hockey
- Gp Training; Officials; Juniors; National team; Under 18; Under 20; Women; Senior men
- ● ET - Exam - Comp - Inf - PL - LG
- < Intl Ice Hockey Fedn; Brit Olympic Assn; UK Sport; Cent Coun for Physical Recreation (CCPR); English / Scottish Ice Hockey Assn(s)
- M 10,000 i, 65 clubs, 3 regions
- ¶ Weekly Media Services; m only.
  Ice Hockey Annual - 1.
- × 1999 (1 July) British Ice Hockey Association

Icelandic Horse Society of Great Britain Ltd   (IHSGB)   1986
- ■ 111 Old Hills, Callow End, WORCESTER, WR2 4TQ.
  (chmn/p)
  01324 411090
  http://www.ihsgb.co.uk
  Chmn: Ian Pugh,   Sec: Heather Dunn
- ▲ Registered Charity
- ○ *B; to encourage, promote & improve the breeding & use of the Icelandic horse
- Gp Breeding; Sports; Youth
- ● Conf - Mtgs - ET - Exhib - Comp - EXpt - Inf - Lib - VE
- < Intl Fedn of Icelandic Horse Assns (FEIF)
- M 300 i
- ¶ Sleipnir (Jnl) - 6; £28 yr m.

ICHCA International Ltd   (ICHCA)   2003
- NR 85 Western Rd (suite 2), ROMFORD, Essex, RM1 3LS.   (hq)
  01708 735295
  Co Sec: Mrs Rosemary Neilson
- ▲ Company Limited by Guarantee
- ○ *T; to promote efficient & economic movement of goods from origin to destination by air, rail, road & sea
- × 2003 International Cargo Handling Co-ordination Association

ICOM Energy Association (ICOM) 2004

■ 36 Holly Walk, LEAMINGTON SPA, Warks, CV32 4LY.   (hq)
  01926 463940   fax 01926 423284
  email petermccree@icomenergyassociation.org.uk
  http://www.bcema.co.uk
  Chief Exec: Peter McCree
▲ Company Limited by Guarantee
○ *T; manufacturers & distributors of combustion equipment
  including boilers, burners, air heaters, radiant heaters,
  controls
Gp Air heaters; Boilers (commercial); Boilers (industrial process);
  Burners; Controls; Radiant heaters; Water heaters
● Mtgs - Stat - LG
M 44 f
✕ 2004 (May) British Combustion Equipment Manufacturers
  Association

ICSA - Irish Cattle & Sheep Farmers Association   (ICSA)

IRL 9 Lyster House, PORTLAOISE, Co Laois, Republic of Ireland.
  (hq)
  353 (57) 866 2120   fax 353 (57) 866 2121
  email info@icsaireland.com
  http://www.icsaireland.com
  Gen Sec: Eddie Punch
○ *F

ICT Ireland (ICT)

IRL Confederation House, 84-86 Lower Baggot St, DUBLIN 2,
  Republic of Ireland.
  353 (1) 605 1527   fax 353 (1) 638 1527
  email info@ictireland.ie
  Dir: Kathryn Raleigh
○ *T; to represent companies in the information &
  communications technology sector
< IBEC
M c 1,000 f

Ideas UK - UK Association of Suggestion Schemes   1987

NR 52 Peveril Bank, Dawley Bank, TELFORD, Shropshire,
  TF4 2BZ.   (hq)
  0870 902 1658   fax 0870 902 1658
  email enquiries@ideasuk.com   http://www.ideasuk.com
  Contact: Steve Procter
▲ Company Limited by Guarantee; Registered Charity
○ *K; to promote the benefits of suggestion schemes to industry,
  commerce & the public sector
Gp Sectors: Financial services, Utilities, Government depts
● Conf - Mtgs - ET - Comp - Stat - Inf
M i, f, government depts
¶ News - 4;   LM;   Annual Survey; all ftm only.
  Suggestion Schemes: the management tool of the 90's (1995).

IGA-UK (IGA) 1994

■ Stonedge, Dunkerton, BATH, Somerset, BA2 8AS.   (hsb)
  01761 437809   fax 01761 432572
  email mb@graphology.org.uk
  http://www.graphology.org.uk
  Principal: Lawrence Warner,   Hon Sec: Martin Baker
▲ Company Limited by Guarantee
Br 2
○ *P; personality assessment through handwriting analysis; tuition
  in such assessment
● Conf - ET - Exam - Res - SG
M 180 i, UK / 20 i, o'seas
¶ The International Graphologist - 4; ftm, £20 nm.

Ileostomy & Internal Pouch Support Group
  see ia: the Ileostomy & Internal Pouch Support Group

Imaginative Book Illustration Society (IBIS) 1995

NR 434 Fulham Palace Rd, LONDON, SW6 6HX.   (hsp)
  020 7381 9113   fax 020 7381 6499
  http://www.bookillustration.org
  Hon Sec: Robin Greer
○ *A; 'to study & research imaginatively illustrated books, mainly
  in the English language'
● Conf - Mtgs - Exhib
M 200 i, 80 f, UK / 80 i, 20 f, o'seas
¶ IBIS Studies - 3.
  IBIS Jnl - 2 yrly.

Imaging Products Group
  on 10 January 2002 merged with the British Imaging & Photographic
  Association, the British Photographic Enterprise Group, the British
  Photographic & Imaging Association & the Photographic Waste
  Management Association to form the **Photo Imaging Council**

Immigration Law Practitioners Association   (ILPA)

■ Lindsey House, 40-42 Charterhouse St, LONDON,
  EC1M 6JN.   (hq)
  020 7251 8383   fax 020 7251 8384
  email info@ilpa.org.uk   http://www.ilpa.org.uk
  Gen Sec: Susan Lowlands
▲ Company Limited by Guarantee
○ *P
● Conf - Mtgs - ET - Res - LG
M 589 i, 398 f, 125 org
¶ [on website}

Imperial Society of Knights Bachelor (ISKB) 1908

■ 1 Throgmorton Avenue, LONDON, EC2N 2BY.   (hq)
  020 7374 8974   fax 020 7374 8968
  email iskb99@supanet.com
  Clerk to the Council: Richard L Jenkins
▲ Registered Charity
○ *W; 'participation by its members in the UK & Commonwealth
  in charitable work compatible with upholding the status &
  dignity of Knights Bachelor'
● Mtgs - Inf - Lib - Annual service of dedication
¶ Chivalry - 1/2; free.
  The Story of the Knights Bachelor; ftm.

Imperial Society of Teachers of Dancing (ISTD) 1904

NR Imperial House, 22-26 Paul St, LONDON, EC2A 4QE.   (hq)
  020 7377 1577
  Chief Exec: Jon Singleton
▲ Registered Charity
Br 10; 37 countries o'seas
○ *D, *P; professional society for teachers of dancing & an
  examination board
Gp Ballroom; Latin-American; Sequence; Classical Greek dance;
  Imperial Ballet; Modern; Tap; National dance; Scottish
  dance; Disco; Freestyle; Rock'n'Roll; Cecchetti ballet; Jazz;
  Dance research; Natural movement
● Conf - Mtgs - ET - Exam - Res - Exhib - Comp - Inf - Lib
< Brit Coun of Ballroom Dancing; Coun for Dance Educ &
  Training; CCPR (movement & dance divn)
M 7,000 i, UK / 2,900 i, o'seas
¶ Dance - 6; ftm only.

Implanted Defibrillator Association of Scotland   (IDAS) 1994

■ 10 Selkirk Ave, PAISLEY, PA2 9JF.   (chmn/p)
  01505 813995
  email hanheart@aol.com
  http://www.defib-scotland.com
  Hon Sec: Michael Hanley
▲ Registered Charity
○ *W; self-help group providing information & advice to people
  having an implanted defibrillator, or those about to have one
  implanted
● Mtgs - Inf - LG
M 157 i
¶ Vital Spark - 4; ftm only.

Imported Tobacco Products Advisory Council (ITPAC) 1974
- ■ Rondle Wood House, Milland, LIPHOOK, Hants, GU30 7LA. (hsp)
  0790 019 7888   fax 0173 082 1397
  email wyndham@carverw.com
  Sec-Gen: Wyndham H Carver
- ▲ Un-incorporated Society
- ○ *T; to represent the interests of importers of cigars, tobaccos & cigarettes to government & other relevant bodies; to provide inforamtion on tobacco & the industry
- ● Mtgs - Res - Inf - LG
- M 11 f, UK / 1 f, o'seas

Imported Tyre Manufacturers' Association (ITMA) 1979
- ■ 5a Pindock Mews, LONDON, W9 2PY. (hsp)
  020 7289 1043   fax 020 7286 9859
  email prt@itma1.freeserve.co.uk
  Dir: Peter Taylor
- ▲ Company Limited by Guarantee
- ○ *T; for tyre importers & manufacturers in the UK
- ● Mtgs - Stat - Inf - LG
- < Eur Tyre Recycling Assn (ETRA); Tyre Ind Coun (TIC); Tyre Ind Fedn (TIF)
- M 20 f

Impotence Association
   2002-3 **Sexual Dysfunction Association**

INCA - Institute for Numerical Computation & Analysis (INCA) 1980
- IRL 19 Silchester Rd, DÚN LAOGHAIRE, Co Dublin, Republic of Ireland.
  353 (1) 402 8535   fax 353 (1) 402 8540
  email jm@incaireland.org
  Sec: D Herlihy
- ○ *Q

Incentive Travel & Meetings Association
   2005 merged with the Corporate Event Association to form **Eventia**

Incontact (INCONTACT) 1989
- ■ United House, North Rd, LONDON, N7 9DP. (hq)
  0870 770 3246   fax 0870 770 3249
  email info@incontact.org   http://www.incontact.org
  Exec Dir: Lesley Woolnough
- ▲ Company Limited by Guarantee; Registered Charity
- Br 3
- ○ *G, *W; to provide information & support to people with bladder & bowel problems &/or diverticular disease
- ● Conf - Mtgs - ET - Inf
- < UK Continence Alliance (UKCA)
- M 14, 785 i
- ¶ Incontact - 4; free.

Incorporated Association of Organists (IAO) 1913
- ■ 17 Woodland Rd, Northfield, BIRMINGHAM, B31 2HU. (hsp)
  0121-475 4408   fax 0121-475 4408
  http://www.iao.org.uk
  Chief Exec: John Stormont
- ▲ Registered Charity
- Br 82; 10 (inc Australia, N Zealand, S Africa)
- ○ *D, *E; to promote the education & enjoyment of all who love the (pipe) organ & its music, players & listeners alike; to encourage training & education to improve standards at all levels
- ● Conf - Mtgs - ET
- M 6,000 i, UK / 1,000 i, o'seas
- ¶ Organists' Review - 4; £3.75 m, £5.25 nm.
  Piping the News - 4; ftm.

Incorporated Association of Preparatory Schools (IAPS) 1892
- ■ 11 Waterloo Place, ROYAL LEAMINGTON SPA, Warks, CV32 5LA. (hq)
  01926 887833   fax 01926 888014
  email hq@iaps.org.uk   http://www.iaps.org.uk
  Gen Sec: J H Morris
- ▲ Company Limited by Guarantee
- ○ *E, *P; 'independent education of boys & girls (up to 13) for entrance to independent secondary schools'
- ● Conf - Mtgs - ET
- < Independent Schools Coun
- M 535 schools, UK / 35 schools, o'seas
- ¶ Independent Schools Ybk.   Prep School Magazine.

Incorporated Guild of Hairdressers, Wigmakers & Perfumers 1882
- ■ Archway House, Langdale Rd, BARNSLEY, S Yorks, S71 1AQ. (hq)
  01226 786555   fax 01226 786555
  email patterson-a@btconnect.com
  Master: Keith Reeve
- ▲ Company Limited by Guarantee
- ○ *P; to promote & advise in the hairdressing industry
- ● Conf - Mtgs - Exam - Comp - Inf - LG
- M 580 i
- ¶ NL - 4;   AR - 1; ftm only.

Incorporated National Association of British & Irish Millers Ltd (NABIM) 1878
- NR 21 Arlington St, LONDON, SW1A 1RN. (hq)
  020 7493 2521
  Sec: N F Bennett
- ▲ Company Limited by Guarantee
- ○ *T; for UK flour millers
- ● Conf - Mtgs - ET - Exam - Stat - Inf - LG
- M 32 f
- ¶ Facts & Figures - 1; ftm.

Incorporated Phonographic Society (IPS) 1872
- ■ c/o The Bishopsgate Institute, 230 Bishopsgate, London, EC2M 4QH. (mtgs)
  020 8907 8249   fax 020 8907 5820
  http://www.the-ips.org.uk address
  Gen Admin: Mary Sorene
- ▲ Company Limited by Guarantee
- ○ *P; to maximise members' skill in all systems of shorthand & typewriting schools
- Gp Reporters; Secretaries; Teachers of secretarial skills; Shorthand users
- ● Mtgs - Exam - SG - Inf
- M 250 i, UK / 50 i, o'seas
- ¶ IPS Jnl - 4; ftm, £5 yr nm.

Incorporated Society of British Advertisers Ltd (ISBA) 1900
- ■ Langham House, 1B Portland Place, LONDON, W1B 1PN. (hq)
  020 7291 9020   fax 020 7291 9030
  email info@isba.org.uk   http://www.isba.org.uk
  Dir Gen: Malcolm Earnshaw
- ▲ Company Limited by Guarantee
- ○ *T; to represent the collective interests of British advertisers to government, regulators & the media; to provide expert advice & guidance on advertising effectively & efficiently
- ● Conf - Mtgs - Inf - LG
- < Wld Fedn of Advertisers; Advertising Assn
- M 400 f
- ¶ AR - 1; free.

Incorporated Society of Musicians (ISM) 1882

■ 10 Stratford Place, LONDON, W1C 1BA. (hq)
  020 7629 4413   fax 020 7408 1538
  email membership@ism.org   http://www.ism.org
  Chief Exec: Neil Hoyle
▲ Company Limited by Guarantee
○ *P; to promote the art of music; to maintain the honour &
  interests of the music profession
Gp Professional private music teachers; Performers & composers;
  Musicians in education
● Conf - Mtgs - ET - LG
M 4,800 i, 120 f, UK
¶ Music Jnl - 12; ftm, £25 nm.
  Register of Performers & Composers - 1; ftm, £13 nm.
  Register of Professional Private Music Teachers - 1; ftm, £16 nm.
  Register of Musicians in Education - 1; ftm, £10 nm.
  Ybk (incl LM) - 1; ftm, £26 nm.   AR - 1; free.
  Publications list available.

Incorporated Society of Organ Builders (ISOB) 1947

NR Smithy Steads, Cragg Vale, HEBDEN BRIDGE, W Yorks,
  HX7 5SQ. (sp/b)
  email dmin@isob.co.uk   http://www.isob.co.uk
○ *P, *T
● Conf - Mtgs - Inf - VE
M 190 i, UK / 9 i, o'seas
¶ Jnl - irreg.   LM - 1; free.   AR; ftm only.

Incorporated Society for Psychical Research (SPR) 1882

NR 49 Marloes Rd, LONDON, W8 6LA. (hq)
  020 7937 8984
  http://www.spr.ac.uk
  Sec: Peter M Johnson
▲ Company Limited by Guarantee; Registered Charity
○ *Q; 'to further systematic, scientific investigation of certain
  paranormal phenomena which are apparently inexplicable
  on any generally recognised hypothesis - telepathy & all
  forms of paranormal cognition, poltergeists, apparitions,
  alleged movement of objects without contact; any other
  phenomena which appear to be paranormal. The Society
  does not hold or express views'
Gp ESP C'ee; Physical phenomena; Research advisory; Publications
● Conf - Lectures - Res - Inf - Lib
M 1,100 i
¶ Jnl - 4.   Proceedings - irreg.
  Paranormal Review Magazine - 4.

Incorporated Society of Registered Naturopaths (ISRN) 1934

NR The Coach House, 70 Kingston Avenue, EDINBURGH,
  EH16 5HW. (hq)
  0131-664 3435
▲ Company Limited by Guarantee
○ *P; alternative therapy offering naturopathic, dietary &
  manipulative advice & therapy
● Conf - ET - Exam
< Brit Naturopathic Assn
M 40 i, UK / 5 i, o'seas
¶ Publications list available.

Incorporation of Plastic Window Fabricators & Installers (IPWFI) 1991

■ Apex House - 172 Blackmoorfoot Rd, Crosland Moor,
  HUDDERSFIELD, W Yorks, HD4 5RE. (hq)
  01484 303900   fax 01484 462463
  email ipwfi@aol.co.uk   http://www.ipwfi.co.uk
  Dir: John Heward
▲ Company Limited by Guarantee
○ *T; for the window industry
Gp Insurance to the consumer of window companies
● Conf - Exhib
M 740 i

Independent Association of Telecommunications Users Ltd
  see **Telecommunications Users' Association (Independent
  Association of Telecommunications Users)**

Independent Banking Advisory Service (IBAS) 1993

■ North View, North Fen, Somersham, HUNTINGDON, Cambs,
  PE28 3WD. (hq)
  01487 843444   fax 01487 740607
  email helpdesk@ibas.co.uk   http://www.ibas.co.uk
  Exec Officer: Sara Cummings
▲ Un-incorporated Society
○ *K; independent advice & case investigation on all matters
  relating to banking, mortgage shortfall, & banking
  procedures & charging structures
● Res - Stat - Inf - LG
M [confidential]

Independent Battery Distributors Association (IBDA) 1991

■ 3 Blakeley Dene, Raby Mere, WIRRAL, Cheshire, CH63 0QE.
  (gsp)
  0151-334 2040   fax 0151-334 2040
  email godfreyferris@lineone.net   http://www.ibda.co.uk
  Gen Sec: J Godfrey Ferris
▲ Company Limited by Guarantee
○ *T; for independent battery distributors in the UK
● Conf - Mtgs - ET - Inf - LG
< Automotive Aftermarket Liaison Gp; Soc of Motor Mfrs &
  Traders (SMMT)
M 2 i, 24 f, 6 mfrs
¶ IBDA NL - 4;   Information Booklets; all ftm only.
  LM - 1; ftm, £10 nm.   Battery User Guides; ftm, £1 nm.
  AR; free.

Independent Broadcasters of Ireland
  see **IBI (Independent Broadcasters Ireland)**

Independent Business League (IBL) 1990

NR Marlborough House (suite 11), 159 High St, WEALDSTONE,
  Middx, HA3 5DX. (hq)
  020 8427 0813   fax 020 8427 0523
▲ Limited Company
○ *K; to promote, protect & reduce the costs to businesses within
  the UK
Gp Computers; Jewellers; Restaurants; Shops
● Inf - Status checks - Legal advice - Debt recovery - Business
  review - Discounts available on group purchase schemes
¶ NL - 2; ftm only.

Independent Children's Homes Association (ICHAC) 2004

■ PO Box 15, WREXHAM, Denbighshire, LL13 0WT. (hq)
  01948 830008   fax 01948 830008
  email admin@icha.org.uk   http://www.icha.org.uk
  Sec: Christine Hamer
○ *W; for all independent providers of social care for children;
  works to raise professional standards through shared work
  experience
● ET - Res - Exhib - SG - Stat
M [not stated]
¶ Ybk - 1.
✕ 2004 National Association of Independent Resources for
  Children

Independent Consultants Consortium Ltd (ICON) 1980

■ 101 Amersham Rd, BEACONSFIELD, Bucks, HP9 2EH. (hsp)
  01494 673581   fax 01494 670083
  email icon@chiltime.co.uk   http://www.icon.uk.net
  Hon Sec: John Holroyd
▲ Un-incorporated Society
Br 2
○ *P, *T; a national umbrella for independent management
  consultants & consultancies
Gp 3 regional groups
● Conf - ET - Inf
M 33 f
¶ ICON NL - 2; free.

Independent Family Brewers of Britain (IFBB) 1993
NR The Ram Brewery, Wandsworth, LONDON, SW18 4JD. (asa)
   Sec: Torquil Sligo-Young
▲ Company Limited by Guarantee
○ *N, *T; to represent nationally & internationally the common
   interests of Britain's independent family-controlled brewers;
   to protect traditional brewery tenancies (the Tied House
   system) from potential EC legislation
< all members are also members of the British Beer & Pub Assn
M f

Independent Federation of Nursing in Scotland (IFON) 1995
NR Huntershill Village, 102 Crowhill Rd, Bishopbriggs, GLASGOW,
   G64 1RP. (hq)
   0141-772 9222   fax 0141-762 3776
   email ifoninscotland@aol.com   http://www.ifon.org
   Gen Sec: Mrs Irenee F O'Neill
Br 6
○ *U; 'is a nursing union with a solely Scottish identity, run by
   health care professionals for health care professionals'
Gp Health care professionals: Un-qualified, Qualified
● Conf - ET - Exhib - Empl
M i
¶ Nursing Scotland - 6; ftm only.

Independent Fire Engineering & Distributors Association
NR Unit 903 Solent Business Centre, Millbrook Rd West, Millbrook,
   SOUTHAMPTON, Hants, SO15 0HW.
   023 8051 3326
○ *T

Independent Food Retailers Confederation
   since 2003 **Independent Retailers Confederation**

Independent Footwear Retailers' Association (IFRA) 1950
■ 3 Burystead Place, WELLINGBOROUGH, Northants, NN8 1AH.
   01933 272999   fax 01933 225009
   email ifra@britfoot.com   http://www.shoeshop.org.uk
   Sec: Niall Campbell
○ *T
● Conf - Mtgs - ET - Exhib - SG - Stat - Lib - VE - Empl
< Footwear Distbrs' Fedn; Soc Shoe Fitters; Nat Shoe Retailers'
   Assn (USA)
M 250 f
¶ NL - 4; ftm only.

Independent Games Developers Trade Association
   see **TIGA: the Independent Games Developers Trade
   Association**

Independent Garage Association
   2000-2 became the Independent Garage Division of the **Retail
   Motor Industry Federation**

Independent Group of Analytical Psychologists (IGAP)
■ PO Box 22343, LONDON, W13 8GP. (hsp)
   020 8933 0353   fax 020 8933 0645
   email office@igap.co.uk   http://www.igap.co.uk
   Sec: Clare Craig
▲ Company Limited by Guarantee; Registered Charity
○ *P; Jungian analysis
● ET - SG
M 49 i, UK / 9 i, o'seas

Independent Healthcare Association
   since 2004 **English Community Care Association**

Independent Midwives' Association (IMA) 1985
■ 89 Green Lane, FARNCOMBE, Surrey, GU7 3TB. (hsp)
   01483 425833
   http://www.independentmidwives.org.uk
   Sec: Andrya Prescott
○ *P; support group for midwives working independently, giving
   women informed choices in childbirth, home, hospital or
   water births
● Mtgs - Exhib - SG - Stat - Inf
< Intl Confedn of Midwives; Assn of Radical Midwives
M 88 i
¶ Register of Independent Midwives - 2 yrly; ftm, send sae nm.

Independent Motor Trade Factors Association Ltd (IFA) 1977
NR 9 Church St, ST AUSTELL, Cornwall, PL25 4AT. (hq)
   01726 70440
   Sec: Gretal Taylor
○ *T
M f

Independent Pilots Association (IPA) 1992
■ The Priory, HAYWARDS HEATH, W Sussex, RH16 3LB. (hq)
   01444 441149   fax 01444 441192
   email office@ipapilot.com   http://www.ipapilot.com
   Sec: Capt Noel Baker
▲ Company Limited by Guarantee
Br 1
○ *P; for aviation pilots & flight engineers
● Conf - Mtgs - ET - Res - Inf - LG
> Indep Pilots Fedn
M 1,230 i, UK / 330 i, o'seas
¶ Skypointer - 6; ftm only.

Independent Print Industries Association (IPIA) 1990
■ Brooklyn House, 44 Brook St, Shepshed, LOUGHBOROUGH,
   Leics, LE12 9RG. (hq)
   01509 600242   fax 01509 600396
   email info@ipia.org.uk   http://www.ipia.org.uk
   Chief Exec: David Sewell
▲ Un-incorporated Society
○ *T; for print managers, brokers, distributors, & outsourcers of
   print as well as trade manufacturers of print & print related
   products & services
Gp Trade printers; Print managers; Brokers; Distributors &
   outsourcers; Software suppliers to the printing industry;
   Suppliers of office & computer consumables; Papermakers &
   merchants
● Conf - Mtgs - ET - Exhib - Inf
< Document Mgt Inds Assn (DMIA)(USA)
M 165 f, UK / 4 f, o'seas
¶ Innovation in Print - 6; free.

Independent Publishers Advisory Council
   a group of the **Periodical Publishers Association**

Independent Publishers Guild (IPG) 1962
NR PO Box 93, ROYSTON, Herts, SG8 5GH. (dir/b)
   01763 247014   fax 01763 246293
   email info@ipg.uk.com   http://www.ipg.uk.com
   Exec Dir: Bridget Shine
▲ Company Limited by Guarantee
○ *T; 'providing a forum for the exchange of ideas & information'
   for directors of independent publishing companies
● Conf - Mtgs - Exhib - Inf - VE - Book industry communication
< National Book Committee
M 419 f
¶ email bulletin- 52; ftm only.

© CBD Research Ltd · Beckenham · BR3 5JS · Tel 020 8650 7745 · Fax 020 8650 0768 · E-mail cbd@cbdresearch.com · www.cbdresearch.com

Independent Retailers Confederation (IRC) 1991
- ■ 21 Baldock St, WARE, Herts, SG12 9DH. (hsb)
  01920 468061 fax 01920 461632
- ○ *N, *T; a group of independent trade associations which meet to exchange information & views on matters affecting small independent retailers
- M 12 trade associations
- ✕ 2003 Independent Food Retailers Confederation

Independent Safety Consultants Association (ISCA) 1985
- ■ PO Box 5940, HINCKLEY, Leics, LE10 1WA. (hsb)
  email services@isca.org.uk http://www.isca.org.uk
  Sec: Mrs Caroline Head, Chmn: Howard Hall
- ▲ Un-incorporated Society
- ○ *P, *T; for safety consultancies giving safety advice & guidance; some consultancies give specialist help for asbestos, construction etc
- ● Mtgs
- M 5 i, 11 f

Independent Schools Association (ISA) 1895
- NR Boys' British School, East St, SAFFRON WALDEN, Essex, CB10 1LS. (hq)
  01799 523619
  Gen Sec: T M Ham
- ▲ Company Limited by Guarantee
- ○ *E; promotion of interests of independent schools
- ● Conf - Mtgs - Comp - SG - Inf
- < Indep Schools Jt Coun; ISIS
- M 300 i (heads of independent schools), UK / 3 i, o'seas
- ¶ Directory - 1.

Independent Schools' Bursars Association (ISBA) 1932
- NR Unit 11-12 Manor Farm, Cliddesden, BASINGSTOKE, Hants, RG25 2JB. (hq)
  01256 330369 fax 01256 330376
  email office@theisba.org http://www.theisba.org.uk
  Gen Sec: J R B Cook
- ▲ Registered Charity
- ○ *P; the advancement of education by the promotion of efficient & effective administration & ancillary services at independent schools
- ● Conf - Mtgs - ET - SG - Inf
- < Indep Schools Coun (ISC)
- M 852 schools, UK / 30 schools, o'seas
- ¶ The Bursar's Review - 3; Bulletin (NL) - 10; both ftm only.

Independent Schools Council (ISC) 1974
- NR St Vincent House, 30 Orange St, LONDON, WC2H 7HH. (hq)
  020 7766 7070 fax 020 7766 7071
  email isc@iscis.uk.net http://www.iscis.uk.net
  Sec: Jonathan Shephard
- ▲ Company Limited by Guarantee
- ○ *E, *N; the policy & management of independent education
- ● ET
- M 1,300 schools within 7 orgs:
  Association of Governing Bodies of Independent Schools
  Girls' Schools Association
  Headmasters' & Headmistresses' Conference
  Incorporated Association of Preparatory Schools
  Independent Schools Association
  Independent Schools Bursars' Association
  Society of Headmasters & Headmistresses of Independent Schools

Independent Schools Council Information Service (ISCIS) 1972
- NR 14 Buckingham Palace Rd, LONDON, SW1W 0QP. (hq)
  020 7798 1560
  Nat Dir: David Woodhead
- ▲ Company Limited by Guarantee
- Br 8
- ○ *G; to provide information to parents, the public, the media, parliamentarians, government departments & opinion formers about independent schools in the UK, in particular those in membership of the Independent Schools Council
- ● Conf - Mtgs - ET - Res - Stat - Expt - Expt - Inf - LG
- < Indep Schools Coun (ISC)
- M 1,300 schools
- ¶ The ISCIS Guide - 1; free.
  The ISCIS Guide (CD-ROM) - 1; £5.99 m, £6.99 nm.
  The ISCIS Annual Census - 1; £12 m, £15 nm.

Independent Sports Retailers Association
  since 2006 **Sports Manufacturers & Retailers Trade Association**

Independent Theatre Council (Ltd) (ITC) 1974
- ■ 12 The Leathermarket, Weston St, LONDON, SE1 3ER. (hq)
  020 7403 1727 fax 020 7403 1745
  email admin@itc-arts.org http://www.itc-arts.org
  Chief Exec: Charlotte Jones
- ▲ Company Limited by Guarantee
- ○ *T; management association for the performing arts
- ● Conf - ET - Advice service & networking for members
- M 644 i, f & org
- ¶ NL - 6; ftm only. AR - 1.
  The ITC Practical Guide for Writers & Companies; £5.
  Working in Schools; £5.
  Equal Opportunities - policy into practice; £5 each (£12 the set):
    Race; Disability; Sexuality; Gender.

Independent Training Standards Scheme & Register (ITSSAR) 1990
- ■ Armstrong House, 28 Broad St, WOKINGHAM, Berks, RG40 1AB. (hq)
  0118-989 3229
  Chmn: Lynda Dobson
- ▲ Company Limited by Guarantee
- ○ *E; fork lift truck accreditation scheme
- ● ET
- M 3,000 i, 200 f

Independent Turner Society 1988
- ■ Turner House, 153 Cromwell Road, LONDON, SW5 0TQ.
  020 7373 5560 fax 020 7373 5560
  email selbywhittingham@hotmail.com
  http://www.jmwturner.org
  Hon Sec: Dr Selby Whittingham
- ▲ Un-incorporated Society
- ○ *K; campaigning for a proper Turner gallery for J M W Turner's bequest
- ● Campaigning
- M [not stated]
- ¶ Jnl - irreg; NL - 2/3; both ftm only.

Independent Tyre Distributors Network
- NR Euroteam House, East St, OKEHAMPTON, Devon, EX20 1AS.
  01837 54243 fax 01837 54043
  Dir: Mrs J Dawe
- ○ *T

Independent Valuers Association
- NR PO Box 12, PAIGNTON, Devon, TQ3 1ZA. (hsp)
  01803 872265
  Founder: Bill Simpson
- ○ *P; for valuers of antiques & works of art & security advisers

Independent Warranty Association   (IWA)   1990

NR   Spring House, 51 Spring Gardens, NORTHAMPTON,
          NN1 1LX.   (hq)
○   *T; to provide insurance protection for home improvements to
          members
M   f

Independent Waste Paper Processors Association   (IWPPA)
1976

NR   Heritage House, Vicar Lane, DAVENTRY, Northants,
          NN11 4GD.   (hq)
          01327 703223
       Sec: M J Limb
○   *T
●   Mtgs - Expt - LG
M   83 f, UK / 4 f, o'seas

Indian Military Historical Society   (IMHS)   1983

■   33 High St, Tilbrook, HUNTINGDON, Cambs, PE28 0JP.   (hsp)
          01480 860437
          email imhs@zetnet.co.uk
       Hon Sec: A N McClenaghan
▲   Un-incorporated Society
○   *G; to act as a forum for the dissemination of knowledge of
          uniforms, medals, badges, buttons & other militaria, as well
          as the history of service in India both before & after
          independence (India, Pakistan & Bangladesh)
●   Res - Inf
M   190 i, 5 org, UK / 80 i, 2 org, o'seas
¶   Durbar - 4; ftm only.

Industrial Agents Society   (IAS)   1975

NR   c/o Mark Webster, Cushman & Wakefield, 43-45 Portman
          Square, LONDON, W1A 3BG.   (chmn/b)
       Chmn: Mark Webster
▲   Un-incorporated Society
○   *P; commercial surveyors & agents whose principal business
          activity is wholly or mainly the buying, selling or development
          of business space, including industrial & warehouse property
●   Conf - Mtgs - VE
M   900 i
¶   NL - 2.   Members Directory - 1.

Industrial Common Ownership Movement Ltd
       2001 (December) merged with the Co-operative Union to form **Co-
       operatives UK Ltd**

Industrial Law Society

NR   18 Graysmead, SIBLE HEDINGHAM, Essex, CO9 3NY.
          01787 463838
○   *L, *P
●   [Hours 1000-1300]

Industrial Locomotive Society   (ILS)   1946

■   Topham, 14 Leigh Lane, Branshall, UTTOXETER, Staffs,
          ST14 5DN.   (hsp)
          email enquiries@industrial-loco.org.uk
          http://www.industrial-loco.org.uk
       Hon Sec: Allen Civil
▲   Un-incorporated Society
○   *G; historical research into railways other than main line
          railways (incl military railways & associated industrial
          archaeology)
●   Mtgs - Res - Lib - PL
M   210 i, 10 org, UK / 30 i, 4 org, o'seas
¶   The Industrial Locomotive - 4; ftm, £3 nm.

** Industrial Marketing Association
       Organisation lost: see Introduction paragraph 3

Industrial Packaging Association   (IPA)   2004

■   PO Box 110, KNARESBOROUGH, N Yorks, HG5 8ZX.   (ceo/b)
          0777 063 3320   fax 01423 867098
          email info@theipa.co.uk   http://www.theipa.co.uk
       Chief Exec: Phil Pease
▲   Un-incorporated Society
○   *T; for the industrial industry - kegs, drums, intermediate bulk
          containers (IBCs)
Gp   Steel / Plastic / Fibre drum manufacturing; IBC Manufacturing;
          Used container; Re-conditioning & recycling
●   Mtgs - ET - Inf
<   Intl Plastics Packaging (ICPP); Eur Steel Drum Mfrs (SEFA); Eur
          Plastics Packaging Assn (EUPC)
M   28 f, UK / 2 f, o'seas
×   2004 (Association of Drum Manufacturers
          (Federation of Drum Reconditioners
          (Rigid Intermediate Bulk Container Association

Industrial Participation Forum
       a group of the **Defence Manufacturers Association**

Industrial Railway Society   (IRS)   1949

NR   4 Fernbrook Drive, HARROW, Middx, HA2 7EB.   (hsp)
          email news@irsociety.co.uk   http://www.irsociety.co.uk
       Hon Sec: Edward Knotwell
▲   Un-incorporated Society
○   *G; study & record all aspects of industrial railways & their uses
Gp   Rail mounted cranes; Non-locomotive worked railway lines &
          small mines; Ex-British Rail locomotives engaged in industrial
          use; Tunnelling contractors using rail transport; Ministry of
          Defence railways; Coal-mining railways
●   Mtgs - Res - Lib - PL - VE (many visits take place abroad)
M   950 i, UK / 50 i, o'seas
¶   Industrial Railway Record - 4.
       Bulletin - 6.   Books.

Industrial Rope Access Trade Association   (IRATA)   1989

■   99 West St, FARNHAM, Surrey, GU9 7EN.   (asa)
          01252 739150   fax 01252 739140
          email info@irata.org   http://www.irata.org
       Sec: John G Fairley
▲   Company Limited by Guarantee
○   *T
●   Conf - Mtgs - ET - Exam - Inf - LG
M   24 i, 44 f, UK / 3 i, 16 f, o'seas
¶   Directory;   Brochure; both free.
       Guidelines: on the use of rope access methods for industrial
          purposes; £10 m, £45 nm.
       International Guidelines: on the use of rope access methods for
          industrial purposes; £10 m, £45 nm.
       General Requirements: for certification of personnel engaged in
          industrial rope access methods; £10 m, £45 nm.

Industrial Society
       in April 2002 the Society was reorganised & changed name to **Work
       Foundation**
       The training & development activity is now owned by Capita plc.

Industrial Tyre Association   (ITA)   1977

NR   33 Marshfield Way, BATH, BA1 6HD.   (sp)
          01225 420577
       Sec: Pul Hayward
▲   Un-incorporated Society
○   *T
●   Mtgs - SG - Stat - Inf
M   f
¶   Guidelines for Industrial Tyres.

**Industry Council for Packaging & the Environment   (Incpen)
1974**
- ■ Soane Point, 6-8 Market Place, READING, Berks, RG1 2EG.
  (hq)
  0118 925 5991
  http://www.incpen.org
- ▲ Company Limited by Guarantee
- ○ *T; to study the environmental & social impacts of packaging;
  members are international companies involved in all aspects
  of the distribution of packaged goods
- Gp Trade; Environment
- ● Conf - Mtgs - ET - Res - Exhib - Stat - Inf - LG
- < Eur Org for Packaging & the Envt (EUROPEN)
- M 25 f
- ¶ NL - 11; ftm only.
  Factsheets;   AR; both free.

Industry Research & Development Group
- IRL Confederation House, 84-86 Lower Baggot St, DUBLIN 2,
  Republic of Ireland.
  353 (1) 605 1608   fax 353 (1) 661 1095
  email irdg@iol.ie   http://www.irdg.ie
  Managing Dir: Dick Kavanagh
- ○ *T; Irish-owned & multinational companies from all
  manufacturing sectors
- < IBEC

Infant & Dietetic Foods Association   (IDFA)   1986
- ■ 6 Catherine St, LONDON, WC2B 5JJ.   (hq)
  020 7420 7112   fax 020 7836 0580
  email idfa@fdf.org.uk   http://www.idfa.org.uk
  Dir Gen: Roger Clarke
- ▲ Un-incorporated Society
- ○ *T; manufacturers & suppliers of dietetic & infant foods
- ● Mtgs - Inf - LG
- < Intl Soc for Dietetic Foods (ISDI); Assn of Infant & Dietetic Foods
  in the EEC (IDACE); Food & Drink Fedn
- M 14 f

Infection Control Nurses Association of GB   (ICNA)   1960
- ■ c/o Fitwise, Drumcross Hall, BATHGATE, W Lothian,
  EH48 4JT.   (asa)
  01506 811077   fax 01506 811477
  email info@fitwise.co.uk   http://www.icna.co.uk
  Hon Sec: Neil Wigglesworth
- ▲ Registered Charity
- Br 11
- ○ *P; infection control in hospital trusts, community trusts (NHS) &
  public health; the advancement of education in the art &
  science of infection control for the benefit of the whole
  community
- Gp Community infection control nurses network; Paediatric
  infection control special interest group; Mental health special
  interest network
- ● Conf - Mtgs - ET - Res - Exhib - SG - LG
- < Intl Fedn of Infection Control (IFIC); Assn for Profls in Infection
  Control & Epidemiology (APIC)(USA); Community & Hospital
  Infection Control Assn (CHICA)(Canada)
- M 1,002 i, 49 f, UK / 36 i, o'seas
- ¶ British Jnl of Infection Control - 4; ftm,
  prices on application nm.
  Infection Control Supplement - Nursing Times - 4; ftm only.
  ICNA News - 6;   AR; both ftm only.
  Glove Usage Guidelines; £20.   Hbk - 1; ftm, £10.95 nm.
  Guidelines for Hand Hygiene; £3.50.

Infertility Network UK
- NR Charter House, 43 St Leonard's Rd, BEXHILL-on-SEA, E Sussex,
  TN40 1JA.   (hq)
  01424 732402
  http://www.infertilitynetworkuk.com
- ▲ Company Limited by Guarantee; Registered Charity
- ○ *K, *W; to provide essential support services & information on
  developments in infertility research; to represent patients'
  views; to campaign to raise awareness of the impact of
  infertility & improve access to treatment
- ● Conf - Mtgs - ET - Res - Stat - Inf - LG
  Support line: 0870 118 8088
- M [not stated]
- ¶ Fact sheets.
  A Journey through Infertility (video).
- × 2003 (CHILD
  (Issue (the National Fertility Association) Ltd

Inflatable Play Manufacturers Association   (IPMA)   1990
- ■ Federation House, STONELEIGH PARK, Warks, CV8 2RF.
  024 7641 4999   fax 024 7641 4990
  Co Sec: Deborah Holt
- ▲ Company Limited by Guarantee
- ○ *T
- ● Mtgs - ET - Stat - Expt - Inf - LG
- M 15 f

Information Technology, Telecommunications & Electronics Association
see **Intellect, the Information Technology,
Telecommunications & Electronics Association**

Inland Shipping Group
a group of the **Inland Waterways Association**

Inland Waterways Association   (IWA)   1946
- NR PO Box 114, RICKMANSWORTH, Herts, WD3 1ZY.   (hq)
  01923 711114
  Exec Dir: Neil Edwards
- ▲ Company Limited by Guarantee; Registered Charity
- Br 35
- ○ *K; to ensure the restoration, conservation, retention &
  development of the navigable waterways of the British Isles &
  their fullest commercial & recreational use
- Gp Inland Shipping Group
- ● Conf - Mtgs - ET - Res - Exhib - Comp - SG - Stat - Inf - VE - LG
  - Conservation & restoration work
- M 18,000 i, 100 f, 200 org, UK / 300 i, f & org, o'seas
- ¶ Waterways - 3.   Inland Waterways Guide - 1.
  Wide variety of regional, local & specialist publications.

Inland Waterways Association of Ireland   1954
- IRL Ballymakenny, DROGHEDA, Co Louth, Republic of Ireland.
  http://www.iwai.ie
  Hon Sec: Carmel Meegan
- ○ *G

Inland Waterways Protection Society Ltd   (IWPS)   1958
- ■ Browside Farm, Mudhurst Lane, Lyme Handley,
  WHALEY BRIDGE, High Peak, Derbys, SK23 7BT.   (chmn/p)
  01663 732493   fax 01663 732895
  email ian@browside.co.uk   http://www.brocross.com/
  iwps/index.htm
  Chmn: Ian Edgar
- ▲ Company Limited by Guarantee; Registered Charity
- ○ *K; for the restoration, preservation & development of the
  inland waterways of Great Britain
- ● Waterway restoration & development (specifically the Bugsworth
  canal basin at the head of the Peak Forest Canal)
- M 300 i, 20 f, 10 org
- ¶ Onward - 2; ftm, £1.50 nm.   174 (NL) - 4; ftm, 50p nm.
  Note: 174 is the number of the last remaining Peak Forest
  Tramway wagon

Inn Sign Society (ISS) 1960

NR 9 Denmead Drive, Wednesfield, WOLVERHAMPTON, W Midlands, WV11 2QS. (hsp)
01902 721808
http://www.bjcurtis.force9.co.uk
Hon Sec: Alan Rose
▲ Un-incorporated Society
○ *G; the study of the inn sign (pub sign), its origin, history, the stories connected with individual signs
● Inf
M 360 i, 5 f, UK / 7 i, o'seas
¶ At the Sign of [...] - 4; ftm only.

Insolvency Lawyers Association (ILA) 1989

■ c/o Allen & Overy, 1 New Change, LONDON, EC4M 9QQ. (sb)
020 7330 2698 fax 020 7330 9999
email info@ilauk.com http://www.ilauk.com
Sec: Ian Field
▲ Company Limited bu Guarantee
○ *P; a special interest group providing a forum for lawyers specialising in insolvency administration
● Conf - Mtgs - ET - Inf - LG
M 291 i, 21 org, UK / 4 i, o'seas
¶ Insolvency Intelligence - 12;   Bulletins [email] - 26.

Insolvency Practitioners Association (IPA) 1961

■ 52-54 Gracechurch St, LONDON, EC3V 0EH. (hq)
020 7623 5108 fax 020 7623 5127
email secretariat@insolvency-practitioners.org.uk
http://www.ipa.uk.com
Chief Exec: N Sabin
○ *P; members act as trustees, liquidators, receivers, administrators etc
no further information supplied

Institiúid Bitheolaíochta na h'Éireann (Institute of Biology of Ireland) 1965

IRL c/o University College Dublin, Belfield, DUBLIN 4, Republic of Ireland.
email ibi@may.ie http://www.may.ie/ibi
Hon Sec: Norma Cahill
○ *P

Institiúid Ceimice na h'Éireann (Institute of Chemistry of Ireland) 1950

IRL PO Box 9322, Cardiff Lane, DUBLIN 2, Republic of Ireland.
email instchem@iol.ie
http://www.instituteofchemistry.org
Hon Sec: Dr J P Ryan
○ *L

INSTITUTE ...

Other than the bodies listed below, organisations entitled 'Institute' that have no voluntary membership structure but carry out serious research will be found in our publication
Centres, Bureaux & Research Institutes

** Institute of Account Executives & Book-keepers

Organisation lost: see Introduction paragraph 3

Institute of Accounting Technicians in Ireland (IATI)

IRL 83 Pembroke Rd, Ballsbridge, DUBLIN 4, Republic of Ireland.
353 (1) 637 7363 fax 353 (1) 637 7357
email info@iati.ie http://www.iati.ie
Sec: Shay Fleming
○ *P

Institute of Acoustics (IoA) 1974

■ 77a St Peter's St, ST ALBANS, Herts, AL1 3BN. (hq)
01727 848195 fax 01727 850553
email ioa@ioa.org.uk http://www.ioa.org.uk
Chief Exec: Kevin Macan-Lind
▲ Company Limited by Guarantee
Br 10
○ *L, *P; the art, science & technology of acoustics
Gp Acoustics: Building, Physical, Musical, Underwater
Noise: Electro, Environmental, Industrial, Speech
● Conf - Mtgs - ET - Exam - Exhib - Lib
< Intl Inst Noise Control - Engg (I-INCE); Intl Congress Acoustics (ICA); Eur Acoustics Assn (EAA)
M 2,600 i, 20 f, 30 org, UK / 300 i, o'seas
¶ Acoustics Bulletin - 6; ftm, £20 each nm.
Register of Members - 1; ftm, £10 nm.
Buyers Guide - 1; ftm; £15 nm.

Institute of Actuaries 1848

■ Staple Inn Hall, High Holborn, LONDON, WC1V 7QJ. (hq)
020 7632 2100 fax 020 7632 2111
email institute@actuaries.org.uk
http://www.actuaries.org.uk
Pres: Nicholas J Dumbreck
Sec-Gen: Caroline M Instance
▲ Incorporated by Royal Charter 1884
Br 2
○ *P; the controlling body (along with the Faculty of Actuaries in Edinburgh) for the actuarial profession
Gp Continuous mortality investigation;
Boards: Life (insurance), Pensions, General insurance, Finance investment & risk management, Education & continuing professional development
● Conf - Mtgs - ET - Exam - Res - Lib - Technical guidance - Issuance of practising certificates - The Education Executive, Careers & Library are at:
4 Worcester St, OXFORD, OX1 2AW. 01865 268200
< Intl Actuarial Assn
> Faculty of Actuaries in Scotland
M 10,270 i, UK / 5,067 i, o'seas
¶ British Actuarial Jnl - 5.
Annals of Actuarial Science - 2.
Manual of Actuarial Practice - updated.

Institute of Administrative Management (IAM) 1915

■ Caroline House, 55-57 High Holborn, LONDON, WC1V 6DX. (hq)
020 7841 1100 fax 020 7841 1119
email info@instam.org http://www.instam.org
Chief Exec: David Woodgate
▲ Registered Charity
○ *P; to promote & develop, for the public benefit, the science of administrative management in all branches
● Conf - ET - Exam - Res - Exhib - Stat - Inf
M 4,500 i, UK / 4,500 i, o'seas
¶ Manager: the British Jnl of Administrative Management - 6; ftm, £45 yr nm. AR - 1.
Publications list available.

Institute of Advanced Motorists Ltd (IAM) 1956

■ 510 Chiswick High Rd, LONDON, W4 5RG. (hq)
020 8996 9600 fax 020 8996 9601
email enquiries@iam.org.uk http://www.iam.org.uk
Chief Exec: C T Bullock
▲ Company Limited by Guarantee; Registered Charity
Br 208
○ *K; to make a major contribution to road safety through the skill, attitude & responsibility, shown by motorists & motorcyclists, in the test for membership
Gp IAM fleet training (for company personnel)
● Exam - IAM Fleet Training Ltd (for training of company personnel) - Advanced Driving (IAM Group Services Ltd)
M 112,000 i, UK / 1,000 i, o'seas
¶ Advanced Driving - 3; ftm.
How to be an Advanced Motorist;
How to be an Advanced Motorcyclist; both £7.99.

© CBD Research Ltd · Beckenham · BR3 5JS · Tel 020 8650 7745 · Fax 020 8650 0768 · E-mail cbd@cbdresearch.com · www.cbdresearch.com

Institute of Advertising Practitioners in Ireland   (IAPI)   1964

IRL   8 Upper Fitzwilliam St, DUBLIN 2, Republic of Ireland.
        353 (1) 676 5991   fax 353 (1) 661 4589
        email info@iapi.com   http://www.iapi.ie
        Chief Exec: Steve Shanahan
○   *P

** Institute for African Alternatives

       Organisation lost: see Introduction paragraph 3

**Institute of Agricultural Secretaries & Administrators   (IAgSA)
1967**

■   National Agricultural Centre, Stoneleigh Park, KENILWORTH,
       Warks, CV8 2LG.   (hq)
       024 7669 6592   fax 024 7641 7937
       email iagsa@iagsa.co.uk   http://www.iagsa.co.uk
       Sec: Mrs Charlotte O'Kane
▲   Company Limited by Guarantee
Br   29
○   *P, *T; to promote & encourage professional excellence in rural
       business administration
Gp   Agriculture
●   Conf - Mtgs - ET - LG
M   900 i, 20 f
¶   Jnl - 1;   Bulletin - 12; both ftm only.
       Directory - 1.

Institute of Amateur Cinematographers   (IAC)   1932

NR   Global House, 1 Ashley Avenue, EPSOM, Surrey, KT18 5AD.
       01372 739672
       Chmn: Linda Gough
▲   Company Limited by Guarantee; Registered Charity
○   *G; 'non-commercial organisation to assist amateur movie
       makers'
●   Comp - Inf - Film & video library
M   2,000 i
¶   Film & Video Maker - 6; ftm only.
       Note: Generally known as IAC - The Film & Video Institute

Institute of Animal Technology   (IAT)   1965

NR   5 South Parade, Summertown, OXFORD, OX2 7JL.
       (asa/regd/office)
       email secretary@iat.org.uk   http://www.iat.org.uk
▲   Company Limited by Guarantee
Br   16
○   *P, *V; to advance & promote excellence in the care & welfare of
       animals in science
●   Conf - ET - Exam
<   Eur Fedn of Animal Technologists (EFAT); Amer Assn of
       Laboratory Animal Science (AALAS)
M   2,100 i, 60 f, UK / 50 i, o'seas
¶   Jnl of Animal Technology & Welfare - 3.
       Bulletin - 12.

Institute of Archeologists of Ireland   (IAI)

IRL   63 Merrion Sq, DUBLIN 2, Republic of Ireland.
        353 (1) 662 9517
        email iaireland@eircom.net
        Chmn: Eoin Halpin
○   *L

Institute of Architectural Ironmongers

■   8 Stepney Green, LONDON, E1 3JU.   (hq)
       020 7790 3431   fax 020 7790 8517
       email info@gai.org.uk   http://www.gai.org.uk
       Sec: Peter Spill
▲   Un-incorporated Society
Br   5
○   *P; interests of individual architectural ironmongers
●   Conf - Mtgs - Exhib - SG - VE
M   350 i
¶   Bulletin - 4; m only.

Institute of Art & Law   (IAL)

NR   1-5 Cank St, LEICESTER, LE1 5GX.   (hq)
       0116-253 8888
       http://www.ial.uk.com
       Dir: Ruth Redmon-Cooper
○   *L, *P; for those interested in all aspects of transacting in art
●   Mtgs - Seminars (speakers incl academics, practitioners,
       government officials & museum directors) - Publishing
M   i, org
¶   Art Antiquity & Law [Jnl] - 4.
       Commentary on the Unidroit Convention by Lyndel V Prott.
       Art Treasures & War by Wojciech Kowalski.

Institute of Asphalt Technology   (IAT)   1966

■   Paper Mews Place, 290 High St, DORKING, Surrey,
       RH4 1QT.   (hq)
       01306 742792   fax 01306 742792
       email secretary@instofasphalt.demon.co.uk
       http://www.instofasphalt.org
       Sec: Anthony Pelham Morter
▲   Company Limited by Guarantee
Br   9; Republic of Ireland
○   *P; to encourage & promote improvements in the practice,
       knowledge & standards of asphalt technology
●   Conf - Mtgs - ET - Exam - Exhib - Lib - PL - VE
M   15,900 i UK / 88 i, o'seas
¶   Asphalt Professional - 6; ftm, on request (tel) nm.
       Sampling Bituminous Materials (training video 1).
       Hot Rolled Asphalt Production Laying & Compaction (training
       video 2).

Institute of Assessors & Internal Verifiers   (IVA)   1998

■   PO Box 148, WIRRAL, Cheshire, CH62 7WB.   (mail/address)
       0151-334 8215   fax 0151-334 2623
       email office@iavltd.co.uk   http://www.iavltd.co.uk
       Chief Exec: Mr Homan
▲   Company Limited by Guarantee
○   *P; for assessors & internal verifiers involved with national
       training / national vocational qualifications (NVQs)
●   Conf - Mtgs - ET - Res - Inf - LG
M   3,500 i, 200 i
¶   Best Practice (Jnl) - 4.
×   2003 Institute of Verifiers & Assessors

Institute of Association Management   (IAM)   1933

■   1 Queen Anne's Gate, Westminster, LONDON, SW1H 9BT.
       (hq)
       0870 330 8624   fax 0870 330 8614
       email iam@iofam.org.uk   http://www.iofam.org.uk
       Pres: Brian Spratt
▲   Un-incorporated Society
○   *P; to represent & support 'executives, managers & staffs of
       trade & professional associations, medical institutes,
       chambers of commerce & similar bodies'
Gp   Computers; Europe; Assn mgt companies; Govt liaison
●   Conf - Mtgs - ET - Inf - VE - LG
M   370 i, 30 f, UK
¶   Association Executive - 4; ftm, £30 nm.   Hbk & LM - 1; ftm.

Institute of Auctioneers & Appraisers in Scotland   1926

■   Rural Centre, West Mains, Ingliston, NEWBRIDGE, Midlothian,
       EH28 8NZ.   (hq)
       0131-472 4067   fax 0131-472 4067
       email iaas@fsmail.net
       http://www.auctioneersscotland.co.uk
       Exec Sec: W Andrew Wright
▲   Company Limited by Guarantee
○   *P; for livestock & fine arts auctioneers, agricultural valuers &
       estate agents
Gp   Land agents; Fine art auctioneers & valuers
●   Conf - ET - LG
<   Eur Assn of Livestock Markets
M   290 i, 35 f

Institute of Automotive Engineer Assessors (IAEA) 1932

NR Brooke House, 24 Dam St, LICHFIELD, Staffs, WS13 6AB. (hq)
    01543 266906
    Sec: John R Morris
▲ Company Limited by Guarantee; Registered Charity
○ *P; to promote & develop for public benefit the science, design, manufacture & related technology of motor vehicles & their repair
M 1,250 i, UK / 50 i, o'seas
¶ ICME Register of Members (Ybk) - 1; free.

Institute of Bankers in Ireland 1898

IRL 1 North Wall Quay, DUBLIN 1, Republic of Ireland. (hq)
    353 (1) 611 6500   fax 353 (1) 611 6565
    http://www.bankers.ie
    Chief Exec: Anthony Walsh
○ *P

Institute of Barristers' Clerks (IBC) 1922

NR 289-293 High Holborn, LONDON, WC1V 7HZ. (admin/b)
    020 7831 7144
    http://www.barristersclerks.com
▲ Registered Charity
○ *P
● Conf - Mtgs - ET - Inf
M 850 i
¶ Mailshot (with job vacancies) - 52; £10 for 6 months.

Institute of Biology (IOB) 1950

■ 9 Red Lion Court, LONDON, EC4A 3EF. (hq)
    020 7936 5900
    Chief Exec: Prof Alan D B Malcolm
▲ Registered Charity
Br 17; Hong Kong
○ *L, *P; to advance the science & practice of the biological sciences; to advance education & encourage the study of the biological sciences & their applications
● Conf - Mtgs - ET - Exam - Exhib - Comp - Inf - VE - LG
< Intl U of Biological Sciences (IUBS); Eur Countries Biologists Assn (ECBA); Science Coun; Royal Instn; Brit Assn for the Advancement of Science; Save Brit Science
M 15,800 i, 6 f, 76 org, UK / 1,331 i, o'seas
¶ Jnl of Biological Education - 4.
    Biologist - 6.   AR - 1.
    Publications list available.

Institute of Biology of Ireland
    see **Institiúid Bitheolaíochta na h'Éireann** (Institute of Biology of Ireland)

Institute of Biomedical Science (IBMS) 1912

NR 12 Coldbath Sq, LONDON, EC1R 5HL. (hq)
    020 7713 0214   fax 020 7436 4946
    email mail@ibms.org   http://www.ibms.org
    Chief Exec: Alan Potter
▲ Registered Charity
Br 48; 5 o'seas
○ *L, *P; promotes the scientific study & development of biomedical science
● Conf - Mtgs - ET - Exam - Res - Comp - Inf - LG
< Eur Professions in Biomedical Science; Eur Confedn of Laboratory Science
M 15,000 i, 74 f, UK / 1,000 i, o'seas
¶ Biomedical Scientist - 12.
    British Jnl of Biomedical Science - 4.
    Science & educational leaflets.   AR.

Institute of Bookbinding & Allied Trades (IBAT) 1904

NR 2 Mount Pleasant Rd, HASTINGS, E Sussex, TN34 3SB.
    Pres: John Ash
▲ Un-incorporated Society
○ *P, *U; to promote the exchange of information within the bookbinding industry & improve the standards of training
● Mtgs - ET - Inf - VE
< Worshipful Company of Stationers
M 130 i
¶ Quarterly Magazine.   LM - 1;   AR; both ftm only.

Institute of Brewing
    in 2001 became the Institute & Guild of Brewing, which in 2005 became the **Institute of Brewing & Distilling**

Institute of Brewing & Distilling (IBD) 1886

■ 33 Clarges St, LONDON, W1J 7EE. (hq)
    020 7499 8144   fax 020 7499 1156
    email enquiries@ibd.org.uk   http://www.ibd.org.uk
    Contact: The Secretary
▲ Registered Charity
○ *P; for the advancement of education & professional development in the science & technology of brewing, distilling & related industries
● Conf - Mtgs - ET - Exam - Exhib - Comp - Lib
M 1,925 i, UK / 1,950 i, o'seas
¶ The Brewer & Distiller - 12; ftm, £60 (£75 o'seas) nm.
    Jnl of the Institute of Brewing - 4; ftm only.
    Brewing & Distilling Directory - 1; ftm only.
✕ 2001 Institute of Brewing
    2005 Institute & Guild of Brewing

Institute of British Foundrymen
    since 2001 **Institute of Cast Metal Engineers**

Institute of British Organ Building

■ 13 Ryefields, THURSTON, Suffolk, IP31 3TD.
    01359 233433
    Admin: Carol Levey
○ *T; for builders of pipe organs
¶ Ybk.

Institute of Broadcast Sound (IBS) 1977

■ PO Box 932, GUILDFORD, Surrey, GU4 7WW. (mail)
    01483 575450   fax 0870 762 2835
    email info@ibs.org.uk   http://www.ibs.org.uk add
    Secretariat: Malcolm Johnson
▲ Registered Charity
○ *P; to promote the excellence of professional sound for radio & television broadcasting; to provide a continuing forum for such objectives
● Conf - Mtgs - ET - Exhib - Inf - Lib - LG
M 800 i, 30 f, UK / 50 i, 1 f, o'seas
¶ Line Up - 5; ftm, £40 nm.

Institute of Builders' Merchants (IBM) 1968

NR Touchwood, 2 Oak View Rise, Harlow Wood, MANSFIELD, Notts, NG18 4UT. (hq)
    01623 633228   fax 01623 427693
    Dir: Dave Saunders
Br 6
○ *P; improvement of technical & general knowledge of persons engaged in the trade of builders' merchant
● ET
< Bldrs Merchants Fedn; Worshipful Company of Bldrs Merchants
M 800 i

Institute of Burial & Cremation Administration (Inc)
    since 2003 **Institute of Cemetery & Crematorium Management**

Institute of Business Administration Ltd (IBA) 1947
NR   16 Park Crescent, LONDON, W1B 1BA.   (hq)
     http://www.ibauk.org
○   *P; for company secretaries & administrators in medium &
     small size organisations

Institute of Business Administration & Management
     no longer in existence

Institute of Business Advisers (IBA) 1989
■   Response House, Queen Street North, CHESTERFIELD, Derbys,
     S41 9AB.   (asa)
     01246 453322   fax 01246 453300
     email enquiries@iba.org.uk   http://www.iba.org.uk
     Chief Exec: Mike Horner
▲   Company Limited by Guarantee; Registered Charity
Br   19; Ireland
○   *P; for business advisers, mentors & trainers who specialise in
     helping small to medium sized businesses
●   Conf - Mtgs - ET - Exhib - Stat - Inf - VE - LG
     Legal advice - Professional indemnity insurance (members only)
M   1,813 i, 15 f, UK / 73 i, o'seas
¶   Business Adviser (Jnl) - 4.   Update - 12.   AR.
     Benefits for business;   Benefits of membership;
     Membership information; all free.

Institute of Business Analysts & Consultants 1983
IRL c/o Administrator, Andrew Kinsella, 7 Forest Park, SWORDS,
     Co Dublin, Republic of Ireland.
     353 (1) 810 7685
     email secretary@inbusans.ie   http://www.inbusans.ie
○   *P

Institute of Business Ethics (IBE) 1986
NR   24 Greencoat Place, LONDON, SW1P 1BE.   (hq)
     020 7798 6040
     Dir: Philippa Foster Back
▲   Registered Charity
○   *T; to clarify ethical issues involved in business; to identify &
     promulgate best business practice
●   Conf - Mtgs - ET - Res - Lib
M   25 i, 60 f, 10 org, UK / 2 f, o'seas
¶   Various publications available.

** Institute of Business Ideas & Solutions
     Organisation lost: see Introduction paragraph 3

Institute of Car Fleet Management (ICFM) 1992
NR   PO Box 314, CHICHESTER, W Sussex, PO20 9WZ.   (hq)
     01462 744914
○   *P
¶   Fleet Excellence (NL) - 6; ftm only.
     Guide to Car Fleet Management (Hbk).

Institute of Career Guidance Ltd (ICG) 1922
NR   Copthall House (3rd floor), 1 New Rd, STOURBRIDGE,
     W Midlands, DY8 1PH.   (hq)
     01384 445630   fax 01384 440830
     email hq@icg-uk.org   http://www.icg-uk.org
     Admin: Ruth Weston
▲   Company Limited by Guarantee
○   *P; awarding body for the career guidance sector
●   Conf - ET - Exhib - Lib
M   3,000 i, 17 f
¶   Careers Guidance Today - 6; ftm, £27.50 yr nm.
     Front-Line - 6; ftm only.
     Vacancy Bulletin (Portico) - 26; £10 m, £40 nm.

Institute of Carpenters (IOC) 1890
NR   35 Hayworth Rd, Sandiacre, NOTTINGHAM, NG10 5LL.   (asa)
     0115-949 0641   fax 0115-949 1664
     email mail@central-office.co.uk
     Sec: David R Winson
○   *P
M   3,000 i
¶   Jnl - 4; ftm.

Institute of Cast Metal Engineers (ICME) 1904
■   National Metalforming Centre, 47 Birmingham Rd,
     WEST BROMWICH, W Midlands, B70 6PY.   (hq)
     0121-601 6979   fax 0121-601 6981
     email info@icme.org.uk   http://www.icme.org.uk
     Operations Mgr: Marian Holland
▲   Registered Charity
Br   7
○   *P; to provide professional development programmes for
     individuals employed in the global cast metal industry
Gp   Working gps (technical, educational & training) investigating
     various topics
●   Mtgs - ET - Inf - Lib - PL
<   Wld Foundrymen Org; Engg Coun
M   1,207 i, UK / 90 i, o'seas
¶   Foundry Trade Jnl - 10; ftm, £179 (237 RoW) nm.
     Diecasting World - 2; £38 (£56 RoW).
     Foundry Ybk & Castings Buyers Guide - 1; £151.
     AR - 1; free.
×   2001 Institute of British Foundrymen

**Institute of Cemetery & Crematorium Management (ICCM)
1913**
■   City of London Cemetery, Aldersbrook Rd, LONDON,
     E12 5DQ.   (hq)
     020 8989 4661   fax 020 8989 6112
     email julie@iccm.fsnet.co.uk   http://www.iccm-uk.com
     Chief Exec: Tim Morris
▲   Company Limited by Guarantee
Br   8
○   *P; to promote professional training, education & consultancy
     for UK burial & cremation authorities
●   Conf - Mtgs - ET - Exam - Exhib - Lib
<   Intl Cremation Fedn
M   680 i, 305 f, UK / 10 i, o'seas
¶   The Jnl - 4; ftm, £4 yr nm.
×   2003 Institute of Burial & Cremation Administration
     2004-05 Confederation of Burial Authorities

Institute of Certified Book-Keepers (ICB) 1996
■   Mill Rd, STOKENCHURCH, Bucks, HP14 3BF.   (hq)
     0845 060 2345
     Chief Exec: Garry Carter
▲   Company Limited by Guarantee
Br   32; 11 countries
○   *P; to set standards in book-keeping
Gp   Members in practice
●   Exam
<   ICB Intl
M   100,000 i, 5 f, 54 colleges & training org, UK / 604 i, o'seas
¶   Invoice - 4.

**Institute of Certified Public Accountants in Ireland (CPA)
1943**
IRL 9 Ely Place, DUBLIN 2, Republic of Ireland.
     353 (1) 676 7353   fax 353 (1) 661 2367
     email cpa@cpaireland.ie   http://www.cpaireland.ie
     Chief Exec: Eamonn Siggins
Br   3 Wellington Park, Belfast, BT9 6DJ.
     048 9092 3390
○   *P

Institute of Charity Fundraising Managers
     since 2002 **Institute of Fundraising**

Institute of Chartered Accountants in England & Wales (ICAEW) 1880
NR   PO Box 433, Chartered Accountants' Hall, Moorgate Place, LONDON, EC2P 2BJ.   (hq)
     020 7920 8100
     Chief Exec: Eric Anstee
▲   Registered Charity
○   *P
M   i, f & org
¶   Accountancy (Jnl) - 12.   LM.   AR.

Institute of Chartered Accountants in Ireland 1888
IRL   83 Pembroke Rd, Ballsbridge, DUBLIN 4, Republic of Ireland.   (hq)
     353 (1) 637 7200   fax 353 (1) 668 0842
     email ca@icai.ie   http://www.icai.ie
     Sec: Judy Fay
Br   11 Donegall Square South, Belfast, BT1 5JE.
     028 9032 1600
○   *P

Institute of Chartered Accountants of Scotland (ICAS) 1854
NR   21 Haymarket Yards, EDINBURGH, EH12 5BH.   (hq)
     0131-347 0100   fax 0131-347 0105
     email enquiries@icas.org.uk   http://www.icas.org.uk
     Chief Exec & Sec: Des Hudson
Br   7 area committees
○   *P
●   Conf - Mtgs - ET - Exam - Res - SG - Inf - Lib - LG
<   Intl Fedn of Accountants (IFAC); Intl Accounting Standards C'ee (IASC); Fédn des Experts Comptables Eur (FEE); Auditing Practices Bd (APB)
M   15,208 i
¶   CA Magazine - 12; ftm.
     Directory of Insolvency Permit Holders - 1.
     Research Publications; prices vary.

Institute of Chartered Foresters (ICF) 1925
NR   7A St Colme St, EDINBURGH, EH3 6AA.   (hq)
     0131-225 2705   fax 0131-220 6128
     email icf@charteredforesters.org
     http://www.charteredforesters.org
     Exec Dir / Sec: Mrs Margaret Dick
▲   Registered Charity
○   *L, *P
●   Conf - ET - Exam - Res - SG - Inf
M   i
¶   The Chartered Forester (Jnl) - 6;
     Register of Consultants - 1;   AR; all ftm.
     Forestry - 4; £40 m, £230 nm.
     Note: is preparing to move to the headquarters of the Confederation of Forest Industries, 5 Dublin Street Lane South, EDINBURGH, EH1 3PX.

Institute of Chartered Secretaries & Administrators (ICSA) 1891
NR   16 Park Crescent, LONDON, W1B 1AH.   (hq)
     020 7580 4741
     Chief Exec: John Ainsworth
▲   Registered Charity
○   *P; law & practice of secretaryship & administration
●   Conf - Mtgs - SG - ET - Stat - Exam - Res - Inf - Lib - LG - Recruitment consultancy
M   21,000 i, UK / 23,000 i, o'seas
¶   Chartered Secretary - 12.
     A series of practice guides in the corporate, not-for-profit & public sectors.
     Directory of Members in Public Practice - 1.

Institute of Chartered Shipbrokers (ICS) 1920
NR   85 Gracechurch St, LONDON, EC3V 0AA.   (hq)
     020 7623 1111
     Dir: Alan Phillips
▲   Royal Charter
○   *P
●   ET - Exam - Lib - LG
M   1,887 i, 149 f, UK / 1,199 i, 1 f, o'seas
¶   The Shipbroker - 4.   Bulletin - 12.
     Reference Book & LM - 1.

Institute of Chemistry of Ireland
     see **Institiúid Ceimice na h'Éireann** (Institute of Chemistry of Ireland)

Institute of Chiropodists & Podiatrists 1938
■   27 Wright St, SOUTHPORT, Merseyside, PR9 0TL.   (hq)
     01704 546141   fax 01704 500477
     email secretary@inst-chiropodist.org.uk
     http://www.inst-chiropodist.org.uk
     Sec: Mrs S M Kirkham
▲   Company Limited by Guarantee
Br   25
○   *P
M   i
¶   The Chiropody Review - 6.

Institute of Civil Defence & Disaster Studies (ICDDS) 1938
NR   PO Box 698, CAMBERLEY, Surrey, GU15 3WY.   (mail/address)
     01305 767560   fax 01305 767560
     email registrar@icdds.org   http://www.icdds.org
     Hon Gen Sec: Gary Silver
▲   Registered Charity
○   *P; advancement of civil defence & civil protection in all its aspects; disaster studies
●   Conf - Res - Lib - LG (Cabinet Office)
<   Intl Civil Defence Org (ICDO)(Geneva)
>   Brit Civil Defence Assn; Brit Geological Soc (BGS); RAF Liaison Officers
M   160 i, 800 i in 4 org, UK / 20 i, o'seas
¶   Alert (Jnl) - 4/6.

Institute of Clay Technology
     2005 has become the International Clay Technology Association, within the Ceramics Division of the **Institute of Materials, Minerals & Mining**

Institute of Clayworkers (ICW)
NR   Federation House, Station Rd, STOKE-ON-TRENT, Staffs, ST4 2SA.   (hq)
     01782 744631   fax 01782 744102
     email bcc@ceramfed.co.uk
     Sec: A McRae
     A benevolent fund, awarding long service medals

Institute of Clerks of Works of Great Britain Inc (ICW) 1882
■   Equinox, 28 Commerce Rd, Lynchwood, PETERBOROUGH, Cambs, PE2 6LR.   (hq)
     01733 405160   fax 01733 405161
     email info@icwgb.co.uk   http://www.icwgb.org
     Chief Exec: Don McGeorge
▲   Company Limited by Guarantee
Br   20; Hong Kong
○   *P; examining & qualifying body for clerks of works in the UK & overseas
Gp   Building construction
●   Conf - Mtgs - Res - Exhib - Inf - VE - LG
>   Brit Standards Inst; Construction Ind Coun
M   1,579 i, UK / 183 i, o'seas
¶   Site Recorder (Jnl) - 12;   LM - 1; both ftm.

© CBD Research Ltd · Beckenham · BR3 5JS · Tel 020 8650 7745 · Fax 020 8650 0768 · E-mail cbd@cbdresearch.com · www.cbdresearch.com

Institute of Clinical Research   (ICR)   1978
- ■ Thames House, Mere Park, Dedmere Rd, MARLOW, Bucks, SL7 1PB.   (hq)
  01628 899755   fax 01628 899766
  http://www.instituteofclinicalresearch.org
  Chief Exec: Dr John Hooper
- ▲ Company Limited by Guarantee
- ○ *P
- ● Conf - Mtgs - ET - Exam - Exhib
- M 3,980 i, UK / 1,048 i, o'seas
- ¶ Clinical Research Focus - 11; ftm only.   AR; free.

Institute of Commercial Management Ltd   (ICM)   1979
- ■ The Fusee, 20a Bargates, CHRISTCHURCH, Dorset, BH23 1QL.   (hq)
  01202 490555   fax 01202 490666
  email icm@icm.ac.uk   http://www.icm.ac.uk
  Chief Exec: Dr Alistair Somerville-Ford
- ▲ Company Limited by Guarantee; Registered Charity
- ○ *E, *P; 'educational foundation supporting business, personal & professional development'
- Gp Provision of expert technical assistance & consultancy services in the fields of trade, tourism & professional development
- ● Conf - ET - Exam
- M 12,400 i

Institute for Communications Arbitration & Forensics   (ICAF)
- NR Ranmore House, The Crescent, LEATHERHEAD, Surrey, KT22 8DY.
  01372 361234
- ○ *P

** Institute of Community Development
   Organisation lost: see Introduction paragraph 3

Institute of Company Accountants
   2003 amalgamated with the **Association of International Accountants**

Institute for Complementary Medicine   (ICM)   1982
- NR PO Box 194, LONDON, SE16 7QZ.   (hq)
  020 7237 5165
  Chief Exec: Michael Endacott
- ▲ Registered Charity
- ○ *P; to make known information, to encourage research & promote high standards in practice & training in complementary medicine
- ● Conf - ET - Inf - LG
- M i, 600 org
- ¶ ICM Update - 4.

** Institute of Computer Technology
   Organisation lost: see Introduction paragraph 3

Institute of Concrete Technology   (ICT)   1972
- NR 4 Meadows Business Park, Blackwater, CAMBERLEY, Surrey, GU17 9AB.   (hq)
  01276 37831   fax 01276 37831
  email ict@ictech.org   http://www.ictech.org
  Pres: R Gaimster,   Hon Sec: C D Nessfield
- ▲ Company Limited by Guarantee
- Br 1; Ireland, South Africa
- ○ *P; to promote the advancement of concrete technology
- ● Conf - Mtgs - ET - Exam
- M 420 i, UK / 210 i, o'seas
- ¶ NL - 4.   Ybk.   Members Hbk.

Institute of Conflict Management   (ICM)   2000
- ■ 840 Melton Rd, Thurmaston, LEICESTER, LE4 8BN.   (hq)
  0116-264 0049   fax 0116-264 0141
  email icm@associationhq.org.uk
  http://www.conflictmanagement.org
  Chief Exec: Stuart Hex
- ▲ Company Limited by Guarantee
- ○ *P; to develop, monitor & promote professional standards for the effective prevention & management of aggression & conflict at work
- ● Conf - Mtgs - ET - Res - Exhib - Inf - LG - Training provision of the National Foundation Certificate for Managing Work-related Violence - Quality award process for training in the management of work related violence
- M 350 i
- ¶ ICM NL - 4.

Institute of Conservation   2005
- NR Downstream Building (3rd floor), 1 London Bridge, LONDON, SE1 9BG.   (hq)
  020 7785 3805   fax 020 7785 3806
  http://www.instituteofconservation.org.uk
  Chief Exec: Alastair McCapra,
  Admin Officer: Diane Copley
- ○ *P
- × 2005 (Care of Collections Forum
   (Institute of Paper Conservation
   (Photographic Materials Conservation Group
   (Scottish Society for Conservation & Restoration
   (United Kingdom Institute for Conservation of Historic & Artistic Works

Institute for the Conservation of Historic & Artistic Works in Ireland   (ICHAWI)
- IRL 4 Castle St, DUBLIN 2, Republic of Ireland.
   353 (1) 476 3801
   email ichawi@eircom.net   http://www.ichawi.org
   Hon Sec: Maighréad McParland
- ○ *P

Institute of Construction Management   (ICM)   1970
- NR 69 Adur Avenue, SHOREHAM-BY-SEA, W Sussex, BN43 5NL.
   01273 453394
   Sec: D Charlton
- ▲ Company Limited by Guarantee
- Br 9; Hong Kong
- ○ P; construction & site management & knowledge of all modern construction methods
- ● Conf - Mtgs - ET - Exam - Inf - VE
- < Construction Ind Coun
- M c 700 i & f
- ¶ Viewpoint (NL) - 4; ftm only.

Institute of Construction Specialists   (IOCS)   2001
- ■ 1 Walpole House, 2 Pickford St, ALDERSHOT, Hants, GU11 1TZ.   (hq)
  01252 312122   fax 01252 343081
  email info@constructionspecialists.org
  http://www.constructionspecialists.org
  Group Dir: A R Gibbs
- ▲ Un-incorporated Society
- ○ *P; for managers & administrative & supervisory staff of specialist construction firms; to focus on training & accreditation
- ● ET - Exam - Comp
- < Construction Specialists Gp
- M i
- ¶ IOCS/CCS NL - 10; ftm only.

Institute of Consumer Affairs   (ICA)   1974
NR   Freshfields, The Hill, PANXWORTH, Norfolk, NR13 6JG.
    (chmn/p)
    01603 270588
    Chmn: Desmond O'Brien
○   *P; a network of consumer advisers & others working in
    consumer protection & consumer affairs. To raise the quality
    of services to consumers through better information, advice &
    education; to improve consumer protection
●   Conf - Mtgs - ET - Inf
M   150 i
¶   Help & Advice - 6; m only.

**Institute of Consumer Sciences (incorporating Home Economics)
(ICSc)   2000**
NR   Lonsdale House, 52 Blucher St, BIRMINGHAM, B1 1QU.   (hq)
    0121-616 5188
    The Executive Officer
▲   Company Limited by Guarantee; Registered Charity
Br   11
○   *P; representing those working in education, industry, services,
    retailing & government in the areas of consumer sciences &
    home economics in order to improve the quality of life for
    individuals, families & communities
Gp   Standards board; Promotions board; School based panel;
    Higher & further education & research based panel; Business
    & professional panel; Corporate forum
●   Conf - Mtgs - ET - Inf - LG
<   Intl Fedn for Home Economics
M   1,400 i, 28 f, UK / 12 i, o'seas
¶   Consumer Sciences Today - 4.

Institute of Contemporary Arts   (ICA)   1947
NR   12 Carlton House Terrace, LONDON, SW1Y 5AH.   (hq)
○   *A, *D; a centre for contemporary cultural activities, incl film,
    theatre, dance, lectures & visual arts

Institute of Continuing Professional Development
NR   35-37 Grosvenor Gardens, LONDON, SW1W 0BS.
    020 7828 1965   fax 020 7828 1967
    http://www.cpdinstitute.org
    Mem Mgr: Jane Guest
○   *E

Institute of Copywriting   (IOC)   1992
§   Overbrook Business Centre, Poolbridge Rd, Blackford,
    WEDMORE, Somerset, BS28 4PA.
    0800 781 1715
    Note: part of the Learning Institute, which offers over 25
    vocational courses.

Institute of Corrosion   (ICorr)   1975
NR   Corrosion House, Vimy Court, Vimy Rd, LEIGHTON BUZZARD,
    Beds, LU7 1FG.   (hq)
    01525 851771
    Hon Sec: Dr Steve Mabbutt
▲   Registered Charity
Br   8; Republic of Ireland
○   *L *P; study & advice concerning corrosion engineering
    problems & corrosion prevention
●   Conf - Mtgs - ET
M   1,450 i, 40 f, UK / 150 i, 1 f, o'seas
¶   Corrosion Science - 12.   Corrosion Management - 6.
    UK Corrosion (conference papers) - 1.

Institute of Cost & Executive Accountants   (ICEA)   1958
■   Akhtar House, 2 Shepherd's Bush Rd, LONDON, W6 7PJ.   (hq)
    020 8749 7126   fax 020 8749 7127
    email icea@enta.net   http://www.icea.enta.net
    Sec Gen: Dr Sushil K das Gupta
▲   Company Limited by Guarantee; Registered Charity
Br   14; 23 o'seas
○   *P; ' modern professional accounting institute, producing
    tomorrow's accountants to take financial decisions'
Gp   Small business; Public practice; Local government
●   Conf - Mtgs - ET - Exam - Res - Exhib - SG - Inf - Lib - LG
<   Eur Accounting Assn; Coun for Educ in the C'wealth; Brit
    Accounting Assn; Foundation for Science & Technology in the
    UK
M   c 2,000 i, UK / c 2,000 i, o'seas
¶   Executive Accountant - 4.

Institute of Couriers
NR   Green Man Tower, 332 Goswell Rd, LONDON, EC1V 7LQ.
    0845 601 0245
    http://www.ioc.uk.com
○   *T

Institute of Credit Management   (ICM)   1939
■   The Water Mill, Station Rd, South Luffenham, OAKHAM,
    Rutland, LE15 8NB.   (hq)
    01780 722900   fax 01780 721333
    email info@icm.org.uk   http://www.icm.org.uk
    Dir Gen: Philip King
▲   Company Limited by Guarantee; Registered Charity
Br   26
○   *P; for those employed in credit management, credit finance &
    ancillary services
●   Conf - Mtgs - ET - Exam - Res - Exhib - Inf - Lib - LG
<   Fedn of Eur Credit Mgt Assns (FECMA)
M   9,000 i, UK / 300 i, o'seas
¶   Credit Management - 12; ftm, £75 yr nm.
    AR - 1; ftm.

Institute of Customer Service   (ICS)   1997
NR   2 Castle Court, St Peter's Street, COLCHESTER, Essex,
    CO1 1EW.   (hq)
    01206 571716   fax 01206 546688
    email enquiries@icsmail.co.uk
    http://www.instituteofcustomerservice.com
    Chief Exec: David Parsons
▲   Company Limited by Guarantee
Br   10
○   *P; to develop & spread authoritative knowledge & good
    practice, define national professional & occupational
    standards & provide professional recognition to individuals in
    the customer service industry
●   Conf - Mtgs - ET - Res - Exhib - Stat - Inf - VE - LG
M   3,000 i, 180 f
¶   Customer First - 5; ftm, £4.95 nm.
    Research publications - irreg; prices vary.

Institute of Decontamination Services   (InstDSc)   2004

■ Chesterfield Royal Hospital, Calow, CHESTERFIELD, Derbys, S44 5BL.   (hsb)
   01246 513069
   email kathleen.saxelby@chesterfieldroyal.nhs.uk
   http://www.idsc-uk.org
   Dir of Admin: Kathleen Saxelby
▲ Un-incorporated Society
Br 8
○ *P; for staff & management in the field of decontamination & sterile services
Gp Conference c'ee; Education
● Conf - Mtgs - ET - Exhib - Promotion of research & development
< Eur Fedn of Hospital Sterile Services
> Eur Fedn of Hospital Sterile Services
M 370 i, 15 f, UK / 8 i, o'seas
¶ Jnl - 4; ftm, £25 each nm.
   Ybk - 1; ftm, £55 nm.
   Technical Vocational Training Programme; £18.
   Standards & Practices; £25.
✕ 2004 Institute of Sterile Services Management

Institute of Demolition Engineers   (IDE)   1971

■ 69 Poplicans Rd, Cuxton, ROCHESTER, Kent, ME2 1EJ.   (hsp)
   01634 294255   fax 01634 294255
   email info@ide.org.uk   http://www.ide.org.uk
   Sec: Mrs Valerie J Stroud
▲ Registered Charity
○ *P; to advance the science of demolition engineering, the use of effective techniques in the industry & safer methods of working; to provide a qualifying body in the industry
● Conf - Mtgs - ET - Exam - Inf - LG
M 267 i, UK / 3 i, o'seas
¶ Demolition Engineer - 3; free, (on website).

Institute of Designers in Ireland   1972

IRL 8 Merrion Sq, DUBLIN 2, Republic of Ireland.
   353 (1) 489 3650
   email idi@indigo.ie
   Pres: Arthur Duff
○ *A, *P

Institute of Direct Marketing   (IDM)   1987

NR 1 Park Rd, TEDDINGTON, Middx, TW11 0AR.   (hq)
   020 8977 5705   fax 020 8943 2535
   email enquiries@theidm.com   http://www.theidm.com
   Managing Dir: Prof Derek Holder
▲ Registered Charity
○ *P; direct marketing training & education for members
● ET - Exam - Lib
< Direct Marketing Assn
M 5,000 i, UK / 200 i, o'seas
¶ Jnl of Interactive Marketing - 4.

Institute of Directors   (IoD)   1903

NR 116 Pall Mall, LONDON, SW1Y 5ED.   (hq)
   020 7839 1233   fax 020 7930 1949
   email join-iod@iod.com   http://www.iod.com
   Chief Operating Officer: Andrew Main Wilson
   Sec: Alan Morkel
▲ Royal Charter
Br 30; 11 countries o'seas
○ *P; commitment to high standards of corporate guidance; development of directors' professional competence; to bring the experience of business leaders to bear on the conduct of public affairs for the common good
● Conf - ET - Exam - Res - Inf - Lib - LG
< Australian Inst Company Dirs; Inst Corporate Dirs Canada; Inst Dirs New Zealand; Inst Dirs Southern Africa
M 54,000 i
¶ IoD News [NL] - 12; ftm.   AR; free.
   Handbooks & guides; prices vary.

Institute of Directors in Ireland

IRL Heritage House, Dundrum Office Park, DUBLIN 14, Republic of Ireland.
   353 (1) 296 4093   fax 353 (1) 296 4127
   email info@iodireland.ie   http://www.iodireland.ie
   Sec: Ralph MacDarby
○ *P

Institute of Domestic Heating & Environmental Engineers   (IDHEE)   1964

■ Unit 32c New Forest Enterprise Centre, Chapel Lane, Totton, SOUTHAMPTON, Hants, SO40 9LA.   (hq)
   023 8066 8900   fax 023 8066 0888
   email admin@idhee.org.uk   http://www.idhee.org.uk
   Exec Chmn: Bill Bucknell
▲ Un-incorporated Society
Br Ireland, New Zealand
○ *P; to raise the standard of domestic heating & environmental engineering
Gp Renewable energy; Consulting & design engineers
● Conf - Mtgs - ET - Exam - Exhib - LG
M 781 i, 31 f, UK / 64 i, 3 f, o'seas
¶ Comfort Engineering - 4; ftm, £5 nm.
   Technical Hbk - 1; ftm, £7.50 nm.

Institute of Ecology & Environmental Management   (IEEM)   1991

■ 45 Southgate St, WINCHESTER, Hants, SO23 9EH.   (hq)
   01962 868626   fax 01962 868625
   email enquiries@ieem.net   http://www.ieem.net
   Exec Dir: Dr Jim R Thompson
▲ Company Limited by Guarantee
Br 5 regional sections
○ *P; to promote & support professionalism in the fields of ecology & environmental management
● Conf - Mtgs - ET - LG
< Intl Consvn U (IUCN); Eur Fedn of Assns of Envtl Profls (EFAEP); Soc for the Envt (SOCENV)
M 2,527 i, UK / 97 i, o'seas
¶ In Practice (Jnl) - 4; ftm; £30 yr UK (£40 o'seas).
   Members Directory - 1; [on website].
   Conference Proceedings - 2; ftm, £21 each nm.

Institute of Economic Affairs Ltd   (IEA)   1957

NR 2 Lord North St, LONDON, SW1P 3LB.   (hq)
   020 7799 3745
   Dir Gen: John Blundell
▲ Registered Charity
○ *L; extension of public understanding of economic principles in their application to practical problems
● Conf - ET - Lib
M 2,000 i, 500 f, UK / 500 i, 5 f, o'seas
¶ Economic Affairs - 4; ftm.   Hobart Papers.
   Hobart Paperbacks.   Research Monographs.
   Series on Environment.   Choice in Welfare.
   Health Series.   Religion 2 Liberty.   Occasional Papers.
   Publications are irreg & prices vary.
   Videos.   Conferences.   Lectures.

Institute of Educational Assessors   2005

NR 29 Bolton St, LONDON, W1J 8GP.   (hq)
   http://www.ioea.org.uk
○ *P

Institute of Electrolysis Ltd
   2004 merged with the British Association of Electrolysists to form the
   British Institute & Association of Electrolysis

Institute of Employment Rights   (IER)   1989

■ 177 Abbeville Rd, LONDON, SW4 9RL.   (hq)
   020 7498 6919   fax 020 7498 9080
   email office@ier.org.uk   http://www.ier.org.uk
   Dir: Carolyn Jones,
   Admin & Publications Officer: Megan Dobney
▲ Company Limited by Guarantee; Registered Charity
○ *Q; 'an independent organisation or think-tank acting as a
   focal point for the spread of new ideas in the field of the
   Labour movement & labour law'
● Conf - ET - Res - Inf - Publishing
M 406 i, 55 f, 290 org, UK / 6 i, 3 f, o'seas
¶ Books on various aspects of labour law - 8; £6.50 m, £20 nm.

Institute of Energy
   July 2003 merged with the Institute of Petroleum to form the **Energy Institute**

Institute of Entertainment & Arts Management   (IEAM)   1982

■ 17 Drake Close, HORSHAM, W Sussex, RH12 4UB.   (admin/p)
   0870 241 7248   fax 0870 241 7248
   email admin@ieam.co.uk   http://www.ieam.co.uk
   Admin: Shirley Carpenter
   Pres: Chris Haylett (Ambassador Theatre Group)
▲ Company Limited by Guarantee
Br Northern & Southern areas
○ *D; for managers & managements throughout local
   government, commercial & subsidised sectors of the arts,
   entertainment & related leisure interests
● Conf - Mtgs - ET - Exhib - Comp - Stat - Inf - VE
M 290 i
¶ NL - 12;   Ybk - 1; both ftm only.

Institute of Environmental Management & Assessment (IEMA)   1999

■ St Nicholas House, 70 Newport, LINCOLN, LN1 3DP.   (hq)
   01522 540069   fax 01522 540090
   email info@iema.net   http://www.iema.net
   Chief Exec: Russell Foster
○ *P; to promote & develop the best practice standards in
   environmental management, auditing & assessment
● Conf - Mtgs - ET - Exam - Exhib - Inf - Lib
M 7,620 i, 310 f, UK / 1,245 i, 26 f, o'seas

Institute of Explosives Engineers   (IExpE)   1974

NR Wellington Hall 289, Cranfield University, Defence Academy of
   the UK, Shrivenham, SWINDON, Wilts, SN6 8LA.   (hq)
   01793 785322   fax 01793 785972
   email info@iexpe.org   http://www.iexpe.org
   Sec: Gillian Bonar
Br 13
○ *P; the qualifying body for explosives engineers
Gp Quarrying; Tunnelling & shaft sinking; Excavation & land
   clearance; Demolition; Underwater work; Pyrotechnics;
   Offshore oil operations; High explosives trials; Film & special
   effects
● Conf - Mtgs - ET - Exam - Res - Exhib - SG - Inf - LG
< Eur Fedn Explosives Engineers
M 758 i, 31 i (company), 20 f, UK / 145 i, 4 f, o'seas
¶ Explosives Engineering - 4.

Institute of Export   (IoE)   1935

■ Export House, Minerva Business Park, Lynch Wood,
   PETERBOROUGH, Cambs, PE2 6FT.   (hq)
   01733 404400   fax 01733 404444
   email institute@export.org.uk
   http://www.international-trade.org.uk
   Dir: Philip Turon
▲ Company Limited by Guarantee; Registered Charity
Br 21; 1 o'seas
○ *P; to enhance the export performance of the UK by setting &
   raising professional standards in international trade
   management & export practice
Gp Education & training; Specialised business information;
   Membership representation
● Conf - Mtgs - ET - Exam - Res - Stat - Expt - Inf - LG
M 3,000 i, 100 f, UK / 500 i, o'seas
¶ Exporting World - 10; ftm, £4 nm.

Institute for Family Business (UK)

NR 36 Park Rd, LONDON, NW1 4SA.   (hq)
   0870 872 8388   fax 0870 872 8387
   http://www.ifb.org.uk
   Dir Gen: Grant E Gordon
○ *T

Institute of Fence Engineers

no longer in existence

Institute of Field Archaeologists   (IFA)   1982

NR SHES, University of Reading, Whiteknights, PO Box 227,
   READING, Berks, RG6 6AB.   (hq)
   0118-931 6446
   Dir: Peter Hinton
▲ Company Limited by Guarantee
Br 7 area groups
○ *L, *P; to promote, maintain & develop professional guidelines
   & standards for archaeology
Gp Buildings; Archaeological resource management; Maritime
   affairs; Finds
● Conf - Mtgs - ET - Res - Exhib - Inf
< Irish Assn Profl Archaeologists; Assn Archaeol Illustrators &
   Surveyors
M 1,597 i, 37 org, UK / 26 i, o'seas
¶ The Archaeologist (Jnl) - 4.   IFA Ybk (incl LM).
   IFA Technical Papers.   AR.   Standards.
   IFA Papers.   Constitutional Documents.

Institute of Financial Accountants   (IFA)   1916

■ Burford House, 44 London Rd, SEVENOAKS, Kent,
   TN13 1AS.   (hq)
   01732 458080
   Chief Exec: J M Dean
▲ Company Limited by Guarantee
○ *P; for accountants in commerce, industry & private practice
M i

Institute of Financial Planning   (IFP)   1987

NR Whitefriars Centre, Lewins Mead, BRISTOL, BS1 2NT.   (hq)
   0117-945 2470   fax 0117-929 2214
   email enquiries@financialplanning.org.uk
   http://www.financialplanning.org.uk
   Chief Exec: Nick Cann
▲ Company Limited by Guarantee
Br 12
○ *P; to promote understanding & recognition of the financial
   planning profession (those who offer objective assistance to
   clients in organising their personal & business affairs)
● Conf - Mtgs - ET - Exam - Res - Exhib - Comp - SG - Inf - Lib -
   LG
< Intl CFP Coun; Financial Planning Assn (FPA)(USA)
M 1,250 i, UK / 50 i, o'seas
¶ Financial Planner - 4; ftm only.

© CBD Research Ltd · Beckenham · BR3 5JS · Tel 020 8650 7745 · Fax 020 8650 0768 · E-mail cbd@cbdresearch.com · www.cbdresearch.com

Institute of Financial Services   (ifs)   1879

NR   4-9 Burgate Lane, CANTERBURY, Kent, CT1 2XJ.   (hq)
         01227 818609
         Chief Exec: Gavin Shreeve
▲   Registered Charity
Br   72 local centres; 6 o'seas
○   *L, *P; education & training of financial services staff
●   Conf - Mtgs - ET - Exam - Res - Exhib - Comp - SG - Inf - Lib
M   42,000 i
¶   Financial World - 12.
         ifs News - 12.   Syllabus.   Catalogue.   AR.
         Publications list available.
         Note: The parent body of the ifs is the Chartered Institute of
         Bankers; the ifs develops & delivers qualifications for which
         the CIB acts as an assessing & awarding body

Institute for Fiscal Studies   (IFS)   1969

■   7 Ridgmount St, LONDON, WC1E 7AE.   (hq)
         020 7291 4800
         email mailbox@ifs.org.uk   http://www.ifs.org.uk
         Dir: Robert Chote
▲   Company Limited by Guarantee; Registered Charity
○   *Q; promotion of research & understanding of the economic &
         social implications of existing taxes & different fiscal systems
●   Conf - ET - Res - SG - Stat - Inf
M   600 i, 100 f, 100 org, UK / 100 i, 50 org, o'seas
¶   Fiscal Studies (Jnl) - 4; ftm, £237 nm.
         Reports & Commentaries - 15; ftm, c £40 each nm.
         Briefing Notes - 15;   NL - 4; Working Papers - 20;
         [last three publications online].

Institute of Fisheries Management   (IFM)   1969

■   22 Rushworth Ave, WEST BRIDGFORD, Notts, NG2 7LF.
         (treas/p)
         0115-982 2317   fax 0115-982 6150
         email valerie@ifmt.fsnet.co.uk   http://www.ifm.org.uk
         Exec Sec: Valerie Holt
▲   Un-incorporated Society
Br   11
○   *L, *P; management of freshwater aquatic environment
●   Conf - Mtgs - ET - Exam - LG
<   is a constituent body of the Soc for the Envt
M   1,010 i, 5 f, 40 org, UK / 40 i, o'seas
¶   Fish - 4; ftm only.

Institute of Food Science & Technology   (IFST)   1964

■   5 Cambridge Court, 210 Shepherds Bush Rd, LONDON,
         W6 7NJ.   (hq)
         020 7603 6316
         email info@ifst.org   http://www.ifst.org
         Chief Exec: Helen G Wild
▲   Company Limited by Guarantee; Registered Charity
Br   7
○   *L, *P; application of science & technology to every aspect of
         food
●   Conf - Mtgs - ET - Exam - VE - LG
<   Intl U of Food Science & Technology (IUFOST); UK Fedn for
         Food Science & Technology (UKFFOST); Parliamentary Food
         & Health Forum; Eur Food Law Assn (UK section); Science
         Coun; Foundation for Science & Technology
M   2,221 f, UK / 335 f, o'seas
¶   International Jnl of Food Science & Technology - 10;
         £21 m (£13 online), £936 yr nm (UK).
         Food Science & Technology - 4; ftm, £96 yr nm.
         Keynote - 11; ftm.

Institute of Food Science & Technology of Ireland   1975

IRL   PO Box 10071, DUBLIN 2, Republic of Ireland.
         email ifsti@hotmail.com   http://www.ifsti.com
         Hon Sec: Dr Lisa O'Connor
○   *L

Institute of Football Management & Administration   (IFMA)   1990

NR   The Camkin Suite, 1 Pegasus House, Pegasus Court,
         Tachbook Park, WARWICK, CV34 6LW.   (hq)
         01926 831556   fax 01926 429781
         email ifma@leaguemanagers.com
         http://www.leaguemanagers.com
         Chmn: Andy Daykin
▲   Registered Trade Union
○   *S; for all key staff in 92 FA Premier & Football League football
         clubs
●   Conf - Mtgs - ET - Exhib - SG - Inf
M   708 i
¶   Centre Circle - 4; free.

Institute of Fundraising   (IF)   1983

NR   Park Place, 12 Lawn Lane, LONDON, SW8 1UD.   (hq)
         020 7840 1000   fax 020 7840 1001
         http://www.institute-of-fundraising.org.uk
▲   Un-incorporated Society
○   *P
M   i, f & org
¶   Update - 11; ftm only.   LM; m only.   Ybk; ftm.
         List of Consultants; ftm.   AR; free.
×   2002 Institute of Charity Fundraising Managers

Institute of Geologists of Ireland

IRL   c/o Dept of Geology, University College Dublin, Belfield,
         DUBLIN 4, Republic of Ireland.
         353 (1) 716 2085   fax 353 (1) 283 7733
         email admin@igi.ie   http://www.igi.ie
         Sec: Geoff Wright
○   *P

Institute of Golf Club Management
         a specialist group of the **Association of Golf Club Secretaries**

Institute of Grocery Distribution   (IGD)   1909

NR   Grange Lane, Letchmore Heath, WATFORD, Herts,
         WD25 8GD.   (hq)
         01923 857141

Institute of Groundsmanship   (IOG)   1934

NR   28 Stratford Office Village, Wolverton Mill East,
         MILTON KEYNES, Bucks, MK12 5TW.   (hq)
         01908 312511   fax 01908 311140
         email iog@iog.org   http://www.iog.org
         Chief Exec: Patrick Gosset
▲   Company Limited by Guarantee
Br   39
○   *P
●   Conf - Mtgs - ET - Exam - Res - Exhib - Inf - Lib - Empl
M   i & org
¶   The Groundsman - 12.

Institute of Group Analysis   (IGA)   1971

NR   1 Daleham Gardens, LONDON, NW3 5BY.   (hq)
         020 7431 2693   fax 020 7431 7246
         email iga@igalondon.org.uk
         http://www.groupanalysis.org
         Hon Sec: Linda Anderson,   Chmn: David Vincent
▲   Company Limited by Guarantee; Registered Charity
Br   8
○   *P; a teaching institution for group-analytic psychotherapy; to
         promote group analysis; to train in group analysis
Gp   Clinical section
●   Conf - Mtgs - ET - Res - SG - Lib
M   300 i
¶   Dialogue (NL) - 3;   AR - 1; both ftm only.

Institute of Guidance Counsellors   (IGC)   1968
IRL   17 Herbert St, DUBLIN 2, Republic of Ireland.
          353 (1) 676 1975   fax 353 (1) 661 2551
          email igc@eircom.net   http://www.igc.ie
          PRO: Marion Quinn
○   *P

Institute & Guild of Brewing
          since 2005 **Institute of Brewing & Distilling**

Institute of Health Care Management   (IHM)   1902
NR   18-21 Morley St, LONDON, SE1 7QZ.   (hq)
          020 7620 1030
▲   Company Limited by Guarantee
○   *M, *N, *P; for those involved in the management of health
          services; to affect health services policy
●   Conf - Mtgs - ET - Exam - Exhib
M   8,500 i, UK / 500 i, o'seas

Institute of Health Food Retailing
          since 2002 **Health Food Institute**

Institute of Health Promotion & Education   (IHPE)   1962
■   Oral Health & Development, University Dental Hospital, Higher
          Cambridge St, MANCHESTER, M15 6FH.   (hsp)
          0161-275 6610   fax 0161-275 6299
          email anthony.blinkhorn@man.ac.uk
          http://www.ihpe.org.uk
          Hon Sec: Prof A S Blinkhorn
▲   Un-incorporated Society
○   *L; for all interested in health promotion & education
Gp   Professional educators
M   600 i, 150 f, UK / 100 i, 50 f, o'seas
¶   Jnl - 4; ftm, £36 yr nm.

**Institute of Health Record & Information Management (UK)
(IHRIM(UK))   1948**
NR   141 Leander Drive, Castleton, ROCHDALE, Lancs,
          OL11 2XE.   (hq)
          01706 868481   fax 01706 868481
          email ihrim@zen.co.uk   http://www.ihrim.co.uk
          Office Mgr: Gordon Nicholson
▲   Un-incorporated Society
○   *P; the promotion of excellence & professionalism in the
          management of health records & information to enable
          delivery of high quality health care professions
●   Conf - ET - Exam - Exhib - SG - Inf
<   Intl Fedn of Health Records Orgs (IFHRO); NHS Inf Authority
M   735 i, 20 f, UK / 50 i, o'seas
¶   Jnl - 4; ftm.
×   2001 Institute of Health Record Information & Management

**Institute of Healthcare Engineering & Estate Management
(IHEEM)   1943**
NR   2 Abingdon House, Cumberland Business Centre,
          PORTSMOUTH, Hants, PO5 1DS.   (hq)
          023 9282 3186
          The Chief Executive
▲   Company Limited by Guarantee; Registered Charity
Br   14; Hong Kong, Ireland
○   *L, *P; for all those working in the healthcare engineering &
          estates field; the Institute is nominated by the Engineering
          Council
Gp   Sterilisation, Architects; Diagnostic imaging section
●   Conf - Mtgs - ET - Exhib - Lib
<   Intl Hospital Fedn; Intl Fedn of Hospital Engg; Engg Coun
M   2,200 i, 60 f, UK / 150 i, 5 f, o'seas
¶   Health Estate Jnl - 10.   Ybk.   AR.
          Guide to Commissioning.

Institute of Heraldic & Genealogical Studies   (IHGS)   1961
■   79-82 Northgate, CANTERBURY, Kent, CT1 1BA.   (hq)
          01227 768664   fax 01227 765617
          email ihgs@ihgs.ac.uk   http://www.ihgs.ac.uk
          Principal: Cecil R Humphery-Smith
▲   Registered Charity
○   *E, *P, *Q; to study the history & structure of the family
          genealogy, heraldry & their applications for historical
          research; family history research for genetical inherited
          diseases
●   ET - Exam - Res - Lib
<   Intl Confedn of Genealogy & Heraldry; Fedn of Family History
          Socs
M   240 i, UK / 30 i, o'seas
¶   Family History (Jnl) - 4; ftm, £15 yr nm.

Institute of Highway Incorporated Engineers   (IHIE)   1965
■   De Morgan House, Russell Square, LONDON, WC1B 4HS.
          (hq)
          020 7436 7487   fax 020 7436 7488
          email information@ihie.org.uk   http://www.ihie.org.uk
          Sec: Miss J M Walker
▲   Company Limited by Guarantee
Br   15
○   *P; interests of incorporated engineers & technicians in
          landbased highways & transportation
●   Conf - Mtgs - Exam - Exhib - Comp - VE
<   Engg Coun; Construction Ind Coun
M   3,000 i, UK / 100 i, o'seas
¶   Transportation Professional - 10; ftm (joint publication with
          Institution of Highways & Transportation).

Institute of Historic Building Conservation   (IHBC)   1981
■   Jubilee House, High St, TISBURY, Wilts, SP3 6HA.   (hsp)
          01747 873133   fax 01747 871718
          Sec: Dr Richard Morrice
○   *P; to promote the successful preservation & enhancement of
          the historic built environment in the UK
M   c 1,500 i
¶   Context - 5; ftm only.

Institute of Holistic Therapies   1976
■   Oakwood, Kirkdale Court, KIRKBYMOORSIDE, N Yorks,
          YO62 6HN.   (hq)
          01751 430626
          Head Tutor: Keith Jones
▲   Un-incorporated Society
○   *P; to train people in the art of holistic or alternative medicine &
          therapies; to provide low cost insurance protection for all
          members of the profession
●   ET - Exam - Res
<   La Roche Intl Coll
M   300 i, 1 org, UK / 250 i, o'seas

Institute of Home Inspectors   (IHI)   2006
■   36 The Chase, BROMLEY, Kent, BR1 3DF.   (hsp)
          020 8464 0563
          email ndengland@aol.com
          Hon Sec: C P England
▲   Company Limited by Guarantee
Br   20
○   *P; licensed home inspectors & those studying to be licensed
          home inspectors
M   6,000 i
¶   email NL.

© CBD Research Ltd · Beckenham · BR3 5JS · Tel 020 8650 7745 · Fax 020 8650 0768 · E-mail cbd@cbdresearch.com · www.cbdresearch.com

Institute of Home Safety   (IHS)   1976

- 56 Barton Rd, LUTON, Beds, LU3 2BB.   (hsp)
  01582 493382
  Chmn: Carol Ainge
- *E, *W; accident prevention in the home & its environs (inc outbuildings, gardens, ponds etc); to provide a forum & point of contact for the development, dissemination & exchange of ideas & information
- Conf - Mtgs - ET - Exhib - Comp - Inf - LG - Organisation of campaigns etc on home safety & accident prevention
- < R Soc for Prevention of Accidents (RoSPA); Child Accident Prevention Trust (CAPT); London Home & Water Safety Coun (LHWSC); Inst of Safety & Public Protection (ISPP); Brit Safety Soc (BSS)
- M   70 i
- ¶   NL - 4.   AR.

Institute of Horticulture   (IOH)   1985

- 14-15 Belgrave Sq, LONDON, SW1X 8PS.   (hq)
  020 7245 6943   fax 020 7245 6943
  email ioh@horticulture.org.uk
  http://www.horticulture.org.uk
  Admin Mgr: Kiersty Darnell
- ▲ Registered Charity
- Br   8
- *P; to promote the profession of horticulture
- Gp Advisory & research; Amenity horticulture; Commercial horticulture; Education
- Conf - Mtgs - ET - Comp - Inf - VE - LG
- M   2,000 i, 10 f, UK / 65 i, o'seas
- ¶   The Horticulturist (Jnl) - 4; ftm, £77 yr nm.
  Come Into Horticulture (careers booklet);
  Education & Training Courses in Horticulture;   AR.

Institute of Ideas

NR Academy of Ideas, Signet House, 49-51 Farringdon Rd, LONDON, EC1M
http://www.3JP.
020 7269 9220   fax 020 7269 9235
email academy@instituteofideas.com
http://www.instituteofideas.com

Institute of Imagination

NR House of William Blake, 17 South Molton St, LONDON, W1K 5QT.
020 7495 5654

Institute of Incorporated Public Accountants

IRL Unit 2 Abbey Moat House, NAAS, Co Kildare, Republic of Ireland.
353 (45) 895936   fax 353 (45) 895830
email info@iipa.ie   http://www.iipa.ie
Pres: John McCarrick
Sec: Brendan Cosgrave
- *P

Institute for Independent Business   (IIB)   1984

NR Clarendon House, Bridle Path, WATFORD, Herts, WD17 1UB.
(hq)
01923 239543
email info@iib.org.uk   http://www.iib.org.uk
Principal: Linden P Dyason
- ▲ Company Limited by Guarantee; Registered Charity
- Br   4; India, USA
- *T; to provide practical advice to the independent business sector
- Gp Small to medium-sized businesses
- Conf - Mtgs - ET - Exam - Res - SG - Expt - Inf - Support for experienced executives wishing to become management consultants
- M   950 f, UK / 30 f, o'seas
- ¶   Independent Business Today - 4.

Institute of Indirect Taxation   (IIT)   1991

- The Stables, Station Road West, OXTED, Surrey, RH8 9EE.   (hq)
  01883 730658   fax 01883 717778
  email enquiries@theiit.org.uk   http://www.theiit.org.uk
  Chief Exec: Terry Davies
- ▲ Company Limited by Guarantee
- *P; to qualify, regulate & represent practitioners & research in VAT, customs, excise, stamp taxes, other direct & indirect taxes
- Conf - ET - Exam - Res - LG
- <   Academy of Experts
- M   550 i, UK / 50 i, o'seas
- ¶   Indirect Tax Voice - 9; ftm.

Institute for Individual Psychology
  see **Adlerian Society (of the United Kingdom) & Institute for Individual Psychology**

Institute of Industrial Engineers   (IIE)

IRL PO Box 790, Sandyford, DUBLIN 18, Republic of Ireland.
353 (1) 294 3131   fax 353 (1) 294 3131
email enquiries@iie.ie   http://www.iie.ie
Hon Sec: Daniel Vaughan
- *P

** Institute of Industrial Selling

Organisation lost: see Introduction paragraph 3

Institute of Information Scientists
  April 2002 merged with the Library Association to become **CILIP: Chartered Institute of Library & Information Professionals**

Institute of Insurance Brokers

- Higham Business Centre, Midland Rd, HIGHAM FERRERS, Northants, NN10 8DW.   (hq)
  01933 410003   fax 01933 410020
  email inst.ins.brokers@iib-uk.com
  http://www.iib-uk.com
  Dir Gen: Andrew Paddick,   Sec: Barbara Bradshaw
- ▲ Company Limited by Guarantee
- *P; for independent insurance broking businesses
- Conf - Mtgs - ET - Exam - Res - Exhib - Comp - SG - Inf - Lib - LG
- M   1,100 f

Institute of Internal Auditors - United Kingdom & Ireland   (IIA-UK)

NR 13 Abbeville Mews, 88 Clapham Park Rd, LONDON, SW4 7BX.
020 7498 0101
email info@iia.org.uk
Chief Exec: Mrs Gail Easterbrook
- *P
- M   i
- ¶   Internal Auditing & Business Risk - 12.
  Various other publications.

Institute of International Licensing Practitioners Ltd   (IILP)   1969

- Oxford Centre for Innovation, Mill St, OXFORD, OX2 0JX.
  (asa)
  01865 812060   fax 01865 793165
  email enquiries.iilp.net   http://www.iilp.net
  Sec: James Hunt,   Chmn: Mike Kerr
- ▲ Company Limited by Guarantee
- *P; assistance to companies, or individuals, to obtain the service of a qualified licensing practitioner; to set, promote & maintain high standards of professional practice amongst those engaged in licensing, technology transfer & commercialising invention; to promote the wider understanding of the value of licensing in international business as a marketing & business development tool
- Conf
- M   i, f, org

Institute of International Trade of Ireland

IRL   28 Merrion Sq, DUBLIN 2, Republic of Ireland.
      353 (1) 661 2182   fax 353 (1) 661 2315
      email iiti@irishexporters.ie   http://www.irishexporters.ie
      Dir: John F Whelan
○   *T

Institute of Inventors   (II)   1964

■   19-23 Fosse Way, Ealing, LONDON, W13 0BZ.   (hq)
      020 8998 3540; 6372
      http://www.instituteofinventors.com
      Pres: Michael V Rodrigues
▲   Un-incorporated Society
○   *L
Gp   Sifting c'ee;
      Depts: Online database patent research, Patent drafting, CAD
        design development
●   Exam - Res - Inf - LG - Patent searching - New invention design
        & development - Invention investor marriage
M   i & f
¶   New Invention List - 12.

Institute of IT Training

NR   Westwood House, Westwood Business Park, COVENTRY, Warks,
        CV4 8HS.   (hq)
      0845 006 8858
      Chief Exec: Colin Steed
▲   Company Limited by Guarantee
○   *P; for IT trainers
●   ET
M   3,500 i, UK / 250 i, o'seas

Institute for Jewish Policy Research   (JPR)   1996

NR   79 Wimpole St, LONDON, W1G 9RY.   (hq)
      020 7935 8266
      Exec Dir: Antony Lerman
▲   Registered Charity
○   *Q; 'an independent think tank which informs & influences
        policy, opinion & decision making on issues affecting Jewish
        life worldwide'
●   Conf - Res - Inf - Development & dissemination of policy
        proposals - Promotion of public debate
M   i & org
¶   Patterns of Prejudice (Jnl) - 4.
      JPR Reports & Policy Papers.
      Antisemitism in the World Today; (Internet publication)

Institute of Leadership & Management   (ILM)   1947

NR   Stowe House, Netherstowe, LICHFIELD, Staffs, WS13 6TJ.   (hq)
      01543 251346
      Chief Exec: Kim Parish
▲   Company Limited by Guarantee; Registered Charity
○   *P; 'education for supervisors & first-line managers, leading to
        management, world class & team leader qualifications'
●   Conf - ET - Exam - Inf
M   24,000 i
¶   Modern Management - 6.

Institute of Legal Cashiers & Administrators   (ILCA)   1978

■   Marlowe House (2nd floor), 109 Station Rd, SIDCUP, Kent,
        DA15 7ET.   (hq)
      020 8302 2867   fax 020 8302 7481
      email info@ilca.org.uk   http://www.ilca.org.uk
      Exec Sec: Margaret Macdonald
○   *P; to promote the status of the legal cashier & administrator
●   Conf - Mtgs - ET - Exam - Res - Exhib - Comp - Inf
<   Inst Legal Accountants Ireland
M   3,000 i
¶   Legal Abacus - 6; ftm, £30 yr nm.

Institute of Legal Executives   (ILEX)   1963

■   Kempston Manor, Kempston, BEDFORD, MK42 7AB.   (hq)
      01234 841000   fax 01234 853982
      email info@ilex.org.uk   http://www.ilex.org.uk
      Sec Gen: Mrs Diane Burleigh
▲   Un-incorporated Society
Br   19; Bermuda, Gibraltar
○   *P; for legal executives (persons employed by, or working for,
        solicitors in private practice, or solicitors employed as such in
        governmental, public, commercial or other departments or
        undertakings)
Gp   Lawyers; Press; Colleges; MP's
●   Conf - Mtgs - Exam - Res - Exhib - Comp
M   22,000 i
¶   Legal Executive Jnl - 12; ftm.
      AR; free.

Institute of Legal Secretaries & PAs   (ILS)   1990

■   9 Unity St, BRISTOL, BS1 5HH.   (hq)
      0117-927 7007   fax 0117-929 3887
      email info@institutelegalsecretaries.com
      http://www.institutelegalsecretaries.com
      Chief Exec: Emma Stacey
▲   Un-incorporated Society
○   *P; to provide for the professional recognition of members by
        the quality of their qualifications, standard, skills & expertise;
        to further the knowledge of law & legal procedure
Gp   Legal: Secretaries, PAs, Receptionists
●   Conf - ET - Exam - Res - Exhib - Inf - LG
<   Nat Assn of Licensed Paralegals
M   c 2,000 i
¶   Dedicated - 4; ftm only.

Institute of Leisure & Amenity Management   (ILAM)   1982

NR   ILAM House, Lower Basildon, READING, Berks, RG8 9NE.
        (hq)
      01491 874800   fax 01491 874801
      email info@ilam.co.uk   http://www.ilam.co.uk
      Chief Exec: Andy Worthington
▲   Registered Charity
Br   13
○   *P; representing the public, private & voluntary sectors of leisure
        - sports centres, arts & entertainment complexes, parks,
        gardens & playgrounds, museums & tourist attractions,
        health & fitness clubs, countryside recreation
Gp   Children's play; Cultural activities; Sports services; Tourism &
        visitor attractions; Leisure education & training; Parks, open
        spaces & countryside
●   Conf - Mtgs - ET - Exam - Res - Exhib - Comp - SG - Stat - Inf -
        Lib - LG
M   5,000 i
¶   Leisure Manager - 12; ftm, £40 yr nm.
      Leisure News & Jobs - 52; ftm, £35 nm.   AR; ftm.
      Note: is in the process of merging with the National Association
        for Sports Development to form the **Institute for Sports,
        Parks & Leisure.**

Institute of Leisure & Amenity Management Ireland Ltd   (ILAM)

IRL   The Old Barracks, Main St, CLANE, Co Kildare, Republic of
        Ireland.
      353 (45) 861201   fax 353 (45) 893195
      email info@ilamireland.ie   http://www.ilamireland.ie
      Chief Exec: Kilian Fisher
○   *P

Institute of Licensed Trade Stock Auditors   (ILTSA)   1953

- ■ Brockwell Heights, Brockwell Lane, Triangle, SOWERBY BRIDGE, HX6 3PQ.   (hsp)
  01422 833003   fax 01422 316641
  email dianeswift@iltsa.co.uk   http://www.iltsa.co.uk
  Sec: Diane Swift
- ▲ Company Limited by Guarantee
- Br 300
- ○ *P; to support licensed trade stock auditors in the UK
- ● Mtg (AGM) - ET - Exam
- M 395 i
- ¶ The Stock Auditor - 6; ftm, £2 each nm.
  Taking Stock Book; £18.   LM - 1; free.

Institute of Linguists
   since 2005-06 **Chartered Institute of Linguists**

Institute of Logistics & Transport
   since 2004 **Chartered Institute of Logistics & Transport in the UK**

Institute of Machine Woodworking Technology Ltd (IMWoodT)   1952

- ■ St Keynes, Bowl Rd, CHARING, Kent, TN27 0HB.   (hsp)
  01233 713768   fax 01233 713768
  email imwoodt@tesco.net   http://www.imwoodt.org.uk
  Hon Sec: Pamela Fryer
- Br 4; 1
- ○ *E, *L; theory & practice of machine woodworking technology
- Gp Health & safety
- ● Conf - Mtgs - ET - Exhib - Comp - Inf - VE
- M i, 1 f
- ¶ Woodworking Technology - 1; ftm.   AR; ftm only.

Institute of Maintenance & Building Management   (IMBM)   1951

- ■ Keets House, 30 East St, FARNHAM, Surrey, GU9 7SW.   (hq)
  01252 710994   fax 01252 737741
  http://www.imbm.org.uk
  Chief Exec: Simon P Sinclair
- ▲ Un-incorporated Society
- ○ *P; the industry lead body for building maintenance & estates services & the effective management of buildings
- M 2,100 i

Institute of Management
   since 2002 **Chartered Management Institute**

Institute of Management Consultancy
   a group of the **Chartered Management Institute**

Institute of Management Consultants in Ireland   (IMCI)

- IRL 329 Gardner House, Wilton Place, DUBLIN 2, Republic of Ireland.
  353 (1) 662 6577   fax 353 (1) 704 8598
  email info@imci.ie   http://www.imci.ie
  Sec: Brian Flanagan
- ○ *P

Institute for the Management of Information Systems   (IMIS)   1978

- ■ 5 Kingfisher House, New Mill Rd, ORPINGTON, Kent, BR5 3QG.   (hq)
  07000 023456   fax 07000 023023
  email central@imis.org.uk   http://www.imis.org.uk
  Chief Exec: Ian M Rickwood
- ▲ Registered Charity
- Br 6; Malta, Malaysia, Zambia, Zimbabwe
- ○ *P; to advance the interests of the management of information systems / information technology profession
- Gp Outsourcing; Women in Technology (WIT)
- ● Conf - Mtgs - ET - Exam - LG
- M 3,255 i, 40 f, UK / 7,411 i, 20 f, o'seas
- ¶ IMIS Jnl - 6; free.
  IT Skills Trend Report Summary; free.

Institute of Management Services   (IMS)   1978

- NR Brooke House, 24 Dam St, LICHFIELD, Staffs, WS13 6AB.   (hq)
  01543 266909
  Management Services Officer: Vivienne Phillips
- ▲ Registered Charity
- ○ *P; productivity improvement; work study; O&M & related areas
- M 4,000 i

Institute of Management Specialists   (IMS)   1971

- ■ Warwick Corner, 42 Warwick Rd, KENILWORTH, Warks, CV8 1HE.   (asa)
  01926 855498   fax 01926 513100
  Pres/Hon Sec: Prof H J Manners
- ○ *P; for those in industrial, business, commercial, professional, educational & technical fields, who provide a service to senior departmental management
- < Academy of Execs & Administrators; Academy of Multi-Skills; Inst of Manufacturing; Profl Business & Technical Mgt
- ¶ The Management Specialist (Jnl) - 3; £2 m, £7 nm.

Institute of Manufacturing   (IManf)   1978

- ■ Warwick Corner, 42 Warwick Rd, KENILWORTH, Warks, CV8 1HE.   (asa)
  01926 855498   fax 01926 513100
  Pres/Hon Sec: Prof H J Manners
- ○ *P; to develop recognition of the professional role of the manufacturer in industry
- ● ET - Exam
- < Inst of Mgt Specialists; Profl Business & Technical Mgt
- ¶ Manufacturing (Jnl) - 1; £2 m, £7 nm.
  Manufacturing Management - 1; £2 m, £7 nm.

Institute of Marine Engineering, Science & Technology (IMarEST)   1889

- NR 80 Coleman St, LONDON, EC2R 5BJ.   (hq)
  020 7382 2600   fax 020 7382 2670
  email info@imarest.org   http://www.imarest.org
  Sec: Keith Read
- ▲ Registered Charity
- Br 14; 33 o'seas
- ○ *L, *P; to promote the scientific development of marine engineering, science & technology: marine, offshore & subsea engineering, naval architecture & ship construction, marine science & marine technology
- Gp Marine, offshore & subsea engineering; Naval architecture & ship construction; Marine science & technology
- ● Conf - Mtgs - ET - Exhib - Inf - Lib - LG
- < Engg Coun (EC); Intl Maritime Org (IMO); W Eur Confedn of Maritime Technology Societies (WEMT)
- M 10,073 i, UK / 6,067 i, o'seas
- ¶ Marine Engineers Review - 10.
  Jnl of Offshore Technology - 6.
  Maritime IT & Electronics - 6.
  Transactions (after each technical meeting).
  IMarEST News - 12.   AR.
  Technical publications & CD ROMs - catalogue available.
     Member prices on request.

Institute of Market Officers

has closed

Institute of Masters of Wine   (IMW)   1953

NR   Mapfre House, 2-3 Philpot Lane, LONDON, EC3M 8AN.   (hq)
020 7621 2830   fax 020 7929 2302
email enquiries@masters-of-wine.org
Exec Dir: Jane Carr
Br   Australia, USA
○   *P; to promote the attainment & maintenance of high standards
of technical knowledge & achievement by those making their
livelihood in the wine & spirit trade
M   229 i
¶   Jnl of Wine Research - 3.   NL - 12.   LM - 1.

Institute of Materials
merged with the Institution of Mining & Metallurgy in 2002 to form
the **Institute of Materials, Minerals & Mining**

Institute of Materials, Minerals & Mining   (IMMM)   1945

NR   1 Carlton House Terrace, LONDON, SW1Y 5DB.   (hq)
020 7451 7300   fax 020 7839 1702
Chief Exec: Dr B A Rickinson
▲   Registered Charity
○   *L, *P; the professional body for all involved in the field of
materials, minerals & mining; to promote the science & study
of all aspects of the science, technology & use of materials &
minerals
Gp   IoP: the Packaging Society; Ceramic divn
●   Conf - Mtgs - ET - Exam - Exhib - Comp - SG - Stat - Expt - Inf
- Lib - VE - Empl
M   i & f
¶   Jnl.   AR.
×   2002 (Institute of Materials
(Institution of Mining & Metallurgy

Institute of Mathematics & its Applications   (IMA)   1964

■   Catherine Richards House, 16 Nelson St, SOUTHEND-ON-
SEA, Essex, SS1 1EF.   (hq)
01702 354020   fax 01702 354111
email post@ima.org.uk   http://www.ima.org.uk
Exec Dir: David Youdan
▲   Registered Charity
Br   6
○   *E, *L, *P; for qualified & practising mathematicians; to
promote mathematics in industry, business, the public sector,
education & research
Gp   Computational fluid dynamics; Computational science &
engineering education; Environment; Numerical analysis;
Management
●   Conf - Mtgs - Comp - LG
<   Eur Mathematical Soc; Coun of Mathematical Sciences
M   5,900 i, UK / 500 i, o'seas
¶   Mathematics Today - 6; ftm, £82 yr nm.
IMA Jnl of Applied Mathematics.
IMA Jnl of Numerical Analysis.
Mathematical Medicine & Biology: a Jnl of the IMA.
IMA Jnl of Mathematical Control & Information.
IMA Jnl of Management Mathematics.
Teaching Mathematics & its Applications: an international Jnl of
the IMA.
[prices vary with print &/or online access & discounts for the
number taken].

Institute of Maxillofacial Prosthetists & Technologists   (IMPT) 1962

NR   Maxillofacial Prosthetics Service, Poole Hospital NHS Trust,
Longfleet Rd, POOLE, Dorset, BH15 2JB.   (hsb)
Contact: Mark Townend
▲   Company Limited by Guarantee; Registered Charity
○   *L, *M, *P; to establish, oversee & maintain the study & science
of maxillofacial prosthetics & technology for the benefit of
patients requiring prosthetic rehabilitation for trauma, burns,
cancer, congenital deformity etc
●   Conf - Mtgs - ET - Exam - Res - SG - Lib - LG
M   i

Institute of Measurement & Control   (InstMC)   1944

NR   87 Gower St, LONDON, WC1E 6AF.   (hq)
020 7387 4949
Sec: Michael J Yates
▲   Registered Charity
Br   20; Hong Kong, Ireland
○   *P; to promote for the public benefit the general advancement
& application of the science & practice of measurement &
control technology
Gp   Aviation; Measurement science & technology; Systems & control
technology; Systems & management; Safety; Standards;
Weighing
●   Conf - Mtgs - ET - Exhib - LG
<   Intl Measurement Confedn (IMEKO); UK Automatic Control
Coun (UKAC); Foundation for Science & Technology
M   4,400 i, 180 f, UK / 350 i, o'seas
¶   Transactions - 5.   Measurement & Control - 10.
Interface (NL) - 2.   Ybk.

Institute of Medical Illustrators   (IMI)   1968

■   Medical & Dental Illustration, Leeds Dental Institute,
Clarendon Way, LEEDS, W Yorks, LS2 9LV.   (hsb)
0113-343 6258   fax 0113-343 6165
email a.j.robertson@leeds.ac.uk   http://www.imi.org.uk
Hon Sec: Angus J Robertson
▲   Registered Charity
○   *T, *P; to promote the role of the medical illustrator as a
professional member of a multi-skilled team offering clinical
illustrative & communication services for the benefit of patient
& client
Gp   Medical photographers; Artists; Video & audio-visual
personnel; Graphic designers; Multi-media specialists
●   Conf - Mtgs - ET - Exam - Exhib - Comp - LG
<   Eur Fedn of the Scientific Image (EFSI); Nat Bd of Registration of
Med Illustrators (NBRMI)
M   370 i, 25 f, UK / 25 i, o'seas
¶   Jnl of Audiovisual Media in Medicine - 4; ftm, £62 nm.
IMI News & Illustrator - 4; free.   LM - 1; ftm only.

Institute of Metal Finishing   (IMF)   1925

■   Exeter House, 48 Holloway Head, BIRMINGHAM, B1 1NQ.
(hq)
0121-622 7387   fax 0121-666 6316
email exeterhouse@instituteofmetalfinishing.org
http://www.uk-finishing.org.uk
Business Devt Mgr: Ken Hoare
▲   Registered Charity
Br   8
○   *L; theory & practice of all aspects of metal finishing
Gp   Aluminium; Organic; Printed circuit; Electroforming
●   Conf - Mtgs - ET - Exam - Exhib - SG - Inf - Lib - VE
M   1,200 i, 62 f, UK / 345 i, 3 f, o'seas
¶   Transactions - 6.

© CBD Research Ltd · Beckenham · BR3 5JS · Tel 020 8650 7745 · Fax 020 8650 0768 · E-mail cbd@cbdresearch.com · www.cbdresearch.com

Institute of Money Advisers   2006
- ■ Office 2 / Voluntary Action Leeds, Stringer House, 34 Lupton St, Hunslet, LEEDS, W Yorks, LS10 2QW.   (hq)
  0113-270 8444   fax 0113-270 2111
  Admin: Carde Robertson
- ▲ Registered Charity
- ○ *P, *W; for money advisers (ie those who advise debtors); to provide a range of services
- ● Conf - Mtgs - ET - Exhib - Stat - Inf - LG
- < NCVO; ASA
- M 600 i
- ¶ Quarterly Account - 4; ftm, £25 nm.   AR - 1; ftm only.
- × 2005 Money Advice Association

Institute of the Motor Industry (Inc)   (IMI)   1920
- ■ Fanshaws, BRICKENDON, Herts, SG13 8PQ.   (hq)
  01992 511521   fax 01992 511548
  email imi@motor.org.uk   http://www.motor.org.uk
  Chief Exec: Sarah Sillars
  Dir Marketing: N C Beaven
- ▲ Company Limited by Guarantee
- Br Australia, Malaysia
- ○ *P
- ● Conf - Mtgs - ET - Exam - Res - Stat - Inf
- M 25,160 i, UK / 3,100 i, o'seas
- ¶ Motor Industry Magazine - 10; ftm, £4 nm.

Institute of Musical Instrument Technology   (IMIT)   1961
- ■ 11 Kendall Avenue South, SOUTH CROYDON, Surrey, CR2 0QR.   (hsp)
  http://www.imit.org.uk
  Hon Sec: Malcolm Dalton
- ▲ Company Limited by Guarantee
- ○ *L, *P; for those engaged in musical instrument design, manufacture, repair or education
- ● Conf - Mtgs - Exam - Lib - VE
- M 215 i, UK / 5 i, o'seas
- ¶ Jnl - c 1;   Soundings - 4;   LM - 1; all ftm.

Institute for Numerical Computation & Analysis
   see **INCA - Institute for Numerical Computation & Analysis**

Institute of Operations Management   (IOM)   1969
- NR University of Warwick Science Park, Sir William Lyons Rd, COVENTRY, Warks, CV4 7EZ.   (hq)
  024 7669 2266   fax 024 7669 2266
  email iom@iomnet.org.uk   http://www.iomnet.org.uk
  Chief Exec: J D Tayler
- ▲ Company Limited by Guarantee; Registered Charity
- Br 10
- ○ *P; operations supply chain & production management in manufacturing & service industries
- Gp Special interest: 1) Pharmaceutical, toiletries & chemicals; 2) Advanced planning & scheduling; 3) Lean & Agile; 4) Product support & services; 5) Retail; 6) Health
- ● Conf - Mtgs - ET - Exam - Inf - Lib - VE - Qualification awarding body
- M 4,000 i, 15 f, UK / 100 i, o'seas
- ¶ Control - 8.

Institute for Optimum Nutrition   (ION)   1984
- ■ Avalon House, 72 Lower Mortlake Rd, RICHMOND, Surrey, TW9 2JY.   (hq)
  0870 979 1122
  http://www.ion.ac.uk
- ▲ Registered Charity
- ○ *K; to help the public achieve optimum nutrition & optimum health through an education programme &/or one-to-one consultations for advanced assessment of personal nutrition needs
- ● Conf - ET - Exam - Res - Exhib - Inf - Lib - Courses
- M 3,700 i
- ¶ Optimum Nutrition - 4.
  Specialised magazine on diet & health; ftm.

Institute for Outdoor Learning   (IOL)   1970
- ■ The Barn, Plumpton Old Hall, Plumpton, PENRITH, Cumbria, CA11 7YE.   (hq)
  01768 885800   fax 01768 885801
  email institute@outdoor-learning.org
  http://www.outdoor-learning.org
  Managing Dir: Karen J Brush
- ▲ Registered Charity
- Br regional groups
- ○ *P; to support, develop & promote learning through outdoor experiences
- Gp Development training; Research forum
- ● Conf - Mtgs - ET - Res - Exhib - SG - Stat - Inf - Lib - LG
- < CCPR; Engl Outdoor Coun; SPRITO
- M 1,100 i, 140 f, 60 org, UK / 36 i, 10 f, 3 org, o'seas
- ¶ Jnl of Adventure Education & Outdoor Learning - 2; £22 m, £25 nm.
  Horizons Magazine - 4; £17.65 m, £26 nm.
  NL - 12; ftm only.
  Outdoor Sourcebook - 1; £8 95 m, £9.95 nm.
  Guide to Careers in Outdoor Learning - 1; £8 m, £9 nm.

Institute of Packaging
   in 2005 became IOP: The Packaging Society (a division of the **Institute of Materials, Minerals & Mining**)

Institute of Paper Conservation
   in 2005 merged with the Care of Collections Forum, Photographic Materials Conservation Group, Scottish Society for Conservation & Restoration & United Kingdom Institute for Conservation of Historic & Artistic Works to form the **Institute of Conservation**

Institute of Paper International
   since 2003-04 **Institute of Paper, Printing & Publishing**

Institute of Paper, Printing & Publishing International   1992
- ■ 83 Guildford St, CHERTSEY, Surrey, KT16 9AP.   (hq)
  0870 330 8625   fax 0870 330 8615
  http://www.ip3.org.uk
  Dir Gen: David J Pryke
- Br Ireland
- ○ *P; for those employed in, or closely associated with, the paper industry
- ● Conf - Mtgs - ET - Exam - Inf - Lib - VE
- M i
- ¶ NL - 4; ftm only.
  Various other publications - details on request.
- × 2002 (Institute of Paper International
       (Institute of Publishing
  2003 (Institute of Paper & Publishing
       (Institute of Printing

Institute of Paper & Publishing
   see **Institute of Paper, Printing & Publishing International**

Institute of Paralegal Training   (ILT)   1976
- ■ The Mill, Climping St, Climping, LITTLEHAMPTON, W Sussex, BN17 5RN.   (hq)
  Sec Gen: A Y Ibberson
- ○ *P; 'for persons of education, ability & experience who desire to qualify as legal secretaries &/or administrators & to secure professional status'
- ● ET - Exam - Inf - Examination Board for Legal Secretaries
- M i
- ¶ Examination Papers.

Institute of Patentees & Inventors (IPI) 1919
NR   PO Box 39296, LONDON, SE2 7WH. (hq)
        0871 226 2091   fax 020 8293 5920
        email enquiries@invent.org.uk
        http://www.invent.org.uk
▲ Company Limited by Guarantee
○ *L; assistance & advice to inventors on protection &
     commercialising of inventions, encouragement of inventive
     talent & industrial innovation
● Mtgs - ET - Exhib - Inf
< Intl Fedn Inventors' Assns (IFIA)
M 830 i, 12 f, UK / 28 i, o'seas
¶ Future & the Inventor - 4; ftm.

Institute of Payroll & Pensions Management (IPPM) 1997
NR   Shelly House, Farmhouse Way, SOLIHULL, W Midlands,
        B90 4EH. (hq)
        0121-712 1000
▲ Company Limited by Guarantee
○ *P
● Conf - Mtgs - ET - Exam - Res - Exhib - Lib - LG
M 4,500 i
¶ Pay Advice - 12.   Members' Hbk - 1.

Institute of Petroleum
     July 2003 merged with the Institute of Energy to form the **Energy Institute**

Institute of Physics (IoP) 1919
NR   76 Portland Place, LONDON, W1B 1NT. (hq)
        020 7470 4800   fax 020 7470 4848
        email physics@iop.org   http://www.iop.org
        Chief Exec: Julia King
▲ Registered Charity
Br 13
○ *L, *P; advancement of knowledge of physics, pure & applied,
     & the elevation of the profession of physicist
Gp 44 specialist subject groups; 4 professional groups
● Conf - Mtgs - ET - Stat - LG
M i
¶ Jnl of Physics:
     A Mathematical & General Physics - 24.
     B Atomic, Molecular & Optical Physics - 24.
     C Condensed Matter - 51.
     D Applied Physics - 12.
     G Nuclear & Particle Physics - 12.
     Publications list on website.

Institute of Physics & Engineering in Medicine (IPEM) 1982
■ Fairmount House, 230 Tadcaster Rd, YORK, YO24 1ES. (hq)
        01904 610821
        http://www.ipem.ac.uk
        Gen Sec: R W Neilson
○ *L; advancement of physics & allied physical sciences applied
     to medicine & biology

Institute of Piping (InstP) 1960
NR   16-24 Otago St, GLASGOW, G12 8JH. (hq)
        0141-334 3587   fax 0141-587 6068
        Hon Sec: Robert Wallace
○ *D; examination & certification of pipers

Institute of Plumbing & Heating Engineering (IPHE) 1906
NR   64 Station Lane, HORNCHURCH, Essex, RM12 6NB. (hq)
        01708 472791
        Chief Exec & Sec: Blaine Judd
▲ Company Limited by Guarantee; Registered Charity
Br 60
○ *L, *P, *T; 'to advance the science & practice of plumbing &
     heating engineering in the public interest'
● Conf - Mtgs - ET - Exhib - Lib - LG
M 13,647 i, 278 f, UK / 526 i, 10 f, o'seas
¶ Plumbing - 6; ftm.   AR; ftm only.
     Plumbing Engineering Services Design Guide.
     Legionnaires Disease - Good Practice Guide for Plumbers.
× 2004 (June) Institute of Plumbing

Institute of Population Registration
     2004 merged with the Conference of Supervisory Registrars & the
     Society of Registration Officers to form the **Association of
     Registration & Celebratory Services**

Institute of Practitioners in Advertising (IPA) 1917
■ 44 Belgrave Sq, LONDON, SW1X 8QS. (hq)
        020 7235 7020   fax 020 7245 9904
        email info@ipa.co.uk   http://www.ipa.co.uk
        Sec: Geoffrey Russell
▲ Company Limited by Guarantee
Br 2
○ *P, *T; the professional & trade organisation for UK advertising
     & marketing agencies
Gp 44 Clubs
● Conf - Mtgs - ET - Res - Exhib - Stat - Inf - Lib - Empl - LG
< Eur Assn of Communications Agencies
M 210 f
¶ IPA Newsfile - 4;   LM - 1; both free.

Institute of Printing
     see **Institute of Paper, Printing & Publishing International**

Institute of Professional Auctioneers & Valuers
IRL   129 Lower Baggot St, DUBLIN 2, Republic of Ireland.
        353 (1) 678 5685   fax 353 (1) 676 2890
        email info@ipav.ie
        Chief Exec: Liam O'Donnell
○ *P
M c 700

Institute of Professional Designers (IPD) 1963
NR   Piccotts End Farm, 117 Piccotts End Rd, HEMEL HEMPSTEAD,
        Herts, HP1 3AU. (hq)
        01442 245513
        Pres/Sec: Gerald Wiedman
▲ Un-incorporated Society
○ *A, *P; environmental design incl architecture, interior design &
     website design
Gp Interior designers; Architects; Landscape architects; Graphic
     designers; Designers
● Inf
M 250 i, UK / 200 i, o'seas
¶ Calendar - 1; free.

Institute of Professional Goldsmiths (IPG) 1984
■ Long Cottage, 17 Acre End St, EYNSHAM, Oxon, OX29 4PE.
        (asa)
        01865 464255   fax 01865 464256
        email enquiries@ipgold.org.uk
        http://www.ipgold.org.uk
        Admin Sec: Carole Parker
○ *P; to establish & maintain the highest standards of
     craftsmanship
● Mtgs - VE
M i

© CBD Research Ltd · Beckenham · BR3 5JS · Tel 020 8650 7745 · Fax 020 8650 0768 · E-mail cbd@cbdresearch.com · www.cbdresearch.com

Institute of Professional Investigators Ltd   (IPI)   1976
- ■ 83 Guildford St, CHERTSEY, Surrey, KT16 9AS.   (hq)
  0870 330 8612
  http://www.ipi.org.uk
- ○ *P
- M i
  no further information supplied

Institute of Professional Sales
2004 has been incorporated into the **Chartered Institute of Marketing**

Institute of Professional Sport   (IPS)
- NR 10 Bow Lane (3rd floor), LONDON, EC4M 9AL   (hq)
  Secretariat: Delores Omosefe
- ▲ Un-incorporated Society
- ○ *P, *S; for professional sports players' organisations
- ● Conf - Mtgs - Res - Stat - LG
- M 14 org

Institute of Professional Willwriters   (IPW)   1991
- ■ Trinity Point, New Rd, HALESOWEN, W Midlands, B63 3JY.
  (hq)
  0845 644 2042   fax 0845 644 2043
  email office@ipw.org.uk   http://www.ipw.org.uk
  Chmn: Paul Sharpe
- ▲ Un-incorporated Society
- ○ *P; for individuals & organisations who specialise in will-writing
- ● Conf - ET - Exam
- < Fedn of Small Businesses
- M 130 i, UK / 2 i, o'seas
- ¶ IPW Jnl - 12; ftm.

Institute of Psychoanalysis   1924
- NR Byron House, 112A Shirland Rd, LONDON, W9 2EQ.   (hq)
  020 7563 5000   fax 020 7563 5001
  http://www.psychoanalysis.org.uk
  Hon Sec: M Mercer
- ▲ Company Limited by Guarantee; Registered Charity
- ○ *L; the theory & practice of Freudian psychoanalytic treatment
- Gp British Psycho-Analytical Society; London Clinic of Psycho-Analysis
- ● Conf - Mtgs - ET - Exam - SG - Inf - Lib - Empl - Clinic
- < Intl Psychoanalytical Assn; Eur Psychoanalytical Fedn
- M 352 i, UK / 97 i, o'seas
- ¶ International Jnl of Psychoanalysis - 6.   AR.

Institute of Public Administration   (IPA)   1957
- IRL 57-61 Lansdowne Rd, DUBLIN 4, Republic of Ireland.   (hq)
  353 (1) 240 3600   fax 353 (1) 668 9135
  email information@ipa.ie   http://www.ipa.ie
  Dir Gen: John Cullen,
  Sec: Margaret Healy
- ○ *P; Irish public sector management development agency
- ● ET - Lib - Res
- ¶ Publications list available

Institute of Public Loss Assessors   (IPLA)   1965
- NR 14 Red Lion St, CHESHAM, Bucks, HP5 1HB.   (hsb)
  01494 782342   fax 01494 774928
  Gen Sec: J D Turberville
- ▲ Company Limited by Guarantee
- ○ *P; for all qualified persons who prepare on behalf of public & corporate bodies claims arising from insured losses, statutory claims, malicious claims & third party claims
- ● Conf - Mtgs - Inf
- M 200 i, UK / 10 i, o'seas

Institute of Public Relations
since 2005 **Chartered Institute of Public Relations**

Institute of Public Rights of Way Officers   (IPROW)
- ■ PO Box 78, SKIPTON, N Yorks, BD23 4UP.   (mail address)
  07000 782318   fax 07000 782319
  email iprow@iprow.co.uk   http://www.iprow.co.uk
  Hon Sec: Miss L S Matthews
- ▲ Un-incorporated Society
- ○ *P; for all working with public rights of way
- ● Conf - ET - Inf - LG
- M 350 i
- ¶ Waymark - 3; ftm only.

Institute of Public Sector Management   (IPSM)   1997
- ■ 17 St Andrews Drive, AXMINSTER, Devon, EX13 5HA.   (hq)
  01297 35423
  email info@ipsm.org.uk   http://www.ipsm.org.uk
  Hon Sec: Derek Wolfe
- ▲ Company Limited by Guarantee
- ○ *P; for managers working in the public services, voluntary bodies & community enterprises
- Gp Risk management; Balanced scorecard
- ● Conf - ET - Res - Inf - LG
- M 300 i
- ¶ Topics - 4; ftm only.

Institute of Publishing
see **Institute of Paper, Printing & Publishing International**

Institute of Qualified Private Secretaries
since September 2003 **Institute of Qualified Professional Secretaries**

**Institute of Qualified Professional Secretaries Ltd   (IQPS)
1957**
- ■ 24-28 St Leonards Rd (Suite 464), WINDSOR, Berks,
  SL4 3BB.   (hq)
  0844 800 0182   fax 01753 775798
  email office@iqps.org   http://www.iqps.org
  Mem Devt Mgr: Jackie Wood
- ▲ Company Limited by Guarantee
- Br 11
- ○ *P; establishment of status of qualified secretaries & administrators within the professions, commerce, industry & colleges
- ● Conf - Mtgs - ET - Exhib - Comp - Inf
- < Intl Assn Admin Profls (US)
- M 1,500 i, UK / 50 i, o'seas
- ¶ Career Secretary (Jnl) - 4; ftm, £60 yr nm.
- × 2003 (September) Institute of Qualified Private Secretaries

Institute of Quality Assurance   (IQA)   1919
- NR 12 Grosvenor Crescent, LONDON, SW1X 7EE.   (hq)
  020 7245 6722   fax 020 7245 6788
  email iqa@iqa.org   http://www.iqa.org
  Dir Gen: Frank Steer
- ▲ Company Limited by Guarantee; Registered Charity
- ○ *L, *P; the advancement of quality management practices; to facilitate the exchange of related information & ideas; to promote the education, training, qualification & professional development of all those involved in quality
- Gp Deming; Engineering; Food industry; Health & social care; Human factors; Integrated management; Medical devices; Management Consultants Register
- ● Conf - Mtgs - ET - Exam - Exhib - Inf - Lib - LG
- < Eur Org for Quality (EOQ); World Quality Council (WQC)
- M 12,000 i, 600 f, UK / 1,000 i, 100 f, o'seas
- ¶ Quality World - 12.

Institute of Quarrying   (IQ)   1917
NR   7 Regent St, NOTTINGHAM, NG1 5BS.   (hq)
    0115-945 3880   fax 0115-948 4035
    email mail@quarrying.org   http://www.quarrying.org
    Sec: Lyn Bryden
▲   Company Limited by Guarantee; Registered Charity
Br   13; Australia, Malaysia, New Zealand, Hong Kong, South
    Africa,
○   *P; to improve the standards of business, technical &
    environmental performance in quarrying
●   Conf - Mtgs - ET - Exam - VE
M   2,850 i, UK / 2,500 i, o'seas
¶   Quarry Management - 12.

Institute of Race Relations   (IRR)   1958
NR   2-6 Leeke St, LONDON, WC1X 9HS.   (hq)
    020 7837 0041
    email info@irr.org.uk   http://www.irr.org.uk
    Sec: Jenny Bourne
▲   Company Limited by Guarantee; Registered Charity
○   *Q; promotion of research, making available information &
    advice on proposals concerned with race relations & racial
    justice in Britain & internationally
Gp   European race audit; Multimedia dept
●   ET - Res - Lib - Publishing
M   120 i
¶   Race & Class - 4.   European Race Bulletin - 4.
    Sage Race Relations Abstracts - 4.
    Books, pamphlets, bibliography.

Institute of Refractories Engineers   (IRE)   1961
NR   Joan Royd Cottage, Penistone, SHEFFIELD, S Yorks, S36 9DA.
    (sp)
    01226 762578   fax 01226 762673
    email alanhey@ireng.org   http://www.ireng.org
    Sec & Treas: Alan Hey
▲   Un-incorporated Society
Br   9; Australia, South Africa
○   *P; promotion of refractories engineering & technology - high
    temperature materials required in: iron & steel, cement,
    chemical & petrochemical, glass, incineration, power,
    ceramics & domestic uses
●   Conf - Mtgs - ET - Inf - Assessment Centre (NVQs in refractories
    installation)
<   Inst of Materials; Soc Glass Technology; Inst of Brit Foundrymen
M   c 600 i, UK / c 420 i, o'seas
¶   Refractories Engineer - 6.

Institute of Refrigeration   (IoR)   1899
NR   76 Mill Lane, CARSHALTON, Surrey, SM5 2JR.   (hq)
    020 8647 7033   fax 020 8773 0165
    email ior@ior.org.uk   http://www.ior.org.uk
    Sec: Miriam Rodway
▲   Registered Charity
Br   8
○   *L, *P; to advance refrigeration standards & services
Gp   Service engineers' section; Intl Refrigeration C'ee
●   Mtgs - ET - Inf
<   Intl Inst Refrigeration; Amer Soc Heating Refrigerating Air
    Conditioning Engrs
M   1,900 i, UK / 200 i, o'seas
¶   Proceedings - 1.   NL.

Institute of Remedial Treatment Surveyors
    since 2005 **Institute of Specialist Surveyors & Engineers**

Institute of Residential Property Management   (IRPM)   2002
■   178 Battersea Park Rd, LONDON, SW11 4ND.   (secretariat)
    020 7622 5092   fax 020 7498 6153
    email info@irpm.org.uk   http://www.irpm.org.uk
    Contact: The Executive Secretary
▲   Un-incorporated Society
○   *P; 'founded as a means of delivering a portable professional
    qualification in residential property management to
    individuals working in the sector, & one which would be
    accepted by all those operating within it'
●   Exam
<   Sponsors: Assn Residential Managing Agents (ARMA), Assn
    Retirement Housing Mgrs(ARHM); Property Mgrs Assn
    Scotland (PMAS)
M   688 i
¶   Members' NL - 3; ftm only.
    [LM on website].

Institute of Revenues, Rating & Valuation   (IRRV)   1882
NR   41 Doughty St, LONDON, WC1N 2LF.   (hq)
    020 7831 3505
○   *P; rating & local revenues administration; valuation for rating
    & general purposes; valuation appeals
M   i

Institute of Risk Management   (IRM)   1986
■   Lloyd's Avenue House, 6 Lloyd's Ave, LONDON, EC3N 3AX.
    (hq)
    020 7709 9808   fax 020 7709 0716
    email enquiries@theirm.org   http://www.theirm.org
    Chief Exec Officer: Steve Fowler
▲   Company Limited by Guarantee
○   *P; 'the world's leading provider of professional risk
    management education'
Gp   Health sector; Innovations, value creation & opportunity;
    Operating & financial review; People; Communication,
    culture, decision making & motivation; Transport & logistics;
    PPP/PFI; Loss management; Strategic risk management
●   Conf - Mtgs - ET - Exam - Exhib - SG - Lib
<   Intl Fedn of Risk Mgt Assns (IFRIMA)
M   2,000 i, UK / 500 i, o'seas
¶   InfoRM - 6; ftm only.

Institute of Road Safety Officers Ltd   (IRSO)   1971
■   Pin Point, 1-2 Rosslyn Crescent, HARROW, Middx, HA1 2SB.
    (hq)
    0870 010 4442   fax 0870 333 7772
    email irso@dbda.co.uk   http://www.irso.org.uk
    Hon Sec: Mrs Kathy Saunders
▲   Company Limited by Guarantee
Br   13
○   *P; to receive, analyse & disseminate information to members
    relating to road safety education, training & publicity
    programmes
●   Conf - Mtgs - ET - Exam - Exhib - LG
<   Parliamentary Advisory Coun on Transport Safety
M   400 i
¶   InRoads (Jnl) - 4; ftm, £50 nm.   AR; free.

Institute of Roofing   (IoR)   1981
■   24 Weymouth St, LONDON, W1G 7BW.   (hq)
    020 7436 0103   fax 020 7636 1287
    email info@instituteofroofing.org.uk
    http://www.instituteofroofing.org.uk
    Co Sec: Brian Clarke
▲   Company Limited by Guarantee
○   *P; for individuals working in the roofing industry
●   Conf - Mtgs - ET - Exam
M   1,086 i, UK / 3 i, o'seas
¶   IoR Bulletin (NL) - 4; ftm only.

Institute of Safety in Technology & Research (ISTR) 1981
NR MRC Corporate Safety, University of Edinburgh Medical School,
     Teviot Place, EDINBURGH, EH8 9AG. (hsb)
     0131-650 3282
     Hon Sec: Dr A R Mitchell
○ *P; for safety professionals working in organisations engaged in
     research activities
● Conf - Mtgs
M 204 i, UK / 1 i, o'seas
¶ ISTR Bulletin - 3;   Ybk; both ftm only.

Institute of Sales & Marketing Management (ISMM) 1966
■ Harrier Court, LOWER WOODSIDE, Beds, LU1 4DQ. (hq)
     01582 840001 fax 01582 849142
     email sales@ismm.co.uk   http://www.ismm.co.uk
     Chmn: Sheila Watson-Challis
▲ Company Limited by Guarantee
○ *P; to represent sales people & companies with a sales force
● Conf - Mtgs - ET - Exam - Res - Government accredited
     awarding body for sales qualifications
M [not divulged]
¶ Winning Edge - 10; ftm, £95 yr nm.

Institute of Sales Promotion Ltd (ISP) 1933
■ Arena House, 66-68 Pentonville Rd, LONDON, N1 9HS. (hq)
     020 7837 5340 fax 020 7837 5326
     email enquiries@isp.org.uk   http://www.isp.org.uk
     Dir-Gen: Edwin Mutton
▲ Company Limited by Guarantee
○ *P; to promote the promotional marketing industry in the UK
Gp Legal advisory service; Coupon c'ee; Education; Promoter's
● Conf - Mtgs - ET - Exam - Res - Exhib - Stat - Inf - Lib - LG
< Eur Promotional Marketing Alliance; Eur Assn of
     Communication Agencies; CBI; Advertising Assn
M 850 i, 250 f
¶ ISP email - 12; ftm only.   AR - 1.

Institute of Science Technology (IST) 1954
NR Brooke House, 24 Dam St, LICHFIELD, Staffs, WS13 6AB. (hq)
     01543 266908
     Hon Sec: A Taylor
▲ Company Limited by Guarantee
○ *L, *P; to advance knowledge of science laboratory techniques;
     to promote professional standing of laboratory technicians
● Conf - ET - Exam - Exhib - Inf
M 1,100 i, UK / 100 i, o'seas
¶ Science Technology - 4; ftm only.

Institute of Scientific & Technical Communicators (ISTC) 1972
■ PO Box 522, PETERBOROUGH, Cambs, PE2 5WX. (hsp)
     01733 390141 fax 01733 390126
     email istc@istc.org.uk   http://www.istc.org.uk
     Sec: Carol Hewitt
▲ Company Limited by Guarantee
○ *P; communication & presentation of scientific & technical
     information
Gp Independent authors (IASIG); Middle East; Irish
● Conf - ET
< Intl Coun for Technical Communication (INTECOM)
M c 1,000 i, 21 f, UK / c 75 i, o'seas
¶ Communicator (Jnl) - 4; ftm, £35 (£40 EU, £43 RoW) nm.
     ISTC Hbk on Professional Communication & Information
     Design; £20 (available through Amazon).

Institute of Security Management (ISecM) 1988
■ 17 Hough Rd, Kings Heath, BIRMINGHAM, B14 6HL. (hsp)
     0121-444 5006
     Nat Sec: David Fell
○ *P; members are from various specialist groups employed in
     the industry incl: Armed forces, UK police services,
     Commercial & industrial security, MOD, Banks, Exhibition,
     Electronic security alarms, PCTV, Radio
● Conf - Mtgs - ET - LG
< Jt Securities Ind Coun (JSIC); Security Systems & Alarms
     Inspection Bd (SSAIB)
M 150 i, UK / 20 i, o'seas
¶ NL - 4.

Institute of Sheet Metal Engineering (ISME) 1946
NR PO Box 2242, STAFFORD, ST17 0WH. (hq)
     01785 716886 fax 01785 716886
     email isme@onetel.com
     Hon Sec: F C Cooper
▲ Registered Charity
○ *L; theory & practice of sheet metal forming & fabrication
Gp Sheet forming technology; Education & training
● Conf - Mtgs - Exhib - Comp - SG - Inf - VE - Lectures
< Confedn of Brit Metalforming
M 104 i, 38 f, UK / 9 i, o'seas
¶ Oracle - 4.

Institute of Shopfitters
NR 35 Hayworth Rd, Sandiacre, NOTTINGHAM, NG10 5LL. (hq)
     0115-949 0641 fax 0115-949 1664
     Sec: David R Winson
○ *P

Institute for Small Business & Entrepreneurship (ISBE) 1993
■ 3 Ripon Rd (2nd floor), HARROGATE, N Yorks, HG1 2SX. (hq)
     01423 500046 fax 01423 500046
     email info@isbe.org.uk   http://www.isbe.org.uk
     Admin: G E Wareham
▲ Company Limited by Guarantee; Registered Charity
○ *Q; to encourage high quality research into the field of small
     business development; to disseminate the results for
     discussion; to assist & inform those responsible for the
     formulation, development, implementation & evaluation of
     enterprise policy
● Conf - Workshops & Seminars
M 232 i, 78 f, 10 org, UK / 32 i, o'seas
¶ Small Business Issues (NL) - 4; ftm, £10 nm.
× 2005 Institute of Small Business Affairs

Institute for Social Inventions 1985
NR 12a Blackstock Mews, Blackstock Rd, LONDON, N4 2BT.
     (mtgs)
     020 7359 8391 fax 020 7354 3831
     http://www.globalideasbank.org address
     Contact: Nick Temple
○ *K; to promote social inventions - new imaginative non-
     technological solutions to social problems
● Conf - Mtgs - ET - Res - Comp - Inf - Lib - Workshop courses in
     state schools - £1,000 awards for best ideas
M 400 members & subscribers
¶ Social Inventions Annual Book - 1; £15 m only.
     Note: The Institute runs the Global Ideas Bank on Internet:
     www.globalideasbank.org

Institute of Sound & Communications Engineers (ISCE)
NR PO Box 7966, READING, Berks, RG6 7WY. (hq)
     0118-954 2175 fax 0118-954 2175
     http://www.isce.org.uk
     Secretariat: Rosalind Wigmore
▲ Company Limited by Guarantee
○ *L, *P; supports technicians, managers & designers in the
     performing arts & public address industries
● Conf - Mtgs - ET - Exam - Exhib - Lib
M 250 i, 16 f, UK / 20 i, o'seas
¶ Public Address (NL) - irreg.

Institute of Specialist Surveyors & Engineers 1989
NR   Essex House, High St, CHIPPING ONGAR, Essex, CM5 9EB.
       (hq)
       0800 915 6363
       Chmn: Derek Spring
▲   Company Limited by Guarantee
○   *P; professional advice on dry rot, woodworm & dampness;
       assistance in finding reliable surveyors & treatment specialists
M   c 200 i
✕   2005 Institute of Remedial Treatment Surveyors

Institute of Spiritualist Mediums   (ISM)   1956
NR   121 Church End Lane, RUNWELL, Essex, SS11 7DN.   (hq)
       Gen Sec: Mrs Dianne Walker
▲   Registered Charity
○   *E; to improve the standard of mediumship & the work of
       spiritualist mediums

Institute of Sport & Recreation Management   (ISRM)   1921
NR   Sir John Beckwith Centre for Sport, Loughborough University,
       LOUGHBOROUGH, Leics, LE11 3TU.   (hq)
       01509 226474
       Chief Exec: Ralph Riley
○   *P; for those involved in sport & recreation facility management
       & operation (including swimming baths)

Institute of Sports, Parks & Leisure   (ISPAL)
NR   ILAM House, Lower Basildon, READING, Berks, RG8 9NE.
       01491 874800

Institute of Spring Technology   (IST)   1997
■   Henry St, SHEFFIELD, S Yorks, S3 7EQ.
       0114-276 0771   fax 0114-252 7997
       email ist@ist.org.uk   http://www.ist.org.uk
       Managing Dir: Andrew Watkinson
▲   Company Limited by Guarantee
○   *E, *L, *P, *Q, *T; sprint design, testing & consultancy
●   ET - Res - Exhib - Inf - Lib - VE
<   Intl Wire & Machinery Assn; Eur Spring Fedn; Fastener & Engg
       Res Assn
M   100 i, UK / 120 i, o'seas
¶   IST Technology NL - 4;   UKSMA NL - 4; both ftm only.
       UKSMA Member Guide - 1;   IST Member Guide - 1; both
       free.

Institute of Sterile Services Management
       since 2004 **Institute of Decontamination Sciences**

Institute of Stock Auditors & Valuers 1972
NR   PO Box 1075, BEAMINSTER, Dorset, DT8 3YA.   (sb)
       01460 727694
▲   Un-incorporated Society
○   *P, *T; to act as a regulatory body for professional stocktakers &
       trade valuers
●   Conf - Mtgs - ET - Exam - Inf - Lib - LG
M   105 i
¶   Count Me In (Jnl) - 4;   Hbk;   LM; all free.
✕   2004 Trade Valuers Institute

Institute of Swimming Pool Engineers Ltd   (ISPE)   1979
NR   PO Box 3083, NORWICH, Norfolk, NR6 7YL.   (hq)
       01603 499959
       Co Sec: Molly W Alcock   Gen Sec: Ross Alcock
▲   Company Limited by Guarantee
○   *P; design, construction & maintenance of swimming pools &
       spas, both public & private
Gp   Education & training to the swimming pool industry
●   Conf - ET - Exam - Exhib - SG - Inf
M   830 i, UK / 30 i, o'seas
¶   ISPE Magazine - 4; free.   Hbk.
       Home study course training manuals.
       Swimming Pool Industry Directory & Specifier (SPidas).
       Technical Papers (20 titles to date; £6-£13) incl:
          Water treatment for pool operators.
          Heat pumps.   Ozone.
          Domestic & commercial spas.
          Heat losses from indoor & outdoor pools.

Institute of Swimming Teachers & Coaches Ltd   (ISTC)   1975
■   Harold Fern House, Derby Square, LOUGHBOROUGH, Leics,
       LE11 5AL.   (hq)
       01509 618746
       email istc@swimming.org.uk
       http://www.swimming.org.uk
       Admin: Jane Nickerson
▲   Company Limited by Guarantee
Br   12; Eire, International
○   *P, *S; for qualified swimming teachers & coaches
●   Conf - Mtgs - ET - Res - Exhib - Inf - Lib - LG
<   Fedn of Water Fitness Profls; Amat Swimming Assn;
       Synchronised Swimming Coaches Assns
M   13,000 i, UK / 1,000 i, o'seas
¶   Swimming Times - 12; ftm, £1.70 nm.   LM - 2 yrly; ftm.

Institute of Trade Mark Attorneys   (ITMA)   1934
■   Canterbury House, 2-6 Sydenham Rd, CROYDON, Surrey,
       CR0 9XE.   (hq)
       020 8686 2052   fax 0202 8680 5723
       email tm@itma.org.uk   http://www.itma.org.uk
       Co Sec: Mrs Margaret J Tyler
▲   Company Limited by Guarantee
○   *P
●   Conf - Mtgs - ET - Exam - LG
M   970 i, UK / 500 i, o'seas
¶   NL - 12;   Information - 12;   AR - 1; all ftm only.
       LM - 1; ftm, £10 nm.

Institute of Traffic Accident Investigators   (ITAI)   1990
■   Babington Lodge, 128 Green Lane, DERBY, DE1 1RY.
       (admin/office)
       01332 292447   fax 01332 290855
       email admin@itai.org   http://www.itai.org
       Admin: Anna Maria Rudy
▲   Company Limited by Guarantee
○   *P; representation, communication, education, & regulation in
       traffic accident investigation
●   Conf - ET - Exam - Res - VE
M   750 i, UK / 60 i, o'seas
¶   Impact (Jnl) - 3; ftm, £10 nm.   Contact (NL) - 6; ftm only.

Institute of Training & Occupational Learning   (ITOL)   2000
NR   The Cotton Exchange (suite 414), Old Hall St, LIVERPOOL,
       L3 9LQ.   (hq)
       0151-236 1271   fax 0151-255 1824
       email admin@itol.co.uk
       http://www.traininginstitute.co.uk
       Dir: Jeffrey Brooks
▲   Un-incorporated Society
○   *P; training, assessment & vocational education
●   ET - Exam - Res - Inf - Lib
¶   British Journal of Occupational Learning - 2.
       TT & HR Magazine - 6.

Institute of Transactional Analysis   (ITA)   1977
- ■ PO Box 1101, WIGTON, Cumbria, CA7 9YH.   (hq)
  0845 009 9101
  email admin@ita.org.uk   http://www.ita.org.uk
  Exec Officer: Eliott Green,   Chmn: Pete Shotton
- ▲ Registered Charity
- ○ *P; the education of the public in the study, theory & practice of transactional analysis - a theory of personality & social psychology within a humanistic tradition
- Gp Clinical; Counselling; Educational; Organisational
- ● Conf - ET - Exam - Res - SG - Inf - LG
- < Eur Assn Transactional Analysis; UK Coun for Psychotherapy
- M 1,40 i, 8 f, UK / 7 i, o'seas
- ¶ ITA News (NL) - 6; ftm, £10 nm.
  Transactions (Jnl) - 2; ftm only.

Institute of Translation & Interpreting   (ITI)   1986
- ■ Fortuna House, South Fifth St, MILTON KEYNES, Bucks, MK9 2EU.   (hq)
  01908 325250
  email info@iti.org.uk   http://www.iti.org.uk
  Chief Exec: Alan Wheatley
- ▲ Company Limited by Guarantee
- ○ *P; for translators & interpreters; has a structure of regional group, language & subject networks
- Gp Subject networks: Medicine, Law, Insurance, Finance & trade, Book translators, Media, arts & tourism, Information technology, Patents, Construction
- ● Conf - Mtgs - ET - Exhib - SG - Expt - Inf
- < Intl Fedn of Translators (FIT)
- M 2,240 i, 93 f, UK / 480 i, 5 f, o'seas
- ¶ ITI Bulletin - 6; ftm.   LM - 1.   AR - 1; free.
  Conference Proceedings - 1.   Leaflets & factsheets - irreg.

Institute of Transport Administration   (IoTA)   1944
- NR IoTA House, 7B St Leonards Rd, HORSHAM, W Sussex, RH13 6EH.   (hq)
  01403 242412   fax 01403 242413
  email director.iota@btclick.com   http://www.iota.org.uk
  Pres; Dr Michael Asteris
- ○ *P; to improve & develop the knowledge & efficiency of members in the skills of transport management
- M i
- ¶ Transport Management (Jnl) - 6.

Institute of Transport Management   (ITM)   1977
- NR Unit 64 / 14-20 George St, BIRMINGHAM, W Midlands, B12 9RG.   (hq)
  0121-440 5222
  Chmn: William Gavin
- ▲ Registered Charity
- Br Belgium
- ○ *P
- ● Conf - Mtgs - ET - Res - Stat - Expt - Inf - Awards
- M c 9,000 i, UK / c 6,300 i, o'seas
- ¶ Transport Journal - 12.

Institute of Travel Management Ltd   (ITM)   1956
- NR Waters Green House, Waters Green, MACCLESFIELD, Cheshire, SK11 6LF.   (hq)
  01625 430472   fax 01625 439183
  email secretariat@itm.org.uk
  Nat Chmn: Louise Innes
- ▲ Company Limited by Guarantee
- Br 6; Ireland
- ○ *P; for those involved in the planning & procurement of business travel services
- Gp Supplier c'ee (representatives of short-haul airlines, international & independent hotels & surface transportation)
- ● Conf - Mtgs - ET - Exhib - SG - LG
- < Chart Inst Purchasing & Supply (CIPS)
- M 312 i, 284 f, UK / 38 i, 16 f, o'seas
- ¶ Newsline - 4;   ITM Ybk - 1; both ftm only.

Institute of Travel & Tourism   (ITT)   1956
- NR PO Box 217, WARE, Herts, SG12 8WY.   (hq)
  0870 770 7960
- ▲ Company Limited by Guarantee
- ○ *P
- ● Conf - Mtgs - ET - Exhib - Comp - SG - Inf - Lib - VE - LG
- M 3,000 i, 200 f
- ¶ Jnl - 6;   Hbk - 1;   AR & accounts; all ftm only.

Institute of Trichologists (Inc)   (IT)   1902
- NR 24 Langroyd Rd (ground floor), LONDON, SW17 7PL.   (regd)
  08706 070602 off
  Chmn: Mrs Marilyn Sherlock
- ▲ Company Limited by Guarantee
- ○ *L, *P; the treatment & care of human hair & scalp in health & disease
- ● ET - Exam - Res
- M 220 i, UK / 20 i, o'seas
- ¶ The Trichologists - 2.

Institute of Value Management   (IVM)   1966
- ■ 1-3 Birdcage Walk, LONDON, SW1H 9JJ.   (mail/address)
  0870 902 0905
  email secretary@ivm.org.uk   http://www.ivm.org.uk
  Hon Sec: Douglas Hurst
- ▲ Company Limited by Guarantee
- Br 6; 1
- ○ *P; 'driving for sustainable worth in all sectors'
- ● Conf - Mtgs - ET - G - Inf - LG
- M 180 i, 16 f, UK / 21 i, o'seas
- ¶ Value Jnl - 3; ftm, £10 nm.

Institute of Vehicle Engineers
   since 2005-06 **Society of Automotive Engineers-UK**

Institute of Vehicle Recovery   (IVR)   1984
- ■ Bignell House (top floor), Horton Rd, WEST DRAYTON, Middx, UB7 8EP.   (hq)
  01895 436426
- ▲ Company Limited by Guarantee
- ○ *P; interests of persons engaged in motor vehicle recovery; to promote technical training & improve the standard of safety in motor vehicle recovery
- ● ET - Exam - Res - Exhib - SG
- M 700 i, UK / 56 i, o'seas
- ¶ NL; ftm.

Institute of Verifiers & Assessors Ltd
   since 2003 **Institute of Assessors & Internal Verifiers**

Institute of Videography   (IOV)   1985
- NR PO Box 625, LOUGHTON, Essex, IG10 3GZ.
  020 8502 3817   fax 020 8508 9211
  email info@iov.co.uk   http://www.iov.co.uk
  Exec Coordinator: Kevin Cook
- Br 16
- ○ *P; video production & training
- ● Conf - Comp - Mtgs - SG - ET - Inf - Exhib - VideoSkills workshops
- M 800 i, 50 f
- ¶ Focus Magazine - 12.

Institute of Vitreous Enamellers incorporating the Vitreous Enamel Association (IVE) 1934

NR 39 Sweetbriar Way, Heath Hayes, CANNOCK, Staffs, WS12 2US. (hsp)
01543 450596
Hon Sec: Angela Nutting
▲ Company Limited by Guarantee
○ *L, *P; exchange of technical information on vitreous enamelling
Gp Standards; Marketing strategy; Ball milling working
● Conf - Mtgs - ET - Inf - Lib - VE - LG - Advice on environment, health & safety
< Intl Enamellers Inst; Eur Enamellers Authority
M 65 i, 29 f, UK / 15 i, 5 f, o'seas
¶ The Vitreous Enameller (Jnl) - 4.
Atlas of Enamel Defects. Buyer's Guide.
Classification of Adhesion of Vitreous Enamel to Steel.

Institute of Wastes Management
since 2002 **Chartered Institution of Wastes Management**

Institute of Welfare (IWO) 1945

NR Newland House (2nd floor), 137-139 Hagley Rd, Edgbaston, BIRMINGHAM, B16 8UA. (hq)
0121-454 8883   fax 0121-454 7873
email info@instituteofwelfare.co.uk
Chmn: Austin Griffiths
○ *P; for welfare officers in industry, commerce, social organisations, national & local government departments
● Conf - Mtgs - ET - Res
M c 2,500 i
¶ Welfare World - 4.
✕ Institute of Welfare Officers

Institute of Welsh Affairs (IWA) 1987

■ St Andrew's House, 24 St Andrew's Crescent, CARDIFF, CF10 3DD. (hq)
029 2066 6606   fax 029 2022 1482
email wales@iwa.org.uk   http://www.iwa.org.uk
Dir: John Osmond
▲ Company Limited by Guarantee; Registered Charity
Br 4
○ *P; to promote the prosperity of Wales, its industry & people by encouraging debate upon & research into economic, social & cultural issues
● Conf - Mtgs - Res
M 1,100 i, 150 f, UK / 50 i, o'seas
¶ The Gregynog Papers - 2.   Agenda - 3.

Institute of Wood Science (IWSc) 1955

■ Stocking Lane, Hughenden Valley, HIGH WYCOMBE, Bucks, HP14 4NU. (hq)
01494 565374   fax 01494 565395
email info@iwsc.org.uk   http://www.iwsc.org.uk
Dir: J M Lumsden
▲ Company Limited by Guarantee; Registered Charity
○ *P; to advance & encourage the scientific, technical, practical & general knowledge of timber & wood-based materials
M i & f
¶ Jnl - 2;   NL - 2.

Institution of Agricultural Engineers (IAgrE) 1938

■ West End Rd, SILSOE, Beds, MK45 4DU. (hq)
01525 861096   fax 01525 861660
email secretary@iagre.org   http://www.iagre.org
Chief Exec: Christopher R Whetnall
▲ Company Limited by Guarantee; Registered Charity
Br 13
○ *L, *P; for engineers, managers, scientists & technologists in agriculture & allied industries (incl forestry, food processing, agrochemicals & amenity industries)
Gp Agro-industrial products; Amenity & ecological engineering; Food technology; Forestry engineering; Horticultural engineering; Machinery management; Overseas development; Pioneering technology; Precision in farming; Renewable energy; Soil & water management; Vehicles; Young engineers
● Conf - Mtgs - Inf - Lib
< Intl Commission of Agricl Engg (CIGR); Eur Soc of Agricl Engrs (EurAgEng)
M 1,700 i, 15 f, UK / 200 i, o'seas
¶ Landwards - 4; ftm, £52 nm.

Institution of Analysts & Programmers (IAP) 1971

NR 36 Culmington Rd, LONDON, W13 9NH. (hq)
020 8567 2118
http://www.iap.org.uk
Dir Gen: Michael Ryan
○ *P; systems analysis & computer programming
M c 3,000 i, UK / c 500 i, o'seas
¶ NL - 4;   LM;   AR.

＊＊ Institution of British Engineers
Organisation lost: see Introduction paragraph 3

Institution of Chemical Engineers (IChemE) 1922

■ Davis Building, 165-189 Railway Terrace, RUGBY, Warks, CV21 3HQ. (hq)
01788 578214   fax 01788 560833
http://www.icheme.org
Chief Exec: Dr Trevor J Evans
▲ Registered Charity
Br Australia, Malaysia, Singapore
○ *L, *P; the professional qualifying body for process & chemical engineers
● Conf - ET - Exhib - Products & services for qualified chemical engineers & those interested in chemical engineering as a career
M 18,168 i, UK / 7,455 i, o'seas
¶ The Chemical Engineer (tce) - 12 ftm, £165 (UK) (£180 RoW) nm.
Chemical Engineering Research & Design - 12;
(members) print & online; £120 (UK) £140 (RoW).
(members) online only; £50 (UK+RoW).
(non-members) print & online £721 (UK) £742 (RoW).
Process Safety & Environmental Protection - 6;
(members) print & online; £80 (UK) £100 (RoW).
(members) online only; £40 (UK+RoW).
(non-members) print & online; £448 (UK) £464 (RoW).
Food & Bioproducts Processing - 4;
(members) print & online; £50 (UK) £70 (RoW).
(members) online only; £30 (UK+RoW).
(non-members) £278 (UK) £294 (RoW).

Institution of Civil Engineering Surveyors   (ICES)   1969
NR   Dominion House, Sibson Rd, SALE, Cheshire, M33 7PP.   (hq)
       0161-972 3100   fax 0161-972 3118
       email admin@ices.org.uk   http://www.ices.org.uk
       Hon Sec: A H Palmer,   Exec Dir: C H Blackwell
▲   Company Limited by Guarantee; Registered Charity
○   *P; the qualification & regulation of geospatial engineering
       surveyors (land surveyors) & commercial managers (quantity
       surveyors)
Gp   Commercial management, including:
       Construction economics; Construction law; Cost engineering;
       Estimating; Planning; Procurement engineering, Project
       management, Quantity surveying.
       Geospatial engineering surveyors, including:
       Cartography; Dimensional control; Geographical information
       systems; Hydrographic surveying; Land / engineering
       surveyors; Photogrammetrists; Remote seeking.
●   Conf - Mtgs - ET - Exam - Res - Exhib - Stat - Inf - Lib
<   Intl Fedn Surveyors (FIG); Construction Ind Coun; Instn Civil
       Engrs
M   3,100 i, UK / 400 i, o'seas
¶   Civil Engineering Surveyor (Jnl) - 12.
       Construction & Law Review - 1.   .
       Reference Manual for Construction Plant - 3/4 yrly.

Institution of Civil Engineers   (ICE)   1818
NR   1-7 Great George St, LONDON, SW1P 3AA.   (hq)
       020 7222 7722
       Chmn: Prof Quentin Leiper
Br   Intl local assns: Australia, France, Hong Kong, India, Indonesia,
       Ireland, Netherlands, Qatar, Saudi Arabia, Sri Lanka, USA
       Branches: Belgium, Cayman Islands, Poland, Switzerland
○   *L, *P
Gp   British Geotechnical Assn; Soc for Earthquake & Civil
       Engineering Dynamics
●   Conf - Mtgs - ET - Exam - Res - Exhib - Comp - Inf - Lib - LG -
       Register of engineers for disaster relief - Dispute resolution
       service - Recruitment subsidiary - Panel for historical
       engineering works - Archives - Audio-visual collection -
       Guided tours of building available - Rooms available for
       external bookings
<   Intl C'ee on Large Dams; Intl Assn for Hydraulic Res; Intl Cmsn
       on Irrigation & Drainage; Intl Soc of Trenchless Technology;
       Permanent Intl Assn of Navigation Congresses; Central
       Dredging Assn; Standing C'ee on Structural Safety
M   60,891 i, UK / 14,162 i, o'seas

Institution of Diagnostic Engineers   1983
NR   7 Weir Rd, Kibworth, LEICESTER, LE8 0LQ.   (hq)
       0116-279 6772   fax 0116-279 6884
       email admin@diagnosticengineers.org
       http://www.diagnosticengineers.org
       Sec: Mrs Josephine Mullins
▲   Company Limited by Guarantee; Registered Charity
○   *P; engineers involved in diagnosing faults in machines, plant,
       & systems.
       Specialist areas: Vibration analysis, condition monitoring,
       engine health
●   Conf - ET - Exhib - VE
M   1,700 i, 10 f, UK / 500 i, o'seas
¶   Diagnostic Engineering - 6; ftm, £60 nm.
       Note: the institution is a registered charity under the name of
       Society of Diagnostic Engineers

Institution of Diesel & Gas Turbine Engineers   (IDGTE)   1913
■   Bedford Heights, Manton Lane, BEDFORD, MK41 7PH.   (hq)
       01234 214340   fax 01234 355493
       email enquiries@idgte.org   http://www.idgte.org
       Dir Gen: J H Blowes
▲   Un-incorporated Society
Br   Canada
○   *L; the advancement of diesel & gas engines, gas turbines &
       related products & technology
Gp   Working gps: Diesel engines, Gas turbines
●   Conf - Mtgs - ET - Exhib - Inf - Lib - VE
M   457 i, 60 f, UK / 101 i, 58 f, o'seas
¶   The Power Engineer - 4; ftm (extra copies £15), £30 nm.
       The Power Engineer (Working Cost & Operational Report) - 1;
       ftm (extra copies £25), £50 nm.

Institution of Economic Development Ltd   (IED)   1983
NR   PO Box 396, HIGH WYCOMBE, Bucks, HP15 6EL.   (hq)
       01494 714201
       Dir of Admin: Stephanie Wakefield
○   *P
M   1,000 i
¶   Economic Development - 4.

Institution of Electrical Engineers
       2006 merged with Institution of Incorporated Engineers to form the
       Institution of Engineering & Technology

Institution of Engineering Designers   (IED)   1945
■   Courtleigh, Westbury Leigh, WESTBURY, Wilts, BA13 3TA.   (hq)
       01373 822801   fax 01373 858085
       email ied@ied.org.uk   http://www.ied.org.uk/
       Sec: E K Brodhurst
▲   Company Limited by Guarantee; Registered Charity
Br   13; Malta, Hong Kong
○   *P; to advance education in engineering, product design &
       CADD; Licensed body of the Engineering Council
Gp   Computer aided design (CAD); Product design
●   Conf - Mtgs - ET - Exhib - Comp - SG - Stat - Inf - Lib - VE
M   4,920 i, UK / 410 i, o'seas
¶   The Engineering Designer - 6; ftm, £39 yr nm.

Institution of Engineering & Technology   (IET)   1871
■   Savoy Place, LONDON, WC2R 0BL.   (hq)
       020 7240 1871   fax 020 7497 7735
       http://www.theiet.org
       Chief Exec: Dr A Roberts
▲   Registered Charity
Br   47; 53 o'seas
○   *L, *P; to promote the advancement of electrical, electronic &
       manufacturing science & engineering; to act as the voice of
       the profession; to set standards of qualifications
Gp   40 technical interest groups grouped under: Communications
       engineering, Computing & control, Electronic systems &
       software, Information professional, Management,
       Manufacturing, Power, Transport
●   Conf - Mtgs - ET - Exhib - Comp - Inf - Lib - PL - VE - LG
M   c 150,000 i & f
¶   Engineering & Technology (Jnl) - 12.
       Communications Engineer.
       Computing & Control.
       Electronic Systems & Software.
       Engineering Management.
       Information Professional.
       Manufacturing Engineer.
       Power Engineer.
       Flipside (for teenagers).
       Student & Graduate Magazine.
✕   2004-05 (Society of Engineers
       2006 (Institution of Electrical Engineers
               (Institution of Incorporated Engineers

Institution of Engineers of Ireland   (Engineers Ireland)   1835
IRL   22 Clyde Rd, DUBLIN 4, Republic of Ireland.
    353 (1) 668 4341   fax 353 (1) 668 5508
    email info@iei.ie   http://www.iei.ie
    Dir Gen: Kevin Kiernan
○   *P
M   c 22,000
    Note: uses Engineers Ireland as the operating name

**Institution of Engineers & Shipbuilders in Scotland   (IESIS)
1857**
NR   Clydeport Building, 16 Robertson St, GLASGOW, G2 8DS.
    (hq)
    0141-248 3721   fax 0141-221 2698
○   *L, *P
M   i

Institution of Environmental Sciences Ltd   (IEnvSc)   1971
NR   38 Ebury St (suite 1), LONDON, SW1W 0LU.   (hq)
    020 7730 5516   fax 020 7730 5519
    Hon Sec: Mrs J R Blumhof
▲   Company Limited by Guarantee; Registered Charity
○   *L, *P; to promote, sponsor, & organise research &
    interdisciplinary action, consultation & coordination into all
    matters concerning environmental sciences
Gp   Education c'ee
●   Conf - ET - Accreditation of university courses - Publications -
    Careers advice
<   Science Coun
M   780 i, 8 f, 6 org, UK / 65 i, o'seas
¶   The Environmental Scientist - 6.
    The Environmental Careers Hbk.

Institution of Fire Engineers   (iFE)   1918
■   London Rd, MORETON-in-MARSH, Glos, GL56 0RH.   (hq)
    01608 812580
    Chief Exec: Ellen Jessett
▲   Company Limited by Guarantee; Registered Charity
Br   20; 18 countries o'seas
○   *L, *P; to promote, encourage & improve the science & practice
    of fire extinction, fire prevention & fire engineering
●   Conf - Mtgs - ET - Exam - Res - Exhib - Inf
M   7,000 i, UK / 4,500 i, o'seas
¶   Fire Engineers Jnl - 6; ftm.
    Hbk for Fire Engineers.   How did it start?
    Fire Technology - Chemistry Combustion.
    Fire Technology - Calculations.
    Dictionary of Fire Technology.
    Guide to Examinations of the IFE.
    Principles of Fire Investigation.

Institution of Gas Engineers & Managers   (IGEM)   1863
NR   Charnwood Wing - Holywell Park, Ashby Rd,
    LOUGHBOROUGH, Leics, LE11 3GR.   (hq)
    01509 282728   fax 01509 283110
    email general@igem.org.uk   http://www.igem.org.uk
    Chief Exec & Sec: John Williams
▲   Registered Charity
Br   10; Brazil, Hong Kong
○   *L, *P; licensed to accredit engineers to Chartered, Incorporated
    & Technician levels; provides a focus & technical standards
    for the gas industry
Gp   Sections: Information, Membership, Technical
●   Conf - Mtgs - ET - Exhib - Comp - SG - Inf - Lib - PL - LG
<   Intl Gas U (IGU); Accredited by Engg Coun (UK)
M   4,846 i, 114 f, UK / 394 i, 12 f, o'seas
¶   International Gas Engineering & Management (Jnl) - 10.
✕   2001 Institution of Gas Engineers

Institution of Highways & Transportation   (IHT)   1930
■   6 Endsleigh St, LONDON, WC1H 0DZ.   (hq)
    020 7387 2525   fax 020 7387 2808
    http://www.iht.org
    Chief Exec: Mary Lewis
▲   Company Limited by Guarantee; Registered Charity
Br   18; Hong Kong, Malaysia, Republic of Ireland
○   *P
●   Conf - Mtgs - ET - Exhib - Expt - Inf - VE - LG
M   9,514 i, 19 f, UK / 1,166 i, o'seas
¶   Transportation Professional - 10; ftm, £58.

Institution of Incorporated Engineers
    2006 merged with Institution of Electrical Engineers to form the
    Institution of Engineering & Technology

Institution of Lighting Engineers   (ILE)   1924
NR   Regent House, Regent Place, RUGBY, Warks, CV21 2PN.   (hq)
    01788 576492
    Chief Exec: Richard Frost
▲   Company Limited by Guarantee; Registered Charity
Br   7 regions
○   *P
Gp   4
●   Conf - Mtgs - ET - Exhib - Comp - SG - Stat - Inf - Lib - VE - LG
<   Commission Intle d'Eclairage
M   2,000 i, 52 f, UK / 50 i, o'seas
¶   Lighting Jnl - 6.   Technical reports.

Institution of Mechanical Engineers   (IMechE)   1847
NR   1 Birdcage Walk, LONDON, SW1H 9JJ.   (hq)
    020 7222 7899
    Dir Gen: Sir Michael Moore
▲   Registered Charity
○   *L, *P; 'to create the natural professional home for all involved
    in mechanical engineering'

Institution of Mining & Metallurgy
    merged in 2002 with the Institute of Materials to form the **Institute of
    Materials, Minerals & Mining**

Institution of Nuclear Engineers   (INucE)   1959
NR   1 Penerley Rd, LONDON, SE6 2LQ.   (hq)
    020 8698 1500 & 4750
    Exec Sec: Mark Askew
▲   Company Limited by Guarantee; Registered Charity
Br   5; S Africa
○   *L, *P; to promote & advance nuclear engineering & allied
    branches of science & engineering
●   Conf - Mtgs - Inf - VE - Scholarships & prizes
<   Eur Nuclear Soc
M   1,155 i, 117 subscribers, UK / 155 i, 115 subscribers, o'seas
¶   The Nuclear Engineer (Jnl) - 6; ftm.

Institution of Occupational Safety & Health   (IOSH)   1945
■   The Grange, Highfield Drive, WIGSTON, Leics, LE18 1NN.
    (hq)
    0116-257 3100   fax 0116-257 3101
    http://www.iosh.co.uk
▲   Incorporated by Royal Charter; Registered Charity
Br   23; 2
○   *P; for those professionally involved in occupational safety &
    health
Gp   Construction; Public services; Offshore; Healthcare
●   Conf - Mtgs - ET - Res - Exhib - Inf - Lib - PL - VE - LG
M   26,500 i, UK / 2,500 i, o'seas
¶   Safety & Health Practitioner - 12.   Jnl - 2 yrly.
    Various other publications.

    © CBD Research Ltd · Beckenham · BR3 5JS · Tel 020 8650 7745 · Fax 020 8650 0768 · E-mail cbd@cbdresearch.com · www.cbdresearch.com

Institution of Planning Supervisors (IPS) 1995
NR   Heriot-Watt Research Park, EDINBURGH, EH14 4AP.   (hq)
        0131-449 4646
        Gen Sec: M Laftavi
▲   Company Limited by Guarantee
○   *P; to improve health & safety in the construction industry
        particularly in relation to the Construction (Design &
        Management) Regulations 1994 (CDM) & to the role of
        planning supervisor
M   i
¶   Newsfile - 4; ftm.

** **Institution of Polymaths**
        Organisation lost: see Introduction paragraph 3

Institution of Professionals, Managers & Specialists
        merged on 1 November 2001 with the Engineers & Managers
        Association to form **Prospect**

Institution of Railway Signal Engineers (IRSE) 1912
NR   1 Birdcage Walk (4th floor), Westminster, LONDON,
        SW1H 9JJ.   (hq)
        020 7808 1180
        Chief Exec: Colin H Porter
▲   Registered Charity
Br   worldwide
○   *L, *P; railway signalling & telecommunications
●   Conf - Mtgs - ET - Exam - Exhib - SG - Inf - Lib - VE
M   2,500 i, UK / 1,000 i, o'seas
¶   NL - 6.   Proceedings - 1.
        Various books.

Institution of Structural Engineers (IStructE) 1908
NR   11 Upper Belgrave St, LONDON, SW1X 8BH.   (hq)
        020 7235 4535   fax 020 7235 4294
        email mail@istructe.org.uk   http://www.istructe.org.uk
        Chief Exec & Sec: Dr Keith J Eaton
▲   Incorporated by Royal Charter; Registered Charity
Br   18; Australia, Barbados, Hong Kong, N Zealand, Nigeria,
        Singapore, S Africa, Trinidad & Tobago
○   *L, *P
●   Conf - Mtgs - ET - Exam - Comp - SG - Inf - Lib
M   16,300 i, UK / 6,600 i, o'seas
¶   The Structural Engineer (Jnl) - 23.
        Publications list available.

Institution of Water Officers Ltd
        since 2001 **IWO**

Instock Footwear Suppliers' Association (IFSA) 1947
NR   Marlow House, Churchill Way, Fleckney, LEICESTER,
        LE8 8UD.   (hq)
        0116-240 3232   fax 0116-240 2762
▲   Un-incorporated Society
○   *T; those distributing footwear (from manufacturers to retailers)
●   Mtgs - LG
M   10 f
¶   NL; ftm only.

Insulated Render & Cladding Association Ltd   1981
NR   PO Box 12, HASLEMERE, Surrey, GU27 3AH.   (hq)
        01428 654011   fax 01428 651401
        Dir: Gillian Allder
▲   Company Limited by Guarantee
○   *T
●   Mtgs - Inf - LG - Seminars
M   58 f
¶   NL; m only.   LM.   Technical literature.

Insurance Financial & Legal Services Association
        a group of the **British Marine Federation**

Insurance Institute of Ireland
IRL   39 Molesworth St, DUBLIN 2, Republic of Ireland.   (hq)
        353 (1) 677 2582   fax 353 (1) 677 2621
        email iii@iol.ie   http://www.insurance-institute.ie
        Chief Exec: Denis Hevey
○   *P

**Intellect, the Information Technology, Telecommunications &
   Electronics Association   1994**
NR   Russell Square House, 10-12 Russell Sq, LONDON, WC1B 5EE.
        020 7331 2000   fax 020 7331 2040
        email john.park@intellectuk.org
        http://www.intellectuk.org
        Co Sec: John Park
▲   Un-incorporated Society
○   *N, *T; interests of the information technology, electronics,
        communications, defence electronics, office technology &
        document management, software & services industries
Gp   Councils for: Telecommunications & radio, Information
        technology, Aerospace & defence, Naval & maritime, Office
        technology, Components & manufacturing;
        Group: Defence policy;
        Advisory groups: Commercial, Engineering services, Publicity,
        Research, Mobile telephone, Skills & training, Health, safety
        & environment
        Business Function Groups: Human Resources, Legal &
        contracts, Marketing, Quality
        Industry Groups: Financial services, Utilities, Defence,
        Government, Healthcare; Justice & emergency services
●   Conf - Mtgs - Exhib - Stat - Expt - Inf - LG
<   EECA; EICTA; FRMB; EDIG; CEN; CENELEC; ETSI; NIAG;
        NATO
M   1,000+ f
¶   Publications list available.
×   2002 (Computing Services & Software Association
        (FEI - Federation of the Electronics Industry

Intellectual Property Lawyers Association   1982
NR   c/o Philip Westmacott, Bristows, 3 Lincoln's Inn Fields,
        LONDON, WC2A 3AA.
○   *P

Intelligent Membrane Trade Association
■   PO Box 74, Stretford, MANCHESTER, M32 0XN.   (sb)
        0161-865 8913   fax 0161-866 9859
        email ima.uk@icopal.com
        Sec: Tony Burke
○   *T

Intensive Care Society (ICS) 1970
■   29b Montague St, LONDON, WC1B 5DH.   (hq)
        020 7291 0690
        email admin@ics.ac.uk   http://www.ics.ac.uk
        Hon Sec: Dr S A Ridley
▲   Registered Charity
○   *P; to promote & develop the medical speciality of intensive
        care
Gp   Conferences; Education & training; Scientific or other systematic
        research
●   Conf - Mtgs - ET - Res - Exhib - Stat - LG
<   Wld Fedn of Socs of Intensive & Critical Care Medicine; Eur Soc
        of Intensive Care; Ir Intensive Care Soc
M   2,000 i, UK / 23 i, o'seas
¶   JICS (Jnl) - 3; ftm only.   AR; free.
        Standards Documents;   Guidelines; both ftm.

Interactive Media in Retail Group (IMRG) 1990
NR   5 Dryden St, Covent Garden, LONDON, WC2E 9NB.
        http://www.imrg.org

INTERFLORA
NR Interflora House, SLEAFORD, Lincs, NG34 7TB.   (hq)
0870 904 5459
○ *T
M f
No further information supplied.

Interior Decorators & Designers Association Ltd
in 2002 merged with the International Interior Design Association (UK chapter) to become **British Interior Design Association**

Interlay, the Association of Block Paving Contractors
a product group of the **British Precast Concrete Federation**

Intermediary Mortgage Lenders Association   (IMLA)   1988
■ 3 Savile Row, LONDON, W1S 3PB.   (hsb)
020 7440 2233
email julie.dover@cml.org.uk
Sec: Julie Dover
▲ Company Limited by Guarantee
○ *T
● Mtgs
M 32 f
¶ LM - 1; free.

International Association of Animal Therapists   (IAAT)   1991
NR Tyringham Hall, Cuddington, AYLESBURY, Bucks, HP18 0AP.
(hsp)
01844 291526   fax 01844 290474
email animalth@aol.com
Principal: Sherry Scott
▲ Company Limited by Guarantee
○ *P, *V
● Mtgs - ET - Exam - Expt
M 40 i, UK / 20 i, o'seas
✕ 2005 National Association of Animal Therapists

International Association of Auto Theft Investigators (UK Branch)   (IAATI)
NR 23 Stirling Drive, Garswood, Ashton-in-Makerfield, WIGAN, WN4 0UG.
01942 724828   fax 01942 207545
email admin@iaati.org.uk   http://www.iaati.org.uk
Pres: Tony Simms,   Sec: Bryan King-Williams
Br Europe (several); Australia, S Africa, USA
○ *P; to provide an exchange of technical information & development; to cooperate with all law enforcement agencies & associations involved in prevention, detection & suppression of vehicle crime
● Conf - VE - ET - LG
< Intl Assn Auto Theft Investigators
M 380 i, UK / 4,000 i, o'seas

International Bond & Share Society   (IBSS)   1978
■ 167 Barnett Wood Lane, ASHTEAD, Surrey, KT21 2LP.   (hsp)
01372 276787
email secretary@scripophily.org
http://www.scripophily.org
Hon Sec: Philip Atkinson
○ *G; the study, buying & selling, exchanging & promoting the knowledge of scripophily (collectable bond, stock & share certificates)
M i

International Cargo Handling Co-ordination Association
since 2003 **ICHCA International**

International Chamber of Commerce - UK National Committee (ICC United Kingdom)   1920
■ 12 Grosvenor Place, LONDON, SW1X 7HH.   (hq)
020 7838 9363
Dir: Andrew Hope
○ *T; to represent interests of world business to governments & intergovernmental organisations
Gp Air transport; Arbitration; Banking technique & practice; Competition law; Computing telecommunications & information policy; Environment; Financial services; Insurance; Intellectual property; International commercial practice; Marketing; Multinationals & investment; Sea Transport; Taxation; Trade policy; Trade regulations
● Conf - Mtgs - LG
M f
¶ Business Bulletin (NL) - 6:   AR; both free.
Publications list available.

International Consulting Economists' Association   (ICEA)   1986
■ 45 Sorrel Bank, Linton Glade, CROYDON, Surrey, CR0 9LW. (hsb)
020 8651 1380
email secretariat@icea.co.uk   http://www.icea.co.uk
Secretariat: Mrs Turhan Donegan
▲ Un-incorporated Society
○ *P; international economic consultancy; economic issues; development aid
Gp Agricultural & rural development; Aid & evaluation; Construction; Education; Energy; Environment & water; EU integration; Finance; Health; Industry; Infrastructure; Irrigation; Manufacture; Migration; Private sector; Tourism; Trade; Transport; Urban; Other
● Mtgs
M 124 i, UK / 19 i, o'seas
¶ NL - 2;   LM - 1; both ftm only.

International General Produce Association Ltd   (IGPA)   1876
■ GAFTA House, 6 Chapel Place, Rivington St, LONDON, EC2A 3SH.
020 7814 9666   fax 020 7814 8383
email igpa@gafta.com   http://www.igpa.com
Sec: Pamela Kirby Johnson
○ *T; a contract issuing body for international trade in herbs, spices, essential oils, aromatic chemicals & general produce
M i, f & org
¶ Hbk.

International Glassfibre Reinforced Concrete Association   (GRCA)   1975
NR c/o The Concrete Society, Riverside House, 4 Meadows Business Park, Station Approach, Blackwater, CAMBERLEY, Surrey, GU17 9AB.   (hq)
01276 607140
▲ Company Limited by Guarantee
Br 2
○ *T; the development of GRC industry for the benefit of suppliers, manufacturers, users & specifiers; GRC is a composite of alkali resistant glass fibres & concrete/sand matrix (thin high strength concrete)
● Conf - Mtgs - ET - Res - Exhib - SG - Inf - LG
< Fachvereinigung Faserbeton (FVF)(Germany); Prestressed Concrete Inst (PCI)(USA)
M 20 f, UK / 60 f, o'seas
¶ GRCA News - 3; free.   LM - 1; free.
Conference Proceedings - 2 yrly.
Specifications & Codes of Practice.
List of publications & price list; free.

International Guild of Knot Tyers   1982
- 16 Egles Grove, UCKFIELD, E Sussex, TN22 2BY.   (hsp)
  01825 760425   fax 01825 761371
  email sec@igkt.net   http://www.igkt.net
  Hon Sec: Nigel Harding
- ▲ Registered Charity
- Br 16; 7
- ○ *G; all aspects of knot-tying & associated ropework
- M 573 i, 5 f, 5 org, UK / 629 i, 1 f, o'seas
- ¶ Knotting Matters (NL) - 4.
  Membership Hbk - 18 months; m only.

International Language [IDO] Society of Great Britain (ILSGB)   1910
- 24 Nunn St, LEEK, Staffs, ST13 8EA.   (hsp)
  Hon Sec: David Weston
- ▲ Un-incorporated Society
- ○ *X; to promote the use of Ido as an international language
- ● Mtgs - Inf
- < Uniono por la Linguo Internaciona Ido
- M 20 i, UK / 16 i, o'seas

International Law Association   (ILA)   1873
- NR Charles Clore House, 17 Russell Sq, LONDON, WC1B 5DR.
  (hq)
  020 7323 2978
  Sec Gen: David Wyld
- ○ *L; study, elucidation & advancement of international law, both public & private
- M c 4,000 i

International Marine Contractors Association   (IMCA)   1972
- NR 5 Lower Belgrave St, LONDON, SW1W 0NR.   (hq)
  020 7824 5520   fax 020 7824 5521
  email imca@imca-int.com   http://www.imca-int.com
  Chief Exec: Hugh Williams
- ▲ Un-incorporated Society
- Br Africa, Americas, Asia, Europe, Middle East, Pacific
- ○ *T
- Gp Marine; Diving; Safety & legislation; ROV; Survey vessels; Training certification & personal competence
- ● Conf - Mtgs - ET - Exam - LG
- M f
- ¶ IMCA NL - 4; free.

International Otter Survival Fund   (IOSF)   1993
- Lower Harapool, BROADFORD, Isle of Skye, IV49 9AQ.   (hq)
  01471 822487   fax 01471 822487
  email iosf@otter.org   http://www.otter.org
  Chief Exec: Grace Yoxon
- ▲ Company Limited by Guarantee; Registered Charity
- Br Belarus, Sri Lanka
- ○ *K, *V; 'to conserve otters by safeguarding areas of good habitat & supporting people working in research & rehabilitation worldwide'
- Gp Toxicology
- ● Conf - ET - Res - Inf - Lib - PL
- M 5,500 i, 25 f, 6 org, UK / 420 i, o'seas
- ¶ IOSF Otter Journal - 1; £35 m, £45 nm.
  Otter News - 4; free.

International Pen Friends   (IPF)   1967
- PO Box 42, BERWICK-upon-TWEED, TD15 1RU.
  (UK/coordinator)
  01289 331335   fax 01289 331335
  email ipfatuk@aol.com
  UK Coordinator: Mrs Pamela Walker
- ▲ Company Limited by Guarantee
- Br worldwide
- ○ *G, *X; promotion of international correspondence for all age groups
- Gp Sections: Youth (schools service); Language students
- ● Comp - Supply of a pen friend service for all age groups; apply in writing to address above
- M 4,000 i, UK / 250,000 i, o'seas
- ¶ People & Places - 2; £5 each.

International Register of Consultant Herbalists & Homoeopaths 1960
- 32 King Edward Rd, SWANSEA, Glam, SA1 4LL.   (hsb)
  01792 655886   fax 01792 655886
  email office@irch.org   http://www.irch.org
  Co Sec: Ifanca H James
- ▲ Company Limited by Guarantee
- ○ *M, *P; to train traditional herbalists & homoeopaths; to hold a register of these members to provide the public with a treatment in herbal &/or homoeopathic medicine
- Gp Herbal; Homoeopathic
- ● Conf - Mtgs - ET - Exam - Res - Exhib - Comp - SG - Inf - Lib - VE
- < Coun of Orgs Registering Herbalists (CORH); Eur Herbal Practitioners Assn (EHPA)
- M 57 i, UK / 7 i, o'seas
- ¶ Jnl of Natural Medicine - 4; ftm, £19.50 (£25.50 o'seas) yr nm.
  Note: trading as General Council & Register of Consultant Herbalists Ltd

International Society of Typographic Designers   (ISTD)   1928
- PO Box 725, TAUNTON, Somerset, TA2 8WE.   (hsp)
  020 7436 0984   fax 020 7637 7352
  email mail@istd.org.uk   http://www.istd.org.uk
  Chmn: Jonathan Doney
- ▲ Company Limited by Guarantee
- Br Ireland, Lebanon, South Africa
- ○ *P; to promote the highest standards of typographic design
- ● Conf - Mtgs - ET - Exam - Exhib - SG - Inf - VE - Student assessment programme for direct entry
- < Intl Congress of Graphic Design Assns
- M 580 i, UK / 75 i, o'seas
- ¶ Typographic - 2; ftm, £12 nm.

International Steel Trade Association   (ISTA)
- Broadway House, Tothill St, LONDON, SW1H 9NQ.   (hq)
  020 7799 2662   fax 020 7799 2468
  email hbailey@steeltrade.co.uk
  http://www.steeltrade.co.uk
  Dir: H W Bailey
- ○ *T; to look after the interests of international steel traders
- ● Mtgs - ET - VE - LG
- M 99 f
- ¶ AR.

International Stress Management Association (UK)   (ISMA (UK))   1984
- PO Box 26, SOUTH PETHERTON, Somerset, TA13 5SW.   (sb)
  0700 078 0430
  email stress@isma.org.uk   http://www.isma.org.uk
  Chmn: Jane Thomas
- ▲ Company Limited by Guarantee; Registered Charity
- Br Australia, Brazil, Hong Kong, India, Netherlands, Russia, USA
- ○ *P; to promote sound knowledge & best practice in the prevention & reduction of human stress
- ● Conf - Mtgs - LG
- M 550 i
- ¶ Stress News - 4; ftm, £35 yr nm.

International Underwriting Association of London   (LIRMA)   1991

NR   London Underwriting Centre, 3 Minster Court, Mincing Lane, LONDON, EC3R 7DD.
020 7617 4444
Chief Exec: Dave Matcham
▲   Company Limited by Guarantee
○   *T; for international reinsurance & non-marine insurance companies in the international wholesale market

Internet Content Rating Association   (ICRA)   1999

NR   22 Old Steine, BRIGHTON, E Sussex, BN1 1EL.
http://www.icra.org.uk

Internet Service Providers Association   (ISPA)   1995

■   23 Palace St, LONDON, SW1E 5HW.   (hq)
020 7233 7234   fax 020 7233 7294
email secretariat@ispa.org.uk   http://www.ispa.org.uk
Gen Sec: Nicholas Lansman
▲   Company Limited by Guarantee
○   *T; to promote the development of the internet industry
●   Conf - Mtgs - Res - LG
<   EuroISPA; IWF
M   130 f
¶   NL (electronic) - 12;   (in hardcopy) - 2; free.

Interpave, the Precast Concrete Paving & Kerb Association
a product association of the **British Precast Concrete Federation**

Interstitial Cystitis Support Group
since 2003 **Cystitis & Overactive Bladder Foundation**

Intumescent Fire Seals Association   (IFSA)   1982

NR   20 Park St, PRINCES RISBOROUGH, Bucks, HP27 9AH.   (hq)
01844 276928
http://www.ifsa.org.uk
Sec: Mrs Christine Barfield
▲   Un-incorporated Society
○   *T; promotion of benefits both technical & commercial arising from the use of intumescent fire & smoke seals
Gp   Representation on BSS, ISO & CEN standards c'ees
●   Conf - Mtgs - ET - Res - Expt - Inf
M   14 f
¶   Technical Information Sheets 1-5 - updated.
IFSA Code.

Inverness Chamber of Commerce   1893

■   PO Box 5512, INVERNESS, Highland, IV2 3ZE.   (hq)
01463 718131   fax 01463 718131
email info@inverness-chamber.co.uk
http://www.inverness-chamber.co.uk
Chief Exec: Simon Cole-Hamilton
▲   Company Limited by Guarantee
○   *C
●   Mtgs - Exhib - LG
<   Aberdeen & Grampian Cham Comm; Scot Chams Comm
M   293 f
¶   inbusiness - 6.   LM; ftm only.
×   2003 (25 March) Inverness & District Chamber of Commerce

Inverness & District Chamber of Commerce
since 25 March 2003 **Inverness Chamber of Commerce**

Investment Management Association   (IMA)   1959

NR   65 Kingsway, LONDON, WC2B 6TD.   (hq)
020 7831 0898
Office Mgr: Carolyn Smith
○   *T; to improve the regulatory, fiscal & legal environment for unit trusts & investment funds; to increase public awareness of collective investments
●   Conf - Mtgs - ET - Exam - Res - Stat - Inf - LG
M   f
×   2002 (Association of Unit Trusts & Investment Funds
(Fund Managers Association

Investment Property Forum   (IPF)   1988

■   New Broad Street House, 35 New Broad St, LONDON, EC2M 1NH.   (hq)
020 7194 7920   fax 020 7194 7921
email ipfoffice@ipf.org.uk   http://www.ipf.org.uk
Exec Dir: Amanda Keane
▲   Company Limited by Guarantee
○   *P; 'to improve the awareness, understanding & efficiency of property as an investment'
●   Conf - Mtgs - ET - Res - VE - LG - Social lunches & dinners
M   1,450 i
¶   Forum View - 3;   Annual Review, Report & Accounts; both ftm.

Investor Relations Society   (IRS)   1980

NR   Bedford House, 3 Bedford St, LONDON, WC2E 9HD.   (hq)
020 7379 1763
Gen Mgr: Tony Workman
▲   Company Limited by Guarantee
○   *N; to promote better communications between companies & their investors
●   Conf - Mtgs - ET - Res - Inf - Lib
<   Intl Investor Relations Fedn (IIRF)
M   320 i, UK / 20 i, o'seas
¶   Informed (Jnl) - 4;   Bulletin (NL) - 12;   AR; all ftm only.
Publications list available.

Involvement & Participation Association   (IPA)   1884

NR   42 Colebrooke Row, LONDON, N1 8AF.   (hq)
020 7354 8040
▲   Company Limited by Guarantee; Registered Charity
○   *E, *Q; improvement of business performance through involving employees in the operation of the organisation
●   Conf - Mtgs - ET - Res - Exhib - Inf - Lib - VE - Empl - LG
M   40 i, 175 f, UK / 10 i, 10 f, o'seas
¶   IPA Magazine (Jnl) - 4.

Iran Society   1936

■   2 Belgrave Sq, LONDON, SW1X 8PJ.   (hq)
020 7235 5122   fax 020 7259 6771
email iransoc@rsaa.org.uk
http://www.iransoc.dircon.co.uk
Hon Sec: Robert McKenzie,
Chmn: Michael Noël Clarke
▲   Registered Charity
○   *X; 'to promote learning & advance education regarding Iran, its people & culture; no contemporary party politics form any part of the Society's activities'
●   Mtgs - VE - Lectures
M   396 i, 10 f
¶   Jnl - 1;   AR - 1; both free.

Irish Airline Pilots' Association   1946

IRL   Corballis Park, DUBLIN AIRPORT, Co Dublin, Republic of Ireland.
353 (1) 844 5272   fax 353 (1) 844 6051
email admin@ialpa.net   http://www.ialpa.net
○   *P

© CBD Research Ltd · Beckenham · BR3 5JS · Tel 020 8650 7745 · Fax 020 8650 0768 · E-mail cbd@cbdresearch.com · www.cbdresearch.com

Irish Amateur Boxing Association   (IABA)
IRL   National Boxing Stadium, South Circular Rd, DUBLIN 8,
        Republic of Ireland.   (hq)
        353 (1) 453 3371   fax 353 (1) 454 0777
        email iaba@eircom.net
        Hon Sec: Séan Crowley
○   *S

Irish Anti-Vivisection Society   1970
IRL   PO Box 13, GREYSTONES, Co Wicklow, Republic of Ireland.
        353 (1) 282 0154
        Sec: Heather Finnegan
○   *K, *V

Irish Association of Corporate Treasurers
IRL   PO Box 10104, LUCAN, Co Dublin, Republic of Ireland.
        353 (1) 610 8574   fax 353 (1) 621 3494
        email info@treasurers.ie   http://www.treasurers.ie
        Sec: Judith Lawless
○   *P

Irish Association for Counselling & Psychotherapy   (IACP)
IRL   8 Cumberland St, DÚN LAOGHAIRE, Co Dublin, Republic of
        Ireland.
        353 (1) 230 0061   fax 353 (1) 230 0064
        email iacp@irish-counselling.ie
        http://www.irish-counselling.ie
        Chief Exec: Yvonne Curtin
○   *P
×   2002 Irish Association for Counselling and Therapy

Irish Association for Cultural, Economic & Social Relations   1938
IRL   PO Box 8417, DUBLIN 14, Republic of Ireland.
        email info@irish-association.org
        http://www.irish-association.org
        Pres: Jean Whyte
○   *K, *X; to foster understanding between Irish people of different
        traditions

Irish Association of Distributive Trades Ltd
IRL   Rock House, Main St, BLACKROCK, Co Dublin, Republic of
        Ireland.
        353 (1) 288 7584   fax 353 (1) 283 2206
        Dir Gen: Tara Buckley
○   *T; represents food wholesalers in Ireland

Irish Association for Economic Geology
IRL   c/o The Geological Survey of Ireland, Beggars Bush,
        Haddington Rd, Ballsbridge, DUBLIN 4, Republic of Ireland.
        353 (1) 678 2000   fax 353 (1) 678 2589
        Sec: Wayne Cox
○   *L; mineral exploration, mining geology & petroleum geology

Irish Association for Industrial Relations   1971
IRL   c/o Dept of Personnel & Employment Relations, University of
        Limerick, LIMERICK, Republic of Ireland.
        353 (61) 202380
        Hon Sec: Dr Noel Harvey
○   *P

Irish Association of International Express Carriers   (IAIEC)
IRL   c/o 28 South Frederick St, DUBLIN 2, Republic of Ireland.
        353 (1) 676 5633   fax 353 (1) 676 5641
        email michael.darcy@darcysmyth.ie
        Chmn : David Canavan
○   *T

Irish Association of Investment Managers   1986
IRL   35 Fitzwilliam Place, DUBLIN 2, Republic of Ireland.
        353 (1) 676 1919   fax 353 (1) 676 1954
        email info@iaim.ie   http://www.iaim.ie
        Sec Gen: Ann Fitzgerald
○   *P; institutional investors in the Irish market

Irish Association of Pension Funds   (IAPF)   1973
IRL   Slane House, 25 Lower Mount St, DUBLIN 2, Republic of
        Ireland.
        353 (1) 661 2427   fax 353 (1) 662 1196
        email info@iapf.ie   http://www.iapf.ie
        Sec: Marie Collins
○   *T

Irish Association of Social Workers   1971
IRL   114-116 Pearse St, DUBLIN 2, Republic of Ireland.
        353 (1) 677 4838   fax 353 (1) 671 5734
        email iasw@eircom.net   http://www.iasw.ie
        Hon Sec: Karen Breen
○   *P

Irish Association for Spina Bifida & Hydrocephalus
IRL   Old Nangor Rd, Clondalkin, DUBLIN 22, Republic of Ireland.
        353 (1) 457 2329   fax 353 (1) 457 2328
        email info@iasbah.ie   http://www.iasbah.ie
        Hon Sec: Clare Gill
○   *W

Irish Astronomical Society   1937
IRL   PO Box 2547, DUBLIN 14, Republic of Ireland.
        email ias1937@hotmail.com
        http://www.irishastrosoc.org
        Hon Sec: Angela O'Connell
○   *L

Irish Auctioneers & Valuers Institute   (IAVI)   1922
IRL   38 Merrion Sq, DUBLIN 2, Republic of Ireland.   (hq)
        353 (1) 661 1794   fax 353 (1) 661 1797
        email info@iavi.ie
        Chief Exec: Alan A Cooke
○   *P

Irish Bankers' Federation
IRL   Nassau House, Nassau St, DUBLIN 2, Republic of Ireland.
        353 (1) 671 5311   fax 353 (1) 679 6680
        email ibf@ibf.ie   http://www.ibf.ie
        Chief Exec: Pat Farrell
○   *P

Irish Basketball Association   1947
IRL   National Basketball Arena, Tymon Park, DUBLIN 24, Republic
        of Ireland.
        353 (1) 459 0211   fax 353 (1) 459 0212
        email info@basketballireland.ie
        http://www.basketballireland.ie
        Chief Exec: Debbie Massey
○   *S
        Note: uses the marketing name of Basketball Ireland.

Irish BioIndustry Association   (IBIA)
IRL   Confederation House, 84-86 Lower Baggot St, DUBLIN 2,
        Republic of Ireland.
        353 (1) 605 1584   fax 353 (1) 638 1584
        email matt.moran@ibec.ie
        Dir: Matt Moran
○   *P
<   IBEC

Irish Book Publishers' Association
        see **CLÉ: the Irish Book Publishers Association**

Irish Bowling Association (IBA) 1904
NR   2 Oronsay Crescent, LARNE, BT40 2HD. (hsp)
     Hon Sec: Tom McGarel
▲   Un-incorporated Society
○   *S; regulating & organising men's outdoor flat green bowls in
     Ireland
Gp   Irish Bowls Coaches Association; Irish Bowls Umpires
     Association
●   Mtgs - Comp - Inf
<   Wld Bowls; Eur Bowls U; Brit Isles Bowls Coun; NI C'wealth
     Games Coun; NI Sports Forum; NI Sports Trust
>   Bowling League of Ireland; NI Bowling Assn; NI Private Greens
     League; NI Provincial Bowling Assn
M   5,200 i, 125 clubs
¶   Ybk.

Irish Bowls Coaches Association
     is a group of the **Irish Bowling Association**

Irish Bowls Umpires Association
     is a group of the **Irish Bowling Association**

Irish Brewers Association
IRL Confederation House, 84-86 Lower Baggot St, DUBLIN 2,
     Republic of Ireland.
     353 (1) 660 1011   fax 353 (1) 660 1717
<   IBEC

Irish Bridge Union
IRL 8 Orchardstown Pk, DUBLIN 14, Republic of Ireland.
     353 (1) 494 7726
     161 Moss Rd, Lambeg, Lisburn, Co Antrim, BT27 4LG.
     Jt Hon Secs: Mrs K Downes & Dr A Hill
○   *G

Irish Business & Employers Confederation (IBEC) 1993
IRL Confederation House, 84-86 Lower Baggot St, DUBLIN 2,
     Republic of Ireland.
     353 (1) 605 1500   fax 353 (1) 638 1500
     http://www.ibec.ie
     Dir Gen: Turlough O'Sullivan
○   *T, *N

Irish Cancer Society 1963
IRL 43-45 Northumberland Rd, DUBLIN 4, Republic of Ireland.
     353 (1) 231 0500   fax 353 (1) 231 0555
     email info@irishcancer.ie   http://www.cancer.ie
     Chief Exec: John McCormack
○   *W

Irish Cattle & Sheep Farmers Association
     see **ICSA - Irish Cattle & Sheep Farmers Association**

Irish Cellular Industry Association
IRL Confederation House, 84-86 Lower Baggot St, DUBLIN 2,
     Republic of Ireland.
     353 (1) 605 1656   fax 353 (1) 638 1656
     email icia@ibec.ie   http://www.icia.ie
     Dir: Tommy McCabe
○   *T
<   IBEC

Irish Chamber of Shipping
IRL Port Centre, Alexandra Rd, DUBLIN 1, Republic of Ireland.
     353 (1) 855 9011   fax 353 (1) 855 9022
     Dir: B W Kerr
○   *N

Irish Chemical Marketers Association (ICMA)
IRL Confederation House, 84-86 Lower Baggot St, DUBLIN 2,
     Republic of Ireland.
     353 (1) 605 1563   fax 353 (1) 638 1563
     Dir: Matt Moran
○   *P
<   IBEC

Irish Chiropodists/Podiatrists Organisation
IRL c/o Ard na Gréine, Flynn's Cross, BALLINCOLLIG, Co Cork,
     Republic of Ireland.
     353 (21) 487 4560
     Gen Sec: Finbarr Dalton
○   *P
×   2000-2002 Society of Chiropodists & Podiatrists (Ireland)

Irish Clothing & Textiles Alliance (ICATA)
IRL Confederation House, 84-86 Lower Baggot St, DUBLIN 2,
     Republic of Ireland.
     353 (1) 605 1560   fax 353 (1) 638 1560
     email icata@ibec.ie   http://www.ibec.ie/icata
     Dir: Susan Doyle
○   *P
<   IBEC

Irish Co-operative Organisation Society Ltd (ICOS)
IRL 84 Merrion Sq, DUBLIN 2, Republic of Ireland.
     353 (1) 676 4783   fax 353 (1) 662 4502
     http://www.icos.ie
     Sec: Seamus O'Donohoe
○   *N; for the co-operative movement in Ireland

Irish Cold Storage Federation
IRL Confederation House, 84-86 Lower Baggot St, DUBLIN 2,
     Republic of Ireland.
     353 (1) 605 1500   fax 353 (1) 638 1500
○   *T
<   IBEC

Irish College of General Practitioners
IRL 4-5 Lincoln Place, DUBLIN 2, Republic of Ireland.
     353 (1) 676 3705   fax 353 (1) 676 5850
     email info@icgp.ie   http://www.icgp.ie
     Hon Sec: Dr Fiona Graham
○   *P
M   2,600

Irish Commercial Horticultural Association
IRL c/o Irish Farm Centre, Naas Rd, DUBLIN 12, Republic of
     Ireland.
     353 (1) 450 0266   fax 353 (1) 456 5146
     http://www.ifa.ie
     Exec Sec: Kieran Leddy
○   *F, *H; for growers of vegetables, fruit & ornamental plants

Irish Computer Society 1972
IRL Crescent Hall, Mount Street Crescent, DUBLIN 2, Republic of
     Ireland.
     353 (1) 644 7820   fax 353 (1) 662 0224
     email info@ics.ie   http://www.ics.ie
     Chief Exec: Jim Friars
○   *P

Irish Concrete Federation
IRL 8 Newlands Business Park, Naas Rd, Clondalkin, DUBLIN 22,
     Republic of Ireland.
     353 (1) 464 0082   fax 353 (1) 464 0087
     email info@irishconcrete.ie   http://www.irishconcrete.ie
     Chief Exec & Sec: John Maguire
○   *T

Irish Concrete Society
IRL　Platin, DROGHEDA, Co Louth, Republic of Ireland.
　　　353 (41) 987 6466　fax 353 (41) 987 6400
　　　Hon Sec: Marie O'Donovan
○　　*P, *T

Irish Conference of Professional & Service Associations　1946
IRL　93 St Stephen's Green, DUBLIN 2, Republic of Ireland.
　　　353 (1) 830 3833　fax 353 (1) 830 3331
　　　Hon Sec: John Healy
○　　*N

Irish Congress of Trade Unions　(ICTU)　1959
IRL　31-32 Parnell Sq, DUBLIN 1, Republic of Ireland.
　　　353 (1) 889 7777　fax 353 (1) 887 2012
　　　email congress@ictu.ie　http://www.ictu.ie
　　　4-6 Donegal St Place, Belfast BT1 2FM.
　　　Gen Sec: David Begg
○　　*N, *U
　　　Note: There are 57 unions affiliated to ICTU; full details are
　　　contained in 'Administration Yearbook & Diary' (see
　　　Introduction 3 (c)).

Irish Contract Cleaning Association
IRL　Confederation House, 84-86 Lower Baggot St, DUBLIN 2,
　　　Republic of Ireland.
　　　Sec: Sonya Higgins
○　　*T; for companies in the commercial cleaning field
<　　IBEC

Irish Corrugated Packaging Association
IRL　Confederation House, 84-86 Lower Baggot St, Dublin 2,
　　　Republic of Ireland.
○　　*T
<　　IBEC

**Irish Cosmetics, Detergents & Allied Products Association
(ICDA)**
IRL　Confederation House, 84-86 Lower Baggot St, DUBLIN 2,
　　　Republic of Ireland.
　　　353 (1) 605 1624　fax 353 (1) 638 1624
　　　email info@icda.ie　http://www.icda.ie
　　　Dir: Marian Byron
○　　*T; to represent the industry & keep it updated on all relevant
　　　EU rules & regulations
<　　IBEC

Irish Council against Blood Sports　1966
IRL　PO Box 88, MULLINGAR, Co Westmeath, Republic of Ireland.
　　　353 (44) 934 9848
　　　email icabs@eircom.net
　　　http://www.banbloodsports.com
　　　PRO: Aideen Yourell
○　　*K

Irish Council for Civil Liberties　(ICCL)　1976
IRL　40-41 Lower Dominick St, DUBLIN 1, Republic of Ireland
　　　353 (1) 878 3136　fax 353 (1) 878 3109
　　　email iccl@iol.ie　http://www.iccl.ie
　　　Admin: Dawn Quinn
○　　*K

Irish Countrywomen's Association　(ICA)　1910
IRL　58 Merrion Rd, DUBLIN 4, Republic of Ireland.　(hq)
　　　353 (1) 668 0453　fax 353 (1) 660 9423
　　　email office@ica.ie　http://www.ica.ie
　　　Hon Sec: Peg McMeel
○　　*G

Irish Creamery Milk Suppliers Association　(ICMSA)
IRL　John Feely House, Dublin Rd, LIMERICK, Republic of Ireland.
　　　353 (61) 314677　fax 353 (61) 315737
　　　email icmsa@eircom.net　http://www.icmsa.ie
　　　Gen Sec: Ciaran Dolan
○　　*F; for family farms

Irish Dairy Industries Association　(IDI)　1971
IRL　Confederation House, 84-86 Lower Baggot St, DUBLIN 2,
　　　Republic of Ireland.
　　　353 (1) 605 1574　fax 353 (1) 638 1574
　　　Dir: Michael Barry
○　　*F

Irish Deaf Society / National Association of the Deaf　1981
IRL　30 Blessington St, DUBLIN 7, Republic of Ireland.
　　　353 (1) 860 1878　fax 353 (1) 860 1960
　　　email info@irishdeafsociety.ie
　　　http://www.irishdeafsociety.ie
　　　Hon Sec: John Bosco Conama
○　　*W

Irish Dental Association　(IDA)　1922
IRL　Unit 2 Leopardstown Office Park, Sandyford, DUBLIN 18,
　　　Republic of Ireland.
　　　353 (1) 283 0499　fax 113 (1) 283 0515
　　　http://www.dentist.ie
　　　Sec Gen: Donal St A Atkins
○　　*P

Irish Direct Marketing Association　(IDMA)
IRL　Sigmund Business Centre, 93A Lagan Rd, Glasnevin,
　　　DUBLIN 11, Republic of Ireland.
　　　353 (1) 830 4752　fax 353 (1) 830 8914
　　　email info@idma.ie　http://www.idma.ie
　　　Chmn: Alex Pigot
○　　*T

Irish Draught Horse Society (GB)　(IDHS(GB))　1980
NR　PO Box 1869, SALISBURY, SP3 5XA.
　　　0845 230 0399　fax 01722 714979
▲　　Registered Charity
○　　*B
M　　i
¶　　NL - 4; free.　Ybk.

Irish Educational Publishers Association
IRL　c/o Gill & Macmillan Ltd, Hume Avenue, Park West,
　　　DUBLIN 12, Republic of Ireland.
　　　353 (1) 500 9509　fax 353 (1) 500 9598
　　　email hmahony@gillmacmillan.ie
　　　Sec: Hubert Mahony
○　　*T

Irish Epilepsy Association
　　　see **Brainwave, the Irish Epilepsy Association**

Irish Exporters Association　(IEA)
IRL　28 Merrion Sq, DUBLIN 2, Republic of Ireland.
　　　353 (1) 661 2182　fax 353 (1) 661 2315
　　　email iea@irishexporters.ie　http://www.irishexporters.ie
　　　Chief Exec: John F Whelan
○　　*T

Irish Family History Society　1984
IRL　PO Box 36, NAAS, Co Kildare, Republic of Ireland.
　　　email ifhs@eircom.net
　　　Chmn: Mary Beglan
○　　*G

Irish Family Planning Association (IFPA) 1969
IRL 60 Amiens St, DUBLIN 1, Republic of Ireland.
    353 (1) 474 0944   fax 353 (1) 474 0945
    email post@ifpa.ie   http://www.ifpa.ie
    Chief Exec: Niall Behan
○ *W

Irish Farmers' Association 1972
IRL Irish Farm Centre, Naas Rd, Bluebell, DUBLIN 12, Republic of
    Ireland.
    353 (1) 450 0266   fax 353 (1) 455 1043
    http://www.ifa.ie
    Gen Sec: Michael Berkery
○ *F

Irish Federation of Sea Anglers 1953
IRL c/o H O'Rorke, 67 Windsor Drive, MONKSTOWN, Co Dublin,
    Republic of Ireland.
    353 (1) 280 6873   fax 353 (1) 280 6873
    email ccifsa@yahoo.ie
    Hon Sec: H O'Rorke
○ *G, *S

Irish Federation of University Teachers (IFUT) 1965
IRL 11 Merrion Sq, DUBLIN 2, Republic of Ireland.
    353 (1) 661 0910   fax 353 (1) 661 0909
    email ifut@eircom.net   http://www.ifut.ie
    Gen Sec: Daltún Ó Ceallaigh
○ *E, *P

Irish Federation of Women's Clubs
IRL 11 St Peter's Rd, Phibsboro, DUBLIN 7, Republic of Ireland.
    353 (1) 868 0080
    Hon Sec: Joan Murnane
○ *W

Irish Field & Country Sports Society
    since 2002 **Countryside Ireland**

Irish Film Institute
IRL 6 Eustace St, Temple Bar, DUBLIN 2, Republic of Ireland.
    353 (1) 679 5744   fax 353 (1) 677 8755
    email info@irishfilm.ie   http://www.irishfilm.ie
    Dir: Mark Mulqueen
○ *A
× 2003 Film Institute of Ireland

Irish Finance Houses Association Ltd
IRL ICB House, Newstead, Clonskeagh Rd, DUBLIN 14, Republic of
    Ireland.
    353 (1) 260 0388   fax 353 (1) 260 0390
    Sec Gen: Séamus Ó Tighearnaigh
○ *T

Irish Fish Processors & Exporters Association
IRL c/o T F Geoghegan, 25 Kincora Ave, Clontarf, DUBLIN 3,
    Republic of Ireland.
    353 (1) 833 7882
    Sec: T F Geoghegan
○ *T

Irish Fish Producers' Organisation
IRL 11 Elgin Rd, DUBLIN 4, Republic of Ireland.
    353 (1) 668 7077   fax 353 (1) 668 4466
    email ifpo@eircom.net
    Chief Exec: Lorcán Ó Cinnéide
○ *T

Irish Fishermen's Organisation Ltd 1974
IRL Cumberland House, Fenian St, DUBLIN 2, Republic of Ireland.
    353 (1) 661 2400   fax 353 (1) 661 2424
    email irishfish@eircom.net
    Sec Gen: Frank Doyle
○ *N, *T

Irish Football Association Ltd (IFA) 1880
NR 20 Windsor Ave, BELFAST, BT9 6EE.   (hq)
   028 9066 9458
   email enquiries@irishfa.com
   Chief Exec: Howard J C Wells
▲ Company Limited by Guarantee
○ *S; governing body for Association football in Northern Ireland
● Mtgs - ET - Exam - LG
< U Eur Football Assns (UEFA); Fédn Intle Football Assns (FIFA)
M c 1,000 clubs
¶ Hbk (rules & regulations) - 1.   AR.
× 2004 (absorbed) Irish Football League

Irish Football League
    2004 was absorbed by the **Irish Football Association**

Irish Franchise Association
IRL 30 Tolka Valley Business Park, Ballyboggan Rd, Glasnevin,
    DUBLIN 11, Republic of Ireland.
    353 (1) 499 1091   fax 353 (1) 830 3913
    http://www.irishfranchiseassociation.com
    Chief Exec: Michael Bradley
○ *T

Irish Genealogical Research Society (IGRS) 1936
IRL 28 Marlfield, Cabinteely, DUBLIN 18, Republic of Ireland.   (.)
    email iclayton@gofree.indigo.ie   http://www.igrsoc.org
Br 1; Eire
○ *L
● Mtgs - Res - Lib
M 350 i, 20 org, UK / 550 i, 20 org, o'seas
¶ The Irish Genealogist - 1; £16.   NL - 2; ftm only.

Irish Geological Association
IRL c/o Beggar's Bush, Haddington Rd, DUBLIN 4, Republic of
    Ireland.
    353 (1) 678 2000
    http://www.ucd.ie/geology/IGA
    Pres: Barry Long
○ *L

Irish Georgian Society (IGS) 1958
IRL 74 Merrion Sq, DUBLIN 2, Republic of Ireland.
    353 (1) 676 7053   fax 353 (1) 662 0290
    email info@igs.ie   http://www.igs.ie
○ *K, *L

Irish Girl Guides
IRL 27 Pembroke Park, DUBLIN 4, Republic of Ireland.
    353 (1) 668 3898   fax 353 (1) 660 2779
    email info@irishgirlguides.ie
    http://www.irishgirlguides.ie
    Chief Exec: Linda Peters
○ *Y

Irish Grain & Feed Association
IRL 19 Carrick Hill, PORTLAOISE, Co Laois, Republic of Ireland.
    353 (57) 866 7022   fax 353 (57) 866 8690
    email info@eorna.ie
    Dir: Deirdre Webb
○ *T; manufacturers of compound animal feed & grain importers
    & traders

Irish Grassland Association
IRL Moneymore Farm, BORRIS-IN-OSSORY, Co Laois, Republic of
     Ireland.
        353 (505) 41025   fax 353 (505) 41025
        email grainne@irishgrassland.com
     Hon Sec: G Dwyer
○   *P
●   Conf
M   c 1,000

Irish Hardware & Building Materials Association
IRL Elmville, Upper Kilmacud Rd, Dundrum, DUBLIN 14, Republic
     of Ireland.
        353 (1) 298 0969   fax 353 (1) 298 6103
        email iha@iol.ie   http://www.irishhardware.ie
     Sec Gen: James Goulding
○   *T

Irish Health Services Management Institute
IRL Hume Street Hospital, DUBLIN 2, Republic of Ireland.
        353 (1) 661 9787   fax 353 (1) 661 9787
        email enquiries@ihsmi.ie
     Hon Sec: Edward J Byrne
○   *P

Irish Hereford Breed Society
IRL Harbour St, MULLINGAR, Co Westmeath, Republic of Ireland.
        353 (44) 934 8855   fax 353 (44) 934 8949
        http://www.irishhereford.com
     Sec: Laurence Feeney
○   *B

Irish Hockey Association   1893
IRL 6A Woodbine Park, BLACKROCK, Co Dublin, Republic of
     Ireland.   (mail/address)
        353 (1) 260 0028   fax 353 (1) 260 0087
        email info@hockey.ie   http://www.hockey.ie
     Sec: Joan Morgan
○   *S
×   2001 (Irish Hockey Union
          (Irish Ladies Hockey Association

Irish Hospital Consultants Association
IRL Heritage House, Dundrum Office Park, DUBLIN 14, Republic of
     Ireland.
        353 (1) 298 9123   fax 353 (1) 298 9395
        email info@ihca.ie
     Sec Gen: Finbarr Fitzpatrick
○   *P

Irish Hospitality Institute   (IHI)   1966
IRL 8 Herbert Lane, DUBLIN 2, Republic of Ireland.
        353 (1) 662 4790   fax 353 (1) 662 4789
        email admin@ihi.ie   http://www.ihi.ie
     Chief Exec: Adrian Cummins
○   *P
×   2005 Irish Hotels & Catering Institute

Irish Hotels & Catering Institute
     since 2005 **Irish Hospitality Institute**

Irish Hotels Federation
IRL 13 Northbrook Rd, DUBLIN 6, Republic of Ireland.
        353 (1) 497 6459   fax 353 (1) 497 4613
        email info@ihf.ie   http://www.ihf.ie
     Chief Exec: John Power
○   *T

Irish Hydro Power Association
IRL c/o Joseph Stewart & Co, Corn Mills, BOYLE, Co Roscommon,
     Republic of Ireland.
        353 (71) 966 2009   fax 353 (71) 966 2739
        http://www.irish-hydro.org
     Chmn: Darrell Nightingale
○   *T; for producers of hydroelectric power; to press for its greater
     use

Irish Institute of Credit Management   (IICM)   1980
IRL 121 Lower Baggot St, DUBLIN 2, Republic of Ireland.
        353 (1) 676 7822
        email iicm@indigo.ie   http://www.iicm.ie
     Chief Exec: Declan Flood
○   *P

Irish Institute of Pensions Managers   1989
IRL Insurance House, 39 Molesworth Street, DUBLIN 2, Republic of
     Ireland.
        353 (1) 662 0320   fax 353 (1) 677 2621
     Sec: Geoffrey McMaster
○   *P

Irish Institute of Purchasing & Materials Management   (IIPMM)
IRL 5 Belvedere Place, DUBLIN 1, Republic of Ireland.
        353 (1) 855 9257   fax 353 (1) 855 9259
        email iipmm@iipmm.ie   http://www.iipmm.ie
     Chief Exec: Des Crowther
○   *P

Irish Institute of Training & Development   1969
IRL Leinster Mills, Osberstown, NAAS, Co Kildare, Republic of
     Ireland.
        353 (45) 881166   fax 353 (45) 881192
        email info@iitd.com   http://www.iitd.ie
     Hon Sec: Pat Power
○   *P

Irish Institution of Surveyors   (IIS)
IRL 36 Dame St, DUBLIN 2, Republic of Ireland.
        353 (1) 677 4797
        email iissecretary@eircom.net
        http://www.irish-surveyors.ie
     Sec: Vera Destac
○   *P
M   c 320

Irish Insurance Federation   (IIF)
IRL Insurance House, 39 Molesworth St, DUBLIN 2, Republic of
     Ireland.
        353 (1) 676 1820   fax 353 (1) 676 1943
        email fed@iif.ie   http://www.iif.ie
     Chief Exec: Michael Kemp
○   *T

Irish International Freight Association
IRL Strand House, Strand St, MALAHIDE, Co Dublin, Republic of
     Ireland.
        353 (1) 845 5411   fax 353 (1) 845 5433
        email iifa@eircom.net   http://www.iifa.ie
     Hon Sec: Michael Slevin
○   *P
×   Institute of Freight Forwarders of Ireland

Irish Internet Association   1997
IRL 10-13 Thomas St, DUBLIN 8, Republic of Ireland.
        353 (1) 453 5707
        email info@iia.ie   http://www.iia.ie
     Chief Exec: Irene Gahan
○   *T
M   c 700 f

Irish Kidney Association   (IKA)
IRL   Donor House, Block 43A Parkwest, Crumlin, DUBLIN 12,
          Republic of Ireland.
          353 (1) 688 9788
          email info@ika.ie   http://www.ika.ie
          Hon Sec: Vera Frisby
Br   24
○   *W

Irish Ladies' Golf Union   1983
IRL   1 Clonskeagh Sq, Clonskeagh Rd, DUBLIN 14, Republic of
          Ireland.
          353 (1) 269 6244   fax 353 (1) 283 8670
          email info@ilgu.ie   http://www.ilgu.ie
          Chief Exec: Sinead Heraty
○   *S

Irish Ladies Hockey Association
          since 2002 **Irish Hockey Association**

Irish Landscape Institute   (ILI)   1993
IRL   6 Merrion Sq, DUBLIN 2, Republic of Ireland.
          353 (1) 662 7409
          Sec: Lucy Carey
○   *P

Irish League of Credit Unions   (ILCU)
IRL   33-41 Lower Mount St, DUBLIN 2, Republic of Ireland.
          353 (1) 614 6700   fax 353 (1) 614 6701
          email info@creditunion.ie   http://www.creditunion.ie
          Sec: John O'Halloran
○   *N

Irish Linen Guild
          Contact on telephone stated that this a virtual organisation with
          no address nor telephone number; email
          info@irishlinen.co.uk

Irish Management Institute   (IMI)   1952
IRL   National Management Centre, Sandyford Rd, DUBLIN 16,
          Republic of Ireland.
          353 (1) 207 8400   fax 353 (1) 295 5150
          email reception@imi.ie   http://www.imi.ie
          Chief Exec: Dr Tom McCarthy
○   *P

Irish Marine Federation
IRL   Confederation House, 84-86 Lower Baggot St, DUBLIN 2,
          Republic of Ireland.
○   *T
<   IBEC

Irish Maritime Law Association   (IMLA)   1963
IRL   Grattan House, Mount St Lower, DUBLIN 2, Republic of Ireland.
          353 (1) 661 9599   fax 353 (1) 662 2941
          Hon Sec: Sean Kelleher
○   *N

Irish Master Printers' Association   1919
IRL   Sheridan House, 33 Parkgate St, DUBLIN 8, Republic of
          Ireland.
          353 (1) 677 9116   fax 353 (1) 677 9144
          email barbara@rnan.ie
          Chief Exec: Neville Galloway
○   *T

Irish Masters of Beagles Association   1949
IRL   3 Iveragh Rd, Whitehall, DUBLIN 9, Republic of Ireland.
          Hon Sec: J O'Sullivan
○   *S

Irish Meat Association
          since 2004 **Meat Industry Ireland**

Irish Medical Devices Association   (IMDA)   1995
IRL   Confederation House, 84-86 Lower Baggot St, DUBLIN 2,
          Republic of Ireland.
          353 (1) 605 1593   fax 353 (1) 638 1593
          email imda@ibec.ie
          Dir: Sharon Higgins
○   *T
<   IBEC

Irish Medical Organisation   (IMO)   1936
IRL   10 Fitzwilliam Place, DUBLIN 2, Republic of Ireland.   (hq)
          353 (1) 676 7273   fax 353 (1) 661 2758
          email imo@imo.ie   http://www.imo.ie
          Chief Exec: George McNeice
○   *P, *U

Irish Mining & Exploration Group
IRL   Confederation House, 84-86 Lower Baggot St, DUBLIN 2,
          Republic of Ireland.
○   *T
<   IBEC

Irish Mining & Quarrying Society
IRL   87-89 Waterloo Rd, DUBLIN 4, Republic of Ireland.
          353 (1) 668 5193
          Hon Sec: Brian Burke
○   *P

Irish Moiled Cattle Society
NR   Oaktree Farm, Buttermilk Lane, Yarningale Common,
          CLAVERDON, Warks, CV35 8HV.   (mail/address)
          01926 842413
          Sec: Louise Smith
○   *B
M   c100

Irish Mortgage Council
IRL   Nassau House, Nassau Street, DUBLIN 2, Republic of Ireland.
          353 (1) 677 7612   fax 353 (1) 677 7652
          email imc@ibf.ie   http://www.mortgagecouncil.ie
          Chmn: Tony Moroney
○   *T
×   2003 Irish Mortgage & Savings Association

Irish Municipal, Public & Civil Trade Union   (IMPACT)
IRL   Nerney's Court, DUBLIN 1, Republic of Ireland.
          353 (1) 817 1500   fax 353 (1) 817 1501
          http://www.impact.ie
          Gen Sec: Peter McLoone
○   *U
M   c 54,000

Irish Museums Association
IRL   c/o Pearse Museum, St Enda's Pk, Rathfarnham, DUBLIN 16,
          Republic of Ireland.
          353 (87) 279 0518
          http://www.irishmuseums.org
          Sec: Karin Stierle
○   *G, *P; for all working or interested in museums

**Irish National Federation against Copyright Theft   (INFACT)
1982**
IRL   PO Box 5344, DUBLIN 7, Republic of Ireland.
          353 (1) 882 8565   fax 353 (1) 882 8594
          email infact@iol.ie
          Dir Gen: Brian Finnegan
○   *T

Irish National Teachers Organisation   (INTO)   1868
IRL   35 Parnell Sq, DUBLIN 1, Republic of Ireland.
         353 (1) 804 7700
         email info@into.ie   http://www.into.ie
         23 College Gardens, BELFAST, BT9 6BS.
         028 9038   1455 fax 028 9066 2803 (Northern office)
         Gen Sec: John Carr
   ○   *P

Irish Naturist Association   (INA)   1965
IRL   PO Box 1077, Churchtown, DUBLIN 14, Republic of Ireland.
         353 (86) 837 0395   fax 353 (86) 837 0395
         email irishnaturist@esatclear.ie
         Pres: Pat Gallagher
   ○   *G

Irish Nurses' Organisation   (INO)
IRL   Whitworth Building, North Brunswick St, DUBLIN 7, Republic of
         Ireland.
         353 (1) 664 0600   fax 353 (1) 664 0466
         email ino@ino.ie   http://www.ino.ie
         Gen Sec: Liam Doran
   ○   *P
   M   c 30,000

Irish Nursing Homes Organisation   (INHO)
IRL   Unit G6 Centrepoint Business Park, Oak Road, DUBLIN/t/12,
         Republic of Ireland.
         353 (1) 429 1843   fax 353 (1) 429 1845
         email inho@iol.ie
   ○   *N

Irish Offshore Operators Association
IRL   Tramway House, Dartry Rd, DUBLIN 6, Republic of Ireland.
         353 (1) 497 5716   fax 353 (1) 497 5886
         email iooa@tramway.ie   http://www.iooa.ie
         Chmn: Fergus B Cahill
   ○   *T

Irish Organic Farmers & Growers Association   (IOFGA)
IRL   Main St, NEWTOWNFORBES, Co Longford, Republic of Ireland.
         353 (43) 42495
         email iofga@eircom.net   http://www.irishorganic.ie
   ○   *F; for those interested in farming organically

Irish Peatland Conservation Council
IRL   Bog of Allen Nature Centre, Lullymore, RATHANGAN, Co
         Kildare, Republic of Ireland.
         353 (45) 860133   fax 353 (45) 860481
         email bogs@ipcc.ie   http://www.ipcc.ie
         Sec: Dr Ruth McGrath
   ○   *K

Irish Pharmaceutical & Chemical Manufacturers Association
         since 2004 **PharmaChemical Ireland**

Irish Pharmaceutical Healthcare Assn   (IPHA)
IRL   Franklin House, 140 Pembroke Rd, DUBLIN 4, Republic of
         Ireland.   (hq)
         353 (1) 660 3350   fax 353 (1) 668 6672
         email info@ipha.ie   http://www.ipha.ie
         Chief Exec: Anne Nolan
   ○   *T

Irish Pharmaceutical Union
IRL   Butterfield House, Butterfield Ave, Rathfarnham, DUBLIN 14,
         Republic of Ireland.
         353 (1) 493 6401   fax 353 (1) 493 6407
         email info@ipu.ie   http://www.ipu.ie
         Sec Gen: Seamus Feely
   ○   *T

Irish Planning Institute   1975
IRL   8 Merrion Sq, DUBLIN 2, Republic of Ireland.
         353 (53) 914 0800   fax 353 (53) 914 0804
         http://www.irishplanninginstitute.ie
         Hon Sec: Philip Jones
   ○   *P

Irish Playwrights & Screenwriters Guild   1969
IRL   Art House, Curved St, Temple Bar, DUBLIN 2, Republic of
         Ireland.
         353 (1) 670 9970   fax 353 (1) 492 3808
         email david.kavanagh@script.ie   http://www.script.ie
         Chief Exec: David Kavanagh
   ○   *P

Irish Printing Federation   (IPF)   1899
IRL   Confederation House, 84-86 Lower Baggot St, DUBLIN 2,
         Republic of Ireland.
         353 (1) 605 1500   fax 353 (1) 638 1500
         Dir: Terry Cummins
   ○   *T
   <   IBEC

Irish Professional Conservators' & Restorers' Association   1982
IRL   PO Box 9185, DUBLIN 4, Republic of Ireland.   (mail)
         http://www.ipcra.org address
   ▲   Un-incorporated Society
   ○   *P

Irish Professional Photographers' Association
IRL   5 Naas Rd Business Park, Muirfield Drive, DUBLIN 12, Republic
         of Ireland.
         353 (1) 429 8648
         email ippa@irishphotographers.com
         Hon Sec: Mick Quinn
   ○   *P

**Irish Property & Facility Management Association   (IPFMA)
1989**
IRL   5 Wilton Place, DUBLIN 2, Republic of Ireland.
         353 (1) 676 5500   fax 353 (1) 676 1412
         email info@ipfma.com
         Sec: Tony Smith
   ○   *P
   ×   2001 Irish Property Managers Association

Irish ProShare Association   (IPSA)
IRL   Confederation House, 84-86 Lower Baggot St, DUBLIN 2,
         Republic of Ireland.
   ○   *P
   <   IBEC

Irish Radio Transmitters Society   (IRTS)   1932
IRL   PO Box 462, DUBLIN 9, Republic of Ireland.
         http://www.irts.ie
         Sec: Noel Walsh
   ○   *G

Irish Real Tennis Association   (IRTA)
IRL   c/o Turnberry, Carrigaline Rd, DOUGLAS, Co Cork, Republic of
         Ireland.
         353 (87) 226 0032
         http://www.irishrealtennis.ie
         Sec: Ted Neville
   ○   *S

Irish Recorded Music Association   (IRMA)
IRL   IRMA House, 1 Corrig Avenue, DÚN LAOGHAIRE, Co Dublin,
        Republic of Ireland.
        353 (1) 280 6571   fax 353 (1) 280 6579
        email info@irma.ie   http://www.irma.ie
        Sec: Clive Leacy
○   *T

Irish Red Cross Society
IRL   16 Merrion Sq, DUBLIN 2, Republic of Ireland.
        353 (1) 676 5135   fax 353 (1) 661 4461
        email info@redcross.ie   http://www.redcross.ie
        Chmn: David Andrews
○   *W

Irish Retail Newsagents Association
IRL   2 Priory Hall, STILLORGAN, Co Dublin, Republic of Ireland.
        353 (1) 288 7817   fax 353 (1) 288 7224
        email irna@iol.ie
        Chief Exec: Vincent Jennings
○   *T

Irish Road Haulage Association   1973
IRL   Unit 12 CGI Building, Blanchardstown Corporate Park,
        DUBLIN 15, Republic of Ireland.
        353 (1) 822 4888   fax 353 (1) 822 4898
        email info@irha.ie   http://www.irha.ie
        Pres: Vincent Caulfield
○   *T

Irish Rugby Football Union   (IRFU)   1874
IRL   62 Lansdowne Rd, DUBLIN 4, Republic of Ireland.   (hq)
        353 (1) 647 3800   fax 353 (1) 647 3801
        http://www.irishrugby.ie
        Chief Exec: P R Browne
○   *S

Irish Sailing Association
IRL   3 Park Rd, DÚN LAOGHAIRE, Co Dublin, Republic of Ireland.
        353 (1) 280 0239   fax 353 (1) 280 7558
        email info@sailing.ie   http://www.sailing.ie
        Sec Gen: Paddy Boyd
○   *S

Irish Security Industry Association   (ISIA)   1972
IRL   21 Waterloo Rd, DUBLIN 4, Republic of Ireland.
        353 (1) 849 3426   fax 353 (1) 849 2402
        email info@isia.ie   http://www.isia.ie
        Exec Dir: Barry Brady
○   *P, *T

Irish Seed Trade Association
IRL   Marina House, Clarence St, DÚN LAOGHAIRE, Co Dublin,
        Republic of Ireland.
        353 (1) 663 8700   fax 353 (1) 663 8704
        email ista@fmco.ie
        Sec: Patrick O'Mara
○   *T

Irish Ship Agents' Association   (ISAA)
IRL   Ormonde House, 26 Harbour Row, CÓBH, Co Cork, Republic
        of Ireland.
        353 (21) 481 3180   fax 353 (21) 481 1849
        email isaa1@eircom.net
        Pres: Monnie Cliffe
○   *T

Irish Small & Medium Enterprises Association   (ISME)
IRL   17 Kildare St, DUBLIN 2, Republic of Ireland.
        353 (1) 662 2755   fax 353 (1) 661 2157
        email info@isme.ie   http://www.isme.ie
        Sec: Helen Johnston
○   *T

Irish Society
    see **Honourable The Irish Society (The)**

Irish Society for Archives   1970
IRL   c/o Dublin City Archive, City Library & Archive, 138-142 Pearse
        St, DUBLIN 2, Republic of Ireland.
        Hon Sec: Olivia McCormack
○   *L

Irish Society for Autism   (ISA)   1963
IRL   Unity Building, 16-17 Lower O'Connell St, DUBLIN 1, Republic
        of Ireland.
        353 (1) 874 4684   fax 353 (1) 874 4224
        email autism@isa.iol.ie   http://www.autism.ie
        Hon Sec: Nuala Matthews
○   *W

Irish Society of Chartered Physiotherapists
IRL   c/o Royal College of Surgeons, St Stephen's Green, DUBLIN 2,
        Republic of Ireland.
        353 (1) 402 2148   fax 353 (1) 402 2160
        email info@iscp.ie   http://www.iscp.ie
        Chief Exec: Helen McGrath
○   *P

Irish Society of Occupational Medicine   (ISOM)
IRL   PO Box 7453, Ballsbridge, DUBLIN 4, Republic of Ireland.
        email isom@eircom.net   http://www.iol.ie/~isom
        Hon Sec: Dr Tom Donnelly
○   *P

**Irish Society for the Prevention of Cruelty to Animals   (ISPCA)
1949**
IRL   Derryglogher Lodge, KEENAGH, Co Longford, Republic of
        Ireland.
        353 (43) 25035   fax 353 (43) 25024
        email info@ispca.ie   http://www.ispca.ie
        Pres: Pegeen McAllister
○   *V

**Irish Society for the Prevention of Cruelty to Children   (ISPCC)
1956**
IRL   20 Molesworth St, DUBLIN 2, Republic of Ireland.
        353 (1) 679 4944   fax 353 (1) 679 1746
        email ispcc@ispcc.ie   http://www.ispcc.ie
        Chief Exec: Paul Gilligan
○   *W

Irish Society of Public Health Medicine
IRL   c/o Dr Pasqueline Lyng, Vergemount Hall, Clonkeagh,
        DUBLIN 6, Republic of Ireland.
        353 (1) 268 0300
        Hon Sec: Dr Elaine Martin
○   *P

Irish Software Association
IRL   Confederation House, 84-86 Lower Baggot St, DUBLIN 2,
        Republic of Ireland.
        353 (1) 605 1582   fax 353 (1) 638 1582
        email isa@ibec.ie   http://www.software.ie
        Dir: Michele Quinn
○   *P
<   IBEC
×   1996-7 Irish Computer Aided Design Association

Irish Sudden Infant Death Association   1976
IRL   Carmichael House, 4 North Brunswick St, DUBLIN 7, Republic
       of Ireland.
         353 (1) 873 2711   fax 353 (1) 872 6056
         email isida@gofree.indigo.ie
       Sec: Frank Dowling
○   *W

Irish Taxation Institute   1967
IRL   19 Sandymount Ave, DUBLIN 4, Republic of Ireland.
         353 (1) 663 1700   fax 353 (1) 668 8387
         email info@taxireland.ie   http://www.taxireland.ie
       Chief Exec: Mark Redmond
○   *P
×   2003 Institute of Taxation in Ireland

Irish Taxi Drivers' Federation
IRL   48 Summerhill Parade, DUBLIN 1, Republic of Ireland.
         353 (1) 855 5682   fax 353 (1) 836 4155
       Sec: Martin J Morris
○   *P

Irish Texts Society (Cumann na Scribheann nGaedhilge)
§   c/o Royal Bank of Scotland, 49 Charing Cross, LONDON,
       SW1A 2DX.   (mail/address)
       *L; publication of manuscripts (covering literature, history etc) in
       the Irish language with English translations

Irish Thoroughbred Breeders Association   (ITBA)
IRL   Greenhills, KILL, Co Kildare, Republic of Ireland.
         353 (45) 877543   fax 353 (45) 877429
         email info@itba.ie   http://www.itba.ie
       Sec: Anne O'Connor
○   *P

Irish Timber Growers Association   (ITGA)   1971
IRL   17 Castle St, DALKEY, Co Dublin, Republic of Ireland.
         353 (1) 235 0520   fax 353 (1) 235 0416
         email itga@eircom.net
       Hon Sec: D Bergin
○   *T; private woodland owners

Irish Tourist Industry Confederation   (ITIC)
IRL   17 Longford Terrace, MONKSTOWN, Co Dublin, Republic of
       Ireland.
         353 (1) 284 4222   fax 353 (1) 280 4218
         email itic@eircom.net   http://www.itic.ie
       Chief Exec: Eamonn McKean
○   *N, *T

Irish Translators and Interpreters Association   1986
IRL   Irish Writers' Centre, 19 Parnell Square, DUBLIN 1, Republic of
       Ireland.
         353 (1) 872 1302   fax 353 (1) 872 6282
         http://www.translatorsassociation.ie
       Chmn: Annette Schiller
○   *P
×   2002 Irish Translators' Association

Irish Travel Agents Association   1971
IRL   Heaton House (3rd floor), 32 South William St, DUBLIN 2,
       Republic of Ireland.
         353 (1) 679 4179   fax 353 (1) 671 9897
         email info@itaa.ie
       Chief Exec: Simon Nugent
○   *P
M   365 f

Irish Tyre Industry Association
IRL   PO Box 5387, DUBLIN 13, Republic of Ireland.
         353 (1) 832 4295   fax 353 (1) 832 3129
       Chief Exec: Jack Farrell
○   *T

Irish Universities Association   (IUA)   1997
IRL   48 Merrion Square, DUBLIN 2, Republic of Ireland.
         353 (1) 676 4948   fax 353 (1) 662 2815
         email iua@iua.ie   http://www.iua.ie
       Dir: Michael McGrath
M   7 universities
×   2005 Conference of Heads of Irish Universities

Irish Vocational Education Association   (IVEA)   1902
IRL   99 Marlborough Rd, Donnybrook, DUBLIN 4, Republic of
       Ireland.
         353 (1) 496 6033   fax 353 (1) 496 6460
         email info@ivea.ie   http://www.ivea.ie
       Gen Sec: Michael Moriaty
○   *E

Irish Wheelchair Association   1960
IRL   Áras Chúchulain, Blackheath Drive, Clontarf, DUBLIN 3,
       Republic of Ireland.
         353 (1) 818 6400   fax 353 (1) 833 3873
         email info@iwa.ie   http://www.iwa.ie
○   *W

Irish Women's Bowling Association   (IWBA)   1947
■   30 Cromlyn Fold, HILLSBOROUGH, Co Down, BT26 6SD.
       (hsp)
         028 9268 8254   fax 028 9268 8808
       Hon Sec: Mrs Jean Fleming
○   *S; to encourage the sport of bowls for women
<   Wld Bowls Ltd; Eur Bowls U; Brit Isles Coun (England, Scotland,
       Wales & Jersey)
M   2,400 i

Irish Writers' Union   1986
IRL   Irish Writers' Centre, 19 Parnell Square, DUBLIN 1, Republic of
       Ireland.
         353 (1) 872 1302   fax 353 (1) 872 6282
       Hon Sec: Sam McAughtry
○   *A

Irish Youth Hostels Association (An Óige)   (IYHA)
IRL   61 Mountjoy St, DUBLIN 7, Republic of Ireland.
         353 (1) 830 4555   fax 353 (1) 830 5808
         email mailbox@anoige.ie   http://www.irelandyha.org
       Hon Sec: Brian Graham
○   *Y

Iron & Steel Trades Confederation
       merged in 2004 with the National Union of Knitwear, Footwear &
       Apparel Trades to become **Community**

IsItFair (Campaign for Reform of Council Tax)
NR   Willow Cottage, Church Lane, Headley, BORDEN, Hants,
       GU35 8PJ.
         01428 712680
         email c@isitfair.co.uk
       Contact: Christine Melsom

Isle of Man Chamber of Commerce   1956
■   17 Drinkwater St, DOUGLAS, Isle of Man, IM1 1PP.   (hq)
     01624 674941   fax 01624 663367
     email enquiries@iomchamber.org.im
     http://www.iomchamber.org.im
     Chief Exec: Mrs Barbara O'Hanlon
▲   Company Limited by Guarantee
○   *C
●   Mtgs - Expt - Inf - Lib - LG - Seminars
<   Brit Chams Comm
M   370 f, 5 org
¶   Members Classified Directory 2004-05; ftm, £25 nm.

**Isle of Man Natural History & Antiquarian Society
(IOMNHAS)   1879**
NR   Stream Cottage, Ballacrye, Ballaugh, ISLE OF MAN, IM7 5AV.
     (hsp)
     Sec: Mrs C J Bryan
▲   Registered Charity
○   *L, 'the advancement of knowledge of natural science, human
     history & cultural development in the Isle of Man & counties
     related thereto'
Gp   Archaeology field walking
●   Mtgs - Res - Lib
M   c 544 i
¶   Proceedings - 2 yrly.

Isle of Wight Chamber of Commerce, Tourism & Industry   1910
NR   Mill Court, Furrlongs, NEWPORT, Isle of Wight, PO30 2AA.
     (hq)
     01983 520777   fax 01983 554555
     email chamber@iwchamber.co.uk
     http://www.iwchamber.co.uk
     Chief Exec: Kevin Smith
▲   Company Limited by Guarantee
○   *C; business support services
●   Conf - Mtgs - ET - Res - Expt - Inf - Lib - PL - VE - LG
<   Brit Chams Comm (BCC)
M   800 f
¶   Island Business - 12; ftm, £2.25 nm.
     Chamber Directory - 1; ftm. [TBA nm].

Isle of Wight Natural History & Archaeological Society   1919
■   Salisbury Gardens, Dudley Rd, VENTNOR, Isle of Wight,
     PO38 1EG.   (hq)
     01983 855385
     Hon Sec: Mrs L Snow
▲   Registered Charity
○   *L; to promote study of the natural history & archaeology of the
     Isle of Wight (incl the conservation of the flora & fauna & all
     objects of special archaeological & geological interest)
Gp   Access to the countryside; Archaeology; Bat; Botany;
     Conservation working parties; Entomology; Geology;
     Mammals, reptiles & amphibians; Marine & freshwater;
     Ornithology
●   Mtgs - ET - Res - SG - Lib - VE - LG - Island Countryside Centre
M   c 700 i, 13 org, 16 schools
¶   Proceedings - 1; ftm, £10 nm.   Bulletins - 1; ftm only.
     Isle of Wight Birds - 1; ftm, £3 nm.

Islington Chamber of Commerce & Trade Ltd   (ICCT)   1924
NR   64 Essex Rd, LONDON, N1 8LR.   (hq)
     020 7226 1593
     Mgr: Andrew Mortimer
▲   Company Limited by Guarantee
○   *C
●   Conf - Mtgs - ET - Exhib - Expt - VE - LG - Local PR &
     promotion
M   550 f
¶   NL - 6; ftm only.   Islington Business Newspaper - 6; free.
     Islington Chamber Members' Directory - 1; ftm, £3 nm.

Issue (the National Fertility Association) Ltd
     December 2003 merged with CHILD to form **Infertility Network
     UK**

Italian Chamber of Commerce & Industry for the UK
■   1 Princes St, LONDON, W1B 2AY.   (hq)
     020 7495 8191   fax 020 7495 8194
     email info@italchamind.org.uk
     http://www.italchamind.org.uk
     Sec: Giorgio Giaccardi
○   *C
M   400 f

ITS United Kingdom   1993
■   Tower Bridge Business Centre (suite 312), 46-48 East Smithfield,
     LONDON, E1W 1AW.   (hq)
     020 7709 3003   fax 020 7709 3007
     email mailbox@its-uk.org.uk   http://www.its-uk.org.uk
     Chief Exec: Mrs Jennie Martin
▲   Company Limited by Guarantee
○   *T; for UK companies involved in Intelligent Transport Systems -
     the use of electronic systems & services to provide online
     route guidance; to improve traffic control & the capacity of
     roads as an alternative to building new ones
Gp   Intelligent transport systems: Education, System architecture,
     Millennium project, Government consultation
●   Conf - Mtgs - ET - Res - Exhib - SG - Expt - Inf - Lib - VE - LG
<   ITS America; Eur Road Transport Informatics Coordination &
     Devt Org (ERTICO)
M   80 f, 25 org, UK / 5 org, o'seas
¶   ITS Focus - 4; ftm.

IWO   (IWO)   1946
■   4 Carlton Court, Team Valley, GATESHEAD, Tyne & Wear,
     NE11 0AZ.   (hq)
     0191-422 0088   fax 0191-422 0087
     email info@iwo.org.uk   http://www.iwo.org.uk
     Gen Sec: Mrs Lynn Cooper
Br   9
○   *P; for people working in the water industry
●   Conf - Mtgs - Exhib - SG - VE
<   Engg Coun; Amer Water Works Assn
M   2,000 i, 40 f, UK / 50 i, o'seas
¶   Jnl - 4; ftm, £25 yr nm.
×   2001 Institution of Water Officers Ltd

J B Priestley Society 1997
NR   54 Framingham Rd, Sale, GREATER MANCHESTER, M33 3RJ.
     (hsp)
     0161-962 1477   fax 0161-962 7538
     email rodslater@ukonline.co.uk
     http://www.jbpriestley-society.com
     Hon Sec: Rod Slater
▲   Un-incorporated Society
○   *A; appreciation of the works of the English writer J B Priestley
     (1894-1984)
●   Mtgs - Exhib - VE - Walks - Archive - Links with drama groups
M   205 i, 2 f, 4 org, UK / 15 i, o'seas
¶   Jnl - 1.   NL - 2.

Jacob Sheep Society Ltd   (JSS)   1969
NR   Oaktree Farm, Buttermilk Lane, Yarningale Common,
     CLAVERDON, Warks, CV35 8HP.
     0870 165 1353   fax 0870 165 1353
     http://www.jacobsheep.freeserve.co.uk
     Sec: Louise Smith
▲   Company Limited by Guarantee; Registered Charity
○   *B
●   Mtgs - Exhib - Expt - Inf - VE
<   Nat Sheep Assn
M   730 i, UK / 24 i, o'seas
¶   Jacob Jnl - 3.   Flock Book - 1; £10.

James Hilton Society   (JHS)   2000
■   49 Beckingthorpe Drive, Bottesford, NOTTINGHAM,
     NG13 0DN.   (hsp)
     Hon Sec: J R Hammond
▲   Un-incorporated Society
○   *A; to promote interest in the life & work of the novelist &
     scriptwriter James Hilton (1900-1954), author of Goodbye
     Mr Chips, Lost Horizon & Random Harvest
●   Conf - Mtgs - Res - VE
<   Alliance of Literary Socs
M   70 i, UK / 5 i, o'seas
¶   James Hilton (NL) - 4; £10 yr m only.

Jane Austen Society   1940
NR   9 Nicola Close, SOUTH CROYDON, Surrey, CR2 6NA.   (hsp)
     http://www.janeaustensociety.org.uk
     Hon Sec: Maureen Stiller
▲   Registered Charity
Br   12; Australia, Canada, USA
○   *A; to foster the appreciation & study of the life, work & times of
     Jane Austen
●   Conf - Mtgs - ET - Res - Comp - SG - VE
<   Jane Austen Memorial Trust
M   1,700 i, UK / 300 i, o'seas
¶   NL - 2;   AR - 1; both ftm only.

Japan Society   1891
■   59 Buckingham Gate, LONDON, SW1E 6AJ.   (hq)
     020 7828 6330   fax 020 7828 6331
     email info@japansociety.org.uk
     http://www.japansociety.org.uk
     Exec Dir: Captain Robert Guy
▲   Company Limited by Guarantee; Registered Charity
○   *T, *X; the better mutual understanding of the cultures, societies
     & businesses of Japan & the UK
●   Conf - ET - Res - Inf - Lib - PL - VE - LG
M   600 i, 300 f, UK / 30 i, o'seas
¶   Proceedings - 1;   NL - 3; both ftm only.
     Books - 1; ftm, £10 each nm:
        British Envoys in Japan.
        Biographical Portraits Vol IV.
        Japan Experiences.
✕   2002 Japan Association (merged)

** Japan Society of Scotland
     Organisation lost: see Introduction paragraph 3

**Japanese Chamber of Commerce & Industry in the United
     Kingdom   (JCCI)   1959**
■   Salisbury House (5th floor), 29 Finsbury Circus, LONDON,
     EC2M 5QQ.   (hq)
     020 7628 0069   fax 020 7374 2280
     email chamber@jcci.org.uk
     Sec-Gen: M Takahashi
▲   Company Limited by Guarantee
○   *C; promotion of UK-Japan economic relations & of the
     interests of Japanese business in the UK
●   Mtgs - ET - Expt - Inf - LG
<   Coun of Foreign Chams Comm in the UK
M   312 f (Japanese owned companies in the UK)
¶   JCCI Review (NL) - 4; free.
     Thames (NL in Japanese) - 4;   Members' Directory - 1;
     Economic Trends UK (report in Japanese) - 4; all ftm only.

Japanese Garden Society
■   Groves Mill, Shakers Lane, LONG ITCHINGTON, Warks,
     CV47 9QB.
     http://www.jgs.org.uk
     Hon Sec: Mrs Kira Dalton
○   *G
M   i
     no further information supplied

Jazz Piano Teachers Association   (JAPTA)   2001
■   70 Culverden Rd, LONDON, SW12 9LS.   (hsp)
     020 8675 0335
     email info@japta.org.uk   http://www.japta.org.uk
     Hon Sec: Robert Webb
▲   Un-incorporated Society
○   *D, *P; for jazz education relating especially to piano
●   ET
M   c 300 i, c 10 f, c 5 org
¶   NL - 2; on web.

Jerome K Jerome Society   1984
■   15 Lichfield St, WALSALL, W Midlands, WS1 1TS.   (hsb)
     01922 627686   fax 01922 721065
     email tonygray@fraser-wood.co.uk
     Hon Sec: Anthony A Gray
▲   Registered Charity
○   *A; to support the Jerome K Jerome birthplace museum at
     Belsize House, Bradford St, Walsall; to research & study
     Jerome's life & works
●   Mtgs - VE
M   140 i, 10 f, UK / 10 i, o'seas
¶   Idle Thoughts (NL); ftm, £1.50 each nm.

Jersey Cattle Society of the UK   (JCS)   1878
NR   Scotsbridge House, Scots Hill, RICKMANSWORTH, Herts,
     WD3 3BB.   (hq)
     01923 695203   fax 01923 695303
     email jcsoffice@jerseycattle.org
     http://www.jerseycattle.org
     Sec: Steve Baker
○   *B
M   700 i

Jersey Chamber of Commerce & Industry Inc   1768
NR   Chamber House, 25 Pier Rd, ST HELIER, Jersey,
     Channel Islands, JE1 4HF.   (hq)
     01534 724536   fax 01534 734942
     Chief Exec: Andrew Goodyear
○   *C
M   f

Jersey Farmers' Union (JFU) 1919
NR 22 Seale St, ST HELIER, Jersey, Channel Islands, JE2 3QG.
      (hq)
        01534 733581   fax 01534 733582
○ *F

Jewellery Distributors' Association of the UK (JDA) 1970
■ 10 Vyse St, BIRMINGHAM, B18 6LT. (hq)
      0121-474 2034 fax 0121-474 2034
      http://www.jda.org.uk
      Sec: Lynn B Snead
▲ Company Limited by Guarantee
○ *T; to represent the wholesalers, importers & distributors of
      precious & fashion jewellery & silverware who sell to high
      street jewellery shops
● Conf - Mtgs - Exhib - Expt - Inf - LG
< Brit Jewellery, Giftware & Finishing Fedn
M 80 f, UK / 2 f, o'seas
¶ The Distributor - 2; free.

Jewish Historical Society of England (JHSE) 1893
NR 33 Seymour Place, LONDON, W1H 5AP. (hq)
      020 7723 5852   fax 020 7723 5852
      email jhse@dircon.co.uk   http://www.jhse.org
      Contact: The Administrator
○ *L; research into Jewish history
● Conf - Mtgs - Res - Comp - Lib
M i
¶ Transactions - 2 yrly.
      Bulletin, AR & Accounts - 1; ftm only.

Jockeys Association of Great Britain Ltd (JAGB) 1969
■ 39b Kingfisher Court, Hambridge Rd, NEWBURY, Berks,
      RG14 5SJ. (hq)
      01635 44102   fax 01635 37932
      email jockeys@jagb.co.uk
      http://www.jockeysassociation.co.uk
      Chief Exec: John Blake
▲ Company Limited by Guarantee
○ *P, *S; to promote facilities for professional jockeys; to negotiate
      on their behalf with racing authorities
● Mtgs - Empl
M c 475 i

Johann Strauss Society of Great Britain 1964
■ 12 Bishams Court, Church Hill, CATERHAM, Surrey,
      CR3 6SE. (hsp)
      01883 349681
      Hon Sec: Mrs V E Coates
▲ Un-incorporated Society
○ *D; recording, study, & appreciation of the music of the Strauss
      family & their Viennese contemporaries
● Mtgs - Exhib - SG - Lib
< 11 sister societies worldwide
M 500 i, UK / 100 i, o'seas
¶ Vienna Music - 2; ftm, £5 nm.   NL - 6; ftm only.

John Bradburne Memorial Society
NR PO Box 32, LEOMINSTER, Herefords, HR6 0YB.
      01568 760632
      http://www.johnbradburne.com
      Chmn: Tim Brigstocke
○ *G, *W; to support the Mutemwa Leprosy Settlement,
      Zimbabwe, in memory of John Bradburne (1921-1979), who
      worked at the settlement; to disseminate information on John
      Bradburne, poet, pilgrim & prophet

John Buchan Society 1979
◼ Greenmantle, 75 Main St, Kings Newton, MELBOURNE,
      Derbys, DE73 8BX. (hsp)
      01332 865315
      email kenjbsoc@moonfleet69.freeserve.co.uk
      http://www.johnbuchansociety.co.uk
      Hon Sec: Kenneth Hillier
▲ Registered Charity
○ *A; to promote a wider understanding & appreciation of the life
      & works of John Buchan (1875-1940)
● Conf - Mtgs - Res - Inf - VE
< Alliance of Literary Socs; Biggar Museum Trust
M 400 i, UK / 70 i, o'seas
¶ The John Buchan Jnl - 2; ftm, £4 nm.   NL - 2; ftm only.

John Clare Society 1981
NR 9 The Chase, ELY, Cambs, CB6 3DR. (hsp)
      01353 668438
▲ Un-incorporated Society
○ *A, *G, *L; to promote the study of the life & work of the poet
      John Clare (1793-1864) & the collection, preservation &
      exchange of items of literary & biographical interest
      associated with him
● Conf - ET - Res - VE
< Alliance of Literary Socs
M i & org

John Curwen Society
      The funding body of the **Curwen Institute**

John Hampden Society (JHS) 1992
NR Little Hampden, Cryers Hill, HIGH WYCOMBE, Bucks,
      HP15 6JS. (hq)
      01494 562279
      email enquiries@johnhampden.org
      http://www.johnhampden.org
      Hon Sec: Mrs Anthea Coles
▲ Registered Charity
Br Australia, New Zealand, USA
○ *G, *L; to make better known the character & achievements of
      the 17th century Parliamentarian John Hampden; to
      stimulate research into his life & times
● Res - Exhib - Inf - Lib - PL - VE - Lectures - Preservation &
      renovation of monuments & artifacts connected with John
      Hampden
< English Civil War Soc; Hampden (Maine) Histl Soc
M 130 i, UK / 12 i, o'seas
¶ The Patriot (NL) - 4.
      John Hampden & His Times (brochure).
      John Hampden of Buckinghamshire: the people's hero.
      The Controversy of John Hampden's Death.
      In the Steps of the Patriot (leaflet).

John Innes Manufacturers Association (JIMA) 1975
◼ PO Box 8, Dept CBD, HARROGATE, N Yorks, HG2 8XB. (asa)
      01423 879208   fax 01423 870025
      email info@johninnes.info   http://www.johninnes.info
      Sec & PRO: Brian L Dunsby
▲ Un-incorporated Society
○ *T; to represent the leading independent UK manufacturers of
      John Innes loam-based composts (or potting mixes)
● Mtgs - Inf - Advertising & PR - Quality standards
M 8 f
¶ Benefits of John Innes loam based compost (leaflet) - 1;
      ftm & consumers.
      Technical Data Sheets (set of 19); ftm & trade enquirers.

John Masefield Society 1992
■ The Frith, LEDBURY, Herefords, HR8 1LW. (chmn/p)
   01531 633800
      email carter-p@btconnect.com
      http://www.sas.ac.uk/ies/Full%20text%20Archive/
      Masefield/Society/jmsws.htm
   Chmn: Peter Carter,   Sec: Robert Vaughan
▲ Registered Charity
○ *A; to stimulate interest in the life & works of the poet & novelist
   John Masefield (1878-1967) Poet Laureate 1930-1967
● Readings - Lectures - Festivals - Screenings - Walks
M 160 i, 2 org
¶ Jnl - 1; ftm, £3 nm.   NL - 2.

John Meade Falkner Society 1999
■ Greenmantle, 75 Main St, Kings Newton, MELBOURNE,
   Derbys, DE73 8BX. (founder/p)
   01332 865315
      email kenjmsoc@moonfleet69.freeserve.co.uk
      http://www.johnmeadefalknersociety.co.uk
   Founder & Hon Sec: Kenneth Hillier
▲ Un-incorporated Society
○ *A; to promote a wider understanding & appreciation of the life
   & works of John Meade Falkner (1858-1932)
● Mtgs - Res - Inf - VE
< Alliance of Literary Societies
M 34 i, UK / 15 i, o'seas
¶ Jnl - 1; ftm, £2 nm.   NL - 3; ftm only.

John Moore Society 1988
■ 3 Normandy Close, Hampton Magna, WARWICK,
   CV35 8UB. (hsp)
   01926 494368
      email phillrobbins@yahoo.co.uk
      http://www.gloster.demon.co.uk/JMCM/jmoore.html
   Mem Sec: Phillip Robbins
▲ Un-incorporated Society
○ *A; to promote the life & works of John Moore, the 20th century
   conservation pioneer & author of the 'Brensham Trilogy',
   who was concerned about threats to the countryside
● Mtgs - ET - Exhib - Inf - Lib - VE
M 150 i, 2 org, UK / 10 i, o'seas
¶ Jnl - 2; ftm, £3.50 nm.

John Polidori Literary Society 1990
■ Automedia Syndications, PO Box 6078, NOTTINGHAM,
   NG16 4HX. (mail) address
   Founder & Pres: Franklin C Bishop
▲ Un-incorporated Society
○ *A; the study of John William Polidori, MD (1795-1821) poet,
   novelist, philosopher & author of 'The Vampyre: a tale'
   (1819) thereby introducing into English literature the icon of
   the vampyre portrayed as a handsome seducer, a cynical
   aristocrat
● Res - Publication
M i
¶ John Polidori- creator of the literary vampire.
   Reprints of rare letters & writings.
   In This Sad Web of Life - biography of John William Polidori.

John Snow Society
NR Royal Institute of Public Health, 28 Portland Place, LONDON,
   W1B 1DE.
   020 7291 8359 fax 020 7291 8383
      http://www.johnsnowsociety.org
○ *L; to promote the life & works of Dr John Snow, the pioneer of
   epidemiological method & celebrated anaesthetist

Johnson Society 1910
■ Johnson Birthplace Museum, Breadmarket St, LICHFIELD,
   Staffs, WS13 6LG. (hq)
   01543 264972
   Hon Gen Sec: Mrs Norma Hooper
▲ Registered Society
○ *L, study of life, works & times of Dr Samuel Johnson,
   preservation of his birthplace, books, manuscripts etc
● Mtgs - VE
M i & org
¶ Transactions - 1; ftm.

Johnson Society of London (JSL) 1928
NR 255 Baring Rd, Grove Park, LONDON, SE12 0BQ. (hsp)
   020 8851 0173
   Hon Sec: Mrs Zandra O'Donnell
▲ Un-incorporated Society
○ *L; 'to 'Johnsonise the land' (Boswell); to promote the study of
   Samuel Johnson, his works, his circle, his contemporaries &
   his times'
M i
¶ The New Rambler - 1.   The New Idler - 3/4.

Joinery Managers Association
NR 35 Hayworth Rd, Sandiacre, NOTTINGHAM, NG10 5LL.
   0115-949 0641
   Dir: David R Winson

**Joint Animal By Products Parliamentary & Advisory Committee
(JABPPAC)**
■ 25 Somersall Lane, CHESTERFIELD, Derbys, S40 3LA. (sb)
   01246 850025 fax 01246 850020
   Sec: D Ashworth
▲ Un-incorporated Society
○ *N, *T; maintaining a watching brief on emerging legislation
   affecting members
● Stat - Inf - LG
M 8 f

Joint Association of Classical Teachers (JACT) 1962
NR Senate House, Malet St, LONDON, WC1E 7HU. (hq)
   020 7862 8706 fax 020 7862 8729
      email croberts@sas.ac.uk   http://www.jact.org
   Hon Sec: Alan Clague
▲ Registered Charity
○ *E, *P; to promote the teaching of the classics in schools; to
   support those who teach classics
● Conf - ET - Exam - LG
< Classical Assn; Assn for Latin Teaching
M 1,450 i, UK / 137 i, o'seas
¶ Jnl of Classic Teaching 3.
   Omnibus - 2.

Joint Association of Geoscientists for International Development
   a group of the **Geological Society**

Joint Association for Quaternary Research
   a group of the **Geological Society**

Joint Committee for Palaeontology
   a group of the **Geological Society**

Joseph Conrad Society (UK)   1973
■ c/o POSK, 238-246 King St, LONDON, W6 0RF.   (hq)
020 8741 1940
email theconradian@aol.com
http://www.josephconradsociety.org
Sec: Hugh Epstein
▲ Registered Charity
○ *A, *L; to promote the study of all aspects of the work & life of
Joseph Conrad (1857-1924)
● Conf - Res - Comp - Lib
< Joseph Conrad Soc(s) of America & France; Tokyo Conrad Gp
(Japan)
M 50 i, UK / 100 i, o'seas
¶ The Conradian - 2; £20.
Note: the hq is run by the staff of the Polish Library.

Josephine Butler Society   (JBS)   1869
■ 4 The Hedges, Penenden Heath, MAIDSTONE, Kent,
ME14 2JW.   (hsp)
01622 679630
Hon Correspondence Sec: Mrs Jenni Paterson
▲ Un-incorporated Society
○ *K; 'to promote an equal, moral standard of morality & sexual
responsibility between men & women; to expose the traffic in
persons & exploitation of prostitution by third parties; to
examine existing & proposed legislation in matters relating to
prostitution'
● Conf - Mtgs - Res - SG - Inf - Lib - LG
< Intl Abolitionist Fedn; Intl Coun Women; C'wealth Countries
League; Nat Coun Women; Women's Coun; Nat Assn
Women's Orgs
M c 80 i
¶ News & Views - 1.

Judo Scotland   1949
NR Adventure Centre, South Platt Hill, Ratho, NEWBRIDGE,
EH28 8AA.   (hq)
0131-333 2981
email info@judoscotland.com
http://www.judoscotland.com
Chief Exec: Colin McIver
▲ Company Limited by Guarantee
○ *S; governing body for Judo in Scotland
● ET - Exam - Comp - Stat
< Brit Judo Assn
M 6,000 i, 125 org
¶ Judo News - 3; ftm only.
✕ 2002 (May) Scottish Judo Federation

Jussi Björling Appreciation Society   (JBAS)   1988
NR Glenaire, 58 Mill Rd, CROWLE, N Lincs, DN17 4LN.   (hsp)
01724 710334
email erikwimbles@lineone.net
Sec: Erik Wimbles
▲ Un-incorporated Society
○ *D; the appreciation of the life, career & recordings of the
Swedish tenor Jussi Björling (1911-1960)
● Conf - VE - Stat - Res
< Jussi Björling Soc, USA
M 50 i, UK / 4 i, o'seas
¶ Jnl - 2;   NL - 2; ftm only.

Justice Awareness & Basic Support   (JABS)   1994
NR 1 Gawsworth Rd, Golborne, WARRINGTON, Cheshire,
WA3 3RF.   (hq)
01942 713565   fax 01942 201323
email jackie@jabs.org.uk   http://www.jabs.org.uk
Founder & Nat Co-ordinator: Jacqueline Fletcher
○ *K; 'JABS neither recommend nor advise against vaccinations
but aim to promote understanding about immunisations &
offer basic support to any parent whose child has a health
problem after vaccination'
● Inf - LG

Justices' Clerks' Society   (JCS)   1839
NR Port of Liverpool Building (2nd floor), Pier Head, LIVERPOOL,
L3 1BY.   (hq)
0151-255 0790   fax 0151-236 4458
email secretariat@jc-society.co.uk
http://www.jc-society.co.uk
Chief Exec: Sid Brighton
▲ Company Limited by Guarantee
Br 16
○ *P; promotion of science of law, especially as administered by
Justices of the Peace in the UK
● Conf - Mtgs - LG
M i
¶ The Justices' Clerk Jnl - 4; ftm.
Good practice guides; prices vary.

© CBD Research Ltd · Beckenham · BR3 5JS · Tel 020 8650 7745 · Fax 020 8650 0768 · E-mail cbd@cbdresearch.com · www.cbdresearch.com

Kaolin & Ball Clay Association (UK)   2000
- ■ Tehidy Centre, Burngullow Lane, High St, ST AUSTELL, Cornwall, PL26 7TQ.   (hsb)
01726 828517   fax 01726 828523
Sec: George Muskett
- ▲ Company Limited by Guarantee
- ○ *T; to represent the interests of both ball clay & china clay producers
- Gp Minerals searches
- ● Mtgs - LG
- M 5 f

Karg-Elert Archive   (KES)   1987
- ■ 38 Lyndhurst Ave, TWICKENHAM, Middx, TW2 6BX.   (hsp)
020 8894 6859   fax 020 8894 6859
email anthony@caldicott247.fslife.co.uk
http://www.karg-elert.archive.org.uk
Chmn: Anthony Caldicott
- ○ *D; to further the appreciation, performance & recording of the music of Sigfrid Karg-Elert (1877-1933) composer & organist
- ● Res - Inf - Performances
- < Karg-Elert Gesellschaft (Germany)
- M 45 i, UK / 15 i, o'seas
- ¶ NL - 2; ftm, 50p nm.   Review - 1; ftm, 50p nm.

Keats-Shelley Memorial Association (Inc)   (KSMA)   1906
- ■ 1 Satchwell Walk, Royal Priors, ROYAL LEAMINGTON SPA, Warks, CV32 4QE.   (hsp)
01926 427400   fax 01926 335133
http://www.users.ox.ac.uk/~scat0385/ksma.html
Hon Sec: David Leigh-Hunt
- ▲ Company Limited by Guarantee; Registered Charity
- Br Italy
- ○ *A; to encourage interest in the works of John Keats & Percy Bysshe Shelley & other Romantic writers; to maintain the house in which Keats died at 26 Piazza di Spagna (Rome), as a museum in honour of romantic poets in Italy
- ● Conf - Mtgs - Comp - Inf - Lib
- < Alliance Literary Socs
- M i
- ¶ Annual Review - 1; price on application.

Keep Fit Association   (KFA)   1956
- NR Suite 105, Astra House, Arklow Rd, LONDON, SE14 6EB.   (hq)
020 8692 9566   fax 020 8692 8383
email kfa@keepfit.org.uk   http://www.keepfit.org.uk
Sec: Lyn Davis
- Br 70
- ○ *G; 'to enable people of all ages to enjoy a total body experience; to be able to sample the vitality, energy & variety, improved stamina, strength & suppleness; develop balance, agility, coordination & rhythm, to participate in the physical & mental challenge'
- Gp Youth Moves (keep fit for ages 5-16)
- ● Conf - Mtgs - ET - Exhib - Comp
- ¶ Quarterly Publication - 3.   NL - 6.
Your Move Magazine - 2.

Keighley & Worth Valley Railway Preservation Society (KWVRPS)   1962
- NR The Railway Station, Haworth, KEIGHLEY, W Yorks, BD22 8NJ.   (hq)
01535 645214; 01535 647777 (speaking timetable)
fax 01535 647317
- ▲ Un-incorporated Society
- ○ *G; preservation of the line as an operating steam passenger railway
- ● Running the railway by volunteers
- M i

Keith Murray Collectors Club
- NR PO Box 2706, ECCLESHALL, Staffs, ST21 6WY.   (hsb)
Hon Sec: Leonard Griffin
- ○ *G; for collectors of ceramics designed by Keith Murray

Kempe Society   1984
- ■ 41 York Avenue, Crosby, LIVERPOOL, L23 5RN.   (hsp)
0151-924 6345
email collins79@hotmail.com
http://www.churchmousewebsite.co.uk
Hon Sec: Philip N H Collins
- ▲ Un-incorporated Society
- ○ *A; to encourage the fitting recognition of Charles Kempe (stained glass painter); to advocate sensitive re-use of glass at risk from redundant or demolished churches
- Gp County recorder section
- ● Conf - Res - Exhib - PL
- < Ecclesiological Soc; Victorian Soc
- M 300 i, UK / 20 i, o'seas
- ¶ Wheatsheaf (NL) - 4; ftm only.
Complete Corpus of Kempe Glass in the UK; £15.

Kendal & South Lakeland Chamber of Commerce, Trade & Industry has become the Kendal Branch of the **Cumbria Chamber of Commerce**

Kennel Club   (KC)   1873
- ■ 1-5 Clarges St, LONDON, W1J 8AB.   (hq)
0870 606 6750
http://www.the-kennel-club.org.uk
Chief Exec: R Smart
- ○ *B; to promote the general improvement of dogs, dog shows, field trials, working trials & obedience classes
- Gp Classification of breeds; Registration of pedigrees, transfers, etc; Registration of societies & associations; Publications; Crufts Dog Show; Discipline; Awards; Discover dogs
- ● Mtgs - Exhib - Inf
- M 700 i
- ¶ Kennel Club Ybk - 1; ftm.   Kennel Gazette - 12; ftm.
Kennel Club Stud Book - 1; ftm.
Breeds Record Supplement (7 groups) - 4; ftm.

Kent Archaeological Society   (KAS)   1857
- ■ The Museum, St Faith's Street, MAIDSTONE, Kent, ME14 1LH.   (hq)
Hon Gen Sec: Andrew Moffat
- ▲ Registered Charity
- ○ *L; 'study & publication of, & education in, all aspects of archaeology & history of the ancient county of Kent'
- Gp Records; Buildings; Fieldwork; Churches; Place names; Education; Library; Visual records
- ● Conf - Res - Exhib - SG - Lib - PL - VE
- < to some 193 UK & overseas institutions
- M C 1,500 I & ORG
- ¶ Archaeologia Cantiana - 1; ftm.   NL - 3; ftm only.
Kent Record Series & Monograph Series - c 1; prices vary.

Kent County Agricultural Society (KCAS) 1923
- ■ County Showground, Detling, MAIDSTONE, Kent, ME14 3JF. (hq)
  01622 630975   fax 01622 630978
  email nfo@kentshowground.co.uk
  http://www.kentshowground.co.uk
  Gen Mgr: David Geoff
- ▲ Company Limited by Guarantee; Registered Charity
- ○ *F, *H; improvement of agriculture, forestry, horticulture & allied industries: rural crafts, breeding of livestock & the demonstration of improved methods
- Gp Livestock; Show jumping; Agricultural demonstrations; Bee garden; English wine; British food; Forestry; Cherry & soft fruit show; Flower show; Crafts; Farming fayre; Trade stands
- ● Conf - Mtgs - ET - Exhib - Organisation of the Kent County Show
- < Assn Show & Agricl Orgs; Breed Socs
- M 2,348 i, 438 f
- ¶ Kent View - 2; ftm, £1 nm.

Kent & East Sussex Railway Co Ltd 1961
- ■ Tenterden Town Station, TENTERDEN, Kent, TN30 6HE. (hq/sb)
  0870 600 6074   fax 01580 765654
  email enquiries@kesr.org.uk   http://www.kesr.org.uk
- ▲ Registered Charity
- ○ *G; operation of steam trains
- Gp Restoration, Maintenance, Supporters groups
- ● Mtgs - Exhib - Inf - Running a tourist railway - Maintenance of rolling stock
- < Heritage Rly Assn; S E England Tourist Bd
- M 2,000 i, UK / 50 i, o'seas
- ¶ Tenterden Terrier - 3.
- ✕ 2004 Tenterden Railway Company Ltd

Kent Invicta Chamber of Commerce   1900
- NR Ashford Business Point, Waterbrook Avenue, Sevington, ASHFORD, Kent, TN24 0LH. (hq)
  01233 503838   fax 01233 503687
  Chief Exec: Chris Capron
- ▲ Company Limited by Guarantee
- Br Canterbury
- ○ *C
- ● Conf - Mtgs - Exhib - Inf - VE - LG
- M 600 f
- ¶ Chamber Update - 12; free.   Diary (inc LM).
- ✕ 2005 Ashford (Kent) Chamber of Commerce

Kent Thames-side Chamber of Commerce
  a branch of **North Kent Chamber of Commerce**

Kentish Cobnuts Association   1991
- NR Apple Trees, Comp Lane, St Mary's Platt, SEVENOAKS, Kent, TN15 8NR. (hsp)
  01732 882734
  http://www.kentishcobnutsassociation.co.uk
  Hon Sec: Alexander Hunt
- ▲ Un-incorporated Society
- ○ *T; to promote the growing & marketing of Kentish cobnuts
- ● Mtgs - ET - Exhib - VE
- M 150 i, UK / 10 i, o'seas
- ¶ The Cobweb (NL) - 4; free.   Information pack; £5.
  Pruning Kentish Cobnuts; £3.
  In a Nutshell by Meg Game; £5.

Kerry Hill Flock Book Society
- ■ Brynteg, Pen-y-Garnedd, Llanrhaeadr ym Mochnant, OSWESTRY, Powys, SY10 0AW. (hsp)
  01691 860336   fax 01691 860571
  Sec: Gillian Napper
- ○ *B; includes marketing of the sheep breed
- ● Mtgs
- M c 150 i
- ¶ Kerry Hill Flock Book Society - 1.

Kesva an Taves Kernewek (Cornish Language Board)
- ■ 16 Trelawney Rd, CALLINGTON, Kernow (Cornwall), PL17 7EE.   (hsp)
  01579 382511
  email mpiercekernow@hotmail.com
  Sec: Mrs M Pierce
- ○ *L; promotion of the Cornish language
- ● Mtgs - ET - Exam - Res - Inf
- M [not stated]
- ¶ Books, dictionaries & academic texts.

Keygraphica   1934
- ■ 3 Eathorpe Park, The Fosse, Eathorpe, ROYAL LEAMINGTON SPA, Warks, CV33 9DX.   (hq)
  01926 632264
  email keygraphica@thesecretariat.co.uk
  Sec: Yasmin Chopin
- ▲ Company Limited by Guarantee
- ○ *T
- Gp EL (Electroluminescence); Technology
- ● Conf - Mtgs
- M 50 f
- ¶ LM - 1.

Kids' Clubs Network
  since 2004 **4children**

Kilvert Society 1948
- ■ Sandalwood, North End Rd, Steeple Claydon, BUCKINGHAM, Bucks, MK18 2PG.   (hsp)
  01296 730498
  email kilvertsociety@here.communigate.co.uk
  Hon Sec: David John Elvins
- ▲ Un-incorporated Society
- ○ *L; to foster an interest in the Rev Francis Kilvert, his work, diary & the countryside he loved
- ● Conf - Mtgs - Res - Inf - Lib (archives) - PL - VE - Church services - Conducted walks
- < William Barnes Soc; Alliance of Literary Socs; John Clare Soc
- M 484 i, 3 socs, 4 libs, UK / 116 i, o'seas
- ¶ Jnl - 3; ftm only.

Kinesiology Federation (KF) 1991
- ■ PO Box 28908, DALKEITH, EH22 2YQ.   (admin/p)
  0870 011 3545
  email kfadmin@kinesiologyfederation.org
  http://www.kinesiologyfederation.org
  Admin: Joyce Couper
- ▲ Company Limited by Guarantee
- ○ *M, *N, *P; an organisation representing the many varied types of kinesiology (a holistic complementary system of natural healing based on muscle testing to identify & facilitate the release of blocks in the body's vital energies, drawing on principles from traditional Chinese medicine)
- ● Inf
- < Brit Complementary Medicine Assn
- M 378 i, 5 org, UK / 7 i, 2 org, o'seas
- ¶ KF Today (NL); ftm only.

King's Army
  a group of the **English Civil War Society Ltd**

© CBD Research Ltd · Beckenham · BR3 5JS · Tel 020 8650 7745 · Fax 020 8650 0768 · E-mail cbd@cbdresearch.com · www.cbdresearch.com

Kingston Chamber of Commerce   (KCoC)   1903

NR   Kingston Innovation Centre, 3 Kingsmill Business Pk,
      Chapel Mill Rd, KINGSTON upon THAMES, Surrey,
      KT1 3GZ.   (hq)
      020 8481 0450   fax 020 8481 0460
      email marketing@kingstonchamber.co.uk
      http://www.kingstonchamber.co.uk
      Chief Exec: Lisa Gagliani
▲   Company Limited by Guarantee
○   *C
Gp   Small/medium businesses
●   Mtgs - ET - Expt
M   500 i & f
¶   Eureka - 6; free.

Kipling Society   1927

■   6 Clifton Rd, LONDON, W9 1SS.   (hsp)
      020 7286 0194   fax 020 7286 0194
      email jane@keskar.fsworld.co.uk
      http://www.kipling.org.uk
      Hon Sec: Jane Keskar
▲   Registered Charity
Br   USA
○   *A, *L; to extend the knowledge of Rudyard Kipling (1865-
      1936), his life & works; for anyone interested in his prose &
      verse
●   Mtgs - Inf - Lib (housed at the City University [London])
M   519 i, 90 universities/libraries
¶   The Kipling Jnl - 4; ftm, £1 nm.
      [membership £22].

Kitchen Bathroom Bedroom Specialists Association   (KBSA)   1977

■   12 Top Barn Business Centre, Holt Heath, WORCESTER,
      WR6 6NH.   (hq)
      01905 621787   fax 01905 621887
      email info@kbsa.co.uk   http://www.kbsa.co.uk
▲   Company Limited by Guarantee
○   *T; for the independent kitchen, bedroom & bathroom specialist
Gp   Kitchens; Bedrooms; Bathrooms; Fitted interiors
●   Conf - Mtgs - ET - Res - Exhib - Inf - LG
<   CBI; METO; NHIC; NKBA
M   i & f
×   2002 Kitchen Specialists Association

Kitchen Specialists Association
      since 2002 **Kitchen Bathroom Bedroom Specialists Association**

Kite Society   (KSGB)   1979

NR   PO Box 2274, Great Horkesley, COLCHESTER, Essex,
      CO6 4AY.   (hsp)
      01206 271489
      email info@thekitesociety.org.uk
      http://www.thekitesociety.org.uk
▲   Un-incorporated Society
Br   5
○   *S; to promote adult kiteflying activities
●   Conf - Res - Exhib - Comp - PL - VE
M   3,500 i, 40 f, UK / 400 i, 30 f, o'seas
¶   The Kiteflier (NL) - 4.

Klinefelter's Syndrome Association   (KSA)

■   3 Coxwell Rd, FARRINGDON, Oxon, SN7 7EB.
      01367 241409
      email secretary@ksa-uk.co.uk   http://www.ksa-uk.co.uk
      Sec: Clare Callanan
▲   Registered Charity
○   *W; gives support & information to adults & parents / carers of
      children with Klinefelter's Syndrome
●   Conf - Mtgs - Inf - Activity weekends
M   140 i
¶   A Guide for Adults; 42p postage.
      A Guide for Parents; 42p postage.
      NL - 4; free.

Kmoch European Bands Society   (KEBS)   1973

■   1 Keelton Close, Bicton Heath, SHREWSBURY, SY3 5PS.   (hsp)
      01743 354784
      Hon Sec: K J Bladon
Br   Czech Republic, Sweden
○   *D; history, performance & all aspects of music played by
      military & brass bands in Central Europe
●   Mtgs - Res - Inf - VE
M   90 i, 2 org, UK / 60 i, 4 org, o'seas
¶   Ceska Muzika (Jnl) - 1; ftm, £4 nm.
      Blasmusik Bulletin - 3.
×   2003 (1 January) František Kmoch Czech Bands Society

Knights of Royal England   (National Jousting Association)   1985

NR   Beechenwood Farm, Spode Lane, Cowden, EDENBRIDGE,
      Kent, TN8 7HP.   (hq)
      01342 850392   fax 01342 850392
      Pres: Jeremy Richardson
▲   Un-incorporated Society
○   *S; to promote, perform & preserve mediaeval jousting & its
      associated history by staging tournaments, educating &
      entertaining
●   Mtgs - ET - Exhib - Comp - Expt - Inf - PL
M   88 i, UK / 19 i, o'seas

Knitting & Crochet Guild   1978

■   108 Park Lane, KIDDERMINSTER, Worcs, DY11 6TB.
      (mem/sec/p)
      01562 754367
      email guild@blueyonder.co.uk
      http://www.knitting-and-crochet-guild.org.uk
      Mem Sec: Mrs Anne Budworth
▲   Registered Charity
Br   33; Australia, Canada, New Zealand, USA
○   *G; for handknitters, machine knitters, crocheters; to preserve
      the best of the old whilst exploring the new
●   ET - Lib
M   850 i, UK / 50 i, o'seas
¶   Slip Knot - 4;   Hbk - 1;   Assorted Supplements - 4;
      all ftm only.

Knitting Industries' Federation   (KIF)   1970

■   12 Beaumanor Rd, LEICESTER, LE4 5QA.   (hq)
      0116-266 3332   fax 0116-266 3335
      email directorate@knitfed.co.uk
      Dir: Mrs Anne Carvell
▲   Company Limited by Guarantee
○   *T; promotion of the interests of the textile knitting & hosiery
      industry in the UK; is a non-profit making organisation
Gp   Dyeing & finishing
●   Mtgs - Expt - Inf - Empl - LG
<   EURATEX; Brit Clothing Ind Assn (BCIA); Brit Apparel & Textile
      Confedn
>   Brit Narrow Fabrics Assn (BNFA)
M   280 f
¶   Bulletin - 6;   IR Bulletins - 4;
      Health & Safety Bulletin - 2; all ftm only.
      Knitstats - 1; ftm.   AR; free.

Knowsley Chamber of Industry & Commerce

NR   Knowsley Business Research Centre, Admin Rd, KNOWSLEY,
      Merseyside, L33 7TX.
      0151-477 1356   fax 0151-549 1357
      http://www.knowsleychamber.org.uk
      Head of Business Services: Keith Lynch
○   *C

L P Gas Association   (LPGA)   1970

- ■ Pavilion 16 Headlands Business Park, Salisbury Rd, RINGWOOD, Hants, BH24 3PB.   (hq)
  01425 461612   fax 01425 471131
  Dir Gen: Tom Fidell
- ▲ Company Limited by Guarantee
- ○ *T
- ● Conf - Mtgs - Exhib - Stat - Inf - LG
- < Eur LPG Assn (AEGPL)
- M 162 f, UK / 2 f, o'seas
- ¶ NL - 4; ftm only.   AR.
  Codes of Practice (36 to date) - irreg; prices on application.

Laban Guild for Movement & Dance

- NR Creekside, LONDON, SE8 3DZ.
  020 8691 8600   fax 020 8691 8400
  email info@laban.org
- ▲ Registered Charity
- ○ *D; the promotion & advancement of the study of human movement recognising the contribution made by Rudolf Laban
- Gp Dance; Movement analysis; Dance notation; Movement/dance therapy; Dance in education; Movement for actors; Action profiling
- ● Conf - Mtgs - ET - Exam - Exhib
- < Motus Humanus (USA); Eurolab (Europe); Foundation for Community Dance (UK)
- M 240 i, 35 org, UK / 60 i, 25 org, o'seas
- ¶ Movement & Dance - 4.

Labologists Society   1958

- ■ 87 Cambridge Rd, BIRMINGHAM, B13 9UG.   (hsp)
  http://www.labology.org.uk
  Chmn/Sec: D C Adams
- ▲ Un-incorporated Society
- ○ *G; research into history of breweries & social history connected with the brewing trade. Collection of beer, wines, spirits & soft drinks labels, as well as advertising matter relating to old breweries

Laboratory Animal Science Association   (LASA)   1976

- ■ PO Box 3993, TAMWORTH, Staffs, B78 3QU.   (asa)
  01827 259130
  Admin: Sue Millington
- ▲ Registered Charity
- ○ *P, *V; welfare of animals in laboratory science; to promote refinement of scientific procedures
- Gp Sections: Management, Animal health & nutrition, Toxicology & pathology, Alternatives, Ethics, Transgenic animals
- ● Conf - Mtgs - ET - Comp - SG - LG
- < Fedn of Eur Laboratory Animal Science Assns
- M 289 i, 14 f, UK / 63 i, 2 f, o'seas
- ¶ Laboratory Animals (Jnl) - 4;   NL - 4;   AR; all ftm only.

Laboratory Animals Veterinary Association
   is a group of the **British Veterinary Association**

Lace Guild   1976

- ▥ The Hollies, 53 Audnam, STOURBRIDGE, W Midlands, DY8 4AE.   (hq)
  01384 390739   fax 01384 444415
  email hollies@laceguild.org   http://www.laceguild.org
  Hon Chmn: Mrs Suzanne Jarvis,   Mem Sec: Mrs Maggie Jenkins
- ▲ Registered Charity
- ○ *G; to promote understanding of all aspects of lace & lacemaking by hand
- ● Conf - Mtgs - ET - Exam - Res - Exhib - Comp - SG - Inf - Lib - PL
- M c 4,888 i, 30 org, UK / c 1,000 i, 20 org, o'seas
- ¶ Lace (NL) - 4; £23 (£27 EU, £31 RoW), m only.   AR - 1; ftm only.
  Young Lacemaker - 4; £5 (£8 EU, £9 RoW), m only.

Lace Society   1968

- ▥ 591 Filton Avenue, Northville, BRISTOL, BS7 0QH.   (mem/sec/p)
  Hon Mem Sec: Mrs S Fortune
- ▲ Un-incorporated Society
- ○ *A; to further the making & collecting of lace (crochet, pillow-lace, tatting, knitted lace & needle-lace)
- ● Conf - ET - Exhib - Inf - Lib
- M 850 i, UK / 36 i, o'seas
- ¶ Lacemaking (NL) - 4;   AR; both ftm only.

Ladder Stabiliser Manufacturers Association
   since 2005 **Ladder Systems Manufacturers Association**

Ladder Systems Manufacturers Association   (LASMA)   1997

- NR PO Box 288, YORK, YO10 4ZE.   (sb)
  01904 623555   fax 01904 673021
  Sec: Brian Wilson
- ▲ Un-incorporated Society
- ○ *T
- ● Inf - LG
- M 3 f
- × 2005 Ladder Stabiliser Manufacturers Association

Ladies' Association of British Barbershop Singers   (LABBS)   1976

- NR 10 Pacific Heights, 79 Park Rd, BECKENHAM, Kent, BR3 1QQ.   (pro/p)
  07813 191945
  http://www.labbs.org.uk
  PRO: Diane Ebden
- ▲ Un-incorporated Society
- ○ *A; to encourage & promote singing in 4-part harmony in the UK, through education & friendship
- ● Mtgs - ET - Exhib - Comp - Inf - Lib
- M 1,700 i, 52 clubs
- ¶ Voice Box - 4; ftm only.

Ladies' Golf Union   (LGU)   1893

- ■ The Scores, ST ANDREWS, Fife, KY16 9AT.   (hq)
  01334 475811   fax 01334 472818
  email info@lgu.org   http://www.lgu.org
  Contact: The Secretary
- Br 4
- ○ *S; the governing body for women's amateur golf in the UK, Ireland & overseas
- ● Mtgs - Lib
- < [too many to list]
- M c 2,750 clubs (representing c 220,000 lady members)
- ¶ The Lady Golfer's Hbk - 1.

Lakeland Dialect Society (LDS) 1939

- ■ Gale View, Main St, Shap, PENRITH, Cumbria, CA10 3NH. (hsp)
  01931 716386
  email lakespeak@galeview.freeserve.co.uk
  http://www.lakelanddialectsociety.org
  Hon Sec: Mrs Jean M Scott-Smith
- ▲ Un-incorporated Society
- ○ *L; to study origins & history of dialect, folklore & songs, local customs & traditions; to encourage interest in the use of dialect speech & writing all particular to the former counties of Cumberland, Westmorland & Furness district of Lancashire (now encompassed by the modern county of Cumbria)
- ● Mtgs - Comp - Inf - Lib - Church service conducted in dialect (2-yrly, next June 2006) - Talks & lectures by arrangement
- > Yorkshire Dialect Soc; Northumbrian Language Soc, Edwin Waugh Soc
- M 264 i, 3 org, 4 colleges & libraries, UK / 9 i, 7 colleges & libraries, o'seas
- ¶ The Jnl - 1; ftm, £1.50 nm.
  Lakeland Treasury 1998; £5 m, £5.50 nm.
  Lakeland Gems 1999; (tape) £5 m, £5.50 nm, (CD) £11 m, £11.50 nm.
  Old Fell Side (Kendal) 1991; £5 m, £5.50 nm.
  Susannah Blamire (18th century poet) 1994; £2 m, £2.50 nm.
  Hoosta Ga'an On?, 2002; £7 m, £7.50 nm.

Lanarkshire Chamber of Commerce 2003

- ■ Barncluith Business Centre, Townhead St, HAMILTON, ML3 7DP.
  01698 426882   fax 01698 891916
  email info@lanarkshirechamber.org
  http://www.lanarkshirechamber.org
  Chief Exec: Douglas Millar
- ○ *C
  Note: was formed in 2003 from a merger of Clyde Vale, Hamilton & Clydesdale, Motherwell & District & East Kilbride Chambers & the Cambuslang & Rutherglen Business Group

Lancashire Authors' Association (LAA) 1909

- ■ 5 Quaker Fields, Westhoughton, BOLTON, Lancs, BL5 2BJ. (sp)
  01942 791390
  Gen Sec: Eric Holt
- ▲ Un-incorporated Society
- ○ *L; for writers & lovers of Lancashire literature & history
- ● Mtgs - Comp - Lib
- M c 220 i, c 30 libraries & org, UK / c 20 i, c 10 libraries & org, o'seas
- ¶ The Record (Jnl) - 4; ftm only.

Lancashire & Cheshire Antiquarian Society (LCAS) 1883

- ■ 59 Malmesbury Rd, Cheadle Hulme, CHEADLE, Cheshire, SK8 7QL. (hsp)
  0161-439 7202
  email morris.garratt@lineone.net
  Hon Sec: Morris Garratt
- ▲ Un-incorporated Society
- ○ *L, *Q; for the study of all aspects of the history of the Counties Palatine of Lancashire & Cheshire, from antiquity to the present day: archaeology, architecture, social, economic & industrial history
- ● Conf - Mtgs - Res - Lib (housed at Manchester Central Reference Library) - VE - Making representations concerning listed buildings, conservation areas & major planning applications
- M 171 i, f & org, UK / c 150 i, f & org, o'seas
- ¶ Transactions - 1; ftm, £15 nm.

Lancashire Parish Register Society (LPRS) 1897

- ■ 19 Churton Grove, Shevington Moor, WIGAN, Lancs, WN6 0SZ. (h/treas/p)
  email akenwright@yahoo.com
  http://www.genuki.org.uk/big/eng/LAN/lprs
  Hon Treas: Alan Kenwright
- ▲ Registered Charity
- ○ *G, L; to transcribe, index & publish the pre-1837 parochial registers of ancient Lancashire
- ● Mtgs - Transcribing & publishing parish registers
- < Fedn Family History Societies
- M 340 i, 60 libraries, UK / 40 i, 30 libraries, o'seas
- ¶ NL - irreg; ftm only.
  Printed Parish Registers - 2; £18 to i, £28 libraries).

Lancashire & Yorkshire Railway Preservation Society (LYRPS) 1960

- NR c/o Haworth Station, Haworth, KEIGHLEY, W Yorks, BD22 8NJ. (hq)
- ▲ Registered Charity
- ○ *G; to seek, preserve &/or restore to working order rolling stock & other items of the Lancashire & Yorkshire Railway, its connections & records
- ● Mtgs

Lancashire & Yorkshire Railway Society (LYRS) 1950

- ■ 31 Enfield Close, Hilton, DERBY, DE65 5HT. (hsp)
  01283 730544
  Hon Sec: Martin Nield
- ▲ Un-incorporated Society
- ○ *G; to create a permanent record of the 75 years existence of The Lancashire & Yorkshire Railway
- ● Mtgs - Exhib - Inf - PL - VE
- M 671 i, 23 org, UK / 27 i, o'seas
- ¶ Focus - 3;   NL - 4; both free.

Lancaster District Chamber of Commerce, Trade & Industry 1897

- ■ Commerce House, Fenton St, LANCASTER, LA1 1AB. (hq)
  01524 381331   fax 01524 389505
  email info@lancaster-chamber.org.uk
  http://www.lancaster-chamber.org.uk
  Pres: M A Harrison
- ▲ Company Limited by Guarantee
- ○ *C
- Gp Industry; Commerce; Retail & retail promotion; Transport policy; Economic
  Policy: Transport, Economic development, Finance, Tourism
- ● Mtgs - ET - Expt - Inf - Lib - LG
- < N & W Lancs Cham Comm
- M 454 f
- ¶ Business Matters - 12; free.

Land Drainage Contractors Association (LDCA) 1985

- ■ National Agricultural Centre, Stoneleigh Park, KENILWORTH, Warks, CV8 2LG. (hq)
  01327 263264   fax 01327 263265
  email secretary@ldca.org   http://www.ldca.org
  Sec: Bruce Brockway
- ▲ Company Limited by Guarantee
- ○ *T; contractors in agricultural drainage, pipeline utilities & highway, & sports turf drainage
- Gp Contractors; Trade manufacturers & suppliers; Consultants
- ● Conf - Mtgs - ET - Exhib - VE - LG - Demonstrations
- M 70 f
- ¶ NL - 4; ftm.
  Specifications (at £25 each) for:
  Field drainage.
  Pipeline re-instatement.
  Sports turf drainage.

Land's End - John O'Groats Association   1983
NR   18 Coberley Ave, Davyhulme, MANCHESTER, Lancs,
       M41 8QE. (h/mem/p)
       http://www.landsendjohnogroats.com
       Mem Sec: Don Dyer
▲   Un-incorporated Society
○   *G, *K; to support, or assist or organise, attempts by the public
       to make a continuous journey from Land's End to John
       O'Groats (or vice versa), in compliance with the law & other
       statutory provisions, for social or recreational purposes
●   Mtgs - Inf
M   c 200 i, UK / 8 i, o'seas
¶   Quo Vadis? (Jnl) - 3; ftm only.   LM - irreg.

Landlife   1975
■   National Wildflower Centre, Court Hey Park, LIVERPOOL,
       L16 3NA. (hq)
       0151-737 1819   fax 0151-737 1820
       email info@landlife.org.uk   http://www.landlife.org.uk
       Chief Exec: Grant Luscombe
▲   Company Limited by Guarantee; Registered Charity
○   *K; a charity taking action for a better environment by creating
       new opportunities for wildlife & encouraging people to enjoy
       them
Gp   Suppliers of wildflower seeds & plants
●   Res - PL - VE
>   Ladybird Johnson; Nat Wildflower Ctr (Texas, USA)
M   200 i
¶   Natterjack News - 2;   AR - 1;
       Wildflower Seed Catalogue - 2 yrly; all free.
       Wildflower Seed & Plant Catalogue - 1.

Landscape Institute   (LI)   1929
NR   33 Great Portland St, LONDON, W1W 8QG.   (hq)
       020 7299 4500   fax 020 7299 4501
       Dir-Gen: Michael Wetherell
○   *L, *P; the advancement of all aspects of the arts & sciences of
       landscape architecture & management
●   Conf - Mtgs - ET - Exam - Exhib - Comp - Stat - Expt - Inf - Lib
M   i
¶   Landscape Design - 10; ftm.

Landscape Research Group   (LRG)   1966
■   PO Box 53, Horspath, OXFORD, OX33 1WX.   (admin)
       email admin@landscaperesearch.org
       http://www.landscaperesearch.org address
       Chmn: Dr George Revill,   Sec: Dr S Shuttleworth
       Admin: Mrs Pauline Graham
▲   Company Limited by Guarantee; Registered Charity
○   *L; to promote the study of & interest in landscape, landscape
       research & the human environment
●   Conf - Res
M   117 i, 40 f, 150 org, UK / 65 i, 5 f, 90 org, o'seas
¶   Landscape Research Jnl - 4; ftm, £35 nm.   LM.
       Landscape Research Extra (NL) - 3; ftm only

Latex Allergy Support Group
NR   PO Box 27, FILEY, N Yorks, YO14 9YH.
       07071 225838
       http://www.lasg.co.uk
○   *W
●   Helpline: 0707 122 5838 (Mon-Fri 1900-2200 hrs)

Latin American Association   1986
NR   Priory House, Kingsgate Place, LONDON, NW6 4TA.   (hq)
       020 7372 8653   fax 020 7372 5650
       email lesas@latinamericanassociation.fsnet.co.uk
       Chmn: Javier Sanchez
▲   Registered Charity
○   *X; to help Latin-American people living in London by providing
       free/low cost services & a space for events
Gp   Legal advice; Nursery; Psychotherapy; Library; English &
       Spanish classes
●   ET - Exhib - Inf - Lib
M   120 i

**Latin Mass Society for the Preservation of the Tridentine Rite of
Mass   (LMS)   1965**
■   11-13 Macklin St, LONDON, WC2B 5NH.   (hq)
       020 7404 7284   fax 020 7831 5585
       email thelatinmasssociety@snmail.co.uk
       http://www.latin-mass-society.org
▲   Registered Charity
Br   22
○   *R; preservation & restoration of the Tridentine Rite of Mass in
       the Catholic Church
●   Arranging masses
<   Intl Fedn of Una Voce (Switzerland)
M   4,000 i, UK / 300 i, o'seas
¶   NL - 4; ftm only; and selected bookshops; £1.95 each.

Laurel & Hardy Appreciation Society - Sons of the Desert   1972
NR   63 Wollaston Close, GILLINGHAM, Kent, ME8 9SH.   (hsp)
       01634 371550
       http://www.laurelandhardy.org
       Pres: Robert S Lewis
▲   Un-incorporated Society
○   *G; founded (in the USA in 1965 & in the UK in 1972) to
       perpetuate the spirit & genius of Laurel & Hardy
●   Conf - VE
<   worldwide Laurel & Hardy Fan Club
M   6,000 i, UK / 10,000 i, o'seas
¶   The Laurel & Hardy Magazine - 4.

Laurence-Moon-Bardet-Biedl Society   (LMBBS)   1988
■   1 Blackthorn Avenue, Southborough, TUNBRIDGE WELLS, Kent,
       TN4 9YA.   (hsp)
       01892 682680
       email julie.sales@lmbbs.org.uk   http://www.lmbbs.org.uk
       Sec: Julie Sales
▲   Registered Charity
○   *W; to support sufferers from the genetic disorder causing
       visual impairment, as well as their families & professionals
●   Conf - Inf
       Helpline: 01633 664163
<   Genetic Interest Gp; Contact-a-Family
M   215 i
¶   NL - 2;   More than meets the eye (medical leaflet);
       The LMBBS child at school;   Introducing LMBBS;   all free.

Law Centres Federation   (LCF)   1978
■   Duchess House, 18-19 Warren St, LONDON, W1T 5LR.   (hq)
       020 7387 8570   fax 020 7387 8368
       email info@lawcentres.org.uk
       http://www.lawcentres.org.uk
       Dir: Steve Hynes
▲   Company Limited by Guarantee
Br   57
○   *N, *W; to encourage the development of publicly funded legal
       services for those most disadvantaged in society; to provide
       support & development services to Law Centres
●   Conf - Inf - LG
<   Advice Services Alliance
M   51 org
¶   Law Centres providing Equal Access for All.   AR.
       LCF Promoting Equal Access for All.

The Law Society of England & Wales   (The Law Society)   1825
NR   Law Society's Hall, 113 Chancery Lane, LONDON,
       WC2A 1PL.   (hq)
       020 7242 1222
       Chief Exec: Janet Paraskeva
○   *E, *L, *P
M   i & f

Law Society of Ireland   1830
IRL   Blackhall Place, DUBLIN 7, Republic of Ireland.   (hq)
       353 (1) 672 4800   fax 353 (1) 672 4801
       email general@lawsociety.ie   http://www.lawsociety.ie
       Pres: Michael Irvine
○   *P

Law Society of Northern Ireland   1922
- ■ 98 Victoria St, BELFAST, BT1 3JZ.   (hq)
  028 9023 1614   fax 028 9023 2606
  email info@lawsoc-ni.org   http://www.lawsoc-ni.org
  Chief Exec: John Bailie
- ○ *L, *P; by Royal Charter & Statute, the governing body of
  solicitors in Northern Ireland
- Gp Association of Collaborative Lawyers; Environment & Planning
  Law Association; Solicitors' Criminal Bar Associaton
  Lawyers: Company & commercial; Employment
- ● Conf - Mtgs - ET - Exam - Res - Stat - Inf - Lib - Empl
- < Intl Bar Assn; C'wealth Bar Assn
- M 2.200 i, 575 f
- ¶ The Writ (NL) - 10; ftm only.
  Solicitors of the Supreme Court of Northern Ireland: List - 2 yrly;
  m only.
  Legal Aid Solicitors List (NL) - 1; free.

Law Society of Scotland   1949
- NR 26 Drumsheugh Gardens, EDINBURGH, EH3 7YR.   (hq)
  0131-226 7411   fax 0131-225 2934
  email lawscot@lawscot.org.uk
  http://www.lawscot.org.uk
  Chief Exec: Douglas Mill
- ○ *L, *P
- M i

Lawn Tennis Association   (LTA)   1888
- ■ The Queen's Club, Palliser Rd, LONDON, W14 9EG.   (hq)
  020 7381 7000   fax 020 7381 3773
  http://www.LTA.org.uk
  Chief Exec: R Draper
- ○ *S; promotion of the game of lawn tennis
- ● Conf - Mtgs - ET - Exam - Res - Exhib - Comp - Stat - Inf
- < Intl Tennis Fedn; Eur Tennis Assn; Brit Olympic Assn; Central
  Coun Physical Recreation
- M 82,000 i, 2,500 clubs, 3,000 schools
- ¶ Ace & Volley - 11.   British Tennis - 11.
  LTA Hbk - 1; ftm.   AR.

Lawn Tennis Writers Association   (LTWA)   1950
- NR Cedar Lodge, Howe Rd, WATLINGTON, Oxon, OX9 5ER.
  (hsp)
  01491 612042   fax 01491 614104
  http://www.ltwa.org.uk
  Hon Sec: Henry Wancke
- ○ *P, *S
- M 50 i

Lead Contractors Association   (LCA)   1984
- ■ Centurion House, 38 London Rd, EAST GRINSTEAD, W Sussex,
  RH19 1AB.   (hq)
  01342 317888   fax 01342 303200
  email rwr@lca.gb.com   http://www.lca.gb.com
  Sec: R W Robertson
- ▲ Un-incorporated Society
- ○ *T; specialist leadwork contractors
- Gp Quality standards; Quality assessment & training
- ● Conf - Mtgs - ET - Comp
- < Lead Sheet Assn; Plumbing & Heating Ind Alliance; Summit
  Skills
- M 90 f
- ¶ Quarterly NL;   Annual Directory; both free.

Lead Sheet Association   (LSA)   1926
- ■ Hawkwell Business Centre, Maidstone Rd, PEMBURY, Kent,
  TN2 4AH.   (hq)
  01892 822773   fax 01892 823003
  email leadsa@globalnet.co.uk
  http://www.leadsheetassociation.org.uk
  Co Sec: B Hawkes
- ▲ Company Limited by Guarantee
- ○ *T
- ● ET - Exam - Res - Stat - Inf - Lib
- M 4 f
- ¶ Publications list available.

Lead Smelters & Refiners Association   (LSRA)   1967
- ■ 17A Welbeck Way, LONDON, W1G 9YJ.   (hq)
  020 7499 8422   fax 020 7493 1555
  email mcdermott@ldaint.org   http://www.ldaint.org
  Sec: Dr David Wilson
- ○ *T
  No further information supplied

League against Cruel Sports Ltd   (LACS)   1924
- NR Sparling House, 83-87 Union St, LONDON, SE1 1SG.   (hq)
  020 7403 6155
- ○ *K, *V; to campaign for the protection of animals from cruel
  sports
- M i

League for the Exchange of Commonwealth Teachers   (LECT)
1901
- NR 7 Lion Yard, Tremadoc Rd, LONDON, SW4 7NQ.   (hq)
  020 7498 1101   fax 020 7720 5403
- ○ *E, *X; to promote friendly & educational understanding
  through the interchange of teachers between countries of the
  Commonwealth
- M i & org

League Managers Association   (LMA)   1990
- NR The Camkin Suite, 1 Pegasus House, Pegasus Court,
  Tachbrook Park, WARWICK, CV34 6LW.   (hq)
  01926 831556   fax 01926 429781
  email lma@leaguemanagers.com
  http://www.leaguemanagers.com
  Chief Exec: John Barnwell
- ▲ Un-incorporated Society
- ○ *P; for managers at all 92 FA Premier & Football League
  football clubs
- ● Mtgs - ET - Exam - SG
- M 150 i
- ¶ Centre Circle - 4; free.   LMA NL - 12; ftm only.

League of Professional Craftsmen Ltd   (LPC)   1988
- NR Marlborough House (suite 111), 159 High St, WEALDSTONE,
  Middx, HA3 5DX.   (hq)
  020 8427 8813   fax 020 8427 0523
- ○ *T; to promote & protect the interests of skilled craftsmen; to
  give protection to the public
- Gp Builders; Carpenters; Decorators; Glazers; Joiners; Plumbers
- ● Inf - Status checks - Legal advice - Arbitration service - Debt
  recovery - Business review - Insurance backed guarantee
- M i & f
- ¶ NL - 2; ftm only.

** **Learning Disabilities Arts Network for London**
  Organisation lost: see Introduction paragraph 3

Learning on Screen: the Society for Screen-Based Learning
  since April 2004 has become part of **British Universities Film &
  Video Council**

Leasehold Enfranchisement Association   (LEA)   1988

NR   52-3 Kingsway Court, 1st Avenue, HOVE, E Sussex,
    BN3 2LQ.   (chief exec/p)
    01273 705432   fax 01273 735101
    email enfranchiseinfo@yahoo.co.uk
    Chief Exec: Shula Rich
▲   Un-incorporated Society
○   *K; 'abolition of leasehold ownership of flats & houses, plus
    easy fair access to freeholds for leaseholders'
●   Conf - Mtgs - ET - Res - SG - Inf - LG
M   8,000 i
¶   Escaping the Leasehold Trap (video); £6 m, £10 nm.

Leather Producers' Association   (LPA)   1919

■   8 Queensberry Rd, KETTERING, Northants, NN15 7HL.   (hq)
    01536 483668   fax 01536 416771
    Sec: Jack Purvis
▲   Company Limited by Guarantee
○   *T; employee relations within the leather producing industry
●   Empl
M   23 f
¶   Leather Technician's Hbk.

Leatherhead International

    is a global organisation & therefore outside the scope of this
    directory

Leeds Chamber of Commerce & Industry   1851

NR   102 Wellington St, LEEDS, W Yorks, LS1 4LT.   (hq)
    0113-247 0000   fax 0113-247 1111
    Chief Exec: Richard Mansell
▲   Company Limited by Guarantee
○   *C
M   1,650 f

Leek Growers' Association Ltd   (LGA)

■   133 Eastgate, LOUTH, Lincs, LN11 9QG.   (asa)
    01507 602427   fax 01507 607165
    email crop.association@pvga.co.uk
    Sec: Mrs Jayne Dyas
○   *T; to provide technical, commercial & marketing information
    for growers
●   Conf - Mtgs - Res - Exhib - Stat - Inf - LG
M   120 f

Left-Handers Association   (LHA)

■   Sterling House, 18 Avenue Rd, BELMONT, Surrey, SM2 6JD.
    (hq)
    020 8770 3722   fax 020 8715 1220
    email enquiries@anythingleft-handed.co.uk
    http://www.anythingleft-handed.co.uk
    Organiser: Lauren Milsom
▲   Un-incorporated Society
○   *G
●   ET - Res - Stat - Inf - LG
<   Left-Handers Club
M   i
¶   The Left-Hander - 12.

Left Handers Club   (LHC)   1990

■   18 Avenue Rd, BELMONT, Surrey, SM2 6JD.   (hq)
    020 8770 3722   fax 020 8715 1220
    email enquiries@anythingleft-handed.co.uk
    http://www.anythingleft-handed.co.uk
    Dir: Lauren Milsom
▲   Un-incorporated Society
○   *G; provide support, advice & information for left-handers to
    increase awareness of their needs, particularly in schools; to
    promote research & consideration in product design &
    manufacture
M   i & schools
¶   The Left-Hander (NL).

Legal Aid Practitioners Group

NR   10 Greycoat Place, LONDON, SW1P 1SB.
    020 7960 6068   fax 020 7960 6168
    http://www.lapg.co.uk
    Kate Comyn
○   *P

Legal Software Suppliers Association   (LSSA)   1996

■   1 Tyler St, STRATFORD-upon-AVON, Warks, CV37 6TY.   (hq)
    01789 296096   fax 01789 294511
    email sec@issa.co.uk   http://www.lssa.co.uk
    Sec: Roger M Hancock
▲   Un-incorporated Society
○   *T; regulatory body for suppliers of software to legal firms &
    businesses
●   Conf - Mtgs - ET - Exhib - Inf
M   25 f
¶   NL - 4; free on website.

Legalise Cannabis Campaign   (LCC)   1978

NR   BM Box 2455, LONDON, WC1N 3XX.   (mail) address
○   *K; to campaign for cannabis law reform; uses & effects of
    cannabis; effects of prohibition

Leicester & County Footwear Manufacturers' Association

    is now Leicester Engineering Training Group, and is now
    outside the scope of this Directory

**Leicester Longwool Sheepbreeders' Association   (LLSBA)
1883**

■   Coppelade, Wallisgate, Whaplode, SPALDING, Lincs,
    PE12 6UB.   (hsp/b)
    01406 424242   fax 01406 424242
    Sec: Barry Enderby
▲   Un-incorporated Society
Br   Australia, New Zealand, America
○   *B; preservation & conservation of the rare breed of which a
    high percentage are scrapie resistant
●   Mtgs - Exhib - Comp - Expt - VE
>   Rare Breeds Survival Trust (RBST); Nat Sheep Assn
M   70 i, UK / 5 i, o'seas
¶   NL - 4; ftm.   Flock Book (LM) -1;   AR - 1; all ftm only.

Leicestershire Agricultural Society Ltd   (LAS Ltd)   1833

■   The Show Office, Dishley Grange Farm, Derby Rd,
    LOUGHBOROUGH, Leics, LE11 5SF.   (hq)
    01509 646786   fax 01509 646787
    email info@leicestershireshow.co.uk
    http://www.leicestershireshow.co.uk
    Show Admin: J A Hardy-Smith
▲   Company Limited by Guarantee; Registered Charity
○   *F, *G
Gp   BSJA showjumping; Cattle; Goats; Horse & pony; Sheep; Dog
    show; Trade stands; Pigeon & poultry; Heavy horse; Private
    driving; Funfair; Army
●   Comp - ET - Leicestershire County Show
<   Various breed socs
M   c 400 i
¶   NL - 2;   AR - 1; both free.

**Leicestershire Archaeological & Historical Society   (LAHS)
1855**

■   The Guildhall, Guildhall Lane, LEICESTER, LE1 5FQ.   (hq)
    0116-270 3031
    Hon Sec: Dr Alan D McWhirr
▲   Registered Charity
○   *L; study of archaeological history & preservation of historical
    buildings in Leicestershire
Gp   Historic buildings; Archaeology
M   i & org
¶   NL - 2; ftm.   Transactions - 1; ftm.

Leicestershire Chamber of Commerce   1860
NR   Charnwood Court, 5b New Walk, LEICESTER, LE1 6TE.   (hq)
        0116-247 1800   fax 0116-247 0430
        email leics@chamberofcommerce.co.uk
        http://www.chamberofcommerce.co.uk
        Managing Dir: Martin Traynor
▲   Company Limited by Guarantee
○   *C
●   Mtgs - ET - Res - Stat - Expt - Inf - LG
<   Brit Chams Comm
M   1,800 f
¶   Chamber News - 12.
        Directory - 1.

Leisure Boat Builders Association
        a group of the **British Marine Federation**

Leisure & Outdoor Furniture Association   (LOFA)
■   113 Worcester Rd, CHICHESTER, W Sussex, PO19 4EE.   (asa)
        01243 839593   fax 01243 839467
        http://www.lofa.com
        Sec: Richard Plowman
○   *T
M   f
        no further information supplied

Leisure Studies Association (LSA)   1975
NR   Chelsea School, University of Brighton, EASTBOURNE, E Sussex,
        BN20 7SP.   (mem)
        01323 640357   fax 01323 644641 sb
        Admin: Myrene McFee
▲   Registered Charity
○   *P; an independent body of researchers, planners,
        policymakers, administrators & practitioners interested in
        leisure issues
M   i & f
¶   LSA NL - 3; ftm only.

Leith Chamber of Commerce   1786
■   Capital House, 2 Festival Square, EDINBURGH, EH3 9SU.
        (hq)
        0131-221 2999   fax 0131-221 2998
        Sec: John Kennedy
○   *C
●   Mtgs - ET
<   Edinburgh Cham Comm
M   f
¶   Business Comment - 4.

Leopold Stokowski Society   1978
NR   12 Market St, DEAL, Kent, CT14 6HS.   (mail/address)
        Sec: Christine Athalie Ducrotoy
▲   Un-incorporated Society
Br   Japan, USA
○   *D; promotion of Leopold Stokowski's work
●   Conf - Mtgs - Res - Exhib - Inf - PL - VE - Production of
        historical recordings of live performances
M   i
¶   Toccata - 2; ftm only.

Let's Face It   (LFI)   1984
■   72 Victoria Avenue, WESTGATE-ON-SEA, Kent, CT8 8BH.
        (hq)
        01843 833724   fax 01843 835695
        email chrisletsfaceit@aol.com
        http://www.lets-face-it.org.uk
        Chief Exec: Christine Piff
▲   Registered Charity
Br   26; 8 o'seas
○   *W; to give patient & family support when coping with facial
        disfigurement; to advise on surgeons, prosthetics & other
        services
        Incl the junior 'Let's Face It'
Gp   Facial cancer; Burns; Accidents; Bells Palsy; Congenital
        disfigurement; Acne; Facial hair; Dysmorphobia
●   Mtgs - SG - Inf
M   c 1,700 i
¶   Lets Face It; £2.50.   NL - 3; £10 yr.
        Me & My Face; 75p.   Leaflets.

Letter Box Study Group   (LBSG)   1976
■   13 Amethyst Ave, Davis Estate, CHATHAM, Kent, ME5 9TX.
        (hsp)
        01634 861714
        email enquiry@lbsg.org   http://www.lbsg.org
        Hon Sec: Mrs Avice Harms
○   *G; to collect, disseminate & record information on letter boxes
        at home & abroad, particularly those of historical importance
        & rarity
●   Conf - Res - Inf
M   c 800 i
¶   NL - 4; ftm only.

Letter File Manufacturers Association
NR   12 Corporation St, HIGH WYCOMBE, Bucks, HP13 6TQ.   (hq)
        0845 450 1565
▲   Un-incorporated Society
○   *T
<   an affiliate of the British Office Supplies & Services Federation
M   f

Leukaemia CARE   1967
■   1 Bush Court, Blackpole Estate, WORCESTER, WR3 8SG.   (hq)
        01905 755977   fax 01905 755166
        email info@leukaemiacare.org.uk
        http://www.leukaemiacare.org.uk
        Chief Exec: Tony Gavin
▲   Registered Charity
○   *W; to provide vital care & support services to those whose lives
        are affected by leukaemia & allied blood disorders, including
        the welfare of families & carers as well as the sufferers
        themselves
●   Mtgs - Inf - Support via CARE line 0800 169 6680
M   6,200 i, 220 f, 600 org
¶   Focus (NL) - 2.
        Booklets: Insight   Care; all free.
        Framework (AR); ftm, charged to nm.

Lewis Carroll Society   1969
■   69 Cromwell Rd, HERTFORD, Herts, SG13 7DP.   (hsp)
        email alanwhite@tesco.net
        http://www.lewiscarrollsociety.org
        Sec: Alan White
▲   Registered Charity
○   *A, *G; to promote interest in the life of Charles Lutwidge
        Dodgson (1832-1898); to study works produced under his
        real name & under his famous pseudonym, Lewis Carroll
●   Conf - Mtgs - ET - Res - Exhib - Comp - SG - Inf - VE
<   Lewis Carroll Socs: Australia, Canada, Japan, N America
M   250 i, UK / 150 i, o'seas
¶   The Carrollian (Jnl) - 2; ftm, £5 issue nm.
        Bandersnatch (NL) - 4; ftm, prices vary nm.
        Lewis Carroll Review - 4; ftm, £1 issue nm.

Lewisham Chamber of Commerce
      in 2004 merged to form **Greenwich, Bexley & Lewisham Chamber of Commerce**

LG Communications
      see **Association of Local Government Communications**

Liberation - incorporating the Movement for Colonial Freedom 1954
NR   9 Arkwright Rd, LONDON, NW3 6AB.   (hq)
      020 7435 4547   fax 020 7435 8745
      email liberation@btinternet.com
      http://www.btinternet.com/~liberation
      Gen Sec: Maggie Bowden
▲   Un-incorporated Society
○   *K; an anti-racist, anti-imperialist organisation for peace & social justice concerned with Africa, Asia, Caribbean & Latin America
Gp UN; NGO; Women; Racism; Somalis; Sudanese
●   Conf - Mtgs - ET - Res
M   c 1,000 i
¶   Liberation - 6.

Libertarian Alliance   1967
NR   2 Lansdowne Row (suite 35), LONDON, W1J 6HL. (accom/add)
      0870 242 1712
      email admin@libertarian.co.uk
      http://www.libertarian.co.uk
      Dir: Dr Sean Gabb
○   *K; 'leading radical pro-free market & civil libertarian group. Campaigning for social & economic freedom'
●   Conf - Mtgs - Seminars
<   Intl Soc for Individual Liberty; Libertarian Intl
¶   Free Life (Jnl) - 4.
      c 700 publications in print - list available.

Liberty: National Council for Civil Liberties   (Liberty)   1934
■   21 Tabard St, LONDON, SE1 4LA.   (hq)
      020 7403 3888   fax 020 7407 5354
      email info@liberty-human-rights.org.uk
      http://www.liberty-human-rights.org.uk
      Dir: Shami Chakrabarti
▲   Registered Charity
○   *K; campaigns to extend & defend civil liberties
●   Conf - Mtgs - Res - Inf - Lib - Lobbying - Test case work in UK & European courts
<   Intl League of Human Rights
M   7,000 i
¶   Liberty - 4; ftm.   AR.
      Publications list available.

Librarians' Christian Fellowship   (LCF)   1976
■   34 Thurlestone Ave, ILFORD, Essex, IG3 9DU.   (hsp)
      020 8599 1310
      email secretary@librarianscf.org.uk
      http://www.librarianscf.org.uk
      Hon Sec: Graham Hedges
▲   Un-incorporated Society
Br 9
○   *R; 'to enable Christian librarians to consider issues in librarianship from a standpoint of the Christian faith...'
Gp C'ee for Overseas Library Development
●   Conf - Mtgs - Res - Exhib - SG - Inf - Lib - VE
<   Chart Inst of Library & Ind Profls; Christian Res Assn; Evangelical Alliance; Universities & Colleges' Christian Fellowship
M   330 i, UK / 30 i, o'seas
¶   Christian Librarian - 4; ftm, £20 nm.

Librarians of Institutes & Schools of Education   (LISE)   1954
NR   Anglia Ruskin University, Rivermead Library, Bishop Hall Lane, CHELMSFORD, Essex, CM1 1SQ.   (chmn/b)
      01245 493131   fax 01245 495920
      http://www.www2.worc.ac.uk/lise/
      Chmn: Alan Bradwell
▲   Registered Charity
Br 28
○   *P; promotes information provision for students, teachers, researchers & others engaged in education
●   Conf - Mtgs - ET - Res
M   c 60 f
¶   Education Libraries Jnl - 3.

Library Association
      April 2002 merged with the Institute of Information Scientists to become **CILIP: Chartered Institute of Library & Information Professionals**

Library Association of Ireland
IRL 53 Upper Mount St, DUBLIN 2, Republic of Ireland.
      353 (87) 776 8054
      http://www.libraryassociation.ie
      Hon Sec: Denis Murphy
○   *P

Library Campaign: supporting friends & users of libraries   1984
■   22 Upper Woburn Place, LONDON, WC1H 0TB.   (mail)
      0870 770 7946   fax 0870 770 7947
      email librarycam@aol.com
      http://www.librarycampaign.com address
      Sec: Andrew Coburn
▲   Registered Charity
○   *K; to advance the lifelong education of the public by the promotion, support, assistance & improvement of libraries throughout the activities of friends & users' groups
●   Conf - Mtgs - LG
<   NASUWT, NUT, UNISON
M   600 i, 10 f, 50 org
¶   The Campaigner (NL) - 2; ftm, £2 each nm.

Licensed Animal Slaughterers & Salvage Association   (LASSA)   1917
■   25 Somersall Lane, CHESTERFIELD, Derbys, S40 3LA.   (hq)
      01246 850025   fax 01246 850020
      Sec: D Ashworth
▲   Un-incorporated Society
○   *T; to represent the knacker industry
●   Mtgs - ET - SG - Inf - LG
<   Jt Animal By-Products Parliamentary & Advy C'ee
M   35 i, 75 f, 1 org
¶   NL - 4; ftm only.

Licensed Taxi Drivers' Association Ltd   (LTDA)   1967
NR   Taxi House, Woodfield Rd, LONDON, W9 2BA.   (hq)
      020 7286 1046   fax 020 7286 2494
○   *W; the wellbeing of taxi drivers & their families
M   i

Licensed Trade Charity   (SLV)   1793
§   Heatherley, London Rd, ASCOT, Berks, SL5 8DR.   (hq)
      01344 884440   fax 01344 884703
      email info@slv-online.org.uk
      http://www.slv-online.org.uk
      Chief Exec: Colin Wheeler
      Originally the Society of Licensed Victuallers this is a registered charity caring for those in need in the licensed drinks industry by provision of a range of benefits, including financial support & advice plus the education of children at the SLV's two schools (Ascot, Berks & Ilkley, W Yorks). Members are also offered a range of lifestyle benefits.

© CBD Research Ltd · Beckenham · BR3 5JS · Tel 020 8650 7745 · Fax 020 8650 0768 · E-mail cbd@cbdresearch.com · www.cbdresearch.com

Licensed Vintners' Association   1817

IRL   Anglesea House, Anglesea Rd, Ballsbridge, DUBLIN 4, Republic of Ireland.
    353 (1) 668 0215   fax 353 (1) 668 0448
    http://www.lva.ie
    Chief Exec: Donal O'Keeffe
○   *T

Licensing Executives Society Ltd   (LES)   1968

■   c/o Northern Networking Ltd, 1 Tennant Avenue, College Milton South, East Kilbride, GLASGOW, G74 5NA. (hsb)
    01355 244966   fax 01355 249959
    email LES@glasconf.demon.co.uk
    http://www.bi.les-europe.org
    Hon Sec: Dr John M Roe
▲   Company Limited by Guarantee
○   *P; the successful commercialisation of technology & intellectual property rights by licensing or transfer
Gp   Brands; Education; EC Laws; Healthcare; IT & commerce
●   Conf - Mtgs - ET - LG
<   Licensing Executives Soc Intl (LESI)
M   635 i, UK/ 10,000 i, o'seas
¶   News Exchange - 6.   Les Nouvelles - 6.
    LM (LESI) -1.   AR (LESI) - 1.

Life   (LIFE)   1970

NR   Life House, Newbold Terrace, ROYAL LEAMINGTON SPA, Warks, CV32 4EA.   (hq)
    01926 421587   fax 01926 336497
    email info@lifeuk.org   http://www.lifeuk.org
    Chief Exec: Martin Foley
▲   Registered Charity
Br   160; Gibraltar, Ireland, Malta
○   *W; full welfare service before, during & after birth including accommodation for homeless mothers; full education service in schools & to other groups; research information on all reproductive issues
Gp   Nurses; Doctors; Anglicans & Evangelicals
●   Conf - Mtgs - ET - Res - Stat - Inf
M   35,000 i
¶   Life News - 4.

Life Academy   1964

■   9 Chesham Rd, GUILDFORD, Surrey, GU1 3LS.   (hq)
    01483 301170   fax 01483 300981
    email info@life-academy.co.uk
    http://www.life-academy.co.uk
    Chief Exec: Stuart Royston
○   *E, *W; planning & preparation for retirement & life change; incl social circumstances, leisure, health, career development & training of trainers to assist such guidance
Gp   Retirement; Mid-life planning; Post retirement; Pre-retirement education
●   Post-graduate certificate & Masters Programme in Pre-Retirement Education & Planning
M   i & corporate
¶   NL.   Your Retirement - 1.   AR.
    Resource lists & other publications available.
×   2005 Pre-Retirement Association

Life Insurance Association Ltd
    2005 merged with the Society of Financial Advisers to form the
    Personal Finance Society

Lifeboat Enthusiasts' Society   (LBES)   1964

■   13 West Way, Petts Wood, ORPINGTON, Kent, BR5 1LN.   (hsp)
    01689 829068
    Hon Sec: John G Francis
▲   Registered Charity
○   *G; to bring together all with a keen interest in lifeboats & the lifeboat service, past & present
●   Res - Stat - PL - Lifeboat modelling
<   R Nat Lifeboat Instn
M   744 i, UK / 29 i, o'seas
¶   NL - 3; ftm only.   Annual Hbk - 1; ftm, £5 nm.

Lift & Escalator Industry Association   (LEIA)   1997

■   33-34 Devonshire St, LONDON, W1G 6PY.   (hq)
    020 7935 3013   fax 020 7935 3321
    email enquiries@leia.co.uk   http://www.leia.co.uk
    Managing Dir: D M Fazakerley
▲   Company Limited by Guarantee
○   *T; interests of manufacturers & distributors of lifts, escalators & passenger conveyors & equipment therefor
Gp   Lifts; Escalators; Passenger conveyors
●   Mtgs - ET - Inf - Technical cooperation on high standard of design & safety - Standardisation
M   f

Lifting Equipment Engineers Association   (LEEA)   1944

■   3 Osprey Court, Kingfisher Way, Hinchingbrooke Business Park, HUNTINGDON, Cambs, PE23 6FN.   (hq)
    01480 432801   fax 01480 436324
    http://www.leea.co.uk
    Chief Exec: Derrick Bailes
▲   Company Limited by Guarantee
○   *T; interests of specialists engaged in design, manufacture, testing, examination, inspection, sale, repair, maintenance & hire of lifting equipment
Gp   Technical; Examination; Registration
●   Conf - Mtgs - ET - Exam - Exhib - SG - Inf - Lib
M   127 f, UK / 73 f, o'seas
¶   Bulletin - 8;   LM;   AR - 1; all ftm only.
    Lifting Engineers Hbk; £8 m, £20 nm.
    Lifting Equipment - a user's pocket guide; £8.
    Code of Practice for Safe Use of Lifting Equipment; £75 m, £125 nm.
    Hand Chain Blocks & Lever Hoists in the Offshore Environment; £10 m, £15 nm.

Light Music Society   1957

NR   Lancaster Farm, Chipping Lane, Longridge, PRESTON, Lancs, PR3 2NB.   (chmn/p)
    01772 783646   fax 01772 786026
    Chmn: Ernest Tomlinson,   Sec: Mrs H Ashton
○   *D; to act as the backing organisation for the Library of Light-Orchestral Music; this music is available for hire by members & provides an archive of the kind of music played by popular orchestras for over a one hundred years
●   Mtgs - Inf - Lib
M   250 i, UK / 10 i, o'seas
¶   NL - 3/4; ftm only.

Light Rail Transit Association   (LRTA)   1938

NR   c/o Haslams, 133 Lichfield St, WALSALL, W Midlands, WS1 1SL.   (mail/address)
    0117-951 7785
    email office@lrta.org   http://www.lrta.org
    Chmn: David F Russell
▲   Un-incorporated Society
○   *K; to advocate the retention & development of public transport, especially light rail transit & tramways
●   Mtgs - Inf - Lib - VE - Duplication of books & videos on tramways
<   Confedn of Passenger Transport (fixed track section); UITP
M   c 1,800 i, UK / c 1,500 i, o'seas
¶   Tramways & Urban Transit - 12.

Lighter Trades Industrial Section
closed 2006

Lighthouse Society of Great Britain
has been terminated

Lighting Association Ltd   (LA)   1970
■   Stafford Park 7, TELFORD, Shropshire, TF3 3BQ.   (hq)
    01952 290905   fax 01952 290906
    email enquiries@lightingassociation.com
    http://www.lightingassociation.com
    Co Sec & Chief Exec: Keven Verdun
▲   Company Limited by Guarantee
○   *T; for all sectors of the lighting industry
Gp Luminaire manufacturers; Lighting distributors; Component
    manufacturers & suppliers; Lamp suppliers & producers
●   Mtgs - ET - Exhib - Comp - SG - Stat - Expt - Inf - Lib - LG -
    Seminars - Accreditation - Certification laboratories
<   C'ee Eur Luminaire Mfrs Assn (CELMA)
>   Furniture Ind Res Assn (FIRA); Profl Lighting & Sound
    Assn (PLASA)
M   218 f, UK / 12 f, o'seas
¶   LA News & Views - 12;   Lighting News - 2;
    Buyers Guide - 1;   AR - 1; all ftm only.

Lighting Industry Federation Ltd   (LIF)   1969
NR Westminster Tower (Ground Floor), 3 Albert Embankment,
    LONDON, SE1 7SL.   (hq)
    Dir: Ernest Magog
○   *T
M   f

Lightweight Cycle Association of GB
is defunct

Lightweight Cycle Manufacturers Association
defunct

Limbless Association   1982
NR Rehabilitation Centre, Roehampton Lane, LONDON,
    SW15 5PN.   (hq)
    020 8788 1777   fax 020 8788 3444
▲   Company Limited by Guarantee; Registered Charity
○   *W; for the welfare of people of all ages who have been born
    without limb(s), or who have had amputations, their carers &
    the professionals involved with their care; to promote policy
    matters & monitor NHS services for limbless people
●   Conf - Res - Inf
<   R Assn for Disability & Rehabilitation
M   3,000 i, 13 f, UK / 100 i, o'seas
¶   Step Forward - 4; ftm, amputees, carers & professionals.

Limerick Chamber of Commerce   1815
IRL 96 O'Connell St, LIMERICK, Republic of Ireland.
    353 (61) 415180   fax 353 (61) 415785
    email info@limchamber.ie   http://www.limchamber.ie
    Chief Exec: Maria Kelly
○   *C

Lincoln Longwool Sheep Breeders' Association   1892
NR Lincolnshire Showground, Grange-de-Lings, LINCOLN,
    LN2 2NA.   (hq)
    01522 511395   fax 01522 730033
    Sec: Mrs L Newboult
▲   Registered Charity
○   *B
●   Mtgs - Exhib - Comp - Stat - Expt - Inf
M   87 i
¶   Jnl - 6.   Flock Book - 1.

Lincoln Record Society   (LRS)   1910
■   Lincoln Cathedral Library, The Cathedral, LINCOLN,
    LN2 1PZ.   (h)
    01522 544544   fax 01522 511307
    http://www.lincoln-record-co.uk treas b
    Hon Editor: Dr Nicholas Bennett
▲   Registered Charity
○   *L; publication of historical records relating to the ancient
    county & diocese of Lincoln
●   Res
M   175 i, 70 org, UK / 9 i, 43 org, o'seas
¶   Lincoln Record Society - 1; £18 m, £25-£30 nm.

Lincoln Red Cattle Society   (LRCS)   1895
NR Lincolnshire Showground, Grange-de-Lings, LINCOLN,
    LN2 2NA.   (hq)
    01522 511395   fax 01522 730033
    http://www.lincolnredcattlesociety.co.uk
    Sec: Mrs L Newboult
▲   Registered Charity
○   *B
●   Mtgs - Exhib - Comp - Stat - Inf
<   Nat Cattle Assn
M   108 i, 1 f, 2 org, UK / 4 i, o'seas
¶   Jnl - 6.   Herd Book - 1.

Lincolnshire Agricultural Society   1869
■   Lincolnshire Showground, Grange-de-Lings, LINCOLN,
    LN2 2NA.   (hq)
    01522 522900 & 524240   fax 01522 520345
    http://www.lincolnshireshowground.co.uk
    Chief Exec & Sec: S A C Frere-Cook
▲   Company Limited by Guarantee; Registered Charity
○   *F; to stage county agricultural shows incl all aspects of
    agriculture, forestry, horticulture & conservation
●   Conf - Mtgs - ET - Exhib - Comp - Annual show
M   i, f, org
¶   Show catalogue.   AR.
    Programme & prize list schedule.

Lincolnshire Chamber of Commerce & Industry   1889
NR Commerce House, Outer Circle Rd, LINCOLN, LN2 4HY.   (hq)
    01522 523333   fax 01522 546667
○   *C
M   c 1000 i, f & org

Lindsay Society for the History of Dentistry   1963
■   Dunelm, Black Dyke Lane, Upper Poppleton, YORK,
    YO26 6PT.   (hsp)
    01904 794929
    email lalage@robson1.fsnet.co.uk
    http://www.bda.org.uk
    British Dental Association (Museum Dept), 64 Wimpole St,
    LONDON, W10 8YS.   hq.
    Hon Sec: Dr J Stuart Robson
▲   Un-incorporated Society
○   *L; to study all aspects of the history of dentistry - the training of
    dentists, the development of treatments to cure oral diseases
    & the historical impact of economic factors on the profession
    & patients
●   Conf - Mtgs - Res - Inf
<   Brit Dental Assn; Brit Soc for the History of Medicine
M   80 i, UK / 20 i, o'seas
¶   Dental Historian Jnl - 2; ftm, £12 nm.

© CBD Research Ltd · Beckenham · BR3 5JS · Tel 020 8650 7745 · Fax 020 8650 0768 · E-mail cbd@cbdresearch.com · www.cbdresearch.com

Linguistics Association of Great Britain   (LAGB)   1959
NR   Dept of Phonetics & Linguistics, University College London,
        Gower St, LONDON, WC1E 6BT.   (hsb)
        020 7679 3154
        Hon Sec: Dr Ad Neeleman
▲   Un-incorporated Society
○   *L; to promote the study of linguistics
Gp   C'ee for linguistics in education; C'ee for endangered
        languages
●   Conf - Mtgs - ET - Res - LG
M   600 i
¶   Jnl of Linguistics - 3.

Linnean Society of London   1788
NR   Burlington House, Piccadilly, LONDON, W1J 0BF.   (hq)
        020 7434 4479   fax 020 7287 9364
        email adrian@linnean.org   http://www.linnean.org
        Exec Sec: Adrian Thomas
▲   Registered Charity
○   *L; the science of natural history in all its branches
●   Conf - Mtgs - Lib
M   1,700 i, UK / 800 i, o'seas
¶   The Linnean - 4; ftm, (internet; free nm).
        Biological Jnl.   Botanical Jnl.   Zoological Jnl.

Lipizzaner National Stud Book Association of Great Britain
NR   Cilyblaidd Manor, Pencarreg, LLANYBYDDER, Carmarthenshire,
        SA40 9QL.   (hsp)
        01570 480090   fax 01570 480012
        email info@lipizzaner.org.uk
        Sec: L D Moran
○   *B
●   Inf
M   i

Lipizzaner Society of Great Britain   1982
NR   Starrock Stud, Underhill Farm, Ludwell, SHAFTESBURY, Dorset,
        SP7 0PW.   (hsp)
        01747 828639   fax 01747 851202
        email una@lipizzaner.co.uk
        http://www.lipizzaner.co.uk
        Chmn: Una Harley
▲   Company Limited by Guarantee
○   *B; breeding of purebred & partbred Lipizzaner horses
●   Mtgs - ET - Res - Exhib - Comp - Inf - Lib - VE - LG -
        Compilation of two stud books
<   Intl Lipizzaner U; Brit Horse Soc (BHS); Spanish Riding School
        (Vienna)
M   c 140 i
¶   Jnl; ftm.

**Liquid Food Carton Manufacturers' Association   (LFCMA)
1986**
■   Churcham House, 1 Bridgeman Rd, TEDDINGTON, Middx,
        TW11 9AT.   (hq)
        020 8977 6116   fax 020 8977 3122
        http://www.drinkscartons.com
        Dir: Jenny Francis
▲   Un-incorporated Society
○   *T; to represent manufacturers of liquid food/beverage cartons;
        to address environmental issues (recovery, re-cycling,
        renewability)
<   Alliance for Beverage Cartons & the Envt (Brussels) [this is the
        umbrella organisation for marketing activities]
M   3 f
¶   Alliance NL - 4; free.
        The Alliance for Beverage Cartons & the Environment
        (brochure); free.

Lisburn Chamber of Commerce   1961
■   3a Bridge St, LISBURN, Co Antrim, BT28 1XZ.   (hq)
        028 9266 6297   fax 028 9266 6297
        email lisburnchamber@btconnect.com
        Hon Sec: S Baird
▲   Un-incorporated Society
○   *C
●   Conf - Mtgs - Inf - VE - LG
<   NI Cham Comm & Ind
M   120 f
¶   News Sheet - 4; free.

List & Index Society   (LIS)   1965
NR   c/o The National Archives, Ruskin Avenue, Kew, RICHMOND,
        Surrey, TW9 4DU.   (sec/b)
        020 8876 3444   fax 020 8878 8905
        email listandindexsociety@nationalarchives.gov.uk
▲   Un-incorporated Society
○   *L; to distribute unpublished Public Record Office search room
        lists & indexes
M   50 i, 50 org, UK / 25 i, 70 org, o'seas
¶   Lists & indexes:
        Standard series - 1;
        Special series - irreg; all prices on application.

Listed Property Owners Club   (LPOC)   1994
■   Lower Dane, Hartlip, SITTINGBOURNE, Kent, ME9 7TE.   (hsp)
        01795 844939   fax 01795 844862
        email info@lpoc.co.uk   http://www.lpoc.co.uk
        Managing Dir: Peter Anslow
▲   Company Limited by Guarantee
○   *G; assistance & information for the owners of listed buildings
Gp   Legal information; VAT information; Insurance policy
●   Conf - Exhib - Inf
M   2,423 i, 229 f
¶   Listed Heritage - 6; ftm only.

**** Liszt Society**
        Organisation lost: see Introduction paragraph 3

Lithuanian Association in Great Britain Ltd   1947
NR   Headley Park Club, Picketts Hill, BORDON, Hants,
        GU35 8TE.   (hq)
▲   Company Limited by Guarantee
Br   19
○   *W; promotion of welfare, social & cultural activities for
        Lithuanians in Great Britain
Gp   Lithuanian Youth Association in GB
●   Conf - Mtgs - Exhib - SG - Lib
<   Lithuanian Wld Community
M   c 800 i, 10 org
¶   Europos Lietuvis - 52.   Lynes (Youth NL) - 4.

Little Theatre Guild of Great Britain   (LTG)   1946
NR   181 Brampton Rd, CARLISLE, Cumbria, CA3 9AX.   (sp)
        01228 522649   fax 01228 522649
        http://www.littletheatreguild.org
        Sec: Barbara Watson
▲   Registered Charity
○   *D; encouragement of establishment & work of little theatres
●   Conf - ET - Comp - Workshops & Seminars
<   Intl Theatre Exchange; Cent Coun for Amateur Theatre;
        Voluntary Arts Network
M   97 org
¶   NL - 4.   Ybk.

Liverpool Chamber of Commerce & Industry   (LCCI)   1850
■   1 Old Hall St, LIVERPOOL, L3 9HG.   (hq)
     0151-227 1234   fax 0151-236 0295
     email chamber@liverpoolchamber.org.uk
     http://www.liverpoolchamber.org.uk
     Chief Exec Officer: Jack Stopforth
▲   Company Limited by Guarantee
Br   2; China
○   *C; represents, promotes & supports the business community of
     Merseyside
●   Conf - Mtgs - ET - Exam - Res - Exhib - Comp - Stat - Expt - Inf
     - Lib - VE - LG
<   Eurochambers; Brit Chams Comm; NW Chams Comm
M   50 i, 1,550 f
¶   Liverpool Chamber - 6; ftm, £3 nm.

Livestock Auctioneers Association   (LAA)   1954
■   Cobblethwaite, Wreay, CARLISLE, Cumbria, CA4 0RZ.   (hq)
     01697 475433   fax 01697 475423
     email chris.dodds@laa.co.uk   http://www.laa.co.uk
     Sec: Chris Dodds
▲   Un-incorporated Society
Br   13
○   *T; 'all matters pertaining to the sale by auction of cattle, sheep
     & pigs in England & Wales'
Gp   Conditions of sale sub-c'ee; (Working parties as required)
●   Mtgs - Stat - Inf - LG
<   Association Européenne des Marchés aux Bestiaux (Brussels)
M   13 i (associates), 216 f
¶   NL - as required; m only.   Report - 1; ftm, postage nm.
     Directory of Markets in England, Wales & Scotland - 3 yrly; ftm,
     £25 nm.
     Conditions of sale - as required; ftm, £10 nm.

Livestock Traders Association of Great Britain Ltd   (LTA)   1918
NR   The Orchard, North Kilworth, LUTTERWORTH, Leics,
     LE17 6HG.   (hsp)
     01858 880714   fax 01858 880714
     Hon Sec: D G W Ward
▲   Company Limited by Guarantee
○   *T; interests of livestock traders & cattle & sheep salesmen in
     the farming industry
●   LG
M   35 i, 15 f

Living Streets (Pedestrians' Association)   1929
NR   31-33 Bondway (3rd floor), LONDON, SW8 1SJ.   (hq)
     020 7820 1010   fax 020 7820 8208
     email info@pedestrians.org.uk
     http://www.livingstreets.org.uk
     Chief Exec: Tom Franklin
▲   Registered Charity
Br   91
○   *K; to promote the interests & safety of people on foot
●   Conf - Mtgs - Res - LG
<   Intl Fedn of Pedestrians; Fedn of Eur Pedestrian Assns
M   c 1,200 i, 50 org
¶   Walk (Jnl) - 4; ftm.   AR; free.
     Note: the registered title of this organisation is Pedestrians'
     Association

Lizard Canary Society
     a member body of the **Society for the Protection of Aviculture**

Llanwenog Sheep Society
     see **Cymdeithas Defaid Llanwenog Sheep Society**

Lleyn Sheep Society
NR   Gwyndy, Bryncroes, Sarn, PWLLHELI, Gwynedd, LL53 8ET.
     01758 730366
     http://www.lleynsheep.com
     Sec: Mrs G Roberts
○   *B
M   c 700 i

Lloyd's Aviation Underwriters' Association
     a member of the **Lloyd's Market Association**

Lloyd's Market Association   (LMA)   2001
NR   Suite 1085, 1 Lime St, LONDON, EC3M 7DQ.
     020 7327 3333   fax 020 7327 4443
     Chief Exec: Simon Sperryn
○   *N, *P; 'to promote the interests of the Society of Lloyds & to
     represent the interests of underwriters, managers & members
     of the Association'
M   4 org:
     Lloyd's Aviation Underwriters Association
     Lloyd's Underwriters Association
     Lloyd's Underwriters' Non-Marine Association
     Lloyds' Underwriting Agents Association

Lloyd's Motor Underwriters Association
     2004 merged with the **Lloyd's Market Association**

Lloyd's Names Association
NR   Stable Court, Kingham, CHIPPING NORTON, Oxon, OX7 6YL.
     01608 658226   fax 01608 658116
     email ll49@dial.pipex.com
     Chmn: Christopher Stockwell

Lloyd's Underwriters' Association
     a member of **Lloyd's Market Association**

Lloyd's Underwriters' Non-Marine Association
     a member of **Lloyd's Market Association**

Lloyd's Underwriting Agents Association
     a member of **Lloyd's Market Association**

LMCA   (LMCA)   1989
■   Unit 212, 16 Baldwins Gardens, LONDON, EC1N 7RJ.   (hq)
     020 7813 3637   fax 020 7813 3640
     email info@lmca.org.uk   http://www.lmca.org.uk
     Admin: Pia Charles
▲   Company Limited by Guarantee; Registered Charity
○   *N; 'an umbrella body working with member organisations
     towards better lives for people with long-term health
     conditions; it aims to gain recognition of people's needs &
     ensure resources are available to meet them'
●   Conf - Mtgs - ET - Res - LG
M   110 org
¶   Connect (NL) - 4;   AR - 1;   LM; all free.
×   2005 Long-term Medical Conditions Alliance

Loan Market Association   (LMA)
NR   10 Upper Bank St, LONDON, E14 5JJ.   (hq)
     020 7006 6007   fax 020 7006 3423
     email lma@cliffordchance.com
     http://www.lma.eu.com
     Exec Dir: Clare Dawson
▲   Company Limited by Guarantee
○   *T; 'embraces all aspects of the primary & secondary
     syndicated loan markets in Europe'
●   Conf - Mtgs - ET - Inf - LG (regulatory & fiscal issues) -
     Seminars - Provision of recommended standard
     documentation & secondary loan pricing data
<   Asia Pacific Loan Market Assn; Loan Syndications & Trading
     Assn Inc
M   77 f, 3 courtesy mems, UK / 122 f, 5 courtesy mems, o'seas
¶   LMA News - 2; free.

© CBD Research Ltd · Beckenham · BR3 5JS · Tel 020 8650 7745 · Fax 020 8650 0768 · E-mail cbd@cbdresearch.com · www.cbdresearch.com

Local Authorities Research & Intelligence Association (LARIA) 1974

■ 9 Cortland Rd, Nunthorpe, MIDDLESBROUGH, TS7 0JX. (hsb)
01642 316576 fax 01642 314892
email lariaoffice@aol.com http://www.laria.gov.uk
Hon Sec: K V Moller
○ *P; to promote the role & practice of research within the field of local government; to provide a supporting network for those conducting or commissioning research
● Conf - ET - Res - SG - LG
< Assn of Local Govt Inf Specialists (ALGIS)
M 1,187 i, 217 local authorities
¶ Laria News - 3; free.
Note: is a Registered Friendly Society.

Local Authority Caterers' Association (LACA) 1990

■ Bourne House, Horsell Park, WOKING, Surrey, GU21 4LY. (hq)
01483 766777 fax 01483 751991
email admin@laca.co.uk http://www.laca.co.uk
Admin: Vic Laws
▲ Un-incorporated Society
Br 9
○ *T; to promote professionalism in local authority catering
Gp Representation on c'ees of relevant professional bodies
● Conf - Mtgs - ET - Exhib - Comp - LG
M 700 i, 250 f
¶ NL - 4; ftm. Reports & Hbk (incl LM) - 1; ftm.

Local Authority Road Safety Officers' Association (LARSOA) 1974

NR Road Safety Group / Traffic & Safety, Guild House, Cross St, PRESTON, Lancs, PR1 8RD. (hsb)
01772 534663
Hon Sec: Alan Fisher
▲ Un-incorporated Society
○ *P; a national forum for road safety education, training, publicity & the School Crossing Patrol Service
M all local authorities except London

Local Education Authorities Research Group
since 7 July 2006 **Children's Services Research Group**

Local Government Association (LGA) 1997

NR Local Government House, Smith Sq, LONDON, SW1P 3HZ. (hq)
020 7664 3131 fax 020 7664 3030
email info@lga.gov.uk http://www.lga.gov.uk
Chief Exec: Brian Briscoe
○ *P; 'to enable local authorities to speak with one voice & promote the cause for democratic local communities which are prosperous, safe, healthy & environmentally friendly'
● Conf - Mtgs - Inf - Empl - LG
M 480 local authorities
¶ First - 52; ftm.

Local Government Reform Society Ltd 1964

■ 14 Princess Ave, BOGNOR REGIS, W Sussex, PO21 2QT. (hsb/p)
Hon Sec: Paul Smith
▲ Company Limited by Guarantee
○ *K; abolition of secrecy in local government; divorce of councillors' business interests from their public duties; improvement of spirit & practice of local government; to encourage a real vocation of public service to the whole community, major expenditure on new projects involving rate increase to be subject to local referendum; admission of press & public to all local authority meetings; all minutes to be available for public inspection
M i, f & org

Local Government Technical Advisers Group (TAG) 1995

■ Roy Fairclough Consultancy, County House, 12-13 Sussex St, PLYMOUTH, Devon, PL1 2HR. (hsb)
01752 213665 fax 01752 222678
email tag@rfconsultancy.org.uk
http://www.t-a-g.org.uk
Gen Sec: Roy Fairclough
▲ Un-incorporated Society
Br 12 regions
○ *P; the provision of coordinated & comprehensive services to local & central government & its agencies in the management & operation of all areas of technical services
Gp Regeneration; Environment; Transportation; Operations; Property & estate management; Coastal management
● Conf - Mtgs - SG - Inf - VE - LG
M c 600 i
¶ Bulletin - 6; ftm.

Locomotive & Carriage Institution (Loco & Carr Inst) 1911

NR 34 Camp St, DERBY, DE1 3SD. (gsp)
01332 295378
Gen Sec: A J Spencer
▲ Un-incorporated Society
Br 2; Germany
○ *L; the advancement of knowledge & information in all aspects of modern railway operation
● Mtgs - VE
M c 450 i, UK / 13 i, o'seas
¶ NL - 4; ftm.

Locomotive Club of Great Britain (LCGB) 1949

NR 5 Canons Close, Wootton, BEDFORD, MK43 9DP. (chmn/p)
http://www.lcgb.net
Chmn: J A Turner
○ *G; railway history & operation & all other aspects
M c 1,000 i

Locomotive 6201 'Princess Elizabeth' Society Ltd (PELS) 1963

■ 39 Newton St, MILLOM, Cumbria, LA18 4DR. (chmn/p)
01229 775215 fax 01229 775215
Chmn: Clive Mojonnier
▲ Company Limited by Guarantee
○ *G; to preserve & operate on British Rail main lines (passed for steam operation) the 'Princess Elizabeth' 6201. This locomotive was preserved because of its record non-stop runs between London-Glasgow-London, 16-17 November 1936 & was the forerunner of non-stop steam operation between the two cities; the locomotive is available for private charter
● AGM - Open days at the East Lancs Railway, Bury - Preservation of the engine
< Mainline Steam Locomotive Operators Ltd; Assn Rly Presvn Socs
M 160 i, UK / 6 i, o'seas
¶ NL - 4; ftm only.

Locus Association

■ c/o Quintus Public Affairs, Buchanan House, 3 St James's Square, LONDON, SW1 4JU. (asa)
020 7930 9730 fax 020 7976 1680
http://www.locusassociation.co.uk
Sec: Harriet Crothwaite
○ *T; to increase opportunities & reduce barriers to fair trade between the public & private sector, particularly in the use of PSI (public sector information)

London Anglers' Association (LAA) 1884

NR   Izaak Walton House, 2A Hervey Park Rd, LONDON, E17 6LJ.
       (hq)
       020 8520 7477   fax 020 8520 7477
       email admin@londonanglers.net
       http://www.londonanglers.net
       Chmn/Sec: A E Hodges
▲   Un-incorporated Society
○   *S; to promote the sport of fair angling & to provide fishing
       facilities for members
●   Comp
M   3,000 i
¶   AR - 1; free.

London Appreciation Society (LAS) 1932

■   45 Friars Avenue, Friern Barnet, LONDON, N20 0XG.
       (chmn/p)
       Chmn: Anthea H Gray
▲   Un-incorporated Society
○   *G; a secular, non-political & non-profit-making organisation
       for adults interested in the past, present & future of London
●   Guided walks, visits & lectures
M   c 580 i
¶   Blue Book (programme of events) - 2; ftm only.
       Note: the Society has a five-year waiting list.

London Bullion Market Association (LBMA) 1987

NR   13 Basinghall St, LONDON, EC2V 5BQ.   (hq)
       020 7796 3067   fax 020 7796 2112
       Chief Exec: Stewart Murray
▲   Company Limited by Guarantee; Registered Charity
○   *T; to promote the interests of the London (gold & silver) bullion
       market
●   Conf - ET - Stat - LG - Liaison with regulatory authority
M   63 f
¶   Alchemist (NL) - 4; free.
       Brochure; ftm, single copy free nm.

London Chamber of Commerce & Industry (incorporating the Westminster Chamber of Commerce) (LCCI) 1881

■   33 Queen St, LONDON, EC4R 1AP.   (hq)
       020 7248 4444   fax 020 7489 0391
       email lc@londonchamber.co.uk
       http://www.londonchamber.co.uk
       Chief Exec: Colin Stanbridge
▲   Company Limited by Guarantee
Br   5 (export documentation only)
○   *C
Gp   Asian Business Assn; Defence & security gp; Property &
       construction gp; Women in business gp
●   Conf - Mtgs - ET - Stat - Expt - Inf - Lib - LG - Networking -
       Seminars
<   Intl Chams Comm; Brit Chams Comm
M   3,000 f
¶   London Business Matters (Jnl) - 12; ftm.
       Directory of Members - 1; ftm, £105 nm.
       AR & Accounts.

London Cornish Association (LCA) 1898

■   26 Sharrow Vale, HIGH WYCOMBE, Bucks, HP12 3HB.   (hsp)
       01494 531703   fax 01494 531703
       email francis@francisdunstan.plus.com
       http://www.londoncornish.co.uk
       Hon Sec: Dr Francis Dunstan
Br   19; Australia, Canada, N Zealand, South Africa, USA
○   *G; to encourage fellowship & social activities among Cornish
       people in London & the Home Counties, & to provide a link
       to Cornish associations worldwide.
Gp   Family History; 'Old Cornwall'
●   Conf - Mtgs - Research - SG - Lib - VE
<   19 in UK and Cornish Associations in Australia, Canada, N
       Zealand, S Africa, & USA
M   230 i, UK / 50 i, o'seas
¶   NL - 3;   Cornish Worldwide - 3; both ftm.
       Ybk (incl LM).

London Cycling Campaign (LCC) 1978

NR   2 Newhams Row (Off Bermondsey St), LONDON, SE1 3UZ.
       (hq)
       020 7234 9310
       email office@lcc.org.uk   http://www.lcc.org.uk
       Dir: Simon Brammer
Br   33
○   *K
●   Conf - Mtgs - Exhib - Inf - Lib - LG
M   c 9,000 i
¶   London Cyclist - 6.

London District Surveyors Association (LDSA)

NR   c/o Trevor McIntosh, London Borough of Merton - Civic Centre,
       London Rd, MORDON, Surrey, SM4 5DX.   (hsb)
       020 8545 3121
       http://www.londonbuildingcontrol.org.uk
       Hon Sec: Trevor McIntosh
Br   34
○   *P; 'uniformity of interpretation & operation of the Building
       Regulations in London'
Gp   C'ees: Education & training, Electrical & mechanical, Fire safety
       & means of escape, LANTAC, Licensing, Management &
       legislation, Publications & seminars, Safety at sports grounds,
       Technical & foundations
●   Mtgs - ET - SG - Inf - LG
<   District Surveyors Assn
M   33 i

London Fish Merchants (Billingsgate) Ltd (LFMA) 1923

NR   Office 36 Billingsgate Market, Trafalgar Way, LONDON,
       E14 5ST.   (hq)
       020 7515 2655   fax 020 7538 2618
○   *T; to promote Billingsgate Market; to help merchants in any
       sphere of their business
M   f
¶   AR.

London Fish & Poultry Retailers Association
       is a branch association of the **National Federation of
       Fishmongers**

London Food Link
       is a group of **Sustain: the Alliance for Better Food & Farming**

London General Shipowners' Society
       is incorporated in **London Shipowners' & River Users' Society**

London Harness Horse Parade Society 1885

■   Oakley Farm, Merstham, REDHILL, Surrey, RH1 3QN.   (hq)
       01737 646132   fax 01737 645121
▲   Company Limited by Guarantee; Registered Charity
○   *V; improvement of general condition & treatment of horses &
       ponies employed for transport
●   Annual parade in Battersea Park on Easter Monday

London Investment Banking Association (LIBA) 1988

■   6 Frederick's Place, LONDON, EC2R 8BT.   (hq)
       020 7796 3606   fax 020 7796 4345
       email liba@liba.org.uk   http://www.liba.org.uk
       Dir Gen: Jonathan Taylor
▲   Un-incorporated Society
○   *T; for firms active in the investment banking & securities
       industry; to represent members' interests to authorities in the
       UK & Europe
●   Mtgs - SG - LG
<   Intl Coun of Securities Assns (ICSA)
M   50 f
¶   AR; free.

London Jute Association (LJA) 1875
NR   33 Haynes Park Court, Slewins Close, HORNCHURCH, Essex,
       RM11 2DE.   (hq)
       01708 453000   fax 01708 453010
       Sec: P W Rosamond
○   *T; buying & selling of raw jute
M   7 f

London Library 1841
■   14 St James's Sq, LONDON, SW1Y 4LG.   (hq)
       020 7930 7705   fax 020 7766 4766
       email membership@londonlibrary.co.uk
       http://www.londonlibrary.co.uk
       Librarian: Inez T P A Lynn
○   *G; a research library of books in the humanities, with lending
       service to subscribing members
●   Res - Lib
M   8,200 i, 250 org
¶   AR; ftm only.

London Mathematical Society (LMS) 1865
■   De Morgan House, 57-58 Russell Sq, LONDON, WC1B 4HS.
       (hq)
       020 7637 3686   fax 020 7323 3655
       email lms@lms.ac.uk   http://www.lms.ac.uk
       Exec Sec: P Cooper
▲   Registered Charity
○   *L; to promote & extend mathematical knowledge
●   Conf - Mtgs - Res - Inf - Lib - Symposia
<   18 mathematical societies in other countries
M   c 1,700 i, UK / c 800 i, o'seas
¶   Proceedings - 6; £60 m, £460 nm.   Jnl - 6; £60 m, £422
       nm.
       Bulletin - 6; £33 m, £193 nm.   NL - 11; ftm only.
       Hbk - 2 yrly; ftm only.

London Mayors' Association (LMA) 1901
■   c/o Freeman Box & Co, 8 Bentinck St, LONDON, W1U 2BJ.
       (chmn/b)
       020 7486 9041   fax 020 7224 1336
       email rjd432@aol.com
       http://www.londonmayors.org.uk
       Chmn: Councillor Robert Davis
▲   Company Limited by Guarantee
○   *P; to represent the Mayors, Lord Mayors & former Mayors &
       Lord Mayors of the London Boroughs
●   Mtgs - VE
M   600 i
¶   NL - 4; free.
       Mayoral Directory - 1; £40 (for 7).

London Medieval Society (LMS) 1945
NR   3 Rothwell St, LONDON, NW1 8YH.   (hsp)
       020 7722 1040
       email groy@britishlibrary.net   http://www.the-lms.org
       Hon Sec: Dr G Roy
▲   Un-incorporated Society
○   *L; promotion of research & study of the culture & civilisation of
       the Middle Ages
●   Conf - Inf
<   Inst of Romance Studies (University of London)
M   130 i, 20 org, UK / 30 i, o'seas
¶   NL - 1.

London & Middlesex Archaeological Society (LAMAS) 1855
■   c/o Museum of London, London Wall, LONDON,
       EC2Y 5HN.   (regd)
       020 7600 3699   fax 020 7600 1058
       http://www.lamas.org.uk address
       Hon Sec: Jackie Keily
▲   Registered Charity
○   *L; to promote the study of the local history & archaeology of
       the metropolitan area of London
Gp C'ees: Archaeological research, Historic buildings, Local history
●   Conf - Mtgs - Res - Inf - Lib - LG
M   651 i
¶   [Visit website for full information]

London Money Market Association (LMMA) 1998
NR   c/o Investec Bank (UK) Ltd, 2 Gresham St, LONDON,
       EC2V 7QP.   (hsb)
       020 7597 4485   fax 020 7597 4491
       Hon Sec: Mrs Kathy Cong
○   *T; to monitor the liquidity of the Sterling Money Market; to
       consider matters of policy interest to members; to promote
       good relations with the Treasury & the Bank of England
●   Mtgs - Inf
M   c 20 f

London Motor Cab Proprietors' Association (LMCPA) 1909
■   c/o Richmond Road Cab Centre, 195 Richmond Rd, LONDON,
       E8 3NJ.   (hq)
       020 7275 7589
       Sec & Treas: K J G Day
▲   Un-incorporated Society
○   *T; taxi fleet proprietors operating within the licensed London
       taxi trade
●   Mtgs - Stat - VE - LG
<   London Taxi Bd
M   50 f

London Natural History Society (LNHS) 1858
NR   19 Mecklenburgh Square, LONDON, WC1N 2AD.   (mail)
       020 7837 7800 address
       Sec: Dr John Edgington
▲   Registered Charity
○   *L, *Q; study of natural history within 20 miles of St Paul's
       Cathedral
Gp Botany; Ecology; Entomology; Geology; Ornithology; Ramblers
       & archaeology; S W Middlesex
●   Conf - Mtgs - Res - Lib
M   1,200 i
¶   The London Naturalist - 1; ftm.
       London Bird Report - 1; ftm.
       Ornithological Bulletin - 6;   NL - 6;   both m only.

**London Private Hire Car Association Ltd   (Graded Private Hire
Companies) 1994**
NR   213 Kenton Rd, HARROW, Middx, HA3 0HD.
       07956 329288   (hq)
       Chmn: Steve Wright
▲   Company Limited by Guarantee
○   *T; for private hire, chauffeur & mini cab companies
M   600 f
¶   Private Hire News - 4; free.

London Record Society 1964

■   c/o Institute of Historical Research, Senate House, LONDON, WC1E 7HU.   (hsb)
01992 300596   fax 020 7862 8793
email londonrecord.society@ntlworld.com
http://www.history.ac.uk/cmh/lrs
Hon Sec: Dr Heather Bradley
▲   Registered Charity
○   *L; publication of an annual series of carefully edited transcripts, abstracts & lists of original sources for the history of London; stimulation of public interest in the archives of London
●   Mtgs
M   141 i, 83 f & org, UK / 24 i, 89 f & org, o'seas
¶   Annual volume; £12 m, (£18 instns), £20 nm.

London Rice Brokers' Association   (LRBA)   1869

NR   4 St Georges Yard, FARNHAM, Surrey, GU9 7LW.   (hq)
01252 741400   fax 01252 727677
email rice@lrba.com
Sec: Michael French
○   *T; establishment of contract forms on which rice business is transacted
M   i & f
¶   Monthly Rice Circular - 12.

London Shellac Trade Association

no longer in existence

London Shipowners' & River Users' Society (incorporating the London General Shipowners' Society)   1811

■   Carthusian Court, 12 Carthusian St, LONDON, EC1M 6EZ.   (hq)
020 7417 2830   fax 020 7600 1534
Sec: D W Chard
○   *T; representative body protecting & promoting the interests of London river users
M   f

London Society   1912

NR   Mortimer Wheeler House, 46 Eagle Wharf Rd, LONDON, N1 7ED.   (hq)
020 7253 9400
email info@londonsociety.org.uk
http://www.londonsociety.org.uk
Hon Sec: Dr John D Hill
▲   Un-incorporated Society
○   *K; to stimulate a wider concern for the beauty of London, the preservation of its amenities & careful consideration of its development
●   Mtgs - Inf - Lib - VE
M   500 i, 10 f, 100 org, UK / 20 i, 10 org, o'seas
¶   Jnl - 2; ftm only.

London Stock Exchange plc   1676

NR   10 Paternoster Square, LONDON, EC4M 7LS.   (hq)
020 7797 1000   http://www.londonstockexchange.com
Chief Exec: Mrs Clara Furse
○   *P; to provide a central market in securities
M   f

London Subterranean Survey Association   (LSSA)   1968

■   98 Cambridge Gardens, LONDON, W10 6HS.   (hsp)
020 7361 2097   fax 020 7361 3463
email plnrm@rbkc.gov.uk
Hon Sec: Roger Morgan
▲   Un-incorporated Society
○   *L; to promote the discovery & recording of natural & man-made features of subterranean London; to promote the utilisation of subterranean space & to minimise its conflict with surface developments
●   Res - Inf - Lib - PL - VE
<   Subterranea Britannica
M   20 i, 1 org

London Swing Dance Society   (LSDS)   1986

■   22 Bessingby Rd, RUISLIP, Middx, HA4 9BX.   (hq)
01895 613703
email swinguk@zetnet.co.uk
http://www.swingdanceuk.com
Dir & Founder: Simon Selmon
▲   Company Limited by Guarantee
○   *D, *G; to support & promote swing dance events, classes & performances
●   Mtgs - Exhib - Comp
M   c 400 i

London Topographical Society   (LTS)   1880

NR   36 Old Deer Park Gardens, RICHMOND, Surrey, TW9 2TL.   (hsp)
020 8940 5419
http://www.topsoc.org
Hon Sec: Patrick Frazer
▲   Registered Charity
○   *L, *Q; publication of facsimiles of scarce printed or manuscript maps & views of London; research on these & other topographical subjects
●   Res - Publication
M   c 1,000 i & f
¶   London Topographical Record (Jnl) - 5 yrly.   NL - 2.

London Underground Railway Society   (LURS)   1961

■   54 Brinkley Rd, Worcester Park, KINGSTON UPON THAMES, Surrey, KT4 8JF.   (sp)
020 8330 1855
http://www.lurs.org.uk
Sec: Eric Felton
▲   Un-incorporated Society
○   *G; study of the railways of London Transport, its predecessors & successors & other underground railways in London
Gp   Modelling; Visits
●   Mtgs - Inf - VE
M   c 900 i, UK / 50 i, o'seas
¶   Underground News - 12; ftm (on sale at the London Transport Museum).

London Welsh Association   (LWA)   1920

NR   157-163 Gray's Inn Rd, LONDON, WC1X 8UE.   (hq)
020 7837 3722   fax 020 7837 6268
○   *G; a centre for the promotion of Welsh cultural activities, the Welsh language & for social discourse
M   1,500 i
¶   London Welshman - 4.

Londonderry Chamber of Commerce   1885

■   Chamber of Commerce House, 1 St Columb's Court, Bishop St, DERRY, BT48 6PT.   (hq)
028 7126 2379   fax 028 7128 6789
email info@londonderrychamber.co.uk
http://www.londonderrychamber.co.uk
Chief Exec: Janice Tracey
▲   Company Limited by Guarantee
○   *C; the business representation body to drive & develop economic development in the Northwest region; areas of interest - tourism, infrastructure, skills business development & information
Gp   Business Information & Guidance Service; NWCCI - Cross Border Lobby Gp
●   Conf - Mtgs - ET - Stat - Expt - Inf - LG
<   Cham of Comm Ireland
M   310 f
¶   NL - 4;   Ybk - 1;   AR - 1; all free.

© CBD Research Ltd · Beckenham · BR3 5JS · Tel 020 8650 7745 · Fax 020 8650 0768 · E-mail cbd@cbdresearch.com · www.cbdresearch.com

Long Distance Walkers Association Ltd   (LDWA)   1972
- ■ 1 Priory Grove, REDCAR, Cleveland, TS10 1QT.   (sb)
  email secretary@ldwa.org.uk   http://www.ldwa.org.uk
  Gen Sec: Edith Moran
- ▲ Company Limited by Guarantee
- Br 40
- ○ *G; furthering the interests of people who enjoy long distance walking
- ● Mtgs - Challenge & social walks, long distance paths
- < Ramblers Assn
- M 6,500 i
- ¶ Strider - 3; ftm only.
  Long Distance Walkers Hbk - 3 yrly; £12.99 (April 2002).

Long-term Medical Conditions Alliance
  since 2005 **LMCA**

Longhorn Cattle Society   1878
- ■ Southcott Farm, Chawleigh, CHULMLEIGH, Devon, EX18 7HP.   (hsp)
  01769 581212   fax 01769 581212
  email longhorns@tiscali.co.uk
  http://www.longhorncattlesociety.com
  Sec: Mrs Sarah Slade
- ▲ Registered Charity
- ○ *B; registration of pedigree longhorn cattle & their promotion, improvement & marketing
- ● Conf - Mtgs - ET - Exhib - Comp - SG - Expt - Inf - PL - VE
- < Nat Cattle Assn (NCA); Rare Breeds Survival Trust (RBST)
- M 410 i, UK / 10 i, o'seas
- ¶ Jnl - 1; ftm.   Herd Book - 1; ftm, £3 nm.
  List of A1 Bulls - 2 yrly;   Rules;   AGM Report; all ftm.

Lonk Sheep Breeders Association   (LSBA)   1905
- ■ 51 Glen View Rd, BURNLEY, Lancs, BB11 2QW.   (hsp)
  01282 433047
  Hon Sec: Mrs Jeanette Shorrock
- ▲ Registered Charity
- ○ *B
- ● Mtgs - Exhib - Shows & sales
- < Nat Sheep Assn
- M 77 i
- ¶ Flock Book - irreg.

LOOK   (LOOK)   1991
- ■ Queen Alexandra College, 49 Court Oak Rd, Harborne, BIRMINGHAM, B17 9TG.   (hq)
  0121-428 5038   fax 0121-428 5038
  http://www.look-uk.org
  Inf Officer: Jane Benham
- ▲ Registered Charity
- ○ *W; the national federation of families with visually impaired children; to support parents &/or carers of children with visual problems
- ● ET - Inf - Lib - Welfare support - Linking families with similar disabilities
- M [not stated]
- ¶ NL - 4; ftm.
- ✕ National Federation of Families with Visually Impaired Children

Lord's Day Observance Society   (LDOS)   1831
- NR Ryelands Rd, LEOMINSTER, Herefordshire, HR6 8NZ.   (hq)
  01568 613740   fax 01568 611473
  email sales@dayone.co.uk   http://www.dayone.co.uk
  Gen Sec: John Roberts
- ▲ Company Limited by Guarantee; Registered Charity
- Br 3
- ○ *K; to preserve Sunday as a national day of rest
- ● Conf - Mtgs - ET - Exhib - SG - Inf - Prison work
- M 379 i, UK / 25 i, o'seas
- ¶ Day One - 3; free.

Lotteries Council   1979
- NR 21 Bristow Close, Great Sankey, WARRINGTON, WA5 8EU.   (mail/address)
  Exec Officer: Mrs Judith Horner (01925 710880)
- ○ *T; for any person or organisation who is engaged in activities connected with the promotion of lawful lotteries
- ● Conf - Mtgs - Inf - LG
- M c 150 i, f & org
- ¶ Lottery Magazine - 4.   Code of Conduct.
  The Acts Combined.

Lovebird (1990) Society
  a member body of the **Society for the Protection of Aviculture**

Low Incomes Tax Reform Group   (LITRG)   1998
- NR 12 Upper Belgrave St, LONDON, SW1X 8BB.   (hq)
  020 7235 9381   fax 020 7235 2562
  Chmn: John Andrews
- ▲ Registered Charity
- ○ *K; the tax problems of those on low incomes
- ● ET - Res - LG
- M 20 i
- ¶ Older People on Low Incomes:
  The case for a friendlier tax system.
  The taxman's response; both irreg.

Low Power Radio Association
  this association is now based in Belgium & is therefore outside the scope of this directory:
  in 2006 telephone 00 32 (2) 714 54 90

Lowe Syndrome Association (UK Contact Group)   (LSA)   1983
- ■ 29 Gleneagles Drive, Penwortham, PRESTON, Lancs, PR1 0JT.   (hsp)
  01772 745070
  email info@lowesyndrome.org
  http://www.lowesyndrome.org
  UK Contact Family: Mr David & Mrs Julie Oliver
- ▲ Un-incorporated Society
- ○ *W; to provide mutual support & information among families; Lowe Syndrome is a rare genetic condition which only affects boys, causing physical & mental handicaps & medical problems
- ● Conf - Res - Inf
- < Contact-a-Family
- M 15 i, UK / 350 i, o'seas
- ¶ NL - 3;   Family Directory - 1; both ftm only.

Loyal Company of Town Criers   (LCTC)   1994
- NR 6 Panton Place, Hoole, CHESTER, Cheshire, CH2 3JE.
  01244 311736   fax 01244 311736
  email chestercrier@city2000.net
  Contact: David Mitchell
- ○ *G; to promote & encourage the appointment of town criers; to maintain the standards & conduct of their ancient office
- ● Conf - Mtgs - Res - Exhib - Comp - Expt - Inf - VE
- < Pacific Northwest Company of Town Criers (Canada); Public Criers of Victoria (Canada)
- M 146 i, UK / 37 i, o'seas
- ¶ The Scroll (NL) - 3; ftm only.

Luing Cattle Society Ltd   1965
- ■ Incheoch Farms, Alyth, BLAIRGOWRIE, Perthshire, PH11 8HJ. (sp)
  01575 560763   fax 01575 560771
  email secretary@luing-cattle.ndo.co.uk
  Sec: Mrs Judy McGowan
- ▲ Registered Charity
- ○ *B; a native beef-breed from the Island of Luing off the west coast of Scotland
- ● Mtgs - Comp - Stat - Inf - VE
- M 320 i, 6 f, UK / 15 i, o'seas
- ¶ The Luing Jnl - 1;   Luing News - 3; both free.
  AR; ftm only.

Lupus UK   1990

■ St James House, Eastern Rd, ROMFORD, Essex, RM1 3NH.
  (hq)
  01708 731251   fax 01708 731252
  email headoffice@lupusuk.co.uk
  http://www.lupusuk.org.uk
  Dir: Chris Maker
▲ Registered Charity
Br 30 regional gps
○ *W; to support those who suffer with the disease Systemic Lupus
  Erythematosus; fundraising for research & welfare support;
  advice for members & those seeking diagnosis
● Conf - Mtgs - Res
< Eur Lupus Fedn; Long Term Medical Conditions Alliance; Brit
  League Against Rheumatism; Brit Assn of Dermatologists
M 7,500 i, UK / 100 i, o'seas
¶ Factsheets; free.   Publications list available.

Lusitano Breed Society (Great Britain)   (LBSGB)   1984

■ Carreg Dressage, Aber Cegir, MACHYNLLETH, Powys,
  SY20 8NW.   (hsp)
  01650 511800
  http://www.lusobreedsociety.co.uk
▲ Company Limited by Guarantee
○ *B; promotion & registration of the Lusitano (Portuguese) horse
Gp Classical riding; Training; Dressage
● ET - Comp - Inf
< Associação Portuguesa de Craidores do Cavalo Puro Sangue
  Lusitano (Lisbon)
M 250 i, UK / 10 i, o'seas
¶ Luso News - 3; ftm, £3.50 each nm.   NL - 3/4.

Lute Society   1956

■ Southside Cottage, Brook Hill, Albury, GUILDFORD, Surrey,
  GU5 9DJ.   (hsp/b)
  01483 202159   fax 01483 203088
  email lutesoc@aol.com   http://www.lutesoc.co.uk
  Sec: Christopher Goodwin
▲ Un-incorporated Society
○ *D; to spread information on the lute, other related instruments
  & their music
● Mtgs - Res - Comp - Inf - PL - Publication of music, working
  drawings of instruments
M 320 i, 10 libraries, UK / 300 i, 50 libraries, o'seas
¶ The Lute (Jnl) - 1; with Lute News - 4; £31 (subscription only).
  Catalogue available of booklets & music.

Lutheran Council of Great Britain   (LC)   1955

NR 30 Thanet St, LONDON, WC1H 9QH.   (hq)
  020 7554 2900   fax 020 7383 3081
  Gen Sec: Rev Tom Bruch
○ *R
M c 25,000 i
¶ Contact - 2.

Lutyens Trust   1985

■ Goddards, Abinger Common, DORKING, Surrey, RH5 6JH.
  (hq)
  01306 730487
  Chmn: Martin Lutyens
▲ Registered Charity
○ *A; to protect the spirit & substance of the work of the architect
  Sir Edwin Lutyens
¶ NL - 3; ftm only.
  Guidebook to Goddards (the Trust's house designed by Sir
  Edwin Lutyens)

Lymphoedema Support Network   (LSN)

NR St Luke's Crypt, Sydney St, London, SW3 6NH.
  020 7351 0990   fax 020 7349 9809
  http://www.lymphoedema.org/lsn
○ *W

Lymphoma Association   1986

■ PO Box 386, AYLESBURY, Bucks, HP20 2GA.   (hq)
  01296 619400   fax 01296 619414
  email information@lymphoma.org.uk
  http://www.lymphoma.org.uk
  Chief Exec: Melanie Burfitt
▲ Registered Charity
○ *W; to provide information & emotional support to anyone with
  Lymphatic cancer, their families, carers & friends
Gp Non-Hodgkin's lymphoma; Hodgkin lymphoma
● Conf - Exhib - Inf - Lib
  Helpline: 0808 808 5555; www.lifesite.info (for young adults)
M 2,125 i
¶ Lymphoma NL - 4;
  Lymphoma Fundraising News - 4; both ftm only.
  Booklets (designed to help patients to cope with their
    illness & treatments):
    Lymphomas (a general booklet for Hodgkin); £2.
    Low Grade Hodgkin Lymphomas; £2 (both; £25 for 15
    copies).
    Hodgkin Lymphoma; £3 (£25 for 10 copies).
  Videos:
    Hodgkin lymphoma & its treatments; £10.
    Understanding non-Hodgkin lymphoma; £10.
  Publications list available.

© CBD Research Ltd · Beckenham · BR3 5JS · Tel 020 8650 7745 · Fax 020 8650 0768 · E-mail cbd@cbdresearch.com · www.cbdresearch.com

Macclesfield Chamber of Commerce & Enterprise   (MCCE) 1994
NR   Churchill Chambers, Churchill Way, MACCLESFIELD, Cheshire, SK11 6AS.   (hq)
      01625 665940   fax 01625 665941
      Chief Exec: John Lamond
▲   Company Limited by Guarantee
○   *C
●   Mtgs - Inf - LG
<   Brit Chams Comm
M   500 f
¶   Chamberlink (NL) - 6.   Directory - 1.

Macedonian Society of Great Britain   1989
NR   The Hellenic Centre, 16 Paddington St, LONDON, W1M 3LB.
      (regd/office)
      020 7487 5060   fax 020 7486 4254
      http://www.macedonia.org.uk
○   *G; for the further education of the public in aspects of Macedonian culture, art, language & life

Machine Tool Technologies Association
   since October 2002 **Manufacturing Technologies Association**

Machinery Users' Association (Inc)   (MUA)   1887
NR   11 Moorfields High Walk, LONDON, EC2Y 9DP.   (hq)
      020 7638 4383
      Managing Dir: Paul Sewell
▲   Company Limited by Guarantee
○   *P; representations to government on property rating & valuation matters
M   5 i, 60 f
¶   NL - 4; ftm only.

Macular Disease Society   (MDS)   1987
■   PO Box 1870, ANDOVER, Hants, SP10 9AD.   (hq)
      01264 350551   fax 01264 350558
      email info@maculardisease.org
      http://www.maculardisease.org
      Chief Exec: Tom Bremridge
▲   Company Limited by Guarantee; Registered Charity
○   *W; to provide information, help, support & practical advice to people with Macular Disease (loss of central vision due to scarring of the retina - the most common cause of registrable blindness in the UK), health professionals & the general public
●   Conf - Mtgs - Res - Exhib - LG
      Helpline: 0845 241 2041
<   AMD Alliance Intl
M   13,000 i in 133 gps
¶   Side View (NL) - 4;   Digest (Jnl) - 1; both ftm only.
      [subscription: i (£15 UK / £30 o'seas), professionals (eyehealth) £50-£100.

Made-up Textiles Association Ltd
   since 2004 **Performance Textiles Association**

Magic Circle   1905
NR   Centre for the Magic Arts, 12 Stephenson Way, LONDON, NW1 2HD.   (hq)
      020 7387 2222   fax 020 7387 5114
      http://www.themagiccircle.co.uk
      Sec: Chris Pratt
○   *A, *P; to advance the art of magic
●   Mtgs - ET - Exam - Res - Comp - Exhib - Lib
M   1,500 i
¶   The Magic Circular - 12; ftm only.

Magic Lantern Society   1976
■   South Park, Galphay Rd, Kirkby Malzeard, RIPON, N Yorks, HG4 3RX.   (hsp)
      email lmh.smith@magiclanternsocy.demon.co.uk
      http://www.magiclantern.org.uk
      Hon Sec: L M H Smith
▲   Un-incorporated Society
○   *G
●   Conf - Mtgs - Res - Exhib - Inf - Lib
<   Magic Lantern Soc US & Canada
M   260 i, 10 f, UK / 120 i, o'seas
¶   Jnl;   NL; both ftm.

Magistrates' Association   1920
NR   28 Fitzroy Sq, LONDON, W1T 6DD.   (hq)
      020 7387 2353   fax 020 7383 4020
      email secretariat@magistrates-association.org.uk
      http://www.magistrates-association.org.uk
      Chief Exec: Sally J Dickinson
▲   Registered Charity (incorporated by Royal Charter)
Br   60
○   *P; supports magistrates in their duties; contributes towards their training
●   Conf - Mtgs - ET - Inf - LG
M   28,500 i
¶   The Magistrate - 10; £24 yr m.   AR.

Magna Carta Society
NR   PO Box 358, HORSHAM, W Sussex, RH13 7FY.
      01403 741334   fax 01403 741736
○   *G

Maidenhead & District Chamber of Commerce
■   Risborough House, 29-31 Risborough Rd, MAIDENHEAD, Berks, SL6 7YT.
      01628 670573   fax 01628 670573
      email admin@maidenhead.org.uk
      http://www.maidenhead.org.uk
      Sec: Lynda Morten
▲   Company Limited by Guarantee
○   *C
      no further information supplied

Maidstone & Mid Kent Chamber of Commerce & Industry   (Maidstone Chamber)
   is a branch of the **Kent Invicta Chamber of Commerce**

Mail Consolidators Association   (MCA)
■   c/o BTB Mailflight Ltd, Wolseley Rd, Kempston, BEDFORD, MK42 7UA.   (chmn/b)
      01234 840222   fax 01234 841041
      email iank@btbmf.co.uk   http://www.mcaonline.net
      Chmn: Ian Kavanagh
○   *T; for consolidators of international mail
●   Mtgs
M   25 f

Mail Order Traders' Association of Great Britain   (MOTA) 1941
■   PO Box 51909, LONDON, SW99 0WZ.   (hsb)
      020 7735 3410   fax 020 7735 9592
      Chief Exec: Mark Hogarth
▲   Un-incorporated Society
○   *T; to represent the major home shopping companies in GB
●   Mtgs - Res - Stat - LG - Operation of a code of practice
<   Eur Mail Order Traders' Assn; Advertising Assn (AA); Brit Retail Consortium (BRC)
M   7 f
¶   LM - as required.

Mail Users' Association Ltd   (MUA)   1975
NR   70 Main Rd, Hermitage, EMSWORTH, Hants, PO10 8AX.
         (hsb)
         01243 370840   fax 01243 370840
         Sec: Jeremy Partridge
○   *T; to work on behalf of its members for improvements in the
         postal services
M   c 50 i, f & org
¶   NL - 6.

Maine-Anjou Cattle Society of the UK
■   20 Mill St, SHIPSTON ON STOUR, Warks, CV36 4AW.   (hsb)
         Sec: J S S Bosley
○   *B
         no further information supplied

** Mainline Steam Locomotive Operators Ltd
         Organisation lost: see Introduction paragraph 3

Maize Growers Association   (MGA)   1988
■   Town Barton Farm, Sandford, CREDITON, Devon, EX17 4LS.
         (hq)
         01363 775040
         Admin: June Howard
▲   Company Limited by Guarantee
○   *F; a farmer managed group providing technology to maximise
         the profitability of growing forage crops, particularly maize
●   Conf - Res - Comp - Inf - VE
M   c 900 i & f
¶   MGA Times - 12;   Maize Grower - 2;
         Technical Notes - agronomy / ruminant - 12; all ftm only.

Major Contractors Group
         is a contractor organisation within the **Construction Confederation**

Major Projects Association   (MPA)   1982
NR   Egrove Park, Kennington, OXFORD, OX1 5NY.   (hq)
         01865 422581   fax 01865 326068
         Admin: Manon Bradley
○   *L, *P; to explore specific, mainly industrial, projects
M   c 70 f

Making Music   1935
NR   2-4 Great Eastern St, LONDON, EC2A 3NW.   (hq)
         0870 903 3780   fax 0870 903 3785
         email info@makingmusic.org.uk
         http://www.makingmusic.org.uk
         Chief Exec: Robin M Osterley
▲   Company Limited by Guarantee; Registered Charity
Br   13
○   *D; to represent & assist the UK's voluntary music sector
Gp   Choirs; Orchestras; Music clubs
●   Conf - ET - Inf - LG
<   Nat Music Coun, Assn Brit Orchestras, Nat Campaign for the
         Arts, Voluntary Arts Network, Scottish Arts Lobby
M   c 2,300 org
¶   Making Music News - 4; free.
         Annual Review;   Guide to Member Services; both ftm.
         Orchestral Catalogue.   Choral Catalogue.
         Chamber Music Catalogue.   Information sheets; ftm only.

Malacological Society of London   (Malsoc)   1893
■   c/o Ecology Research Group, Canterbury Christ Church
         University College, North Holmes Rd, CANTERBURY, Kent,
         CT1 1QU.   (hsb)
         01227 767700   fax 01227 470442
         email g.b.dussart@canterbury.ac.uk
         http://www.malacsoc.org.uk
         Hon Sec: Prof G B J Dussart
▲   Registered Charity
○   *L; study of molluscs from pure & applied aspects
●   Conf - Res
M   c 330 i
¶   Jnl of Molluscan Studies - 4 (with supplements); ftm.
         Bulletin - 2; ftm only.

Malcolm Muggeridge Society   2003
■   Pilgrim's Cottage, Pike Rd, EYTHORNE, Kent,CT15 4DJ.   (sb/p)
         01304 831964
         email info@malcolmmuggeridge.org
         http://www.malcolmmuggeridge.org
         Sec: David Williams
▲   Un-incorporated Society
○   *G; to promote the work of the author, journalist, broadcaster,
         Christian apologist & soldier/spy, Malcolm Muggeridge
         1903-1990
●   Conf - Mtgs - Inf - Lib - VE
M   105 i, UK / 110 i, o'seas
¶   The Gargoyle (Jnl) - 4; ftm, £5 nm.

Malcolm Saville Society   1994
■   78a Windmill Rd, MORTIMER, Berks, RG7 3RL.   (msp)
         email mystery@witchend.com   http://www.witchend.com
         Chmn: Richard Griffiths
▲   Un-incorporated Society
○   *A, *G; to celebrate the life & work of this popular children's
         author (1901-1982); to stimulate awareness of his books
●   Mtgs - Lib - Themed walks based on the novels - Book search
         service
M   370 i, UK / 12 i, o'seas
¶   Acksherley! - 3;   Peewit! (LM) - 1; both ftm only.
         AGM Souvenir programme; price varies.

Malone Society   1906
■   c/o Dr Wim Van Mierlo, University of London, School of
         Advanced Study, Senate House, Malet St, LONDON,
         WC1E 7HU.   (hq)
         020 7862 8679
         email wim.van-mierlo@sas.ac.uk   http://www.sas.ac.uk/
         ies/malone
         Exec Sec: Prof John Creaser
▲   Registered Charity
Br   Australia, Canada, Japan, Switzerland
○   *A, *D, *L; publishing editions of 16th & 17th Century plays
         from manuscript, photographic facsimile editions of original
         documents relating to the Renaissance theatre & drama
●   ET - Inf - Lib
<   Shakespeare Assn of America
M   238 i, UK / 432 i, o'seas
¶   Books - 1 or 2 yr; ftm.   AR - 1; free.
         [subscription £20]

Malt Distillers Association of Scotland   (MDAS)   1874
■   1 North St, ELGIN, Moray, IV30 1UA.   (asa)
         01343 544077   fax 01343 548523
         email mdas@grigor-young.co.uk
         Secs: Grigor & Young (solicitors & estate agents)
○   *T; interests of the pot still malt whisky industry
M   f

© CBD Research Ltd · Beckenham · BR3 5JS · Tel 020 8650 7745 · Fax 020 8650 0768 · E-mail cbd@cbdresearch.com · www.cbdresearch.com

Maltsters' Association of Great Britain   (MAGB)   1827
NR   31b Castle Gate, NEWARK, Notts, NG24 1AZ.   (hq)
   01636 700781
     email info@magb.org.uk   http://www.ukmalt.com
   Dir Gen: Ivor Murrell
▲   Un-incorporated Society
○   *T; 'to promote & safeguard the UK malting industry'
Gp   Malt exporters
●   Conf - Mtgs - ET - Exam - Res - Stat - Expt - LG
<   Euromalt
M   14 f
¶   AR; ftm only.

Mammal Society   1954
■   2B Inworth St, LONDON, SW11 2EP.   (hq)
   020 7350 2200
     email enquiries@mammal.org.uk
     http://www.mammal.org.uk
   Admin Officer: Sarah Gardner
▲   Company Limited by Guarantee; Registered Charity
○   *L, *Q; to protect British mammals, halt the decline of
   threatened species & advise on all issues affecting British
   mammals; to study mammals, identify the problems they
   face & promote conservation & other policies based on
   sound science
●   Conf - Mtgs - ET - Res - Inf - Study of conservation needs of
   threatened species - Trap loan scheme for members
<   IVCN; Wildlife & Countryside Link
M   2,200 i, UK / 100 i, o'seas
¶   Mammal Review - 4.   Mammal News - 4.
   Mammalaction News [youth group NL] - 4.
   Other publications.

Management Consultancies Association   (MCA)   1956
■   60 Trafalgar Sq, LONDON, WC2N 5DS.   (hq)
   020 7321 3990   fax 020 7321 3991
     email mca@mca.org.uk   http://www.mca.org.uk
   Chief Exec: Peter Hill
▲   Company Limited by Guarantee
○   *P, *T; to maintain standards within the UK management
   consultancy sector
Gp   HR directors; Marketing director; Finance directors; Public
   sector interest; Statistics interest
●   Conf - Mtgs - ET - Res - Exhib - Stat - Inf - LG
<   Eur Fedn of Mgt Consultancy Assns (FEACO)
M   65 f
¶   Spectra (Jnl) - 4;   Electronic NL - 12;   Careers Guide;
   Corporate brochure; all free.
   The UK Consulting Industry Report - 1.
   MCA book series; £16.99 (published by Hodder & Stoughton).

Managing & Marketing Sales Association   (MAMSA)   1979
NR   PO Box 11, SANDBACH, Cheshire, CW11 3GE.   (sp)
   01270 526339   fax 01270 526339
     email mamsas@mamsasbp.com
     http://www.mamsasbp.com
   Chief Exec: M Whitaker
○   *P; examination board for sales marketing; management;
   business studies & communications
●   ET - Exam - Inf - Correspondence courses
M   2,600 i, UK / 16,000 i, o'seas

Manchester Chamber of Commerce & Industry
   2004 merged with Chamber Business Connections to form the
   Greater Manchester Chamber of Commerce

Manchester Geographical Society   1884
■   Friends Meeting House, 6 Mount St, MANCHESTER, M2 5NS.
   (hq)
   0161-834 2965
     email mgs@mangeogsoc.fsnet.co.uk
     http://www.mangeogsoc.org.uk
   Sec: Mrs J Concannon,   Hon Sec: Dr B P Hindle
▲   Registered Charity
○   *E, *L, *Q; to promote all branches of geographical science
●   Mtgs - Inf - Library on permanent loan to the University of
   Manchester
<   R Geographical Soc; Geographical Assn
M   160 i
¶   North-West Geography (Jnl) - 4; free.   AR - 1; ftm only.

Manchester Literary & Philosophical Society   (LIT & PHIL)
1781
NR   Loxford Tower, Lower Chatham St, MANCHESTER, M15 6BS.
   (hq)
   0161-247 6774   fax 0161-247 6773
     http://www.manlitphil.co.uk
   Hon Sec: Mrs Patricia Verdin
▲   Company Limited by Guarantee; Registered Charity
○   *A, *L; 'to promote the advancement of education & the
   widening of public interest in, & appreciation of, any form of
   literature, science, the arts & public affairs...'
Gp   Sections: Arts, Science & technology, Social philosophy, Young
   people
●   Conf - Mtgs - Lib
M   c 500 i
¶   Manchester Memoirs - 1.   NL - 12.   AR.
   John Dalton Bibliography, Vol 2.

Manchester Medical Society   (MMS)   1834
■   John Rylands University Library, Oxford Rd, MANCHESTER,
   M13 9PP.   (hq)
   0161-273 6048   fax 0161-272 8046
     email admin@mcr-med-society.u-net.com
     http://www.mms.org.uk
   Chmn: Prof J A Morris
▲   Registered Charity
○   *L, *M; to cultivate & promote all branches of medicine, & of all
   related schemes
Gp   Medicine; Anaesthesia; Odontology; Primary care; Surgery;
   Pathology; Paediatrics; Psychiatry; Public health medicine;
   Imaging
●   Mtgs - ET - Lib
M   2,100 i

Manic Depression Fellowship Ltd
   since 2005 **MDF - the Bipolar Organisation**

Manila Hemp Association   (MHA)   1910
NR   c/o John Harrison, 25 Beaufort Court, Admirals Way,
   LONDON, E14 9XL.   (hsb)
   020 7538 5383   fax 020 7538 2007
   Chmn: John Harrison
○   *T; trading in manila hemp & abaca
M   20 i, 12 f, UK / 3 i, 3 f, o'seas
¶   AR; free.

Manorial Society of Great Britain (MSGB) 1906
■ 104 Kennington Rd, LONDON, SE11 6RE.   (hq)
   020 7735 6633   fax 020 7582 7022
   email manorial@msgb.co.uk   http://www.msgb.co.uk
   Hon Exec Chmn: Robert A Smith
○ *L; historical research, manorial rights, legal liability, insurance,
   estate management, genealogy, armigerous devices
● Conf
M i & f
¶ Bulletin - 2; ftm only.   NL - 12; m only.
   Labour & the House of Lords (1998); (proceedings of a
      conference with The Daily Telegraph).
   Britain & Europe (1999); (proceedings of conference with
      The Daily Telegraph).
   Millennium Book (2000).
   The Land Registration Bill (2002).
   Blood Royal, Queen's Golden Jubilee.
   The Land Registration Act (2005).

Manpower Society Ltd
   since 2002 **HR Society**

Mansfield & District Chamber of Trade & Commerce (COT) 1922
NR PO Box 155, MANSFIELD, Notts, NG18 1DG.   (sb)
   01623 622347
   email enquiries@mansfieldchamber.co.uk
   http://www.mansfieldchamber.co.uk
   Admin Officer: June Stendall
▲ Un-incorporated Society
○ *C
● Mtgs

Manufacturers' Agents' Association of Great Britain & Ireland Inc (MAA) 1908
■ Unit 16 Thrales End, HARPENDEN, Herts, AL5 3NS.   (hq)
   01582 767618   fax 01582 769243
   email prw@themaa.co.uk   http://www.themaa.co.uk
   Sec: Paul Wakeling
▲ Company Limited by Guarantee
○ *T; independent manufacturers' (commission) agents
● Conf - Mtgs - ET - Stat - Res - Inf - LG - Legal advice
< Intl U of Comml Agents & Brokers (Amsterdam)
M 500 i
¶ Agents News - 12.
   The Commission Agent.   20 Legal Questions Agents Ask.

Manufacturers of Domestic Unvented Systems (MODUS) 1977
■ 17 Victoria Rd, SALTAIRE, W Yorks, BD18 3LQ.   (sb)
   01274 583355   fax 01274 583355
   email info@modus-uk.org   http://www.modus-uk.org
   Sec: David Walker
▲ Un-incorporated Society
○ *T; direct mains water supply in domestic property: boilers, hot
      water heating apparatus, control valves, taps, plumbing
● Mtgs - ET - Inf
< Plumbing & Heating Ind Alliance; Inst of Plumbing
M 12 f
× 2002 Manufacturers of Domestic Unvented Supply Systems
      Equipment

Manufacturing Science Finance Union
   in January 2004 became **Amicus**

Manufacturing Technologies Association (MTA) 1919
NR 62 Bayswater Rd, LONDON, W2 3PS.   (hq)
   020 7298 6400
   http://www.mta.org.uk
   Dir Gen: Andrew Manly
▲ Company Limited by Guarantee
○ *T; machine tools & equipment
Gp Equipment; Importers; Manufacturers
● Mtgs - ET - Exhib - Comp - Stat - Expt - LG - Technical / Health
      & safety
M 230 f
¶ Various technical publications.
× 2002 (October) Machine Tool Technologies Association

Manx Gaelic Society
   see **Cheshaght Ghailckagh (Yn) (the Manx Gaelic Society)**

Manx Loaghtan Sheep Breeders Group (MLSBG) 1988
NR 8 Austin Rd, The Beeches, CIRENCESTER, Glos, GL7 1BT.
   (hsp)
   01285 654297
   Sec: Joan Hughes
▲ Un-incorporated Society
○ *B
● Workshops
< Rare Breed Survival Trust
M 72 i, 3 f, 1 org, UK / 1 i, o'seas
¶ NL - 3; ftm only.

Manx National Farmers' Union (MNFU) 1947
NR Agriculture House (ground floor), Ballafletcher Farm Rd,
      TROMODE, Isle of Man, IM4 4QL.   (sp)
   01624 662204   fax 01624 662204
   email manx-nfu@talk21.com   http://www.manx-nfu.org
▲ Un-incorporated Society
Br 3
○ *F
● Mtgs - LG
M c 360 i

Map Curators Group
   a group of the **British Cartographic Society**

Marchigiana Cattle Society
NR 17 Jubilee Crescent, BRIDGEND, Glam, CF31 3AY.   (hsp)
   01656 653029
   Sec: Andrew Shackell
○ *B

Marfan Association UK 1984
■ Rochester House, 5 Aldershot Rd, FLEET, Hants, GU51 3NG.
   (hq)
   01252 810472   fax 01252 810473
   email marfan@tinyonline.co.uk
   http://www.marfan.org.uk
   Chmn: Mrs Diane Rust
▲ Registered Charity
○ *W; offering support to patients with Marfan syndrome, which
      affects the cardiovascular system, causing near-sightedness &
      skeletal abnormalities; working alongside the many medical
      sectors involved in patient care; educating patients, doctors,
      the public, the Dept of Health & the Government;
      undertaking & sponsoring research projects
● Conf - ET - Res - Exhib - Stat - Inf - LG
< Intl Fedn of Marfan Syndrome Orgs; Eur Marfan Support
      Network
M 1,500 families
¶ In Touch (Jnl) - 2.
   Publications list available.

Margarine Manufacturers Association of Ireland   (IMDA)   1995
IRL   Confederation House, 84-86 Lower Baggot St, DUBLIN 2,
      Republic of Ireland.
○   *T
<   IBEC

Margarine & Spreads Association   (MSA)
■   6 Catherine St, LONDON, WC2B 5JJ.   (hq)
    020 7836 2460   fax 020 7836 0580
    Sec: Juliet Howarth
▲   Un-incorporated Society
○   *T
<   Intl Fedn Margarine Assns (IFMA); EEC Margarine Mfrs Assn
    (IMACE); Food & Drink Fedn
M   8 f
¶   AR; ftm only.

Margery Allingham Society   1987
■   9 Bailey St, Castle Acre, KING'S LYNN, Norfolk, PE32 2AG.
    (gen/sec)
    http://www.margeryallingham.org.uk
    2B Hiham Green, WINCHELSEA, E Sussex, TN36 4HB.
    01797 222363   fax 01797 222363. (hon/mem/sec).
    Gen Sec: Mrs Marianne Van Hoeven
▲   Un-incorporated Society
○   *A, *G; to bring together all interested in the life & work of
    Margery Allingham, a queen of crime & one of the greatest
    detective story writers of the 'Golden Age'
●   Conf - VE
M   120 i, UK / 12 i, o'seas
¶   The Bottle Street Gazette - 2; ftm.

Margery Kempe Society   1999
NR   1a Auckland Rd, LONDON, SW11 1EW.   (hsp)
     020 7924 5868
     Hon Sec: Carole Madden
○   *G; to further learned research into the English mystic Margery
    Kempe (c1373-c1440); to further historical & literary
    research in this field
●   Conf
M   30 i

Marie Stuart Society   1992
■   Copeland, 3 Barley Close, Little Eaton, DERBY, DE21 5DJ.
    (hsp)
    email syd@internet.co.uk   http://www.marie-stuart.co.uk
    Sec: Syd Whitehead
▲   Registered Charity
Br 3
○   *G; study & research into the life & times of Mary Queen of
    Scots (1542-1587)
●   Mtgs - Res - Exhib - Comp - Inf - Lib - PL - LG
M   134 i, UK / 30 i, o'seas
¶   Jnl - 3; ftm only.

**Marine Biological Association of the United Kingdom
(MBAUK)   1884**
■   The Laboratory, Citadel Hill, PLYMOUTH, Devon, PL1 2PB.
    (regd/office)
    01752 633207   fax 01752 633102
    email sec@mba.ac.uk   http://www.mba.ac.uk
    Dir & Sec: Prof Stephen J Hawkins
▲   Company Limited by Guarantee; Registered Charity
○   *L, *Q; studies in various aspects of marine biology &
    biological oceanography, pollution, taxonomy, physiology,
    molecular biology & biochemistry
Gp Biochemists; Biologists; Library; Molecular biologists;
    Physiologists
●   Mtgs - ET - Res - Inf - Lib - SG - VE
M   983 i, 11 f, UK / 286 i, 1 f, o'seas
¶   Jnl - 6; ftm, £445 yr nm.
    NL - 2;   AR - 1; both ftm only.
    [subscription £95 yr].

Marine Conservation Society   (MCS)   1983
NR   Unit 3 Wolf Business Park, Alton Rd, ROSS-ON-WYE,
     Herefords, HR9 5BU.   (hq)
     01989 566017   fax 01989 567815
     email info@mcsuk.org   http://www.mcsuk.org
     Dir of Consvn: Mrs Samantha Fanshawe
     Operations Mgr: Mrs Pamela Bridgewater
▲   Company Limited by Guarantee; Registered Charity
○   *K, *L; 'the only UK based charity devoted exclusively to the
    protection of the marine environment; it believes that
    decisions affecting our seas & coasts should be based on
    sound scientific principles & implemented by environmentally
    sensitive management'
●   Conf - ET - Res - Inf - PL - VE - LG - Volunteer work
<   Sea at Risk; Sea Turtle Survival; Wildlife & Countryside Link
M   5,200 i, UK / 200 i, o'seas
¶   Marine Conservation (Jnl) - 4; ftm.

**Marine Engine & Equipment Manufacturers' Association
(MEEMA)   1960**
NR   56 Braycourt Ave, WALTON-on-THAMES, Surrey, KT12 2BA.
     (hsp)
     01932 224910
     Sec: Mrs Alison Banks
○   *T; manufacturers, wholesalers & retailers of marine engines &
    related equipment including personal watercraft
<   a group association within the British Marine Federation
M   100 f
¶   LM; ftm, on request nm.

Marine Institute   1941
IRL   80 Harcourt St, DUBLIN 2, Republic of Ireland.
      353 (1) 476 6500
      email institutemail@marine.ie   http://www.marine.ie
      Pres: Desmond Branigan   (353 (1) 660 0737)
○   *G; to promote greater awareness among the people of Ireland
    of their maritime history & of the sea
    Maritime Institute of Ireland

Marine Leisure Association   2005
■   Burrwood, 24 Peterscroft Avenue, Ashurst, SOUTHAMPTON,
    Hants, SO40 7AB.   (hq)
    023 8029 3822   fax 023 8029 3888
    email info@marineleisure.co.uk
    http://www.marineleisure.co.uk
    Gen Sec: Mrs Brigid Howells
▲   Company Limited by Guarantee
○   *S, *T; to market & promote training, charter & holidays afloat
Gp Training; Charter; Holidays
●   Conf - Mtgs - ET - Exam - Exhib - Stat - Expt - Inf - LG
<   Brit Marine Fedn (BMF); R Yachting Assn (RYA) - training only;
    Air Travel Organiser Licence (ATOL) - holidays only
M   150 f, UK / 25 f, o'seas
¶   Brochure - 1; free.
✕   2005 (Association of Bonded Sailing Companies
         (National Federation of Sea Schools
         (Yacht Charter Association
         all merged September 2005

Marine Society & Sea Cadets   (MSSC)   2004
- ■ 202 Lambeth Rd, LONDON, SE1 7JW.   (hq)
  020 7654 7000   fax 020 7928 8914
  email info@ms-sc.org   http://www.sea-cadets.org
  Chief Exec: Jeremy Cornish
- ▲ Registered Charity
- Br 400
- ○ *E, *W; to raise public awareness of the Royal & Merchant
  Navies, & the maritime world in general; to provide support
  for those who go to sea & enhance the well-being of
  professional sailors; to be responsible for the activities of the
  Sea Cadet Corps, open to young people 10-18 years old
- Gp Seafarers libraries; College of the Sea; Sea lines; Sea training
  ship
- ● ET - Lib - Nautical/maritime youth training (sponsored by Royal
  Navy training ships)
- < Intl Sea Cadet Assn (ISCA)
- M 16,000 i, UK / 1,200 i, o'seas
- ¶ The Seafarer (Jnl) - 6; £25 yr m, £3 each nm.
  AR - 1; ftm only.
- × 2004 (Marine Society
      (Sea Cadet Associaton (merged November)

Marine Trades Association   (MTA)   1960
- NR The Maples, Lower Chase Rd, WALTHAM CHASE, Hants,
  SO32 2LH.   (sp)
  01489 896559
  http://www.britishmarine.co.uk
  Sec: Maria Hassall
- ▲ Un-incorporated Society
- ○ *T; retailing, distributing, wholesaling & manufacturing marine
  equipment
- ● Conf - ET - Exhib (annual 2-day) - Expt
- < an association within the British Marine Federation
- M 312 f
- ¶ Ybk.

Marineco   1975
- NR Parade House, The Parade, LISKEARD, Cornwall, PL14 6AF.
  (hq)
  01579 340455
  http://www.marineco.co.uk
  Managing Dir: C J Dinham
- Br 2
- ○ *N; group buying of commercial fishing gear
- ● Mtgs - Exhib
- M c 30 f
- × 2001 (November) Fishing Co-operatives (UK) Ltd

Maritime Information Association   (MIA)   1971
- NR 18 Durrington Avenue, London, SW20 8NT.   (sec/p)
  http://www.maritime-information.net
  Chmn: Michael Naxton
- ▲ Un-incorporated Society
- ○ *L; contact with marine librarians, information workers & others
  with an interest in the maritime world
- ● Conf - Mtgs - VE - Lectures
- ¶ NL - 4;   LM - 1.
  Maritime Information: a guide to sources.

Maritime Interest Group
  a group of the **Defence Manufacturers Association**

Maritime Trust   1969
- NR 2 Greenwich Church St, LONDON, SE10 9BG.   (hq)
  020 8858 2698   fax 020 8858 6976
  email info@cuttysark.org.uk
  http://www.cuttysark.org.uk
  Hon Sec: Richard Doughty
- ▲ Registered Charity
- ○ *G; preservation & restoration of historic British ships
- M c 600 i
- ¶ NL - 2;   AR; both ftm only.

**Market Research Quality Standards Association   (MRQSA)
1996**
- NR Pendowrick, Pendower Rd, Veryan, TRURO, Cornwall,
  TR2 5QL.   (hsp)
  01872 501373
  email pettrevjac@aol.com
  Sec: Peter Jackson
- ▲ Company Limited by Guarantee
- ○ *P; to develop quality standards for market research services; to
  develop schemes by which organisations can be assessed to
  these standards
- ● Conf - liaison with bodies in associated fields
- M 5 org

Market Research Society   (MRS)   1946
- NR 15 Northburgh St, LONDON, EC1V 0JR.   (hq)
  020 7490 4911   fax 020 7490 0608
  email info@marketresearch.org.uk
  http://www.mrs.org.uk
  Dir Gen: David Barr
- ▲ Company Limited by Guarantee
- Br Scotland
- ○ *P; for professional researchers & other engaged (or interested)
  in market, social & opinion research
- ● Conf - Mtgs - ET - Exam - Res - Exhib - Inf - Lib - LG
- < Intl Cham Comm (UK): Advertising Assn; Marketing Coun
- M 7,300 i, UK / 700 i, o'seas
- ¶ Research - 12; ftm.   MRS News - 8; ftm only.
  International Jnl of Market Research - 4; ftm.
  Research Buyers Guide - 1; ftm.   AR - 1; ftm only.
- × 2006 (incorporated) British Market Research Association

Marketing Communication Consultants Association   1989
- NR 3-4 Bentinck St, LONDON, W1U 2EH.   (hq)
  020 7935 3434   fax 020 7935 6464
  email info@mcca.org.uk
  Chmn: Graham Kemp
- ○ *T; practitioners in promotional marketing & communication
- M c 50 f
- × 2002 Sales Promotion Consultants Association

Marketing Institute [Ireland]
- IRL South County Business Park, Leopardstown, DUBLIN 18,
  Republic of Ireland.
  353 (1) 295 2355   fax 353 (1) 295 2453
  email info@mii.ie   http://www.mii.ie
  Chief Exec: Ed McDonald
- ○ *P

Marketing Society
- IRL PO Box 58, BRAY, Co Wicklow, Republic of Ireland.
  353 (1) 276 1995
  email info@marketingsociety.ie
  http://www.marketingsociety.ie
  Chmn: Damien Loscher
- ○ *P

Marketing Society Ltd   1959
- NR 1 Park Rd, TEDDINGTON, Middx, TW11 0AR.   (hq)
  020 8973 1700
  Chief Exec: Hugh Burkitt
- ▲ Company Limited by Guarantee
- ○ *P; 'for senior marketers'
- ● Conf - Mtgs - Inf
- M 3,500 i
- ¶ Market Leader - 4.

Marlowe Society   1955

NR   9 Middlefield Gardens, Hurst Green Rd, HALESOWEN,
     W Midlands, B62 9QH.   (h/mem/sp)
     0121 421 1482
     email marsoct@ntlworld.com
     http://www.marlowe-society.org
     Hon Mem Sec: Frieda Barker,   Chmn: Mike Frohnsdorff
▲   Company Limited by Guarantee; Registered Charity
○   *A, *G; to present Christopher Marlowe in his true light as a
     great poet-dramatist; to stimulate research into his life &
     work, into the lives of his friends & associates & the era in
     which he lived
●   Conf - Mtgs - ET - Res - Exhib - SG - Inf - Lib - VE - Holding
     Marlowe Day annually in Canterbury
M   110 i, 2 schools (King's, Canterbury + Alleyn's, Dulwich), UK /
     25 i, o'seas
¶   NL - 3; ftm, £1 nm.
     Research Jnl - irreg.
     Note: 'this is not the same as the Marlowe [Dramatic] Society of
     Cambridge which was founded by Rupert Brooke & is
     devoted to performing plays'.

MARQUES the Association of European Trade Mark Owners (MARQUES)   1988

■   840 Melton Rd, Thurmaston, LEICESTER, LE4 8BN.   (sb)
     0116-264 0080   fax 0116-264 0141
     email info@marques.org   http://www.marques.org
     Co Sec: Robert Seager
▲   Company Limited by Guarantee
○   *T; representing on a Pan-European basis the interests of
     owners of trade marks & associated intellectual property
●   Conf - Mtgs - Inf - LG
M   50 f, UK / 250 f, o'seas
¶   Marques News Sheet - 10; ftm only.
✕   Association of European Brand Owners

Marquetry Society   1952

■   13 Cavendish Rd, FELIXSTOWE, Suffolk, IP11 2AR.   (hsp)
     01394 278453   fax 01473 257329
     email warrenashley@btopenworld.com
     http://www.marquetry.org
     Hon Gen Sec: Ashley Warren
▲   Un-incorporated Society
Br   29; 8
○   *G; to foster the craft of marquetry
●   Mtgs - Exhib (annual + members competitions) - Inf - PL
<   Crafts Coun; Voluntary Arts Network
M   c 500 i, UK / c 150 i, o'seas
¶   The Marquetarian - 4; ftm, £2 nm.

Martial Arts Development Commission (MADEC)   1992

NR   PO Box 416, WEMBLEY, Middx, HA0 3WD.   (hq)
     0870 770 0461
     Chmn: Richard Thomas
▲   Un-incorporated Society
○   *S; to act as a forum for the martial arts; to promote & develop
     the practice & administration of the martial arts within the UK
     & Northern Ireland
Gp   Aikido, Budo, Capoeira, Judo, Ju jitsu, Karate, Kalarippayat,
     Kendo, Kobudo, Kyudo, Kung fu, Tai chi, Taekwondo, Tang
     soo do, Thai boxing, Kick boxing, Wu shu, Wing Chun
●   Conf - Mtgs - ET - Comp - Inf
<   Nat Coun for Voluntary Orgs (NCVO); Sport & Recreation Ind
     Trg Org (SPRITO)
M   14,000 i, 100 org
¶   Various leaflets on: Disciplines, Safety, Weapons (send
     large sae).

Mary Rose Society   1978

NR   c/o The Mary Rose Trust, College Rd, HM Naval Base,
     PORTSMOUTH, Hants, PO1 3LX.   (hq)
     023 9275 0521
     http://www.maryrose.org
     Chmn: Nicholas Braddock
○   *G; support of the Mary Rose (King Henry VIII's flagship)

Mary Webb Society   1972

■   8 The Knowe, Willaston, NESTON, Cheshire, CH64 1TA.   (hsp)
     0151-327 5843
     email suehigginbotham@yahoo.co.uk
     http://www.marywebb.vze.com
     Sec: Sue Higginbotham
▲   Un-incorporated Society
○   *A, *G; to honour the memory of the author Mary Webb; to
     further appreciation of her works & the Shropshire
     countryside about which she wrote
●   Mtgs - Exhib - VE
<   Alliance of Literary Socs
M   157 i, UK / 9 i, o'seas
¶   Jnl - 1; ftm, £3 nm.   NL - 2/3; free.

Masham Sheep Breeders Association (MSBA)   1986

■   Oak Bank, Bentham, LANCASTER, LA2 7DW.
     01524 261606
     Sec: Mrs V J Lawson
▲   Company Limited by Guarantee
○   *B; 'quality female sheep'
●   Mtgs - Exhib
<   Nat Sheep Assn
M   80 i
¶   NL - 4; ftm only.   LM; ftm.

Massenet Society   1972

NR   Flat 2, 79 Linden Gardens, LONDON, W2 4EU.
     020 7229 7060
     Founder & Dir: Stella J Wright
Br   USA
○   *D; to promote a wider knowledge of the music of Jules
     Massenet (1842-1912) the French composer
●   Lib
¶   NL.   Jnl.

Mast Action UK: the National Campaign for the Sensible Siting of Masts (MAUK)   2000

NR   PO Box 312, WALTHAM CROSS, Herts, EN7 5ZE.
     0170 787 2920
     email headoffice@mastaction.co.uk
     http://www.mastaction.co.uk
     Coordinators: Chris Mangat,   Julie Matthew
○   *K; for control in the raising of masts for telephone & other
     purposes

Master Carvers' Association (MCA)   1897

■   Unit 20, 21 Wren St, LONDON, WC1X 0HF.   (hsb)
     020 7278 8759   fax 020 7278 8759
     email info@mastercarvers.co.uk
     http://www.mastercarvers.co.uk
     Hon Sec: Paul Ferguson
▲   Un-incorporated Society
○   *A, *T; promotion & protection of the interests of wood carving,
     stone carving & modelling generally
●   Conf - Inf - Empl
M   37 f, UK / 2 f, o'seas
¶   NL - irreg; ftm only.   LM; free.

Master Chefs of Great Britain (MCGB)   1980

■   Woodmans, Brithem Bottom, CULLOMPTON, Devon,
     EX15 1NB.   (hsp)
     01884 35104   fax 01884 35105
     email mcgb@masterchefs.co.uk
     http://www.masterchefs.co.uk
     Chmn: Peter Jukes Sec: Susan M McGreever
○   *P; to provide a forum for the exchange of culinary ideas; to
     further the profession through the training & guidance of
     young chefs; to promote all that is best about British cuisine
     & the produce available
●   Mtgs - ET - Culinary demonstrations
M   240 i, 22 f, UK / 5 i, o'seas
¶   Masterchefs - 4; ftm, £3 nm.

Master Craftsmen's Association & Retail Export Group   (MCA)

NR c/o Henry Poole & Co Ltd, 15 Savile Row, LONDON,
      W1S 3PJ.   (hsb)
      020 7734 5985   fax 020 7287 2161
      Sec: Alex Cook
▲ Un-incorporated Society
○ *T; to export 'bespoke' handmade gentlemen's suits, shirts,
      shoes etc
Gp Bespoke: tailors, shoemakers, shirtmakers; Woollen / trimming
      merchants
● ET - Expt
M 35 f

Master Locksmiths' Association   (MLA)   1958

■ 5d Great Central Way, Woodford Halse, DAVENTRY, Northants,
      NN11 3PZ.   (hq)
      01327 262255   fax 01327 262539
      email admin@locksmiths.co.uk
      http://www.locksmiths.co.uk
      Chief Exec: Lorraine Stanley
▲ Company Limited by Guarantee
○ *P, *T
● Conf - Mtgs - ET - Exam - Exhib - Inf - Lib - LG - Locktesting -
      Professional consultancy
M 1,000 i, 350 f, UK / 100 i, o'seas
¶ Keyways - 6; ftm only.

Master Photographers Association Ltd   (MPA)   1952

■ 1 Chancery Lane, DARLINGTON, Co Durham, DL1 5QP.   (hq)
      01325 356555   fax 01325 357813
      email enquiries@mpauk.com   http://www.mpauk.com
      Chief Exec: Colin R Buck
○ *T; represents professional photographers
M f
      no further information supplied

Masters of Deerhounds Association   (MDHA)   1951

■ Broford Farm, DULVERTON, Somerset, TA22 9DW.   (hsp)
      Sec: Guy Everard
▲ Company Limited by Guarantee; Registered Charity
○ *S; control & regulation of deer hunting with hounds
M 3 hunts in England (Devon & Somerset, Tiverton, Quantock)

Masters of Foxhounds Association   (MFHA)   1881

■ The Old School, Bagendon, CIRENCESTER, Glos, GL7 7DU.
      (hq)
      01285 831470
      http://www.mfa.co.uk
      Dir: A Jackson
○ *S; the governing body of foxhunting
M i (past & present masters of foxhounds only)

Mastic Asphalt Council   (MAC)   1995

■ PO Box 77, HASTINGS, E Sussex, TN35 4WL.   (hq)
      01424 814400   fax 01424 814446
      email masphaltco@aol.com
      Dir & Sec: J K Blowers
▲ Company Limited by Guarantee
○ *T; represents mastic asphalt contractors & manufacturers
      providing a free technical service to specifiers
Gp Specialist mastic asphalt contractors
● Conf - Mtgs - ET - Exhib - Comp - SG - Inf - VE - Empl - LG
      (via NSCC)
< Eur Mastic Asphalt Assn (EMAA); Nat Specialist Contrs
      Coun (NSCC)
M 72 f (contractors), 6 f (manufacturing), 21 associates
¶ The New Technical Guide (incl Roofing, Flooring, Paving,
      Tanking); ftm, £30 nm.
      [the Guide is produced as an A4 loose-leaf ring-binder]

Materials & Components Developing & Testing Association
(MACDATA)   1968

§ University of Paisley, High St, PAISLEY, Renfrewshire, PA1 2BE.
      Being wound down (August 2006)

Materials Handling Engineers Association   (MHEA)   1939

■ 19 Marrick Rd, STOCKTON-on-TEES, Cleveland, TS18 5LW.
      (hq)
      01642 570045   fax 01642 570045
      http://www.mhea.co.uk
      Sec: Dr Harold Wright
▲ Un-incorporated Society
○ *T; manufacturers & users of bulk & continuous handling eqpt
● Conf - Mtgs - Expt through ISHAB - LG
< permanent member of Intl Solids Handling Advy Bd (ISHAB)
M 27 f
¶ Online NL - 3; ftm.
      Recommended Practice for Troughed Belt Conveyors.

Maternity Alliance

Closed 2005

MatheMagic   1999

■ 1 Straylands Grove, YORK, YO31 1EB.
      email info@mathemagic.org + qed@enterprise.net
      http://www.mathemagic.org
      Dir: John Bibby
▲ Un-incorporated Society
○ *E; to popularise maths & numeracy
Gp Adult basic skills; Multicultural mathematics
● Conf - Exhib - Comp - PL - VE - Maths Funfairs
< Adults Learning Mathematics
M 300 i, UK / 20 i, o'seas
¶ NL

Mathematical Association   (MA)   1871

■ 259 London Rd, LEICESTER, LE2 3BE.   (hq)
      0116-221 0013   fax 0116-212 2835
      http://www.m-a.org.uk
      Admin: Marcia Murray
▲ Registered Charity
Br 20
○ *E, *P; to improve mathematical education
Gp Library; Publications; Teaching; Problem bureau; Careers;
      Schools & industry; Diplomas; Universities; Society of Young
      Mathematicians
● Conf - Mtgs - ET - Exam - Exhib - Comp - Lib - LG
< Intl Congress on Mathematical Educ; Coun of Subject Teaching
      Assns; R Soc Mathematical Instruction (sub c'ee); Standing
      Conf of Assns concerned with Mathematical Education in
      Schools
M 5,000 i worldwide UK / 500 i, 300 f, o'seas
¶ [publishes a range of mathematics books & jnls].

Max Wall Society   2003

■ 11 Cecil Court, Charing Cross Rd, LONDON, WC2N 4EZ.
      (hsb)
      020 7836 1142   fax 020 7836 1142
      email drummond@popt.fsnet.co.uk
      Sec: David Drummond
▲ Un-incorporated Society
○ *G; for all interested in the life & performing career of Max[well
      George Lorimer] Wall (1908-1990), actor & comedian & to
      perpetuate his memory
● Exhib - Lectures - Annual dinner
M c 150 i
¶ Wallpaper; ftm only.

McCarrison Society 1965

NR c/o IBCHN, London Metropolitan University, North London
    Campus, 166-222 Holloway Rd, LONDON, N7 8DB.
    (chmn/b)
    020 7133 2440   fax 020 7133 2453
    email michael@macrawf.demon.co.uk
    Chmn: Prof Michael A Crawford
▲ Registered Charity
Br 2
○ L, *P; research & dissemination of knowledge on nutrition &
    health; areas of interest include the rise in mortality from
    non-communicable diseases, mental ill-health & the
    widening inequality of health
Gp Dietetics; Nutrition; Cardiology; Cancer; Comparative
    pathology; Epidemiology; Diseases of Western & developing
    countries
● Conf - Mtgs - ET - Res - Comp - SG - LG
< Mother & Child Foundation
M 250 i, UK / 50 i, o'seas
¶ Nutrition & Health - 4.

MCPS-PRS Alliance

NR 29-33 Berners St, LONDON, W1T 3AB.   (hq)
    020 7580 5544   fax 020 7306 4455
○ *T; collection of royalties for the music industry
M 2 org:
    Mechanical Copyright Protection Society Ltd
    Performing Right Society Ltd

McTimoney Chiropractic Association   (MCA)   1979

■ WALLINGFORD, Oxon, OX10 8DJ.   (hq)
    01491 829211   fax 01491 829492
    email services@mctimoney-chiropractic.org
    http://www.mctimoney-chiropractic.org
    Sec: Christine Chalmers,   Chmn: Dr Christina Cunliffe
○ *P; promotion of McTimoney chiropractic
Gp Chiropractic; Private sector education (McTimoney chiropractic
    college)
● Conf - ET - Exam - Res - Exhib - Inf - PL
M 500 i, UK / 10 i, o'seas
¶ Background (NL) - 4; ftm only.
    Directory of Practitioners - 1; ftm, £7.10 nm.
    Information leaflets & college prospectus.

MDA Europe   (MDA)   1977

■ The Spectrum Building, The Michael Young Centre, Purbeck Rd,
    CAMBRIDGE, CB2 2PD.   (hq)
    01223 415760
    email infp@mda.org.uk   http://www.mda.org.uk
    Dir: Nick Poole
▲ Company Limited by Guarantee
○ *T; to support education by promoting standards & best
    practice in museums
● Mtgs - ET - Res - Inf - Standards
M 671 i & f, 5 org
¶ Collections News - 4;   AR - 1; both free.

MDF - the Bipolar Organisation   (MDF)   2005

NR Castle Works, 21 St George's Rd, LONDON, SE1 6ES.   (hq)
    0845 634 0540   fax 020 7793 2639
    email mdf@mdf.org.uk   http://www.mdf.org.uk
▲ Company Limited by Guarantee; Registered Charity
○ *W; to support those with manic depression & their carers &
    friends; to encourage research into the illness; to educate the
    public & caring professions
M c 150 self-help groups
¶ Pendulum - 4; ftm.
    Group News.
    Factsheets & literature.
× 2005 Manic Depression Fellowship Ltd

Meat Industry Ireland

IRL Confederation House, 84-86 Lower Baggot St, DUBLIN 2,
     Republic of Ireland.
     Chief Exec: Cormac Healy
○ *T
< IBEC
    2004 Irish Meat Association

MeCCSA with AMPE   1999

■ c/o Prof Peter Golding, Dept of Social Sciences, Loughborough
    University, LOUGHBOROUGH, Leics, LE11 3TU.   (hsb)
    01509 223390
    email p.golding@lboro.ac.uk
    Hon Sec: Prof Peter Golding
○ *P
× 2006 (Association of Media Practice Educators
          (Media Communication & Cultural Studies Association

Mechanical Copyright Protection Society Ltd
a member of the **MCPS-PRS Alliance**

Mechanical & Metal Trades Confederation   (METCOM)   1989

NR Mirren Court (One), 119 Renfrew Rd, PAISLEY, Renfrewshire,
    PA3 4EA.   (hq)
    0141-847 1265
    email glasgow@metcom.org.uk
    http://www.metcom.org.uk
    Carlyle House, 235-237 Vauxhall Bridge Rd, London,
    SW1V 1EJ.
       020 7233 7011   fax 020 7828 0667
       email london@metcom.org.uk
    The McLaren Building, 35 Dale End, Birmingham, B5 4JP.
       0121-200 2100   fax 0121-200 1306
       email birmingham@metcom.org.uk
    Managing Dir: B Huxley (Birmingham),
       email bhuxley@metcom.org.uk
    Exec Dir: Keith Warren (London)
       email keith.warren@metcom.org.uk
▲ Company Limited by Guarantee
Br 2
○ *N; a federation of trade associations in the mechanical
    engineering & metal industries. Represents members on
    issues of common interest & on government & EEC policies
Gp Personnel services (incl industrial relations advisory service);
    Training (incl training needs analysis)
    London: Representational division (all subjects affecting
       members' interests)
    Birmingham: Contract services; Consultancy service for: Quality
       assurance; Energy; Management; Marketing; Business
       planning; Exporting
● Mtgs - ET - Exhib - Stat - Expt - Inf - Empl - LG
< ORGALIME (Brussels)
M 4,000 f, 34 org

Mechanical Organ Owners Society   (MOOS)   1976

NR 27 Silvergate, Blickling, NORWICH, Norfolk, NR11 6NN.
    (secs/p)
    01263 732776
    email info@moos.org.uk   http://www.moos.org.uk
    Sec: Robert Wichall
▲ Un-incorporated Society
○ *G; to promote an interest in all types of mechanical organs
    (fair, street & dance); to protect owners' interests regarding
    the playing & legislation of organ display vehicles
● Res - Exhib - Inf - VE - LG
< Kring van Draaiorgelvrienden (Dutch Organ Soc); Fair Organ
    Presvn Soc
M 250 i, UK / 30 i, 1 org (Nat Museum of Mechanical Musical
    Instruments (Netherlands)
¶ Vox Humana (Jnl) - 4; ftm. (subscription £12 (£15 o'seas)).

Medau Society   1952
■   8B Robson House, East St, EPSOM, Surrey, KT17 1HH.   (hq)
     01372 729056   fax 01372 729056
     email office@medau.org.uk   http://www.medau.org.uk
     Admin: Lynda Bridges
▲   Company Limited by Guarantee
○   *G, *S; to train & support Medau Movement teachers; (for
     women (devised by Hinrich Medau) using hoops, clubs &
     balls)
●   Mtgs - ET - SG - Inf
<   Sport England; Cent Coun of Physical Recreation (CCPR)
M   2,200 i, UK / 7 i, o'seas
¶   Medau News - 2;   AR; both ftm only.

Media Communication & Cultural Studies Association
     2006 merged with the Association of Media Practice Educators to
     form **MeCCSA with AMPE**

Media Research Group
NR   Rowan House, Gunville Rd, WINTERSLOW, Wilts, SP5 1PP.
     (admin/p)
     01980 862248
     http://www.mrg.org.uk
     Admin: Sally Hiddleston
○   *P; 'to recognise & promote importance of media research, its
     validity, directness & development'

Media Society Ltd   (MS)   1973
NR   Flat 1, 24 Park Rd, LONDON, NW1 4FH.   (hsp)
     020 7723 5059   fax 020 7723 6698
     Admin: Dorothy Josem
▲   Registered Charity
○   *P; for people working in the media & public life
●   Mtgs
<   Chart Inst of Journalists
M   300 i

Mediators Institute Ireland   1992
IRL   Montana House, Whitechurch, DUBLIN 16, Republic of Ireland.
     353 (1) 201 7526   fax 353 (1) 201 7526
     email 09>mediatorsinstiteireland.com
     Chmn: Polly Fillimore

mediawatch-uk   1965
■   3 Willow House, Kennington Rd, ASHFORD, Kent,
     TN24 0NR.   (hq)
     01233 633936   fax 01233 633836
     email info@mediawatchuk.org
     http://www.mediawatchuk.org
     Dir: John C Beyer
▲   Un-incorporated Society
Br   40; Australia
○   *K; 'to uphold good standards of programme content in TV &
     radio; to strengthen the law against obscenity in the media'
●   Conf - ET - Res - Inf - LG
M   8,000 i, 175,000 org, UK / 100 i, o'seas
¶   newsbrief - 3; 50p.

Medical Action for Global Security   (MEDACT)   1992
NR   The Grayston Centre, 28 Charles Sq, LONDON, N1 6HT.   (hq)
     020 7324 4739   fax 020 7324 4734
     email info@medact.org   http://www.medact.org
○   *K; for doctors & other health professionals committed to
     preventing war & promoting peace & global security
M   i
¶   Medicine & War (Jnl) - 4.   Communiqué - 3.

**Medical Artists Association of Great Britain & Northern Ireland
(MAA)   1949**
NR   Unit of Anatomy & Forensic Anthropology, Life Sciences Bldg,
     University of Dundee, Dow St, DUNDEE, DD1 5EH.   (hsb)
     01382 386324 & 348627
     Hon Sec: Caroline Wilkinson
○   *A; to promote & facilitate the acquisition & dissemination of
     knowledge of the graphic & plastic arts as applied to the
     illustration of medicine
M   c 80 i

Medical Council on Alcohol   1967
NR   3 St Andrew's Place, LONDON, NW1 4LB.   (hq)
     020 7487 4445   fax 020 7935 4479
     email mca@medicouncilalcol.demon.co.uk
     http://www.medicouncilalcol.demon.co.uk
     Exec Dir: Dr G E Ratcliffe
▲   Registered Charity
○   *L, *M, *P; to reduce alcohol related harm by educating the
     medical & associated professions about the effects of alcohol
     upon health; to assist in helping medical colleagues who
     have alcohol problems
Gp   C'ees: Education, Executive, Finance, Journal
●   Conf - Mtgs - ET - Comp - Lib - PL
<   Eur Soc Biological Res into Alcoholism
M   340 i, 60 f, UK / 10 i, o'seas
¶   Alcohol & Alcoholism (Jnl) - 6.
     Alcoholism (NL) - 6.
×   2001 (July) Medical Council on Alcoholism

Medical Defence Union   (MDU)   1885
NR   230 Blackfriars Rd, LONDON, SE1 8PJ.   (hq)
     020 7202 1500   fax 020 7202 1666
     http://www.the-mdu.com
     Chief Exec: Dr Michael Saunders
▲   Company Limited by Guarantee
○   *N; provision of medico-legal advice, assistance & indemnity to
     doctors, dentists, nurses & other healthcare professionals in
     the UK & Eire
●   Conf - ET - LG - Workshops - Presentations
M   c 90,000 i
¶   Jnl - irreg; ftm only.   AR; free.
     Training packages; m only.

Medical & Dental Defence Union of Scotland   (MDDUS)   1902
NR   Mackintosh House, 120 Blythswood St, GLASGOW, G2 4EA.
     (hq)
     0141-221 5858   fax 0141-228 1208
     email info@mddus.com   http://www.mddus.com
     Chief Exec: Prof Gordon Dickson
▲   Company Limited by Guarantee
○   *M; professional indemnity for doctors & dentists
Gp   Risk management; Education for primary care staff
●   Conf - ET - Inf - LG
<   Physician Insurers Assn of America (PIAA)
M   22,000 i
¶   Summons (Jnl) - 4;   AR; both free.

Medical Equestrian Association   (MEA)   1984
■   c/o Dr J M Salusbury-Trelawny, Ravenscroft Hall, King St, Byley,
     MIDDLEWICH, Cheshire, CW10 9LE.   (hsp)
     01606 835480
     email honsec@medequestrian.co.uk
     http://www.medequestrian.co.uk
     Hon Sec: Dr Joanna M S Trelawny
▲   Registered Charity
Br   links with similar gps in Eire, Australia, New Zealand, Sweden,
     USA
○   *K, *M; to maintain & improve medical cover at equestrian
     events - Pony Club, riding clubs, British eventing, carriage
     driving, flat & jump racing
●   Mtgs - ET - VE
M   150 i, UK / 50 i, o'seas

Medical Ethics Alliance   (MAEA)   1999
◼ PO Box 11582, Edgbaston, BIRMINGHAM, B16 9XE.
  (mail/address)
  01905 352967   fax 01905 352967
  email worcestercoles@aol.com
  http://www.medethics-alliance.org
  Hon Sec: Dr F Leahy
▲ Registered Charity
○ *K, *P; to promote discussion on medical ethics within & without
  the medical profession
● Conf - Mtgs - Exhib - SG - Inf - LG
< affiliated to all organisations listed as members
M 60 i, 3,000 f via 6 org:
  Guild of Catholic Doctors
  First Do No Harm
  HOPE (Healthcare Opposed to Euthanasia)
  Muslim Doctors & Dentists Association
  Nurses Opposed to Euthanasia
  World Federation of Doctors
¶ Ethics & Wisdom in Medicine - 3; [online Jnl].
  Conferences papers - 2; prices vary.

Medical Journalists' Association   (MJA)   1967
◼ Fairfield, Cross in Hand, HEATHFIELD, E Sussex, TN21 0SH.
  (hsp)
  01435 868786   fax 01435 865714
  email pigache@tiscali.co.uk   http://www.mja-uk.org
  Hon Sec: Philippa Pigache
▲ Un-incorporated Society
○ *M, *P; to improve the quality of medical journalism &
  understanding between medical healthcare professionals, the
  media & the public
● Mtgs - ET - Awards
M 390 i, UK / 2 i, o'seas
¶ MJA News (NL) - 5; ftm only.
  Directory of Members with contacts - 1; ftm,
      £450 (commercial), £200 (charities & academics).

Medical Officers of Schools Association   (MOSA)   1884
◼ Amherst Medical Practice, 21 St Botolph's Rd, SEVENOAKS,
  Kent, TN13 3AQ.   (hsb)
  01732 459255   fax 01732 450751
  email honsec@mosa.org.uk   http://www.mosa.org.uk
  Hon Sec: Dr Neil Arnott
▲ Un-incorporated Society
○ *L, *P; promotion of school health
● Conf - Mtgs - ET - Inf - Empl
< Eur U of School & University Health & Medicine
M c 400 i
¶ NL - 4; free.
  Handbook of School Health - 5-6 yrly.

Medical Protection Society Ltd   (MPS)   1892
NR Granary Wharf House, LEEDS, W Yorks, LS11 5PY.   (hq)
  0113-243 6436   fax 0113-241 0500
  http://www.medicalprotection.org
▲ Company Limited by Guarantee
○ *P; a not-for-profit mutual association run exclusively for, &
  largely by, doctors, dentists & other healthcare professionals
● ET - Inf - Wide range of medico-legal services (professional
  indemnity for adverse awards of costs & damages in medical
  negligence cases)
< Physician Insurers Assn of America
M 100,000 i UK / 125,000 i, o'seas
¶ Casebook (Jnl) - 2;   Medico-legal booklets;   AR; all free.

Medical Research Society   (MRS)
NR Renal Medicine (Box 118) Dialysis Centre, Addenbrooke's
  Hospital, Hills Rd, CAMBRIDGE, CB2 2QQ.   (hsb)
  01223 217828   fax 01223 586506
  http://www.medres.org
  Academic Sec: Dr Afzal Chaudhry
▲ Registered Charity
○ *L; exchange of information on medical research
Gp Association of Young Medical Scientists (AYMS)
● Conf - Mtgs - ET - Comp - LG
< Biological Coun
M 350 i
¶ Clinical Science - 12; ftm, £90 yr nm.

Medical Sciences Historical Society   (MSHS)   1982
◼ 117 Woodland Drive, Cassiobury, WATFORD, Herts,
  WD17 3DA.   (hsp)
  01923 231704
  Hon Sec: Hilda Taylor
▲ Registered Charity
○ *L; to further education in the history of diagnostic medical
  sciences; to provide a forum for everyone with an interest in
  the history of the medical laboratory
● Mtgs
< Brit Soc History Medicine
M 80 i, UK / 4 i, o'seas
¶ Medical Science History - 1.   NL - 2.

Medical Society of London   1773
◼ Lettsom House, 11 Chandos St, LONDON, W1G 9EB.   (hq)
  020 7580 1043
  Registrar: Col Richard Kinsella-Bevan
○ *L; the advancement of medicine & surgery
● Mtgs - Inf
M i
¶ Transactions - 1.

Medical Society for the Study of Venereal Diseases
  2003 merged with the Association for Genito-Urinary Medicine to
  form the **British Association for Sexual Health & HIV**

Medical Women's Federation   (MWF)   1917
NR Tavistock House North, Tavistock Sq, LONDON, WC1H 9HX.
  (hq)
  020 7387 7765   fax 020 7388 9216
  email mwf@btconnect.com
  Pres: Dr Melanie Davies
○ *P; to further the careers of women doctors
M i
¶ Medical Woman.   AR; both ftm.

Medico-Legal Society   1901
NR c/o Hempson's Solicitors, 40 Villiers St, LONDON, WC2N 6NJ.
  020 7839 0278
▲ Registered Charity
○ *L; the dissemination of medico-legal knowledge in all its
  aspects

Medieval Dress & Textile Society   (MEDATS)
NR c/o Senior Curator of Armour, Royal Armouries, Armouries
  Drive, LEEDS, LS10 1LT.   (sec)
  0113-220 1852   http://www.medats.org.uk
  Sec: Karen Watts
○ *L
● Mtgs
M 200 i
¶ NL - 3.

Medieval Settlement Research Group (MSRG) 1986

■ School of Archaeology & Ancient History, University of Leicester,
University Rd, LEICESTER, LE1 7RH. (hsb)
0116-252 2617   fax 0116-252 5005
email njc10@le.ac.uk
Hon Sec: Dr Neil Christie
▲ Registered Charity
○ *L; to advance knowledge of settlements, especially those
dating between the 5th & 16th centuries; to offer advice &
information to those conducting research into settlement
history; to influence national policy on the survey,
conservation & excavation of medieval settlement sites; to
encourage the preservation of settlement sites wherever
possible.
● Conf - Mtgs - Res - Inf - VE - LG - Seminars - Sponsorship of
original research
M 430 i, 55 org
¶ AR; ftm, £5 nm.

Meet-a-Mum Association (MAMA) 1979

NR 54 Lillington Rd, RADSTOCK, BA3 3NR. (hq)
0845 120 6162
http://www.mama.co.uk
▲ Registered Charity
Br 68
○ *W; to support mums & mums-to-be feeling isolated or
suffering with post-natal depression by putting them in touch
with others; offers support through the national helpline
020 8768 0123 (Mon-Fri 0700-2200)
● Mtgs - ET - Exhib - SG - Inf - LG
< Telephone Helplines Assn
M 3,000 i
¶ Behind the Painted Smile: an insight into postnatal depression.
Lifting the Veil of Silence on Emotional Problems after
Childbirth.
Publications list available.

Meetings Industry Association (MIA) 1991

■ PO Box 515, KELMARSH, Northants, NN6 9XW. (hq)
0845 230 5508   fax 0845 230 7708
email info@mia-uk.org   http://www.mia-uk.org
Chief Exec: Jane Evans
▲ Company Limited by Guarantee
○ *P, *T; meetings & conference industry
● Conf - Mtgs - ET - Res - Exhib
M 450 f
¶ NL - 12;   Magazine - 4; both free.
UK Conference Market Survey - 1; £135 m, £165 nm.
Buyers' Directory of Members - 1; free.   AR - 1; ftm only.

Megalithic Society (incorporating the Stonehenge Society) 1997

NR Whitehill Villa, 25A Whitehill, BRADFORD-ON-AVON, Wilts,
BA15 1SQ. (hq)
01225 862482
email terence.meaden@stonehenge-avebury.net
http://www.stonehenge-avebury.net
Chief Exec: Terence Meaden
▲ Un-incorporated Society
Br 2
○ *G, *K; to promote interest in & the preservation & security of
the ancient stones of Britain; is also concerned with crop
circles
Gp Avebury; Stonehenge
● Mtgs - ET - Res - Inf - PL - VE
< Stonehenge Soc
M 50 i
¶ The Complete Guidebook to Avebury; £8 m, £10 nm.

Melton Mowbray Pork Pie Association

■ PO Box 5540, MELTON MOWBRAY, Leics, LE13 1YU.
01664 569388
Chmn: Matthew O'Callaghan
○ *T; makers of Melton Mowbray pork pies
M 7 f

Men of the Stones (MOS) 1947

NR Beechcroft, Weston-under-Lizard, SHIFNAL, Shropshire,
TF11 8JT. (chmn/p)
01952 850269
http://www.menofthestones.org.uk
Chmn: Michael Tebbutt
▲ Registered Charity
○ *K; a society advocating the use of stone & other natural &
local building materials; to encourage craftsmanship &
preservation of the good architectural qualities of Stamford &
other places in the limestone belt
Gp Stone roof slating; Training (incl conservation architects)
● Mtgs - VE
< Soc Protection Ancient Bldgs; Georgian Gp; Ancient
Monuments Soc; Civic Trust
M c 475 i & f
¶ Ybk (incl LM, lists of work done, aims & rules); ftm.

MENCAP: Royal Society for Mentally Handicapped Children & Adults (MENCAP) 1946

NR 123 Golden Lane, LONDON, EC1Y 0RT. (hq)
020 7454 0454   fax 020 7696 5540
email information@mencap.org.uk
http://www.mencap.org.uk
Chief Exec: Jo Williams
▲ Registered Charity
○ *W; 'is the leading charity working with children & adults with
learning disabilities in England, Wales & Northern Ireland; it
campaigns to ensure that persons with such a disability live
the fullest life possible; it undertakes research into issues
affecting people with a learning disability
Gp Services: Support & Advice through family adviser service;
Housing advice; Residential; Employment via pathway
employment service; Holiday advice; Leisure; Education at
Mencap's 3 FE colleges; Bookshop
Divn: National Federation of Gateway Clubs
● Conf - Mtgs - ET - Res - Exhib - Inf - LG
< Intl League of Socs for Persons with Mental Handicaps
M 14,500 i, c 1,000 affiliated gps
¶ Publications list available.
✕ 2005 English Sports Association for People with Learning
Disabilities (merged)

Ménière's Society 1984

■ The Rookery, Surrey Hills Business Park, Wotton, DORKING,
Surrey, RH5 6QT. (hq)
01306 876883   fax 01306 876057
email info@menieres.org.uk
http://www.menieres.org.uk
Dir: Mrs Natasha Harrington-Benton
▲ Registered Charity
○ *W; to help those with the symptoms of Ménière's disease:
vertigo (nausea), fluctuating & increasing deafness & tinnitus
● Conf - Mtgs - Res - Stat - Inf
Helpline: 0845 120 2975
M 5,400 i, 139 org, UK / 53 i, 10 org, o'seas
¶ NL - 4;   Contact List - 4;   Information sheets;
AR; all ftm only.

Meningitis Association of Scotland 1991

NR Flat 21, 7 Craigielea St, GLASGOW, G31 2TJ.
0141-554 6680
Chmn: Mrs E E McKiernan

© CBD Research Ltd · Beckenham · BR3 5JS · Tel 020 8650 7745 · Fax 020 8650 0768 · E-mail cbd@cbdresearch.com · www.cbdresearch.com

Meningitis Research Foundation   1989
■   Midland Way, Thornbury, BRISTOL, BS35 2BS.   (hq)
      01454 281811   fax 01454 281094
      email info@meningitis.org   http://www.meningitis.org
      Chief Exec: Denise Vaughan
▲   Registered Charity
Br 3; Republic of Ireland
○   *M, *Q; to promote research into the causes & treatment of all
      forms of meningitis & associated infections, & the
      dissemination of knowledge gained by such research; to
      advance the education of the public in the causes, treatment
      & prevention of meningitis & associated infections; to help
      relieve distress to individuals & families caused by death &
      damage through meningitis & associated infections
●   Conf - ET - Res - Exhib - Inf - PL - LG
<   Assn of Med Res Charities (AMRC); Telephone Helplines
      Assn (THA)
M   5,500 i, UK / 100 i, o'seas
¶   Microscope (NL) - 4;   AR - 1; both free.
      Awareness Literature:
         Baby Watch; Tot Watch; Get it Sussed;
         Race against Time; Symptoms
      Materials for health professionals to help in the diagnosis &
      treatment of meningitis & septicaemia.

Mental After Care Association
      since July 2005 **Together: working for wellbeing**

Mental Health Ireland
IRL 6 Adelaide St, DÚN LAOGHAIRE, Co Dublin, Republic of
      Ireland.
      353 (1) 284 1166   fax 353 (1) 284 1736
      email info@mentalhealthireland.ie
      http://www.mentalhealthireland.ie
      Hon Sec: Brian Glanville
○   *W

Mental Health Nurses Association   (MHNA)   1975
■   Cals Meyn, Grove Lane, Hinton, CHIPPENHAM, Wilts,
      SN14 8HF.   (hq)
      0786 070 2303
      email brian.rogers@amicustheunion.org
      http://www.amicus-mhna.org
      Profl Officer: Brian Rogers
○   *P, *U; representing the professional & labour relations needs of
      community mental health nurses
●   Conf - Mtgs - ET - Res - Inf - Lib - Empl - LG
<   AMICUS; Jt C'ee of Profl Nursing, Midwifery & Health Visiting
      Assns (England, Wales & N Ireland branches)
M   2,000 i
¶   Mental Health Nursing - 6; ftm, £63 yr nm.   Hbk; ftm.
×   2003 (April) Community Psychiatric Nurses' Association

**Merchant Navy Locomotive Preservation Society Ltd
(MNLPS)   1965**
NR 12 Inglewood Ave, Heatherside, CAMBERLEY, Surrey,
      GU15 1RJ.   (hsp)
      01276 514000
      Sec: R F Abercrombie
▲   Registered Charity
○   *G, *K; to preserve, maintain, operate & foster an interest in the
      ex-British Railways Southern Region 'Merchant Navy' Class
      locomotive no. 35028 'Clan Line'
●   Mtgs - ET - Exhib - Comp - Maintenance of the locomotive -
      Special excursion runs
M   i
¶   Southern Express (Jnl).

Mercia Cinema Society   1980
NR 29 Blackbrook Court, LOUGHBOROUGH, Leics, LE11 5UA.
      (Admin/p)
      01509 218393
      email Mervyn.Gould@virgin.net
      http://www.merciacinema.org.uk
      Administrator: Mervyn Gould
▲   Registered Charity
○   *G; for the promotion & publication of research into cinema
      history
●   Conf - Res - Inf - Lib - Publishing
M   c 180 i
¶   The Mercia Bioscope - 4; ftm.
      Various books on cinemas of specific areas.

Merioneth Agricultural Society   (MAS)   1868
■   Tir y Dail, Cader Rd, DOLGELLAU, Gwynedd, LL40 1SG.   (hsp)
      01341 422837   fax 01341 422837
      email sioesir@aol.com   http://www.sioesir.org.uk
      Hon Sec: E Douglas Powell
▲   Registered Charity
○   *F; promotion of agriculture by staging an annual county show
●   Exhib - Comp - Merioneth County Show
M   400 i
¶   Show catalogue - 1; £2.

Merseyside Industrial Heritage Society   (MIHS)   1970
NR c/o Merseyside Maritime Museum, Albert Dock, LIVERPOOL,
      L3 4AQ.
▲   Un-incorporated Society
○   *K, *L; to foster an interest in the study & conservation of the
      industrial heritage of Merseyside
M   i & org

Merton Chamber of Commerce   1992
■   Tuition House (5th floor), 27-37 St George's Rd, LONDON,
      SW19 4EU.
      020 8944 5501   fax 020 8286 2552
      email info@mertonchamber.co.uk
      http://www.mertonchamber.co.uk
      Chief Exec: Diana Sterck
▲   Company Limited by Guarantee
○   *C
●   Mtgs - ET - Exhib - Inf - LG - Business support services
M   350 f
¶   NL - 4; free.   LM - 1; ftm, £5 nm.

**Metal Cladding & Roofing Manufacturers Association Ltd
(MCRMA)**
NR 18 Mere Farm Rd, Prenton, WIRRAL, Cheshire, CH43 9TT.
      0151-652 3846   fax 0151-653 4080
      email mcrma@compuserve.com
      http://www.mcrma.co.uk
      Dir: Clifford E Dyer
○   *P

Metal Finishing Association
      is a group of the **Surface Engineering Association**

Metal Gutter Manufacturers Association Ltd   (MGMA)
NR 18 Mere Farm Rd, Prenton, WIRRAL, Cheshire, CH43 9TT.
      0151-652 3846   fax 0151-653 4080
      http://www.mgma.co.uk
      Sec: Clifford E Dyer
○   *T

Metal Packaging Manufacturers Association   (MPMA)   1914
- ■ Soane Point, 6-8 Market Place, READING, Berks, RG1 2EG. (hq)
     0118 925 5520   fax 0118 925 5888
     email enquiries@mpma.org.uk
     http://www.mpma.org.uk
     Dir: A R Woods
- ▲ Company Limited by Guarantee
- ○ *T; interests of companies involved directly, or indirectly, in the production of light metal containers, closures & components
- Gp Business c'ees: Open top, Closures, General line, Technical, Food contact
     Service/advisory c'ees: Environment, Health & safety, Public relations
- ● Mtgs - Exhib - Stat - Inf
- < Secrétariat Eur des Fabricants d'Emballages Métalliques Légers (SEFEL)
- M 23 f (full), 19 f (associate)

Metalforming Machinery Makers Association Ltd   (MMMA)
- ■ McLaren Building, 35 Dale End, BIRMINGHAM, B4 7LN.   (hq)
     0121-200 2100   fax 0121-200 1306
     email enquiries@mmma.org.uk
     http://www.mmma.org.uk
     Sec: David Brotherton
- ▲ Company Limited by Guarantee
- ○ *T
- ● Exhib - Expt - Inf - LG
- < a METCOM organisation
- M 34 f
- ¶ Hbk.

Metalworking Fluid Product Stewardship Group
    a group of the **UK Lubricants Association Ltd**

Metamorphic Association   1979
- NR PO Box 32368, LONDON, SW17 8YB.   (hq)
     0870 770 7984 (recorded information only)
     email metamorphicassoc@cs.com
     http://www.metamorphicassociation.org.uk
     Dir: Gaston Saint-Pierre
- ▲ Registered Charity
- ○ *P; to promote awareness, understanding & use of the metamorphic technique - a unique & simple approach to self-healing & personal development
- ● Conf - Mtgs - ET - Exhib - Inf
- M c 350 i
- ¶ NL - 4;   Bulletin - 4; both ftm only.
     Programme of Activities - 2; ftm, on request for sae.

Metaphysical Research Group
    the business group of the **Society of Metaphysicians**

Metropolitan Drinking Fountain & Cattle Trough Association 1859
- ■ Oaklands, 5 Queenborough Gardens, CHISLEHURST, Kent, BR7 6NP.   (hsp)
     020 8467 1261
     email dfa@tesco.net
     Sec: Ralph P Baber
- ▲ Registered Charity
- ○ *G; to promote the provision of drinking water for people & animals in the UK & overseas; to keep an archive of materials, artifacts, drinking fountains, cattle troughs & other installations
- M 25 i
     Note: Also known as the Drinking Fountain Association.

Metropolitan Public Gardens Association   (MPGA)   1882
- NR 348 London Rd, MITCHAM, Surrey, CR4 3ND.   (sp)
     020 8648 9469
     Sec: Mrs J K Bellamy
- ▲ Registered Charity
- ○ *G; the protection, preservation & acquiring for permanent preservation for public use of gardens, disused burial grounds, churchyards, open spaces, areas of land adjoining roads & footpaths, or any land situated within the Metropolitan Police District; the encouragement of window boxes, provision of seats & the planting of trees
- ● AGM - Res - Exhib - Comp (via London in Bloom) - SG - LG
- < London in Bloom
- M 100 i
- ¶ Ybk (AR) - 1; free.

Meuse Rhine Issel Cattle Society of the United Kingdom (MRI)   1971
- NR Castlemoor Farm, Four Oaks, NEWENT, Glos, GL18 1LU. (sp/b)
     01531 890730   fax 01531 890939
     email office@mri.org.uk   http://www.mri.org.uk
     Sec: Mrs Niki Ford
- ▲ Registered Charity
- Br N Zealand
- ○ *B, *F
- ● Conf - Mtgs - Exhib - Stat - Expt - Inf - Semen sales
- < R Assn Brit Dairy Farmers; Nat Cattle Assn (Dairy)
- M 72 i, UK / 3 i, o'seas
- ¶ MRI NL - 3;   Herdbook - 1; £10; both m only.

Meyrick Society   1890
- ■ 38 Downs Hill, BECKENHAM, Kent, BR3 5HB.   (hsp)
     020 8650 4527   fax 020 7930 2223
     email robin@peterdaleltd.com
     Hon Sec: Robin Dale
- ○ *G, *L; promotion of the study of antiques, arms & armour
- ● Mtgs
- M 25 i

Micro & Anophthalmic Children's Society   (MACS)   1993
- NR 22 Lower Park St, HOLYHEAD, Anglesey, LL65 1DU.   (hsp)
     0870 600 6227
     email enquiries@macs.org.uk   http://www.macs.org.uk
     Sec: Lynda Rhodes
- ▲ Registered Charity
- ○ *W; a support group for children born with anophthalmia (absence of eyes), microphthalmia (small eyes) & coloboma (a structural defect of the eyes)
- ● Conf - Mtgs
- < Contact a Family
- M 300 i, UK / 120 i, o'seas
- ¶ NL - 3;   AR; both free.

Microtome Manufacturers Association   (MMA)   1976
- ■ 10 Montcalm Close, Hayes, BROMLEY, Kent, BR2 7LZ.   (hsp)
- ▲ Un-incorporated Society
- ○ *T
- ● Mtgs - Stat
- M 34 f
- ¶ Notes - 2/3;   Report - 1.

© CBD Research Ltd · Beckenham · BR3 5JS · Tel 020 8650 7745 · Fax 020 8650 0768 · E-mail cbd@cbdresearch.com · www.cbdresearch.com

Microwave Technologies Association   (MTA)   1978
- ■ Norfolk Glen, Love Lane, IVER, Bucks, SL0 9QZ.   (hq)
  01753 652939   fax 01753 652939
  email jennipher@microwaveassociation.org.uk
  http://www.microwaveassociation.org.uk
  Chmn: Jennipher Marshall-Jenkinson
- ▲ Un-incorporated Society
- ○ *T; to promote & advise on all aspects of microwave & microwave related products to trade, hotels, caterers & consumers
- Gp Individual membership; Corporate membership
- ● Mtgs - ET - Exhib - Inf
- < Food Standards Authority
- M 50 i, 20 f
- ¶ NL - 6; ftm only.
- × 2001 (July) Microwave Association

Mid Essex Chamber of Commerce (Westcliff-on-Sea)
  a branch office of **Essex Chambers of Commerce**

Mid Yorkshire Chamber of Commerce & Industry Ltd   (MYCCI) 1853
- ■ Commerce House, Wakefield Rd, Aspley, HUDDERSFIELD, W Yorks, HD5 9AA.   (hq)
  01484 438800   fax 01484 514199
  http://www.mycci.co.uk
  Chief Exec: Eddie Rogers
- ▲ Company Limited by Guarantee
- Br Bulgaria
- ○ *C
- Gp Child nurseries; Consultancy; Corporate events; Enterprise agency; International trade; Policy & representation; Publishing; Training
- ● Conf - Mtgs - ET - Res - Exhib - SG - Stat - Expt - Inf - LG - Payroll bureau - Trade missions - Trade documentation
- < Eurochambres
- M 1,800 f
- ¶ Close-Up - 12; free.

Middle East Association   (MEA)   1961
- ■ 33 Bury St, St James's, LONDON, SW1Y 6AX.   (hq)
  020 7839 2137   fax 020 7839 6121
  email mail@the-mea.co.uk   http://www.the-mea.co.uk
  Sec: Graham Green
- ▲ Company Limited by Guarantee
- ○ *T; to promote trade & investment between the UK & the Middle East (all Arab states, Iran, Turkey, Afghanistan, Ethiopia & Eritrea) on behalf of its members
- Gp Law sub group
- ● Conf - Mtgs - Exhib - Stat - Expt - Inf - Lib - VE - LG
- M c 70 i, 350 f
- ¶ Information Digest - 24;   Hbk - 1;   AR; free. Information sheets.

Midlands Association of Chefs
  2005 merged with Chefs & Cooks Circle to form the **British Culinary Federation**

Midlands Asthma & Allergy Research Association   (MAARA) 1968
- ■ Kingsway House, Kingsway, DERBY, DE22 3HL.   (hq)
  01332 362461   fax 01332 362462
  email enquiries@maara.org   http://www.maara.org
  Hon Sec: Jeremy M Barlow
- ▲ Registered Charity
- ○ *Q; to research into asthma & allergy
- Gp Aerobiology research
- ● Mtgs - Res
- < Intl Assn of Aerobiology; Brit Aerobiology Fedn
- M 300 i
- ¶ [see website]

Midlands Club Cricket Conference   (MCCC)   1947
- ■ 4 Silverdale Gardens, Wordsley, STOURBRIDGE, W Midlands, DY8 5NU.   (hsp)
  01384 278107   fax 01384 835687
  email davidr.thomas@blueyonder.co.uk
  http://www.mccc.co.uk
  Hon Sec: David R Thomas
- ▲ Un-incorporated Society
- ○ *S; to foster & maintain club cricket in the Midlands
- Gp Fixture bureau; Tours bureau; Club insurance; Competitions for various age groups
- ● Comp - Inf
- < England & Wales Cricket Bd
- M c 500 clubs and leagues
- ¶ NL - 3;   Ybk - 1

Migraine Action Association   1958
- NR Unit 6 Oakley Hay Lodge Business Park, Great Folds Rd, GREAT OAKLEY, Northants, NN18 9AS.   (hq)
  01536 461333   fax 01536 461444
  email info@migraine.org.uk
  http://www.migraine.org.uk
  Dir: Mrs Ann Turner
- ▲ Registered Charity
- ○ *Q; promotion of research into causes & cure of migraine; information & assistance to sufferers
- ● Conf - Res - Inf - Migraine Action Week (September)
- M c 36,000 i
- ¶ NL - 4.   Various booklets & leaflets.

Milestone Society   2001
- ■ The Oxleys, Tenbury Road, Clows Top, KIDDERMINSTER, Worcs, DY14 9HE.   (hsp)
  01299 832358   fax 01299 832162
  email terry-keegan@supanet.com
  http://www.milestone-society.co.uk
  Sec: Terry E Keegan
- ▲ Registered Charity
- ○ *G; to identify, record, research, conserve & interpret for public benefit the milestones & other waymarkers of the British Isles
- ● Conf - Mtgs - Res - Inf - PL
- M 400 i, UK / 4 i, o'seas
- ¶ Milestones & Waymakers; ftm, £3.50 nm. NL - 2; ftm only.

Military Heraldry Society (The Cloth Insignia Research & Collectors Society)   (M Her S)   1951
- ■ Windyridge, 27 Sandbrook, Ketley, TELFORD, Shropshire, TF1 5BB.   (publicityofficer)
  01952 270221
  email billbowbagins@hotmail.com
  Contact: The Publicity Officer
- ▲ Un-incorporated Society
- ○ *G; collectors of cloth formation signs (shoulder sleeve insignia, shoulder titles, regimental & unit flashes & similar items)
- ● Mtgs - Res - Inf - Lib
- M 250 i, UK / 140 i, o'seas
- ¶ The Formation Sign - 4; free.

Military Historical Society   (MHS)   1948
- NR c/o National Army Museum, Royal Hospital Rd, LONDON, SW3 4HT.
  020 7730 0717
  99 Douglas Rd SURBITON, Surrey, KT6 7SD.   (mem/sec).
  Mem Sec: W J Herbert
- Br 4
- ○ *G; to promote the collection of objects of military historical interest
- ● Mtgs - ET - Res - Exhib - VE
- M 800 i, 50 org, UK / 300 i, 25 org, o'seas
- ¶ Bulletin - 3; ftm, £2.50 each nm. Special publication - 1; ftm, £5-£15 nm.

Military Vehicle Trust   (MVT)   1970
- ◼ Meadowhead Cottage, Beaumaris Ave, BLACKBURN, Lancs, BB2 4TP.   (hsp)
   01254 202253
   http://www.mvt.org.uk
   Gen Sec: Simon P Bromley
- ▲ Company Limited by Guarantee; Registered Charity
- Br 43
- ○ *G; preservation & restoration of military vehicles
- ● Mtgs - Exhib - Inf - Lib - PL - VE - LG - Shows - Film hire
- < Danish Soc Military Vehicle Presvn (FMKB), Belgian Military Vehicle Trust, MOVT, Swiss Club Romand, VHSP
- M 5,6761 i, UK / 609 i, o'seas
- ¶ Windscreen - 4; ftm, £3.50 nm.
   Greensheet (NL) - 6; ftm only.

Milking Machine Manufacturers' Association   (MMMA)   1941
- ◼ Samuelson House, Paxton Rd, Orton Centre, PETERBOROUGH, Cambs, PE2 5LT.   (hq)
   01733 362925   fax 01733 370664
   email dg@aea.uk.com
   Sec: Jake Vowles
- ▲ Company Limited by Guarantee
- ○ *T; representing manufacturers of equipment used by the dairy farming industry
- M 5 f

Milton Keynes & North Buckinghamshire Chamber of Commerce   1994
- NR 599 Avebury Boulevard, CENTRAL MILTON KEYNES, Bucks, MK9 3HR.   (hq)
   01908 259000   fax 01908 246799
   Managing Dir: Sean Hickey
- ○ *C
- ● ET - Inf
- < Brit Chams Comm; TEC Nat Coun
- M 1,500 f
- ¶ Opportunity (Jnl) - 6.   AR - 1; both free.

Mind (the Mental Health Charity)   (MIND)   1946
- NR Granta House, 15-19 Broadway, LONDON, E15 4BQ.   (hq)
   020 8519 2122   fax 020 8522 1725
   email contact@mind.org.uk   http://www.mind.org.uk
   Contact: The Chief Exec
- ▲ Registered Charity
- ○ *W; works for everyone with experience of mental distress
- ● Conf - ET - Res - Exhib - Inf - Lib - LG - Advice service & legal network
   MINDinfoline: 020 8522 1728   (Outer London 0845 766 0163)
- < Wld Fedn for Mental Health
- M c 1,200 i
- ¶ Publications list available.

Mineral Industry Research Organisation   (MIRO)   1974
- NR Atlas House (3rd floor), 31 King St, LEEDS, W Yorks, LS1 2HL. (hq)
   0113-245 8006   fax 0133-245 7451
   email mail@mito.co.uk
   Contact: The Director
- ▲ Company Limited by Guarantee
- ○ *Q; technology brokerage that identifies, promotes & manages innovative technology research projects on exploration, mining, extraction & processing of primary & secondary raw materials, wherever possible by obtaining co-funding from European, national or regional agencies
- Gp Research executive committee & sub-panels
- ● Conf - Mtgs - Res - Inf - LG
- < Assn Indep Res & Technology Orgs
- M 45 f
- ¶ Miro News - 6;   AR; both ftm.   Publications list available.

Mineralogical Society of Great Britain & Ireland   (MINSOC) 1876
- ◼ 41 Queen's Gate, LONDON, SW7 5HR.   (hq)
   020 7584 7516   fax 020 7823 8021
   email info@minersoc.org   http://www.minersoc.org
   Gen Sec: Dr Mark Hodson
- ▲ Registered Charity
- ○ *L; advancing the knowledge of the science of mineralogy & its application to other subjects including crystallography, geochemistry, petrology, environmental science & economic geology
- Gp Clay minerals; Geochemistry; Applied mineralogy; Metamorphic studies; Mineral physics; Volcanic & magmatic studies
- ● Conf - Mtgs - ET - SG - Exhib - Inf - Lib - VE - LG
- < Intl Mineralogical Assn; Eur Mineralogical U; Foundation for Science & Technology; Geological Soc; R Society
- M c 900 i
- ¶ Publications list available on request.

Minerals Engineering Society   (MES)   1958
- ◼ 2 Ryton Close, Blyth, WORKSOP, Notts, S81 8DN.   (hsp)
   01909 591940
   email hon.sec.mes@lineone
   http://www.mineralsengineering.org
   Hon Sec: A W Howells
- ▲ Company Limited by Guarantee; Registered Charity
- Br 7
- ○ *L, *P; minerals processing, extractive metallurgy, coal preparation
- ● Conf - Mtgs
- M c 600 i
- ¶ MQR - 10; ftm.

Miners' & Industrial Lamp Manufacturers' Association (MILMA)   1934
- ◼ c/o Wolf Safety Lamp Co, Saxon Road Works, 62-92 Saxon Rd, SHEFFIELD, S Yorks, S8 0YA.   (sec/b)
   0114-255 1051   fax 0114-255 7988
   Sec: John N M Jackson
- ▲ Un-incorporated Society
- ○ *T; manufacturers of mining & industrial portable lamps - including safety lamps
- ● Mtgs - Expt - LG - Participation in British, European & International Standards Committees
- M 6 f

Miniature Armoured Fighting Vehicles Association   (MAFVA) 1965
- ◼ 45 Balmoral Drive, HOLMES CHAPEL, Cheshire, CW4 7JQ. (hsp)
   01477 535373   fax 01477 535892
   email mafvahq@aol.com   http://www.mafva.org.uk
   Pres & Sec: G E Gary Williams
- ▲ Un-incorporated Society
- Br 52; 59 o'seas
- ○ *G; for makers & collectors of model AFVs & other military vehicles & equipment
- ● Mtgs - Res - Exhib - Comp - Stat - Inf - VE
- M 4,060 i, f & org, UK / 2,600 i, f & org, o'seas
- ¶ Tankette - 6.
   NL (county groups) - 7; ftm only.

© CBD Research Ltd · Beckenham · BR3 5JS · Tel 020 8650 7745 · Fax 020 8650 0768 · E-mail cbd@cbdresearch.com · www.cbdresearch.com

Miniature Mediterranean Donkey Association   (MMDA)   1996
- ■ Fox Hollow, Blacklands Lane, Sudbourne, WOODBRIDGE, Suffolk, IP12 2AX.   (hsp)
  01394 450615
  http://www.miniature-donkey-assoc.com
  Sec: Jill Allen-Melvin
- ▲ Company Limited by Guarantee
- ○ *B; care, welfare, education & promotion of the breed
- Gp Register & stud book of the UK
- ● ET - Stat - Expt - Inf - Lib - LG
- < Nat Miniature Donkey Assn (USA)
- M 150 i, UK / 4 i, o'seas
- ¶ Little People (NL) - 6; ftm only.

Mining Association of the United Kingdom   (MAUK)   1946
- ■ 78 Copt Heath Drive, Knole, SOLIHULL, B93 9PV.   (hq)
  01564 205079   fax 01564 205078
  email mauk@mauk.org.uk
  Sec: Robert (Bob) A Fenton
- ▲ Company Limited by Guarantee
- ○ *T; to promote & foster the industry of mining metals & minerals worldwide
- ● General representation & coordinated action on matters such as European interests, health & safety & government policy
- < Euromines (Brussels); Eurométaux (Brussels); CBI Minerals C'ee
- M 3 i, 15 f, 1 org
- ¶ LM - 1.   AR; free.

Minor Counties Cricket Association   (MCCA)   1895
- ■ Blueberry Haven, 20 Boucher Rd, BUDLEIGH SALTERTON, Devon, EX9 6JF.   (sp)
  01395 445216   fax 01395 445216
  email geoffe1@btinternet.com
  Sec: G R Evans
- ▲ Un-incorporated Society
- ○ *S
- ● Cricket matches
- < England & Wales Cricket Bd
- M 280 i, 20 county cricket clubs
- ¶ Minor Counties Cricket Annual - 1; ftm, £8 nm.

Minor Metals Trade Association   1973
- ■ Tamesis House, 35 St Philips Avenue, WORCESTER PARK, Surrey, KT4 8JS.   (asa)
  020 8330 7456   fax 020 8330 7447
  email secretariat@mmta.co.uk
  Sec: N Barry Jaynes
- ▲ Company Limited by Guarantee
- ○ *T; regulation of trading relationships in the trading of minor metals
- ● Conf - Mtgs - LG
- M 35 f, UK / 35 f, o'seas

MIRA Ltd   (MIRA)   1946
- NR Watling St, NUNEATON, Warks, CV10 0TU.   (hq)
  024 7635 5000   fax 024 7635 5355
  http://www.mira.co.uk
  Managing Dir: J R Wood
- ▲ Company Limited by Guarantee
- ○ *Q
- Gp Aerodynamics; Durability; Noise; Vehicle safety; Ride & handling; Engines & transmissions; Vehicle analysis; Proving ground
- ● Conf - Mtgs - Res - SG - Inf - Lib
- < Assn Indep Res & Technology Orgs
- M 85 f
- ¶ Automobile Abstracts - 12.
  Automotive Business News - 25.
  Research Reports; ftm.   AR; free.
- × 2001 Motor Industry Research Association

MIRAD, the Institute of Registration Dealers & Agents   (MIRAD)
- NR PO Box 333, SOUTHPORT, Merseyside, PR9 7GW.
  07703 456789   fax 01704 534333
  email enquiries@mirad.co.uk   http://www.mirad.co.uk
- ○ *T; dealers in vehicle registration number plates

Miscarriage Association   (MA)   1982
- ■ c/o Clayton Hospital, Northgate, WAKEFIELD, W Yorks, WF1 3JS.   (hq)
  01924 200799   fax 01924 298834
  email info@miscarriageassociation.org.uk
  http://www.miscarriageassociation.org.uk
  Nat Dir: Ruth Bender Atik
- ▲ Company Limited by Guarantee; Registered Charity
- Br 50+
- ○ *M, *W; to provide information & support to women & their partners who have had a miscarriage, ectopic or molar pregnancy; to promote good practice in the way pregnancy loss is managed in hospitals & the community
- Gp Special register
- ● Support group meetings - Inf
- M 200 volunteer support contacts, 45 support gps
- ¶ NL - 4; ftm.   AR.
  Information leaflets; prices vary.

Mixed Wood-chip Suppliers Association   (MWSA)
- ■ Kingsway House, Wrotham Rd, Meopham, GRAVESEND, Kent, DA13 0AU.   (sp)
- ○ *T
- ● Mtgs - ET - Stat
- M 7 f

Mobile Data Association   (MDA)   1994
- ■ 13 Foster Way, Great Cambourne, CAMBRIDGE, CB3 6BP.   (asa)
  07041 340235
  email info@mda-mobiledata.org
  http://www.mda-mobiledata.org
  Dir: Martin Ballard
- ▲ Company Limited by Guarantee
- ○ *T; to increase awareness of mobile data amongst users & their advisers
- ● Conf - Mtgs - ET - Exhib - Stat - Inf - LG
- M 68 f, UK / 8 f, o'seas
- ¶ Mobile Data: beyond the wire [Hbk] - 1; ftm, £25 nm.

Mobile Electronics & Security Federation   (MESF)   1977
- NR PO Box 3750, BRAINTREE, Essex, CM77 8DZ.   (hq)
  01376 561040   fax 01376 561062
  email mobilefed@aol.com   http://www.mesf.org.uk
  Gen Sec: Jeff Marshall
- ▲ Company Limited by Guarantee
- ○ *T; 'for the aftermarket mobile electronics industry' (electronic items added to vehicles after purchase, including radios & CD/cassette players, telephones, security systems, navigation, tracking, telematics, multimedia)
- Gp Mobile electronics certification programme (MECP)
- ● Mtgs - ET - Exam - Exhib - Comp - Inf - LG
- M c 800 i, c 70 org
- ¶ Mobile Electronics - 6; ftm only.

Mobile Industry Crime Action Forum   (MICAF)   2000
- NR PO Box 28353, LONDON, SE20 7WJ.
  020 8778 9864   fax 020 8659 9561
  email micaf@tuff.co.uk   http://www.micaf.co.uk
  Exec Sec: Jack Wraith
- ▲ Un-incorporated Society
- ○ *T; to provide a forum for the exchange of information & research in mobile handset abuse & theft
- Gp Administrative Board;
  Mobile phone & theft technical group; Crime prevention group; Cooperation working group
- ● Conf - Mtgs - ET - SG - Stat - Inf - LG
- < TUFF Ltd
- M 30 i, 14 f

Mobile Marketing Association (UK)
NR c/o Charles Horder, Everett & Son, 35 Paul St, LONDON, EC2A 4UQ.   (hsb)
   Chmn: Nick Wiggin
▲ Company Limited by Guarantee
○ *T; to develop marketing via mobile phones & wireless technology
● Conf - Mtgs - ET - Res - Exhib - Inf - LG
M c 500
¶ NL - 4; free.

Mobile Operators Association   2003
NR Russell Square House, 10-12 Russell Square, LONDON, WC1B 5EE.
   020 7331 2015   fax 020 7931 2047
   email info@ukmoa.org
○ *T; mobile phone network operators
M 5f

Mobile & Outside Caterers Association
   since 2005 **Nationwide Caterers Association**

Mobilise Organisation   1922
■ Cottingham Way, THRAPSTON, Northants, NN14 4PL.   (hq)
   01832 734724   fax 01832 733816
   http://www.ddmc.org.uk
   Chmn: Douglas Campbell
▲ Company Limited by Guarantee
Br 50 area representatives
○ *W; to promote & protect the interests & welfare of physically disabled drivers; assistance regarding car conversions, ferry concessions, reduced RAC subscriptions, general information
● Mtgs - ET - Exam - LG
M 14,500 i, 7 f
¶ The Disabled Motorist - 6; ftm, £2 each nm.
✕ 2005-6 (Disabled Drivers Association
     (Disabled Drivers Motor Club

Model Electronic Railway Group   (MERG)   1967
■ Dingle Bank, Elmhurst Walk, Goring-on-Thames, READING, Berks, RG8 9DE.   (hsp)
   01491 872566
   email secretary@merg.org.uk   http://www.merg.org.uk
   Hon Sec: Howard Watkins
▲ Un-incorporated Society
○ *G; to promote & foster interest in the application of electronics, including computers, to railway modelling
● Mtgs - ET - Exhib - Inf - Lib - VE
M 800 i, UK / 80 i, o'seas
¶ Jnl - 4;
   Technical Bulletins (downloadable from web) - irreg; both ftm only.

Model Railway Club   (MRC)   1910
■ Keen House, 4 Calshot St, LONDON, N1 9DA.   (hq)
   020 7837 2542
   http://www.themodelrailwayclub.org
   Chmn: Peter Mann
▲ Company Limited by Guarantee
○ *G; the modelling & study of railways
● Conf - Mtgs - ET - Exhib - SG - Inf - Lib
< Chiltern Model Rly Assn
M c 200 i
¶ Bulletin - 6; ftm only.

Model Yachting Association   (MYA)   1911
NR Five Oaks, Church Lane, OAKLEY, Beds, MK43 7RU.   (chmn/p)
   01234 822408   fax 01234 822699
   http://www.mya-uk.org.uk
   Chmn: Chris Durant
▲ Un-incorporated Society
○ *G, *S; to promote the design, construction & racing of model sailing boats; to act as the model yacht racing authority for the UK
● Mtgs - Comp - Settling conditions, venues & dates for national & international competitions
< Intl Sailing Fedn/Radio Sailing Divn (ISAF/RSD); R Yachting Assn; Cent Coun of Physical Recreation (Water Recreation Divn)
M 1,600 i & clubs
¶ Acquaint - 4;   Ybk - 1; both ftm, £2.50 each nm.

Modern Churchpeople's Union   (MCU)   1898
■ MCU Office, 9 Westward View, Aigburth, LIVERPOOL, Merseyside, L17 7EE.   (hq)
   0151-726 9730
   email office@modchurchunion.org
   http://www.modchurchunion.org
   Gen Sec: Revd Jonathan Clatworthy
▲ Registered Charity
○ *R; an Anglican society for the study & advancement of liberal theological thought
● Conf - Mtgs - ET - SG
< Inclusive Church
M 550 i, 130 org, UK / 10 i, 90 org, o'seas
¶ Modern Believing - 4; ftm, £6 each nm.
   Signs of the Times (NL) - 4; ftm, 50p each nm.

Modern Humanities Research Association   (MHRA)   1918
NR 1 Carlton House Terrace, LONDON, SW1Y 5DB.   (hsb)
   Hon Sec: Dr D C Gillespie
▲ Registered Charity
Br Washington (DC)
○ *L, *Q; advanced studies & research in modern & medieval languages & literature (incl English)
● Res - Inf
< Intl Fedn Modern Languages Literatures
M i
¶ Modern Language Review - 4.
   Publications list available on request.

Modern Masonry Alliance
   a product association of the **British Precast Concrete Federation**

Modern Pentathlon Association of Great Britain   (MPAGB)   1948
NR Norwood House, University of Bath, Claverton Down, BATH, BA2 7AY.   (hq)
   01225 386808   fax 01225 386995
   email admin@mpagb.org.uk
   http://www.mpagb.org.uk
   Admin Sec: Liz Hunt,   Chief Exec: Peter Hart
○ *S; organisation of modern pentathlon (a compilation of 5 different events, fencing, swimming, shooting, cross-country running & riding)
● Mtgs - ET - Exam - Comp - Stat - Inf - Lib - VE
< U Intle Pentathlon Moderne (UIPM)
M 2,000 i, 86 clubs, UK / 6 i, o'seas
¶ Broadsheet - 4; ftm only.

Modern Studies Association   (MSA)   1972
NR 14 Fontstane St, Monifieth, DUNDEE, Angus, DD5 4LE.   (sp)
   http://www.msa-scotland.org.uk
   Chmn: Irene Morrison
▲ Un-incorporated Society
○ *E, *P; to promote & enhance teaching of modern studies in Scottish schools
● Conf - ET - Res - Comp
M 468 i
¶ Most (Jnl) - 1;   NL - 2;   Ybk - 1; all ftm only.

© CBD Research Ltd · Beckenham · BR3 5JS · Tel 020 8650 7745 · Fax 020 8650 0768 · E-mail cbd@cbdresearch.com · www.cbdresearch.com

Modular & Portable Building Association Ltd (MPBA) 1938

■ PO Box 99, CAERSWS, Powys, SW17 5WR. (hsp)
　0870 241 7687　fax 0870 241 7475
　email mpba@mpba.biz　http://www.mpba.biz
　Gen Mgr: Mrs Jackie Maginnis
▲ Company Limited by Guarantee
○ *T; to promote the modular & portable buildings industry & companies involved in the supply of products & services to the industry
Gp C'ees: Technical, Health & safety & hire
● Conf - Mtgs - ET - Res - Exhib - LG
M c 110 f
✕ 2004 (March) National Prefabricated Building Association

Momentum - the Northern Ireland ICT Federation (MOMENTUM)

NR NiSoft House, Ravenhill Business Pk, Ravenhill Rd, BELFAST, BT6 8AW.
　028 9045 0101　fax 028 9045 2123
　http://www.momentumni.org

Monarchist League 1943

■ PO Box 5307, BISHOPS STORTFORD, Herts, CM23 3DZ. (mail/address)
　01279 465551　fax 01279 466111
　http://www.monarchy.net
　Contact: The Secretary
▲ Un-incorporated Society
Br 22; Australia, USA
○ *G; to promote, support & defend the monarchical system of government in the UK & abroad
Gp Bulgaria; Egypt; Portugal; Heraldry
● Mtgs - Inf - Lib - LG
< cooperates with c 100 monarchist organisations worldwide
M 4,500 i, UK / 500 i, o'seas
¶ Monarchy (Jnl) - 4.　The Crown (Jnl) - 4.
　Note: The Constitutional Monarchy Association is part of the League.

Money Advice Association
　since 2005 **Institute of Money Advisers**

Monmouthshire Show Society Ltd 1790s

NR Parclands House, Raglan, USK, Monmouthshire, NP15 2BX. (hsb)
　01291 691160　fax 01291 691161
　http://www.monmouthshow.co.uk
　Management Sec: Mrs K Spencer
▲ Registered Charity
○ *F; to produce the Monmouthshire agricultural show; to promote the welfare of animals
● Mtgs - ET - Exhib - Comp
M 350 i

Montessori Society (AMI) UK (Mont Soc) 1935

■ 26 Lyndhurst Gardens, LONDON, NW3 5NW. (hq)
　020 7435 7874
　Mem Sec: Mrs Elizabeth Hood
▲ Un-incorporated Society
○ *E; promotion of the philosophy of Dr Maria Montessori with regard to child development & general attitude to life
● Conf - Exhib - Inf
< Assn Montessori Intle (AMI)
M 300 i, UK / 50 i, o'seas
¶ Montessori Direction - 2; free.
　The Montessori Review - 1; ftm, £1 back numbers.
　List of Schools run by AMI Trained Teachers - 1; free.

Monumental Brass Society 1887

NR Lowe Hill House, STRATFORD ST MARY, Suffolk, CO7 6JX. (hsp)
　01206 337239 or 020 8520 5249　fax 020 8521 8387
　email martin.stuchfield@intercitygroup.co.uk
　http://www.mbs-brasses.co.uk
　Hon Sec: H Martin Stuchfield
Br 12; 2 in USA
○ *L; study & preservation of monumental brasses, indents of lost brasses & incised slabs
● Conf - Mtgs - Res - Stat - Inf - VE - Advice & assistance to Church authorities on care & repair of brasses
M c 500 i, 50 org
¶ Portfolio - irreg;　Transactions - 1;　Bulletin - 3;
　AR - 1;　LM - irreg; all ftm only.

Moorland Association 1987

NR 16 Castle Park, LANCASTER, LA1 1YG. (hsb)
　01524 846846
　http://www.moorlandassociation.org
　Sec: R M N Gillibrand
▲ Un-incorporated Society
○ *K; to conserve heather moorland in England & Wales
● Conf - Mtgs - ET
M i & f

Morgan Horse Association 1975

NR Pampisford Place, PAMPISFORD, Cambs, CB2 4EW. (hq)
　01223 833186　fax 01223 836505
　email info@mha-uk.org
　Sec: Sylvia Sullivan
○ *B
M c 100 i

Morganatic Society

NR 191 Westcombe Hill, LONDON, SE3 7DB.
○ *G; 'for mutual sympathy for the lesser-born persons in morganatic relationships''
● Mtgs

Morris Federation (MF) 1971

■ 28 Fairstone Close, HASTINGS, E Sussex, TN35 5EZ. (hsp)
　01424 436052
　email sec@morrisfed.org.uk
　http://www.morrisfed.org.uk
　Hon Sec: Fee Lock
▲ Un-incorporated Society
Br 400+; 6
○ *D, *G; to encourage & maintain interest in Morris dancing
Gp Notation; Archive; Publicity; Step-dance
● Conf - Mtgs - Res - Inf - Lib - PL - LG - Public dance displays
< Folk Arts England; Engl Folk Dance & Song Soc
M 30 i, 350 org, UK / 2 i, 3 org, o'seas
¶ NL - 4; ftm only.

Morris Ring 1934

■ 70 Greengate Lane, Birstall, LEICESTER, LE4 3DL. (hsp)
　Bagman: Charlie Corcoran
○ *G; practice & performance of English men's ritual dance (Morris, sword-dancing & mumming)
● Conf - Mtgs - ET - Res - Exhib - SG - Inf
M 180 clubs & 60 associates, UK / 6 o'seas
¶ Ring Directory (list of clubs) - 1.
　List of books, tapes & equipment available.

Mortar Industry Association (MIA) 1998
NR Gillingham House, 38-44 Gillingham St, LONDON,
       SW1V 1HU. (hq)
       020 7963 8000
       Chmn: Neil Beningfield
▲ Company Limited by Guarantee
○ *T; the manufacture, use & applications of building mortars
Gp C'ees: Technical, Marketing
● Mtgs - Res - SG - Inf - LG
< UK Cast Stone Assn; Eur Mortar Industry Assn
M 30 f
¶ Various publications & guides to the uses of mortar; free.
       Video.

Mothers Apart from Their Children (MATCH) 1979
■ c/o BM Problems, LONDON, WC1N 3XX. (mail)
       email enquiries@matchmothers.org
       http://www.matchmothers.org address
       Chmn: Marion Jayawardene
▲ Un-incorporated Society
○ *G, *W; 'to offer emotional support to mothers who are
       separated from their children regardless of the reasons for
       the separation
● Mtgs - LG - Penpals - Private web forum for members
< Equal Parenting Coalition
M 220 i
¶ NL - 4; ftm, £1 nm.

Mothers' Union (MU) 1876
§ 24 Tufton St, LONDON, SW1P 3RB. (hq)
       020 7222 5533   fax 020 7222 1591
       email mu@themothersunion.org
       http://www.themothersunion.org
       Chief Exec: Reg Bailey
       a Christian organisation with over 1,000,000 members
       worldwide promoting the well-being of families

Motor Accident Solicitors Society (MASS) 1991
NR 54 Baldwin St, BRISTOL, BS1 1QW. (hq)
       0117-929 2560   fax 0117-904 7220
       email office@mass.org.uk   http://www.mass.org.uk
       Exec Dir: Jane Loney
▲ Un-incorporated Society
○ *P; for solicitors who specialise in road traffic accident claims,
       providing advice & assistance to claimants; 'MASS promotes
       the highest standards of legal services through education &
       representation in the pursuit of justice for the victims of road
       traffic accidents'
● Conf - Mtgs - ET - Inf - LG
M 160 f
¶ MASS Newsletter - 4; ftm, £50 nm.
       MASS Directory of Services - 1;   Accident Advice Leaflets;
       Accident Report Forms;   all ftm.

Motor Caravanners' Club Ltd 1960
■ 22 Evelyn Close, TWICKENHAM, Middx, TW2 7BN. (hq)
       020 8893 3883   fax 020 8893 8324
       email info@motorcaravanners.org.uk
       http://www.motorcaravanners.org.uk
       Sec: Colin Reay
▲ Company Limited by Guarantee
Br 27; Europe & rest of world
○ *G; to promote & develop motor-caravanning
Gp Walking; American motor homes; Photography; European
       rallies
● Mtgs - Exhib - Inf - VE - LG
< Fédn Intle de Camping & de Caravanning
M 11,500 i, UK / 100 i, o'seas
¶ Motor Caravanner - 12;   Buyers Guide;   Sites List - 1; all ftm.

Motor Cycle Industry Association Ltd (MCIA) 1973
NR Starley House, Eaton Rd, COVENTRY, Warks, CV1 2FH. (hq)
       024 7625 0800
       http://www.mcia.co.uk
       Chief Exec: Mark Foster
▲ Company Limited by Guarantee
○ *T
Gp Manufacturers & importers of machines; Accessory &
       component manufacturers; Factors; Associates
● Conf - Mtgs - Res - Exhib - Stat - Expt - Inf - LG
< Intl Motorcycle Mfrs Assn; Nat Motorcycle Coun; RoSPA; ACEM
M 150 f
¶ Revolutions (NL) - 4; ftm.   LM.   AR.

Motor Industry Public Affairs Association Ltd (MIPAA) 2005
■ Little Grange, Church St, West Grimstead, SALISBURY, Wilts,
       SP5 3RE. (gsp)
       01722 711295   fax 01722 711295
       email hyaxley@supanet.com   http://www.mipaa.com
       Gen Sec: Heather Yaxley
▲ Company Limited by Guarantee
○ *P; for those engaged in communications in the motor industry
● Mtgs - ET - SG - Inf - VE - Job search service - Mentoring
       programme
M 460 i, UK / 10 i, o'seas
¶ The News (NL) - 4;   Directory - 1; both ftm.
× 2005 (November) Motor Industry Public Affairs Association

Motor Industry Research Association
       since 2001 **MIRA Ltd**

Motor Neurone Disease Association 1979
■ PO Box 246, NORTHAMPTON, NN1 2PR. (hq)
       01604 250505   fax 01604 624726
       Chief Exec: Dr Kirstine Knox
▲ Registered Charity
Br 100
○ *W; the support of people with MND & their carers; to research
       into the causes & treatment of the disease
● Conf - Mtgs - ET - Res - Inf - Lib - Loan of equipment - Helpline
< Intl Alliance of ALS/MND Assns; Assn of Medical Res Charities
M c 6,500 i
¶ Thumbprint (NL) - 4; free.
       MND Association News (NL) - 12; ftm only.   AR - 1; free.
       International Exchange (NL) - 3.

Motor Schools Association of Great Britain Ltd (MSA) 1935
NR 101 Wellington Road North, STOCKPORT, Cheshire, SK4 2LP.
       (hq)
       0161-429 9669
       email mail@msagb.co.uk   http://www.msagb.co.uk
       Gen Mgr: John R Lepine
▲ Company Limited by Guarantee
Br 10
○ *T; all aspects of learning to drive, driving, advanced driving &
       road safety
● Conf - Mtgs - ET - Exam - Res - Comp - SG - Stat - Inf - Lib -
       VE - LG
< Europäische Fahrlehrer Assoziation (EFA); Eur Safe Vehicle
       Alliance (ESVA); Approved Driving Instructor Training
       Establishments Mgt C'ee; Parliamentary Advy C'ee on
       Transport Safety
M 6,250 i
¶ MSA Newslink - 11;   AR & Ybk - 1;
       The Northern Instructor - 11;
       The Midlands & Eastern Instructor - 11;
       The Southern Instructor - 11;   all ftm only.

© CBD Research Ltd · Beckenham · BR3 5JS · Tel 020 8650 7745 · Fax 020 8650 0768 · E-mail cbd@cbdresearch.com · www.cbdresearch.com

Motor Sports Association UK   (MSAUK)   1979

NR   Motor Sports House, Riverside Park, Colnbrook, SLOUGH,
       Berks, SL3 0HG.   (hq)
       01753 765000   fax 01753 682938
       http://www.msauk.org
▲   Company Limited by Guarantee
○   *S; the governing body for motor sport in the UK
●   Exhib - Comp - Inf
<   Fédn Automobile Intle (FIA)

Motor Vehicle Dismantlers Association of Great Britain
(MVDA)   1943

■   33 Market St, LICHFIELD, Staffs, WS13 6LA.   (hq)
       01543 254254   fax 01543 254274
       email mail@mvda.org.uk   http://www.mvda.org.uk
       Sec: Duncan Wemyss
▲   Un-incorporated Society
○   *T
●   Conf - Mtgs - ET - Inf - LG
<   Eur Vehicle Dismantlers Assn (EGARA)
M   217 f, UK / 8 f, o'seas
¶   Automotive Recycling & Disposal UK - 4; free.

Motor Vehicle Repairers Association
   since 2002-03 **MVRA Ltd**

Motorcycle Action Group   (MAG(UK))   1973

■   PO Box 750, RUGBY, Warks, CV21 3ZR.   (hq)
       0870 444 8448   fax 0870 444 8449
       http://www.mag-uk.org
▲   Company Limited by Guarantee
○   *K; to protect the rights & interests of motorcyclists; to
       safeguard the tradition & future of motorcycling in the UK; to
       promote positive aspects of motorcycling
●   Conf - Mtgs - Res - Exhib - SG - Stat - Inf - LG
<   Intl Coalition of Motorcyclists (ICOM); Fédn Eur de
       Motocyclistes Assns (FEMA); links with other motorcycle assns
       & gps worldwide
M   25,000 i, 40 f, 270 clubs, / 80 i, o'seas
¶   The Road - 6; ftm, £2 nm.
       Network for Regions (NL) - 12; ftm, £10 yr nm.

Motorcycle Rider Training Association
   a group of the **Retail Motor Industry Federation**

Motoring Organisations' Land Access & Recreation Association
(LARA)   1986

■   PO Box 20, MARKET DRAYTON, Shropshire, TF9 1WR.
       (devt/offr/p)
       01630 657627   fax 01630 658928
       email larahq@aol.com
       Admin: Mary Stevens;   Motor Recreation Devt Officer: Tim
       Stevens
▲   Un-incorporated Society
○   *N, *S; an umbrella organisation of motor sport groups -
       promoting responsible use of the environment for motor
       sports & recreation
●   Conf - Mtgs - Res - Inf - LG - Liaison with local & county
       authorities & with sporting, recreational & rights of way
       groups
M   330,000 i, in 11 org
¶   Access Guide; ftm.   Conference papers.   Leaflets; free.
       Codes of Conduct; free.

Motorsport Industry Association Ltd   (MIA)   1994

■   Federation House, STONELEIGH PARK, Warks, CV8 2RF.   (hq)
       024 7669 2600   fax 024 7669 2601
       email info@the-mia.com   http://www.the-mia.com
       Chief Exec: Chris Aylett
▲   Company Limited by Guarantee
Br   USA
○   *T; to represent, promote & protect the interests of the British
       motorsport industry
Gp   Motorsport Education & Training Council
●   Conf - Mtgs - ET - Exhib - Expt - Inf - VE - LG
M   220 f
¶   NL [email] - 52;   LM;   AR - 1; all ftm.

Mountain Bothies Association   (MBA)   1965

■   c/o Henderson, Black & Co, 22 Crossgate, CUPAR, Fife,
       KY15 5HW.   (asa)
       01334 656666   fax 01334 656278
       email mba@hendersonblack.co.uk
       http://www.mountainbothies.org.uk
       Gen Sec: Peter King
▲   Company Limited by Guarantee; Registered Charity
Br   9 areas
○   *W; to maintain simple shelters in remote country for the use &
       benefit of all who love wild & lonely places
Gp   Renovation work on old & derelict buildings in remote areas
●   Renovation & maintenance work parties
<   Scot Rights of Way & Access Soc; Mountaineering Coun
       Scotland; NE Mountain Trust
M   c 3,000 i
¶   NL - 4; ftm.   AR - 1; ftm, on request nm.
       Members Hbk - 1; ftm only.
       Volunteer's Hbk - 1; ft volunteers, on request nm.

Mountain Training Board
   is a group of the **Mountaineering Council of Ireland**

Mountaineering Council of Ireland   (MCI)   1972

IRL   Sport HQ, 13 Joyce Way, Park West Business Park, DUBLIN 12,
       Republic of Ireland.   (hq)
       353 (1) 625 1115   fax 353 (1) 625 1116
       email mci@eircom.net   http://www.mountaineering.ie
       Hon Sec: Rita Connell
▲   Company Limited by Guarantee
Br   N Ireland
○   *S; promotes mountaineering which includes walking &
       climbing; to preserve & maintain the mountaineering
       environment
Gp   Mountain Training Board; Environmental protection
●   Conf - ET - Comp - Inf - Lib - LG
<   U Intle des Assns d'Alpinisme; Eur Ramblers Assn
M   c 1,100 i, 8,000 club members
¶   Irish Mountain Log - 4; ftm.

Mountaineering Council of Scotland   (MCofS)   1970

NR   The Old Granary, West Mill St, PERTH, PH1 5QP.   (hq)
       01738 638227   fax 01738 442095
       email info@mountaineering-scotland.org.uk
       Nat Officer: Kevin Howett
▲   Un-incorporated Society
○   *S; the governing body of the sport in Scotland; interests of
       mountaineers, walkers, climbers & cross-country skiers
M   i, f & clubs
¶   NL - 5; ftm only.   Scottish Clubs' Huts - 1; ftm.
       Independent Hostel Guide - 1.
       Heading for the Scottish Hills (access during stalking period) -
       updated.
       Guidance Notes for clubs & other organisations (Liability &
       Safety).

Mounted Games Association of Great Britain   (MGAGB) 1984

■   The Paddocks, Croft Lane, CHIPPERFIELD, Herts, WD4 9DX. (hsb)
 01298 24292   fax 01298 24292
 email mary@mgagb.co.uk   http://www.mgagb.co.uk
 Chief Exec: Mrs Mary Worth
▲   Company Limited by Guarantee
○   *S, *Y; to organise & promote mounted games events for young riders
●   Mtgs - Comp
<   Intl Mounted Games Assn (IMGA)
M   1,400 i
¶   Pony Express - 4; ftm.   Hbk - 1.

Movement for Colonial Freedom
 see **Liberation - incorporating Movement for Colonial Freedom**

Movers Institute (TMI)   (TMI)   1937

NR   Tangent House, 62 Exchange Rd, WATFORD, Herts, WD18 0TG.   (hq)
 01923 699480   fax 01923 699481
 email info@bar.co.uk   http://www.bar.co.uk
 Sec: Robert D Syers
▲   Company Limited by Guarantee
○   *T; training, educational & accreditation for the removals & storage industry
Gp   National & European domestic moves; Overseas; Commercial
●   Conf - Mtgs - ET - Exam - Comp - SG - Inf - VE
<   Brit Assn of Removers (BAR)
M   1,300 i
¶   Moving News - 4; ftm only.

Moving Image Society
 see **BKSTS - the Moving Image Society**

Mull & Iona Chamber of Commerce   1992

NR   Ceann Cuin, DERVAIG, Isle of Mull, PA75 6QR.   (sb)
 email georgia@oopspardon.freeserve.co.uk
 http://www.mullchamber.org
 Sec: Georgia O'Neill
○   *C

Multi Vintage Wine Growers Society   (MVWGS)   1985

■   191 Westcombe Hill, LONDON, SE3 7DR.   (hsp)
▲   Un-incorporated Society
○   *G; for anyone interested in wine growing techniques
●   Mtgs - Stat - VE - LG
M   23 i
¶   Jnl - irreg; m only.

Multiple Births Foundation   (MBF)   1988

■   Hammersmith House (level 4), Queen Charlotte's & Chelsea Hospital, Du Cane Rd, LONDON, W12 0HS.   (hq)
 020 8383 3519   fax 020 8383 3041
 email mbf@hhnt.nhs.uk
 http://www.multiplebirths.org.uk
 Dir: Jane Denton,   Admin: Marion Paterson
▲   Registered Charity
○   *P, *W; to offer support to parents of twins & triplets (& more); to offer advice & training to the professions concerned with them
Gp   Medical (paediatricians, obstetricians, GPs); Nursing (midwives, health visitors); Education (teachers, psychologists)
●   Conf - Mtgs - ET - Stat - Inf - Lib - PL
¶   NL - 4; £10/£15 yr m.   AR.   Publications list available.

Multiple Sclerosis National Therapy Centres   1993

■   Bradbury House, 155 Barkers Lane, BEDFORD, MK41 9RX. (MS/Centre)
 01234 325781   fax 01234 365242
 email info@ms-selfhelp.org
 http://www.ms-selfhelp.org
 Admin: Mrs V Woods
▲   Company Limited by Guarantee; Registered Charity
○   *N, *W; to administer the MS therapy centres throughout the country which provide therapy, support & information to all MS sufferers & their families
●   ET - Inf
M   35 centres
¶   NL (to all MS centres) - 2/3.
×   2002 Federation of Multiple Sclerosis Therapy Centres
 2003 National Multiple Sclerosis Therapy Centres

Multiple Sclerosis Society of Great Britain & Northern Ireland (MS Society)   1953

NR   372 Edgware Rd, LONDON, NW2 6ND.   (hq)
 020 8438 0700   fax 020 8438 0701
 email info@mssociety.org.uk
 http://www.mssociety.org.uk
 Chief Exec: Mike O'Donovan
▲   Registered Charity
Br   360
○   *M, *W; to advise & assist anyone affected by MS
●   Conf - Mtgs - Res - Inf
>   MS Trust
M   c 44,000 i
¶   MS Matters - 6; ftm.
 Publications list available.

Multiple Sclerosis Society of Ireland

IRL   80 Northumberland Rd, DUBLIN 4, Republic of Ireland.
 353 (1) 678 1600   fax 353 (1) 678 1601
 email info@ms-society.ie   http://www.ms-society.ie
 Chief Exec: Dr Graham Love
○   *W

MultiService Association   (MSA)

NR   St Crispin's House, 21 Station Rd, DESBOROUGH, Northants, NN14 2SA.   (hq)
 01536 760374
 email info@msauk.biz
 Chief Exec: Trevor Griffiths
▲   Company Limited by Guarantee
○   *T; the national association for the shoe repair industry; extra services provided by members include key cutting, engraving & watch repairs
●   Conf - Mtgs - ET - Exhib - Comp - Inf - Empl - LG
<   Europäische Vereinigung des Schuhmacherhandwerks
M   i, f & org
×   2003 (November) Society of Master Shoe Repairers

Murray Grey Beef Cattle Society Ltd   1973

■   Pen-Twyn, Llangenny, CRICKHOWELL, Brecknockshire, NP8 1HD.   (hq)
 01873 810547   fax 01873 810547
 email murray.grey@virgin.net
 http://www.murray-grey.co.uk
 Sec: Mrs Rosemary Kent
▲   Company Limited by Guarantee; Registered Charity
○   *B; to promote research into improvement of the breed; to maintain the purity of the breed
●   Mtgs - Exhib - Comp - VE
M   50 i, UK / 4 i, o'seas
¶   NL - 3;   Herdbook - 1;   Ybk - 1.

Muscular Dystrophy Campaign   1961
- ■ 7-11 Prescott Place, LONDON, SW4 6BS.   (hq)
  020 7720 8055   fax 020 7498 0670
  http://www.muscular-dystrophy.org
- ▲ Company Limited by Guarantee; Registered Charity
- ○ *M, *W; to raise funds for & to manage medical research into
  muscular dystrophy & allied neuromuscular diseases;
  practical advice & support to affected families
- < Eur Alliance of Muscular Dystrophy Assns
- M c 2,000 i
- ¶ Target MD (NL) - 4; ftm.   AR; free.

Muscular Dystrophy Ireland
- IRL 71-72 North Brunswick St, DUBLIN 7, Republic of Ireland.
  353 (1) 872 1501   fax 353 (1) 872 4482
  email info@mdi.ie   http://www.mdi.ie
  Chmn: Florence Dougall
- ○ *W
- × 2000-2002 Muscular Dystrophy Society of Ireland

Museum Ethnographers Group   (MEG)   1976
- ■ Cambridge University Museum of Archaeology & Anthropology,
  Downing St, CAMBRIDGE, CB2 3DZ.   (hsb)
  01223 765659   fax 01223 333517
  email TC10006@cam.ac.uk
  http://www.museumethnographersgroup.org.uk
  Hon Sec: Tabitha Cadbury
- ▲ Registered Charity
- ○ *P; to encourage good practice in the curatorship of
  ethnographic collections in the UK; to encourage research &
  the exchange of information
- ● Conf - Mtgs - ET - Inf - VE
- M [not stated]
- ¶ Jnl of Museum Ethnography - 1; ftm, £25 nm.
  MEG NL - 4; ftm only.   Occasional Papers; prices vary.

Museum of Garden History   1977
- ■ Lambeth Palace Rd, LONDON, SE1 7LB.   (hq)
  020 7401 8865   fax 020 7401 8869
  email info@museumgardenhistory.org
  http://www.museumgardenhistory.org
  Chief Exec: Victoria Farrow
- ▲ Company Limited by Guarantee; Registered Charity
- ○ *H; a museum devoted to the history of gardens & techniques
  of gardening.   A 17th century knot garden is on site
- ● ET - Exhib - Inf - Lib - PL - VE
- < R Oak Foundation of the USA
- M 1,500 i, UK / 100 i, o'seas
- ¶ Jnl - 3; ftm, £2.50 nm.

Museum Professionals Group   (MPG)   1937
- NR Northampton Museums, 13 Guildhall Rd, NORTHAMPTON,
  NN1 1DP.   (chmn/b)
  01604 837279
  email wbrown@northampton.gov.uk
  Chmn: Will Brown
- ▲ Un-incorporated Society
- ○ *P; to campaign on issues relevant to all junior museum
  professionals
- ● Conf - Mtgs - ET - Res
- M 100 i, 40 org, UK / 10 org, o'seas

Museums Association   (MA)   1889
- ■ 24 Calvin St, LONDON, E1 6NW.   (hq)
  020 7426 6970   fax 020 7426 6961
  email info@museumsassociation.org
  http://www.museumsassociation.org
  Dir: Mark Taylor
- ▲ Registered Charity
- ○ *A, *P; the interests of museum people, museums & their
  collections
- ● Conf - Mtgs - ET - Inf - LG
- M 5,000 i, 250 f, 600 instns, UK & o'seas
- ¶ Museums Jnl - 12.   Museum Practice - 4.
  Museums Ybk (a directory of museums & galleries of the British
  Isles).
  Ethics Guidelines.   Museum briefings.   AR.

Mushroom Growers' Association   (MGA)   1945
- NR PO Box 192, Ketton, STAMFORD, Lincs, PE9 3ZT.   (hq)
  01780 722074   fax 01780 729006
  http://www.mushroomgrowers.org
  Contact: Melissa Nairn
- ▲ Un-incorporated Society
- ○ *F, *T; for growers, suppliers, scientists & academic institutions;
  provides technical advice & information
- ● Conf - Mtgs - Exhib - Stat - Inf - VE - LG
- M c 250 f
- ¶ Mushroom Jnl - 6.

Music Education Council   (MEC)   1975
- NR 54 Elm Rd, Hale, ALTRINCHAM, Cheshire, WA15 9QP.
  (admin/p)
  0161-928 3085   fax 0161-929 9648
  email ahassan@easynet.co.uk   http://www.mec.org.uk
  Admin: Anna Hassan
- ▲ Registered Charity
- ○ *D, *E; promote & advance the education & training of the
  public in music
- ● Conf - Inf
- < Intl Soc for Music Educ (ISME)
- M c 50 i, 170 org
- ¶ NL - 6.

Music Industries Association   (MIA)   1882
- NR Ivy Cottage Offices, Finch's Yard, Eastwick Rd,
  GREAT BOOKHAM, Surrey, KT23 4BA.   (hq)
  01372 750600   fax 01372 750515
  email enquiries@mia.org.uk
  Dir Gen: Paul McManus
- ▲ Company Limited by Guarantee
- ○ *D, *T; for manufacturers, distributors, importers & retailers of
  musical instruments, accessories & amplification eqpt
- Gp Sector groups: Pianos, Band & orchestral instruments,
  Keyboards, Guitars, Amplification; Music education;
  Promotions; Trade & public exhibitions; Statistics; E-
  commerce
- ● Conf - Mtgs - ET - Res - Exhib - Stat - Expt - Inf - LG
- < Nat Music Coun; Music Education Coun; Confedn Brit Ind; Brit
  Chams Comm
- M 300 f
- ¶ Business to Business - 12.
  List of publications on request.

Music Masters' & Mistresses' Association   (MMA)   1903
- NR St Edmund's School, CANTERBURY, Kent, CT2 8HU.
  (admin/b)
  01227 475600
  Admin: Carol Hawkins
- ▲ Company Limited by Guarantee
- ○ *E, *P; advancement of musical education in independent
  schools; a professional forum for teachers of music
- ● Conf - Mtgs - Inf
- M c 950 i, UK / c 10 i, o'seas
- ¶ Jnl - 3;   LM - 1; both ftm only.

Music Producers Guild Ltd   (MPG)   1986
NR   71 Avenue Gardens, LONDON, W3 8HB.   (mail)
         020 3110 0060 address
         Co Sec: Penny Ganz,   Chmn: Mike Howlett
▲   Company Limited by Guarantee
Br   affiliates in 10 countries o'seas
○   *T; to represent people in the production of music (record
         producers, sound engineers)
Gp   Special interest gps
●   Conf - Mtgs - ET - Inf - Empl
<   Eur Sound Directors Assn (ESDA); Music Producers Gld of
         America (MPGA)
M   c 400 i
¶   NL - 4.   A&R Guide - 1.

Music Publishers' Association Ltd   (MPA)   1881
■   British Music House (6th floor), 26 Berners St, LONDON,
         W1T 3LR.   (hq)
         020 7580 0126   fax 020 7637 3929
         email info@mpaonline.org.uk
         http://www.mpaonline.org.uk
         Chief Exec: Stephen Navin
▲   Company Limited by Guarantee
○   *T; to represent the interests of music publishers to government,
         the music industry, the media & the public
●   Conf - Mtgs - ET - Inf - LG
<   Intl Confedn of Music Publishers; Brit Music Rights
M   c 200 f
¶   Music Copyright Matters - 4; ftm only.
         Distributor's List - 1; ftm, £10 nm.
         LM - 1; ftm, £10 nm.   Code of Fair Practice.

Musical Box Society of Great Britain   (MBSGB)   1962
NR   PO Box 373, WELWYN GARDEN CITY, Herts, AL6 0WY.   (hsb)
         http://www.mbsgb.org.uk
○   *D, *G; preservation of musical boxes & all other forms of
         mechanical musical instruments, including automata;
         research into their history & development
●   Conf - Mtgs - Res - Exhib - SG - Inf - VE
M   c 250 i, UK / 350 i, o'seas
¶   The Music Box - 4; ftm, £8.50 each nm.

Musicians' Union   (MU)   1893
NR   60-62 Clapham Rd, LONDON, SW9 0JJ.   (hq)
         020 7582 5566   fax 020 7582 9805
         email info@musiciansunion.org.uk
         http://www.musiciansunion.org.uk
         Gen Sec: John F Smith
Br   74
○   *U
Gp   Sections: Folk, Jazz, Session, Theatre; Freelance orchestral;
         Teachers' register;
         British Music Writers' Council
●   Conf - Mtgs - ET - Exhib - Stat - Inf - Empl - LG - Careers
         service - Lobbying
<   Intl Fedn Musicians (FIM)
M   31,000 i
¶   Musician (Jnl) - 4; free.
         Section NL - 4;   Branch NL - 12; both ftm only.

Mutton Renaissance Campaign   2004
■   10-12 Picton St, BRISTOL, BS6 5QA.
         0870 242 3219
         http://www.muttonrenaissance.org.uk
○   *K

Muzzle Loaders Association of GB   (MLAGB)   1952
NR   82A High St, SAWSTON, Cambs, CB2 4HJ.   (mem/sb)
         01223 830665   fax 01223 839804
         Mem Sec: David Cole,   Sec: Charles Higginbottom
Br   29
○   *G; for collectors, shooters & students of muzzle loading
         firearms
Gp   Rifle; Pistol; Clay pigeon
●   Mtgs - Comp
<   Muzzle Loading Assns Intl C'ee (Paris); Brit Shooting Sports
         Coun; Nat Rifle Assn
M   1,900 i, 180 clubs, UK / 17 i, 3 clubs, o'seas
¶   Black Powder (NL) - 4; ftm.

MVRA Ltd   (MVRA Ltd)   1988
NR   Glenfield Business Park, Philips Rd, BLACKBURN, Lancs,
         BB1 5QH.   (hq)
         0870 458 3051   fax 0870 458 3052
         email enquiry@mvra.com   http://www.mvra.com
         Managing Dir: Mike Monaghan,
         PR & Communications: Barbara Herbert
▲   Company Limited by Guarantee
○   *T; a motor trade body representing motor vehicle repairers
Gp   Car; Commercial; Motorcycle
●   LG
M   2,200 i
✕   2002-03 Motor Vehicle Repairers' Association

Myalgic Encephalopathy Association   (MEA)   1976
■   4 Top Angel, Buckingham Industrial Park, BUCKINGHAM,
         MK18 1TH.   (hq)
         0870 444 8233   fax 01280 821602
         email lucy.kingham@meassociation.org.uk
         http://www.meassociation.org.uk
         Chief Exec: Neil Riley
▲   Company Limited by Guarantee; Registered Charity
○   *W; to serve the needs of people with ME/CFS & their families
         & carers
●   Conf - Res
<   Nat Coun of Voluntary Orgs (NCVO); Long-Term Med
         Conditions Alliance (LMCA)
M   6,800 i
¶   Perspectives - 4.
         [subscription £18]

Myasthenia Gravis Association   (MGA)   1976
■   Southgate Business Centre (1st floor), Normanton Rd, DERBY,
         DE23 6UQ.   (hq)
         01332 290219   fax 01332 293641
         email mg@mga-charity.org   http://www.mgauk.org
         Chmn: Peter Finney
▲   Registered Charity
○   *W; to provide advice & support for sufferers, carers & the
         medical profession; to fund research into improved
         treatment; (an auto-immune disease characterised by
         fluctuating, sometimes fatal, muscle weakness)
●   Conf - Mtgs - ET - Res - Exhib - Inf
         Helpline: 0800 919922
<   Neurological Alliance
M   9,000 i, UK / 270 i, o'seas
¶   MGA News - 4; free.   Medical Companion; ftm, £2.50 nm.
         AR; ftm only.   Information leaflets; free.

© CBD Research Ltd · Beckenham · BR3 5JS · Tel 020 8650 7745 · Fax 020 8650 0768 · E-mail cbd@cbdresearch.com · www.cbdresearch.com

Myositis Support Group
NR 146 Newtown Rd, Woolston, SOUTHAMPTON, Hants,
      SO19 9HR.
      023 8044 9708   fax 023 8039 6402
      email info@myositis.org.uk   http://www.myositis.org.uk
○   *W; inflamation of muscles

Myotonic Dystrophy Support Group   (MDSG)   1985
■   35a Carlton Hill, Carlton, NOTTINGHAM, NG4 1BG.
      0115-987 5869   fax 0115-987 6462
      email mdsg@tesco.net   http://www.mdsguk.org
      Nat Co-ordinator: Margaret Bowler
▲   Registered Charity
○   *W; to give support to families & professionals concerning
      myotonic dystrophy
●   ET - Res - Exhib - Helpline
<   Muscular Dystrophy Campaign; Contact-a-Family; LMCA;
      NCVO
M   35 i, UK / 20 i, o'seas
¶   NL - 3; ftm.

Naace (Naace) 1985
NR PO Box 6511, NOTTINGHAM, NG11 8TN. (hq)
 0870 240 0480 fax 0870 241 4115
 email office@naace.org http://www.naace.org
 Gen Sec: Mary Barker
▲ Company Limited by Guarantee; Registered Charity
○ *P; 'advancing education through ICT'
● Conf - Mtgs - ET - Res - Exhib - SG - Inf - LG
M 3,100 i, 115 f
¶ NL - 52; Jnl - 2; both ftm only.
✕ 2004 (Computer Education Group
 (Micros & Primary Education

NABAS (the Balloon Association) Ltd (NABAS) 1988
■ Katepwa House, Ashfield Park Ave, ROSS-ON-WYE, Herefords,
 HR9 5AX. (regd/office)
 01989 762204 fax 01989 567676
 email admin@nabas.co.uk http://www.nabas.co.uk
 Admin: Gillian Hinton
▲ Company Limited
○ *T; to coordinate the party & promotional balloon decorating
 industry, both latex & foil
Gp Decorators; Retailers; Manufacturers; Wholesalers
● Conf - Mtgs - ET - Exhib - Comp - Inf
M 720 f
¶ Balloonies (NL) - 12; LM - 2; both ftm.

**NACRO - National Association for the Care & Resettlement of
Offenders 1966**
NR 169 Clapham Rd, LONDON, SW9 0PU. (hq)
 020 7582 6500 fax 020 7735 4666
 http://www.nacro.org.uk
 Chief Exec: Paul Cavadino
○ *W

**NAGALRO: Professional Association for Family Court Advisers &
Independent Social Work Practitioners & Consultants
(NAGALRO) 1989**
■ PO Box 264, ESHER, Surrey, KT10 0WA.
 01372 818504 fax 01372 818505
 email nagalro@globalnet.co.uk
 http://www.nagalro.com
 Principal Admin: Karen Harris
▲ Company Limited by Guarantee
○ *P
● Conf - Mtgs - Inf - LG
M 900 i
¶ Seen & Heard - 4; ftm.
✕ 2002 National Association of Guardians ad Litem & Reporting
 Officers

Nansen Highland 1991
NR Redcastle Station, MUIR of ORD, Inverness, IV6 7RX. (hq)
 01463 871255 fax 01463 870258
 email nansen@highlandhq.freeserve.co.uk
 http://www.nansenhighland.co.uk
 Dir: Bart Lafere
▲ Company Limited by Guarantee; Registered Charity
○ *E; a non-governmental organisation specialising in youth &
 social training; the Society is named for Fridtjof Nansen the
 Norwegian arctic explorer, zoologist & statesman
● ET
¶ AR.

**Napaeo - the Association for Land Based Colleges
(Napaeo) 1950**
■ 67 The Meadows, Cherry Burton, BEVERLEY, E Yorks,
 HU17 7RL. (hsp/b)
 01964 550736 fax 01964 550736
 email howardpetch@btinternet.com
 Chief Exec: Howard W Petch
▲ Un-incorporated Society
○ *P; to support the role & work of UK colleges engaged in the
 provision of further & higher education & training in land
 based & associated subjects
● Conf - Mtgs - ET - SG - Inf - LG
< Assn of Colleges
M 45 i

Napoleonic Association Ltd (NA) 1975
■ 16 Little Kimble Walk, Hedge End, SOUTHAMPTON, Hants,
 SO30 0JQ. (sec/p)
 01489 783224
 email celia.norris@ntlworld.co http://www.n-a.co.uk
 Co Sec: Celia Norris
▲ Company Limited by Guarantee
○ *G, *L; to promote interest & study in military history 1792-
 1815 & to re-enact such history
Gp Research; Wargames; Re-enactment
● Res - Battle re-enactment & shows - Research conferences
< Muzzle Loaders Assn of GB
M 600 i, UK / 20 i, o'seas

Napoleonic Society 1969
■ 157 Vicarage Rd, LONDON, E10 5DU. (hq)
 020 8539 3876 fax 020 8539 3876
 email napoleon-owner@smartgroups.com
 http://www.smartgroups.com/vault/napoleon
 Sec: Ronald King
▲ Un-incorporated Society
○ *L, *Q; to foster interest & understanding of French history
 1756-1945
● Res - SG - Inf - Lib - PL
¶ Napoleon.
 Note: Please note this is NOT a re-enactment or fancy costume
 society.

Narcolepsy Association United Kingdom (UKAN) 1981
■ PO Box 13842, PENICUIK, EH26 8WX. (mail/address)
 0845 450 0394
 email info@narcolepsy.org.uk
 http://www.narcolepsy.org.uk
 Business Mgr: Margaret Roxburgh
▲ Registered Charity
Br 20
○ *W; to support research into the causes & treatment of
 narcolepsy (a sleep disorder characterised by excessive
 daytime sleepiness); to provide support & information for
 sufferers & their families; to press for recognition of
 narcolepsy as a disability by the DoE & DSS
● Inf - LG
< Eur Narcolepsy Assn (ENA); Neurological Alliance; Long-term
 Med Conditions Alliance (LMCA); Genetic Interest Gp (GIG);
 Nat Coun of Voluntary Orgs (NCVO)
M 700 i, 1 f, 4 org, UK / 50 i, o'seas
¶ Catnap (Jnl) - 4; ftm, 50 p each nm.
 Reports:
 1. Medication for Narcolepsy; £1.50 m, £2.25 nm.
 2. Narcolepsy: a layman's guide; £1 m, £1.50 nm.
 3. Narcolepsy: care & treatment; £1.80 m, £2.70 nm.
 Personal Experiences; £2 m, £3 nm.

Narrow Bandwidth Television Association   (NBTVA)   1975
- ■ 1 Burnwood Drive, Wollaton, NOTTINGHAM, NG8 2DJ.   (hsp)
   0115-928 2896
   http://www.nbtv.org
   Chmn: D B Pitt
- ▲ Un-incorporated Society
- ○ *G; for those interested in amateur television - construction of apparatus, transmission & reception & the history of television
- ● Conf - ET - Res - Exhib
- < Brit Amat TV Club
- M 100 i, UK / 50 i, o'seas
- ¶ NBTV (NL) - 4; £5 yr m.

Narrow Gauge Railway Society   (NGRS)   1951
- NR 34 East St, FAREHAM, Hants, PO16 0BY.   (hsp)
   Hon Sec: Brian Gent
- ▲ Un-incorporated Society
- ○ *G
- ¶ Narrow Gauge - 4.   Narrow Gauge News - 6.

nasen   (nasen)   1992
- ■ Nasen House 4-5 Amber Business Village, Amber Close, Amington, TAMWORTH, Staffs, B77 4RP.   (hq)
   01827 311500   fax 01827 313005
   email welcome@nasen.org.uk
   http://www.nasen.org.uk
   Chief Exec Officer: Lorraine Peterson
- ▲ Company Limited by Guarantee; Registered Charity
- Br 65
- ○ *E, *P; to promote the development of children & young people with special educational needs
- ● Conf - Mtgs - ET - Res - Exhib - SG - Inf - LG
- < NCVO; COSTA; Nat Children's Bureau
- M 7,000 i, 3,000 schools
- ¶ British Journal for Special Education - 4; ftm.
   Support for Learning - 4; ftm.
   Special (NL) - termly; ftm, £12 nm (£15 o'seas).
   Publications list available.
- ✕ 2004-05 National Association for Special Educational Needs

NATFHE - the University & College Lecturers' Union   (NATFHE)   1976
- ■ 27 Britannia St, LONDON, WC1X 9JP.   (hq)
   020 7837 3636   fax 020 7837 4403
   email hq@natfhe.org.uk   http://www.natfhe.org.uk
   Gen Sec: Paul Mackney
- Br 700
- ○ *E, *P, *U; lecturers in post-school, further, higher, penal & agricultural education
- ● Conf - ET - Res - Exhib - Stat - Empl - LG
- < Eur Trades U C'ee for Educ; TUC
- M 68,000 i
- ¶ Jnl of Further & Higher Education - 3; £13 m, £100 institutions, £32 nm.
   The Lecturer - 6; ftm, £12 nm.   Publications list.
   Note: amalgamated on 1 June 2006 with the Association of University Teachers to form the University & College Union; a transitional year will exist until full operational unity is achieved in June 2007.

National Abortion Campaign
   2003 merged with the Abortion Law Reform Association to form
   Abortion Rights

National Access & Scaffolding Confederation   (NASC)   1943
- ■ Carthusian Court, 12 Carthusian St, LONDON, EC1M 6EZ.
   (hq)
   020 7397 8120
   email enquiries@nasc.org.uk   http://www.nasc.org.uk
   Managing Dir: Robin James
- ▲ Company Limited by Guarantee
- ○ *T; for the access & scaffolding industry; members provide products & services including the supply & erection, hire, sale & manufacturing of: access & scaffolding equipment, formwork & falsework & temporary suspended access systems
- ● Inf - LG
- < Nat Specialist Contrs Coun; Access Ind Forum
- > Specialist Access Engg & Maintenance Assn (SAEMA); Fall Arrest Safety Eqpt Training (FASET)
- M 180 f
- ¶ NASC Ybk (incl LM - 1.
   SG4:05 - Preventing falls in scaffolding & falsework; £25.
   SG4: You - User guide to SG4:05; £5.
   Guide to Good Practice for Scaffolding with Tubes & Fittings; £105.
   Technical & Safety Guidance Notes; prices vary.

National Accordion Organisation of the United Kingdom   (NAO)   1947
- ■ 112 Countesthorpe Rd, South Wigston, LEICESTER, LE18 4PG.   (hsb)
   0116-241 2856; 0116-278 4094
   email naouk@accordions.com
   http://www.accordions.com/nao
   Hon Sec: Miss Pauline Noon,   Chmn: Raymond Bodell
- ▲ Registered Charity
- ○ *D; to promote accordion playing competitions
- ● Comp - ET (through the British Academy of Accordionists (BCA) at address above)
- < Confédn Intle des Accordéonistes (CIA)
- M 700 i
- ¶ NL - 6;   Ybk - 1; m only.

National Acquisitions Group   (NAG)   1986
- ■ 12 Holm Oak Drive, MADELEY, Cheshire, CW3 9HR.   (hq)
   01782 750462   fax 01782 750462
   email nag@btconnect.com   http://www.nag.org.uk
   Hon Sec: Eileen Hiller
- ▲ Un-incorporated Society
- ○ *P; to stimulate, coordinate & publicise developments concerning the acquisition of library materials; to provide a forum for their discussion
- ● Conf - Mtgs - ET - Res - VE
- M 5 i, 450 f, UK / 15 f, o'seas
- ¶ Directory of Acquisitions Librarians; £60 m, £80 nm.
   Publications list available.

National Acrylic Painters' Association   (NAPA)   1985
- ■ 134 Rake Lane, Wallasey, WIRRAL, Merseyside, CH45 1JW.
   (hq)
   0151-639 2980   fax 0151-639 2980
   http://www.art-arena.com/napa + napauk.org
   Sec: Anthony F Patrick
   (email:anthony@patrick1766.freeserve.co.uk)
- ▲ Un-incorporated Society
- Br USA
- ○ *A, *G, *P; the promotion of the use of acrylic paint as a medium of excellence & innovation for professional fine art painters
- ● Exhib - PL
- < Fine Art Tr Gld
- M 100 i, UK / 300 i, ISAP, o'seas
- ¶ International (NL) - 2; ftm, £1 nm.
   Exhibition Catalogue - 1; £1.

National Acupuncture Detoxification Association   (NADA) 1988
NR   The People's Centre, 50-54 Mount Pleasant, LIVERPOOL, L3 5SD.
  0151-708 8107
▲   Un-incorporated Society
Br   Europe, Australia, Canada, India, Mexico, Nepal, Russia, Trinidad, USA
○   *P; to treat substance abuse, compulsive behaviour, attention deficient disorder & stress management
M   1,000 i, UK / 10,000 i, o'seas
¶   NL - 2; ftm only.
✕   2001-02 National Auricular Acupuncture Detoxification Association

National Adult School Organisation   (NASO)   1899
NR   Riverton, 370 Humberstone Rd, LEICESTER, LE5 0SA.   (hq)
  0116-253 8333   fax 0116-251 3626
  email gensec@naso.org.uk   http://www.naso.org.uk
  Gen Sec: Mrs Patricia C Dean
▲   Registered Charity
Br   10
○   *E; to promote learning for life for those aged 50+ through the medium of informal, non-vocational study in discussion groups
●   Conf - Mtgs - ET - Exhib - SG - VE - Residential schools
<   Nat Coun Voluntary Orgs (NCVO)
M   1,078 i
¶   One & All - 10.   AR.
  Study Hbk (title varies) - 1.
  Discussion leaflets & Training papers - sets of 12.

National Advisory Service for Parents of Children with a Stoma (NASPCS)   1988
NR   51 Anderson Drive, Valley View Park, DARVEL, E Ayrshire, KA17 0DE.   (chmn)
  01560 322024
  email john@stoma.freeserve.co.uk
  http://www.naspcs.co.uk p
  Chmn: John Malcolm
▲   Registered Charity
○   *W; parental self-help group for those with children who have serious bladder & bowel problems
●   Res - Stat - Inf
<   Intl Ostomy Assn
M   440 i, 12 f, 60 org, UK / 20 i, 4 org, o'seas
¶   NL - 4; free.   Contact list - 1; ftm only.

National Alliance of Women's Organisations   (NAWO)   1989
NR   1-3 Berry St, LONDON, EC1V 0AA.   (hq)
  020 7490 4100
▲   Registered Charity; Un-incorporated Society
○   *N; brings widely diverse women's organisations together to achieve equality & justice for all women
M   org

National Amateur Bodybuilders Association   (NABBA)   1950
NR   PO Box 1186, BRIERLEY HILL, Staffs, DY5 2GL.   (hq)
  01384 898578   fax 01384 898579
  http://www.nabba.co.uk
  Sec: Mrs V Charles
▲   Un-incorporated Society
○   *S; the controlling body for bodybuilding contests for men & women; promotion of weight-training as a means of health & fitness
M   i & clubs

National Ankylosing Spondylitis Society   (NASS)   1976
■   PO Box 179, MAYFIELD, E Sussex, TN20 6ZL.   (hq)
  01435 873527   fax 01435 873027
  email nass@nass.co.uk   http://www.nass.co.uk
  Dir: Fergus Rogers
▲   Registered Charity
Br   110
○   *W; patient education & support
●   Conf - Mtgs - ET - Res - Inf
<   Ankylosing Spondylitis Intl Fedn; Brit League against Rheumatism; Brit Soc of Rheumatology
M   7,000 i, UK / 400 i, o'seas
¶   AS News - 2; free.
  Guidebook for Patients - 1; free.
  Living with Ankylosing Spondylitis.
  Physiotherapy (cassette tape).
  Fight Back (physiotherapy video + DVD); £12
  Other publications available.

National Anti-Vivisection Society Ltd   (NAVS)   1875
§   261 Goldhawk Rd, LONDON, W12 9PE.   (hq)
  020 8846 9777
  http://www.navs.org.uk
  Dir: J Creamer
  'a campaign body promoting awareness of experiments or procedures on living animals; to provide evidence of the misleading & dangerous results of these when applied to people...'
  The society is affiliated to The Animal Defenders & Animal + World Show.

National Arabidopsis Society   (NAS)   1999
■   81 Park View, Collins Rd, LONDON, N5 2UD.   (asa)
○   *L
●   Conf - Mtgs - VE
M   i

National Arenas Association   (NAA)   1991
NR   27 Friary Avenue, Shirley, SOLIHULL, W Midlands, B90 4FZ.   (hq)
  0121-744 2211
  email naa@blueyonder.co.uk   http://www.ilmc.com/naa
  Admin: Eileen Naughton
○   *T; owners of concert venue type arenas
M   15 venues

National Art Collections Fund (The Art Fund)   1903
■   Millais House, 7 Cromwell Place, LONDON, SW7 2JN.   (hq)
  020 7225 4800   fax 020 7225 4848
  email info@artfund.org   http://www.artfund.org
  Dir: David Barrie
▲   Registered Charity
○   *A; the UK's leading art charity; to help museums, art galleries, historic houses & other public collections to acquire works of art, either by grants or through gifts & bequests.
  The Art Fund is independent of government & receives no public funding
●   Funding
M   80,000 i
¶   Art Quarterly - 4;   Review - 1; both ftm only.

National Association for Able Children in Education   (NACE)
NR   PO Box 242, Arnolds Way, OXFORD, OX2 9FR.
  01865 861879   fax 01865 861880
  email info@nace.co.uk   http://www.nace.co.uk
  Dir: Joanna Raffan
○   *E; to help education professionals to improve classroom practice for able, gifted & talented pupils
M   c 2,000 i

© CBD Research Ltd · Beckenham · BR3 5JS · Tel 020 8650 7745 · Fax 020 8650 0768 · E-mail cbd@cbdresearch.com · www.cbdresearch.com

National Association of Accordion & Fiddle Clubs

- ■ 7 Lathro Lane, KINROSS, KY13 8RX.
  01577 862337
  Sec: Lorna Mair
- ○ *D
- M 76 clubs
  no further information supplied

National Association of Administrative Staff in Schools & Colleges
  since 2002 a group of **Professionals Allied to Teaching**

National Association of Adult Placement Services (NAAPS)

- NR 602 The Cotton Exchange, Old Hall St, LIVERPOOL, L3 9LQ.
  (hq)
  0151-227 3499 fax 0151-236 3590
  http://www.naaps.co.uk
  Chief Exec: Sian Lockwood
- ▲ Registered Charity
- ○ *W; to promote & develop adult placement as a resource
  offering vulnerable adults the opportunity to live in a normal
  domestic setting, as part of a family & of a local community
- ● Conf - Mtgs - ET - Inf
- M 2,000+ i, 150+ SSDs
- ¶ Publications list available.

National Association of Advanced Motorcycle Instructors (NAAMI)

- ■ 376 Alcester Road South, Kings Heath, BIRMINGHAM,
  B14 6EW. (regd/office)
  0121-444 0440 fax 0121-444 0440
  email info@naami.co.uk http://www.naami.co.uk
  Sec & Dir: Charles Davis
- ▲ Company Limited by Guarantee
- ○ *P; to promote & maintain high & consistent standards of
  advanced motorcycle instruction, & increased awareness of
  the safety & other benefits of advanced motorcycle training
- ● Conf - Mtgs - ET - Res - SG - Inf - LG
- M 34 i
- ¶ NAAMI News (NL) - 4; ftm.

National Association of Advisers for Computers in Education
  *merged in 2004 with Micros & Primary Education & Computer
  Education Group to form* **Naace**

National Association of Advisers & Inspectors in Design & Technology (NAAIDT) 1992

- NR Hallgate, 26 Back Lane, Glapwell, CHESTERFIELD, Derbys,
  S44 5PX. (hsp)
  07887 523895
  email john.culpin@naaidt.org.uk
  http://www.naaidt.org.uk
  Admin Officer: John Culpin
- ▲ Un-incorporated Society
- ○ *P; promotes the teaching of design & technology in schools
- < Standing Conf Schools' Science & Technology
- M 315 i & f
- ¶ NL. Conference Report - 1.
  Safety Training for Teachers. Occasional papers.

National Association of Advisory Officers for Special Educational Needs (NAAOSEN) 1983

- NR Maryland, Princes St, TUNBRIDGE WELLS, Kent, TN2 4SL.
  (hsp)
  Contact: Diana Robinson
- ○ *P
- ● Conf - LG
- < Nat Assn Educl Inspectors, Advisers & Consultants
- M i
- ✕ 2005-06 National Association of Advisory Officers for Special
  Education

National Association of Aerial Photographic Libraries (NAPLIB) 1989

- ■ c/o RCAHMS, John Sinclair House, 16 Bernard Terrace,
  EDINBURGH, EH8 9NX. (hq)
  http://www.naplib.org
  Hon Sec: Kevin McLaren
- ○ *L; promote the use & preservation of aerial photography
- ● Conf - Inf - VE
- < Remote Sensing & Photogrammetry Soc
- M 47 i, 31 f, UK / 1 i, o'seas
- ¶ NAPLIB Flyer - 4; ftm only.
  NAPLIB Directory of Aerial Photographic Collections in the
  UK; £10 m, £15 nm.
  The Care & Storage of Photographs: recommendations for
  good practice; £2.50 m, £5 nm.

National Association of Agricultural Contractors (NAAC) 1893

- ■ Samuelson House, Paxton Rd, Orton Centre, PETERBOROUGH,
  Cambs, PE9 4RP. (hq)
  01733 362920 fax 01733 362921
  email jill.hewitt@naac.co.uk http://www.naac.co.uk
  Chief Exec: Mrs Jill Hewitt
- ▲ Company Limited by Guarantee
- ○ *F,*H, *T; for UK contractors who supply land-based services to
  farmers, government, local authorities, sports & recreational
  facilities
- Gp Crop spraying; Amenity; Livestock; Mobile feed mill+mix;
  Mobile seed processors
- ● Conf - Mtgs - ET - Inf & advice - LG
- < Confédn Eur des Entrepreneurs de Travaux Techniques
  Agricoles et Rurales (CEETAR)
- M i & f (numbers confidential)
- ¶ Contracting Bulletin - 12; ftm only.
  ProContractor - 2; free.
  Contractors Directory [Ybk] - 1; ftm only.

National Association of Alcohol & Drug Abuse Counsellors (UK) (NAADAC) 1984

- NR Unit 84, 95 Wilton Rd, LONDON, SW1V 1BZ. (hq)
  0873 763 6139
  Chief Exec: Simon Shephard
- ▲ Company Limited by Guarantee
- ○ *P, *W; to contribute to the relief of poverty, sickness & distress
  among persons suffering from addiction to drugs of any
  kind; to develop alcohol & drug abuse counselling as a
  professional specialism
- ● Conf - Mtgs - ET - Inf - LG
- M c 1,000 i
  Note: since 2000 has used the trade name of Federation of
  Drug & Alcohol Professionals

National Association of Almshouses 1946

- ■ Billingbear Lodge, Carters Hill, WOKINGHAM, Berks,
  RG40 5RU. (hq)
  01344 452922 fax 01344 862062
  email naa@almshouses.org
  http://www.almshouses.org
  Dir: A P De Ritter
- ▲ Registered Charity
- ○ *W; to advise members on any matters concerning almshouses
  & the welfare of the elderly
- ● Conf - Mtgs - Res - Exhib - SG - VE - LG
- < Age Concern; Charities Working Party
- M 1,800 almshouses
- ¶ The Almshouses Gazette - 4; £1; AR - 1; £1.
  Also known as the Almshouse Association.

National Association of Animal Therapists
  since 2005 has changed title to **International Association of
  AnimalTherapists** *although remaining a UK association*

National Association for Areas of Outstanding Natural Beauty (NAAONB)
NR The Old Police Station, Cotswold Heritage Centre, NORTHLEACH, Glos, GL54 3JH.
01451 862007
Sec: Jill Smith

National Association of Bank & Insurance Customers (NABIC) 1992
NR PO Box 15, Caldicot, NEWPORT, Monmouthshire, NP26 5YD. (sb)
email enquiries@lemonaid.net   http://www.lemonaid.net
Sec: Janet Saunders
▲ Un-incorporated Society
Br 3; France, Germany, Holland, Italy, Spain, USA
○ *K, *N; 'independent watchdog group for private & commercial users of bank & insurance services'
Gp Banks; Banking; Insurance; Customer protection; Consumer protection
● Conf - ET - Res - SG - Stat - Inf - Lib - LG
< Eur U of Financial Service Users; Nat Assn of Mortgage Victims; Anti-poverty Forum
M 5,000 i, 15,000 f, 100 org, UK / 100 i, 250 f, 10 org, o'seas
¶ Money Minder - 12; ftm only.
Reports & Statistics - irreg; on application.

National Association for Bikers with a Disability   (NABD) 1991
■ Unit 20 The Bridgewater Centre, Robson Avenue, Urmston, MANCHESTER, Lancs, M41 7TE. (hq)
0870 759 0603
email office@thenabd.org.uk   http://www.nabd.org.uk
▲ Registered Charity
Br 32; Republic of Ireland
○ *W; to help disabled people enjoy motorcycling to the full; to organise & finance adaptions to motorcycles, trikes & scooters to suit the disability of the rider; help with licensing, insurance & general access to motorcycling events; to ensure that when it comes to motorcycling 'a disability is not a handicap'.
● Conf - Mtgs - ET - Res - Exhib - Comp - Inf - VE - LG - Annual National Rally
< Motorcycle Action Group (MAG); Brit Motorcyclist Fedn (BMF)
M 2,000 i, 30 f, 70 org, UK / 20 i, o'seas
¶ Open House - 4; ftm, donation nm.

National Association of Boat Owners   (NABO) 1991
NR 48 Old Lane, Bramhope, LEEDS, W Yorks, LS16 9AZ. (hsp)
0113-284 2046
email gen.sec@nabo.org.uk   http://www.nabo.org.uk
Freepost (BM8367), B31 2BR.
Gen Sec: Carole Sampson
▲ Un-incorporated Society
○ *G; representation of private boat owners on Britain's inland waterways
● Stat - Inf - LG & representation to statutory bodies & waterway authorities
< Intl Navigation Assn
M 2,500 i & org
¶ NABO News - 7; ftm only.

National Association of Bookmakers Ltd   (NAB) 1932
NR 19 Culm Valley Way, UFFCULME, Devon, EX15 3XZ. (hq)
01884 841859
○ *T; for on-course bookmakers

National Association of Brass Band Conductors   (NABBC) 1946
■ 30 Havant Rd, HORNDEAN, Hants, PO8 0DT. (hsp)
023 9259 8162
Hon Sec: Ted Howard
▲ Un-incorporated Society
Br 6
○ *G; the promotion of brass band music & conductors
● Conf - Mtgs - Comp - Lib - Assistance to members wishing to study adjudication
M 300 i
¶ The Conductor - 4; ftm, £2.50 yr nm.

National Association of British & Irish Millers
see **Incorporated National Association of British & Irish Millers**

National Association of British Market Authorities   (NABMA) 1919
NR The Guildhall, OSWESTRY, Salop, SY11 1PZ. (hq)
01691 680713   fax 01691 671080
email nabma@nabma.com   http://www.nabma.com
Chief Exec: G Wilson
○ *N, *T; to constitute a medium of communication between members & others in promoting & administering matters of common interest relating to markets, fairs, abattoirs & cold stores
Gp Section c'ees: Livestock & abattoirs, Retail markets, Wholesale markets
● Conf - Mtgs - Exhib - Inf - VE - LG
< Assn of Town Centre Mgt; Eur Assn of Livestock Markets; Wld U of Whls Markets
M 135 local authorities
¶ AR; ftm.

National Association of Building Co-operatives Society Ltd (NABCO)
IRL 50 Merrion Square East, DUBLIN 2, Republic of Ireland.
353 (1) 661 2877   fax 353 (1) 661 4462
http://www.nabco.ie
Gen Sec: Bernard Thompson
○ *N

National Association for the Care & Resettlement of Offenders
see **NACRO - National Association for the Care & Resettlement of Offenders**

National Association of Careers & Guidance Teachers
since 2004 **Association for Careers Education & Guidance**

National Association of Catering Butchers   (NACB) 1983
NR 224 Central Markets, LONDON, EC1A 9LH. (hq)
020 7248 1896   fax 020 7329 0658
Sec: Liz Murphy
○ *T
M c 30 f

National Association of Child Contact Centres   (NACCC) 1985
■ Minerva House, Spaniel Row, NOTTINGHAM, NG1 6EP. (hq)
fax 0845 450 0420
email contact@naccc.org.uk   http://www.naccc.org.uk
Chief Exec [interim]: Gordon Anderson
▲ Company Limited by Guarantee; Registered Charity
○ *N, *W; to keep over 2,000 children a week in touch with both parents through a network of child contact centres
● Helpline: 0845 450 0280 (0900-1300 Mon-Fri)
M c 300 centres
¶
Ben's Story: an introduction to child contact centres (a children's book); £2 m, £2.50 nm.
AR.

National Association for Child Support Action (NACSA) 1993
NR PO Box 4454, DUDLEY, W Midlands, DY1 9AN.
      (mail/address)
      email admin@nacsa.co.uk   http://www.nacsa.co.uk
▲   Company Limited by Guarantee
○   *K; to help & support parents who have problems with the
      Child Support Agency
Gp specialist advisers
●   Res - Inf - LG
¶   NACSA News - 4; ftm only.

National Association for Children of Alcoholics   (NACOA)
§   P O Box 64, Fishponds, Bristol, BS16 2YY.
      0800 358 3456(helpline)
      email nacoa.org.uk
      a non-membership body

National Association of Chimney Engineers Ltd (NACE) 1982
NR PO Box 849, LINCOLN, LN4 3WU.   (hq)
      01526 322555   fax 01526 323181
      email info@nace.org.uk   http://www.nace.org.uk
      Sec: Michael Carr
▲   Company Limited by Guarantee
○   *T; to promote & develop the safe installation & construction of
      all types of chimney & chimney lining in domestic properties
Gp Competent persons register; Code of practice development
●   ET - Exhib - Inf - LG
M   c 30 f, 10 associate
¶   Flueways (NL) - 4; ftm only.
✕   2001 National Association of Chimney Lining Engineers

National Association of Chimney Sweeps (NACS) 1982
◼   Unit 15 Emerald Way, Stone Business Park, STONE, Staffs,
      ST15 0SR.   (hq)
      01785 811732   fax 01785 811712
      email nacs@chimneyworks.co.uk
      http://www.nacs.org.uk
      Admin: Mrs Patricia Coulthard-Jones
○   *T; to promote the use of professional sweeps to clean &
      maintain chimneys; to advise public of chimney safety
●   Conf - Mtgs - ET - Exam - Exhib - LG
<   Europäische-Schornsteinfegermeister-Föderation; Co-Gas
      Safety; HETAS; OFTEC; Solid Fuel Assn; Nat Fireplace Assn;
      Nat Energy Foundation
M   235 i, 16 f, UK / 2 f, o'seas
¶   Chimney Jnl - 3; ftm.

National Association of Choirs (NAC) 1920
◼   612 Lightwood Rd, Lightwood, STOKE-on-TRENT, Staffs,
      ST3 7EQ.   (hsp)
      email rhodeswf@ntlworld.com
      http://www.ukchoirsassn.co.uk
      Gen Sec: Frank Rhodes
▲   Registered Charity
Br 25 areas
○   *D, *N; to promote, develop & maintain public education in, &
      appreciation of, the art & science of music & in particular
      choral music
●   Conf - Mtgs - Inf - Lib
<   Tonsil
M   13 i, 16 f, 500 org
¶   NAC News & Views - 3; ftm, £2 nm.
      NAC Ybk - 1; ftm, £2 nm.

National Association of Cider Makers (NACM) 1920
◼   6 Catherine St, LONDON, WC2B 5JJ.   (hq)
      020 7836 2460   fax 020 7836 0580
      email bob.price@fdf.org.uk
      Sec: R D Price
▲   Un-incorporated Society
○   *T; interests of makers of cider & perry
Gp Technical (incl manufacture, packaging & labelling)
●   Mtgs - LG
<   Assn des Inds des Cidres et Vins de Fruits de l'EU (AICV); Food
      & Drink Fedn
M   8 f, 2 affiliated org
      SW of England Cidermakers Association
      Three Counties Cider & Perry Association
¶   Cider - 2.   LM; on request.

**National Association of Cigarette Machine Operators
(NACMO) 1968**
◼   Cherwell Tobacco, Unit 2 Waymills Industrial Estate,
      WHITCHURCH, Shropshire, SY13 1TT.   (hsb)
      01948 663322   fax 01948 663671
      Gen Sec: Michael G White
▲   Company Limited by Guarantee
Br 5
○   *T; for cigarette vending machine operators
●   Conf - Mtgs - Exhib - Inf
M   5 i, 295 f
¶   Bulletin - 12.

National Association of Citizens Advice Bureaux
since 2003 **Citizens Advice Bureau**

National Association of Clinical Tutors (NACT) 1969
◼   56 Queen Anne St, LONDON, W1G 8LA.   (hq)
      020 7317 3109   fax 020 7317 3110
      email office@nact.org.uk   http://www.nact.org.uk
      Exec Mgr: Mrs Jane Litherland
▲   Registered Charity
○   *E, *P; to support medical education in running postgraduate
      medical education in teaching hospitals
Gp Clinical tutors; Foundation programme training directors
●   Conf - Mtgs - ET
M   480 i
¶   Directory of Postgraduate Medical Centres (with gazetteer) - 1;
      ftm, £60 nm.

**National Association of Clubs for Young People (NACYP)
1925**
NR 371 Kennington Lane, LONDON, SE11 5QY.   (hq)
      020 7793 0787   fax 020 7820 9815
      email office@nacyp.org.uk   http://www.nacyp.org.uk
      Chief Exec: Simon Antrobus
▲   Registered Charity
○   *Y; to enable young men & young women to achieve their
      potential by providing them with opportunities to develop
      their personal & social education from activities delivered
      through a network of affiliated clubs
M   400,000 i, 3,500 clubs
¶   Annual review.   AR.   Ybk.   NL - 4.
      Various booklets & leaflets.

National Association for Colitis & Crohn's Disease (NACC) 1979
NR 4 Beaumont House, Sutton Rd, ST ALBANS, Herts, AL1 5HH. (hq)
01727 830038 fax 01727 862550
http://www.nacc.org.uk
Dir: Richard Driscoll
▲ Registered Charity
Br 70
○ *W; to provide support & information to patients & families with ulcerative colitis & Crohn's disease; to fund research into the cause & cure of these conditions
Gp NACC in contact listening ear service; Welfare fund
● Conf - Mtgs - Res - Inf
Infoline: 0845 130 2233
M c 30,000 i
¶ NL - 4. AR; free.

National Association Commercial Finance Brokers (NACFB) 1993
NR 17 Gandy St, EXETER, Devon, EX4 3LS. (hq)
01392 491551 fax 01392 498090
email admin@nacfb.org http://www.nacfb.org
Chief Exec: Keith Heron
▲ Company Limited by Guarantee
○ *P; for commercial mortgage, lease & asset finance, factoring & invoice discounting brokers
● Conf - Mtgs - ET - Exhib - LG
M 500 i, 350 f
¶ Niche Commercial - 12.

National Association of Complaints Personnel, Health Ltd (NACP) 1996
NR c/o Blythens Ltd, Haydn House, 309-329 Haydn Rd, Sherwood, NOTTINGHAM, NG5 1HG. (regd/off)
▲ Company Limited by Guarantee
○ *P; to act as a communication channel between policy makers, overseeing bodies & those working directly, or indirectly, in NHS Complaints

National Association of Cooperative Officials (NACO) 1917
NR 6a Clarendon Place, HYDE, Cheshire, SK14 2QZ. (hq)
0161-351 7900 fax 0161-366 6800
Gen Sec: L W Ewing
▲ Registered Trade Union
Br 41 (5 sections)
○ *U
● Conf - ET - Res - Empl - LG
< TUC; Soc for Cooperative Studies; Labour Research
M c 2,500 i & constituent org
¶ Cooperative Official - 5; ftm only.

National Association of Councillors 1959
NR Gateshead Civic Centre, GATESHEAD, Tyne & Wear, NE8 1HH. (hsb)
0191-433 3000 fax 0191-477 9253
email cllr.pmole@gateshead.gov.uk
Nat Sec: Councillor Peter Mole
○ *P; to represent the interests of local government councillors
¶ The Councillor - 2. Bulletin - 2.

National Association of Councils for Voluntary Service
since 14 June 2006 **National Associaton for Voluntary & Community Action**

National Association of Counsellors, Hypnotherapists & Psychotherapists (NACHP) 1977
■ PO Box 719, Burwell, CAMBRIDGE, CB5 0NX. (hq)
01638 741363 fax 01638 744190
email mail@nachp.org http://www.nachp.org
Chmn: James Hammond, Co Sec: Sarah Anderson
▲ Company Limited by Guarantee; Registered Charity
○ *P; to provide information to the general public in the fields of counselling, hypnotherapy & psychotherapy; to provide accreditation of qualified & ethical persons
Gp Counsellors; Hypnotherapists; Psychotherapists; Trans-gender issues; Education/training; Information
● Conf - Mtgs - ET - Inf
< UK Confedn of Hypnotherapy Orgs
M 102 i, UK / 2 i, o'seas
¶ NL - 4; ftm only.

National Association of Credit Hire Operators
NR 1 Garston Gardens, KENLEY, Surrey, CR8 5AN.
020 8660 9907
http://www.nacho.org.uk
○ *T

National Association of the Deaf
see **Irish Deaf Society / National Association of the Deaf**

National Association for Deaf People (NAD) 1963
IRL 35 North Frederick St, DUBLIN 1, Republic of Ireland.
353 (1) 872 3800 fax 353 (1) 872 3816
email nad@iol.ie http://www.nadp.ie
Chief Exec: Niall Keane
○ *W

National Association of Deafened People (NADP) 1984
■ PO Box 50, AMERSHAM, Bucks, HP6 6XB. (mail/address)
01227 379538 01227 762879 (text) fax 01227 379538
email enquiries@nadp.org.uk http://www.nadp.org.uk
Hon Sec: Gillian Hadfield
▲ Registered Charity
○ *W; to promote the interests & welfare of people with a profound or total acquired hearing loss
● Conf - Exhib - Inf - Local support groups
< member of UK Council on Deafness
M 500 i
¶ Network (NL) - 4; ftm only.
Information Booklet; ftm, £2.50 nm.
An Introduction to Cochlear Implants; ftm, £5 nm.
[membership; £15]

National Association of Decorative & Fine Arts Societies (NADFAS) 1968
NR NADFAS House, 8 Guilford St, LONDON, WC1N 1DA. (hq)
020 7430 0730 fax 020 7242 0686
email enquiries@nadfas.org.uk
http://www.nadfas.org.uk
▲ Company Limited by Guarantee; Registered Charity
○ *A; 'for the aesthetic education of the public in the cultivation, appreciation & study of the decorative & fine arts; gives aid for the preservation of the artistic heritage of the UK & other countries for the benefit of the public''
Gp Church recorders; Heritage volunteers; Young arts
● ET - SG - VE
M c 90,000 i, 370 societies
¶ NADFAS News (Jnl) - 2; Annual Review; both ftm only.

© CBD Research Ltd · Beckenham · BR3 5JS · Tel 020 8650 7745 · Fax 020 8650 0768 · E-mail cbd@cbdresearch.com · www.cbdresearch.com

National Association for Dentistry in Health Authorities & Trusts (NADHAT) 1975
NR Dental Dept - Zetland House, Friarage Hospital,
    NORTHALLERTON, N Yorks, DL6 1JG.   (hsb)
    01609 764112
    Hon Sec: Patricia Ludiman
○ *P; networking & forum for dental managers who commission
    & provide community hospital dental services
● Conf - Res - ET - Inf
M c 100
¶ LM - 1; £3.

National Association of Deputising Doctors   (NADD)   1983
◼ 8 Dartmouth Park Hill, LONDON, NW5 1HL.   (hsb)
    020 7272 1337   fax 020 7561 1494
    Hon Sec: Dr C Fleming
Br 2
○ *P; to protect & promote the interests of doctors working in 'out-
    of-hours' medical services
● Conf - Mtgs
< Brit Medical Assn
M 2,000 i

National Association for the Development of Work with Sex Offenders
    since 2001 **National Organisation for the Treatment of Abusers**

National Association of Early Years Professionals
    dissolved 2004

National Association for the Education of Sick Children (NAESC)   1993
§ Regus House, Herald Way - Pegasus Business Park, CASTLE
    DONNINGTON, Derbys, DE74 2TZ.   (hq)
    01332 638586   fax 01332 638206
    a non-membership body which works exclusively to: improve
    educational opportunities across the UK for all children
    whose education is disrupted by illness; mount projects to
    improve the provision of education for sick children; define &
    gain acceptance of standards of education by health
    professionals; support the training of teachers

National Association for the Education, Training & Support of Blind & Partially Sighted People   (OPSIS)   1992
◼ c/o Queen Alexandra College, Court Oak Rd, Harborne,
    BIRMINGHAM, B17 9TG.   (hq)
    0121-428 5037   fax 0121-428 5048
    email opsis@dircon.co.uk   http://www.opsis.org.uk
    Chief Exec: Mike Brace
○ *N, *W; to exert influence on policymakers, raise standards &
    improve the quality of services for visually impaired people
Gp Housing; Schools
● Conf - Mtgs - ET - Exhib - Inf - LG - Welfare & support for
    visually impaired people
< VISION 2020
M 7 org

National Association of Educational Guidance for Adults (NAEGA)   1982
NR PO Box 36, Offley, HITCHIN, Herts, SG5 3BB.   (mail)
    01462 769400   fax 01462 769400
    email admin@naega.org.uk
    http://www.naega.org.uk address
    Admin: Di Middleditch
Br 8
○ *E; to encourage the formation & development of client-centred
    educational guidance provision for adults
Gp Guidance practitioners; Managers in guidance organisations;
    Others with an interest in promoting life-long learning
● Conf - Mtgs - ET - Exhib - Inf - LG
< Standing Conf Assns for Guidance in Educl Settings; Nat Advy
    Coun Careers & Educl Guidance
M 177 i, 156 f
¶ News & Views - 4; ftm, £5 nm.   AR; ftm, £2.50 nm.
    Occasional papers - irreg; ftm, price varies nm.

National Association of Educational Inspectors, Advisers & Consultants
    since November 2005 **Association of Professionals in Education & Children's Trusts**

National Association for Environmental Education (UK) (NAEE)   1960
◼ University of Wolverhampton, Walsall Campus, Gorway Rd,
    WALSALL, W Midlands, WS1 3BD.   (hq)
    01922 631200
    email info@naee.org.uk   http://www.naee.org.uk
    Hon Sec: Sue Fenoughty
▲ Registered Charity
○ *E, *L, *P; 'for all interested in education & the environment'
● Conf - Mtgs - ET - Res - SG - Inf
M 2,000 i, 12 local org, UK / i, o'seas
¶ Environmental Education - 3; £25 yr m, £6 each nm.
    subscription: UK i/£25, f/£30; o'seas i/£40, f/£50

National Association of Estate Agents   (NAEA)   1962
◼ Arbon House, 21 Jury St, WARWICK, CV34 4EH.   (hq)
    01926 496800   fax 01926 400953
    email info@naea.co.uk   http://www.naea.co.uk
    Chief Exec: Peter Bolton King
▲ Company Limited by Guarantee
Br 48
○ *P; cooperation among estate agents & protection of public
    against fraud, misrepresentation & malpractice
Gp Residential sales; Residential lettings; Commercial sales;
    Commercial lettings; Property management; International
    property
● Conf - Mtgs - ET - Exam - Res - Exhib - Comp - Stat - Inf - VE -
    LG
< Nat Assn of Realtors (USA); Maklarsmafundet (Sweden); Assn of
    Real Estate Agents [in] Romania / Japan; Estate Agents Bd of
    S Africa; Inst of Profl Auctioneers & Estate Agents, Southern
    Ireland
M 9,500 i
¶ The Estate Agent - 8; ftm.
    A Simplified Guide to the Estate Agents Act 1979 & its Orders &
    Regulations.
    An Introduction to Commercial & Business Transfer Agency.
    A Practitioner's Guide to Residential Letting & Property
    Management.
    An Estate Agent's Guide to the Property Misdescriptions Act.
    International Manual.   International Directory.

National Association of Ex-Offenders
    see **Unlock - National Association of Ex-Offenders**

National Association of Farmers' Markets
    in 2004 merged with the Farm Retail Association to form the
    National Farmer's Retail & Markets Association

National Association of Farriers, Blacksmiths & Agricultural Engineers (NAFB&AE) 1902
- ■ The Forge, Avenue B / 10th Street, National Agricultural Centre, STONELEIGH PARK, Warks, CV8 2LG. (hq)
  024 7669 6595   fax 024 7669 6708
  Nat Organiser: Miss L Scrannage
- Br 28
- ○ *T
- ● Conf - Mtgs - ET - Exhib - Comp - Inf - Empl
- M 1,300 i
- ¶ Forge - 6; ftm, £5.90 nm.

National Association of Field Studies Officers (NAFSO) 1969
- NR CEES Stibbington Centre, Church Lane, Stibbington, PETERBOROUGH, Northants, PE8 6LP. (hsb)
  01780 782386   fax 01780 783835
  email office@nafso.org.uk
  Hon Sec: Tricia Zimmerman
- ▲ Un-incorporated Society
- ○ *P; for field studies officers in education & all interested in the environment, natural history & historical sites & buildings
- Gp Field studies; Education; Environmental; Heritage education; Ecology; Geography; History; Outdoor education; Geology
- ● Conf - Mtgs - ET (weekend courses) - Stat - Inf
- < Outdoor Council
- M c 300 i
- ¶ Jnl - 1; ftm.   NL - 3 (termly); ftm only.   Papers.

National Association of Fire Officers (NAFO) 1942
- NR Hayes Court, West Common Rd, HAYES, Kent, BR2 7AU. (hq)
  020 8462 7755   fax 020 8315 8234
  http://www.nafo.org.uk
- Br 63
- ○ *U
- ● Conf - Empl - LG
- M 5,000 i
- ¶ Magazine - 4;   Ybk; both ftm.

National Association of Fisheries & Angling Consultatives (NAFAC)
- NR 106 Icknield Port Rd, Edgbaston, BIRMINGHAM, B16 0AA.
  0121-454 2886
  http://www.nafac.co.uk
  Sec: John Williams
- ○ *G

National Association of Flower Arrangement Societies of Great Britain (NAFAS) 1959
- NR Osborn House, 12 Devonshire Square, LONDON, EC2M 4TE. (hq)
  020 7247 5567   fax 020 7247 7232
  email flowers@nafas.org.uk   http://www.nafas.org.uk
- ▲ Registered Charity
- Br 1,500
- ○ *A; promotion of the art & practice of flower arranging
- Gp Demonstrators; Teachers; Judges & speakers
- ● Conf - Mtgs - ET - Exam - Exhib - Comp - SG - Lib - PL - VE
- < Wld Assn of Flower Arrangers (WAFA); R Horticl Soc
- M 80,000 i, UK / 500 i, o'seas
- ¶ The Flower Arranger - 4.

National Association of Funeral Directors (NAFD) 1905
- ■ 618 Warwick Rd, SOLIHULL, W Midlands, B91 1AA. (hq)
  0845 230 1343   fax 0121-711 1351
  email info@nafd.org.uk   http://www.nafd.org.uk
  Chief Exec: Alan Slater
- ○ *T
- ● Conf - ET - Exam - Exhib - Stat - Inf - LG
- < Eur Fedn Funeral Services; Fédn Intle des Assns de Thanatologues; Nat Assn Pre-paid Funeral Plans; Coun of Brit Funeral Services
- M 3,200 f
- ¶ Funeral Director (Jnl) - 12; ftm.

National Association of Gallery Education
   see **engage: National Association of Gallery Education**

National Association for Gifted Children (NAGC) 1967
- ■ Challenge House (suite 14), Sherwood Drive, Bletchley, MILTON KEYNES, Bucks, MK3 6DP. (hq)
  0870 770 3217   fax 0870 770 3219
  email amazingchildren@nagcbritain.org.uk
  http://www.nagcbritain.org.uk
  Dir: Stephen Tommis
- Br 26
- ○ *W; to help, support & encourage gifted & talented children & their families & all others involved in their education & welfare
- M c 2,000 i, 500 schools
- ¶ Gifted & Talented (Jnl) - 1.
  NL - 3;   AR - 1; both ftm only.

** National Association for Gifted Children in Scotland
   Organisation lost: see Introduction paragraph 3

National Association of Goldsmiths of GB & Ireland (N.A.G.) 1894
- NR 78a Luke St, LONDON, EC2A 4XG. (hq)
  020 7613 4445   fax 020 7613 4450
  email nag@jewellers-online.org.
  http://www.jewellers-online.org
  Chief Exec: Michael J Hoare
- ▲ Company Limited by Guarantee
- ○ *T; to represent the interests of retail jewellers (incl goldsmiths, silversmiths & horologists) in the UK & Ireland
- Gp Jewellery sector
- ● Conf - ET - Res - Exhib - Inf - Lib - LG - Promotional services
- M 3,000 f
- ¶ The Jeweller (Jnl) - 6; ftm.
  n:gauge (NL) - 12.
  Note: The abbreviation for this association must have full stops.

National Association of Governors & Managers
   in 2005 became National Association of School Governors, which merged in 2006 with the **National Governors' Association**

National Association of GP Cooperatives
   closed

National Association of Head Teachers (NAHT) 1897
- NR 1 Heath Sq, Boltro Rd, HAYWARDS HEATH, W Sussex, RH16 1BL. (hq)
  01444 472472   fax 01444 472473
  email info@naht.org.uk   http://www.naht.org.uk
  Gen Sec: Mick Brookes
- ○ *E, *P, *U; for head teachers, deputy head teachers & leaders, principals & vice-principals, of schools & colleges in state maintained & the private sector from nursery to tertiary level
- M c 30,500 i

National Association for Heads of Hospitality Education
   since 2003 **PACE: Professional Association for Catering Education**

National Association of Health Stores (NAHS) 1931
- NR 37 Spencer Rd, DERRY, BT47 6AA. (sb)
  028 7134 2865
  email info@nahs.co.uk   http://www.nahs.co.uk
  Co Sec: Anne Munro
- ▲ Un-incorporated Society
- ○ *T; for independent & other specialist health food retailers
- ● Mtgs - ET - Stat - Inf - Empl - LG
- M i representing retail outlets
- ¶ NL - 4/8 weekly; free.

National Association for Healthcare Security
NR c/o Gareth Hughes, Countess of Chester Hospital NHS Trust,
     Liverpool Rd, CHESTER, CH2 1UL.
     01244 364258
     email enqs@nahs.org.uk
     Sec: Gareth Hughes
○   *P
M   c 70 i

National Association for Higher Education in the Moving Image (NAHEMI) 1963
NR Sir John Cass Dept of Art, Media & Design, London
     Metropolitan University, 59-63 Whitechapel High St,
     LONDON, E1 7PH. (chmn/b)
     020 7320 1000   fax 020 7320 1163
     Chmn: Yossi Balanescu-Bal
○   *A, *E

National Association of Homeopathic Groups (NAHG) 1982
NR 11 Wingle Tye Rd, BURGESS HILL, W Sussex, RH15 9HR. (hsp)
     01444 236848   fax 01444 236848
     email homoeopathy@platform11.org.uk
     Nat Admin: Mrs Mary Mitchell
▲   Un-incorporated Society
○   *K, *M, *N
●   Conf - Inf
M   20 i, 10 org
¶   NL - 2/3;
     Homeopathy for Today & the Future - 2; both ftm only.

National Association of Hospital Broadcasting Organisations (NAHBO) 1970
NR PO Box 76, ELY, Cambs, CB6 3ET. (pres/p)
     0870 521 6009
     email president@hbauk.com   http://www.hbauk.com
     Pres: June Snowden
▲   Company Limited by Guarantee; Registered Charity
○   *W; the relief of sickness & infirmity through the formation,
     provision & extension of hospital broadcasting & allied
     services
●   Conf - Mtgs - Media seminars & workshops - Promotion &
     support of hospital radio - Liaison
M   c 270 org
¶   On Air - 6.
     Note: the trading name of this association is Hospital
     Broadcasting Association

National Association of Hospital & Community Friends
     since 2005 **Attend**

National Association of Hospital Fire Officers (NAHFO) 1973
NR c/o Royal Bolton Hospital, Farnworth, BOLTON, Lancs,
     BL4 0JR. (hsb)
     01204 390905   fax 01204 390908
     email ken.bullas@boltonh-tr.nwest.nhs.uk
     http://www.nahfo.org.uk
     Gen Sec: Ken Bullas
Br   13
○   *P; to promote & encourage the highest standards of fire safety
     in Health Service premises
●   Conf - Mtgs - ET - SG - Stat - VE - LG - Liaison with NHS
     Estates & Fire & Local Authorities on development of
     legislation & all matters relating to fire safety in healthcare
<   Brit Fire Services Assn; UNISON
M   c 370 i
¶   NL - 4.

National Association of Hospital Play Staff (NAHPS) 1975
NR Fladgate, Forty Green, BEACONSFIELD, Bucks, HP9 1XS.
     (inf/officer/p)
     Admin: Sue Pallot
▲   Registered Charity
○   *W; support & information for staff who lead therapeutic play
     for hospital patients under 21 years; to campaign & advise
     on high quality hospital play services
●   Conf - Mtgs - ET - Inf - Empl
M   c 450 i
¶   Jnl - 2.   NL - 2.   AR.
     Expert Articles & Reading List.
     Salary & other information; free.

National Association of Hot Foil Printers
     see **Association of Hot Foil Printers**

National Association of Independent Resources for Children
     since 2004 **Independent Children's Homes Association**

National Association of Independent Travel Agents Ltd
     since May 2005 **Advantage**

National Association of Investigators & Process Servers (NAIPS)
■   Jowitt House, 153 Sunbridge Rd, BRADFORD, W Yorks,
     BD1 2PA. (hsb)
     01274 730444   fax 01274 494042
     email roy@checkserv.demon.co.uk
     Hon Sec: Roy Sykes
○   *P
●   Conf - Mtgs
<   Assn Brit Investigators; Nat Assn Retired Police Officers
M   20 i

National Association of Karate & Martial Art Schools (NAKMAS) 1990
NR Rosecraig, Bullockstone Rd, HERNE BAY, Kent, CT6 7NL. (hq)
     01227 370055
     http://www.nakmas.org.uk
     Dir of Operations: Miss Sandra J Beale
▲   Un-incorporated Society
○   *S; to act as the governing body for martial arts; to provide
     training courses & vocational & NVQ qualifications
Gp NVQ national accreditation team
●   Conf - Mtgs - ET - Exam - Res - Exhib - Comp - SG - Inf - Lib -
     LG
<   Brit Quality Foundation (BQF); Brit Standards Instn (BSI); Nat Trg
     Org
M   54,000 i, 500 org, UK / 1,500 i, o'seas
¶   NAKMAS Jnl - 4.
     Introduction to Martial Arts.
     Martial Arts Code of Safety.
     Codes of Ethics & Child Protection Procedures.

National Association of Ladies' Circles of Great Britain & Ireland (NALC) 1936
■   Provincial House, Cooke St, KEIGHLEY, W Yorks, BD21 3NN.
     (hq)
     01535 607617   fax 01535 662312
     http://www.ladies-circle.org.uk
Br   650
○   *W; 'non-political, non-sectarian organisation for women aged
     18-45 for social contact'
●   Conf - Mtgs - VE - Social activities - Fund-raising - Community
     service projects
<   Ladies' Circle Intl
M   3,750 i
¶   The Circler - 2; ftm, £2 nm.

National Association of Language Advisers   (NALA)   1969
- ■ c/o Redcar & Cleveland ICT Centre, Corporation Rd, REDCAR, Cleveland, TS10 1HA.   (hsb)
  01642 286688
  Hon Sec: Jim McElwee
- ○ *P; for modern foreign language (MFL) advisers, consultants & inspectors (public & private sectors) who work with schools & colleges in the UK to promote the quality of MFL teaching & learning
- ● Conf - Mtgs - ET - Res - Inf - LG
- M   c 250 i
- ¶ NALA Update - 3; ftm only.
  Report on Members' Annual Trends Survey - 1; ftm; (from Centre for Information on Language Teaching & Research, 20 Bedfordbury, London, WC2N 4LB).

National Association of Laryngectomee Clubs   (NALC)   1976
- ■ 152 Buckingham Palace Rd, LONDON, SW1W 9TR. U.   (hq)
  020 7730 8585   fax 020 7730 8584
  http://www.naic.co.uk
  Gen Sec: Vivien Reed
- ▲ Registered Charity
- Br 94
- ○ *W; to promote the welfare & rehabilitation of laryngectomy patients & their families; to be of assistance to professionals working in the field
- Gp Cancer of the larynx
- ● Conf - Mtgs - ET - Inf - Seminars - Counselling, help & referral service
- < MacMillan Cancer Relief
- M 4,000 i, 94 clubs
- ¶ Clan (NL) - 4.
  Publications list available.

National Association of the Launderette Industry Ltd   (NALI)   1955
- ■ 146 Welling Way, WELLING, Kent, DA16 2RS.   (sp)
  020 8856 9798   fax 020 8856 9394
  Sec: G W Bricher
- ▲ Company Limited by Guarantee
- ○ *T; for launderette operators & supplier companies to the trade
- ● Mtgs - Exhib - SG - Stat - Inf - LG
- M 586 i, 56 f
- ¶ Launderette & Cleaning World - 4; ftm.

National Association for Leisure Industry Certification (NAFLIC)   1988
- ■ PO Box 752, SUNDERLAND, Co Durham, SR3 1XX.   (hsp)
  0191-523 9498   fax 0191-523 9498
  email mccleisure@lineone.net   http://www.naflic.org.uk
  Gen Sec: Neil R McCullough
- ▲ Un-incorporated Society
- ○ *T; to promote safety in the leisure industry
- ● Conf - Mtgs - Exhib - Inf - LG
- M 34 f, UK / 2 f, 1 org, o'seas

National Association of Licensed Opencast Operators (NALOO)   1988
- ■ c/o H J Banks & Co Ltd, Inkerman Rd, Tow Law, BISHOP AUCKLAND, Co Durham, DL13 4HG.   (hsb)
  01740 658500
  Sec: Ian Parkin
- ▲ Company Limited by Guarantee
- ○ *T; to promote the interests of those concerned with licensed opencast coal mining operations
- M f

National Association of Licensed Paralegals   (NALP)   1989
- ■ 9 Unity St, BRISTOL, BS1 5HH.   (hq)
  0117-927 7077   fax 0117-929 3887
  email legalnapl@aol.com
  http://www.nationalparalegals.com
  Gen Sec: John C Stacey-Hibbert
- ▲ Un-incorporated Society
- Br 3
- ○ *P; national regulatory & professional body for paralegals; provides educational & qualifying requirements, training, professional status & licensing to all those working or seeking to work as paralegals in solicitors' offices or within commerce, industry or the public sector
- Gp Community & voluntary sector paralegals group; Paralegal advocacy group; Private paralegal practitioners; Vocational training
- ● Conf - Mtgs - ET - Exam - Res - Exhib - SG - Inf - VE - Empl - LG
- > Inst Legal Secs & PAs
- M c 4,000 i, UK / c 250 i, o'seas
- ¶ The Paralegal (Jnl) - 4; ftm only.
- × 2005 National Association of Paralegals

National Association for Literature Development   (NALD)   1994
- NR PO Box 49657, LONDON, N8 7YZ.   (co-ord/office)
  020 8348 3846
  email dara@nald.info   http://www.nald.org
  Co-ordinator: Steve Deardon
- ▲ Un-incorporated Society
- ○ *P; 'for all most involved in developing writers, readers & literature audiences'
- ● Conf - Mtgs - ET - Res - Inf
- M c 80 i, 110 f
- ¶ ELATEST (NL) - 12; ftm only.

National Association of Local Councils   (NALC)   1947
- NR 109 Great Russell St, LONDON, WC1B 3LD.   (hq)
  020 7637 1865   fax 020 7436 7451
  email nalc@nalc.gov.uk   http://www.nalc.gov.uk
- ▲ Un-incorporated Society
- ○ *N; to promote interests of parish, community & town councils; to assist them in the performance of their duties; to promote social, cultural & recreational life of parishes & villages
- ● Conf - Mtgs - ET - Exhib - Inf - Empl - LG
- < Intl U Local Authorities
- M 10,000 parish, community & town councils in England & Wales
- ¶ Local Council Review.   Various other publications.

National Association of Local Councils in Wales
  in 2004 joined with the Wales Association of Community & Town Councils to form **One Voice Wales**

National Association of Local Government Arts Officers (NALGAO)   1997
- NR c/o Pete Bryan, 36 Gwendolin Ave, Birstall, LEICESTER, LE4 4HD.   (hq)
  0116-267 1441   fax 0116-267 1441
  email nalgao@aol.com   http://www.nalgao.org
  Admin: Pete Bryan
- ▲ Un-incorporated Society
- ○ *A, *P; for logal government arts officers & those in the creative industries sector
- Gp Local authority arts officers; Creative industries sector
- ● Conf - Mtgs - ET - Res - SG - Stat - Inf - LG
- M 325 i & local authorities
- ¶ NL - 3; ftm only.

National Association for Managers of Student Services
- NR PO Box 26311, CREIFF, Perthshire, PH7 3YU.
  01764 650363   fax 01764 650363
  Admin: Tina Philp
- ○ *P

© CBD Research Ltd · Beckenham · BR3 5JS · Tel 020 8650 7745 · Fax 020 8650 0768 · E-mail cbd@cbdresearch.com · www.cbdresearch.com

National Association of Master Bakers   (NAMB)   1887
■   21 Baldock St, WARE, Herts, SG12 9DH.   (hq)
      01920 468061   fax 01920 461632
      Chief Exec: David Smith
○   *T; to represent craft bakery businesses in England & Wales
M   f

**National Association of Master Letter Carvers   (NAMLC)
1920**
■   c/o NAMM, 1 Castle Mews, RUGBY, Warks, CV21 2XL.   (hq)
      01788 542264   fax 01788 542276
      Sec: John Smith
▲   Un-incorporated Society
○   *P; to preserve & promote hand carved lettering in stone,
      marble & granite
●   Mtgs - Empl
M   50 i
¶   LM; free.

National Association of Mathematics Advisers   (NAMA)   1974
NR   PO Box 51, Glos, GL12 7XA.
      http://www.nama.org.uk
▲   Un-incorporated Society
○   *E, *P; to disseminate information & ideas on all subjects
      relating to maths education; to promote specific policies on
      maths education
●   Conf - ET - SG - LG
M   350 i
¶   NL - 3; ftm.

**National Association for Medical Education Management
(NAMEM)   1975**
■   PO Box 375, YORK, YO10 3WQ.   (hsp)
      01904 414832
      email ruth.bycroft@btinternet.com
      http://www.namem.org.uk
      Exec Sec: Mrs Ruth Bycroft
○   *N, *P; organisation & administration of postgraduate medical
      training for dentists & doctors
●   Conf - Mtgs - ET - SG
<   Nat Assn Clinical Tutors (NACT)
>   NAMPS; Middlesex University
M   250 i
¶   NL - 2.   AR - 1.   LM - 1.
      Reference Hbk - 1.   Training Programme 3-yr course; £1,200.
      Council Hbk - 1.
×   2002 (January) National Association of Postgraduate Medical
      Education Centre Administrators

National Association of Memorial Masons   (NAMM)   1907
■   1 Castle Mews, RUGBY, Warks, CV21 2XL.   (hq)
      01788 542264   fax 01788 542276
      email enquiries@namm.org.uk
      http://www.namm.org.uk
      Pres: Keith Rackham
▲   Company Limited by Guarantee
○   *T; interests of memorial masonry industry (natural stone
      memorials)
●   Conf - Mtgs - ET - Exam - Res - Exhib - Comp - Inf - VE - Empl
      - LG
<   Intl Monument Fedn; EURO-ROC; Coun of Brit Funeral
      Services; Confedn of Burial Authorities (UK)
M   25 i, 400 f, UK / 5 i, 25 f, o'seas
¶   Review (Jnl) - 4; ftm only.

**National Association for Mental After-Care in Residential Care
Homes   (MARCH)   1989**
■   10 Holmwood Avenue, UDDINGSTON, Lanarkshire,
      G71 7AJ.   (hq)
      01698 815400
      email ian@silverwellshouse.co.uk
      http://www.march.org.uk
      Sec: Ian Strachan
▲   Company Limited by Guarantee; Registered Charity
○   *W; to relieve those persons who are, or who have been,
      suffering from a mental disorder; to secure & enhance their
      quality of life & assist in the prevention of further episodes of
      acute illness
Gp   Dementia care (EMI); Respite care
●   Conf - Mtgs - ET - Res - Exhib - SG - Stat - Inf - LG
M   70 i
¶   MARCH Mental Health Circular - 4; ftm, £2.50 nm.

**National Association for the Mentally Handicapped of Ireland
(NAMHI)**
IRL   5 Fitzwilliam Place, DUBLIN 2, Republic of Ireland.
      353 (1) 676 6035   fax 353 (1) 676 0517
      email info@namhi.ie   http://www.namhi.ie
      Chief Exec: Deirdre Carroll
○   *W

National Association of Microwave Engineers   (NAME)
■   5 Bournemouth Drive, SEAHAM, Co Durham, SR7 8HB.
      0191-581 7964
      email nameoffice@ntlworld.com
○   *T
      no further information supplied.

**National Association of Mining History Organisations
(NAMHO)   1979**
■   c/o Peak District Mining Museum, The Pavilion,
      MATLOCK BATH, Derbys, DE4 3NR.   (hq)
      01629 583834
      http://www.namho.org
      Hon Sec: S Bassham
▲   Registered Charity
○   *L, *N; for learned & research organisations; to promote
      development of knowledge of mining history
●   Conf - Res - SG - Inf - VE - LG - Field meetings - Formation of
      codes of practice
<   Assn of Indl Archaeology; Brit Cave Res Assn; Nat Caving Assn
M   7 f, 73 org, UK / 1 org, o'seas
¶   NL - 3; ftm, £1 nm.   Mining Heritage Guide; £5 m, £6 nm.
      Code of Practice for: Mineral collecting, Removal of artefacts,
      Mine exploration; free for sae please.   Publicity leaflet.

National Association of Music Educators   (NAME)   1947
■   Gordon Lodge, Snitterton Rd, MATLOCK, Derbys, DE4 3LZ.
      (hq)
      01629 760791   fax 01629 760791
      email musiceducation@name.org.uk
      http://www.name.org.uk
      Admin: Helen Fraser
▲   Un-incorporated Society
○   *D, *E; for all involved in the furtherance of musical education
Gp   Music curriculum: Primary, Secondary; Initial teacher training &
      higher education; Advisers, inspectors, consultants;
      Corporate members
●   Conf - Mtgs - ET - Res - Inf - LG
<   Music Educ Coun; Fedn of Music Services; Scot Assn of Music
      Educators; Welsh Music Inf Centre (CAGAC)
M   556 i, 53 org, UK / 4 i, o'seas
¶   Name magazine - 3; ftm, £3.50 nm.
      Postbag (NL) - 4; ftm, £1 nm.

National Association of Musical Instrument Repairers (NAMIR) 1993
- ■ 42 Marine Parade, HYTHE, Kent, CT21 6AN. (hsp)
  email secretary@namir.org.uk   http://www.namir.org.uk
  Hon Sec: C McNeilly
- ▲ Un-incorporated Society
- ○ *P; to encourage a high standard of workmanship & customer care; to provide a means of information exchange on techniques & parts availability; to provide technical backup where required; to advance technical skills by cooperation with manufacturers; to act as arbitrator in the event of a dispute between repairer & customer
- Gp Woodwind; Brass; Strings; Baroque instruments; Suppliers
- ● Conf - Mtgs - ET - Inf - VE
- < Nat Assn of Profl Band Instrument Repair Technicians (NAPBIRT (USA))
- M 136 i, 6 f, UK / 12 i, o'seas
- ¶ The Intrepid Repairer - 4; ftm.

National Association of Nappy Services (NANS) 1992
- NR 271 Holdbrook Court, Holdbrook South, WALTHAM CROSS, Herts, EN8 7SL. (hsb)
  http://www.changeanappy.co.uk
  Contact: Ian Rapley
- ▲ Un-incorporated Society
- ○ *T; for cotton nappy laundering services
- ● Conf - Mtgs - Exhib - Inf - LG
  Helpline: 0121-693 4949
- < Real Nappy Assn
- M 30 f

National Association of Natural Family Planning Teachers
  since 2002 **Natural Family Planning Teachers Association**

National Association of NFU Group Secretaries (NAGS) 1947
- NR Woodside Industrial Estate, Llanbadoc, USK, Gwent, NP15 1SS. (hsb)
  01291 672715   fax 01291 673835
  Gen Sec: Andy Hilditch
- ▲ Un-incorporated Society
- ○ *T; 'to represent the business & welfare interests of agents of the NFU Mutual & Farming Union Secretaries to their principals, & otherwise promote the prosperity of their business'
- Gp Education; Financial services; Insurance; IT & group services
- ● Conf - Mtgs - ET - SG - Stat - Inf - Empl
- M 430 i, 300 f
- ¶ NL - 4; ftm.

National Association of Non-Principals
  since 2004 **National Association of Sessional GPs**

National Association of Nurses for Contraception & Sexual Health
- NR 9 Church Close, Drayton Bassett, TAMWORTH, Staffs, B78 3UJ.
  01827 260117   fax 01827 260154
  email office@nancsh.org.uk   http://www.nancsh.org.uk
- ○ *M, *P

National Association of Official Prison Visitors (NAOPV) 1924
- NR 32 Newnham Avenue, BEDFORD, MK41 9PT. (hsb)
  01234 359763   fax 01234 359763
  Gen Sec: Mrs A G McKenna
- Br 40
- ○ *W
- ● Conf - Mtgs - LG (Home Office)
- M 1,400 i
- ¶ NL - 2; ftm.
- × 2003 National Association of Prison Visitors

National Association of Ovulation Method Instructors UK (NAOMI) 1978
- ■ The Billings Method Centre, 4 Southgate Drive, CRAWLEY, W Sussex, RH10 6RP. (p/pres/p)
  01444 881744   fax 01444 881744
  http://www.billingsnaomi.org
  Pres: Dr Helen Davies
- ▲ Registered Charity
- ○ *P; to provide information & authentic literature on the Billings Ovulation Method of natural family planning to achieve, or avoid, a pregnancy
- ● ET (for qualifications to instruct) - Inf - Lib
- < Wld Org of the Ovulation Method Billings (WOOMB)
- M i

National Association of Paper Merchants   (NAPM) 1920
- NR PO Box 2850, NOTTINGHAM, NG5 2WW. (hq)
  0115-841 2129
  email info@napm.org.uk   http://www.napm.org.uk
  Dir: Tim Bowler
- ▲ Un-incorporated Society
- ○ *T
- ● Conf - Mtgs - Stat - Inf - Lib - LG
- M 21 f

National Association of Paralegals
  since 2005 **National Association of Licensed Paralegals**

National Association of Park Home Residents   (NAPHR) 1982
- ■ Flat B / 38 Abergele Rd, COLWYN BAY, LL29 7PA. (hq)
  01492 535677
  email jim@naphr.co.uk   http://www.naphr.org.uk
  Chmn: Jim Winchester
- ▲ Un-incorporated Society
- ○ *G; voluntary advisory group serving the interests of park home / mobile home owner occupiers on permanently licensed parks
- Gp Mobile home law
- ● Inf
- M 10,000 i
- ¶ NAPHR NL - irreg; ftm.

National Association for Pastoral Care in Education   (NAPCE) 1982
- ■ c/o Institute of Education, COVENTRY, Warks, CV4 7AL. (hq)
  024 7652 3810   fax 024 7657 4110
  email base@napce.org.uk   http://www.napce.org.uk
  Chmn: Jae Bray
- ▲ Registered Charity
- Br 13
- ○ *E, *W; 'promoting pastoral care & personal-social education'
- ● Conf - Mtgs - ET - Res - Comp - Inf
- M 800 i, 1,200 org, UK / 50 i, o'seas
- ¶ Pastoral Care in Education (Jnl) - 4; ftm, £4 each nm.
  AR; free.

National Association for Patient Participation   (N.A.P.P.) 1978
- NR 10 Rosegarth Avenue, Aston, Sheffield, S26 2DD.
  (mail/address)
  Hon Sec: Audrey Hoggard
- ▲ Registered Charity
- ○ *W; to develop & maintain patient participation at surgeries & health care centres; to facilitate improved networking of patients within primary care groups; individuals can affiliate
- ● Conf - Mtgs - ET - LG
- M c 200 groups
- ¶ NL - 4; m only.
  Note: it is a legal requirement that this Association uses full stops in its abbreviation

© CBD Research Ltd · Beckenham · BR3 5JS · Tel 020 8650 7745 · Fax 020 8650 0768 · E-mail cbd@cbdresearch.com · www.cbdresearch.com

National Association of Pension Funds Ltd   (NAPF)   1923
NR   NIOC House, 4 Victoria St, LONDON, SW1H 0NX.   (hq)
       020 7808 1300   fax 020 7222 7585
       http://www.napf.co.uk
       Chief Exec: Christine Farnish
○   *T
M   c 1,400 org

**National Association for People Abused in Childhood
(NAPAC)   1997**
NR   42 Curtain Rd, LONDON, EC2A 3NH.
▲   Registered Charity
○   *W
●   Helpline: 0800 085 3330
       no further information supplied

National Association of Percussion Teachers   (NAPT)   1984
■   11 Mallard Close, Kempshott, BASINGSTOKE, Hants,
       RG22 5JP.   (hsp)
       01256 329009
       email wendy@waba4.co.uk   http://www.napt.org.uk
       Hon Sec: Wendy Harding
○   *D, *P; for teachers, instructors & players of percussion
       instruments
Gp   Percussion teachers & performers
●   Conf - ET - Lib
M   200 i, 8 f, UK / 10 i, o'seas
¶   NL - 3; ftm only.

*National Association of Postgraduate Medical Education Centre
    Administrators*
    since January 2002 **National Association for Medical Education
    Management**

National Association of Poultry Suppliers
    has closed

**National Association for Pre-Paid Funeral Plans   (NAPFP)
1993**
NR   15 Riverside Drive, SOLIHULL, W Midlands, B91 3HH.   (hq)
       0121-715 5133
       Sec: Nigel Burton
▲   Un-incorporated Society
○   *T; to serve the interests of members in providing pre-paid
       funeral plans for clients (incl ensuring the security of funds
       entrusted for this purpose) & maintaining a high standard of
       integrity in the marketing & selling of such plans
●   Inf - LG
M   9 f
¶   Code of Practice - 1;   AR - 1;
       Independent Chairman's Report on Adherence to Code of
       Practice - 1; all ftm.

**National Association for Premenstrual Syndrome   (NAPS)
1984**
■   41 Old Rd, EAST PECKHAM, Kent, TN12 5AP.   (hq)
       0870 777 2178   fax 0870 777 2178
       email naps@pms.org.uk   http://www.pms.org.uk
       Chief Exec: Christopher Ryan
▲   Registered Charity
○   *W; to provide support, help & information to women who
       suffer pre-menstrual syndrome & theirfamilies; works to
       promote better understanding of the condition & its treatment
●   Conf
       Helpline: 0870 777 2177
<   Long-term Med Conditions Alliance
M   c 850 i
¶   NL - 12;   Understanding PMS.
       Diet books & other publications.

National Association of Press Agencies Ltd   (NAPA)   1983
■   41 Lansdowne Crescent, ROYAL LEAMINGTON SPA, Warks,
       CV32 4PR.   (asa)
       0870 609 1935   fax 01926 424760
       http://www.napa.org.uk
       The Administrator
▲   Company Limited by Guarantee
Br   46; 3
○   *T; for news & photographic agencies, established
       correspondents for all leading newspapers, magazines, TV &
       broadcasting outlets
●   Conf - Mtgs
M   46 f, UK / 3 f, o'seas
¶   NAPA Hbk - 1.

National Association of Primary Care   (NAPC)   1998
NR   Lettsom House, 11 Chandos St, Cavendish Sq, LONDON,
       W1G 9DP.   (hq)
       020 7636 7228   fax 020 7636 1601
       email napc@napc.co.uk   http://www.napc.co.uk
○   *N; for all practices working as Primary Care Groups
●   Conf - ET - Inf (& training resources on secure website) - LG -
       Workshops
       Helpline: 020 7636 1677, Mon-Fri 0900-1700)
M   org
¶   Jnl
       Simple Guide to CGs
       Making Sense of Health Improvement Programmes.

**National Association of Primary Care Educators UK   (NAPCE)
1990**
NR   Carne House (1st floor), Parsons Lane, BURY, Lancs, BL9 0JT.
       (hq)
       0161-272 0110   fax 0161-763 9278
       email napce@btinternet.com   http://www.napce.net
       Chmn: Dr Stephen Holmes
▲   Registered Charity
○   *E, *M, *P
●   Conf - Mtgs - ET
¶   NL - 4; free.
       List of publications available.

National Association for Primary Education   (NAPE)   1980
NR   NAPE National Office, Moulton Rd, Moulton, NORTHAMPTON,
       NN3 7RR.   (hq)
       01604 647646   fax 01604 647660
       email nationaloffice@nape.org.uk
       http://www.nape.org.uk
       Hon Gen Sec: Diana B Butt
▲   Registered Charity
○   *E; partnership between parents & teachers & any other
       interested individuals, in the promotion & provision of
       primary & pre-school education
●   Conf - Mtgs - ET - Res - Exhib - Comp - SG - Stat - Inf - LG
<   Eur Parents Assn; Home & School Coun; Coll of Teachers
M   300 i, 5 f, 300 schools, UK / 3 i, 4 schools, o'seas
¶   Newsbrief (NL) - 4; ftm only.

National Association of Prison Visitors
    2003 has become **National Association of Official Prison
    Visitors**

National Association of Private Ambulance Services (NAPAS) 1987

■ 21 Bassenhally Rd, WHITTLESEY, Cambs, PE7 1RN.   (hsp)
   01733 350916   fax 01733 350112
   email napas@ambulanceservices.co.uk
   http://www.ambulanceservices.co.uk
   Nat Dir: Peter A Littledyke

▲ Un-incorporated Society
Br 53; 3 Republic of Ireland
○ *P; to ensure standards in the provision of independent, private
   & professional ambulance & ambulance aid in the UK &
   throughout Europe
Gp Equestrian; Boxing; Motor sport; Pop concerts; Repatriation;
   NHS contracting; Rave parties; Club medics;
   Ambulance services: Air, Rail, Road, Ice sports;
   Advisory & contingency for all events & business
● Conf - Mtgs - ET - Res - SG - Stat - Inf - Lib - PL - LG
< Brit Ambulance Services Panel; DTI Foresight
M 53 f, UK / 3 f, o'seas
¶ NAPAS News & Views - 4; ftm only.
   NAPAS Code of Practice & Annual Members Audit - 1; ftm,
   4x1st class stamps, nm.

National Association of Probation & Bail Hostels   (NAPBH) 1942

NR Baltic Wharf, St Peter's Quay, TOTNES, Devon, TQ9 5EW.
   01803 864781   fax 01803 866265
   email office@napbh.org.uk   http://www.napbh.org.uk
   Sec: Eunice Dunkley
M c 300 i

National Association of Probation Officers   (NAPO)   1912

NR 3-4 Chivalry Rd, LONDON, SW11 1HT.   (hq)
   020 7223 4887   fax 020 7223 3503
   email info@napo.org.uk   http://www.napo.org.uk
   Gen Sec: Judy McKnight
○ *P, *U
M 7,500 i
¶ Probation Journal - 12.

National Association for Providers of Activities for Older People (NAPA) 1997

■ Bondway Commercial Centre (5th floor), Unit 512,
   71 Bondway, LONDON, SW8 1SQ.   (hq)
   020 7078 9375   fax 020 7735 9634
   email sylvie@napa-activities.co.uk
   http://www.napa-activities.net
   Strategic Dir: Mrs Sylvie Silver
▲ Company Limited by Guarantee; Registered Charity
○ *W; to provide activities for older people, essential to the
   maintenance of physical & psychological health & wellbeing; to provide education & training; to support individuals
   who provide activities, whether in home or care settings
● ET - Res - Inf
M 660 i
¶ NAPA NL - 3; ftm.

National Association of Public Golf Courses   (NAPGC)   1927

■ 12 Newton Close, REDDITCH, Worcs, B98 7YR.   (hsp)
   01527 542106   fax 01527 455320
   email eddiemitchell@blueyonder.co.uk
   http://www.napgc.org.uk
   Hon Sec: Ed Mitchell
▲ Un-incorporated Society
○ *S; to represent public pay & play golf courses in the UK
M 100 clubs & members
¶ Annual Competitions Review - 1; ftm.   Ybk.

National Association of Railway Clubs

■ 4 Belmont, BRIGHTON, E Sussex, BN1 3TF.
   01273 462977
   Sec: M Edwards
○ *N

National Association of Range Manufacturers   1933

NR c/o Preston & Thomas Ltd, Woodville Engineering Works,
   Heron Rd, Rumney, CARDIFF, Glam, CF3 3YF.   (sb)
   029 2079 3331   fax 029 2077 9195
   Sec: Simon Preston
○ *T; interests of makers & suppliers of equipment for fried fish &
   chip restaurants
M f
¶ Fish Trader - 52.

National Association of Re-enactment Societies   (NARES) 1991

NR Alma House, 72 Cow Close Rd, LEEDS, W Yorks, LS12 5PD.
   (hsp)
   0113-229 6759
   email des1622@ntlworld.com
   Sec: Des Thomas
▲ Un-incorporated Society
○ *G, *N; to represent the interests of British re-enactors
● Conf - Mtgs - ET - Res - Exhib - SG - Inf - PL
M 5,000 i, 25 f
¶ Retrospection - 4; ftm, £1 nm.

National Association of Registered Petsitters

NR Priory Leasow, Titley, KINGTON, Herefords, HR5 3RS.
   0870 350 0543
   email info@dogsit.com   http://www.dogsit.com
   Chmn: Robin Taylor
○ *G

National Association for the Relief of Paget's Disease (NARPD) 1973

NR 323 Manchester Rd, Walkden, Worsley, MANCHESTER,
   M28 3HH.   (hq)
   0161-799 4646   fax 0161-799 6511
   email director@paget.org.uk   http://www.paget.org.uk
   Dir: Marilyn McCallum
▲ Registered Charity
○ *W; to support & inform sufferers of Paget's disease of bone, &
   their carers; to raise awareness of the disease among the
   medical profession & the public at large; to support & raise
   funds for research
M c 2,400 i
¶ NL - 4;   AR;   Information booklets; all free.

National Association of Retired Police Officers   (NARPO) 1919

NR 38 Bond St, WAKEFIELD, W Yorks, WF1 2QP.   (hq)
   01924 362166   fax 01924 372088
   email narpo.org.uk
   Chief Exec: Mike Thornton
▲ Un-incorporated Society
Br 120
○ *P; 'to safeguard the rights of members & promote measures
   for their welfare with particular regard to pensions'
● Conf - Mtgs - Inf - Pension matters - Appeals & benefits
< Public Services Pensioners Coun
M 100,000 i
¶ Magazine - 4; ftm only.

National Association of Road Transport Museums   (NARTM) 1982
- ■ Museum of Transport, Boyle St, Cheetham, MANCHESTER, M8 8UW.   (chmn/b)
  0161-205 2122   fax 0161-202 1110
  http://www.nartm.org.uk
  Chmn: Dennis Talbot
- ▲ Un-incorporated Society
- Br 25
- ○ *G, *N; to assist the development of volunteer-operated road transport museums by the exchange of information & expertise. To monitor the introduction of legislation which may affect the continued operation of historic road vehicles
- Gp Vehicle database - listing historic buses & coaches in collections
- ● Mtgs - Stat - Inf - VE - LG
- < Fedn Brit Historic Vehicle Clubs
- M c 60 org
- ¶ The Bulletin - 4; ftm only.

National Association of Rooflight Manufacturers   (NARM) 1988
- NR 43 Clare Croft, Middleton, MILTON KEYNES, MK10 9HD.   (hq)
  01908 692325
  email admin@narm.org.uk   http://www.narm.org.uk
  Sec: Lorraine Cookham
- ○ *T; represents manufacturers of rooflights & raw materials in the UK; to enhance & improve standards within the UK & Europe on all types of rooflight products; to provide assistance to architects & other specifiers
- Gp Technical c'ee
- ● Mtgs - Stat - Inf - LG
- < Eurolux
- M 9 f, 5 associates
- ¶ LM.
- ✕ 2002-04 Association of Rooflight Manufacturers

National Association of Round Tables of Great Britain & Ireland   (RTBI)   1927
- ■ 4 Embassy Drive, Edgbaston, BIRMINGHAM, B15 1TP.   (hq)
  0121-456 4402
  email hq@roundtable.org.uk
  Sec: John Handley
- ○ *W, *X; service to community through cultivation of highest ideals in business, professional & civic traditions
- M c 10,000 i

National Association of Scaffolding Contractors last in D17 (04)
   see **National Access & Scaffolding Confederation**

National Association of School Business Managers
   is a subsidiary of the **National Bursars Association**

National Association of School Governors
   since 2006 **National Governors' Association**

National Association of Schoolmasters Union of Women Teachers   (NASUWT)   1919
- ■ Hillscourt Education Centre, Rose Hill, Rednal, BIRMINGHAM, B45 8RS.   (hq)
  0121-453 6150   fax 0121-457 6208
  email nasuwt@mail.nasuwt.org.uk
  http://www.teachersunion.org.uk
  Gen Sec: Chris Keates
- Br 360; Cyprus, Germany, Gibraltar
- ○ *E, *P, *U
- ● Conf - Mtgs - ET - Res - Inf - Empl - LG
- < Educ Intl
- M 223,486 i
- ¶ Teaching Today - termly; ftm.

National Association of Screen Make-up Artists & Hairdressers   (NASMAH)   2000
- ■ 68 Sarsfield Rd, PERIVALE, Middx, UB6 7AG.   (chmn/p)
  020 8998 7494   fax 020 8998 7494
  email info@nasmah.org.uk   http://www.nasmah.org.uk
  Sec: Angela Seyfang,   Chmn: Sandra Exelby
- ○ *P; to raise the standards of make-up artists & hairdressers in this country; to improve training & raise the profile of members in the media industry
- Gp Training; Seminars; Master classes; Courses
- ● Mtgs - ET - Exhib - Inf
- M 200 i
- ¶ NL - 6; free.   Directory - 2 yrly; ftm, £10 nm.

National Association of Security Dog Users   (NASDU)   1996
- ■ Unit 11 Boundary Business Centre, WOKING, Surrey, GU21 5DH.   (mailink/address)
  01483 888588   fax 01483 486335
  email info@nasdu.co.uk   http://www.nasdu.co.uk
  Co Sec: Steve Hill
- ▲ Company Limited by Guarantee
- ○ *P; to achieve, promote & maintain national standards for all trainers, handlers & dogs within the security industry; for those who are concerned the care, health, safety & welfare of dogs within the industry
- Gp Training sub-c'ee; Detection dogs (incl drugs & explosives)
- ● Conf - Mtgs - ET - Exam - Res - Inf - LG - Annual working security dogs trials
- < Brit Inst of Profl Dog Trainers; Skills for Security
- M 200+ i, 60 f, 10 org, UK / 10 i, o'seas
- ¶ NL - 4; ftm, £2 nm.   Code of Practice; £25.
  Pocket Reference Guide; £5.
  Underpinning Knowledge Pack; £25 m, £32.50 nm.
  Trainers Pack; £150 m only.

National Association of Seed Potato Merchants
   2006 merged with the Scottish Potato Trades Association to form the
   British Potato Trades Association

National Association of Sessional GPs   (NASGP)   1997
- ■ PO Box 188, CHICHESTER, W Sussex, PO19 2ZA.   (hsp)
  fax 01243 536428
  email info@nasgp.org.uk   http://www.nasgp.org.uk
  Chie Exec Officer: Richard Fieldhouse
- ▲ Company Limited by Guarantee
- ○ *P; voluntary organisation supporting sessional (salaries & freelance) general practitioners
- Gp GPs: salaried; Freelance/locum
- ● Inf
- M 1,500 i
- ¶ The Sessional GP - 6; ftm, £5 nm.
- ✕ 2004 National Association of Non-Principals

National Association of Shopfitters   (NAS)   1919
- NR 411 Limpsfield Rd, The Green, WARLINGHAM, Surrey, CR6 9HA.   (hq)
  01883 624961
  http://www.shopfitters.org
  Dir: R Hudson
- Br 4
- ○ *T
- ● Conf - Mtgs - Comp - Stat - Expt - Inf
- < Intl Shopfitting Org; Australian Shopfitters Assn; NZ Shopfitters Assn
- M f

National Association for Small Schools (NASS) 1978
- ◼ Cloudshill Cottage, High St, Shutford, BANBURY, Oxon, OX15 6PQ. (nat/coord/p)
  01295 780225   fax 01295 780308
  email mbenford@bigfoot.com
  http://www.smallschools.org.uk
  Inf Officer: Mervyn Benford
- ○ *E, *K, *N; to advance the case for retaining small local schools, mainly those threatened with closure; to promote good practice in both school & community
- ● Conf - Res - Inf
- < Interskola (education in sparsely populated areas)
- > Human Scale Education; Village Retail Services Assn
- M 600 i & gps, UK / 15 i & gps, o'seas
- ¶ NL - 2.

National Association of Social Workers in Education (NASWE) 1884
- NR c/o National Children's Bureau, Wakley St, LONDON, EC1V 7QE. (gsp)
  020 7843 6000
  http://www.naswe.org.uk
  Gen Sec: Jacqui Newvell
- ▲ Un-incorporated Society
- ○ *E, *P; for all education welfare officers & education social workers working for a local education authority
- ● Conf - Mtgs - ET - LG
- < UNISON
- M c 500 i
- ¶ The Education Social Worker - 3; ftm, on request nm.

National Association of Sole Practitioners (NASP)
- NR Buckland Manor, LYMINGTON, Hants, SO41 8NP. (hsp)
  01590 672595
  Hon Sec: Clive Sutton
- ▲ Un-incorporated Society
- ○ *P; sole practitioner solicitors in general practice
- ● Inf - Lib
- M c 70 i
- ¶ NL - 2; ftm only.

National Association for Special Educational Needs
  since 2004-05 **nasen**

National Association of Specialist Computer Retailers (NASCR) 1988
- NR 13 New St, LOUTH, Lincs, LN11 9PT. (hq)
  0845 644 0715   fax 0845 644 0716
  http://www.nascr.org
  Dir: Geoff Carr
- ▲ Un-incorporated Society
- ○ *T; to represent computer retailers & other companies involved in the computer industry; to promote fair practices within the industry & for the consumer
- ● Mtgs - Res - Exhib - Stat - Inf - VE - LG
- M 200 f
- ¶ NASCR Update - 52;   NASCR Ybk - 1; both free.

National Association for Staff Development in the Post-16 Sector (NASD) 1978
- ◼ Acacia House, 83 Underdale Rd, SHREWSBURY, Shropshire, SY2 5EF. (hsb)
  01743 340237
  email steven@sbloor.freeserve.co.uk
  Sec: Joy Shand
- ▲ Un-incorporated Society
- ○ *E; to improve the effectiveness of staff development in the post 16 sector of education in a manner that is responsive to national & college issues
- ● Conf - ET - Inf
- M 30 i, 200 f
- ¶ Jnl - 2; £6 yr.

National Association of Steel Stockholders (NASS) 1928
- ◼ McLaren Building (6th floor), Dale End, BIRMINGHAM, B4 7LN. (hq)
  0121-200 2288   fax 0121-236 7444
  email info@nass.org.uk   http://www.nass.org.uk
  Dir Gen: Bryan Holden
- ○ *T
- Gp Product Gps: General steels, Strip mill coil & sheet, Bright & engineering steels, Stainless steels, Tubes, Plate & processing
  Specialist c'ee: Health & safety
- ● Conf - Mtgs - ET - Exhib - SG - Stat - Inf - VE - LG
- < EUROMETAL; is a member of Metals Forum
- M 113 f
- ¶ NASS News (NL) - 4.   LM.   AR.
  Steel & Its Distribution.
  Safety Guidelines for Steel Stockholders & Processors.
  Beating the Odds [&] Moving Steel by Crane (health & safety video).

National Association for the Support of Victims of Stalking & Harassment (NASH) 1993
- NR PO Box 1309, KENILWORTH, Warks, CV8 2YJ.
  01926 850089
  Dir: Evonne von Heussen-Countryman
- ○ *W; to support & advise the victims of stalking & harassment, in any circumstances, & their families; to provide expert witnesses in court cases
  Note: Please enclose an SAE when writing to the Association.

National Association of Supported Employment
  2006 merged with the Association for Supported Employment to form the **British Association for Supported Employment**

National Association of Supporting Artistes Agents (NASAA)
- NR 373-377 Clapham Rd, LONDON, SW9 9BT.
  email chair@nasaa.org.uk
  Chmn: Sarah Dickinson
- ○ *T

National Association of Swimming Clubs for the Handicapped (NASCH) 1965
- NR The Willows, Mayles Lane, WICKHAM, Hants, PO17 5ND. (hsb)
  01329 833689
  Contact: Mike O'Leary
- ▲ Registered Charity
- ○ *S; to promote swimming & swimming clubs for people with disabilities
- ● Conf - Inf
- < Nat Coordinating C'ee on Swimming for the Disabled
- M c 10,000 i, 100 clubs
- ¶ Register of Swimming Sessions for Disabled People - 2 yrly.
  Ybk - 1; free.

National Association of Teachers of Dancing Ltd (NATD) 1906
- ◼ 44-47 The Broadway, THATCHAM, Berks, RG19 3HP. (hq)
  01635 868888   fax 01635 872301
  email info@natd.org.uk   http://www.natd.org.uk
  Sec: Mrs Lyn Foster
- ▲ Company Limited by Guarantee
- Br worldwide
- ○ *D, *P; to promote & improve the art of dancing in all its forms - ballroom, theatrical & social
- Gp Ballroom; Latin American; Classic & sequence; Ballet; Tap; Modern stage; Acrobatic; Disco free-style; Rock'n'roll; National dance; Dance & exercise; Country & Western; Contemporary dance
- ● Conf - Mtgs - ET - Exam
- M 2,500 i, UK / 500 i, o'seas
- ¶ NL - 4; free.   AR - 1; ftm only.
  Mail shots - new dances etc - irreg; ftm.

© CBD Research Ltd · Beckenham · BR3 5JS · Tel 020 8650 7745 · Fax 020 8650 0768 · E-mail cbd@cbdresearch.com · www.cbdresearch.com

National Association of Teachers of Travellers   (NATT)   1980
- ■ 16 Carlyon Rd, ST AUSTELL, Cornwall, PL25 4AJ.   (pres/b)
  01726 77113   fax 01726 77113
  email gharrisonwhite@cornwall.gov.uk
  http://www.natt.org.uk
  Pres: Ginny Harrison-White
- ▲ Company Limited by Guarantee; Registered Charity
- ○ *E, *P; to promote access to educational opportunities for Gypsies & Travellers as a recognised ethnic group under the Race Relations Act
- ● Conf - Mtgs - Inf
- < Eur Fedn Educ Children Occupational Travellers (EFECOT)
- M 200 i
- ¶ NL - 3; free.   Information Mail Out - 3; ftm only.

National Association for the Teaching of Drama   (NATD)   1977
- ■ The Kingstone School, Broadway, BARNSLEY, S70 6RB.
  01226 738598
  email j.atkinson1@barnsley.org
  Admin: Julie Atkinson
- ○ *A, *E; the advancement of young people through drama; to encourage & promote the development of drama at all levels of education; to provide support for all involved with drama in education
- ● Conf - Mtgs - ET - SG - LG
- < Standing Conf of Young Peoples Theatre (SCYPT)
- M c 120 i
- ¶ Jnl for Drama in Education - 2; ftm.
  Publication arising from Annual Conference.
  Other occasional publications.

National Association for the Teaching of English   (NATE)
- NR 50 Broadfield Rd, Broadfield Business Centre, SHEFFIELD, S Yorks, S8 0XJ.   (hq)
  0114-255 5419   fax 0114-255 5296
  email natehq@btconnect.com   http://www.nate.org.uk
  Hon Sec: Moyra Beverton
- ▲ Company Limited by Guarantee; Registered Charity
- Br 13 regions
- ○ *E, *P; to improve the teaching of English at all levels of education; to provide a national voice on all aspects of education concerning English concerning English
- ● Conf - Mtgs - Exhib - SG - Inf
- < Intl Fedn for the Teaching of English; Coun of Subject Teaching Assns
- M i, schools & colleges
- ¶ English in Education (Jnl) - 3;   Natenews - 5;
  The English & Media Magazine - 2; all ftm.

National Association for Teaching English & other Community Languages to Adults   (NATECLA)   1976
- ■ NATECLA National Centre, South Birmingham College, Room HB110 Hall Green Campus, Cole Bank Rd, BIRMINGHAM, B28 8ES.   (hq)
  0121-688 8121   fax 0121-694 5062
  email co-ordinator@natecla.fsnet.co.uk
  http://www.natecla.org.uk
  Coordinator: Cathy Burns
- ▲ Un-incorporated Society
- Br 10
- ○ *E, *K, *P; campaigning, information, training for ESOL & other language tutors
- ● Conf - ET - Inf - LG
- M 489 i, 122 org
- ¶ NATECLA News - 3; ftm, £2 nm.
  Language Issues [Jnl] - 2; £10 m (£20 instns), £15 nm (£30 instns).

National Association of Tenants Organisations   (NATO)
- IRL 35 Meath Place, DUBLIN 8, Republic of Ireland.
  353 (1) 454 3842   fax 353 (1) 454 3842
  Gen Sec: Matt Larkin
- ○ *G

National Association of Theatre Nurses
  since 2004-05 **Association for Perioperative Practice**

National Association for Therapeutic Education   (NATE)   1995
- ■ 59 Birdham Rd, CHICHESTER, W Sussex, PO19 8TB.   (hsp)
  01243 776042
  email john.tierney@virgin.net
  Dir: John Tierney
- ▲ Un-incorporated Society
- ○ *E, *P; to promote understanding of therapeutic education; to provide a focus for workers in the field
- ● Mtgs - Res - LG - Lobbyists
- M c 95 i

National Association of Toastmasters   (NAT)   1974
- NR 33 Woolhampton Way, CHIGWELL, Essex, IG7 4QQ.   (hsp)
  0845 838 2814
  email secretary@natuk.com   http://www.natuk.com
  Hon Sec: Robert Pursell
- ▲ Un-incorporated Society
- ○ *P; provision of toastmasters for all types of functions
- ● Mtgs - ET
- M 60 i

** National Association of Tool Dealers
  Organisation lost: see Introduction paragraph 3

National Association of Toy & Leisure Libraries   (Play Matters)   1972
- NR 68 Churchway, LONDON, NW1 1LT.   (hq)
  020 7255 4600   fax 020 7255 4602
  email admin@playmatters.co.uk
  http://www.natll.org.uk
- ▲ Registered Charity
- ○ *W; to promote the principle that play DOES matter for the developing child; to offer a supportive service to parents & extend the opportunity for shared play in the home;   Leisure libraries extend this concept to adults with special needs
- ● Conf - ET - Exhib - Inf - Making available & lending appropriate toys at local level, through toy libraries
- < Intl Toy Libraries Assn
- M c 1,000 libraries
- ¶ Play Matters (Jnl) - 4; ftm, £1 nm.   AR.
  Publications list available.

National Association of Tripe Dressers   (NATD)
- NR 1 Tuscan Court - 18 The Esplanade, TELSCOMBE CLIFFS, E Sussex, BN10 7HF.   (hsp)
  01273 585422
  Hon Sec: Mrs Jean Beavis
- ○ *T
- ● Mtgs
- M 4 f

National Association of Valuers & Auctioneers in England, Wales & Scotland   (NAVA)   1988
- ■   c/o John Pye & Sons Ltd, James Shipstone House, Radford Rd, NOTTINGHAM, NG7 7FN.   (hq)
    0115-970 6060/6363   fax 0115-942 0100
    http://www.nava.org.uk
    Warwick Auctions of Coventry, 3 Queen Victoria Rd, COVENTRY, Warks, CV1 3JS.
    024 7623 0992.   (hsb)
    Hon Sec: Robert Beaumont,   CEO: Steven Denley Hill
- ▲   Un-incorporated Society
- ○   *P; valuers & auctioneer firms giving independent, impartial valuation advice & asset sales services to business & the public, for finance, company restructuring, insurance, insolvency, asset transfer & probate purposes (covers everything from drawing pins through antiques, plant, machinery to aeroplanes)
- Gp   Insolvency; Fine arts & antiques; Plant & machinery
- ●   Conf - Mtgs - ET - Exam - Res - Lib
- M   186 i, 64 f
- ¶   Gavel (NL) - 4; free.

** National Association for Victims of Fraud & Banking Malpractice
    Organisation lost: see Introduction paragraph 3

National Association of Victims Support Schemes   (Victim Support)   1979
- ■   Cranmer House, 39 Brixton Rd, LONDON, SW9 6DZ.   (hq)
    020 7735 9166
    email contact@victimsupport.org.uk
    http://www.victimsupport.org
    Chief Exec: Gillian Guy
- ▲   Registered Charity
- ○   *N, *W; to provide victims of crime with appropriate & sufficient recognition, support & information to assist them in dealing with the crimes which they have experienced; to ensure that the rights of victims of crime are acknowledged & advanced in all aspects of criminal justice & social policy
- ●   Conf - ET - Res - Inf - Lib - LG
- <   Eur Forum for Victims Orgs; Nat Coun for Voluntary Orgs (NCVO)
- M   374 schemes, 86 crown court witness services
- ¶   Publications list available.

National Association for Voluntary & Community Action   (NACVS)   1991
- ■   Arundel Court, 177 Arundel St, SHEFFIELD, S Yorks, S1 2NU.   (hq)
    0114-278 6636   fax 0114-278 7004
    email nacvs@nacvs.org.uk   http://www.nacvs.org.uk
    Chief Exec: Kevin Curley
- ▲   Company Limited by Guarantee; Registered Charity
- ○   *N, *W; to promote, support & develop an effective local voluntary sector; the national forum of local infrastructure organisations
- ●   Conf - Mtgs - ET - Inf - LG
- <   Nat Coun Voluntary Orgs (NCVO); Standing Conf for Community Devt (SCCD)
- M   350 local infrastructure org
- ¶   NACVS Circulation - 6.
    AR; free.   Occasional publications.
- ✕   2006 (14 June) National Association of Councils for Voluntary Service

National Association of Voluntary Service Managers   (NAVSM)   1968
- NR   c/o Simon Needham (Voluntary Services Manager), Nottingham City Hospital, Hucknall Rd, NOTTINGHAM, NG5 1PB.   (chmn/b)
    0115 962 7912
    Chmn: Simon Needham
- ▲   Un-incorporated Society
- ○   *P, *W; for voluntary managers & volunteers in the field of health & social care
- ●   Conf - Mtgs - ET - Stat - Inf - LG
- <   Volunteer Centre UK
- M   135 i
- ¶   NL - 6; free.   AR.

National Association of Waste Disposal Officers
- NR   Assistant Director of Environmental Services, North Yorkshire County Council, County Hall, Racecourse Lane, Northallerton, N Yorks, DL7 8AH.
    01609 532161
    Sec: Ian Flelding
- ○   *P
- M   i

National Association of Widows   (NAW)   1971
- ■   48 Queen's Rd (3rd floor), COVENTRY, Warks, CV1 3EH.   (hq)
    024 7663 4848   fax 0845 838 2261
    email inf@nawidows.org.uk
    http://www.nawidows.org.uk
    Nat Chmn: Jean Sargent
- ▲   Company Limited by Guarantee; Registered Charity
- Br   34
- ○   *W; run by widows for widows; to provide friendship & support; there are local branches nationwide & headquarters membership is available where there is no local branch
- ●   Conf - Mtgs - Comp - LG
    Office hours: 0900-1600 Mon, Tues, Thurs, Fri
- M   3,000 i

National Association of Wine & Beermakers (Amateur)   (NAWB(A))   1961
- NR   20 Stable Row, Priorslee Village, TELFORD, Shropshire, TF2 9NW.   (memsec/p)
    http://www.nawb.org.uk
    Mem Sec: Mrs Audrey Atwell
- ▲   Un-incorporated Society
- ○   *G; to promote the art of home wine & beermaking
- ●   Conf - Mtgs - ET - Comp
- M   450 i, 12 regional org, 60 local org
- ¶   NL - 4; ftm only.

National Association of Women's Clubs   (NAWC)
- NR   5 Vernon Rise, King's Cross Rd, LONDON, WC1X 9EP.   (hq)
    020 7837 1434   fax 020 7713 0727
    Chmn: Christine Burton
- Br   300
- ○   *E; to advance education & provide facilities for recreation or other leisure time occupations for women, without distinction of political, religious or other opinions
- ●   Conf - Mtgs - Comp - SG
- <   NCVO; Nat Coun Women; Women's Nat Commission
- M   c 7,000 i
- ¶   NL - 6; ftm.   Club History; 75p m.   AR; ftm, 50p nm.

© CBD Research Ltd · Beckenham · BR3 5JS · Tel 020 8650 7745 · Fax 020 8650 0768 · E-mail cbd@cbdresearch.com · www.cbdresearch.com

National Association of Women Pharmacists (NAWP) 1905
■ c/o The Office Manager, Royal Pharmaceutical Society of GB,
   1 Lambeth High St, LONDON, SE1 7JN.   (mail)
   01453 759516
   email enquiries@nawp.org.uk
   http://www.nawp.org.uk address
   Hon Sec: Mrs Brenda Ecclestone
▲ Un-incorporated Society
Br 3
○ *P
● Conf - ET - VE
M c 300 i
¶ NL - 4; ftm.

National Association of Writers in Education (NAWE) 1987
NR PO Box 1, Sheriff Hutton, YORK, YO60 7YU.   (mail/address)
   01653 618429
   email info@nawe.co.uk   http://www.nawe.co.uk
   Dir: Paul Munden
▲ Company Limited by Guarantee
○ *A; to promote & support the development of creative writing of
   all genres in all educational settings
● Conf - ET - Res - Inf - LG
M c 800 i, c 100 f
¶ Writing in Education - 3; ftm only.

National Association of Writers' Groups (NAWG) 1995
■ 40 Burstall Hill, BRIDLINGTON, E Yorks, YO16 7GA.   (hq)
   01262 609228
   Chmn: Mike Wilson
▲ Registered Charity, Un-incorporated Society
○ *A, *N; to support writers' groups
● Conf - Mtgs - ET - Comp - SG - Inf
M 160 i, f & org
¶ Link Magazine - 6; ftm only.

**National Association of Youth & Community Education Officers
(NAYCEO) 1942**
NR c/o Barbican Post Office, Barbican Rd, LOOE, Cornwall,
   PL13 1EZ.
   01503 265300
   Exec Sec: Mike Williams
▲ Un-incorporated Society
○ *E, *P, *Y
Gp Professional Services; Social Action; International; Women's
   Issues
● Conf - Mtgs - ET - Exhib - Inf - VE - Empl
< Nat U of Teachers
M i
¶ AR; ftm.   Policy statements - irreg; ftm.

National Association for Youth Drama (NAYD)
IRL 34 Upper Gardiner St, DUBLIN 1, Republic of Ireland.
   353 (1) 878 1301   fax 353 (1) 878 1302
   email info@nayd.ie   http://www.youthdrama.ie
   Dir: Orlaith McBride
○ *D, *Y

National Association for Youth Justice (NAYJ) 1995
■ Bitter End, 4 Spring Close, Ratby, LEICESTER, LE6 0XD.   (hsp)
   0116-238 8354   fax 0116-238 7028
   email nayjken@aol.com   http://www.nayj.org.uk
   Admin & Devt: Ken Hunnybun
○ *K; to promote the rights of, & justice for, children in trouble; to
   campaign for the development & implementation of policies
   & practice consistent with this purpose
● Conf - Mtgs - ET - Liaison with children's orgs
> Regional organisations & observers from NI, Scotland & Wales
M 200 i, associated regional orgs
¶ Youth Justice; ftm, £30 nm. (published jointly with Russell
   House Publishing).

National Association of Youth Orchestras (NAYO) 1961
■ Central Hall, West Tollcross, EDINBURGH, EH3 9BP.   (hq)
   0131-221 1927   fax 0131-229 2921
   email admin@nayo.org.uk   http://www.nayo.org.uk
   Gen Mgr: Susan White
▲ Registered Charity
○ *D; to represent youth orchestras throughout the UK; to foster
   their development
Gp Festivals of British Youth Orchestras; European Youth Music
   Week
● Conf - Mtgs - ET - Comp - Inf - Lib - VE - LG
< Intl Arbeitskreis für Musik; Eur Assn Youth Orchestras; Brit Assn
   of Symphonic Bands & Wind Ensembles; Scot Arts Lobby;
   Music Educ Coun; Assn of Brit Orchestras; Voluntary Arts
   Network; Inc Soc of Musicians
M 4 i, 12 f, 128 org, UK / 1 i, 2 org, o'seas
¶ Full Orchestra (NL) - 3; ftm only.   AR - 1.
   Directory of Youth & Student Orchestras, 2002; ftm, £5.50 nm.
   Youth Orchestra Tours Guide; ftm only.

National Association of Youth Theatres (NAYT) 1982
■ The Arts Centre, Vane Terrace, DARLINGTON, Co Durham,
   DL3 7AX.   (hq)
   01325 363330   fax 01325 363313
   email nayt@btconnect.com   http://www.nayt.org.uk
   Dir: Ben Ayrton
▲ Company Limited by Guarantee; Registered Charity
○ *D; supports the development of Youth Theatre activity; is open
   to any group or individual using theatre techniques in their
   work with young people, outside of formal education
● Conf - ET - Inf - Big Youth Theatre Festival (4-day workshop &
   performance programme)
< Nat Coun for Voluntary Youth Service (NCVSI); Nat Assn of
   Clubs for Young People (NACYP); Nat Operatic & Dramatic
   Assn (NODA); Nat Assn Youth Drama (NAYD); Promote Youth
   Theatre Scotland; Nat Coun of Voluntary Orgs (NCVO)
M 300 i, youth theatres & groups
¶ Bulletin - 12;   AR; both ftm only.
   The Big Youth Theatre Manual; £19.99.
   Playing a Part: a study of the impact of youth theatre on the
   personal, social & political development of young
   people; £10.

National Asthma Campaign
   since 2004 **Asthma UK**

**National Auricula & Primula Society (Midland & West Section)
(NAPS) 1901**
NR 9 Church St, Belton, LOUGHBOROUGH, Leics, LE12 9UG.
   (hsp)
   01530 222458   fax 01530 222458
   email david.tarver@btinternet.com
   http://www.auriculaandprimula.org.uk
   Hon Sec: David Tarver
▲ Un-incorporated Society
Br 3 sections
○ *H; to encourage & extend the cultivation of auriculas &
   primulas; to preserve & improve accepted standards
● Conf - Mtgs - Res - Exhib - Comp - Inf - PL - LG
< R Horticl Soc
M c 600 i
¶ NL - 2; 25p.   Argus [Ybk] - 1.

National Auricula & Primula Society (Northern) 1872
■ 27 Temple Rhydding Drive, Baidon, SHIPLEY, W Yorks,
   BD17 5PX.   (hsp)
   http://www.auriculas.org.uk
   Hon Sec: R Taylor
▲ Un-incorporated Society
○ *H; to encourage the growing & exhibition of Auriculas &
   Primulas
¶ Ybk.

National Auricula & Primula Society (Southern)   1876
- ■ 67 Warnham Court Rd, CARSHALTON BEECHES, Surrey, SM5 3ND.   (hsp)
  Hon Sec: L E Wigley
- ○ *H; breeding & cultivation of auriculas, primroses, polyanthuses & other hardy primula species
- ● Exhib - Comp - Inf - Plant sales
- M 400 i, UK / 10 i, o'seas
- ¶ Offsets (NL) - 1; free.   Ybk; ftm, £4 nm.

National Autistic Society   (NAS)   1962
- NR 393 City Rd, LONDON, EC1V 1NG.   (hq)
  020 7833 2299   fax 020 7833 9666
  email nas@nas.org.uk   http://www.nas.org.uk
  Chief Exec: Vernon Beauchamp
- ▲ Company Limited by Guarantee; Registered Charity
- Br 45
- ○ *W; to provide: 1) specialist schools & adult services for people with autistic spectrum disorder, 2) supported employment; to promote awareness with central government & the public; to offer information, advice & support to people with autism & their families & carers
- ● Conf - ET · Inf - Lib - LG
- < Autism Europe
- M c 12,000 i & org
- ¶ Communication (Jnl) - 3.
  Publications list available.

National Backpain Association   (BackCare)   1968
- ■ 16 Elmtree Rd, TEDDINGTON, Middx, TW11 8ST.   (hq)
  020 8977 5474   fax 020 8943 5318
  email info@backcare.org.uk
  http://www.backcare.org.uk
  Chief Exec: Mrs Nia Taylor
- ▲ Company Limited by Guarantee; Registered Charity
- Br 30
- ○ *Q, *W; to educate people on how to avoid preventable back pain; to support those living with back pain; to promote research into causes & treatment of back pain
- ● ET - Res - Inf - LG
- < NCVO; Assn of Medical Res Charities (AMRC); Long-term Medical Conditions Alliance (LMCA); Arthritis & Musculo-Skeletal Alliance (ARMA)
- M 4,000 i, 200 f, UK / 100 i, o'seas
- ¶ Talkback - 4; ftm, £3.95 nm.
  Various books & leaflets.

National Baton Twirling Association   (NBTA)   1982
- NR 17 Gard Close, TORQUAY, Devon, TQ2 8QU.   (hsp)
  01803 324175
  http://www.nbta.org.uk
  Sec: Denise Pearse
- ○ *S; to promote the sport of baton twirling & associated activities
- ● Mtgs - ET - Exam - Comp
- < Nat Baton Twirling Assn Europe; Nat Baton Twirling Assn Intl (USA)
- M c 1,500 i
- ¶ News Direct (NL) - 4; ftm only.

National Bed Federation Ltd   (NBF)   1912
- ■ Victoria House, Victoria St, TAUNTON, Somerset, TA1 3FA.   (hq)
  01823 368008   fax 01823 350526
  email info@bedfed.org.uk   http://www.bedfed.org.uk
  Chief Exec: Patrick Quigley
- ▲ Company Limited by Guarantee
- ○ *T; interests of manufacturers of beds & mattresses & their suppliers
- ● Conf - Mtgs - Exhib - Stat - Inf - VE - LG
- M 112 f, UK & o'seas

National Beef Association   (NBA)   1998
- NR Mart Centre, Tyne Green, HEXHAM, Northumberland, NE46 3SG.   (hq)
  01434 601005   fax 01434 601008
  email helen@natbeef.demon.co.uk
  Sec: Helen Dobson,   Chief Exec: Robert Forster
- ▲ Company Limited by Guarantee
- ○ *F,*T; development & sustainability of beef cattle production within the UK
- ● Conf - Mtgs - LG
- M 2,600 i, 70 f, 32 org
- ¶ Beef Farmer - 4; ftm only.

National Begonia Society   (NBS)   1948
- NR 7 Brabraham Rd, Sawston, CAMBRIDGE, CB2 4DQ.   (hsp)
  01223 834202
  http://www.national-begonia-society.co.uk
  Hon Sec: Alan Harris
- ○ *H; improved cultivation of begonias & their hybridisation
- ● Mtgs - ET - Comp
- < R Horticl Soc
- M c 500 i, f & org
- ¶ Bulletin - 3; ftm only.

National Bingo Game Association Ltd   (NBGA)   1986
- NR 75 High Street North, DUNSTABLE, Beds, LU6 1JF.   (hq)
  01582 860900
  email info@nationalbingo.co.uk
  http://www.nationalbingo.co.uk
  Chief Exec: Paul Talboys
- ▲ Company Limited by Guarantee
- ○ *T; administration of the game
- ● Administration
- M f
- ¶ AR.

National Brickmakers Federation   1918
- ■ Apartment No 4 Bryn Cregin, Ty Mawr Rd, DEGANWY, Conwy, LL31 9UR.   (sp)
  01492 585118
  Sec: J H Mosedale
- ▲ Un-incorporated Society
- ○ *N; provides a forum for meetings of the UK brick industry with reports from various bodies &/or speakers of relevance
- ● Conf - Mtgs
- M 26 f
- × 2003 (Northern Brick Federation
        (Southern Brick Federation

National Bursars Association
- NR 140 Wood St, RUGBY, Warks, CV21 2SP.   (hq)
  01788 573300   fax 01788 571812
  email bursarsassoc@btinternet.com
  http://www.nba.org.uk
  Chief Exec: William Simmonds
- ○ *P; for school bursars, business managers & administrators
- M i

National Campaign for the Arts Ltd   (NCA)   1985
- NR 1 Kingly St, LONDON, W1B 5PA.   (hq)
  020 7287 3777   fax 020 7287 4777
  email nca@artscampaign.org.uk
  http://www.artscampaign.org.uk
  Dir: Victoria Todd
- ▲ Company Limited by Guarantee
- ○ *A, *D, *K; the only independent lobbying organisation which exists to represent the interests of the whole arts sector in all its diversity. It is funded entirely by its members to ensure its independence
- ● Conf - ET - Res - LG
- M c 500 i, 500 org
- ¶ Arts News - 4; ftm.   Facts About the Arts.
  Arts Care (NL) - 10; ftm.

National Campaign for Firework Safety   (NCFS)   1969
- 118 Long Acre, Covent Garden, LONDON, WC2E 9PA.   (hq)
  020 7836 6703
  email ncfs@cgsystem.co.uk   http://www.cgsystem.co.uk
  Dir: Noël Tobin
▲ Registered Charity
Br 12; N Zealand
○ *K; to amend the 1875 Explosives Act & 1976 & 1992
  Fireworks Acts; to license fireworks for use by trained people
  for organised displays only, to dis-allow sale of fireworks to
  un-licensed individuals
Gp Fireworks; Consumers; Safety
● Conf - Mtgs - Res - Exhib - Stat - Inf - LG
< Fire Brigades U; Age Concern; Cats Protection League; Canine
  Defence League; Nat Civil Defence Org
> Confedn of Brit Ind (CBI)
M 100,000 i, 15 org
¶ [see website].

National Campaign for the Homeless
  see **Shelter: National Campaign for the Homeless**

National Campaign for real Nursery Education   (NCNE)   1965
NR c/o Tachbrook Nursery School, Aylesford St, LONDON,
  SW1V 3RN.   (mail)
  email ncea@yahoo.co.uk address
  Contact: Tess Robson
○ *E, *K; promoting & defending state funded nursery education
  nationally
M i
× 2003 National Campaign for Nursery Education

National Campaign for the Sensible Siting of Masts
  see **Mast Action: the National Campaign for the Sensible
  Siting of Masts**

National Campaign for Water Justice   (NCWJ)   1992
- 25 Brooklyn Close, CARSHALTON, Surrey, SM5 2SL.   (hq)
  020 8773 9743   fax 020 8773 9743
  Gen Sec: Tony May,   Chmn: Neil Fishpool
Br 40; Canada, France, USA
○ *K; 'for the re-instatement of the core business of water supply
  & sewerage services into public hands; for the lowering of all
  water charges; to stop the abuses of the water industry such
  as high salaries to the selected few; to campaign against the
  bringing in of measured water & forced installation of water
  meters where they are not wanted'
Gp Advice on: Water law, Political (legislative issues), Complaints
  against the industry, Matters related to people on state
  benefits, the retired & aged, & water matters overseas
● Conf - Mtgs - Res - Stat - Inf - Lib - LG
< U Associates US; Canadian Envtl Law Assn; Nat Consumer
  Coun
M 38,250 i, 18 f, 36 org, UK / 14 i, o'seas
¶ Justice Bulletin - irreg; free.
  Membership Joining Book - 4; free.

National Cancer Alliance   (NCA)   1995
NR PO Box 579, OXFORD, OX4 1LB.   (hq)
  01865 793566   fax 01865 251050
  email nationalcanceralliance@btinternet.com
  http://www.nationalcanceralliance.co.uk
  Chief Exec: Dr Becky Miles
▲ Company Limited by Guarantee; Registered Charity
○ *N; an alliance of patients, carers & health professionals
  working together to improve the treatment & care of all
  cancer patients in Britain
M i

National Candida Society   1997
NR PO Box 151, ORPINGTON, Kent, BR5 1UJ.
  01689 813039
  email info@candida-society.org.uk
  http://www.candida-society.org.uk
  Dir: Dr Christine Tomlinson
○ *M

National Canine Defence League
  since November 2003 **Dogs Trust**

National Caravan Council Ltd   (NCC)   1939
- Catherine House, Victoria Rd, ALDERSHOT, Hants,
  GU11 1SS.   (hq)
  01252 318251   fax 01252 322596
  email info@nationalcaravan.co.uk
  http://www.nationalcaravan.co.uk
  Dir Gen: Graham Beacon
▲ Company Limited by Guarantee
○ *G, interests of the caravan industry
Gp National Park Homes Council; Manufacturers; Traders; Park
  operators; Supplies & services; Holiday caravan distributors
● Conf - Mtgs - ET - Exhib - Stat - Inf - LG
< Eur Caravan Fedn
M 23 i, 500 f, UK / 10 f, o'seas
¶ The Business - 4;   NL - 12; AR; all ftm.

National Care Association   (NCA)   1981
- 45-49 Leather Lane, LONDON, EC1N 7TJ.   (hq)
  020 7831 7090   fax 020 7831 7040
  email info@ncha.gb.com   http://www.ncha.gb.com
  Chief Exec: Sheila Scott
▲ Company Limited by Guarantee
○ *N, *T; to represent providers of care to local & national
  government; to provide services to members to allow them to
  concentrate on the people they care for
Gp Children's services; Domiciliary care; Nursing care; Older
  people; Younger adults
● Conf - Mtgs - ET - Exhib - Inf - LG
M 2,000 i
¶ NL - 12;   Homeowners Manual;   Health & Safety Manual;
  Working Safely (Employees' Hbk).
× 2005 National Care Homes Association

National Care Homes Association
  since 2005 **National Care Association**

**National Carnival Guild - the National Federation of Carnival
  Associations & Committees   (Carnival Guild)   1964**
NR 54 Rokesley Avenue, LONDON, N8 8NR.   (chmn/p)
  020 8340 7339
  Chmn: Gordon P Rathbone
○ *G; promotion of carnival; cooperation between carnival
  associations

National Carpet Cleaners Association Ltd   (NCCA)   1968
NR 62c London Rd, OADBY, Leics, LE2 5DH.   (hq)
  0116-271 9550   fax 0116-271 9588
  email info@ncca.co.uk   http://www.ncca.co.uk
  Co Sec: Paul Pearce
▲ Limited Company
Br 3
○ *T; as well as carpets also incl soft furnishings (curtains &
  upholstery), fire & flood restoration
Gp Fire & flood divn
● Conf - ET - Exam - Res - Exhib - Inf - Lib - PL - LG
< Brit Cleaning Coun; Carpet & Upholstery Cleaners Assn of
  Australia [& South Africa]; Assn of Specialists in Cleaning &
  Restoration (USA)
M c 550 f
¶ NL - 12; ftm.

National Cattle Association (Dairy)
- ■ Brick House, Risbury, LEOMINSTER, Herefords, HR6 0NQ.
01568 760632   fax 01568 760523
email timbrigstock@hotmail.com
Sec: Tim Brigstocke
- ▲ Un-incorporated Society
- ○ *B, *N; to represent the interests of dairy cattle breed societies
- ● Conf - Mtgs - Et - Stat - Inf - LG
- M 11 breed societies
no further information supplied

National Caving Association
   since 2004 **British Caving Association**

National Cavy Club   (NCC)   1890
- ■ 79 Thornhill Gardens, HARTLEPOOL, TS26 0JF.   (hsp)
01429 264294
email nationalcavyclub@yahoo.co.uk
http://www.nationalcavyclub.co.uk
Hon Sec: Mrs Pauline Avery
- ▲ Un-incorporated Society
- ○ *G, *V; to promote & encourage the breeding, keeping & exhibiting of all varieties of cavies (guinea pigs)
- ● Mtgs - Exhib - Comp - Inf
- M c 575 i, UK / 5 i, o;seas
- ¶ Newsflash (NL) - 2; ftm only.   NCC Hbk - 2 yrly; ftm, £4 nm.
Cavies (Jnl) - 12; £30 yr (the official organ for the club but not published by it).

National Charity for the Newborn
   see **BLISS - National Charity for the Newborn**

National Childbirth Trust   (NCT)   1956
- NR Alexandra House, Oldham Terrace, LONDON, W3 6NH.   (hq)
0870 770 3237 (admin), 0870 444 8707 (enquiries)
fax 0870 770 3237
email enquiries@national-childbirth-trust.co.uk
http://www.nctpregnancyandbabycare.com
Chief Exec: Belinda Phipps
- ▲ Registered Charity
- Br 336
- ○ *W; 'the NCT wants all parents to have an experience of pregnancy, birth & early parenthood that enriches their lives & gives them confidence in being a parent; it runs antenatal classes & provides information on maternity issues, breastfeeding & postnatal support'
- Gp Postnatal support; Home birth; Caesarean
- ● Mtgs - ET - Res - Exhib - Inf - LG
- < Intl Childbirth Education Assn; Unicef Baby Friendly Initiative; Baby Milk Action; Consumer Congress; Nat Alliance Women's Orgs; Nat Children's Bureau; Nat Coun Voluntary Orgs (NCVO); Nat Coun Women; Women's Nat Cmsn
- M 42,000 i
- ¶ New Generation (Jnl) - 4;   Local NLs - varies; all ftm.
NCT Sales Catalogue (with sales goods); free.

National Childminding Association   (NCMA)   1977
- NR Royal Court, 81 Tweedy Rd, BROMLEY, Kent, BR1 1TG.   (hq)
0845 880 0044
email info@ncma.org.uk   http://www.ncma.org.uk
Chief Exec: Liz Bayram
- ▲ Registered Charity
- Br 2 (North & South)
- ○ *W; promotes quality registered childminding for children, families & communities
- ● Conf - Mtgs - ET - Res - SG - Inf - Lib - VE - LG
- M c 47,000 i
- ¶ Who Minds - 4; ftm.   AR.
Publications list available.

National Children's Nurseries Association   1988
- IRL Unit 12C, Bluebell Business Park, Old Naas Rd, DUBLIN 12, Republic of Ireland.
353 (1) 460 1138   fax 353 (1) 460 1185
email info@ncna.ie   http://www.ncna.net
Sec: Sharon Regan
- ○ *P

National Children's Wear Association of Great Britain & Northern Ireland   (NCWA)   1940
- NR 5 Portland Place, LONDON, W1B 1PW.   (hq)
020 7631 5445   fax 020 7631 3443
email info@ncwa.co.uk   http://www.ncwa.co.uk
Co Sec: Elizabeth Fox
- ▲ Company Limited by Guarantee
- ○ *T; all sectors of the children's wear industry
- Gp Retailers; Manufacturers; Distributors; Accredited agents
- ● Conf - Mtgs - ET - Exhib - Inf - LG - Seminars
- < BKCEC; BSSA; BCIA
- M c 600 f

National Chinchilla Society   (NCS)   1955
- ■ 101 Simmondley Lane, GLOSSOP, Derbys, SK13 6LU.   (sp)
01457 856945   fax 01457 856945
http://www.natchinsoc.freeuk.com
Hon Sec: Paul S Spooner
- ▲ Un-incorporated Society
- ○ *B; to promote good husbandry practice in the breeding of chinchillas
- ● Mtgs - ET - Exhib - Inf
- M c 150 i
- ¶ Gazette - 6; ftm only.
Guide to Quality Chinchilla;   Show Rules.

National Chrysanthemum Society   (NCS)   1846
- NR 317 Plessey Rd, BLYTH, Northumberland, NE24 3LJ.
01670 353580
http://www.ncsuk.info
Mem Sec: Peter Fraser
- ▲ Registered Charity
- Br 6
- ○ *H; to encourage the growing of chrysanthemums to the highest standard
- ● Conf - Mtgs - Exam - Exhib - Comp - SG - National Register of Chrysanthemums
- < R Horticl Soc
- M 4,000 i, 1,000 org, UK / 300 i, o'seas
- ¶ Bulletin - 2.   Ybk.
List of specialist publications available.

National Coastwatch Institution
- NR Heron's Flight, Church Lane, Fritton, GREAT YARMOUTH, Norfolk, NR31 9EZ.   (hq)
0870 787 2147
email jwt.fritton@btinternet.com   http://www.nci.org.uk
Gen Sec: John Turlington
- ○ *K; set up by the Sea Safety Group (UK) to re-open the coastal look-out stations closed by the government as a money-saving idea in the 'age of satellite installations'

National Cochlear Implant Users Association   (NCIUA)
- ■ PO Box 260, HIGH WYCOMBE, Bucks, HP11 1FA.
     (mail/address)
     email alison.Heath@hotmail.com
     http://www.nciua.demon.co.uk
     Sec: Alison Heath
- ▲ Registered Charity
- Br 10 local support groups for parents & users
- ○ *K; campaigning for adequate funds for cochlear implants for the deaf; to support users
- ● Conf - Inf
- < EURO-CIU
- M 403 i, 12 f, 10 org
- ¶ NCIUA NL - 4; ftm only.
     Cochlear Implants: a collection of experiences of users of all ages; ftm, £2 nm.

NATIONAL COMMITTEE …
For details of bodies whose names begin thus see the companion volume **'Councils, Committees & Boards' (Introduction paragraph 6)**

National Community Boats Association   1985
- NR c/o The Yorkshire Waterways Museum, Dutch River Side, GOOLE, E Yorks, DN14 5TB.   (hq)
     01405 765704   fax 01405 765704
     email staff@national-cba.co.uk
     http://www.national-cba.co.uk
- ○ *W; to provide community groups (schools, hospitals, youth clubs, etc) with access to the UK & European inland waterways

National Community Music Association
    see **Sound Sense: National Community Music Association**

National Confederation of Parent-Teacher Associations (NCPTA)   1956
- ■ 18 St John's Hill, SEVENOAKS, Kent, TN13 3NP.   (hq)
     01732 748850   fax 01732 748851
     email info@ncpta.org.uk   http://www.ncpta.org.uk
     Chief Exec: D W Butler
- ▲ Company Limited by Guarantee; Registered Charity
- ○ *E, *K; to promote cooperation between home & school
- ● Conf - ET - Res - LG
- < Eur Parents Assn
- M 12,000 org
- ¶ PTA - 3;   News & Views - 3;   AR; all ftm only.

National Consortium for Sheltered Housing
    see **ERoSH, the National Consortium for Sheltered Housing**

National Consumer Federation   (NCF)   2001
- ■ 180 High St, WEST MOLESEY, Surrey, KT8 2LX.   (hsp)
     020 8941 2513   fax 020 8979 0871
     email secretary@ncf.info@ncf.info
     Hon Sec: Mrs Stella Nicholas
- ▲ Company Limited by Guarantee; Registered Charity
- Br 6
- ○ *K, *N; to promote grassroot consumer interests & provide a channel for consumer opinion & representation
- Gp Food; Personal finance; Consumer affairs; Communications
- ● Conf - Mtgs - SG - VE - LG
- M 130 i, 32 f, 54 org, UK / 1 i, o'seas
- ¶ Consumer News - 4; ftm, £6 nm.   AR - 1.

National Contractors Federation
    is a contractor organisation within the **Construction Confederation**

National Cooperage Federation   (NCF)   1919
- ■ 34 Maitland Rd, KIRKLISTON, W Lothian, EH29 9AP.   (hsp)
     0131-333 3314
     email john@gaffney113.wanadoo.co.uk
     Hon Sec: John Gaffney
- ▲ Un-incorporated Society
- ○ *T; interests of employers of coopers in the UK
- ● Mtgs - Trade tests for apprentices
- M 42 f
- ¶ AR - 1; free.

NATIONAL COUNCIL …
For details of bodies whose names begin thus, other than the following, see the companion volume **'Councils, Committees & Boards' (Introduction paragraph 6)**

National Council for Aviculture Ltd   (NCA)   1945
- NR 4 Haven Crescent, Werrington, STOKE-on-TRENT, Staffs, ST9 0EY.   (hsp)
     01782 305042   fax 01782 305042
     Admin: Brian Hughes
- ○ *N; coordination body for aviculturists
- M 20, 000 i

National Council for Civil Liberties
    see **Liberty: National Council for Civil Liberties**

National Council for the Conservation of Plants & Gardens (NCCPG)   1978
- ■ Stable Courtyard, Wisley Garden, WOKING, Surrey, GU23 6QP.   (hq)
     01483 211465   fax 01483 212404
     email info@nccpg.org.uk   http://www.nccpg.com
     Gen Administrator: Genevieve Melbourne Webb
- ▲ Company Limited by Guarantee; Registered Charity
- Br 41
- ○ *H, *N; to conserve the heritage of our garden plants built up during the past 400 years.   This is achieved through NCCPG's 600 National Plant Collections in which some 50,000 garden plants are maintained in safe cultivation
- Gp c 600 National Collections
- ● Mtgs - Res - Exhib - Inf - PL - VE
- < works closely with RBG, Kew, R Horticl Soc, NTS & Engl Heritage
- M 7,000 i, 12 f, UK / 60 i, o'seas
- ¶ Plant Heritage (Jnl) - 2.
     The National Plant Collections Directory.
     Publications list available.

National Council for the Divorced & Separated   (NCDS)   1974
- ■ 14 Abbots Drive, HUCKNALL, Notts, NG15 6QW.   (hsp)
     07041 478120
     email info@ncds.org.uk   http://www.ncds.org.uk
     Hon Sec: [name withheld]
- ▲ Registered Charity
- Br 75; Ireland
- ○ *W; welfare of all persons, divorced or separated, widowed & widowers
- ● Conf - Mtgs - Inf - VE
- < NCDS Trust (a charity)
- M 6,000 i
- ¶ NL - 4.

National Council for Housing & Planning
    see **ROOM, the National Council for Housing & Planning**

National Council for Hypnotherapy (including the Hypnotherapy Register) (NCH) 1973
NR PO Box 421, Charwelton, DAVENTRY, Northants, NN11 1AS. (admin)
    01327 264464
    email admin@hypnotherapists.org.uk
    Admin: Su Ricks
▲ Un-incorporated Society
○ *P; to provide a register of competent hypnotherapists
Gp Hypnotherapists
● Conf - Mtgs - ET - Exam - Res - Inf - LG - Referrals register
< Foundation for Integrated Medicine; Nat Gld of Hypnotists
M c 800 i
¶ Jnl - 4. LM. AR.

** National Council on Inland Transport
    Organisation lost: see Introduction paragraph 3

National Council for Metal Detecting (NCMD) 1981
■ 51 Hilltop Gardens, Denaby, DONCASTER, S Yorks, DN12 4BA. (sp)
    01709 868521
    email trevor.austin@ncmd.co.uk   http://www.ncmd.co.uk
    Gen Sec: Trevor Austin
▲ Un-incorporated Society
Br 150; USA
○ *G; the encouragement & defence of the hobby of recreational metal detecting
● Mtgs - Comp - LG
< Cent Coun Physical Recreation (CCPR)
M 5,000 i, UK / 150 i, o'seas
¶ Reports of Executive Committee Meetings - 3/4; free. Reports of meetings with government bodies.

National Council of Psychotherapists (NCP) 1971
■ PO Box 6072, NOTTINGHAM, NG6 9BW. (hsb)
    0845 230 6072   fax 0115-913 1382
    email ncphq@ntlworld.com
    http://www.natcouncilofpsychotherapists.org.uk
    Sec: Brian Jackson
▲ Un-incorporated Society
○ *P; to represent & protect registered members & the general public in the field of psychotherapy & hypnotherapy
Gp Psychotherapy; Hypnotherapy; Critical incident de-briefing
● Conf - ET - Exam - Res
M c 300 i, 12 f, UK / c 20 i, o'seas
¶ Fidelity (Jnl) - 4; ftm, £2.50 nm. AR; ftm only.

National Council for the Welfare of Prisoners Abroad
    since April 2003 **Prisoners Abroad**

National Courier Association (NCA) 1989
■ 7 Canons Rd, Old Wolverton, MILTON KEYNES, Bucks, MK12 5TL. (hq)
    01908 317892   fax 01908 314000
    email ncaadmin@london-link.co.uk
    http://www.thenca.co.uk
    Chmn: Alan Savage
▲ Company Limited by Guarantee
○ *T; network of independent courier companies completing same-day work throughout the UK, which intertrade with each other
● Conf - Mtgs
M 98 f

National Dahlia Society (NDS) 1881
NR 48 Vickers Rd, Ash Vale, ALDERSHOT, Hants, GU12 5SE. (sp)
    01252 693003
    Gen Sec: David Kent
▲ Registered Charity
○ *H; to encourage, improve & extend the cultivation of the dahlia
● Conf - Exam - Exhib - Comp - Inf
< R Horticl Soc; several societies o'seas
M 3,000 i, 950 org, UK / 300 i, 30 org, o'seas
¶ List of publications available.

National Dance Teachers Association (NDTA) 1988
■ PO Box 4099, LICHFIELD, Staffs, WS13 6WX. (hq)
    01543 308618   fax 01543 308618
    email office@ndta.org.uk   http://www.ndta.org.uk
    Chmn: Veronica Jobbins, Vice-Chmn: Carolyn Woolridge
    Sec: Judy Evans
▲ Company Limited by Guarantee; Registered Charity
○ *D, *P; to support teachers in schools & colleges to deliver dance within the school curriculum
● Conf - Mtgs - ET - Inf - LG
M 656 i, 369 schools, UK / 9 i, 3 schools, o'seas
¶ Dance Matters - 3; ftm.

National Day Nurseries Association (NDNA) 1991
■ Oak House, Woodvale Rd, BRIGHOUSE, W Yorks, HD6 4AB. (hq)
    0870 774 4244   fax 0870 774 4243
    email info@ndna.org.uk   http://www.ndna.org.uk
    Chief Exec: Purnima Tanuku
▲ Company Limited by Guarantee; Registered Charity
Br 5
○ *T; to enhance the development & education of children in their early years; to maintain high standards in care & education for the benefit of children, their families & communities
● Conf - Mtgs - ET - Inf - LG
M 2,000 f
¶ Nursery News - 4; AR - 1.

National Deaf Children's Society (NDCS) 1944
NR 15 Dufferin St, LONDON, EC1Y 8UR. (hq)
    020 7490 8656   fax 020 7251 5020
    email ndcs@ndcs.org.uk   http://www.ndcs.org.uk
    Chief Exec: Susan Daniels
▲ Company Limited by Guarantee; Registered Charity
Br 120
○ *E, W, *Y; to inform & advise deaf children & young people & their carers
Gp Technology Inf Centre (London); Services delivery (London)
● Conf - ET - Res - Exhib - Inf - Lib
    Helpline: 0808 800 8880 (Mon-Fri 0010-1700, Tues-1900)
M 14,000 i
¶ Talk - 6; £10. AR. Publications list available.

National Deafblind & Rubella Association
    see **Sense - National Deaf-Blind & Rubella Association**

National Dog Wardens Association (NDWA) 1987
NR Haffield Lodge, Gloucester Rd, Corse, STAUNTON, Glos, GL19 3RA.
    Pres: Sue Bell
Br 12; Bermuda, France, Gibraltar, USA
○ *P; for workers in the field of animal control
● Conf - Mtgs - ET - Res - Exhib - Stat - Inf - VE - LG
< Nat Animal Control Assn America
M i, f, & org
¶ Dog Warden News - 4.

National Drama   (ND)   1989

NR West Barn, Church Farm, Happisburgh, NORWICH, Norfolk,
      NR12 0OY.   (chmn/p)
      01692 650066
      http://www.nationaldrama.co.uk
      Chmn: Patrice Baldwin
▲ Un-incorporated Society
○ *D, *P; for people who work with young people (all ages) in
      drama & theatre
Gp Teachers (all sectors of education); Theatre educators; Theatre
      workers; Workers with people with special needs
● Conf - Mtgs - ET - Res - Inf - LG
M c 650 i, UK & o'seas
¶ Drama (Jnl) - 2; ftm.   Reflections (NL) - 3; ftm only.
      Drama Research.

National Drama Festivals Association   (NDFA)   1964

■ Bramleys, Main St, Shudy Camps, CAMBRIDGE, CB1 6RA.
      (hsp)
      01799 584920
      email tonybroscomb@compuserve.com
      Hon Sec: A R (Tony) Broscomb
▲ Registered Charity
○ *D; to encourage & support the amateur theatre in all its forms
      & through the organisation of drama festivals
● Drama festivals - Play writing competitions - Representation,
      coordination & liaison
< Cent Coun for Amat Theatre
M 37 i, 51 festival organisers, 23 associate org
¶ NL - 4;   Directory (incl list of festivals) - 1; both ftm.

National Dried Fruit Trade Association (UK) Ltd   (NDFTA)   1942

■ PO Box 54905, LONDON, W3 8XX.   (hq)
      020 8992 5655   fax 020 8992 9571
      email john@ndfta.co.uk   http://www.driedfruit-info.com
      Sec Gen: John R Corner
▲ Company Limited by Guarantee
○ *T; all matters connected with the dried fruit trade (mainly
      currants, sultanas, raisins, apricots, peaches, pears, dates &
      prunes)
Gp Sub-c'ees: Technical, Public relations
● Conf - Mtgs - Res - Stat - Inf - VE - LG
< Fédn Eur du Commerce en Fruits Secs, Conserves, Epices et
      Miel (FRUCOM);
M 22 f, UK / 14 f, o'seas

National Early Music Association   (NEMA)   1981

NR 137 Preston Rd, WEMBLEY, Middx, HA9 8NW.   (admin/p)
      020 8904 1076   fax 020 8723 7787
      http://www.nema-uk.org
      Hon Treas: Mark Windisch
▲ Registered Charity
Br 11
○ *D, *N; to bring together organisations & individuals, both
      professional & amateur, involved in the whole range of early
      music
Gp Dance; Music; Theatre; Coordinating bodies
● Conf - ET - Inf
< UK Early Music Forum
M c 300 i, f & org
¶ Early Music Performer - 2.

National Eczema Society   (NES)   1976

NR Hill House, Highgate Hill, LONDON, N19 5NA.   (hq)
      020 7281 3553   fax 020 7281 6395
      http://www.eczema.org
      Exec: Margaret Cox
▲ Registered Charity
○ *W; to provide information & support for eczema patients &
      their carers; to provide education & support for health
      professionals; to raise public awareness about the condition
● ET - Inf
M 12,000 i
¶ Exchange (Jnl) - 4; ftm.

National Edible Oil Distributors Association   (NEODA)

NR PO Box 259, BECKENHAM, Kent, BR3 3YA.   (hq)
      020 8776 2644   fax 020 8249 5402
      Sec: Lynda Simmons
▲ Un-incorporated Society
○ *T; of trades concerned in the supply of frying media & suchlike
      material
● Conf - Mtgs - Inf
< Food & Drink Fedn; Fedn Oils, Seeds Fats Assns (FOSFA)
M 70 f
¶ LM; ftm only.   AR.

National Egg Marketing Association Ltd   (NEMAL)   1935

NR 89 Charterhouse St (2nd floor), LONDON, EC1M 6HR.   (hq)
      020 7608 3760   fax 020 7608 3860
      email Louisa.Platt@britisheggindustrycouncil.com
      http://www.britegg.co.uk
      Sec: Louisa Platt
▲ Company Limited by Guarantee
○ *T; interests of those who pack & market eggs
● Mtgs - LG
< Brit Egg Ind Coun
M 53 f

National Endometriosis Society   (NES)   1981

■ 50 Westminster Palace Gardens, 1-7 Artillery Row, LONDON,
      SW1P 1RR.   (hq)
      020 7222 2781   fax 020 7222 2786
      http://www.endo.org.uk
      Chief Exec: Robert Music
▲ Company Limited by Guarantee
Br 50+
○ *K; support for women suffering from endometriosis; raising
      money for research into the disease; information to health
      professionals
● Conf - Mtgs - Res - Inf
      Helpline: 0808 808 2227
M c 2,500 i
¶ NL - 4;   AR - 1; both ftm only.
      Publications list available.

National Energy Action   (NEA)   1981

NR St Andrew's House, 90-92 Pilgrim St,
      NEWCASTLE UPON TYNE, NE1 6SG.   (hq)
      0191-261 5677   fax 0191-261 6496
      email info@nea.org.uk   http://www.nea.org.uk
      Chief Exec: William Gillis
▲ Registered Charity
○ *K; promotes energy efficiency services to tackle the heating &
      insulation problems of low-income households
● Conf - Mtgs - ET - Res - Lib
< Nat Coun of Voluntary Orgs
M 242 org
¶ Energy Action - 4; ftm, £25 nm.   NL - 6; ftm only.
      AR - 1; free.   Other publications.

National Entertainment Agents Council   (NEAC)   1978

■ PO Box 112, SEAFORD, E Sussex, BN25 2DQ.   (gsb)
      0870 755 7612   fax 0870 755 7613
      email info@neac.org.uk   http://www.neac.org.uk
      Gen Sec: Chris Bray
▲ Un-incorporated Society
Br 4
○ *P, *T
● Conf - Mtgs - ET - Inf - LG
< Nat Outdoor Events Assn
M 100 f
¶ The Agent - 24; ftm only.

National Exhibitors Association (NEA) 1988

- ■ 29a Market Sq, BIGGLESWADE, Beds, SG18 8AQ. (hq)
  01767 316255 fax 01767 316430
  http://www.eou.org.uk
  Sec Gen: Peter Cotterell
- ▲ Un-incorporated Society
- ○ *T
- ● Conf - ET
- M 70 f

National Family Mediation (NFM) 1982

- ■ Devon & Exeter Institution, 7 The Close, EXETER, Devon,
  EX1 1EZ. (hq)
  01392 668090/091 fax 01392 204227
  email general@nfm.org.uk http://www.nfm.u-net.com
  Chief Exec: Jane Robey
- ▲ Registered Charity
- Br 50
- ○ *W; to help those involved in family breakdown to
  communicate better with one another & reach their own
  decisions about some or all of the issues arising from
  separation, divorce, children, property & finance
- Gp Divorce; Mediation; Families
- ● ET - Mediation
- M 60 services
- ¶ The Bulletin - 4; free. AR - 1.

National Fancy Rat Society (NFRS) 1976

- NR PO Box 24207, LONDON, SE9 5ZF. (hsb)
  email secretary@nfrs.org http://www.nfrs.org
  Hon Sec: Estelle Sandford
- ▲ Un-incorporated Society
- ○ *B; to promote the care of the Fancy Rat (Domesticus Rattus
  Norvegicus) as a pet & exhibition animal
- ● Conf - Mtgs - ET - Res - Exhib - Comp - Inf - Lib
- < Amer Fancy Rat & Mouse Assn; Amer Rat, Mouse & Hamster
  Soc; Svenska Råttssällskapet; Sydsveriges Maädjursvänner;
  Finnish Rat Soc
- M c 800 i
- ¶ Pro-rat-a (NL) - 6; ftm, £3 nm.

National Farmers' Retail & Markets Association Ltd (FARMA) 1979

- NR The Greenhouse, PO Box 575, SOUTHAMPTON, Hants,
  SO15 7BZ. (hq)
  0845 458 8420 fax 0845 456 5156
  email justask@farma.org.uk http://www.farma.org.uk
  Exec Sec: Rita Exner
- ▲ Co-operative under Industrial & Provident Society rules
- ○ *F, *K, *T; 'representing direct sales to customers through farm
  shops, pick-your-own, farmers' markets, home delivery, on-
  farm catering & farm entertainment'
- ● Conf - Mtgs - ET - Res - Exhib - Comp - SG - Stat - Inf - Lib - PL
  - VE - LG
- M 650 f, UK / 10 f, o'seas
- ¶ Retail Farmer - 4; ftm only.
- × 2004 (Farm Retail Association
  (National Association of Farmers' Markets

National Farmers Union of England & Wales (NFU) 1908

- ■ Agriculture House, Stoneleigh Park, STONELEIGH, Warks,
  CV8 2TZ. (hq)
  024 7685 8500 fax 020 7685 8501
  http://www.nfuonline.com
  Dir Gen: Richard Macdonald, Sec: Lucilla Evers
- ▲ Un-incorporated Society
- Br 8; Brussels
- ○ *F, *H; to represent & promote the interests of farmers &
  growers & others with an interest in agriculture, horticulture &
  the countryside
- ● Conf - Mtgs - ET - Res - Exhib - Comp - SG - Stat - Inf - VE - LG
- < Intl Fedn of Agricl Producers (IFAP); Gen Confedn of Agricl Co-
  operatives in the EU (COGECA); Eur Confedn of
  Agriculture (CEA); Nat Pig Assn; Taste of the West; Dairy
  Coun
- M 136,573 i (incl countryside mems)
- ¶ British Farmer & Grower - 12; ftm, £55 yr nm.
  NFU Horticulture - 3; NFU Professional - 12;
  NFU Countryside - 12; NFU Farming Wales - 12; all ftm only.
  nfuonline.com (hosting various publications).

National Farmers' Union of Scotland
   see **NFU Scotland**

National Federation of Access Centres
   since c 2006 **National Network of Assessment Centres**

National Federation of Anglers (NFA) 1903

- ■ National Water Sports Centre, Adbolton Lane, Holme
  Pierrepont, NOTTINGHAM, NG12 2LU. (hq)
  0115-981 3535 fax 0115-981 9039
  email office@nfadirect.com http://www.nfadirect.com
  Chief Exec Officer: Paul Baggaley
- ▲ Un-incorporated Society
- Br 8 regions
- ○ *G, *K, *S; the governing body for freshwater angling; to
  promote & protect angling through education, development
  & performance programmes; to promote the conservation &
  development of fisheries; to represent freshwater angling at
  local, national & international levels
- ● Conf - Mtgs - Comp
- < Confédn Intle de la Pêche Sportive (CIPS); FIPS
- M 3,320 i (direct members), 330 clubs (with individual members)
- ¶ Link (NL) - 4; ftm only. AR - 1; free.

National Federation of Badger Groups (NFBG) 1986

- NR 2b Inworth St, LONDON, SW11 3EP. (hq)
  020 7228 6444 fax 020 7228 6555
  email enquiries@nfbg.org.uk
  http://www.badger.org.uk
- ▲ Registered Charity
- ○ *K, *V; to develop & support a network of badger protection
  groups in the UK; to campaign for the protection of badgers
  & against persecution, including snares
- Gp Badgers & TB; Badgers & roads; Badgers' rehabilitation &
  welfare
- ● Conf - Mtgs - Inf
- M 15 i, 81 groups
- ¶ NL - 2. AR.
  Report of Annual Conference - 1.
  Occasional papers & guidance notes - irreg; ftm.
  the working name of the Federation is the Badger Trust.

National Federation for Biological Recording   (NFBR)   1985
NR   c/o CEH Monks Wood, Abbots Ripton, HUNTINGDON,
    Cambs, PE28 2LS.
    01487 772405   fax 01487 773467
    http://www.nfbr.org.uk
    Sec: P T Harding
▲   Un-incorporated Society
○   *G, *P; wildlife recording - the recording of the natural world
    (species & habitats)
●   Conf - Mtgs - ET - Res
M   c 200 i
¶   NL - 3;   Conference Proceedings - 1; both ftm.

**National Federation of the Blind of the United Kingdom
    (NFBUK)   1947**
■   Sir John Wilson House, 215 Kirkgate, WAKEFIELD, W Yorks,
    WF1 1JG.   (hq)
    01924 291313   fax 01924 200244
    email nfbuk@nfbuk.org   http://www.nfbuk.org
▲   Registered Charity
Br   24
○   *K, *W; for the welfare of all blind people
●   Conf - Mtgs - Exhib - Comp - SG - Inf
<   Wld Blind U; Eur Blind U; NCVO; Disability Alliance; RNIB;
    Disabled Living Foundation
M   c 1,400 i & associates
¶   Viewpoint - 4;   Fedtalk tape - 4;   AR; free.

National Federation of Bridleway Associations   (NFBA)   1989
NR   The Barn, Mankinholes, TODMORDEN, Lancs, OL14 6HR.
    (chmn/p)
    01706 815598
    email nfba@righttoride.org.uk
    http://www.rightsofway.org.uk
    Chmn: Sue Hogg
▲   Un-incorporated Society
○   *K; to protect & defend existing & non-definitive bridleways &
    higher rights of way; to encourage the formation of bridleway
    groups throughout England & Wales; to pursue claims for
    statutory definition of bridleways
●   Mtgs - Res - Inf - LG
<   Rights of Way Review Committee
>   Local Bridleway Assns; Local Riding Gps
M   6 i, 20 org
¶   Seminar Proceedings - 1; £5.

National Federation of Builders
    is a contractor organisation within the **Construction Confederation**

National Federation of Bus Users
    since 2005 **Bus Users UK**

National Federation of Carnival Associations
    see **National Carnival Guild - the National Federation of
    Carnival Associations**

National Federation of Cemetery Friends   (NFCF)   1986
■   42 Chestnut Grove, SOUTH CROYDON, Surrey, CR2 7LH.
    (sec/p)
    020 8651 5090
    email gwyneth1@btinternet.com
    http://www.cemeteryfriends.fsnet.co.uk
    Hon Sec: Gwyneth Stokes
▲   Un-incorporated Society
○   *N; provides a forum for the exchange of information & views
    on the conservation of cemeteries & their appropriate
    development for educational & recreational purposes
●   Inf - Advises potential groups
M   63 groups (Friends)
¶   NL - 1; ftm only.   Notes on saving cemeteries; £3.

**National Federation of Community Organisations   (Community
Matters)   1945**
■   12-20 Baron St, LONDON, N1 9LL.   (hq)
    020 7837 7887   fax 020 7278 9253
    email communitymatters@communitymatters.org.uk
    http://www.communitymatters.org.uk
    Nat Dir: David Tyler
▲   Company Limited by Guarantee; Registered Charity
○   *N, *W; to promote & support action by ordinary people in
    response to society, education & recreational needs in their
    neighbourhood & community, resulting in healthy,
    sustainable communities in which everyone can play their full
    part
Gp   Local Federation of Community Organisations
●   Conf - Mtgs - ET - Res - Inf - LG - Advice & consultancy
<   Nat Coun for Voluntary Orgs; Charity Tax Reform Gp; Wales
    Coun for Voluntary Assns
M   over 1,200 org
¶   Community - 6; ftm, £15 nm.
    Community Extra; ftm, £15 nm.   NL; free.
    ther publications available.

National Federation of Demolition Contractors   (NFDC)   1941
■   Resurgam House, 1A New Rd, The Causeway, STAINES, Middx,
    TW18 3DH.   (hq)
    01784 456799   fax 01784 461118
    email info@demolition-nfdc.com
    http://www.demolition-nfdc.com
    NAt Sec: Howard Button
▲   Company Limited by Guarantee
○   *T; for employers in the demolition & dismantling industry
●   Conf - Mtgs - ET - Inf - Empl - LG
<   Eur Demolition Assn
M   190 f
¶   Demolition & Dismantling Jnl - 4;   Ybk - 1;   LM - 2 yrly;
    all free.
    Form of Direct Contract.   Working Rule Agreement - 1.

National Federation of Eighteen Plus Groups   (18 plus)   1941
NR   Church St Chambers, 8-10 Church St, NEWENT, Glos,
    GL18 1PP.   (hq)
    01531 821210   fax 01531 821474
    email office@18plus.org.uk
    Admin Officer: Mrs Christine George
    Hon Gen Sec: Francis Wellington
Br   50 gps
○   *N, *Y; a multi-activity social group for ages 18-29, run by
    members for the members
●   Conf - Mtgs - ET - VE
M   c 1,000 i
¶   Plus News - 4; ftm only.

National Federation of Enterprise Agencies   (NFEA)   1993
■   12 Stephenson Court, Fraser Rd, Priory Business Park,
    BEDFORD, MK44 3WH.   (hq)
    01234 831623   fax 01234 831625
    email enquiries@nfea.com   http://www.nfea.com +
    smallbusinessadvice.org.uk
    Chief Exec: George Derbyshire
○   *N; for local enterprise agencies & other like-minded
    organisations, in England; it forms a network of independent
    not-for-profit local agencies committed to responding to the
    needs of small & growing businesses by providing a
    comprehensive range of quality services
Gp   Business Volunteer Mentors Association
M   c 130 f
¶   Best Practices Jnl - 1.   NL - 4.   Bulletin - 12.
    Various publications.

National Federation of Families with Visually Impaired Children
    see **LOOK**

National Federation of Fish Friers Ltd (NFFF) 1913
NR New Federation House, 4 Greenwood Mount, Meanwood, LEEDS, W Yorks, LS6 4LQ. (hq)
0113-230 7044 fax 0113-230 7010
email mail@federationoffishfriers.co.uk
http://www.federationoffishfriers.co.uk
Gen Sec: Mrs A M Kirk
▲ Company Limited by Guarantee
○ *T
● Conf - Mtgs - ET - Exhib - Inf - LG
M c 2,500 i
¶ Fish Friers Review - 12; ftm.

National Federation of Fishermen's Organisations (NFFO) 1977
NR Marsden Rd, GRIMSBY, Lincs, DN31 3SG. (hq)
01472 352141
email nffo@nffo.org.uk http://www.nffo.org.uk
Chief Exec: Barry C Deas
○ *T; to represent fishermen & their interests, locally, nationally & within the European Community
M c 1,200 i in 40 org
¶ NL - 6. NFFO Official Ybk & Diary - 1.

National Federation of Fishmongers Ltd (NFF) 1932
NR Pisces, London Rd, Feering, COLCHESTER, Essex, CO5 9ED. (hq)
01376 571391 fax 01376 571391
Sec: Mrs Leftwich
▲ Company Limited by Guarantee
Br London Fish & Poultry Retailers Assn
○ *T; interests of retail fishmongers
● Conf - Mtgs - ET - Exam - Exhib - Comp - Inf - LG
< Confedn of Indep Food Retailers
M c 800 i & f

National Federation of Football Supporters' Clubs
2002 merged with the Football Supporters Association to become the **Football Supporters Federation**

National Federation of Gateway Clubs
is a division of **MENCAP: Royal Society for Mentally Handicapped Children & Adults**

National Federation of Glaziers (NFG) 1991
■ 27 Old Gloucester St, LONDON, WC1N 3XX. (hq)
020 7404 3099
Chmn: A C Jones
▲ Un-incorporated Society
○ *T; to provide information & assistance on glass products in relation to window & conservatory installation
● Inf - Vetting of individuals & companies in the field - Arrangement of insured guarantees (as introducer) of approved schemes - Helpline for members
M 170 f
¶ Commitment to Good Practice.

National Federation of Inland Wholesale Fish Merchants (NFIWFM)
NR Office 36 Billingsgate Market, Trafalgar Way, LONDON, E14 5ST.
020 7515 2655 fax 020 7517 3531
○ *T; to promote inland fish merchants
M f

National Federation of Kidney Patients' Associations
the registered name with the Charity Commissioners of the **National Kidney Federation**

National Federation of Master Steeplejacks & Lightning Conductor Engineers
since November 2003 **Association of Technical Lightning & Access Specialists**

National Federation of Master Window & General Cleaners
since 1 January 2006 **Federation of Window Cleaners**

National Federation of Meat & Food Traders 1888
NR 1 Belgrove, ROYAL TUNBRIDGE WELLS, Kent, TN1 1YW. (hq)
01892 541412 fax 01892 535462
email info@nfmft.co.uk
Chief Exec: Graham Bidston
○ *T
M f
¶ Food Trader - 10; ftm. Ybk.

National Federation of Residential Landlords (NFRL) 1996
NR PO Box 11107, LONDON, SW15 6ZE. (exec/office)
0845 456 0357 fax 0845 456 0357
email info@nfrl.org.uk http://www.help4landlords.org
Exec Office Representative: Richard Price
▲ Un-incorporated Society
○ *N; as the national voice of private landlords is recognised by government to promote a viable private rented sector as a major source of accessible, good value rented housing in the UK
● Conf - Mtgs - ET - Res - Inf - LG
< U Intle de la Propriété Immobilière (UIPI)
M 12,000 i in 40 landlords assns
¶ Residential Renting (Jnl) - 4; ftm only.

National Federation of Retail Newsagents 1919
■ Yeoman House, Sekforde St, LONDON, EC1R 0HF. (hq)
020 7253 4225 fax 020 7250 0927
email info@nfrn.org.uk http://www.nfrn.org.uk
Nat Pres: Mahendra Jadeja
▲ Un-incorporated Society
Br 209; 20 o'seas (incl Republic of Ireland)
○ *T
● Conf - Mtgs - ET _ Res - Exhib - Stat - Inf - LG - CTN World Exhib
M 18, 603 i, UK / 469 i, o'seas
¶ Retail Newsagent - 52; £1.50.
Retail Express - 26; free. The FED - 12; ftm, £1.95 nm.
Members Business Guide - 1; AR - 1; both ftm only.

National Federation of Retirement Pensions Associations (Pensioners' Voice) 1940
NR Thwaites House, Railway Rd, BLACKBURN, Lancs, BB1 5AX. (hq)
01254 52606 fax 01254 52606
Gen Sec: Robert Stansfield
○ *K; to improve the quality of life of the elderly
M 900 i, 250 branches (social groups)
¶ Pensioner's Voice - 6.

National Federation of Roofing Contractors (NFRC) 1943
■ 24 Weymouth St, LONDON, W1G 7LX. (hq)
020 7436 0387 fax 020 7637 5215
email info@nfrc.co.uk http://www.nfrc.co.uk
Chief Exec: Ray Horwood
Br 6; Ireland
Scottish section: PO Box 28011, Edinburgh, EH16 6WN.
0131-448 0266 fax 0131-440 4032
email jmckinney@support-services.fsbusiness.co.uk
Sec: John McKinney
○ *T; for the roofing trade (includes manufacturers, suppliers & service providers); ensures (through its vetting procedure & code of practice) that high standards of workmanship & high quality materials are used
Gp Construction; Roofing
● Conf - Mtgs - ET - Res - Comp - Inf - VE - Empl - LG
< Intl Fedn of Roofing Contrs (IFD); Nat Home Improvement Coun (NHIC); Nat Specialist Contrs Coun (NSCC); Constructors' Liaison Gp (CLG)
M c 900 f
¶ Update (NL) - 6; ftm only.
Annual Directory - 1; ftm, £35 nm.
Technical Bulletins; prices vary. AR - 1; free.

National Federation of Sea Anglers (NFSA) 1904
NR   Hamlyn House (Level 5), Mardle Way, BUCKFASTLEIGH,
      Devon, TQ11 0NS.   (hq)
      01364 644643   fax 01364 644486
      email ho@nfsa.org.uk   http://www.nfsa.org.uk
      Devt Officer: David Rowe
○   *S; the recognised governing body for the sport of sea angling;
      to look after sea anglers & clubs
M   i in clubs
¶   NL - 4; free.

National Federation of Sea Schools
      in September 2005 merged with the Association of Bonded Sailing
      Companies & the Yacht Charter Association to form the **Marine
      Leisure Association**

**National Federation of Services for Unmarried Parents & their
      Children (TREOIR) 1976**
IRL   14 Gandon House, Custom House Sq, IFSC, DUBLIN 1,
      Republic of Ireland.
      353 (1) 670 0120   fax 353 (1) 670 0199
      email infotreoir.ie
      Chief Exec: Margaret Dromey
○   *W
✕   2005-06 Federation of Services for Unmarried Parents & their
      Children

National Federation of Shopmobility (NFS) 1987
NR   Enham Place, Enham Alamein, ANDOVER, Hants, SP11 6JS.
      (hq)
      0845 644 2446   fax 0845 644 4442
      email info@shopmobilityuk.org.uk
      http://www.justmobility.co.uk
○   *K; to assist groups to establish shopmobility schemes
      throughout the country by providing information, advice &
      contacts
      Shopmobility is a free mobility equipment loan scheme -
      equipment is loaned daily
●   Conf - Mtgs - Inf
M   300 schemes representing 720,000 users
¶   NFS Review - 2;   AR; both ftm only.
      NFS Directory - 2.   NFS Guidelines - 1.

National Federation of Solo Clubs (Solo NFSC) 1965
■   PO Box 2278, NUNEATON, Warks, CV11 5YX.   (sp)
      024 7673 6499
      Nat Sec: Mavis Marsden
▲   Registered Charity
Br   53
○   *W; to provide friendship, social activities & welfare facilities for
      widowed, divorced, separated & single people over 21; to
      offer help & comfort to the bereaved & lonely
●   Mtgs - Holidays - Day trips - Dancing - Skittles - Ten pin
      bowling - Social gatherings
M   3,500 i

National Federation of Spiritual Healers (NFSH) 1955
NR   Old Manor Farm Studio, Church St, SUNBURY-on-THAMES,
      Middx, TW16 6RG.   (hq)
      01932 7831647
      email office@nfsh.org.uk   http://www.nfsh.org.uk
▲   Registered Charity
○   *P; for potential & established spiritual healers; 'NFSH is not
      associated with any religion'
●   Conf - Mtgs - Res - Exhib - SG - Inf - National Healer Referral
      Service - Distance healing
      Helpline: 0845 123 2777
M   c 5,000 i
¶   Healing Today (Jnl) - 4;   Regional NLs - 4;   AR; all ftm.

National Federation of Sub-Postmasters (NFSP) 1897
NR   Evelyn House, 22 Windlesham Gardens, SHOREHAM-by-SEA,
      W Sussex, BN43 5AZ.   (hq)
      01273 452324   fax 01273 465403
      email admin@nfsp.org.uk   http://www.nfsp.org.uk
      Gen Sec: Colin Baker
▲   Un-incorporated Society
Br   95
○   *U
●   Conf - Mtgs - ET - Res - Exhib - Inf - Empl - LG
M   c 14,000 i
¶   The Subpostmaster (Jnl) - 12.   Hbk - 3 yrly.
      Branch Secretaries Circular - 24.   AR.

National Federation of Swimschools
NR   c/o STA, Anchor House, Birch St, WALSALL, W Midlands,
      WS2 8HZ.
      01922 748394
      http://www.nfswimschools.co.uk
○   *S

**National Federation Terrazzo Marble & Mosaic Specialists
      (NFTMMS) 1932**
NR   PO Box 2843, LONDON, W1A 5PG.   (hsp)
      0845 609 0050   fax 0845 607 8610
      email info@nftmms.co.uk   http://www.nftmms.co.uk
      Sec: Donald Slade
▲   Un-incorporated Society
○   *T; interests of manufacturers & fixers of terrazzo tiles, working
      & laying of natural stone & mosaic
Gp   Associate membership for suppliers of goods & services to full
      members
●   Mtgs - Inf - VE - Provision of technical information (free) -
      Technical Inspection service (chargeable)
<   Brit Standards Inst; Trade Assn Forum
M   c 50 f
¶   Technical Specifications for Terrazzo & Marble - irreg; free.

National Federation of Women's Institutes (NFWI) 1915
■   104 New Kings Rd, LONDON, SW6 4LY.   (hq)
      020 7371 9300   fax 020 7736 3652
      email hq@nfwi.org.uk
      http://www.womens-institute.co.uk
      Gen Sec: Mrs Jana Osborne
▲   Registered Charity
○   *G; educational, social & community work
●   Conf - Mtgs - ET - Exam - Exhib - Comp - SG - Stat - Inf
M   230,000 i
¶   NF News - 10.   WI Life - 8.
      Hbk.   AR.
      Wide range of publications on home economics, arts & crafts
      training & general interest.

**National Federation of Young Farmers' Clubs (England &
      Wales) (NFYFC) 1932**
NR   YFC Centre, NAC, Stoneleigh Park, KENILWORTH, Warks,
      CV8 2LG.   (hq)
      024 7685 7200   fax 024 7685 7229
      email post@nfyfc.org.uk   http://www.nfyfc.org.uk
      Contact: The Chief Exec
▲   Registered Charity
○   *F, *Y; to advance knowledge of agriculture, rural life,
      countryside issues & home crafts
●   Conf - Mtgs - Comp - LG
M   c 20, 500 i
¶   Ten 26 - 4; ftm only.

National Federation of Youth Action Agencies
      since 2002 **Youth Action Network**

National Ferret Welfare Society (NFWS) 1989
NR Croit Cullach, 4 Durnamuck, Dundonnell, GARVE, Ross-shire, IV23 2QZ. (mem/sec)
PRO: Prof June McNicholas
○ *V; to promote the welfare of ferrets
● Inf - Annual show (m only)
< Countryside Alliance (CA)
M c 300
¶ NFWS News - 4.   Mustelid Meanderings - 1/2.

National Fertility Association
December 2003 merged with CHILD to form **Infertility Network UK**

National Field Archery Society (NFAS) 1973
■ 3 Coombe St, BRUTON, Somerset, BA10 0EP. (hsp)
01749 813056
email general.secretary@nfas.net   http://www.nfas.net
Gen Sec: Ralph Ashdown
▲ Company Limited by Guarantee
○ *S; promotion of archery in woodland
● Exhib - Comp
M c 4,500 i
¶ NFAS NL - 6; ftm only.

National Fillings Association (NFA) 1963
■ c/o HLM Secretaries Ltd, St James's (9th floor), 79 Oxford St, MANCHESTER, M1 6FQ. (asa)
0161-236 8006   fax 0161-236 8306
email nfa@hlmsecretaries.co.uk
Sec: Chris Varley
▲ Un-incorporated Society
○ *T; upholstery fibre processors & manufacturers of curled hair, cotton felt, flock & felt, polyester fibre
● Mtgs - ET
M 10 f

National Fireplace Association (NFA) 1970
■ McLaren Building (6th floor), 35 Dale End, BIRMINGHAM, B4 7LN. (hq)
0121-200 1310   fax 0121-200 1306
email enquiries@nfa.org.uk   http://www.nfa.org.uk
Dir: David C Brotherton
○ *T; advertising & promotion for the fireplace industry
● Mtgs - Inf
< a METCOM organisation
M 260 f, org
¶ Fireplace Ybk - 1; ftm, £5 nm.
Technical leaflets; ftm, £3 each nm:
Open fires for coal & wood.
Chimney problems & how to cure them.
Air supply for open fires.
Lining old chimneys.
Fuels for your fire.
Coal & log effect gas fires.
Roomheaters & stoves.
Fireplace safety, maintenance & chimney sweeping.
Masonry chimneys, their design & construction.
Fireplace surrounds, their construction & installation.

National Forum of Engineering Centres (NFEC) 1993
NR Unit 720 The Big Peg, 120 Vyse St, BIRMINGHAM, B18 6NF. (hq)
0121-200 3048   fax 0870 705 9881
▲ Registered Charity
○ *E
M f & org
✕ 2003 National Forum for Engineering in Colleges

National Forum for Risk Management in the Public Sector
see **ALARM: the National Forum for Risk Management in the Public Sector**

National Foundation for Educational Research in England & Wales (NFER) 1946
NR The Mere, Upton Park, SLOUGH, Berks, SL1 2DQ. (hq)
01753 574123   fax 01753 691632
email enquiries@nfer.ac.uk   http://www.nfer.ac.uk
Sec: A B Clark
▲ Company Limited by Guarantee; Registered Charity
Br 2
○ *E, *Q; provision of educational research services, information & results; development of assessment tests & methods
● Conf - Mtgs - ET - Res - Inf - Lib
M c 200 org
¶ Publications list available.

National Fox Welfare Society (NFWS) 1993
NR 135 Higham Rd, RUSHDEN, Northants, NN10 6DS. (coordinators/p)
01933 411996
○ *V; to rescue & rehabilitate sick & injured foxes; to provide advice to the public on any aspect of fox behaviour or problems; to recommend, or provide, an effective deterrent

National Franchised Dealers Association
a group of the **Retail Motor Industry Federation**

National Franchisee Forum
'kindly delete'

National Fruit Wine, Mead & Liqueur Producers Association 2003
■ 3 Grange Rd, TRING, Herts, HP23 5JP. (hsp)
01442 823993   fax 01442 823993
email bsreid@aol.com
Hon Sec: Brian S Reid
▲ Un-incorporated Society
○ *T; 'to improve the quality & image of fruit wines, meads & liqueurs in the UK'
● Mtgs - Exhib - Comp - VE
< Intl Assn Cider & Fruit Wine Producers
M 12 f

National Game Dealers' Association (NGDA) 1979
■ Pollards Farm, Clanville, ANDOVER, Hants, SP11 9JE. (chmn/b)
01264 730294   fax 01264 730780
Chmn: Chris Chappel
▲ Un-incorporated Society
Br Scotland
○ *T; to safeguard & promote the commercial interests of the members; to encourage best practice in the industry
● Conf - Mtgs - ET - Res - Exhib - Stat - Expt - Inf - LG
M 1 i, 36 f, 1 org
¶ Various publications.

National Gamekeepers Organisation (NGO) 1997
NR PO Box 107, BISHOP AUCKLAND, Co Durham, DL14 9YW. (hq)
01388 665899   fax 01388 665899
http://www.nationalgamekeepers.org.uk
Mem Sec: Ann Robinson-Ruddock
○ *P
Gp Moorland branch
M c 10,000 i

© CBD Research Ltd · Beckenham · BR3 5JS · Tel 020 8650 7745 · Fax 020 8650 0768 · E-mail cbd@cbdresearch.com · www.cbdresearch.com

National Gardens Scheme Charitable Trust (NGS) 1927

■ Hatchlands Park, East Clandon, GUILDFORD, Surrey,
GU4 7RT.   (hq)
01483 211535   fax 01483 211537
email ngs@ngs.org.uk   http://www.ngs.org.uk
Chief Exec: Mrs Julia Grant

▲ Registered Charity

○ *G, *H, *W; a non-membership body raising money for:
1) Queen's Nursing Institute, 2) training of Macmillan Cancer
Relief nurses, 3) the careership scheme & gardens fund of the
National Trust, 4) Perennial & Royal Gardeners Orphans
Fund, 5) the Nurses' Welfare service, 6) Crossroads, 7) Help
the Hospices, (8) Marie Curie Cancer Care; & many charities
chosen by garden owners

● Exhib - PL - arrangement of opening (to the public) of nearly
3,500, mostly private, gardens in England & Wales on
certain days to raise money

¶ The Yellow Book, 2006; £7.99. (formerly known as Gardens of
England & Wales open for Charity).

National Gerbil Society (NGS) 1971

■ 373 Lynmouth Ave, MORDEN, Surrey, SM4 4RY.   (sp)
020 8241 8942   fax 0870 160 0843
email jackie@gerbils.co.uk   http://www.gerbils.co.uk
Sec: Jackie Roswell

▲ Un-incorporated Society

○ *G; to promote Gerbils & Jirds as pets, breeding & exhibition
animals

● Mtgs - Exhib - Comp - Inf - PL - VE

< Intl Gerbil Fedn

M 200 i, 1 f, UK / 11 i, 3 org, o'seas

¶ The Nibbler - 4;   Ybk; both ftm only.

National Golf Clubs' Advisory Association (NGCAA) 1922

NR Tranzart Business Centre, Owl Gate, Hanley Swan,
WORCESTER, WR8 0DT.   (hq)
01684 311353   fax 01684 311924
http://www.ngcaa.org.uk
Sec: Michael Shaw

▲ Un-incorporated Society

○ *N, *S; provision of advice, especially legal advice, to affiliated
golf clubs

● Inf

M 1,200 golf clubs

¶ NL - 6;   Ybk (incl AR & LM); both ftm only.

National Governors' Association 1970

NR SBQ1 (2nd floor), 29 Smallbrook Queensway, BIRMINGHAM,
B5 4HG.   (hq)
0121-643 5787   fax 0121-633 7141
http://www.nga.org.uk
Chief Exec: Jean McEntire

▲ Company Limited by Guarantee; Registered Charity

○ *E; to represent the governor's view

Gp Governing bodies of schools

● Publications

M c 6,000 i, 600 org

✕ 2006 (merged) National Association of School Governors 2005
National Association of Governors & Managers

National Grammar Schools Association (NGSA) 1986

NR c/o SBS Ltd, 6 Banbury Rd, BRACKLEY, Northamptonshire,
NN13 6AU.   (sb/p)
C1543 2515172
http://www.ngsa.org.uk
Sec: Jenny Jones

▲ Un-incorporated Society

○ *K; to support selective education as a parental option within
the State education sector; to offer support & advice to
grammar schools under threat of closure or reorganisation

M schools

National Greyhound Racing Club Ltd (NGRC) 1928

NR Twyman House, 16 Bonny St, LONDON, NW1 9QD.   (hq)
020 7267 9256   fax 020 7482 1023
email mail@ngrc.org.uk   http://www.ngrc.org.uk
Chairmen: Peter Cadman & David Phillips

▲ Company Limited by Guarantee

○ *S; the judicial & administrative body for greyhound racing

M racecourses

¶ Various publications.

National Group on Homeworking (NGH) 1984

NR 30-38 Dock St (office 26), LEEDS, W Yorks, LS10 1JF.   (hq)
0113-245 4273   fax 0113-246 5616
Dir: Linda Devereux

▲ Company Limited by Guarantee

○ *K, *N; an independent voluntary organisation representing
homeworkers in the UK; campaigns for equal employment
rights for those working from home

¶ Publications available.

National Guild of Removers & Storers 1993

NR 3 High St, CHESHAM, Bucks, HP5 1BG.   (hq)
01494 792279   fax 01494 792111
http://www.ngrs.org.uk
Hon Chmn: Jonathan Bramwell

○ *T

● Conf - Mtgs - LG

< Assn Relocation Agents; Nat Register of Approved Removers &
Storers

M c 200 f

¶ The Professional Remover - 6; free.

National Hairdressers' Federation (NHF) 1942

■ 1 Abbey Court, Fraser Rd, Priory Business Park, BEDFORD,
MK44 3WH.   (hq)
0845 345 6500   fax 01234 838875
email enquiries@nhf.info   http://www.nhf.biz
Gen Sec: Ray J Seymour

▲ Un-incorporated Society

Br 52

○ *T; for self-employed hairdressing, beauty therapists & salon
owners

● Conf - Mtgs - Comp - SG - Empl - LG

< Org Mondiale de la Coiffure

M 7,250 i, 30 f, UK / 30 i, o'seas

¶ Headline News - 6; ftm only.

National Harmonica League (NHL) 1975

■ 112 Hag Hill Rise, Taplow, MAIDENHEAD, Berks, SL6 0LT.
(chmn/p)
01628 604069
Chmn: Dr Roger Trobridge

▲ Un-incorporated Society

○ *D; for anyone interested in the harmonica, whether a player or
not

● Mtgs - ET - Comp - Inf

< Intl Harmonica Org

M c 400 i

¶ Harmonica World - 6; ftm, £1.50 nm.

National Health Service Consultants' Association 1976

NR Hill House, Great Bourton, BANBURY, Oxon, OX17 1QH.
(chmn)
01295 750407   fax 01295 750407
email nhsca@pop3.poptel.org.uk
http://www.nhsca.org.uk p
Pres: Peter Fisher,   Chmn: Prof Allyson Pollock

○ *P

M c 650 i

¶ Publications list available on request.

National Hedgelaying Society (NHLS) 1978
NR 88 Manor Rd, TODDINGTON, Beds, LU5 6AJ. (hsb)
    01525 873795
    email allan.portas@farmersweekly.net
    http://www.hedgelaying.org.uk
    Hon Sec: Allan Portas
▲ Registered Charity
○ *F, *K; to encourage the art of hedge laying & to keep local
    styles in existence; to encourage landowners to manage
    hedges by laying
● Comp - Inf
M 250 i
¶ NL - 3; free. Hedgelaying Explained.

**National Heritage: the Museums Action Movement (NH)
1971**
§ NH Administration Centre, Rye Rd, HAWKHURST, Kent,
    TN18 5DW. (hq)
    01580 752052 fax 01580 755670
    email liz@lizm.eclipse.co.uk
    http://www.nationalheritage.org.uk
    Admin: Liz Moore
▲ Registered Charity
○ *A, *G; to support museums & galleries in the United Kingdom;
    to represent their visitors & users
● Mtgs - Inf - Research/survey collection
M i, f, museums
¶ Museum News. AR.

National Hillclimb Association
■ 205A Berrow Rd, BURNHAM ON SEA, Somerset, TA8 2JG.
    (mem/sp)
    01278 786377
    Mem Sec: Pete Isaac
○ *S; motor-cycle hillclimbs
    No further information supplied

National Historic Ships (NHSC) 1992
NR National Maritime Museum, Greenwich, LONDON,
    SE10 9NF. (hq)
    020 8312 6486 fax 020 8312 6665
    email nrhv@nmm.ac.uk http://www.nhsc.org.uk
    Head of Secretariat: Martyn Heighton
○ *L; to secure the long time preservation of a sample of ships
    representing important aspects of UK maritime history
Gp Technical c'ee (people with specialist skills & knowledge in ship
    preservation)
● Conf - Mtgs - Res - Inf - PL - LG
< Nat Maritime Museum
M [not stated]
× 2006 National Historic Ships Committee

National Home Improvement Council (NHIC)
NR Carlyle House, 235-237 Vauxhall Bridge Rd, LONDON,
    SW1V 1EJ. (hq)
    020 7828 8230 fax 020 7828 0667
    email info@nhic.org.uk http://www.nhic.org.uk/
    Exec Dir: Graham S Ponting
▲ Company Limited by Guarantee
○ *T; to encourage a vibrant modernisation & renovation market
    in the private & public sectors, both to improve housing stock
    & business opportunities for members
● Mtgs - ET - Stat - Inf - LG
M c 80 org
¶ Progress - 2.

National Hop Association (NHA)
NR The Basement, 754 Fulham Rd, LONDON, SW6 5SH.
    (press/office)
    020 7384 1333 fax 020 7384 0335
    email rupert@randr.co.uk http://www.hops.co.uk
○ *F, *N; to represent the hop growers of England, through the 5
    producer groups
● Mtgs - Res - Stat - Expt - Inf - PL
M 5 gps

National Horse Brass Society (NHBS) 1975
NR Woodbine Cottage, Tarrington, HEREFORD, HR1 4HZ. (hq)
    01432 890404
    http://www.horse-brass-society.org.uk
    Gen Sec: Steve Pink
▲ Un-incorporated Society
○ *G; to bring together people interested in horse brasses
● Mtgs - VE - Archives
M c 450 i
¶ Jnl - 2; NL - 2; Directory - 1; all ftm.
    Reference works - 1$\frac{1}{2}$-2 yrly; c £10.

National Housing Federation 1935
NR 25 Procter St, LONDON, WC1V 6NY. (hq)
    020 7067 1010 fax 020 7067 1011
    email info@housing.org.uk http://www.housing.org.uk
    Chief Exec: Jim Coulter
▲ Company Limited by Guarantee
Br 10
○ *N; to promote housing associations; to provide advice in
    formation
● Conf - Mtgs - ET - Res - Exhib - Stat - Inf - LG
< Intl Fedn Housing & Planning; Comité Européen Co-ordination
    de l'Habitat Social
M 1,380 housing assns
¶ Housing Today - 51; ftm, prices on application nm.
    Ybk. AR; free.

National Ice Skating Association of UK Ltd (NISA) 1879
■ National Ice Centre, Lower Parliament St, NOTTINGHAM,
    NG1 1LA. (hq)
    0115-988 8060 fax 0115-988 8061
    email nisa@iceskating.org.uk
    http://www.iceskating.org.uk
    Chief Exec: Keith Horton
▲ Company Limited by Guarantee
○ *S; to develop ice skating in all its disciplines; to optimise
    individual achievement at every level
● Comp - Inf
< Intl Skating U (ISU)(Switzerland)
M 4,500 i, 84 clubs
¶ Ice Link (Jnl) - 6; free.

National Independent Supermarket Association
    see**NISA Today's Holdings Ltd**

National Information Forum (NIF) 1981
■ Post Point 905 BT Burne House, Bell St, LONDON, NW1 5BZ.
    (hq)
    020 7402 6681 fax 020 7402 1259
    email info@nif.org.uk http://www.nif.org.uk
    Dir: Ann Darnbrough
▲ Company Limited by Guarantee; Registered Charity
○ *K; 'committed to making information more accessible &
    available to all disabled or elderly people, refugees & any
    other groups who have difficulty in getting information'
● Conf - Mtgs - ET - Inf - LG
M 250 org
¶ Innovations in Information (Jnl) - 3; £15.
    Other publications available on request.

National Institute of Adult Continuing Education (England & Wales)   (NIACE)   1949
- ■ Renaissance House, 20 Princess Road West, LEICESTER, LE1 6TP.   (hq)
  0116-204 4200
  email enquiries@niace.org.uk   http://www.niace.org.uk
  Dir: Alan Tuckett
- ▲ Company Limited by Guarantee; Registered Charity
- ○ *E, *N; a national centre for cooperation, enquiry, research, information & consultation in the field of continuing education for adults
- ● Conf - Mtgs - Res - Exhib - SG - Stat - Inf - Lib - LG
- < Eur Assn of Adult Educ; Intl Coun of Adult Educ
- M c 250 i, 480 org
- ¶ Publications list available.

National Institute of Carpet & Floorlayers Ltd   (NICF)   1978
- ■ 4d St Mary's Place, The Lace Market, NOTTINGHAM, NG1 1PH.   (hq)
  0115-958 3077   fax 0115-941 2238
  email info@nicfltd.org.uk   http://www.nicfltd.org.uk
- ○ *T; to give competent fitters a form of recognition so that retailers, contractors & customers can identify them
- ● ET - Exam - Exhib - Inf - Conciliation of complaints
- M 500 i, 100 f (manufacturers as patrons, retailers as associates)
- ¶ Installation Manual; £50 m, £75 nm.

National Institute of Medical Herbalists Ltd   (NIMH)   1864
- ■ Elm House, 54 Mary Arches St, EXETER, Devon, EX4 3BA.   (hq)
  01392 426022   fax 01392 498963
  email nimh@ukexeter.freeserve.co.uk
  http://www.nimh.org.uk
  Hon Sec: Paul Chenery
- ▲ Company Limited by Guarantee
- ○ *L, *P, *Q; a professional body of practising medical herbalists; research & education in herbal medicine
- ● Conf - Mtgs - ET - Res - Inf - Lib - LG
- < Eur Herbal Practitioners Assn; Brit Herbal Medicine Assn
- M 575 i, UK / 120 i, o'seas
- ¶ European Jnl of Herbal Medicine - 3; ftm, £24.50 nm (UK). Herbal Thymes (NL) - 4; ftm only.   LM - 1; free.

National Insulation Association   (NIA)   2002
- NR CIGA House, 3 Vimy Court, Vimy Rd, LEIGHTON BUZZARD, Beds, LU7 1FG.   (hq)
  01525 383313   fax 01525 385926
  http://www.insulationassociation.org.uk
  Exec Dir: Gillian A Allder
- ▲ Company Limited by Guarantee
- ○ *T; for the insulation industry: cavity wall insulation, loft insulation, draught proofing & insulated thermal linings
- ● Conf - Mtgs - ET - Res - Exhib - Inf - Lib - PL - LG
- < Bldgs Energy Efficiency Fedn (BEEF)
- M 124 f
- ¶ The Installer - 3;   In-House NL - 6/10; both ftm only. LM - updated; free.
- × 2002 National Cavity Insulation Association

National Irish Safety Organisation   (NISO)
- IRL A11 Calmount Park, Ballymount, DUBLIN 12, Republic of Ireland.
  353 (1) 465 9760   fax 353 (1) 465 9765
  email info@niso.ie
  Chief Exec: Ted O'Keefe
- ○ *P

National Joint Utilities Group   (NJUG)   1977
- NR 59-60 Russell Sq, LONDON, WC1B 4HP.   (hq)
  0870 801 8007   fax 0870 801 8008
  email info@njug.co.uk
  Nat Coordinator: Mrs Irene Elsom
- ○ *N, *T; the forum for objects of mutual interest in distribution engineering activities for the gas, electricity, water & cable / telecommunications industries; to coordinate reports / responses on behalf of the utilities
- Gp Electricity industry; Gas industry; Telecommunications; Water industry
- ● Conf - Mtgs - Res - Exhib
- < Assn Geographic Inf
- M f & org
- ¶ Bulletin - 2; free.
  Specialist reports; prices vary (free to £10).   AR.

National Jousting Association
see **Knights of Royal England (National Jousting Association)**

National Jumblers Federation   (NJF)
- NR 347 Kingston Rd, Ewell, EPSOM, Surrey, KT19 0BS.   (hsp)
  020 8393 3342
  email truedvd@aol.com
  Sec: David True
- ○ *G, *T; acts in the interests of autojumblers, bike jumblers & boat jumblers
- M i & f
- ¶ Jnl - 6.

National Karting Association Ltd   (NKA)   1993
- ■ Devonia, Long Road West, Dedham, COLCHESTER, Essex, CO7 6ES.   (hsp/b)
  01206 322726   fax 01206 322726
  email nka@nationalkarting.co.uk
  http://www.nationalkarting.co.uk
  Co Sec: Mrs Linda D Barton
- ▲ Company Limited by Guarantee
- Br USA
- ○ *S, *T; to help circuit owners in the aspects of health & safety & promotion
- Gp Safety coordination
- ● Mtgs - ET - LG
- < Motor Activities Trg Coun; [& a proposed Kart Forum body]
- M c 100 i
- ¶ NL - 4;   NKA Guideline; both ftm.

National Kidney Federation   1978
- ■ 6 Stanley St, WORKSOP, Notts, S81 7HX.   (hq)
  01909 487795   fax 01909 481723
  email nkf@kidney.org.uk   http://www.kidney.org.uk
  Chief Exec: Timothy F Statham
- ▲ Registered Charity
- ○ *W; to promote the welfare of persons suffering from kidney disease or renal failure & those relatives & friends who care for them
- ● Conf - Inf - LG
  Helpline: 0845 601 0209
- < Eur Kidney Patients' Assn (CEAPIR)
- M 500 i, 65 org
- ¶ Kidney Life - 4; £12.
  Conference Report - 1;   AR & Accounts - 1; both free.

National Landlords' Association (NLA) 1973

NR 22-26 Albert Embankment, LONDON, SE1 7TJ. (hq)
0870 241 0471
http://www.landlords.org.uk
Chmn: David Salusbury
▲ Company Limited by Guarantee
○ *K; to protect & promote the interests of private landlords of
residential property
● Mtgs - SG - Inf - LG
< Nat Fedn of Residential Landlords
M 4,750 i
2004 Small Landlords Association
¶ Jnl - 4; NL - 6; both ftm only.

National Library for the Blind (NLB) 1882

■ Far Cromwell Rd, Bredbury, STOCKPORT, Cheshire,
SK6 2SG. (hq)
0161-355 2000 fax 0161-355 2098
email enquiries@nlbuk.org http://www.nlbuk.org
Chief Exec: Helen Brazier
▲ Company Limited by Guarantee; Registered Charity
○ *K, *W; to work towards equal access to information &
literature for visually impaired people; membership is open
to anyone who needs to use the services (the visually
impaired, teachers, librarians, parents)
Gp Braille & Moon libraries; Braille music library
● Res - Exhib - Inf - Lib (free postal service worldwide to blind &
partially sighted)
Helpline: 0161-355 2000 (Mon-Fri 0830-1630 hrs)
< Intl Fedn of Library Assns (IFLA); Share the Vision (STV); Chart
Inst of Library & Inf Profls (CILIP)
M 5,000 i, 500 org, UK & o'seas
¶ Focus (supporters NL) - 4; Annual Review;
Read On (readers magazine) - 4;
New Reading Catalogue (books added to stock) - 4;
SoapBox (campaigners' network NL) - 4; all free.

National Limousine Association

■ Bel-Air Limousines, 26 Alma Rd, ROTHERHAM, S Yorks,
S60 2HZ. (chmn/b)
01709 838159
http://www.nlauk.co.uk
Chmn: Harvey Muxlow
○ *T

National Literacy Association (NLA) 1993

■ Leonard House (1st floor), 321 Bradford St, BIRMINGHAM,
B6 6ET. (hq)
0121-622 5143 fax 0121-622 5143
email mail@nla.org.uk http://www.nla.org.uk
Dir & Sec: Jo Klaces
▲ Registered Charity
○ *K; a charity working to eliminate illiteracy amongst children &
young people
● ET - Res - Stat - Inf - Lib - LG
< Assn Educl Psychologists; Assn of Teachers & Lecturers; Brit
Dyslexic Assn; Brit Educl Suppliers Assn [& 9 other
educational bodies]
M 64 i, 298 org
¶ NL - 4; free. AR - 1; board members only.
The Guide to Literacy Resources 7th ed - 1.
Literacy & ICT: cutting edge practice in the primary school - 1.

National Market Traders Federation (NMTF) 1899

■ Hampton House, Hawshaw Lane, Hoyland, BARNSLEY, S Yorks,
S74 0HA. (hq)
01226 749021 fax 01226 740329
email enquiries@nmtf.co.uk http://www.nmtf.co.uk
Gen Sec: D E Feeny
▲ Un-incorporated Society
Br 172
○ *T; representation of market traders at local, national &
international level
● Conf - Mtgs - Exhib - Provision of business insurance for market
traders
< U Eur de Commerce Ambulant
M 32,000 i
¶ Federation News - 6; free.

National Metal Trades Federation (NMTF) 1912

NR Mirren Court (One), 119 Renfrew Rd, PAISLEY, Renfrewshire,
PA3 4EA. (hq)
0141-847 1265
http://www.nationalmetaltradesfederation.org.uk
Sec: A Shaw, Dir: A G MacDonald
▲ Un-incorporated Society
○ *T
● Conf - Mtgs - ET - SG - Inf - Empl
< METCOM
M c 70 f
¶ Circulars; m only.

National Microelectronics Institute (NMI) 1997

NR Geddes House (suite 2), Kirkton North, LIVINGSTONE,
West Lothian, EH54 6GU. (hq)
email info@nmi.org.uk http://www.nmi.org.uk
Chief Exec: Derek Boyd
▲ Company Limited by Guarantee
○ *N, *T; to provide a mechanism for collaboration between
members, educational organisations, regional bodies &
government
● Mtgs - ET - LG
M [not stated]

National Motorcycle Council (NMC) 1985

NR Starley House, Eaton Rd, COVENTRY, Warks, CV1 2FH. (hq)
0870 330 7820
http://www.nmc.org.uk
Secretariat: Craig Carey-Clinch
○ *N; liaison between various sectional interests within
motorcycling
● Inf - LG
< Parliamentary Advisory C'ee on Transport Safety (PACTS)
M i, f & org

National Mouse Club (NMC) 1895

NR 44 Speeton Avenue, BRADFORD, W Yorks, BD7 4NQ. (hsp)
01274 574205
Hon Sec: Brian Cookson
▲ Un-incorporated Society
○ *B; to promote breeding & exhibition of fancy mice
● Mtgs - Exhib - Comp - Inf
M 150 i, UK / 5 i, o'seas
¶ NMC News - 12; £20 yr m, £2 each nm. Ybk; ftm only.

National Multiple Sclerosis Therapy Centres
since 2003 **Multiple Sclerosis National Therapy Centres**

National Music Disability Information Service
a group of **Sound Sense: National Community Music
Association**

National Neighbourhood Watch Association

has closed

© CBD Research Ltd · Beckenham · BR3 5JS · Tel 020 8650 7745 · Fax 020 8650 0768 · E-mail cbd@cbdresearch.com · www.cbdresearch.com

National Network of Assessment Centres   (NNAC)
NR   The Royal National College, College Rd, HEREFORD,
         HR1 1EB.   (hq)
         01432 476630   fax 01432 376630
○   *n, *w; for physically or sensorily disabled people; to advise
      colleges & universities about teaching, learning strategies &
      enabling devices to ensure access to the curriculum for all
      students
M   centres
×   2006 National Federation of Access Centres

National Newspapers of Ireland   (NNI)
IRL   Clyde Lodge, 15 Clyde Rd, DUBLIN 4, Republic of Ireland.
         353 (1) 668 9099   fax 353 (1) 668 9872
         email nni@cullencommunications.ie   http://www.nni.ie
         Co-ordinating Dir: Frank Cullen
○   *T; the representative body of Ireland's daily & weekly
      newspapers

National Off-Licence Association
IRL   1-3 Sandford Rd, Ranelagh, DUBLIN 6, Republic of Ireland.
         353 (1) 497 9286   fax 353 (1) 491 0172
         email admin@noffla.ie   http://www.noffla.ie
         Chief Exec: Reggie Walsh
○   *T

National Office of Animal Health Ltd   (NOAH)   1986
■   3 Crossfield Chambers, Gladbeck Way, ENFIELD, Middx,
      EN2 7HF.   (hq)
      020 8367 3131   fax 020 8363 1155
      email noah@noah.co.uk   http://www.noah.co.uk
      Chief Exec: Philip Sketchley
▲   Company Limited by Guarantee
○   *T, *V; for manufacturers of licensed animal medicines in the
      UK (incl pet & farm animals)
Gp   Code of Practice C'ee for the Promotion of Animal Medicines
●   Conf - Mtgs - ET - Res - Exhib - Stat - Inf - LG - Conducts
      research sales survey on behalf of members & non-members
      - Media relations on behalf of members
<   Intl Fedn Animal Health (IFAH); Intl Fedn Animal Health (IFAH-
      Europe)
M   32 i, 12 f
¶   Compendium of Data Sheets IOC Animal Medicines - 1.
      (also available online: www.noahcompendium.co.uk).
      Poisoning in Veterinary Practice, 1992; £3.
      Animal Medicine Record Book, 1999; £3.50.
      Briefing documents & reports; free.

National Operatic & Dramatic Association   (NODA)   1899
■   58-60 Lincoln Rd, PETERBOROUGH, Cambs, PE1 2RZ.   (hq)
      0870 770 2480   fax 0870 770 2490
      email everyone@noda.org.uk   http://www.noda.org.uk
      Chief Exec: Mark Pemberton
▲   Registered Charity
○   *A, *D, *N; 'national umbrella body for amateur operatic &
      dramatic societies'
●   Conf - Mtgs - ET (Summer school for amateur operatic &
      dramatic students with professional tutors)
<   Intl Theatre Exchange (UK branch of IATA)
M   2,500 i, 2,500 org
¶   NODA National News - 4; ftm, £2.50 each nm.

National Organisation of Beaters & Pickers-up   2005
NR   The Cabin, 14 Kickdom Close, The Downs, AMESBURY, Wilts,
         SP4 7XB.
         07799 337995
         http://www.nobs.org.uk
         Contact: Mark Elliott

National Organisation for Counselling Adoptees & their Parents
   since 2004-05 **Supporting Adults affected by Adoption**

**National Organisation for Phobias, Anxiety, Neuroses,
   Information & Care   (NO PANIC)**
■   93 Brands Farm Way, TELFORD, Shropshire, TF3 2JQ.   (hsp)
      01952 590005   fax 01952 270962
      email ceo@nopanic.org.uk   http://www.nopanic.org.uk
      Chief Exec: Colin M Hammond
▲   Registered Charity
Br   Ireland
○   *W; the relief & rehabilitation of those people suffering from
      panic attacks, phobias, obsessive compulsive disorder,
      related anxiety disorders & tranquilliser withdrawal; to
      provide support to sufferers & their families &/or carers
●   Conf - ET - Inf - Telephone recovery course - Advice & support
      Helpline: 0808 808 0545 (0010-2200 daily)
M   2,700 i, UK / 100 i, o'seas
¶   NL - 24; ftm.
      No Panic: the facts [about the charity].
      Information booklets [on specific problems]; £1.50 each.
      Books; £5 - £12 each.   Audio & Visual aids; £2 - £14.

**National Organisation for the Treatment of Abusers   (NOTA)
1991**
NR   PO Box 356, HULL, HU12 8WR.   (hq)
         01482 896990   fax 01482 896990
         email notaoffice@aol.com   http://www.nota.co.uk
▲   Registered Charity
Br   12; Eire
○   *K, *P; to protect potential victims of sexual aggression through
      developing & promoting professional practice with both sex
      offenders (regardless of their age or gender)... & by direct
      work with their victims & non-abusing family members
●   Conf - Mtgs - ET - Res - LG
<   Assn for the Treatment of Abusers (USA)
M   c 1,200 i
¶   Jnl of Sexual Aggression - 2.   NOTA News - 4.
      Annual Conference Audio Tapes - 1.
×   2001 National Association for the Development of Work with
      Sex Offenders

National Orthophobics Group
■   81 Park View, Collins Rd, LONDON, N5 2UD.
○   *W
M   5 i

National Osteoporosis Society   (NOS)   1986
NR   Camerton, BATH, Somerset, BA2 0PJ.   (hq)
         01761 471771   fax 01761 471104
         email info@nos.org.uk   http://www.nos.org.uk
         Chief Exec: Prof C Cooper
▲   Registered Charity
Br   130 regional support groups
○   *W; to provide help & support for sufferers of osteoporosis; to
      encourage the medical professions, government etc to work
      together towards improving treatment & prevention; to
      support research
●   Conf - Mtgs - Res - Exhib - Stat - Inf - LG - National telephone
      helpline
<   Eur Foundation for Osteoporosis & Bone Disease; Intl
      Osteoporosis Foundation; Nat Coun Women
M   c 27,000 i
¶   Osteoporosis News (NL) - 4; ftm only.
      Osteoporosis Review - 4; ftm only.   AR; free.

National Outdoor Events Association   (NOEA)   1979
■   7 Hamilton Way, WALLINGTON, Surrey, SM6 9NJ.   (hq)
      020 8669 8121   fax 020 8647 1128
      email secretary@noea.org.uk   http://www.noea.org.uk
      Gen Sec: John W Barton
▲   Un-incorporated Society
○   *T; for local authorities, show organisers & suppliers of
      equipment & services for the outdoor events industry
M   262 f
¶   Ybk; free.   Code of Practice for Outdoor Events; £22.

National Outsourcing Association   (NOA)
NR   44 Wardour St, LONDON, W1D 6QZ.   (hq)
       020 7292 8686   fax 020 7287 2905
       email admin@noa.co.uk   http://www.noa.co.uk
       Admin: Emma Peacock
▲   Company Limited by Guarantee
○   *T; to develop experience & professionalism in all areas of
       business technology outsourcing - in particular outsourcing of
       telecommunications & computing networks; to promote the
       business advantages of outsourcing
●   Conf - Mtgs - Res - Inf - LG - Promotion & lobbying
M   f
¶   Business Technology Outsourcer - 2; free.
✕   2001 (December) Network Outsourcing Association

National Packaging Council   (NPC)   1999
NR   24 Grange St, KILMARNOCK, E Ayrshire, KA1 2AR.   (hq)
       01563 570518   fax 01563 572728
       email npc@natpack.org.uk   http://www.natpack.org.uk
       Sec: Allan Glen
○   *N, *P; administrative & management services for trade
       associations involved in the packaging industry
Gp   British Packaging Association; ETAPS (Environmental &
       Technical Association for Paper Sack Industry); Foodservice
       Packaging Association; Sheet Plant Association
●   Conf - Mtgs - ET - Exhib - Comp - Inf - VE - LG
M   180 f, UK / 10 f, o'seas

National Panel Products Association
       is the Hardwood & Panel Products division of the **Timber Trade
       Federation**

National Park Homes Council
       is a group of the **National Caravanners Council**

National Pawnbrokers Association   (NPA)   1892
NR   Kildare House (7th floor), 3 Dorset Rise, LONDON,
       EC4Y 8EN.   (asa)
       020 7242 1114   fax 020 7405 4266
       http://www.thenpa.co.uk
       Sec Gen: Timothy G Ford
▲   Company Limited by Guarantee
○   *T
●   Conf - Mtgs - Res - Exhib - Comp - Stat - Inf - VE - LG -
       Insurance - Legal, financial, operations, publicity advice -
       New business promotion & assistance
<   Nat Cham Tr; Soc Assn Execs: Glasgow Pawnbrokers Assn
M   c 450 f
¶   NPA Times - 4;   AR & Accounts - 1; both free.
       Leaflets:
       Pawnbrokers Guide;   Using a Pawnbroker; both ftm.

National Pensioners' Convention   (NPC)   1990
■   19-23 Ironmonger Row, LONDON, EC1V 3QP.   (hq)
       020 7553 6510   fax 020 7553 6511
       email admin@npcuk.org   http://www.npcuk.org
       Gen Sec: Joe Harris
       Admin: Alison Purshouse
▲   Un-incorporated Society
Br   500 affiliated groups
○   *K, *N; umbrella organisation for pensioner organisations,
       regional pensioner liaison forums, charities & trade union
       retired members associations
●   Mtgs - ET - Res - Inf - LG
<   AGE: the Eur Older People's Platform
M   1,200 i, 100 f, 400 org
¶   The Message - 4; ftm, 10p per copy nm.
       Pension credit for beginners; 50p.
       Women - 'Wise-up' on Pensions; £1.

National Pest Technicians Association   (NPTA)   1993
■   NPTA House, Hall Lane, Kinoulton, NOTTINGHAM,
       NG12 3EF.   (hq)
       01949 81133   fax 01949 823905
       email officenpta@aol.com   http://www.npta.org.uk
       Sec: John A Davison
       Admin Officer: Mrs Julie Gillies
▲   Company Limited by Guarantee
○   *P; to promote the role of pest controller
●   Conf - Mtgs - ET - Exhib - Inf
M   c 900 i & f
¶   Today's Technician - 4; ftm, £4 each nm.

National Pharmacy Association   (NPA)   1921
NR   38-42 St Peter's Street, ST ALBANS, Herts, AL1 3NP.   (hq)
       01727 832161   fax 01727 840858
       email npa@npa.co.uk   http://www.npa.co.uk
       Sec: J D'Arcy
▲   Company Limited by Guarantee
○   *T; for community retail pharmacists
●   Conf - ET - Exam - Exhib - Inf - Lib - VE - Empl - LG
<   Eur Pharmacy Gp
M   11,000 f
¶   The Supplement - 12; free.
✕   2005 National Pharmaceutical Association

National Philatelic Society   (NPS)   1899
■   The British Philatelic Centre, 107 Charterhouse St, LONDON,
       EC1M 6PT.   (hq)
       020 7490 9610
       email nps@ukphilately.org.uk
       http://www.ukphilately.org.uk/nps
       Hon Gen Sec: Peter Mellor
▲   Un-incorporated Society
○   *G; promotion & encouragement of philately
●   Mtgs - Lib
<   Assn of Brit Philatelic Socs
M   600 i, 1 org, UK / 50 i, o'seas
¶   The Stamp Lover - 6; ftm, £17 yr nm.

National Phobics Society   (NPS)   1970
■   Zion CRC, 339 Stretford Rd, Hulme, MANCHESTER,
       M15 4ZY.   (hq)
       0870 122 2325   fax 0161-227 9862
       email nationalphobic@btconnect.com
       http://www.phobics-society.org.uk
       Chief Exec: Glenmoure Kingsley-Nunes
▲   Registered Charity
Br   self-help groups & therapists
○   *W; to support anyone affected by anxiety disorders (phobias,
       panic attacks, obsessive/compulsive disorders)
Gp   Mental health; Anxiety disorders
●   Conf - ET - Inf - Support groups - One to one therapy services -
       Helpline services - Co-hosts a national Anxiety Disorders
       Conference each year, see www.anxietyconference.org.uk
M   6,000 i, 1,000 f, 20 self-help gps, UK / 25 i, o'seas
¶   Don't Panic (NL) - 4; ftm only.

National Piers Society   (NPS)   1979
■   4 Tyrrell Rd, SOUTH BENFLEET, Essex, SS7 8DH.   (pro/p)
       01472 350404
       email timmickleburgh2002@yahoo.co.uk
       http://www.piers.co.uk
       PRO: Tim Wardley
▲   Company Limited by Guarantee; Registered Charity
○   *G, *K; promoting interest in the preservation & continued
       enjoyment of seaside piers
●   Res - Inf - PL - VE - LG
<   Paddle Steamer Preservation Soc
M   i & f
¶   Piers (Jnl) - 4; ftm.   Good Piers Guide.
       Guide to British Piers, 3rd ed.

National Pig Association (NPA) 1999
NR Agriculture House, STONELEIGH PARK, Warks, CV8 2LZ. (hq)
    024 7685 8784 fax 024 7865 8786
    email npa@npanet.org.uk   http://www.npa-uk.net
    Chief Exec: Stewart Houston
▲ Company Limited by Guarantee
○ *B, *T; for the UK pig industry
Gp Allied industry; Campaigns
● Conf - Mtgs - ET - LG
M 1,300 i, 100 f

National Pigeon Association (NPA) 1918
NR Bridge Villa, Main St, Pollington, GOOLE, Yorks, DN14 0DW.
    (hsp)
    01405 869516
    Sec: Mrs Tracey Edwards
▲ Un-incorporated Society
○ *B, *G; organising body for issue of rings & exhibitions of fancy
    pigeons (NOT racing pigeons)
● Mtgs - Exhib
< Entente Européenne d'Aviculture et de Cuniculture
M c 150 org
¶ Feathered World - 12; £21 yr.

National Pipe Organ Register
    a group of the **British Institute of Organ Studies**

National Plant Societies Federation
    no longer in existence

National Playbus Association 1974
NR Brunswick Court, Brunswick Square, BRISTOL, BS2 8PE. (hq)
    0117-916 6580 fax 0117-916 6588
    email playbus@playbus.org.uk
    http://www.playbus.org.uk
    Chief Exec: Geoffrey Riddick
▲ Company Limited by Guarantee; Registered Charity
○ *N, *W, *Y; a national umbrella organisation which supports the
    work of locally based community groups who make use of
    covered vehicles to provide services
● Conf - ET - Inf - Project support & development
< Nat Coun Voluntary Orgs (NCVO); Scot Coun Voluntary
    Orgs (SCVO); Nat Coun Voluntary Child Care
    Orgs (NCVCCO)
M c 230 org
¶ Busfare - 3. AR.
    Information sheets & specialist publications; prices vary.

National Playing Fields Association (NPFA) 1925
■ Stanley House, St Chad's Place, LONDON, WC1X 9HH. (hq)
    020 7833 5360
    Dir: Alison Moore-Gwyn
▲ Registered Charity
Br 4
○ *K; charity committed to the protection & preservation of
    recreational space
● Conf - ET - Inf - LG
M 600 i, f & org
¶ The Six Acre Standard; £25. Taking a Lead; £12.95.
    Playwork - a guide for trainers; £10.
    Impact Absorbing Surfaces for Children's Playgrounds; £15.
    Play Safety Guidelines; £11.95. NPFA Cost Guide; £25.

National Pony Society (NPS) 1893
NR 7 The Windmill, St Mary's Close, Turk St, ALTON, Hants,
    GU34 1EF. (hq)
    01420 88333 fax 01420 80599
    email secretary@nationalponysociety.org.uk
    http://www.nationalponysociety.org.uk
    Exec Sec: Mrs L Wilkins
▲ Registered Charity
○ *B, *V; to encourage the breeding, registration & improvement
    of British riding ponies (incl mountain & moorland ponies); to
    foster the welfare of ponies in general
Gp Breed societies; Veterinary & animal welfare gps
● Conf - Mtgs - ET - Exam - Exhib - Comp - SG - Inf - Stud book,
    register & appendix
< Brit Driving Soc; Brit Show Pony Soc; Brit Equine Welfare C'ee;
    Central Prefix Register
M 3,000 i
¶ Review - 1; ftm.   NL - 3; ftm only.
    Stud Book.   AR; free.   Judges List & Rules.
    Show Schedule; free.   Show Catalogue.

National Portage Association (NPA) 1983
■ PO Box 3075, YEOVIL, Somerset, BA21 3FB. (admin/p)
    01935 471641 fax 01935 471641
    email npa@portageuk.freeserve.co.uk
    http://www.portage.org.uk
    Admin: Brenda Paul
▲ Company Limited by Guarantee; Registered Charity
Br Regional
○ *E, *W; to support families caring for children with special
    needs by promoting & supporting portage educational home
    visiting services
Gp Training & Monitoring; Information & Publicity; Ethics
● Conf - Mtgs - ET - Exhib - Inf
M 400 i, 77 groups, UK / 3 i, 1 group, o'seas
¶ Portage Post NL - 3; ftm.   AR - 1; free.
    Conference Proceedings - 1; £11.74.
    Publications list available.

National Portraiture Association (NPA) 1972
NR 59-60 Fitzjames Avenue, LONDON, W14 0RR. (hq)
    020 7602 0892 fax 020 7602 6705
    email enquiries@natportrait.com
    http://www.natportrait.com
    Dir: William H Deeves
▲ Un-incorporated Society
○ *A; acquisition of fine portrait commissions in all media
● Bursaries for talented children

National Pot Leek Society 1978
NR 147 Sea Rd, Fulwell, SUNDERLAND, SR6 9EB. (hsp)
    0191-549 4274
    Hon Sec: Derek Richardson
○ *H; culture, knowledge & research into growth & diseases of
    pot grown leeks
● ET - Res - Exhib - Stat - Inf
M i
¶ Jnl - 4; ftm.   NL.

National Prefabricated Building Association Ltd
    since 2004 **Modular & Portable Building Association**

National Private Hire Association (NPHA) 1993
■ 8 Silver St, BURY, Lancs, BL9 0EX. (hq)
    0161-280 2800 fax 0161-280 7787
    Gen Sec: Bryan M Roland
▲ Company Limited by Guarantee
○ *T; for private hire & hackney carriage companies & drivers; to
    raise standards in the trade, both actual & as perceived by
    the public
Gp NPH QA - ISO 9002 consultancy
● Conf - ET - Exhib - Inf - LG - Legal guidance - Representations
    in court
M 50 i, 600 f, 66 local org
¶ Private Hire & Taxi Monthly - 12.

National Pure Water Association   1960
NR   42 Huntington Rd, YORK, N Yorks, YO31 8RE.
   020 8220 9168
   http://www.npwa.freeserve.co.uk
○   *K; to oppose the use of public water supplies for the purpose
   of mass medication, particularly fluoridation; to protect the
   public water supplies from any form of pollution or
   contamination, deliberate or accidental
●   Inf
¶   NL - 4; ftm.

National Quoits Association   (NQA)   1986
NR   54 Park Avenue, Shiremoor, NEWCASTLE upon TYNE,
   NE27 0LG.   (hsp)
   0191-253 2646
   Pres: Peter Brown
○   *S; the governing body for the traditional & ancient game of
   quoits
M   i & leagues

National Register of Access Consultants   (NRAC)   2000
■   70 South Lambeth Rd, LONDON, SW8 1RL.   (hq)
   020 7735 7845   fax 020 7840 5811
   email info@nrac.org.uk   http://www.nrac.org.uk
   Chief Exec: Sarah Langton-Lockton
○   *P; accreditation of individuals in the access/inclusive
   environments sector
Gp   Specialists for building types; Countryside; Designer; Expert
   witness; Policy & strategy; Signage & wayfinding; Trainer;
   Transport; Web accessibility
●   Conf - Accreditation of individuals - Services to members
M   200 i, + 150 affiliates (i & org)
¶   email NL - m only.

**National Register of Hypnotherapists & Psychotherapists
(NRHP)   1985**
■   12 Cross St (room B), NELSON, Lancs, BB9 7EN.   (hq)
   01282 716839   fax 01282 698633
   email nrhp@btconnect.com   http://www.nrhp.co.uk
   The Secretary
▲   Company Limited by Guarantee
○   *P; for students & graduates of the National College of
   Hypnosis & Psychotherapy
●   Conf - ET - Res - Stat - Inf - LG
<   Eur Assn for Psychotherapy; UK Coun for Psychotherapy
M   350 i, UK / 5 i, o'seas
¶   NL - 3; ftm only.   LM (by area); free on request.
   Directory of Practitioners - 1; ftm, £5 nm.

National Register of Personal Trainers   (NRPT)   1991
NR   PO Box 3455, MARLOW, Bucks, SL7 1WG.
   0870 200 6010
   email info@nrpt.co.uk   http://www.nrpt.co.uk
○   *P
M   c 600 i

National Register of Property Preservation Specialists
■   11 Greenland Rd, BARNET, Herts, EN5 2AL.
   0500 223505
   http://www.nrpps.co.uk
   Contact: Mr Smith
○   *P
M   c 180 i

National Renderers Association   (NRA)
■   52 Packhorse Rd, GERRARDS CROSS, Bucks, SL9 8EF.   (hq)
   01753 895414   fax 01753 880686
   email nralondon@renderers.org
   http://www.renderers.org
   Regional Dir: Neville Chandler
▲   Company Limited by Guarantee
Br   1; Hong Kong, Mexico, USA
○   *T; to promote the use of rendered products
●   ET - Expt - LG
M   f
¶   The Bulletin - 4; free.

National Rheumatoid Arthritis Society   (NRAS)   2001
■   Unit B4 Westacott Business Centre, Littlewick Green,
   MAIDENHEAD, Berks, SL6 3RT.   (hq)
   01628 823524
   email enquiries@rheumatoid.org.uk
   http://www.rheumatoid.org.uk
   Chmn: Ailsa Bosworth
▲   Registered Charity
○   *G, *K; is patient-led & focuses on rheumatoid arthritis; to
   provide an advisory & information service on all aspects of
   the disease
Gp   Expert patient network
●   Inf
M   c 850 i
¶   NL - 3; ftm only (subscription £15).   AR.
   Information leaflet.

National Rifle Association   (NRA)   1860
■   c/o National Shooting Centre, Bisley Camp, Brookwood,
   WOKING, Surrey, GU24 0PB.   (hq)
   01483 797777   fax 01483 797285
   email info@nra.org.uk   http://www.nra.org.uk
   Chmn: John Jackman,   Sec Gen: Glynn Algar
▲   Registered Charity
○   *S; to promote rifle & pistol shooting
●   Mtgs - ET - Exhib - Comp - Stat - Inf - Lib - PL - LG
<   Brit Shooting Sports Coun; GB Target Shooting Fedn
M   4,500 i, 1,100 org, UK / 42 org, o'seas
¶   Jnl - 3; ftm.

National Roller Canary Society
   a member body of the **Society for the Protection of Aviculture**

**National Roller Hockey Association of England Ltd   (NRHA)
1909**
NR   136 Canterbury Rd, HERNE BAY, Kent, CT6 5RX.   (sp)
   http://www.nrha.co.uk
   Sec: Aileen Barker
○   *S; governing body for roller hockey
M   i & clubs
¶   NL - 12.   Coaching Manual.   AR.

National Rounders Association   (NRA)   1943
NR   55 Westland Gdns, Westfield, SHEFFIELD, S Yorks, S20 8ES.
   (office/address)
   0114-248 0357   fax 0870 052 0396
   email nraoffice@btopenworld.com
   http://www.nra-rounders.co.uk
   Contact: Alan Fergus
▲   Voluntary Organisation
○   *S; national governing body for game of rounders; trustees of
   the rules of rounders worldwide
Gp   International teams at 8 age groups (ladies)
●   Mtgs - ET - Exam - Res - Comp - Inf - LG
<   Cent Coun for Physical Recreation (CCPR); Sports Coach
   UK (SCUK)
M   c 10,000 i, c 800 org
¶   Publications list on request.

© CBD Research Ltd · Beckenham · BR3 5JS · Tel 020 8650 7745 · Fax 020 8650 0768 · E-mail cbd@cbdresearch.com · www.cbdresearch.com

National Sawmilling Association   (NSA)   1946
NR   26-27 Oxendon St, LONDON, SW1Y 4EL.   (hq)
         020 7839 1891   fax 020 7930 0094
         http://www.ttf.co.uk
○   *T; to represent sawmilling employers & importers in
         negotiations
         The sawmilling industry in general, is represented by the UK
         Forest Products Association (qv)
<   a division of the Timber Trade Federation
M   c 100 f (all members of the TTF)

National Schizophrenia Fellowship
         since July 2002 **Rethink severe mental illness**

National School Band Association   (NSBA)   1952
■   10 Wychwood Close, The Slade, CHARLBURY, Oxon,
         OX7 3TB.   (sec/p)
         01608 811837   fax 01608 811837
         http://www.nsba.org.uk
         Exec Officer: Dr Thomas Chatburn
▲   Registered Charity
○   *D; to encourage an interest in music, through the playing of
         brass & woodwind instruments in schools
M   i & schools

National Secular Society   (NSS)   1866
■   25 Red Lion Sq, LONDON, WC1R 4RL.   (hq)
         020 7404 3126   fax 0870 762 8971
         email admin@secularism.org.uk
         http://www.secularism.org.uk
         Exec Dir: Keith Porteus Wood
▲   Company Limited by Guarantee
○   *K; to campaign for secularism (incl free speech, freedom from
         religious discrimination & other civil liberties) & for an end to
         religious privilege (incl no public finding of an established
         church, of sectarian schools & of faith-based social services)
●   LG - Campaigning
<   Intl Ethical & Humanist U; Liberty; Amnesty Intl; Abortion Law
         Reform Assn; Network for Peace
M   2,090 i, 31 org, UK / 45 i, o'seas
¶   Bulletin - 3;   Newsline (email) - 52;   AR - 1; all free.
✗   2001 National Secular Society Ltd

National Security Inspectorate   (NSI)   2001
■   Sentinel House, 5 Reform Rd, MAIDENHEAD, Berks, SL6 8BY.
         (hq)
         0845 006 3003   fax 01628 773367
         email nsi@nsi.org.uk   http://www.nsi.org.uk
         Chief Exec: Tom Mullarkey
▲   Company Limited by Guarantee
○   *N; an independent regulatory & certification body approving &
         regulating firms concerned with installation, service &
         maintenance of all security systems - intruder alarms, CCTV,
         access control, & alarm receiving centres; inspection of
         companies providing 'people based' services in the security
         industry; inspection of companies designing, installing,
         commissioning & maintaining fire detection systems
●   Conf - Mtgs - Exhib - Inf - LG - Inspection services
<   BSI; Security Ind Training Org; Security Ind Bd; Jt Security Ind
         Coun
M   1,100 f
¶   Network NL - 3;
         2 directories of approved companies - 1; all free.
         Technical Memoranda - irreg; ftm only.
         Regulatory Documents - irreg; £9.

** **National Service Veteran Alliance**
         Organisation lost: see Introduction paragraph 3

National Sewerage Association   (NSA)   1995
■   98 Alric Ave, NEW MALDEN, Surrey, KT3 4JW.   (hsp)
         020 8942 9391   fax 020 8942 9391
         email nsa@tinyonline.co.uk   http://www.sewerage.org
         Sec: Mrs V A Gibbens
▲   Un-incorporated Society
○   *T; to improve the professional standards of firms carrying out
         sewer surveys, cleaning, monitoring, repairs & renovation
Gp   Contractors: CCTV sewer inspection, Flow monitoring,
         Blockage clearance & cleaning; Associated manufacturers
●   Mtgs - ET - Inf - LG - Liaison with water companies & WRc on
         national standards for the industry
M   32 f
¶   Members Directory - on request; free.

National Sheep Association   (NSA)   1892
NR   The Sheep Centre, MALVERN, Worcs, WR13 6PH.   (hq)
         01684 892661
○   *B, *T; expansion of UK sheep industry
M   f

National Small-Bore Rifle Association   (NSRA)   1903
NR   Lord Roberts Centre, Bisley Camp - Brookwood, WOKING,
         Surrey, GU24 0NP.   (hq)
         0845 130 6772   fax 01483 476392
         email info@nsra.co.uk   http://www.nsra.co.uk
         Sec: D Lattimore
▲   Registered Charity
○   *S; promotion of .22 target shooting & air rifle shooting & .177
         airgun shooting
●   Mtgs - ET - Comp - Stat - Inf - Lib
<   U Intle de Tir; Eur Shooting Fedn; GB Target Shooting Fedn
M   c 6,300 i, 1,000 clubs
¶   The Rifleman - 4; ftm.

National Society of Allied & Independent Funeral Directors
         this is the registered title of the organisation known as the **Society of**
         Allied & Independent Funeral Directors

National Society of Allotment & Leisure Gardeners Ltd
(NSALG)   1930
■   O'Dell House, Hunters Rd, CORBY, Northants, NN17 5JE.
         (hq)
         01536 266576   fax 01536 264509
         email natsoc@nsalg.org.uk   http://www.nsalg.org.uk
         Sec: Geoff Stokes
○   *G, *H; to ensure that allotments & leisure gardens are
         available to all who require them
●   Conf - Inf
<   NCVO
M   85,000 i, 1,700 org
¶   Allotment & Leisure Gardener - 4; ftm, £2 nm.

National Society (Church of England) for Promoting Religious
Education   1811
■   Church House, Great Smith St, LONDON, SW1P 3NZ.   (hq)
         020 7898 1518
         http://www.natsoc.org.uk
         Gen Sec: Canon John Hall
▲   Registered Charity
○   *R; to support all involved in religious education in schools,
         colleges & churches in England & Wales
M   i & schools

National Society for Clean Air & Environmental Protection (NSCA) 1899

- ■ 44 Grand Parade, BRIGHTON, E Sussex, BN2 9QA.   (hq)
    01273 878770   fax 01273 606626
    email admin@nsca.org.uk   http://www.nsca.org.uk
    Chief Exec: Martin Joseph
- ▲ Registered Charity
- Br 10
- ○ *K; to promote clean air through the reduction of air, water & land pollution, while having due regard to the environment
- ● Conf - ET - Res - Exhib - Inf
- < Intl U of Air Pollution Prevention & Envtl Protection Assns (IUAPPA); Eur Envt Bureau (EEB)
- M i, f, & local authorities
- ¶ Pollution Hbk - 1.   Leaflets.

National Society for Education in Art & Design (NSEAD) 1888

- NR The Gatehouse, Corsham Court, CORSHAM, Wilts, SN13 0BZ.   (hq)
    01249 714825   fax 01249 716138
    email johnsteers@nsead.org   http://www.nsead.org
    Sec: Dr John Steers
- ▲ Un-incorporated Society
- ○ *E, *P, *U; to promote & defend art & design education & the interests of teachers
- Gp Boards: Editorial, Teacher education, Information & communications technology
- ● Conf - ET - Res - Inf - Empl
- < Intl Soc for Educ through Art
- M c 2,500 i
- ¶ International Jnl of Art & Design Education - 3; ftm. Start - 6; ftm.

National Society for Epilepsy (NSE) 1892

- ■ Chesham Lane, CHALFONT ST PETER, Bucks, SL9 0RJ.   (hq)
    01494 601300   fax 01494 871927
    Chief Exec: Graham Faulkner
- ▲ Company Limited by Guarantee; Registered Charity
- ○ *W; to advance research, treatment, care, understanding & support for people with epilepsy
- ● ET - Res - Exhib - Inf
    Helpline: 01494 601400
- M i
- ¶ Epilepsy Review (Jnl) - 3; ftm only.   AR - 1; free.

National Society of Master Thatchers (NSMT) 1977

- ■ 13 Parkers Hill, Tetsworth, THAME, Oxon, OX9 7AQ.   (hsp)
    01844 281208   fax 01844 281208
    Sec & Chief Exec: Marjorie Sanders
- ▲ Company Limited by Guarantee
- ○ *T; the protection & promotion of thatch for the benefit of members & the thatch owning public
- Gp Thatching; Thatched property ownership; Thatching advice
- ● Conf - Mtgs - ET
- M 120 i, 3 f, 3 org
- ¶ The Thatcher's Standard - 4; ftm, £12.50 yr nm.
    Guidance Notes:
      Fire & Thatch; £5.50.
      Conservation Issues & the Maintenance of Cereal
        Varieties for Thatching; £5.50.

National Society of Painters, Sculptors & Printmakers (NS) 1930

- ■ 122 Copse Hill, LONDON, SW20 0NL.   (hsp)
    020 8946 7878
    http://www.nationalsociety.org
    Hon Sec: Gwen Spencer
- ▲ Registered Charity
- ○ *A; 'formed in 1930 to meet a growing desire among artists of every creed & outlook for an annual exhibition in London which would embrace all aspects of art under one roof, without prejudice or favour to anyone'
- ● Mtgs - Exhib
- M 81 i, UK / 2 i, o'seas
- ¶ NL - 2; ftm only.

National Society for Phenylketonuria (United Kingdom) Ltd (NSPKU) 1973

- ■ PO Box 26642, LONDON, N14 4ZF.   (hq)
    0845 603 9136
    email info@nspku.org.   http://www.nspku.org
    Chmn: Dave Stening
- ▲ Company Limited by Guarantee; Registered Charity
- ○ *W; the welfare of persons suffering from Phenylketonuria & allied (amino acid) disorders, their families & carers
- Gp Medical advisory panel (provides a link with the medical profession & a voice in decisions on standards on PKU treatment)
- ● Conf - Mtgs - Inf
- < Eur Soc for Phenylketonuria (ESPKU); Genetic Interest Gp (GIG)
- M 1,130 i, 5 f, 1 org, UK / 50 i, 10 org, o'seas
- ¶ News & Views (NL) - 4; ftm, £1 nm.
    Treatment of Phenylketonuria; ftm, £5.
    Leaflets (on diet, recipes & cookery); 25p - £5.

National Society for the Prevention of Cruelty to Children (NSPCC) 1884

- ■ 42 Curtain Rd, LONDON, EC2A 3NH.   (hq)
    020 7825 2500   fax 020 7825 2525
    email info@nspcc.org.uk   http://www.nspcc.org.uk
    Dir & Chief Exec: Mary Marsh
- ▲ Registered Charity
- ○ *K, *W; to prevent child abuse & neglect in all its forms
- ● ET - Res - Inf - Lib - LG
    Child protection helpline: 0800 800 5000
- M voluntary workers
- ¶ Publications catalogue & some full text publications available on website.

National Society of Professional Hypnotherapists (NSPH) 1990

- ■ Kennard, Shawfield Lane, BLAIRGOWRIE, Perthshire, PH10 6GW.   (hq)
    01250 874384
    email nwblair@nsph-hypnotherapy.co.uk
    http://www.nsph-hypnotherapy.co.uk
    Hon Sec: Neil Watson
- ▲ Un-incorporated Society
- ○ *P
- ● Mtgs - ET - Exam - Res - Exhib - SG - Inf
- M 100 i, UK / 6 i, o'seas
- ¶ NSPH Members Jnl - 4; ftm only.

National Society for the Promotion of Punctuality (NSPP)

- ■ 81 Park View, Colins Rd, LONDON, N5 2UD.   (asa)
- ○ *K; to increase public awareness of the importance of punctuality; 'being late may be fashionable but it is also rude'
- ● Mtgs - Stat - VE
- M 52 i
- ¶ Stopwatch (Jnl) - 12.

© CBD Research Ltd · Beckenham · BR3 5JS · Tel 020 8650 7745 · Fax 020 8650 0768 · E-mail cbd@cbdresearch.com · www.cbdresearch.com

National Society for Research into Allergy   (NSRA)   1980
- ■ 2 Armadale Close, Hollycroft, HINCKLEY, Leics, LE10 0SZ. (hsp/b)
  01455 250715
  email eunicerose@donald.com
  http://www.all-allergy.co.uk
  Hon Sec: Mrs Eunice L Rose
- ▲ Registered Charity
- Br New Zealand, USA
- ○ *K, *Q; to promote the awareness of allergic diseases; to research into the causes of allergic diseases & methods of safe treatment; to offer help & advice to people suffering from allergy-intolerance
- Gp Asthma; Eczema; Migraine; Crohn's; ME; Food & chemical intolerance; Allergy
- ● Mtgs - ET - Res
- M c 1,000 i, UK / c 100 i, o'seas
- ¶ Reaction - 3; ftm, £5 nm.
  Is it anything you ate? - 1; ftm (on joining), £10 nm.
  Publications list available.

National Society of Teapot Collectors
- NR 81 Park View, Collins Rd, LONDON, N5 2UD.
- ○ *G
- Gp Miniature teapots
- ● Mtgs - Exhib
- M 44 i
- ¶ The Spout (Jnl) - 6; ftm only.

National Specialist Contractors Council   (NSCC)   1992
- ■ Carthusian Court, 12 Carthusian St, LONDON, EC1M 6EZ. (hq)
  0870 429 6351   fax 0870 429 6352
  Chief Exec Officer: Suzannah Nichol
- ▲ Company Limited by Guarantee
- Br Scottish section: PO Box 28011, Edinburgh, EH16 6WN.
  0131-448 0266   fax 0131-440 4032
  Sec: Alan McKinney
- ○ *T; the sub-contract sector of the construction industry
- ● Conf - Mtgs - ET - Res - SG - Stat - Inf - LG
- M 30 associations
- ¶ Bulletin - 2;   AR; both ftm only.
  Check It - 2; ftm, £10 nm.

National Sprint Association Ltd   (NSA)   1958
- NR 8 King George Gardens, Chapel Allerton, LEEDS, W Yorks, LS7 4NS.   (chmn/p)
  0113-295 6949
  Chmn: Tony Hodgson
- ○ *S; organisation of motorcycle & three-wheeler standing-start quarter-mile sprints (& record attempts) in a straight line, not circuits
- < Auto-Cycle U

National Street Rod Association
- NR 8 Punchbowl Lane, BOSTON, Lincs, PE21 8HU.   (contact/p)
  01205 310885   fax 01205 354819
  email hotrods@ukgateway.net   http://www.nsra.org.uk
  Contact: Dave Biggadyke
- ○ *G
- M 2,000 i

National Sulphuric Acid Association Ltd
  is a sector group of the **Chemical Industries Association**

National Support Group for Victims of Failed Home Income Plans   (HIPS(97))   1997
- ■ White Cottage, Elstronwick, Burton Pidsea, HULL, HU12 9BP. (hsp)
  01964 670614   fax 01964 670614 (phone first)
  email abcraven@breathe.com
  Organiser: A B Craven
- ○ *G, *K; to support victims of failed home income plans (HIPS) originally set up in 1991; & is also involved in modern equity release schemes (known as home reversion schemes) which as yet, are un-regulated
- ● Inf - LG
- < Nat Pensioners Convention
- M 120 i
- ¶ HIPS (97) NL - 4; free.

National Sweet Pea Society   (NSPS)   1900
- NR 8 Wolseley Rd, Parkestone, POOLE, Dorset, BH12 2DP.   (hsp)
  Hon Sec: Janet Bulstrode
- ▲ Registered Charity
- ○ *H; to promote the growing of the sweet pea & to further its development
- ● Conf - Exhib - Comp
- < R Horticl Soc
- M 1,100 i, 10 f, 300 affiliated socs, UK / 50 i, o'seas
- ¶ NSPS Annual.   Bulletin (Spring & Autumn) - 2.
  Schedule of Exhibitions - 1.   Judges' Rules.
  Enjoy Sweet Peas.

National Taxi Association   (NTA)   1960
- NR Infirmary St, Newtown, CARLISLE, Cumbria, CA2 7AA.   (hsb)
  01228 598740
  email secretary@national-taxi-association.co.uk
  Admin Officer: Wayne Casey
- ▲ Company Limited by Guarantee
- ○ *N, *P, *T; the Hackney carriage trade
- ● Conf - Mtgs - Exhib - LG
- M c 70 trade org

National Tortoise Club of Great Britain   1975
- ■ 2 Laith Close, Cookridge, LEEDS, W Yorks, LS16 6LE. (chief/exec/p)
  0113-267 7587
  Chief Exec: Mrs B Waller
- Br worldwide
- ○ *B, *G; exchange of information on all aspects of tortoise keeping & breeding (incl the American Box, Greek & all Mediterranean & other species)
- ● Mtgs - ET - SG - Inf - Talks - Box Tortoise (help & advice) - Speaker available for talks incl radio & TV
- M i (numbers expanding)
- ¶ Care sheets & data; prices on application.   [NL under review].
  Note: as this is a voluntary body run by experts all enquiries must be accompanied by a pre-paid envelope &/or donation.

National Traction Engine Trust   1954
- ■ 153 Micklefield Rd, HIGH WYCOMBE, Bucks, HP13 7HA. (hsp)
  01494 521727   fax 01494 521727
  email suejackson@themutual.net
  Gen Sec: Mrs Susan Jackson
- ▲ Registered Charity
- ○ *G; preservation, restoration & maintenance of steam driven traction engines & steam driven road vehicles; training in operation & maintenance of steam driven vehicles
- ● Conf - Mtgs - Res - Exhib - Comp - Inf - VE
- < Fedn of Brit Historic Vehicle Clubs
- M 3,100 i, 60 affiliated gps
- ¶ Steaming - 4; ftm, £22 nm.
  Code of Practice for the better organisation of Traction Engine rallies, incorporating the Rally Authorisation Scheme.
  Code of Practice for Traction Engines & Similar Vehicles.

National Trailer & Towing Association Ltd   (NTTA)   1976
■   1 Alveston Place, ROYAL LEAMINGTON SPA, Warks,
     CV32 4SN.
     01926 335445   fax 01926 335445
     email info@ntta.co.uk   http://www.ntta.co.uk
     Exec Admin: David Millington
▲   Company Limited by Guarantee
○   *T; to represent the trailer & towbar industries on British,
     European & Industrial Standards Committees
Gp Training courses; NVQ qualifications; Consultancy; Expert
     witness; Inspection & report
●   Conf - Mtgs - ET - Exhib - Inf - LG
<   BSI; ISO; SMMT
M   151 f, 2 org
¶   NTTA News - 4; ftm only.

National Trainers Federation   (NTF)   1975
NR 9 High St, LAMBOURN, Berks, RG17 8XN.   (hq)
     01488 71719   fax 01488 73005
     email info@racehorsetrainers.org
     http://www.racehorsetrainers.org
     Chief Exec: Rupert Arnold
○   *T; to promote the interests of racehorse trainers within the
     racing industry
M   c 550 i

National Training Federation
     see **Association of Learning Providers**

National Trolleybus Association   (NTA)   1963
■   49 Alzey Gardens, HARPENDEN, Herts, AL5 5SY.   (editor/p)
     http://www.trolleybus.co.uk/nta
     Editor: R T E Box
▲   Company Limited by Guarantee; Registered Charity
○   *G; to preserve & to promote interest in trolleybuses
●   Mtgs - Stat - PL
<   Transport Trust; Assn of Indep Museums
M   554 i, f & org
¶   Trolleybus Magazine - 6; ftm only.
     Is involved in Trolleybooks, a joint publishing venture with the
     British Trolleybus Society.

National Trust for Ireland   (An Taisce)   1948
IRL Tailor's Hall, Back Lane, DUBLIN 8, Republic of Ireland.
     353 (1) 454 1786   fax 353 (1) 453 3255
     email info@antaisce.org   http://www.antaisce.org
     Chmn: Frank Corcoran
○   *G

National Trust for Places of Historic Interest or Natural Beauty
     1895
NR Heelis, Kemble Drive, SWINDON, Wilts, SN2 2NA.   (hq)
     01793 817400   fax 01793 817401
     email enquiries@thenationaltrust.org.uk
     http://www.nationaltrust.org.uk
     Dir: Fiona Reynolds
▲   Registered Charity
○   *G; to preserve places of historic interest or natural beauty
     permanently for the nation to enjoy; as a charity independent
     of government, the Trust protects forests, woods, fens,
     farmland, downland, moorland, islands, archaeological
     remains, villages - for ever, for everyone
M   c 3,500,000 i

National Trust for Scotland   (NTS)   1931
NR 28 Charlotte Sq, EDINBURGH, EH2 4ET.   (hq)
     0131-243 9300   fax 0131-243 9301
     email information@nts.org.uk   http://www.nts.org.uk
     Chmn: Shonaig MacPherson
▲   Registered Charity
○   *G; to protect & promote Scotland's national & cultural heritage
     for present & future generations to enjoy
●   Care of properties & opening them to the public - Inf (on
     matters relating to the Trust only) - VE
<   Europa Nostra
M   270,000 i
¶   Jnl - 4;   Ybk - 1; both ftm only.

National Tyre Distributors Association   (NTDA)   1930
NR 8 Temple Square, AYLESBURY, Bucks, HP20 2QH.   (hq)
     0870 900 0600   fax 0870 900 0610
     email mail@ntda.co.uk   http://www.ntda.co.uk
     Dir: Richard Edy
○   *T; for companies in the tyre specialist & fast fit trade
Gp Divisions: Training services; Technical services;
     Specialist c'ees: Tyre Wholesalers Group; Approved tyre
     repairers
●   Conf - Mtgs - ET - Exhib - Comp - Stat - Inf - LG
<   BIPAVER
M   450 f, UK / 1 f, o'seas
¶   NTDA News - 12;   AR; both ftm only.
     Directory of Members & Ybk - 1; ftm, £25 nm.

National Union of Journalists   (NUJ)   1907
NR 308-312 Gray's Inn Rd, LONDON, WC1X 8DP.   (hq)
     020 7278 7916   fax 020 7837 8143
     email info@nuj.org
     Gen Sec: Jeremy Dear
○   *U
M   c 35,000 i

National Union of Knitwear, Footwear & Apparel Trades
     merged in 2004 with the Iron & Steel Trades Confederation to
     become **Community**

National Union of Lock & Metal Workers
     in 2004 merged with the **Transport & General Workers' Union**

National Union of Marine, Aviation & Shipping Transport
     Officers   (NUMAST)   1936
■   Oceanair House, 750-760 High Rd, LONDON, E11 3BB.   (hq)
     020 8989 6677   fax 020 8530 1015
     email info@numast.org   http://www.numast.org
     Gen Sec: Brian Orrell
▲   Un-incorporated Society
○   *U
●   ET - Res - Inf - Empl - LG
<   Eur Transport Workers' Fedn (ETF); Intl Transport Workers'
     Fedn (ITF)
M   19,100 i
¶   The Telegraph - 12; ftm, £40 nm.

National Union of Mineworkers   (NUM)   1944
NR Miners' Offices, 2 Huddersfield Rd, BARNSLEY, S Yorks,
     S70 2LS.   (hq)
     01226 215555
     Sec: Steve Kemp
○   *U
●   Conf - Mtgs
<   TUC; Labour Party
M   c 3,500 i
¶   The Miner - 4; ftm.

National Union of Residents' Associations   (NURA)   1921
- ■ 20 Park Drive, ROMFORD, Essex, RM1 4LH.   (chmn/p)
      01708 749119   fax 01708 736213
      Chmn: Ian Wilkes
- ○ *K
- ● Mtgs - LG
- M c150 org
- ¶ NURA NL - irreg; ftm.

National Union of Students   (NUS)   1922
- NR Centro 3 (2nd floor), 19 Mandela St, LONDON, NW1 0DU.
      (hq)
      0871 221 8221   fax 020 7263 5713
      email nusuk@nus.org.uk   http://www.nusonline.co.uk
      Nat Dir: Nick Gash
- ▲ Un-incorporated Society
- ○ *U
- Gp Scotland; Wales; N Ireland
- ● Conf - Res - Inf - LG - Campaigns
- M 5,000,000 i in 700+ student unions

National Union of Teachers   (NUT)   1870
- NR Hamilton House, Mabledon Place, LONDON, WC1H 9BD.
      (hq)
      020 7388 6191
      Gen Sec: Steve Sinnott
- ▲ Un-incorporated Society
- ○ *U; to promote state education & protect & improve the
      salaries, working conditions & status of the teaching
      profession in England & Wales
- ● Conf - ET - Res - Exhib - Inf - Empl - LG
- < Educ Intl; TUC
- M c 250,000 i
- ¶ The Teacher - 8.   Education Review - 2.

National Vegetable Society   (NVS)   1960
- ■ 5 Whitelow Rd, Heaton Moor, STOCKPORT, Cheshire,
      SK4 4BY.   (hsp)
      0161-442 7190
      email d.hampsey@ntlworld.com
      http://www.nvsuk.org.uk
      Nat Webmaster: David Hampsey
- Br 5
- ○ *H; to advance the education of the public in the cultivation &
      improvement of vegetables
- ● Mtgs - Exam - Exhib - Comp - Inf - Lib - Displays at shows
- < R Horticl Soc
- M 2,500 i
- ¶ Bulletin - 4;   Directory - 1;   AR; all ftm.
      Growing leaflets (13); 40p each m.
      Judges Guide; £3.50 m.

National Vintage Tractor & Engine Club   (NVTEC)   1965
- ■ Eastfields, Eastfield, North Wheatley, RETFORD, Notts,
      DN22 9BX.   (hsp)
      01427 880238
      email p.scarborough@lineone.net
      http://www.nvtec.co.uk
      Hon Sec: Pat Scarborough
- ▲ Un-incorporated Society
- Br 33; France, Germany, Norway, USA
- ○ *G; study & preservation of agricultural tractors, machines &
      implements & all associated equipment
- ● Cobnf - Mtgs - ET - Exhib - Comp - Inf - VE - LG
- < Soc Ploughmen; Traction Engine Trust; Nat Farmers' U
- M 61000 i
- ¶ Vaporising - 4; ftm only.

National Wardens' Association
      since 2005 **NWA - an association of housing & support**
      managers

National Whippet Association
- NR 36 New Waverley Rd, Laindon, BASILDON, Essex, SS15 4BH.
      01268 288091
      http://www.nationalwhippetassoc.uk.com
      Hon Sec: Mrs Maureen Blanks
- ○ *B

National Women's Register   (NWR)   1960
- NR 3A Vulcan House, Vulcan Road North, NORWICH, Norfolk,
      NR6 6AQ.   (hq)
      01603 406767   fax 01603 407003
      email office@nwr.org   http://www.nwr.org
      Co Sec & Organiser: Gaynel Munn
- ▲ Company Limited by Guarantee; Registered Charity
- Br c 450; Australia, Belgium, South Africa, Zimbabwe
- ○ *G; for women of all ages who wish to participate in wide-
      ranging discussions leading to friendship & other activities
- Gp Correspondence magazine; Penfriends; House exchange;
      Research bank; Postal Book
- ● Conf - Mtgs - ET - Res - Exhib - Comp
- M c 7,500 i
- ¶ Register - 2; ftm only.

National Wool Textile Export Corporation   (NWTEC)   1940
- ■ Lloyds Bank Chambers, 43 Hustlergate, BRADFORD, W Yorks,
      BD1 1PH.   (hq)
      01274 724235   fax 01274 723124
      email mailbox@bwtec.co.uk   http://www.bwtec.co.uk
      Dir: R Peter Ackroyd
- ▲ Company Limited by Guarantee
- ○ *T; promotion & protection of the export trade of the British
      wool textile industry
- M c 250 f
- ¶ 'All publications for m only'.

National Youth Council of Ireland   (NYCI)
- IRL 3 Montague St, DUBLIN 2, Republic of Ireland.
      353 (1) 478 4122   fax 353 (1) 478 3974
      email info@nyci.ie   http://www.youth.ie
      Dir: Mary Cunningham
- ○ *Y
- M c 40 orgs

National Youth Federation
- IRL 20 Lower Dominick St, DUBLIN 1, Republic of Ireland.
      353 (1) 872 9933   fax 353 (1) 872 4183
      email info@nyf.ie
      Chief Exec: Diarmuid Kearney
- ○ *Y

Nationwide Association for Information Destruction
      in 2001 became the Information Destruction Section of the **British**
      Security Industry Association

Nationwide Caterers Association Ltd   (NCASS)   1987
- ■ Association House, 89 Mappleborough Rd, Shirley, SOLIHULL,
      W Midlands, B90 1AG.   (hq)
      0121-603 2524   fax 0121-474 3938
      email enq@ncass.org.uk   http://www.ncass.org.uk
      Sec: Robert Fox
- ▲ Company Limited by Guarantee
- ○ *T; for caterers & suppliers - mobile caterers, static caterers
      (sandwich bars, takeaways) & suppliers to the trade
- Gp Technical c'ee
- ● ET - Exam - Comp - Inf - Lib - LG- LG
- M 600 i, 100 f
- ¶
      NL - 4; free.
      Profitable Mobile Catering - 1; £20.
      The Events Directory - 1; £20 m, £40 nm.
      Annual Industry Guide - 1; £20.
      [subscription: £174 i, £350 f].
- × 2005 Mobile & Outside Caterers Association

Natural Family Planning
    see **Fertility Care Scotland (Natural Family Planning)**

Natural Family Planning Teachers Association   (NFPTA)   1982
NR   218 Heathwood Rd, CARDIFF, Glam, CF14 4BS.   (sec/p)
        029 2075 4628
        email norman@cardiff80.freeserve.co.uk
        Chmn: Mrs C Norman
○   *P
M   c 200 i
✕   2002 National Association of Natural Family Planning Teachers

Natural Gas Vehicle Association   (NGVA)   1992
■   36 Holly Walk, ROYAL LEAMINGTON SPA, Warks, CV32 4LY.
        (hq)
        01926 462900   fax 01926 462919
        email info@ngva.co.uk   http://www.ngva.co.uk
        Marketing Mgr: Caroline Haine
▲   Company Limited by Guarantee
Br   Brussels
○   *T; to promote the use of natural gas as an environmentally
        safe & economic vehicle fuel
Gp   C'ees: Technical; Marketing; Government relations
●   Conf - Mtgs - ET - Res - Expt - Inf
<   Intl Natural Gas Vehicle Assn; Eur Natural Gas Vehicle Assn;
        Japan & USA Gas Vehicle Assn
M   30 f
¶   NGV News - 4.

Natural History Society of Northumbria   (NHSN)   1829
■   The Hancock Museum, Barras Bridge, NEWCASTLE UPON
        TYNE, NE2 4PT.   (hq)
        0191-232 6386   fax 0191-232 2177
        email nhsn@ncl.ac.uk   http://www.nhsn.ncl.ac.uk
        Sec: David C Noble-Rollin
▲   Registered Charity
○   *L; to encourage the study of natural history in all its branches;
        to protect the natural environment & local flora & fauna
Gp   Botany; Entomology; Geology; Mammals; Ornithology
●   Mtgs - Res - Lib (open for public access) - VE - LG - Field mtgs -
        Lectures
M   900 i, UK / 4 i, o'seas
¶   Bulletin - 3.   Transactions - 3 (2-yrly);   AR; all ftm.

Natural Medicines Society
        closed down and ceased trading in November 2004

Natural Sausage Casings Association   (NSCA)   1953
■   Wychwood Cottage, 38 High St, RISELEY, Beds, MK44 1DX.
        (asa)
        01234 709022   fax 01234 709749
        Sec: Digby Morgan-Jones
○   *T; for those involved in the natural casings industry in the UK;
        to cooperate with any other organisation worldwide with
        similar objectives
●   Mtgs - LG - Statistical information for members
<   Eur Natural Casings Assn
M   13 f + 1f (Eire)

Natural Sciences Collections Association   (NatSCA)   2003
NR   c/o The Natural History Museum, Cromwell Rd, LONDON,
        SW7 5BD.   (hsb)
        020 7942 5196
        email p.brown@nhm.ac.uk
        Hon Sec: Paul Brown
▲   Registered Charity
○   *L, *P; to act as a forum for natural sciences curators; to
        promote the care, use & development of natural sciences
        collections in the UK & overseas
●   Conf - Mtgs - ET - Inf - VE - LG
M   c 200 i, c 50 org
¶   NatSCA News - 2; ftm, £5 nm.
✕   2003 (Biology Curators Group
            (Natural Sciences Conservation Group

Natural Sciences Conservation Group
        merged in 2003 with the Biology Curators Group to form the
        Natural Sciences Collections Association

Nature in Art Trust   1982
NR   Wallsworth Hall, Twigworth, GLOUCESTER, GL2 9PA.   (hq)
        01452 731422   fax 01452 730937
        email ninart@globalnet.co.uk
        http://www.nature-in-art.org.uk
        Chmn: Dr David H Trapnell
▲   Company Limited by Guarantee; Registered Charity
○   *A; to collect & display fine, decorative & applied art inspired
        by nature in all media & from any period or culture; to
        provide learning opportunities for young people & adults
●   Conf - Mtgs - ET - Exhib - Comp - SG - Inf - Lib - VE
<   Museums & Galleries Commission (a fully registered museum)
M   c 1,200 i
¶   Nature in Art - 4; ftm.

Nautical Archaeology Society   (NAS)   1972
■   Fort Cumberland, Fort Cumberland Rd, PORTSMOUTH, Hants,
        PO4 9LD.   (hq)
        023 9281 8419   fax 023 9281 8419
        email nas@nasportsmouth.org.uk
        http://www.nasportsmouth.org.uk
        Chmn: George Lambrick
▲   Registered Charity
Br   7; 20 countries
○   *G, *L, *Q; to further research into all aspects of nautical &
        maritime archaeology; to bring together all people interested
        in our maritime heritage
Gp   Ancient technologists; Archaeologists; Avocationals;
        Conservators; Historians; Naval architects; Researchers;
        Sports divers; Students
●   Conf - Mtgs - ET - Res - Exhib - Comp - Inf - Lib - VE - LG
<   Inst of Naval Archaeology (INA)
>   The Dive Connection (TDC)
M   500 i, 50 f, UK / 300 i, 25 f, o'seas
¶   International Jnl of Nautical Archaeology - 2; ftm, £16 each
        nm.
        Nautical Archaeology NL - 4; ftm.
        NAS Monograph Series - irreg.
        [subscription £45].

Nautical Institute   (NI)   1972
NR   202 Lambeth Rd, LONDON, SE1 7LQ.   (hq)
        020 7928 1351   fax 020 7401 2817
        email sec@nautinst.org   http://www.nautinst.org
        Chief Exec: C P Wake
▲   Company Limited by Guarantee; Registered Charity
Br   40 worldwide
○   *P; to promote a high standard of knowledge among those in
        control of sea-going vessels including non-displacement
        craft. Open to all qualified mariners
●   Conf - ET - Inf - Lib
<   Sea Vision UK; UK Maritime Forum
M   6,500 i in 110 countries
¶   Publications list available.

Naval Historical Collectors & Research Association   (NHCRA)   1988
■   30 Compit Hills, CROMER, Norfolk, NR27 9LJ.   (mem/sp)
        01263 519594
        email wilkinsonA44@hotmail.com
        http://www.nhcra-online.org
        Mem Sec: Anthony C Wilkinson
▲   Un-incorporated Society
○   *G; collecting naval medals & memorabilia; research into
        naval battles, ships & personnel
●   Scientific, systematic research - PL
M   400 i, 5 f, 12 org, UK / 40 i, o'seas
¶   The Review (Jnl) - 4; ftm, £15 nm (£17 EU) (£20 o'seas)
        or £3.50 each.
        Note: the association is a non-profit-making body in support of
        worthy naval causes & charities

      © CBD Research Ltd · Beckenham · BR3 5JS · Tel 020 8650 7745 · Fax 020 8650 0768 · E-mail cbd@cbdresearch.com · www.cbdresearch.com

Navy Records Society   (NRS)   1893

- ■ c/o Pangbourne College, PANGBOURNE, Berks, RG8 8LA. (hsb)
  Hon Sec: R H A Brodhurst
- ▲ Registered Charity
- ○ *L; editing & publishing manuscripts & rare works illustrating the history, administration, organisation or social life of the Navy
- ● Publishing
- M c 650 i, c 150 org
- ¶ NL - 1;   AR - 1.
  1 or 2 vols each year.

Needleloom Underlay Manufacturers' Association   (NUMA) 1957

- NR Tower House, 269 Walmersley Rd, BURY, Lancs, BL9 6NX. (asa)
  0161-761 5231   fax 0161-761 3001
  Sec & Treas: C A Nuttall
- ▲ Un-incorporated Society
- ○ *T; manufacturers of needled underfelts & allied industries
- ● Conf - Mtgs - Inf
- < BSI
- M 5 f

Neil Munro Society   1996

- ■ 8 Briar Rd, Kirkintilloch, GLASGOW, G66 3SA.   (hsp)
  0141-776 4280   fax 0141-776 4280
  email brian@bdosborne.fsnet.co.uk
  http://www.neilmunro.co.uk
  Sec: Brian D Osborne
- ▲ Un-incorporated Society
- ○ *A; to promote interest in the life & works of Neil Munro (1863-1930) Scottish novelist, journalist & poet
- ● Conf - Mtgs - Res - Exhib - Comp - Lib - VE
- < Alliance of Literary Societies
- M 160 i, 2 f, UK / 15 i, o'seas
- ¶ Paragraphs (NL) - 2; ftm only.

Nelson Society   1981

- NR 68 Stamshaw Rd, PORTSMOUTH, Hants, PO2 8LS.   (mail address)
  Mem Sec: Andrea Green
- ▲ Registered Charity
- Br 6
- ○ *G; to promote interest in, & appreciation of, the outstanding qualities of leadership & patriotism displayed by Admiral Lord Nelson
- ● Conf - Mtgs - Res - Exhib - Lib - VE
- M c 1,000 i
- ¶ The Nelson Dispatch - 4.

Neonatal Society   (NNS)   1959

- NR c/o Dr Nikki Robertson, UCL, Dept of Obstetrics & Gynaecology, 86-96 Chenies Mews, LONDON, WC1E 6HX.   (hsb)
  020 7679 6052
  Sec: Dr Nikki Robertson
- ○ *Q; 'a research society with members from clinical & basic science disciplines relating to perinatology'
- ● Conf - Mtgs - Res - Exhib
- M c 280 i, UK / c 90 i, o'seas
- ¶ NL - 3. Hbk.

Nerine & Amaryllid Society   (NAAS)   1997

- ■ 2 The Grove, Ickenham, UXBRIDGE, Middx, UB10 8QH.   (hsp)
  01895 464694   fax 0870 052 9312
  http://www.nerine.org.uk
  Sec: Dr Roger D Beauchamp
- ▲ Un-incorporated Society
- ○ *H; for the general study & promotion of interest in, the plant family Amaryllidaceae
- ● Exhib - Inf - is the International Cultivar Registration Authority (ICRA) for Nerine
- < R Horticl Soc
  is an Agency of the Intl Soc for Horticl Science (ISHS)
- M c 130 i, UK / c 5 i, o'seas
- ¶ Amaryllids - 3;   LM - 1;   AR; all ftm only.
  [subscription; £10 single, £15 joint & overseas].

Netball Northern Ireland   (NINA)   1951

- NR House of Sport, Upper Malone Rd, BELFAST, BT9 5LA.   (hq)
  028 9038 3806   fax netball@houseofsportni.net
  Sec: Ann Corran
- ○ *S; to develop netball in NI
- < Intl Fedn Netball Assns (IFNA); Fedn Eur Netball Assns (FENA)
- > NI Clubs Netball Assn (NICNA); NI Schools Netball Assn (NISNA)
- M c 1,500 i, 30 clubs

Netball Scotland   1946

- NR Central Chambers (suite 196), 93 Hope St, GLASGOW, G2 6LD.   (hq)
  0141-572 0114   fax 0141-248 5566
  http://www.netballscotland.com
- ▲ Un-incorporated Society
- ○ *S; promotion & playing of netball in Scotland
- M c 2,000 i & org

Netherlands-British Chamber of Commerce   1891

- ■ Imperial House, 15-19 Kingsway, LONDON, WC2B 6UN. (hq)
  020 7539 7960
  email info@nbcc.co.uk   http://www.nbcc.co.uk
  Dir: M van Deursen
- Br 2; Netherlands
- ○ *C
- ● Conf - Mtgs - Res - Exhib - Expt - Inf - VE
- M 200 i, UK / 200 i, o'seas
- ¶ In Touch - 4; ftm.   Ybk; ftm.
  Other publications & directories.

Network for Alternative Technology & Technology Assessment (NATTA)   1976

- ■ c/o EERU, Faculty of Technology, Open University, Walton Hall, MILTON KEYNES, Bucks, MK7 6AA.   (hq)
  01908 654638 (24-hr answering machine)
  fax 01908 654052
  email s.j.dougan@open.ac.uk
  http://www.eeru.open.ac.uk/natta/rol.html
  Coordinator: Ms Tam Dougan,
  Editor: Prof David Elliott
- ▲ Un-incorporated Society
- ○ *E; renewable energy (water, solar, wind power) & related energy issues
- ● Conf - ET
- M 500 i
- ¶ Renew (NL) - 6; (prices to m = £18 waged, £12 non-waged, £50 libs & instns, £6 airmail supplement).
  Renewables, Past, Present & Future: a review of government policy & the development of the UK Renewable Energy Programme 1994-97 by Dave Elliott; £10.
  Various other publications.

Network of Government Library & Information Specialists (NGLIS) 1925

■ c/o Kate Pritchard, Library & Records Management, Veterinary Laboratories Agency, WEYBRIDGE, Surrey, KT15 3NB. (sb)
  01932 357715   fax 01932 357608
  email k.pritchard@via.defra.gli.gov.uk
  Sec: Kate Pritchard
▲ Un-incorporated Society
○ *P; to promote networking with colleagues working in the information sector
● Conf - Mtgs - ET - Inf - VE
< C'ee of Departmental Librarians (CDL); Govt Libaries & Inf Gp (GLIG)
M 494 i
¶ State Librarian (Jnl) - 2; ftm.
✕ 2005 Circle of State Librarians

Network of Independent Forensic Accountants (NIFA) 1999

■ 4 Pavilion Court, 600 Pavilion Drive, Brackmills, NORTHAMPTON, NN4 7SL. (sb)
  0845 609 6091   fax 01604 662681
  email nifa@nifa.co.uk   http://www.nifa.co.uk
  Sec: Clive Adkins
▲ Company Limited by Guarantee
○ *P, *T; to provide forensic accounting & litigation support services
● Conf - Mtgs - ET
M 15 i, 15 f
¶ NIFA News - 4; free.

Network Outsourcing Association
  since December 2001 **National Outsourcing Association**

Neuroblastoma Society 1982

■ Beverley House, Frilford, ABINGDON, Oxon, OX13 5NU. (chmn/p)
  01865 391207
  email info@nsoc.co.uk   http://www.nsoc.co.uk
  Chmn: Mrs Antonya Cooper,   Hon Sec: Dr Tony Beechcroft
▲ Registered Charity
○ *K, *W; to raise funds for UK based research into neuroblastoma (a children's cancer); to offer support for families affected by neuroblastoma
● Res - SG - Social fundraising events
M c 350-400 i
¶ Neuroblastoma News - 4.
  Neuroblastoma - a booklet for parents - every 3-4 years.

Neurofibromatosis Association 1981

NR Quayside House, 38 High St, KINGSTON upon THAMES, Surrey, KT1 1HL. (hq)
  020 8439 1234   fax 020 8439 1200
  Gen Sec: Mark Stevens
▲ Registered Charity
○ *W; a self-help group providing advice & information; to establish & maintain a network of family support workers; to sponsor research through fund raising
< Intl Neurofibromatosis Assn (NFA); Neurological Alliance; Genetic Interest Gp; Neurofibromatosis Assn Australia (NFAA)
M 1,667 i, UK / 31 i, o'seas
¶ Factsheets & videos.   Publications list available.

Neurological Alliance 1994

NR Stoke House, 240 City Rd, LONDON, EC1V 2PR. (hq)
  020 7566 1540
  email admin@neural.org.uk
  Co-Chmn: Maggie Alexander,   Andrew Russell
▲ Company Limited by Guarantee; Registered Charity
○ *N, *W; unites charities working to raise the profile of conditions & needs of people with neurological conditions & their carers; to raise the standards of care & improve lives
● Conf - Mtgs - LG - Lobbying/campaigning
M c 60 org
¶ Publications list available.

Neutral Alcohol Producers Association   (NAPA)   1982

■ 4 Stour Close, KESTON, Kent, BR2 6BX.   (hsb)
  01689 889583
  email dhw@dhward.com
  Sec: David H Ward (mobile 0783 141 6335)
  Chmn: David Rae
▲ Un-incorporated Society
○ *T; UK producers of neutral alcohol for drinks & industrial use. Neutral alcohol is distilled from agricultural crops, the main market being in the production of spirit drinks (gin & vodka) & a growing potential for use in biofuel production
● Conf - Mtgs - SG - Stat - Inf
< U Eur des Producteurs d'Alcools (UEPA); Confédn Eur des Producteurs de Spiritueux (CEPS); Gin & Vodka Assn; Scotch Whisky Assn
M 7 f, 4 associate f

New Approaches to Cancer 1981

§ PO Box 194, CHERTSEY, Surrey, KT16 0WJ. (hq)
  0800 389 2662
  email help@anac.org.uk   http://www.anac.org.uk
  Admin Volunteer: Britt Leamy
  a registered charity which promotes self-help to cancer patients & their families by supplying free information packs on herbal remedies, diet & complementary therapies; it also holds yoga classes & talks, has support groups & publishes a free NL 'Hands On' 3 times a year.

New Canterbury Literary Society - Richard Aldington Society (NCLS) 1973

NR Old Post Office Garage, Chapel St, ST IVES, Cornwall, TR26 2LR. (hsp)
  01736 795616
  Hon Sec: David Wilkinson
○ *A; to promote interest in the life & writings of the author Richard Aldington (1892-1962)

New English Art Club
  a member body of the **Federation of British Artists**

New Forest Agricultural Show Society 1920

NR The Showground, New Park, BROCKENHURST, Hants, SO42 7QH. (hq)
  01590 622400   fax 01590 622637
  email info@newforestshow.co.uk
  http://www.newforestshow.co.uk
  Chief Exec: Richard Cozens
▲ Company Limited by Guarantee; Registered Charity
○ *F, *H; to promote & encourage the development of agriculture, forestry, equestrianism & horticulture. . . & to encourage the breeding of stock

New Forest Pony Breeding & Cattle Society   (NFPB&CS) 1891

NR The Corner House, Ringwood Rd, BRANSGORE, Dorset, BH23 8AA. (hsp)
  01425 672775
  Sec: Jane Murray
▲ Company Limited by Guarantee; Registered Charity
○ *B
● Mtgs - Exhib - Comp - Expt
< Stud Book Societies in: Australia, Belgium, Denmark, Finland, France, Germany, Holland, Norway, Sweden, USA
M c 1,400 i
¶ Stud Book - 1.   Leaflets.   AR.
  Celebration of New Forest Ponies.

New Producers Alliance   (NPA)   1992
NR   The Tea Building, 56 Shoreditch High St, LONDON, E1 6JJ.
    (hq)
    020 7613 0440
    email queries@npa.org.uk
    http://www.newproducer.co.uk
    Chief Exec: David Pope
▲   Registered Charity
○   *P; to train & support new filmmakers
●   Mtgs - ET - Inf - Lib
<   Brit Film Inst
M   1,000 i
¶   New Producer - 12; ftm only.

Newark Area Chamber of Commerce
    is a branch of **Nottinghamshire Chamber of Commerce &
Industry**

Newark & Nottinghamshire Agricultural Society   1799
■   The County Showground, Winthorpe, NEWARK, Notts,
    NG24 2NY.   (hq)
    0870 224 1035   fax 0870 224 1036
    email info@newarkshowground.com
    http://www.newarkshowground.com
    Chief Exec: Adrian M Johnston
▲   Company Limited by Guarantee; Registered Charity
○   *F; to promote agriculture through the County Show, held
    annually on the 2nd weekend of May
●   Annual show - Hire of venue, halls & catering business
<   Assn Show & Agricl Orgs; Nottinghamshire Cham Comm;
    Newark Business Club
M   500 i, 40 f, 40 org
¶   NL - 2; free.   AR - 1; ftm only.

**Newcomen Society for the Study of the History of Engineering &
Technology   (The Newcomen Society)   1920**
NR   Science Museum, LONDON, SW7 2DD.   (hq)
    020 7371 4445   fax 020 7371 4445
    email office@newcomen.com
    http://www.newcomen.com
    Exec Sec: R M Swann
▲   Company Limited by Guarantee; Registered Charity
Br   7
○   *L; the study of the history of engineering & technology
●   Conf - Mtgs - SG - Inf - VE
M   c 900 i, 100 org
¶   Transactions - 2; ftm, £40 nm.   Bulletin - 3; ftm only.

Newman Association   1942
NR   20-22 Bedford Row, LONDON, WC1R 4JS.   (mail/address)
    email secretary@newman.org.uk
    http://www.newman.org.uk
    Contact: The Secretary
▲   Company Limited by Guarantee; Registered Charity
Br   20
○   *E, *R; educational & religious organisation
●   Conf - Mtgs
<   Pax Romana
M   830 i
¶   The Newman - 3; ftm, £1 nm.

**Newport & Gwent Chamber of Commerce, Enterprise &
Industry   (ngb2b)   1870**
■   Unit 30 Enterprise Way, NEWPORT, Monmouthshire,
    NP20 2AQ.   (hq)
    01633 222664   fax 01633 222301
    email info@ngb2b.co.uk   http://www.ngb2b.co.uk
    Managing Dir: David Russ
▲   Company Limited by Guarantee
○   *C
●   Conf - Mtgs - ET - Exhib - Expt - Inf - Lib - VE - LG -
    Commercial services
<   Brit Chams Comm; Chamber Wales; SW Chams Gp
>   Chambers of Commerce: Chepstow & Monmouth; Newport
    Cham Tr
M   c 450 org
¶   Chamber Chat - 4; free.   AR - 1; free.
    South Wales Business Directory - 1; ftm.
    Note: since May 2000 trades under the name ngb2b at the
    same address.
×   2005 Newport & Gwent Chamber of Commerce & Industry

Newspaper Conference   1920
NR   74-77 Great Russell St, LONDON, WC1B 3DA.   (hq)
    020 7693 0441   fax 020 7580 7167
    http://www.newspapersoc.org.uk
    Contact: Martha Leary-Tanner
○   *P; comprises London editors & political correspondents of
    regional newspapers in membership of the Newspaper
    Society; meets 3 or 4 times a year with senior politicians
●   Conf - Mtgs
M   23 i

Newspaper Publishers Association Ltd   (NPA)   1906
NR   34 Southwark Bridge Rd, LONDON, SE1 9EU.   (hq)
    020 7928 6928   fax 020 7928 2067
    Dir: Steve Oram
○   *T; for national morning, evening & Sunday newspapers incl
    their Manchester editions
M   f

Newspaper Society   1836
NR   Bloomsbury House, 74-77 Great Russell St, LONDON,
    WC1B 3DA.   (hq)
    020 7636 7014   fax 020 7631 5119
    email ns@newspapersoc.org.uk
    http://www.newspapersoc.org.uk
    Dir: David Newell
▲   Un-incorporated Society
○   *P, *T; 'the voice of Britain's regional press; to represent &
    promote the interests of over 1,300 local & regional titles'
Gp   Political, Editorial & Regulatory Affairs (PERA); Marketing;
    Communications; Finance & administration
●   Conf - Mtgs - ET - Res - Exhib - SG - Stat - Inf - LG - Legal
    advice - Issuing of press ID cards - Press/Rota passes
<   Wld Assn Newspapers (WAN); Eur Newspaper Publishers Assn
    (ENPA); Advertising Assn (AA); Newspaper Conf; Young
    Newspaper Executives Assn (YNEA)
M   f
¶   NS News (NL) - 52.   Headlines (Magazine) - 6.
    Production Jnl - 12.   Commercial Update - 4.
    Headlines & Production Jnl are both available by annual
    subscription.

NFU Scotland   (NFUS)   1913
■   Rural Centre, West Mains, Ingliston, NEWBRIDGE, Midlothian,
    EH28 8LT.   (hq)
    0131-472 4000   fax 0131-472 4010
    Chief Exec: A J Robertson
Br   72
○   *F, *H, *P; agriculture in all its branches
●   Conf - Mtgs - ET - Res - Exhib - Comp - SG - Stat - Inf - Lib - VE
    - Empl - LG
<   C'ee Agricl Orgs in the EU (COPA); Intl Fedn Agricl Producers
M   12,000 i
¶   Scottish Farming Leader Update - 4/6; ftm.

NHS Alliance   1998
NR   Goodbody's Mill, Albert Rd, RETFORD, Notts, DN22 6JD.   (hq)
       01777 869080   fax 01777 869081
       http://www.nhsalliance.org
       Chief Officer: Michael Sobanja
▲   Un-incorporated Society
○   *P; to represent primary care groups & trusts to government; to
     provide networking opportunities & develop & spread good
     practice
Gp   Managers; Lay members
●   Conf - Res - SG - Inf - Empl - LG
M   500 i, 300 primary care trusts
¶   Publications; irreg.

NHS Confederation   (NHSC)   1997
NR   29 Bressenden Place, LONDON, SW1E 5DD.   (hq)
       020 7074 3200   fax 020 7074 3201
       Chief Exec: Dr G Morgan
▲   Registered Charity
Br   4
○   *N; to represent the interests of all NHS bodies across the UK;
     includes over 95% of NHS trusts, health authorities & boards
●   Conf - Exhib - Empl - LG
M   Trusts, Health authorities
¶   Interchange News - 12.   Briefings/Updates - irreg.
     Wellards NHS Hbk - 1.
     Various Reports.   AR.

NHS Support Federation   1989
NR   113 Queens Rd, BRIGHTON, E Sussex, BN1 3XG.   (hq)
       01273 234822
       http://www.nhscampaign.org
○   *K
M   c 5,000 i in groups

NHS Trusts Association   (NHSTA)
NR   PO Box 45734, LONDON, SW16 5JW.
       020 8679 2471   fax 020 8765 4818
       http://www.nhsta.org.uk
       Chief Exec: David Tod
✕   2006 Association of Primary Care Groups & Trusts

NIAB   (NIAB)   1919
NR   Huntingdon Rd, CAMBRIDGE, CB3 0LE.   (hq)
       01223 342200   fax 01223 277602
       email info@niab.com   http://www.niab.com
       Dir: Prof W Powell
Br   8 regional trials centres
○   *F, *H, *Q; improvement of crop varieties & seeds
●   Conf - Mtgs - ET - Exam - Res - Exhib - Stat - Inf - Lib - PL - LG
M   c 4,300 i
¶   Jnl.   AR.
     Publications list available.

NISA Today's Holdings Ltd   (NISA)   1978
NR   PO Box 58, SCUNTHORPE, Lincs, DN15 8QP.
       01724 282028   fax 01724 864835
       Exec Chmn: Dudley Ramsden
○   *T
M   f
     Note: is a buying consortium for independent supermarkets etc;
     was previously known as the National Independent
     Supermarkets Association.

NO2ID   (NO2ID)   2004
■   Box 412, 78 Marylebone High St, LONDON, W1U 5AP.
     (mail/add)
     07005 800651
     email enquiries@no2id.net   http://www.no2id.net
     Nat Co-ordinator: Phil Booth
▲   Un-incorporated Society
○   *K; 'to research, evaluate & raise public awareness of the issues
     around ID cards, identity registers & unique identifiers,
     including biometrics; to lobby & campaign against any such
     legislation or schemes that would prove detrimental to UK
     citizens, including initiatives that would involve
     comprehensive data sharing without the fully informed &
     explicit consent of the individual'
●   Conf - Mtgs - ET - Res - Exhib - Comp - Stat - Inf - LG
<   Eur Social Forum
M   20,000 i, 80 org
¶   NO2ID (email NL) - 26; free.

Noise Abatement Society   (NAS)   1959
NR   44 Grand Parade, BRIGHTON, E Sussex, BN2 9QA.   (hq)
       01273 682223
       email nas@noiseabatementsociety.fsnet.co.uk
       http://www.noiseabatementsociety.com
       Dir: Peter Wakeham
▲   Registered Charity
○   *K; to reduce noise from all sources to tolerable & reasonable
     levels
Gp   Helpline: 0800 389 1380
●   Conf - Mtgs - ET - Res - Exhib - SG - Stat - Inf - LG
M   11,000 i, 128 f, 250 org
¶   NL - 4; ftm only.

Non-Administrative Receivers Association   (NARA)   1995
■   PO Box 553, WORCESTER, Worcs, WR2 6WY.   (admin/sb)
     0870 600 1925   fax 0870 600 1925
     Contact: Dag Smith
○   *P; to promote the interests of receivers who are NOT
     administrative receivers; incl LPA & fixed charge receivers
     (agricultural receivers, receivers of book debt & court
     appointed receivers)

Non-Ferrous Alliance   (NFA)   1995
■   Broadway House, Calthorpe Rd, Five Ways, BIRMINGHAM,
     B15 1TN.   (hq)
     0121-456 1103   fax 0121-456 2274
     Sec: Will Savage
▲   Un-incorporated Society
○   *T; UK non-ferrous metals
●   Conf - Mtgs - ET - Stat - LG
M   280 f in 9 org:
       Aluminium Federation
       British Non-Ferrous Metals Federation
       Cobalt Development Institute
       International Molybdenum Association
       International Tungsten Industry Association
       Lead Development Association International
       Nickel Institute
       Titanium Information Group
       Zinc Information Centre

Norfolk Chamber of Commerce & Industry   1896
NR   9 Norwich Business Park, Whiting Rd, NORWICH, Norfolk,
        NR4 6DJ.   (hq)
        01603 625977   fax 01603 633032
        email info@norfolkchamber.co.uk
        http://www.norfolkchamber.co.uk
        Chief Exec: Caroline Williams
▲   Company Limited by Guarantee
Br   Great Yarmouth, King's Lynn
○   *C
Gp   C'ees: Tax & business finance, Business law, Transportation,
        International trade, POAC, TAC
●   Mtgs - Stat - Expt - Inf - LG - Interpreting
<   Brit Netherlands Cham Comm; Brit Chams Comm (BCC)
M   2,000 f
¶   Business Magazine - 12; ftm.   AR; free.
×   2001 Norfolk & Waveney Chamber of Commerce & Industry

Norfolk Naturalists' Trust
        the registered name of the **Norfolk Wildlife Trust**

Norfolk & Norwich Archaeological Society   1846
■   c/o 30 Brettingham Avenue, Cringleford, NORWICH, Norfolk,
        NR4 6XG.   (hsp)
        01603 455913
        http://www.nnas.info
        Hon Sec: Roger Bellinger
▲   Registered Charity
○   *L; study of the archaeology, history, architecture & antiquities
        of Norfolk
●   Mtgs - ET - Lib (at 64 The Close, Norwich) - VE - Lectures
<   Coun Brit Archaeology
M   400 i, 50 f, UK / 50 i, o'seas
¶   Norfolk Archaeology - 1; £20.

Norfolk Record Society   (NRS)   1923
■   29 Cintra Rd, NORWICH, Norfolk, NR1 4AE.   (hsp)
        01603 436046
        email nrs@norfolkrecordsociety.org.uk
        http://www.norfolkrecordsociety.org.uk
        Hon Sec: Dr G A Metters
▲   Registered Charity
○   *L; publication of historical record material relating to the
        County of Norfolk
●   Lectures to accompany launch of each new volume
<   Fedn of Norfolk Historical & Archaeol Socs
M   c 350 i
¶   1 publication each year; ftm, £18 nm.

Norfolk & Waveney Chamber of Commerce & Industry
        since 2001 **Norfolk Chamber of Commerce & Industry**

Norfolk Wildlife Trust   (NWT)   1926
NR   Bewick House, 22 Thorpe Rd, NORWICH, Norfolk, NR1 1RY.
        (hq)
        01603 625540
        http://www.norfolkwildlifetrust.org.uk
        Dir: Brendan Joyce
▲   Registered Charity
○   *E, *G; to protect & enhance Norfolk's wildlife & wild places;
        the trust looks after 40 nature reserves & owns 10 km of
        coastline, 9 Norfolk Broads & 5 ancient woodlands
●   Mtgs - ET - Exhib - Stat - Inf - VE
<   The Wildlife Trusts (R Soc Nature Consvn)
M   17,500 i, c 100 f
¶   Tern (NL) - 3;   Events Listings - 3;   AR; all free.
        Note: the registered name is the Norfolk Naturalists' Trust

North Country Cheviot Sheep Society   1946
■   16 St Vincent Rd, TAIN, Ross-shire, IV19 1JR.   (sp)
        01862 894014   fax 01862 894014
        email secretary@nc-cheviot.co.uk
        http://www.nc-cheviot.co.uk
        Sec: William Morrison
▲   Registered Charity
○   *B
●   Mtgs - Exhib - Comp - Inf - Shows
<   Nat Sheep Assn
M   400 i, UK / 6 i, o'seas
¶   Flock Book - 1; £5 m, £7.50 nm.   Brochures.

North Derbyshire Chamber of Commerce & Industry
        in 2003 merged with South Derbyshire Chamber of Commerce &
        Industry to form the **Derbyshire Chamber & Business Link**

**North Devon Chamber of Commerce & Industry   (NDCCI)
        1994**
■   5 The Quay, BIDEFORD, Devon, EX39 2XX.   (hq)
        01237 426420   fax 01237 426426
        email infondcci.com   http://www.ndcci.com
        Co Sec: Mrs Sophia Mayo
▲   Company Limited by Guarantee
○   *C
Gp   Manufacturers; Directors; Tourism & services
●   Conf - Mtgs - ET - Exhib - Stat - Inf - Empl - LG
<   SW Cham Comm; Brit Chams Comm
M   258 f
¶   NL - 4;   AR; both free.   LM; £15 m, £60 nm.

North East Chamber of Commerce, Trade & Industry   1995
NR   Aykley Heads Business Centre, Aykley Heads, DURHAM,
        DH1 5TS.   (local/office)
        0191-386 1133   fax 0191-386 1144
        email information@ne-cc.com
        Chief Exec: George Cowcher
▲   Company Limited by Guarantee
Br   offices also in Newcastle, South Tyneside, Sunderland &
        Teesside
○   *C
●   Conf - Mtgs - ET - Res - Exhib - Stat - Expt - Inf - VE - LG
<   Brit Chams Comm
M   5,000 f
¶   Business Contact magazine - 12;
        Chamber Business Directory - 1; both ftm only.

North of England Horticultural Society   (NEHS)   1911
NR   4A South Park Rd, HARROGATE, N Yorks, HG1 5QU.   (hq)
        01423 561049   fax 01423 536880
        email info@flowershow.org.uk
        http://www.flowershow.org.uk
        Co Sec: Jane Kitchen
▲   Registered Charity
○   *G, *H; organisation of Harrogate spring & autumn flower
        shows
●   Exhib
M   150 i
¶   Show leaflet - 2; free.   Show Catalogue - 2.

**North of England Institute of Mining & Mechanical Engineers
        (NEIMME)   1852**
NR   Neville Hall, Westgate Rd, NEWCASTLE UPON TYNE,
        NE1 1SE.   (hq)
        0191-232 2201   fax 0191-232 2201
        email office@mininginstitute.org
        http://www.mininginstitute.org.uk
        Hon Sec & Treas: J S Porthouse
▲   Registered Charity
○   *L, *Q; to advance & promote the science & technology of
        mining engineering & other allied branches of engineering,
        particularly coal mining
●   Conf - Mtgs - SG - Lib - VE
<   Inst of Materials, Minerals & Mining (NE)
M   c 400 i

North of England Mule Sheep Association   (NEMSA)   1980
■   Eslaforde, Wear View, Frosterley, BISHOP AUCKLAND,
     Co Durham, DL13 2RB.   (regd)
     01388 527411   fax 01388 526728
     email info@nemsa.co.uk   http://www.nemsa.co.uk off
     Sec: Mrs Dorothy L Bell
Br   9
○   *B; to promote the North of England mule ewe lamb as a
     breeding sheep (a cross of 2 contrasting pure breeds; a
     Bluefaced Leicester ram to either a Swaledale or
     Northumberland type Blackface dam)
●   Mtgs - Exhib - Comp - Stat - Expt - Inf
<   Nat Sheep Assn
M   c 1,000 i
¶   Mule News (Jnl) - 1;   Sales booklet - 1; both free.

**North of England Rose, Carnation & Sweet Pea Horticultural
     Society   (ROSECARPE)   1938**
■   6 Stoneylea Close, Crawcrook, RYTON, Tyne & Wear,
     NE40 4EZ.   (hsp)
     0191-413 3634
     email morris@morrosa.fsnet.co.uk
     http://www.rosecarpe8k.com
     Sec: Mrs Rosemary Robinson
▲   Un-incorporated Society
○   *H; to encourage, improve & extend the cultivation of flowers &
     the art of flower arranging, information on show exhibits &
     on all garden enquiries
Gp   Carbations; Daffodils; Roses; Sweet peas
●   Mtgs - Exhib - Inf - VE - Spring bulb show
     Show Sec: Morris Robinson, 0191-413 8026
<   Nat Rose Soc; Nat Sweet Peas Soc; Brit Nat Carnation Soc;
     Nthn Daffodil Soc
M   150 i
¶   Ybk - 1; ftm.   AR.
     [subscriptions £3 yr, or £30 life].

North of England Zoological Society   (Chester Zoo)   1934
■   Zoological Gardens, UPTON BY CHESTER, Cheshire,
     CH2 1LH.   (hq)
     01244 380280   fax 01244 371273
     email marketing@chesterzoo.co.uk
     http://www.chesterzoo.org
     Chief Exec: Prof Gordon McGregor Reid
▲   Company Limited by Guarantee; Registered Charity
○   *B, *E, *V; a conservational & educational charity dedicated to
     breeding & supporting rare & endangered species &
     increasing knowledge of fauna & flora worldwide
●   Conf - Mtgs - ET - Res - SG - Lib - VE
<   Wld Assn Zoos & Aquariums (WAZA); Intl U Conservation of
     Nature (IUCN); Eur Assn Zoos & Aquaria (EAZA); Assn
     Leading Visitor Attractions (ALVA); Fedn Zoological Gardens
     GB & Ireland
M   10,000+ i
¶   Chester Zoo Life (Jnl) - 4; ftm, £1 nm.
     Guide Book & Map; £3 (£4 by post).   AR; ftm, £5 nm.

**North Hampshire Chamber of Commerce & Industry
     (NHCCI)   1998**
NR   Business Support Centre, Deanes Bldg, London Rd,
     BASINGSTOKE, Hants, RG21 7YP.   (hq)
     01256 352275   fax 01256 479391
     email office@nhcci.co.uk   http://www.nhcci.co.uk
     Co Sec: Valerie Cloke,   Chief Exec: John Horrocks
▲   Company Limited by Guarantee
Br   2
○   *C; representation, networking, business briefings, training,
     information, international trade, export services
Gp   Business network; Business health advisory; Women in business
●   Conf - Mtgs - ET - Res - Exhib - SG - Stat - Expt - Inf - Lib - VE -
     LG
<   Brit Chams Comm
M   1,000 f
¶   Chamber News - 12;   Chamber Voice - 4; both free.
     Directory - 1; ftm, £25 nm.

North of Ireland Potato Breeders Association   (NIPBA)   1996
NR   38-40 Carnlea Rd, BALLYMENA, Co Antrim, BT43 6TS.   (hq)
     028 2568 5533
     Chmn: R J Cherry
▲   Company Limited by Guarantee
○   *T; interests of breeders of new varieties of potatoes for home &
     overseas markets
●   Mtgs - Res - SG - Inf - VE - LG
M   14 i

North of Ireland Potato Marketing Association   1935
NR   Grove View Farm, GARVAGH, Co Londonderry, BT51 5NX.
     (hq)
     028 2955 7070
     Sec: Amanda Laughlin
▲   Company Limited by Guarantee
○   *T; interests of potato merchants & exporters (both ware & seed
     potatoes)
●   Mtgs - Exhib - Expt - Inf - VE
<   Eur U Potato Merchants; Brit Potato Trs Consortium
M   10 f
¶   NL - 5-6; ftm only.   LM - 1.   AR; ftm only.

North Kent Chamber of Commerce   1891
■   Stirling House, Sunderland Quay, Culpeper Close, Medway City
     Estate, ROCHESTER, Kent, ME2 4HN.   (hq)
     01634 311411   fax 01634 311450
     email general@northkentchamber.org
     Managing Dir: T Manley
▲   Company Limited by Guarantee
Br   Kent Thames-side Division:
     The Business Centre, Upper Rose Gallery, Bluewater,
     GREENHITHE, Kent, DA9 9ST.
     01322 381333   fax: 01322 381555
     Swale Division:
     Unit B1, St George's Business Park, Castle Rd,
     SITTINGBOURNE, Kent, ME10 3TB.
     01795 432602
○   *C
●   Conf - Mtgs - ET - Expt
<   Brit Chams Comm
M   c 400 f
¶   Business Chat - 6;   Diary - 1; both free.

North London Chamber of Commerce
■   Enfield Business Centre, 201 Hertford Rd, ENFIELD, Middx,
     EN3 5JH.
     020 8443 4464   fax 020 8443 3822
     email chamber@nlcc.co.uk   http://www.nlcc.co.uk
○   *C

North of Scotland Grassland Society   1961
NR   Gowanwell, Crudie, TURRIFF, Aberdeenshire, AB53 5QR.
     (hsp)
     01261 851416   fax 01261 851416
     Hon Sec: Iain Taylor
▲   Registered Charity
○   *F; research into methods & management of grass & forage
     crops
●   Conf - Mtgs - ET - Res - Comp
<   Brit Grassland Soc
M   C 320 I
¶   Norgrass - 1; ftm only.

© CBD Research Ltd · Beckenham · BR3 5JS · Tel 020 8650 7745 · Fax 020 8650 0768 · E-mail cbd@cbdresearch.com · www.cbdresearch.com

North Somerset Agricultural Society   1840
- ■ Hippisleys Farm, Wick St Lawrence, WESTON-super-MARE, Somerset, BS22 7YG.   (sp)
    0845 634 2464   fax 01934 514764
    email office@nsas.org.uk   http://www.nsas.org.uk
    Sec: Miss Katie Hutchings
- ▲ Company Limited by Guarantee; Registered Charity
- ○ *F; to promote agriculture & rural issues
- Gp Annual agricultural show; Annual ploughing match & produce show
- ● Mtgs - ET - Exhib (agricultural & produce shows) - Comp (ploughing match)
- < Assn of Show & Agricl Orgs (ASAO)
- M 500 i
- ¶ NL - 12; ftm, £15 nm.
    [subscription £15].

North Staffordshire Chamber of Commerce & Industry (NSCCI)   1861
- ■ Commerce House, Festival Park, STOKE-on-TRENT, Staffs, ST1 5BE.   (hq)
    01782 202222   fax 01782 202448
    email membership@nscci.co.uk   http://www.nscci.co.uk
    Membership Services Mgr: Mark Brammar
- ▲ Company Limited by Guarantee
- ○ *C
- Gp Export club; Manufacturing; Professional services network
- ● Mtgs - ET - Res - Expt - Inf - LG
- < Brit Chams Comm
- M 1,070 f
- ¶ Focus - 4; ftm, £30 nm.
    International Trade News;
    Business Bulletin - 6; both ftm only.

North West Area Board Association   (NWABA)   1957
- ■ c/o HLM Secretaries Ltd, St James's (9th floor), 79 Oxford St, MANCHESTER, M1 6FQ.   (asa)
    0161-236 8006   fax 0161-236 8306
    email nwaba@hlmsecretaries.co.uk
    Sec: Chris Varley
- ▲ Un-incorporated Society
- ○ *T; manufacture & supply of wood-based boards, panels & other products
- ● Mtgs - ET - VE
- M 20 f

North West Chambers of Commerce
    since 2005 **Chamber of Commerce North West Ltd**

North West London Chamber of Commerce Ltd
- NR Enterprise House, 297 Pinner Rd, HARROW, Middx, HA1 4HS.   (hq)
    020 8427 2884   fax 020 8861 5709
    email info@chamber.org.uk
- ○ *C

North West Timber Trade Association   (NWTTA)   1972
- ■ c/o HLM Secretaries Ltd, St James's (9th floor), 79 Oxford St, MANCHESTER, M1 6FQ.   (asa)
    0161-236 8006   fax 0161-236 8306
    email nwtta@hlmsecretaries.co.uk
    Sec: Chris Varley
- ▲ Un-incorporated Society
- ○ *T; importers, agents & merchants for timber
- ● Mtgs - Stat - Inf - VE
- < Timber Tr Fedn
- M 64 f

North & Western Lancashire Chamber of Commerce (NWLCC)   1916
- NR 9-10 Eastway Business Village, Oliver's Place, Fulwood, PRESTON, Lancs, PR2 9WT.   (hq)
    01772 653000   fax 01772 655544
    email info@lancschamber.co.uk
    http://www.lancschamber.co.uk
    Chief Exec: Babs Murphy
- ▲ Company Limited by Guarantee
- ○ *C
- Gp Export; Marketing
- ● Conf - Mtgs - ET - Res - Exhib - Stat - Expt - Inf - Lib - Empl - LG
- < ABCC; Coun Brit Chams Comm Continental Europe
- M 1,200 f
- ¶ Chacom - 12.   Network - 4; ftm, on request nm.
    Classified Directory - 1; ftm.   AR; free.
- × 2004 Central & West Lancashire Chamber of Commerce & Industry

North Western Model Railway Clubs Association   (NWMRCA)   1968
- NR 58 Greengate Lane, KENDAL, Cumbria, LA9 5LL.   (hsp)
    01539 726285
    http://www.nwmrca.org.uk
    Chmn: Malcolm Conway
- ▲ Un-incorporated Society
- ○ *G, *N; to provide a link between model railway clubs in the North West
- ● Conf - Exhib - Conf - Inf
- M c 50 clubs
- ¶ North West Notes - 12;   NL - 4; both ftm.

North Yorkshire Moors Historical Railway Trust   (NYMR)   1967
- NR Pickering Station, PICKERING, N Yorks, YO18 7AJ.   (hq)
    01751 473799   fax 01751 476970
    email admin@nymrpickering-fsnet.co.uk
    http://www.northyorkshiremoorsrailway.com
    Gen Mgr: Philip Benham
- ▲ Registered Charity
- ○ *G; to advance the education of the public in the history & development of railway locomotion by the maintenance, in working order, of the historic & scenic railway line between Grosmont & Pickering
- ● ET
- < Assn of Rly Presvn Socs
- M c 7,225 i, 50 f
- ¶ Moors Line - 4; ftm, £1.20 nm.

Northamptonshire Chamber of Commerce, Training & Enterprise   1991
- NR Opus House, Anglia Way, Moulton Park, NORTHAMPTON, NN3 6Ja.   (hq)
    01604 490490   fax 01604 670362
    Chief Exec: Stephen Smith
- ○ *C
- M c 1,300 i & f

Northamptonshire Footwear Manufacturers' Association
    merged in April 2003 with the **British Footwear Association**

Northamptonshire Natural History Society   1876
- NR The Humfrey Rooms, 10 Castilian Terrace, NORTHAMPTON, NN1 1LD.   (hq)
    01604 604529
    Sec: C T Sampson
- ○ *G; to promote research into the natural history & allied sciences of the County
- ● Mtgs - Res
- M i & org
- ¶ Jnl.

Northamptonshire Record Society   1920
NR   Wootton Hall Park, NORTHAMPTON, NN4 8BQ.   (hq)
      01604 762297
      http://www.northamptonshirerecordssociety.org.uk
      Sec: Leslie C Skelton
▲   Registered Charity
○   *L, *Q; the pursuit of the history of Northamptonshire in all its
      forms
●   Mtgs - Lib - Lectures
M   500 i, 130 org, UK / 80 families, o'seas
¶   Northamptonshire Past & Present (Jnl) - 1; £3.
      Publications list available.

Northern Cricket Union of Ireland   (NCU)   1886
NR   c/o House of Sport, Upper Malone Rd, BELFAST, BT9 5LA.
      (hq)
      028 9038 3805
      Gen Sec: W J McCarroll
▲   Un-incorporated Society
○   *S; the governing body for cricket in Belfast & Counties Antrim,
      Down & Armagh
●   ET (coaches, umpires & scorers) - Exam (umpires) - Comp - Stat
      - Inf - Mtgs - VE
<   Ir Cricket U; England & Wales Cricket Bd
M   50 clubs, 44 schools
¶   Hbk - 1; ftm, £2 nm.

**Northern Ireland Amusement Caterer's Trade Association
      (NIACTA)**
NR   58 Mallusk Rd, Hyde Park Industrial Estate, NEWTOWNABBEY,
      Co Antrim, BT36 4PX.
      028 9084 8731   fax 028 9083 3104
      Hon Sec: Jon Sander
○   *T
M   c35 i

Northern Ireland Archery Society   (NIAS)
NR   PO Box 282, CRAIGAVON, Co Armagh, BT67 0YA.   (mail)
      email admin@nias.co.uk add
      Chmn: Hugh Irvine
○   *S; governing body of the sport of archery in NI
M   i & clubs
¶   Archery Bulletin (NL) - 12, ftm.

**Northern Ireland Association for the Care & Resettlement of
      Offenders   (NIACRO)   1971**
NR   169 Ormeau Rd, BELFAST, BT7 1SQ.   (hq)
      028 9032 0157
      http://www.niacro.org
      Chief Exec: Olwyn Lyner
○   *W; to assist with the rehabilitation of offenders; to work with
      those at risk of criminal involvement & thereby prevent crime

Northern Ireland Association for Mental Health   1959
NR   80 University St, BELFAST, BT7 1HE.   (hq)
      028 9032 8474
      email info@niamh.co.uk
      Chief Exec: Alan Ferguson
▲   Company Limited by Guarantee
Br   32
○   *W; all aspects of mental health & mental illness
●   ET - Inf - Day care facilities - Self-help groups
M   c 150 i
¶   Mental Health Matters - 4; ftm.   AR; free.

**Northern Ireland Association for the Study of Psychoanalysis
      (NIASP)   1988**
NR   c/o Dr J Finlay, Holywell Hospital, Steeple Rd, ANTRIM, BT41
      2RJ.
      028 9446 5211   fax 028 9446 1903
      Sec: Dr John Finlay
▲   Registered Charity
○   *P
Gp   Child psychotherapy; Group psychotherapy
●   Conf - Mtgs - ET - Res - SG
<   Brit Confedn Psychotherapy (BCP); Intl Psychoanalytic Assn (IPA)
M   c 20 i

Northern Ireland Athletic Federation   (NIAF)   1935
NR   Athletics House, Old Coach Rd, BELFAST, BT9 5PR.   (hq)
      028 9060 2707   fax 028 9030 9939
      email info@niathletics.org   http://www.niathletics.org
      Hon Sec: John Allen
○   *S; men's & women's athletics in NI
<   Intl Assn of Athletic Fedns; UK Athletics
M   45 clubs
¶   Ybk.   AR.

Northern Ireland Bankers' Association   (NIBA)   1947
■   Stokes House, 17-25 College Square East, BELFAST,
      BT1 6DE.   (hq)
      028 9032 7551   fax 028 9033 1449
      Sec: Bill McAlister
▲   Un-incorporated Society
○   *P; a forum for interbank discussion of items of common
      interest
M   4 f

Northern Ireland Bat Group   (NIBG)   1985
■   c/o Ulster Museum, Botanic Gardens, BELFAST, BT9 5AB.
      (contact/point)
      028 9038 3144   fax 028 9038 3103
      Contact: Mrs Lynne Rendle
▲   Un-incorporated Society
○   *V; to promote bat conservation in Northern Ireland by
      educating & advising the public; to monitor numbers &
      investigate aspects of bat biology
●   ET - Res - Exhib - LG
M   71 i
¶   NL - 4; ftm only.

**Northern Ireland Chamber of Commerce & Industry   (NICCI)
      1783**
NR   22 Great Victoria St, BELFAST, BT2 7BJ.   (hq)
      028 9024 4113   fax 028 9024 7024
      email mail@northernirelandchamber.com
      http://www.northernirelandchamber.com
      Chief Exec: Frank Hewitt
○   *C
M   c 4,000 i & f
¶   The Business Connections - 6.

Northern Ireland Childminding Association   1990
NR   16-18 Mill St, NEWTOWNARDS, BT23 4LU.
      028 9181 1015   fax 028 9182 0921
      http://www.nicma.org
      Dir: Bridget Nodder
○   *P
M   c 2,500 i

Northern Ireland Council for Voluntary Action   (NICVA)   1938
NR   61 Duncairn Gardens, BELFAST, BT15 2GB.   (hq)
      028 9087 7777   fax 028 9087 7799
      http://www.nicva.org
      Chief Exec: Seamus McAleavey
▲   Company Limited by Guarantee; Registered Charity
○   *N, *W; resource & development body serving the voluntary
      sector in Northern Ireland
M   i, f & org

© CBD Research Ltd · Beckenham · BR3 5JS · Tel 020 8650 7745 · Fax 020 8650 0768 · E-mail cbd@cbdresearch.com · www.cbdresearch.com

Northern Ireland Countryside Staff Association   (NICSA) 1992
NR   c/o Park Amenities Dept, Belfast City Council, Malone House, Barnett Demesne, BELFAST, BT9 5PB.   (chmn/b)
028 9066 2259
http://www.nicsa.co.uk
Chmn: Orla Maguire
○   *P; for all staff involved in promotion & conservation of the natural heritage of Northern Ireland
●   Conf - Mtgs - ET - VE
<   Intl Ranger Fedn; Scot Countryside Rangers Assn; Countryside Mgt Assn
M   c 80 i
¶   NICSA News (NL) - 3; free.

Northern Ireland Cycling Federation   (NICF)   1949
NR   21 Rossdale Rd, BANGOR, Co Down, BT19 6BE.   (hsp)
028 9146 4102   fax 028 9146 4102
Hon Sec: Suzanne Hamilton
○   *S; sporting body for cyclists in Northern Ireland
●   Comp
<   Brit Cycling
M   c 500 i in c 20 clubs
¶   Ybk; ftm.

Northern Ireland Dairy Association
since 2005 is the Northern Ireland branch of **Dairy UK**

Northern Ireland Deer Society   (NIDS)   1989
NR   14 Glenaan Park, BANGOR, Co Down, BT20 4SN.   (h/treas/p)
028 9145 5818
Sec: Dave McCullough
▲   Un-incorporated Society
○   *V; to protect the welfare of deer & their habitat; to advance the study of deer, their distribution & ecology for their better management & humane control
●   Mtgs - Res - Exhib - Inf - VE
M   i

Northern Ireland Federation of Housing Associations (NIFHA)   1977
■   38 Hill St, BELFAST, BT1 2LB.   (hq)
028 9023 0446   fax 028 9023 8057
email info@nifha.org   http://www.nifha.org
Dir & Co Sec: Christopher Williamson
▲   Company Limited by Guarantee
○   *N; 'to represent & promote housing associations in Northern Ireland; to support them in the provision of high quality, affordable housing for the benefit of the community'
●   Conf - Mtgs - ET - Res - Exhib - SG - Stat - Inf - VE - LG
<   Intl Co-operative Alliance; Eur Liaison C'ee for Social Housing (CECODHAS)
M   45 housing org
¶   AR.

Northern Ireland Fruit Growers' Association (incorporating Ulster Apple Exporters Association)   (NIFGA)   1942
NR   52 Teaguy Rd, Annaghmore, PORTADOWN, Co Armagh, BT62 1LX.   (hsp/b)
0778 715 0512 (mobile)
Sec: Dermot Morgan
○   *T; promotion of fruit growing
●   Conf - Mtgs - Comp - SG - Inf (m) - VE
<   Ulster Farmers U; Brit Farm Produce Coun
M   c 100 i & f

Northern Ireland Grain Trade Association Ltd   (NIGTA)   1966
NR   c/o Doris Leeman, 27 Berwick View, MOIRA, Co Down, BT67 0SX.   (hq)
028 9261 1044   fax 028 9261 1979
email doris@leemanpr.demon.co.uk
Sec: Doris Leeman
○   *T
M   30 f

Northern Ireland Hotels Federation   1922
NR   Midland Building, Whitla St, BELFAST, BT15 1JP.   (hq)
028 9035 1110   fax 028 9035 1509
email office@nihf.co.uk
Chief Exec: Janet Gault
▲   Un-incorporated Society
○   *T; private sector business in the hospitality industry - hotel, guesthouses, restaurants, commercial & trade suppliers
●   Conf - Mtgs - ET - Exhib - Comp - Expt - LG
<   Brit Hospitality Assn
M   [not stated]
¶   NL - 4.   AR & Accounts.

Northern Ireland Local Government Association   (NILGA) 1973
■   123 York St, BELFAST, BT15 1AB.   (hq)
028 9024 9286   fax 028 9023 3328
email office@nilga.org   http://www.nilga.org
Chief Exec: Heather Moorhead
▲   Un-incorporated Society
○   *N; represents the interests of local authorities in Northern Ireland
●   Conf - Mtgs - SG - Empl - LG
<   LEIB; Local Authorities Coordinating Body on Food & Trading Standards (LACOTS)
M   c 150 icils
¶   The Councillors' Hbk - 4 yrly; free.
NL - 4;   AR - 1; both free.

Northern Ireland Master Butchers Association   (NIMBA) 1937
■   38 Oldstone Hill, MUCKAMORE, Co Antrim, BT41 4SB.   (sp)
028 9446 5180
Sec: Harry Marquess
▲   Un-incorporated Society
○   *T
●   Mtgs - Comp - Inf - Empl - LG
M   200 i
¶   N.I. Master Butchers - 4.

Northern Ireland Master Plumbers' Association   (NIMPA) 1931
■   38 Hill St, BELFAST, BT1 2LB.   (asa)
028 9032 1731   fax 028 9024 7521
email crawfordsedgwick@excite.com
Sec: W A Crawford
▲   Un-incorporated Society
○   *T
●   Conf - Mtgs - ET - Empl
<   Scot & NI Plumbing Employers' Fedn
M   118 f
¶   Plumbheat - 10; ftm only.

Northern Ireland Meat Exporters Association   (NIMEA)   1980
NR   24 Ballydown Rd, BANBRIDGE, Co Down, BT32 3RP.   (hq)
028 4062 6338   fax 028 4062 6083
email nimea@aol.com   http://www.nimea.co.uk
Chief Exec: Cecil Mathers
▲   Company Limited by Guarantee
○   *T; to represent all EU approved meat exporting companies in Northern Ireland
Gp   Plants: Slaughter, Cutting, Processing
●   Conf - Mtgs - ET - Expt - Inf - LG
<   UECBV (Brussels, Belgium)
M   17 f

Northern Ireland Mixed Marriage Association   (NIMMA) 1974
- ■ 28 Bedford St, BELFAST, BT2 7FE.
  028 9023 5444   fax 028 9043 4544
  email nimma@nireland.com   http://www.nimma.org.uk
- ▲ Registered Charity
- ○ *W; for the mutual support & help of people involved in or
  about to be involved in a mixed (Catholic / Protestant)
  marriage
- ● Inf - 'helping the clergy to understand the concept &
  practicalities of mixed marriage' - Influencing the attitudes of
  the community to mixed marriage
- < Assn Interchurch Families
- M 80 i
- ¶ Newssheet / Update - 4; ftm only.
  Mixed Marriage in Ireland: A companion to those involved, or
  about to be involved, in a mixed marriage; £3.50.

Northern Ireland Plastics Association
  since 2002 **Northern Ireland Polymer Association**

Northern Ireland Polymer Association   2002
- NR c/o Polymer Processing Research Centre, Queen's University of
  Belfast, Ashby Bldg, Strandmills Rd, BELFAST, BT9 5AH.
  Chmn: Brian McCann
- ○ *T
- × 2002 Northern Ireland Plastics Association

Northern Ireland Poultry Federation
- NR c/o O'Kane Poultry Ltd, 170 Larne Rd, BALLYMENA, Co Antrim,
  BT42 9XX.   (chmn/b)
  028 2564 1111   fax 028 2565 8498
  Chmn: W P O'Kane
- ○ *T
- M f

Northern Ireland Public Service Alliance   (NIPSA)   1971
- ■ 54 Wellington Park, BELFAST, BT9 6DP.   (hq)
  028 9066 1831   fax 028 9066 5847
  http://www.nipsa.org.uk
  Gen Sec: John Corey
- Br 250
- ○ *U; representing non-industrial grades of civil & public servants
- ● Conf - Mtgs - ET - Inf - Lib - Empl
- M 44,000 i
- ¶ NIPSA News (newspaper) - 11;   Bulletins;   AR;
  Rule Book & Constitution - 1; all free.

Northern Ireland Shows' Association   (NISA)   1983
- ■ The King's Hall, Balmoral, BELFAST, BT9 6GW.   (hsb)
  028 9066 5225   fax 028 9066 1264
  email karen@kingshall.co.uk
  Hon Sec: Colin McDonald
- ○ *F, *N; to represent all agricultural shows in Northern Ireland
- ● Conf - Mtgs - ET - Exhib - Comp
- M 15 agricultural org (N Ireland)

Northern Ireland Textile & Apparel Association Ltd
  reported to us as having closed - we should appreciate
  confirmation.

Northern Ireland Timber Trade Association   (NITTA)   1939
- NR 13 Churchill Drive, CARRICKFERGUS, Co Antrim, BT38 7LH.
  (hsp/b)
  028 9336 2784   fax 028 9332 9011
  Liaison Officer: T G Rankin
- ▲ Un-incorporated Society
- ○ *T; to promote the imported timber industry
- ● Conf - Mtgs - ET - Stat - Empl
- < Timber Trade Fedn UK; Nat Sawmill Assn; Timber Res & Devt
  Assn
- M 17 f

Northern Ireland Transplant Association   1991
- ■ Eagle Lodge, 51 Circular Rd, BELFAST, BT4 2GA.   (hq)
  028 9076 1394
  email nitransplants@email.com   http://www.nita.org.uk
  Hon Sec: Beverly Robinson
- ▲ Registered Charity
- ○ *W; to give support, advice & aid to those concerned with
  organ transplantation; to promote the organ donor card &
  registration scheme
- ● Conf - Mtgs - ET - Inf - VE - LG
- M 160 i (NI only)
- ¶ NL - 2; ftm only.

Northern Ireland Volleyball Association   (NIVA)   1970
- ■ 21 Broughton Park, Raventill Rd, BELFAST, BT6 0BD.   (mail)
  http://www.nivb.com address
  Pres: Paddy Murphy
- ○ *S; the organisation of the sport of volleyball in Ireland
- ¶ Hbk - 1; ftm.

Northern Ireland Women's Aid Federation   (NIWAF)   1978
- NR 129 University St, BELFAST, BT7 1HP.   (hq)
  028 9024 9041   fax 028 9023 9296
  email info@womensaidni.org
  Dir: Annie Campbell
- ▲ Company Limited by Guarantee; Registered Charity
- ○ *K, *W; to challenge attitudes & beliefs which perpetuate
  domestic violence; it seeks to promote healthy & non-abusive
  relationships
- Gp Advice; Outreach; Refuge; Aftercare; Education & awareness
  on domestic violence
- ● Conf - Mtgs - ET - Exhib - Stat - Inf - Lib - LG
  Helpline 0800 917 1414 (24-hr)
- < Eur Women's Lobby (EWL); Women against Violence (WAVE);
  Women's Aid Fedn England / Scotland / Wales / Eire
- M 11 groups
- ¶ List of publications on request.

Northern Mill Engine Society   (NMES)   1966
- ■ 84 Watkin Rd, Clayton-le-Woods, CHORLEY, Lancs, PR6 7PX.
  (hsp)
  01257 265003
  http://www.nmes.org
  Hon Sec: John Phillp
- ▲ Company Limited by Guarantee; Registered Charity
- ○ *G, *L; preservation of steam engines used to drive the textile
  mills of Lancashire & Yorkshire
- ● Mtgs - Exhib - Operation of Bolton Steam Museum
- M 230 i, 4 f, 4 org, UK / 5 i, 1 org, o'seas
- ¶ The Flywheel - 3;   NL - 4; both ftm.

Northern Mine Research Society   (NMRS)   1960
- NR 3 Leebrook Drive, Owlthorpe, SHEFFIELD, S20 7QG.   (hq)
  Pres: John Hunter
- ▲ Registered Charity
- ○ *G, *L; encourages research & publication covering all aspects
  of mining history & related topics in Britain
- ● Conf - Mtgs - Res - Inf - Lib - VE
- < Nat Assn of Mining History Orgs (NAMHO); Assn Indl
  Archaeology (AIA)
- M 425 i, UK / 8 i, o'seas
- ¶ NL - 4; ftm only.
  British Mining Monograph - 1; ftm, £13 nm.
  British Mining Memoirs - 1; ftm, £13 nm.

Northern Offshore Federation   (NOF)   1988
- ■ Pennine House (3rd floor), District 1, WASHINGTON, Tyne &
  Wear, NE37 1EP.   (hq)
  0191-417 4254   fax 0191-417 4257
  email nof@nof.co.uk   http://www.nof.co.uk
  Dir: G Rafferty
- ○ *T; for the oil, gas & associated energy related industries; to
  promote the North of England as an area of expertise in
  these industries
- M c 230 f

© CBD Research Ltd · Beckenham · BR3 5JS · Tel 020 8650 7745 · Fax 020 8650 0768 · E-mail cbd@cbdresearch.com · www.cbdresearch.com

Northumberland & Newcastle Society   1924
NR   Jesmond Methodist Church, St George's Terrace, Jesmond,
      NEWCASTLE UPON TYNE, NE2 2DL.   (hq)
      0191-281 6266
      email secretary@nandnsociety.org.uk
      http://www.nandnsociety.org.uk
      Sec: Mrs Ros Hall
○   *G; conservation & preservation of buildings & the countryside
●   Mtgs - ET - Exhib - SG - Stat - Inf - VE
M   i, f & org
¶   City & County (Jnl) - 4;   AR; both free.

Northumbrian Pipers' Society   (NPS)   1928
■   Park House, Lynemouth, MORPETH, Northumberland,
      NE61 5XQ.   (hsp)
      01670 860215
      email secretary@northumbrianpipers.org.uk
      http://www.northumbrianpipers.org.uk
      Hon Sec: Julia Say
▲   Un-incorporated Society
○   *D; to foster & encourage the playing, study, manufacture &
      development of Northumbrian pipes & their music &
      traditional Northumbrian music in general
●   Mtgs - ET - Res - Comp
M   650 i, UK / 150 i, o'seas
¶   NPS NL - 4; ftm only.   NPS Magazine - 1; ftm, £4 nm.

Norwegian-British Chamber of Commerce   1906
NR   Charles House, 5 Lower Regent St, LONDON, SW1Y 4LR.   (hq)
      020 7930 0181   fax 020 7930 7946
      http://www.norwegian-chamber.co.uk
      Gen Mgr: Anni Glesaaen
▲   Company Limited by Guarantee
○   *C
●   Conf - Mtgs
M   c 800 i & f
¶   Ybk & LM - 1; ftm, £25 nm.

Not Forgotten Association   1920
§   2 Grosvenor Gdns, LONDON, SW1W 0DH.   (hq)
      020 7730 2400   fax 020 7730 0020
      http://www.nfassociation.org
      a service charity which acts for the benefit of disabled ex-service
      men & women; in particular provision of televisions,
      holidays, outings & entertainment

Notaries' Society   1907
NR   PO Box 226, WOODBRIDGE, Suffolk, IP12 1WX.   (hq)
      01394 380436   fax 01394 383772
      email NotariesSociety@compuserve.com
      http://www.thenotariessociety.org.uk
      Sec: Christopher VAughan
▲   Company Limited by Guarantee
○   *P; for public notaries
●   Conf - Mtgs - ET - Res - Inf - LG
M   793 i
¶   The Notary; m & registered correspondents only.

Nottinghamshire Chamber of Commerce & Industry   1860
NR   Abbeyfield House, Abbeyfield Rd, NOTTINGHAM, NG7 2SZ.
      (hq)
      0115-933 0033
      email marketing@nottschamber.co.uk
      http://www.nottschamber.co.uk
      Chief Exec: G W Hulse,   Sec: M Archer
▲   Company Limited by Guarantee
Br   6 area chambers
○   *C; business support services incl training, business
      development & networking
●   Mtgs - ET - Res - Exhib - Expt - Inf - Lib - LG
<   Brit Chams Comm; E Midlands Cham Comm
M   2,941 f
¶   Network Nottinghamshire - 10; ftm.
      Quarterly Economic Survey - 4.
      Nottinghamshire Business Directory - 1; ftm.
      East Midlands Business Directory - 1; ftm.
      Salaries & Benefits Survey - 1.   Diary - 1.

Nottinghamshire Local History Association   (NLHA)   1953
■   6 The Maltings, Blyth, WORKSOP, Notts, S81 8HD.   (hsp)
      01909 591427
      Chmn: Margaret Woodhead,   Hon Sec: Colin Witham
▲   Registered Charity
○   *G; to encourage interest in the local history of
      Nottinghamshire
●   Mtgs - Publishing works on Nottinghamshire local history
M   149 i, 51 org
¶   Nottinghamshire Historian (Jnl) - 2; ftm, £2 nm.

Nuclear Industry Association   (NIA)   1962
■   Carlton House, 22A St James's Square, LONDON,
      SW1Y 4JH.   (hq)
      020 7766 6640   fax 020 7839 1523
      email info@niauk.org   http://www.niauk.org
      Chief Exec: Keith Parker
▲   Company Limited by Guarantee
○   *T; UK civil nuclear industry
●   Conf - Mtgs - ET - Exhib - Expt - Inf - LG
<   Brit Energy Assn
M   87 f
¶   Industry Link (NL) - 4;   Trade Directory - 1;
      Educational Booklets;   AR; all free.
×   2003 (June) British Nuclear Industry Forum

Nuclear Stock Association Ltd   (NSA)   1952
■   PO Box 65, Walpole St Peter, WISBECH, Cambs, PE14 7ZZ.
      (hq)
      01945 781148   fax 01945 781149
      email nsagrant@aol.com
      Sec: A J Grant
○   *H, *T; the maintenance & supply of high health status indexed
      propagation material for soft & tree fruit propagation
Gp   Working gps: Strawberry, Rubus & ribes; Tree fruits c'ee
●   Mtgs - VE - LG
M   i
¶   AR - 1; ftm only.
      Note: is a limited company registered as a Friendly Society

Nutrition Society   1941
NR   10 Cambridge Court, 210 Shepherds Bush Rd, LONDON,
      W6 7NJ.   (hq)
      020 7602 0228   fax 020 7602 1756
      email office@notsoc.org.uk
      Chief Exec: Frederick Whitworth-Bowyer
○   *L, *P; to advance the scientific study of nutrition & its
      application to the maintenance of human & animal health
M   c 2,700 i
¶   Proceedings (1 vol in 3 parts).
      British Jnl of Nutrition (2 vols in 3 parts).
      Publications list available.

NWA - an association of housing & support managers (NWA) 1985

■ Katepwa House, Ashfield Pk, ROSS-ON-WYE, Herefordshire, HR9 5AX. (hq)
  01989 566699   fax 01989 567676
  email nwa@assocmanagement.co.uk
  http://www.shelteredhousingmanagers.co.uk
  Sec: Gwen Hassall
  Admin: Gill Hinton
▲ Un-incorporated Society
○ *P; for the support of wardens & scheme managers of sheltered housing & for people with an interest in older people
● Conf - Mtgs - Inf (members only) - VE - LG
M 1,350 i, 66 f
¶ The Voice - 4; ftm, £1 nm.

Nystagmus Network   1984

NR 13 Tinsley Close, Claypole, NEWARK, Notts, NG23 5BS.
  (Inf/Offr/p)
  01636 627004
  email info@nystagmusnet.org
  http://www.nystagmusnet.org
  Information Officer: Paul White
▲ Registered Charity
○ *W; to promote help, support & information to all those affected by the eye condition Nystagmus (characterised by jerky eye movements which nearly always impair vision)
● Conf - ET - Res - Exhib - Inf
  Helpline: 01392 272573
< Look; Contact a family; Albino Fellowship
M 500 i, 20 org
¶ Focus (NL) - 4;   Parent Pack; both ftm only.
  Understanding Nystagmus (booklet); ftm.
  Tales of Northwick (book).   Information sheets; ftm.
  Publications list available.

© CBD Research Ltd · Beckenham · BR3 5JS · Tel 020 8650 7745 · Fax 020 8650 0768 · E-mail cbd@cbdresearch.com · www.cbdresearch.com

Observer's Pocket Series Collectors' Society   (OPSCS)   1993
■ 10 Villiers Rd, KENILWORTH, Warks, CV8 2JB.   (hsp)
01926 857047
Hon Sec: Alan Sledger
▲ Un-incorporated Society
○ *G; 'to promote the interest in & collecting of Observer's &
other related books published by F Warne'
● Mtgs
M 550 i, UK / 15 i, o'seas
¶ OPSCS Magazine - 4; ftm only.

Obsessive Action
since January 2002 **OCD Action**

Obstetric Anaesthetists Association   (OAA)   1969
■ PO Box 3219, LONDON, SW13 9XR.   (regd off)
020 8741 1311   fax 020 8741 0611
email secretariat@oaa-anaes.ac.uk
http://www.oaa-anaes.ac.uk
▲ Registered Charity
○ *P; highest standards of anaesthetic practice in the care of
mother & baby
● Conf - Mtgs - ET - Res - Exhib - Advice & policies relating to the
provision of anaesthetic services on request
M 1,645 i, UK / 372 i, o'seas
¶ Pencil Point (NL) - 4; ftm only.
International Jnl of Obstetric Anaesthesia - 4; ftm, £95 nm.

Occupational & Environmental Diseases Association   (OEDA)   1993
■ PO Box 26, ENFIELD, Middx, EN1 2NT.   (sp)
020 8360 8490
http://www.oeda.demon.co.uk
Mgt C'ee: Dr Nancy Tait
▲ Registered Charity
○ *W; to help those suffering from, & those working to identify &
prevent, industrial diseases
● Res - SG - Inf
¶ Asbestos Facts;   Publications list available.

Occupational Pensioners Alliance   (OPA)   2003
NR Carlton House, 42-44 West St, DUNSTABLE, Beds, LU6 1TA.
(exec/b)
01582 663880   fax 01582 475775
email rogerturner@pensioneronline.com
http://www.opalliance.org.uk
Exec Officer: Roger Turner
▲ Un-incorporated Society
○ *K; to develop & promote policies that are in the interests of
occupational pension schemes; to influence national &
European policy making
● Mtgs - LG - Campaigning to government on all issues affecting
occupational pensions
< Nat Pensioners' Convention
M [not stated]
✕ 2003 (Alliance of Occupational Pensioners
(Confederation of Occupational Pensioner Associations

OCD Action   1991
■ Units 107-109 Aberdeen Centre, 22-24 Highbury Grove,
LONDON, N5 2EA.   (hq)
0845 390 6237   fax 020 7228 0828
email info@ocdaction.org.uk
http://www.ocdaction.org.uk
Chmn: Piers Watson
▲ Registered Charity
○ *W; to advance awareness, research, understanding &
treatment of obsessive compulsive disorder & associated
disorders; to offer support & advice to sufferers, their families
& interested professionals
● Conf - Inf
M 1,200 i
¶ NL - 3;   Information booklet; free.
Challenging OCD - 1; free.
[subscription £17 yr].

Ocean Liner Society   (OLS)   1987
■ 27 Old Gloucester St, LONDON, WC1N 3XX.   (hsp)
▲ Un-incorporated Society
○ *G; to promote interest in passenger ships past & present (incl
line service or cruising, ferries with overnight accommodation
& sailing or cargo ships carrying passengers)
● Mtgs - Res - Exhib - Lib - PL - VE
M 400 i, 40 f, 10 org, UK / 200 i, 20 f, 5 org, o'seas
¶ Sea Lines (Jnl) - 4; ftm.

Oesophageal Patients Association   1985
NR 22 Vulcan House, Vulcan Rd, SOLIHULL, West Midlands,
B91 2JY.
0121-704 9860
Chief Exec: David Kirby
○ *W; support group for people with oesophageal cancer

Offa's Dyke Association   (ODA)   1969
■ West St, KNIGHTON, Radnorshire, LD7 1EN.   (hq)
01547 528753
Chmn: Dr Ian Dormor,   Hon Sec: Peter Weetman
▲ Registered Charity
○ *G; to provide a link between walkers, tourists, historians,
conservationists & those who live & work on the Welsh
Border; to provide visitors with information about the area &
specifically the Offa's Dyke Path
Gp 'linesmen' who monitor, carry out minor maintenance & report
on problems in their section
● Mtgs - ET - Res - Exhib - Comp - SG - Inf - Lib - PL - Footpath
maintenance - Tourist Information centre (on behalf of the
Wales Tourist Board)
< None formal but close links with: Ramblers Assn; YHA;
National trail protection orgs, local authorities, Countryside
Coun for Wales.
M 1,000 i & org
¶ NL - 3; ftm only.   Accommodation list - 1; ftm, £4 nm.
Strip maps of Offa's Dyke Path; £5 a set of 10.
Route Notes N to S, S to N; £2 each.
List available of other publications.

Offenders Tag Association   (OTA)   1982
■ 128 Kensington Church St, LONDON, W8 4BH.   (hq)
020 7221 7166   fax 020 7792 9288
email ota@stacey-international.co.uk
http://www.offenderstag.co.uk
Chmn: Tom Stacey,   Sec: M A Carruthers
▲ Un-incorporated Society
○ *K; penal reform lobby group
● Inf - LG
M 30 i

Office Products & Stationery Association
NR   12 Corporation St, HIGH WYCOMBE, Bucks, HP13 6TQ.
      0845 450 1565
▲   Un-incorporated Society
○   *T
<   an affiliate of the British Office Supplies & Services Federation
M   f

Officers' Association (OA) 1920
§   48 Pall Mall, LONDON, SW1Y 5JY. (hq)
      020 7389 5204
      http://www.officersassociation.org.uk
      For the relief of distress amongst those who have, or have had,
      commission in HM Forces, or their families; is a registered
      charity

Offshore Contractors' Association (OCA) 1995
■   58 Queens Rd, ABERDEEN, AB15 4YE. (hq)
      01224 326070   fax 01224 326071
      email admin@oca-online.co.uk
      http://www.oca-online.co.uk
      Chief Exec: Bill Murray
▲   Company Limited by Guarantee
○   *T; to represent the UK's Oil & gas contracting industry
●   Mtgs - Res - Exhib - Stat - Inf - Lib -Empl - LG
M   c 70 f
¶   NL - 12;   Brochure; both free.
      Guidance Notes - irreg; prices vary.

Offshore Engineering Society (OES) 1987
NR   1-7 Great George St, LONDON, SW1P 3AA. (hq)
      020 7665 2239
      email janice.leung@ice.org.uk   http://www.oes.org.uk
      Sec: Janice Leung
○   *P, *T; offshore engineering
M   200 i, 30 f
¶   List of publications available.

Offshore Industry Liaison Committee (OILC) 1992
■   49 Carmelite St, ABERDEEN, AB11 6NQ. (hq)
      01224 210118   fax 01224 210095
      email gensec@oilc.org   http://www.oilc.org
      Gen Sec: Jake Molloy
○   *U; for offshore workers
●   Conf - ET
M   i [not stated]
¶   Blowout (Jnl) - 4; ftm, £1 nm.
      Flareoff (supplement) - 4; free.

Oil & Colour Chemists' Association (OCCA) 1918
■   967 Harrow Rd, WEMBLEY, Middx, HA0 2SF. (hq)
      020 8908 1086
      Gen Sec: C Pacey-Day
▲   Company Limited by Guarantee; Registered Charity
Br   12; 7 o'seas
○   *L; science & technology of paint, printing ink & allied
      industries
●   Conf - Mtgs - ET - Exhib
<   Coating Socs Intl (CSI)
M   1,550 i, UK / 1,650 i, o'seas
¶   Surface Coatings International:
      Part A - 8.
      Part B - 4.
      UK Surface Coatings Hbk - 1.

Oil Firing Technical Association for the Petroleum Industry (OFTEC) 1991
■   Foxwood House, Dobbs Lane, Kesgrave, IPSWICH, Suffolk,
      IP5 2QQ. (hq)
      0845 658 5080   fax 0845 658 5181
      email enquiries@oftec.org   http://www.oftec.org
      Chief Exec: Richard Gales
▲   Company Limited by Guarantee
Br   Republic of Ireland
○   *T; to provide technical services for the oil firing industry
Gp   Oil: companies, distbrs, eqpt mfrs
●   Conf - Mtgs - ET - Exam - Exhib - Stat - LG - Testing & approval
      of oil firing equipment - Register of approved technicians
<   Eurofuel
M   150 f, UK / 1 f, o'seas

Oil Recycling Association (ORA) 1998
■   62 Lower St, STANSTED, Essex, CM24 8LR. (hsp)
      01279 814035   fax 01279 814035
      email oilrecyclingasso@aol.com
      Hon Sec: Roger Creswell
▲   Company Limited by Guarantee
○   *T; for those engaged in the recovery & recycling of lubricants,
      fuels & other liquid wastes which are no longer fit for their
      original purpose and arise mainly from the servicing of
      automotive engines & other mechanical equipment;
      The recovery & recycling of other garage wastes such as oil
      filters, catalysts, batteries & other products
Gp   Allied shipping services
●   Mtgs - Res - Stat - Inf - LG
M   29 f
¶   NL - 4; ftm only.

Old Bottle Club of Great Britain (OBCofGB) 1975
NR   2 Strafford Ave, Elsecar, BARNSLEY, S Yorks, S74 8AA. (hsp)
      01226 745156
      Hon Sec: Alan Blakeman
Br   40
○   *G; recovery & study of antique bottles & containers pre 1911
●   Conf - Mtgs - Res - ET - Exhib - Comp - Inf - VE
M   c10,000 i
¶   British Bottle Review - 4.

Old Gaffers Association
NR   6 Chatham Place, RAMSGATE, Kent, CT11 7PT. (hsp)
      01843 582997
      Hon Sec: Robert Holden
○   *G; for owners of 'gaff-rigged' (mainly 19th century) sailing
      craft

Old Lawn Mower Club 1990
■   c/o Milton Keynes Museum, McConnell Drive, Wolverton,
      MILTON KEYNES, Bucks, MK12 5EL. (mail)
      01908 316222
      email enquiry@oldlawnmowerclub.co.uk
      http://www.oldlawnmowerclub.co.uk address
      Sec: Bernard Robinson
▲   Un-incorporated Society
○   *G; promotes the collection, preservation & display of old
      lawnmowers
●   Mtgs - Exhib - Inf
M   300 i, UK / 15 i, o'seas
¶   Grassbox (NL) - 4; ftm only.

Old Time Dance Society 1984
- ■ 31 Dexter Way, MIDDLEWICH, Cheshire, CW10 9GH. (hsp)
  01606 834492 fax 01606 834693
  email oldtimefred@supanet.com
  http://www.oldtimedance.co.uk
  Hon Sec: Fred Boast
- ▲ Un-incorporated Society
- ○ *D; to keep Old Time Dancing & its music alive; to help form new old time dance clubs
- ● Conf
- M 1,450 i, UK / 40 i, o'seas
- ¶ NL - 8; AR; both ftm only.
- × 2005 Society for the Preservation & Appreciation of Old Time Music & Dancing (Old Time Society)

Old Time Society
originally the shortened title of the Society for the Preservation & Appreciation of Old Time Music & Dancing, which in 2005 changed its name to **Old Time Dance Society**

Omnibus Society (OS) 1929
- ■ 185 Southlands Rd, BROMLEY, Kent, BR2 9QZ.
  http://www.omnibussoc.org
  Hon Sec: A J Francis
- ▲ Registered Charity
- Br 5
- ○ *G; study of passenger road transport; understanding of traffic, engineering & methods of operating buses, coaches, trolleybuses & tramcars
- Gp Photographic register; Central timetable collection; Ticket collection; Route recording schemes; Historical research
- ● Mtgs - Res - SG - Inf - Lib - VE
- M 960 i, UK / 10 i, o'seas
- ¶ The Omnibus Magazine - 6;   Members' Bulletin - 6; both ftm.

On Site Massage Association (OSMA) 1992
- ■ Avon Rd, WOTTON-UNDER-EDGE, Glos, GL12 8TT. (hq)
  01454 269269 fax 01454 261900
  email all@aosm.co.uk http://www.aosm.co.uk
  Principals: David & Helen Woodhouse
- ○ *P; 'a form of acupressure massage where the client sits on a specially designed chair, with no clothes removed or aids used. The sequence takes just 20 minutes & leaves the client feeling relaxed & alert'
- ● Conf - ET - Exhib - Work in therapy centres & offices
- < Brit Complementary Medicine Assn (BCMA); Complementary Medicine Assn (CMA); Gld Complementary Practitioners
- M 550 i
- ¶ In Touch (NL) - 4; £15 m, £20 nm.

One Parent Families Scotland (OPFS) 1944
- NR 13 Gayfield Sq, EDINBURGH, EH1 3NX. (hq)
  0131-556 3899
  http://www.opfs.org.uk
  Dir: Sue Robertson
- ▲ Registered Charity
- ○ *W; to promote & provide support, information & services for single parent families within Scotland
- ● Conf - ET - Res - Inf - Counselling - Campaigns
  Helpline: 0800 018 5026
- M c 430 i & org
- ¶ AR;   Leaflets & publications; all free.

One Voice Wales (OVW) 2004
- ■ Unit 5 Betws Business Park, Park St, AMMANFORD, Carmarthenshire, SA18 2ET. (hq)
  01269 595400 fax 01269 595400
  email admin@onevoicewales.org.uk
  http://www.onevoicewales.org.uk
  Chmn: Cllr David Street,   Chief Exec: Iwan W Richards
- ▲ Un-incorporated Society
- Br 13 area committees
- ○ *N; coordinating body for local councils in wales; to promote good government
- ● Mtgs - Inf - LG
- M 556 towns & community councils
- ¶ The Voice - 4; ftm only.
- × 2004 (National Association of Local Councils in Wales (Wales Association of Community & Town Councils

One World Linking Association (UKOWLA)
- ■ The Upper Office, The Dutch Barn, Manton, MARLBOROUGH, Wilts, SN8 1PS.
  01672 861001 fax 01672 861081
  http://www.ukowla.org.uk
- ○ *X; 'to support, promote & encourage communities in the UK to develop partnership links with communities in the South (Africa, Asia, Latin America, the Caribbean'

Online Content UK 2001
- ■ Mayfair House, 14-18 Heddon St, LONDON, W1B 4DA. (hq)
  0845 123 5717
  http://www.onlinecontentuk.org
  Dir: Elizabeth Varley
- ▲ Un-incorporated Society
- ○ *P; for UK based new media editorial professionals; to support the editorial community within the new media & technology industries
- ● Conf - Mtgs - ET - Email discussion list - Industry job & resources lists
- M 215 i, UK / 10 i, o'seas

Online User Group
is a group of **CILIP**

Onsite Communications Association (OSCA) 1963
- NR 25 Shelley Lane, HAREFIELD, Middx, UB9 6HP. (sb/p)
  01895 473551 fax 0870 831 6161
  Sec Gen: Derek Banner
- ▲ Un-incorporated Society
- ○ *T; manufacturers & suppliers of radio paging & local communications eqpt
- ● Conf - Mtgs - Exhib - Inf - LG
- M i & f

Open Spaces Society
the working title of the **Commons, Open Spaces & Footpaths Preservation Society**

Operational Research Society (ORSoc) 1948
- NR Seymour House, 12 Edward St, BIRMINGHAM, B1 2RX. (hq)
  0121-233 9300
  Admin: Helen Wilkes
- ▲ Company Limited by Guarantee; Registered Charity
- Br 1
- ○ *L; the advancement of the knowledge & applications of operational research
- ● Conf - Mtgs - ET - Res - SG - Inf - Lib - Careers inf - Publicity for OR - Grants
- M i
- ¶ Jnl - 12;   OR NL - 12;   OR Insight - 4; all ftm.
  European Jnl of Information Systems - 4; prices on application.

Ophthalmic Lens Manufacturers' & Distributors' Association (OLMADA) 1950
- ■ 199 Gloucester Terrace, LONDON, W2 6LD. (hq)
  020 7298 5123   fax 020 7298 5120
  email info@fmo.co.uk
- ▲ Company Limited by Guarantee
- ○ *T; prescription spectacles
- ● Conf - Mtgs - Exhib - Inf - LG
- < Fedn Mfrg Opticians
- M 85 f
- ¶ AR; ftm only.

Ophthalmological Products Trade & Industry Conference (OPTIC (UK)) 1984
- ■ PO Box 363, DORKING, Surrey, RH4 3XQ. (hq)
  01306 741367
  Contact: Mrs M Wright
- ○ *N
  no further information supplied

OPTIC (UK)
  see **Ophthalmological Products Trade & Industry Conference**

Optical Equipment Manufacturers' & Suppliers' Association (OEMSA) 1990
- ■ 199 Gloucester Terrace, LONDON, W2 6LD.
  020 7298 5123   fax 020 7298 5120
  email info@fmo.co.uk
  Contact: the Hon Sec
- ▲ Un-incorporated Society
- ○ *T
- ● Mtgs
- < Fedn Mfrg Opticians
- M 18 f

Optical Frame Importers' & Manufacturers' Association (OFIMA) 1983
- ■ 199 Gloucester Terrace, LONDON, W2 6LD. (hq)
  020 7405 8101   fax 020 7831 2797
  email info@fmo.co.uk
  Contact: the Hon Sec
- ○ *T; companies importing & distributing spectacle frames manufactured outside the UK
- ● Mtgs
- < Fedn Mfrg Opticians
- M 45 f
- ¶ AR; ftm only.

Optra Exhibitions UK (OEUK) 1968
- ■ 199 Gloucester Terrace, LONDON, W2 6HX. (hq)
  020 7298 5123   fax 020 7298 5120
  email info@fmo.co.uk
  Contact: the Hon Sec
- ▲ Un-incorporated Society
- ○ *T; formulating the ophthalmic optical trades policy on exhibitions
- ● Mtgs - Exhib
- < Fedn Mfrg Opticians
- M c 40 f

Oral History Society
- ■ c/o Dept of History, University of Essex, COLCHESTER, Essex, CO4 3SQ. (hq)
  email rob.perks@bl.uk   http://www.oralhistory.org.uk
  c/o British Library Sound Archive, 96 Euston Rd, LONDON, NW1 2DB.
    020 7412 7405   fax 020 7412 7441 (hsb)
  Sec: Robert Perks
- ▲ Registered Charity
- ○ *L; study & writing of history through the words of people who experienced it
- Gp Local history; Social history; Political history; Reminiscence; Care of the elderly; Archives
- ● Conf - Mtgs - Res - Inf
- M 600 i, 300 org
- ¶ Oral History - 2.

Orchid Society of Great Britain (OSGB) 1950
- ■ 16 The Rise, AMERSHAM, Bucks, HP7 9AG. (hsp)
  01494 434730
  email annerutter@dsl.pipex.com
  http://www.orchid-society-gb.org.uk
  Hon Sec: Anne Rutter
- ▲ Registered Charity
- Br 3
- ○ *H; support & encouragement in amateur orchid growing; orchid conservation
- ● Mtgs - Exhib - Comp - Inf - Lib - PL - VE - Conservation of orchids by redistribution of deceased members' plants
- < R Horticl Soc; American Orchid Soc; Barbara Everard Trust for Orchid Consvn
- M 1,011 i, 25 org, UK / 69 i, 45 org, o'seas
- ¶ Jnl - 4; ftm only.
  Orchid Cultivation Booklet; ftm, £3 nm.

Order of Malta 1174
- IRL St John's House, 32 Clyde Rd, DUBLIN 4, Republic of Ireland.
  353 (1) 614 0033   fax 353 (1) 668 5288
  email omac@orderofmalta.ie
  http://www.orderofmalta.ie
  Chancellor: Kevin Cunnane
- ○ *W

Order of Woodcraft Chivalry (OWC) 1916
- ■ 7 The Enterdent, GODSTONE, Surrey, RH9 8EG. (hsp)
  01883 744200
  Hon Sec: Vivienne Cluff
- ▲ Un-incorporated Society
- Br 3
- ○ *G; family outdoor activities as a means of character development, self-sufficiency & initiative in adults as well as children
- Gp Camping in adverse conditions for survival skills; Country dancing; Woodcraft
- ● Inf - VE
- ¶ Pine Cone (Jnl) - 4; ftm, £6 nm.

Orders & Medals Research Society (OMRS) 1942
- ■ PO Box 1904, SOUTHAM, Warks, CV47 2ZX. (hsb)
  01295 690009
  email generalsecretary@omrs.org.uk
  http://www.omrs.org.uk
  Gen Sec: P M R Helmore
- ▲ Un-incorporated Society
- Br 10; Australia, Canada, Hong Kong, New Zealand
- ○ *G; to foster an interest in orders, decorations & campaign medals; to publish the results of members' researches
- Gp Ribbon collectors; Miniature medal collectors
- ● Mtgs - Res - Lib - Annual convention
- M 1,850 i, 63 f, 39 org, UK / 753 i, 17 f, 22 org, o'seas
- ¶ Orders & Medals - 4;   LM - 2 yrly; both ftm only.

© CBD Research Ltd · Beckenham · BR3 5JS · Tel 020 8650 7745 · Fax 020 8650 0768 · E-mail cbd@cbdresearch.com · www.cbdresearch.com

Ordnance Society (OS) 1988
NR   3 Maskell Way, FARNBOROUGH, Hants, GU14 0PU.
        Membership Sec: Ian McKenzie
▲   Un-incorporated Society
○   *G; to study all aspects of the history of ordnance, artillery &
        ammunition

Orff Society UK   1964
■   7 Rothesay Ave, RICHMOND, Surrey, TW10 5EB.   (hsp)
        020 8876 1944   fax 020 8876 1944
        Hon Sec: Margaret Murray
▲   Un-incorporated Society
○   *D, *E; to promote the experience & understanding of Carl
        Orff's approach to music education; a creative way of
        teaching music to groups using voices in speech/singing,
        movement/dance & all percussion in early stages
●   Conf - ET - Exam - Inf - Lib - Workshops
<   Carl-Orff & Orff-Schulwerk associations & societies worldwide
M   135 i, 1 f, 8 universities, UK / 11 i, 2 universities,
        9 schools, o'seas
¶   Orff Times - 2; ftm only.

The Organ Club   1926
■   48 Cloudesley Mansions, Cloudesley St, LONDON, N1 0ED.
        (memsec/p)
        Mem Sec: Steve Dunk
○   *D; to promote & develop public education in organs & organ
        music; to promote study & research
●   Mtgs - Inf - Lib - PL - VE
M   500 i, UK / 60 i, o'seas
¶   Jnl - 3.   NL - 6;   AR - 1;   Hbks - irreg.

Organic Food Federation (OFF) 1986
NR   31 Turbine Way, Eco Tech Business Park, SWAFFHAM, Norfolk,
        PE37 7XD.   (hq)
        01760 720444
        http://www.organicfoodfed.com
        Exec Sec: Julian Wade
▲   Company Limited by Guarantee
○   *F, *T; for processors, producers & retailers of organic food
●   Mtgs - ET - Exhib - Stat - LG
<   UK Register of Organic Food Standards ([UKROPS] A division of
        DEFRA)
M   c 380 f

** **Organic Living Association**
        Organisation lost: see Introduction paragraph 3

Organic Organisation
        is an alternative title for the **Henry Doubleday Research
        Association**

Organisation of Horsebox & Trailer Owners
NR   Whitehill Farm, Hamstead Marshall, NEWBURY, Berks,
        RG20 0HP.   (hq)
        01488 657651
        email info@horsebox-rescue.co.uk
        Managing Dir: Jon Phillips
○   *G

Organisation for Timeshare in Europe
▲   Un-incorporated Society
        the only office for this organisation is now in Belgium, it is
        therefore outside scope of this directory

Oriental Ceramic Society (OCS) 1921
■   PO Box 517, CAMBRIDGE, CB1 0BF.   (hq)
        01223 881328   fax 01223 881328
        email ocslondon@btinternet.com
        http://www.ocs-london.com
        The Society of Antiquaries, Burlington House, LONDON,
        W1J 0BF.   (regd/office)
        Admin: Mrs Mary Painter
▲   Company Limited by Guarantee; Registered Charity
○   *A, *G; to increase the knowledge & appreciation of ceramics
        & all the arts of Asia; to provide a link between collectors,
        curators, scholars & others with like interests
●   Conf - Mtgs - Res - Exhib - SG - VE
M   440 i, UK / 500 i, o'seas, & Libraries, museums & other
        ceramic societies
¶   Transactions - 1; ftm only.
        [subscription, £55 (home), £50 (o'seas), £100 (corporate),
        £25 (under-25 & curators)].

Original Pearly King's & Queen's Association   (OPKA) 1975
§   c/o St Martin's in the Field, Trafalgar Square, LONDON,
        WC2N 4JJ.
○   *G; charity fund workers - spare time

Orkney Chamber of Commerce
NR   PO Box 6202, Hatston Industrial Estate, KIRKWALL, Orkney,
        KW15 1YG.
○   *C
        No further information supplied

Ornamental Aquatic Trade Association (OATA) 1991
NR   Wessex House (1st floor office suite), 40 Station Rd, WESTBURY,
        Wilts, BA13 3TN.   (hq)
        0870 043 4013
        Sec: Keith Davenport
▲   Company Limited by Guarantee
○   *T; for the ornamental fish industry
●   ET - Stat - Inf
M   c 700 f
¶   The Voice (NL) - 4;   OATA Worldwide NL - 12;
        LM - 1; all ftm only.   Handbooks.
        Publications list available.

**Ornamental Pool & Fountain Constructors & Maintainers
Association (OPFCA) 1981**
■   Kingsway House, Wrotham Road, MEOPHAM, Kent,
        DA13 0AV.   (hsp)
▲   Un-incorporated Society
○   *T
●   Conf - Mtgs - Inf - VE
M   1 i, 11 f.

Ornithological Society of the Middle East (OSME) 1967
■   c/o The Lodge, SANDY, Beds, SG19 2DL.   (mail/address)
        01636 703512   fax 01442 822623
        email secretary@osme.org   http://www.osme.org
        Sec: John Bartlet,   Chmn: Keith Betton
▲   Registered Charity
○   *G; recording, conservation study of wild birds in the Middle
        East
●   Conf - ET - Res - SG - Lib - LG
M   429 i, 3 f, 68 org, UK / 325 i, o'seas
¶   Sandgrouse - 2; ftm, £5 nm.

Orthodontic Technicians Association   (OTA)   1971
- Maxillofacial & Orthodontic Laboratory, Royal Lancaster Infirmary, Ashton Rd, LANCASTER, LA1 4RP.   (hsb)
  01524 583410   fax 01524 583719
  email paul.mallett@mbht.nhs.uk
  http://www.orthota.co.uk
  Hon Sec: Paul A Mallett
- ▲ Un-incorporated Society
- ○ *P; to encourage the study, improve the practice & advance the knowledge of the science of orthodontic laboratory techniques
- Gp Education sub-c'ee
- ● Conf - Mtgs - ET - Exhib - Comp - Inf - PL - Empl - LG
- < Brit Orthodontic Soc (BOS)
- M 250 i, UK / 5 i, 3 f, o'seas
- ¶ NL - 4;   Proceedings - 1; both ftm only.

Oscar Wilde Society   (OWS)   1992
- NR 100 Peacock St, GRAVESEND, Kent, DA12 1EQ.   (hsp)
  01474 535978
  Hon Sec: Vanessa Harris
- ▲ Un-incorporated Society
- ○ *A; to further interest in & knowledge of, the life & works of Oscar Wilde
- ● Conf - Mtgs - ET - Res - Exhib - Comp - Inf - VE - Lib
- < Alliance of Literary Socs
- M 210 i, UK / 75 i, o'seas
- ¶ The Wildean (Jnl) - 2; ftm, £6 nm.
  Intentions (NL) - 5; ftm only.

Osteopathic Sports Care Association   (OSCA)   1995
- NR PO Box 6236, LEIGHTON BUZZARD, Beds, LU7 3YH.   (mail)
  0791 712 5923
  email osca.org.uk address
  Hon Sec: Helen White
- ▲ Un-incorporated Society
- ○ *M; osteopathic education, promotion & sports care
- Gp Sub-c'ees: Conferences, Periodical, Post graduate education
- ● Conf - Mtgs - ET - Res - Inf - VE
- < in partnership with Nat Sports Medicine Inst
- M c 250 i
- ¶ Still Improving Sport - 4.

Outdoor Advertising Association of Great Britain Ltd   (OAA) 1982
- Summit House, 27 Sale Place, LONDON, W2 1YR.   (hq)
  020 7973 0315   fax 020 7973 0318
  email enquiries@oaa.org.uk   http://www.oaa.org.uk
  Chief Exec: Alan James
- ○ *T; for UK poster contractors
- M f
  No further information supplied

Outdoor Advertising Council
- Collingwood, 2 Bell Barn Rd, Stoke Bishop, BRISTOL, BS9 2DA.   (hsp)
  0117-904 7235   fax 0117-904 7236
  Sec: Chris Thomas
- ▲ Un-incorporated Society
- ○ *N
- ● Conf - Mtgs - ET - LG
- M c 300 f

Outdoor Industries Association
  see **Go Outdoors - Outdoor Industries Association**

Outdoor Media Association
- IRL 3 Waverly Church Road, GREYSTONES, Co Wicklow, Republic of Ireland.
  353 (1) 201 6760
  Dir: Su Duff

Outdoor Writers' Guild   (OWG)   1980
- NR PO Box 118, TWICKENHAM, Middx, TW1 2XB.   (hsp)
  020 8538 9468
  email info@owg.org.uk   http://www.owg.org.uk
  Hon Sec: Hazelle Jackson
- ▲ Un-incorporated Society
- ○ *P; to promote a high professional standard among writers who specialise in outdoor activities; to provide a forum for members to meet, includes writers, photographers, illustrators, broadcasters
- ● ET - VE - Awards to members - Press trips
- M 200 i, UK / 5 i, o'seas
- ¶ Bootprint - 4;   Electronic Media Bulletin - 6; both ftm only.

Ovacome   1996
- Elizabeth Garrett Anderson Hospital, Huntley St, LONDON, WC1A 2DH.   (hq)
  020 7380 9589
  Dir: Louise Bayne
- ▲ Registered Charity
- ○ *W; a nationwide support group for those concerned with ovarian cancer: sufferers, families, carers & health professionals
- Gp Fone friends network
- ● Support & fund-raising events
- M 1,700 i, 100 hospitals, care professionals
- ¶ NL - 4;   AR; both free.

Over Fifties Association   (TOFFS)   1990
- NR 29 Hill Court, The Ridings, LONDON, W5 3DF.   (hq)
  020 8998 2065
  Chmn: Eric Bellenie
- ▲ Un-incorporated Society
- ○ *K; to abolish age discrimination; to establish training centres; to encourage cooperative commercial ventures
- ● ET - Res - Stat - Inf - LG
- M c 10,000 i, 50 f
- ¶ Toffs (Jnl/NL) - 4; ftm.

Overeaters Anonymous   (OA)   1960
- PO Box 19, Stretford, MANCHESTER, M32 9EB.   (mail)
  0700 078 4985
  http://www.oagb.org address
- Br 200; worldwide
- ○ *W; to help compulsive eaters & people with eating disorders to recover using the 12 steps adopted from Alcoholics Anonymous
- ● Conf - Mtgs
- M i [unknown]
- ¶ Lifeline - 12.

Overseas Press & Media Association   (OPMA)   1965
- NR 15 Magrath St, CAMBRIDGE, CB4 3AH.   (asa)
  01223 512631
  Hon Sec: Ramesh Rajakrishnen
- ▲ Company Limited by Guarantee
- ○ *T; to promote the interests of advertising representatives of media from overseas
- ● Mtgs - ET
- M c 150 f
- ¶ Overseas Press & Media Guide - 1.

Overseas Territories Association
  see **United Kingdom Overseas Territories Association**

Owner Drivers Society   (ODS)   1948
- NR 21 Buckingham Palace Rd, LONDON, SW1W 0PN.   (hq)
  020 7834 6541   fax 020 7931 0822
  Sec: T Owen
- ▲ Un-incorporated Society
- ○ *T; taxi drivers' representatives
- ● LG
- < Nat Taxi Assn
- M 1,800 i

Oxford Down Sheep Breeders Association   (ODSBA)   1889
■ Bishop's Gorse, Lighthorne, WARWICK, CV35 0BB.   (hsp)
   01926 651273
   email john.brigg@virgin.net
   http://www.oxforddownsheep.org.uk
   Sec: John S Brigg
▲ Company Limited by Guarantee; Registered Charity
○ *B
● Mtgs - Exhib - Comp - Stat - Inf
< Nat Sheep Assn
M 70 i, 2 f, UK / 1 i, o'seas
¶ Flock Book - 1; £7.
   The Oxford Down - One Hundred Years of Breeding; £5.

Oxford Sandy & Black Pig Society   (OSB)   1985
NR Tadneys Farm, Fox Lane, Kempsey, WORCESTER, WR5 3QD.
   (hsp)
   01926 650150   fax ronaldannetts@aol.com
   Hon Sec: Ron Annetts
○ *B; to promote one of the oldest British pig breeds
● Mtgs - Exhib - Comp - Inf - Agricultural shows
M c 100 i
¶ NL - 6/8; free.   Herdbook - 1; ftm.

Oxford University Archaeological Society   (OUAS)   1911
■ Institute of Archaeology, Beaumont St, OXFORD, OX1 2PG.
   (mail)
   email archsoc@herald.ox.ac.uk
   http://www.geocities.com/ouarchsoc address
   Sec: 'office only held for one academic term'
▲ Un-incorporated Society
○ *L; investigation of local antiquities
Gp Excavations; Roman / Anglo-Saxon / Mediaeval archaeology
● Conf - Mtgs - Res - VE - Excavations
< Oxfordshire Architectural & Histl Soc
M 150 i

Oxfordshire Architectural & Historical Society   (OAHS)   1839
■ 53 Radley Rd, ABINGDON, Oxon, OX14 3PN.   (hsb)
   01235 525960   fax 0871 433 5058
   email tony@oahs.org.uk   http://www.oahs.org.uk
   Sec: Dr A J Dodd
▲ Registered Charity
○ *L; study of local history, archaeology & architecture
Gp Victorian; Listed buildings c'ee; Oxford City & County
   Archaeological Forum
● Mtgs - Lib - VE
< Coun Brit Archaeology
M 600 i, 150 org, UK / 10 i, 10 org, o'seas
¶ Oxoniensia (Jnl) - 1; ftm, £12 nm.

Oxfordshire Record Society   (ORS)   1919
NR Bodleian Library, OXFORD, OX1 3BG.   (mail) add
▲ Registered Charity
○ *L; to publish edited texts of local history documents relating to
   Oxfordshire

P G Wodehouse Society (UK) 1995
NR 26 Radcliffe Rd, CROYDON, Surrey, CR0 5QE.   (mem/sp)
   http://www.eclipse.co.uk/wodehouse
   Mem Sec: Christine Hewitt
▲ Un-incorporated Society
○ *A; to promulgate the enjoyment of the writings of
   P G Wodehouse (1881-1975)
● Mtgs - VE
< Other Wodehouse societies in Belgium, India, Netherlands,
   Russia, Sweden & USA
M 500 i, UK / 100 i, o'seas
¶ Wooster Sauce - 4; ftm only.

PACE: Professional Association for Catering Education   (PACE)
2003
■ Thomas Danby College, Roundhay Rd, LEEDS, W Yorks,
   LS7 3BG.   (sb)
   0113-284 6408   fax 0113-240 1967
   email jim.armstrong@thomasdanby.co.uk
   http://www.keepinpace.org.uk
   Chief Exec: Jim Armstrong
▲ Company Limited by Guarantee
Br 6 regional
○ *N, *P; to encourage catering educational institutions to work
   together to manage the challenges of continual change
   within hospitality & catering education
● Conf - Mtgs - ET - Res - Exhib - Comp - Inf - LG
M c 500 i, f & org
   Note: PACE is the trading name of Keep in Pace Ltd
× 2003 National Association for Heads of Hospitality Education

Pacific Islands Society of the United Kingdom & Ireland
(PISUKI) 1981
NR The Great House, Llandewi, RHYDDERCH, Monmouthshire,
   NP7 9UY.   (chmn/p)
   Chmn: Michael Walsh
▲ Un-incorporated Society
○ *X; for Pacific Islanders in the UK & Ireland & to bring together
   all those interested in, or concerned with, the islands
● Conf - Mtgs - Inf - Social activities especially for islanders
   temporarily in UK
M c 300 i & f, 16 org
¶ The Outrigger (NL) - 3/4; ftm.

Packaging Federation (PF) 1995
■ Vigilant House, 120 Wilton Rd, LONDON, SW1V 1JZ.
   (regd/office)
   020 7808 7217   fax 020 7808 7218
   email iandent@packagingfedn.co.uk
   Chief Exec: Ian Dent
▲ Company Limited by Guarantee
○ *T; to represent members, who are the major packaging firms,
   on economic & environmental issues
● Mtgs - LG
M f

Packaging & Industrial Films Association (PIFA) 1973
■ 2 Mayfair Court, North Gate, New Basford, NOTTINGHAM,
   NG7 7GR.   (hq)
   0115-942 2445   fax 015-942 2650
   email pifa@pifa.co.uk   http://www.pifa.co.uk
   Chief Exec: David Tyson
▲ Company Limited by Guarantee
○ *T; producers & distributors of plastic packaging & industrial
   films
● Mtgs - ET - Stat - LG
< Plast Euro Film; Brit Plastics Fedn; Packaging Fedn
M 55 f, UK / 4 f, o'seas
¶ PIFA Annual review - 1; ftm, £25 nm.
   PIFA Annual Statistical Report - 1; £25 m, £50 nm.

Paddle Steamer Preservation Society   (PSPS) 1959
■ PO Box 365, WORCESTER, WR3 7WH.   (asa)
   Hon Sec: John Anderson
▲ Company Limited by Guarantee; Registered Charity
Br 5
○ *G, *K; to encourage interest in paddle steamers; retention of
   existing services & preservation of the society's own steamers
Gp Models
● Conf - Mtgs - Res - Exhib - VE - Special cruises
< Transport Trust
M 3,400 i, UK / 100 i, o'seas
¶ Paddle Wheels - 4; ftm.

Pagan Federation   (PF) 1971
NR BM 7097, LONDON, WC1N 3XX.   (mail)
   0798 603 4378 address
   Contact: Lindsey J Heffern
▲ Un-incorporated Society
Br 13 districts, UK; 1 district, o'seas
○ *G; to provide information on the pagan religions; to fight
   discrimination & enable Pagans to follow their chosen
   spiritual paths
● Conf - Mtgs - ET - Inf - VE - LG
M c 4,000 i, UK / 200 i, o'seas
¶ Pagan Dawn - 4;   AR; ftm.
   Various information packs.

Paget Gorman Society
■ 43 Westover Rd, FLEET, Hants, GU51 3DB.   (hq)
   01252 621183
   email contact.pgs@ntlworld.com   http://www.pgss.org
   Admin Sec: Mike Simpson
▲ Registered Charity
○ *W; to support the use of Paget Gorman signed speech by
   speech therapists in schools, special schools, special units &
   hospital units
● Conf - Mtgs - ET - Exam - Res - Awarding of qualifications
M 1,000 i, UK / 100 i, o'seas
¶ NL - 1; free.

Pain Society (the British Chapter of IASP)
   since 2004 **British Pain Society**

Paint & Powder Finishing Association
   is a group of the **Surface Engineering Association**

Paint Research Association   (PRA) 1926
NR 14 Castle Mews, High St, HAMPTON, Middx, TW12 2NP.   (hq)
   020 8487 0800   fax 020 8487 0805
   http://www.pra-org.uk
   Managing Dir: Jonathan Bourne
▲ Company Limited by Guarantee
○ *Q; research, technology & information services for the
   coatings & related industries
● Conf - Mtgs - ET - Res - Exhib - Stat - Inf - Lib
< Assn Indep Res & Technology Orgs
M 100 f, UK / 75 f, o'seas

Painting & Decorating Association 2002
■ 32 Coton Rd, NUNEATON, Warks, CV11 5TW.   (hq)
   024 7635 3776   fax 024 7635 4513
   http://www.paintingdecoratingassociation.co.uk
▲ Un-incorporated Society
○ *T; for professional painters & decorators in GB
● Conf - Mtgs - ET - Exhib - Comp - LG
M 2,400 f
× 2002 (British Decorators Association
         (Painting & Decorating Federation

Palaeontographical Society   1847
NR   Dept of Palaeontology, Natural History Museum, Cromwell Rd,
       LONDON, SW7 5BD.   (hsb)
       020 7942 5195   fax 020 7942 5546
       email p.ensom@nhm.ac.uk
       Sec: Dr S Long
▲   Registered Charity
○   *L, *Q; promotion of study of geology through publications
       figuring & describing British fossils
●   Publication
M   144 i, 145 org
¶   Monographs - 1.

Palaeontological Association   1957
■   Dept of Earth Sciences, University of Durham, Science Site,
       DURHAM, DH1 3LE.   (hsb)
       0191-334 2320   fax 0191-334 2301
       email h.a.armstrong@durham.ac.uk
       http://www.palass.org
       Sec: Dr H A Armstrong
▲   Registered Charity
○   *L, *Q; to study palaeontology (life of the past) & its allied
       sciences
●   Conf - Mtgs - Res - Inf - PL
M   c 1,200 i, c 700 f, UK / c 500 i, o'seas
¶   Palaeontology - 6; £28 yr m, £55 per part nm.

Pali Text Society   (PTS)   1881
NR   c/o Gazette, White Cross Mills, Hightown, LANCASTER,
       LA1 4XS.   (hq)
       01524 528530   fax 01524 63232
       email pts@palitext.com   http://www.palitext.com
       Pres: Dr R M L Gethin
▲   Registered Charity
○   *L, *Q, *R; promoting the study of Pali by publishing Pali texts in
       Roman characters, translations & ancillary work; funding
       research students
●   Res - Inf - Lib - Publishing
M   c 570 i
¶   Jnl - irreg.   List of Issues; free.
       NL - 2;   AR; both ftm only.

Palmerston Forts Society   (PFS)   1984
NR   Fort Nelson, Portsdown Hill Rd, FAREHAM, Hants,
       PO17 6AN.   (hq)
       023 9266 0261 (0900-1700 hrs)   (chmn/b)
       Chmn: Geoffrey M Salvetti
▲   Registered Charity; Un-incorporated Society
○   *G, *L; a forum for research into the field of Victorian
       fortification & artillery; to offer advice to government & local
       authorities on Victorian fortifications
Gp   Portsdown artillery volunteers
●   Conf - Mtgs - ET - Res - Exhib - SG - Inf - Lib - PL - Artillery re-
       enactment (authentic Victorian gun drills on period pieces)
M   i

Pancreatic Society of GB & Ireland
NR   c/o Mr Ross Carter, West of Scotland Pancreatic Unit, Glasgow
       Royal Infirmary, Alexandra Parade, GLASGOW, G31 2ER.
       (sb)
       0141-211 5129
       Sec: Ross Carter
▲   Registered Charity
○   *L
●   Conf - ET - Res - SG
M   180 i, UK / 20 i, o'seas

Paper Agents Association   (PAA)   1924
■   Imp House, 64 Dinorben Ave, FLEET, Hants, GU52 7SH.   (sp)
       01252 680449   fax 0709 238 6132
       email info@paa.org.k   http://www.paa.org.uk
       Sec: John R Paine
▲   Un-incorporated Society
○   *T; to promote a better & closer understanding among
       accredited agents & mill owned sales offices in the UK & Eire
       representing overseas paper & board makers; to represent
       legitimate overall best interests in the local market
Gp   Publications & fine papers; Corrugated case materials;
       Packaging, industrial & other papers; Carton boards,
       industrial & other boards
●   Mtgs - Stat - LG
<   Confedn Paper Inds
M   39 f

Paper Federation of Great Britain Ltd
       since 2004 the Papermaking group of the **Confederation of Paper
       Industries**

Paper Industry Technical Association Ltd   (PITA)   1920
■   5 Frecheville Court, BURY, Lancs, BL9 0UF.   (hq)
       0161-764 5858   fax 0161-764 5353
       email info@pita.co.uk   http://www.pita.co.uk
       Exec Dir: John Clewley
▲   Company Limited by Guarantee; Registered Charity
○   *P; for all involved in the pulp, paper, converting & allied
       industries
Gp   Environmental; Engineering; Papermaking; Raw materials;
       Coating; Finishing
●   Conf - Mtgs - ET - SG - Inf - VE
M   1.097 i, 138 f, UK / 150 i, o'seas
¶   Paper Technology - 12; ftm, £100 yr nm.
       PITA Ybk - 1; ftm only.
       The Essential Guide to Aqueous Coating of Paper & Board
       (textbook); £75 m, £85 nm.

Paper Makers' Allied Trades Association   (PMATA)   1931
■   24 Beatrice Rd, Worsley, MANCHESTER, M28 2TN.   (hsp)
       0161-794 5734   fax 0161-793 0827
       Hon Sec: D G McNay
▲   Un-incorporated Society
○   *T; fostering good relations between the paper industry & its
       suppliers
●   Golf competitions - Annual dinners
M   200 i, 78 f

Paperweight Collectors Circle   1981
NR   PO Box 941, Comberton, CAMBRIDGE, CB3 7GQ.
       http://www.kevh.clara.net/index.htm
▲   Un-incorporated Society
○   *G; for collectors of paperweights
●   Mtgs - Exhib
M   200 i, UK / 30 i, o'seas
¶   NL - 4; m only.
×   2003-04 Cambridge Paperweight Circle

Parallel Traders Association
NR   c/o Clintons, 55 Drury Lane, LONDON, WC2B 5SQ.
       020 7379 6080
       Contact: Gary Lux
○   *T

Parapet & Safety Fence Manufacturers Association
       since 2003-04 **Vehicle Restraint Manufacturers Association**

Parenteral Society
       since March 2006 **Pharmaceutical & Healthcare Sciences
       Society**

Parents against Oral Contraception for Children   1996
- 208 Allerton Rd, Allerton, BRADFORD, W Yorks, BD15 7AA. (hsp)
  01274 499328
  email paocfc@aol.com   http://www.hometown.aol.com/paocfc/paocfc.html
  Hon Sec: Mrs Jenny Bacon
- ▲ Un-incorporated Society
- ○ *K; to make parents aware that their children can obtain oral contraceptives without their permission; to raise awareness of the dangers of giving oral contraceptives to children & minors without consulting their parents
- ● Campaigning - ET - Inf
- < Human Life Intl; Life; Family & Youth Concern; Parents Network; Soc Protection Unborn Child
- M c 11,500 i (sympathisers)

Parents at Work
in 2004 merged with New Ways to Work to form **Working Families**

Parity   1986
- Constables, Windsor Rd, ASCOT, Berks, SL5 7LF.   (hsp)
  01344 621167
  Hon Sec: David Yarwood
- ▲ Registered Charity
- ○ *K; to promote & protect the equal rights of men & women to the enjoyment of all civil, political, economic, social & cultural rights under the law
- Gp Human rights; Legal; Parliamentary; Pensions; Research
- ● Mtgs - Res - Inf - Identifying & monitoring unequal treatment of men & women under law - Promoting legal activities
- M c 300 i, 2 trade unions, UK / c 5 i, o'seas
- ¶ NL - 4.   Information sheets - irreg.

Parking Enforcement Agency
see**UK Parking Enforcement Agency**

Parkinson's Disease Society of the United Kingdom   (PDS)   1969
- 215 Vauxhall Bridge Rd, LONDON, SW1V 1EJ.   (hq)
  020 7931 8080
  Chief Exec: Linda Kelly
- ▲ Company Limited by Guarantee; Registered Charity
- Br 250
- ○ *W; welfare, research, education of the public & help to patients & their relatives
- Gp YAPPERS: Young Alert Parkinsonians, Partners & Relatives (a support group)
- ● Conf - Mtgs - ET - Res - Stat - Inf - Lib - PL
- < Eur Parkinson's Disease Soc (EPDA)
- M 27,000 i

Parrot Society UK   1967
- 92a High St, BERKHAMSTED, Herts, HP4 2BL.   (hq)
  01442 872245   fax 01442 872245
  email les.rance@theparrotsocietyuk.org
  http://www.theparrotsocietyuk.org
  Sec: Les A Rance
- ▲ Registered Charity
- ○ *B, *G; to promote the breeding & keeping of all parrot-like birds
- ● Conf - Mtgs - Exhib - Inf - VE - LG
- < Soc for the Protection of Aviculture
- M 4,777 i, UK / 171 i, o'seas
- ¶ The Magazine of the Parrot Society UK - 12; £16 yr m only.

Parson Woodforde Society   1968
- 22 Gaynor Close, WYMONDHAM, Norfolk, NR18 0EA.   (hsp)
  email mabrayne@supanet.com
  http://www.parsonwoodforde.co.uk
  Mem Sec: Mrs A Elliott
- ▲ Registered Charity
- ○ *A; to extend & develop the knowledge of the life of the eighteenth century diarist James Woodforde (1740-1803) & of the society in which he lived
- ● Mtgs - Res
- < Alliance of Literary Societies
- M 390 i, UK / 10 i, o'seas
- ¶ Jnl - 4;   NL - 4; both ftm only.
  [15 volumes of diary material]; £20-£25 (available from the President).

Partially Sighted Society   (PSS)   1973
- NR PO Box 322, DONCASTER, S Yorks, DN1 2XA.   (hq)
  01302 323132
  email info@partsight.org.uk
  Sec: Norman Stenson
- ▲ Company Limited by Guarantee
- Br 10
- ○ *W; to help visually impaired people to make the best use of remaining sight; to raise public awareness of the problems associated with visual impairment
- ● Inf - Supply of aids & equipment to help in daily living
- M i, f & clubs
- ¶ Oculus - 4.   AR.

Passenger Shipping Association   (PSA/PSARA)   1958
- Walmar House (4th floor), 288-292 Regent St, LONDON, W1B 3AL.   (hq)
  020 7436 2449   fax 020 7636 9206
  email admin@psa-psara.org
  http://www.psa-psara.org
  Dir: William Gibbons
- ▲ Company Limited by Guarantee
- ○ *T; for cruise lines & ferry operators
- Gp Passenger Shipping Association Retail Agents Scheme (PSARA): training & education for travel agents
- ● Mtgs - ET - Inf - VE
- M [not stated]
- ¶ Get Cruisewise - 4; free to PSARA m only.

Passive Fire Protection Federation   (PFPF)   1995
- 99 West St, FARNHAM, Surrey, GU9 7EN.   (asa)
  01252 739152   fax 01252 739140
  email info@associationhouse.org.uk
  http://www.associationhouse.org.uk
  Sec: John G Fairley
- ○ *T
- M 21 f
- × 2002-03 Passive Fire Protection Association

Pastel Society
a member organisation of the **Federation of British Artists**

Pathological Society of Great Britain & Ireland   1906
- NR 2 Carlton House Terrace, LONDON, SW1Y 5AF.   (sb)
  020 7976 1260
  Pres: Prof N A Wright,   Admin: Mrs R A Pitts
- ○ *L; advance study of pathology & facilitate communication between pathologists
- ● Conf
- M c 1,200 i
- ¶ Jnl of Pathology - 12.

© CBD Research Ltd · Beckenham · BR3 5JS · Tel 020 8650 7745 · Fax 020 8650 0768 · E-mail cbd@cbdresearch.com · www.cbdresearch.com

Patient Information Forum   (PiF)   1997
■ Handel House, 13 Park Rd, MANCHESTER, M8 4HT. M8 4HT.
   (chmn/p)
   07985 639887
   email secretary@pifonline.org.uk
   http://www.pifonline.org.uk
   Chmn: Mark Duman
▲ Un-incorporated Society
Br 10
○ *M, *N; for those producing, developing, disseminating &
   researching high quality information for patients, carers, their
   families & others
● Conf - Mtgs - ET - Res - Inf - LG - Quality, appraisal,
   accreditation - Consulting
M 305 i, UK / 2 i, o'seas
¶ [subscription, £50 yr].
✕ 2005 (December) Consumer Health Information Consortium
   (merged)

Patients Association   1963
§ PO Box 935, HARROW, Middx, HA1 3YJ.   (hq)
   020 8423 9111   fax 020 8423 9119
   email mailbox@patients-association.com
   http://www.patients-association.com
● Helpline: 0845 608 4455
   Advice service & collective voice for patients to promote
   goodwill between patients & the medical service

Patients' Voice for Medical Advance
NR PO Box 504, DUNSTABLE, Beds, LU6 2LU.
   01582 873108
   http://www.patientsvoice.org.uk
○ *K; 'a patients' group which supports the humane use of
   animals & genetic technology, where necessary, in medical
   research'
✕ 2005 Seriously Ill for Medical Research

Pattern, Model, & Mould Manufacturers Association
   (PMMMA)   1954
NR National Metalforming Centre, 47 Birmingham Rd,
   WEST BROMWICH, W Midlands, B70 6PY.   (hq)
   0121-601 6976
   Sec: Andrew Turner
▲ Un-incorporated Society
○ *T
Gp Mould makers; Pattern makers
● Mtgs - Exhib - Inf - LG
< Wld Foundrymen Org; Inst Cast Metals Engrs
M 40 i & f
¶ Patternmaking News - 4.

Patton Historical Society   1985
■ Clatterwick House, Little Leigh, NORTHWICH, Cheshire,
   CW8 4RJ.
   01606 891303 & 781731 (evgs)   (hsp)
   Hon Sec: Kenneth N Oultram
○ *L; to commemorate the life & times of US General George S
   Patton who was based in Cheshire in World War II
✕ 2000-02 British Patton Historical Society

Payroll Alliance   1985
NR Tolley House, 2 Addiscombe Rd, CROYDON, Surrey,
   CR9 5AF.   (hq)
   020 8401 1828
   Commercial Mgr: Coral Lewis
○ *P; to enhance the professionalism of payroll staff
M f
¶ Payroll Managers Magazine - 12.   Hbk - 1.

Peace Pledge Union   (PPU)   1934
NR 1 Peace Passage, LONDON, N7 0BT.   (hq)
   020 7424 9444
   Admin: Annie Bebington
▲ Un-incorporated Society
○ *K; promotion of pacifism & nonviolent solution to
   international, national & local conflict

Peak District Mines Historical Society Ltd   (PDMHS)   1959
■ Peak District Mining Museum, The Pavilion, South Parade,
   Matlock Bath, MATLOCK, Derbys, DE4 3NR.   (regd)
   01629 583834
   email mail@peakmines.co.uk   http://www.pdmhs.com +
   peakmines.com office
   Hon Sec: Nigel Nix
▲ Company Limited by Guarantee; Registered Charity
○ *L; to promote, encourage & further the study of & research
   into the mines & mineralogy of the Peak district & adjacent
   areas in England; to catalogue, collect, collate, publish & sell
   material & inforamtion & service, or interest to the members
   & general public
Gp Mining museum; Archaeology & conservation
● Mtgs - Res - Exhib - Inf - Lib - VE - Preservation of artifacts -
   Peak District Mining Museum
< Nat Assn of Mining Hist Orgs (NAMHO)
M 450 i, 10 org, UK / 12, o'seas
¶ Mining History (Jnl) - 2; ftm, £8 nm.   NL - 4; ftm only.

Peak & Northern Footpaths Society   (PNFS)   1894
■ Taylor House, 23 Turncroft Lane, Offerton, STOCKPORT,
   Cheshire, SK1 4AB.   (hq)
   0161 480 3565   fax 0161 429 7279
   email mail@peakandnorthern.org.uk
   http://www.peakandnorthern.org.uk
   Chmn: David Bratt
▲ Registered Charity
○ *K; preservation, maintenance & defence of public rights of
   way, commons & open spaces in the Northern & Midland
   counties of England
● Conf - Mtgs - Inf - LG
< Brit Trust for Consvn Volunteers (BTCV); Open Spaces Soc;
   Ramblers Assn; NW Coun for Sport; Byways & Bridleways
   Trust
M c 1,000 i, 80 org
¶ Signpost - 4; ftm.   AR; ftm, £2 nm.

Peat Producers Association
   since 2002 **Growing Media Association**

Pedestrians' Association
   see **Living Streets (the Pedestrians Association)**

Peel Society
NR 2 Sunningdale, TAMWORTH, Staffs, B77 4NW.
   http://www.thepeelsociety.org.uk
○ *G; Sir Robert Peel (1788-1850), founder of the Metropolitan
   Police; hence the names 'Bobbies' & 'Peelers'

Pembrokeshire Agricultural Society   (PAS)   1784
■ Show Office, County Showground, Withybush,
   HAVERFORDWEST, Pembrokeshire, SA62 4BP.   (hq)
   01437 764331   fax 01437 767203
   Gen Mgr: Malcolm Crossman
▲ Registered Charity
○ *F, *H; agricultural show
● Conf - Mtgs - Exhib
M i

Pembrokeshire Chamber of Commerce   1990
NR   Portcullis House, Old Hakin Rd, HAVERFORDWEST,
       Pembrokeshire, SA61 1XE.   (hq)
       01437 779914
       Contact: Helen Scourfield
▲   Un-incorporated Society
○   *C
Gp   various sub-c'ees
●   Conf - Mtgs - ET - Res - Exhib - SG - Expt - Inf - VE - LG - Web
       sites/pages for members
<   Brit & Eur Cham Comm; Cham Wales
M   c 100 f

Pembrokeshire Historical Society   (PHS)   1983
■   Dolau, Dwrbach, FISHGUARD, Pembrokeshire, SA65 9RN.
       (hsp)
       01348 873316
       Sec: Mrs Anne Eastham
▲   Un-incorporated Society
○   *L, *Q; to promote interest in & research into subjects of
       historical, archaeological, artistic, genealogical &
       architectural importance in the heritage of Pembrokeshire
●   Conf - Mtgs - VE
>   Pembrokeshire Family History Soc; Pembrokeshire local history
       societies
M   250 i
¶   PHS Jnl - 1; £5 m, £6 nm.

Penguin Collectors' Society   (PCS)   1974
NR   31 Myddelton Sq, LONDON, EC1R 1YB.   (hsp)
       020 7278 8064
       Sec/Treas: Michael Fowle
▲   Company Limited by Guarantee
Br   Australia, Canada, USA etc
○   *G; to encourage the study, research & collection of Penguin
       books; to publish relevant material
●   Conf - Res - Publication
M   350 i, UK / 50 i, o'seas
¶   The Penguin Collector - 2.
       List of publications available on request.

Pensioners' Voice
       the 'shorter' name for the **National Federation of Retirement
       Pensions Associations**

Pensions Action Group
NR   36 Seaside Avenue, Minster on Sea, SHEERNESS, Kent,
       ME12 2NN.
       01795 875835
       Andrew Parr

Pensions Management Institute   (PMI)   1976
■   PMI House, 4/10 Artillery Lane, LONDON, E1 7LS.   (hq)
       020 7247 1452   fax 020 7375 0603
       http://www.pensions-pmi.org.uk
       Chief Exec: Roger Booth
▲   Company Limited by Guarantee
Br   10
○   *P
●   Conf - Exam - Exhib - VE
M   4,431 i, UK / 200 i, o'seas
¶   PMI News - 12;   PMI Technical News - 4;
       PMI Trustee Group News - 6; all ftm only.

People & Dogs Society   (PADS)   1988
■   45B Ashgap Lane, NORMANTON, W Yorks, WF6 2DT.   (hsp)
       01924 897732   fax 01977 677968
       email pads@btinternet.com   http://www.padsonline.org
       Hon Sec: Mrs K Le Seelleur
▲   Registered Charity
○   *V; to encourage high standards of dog ownership; to help
       people with problem dogs or dog-related problems
●   ET - Exhib - Comp - Inf - Dog shows - Confidential advice line
<   Telephone Helplines Assn (associate mem)
M   [not stated]
¶   Pawprints - 3; m only.
       Code of Caring (leaflets on dog care);   Factsheets; both free.

PEP & ISA Managers' Association   (PIMA)   1998
NR   Cleveland Business Centre, 1 Watson St, MIDDLESBROUGH,
       N Yorks, TS1 2RQ.   (hq)
       01642 207202
       Dir Gen: Tony Vine-Lott
▲   Company Limited by Guarantee
○   *P; to encourage consultation on existing & future regulations
       with government, HM Treasury, Inland Revenue, statutory
       regulating authorities & other relevant organisations
●   Conf - Mtgs - ET - Res - Stat - Inf - LG
M   c 115 f
¶   Pimatters (NL) - 4; free.

PERA   1946
NR   Pera Innovation Park, MELTON MOWBRAY, Leics, LE13 0PB.
       (hq)
       01664 501501
       http://www.peta.com
       Chief Exec: Dr Peter Davies
▲   Company Limited by Guarantee
○   *Q; to promote innovation & productivity within technology &
       manufacturing led organisations through the application of
       current & future thinking & technology transfer practices
M   c 500 f
¶   Pera Abstracts - 5;   Technical Reports - irreg; both ftm only.

Percussive Arts Society   (PAS)
NR   25 Copperfield Rd, Cheadle Hulme, CHEADLE, Cheshire,
       SK8 7PN.   (msp)
       0161-439 5757
       Mem Sec: Ron Baker
○   *D, *P; for teachers, instructors & players of percussive
       instruments
●   ET - Inf
<   Percussive Arts Soc (USA)
M   i
¶   Percussive Notes - 4; ftm.

Percy Grainger Society   (PGS)   1978
■   6 Fairfax Crescent, AYLESBURY, Bucks, HP20 2ES.   (hsp)
       01296 428609   fax 01296 581185
       email pgsoc@percygrainger.org.uk
       http://www.percygrainger.org.uk
       Sec: Barry P Ould
▲   Un-incorporated Society
○   *D; to promote & develop interest in the life & works of the
       Australian composer & pianist Percy Aldridge
       Grainger (1882-1961)
●   Inf - Lib (music & sound archives) - PL
<   Intl Percy Grainger Soc (USA); Friends of Percy Grainger
       Museum (Melbourne, Australia)
M   120 i, 10 f, UK / 300 i, 15 f, o'seas
¶   The Grainger Society Jnl - 2;   Random Round (NL) - 2;
       In a Nutshell - 4;   (subscription for all 3, £14 m, £18 nm).

Performance Textiles Association Ltd   (PERTEXA)   1919
NR   42 Heath St, TAMWORTH, Staffs, B79 7JH.   (asa)
    01827 52337
    Sec: Michael Skelding
○   *T; manufacture, repair & making up of tents, tarpaulins,
    marquees, covers etc; coaters & sailmakers, flag, banner &
    bunting manufacturers
Gp   Association of Load Restraint Equipment Manufacturers
●   Conf - Mtgs - Res - Exhib
M   276 f
¶   Industrial Textiles - 4; ftm, £33 nm.
✕   2004 Made-up Textiles Association

Performing Artists' Media Rights Association   (PAMRA)   1995
NR   161 Borough High Street (3rd floor), LONDON, SE1 1HR.
    (hq)
    020 7940 0413
    email office@pamra.org.uk
    Exec Dir: Sabine Schlag
▲   Company Limited by Guarantee
○   *T; a collecting society
M   c 17,000 i

Performing Right Society Ltd
    a member of the **MCPS-PRS Alliance**

Periodical Publishers Association - Interactive   (PPAi)   1998
NR   Queen's House, 28 Kingsway, LONDON, WC2B 6JR.   (hq)
    020 7404 4166
○   *T; for online content providers
<   Is a division of the Periodical Publishers Association & a
    member of theAssociation of Online Publishers

Periodical Publishers Association Ltd   (PPA)   1913
◼   Queen's House, 28 Kingsway, LONDON, WC2B 6JR.   (hq)
    020 7404 4166   fax 020 7404 4167
    email info1@ppa.co.uk   http://www.ppa.co.uk
    Chief Exec: Ian Locks
▲   Company Limited by Guarantee
○   *T; interests of the UK magazine publishing industry
Gp   Association of Publishing Agencies; PPA Scotland; PPA Ireland
    C'ees: Ad marketing, B2B media, Copyright, Credit
    management, Editorial public affairs, Environmental,
    Finance, Newstrade, PPA Interactive, Parliamentary & legal
    affairs, Production & technology, Subscriptions
    Postal contract gp; Independent Publishers Advisory Council
●   Conf - Mtgs - ET - Res - Exhib - Comp - SG - Stat - Expt - Inf -
    Lib - PL - VE - LG
<   is linked with: Publishers Assn (books), Newspaper Soc
    (newspapers), Newspaper Pubrs Assn (daily newspapers) to
    form the UK Publishing Media
    Online Publishing Assn (US)
M   c 400 f
¶   List of publications available.

Permaculture Association (Britain)   (PcA)   1984
◼   BCM Permaculture Association, LONDON, WC1N 3XX.   (mail
    address)
    0845 458 1805
    Coordinator: Andrew Goldring
▲   Registered Charity
○   *F; sustainable design & implementation in agriculture, forestry,
    housing & energy
Gp   Projects network; Designers' register; Teachers' register;
    Permaculture design courses; Permaculture diploma
●   Conf - ET - Res - Exhib - Inf
M   800 i, UK / 50 i, o'seas
¶   Permaculture Works (Jnl) - 4; ftm.

Permanent Way Institution   (PWI)   1884
NR   11 Caraway Place, Meir Park, STOKE-on-TRENT, Staffs,
    ST3 7FE.   (hq)
    01782 397880
    Gen Sec: Brian Newman
▲   Company Limited by Guarantee
Br   20; Australia, Ireland, Malaysia, S Africa
○   *L, *P; management, construction & maintenance of railway
    permanent way & works
Gp   Sub-c'ees: Technical (training & education), Textbooks
●   Conf - Mtgs - Exhib - VE
<   Verband Deutscher Eisenbahn-Ingenieure (VDEI); Weg en
    Werken Vereniging (WWV); U of Eur Railway Engineer
    Assns (UEEIV)
M   c 4,000 i
¶   Jnl & Report of Proceedings - 4.   British Railway Track.
    The Permanent Way Institution - the first 100 years, 1884-
    1984.
    New Tracks to the Cities.   Evolution of Permanent Way.

Permit Trainers Association   1973
◼   151 Shaftesbury Avenue, LONDON, WC2H 8AL.   (hq)
    Drewitts, Warninglid, HAYWARDS HEATH, W Sussex, RH17 5TB.
      01444 461235   fax 01444 461485   (chmn/p)
    email freddie.gray@tiscali.co.uk
    Chmn: Frederick Gray
    Hon Sec: J Payne (01398 371244)
▲   Company Limited by Guarantee
○   *P; for racehorse owners & trainers; training of National Hunt
    racehorses which are family owned
M   300 i

Personal Computer Association
    since 2004 **Professional Computing Association**

Personal Computer Direct Marketers' Association
    a group of the **Professional Computing Association**

Personal Finance Society   (PFS)   1972
NR   20 Aldermanbury, LONDON, EC2V 7HY.   (hq)
    020 8530 0852   fax 020 7796 3882
    http://www.thepfs.org
    Chief Exec: Tim Eadon
▲   Company Limited by Guarantee
○   *P; representing the interests of all those who give & support
    personal financial advice
●   Conf - Mtgs - ET - SG - LG
✕   2005 (Life Insurance Association Ltd
        (Society of Financial Advisers

Personal Injuries Bar Association   (PIBA)   1995
NR   No 5 Chambers, Fountain Court, Steelhouse Lane,
    BIRMINGHAM, B4 6DR.   (sb)
    0121-606 0500   fax 0121-606 1501
    email tn@no5.com   http://www.piba.org.uk
    Sec: Tim Newman
▲   Un-incorporated Society
○   *P; to represent the Personal Injury Bar of England & Wales; to
    provide education & training to barristers in the field of
    personal injuries
●   Conf - Mtgs - ET - Inf - LG
M   c 1,100 i
¶   NL - 3/4; ftm.
    Personal Injuries Hbk (published by Sweet & Maxwell).

Personal Managers Association Ltd (PMA) 1950
■ 1 Summer Rd, EAST MOLESEY, Surrey, KT8 9LX. (hq)
    020 8398 9796   fax 020 8398 9796
    email info@thepma.com
    Liaison Sec: Angela Adler
○ *P; for those variously operating in the entertainment &
    publishing industries as personal managers, theatrical
    agents, literary or authors' agents
● Mtgs
M 125 f

Personal Safety Association (PSA)
NR 32 Cheam Place, CARDIFF, Glam, CF14 5DD. (hq)
    029 2075 2508
    email mark@ppts.co.uk
    Sec: L Hicks
○ *P; 'to offer the UK & Ireland's only open college network
    accreditations & BTEC qualifications in conflict management
    & personal safety'
● ET - Exam - Res - Inf
M i, f & org
¶ NL - 6; ftm only.

Personal Safety Manufacturers Association 1959
■ c/o British Safety Industry Federation, St Asaph Business Park,
    ST ASAPH, Denbighs, LL17 0LJ. (asa)
    01745 585600   fax 01745 585800
    email info@bsif.co.uk
    Sec: G R Hooke
▲ Company Limited by Guarantee
○ *T; manufacturers of personal protective equipment
● Mtgs - LG - Liaison with EU - Standards liaison & development
< Brit Safety Ind Fedn
M 60 f
¶ C[ommunauté] E[uropéenne] Marked Products Directory (within
    the Directive); free for an A5 sae with a 1st class stamp.

Perthes Association 1976
NR PO Box 773, GUILDFORD, Surrey, GU1 1XN.
    01483 306637 (admin) 01483 534431 (helpline)   (hq)
    email admin@perthes.org.uk   http://www.perthes.org.uk
    Dir: Lisa Grant
▲ Registered Charity
○ *W; to help & advise families with children suffering from
    Perthes disease (a potentially crippling disease of the hip) &
    other forms of osteochondritis as well as multiple epiphyseal
    dysplasia
● Comp - Inf - VE - Children's Christmas party - Contact register
    - Equipment loan for members (subject to availability)
< Contact a Family
M c 1,000 i
¶ NL - 4; ftm only.   Hbk; ftm.
    Layman's Guide to Osteochondritis; ftm.
    Your Child in an Immobilising Plaster: a few hints; ftm.
    Leaflets; ftm, one free copy nm.

Perthshire Agricultural Society (PAS) 1867
■ 26 York Place, PERTH, PH2 8EH. (hq)
    01738 623780   fax 01738 621206
    email secretary@perthshow.co.uk
    http://www.perthshow.co.uk
    Sec: Neil C Forbes
▲ Company Limited by Guarantee
○ *F; promotion of agriculture & organisation of 2-day
    agricultural show
● ET - Agricultural show
M 750 i

Perthshire Chamber of Commerce (PCC) 1871
NR The Atrium, 137 Glover St, PERTH, PH2 0JB. (hq)
    01738 637626
    http://www.perthshirechamber.co.uk
    Business Mgr: Marilyn Wallace
▲ Company Limited by Guarantee
○ *C
● Mtgs - Expt - Inf - Lib - LG
< Scot Cham Comm
M c 400 f
¶ NL - 12;   AR; both ftm.

Perthshire Society of Natural Science (PSNS) 1867
■ Perth Museum & Art Gallery, George St, PERTH, PH1 5XX.
    (mail/address)
    Hon Sec: Miss R Fothergill
▲ Registered Charity
○ *L; the study & research of natural history & natural sciences
    incl photography, archaeology, history, botany, ornithology;
    the study of the natural environment & its conservation
M i

** Pet Allergy Association
▲ Registered Charity
    Organisation lost: see Introduction paragraph 3

Pet Care Trust 1951
■ Bedford Business Centre, 170 Mile Rd, BEDFORD, MK42 9TW.
    0870 062 4400
    Chief Exec: Janet Nunn
▲ Registered Charity
○ *T; retail pet trade; manufacturers & wholesalers of pet foods &
    accessories; dog groomers; boarding kennels & catteries
Gp Manufacturers; Retailers; Wholesalers; Groomers; Boarding
    kennels & catteries
● Conf - Mtgs - ET - Exam - Exhib - Stat - Expt - LG
M 1,500 f
¶ NL - 6.   Ybk.

Pet Food Manufacturers' Association Ltd (PFMA) 1969
■ 20 Bedford St, Covent Garden, LONDON, WC2E 9HP. (hq)
    020 7379 9009   fax 020 7379 8008
    email info@pfma.org.uk   http://www.pfma.com
    Chief Exec: Michael Bellingham
▲ Company Limited by Guarantee
○ *T
● Mtgs - Inf - VE - LG - Seminars - Symposia
< Eur Pet Food Mfrs Assn (FEDIAF)
M 50 f

Pet Fostering Service Scotland (PFSS) 1985
■ PO Box 6, CALLANDER, Perthshire, FK17 8ZU. (mail)
    01877 331496 (referral phone) address
    Chmn: Anne Docherty
▲ Registered Charity
○ *G, *W; provision of short-term care of pets belonging to
    people who have to go into hospital or other short-term care
    in emergencies
● ET - Inf
< SCAS; BSAVA
M 300 i
¶ Booklet.

Pet Health Council   (PHC)   1979
NR   1 Bedford Avenue, LONDON, WC1B 3AU.   (hq)
    020 7255 5408
    Sec: Hannah O'Neill
▲   Company Limited by Guarantee
○   *N; *V; to promote pet health in relation to human health
●   Inf
M   9 org:
    Associaton of Pet Behaviour Counsellors
    British Small Animal Veterinary Association
    British Veterinary Association
    National Office of Animal Health
    National Pharmacy Association
    Pet Food Manufacturers Association
    Royal College of Nursing -Complementary Therapies
      Forum
    Royal Pharmaceutical Society of GB
    Society for Companion Animal Studies
¶   Leaflets.

Pet Product Retail Association
    a group of the **British Hardware Federation**

Peter Warlock Society   1963
NR   Jubilee Cottage, 30 The Hill, GARSINGTON, Oxon,
    OX44 9DG.   (hsp)
    01865 368461
    http://www.peterwarlock.org
    Hon Sec: Chris Sreeves
▲   Registered Charity
○   *D; to increase the knowledge of all aspects of the life & works
    of composer Peter Warlock (1894 - 1930)
●   Mtgs - Comp - Inf - Lib - Publishing complete edition of
    Warlock's works
M   250 i, UK / 35 i, o'seas
¶   NL - 2.   Society Edition of Songs, 9 vols.

Peterborough Royal Foxhound Show Society   (PRFSS)   1878
■   East of England Showground, PETERBOROUGH, Cambs,
    PE2 6XE.   (hq)
    01733 234451   fax 01733 370038
    Sec: Andrew Mercer
○   *B; breeding & showing of foxhounds

Petfood Manufacturers Association of Ireland   (IMDA)   1995
IRL   Confederaton House, 84-86 Lower Baggot St, DUBLIN 2,
    Republic of Ireland.
○   *T
<   IBEC

Petrol Retailers Association
    a group of the **Retail Motor Industry Federation**

Petroleum Exploration Society of Great Britain   (PESGB)   1965
NR   9 Berkeley St (5th floor), LONDON, W1J 8DW.   (hq)
    020 7408 2000
    http://www.pesgb.org.uk
    Pres: Chris Flavell
▲   Registered Charity
○   *L; to promote, for the public benefit, education in the scientific
    & technical aspects of petroleum
●   Conf - ET - Exhib - Inf - VE
<   Amer Assn Petroleum Geologists (AAPG); SEG
M   5,300 i, UK / 600 i, o'seas
¶   NL - 12; ftm only.

Pewter Society   1918
■   Llananant Farm, Penallt, MONMOUTH, Monmouthshire,
    NP25 4AP.   (hsp)
    email secretary@pewtersociety.org
    http://www.pewtersociety.org
    Hon Sec: Peter Hayward
▲   Un-incorporated Society
○   *A, *G; to stimulate interest in, & preservation of, old pewter
●   Mtgs - Res - Inf - Lib
M   150 i, 10 org, UK / 90 i, o'seas
¶   Jnl - 2;   NL - 2;   LM; all ftm only.

Pharmaceutical & Healthcare Sciences Society   1981
NR   99 Ermin St, Stratton St Margaret, SWINDON, Wilts,
    SN3 4NL.   (hq)
    01793 824254
    http://www.phss.co.uk
    Business Devt Mgr: Mrs June T Prout
▲   Un-incorporated Society
○   *L, *P; for those individuals employed in the field of injectable &
    implantable drugs & devices; interests cover: research &
    development, manufacturing, quality control, engineering,
    the practice of medicine, nursing care & related activities
Gp   Freeze drying; Biotechnology; LAL
M   i & f
    2006 (March) Parenteral Society

**Pharmaceutical Information & Pharmacovigilance Association
(PIPA)   1980**
NR   PO Box 254, HASLEMERE, Surrey, GU27 7XT.   (mail)
    email pipa@pipaonline.org address
○   *P; to maintain & develop professional standards in all aspects
    of information work in the pharmaceutical industry
M   i
×   2005 Association of Information Officers in the Pharmaceutical
    Industry

Pharmaceutical Society of Ireland   1875
IRL   18 Shrewsbury Rd, DUBLIN 4, Republic of Ireland.
    353 (1) 218 4000   fax 353 (1) 283 7678
    email info@pharmaceuticalsociety.ie
    Admin Sec: Dr Ambrose McLoughlin
○   *T

Pharmaceutical Society of Northern Ireland   (PSNI)   1925
NR   73 University St, BELFAST, BT7 1HL.   (hq)
    028 9032 6927
    Dir: Raymond Blaney
▲   Statutory body
○   *P; registration & educational body for the practice of the
    profession of pharmacy in Northern Ireland
●   Mtgs - ET - Exam - LG
<   Intl Pharmaceutical Fedn; C'wealth Pharmaceutical Assn
M   1,700 i

PharmaChemical Ireland
IRL   Confederation House, 84-86 Lower Baggot St, DUBLIN 2,
    Republic of Ireland.
    353 (1) 605 1584   fax 353 (1) 638 1584
    email matt.moran@ibec.ie
    Dir: Matt Moran
○   *T
<   IBEC
×   2004 Irish Pharmaceutical & Chemical Manufacturers
    Association

Philatelic Traders Society Ltd   (PTS)   1946

- ■ PO Box 371, FLEET, Hants, GU52 6ZX.   (hq)
  01252 628006   fax 01252 684674
  email info@philatelic-traders-society.co.uk
  http://www.philatelic-traders-society.co.uk
  Sec: J M Czuczman
- ▲ Company Limited by Guarantee
- ○ *G, *T; organisation of stamp dealers, auctioneers, philatelic
  publishers & philatelic accessory dealers; to promote the
  hobby of philately
- ● organisation of two national stamp exhibitions in London by
  Stampex Ltd (a wholly owned subsidiary)
- M 300 f, UK / 200 i, o'seas
- ¶ PTS News - 6; ftm only.   Directory - 1; ftm, £10 nm.

Philip Larkin Society   (PLS)   1995

- ■ c/o Dept of English, University of Hull, HULL, HU6 7RX.   (sb)
  01482 465637   fax 01482 465640
  email j.booth@hull.ac.uk   http://www.philiplarkin.com
  Hon Sec: Carole Collinson
- ▲ Registered Charity
- ○ *A, *G; to promote awareness of the life & work of the poet,
  writer & Hull University librarian Philip Larkin (1922-1985) &
  his literary contemporaries
- Gp Publishing sub-c'ee
- ● Conf - Mtgs - Res - Exhib - VE
- < Alliance Literary Socs
- M 250 i, UK / 50 i, o'seas
- ¶ About Larkin - 2; ftm, £7 each nm.   Monographs.

Philological Society   1842

- ■ SOAS/University of London, Thornhaugh St, LONDON,
  WC1H 0XG.   (hsb)
  email lm5@soas.ac.uk   http://www.lings.ln.man.ac.uk/
  More/Philsoc
  Hon Sec: Dr Lutz Marten
- ▲ Company Limited by Guarantee; Registered Charity
- ○ *L, *Q; the study of the structure, the affinities & the history of
  languages
- ● Conf - Mtgs - Res
- M 618 i
- ¶ Transactions - 3.
  Publications of the Philological Society - irreg.

Philosophical Society of England   (PhS)   1913

- ■ 6 Craghall Dene Avenue, NEWCASTLE upon TYNE,
  NE3 1QR.   (hsb)
  0191-284 1223
  email thephilosophicalsociety@yahoo.co.uk
  http://www.philsoc.co.uk
  http://www.atschool.eduweb.co.uk/cite/staff/
  philosopher/philsocindex.htm
  Chmn: Michael Bavidge
- ○ *L, *R; the study & discussion of the philosophy of religion &
  'English thought'
- M 110 i, UK / 60 i, o'seas
- ¶ The Philosopher - 2; ftm, £15 m.

Phoenix Camping Club   1999

- ■ Apple Croft, 3 Station Rd, Marsh Gibbon, BICESTER, Oxon,
  OX27 0HN.
  01869 278345   0771 914 6822 (mobile)   (hsp)
  email mikeapple2@aol.com
  Sec: Mike Appleby
- ▲ Un-incorporated Society
- ○ *G; 'offers friendship & company via a programme of 3-7 day
  meets on campsites throughout the UK, for single, divorced
  or widowed campers who live without a partner & camp in
  their own motor caravan, caravan, tent or trailer tent
- ● Mtgs
- M c 150 i
- ¶ NL - c 9; ftm only.
  Note: Please enclose a large SAE with all enquiries

Phonographic Performance (Ireland) Ltd   (PPI)   1968

- IRL 1 Corrig Avenue, DÚN LAOGHAIRE, Co Dublin, Republic of
  Ireland.
  353 (1) 280 5977   fax 353 (1) 280 6579
  email info@ppiltd.com   http://www.ppiltd.com
  Chief Exec: Dick Doyle
- ○ *T; collects royalties originating from the broadcasting of sound
  recordings

Phonographic Performance Ltd   (PPL)   1934

- NR 1 Upper James St, LONDON, W1F 9DE.   (hq)
  020 7534 1000
- ▲ Company Limited by Guarantee
- ○ *T; 'licensing of the public performance & broadcasting of
  sound recordings in the UK pursuant to the provisions of the
  Copyright Act 1956'
- M i & f

Photo Imaging Council   (PIC)   2002

- ■ Orbital House, 85 Croydon Rd, CATERHAM, Surrey,
  CR3 6PD.   (hq)
  01883 334497
  email pic@admin.co.uk   http://www.pic.uk.net
  Co Sec: Mrs Pamela Hyde
- ▲ Company Limited by Guarantee
- ○ *T; to represent & promote the interests of the photographic &
  imaging industry in the UK to government, the media,
  external organisations & the general public
- Gp Manufacturing; Marketing; Photo wastes; Export
- ● Conf - Mtgs - Exhib - Comp - Stat - Expt - LG
- < Brit Brands Gp
- M 110 f
- × 2002 (British Imaging & Photographic Association
  (British Photographic Enterprise Group
  (British Photographic & Imaging Association
  (Imaging Products Group
  (Photographic Waste Management Association
  (all merged 10 January 2002)

Photographic Alliance of Great Britain   (PAGB)   1930

- ■ 30 Merle Avenue, Harefield, UXBRIDGE, Middx, UB9 6DG.
  01895 822202
  email graham_laughton@yahoo.co.uk
  http://www.pagb-photography-uk.co.uk
  Hon Sec: Graham A Laughton
- ▲ Un-incorporated Society
- ○ *N; to coordinate the interests of the 15 photographic societies
  in the UK
- ● Mtgs - Exhib - Comp - SG - Inf - Provision of services & awards
  to the Federations - Confers patronage to exhibitions
- < Fédn Intle de l'Art Photographique (FIAP)
- > c 1,000 UK Camera Clubs
- M 25 i, 15 federations
- ¶ NL - 2; ftm, £5 nm.   Hbk - 2; ftm, £10 nm.

Photographic Collectors Club of Great Britain   (PCCGB)   1977

- NR 5 Buntingford Rd, Puckeridge, WARE, Herts, SG11 1RT.
  (mem/office)
  01920 821611
  Mem Sec: Diana Balfour
- ▲ Un-incorporated Society
- ○ *A, *G; to promote the study & collection of historical
  photographic equipment & images
- ● Mtgs - Exhib - SG - Inf - Major Fair (London, May)
- < Exacta Circle; Half Frame Gp; Voigtlander Verein; Kodak
  Brownie
- M 1,150 i, UK / 50 i, o'seas
- ¶ Photographica World (Jnl) - 4;   Tailboard (NL) - 6;
  Postal Auction - 4;   Members' Hbk (LM) - 1; all ftm only.

Photographic Materials Conservation group
in 2005 merged with the Care of Collections Forum, the Institute of
Paper Conservation, the Scottish Society for Conservation &
Restoration & the United Kingdom Institute for Conservation of
Historic & Artistic Works to form the **Institute of Conservation**

Photographic Waste Management Association
on 10 January 2002 merged with the British Imaging & Photographic Association, the British Photographic Enterprise Group, the British Photographic & Imaging Association & the Imaging Products Group to form the **Photo Imaging Council**

Photoluminescent Safety Products Association   (PSPA)   1991
NR   c/o Sealand Centre, 3-5 Holmethorpe Avenue, REDHILL, Surrey, RH1 2LZ.   (mail)
01737 763400   fax 01737 728818
http://www.pspa.org.uk add
Contact: Terry Egan
▲   Company Limited by Guarantee
○   *T; promotes use & knowledge of photoluminescent products in the field of safety
M   14 f, UK / 8 f, o'seas

Photonics Cluster
NR   Faraday Wharf, Holt St, Aston Science Pk, BIRMINGHAM, B7 4BB.
0121-260 6020
http://www.photonicscluster.org
○   *T; photonics industry

Physical Education Association of the United Kingdom
this association was dissolved in March 2006 and has been replaced by the **Association for Physical Education**

Physiological Society   1876
NR   PO Box 11319, LONDON, WC1X 8WQ.   (hq)
020 7269 5710
http://www.physoc.org
Chief Exec: Dr Michael Collis
▲   Company Limited by Guarantee; Registered Charity
○   *L, *M; to promote the advancement of physiology; to contribute to the understanding of biomedical & related sciences; to aid the prevention & treatment of disease, disability & malfunction of physical processes in all forms of life
●   Mtgs - ET - Res - SG - LG
M   c 2,000 i, UK / c 500 i, o'seas
¶   Jnl of Physiology - 24.   Experimental Physiology - 6.
Magazine - 6;   AR;   Monographs;   Study guides;   Books; prices vary.

Pianoforte Tuners' Association   (PTA)   1913
■   10 Reculver Rd, HERNE BAY, Kent, CT6 6LD.   (hsp)
01227 368808   fax 01227 368808
http://www.pianotuner.org.uk
Admin Sec: Mrs Valerie Addis
▲   Un-incorporated Society
○   *P
●   Conf - Mtgs - ET - Exam - Inf - Lib - VE
M   200 i, UK / 10 i, o'seas
¶   NL - 12; ftm.   Ybk; ftm, £2 nm.

Pick's Disease Support Group   (PDSG)   1993
■   3 Fairfield Park, LYME REGIS, Dorset, DT7 3DS.   (hsp)
01297 445488
email penelope@pdsg.org.uk   http://www.pdsg.org.uk
Hon Sec: Penelope K Roques
▲   Registered Charity
○   *W; for carers of people with frontotemporal dementia - Pick's disease, frontal lobe degeneration, corticostal degeneration & alcohol related dementia
●   Conf - Mtgs - ET - VE
<   Nat Hospital Devt Foundation
M   600 i, 50 org, UK / 700 i, 50 org, o'seas
¶   NL - 4; free.

Pickles & Sauces Association
is an association within the **Food Processors' Association**

Picon Ltd   1993
■   St Christopher's House, Holloway Hill, GODALMING, Surrey, GU7 1QZ.   (hq)
01483 412000   fax 01483 412001
email info@picon.co.uk   http://www.picon.com
Chief Exec: J Brazier
▲   Company Limited by Guarantee
○   *T; for manufacturers of printing, paper-making & converting machinery (processing paper & plastic films to add value)
Gp   Pulp & paper executive; Chemicals; Environmental
●   Mtgs - ET - Res - Exhib - Stat - Inf - Expt - VE - LG
<   Eur C'ee of Printing & Paper Converting Machinery Mfrs (EUMAPRINT); Paper Ind Technical Assn (PITA)
M   150 f
¶   Paper & Converting Machinery News - 4; on subscription.
AR - 1; m only.
Various other publications - m only.

Pictish Arts Society   (1988)
■   Pictavia, Haughmuir, BRECHIN, Angus, DD9 6RL.
(visitor/centre)
email admin@pictarts.org   http://www.pictarts.org
Hon Sec: Stewart Mowatt
○   *G; the study, research, development & preservation of Pictish arts, crafts & language; to advance the education of the public in all aspects of the early history of Scotland & in particular the Picts in Scotland
●   Conf - Mtgs (Winter) - ET - Lib - VE
M   200 i, 10 org, UK / 18 i, o'seas
¶   Jnl - 1; ftm, £5 nm.   NL - 4; ftm only.

Picture Research Association   (PRA)   1977
■   c/o Scala, 1 Willow Court, off Willow St, LONDON, EC2A 4QB.   (mail/address)
020 7739 8544
Chmn: Charlotte Lippmann
○   *P; for all those involved in picture research, editing, management & supply
Gp   Freelance register; Members advisory service
●   Conf - Mtgs - ET - Inf
M   250 i, UK / 30 i, o'seas
¶   Montage - 4.   Bulletin (NL) - 12.

Pig Veterinary Society
a group of the **British Veterinary Association**

Pigging Products & Services Association   (PPSA)   1990
■   PO Box 2, STROUD, Glos, GL6 8YB.   (hsb)
01285 760597   fax 01285 760470
email ppsa@ppsa-online.com
http://www.ppsa-online.com
Exec Sec: Gill Hornby
▲   Company Limited by Guarantee
Br   USA
○   *T; to promote the knowledge of pipeline pigging & its related products & services by providing a channel of communication between members themselves, users & other interested parties
Pigs are devices inserted into & travel throughout the length of a pipeline driven by the product flow
●   Conf - ET - Inf - PL
M   10 i, 17 f, UK / 5 i, 49 f, o'seas
¶   Pigging Industry News - 3; free.
Buyers' Guide & Directory of Members - 1; free.
An Introduction to Pipeline Pigging; ftm, £25 ($50 o'seas).

The Pilgrims   1902
- ■ Allington Castle, MAIDSTONE, Kent, ME16 0NB.   (hq)
  01622 606404   fax 01622 606402
  email sec@pilgrimsociety.org
  Hon Sec: M P S Barton
- ▲ Un-incorporated Society
- ○ *X; promotion of Anglo-American good fellowship
- ● Dinners & receptions
- < The Pilgrims of the USA
- M 1,000 i, UK / 50 i, o'seas
- ¶ NL - 2;   LM & Rules - 2 yrly; free.

Pinball Owners' Association   (POA)   1976
- ■ Kilndown, 31 Earlsmead Crescent, Cliffsend, RAMSGATE, Kent,
  CT12 5LQ.   (mail)
  email poa@dial.pipex.com
  http://www.dspace.dial.pipex.com/poa/ address
  Mem Sec: Philip Crow
- ▲ Un-incorporated Society
- ○ *G, *S; to promote the playing, collecting & ownership of
  pinball & other coin operated machines
- ● Comp - Exhib (Annual show) - Inf - Spares & specialist goods
  sales
- M 470 i, 15 f, UK / 50 i, 10 f, o'seas
- ¶ Pinball Player - 10; £16 m, £20 nm.

Piobaireachd Society   1902
- NR 16-24 Otago St, GLASGOW, G12 8JH.   (hq)
  0141-334 3587   fax 0141-587 6068
  Hon Sec: Dugald MacNeill
- ▲ Un-incorporated Society
- ○ *D, *G; the encouragement & dissemination of the
  piobaireachd & its playing

Pipe Jacking Association   (PJA)   1973
- ■ 10 Greycoat Place, LONDON, SW1P 1SB.   (hq)
  0845 070 5201   fax 0845 070 5202
  email secretary@pipejacking.org
  http://www.pipejacking.org
  Sec: Andrew K Marshall
- ▲ Company Limited by Guarantee
- ○ *T; to represent the leading contractors, pipe suppliers &
  machine manufacturers in the pipe jacking & microtunnelling
  industry in the UK
- Gp Tunnelling; Tunnelling machinery; Pipe manufacture
- ● Conf - Mtgs - ET - Inf
- M 21 f
- ¶ NL - 2.
  Guide to Best Practice for the Installation of Pipe Jacks &
  Microtunnels; £35 nm.
  An Introduction to Pipe Jacking & Microtunnelling
  Design £9.50 nm.

Pipe Roll Society   1883
- ■ c/o The National Archive, Ruskin Avenue, KEW, Surrey,
  TW9 4DU.
  020 8876 3444   fax 020 8878 8905
  Contact: David Crook
- ▲ Registered Charity
- ○ *L; 'the enlargement of the public knowledge of medieval
  English history by the publication of the Pipe Rolls &
  associated records of medieval English government & other
  manuscripts of national importance prior to 1350'
  No further information supplied.

Pipedown
  see **Campaign for Freedom from Piped Music**

Pipeline Industries Guild Ltd   (PIG)   1957
- ■ 14-15 Belgrave Sq, LONDON, SW1X 8PS.   (hq)
  020 7235 7938   fax 020 7235 0074
  email hqsec@pipeguild.co.uk
  http://www.pipeguild.co.uk
  Dir Gen: Richard Glenister
- ▲ Company Limited by Guarantee
- Br 6; Republic of Ireland; Balkan & Black Sea
- ○ *T; science & practice of aspects of the pipeline engineering
- Gp Technical panels: Onshore, Offshore, Utilities
- ● Conf - Mtgs - ET - Exhib - Comp/Awards - Expt - Inf - Lib - LG
- < Fedn of Wld Pipeline Assns
- M 1,000 i, 220 f, UK / 300 i, 20 f, o'seas
- ¶ Pipeline Industry Directory - 1; ftm, £50 nm.

Pipers' Guild   1932
- NR 25 Dorothy Curtice Court, London Rd, Copford, COLCHESTER,
  Essex, CO6 1DX.   (sb/p)
  email sec@pipersguild.org
  Sec: Anne Jones
- ○ *G

Pira International   1929
- ■ Cleeve Rd, LEATHERHEAD, Surrey, KT22 7RU.   (hq)
  01372 802000   fax 01372 802238
  email infocentre@pira.co.uk   http://www.piranet.com
  Managing Dir: Michael Hancock
- ▲ Company Limited by Guarantee
- ○ *Q; consultancy & research into paper, packaging, printing &
  publishing
- Gp Printing & publishing; Paper & board; Packaging
- ● Conf - ET - Res - Inf - Lib
- ¶ [Publications catalogue on website].

Pizza, Pasta & Italian Food Association   (PAPA)   1977
- ■ Archway House, Moor St, CHEPSTOW, Monmouthshire,
  NP16 5DB.   (hq)
  01291 636338   fax 01291 630402
  email enq@papa.org.uk   http://www.papa.org.uk
  Dir: Jim Winship
- ○ *T; to promote better standards & knowledge in the industry
- ● Mtgs - Inf - VE - Promotions - Insurance schemes - Financial
  advice
- < Nat Assn of Pizza Operators (USA)
- M 52 i, 680 f, UK / 13 i, 36 f, o'seas
- ¶ Magazine - 6; ftm, £48 nm.   PAPA Ybk - 1; ftm.

Plain English Campaign 1979   (PEC)
- ■ PO Box 3, NEW MILLS, High Peak, Derbys, SK22 4QP.   (hq)
  01663 744409   fax 01663 747038
  email info@plainenglish.co.uk
  http://www.plainenglish.co.uk
  Mgr: Tony Maher
- ▲ Company Limited by Guarantee
- ○ *K; to persuade government departments, local councils &
  companies to write forms, leaflets, letters & agreements
  clearly & to set them out clearly & logically
- ● Conf - ET - Res - Exhib - Comp - LG
- M 1,000 i, 500 f
- ¶ Plain English (Jnl) - 4; free.
  List available on request.

Plainsong & Mediæval Music Society   (PMMS)   1888
- ■ 19 The Close, SALISBURY, Wilts, SP1 2EB.   (hq)
  email pmms@rscm.com
  Chmn: Prof John Harper
- ▲ Registered Charity
- ○ *D, *L; the advancement of education in plainsong & mediæval
  music
- ● Publication of scholarly books & facsimiles
- M i & libraries
- ¶ Plainsong & Medieval Music (Jnl) - 2; ftm.

© CBD Research Ltd · Beckenham · BR3 5JS · Tel 020 8650 7745 · Fax 020 8650 0768 · E-mail cbd@cbdresearch.com · www.cbdresearch.com

Planning Officers Society   1997
NR   PO Box 411, FLEET Hants, GU59 5AP.   (sb)
       0791 770 7310   fax 01252 671304
       http://www.planningofficers.org.uk
       Sec: Chris Swanwick
○   *P

**Plantagenet Medieval Archery & Combat Society
  (Plantagenet Society)   1976**
■   37 Willowslea Rd, WORCESTER, WR3 7QP.   (sp)
       01905 455192
       email mike@mkerslake.freeserve.co.uk
       http://www.the-plantagenets.freeserve.co.uk
       Sec: Mike Kerslake
▲   Un-incorporated Society
○   *G; re-enactment of medieval tourneys, sieges, foot combat,
       archery, music & dance
Gp   Archers; Knights; Musicians; Dancers
●   Re-enactments & entertainment
M   60 i

Plantlife International: the wild plant conservation charity
■   14 Rollestone St, SALISBURY, Wilts, SP1 1DX.   (hq)
       01722 342730
       email enquiries@plantlife.org.uk
       http://www.plantlife.org.uk
       Devt Mgr: Lisa Clements
▲   Registered Charity
○   *K; 'the in-situ conservation of wild plants'
●   Res - LG - Conservation of wild plants
M   125,000 i
¶   Plantlife - 3; ftm, on request nm.

Plastic Installers Federation
       it has been reported to us that this organisation has gone out of
       business - we should be grateful for confirmation

Plastics & Board Industries Federation   (PBIF)   2001
■   Rock House, Maddacombe Rd, Kingskerswell,
       NEWTON ABBOT, Devon, TQ12 5LF.   (hq)
       01803 403303   fax 01803 873167
       email pbifoffice@aol.com   http://www.pbif.co.uk
       Chief Exec: Alison Ainsworth
▲   Company Limited by Guarantee
○   *T; for companies who either manufacture products which
       involve high frequency welding of PVC, or converting other
       types of plastic or board, or who are suppliers to those
       manufacturers
●   Mtgs - ET - Exhib - Inf
<   Binding Inds of America (BIA); Australian Plastic Fabricators
       Assn (APFA); Australian Canvas & Synthetic Products Assn
M   6 i, 114 f, UK / 1 i, 26 f, o'seas
¶   PBIF Magazine (Jnl) - 4; ftm, £35 nm (£45 EU, £55 Intl).

Plastics Historical Society   (PHS)   1986
■   31A Maylands Drive, SIDCUP, Kent, DA14 4SB.   (hsp)
       020 8302 0684
       email r_chambers@lineone.net
       http://www.plastiquarian.com
       Hon Sec: Richard Chambers
▲   Un-incorporated Society
○   *L; to study all historical aspects of plastics & other polymers; to
       record current developments
●   Conf - Mtgs - Res - Exhib - Inf - Lib - VE
<   Inst Materials, Minerals & Mining
M   175 i, 25 org, UK / 50 i, o'seas
¶   Plastiquarian - 2; ftm, £10 nm.   NL - 6; ftm, £3 nm.

Plastics Ireland
IRL Confederation House, 84-86 Lower Baggot St, DUBLIN 2,
       Republic of Ireland.
○   *T
<   IBEC
       Plastics Industries Association

Plastics Window Federation
NR   Federation House, 85-87 Wellington St, LUTON, Beds,
       LU1 5AF.   (hq)
       01582 456147
       http://www.inf@pwfed.co.uk
       Dir: Kenneth A Wiltsher
▲   Company Limited by Guarantee
○   *T; manufacturers & installers of plastics (PVCU) windows for
       domestic & commercial use
●   Exam - Arbitration & technical services - Insurance for
       consumers
M   c 600 f

Play Matters
       see **National Association of Toy & Leisure Libraries**

Play Providers Association   (PPA)   2005
■   Federation House, STONELEIGH PARK, Warks, CV8 2RF.   (hq)
       024 7641 4999   fax 024 7641 4990
       email ppa@playproviders.org
       http://www.playproviders.org.uk
▲   Company Limited by Guarantee
○   *T; for indoor operators of children's play centres
●   Mtgs
<   a group of the Federation of Sports & Play Assns (FSPA)
M   f

Player Piano Group   (PPG)   1959
■   93 Evelyn Ave, RUISLIP, Middx, HA4 8AH.   (hsp)
       01895 634288
       Hon Sec: Tony Austin
▲   Un-incorporated Society
○   *D, *G; to foster interest in the player piano & the reproducing
       piano; their history, mechanisms & musical virtues
●   Mtgs - VE
<   Automatic Musical Instrument Collectors Assn Intl (AMICA); Ned
       Pianola Vereniging; NW [& S Wales & the West] Player Piano
       Assn[s]; Gesellschaft Selbspielende Musikinstrumente eV;
       Australian Collectors Mechanical Musical Instruments;
       Perferons la Musique; Pianola Inst
M   273 i, 5 org, UK / 26 i, 5 org, o'seas
¶   The Bulletin - 4; ftm only.

Player-Playwrights   1947
■   9 Hillfield Park, LONDON, N10 3QT.
       020 8883 0371
       email p-p@dial.pipex.com
       Hon Sec: Peter Thompson
○   *A; for people interested in playwriting & drama
M   c125

Playlink
       is in process of winding down. Its successor body Playlink (not
       for profit) is not considered as an association, website:
       freeplaynetwork.org.uk.

Pleasure Horse Society Ltd   2003
NR   Victoria House, Desborough St, HIGH WYCOMBE, Bucks,
       HP11 2NF.
       01494 601042
       email info@pleasurehorsesociety.co.uk
       Contact: Chris Stroud
○   *G; for all horse owners

Plymouth Chamber of Commerce & Industry   (PCCI)   1813
NR   22 Lockyer St, PLYMOUTH, Devon, PL1 2QW.   (hq)
    01752 220471
    http://www.plymouth-chamber.co.uk
    Dir of Operations & Co Sec: Sally Perdrisat
▲   Company Limited by Guarantee
○   *C
Gp   Membership consultation, policy & representation; Membership
    services & marketing
●   Mtgs - ET - Res - Exhib - Expt - Inf - VE - LG - Representation of
    members' views
M   900 f
¶   NL - 12.   LM - 12.   Ybk.

Poetry Society (Inc)   (PS)   1909
NR   22 Betterton St, LONDON, WC2H 9BX.   (hq)
    020 7420 9880   fax 020 7240 4818
    email info@poetrysociety.org.uk
    http://www.poetrysociety.org.uk
    Dir: Jules Mann
▲   Company Limited by Guarantee; Registered Charity
○   *A; promotion of poets & poetry
●   ET - Res - Exhib - Comp - Inf
M   c 4,000 i & org
¶   The Poetry Review - 4.   The Poetry News - 4.

Point-to-Point Owners & Riders Association   (PPORA)   1977
NR   The Coach House, Mill Rd, Sturry, CANTERBURY, Kent,
    CT2 0AJ.   (hsb)
    01227 713080   fax 01227 713088
    http://www.pointtopointownersandriders.co.uk
    Hon Sec: Jeanette Dawson
▲   Un-incorporated Society
○   *G, *S
●   Mtgs - Inf
M   2,000 i
¶   Between the Flags - 2.

** **Poldark Appreciation Society**
    Organisation lost: see Introduction paragraph 3

Police Federation of England & Wales   1919
NR   15-17 Langley Rd, SURBITON, Surrey, KT6 6LP.   (hq)
    020 8399 2224   fax 020 8390 2249
    email polfed@polfed.org   http://www.polfed.org
    Gen Sec: John Francis
Br   43 (Joint Branch Boards)
○   *U; 'professional involvement in all aspects of policing &
    legislation'
●   Conf - Mtgs - ET - Res - SG - Stat - Inf - Lib - VE - Empl - LG
M   i
¶   Police - 12; free to branches.

Police Federation for Northern Ireland   (PFNI)   1971
■   77-79 Garnerville Rd, BELFAST, BT4 2NX.   (hq)
    028 9076 4200
    Sec: Terry Spence
▲   Un-incorporated Society
○   *P; representative body concerned with welfare & efficiency of
    police
●   Conf - Mtgs - ET - Res - Lib - Empl - LG
<   Standing C'ee of Police in Europe
M   11,189 i
¶   Police Beat - 12; m only.

Police History Society   (PHS)   1985
■   64 Nore Marsh Rd, WOOTTON BASSETT, Wilts, SN4 8BH.
    (hsp)
    01793 853635
    email stevebridge100@btinternet.com
    http://www.policehistorysociety.co.uk
    Hon Sec: Steve Bridge
▲   Registered Charity
○   *G; promotion of interest in police history
Gp   Police museum curators
●   Conf - Res - Re-publication of historical sources of police
    history
M   c350 i
¶   Jnl - 1; ftm, £5 nm.   NL - 4;   LM - 2/3 yrly; both ftm only.
    Monographs - irreg; prices vary.

Police Insignia Collectors Association of Great Britain   (PICA GB)   1975
■   8 Foxon Lane Gdns, CATERHAM, Surrey, CR3 5SN.   (hmsp)
    http://www.pica.co.uk
    Hon Mem Sec: Tony Collman
○   *G; to foster comradeship through a mutual interest in police
    insignia; to instruct, inform & interest all collecting police
    insignia
●   Swap mtgs
M   600 i / 150 i, o'seas.
¶   PICA Magazine - 3; ftm only.

Police Professional Network
    a group of the **Chartered Management Institute**

Police Superintendents' Association of England & Wales   1921
■   67a Reading Rd, PANGBOURNE, Berks, RG8 7JD.   (hq)
    0118-984 4005   fax 0118-984 5642
    email enquiries@policesupers.com
    http://www.policesupers.com
    Nat Sec: Chief Superintendent Philip Aspey
    Pres: Chief Superintendent Rick Naylor
Br   44
○   *P; for police superintendents & chief superintendents in
    England & Wales
Gp   Business Areas: BCU (Basic Command Unit) liaison; Command
    resilience; Crime; Diversity; Human resources; Operational
    policing; Panel of friends; Roads policing
●   Conf - Mtgs - Res - Stat - Inf - Empl - LG
M   1,510 i
¶   The Superintendent - 3; free.

Polish Society   1996
■   Ashcroft House, Chalton Rd, BRIDGE OF ALLAN, Stirlingshire,
    FK9 4EF.   (chmn/p)
    01786 832793
    Chmn: Prof Peter D Stachura
▲   Un-incorporated Society
○   *L, *X; an academic discussion forum for Polish history, culture
    & contemporary affairs
●   Conf - Mtgs - ET - Res
M   25 i
¶   NL - 3; ftm only.

Polite Society
    see **Campaign for Courtesy (Polite Society)**

© CBD Research Ltd · Beckenham · BR3 5JS · Tel 020 8650 7745 · Fax 020 8650 0768 · E-mail cbd@cbdresearch.com · www.cbdresearch.com

Political Studies Association of the United Kingdom   (PSA) 1950
NR   School of Policy Studies, University of Ulster, NEWTOWNABBEY, Co Antrim, BT37 0QB.   (hq)
028 9036 8896   fax 028 9036 6847
http://www.psa.ac.uk
Hon Sec: Prof Paul Carmichael
▲   Registered Charity
○   *L; promotion of the development of political studies
●   Conf - Mtgs - ET - Res - SG - Stat - LG
M   i & f
¶   Many publications available

Politics Association   (PA)   1969
NR   Old Hall Lane, MANCHESTER, M13 0XT.   (hq)
0161-256 3906   fax 0161-256 3906
email politic@enablis.co.uk
http://www.politics-association.org.uk
Gen Sec: Vanessa Pryce
▲   Registered Charity
Br   6
○   *E; to promote the study & teaching of the theory & practice of politics
Gp   Politics Association Resources Centre (PARC) - teaching resources, publishing, printing
●   Conf - Mtgs - ET - Exam - Res - Comp - Inf - LG
<   Hansard Soc for Parliamentary Government
M   c 1,300 i
¶   Talking Politics (Jnl) - 4.

Poll Holstein Breeders Club   (Poll Club)   1975
■   Gatesgarth, Periton Rd, MINEHEAD, Somerset, TA24 8DR. (hsp)
01643 702130
Hon Sec: Mrs Doreen M Fuller
▲   Un-incorporated Society
○   *B; to promote the breeding of poll cattle (ie cattle without horns)
●   Mtgs - VE
<   Holstein UK
M   30 i

Polymer Machinery Manufacturers' & Distributors' Association Ltd   (PMMDA)   1966
■   PO Box 2539, RUGBY, Warks, CV23 9YF.   (c'ee/sp)
0870 241 1474   fax 0870 241 1475
email pmmda@pmmda.org.uk
http://www.pmmda.org.uk
C'ee Sec: Sandy Weaver,   Pres: Brian Stinton
▲   Company Limited by Guarantee
○   *T; support to plastics machinery suppliers in the UK
Gp   Export; Technical; Health & safety
●   ET - Exhib - SG - Stat - Expt - Inf - LG - Sponsorship of 'Modern Apprentice'
<   Brit Plastics Fedn
M   c 80 f
¶   Buyers Guide to...
Granulators;   Chillers;   Robots;   Dryers;   Temperature Control;   all 2 yrly; free.

Ponies Association (UK) Ltd   (Ponies(UK))   1988
■   Chesham House, 56 Green End Rd, SAWTRY, Cambs, PE28 5UY.   (hq)
01487 830278   fax 01487 832086
email info@poniesuk.org   http://www.poniesuk.org
Chmn: Mrs Davina Whiteman
▲   Company Limited by Guarantee; Registered Charity
○   *G; to promote equestrian events & the training of horse & rider
●   Conf - ET - Comp
M   4,500 i
¶   NL - 2 + by email; ftm only.

The Pony Club   (Pony Club)   1929
■   Stoneleigh Park, KENILWORTH, Warks, CV8 2RW.   (hq)
024 7669 8300
http://www.pcuk.org
Chief Exec: Mrs Judy E Edwards
▲   Registered Charity
Br   360; 15 countries
○   *S, *Y; an international voluntary youth organisation for those interested in ponies & riding
Gp   Mounted games; Tetrathlon; Polo; Polocrosse; Show jumping; Eventing; Dressage; Racing
●   Conf - ET - Exam - Exhib - Comp - VE
M   36,000 i, UK / 104,500 i, o'seas
¶   Ybk.   Instructors Hbk.
Manual of Horsemanship.   All Rule Books - 1.

Pool Promoters Association   (PPA)   1933
NR   100 Old Hall St, LIVERPOOL, L3 9TD.   (asa)
0151-237 7777   fax 0151-237 7676
Sec: W Roger S Calvert
▲   Un-incorporated Society
○   *T; to coordinate dealings with the government & football authorities; to deal generally with enquiries from the public & the media
●   Mtgs - Comp - Stat - Inf - LG
M   2 f

Pop & Rock Fans' Association   (PRFA)   1997
■   11 South Block Peabody Buildings, Brodlove Lane, LONDON, E1W 3DY.   (hsb)
0798 047 7454
email gothamcity8@yahoo.co.uk
Pres: Michael Blackett
▲   Un-incorporated Society
○   *D, *K; to give record buying fans a voice & platform within the music industry on a wide variety of interests - CD prices, tickets, merchandise, venue conditions etc
●   Conf - Mtgs - Campaigning/marching
M   20+ i

Popular Flying Association   (PFA)   1946
NR   Turweston Aerodrome, BRACKLEY, Northants, NN13 5YD. (hq)
01280 846786   fax 01280 846780
email office@pfa.org.uk   http://www.pfa.org.uk
Chmn: Roger Hopkinson,   Sec: Stewart Jackson
▲   Company Limited by Guarantee
○   *G, *S; the representative body in the UK for amateur aircraft construction, recreational & sport flying; encourages amateur design; promotes clubs & light aviation's infrastructure
Gp   Engineering (to administer & regulate amateur aircraft construction)
●   Conf - Mtgs - ET - Res - Inf - Lib - LG - Annual international air rally
<   R Aero Club; Sports Council
M   8,500 i
¶   Popular Flying (Jnl) - 6; ftm, £5 each nm.

Portable Electric Tool Manufacturers Association   (PETMA) 1942
■   PO Box 35084, LONDON, NW1 4XE.   (asa)
020 7935 8532   fax 020 7935 8532
email office@petma.org.uk
Sec: C Dunn-Meynell
○   *T
●   Mtgs - Res - Inf
<   Eur Portable Tool Assn (EPTA)
M   2 f

Portman Group   (TPG)   1990
- 7-10 Chandos St, LONDON, W1G 9DQ.   (hq)
  020 7907 3700   fax 020 7907 3710
  email info@portmangroup.org.uk
  http://www.portmangroup.org.uk
  Chief Exec: Jean Coussins
- ○ *K; a drinks industry initiative against alcohol misuse
- ● Conf - Mtgs - ET - Res - Stat - Inf
- M 8 f, 2 org

Portsmouth & South East Hampshire Chamber of Commerce & Industry   (P&SEHCC&I)   1879
- Regional Business Centre, Harts Farm Way, HAVANT, Hants, PO9 1HR.   (hq)
  023 9244 9449   fax 023 9244 9444
  email sehants@chamber.org.uk
  http://www.chamber.org.uk
  Chief Exec: Maureen Frost
- ▲ Company Limited by Guarantee
- ○ *C
- ● Conf - Mtgs - ET - Res - Exhib - Expt - Inf - Lib - LG - Networking - Commercial services
- < Brit Chams Comm
- > E Hants Cham Comm
- M 800 f, 100 org
- ¶ Business News - 10; ftm, £2.90 each nm.

Portuguese Chamber - the Portuguese UK Business Network   1980
- 11 Belgrave Square (4th floor), LONDON, SW1X 8PP.   (hq)
  020 7201 6638
  Chief Exec: John Newgas
- ▲ Company Limited by Guarantee
- Br representative offices in Midlands & Scotland; Lisbon (Portugal)
- ○ *C
- Gp Industry; Financial; Construction; Import/Export; Legal; Consultancy; Design; Marketing; Freight/Transport; Services
- ● Conf - Mtgs - Res - SG - Stat - Expt - Inf - LG
- M 240 f & org, UK / 105 f & org, o'seas
- ¶ Tradewinds (NL) - 3; ftm.
  Directory & Ybk; ftm.

Post-tensioning Association   (PTA)   1984
- NR c/o David Collings, Benaim (UK) Ltd, Dilke House, 1 Malet St, LONDON, WC1E 7JN.   (chmn/b)
  020 7580 6000   fax 020 7580 69090
  Chmn: David Collings
- ▲ Un-incorporated Society
- ○ *T; post-tensioned concrete
- ● Mtgs - SG - Technical developments in conjunction with other technical committees & bodies
- M 10 f
  Note: a new chairman is due to be elected in January 2007

Post Office Vehicle Club   (POVC)   1962
- NR 32 Russell Way, LEIGHTON BUZZARD, Beds, LU7 3NG.
  01525 382129
  email povehclub@aol.com   http://www.povehclub.org.uk
  Hon Sec: Frank Weston
- ○ *G; for people interested in vehicles operated by the General Post Office & its successors, the Post Office, BT & Royal Mail
- ● Mtgs - Res - Exhib - Inf - VE
- < Roads & Road Transport Hist Assn
- M 200 i
- ¶ Post Horn - 12.

Postal History Society   (PHS)   1936
- 36 Salmons Lane, WHYTELEAFE, Surrey, CR3 0AN.   (sp)
  020 8763 0146
  Sec: Jay Walmsley
- ○ *G, *L, *Q; the study of written communication, with special emphasis on the postal services of the world
- ● Conf - Mtgs - Exhib - Comp - Inf - Lib - Publications
- M c 370 i
- ¶ Postal History - 4; ftm, £7 nm.

Postcard Traders' Association   (PTA)   1976
- 11 Richard Close, Upton, POOLE, Dorset, BH16 5PF.   (hsp)
  01202 623300   fax 01202 631149
  email magpiebillpipe@freeserve.com
  http://www.postcard.co.uk
  Hon Sec: Bill Pipe
- ▲ Un-incorporated Society
- ○ *T; to encourage the hobby of picture postcard collecting worldwide
- ● Exhib - Comp - Inf - Organisation of the Picture Postcard Show
- M 160 f, UK / 21 f, o'seas
- ¶ News - 4; ftm only.

Potato Processors Association   (PPA)
- NR 6 Catherine St, LONDON, WC2B 5JJ.   (hq)
  020 7836 2460   fax 020 7836 0580
- ▲ Un-incorporated Society
- ○ *T
- ● Mtgs
- < U Eur Inds Transformation Pomme de Terre; Food & Drink Fedn
- M 11 f, 1 org

Poultry Club of Great Britain   (PCGB)   1877
- NR South Lodge, Creeton Rd, Swinstead, GRANTHAM, Lincs, NG33 4PG.   (hsb)
  01476 550067
  email info@poultryclub.org   http://www.poultryclub.org
  Gen Sec: Mrs A Bachmet
- ▲ Registered Charity
- ○ *B, *F; to promote high standards in the keeping & breeding of purebred poultry
- ● ET - Exhib - Inf
- M c 1,400 i & org
- ¶ NL - 4;   Ybk - 1; both ftm only.

Powder Actuated Systems Association
  this organisation is now dormant

Power Fastenings Association Ltd   (PFA)   1978
- NR 42 Heath St, TAMWORTH, Staffs, B79 7JH.   (hq)
  01827 52337
  Sec: A D Skelding
- ▲ Company Limited by Guarantee
- ○ *T; portable, compressed air actuated tools for driving fasteners into another object by means of a single blow
- ● Mtgs - Stat
- < ATACI (France); ISANTA (USA)
- M 6 i

Powered Access Interest Group
  a special interest group of the **Construction Plant-hire Association**

Powys Society   1967
- 25 Mansfield Rd, TAUNTON, Somerset, TA1 3NJ.   (hsp)
  01823 278177
  http://www.powys-society.org
  Hon Sec: Peter Lazare
- ▲ Registered Charity
- ○ *A, *G; to establish public recognition of the writings, thought & contribution to the arts of the Powys family, particularly the brothers John Cowper, Theodore & Llewelyn & their close circle of friends: Louis Wilkinson, James Hanley, T E Lawrence & Sylvia Townsend Warner
- ● Conf - Mtgs - Lib
- < Powys Soc of N America
- M 200 i, UK / 150 i, o'seas
- ¶ The Powys Journal - 1.   The Powys NL - 3.   LM - 3 yrly.
  A Powys Checklist (list of publications by the Powys family & circle) - irreg.

© CBD Research Ltd · Beckenham · BR3 5JS · Tel 020 8650 7745 · Fax 020 8650 0768 · E-mail cbd@cbdresearch.com · www.cbdresearch.com

Prader-Willi Syndrome Association (UK)   (PWSA (UK))   1981
- ■ 125a London Rd, DERBY, DE1 2QQ.   (welfare/coord/p)
  01332 365676   fax 01332 360401
  email info@pwsa-uk.demon.co.uk
  http://www.pwsa.co.uk
  Welfare Services Coordinator: Jacquie Wood
  Hon Sec: Julian Courtauld
- ▲ Registered Charity
- Br 6
- ○ *W; to promote care, welfare & treatment of people with
  Prader-Willi syndrome; to offer support & information to
  carers & professionals
- ● Conf - Mtgs - ET - Inf - Lib
- < Intl Prader-Willi Syndrome Org
- M 1,300 i, UK / 90 i, o'seas
- ¶ Publications list available.

Prayer Book Society   (PBS)   1975
- NR The Studio, Copyhold Farm, Lady Grove, Goring Heath,
  READING, Berks, RG8 7RT.   (chmn/b)
  0118-984 2582
  http://www.prayerbook.org.uk
  Chmn: Roger Evans
- ▲ Registered Charity
- Br 44; Portugal, S Africa
- ○ *R; to uphold the worship & doctrine of the Church of England
  as enshrined in the Book of Common Prayer; to spread the
  use of the Book of Common Prayer & to see that it is used
- ● Conf - Mtgs - ET - Comp - Inf
- M i
- ¶ NL - 4.   Faith & Heritage - 2.   Faith & Worship - 2.

PRCA Ireland - Public Relations Consultants Association Ireland   (PRCA)
- IRL 78 Merrion Sq, DUBLIN 2, Republic of Ireland.
  353 (1) 676 4565   fax 353 (1) 676 4562
  email info@prca.ie   http://www.prca.ie
  Chmn: Carol Flynn,   Chief Exec: Gerry Davis
- ○ *P

Pre Eclampsia Society   (PETS)   1981
- ■ Meadowside, 185 Greenward Lane, HOCKLEY, Essex,
  SS5 5JN.   (trustee/p)
  01702 205088
  email dawnjames@clera.co.uk
  http://www.pre-eclampsia-society.org.uk
  Founder: Dawn James,   Trustee: Sharon Copping
- ▲ Registered Charity
- ○ *W; self-help & support group for women suffering from, or
  who have suffered from, pre-eclampsia / eclampsia, &
  others interested in the condition
- ● Res - Comp - Stat - Inf - Lib
- M 200 i
- ¶ NL - 4; ftm only.

Pre-Raphaelite Society   (PRS)   1988
- ■ 37 Larchmere Drive, Hall Green, BIRMINGHAM, B28 8JB.
  (sp)
  email info@pre-raphaelitesociety.org
  http://www.pre-raphaelitesociety.org
  Sec: Barry C Johnson
- ▲ Registered Charity
- ○ *A; the study of the lives & art of the Pre-Raphaelite
  Brotherhood
- ● VE - Lectures - Seminars
- M 350 i, UK & o'seas
- ¶ The Review of the PRS - 3.

Pre-Retirement Association of Great Britain & Northern Ireland
  since 2005 **Life Academy**

Pre-School Learning Alliance   (PLA)   1961
- NR 188 York Way, LONDON, N7 9AD.   (hq)
  020 7697 2534   fax 020 7700 0319
  email info@pre-school.org.uk
  http://www.pre-school.org.uk
  Chmn (Nat Exec C'ee): Judith Thompson
- ▲ Registered Charity
- Br 300
- ○ *E; links 16,000 pre-schools & 500,000 young children & their
  families in England
- ● Conf - Mtgs - ET - Exam - Res - Exhib - Comp - Stat - Inf - Lib -
  PL - VE - Empl - LG
- < Wld Org for Early Childhood Education (OMEP)
- M 500,000 i (children), 16,000 gps
- ¶ Under Five (NL) - 10.   AR; free.
  Guide to Training [lists courses] - 1.
  Leaflets; free.   Publications list available.

Precast Concrete Paving & Kerb Association
  see Interpave, the Precast Concrete Paving & Kerb Association - a
  product association of the **British Precast Concrete Federation**

Precast Flooring Federation
  a product association of the **British Precast Concrete Federation**

Prefabricated Access Suppliers' & Manufacturers' Association   (PASMA)   1978
- ■ PO Box 168, LEEDS, LS11 9WW.   (hsp)
  0845 230 4041   fax 0845 230 4042
  email info@pasma.co.uk   http://www.pasma.co.uk
  Gen Mgr: Peter Bennett
- ▲ Company Limited by Guarantee
- ○ *T; the safe use of aluminium towers
- ● Conf - Mtgs - ET - Exam - Exhib
- < Access Ind Forum
- M 40 i, 220 f
- ¶ Operators Code of Practice; £5.
  Guide to Safe Use of Mobile Access (DVD); £35.

Prehistoric Society   1935
- NR c/o University College London, Institute of Archaeology, 31-34
  Gordon Sq, LONDON, WC1H 0PY.   (mail) address
  Admin Sec: Dr Tessa Machling
- ▲ Company Limited by Guarantee; Registered Charity
- ○ *L; study of prehistory & its interpretation & conservation
- ● Conf - Mtgs - Res
- < Coun Brit Archaeology
- M 1,700 i, 200 org, UK / 300 i, 200 org, o'seas
- ¶ Proceedings - 1.   PAST (NL) - 3.

Premature Menopause Support Group
  see full title **Daisy Network Premature Menopause Support Group**

Premenstrual Society   (Premsoc)   1986
- NR PO Box 429, ADDLESTONE, Surrey, KT15 1DZ.   (h)
  01932 872560 (1100-1800 hrs) chmn b
  Chmn: Dr Michael G Brush
- Br 10
- ○ *W; information & support for individual sufferers from
  premenstrual syndrome (PMS) & period pains
  (dysmenorrhoea)
- ● Conf - ET - Res - Inf
- M 500 i
- ¶ NL - 2; ftm only.   Leaflets.
  Selfhelp for PMS (booklet); free (sae please).

Premium Rate Association   (PRA)   1997
NR   Elite House, 25 South St, READING, Berks, RG1 4QU.   (hq)
0118-956 7956
Chief Exec: Suzanne Gillies
▲   Company Limited by Guarantee
○   *T; for companies involved in the premium rate telephone industry
Gp   Telecommunications
●   Mtgs - Res - LG - Liaison with regulators (ICSTIS, OFCOM)
M   35 f
¶   NL - 4.

Presbyterian Historical Society of Ireland   (PHSI)   1906
■   Church House, Fisherwick Place, BELFAST, BT1 6DW.   (hq)
028 9032 2284   fax 028 9041 7307
Hon Secs: Dr A W G Brown & James Moffett
▲   Registered Charity
○   *L; to collect & preserve the materials & to promote knowledge of the history of the Presbyterian Church in Ireland & of its constituent congregations
●   Mtgs - Lib
M   400 i, UK / 50 i, o'seas
¶   Bulletin - 1; ftm, £2 nm.
Fasti of the General Assembly of the Presbyterian Church in Ireland 1840-1910; 3 parts; £2 per part.
Publications list available.

Press Standards Board of Finance Ltd   (PRESSBOF)   1990
NR   48 Palmerston Place, EDINBURGH, EH12 5DE.   (sb)
0131-240 3270   fax 0131-220 4344
Sec & Treas: J B Raeburn
▲   Company Limited by Guarantee
○   *N, *T; coordination & finance of self-regulation in the newspaper & magazine publishing industry in the UK
●   Mtgs - LG
M   5 org
¶   Code of Practice; ftm.

Pressed Flower Guild   1983
NR   383 Leasowe Rd, Moreton, WIRRAL, Merseyside, CH46 2RF.   (hsp)
0151-638 1706
Hon Sec: Mrs C Foster
▲   Un-incorporated Society
○   *H; to raise the standard of pressed flowers; to arrange teaching & seminar facilities
●   Conf - Mtgs - ET - Exam - Res - Exhib - Comp - SG - Inf - Lib - VE
<   R Horticl Soc
M   c 150 i
¶   NL - 4;   LM - 1; both ftm only.
✕   2000-02 Pressed Flower Craft Guild

Pressure Gauge & Dial Thermometer Association   (BPGMA)   1951
■   Heathcote House, 136 Hagley Rd, BIRMINGHAM, B16 9PN.   (asa)
0121-454 4141   fax 0121-454 4949
email info@pgdt.org   http://www.pgdt.org
Exec Sec: Mrs Sharon J Parker
▲   Un-incorporated Society
○   *T; to promote the industry; to participate in the preparation & amendment of European & inter-nation standards
●   Mtgs - Stat
M   16 f
✕   2003-04 British Pressure Gauge Manufacturers Association

Pressure Sensitive Manufacturers Association   (PSMA)   1974
NR   c/o BPIF, Farringdon Point, 29-35 Farringdon Rd, LONDON, EC1M 3JF.   (hsb)
020 7915 8334
Sec: Sue Bridger
○   *T
●   Mtgs
<   a special interest group within the British Printing Industries Federation
M   9 f

Prestressed Concrete Association
a product association of the **British Precast Concrete Federation**

Primary Care Dermatology Society   (PCDS)   1994
■   Gable House, 40 High St, RICKMANSWORTH, Herts, WD3 1ER.   (secretariat)
01923 711678   fax 01923 778131
email pcds@pcds.org.uk   http://www.pcds.org.uk
Chmn: Dr Stephen Kownacki,   Dr Elizabeth Ogden
▲   Company Limited by Guarantee
Br   Republic of Ireland
○   *M
●   Conf - Mtgs - ET
<   Brit Assn Dermatologists
M   580 i, 13 f, UK / 80 i, o'seas
¶   PCDS Bulletin - 4; free.

Primary Care Rheumatology Society
NR   PO Box 42, NORTHALLERTON, N Yorks, DL7 8YG.
01609 774794   fax 01609 774726
http://www.pcrsociety.org.uk

Primary Immunodeficiency Association   (PiA)   1989
■   Alliance House, 12 Caxton St, LONDON, SW1H 0QS.   (hq)
020 7976 7640   fax 020 7976 7641
email info@pia.org.uk   http://www.pia.org.uk
Chief Exec: Chris Hughan
▲   Registered Charity
○   *W; to promote the wellbeing of people with primary immunodeficiencies
Gp   Personal support; Medical advisory panel
●   Conf - Mtgs - Res - Inf - LG
<   Intl Patient Org for Primary Immunodeficiencies (IPOPI); AMRC
M   c 1,500
¶   Insight - 4; subscription only.
Various publications; ftm, 50p - £2 nm.

Primate Society of Great Britain   (PSGB)   1967
■   c/o Dr Colleen Schaffner, Psychology Dept, University of Chester, CHESTER, CH1 4BJ.   (hsb)
01244 513476   fax 01244 392823
email secretary:@psgb.org   http://www.psgb.org
Sec: Dr Colleen Schaffner,
Pres: Prof Ann MacLaren
▲   Registered Charity
○   *L; research into & general awareness of primate biology, evolution, conservation & management
Gp   Working parties: Conservation, Captive care
●   Conf - Mtgs - ET - Res - Inf - LG
<   Intl Primatological Soc; Eur Primatological Fedn; Inst Biology
M   265 i, 10 f, UK / 20 i, 10 f, o'seas
¶   Primate Eye - 3; £25 m, £30 nm.

© CBD Research Ltd · Beckenham · BR3 5JS · Tel 020 8650 7745 · Fax 020 8650 0768 · E-mail cbd@cbdresearch.com · www.cbdresearch.com

Principals' Professional Council   1920
NR   1 Heath Sq, Boltro Rd, HAYWARDS HEATH, W Sussex,
    RH16 1BL.   (hsb)
    01444 472499
    Sec: Ken Clarke
▲   Un-incorporated Society
Br   9
○   *E, *P; committed to the strong mutual support of its members
    working with other organisations for the promotion &
    development of the further education sector
Gp   Colleges of Agriculture & Horticulture
●   Conf - Mtgs - ET - LG
<   a council of the Association of Colleges
M   750 i
¶   Newslink (NL) - 5;   Life Members (NL) - 2;
    Hbk (incl LM) - 1; all ftm only.

Printed Postage Impression Study Circle
    a group of the**British Postmark Society**

Printing Historical Society   (PHS)   1964
■   c/o St Bride Library, Bride Lane, Fleet St, LONDON,
    EC4Y 8EE.   (hq)
    email secretary:printinghistoricalsociety.org.uk
    Hon Sec: Philip Wickens
▲   Registered Charity
○   *L; history of printing & preservation of historical printing
    equipment; history of the book
●   Conf - Mtgs - ET - Res - VE - Recording & preserving antique
    equipment
M   i & libraries
¶   Jnl - 2;   NL - irreg; both ftm.

Printmakers Council   (PMC)   1965
NR   Ground Floor Unit, 23 Blue Anchor Lane, LONDON,
    SE16 3UL.   (hq)
    020 7237 6789
▲   Registered Charity
○   *A; promotion of printmaking & the art & work of
    contemporary printmakers & new & experimental techniques;
    to aid young & unestablished artists
●   Mtgs - Exhib - Comp - Inf - Lib (slides)
M   300 i, UK / 20 i, o'seas
¶   Imprint - 4; ftm only.

Prison Advice & Care Trust   (PACT)   1975
NR   C5 City Cloisters, 196 Old St, LONDON, EC1V 9FR.   (hq)
    020 7490 3139
    Dir: Andy Keen-Downs
▲   Company Limited by Guarantee; Registered Charity
○   *W; to offer advice, information & emotional support to families
    & friends of those in prison
●   Mtgs
M   i
¶   Leaflets;   Information booklets;   AR.
×   2001 Prisoners' Wives & Families Society

Prison Governors Association   (PGA)   1987
NR   Horseferry House (Rm 405), Dean Ryle St, LONDON,
    SW1P 2AW.   (hq)
    020 7217 8591   fax 020 7217 8923
    http://www.prisongovernors.org.uk
    Gen Sec: C P A Bushell
▲   Un-incorporated Society
Br   c 150
○   *P; to represent the industrial relations & professional interests
    of prison governors (operational managers & senior
    operational managers in England, Wales, Scotland &
    Northern Ireland
Gp   Northern Ireland (separate prison services), Scotland
●   Conf - Mtgs - Empl - LG
M   1,200 i
¶   The Key - 4; ftm only.

Prison Officers' Association   (POA)   1939
NR   245 Church St, LONDON, N9 9HW.   (hq)
    020 8803 0255
    Gen Sec: B Caton
Br   1; N Ireland
○   *U
Gp   Prison officers; Nurses & ancillary staff in special hospitals
●   Conf - Mtgs - ET - Res - Stat - Inf - Lib - VE - Empl
<   TUC; Coun Civil Service Us; EUROFEDOP
M   c 35,000 i
¶   Gatelodge - 6.
×   2001 Prison Officers Association of Scotland (merged)

Prisoners Abroad   1978
■   89-93 Fonthill Rd, LONDON, N4 3JH.   (hq)
    020 7561 6820   fax 020 7561 6821
    email info@prisonersabroad.org.uk
    http://www.prisonersabroad.org.uk
    Chief Exec: Pauline Crowe
▲   Registered Charity
○   *W; to offer support for British nationals in prison outside the
    UK & their families. Information on foreign criminal justice
    systems, prison conditions & transfer
●   Inf - Practical support - Survival grants - Pen-pal scheme -
    Resettlement assistance
¶   NL - 3;   AR - 1; both free.
×   2003 (April) National Council for the Welfare of Prisoners
    Abroad

Prisoners Wives & Families Society
    2001 merged with the Bourne Trust to form the **Prison Advice &
    Care Trust**

Private Libraries Association   (PLA)   1956
■   Ravelston, South View Road, PINNER, Middx, HA5 3YD.
    email dchambrs@aol.com   http://www.plabooks.org
    Hon Sec: S J Brett,   Hon Ed: David Chambers
▲   Registered Charity; Un-incorporated Society
○   *A, *G; encouragement of buying & private ownership of
    books; publication of books of relevance to book collectors
●   Mtgs - VE
<   [in liaison with the Chart Inst of Library & Inf Profls]
M   370 i, 30 f, UK / 150 i, 100 f, o'seas
¶   The Private Library - 4; ftm, £25 nm.   NL - 4.
    Private Press Books (check list of work of private presses in the
    western world) - 1; £10 m, £16 nm.
    Members' Volume - 2/3 yrly; ftm, £30-£50 nm.
    Exchange List - 4.

Private Wagon Federation   (PWF)   1977
NR   Homelea - Westland Green, Little Hadham, WARE, Herts,
    SG11 2AG.   (hsp)
    01279 843487
    email geoffrey.prattbtconnect.com
    Sec Gen: G Pratt
○   *T
Gp   Railway wagon: Building; Hiring; Owners; Repairers
M   5 org

Probation Boards' Association   2002
NR   83 Victoria St, LONDON, SW1H 0HW.   (hq)
    020 3008 7930   fax 010 3008 7931
    Chief Exec: Martin Wargent
○   *T
M   42 probation boards

Probation Managers Association (PMA) 1980
NR Hayes Court, West Common Rd, HAYES, Kent, BR2 7AU. (sb)
020 8462 7755
Br 39
○ *U; for managers in probation service - provides professional
advice & support & full range of trade union functions
● Conf - Mtgs - ET - Inf - NG - LG
M 600 i
¶ The Probation Manager - 4; ftm.

Processed Vegetable Growers' Association Ltd (PVGA) 1970
■ 133 Eastgate, LOUTH, Lincs, LN11 9QG. (hq)
01507 602427   fax 01507 600689
email postbox@pvga.co.uk
Chief Exec: M P Riggall
○ *F, *H
● Mtgs - Res - Stat - Expt - Inf - LG - Provision of administration &
secretarial services - Contract negotiation support
M [i, f]
¶ Specialist market surveys in UK & Europe - prices vary.

**Processing & Packaging Machinery Association (PPMA)
1987**
■ New Progress House, 34 Stafford Rd, WALLINGTON, Surrey,
SM6 9AA. (hq)
020 8773 8111   fax 020 8773 0022
email admin@ppma.co.uk   http://www.ppma.co.uk
Chief Exec: Chris Boxton
▲ Company Limited by Guarantee
○ *T; for manufacturers of machinery used in processing &
packaging food, cosmetics, pharmaceuticals, beverages etc
● Conf - Mtgs - ET - Exhib - Stat - Expt - Inf - Lib - PL - LG
< Confedn Packaging Machinery Assns (COPAMA); European
Sector Gp (EUROPAMA)
M c 330 f
¶ PPMA Machinery Directory - 1; ftm.
Machinery Update - 6; ftm.

Processors & Growers Research Organisation (PGRO) 1944
■ The Research Station, Great North Rd, THORNHAUGH,
Cambs, PE8 6HJ. (hq)
01780 782585   fax 01780 783993
email info@pgro.co.uk   http://www.pgro.co.uk
Dir & Sec: G P Gent
▲ Registered Charity
○ *H, *Q; research into the production & harvesting of peas &
beans for both vegetable & protein use
Gp Agronomy; Biology; Botany
● Conf - ET - Res - SG - Inf - Lib - VE - Advisory & technical
services
M 3,003 i, 135 f, 30 org, UK / 8 i, 33 f, 17 org, o'seas
¶ NL - 2; ftm.   AR; ftm, £2 nm.
Information sheets - 8/10; m only.

Procurators Fiscal Society 1930
NR Procurator Fiscal's Office, Carlyle House, Carlyle Rd,
KIRKCALDY, Fife, KY1 1DB. (hsb)
01592 268661
Sec: Valerie Bremner
○ *P; [in Scotland the Procurator Fiscal is the name for the public
prosecutor who also does the same work as a Coroner
elsewhere]
is a division of the Association of First Division Civil Servants

Producers Alliance for Cinema & Television (PACT) 1991
NR Procter House, 1 Procter St, LONDON, WC1V 6DW. (hq)
020 7067 4367
○ *P, *T; for independent film & television producers in the UK
M f

Production Managers Association   1991
NR Ealing Studios, Ealing Green, LONDON, W5 5EP. (hq)
020 8758 8699
Admin: Caroline Fleming
○ *P; for film, TV & video production managers
< Producers Alliance for Cinema & Television (PACT)
M c 180 i
¶ The Bottom Line - 6.
Directory of Members - 1.

Production Services Association (PSA) 1994
NR PO Box 2709, BATH, BA1 3YS. (hq)
01225 332668   fax 01225 332701
email admin@psa.org.uk   http://www.psa.org.uk
Gen Mgr: Andy Lenthal;
▲ Company Limited by Guarantee
○ *T; to make representations to government & the EU on matters
affecting the live music, events & entertainment industry
Gp Training & qualification development in the BTEC award system
● Conf - ET - Exhib - LG
M c 500

Professional Anglers Association Ltd   (PAA)
■ Federation House, STONELEIGH, Warks, CV8 2RF. (hq)
024 7641 4999   fax 024 7641 4990
email paa@sportsandplay.com   http://www.paauk.com
Sec: Shaun Gilbert
▲ Company Limited by Guarantee
○ *P; to represent accredited angling coaches
● ET
< a group of the Fedn of Sports & Play Assns (FSPA)
M 130 i

Professional Association of Alexander Teachers (PAAT) 1987
■ 18 Hilton Ave, BIRMINGHAM, B28 0PE. (hsp)
0121-745 7707
http://www.paat.org.uk
Hon Sec: Angela Coates
▲ Un-incorporated Society
Br 14
○ *P; to support members who are teachers of the Alexander
Technique; to promote the Alexander Technique which
provides a practical means for change by bringing about an
improvement in physical balance & coordination
● ET - Exam - Res - Exhib - SG - Inf - Evening classes -
Introductory courses - 4-year teachers training course
M 43 i
¶ Pamphlets.

Professional Association for Catering Education
see **PACE: Professional Association for Catering Education**

Professional Association of Clinical Therapists
see note under **Federation of Holistic Therapists**

*Professional Association for Family Court Advisers & Independent Social
Work Practitioners & Consultants*
see **NAGALRO: Professional Association for Family Court
Advisers & Independent Social Work Practitioners &
Consultants**

© CBD Research Ltd · Beckenham · BR3 5JS · Tel 020 8650 7745 · Fax 020 8650 0768 · E-mail cbd@cbdresearch.com · www.cbdresearch.com

Professional Association of Nursery Nurses   (PANN)   1982
NR   2 St James' Court, Friar Gate, DERBY, DE1 1BT.
        01332 372337   fax 01332 290310 & 292431   (hq)
        email pann@pat.org.uk   http://www.pat.org.uk
        Gen Sec: Jean Gemmell,
        Profl Officer: Tricia Pritchard
Br   12
○   *P, *U; an independent trade union, with a no-strike rule
        promoting professionalism; members include nursery nurses,
        nannies & other childcarers
●   Conf - Mtgs - Exhib - Inf
<   since 1.9.1995 a section of the Profl Assn of Teachers
M   3,600 i
¶   Professionalism in Practice - 4; ftm, £2 nm.
        Members' Hbk [with PAT] - 1; ftm only.

Professional Association of Teachers   (PAT)   1970
NR   2 St James' Court, Friar Gate, DERBY, DE1 1BT.   (hq)
        01332 372337   fax 01332 290310 & 292431
        email hq@pat.org.uk   http://www.pat.org.uk
        Gen Sec: Philip Parkin
Br   165
○   *E, *P, *U; a professional association of teachers, lecturers &
        head teachers in all parts of the UK, from nursery school to
        tertiary institutions, in both the maintained & independent
        sectors.   Is strictly independent & has a no-strike rule
●   Conf - Mtgs - ET - Res - Exhib - Stat - Inf - LG
M   35,000 i, UK / 100 i, o'seas
¶   Professionalism in Practice - 4; ftm, £2 nm.
        Members' Hbk (incl LM) - 1; ftm only.

Professional Associations Research Network   (PARN)   1998
■   49 Park St, BRISTOL, BS1 5NT.   (hq)
        0117-929 4515   fax 0117-934 9623
        email info@parn.org.uk   http://www.parn.org.uk
        Dir: Prof Andy Friedman
▲   Company Limited by Guarantee
○   *N, *P; 'to be the centre of expertise on issues relating to
        professionalism & the professionalisation of the professional
        associations. To provide a research enriched network for
        professional associations & a range of specialist knowledge
        based services'
Gp   CPD Network; Consultancy & information services
●   Conf -ET - Res - Inf - Lib - Consultancy - Publications -
        Networking
M   108 org, UK / 11 (Ireland)
¶   CPD Spotlight (NL) - 12; ftm only.
        PARN Members News Update - 12; ftm only
        PARN Research Publications - 2; ftm, £50-£95 nm.

Professional Boatmans Association   1991
NR   48 Loveys Rd, Yapton, ARUNDEL, W Sussex, BN18 0HG.   (hq)
        01243 551927
        http://www.pba.org.uk
        Sec: Daniel Parker

Professional Bodyguard Association   (PBA)   1985
NR   The White House, 24 Cumberland Terrace, WILLINGTON,
        Co Durham, DL15 0PB.   (hq)
        01388 745645
        Hon Sec: M J Tombs
▲   Un-incorporated Society
○   *P; for the training of bodyguards
●   ET
<   ASLET; Amer Soc of Law Enforcement Trainers; ASLET
M   1,000 i, UK / 300 i, o'seas

**Professional Business & Technical Management   (ProfBTM)
1983**
■   Warwick Corner, 42 Warwick Rd, KENILWORTH, Warks,
        CV8 1HE.   (asa)
        01926 855498   fax 01926 513100
        Pres/Hon Sec: Prof H J Manners
○   *P; to provide a link between business & technology; to keep
        members informed of new developments, controls, methods,
        techniques & education in business & technical fields
Gp   Business; Technology; Management
●   ET - Exam
<   Inst Management Specialists; Inst Manufacturing
¶   Professional Business & Technical Management (Jnl) - 3; £2 m,
        £7 nm.

Professional Charter Association   (PCA)   1991
■   c/o The Glass Works, Penns Road, PETERSFIELD, Hants,
        GU23 2EW.   (hq)
        01730 710425   fax 01730 710423
        email info@ybdsa.co.uk   http://www.ybdsa.co.uk
        Chmn: Robin Milledge
○   *T; to represent professional skippers & vessel owmers whose
        principal activity is shippered charter in domestic waters
●   Mtgs - LG - Social events
<   Yacht Brokers, Designers & Surveyors Assn
M   25 f
¶   [in the YBDSA Ybk - 2 yrly.]

Professional Coarse Fisheries Association   (PCFA)
■   c/o Tingrith Fishery, TINGRITH, Beds, MK17 9EW.   (chmn/p)
        01525 714012
        email pcfa@fisheries.co.uk   http://www.fisheries.co.uk/
        pcfa
        Chmn: Ann Freeman
▲   Un-incorporated Society
○   *T
●   Mtgs - Inf - LG
M   60 f
×   2005-06 Commercial Coarse Fisheries Association

Professional Computing Association   (PCA)   1993
■   PO Box 48, ROYSTON, Herts, SG8 6JS.   (hq)
        01763 262987   fax 01763 261907
        email admin@pcauk.org   http://www.pcauk.org
        Exec Dir: Keith Warburton
▲   Company Limited by Guarantee
○   *T; to promote, represent & provide services & information for
        businesses in the personal computer marketplace; to provide
        consumer advice & protection
Gp   Personal Computer Direct Marketers' Association; Payment
        protection scheme
●   Conf - Mtgs - ET - Inf - LG
M   155 f, 2 org
¶   Interface (NL) - 12; ftm, £50 nm.   AR; ftm.
        EMC Guidance Notes (notes on EC Guidelines); ftm, £30 nm.
×   2004 Personal Computer Association

Professional Contractors Group Ltd   (PCG)   1999
NR   Sovereign Court, 635 Sipson Rd, WEST DRAYTON, Middx,
        UB7 0JE.   (hq)
        0845 125 9899   fax 020 8622 3200
        email admin@pca.org.uk   http://www.pca.org.uk
        Chmn: David Ramsden
▲   Company Limited by Guarantee
○   *T; to represent the interests & to promote the use of
        independent contractors & consultants, & to ensure the sector
        retains a professional image; to make representations to
        Government for legislation affecting independent contractors;
        to help members cope with the burden of new legislation,
        particularly IR35; to oppose IR35
Gp   Aberdeen Working Party (AWP); Associate members
●   Conf - Mtgs - LG - Legal / accounting / tax technical advice
<   Assn Technology Staffing Cos (ATSCO); Confedn Brit Ind (CBI);
        Fedn Small Businesses (FSB); Inst Chart Accountants (ICAEW);
        Inst Directors (IoD); Recruitment & Employment
        Confedn (REC); Tax Faculty / Inst Taxation
M   c 14,000 f
¶   NL (email only) - irreg; ftm.

Professional Council for Religious Education   (PCFRE)   1985
■   1020 Bristol Rd, Selly Oak, BIRMINGHAM, W Midlands,
        B29 6LB.   (hq)
        0121-472 4242   fax 0121-472 7575
        email lat@retoday.org.uk   http://www.retoday.org.uk
        Gen Sec: Peter Fishpool
▲   Un-incorporated Society
○   *E, *P, *R; for teachers of religious education in schools &
        colleges
Gp   Examinations & assessment
●   Conf - Mtgs - ET - Res - Comp - LG
<   Eur Fedn Teachers of Religious Educ
M   1,000 i, 50 f, 1,000 schools, UK / 100 i, 23 f, o'seas
¶   Resource - 3; ftm only.

Professional Cricketers' Association   (PCA)   1967
NR   338 Euston Rd (3rd floor), LONDON, NW1 3BT.   (hq)
        020 7544 8668   fax 020 7544 8515
        Chief Exec: Richard Bevan
○   *S; for current & past professional cricketers
M   420 i

Professional Darts Players Association   (PDPA)
■   Federation House, STONELEIGH PARK, Warks, CV8 2RF.   (hq)
        024 7641 4999 ext 207   fax 024 7641 4990
        email jacquib@sportsandplay.com
        http://www.sportsandplay.com
        Assn Mgr: Mrs Jacqui Baldwin
○   *P
<   a group of the Fedn of Sports & Play Assns (FSPA)
M   i

Professional Footballers Association   (PFA)   1907
■   20 Oxford Court, Bishopsgate, MANCHESTER, M2 3WQ.   (hq)
        0161-236 0575   fax 0161-228 7229
        email info@thepfa.co.uk
        http://www.givemefootball.com
        Chief Exec: Gordon Taylor
○   *U
●   Conf - Mtgs - ET - Res - Empl - LG
<   Intl Assn of Football Players Us (FIFPro)
M   4,000 i
¶   The Players Jnl - 4;   The Players Club - 4;   AR; all ftm only.

Professional Gardeners' Guild   (PGG)   1977
■   c/o Mrs Deb Goodenough - Head Gardener, Osborne House,
        EAST COWES, Isle of Wight, PO32 6JY.   (hsp/b)
        01983 299747 (am), 280431 (pm)   fax 01983 297281
        email goodenoughs@btinternet.com
        http://www.pgg.org.uk
        Hon Sec: Mrs Deb Goodenough
▲   Un-incorporated Society
Br   4; Ireland, USA, worldwide
○   *H, *P; to promote & encourage professional contact,
        communication & cooperation between gardeners,
        exchanging ideas & information on all aspects of
        professional gardening, including the use of both new
        technology & traditional skills; to promote gardening as a
        profession, & the better management & maintenance of
        gardens & designed landscapes, especially those of historic,
        horticultural & botanical value
●   Conf - Mtgs - ET - Res - Exhib - Comp - SG - Stat - Inf - VE -
        Empl - LG - Training bursary - Job opportunities - Advice -
        Industry representation
<   Historic Houses Assn; Nat Trust; English Heritage; Garland
M   800+ i, c 10 f, c 30 org, UK / 100+ i, o'seas
¶   The Professional Gardener (Jnl) - 4; £20 m, £36 nm,
        £40 companies, £48 libraries.

Professional Golfers' Association   (PGA)   1901
■   Centenary House, The Belfry, SUTTON COLDFIELD,
        W Midlands, B76 9PT.   (hq)
        01675 470333   fax 01675 477888
        Chief Exec: Sandy Jones
Br   7 regions
○   *P, *S; to promote interest in golf
Gp   Tournament section; Membership services; Development section
●   Conf - Mtgs - ET - Exam - Comp - Stat - Inf - Lib - PL - Empl -
        Securing sponsorship for members tournaments
M   6,500 i, 1,200 trainees, UK / 900 i, o'seas
¶   Profile (Jnl) - 12; ftm, £35 yr nm.
        The PGA Ybk - 1; ftm only.   Regional Hbks - 1; ftm only.

Professional Lighting & Sound Association   (PLASA)   1977
■   38 St Leonards Rd, EASTBOURNE, E Sussex, BN21 3UT.   (hq)
        01323 410335   fax 01323 646905
        email info@plasa.org   http://www.plasa.org
        Exec Dir: Ruth Rossington
▲   Company Limited by Guarantee
○   *T; to serve the entertainment, leisure, communication &
        architectural industries
●   Exhib - Expt - Inf - Lib - VE - LG - Members deliver technical &
        creative solutions to clients & projects worldwide
<   Wld Entertainment Technology Fedn (WETF)
M   50 i, 350 f, UK / 70 f o'seas
¶   Lighting & Sound International - 11; ftm, £30 yr nm.
        Lighting & Sound America - 12; ftm, controlled nm.
        Membership News - 12;   Standards News - 12; both ftm only.
        PLASA Industry Directory - 1; ftm, controlled nm.
        Ybk - 1; free.   AR; ftm.

**Professional Photographic Laboratories Association   (PPLA)
1984**
NR   Wisteria House, 28 Fulling Mill Lane, WELWYN, Herts,
        AL6 9NS.
        0870 240 4542
▲   Company Limited by Guarantee
○   *P, *T; to support professional photographic & imaging centres
●   Conf - Exhib - Inf - Lib - VE
<   Photo Marketing Assn Intl (USA)
M   250 f
¶   Lablink (NL) - 6; ftm.

Professional Plant Users Group   (PPUG)
NR   c/o Landscape Institute, 33 Great Portland St, LONDON,
        W1W 8QG.
        020 7299 4500
○   *H, *P; professional & trade bodies using plants in landscaping

© CBD Research Ltd · Beckenham · BR3 5JS · Tel 020 8650 7745 · Fax 020 8650 0768 · E-mail cbd@cbdresearch.com · www.cbdresearch.com

Professional Rugby Players Association   (PRA)   1998
NR   Parkshot House, 5 Kew Rd, RICHMOND, Surrey, TW9 2PR.
     (hq)
     020 8334 8019
     Chief Exec: Damien Hopley
○   *P, *S; to represent professional Rugby Union players
●   Mtgs
M   i

Professional Services Marketing Group
NR   PO Box 131, SAFFRON WALDEN, Essex, CB11 4ZN.   (asa)
     01799 528227   fax 01799 528429
     http://www.psmg.co.uk
     Admin: Carol Strath
○   *P; 'for all those with marketing responsibilities within
     professional service suppliers in the UK & internationally'
●   Conf - Mtgs - ET - Inf - Workshops - Networking - Liaison with
     other professional bodies
¶   List available on request.

Professional Speakers Association   (PSA)
NR   The Counting House, Mill Road, Cromford, MATLOCK, Derbys,
     DE4 3RQ.   (hq)
     01629 826996   fax 01629 826997
○   *T
●   Mtgs
M   i

Professionals Allied to Teaching   (PAtT)   2000
NR   2 St James' Court, Friar Gate, DERBY, DE1 1BT.   (hq)
     01332 372337   fax 01332 290310
     email patt@pat.org.uk   http://www.pat.org.uk
     Gen Sec: Jean Gemmell
▲   Trade Union Section
○   *P; a section of PAT union for education support staff working in
     schools or colleges or peripatetic staff
●   Conf - Mtgs - ET - Exhib
>   Nat Assn of Admin Staff in Schools & Colleges
¶   Professionalism in Practice - 4; ftm, £2 nm.
     Hbk (with PAT) - 1; ftm only.

**Promota (UK) Ltd (Promotional Merchandise Trade Association)
1958**
NR   Forum Court, 83 Copers Cope Rd, BECKENHAM, Kent,
     BR3 1NR.   (asa)
     020 8639 0358   fax 020 8663 0949
     email info@promota.co.uk   http://www.promota.co.uk
     Sec: Mrs Lesley Reid
▲   Company Limited by Guarantee
○   *T; manufacturers, importers & distributors of promotional
     merchandise
●   Conf - Mtgs - Res - Exhib - SG
M   750 f, UK / 60 f, o'seas
¶   Bulletin - 6; ftm.

Promotional Finishers Association
     since 2005 BPIF promotional finishers, a group of the **British
     Printing Industries Federation**

Promotional Merchandise Trade Association
     see **Promota (UK) Ltd (Promotional Merchandise Trade
     Association)**

Property Care Association
     is a group of the **British Wood Preserving & Damp-proofing
     Association**

Property Consultants Society Ltd   (PCS)   1954
NR   107a Tarrant St, ARUNDEL, W Sussex, BN18 9DP.   (hq)
     01903 883787   fax 01903 889590
     email pcs@p-c-s.org.uk
     Sec: David J May
▲   Company Limited by Guarantee
○   *P; a central organisation for qualified surveyors, architects,
     valuers, auctioneers, land & estate agents, master builders &
     constructional engineers who practise as consultants
●   Stat - Inf
M   550 i, UK / 70 i, o'seas
¶   NL - 4;   LM - irreg;   AR - 1; all ftm only.

Proprietary Association of Great Britain   (PAGB)   1919
■   Vernon House, Sicilian Ave, LONDON, WC1A 2QS.   (hq)
     020 7242 8331   fax 020 7405 7719
     email info@pagb.co.uk   http://www.pagb.co.uk
     Co Sec: Marion Fergusson
▲   Company Limited by Guarantee
○   *T; to represent manufacturers of branded over-the-counter
     (OTC) medicines & food supplements
●   Conf - Mtgs - ET - Exam - Res - Inf - LG
M   46 f, 54 f associates
¶   This Week (NL) - 52; ftm only.
     Bulletin - 4;   AR; both free.

Proprietary Crematoria Association
     since 2003 **Association of Private Crematoria & Cemeteries**

ProShare Association
     in 2005 part of this organisation was acquired by the **Institute
     of Financial Services** and part joined Digital Look.

Prospect   2001
NR   75-79 York Rd, LONDON, SE1 7AQ.   (hq)
     020 7902 6600
     http://www.prospect.org.uk
     Gen Sec: Paul Noon
○   *P, *U; interests & professional knowledge of members in the
     UK Civil Service & public & private sectors
●   Conf - Mtgs - ET - Res - Inf - Lib - Empl - Campaigning
M   c 102,000 i
×   2001 (Engineers' & Managers' Association
          (Institution of Professionals, Managers & Specialists
          (merged 1 November)

Prostate Cancer Support Association   (PSA)   1995
■   BM Box 9434, LONDON, WC1N 3XX.   (asa)
     0845 601 0766
     email psasec@atlworld.com
     http://www.prostatecancersupport.info
     Hon Sec: Philip Barnard
▲   Registered Charity
Br   4
○   *N, *W; regional & local self-help & support groups; it is
     managed by & for men with prostate cancer, their families &
     those who are interested in improving the care & support of
     those affected by this form of cancer
●   Mtgs - Inf
<   USTOO! Intl
M   253 i
¶   NL - 6; free.

Protestant Alliance   (PA)   1845
NR   77 Ampthill Rd, FLITWICK, Beds, MK45 1BD.   (hsp/b)
     01525 712348   fax 01525 712348
     Sec: Dr S J Scott-Pearson
○   *R; Protestant theology & history
M   i

Protestant Reformation Society   (PRS)   1827
NR   PO Box 47, RAMSGATE, Kent, CT11 9XB.   (hsp)
    01843 580542
    Gen Sec: Dr D A Scales
○   *R; to promote the religious principles of the Reformation
M   i
¶   NL - 3.

Protestant Truth Society (Inc)   (PTS)   1889
NR   184 Fleet St, LONDON, EC4A 2HJ
    020 7405 4960
    email info@protestant-truth.org
    Sec: G Rae
▲   Company Limited by Guarantee; Registered Charity
○   *K, *R; 'for the promotion & protection of the Protestant
    reformed faith'
●   Conf - Mtgs - Exhib - Comp - VE - Providing preachers for
    church services & deputation meetings
M   55 i
¶   Protestant Truth - 6.

Provincial Booksellers Fairs Association   (PBFA)   1974
■   The Old Coach House, 16 Melbourn St, ROYSTON, Herts,
    SG8 7BZ.   (hq)
    01763 248400   fax 01763 248921
    email info@pbfa.org   http://www.pbfa.org
    Admin: Ms Becky Wears
▲   Un-incorporated Society
○   *T; to promote interest in the collection & sale of antiquarian &
    secondhand books by organising book fairs, exhibitions,
    lectures & seminars; to publish books on book collecting
●   Conf - Exhib - Inf - Book fairs
    Book fairs information: 01763 249212
M   703 f, UK / 47 f, o'seas
¶   NL - 10; ftm only.
    Calendar of Book Fairs - 1; Fair Catalogues; both free.
    Book Collecting; ABC of Book Collecting; both £12.95
    Directory of Antiquarian & Second Hand Booksellers - 1; ftm,
    £4.00 nm.

Provincial Hospital Services Association   (PHSA)   1919
§   14 St Cuthbert's Street, BEDFORD, MK40 3JU.   (hq)
    01234 267371
    http://www.medicaid.org.uk
    Private medical & hospital cash scheme insurers

Provision Trade Federation   (PTF)   1976
■   17 Clerkenwell Green, LONDON, EC1R 0DP.   (hq)
    020 7253 2114   fax 020 7608 1645
    email info@provtrade.co.uk
    http://www.provtrade.co.uk
    Dir Gen: Mrs Clare Cheney
▲   Company Limited by Guarantee
○   *T; for the provision trade & allied trades in the UK
Gp   Bacon & pigmeat; Canned foods; Chilled & processed meats;
    Dairy products; Export; Speciality cheese; Yoghurt & short life
    dairy products
●   Mtgs - Stat - Inf - LG - Annual dinner
<   Food & Drink Fedn (FDF); EUCOLAIT; Tr Assn Forum
M   130 f
¶   Ybk; free.

Psoriasis Association   1968
■   Milton House, 7 Milton St, NORTHAMPTON, NN2 7JG.   (hq)
    01604 711129   fax 01604 792894
    email mail@psoriasis.demon.co.uk
    Chief Exec: Mrs Gladys Edwards
▲   Registered Charity
Br   12
○   *W; all matters relating to psoriasis & psoriatic arthritis
●   Conf - Res - Inf - LG
<   Eur Psoriasis Assns (EUROPSO); Assn Med Res
    Charities (AMRC); Long Term Med Conditions Alliance
    (LMCA); Nat Coun Voluntary Orgs
M   5,020 i, 10 f, UK / 80 i, o'seas
¶   Psoriasis (Jnl) - 4; ftm.

Psoriatic Arthropathy Alliance   (PAA)   1993
NR   PO Box 111, ST ALBANS, Herts, AL2 3JQ.   (hq)
    0870 770 3212   fax 0870 770 3213
    email info@paalliance.org   http://www.paalliance.org
    Chief Exec: Julie Chandler
▲   Company Limited by Guarantee; Registered Charity
○   *W; to raise awareness of & help people with psoriatic arthritis
    & its associated skin disorder, psoriasis
●   Conf - ET - Exhib - Inf - LG
<   Intl Fedn Psoriasis Assns; All Party Parliamentary Gp for Skin;
    Brit League against Rheumatism
M   [subscribers]
¶   Skin 'n' Bones Connection (Jnl) - 2; £3.
    Psoriatic Care Fact File - ongoing; £9.50.
    Leaflets & booklets.

Psychiatric Rehabilitation Association   (PRA)   1959
■   The Groupwork Centre, Bayford Mews, Bayford St, LONDON,
    E8 3SF.   (hq)
    020 8985 3570   fax 020 8986 1334
    email ppra528898@aol.com
    http://www.pra-services.4mg.com
    Chief Exec: Mirella Manni
▲   Registered Charity
Br   14
○   *W; to promote mental health & improve attitudes towards the
    mentally ill
Gp   Art training; Computer training; Counselling; European
    networking; Stress management
●   ET - Exam - Res - Exhib - SG - Inf - VE - Provision of day
    centres, work programmes, residential care
M   2,000 i
¶   NL - 4; ftm, £10 yr nm.   AR - 1; free.

Psychological Society of Ireland   1970
IRL   CX House, 2A Corn Exchange Place, Poolbeg St, DUBLIN 2,
    Republic of Ireland.
    353 (1) 474 9160   fax 353 (1) 474 9161
    email info@psihq.ie   http://www.psihq.ie
    Chief Exec: Adrienne Harrington
○   *P

Public & Commercial Services Union   (PCS)   1998
■   160 Falcon Rd, LONDON, SW11 2LN.   (hq)
    020 7924 2727   fax 020 7924 1847
    email info@pcs.org.uk   http://www.pcs.org.uk
    Gen Sec: Mark Serwotka
▲   Un-incorporated Society
Br   1,000
○   *U; to represent civil & public servants
●   Conf - Mtgs - ET - Res - Inf - Empl - LG
<   Public Services Intl (PSI); Trade Union Congress (TUC)
M   320,000 i
¶   PCS View - 12; ftm only.   AR - 1; free.
×   2005 (merged) Association of Magisterial Officers

Public Contractors Association   (PCA)   1995
NR   20 Cleveland Gardens, LONDON, SW13 0AG.   (hq)
         020 8487 9580
         email pca@cdcpublicaffairs.com
         Sec: Cliff Davis-Coleman
○   *T; a political group lobbying for free & open competition
         between the public & private sector
Gp   Housing Management Contractors Association (HMCA)
●   Conf - Mtgs - Res - LG
M   12 f, UK / 6 f, o'seas

Public Fundraising Regulatory Association   (PFRA)   2001
■   Unit 11 Europoint, 5-11 Lavington St, LONDON, SE1 0NZ.
         (hq)
         020 7401 8452   fax 020 7928 2925
         email info@pfra.org.uk   http://www.pfra.org.uk
         Sec: Sue Brumpton
▲   Company Limited by Guarantee
○   *K; to regulate the 'face-to-face' fundraising by charities &
         professional fundraising organisations; works with local
         authorities to ensure that fundraising sites are used
         appropriately
●   Mtgs - Inf - LG - Accreditation scheme - Monitoring of
         members' compliance
M   121 f
¶   Voice (NL) - 3; free.

Public Management & Policy Association   (PMPA)   1998
NR   3 Robert St, LONDON, WC2N 6RL.
         020 7543 5600
○   *P; for managers & policy-makers within the public services

Public Monuments & Sculpture Association   (PMSA)   1991
■   72 Lissenden Mansions, Lissenden Gardens, LONDON,
         NW5 1PR.   (hq)
         020 7485 0566   fax 020 7267 1742
         email pmsa@pmsa.org.uk   http://www.pmsa.org.uk
         Chief Exec: Jo Darke,   Chmn: Loyd Grossman
▲   Company Limited by Guarantee; Registered Charity
○   *A, *G, *L; to record, preserve, research & enhance public
         appreciation of all aspects of public sculpture & monuments
Gp   National Recording Project (NRP); Save our Sculpture
         Campaign; Custodians Handbook; The Sculpture Journal;
         the Marsh Award for public sculpture
●   Conf - Mtgs - Res - Inf - VE
<   Ancient Monuments Soc; Art & Architecture; Brit Sundial Soc;
         Fountain Soc; Historic Gardens Foundation; R Brit Soc of
         Sculptors; Soc of Portrait Sculptors
M   228 i, UK / 10 i, 35 f, o'seas
¶   The Sculpture Jnl - 2; ftm, £25 nm.
         Public Sculpture of Britain (a series of volumes describing in
         detail the national heritage of public sculpture); £19.95 -
         £52.95.

Public Relations Consultants Association   (PRCA)   1969
NR   Willow House, Willow Place, LONDON, SW1P 1JH.   (hq)
         020 7233 6026
         http://www.prca.org.uk
         Dir Gen: Patrick Barrow
▲   Company Limited by Guarantee
○   *P; the maintenance of ethics & standards throughout the
         industry
Gp   Government; Market sector; Finance directors c'ee; Scottish
         Public Relations Consultants Assn
●   Conf - Mtgs - ET - Res - Comp - Inf - Lib - Empl
<   Intl C'ee of Public Relations Consultancies Assns Ltd (ICO)
M   127 f
¶   Public Relations Consultancy (Ybk) - 1.

Public Relations Consultants Association Ireland
       see **PRCA Ireland**

Public Relations Institute of Ireland   (PRII)   1953
IRL   78 Merrion Sq, DUBLIN 2, Republic of Ireland.
         353 (1) 661 8004   fax 353 (1) 676 4562
         email info@prii.ie   http://www.prii.ie
         Pres: Pat Montague,   Chief Exec: Gerry Davis
○   *P

Public Sector People Managers' Association   (PPMA)   1975
NR   81 Sea Rd, WESTGATE, Kent, CT8 8QG.   (hq)
         01843 834824
         email john.tonks@ppma.org.uk   http://www.ppma.org.uk
         Sec: John Tonks
▲   Un-incorporated Society
Br   17
○   *P
Gp   Recruitment training & development; Industrial relations &
         conditions of service; Performance review organisation &
         planning; Equal opportunities
●   Conf - Mtgs - ET - Res - Exhib - Comp - SG - Stat - Inf - Empl
<   Inst Personnel Managers Assn (USA)
M   500 i
¶   NL - 4;   AR; both free.   Various technical publications.
×   2006 Society of Chief Personnel Officers in Local Government

Public Services Network   (PSnet)   2001
■   19 Shepperton Close, Great Billing, NORTHAMPTON,
         NN3 9NT.   (dir/p)
         01604 401726   fax 01604 414366
         email ossiedodds@psnet.org.uk
         http://www.psnet.org.uk
         Director: Oswald A Dodds
▲   Un-incorporated Society
Br   12
○   *P; to promote internally provided public services &
         professionalism & good practice in their management
●   Conf - ET - Res - Exhib - Stat - Inf - LG
M   210 f
¶   Contract - 6; free.

Publicity Club of Ireland   1923
IRL   c/o 79 Bettyglen, Raheny, DUBLIN 5, Republic of Ireland.
         353 (1) 831 3320   fax 353 (1) 494 1071
         email msohaodha@yahoo.co.uk
         Sec: Frank McGouran
○   *P

Publicity Club of London   (PCL)   1913
NR   Sheraton House, 15-19 Great Chapel St, LONDON,
         W1F 8FN.   (chmn/b)
         020 7734 5666   fax 020 7734 9666
         http://www.thepcl.co.uk
○   *P; a cross-discipline organisation with members from
         advertising, direct marketing, marketing, new media, PR &
         the media in the London area
●   Mtgs - Exhib - VE
M   500 i

Publishers Association   (PA)   1896
■   29b Montague St, LONDON, WC1B 5BW.   (hq)
         020 7691 9191   fax 020 7691 9199
         email mail@publishers.org.uk
         http://www.publishers.org.uk
         Chief Exec: Ronnie Williams
▲   Company Limited by Guarantee
○   *T; to represent interests of UK publishers in books, book
         related material & journals to governments, other bodies in
         the trade & the public at large
Gp   Educational Publishers Council (EPC); Coun Academic &
         Professional Publishers (CAPP); Trade Publishers Council;
         Book Development Council International (BDCI)
●   Conf - Mtgs - Exhib - Stat - Expt - Inf - LG
M   180 f
¶   LM (CAPP) - 1;   LM (EPC) - 1; both free.
         Book Trade Year Book - 1; £10 m, £50 nm.

Publishers Licensing Society   (PLS)   1981
- ■ 37-41 Gower St, LONDON, WC1E 6HH.   (hq)
  020 7299 7730   fax 020 7299 7780
  email pls@pls.org.uk   http://www.pls.org.uk
  Chief Exec: Dr Alicia Wise,   Mgr: Caroline Elmslie
- ▲ Company Limited by Guarantee
- ○ *T; formed jointly by the Association of Learned & Professional
  Society Publishers, the Periodical Publishers Association & the
  Publishers Association to protect & enforce publishers' rights
  in copyright of all published works (by means of
  reprographic reproduction); to distribute royalties from such
  reproduction
- < Intl Fedn of Reproduction Rights Orgs; Copyright Licensing
  Agency
- M 1,800 f
- ¶ PLS Plus (NL) - 3;   AR - 1; both ftm only.

Pugin Gild   1974
- ■ 157 Vicarage Rd, LONDON, E10 5DU.   (hq)
  020 8539 3876   fax 020 8539 3876
  email pugin-owner@smartgroups.com
  http://www.smartgroups.com/vault/pugin
  Sec: Ronald King
- ▲ Un-incorporated Society
- ○ *L; to promote Christian architecture, crafts & guild system
- ● Res - SG - Inf - Lib - PL

Pugin Society   1995
- NR 33 Montcalm House, Westferry Rd, LONDON, E14 3SD.   (hsp)
  020 7515 9474
  Hon Sec: Pam Cole
- ▲ Registered Charity
- ○ *G; to promote as extensively as possible knowledge of the life,
  buildings, designs & writing of Augustus Welby Pugin (1812-
  1852); to protect, where possible, threatened buildings or
  artifacts designed by him

Pullet Hatcheries Association   (PHA)   1985
- NR 89 Charterhouse St (2nd floor), LONDON, EC1M 6HR.   (hq)
  020 7608 3760   fax 020 7608 3860
  email Louisa.Platt@britisheggindustrycouncil.com
  http://www.britegg.co.uk
  Sec: Louisa Platt
- ▲ Company Limited by Guarantee
- ○ *T
- ● Mtgs - LG
- M 8 f

Pullet Rearers Association   1983
- NR 89 Charterhouse St (2nd floor), LONDON, EC1M 6HR.   (hq)
  020 7608 3760   fax 020 7608 3860
  email Louisa.Platt@britisheggindustrycouncil.com
  http://www.britegg.co.uk
  Sec: Louisa Platt
- ▲ Company Limited by Guarantee
- ○ *T; for pullet rearers & shell egg producers
- ● Mtgs - LG
- < Brit Egg Ind Coun; Pullet Hatcheries Assn
- M 13 f

Pulmonary Hypertension Association   (PHA)
- NR The Brampton Centre, Brampton Rd, Wath Upon Dearne,
  ROTHERHAM, S Yorks, S63 6BB.
  01709 761450   fax 01709 761450
  http://www.pha-uk.com
- ○ *M

Pulp & Paper Fundamental Research Society   (FRC)   c1984
- ■ 5 Frecheville Court, BURY, Lancs, BL9 0UF.   (hq)
  0161-764 5858   fax 0161-764 5353
  email frc@pita.co.uk   http://www.ppfrs.org.uk
  Admin: John Clewley
- ▲ Company Limited by Guarantee; Registered Charity
- ○ *Q; to promote research & education in the pulp & paper
  industry; its principal activity is the organising of four-yearly
  symposia, alternately in the universities of Oxford &
  Cambridge
- ● Conf
- M 10 i, UK / 6 i, o'seas
- ¶ Proceedings of each symposia - 4 yrly; £135.

Pump Distributors Association   (PDA)   1985
- ■ c/o 5 Chapelfield, Orford, WOODBRIDGE, Suffolk,
  IP12 2HW.   (chief exec/p)
  fax 01394 450181
  email pumps@the-pda.com   http://www.the-pda.com
  Chief Exec: Ian Castle
- ▲ Un-incorporated Society
- ○ *T; to represent firms who distribute industrial pumps, install
  pumps & repair them
- Gp Pump training in conjunction with the British Pump
  Manufacturers' Association
- ● Conf - Mtgs - ET - Inf
- M 28 f, UK / 1 f, o'seas
- ¶ NL - 2; free.

Punch & Judy College of Professors
- NR Punch's Oak, Cleobury Rd, Far Forest, Rock, KIDDERMINSTER,
  Worcs, DY14 9EB.
  01299 266634
  http://www.punchandjudy.org
  Coordinator: Glyn Edwards
- ○ *D
- < Worldwide Friends of Punch & Judy
- M 12 i

Purine Metabolic Patients Association   (PUMPA)   1992
- NR Purine Research Unit / Thomas Guy House (5th floor), Guy's
  Hospital, LONDON, SE1 9RT.   (hq)
  020 7188 1276
  email info@pumpa.org   http://www.pumpa.org
  Contact: Dr Anne Simmonds
- ▲ Registered Charity
- ○ *W; to increase awareness of the 28 genetic nucleotide
  disorders under the PUMPA umbrella which include
  compulsive self-biting, kidney disease & fatal infections; to
  improve diagnosis & develop treatments Europe-wide by the
  establishment of a centre - the Princess Margaret Nucleotide
  Centre (PMNC)
- Gp Patient contact Lesch-Nyhan disease; Familial juvenile gout
- ● Conf - Mtgs - ET - Res
- < Intl Fedn of Clinical Chemists; Contact a Family; Lesch-Nyhan
  Action C'ee
- M i
- ¶ Publications list available on request.

© CBD Research Ltd · Beckenham · BR3 5JS · Tel 020 8650 7745 · Fax 020 8650 0768 · E-mail cbd@cbdresearch.com · www.cbdresearch.com

Pushkin Club   1954

■ Pushkin House, 46 Ladbroke Grove, LONDON, W11 2AP.
   (meeting)
   020 7221 1981 room
   Co-Chmn: Lucy Daniels,   Richard McKane
▲ Un-incorporated Society
○ *A; Russian culture, particularly literature
● Mtgs - Inf - Lectures - Recitals [in English, in Russian or
   bilingual]
M c 80 i
¶ Programme - 1; free.
   Note: In 2007 will move to: 5a Bloomsbury Sq, LONDON,
   WC1A 2LP.

Pygmy Goat Club   1982

NR Solomons Farm, Latchley, GUNNISLAKE, Cornwall,
   PL18 9AX.   (sp)
   01822 834474   http://www.pygmygoatclub.org
   Sec: Mrs Margaret Thompson
▲ Un-incorporated Society
○ *B
● Mtgs - Exhib - Inf - Shows
M 500 i, org, UK / 4 i, o'seas
¶ Pygmy Goat Notes - 4; ftm only.   Herdbook - 1.
   Pygmy Goat Hbk.   Members Hbk - 1; ftm only.

Quality British Celery Association   (QBC)
- ■ 133 Eastgate, LOUTH, Lincs, LN11 9QG.   (asa)
  01507 602427   fax 01507 607165
  email crop.association@pvga.co.uk
  Sec: Mrs Jayne Dyas
- ○ *T; to provide technical, commercial & marketing information
  for growers
- ● Conf - Mtgs - Res - Exhib - Stat - Inf - LG
- M 120 f

Quality Guild   (QG)   1993
- ■ Capital Building, Hilltop Heights, London Rd, CARLISLE,
  Cumbria, CA1 2NS.   (hq)
  0870 757 1188
  Mgr: Joe Tomlinson
- ▲ Company Limited by Guarantee
- ○ *T; quality assessed business operating throughout Cumbria,
  South West Scotland, the Borders, Lancashire & North East
- ● Mtgs - ET - Exam
- M 400 f
- ¶ Business Networking Magazine - 6;
  Quality Guild Directory - 1; both ftm.

Quality Meat Scotland   (QMS)   2000
- NR Rural Centre - West Mains, Ingliston, NEWBRIDGE, Midlothian,
  EH28 8NZ.   (hq)
  0131-472 4040
  email info@qmscotland.co.uk
  Chief Exec: Uel Morton
- ▲ Company Limited by Guarantee
- ○ *T; to promote sales of Scottish meat products
- ● Conf - Mtgs - ET - Res - Exhib - Comp - Stat - Expt - Inf - PL -
  VE - LG
- ¶ Strategic Plan - 3 yrly; free.

Quality Methods Association   (QMA)   1993
- ■ PO Box 486, DERBY, DE22 2ZS.   (mail/address)
  01332 557900   fax 01332 557900
  email info@qma.co.uk   http://www.qma.co.uk
  Admin: Marion Jacques
- ○ *P; for quality improvement in business management
- ● Mtgs - ET - VE
- ¶ Tell Me (NL) - irreg; ftm only.

Quality Milk Producers Ltd   1954
- NR Scotsbridge House, Scots Hill, RICKMANSWORTH, Herts,
  WD3 3BB.   (hq)
  01923 695266
  Chmn: David Shaw,   Sec & Gen Mgr: Steve Baker
- ▲ Company Limited by Guarantee
- ○ *T; marketing, advertising & representation for Channel Islands
  (Gold Top) milk producers
- ● Conf - Exhib - Comp - Stat - Expt - Inf - Promotion
- M 600 i
- ¶ Gold Top News - 3; m only.

Quality Trout UK
  a group of the **British Trout Association**

Quarry Products Association   (QPA)   1982
- ■ Gillingham House, 38-44 Gillingham St, LONDON,
  SW1V 1HU.   (hq)
  020 7963 8000
  email info@qpa.org   http://www.qpa.org
  Dir Gen: Simon van der Byl
- ▲ Company Limited by Guarantee
- Br 3
- ○ *T; for the aggregates, asphalt, ready-mixed concrete, mortar,
  lime & silica-sand industries
- ● Conf - Mtgs - ET - Res - Exhib - Stat - Inf - Lib - PL - LG
- < Eur Asphalt Producers Assn; Eur Ready-Mixed Concrete Org;
  Eur Aggregates Assn
- M c 140 f
- ¶ The Aggregates Industry at a Glance (fact file).
  Voice of the Quarrying Industry (a profile of the QPA & its
  work).
  General:
    What's in a Quarry (Video); £15.
    Quarrying in Depth - recycling.
  Environmental:
    Directory of Restoration: a compendium of examples.
    Shifting Ground (Video); £35.
    Managers' Guide to the video; £3.25.
  Lime:
    Lime Stabilisation Manual; £6.   Leaflets.
  Marine:
    Aggregates from the Sea (video) & (booklet); free.
  Health & Safety:
    Clearing Blocked Crushers; £6.75.
    Code of Practice for Safeguarding Machinery; £7.50.
    Record Book for the Recording of Explosives kept in:
      Quarries' Blasting Sites; £3.
      Quarries' Explosives Stores; £3.
  Safety booklets; 30p each.
  Publications list available.

Quarry Products Association of Northern Ireland
  is a branch of the **Quarry Products Association**

Quaternary Research Association
  a group of the **Geological Society**

Queen's English Society   (QES)   1972
- NR The Clergy House, Hide Place, LONDON, SW1P 4NJ.   (hsp)
  020 7630 1819
  http://www.queens-english-society.com
  Hon Sec: G J Hardwick
- ▲ Registered Charity
- Br 4
- ○ *K; to promote & uphold the use of good English; to encourage
  the enjoyment of the language; to defend the precision,
  subtlety & richness of the language against debasement,
  ambiguity & other forms of misuse
- ● Conf - Mtgs
- M 695 i, UK / 84 i, o'seas
- ¶ Quest (Jnl) - 4.

Queen's Nursing Institute   (QNI)   1887
- § 3 Albemarle Way, LONDON, EC1V 4RQ.
  020 7490 4227   fax 020 7490 1269
  email qni@aol.com   http://www.qni.org.uk
  An independent non-membership body to provide the highest
  standards of nursing for the benefit of the community &
  public health; is a registered charity

Quekett Microscopical Club (QMC) 1865
- ■ 90 The Fairway, SOUTH RUISLIP, Middx, HA4 0SQ.
  (subn/manager/p)
  email secretary@queckett.org.   http://www.queckett.org
  Subscription Manager: Peter Thomas
- ▲ Registered Charity
- ○ *L; all aspects of light microscopes
- ● Mtgs
- M 360 i, UK / 60 i, o'seas
- ¶ The Quekett Jnl of Microscopy - 2.   Bulletin - 2.

Quilling Guild   1982
- NR 1 Clark Close, Woolavington, BRIDGWATER, Somerset,
  TA7 8HE.   (hsp)
  Enquiries Officer: Sharon Nattress
- ▲ Un-incorporated Society
- ○ *G; to promote the ancient art of quilling (rolled paper work or
  paper filigree); to record the history of quilling
- ● Conf - Mtgs - Comp - Inf - PL
- M 770 i, UK / 180 i, o'seas
- ¶ Quillers Today (NL) - 3.   Quilling Wise - 3.

Quilt Art
   is a group of the **Quilters' Guild of the British Isles**

Quilt Association   1995
- ■ The Minerva Arts Centre, High St, LLANIDLOES, Powys,
  SY18 6BY.
  01686 413467
  email quilts@ic24.net   http://www.quilt.org.uk
  Exhib Organiser: Mrs Doreen Gough
- ▲ Company Limited by Guarantee; Registered Charity
- ○ *G; the exhibition of Welsh quilts, both antique &
  contemporary; education connected with quilting, its history &
  artistry
- ● Conf - Mtgs - ET - Exhib - SG - VE
- > Mid-Wales branch of Embroiderers' Gld; Welsh Heritage
  Quilters
- M 150 i, UK / 25 i, o'seas
- ¶ NL - 2;   AR;   both ftm only.

Quilters' Guild of the British Isles   1979
- NR Room 190 Dean Clough, HALIFAX, W Yorks, HX3 5AX.   (hq)
  01422 347669
  Admin Sec: Jane Fellows
- ▲ Company Limited by Guarantee; Registered Charity
- Br 17 regions
- ○ *G; to promote the study & art of the techniques & heritage of
  patchwork, quilting & appliqué & of their future use &
  development
- Gp British Quilt Study Group; Quilt Art
- ● Conf - ET - Res - Exhib - Comp - SG - Inf - Lib - VE
- < Eur Quilting Assn
- M c 6,500 i, UK / c 200 i, o'seas
- ¶ The Quilter - 4;   Hbk - 1;   NL (Regional) - 3; all ftm only.

Quoted Companies Alliance   (QCA) 1992
- NR 6 Kinghorn St, LONDON, EC1A 7HW.
  020 7600 3745
  email mail@qcanet.co.uk
  Chief Exec: John Pierce
- ○ *P; for Smaller Quoted Companies (SQCs) which are listed on
  the London Stock Exchange & are outside the FTSE 350 Index
- ¶ QCA Voice - 4.

R L Stevenson Club
    see **Robert Louis Stevenson Club**

R S Surtees Society   (RSSS)   1983
NR   Manor Farm House, Nunney, FROME, Somerset, BA11 4NJ.
        01373 836937
        http://www.r.s.surteessociety.org
        Chief Exec: Helen Lady Pickthorn,   Sec: Jeremy Lewis
▲   Un-incorporated Society
Br   USA
○   *A, *L; for those interested in the life & works of R S Surtees
        (1803-64), the sporting writer of the 'Jorrocks' stories;
        keeping the works in print
●   Exhib - Publishing
<   Selwood Foundation
M   c 4,000 i

Rabbit Welfare Association   (RWA)   1996
NR   PO Box 603, HORSHAM, W Sussex, RH13 5WL.
        (mail/address)
        0870 046 5249 (helpline)
        Chief Exec: Rachel Todd
▲   Un-incorporated Society
○   *B; to promote the keeping of rabbits as house pets; to raise
        interest in rabbit medicine within the veterinary profession
Gp   Coordinators: Rabbits; Pets; Houserabbits
●   Conf - Mtgs - ET - Exhib - Inf
M   3,500 i, f & org
¶   Rabbiting On - 4;   Hbk; both ftm.

Race Walking Association   (RWA)   1907
■   Hufflers, Heard's Lane, Shenfield, BRENTWOOD, Essex,
        CM15 0SF.   (hsp)
        01277 220687   fax 01277 212380
        email racewalkingassociation@btinternet.com
        http://www.racewalkingassociation.btinternet.co.uk
        Hon Gen Sec: Peter J Cassidy
▲   Un-incorporated Society
○   *S; organisation, management, control & development of race
        walking (within the territory of the Amateur Athletic
        Association - England, the Isle of Man & the Channel Islands)
●   Conf - Mtgs - ET - Exam - Comp - SG - Stat - Inf - VE
<   Amat Athletic Assn of England
M   120 clubs & county org
¶   Race Walking Record - 12; £20 (UK), £30 (Europe),
        £40 (o'seas).
        Hbk.

Racecourse Association Ltd   (RCA)   1907
NR   Winkfield Rd, ASCOT, Berks, SL5 7HX.   (hq)
        01344 625912
        Chmn: David Thorpe
▲   Company Limited by Guarantee
○   *S, *T; to promote & represent the interests of racecourse
        owners
Gp   Publicity & Marketing
●   Mtgs - Exhib - Inf
M   58 f (racecourses)
¶   AR; free.

Racehorse Owners Association Ltd   (ROA)   1945
■   60 St James St, LONDON, SW1A 1LE.   (hq)
        020 7408 0903   fax 020 7408 1662
        email info@roa.co.uk   http://www.racehorseowners.net
        Sec: Keeley Brewer
▲   Company Limited by Guarantee
○   *S; representation of all racehorse owners in negotiation with
        the British Horseracing Board, Jockey Club, Horserace
        Betting Levy Board, the government & other bodies in racing
        in the UK & abroad
●   Conf - Mtgs - Res - SG - Stat - Inf - LG
M   c 7250 i & f
¶   Owner Magazine - 6; ftm, £6 nm.

Racehorse Transporters Association   (RTA Ltd)   1967
■   Folly House, Lambourn, HUNGERFORD, Berks, RG17 8QG.
        (chmn/p)
        01488 71700   fax 01488 73208
        email merrick@lrtltd.demon.co.uk
        Chmn: Merrick E D Francis,
        Sec: Miss Philippa Gillie (00 353 872 116719)
▲   Company Limited by Guarantee
○   *T; 'the RTA is the trade association member of the British
        Horseracing Board Industry Committee, which represents the
        majority of all UK & Irish transporters & shipping agents; the
        association is available to help & advise members on any
        subject of horse transport'
●   Mtgs - ET - Inf - LG
<   Brit Horseracing Bd Ind C'ee Ltd; Nat Trainers Fedn;
        Thoroughbred Breeders Assn
M   90 f, UK / 15 f, Republic of Ireland

Rachmaninoff Society   1990
NR   2 Boundary Lane, Mossley, CONGLETON, Cheshire,
        CW12 3HZ.   (memsec/p)
        01260 272073
        Mem Sec: Charles McAllister
▲   Un-incorporated Society
Br   North America
○   *D; to promote an interest in & appreciation of, the life & work
        of Sergei Rachmaninoff (1873-1943) Russian composer,
        pianist & conductor
●   Conf - Res - Inf
M   c 120 i, UK / 140 i, o'seas
¶   NL - 4;   LM - 1; both ftm only.

Racket Sports Association
    since 2006 **Sports Manufacturers & Retailers Trade
    Association**

Radical Statistics Group   1975
■   27/2 Hillside Cescent, EDINBURGH, EH7 5EF.
        email radstats@mailbase.ac.uk
        http://www.radstats.org.uk
        Admin: Alistair Cairns
▲   Un-incorporated Society
○   *P; for statisticians & research workers with a common concern
        about the political assumptions & implications of much of
        their work & an awareness of the actual & potential use of
        statistics & its techniques. The group is independent from
        other organisations... members are radical in the sense of
        being committed to helping to build a more free, egalitarian
        & democratic society
Gp   Radical Statistics Health Gp
●   Conf - Res - SG - Stat
M   c 300 i, 30 librarians
¶   Radical Statistics - 3; £12.
        Jnl;   NL.

Radio Academy   1983

NR   5 Market Place, LONDON, W1W 8AE.   (hq)
       020 7255 2010   fax 020 7255 2029
       email info@radioacademy.org
       http://www.radioacademy.org
       Dir: John Bradford
▲   Registered Charity
Br   11
○   *P; dedicated to the encouragement, recognition & promotion
       of excellence throughout the UK radio industry
Gp   Administrates for: Student Radio Association
●   Conf - Mtgs - ET - Res - Comp
>   Student Radio Assn
M   c 1,800 i & f
¶   Off Air (NL) - 4; ftm only.   AR - 1; free.
       Directory - 1; ftm.

Radio, Electrical & Television Retailers' Association Ltd (RETRA)   1942

NR   RETRA House, St John's Terrace, 1 Ampthill St, BEDFORD,
       MK42 9EY.   (hq)
       01234 269110
       Chief Exec: Fred Round
▲   Company Limited by Guarantee
○   *T; for electrical & electronics retailers, renters & service
       businesses; to represent small independents together with
       regional & national multiples
Gp   Conference; Training; Legal; Advice; Representation; Lobbying;
       Visits & excursions; Stationery & business supplies;
       Information; Meetings
●   Conf - Mtgs - ET - Comp - Inf - VE - LG
<   Eur Fedn Electronics Retailers (EFER); Retailers' Forum
M   1,500 i, 4,000 f
¶   Alert (NL) - 10.   Ybk.   AR.
       Safety in Electrical Testing.   Directory - 1.

Radio Society of Great Britain   (RSGB)   1913

NR   LAMBDA House, Cranborne Rd, POTTERS BAR, Herts,
       EN6 3JE.   (hq)
       0870 904 7373   fax 0870 904 7374
       http://www.rsgb.org.uk
       Gen Mgr: Peter A Kirby
▲   Company Limited by Guarantee
○   *G; all activities concerned with the advancement of amateur
       radio & the science of communication
●   Conf - Mtgs - ET - Exam - Res - Exhib - Comp - SG - Inf - Lib -
       PL - LG
<   Intl Amat Radio U (IARU); Inst of Electrical Engrs
M   c 26,000 i, UK / c 2,500 i, o'seas, 700 affiliated clubs & org
¶   Radcom - 12.   Various other publications.

Radionic Association Ltd   (RA)   1943

■   Baerlein House, Goose Green, Deddington, BANBURY, Oxon,
       OX15 0SZ.   (hq)
       01869 338852   fax 01869 338852
       email radionics@association.freeserve.co.uk
       http://www.radionic.co.uk
       Sec: Mrs P Harris
▲   Company Limited by Guarantee
○   *P, *Q; to promote the study & practice of radionics
●   ET - Res - SG - Inf - Lib
<   Brit Complementary Medicine Assn; Confedn of Healing Orgs
M   214 i, 5 f, UK / 28 i, 2 f, o'seas
¶   Jnl - 4; ftm only.
       (subscription £25).

Radnorshire Society   1930

■   Pool House, Discoed, PRESTEIGNE, Powys, LD8 2NW.   (mail)
       http://www.radnorshiresociety.org.uk address
       Hon Sec: Mrs S Cole
▲   Registered Charity
○   *L; history & culture of Radnorshire (pre-1974 county, now
       Powys)
●   Mtgs - Lib
M   350 i, 20 org, UK / 10 i, o'seas
¶   Transactions - 1; ftm, back issues £1 m, £5 nm.

Rail Freight Group   (RFG)   1990

■   17 Queen Anne's Gate, LONDON, SW1H 9BU.   (hq)
       020 7233 3177
       http://www.rfg.org.uk
       Admin Mgr: Phillippa O'Shea
▲   Company Limited by Guarantee
○   *K; promotion & development of freight by rail
●   Conf - Mtgs - Res - Inf - Lib - LG - Media relations - Press
       releases - Political lobbying
M   145 f, UK / 5 f, o'seas
¶   Rail Freight Group News - 6; free.   Hbk - 1; ftm.

Rail Industry Contractors Association   (RICA)   1999

NR   Gin Gan House, Thropton, MORPETH, Northumberland,
       NE65 7LT.
       01669 620569
       http://www.rica-uk.com
       Indep Chmn: Colin Wheeler
○   *T; to represent suppliers of labour & other suppliers & services
       to the railway industry
●   Mtgs - Liaison within rail industry - Lobbying
M   50 f
×   2006 Association of On-Track Labour Suppliers

Rail, Maritime & Transport Union   (RMT)

NR   39 Chalton St, LONDON, NW1 1JD.
       020 7387 4771
       http://www.rmt.org.uk
       Gen Sec: Bob Crow
○   *U
M   c 73,000 i

Rail Plant Association
       is a group of the **Construction Plant-hire Association**

Railfuture
       from 2000 (May) is the title used for campaigning purposes by the
       Railway Development Society

Railway & Canal Historical Society   (R&CHS)   1954

■   3 West Court, West St, OXFORD, OX2 0NP.   (hsp)
       01865 240514
       email ms@bodley.ox.ac.uk   http://www.bodley.ox.ac.uk/
       external/rchs
       Hon Sec: Matthew Searle
▲   Company Limited by Guarantee; Registered Charity
Br   6
○   *G, *L; to encourage the study of the history of transport, with
       particular reference to railways & canals but including
       associated modes of transport such as river navigations,
       roads, docks, coastal shipping, ferries & by air
Gp   Road transport; Tramroads; Waterways; Air transport; Railway
       chronology; Pipelines
●   Mtgs - Res - Inf - PL - VE
M   780 i, 2 f, 3 org, UK / 16 i, 1 org, o'seas
¶   Jnl - 3;   Bulletin - 6; both ftm.

Railway Correspondence & Travel Society   (RCTS)   1928
NR   6 Sandpiper Rd, IPSWICH, Suffolk, IP2 9HX.
     01473 404683
        http://www.rcts.org.uke.freeserve.co.uk   (hsp)
        http://www.rcts.org.uk
        Hon Sec: John Day
▲   Un-incorporated Society
Br   27
○   *G; railway history, operation & development
Gp   Photographic
●   Conf - Mtgs - Exhib - Stat - Inf - Lib - VE - Publication of
        specialist histories involving research on locomotives
<   6 railway socs in UK; 30 o'seas
M   3,000 i
¶   The Railway Observer - 12; ftm.
        A wide range of books on railway subjects.

Railway Development Society Ltd   (RDS)   1978
■   18A Grantham Rd, Bracebridge Heath, LINCOLN, LN4 2LD.
     (hq)
        email info@railfuture.org.uk   http://www.railfuture.org.uk
        Chmn: Mike Crowhurst
▲   Company Limited by Guarantee
Br   17
○   *K; to gain improvements to the railways; to provide the public
        with a modern joined-up transport system; to fight for
        environmentally friendly transport
Gp   Freight; Passenger; International; Reopenings; Policy & lobbying
●   Conf - Mtgs - SG - Inf - VE - LG
<   Transport 2000
M   3,400 i, 10 f, 80 org, UK / 10 i, o'seas
¶   Railwatch - 4.
        Note: Uses title Railfuture for all campaigning purposes.

Railway Enthusiasts Society (Rail Europe)   1963
■   PO Box 1, Allerton, BRADFORD, W Yorks, BD15 9BU.   (hsp)
        email raileurope@onetel.com
        http://www.rail-europe.co.uk
        Hon Sec: Dale W Fickes
▲   Un-incorporated Society
○   *G; to further an interest in railways, particularly modern
        traction, with similar enthusiasts throughout Europe
●   VE
<   Utd Travel Associates
M   100 i, UK / 1 i, o'seas
¶   European Rail News (NL) - 5/6; £15 m (2004).

Railway Forum
■   12 Grosvenor Place, LONDON, SW1X 7HH.   (hq)
        020 7259 6543   fax 020 7259 6544
        email railinfo@railwayforum.com
        http://www.railwayforum.com
○   *T; 'railway industry strategic think tanks & lobby group
        representing passenger & freight train operating companies,
        infrastructure providers, service companies & equipment
        suppliers'

Railway Industry Association   (RIA)   1875
■   22 Headfort Place, LONDON, SW1X 7RY.   (hq)
        020 7201 0777   fax 020 7235 5777
        email ria@riagb.org.uk   http://www.riagb.org.uk
        Dir Gen: Jeremy Candfield,   Dir: G Coomb
▲   Un-incorporated Society
○   *T; to promote the interests of British rail industry
        manufacturers, contractors & specialist service providers,
        both in the UK & overseas
●   Conf - Mtgs - Exhib - Expt - Inf - LG
<   Eur Fedn of Rly Trackworks Contrs; U des Inds Ferroviaires Eur;
        Confedn Brit Ind; Rly Forum
M   140 f
¶   UK Railway Suppliers Directory.
        Technical Specifications.

Railway Preservation Society of Ireland   (RPSI)   1964
■   22 Castleview Rd, WHITEHEAD, Co Antrim, BT38 9NA.   (regd)
        028 2826 0803   fax 028 2826 0803
        email rpsitrains@hotmail.com
        http://www.rpsi-online.org office
        Hon Sec: Paul McCann
▲   Company Limited by Guarantee; Registered Charity
Br   Republic of Ireland
○   *G, *K; to preserve, maintain & operate mainline steam
        locomotives & vintage rolling stock on the main line railways
        of Ireland
●   Mtgs
<   Heritage Rly Assn (HRA)
M   700 i, UK / 300 i, o'seas
¶   Five Foot Three (Jnl) - 1; ftm, £3 nm.

Railway Society of Scotland
        this society has been disbanded

Railway Study Association   (RSA)   1909
■   37 Charlwood Rd, BURGESS HILL, W Sussex, RH15 0RJ.   (hsp)
        01444 246379   fax 01444 246392
        email info@railwaystudyassociation.org
        http://www.railwaystudyassociation.org
        Hon Sec: Steven Saunders
▲   Un-incorporated Society
○   *G; 'to be the most effective forum in Great Britain for
        promoting a broad understanding of all aspects of the
        railway industry'
●   Conf - Mtgs - VE
M   830 i, 32 f, UK / 12 i, o'seas
¶   NL - irreg.   Ybk.

Ramblers' Association   (RA)   1935
■   Camelford House (2nd floor), 87-90 Albert Embankment,
        LONDON, SE1 7TW.   (hq)
        020 7339 8500   fax 020 7339 8501
        email ramblers@ramblers.org.uk
        http://www.ramblers.org.uk
        Chief Exec: Nick Barrett
▲   Registered Charity
○   *G, *K, *S; to encourage walking; to protect footpaths; to
        campaign for freedom to roam in open country; to defend
        the beauty of the countryside
●   Conf - Mtgs - ET - Res - Exhib - Inf - Lib (maps) - LG
M   i

Randolph Caldecott Society   1983
■   Clatterwick House, Little Leigh, NORTHWICH, Cheshire,
        CW8 4RJ.
        01606 891303 & 781731 (evgs)   (hsb)
        Hon Sec: Kenneth N Oultram
○   *A, *G; to promote the work of Randolph Caldecott, the 19th
        century artist & illustrator; to liaise with the American-based
        society

Ranulf Higden Society   1992
NR   5 Beechwood Drive, Alsager, STOKE-ON-TRENT, Staffs,
        ST7 2HG.   (hsp)
        01270 878787
        Hon Sec: J C Sutton
○   *A; to promote interest, understanding & research into
        documents written in Medieval Latin & Anglo Norman (with
        particular emphasis on north western England).   Ranulf
        Higden was a Benedictine monk & English chronicler who
        died in 1364
M   c 75 i

© CBD Research Ltd · Beckenham · BR3 5JS · Tel 020 8650 7745 · Fax 020 8650 0768 · E-mail cbd@cbdresearch.com · www.cbdresearch.com

Ranunculaceae Society   2003
- ■ 24 Lambourne Wood, Brennanstown Rd, Cabinteely, DUBLIN 18, Republic of Ireland.   (hsp)
  353 (1) 289 2721   fax 353 (1) 289 2721
  email ranunculaceae@eircom.net
  http://www.buttercupsonline.com
  Admin Sec: Claire Gloster
- ○ *H; to foster interest in plants belonging to the buttercup family - Ranunculaceae
- ● Conf - Mtgs (irreg) - VE
- < R Horticl Soc
- M 15 i, 1 f, 1 org, Republic of Ireland / 65 i, o'seas
- ¶ NL - 4; ftm, £2 nm.

Rapid Prototyping & Manufacturing Association   1995
- NR Institution of Mechanical Engineers, 1 Birdcage Walk, LONDON, SW1H 9JJ.
  020 7304 6864
- ○ *T
- M 250 i

Rapra Technology Ltd   1919
- NR Shawbury, SHREWSBURY, Shropshire, SY4 4NR.   (hq)
  01939 250383   fax 01939 251118
  email info@rapra.net   http://www.rapra.net
- ▲ Private Limited Company
- ○ *Q; 'independent research, technology & information consultancy specialising in plastics & rubber'
- ● Conf - ET - Res - Inf
- < Assn of Indep Res & Technology Orgs (AIRTO)
- M f
- ¶ over 1,200 titles.

Rare Breeds Survival Trust   (RBST)   1973
- ■ Stoneleigh Park, KENILWORTH, Warks, CV8 2LG.   (hq)
  024 7669 6551   fax 024 7669 6706
  email enquiries@rbst.org.uk   http://www.rbst.org.uk
  Exec Dir: Robert Terry
- ▲ Company Limited by Guarantee; Registered Charity
- ○ *B, *K; the preservation, conservation & promotion of native breeds of British farm livestock
- ● Conf - Res - Exhib - SG - Stat - Inf - Lib - PL - LG
- < Rare Breeds Intl
- M 9,500 i, 114 org, UK / 260 i, o'seas
- ¶ The Ark - 4; ftm.

Rare Poultry Society   (RPS)   1969
- NR Danby, The Causeway, Congresbury, BRISTOL, BS49 5DJ.   (hsp)
  01934 833619
  Hon Sec: Mrs Anne Merriman
- ▲ Un-incorporated Society
- ○ *G, *K; for the preservation of over 50 rare & endangered breeds of poultry & turkeys
- ● Mtgs - Exam - Res - Exhib - Comp - Stat - Inf
- < Poultry Club of GB
- M c 290 i
- ¶ NL;   LM - 1;   Breeders lists - 1; all ftm.

Rating Surveyors Association   1909
- ■ c/o Montagu Evans, 44-48 Dover St, LONDON, W1S 4AZ.   (hsb)
  020 7312 7517   fax 020 7312 7535
  email mark.higgin@montagu-evans.co.uk
  http://www.ratingsurveyorsassociation.org
  Hon Sec: Mark Higgin
- ▲ Un-incorporated Society
- ○ *P; to represent individuals engaged in rating in both the public & private sector
- ● Mtgs - Inf - VE - LG
- < R Instn of Chart Surveyors
- M 440 i
- ¶ NL - 2;   LM;   President's Report (AR) - 1.

Rationalist Association   (RPA)   1899
- ■ 1 Gower St, LONDON, WC1E 6HD.   (hq)
  020 7436 1151
  email info@newhumanist.org.uk
  http://www.newhumanist.org.uk
  Editor: Caspar Melville
- ▲ Registered Charity
- ○ *K; publishing & campaigning in the area of secular humanism & non-religious thought; for artists, non-religious, free thinkers - philosophy, science & culture
- ● Conf - Publishing
- M 2,190 UK / 310 i, o'seas
- ¶ The New Humanist (Jnl) - 6; £18.
- ✕ 2005-06 Rationalist Press Association

Rationalist Press Association Ltd
  since 2005-06 **Rationalist Association**

Ray Society   1844
- ■ c/o Dept of Zoology, Natural History Museum, South Kensington, LONDON, SW7 5BD.   (hsb)
  020 7942 5532   fax 020 7942 5433
  email nje@nhm.ac.uk
  http://www.books.free-online.co.uk
  Hon Sec: Dr Nicholas John Evans
- ▲ Registered Charity
- ○ *L; publication of original texts of scientific interest & merit which would not otherwise be published because of lack of commercial; works usually (but not specifically) relate to British flora & fauna
  Founded in memory of English naturalist John Ray (1627-1705)
- ● ET - Res - Publication of scientific books/monographs of original works, translations & facsimiles on natural history
- M c 200 i, UK / c 50 i, o'seas
- ¶ Volumes (bound books 700-900 pages) - c 1; prices vary.
  AR - 1; ftm, £1 nm.

Raynaud's & Scleroderma Association   1982
- ■ 112 Crewe Rd, ALSAGER, Cheshire, ST7 2JA.   (hq)
  01270 872776   fax 01270 883556
  email info@raynauds.org.uk
  http://www.raynauds.org.uk
  Dir: Mrs Anne H Mawdsley
- ▲ Registered Charity
- ○ *W; to promote better communication between doctors & patients; to put patients in touch with each other in order to exchange ideas; to raise funds for research
- Gp Sufferers; Health professionals; General public
- ● Conf - Mtgs - Res
- < Brit Soc of Rheumatology; Arthritis & Musculoskeletal Alliance (ARMA)
- M 6,000 i
- ¶ Hot News (NL) - 4; ftm.
  Raynaud's: your questions answered; £4.
  Journey of Discovery; £13.50.

Re-Solv (the Society for the Prevention of Solvent & Volatile Substance Abuse)   (Re-Solv)   1984
- NR 30A High St, STONE, Staffs, ST15 8AW.
  01785 817885
  http://www.re-solv.org
  Chmn: Gerald Soane,   Dir: Warren Hawksley
- ▲ Company Limited by Guarantee; Registered Charity
- Br 3 regions
- ○ *K; the only national charity dealing with all aspects of solvent & volatile substance abuse (VSA)
- ● Conf - ET - Res - Inf
- M c 30 i, 50 assns, 220 health authorities etc
- ¶ NL - 6; free.
  Publications & videos, list available.

REACH: the Association for Children with Hand or Arm Deficiency (REACH) 1978
- ■ PO Box 54, HELSTON, Cornwall, TR13 8WD. (coordinator/p)
  0845 130 6225   fax 0845 130 0262
  email reach@reach.org.uk   http://www.reach.org.uk
  Nat Coordinator: Mrs Sue Stokes
- ▲ Registered Charity
- Br 15; Eire
- ○ *W; to support families of upper limb deficient children
- ● Conf - Mtgs - Exhib - Inf
- M 1,053 i, UK / 53 i, o'seas
- ¶ Within Reach - 4;   Introductory Booklet;
  Guide to Artificial Arms;   AR; all free.

Reading Association of Ireland
- IRL Education Dept, St Patrick's College, Drumcondra, DUBLIN 9, Republic of Ireland.
  353 (1) 884 2072
  Sec: Celine Fitzpatrick
- ○ *K

Real Nappy Association
  no longer in existence

Record Society of Lancashire & Cheshire (LCRS) 1878
- NR John Rylands University Library of Manchester, Oxford Rd, MANCHESTER, M13 9PP. (hsb)
  Hon Sec to Council: Dorothy J Clayton
- ○ *L; publication of original documents relating to the two counties

Records Management Society of Great Britain (RMS) 1983
- ■ Woodside, Coleheath Bottom, Speen, PRINCES RISBOROUGH, Bucks, HP27 0SZ. (regd/office/hsp)
  01494 488566
  Chmn: PAul Duller,   Sec: Lawrence Rodgers
- ▲ Un-incorporated Society
- Br 7 regional groups
- ○ *P; 'to encourage the highest standards in records management: the systematic control, organisation, access & protection of an organisation's information (whether it be on tape, disk, paper or film) from its creation through its use to its permanent retention or legal destruction'
- Gp Orgs covered by the Public Record Acts
- ● Conf - Mtgs - ET - Exhib - SG - VE - LG
- M 700 i, 250 f
- ¶ Bulletin - 6.   NL - 6.

Records Racing & Rally Association
  see **Royal Aero Club Records Racing & Rally Association**

Recreation Managers' Association of Great Britain (RMA) 1956
- ■ PO Box 2437, Kidsgrove, STOKE-on-TRENT, Staffs, ST7 4ZQ. (hq)
  01782 788111
  email glennrma@msn.com   http://www.rma-gb.org
  Chief Exec: Clive Ashley
- ○ *P; promotion of interests of secretaries & managers (& assistant secretaries & managers) of recreation clubs associated with commerce & industry, the armed forces, civil services, public services, & educational establishments
- ● Conf - ET - SG - LG
- < Sports Coun; Cent Coun Physical Recreation; Nat Playing Fields Assn; Eur Fedn Company Sports; Secs & Managers Australia; Club Managers Assn Amer
- > Business in Sport & Leisure (BISL)
- M 80 f
- ¶ Review - 4; ftm.   NL - 10; free.   Ybk - 1; m only.

Recruitment & Employment Confederation (REC) 1963
- NR 36-38 Mortimer St, LONDON, W1W 7RG.   (hq)
  020 7462 3289
  email info@rec.uk.com   http://www.rec.uk.com
  Chief Exec: Marcia Roberts
- ▲ Company Limited by Guarantee
- Br 2
- ○ *P; recruitment industry training & education
- ● Conf - Mtgs - ET - Exam - Res - Inf - LG
- M c 5,000 i, c 7,000 f
- ¶ Recruitment Matters - 6.

Recruitment Society 1978
- ■ 211 Piccadilly, LONDON, W1J 9HF.   (hsb)
  020 7917 1728
  email admin@recruitmentsociety.org.uk
  http://www.recruitmentsociety.org.uk
  Admin: Richard Taylor,   Chmn: Steve Huxham
- ▲ Un-incorporated Society
- ○ *P; to provide a forum for discussion of best practice in recruitment
- ● Conf - Mtgs
- M 300 i

Recyclatex
  a group of the **Textile Recycling Association**

Recyclers Great Britain
  trades as **United Kingdom Cartridge Remanufacturers' Association**

Red Poll Cattle Society 1888
- ■ 52 Border Cot Lane, Wickham Market, WOODBRIDGE, Suffolk, IP13 0EZ.   (hq)
  01728 747230   fax 01728 748226
  email secretary@redpoll.co.uk   http://www.redpoll.org
  Sec: Mrs T J Booker
- ▲ Registered Charity
- ○ *B
- ● Stat - Expt - Inf
- M 314 i, f & org, UK / 31 i, f & org, o'seas
- ¶ NL - 4; m only.   Herd Book - 1; ftm, £10 nm.

Redbridge Chamber of Commerce
- NR Teachers' Centre, Melbourne Rd, ILFORD, Essex, IG1 4HT. (hq)
  020 8514 5364   fax 020 8514 8488
  email chamber@redbridgechamber.co.uk
  http://www.redbridgechamber.co.uk
  Sec: Debbie Thomas,   Chmn: Julie Woodward
- ▲ Company Limited by Guarantee
- ○ *C

RedR - Engineers for Disaster Relief (RedR-IHE) 1980
- ■ 1 Great George St, LONDON, SW1P 3AA.   (hq)
  020 7233 3116
  email info@redr.org   http://www.redr.org/london
  Chief Exec: Bobby Lambert
- ▲ Company Limited by Guarantee; Registered Charity
- Br Sri Lanka, Pakistan, Sudan
- ○ *W; an international NGO providing recruitment & support services for humanitarian, professionals across the world; RedR London & international health exchanges
- Gp The security programmes; Recruitment; General training; Membership
- ● ET - Res - Inf - PL
- < RedR Intl; People in Aid
- M c 200 i
- ¶ NL - 3.   AR.
  Engineering in Emergencies: a practical guide.
- × 2003 RedR-IHE

© CBD Research Ltd · Beckenham · BR3 5JS · Tel 020 8650 7745 · Fax 020 8650 0768 · E-mail cbd@cbdresearch.com · www.cbdresearch.com

Referees' Association   (The RA)   1908
NR   1 Westhill Rd, Coundon, COVENTRY, Warks, CV6 2AD.   (hq)
        024 7660 1701   fax 024 7660 1556
        email ra@footballreferee.org
        http://www.footballreferee.org
        Gen Sec: Arthur W S Smith
▲   Registered Charity
Br   340; worldwide
○   *S; interests of all grades of Football Association registered
        referees & assistant referees
●   Conf - Mtgs - ET - Exhib
M   c 35,000 i
¶   The Football Referee - (September to April); 90p.

Referenda Society   1991
NR   29 Cleeves Walk, ILFORD, Essex, IG6 2NQ.   (Regd)
        929 8500 4074 office
        Dir: G Monnery
○   *K; to campaign for the introduction of a referenda voting
        system by which the electorate can express an opinion on
        issues of public concern & interest & secure the appropriate
        legislation
●   Campaigning
M   i
¶   Introducing Direct Democracy; free for sae.

Refined Bitumen Association Ltd   (RBA)   1968
NR   Crowthorne House, Nine Mile Rd, WOKINGHAM, Berks,
        RG40 3GA.   (hq)
        email asphalt@hmpr.co.uk
        14a Eccleston St, LONDON, SW1W 9LT.
        020 7730 1100   fax 020 7730 2213.   (press office)
        Sec: Dr Tony Harrison
▲   Company Limited by Guarantee
○   *T; to represent the bitumen supply industry in the UK; to
        increase knowledge of the engineering properties of bitumen
        & the development of the applications in which bitumens are
        used
Gp   Technical c'ee
●   Mtgs - ET - Res - SG - Inf - LG - Sponsoring research into
        bituminous materials for use in the construction &
        maintenance of highways & airfields
<   Eurobitume; Quarry Products Assn; Road Surface Dressing Assn
        (RSDA)
M   8 f
¶   Technical bulletins on specific subjects - irreg; free.

Refined Sugar Association   (RSA)   1891
■   15-18 Lime St (4th floor), LONDON, EC3M 7AQ.   (hq)
        020 7626 1745   fax 020 7283 3831
        email moond@sugar-assoc.co.uk
        Sec: N Durham
○   *T; rules & contract conditions for the white sugar trade
Gp   Arbitrators; Rules & contract conditions
●   Mtgs - ET - Inf - Empl - LG
M   40 f, UK / 70 f, o'seas
¶   Rules & Regulations; £35 m, £60 nm.

Refractories Association of Great Britain
        merged in June 2002 with the British Industrial Ceramic
        Manufacturers Association to form **British Refractories &
        Industrial Ceramics**

Refractory Users Federation   (RUF)   1945
NR   Broadway House (5th floor), Tothill St, LONDON, SW1H 9NS.
        (asa)
        020 7799 2000
▲   Un-incorporated Society
○   *T; for contractors involved in refractory work of all types incl
        furnace installation & boiler setting
●   Mtgs - ET - Inf - Empl - LG
<   Engg Construction Ind Assn
M   10 f

Refrigerant Users' Group
        is a group of the **Halon Users National Consortium Ltd**

Refrigerated Transport Information Society
        a group of **Cambridge Refrigeration Technology**

Regency Society of Brighton & Hove   1945
NR   85 Furze Croft, Furze Hill, HOVE, E Sussex, BN3 1PE.   (hsp)
        01273 737434   fax 01273 736042
        email john-small@lineone.net
        http://www.regencysociety.org
        Hon Sec: John Small
▲   Registered Charity
○   *A, *K; preservation of historic architecture of Brighton & Hove;
        to promote interest in architecture & urban design
●   Mtgs - Res - Exhib - VE
<   Georgian Gp; Civic Trust; Fedn of Sussex Amenity Socs; 20th
        Century Soc; Victorian Soc
M   c 400 i, 5 org
¶   AR; free.

Regia Anglorum   (Regia)   1980
NR   9 Durleigh Close, Headley Park, BRISTOL, BS13 7NQ.   (hq)
        0117-964 6818
        email events@regia.org   http://www.regia.org
        Business Mgr: J Kim Siddorn
▲   Un-incorporated Society
Br   40; Australia, Canada, Denmark, Germany, Italy, N Zealand,
        USA
○   *D, *G; to accurately re-create the life & times of the Saxons,
        Vikings, Cymru, Scots, Normans & other inhabitants of the
        islands of Britain between the reigns of Alfred the Great &
        Richard the Lionheart
Gp   Archery; Arms & armour; Battle re-enactment; Carpentry &
        house-building techniques; Early music; Folkdance; Hunting;
        Permanent site in Kent; Ships & the sea
●   Conf - Mtgs - ET - Res - Exhib - Inf - PL - LG
<   Nat Assn Re-enactment Socs; Engliscan Gesíþas; York
        Archaeological Trust
M   650 i, UK / 100 i, o'seas
¶   Chronicle (NL) - 4; ftm only.   Clamavi - irreg.

Regional Newspapers Association of Ireland   (RNAI)   1919
IRL   Sheridan House, 33 Parkgate St, DUBLIN 8, Republic of Ireland.
        353 (1) 677 9116   fax 353 (1) 677 9144
        email barbara@rnan.ie   http://www.rnan.ie
        Admin: Barbara Sheridan
○   *T; the representative body of Ireland's weekly regional
        newspapers

Regional Studies Association   (RSA)   1965
■   PO Box 2058, SEAFORD, E Sussex, BN25 4QU.   (hq)
        01323 899698   fax 01323 899798
        email rsa@mailbox.ulcc.ac.uk
        http://www.regional-studies-assoc.ac.uk
        Chief Exec: Sally Hardy
▲   Registered Charity
Br   11; Ireland, Poland, Hungary
○   *E, *L; to promote education & studies in regional planning
Gp   International regional research
●   Conf - Mtgs - SG - Inf
M   450 i, 170 org, UK / 110 i, 17 org, o'seas
¶   Regional Studies - 9;   NL - 6;   AR; all ftm.

Register of Apparel & Textile Designers   (RATD)   1985
NR   5 Portland Place, LONDON, W1B 1PW.   (hq)
　　020 7636 5577   fax 020 7636 7515
　　Mgr: Laurian Davies
○　*T; to assist manufacturers of clothing & textiles in the UK &
　　overseas; to offer a help & advice service to designers by
　　holding up-to-date lists of designers by speciality;
　　The Register is jointly sponsored by the British clothing industry
　　& UK Fashion Exports
●　Conf - Mtgs - ET - Res - Exhib - Expt - Inf - Lib - VE - Empl - LG
M　i
¶　NL - 12; ftm only.

Register of Chinese Herbal Medicine   (RCHM)   1987
■　Office 5 Ferndale Business Centre, 1 Exeter St, NORWICH,
　　NR2 4QB.   (hq)
　　01603 623994   fax 01603 667557
　　email herbmed@rchm.co.uk   http://www.rchm.co.uk
　　Pres: Tony Booker
○　*P; to register & regulate fully qualified practitioners of
　　traditional Chinese herbal medicine across the UK; to
　　safeguard & promote their interests
●　LG
<　Eur Herbal Practitioners Assn (EHPA)
M　400 i, UK / 30 i, o'seas
¶　RCHM Jnl - 2; ftm, £25 yr nm.
　　LM - on request; free.

**Register of Independent Professional Turfgrass Agronomists
(RIPTA)   2002**
NR　21 Grove Park, WALSHAM-le-WILLOWS, Norfolk, IP31 3AE.
　　(hsb)
　　01359 259361
　　email tim.lodge@stri.co.uk   http://www.ripta.co.uk
　　Keeper of the Register: Dr Tim Lodge
▲　Un-incorporated Society
○　*P; ; to give independent advice on growing & tending turf
●　Inf
M　16 i

Register of Professional Turners
NR　The Workshop, Moor Close Lane, Over Kellet, CARNFORTH,
　　Lancs, LA6 1DF.   (chmn/p)
　　01524 735882
　　Chmn: Malcolm Cobb
○　*P; woodturners
M　215 i

Registered Nursing Home Association Ltd   (RNHA)   1968
■　15 Highfield Rd, Edgbaston, BIRMINGHAM, B15 3DU.   (hq)
　　0121-454 2511   fax 0121-454 0932
　　http://www.rnha.co.uk
　　Chief Exec: Frank E Ursell
▲　Company Limited by Guarantee
Br　35
○　*P; improvement of standards of care & techniques in
　　registered nursing homes
●　Conf - Mtgs - ET - Res - SG - Stat - Inf - VE - Joint efforts with
　　DH & DSS.
M　1,600 nursing homes, clinics & hospitals
¶　Courier (NL) - 6;　Nursing Home News - 6; both ftm only.
　　Reference Book - 1; ftm.
　　Care Assistant Training Manual; ftm, £50 nm.
　　Business Management / Nursing Management Manuals; both
　　ftm only.

Reiki Association   (TRA)   1991
■　2 Spa Terrace, Fenny Bridge, HUDDERSFIELD, W Yorks,
　　HD8 0BD.   (coordinator/p)
　　0770 427 0727
　　email co-ordinator@reikiassociation.org.uk
　　http://www.reikiassociation.org.uk
　　Coordinator: Sally Smith
▲　Company Limited by Guarantee
○　*P, *W; for Reiki practitioners & masters with the focus of Usui
　　Shiki Ryoho Reiki; to offer information to the public about
　　Reiki treatments
●　Conf - Mtgs - ET - Exhib - Inf
M　936 i, UK / 31 i, o'seas
¶　Touch - 4; ftm only.
　　Reiki Magazine International - 6; £26 yr m, £45 yr nm.

Relatives & Residents Association   1992
NR　24 The Ivories, 6-18 Northampton St, LONDON, N1 2HY.
　　(hq)
　　020 7359 8148   fax 020 7226 6603
　　email advice@relnes.org   http://www.relres.org.uk
　　Chief Exec: Gillian Dalley
▲　Company Limited by Guarantee; Registered Charity
○　*W; to support & advise older people, & their relatives &
　　friends, who are in, or considering, long term care; to
　　promote good practice in homes through local groups,
　　publications & training
●　Conf - Mtgs (local gps) - ET - Inf
　　Advice line: 020 7359 8136
M　c 300 i
¶　NL - 2; ftm, £1 nm.
　　Involving Relatives & Friends: a good practice guide for homes
　　for older people.
　　Gardening in Homes.
　　Dental Care for People in Homes (book).
　　Publications list available.

Religious Drama Society of GB   (Radius)   1929
■　58-60 Lincoln Rd, PETERBOROUGH, Cambs, PE1 2RZ.   (hq)
　　01733 565613
　　email office@radius.org.uk   http://www.radius.org.uk
　　Hon Office Mgr: Anne Giles
▲　Registered Charity
○　*R; to promote drama which explores faith & the human
　　condition
●　Conf - ET - Comp - Inf - Lib - VE
M　200 i, 30 org, UK / 20 i, o'seas
¶　Radius Performing (Jnl) - 4; ftm, £1 nm.

Religious Society of Friends (Quakers)   (Quakers)   1650
NR　173-177 Euston Rd, LONDON, NW1 2BJ.   (hq)
　　020 7663 1000
　　Recording Clerk: Elsa Dicks
▲　Registered Charity
Br　475; Worldwide
○　*R; pastoral work; witness to Quaker beliefs
●　Conf - Mtgs - Inf - Lib - Supporting international representatives
M　16,978 i, (13,309 attenders)
¶　Quaker News - 4.　Quaker Monthly - 12.
　　Quaker Projects - 2;　Books - irreg.

Remote Gambling Association   (RGA)   2005
NR　Regency House, 1-4 Warwick St, LONDON, W1B 5LT.
　　020 7479 4040
　　http://www.rga.eu.com
　　Chief Exec: Clive Hawkswood
○　*T
M　34 online betting and poker sites

Remote Imaging Group   (RIG)

■ PO Box 2001, DARTMOUTH, Devon, TQ6 9QN.   (msp)
   01454 773387   fax 01454 887880
   email membership@rig.org.uk   http://www.rig.org.uk
▲ Company Limited by Guarantee
○ *G; to promote interest & disseminate information pertaining to
   the reception & display of 'remote images' namely weather
   satellites; to liaise with official bodies, eg AMSAT-UK, the
   Dept of Trade & Industry, the European Space Agency, Nat
   Oceanic & Atmospheric Administration (US), the Radio
   Society of Great Britain, etc
● Conf - Exhib - Inf
M 1,250 i, UK / 536 i, o'seas
¶ RIG Jnl - 4; ftm only.

Remote Sensing & Photogrammetry Society   (RSPSoc)   2001

■ School of Geography, University of Nottingham,
   NOTTINGHAM, NG7 2RD.   (hq)
   0115-951 5435   fax 0115-951 5249
   email rspsoc@nottingham.ac.uk   http://www.rspsoc.org
   Hon Gen Sec: Dr Philippa Mason
▲ Registered Charity
○ *L; to promote the knowledge & understanding of remote
   sensing & photogrammetry
Gp Special interest: Archaeology, Education, Geological remote
   sensing, GIS, Modelling & advanced techniques, Ocean
   colour, Synthetic aperture radar
● Conf - Mtgs - ET - Inf
< Intl Soc of Photogrammetry & Remote Sensing (ISPRS)
M 1,200 i, 65 f
¶ RSPSoc NL - 4;   AR; both ftm only.
   International Jnl of Remote Sensing - 22; £55 m (2003).
   The Photogrammetric Record - 4; ftm, £150 nm.
   Annual Conference Proceedings (CD-ROM) - 1; ftm, £10 nm.

Renal Association   1950

NR Triangle House (Unit 2), Broomhill Rd, LONDON,
   SW18 4HX.   (secretariat)
   020 8875 2413
   Hon Sec: Prof Adrian Woolf
▲ Company Limited by Guarantee; Registered Charity
○ *L; to advance, collate & disseminate knowledge of renal
   function & structure; to seek means for the prevention &
   treatment of renal disorders
● Conf - Mtgs - ET - Exhib
M 700 i, 11 f

Renewable Energy Association   (REA)   2001

■ 17 Waterloo Place, LONDON, SW1Y 4AR.   (hq)
   020 7747 1830   fax 020 7925 2715
   email info@r-e-a.net   http://www.r-e-a.net
   Chief Exec: Philip Wolfe
▲ Company Limited by Guarantee
○ *T; to secure the best legislative & regulatory controls for
   expanding renewable energy production in the UK
Gp Biomass; Bioenergy; Solar; Ocean energy; Renewable transport
   fuels
● Conf - Mtgs - SG - Stat - LG
M 400 i, f & org
¶ Renewbles Ybk - 1.
✕ 2005 (British BioGen
       (Renewable Power Association (December)
   2006 (British Assocaition of Biofuels & Oils
       (British Photovoltaic Association (April)

Renfrewshire Chamber of Commerce   1964

NR Bute Court, St Andrews Drive, Glasgow Airport, PAISLEY,
   Renfrewshire, PA3 2SW.
   0141-847 5450
   http://www.renfrewshirechamber.com
   Chief Exec: Norman Simpson
▲ Company Limited by Guarantee
○ *C
   no further information supplied

Repetitive Strain Injury Association

   liquidated 2005

Research Defence Society   (RDS)   1908

■ 25 Shaftesbury Ave, LONDON, W1D 7EG.   (hq)
   020 7287 2818   fax 020 7287 2627
   email admin@rds-net.org.uk
   http://www.rds-net.org.uk
   Exec Dir: Dr Simon Festing
▲ Industrial & Provident Society
○ *L; 'to make known the facts about experimental research
   involving use of animals; to emphasise importance &
   necessity of such experiments; to give guidance on the
   prevention of suffering of experimental animals'
● Inf - LG - Public education
< Eur Biomedical Res Assn
M 10,000 i, 50 f, 100 org
¶ NL - 4; free.

Research & Development Society   (R&D)   1962

NR c/o Royal Society, 6-9 Carlton House Terrace, LONDON,
   SW1Y 5AG.
   020 7451 2513   fax 020 7930 2170
   Admin Sec: Scott Keir
▲ Company Limited by Guarantee
○ *P; 'to promote networking between people involved in R & D
   management & related professions over the whole range of
   science, engineering & technology; to disseminate current
   new ideas in science & technology, related management &
   business development, & science policy'
● Mtgs
M c 450 i, f & org
   Note: the society was incorporated in 1961

Residential Boat Owners Association   (RBOA)   1963

■ Narrowboat Wasp, Sorrel Crafts (off Barons Way),
   MOUNTSORREL, Leics, LE12 7EA.   (mail)
   07710 029247
   http://www.rboa.org.uk add
   Chmn: Beryl McDowall
▲ Un-incorporated Society
○ *K; to further the interests of boat dwellers on the coasts, rivers
   & canals of Britain; to safeguard & increase the number of
   residential moorings; to encourage high standards of safety
   of boats & their moorings & good relations between
   members & landlords & local authorities; to encourage
   mobile boats to cruise
● Mtgs
M i, f & org
¶ Soundings (NL) - 4; ftm.   Living Afloat; £8.50.
   A Home Afloat (leaflet); free.

Residential Landlords Association

NR 1 Roebuck Lane, SALE, Cheshire, M33 7SY.
   0845 666 5000   fax 0845 665 1845
   http://www.rla.org.uk

Residential Sprinkler Association Ltd
   since 2002-03 **Fire Sprinkler Association**

Residential Ventilation Association   (RVA)   2000

■ 2 Waltham Court, Milley Lane, Hare Hatch, READING, Berks,
   RG10 9TH.   (hq)
   0118-940 3416   fax 0118-940 6258
   email info@feta.co.uk   http://www.feta.co.uk
   Dir Gen: Cedric Sloan
○ *T; the responsible provision of suitable ventilation products for
   all applications in the home
● Mtgs - SG - Inf
< Heating & Ventilating Mfrs' Assn (HEVAC); Fedn Envtl Trade
   Assns (FETA)
M 19 f

Resin Flooring Association
  see **FeRFA: the Resin Flooring Association**

Resolution   (SFLA)   1982
NR   PO Box 302, ORPINGTON, Kent, BR6 8QX.   (hq)
      01689 820272   fax 01689 896972
      Chmn: Kim Beatson,   Sec: Godfrey Freeman
Br   29 regional groups
○   *P; solicitors working in the area of family law & marriage
      break down, who have adopted a conciliatory, rather than a
      litigious approach to family law
Gp   Working parties & c'ees: Mediation, Legal aid, Education,
      Training, Procedure, Children; Child Support Act
M   c 5,000 i
¶   NL - 6.   Precedents for Consent Orders - updated.
×   2005 Solicitors Family Law Association

Resource Use Institute Ltd   (RUI)   1969
NR   19 West End, Kinglassie, LOCHGELLY, Fife, KY5 0XG.   (hsb)
      01592 882248
      http://www.rui.co.uk
      Sec: Miss Isabel Soutar
▲   Company Limited by Guarantee
Br   3
○   *L; to encourage new thinking, especially in science, technology
      & economics; the management of innovation
Gp   Clay minerals; Resource economics; Mathematical chemistry;
      Land utilisation
●   Res
M   18 i, UK / 1 i, o'seas

Restaurant Association   (RAGB)   1968
NR   Queen's House, 55-56 Lincoln's Inn Fields, LONDON,
      WC2A 3BH.   (hq)
      020 7404 7744   fax 020 7404 7799
      email info@ragb.co.uk   http://www.ragb.co.uk
      Dir: David Harrold
▲   Company Limited by Guarantee
○   *P, *T; to educate, inform & represent member restaurateurs
●   Conf - Mtgs - ET - Exhib - Comp - Inf - LG
M   3,000 f
¶   Dine Out - 4.   Digest - 10.

Restaurant Property Advisors Society   (RPAS)   1990
NR   c/o CBRE, 80 New Bond St, LONDON, W1S 1SB.   (sb)
      020 7663 5555
      http://www.rpas.org.uk
      Sec: Jason Grant
▲   Un-incorporated Society
○   *P; 'professionals specialising in the sale, acquisition, letting,
      valuation, rent review & lease renewal advice on restaurants
      & other licensed properties'
●   Conf - Mtgs
M   60 i

Restaurants Association of Ireland
IRL   11 Bridge Court, City Gate, Saint Augustine St, DUBLIN 8,
      Republic of Ireland.
      353 (1) 677 9901   fax 353 (1) 671 8414
      email info@rai.ie
      Chief Exec: Henry O'Neill
○   *T

Restricted Growth Association   (RGA)   1970
NR   PO Box 4008, YEOVIL, Somerset, BA20 9AW.   (mail/address)
      01935 841364
      email office@restrictedgrowth.co.uk
      Assn Mgr: Ruth Morgan
▲   Registered Charity
○   *Q, *W; to promote the general welfare of persons of restricted
      growth; to investigate the causes & mitigate their medical
      condition
M   i

**Retail Book, Stationery & Allied Trade Employees Association
(RBA)**
NR   22 Borough Fields Shopping Centre, Wootton Bassett,
      SWINDON, Wilts, SN4 7AX.
      01793 841414
      http://www.the-rba.org
      Nat Officer: Paul Lee,   Pres: David Pickles
○   *U
M   c 4,500 i
¶   Jnl;   Newssheets; both m only.   AR.
      Note: Generally known as the Retail Book Association

Retail Bridalwear Association Ltd   (RBA)   1995
NR   106 Broad Street Mall, READING, Berks, RG1 7QA.   (hq)
      01494 445155   fax 01494 445155
      email rba@fsmail.net(09)rbaltd.org.uk
      Sec: Philip Rathkey
▲   Company Limited by Guarantee
○   *T; an association of independent bridal & formalwear retailers
      committed to the highest standards of customer service
      where the bride & groom can buy confidence
●   Mtgs - ET - SG - VE - LG - Annual awards
>   Brit Bridalwear Assn
M   100 i
¶   LM on website

**Retail Confectioners & Tobacconists Association Ltd   (RCTA)
1976**
NR   c/o Levicks, 3 Lloyd Rd, BROADSTAIRS, Kent, CT10 1HY.   (hq)
      Contact: Michael Collier
○   *T; 'providing a distribution service of product to members;
      liaison with trade & industry on issues parochial to the CTN
      sector in tobacco, confectionery & ancillary fields'

Retail Grocery, Dairy & Allied Trades Association [Ireland]
  see **RGDATA - Retail Grocery, Dairy & Allied Trades
  Association**

Retail Motor Industry Federation   (RMI)   1913
NR   201 Great Portland St, LONDON, W1W 5AB.   (hq)
      020 7580 9122
      Chief Exec: Matthew Carrington
Br   8
○   *T; interests of those selling & servicing new & used cars, trucks
      & motorcycles & other related activities
Gp   Cherished Number Dealers Association; Independent Garage
      Association; Motorcycle Retailers Association; Motorcycle
      Rider Training Association; National Franchised Dealers
      Association; Petrol Retailers Association; Society of Motor
      Auctions;
      Bodyshop Services division
M   12,000 f
¶   Motor Retailer - 12.
      Forecourt - 12.
      Recovery Operator - 4.

Rethink   (Rethink)   1972
■   Royal London House (5th floor), 22-25 Finsbury Sq, LONDON,
      EC2A 1DX.   (hq)
      0845 456 0455   fax 01622 683278
      email info@rethink.org   http://www.rethink.org
      Chief Exec: Paul Jenkins
▲   Registered Charity
Br   9 in England, 1 Northern Ireland
○   *W; to help everyone affected by severe mental illness, recover
      a better quality of life
Gp   350 mental health services; 30 local support groups; National
      advice service
●   Mtgs - Res - Inf - LG
<   Mental Health Providers' Forum; Mental Health Alliance; NHS
      Confedn
M   c 6,000 i
¶   Publications list on WWW.mentalhealthshop.org

Retread Manufacturers Association   (RMA)   1938
NR   PO Box 320, CREWE, Cheshire, CW2 6WY.   (hq)
　　　01270 561014   fax 01270 668801
　　　Dir: D Wilson
▲　　Un-incorporated Society
○　　*T; for the UK retread tyre industry & associated businesses
●　　Conf - Mtgs - ET - Exam - Res - Exhib - SG - Stat - Inf - VE - LG
<　　Intl Assn of Retreading & Dealer Assns (BIPAVER); Eur Tyre
　　　Recycling Assn (ETRA); Soc of Assn Execs (SAE); Tyre Ind
　　　Coun (TIC); Brit Tyre Ind Fedn (BTIF)
M　　110 f, UK / 6 f, o'seas
¶　　The Retreader (published in Tyres & Accessories) - 12.
　　　LM - updated.   AR.
　　　Manual of Operating Standards.

Retreat Association   (RA)   1989
◼　　The Central Hall, 256 Bermondsey St, LONDON, SE1 3UJ.
　　　(hq)
　　　020 7357 7736   fax 020 7357 7724
　　　email info@retreats.org.uk   http://www.retreats.org.uk
　　　Exec Officer: Paddy Lane
○　　*G, *N, *R; a federation of Christian retreat groups
●　　Inf - Coordinates information on training courses
M　　7 retreat gps each with own members:
　　　Association for Promoting Retreats
　　　Baptist Union Retreat Group
　　　Catholic Network for Retreats & Spirituality
　　　Methodist Retreat & Spirituality Network
　　　Quaker Retreat Group
　　　United Reformed Church Silence & Retreat Network
　　　affiliates of the Retreat Associaton
¶　　Retreats - 1.   NL; m only.   AR - 1.
　　　Information leaflets.

**Retroreflective Equipment Manufacturers' Association
(REMA)   1977**
◼　　1 Wine St, BRADFORD-ON-AVON, Wilts, BA15 1NS.   (hsp)
　　　01225 862625   fax 01225 862625
　　　email info@rema.org.uk   http://www.rema.org.uk
　　　Hon Sec: Peter Slade
▲　　Un-incorporated Society
○　　*T; manufacturers of road & other safety products that employ
　　　wholly retroreflective surfaces in their construction or form
Gp　Road studs; Temporary markings; High visibility clothing; Road
　　　cones & cylinders; Road danger lamps; Retroreflective
　　　materials; Barriers & temporary signs; Marker posts & street
　　　furniture
●　　Mtgs - SG - Inf - LG
M　　32 f
¶　　LM - 1; free.

Rett Syndrome Association   (RSA)   1985
◼　　113 Friern Barnet Rd, LONDON, N11 3EU.
　　　0870 770 3266 (0900-1700) 24-hr answerphone
　　　fax 0870 770 3265
　　　email info@rettsyndrome.org.uk
　　　http://www.rettsyndrome.org.uk
　　　Hon Chmn: Linda Partridge
▲　　Registered Charity
○　　*M, *W; 'Rett syndrome is a complex neurological disorder that
　　　occurs mostly in females; the charity offers help & advice to
　　　all families & professionals; to raise funds for research'
●　　Fund raising - Specialist clinics - Facilitates local support groups
<　　Intl Rett Syndrome Assn
M　　i
¶　　NL - 4.

Returned Volunteer Action   (RVA)   1966
NR   1 Amwell St, LONDON, EC1R 1TH.   (hq)
　　　020 7247 6406
　　　email retvolact@lineone.net
　　　Hon Sec: A C Symes
▲　　Company Limited by Guarantee; Registered Charity
○　　*W; to help returned volunteers & development workers
　　　evaluate their overseas experience; to encourage those
　　　seeking overseas placements to examine their personal
　　　expectations & motivations
●　　ET - Inf
M　　350 i, 250 org
¶　　Development Action (NL) - 12; ftm, £5 yr nm.
　　　Introduction to Volunteering Overseas; £4.
　　　Publications list available; free.

**RGDATA - Retail Grocery, Dairy & Allied Trades Association
(RGDATA)**
IRL   Rock House, Main St, BLACKROCK, Co Dublin, Republic of
　　　Ireland.
　　　353 (1) 288 8313   fax 353 (1) 283 2206
　　　email rgdata@rgdata.ie   http://www.rgdata.ie
　　　Dir Gen: Tara Buckley
○　　*T

Rhea & Emu Association   (REA)
NR   31 Newbold Rd, KIRKBY MALLORY, Leics, LE9 7QG.   (hsp)
　　　01455 823344   fax 01455 823344
　　　Sec: Margaret Dover
○　　*B
●　　Mtgs
M　　40 i, UK / 1 i, o'seas

Rheumatoid Arthritis Surgical Society
　　　a specialist society of the **British Orthopaedic Association**

Rice Association   (RA)   1989
NR   21 Arlington St, LONDON, SW1A 1RN.   (hq)
　　　020 7493 2521
▲　　Un-incorporated Society
○　　*T; processors, packers & users of rice in the UK
●　　Mtgs - LG
<　　Food & Drink Fedn
M　　16 f
¶　　LM; free.

Richard Aldington Society
　　　see **New Canterbury Literary Society - Richard Aldington
　　　Society**

Richard III Society - Fellowship of the White Boar   1924
◼　　4 Oakley St, LONDON, SW3 5NN.   (hsp)
　　　01689 823569
　　　email information@richardiii.net   http://www.richardiii.net
　　　Hon Sec: Miss Elizabeth M Nokes
▲　　Un-incorporated Society
Br　　15; America, Australia, Canada
○　　*G, *L; to promote historical research into life & times of King
　　　Richard III & to secure re-assessment of his role in English
　　　history
●　　Conf - Mtgs - Res - Inf - Lib - VE
M　　3,000 i, UK / 1,000 i, o'seas
¶　　The Ricardian - 1; ftm, £16 nm.
　　　The Ricardian Bulletin - 4; ftm only.

Richard Jefferies Society   1950
NR   Pear Tree Cottage, Longcot, FARINGDON, Oxon, SN7 7SS.
     (hsp)
     01793 783040
     Hon Sec: Jean Saunders
▲   Registered Charity
○   *A; to promote study & interest in the life & works of Richard
     Jefferies, naturalist & writer, & concern for places intimately
     connected with him in Wiltshire, Sussex & Surrey
●   Mtgs - Res - Inf - Lib - PL - VE - Book sales - Care of memorials
M   c 300 i & org
¶   Jnl - 1; ftm, £1.50 nm.   NL - 2;   AR; both ftm.

Richard Strauss Society   1991
■   19 North Rd, LONDON, N6 4BD.   (sp)
     020 8245 3064   fax 020 8245 3064
     email dfad29@blueyonder.co.uk
     http://www.richard-strauss-society.co.uk
     Hon Sec: David Davidson
▲   Registered Charity; Un-incorporated Society
○   *D; the life & works of Richard Strauss
●   Conf - SG - VE
M   100 i, UK / 2 i, o'seas
¶   NL - 3/4; ftm only.

Richmond Chamber of Commerce   1908
NR   York House (Room 706), Richmond Rd, TWICKENHAM, Middx,
     TW1 3AA.   (hq)
     020 8891 7457
     http://www.richmondchamberofcommerce.co.uk
     Pres: Maurice Press
○   *C
●   Conf - Mtgs - ET - Stat - Inf - LG
<   West London Enterprise Agency; Richmond in Business
×   2005 Richmond Borough Chamber of Commerce

Rider Haggard Society   (RHS)   1984
■   27 Deneholm, Monkseaton, WHITLEY BAY, Tyne & Wear,
     NE25 9AU.   (hsp)
     0191-252 4516   fax 0191-252 4516
     email rb27allen@aol.com
     Hon Sec: Roger Allen
▲   Un-incorporated Society
○   *A; for all who appreciate Rider Haggard's works
●   Mtgs - Res - Buying/selling Haggard's books
<   Alliance of Literary Socs
M   90 i, UK / 21 i, o'seas
¶   The Haggard Jnl - 4; ftm.
     Illustrated Guide to Fiction; £15.
     Illustrated Guide to Non-Fiction; £16.
     Haggardiana (ephemera folder); £16 m, £25 nm.

Riding for the Disabled Association   1969
■   Lavinia Norfolk House, Avenue R, STONELEIGH PARK, Warks,
     CV8 2LY.   (hq)
     0845 658 1082   fax 0845 658 1083
     email info@rda.org.uk   http://www.rda.org.uk
     Chief Exec: Ed Bracher
▲   Company Limited by Guarantee; Registered Charity
○   *W; to improve the lives of people with special needs, by
     enabling them to ride &/or carriage drive for the benefit of
     their health & general wellbeing
●   Conf - Mtgs - ET - Exam - Comp - LG
<   Fedn of Riding for the Disabled Intl; Brit Equestrian Fedn; Nat
     Equine Welfare Coun
M   18,500 i (volunteers), 25,000 i (riders)
¶   RDA News - 4; free (not Summer).

Rights of Women   (ROW)   1975
■   52-54 Featherstone St, LONDON, EC1Y 8RT.   (hq)
     020 7251 6575/6   textphone 020 7490 2562
     fax 020 7490 5377
     email info@row.org.uk
     http://www.rightsofwomen.org.uk
     Dir: Ranjit Kaur
▲   Un-incorporated Society
○   *K; to advise & inform women of their legal rights & promote
     the interests of women in relation to the law
●   Conf - Mtgs - Res - Inf - Legal advice/referral
<   Advice UK
M   150 i, 50 f

Rigid Intermediate Bulk Container Association
     in 2004 merged with the Association of Drum Manufacturers & the
     Federation of Drum Reconditioners to form the **Industrial
     Packaging Association**

Ring of Tatters   1980
■   37 Manor Abbey Rd, HALESOWEN, W Midlands, B62 5AQ.
     (chmn/p)
     0121-422 5425   fax 0121-423 1948
     http://www.ringoftatters.org.uk
     Chmn: Mrs Brenda Rewhorn
○   *G; to promote interest in & knowledge of the lacemaking craft
     of tatting
●   Mtgs - ET - Exhib - Comp - Lib
M   800 i, 400 i
¶   NL - 2; £6.75 m only.

**River Association for Freight & Transport (incorporating
AMLBO)   (RAFT)   2000**
NR   Tamesis House, 35 St Philips Avenue, WORCESTER PARK,
     Surrey, KT4 8JS.   (hq)
     020 8330 6446   fax 020 8330 7447
     email raft@tamgroup.co.uk
     Sec: N Barry Jaynes
○   *T; for operation on & around the River Thames
Gp   Lighterage; Passenger boats; Wharves
●   Mtgs - Comp - LG
M   12 f

River Thames Society   (RTS)   1962
NR   Side House, Middle Assendon, HENLEY-on-THAMES, Oxon,
     RG9 6AP.   (admin)
     01491 571476
     http://www.riverthamessociety.org.uk p
     Admin: Mrs Alix Horne
▲   Company Limited by Guarantee; Registered Charity
Br   5
○   *K; encouragement of interest in the river & preservation &
     development of its amenities & natural beauty
●   Conf - Mtgs - Exhib - Lib (at River & Rowing Museum, Henley-
     on-Thames)
<   Inland Waterways Assn; Ramblers Assn
M   c 1,200 i, f & org, UK / 2 i, o'seas
¶   Thames Guardian - 4.

RNID (RNID) 1911
NR   19-23 Featherstone St, LONDON, EC1Y 8SL.   (hq)
       0808 808 0123 (voice)   0808 808 9000 (textphone)
       fax 020 7296 8199
       email informationline@rnid.org.uk
       http://www.rnid.org.uk
       Chief Exec: Dr John Low
▲   Registered Charity
Br   7 offices
○   *W; works to provide services for deaf & hard of hearing
       people; seeks to raise public awareness of the issues
       surrounding deafness
●   ET - Res - Exhib - Inf - Lib
       Services for deaf people: Typetalk, the national telephone relay
       service; Sound Advantage, providing assistive devices
M   37,624 i & org
¶   One in Seven - 6
✕   2002 Royal National Institute for Deaf People

Road Block
NR   PO Box 100, 12-18 Hoxton St, LONDON, N1 6NG.
       020 7729 6973
       http://www.roadblock.org.uk
○   *K; to campaign against road-building

Road Emulsion Association Ltd   (REAL)   1928
NR   September House, Plantation Way, STORRINGTON, W Sussex,
       RH20 4JF.   (hq)
       01903 746584
       http://www.rea.org.uk
       Consultant & Sec: John Keayes
▲   Company Limited by Guarantee
○   *T; to promote the interests of producers & suppliers of road
       emulsion materials
●   Conf - Mtgs - Inf - LG
<   Intl Bitumen Emulsion Fedn (IBEF); Asphalt Emulsion Mfrs
       Assn (AEMA)
M   6 f

Road Haulage Association Ltd   (RHA)   1945
NR   35 Monument Hill, WEYBRIDGE, Surrey, KT13 8RN.   (hq)
       01932 841515
       Chief Exec: Roger King
▲   Company Limited by Guarantee
Br   4
○   *T; to represent Britain's professional hire-or-reward hauliers
●   Conf - Mtgs - ET - Exhib
<   Intl Road Transport U
M   10,000 f
¶   Roadway - 12; ftm.   Road Haulage Manual - 2 yrly; ftm.

Road Locomotive Society   (RLS)   1937
NR   PO Box 1878, ANDOVER, Hants, SP10 9AU.
       01332 781485
▲   Registered Charity
○   *G; to encourage education & research into the history of self
       propelling steam engines & vehicles (other than those
       running on rails) & portable engines
●   Mtgs - Res - Inf - Lib - PL - VE - LG
M   c 700 i & f
¶   Journal - 4; ftm. Various specialist publications.

Road Records Association   (RRA)   1888
NR   4 Scholars Walk, GUILDFORD, Surrey, GU2 7TR.   (chmn/p)
       01483 855815
       Chmn: Tim Dadswell
○   *S; verification of road cycling records
●   Dinner (triennial)
M   500 i, UK / 6 i, o'seas

Road Rescue Recovery Association   (RRRA)   1987
■   Hubberts Bridge Rd, Kirton Holme, BOSTON, Lincs,
       PE20 1TW.   (hq)
       01205 290622   fax 01205 290611
       email linda@recovery.co.uk   http://www.recovery.co.uk
       Chmn: Nigel Howarth
▲   Company Limited by Guarantee
○   *T;
●   Mtgs - ET - Exam - Res - Exhib - Inf - LG - Shows
M   31 i, 448 f
¶   Jnl - 4; ftm, £2.95 nm.   NL - 2; ftm only.
       Ybk - 1; free.   LM - irreg.   AR; ftm only.

Road Roller Association   (RRA)   1974
NR   Invicta, 9 Beagle Ridge Drive, Acomb, YORK, E Yorks,
       YO24 3JH.   (memsec/p)
       email info@r-r-a.org.uk   http://www.r-r-a.org.uk
       Mem Sec: Mrs D Rayner
○   *G; preservation, study of history & manufacture of road rollers
       & road making equipment, especially steam road rollers
●   Mtgs - ET - Res - Exhib - Inf - Lib - PL - VE
<   Nat Traction Engine Trust; Transport Trust; Fedn British Historic
       Vehicles Clubs
M   500 i, 8 f
¶   Rolling - 4; ftm.

Road Runners Club   (RRC)   1951
NR   The Firs, 15 Pinewood Rd, LONDON, SE2 0RY.   (hsp)
       Hon Sec: Dan Coffey
○   *S; road running & long distance running & racing
●   Mtgs - Comp - Road running course measurement - Standards
       scheme for road runners - Insurance for road runners
M   i
¶   NL - 3; ftm only.

Road Safety Markings Association   (RSMA)   1976
IRL   Unit 23 Bury Business Centre, Kay St, BURY, Lancs, BL9 6BU.
       (hq)
       0161-763 7711   fax 0161-763 7722
       email rsma@dial.pipex.com
       Nat Dir: George A Lee
▲   Un-incorporated Society
○   *T; provision of road/traffic safety markings, both vertical &
       horizontal (incl: thermoplastic, paint, road studs, road tapes)
       Is an NVQ assessment centre
Gp   Road marking forum; Client/contractor partnership gp; Health
       & safety forum; Promoting health & safety to industry;
       Marketing; Technical; Contracting; Ad hoc projects
●   Conf - Mtgs - ET - Res - Exhib - SG - Stat - Inf - LG
<   Intl Road Fedn
M   75 f, 5 org
¶   Standard Issue (NL) - 4.
       Update your Road Markings (CD); ftm.
       Whose Job is it Anyway? (video).
       Top Marks - 1;   Stanspec 2006 (CD).
       RSMA Safety Code of Practice (CD) - 1.

Road Surface Dressing Association Ltd   (RSDA)   1942
■   Westwood Park, London Rd, Little Horkesley, COLCHESTER,
       Essex, CO6 4BS.   (hq)
       01206 274052
       Consultant Dir & Sec: John Baxter
▲   Company Limited by Guarantee
○   *T; surface dressing of roads, footpaths & other ground
       surfaces
●   Conf - Mtgs - ET
M   30 f, 6 f (associates)
¶   AR; free.   Publications list available.

Road Time Trials Council
   since 2002 **Cycling Time Trials**

Road Transport Fleet Data Society   (Fleet Data)   1980
NR   18 Poplar Close, BIGGLESWADE, Beds, SG18 0EW.   (hsp)
       email info@fleetdata.co.uk
       Hon Sec: P Jarman
▲   Un-incorporated Society
○   *G; interest in vehicles of local & national government, public
       service fleets, power & water industries etc; research on
       vehicles & operators which no longer exist
●   Res - SG - Inf - Lib - PL - VE - Compilation of photographic &
       related items
M   90 i
¶   Council Vehicle News - 4;   Ybk - irreg;
       Public Utilities Bulletin - 4; all ftm only.
       Vehicle Operator Lists - irreg.
       British Military Serials - irreg.
       Note: NO trade enquiries please!

RoadPeace, UK's charity for road crash victims   1992
■   PO Box 2579, LONDON, NW10 3PW.   (hq)
       0845 450 0355   fax 020 8838 5103
       email info@roadpeace.org   http://www.roadpeace.org
       Chmn: Zoë Stow
▲   Registered Charity
○   *K, *W; offers vital information & assistance to bereaved &
       injured road victims; advocates for their rights & justice;
       highlights road danger issues
●   Conf - Mtgs - ET - Res - Exhib - Stat - Inf - Lib - LG
<   Eur Fedn of Road Crash Victims (NGO of UN); PACTS;
       Transport 2000; Safer Streets Coalition, Slower Speeds
       Initiative
M   2,000 i, 300 f, 50 org, UK / 30 i, o'seas

Roads & Road Transport History Association Ltd   1992
■   124 Shenstone Ave, Norton, STOURBRIDGE, W Midlands,
       DY8 3EJ.   (hsp)
       01384 394832   fax 01384 394832
       email RoadsandRTHA@aol.com
       http://www.rrtha.org.uk
       Hon Sec: Christopher Hogan
▲   Company Limited by Guarantee
○   *G
●   Conf - Mtgs - Res - SG - Inf - VE
M   80 i, 16 org, UK / 3 i, o'seas
¶   NL - 4; m only.   Symposium Papers - 1; £3.

Robert Burns World Federation Ltd (Burns Federation)   1885
■   Dean Castle Country Park, KILMARNOCK, E Ayrshire,
       KA3 1XB.   (hq)
       01563 572469   fax 01563 572469
       email member@kilmarnock26.freeserve.co.uk
       http://www.worldburnsclub.com
       Chief Exec: Mrs Shirley Bell
▲   Company Limited by Guarantee; Registered Charity
○   *A, *E; to stimulate the teaching & study of Scottish literature,
       history, art, music & language through competitions; to
       conserve buildings & places associated with Robert
       Burns (1759-1796) & his contemporaries
●   Conf - Mtgs - ET - Comp - Inf - LG
M   356 i, 6 f, 249 org, UK / 67 i, 54 org, o'seas
¶   Burns Chronicle - 3; ftm, £5 nm.   AR.

Robert Farnon Society   (RFS)   1956
■   Stone Gables, Upton Lane, Seavington St Michael, ILMINSTER,
       Somerset, TA19 0PZ.   (hsp)
       01460 242226   fax 01460 242226
       http://www.rfsoc.org.uk
       Hon Sec: David Ades
▲   Un-incorporated Society
○   *D; a musical appreciation society for lovers of light orchestral
       & film music; to keep members informed of all aspects of
       Robert Farnon's work in radio, TV, films, records etc; to
       encourage & publicise the work of other similar musicians
       from light classics to jazz
●   Mtgs (in London April & November) - Res - Stat - Inf
M   750 i, UK / 100 i, o'seas
¶   Journal into Melody - 4; £15 yr.

Robert Louis Stevenson Club   (RLS Club)   1920
■   12 Dean Park, LONGNIDDRY, E Lothian, EH32 0QR.   (hsp)
       01875 852976   fax 01875 853328
       email alan@amarchbank.freeserve.co.uk
       http://www.rlsclub.org.uk
       Hon Sec: Alan Marchbank
▲   Registered Charity
○   *A, *G; to foster an interest in the life & works of Robert Louis
       Stevenson (1850-94)
●   Mtgs - Inf - VE
M   282 i, 2 f, UK / 64 i, 2 org, o'seas
¶   RLS Club News - 2; ftm only.

Roller Coaster Club of Great Britain   (RCCGB)   1988
■   PO Box 235, UXBRIDGE, Middx, UB10 0TF.   (hq)
       01895 259802   fax 01895 259802
       email rccgb@rccgb.co.uk
       Chmn: Andrew Hine
○   *G; to unite roller-coaster enthusiasts from all over the world; to
       encourage amusement parks & manufacturers to create &
       build new, exciting & daring rides
Gp   Historians photo library
●   Mtgs - Res - Exhib - Comp - Stat - Inf - PL - Annual coach tour
       of coasters in Europe & the USA
<   Intl Assn of Amusement Parks & Attractions (IAAPA)
M   1,300 i, 21 f, 1 org, UK / 100 i, 17 f, 1 org, o'seas
¶   AIRtime (Jnl) - 6; ftm only.
       Yearly Survey (Report) - 1; ftm, £3 nm.

Roman Society
   see **Society for the Promotion of Roman Studies**

Romantic Novelists Association   (RNA)   1960
■   Bonnyton House, ARBIRLOT, Angus, DD11 2PY.   (hsp)
       01241 874131   fax 01242 874131
       email eileen@eileenramsay.f9.co.uk
       http://www.rna-uk.org
       Chmn: Jenny Haddon,   Hon Sec: Eileen Ramsay
▲   Un-incorporated Society
○   *A; to raise the prestige of the genre & the professionalism of
       romantic novelists
Gp   New Writers Scheme (for unpublished writers)
●   Conf - Mtgs - Comp - Inf
M   700 i, UK / 20 i, o'seas
¶   RNA News - 4.

Romany Guild
   no longer exists, the secretary has died

Romany Society   1996

- ■ 10 Haslam St, BURY, Lancs, BL9 6EQ.   (hsp)
  0161-764 7078   fax 01625 504515
  email romany@macclesfield.gov.uk
  Hon Sec: John Thorpe
- ▲ Un-incorporated Society
- ○ *G; to celebrate the life & work of the Rev G Bramwell Evens -
  'Romany of the BBC'; to ensure that his ground-breaking
  natural history broadcasting is remembered by future
  generations; to promote interest in the natural world by all &
  particularly the young
- ● Mtgs - Res - Inf - Lib - VE
- < Alliance Literary Socs
- M 241 i, 3 org, UK / 2 i, o'seas
- ¶ Romany Magazine - 1;   NL - seasonal; both ftm only.

Romney Sheep Breeders' Society   1895

- NR 2 Woodland Close, WEST MALLING, Kent, ME19 6RR.   (sp)
  01732 845637
  email alan.t.west@btinternet.com
  http://www.romneyshhepuk.co.uk
  Sec: Alan West
- ▲ Company Limited by Guarantee
- ○ *B
- Gp Registration of members; Registration of animals; Official
  society records; Export promotion
- ● Mtgs - Exhib - Expt
- < Nat Sheep Assn
- M 120 i, 60 org
- ¶ The Romney Flock Book - 1;   The Romney Hbk - irreg;
  both free.

Ronald Stevenson Society   (RSS)   1993

- ■ 3 Chamberlain Rd, EDINBURGH, EH10 4DL.   (hsp)
  fax 0131-229 9298
  http://www.ronaldstevensonsociety.org.uk
  Chmn: P Hutton,   Hon Sec: Iain Colquhoun
- ▲ Un-incorporated Society
- Br Luxembourg, Switzerland
- ○ *D; to publish & promote the performance & recording of the
  music of Ronald Stevenson, Scottish composer, pianist &
  writer
- Gp Pianists; Singers; Chamber players; Conductors
- ● Conf - Res - Summer piano school - Concerts & recitals -
  Publication of Stevenson's music
- < Centro studi musicali Busoni (Empoli, Italy); Scot Music Inf
  Centre; Nat Lib Scotland; Scot Poetry Lib; Scot Arts Coun
- M 105 i, 3 org, UK / 25 i, o'seas
- ¶ NL - 3; ftm, subscribers only nm.
  Catalogue of Publications.

Roofing Industry Alliance   (RIA)   1997

- ■ Fields House, Gower Rd, HAYWARDS HEATH, W Sussex,
  RH16 4PL.   (hq)
  01444 440027
  Co Sec: William A Jenkins
- ▲ Company Limited by Guarantee
- ○ *N, *T; to bring together designers, specifiers, contractors,
  merchants, manufacturers & clients to focus on the issues
  affecting the industry
- ● ET - Inf - LG - Registration & certification scheme

ROOM, the National Council for Housing & Planning (ROOM)   1900

- NR RoomatRTPI, 1 Botolph Lane, LONDON, EC3R 8DL.   (hq)
  020 7929 9494
  Dir: Prof Kelvin MacDonald
- ▲ Registered Charity
- Br 13
- ○ *K, *N; to achieve better standards & conditions in: housing,
  town & country planning, the physical & community
  regeneration of our cities, towns & countryside
- ● Conf - Mtgs - ET - Res - Exhib - SG - VE - LG
- M 100 i, 150 f, 300 org, UK / 20 i, o'seas
- ¶ Axis, the Jnl of Housing, Planning & Regeneration; ftm.
  Publications list available.

Rotating Electrical Machines Association
  as part of BEAMA Power is a group of **BEAMA**

Rotherham Chamber of Commerce   1909

- ■ 2 Genesis Business Park, Sheffield Rd, ROTHERHAM, S Yorks,
  S60 1DX.   (hq)
  01709 386200   fax 01709 839271
  http://www.rotherhamchamber.org.uk
  Chief Exec: John Lewis
- ▲ Company Limited by Guarantee
- ○ *C
- ● Expt - Inf
- < Brit Chams Comm
- M 1,200 f
- ¶ Chamber Matters (NL) - 5;   Diary inc LM - 1;
  AR;   all ftm only.

Rough Fell Sheep Breeders Association   (RFSBA)   1926

- ■ Weasdale Farm, Newbiggin on Lune, KIRKBY STEPHEN,
  Cumbria, CA17 4LY.   (sp)
  01539 623238
  http://www.roughfellsheep.co.uk
  Sec: Mrs P Tyson
- ○ *B
- ● Mtgs - Res - Exhib - Inf
- M c 200 i
- ¶ Flock Book - 1.

Rough & Smooth Collie Training Association   (RSCTA)   1991

- ■ 1 Leigh Lane, BRAMSHALL, Staffs, ST14 5DN.   (hsp)
  01889 568090
  email collies@rscta.free-online.co.uk
  http://www.rscta.free-online.co.uk
  Hon Sec: Mrs Jean Tuck
- ▲ Un-incorporated Society
- ○ *B; to preserve, promote & enhance the Collie as a working
  breed through the establishment & support of working events
  & tests
- ● ET - Comp - Inf - Promotion of responsible dog breeding
- < Kennel Club
- M 75 i
- ¶ Collie-Active (NL) - 2/3; ftm, 50p nm.   LM - irreg; ftm.

Round Tower Churches Society   (RTCS)   1973

- ■ Crabbe Hall, Burnham Market, KING'S LYNN, Norfolk,
  PE31 8EN.   (hsp)
  01328 738237
  http://www.roundtowers.org.uk
  Hon Sec: Mrs E M Stilgoe
- ▲ Registered Charity
- ○ *G; promotion of interest, research & preservation of round
  tower churches
- ● Res - Exhib - SG - Inf - Lib - VE - Lectures, slide shows &
  organised tours to churches
- M 520 i, 55 parochial church councils, UK / 6 i, o'seas
- ¶ Magazine - 4; ftm, 50p nm.

Roundhead Association
  a group of the **English Civil War Society Ltd**

Roussin Sheep Society   1989

NR   Glentara, The Park, THORNHILL, Dumfriesshire, DG3 5JT.
      (sp)
      01848 331640
      Sec: Mr A Wright
○   *B
<   Nat Sheep Assn

Routemaster Operators & Owners Association   (Routemaster Association)   1988

NR   23 Oakhurst Drive, CREWE, Cheshire, CW2 6UE.
      http://www.routemaster.org.uk
      Sec: Graham Meadows
○   *G; for operators & owners of Routemaster buses, suppliers of
      parts or services & anyone else with a genuine interest in
      their operation or preservation
M   c 400

Royal Academy of Arts   (RA)   1768

NR   Burlington House, Piccadilly, LONDON, W1J 0BD.   (hq)
      020 7300 8000   fax 020 7300 8001
      http://www.royalacademy.org.uk
      Acting Sec: Mary Ann Stevens
▲   Registered Charity
○   *A; promotion of the visual arts
Gp Friends of the Royal Academy
●   ET - Exhib - Lib
<   Amer Associates of the R Academy Trust; R Scot Academy; R
      Hibernian Academy
M   80 i & c 85,000 friends
¶   R A Magazine - 4; ftm.   AR.

Royal Academy of Dance incorporating the Benesh Institute (RAD)   1920

■   36 Battersea Sq, LONDON, SW11 3RA.   (hq)
      020 7924 3129   fax 020 7924 3129
      email info@rad.org.uk   http://www.rad.org.uk
      Chief Exec: Luke Rittner
▲   Registered Charity
Br 83 o'seas
○   *D, *E, *P; to improve the standards of dance teaching
      worldwide; to provide the opportunity for largest number of
      children to learn & enjoy ballet
●   Conf - ET - Exam - Comp - Inf - Lib - PL
M   5,000 i, UK / 10,000 i, o'seas
¶   Dance Gazette - 3.
      UK Diary (with Dance Gazette).   AR.

Royal Academy of Dramatic Art   (RADA)   1904

§   62-64 Gower St, LONDON, WC1E 6ED.   (hq)
      020 7636 7076   fax 020 7323 3865
      http://www.rada.org
      To train actors, stage managers & technical staff for
      professional stage, film & television

Royal Academy of Engineering   1976

NR   29 Great Peter St, LONDON, SW1P 3LW.   (hq)
      020 7227 0500   fax 020 7233 0054
      email administrator@raeng.co.uk
      http://www.raeng.org.uk
      Chief Exec: P D Greenish
▲   Registered Charity
○   *L, *N; 'the pursuit, encouragement & maintenance of
      excellence in the whole field of engineering for the benefit of
      the people of the UK'
Gp Standing c'ees: Engineering, Education, Awards, International
      activities
●   Conf - Mtgs - ET - Res - SG - VE - LG
<   Eur Coun of Applied Sciences & Engg (Euro-CASE); Coun of
      Academies of Engg & Technological Services (CAETS)
M   c 1,300 i
¶   NL - 4;   Ingenia - 4;   AR;
      Lectures & Conference Proceedings - 5; all free.
      Note: Fellows of the Academy will use the designatory letters
      'FREng'

Royal Academy of Medicine in Ireland   1882

IRL 20-22 Hatch St, DUBLIN 2, Republic of Ireland.
      353 (1) 661 6677   fax 353 (1) 676 2920
      email secretary@rami.ie   http://www.rami.ie
      Gen Sec: Dr John O'Connor
○   *M, *P

Royal Academy of Music   (RAM)   1822

NR   Marylebone Rd, LONDON, NW1 5HT.   (hq)
      020 7873 7373
      http://www.ram.ac.uk
      Principal: Prof Curtis Price
▲   Registered Charity
○   *D, *P; the further education & training of musicians
      (performers of classical music & jazz, opera & music theatre;
      composers)
●   ET - Res - Exhib - Inf - Lib - VE - Public concerts
<   University of London
M   i
¶   Diary of Events - 3; free.
      Prospectus (details of classes & entry arrangements); free.

Royal Aero Club Records Racing & Rally Association   (3R's)   1982

■   20 Woodlands Drive, Colsterworth, GRANTHAM, Lincs,
      NG33 5NH.   (sp)
      01476 860606   fax 01476 860606
      email judyhanson3rs:aol.com
      http://www.airraceuk.com
      Sec: Judy Hanson
▲   Company Limited by Guarantee
○   *S; national handicap air racing
●   Comp
<   Fédn Aeronautique Intl; R Aero Club
M   59 i

Royal Aero Club Trust   (RAeC Trust)   1997

■   Kimberley House, Vaughan Way, LEICESTER, LE1 4SG.   (hq)
      0116-253 1051   fax 0116-251 5939
      email administrator@royalaeroclubtrust.org
      http://www.royalaeroclubtrust.org
      Hon reas & Sec: Peter Crispin
▲   Company Limited by Guarantee; Registered Charity
○   *G; to advance the course of air sport & aviation
Gp Flying for youth: Bursary scheme, Airsport information data
      bank; Conservation of memorabilia; National photographic
      competition
●   Conf - ET - Res - Comp - SG - PL
<   R Aero Club UK
¶   AR

Royal Aero Club of the UK

■   Radford Barn, Radford Semele, ROYAL LEAMINGTON SPA,
      Warks, CV31 3UT.   (hq)
      01926 332713   fax 01926 335206
      email secretary@royalaeroclub.org
      http://www.royalaeroclub.org
      Sec: Diana M King
▲   Company Limited by Guarantee
○   *G, *N, *S; the coordinating body of British airsport
●   Comp - LG
<   EAS; FAI
M   160 i, 6 f, 20 org, UK / 5 i, o'seas
¶   NL - 4; ftm.
      Annual Award Ceremony Report - 1; ftm (on application nm).

Royal Aeronautical Society (RAeS) 1866
- ■ 4 Hamilton Place, LONDON, W1J 7BQ. (hq)
  020 7670 4300   fax 020 7499 6230
  email raes@raes.org.uk   http://www.aerosociety.com
  Chief Exec: Keith Mans
- ▲ Registered Charity
- Br 37; Australia, Cyprus, France, Germany, Hong Kong, Ireland, Kenya, Malaysia, New Zealand, Pakistan, Singapore, South Africa, UAE, Zimbabwe
- ○ *L, *P; for the global aerospace community; for the general advancement of aeronautical art, science & engineering & for promoting that species of knowledge which distinguishes the profession of aeronautics
- Gp Air law; Air transport; Space; Guided flight; Historical; Light aviation; Humanpowered aircraft; Management studies; Rotorcraft; Test pilots; Graduates & students; Aviation medicine; Propulsion; Aerodynamics; Avionics systems; Flight simulation; Structures & materials; Flight operations; Human factors
- ● Conf - Mtgs - ET - Res - Comp - Inf - Lib - PL - VE - LG - Careers service
- M 15,000 i, 101 f, UK / 4,500 i, 15 f, o'seas
- ¶ Aeronautical Jnl - 12; £39 yr m, £25 yr nm.
  Aerospace International - 12; ftm, £95 yr nm.
  Aerospace Professional - 12; ftm only.

Royal African Society 1901
- NR SOAS/University of London, Thornhaugh St, LONDON, WC1H 0XG. (hq)
  020 7898 4390   fax 020 7898 4389
  email ras@soas.ac.uk
  Sec: Lindsay Allan
- Br 3
- ○ *X; to spread information about the peoples & countries of Africa; to develop public interest in African problems; to serve as a link between the peoples of UK & Africa
- ● Conf - Mtgs - Lib
- M 599 i, 23 f, UK / 157 i, 2 f, o'seas
- ¶ African Affairs - 4.

Royal Agricultural Society of the Commonwealth (RASC) 1957
- ■ 2 Grosvenor Gardens, LONDON, SW1W 0DH. (hq)
  020 7259 9678   fax 020 7259 9675
  email rasc@commagshow.org
  http://www.commagshow.org
  Hon Sec: Charles Runge
- ▲ Company Limited by Guarantee; Registered Charity
- Br 1
- ○ *F, *N; a federation of national agricultural societies within the British Commonwealth, to encourage interchange of knowledge & experience in the practice & science of agriculture
- ● Conf - Organising cooperation & exchange between member societies
- M 12 org, UK / 31 org, o'seas
- ¶ NL - 4; ftm.   Biennial Conference Report - 2 yrly.

Royal Agricultural Society of England (RASE) 1840
- ■ Stoneleigh Park, KENILWORTH, Warks, CV8 2LZ. (hq)
  024 7669 6969   fax 024 7669 6900
  email info@rase.org.uk   http://www.rase.org.uk
  Chief Exec: Prof John Moverley
- ▲ Registered Charity
- ○ *F; to promote the practice & science of agriculture
- Gp International Agri-technology Centre; Arthur Rank Centre; Haymarket Land events; Farming & countryside education
- ● Conf - ET - Res - Exhib - Lib - LG
- M 6,754 i, UK / 7 i, o'seas
- ¶ Jnl of the RASE - 1; ftm, £35 nm.
  Rural Matters - 4; ftm only.

Royal Air Force Historical Society (RAFHS) 1986
- ■ Silverhill House, Coombe, WOTTON-UNDER-EDGE, Glos, GL12 7ND. (hsp)
  01453 843362
  Mem Sec: Dr Jack Dunham
- ▲ Registered Charity
- ○ *L; to serve as a focus of interest in the history of the Royal Air Force & its precursor services, their operations, policies & personalities
- ● Seminars (2 a yr) - AGM
- M 860 i, UK / 55 i, o'seas
- ¶ Jnl (proceedings of seminars & AGM) - 2/3; ftm, back issues £10 (hardback), £5 (softback).

Royal Air Forces Association (RAFA) 1943
- NR 117½ Loughborough Rd, LEICESTER, LE4 5ND. (hq)
  0116-266 5224
  http://www.rafa.org.uk
  Sec Gen: Edward Jarron
- ▲ Un-incorporated Society
- Br 571; 27 countries o'seas
- ○ *W; the welfare of serving & ex-serving members of the Commonwealth Air Forces & their dependents
- ● Conf - Mtgs - ET
- M 100,000 i
- ¶ Air Mail - 4;   AR; both free.

Royal & Ancient Golf Club (R&A) 1754
- NR St Andrews, FIFE, KY16 9JD. (hq)
  01334 460000   fax 01334 460001
  http://www.randa.org
  Sec: Peter Dawson
- ▲ Un-incorporated Society
- ○ *S; governing body for rules of golf & amateur status for all countries of the world apart from the USA & Canada
- Gp Organisers of golf championships; Rules of golf seminars
- ● Conf - Mtgs - Exam - Exhib - Comp - Lib - PL
- < Wld Amat Golf Coun
- M 2,400 unions & assns worldwide
- ¶ R&A News Bulletin - 2; free.
  A Course for all Seasons: a guide to golf course management.
  Practical Greenkeeping (textbook) by J Arthur.

Royal Anthropological Institute of Great Britain & Ireland (RAI) 1843
- NR 50 Fitzroy St, LONDON, W1T 5BT. (hq)
  020 7387 0455
  http://www.therai.org.uk
  Hon Sec: Dr Eric Hirsch
- ▲ Company Limited by Guarantee; Registered Charity
- ○ *L; to promote the study of the science of man
- ● Conf - Res - Inf - Lib - PL - Fundraising
- M c 1,000 i, UK / c 500 i, o'seas
- ¶ Jnl - 4.   Anthropology Today - 6.
  Anthropological Index Online (free Internet bibliographic service).

Royal Archaeological Institute (RAI) 1844
- ■ c/o Society of Antiquaries, Burlington House, Piccadilly, LONDON, W1J 0BE. (hq)
  020 7479 7092   fax 0116-243 3839
  email admin@royalarchaeolinst.org
  http://www.royalarchaeolinst.org
  Admin: Caroline Raison
- ▲ Registered Charity
- ○ *L; all aspects of archaeology & history of architecture but mainly that of GB
- ● Conf - Mtgs - Res - Comp - VE
- M c 1,700 i, 384 libraries & org
- ¶ Archaeological Jnl - 1; ftm; £40 nm.   NL - 2; free.
  Index to Jnl; prices on application.

Royal Asiatic Society of Great Britain & Ireland (RAS) 1823
NR 14 Stephenson Way, LONDON, NW1 2HD.   (hq)
    020 7388 4539
    email info@royalasiaticsociety.org
    http://www.royalasiaticsociety.org
    Exec Officer: Camilla Larsen
▲ Registered Charity
○ *L; dissemination & publication of information about Asia up to
    1950 (not current affairs)
● Mtgs - Lib
M c 500 i, UK / c 300 i, o'seas
¶ Jnl - 3; ftm.

Royal Association of British Dairy Farmers (RABDF) 1876
■ Dairy House, Unit 31, Stoneleigh Deer Park, Stareton,
    KENILWORTH, Warks, CV8 2LY.   (hq)
    0845 458 2711   fax 0845 458 2755
    email office@rabdf.co.uk   http://www.rabdf.co.uk
▲ Registered Charity
○ *T, *V; to represent the interests of dairy farmers & the dairy
    farming industry
● Conf - Mtgs - Exam - Exhib - Comp - SG - Inf - VE - LG - Dairy
    Event (http://www.dairyevent.co.uk)
M 2,000 i
¶ Milk Digest - 6;
    Dairy Farming Event Showguide - 1; both ftm.

Royal Association for Deaf People (RAD) 1841
§ Walsingham Rd, COLCHESTER, Essex, CO2 7BP   (hq)
    01206 509509   fax 01206 769755
    email info@royaldeaf.org.uk
    http://www.royaldeaf.org.uk
    a registered charity & non-membership body promoting the
    spiritual, social & general welfare of deaf people

**Royal Association for Disability & Rehabilitation (RADAR)
1977**
NR 12 City Forum, 250 City Rd, LONDON, EC1V 8AF.   (hq)
    020 7250 3222
    http://www.radar@radar.org.uk
    Chief Exec: Kate Nash
▲ Registered Charity
○ *K, *N, *W; works with & for physically disabled people
● Inf
M c 600 i & org
¶ Bulletin - 12.   A Guide to RADAR.   AR & Accounts.
    Publications list available.

Royal Astronomical Society (RAS) 1820
■ Burlington House, Piccadilly, LONDON, W1J 0BQ.   (hq)
    020 7734 4582; 3307   fax 020 7494 0166
    email info@ras.org.uk   http://www.ras.org.uk
    Exec Sec: David Elliott
▲ Registered Charity
○ *L; the leading UK body for astronomy & astrophysics,
    geophysics, solar & solar-terrestrial physics & planetary
    sciences
● Conf - Mtgs - Res - Comp - Lib - PL - Empl - LG - Support for
    educational activities - Awards grants & prizes
< IAU; EAS; Science Coun
> Brit Sundial Soc; Brit Geophysical Assn (BGA)
M 2,037 i, UK / 1,236 i, o'seas
¶ Astronomy & Geophysics (Jnl) - 6; ftm.
    Monthly Notices - 36 [9 volumes of 4 issues each];
    Geophysical Journal International - 12 [4 volumes of
    3 issues each]; prices for both on application.

Royal Bath & West of England Society (Bath) & West 1777
NR The Showground, SHEPTON MALLET, Somerset, BA4 6QN.
    (hq)
    01749 822200   fax 01749 823169
    http://www.bathandwest.co.uk
    Chief Exec: Dr Jane Guise
▲ Company Limited by Guarantee; Registered Charity
○ *F; for the encouragement of agriculture, arts, manufacture,
    commerce
● Conf - Exhib (agricultural shows) - Events & exhibition centre
M 2,141 i
¶ NL - 2;   Annual Review & Report - 1; both free.
    Show Programme - 1;   Show Catalogue; both ftm.

Royal Birmingham Society of Artists (RBSA) 1814
■ Dakota House, 4 Brook St, St Paul's, BIRMINGHAM, B3 1SA.
    (hq)
    0121-236 4353   fax 0121-236 4555
    email secretary@rbsa.org.uk   http://www.rbsa.org.uk
    Hon Sec: Graham Blaine
▲ Registered Charity
○ *A; to advance the public education in (& the practice of) art,
    particularly painting, sculpture, ceramics & printing
● Mtgs - ET - Res - Exhib - Inf
M 127 i & associates
¶ NL - 4; ftm & Friends.

**Royal Botanical & Horticultural Society of Manchester & the
Northern Counties (RBS) 1827**
§ 60 Glebelands Rd, KNUTSFORD, Cheshire, WA16 9DZ.   (sb)
    01565 633917
    Hon Sec: James R Goodchild
    a charity providing funds for the Tatton Garden Society & local
    horticultural societies, as well as judges for local shows,
    speakers, advice etc

Royal British Legion 1921
NR 48 Pall Mall, LONDON, SW1Y 5JY.   (hq)
    020 7973 7200
    Sec-Gen: Ian Townsend
▲ Registered Charity
Br 3,232; 57 o'seas
○ *K, *W; to assist needy ex-servicemen & women & their
    families; to ensure the maintenance of war pensions, war
    widows pensions & associated allowances
Gp Attendants company (security & car parking); RBL poppy
    factory; Disabled industries; Poppy appeal; Training company
● Conf - Mtgs - Comp - Inf
< Brit C'wealth Ex-Services League; Wld Veterans Fedn; Coun of
    British Service & Ex-service Orgs
M 658,000 i, UK & o'seas
¶ The Legion (Jnl) - 12;   AR;   Publicity leaflets &
    posters; all free.

Royal British Legion Scotland (RBLS) 1921
■ New Haig House, Logie Green Rd, EDINBURGH, EH7 4HR.
    (hq)
    0131-550 1563   fax 0131-557 5879
    email admin@rblscotland.org
    http://www.rblscotland.org
    Gen Sec: H Nicholson
▲ Registered Charity
Br 214 in Scotland
○ *K, *W; to safeguard the welfare, interests & memory of those
    who have served in the armed forces, & their dependents
Gp War pensions claims & appeals
● Conf - Mtgs - Inf - VE _ LG
< Brit C'wealth Ex-Services League; Earl Haig Fund (Scotland);
    Officers Assn Scotland; Scot Ex-Services Charitable Orgs
M 50,000 i, 88 private clubs
¶ Scottish Legion News - 4; ftm.

Royal British Society of Sculptors   (RBS)   1904
NR   108 Old Brompton Rd, LONDON, SW7 3RA.   (hq)
     020 7373 5554
     email info@rbs.org.uk
     Dir: Anne Rawcliffe-King
▲   Registered Charity
○   *A, *P; the promotion of sculpture
●   Mtgs - Exhib - Inf - Lib
M   c 500 i

Royal Caledonian Curling Club   (RCCC)   1838
■   Cairnie House, Ingliston Showground, NEWBRIDGE,
     Midlothian, EH28 8NB.   (hq)
     0131-333 3003   fax 0131-333 3323
     email office@royalcaledoniancurlingclub.org
     http://www.royalcaledoniancurlingclub.org
     Chief Exec Officer: Colin Grahamslaw
     Admin Mgr: W J Duthie Thomson
▲   Company Limited by Guarantee
Br   Canada
○   *S; governing body for the sport of curling throughout Scotland
     & mother club of curling throughout the world
●   Conf - Mtgs - ET - Comp - Stat - Lib
<   Wld Curling Fedn (WCF); Eur Curling Fedn (ECF)
M   14,000 i, 569 clubs, UK / 20 assns, o'seas
¶   RCCC Annual - 1; £9.   RCCC Rules of the Game - 1; £1.

Royal Caledonian Horticultural Society   (RCHS)   1809
NR   6 Kirkliston Rd, SOUTH QUEENSFERRY, W Lothian, EH30 9LT.
     (hsp)
     0131-331 1011
     Sec: Tom Mabbott
▲   Registered Charity
○   *H; the encouragement & advancement of horticulture in all its
     forms
●   Mtgs - Exhib - Comp - Inf - VE - Lectures - Awards
<   R Horticl Soc (London)
M   550 i, 7 f, 34 org
¶   Preview - 3.   Caledonian Gardener - 1.

Royal Cambrian Academy of Art   (RCA)   1881
■   Crown Lane, CONWY, Caernarfonshire, LL32 8AN.   (hq)
     01492 593413   fax 01492 593413
     email rca@rcaconwy.org   http://www.rcaconwy.org
     Hon Sec: Tim Pugin,   Curator: Gill Bird
▲   Company Limited by Guarantee; Registered Charity
○   *A; to promote the arts of painting, engraving & sculpture &
     other forms of art in Wales
●   Mtgs - Exhib - Art classes
M   120 i
¶   Summer Exhibition Catalogue - 1; £1.   AR 1; ftm, £1 nm.

Royal Celtic Society   1820
■   23 Rutland St, EDINBURGH, EH1 2RN.   (asa)
     0131-228 6449   fax 0131-229 6987
     email gcameron@stuartandstuart.co.uk
     Hon Sec & Treas: J Gordon Cameron
▲   Registered Charity
○   *G; to promote interest in the history, traditions, arts & music of
     Scotland & in Scottish Gaelic
●   Mtgs - One-off grants to assist with the aims of the society
M   200 i, UK / 10 i, o'seas
¶   AR; m only.

Royal Choral Society   (RCS)   1872
■   Studio 9, 92 Lots Rd, LONDON, SW10 0QD.   (hq)
     020 7376 3718   fax 020 7376 3719
     email helenbody@royalchoralsociety.co.uk
     http://www.royalchoralsociety.co.uk
     Admin: Helen Body
▲   Registered Charity
○   *D; 'we are an amateur choir, singing to a professional
     standard; we work with professional orchestras & promoters'
●   Mtgs - Concerts
<   Making Music (Nat Fedn Music Socs)
M   c 200 i
¶   Summer NL.

Royal College of Anaesthetists   1948
NR   Churchill House, 35 Red Lion Square, LONDON,
     WC1R 4SG.   (hq)
     020 7092 1500
     email info@rcoa.ac.uk
○   *L; advancement of art & science of anaesthetics
M   c 13,000 i
¶   Bulletin - 6; ftm.

Royal College of General Practitioners   (RCGP)   1952
■   14 Prince's Gate, LONDON, SW7 1PU.   (hq)
     020 7581 3232   fax 020 7225 3047
     email info@rcgp.org.uk   http://www.rcgp.org.uk
     Hon Sec: Dr Maureen Baker
▲   Registered Charity
○   *L, *P; to encourage & maintain high standards of general
     medical practice
●   Conf - Mtgs - ET - Exam - Res - Exhib - SG - Inf - Lib - LG
M   17,500 i, UK / 1,300 i, o'seas
¶   Jnl - 12; ftm, £124 nm.   Members' Reference Book - 1; ftm.

Royal College of Midwives   (RCM)   1881
NR   15 Mansfield St, LONDON, W1G 9NH.   (hq)
     020 7312 3535
     Gen Sec: Dame Karlene Davis
▲   Company Limited by Guarantee; Registered Charity
Br   5
○   *P, *U; to advance the art & science of midwifery
●   Conf - Mtgs - ET - Inf - Lib - VE - Empl - LG
<   Intl Confedn Midwives; WHO Collaborating Centre for
     Midwifery
M   c 36,000 i, UK / 7000 i, o'seas
¶   Jnl - 12.

Royal College of Nursing of the United Kingdom   (RCN)   1916
NR   20 Cavendish Sq, LONDON, W1G 0RN.   (hq)
     020 7409 3333
     http://www.rcn.org.uk
     Gen Sec: Dr Beverly Malone
▲   Registered Charity
○   *M, *P; to act as the voice of nursing in the UK; to campaign on
     behalf of nurses & nursing; to promote the interests of nurses
     & patients by working with government, the professional
     bodies, trade unions & voluntary organisations
Gp   Over 80; grouped by:
     Children & young people; Mental health; Learning disabilities;
     Older people; Midwifery; Primary care & public health;
     Nursing therapeutics; Clinical & supportive care; Acute
     intervention; Management & leadership; Education; Work &
     environment; Ethics; Research, informatics & quality
●   Conf - ET - Res - Exhib - Lib - Empl - LG
<   Intl Coun of Nurses (ICN); Eur Fedn of Public Service Us (EPSU);
     C'wealth Nurses Fedn (CNF); Standing C'ee of Nurses (PCN)
M   390,000 i
¶   Nursing Standard - 52.   RCN Bulletin - 26; both ftm.

Royal College of Obstetricians & Gynaecologists   (RCOG) 1929

- ■ 27 Sussex Place, LONDON, NW1 4RG.   (hq)
    020 7772 6200   fax 020 7772 6359
    email coll.sec@rcog.org.uk   http://www.rcog.org.uk
    Chief Exec: Helen Moffatt
- ▲ Registered Charity
- ○ *L, *Q
- ● Conf - Mtgs - ET - Exam - Res - Exhib - SG - Stat - Inf - Lib - LG
- M 4,000 i, UK / 6,000 i, o'seas
- ¶ British Jnl of Obstetrics & Gynaecology - 12.
    The Obstetrician & Gynaecologist - 4.

Royal College of Ophthalmologists   1988

- ■ 17 Cornwall Terrace, LONDON, NW1 4QW.   (hq)
    020 7935 0702
    Hon Sec: L Benjamin
- ○ *L; advancement of study & practice of ophthalmology
- Gp Ophthalmology; Medicine
- ● Conf - Mtgs - ET - Exam
- M 2,800 i, UK / 950 i, o'seas
- ¶ Eye (Jnl) - 6.   College News (NL) - 4.   LM - 1.

Royal College of Organists   (RCO)   1864

- ■ Millennium Point, Curzon St, BIRMINGHAM, B4 7XG.
    0121-331 7222   fax 0121-331 7220
    email admin@rco.org.uk
    Gen Mgr: Mrs Kim Gilbert
- ▲ Registered Charity
- Br 4
- ○ *D; to promote the arts of organ-playing, choir-training & related activities
- ● Conf - Mtgs - ET - Exam - Res - Exhib - Comp - SG - Inf - Lib - PL - VE - Empl
- < Inc Soc of Musicians (corporate member); R School of Church Music
- M 2,479 i, 102 f, UK / 836 i, o'seas
- ¶ RCO News (Jnl) - 4.

Royal College of Paediatrics & Child Health   (RCPCH)   1996

- ■ 50 Hallam St, London, W1W 6DE.   (hq)
    020 7307 5600   fax 020 7307 5601
    email enquiries@rcpch.ac.uk   http://www.rcpch.ac.uk
    Chief Exec: Len Tyler
- ▲ Registered Charity
- ○ *L; to advance education in child health & paediatrics; to relieve sickness by promoting improvements in paediatric practice; to promote research & publish the results
- Gp Accident & emergency; Allergy; Computer information & technology; Clinical genetics; Immunology & infectious diseases; International child health; Nutrition & metabolism; Oncology & haematology; Psychiatry & psychology; Radiology & imaging
    British Paediatric Cardiac Association; British Association for Community Child Health; British Society for Paediatric Dermatology; British Society for Paediatric Endocrinology & Diabetes; British Society for Paediatric Gastroenterology & Nutrition; British Association for Paediatric Nephrology; British Paediatric Neurology Association; British Paediatric Pathology Association; British Association of Perinatal Medicine; British Paediatric Respiratory Society
- ● Conf - Mtgs - ET - Exam - Res
- < Intl Paediatric Assn; Conf of Eur Specialists in Paediatrics
- M 7,194 i, UK / 1,625 i, o'seas
- ¶ NL - 4; ftm.   Hbk; ftm, £20 nm.
    Archives of Disease in Childhood - 12; ftm, £218 (£95+VATonline) nm.
    Cherub Bulletin - 4;   Guideline Appraisal - irreg;   AR - 1; all free.
    British National Formulary for Children - 1: free to those prescribing to children.

Royal College of Pathologists   (RCPath)   1962

- NR 2 Carlton House Terrace, LONDON, SW1Y 5AF.   (hq)
    020 7451 6700   fax 020 7451 6701
    email info@rcpath.org   http://www.rcpath.org
    Chief Exec: Daniel Ross
- ▲ Registered Charity
- ○ *P, *Q; to advance the science & practice of pathology
- ● Conf - Exam
- M 5,000 i, UK / 2,500 i, o'seas
- ¶ Bulletin - 4; ftm, £60 nm.   Hbk - 2 yrly; ftm only.

Royal College of Physicians of Edinburgh   1681

- NR 9 Queen St, EDINBURGH, EH2 1JQ.   (hq)
    0131-225 7324   fax 0131-220 3939
    http://www.rcpe.ac.uk
    Pres: Prof Neil Douglas
    Sec: John Collins
- ▲ Registered Charity
- ○ *L, *P; to promote the highest standards of practice in internal medicine & related specialities wherever its fellows, collegiate members & members practise
- ● Conf - Mtgs - ET - Exam - Res - Exhib - Lib - VE - LG
- M 2,168 fellows, 1,917 collegiate m, 73 affiliates, UK / 2,623 fellows, 609 collegiate m, 7 affiliates, o'seas
- ¶ The Journal - 4;   The Bulletin (NL) - 12 (online); both ftm.

Royal College of Physicians of Ireland

- IRL International House, 20-22 Lower Hatch St, DUBLIN 2, Republic of Ireland.
    353 (1) 661 6677   fax 353 (1) 676 3989
    email info@rcpi.ie   http://www.rcpi.ie
    Sec: J W Bailey
- ○ *M, *P

Royal College of Physicians of London   (RCP)   1518

- ■ 11 St Andrew's Place, Regent's Park, LONDON, NW1 4LE. (hq)
    020 7224 1539   fax 020 7487 5218
    email info@rcplondon.ac.uk
    http://www.rcplondon.ac.uk
    Chief Exec: Martin Else
- ▲ Registered Charity
- Br 12
- ○ *L, *P; to set & improve standards in education & training; to ensure quality of care for patients; to influence the delivery of care; to provide professional leadership & influence government; to involve patients & the public
- Gp Faculty of Occupational Medicine; Faculty of Public Health; Faculty of Pharmaceutical Medicine; Faculty of Forensic Medicine;
    Jt C'ee for Higher Medical Training
- ● Conf - Mtgs - ET - Exam - Exhib - Inf - Lib - LG
- < Eur Assn of Med Specialists (EUMS)
- M 18,900 i (fellows & members), UK / 2,700 i (fellows), o'seas
- ¶ Clinical Medicine (Jnl) - 6; ftm, £120 nm (UK).
    LM - 1; ftm, price on application nm.   AR; free.

Royal College of Physicians & Surgeons of Glasgow (RCPSGlasg)   1599

- NR 232-242 St Vincent Street, GLASGOW, G2 5RJ.   (hq)
    0141-221 6072
    http://www.rcpglas.ac.uk
    Chief Exec: Dr James Miller
- ▲ Registered Charity
- ○ *L, *P; to set & maintain standards of practice in medicine, surgery & dental surgery; to conduct postgraduate examinations & organise training & educational events for physicians, surgeons & dentists at all stages of their careers
- Gp Dental faculty
- ● Mtgs - ET - Exam - Res - Lib
- < Intl Assn of Coll & Academy Presidents; Fedn of R Colls of Physicians in the UK; Senate of Surgery of GB & Ireland
- M c 4,100 i, UK / 2,300 i, o'seas
- ¶ Bulletin - 3; ftm, on application nm.
    News & Views - 3;   AR; both free.

Royal College of Psychiatrists   (RCPsych)   1971
■   17 Belgrave Sq, LONDON, SW1X 8PG.   (hq)
        020 7235 2351
        Sec: Mrs V Cameron,   Registrar: Prof S Bailey
▲   Registered Charity
○   *L, *M, *P; advance the science & practice of psychiatry &
        related subjects
Gp Psychiatry: Child & adolescent, Forensic, General adult,
        Learning disabilities, Liaison, Old age, Rehabilitation,
        Substance misuse
        Psychotherapy
●   Conf - ET - Exam - Res - Inf - VE - LG
<   Wld Psychiatric Assn
M   6,941 i, UK / 1,729 i, o'seas
¶   British Journal of Psychiatry - 12.
        Psychiatric Bulletin - 12.
        Advances in Psychiatric Treatment - 6.

Royal College of Radiologists   1975
NR 38 Portland Place, LONDON, W1B 1JQ.   (hq)
        020 7636 4432   fax 020 7323 3100
        email enquiries@rcr.ac.uk   http://www.rcr.ac.uk
        Exec: Andrew Hall
○   *L, *M, *P; the science & practice of radiology & oncology
M   c 4,400 i, UK / c 1,100 i, o'seas
¶   Clinical Radiology - 12.   Clinical Oncology - 8.

**Royal College of Speech & Language Therapists   (RCSLT)
1945**
NR 2 White Hart Yard, LONDON, SE1 1NX.   (hq)
        020 7378 1200   fax 020 7403 7254
        email postmaster@rcslt.org   http://www.rcslt.org
        Chief Exec: Kamini Gadhok
▲   Registered Charity
○   *P; the governing body for speech & language therapy in the
        UK
Gp all acquired or developmental conditions affecting
        communication
●   Conf - Mtgs - ET - Exam - Res - Exhib - SG - Stat - Inf - Lib - PL
        - Empl
<   Intl Assn of Logopedics & Phoniatrics (AILP); Standing Liaison
        C'ee of EC Speech & Language Therapists & Logopedists
        (CPLOL)
M   10,031 i, UK / 418 i, o'seas
¶   European Journal of Disorders of Communication - 4; ftm.
        Communicating Quality (professional standards).
        Bulletin - 12 (supplements - 24); ftm.
        LM.   AR; ftm only.
        Publications list available.

Royal College of Surgeons of Edinburgh   (RCSEd)   1505
NR Nicolson St, EDINBURGH, EH8 9DW.   (hq)
        0131-527 1600   fax 0131-557 6406
        email information@rcsed.ac.uk   http://www.rcsed.ac.uk
        Hon Sec: P K Datta
▲   Registered Charity
○   *L, *P; a body incorporated by royal charter, concerned with
        education & training for medical & surgical practice & the
        maintenance of high standards of professional competence
        & conduct; includes both surgery & dental surgery
Gp Faculties: Dental surgery, Pre-hospital care, Health informatics
●   Conf - ET - Exam - Inf - Lib - LG
M   7,800 i, UK / 5,500 i, o'seas
¶   Jnl - 6;   NL - 4.

Royal College of Surgeons of England   (RCS)   1800
NR 35-43 Lincoln's Inn Fields, LONDON, WC2A 3PE.   (hq)
        020 7405 3474
        http://www.rcseng.ac.uk
        Chief Exec: David Munn
▲   Registered Charity
○   *L, *P; an independent professional body committed to
        promoting & advancing the highest standards of surgical
        care for patients
M   i

Royal College of Surgeons in Ireland   (RCSI)   1784
IRL 123 St Stephen's Green, DUBLIN 2, Republic of Ireland.   (hq)
        353 (1) 402 2100   fax 353 (1) 402 2460
        http://www.rcsi.ie
        Chief Exec: Michael Horgan
○   *P

Royal College of Veterinary Surgeons   (RCVS)   1844
■   Belgravia House, 62-64 Horseferry Rd, LONDON,
        SW1P 2AF.   (hq)
        020 7222 2001   fax 020 7222 2004
        email admin@rcvs.org.uk   http://www.rcvs.org.uk
        Registrar: Miss J C Hern
▲   Incorporated Statutory Body
○   *L, *P, *V
●   ET - Exam - Stat - Inf - Lib
M   16,785 i, UK / 4,772 i, o'seas
¶   NL - 3; ftm & online.   Register of Members - 1; ftm, £40 nm.
        Directory of Veterinary Practices - 1; £65.
        Guide to Professional Conduct - 1; free online; printed
            copies £15 m, £20 nm.
        List of Veterinary Nurses - 1; £10.   AR; free.

Royal Cornwall Agricultural Association   (RCAA)   1793
■   The Royal Cornwall Showground, WADEBRIDGE, Cornwall,
        PL27 7JE.   (hq)
        01208 812183   fax 01208 812713
        email info@royalcornwall.co.uk
        http://www.royalcornwall.co.uk
        Sec: C P Riddle
▲   Registered Charity
○   *F; to promote agriculture
Gp C'ees for: Poultry, Dogs, Fur, Bees, Honey, Pigeons, Cage birds,
        Goats, Horticulture
●   Mtgs - Exhib - Comp
<   Most livestock breed societies
M   6,500 i, c 750 f
¶   Show Catalogue - 1; £3.50.   AR; ftm only.
        Souvenir Programme - 1; £2.50.

Royal Dublin Society   (RDS)   1731
IRL Ballsbridge, DUBLIN 4, Republic of Ireland.   (hq)
        353 (1) 668 0866   fax 353 (1) 660 4014
        email info@rds.ie   http://www.rds.ie
        Chief Exec: Michael Duffy
○   *L

Royal Economic Society   (RES)   1890
■   Dept of Economics, London Business School, Sussex Place,
        Regent's Park, LONDON, NW1 4SA.   (hsb)
        020 7262 5050
        Sec-Gen: Prof Richard Portes
▲   Registered Charity
○   *L
●   Conf - ET - Res - Inf
<   Intl Economic Assn
M   1,500 i, UK / 1,700 i, o'seas
¶   The Economic Jnl - 8.   NL - 4; both ftm.
        New editions of economic classics.

Royal Entomological Society of London   (REntSoc)   1833
NR 41 Queen's Gate, LONDON, SW7 5HR.   (hq)
        020 7584 8361   fax 020 7581 8505
        email royensoc.co.uk
        Registrar: W H F Blakemore
○   *L
M   i

Royal Environmental Health Institute of Scotland (REHIS) 1983

- 3 Manor Place, EDINBURGH, EH3 7DH. (hq)
  0131-225 6999 fax 0131-225 3993
  email contact@rehis.org http://www.rehis.org
  Sec & Chief Exec: Tom Bell
- ▲ Incorporated by Royal Charter
- ○ *P; covers food safety, housing, health & safety, pollution, public health, waste management
- ● Conf - Mtgs - ET - Exam - Res - Exhib - SG - Stat - Inf - Lib - VE - LG
- < Intl Fedn of Envtl Health
- M 1,000 i, UK / 100 i, o'seas
- ¶ Environmental Health Scotland - 6;
  Congress Proceedings - 1; AR; all ftm only.

Royal Faculty of Procurators in Glasgow (RFPG) 1796

NR 12 Nelson Mandela Place, GLASGOW, G2 1BT. (hq)
  0141-331 0533 fax 0141-332 4714
  email library@rfpg.org http://www.rfpg.org
  Gen Mgr: I Pearson
- ▲ Royal Charter
- ○ *P; to provide a first class library for faculty members; to promote legal education at the universities in Glasgow
- Gp solicitors in Glasgow & surrounding area
- ● ET - Lib - Seminars on legal topics - Management of charitable funds
- M 1,400 i, 200 f
- ¶ Report & Accounts - 1.

Royal Forestry Society of England, Wales & Northern Ireland (RFS) 1882

- 102 High St, TRING, Herts, HP23 4AF. (hq)
  01442 822028 fax 01442 890395
  email rfshq@rfs.org.uk http://www.rfs.org.uk
  Chief Exec: Dr J E Jackson
- ▲ Company Limited by Guarantee; Registered Charity
- Br 21 divisions
- ○ *L; promoting the wise management of trees & woods; advancement of knowledge & practice of forestry & arboriculture; promotion of sustainable forestry
- ● Mtgs - Exam - Lib - VE
- M 4,235 i, 280 f
- ¶ Quarterly Jnl of Forestry - 4; ftm, £2.50 nm.

Royal Geographical Society (with the Institute of British Geographers) (RGS-IBG) 1830

NR 1 Kensington Gore, LONDON, SW7 2AR. (hq)
  020 7591 3000
  Dir & Sec: Dr Rita Gardner
- ▲ Registered Charity
- ○ *L, *Q; advancement of geographical science
- M i, f & org

Royal Glasgow Institute of the Fine Arts (RGI) 1861

- 5 Oswald St, GLASGOW, G1 4QR. (asa)
  0141-248 7411 fax 0141-221 0417
  email rgi@robbferguson.co.uk
  http://www.rgiscotland.co.uk
  Sec: Gordon C McAllister, CA
- ▲ Company Limited by Guarantee; Registered Charity
- ○ *A; to encourage & promote contemporary art
- ● Exhib
- M 1,250 i

Royal Guernsey Agricultural & Horticultural Society

NR 3 Cornet St, ST PETER PORT, Guernsey, GY1 1BZ.
  01481 720711
  Sec: Joan de Garis
- ○ *F, *H
- M c 100 i

Royal Highland & Agricultural Society of Scotland (RHASS) 1784

NR Royal Highland Centre, Ingliston, EDINBURGH, W Lothian, EH28 8NF. (hq)
  0131-335 6200 fax 0131-333 5236
  email info@rhass.org.uk http://www.rhass.org.uk
  Chief Exec: R J Jones, Sec: Mrs G M Lamont
- ▲ Registered Charity
- ○ *F; promotion of agriculture & allied industries in Scotland
- ● Exhib - Comp - Lib - LG
- < R Agricl Soc of the C'wealth
- M 14,000 i, UK / 50 i, o'seas
- ¶ Royal Highland Review - 3.
  Royal Highland Show Guide - 1.
  Royal Highland Show Catalogue - 1.

Royal Highland Education Trust (RHET) 1999

NR Royal Highland Centre, Ingliston, EDINBURGH, W Lothian, EH28 8NF. (hq)
  0131-335 6227 fax 0131-333 5236
  email rhet@rhass.org.uk http://www.rhet.rhass.org.uk
  Chmn: J L Morison, Sec: G M Barwick
- ▲ Registered Charity
- ○ *F; information service for schools & the public about the economic & environmental realities of farming, forestry & food production in Scotland
- Gp Local initiative bodies available for school-farm links
- ● Inf
- ¶ Sprouts (NL) - 3.

Royal Historical Society (RHistS) 1868

NR University College London, Gower St, LONDON, WC1E 6BT. (hq)
  020 7387 7532
  Exec Sec: Susan Carr
- ○ *L; promote the study of history by the publication of documentary, bibliographical & reference material
- ● Conf - Mtgs - Essay comp - Publishing
- M c 3,000 l
- ¶ Transactions - 1. Camden series - 1 or 2 vol yr.
  Guides & Handbook Series - (irreg).

Royal Horticultural Society (RHS) 1804

- 80 Vincent Sq, LONDON, SW1P 2PE. (hq)
  020 7834 4333 fax 020 7821 3020
  Dir Gen: A J Colquhoun
- ▲ Registered Charity
- Br RHS Garden, Wisley (Surrey); Harlow Carr (Yorks); Hyde Hall (Essex); Rosemoor (Devon)
- ○ *H; the encouragement & improvement of the science, art & practice of horticulture in all its branches
- ● Conf - Mtgs - ET - Exam - Res - Exhib - Comp - Inf - Lib
- M 335,000 i, 3,000 org, UK & o'seas
- ¶ The Garden (Jnl) - 12; ftm, £3.50 each nm.
  Numerous manuals & reference works.

Royal Horticultural Society of Ireland (RHSI) 1830

IRL Cabinteely House, The Park, Cabinteely, DUBLIN 18, Republic of Ireland.
  353 (1) 235 3912 fax 353 (1) 235 3912
  email info@rhsi.ie http://www.rhsi.ie
  Sec: Brid Ni Threasaigh
- ○ *H

Royal Humane Society   (RHS)   1774
NR   Brettenham House, Lancaster Place, LONDON, WC2E 7EP.
      (hq)
      020 7836 8155   fax 020 7836 8155
      email info@royalhumanesociety.org
      http://www.royalhumane.org
      Sec: David Pennefather
▲   Registered Charity
○   *W; to encourage the saving of human life; to present awards
      for bravery in so doing
●   Mtgs - Res - Lib
<   R Humane Socs: Australasia, New South Wales, New Zealand
M   i & f
¶   Short History of the Society;   Medals of the Society.
      Saved from a Watery Grave;   AR.

Royal Incorporation of Architects in Scotland   (RIAS)   1916
■   15 Rutland Sq, EDINBURGH, EH1 2BE.   (hq)
      0131-229 7545   fax 0131-228 2188
      email admin@rias.org.uk   http://www.rias.org.uk
      Chief Exec: Mrs Mary Wrenn
▲   Registered Charity
○   *L, *P; for architects, professional advisory services
Gp Competitions; Exhibitions; Bookshop & gallery; Library;
      Professional section for architects & public
●   Conf - Mtgs - ET - Res - Exhib - Comp - Lib - PL - LG
<   R Inst Brit Architects (RIBA)
M   3,000 i, 500 f, 6 org
¶   Chartered Architect - 5.   e-bulletins - 12.

Royal Institute of the Architects of Ireland   (RIAI)   1839
IRL 8 Merrion Sq, DUBLIN 2, Republic of Ireland.
      353 (1) 676 1703   fax 353 (1) 661 0948
      email info@riai.ie   http://www.riai.ie
      Dir: John Graby
○   *P

Royal Institute of British Architects   (RIBA)   1834
■   66 Portland Place, LONDON, W1B 4AD.   (hq)
      020 7580 5533   fax 020 7255 1541
      email info@inst.riba.org   http://www.architecture.com
      Dir Gen: Richard Hastilow
○   *L, *P; to advance architecture by demonstrating public benefit,
      & promoting excellence in the profession
●   Conf - Exam - Exhib - Comp - Inf - Lib - PL - LG
M   30,000 i
¶   RIBA Jnl - 12; ftm.   AR - 1; free.
      Architecture Periodicals Index - 4.
      RIBA Directory of Practices - 1 (printed & on-line).
      RIBA Directory of Members - 1; ftm (on-line only).
      RIBA International Directory of Practices - 1 (on-line only).

Royal Institute of International Affairs   (RIIA)   1920
■   Chatham House, 10 St James's Sq, LONDON, SW1Y 4LE.
      (hq)
      020 7957 5700   fax 020 7957 5710
      http://www.chatham.org.uk
      Dir: Prof Victor Bulmer-Thomas
▲   Registered Charity
○   *L; for the discussion, research & analysis of international
      affairs; the provision of information on & analysis of
      international issues with the object of stimulating informal
      debate among decision-makers & the wider public
Gp Europe; Middle East; Russia & Eurasia; Asia; Americas; Africa;
      International economics; New security issues; Sustainable
      development; International law
●   Conf - Mtgs - Res - SG - Lib
<   Instns of international affairs
M   1,700 i, 300 f
¶   The World Today (Jnl) - 12.
      International Affairs (Jnl) - 6; ftm.
      Chatham House NL - 12.   AR.
      Publications list available.

Royal Institute of Navigation   (RIN)   1947
NR   at the Royal Geographical Society, 1 Kensington Gore,
      LONDON, SW7 2AT.   (hq)
      020 7591 3130
      Dir: Gp Capt D W Broughton
▲   Registered Charity
Br   2
○   *L; the advancement of the art & science of navigation by land,
      sea, air & in space (includes animal & bird navigation)

Royal Institute of Oil Painters
      a member organisation of the **Federation of British Artists**

Royal Institute of Painters in Water Colours
      a member organisation of the **Federation of British Artists**

Royal Institute of Philosophy   1925
NR   14 Gordon Sq, LONDON, WC1H 0AR.   (hq)
      020 7387 4130
      Sec: James Garvey
▲   Company Limited by Guarantee; Registered Charity
Br   3
○   *L; to promote the study of philosophy & the encouragement of
      original work
●   Conf - Lectures
M   650 i
¶   Philosophy - 4;   Think - 4; both ftm.

Royal Institute of Public Health   (RIPH)   1886
NR   28 Portland Place, LONDON, W1B 1DE.   (hq)
      020 7580 2731
      The Chief Executive
○   *P
×   2002 Royal Institute of Public Health & Hygiene

Royal Institution of Chartered Surveyors   (RICS)   1868
NR   12 Great George St, LONDON, SW1P 3AD.   (hq)
      0870 333 1600
      Chief Exec: John Armstrong
○   *P
M   i & f

Royal Institution of Cornwall   (RIC)   1818
■   Royal Cornwall Museum, 25 River St, TRURO, Cornwall,
      TR1 2SJ.   (hq)
      01872 272205   fax 01872 240514
      email enquiries@royalcornwallmuseum.org.uk
      http://www.royalcornwallmuseum.org.uk
      Dir: Hilary Bracegirdle
▲   Registered Charity
○   *L; furtherance of Cornish studies; maintenance of the Museum
●   Mtgs - ET - Exhib - Inf - Lib - PL - VE
M   714 i, UK / 25 i, o'seas
¶   RIC Jnl - 1;   NL - 2; both ftm.

Royal Institution of Great Britain   (RI)   1799
NR   21 Albemarle St, LONDON, W1S 4BS.   (hq)
      020 7409 2992
      Dir: Baroness Susan Greenfield
Br   Davy Faraday Research Laboratory
○   *L, *Q; advancement of the public understanding of science; to
      research into solid state chemistry
Gp History of Science; Royal Institution Discussion Evenings
M   i & f
¶   Elements - 4.

Royal Institution of Naval Architects   (RINA)   1860
NR   10 Upper Belgrave St, LONDON, SW1X 8BQ.   (hq)
          020 7235 4622
          Chief Exec: Trevor Blakeley
▲   Registered Charity
Br   Europe (14), Asia Pacific, Australia, Middle East
○   *L, *P; advancement of the art & science of naval architecture,
          as applied to ship design & other related activities
Gp   Small craft; High speed craft; Historical; Young members
●   Conf - Mtgs - ET - Exhib - Comp - SG - Inf - Lib - LG
<   W Confedn of Maritime Technology Socs (WEMT)
M   4,100 i, UK / 2,400 i, o'seas
¶   The Naval Architect - 10.   Ship & Boat Intl - 10.
          Offshore Marine Technology - 4.
          Warship Technology - 5 (included with The Naval Architect).
          Ship Repair & Conversion Technology - 4.
          Significant Ship - 1.   Significant Small Craft - 1.

Royal Institution of South Wales   (RISW)   1835
■   c/o Swansea Museum, Victoria Rd, SWANSEA, Glam,
          SA1 1SN.   (regd/off)
          01792 653763   fax 01792 652585
          Hon Sec: Jennifer Sabine,   Pres: Gwyneth Davies
▲   Registered Charity
○   *L; created as a literary & philosophical institution; nowadays,
          acts as a friends group of Swansea Museum
●   Mtgs - Res - Inf - Fundraising for Swansea Museum - Public
          lectures
<   Brit Assn Friends Museums
M   c 350 i
¶   Minerva: Jnl of Swansea History - 1; £5 m, £6 nm.
          The Remarkable James Livingstone; £5.
          Welsh Ceramics In Context: Pt 1; £27.50 (softback),
          £39.95 (hardback).
          Welsh Ceramics in Context: Pt 2; £39.50 (softback),
          £55 (hardback).

Royal Irish Academy   (RIA)   1785
IRL   19 Dawson St, DUBLIN 2, Republic of Ireland.   (hq)
          353 (1) 676 2570   fax 353 (1) 676 2346
          email admin@ria.ie   http://www.ria.ie
          Sec: Prof J A Slevin
○   *L
M   320

Royal Irish Academy of Music   (RIAM)   1848
IRL   36 Westland Row, DUBLIN 2, Republic of Ireland.
          353 (1) 676 4412   fax 353 (1) 662 2798
          email info@riam.ie   http://www.riam.ie
          Sec: Dorothy Shiel
○   *D, *E

Royal Irish Automobile Club   (RIAC)   1901
IRL   34 Dawson St, DUBLIN 2, Republic of Ireland.
          353 (1) 677 5141 (Motor Sport Dept: 677 5628)
          fax 353 (1) 671 0793
          email info@riac.ie   http://www.motorsportireland.com
          Sec: A T M Sinclair
○   *G

**Royal Isle of Wight Agricultural Society / I.W.Show Ltd
   (RIWAS)   1882**
NR   Central House, 48-49 High St, NEWPORT, Isle of Wight,
          PO30 1SE.   (hq)
          01983 826275
          email info@riwas.org.uk
          Hon Sec: Mrs Rosemary Edwards
▲   Company Limited by Guarantee; Registered Charity
○   *F; to promote farming & agriculture & organisation of local
          County show
●   Exhib - Shows
M   540 i, UK / 1 i, o'seas
¶   NL - 4;   AR; both ftm only.

**Royal Jersey Agricultural & Horticultural Society   (RJA&HS)
   1833**
■   Royal Jersey Showground, La Route de la Trinité, TRINITY,
          Jersey, Channel Islands, JE3 5JP.   (hq)
          01534 866555   fax 01534 865619
          email society@royaljersey.co.uk
          http://www.royaljersey.co.uk
          Chief Exec: James W Godfrey
▲   Registered Charity
○   *B, *F, *H
●   Conf - Mtgs - Exhib - Comp - Expt - Inf - LG
M   1,000 i, 20 f, 10 org, UK / 200 i, o'seas
¶   Jersey at Home - 1; ftm, £5 nm.

Royal Lancashire Agricultural Society   (RLAS)   1767
■   5 Windmill Cottages, Preston New Rd, BLACKBURN, Lancs,
          BB2 7NT.   (hq)
          01254 813769   fax 01254 812522
          email info@rlas.co.uk   http://www.rlas.co.uk
          Hon Sec: John Thompson
▲   Company Limited by Guarantee; Registered Charity
○   *F; promotion of agriculture; to organise the annual show
●   Exhib (annual show)
M   450 i
¶   Rural Review (NL) - 2; m only.   Show Catalogue - 1.   AR.

Royal Life Saving Society UK   (Lifesavers)   1891
NR   River House, High St, BROOM, Warks, B50 4HN.   (hq)
          01789 773994   fax 01789 773995
          email lifesavers@rlss.org.uk
          http://www.lifesavers.org.uk
          Chief Exec: Di Standley
▲   Company Limited by Guarantee; Registered Charity
Br   50
○   *K, *W; educating people in preventing the loss of life through
          drowning, choking & heart attacks
●   ET - Comp - Inf - LG
<   Intl Lifesaving Fedn; Inst Sport & Recreational Mgt
M   13,000 i, 1,400 org
¶   Lifesavers Magazine - 4; ftm & supporters.

Royal Manx Agricultural Society   (Royal Manx)   1858
■   Vesper Gate, Sulby Bridge, LEZAYRE, Isle of Man, IM7 2ET.
          (sp)
          01624 898229   fax 01624 898229
          email royalmanx@manx.net
          Sec: Ian D Corkill
▲   Company Limited by Guarantee; Registered Charity
○   *F, *H; to promote agriculture & horticulture to the general
          public through exhibitions & shows
●   Mtgs - Exhib - Comp - VE - LG - Schools competition with
          'greenfingers' bias
<   Brit Show Jumping Assn; Clydesdale Horse Soc of GB &
          Ireland; Shire Horse Assn; Holstein UK Premier Show; R
          Gardeners Benevolent Assn
M   70 i

Royal Martyr Church Union   (RMCU)   1906
■   7 Nunnery Stables, ST ALBANS, Herts, AL1 2AS.   (hsp)
          01727 856626
          Hon Sec & Treas: E D Roberts
▲   Un-incorporated Society
○   *G, K; to promote the restoration of King Charles I's name to
          its proper place & fitting observance in the worldwide
          church's calendar; to maintain the principles of faith, liberty
          & loyalty for which the King died; to bring together
          descendants of cavalier officers & men, and anyone
          interested in Caroline history
●   Mtgs (AGM follows London service) - Annual remembrance
          service on 30 January (or the nearest Thursday, if 30 January
          falls at a weekend) at St Mary's Cathedral, Palmerston Place,
          Edinburgh & on the nearest Saturday to 30 January in
          St Mary-le-Strand, Strand, London WC2
M   79 i, UK / 10 i, o'seas
¶   Royal Martyr Annual - 1; ftm, on application nm.

Royal Medical Society   (RMS)   1736
■   Potterrow, 5/5 Bristo Sq, EDINBURGH, EH8 9AL.   (hq)
     0131-650 2672   fax 0131-650 2672
     email enquiries@royalmedical.co.uk
     http://www.royalmedical.co.uk
     Sec: Mrs Elizabeth Singh,   Snr Pres: Joanne Sells
▲   Registered Charity
○   *L; the medical student society of Edinburgh
Gp   Museum; Library; Learning resource centre
●   Mtgs - ET - Comp - SG - Inf - Lib - PL
M   300 i
¶   Res Medica (Jnl) - 2.

Royal Meteorological Society   (RMetSoc)   1850
NR   104 Oxford Rd, READING, Berks, RG1 7LL.   (hq)
     0118-956 8500
     email info@rmets.org
     Exec Dir: R E W Pettifer
▲   Registered Charity
○   *L; promotion of all aspects of the science of meteorology
Gp   Climatology; Dynamical problems; Agricultural meteorology;
     History of meteorology & physical oceanography;
     Atmospheric chemistry; Meteorological observing systems
●   Conf - Mtgs - ET - VE
M   i, f & org
¶   Jnl - 8.   Weather - 12.   Meteorological Applications - 4.
     International Jnl of Climatology - 15.

Royal Microscopical Society   (RMS)   1839
NR   37-38 St Clements, OXFORD, OX4 1AJ.   (hq)
     01865 248768   fax 01865 791237
     email info@rms.org.uk   http://www.rms.org.uk
     Exec Dir: Rob Flavin
▲   Registered Charity
○   *L; 'publication & discussion of research in fields of
     improvement in construction & mode of application of
     microscopes, & those branches of science where microscopy
     is important'
Gp   Cytometry; Cell biology; Electron microscopy; Light microscopy;
     Materials science
●   Conf - Mtgs - ET - Exhib
<   Intl Fedn Socs Histochemistry & Cytochemistry; Intl Fedn Socs
     Electron Microscopy
M   c 900 i, UK / 500 i o'seas
¶   Jnl of Microscopy - 12.
     In Focus - 4; ftm.

Royal Miniature Society
     see **Royal Society of Miniature Painters, Sculptors &
     Engravers**

Royal Musical Association   (RMA)   1874
■   4 Chandos Rd, Chorlton-cum-Hardy, MANCHESTER,
     M21 0ST.   (hsp/b)
     0161-861 7542   fax 0161-861 7543
     email jeffrey.dean@stingrayoffice.com
     http://www.rma.ac.uk
     Sec: Dr Jeffrey Dean
▲   Company Limited by Guarantee; Registered Charity
Br   2
○   *D, *L; art, science & history of music
●   Conf - Mtgs
<   Amer Musicological Soc; Soc for Musicology in Ireland
M   900 i, UK / 85 i, o'seas
¶   Jnl - 2; ftm, £99 nm.
     NL - 2; ftm, £8 nm.
     RMA Research Chronicle - 1; price varies.
     RMA Monographs; price varies.

Royal National Institute of the Blind   (RNIB)   1868
NR   105 Judd St, LONDON, WC1H 9NE.   (hq)
     020 7388 1266
     http://www.rnib.org.uk
     Dir Gen: Lesley-Anne Alexander
▲   Registered Charity
Br   9
○   *W; 'works for blind & partially sighted people throughout the
     UK.   We have over 60 different services to help people at
     all stages of their lives'
●   Inf - Talking book service - Tape & braille services - Holidays -
     Residential homes - Training, rehabilitation & help in finding
     jobs
M   subscribers

Royal National Institute for Deaf People
     since 2002 **RNID**

Royal National Lifeboat Institution   (RNLI)   1824
NR   West Quay Rd, POOLE, Dorset, BH15 1HZ.   (hq)
     0845 122 6999
     http://www.rnli.org.uk
     Chief Exec: Andrew Freemantle
○   *W; to save lives at sea around the coasts of UK & Ireland
●   Conf - Mtgs - Exhib - Inf - PL - VE
<   Intl Lifeboat Fedn
M   200,000+ i
¶   The Lifeboat - 4; ftm.   AR; free.

Royal National Rose Society   (RNRS)   1876
NR   Gardens of the Rose, Chiswell Green, ST ALBANS, Herts,
     AL2 3NR.   (hq)
     01727 850461   fax 01727 850360
     http://www.rnrs.org
     Gen Mgr: Brian Gill
▲   Company Limited by Guarantee; Registered Charity
○   *H
●   Res - Exhib - Inf - Lib - PL
M   c 10,000 i & org
¶   The Rose (Jnl) - 3.
     How to Grow Roses - irreg.

Royal Naval Association   (RNA)   1950
NR   82 Chelsea Manor St, LONDON, SW3 5QJ.   (hq)
     020 7352 6764
     Gen Sec: Commodore Barry Leighton
▲   Registered Charity
Br   450; 10 o'seas
○   *W; 'to further the efficiency of the Service in which members of
     the association have served or are serving, by fostering the
     esprit de corps & preserving the traditions of the Service; . . .
     to relieve members of the association who are in conditions
     of real hardship or distress'
●   Conf - Mtgs - VE
M   i
¶   NL - 4;   Circular - 11;   Ybk;   AR; all ftm.

Royal Naval Bird Watching Society   (RNBWS)   1946
■   16 Cutlers Lane, Stubbington, FAREHAM, Hants, PO14 2JN.
     (hsp)
     0771 736 8300
     email francisward@btopenworld.com
     http://www.rnbws.org.uk
     Hon Sec: Cdr Frank S Ward
▲   Registered Charity
○   *G; forum for exchange of information & observation of
     seabirds & land birds at sea & onboard ships whilst at sea
Gp   Seabird distribution database
●   Res - PL of seabirds: c/o Lt Cmdr G D Lewis RN,
     40 Pondfield Rd, Saltash, Cornwall, PL12 4UA.
M   180 i, org, UK / 60 i, org, o'seas
¶   NBWS Bulletin - 2; ftm, £1 each nm.
     Sea Swallow - 1; ftm, £8 nm.

Royal Navy Enthusiasts' Society   (RNES)   1977
- ■   5 Midways, STUBBINGTON, Hants, PO14 2DA.   (hq)
     01329 668139
     Chmn: D J Maxted
- ▲   Un-incorporated Society
- ○   *G; collection of memorabilia & ephemera of the Royal Navy
     from 1600 to the present day
- Gp   Collectors: cap tallies, branch badges; Historians: Nelson, his
     ships & men, World Wars I & II; Photographs of ships; the
     Royal Navy & other navies
- ●   Mtgs - Res
- <   Fedn of Naval Assns
- M   145 i, UK / 4 i, o'seas
- ¶   Excalibur (NL) - 12; free.

Royal Norfolk Agricultural Association   (RNAA)   1847
- ■   Norfolk Showground, Dereham Rd, New Costessey,
     NORWICH, Norfolk, NR5 0TT.   (hq)
     01603 748931   fax 01603 748729
     Show Mgr: Mrs Sarah de Chair
- ○   *F; the improvement of livestock & plants, agricultural machines
     & implements; encouragement of skills & education in
     agriculture & horticulture
- ●   ET - Res - Exhib - Comp - Annual show covering livestock
     (horses, cattle, pigs, sheep, goats, driving & showjumping);
     Small livestock (poultry, rabbits, cavies, cage birds & dogs);
     Agricultural machinery & general trade stands
- <   Assn Show & Agricl Orgs (ASAO); Breed Socs
- M   4,000 i
- ¶   Jnl;   Prize List - 1;   NL;   AR; all ftm.
     Catalogue - 1; £5.

Royal Northern Agricultural Society   (RNAS)   1845
- ■   Knappyround, LUMPHANAN, Aberdeenshire, AB31 4QL.   (sp)
     01339 883632
     Sec: Scott Raeburn
- ▲   Registered Charity
- ○   *F; farming & agriculture
- ●   Conf - Res - Exhib - VE
- M   525 i

Royal Numismatic Society   (RNS)   1836
- ■   c/o Dept of Coins & Medals, British Museum, LONDON,
     WC1B 3DG.   (hsb)
     020 7323 8173   fax 020 7323 8267
     email rns@dircon.co.uk   http://www.rns.dircon.co.uk
     Jt Secs: Vesta Sarkhosh Curtis,   Catherine Eagleton
- ▲   Registered Charity
- ○   *L
- ●   Mtgs - Lib
- M   420 i, 21 org, UK / 500 i, 54 org, o'seas
- ¶   The Numismatic Chronicle (Jnl) - 1; £35.
     Coin Hoards - 1; price varies.   Jnl - irreg.
     Special publications - irreg.

Royal Over-Seas League   (ROSL)   1910
- NR   Over-Seas House, Park Place, St James's St, LONDON,
     SW1A 1LR.   (hq)
     020 7408 0214   fax 020 7499 6738
     email info@rosl.org.uk   http://www.rosl.org.uk
     Dir Gen: Robert F Newell
- ▲   Royal Charter
- Br   12; Australia, Canada, Hong Kong, New Zealand
- ○   *X; private membership-based London club which encourages
     the arts in the youth of the Commonwealth; to increase the
     knowledge & interest in the Commonwealth
- ●   Conf - Mtgs - Comp (music & art) - Exhib - VE - Residential
     club-house - Lectures
- M   12,814 i, UK / 10,038 i, o'seas
- ¶   Overseas - 4; ftm, £7.50 nm (£10 o'seas).

Royal Pharmaceutical Society of Great Britain   (RPSGB)   1841
- NR   1 Lambeth High St, LONDON, SE1 7JN.   (hq)
     020 7735 9141
     email enquiries@rpsgb.org
     Sec & Registrar: Ann M Lewis
- ▲   Un-incorporated Society
- Br   130
- ○   *L, *P; the professional & statutory body for Britain's
     pharmacists; to maintain the register of pharmaceutical
     chemists; to promote good practice in pharmacy
- Gp   Pharmacists: Agricultural & veterinary, Community, Hospital,
     Industrial;
     Academic pharmacy; Joint Pharmaceutical analysis;
     Pharmaceutical sciences; British Pharmaceutical Students
     Association
- ●   Conf - Mtgs - ET - Exam - Res - Exhib - Inf - Lib - LG
- M   c 40,000 i, UK / 2,500 i, o'seas
- ¶   Pharmaceutical Jnl - 52.   Hospital Pharmacist - 10.
     Jnl of Pharmacy & Pharmacology + Pharmacy & Pharmacology
     Communities - 12.
     International Jnl of Pharmacy Practice - 4.
     Publications list available of pharmacopoeia, textbooks &
     handbooks on various aspects of pharmacy practice.

Royal Philatelic Society London   (RPSL)   1869
- ■   41 Devonshire Place, LONDON, W1G 6JY.   (hq)
     020 7486 1044
     Hon Sec: Brian Trotter
- ○   *L; for amateur collectors; research & advancement of the
     science of philately
- ●   Mtgs - Lib
- M   c 2000 i
- ¶   The London Philatelist (Jnl) - 10; ftm.

Royal Philharmonic Society   (RPS)   1813
- ■   10 Stratford Place, LONDON, W1C 1BA.   (hq)
     020 7491 8110   fax 020 7493 7463
     email admin@royalphilharmonicsociety.co.uk
     http://www.royalphilharmonicsociety.org.uk
     Gen Admin: Rosemary Johnson
- ▲   Registered Charity
- ○   *D; to promote excellence, creativity & understanding in
     classical music
- ●   Lectures - Scholarships - Awards - Commissioning new music
- <   Intl Mendelssohn Foundation
- M   700 i, 8 f, UK / 30 i, o'seas
- ¶   Fanfare [NL] - 2.   RPS Annual Lecture Text - 1.

Royal Philosophical Society of Glasgow   (RPSG)   1802
- NR   PO Box NAT8268, GLASGOW, G46 7BR.   (sb)
     0141-946 4358
     Sec: Mrs Mairi Mitchell
- ▲   Company Limited by Guarantee; Registered Charity
- ○   *L; lectures & discussion on all branches of arts & science
- ●   Mtgs - VE - Annual dinner
- M   i
- ¶   NL - 12;   AR; both ftm.
     [website includes précis of lectures].

© CBD Research Ltd · Beckenham · BR3 5JS · Tel 020 8650 7745 · Fax 020 8650 0768 · E-mail cbd@cbdresearch.com · www.cbdresearch.com

Royal Photographic Society of Great Britain   (RPS)   1853
- ■ Fenton House, 122 Wells Rd, BATH, Somerset, BA2 3AH.   (hq)
  01225 325733   fax 01225 448688
  http://www.rps.org
  Pres: Ralph Jacobsen
- ▲ Company Limited by Guarantee; Registered Charity
- Br 16; contacts in: Australia, Hong Kong, Japan, Russia
- ○ *L; to promote the art & science of photography in all aspects
- Gp Archaeology & heritage; Audio-visual; Colour; Contemporary;
  Creative; Digital imaging; Film & video; Historical;
  Holography; Imaging science & technology; Medical; Nature;
  Pictorial; Travel; Visual journalism
- ● Mtgs - ET - Res - Exhib - Comp - Inf
- M 7,972 i, 102 f, UK / 1,271 i, 104 f, o'seas
- ¶ RPS Journal - 10; ftm, £65 yr nm (£70 o'seas).
  Imaging Science Journal - 4; ftm.
  Group & Regional NLs - 1/2; ftm only.

Royal Pigeon Racing Association   (RPRA)   1896
- ■ The Reddings, CHELTENHAM, Glos, GL51 6RN.   (hq)
  01452 713529   fax 01452 857119
  email gm@rpra.org   http://www.rpra.org
  Gen Mgr: Peter Bryant
- Br 13
- ○ *B, *S; control & administration of long distance pigeon racing
- ● Conf - Mtgs - Exhib - Comp - Stat - Inf - LG
- < Fédn Colombophile Intle (FCI); Confedn of Long Distance
  Pigeon Us of GB (CLDPUGB)
- M 48,000 i, 2,400 clubs
- ¶ The British Homing World - 52, 49p.

Royal School of Church Music   (RSCM)   1927
- ■ 19 The Close, SALISBURY, Wilt, SP1 2EB.   (hq)
  email enquiries@rscm.com   http://www.rscm.com
  Dir: Prof J Harper
- ▲ Company Limited by Guarantee; Registered Charity
- Br 43; Australia, Canada, N Zealand, S Africa, USA
- ○ *D, *L; training, advice & resources for all concerned with music
  in worship - singers, organists, instrumentalists, clergy &
  congregation
- ● ET - Exam - Comp - SG - Inf - Lib - Publishing & retailing
  church music & training material
- M 2,509 i, 5,547 org, UK / 1,492 i, 2,003 org, o'seas
- ¶ Church Music Quarterly - 4; ftm.   AR.

Royal Scottish Academy of Art & Architecture   (RSA)   1826
- ■ The Mound, EDINBURGH, EH2 2EL.   (hq)
  0131-225 6671   fax 0131-220 6016
  email info@royalscottishacademy.org
  http://www.royalscottishacademy.org
  Admin Sec: Bruce Laidlaw
- ▲ Registered Charity
- ○ *A; promotion & furtherance of the fine arts in Scotland
  (painting, sculpture, architecture & printmaking)
- ● Exhib - Comp - Lib
- M 90 i
- ¶ Exhibition Catalogue - 1.
- ✕ 2006 Royal Scottish Academy of Painting, Sculpture &
  Architecture

Royal Scottish Academy of Music & Drama   (RSAMD)   1847
- NR 100 Renfrew St, GLASGOW, G2 3DB.   (hq)
  0141-332 4101   fax 0141-332 8901
  email registry@rsamd.ac.uk   http://www.rsamd.ac.uk
  Principal: John Wallace
- ▲ Company Limited by Guarantee; Registered Charity
- ○ *D; an international conservatoire for degree courses in music
  & drama; to act as an arts & conference venue
- < St Andrews University; Glasgow University; The Piping Centre
- M [none]
- ¶ Drama NL - 4;   Events Brochure - 4;
  Events Brochure - 4;   Prospectus - 1; all free.

Royal Scottish Academy of Painting, Sculpture & Architecture
  since 2006 **Royal Scottish Academy of Art & Architecture**

Royal Scottish Automobile Club (Motor Sport) Ltd
since 2004-05 **RSAC Motorsport Ltd**

Royal Scottish Country Dance Society   (RSCDS)   1923
- NR 12 Coates Crescent, EDINBURGH, EH3 7AF.   (hq)
  0131-225 3854   fax 0131-225 7783
  email info@rscds.org   http://www.rscds.org
  Sec: Elspeth Gray
- ▲ Registered Charity
- Br 170
- ○ *D; to preserve & further the practice of traditional Scottish
  country dancing
- ● Mtgs - Exam
- M c 17,000 i
- ¶ Bulletin - 1; ftm.   Scottish Country Dancer - 2.

Royal Scottish Forestry Society   (RSFS)   1854
- ■ Hagg-on-Esk, CANONBIE, Dumfriesshire, DG14 0XE.   (hsb)
  01387 371518   fax 01387 371418
  email rsfs@lumison.co.uk   http://www.rsfs.org
  Admin Dir: Andrew G Little
- ▲ Registered Charity
- Br 6
- ○ *H, *L; to advance all areas of forestry
- Gp Silviculture; Trees, woods & people; Forest for a 1000 years
- ● Conf - Mtgs - ET - Exhib - Comp - SG - Lib - VE - LG
- < Forestry Ind Coun (FIC)
- M 950 i, 50 f, UK / 50 i, 10 f, o'seas
- ¶ Scottish Forestry - 4; ftm, £52 (£67 o'seas).

Royal Scottish Geographical Society   (RSGS)   1884
- ■ 40 George St, GLASGOW, G1 1QE.   (hq)
  0141-552 3330   fax 0141-552 3331
  email rsgs@strath.ac.uk   http://www.rsgs.org
  Sec: Dr David M Munro
- ▲ Registered Charity
- Br 14
- ○ *E, *L; the advancement of the study of geography
- ● Conf - Mtgs - ET - Exhib - Comp - Inf - Lib - PL - VE - LG
- M 3,076 i, 22 org, UK / 30 i, o'seas
- ¶ Scottish Geographical Jnl - 4; ftm, £44 nm (£95 instns).
  GeogScot (NL) - 3; ftm, £2 nm.   AR.

Royal Scottish Pipe Band Association   (RSPBA)   1930
- NR 45 Washington St, GLASGOW, G3 8AZ.   (hq)
  0141-221 5414
  http://www.rspba.org
  Chief Exec: Ian Embelton
- ▲ Registered Charity
- Br 12
- ○ *D, *G
- ● Conf - ET - Comp - Lib
- M c 650 pipe bands
- ¶ The Pipe Band - 4.

Royal Scottish Society of Arts (Science & Technology)   (RSSA)   1821
- ■ 29/3 East London St, EDINBURGH, EH7 4BN.   (hsp)
  0131-556 2161
  email secretary@rssa.org.uk   http://www.rssa.org.uk
  Hon Sec: Mrs Jane Ridder-Patrick
- ▲ Registered Charity
- ○ *L; 'for the promotion of the 'useful arts' - science, technology,
  engineering, manufacturing' & concerned with the
  application of science & technology)
- ● Mtgs - VE
- M 163 i

Royal Scottish Society of Painters in Water Colours (RSW) 1878

■ 5 Oswald St, GLASGOW, G1 4QR. (asa)
0141-248 7411 fax 0141-221 0417
email rsw@robbferguson.co.uk
http://www.thersw.org.uk
Sec: Gordon C McAllister, CA
▲ Registered Charity
○ *A; to develop & encourage the art of painting in watercolour
● Exhib
M 112 i

Royal Scottish Society for the Prevention of Cruelty to Children
see **Children 1st (Royal Scottish Society for Prevention of Cruelty to Children)**

The Royal Society 1660

NR 6 Carlton House Terrace, LONDON, SW1Y 5AG. (hq)
020 7451 2500
Exec Sec: Stephen Cox
▲ Registered Charity
○ *L, *Q; 'to recognise excellence in science; to support leading edge scientific research & its applications: to stimulate international interaction; to further the role of science, engineering & technology in society; to promote education & the public's understanding of science; to provide independent authoritative advice on matters relating to science; to encourage research into the history of science
● Mtgs - Res - Exhib - SG - Stat - Inf - Lib - PL - Grants for research & travel overseas - Appointments
< Intl Coun for Science (ICSU); Eur Science Foundation (ESF)
M 1,200 i, UK / 100 i, o'seas
¶ Philosophical Transactions:
(Series A - Mathematical & Physical Sciences.
(Series B - Biological Sciences); prices vary.
Proceedings (Series A & B); prices vary.
Science & Public Affairs - 1.   NL; ftm.
Notes & Records - 2; ftm.   Ybk.
Biographical Memoirs of Fellows - 1.
List of Fellows 1660-2000.
Obituaries of Fellows 1830-2000.
Numerous reports & papers.

Royal Society of Antiquaries of Ireland (RSAI) 1849

IRL 63 Merrion Sq, DUBLIN 2, Republic of Ireland.
353 (1) 676 1749 fax 353 (1) 676 1749
Exec Sec: Colette Ellison
○ *L

Royal Society of Architects in Wales

■ Bute Building, King Edward VII Avenue, Cathays Park, CARDIFF, Glam, CF10 3NB.
029 2087 4753 fax 029 2087 4926
email rsaw@inst.riba.org
http://www.architecture-wales.com
Dir: Mary Wrenn
▲ Registered Charity
○ *P
● Conf - Mtgs - Comp - LG
< R Inst Brit Architects
M 854 i
¶ Touchstone - 2; £5.

Royal Society for the encouragement of Arts, Manufactures & Commerce (RSA) 1754

■ 8 John Adam St, LONDON, WC2N 6EZ. (hq)
020 7930 5115 fax 020 7839 5805
email general@rsa.org.uk   http://www.thersa.org
Exec Dir: Penny Egan
▲ Registered Charity
Br 11; 4 o'seas
○ *A, *E, *L, *P; the RSA's 21st century mission is to:
encourage enterprise
move towards a zero waste society
develop a capable population
foster resilient communities
advance global citizenship
Gp Examples of projects: Design Directions; Environment Awards Forum; Intellectual Property Charter; Opening Minds
● Conf - Mtgs - Res - Exhib - Comp - SG - Lib - Archive (200 years of RSA history) - Lectures
M 20,500 i, 15 f, UK / 2,500 i, o'seas
¶ The RSA Jnl - 5.
Note: Also known as the Royal Society of Arts.

Royal Society for Asian Affairs 1901

■ 2 Belgrave Sq, LONDON, SW1X 8PJ. (hq)
020 7235 5122
Sec: Norman Cameron
▲ Registered Charity
○ *L; culture & current affairs of Asian countries, from the Near East to China & Japan
● Conf (occasional) - Mtgs - Lib - PL
¶ Asian Affairs (Jnl) - 3; ftm, £55 i (£125 instns), nm.

Royal Society of British Artists
a member organisation of the **Federation of British Artists**

Royal Society of British Sculptors
since 2003 **Royal British Society of Sculptors**

© CBD Research Ltd · Beckenham · BR3 5JS · Tel 020 8650 7745 · Fax 020 8650 0768 · E-mail cbd@cbdresearch.com · www.cbdresearch.com

Royal Society of Chemistry (RSC) 1980

■ Burlington House, Piccadilly, LONDON, W1J 0BA. (hq)
020 7437 8656   fax 020 7437 9798
email library@rsc.org   http://www.rsc.org
Sec Gen: Dr Richard Pike
▲ Registered Charity
Br 35; 8 o'seas
○ *L; to advance the chemical sciences
Gp Specialist subject groups are controlled by the following
divisions:
Analytical, Dalton, Education, Faraday, Industrial, Perkin
● Conf - Mtgs - ET - Exam - SG - Stat - Inf - Lib
< Intl U of Pure & Applied Chemistry; Fedn of Eur Chemical Socs;
Eur Communities Chemistry Coun
M 34,721 i, UK / 7,714 i, o'seas
¶ The Analyst.   Analytical Abstracts.
Annual Reports on the Progress of Chemistry:
Section A;   Section B;   Section C.
Catalysts & Catalysed Reactions.   Chemical Communications.
Chemical Hazards in Industry.
Physical Chemistry Chemical Physics.
Chemical Society Reviews.   Chemical World.
Chromatography Abstracts.   CrystEngComm.
Dalton Transactions.   Education in Chemistry.
Faraday Discussions.   Geochemical Transactions.
Green Chemistry.   Hazards in the Office.
Issues in Environmental Science & Technology.
Jnl of Analytical Atomic Spectrometry.
Jnl of Environmental Monitoring.
Jnl of Materials Chemistry.   Lab on a Chip.
Laboratory Hazards Bulletin.   Mass Spectrometry Bulletin.
Methods in Organic Synthesis.   Natural Products Reports.
Natural Products Updates.   New Jnl of Chemistry.
Organic & Biomolecular Chemistry.   New Pesticide Outlook.
Photochemical & Photobiological Sciences.
PhysChemComm.   Russian Chemical Reviews.
University Chemistry Education.
[Reduced member prices are available for all RSC
publications].

Royal Society of Edinburgh (RSE) 1783

NR 22-26 George St, EDINBURGH, EH2 2PQ. (hq)
0131 240 5000
Gen Sec: Prof Gavin McCrone
▲ Registered Charity
○ *L; the achievement of learning & useful knowledge in
Scotland.   'The Society is unique in the UK as it
encompasses all branches of learning - science, arts, letters,
the professions, technology, industry & commerce'
● Conf - Mtgs - SG - LG - Awards research fellowship, prizes &
prize lectureships - Schemes to interest young people in
science & technology
M c 1,200 i (fellows by election only)
¶ Transactions: Earth Sciences - 4.
Proceedings Section A (Mathematics) - 6.
RSE News - 4;   AR.   Ybk (inc LM).

Royal Society of Health
see **Royal Society for the Promotion of Health** (full title)

Royal Society of Literature of the United Kingdom (RSL) 1820

■ Somerset House, Strand, LONDON, WC2R 1LA. (hq)
020 7845 4676   fax 020 7845 4679
email info@rslit.org   http://www.rslit.org
Sec: Mrs Maggie Fergusson,   Chmn: Maggie Gee
▲ Registered Charity
○ *A; to sustain & encourage all that is perceived as best, whether
traditional or experimental, in English letters
● Conf - Mtgs - Comp
M 465 fellows, 420 members, 10 org
¶ News from the RSL - 1.

Royal Society of Marine Artists
a member organisation of the **Federation of British Artists**

Royal Society of Medicine (RSM) 1805

NR 1 Wimpole St, LONDON, W1G 0AE. (hq)
020 7290 2900   fax 020 7290 2909
email library@rsm.ac.uk   http://www.rsm.ac.uk
Chief Exec: Stephen Dodd
▲ Registered Charity
○ *L; 'for the cultivation & promotion of physic & surgery & of the
branches of science connected with them'
Gp Sections:
Accident & emergency medicine, Anaesthesia, Black & ethnic
minority health, Cardiothoracic, Catastrophes & conflict,
Clinical, Clinical forensic & legal medicine, Clinical
immunology & allergy, Clinical neurosciences,
Coloproctology, Communication in healthcare, Comparative
medicine, Dermatology, Endocrinology & diabetes,
Epidemiology & public health, Food & health, General
practice with primary healthcare, Geriatrics & gerontology,
History of medicine, Hypnosis & psychosomatic medicine,
Laryngology & rhinology, Learning disability, Lipids in clinical
medicine, Maternity & the newborn, Medical genetics,
Nephrology, Obstetrics & gynaecology, Occupational
medicine, Odontology, Oncology, Open, Ophthalmology,
Orthopaedics, Otology, Paediatrics & child health, Palliative
care, Pathology, Pharmaceutical medicine & research, Plastic
surgery, Psychiatry, Quality in health care, Radiology,
Respiratory medicine, Rheumatology & rehabilitation, Sexual
health & reproductive medicine, Sleep medicine, Sports &
exercise medicine, Surgery, Telemedicine & e-health,
Transplantation, United services, Urology, Vascular medicine,
Venous
● Conf - Mtgs - ET - Lib
M 14,774 i, UK / 2,292 i, o'seas
¶ Jnl - 12;   Calendar - 1;   AR; all ftm only.

Royal Society for Mentally Handicapped Children & Adults
see **MENCAP: Royal Society for Mentally Handicapped
Children & Adults**

Royal Society of Miniature Painters, Sculptors & Gravers (RMS) 1895

NR 1 Knapp Cottages, Wyke, GILLINGHAM, Dorset, SP8 4NQ.
(hsp)
01747 825718
email hendersons@dial.pipex.com
http://www.royal-miniature-society.org.uk
Exec Sec: Mrs Pamela Henderson
▲ Registered Charity
○ *A, *P; the practice & exhibition of miniature art
● Exhib
M c 120 i
¶ 100th Anniversary Book; £40.
Annual Exhibition Catalogue - 1; £3.50.
Note: is more usually known as the Royal Miniature Society.

Royal Society of Musicians of Great Britain (RSM) 1738

§ 10 Stratford Place, LONDON, W1C 1BA. (hq)
020 7629 6137   fax 020 7629 6137
a charity for the relief of poverty in the musical profession due
to illness, accident or bereavement

Royal Society for Nature Conservation
since 2004 **Royal Society of Wildlife Trusts**

Royal Society of Painter-Printmakers (RE) 1884

NR 48 Hopton St, LONDON, SE1 9JH. (hq)
020 7928 7521
▲ Registered Charity
○ *A; to promote printmaking through exhibitions
● ET - Exhib - SG - Inf - Lib
M i

Royal Society of Portrait Painters
a member organisation of the **Federation of British Artists**

Royal Society for the Prevention of Accidents   (RoSPA)   1916

■   Edgbaston Park, 353 Bristol Rd, BIRMINGHAM, B5 7ST.   (hq)
         0121-248 2000
▲   Company Limited by Guarantee; Registered Charity
Br   3
○   *E, *K; accident prevention
●   Conf - Mtgs - ET - Exam - Exhib - Stat - Inf - Lib - PL - LG
<   La Prévention Routière Intle
M   6,905 i, f & org
¶   RoSPA Bulletin - 12.
     Occupational Safety & Health - 12.
     Safety Express - 6.   Staying Alive - 4.
     Care on the Road - 6.   Safety Education - 3.

**Royal Society for the Prevention of Cruelty to Animals
(RSPCA)   1824**

■   Wilberforce Way, HORSHAM, W Sussex, RH13 9RS.   (hq)
         0870 010 1181
         http://www.rspca.org.uk
     Dir Gen: Jackie Ballard
▲   Registered Charity
Br   177
○   *K
●   Inf - PL - LG
M   35,561 i
¶   Animal Action - 6; £8 m.   Animal Life - 4; £17.50 m.
     Science Review - 1;   AR; both ftm.

Royal Society for the Promotion of Health   1876

NR   38a St George's Drive, LONDON, SW1V 4BH.   (hq)
         020 7630 0121   fax 020 7976 6847
         email rshealth@rshealth.org.uk   http://www.rsph.org
     Chief Exec: Stuart Royston
▲   Registered Charity
○   *E, *L; to promote the continuous improvement of human
     health worldwide through education, communication &
     encouragement of scientific research
●   Conf - Exam
<   Wld Fedn of Public Health Assns; Amer Public Health Assn
M   5,000 i, UK / 1,000 i o'seas
¶   Jnl - 4.   Hygeia - 4.
     Audit - 3.   Annual Review.
     Note: This organisation is more usually called the Royal Society
     of Health

Royal Society for the Protection of Birds   (RSPB)   1889

NR   The Lodge, SANDY, Beds, SG19 2DL.   (hq)
         01767 680551   fax 01767 692365
         http://www.rspb.org.uk
     Chief Exec: Graham Wynne
▲   Registered Charity
○   *G, *K; conservation & protection of wild birds; 'RSPB works for
     a healthy environment rich in birds & wildlife'
●   Conf - Res - Lib - PL
<   Birdlife Intl
M   1,036,869 i
¶   Birds - 4.

Royal Society of St George   1894

■   127 Sandgate Rd, FOLKESTONE, Kent, CT20 2BH.   (hq)
         01303 241795   fax 01303 211710
         email info@rssg.u-net.com
         http://www.royalsocietyofstgeorge.com
     Hon Sec: Dr Ivor Wilson
▲   Registered Charity
Br   40; c 40
○   *K, *W; 'the premier patriotic society of England, standing for
     loyalty & patriotic service to our nation & within our
     communities, with duty to our sovereign who as head of state
     transcends all party, political & personal ego & ambitions'
Gp   C'ees: Policy, Events; Charitable trust
●   Conf - Mtgs - ET - Lib - VE
<   about 40 affiliated socs o'seas
M   10,000 i
¶   England's Standard - 3; ftm, £2.50 nm.

**Royal Society of Tropical Medicine & Hygiene   (RSTM&H)
1907**

■   50 Bedford Square, LONDON, WC1B 3DP.   (hq)
         020 7580 2127   fax 020 7436 1389
         email mail@rstmh.org   http://www.rstmh.org
     Admin: Caryl Guest
▲   Registered Charity
○   *L; 'study of diseases & hygiene of man & other animals in
     warm climates'
●   Mtgs
M   827 i, UK / 2,067 i, o'seas
¶   Transactions - 12;   Ybk - 1; both ftm.

Royal Society of Ulster Architects   (RSUA)   1901

■   2 Mount Charles, BELFAST, BT7 1NZ.   (hq)
         028 9032 3760   fax 028 9023 7313
         email info@rsu.org.uk   http://www.rsu.org.uk
     Sec: Gillian Lendrum
▲   Registered Charity
○   *P
●   Conf - Mtgs - ET - Exhib - Comp - VE
<   R Inst Brit Architects
M   750 i
¶   Perspective (Jnl) - 6; ftm, £4.50 nm.   Ybk; ftm, £25 nm.

Royal Society of Wildlife Trusts   (RSWT)   1912

■   The Kiln, Waterside, Mather Rd, NEWARK, Notts, NG24 1WT.
     (hq)
         0870 036 1000   fax 0870 036 0101
         http://www.rsnc.org
     Chief Exec: Stephanie Hilborne
▲   Registered Charity
Br   47 wildlife trusts
○   *K, *N; to promote wildlife conservation in the UK; The Wildlife
     Trusts manage more than 2,500 nature reserves
Gp   Wildlife watch
●   Conf - Mtgs - ET - Res - Stat - Inf - LG - Land management
<   Eur Envtl Bureau; NCVO; Wildlife Link
M   c 260,000 i
¶   Natural World - 3;   Watchword - 3; both ftm only.   AR.
     Note: since 1994 has become known as The Wildlife Trusts.
✕   2004 Royal Society for Nature Conservation

Royal Statistical Society   (RSS)   1834

NR   12 Errol St, LONDON, EC1Y 8LX.   (hq)
         020 7638 8998
         http://www.rss.org.uk
     Dir Gen: Ivor J Goddard
▲   Registered Charity
○   *L
Gp   Business & industrial; Medical; Computing; Official statistics;
     Social statistics; General applications; Research; Statistics
     User Forum
●   Conf - Mtgs - ET - Exam - SG
<   Intl Statistical Inst; Intl Assn for Statistical Educ
M   c 4,700 i, UK / 1,800 i, o'seas
¶   Jnl (4 series) - 3/4 (each series); available on request.
     RSS News - 10; ftm only.

Royal Stuart Society & Royalist League   1926
- ■ 24 Park St, SALISBURY, Wilts, SP1 3AU.   (hsp)
  http://www.royalstuartsociety.com
  Principal Sec: Roger Davies
- ▲ Un-incorporated Society
- ○ *G, *K; for all who have an interest in the members of the
  Royal House of Stuart, their descendants & supporters; to
  promote research in, & further knowledge of, Stuart history;
  to uphold rightful monarchy & oppose republicanism; to
  arrange sommemorations, lectures & other activities as shall
  advance these objects
- ● Conf - Mtgs - Res - VE - LG - Lectures - Commemorative &
  social events
- < Intl Monarchist League
- M i
- ¶ NL - 3; ftm only.
  Royal Stuart Papers - 2; ftm, £3 each nm.
  Royal Stuart Review - 1; ftm, £3 each nm.

Royal Surgical Aid Society   (AgeCare)   1862
- § 47 Great Russell St, LONDON, WC1B 3PB.   (hq)
  020 7637 4577   fax 020 7323 6878
  email enquiries@agecare.org.uk
  A charity for the foundation & maintenance of homes for aged
  persons of limited means

Royal Television Society   (RTS)   1927
- NR Kildare House (5th floor), 3 Dorset Rise, LONDON,
  EC4Y 8EN.   (hq)
  020 7822 2810   fax 020 7822 2811
  http://www.rts.org.uk
  Chief Exec: Simon Albury
- ▲ Company Limited by Guarantee; Registered Charity
- Br 15; USA
- ○ *L; the art, science & politics of television
- Gp Craft & design; Education; History & archives; Technologies;
  News & current affairs; Press PR & marketing; Technical
  operations
- ● Conf - Mtgs - ET - Comp - Awards
- M 3,000 i, 100 f, UK / 250 i, o'seas
- ¶ Jnl - 8.   Hbk - 1.   AR.
  Various books & monographs.

Royal Town Planning Institute   (RTPI)   1914
- NR 41 Botolph Lane, LONDON, EC3R 8DL.   (hq)
  020 7929 9494   fax 020 7929 9490
  email online@rtpi.org.uk   http://www.rtpi.org.uk
  Sec Gen: Robert Upton
- ▲ Registered Charity
- Br 13; various countries o'seas
- ○ *L, *P; to advance the science & art of town planning in all its
  aspects (including local, regional & national planning) for the
  benefit of the public
- Gp Planning service
- ● Conf - Mtgs - ET - Res - SG - Inf - Lib - LG
- < Eur Coun of Town Planners; C'wealth Assn of Planners; Urban
  Design Alliance
- M 18,000 i
- ¶ Various papers.

Royal Ulster Agricultural Society   (RUAS)   1826
- ■ The King's Hall, Balmoral, BELFAST, BT9 6GW.   (hq)
  028 9066 5225   fax 028 9066 1264
  email general@kingshall.co.uk
  Chief Exec: Colin McDonald
- ▲ Registered Charity
- ○ *F; to promote agriculture, industries, sciences & the arts
- ● Conf - Exhib - Organisation of the Balmoral Show (the national
  agricultural show in NI) & of the Royal Ulster Winter Fair, a
  dairy orientated event
- < R Agricl Soc of the C'wealth
- M 3,500 i
- ¶ NL.   Hbk.   AR.

**Royal United Kingdom Beneficent Association   (RUKBA)
1863**
- § 6 Avonmore Rd, LONDON, W14 8RL.   (hq)
  020 7605 4200   fax 020 7605 4201
  email charity@rukba.org.uk   http://www.rukba.org.uk
  Provision of annuities, homes accommodation, relief grants,
  clothing etc to persons of the professional & kindred classes
  who are aged, in need or infirm

**Royal United Services Institute for Defence & Security Studies
(RUSI)   1857**
- ■ Whitehall, LONDON, SW1A 2ET.   (hq)
  020 7930 5854   fax 020 7321 0943
  email defence@rusi.org   http://www.rusi.org
  Dir: Rear Admiral Richard Cobbold
- ▲ Registered Charity
- ○ *L, *P, *Q; the study, analysis & debate of matters concerning
  natural & international defence & security; is a professional
  association of the Armed Forces
- Gp International security studies; Military sciences & homeland
  security & resilience
- ● Conf - Mtgs - Res - SG - Inf - Lib - LG
- M 4,500 i, 300 f, 200 org, UK / 1,000 i, 50 f, 32 org, o'seas
- ¶ RUSI Jnl - 6.   Security Monitor - 10;
  RUSI Defence Systems - 3.   Whitehall Papers - 6.
  Various other publications.

Royal Warrant Holders Association   1840
- ■ 1 Buckingham Place, London, SW1E 6HR.   (hq)
  020 7828 2268   fax 020 7828 1668
  email warrants@rwha.co.uk
  http://www.royalwarrant.org
  Sec: Col Christopher Pickup
- ○ *T; to unite in one body all who hold a Royal Warrant of
  Appointment; the maintenance of the highest standards of
  craftsmanship & service
- M c 870 f

Royal Watercolour Society   (RWS)   1804
- ■ 48 Hopton St, LONDON, SE1 9JH.   (hq)
  020 7928 7521   fax 020 7928 2820
  email info@banksidegallery.com
  http://www.banksidegallery.com
  Pres: Trevor Frankland
- ▲ Registered Charity
- ○ *A; to spread the knowledge of watercolour painting; to act as
  a showcase for the best of watercolour either by members or
  annually by non-members in open competition
- Gp Friends of the RWS
- ● ET - Exhib
- M 84 i
- ¶ NL - 4; ftm only.

**Royal Welsh Agricultural Society Ltd   (Cymdeithas Amaethyddol
Frenhinol Cymru Cyf)   (RWAS)   1904**
- ■ Royal Welsh Showground, Llanelwedd, BUILTH WELLS, Powys,
  LD2 3SY.   (hq)
  01982 553683   fax 01982 553563
  email requests@rwas.co.uk   http://www.rwas.co.uk
  Chief Exec: David Walters,   Sec: Barrie Jones
- ▲ Company Limited by Guarantee
- ○ *B, *F, *H; to promote agriculture, horticulture, forestry &
  conservation in Wales
- Gp R Welsh Agricl Winter Fair; R Welsh Smallholders' & Garden
  Festival
- ● Conf - Mtgs - Exhib - Comp - Agricultural shows
- M 12,500 i
- ¶ Jnl - 1;   Show Programme; both ftm.
  Show Catalogue.

Royal Yachting Association (RYA) 1875
NR RYA House, Ensign Way, HAMBLE, Hants, SO31 4YA. (hq)
      0845 345 0400 fax 0845 345 0329
      email admin@rya.org.uk http://www.rya.org.uk
      Chief Exec: Rod Carr
▲ Company Limited by Guarantee
○ *S; to protect & promote all forms of boating
Gp Yacht racing; Power boating (incl racing); Cruising; Training;
      Windsurfing
● Mtgs - ET - Exam - Exhib - Comp - Inf
< Intl Sailing Fedn; Offshore Racing Coun; U Intle Motonautique
M c 100,000 i, 1,600 clubs, 2,300 training centres
¶ RYA News - 4; ftm. AR.

Royal Yachting Association Scotland (RYAS)
NR Caledonia House, South Gyle, EDINBURGH, EH12 9DQ.
      0131-317 7388
○ *S; the promotion of sailing in Scotland
¶ Ybk.
      no further information supplied

Royal Zoological Society of Scotland (RZSS) 1909
■ 134 Corstorphine Rd, EDINBURGH, EH12 6TS. (hq)
      0131-334 9171 fax 0131-314 0384
      http://www.edinburghzoo.org.uk
      Chief Exec: David Windmill
▲ Registered Charity
○ *L, *V; 'to promote, facilitate & encourage the study of zoology
      & kindred subjects; to foster an interest in animal life'
Gp Edinburgh Zoo; Highland Wildlife Park
● Mtgs - ET - VE - Care & conservation of wildlife
< Intl U Consvn Nature & Natural Resources; World Assn Zoos &
      Aquariums; Eur Assn Zoos & Aquaria; Fedn Zoological Gdns
      of GB & I.
M 15,000 i, 85 f
¶ Life Links (NL) - 3; free. Guide Book; £5. AR; free.

Royalist League
     see **Royal Stuart Society & Royalist League**

RSAC Motor Sport Ltd (RSAC(MS)) 1982
■ St James Business Centre, Linwood Road, PAISLEY,
      Renfrewshire, PA3 3AT. (hq)
      0141-887 9905
      http://www.rsacmotorsport.co.uk
▲ Company Limited by Guarantee
○ *S; for the development of motor sport in Scotland;
      authorisation of motoring events on the public highway in
      Scotland
Gp Development; Event organising c'ees
● Mtgs - Comp - Inf
< Motor Sports Assn UK
M 2 f, 40 clubs
      since 2004-05 **RSAC Motorsport Ltd**
¶ NL - 2. Ybk.

Rubber Stamp Manufacturers' Guild (RSMG)
NR 12 Corporation St, HIGH WYCOMBE, Bucks, HP13 6TQ. (hq)
      020 7637 7692
      email info@rsmg.org.uk http://www.rsmg.org.uk
      Sec: Angela Mackay
▲ Company Limited by Guarantee
○ *T; rubber stamps, daters, marking devices
● Conf - Mtgs - Exhib - SG - Inf
< an affiliate of the British Office Supplies & Services Fedn
M f

Rudolf Kempe Society
NR 58 Waterside, STRATFORD-upon-AVON, Warks, CV37 6BA.
      (dir/p)
      01789 298869
      Artistic Dir: Cordula Kempe
○ *D; for those interested in the life & work of Rudolf Kempe
      (1910-1976), the German conductor

Rugby Fives Association (RFA) 1927
■ 32 Ashbourne Grove, East Dulwich, LONDON, SE22 8RL.
      020 8693 0488
      email ianfuller0@lycos.com http://www.rfa.org.uk
      Gen Sec: Ian Fuller
▲ Company Limited by Guarantee
○ *S; governing body of the game of Rugby fives
● Exhib - Comp - Inf - LG
M 600 i, 100 org
¶ NL - 2; Hbk - 1; Pocket Book - 1; all ftm only.

Rugby Football League (RFL) 1895
NR Red Hall, Red Hall Lane, LEEDS, W Yorks, LS17 8NB. (hq)
      0113-232 9111
      email enquiries@rfl.uk.com
      Exec Chmn: Richard Lewis
○ *S; governing body of Rugby League football in the UK
Gp Brit Amat Rugby League Assn (BARLA)
< Rugby League Intl Fedn
M professional clubs
¶ Guide - 1; ftm.

Rugby Football Union (RFU) 1871
NR Rugby Rd, TWICKENHAM, Middx, TW1 1DS. (hq)
      0870 405 2000 fax 0870 405 2009
      http://www.rfu.com
      Chief Exec: Francis Baron
○ *S; promotion, encouragement & extension of Rugby Union
      football
● Conf - Mtgs - ET - Exam - Comp - Inf - Organisation of
      international matches
< Intl Rugby Football Bd
M 2,000 clubs, 3,500 schools, UK / 70 unions & clubs, o'seas
¶ RFU Hbk (incl Laws of the Game). Laws of the Game.
      Numerous specialised publications.

Rugby Memorabilia Society
NR PO Box 57, HEREFORD, HR1 9DR.
      http://www.rugby-memorabilia.co.uk
○ *G, *S

Rupert Bear Society
     see **Followers of Rupert**

Rural Crafts Association (RCA) 1970
■ Heights Cottage, Brook Rd, Wormley, GODALMING, Surrey,
      GU8 5UA. (hq)
      01428 682292 fax 01428 685969
      email ruralcraftsassociation@btinternet.com
      http://www.ruralcraftsassociation.co.uk
      Chief Exec: Trevor Sears
▲ Company Limited by Guarantee
○ *A; to encourage men & women to make & sell their work &
      skills; to uphold the quality of work; to encourage the growth
      of small craft businesses & provide employment on a long-
      term basis
● Exhib - Inf - Provision of a forum for the sale members' work
M 600 i, UK / 15 i, o'seas
¶ NL - 6. Directory - 1.

Rural Design & Building Association
     since 2004 **Rural & Industrial Design & Building Association
     Ltd**

© CBD Research Ltd · Beckenham · BR3 5JS · Tel 020 8650 7745 · Fax 020 8650 0768 · E-mail cbd@cbdresearch.com · www.cbdresearch.com

Rural & Industrial Design & Building Association Ltd   (RIDBA) 1956
■   ATSS House, Station Rd East, STOWMARKET, Suffolk,
    IP14 1RQ.   (hq)
    01449 676049   fax 01449 770028
    email secretary@ridba.org.uk   http://www.ridba.org.uk
    Nat Sec: A M Hutchinson
▲   Company Limited by Guarantee
Br   4
○   *F, *T; an independent organisation covering all aspects of rural
    building, both industrial & agricultural
Gp   Construction group
●   Conf - Mtgs - SG - Inf - VE - LG
<   Nat Specialist Contractors Coun; Advy C'ee on Roofwork
M   240 i, 60 f, UK / 4 i, o'seas
¶   Countryside Building - 4; ftm, £25 nm.
✕   2004 Rural Design & Building Association

Rural Shops Alliance   (RSA)   2000
NR   The Little Keep, Bridport Rd, DORCHESTER, Dorset,
    DT1 1SQ.   (hq)
    01305 259911   fax 01305 259384
    http://www.rural-shops-alliance.co.uk
    Chief Exec: Sean Carter
▲   Un-incorporated Society
○   *T; the national voice for rural retailers working to benefit
    village shops & communities; professional enhancement of
    businesses
●   Mtgs - ET - Res - SG - Inf - LG
M   7,400 i, 19 f, 34 org
✕   2005 VIRSA Rural Shops Alliance

Rural Theology Association   (RTA)   1981
■   The Vicarage, Rudston, DRIFFIELD, E Yorks, YO25 4XA.
    (hsp/b)
    01262 420313
    email stephen.cope@dial.pipex.com
    http://www.rural-theology.org.uk
    Sec: Stephen Cope
▲   Registered Charity
○   *R
●   Conf - Res - SG - Inf
M   i & org
¶   Rural Theology (Jnl) - 2; ftm, £5 nm.
    NL - 4;   LM - 1; both ftm.

ruralScotland
    the trading name of the **Association for the Protection of Rural Scotland**

Ruskin Society   1997
■   49 Hallam St, LONDON, W1W 6JP.   (hsp)
    020 7580 1894
    email cgamble@britishlibrary.net
    http://www.lancs.ac.uk/depts/ruskin/links.htm
    Hon Sec: Dr C J Gamble,   Chmn: Prof Michael Wheeler
▲   Un-incorporated Society
○   *A; to promote an interest in the life & ideals of John Ruskin
    (1819-1900) & to relate his thought to the present day
●   Mtgs - VE
<   The Ruskin Foundation (Bowland College, University of
    Lancaster)
M   130 i, UK / 5 i, o'seas
¶   NL - irreg; ftm only.

Ruskin Society of London   1985
NR   20 Parmoor Court, Summerfidle Rd, Summertown, OXFORD,
    OX2 7XB.   (hsp/b)
    01865 310987
    Hon Sec: Miss O Forbes-Madden
▲   Un-incorporated Society
○   *A, *L; to promote interest in John Ruskin (1819-1900); in his
    philosophy, artistic guidance & economic recommendations;
    his connection with his contemporaries
●   Res - SG - Inf - VE
<   Brit-Italian Soc; R Soc Literature
M   c 35 i
¶   The Ruskin Gazette - 1; ftm.

Russo-British Chamber of Commerce   (RBCC)   1916
NR   42 Southwark St, LONDON, SE1 1UN.   (hq)
    020 7403 1706
    Exec Dir: Godfrey Cromwell
▲   Company Limited by Guarantee
Br   Russia
○   *C; facilitation & promotion of trade between Russia & Britain
●   Conf - Mtgs - ET - Exam - Exhib - Comp - Expt - Inf - VE - LG
<   Russian Cham Comm & Ind
M   150 f, UK / 2,000 f, Russia
¶   Bulletin - 10/12.
    RBCC observer - 52 (email).

Rutland Agricultural Society   1830
NR   Chard Farm, Main St, TILTON on the HILL, Leics, LE7 9LF.   (hq)
    0116-259 7466
    email jo@rutlandshow.fsnet.co.uk
    Sec: Mrs J Morley
○   *F; organise Rutland county show
●   Mtgs
M   i

Rutland Boughton Music Trust   1978
■   25 Bearton Green, HITCHIN, Herts, SG5 1UN.   (hsp)
    01462 434318 & 0770 358 4152 (mobile)
    email ianrboughton@aol.com
    http://www.rutlandboughtonmusictrust.org.uk
    Admin: Ian Boughton,   Pres: Dr Vernon Handley
▲   Registered Charity
○   *D; to promote an interest in the composer Rutland Boughton
    (1878-1960) by encouraging performances & sponsoring
    recordings of his finest works
●   Mtgs - Exhib - Lib
M   150 i
¶   NL - 1/2; free.

Ryeland Flock Book Society   (RFBS)   1900
■   Holly Cottage, Redmarley, GLOUCESTER, GL19 3NB.
    (hq/hsp)
    01531 650400
    Sec: Mrs Anne M Jones
▲   Company Limited by Guarantee
○   *B
●   Mtgs - Exhib - Inf
<   Nat Sheep Assn
M   300 i, UK / 7 i, o'seas
¶   NL - 4;   AR - 1; both ftm only.
    Hbk; ftm, £5.10 nm.   Flock Books - 1; ftm, £5. nm.

SAA (Society for All Artists) 1992

■ PO Box 50, NEWARK, Notts, NG23 5GY.   (hq)
      01949 844050   fax 01949 844051
      http://www.saa.co.uk
      Sec: Linda Phillips
▲ Un-incorporated Society
○ *A; to inform, encourage & inspire all who want to paint, from
      the complete beginner to those whose profession depends on
      it
● Exhib - Comp - Inf
M 15,063 i, 178 clubs, UK / 511 i, o'seas
¶ Paint (NL) - 6;   SAA Home Shopping Catalogue - 4; both ftm
      only.

SACRO, safeguarding communities - reducing offending
(SACRO) 1971

NR 1 Broughton Market, EDINBURGH, EH3 6NU.   (hq)
      0131-624 7270
      Chief Exec: Susan Matheson
▲ Company Limited by Guarantee; Registered Charity
Br 10 (all in Scotland)
○ *K, *W; to make communities safer in Scotland by reducing
      conflict & offending & by influencing change in criminal
      justice & social policy
Gp Supported accommodation; Throughcare; Bail; Mediation &
      reparation; Young offenders; Community mediation;
      Groupwork services
● Conf - ET - Inf - Lib - LG - Service provision
M 17 i
¶ SACROsanct (in-house NL for staff & volunteers only) - 4.
      Conference Papers - 1.   Strategic Plan - 2 yrly.
      McClintock Lecture Series - 1.   AR.

SAD Association (SADA) 1987

■ PO Box 989, STEYNING, W Sussex, BN44 3HG.   (mail)
      01903 814942   fax 01903 879939
      http://www.sada.org.uk address
      Sec: Marie Walters
▲ Registered Charity
○ *W; to offer advice & support for sufferers of Seasonal Affective
      Disorder (SAD)
● Inf
< Mind; R Coll of Psychiatry
M c 2,250 i, UK / i, o'seas
¶ NL - 3; ftm.

Safe Home Income Plans (SHIP) 1994

■ 20 College St, ST ALBANS, Herts, AL3 4PN.   (hsp)
      01727 836063   fax 01772 840280
      email info@ship-ltd.org   http://www.ship-ltd.org
      Sec: I M McNeill
▲ Company Limited by Guarantee
○ *T; a non-profit trade association dedicated to safe equity
      release plans including lifetime mortgages & home
      reversions
● Mtgs - Stat - Inf - LG
M 18 f

Safe Speed

NR Coast View, Hunting Hill, near TAIN, Ross-shire, IV19 1PE.
      01862 893030
      Founder: Paul Smith
○ *K; campaigning for the removal of speed cameras, for
      improved driving standards & safe speeds set by drivers
M 150 i

Safety Assessment Federation   (SAFed) 1995

■ Nutmeg House, 60 Gainsford St, LONDON, SE1 2NY.   (hq)
      020 7403 0987   fax 020 7403 0137
      email info@safed.co.uk
      Chief Exec: Richard Hulmes
▲ Company Limited by Guarantee
○ *T; representing companies that undertake independent safety
      inspection & certification of engineering & manufacturing
      plant & equipment
Gp SAFed Type Approval Service (STAS)
● Mtgs - Stat - LG
< Eur Confedn of Orgs for Testing, Inspection, Certification &
      Prevention (CEOC)
M 13 f, UK / 2 f, o'seas
¶ Guidelines on/for:
      the Thorough Examination & Testing of Lifts (LG1).
      Periodicity of Examinations of Pressure Systems
         (PSG1).
      the Periodic Testing & Examination of Fixed Low
         Voltage Electrical Installations at Quarries.
      Shell Boilers - Guidelines for the Examination of:
      Longitudinal Seams of Shell Boilers.
      Welding Procedures & Welding Guidelines on Approval Testing.

Safety & Reliability Society 1980

NR Clayton House, 59 Piccadilly, MANCHESTER, M1 2AQ.   (hq)
      0161-228 7824
      Sec: Prof M Preston
Br 5
○ *P; to provide a forum for the exchange of information on
      safety & reliability engineering; to establish professional &
      educational standards for safety & reliability engineers

Sailing Barge Association (SBA)

NR PO Box 5191, BOURNEMOUTH, Dorset, BH1 3WZ.
      (mail/address)
      01202 552582   fax 01202 552582
      email sba@ffbs.co.uk
      http://www.sailingbargeassociation.co.uk
      Sec: F Morris
▲ Un-incorporated Society
○ *T; to keep sailing barges working
M 28 i, 13 f, 3 org
¶ NL - 4; ftm only.

Saint

In the entries below Saint is put in full (rather than St) in order
to keep them in their correct alphabetical order in the
directory.

Saint Albans District Chamber of Commerce 1990

■ Suite 19 Stanta Business Centre, 3 Soothouse Spring,
      ST ALBANS, Herts, AL3 6PF.   (hq)
      01727 863054   fax 01727 851200
      email office@stalbans-chamber.co.uk
      http://www.stalbans-chamber.co.uk
      Mgr: Tonia Harvey
▲ Company Limited by Guarantee
○ *C
● Mtgs - Conf - Inf
M 200 f & org
¶ NL;   Ybk - 1; both ftm only.

Saint Albans & Hertfordshire Architectural & Archaeological Society (SAHAAS) 1845

■ 24 Monks Horton Way, ST ALBANS, Herts, AL4 9AF. (hsp)
01727 851734
Hon Sec: B R Hanlon
▲ Registered Charity
○ *L; to preserve, record & disseminate information about sites & buildings of archaeological & historical importance as well as historical documents & records
Gp Archaeology; Architecture & local history; 17th century research
● Conf - Mtgs - Res - Exhib - SG - Inf - Lib - PL - VE
< Coun Brit Archaeology; Brit Assn Local History
M 500 i, 10 org, UK / 5 i, o'seas
¶ Hertfordshire Archaeology - 1; ftm, prices vary nm.
NL - 3; ftm only.
History of the Society 1845-1995; £2 m, £3 nm.
Research Reports - irreg; prices vary.

Saint Andrew's Ambulance Association (StAAA) 1882

■ St Andrew's House, 48 Milton St, GLASGOW, G4 0HR. (hq)
0141-332 4031   fax 0141-332 6582
email firstaid@staaa.org.uk   http://www.firstaid.org.uk
Chief Exec: Brendan Healy
▲ Registered Charity
Br 13
○ *W; the premier provider of first aid training & services in Scotland
● ET - Provision of first aid cover, services & supplies at events
M 2,000 i
¶ The Bulletin - 2/4; ftm only.   Emergency Booklet; £1.50.
First Aid Manual (8th edition); £9.90.
History of St Andrew's Ambulance Association; £4.99.

Saint Andrew Society 1902

NR PO Box 84, EDINBURGH, EH3 8LG.   (mail) add
○ *K, *N; the society acts as an international 'umbrella' (to which other Scottish societies are affiliated) to uphold the rights & privileges of Scotland & of the Scottish people; to support the study of Scottish languages, history & arts
● Mtgs - Inf - VE - St Andrew's Day dinner
M 150 i
¶ NL - 1.

Saint Dunstan's 1915

§ 12-14 Harcourt St, LONDON, W1H 4HD.   (hq)
020 7723 5021
email enquiries@st-dunstans.co.uk
http://www.st-dunstans.co.uk
Rehabilitation, training & settlement of men & women blinded on war service

Saint Helens Chamber Ltd 1989

■ Technology Campus, ST HELENS, Merseyside, WA9 1UE. (hq)
01744 742000   fax 01744 742001
http://www.sthelenschamber.com
Chief Exec: Kath Boullen
▲ Company Limited by Guarantee
○ *C
● Conf - Mtgs - ET - Inf - Business advice
< Brit Chams Comm
M 1,100 f
¶ Comment - 3;   Comment Extra - 8;   AR; all free.

Saint John Ambulance 1887

NR 27 St John's Lane, LONDON, EC1M 4BU.   (hq)
0870 0104 950
Chief Exec: Roger Holmes
▲ Company Limited by Guarantee; Registered Charity
Br 1917 divns, 48 county hqs; 42 o'seas
○ *W; the first aid, transport & care charity; to provide caring services in support of community needs
● Conf - Mtgs - ET - Exam - Comp - SG - Inf - Lib - LG
M 50,000 i, UK / 250,000 i, o'seas
¶ St John Life - 4.

Saintpaulia & Houseplant Society 1956

■ 33 Church Rd, Newbury Park, ILFORD, Essex, IG2 7ET.   (hsp)
020 8590 3710
Hon Sec & Treas: Mrs F B F Dunningham
▲ Un-incorporated Society
Br 2
○ *H; for all people interested in growing plants in their homes; special interest is shown in Saintpaulias (African violets) & the very wide range of houseplants now available
● Mtgs - Comp - Lib - Annual show
< Gesneriad Soc Intl Inc; R Horticl Soc; African Violet Soc of America; Amer Gloxinia & Gesneriad Soc; African Violet Soc of Australia
M 550 i, UK / 34 i, o'seas
¶ Bulletin - 4; ftm only.
Success with Houseplants (11 leaflets on specific plants); 20p each.

Salers Cattle Society of the United Kingdom & Ireland 1986

■ Brook House Farm, Norbury, WHITCHURCH, Shropshire, SY13 4HY.   (sp)
01948 667223   fax 01948 667448
email johncrowe@salers-cattle-society.co.uk
http://www.salers-cattle-society.co.uk
Sec: John M Crowe
▲ Company Limited by Guarantee
○ *B
● Conf - Mtgs - Exhib - Comp - Inf - VE
< Intl Salers Fedn; Nat Beef Assn
M 180 i
¶ Salers Jnl - 1; free.
NL - 4;   Herd Book - 1; both ftm only.

Sales Institute of Ireland

IRL 68 Merrion Sq, DUBLIN 2, Republic of Ireland.
353 (1) 662 6904   fax 353 (1) 662 6968
email info@salesinstitute.ie   http://www.salesinstitute.ie
Chief Exec: Michael J Rogers
○ *P

Sales Promotion Consultants Association
since 2002 **Marketing Communications Consultants Association**

Salisbury & District Chamber of Commerce & Industry (1912) 1012

■ 7 Scots Lane, SALISBURY, Wilts, SP1 3TR.   (hq)
01722 322708   fax 01722 341508
email mail@salisburychamber.org.uk
http://www.salisburychamber.org.uk
Chief Exec: Mrs Delia Henbury
▲ Company Limited by Guarantee
○ *C
● Mtgs - ET - Exhib - Inf - VE - LG - Networking - Economic partner with local government - Lobbying
M 350 f
¶ Journal Business - 4;   enewsletter - 12; both free.

Salmon & Trout Association (S&TA) 1903

■ Fishmongers' Hall, London Bridge, LONDON, EC4R 9EL. (hq)
020 7283 5838   fax 020 7626 5137
email hq@salmon-trout.org
http://www.salmon-trout,org
Exec Dir: Paul Knight
▲ Company Limited by Guarantee
○ *S; safeguarding the salmon & trout fisheries of the UK & game fishing &angling
M i, f & org

Salt Manufacturers' Association   (SMA)   1970
NR   PO Box 125, KENDAL, Cumbria, LA8 8XA.   (hsp)
    01539 568005   fax 01539 568999
    http://www.saltsense.co.uk
    Sec: Peter R Sherratt
▲   Un-incorporated Society
○   *T; promoting the use of salt for domestic, industrial, catering,
    & de-icing uses; to monitor related medical & environmental
    issues
●   Mtgs - Res - Stat - Inf - LG - Promoting the use of salt
<   Eur Salt Producers Assn; Salt Inst (USA); Food & Drink Fedn
M   6 f
¶   Facts on Salt; free.

Saltire Society   1936
■   9 Fountain Close, 22 High St, EDINBURGH, EH1 1TF.   (hq)
    0131-556 1836   fax 0131-557 1675
    email saltire@saltiresociety.org.uk
    http://www.saltiresociety.org.uk
    Admin: Mrs Kathleen Munro
▲   Registered Charity (Scotland)
Br   9
○   *K; preservation of the best in Scottish tradition &
    encouragement of development of Scottish cultural life
Gp   Publications; Housing design; Education; Literature; Arts &
    crafts; Civil engineering; Science
●   Conf - Mtgs - Exhib - SG - Scots Songs
M   1,057 i, 35 f
¶   NL - 2;   AR; both ftm.

Salvage Association
§   37-39 Lime St, LONDON, EC3M 7AY.
    020 7234 9120   fax 020 7234 9168
    email salvage@wreckage.org
    http://www.wreckage.org
    The survey of damage to merchant ships' hulls, machinery &
    equipment in which marine underwriters may be concerned

Salvation Army   1865
§   101 Newington Causeway, LONDON, SE1 6BN.   (hq)
    020 7367 4500   fax 020 7367 4728
    email webmajor@salvationarmy.org.uk
    http://www.salvationarmy.org.uk
    A Christian, international relief agency, social service & medical
    educational charity

The Samaritans   1953
§   The Upper Mill, Kingston Rd, EWELL, Surrey, KT17 2AF.   (hq)
    020 8394 8300   fax 020 8394 8301
    email admin@samaritans.org.uk
    http://www.samaritans.org.uk
    Chief Exec: David King
    To help the suicidal & despairing by listening & befriending

SAMM National (Support after Murder & Manslaughter)
■   Cranmer House, 39 Brixton Rd, LONDON, SW9 6DZ.   (hq)
    020 7735 3838   fax 020 7735 3900
    email samm@victimsupport.org.uk
    http://www.samm.org.uk
    Training & Devt Officer: Rose Dixon
▲   Registered Charity
○   *W; to offer understanding & support to families & friends who
    have been bereaved as a result of murder & manslaughter,
    through the mutual support of others who have suffered a
    similar tragedy
●   ET - Inf - LG
M   2,000 i
¶   Report & Financial Statement.

SANE   (SANE)   1986
■   Cityside House (1st floor), 40 Adler St, LONDON, E1 1EE.
    (hq)
    020 7375 1002   fax 020 7375 2162
    email info@sane.org.uk   http://www.sane.org.uk
    Chief Exec: Marjorie Wallace
▲   Registered Charity
○   *K, *W; to raise awareness of mental illness & campaign to
    improve services; to initiate & fund research into the causes
    of serious mental illness; to provide information & support to
    those experiencing mental health problems through its
    helpline, SANELINE
Gp   SANELINE: 0845 767 8000 (1200-2300 hrs Mon-Fri, 1200-
    1800 hrs Sat-Sun)
    Prince of Wales International Centre for SANE Research,
    Warneford Hospital, Oxford
●   Res - Inf - Helpline
¶   SANE News - NL;   Medical Methods of Treatment;
    Talking Treatments;   Schizophrenia;
    Manic Depression;   Phobias;   Obsessions;
    Depression;   Anxiety;   all free.

**Sanitary Medical Disposal Services Association   (SMDSA)
1992**
■   111 Wollaston Rd, IRCHESTER, Northants, NN29 7DD.   (hsb)
    01933 311223
    Sec: Martin Foulser
▲   Company Limited by Guarantee
○   *T; interests of companies involved in the collection & disposal
    of sanitary & medical waste materials
M   f

**Sapere (Society for the Advancement of Philosophical Enquiry &
Reflection in Education)   (SAPERE)   1992**
NR   Westminster Institute of Education, Oxford Brookes University,
    Harcourt Hill Campus, OXFORD, OX2 9AT.   (hq)
    01865 488340   fax 01865 488356
    email admin@sapere.net   http://www.sapere.net
    C'ee Chmn: Paul Cleghorn
▲   Registered Charity
○   *E; to promote philosophy for children; to train teachers
Gp   Education; Thinking skills; Teaching; Emotional literacy;
    Citizenship education
●   Conf - ET - Res - Inf - Teacher training - Projects - Courses
<   Intl Coun for Philosophical Inquiry with Children
M   650 i
¶   NL - 4; ftm only.

Sarcoidosis & Interstitial Lung Association   (SILA)   1993
■   c/o Chest Clinic Office, 2nd floor Admin Block, King's College
    Hospital, Denmark Hill, LONDON, SE5 9RS.
    020 7237 5912 (hsp)   (mail/address)
    email info@sarcoidosis.org.uk   http://www.sila.org.uk
    Hon Sec: Heather Walker
▲   Registered Charity25
○   *W; to raise public awareness of sarcoidosis & the effect it has
    on sufferers, patients & friends; to give support & practical
    advice to those affected; to promote research & to identify
    those most at risk
●   Mtgs - Res - Stat - Inf
<   Eur Assn of Patients Orgs for Sarcoidosis & Other
    Granulomatous Disorders (EPOS); Sarcoidosis organisations
    in Germany, Netherlands, Switzerland
M   130 i
¶   NL - 3; ftm, (free for sae nm).
    So You Have Sarcoidosis! by Rose Bartholomew-Thomas;
    ftm, £1 nm.

© CBD Research Ltd · Beckenham · BR3 5JS · Tel 020 8650 7745 · Fax 020 8650 0768 · E-mail cbd@cbdresearch.com · www.cbdresearch.com

Satellite & Cable Broadcasters' Group (SCGB) 1983
- ■ 29 Harley St, LONDON, W1G 9QR. (hq)
  020 7016 2608
  Exec Dir: Charlotte Wright
- ▲ Un-incorporated Society
- ○ *T; for satellite & cable programme providers
- ● Mtgs - Res - LG
- < Advertising Assn; Brit Screen Advy Coun; Skillset
- M 20 f

Saudi British Society 1986
- NR Green Gables, Clee Hill Rd, TENBURY WELLS, Worcs,
  WR15 8HJ. (sp)
  email secretary@saudibritishsociety.org.uk
  Sec: Lisa Bowcock
  Hon Sec: Ionis Thompson
- ▲ Registered Charity
- Br Saudi Arabia
- ○ *X; to promote Saudi-British understanding & educational &
  cultural contacts
- ● Mtgs - ET
- M 200 i, 50 f, UK / 50 i, 8 f, o'seas

Save Britain's Heritage (SAVE)]975
- ■ 70 Cowcross St, LONDON, EC1M 6EJ. (hq)
  020 7253 3500
  Sec: Adam Wilkinson
- ▲ Registered Charity
- ○ *K; to campaign for the preservation & re-use of historic
  buildings; to prevent their loss through demolition or neglect
- ● Res - Exhib
- M c 350 i
- ¶ NL - 1; ftm only.
  SAVE Britain's Heritage 1975-2005: thirty years of
  campaigning; £20.
  Who Cares Wins: the Buildings at Risk Register (2004); £12.
  Publications list available.

Save British Science Society
    since 2005 **Campaign for Science & Engineering in the UK**

Save our Building Societies (SoBS) 2000
- NR 8 Belmont Court, Belmont Hill, ST ALBANS, Herts, AL1 1RB.
  (hsp)
  01727 847370
  email info@sobs.org.uk   http://www.sobs.org.uk
  Coordinator: Bob Goodall
- ○ *K; to save mutual building societies from demutualisation; a
  mutual organisation is owned by its members -
  demutualisation turns it into a plc/bank with shareholders,
  thus changing the ethos from serving its members to making
  profits for shareholders
- ● ET - LG - Lobbying - Publicity - Information resource on
  mutuality & related issues
- M 1,000 i
- ¶ NL - irreg;   Press releases; both free.

Save our Parsonages (SOP) 1994
- ■ Flat Z / 12-18 Bloomsbury St, LONDON, WC1B 3QA. (dir/p)
  020 7636 4884
  email ajsjennings@hotmail.com
  Dir: Anthony J S Jennings
- ▲ Un-incorporated Society
- ○ *K; a support group for historic, or traditional, parsonages
  remaining in church use
- ● Conf - Mtgs - Res - Inf
- < Rural Theology Assn; Engl Clergy Assn
- M 150 i, UK / 1 i, o'seas
- ¶ NL - 1; ftm, £2 nm.

Schizophrenia Association of Great Britain (SAGB) 1970
- NR International Schizophrenia Centre, Bryn Hyfryd, The Crescent,
  BANGOR, Gwynedd, LL57 2AG. (hq)
  01248 354048   fax 01248 353659
  email info@sagb.co.uk   http://www.sagb.co.uk
  Hon Sec: Mrs Gwynneth Hemmings
- ▲ Company Limited by Guarantee; Registered Charity
- ○ *W; to carry out research into the biochemical causes of
  schizophrenia - welfare & treatment (including dietary factors)
- ● Res - Inf - Helpline
- M 2,500 i, 100 f, 900 org, UK / 400 i, 30 org, o'seas
- ¶ NL - 2; ftm.   Reports & leaflets.
  Large free information pack.

Schizophrenia Ireland
- IRL 38 Blessington St, DUBLIN 7, Republic of Ireland.
  353 (1) 860 1620   fax 353 (1) 860 1602
  email info@sirl.ie   http://www.sirl.ie
  Dir: John Saunders
- ○ *W
- ✕ 1997 Schizophrenia Association of Ireland

School Journey Association (SJA) 1911
- § 48 Cavendish Rd, LONDON, SW12 0DH. (hq)
  0845 658 1063   fax 0845 658 1064
  A non-membership body promoting travel & educational
  opportunities to schools within the UK (& help with arranging
  visits in the UK & abroad) in order to bring a greater
  understanding of the languages, history, architecture &
  literature of other countries & a compassionate
  understanding of other cultures

School Library Association (SLA) 1937
- ■ Unit 2 Lotmead Business Village, Lotmead Farm, Wanborough,
  SWINDON, Wilts, SN4 0UY. (hq)
  0870 777 0979   fax 0870 777 0987
  email info@sla.org.uk   http://www.sla.org.uk
  Chief Exec: Kathy Lemaire
- ▲ Company Limited by Guarantee; Registered Charity
- Br 15
- ○ *E; promotion of development of the school library as central to
  literacy & the curriculum
- ● Conf - Mtgs - ET - Publications - Advisory service
- < Intl Assn School Libraries (IASL); Intl Fedn Library Assns (IFLA)
- M 3,500 i
- ¶ The School Librarian (reviewing jnl) - 4; ftm, £85 nm.
  Practical guidelines.   Booklists.

Schoolhouse Home Education Association
- NR PO Box 18044, GLENROTHES, Fife, KY7 9AD.
  01307 463120
- ○ *E; home education in Scotland

Schools Music Association (SMA) 1938
- ■ 71 Margaret Rd, NEW BARNET, Herts, EN4 9NT. (hsp)
  020 8440 6919   fax 020 8440 6919
  email maxwellpryce@educamas.free-online.co.uk
  Hon Sec: J Maxwell Pryce
- ▲ Registered Charity
- Br 14 regions
- ○ *D, *E; to promote the musical education of young people by
  supporting those who work with them
- ● Conf - Mtgs - ET - Res - SG - Inf
- < Inc Soc Musicians (ISM), Music Educ Coun (MEC)
- M i, f & org
- ¶ Bulletin - 3;   Register of Members - 1;   AR; all ftm only.

Schubert Society of Britain

- ■ German YMCA, 35 Craven Terrace, LONDON, W2 3EL.   (sb)
    020 7723 9276   fax 020 7706 2870
    email y-services@german-ymca.org.uk
    http://www.german-ymca.org.uk
    Sec: Udo Bauer
- ▲ Registered Charity
- ○ *D; for those interested in the life & works of the Austrian composer Franz Schubert (1797-1828)
- ● Schubertiades - Gives young musicians an opportunity to perform in London
- < sponsored by the German YMCA in London
- M 60 i, 5 org
- ¶ Concert programmes.

Schumacher UK
    see **Doctor E F Schumacher Society**

Science, Engineering & Manufacturing Technologies Alliance

- NR 14 Upton Rd, WATFORD, Herts, WD18 0JT.
    01923 238441
    http://www.semta.org.uk
    Chief Exec: Philip Whiteman
- ○ *T

Science, Technology, Engineering, Medicine Public Relations Association   (STEMPRA)   1992

- NR c/o Dr Faye Stokes, SGM, Marlborough House, Basingstoke Rd, Spencers Wood, READING, Berks, RG7 1AG.
    0118-988 1843
    Sec: Dr Faye Stokes
- ▲ Un-incorporated Society
- ○ *P; for press & public relations people who work in, with, or for, all the scientific societies
- ● Mtgs - ET - VE
- M 88 i
- ¶ Newsletter - 4.

Scientific Exploration Society Ltd   (SES)   1969

- NR Expedition Base, Motcombe, SHAFTESBURY, Dorset, SP7 9PB. (hq)
    01747 853353   fax 01747 851351
    email brenda@ses-explore.org
    http://www.ses-explore.org
    Exec Sec: Lucy Thompson; Chmn: Col John Blashford-Snell
- ▲ Registered Charity
- ○ *L; 'a leading organisation in the field of scientific exploration & endeavour'
- ● Mtgs - Res
- M i, f & org
- ¶ Sesame (Jnl) - 2; ftm only.

Scientific Instrument Society   (SIS)   1983

- ■ 90 The Fairway, SOUTH RUISLIP, Middx, HA4 0SQ.   (hq)
    http://www.sis.org.uk
    Exec Officer: Peter Thomas
- ▲ Registered Charity
- ○ *G, *L; for all interested in scientific instruments from antiques to the latest electronic devices (collectors, antiques trade, museum staff, professional historians & enthusiasts)
- ● Conf - Mtgs - VE - Lectures
- M 250 i, UK / 350 i, o'seas
- ¶ Bulletin - 4; ftm.

Scientists for Global Responsibility   (SGR)   1992

- NR P O Box 473, FOLKESTONE, CT20 1GS.   (hq)
    07771 883696
    Dir: Dr Stuart Parkinson
- ▲ Un-incorporated Society
- ○ *K, *Q; promoting ethical science & technology
- Gp Arms & arms control; Climate change & energy; Genetic engineering; Science policy; Population, consumption & values
- ● Conf - Res - SG - Inf
- < Intl Network of Engrs & Scientists for Global Responsibility (INES)
- M 600 i, UK / 25 i, o'seas
- ¶ NL - 3.   AR.   Publications list available.

Scleroderma Society   1982

- NR 3 Caple Rd, LONDON, NW10 8AB.   (chmn/p)
    020 8961 4912
    Chmn: Kim Fligelstone
- ○ *W
- M 300 i
- ¶ NL - 4; ftm only.

Scoliosis Association (UK)   (SAUK)   1981

- ■ 2 Ivebury Court, 323-327 Latimer Rd, LONDON, W10 6RA. (hq)
    020 8964 5343
    Chmn: Stephanie Clark
- ▲ Registered Charity
- Br Regional
- ○ *W; to put people with scoliosis (curvature of the spine) in touch with each other; to make available to parents of children with scoliosis the experience of others in this field
- ● Mtgs - Inf
    Helpline: 020 8964 1166
- M 2,000 i, UK / 50 i, o'seas
- ¶ NL - 2.   NL Index.   AR.
    Scoliosis Hbk.   Shona's Story.
    Clothes to Suit.   A Twist of Fate.

Scope   1952

- NR 6 Market Rd, LONDON, N7 9PW.   (hq)
    020 7619 7100
    Co Sec: Sue Bell
- ▲ Company Limited by Guarantee; Registered Charity
- Br 240 local groups (not Scotland)
- ○ *E, *W; (for England & Wales only) to offer assistance for the welfare, treatment, education, employment & advancement of people with cerebral palsy (spasticity); to support parents & carers
- ● Conf - Res - Exhib - Inf - Lib - Campaigns
    Helpline: 0808 800 3333
- < Scot Coun for Spastics; N Ireland Coun for Orthopaedic Devt
- M 208 groups
- ¶ Disability Now - 12; ftm.   Reports.   AR; free.
    Publications list available.

Scotch Half Bred Association   (SHBA)

- NR Greenend Farm, St Boswells, MELROSE, Roxburghshire, TD6 9ES.   (chmn/p)
    01835 824207
    Sec: Nesta Todd
- ○ *B
- ● Promotional
- < Nat Sheep Assn
- M 50 f

© CBD Research Ltd · Beckenham · BR3 5JS · Tel 020 8650 7745 · Fax 020 8650 0768 · E-mail cbd@cbdresearch.com · www.cbdresearch.com

Scotch Malt Whisky Society Ltd   (SMWS)   1983
NR   The Vaults, 87 Giles St, EDINBURGH, EH6 6BZ.   (hq)
        0131-554 3451
        Chmn: Willie Philips,   Managing Dir: Richard Gordon
▲   Company Limited by Guarantee
Br   2; 6
○   *G; club for anyone who enjoys single malt whisky
●   Mtgs - ET - Inf - Whisky tastings - Whisky school
M   15,000 i, UK / 6,000 i, o'seas
¶   NL - 3;   Bottling List - 6;   Hbk (guide); all ftm only.

Scotch Mule Association
NR   Bogside Cottage, Ochiltree, CUMNOCK, KA18 2QF.   (hsp)
        01292 591821
        Sec / Treas: George W Allan
▲   Registered Charity
○   *B; to promote the breed of Mule sheep
●   Mtgs - Exhib - Inf
<   Nat Sheep Assn
M   400 i
¶   NL - 1; free.

Scotch Whisky Association   (SWA)   1943
◼   20 Atholl Crescent, EDINBURGH, EH3 8HF.   (hq)
        0131-222 9200   fax 0131-222 9237
        email contact@swa.org.uk
        http://www.scotch-whisky.org.uk
        Chief Exec: Gavin Hewitt
▲   Company Limited by Guarantee
Br   2
○   *T; protection promotion of Scotch whisky; including legal
        protection, public affairs, international trade issues &
        promoting responsible attitudes to alcohol
●   Conf - Mtgs - ET - Res - Exhib - Stat - Expt - Inf - VE - LG
<   Confédn Eur des Producteurs de Spiritueux (CEPS); CBI; Scot
        Coun Devt & Ind; Scotland Europa
M   58 f
¶   Scotch Whisky: questions & answers.   Annual Review - 1.
        Scotch at a Glance.   Statistical report - 1.
        Distilleries to Visit Guide.   Distillery Map - 1.
        Scotch Whisky: matured to be enjoyed responsibly.

Scotland-Russia Forum   2003
◼   50 Marchmont Crescent, EDINBURGH, EH9 1HE.
        0131-662 9149
        email scotrussforum@blueyonder.co.uk
        http://www.scotlandrussiaforum.org
        Dir: Jenny Carr
○   *X

** Scotland Russia Society   1945
        Organisation lost: see Introduction paragraph 3

ScotlandIS   2000
NR   Geddes House (Suite 41), LIVINGSTON, W Lothian,
        EH54 6GU.   (hq)
        01506 472200
        Exec Dir: Polly Purvis
▲   Company Limited by Guarantee
Br   2
○   *T; design & development of Scottish quality software
Gp   Quality; Aberdeen area; Advanced technologies; Year 2000
●   Conf - Mtgs - ET - Res - Exhib - Comp - SG - Stat - Expt - Inf -
        LG
M   344 f

Scots Language Society   (SLS)   1972
◼   Blackford Lodge, Blackford, AUCHTERADER, Perthshire,
        PH4 1QP.   (admin/p)
        01764 682315   fax 0870 428 5086
        email mail@lallans.co.uk   http://www.lallans.co.uk
        Admin: John Law
▲   Registered Charity
Br   2
○   *L; celebration & preservation of the Scots language
●   Conf - Mtgs - Res - Comp - Inf
<   Scot Poetry Lib Assn
M   350 i, 30 org, UK / 50 i, 10 org, o'seas
¶   Lallans (Jnl, in Scots Language) - 2; ftm, £6.50 each nm.

Scottish Adoption Association Ltd   1923
§   16 Constitution St, Leith, EDINBURGH, EH6 7DF.   (hq)
        0131-553 5060   fax 0131-553 6422
        http://www.scottishadoption.org
        A charity concerned with counselling pregnant women & the
        placement of young babies & young children for adoption

Scottish Aeromodellers Association   (SAA)   1943
NR   PO Box 1621, JOHNSTONE, Renfrewshire, PA9 1YN.   (mail)
        http://www.saaweb.org.uk add
        Sec: Stuart Savage
○   *G; flying radio controlled model aircraft
●   Mtgs - Exam - Exhib - Comp - Inf - VE
<   Brit Model Flying Assn; Scottish Sports Council
M   1,800 i in 55 clubs, UK / 150 i, o'seas
¶   Airtime - 4; ftm.

Scottish Agricultural Arbiters Association   (SAAA)   1926
NR   c/o Princes Exchange, 1 Earl Grey St, EDINBURGH, EH3 9EE.
        (asa)
        0131-228 8111
        Sec: M G Strang Steel
▲   Un-incorporated Society
○   *F, *P; professional interests of agricultural arbiters & valuers
Gp   Agricultural arbiters & valuers
●   Conf - Mtgs - ET - LG
M   243 i, 5 org
¶   LM - 1; ftm only.

Scottish Agricultural Organisation Society Ltd   (SAOS)   1905
◼   The Rural Centre, West Mains, Ingliston, NEWBRIDGE,
        Midlothian, EH28 8NZ.   (hq)
        0131-472 4100
        Chief Exec: James Graham
○   *F, *N, *T; to promote agriculture & rural cooperation in
        Scotland
M   15 i (personal), 80 i (business)
¶   NL - 4;   AR (incl LM) - 1.

Scottish Amateur Boxing Association
        since 2000 **Amateur Boxing Scotland**

Scottish Amateur Brass Band Association
        since 2002-03 **Scottish Brass Band Association**

Scottish Amateur Football Association   (SAFA)   1909
NR   Hampden Park, GLASGOW, G42 9DB.   (hq)
        0141-620 4550
        Sec: Hugh Knapp
○   *S
Gp   Association football as played by amateurs: Saturday, Sunday,
        Youth, Summer
●   Mtgs - Comp - Inf
<   Scot Football Assn
M   65,000 i, 3,000 clubs
¶   Hbk - 1.   AR; ftm only.

Scottish Amateur Music Association   (SAMA)   1956

§   18 Craigton Crescent, ALVA, Clackmannanshire, FK12 5DS.
     (hsp)
     01259 760249
     email secretary@sama.org.uk   http://www.sama.org.uk
     Hon Sec: Miss Margaret W Simpson
▲   Registered Charity
     a non-membership body promoting amateur music making in
         Scotland; courses are run annually for the National Youth
         Brass Band of Scotland, the National Youth Wind Ensemble
         of Scotland, the National Youth String Orchestra of Scotland
         & Training School, the Scots Fiddle School, String Chamber
         Music Weekend, & the National Recorder School of Scotland.

Scottish Amateur Rowing Association   (SARA)   1881

NR   41 Dumyat Ave, Cambuspark, Tullibody,
       CLACKMANNANSHIRE, FK10 2RY.
       Pres: Mary Massaro
▲   Un-incorporated Society
○   *S; governing body for rowing in Scotland
●   Conf - Mtgs - Exam - Comp - VE
<   represented internationally by the Amateur Rowing Association
       (ARA)
M   32 clubs
¶   Rowing Action - 4; free (donations from nm please).

Scottish Amateur Swimming Association
     since 2002-03 **Scottish Swimming Ltd**

Scottish Anglers National Association   (SANA)   1880

■   The National Game Angling Academy, The Pier, Loch Leven,
       KINROSS, KY13 8UF.   (hq)
       01577 861116   fax 01577 864769
       email admin@sana.org.uk   http://www.sana.org.uk
       Sec/Treas: Douglas Beckett
▲   Un-incorporated Society
○   *S; governing body for game angling in Scotland
●   Conf - Mtgs - ET - Exam - Exhib - Comp - Inf - LG
<   FIPS Mouche; Scot Sports Assn
M   195 i, 20 f, 420 org
¶   Alliance News (NL) - 4; free.
     SANA Hbk - 1; ftm,£1.20 nm.

Scottish Archery Association   (SAA)   1949

■   48 Ministers Park, KITTOCH MUIR, East Kilbride, G74 5BX.
       (hsp)
       01355 268211
       email ronamather@btopenworld.com
       http://www.scottisharchery.org.uk
       Hon Sec: Rona E Mather
▲   Un-incorporated Society
○   *S; to promote the sport of archery incl target, field, flight, clout
       & all types of bow including Olympic, compound & longbow
Gp   Archery in schools; Disabled archery
●   Mtgs - Comp
<   Grand Nat Archery Soc (GNAS)
M   1,300 i
¶   AR - 1; ftm only.   [see website]

Scottish Assessors' Association   (SAA)   1854

■   c/o Lanarkshire Valuation Joint Board, North Stand, Cadzow
       Avenue, HAMILTON, Lanarks, ML3 0LU.   (sb)
       01698 476078   fax 01698 476076
       email assessors@southlanarkshire.gov.uk
       http://www.saa.gov.uk
       Sec: Michael A Lithgow
▲   Un-incorporated Society
○   *P; to promote uniformity in operating the provisions of the
       Lands Valuation (Scotland) Acts & the Representation of the
       People Acts
●   Conf - Mtgs - LG
M   94 i

Scottish Association for Country Sports   (SACS)   1994

■   River Lodge, Trochry, DUNKELD, Perthshire, PH8 0DY.   (hq)
       01350 723259   fax 01350 723259
       http://www.sacs.org.uk
       Dir: David S P Cant
▲   Un-incorporated Society
○   *K, *S; political representation for all those involved in country
       sports in Scotland & Northern Ireland who use gun, rifle, rod,
       horse, hawk/falcon, or gundog
●   Exhib - Inf - LG
<   Scot Countryside Inf Exchange
M   8,000 i, UK / c 500 i, o'seas
¶   SACS Magazine - 4.

Scottish Association of Directors of Leisure Services
     since 2002-04 **Voice of Chief Officers of Culture, Community &
     Leisure Services in Scotland**

** Scottish Association of Family History Societies
     Organisation lost: see Introduction paragraph 3

Scottish Association of Geography Teachers   (SAGT)   1970

■   42 Culzean Crescent, Newton Mearns, GLASGOW,
       G77 5TA.   (hsp)
       0141-639 8134   fax 0141-943 0216
       email ssmith@boclair.e-dunbarton.sch.uk
       Gen Sec: Sheree Smith
▲   Registered Charity
○   *E, *P; geographical education
●   Conf - Comp - VE
<   Coun for Brit Geography
M   670 i, UK / 10 i, 20 org, o'seas
¶   Jnl - 1.   NL - 3.   Occasional Papers - 1.

Scottish Association of Health Councils
     has been replaced by the Scottish Health Council, for further
         details see the companion volume 'Councils, Committees &
         Boards' (Introduction paragraph 6)

Scottish Association of Landlords

■   22 Forth St, EDINBURGH, EH1 3LH.   (hq)
       0131-270 4774
       email info@scottishlandlords.com
       http://www.scottishlandlords.com
▲   Company Limited by Guarantee
○   *T
     no further information supplied

Scottish Association of Law Centres   (SALC)   1993

■   c/o Govan Law Centre, 47 Burleigh St, GLASGOW,
       G51 3LB.   (sb)
       0141-440 2503
       Sec: Mike Dailly
▲   Un-incorporated Society
○   *P
●   Conf - Mtgs - ET - Inf - LG
<   Advice Services Alliance
M   4 f, 10 org
¶   SALC Briefing - 1; free.

Scottish Association of Local Sports Councils   (SALSC)   1979

NR   1 Lumsdaine Drive, DALGETY BAY, Fife, KY11 9YU.   (hsb)
       Admin: David Arnott
○   *N, *S
M   district sports councils in Scotland

© CBD Research Ltd · Beckenham · BR3 5JS · Tel 020 8650 7745 · Fax 020 8650 0768 · E-mail cbd@cbdresearch.com · www.cbdresearch.com

Scottish Association for Marine Science   (SAMS)   1885
NR   Dunstaffnage Marine Laboratory, Dunbeg, OBAN, Argyllshire,
       PA37 1QA.   (hq)
       01631 559000
       Dir: Prof G B Shimmield
▲   Company Limited by Guarantee; Registered Charity
○   *Q; research & education in marine science
●   Conf - Mtgs - ET - Exam - Res - Exhib - Lib - VE - LG
<   UHI Millennium Institute
M   409 i, 10 f, 21 org, UK / 42 i, 1 org, o'seas
¶   SAMS Newsletter - 2;   AR; both ftm only.

Scottish Association of Master Bakers   (SAMB)   1891
NR   Atholl House, 4 Torphichen St, EDINBURGH, EH3 8JQ.   (hq)
       0131-229 1401
       Chief Exec: Kirk Hunter
▲   Company Limited by Guarantee
○   *T; craft bakery trade & employers association
Gp   Training & education; Industrial relations; Technical; Member
       services
●   Conf - Mtgs - ET - Res - Comp - SG - Inf - Lib - VE - Empl - LG
<   CBI; UK Baking Ind Consultative C'ee
M   600 i, 400 f, UK / 10 i, o'seas
¶   NL - c17.   Ybk.

Scottish Association of Meat Wholesalers   (SAMW)   1977
■   20 Spoutwells Ave, Scone, PERTH, PH2 6RP.   (hsb)
       01738 562736   fax 01738 562736
       email spoutwellsconsultancy@blueyonder.co.uk
       http://www.scottish-meat-wholesalers.org.uk
       Exec Mgr: Alistair Donaldson
▲   Limited Company (1998)
○   *T; to represent the views of members, on issues affecting the
       Scottish meat industry, to government & other agencies
●   Conf - Mtgs - Expt - Inf - LG
<   Eur Livestock & Meat Trading U (UECBV)
M   39 f

Scottish Association for Mental Health   (SAMH)   1967
§   Cumbrae House, 15 Carlton Court, GLASGOW, G5 9JP.   (hq)
       0141-568 7000
       Chief Exec: Shona Neil
       a registered charity campaigning for better hospital &
       community services for those with mental problems

Scottish Association for Metals   (SAM)   1974
NR   11 Craig's Court, TORPHICHEN, W Lothian, EH48 4NU.   (hsp)
       01506 634184
       Hon Sec: Jim Haywood
▲   Registered Charity
○   *L; the development, performance & processing of metals &
       related materials
●   Conf - Mtgs - VE
<   Inst of Materials
M   180 i

Scottish Association of Painting Craft Teachers   (SAPCT)   1955
■   16 Riverside Gardens, MUSSELBURGH, Midlothian,
       EH21 6NW.   (hsp)
       0131-665 2735
       email brownjeff178@aol.com   http://www.sapct.org
       Nat Sec: Jeff Brown
▲   Un-incorporated Society
○   *P; to advance education of painting & decorating; to liaise with
       other relevant bodies
●   Mtgs - ET - Exhib - Comp - VE
<   Painting Craft Teachers Assn
M   57 i
¶   Artisan - 3; ftm (in liaison with the PCTA in England).

Scottish Association for Public Transport   (SAPT)   1970
■   11 Queens Crescent, GLASGOW, G4 9AS.   (hq)
       0776 038 1729
       email mail@sapt.org.uk   http://www.sapt.org.uk
       Chmn: Dr John McCormick,   Sec: Alastair Reid
▲   Un-incorporated Society
Br   2
○   *K; to promote an integrated, socially inclusive, public transport
●   Conf - Mtgs
<   Transport 2000; Transform Scotland
M   120 i, 20 f, 10 org
¶   Scottish Transport Matters - 4; ftm, £80 yr nm.
       Transport Papers; £1.   AR - 1; ftm only.

**Scottish Association of Sign Language Interpreters   (SASLI)
1981**
■   Donaldsons' College, West Coates, EDINBURGH, EH12 5JJ.
       (hq)
       0131-347 5601
       Dir: Iain Whyte
▲   Registered Charity
○   *P
●   Conf - Mtgs - ET - Exam - Stat
<   Eur Forum of Sign Language Interpreters
M   38 i

Scottish Association of Spiritual Healers   (SASH)   1975
■   36 Ambrose Rise, Dedridge, LIVINGSTONE, W Lothian,
       EH54 6JT.   (hsp)
       01506 413746
       Hon Sec: Mrs E M Philp
▲   Registered Charity
○   *P, *W; to provide spiritual healing, support & guidance
●   Mtgs
<   Brit Alliance of Healers Assn; Confedn of Healers Org; UK
       Healers
M   92 i

**Scottish Association for Volunteer Management   (SAVM)
1996**
■   Room 31 Enterprise House, Springkerse Business Park,
       STIRLING, FK7 7UF.   (hq)
       01786 471100   fax 01786 472659
       email admin@savm.org.uk   http://www.savm.org.uk
       Exec Dir: Ann Bain
▲   Company Limited by Guarantee; Registered Charity
○   *P; to offer support & development for managers of volunteers
●   Conf - Mtgs - ET - Res - Inf
<   Intl Assn of Volunteers Administrators
M   350+ i
¶   NL;   Members' Directory - 1; both ftm only.
       A Good Practice Guide for Employers of Volunteers Managers;
       £7.50.
       Voluntary Sector Acronyms; £1 m, £1.50 nm.
×   Scottish Association of Volunteers Managers

Scottish Association of Young Farmers' Clubs   (SAYFC)   1938
NR   Young Farmers' Centre, Ingliston, Newbridge, EDINBURGH,
       EH28 8NE.   (hq)
       0131-333 2445
       Nat Sec: Fiona Bain
○   *F, *Y
M   c 5,000 i
¶   NL - 4.   Hbk - 1.   AR.
       Training publications (as required).

Scottish Athletics Ltd   (SA)   1992
■   9a South Gyle Crescent, EDINBURGH, EH12 9EB.   (hq)
     0870 145 1500
     email admin@scottishathletics.org.uk
     http://www.scottishathletics.org.uk
     Chief Exec: Geoff Wightman
▲   Company Limited by Guarantee
○   *S; governing body for athletics in Scotland (incl track & field,
     road running, cross country & hill running)
Gp Athletes; Coaches; Officials
●   Mtgs
M   6,500 i, 200 clubs
¶   PB (NL) - 4.   AR - 1.

Scottish Auto-Cycle Union   (SACU)   1913
NR 28 West Main St, UPHALL, W Lothian, EH52 5DW.   (hq)
     01506 858354
     Sec: John Davies
▲   Company Limited by Guarantee
○   *S; to promote & license motorcycle sport in Scotland (incl
     Racing/sprints, moto X, grasstrack, trials, enduros)
●   Mtgs - ET - Exam - Exhib - Comp - Stat - Inf
<   Fédn Intle Motocyclisme (FIM); Auto-Cycle U
M   c 2,500 i, 45 clubs
¶   Hbk - 1.   Fixtures List - 1; free.

Scottish Badminton Union   (SBU)   1901
■   40 Bogmoor Place, GLASGOW, G51 4TQ.   (hq)
     0141-445 1218   fax 0141-425 1218
     email enquiries@badmintonscotland.org.uk
     http://www.badmintonscotland.org.uk
     Chief Exec: Miss Anne Smillie
○   *S
Gp SBU Coaching C'ee; Scottish Schools Badminton Union
●   Mtgs - Comp
<   Intl Badminton Fedn; Eur Badminton U
M   c 12,000 i, 560 clubs
¶   Scottish Badminton - 4 (each season); free to clubs, £6 nm.

Scottish Basketball Association   (SBA)   1947
NR Caledonia House, South Gyle, EDINBURGH, EH12 9DQ.   (hq)
     0131-317 7260
     Chief Exec: Kevin Pringle
▲   Un-incorporated Society
○   *S; to develop & promote basketball in Scotland
Gp Sports development gps: Strathclyde, Highland, Central,
     Tayside, Edinburgh
●   Conf - Mtgs - ET - Exhib - Comp - Stat - Inf - LG
<   Intl Fedn Basketball (FIBA); Brit & Ir Basketball Fedn
M   3,200 i, 120 org
¶   Scottish Basketball (NL) - 4;   AR; both free.
     Note: uses the marketing name of Basketball Scotland.

Scottish Beekeepers' Association   (SBA)   1912
■   Milton House, Main St, SCOTLANDWELL, Kinross-shire,
     KY13 9JA.   (PRO)
     01592 840582
     http://www.scottish-beekeepers.org.uk
     Publicity Convener: Enid Brown
▲   Registered Charity
Br 40
○   *G; to promote beekeeping within Scotland
●   Conf - Mtgs - ET - Exam - Res - Exhib - Comp - SG - Stat - Inf -
     Lib - VE - LG
<   Coun of Nat Beekeepers Assns (CONBA)
M   1,200 i, UK / 40 i, o'seas
¶   The Scottish Beekeeper - 12; ftm only.

Scottish Beer & Pub Association   1906
NR 6 St Colme St, EDINBURGH, EH3 6AD.
     0131-225 4681
     email patrick@geoghegans.co.uk
     Chief Exec: Patrick Browne
○   *T
●   Mtgs - Inf
<   Brit Beer & Pub Assn
M   14 f
¶   LM.
×   2002 Brewers & Licensed Retailers Association

Scottish Biomedical Association
     has merged with the **BioIndustry Association** & is the Scottish
     branch & known as BIA Scotland

Scottish Bowling Association   (SBA)   1892
■   National Centre for Bowling Northfield, Hunters Avenue, AYR,
     KA8 9AL.   (hq)
     01292 294623
     email scottishbowling@aol.com
     Sec: Ian Pickavance
○   *S; to control & foster the level green game of bowls
●   Comp
<   Brit Isles Bowling Coun; Wld Bowls Bd
M   c 75,000 i, 900 org
¶   Bowls for the Beginner - 1.
     Ybk - 1.   Laws of the Game - 1.

Scottish Brass Band Association   (SBBA)
NR 71 Tantallon Drive, PAISLEY, Renfrewshire, PA2 9HS.   (sp)
     http://www.sbba.org.uk
     Sec: Tom Allan
▲   Registered Charity
○   *D; the development of brass bands in Scotland
●   Mtgs - ET - Res - Exhib - Comp
<   Eur Brass Band Assn
>   Nat Youth Brass Bands of Scotland; Scot Borders Brass Band
     Assn; Nthn Counties Brass Band Assn
M   2,500 i, 80 brass bands, 15 youth bands
¶   SBBA Ybk - 1; £10 m.
×   2002-03 Scottish Amateur Brass Band Association

Scottish Building
■   Carron Grange, Carron Grange Ave, STENHOUSEMUIR,
     Falkirk, FK5 3BQ.   (hq)
     01324 555550   fax 01324 555551
     Chief Exec: Michael Levack
○   *N, *T
●   Conf - Mtgs - ET - Exhib - SG - Inf - Empl
<   Construction Confedn
M   c 800 f
¶   Magazine - 4;   Bulletin - 36;   Directory; all ftm;   AR.

Scottish Building Contractors Association   (SBCA)   1869
NR 4 Woodside Place, GLASGOW, G3 7QF.   (hq)
     0141-353 5050   fax 0141-332 2928
     email smith@sbca.freeserve.co.uk
     http://www.scottishcontractors.com
     Pres: Rod Jones
▲   Un-incorporated Society
○   *T
●   Conf - Mtgs - Inf - VE
<   Scot Construction Industry Gp
M   21 i, 37 f
¶   NL - 4;   AR; both ftm only.   LM; free.

Scottish Business in the Community   (SBC)   1982
NR   Livingstone House (1st floor east), 43 Discovery Terrace, Heriot-
        Watt Research Park, EDINBURGH, EH14 4AP.   (hq)
        0131-451 1100   fax 0131-451 1127
        email info@sbcscot.com
        Chief Exec: Samantha Barber
▲   Company Limited by Guarantee; Registered Charity
○   *K, *T; to encourage business to take a responsibility for
        supporting communities at a disadvantage
Gp   Business support; Professional firms; Senior executive
        programme; Partners in leadership; Development assignment
        programme
●   Conf - ET - LG
<   Business in the Community
M   250 f
¶   NL - 3;   LM;   AR - 1; all free.

Scottish Canoe Association   (SCA)   1939
■   Caledonia House, 1 Redheughs Rigg, South Gyle,
        EDINBURGH, EH12 9DQ.   (hq)
        0131-317 7314   fax 0131-317 7319
        email general.office@canoescotland.com
        http://www.canoescotland.com
        Admin: Mrs Margaret Winter
○   *S; governing body of the sport of canoeing in Scotland
Gp   Access; Canoe polo; Canoe surf; Coaching; Marathon racing;
        Slalom; Sprint; Touring; White water racing; Canoe sailing
●   Mtgs - ET - Comp - Inf - Coaching - Tests, proficiency
        certificates & instructors' awards
<   Brit Canoe U; C'wealth Canoe Fedn; Intl Canoe Fedn
M   2,200 i & org
¶   Scottish Paddler - 4; ftm.   Ybk.

Scottish Carriage Driving Association
NR   East Overhill, STEWARTON, Ayrshire, KA3 5JT.
        0845 226 9498
        Sec: Mary Kusin
○   *S

Scottish Cashmere Producers Association   (SCPA)   1986
NR   11 Birley Court, St Boswell's, MELROSE, Roxburghshire,
        TD6 0DT.   (hsp)
        01835 824754   fax 01835 824754
        email scparhu@aol.com
        Sec: John D Barker
▲   Company Limited by Guarantee
○   *T; to set & encourage the acceptance of quality standards for
        Scottish cashmere goats
●   Mtgs - ET - Comp - Inf - LG
M   50 i, 4 f, UK / 2 i, o'seas
¶   SCPA Bulletin - 2; ftm only.

Scottish Catholic Historical Association   (SCHA)   1950
■   c/o Kenneth Dunn, Dept of Manuscripts, National Library of
        Scotland, George IV Bridge, EDINBURGH, EH1 1EW.   (sb)
        Sec: Kenneth Dunn
▲   Registered Charity
○   *L; to study the history of the Catholic church in Scotland
●   Conf - Res
M   270 i, c 80 org, UK / c 30 i, o'seas
¶   Innes Review - 2.

Scottish Centres
        see **Scottish Environmental & Outdoor Education Centres
        Association Ltd**

Scottish Chambers of Commerce   1946
NR   30 George Square, GLASGOW, G2 1EQ.   (hq)
        0141 204 8316   fax 0141 221 2336
        email mail@scottishchambers.org.uk
        http://www.scottishchambers.org.uk
        Dir: Liz Cameron
▲   Un-incorporated Society
Br   20
○   *C, *N; business support
●   Conf - Mtgs - LG
<   Scotland Europa
M   9,000 f
¶   Business Survey - 4; ftm, varies nm.   AR - 1; free.
        National Directory - 1.

Scottish Chess Association
        since 2001 **Chess Scotland**

Scottish Childminding Association   (SCMA)   1990
■   7 Melville Terrace, STIRLING, FK8 2ND.   (hq)
        01786 445377   fax 01786 449062
        email info@childminding.org
        http://www.childminding.org
        Chief Exec: Anne McNellan
▲   Company Limited by Guarantee; Registered Charity
○   *P; 'to promote quality childminding; building confident
        children within a family childcare experience'
●   Conf - Mtgs - ET - Exhib - Stat - Inf - LG
<   Intl Family Day Care Org
M   i
¶   Childminding - 4;   AR; both free.

Scottish Chiropractic Association
NR   Laigh Hatton Farm, Old Greenock Rd, BISHOPTON,
        Renfrewshire, PA7 5PB.
        01505 863151
○   *P

Scottish Church History Society   (SCHS)   1922
■   c/o 48 Corbiehill Crescent, Davidson's Mains, EDINBURGH,
        EH44 5BD.   (hsp)
        0131-336 4071
        email w.d.graham@btinternet.com
        Hon Sec: Rev William D Graham
▲   Registered Charity
○   *L; to promote the study of the history of the Church in Scotland
        & to publish the results
●   Conf - Mtgs
M   175 i, 40 libraries, UK / 45 i, 45 libraries, o'seas
¶   Records of the Scottish Church History Society - 1; £15 ($32).

Scottish Clay Target Association Ltd   (SCTA)   2000
NR   PO Box 246, Wide Open, NEWCASTLE UPON TYNE,
        NE13 6AS.   (hsp)
        0191-236 5326
        Hon Sec: R R Wright
▲   Company Limited by Guarantee
○   *S; 'to promote the art of clay target shooting in Scotland at all
        levels, from novice to international'
●   ET - Comp - Organised series of shoots & selection shoots for
        team selection for national team
<   Intl Coun Clay Pigeon Shooting GB & I; Brit Intl Clay Target
        Shooting Fedn; Scot Target Shooting Fedn
M   1,080 i
¶   NL - 4;   Annual Bulletin; both ftm only.

Scottish Committee of Optometrists (SCO) 1935
- ■ 5 St Vincent St, EDINBURGH, EH3 6SW. (hsb)
  0131-220 4542
  Sec: David S Hutton
- ▲ Un-incorporated Society
- ○ *P; represents interests of optometrists in Scotland
- ● Conf - Mtgs - ET - Res - LG
- < General Optical Coun; Brit Coll Optometrists; Assn
  Optometrists; Eyecare Information Service
- M 740 i
- ¶ Look North - 4; free.

Scottish Community Drama Association (SCDA) 1926
- ■ 5 York Place, EDINBURGH, EH1 3EB. (hq)
  0131-557 5552   fax 0131-557 5552
  email headquarters@scda.org.uk
  http://www.scda.org.uk
- ▲ Registered Charity
- Br 4
- ○ *G; development of amateur & community theatre in Scotland
- Gp Youth Network
- ● Conf - ET - Comp - Inf - Lib (playscripts) - Drama festivals
- < Intl Amat Theatre Assn (IATA); Intl Theatre Exchange (ITE);
  Central Coun for Amateur Theatre (CCAT)
- M 1,200+ i & clubs
- ¶ Jnl - 4; ftm, £10 nm.

Scottish Core of Retired Executives
   since 2001 is the Senior Executive Programme of **Scottish Business in the Community**

Scottish Corn Trade Association Ltd (SCTA) 1969
- NR 77/2 Hanover St, EDINBURGH, EH2 1EE. (asa)
  0131-225 7773   fax 0131-226 4448
- ▲ Company Limited by Guarantee
- ○ *T; promotion of the interests of the grain trade
- ● Mtgs - LG - Annual dinner
- < UKASTA; GAFTA
- M 80 f

Scottish Correspondence Chess Association
   a group of **Chess Scotland**

SCOTTISH COUNCIL . . .
   For details of bodies whose names begin thus, other than those entered below, see the companion volume **'Councils, Committees & Boards' (Introduction paragraph 6)**

Scottish Council on Deafness (SCOD) 1927
- ■ Central Chambers (suite 62 1st floor), 93 Hope St, GLASGOW,
  G2 6LD. (hq)
  0141-248 2474 & 0141-248 2477 (text)
  fax 0141-248 2479
  email admin@scod.org.uk   http://www.scod.org.uk
  Dir: Lilian Lawson
- ▲ Registered Charity
- ○ *N, *W; to act on behalf of agencies & organisations working
  with deaf people in Scotland by forming strategic alliances,
  developing policy initiatives & using them to improve the
  human & civil rights of deaf people living in Scotland
- ● Conf - Mtgs - ET - Res - Inf - LG
- M 80 org
- ¶ NL - 4; ftm only.   Bulletin - 12; ftm, £5 yr nm.
  Directory; £5.   AR - 1; ftm.

Scottish Council for Development & Industry (SCDI) 1931
- ■ 17 Park Circus Place, GLASGOW, G3 6AH. (hq)
  0141-332 9119   fax 0141-333 0039
  email enquiries@scdi.org.uk   http://www.scdi.org.uk
  Chief Exec: Alan Wilson
- ▲ Company Limited by Guarantee
- Br 4
- ○ *K; an independent membership network which strengthens
  Scotland's competitiveness by influencing government
  policies to encourage sustainable economic prosperity
- Gp Business inf; Public policy; Trade devt; Education/industry links
- ● Conf - Mtgs - Res - Stat - Expt - Inf - LG
- M 1,300 f
- ¶ Pointer - 10; £45 m, £90 nm.
  Indicator - 6; ftm only.   AR; free.
  Annual Survey of Scottish Export Sales - 1; ftm only.
- × 2002-03 Scottish Council (Development & Industry)

Scottish Council for National Parks (SCNP) 1989
- NR The Barony, Glebe Rd, KILBIRNIE, Ayrshire, KA25 6HX.
  (chmn/p)
  01505 682447
  Chmn: Robert Maund,   Sec: Kate Walsham
- ▲ Registered Charity
- ○ *F, *K; to promote the establishment of National Parks in
  Scotland with adequate powers & finance to ensure good
  management of the landscape, tourism & the local economy
- ● Mtgs - Inf - PL - LG
- < Intl U for the Consvn of Nature; Europarc
- M 170 i, 14 org, UK / 6 i, 1 org, o'seas
- ¶ NL - 4.

Scottish Council for Single Homeless (SCSH) 1974
- NR Wellgate House, 200 Cowgate, EDINBURGH, EH1 1NQ. (hq)
  0131-226 4382
  email enquiries@scsh.demon.co.uk
  http://www.scsh.co.uk
  Dir: Robert Aldridge
- ▲ Registered Charity
- ○ *K, *W; to promote awareness about the causes, nature &
  extent of single homelessness; to identify means of
  preventing & alleviating homelessness & to collaborate with
  all appropriate agencies
- ● Conf - Mtgs - ET - Res - Exhib - Inf - Lib - LG
- < Fédn Eur des Assns Nationaux Travaillant avec les Sans-
  Abris (FEANTSA); Shelter; Age Concern Scotland
- M 90 i, 200 org, UK / 5 org, o'seas
- ¶ Briefing Papers; free.
  Publications list available.

Scottish Council for Voluntary Organisations (SCVO) 1943
- ■ 15 Mansfield Place, EDINBURGH, EH3 6BB. (hq)
  0131-556 3882   fax 0131-556 0279
  email enquiries@scvo.org.uk   http://www.scvo.org.uk
  Chief Exec: Martin Sime
- ▲ Company Limited by Guarantee; Registered Charity
- Br 3
- ○ *N, *W; an independent organisation working at a national
  level to provide services to voluntary & community groups
  throughout Scotland
- Gp Parliamentary information & advisory service; Policy officers
  network; Social inclusion partnership team; Equal project
  strengthening the social economy; Voluntary management
  development unit; New deal; IT services
- ● Conf - Mtgs - ET - Res - Stat - Inf - Lib - LG
- < Scotland Europa; Civicus
- M 1,200 i & org
- ¶ Third Force News & Inform (jt information pack) - 48;
  ftm, £110 nm.
  Work packs;   Handbooks;   Directories;   AR.
  Publications list available.

Scottish Countryside Activities Council
   was wound up early 2005

   © CBD Research Ltd · Beckenham · BR3 5JS · Tel 020 8650 7745 · Fax 020 8650 0768 · E-mail cbd@cbdresearch.com · www.cbdresearch.com

Scottish Countryside Rangers Association   (SCRA)   1974
NR   Pitcairn Centre, Moidart Drive, Coul, GLENROTHES, Fife,
        KY7 6ET.   (admin)
        Admin Assistant: Claire McGhee
▲   Un-incorporated Society
Br   8
○   *P; countryside ranger services in Scotland
Gp   Study group on access & other provision for people with
        disabilities
●   Conf - ET - Res - Exhib - SG - Stat - Inf - Empl - LG
<   Intl Rangers Fedn
M   i & f
¶   Scramble (Jnl) - 2;   Scribble (regional NL) - 4; both ftm only.
        Conference Reports.

Scottish Covenanter Memorials Association   1966
■   Lochnoran House, AUCHINLECK, Ayrshire, KA18 1LX.   (hsp)
        01290 425594
        email info@covenanter.org.uk
        http://www.covenanter.org.uk
        Hon Sec: Dane Love
▲   Registered Charity
○   *G; to preserve monuments & memorials to the Scottish
        Covenanters (mainly 1638-1689); to erect new memorials to
        commemorate Covenanters or events
●   Lib - Annual mtg - Annual dinner - Irregular religious services
        (Conventicles)
M   360 i, UK / 40 i, o'seas
¶   NL - 3; ftm only.

Scottish Cricket Union
        since 2004 **Cricket Scotland**

Scottish Crofting Foundation   (SCF)   1986
NR   Lochalsh Business Park, AUCHTERTYRE, Kyle of Lochalsh,
        IV40 8EG.   (hq)
        01599 566365
        Chief Exec: Patrick Krause
▲   Un-incorporated Society
Br   58
○   *F; to promote the interests of crofters (small tenant farmers) in
        Highlands & Islands of Scotland
●   Conf - Mtgs - Res - LG
M   4,600 i, 31 f, 80 org, UK / 31 i, o'seas
¶   The Crofter - 4.
        Crofter Forestry Hbk.   Crofter Forestry Experiences.
×   2001 (November) Scottish Crofters Union

Scottish Croquet Association   (SCA)   1974
NR   2 (2F3) St Leonard's Bank, EDINBURGH, EH8 9SQ.
        (matchsec/p)
        Match Sec: Fergus McInnes
▲   Un-incorporated Society
○   *S; promotion, development & organisation of croquet in
        Scotland
●   ET - Comp
<   Wld Croquet Fedn; Eur Croquet Fedn
M   130 i, 9 org
¶   Bulletin - 4.   Ybk.

Scottish Cycling (Ltd)   (SC)   1953
■   The Velodrome, London Rd, EDINBURGH, EH7 6AD.   (hq)
        0131-652 0187   fax 0131-661 0474
        email info@scottishcycling.com
        http://www.scottishcycling.com
▲   Company Limited by Guarantee
○   *S; governing body for cycle sport in Scotland
Gp   Cycling; Mountain biking; Sports; Coaching
●   ET - Comp - Inf - Coaching & leadership - Scottish Mountain
        Bike Leader Award (SMBLA) Scheme
<   Brit Cycling; Sportscotland
M   c 2,4000 i, 100 clubs
¶   NL - 12; free.   Hbk - 1.   AR.
×   2004 Scottish Cyclists Union

Scottish Daily Newspaper Society   (SDNS)   1915
■   48 Palmerston Place, EDINBURGH, EH12 5DE.   (hq)
        0131-220 4353   fax 0131-220 4344
        email info@sdns.org.uk
        Dir: J B Raeburn
○   *T; represents daily & Sunday newspapers in Scotland
●   Mtgs - LG
M   8 f

Scottish Dairy Association
        since 2005 the Scottish branch of **Dairy UK**

Scottish Dance Teachers' Alliance   (SDTA)   1934
■   101 Park Rd, GLASGOW, G4 9JE.   (hq)
        0141-339 8944   fax 0141-357 4994
        email sdta@btconnect.com   http://www.thesdta.com
        Chief Exec: Warren Brown
○   *D, *P; for professional teachers of dancing: ballet, tap,
        modern, jazz, highland, Scottish national, sequence,
        ballroom, Latin American, line-dancing, baton twirling &
        cheerleading, disco; rock'n'roll
●   Conf - Mtgs - ET - Exam - Comp - SG - Expt - Inf - Provision of
        examinations in all forms of [above] dancing
<   Scot Official Bd of Highland Dancing (SOBHD); Brit Dance
        Coun (BDC); Coun for Dance Educl Trg (CDET)
M   500 i, UK / 450 i, o'seas
¶   Alliance News - 4;   AR; both ftm only.

Scottish Dancesport
        since 2006 **Dancesport Scotland**

Scottish Darts Association   (SDA)   1971
NR   213 Bonnyview Drive, ABERDEEN, AB16 7EY.   (regd)
        01224 692535 office
        Gen Sec: Len Mutch
○   *S

Scottish Decorators Federation   (SDF)   1878
■   222 Queensferry Rd, EDINBURGH, EH4 2BN.   (hq)
        0131-343 3300   fax 0131-315 2289
        http://www.scottishdecorators.co.uk
        Chief Exec: Ian H Rogers
○   *T
●   Conf - Mtgs - ET - Comp - Inf - Lib - Empl - LG
M   f
¶   NL - 4; free.   Ybk - 1; ftm.
        Wage agreement information - 1; free.

Scottish Disability Sport   (SDS)   1963
■   Caledonia House, South Gyle, EDINBURGH, EH12 9DQ.   (hq)
        01592 415700   fax 01592 415710
        email ssadsds@aol.com
        http://www.scottishdisabilitysport.com
        Fife Sports Institute, Viewfield Rd, GLENROTHES, Fife,
        KY6 2RB.
        Admin: Joanne Riordan, Chief Exec: Gavin MacLeod
▲   Company Limited by Guarantee; Registered Charity
Br   17
○   *S, *W; national governing & coordinating body of all sports for
        all people with a disability in Scotland
Gp   Committees: Local development; Sports; Athletes; Medical
●   Conf - Mtgs - ET - Comp - Inf
<   Brit Paralympic Assn; C'wealth Games Coun for Scotland
M   c 8,000 i, 8 org
¶   Changing With The Times (NL) - 3;   AR; both free.

Scottish Down's Syndrome Association
        since September 2001 **Down's Syndrome Scotland**

Scottish Dyslexia Association
        since 2004 **Dyslexia Scotland**

Scottish Ecological Design Association (SEDA) 1991
NR Icosis Architects, 28 Albert St, EDINBURGH, EH9 1SH.
　　http://www.seda2.org
　　Sec: Sarah Worrall
○ *K

Scottish Economic Society 1954
NR Dept of Economics, University of Glasgow, GLASGOW,
　　G12 8QQ. (sec/b)
　　0141-330 5534
　　Sec: F G Hay
○ *L; study of economic & social problems. . . in accordance with
　　the Scottish tradition of political economy inspired by Adam
　　Smith

Scottish Educational Research Association (SERA) 1971
NR c/o PDU, Strathclyde University, Jordanhill Campus,
　　76 Southbrae Drive, GLASGOW, G13 1PP.
○ *E; to support teachers with research activities; to disseminate
　　research to the educational community

Scottish Employers' Council for the Clay Industries (SECCI)
NR c/o Raeburn Brick Ltd, East Ave, Priestfield Industrial Estate,
　　HIGH BLANTYRE, S Lanarks, G72 0JB. (pres/b)
　　01698 828888
　　Pres: J M Raeburn
○ *T; manufacturers of all types of bricks, building & refractory,
　　field drain pipes etc
M f

Scottish Engineering 1991
■ 105 West George St, GLASGOW, G2 1QL. (hq)
　　0141-221 3181   fax 0141-204 1202
　　email consult@scottishengineering.org.uk
　　http://www.scottishengineering.org.uk
　　Chief Exec: Peter T Hughes
○ *T; employers' association
Gp Representation; Employment law; Industrial tribunal advice &
　　representation; Personnel procedures & practices; Health &
　　safety advice/consultation; Employment information &
　　statistics; Supervisor & management development
● Mtgs - ET - SG - Stat - Inf - Lib - VE - Empl - LG - Forums &
　　seminars
< Engg Employers' Fedn
M 350 f
¶ Quarterly Review.   Hbk.   Information sheets.   AR.

Scottish Environment Link 1987
NR 2 Grosvenor House, Shore Road, PERTH, PH2 8BD. (hq)
　　01738 630804   fax 01738 643290
　　Chief Officer: Jen Anderson
▲ Registered Charity
○ *N; 'voluntary organisations working together to care for &
　　improve Scotland's heritage for people & nature'
¶ The Link (NL) - 4.

**Scottish Environmental & Outdoor Education Centres Association
　　Ltd (Scottish Centres) 1947**
§ Loaningdale House, Carwood Rd, BIGGAR, S Lanarks,
　　ML12 6LX. (hq)
　　01899 221115   fax 01899 220644
　　email enquiries@scottish-centres.org.uk
　　http://www.scottish-centres.org.uk
　　Chief Exec: Dave Spence
　　a non-membership body for the operation of outdoor
　　education centres; to promote the personal & social
　　development of the community in general & young people in
　　particular
　　is also known as Scottish Centres

**Scottish Esperanto Association   (Esperanto-Asocio de
　　Skotlando) (SEA) 1908**
■ 47 Airbles Crescent, MOTHERWELL, Lanarks, ML1 3AP. (hsp)
　　01698 263199
　　email secretary@skotlando.org   http://www.skotlando.org
　　Hon Sec: David W Bisset
▲ Registered Charity
○ *E, *X; to promote & teach Esperanto
Gp Young people
● Conf - Mtgs - ET - Exam - Res - Exhib - SG - Inf - Lib - LG
< Esperanto Assn of Britain
> Scot Esperanto Study Weekend
M 100 i, 10 org, UK / 10 i, o'seas
¶ Scottish Esperanto Bulletin - 2; ftm, £1 nm.
　　Esperanto en Skotlando - 2; ftm, £4 nm.

** Scottish Exhibitions Study Group
　　Organisation lost: see Introduction paragraph 3

Scottish Federation of Housing Associations Ltd (SFHA) 1976
NR 38 York Place, EDINBURGH, EH1 3HU. (hq)
　　0131-556 5777   fax 0131-557 6028
　　email sfha@sfha.co.uk   http://www.sfha.co.uk
　　Chief Exec: Jacqui Watt
▲ Company Limited by Guarantee
Br Glasgow, Dundee
○ *N; advisory & representative body for housing associations in
　　Scotland
Gp Teams: Policy & practice, Consultancy, Training & events; Lintel
　　Trust (charitable)
● Conf - Mtgs - ET - Exhib - Inf - LG
M 400 f, 100 org
¶ Federation Focus (Jnl) - 10.
　　Federation Digest - 10.
　　SFHA Directory - 1.   SFHA Diary - 1.

**Scottish Federation of Meat Traders Associations (Inc)
　　(SFMTA) 1917**
■ 8-10 Needless Rd, PERTH, PH2 0JW. (hq)
　　01738 637472   fax 01738 441059
　　email info@sfmta.co.uk   http://www.sfmta.co.uk
　　Chief Exec: Douglas Scott
▲ Company Limited by Guarantee
○ *T; for independent meat retailers in Scotland
　　In 2000 the SFMTA Training organisation became Food
　　Training Services, which in 2003 became Scottish Meat
　　Training
● Conf - Mtgs - ET - Exam - Exhib - Comp - Inf - Empl - LG
M 420 f
¶ NL - 12; ftm only.

Scottish Federation of Sea Anglers (SFSA) 1960
■ Unit 6 Evans Business Centre, Mitchelston Drive, Mitchelston
　　Industrial Estate, KIRKCALDY, KY1 3NB. (hq)
　　01592 657520   fax 01592 657520
　　Sec/Admin: Mrs Margaret McCallum
▲ Un-incorporated Society
○ *S; governing body of the sport of sea angling in Scotland
Gp Competitions; Coaching; Conservation
● Mtgs - ET - Comp - Inf - LG
< Sportscotland
M 155 i, 30 clubs
¶ NL - 4; ftm.   SFSA Hbk - 1; ftm, £4 nm.

Scottish Fencing
NR 589 Lanark Rd, EDINBURGH, EH14 5DA.
　　0131-453 9074
　　The Administrator
○ *S; the governing body in Scotland for the sport of fencing
M c750 i

© CBD Research Ltd · Beckenham · BR3 5JS · Tel 020 8650 7745 · Fax 020 8650 0768 · E-mail cbd@cbdresearch.com · www.cbdresearch.com

Scottish Field Archery Association   (SFAA)   1966
- ■ 7 The Cottages, Threemiletown, LINLITHGOW, W Lothian, EH49 6NG.   (hsp)
  01506 830063   fax 01506 830063
  email jimgreig@msn.com
  http://www.scottishfieldarchery.co.uk
  Hon Sec: James B Greig
- ▲ Company Limited by Guarantee
- ○ *S; 'to foster & encourage good fellowship among those who take up the sport of field archery'
- ● Mtgs - ET - Comp
- < Intl Field Archery Assn
- M 250 i, 12 clubs
- ¶ NL - 4; ftm only.

Scottish Field Studies Association Ltd   (SFSA)   1964
- NR Kerrera, 48 Almond View, PERTH, Perthshire, PH1 1QQ. (regd/office)
  01738 444166
  Hon Treas: William Monks
- ▲ Registered Charity
- ○ *E; to study all aspects of natural sciences, natural history & conservation
- < is responsible for the Kindrogan Field Centre, Enochdhu, Blairgowrie, Perthshire, PH10 7PG.
- M i & org
- ¶ NL; free.

Scottish Fish Merchants Federation Ltd
  since 2003 **Scottish Seafood Processors Federation**

Scottish Fishermen's Federation   (SFF)   1973
- NR 24 Rubislaw Terrace, ABERDEEN, AB10 1XE.   (hq)
  01224 646944
  Chief Exec: Bertie Armstrong
- ▲ Un-incorporated Society
- ○ *N, *T; to promote & protect the interests of share fishermen (vessel owners & crew members) engaged in the Scottish fishing industry
- ● Mtgs - LG
- < Assn Nat Fishing Orgs EEC (EUROPECHE)
- M 8 org (1,100 individually owned fishing vessels)
- ¶ Ybk & Diary; ftm only.

Scottish Fishermen's Organisation
- NR Braehead, 601 Queensferry Rd, EDINBURGH, EH4 6EA.
  0131-339 7972
  Chief Exec: Ian McSween
- ○ *N
- M 380 i

Scottish Flour Millers Association   (SFMA)   1920
- NR 15 Midmar Gardens, EDINBURGH, EH10 6DY.   (hsp)
  Sec: Brian Tudor
- ▲ Un-incorporated Society
- ○ *T; for flour millers operating in Scotland
- M f

Scottish Food & Drink Federation   (SFDF)   1999
- NR 4a Torphichen St, EDINBURGH, EH3 8JQ.   (hq)
  0131-229 9415   fax 0131-229 9407
  email sfdf@sfdf.org.uk   http://www.sfdf.org.uk
  Dir: Flora A McLean
- ○ *T
- ● Conf - Mtgs - Inf - LG
- < Food & Drink Fedn; Scot Civic Forum
- M f
- ¶ NL - 12;   AR; both ftm.

Scottish Food Trade Association   (SFTA)   1886
- ■ c/o Mairi McTear, Glasgow Metropolitan College, 230 Cathedral St, GLASGOW, G1 2TG.   (hsb)
  0141-773 2100
  email accreditedtraining@firemail.co.uk
  Sec: Mrs Mairi McTear
- ▲ Un-incorporated Society
- Br 4
- ○ *T; the networking platform for the Scottish food industry
- ● Mtgs
- M 100 i, 50 f

Scottish Football Association Ltd   (SFA)   1873
- ■ Hampden Park, GLASGOW, G42 9AY.   (hq)
  0141-616 6000   fax 0141-616 6001
  email info@scottishfa.co.uk   http://www.scottishfa.co.uk
  Chief Exec: David Taylor
- ▲ Company Limited by Guarantee
- ○ *S
- ● Conf - Mtgs - ET - Exam - Comp - Stat - Inf
- < FIFA; UEFA
- M 77 clubs
- ¶ Hbk; ftm, £10 nm (£2p&p).
  Laws of the Game; ftm, £4 nm.   AR; ftm, £5 nm.

Scottish Football League   (SFL)   1890
- ■ Hampden Park, GLASGOW, G42 9EB.   (hq)
  0141-620 4160   fax 0141-620 4161
  email info@scottishfootballleague.com
  http://www.scottishfootballleague.com
  Sec: Peter Donald
- ▲ Un-incorporated Body
- ○ *S; to promote & extend the game of Association Football in Scotland
- ● Conf - Mtgs - ET - Res - Comp - Stat - Inf - Provision of League championships & League cup competitions
- < Intl Football League Bd; Scot Football Assn
- M 30 clubs
- ¶ Hbk (incl list of clubs & referees) - 1; £10.
  Scottish Football Review Book - 1; £9.95.
  Fixture Book - 1; £3.

Scottish Freshwater Group
- NR c/o Dr Colin Adams, University Field Station, Rowardennan, GLASGOW, G63 0AW.
  01360 870271
  Sec: Dr Colin Adams
- ○ *P

Scottish Further & Higher Education Association
  in 2003 merged with the **Educational Institute of Scotland**

Scottish Gaelic Texts Society   (SGTS)   1934
- ■ c/o McLeish Carswell, 29 St Vincent Place, GLASGOW, G1 2DT.   (hsb)
  0141-248 4134   fax 0141-226 3118
  http://www.sgts.org.uk
  Hon Sec: Miss A F Wilson
- ▲ Registered Charity
- ○ *L; to promote the publication of texts in the Scottish Gaelic language, accompanied by introductions, English translations & glossaries
- ● Res
- M 120 i, 10 org, UK / 20 i, 10 org, o'seas
- ¶ Various publications.

Scottish Gamekeepers' Association   (SGA)   1998
NR   PO Box 7477, PERTH, PH2 7YE.   (hsp)
         01738 587515
         Sec: Sabine Dey
▲   Un-incorporated Society
○   *P; gamekeepers, deer management & fisheries
●   Conf - Mtgs - ET - Res - Comp - Inf - VE - LG
M   2,500 i, 500 f, 25 org, UK / 500 i, o'seas
¶   Scottish Gamekeeper (Jnl) - 4.

Scottish Games Association   (SGA)   1946
NR   Ashleigh, Church St, HALKIRK, KW12 6YD.   (hsp)
         http://www.highlandgames-sga.com
         Hon Sec: Charlie Miller
▲   Company Limited by Guarantee
○   *S; to encourage & foster the highest standards of ethics &
         performance in open athletics & traditional Highland games
●   Mtgs - Comp
M   65 full members, 5 associate members, 4 committees
¶   Ybk.

Scottish Genealogy Society   1953
■   Library & Family History Centre, 15 Victoria Terrace,
         EDINBURGH, EH1 2JL.
         0131-220 3677
         Hon Sec: Ken Nisbet
▲   Registered Charity
○   *L, *Q; to promote research into Scottish family history
●   Mtgs - Inf - Lib
M   i, org
¶   The Scottish Genealogist - 4; ftm.
         Lists of pre 1855 Monumental Inscriptions.

Scottish Gliding Union Ltd   (SGU)   1934
■   The Scottish Gliding Centre, Portmoak Airfield, Scotlandwell,
         KINROSS, KY13 9JJ.   (hq)
         01592 840543
         Hon Sec: Bruce Marshall,   Chmn: John Williams
▲   Company Limited by Guarantee
○   *S; provision & promotion of gliding activities to members & the
         public
Gp   Disabled facilities; Flying for disabled
●   ET (training of glider pilots) - Trial flight option for members of
         the public
<   Brit Gliding Assn
M   250 i
         Note: The trading name is the Scottish Gliding Centre.

Scottish Golf Union Ltd   (SGU)   1920
■   PO Box 29212, ST ANDREWS, Fife, KY16 0YG.   (hq)
         01382 549500
         email sgu@scottishgolfunion.org
         http://www.scottishgolfunion.org
         Chief Exec: Hamish Grey
○   *S; governing body of amateur golf in Scotland
●   Mtgs - ET - Comp - VE - LG
<   Intl Golf Fedn; Eur Golf Assn; Coun of Nat Golf Us
>   Scot Golf Envt Gp (wholly owned subsidiary)
M   260,000 i, 650 clubs in Scotland
¶   Scottish Golfer - 8;   Ybk; both free.
×   2004 (February) Scottish Golf Union

Scottish Grocers' Federation   (SGF)   1918
■   222 Queensferry Rd, EDINBURGH, EH4 2BN.   (hq)
         0131-343 3300   fax 0131-343 6147
         email scotgrocersfed@compuserve.com
         http://www.scottish-grocers-federation.co.uk
         Chief Exec: John Drummond
▲   Company Limited by Guarantee
○   *T; for independent convenience retailers in Scotland
●   Conf - Mtgs - ET - SG - Stat - Inf - LG
<   Intl Fedn of Grocers' Assns (IFGA)
M   600 f
¶   Retail News - 12;   Retail Outlook (Ybk) - 1.

Scottish Gymnastics Association   (SGA)   1890
NR   2 Lint Riggs, FALKIRK, FK1 1DG.   (hq)
         01324 886506
         http://www.scottishgymnastics.com
○   *S
●   Conf - ET - Exam - Comp
<   British Amateur Gymnastics Assn
M   c 8,000 i
×   2004 (July) Fitness Scotland (merged)

** Scottish Gypsy Traveller Association**
         Organisation lost: see Introduction paragraph 3

Scottish Hang Gliding & Paragliding Federation   (SHPF)
1973
NR   11 Lyttleton, Westwood, E KILBRIDE, Lanarks, G75 9BP.
         (chmn/p)
         Chmn: Dave Thomson
○   *S; to promote the sports of hang gliding & paragliding in
         Scotland
M   i & clubs
¶   The Flying Scot (NL) - 4.
×   1996-97 Scottish Paragliding & Hang Gliding Federation

Scottish Hazards Campaign Group
NR   c/o Lothian TUCRC, 26-28 Albany St (basement), EDINBURGH,
         EH1 3QH.   (treas/b)
         0131-556 7318
         Hon Treas: Karen Rennie
▲   Un-incorporated Society
○   *K; to campaign for improvements in health & safety in the
         workplace; to act as a forum for the exchange of information
         between trade union safety representatives, trade union
         officials, occupational health professionals &
         environmentalists
●   Conf - Mtgs - ET - Res
M   30 i, 10 org

Scottish Hereford Breeders Association   1950
NR   Barncleugh, Irongray, DUMFRIES, DG2 9SE.   (hsp)
         Sec: K A Kelly
○   *B; Hereford cattle in Scotland

Scottish History Society   (SHS)   1886
NR   c/o Dr Michael Penman, Dept of History, University of Stirling,
         FK9 4LA.   (hsb)
         Hon Sec: Dr M Penman
▲   Un-incorporated Society
○   *L; 'to discover & print, in a series of annual volumes,
         unpublished documents illustrating the history of Scotland'
●   Conf
<   R Histl Soc (Brit Nat C'ee)
M   430 i, 125 org
¶   Annual Volume (back copies available; prices vary).

Scottish Hockey Union   (SHU)   1989
■   589 Lanark Rd, EDINBURGH, EH14 5DA.   (hq)
         0131-453 9070   fax 0131-453 9079
         email info@scottish-hockey.org.uk
         http://www.scottish-hockey.org.uk
         Chief Exec: Brent Deans
▲   Company Limited by Guarantee
○   *S; the national governing body for the sport of hockey in
         Scotland
Gp   Youth Commission
●   Mtgs - ET - Exam - Exhib - Comp - Inf - LG
<   Intl Hockey Fedn (FIH); Eur Hockey Fedn (EHF)
M   6,000 i, 165 clubs
¶   Hockey Scotland - 2; free.

© CBD Research Ltd · Beckenham · BR3 5JS · Tel 020 8650 7745 · Fax 020 8650 0768 · E-mail cbd@cbdresearch.com · www.cbdresearch.com

Scottish Homing Union   (SHU)
NR   231a Low Waters Rd, HAMILTON, Lanarks, ML3 7QN.   (hq)
⠀⠀⠀01698 286983
⠀⠀⠀Sec: Mrs L Brooks
○   *N, *S; homing pigeons

Scottish Huntington's Association   1989
NR   Thistle House, 61 Main Rd, ELDERSLIE, Renfrewshire,
⠀⠀⠀PA5 9BA.   (hq)
⠀⠀⠀01505 322245   fax 01505 382980
⠀⠀⠀email sha-admin@hdscotland.org
⠀⠀⠀http://www.hdscotland.org
⠀⠀⠀Sec: Ann Carruthers
▲   Company Limited by Guarantee; Registered Charity
Br   9
○   *W; to help sufferers of Huntington's disease & their families; to
⠀⠀⠀help people at risk of developing the disease
●   Conf - Mtgs - ET - Res - Inf - Lib
<   Intl Huntington's Disease Assn
M   1,000 i
¶   Books:
⠀⠀⠀A Physician's Guide to the Management of Huntington's
⠀⠀⠀⠀Disease.
⠀⠀⠀Behavioural Problems in Huntington's Disease.
⠀⠀⠀Huntington's Disease: What's it all about? A guide for young
⠀⠀⠀⠀people (aged 14+).
⠀⠀⠀Other publications available.

Scottish Ice Skating Association   (SISA)
NR   c/o Ice Sports Centre, Riversdale Crescent, EDINBURGH,
⠀⠀⠀EH12 5XN.   (hq)
⠀⠀⠀0131-337 3976
⠀⠀⠀Gen Admin: John Macdonald,⠀⠀Pres: William Findlay
▲   Un-incorporated Society
○   *S; promotion of amateur ice skating in Scotland
Gp   Skating: Recreational; Ice dancing; Figures & free; Pairs;
⠀⠀⠀Exhibition; Show; Precise
●   Exam - Exhib - Comp - Courses & grade test
<   Nat Ice Skating Assn UK Ltd
M   546 i, 22 affiliated clubs
¶   Scottish Skate Update - 4.
⠀⠀⠀Members' Hbk - 1.⠀⠀Event Programme - 4.

Scottish Icelandic Horse Association
NR   Wellbank, Main St, EAST SALTOUN, E Lothian, EH34 5AB.
⠀⠀⠀01875 340105
⠀⠀⠀email info@siha.org.uk⠀⠀http://www.siha.org.uk
⠀⠀⠀Sec: Jill Brennan
○   *B

Scottish Independent Advocacy Alliance   (SIAA)
NR   138 Slateford Rd, EDINBURGH, EH14 1LR.
⠀⠀⠀0131-455 8183   fax 0131-455 8184
⠀⠀⠀http://www.siaa.org.uk

Scottish Independent Nurseries Association
⠀⠀⠀closed 2005

Scottish Indoor Bowling Association   (SIBA)   1936
■   1 Nursery Lane, MAUCHLINE, Ayrshire, KA5 6EH.   (hsp)
⠀⠀⠀01290 551067   fax 01290 551067
⠀⠀⠀Hon Sec: Gordon Woods
▲   Un-incorporated Society
○   *S
●   Mtgs - Comp
<   Wld Indoor Bowls Coun; Brit Isles Indoor Bowls Coun
M   60,000 i (Scotland only)
¶   Bowls International - 12.
⠀⠀⠀World Bowls - 12.⠀⠀Scots Bowler - 12.

Scottish Industrial Heritage Society   (SIHS)   1984
NR   55/57 Queen St, EDINBURGH, EH3 3PA.   (regd/add)
▲   Company Limited by Guarantee; Registered Charity
○   *L; the study of the history & development of industry in
⠀⠀⠀Scotland
●   Conf - Mtgs - Inf - VE
<   Assn for Indl Archaeology
M   120 i, 10 f, 5 org, UK / 1 i, 1 f, o'seas
¶   SIHS Review (NL) - 2.
⠀⠀⠀Guide to Scottish Industrial Heritage (Hbk).

Scottish Inland Waterways Association   (SIWA)   1971
■   Kilnside, Armour Place, JOHNSTONE, Renfrewshire,
⠀⠀⠀PA5 8HH.   (hsp)
⠀⠀⠀Sec: Alan Muir
▲   Registered Charity
○   *G, *K, *N; to preserve & rehabilitate Scottish inland
⠀⠀⠀waterways; to coordinate local canal societies; to promote
⠀⠀⠀the use of waterways for leisure & commercial purposes
●   Mtgs - Exhib - Inf - VE
<   Inland Waterways Assn
M   137 i, 18 org

Scottish Ju-Jitsu Association   (SJJA)   1979
NR   3 Dens St, DUNDEE, DD4 6BU.   (hq)
⠀⠀⠀01382 458262   fax 01382 458262
⠀⠀⠀email scottishjujitsu@aol.com
⠀⠀⠀http://www.scottish-jujitsu.com
⠀⠀⠀Gen Sec: Robert G Ross
▲   Un-incorporated Society
Br   20; Spain, USA
○   *S; governing body for the sport in Scotland
Gp   Ju Jitsu (un-armed combat); Ko-Ryu (traditional schoools of
⠀⠀⠀combat)
●   Conf - Mtgs - ET - Exam - Res - Exhib - Comp - Inf - Lib - VE -
⠀⠀⠀LG
<   Nippon Jujitsu & Kobudo Intl; Amer Self-Defence Assn; Hon Tai
⠀⠀⠀Yoshin Ryu; Scot Sports Coun; Sportscotland; Scot Sports
⠀⠀⠀Assn; Fedn of Scot School Sports Assn
M   800 i, 20 org, UK / 150 i, 3 org, o'seas
¶   Samuri NL - 6;⠀⠀Scottish Jujitsu - 4; both ftm only.

Scottish Judo Federation
⠀⠀⠀since May 2002 **Judo Scotland**

Scottish Kennel Club   (SKC)   1881
NR   Eskmills Park, Station Rd, MUSSELBURGH, Lothian,
⠀⠀⠀EH21 7PQ.   (hq)
⠀⠀⠀0131-665 3920
⠀⠀⠀Office Mgr: Myra Orr
▲   Un-incorporated Society
○   *B; to promote dogs, canine education & responsible dog
⠀⠀⠀ownership
Gp   Dog showing; Obedience; Agility; Working trials
●   Conf - Mtgs - ET - Exhib - SG - Stat - Inf - Lib - LG
<   The Kennel Club
M   2,500 i
¶   Show Schedule - 2.⠀⠀Show Catalogue - 2.
⠀⠀⠀List of Scottish Show Dates - 4.⠀⠀AR.

Scottish Labour History Society   (SLHS)   1961
NR   10 Fountainhall Rd, EDINBURGH, EH9 2NN.   (treas/p)
⠀⠀⠀Treasurer: Jim Cranstoun,⠀⠀Sec: George Rawlinson
○   *G; study, discussion, publication & exhibition of the history of
⠀⠀⠀the Scottish, British & international labour & working class
⠀⠀⠀movements
●   Conf - Exhib - SG
M   200 i, 80 org, UK / 2 i, 20 org, o'seas
¶   Scottish Labour History - 1.

Scottish Ladies' Golfing Association   (SLGA)   1904
NR   The Den, 2 Dundee Rd, PERTH, PH2 7DW.   (hq)
    01738 445357   fax 01738 442380
    email slga@scottishgolf.com
    http://www.scottishgolf.com
    Sec: Sheila A Hartley
○   *S
●   ET - Comp - Inf
<   Ladies' Golf U
M   38,000 i, 420 org
¶   Ybk; £3.

Scottish Landowners' Federation
    since 2004 **Scottish Rural Property & Business Association**

Scottish Language Dictionaries   (SLD)
■   27 George Sq, EDINBURGH, EH8 9LD.   (hq)
    0131-650 4149   fax 0131-650 4149
    email mail@scotsdictionaries.org.uk
    http://www.scotsdictionaries.org.uk
    Dir: Dr Christine Robinson
▲   Registered Charity
○   *L, *Q; 'we research Scots language as it is spoken & used in
    writing, & use our results to update the nation's record of one
    of Scotland's indigenous languages; we also support the use
    of Scots in the community & promote it internationally as part
    of Scottish culture'
●   Res - Inf
M   135 i, 4 org, UK / 6 i, o'seas
¶   NL - 2.
    Compact Scottish National Dictionary (hardback) £157.50 m,
      £175 nm / (paper) £108 m, £120 nm.
    Concise Scots Dictionary (hardback) £22.50 m, £25 nm /
      (paper) £13.50 m, £14.99 nm.
    Scots Thesaurus (paper) £13.50 m, £14.99 nm.
    Pocket Scots Dictionary (paper); £5.40 m, £5.99 nm.
    Essential Scots Dictionary (paper); £7.20 m, £7.99 nm.
×   2002 Scottish National Dictionary Association

Scottish Law Agents Society   (SLAS)   1884
NR   c/o Sheridans, 166 Buchanan St, GLASGOW, G1 2LW.   (sb)
    0141-352 4522   fax 0141-353 3819
    email secretary@slas.co.uk   http://www.slas.co.uk
▲   Un-incorporated Society
○   *P; for Scottish solicitors
Gp   Conveyancing; Court; Legal aid
●   Conf - Mtgs - ET - Res - SG - VE - LG
<   Links with Legal Defence U
M   2,000 i, & Gazette subscribers
¶   The Scottish Law Gazette - 6.
    Memorandum Book - 1.

Scottish Legal Action Group   (Scolag)   1975
■   173 Crossloan Rd, GLASGOW, G51 3QE.   (admin/office)
    0141-445 6451   fax 0141-445 2853
    email admin@scolag.org.uk   http://www.scolag.org.uk
    Convenor: Robert Sutherland
▲   Company Limited by Guarantee; Registered Charity
○   *P; to explain the law; to promote the use of legal services (&
    changes in the law & legal system) so as to benefit
    disadvantaged members of society & promote equal access
    to justice
●   Conf - LG
M   [not stated]
¶   SCOLAG (Jnl) - 12; £42 i, (£18 students, £68 business,
    £47 voluntary orgs).

Scottish Library Association
    is a division of **CILIP**

Scottish Licensed Trade Association   (SLTA)   1880
NR   10 Walker St, EDINBURGH, EH3 7LA.   (hq)
    0131-225 5169
    Sec: Colin A Wilkinson
▲   Un-incorporated Society
Br   6
○   *T; represents all sections of the licensed trade in Scotland
●   Conf - Mtgs - ET - Exam - Exhib - Inf - LG
<   UK & Ireland Licensed Tr Assn
M   3,000 i, 40 f
¶   Scottish Licensee (Jnl) - 4; free.

**Scottish Local Authority Network of Physical Education
(SLANOPE)   1974**
■   Auchterderran Centre, Woodend Rd, CARDENDEN, Fife,
    KY5 0NE.   (hsb)
    01592 414675   fax 01592 414641
    Hon Sec: David Maiden
○   *P; to facilitate physical education networking in local authority
    education departments in Scotland
●   Conf - Mtgs - ET
M   84 i, 31 local authorities, 9 associates

Scottish Local History Forum
NR   c/o Dept of Scottish History, University of Edinburgh, 17
    Buccleuch Place, EDINBURGH, EH8 9LN.   (hsb)
    fax 0131-650 4042
    http://www.slhf.gcal.ac.uk
○   *N; for Scottish local history societies & local historians

Scottish Massage Therapists Organisation Ltd   (SMTO)   1992
■   70 Lochside Rd, Bridge of Don, ABERDEEN, AB23 8QW.   (hsb)
    01224 822960   fax 01224 822960
    email smto@scotmass.co.uk
    http://www.scotmass.co.uk
    Chmn: Maggie Brooks-Carter,   Sec: Nicola Brooks
▲   Company Limited by Guarantee
○   *M, *P; for massage therapists, remedial & sports massage
    therapists, advanced remedial massage therapists,
    manipulative therapists, on-site massage therapists, clinical
    aromatherapists & reflexologists in the UK, primarily in
    Scotland
●   Conf - Mtgs - ET - Res - Exhib - Inf - Continuing professional
    development for members
>   Black Isle Complementary Therapies; Scottish Massage Schools
    Ltd; Western School of Massage
M   500 i, 5 org, UK / 5 i, o'seas
¶   On the Massage Scene - 3; ftm, £2.50 nm.
    Directory of therapists.

**Scottish Master Wrights & Builders Association   (SMWBA)
1885**
NR   Blairtummock Lodge, Campsie Glen, GLASGOW, G66 7AR.
    (asa)
    01360 770583
    Sec / Treas: David C Milliken
○   *T
●   Mtgs - ET - Inf
<   Scot Building Emplrs Fedn
M   i

Scottish Medievalists
    see the **Colloquium for Scottish Medieval & Renaissance
    Studies (the Scottish Medievalists)**

Scottish Military Historical Society   (SMHS)   1967
NR   4 Hillside Cottages, GLENBOIG, N Lanarks, ML5 2QY.   (hsp)
    Hon Sec: Thomas W Moles
○   *G, *L; study of Scottish military history (collecting: information,
    badges, uniforms, medals, books & ephemera)
●   Mtgs - Res - Exhib - Inf - Lib - PL
M   c 400 i

© CBD Research Ltd · Beckenham · BR3 5JS · Tel 020 8650 7745 · Fax 020 8650 0768 · E-mail cbd@cbdresearch.com · www.cbdresearch.com

Scottish Modern Pentathlon Association   (SPMA)   1990
■   Currie Gilmour & Co, 41-43 Warrender Park Rd, EDINBURGH,
      EH9 1EU.   (dir)
      0177 164 4855
      http://www.pentathlon-scotland.co.uk p
      Dir/Admin: Rachel Caughey
▲   Company Limited by Guarantee
○   *S; the governing body in Scotland of the sport & the sports
      pursuits which comprise the modern pentathlon; to provide
      services to individuals, clubs & other bodies with an interest
      in such sports
●   ET - Comp - Coaching
<   Modern Pentathlon Assn GB
M   i

Scottish Motor Neurone Disease Association   1981
■   76 Firhill Rd, GLASGOW, G20 7BA.   (hq)
      0141-945 1077   fax 0141-945 2578
      email info@scotmnd.co.uk   http://www.scotmnd.org.uk
      Chief Exec: Craig Stockton
▲   Company Limited by Guarantee; Registered Charity
Br   4 (Scotland)
○   *W; to help the motor neurone disease patient live as full &
      normal a life as possible
●   Conf - Mtgs - ET - Res - Inf - Lib - Care research - Equipment
      loan service - Fundraising - Counselling service - Holiday
      caravan - Small grants scheme
<   Intl Alliance of MND Assns
M   800 i
¶   Aware (NL) - 3; ftm.   AR; ftm.
      Infofact (leaflets); free.
      Publications list available.

Scottish Motor Racing Club Ltd   (SMRC)   1946
NR   Birch House, Duncrievie, By GLENFARG, Perthshire & Kinross,
      PH2 9PD.   (sp)
      Competition Sec: Chris Edwards
▲   Company Limited by Guarantee
○   *S; organisation of motor racing at Knockhill & Ingliston race
      circuits
●   Mtgs - Comp
M   i

Scottish Motor Trade Association Ltd   (SMTA)   1903
■   Palmerston House, 10 The Loan, SOUTH QUEENSFERRY,
      EH30 9NS.   (hq)
      0131-331 5510   fax 0131-331 4296
      email info@smta.co.uk   http://www.smta.co.uk
      Chief Exec: Douglas Robertson
▲   Company Limited by Guarantee
○   *T
●   Conf - LG
M   i & f
¶   Monthly Bulletin;   AR & Accounts;   both ftm only.

**Scottish Music Hall & Variety Theatre Society, incorporating the Sir
Harry Lauder Society   (SMH&VTS)   1975**
■   69 Langmuirhead Rd, Auchinloch, KIRKINTILLOCH,
      G66 5DJ.   (hsp)
      0141-578 4108
      email bob.bain@ntlworld.com
      Hon Sec: Bob Bain
▲   Un-incorporated Society
○   *A; the Scottish variety theatre & music hall - past, present &
      future
●   Exhib - VE - Staging shows
M   260 i, UK / 16 i, o'seas
¶   Stagedoor - 4; ftm only.
✕   2002-03 Scottish Music Hall Society

Scottish Musical Instrument Retailers Association
NR   15 Lambie Crescent, GLASGOW, G77 6JU.
      0141-577 5330
      Admin: Fred Meil
○   *T
M   f

Scottish National Chess League
      a group of the **Chess Scotland**

Scottish National Dictionary Association Ltd
      since 2002 **Scottish Language Dictionaries**

**Scottish National Federation for the Welfare of the Blind
(SNFWB)   1917**
■   Redroofs, Balgavies, FORFAR, Angus, DD8 2TD.   (hsp)
      01307 830265   fax 01307 830265
      email snfwb@care4free.net
      Sec/Treas: John Duncan
▲   Registered Charity
○   *W; to promote the education & interest of the blind & partially
      sighted community in Scotland
●   Conf - ET - LG
>   most local authorities & volunteer organisations dealing with
      the visually impaired in Scotland
M   52 org
¶   AR; free.

Scottish Neuroscience Group   (SNG)   1971
NR   Dept of Biology, St Andrew's University, ST ANDREW'S, Fife,
      KY16 9TS.   (sb)
      01334 463503
      Sec & Treas: Prof Keith Sillar
○   *L, *P; incl neuroethology, electrophysiology, neuroanatomy,
      neurochemistry, pharmacology, muscle physiology
M   c 60 i

Scottish Newspaper Publishers Association   (SNPA)   1920
■   48 Palmerston Place, EDINBURGH, EH12 5DE.   (hq)
      0131-220 4353   fax 0131-220 4344
      email info@snpa.org.uk   http://www.snpa.org.uk
      Dir: J B Raeburn
▲   Un-incorporated Society
○   *T; representing the weekly newspaper industry in Scotland
●   Conf - Mtgs - ET - Res - Empl - LG
<   Newspaper Soc
M   26 f
¶   NL - 2; free.   LM (on Internet).   AR; free.

**Scottish & Northern Ireland Plumbing Employers' Federation
(SNIPEF)   1923**
NR   2 Walker St, EDINBURGH, EH3 7LB.   (hq)
      0131-225 2255
      Dir & Sec: Robert D Burgon
▲   Company Limited by Guarantee
○   *T; the national trade association for all types of firms involved
      with the plumbing & domestic heating industry
Gp   Association of Installers of Unvented Hot Water Systems
      (Scotland & NI)
●   Conf - Mtgs - ET - Exhib - Comp - Inf
M   946 f
¶   Plumb Heat - 3.   SNIPEF Ybk.

Scottish Optoelectronics Association (SOA) 1994
NR Geddes House, Kirkton North, LIVINGSTON, Midlothian,
      EH54 6GU.   (hq)
      01506 497228   fax 01506 497229
      email soa@optoelectronics.org.uk
      http://www.optoelectronics.org.uk
      Chief Exec: Chris Gracie
▲ Un-incorporated Society
○ *T; to represent the optoelectronics community in Scotland
Gp Displays; Optical communications; Scientific; Industrial
● Mtgs - Exhib - SG - Stat - Expt - Inf - LG
< Optoelectronics Ind Devt Assn (USA); Optoelectronics Ind &
      Technology Devt Assn (Japan); Photonics Ind Devt
      Assn (Taiwan); Photonics Assn Singapore; UK Consortium for
      Photonics & Optics
M 66 f, 22 universities & research org, UK / 1 org, o'seas
¶ Optonews - 4;   Membership Directory; both ftm only.

Scottish Organic Producers Association (SOPA) 1988
NR Scottish Organic Centre, 10th Avenue, Royal Highland Centre,
      Ingliston, EDINBURGH, EH28 8NF.
      0131-335 6606
      Chmn: John Hamilton
○ *T
● Mtgs
M c 450 i

Scottish Orienteering Association (SOA) 1962
NR 6 Newark Crescent, DOONFOOT, Ayr, KA7 4HP.   (hsp)
      http://www.scottish-orienteering.org
      Hon Sec: Mel Perry
▲ Un-incorporated Society
○ *S; to promote & coordinate the sport of orienteering in
      Scotland
● Comp
< Brit Orienteering Fedn; Intl Orienteering Fedn
M 1,400 i, UK / 15 i, o'seas
¶ Score (NL) - 6.   AR.

Scottish Ornithologists' Club (SOC) 1936
NR Scottish Birdwatching Resource Centre, Waterston House,
      ABERLADY, E Lothian, EH32 0PY.   (hq)
      0131-653 0653
      http://www.the-soc.org.uk
      Admin Officer: Kate Walshaw
▲ Registered Charity
Br 14
○ *L; study of Scottish ornithology & protection of rare birds
● Conf - Mtgs - Res - SG - Lib
M 2,800 i, 100 org, UK / 300 i, 50 org, o'seas
¶ Scottish Birds (Jnl).   Raptor Round up.
    Scottish Bird News.   Scottish Bird Report.

Scottish Otolaryngological Society (SOS) 1910
NR c/o David Simpson - ENT Dept, Stobhill Hospital, 133
      Balornock Rd, GLASGOW, G21 3UZ.   (hsb)
      0141-201 3161
      Sec: David Simpson
▲ Registered Charity
○ *P; the study & advancement of otology, rhinology &
      laryngology & all allied branches of medical science by the
      continuing education of members & their trainees
● Conf - Mtgs - ET - Acting as an advisory body on
      otolaryngological matters to other organisations
M 90 i

Scottish Pelagic Fishermen's Association (SPFA) 1932
NR 1 Frithside St, FRASERBURGH, Aberdeenshire, AB43 9AR.   (hq)
      01346 510714
      Sec: Derek Duthie
▲ Company Limited by Guarantee
Br 3
○ *T; to promote & protect the interests of owners of boats
      engaged in fishing for pelagic fish
● Mtgs - LG
< Scot Fishermen's Fedn
M 51 i
¶ NL - 4; ftm.   AR.

Scottish Pensions Association (SOAPA)
NR 207 The Pleasance, EDINBURGH, EH8 9RU.   (hq)
      0131-668 1001
      Pres: John C Wilson
Br 112
○ *K, *W
● Conf - Inf - LG - Lobbying
M 11,000 i
¶ NL - 6.   Campaign Updates.

Scottish Pétanque Association (SPA) 1985
NR 21 Ardmore Gardens, DRYMEN, G63 0BD.   (sp)
      01360 660723
      email john@scottishpetanque.org
      http://www.scottishpetanque.org
      Sec: John Cameron
○ *S; the governing body in Scotland for the playing of pétanque
M i
¶ NL - 3; free.

Scottish Pharmaceutical Federation (SPF) 1919
NR 168 Bath St, GLASGOW, G2 4TQ.   (asa)
      0141-270 9070
      Sec: F E J McCrossin
○ *T; for retail pharmacists in business in Scotland
Gp Community pharmacists
< Nat Pharmaceutical Assn
M 1,044 i
¶ NL - 3;   Annual Financial Statement; both ftm only.

Scottish Pipers Association (SPA) 1920
▨ 69 Kirkland St, GLASGOW, G20 6SU.   (pres/p)
      0141-946 2137
      Pres: Miss J E Campbell
▲ Un-incorporated Society
○ *D; 'the study & practice of the great Highland bagpipe'
● Mtgs - Comp - Recitals of bagpipe music - Ceilidhs
M 120 i, UK / 20 i, o'seas

Scottish Piping Society of London (SPSL) 1932
NR 58 Scotland Farm Rd, Ash Vale, ALDERSHOT, Hants,
      GU12 5JB.   (pipemajor/p)
      Pipe Major: Roger Huth
▲ Registered Charity
○ *G; to further interest in solo piping of the great Highland
      bagpipe
● Mtgs - ET - Comp
M 250 i, 6 i, o'seas
¶ NL - 12; free.

Scottish Place-Name Society (SP-NS) 1996
▨ c/o School of Celtic & Scottish Studies, University of Edinburgh,
      27 George Square, EDINBURGH, EH8 9LD.   (hsb)
      http://www.st-and.ac.uk/institutes/sassi/spns
      No further information supplied

© CBD Research Ltd · Beckenham · BR3 5JS · Tel 020 8650 7745 · Fax 020 8650 0768 · E-mail cbd@cbdresearch.com · www.cbdresearch.com

Scottish Plant Owners Association (SPOA) 1951
NR 302 St Vincent St, GLASGOW, G2 5RZ. (sb)
    0141-248 3434
    http://www.spoa.org.uk
    Sec: Graham Bell
○ *T; for civil engineering, building & plant hire contractors
● Maintains a schedule of rates prepared from an annual survey
    of rates obtained in the market by members - Sponsors a
    form of agreement suitable for the transaction of plant hire
M 260 f
¶ Schedule of Rates & Handbook - 1.

Scottish Plastering & Drylining Association
    2005-6 merged with the **Federation of Plastering & Drywall
    Contractors**

Scottish Poetry Library (SPL) 1984
NR 5 Crichtons Close, Canongate, EDINBURGH, EH8 8DT. (hq)
    0131-557 2876 fax 0131-557 8393
    email inquiries@spl.org.uk http://www.spl.org.uk
    Dir: Dr Robyn Marsack
▲ Registered Charity
Br 9
○ *A, *E; a reference & lending library (free to public) for Scottish
    & international poetry, mainly of the 20th century
● Lib - Events during the Edinburgh International Festival - Visits
    to schools & other orgs - Monthly workshops for practising
    poets
< Scot Lib Inf Coun (SLIC)
M 700 i, 100 schools, colleges & libraries, UK / 50 i, o'seas
¶ NL - 2; ftm, (donation) nm.
    Scottish Poetry Index (ongoing series indexing poetry
    magazines) - irreg.

Scottish Police Federation (SPF) 1919
NR 5 Woodside Place, GLASGOW, G3 7QF. (hq)
    0141-332 5234
    Gen Sec: Joe Grant
Br 8
○ *P; a staff association covering constable to chief inspector
● Conf - Mtgs - Empl - LG - Legal advice
M 14,000 i
¶ AR.

Scottish Potato Trades Association
    2006 merged with the National Association of Seed Potato Merchants
    to form the **British Potato Trades Association**

Scottish Potters' Association
NR Wester Golford, Moyness, NAIRN, Highland, IV12 5QQ.
    (chmn/p)
    email chairman@scottishpotters.org
    http://www.scottishpotters.org
    Chmn: Veronica Newman
▲ Un-incorporated Society
○ *G, *P; the promotion of Scottish potters & ceramics; open to
    professional & amateur potters
● Mtgs - Exhib - VE - Workshops
M 175 i
¶ NL - 4; ftm.

Scottish Prayer Book Society (SPBS)
■ 32 Compton Avenue, GLASGOW, G44 5TH. (hsp)
    Hon Sec: Mrs Paula R Fleetwood
▲ Registered Charity
○ *G, *K, *R; to keep in print & promote the use of the 1929
    Scottish Prayer Book, one of the official service books of the
    Scottish Episcopal Church
● Mtgs
< Prayer Book Soc
M 175 i
¶ Scottish NL - 4.

Scottish Pre-School Play Association (SPPA) 1967
■ 45 Finnieston St, GLASGOW, G3 8JU. (hq)
    0141-221 4148 fax 0141-221 6043
    email info@sppa.org.uk http://www.sppa.org.uk
    Chief Exec: Ian McLaughlan
▲ Company Limited by Guarantee; Registered Charity
Br 5
○ *W; to promote the development of quality care & education in
    pre-school groups which respect the rights, responsibilities &
    needs of all children & their parents
Gp Information & advice; Insurance; Grants; Training; Field staff;
    Publications
● Conf - Mtgs - ET - Res - Comp - Inf - Empl - LG
< Pre-School Assns of England / Wales / Nthn Ireland / Ireland;
    Pre-School Learning Alliance
M 15 i, 26 f, 1,400 member gps
¶ First Five - 4; ftm.
    Learning & Development: an introduction to childcare in an
    early years setting; £38 m, £58 nm.
    Publications list available.

Scottish Print Employers Federation (SPEF) 1910
■ 48 Palmerston Place, EDINBURGH, EH12 5DE. (hq)
    0131-220 4353 fax 0131-220 4344
    email info@spef.org.uk http://www.spef.org.uk
    Dir: J B Raeburn
▲ Un-incorporated Society
Br 4
○ *T
Gp Printing; Binding; Ancillary
● Conf - Mtgs - ET - Inf - Lib - Empl - LG - Legal advisory service
< Intergraf
M 100 f
¶ NL - 2; Directory (on internet); AR; all free.

Scottish Prison Officers' Association
    changed name to Prison Officers Association of Scotland & merged in
    2001 with the **Prison Officers Association**

Scottish Public Relations Consultants Association
    a regional group of the **Public Relations Consultants Association**

Scottish Publishers Association (SPA) 1973
■ Scottish Book Centre, 137 Dundee St, EDINBURGH,
    EH11 1BG. (hq)
    0131-228 6866 fax 0131-228 3220
    email enquiries@scottishbooks.org
    http://www.scottishbooks.org
    Dir: Lorraine Fannin
▲ Registered Charity
○ *T; to provide information, advice, consultancy, training,
    marketing & promotional services
Gp Scot Book Marketing Gp (publicity & marketing service for
    booksellers in Scotland)
● ET - Inf - LG - Attending bookfairs, both domestic & overseas;
    Marketing & export advice; Promotional services
M 72 f
¶ Directory of Publishing in Scotland - 1; £9.99.

Scottish Pure Water Association (SPWA) 1970
NR 108 Millfield Hill, ERSKINE, Renfrewshire, PA8 6JJ. (hsp)
    Hon Sec: Mrs Marion Munro
▲ Un-incorporated Society
○ *K; to oppose the use of public water supply for mass
    medication
● INF
< Nat Pure Water Assn
M [not stated]
¶ NL - irreg; ftm.

Scottish Quality Salmon   (SQS)
NR   Durn, Isla Rd, PERTH, PH2 7HG.   (hq)
      01738 587000
      Chmn: Lord Lindsay
○   *B, *T
M   f

Scottish Railway Preservation Society   (SRPS)   1961
■   The Station, Union St, BO'NESS, W Lothian, EH51 9AQ.   (hq)
      01506 822298   fax 01506 828766
      http://www.srps.org.uk
      Hon Sec: Iain Gent,   Admin: Margaret Haynes
▲   Registered Charity
○   *G; 'to obtain, restore, display & run a working railway; to
      preserve all aspects of Scottish railway history'
      The railway operates under title of Bo'ness & Kinnel Railway
●   Mtgs - Exhib - SG - Operating the railway
<   Heritage Rly Assn
M   1,200 i
¶   Blastpipe - 4; ftm.

Scottish Record Society   (SRS)   1897
NR   Lyon Office, New Register House, EDINBURGH, EH1 3YT.
      (regd/add)
▲   Registered Charity
○   *L; to publish calendars, indices of public records & private
      muniments relating to Scotland for the use of historians &
      genealogists
      The Society DOES NOT undertake private research

Scottish Records Association   (SRA)   1977
NR   Royal College of Physicians & Surgeons, 232-242 St Vincent St,
      GLASGOW, G2 5RJ.   (hsb)
      0141-227 3234   fax 0141-221 1804
      email carol.parry@rcpsglasg.ac.uk
      http://www.scottishrecordsassociation.org
      Sec: Mrs Carol Parry
▲   Registered Charity
○   *L; the preservation & use of historical records in Scotland
●   Conf - Inf - VE
<   Scot Coun on Archives; Nat Coun on Archives
M   276 i, 67 org, UK / 8 i, 11 org, o'seas
¶   Scottish Archives (Jnl) - 1; ftm, £25 nm.   NL - 2.

Scottish Reformation Society   (SRS)   1851
NR   41 Cowgate, EDINBURGH, EH1 1JR.   (hq)
      0131-220 1450   fax 0131-220 1450
      email ashbethany35@hotmail.com
      http://www.scottishreformation.co.uk
      Sec & Lecturer: Rev A Sinclair Horne
▲   Registered Charity
Br   2
○   *R; 'to promote & propagate the Reformation in its history,
      theology & principles'
●   Mtgs - ET - Res - SG - Inf - VE - Reformation tours
<   Utd Protestant Coun
M   400 i, UK / 40 i, o'seas
¶   The Bulwark - 4.

Scottish Renewables Forum
NR   Central Chambers, 93 Hope Street, GLASGOW, G2 6LD.
      0141-222 7921
      http://www.scottishrenewables.com
      Contact: The Administrator
○   *T
<   Renewables Scotland

Scottish Retail Consortium
NR   PO Box 13737, GULLANE, Lothian, EH31 2WX.
      0870 609 3631
M   f

Scottish Rifle Association   (SRA)   1886
■   164 Ledi Drive, Bearsden, GLASGOW, G61 4JX.   (hsp)
      0141-942 2390
      email mabooonscotland@ntlworld.com
      http://www.scottishrifleassociation.org.uk
      Hon Sec: Alan Mabon
▲   Un-incorporated Society
○   *S; the governing body for target rifle shooting (full bore) in
      Scotland
●   Comp
<   Nat Rifle Assn; Scot Target Shooting Fedn
M   180 i, 20 org

Scottish Rights of Way & Access Society   (ScotWays)   1845
■   24 Annandale St, EDINBURGH, EH7 4AN.   (hq)
      0131-558 1222   fax 0131-558 1222
      email info@scotways.com   http://www.scotways.com
      Sec: Tom Titterton
▲   Company Limited by Guarantee; Registered Charity
○   *G, *K; protection of public rights of way in Scotland & general
      access matters
Gp   Legal; Fund-raising; Publicity; Projects; Walks
●   ET - Res - Stat - Inf - PL - VE - LG - Liaison with local authorities
      - Updating record of rights of way - Signposting
M   2,105 i, 463 org
¶   NL - 1;   AR - 1; both free.   Maps.
      Guide to the Law on Rights of Way in Scotland.
      Scottish Hill Tracks 5th ed, 2004.
      The Authority of Case Law.
      Various leaflets to Rights of Way, Catalogue etc; free.

Scottish Rock Garden Club   (SRGC)   1933
■   PO Box 14063, EDINBURGH, EH10 4YE.   (mail)
      http://www.srgc.org.uk address
      Sec: L Mills
▲   Registered Charity
Br   affiliated groups
○   *H; to promote the cultivation of alpine & peat garden plants
●   Conf - Mtgs - Exhib - Comp - SG - Inf - Lib - PL - VE
<   Amer Rock Garden Soc; Caledonian Horticl Soc; R Horticl Soc;
      Nthn Horticl Soc; Alpine Garden Soc
M   4,500 i, UK / in 38 countries o'seas
¶   The Rock Garden (Jnl) - 2;   Secretary's Page - 2;   Ybk - 1;
      all ftm only.

Scottish Rugby Union plc   (SRU)   1873
■   Murrayfield Stadium, EDINBURGH, EH12 5PJ.   (hq)
      0131-346 5000
      Sec: Graham Ireland
○   *S; administration of Rugby in Scotland; the development of the
      game at all levels in schools, clubs, district, national &
      international
M   i & clubs
¶   SRU Hbk - 1.   SRU Laws Book - 1.

Scottish Rural Property & Business Association   (SRPBA)   1906
NR   Stuart House, Eskmills Business Park, MUSSELBURGH,
      Midlothian, EH21 7PB.   (hq)
      0131-653 5400   fax 0131-653 5401
      http://www.srpba.com
▲   Un-incorporated Society
Br   5
○   *F; 'working for: high standards of land management; the
      owners of rural land in Scotland; the rural economy & those
      who depend upon it'
●   Conf - Mtgs - Inf - VE - LG
<   Eur Landowners Org (ELO)
M   3,600 i, 200 f
¶   Landowning in Scotland - 6; ftm only.
✕   2004 Scottish Landowners Federation

© CBD Research Ltd · Beckenham · BR3 5JS · Tel 020 8650 7745 · Fax 020 8650 0768 · E-mail cbd@cbdresearch.com · www.cbdresearch.com

Scottish Salmon Smokers Association   (SSSA)   1986
NR   20 Beaufort Rd, INVERNESS, Highland, IV2 3NP.   (hsb)
         01463 712902
         Sec: Doug Ritchie
▲   Un-incorporated Society
○   *T; to improve product integrity & quality in the Scottish smoked
         salmon industry
●   SG - Stat - Inf
<   Chilled Food Assn
M   20 f

Scottish School Board Association   (SSBA)   1992
■   Newall Terrace, DUMFRIES, DG1 1LW.   (hq/regd/office)
         01387 260428
         Office Mgr: Jennifer Gallacher
▲   Company Limited by Guarantee; Registered Scottish Charity
○   *E; to promote & encourage partnership in education; the
         Association is run by an elected executive board made up
         from 1 member each of Scotland's 32 local authorities & 1
         member from a Special Education Needs school
●   Conf - Mtgs - ET - Res - Exhib - Comp - SG - Inf - VE - LG -
         Provision of School Board training to school boards,
         teachers, head teachers & councillors
M   1,975 school boards in Scotland
¶   Safe School Travel Booklet.   SB Training Booklets.
         A Practical Guide to Safe School Trips Booklet.
         Getting the best out of a School Board Hbk.
         Working with your School Board Hbk for Headteachers.

Scottish Schoolsport Federation   (SSF)   1988
NR   Active Schools Manager, Highland Council, Council Offices,
         DINGWALL, Highlands, IV15 9QN.   (hsb)
         01349 868616
         Sec: Alan Clark
○   *N, *S; concerned largely with extra-curricular / extended
         curriculum school sport; acts as 'holding agency' in Scotland
         for International Schoolsport Federation (ISF) events
Gp   Education; Schools organisations; Sports organisations
●   Conf - Mtgs - Et - Comp - LG
<   Intl Schoolsport Fedn (ISF)
M   14 assns, 18 local authorities

Scottish Seafood Processors Federation Ltd   1986
NR   South Esplanade West, ABERDEEN, AB11 2FJ.   (hq)
         01224 897744   fax 01224 871405
         Chief Exec: Robert Milne
▲   Company Limited by Guarantee
Br   7
○   *T
●   Mtgs - ET - LG
M   180 f
¶   Ybk & Diary.
✕   2003 Scottish Fish Merchants Federation

Scottish Secondary Teachers' Association   (SSTA)   1946
NR   14 West End Place, EDINBURGH, EH11 2ED.   (hq)
         0131-313 7300   fax 0131-346 8057
         email info@ssta.org.uk
         Gen Sec: David Eaglesham
Br   32
○   *E, *U
●   Conf - Mtgs - ET - Res - SG - Inf - Empl - LG
<   Education Intl (EI); Eur Tr U C'ee for Education (ETUCE); Scot Tr
         U Congress
M   9,000 i
¶   Secondary Teacher - 4/5;   Bulletin - 5/6.

Scottish Security Association   (SSA)   1996
NR   PO Box 308, GLASGOW, G44 4BH.   (mail)
         http://www.scottishsecurityassociation.co.uk address
         Sec: George Glennie
▲   Un-incorporated Society
○   *P; to develop & foster members engaged in all aspects of
         security & safety
●   Conf - Mtgs - Exhib - Comp - Lib - VE - LG - Social events
M   50 i (Scotland)
¶   LM - 1; ftm only.

Scottish Seed & Nursery Trade Association   (SSNTA)   1917
NR   34 Ferguson Drive, PERTH, PH1 1SR.
         01738 442950
         Sec: Donna McNicol
▲   Un-incorporated Society
○   *T; for all those involved in the Scottish seed trade (agricultural,
         horticultural, wholesale, retail, nursery traders & landscape
         contractors)
●   Mtgs - VE
<   Attends mtgs of UK Agricl Supply Trade Assn (UKASTA) & UK
         Plant Varieties & Seeds Advisory Body (UKSAB)
M   f

Scottish Ship Chandlers Association   (SSCA)   1955
NR   McColl & Associates Ltd, 11 Burns Rd, ABERDEEN,
         AB15 4NT.   (asa)
         01224 313473   fax 01224 310385
         email roddy@mccollassociates.com
         Secs: McColl & Associates Ltd
○   *T; trade protection
●   Mtgs
M   20 f

Scottish Ski Club   (SSC)   1907
NR   11 Frogston Terrace, EDINBURGH, EH10 7AE.   (pres/p)
         0131-477 3888
         email w.aitken@blueyonder.co.uk
         http://www.scotski.org.uk
         Pres: W Aitken
▲   Un-incorporated Society
○   *S; promotion of skiing; support for competitive ski racing
Gp   Alpine; Nordic; Racing; Touring; Freestyle
●   Mtgs - ET - Comp - Inf - VE
<   Snowsport GB; Snowsport Scotland
M   1,300 i, UK / 50 i, o'seas
¶   Jnl - 1;   NL - 4; both ftm only.

Scottish Society for Autism   1968
NR   Hilton House, Alloa Business Park, Whins Rd, ALLOA,
         Clackmannanshire, FK10 3SA.   (hq)
         01259 720044   fax 01259 720051
         email autism@autism-in-scotland.org.uk
         http://www.autism-in-scotland.org.uk
         Chief Exec: John McDonald
▲   Registered Charity
○   *W; to provide care, support & education for peoples of all
         ages with autism throughout Scotland
●   Conf - Mtgs - ET - Inf - Lib - Residential school for children -
         Respite care & family support - Adult accommodation &
         community houses
M   662 i, 37 schools & housing org
¶   In Touch (Jnl) - 2; ftm, £3 nm.
         Jigsaw (NL) - 3;   AR - 1; both free.

Scottish Society for Conservation & Restoration
         in 2005 merged with the Care of Collections Forum, Institute of Paper
         Conservation, Photographic Materials Conservation Group, United
         Kingdom Institute for Conservation of Historic & Artistic Works to form
         the **Institute of Conservation**

Scottish Society for Contamination Control   (S2C2)   1986
NR   James Watt Building, Glasgow University, GLASGOW,
         G12 8QQ.   (hsb)
         0141-330 3699
▲   Registered Charity
Br   1
○   *K; to advance the education of the public in matters relating to
         the practice & science of contamination control
M   i

Scottish Society for Crop Research   (SSCR)   1981
NR   c/o Scottish Crop Research Institute, Invergowrie, DUNDEE,
         DD2 5DA.   (hq)
         01382 562731
○   *F, *H; incl arboriculture
Gp   Cereals; Potatoes; Soft fruits; Brassicas
●   Conf - Mtgs - Inf
¶   SCRI Staff Scientific Papers - irreg; free.
         Bulletins - irreg; ftm.   AR.
         Note: is a Registered Friendly Society

Scottish Society of the History of Medicine   (SSHM)   1948
NR   Red Gable, Denhead, ST ANDREWS, Fife, KY16 8PB.
▲   Registered Charity
○   *L; to further the general history of medicine, with special
         reference to Scottish medicine
●   Mtgs - Administration of Guthrie Trust to fund research &/or
         publications in the field of medical history - Annual lecture &
         dinner
<   Intl (& Brit) Soc(s) for the History of Medicine
M   198 i, UK / 5 i, o'seas
¶   NL - 1.   Report of the Proceedings - 2.

Scottish Society for Northern Studies   (SSNS)   1967
NR   c/o School of Celtic & Scottish Studies, University of Edinburgh,
         27 George Sq, EDINBURGH, EH8 9LD.   (hq)
○   *L; the study of all aspects of Scandinavian culture, history &
         the historical development of Scandinavian cultural effects in
         North Britain
M   i & org
¶   Northern Studies (Jnl) - 1.

**Scottish Society for the Prevention of Cruelty to Animals
(ScottishSPCA)   1839**
NR   Braehead Mains, 603 Queensferry Rd, EDINBURGH,
         EH4 6EA.   (hq)
         0131-339 0222   fax 0131-339 4777
         email fundraising@scottishspca.org
         http://www.scottishspca.org
         Chief Exec: Ian Gardiner
▲   Registered Charity
Br   55
○   *K, *V; to prevent cruelty to animals & to promote kindness in
         their treatment
●   ET - Inf - PL - Inspectors investigate complaints of cruelty -
         Animal welfare centres - Education officers give talks to
         schools
<   Wld Soc for the Protection of Animals - Eurogroup for Animal
         Welfare
M   9,400 i
¶   SSPCA News - 4;   Animal Express (junior members) - 4;
         Information leaflets;   AR; all free.

Scottish Society for the Protection of Wild Birds   1927
NR   Foremount House, KILBARCHAN, Renfrewshire, PA10 2EZ.
         01505 702419
         Sec: Dr J A Gibson
○   *K, *L
         no further information supplied

Scottish Society for Psychical Research
■   5 Church Wynd, Kingskettle, CUPAR, Fife, KY15 7PS.   (sp)
         01337 830387   fax 01337 830387
         email archie.lawrie@ukgateway.net
         Flat 2/2, 4 Raeberry St, GLASGOW, G20 6AJ.
             0141-579 2512   (chmn/p)
         Chmn: Patricia Robertson,   Sec: Archie Lawrie
▲   Registered Charity
○   *Q; investigating the paranormal in Scotland
Gp   Investigation; Historical research
●   Mtgs - Res - SG - Inf - Library including audio & video tapes
M   225 i, UK / 5 i, o'seas
¶   Psi Report - 9; ftm, £1 nm.

Scottish Society of Rehabilitation   (SSR)   1988
NR   24 Kingsland Drive, GLASGOW, G52 2NE.   (hsp)
         0870 770 5865
         email ssrehabilitation@aol.com   http://www.ssr.org.uk
         Admin Sec: Moira Colvan
▲   Registered Charity
○   *P; to increase awareness & understanding of acute & chronic
         disabling conditions & of their consequent impairments,
         disabilities & handicaps; to promote improvements in
         rehabilitation practice by promoting awareness of effective
         rehabilitation & emphasising multi-disciplinary teamwork
●   Conf - Mtgs - ET
M   100 i
¶   SSR NL - 2; free.

Scottish Solar Energy Group   (SSEG)   1980
NR   c/o Dr Tom Grassie, Room C106, School of Engineering,
         Napier University, Merchiston Campus, 10 Colinton Rd,
         EDINBURGH, EH10 5DT.   (hsb)
         email t.grassie@napier.ac.uk
         Sec: Dr Tom Grassie
○   *P; to encourage the use of solar energy in Scotland
●   Conf - Mtgs - VE - Seminars
M   i
¶   NL - 1.
         Published papers.

Scottish Spina Bifida Association   (SSBA)   1964
NR   The Dan Young Building, 6 Craighalbert Way, CUMBERNAULD,
         G68 0LS.   (hq)
         01236 794500   fax 01236 736435
         email mail@ssba.org.uk   http://www.ssba.org.uk
         Exec: Andrew H D Wynd
▲   Registered Charity
Br   5
○   *W; to increase public awareness & understanding of
         individuals with spina bifida, hydrocephalus & related
         disorders; to aim to secure provision for their special needs &
         those of their families
Gp   Spina bifida; Hydrocephalus
●   Mtgs - ET - Res - Exhib - SG - Inf - VE - Empl - LG
         Family support services: 0845 911 1112
<   Intl Fedn for Spina Bifida & Hydrocephalus; Assn for Spina
         Bifida & Hydrocephalus
M   3,800 i, 20 f, 10 org, UK / 20 i, o'seas
¶   talkBACK - 4; ftm, on request nm.
         Publications list available.

Scottish Sporting Car Club   (SSCC)   1932
NR   18 Ayr Road, Giffnock, GLASGOW, G46 6RY.   (sp)
         Sec: Charles Turner
○   *S; organisation of motor sport events
M   i
¶   Top Gear (NL) - 12; ftm only.

© CBD Research Ltd · Beckenham · BR3 5JS · Tel 020 8650 7745 · Fax 020 8650 0768 · E-mail cbd@cbdresearch.com · www.cbdresearch.com

Scottish Sports Association (SSA) 1983

■ Caledonia House, South Gyle, EDINBURGH, EH12 9DQ.   (hq)
  0131-339 8785   fax 0131-339 5168
  email mail@info-ssa.org.uk
  http://www.scottishsportsassociation.org.uk
  Policy Director: Chris Robison
▲ Company Limited by Guarantee
○ *N, *S; to promote cooperation among governing bodies &
  organisations of sport in Scotland in consultation with (& as
  an independent consultative body to) the Scottish Sports
  Council
● Conf - Mtgs - Res - Inf - LG
M c 80 org
¶ Bulletin - 26; ftm only.

Scottish Squash Ltd 1937

■ Caledonia House, 1 Redheughs Rigg, South Gyle,
  EDINBURGH, EH12 9DQ.   (hq)
  0131-317 7343   fax 0131-317 7734
  email info@scottishsquash.org
  http://www.scottishsquash.org
  Chief Operating Officer: Kim Atkinson
▲ Company Limited by Guarantee
○ *S; the national governing body for the sport of squash in
  Scotland
< Wld Squash Fedn (WSF); Eur Squash Fedn (ESF); Scot Sports
  Assn (SSA)
M i & clubs

Scottish Stone Liaison Group

NR Pentlandfield Business Park (Room 133), The Bush, ROSLIN,
  Midlothian, EH25 9RE.   (hsb)
  0131-448 0313
  Sec: Alan McKinney
○ *G; to ensure the availability of indigenous building materials
  for repair work on local structures

Scottish Sub Aqua Club (ScotSAC) 1953

■ Cockburn Centre, 40 Bogmoor Place, GLASGOW, G51 4TQ.
  (hq)
  0141-425 1021   fax 0141-425 1021
  email ab@hqssac.demon.co.uk
  http://www.scotsac.com
  Admin Officer: Mrs Alicia Bannon
▲ Un-incorporated Society
Br 70+; Eire
○ *S; governing body for sub-aqua diving in Scotland
Gp Boat handling (rigid inflatable boats)
● Conf - Mtgs - ET - Exam - Comp - Lib
< Scot Sports Coun
M c 2,000 i
¶ Scottish Diver Magazine - 6; ftm, £2.50 nm.

Scottish Subsea Technology Group
  was dissolved in 2003 & transferred its assets to **Subsea UK**

Scottish Support for Learning Association (SSLA)

NR 14 Lochinblair Gardens, BLAIRGOWRIE, Perthshire,
  PH10 6GA.   (mail) address
  Contact: Ann Paterson
▲ Registered Charity
○ *P; to support professionals working with children & young
  people
● Conf - Mtgs - ET - Inf - LG
< Ir Support for Learning Assn (ISLA); Scot Dyslexia Assn; Afasic
  Scotland; Enquire
> Ir Support for Learning Assn (ISLA); Enquire; Dyslexia Assn;
  Afasic Scotland
M c 200 i, c 16 f, 4 org

Scottish Surfing Federation (SSF) 1976

NR Mybster Croft, SPITTAL, Caithness, KW1 5XR.   (chmn/p)
  01847 841300
  Chmn: Andrew Bain
○ *S; promotion of surfing in Scotland, both at recreation &
  contest levels

Scottish Swimming Ltd (SASA) 1888

■ National Swimming Academy, University of Stirling, STIRLING,
  FK9 4LE.   (hq)
  01786 466520   fax 01786 466521
  email info@scottishswimming.com
  http://www.scottishswimming.com
  Chief Exec: Ashley Howard
▲ Company Limited by Guarantee
○ *S; governing body for aquatic sport in Scotland
Gp Diving, Education, Medical, Technical training development,
  Water polo
  Swimming: Masters, Open water, Speed, Synchronised
● Mtgs - ET - Exam - Comp - Inf
< Fédn Intle de Natation Amateur (FINA); League Eur de
  Natation (LEN); C'wealth Games Coun for Scotland (CGCS);
  Amat Swimming Fedn of GB (ASFGB); Sportscotland; Scot
  Sports Coun (SSC)
M 160 clubs
¶ Bank of Scotland Learn to Swim Syllabus; £29.99.
  Bank of Scotland Learn to Swim (Adult & Child Syllabus); £35.
  National Swimming Award Pack; £10 m.
× 2002-03 Scottish Amateur Swimming Association

Scottish Table Tennis Association (STTA) 1936

NR Caledonia House, South Gyle, EDINBURGH, EH12 9DQ.   (hq)
  0131-317 8077
▲ Un-incorporated Society
○ *S; governing body for table tennis in Scotland
Gp Veterans
● ET - Comp - Stat - Inf
< Intl Table Tennis Fedn; Eur Table Tennis U; C'wealth Table
  Tennis Fedn
M 1,500 i,
¶ The Bulletin - 5/6.
  Note: trades as Table Tennis Scotland.

Scottish Target Shooting Federation 1886

NR 77 Malbet Pk, Liberton, EDINBURGH, EH16 6WB.   (hsp)
  0131-664 9674
  Hon Sec: Colin R Aitken
○ *S
  No further information supplied

Scottish Tenants Organisation

  not currently operating as a constituted body

Scottish Text Society (STS) 1882

■ School of English, University of Nottingham, University Park,
  NOTTINGHAM, NG7 2RD.   (editorial/sb)
  0115-957 5922
  email sts@arts.gla.ac.uk
  Editorial Sec: Dr Nicola P Royan
▲ Registered Charity
○ *L; to further the study & teaching of Scottish literature by
  publishing editions of original texts (mediaeval period to the
  18th century)
● AGM
M 45 i, 52 f, UK / 17 i, 120 f, o'seas
¶ Annual volume; ftm, £30 nm.   AR; ftm only.

Scottish Timber Trade Association   (STTA)   1910
NR   Office 14 John Player Building, Stirling Enterprise Park,
    Springbank Rd, STIRLING, FK7 7RP.   (asa)
    01786 451623   fax 01786 473112
    email mail@stta.org.uk   http://www.stta.org.uk
    Sec: David Sulman
○   *T
M   f
    Note: is a regional association of the Timber Trade Federation.

Scottish Tourism Forum   1994
■   29 Drumsheugh Gardens, EDINBURGH, EH3 7RN.   (hq)
    0131-220 6321
    Chief Exec: Alan Rankin
▲   Company Limited by Guarantee
○   *N; to represent tourism industry interests with government &
    public agencies
●   Mtgs - Res - LG
M   20 f, 80 org
¶   email NL - 26.   Research Results - 4.

Scottish Tourist Guides Association   (STGA)   1960
■   Old Town Jail, St John Street, STIRLING, FK8 1EA.   (hq)
    01786 447784   fax 01786 447784
    email info@stga.co.uk   http://www.stga.co.uk
    Admin: Doreen Boyle, Chief Exec: Stewart Noble
▲   Company Limited by Guarantee
Br   4
○   *P; providing guiding services throughout Scotland (offers
    guiding in 17 languages)
Gp   Blue Badge members; Regional affiliates; Site affiliates
●   Conf - ET - Exhib - SG - Inf - VE
<   Wld Fedn Tourist Guide Assns; Fedn Eur Guides
>   Scot Tourism Forum
M   475 i
¶   Guidelines (NL) - 6.   LM - 1.

Scottish Trades Union Congress   (STUC)   1897
NR   333 Woodlands Rd, GLASGOW, G3 6NG.   (hq)
    0141-337 8100
    email info@stuc.org.uk
    Gen Sec: Bill Speirs
○   *U
●   Conf
M   c 700,000 i
¶   AR.   LM.   Agenda.

Scottish Transport Studies Group   (STSG)   1984
NR   26 Palmerston Place, EDINBURGH, EH12 5AL.   (mail)
    0870 350 4202 address
    Sec: Iain Docherty
▲   Registered Charity
○   *G, *L, *N; to stimulate interest in, & awareness of, the
    transport function & its importance for the Scottish economy
●   Conf - Mtgs - Res - SG - Stat - Inf
M   55 i, 39 f, 10 org
¶   Scottish Transport Review - 4.   Occasional Papers.

Scottish Tug-of-War Association   (STOWA)   1981
NR   47 Finlay Ave, EAST CALDER, W Lothian, EH53 0RP.   (hsp)
    0131-451 4030
    http://www.scottish-tug-of-war.co.uk
    Sec: Gary Gillespie
○   *S
●   Comp
<   Tug-of-War Intl Fedn (TWIF)
M   100 i, 12 teams
¶   Yearbook - 1.

Scottish Volleyball Association   (SVA)   1963
NR   48 The Pleasance, EDINBURGH, EH8 9TJ.   (hq)
    0131-556 4633
    Chief Exec: Kenny Barton
○   *S; to promote, develop & control volleyball in Scotland
M   i, schools & clubs
¶   NL - 5.   Magazine - 2.   AR.
    Fixture List/Hbk - 1.   Referees Hbk - 1.

Scottish White Fish Producers' Association Ltd   (SWFPA)   1944
NR   c/o MacRae Stephen & Co, 40 Broad St, FRASERBURGH,
    Aberdeenshire, AB43 9AH.   (asa)
    01346 514545   fax 01346 518075
    http://www.swfpa.org.uk
    Sec: George A MacRae
▲   Company Limited by Guarantee
○   *T; trade protection - catching sector fishing industry
●   Conf - Mtgs - Res - SG - LG
M   214 vessels
¶   [all press releases are on the website].

Scottish Wholesale Association   (SWA)   1940
NR   30 McDonald Place, EDINBURGH, EH7 4NH.   (hq)
    0131-556 8753
    Exec Dir: Kate Salmon
○   *T; food, grocery & drink wholesale industry in Scotland
Gp   Licensed c'ee; Non-licensed c'ee; Security circle
●   Conf - Mtgs - ET - LG
<   Fedn Whls Distbrs; Scot Grocers' Fedn; Scot Licensed Tr Assn
M   36 f, 120 associate members
¶   NL - 4; Ybk; both free.

Scottish Wild Boar Association
    no longer in existence

Scottish Wild Land Group   (SWLG)   1982
■   8 Hartington Place, EDINBURGH, EH10 4LE.   (hsp)
    0131-229 2094   (evenings)
    email enquiries@swlg.org.uk   http://www.swlg.org.uk
    Co-ordinator: Alistair Cant
▲   Registered Charity; Un-incorporated Society
○   *K; to protect wild land in Scotland against intrusive
    developments; to ensure any development is done sensitively
    & sustainably
<   Scot Envt Link
M   450 i, UK / 10 i, o'seas
¶   Wild Land News - 3; ftm, 50p nm.

Scottish Wildlife Trust Ltd   (SWT)   1964
NR   Cramond House, Kirk Cramond, Cramond Glebe Rd,
    EDINBURGH, EH4 6NS.   (hq)
    0131-312 7765   fax 0131-312 8705
    email enquiries@swt.org.uk   http://www.swt.org.uk
    Chief Exec: Simon Milne
▲   Registered Charity
Br   3 regional offices
○   *K; to conserve all forms of wild life & habitats in Scotland
●   ET - Res - Management of wildlife reserves
<   UK Wildlife Trusts
M   19,000 i, 34 f, 51 org
¶   Scottish Wildlife - 3.   AR.

Scottish Wirework Manufacturers' Association   (SWMA)   1908
NR   c/o Wm Reid & Sons (Wireworkers) Ltd, 162 Glenpark St,
    GLASGOW, G31 1PG.   (hsb)
    0141-554 6987   fax 0141-556 4483
    Sec: Ian W Reid
○   *T
M   17 f

© CBD Research Ltd · Beckenham · BR3 5JS · Tel 020 8650 7745 · Fax 020 8650 0768 · E-mail cbd@cbdresearch.com · www.cbdresearch.com

Scottish Women's Bowling Association   1936

NR   c/o Anna Marshall, Unit 76, STEP, John Player Building,
       STIRLING, FK7 7RP.   (hsp)
       01786 449012
       Sec: Ms Anna Marshall
○   *S
       No further information supplied.

Scottish Women's Football   (SWF)   1972

■   Hampden Park, GLASGOW, G42 9DF.   (hq)
       0141-620 4580   fax 0141-620 4581
       email swf@scottish-football.com
       http://www.scottishwomensfootball.com
       Exec Admin: Maureen McGonigle
○   *S
Gp   Leagues: Senior, Universities, Under 19, Under 17, Under 13,
       Schools
●   Conf - Mtgs - ET - Comp
M   4,000 i
¶   NL - 2;   Club Secretary Lists - irreg; both free.

Scottish Women's Indoor Bowling Association   (SWIBA)   1961

■   Troscons, Watson St, Letham, FORFAR, DD8 2QB.   (hsp)
       01307 818238
       Hon Sec: Anne Easton
▲   Un-incorporated Society
○   *S
●   Mtgs - Comp - National & international championship teams
<   Brit Isles Women's Indoor Bowls Coun; Wld Indoor Bowls Coun
M   18,000 i, 56 clubs
¶   Ybk.

Scottish Women's Rural Institutes   (SWRI)   1917

■   42 Heriot Row, EDINBURGH, EH3 6ES.   (hq)
       0131-225 1724   fax 0131-225 8129
       email swri@swri.demon.co.uk
       Gen Sec: Mrs Anne Peacock
▲   Registered Charity
Br   905
○   *G; non-political, non-sectarian organisation providing
       educational, recreational & social opportunities for those who
       live & work in the country or are interested in country life
●   Conf - Mtgs - ET - Exhib - Comp - Lib
<   Associated Countrywomen of the World
M   23,000 i
¶   Scottish Home & Country - 12; £1.

** Scottish Wrestling Association

Organisation lost: see Introduction paragraph 3

Scottish Youth Hostels Association   (SYHA)   1932

■   7 Glebe Crescent, STIRLING, FK8 2JA.
       01786 891400
       Gen Sec: Keith Legge
Br   5
○   *Y; provision of low cost hostel accommodation
●   Conf - Mtgs - Exhib - Comp - Stat - Inf - Empl - Activity holidays
       - Foreign travel
M   44,745 i, 1,000 org, clubs & schools
¶   AR; free.   Guides & books.   Publicity pamphlets.

Scout Association   1908

NR   Gilwell Park, Bury Rd, LONDON, E4 7QW.   (hq)
       020 8433 7100   fax 020 8433 7103
       email info.centre@scout.org.uk
       http://www.scouts.org.uk
       Sec: D J C Shelmerdine
▲   Registered Charity
Br   10,000
○   *Y; 'to promote the development of young people in achieving
       their full physical, spiritual, intellectual & social potentials, as
       individuals, as responsible citizens & as members of their
       local, national & international communities'
Gp   Beaver Scouts (6-8); Cub Scouts (8-10½); Scouts (10½-15);
       Explorer Scouts (14½-18); Scout Network (18-25)
●   Conf - Mtgs - ET - Exhib - Comp - Stat - Inf - Expeditions -
       Camping - Games - Outings - Water activities - Mountain &
       hill activities - Air activities
<   Wld Scout Org
M   c 600,000 i
¶   Scouting - 12.

Scout Association of Ireland
       merged in 2003 with Scouting Ireland CSI to form **Scouting Ireland**

Scout & Guide Graduate Association   (SAGGA)   1957

■   15 Weatheroak Close, Webheath, REDDITCH, Worcs,
       B97 5TF.   (hsp)
       0701 070 7442
       email secretary@sagga.org.uk   http://www.sagga.org.uk
       Chmn: Sally Payne
▲   Registered Charity
Br   6
○   *N, *Y; to provide service to the scout & guide movements; to
       promote scout & guide cooperation
●   Conf - Mtgs - ET - SG - VE - Service work
<   Scout Assn; Girl Guiding UK
M   210 i, UK / 10 i, o'seas
¶   News & Ideas - 4; ftm only.

Scouting Ireland   2004

IRL   Larch Hill, DUBLIN 16, Republic of Ireland.
       353 (1) 495 6300   fax 353 (1) 495 6301
       http://www.scouts.ie
       Nat Sec: Mark O'Callaghan
○   *Y
×   2003 (Scout Assn of Ireland
       (Scouting Ireland CSI (merged)

Scrabble Clubs (UK)   1993

■   Mattel House, Vanwall Business Park, Vanwall Rd,
       MAIDENHEAD, Berks, SL6 4UB.   (hq)
       01628 500000   fax 01628 500118
       email philip.nelkon@mattel.com
       Mgr: Philip Nelkon
○   *G
●   Conf - Comp - Inf
M   500 clubs, UK / 400 clubs, o'seas
¶   Scrabble Club News - 4; ftm.

Screen Printing Association (UK) Ltd   (SPA(UK)Ltd)   1934

■   Association House, 7a West St, REIGATE, Surrey, RH2 9BL.
       (hq)
       01737 240792   fax 01737 240770
       email info@spauk.co.uk   http://www.spauk.co.uk
       Dir: Michael Turner
▲   Company Limited by Guarantee
○   *T; advancement of the screen printing & digital imaging
       processes
●   Conf - Mtgs - ET - Res - Exhib - Comp - Stat - Expt - Inf
<   Fedn of Eur Screen Printers Assn (FESPA)
M   200 f, UK / 3 f, o'seas
¶   NL - 4;   LM - 1; both ftm only.   Ybk; free.
       Impact of Digital / Non-Impact Printing on Industry.
       Technical documents & other publications.

Screen Producers Ireland   1987

IRL   The Studio Building, Meeting House Sq, DUBLIN 2, Republic of
      Ireland.
         353 (1) 671 3525   fax 353 (1) 671 4292
         http://www.screenproducersireland.com
      Chief Exec: David McLoughlin
○   *T
×   2003 Film Makers Ireland

Sculptors' Society of Ireland   (SSI)

IRL   Corner Halston St & St Mary's Lane, DUBLIN 7, Republic of
      Ireland.
         353 (1) 872 2296   fax 353 (1) 872 2364
         email info@sculptors-society.ie
         http://www.sculptors-society.ie
      Dir: Toby Dennett
○   *A; to promote contemporary sculpture
M   420

Scurry Driving Association   (SDA)

NR   Granados, East Woodlands Rd, Blatchbridge, FROME,
      Somerset, BA11 5EL.   (regd/add)
         http://www.scurrydrivers.co.uk
▲   Company Limited by Guarantee
○   *S; a competitive sport in which a driven pair of ponies
         complete a course of obstacles, the winner being the pair
         with the fastest overall time
●   ET - Exhib - Comp - Inf
M   40 i
¶   NL - 3; ftm, £3 nm.
         Leaflet with rules.
×   2005 Double Harness Scurry Driving

Sea Cadet Association
      in November 2004 merged with the Marine Society to form the
      Marine Society & Sea Cadets

Sea Cadet Corps   (SCC)   1899

NR   202 Lambeth Rd, LONDON, SE1 7JF.   (hq)
         020 7928 8978
      Contact: Commodore L Brokenshire
○   *Y; to develop self discipline, leadership & responsibility to
         others based on naval ways & traditions
<   Sea Cadet Corps in many other countries; the Navy Leagues
         of: Australia, Canada, N Zealand, S Africa, USA
M   i
¶   Navy News - 12.   AR; free.

Sea of Faith Network (UK)   (SoF)   1989

◼   Gospel Hill Cottage, Chapel Lane, Whitfield, BRACKLEY,
      Northants, NN13 5TF.   (mail)
         http://www.sofn.org.uk add
      Hon Sec: Oliver Essame
▲   Un-incorporated Society
Br   26 groups
○   *L, *R; exploring & promoting religious faith as a human
         creation
●   Conf - Local group meetings for study & discussion
<   Sea of Faith Networks Australia, NZ
M   526 i, UK / 47 i, o'seas
¶   sof - 6; ftm, £15 nm.   NL - 6.
         Agenda of Faith; £2.50.
         A Reasonable Faith: introducing the Sea of Faith
            Network; £2 m, free nm.
         Time and Tide: Sea of Faith beyond the Millennium; £7.

Seabird Group   1966

NR   2 Burgess Terrace, EDINBURGH, EH9 2BD.
         http://www.seabirdgroup.org.uk
      Sec: Alan Leitch
▲   Registered Charity
○   *L; promotion of liaison in the study of seabirds, mainly of
         Britain & Ireland
M   i, f & org
¶   Atlantic Seabirds (Jnl) - 4.   NL - 3.

Seafood Scotland

NR   18 Logie Mill, Logie Green Rd, EDINBURGH, EH7 4HG.
         0131-557 9344
         email enquiries@seafoodscotland.org
         http://www.seafoodscotland.org
      Chief Exec: Libby Woodhatch
○   *T

Seafood Shetland

NR   Shetland Seafood Centre, Stewart Building, LERWICK, Shetland,
      ZE1 0LL.
         01595 693644   fax 01595 696126

Sealed Knot Ltd   (SK)   1968

NR   PO Box 2000, NOTTINGHAM, NG2 5LH.
○   *G; re-enactment of 17th century English Civil War battles, life
         & times

Seasonal Affective Disorder Association
      see **SAD Association**

Seasoning & Spice Association   (SSA)   1992

NR   6 Catherine St, LONDON, WC2B 5JJ.   (hq)
         020 7836 2460
▲   Un-incorporated Society
○   *T; represents seasoning & spice processors based in the UK
●   Mtgs
<   Eur Spice Assn (ESA); Food & Drink Fedn
M   22 f

**Sebda - the Social, Emotional & Behavioural Difficulties
Association   (SEBDA)   1952**

◼   Church House, 1 St Andrew's View, PENRITH, Cumbria,
      CA11 7YF.   (hq)
         01768 210510   fax 01768 210512
         email admin@sebda.org
      Exec Dir: Ted Cole
▲   Registered Charity
Br   6
○   *P; for all professionals working with children with emotional &/
         or behavioural difficulties & their families
●   Conf - Mtgs - ET - LG
<   Nat Children's Bureau; Young Minds
M   1,100 i, UK / 60 i, o'seas
¶   Emotional & Behavioural Difficulties (Jnl) - 3; ftm.
         Sebda News - 12.
         Publications list available.
×   2003 (Feb) Association of Workers for Children with Emotional
         & Behavioural Difficulties

**Second World War Aircraft Preservation Society   (SWWAPS)
1976**

NR   Lasham Airfield, ALTON, Hants, GU34 5SS.   (hq)
▲   Un-incorporated Society
○   *G; a private collection available to the public to preserve
         aircraft, in a museum environment, that would otherwise be
         lost to our aviation heritage; includes artifacts & components
●   Mtgs - ET - Inf - Lib
<   Brit Aviation Presvn Coun (BAPC)
M   43 i

Secondary Heads Association
      since 2006 **Association of School & College Leaders**

Sectional Chamber Association
    a product association of the **British Precast Concrete Federation**

Securities & Investment Institute   1992
NR Centurion House, 24 Monument St, LONDON, EC3R 8AQ.
    (hq)
    020 7645 0600   fax 020 7645 0601
    http://www.securities-institute.org.uk
    Chief Exec: Simon Culhane
▲   Company Limited by Guarantee; Registered Charity
○   *P; for qualified & experienced practitioners of good standing in
    securities, derivatives & related areas of investment business;
    to set & improve standards through training & qualifications
●   Conf - Mtgs - ET - Exam - Res - Lib - LG
M   16,000 i, UK / 1,000 i, o'seas
¶   Securities & Investment Review (Jnl) - 6; ftm.
    LM - 2; ftm.   Report & Accounts - 1; free.
×   2004 Securities Institute

Security Institute of Ireland   1981
IRL Donnelly Court, Cork St, DUBLIN 8, Republic of Ireland.
    353 (1) 454 0439   fax 353 (1) 454 0438
    email sii@eircom.net   http://www.sii.ie
    Sec: John Byrne
○   *P

Security Manufacturers' Export Council
    a group of the **British Security Industry Association**

Seed Crushers & Oil Processors Association
NR PO Box 259, BECKENHAM, Kent, BR3 3YA.   (hq)
    020 8776 2644; 020 8398 5955   fax 020 8249 5402
    Sec: Angela Bowden
▲   Un-incorporated Society
○   *T
<   Intl Assn Seed Crushers (IASC); Eur Seed Crushers & Oil
    Processors' Assn (FEDIOL); FOSFA; Food & Drink Fedn
M   13 f
¶   AR.

Seeing Dogs Alliance   1978
NR 116 Potters Lane, Send, WOKING, Surrey, GU23 7AL.   (hq)
    01483 765556
    http://www.seeingdogs.org.uk
    Hon Sec: Mrs Christine Parker
▲   Registered Charity
○   *W; to train guide dogs for blind people; to give instruction in
    the use of alternative mobility aids where guide dogs are not
    suitable
Gp Study of breeds of dog most suited to guide dog training
●   Mtgs - ET - Res - Inf - Lib
M   c 50 i
¶   Occasional papers - 1; free.
×   2001 Mobility Aid & Guide Dog Alliance

Sefton Chamber of Commerce & Industry Ltd   1993
NR 22 Hoghton St, SOUTHPORT, Merseyside, PR9 0PA.   (hq)
    01704 531710   fax 01704 539255
    email mail@seftonchamber.com
    http://www.seftonchamber.com
    Chief Exec: Steve Dickson
▲   Company Limited by Guarantee
○   *C
●   Conf - Mtgs - ET - Res - Exhib - SG - Stat - Expt - Inf - Lib - VE -
    LG - Video Conference; 01704 549673
<   NI Cham Comm; Business Link Merseyside
M   600 f, 6 org
¶   Chamber News - 6; ftm only.
    Business to Business Flyer - 12.
    Sefton Business Directory - 2; ftm.

Selborne Society   1885
■   89 Daryngton Drive, GREENFORD, Middx, UB6 8BH.
    (regd/add)
    020 8578 3181
    http://www.biochem.ucl.ac.uk/~dab/selborne.html
    Hon Sec: R.J. Hall
▲   Company Limited by Guarantee; Registered Charity
○   *E, *G; to promote interest in conservation & natural history,
    especially among children; to maintain Perivale Wood Nature
    Reserve
●   Mtgs - Res - Exhib - Lib - VE
M   800 i
¶   Jnl Pioneers of Conservation (2004); £2 m, £3 nm. Wildlife in
    the Suburbs (3rd ed); £2 m,£3 nm.

Selden Society   1887
■   c/o Law Building, Queen Mary University of London,
    Mile End Rd, LONDON, E1 4NS.   (hq)
    020 7882 5136   fax 020 8981 8733
    email selden-society@qmul.ac.uk
    http://www.selden-society.qmul.ac.uk
    Sec: Victor Tunkel
▲   Registered Charity
○   *L, *Q; history of English law
●   Res - Inf - Advice to public bodies, libraries, the media &
    general public on questions of legal history, history of courts,
    the profession, institutions, manuscripts, family & local
    history, etc
<   Assn Intle de l'Histoire de Droit
M   380 i, 165 f & org, UK / 1,080 i, f & org, o'seas
¶   Main series - annual volume.
    Volumes in supplementary series - irreg; prices vary.
    Hbk (incl LM & Rules) - 5 yrly.
    Lectures - irreg.   AR - 1.

SELECT   1900
NR The Walled Garden, BUSH ESTATE, Midlothian, EH26 0SB.
    (hq)
    0131-445 5577
    Managing Dir: D N McGuiness
▲   Un-incorporated Society
Br 7
○   *T; to represent the electrical, electronic & communications
    systems industry in Scotland; membership categories incl
    electrical installation, safety & security systems, information
    technology, telecommunications, electronics & controls
●   Conf - Mtgs - ET - Exhib - Comp - SG - Inf - Empl - LG
<   Intl Assn of Electrical Contractors
M   550 f
¶   Cabletalk - 6.   NL - 12.   AR.   LM - 1.

Self Storage Association Ltd   (SSAUK)
■   Priestley House, The Gullet, NANTWICH, Cheshire, CW5 5SZ.
    01270 623150
    http://www.ssauk.com
    Chief Exec: Rodney Walker
○   *T
●   Conf - Mtgs - Inf
M   320 i
¶   Focus Magazine - 4; ftm (£2 extra copies); £4 nm.

Sense - National Deafblind & Rubella Association   1955
■   11-13 Clifton Terrace, LONDON, N4 3SR.   (hq)
    020 7272 7774   fax 020 7272 6012
    email enquiries@sense.org.uk   http://www.sense.org.uk
    Chief Exec: Dr A Best
▲   Registered Charity
Br 11 regions
○   *E, *W; to provide advice & support to deafblind & rubella
    handicapped children & adults & their families
●   Mtgs - ET - Res - Inf - Lib - LG
M   350 i
¶   Talking Sense - 3; ftm, £15 nm.

Seriously Ill for Medical Research
 since 2005 **Patients' Voice for Medical Advance**

Services Industrial Professional & Technical Union
 see **SIPTU (Services Industrial Professional & Technical Union)**

Sevenoaks & District Chamber of Commerce   1910
NR   The Quadrant, 5 Victoria Rd, SEVENOAKS, Kent, TN13 1YD.
      (hq)
      01732 455188
      Chief Exec: Carol Robinson
▲   Company Limited by Guarantee
○   *C
●   Conf - Mtgs - Exhib - Stat - Expt - Inf - LG
M   185 f
¶   NL - 6; ftm.
      Business Directory - 1; published jointly with the local District
      Council & covers businesses within the Sevenoaks & District
      area.

Seventeen Fortyfive / 1745 Association   1946
■   Ferry Cottage, Corran, Ardgour, FORT WILLIAM, Highland,
      PH33 7AA.   (hsp)
      01855 841306
      http://www.1745Association.org.uk
      Hon Sec: Miss C W H Aikman
▲   Registered Charity; Un-incorporated Society
○   *L; the study of Jacobite history; erection of memorials on
      historical sites
●   Conf - VE
M   350 i, 1 f, UK / 50 i, 1 org (Alliance France-Ecosse), o'seas
¶   The Jacobite - 3;   AR - 1; ftm only.

Seventeenth Century Life & Times   2000
■   Fern Cottage, 91 High St, ALTON, Hants, GU34 1LG.
      (chmn/p)
      01420 541731
      http://www.17thcenturylifeandtimes.com
      Chmn: Geoffrey Michael Thorne
▲   Un-incorporated Society
○   *G; 17th century (mainly English civil war) civilian & military
      living history re-enactment
●   Mtgs - ET - Res - Exhib - SG - Inf - VE
<   Nat Assn Re-enactment Socs
M   130 i
¶   The Scrichowl - 2; ftm only.

Sewing Machine Trade Association Ltd   (SMTA)   1939
■   83 Guildford St, CHERTSEY, Surrey, KT16 9AS.   (hq)
      0870 330 8610   fax 0870 330 8611
○   *T; interests of sewing machine dealers & allied interests in the
      UK & Eire
●   Conf - Mtgs - ET - Exhib - Inf - VE
M   360 f, UK / 3 f, o'seas
¶   Shuttle Plus - 4; free.

Sexaholics Anonymous
■   PO Box 1914, BRISTOL, BS99 2NE.   (mail/address)
      0700 072 5463
      http://www.sa.org + sauk.org
▲   Un-incorporated Society
○   *M, *W; offers a 12-step programme of recovery for those who
      want to stop their self-destructive sexual thinking & behaviour
●   Mtgs

Sexual Dysfunction Association   1995
■   Windmill Place Business Centre, 2-4 Windmill Lane,
      SOUTHALL, Middx, UB2 4NJ.   (hq)
      0870 774 3571   fax 0870 774 3572
      email info@sda.uk.net   http://www.sda.uk.net
      Dir: Ann Tailor
▲   Registered Charity
○   *M, *W; to raise awareness of the causes & treatments of male
      & female sexual dysfunction
●   Inf
<   Eur Sexual Dysfunction Alliance (ESDA)
¶   NL - 3; £15 m only.   AR; free.
✕   2002-3 Impotence Association

Sexual Freedom Coalition   (SFC)   1996
■   BCM Box Lovely, LONDON, WC1N 3XX.   (hsb)
      0777 088 4985
      email mail@sfc.org.uk   http://www.sfc.org.uk
      Chair: Dr Tuppy Owens
▲   Un-incorporated Society
○   *K; 'to represent supporters & campaign groups who revere sex
      & want to be free to enjoy seeing, hearing, reading & doing
      as we please, so long as nobody is exploiting anyone else'
●   Conf - LG
>   TLC; Outsiders Trust; Leydig Trust

Shaftesbury Society   1844
§   16 Kingston Rd, LONDON, SW19 1JZ.   (hq)
      0845 330 6033   fax 020 8239 5580
      email info@shaftesburysoc.org.uk
      http://www.shaftesburysoc.org.uk
      A charity caring in the name of Christ, for the physically &
      mentally handicapped & the socially disadvantaged

Shakespeare Reading Society   (SRS)   1874
■   123 Lynton Rd, LONDON, W3 9HN.   (hsp)
      020 8992 0772
      Hon Sec: Mrs Frances J Hughes
▲   Un-incorporated Society
○   *A, *L; to read & study the works of Shakespeare
●   Mtgs - Res - VE - Reading of plays - Lectures - Acting
      workshops
M   50 i
¶   Annual programme; free.

Shared Care Network   1988
NR   Units 63-66 Easton Business Centre, Felix Rd, BRISTOL,
      BS5 0HE.   (hq)
      0117-941 5361
      Chief Execs: Vicky Jones & Candy Smith
▲   Registered Charity
Br   8
○   *N, *W; to support the development of family based short-term
      care services in England, Wales & Northern Ireland
      Family based care services link disabled children to support
      families willing to offer occasional care. The network
      supports 300 schemes organising family based short breaks
●   Conf - Res - Inf - Campaigning
M   300 services
¶   Consolidation or Change? A second survey of Family Based
      Respite Care Services in the UK (1993).
      Getting better all the time: delivering & receiving quality
      services (1995).
      Family Based Short-term Care: the future challenges (1992).

Shark Angling Club of Great Britain   (SACGB)   1953
NR   The Quay, EAST LOOE, Cornwall, PL13 1DX.   (hq)
       01503 262642   fax 01503 262642
       email sacgb@bigfoot.com
       http://www.sharkanglingclubofgreatbritain.org.uk
       Sec: Linda Reynolds
▲   Un-incorporated Society
○   *S; to promote shark angling in GB
●   Comp - SG - Stat - Inf
<   Intl Game Fishing Assn
M   500 i, UK / 50 i, o'seas
¶   NL - 3; ftm only.

Shaw Society   1941
■   51 Farmfield Rd, Downham, BROMLEY, Kent, BR1 4NF.   (hsp)
       020 8697 3619   fax 020 8697 3619
       email anthnyellis@aol.com
       Hon Sec: Miss Barbara Smoker
▲   Un-incorporated Society
○   *A, *L; study of the life & work of George Bernard Shaw; to
       promote interest in his work & provide 'a rallying point for
       the cooperation & education of kindred spirits & a forum for
       their irreconcilable controversies'
●   Mtgs - Inf - Performances at Shaw's house at Ayot St Lawrence
       (Herts)
M   c 90 i, 10 libraries, UK / c 40 i, 100 libraries, o'seas
¶   The Shavian - 2; ftm, donation nm.   NL - 3; ftm.
       News-sheet for meetings - 10; free to attendees.

SHBA Ltd (Homes for Scotland)
       since 2003 **Homes for Scotland**

Sheep Veterinary Society
       a group of the **British Veterinary Association**

Sheet Plant Association   (SPA)
NR   24 Grange St, KILMARNOCK, E Ayrshire, KA1 2AR.   (hq)
       01563 570518   fax 01563 572728
       email npc@natpack.org.uk
       http://www.sheetplant.org.uk
       Sec: Allan Glen
○   *T; to represent the interests of corrugated converters
●   Conf - ET - Exhib - Comp - Inf
<   Fédn Français du Cartonnage; Assn of Indep Corrugated
       Converters (USA)
M   65 f, UK / 5 f, o;seas

Sheffield Chamber of Commerce & Industry   (SCCI)   1857
■   Albion House, Savile St, SHEFFIELD, S Yorks, S4 7UD.   (hq)
       0114-201 8888   fax 0114-201 2963
       http://www.scci.org
       Co Sec: Stephen Mitchell,
       Chief Exec: Nigel Tomlinson
▲   Company Limited by Guarantee
○   *C
Gp   Black & minority ethnic; Manufacturers; Retailers; Women in
       business
●   Conf - ET - Res - Expt - Inf - VE
<   Brit Chams Comm
M   1,800 f
×   2004 City of Sheffield & District Chamber of Trade (merged)

Sheila Kaye-Smith Society   (SK-S)   1987
■   22 The Cloisters, St Johns Rd, ST LEONARDS-on-SEA, E Sussex,
       TN37 6JT.   (hsp)
       01424 422139
       Hon Sec: Miss Christine Hayward
○   *A; to stimulate & widen interest in the life & work of this
       English writer & novelist (1887-1956)
●   Mtgs - VE
<   Alliance of Literary Societies (ALS)
M   56 i
¶   The Gleam (Jnl) - 1;   NL - 1.
       Occasional papers & books.

Shellfish Association of Great Britain   1908
NR   Fishmongers' Hall, London Bridge, LONDON, EC4R 9EL.   (hq)
       020 7283 8305
       Dir: Dr Peter Hunt
○   *T; for the UK shellfish industry (catching, cultivating & selling)
M   f

Shelter: the National Campaign for the Homeless   1966
§   88 Old St, LONDON, EC1V 9HU.   (hq)
       020 7505 2000   fax 020 7505 2169
       email info@shelter.org.uk   http://www.shelter.org.uk
       Dir: Adam Sampson
       a non-membership body seeking 'to play a creative part in the
       life of the nation by relieving human suffering... hardship &
       distress amongst the homeless & those living in adverse
       housing conditions...'

Sheltered Housing Owners' Confederation of Scotland
       has closed

**Sheltered / Retirement Housing Owners' Confederation
(SHOC)   1991**
§   PO Box 321, EDINBURGH, EH9 2QA.   (hq)
       Sec: Mrs M Thomson
       A non-membership body promoting awareness of possible
       pitfalls when buying a sheltered / retirement house

Sherlock Holmes Society of London   1951
■   64 Graham Rd, Wimbledon, LONDON, SW19 3SS.   (pro/p)
       020 8540 7657   fax 020 8540 7657
       email shsl221b@aol.com
       http://www.sherlock-holmes.org.uk
       13 Crofton Avenue, ORPINGTON, Kent, BR6 8DU.
          01689 811314.   (mem/sp).
       PRO: Heather Owen,   Mem Sec: Robert Ellis
▲   Un-incorporated Society
○   *A, *G; 'a spoof literary society devoted to the lives & works of
       Sherlock Holmes & Dr John Watson'
●   Mtgs - VE
M   c 1,000 i
¶   Sherlock Holmes Journal - 2; ftm only.

Shetland Agricultural Association
       since 2003 part of the **Shetland Livestock Marketing Group**

Shetland Cattle Herd Book Society
NR   c/o Shetland Rural Centre, Staneyhill, LERWICK, Shetland,
       ZE1 0NA.
       01595 696300
       Chmn: Mrs Jackie Symes
▲   Registered Charity
○   *B
●   Mtgs
M   i
¶   NL - 2; ftm only.

Shetland Cheviot Marketing Society   1986
■   Fairview, VIDLIN, Shetland, ZE2 9QB.   (hq)
       01806 577227
       Sec: James A Johnson
▲   Un-incorporated Society
○   *B
●   Mtgs
M   100 i

Shetland Flock Book Society   1926

NR   Lonabrek, Aith, BIXTER, Shetland, ZE2 9ND.   (hsp)
     01595 810343
     Sec: James P Nicolson
▲   Registered Charity
○   *B; to encourage the breeding of pure Shetland sheep; to
     ensure that all Shetland Flock Book sheep comply with the
     breed standards
●   Mtgs - Comp
M   116 i

Shetland Knitwear Trades Association

     has closed

Shetland Livestock Marketing Group   (SLMG)

NR   Shetland Rural Centre, Staneyhill, LERWICK, Shetland,
     ZE1 0NA.   (hq)
     01595 696300
○   *F, *V
●   Mtgs - Inf - LG
<   Shetland Flock Health Assn
✕   2003 Shetland Agricultural Association

Shetland Pony Stud Book Society   (SPSBS)   1890

■   22 York Place, PERTH, PH2 8EH.   (asa)
     01738 623471
     Sec: Mrs E Ward
▲   Company Limited by Guarantee; Registered Charity
○   *B
Gp   Pony Breeders of Shetland; Ridden & Driven Performance
     Award Schemes
●   Expt - Inf
M   2,200 i, UK / 120 i, o'seas
¶   Shetland Pony Stud Book - 1.   Magazine - 1.

Shetland Sheep Breeders Group
     since 2002 **Shetland Sheep Society**

Shetland Sheep Society   1986

NR   Turvin Farm, Cragg Vale, HEBDEN BRIDGE, W Yorks,
     HX7 5TN.   (hsp)
     Hon Sec: Mrs Barbara Burrows
○   *B; promotion of Shetland sheep & their products, meat & wool
●   Conf - Mtgs - ET - Exhib - Comp - Expt - Inf - VE
M   375 i, UK / 25 i, o'seas
¶   The Shetland Breed - 4; ftm only.
✕   2002 (October) Shetland Sheep Breeders Group

Shiatsu Society (UK)   1981

■   Eastlands Court, St Peters Rd, RUGBY, Warks, CV21 3QP.   (hq)
     0845 130 4560   fax 01788 555052
     email admin@shiatsusociety.org
     http://www.shiatsusociety.org
     Chmn: David Home
▲   Company Limited by Guarantee
○   *P; for students, practitioners & teachers of Shiatsu - the use of
     finger &/or palm pressure - as a natural healing discipline
●   Conf - Mtgs - ET - Exam - Res - Exhib - Comp - SG - Stat - Inf -
     Lib - PL - Empl - VE - LG
<   Eur Shiatsu Fedn
M   1,850 i, UK / 52 i, o'seas
¶   NL - 4; £43 yr.   Guide to Shiatsu.
     Shiatsu in the NHS.   Schools Booklet.

Shingles Support Society
▲   Registered Charity
     A registered charity supplying information on drug therapy &
     self-help for post-herpetic neuralgia (PIN) following shingles.
     The Society is a group of the Herpes Virus Association.

Ship Stamp Society   (SSS)   1970

■   10 Heyes Drive, LYMM, Cheshire, WA13 0PB.   (hsp)
     01925 758435
     email brad666sss@freenetname.co.uk
     http://www.sron.ruu.nl/erikp/stamps.html
     Hon Sec: T Broadley
▲   Un-incorporated Society
Br   1
○   *G; for collectors of postage stamps with ship interest
●   Mtgs - Res - Exhib - Inf
<   Intl Fedn of Maritime Philately; Brit Thematic Assn
M   180 i, UK / 108 i, o'seas
¶   The Log Book - 12.   LM & Reports; m only.

Shipbuilders & Shiprepairers Association   (SSA)   1989

NR   Meadlake Place, Thorpe Lea Rd, EGHAM, Surrey, TW20 8BF.
     (hq)
     01784 223770   fax 01784 223775
     email director@ssa.org.uk   http://www.ssa.org.uk
     Dir: N W Granger
○   *T; trade & employers' organisation representing UK ship
     repairing & ship building
●   ET - Exhib - Stat - Expt - Inf - Empl
M   45 f
¶   Membership guide; free.   AR; m only.

Shire Horse Society   (SHS)   1878

■   East of England Showground, PETERBOROUGH, Cambs,
     PE2 6XE.   (hq)
     01733 234451   fax 01733 370038
     Sec: Andrew Mercer
○   *B; to promote the breed of English cart-horse
Gp   Judges: In-hand, Turnout
●   Mtgs - ET - Exhib - Comp - Stat - Expt - Inf - VE - LG - National
     Shire Horse Show
M   i, f & org
¶   List of Breeders, Exhibitors & Local Societies - 2;
     NL;   List of Shows - 1;   AR;
     Panel of Judges - 1;
     Notes for Overseas Breeders - irreg; all free.

Shooters' Rights Association   (SRA)   1984

■   PO Box 3, CARDIGAN, Ceredigion, SA43 1BN.   (hq)
     01239 698607   fax 01239 698614
     Sec: Richard Law
▲   Un-incorporated Society
○   *K; provision of public liability & legal costs insurance;
     assistance in difficulties encountered with respect to gun
     licence grant or renewal
●   Res - Exhib - Comp - Inf - Lib
M   3,285 i, 85 f, 115 org, UK / 29 i, o'seas

Shop & Display Equipment Association   (SDEA)   1947

■   24 Croydon Rd, CATERHAM, Surrey, CR3 6YR.   (hq)
     01883 348911   fax 01883 343435
     email enquiries@sdea.co.uk
     http://www.shopdisplay.org
     Dir: Lawrence Cutler
▲   Un-incorporated Society
○   *T; for manufacturers, distributors & importers of shop fittings &
     retail display equipment
●   Conf - Mtgs - Exhib - Stat - Expt - Inf - LG
M   202 f
¶   Shoptalk (NL) - 4;   LM - 1;   PR Planner - 1;
     Confidential Circulars - 52;   all ftm only.
     SDEA Directory of Shopfittings & Display - 1; ftm, £10 nm.

Shoring Technology Interest Group
     a special interest group of the **Construction Plant-hire
     Association**

Short Sea Committee, Chamber of Shipping
     is part of the **Chamber of Shipping**

© CBD Research Ltd · Beckenham · BR3 5JS · Tel 020 8650 7745 · Fax 020 8650 0768 · E-mail cbd@cbdresearch.com · www.cbdresearch.com

Shorthorn Society of the United Kingdom of GB & I   1875
NR   4th Street, Stoneleigh Park, KENILWORTH, Warks, CV8 2LG.
     (hq)
     024 7669 6549   fax 024 7669 6729
     email shorthorn@shorthorn.co.uk
     http://www.shorthorn.co.uk
     Sec: Frank Milnes
○   *B
Gp   Red Cattle Genetics (semen company)
●   Mtgs - Res - Exhib - Comp - Stat - Expt - Inf - PL - VE - Empl -
     Breed societies
<   Wld Shorthorn Coun
M   280 i, UK / 250 i, o'seas
¶   Shorthorn Jnl - 1.   NL - 4.
     Coates Herd Book - 1.

Showmen's Guild of Great Britain   1889
NR   41 Clarence St, STAINES, Middx, TW18 4SY.
     01784 461805
     Gen Sec: Keith Miller
○   *T; interests of travelling showmen & protection of the industry
M   f

Shrievalty Association   1970
■   PO Box 198, LETCHWORTH, Herts, SG6 3ZQ.   (hsb)
     01462 629914   fax 01462 618247
     email secretary@highsheriffs.com
     Hon Sec: Michael McCartney
▲   Company Limited by Guarantee
○   *P; to protect, promote & strengthen the ancient Office &
     traditions of the High Sheriffs
●   Conf - Mtgs - ET - Comp - SG - Inf - LG
M   950 i, UK / 3 i, o'seas
¶   The High Sheriff - 2; ftm, £20 yr nm.
     Note: the association trades under the name of The High
     Sherrifs' Association of England & Wales.

Shropshire Archaeological & Historical Society   (SAHS)   1877
■   Lower Wallop Farm, Westbury, SHREWSBURY, Shropshire,
     SY5 9RT.   (hsp)
     01743 891215
     Sec: Mrs M Roberts
▲   Registered Charity
○   *L; archaeological research, local history & publication of
     parish registers
●   Mtgs - Lib - VE
<   Coun Brit Archaeology
M   345 i, 34 org, UK / 2 i, 12 org, o'seas
¶   Transactions SAHS - 1.   NL - 2.

Shropshire Chamber of Commerce & Enterprise   1962
■   Trevithick House, Stafford Park 4, TELFORD, Shropshire,
     TF3 3BA.   (hq)
     01952 208200   fax 01952 208208
     email enquiries@shropshire-chamber.co.uk
     http://www.shropshire-chamber.co.uk
     Managing Dir: Nick Graham
▲   Company Limited by Guarantee
○   *C
Gp   Key Dimensions (training divn); Networking; Policy &
     representation
●   Conf - Mtgs - ET - Res - Stat - Expt - Inf - Lib - LG - 50%
     ownership of Business Link West Mercia Franchise (operated
     on behalf of Advantage West Midlands)
<   Brit Chams Comm; Confedn W Midlands Chams Comm; Euro
     Chambres
M   1,300 f
¶   Shropshire Business Matters - 4; free.
✗   2001 Shropshire Chamber of Commerce, Training & Enterprise
     2004 Shropshire Chamber & Business Link

**Shropshire Sheep Breeders Association & Flock Book Society
(SSBA)   1882**
■   Stable Views, Alderton, MONTFORD BRIDGE, Shropshire,
     SY4 1AW.   (hsp)
     01743 741689   fax 01743 741113
     email psellwood@aol.com
     http://www.shropshire-sheep.co.uk
     Sec: Pippa Geddes
▲   Registered Charity
○   *B
●   Mtgs - ET - Exhib - Comp - Expt - Inf - PL - LG
M   110 i, UK / 1 i, o'seas
¶   Shroptalk (NL) - 4; ftm; £10 yr nm.

**Shropshire & West Midlands Agricultural Society   (SWMAS)
1875**
■   Agricultural Showground, Berwick Rd, SHREWSBURY,
     Shropshire, SY1 2PF.   (hq)
     01743 289831   fax 01743 289920
     Chmn: David R Tudor
▲   Company Limited by Guarantee; Registered Charity
○   *F; to promote agriculture & industry
Gp   Horse; Cattle; Sheep; Machinery & arable farming;
     Horticulture; Conservation
●   Exhib - Comp - 2 day county show
M   4,000 i, 400 f, 50 org
¶   Show Programme - 1; ftm, £2 nm.   AR; ftm; £2 nm.
     Schedule(s) - 1; free.   Catalogue - 1; £2.50.

Siambr Fasnach Gorllewin Cymru
see **West Wales Chamber of Commerce   (Siambr Fasnach
Gorllewin Cymru)**

Sickle Cell Society   1979
NR   54 Station Rd, LONDON, NW10 4UA.   (hq)
     020 8961 7795
     Dir: Dr Asa'ah Nkohkwo
▲   Registered Charity
○   *W; to help & support families affected by sickle cell disorders;
     to educate the general public & health professionals about
     the problems of sickle cell disorders
●   Conf - Exhib - Inf - Provides financial assistance, educational
     grants & holiday & recreational opportunities
M   150 i
¶   News Review - 4.   AR.
     Information leaflets (publications list available); free.

Side Saddle Association   (SSA)   1974
NR   Nightingale Cottage, Valentine Rd, ABERSYCHAN, Gwent,
     NP4 8QP.   (hsp)
     01495 772212   fax 01495 772212
     http://www.sidesaddleassociation.co.uk
     Hon Enquiries Sec: Mrs A Say
▲   Un-incorporated Society
Br   15; Australia, Austria, Belgium, Canada, Eire, France,
     Germany, Japan, Netherlands, New Zealand, Northern
     Ireland, South Africa, Spain, Sweden, USA
○   *G; to encourage & promote the art of riding side saddle, & the
     furtherance of the interests of side saddle riders all over the
     world
●   Conf - Mtgs - ET - Exam - Exhib - Comp - Inf
<   Brit Horse Soc
M   1,300 i
¶   NL - 3.   Shows & Fixture List - 1.
     Members' Hbk - 1.

Siege Group   (SG)   1988
NR   1 Tyler Ave, LOUGHBOROUGH, Leics, LE11 5NL.   (hsp)
     Sec: David Carvell
○   *G; historical re-enactment of the mid 17th century English
     Civil Wars
●   ET - Res - Exhib - Battle re-enactment - Living history
<   Nat Assn of Re-enactment Socs
M   140 i
¶   The Culverin (NL) - 5/6; ftm.

SIESO (SIESO) 1973
- ■ The Oaks, Thames Lane, CRICKLADE, Wilts, SN6 6BH. (sp)
  01793 759225
  email sieso@sieso.org.uk   http://www.sieso.org.uk
  Sec: Derek F Heathcote
- ▲ Un-incorporated Society
- Br 4
- ○ *P; for managers & those involved in the prevention, of & response to, industrial & commercial emergencies
- Gp Industrial safety: health, safety & environment; Crisis management; Risk assessment; Statutory regulations; EU & government legislation
- ● Conf - ET - Exhib - SG - Inf - VE - LG
- < Nat Steering C'ee for Warning & Informing the Public; Civil Contingencies Coordination Alliance
- M 300 i, UK / 20 i, o'seas
- ✗ 2004-05 Society of Industrial Emergency Services Officers

SIFA (SIFA) 1994
- NR 10 East St, EPSOM, Surrey, KT17 1HH.
  01372 721172
  http://www.sifa.co.uk
  Managing Dir: Ian Muirhead
- M c200 i
- ✗ 2003-04 Solicitors for Independent Financial Advice

Silhouette Collectors Club 1965
- ■ Flat 5/13 Brunswick Sq, HOVE, E Sussex, BN3 1EH. (hsp)
  01273 735760
  Hon Sec: Miss Diana B Joll
- ○ *G; for collectors & anyone interested in the silhouette from 1760 to the present
- ● Res - VE
- M 68 i, UK / 3 i, o'seas
- ¶ NL - 3; ftm only.

Silica & Moulding Sands Association (SAMSA) 1941
- NR Gillingham House, 38-44 Gillingham St, LONDON, SW1V 1HU. (hq)
  020 7963 8000
  Dir: Dr C Kirby,   Sec: B James
- ▲ Company Limited by Guarantee
- ○ *T; to promote the continuity of supply of indigenous silica & industrial sand for the consumer industries
- Gp Environment & planning; Health & safety training
- ● Conf - Mtgs - Stat - Inf - LG
- < Assn of Eur Producers of Silica (EUROSIL); Indl Minerals Assn of Europe (IMA-EUROPE)
- M 11 f

Silk Association of Great Britain (SAGB) 1970
- NR 5 Portland Place, LONDON, W1B 1PW. (hq)
  020 7636 7788   fax 020 7636 7515
  email sagb@dial.pipex.com   http://www.silk.org.uk
  Sec: Adam Mansell
- ▲ Company Limited by Guarantee
- ○ *T; to promote the use of & knowledge of real silk
- ● Mtgs - Stat - Inf - LG
- < Intl Silk Assn; Brit Apparel & Textile Confedn
- M 35 f
- ¶ Serica (NL) - 4; ftm.

Silver Spoon Club of Great Britain (SSC) 1989
- NR Bexfield Antiques, 26 Burlington Arcade, LONDON, W1J 0PU. (ed/b)
  Jnl Editor: Daniel Bexfield
- ▲ Un-incorporated Society
- ○ *G; to assist & support connoisseurs & collectors of antique & other fine silver spoons & related table silver
- Gp Historical; Research; Marketing; Instruction
- ● Res - Comp - SG - Stat - Inf - Lib
- M 175 i, UK / 25 i, o'seas
- ¶ The Finial (Jnl) - 6.
  Note: all activities are carried out by post.

Simplified Spelling Society (SSS) 1908
- ■ 4 Valletta Way, Wellesbourne, WARWICK, CV35 9TB. (mem/sp)
  Mem Sec: Jack Gledhill
- ▲ Un-incorporated Society
- Br Australia, Germany, New Zealand, USA
- ○ *K; 'working for planned change in English spelling for the benefit of learners & users'
- Gp Internet discussion group for members
- ● Conf - Mtgs - SG - Lib
- M 99 i, UK / 47 i, o'seas
- ¶ Jnl - 2; ftm, £15 nm.

Sing for Pleasure 1964
- NR Bolton Music Centre, New York, BOLTON, Lancs, BL3 4NG. (hq)
  0800 018 4164
  http://www.singforpleasure.org.uk
  Mgr: Vicky Williams
- ▲ Registered Charity
- Br Regional c'ees
- ○ *D, *G; for conductors, teachers, singers & children interested in choral music
- ● Conf - Mtgs - ET - SG - Inf - VE
- < À Coeur Joie; Europa Cantat; Brit Fedn Young Choirs; NCVO; Tonsil
- M 650 i, 100 choirs
- ¶ NL - 2; ftm.   Sheet Music - 3; ftm.
  AR; ftm.   Summer & Weekend Course Brochures.

Single Ply Roofing Association (SPRA) 1994
- NR The Building Centre, 26 Store St, LONDON, WC1E 7BT.
  0115-914 4445   fax 0115-974 9827
  email enquiries@spra.co.uk   http://www.spra.co.uk
  Sec: Jim Hooker
- ▲ Un-incorporated Society
- ○ *T; to provide independent technical advice to clients & designers on polymeric roofing membranes & to ensure the membership comply with membership criteria
- ● Mtgs - ET - Comp - Inf
- < Brit Flat Roofing Coun; Construction Products Assn; Nat Specialist Contrs Coun; Roofing Ind Alliance; RIBA CPD Providers Network
- M 75 f
- ¶ Brochure;   Design Guide; both free.

Single Travellers' Action Group (STAG) 1994
- ■ 14 Church Lane, Sharnbrook, BEDFORD, MK44 1HR. (hsp/b)
  01234 782415
  email vivstag@aol.com
  Founder: Mrs Jean Jewell
- ▲ Un-incorporated Society
- Br Regional representatives
- ○ *K; 'to endeavour to abolish the single travller's room supplement on the grounds that it is discriminating'
- ● Res - Inf
- M c 2,000 i, UK / 10 i, o'seas
- ¶ Single Travellers Action Group - 3; £12 m only.

SIPTU (Services Industrial Professional and Technical Union)
- IRL Liberty Hall, DUBLIN 1, Republic of Ireland.
  353 (1) 858 6300   fax 353 (1) 874 9466
  Gen Sec: Joe O'Flynn
- ○ *U
- M c 200,000 i

© CBD Research Ltd · Beckenham · BR3 5JS · Tel 020 8650 7745 · Fax 020 8650 0768 · E-mail cbd@cbdresearch.com · www.cbdresearch.com

Sir Arthur Sullivan Society   (SASS)   1977
- ■ 2 Wherry Way, Dobwalls, LISKEARD, Cornwall, PL14 4NS.   (sp)
  email shturnbull@aol.com
  http://www.sirarthursullivansociety.co.uk
  Sec: Stephen H Turnbull
- ▲ Registered Charity
- ○ *A, *D, *G, *L; to advance the education of the public in &
  promote the performance of, the music of Sir Arthur Sullivan
  (1842-1900) & other contemporary British composers
- ● Conf - Mtgs - ET - Res - Exhib - Inf - Lib - VE - Concerts -
  Recordings - Discography
- < Intl Gilbert & Sullivan Assn
- M 400 i, 15 org, UK / 80 i, 5 org, o'seas
- ¶ Magazine - 2; ftm, £2 nm.   Booklets.   AR; free.
  NL - 3/4;   Ybk;   Discography; all ftm only.

Sir Harry Lauder Society
> see **Scottish Music Hall Society (incorporating the Sir Harry
> Lauder Society)**

Sira Ltd   1918
- ■ South Hill, CHISLEHURST, Kent, BR7 5EH.   (hq)
  020 8467 2636   fax 020 8468 1705
  email info@sira.co.uk   http://www.sira.co.uk
  Chief Exec: Steve Pickering
- ▲ Company Limited by Guarantee
- ○ *Q; Design, manufacture, marketing of instrumentation &
  control equipment; Innovation of new instrumentation
  techniques; Development of solutions to instrument &
  measurement problems; Electro optical design; Safety
  certification
- ● Conf - ET - Res
- < airto
- M c 40 f, UK / 10 f, o'seas

Sittingbourne & Kemsley Light Railway Ltd   (SKLR)   1969
- ■ 51 Russell Drive, WHITSTABLE, Kent, CT5 2RG.   (hsp)
  01227 792498   fax 01277 794963
  email mail@nickw.enterprise-plc.com
  http://www.sklr.net
  Hon Sec: N G Widdows
- ▲ Registered Charity
- ○ *G; railway preservation & operation
- ● Exhib - Railway operation
- < Heritage Rly Assn; Kent [& Swale] Museum[s] Gp; Swale
  Heritage Assn; Swale Tourism Assn
- M 350 i
- ¶ NL - 6; ftm.

Ski Club of Great Britain   (SCGB)   1903
- NR The White House, 57-63 Church Rd, Wimbledon, LONDON,
  SW19 5SB.   (hq)
  020 8410 2000 or 0845 458 0780
  Chief Exec: Miss Caroline Stuart-Taylor
- ○ *S; sport & recreation of skiing - cross-country, downhill, ski
  mountaineering & snowboarding
- M c 26,000 i, f & org

Skibob Association of Great Britain   (SAGB)   1966
- ■ 2-4 Langhorne Gardens, FOLKESTONE, Kent, CT20 2EA.
  (regd)
  01303 251444   fax 01303 255167
  email french@metronet.co.uk
  http://www.skibob.org.uk office
  Chmn: Richard Platt
- ▲ Un-incorporated Society
- ○ *S; promoting the sport of skibobbing
- ● ET - Comp - VE
- < Fédn Intle de Skibob
- M 500 i
- ¶ NL - 1; free.

Sleep Apnoea Trust Association
- NR 12a Bakers Piece, KINGSTON BLOUNT, Oxon, OX39 4SW.
  0845 606 0685   fax 0845 606 0685
  email satrust@aol.com   http://www.sleepmatters.org
  Contact: The Chmn
- ○ *W

Sleep Council   1995
- NR High Corn Mill, Chapel Hill, SKIPTON, N Yorks, BD23 1NL.
  (hq)
  01756 791089
  Head of Marketing: Jessica Alexander (Alexander King
  Associates)
- ▲ Company Limited by Guarantee
- ○ *T; 'promotes the benefits of a good bed to a good night's
  sleep to the consumer & media on behalf of bed
  manufacturers & retailers'
- ● Inf - Advertising
- M 5,000 f
- ¶ Marketing Newz - 3; free.

**Sliding Glass Window Distributors Association   (SGWDA)
1980**
- ■ 10 Montcalm Close, Hayes, BROMLEY, Kent, BR2 7LZ.
  (mail) address
- ○ *T
- ● Conf
- M f
- ¶ Runners - 4; ftm only.

**SMAE Fellowship (Association of British Physiotherapists)
(SMAE)   1919**
- NR The New Hall, 149 Bath Rd, MAIDENHEAD, Berks, SL6 4LA.
  (hq)
  01628 621100
  Principal: M J Batt
- ▲ Un-incorporated Society
- ○ *P; to promote professionalism & training in physiotherapy &
  sports injuries; covers surgical chiropody, podiatric medicine
  & complementary medicine
- ● Conf - Mtgs - ET - Exam - Res - Exhib - SG - Inf - LG
- < SMAE Institute (1919)
- M 2,000 i
- ¶ SMAE Jnl - 4.

**Small Electrical Appliance Marketing Association   (SEAMA)
1981**
- NR Orbital House, 85 Croydon Rd, CATERHAM, CR3 6PD.   (asa)
  01883 334496
  email seama@admin.co.uk
  Sec: T Faithfull
- ▲ Un-incorporated Society
- ○ *T
- ● Conf - Mtgs - SG - Stat - Inf - LG
- M 12 f (22 brand names)
- ¶ LM; free.   Retailers Guide to Service - 1; ftm & retailers.

Small Farms Association   (SFA)   1987
- NR Ley Coombe Farm, Modbury, IVYBRIDGE, Devon, PL21 0TU.
  (chmn/p)
  01548 830302
  Chmn: Philip Hosking
- ▲ Un-incorporated Society
- ○ *F; for those who are interested in the conservation of the
  countryside, particularly farmers who farm less than 250
  acres, & also practise less intensive traditional methods of
  farming that are sympathetic to the needs of the environment
  & its wildlife
- Gp Steering group for marketing
- ● Conf - Mtgs - ET - VE - LG
- M 250 i
- ¶ NL - 12; ftm, on request nm.

Small Firms Association
IRL Confederation House, 84-86 Lower Baggot St, DUBLIN 2,
      Republic of Ireland.
      353 (1) 605 1500   fax 353 (1) 661 2861
      email info@sfa.ie   http://www.sfa.ie
      Dir: Pat Delaney
○   *T
<   IBEC

Small Landlords' Association
      since 2004 **National Landlords' Association**

Small Practices Association
NR The Vicarage, 9 York St, HEYWOOD, Lancs, OL10 4NN.
      01706 620920   fax 01706 620780
      http://www.smallpractices.org.uk
      Nat Mgr: Moira Auchterlonie
○   *M, *T; GP (General practitioner) practices with up to 3 GP
      principals or up to 7,000 registered patients

Small Practitioners Association
      since November 2002 **Society of Professional Accountants**

Small Woods Association (SWA) 1988
NR The Old Bakery, Main Rd, PONTESBURY, Shropshire,
      SY5 0RR. (hq)
      01743 792644   fax 01743 792655
      http://www.smallwoods.org.uk
      Exec Dir: Russell Rowley
▲   Company Limited by Guarantee; Registered Charity
○   *K, *N; to advance education in the conservation of small
      woodlands
Gp Policy development; Training; Marketing; Information line
●   Conf - Mtgs - ET - Exhib - SG - Inf - VE - LG
M   700 i, 100 f, 50 org, UK / 10 i, 5 org, o'seas
¶   Smallwoods - 4.
      Small Woods Information Pack.
      Woodland Initiatives Register.

Smoke Control Association (SCA)
■   2 Waltham Court, Milley Lane, Hare Hatch, READING, Berks,
      RG10 9TH. (hq)
      0118-940 3416   fax 0118-940 6258
      email info@feta.co.uk   http://www.feta.co.uk
      Dir-Gen: C Sloan
○   *T; specialist smoke control section of the HEVAC
      Association. Develops & promotes high standards of
      quality, design, safety & workmanship in the industry &
      publishes standards for smoke control
Gp Technical
●   Mtgs - Exhib - Stat - LG
<   Fedn Envtl Tr Assns (FETA)
M   25 f
×   2001 Smoke Ventilation Association

Smoke Ventilation Association
      since 2001 has become **Smoke Control Association**

**Snack, Nut & Crisp Manufacturers Association Ltd
    (SNACMA) 1983**
■   6 Catherine St, LONDON, WC2B 5JJ. (hq)
      020 7420 7220   fax 020 7420 7221
      email esa@esa.org.uk   http://www.esa.org.uk
      Dir Gen: Steve Chandler
▲   Company Limited by Guarantee
○   *T; to liaise, on behalf of industry, with government
      departments, news organisations, news media, the medical
      profession & food research bodies
Gp Working groups: Climate change, Commercial, Technical
●   Mtgs - ET - Stat - Inf - LG
<   Confedn Food & Drink Inds EU (CIAA); Food & Drink Fedn
M   7 f
¶   NL - 12; ftm.

Snowsport England (ESC) 1979
■   Area Library Building, Queensway Mall, The Cornbow,
      HALESOWEN, W Midlands, B63 4AJ. (hq)
      0121-501 2314   fax 0121-585 6448
      email info@snowsportengland.org.uk
      http://www.snowsportengland.org.uk
      Chief Exec: Trich Ball
▲   Company Limited by Guarantee
○   *S; governing body of the sport in England; to promote &
      develop the sport within England & for English skiers
●   Conf - Mtgs - ET - Exam - Exhib - Comp - Inf - VE - National
      Coaching Scheme (training & coaching instructors, officials &
      competitors) - Responsibility for standards, rules &
      regulations for the sport within England
<   Snowsport GB
M   3,000 i, 15 f, 150 org
      Note: Snowsport England is the trading name of the English Ski
      Council Ltd

Snowsport GB 1981
■   Hillend, Biggar Rd, EDINBURGH, Midlothian, EH10 7EF. (hq)
      0131-445 7676   fax 0131-445 4949
      email info@snowsportgb.com
      http://www.snowsportgb.com
      Chuif Exec: Jason Cockburn
▲   Company Limited by Guarantee
○   *S; governing body for skiing & snowboarding in the UK
      The primary role is the selection, training & management of
      British teams
●   ET
<   Intl Ski Fedn (FIS)
>   Snowsport England; Snowsport Scotland; Snowsport Wales
M   org
¶   Year Planner; free.
      Note: Snowsport GB is the trading name of the British Ski &
      Snowboard Federation.

Snowsport Industries of Great Britain (SIGB) 1987
■   17 Calton Rd, EDINBURGH, EH8 8DL. (asa)
      0131-557 3012   fax 0131-557 9466
      email sigb@raremanagement.co.uk
      http://www.snowlife.org.uk
      Mgrs: (Rare Management) Mike Jardine & Lesley Beck
▲   Company Limited by Guarantee
○   *T
Gp Skiing; Snowboarding
●   Res - Exhib (SOLTEX) - Comp - Stat - Inf - LG
M   200 f, UK / 14 f, o'seas.
¶   NL - 4; free.   Trade Directory - 1; ftm, £5 nm.

Snowsport Scotland (SNSC) 1963
■   Hillend, Biggar Rd, EDINBURGH, Midlothian, EH10 7EF. (hq)
      0131-445 4151
      Devt Manager: Bruce Crawford
▲   Company Limited by Guarantee
○   *S; national governing body for skiing & snowboarding
Gp Clubs (include) Skiing: Disabled, nordic, alpine, freestyle;
      Snowboarding
●   Mtgs - ET - Exam - Comp - LG
<   Fédn Intle de Ski; Brit Ski & Snowboard Fedn; Scot Sports Assn
M   7,000 i, 10 f, 40 clubs, UK / 20 i, o'seas
¶   Snowsport News - 4.
      Scottish Snowsport Hbk - 1.   AR.

Snuff Bottle Society 1969
NR 3 Pitts Deep, CHRISTCHURCH, Dorset, BH23 1BU. (hq)
      01202 469050   fax 01202 469050
      Pres: Michael Kaynes
▲   Un-incorporated Society
○   *G; for all interested in the collecting, sale & exchange of snuff
      bottles
●   Conf - Exhib - Inf
M   50 i, UK / 40 i, o'seas
¶   Snuff Bottle Review - irreg.

Snuff - Narcotic Inhaler Followers & Aficionados
■ 191 Westcombe Hill, LONDON, SE3 7DR.
Gp Snuff Users
● Mtgs
M 10 i
¶ The Sniffer (Jnl) - 6; ftm only.

Social Care Association (SCA) 1949
■ Thornton House, Hook Rd, SURBITON, Surrey, KT6 5AN. (hq)
   020 8397 1411   fax 020 8397 1436
   email sca@scaed.demon.co.uk
   http://www.socialcaring.co.uk
   Chief Exec: Nicholas Johnson
▲ Company Limited by Guarantee
Br 2
○ *P; to promote high standards in social care services
● Conf - ET - Exhib - Inf - LG
M 4,000 i, 100 f
¶ Social Caring - 4.

Social, Emotional & Behavioural Difficulties Association
   see **Sebda - the Social, Emotional & Behavioural Difficulties Association**

Social History Curators Group (SHCG) 1975
NR c/o Discovery Museum, Blandford Sq, NEWCASTLE UPON TYNE, NE1 4NA. (treas/b)
   email enquiry@shcg.org.uk   http://www.shcg.org.uk
   Chmn: Zelda Baveystock
▲ Registered Charity
○ *P; to raise standards of curatorship in museums; interest in all aspects of social history
● Conf - ET - SG - VE - LG
< Museums Assn
M 450 i, UK / 80 i, o'seas
¶ Jnl - 1; ftm, £7.50 nm.   News - 3; ftm only.

Social History Society (SHS) 1976
■ Furness College, LANCASTER, LA1 4YG. (hq)
   01524 592547   fax 01524 846102
   email l.persson@lancaster.ac.uk
   http://www.socialhistory.org.uk
   Admin Sec: Linda Persson
▲ Registered Charity
○ *P; to encourage the study of the history of society
● Conf
M 250 i, UK / 100 i, o'seas
¶ Cultural & Social History - 3; ftm only.

Social Research Association (SRA) 1978
■ 175-185 Gray's Inn Rd, LONDON, WC1X 8UE. (hq)
   020 7812 0634
   email admin@the-sra.org.uk   http://www.the-sra.org.uk
   Chmn: Barbara Dolf
▲ Company Limited by Guarantee; Registered Charity
Br 3
○ *P; to advance the conduct, application & development of social research
Gp C'ees: Training, Events;
   Working gps: Commissioning & funding, Dissemination
● Conf - Mtgs - ET - Res
M 1,000 i, UK / 30 i, o'seas
¶ SRA News (NL) - 4;   e-bulletin - 12; both ftm only.
   Ethical Guidelines; ftm, £10 nm.
   Data Protection Act 1998: guidelines for social research; ftm, £10 nm.
   Commissioning Social Research: a good practice guide; ftm, £10 nm.

Socialist Business Values Association (SBVA) 2000
■ 6 Southgate Green, BURY ST EDMUNDS, Suffolk, IP33 2BL. (hq)
   01284 754123   fax 01284 704121
   email robertcorfe@tiscali.co.uk
   Hon Sec: Robert Corfe
▲ Un-incorporated Society
○ *K; 'to create a pro-business philosophy embracing macro- & micro-economic factors, which fall in alignment with new socialism, the needs of the majority, & those of a modern Labour party; to encourage the formation of discussion groups amongst all constituency Labour party & trades union branches'
Gp Research groups established on an ad hoc basis
● Conf - Mtgs - ET - Res - Exhib - SG
< Campaign for Industry
M i
¶ Re-inventing Democratic Socialism; £16.99.
   Foundations of New Socialism; £14.99
   New Socialist Business Values; £17.99.

Socialist Environment & Resources Association (SERA) 1973
■ 11 Goodwin St, LONDON, N4 3HQ. (hq)
   020 7263 7389   fax 020 7263 7424
   email enquiries@sera.org.uk   http://www.sera.org.uk
   Nat Co-ordinator: Emma Burnell
▲ Company Limited by Guarantee
○ *K; 'an environmental pressure group, affiliated to the Labour Party'
Gp Transport; Energy; Waste
● Conf - Mtgs - Inf - LG
< Labour Party
M 992 i, 23 f, 45 org, UK
¶ New Ground - 2; ftm.

Socialist Health Association (SHA) 1930
■ 22 Blair Rd, East Chorlton, MANCHESTER, Lancs, M16 8NS. (hq)
   0870 013 0065
   email admin@sochealth.co.uk
   http://www.sochealth.co.uk
   Dir: Martin Rathfelder
▲ Un-incorporated Society
Br 6
○ *K; to defend & extend the NHS; to develop the Labour Party's health policies; to encourage debate about politics & health
● Conf - Mtgs - SG
< Brit Labour Party
M 800 i, 100 org, UK / 10 i, o'seas
¶ Socialism & Health (Jnl) - 2/3; free.

La Société Guernesiaise 1882
■ Candie Gardens, ST PETER PORT, Guernsey, Channel Islands, GY1 1UG. (hq)
   01481 725093   fax 01481 726248
   email societe@cwgsy.net   http://www.societe.org.gg
   Sec: Mrs Lawney Martin
▲ Incorporated Society
○ *L; all aspects of natural science, archaeology, history, folklore, language, geography, geology, genealogy, nature conservation, etc of Guernsey & its islands
Gp Archaeology; Astronomy; Botany; Cetacean; Entomology; Family history; Geology & geography; Historic buildings; History; Marine; Nature conservation; Ornithology
● Res - Lib - VE - LG
< Alderney Wildlife Trust; Bat Gp; Friends of Priaulx Library; Guernsey Conservation Volunteers; La Comité d'la Guernésiaise; La Société Sercquiaise; Meteorological Observatory; NCCPG (Guernsey gp)
M 1,150 i, 65 f, (260, UK / 110, foreign)
¶ Transactions - 1; ftm, £10 nm.   NL - 3; ftm only.

Société Jersiaise 1873

■ 7 Pier Rd, ST HELIER, Jersey, Channel Islands, JE2 4XW. (hq)
01534 758314 fax 01534 888262
email societe@societe-jersiaise.org
http://www.societe-jersiaise.org
Sec: Mrs Pauline J Syvret
▲ Registered Charity
○ *L; the study of the history, language, geology, natural history & antiquities of Jersey
Gp Archives; History; Bibliography; Numismatics; Garden history
● Mtgs - ET - Res - Exhib - SG - Inf - Lib - VE - Preservation
< Museums Assn
M 3,500 i
¶ Bulletin - 1; ftm, £15 nm.

Society of Academic & Research Surgery (SARS) 1953

NR at the Royal College of Surgeons, 35-43 Lincoln's Inn Fields, LONDON, WC2A 3PE. (hsb)
020 7869 6640 fax 020 7869 6644
Hon Sec: Linda Slater
○ *L; for the interchange of information about research work embracing all aspects of surgical science & practice
● Conf - Mtgs - Res
M 600 i
¶ Summaries of papers given at meetings are published in the British Journal of Surgery.

Society for Advanced Legal Studies 1997

NR Charles Clore House, 17 Russell Square, LONDON, WC1B 5DR. (hq)
020 7862 5865 fax 020 7862 5855
email sals@sas.ac.uk http://www.ials.sas.ac.uk/sals/society.htm
Sec: Julian Harris
○ *Q; to facilitate legal research at an advanced level; to engender collaboration between scholars & those involved in the practice of law
M 1,000+ i
¶ Amicus Curiae (Jnl) - 6; ftm, £75 nm.

Society for the Advancement of Anaesthesia in Dentistry (SAAD) 1957

NR 21 Portland Place, LONDON, W1B 1PY. (hq)
020 7631 8893
email saad@aagbi.org http://www.saaduk.org
Hon Sec: Dr Derek Debuse
▲ Registered Charity
○ *L; to research into the applications of methods of pain & anxiety control in dentistry
● Conf - ET - Courses - Lectures
< Intl Fedn of Dental Anaesthesiology Socs
M 1,700 i, UK / 300 i, o'seas
¶ SAAD Digest - 4.

Society for Advancement of Games & Simulations in Education & Training 1970

■ 11 Lloyd St, RYTON, Tyne & Wear, NE40 4DJ. (hsp)
0191-413 2262 fax 0191-413 2262
email peter@j-walsh.freeserve.co.uk
Admin: Peter Walsh
▲ Un-incorporated Society
○ *E; to develop games, simulations & all forms of interactive learning in education & training
● Conf - Mtgs - ET - Inf
< ISAGA, ABSEL
M 71 i, 26 f & org, UK / 26 i, 23 f & org, o'seas
¶ Interact - 3.
International Simulation & Gaming Research Ybk.
Note: is also known as the Society for Interactive Learning

Society for the Advancement of Philosophical Enquiry & Reflection in Education
see**Sapere (Society for the Advancement of Philosophical Enquiry & Reflection)**

Society for All Artists
see **SAA (Society for All Artists)**

Society of Allied & Independent Funeral Directors (SAIF) 1989

■ SAIF Business Centre, 3 Bullfields, SAWBRIDGEWORTH, Herts, CM21 9DB. (hq)
01279 726777 fax 01279 726300
email info@saif.org.uk http://www.saif.org.uk
▲ Un-incorporated Society
○ *P, *T; promote, project & assist the interests of independent funeral directors
● Conf - Mtgs - ET - Res - Exhib - SG - LG
< Independent Funeral Directors College
M 600 f
¶ SAIFinsight (NL) - 12; free.
Note: the official name of this society is the National Society of Allied & Independent Funeral Directors

Society for Anaerobic Microbiology 1975

NR c/o Dr Mark Wilks, Dept of Medical Microbiology, St Bartholomew's Hospital, West Smithfield, LONDON, EC1A 7BE. (treas/b)
Treas: Dr Mark Wilks
▲ Company Limited by Guarantee
○ *P
● Conf - Mtgs - ET
M 200 i, UK / 68 i, o'seas
¶ NL - 2; free.
Proceedings of Biennial Meetings - 1/2 yrly; free to delegates, £20.

Society of Ancients (SOA) 1965

■ Twin Oaks, The Drive, Ifold, LOXWOOD, W Sussex, RH14 0TE. (hsp)
01403 752973
email davidedwards30@hotmail.com
http://www.soa.org.uk
Sec: David Edwards
▲ Un-incorporated Society
○ *G; to promote the study of ancient & mediæval military history & wargaming therein
● Conf - Exhib - Comp
M 872 i, UK / 446 i, o'seas
¶ Slingshot - 6.

Society for Anglo-Chinese Understanding Ltd (SACU) 1965

NR 16 Portland St, CHELTENHAM, Glos, GL52 2PB. (hq)
01229 472010
http://www.sacu.org.uk
Chmn: Jane Hadley
▲ Company Limited by Guarantee; Registered Charity
Br 5
○ *X; to promote friendship & understanding between the peoples of Britain & China
● Mtgs - ET - Lib - PL - VE - Inf on China related events in Britain - Inf about China for schools, playgroups & local groups
M 400 i, UK / 20 i, o'seas
¶ China in Focus (Jnl) - 2; ftm, £2.50 nm.
NL - 4. AR - 1; Phrase Book.

Society of Antiquaries of London 1707

NR Burlington House, Piccadilly, LONDON, W1J 0BE. (hq)
020 7734 0193
Gen Sec: David Gaimster
▲ Registered Charity
○ *L; promotion of antiquarian interests, particularly archaeological investigation & the preservation of historic buildings
● Conf - Mtgs - Res - Lib
M 1,700 i, UK / 300 i, o'seas
¶ Antiquaries Jnl - 1.
Research reports; Occasional papers; prices vary.

© CBD Research Ltd · Beckenham · BR3 5JS · Tel 020 8650 7745 · Fax 020 8650 0768 · E-mail cbd@cbdresearch.com · www.cbdresearch.com

Society of Antiquaries of Newcastle upon Tyne (SANT) 1813
■ The Black Gate, Castle Garth, NEWCASTLE UPON TYNE, NE1 1RQ. (hq)
    0191-261 5390
    email admin@newcastle-antiquaries.org.uk
    http://www.newcastle-antiquaries.org.uk
    Sec: Dr N Hodgson,   Mem Sec: Mrs S Walter
▲ Registered Charity
○ *L; the study & preservation of antiquities & historical records particularly relating to the old counties of Northumberland & Durham & Newcastle upon Tyne
● Conf - Mtgs - Res - Lib - VE - One-day workshop (annual) - Workshops (10 evenings)
M 600 i, 100 f, UK / 20 i, 20 f, o'seas
¶ Archaeologia Aeliana - 1.
    Occasional research publications & guide books.

Society of Antiquaries of Scotland 1780
■ Royal Museum, Chambers St, EDINBURGH, EH1 1JF. (hq)
    0131-247 4115 & 4133   fax 0131-247 4163
    email administration@socantscot.org
    http://www.socantscot.org
    Dir: Andrea N Smithre
▲ Registered Charity
○ *L; archaeology, history & antiquities of Scotland
● Conf - Mtgs - Res - VE - LG
< Built Environments Forum Scotland; The Archaeology Forum
M 3,000 i, UK / 600 i, o'seas
¶ Proceedings - 1; ftm, £49 nm.   NL - 2; ftm only.
    Books - irreg; prices vary.

Society for Applied Microbiology (Sfam) 1931
NR The Blore Tower, The Harpur Centre, BEDFORD, MK40 1TQ. (hq)
    01234 326661   fax 01234 326678
    email info@sfam.org.uk   http://www.sfam.org.uk
    Chief Exec Officer: Philip Wheat
▲ Registered Charity; Un-incorporated Society
○ *L; to advance the study of microbiology, in its application to the environment, agriculture & industry
Gp Special interest groups: Bioengineering, Educational development, Environmental, Food safety & technology, Infection, Prevention & treatment, Molecular biology
● Conf - Publishing
< Intl U Microbiology Socs; Fedn Eur Microbiology Socs; Inst of Biology; Foundation for Science & Technology; UK Nat C'ee for Microbiology
M 1300 i, UK / 500 i, o'seas
¶ Jnl of Applied Microbiology - 12; [with] Letters in Applied Microbiology - 12.
    NL - 4.   Environmental Microbiology - 6.

Society for Applied Philosophy (SAP) 1982
NR c/o Jon Cameron, Humanity Manse, University of Aberdeen, ABERDEEN, AB24 3UG. (admin)
    01224 272343
    Admin Assistant: Jon Cameron
▲ Registered Charity
○ *L; to promote philosophical research into practical problems of social & ethical concern
● Conf - Mtgs
M i

Society of Archer-Antiquaries (SAA) 1956
■ Yew Corner, 29 Batley Court, OLDLAND, S Glos, BS30 8DZ. (hsp/b)
    0117-932 3276
    email bogaman@btinternet.com
    http://www.societyofarcher-antiquaries.org
    Hon Sec: Hugh D Hewitt Soar
▲ Registered Charity
Br Australia, Germany, Italy, Netherlands, USA
○ *L; 'study of the history of the bow & arrow across the world'
● Mtgs - Res - Inf - Lib
M 227 i, UK / 161 i, o'seas
¶ Jnl - 1;   NL - 3; both ftm only.

Society of Architectural Historians in Great Britain (SAHGB) 1956
NR c/o RCAHMS, 16 Barnard Terrace, EDINBURGH, EH8 9NX. (hsp)
    email secretary@sahgb.org.uk   http://www.sahgb.org.uk
    Hon Sec: Simon Green
○ *L
● Conf - Mtgs - Comp - Inf - VE
< Soc Architectural Historians (USA)
M i, universities & libraries
¶ Architectural History (Jnl) - 1; ftm.
    NL - 3; ftm.   LM - occasional.

Society of Architectural Illustration Ltd (SAI) 1975
NR Rosemary Cottage, Bletchinglye Lane, ROTHERFIELD, E Sussex, TN6 3NN. (hq)
    01892 852578
    email info@sai.org.uk   http://www.sai.org.uk
    Admin: Heather Coe
▲ Registered Charity
○ *A, *P; for members of the design profession specialising in illustration of architectural subjects
Gp Illustrators; Photographers; Model makers
● Conf - Mtgs - ET - Exhib - Comp
M 178 i, UK / 8 i, o'seas
¶ Viewpoint - 2;   NL - 4; both free.
    LM; on application & by region.   AR.
✕ Society of Architectural Illustrators

Society of Archivists 1947
NR Prioryfield House, 20 Canon St, TAUNTON, Somerset, TA1 1SW. (hq)
    01823 327030   fax 01823 371719
    Office Mgr: Marian Evans
▲ Company Limited by Guarantee; Registered Charity
Br 10; Republic of Ireland
○ *P; for archivists, archive conservators & records managers; for the effective management of record systems including the retrieval of information from them
Gp Records management; Preservation & conservation; Specialist repositories; Film & sound; Archives in education; Information technology
● Conf - Mtgs - ET - Exam - Res - Exhib - Stat - Inf - Lib - VE - Empl - LG
< Intl Coun Archives
M 1,915 i
¶ Jnl - 2.   NL - 12.   Career Opportunities - 26.

Society for Army Historical Research (SAHR) 1921
■ c/o National Army Museum, Royal Hospital Rd, LONDON, SW3 4HT. (accom) address
▲ Registered Charity
○ *L; research into the history & traditions of the British Army, the land forces of the Empire, Dominions & Commonwealth & ancillary units attached thereto
● Mtgs - Res - VE - Publishing members' research - Lecture series
M 930 i, 20 org, UK / 40 i, 10 org, o'seas
¶ Jnl - 4.   Special issues - irreg; ftm only.

Society of Artists' Agents   (SAA)   1992
NR   21c Montpelier Row, LONDON, SE3 0RL.   (admin/p)
      Admin: Jennifer Ward
▲   Un-incorporated Society
○   *T; to promote the use of illustration & improve the working
      practices between clients, agents & artists
●   Mtgs - ET - Inf - SAA Illustration Awards
M   18 f
¶   Originals - 1; ftm.

**Society of Assistants Teaching in Preparatory Schools Ltd
(SATIPS)   1953**
NR   Cherry Trees, Stebbing, GREAT DUNMOW, Essex, CM6 3ST.
      (admin/p)
      01371 856823   fax 01371 856823
      http://www.satips.com
      Admin: Mrs P M Harrison,
      Gen Sec: E R Andrew Davis (01580 752954)
▲   Company Limited by Guarantee; Registered Charity
○   *E; professional support for staff in independent schools
Gp   Art; Classics; Design & technology; Drama; English;
      Geography; History; Information & communications
      technology; Key Stage 2; Maths; Modern languages; Music;
      Personal & social education with health; Physical education;
      Pre-prep & nursery; Religious studies; Science; Senior
      management; Special needs
●   Conf - Mtgs - ET - Exhib - Comp - SG - Inf
M   c 150 i, c 450 schools, UK / c 10 i, c 20 schools, o'seas
¶   Prep School - 3; ftm, £10 yr nm. (published with the Inc Assn of
      Preparatory Schools).
      NL - 3; ftm only.   Broadsheets - 3; ftm, £5 each nm.

Society of Authors   (SoA)   1884
NR   84 Drayton Gardens, LONDON, SW10 9SB.   (hq)
      020 7373 6642   fax 020 7373 5768
      email info@societyofauthors.org
      http://www.societyofauthors.org
      Gen Sec: Mark Le Fanu
○   *U
Gp   Academic writers; Broadcasting; Children's writers & illustrators;
      Educational writers; Medical writers; Translators Association
●   Conf - Mtgs - Inf - Empl - LG
M   8,000 i
¶   The Author - 4.

Society of Authors in Scotland
■   8 Briar Rd, Kirkintilloch, GLASGOW, G66 3SA.   (hsp)
      0141-776 4280   fax 0141-776 4280
      email brian@bdosborne.fsnet.co.uk
      Sec: Brian D Osborne
▲   Company Limited by Guarantee
○   *A; the Scottish branch of the Society of Authors
●   Mtgs - ET - VE
<   Soc Authors
M   450 i
¶   Occasional NL - irreg.

Society for the Autistically Handicapped
      see **Autism Independent UK (Society for the Autistically
      Handicapped)**

Society of Automotive Engineers - UK   (SAE-UK)   1881
■   31 Redstone Farm Rd, Hall Green, BIRMINGHAM, W Midlands,
      B28 9RU.   (hq)
      0121-778 4354
      email info@sae-uk.org   http://www.sae-uk.org
      Chief Exec: Dr Anthony McDonagh-Smith
▲   Registered Charity
○   *L; dedicated to the furtherance of mobility engineering in the
      fields of automotive, aerospace, naval, agricultural & others
●   Conf - Mtgs - ET - Comp - Inf
<   Soc of Automotive Engrs-Intl
>   Soc of Automotive Engrs - Intl (SAE-Intl)
M   2,000 i, 100 f, 20 org
¶   Vehicle Technology - 4; £60 m.   Members' Hbk - 1; ftm only.
×   2005-06 Institute of Vehicle Engineers

Society of Automotive Historians in Britain   (SAH)   1977
■   The Old Schoolhouse, Cenarth, NEWCASTLE EMLYN,
      Carmarthenshire, SA38 9JL   (chmn/p)
      Chmn: Michael Worthington-Williams
▲   Un-incorporated Society
○   *G; to encourage research, preservation, recording,
      compilation & publication of historical facts concerning the
      worldwide development of the automobile & related items
●   Conf - Res - Inf - Annual awards for books & features
<   Soc of Automotive Historians Inc (USA)
M   75 i, UK / 675 i, o'seas
¶   Jnl - 6;   Automotive History Review - irreg; both free.

Society for Back Pain Research   (SBPR)   1971
■   British Orthopaedic Association, Royal College of Surgeons,
      35-43 Lincoln's Inn Fields, LONDON, WC2A 3PN.   (hsb)
      020 7405 6507   fax 020 7831 2676
      email secretary@boa.ac.uk   http://www.boa.ac.uk/sbpr
      Hon Sec: Mr John O'Dowd
▲   Registered Charity
○   *L, *Q; 'a multidisciplinary society dedicated to the investigation
      of the causes & treatment of pain arising in the spine'
●   Conf - Mtgs - Res
<   Brit Orthopaedic Assn
M   c 200 i
¶   [Abstracts published in Jnl of Bone & Joint Surgery suppts].

Society of Batrachologists   1995
■   3 Hughes Stanton Way, MANNINGTREE, Essex, CO11 2HQ.
      (hsp)
○   *L
●   Conf - VE
M   85 i, 1 org
¶   Ribbit (Jnl) - 4.

Society of Bookbinders   (SOB)   1974
NR   6 Broadway, Fulford, YORK, N Yorks, YO10 4JW.   (sp)
      Correspondence Sec: Peri Hill
▲   Registered Charity
Br   7
○   *E, *L, *T; to advance the art, craft & science of bookbinding,
      book restoration & conservation
Gp   Education & training
●   Conf - Mtgs - ET - Exhib - Comp - Inf - VE
M   528 i, 23 f, UK / 40 i, 8 org, o'seas
¶   Bookbinder (Jnl) - 1.
      NL - 3;   Regional NL - 3; both ftm only.
      Educational & training booklets.

** **Society of Bookmen**
      Organisation lost: see Introduction paragraph 3

© CBD Research Ltd · Beckenham · BR3 5JS · Tel 020 8650 7745 · Fax 020 8650 0768 · E-mail cbd@cbdresearch.com · www.cbdresearch.com

Society of Border Leicester Sheep Breeders   1896
NR   Greenend Farm, St Boswells, MELROSE, Roxburghshire,
        TD6 9ES.   (hsp)
        01835 824207
     Sec: Nesta Todd
▲   Registered Charity
○   *B
●   Mtgs - Exhib - Expt - Inf
<   Nat Sheep Assn
M   250 i, 10 f, UK / 5 i, o'seas
¶   Jnl - 1.   Flock Book - 1; £15.   AR.

Society of Botanical Artists   (SBA)   1985
NR   1 Knapp Cottages, Wyke, GILLINGHAM, Dorset, SP8 4NQ.
        (hsp)
        01747 825718   fax 01747 826835
        email pam@soc-botanical-artists.org
        http://www.soc-botanical-artists.org
     Exec Sec: Mrs Pamela Henderson
▲   Registered Charity
○   *A, *P; to paint & record for the benefit of art, botany,
        conservation & horticulture
●   Exhib
M   140 i, UK / 13 i, o'seas
¶   Annual Exhibitions Catalogue - 1; £3.50.

Society of British Aerospace Companies Ltd   (SBAC)   1916
NR   Salamanca Square, 9 Albert Embankment, LONDON,
        SE1 7SP.   (hq)
        020 7091 4500   fax 020 7091 4545
        email post@sbac.co.uk   http://www.sbac.co.uk
     Pres: Chris Geoghegan
▲   Un-incorporated Society
○   *T; UK aerospace & overseas airport development industries
●   Conf - Mtgs - Res - Exhib - Stat - Expt - Inf - Lib - PL - VE - LG -
        Organises the Farnborough Intl Air Show
<   Eur Assn of Aerospace Inds (AECMA)
M   250 f
¶   What's New in UK Aerospace (NL) - 4; Capability Brochure - 1;
        Members' E-Bulletin - 26;   Annual Review; all ftm.

Society of British Gas Industries   (SBGI)   1905
■   36 Holly Walk, ROYAL LEAMINGTON SPA, Warks, CV32 4LY.
        (hq)
        01926 334357   fax 01926 450459
        email mail@sbgi.org.uk   http://www.sbgi.org.uk
     Chief Exec: John Stiggers
○   *T; 'represents virtually all the major players in the UK gas
        industry'
Gp   Appliance manufacturers; Gas suppliers, shippers &
        transporters; Distribution & transmission equipment
        manufacturers & contractors; Service providers; Metering &
        control manufacturers; Ancillary products
●   Conf - Mtgs - Exhib - Stat - Expt - LG - Provides a wide range of
        support services
M   170 f
¶   Gas Business - 4.   Review of Activities - 1.
        Directory of Products & Services - 1.

Society of British Neurological Surgeons   (SBNS)   1926
■   at the Royal College of Surgeons, Lincoln's Inn Fields,
        LONDON, WC2A 3PE.   (hq)
        020 7869 6892   fax 020 7869 6890
        email admin@sbns.freeserve.co.uk
        http://www.sbns.org
     Hon Sec: P van Hille
○   *P; interests of neurosurgery & neurosurgeons
●   Conf - Mtgs - Exam - Res - LG
<   WFNS; EANS
M   c 400 i
¶   NL - 3.

Society of British Theatre Designers   (SBTD)   1971
NR   55 Farringdon Rd (4th floor), LONDON, EC1M 3JB.
        020 7242 9200
     Hon Sec: Peter Ruthven Hall
▲   Registered Charity
○   *P
●   Conf - Exhib - Inf
<   Org Intle de Scénographes, Techniciens et Architects de
        Théâtre OISTAT); Assn Brit Theatre Technicians
M   420 i, 4 org, UK / 12 i, o'seas
¶   Blue Pages (NL) - 4.
        Time + Space, design for performers 1995-1999 (1999).
        Make Space! design for theatre & alternative spaces (1994).
        Register of Stage Designers - 1.

**Society of British Water & Wastewater Industries   (SBWWI)
1986**
■   38 Holly Walk, ROYAL LEAMINGTON SPA, Warks, CV32 4LY.
        (hq)
        01926 831530   fax 01926 831931
        email hq@sbwwi.co.uk   http://www.sbwwi.co.uk
     Exec Dir: Carol Hickman
▲   Un-incorporated Society
○   *T; for manufacturers, contractors, suppliers, consultants &
        other organisations involved in the UK water & wastewater
        industry
Gp   Sections: Contractors, Leakage, Pipeline equipment, Waste
        water;
        Groups: Export, Mechanical fittings, Metering, Plastic pipes
        (standards), Valves
●   Conf - Mtgs - Exhib - Stat - Inf - LG
M   80 f

Society of Business Economists   (SBE)   1953
■   Dean House, Vernham Dean, ANDOVER, Hants, SP11 0JZ.
        (execs/p)
        01264 737552
        email admin@sbe.co.uk   http://www.sbe.co.uk
     Sec: Katie Abberton,   Chmn: David Walton
▲   Company Limited by Guarantee
○   *P; applications of economics in business & industry
Gp   Forecasting; Statistics; Industrial economics
●   Conf - Mtgs - SG
<   Intl Fedn Assns Business Economists (IFABE); Assn Française
        Economistes d'Entreprise (AFEDE); Canadian Assn Business
        Economists (CABE); Nat Assn Business
        Economists (NABE)(USA)
M   600 i, UK / 50 i, o'seas
¶   The Business Economist (Jnl) - 3; ftm, £38 nm (£45 outside
        Europe).

Society of Business Practitioners   (SBP)   1956
NR   PO Box 11, SANDBACH, Cheshire, CW11 0GD.
        (mail/address)
        01270 526339   fax 01270 526339
     Pres: Dr M Whitaker
▲   Company Limited by Guarantee
Br   4; Australia, Cyprus, EU, Hong Kong, Singapore, USA
○   *P; for people in business & students of business disciplines
●   ET - Exam - Res - SG
M   2,000 i, UK / 4,000 i, o'seas
¶   The Business Practitioner - 2;   NL - 2; both free.

Society of Cable Telecommunication Engineers   (SCTE)   1945
NR   Fulton House Business Centre, Fulton Rd, WEMBLEY PARK,
        Middx, HA9 0TF.   (hq)
        020 8902 8998
     Sec: Mrs Beverley K Allgood
▲   Un-incorporated Society
○   *L, *P; cable telecommunication & other related industries
●   Mtgs - ET - Exam - Exhib - Inf
<   Intl SCTE (America)
M   c 700 i, 100 f
¶   CTE (Jnl) - 4;   Ybk; both free.

Society Campaigning for the Removal of Exasperating Automated Switchboards (SCREAMS) 2003
NR 191 Westcombe Hill, LONDON, SE3 7DR.
○ *K
M 40 i
¶ Human Voices (NL) - 4.

Society for Cardiological Science & Technology (SCST) 1948
NR 9 Fitzroy Square, LONDON, W1T 5HW. (admin)
      0121-354 6812
      ∪
▲ Registered Charity
Br 3
○ *P; to advance for the public benefit the science & practice of cardiological science by the promotion of improved standards of education & training
Gp Echocardiographers; Nuclear medicine
● Conf - Mtgs - ET - Exam - Res - Exhib - SG - LG - Maintenance of register of persons whom the society considers qualified to practice
< Brit Cardiovascular Soc; Brit Pacing & Electrophysiology Gp; Brit Soc of Echocardiography
M 1,000 i
¶ SCST Update - 12; ftm.   SCST Jobfinder - 12; free.

Society for Cardiothoracic Surgery of Great Britain & Ireland (SCTS) 1933
■ c/o RCS, 35-43 Lincoln's Inn Fields, LONDON, WC2A 3PE. (asa)
      020 7869 6893   fax 020 7869 6890
      email sctsadmin@scts.org   http://www.scts.org
      Hon Sec: James Roxburgh
▲ Registered Charity
○ *P; cardiothoracic surgery
● Conf - ET - Exhib - Empl - LG
M 492 i, UK / 53 i, o'seas
✕ Society of Cardiothoracic Surgeons of Great Britain & Ireland

Society of Chartered Surveyors (SCS)
IRL 5 Wilton Place, DUBLIN 2, Republic of Ireland.
      353 (1) 676 5500   fax 353 (1) 676 1412
      email info@scs.ie   http://www.scs.ie
      Hon Sec: Lena Clarke
○ *P

Society of Cheese Connoisseurs (SCC) 1985
■ 10 Montcalm Close, Hayes, BROMLEY, Kent, BR2 7LS. (mail) address
○ *G
● Mtgs - VE - Tastings
M 25 i
¶ Mousetrap! (incl AR) - 1;   NL - 4; both ftm only.

Society of Chemical Industry (SCI) 1881
NR 14-15 Belgrave Square, LONDON, SW1X 8PS. (hq)
      020 7598 1500
      Gen Sec: Andrew Ladds
▲ Registered Charity; Incorporated by Royal Charter 1907
Br 12 sections; Australia, Canada, Republic of Ireland, USA
○ *L; 'an interdisciplinary network connecting industry, research & consumer affairs at all levels throughout the world; provides opportunities for forward-looking people in the process & materials technologies, energy, water, agriculture, food, pharmaceuticals, materials, construction & environmental protection areas to exchange ideas & gain new perspectives on markets, technologies, strategies & people'
Gp Agriculture & environment; Bioactive sciences; Biotechnology; Business strategy; Carbon; Colloid & surface chemistry; Construction materials; Consumer & sensory research; Electrochemical technology; Environment; Environmental biotechnology; Fine chemicals; Fire chemistry; Food commodities & ingredients; Food engineering; Health & safety; Macro; Materials chemistry; Oils & fats; Pest management; Process engineering; Separation science & technology; Young chemists panel
● Conf - Mtgs - ET - Exhib - Inf - VE - Premises & facilities available to other societies
< Eur Fedn of Biotechnology (EFB)
M 4,700 i, UK / 2,000 i, o'seas
¶ Chemistry & Industry - 24.   SCI News - 12.   AR.
    Jnl of Chemical Technology & Biotechnology - 12.
    Jnl of the Science of Food & Agriculture - 15.
    Pest Management Science - 12.   Polymer International - 12.

Society of Chief Architects of Local Authorities (SCALA) 1973
■ Hillside, St Mary Church, COWBRIDGE, Vale of Glamorgan, CF71 7LT. (hq)
      01446 771209   fax 01446 772580
      email policy@scala.org.uk   http://www.scala.org.uk
      Sec: Stephen Dodsworth
▲ Company Limited by Guarantee
○ *P; development, design & management of the public sector estate
Gp Design forum: design & related issues; Practice forum: Professional & legal issues
● Conf - Mtgs - ET - LG
M 290 i
¶ SCALA News (NL) - 5; ftm only.
    Building Maintenance Expenditure by Local Authorities; £60 m, £80 nm.
    Appointment of Consultants Document; £30 m, £38 nm.

Society of Chief Librarians in England & Wales (SCL) 1996
■ Tony Durcan, Head of Culture Libraries & Lifelong Learning, Newcastle City Council, Princess Sq, NEWCASTLE upon TYNE, NE99 1DX. (hsb)
      0191-277 4152
      http://www.chieflib.org
      Hon Sec: Tony Durcan
▲ Un-incorporated Society
○ *P; the development of the public library service; to influence statutory, financial & other decisions which relate to the effectiveness of public library services
● Conf - Mtgs - Res - SG - Stat - LG
< Quality Forum [for library & information services]; Share the Vision
M 122 i
¶ Fines & Charges in Public Libraries in England & Wales - 1.

© CBD Research Ltd · Beckenham · BR3 5JS · Tel 020 8650 7745 · Fax 020 8650 0768 · E-mail cbd@cbdresearch.com · www.cbdresearch.com

Society of Chief Officers of Trading Standards in Scotland   1975
NR   Trading Standards & Environmental Services, Council Offices,
        Sandwick Rd, STORNOWAY, Isle of Lewis, PA87 2BW.   (hsb)
        Sec: Harry Miller
▲   Un-incorporated Society
○   *P; coordination of trading standards & consumer protection in
        Scotland
Gp   Metrology; Quality standards; Fair trading; Safety
●   Mtgs - LG
<   Inst of Trading Standards Administration
M   33 i

Society of Chief Personnel Officers in Local Government
        since 2006 **Public Sector People Managers' Association**

Society of Chief Quantity Surveyors in the Public Sector
        since 2005 **Society of Construction & Quantity Surveyors in the
        Public Sector**

Society of Chiropodists & Podiatrists   1945
NR   1 Fellmonger's Path, Tower Bridge Rd, LONDON, SE1 3LY.
        (hq)
        020 7234 8620
        Chief Exec: Joanna Brown
▲   Un-incorporated Society
○   *P, *U; promotion of chiropody/podiatry; information on state
        registered chiropodists & podiatrists
Gp   External relations; Internal relations; Education; Membership
●   Conf - Mtgs - ET - Exam - Exhib - Stat - Expt - Empl - LG
M   8,000 i
¶   Podiatry Now - 12.   British Journal of Podiatry.

Society of Cirplanologists   1955
■   26 Roe Cross Green, Mottram, HYDE, Cheshire, SK14 6LP.
        (hsp)
        01457 763485
        Sec: E A Rose
▲   Un-incorporated Society
○   *L; study, collection, preservation of circuit plans, mainly
        Methodist
●   Informal annual mtg
M   100 i, UK / 5 i, o'seas
¶   Cirplan - 2; £1.50.

**Society of Clinical Perfusion Scientists of Great Britain & Ireland
1974**
■   Royal College of Surgeons, 35-43 Lincoln's Inn Fields,
        LONDON, WC1A 3PN.   (hq)
        020 7869 6891
        Admin: Ms Valerie Campbell
○   *P
✕   2001 Society of Perfusionists of Great Britain & Ireland

Society of Clinical Psychiatrists   (SCP)   1958
NR   Keepers Cottage, Barrock Park, Southwaite, CARLISLE,
        Cumbria, CA4 0JS.   (hsp)
        01697 473461
        email mtwomey@ukonline.co.uk   http://www.scpnet.com
        Hon Sec: Dr Michael P K Twomey
▲   Un-incorporated Society
○   *P; to promote good practice in psychiatry; to undertake studies
        in related matters
Gp   NHS doctors suspensions group
●   Mtgs - Res - SG
M   80 i, UK / 5 i, o'seas
¶   British Journal of Clinical & Social Psychiatry - 4.
        Psychiatry for the Millennium.

Society for Co-operative Studies   (SCS)   1967
NR   c/o Michael Shepherd, Co-operatives UK Ltd, Holyoake House,
        Hanover St, MANCHESTER, M60 0AS.   (mem)
        0161-246 2975
        email michael.shepherd@cooperatives-uk.coop sec/p
        Mem Sec & Treas: Iain Williamson
○   *L, *Q; to promote the study of cooperatives & help in
        identifying such work being undertaken in universities &
        colleges; to build links between cooperatives & academics
●   Conf - Mtgs - Res
M   184 i, 42 org
¶   Jnl - 3; ftm, £10 nm.

Society of Coat Hook Collectors   (SCHC)   1976
■   76c The Avenue, BECKENHAM, Kent, BR3 5EF.   (hsp)
▲   Un-incorporated Society
○   *G
●   Conf - Mtgs - Exhib
M   i

Society for Companion Animal Studies   (SCAS)   1979
■   The Blue Cross, Shilton Rd, BURFORD, Oxon, OX18 4PF.   (hq)
        01993 825597   fax 01993 825598
        email info@scas.org.uk   http://www.scas.org.uk
        Dir: Jo-Ann Donoty
▲   Registered Charity
Br   Australia, France, Japan, Netherlands, New Zealand,
        Singapore, Spain & USA
○   *E, *V, *W; to study the nature of the bond between people &
        companion animals
Gp   Pet bereavement support; Research advisory panel
●   Conf - ET - Res - Exhib - Inf - Lib
<   Intl Assn of Human-Animal Interaction Orgs (IAHAIO)
M   361 i, 58 f, UK / 25 i, o'seas
¶   Jnl - 4; ftm, £2.50 nm.
        When a Pet Dies [learning pack]; £58.
        Children & Pets; £5.99.

Society for Computers & Law   1973
NR   10 Hurle Crescent, Clifton, BRISTOL, BS8 2TA.   (hq)
        0117-923 7393
        Gen Mgr: Ruth Baker
○   *L; to bring together lawyers & computer experts in order to
        study problems of common interest
●   Conf - Mtgs - ET - Res - Exhib - Inf - Lib - VE
M   1,400 i, 185 f, UK / 194 i, 5 f, o'seas
¶   Computers & Law - 6.   Publications list available.

**Society for Computing & Technology in Anaesthesia   (SCATA)
1987**
■   21 Portland Place, LONDON, W1B 1PY.   (hq)
        email mail@scata.org.uk   http://www.scata.org.uk
        Hon Sec: Dr Andrew Donnavan
▲   Registered Charity
○   *L, *M, *P; to promote research into the use of computing &
        technology in anaesthetic practice
●   Conf - Mtgs - ET - Res - SG - LG
<   Eur Soc for Computing & Technology Anaesthesia & Intensive
        Care; Assn Anaesthetists GB & Ireland
M   325 i, UK / 25 i, o'seas

Society for Conservation in Aviculture
        a member body of the **Society for the Protection of Aviculture**

Society of Construction Law   (SCL)   1983
■   67 Newbury St, WANTAGE, Oxon, OX12 8DJ.   (hq)
        01235 770606
        Admin Sec: Mrs Jackie Morris
▲   Registered Charity
○   *L; to promote the study & advancement of education in the
        theory & practice & application of construction law
<   Eur Soc Construction Law
M   i
¶   NL - 9; ftm only.   Papers (after meetings); ftm.

Society of Construction & Quantity Surveyors in the Public
Sector (SCQS) 1973
- ■ 24 Pennine Rise, Scissett, HUDDERSFIELD, W Yorks, HD8 9JE. (ch/exec/p)
  01484 863686
  http://www.scqs.org.uk
  Chief Exec: Brian Kirkham
- ▲ Company Limited by Guarantee
- ○ *P; interchange of information on quantity surveying, building economics, types of contract, government regulations & all other matters affecting the built environment in the public sector
- ● Conf - Mtgs - ET - Res - SG - Stat - LG
- < Fedn Property Socs
- M 224 i
- ¶ NL - 4; free. Ybk - 1; ftm, £5 nm.
- ✕ 2005 Society of Chief Quantity Surveyors in the Public Sector

Society of Consulting Marine Engineers & Ship Surveyors 1920
- NR 202 Lambeth Rd, LONDON, SE1 7JW. (hq)
  020 7261 0869 fax 020 7261 0871
  email sec@scmshq.org http://www.scmshq.org
  Sec: Paul Owen
- Br 4
- ○ *P; for consulting marine engineers, naval architects & ship surveyors
- ● Mtgs - Inf - Social events
- M 332 i, UK / 155 i, o'seas
- ¶ Jnl; m only.

Society for Cooperation in Russian & Soviet Studies (SCRSS)
1924
- ■ 320 Brixton Rd, LONDON, SW9 6AB. (hq)
  020 7274 2282 fax 020 7274 3230
  email ruslibrary@scrss.org.uk http://www.scrss.org.uk
  Sec: Jean S F Turner
- ▲ Registered Charity
- ○ *X; to promote studies in the language, culture & history of Russia & other nationalities formerly constituting the USSR
- Gp Music; Russian/Soviet literature; History; Art; Visual aids; Lawyers & architects
- ● Conf - Mtgs - ET - Res - Exhib - Inf - Lib - PL - VE
- < Russian State Centre for Intl Co-operation in Science & Culture
- M 1,000 i, 10 f, 20 org, UK / 10 i, o'seas
- ¶ SCRSS Information Digest - 3; ftm, £10 yr nm.
  NL - 3; ftm only.
  SCRSS Russian Information Guide - 1; £4.95.

Society of Cosmetic Scientists (SCS) 1948
- ■ 10 House, 24-26 Rothesay Rd, LUTON, Beds, LU1 1QX. (hq)
  01582 726661 fax 01582 405217
  email ifscc.scs@btconnect.com http://www.scs.org.uk
  Sec Gen: Mrs Lorna Weston
- ▲ Un-incorporated Society
- ○ *P; to promote the scientific status of the cosmetic industry
- ● Conf - Mtgs - ET (courses) - Exam - Exhib
- < Intl Fedn Socs Cosmetic Chemists (IFSCC)
- M 950 i
- ¶ International Jnl of Cosmetic Science - 6;
  NL - 9/10; AR; all ftm only.

Society of County Treasurers (SCT) 1903
- NR c/o David Clarke, County Treasurer, Shire Hall, WARWICK, CV34 4RA. (hsb)
  01926 410410
  Hon Sec: David Clarke
- ▲ Un-incorporated Society
- ○ *P; financial management, personnel & other matters affecting local government in England & Wales
- Gp Local government finance
- ● Mtgs - SG - Stat - LG
- M c 50 i
- ¶ Standard Spending Indicators - 1.
  Precept Return - 1. AR.

Society for Court Studies 1995
- ■ PO Box 5388, LONDON, W1A 2WL. (hq)
  Mem Admin: June Prunty
- ▲ Un-incorporated Society
- Br USA
- ○ *L; stimulate the study of royal courts from 1400 to the present
- ● Conf - Mtgs
- M 240 i & f
- ¶ The Court Historian (Jnl) - 2.

Society of Crisp Packet Collectors (SCPC)
- ■ 81 Park View, Collin's Road, LONDON, N5 2UD.
  Hon Sec: V Salis
- ○ *G
- ● Mtgs - Exhib
- M 12 i
- ¶ Blue Bag - irreg, ftm only.

Society of Dairy Technology (SDT) 1943
- NR PO Box 12, APPLEBY in WESTMORLAND, Cumbria, CA16 6YJ. (hq)
  Exec Dir: Maurice Walton
- ▲ Company Limited by Guarantee; Registered Charity
- Br 15; 1
- ○ *L, *F, *P; the advancement of dairy science & technology
- Gp Milk & milk products processing, manufacture & distribution; Supply of dairy plant & equipment; Dairy - education, advisory, research
- ● Conf - Mtgs - ET
- < Intl Dairy Fedn (through the UK Dairy Assn)
- M 450 i, UK / 30 i, o'seas
- ¶ International Jnl of Dairy Technology - 4; ftm, £230 nm. NL - 4; AR; both ftm only

Society for Dance Research (SDR) 1983
- NR c/o LABAN, Creekside, LONDON, SE8 3DZ. (mail)
  020 8691 8600 fax 020 8691 8400
  http://www.sdr-uk.org address
  Hon Sec: Peter Bassett
- ▲ Registered Charity
- ○ *D; to further research in dance history, anthropology, analysis & criticism in both theatre & social forms
- Gp Dance heritage working party
- ● Conf - Mtgs - ET - Res - Inf
- M c 160 i
- ¶ Dance Research Journal - 2; ftm.
  NL - 2; LM - 1; both ftm only.

Society of Decorative Art Curators
- ■ 127 Dale St, LIVERPOOL, L2 2JH. (hsb)
  0151-478 4262
  Mem Sec: Pauline Rushton
- ▲ Un-incorporated Society
- ○ *P
  No further information supplied.

Society of Designer Craftsmen (SDC) 1888
- NR 24 Rivington St, LONDON, EC2A 3DU. (hq)
  020 7739 3663
  email info@societyofdesignercraftsmen.org.uk
  Secs: Alicia Merrett & Jo Hayes
- ▲ Registered Charity
- ○ *A; to promote professional practice by designer-craftsmen of all kinds
- ● Conf - Res - Exhib - SG - Inf
- M 800 i, UK / 13 i, o'seas
- ¶ The Designer Craftsman - 1; Newssheet - 6; both ftm only.

Society of Diagnostic Engineers
  an alternative title of the **Institution of Diagnostic Engineers**

Society of District Council Treasurers

NR c/o Resource & Financial Management, East Staffordshire
Borough Council, Town Hall, BURTON on TRENT, Derbyshire,
DE14 2EB.
01283 508000
Sec: Gareth Moss
○ *P

Society of Dyers & Colourists   (SDC)   1884

NR PO Box 244, 82 Grattan Rd, BRADFORD, W Yorks, BD1 2JB.
(hq)
01274 725138
Gen Sec & Chief Exec: Kenneth M McGhee
○ *L, *P; science & technology of colour & colouration
M 792 i, UK / 762 i, o'seas
¶ Jnl - 10.   Colour Index International.
Textbooks & technical publications.

Society for Earthquake & Civil Engineering Dynamics   (SECED)

NR c/o Institution of Civil Engineers, 1-7 Great George St,
LONDON, SW1P 3AA.   (hq)
020 7222 7722
email seced@ice.org.uk   http://www.seced.org.uk
The Secretary
○ *L, *Q; the better design of structures subject to dynamic loads
from earthquakes & other sources
M i & org
¶ NL.   LM; m only.   AR.

Society for Economic Analysis Ltd   (SEAL)   1933

NR c/o Dr C Wallace, Dept of Economics, Manor Road Building,
Manor Rd, OXFORD, OX1 3UQ.   (sb)
Sec: Dr C C Wallace
▲ Registered Charity
○ *L; research in economics
● Conf - Mtgs - ET - Res
M 35 i
¶ The Review of Economic Studies - 4; ftm.

Society of Editors   1999

■ University Centre, Granta Place, Mill Lane, CAMBRIDGE,
CB2 1RU.   (hq)
01223 304080
Exec Dir: Bob Satchwell
▲ Company Limited by Guarantee
Br 11
○ *P; to represent editors in national, regional & local
newspapers, magazines, broadcasting, new media,
journalism, education & media law; to protect & promote the
freedom of the media & the general right to the freedom of
expression
● Conf - Mtgs - ET - Res - LG
< Wld Assn of Newspapers
M 475 i
¶ Briefing - 12; ftm only.

Society for Editors & Proofreaders   (SfEP)   1988

■ Riverbank House, 1 Putney Bridge Approach, LONDON,
SW6 3JD.   (hq)
020 7736 3278   fax 020 7736 3318
email administration@sfep.org.uk
http://www.sfep.org.uk
Co Sec: Valerie Rice
▲ Un-incorporated Society
○ *P; to foster & encourage high standards of editing &
proofreading
● Conf - Mtgs - ET
M 1,315 i, 49 f, 30 org, UK / 35 i, 2 f, 5 org, o'seas
¶ NL - 6; ftm only.   Directory - 1; free.
× 2002 Society of Freelance Editors & Proofreaders

Society of Education Consultants   (SEC)   1990

■ 25 Dickenson Rd, LONDON, N8 9ER.   (hsb)
0845 345 7932
email enquiries@sec.org.uk   http://www.sec.org.uk
Hon Sec: Patrick Allan
▲ Un-incorporated Society
○ *P; to support education management consultants
● Conf - ET
M 140 i, 12 f, UK / 10 i, o'seas
¶ NL - 6; 'Education' - weekly; both ftm only.

**Society for Education, Music & Psychology Research
(SEMPRE)   1972**

NR Royal National Institute for the Blind, Education & Employment
Division, 105 Judd St, LONDON, WC1H 9NE.   (hsb)
020 7391 2149
Hon Sec: Dr Adam Ockelford
○ *D, *N; to bring together researchers in the field of music
education & similar fields
● Conf - Res
M 157 i, 82 f, UK /130 i, 461 f, o'seas
¶ Psychology of Music (Jnl) - 2; ftm only.
× 2003 Society for Research in the Psychology of Music & Music
Education

Society of Education Officers
see **Confederation of Children's Services Managers**

Society for Effective Affective Learning   (SEAL)   1983

■ 37 Park Hall Rd, LONDON, N2 9PT.   (hq)
020 8365 3869   fax 020 8444 0339
email seal@seal.org.uk   http://www.seal.org.uk
Hon Sec: Rita Baker,
Chief Exec Officer: Hugh L'Estrange
▲ Company Limited by Guarantee; Registered Charity
○ *K; founded to promote learning methods which draw on the
full capacity of the individual - body, emotions, mind & spirit
- in particular accelerated learning
● Conf (2 yrly) - ET - Inf
< Intl Assn of Teachers of English as a Foreign Language; Intl
Alliance for Learning (IAL); Deutsche Gesellschaft für
Suggestopedie Lehren und Lernen (DGSL); Conseil des
Nouveaux Systèmes d'Apprentissage; Föreningen för
Suggestopedi och Holistiskt Läraude (SOHL)
M 428 i, UK / 274 i, o'seas
¶ (A) The Learning Spiral (Jnl); ftm, £10 each nm.
(B) Conference Proceedings; ftm, £10 each nm.
A - 2 issues in non-conference year.
A+B - 1 of each in conference year.
Transforming Learning; ftm (on joining), £15 nm.

Society for Endocrinology   1946

NR 22 Apex Court, Woodlands, Bradley Stoke, BRISTOL,
BS32 4JT.   (hq)
01454 642200
Chmn: Prof John Wass
▲ Registered Charity
○ *L; advancement of public education in endocrinology
● Conf - ET - Exhib - Publishing
< Intl Soc of Endocrinology; Eur Fedn of Endocrine Socs; Brit
Endocrine Socs; The Pituitary Foundation; BioScientifica Ltd
M 1,400 i, UK / 400 i, o'seas
¶ Jnl of Endocrinology - 12.   Endocrine Related Cancer - 4.
Jnl of Molecular Endocrinology - 6. The Endocrinologist - 4.

Society of Engineers
▲ Company Limited by Guarantee
In 2004-05 merged with Institution of Electrical Engineering,
which in 2006 merged with the Institution of Incorporated
Engineers, to form the **Institution of Engineering
Technology**

Society of Environmental Engineers (SEE)

■ The Manor House, High St, BUNTINGFORD, Herts, SG9 9AB. (asa)
01763 271209   fax 01763 273255
email office@environmental.org.uk
http://www.environmental.org.uk
Chief Exec: Prof Raymond Clark
○ *P; engineering & technical aspects of the environment
M i & f
¶ Jnl - 4.   NL - 9/10.

Society for Environmental Exploration (FRONTIER) 1989

NR 50-52 Rivington St, LONDON, EC2A 3QP. (hq)
020 7613 2422
Managing Dir: Ms Eibleis Fanning
▲ Company Limited by Guarantee
○ *L, *N, *Q; an international environmental research, conservation & natural resource development non-governmental organisation (NGO), operating long-term biodiversity & socio-economic field programmes in important threatened tropical habitats
● ET - Res - Stat - Inf - VE - LG - Provision of training for volunteers
M 7 i, UK / 34 i, o'seas
¶ NL - 2; ftm;   Technical Reports - irreg.
Publication list available.

Society of Equestrian Artists (SEA) 1978

■ 26 Doglands Farm, Newton by Toft, MARKET RASEN, Lincs, LN8 3NG. (sp)
01673 885537
email enquiries@equestrianartists.co.uk
http://www.equestrianartists.co.uk
Acting Sec: Susan M Millis
▲ Registered Charity
○ *A
● Mtgs - ET - Exhib - Comp - Inf
M c 450 i, UK / c 25 i, o'seas
¶ NL - 3/4; ftm only.

Society of Euphobics 1997

■ 311 Courtenay House, 9-15 New Park Rd, LONDON, SW2 4UN. (mail/add)
○ *W; for people with a fear of good news
● Mtgs - Lib - VE
M i

Society of Event Organisers (SEO) 1996

■ 29a Market Sq, BIGGLESWADE, Beds, SG18 8AQ. (hq)
01767 316255 fax 01767 316430
http://www.eou.org.uk
Gen Mgr: Peter Cotterell
▲ Un-incorporated Society
○ *P, *T; for organisers of events in companies & associations; events include meetings, conferences, exhibitions, incentive travel, training, corporate hospitality etc
● Conf - Mtgs - ET - Inf - VE - Seminars
M 350 f
¶ Event Organisers Update - 24; free to anyone involved in events.

Society for Existential Analysis 1988

NR BM Existential, LONDON, WC1N 3XX. (mail)
email info@existentialanalysis.co.uk
http://www.existentialanalysis.co.uk address
Chmn: Paul Smith-Pickard
▲ Registered Charity
○ *L; a forum for the analysis of existence from philosophical & psychological perspectives (membership consists mostly of psychotherapists, counsellors, psychologists & philosophers)
● Conf - Inf - Directory of Existential Psychotherapists
M 350 i, UK / 25 i, o'seas
¶ Jnl - 2.

Society for Experimental Biology (SEB) 1923

NR 3 The Carronades, New Rd, SOUTHAMPTON, Hants, SO14 0AA. (hq)
023 8022 4824   fax 023 8022 6312
http://www.sebiology.org
Senior Exec Officer: Christine Trimmer
▲ Company Limited by Guarantee; Registered Charity
Br 2
○ *L, *Q; to embrace all disciplines of experimental biology; to support & promote experimental biology in all its branches, to both the scientific community & the general public
● Conf - Mtgs - ET - Exhib - LG
M 1,350 i, UK / 450 i, o'seas
¶ Jnl of Experimental Botany.   The Plant Jnl.
Bulletin (NL).   Plant Biotechnology.
Publications list available.

Society of Expert Witnesses (SEW) 1996

■ PO Box 345, NEWMARKET, Suffolk, CB8 7TU. (hq)
0845 702 3014   fax 01638 668656
email helpline@sew.org.uk   http://www.sew.org.uk
Sec: Richard Cory-Pearce
▲ Company Limited by Guarantee
○ *P; to promote excellence in all aspects of the service provided by expert witnesses; to cooperate with other bodies with similar aims
● Conf - SG - Inf
M 1,013, i, UK / 20 i, o'seas
¶ Quaterly Jnl - 4.

Society of Financial Advisers
2005 merged with the Life Insurance Association to form the
Personal Finance Society

Society of Fine Art Auctioneers & Valuers (SOFAA) 1973

NR London Rd, Send, WOKING, Surrey, GU23 7LN. (hq)
01483 225891   fax 01483 222171
email chairman@sofaa.org   http://www.sofaa.org
Chmn: Christopher T J Ewbank
▲ Un-incorporated Society
○ *P; promotion & maintenance of standards in the valuation & sale of antiques & fine art
● Conf - Mtgs - ET - Inf - LG
M 60 i, 43 f
¶ LM - updated; free.
✕ 2002 (December) Society of Fine Art Auctioneers

Society of Floristry Ltd (S of F Ltd) 1951

■ The Ridings, East Ashling, CHICHESTER, W Sussex, PO18 9AR. (sb)
0870 241 0432
Sec: Sue Stones
▲ Company Limited by Guarantee
○ *H, *P; for professional florists
● Conf - Mtgs - Exam - Exhib - Comp - SG - Inf
M 1,044 i, UK / c 20 i, o'seas
¶ Focal Point - 4; ftm only.   Hbk.
Publications list available.

Society for Folk Life Studies 1961

NR 548 Wilbraham Rd, MANCHESTER, M21 9LB. (hsb)
0161-881 8640
Hon Sec: Dr Eddie Cass
○ *L; to study traditional & changing ways of life in Great Britain & Ireland with particular interest in regional culture
● Conf - Res - SG
M c 400 I & instns
¶ Folk Life: a jnl of ethnological studies - 1; ftm.   NL.

Society of Food Hygiene Technology   (SOFHT)   1979
- ■ PO Box 37, LYMINGTON, Hants, SO41 9WL.
    01590 671979   fax 01590 671359
    email admin@sofht.co.uk   http://www.sofht.co.uk
    Exec Sec: Mrs H A Hyde
- ▲ Company Limited by Guarantee
- Br 1
- ○ *L, *P
- ● Mtgs - ET - Exhib - Inf
- M 700 i, 130 f, UK / 30 i, o'seas
- ¶ SOFHT Focus (Jnl) - 3;   Diary; both ftm only.   NL.

Society of Freelance Editors & Proofreaders
    since 2002 **Society of Editors & Proofreaders**

Society for French Studies   (SFS)   1947
- NR c/o Dr Sarah Cooper, Trinity Hall, CAMBRIDGE, CB2 1TJ.
    (hsb)
    email sjc28@cus.cam.ac.uk
    Hon Sec: Dr Sarah Cooper
- ○ *L; to promote French studies in universities & institutions of
    comparable standing in the British Isles & Commonwealth
- M i & org
- ¶ French Studies (with French Studies Bulletin) - 4.

Society of Friends of King Richard III
- ■ 121 Windsor Drive, Wigginton, YORK, YO32 2RZ.   (sp)
    01904 762492
    email dorothy@silverboar.org   http://www.silverboar.org
    Founder Member: Dorothy Mitchell
- ▲ Un-incorporated Society
- ○ *G; research into the period of Richard III & the Wars of the
    Roses
- ● Mtgs
- M 300 i, UK / 50 i, o'seas
- ¶ Richard III & York;   Richard III & Council of the North;
    both £2.50 m, £3 nm.

**Society of the Friends of St George's & Descendants of the
    Knights of the Garter   1931**
- ■ 1 The Cloisters, Windsor Castle, WINDSOR, Berks, SL4 1NJ.
    (hsb)
    01753 860629   fax 01753 620165
    email riends@stgeorges-windsor.org
    http://www.stgeorges-windsor.com
    Hon Sec: Nigel Hill
- ▲ Registered Charity
- Br Australia, Canada, New Zealand, USA
- ○ *G; to help maintain the fabric & beauty of St George's
    Chapel, Windsor Castle; to promote interest & knowledge of
    the history & traditions of the Order of the Garter
- M 3,800 i, UK / 1,500 i, o'seas
- ¶ AR - 1; ftm, £2.

Society of Garden Designers   (SGD)   1981
- ■ Katepwa House, Ashfield Park Avenue, ROSS-ON-WYE,
    Herefords, HR9 5AX.   (hq)
    01989 566695   fax 01989 567676
    email info@sgd.org.uk   http://www.sgd.org.uk
    Admin: Gill Hinton
- ▲ Company Limited by Guarantee
- Br 10 regional groups
- ○ *P; to promote professional standards in garden design
- Gp Education policy c'ee
- ● Conf - Mtgs - ET - Exhib - Inf - Lib - VE
- < R Horticl Soc
- M 1,310 i, UK / 45 i, o'seas
- ¶ Garden Design Jnl - 10; ftm, £40 nm.

Society of Garlic Growers, Processors & Packers   (SGPP)   1998
- ■ 191 Westcombe Hill, LONDON, SE3 7DR.
- ○ *T
- ● Mtgs - Tastings
- M i
- ¶ NL - 3; ftm only.

Society of Genealogists   (SoG)   1911
- ■ 14 Charterhouse Buildings, Goswell Rd, LONDON,
    EC1M 7BA.   (hq)
    020 7553 3290   fax 020 7250 1800
    email events@sog.org.uk   http://www.sog.org.uk
    Acting Dir: June M Perrin
- ▲ Company Limited by Guarantee; Registered Charity
- ○ *G, *L; to promote & foster the study of genealogy
- Gp Computers in genealogy
- ● Conf - Mtgs - ET - Lib - VE
- < Fedn of Family History Socs
- M 13,500 i, UK / 1,500 i, o'seas
- ¶ Genealogists' Magazine - 4.
    Computers in Genealogy - 4.   AR.

Society for General Microbiology   (SGM)   1945
- ■ Marlborough House, Basingstoke Rd, Spencers Wood,
    READING, Berks, RG7 1AG.   (hq)
    0118-988 1800   fax 0118-988 5656
    email admin@sgm.ac.uk   http://www.sgm.ac.uk
    Exec Sec: Dr R S S Fraser
- ▲ Company Limited by Guarantee; Registered Charity
- Br Ireland
- ○ *L; to promote the art & science of microbiology
- Gp Cells & cell surfaces; Clinical microbiology; Clinical virology;
    Education; Environmental microbiology; Eukaryotic
    microbiology; Fermentation & bioprocessing; Food &
    beverages; Microbial infection; Physiology, biochemistry &
    molecular genetics; Systematics & evolution; Virus
- ● Conf - Mtgs - Exhib - Inf - LG
- < Fedn of Eur Microbiological Socs (FEMS); Intl U of
    Microbiological Socs
- M 3,925 i, UK / 1,380 i, o'seas
- ¶ Jnl of General Virology - 12; £94 m, £825 nm.
    Microbiology - 12; £94 m, £825 nm.
    Microbiology Today - 4; ftm, £55 nm.
    Jnl of Medical Microbiology - 12; £50 m, £655 nm.
    International Journal of Systematic & Evolutionary Microbiology
    - 6; £50 m, £655 nm.

Society of Glass Technology   (SGT)   1916
- ■ 12 O'Clock Court (Unit 9), 21 Attercliffe Rd, SHEFFIELD,
    S4 7WW.   (hq)
    0114-263 4455   fax 0114-263 4411
    email info@sgt.org   http://www.sgt.org
    Hon Sec: John Henderson
- ▲ Registered Charity
- Br 6; India, USA
- ○ *L; all aspects of the history, art, science, manufacture, after-
    treatment & use of glass of any & every kind
- Gp Technical c'ees - Analysis & properties; Basic science &
    technology; Engineering; Glass batch, furnaces &
    refractories; Handmade glassware
- ● Conf - Mtgs - Lib - VE
- < Intl Cmsn on Glass; Eur Soc Glass Science & Technology
- M 350 i, 70 f, UK / 150 i, 20 f, o'seas
- ¶ Glass Technology - 6.
    Physics & Chemistry of Glasses - 6.
    Borate Glasses, Crystals & Melts 4; £40 m. £60 nm.
    Ceramics & Glass: a basic technology.
    Bosc D'Antic on Glassmaking; £20 m, £25 nm.
    Early 19th Century Glassmaking in Austria & Germany; £20 m,
    £25 nm.
    Crystallisation 2003; £40 m, £60 nm.
    ESG 2004; £40 m, £60 nm.
    Monographs & Topical issues in glass.
    Specialist publications on aspects of glass technology.

Society of Graphic Fine Art (SGFA) 1919

NR PO Box 7727, MALDON, Essex, CM9 3HL. (mail)
     01707 880615 address
     Pres: David Brooke
○ *P; to promote good drawing skills through exhibitions
● Exhib
M i

Society of Greeting Card Collectors (SGCC) 1986

■ 76c The Avenue, BECKENHAM, Kent, BR3 5EF.
▲ Un-incorporated Society
○ *G
● Mtgs - Exhib
M i

Society of Greyhound Veterinarians
    a group of the **British Veterinary Association**

Society of Headmasters & Headmistresses of Independent Schools (SHMIS) 1961

NR 12 The Point, Rockingham Rd, MARKET HARBOROUGH, Leics,
    LE16 7QU. (hq)
    01858 433760
    Gen Sec: Dr David Richardson
▲ Company Limited by Guarantee
○ *E, *P; to maintain high standards of education in member
    schools; to facilitate the sharing of ideas; to ensure genuine
    independence
● Conf - Mtgs - ET - Inf - LG
< Indep Schools Coun (ISC)
M 91 i
¶ NL - 1;   LM - 1;   Hbk - 1.

Society of Health Advisers in Sexually Transmitted Diseases
    since 2002-03 **Society of Sexual Health Advisers**

Society of Health Education & Health Promotion Specialists (SHEPS) 1982

NR c/o University of Central England, Baker Building (7th floor),
    Perry Barr, BIRMINGHAM, B42 2SU. (admin)
▲ Un-incorporated Society
○ *P; 'policy & practice of health promotion & public health'
● Conf - Mtgs - ET - Res - SG - Inf - Empl - LG
< UK Public Health Assn
M 300-400 i
¶ 'A range of ad hoc publications are produced - often in the
    form of policy / discussion papers'

Society of Heraldic Arts (SHA) 1987

NR 26 Paternoster Row, OTTERY St MARY, Devon, EX11 1DP. (hsp)
    01404 815346
    Hon Sec: Kevin Arkinstall
▲ Un-incorporated Society
○ *P; for heraldic artists & craftsmen
● Mtgs - Res - Inf - VE
M i
¶ The Heraldic Craftsman - 4; ftm, £1.50 nm.

Society for the History of Alchemy & Chemistry (SHAC) 1937

■ c/o Dr Anna Simmons, Dept of History of Science, Technology
    & Medicine, The Open University, Walton Hall,
    MILTON KEYNES, Bucks, MK7 6AA. (hsb)
    email a.e.simmons@open.ac.uk   http://www.ambix.org
    Hon Sec: Anna Simmons
▲ Registered Charity
○ *L; all aspects of the history of alchemy & chemistry from the
    earliest times
● Mtgs - Res - Comp
M c 100 i, c 35 f, UK / c 150 i, c 225 f, o'seas
¶ Ambix - 1 volume in 3 parts each yr; £27 m, £109 nm.

Society for the History of Astronomy
    is a group of the **Birmingham & Midland Institute**

Society for the History of Natural History 1936

NR The Natural History Museum, Cromwell Rd, LONDON,
    SW7 5BD. (hsb)
    email secretary@shnh.org   http://www.shnh.org
    Admin: Sadiah Qureshi
▲ Registered Charity
○ *L; study of the history & bibliography of all branches of natural
    history
● Conf
M 600 i
¶ Archives of Natural History - 2.   NL - 3.
    Sherborn Facsimiles (of rare natural history texts) - irreg; price
    varies.
    Special publications & conference papers.

Society of Homeopaths 1978

■ 11 Brookfield, Duncan Close, Moulton Park, NORTHAMPTON,
    NN3 6WL. (hq)
    0845 450 6611   fax 0845 450 6622
    email info@homeopathy-soh.org
    http://www.homeopathy-soh.org
    Chief Exec: Paula Ross,   Hon Sec: Francis Treuherz
▲ Company Limited by Guarantee
○ *P; to promote homeopathy in the Hahnemannian tradition
● Conf - Mtgs - ET - Res - Inf - LG
< Coun for Complementary & Alternative Medicine; Eur Coun for
    Classical Homeopathy; Intl Coun for Classical Homeopathy
M 2,250 i, UK / 85 i, o'seas
¶ Register of Homeopaths (LM).

Society of Hospital Linen Service & Laundry Managers (SHLM) 1951

■ c/o Linen Service Manager, Queenspark Hospital,
    Haslingden Rd, BLACKBURN, Lancs, BB2 3HH.
    01254 294886
    Nat Sec: Lynn Fort
▲ Un-incorporated Society
Br 7 regions & NI
○ *P
● Conf - Mtgs - ET - Exam - Res - Exhib - SG - Stat - Inf - VE -
    Empl
M 170 i
¶ Hbk - 1.

Society of Incentive & Travel Executives

§ c/o Spectra, 12-15 Hanger Green, LONDON, W5 3EL. (hq)
    020 8601 2400
    Dir: Paul Miller
    a registered charity & the Scottish Chapter of S.I.T.E. a
    worldwide organisation promoting excellence in the
    conference & incentive industry through educational,
    networking & code of ethics for professionals on both
    supplier & buyer side of business

Society of Independent Brewers (SIBA) 1980

NR PO Box 101, THIRSK, N Yorks, YO7 4WA. (asa)
    0845 337 9158
    email secretariat@siba.co.uk   http://www.siba.co.uk
    Coordinator: Lucy Hunter
▲ Company Limited by Guarantee
Br 7 regions
○ *T; to represent the small independent brewers
Gp Training; Marketing; Political; Commercial
● Conf - Mtgs - ET - Comp - Inf - LG
< Food & Drink Fedn
M 220 f
¶ SIBA Jnl - 6; ftm only.

Society of Independent Roundabout Proprietors (SIRP) 1985
- ■ 66 Carolgate, RETFORD, Notts, DN22 6EF. (hsb)
  01777 702872
  Sec: Jack Schofield
- ○ *G, *T; owners & operators (both professional & semi-professional) of vintage fairground equipment (wood-framed, hand-turned, steam driven, pre-war) & vintage slot-machines
- ● Mtgs
- M 100 i

Society of Indexers (SI) 1957
- ■ Blades Enterprise Centre, John St, SHEFFIELD, S Yorks, S2 4SU. (hq)
  0114-292 2350   fax 0114-292 2351
  email admin@indexers.org.uk
  http://www.indexers.org.uk
  Sec: Mrs Ann Kingdom,   Admin: Wendy Burrow
- ▲ Un-incorporated Society
- ○ *L, *P; promotes standards & instruction on techniques for all forms of indexing
- ● Conf - Mtgs - ET - Exam - Inf - Register of Indexers
- < Soc of Indexers in: Australia / America / China / South Africa; Indexing & Abstracting Soc of Canada
- M 850 i, 16 f, UK / 60 i, 1 f, o'seas
- ¶ The Indexer - 2; ftm, £50 yr nm.
  SIdelights - 4;   LM - 1; both ftm only.
  Indexers Available - 1; free to publishers, £4.50 nm.
  Occasional papers on aspects of indexing - irreg; prices vary.

Society for Individual Freedom (SIF) 1945
- ■ PO Box 744, BROMLEY, Kent, BR1 4WG. (chmn/p)
  01424 713737
  http://www.individualist.org.uk
  Chmn: M Plumbe
- ▲ Un-incorporated Society
- ○ *K; to campaign & lobby on issues of personal freedom
- ● Conf - Mtgs
- M c 200 i
- ¶ The Individual - 3/4; ftm, £1 nm.
  Books & tracts - irreg.

Society of Industrial Emergency Service Officers
  see **SIESO**

Society of Information Technology Management (SOCITM) 1986
- NR PO Box 121, NORTHAMPTON, NN4 6TG. (hq)
  01604 674800
  Chief Exec: Kate Mountain
- ▲ Un-incorporated Society
- ○ *P
- ● Conf - Mtgs - ET - Res - Exhib - Stat - Inf - LG
- M 1,150 i
- ¶ NL - 4.   Ybk.   IT Trends Year Book.

Society for Interactive Learning
  see **Society for Advancement of Games & Simulations in Education & Training**

Society for International Folk Dancing   (Interfolk) (SIFD) 1946
- NR Oak Cottage, 92 Rose Green Rd, BOGNOR REGIS, W Sussex, PO21 3EG. (contact/p)
  01243 265010
  email mail@sifd.org   http://www.sifd.org
  Contact: Janet Douglas
- ▲ Registered Charity
- ○ *D: to preserve folk dances of all peoples & to make them known; to encourage the practice of them in traditional form
- ● Mtgs - ET - Public dances - Day & summer schools
- < Cent Coun of Physical Recreation; English Folk Dance & Song Soc
- > Israel Dance Inst; Welsh Circle Dance Assn
- M 400 i
- ¶ SIFD News - 12; ftm only.

Society of International Treasurers (SIT) 1977
- NR 2 Tereslake Green, Westbury-on-Trym, BRISTOL, BS10 6LT. (dir/gen/b)
  0117-950 8019   fax 0117-950 8019
  Dir-Gen: Brian Lowe
- ▲ Un-incorporated Society
- ○ *P; to provide a forum for the privileged & confidential interchange of views, opinions & experiences between senior treasury officials of major corporations
- ● Conf - Mtgs - Annual dinner
- M f
- ¶ LM - 1; ftm only.

Society of Irish Foresters 1942
- IRL Enterprise Centre, BALLINTOGHER, Co Sligo, Republic of Ireland.
  353 (71) 916 4434   fax 353 (71) 913 4904
  email sif@eircom.net
  http://www.societyofirishforesters.ie
  Sec: Clodagh Duffy
- ○ *P; to advance & spread the knowledge of forestry in all its aspects

Society of the Irish Motor Industry (SIMI)
- IRL 5 Upper Pembroke St, DUBLIN 2, Republic of Ireland.
  353 (1) 676 1690   fax 353 (1) 661 9213
  email info@simi.ie   http://www.simi.ie
  Sec: Brian Cooke
- ○ *T

Society for Italic Handwriting (SIH) 1952
- ■ 22 Endwood Court, 1 Handsworth Wood Rd, Handsworth Wood, BIRMINGHAM, B20 2RZ. (hsp)
  0121-554 7072
  email nickthenibs@freeserve.co.uk
  http://www.nickthenibs.co.uk
  Sec: Nicholas Caulkin
- ▲ Registered Charity
- ○ *A; to promote the use of Italic handwriting
- ● Mtgs - Exhib - Comp - SG - Inf - Lib
- M 500 i, 3 f, 30 schools, UK / 200 i, o'seas
- ¶ Jnl - 4.

Society of Jewellery History (SJH) 1977
- NR c/o Dept of Scientific Research, British Museum, LONDON, WC1B 3DG. (mail) address
  Mem Sec: Mrs A Stephens
- ○ *L; to stimulate interest in all aspects of jewellery (historical, archaeological, artistic, cultural & technological)
- M i, f & org
- ¶ Jewellery Studies - 1.
  Gems & Jewellery - 4; ftm only. (jt publication with the Gemmological Association).

Society of King Charles the Martyr   (SKCM)   1894
- ■ 22 Tyning Rd, Winsley, BRADFORD-on-AVON, Wilts,
    BA15 2JJ.   (hsp)
    01225 862965
    Chmn: Robin Davies
- ▲ Un-incorporated Society
- Br Australia, USA
- ○ *R; observance of 30 January in commemoration of King
    Charles I's martyrdom & upholding the principles (the prayer
    book & episcopacy) for which he died
- ● Mtgs - Services
- M 150 i, UK / 350 i, o'seas
- ¶ Church & King - 2; ftm.

Society for Landscape Studies   (SLS)   1979
- ■ c/o Dept of Geography, University of Exeter, Amory Buildings,
    North Park Rd, EXETER, Devon, EX4 4QE.   (hsp)
    01392 263330   fax 01392 264358
    email d.c.harvey@exeter.ac.uk
    http://www.landscapestudies.com
    Hon Sec: Dr David Harvey
- ▲ Registered Charity
- ○ *G, *L; 'to secure a more penetrating comprehension of
    landscape evolution & an overall narrative account of
    landscape, prehistory & history, together with an
    understanding of how this has influenced & may usefully
    guide the management of the present-day landscape'
- ● Conf
- < Coun Brit Archaeology
- M 370 i, 140 org, UK / 14 i, o'seas
- ¶ Landscape History - 1.

Society of Laundry Engineers & Allied Trades Ltd   (SLEAT)   1907
- ■ Suite 7 Southernhay, 207 Hook Rd, CHESSINGTON, Surrey,
    KT9 1HJ.   (asa)
    020 8391 2266   fax 020 8391 4466
    email admin@sleat.co.uk   http://www.sleat.co.uk
    Sec: David M Hart
- ▲ Company Limited by Guarantee
- ○ *T; suppliers to the laundry & dry cleaning industry (machinery
    & chemical manufacturers & distributors)
- ● Exhib - LG
- < Eur Laundry & Dry Cleaning Machinery Mfrs Org
- M 45 f

Society of Law Accountants in Scotland
- NR 3 Fintray Rd, Craigiebuckler, ABERDEEN, AB15 8HL.
    Admin: Sheila Dickson
- ○ *P

Society of Leather Technologists & Chemists Ltd   (SLTC)   1897
- NR c/o Tova Irving, William Cowley Vellum & Parchment Works,
    97 Caldecote St, NEWPORT PAGNELL, Bucks, MK16 0DB.
    (hsp)
    01908 610038
    email tova.irving@talktalk.net   http://www.sltc.org
    Hon Sec: Mrs Tova Irving
- ▲ Company Limited by Guarantee; Registered Charity
- Br 2; Australia, S Africa
- ○ *L; 'to assist & encourage the application of science &
    technology to the manufacture & utilisation of leather &
    related products'
- Gp Technical sub c'ee for official methods; Professional grades c'ee
- ● Conf - Mtgs - Collaboration in devising & publishing official
    methods of analysis, national & international - Conferring
    professional grade status
- < Intl U Leather Technologists & Chemists Socs (IULTCS)
- M 270 i, 30 org, UK / 360 i, 210 org, o'seas
- ¶ Jnl - 6.   Official Methods of Analysis.
    Leather Technologists Pocket Book.

Society of Legal Scholars in the United Kingdom & Ireland   (SLS)   1908
- ■ Faculty of Law, University of Southampton, Highfield,
    SOUTHAMPTON, SO17 1BJ.   (hsb)
    023 8059 4039   fax 023 8059 3024
    email s.j.thomson@soton.ac.uk
    http://www.legalscholars.ac.uk
    Hon Sec: Prof N J Wikeley, Admin Sec: Mrs S J Thomson
- ▲ Registered Charity
- ○ *P; to advance legal research & education
- Gp Law: Company, Comparative, Competition, Consumer,
    Contract & commercial, Criminal justice, Environmental,
    European, Family, Human rights & civil liberties, Immigration
    & refugee, Information technology, Intellectual property,
    International, Jurisprudence, Labour, Legal education, Legal
    history, Maritime media, Medical, Practice, Profession &
    ethics, Property & trusts, Public, Restitution, Tax, Torts
- ● Conf - Mtgs - ET - Res - LG
- M 2,400 i, 28 f, UK / 170 i, o'seas
- ¶ Legal Studies (Jnl) - 4;   The Reporter (NL) - 2; both ftm only.

Society of Leisure Consultants & Publishers   (SOLCAP)   1989
- ■ 1 Sandringham Close, Sandringham Park, TARLETON, Lancs,
    PR4 6UZ.   (dir/b)
    01772 816046
    Dir: J B A Sharples
- ▲ Un-incorporated Society
- ○ *T; to represent consultants, publishers & commercial interests
    in the leisure industry (entertainment, recreation, tourism,
    hotels, catering, marketing, publicity, sport & public relations)
- ● Conf - Mtgs - Exhib - Inf - VE
- M 38 i, 10 f, UK / 1 i, 1 f, o'seas
- ¶ NL - 2; ftm, £2 nm.   LM - 1; ftm, £5 nm.

Society of Ley Hunters   (SOL)   2000
- ■ 9 Mawddwy Cottages, Minllyn, Dinas Mawddwy,
    MACHYNLLETH, SY20 9LW.   (hsp)
    01650 531354
    email landcare@btinternet.com
    http://www.leyhunter@ntlworld.com
    7 Mildmay Rd, ROMFORD, Essex, RM7 7DA.   mem/s/p.
    Sec: Laurence Main,   Mem Sec: Adrian Hyde
- ▲ Un-incorporated Society
- ○ *G; the study of leys (straight alignments of ancient sites in the
    landscapes - their meanings & purposes & other related
    mysteries
- ● Mtgs - VE
- M 140 i, UK / 15 i, o'seas
- ¶ NL - 3/4; ftm only.

Society for Libyan Studies   1969
- ■ c/o Institute of Archaeology, 31-34 Gordon Sq, LONDON,
    WC1H 0PY.   (pt-time)
    email sstrong@btclick.com   http://www.britac.ac.uk/
    institutes/libya/form.html
    Sec: Mrs S K Strong
- ▲ Registered Charity
- ○ *L; study & research into history, archaeology, geography &
    geology of Libya
- ● Conf - Mtgs - Res - Exhib - SG - Inf
- M 200 i, 25 org, UK / 100 i, 62 org, o'seas
- ¶ Libyan Studies (AR); £20 m.

Society of Licensed Conveyancers   1988
- NR Chancery House, 110 High St, CROYDON, Surrey,
    CR0 1ND.   (hq)
    020 8681 1001
    Chief Exec: N F Ewert Evans
- ▲ Company Limited by Guarantee
- ○ *P; for licensed conveyancers in England & Wales
- ● Conf - Mtgs - Inf - LG - Referral of the public to a local licensed
    conveyancer - Provision of compulsory professional
    development courses
- M 400 i
- ¶ The Licensed Conveyancer - 4.

© CBD Research Ltd · Beckenham · BR3 5JS · Tel 020 8650 7745 · Fax 020 8650 0768 · E-mail cbd@cbdresearch.com · www.cbdresearch.com

Society of Licensed Victuallers
    Now known as **Licensed Trade Charity**

Society of Limners   (SLm)   1986
- ■ 16 Tudor Close, HOVE, E Sussex, BN3 7NR.   (admin/p)
      01273 770628
        email rgeast.limners@ntlworld.com
      Administrator: Richard East
- ▲ Un-incorporated Society
- ○ *A; to promote & encourage interest in miniature painting & calligraphy
- ● Conf - ET - Exhib
- < Wld Fedn Miniaturists
- M 140 i, 2 org, UK / 5 i, 1 org, o'seas
- ¶ NL - 3, ftm, £1.50 nm.

Society for Lincolnshire History & Archaeology   (SLHA)   1974
- ■ Jews' Court, Steep Hill, LINCOLN, LN2 1LS.   (hq)
      01522 521337   fax 01522 521337
      Chmn: Pearl Wheatley
- ▲ Registered Charity
- Br 2
- ○ *L; local history, archaeology & industrial archaeology of Lincolnshire
- Gp Archaeology; Industrial archaeology; Local history; Publications
- ● Conf - Mtgs - Res - SG - Lib - VE
- < Coun for Brit Archaeology; Brit Assn for Local History; Assn for Indl Archaeology
- M 550 i, 65 f, UK / 3 i, 22 f, o'seas
- ¶ Jnl - 1; ftm, £10 nm.   Magazine - 4; ftm, £1.60 nm.
      Bulletin - 4;   AR - 1; both ftm only.

Society of Local Authority Chief Executives & Senior Managers   (SOLACE)   1973
- NR Hope House, 45 Great Peter St, LONDON, SW1P 3LT.   (hq)
      0845 601 0649
      Dir Gen: David Clark
- ▲ Company Limited by Guarantee; Registered Charity
- Br 12
- ○ *P; for senior managers in local government in the UK; to develop & strengthen the UK local government sector
- Gp Ad hoc enquiries; E-Government & IT; Electoral matters; Health; Human resources; International; Management practice; Transformational change; Urban planning & policy
- ● Conf - Mtgs - ET - Res - Exhib - SG - Empl - LG
- < Local Govt Mgrs Australia; Soc Local Govt Mgrs (NZ); Inst Local Govt Mgrs (S Africa); Intl City Mgrs Assn (USA)
- M 930 i, 8 f, UK / 20 i, o'seas
- ¶ Running Elections.   Healthy Living Report.
      Sing When You're Winning - E-Government.
      Chance or Choice - Risk Management.

Society of Local Council Clerks   (SLCC)   1974
- ■ 1 The Crescent, TAUNTON, Somerset, TA1 4EA.   (hq)
      01823 253646   fax 01823 253681
        email admin@slcc.co.uk   http://www.slcc.co.uk
      Chief Exec: Nick Randle
- ▲ Un-incorporated Society
- Br 34
- ○ *P
- ● Conf - ET - Exam - Inf - Empl - LG
- M 3,500 i
- ¶ The Clerk (Jnl) - 6; ftm, £5 nm.

Society of Local Government Electrical & Mechanical Engineers   (SCEME)   1951
- ■ c/o Charles Tanswell, 1 Lenfield Ave, MAIDSTONE, Kent, ME14 5DU.   (hsb)
      01622 202233
      Hon Sec: Charles Tanswell
- ○ *P; representing all aspects of building service engineering in local authorities in the UK
- Gp Sub-c'ees: Electrical, Energy, Maintenance, Professional matters
- ● Conf - Mtgs - SG - Inf - LG
- M 75 i

Society of London Art Dealers (representing fine art dealers throughout the United Kingdom)   (SLAD)   1932
- ■ Ormond House, 3 Duke of York St, LONDON, SW1Y 6JP.   (hq)
      020 7930 6137   fax 020 7321 0685
        email office@slad.org.uk   http://www.slad.org.uk
      Dir Gen: Christopher Battiscombe
- ▲ Un-incorporated Society
- ○ *T; to promote & protect the good name & interests of the art trade & to enhance public confidence in responsible art dealing
- ● Mtgs - ET - Exhib - Inf - LG - Seminars - VAT & Droit de Suite helpline
- < Confédn Intle Négociants en Oeuvres d'Art (CINOA); Fedn Eur Art Galleries Assns (FEAGA)
- M 115 f
- ¶ NL - 4; ftm only.
      Society of London Art Dealers Directory - 1; free.
      Society of London Art Dealers Survey - 2 yrly; ftm only.

Society of Maritime Industries   1966
- ■ 30 Great Guildford St (4th floor), LONDON, SE1 0HS.   (hq)
      020 7928 9199
      Chief Exec: John C Murray
- ▲ Company Limited by Guarantee
- ○ *T; 'the voice of the UK's maritime business sector, promoting & supporting companies which build, refit & mordernise warships, & which supply equipment & services for all types of commercial & naval ships, ports & terminals infrastructure, offshore oil & gas, & marine science & technology
- Gp Association of British Offshore Industries; Association of Marine Scientific Industries; British Marine Equipment Association; British Naval Equipment Association; Ports & terminals group
- ● Conf - Mtgs - ET - Exhib - SG - Stat - Expt - LG
- M f
- × 2001 British Marine Equipment Council

** Society of Marriage Bureaux
    Organisation lost: see Introduction paragraph 3

Society of Martial Arts
- NR PO Box 34, MANCHESTER, M9 8DN.
        http://www.societyofmartialarts.co.uk
- ▲ Company Limited by Guarantee
- ○ *E, *Q; to promote the educational & research aspects of martial arts; to offer degrees & postgraduate qualifications in martial arts

Society of Master Saddlers (UK) Ltd   1966
- NR Green Lane Farm, Stonham, STOWMARKET, Suffolk, IP14 5DS.   (hq)
      01449 711642   fax 01449 711642
        http://www.mastersaddlers.co.uk
      Chief Exec: Mrs H Morley
- ▲ Company Limited by Guarantee
- ○ *T; representing manufacturers, retail & craft saddlers without retail premises; training & apprenticeship
- Gp Registered qualified saddle fitters
- ● ET - Exhib - Comp - Inf
- M 300 f
- ¶ NL - 2.   Members List & Ybk - 1.
      Leaflets.

Society of Medical Writers (SOMW) 1985
NR   Devils End, All Saints Way, BEACHAMWELL, Norfolk,
       PE37 8BT.   (hsp)
       http://www.somw.org.uk
       Hon Sec: Mrs Irene Ranner
       Chmn: Prof Brian McGuinness
▲   Un-incorporated Society
○   *A; to encourage good standards of writing within the medical
       professions
●   Conf - ET - Comp
<   Assn Broadcasting Doctors; Media Medics
M   200 i, UK / 25 i, o'seas
¶   The Writer (Jnl) - 2; ftm only.
✕   2001 General Practitioners Writers Association

Society for Medicines Research (SMR) 1966
■   Stuart Hex, Association Enterprises, 840 Melton Rd,
       Thurmaston, LEICESTER, LE4 4BN.   (asa)
       0116-264 0083
       email ae@association.hq.org + smr@association.org.uk
▲   Registered Charity
○   *P; to provide a common meeting for all who are interested or
       involved in drug research; to further the education of such
       persons to the ultimate benefit of the general public in the
       field of the relief of sickness
Gp   Medicinal chemistry; Biology; Pharmacology; Medicine;
       Pharmacy; Toxicology; Clinical
●   Conf - Mtgs - ET (one-day scientific mtgs)
<   Eur Fedn of Medicinal Chemistry (EFMC)
M   525 i, UK / 25 i, o'seas
¶   SMR NL - 2; ftm only.

Society for Medieval Archaeology (SMA) 1957
NR   c/o Dr Andrew Reynolds, Institute of Archaeology,
       University College London, 31-34 Gordon Sq, LONDON,
       WC1H 0PY.   (hsb)
       Hon Sec: Dr Andrew Reynolds
▲   Registered Charity
○   *L; archaeology in the British Isles in the post-Roman period
M   i & org
¶   Medieval Archaeology - 1; ftm.   NL - 2; free.

Society of Messengers-at-Arms & Sheriff-Officers 1922
NR   11 Alva St, EDINBURGH, EH2 4PH.   (hq)
       0131-225 9110   fax 0131-220 3468
       email admin@smaso.ednet.co.uk
       http://www.ednet.co.uk/~smaso
       Admin Sec: Alan Hogg,   Sec: Dorothy Lowe
○   *P; professional officers of court (messengers-at-arms or sheriff-
       officers) who are employed by private firms dealing with
       service & enforcement of court papers & decrees
●   Mtgs - Inf
<   U Intle des Huissiers de Justice & Officiers Judiciaires
M   c 200 i & f
¶   NL.   Magazine - 1.   LM.   Information Leaflet.

Society of Metaphysicians Ltd (SOM) 1944
■   Archers' Court, Stonestile Lane, The Ridge, HASTINGS,
       E Sussex, TN34 4PG.   (hq)
       01424 751577   fax 01424 751577
       email newmeta@btinternet.com
       http://www.metaphysicians.org.uk
       Founder-Pres: Dr John J Williamson
▲   Company Limited by Guarantee
Br   51 o'seas
○   *L; development & application of fundamental principles of
       metaphysics
Gp   Bio-energy; Aura research; Electro-imaging; Empathy; Psychic
       science;
       Metaphysical Research Gp (business section of the Society)
●   ET - Exam - Res - SG - Inf - Lib
M   1,200 i, UK / 1,891 i, o'seas
¶   Neometaphysical Digest - 4; ftm, £2.50 nm.
       NL - 12; ftm only.   AR; free.
       Borderline Science Reports (Neometaphysics, Current Affairs,
          Esoteric) - irreg; ftm, prices vary nm.
       Educational Neometaphysical Lessons - 6/weekly; ftm only.

Society of Model Aeronautical Engineers Ltd
       trades under the title **British Model Flying Association**

Society of Model & Experimental Engineers (SMEE) 1898
NR   Marshall House, 28 Wanless Rd, LONDON, SE24 0HW.   (hq)
○   *G; the promotion of excellence in model engineering

Society of Model Shipwrights (SMS) 1975
NR   5 Lodge Crescent, ORPINGTON, Kent, BR6 0QE.   (hsp)
       01689 827213
       Hon Sec: Peter Rogers
▲   Un-incorporated Society
○   *G; to promote research into & construction of true scale
       models of ships & boats of all periods; to preserve the skills
       of model shipwrightry
●   Mtgs - Res - Exhib - Comp
M   c 80 i, UK / 3 i, o'seas
¶   The Log (NL) - 12; ftm only.

Society of Motor Auctions
       is a group of the **Retail Motor Industry Federation**

Society of Motor Manufacturers & Traders Ltd (SMMT) 1902
NR   Forbes House, Halkin St, LONDON, SW1X 7DS.   (hq)
       020 7235 7000
       Chief Exec: Christopher MacGowan
○   *T; 'the leading trade association for the motor industry in the
       UK; to provide a range of products & services; to represent
       the industry to government in the UK & to overseas
       bodies...'
M   f

Society for Mucopolysaccharide Diseases (MPS) 1982
NR   MPS House, Repton Place, White Lion Rd, AMERSHAM, Bucks,
       HP7 9LP.   (hq)
       0845 389 9901   fax 0845 389 9902
       email mps@mpssociety.co.uk
       http://www.mpssociety.co.uk
       Chief Exec: Mrs Christine Lavery
▲   Registered Charity
Br   12 networks; 25 networks
○   *W; to support those affected by the disease, their families &
       carers; to bring about public awareness of MPS & related
       diseases; to support research
●   Conf - ET - Res - Exhib - Stat - Inf - VE
<   Nat Coun for Voluntary Orgs
M   800 families, 6 f, 12 org, UK / 100 i, 3 f, o'seas
¶   NL - 4.   AR.
       Booklets on specific diseases: Hurler, Scheie & Hurler/Scheie,
          Morquio, Sanfilippo, Maroteaux/Lamy etc.

Society of Museum Archaeologists (SMA) 1976
- ■ c/o Dept of Archaeology & Numismatics, National Museum & Gallery, Cathays Park, CARDIFF, CF10 3NP.   (hsb)
  029 2057 3274
  Hon Sec: Elizabeth Walker
- Br 1 regional group in Scotland
- ○ *P; to promote the archaeology profession in museums; to promote archaeology to the public
- ● Conf - SG
- < Museums Assn
- M 250 i, 60 org, UK / 2 i, 2 org, o'seas
- ¶ The Museum Archaeologist - 1; ftm.   NL - 2; ftm.
  Publications list available.

Society for Music Analysis
- NR Dept of Music, School of Humanities, University of Birmingham, Edgbaston, BIRMINGHAM, B15 2TT.
  http://www.lancs.ac.uk/sma
  Admin: Dr Matthew Riley
- ○ *P

Society for Name Studies in Britain & Ireland (SNSBI) 1991
- ■ Medical Library, School of Medical Sciences, University of Bristol, University Walk, BRISTOL, BS8 1TD.   (hsb)
  Hon Sec: Miss Jennifer Scherr
- ○ *L; to research into place-names & personal names of GB & Ireland
- ● Conf - Res - Comp - SG - Inf
- M 200 i, 5 org, UK / i & org, o'seas
- ¶ NOMINA (Jnl) - 1.   NL.

Society for Nautical Research (SNR) 1910
- ■ 6 Ashmeadow Rd, Arnside, CARNFORTH, Lancs, LA5 0AE.
  (hsb)
  01524 761616   fax 01524 761616
  email honsecretary.snr@btinternet.com
  http://www.snr.org
  National Maritime Museum, Greenwich, LONDON, SE10 9NF. (regd office).
  Hon Sec: Peter Winterbottom
- ▲ Company Limited by Guarantee; Registered Charity
- ○ *L, *Q; to research into all matters relating to seafaring & shipbuilding in all ages & among all nations & into the language & customs of the sea & other subjects of nautical interest
- Gp Provides tbe Chairman of the HMS Victory Advisory Technical C'ee, & in partnership with the Royal Navy oversees the continuing preservation, restoration & conservation of the ship
- ● Conf (with the British Commission for Maritime History) - Res - EXhib - LG - Sponsorship of N A M Rodger's Naval History of Britain (in 3 vol) - The recording of small watercraft
- M 1,000 i, 95 org, UK / 300 i, 220 org, o'seas
- ¶ The Mariners Mirror - 4; ftm, £12.95 each nm.
  NL - 4; ftm only.
  Bibliography of Mariner's Mirror (index) - 5 yrly.
  membership; £37 yr.

Society of Numismatic Artists & Designers (SNAD) 1992
- NR 108 Brompton Rd, LONDON, SW11   (hsp)
  020 7373 5554
  Sec: Jane McAdam-Freud
- ▲ Un-incorporated Society
- ○ *P; to raise the quality of coin design in the UK
- ● Mtgs - Exhib - Empl
- M 20 i, UK / 3 i, o'seas

Society of Nursery Nursing (SNN) 1991
- ■ 40 Archdale Rd, LONDON, SE22 9HJ.   (hq)
  020 8693 0555   fax 0709 234 2170
  email info@snn.uk.com   http://www.snn.uk.com
  Chief Exec: Prof R A Herbert-Blankson
- Br 4; 12 o'seas
- ○ *P; 'the only professional body in the field of nursery nursing'
- Gp Graduates (GSNN); Associates (ASNN); Fellows (FSNN)
- ● Conf - Mtgs - ET - Exam - Res - SG - Lib
- < Soc of Sales & Marketing
- M 90 i, UK / 200 i, o'seas
- ¶ The Nursery Nursing Jnl; free.

Society of Occupational Medicine (SOM) 1935
- ■ 6 St Andrews Place, LONDON, NW1 4LB.   (hq)
  020 7486 2641   fax 020 7486 0028
  email admin@som.org.uk   http://www.som.org.uk
  Chief Exec: Hilary Toddht
- ▲ Registered Charity
- Br 10 regional gps
- ○ *L; for doctors working in any capacity in occupational health in any field (incl government agencies & the armed forces) concerned with the protection of the health of people at work & the prevention of occupational diseases & injuries
- ● Conf - Mtgs - Res - Exhib - Inf - VE - LG
- M 1,800 i, UK / 100 i, o'seas
- ¶ Occupational Medicine Journal - 8; ftm.
  NL - 4;   Hbk - 2 yrly;   AR - 1; all ftm only.

Society for Old Testament Study (SOTS) 1917
- ■ St Stephen's House, 16 Marston St, OXFORD, OX4 1JX.   (hsb)
  01865 432298   fax 01865 794338
  email hogn.jarick@theology.ox.ac.uk
  http://www.sots.ac.uk
  Hon Sec: Dr John Jarick
- ▲ Un-incorporated Society
- ○ *L; the promotion & coordination of Old Testament studies in GB & Ireland
- ● Conf
- M 299 i, UK/ 144 i, o'seas
- ¶ NL & LM - 1; ftm only.   Book List - 1; ftm, £22 nm.

Society of Olympic Collectors (SOC) 1984
- ■ 19 Hanbury Path, Sheerwater, WOKING, Surrey, GU21 5RB.
  (hsp)
  Hon Sec: Miss P Burger
- ▲ Un-incorporated Society
- ○ *G; to collect, collate & distribute information about philatelic & other memorabilia items related to the Olympic games
- ● Res - Exhib - Inf - Lib - VE
- < Assn Brit Philatelic Socs
- M 91 i, UK / 117 i, o'seas
- ¶ Torch Bearer (Jnl) - 4; ftm, £2 each nm.

Society of Operations Engineers 2000
- ■ 22 Greencoat Place, LONDON, SW1P 2PR.   (hq)
  020 7630 1111
  Chief Exec: Tracey Shelley
- ▲ Company Limited by Guarantee; Registered Charity
- ○ *P; plant inspection, maintenance, service & works engineering in all industries
- Gp Professional sectors: Institute of Road Transport Engineers, Institution of Plant Engineers; Bureau of Engineer Surveyors
- ● Conf - Mtgs - ET - Comp - Inf - VE
- < Engg Coun; NICEIC; NCSIIB
- M 4,862 i, 16 f, UK / 684 i, o'seas
- ¶ The Plant Engineer (Jnl) - 6.
  Transport Engineer (Jnl).
  Various guides.   AR.

Society of Orthopaedic Medicine Ltd   1983
■   PO Box 223, Patchway, BRISTOL, BS32 4XD.   (admin/p)
    01454 610255   fax 01454 610255
    email admin@somed.org   http://www.somed.org
    Admin Dir: Amanda Sherwood
▲   Company Limited by Guarantee; Registered Charity
○   *P; to promote orthopaedic medicine through education & the
    funding of research
●   Conf - Mtgs - ET - Res
>   Cyriax Org; Orthopaedic Medicine Intl; Ir Soc of Orthopaedic
    Medicine
M   1,000 i, UK / 300 i, o'seas
¶   Jnl of Orthopaedic Medicine - 3; £30.   NL - 2; ftm only.

Society of Parliamentary Agents   (SPA)   1844
NR   c/o Alastair Lewis, Sharpe Pritchard, Elizabeth House,
    Fulwood Place, LONDON, WC1V 6HG.   (hsb)
    020 7405 4600
    Hon Sec: Alastair Lewis
▲   Un-incorporated Society
○   *P
    No further information supplied.

Society of Parsley Cultivators
■   191 Westcombe Hill, LONDON, SE3 7RR.
○   *H
●   Mtgs - Stat - VE
M   f

Society for Pattern Recognition
      see full title **British Machine Vision Association & Society for
      Pattern Recognition**

Society of Pension Consultants   (SPC)   1958
■   St Bartholomew House, 92 Fleet St, LONDON, EC4Y 1DG.
    (hq)
    020 7353 1688   fax 020 7353 9296
    email john.mortimer@spc.uk.com
    http://www.spc.uk.com
    Sec: John Mortimer
▲   Company Limited by Guarantee
Br   3
○   *T; interests of organisations providing advice on & services to
    schemes & funds for the provision of retirement benefits
Gp   Compliance forum
●   Mtgs - Inf - LG
<   Occupational Pension Schemes Jt Working Gp
M   133 f
¶   SPC News - 6; ftm only.   LM - 1;   AR; both free.

Society of Perfusionists of Great Britain & Ireland
      since 2001 **Society of Clinical Perfusion Scientists of Great
      Britain & Ireland**

Society of Pharmaceutical Medicine   (SPM)   1987
NR   c/o Institute of Biology, 9 Red Lion Court, LONDON,
    EC4A 3EF.   (hq)
    020 7936 5900
    Hon Sec: Graham Belgrave
▲   Registered Charity
○   *P; to promote the acquisition & dissemination of knowledge
    concerning the action & development of medicinal agents &
    their application in therapeutics
●   Conf
M   100 i, UK / 20 i, o'seas
¶   International Jnl of Pharmaceutical Medicine - 4.

Society of Ploughmen Ltd   1972
■   Quarry Farm, Loversall, DONCASTER, S Yorks, DN11 9DH.
    (hq)
    01302 852469   fax 01302 859880
    email info@ploughmen.co.uk
    http://www.ploughmen.co.uk
    Exec Dir: Ken Chappell
▲   Company Limited by Guarantee
○   *F; to promote the art & skill of ploughing the land; to promote
    the annual British National Ploughing Championship
●   Comp
<   Wld Ploughing Org
M   800 i, 250 org
¶   NL - 2; ftm only.

Society for Popular Astronomy   (SPA)   1953
■   36 Fairway, Keyworth, NOTTINGHAM, NG12 5DU.   (hsp)
    email info@popastro.com   http://www.popastro.com
    Hon Sec: Guy Fennimore
○   *G, *L; to promote the knowledge & study of astronomy in a
    popular manner
Gp   Sections: Meteors, Comets, Aurorae, Planets, Moon, Sun,
    Variable stars, Deep-sky objects, Lunar occultations
●   Mtgs - ET - Res - Comp - Stat - Inf - VE - Weekend courses
<   Brit Astronomical Assn
M   3,100 i, 60 org, UK / 70 i, 4 org, o'seas
¶   Popular Astronomy (Jnl) - 4; ftm, price on application nm.
    Circular (NL) - 6; ftm only.

Society of Portrait Sculptors   (SPS)   1953
■   27 Winchester St, LONDON, W3 8PA.
    01825 750485   fax 01825 750411
    email sps@portrait-sculpture.org
    http://www.portrait-sculpture.org
    Hon Sec: David Houchin
▲   Registered Charity
○   *A; 'portrait & figurative sculpture'
●   Exhib (annual)
M   30 i, UK / 2 i, o'seas
¶   Catalogue - 1; ftm, £5 nm.

Society for Post-Medieval Archaeology   (SPMA)   1967
■   c/o 267 Kells Lane, Low Fell, GATESHEAD, Tyne & Wear,
    NE9 5HU.
    0191-482 1037
    http://www.spma.org.uk
    Hon Sec: David Cranstone
▲   Company Limited by Guarantee
○   *L; to study evidence of British & Colonial history of the post-
    medieval period before industrialisation
●   Conf - Res - Lib - VE - LG
<   Soc Histl Archaeology (USA)
M   462 i, 219 org
¶   Post-Medieval Archaeology (Jnl); ftm.   NL - 2; free.

Society of Practising Veterinary Surgeons
      a group of the **British Veterinary Association**

*Society for the Preservation & Appreciation of Old Time Music & Dancing
(Old Time Society)*
      since 2005 **Old Time Dance Society**

© CBD Research Ltd · Beckenham · BR3 5JS · Tel 020 8650 7745 · Fax 020 8650 0768 · E-mail cbd@cbdresearch.com · www.cbdresearch.com

Society for the Preservation of Beers from the Wood   (SPBW) 1963
NR   The Rook, High St, Rowde, DEVIZES, Wilts, SN10 2QF.
      (chmn/p)
      01380 726378
      Chmn: Chris Callow
▲   Un-incorporated Society
Br   17; USA
○   *K; to stimulate the brewing & encourage the drinking of
      traditional draught beers, drawn direct from the cask by
      gravity or by handpump or other approved methods & to
      support those brewers who, by their policy, assist in the
      society's aims.
●   Exhib
M   600 i, UK / 300 i, o'seas
¶   Pint in Hand - 4; ftm only.

Society for the Prevention of Solvent & Volatile Substance Abuse
      see **Re-Solv (Society for the Prevention of Solvent & Volatile
      Substance Abuse)**

Society of Procurement Officers in Local Government   (SOPO) 1997
■   SBV Ltd, Rosecroft, Holbrook Rd, Harkstead, IPSWICH, Suffolk,
      IP9 1BP.   (hsp/b)
      01473 327952
      Chief Exec: Peter Howarth
▲   Company Limited by Guarantee
Br   12 regions
○   *P; to provide procurement guidance & promote strategic
      procurement within local government; to provide a forum &
      network
●   Conf - Mtgs - ET - Exhib - Inf - LG
<   Chart Inst of Purchasing & Supply
M   2,400 i, 13 f
¶   enewsletter - 52; free.   Annual Ybk - 1; ftm, £175 nm.
✕   2002-04 Society of Purchasing Officers of Local Government

Society for Producers & Composers of Applied Music   (PCAM) 1982
NR   Birchwood Hall, Storridge, MALVERN, Worcs, WR13 5EZ.
      (admin/p/b)
      01886 884204   fax 01886 884204
      email bfromer@netcomuk.co.uk
      http://www.pcam.co.uk
      Admin: Bob Fromer
▲   Un-incorporated Society
○   *T; music producers &/or composers working primarily in
      commissioned film, advertising & television programme
      music
Gp   Television c'ee
●   Mtgs - ET - Res - Inf
<   sister organisations in Australia, Germany, Spain, USA
M   90 f, UK / 3 f, o'seas
¶   The Bugle (NL) - 4.   PCAM Directory - 1.

Society of Professional Accountants   (SPA)   1996
NR   95 High St, GREAT MISSENDEN, Bucks, HP16 0AL.   (hq)
      01494 864414   fax 01494 864454
      email mail@spa.org.uk   http://www.spa.org.uk
      Chmn: Peter J D Mitchell
▲   Un-incorporated Society
○   *P; for chartered accountants who have a qualification issued
      by a recognised professional accountancy institute (ICAEW,
      ICAI, IAS, ACCA, CIMA); such individuals in practice
●   Inf - LG
<   ICAEW
M   1,800 i, 1,500 f
¶   SOA News - 8;   Members Ybk - 1; both ftm only.
✕   2002 (November) Small Practitioners Association

Society of Professional Engineers Ltd   (SPE)   1969
■   Lutyens House, Billing Brook Rd, Weston Favell,
      NORTHAMPTON, NN3 8NW.   (regd/off)
      01604 415729
      email gillian.stacey@abe.org.uk
      http://www.professionalengineers-uk.com
      Chief Exec: David R Gibson
▲   Company Limited by Guarantee
○   *P; 'to promote the concept of the professional engineer & to
      place on a register those deemed to be so qualified'
M   150 i, UK / 400 i, o'seas
¶   The Professional Engineer - 4; ftm.

Society of Professional Licensed Taxi Drivers
NR   Unit 4 Bush Industrial Estate, Station Rd, LONDON,
      N19 5UW.   (hq)
      020 7281 7676   fax 020 7272 7622
○   *T

Society for Promoting Christian Knowledge   (SPCK)   1698
§   36 Causton St, LONDON, SW1P 4ST.   (hq)
      020 7592 3900   fax 020 7592 3939
      a missionary society providing grants for Christian literature
      enterprises overseas & acting as publishers & booksellers in
      the UK

Society for Promoting the Training of Women   (SPTW)   1859
NR   2 Barons Court Mews, Hollist Lane, Easebourne, MIDHURST,
      W Sussex, GU29 9RS.   (hsp)
      01730 817881
      email sec_sptw@ntlworld.com   http://www.sptw.org
      Hon Sec: Mrs Morgan Thompson
▲   Registered Charity
○   *W; to make interest free loans to women (18+) undertaking
      full time (very occasionally part-time) training for a career
●   ET
M   50 i
¶   AR; ftm, free nm (for sae).

Society for the Promotion of Byzantine Studies   (SPBS)   1983
NR   c/o Dr Antony Eastmond, Courtauld Institute of Art,
      Somerset House, Strand, LONDON, WC2R 0RN.   (hsb)
      Hon Sec: Dr Antony Eastmond
▲   Registered Charity
○   *L; to further the study & knowledge of the history of the
      Byzantine Empire & its neighbours
●   Conf - Mtgs - Res - PL - VE
<   Assn Intle des Etudes Byzantines (AIEB)
M   i
¶   Bulletin - 1.

Society for the Promotion of Hellenic Studies   (Hellenic Society)   1879
NR   Senate House, Malet St, LONDON, WC1E 7HU.   (hq)
      020 7862 8730   fax 020 7862 8731
      Sec: Russell Shone
▲   Registered Charity
○   *L; to study the Greek language, literature, history & art in the
      ancient, Byzantine & modern periods
●   Mtgs - Lib
M   3,000 i, UK / 1,000 org, o'seas
¶   Jnl of Hellenic Studies (with suppt Archaeological Reports) - 1.
      Note: the Library is owned in common with the Society for the
      Promotion of Roman Studies & the Institute of Classical
      Studies of the University of London.

Society for the Promotion of New Music   (SPNM)   1943
NR   St Margaret's House, 18-20 Southwark St (4th floor),
      LONDON, SE1 1TJ.   (hq)
      020 7407 1640   fax 020 7403 7652
      email spnm@spnm.org.uk   http://www.spnm.org.uk
      Admin: Katy Kirk, Exec Dir: Abigail Pogson
▲   Registered Charity
○   *D; to help composers by presenting new works in workshop &
      concert performances
●   Conf - ET - Exhib - Comp - SG - Inf
<   Intl Soc for Contemporary Music (ISCM)(British section)
M   1,500 i, f & org, UK / 100 i, f & org, o'seas
¶   New Notes (contemporary music brochure) - 12.
      Beat Magazine - 4.

Society for the Promotion of Roman Studies   (Roman Society)
1910
■   Senate House, Malet St, LONDON, WC1E 7HU.   (hq)
      020 7862 8727   fax 020 7862 8728
      email office@romansociety.org
      http://www.romansociety.org
      Sec: Dr Helen M Cockle
▲   Company Limited by Guarantee; Registered Charity
○   *L; to promote the study of the history, archaeology, literature &
      art of Italy & the Roman Empire, from the earliest times down
      to c AD 700
●   Conf - Mtgs - Lib
<   Fédn Intle des Assns d'Études Classiques
M   2,100 i, 250 org, UK / 650 i, 950 org, o'seas
¶   Jnl of Roman Studies - 1; ftm, £45 yr nm.
      Jnl of Roman Studies Monographs - irreg; prices vary.
      Britannia - 1; ftm, £45 yr nm.
      Britannia Monographs - irreg; prices vary.   AR; free.

Society of Property Researchers   (SPR)   1987
■   St Mary's, Gandish Rd, EAST BERGHOLT, Suffolk, CO7 6UR.
      (mem/sp)
      01206 298205   fax 01206 298683
      email ftrott@sprweb.com   http://www.sprweb.com
      Mem Sec: Fiona Trott
▲   Un-incorporated Society
○   *P
Gp   Property occupiers; European; Investment; Retail; Geographic
      information in property; New Zealand; Sustainable
      development
●   Mtgs - Res - VE
M   500 i, UK / 30 i, o'seas
¶   LM - 1;   SPR Property Review & Digest No 1 & 2 (1993);
      both ftm only.
      The Adequacy & Accuracy of Commercial Property Data,
      Working Paper No 1: The Need for Property Data (1995);
      Local Area Analysis & Portfolio Construction (1994);
      Property Indices Report (1994);   all ftm, £20 nm.
      Survey of Salaries & Benefits - 2 yrly; ftm, £30 nm.

Society for the Protection of Ancient Buildings   (SPAB)   1877
■   37 Spital Sq, LONDON, E1 6DY.   (hq)
      020 7377 1644   fax 020 7247 5296
      email info@spab.org.uk   http://www.spab.org.uk
      Sec: Philip Venning
▲   Registered Charity
○   *K, *L; to promote the conservative repair of historic buildings;
      the SPAB must be notified of all applications to demolish in
      whole or part any listed building in England & Wales
Gp   Mills section; SPAB in Scotland
●   Conf - Mtgs - ET - Exhib - Inf - Lib - VE - LG
<   Jt C'ee of Nat Amenity Socs
M   8,500 i
¶   SPAB News - 4;   Wind & Watermill - 4; both ftm.

Society for the Protection of Aviculture   (SPA)   2002
NR   Spring Gardens, NORTHAMPTON, NN1 1DR.   (hq)
      01604 624549   fax 01604 627108
      http://www.spauk.net
      Gen Sec & Treas: Dave Whittaker
○   *G, *K, *N; to bring together aviculturalists within the UK; to
      promote education to all bird fanciers for the better welfare
      of birds kept in aviaries & cages
●   Exhib - Inf
>   Australian Finch Society; Budgerigar Soc; Cockatiel Soc;
      Foreign Bird Assn; Foreign Bird League; Gloster Convention;
      Lizard Canary Assn; Lovebird (1990) Soc; Nat Roller Canary
      Soc; Parrot Soc; Soc for Consvn in Aviculture; Zebra Finch
      Soc
M   14 org

Society for the Protection of Life from Fire   1836
§   c/o V Rance, PPIAB, 29 Queen Anne's Gate, LONDON,
      SW1H 9BU.   (hq)
      Sec: E H Gledhill
      further details are available from Mr E H Gledhill at the above
      address

Society for the Protection of Unborn Children   (SPUC)   1967
■   5-6 St Matthew St, LONDON, SW1P 2JT.   (hq)
      020 7222 5845
      http://www.spuc.org.uk
      Gen Sec: Paul Tully
○   *K; 'to affirm & defend the value of all human life - from
      conception to natural death. Our work crystallises in
      opposition to abortion'
Gp   Divisions: Evangelical, Handicap, Muslim, Nurses, Students,
      Tory
●   Conf - Mtgs - ET - Res - Comp - Inf - LG
M   45,000 i
¶   Pro-Life Times.

Society for Psychical Research
      see **Incorporated Society for Psychical Research**

Society of Public Information Networks   (SPIN)
■   PO Box 7202, LOUGHBOROUGH, Leics, LE11 5WS.   (sb)
      Sec: David Thompson
▲   Company Limited by Guarantee
○   *P; to promote current awareness & best practice in the field of
      electronic public information, including Internet, Intranet,
      multimedia, DTV, public access kiosks, mobile phones etc
●   Conf - Res - Exhib - Inf - LG
M   240 f, 40 org
¶   Electronic Public Information - 4.
      Spin Bulletin (email) - 1.

Society of Publishers in Ireland   (SPI)   2002
IRL   c/o Verba Editing House, 4 Donore Rd Industrial Estate,
      DROGHEDA, Co Louth, Republic of Ireland.
      353 (41) 987 1000   fax 353 (41) 987 1000
      email info@the-spi.com   http://www.the-spi.com
      Sec: Rachel Pierce
○   *T

Society of Purchasing Officers in Local Government
      since 2002-04 **Society of Procurement Officers in Local**
      Government

Society of Radiographers   (SoR)   1920
■   207 Providence Square, Mill St, LONDON, SE1 2EW.   (hq)
     020 7740 7200   fax 020 7740 7204
     email info@sor.org   http://www.sor.org
     Chief Exec: Richard Evans
▲   Company Limited by Guarantee
○   *P, *U; the Society, & its directly owned subsidiary the College of
     Radiographers, exist to promote & develop the science &
     practice of radiography (including both diagnostic &
     therapeutic disciplines); it is the recognised trade union for
     those engaged in radiography & related activities
●   Conf - Mtgs - ET - Exam - Res - Exhib - Comp - SG - Stat - Lib -
     VE - Empl - LG
<   Intl Soc Radiographers & Radiological Technologists; Alliance
     Health Profls
M   21,729 i, UK / 244 i, o'seas
¶   Radiography (Jnl) - 4;   Synergy (NL) - 12; both ftm.
     Imaging & Oncology - 1; free to all in radiological &
     oncological communities.

Society for Radiological Protection   (SRP)   1963
■   PO Box 117, BUCKFASTLEIGH, Devon, TQ11 0WA.
     (admin/off)
     01364 644487   fax 01364 644492
     email admin@srp-uk.org   http://www.srp-uk.org
     Hon Sec: Bryan Smith
▲   Registered Charity
○   *L, *P; the scientific, technological, medical & legal aspects of
     radiological protection
●   Conf - Mtgs
<   Intl Radiation Protection Assn
M   1,357 i, f & org
¶   Jnl - 4; ftm, £243 yr nm.

Society of Recorder Players   (SRP)   1937
NR   6 Upton Court, 56 East Dulwich Grove, LONDON,
     SE22 8PS.   (hsp)
     020 8693 4319
     Hon Sec: J Alistair Read
▲   Registered Charity
Br   50; Eire
○   *D; 'education of the public in the study, practice &
     appreciation of the art of music & in particular the repertoire
     & playing of recorders'
●   Conf - Mtgs - ET - SG - Exams for certificate for teaching &
     conducting - Workshops - Biennial competition for young
     professionals
M   1,250 i, 4 org, UK / 30 i, o'seas

Society of Registered Naturopaths
     see **Incorporated Society of Registered Naturopaths**

Society of Registration Officers - Births, Deaths & Marriages
     2004 merged with the Conference of Supervisory Registrars & the
     Institute of Population Registration to form the **Association of
     Registration & Celebratory Services**

Society for Renaissance Studies   (SRS)   1967
NR   c/o Prof Claire Jowitt, School of Arts, Communication &
     Culture, Nottingham Trent University, Clifton Lane,
     NOTTINGHAM, NG11 8NS.   (hsb)
     Hon Sec: Prof Claire Jowitt
▲   Registered Charity
Br   3
○   *L; study of all aspects of the Renaissance
●   Conf - ET - Res - Exhib
M   c 600 i
¶   Renaissance Studies (Jnl).
     Bulletin - 2.

Society for Reproduction & Fertility   1950
NR   Procon Conferences Ltd, Tattersall House, East Parade,
     HARROGATE, N Yorks, HG1 5LT.   (hq)
     01423 564488
     Gen Sec: Pat Neill
○   *L; study of biological & medical aspects of fertility
M   c 1,100 i

Society for Reproductive & Infant Psychology   (SRIP)   1980
NR   School of Healthcare Studies, Baines Wing, University of Leeds,
     LEEDS, W Yorks, LS2 9UT.   (hsb)
     0113 343 1281
     Sec: Janet Hirst
▲   Registered Charity
○   *M; to provide an international forum for discussion of the
     psychological aspects of human reproduction & infant
     development
●   Conf - Mtgs - ET - Res - Comp
M   140 i, UK / 38 i, o'seas
¶   Journal of Reproductive & Infant Psychology - 4.

Society for Research into Higher Education Ltd   (SRHE)   1964
NR   76 Portland Place, LONDON, W1B 1NT.   (hq)
     020 7637 2766
     Chmn: Prof Ron Barnett
○   *L; research & development into all forms of higher education
Gp   Continuing education; Excellence in learning & teaching; Staff
     development; Teacher education; Women in higher
     education
●   Conf - Mtgs - Exhib
M   c 1,000 i & org

**Society for Research into Hydrocephalus & Spina Bifida
(SRHSB)   1957**
NR   Gagle Brook House, Chesterton, BICESTER, Oxon,
     OX26 1UF.   (hsb)
     email hsec@srhsb.org   http://www.srhsb.org
     Hon Sec: Dr Hazel C Jones
▲   Registered Charity
○   *L, *Q; to advance education & promote research into
     hydrocephalus & spina bifida; to bring together workers in
     different fields so that they may be aided in their joint effort
     to prevent, cure or alleviate these conditions
●   Conf - Res
M   56 i, UK / 200 i, o'seas
¶   European Jnl of Pediatric Surgery - 1;   NL - 3;   AR - 1;
     Prospectus - 1; m only, £60 yr (£30 yr senior members).

Society for Research in the Psychology of Music & Music Education
     since 2003 **Society for Education, Music & Psychology
     Research**

**Society for the Responsible Use of Resources in Agriculture & on
the Land   (RURAL)   1983**
■   Chester House 12 Hillbury Rd, Alderholt, FORDINGBRIDGE,
     Hants, SP6 3BQ.   (hq)
     01425 652035
     http://www.rural.org.uk
     Dir: Brig H J Hickman
○   *F; to assist the policy makers in the field of land use,
     agricultural & rural management; to form opinions; to
     reconcile competing rural interests; information policy
     development
●   Conf - Mtgs - SG - Discussion groups
M   180 i, 29 f
¶   RURAL Briefing; £15 yr.   Network opportunities.

Society of Retreat Conductors
     has closed

Society for Sailing Barge Research (SSBR) 1963
- ■ 5 Cox Rd, Alresford, COLCHESTER, Essex, CO7 8EJ. (hsp)
     01206 825317
     email john.white6@talk21.com
     http://www.sailingbargeresearch.org.uk
     Hon Sec: John White
- ▲ Un-incorporated Society
- ○ *G; research into the sailing barge, the men who built & sailed
     them & the ports from which they sailed
- ● Res - Exhib - PL
- M 340 i, 10 org, UK / 10 i, o'seas
- ¶ Topsail (Jnl) - 1;   NL - 2; both ftm only.

Society of Sales & Marketing (SSAM) 1980
- ■ 40 Archdale Rd, LONDON, SE22 9HJ. (hq)
     020 8693 0555   fax 0709 234 2170
     email info@ssam.co.uk   http://www.ssam.co.uk
     Chief Exec: Prof R A Herbert-Blankson
- ▲ Company Limited by Guarantee
- Br 15; 120 o'seas
- ○ *P; 'is the only professional society specialising exclusively in all
     four branches of selling - selling & sales management,
     marketing, retailing & international trade'
- ● Conf - Mtgs - ET - Exam - Res - Lib
- < Soc of Nursery Nursing
- M 1,600 i, 20 f, UK / 4,000 i, o'seas
- ¶ SSAM Jnl.

Society of Schoolmasters & Schoolmistresses (SOSS) 1798
- ■ c/o Miss Sarah Brydon, SGBI, Queen Mary House, Manor Park
     Rd, CHISLEHURST, Kent, BR7 5PY. (hsb)
     020 8468 7997   fax 020 8468 7200
     email sgbi@sgbi.freeserve.co.uk
     Case Officer: Miss Sarah Brydon
- ▲ Registered Charity
- ○ *W; 'to give assistance to necessitous schoolmasters,
     schoolmistresses & their dependents'
- ● Mtgs
- M 14 i

Society of Scottish Artists (SSA) 1891
- ■ 18 Clarence St 1F1, EDINBURGH, EH3 5AF. (sp)
     0131-220 3977
     email ssa@soroka.plus.com   http://www.s-s-a.org
     Sec: Joanne Soroka
- ▲ Registered Charity
- ○ *A; to mount an annual exhibition reflecting the adventurous
     spirit of Scottish art; to promote international exhibition &
     exchange
- ● Exhib
- M 350 i, UK / 10 i o'seas
- ¶ SSA NL - 4; free.
     The SSA: the last 100 years; £15.
     Exhibition Catalogue (incl LM) - 1.

Society of Scribes & Illuminators (SSI) 1921
- ■ 6 Queen Sq, LONDON, WC1N 3AT. (mail)
     email scribe@calligraphyonline.org
     http://www.calligraphyonline.org address
     Mem Sec: Nicky Tait
- ▲ Un-incorporated Society
- ○ *A; to perpetuate a tradition of craftsmanship in the production
     of manuscript books & documents; to encourage the practice
     & influence of calligraphy & fine letterings
- Gp 64 fellows; 28 advanced calligraphers on 3-yr scheme
- ● Mtgs - ET - Exhib - SG - Inf - Lib
- M 700 i, UK / 200 i, o'seas
- ¶ The Scribe (Jnl) - 1; ftm.   NL.   LM.

Society of Sexual Health Advisers   (SSHA)
- ■ MSF Centre, 33-37 Moreland St, LONDON, EC1V 8HA.   (hq)
     020 7780 4061
     email carol.english@amicustheunion.org
     http://www.ssha.info
     Pres: James Hardie,   Hon Sec: Ronald Seery
- ▲ Company Limited by Guarantee
- ○ *P, *U; for health advisers working in GUM
- ● Conf - Mtgs - ET - Res - Empl - LG - Professional website
- < a professional section of AMICUS - the union
- M 360 i
- ¶ SSHA NL - 2; ftm only.
- ✕ 2002-03 Society of Health Advisers in Sexually Transmitted
     Disease

Society of Share & Business Valuers   1996
- NR 8 Baker St, LONDON, W1U 3LL. (hsb)
       020 7893 2407   fax 020 7487 3686
       Sec: J W Hallam
- ○ *P

Society of Shoe Fitters   1958
- ■ 3 Burystead Place, WELLINGBOROUGH, Northants,
     NN8 1AH. (sb)
     01933 229005   fax 01933 225009
     email ssf@britfoot.com   http://www.shoefitters-uk.org
     Sec: Mrs Laura West
- ▲ Un-incorporated Society
- ○ *P; training shoe fitters (entrance via examination &/or
     specialised training course only); assists public in finding
     shoes to fit
- ● Mtgs - ET - Exam - Exhib - Inf - VE
- M 240 i
- ¶ NL - 4; ftm only.   Register of Members - 1; £3.

Society for the Social History of Medicine (SSHM) 1969
- ■ Amory Bldg (Room 330), University of Exeter, EXETER, Devon,
     EX4 4RJ. (hsb)
     email pamela.l.dale@exte.ac.uk   http://www.sshm.org
     Sec: Dr PAmela Dale
- ▲ Registered Charity
- ○ *L; to promote the study of all aspects of the social history of
     medicine, having reference to the patients as well as the
     practitioner & to health as well as disease
- ● Conf - Mtgs - ET - Res - Comp - SG - Inf
- M 189 i, UK / 158 i, o'seas
- ¶ Social History of Medicine (Jnl) - 3; £35 m, £101 nm, (2005).

Society for Social Medicine (SSM) 1957
- ■ Northern & Yorkshire Cancer Registry & Information Service,
     Arthington House, Cookridge Hospital, LEEDS, W Yorks,
     LS16 6QB (hsb)
     0113-392 4174   fax 0113-392 4132
     email admin@socsocmed.org.uk
     http://www.socsocmed.org.uk
     Hon Sec: Dr Amy Downing
- ▲ Un-incorporated Society
- ○ *L; concerned with all aspects of social medicine including
     epidemiology & the study of medical & health needs of
     society, provision & organisation of health services &
     prevention of disease
- ● Conf - Mtgs
- < Eur Public Health Assn
- M 1,250 i, UK / 70 i, o'seas
- ¶ NL - 4;   AR; both ftm only.

© CBD Research Ltd · Beckenham · BR3 5JS · Tel 020 8650 7745 · Fax 020 8650 0768 · E-mail cbd@cbdresearch.com · www.cbdresearch.com

Society of Solicitors in the Supreme Courts of Scotland (SSCSoc) 1784
- ■ SSC Library, Parliament House, 11 Parliament Sq, EDINBURGH, EH1 1RF. (hq)
  0131 225 6268   fax 0131 225 2270
  email enquiries@ssclibrary.co.uk
  http://www.ssclibrary.co.uk
  Sec: Ian L S Balfour
- ○ *P; to maintain a practitioners' law library; to express opinions on current legal questions; to maintain a fund for widows & orphans
- ● Inf - Lib
- < part of the College of Justice in Scotland
- M 300 i, UK / 6 i, o'seas

Society for South Asian Studies   (SSAS)   1972
- ■ 73 Collier St, LONDON, N1 9BE.   (hq)
  020 7812 1422
  email secretary@societyforsouthasianstudies.org
  http://www.societyforsouthasianstudies.org
  Asst Sec: Mrs B McGregor
- ▲ Registered Charity
- ○ *L; to promote & support study & research in the history, archaeology, ethnography, languages, literature, art, culture & geography of the countries of South Asia
- ● Conf - Mtgs - Res
- < British Academy
- > Indian Art Circle
- M 210 i, 90 f, UK / 45 i, o'seas
- ¶ South Asian Studies (Jnl) - 1; £30 (individuals), £40 (insts).

Society of Sports Therapists   1990
- NR 16 Royal Terrace, GLASGOW, G3 7NY.   (hq)
  0845 600 2613   fax 0141-332 5335
  email admin@society-of-sports-therapists.org
  http://www.society-of-sports-therapists.org
  Chmn: Prof Graham N Smith
- ▲ Company Limited by Guarantee
- ○ *P; *S
- ● Mtgs - Exam - LG
- M 3,500 i
- ¶ Sports Therapy (Jnl) - 1.   NL - 6.

Society of Stars   1995
- NR 55 Denham Lane, Chalfont St Peter, GERRARDS CROSS, Bucks, SL9 0EW.   (hq)
  01494 872817
  Exec Dir: Carol M Hehir
- ▲ Company Limited by Guarantee; Registered Charity
- ○ *W; celebrity support for children & adults with cerebral palsy
- ● Mtgs - Fundraising - Promotional appearances
- < Intl Cerebral Palsy Soc (ICPS); Nat Coun Voluntary Orgs (NCVO); Inst Charity Fund Raising Mgrs (ICFM)
- M 200 i, 60 f
- ¶ Society Newsletter - 1;   Society Leaflet - 1; Annual Accounts & Report; all free.

Society for Storytelling   (SfS)   1993
- ■ PO Box 2344, READING, Berks, RG6 7FG.   (hsp)
  0118-935 1381
  email sfs@fairbruk.demon.co.uk   http://www.sfs.org.uk
  Sec: David England
- ▲ Company Limited by Guarantee; Registered Charity
- ○ *A; to increase awareness of the art, practice & value of oral storytelling; to provide information of storytelling, storytellers & events
- Gp Education; Health & therapy; Storytelling in organisations
- ● Conf - ET - Inf - Lib - Co-ordination of events
- < Assn Festival Organisers; FATE; Lapidus; Mythstories Museum; Scottish Storytelling Centre; The Telling Place
- > ACE; Bit Crack; FATE; Fibs & Fables; Mythstories Museum; Scot Storytelling Centre; The Telling Place
- M 569 i, 16 org, UK / 18 i, o'seas
- ¶ Storylines Magazine - 4; ftm only.
  Directory of Storytellers - 1 £7.50 m, £11.50 nm.
  Talkshop Catalogue - 1; free.
  Booklets on the theory & practice of storytelling - irreg.
  Factsheets of useful information & booklists - irreg; £1.35.

Society for the Study of Addiction to Alcohol & other Drugs (SSA)   1884
- NR Leeds Addiction Unit, 19 Springfield Mount, LEEDS, LS2 9NG.   (hq)
  0113-295 1315   fax 0113-295 2770
  Exec Officer: Paula Singleton
- ○ *L; to promote scientific understanding of addiction
- ● Conf - Mtgs - Res - SG
- M c 300 i, UK / c 1,500 i o'seas
- ¶ Addiction Biology - 4.   Addiction - 12.

Society for the Study of Animal Breeding
  a group of the **British Veterinary Association**

Society for the Study of Artificial Intelligence & Simulation of Behaviour   (SSAISB)   1964
- NR CASA-Conference Services, School of Science & Technology, University of Sussex, Falmer, BRIGHTON, E Sussex, BN1 9QH.
  01273 678448
  http://www.aisb.org.uk

Society for the Study of Human Biology   (SSHB)   1958
- ■ Hull York Medical School, University of Hull, Cottingham Rd, HULL, HU6 7RX.   (hsb)
  0870 124 5500   fax 01904 321696
  email sarah.elton@hyms.ac.uk
  http://www.sshb.lboro.ac.uk
  Hon Sec: Dr Sarah Elton
- ▲ Company Limited by Guarantee
- ○ *L; to advance the study in all its branches, of the biology of human populations & of humans as a species, particularly human variability, adaptability & ecoloy, auxology, environmental physiology, epidemiology & ageing
- ● Conf - Mtgs - Symposium
- < Inst Biology
- M 114 i, UK / 66 i, o'seas
- ¶ Annals of Human Biology - 6; ftm, £36 yr nm.
  Symposium Proceedings - 1; price varies (published by Taylor & Francis).

Society for the Study of Labour History (SSLH) 1960

- ■ c/o Dr Joan Allen, School of Historical Studies,
  University of Newcastle, NEWCASTLE upon TYNE, NE1 7RU.
  (hsb)
  0191-222 6701
  email jean.allen@ncl.ac.uk   http://www.facstaff.uww.edu/
  sslh/home.html
  Hon Sec: Dr Joan Allen
- ▲ Registered Charity
- ○ *L; 'an exploration into the working lives & politics of 'ordinary'
  people; the emphasis is on British labour history, though
  comparative & international studies are not neglected';
  preservation of labour archives
- Gp Archives & resources c'ee; Editorial Advy Bd (Labour History
  Review)
- ● Conf - Mtgs - Res - Comp - SG
- ¶ Labour History Review - 3; £24 m.

Society for the Study of Subterranean Survival (SSSS) 1982

- ■ Beau Lodge, Kelsey Lane, BECKENHAM, Kent, BR3 3NF.   (hsp)
- ▲ Un-incorporated Society
- ○ *L
- ● Conf - Mtgs - SG - Lib - VE
- ¶ Survival Underground - 2; ftm only.

Society of Sussex Downsmen
        since 2005 **South Downs Society**

Society of Teachers of the Alexander Technique (STAT) 1958

- NR Linton House (1st floor), 39-51 Highgate Rd, LONDON,
  NW5 1RS.   (hq)
  0845 230 7828
  Admin: Marie Ryan
- ▲ Registered Charity
- Br Australia, Belgium, Brazil, Canada, Denmark, Finland, France,
  Germany, Holland, Israel, USA, S Africa, Switzerland
- ○ *P; to promote increased awareness & understanding of the
  Alexander technique
- ● Mtgs - ET - Inf
- < to similar societies in 10 countries worldwide
- M 822 i, UK / 330 i, o'seas
- ¶ Stat News - 3; ftm only.

Society of Teachers of Speech & Drama (STSD) 1951

- ■ 73 Berry Hill Rd, MANSFIELD, Notts, NG18 4RU.   (regd/office)
  01623 627636
  email ann.k.Jones@btinternet.com
  http://www.stsd.org.uk
  Gen Sec: Mrs Ann K Jones
- ▲ Company Limited by Guarantee
- Br 34; 16 countries o'seas
- ○ *E; the teaching of speech & drama & other theatrical skills; to
  support & encourage students in training
- Gp Teaching: Communication skills, Speech & drama, Theatre
  skills;
  Business communication & presentation; Correction of speech
  problems; Lecturing; Workshops; Conferences; Amateur &
  professional theatre
- ● Conf - ET - Exhib - Comp - SG - Inf
- < Nat Campaign for the Arts; Central Coun of Amat Theatre
- > Voice Network; Engl Speaking Bd; Gld of S African Teachers of
  Speech & Drama;Australian Speech & Drama Assns; New
  Zealand Speech Assn
- M 750 i, 18 f, UK / 98 i, 1 f, o'seas
- ¶ Speech & Drama (Jnl) - 2; ftm, £7 nm.   NL - 3; ftm only.

Society of Technical Analysts Ltd (STA) 1969

- NR Dean House, Vernham Dean, ANDOVER, Hants, SP11 0LA.
  (hq)
  0700 071 0207
  Chmn: Adam Sorab
- ▲ Company Limited by Guarantee
- Br 2
- ○ *P; to promote the use & understanding of technical analysis
  amongst the public & investment community; to maintain
  professional standards in the subject & to set an examination
  to allow competency to be measured & proven

Society of Television Lighting Directors (STLD) 1974

- NR Longwall, Crayburne, BETSHAM, Kent, DA13 9PB.   (hsb)
  email secretary@stld.org.uk
  Hon Sec: Stuart Gain
- ▲ Un-incorporated Society
- ○ *P; an apolitical society for the free exchange of ideas in all
  aspects of the television profession (incl techniques & reports
  on the use & design of equipment both to manufacturers &
  members)
- ● Mtgs (also regional) - ET - Exhib - VE
- M i
- ¶ Television Lighting - 4; ftm only.

Society of Theatre Consultants 1964

- NR 55 Farringdon Rd, LONDON, EC1M 3JB.   (hq)
  020 7242 9200
  Chmn: Anne Minors
- ○ *P; for those practising as consultants on technical problems
  involved in the designing of new theatres & other buildings
  for entertainment & the conversion & modernisation of
  existing ones
- M i
- ¶ LM - irreg; free.

Society of Theatre Designers
        a group of **Association of British Theatre Technicians**

Society for Theatre Research (STR) 1948

- NR c/o The Theatre Museum, 1E Tavistock St, LONDON,
  WC2E 7PR.   (mail) address
  Jt Hon Sec: Eileen Cottis
- ▲ Registered Charity
- Br Northern
- ○ *L, *Q; to foster research into the history & practice of the
  British theatre
- ● Mtgs - Res - SG - VE - Research awards (£4,000 yr) - Annual
  Theatre Book Prize - Administration of annual William Poel
  Festival & the Edward Gordon Craig memorial lecture
- < Intl Fedn for Theatre Res; Theatres Trust
- M 400 i, 80 f, UK / 150 i, 150 f, o'seas
- ¶ Theatre Notebook - 3; £18 m (£19.50 o'seas),
  £6 back issue nm.
  NL - 2;   AR; both ftm only.
  Books on various aspects of the British theatre.

Society of Trust & Estate Practitioners (STEP) 1991

- NR 26 Grosvenor Gardens, LONDON, SW1W 0GT.   (hq)
  020 7838 4890
  Chief Exec: David Harvey
- ▲ Company Limited by Guarantee
- Br 29; Asia, Australia, Canada, Caribbean, Europe, USA
- ○ *P; for those involved at senior level with trusts & estates - from
  the legal, accountancy, corporate trust, banking, insurance &
  related professions
- ● Conf - Mtgs - ET - Exam - SG - LG
- M 3,861 i, UK / 3,913 i, o'seas
- ¶ Jnl - 4;   Membership Directory - 1; both ftm only.
  List of Members for the Public;   AR; both free.

© CBD Research Ltd · Beckenham · BR3 5JS · Tel 020 8650 7745 · Fax 020 8650 0768 · E-mail cbd@cbdresearch.com · www.cbdresearch.com

Society of Turnaround Professionals   (STP)   2000
- ■ 120 Aldersgate St (8th Floor), LONDON, EC1A 4JQ.
  020 7566 4222   fax 020 7566 4224
  email info@stp.org.uk
  Chief Exec: Nick Ferguson
- ○ *P; for rehabilitators of under-performing organisations

Society for Underwater Technology Ltd   (SUT)   1966
- NR 80 Coleman St, LONDON, EC2R 5BJ.   (hq)
  020 7382 2601   fax 020 7382 2684
  email admin@sutadmin.demon.co.uk
  http://www.sut.org.uk
  Exec Sec: Ian Gallett
- ▲ Registered Charity
- Br 2
- ○ *L; to promote the understanding & use of the underwater
  environment; the development of the techniques & tools to
  explore, study & exploit the oceans & the earth beneath
- Gp Underwater science; Underwater robotics; Diving &
  submersibles; Environmental forces; Offshore site
  investigation & geotechnics; Ocean resources; Educational
  support fund management; Publications; Executive;
  Education & training
- ● Conf - Mtgs - ET - Inf - LG
- M 868 i, 109 f
- ¶ Underwater Technology (Jnl) - 4.
  SUT News - 8.   Ybk - 2 yrly.
  Conference proceedings - irreg.

Society for Veterinary Epidemiology & Preventive Medicine
  is an international society & therefore outside the scope of this
  Directory

**Society of Wedding & Portrait Photographers   (SWPP/BPPA)
1988**
- NR 6 Bath St, RHYL, LL16 3EB.   (hq)
  01745 356935
  email enquiries@swpp.co.uk
  Chief Exec: Phil Jones
- ▲ Company Limited by Guarantee
- ○ *P
- ● Conf - Mtgs - ET - Exam - Exhib - Comp - Inf
- M 2000 i
- ¶ Professional Imagemaker.

Society for the Welfare of Horses & Ponies   (SWHP)   1974
- ■ The Horse Hospital, Coxstone, ST MAUGHANS, Monmouth,
  NP25 5QF.   (hq)
  01600 750233   fax 01600 750468
  email swhp@swhp.co.uk   http://www.swhp.co.uk
  Chmn: Mrs J S McGregor
- ▲ Registered Charity
- ○ *G, *K; to take into care sick, injured & abused horses &
  ponies, returning them to health & loaning them to homes
  suitable for their age, fitness & capabilities
- ● SG - LG - Care of horses on site & on loan
- < NAt Equine Welfare Coun
- M 1,200 i, UK / 10 i, o'seas
- ¶ NL - 2; free.

**Society of West Highland & Island Historical Research
(SWHIHR)   1972**
- NR Breachachadh Castle, ISLE OF COLL, Argyll, PA78 6TB.   (hsp)
  01879 230444   fax 01879 230357
  email swhihr@ntlworld.com
  Sec: Douglas Young
- ▲ Un-incorporated Society
- ○ *L; to encourage research into the history of the West Highlands
  of Scotland; to make the results available to the public in an
  attractive format
- ● Res - (Submissions of work are welcomed)
- M 120 i, UK / 35 i, o'seas
- ¶ West Highland Notes & Queries - 2.

Society of Wildlife Artists
  a member organisation of the **Federation of British Artists**

Society of Will Writers & Estate Planning Practitioners   1994
- ■ Eagle House, Exchange Rd, LINCOLN, LN6 3JZ.   (hq)
  01522 687888   fax 01522 694666
  email info@willwriters.com   http://www.willwriters.com
  Dir Gen: Brian W McMillan
- ▲ Company Limited by Guarantee
- Br 13
- ○ *P; 'a non-profit-making self-regulatory organisation whose
  primary objects are the advancement, education & ethical
  standards within the will-writing profession'
- ● Conf - Mtgs - ET - Exam - Res - SG - Inf - LG
- M 1,600 i, UK / 10 i, o'seas
- ¶ Testament (NL) - 12; ftm only.

Society of Women Artists   (SWA)   1855
- NR 1 Knapp Cottages, Wyke, GILLINGHAM, Dorset, SP8 4NQ.
  (hq)
  01747 825718   fax 01747 826835
  email hendersons@dial.pipex.com
  http://www.society-women-artists.org.uk
  Exec Sec: Mrs Pamela Henderson
- ▲ Company Limited by Guarantee; Registered Charity
- ○ *A; a non-political, non-feminist society for the encouragement
  of women artists
- Gp Painting in all media; Drawing; Sculpture in all media;
  Engraving; Lithography; Ceramics; Miniature work
- ● Exhib
- M 142 i
- ¶ Illustrated Exhibition Catalogue - 1; ftm, £3.50 nm.

Society of Wood Engravers   (SWE)   1920
- NR 3 West St, OUNDLE, Northants, PE8 4EJ.   (gsp)
  01832 275028
  Gen Sec: Geraldine Waddington
- ▲ Un-incorporated Society
- Br 1 o'seas
- ○ *A; for those interested in all aspects of wood engraving
- ● Conf - Mtgs - ET - Res - Exhib - Inf - Publications
- M 70 i, UK / 10 i, o'seas
  (subscribers: 350 i, 30 org, UK / 50 i, 30 org, o'seas)
- ¶ Multiples (NL) - 6.

Society of Writers to Her Majesty's Signet   (WSSociety)   1594
- NR Signet Library, Parliament Sq, EDINBURGH, EH1 1RF.   (hq)
  0131-225 4923 & 220 3426 (general enquiries)
  fax 0131-220 4016
  email library@wssociety.co.uk
  http://www.signetlibrary.co.uk
  Chief Exec: Robert Pirrie
- ▲ Un-incorporated Society
- ○ *P; private society of qualified Scottish solicitors
- Gp Signet Library (mainly Scottish law); Training & education
  (courses & seminars for members & non-members); Function
  & conference facilities letting
- ● Conf - ET - SG - Inf - Lib (current & historical material, mainly
  appertaining to Scotland) - Liaison with other legal bodies
- M 1,000 i, UK / 10 i, o'seas
- ¶ Signet NL - 3; ftm only.   AR.

Society of Young Mathematicians
  the youth group of the **Mathematical Association**

Socio-Legal Studies Association   (SLSA)   1989
- NR c/o Sally Wheeler, School of Law, Queen's University Belfast,
  BELFAST, BT7 1NN.   (hsb)
  Sally Wheeler
- ▲ Un-incorporated Society
- ○ *E, *L
- ● Conf - ET - SG
- M i
- ¶ Socio-legal NL - 3; ftm only.   LM - 1.

Sociological Association of Ireland

IRL   Department of Sociology, UCD, DUBLIN 4, Republic of Ireland.
       353 (1) 716 8615
       email sai@ucd.ie   http://www.ucd.ie/sai/
○   *P; for all concerned with theoretical & empirical issues in the
       social sciences

Soil Association Ltd   1946

■   Bristol House, 40-56 Victoria St, BRISTOL, BS1 6BY.   (hq)
       0117-314 5000   fax 0117-314 5001
       email info@soilassociation.org
       http://www.soilassociation.org
       Dir: Patrick Holden,   Sec: Mrs Katherine A Burton
▲   Registered Charity
Br   5
○   *E, *F, *H; 'plays a crucial role in transforming attitudes to food
       & farming in the UK & internationally; we work with the
       public, farmers, growers, food processors, retailers,
       consumers & policy makers. Our mission is to bring about
       change by creating a growing body of public opinion that
       understands the links between farming practice & food &
       between plant, animal, human & environmental health'
●   Conf - ET - Res - Stat - Inf - Lib - PL - LG
<   Intl Fedn Organic Agricl Movements
M   18,000 i, 4,500 f, UK / 100 f, o'seas
¶   Living Earth - 3; ftm, £2 nm.
       Organic Farming - 4; ftm only.

SOLACE (Society of Local Authority Chief Executives & Senior Managers)
       see **Society of Local Authority Chief Executives & Senior
       Managers**

Solar Energy Society   (UK-ISES)   1974

NR   PO Box 489, ABINGDON, Oxon, OX14 4WY.   (hq)
       07760 163559   fax 01235 484684
       email info@uk-ises.org   http://www.thesolarline.com
       Chmn: Prof M G Hutchins
▲   Registered Charity; Un-incorporated Society
Br   worldwide
○   *L, *P; as the UK section of the International Energy Society it
       aims to further the use of all forms of renewable energy
Gp   all renewable energy technologies
●   Conf - Mtgs - ET - Inf - LG
<   Intl Solar Energy Soc
M   250 i, 10 f, UK / 3 i, o'seas
¶   Solar Energy Jnl - 12.
       NL - 4.   Hbk - 1.
       Proceedings of Conferences - 2.

Solar Trade Association Ltd   (STA)   1978

■   National Energy Centre, Davy Avenue, Knowlhill, MILTON
       KEYNES, Bucks, MK5 8NG.   (hq)
       01908 442290   fax 0870 052 9194
       email enquiries@solartradeassociation.org.uk
       http://www.solartradeassociation.org.uk
       Chmn: John Blower
▲   Company Limited by Guarantee
○   *T; to promote widespread use of solar energy technology; to
       encourage excellence within the UK solar energy industry
●   Mtgs - Exhib - Stat - Expt - Inf - Lib - LG - Public call centre
M   30 f
¶   Code of Practice for Solar Industry - irreg;
       Solar Energy - Info Sheet 1 - irreg; both free.

**Soldiers', Sailors' & Airmen's Families Association   (SSAFA)
1885**

§   19 Queen Elizabeth St, LONDON, SE1 2LP.   (hq)
       020 7403 8783   fax 020 7403 8815
       http://www.ssafa.org.uk
       Chief Exec: Andrew Cumming
       An independent voluntary organisation, operating worldwide &
       devoted to the welfare of families of Service & ex-Service men
       & women & reserve forces.
       It operates in cooperation with Lord Robert's Workshops & the
       Forces Help Society

Solicitors' Criminal Bar Association
       a group of the **Law Society of Northern Ireland**

Solicitors Family Law Association
       since 2005 **Resolution**

Solicitors for Independent Financial Advice
       since 2003-04 **SIFA**

Solid Fuel Association   (SFA)   1993

■   7 Swanwick Court, ALFRETON, Derbys, DE55 7AS.   (hq)
       01773 835400   fax 01773 834351
       http://www.solidfuel.co.uk
       Gen Manager: Mrs J Heginbotham
▲   Company Limited by Guarantee
○   *T; promotion of solid fuel
Gp   Approval Coal Merchants Scheme - coal trade code to
       guarantee service to domestic solid fuel customers
●   Mtgs - ET - Exam - Res - Exhib - Stat - Inf - Lib - LG - Advice on
       solid fuel heating
M   2 f
¶   Various technical publications & videos.

Solids Handling & Processing Association Ltd   (SHAPA)   1981

■   20 Elizabeth Drive, OADBY, Leics, LE2 4RD.   (hq)
       0116-271 3704   fax 0116-271 3704
       email shapaltd@aol.com   http://www.shapa.co.uk
       Gen Sec: John Whitehead
▲   Company Limited by Guarantee
○   *T; representing companies/universities involved in the
       handling & processing of particulate solids particularly in the
       process industries; members interests incl: Abrasion resistant
       equipment; Blowers/compressors; Bulk storage & handling;
       Centralised vacuum cleaning; Control systems; Dryers/
       coolers; Dust filters; Feeders; Grinding & milling machinery;
       Instrumentation; Intermediate bulk containers; Load cells;
       Mechanical conveyors/elevators; Mixers; Pneumatic
       handling; Process plant; Sack/bag systems; Sieves/screens;
       Silos, hoppers, bins & tanks & dischargers; Valves; Weighing
       machinery
Gp   Marketing; Technical; Commercial
●   Mtgs - Expt - LG - Scholarship award
<   permanent member of Intl Solids Handling Advy Bd (ISHAB)
M   97 i, 94 f, 3 universities
¶   NL - 3.

Solihull Chamber of Commerce & Industry   (SCCI)   1990

■   Wellington House, Birmingham International Park, Starley Way,
       SOLIHULL, W Midlands, B37 7HE.   (hq)
       0121-781 7384   fax 0121-781 7385
       email info@solihull-chamber.com
       http://www.solihull-chamber.com
       Dir: Jane Jackson
▲   Company Limited by Guarantee
○   *C
●   Conf - Mtgs - ET - Res - Exhib - Stat - Expt - Inf - VE - LG
<   Birmingham Cham Comm; Brit Chams Comm
M   400 f
¶   Chamberlink - 10;   AR; both ftm.
       Birmingham & West Midlands Chamber Directory - 1; ftm,
       £90 nm.
       Birmingham & Solihull Business Guide & Directory - 1; ftm,
       £75 nm.

** Solvent Industries Association

       Organisation lost: see Introduction paragraph 3

© CBD Research Ltd · Beckenham · BR3 5JS · Tel 020 8650 7745 · Fax 020 8650 0768 · E-mail cbd@cbdresearch.com · www.cbdresearch.com

Somerset Archaeological & Natural History Society   (SANHS) 1849
- ■ The Castle, Castle Green, TAUNTON, Somerset, TA1 4AA. (hq)
  01823 272429
- ▲ Registered Charity
- ○ *L
- Gp Archaeology; Local history; Historic buildings; Natural history
- ● Conf - Mtgs - ET - Res - SG - Lib - PL - VE
- M 654 i, 42 org, UK / 4 i, 14 org, o'seas
- ¶ Proceedings - 1.   NL - 2.

Somerset Record Society   1889
- ■ c/o Somerset Studies Library, Paul St, TAUNTON, Somerset, TA1 3XZ.   (hsb)
  01823 340300   fax 01823 340301
  Hon Sec: David Bromwich
- ▲ Registered Charity; Un-incorporated Society
- ○ *L; publication of historical records (not parish registers) of Somerset
- ● Annual mtg
- M 121 i, 53 org, UK / 4 i, 68 org, o'seas
- ¶ Occasional volume - c 1; ftm, prices vary nm.

Songbird Survival   (SBS)
- ■ PO Box 311, DISS, Norfolk, IP22 1WW.   (hq)
  01379 641715   fax 0560 076 5944
  email dawn-chorus@songbird-survival.org.uk
  http://www.songbird-survival.org.uk
  Dir: K A McDougall
- ▲ Registered Charity
- ○ *K; to protect & enhance the population of UK songbirds & other small birds by research & education
- ● Mtgs - Res - Exhib - Stat - Inf - VE - LG
- M 1,800 i
- ¶ Songbird Survival (NL) - 4; ftm only.

Sonic Arts Network   (SAN)   1979
- NR The Jerwood Space, 171 Union St, LONDON, SE1 0LN.   (hq)
  020 7928 7337   fax 020 7928 7338
  email phil@sonicartsnetwork.org
  http://www.sonicartsnetwork.org
  Chief Exec: Phil Hallett
- ▲ Registered Charity
- ○ *D; a performance, information & education resource for those interested in experimental approaches to sound & the ways in which new technology is transforming the nature & practice of music; aims to raise awareness & innovate new approaches to sonic art
- ● Conf - ET - Exhib - Inf - 'Commissioning, encouraging & promoting new & exciting work' - 'Raising awareness of sonic art through information, opportunity & education'
- M 400 i, 50 f, UK / 100 i, 20 f, o'seas
- ¶ Diffusion - 12;   Jnl - 1; both ftm.

Sound Sense: National Community Music Association   1997
- NR 7 Tavern St, STOWMARKET, Suffolk, IP14 1PJ.   (hq)
  01449 673990   fax 01449 673994
  email info@soundsense.org
  http://www.soundsense.org
  Dir: Kathryn Deane
- ▲ Company Limited by Guarantee; Registered Charity
- ○ *D, *G, *N; the national development agency for community & other forms of participatory music
- Gp National Music Disability Information Service (NMDIS)
- ● Conf - Mtgs - Res - Exhib - Stat - Inf - LG
- M 192 i, 87 f, 25 org, UK / 6 i, o'seas
- ¶ Sounding Board - 4; ftm [back issues £5].
  Bulletin Board - 8/10; ftm.
  Publications list available.

Soup, Gravy & Produce Processors' Association
is an association within the **Food Processors' Association**

Source Testing Association   (STA)   1996
- NR Unit 11 Theobald Business Centre, Knowl Piece, Wilbury Way, HITCHIN, Herts, SG4 0TY.   (hq)
  01462 457535   fax 01462 457157
  email dave.curtis@s-t-a.org   http://www.s-t-a.org
  Dir: Dave Curtis
- ▲ Company Limited by Guarantee
- ○ *T; research into aspects of emission monitoring
- Gp Task Groups: Health & safety, Management, Quality, Small business, Technical, Training & personal development
- ● Conf - Mtgs - ET - Res - Exhib - Inf - Seminars - Company endorsement
- M 102 f, UK / 3 f, o'seas
- ¶ STA Communicator (NL) - 2; free.

South Cheshire Chamber of Commerce & Industry Ltd   2001
- NR Enterprise House, Wistaston Road Business Centre, CREWE, Cheshire, CW2 7RP.   (hq)
  01270 504700
  Chief Exec: John Dunning
- ▲ Company Limited by Guarantee
- ○ *C
- ● Mtgs - ET - Exhib - Stat - Expt - Inf - Lib
- < Brit Chams Comm
- M 375 f
- ¶ South Cheshire Business - 4.

South Derbyshire Chamber of Commerce & Industry
2003 merged with North Derbyshire Chamber of Commerce & Industry to form the **Derbyshire Chamber & Business Link**

South Devon Chamber of Trade & Commerce   (SDCC)   1995
- ■ Compton House (Unit 3b, 1st floor), PAIGNTON, Devon, TQ4 5JX.   (chmn/b)
  01803 523272   fax 01803 523272
  email info@southdevonchamber.co.uk
  http://www.southdevonchamber.co.uk
  Admin: Brenda Hooper,   Chmn: Douglas Roxburgh
- ▲ Company Limited by Guarantee
- ○ *C
- Gp Branches: Brixham, Paignton, Torquay
- ● Conf - Mtg - Inf
- M 200 f
- ¶ NL - 4;   Directory/Ybk - 5 yrly; both ftm, prices on application nm.

South Devon Herd Book Society   (SDHBS)   1891
- NR Westpoint, Clyst St Mary, EXETER, Devon, EX5 1DJ.   (hq)
  01392 447494   fax 01392 447495
  email info@sdhbs.org.uk   http://www.sdhbs.org.uk
  Breed Sec: Caroline Poultney
- ▲ Registered Charity
- Br Australia, Canada, New Zealand, South Africa, USA
- ○ *B
- ● Conf - Mtgs - Res - Exhib - Comp - Stat - SG - Expt - Inf - VE - LG
- < S Devon Cattle Socs in: Australia, Canada, New Zealand, S Africa, USA
- M 630 i, UK / 10 i, o'seas
- ¶ Jnl - 1.   NL - 12.   Herd Book - 2 yrly.

South Downs Society   (SDS)   1923

NR   2 Swan Court, Station Rd, PULBOROUGH, W Sussex,
    RH20 1RL.   (hq)
    01798 875073   fax 01798 873108
    http://www.southdownssociety.org.uk
    Gen Sec: Michael Thomas
▲   Company Limited by Guarantee; Registered Charity
○   *G; preservation of character & beauty of the South Downs,
    including their ancient monuments & public rights of way
Gp   Walks; C'ees: Preservation, Membership & publicity
●   Conf - Mtgs - Exhib - Lib - VE - Illustrated talks
<   Fedn of Sussex Amenity Socs; Open Spaces Soc; Brit Trust for
    Consvn Volunteers
M   2,687 i, UK / 20 i, o'seas
¶   Newsheet - 4; free.   AR; ftm.
✕   2005 Society of Sussex Downsmen

South of England Agricultural Society   (SEAS)   1967

NR   The South of England Centre, Ardingly, HAYWARDS HEATH,
    W Sussex, RH17 6TL.   (hq)
    01444 892700   fax 01444 892888
    email seas@btclick.com   http://www.seas.org.uk
    Dir: Mrs Deborah Barber
▲   Registered Charity
○   *H, *F; to promote agriculture, horticulture & forestry
●   Conf - Mtgs - ET - Exhib - Spring Garden Show (May) - South of
    England Show (June) - Autumn Show (October) - Fast Food &
    Drink (December)
M   3,000 i, 1,000 f
¶   Four Seasons News - 2; ftm only.

South Essex Chamber of Commerce (Westcliff-on-Sea)
    is a branch office of the **Essex Chambers of Commerce**

South Gloucestershire Chamber of Commerce

NR   8 Badminton Rd, Downend, BRISTOL, BS16 6BQ.
    0117-910 9200   fax 0117-910 9211
    email sglous.chamber@virgin.net
    http://www.sg-cc.org.uk
    Assistant Mgr: Mrs Laura Bricknell
○   *C
<   is part of Business West

South Place Ethical Society   (SPES)   1793

NR   Conway Hall, 25 Red Lion Sq, LONDON, WC1R 4RL.   (hq)
    020 7242 8034   fax 020 7242 8034
    http://www.ethicalsoc.org.uk
▲   Registered Charity
○   *L; study & dissemination of ethical principles based on
    humanism; the cultivation of a rational & humane way of life
M   i & org
¶   Ethical Record - 10; ftm.   AR.
    Conway Memorial Lecture - 1; ftm.

** **South Wales Mountain Sheep Breeders' Society**
    Organisation lost: see Introduction paragraph 3

South West Coast Path Association   (SWCPA)   1973

■   Windlestraw, Penquit, ERMINGTON, Devon, PL21 0LU.   (hsp)
    01752 896237   fax 01752 896237
    email info@swcp.org.uk   http://www.swcp.org.uk
    Hon Sec: Eric Wallis
▲   Registered Charity
○   *K; to promote the interests of users of the South West coast
    path, Britain's longest national trail
●   Mtgs - Exhib - Inf - PL - LG
M   4,000 i, 20 org, UK / 150 i, o'seas
¶   The South West Coast Path Guide - 1; ftm, £7 nm.
    NL - 2;   AR; both ftm only.

South Western Circle   1962

■   21 Gilbert Close, SPONDON, Derbys, DE21 7GP.   (hsp)
    01332 675559
    email peterswiftderby@tiscali.co.uk
    http://www.lswr.org.uk
    Sec: Peter Swift
▲   Un-incorporated Society
○   *G; historical society for the London & South Western Railway &
    its successors
●   Mtgs - Res - Inf - PL
M   500 i, UK / 25 i, o'seas
¶   South Western Circular - 4;   Monographs; both ftm.

**Southampton & Fareham Chamber of Commerce & Industry
(SFCCI)   1851**

NR   Bugle House, 53 Bugle St, SOUTHAMPTON, Hants,
    SO14 2LF.   (hq)
    023 8022 3541   fax 023 8022 7426
    email info@soton-chamber.co.uk
    http://www.soton-chamber.co.uk
    Dir Gen: Jimmy Chestnut
▲   Company Limited by Guarantee
Br   China representative office
○   *C
●   Mtgs - ET - Res - Exhib - Expt - Inf - Lib - LG
M   2,000 i & f
¶   Chamber of Commerce News - 12; ftm, £7.20 yr nm.

Southdown Sheep Society   1890

■   Meens Farm, Capps Lane, All Saints, HALESWORTH, Suffolk,
    IP19 0PD.   (hsp)
    01986 782416
    email secretary@southdownsheepsociety.co.uk
    http://www.southdownsheepsociety.co.uk
    Sec: Gail Sprake
▲   Company Limited by Guarantee; Registered Charity
○   *B
●   Res - Exhib - Expt - Inf - LG
<   Nat Sheep Assn; Rare Breeds Survival Trust
M   300 i
¶   The Southdown Flock Book - 2 yrly; ftm, £15 nm.
    The Southdown Year Book - 1; ftm, £5 nm.
    The Southdown Sheep; £20+£5p&p

Southern Counties Folk Federation   (SCoFF)   1966

NR   11 Redmoor Close, Bitterne, SOUTHAMPTON, Hants,
    SO19 4DH.   (sp)
    Sec: David Nixon
○   *D, *G, *N

Southern Counties Heavy Horse Association   (SCHHA)   1970

■   74 Burnham Rd, Durrington, WORTHING, E Sussex,
    BN13 2NJ.   (hsp)
    01903 692532
    Hon Sec: Sharon Rumbelow
▲   Un-incorporated Society
○   *B, *F, *G, *V; to promote the heavy horse & preserve the art of
    horse ploughing
Gp   Show horses & drays for promotional work; Working horses for
    ploughing & working demonstrations
●   Mtgs - Exhib - Working demonstrations - Members' events
<   Shire Horse Soc
M   c 400 i & org
¶   NL - 4.   AR.

© CBD Research Ltd · Beckenham · BR3 5JS · Tel 020 8650 7745 · Fax 020 8650 0768 · E-mail cbd@cbdresearch.com · www.cbdresearch.com

Southern Counties Historic Vehicle Preservation Trust (SCHVPT) 1962

- ■ 2 Dower Walk, Gossops Green, CRAWLEY, W Sussex, RH11 8EN.   (inf officer/p)
  01293 529264
  Inf Officer: A Urben
- ▲ Registered Charity
- ○ *G, *L; to preserve historic vehicles & machinery
- ● Mtgs - Exhib - Inf - Lib - PL
- < Nat Traction Engine Trust; Transport Trust; Historic Vehicles Clubs Jt C'ee; Historic Comml Vehicles Soc
- M 300 i, 2 f, 3 org, UK / 2 i, o'seas
- ¶ News Circular - 12; ftm only.
  Traction Engine Register - 3 yrly; £4 m only.

Southern Staffordshire Chamber of Commerce & Industry 1888

- NR Ridings House, Ridings Park, Eastern Way, Hawks Green, CANNOCK, Staffs, WS11 7FH.
  01543 460050
  Chief Exec: Peter Reid
- ▲ Company Limited by Guarantee
- ○ *C
- M f
- ✕ 2001 (26 March) East Mercia Chamber of Commerce & Industry

Southwark Chamber of Commerce

- NR The Town Hall, 31 Peckham Rd, LONDON, SE5 8UB.
  http://www.southwarkcommerce.com
  Chamber Sec: Nancy Hammond
- ○ *C

SOVA (SOVA) 1975

- NR Chichester House, 37 Brixton Rd, LONDON, SW9 6DZ.   (hq)
  020 7793 0404
  Chief Exec: Gill A Henson
- ▲ Registered Charity
- Br 41
- ○ *W; 'to train local volunteers & involve them in work with offenders, ex-offenders & their families; we believe that everybody is touched by crime & that members of the community have a contribution to make in preventing & reducing crime'
- Gp Literacy & numeracy tuition; Employment training; Befriending
- ● Conf - ET - Stat
- M 644 i
- ¶ AR; free.

Soya Protein Association (SPA) 1973

- NR 6 Catherine St, LONDON, WC2B 5JJ.   (hq)
  020 7836 2460   fax 020 7836 0580
- ▲ Un-incorporated Society
- ○ *T; to disseminate information on vegetable proteins for human consumption
- ● Mtgs - Inf
- < Eur Vegetable Protein Fedn (EUVEPRO); Food & Drink Fedn
- M 5 f

Spa Business Association (SpaBA) 1921

- ■ c/o Pennyhill Park Hotel, London Rd, BAGSHOT, Surrey, GU19 5EU.   (hq)
  01276 478647
  email info@spabusinessassociation.co.uk
  http://www.spabusinessassociation.co.uk
  Office Mgr: Gloria Barnard
- ▲ Company Limited by Guarantee
- ○ *T; promotion of British spa heritage towns & assistance on a national basis in creation of climate for investment in those towns in order to revive & reinstate operating thermal & mineral waters to full spa use
- Gp Marketing; Medical advisory c'ee
- ● Mtgs - Res - VE - LG
- < Eur Spas Assn
- ✕ 2004 British Spas Federation

Spanish Chamber of Commerce in Great Britain

- NR 126 Wigmore St, LONDON, W1U 3RZ.
  020 7009 9070   fax 020 7009 9088
  email info@spanishchamber.co.uk
  http://www.spanishchamber.co.uk
  Sec Gen: José Fernández Bragado
- ○ *C
- ● Inf - Consultancy - Logistic & administrative support - Commercial promotion - Seminars - Presentations
- M 225 i & f, UK / 118 i & f, Spain
- ¶ British Companies with Commercial Interests in Spain; £55 m, £100 nm.
  British Business Presence in Spain; £26 m, £52 nm.
  Spanish Business Presence in the UK; £44 m, £58 nm.
  Doing Business in Spain; ftm, £11 nm.
  LM; ftm, £23.50 nm.   NL - 6; ftm only.
  Guide to Doing Business In the UK.

Speakability 1979

- ■ 1 Royal St, LONDON, SE1 7LL.
  020 7261 9572   fax 020 7928 9542   (hq)
  email speakability@speakability.org.uk
  http://www.speakability.org.uk
- ▲ Company Limited by Guarantee
- Br 92
- ○ *K, *W; to support people & carers living with aphasia (loss of communication skills as a result of a stroke, head injury or other neurological condition)
- Gp Nationwide network of support groups; Working parties of people with aphasia & professionals on issues such as employment, leisure, etc
- ● ET - SG - Inf - LG - Campaigning for improved services for people with communication impairments
- < Intl Aphasia Assn (AIA)
- M 3,953 i, 26 f, 509 org, UK / 38 i, o'seas
- ¶ Speaking Up (NL) - 6; ftm, £1.50 nm.
  Annual Review; free.
  Publications & videos list available.

Specialised Organic Chemicals Sector Association (SOCSA) 1993

- NR c/o Chemical Industries Association, Kings Buildings, Smith Sq, LONDON, SW1P 3JJ.   (hq)
  020 7834 3399   fax 020 7834 4469
  email scott@cia.org.uk   http://www.socsa.org.uk
- ○ *T; for those interested in the manufacture of specialised organic chemicals
- M f

Specialist Access Engineering & Maintenance Association (SAEMA) 1972

- ■ Carthusian Court, 12 Carthusian St, LONDON, EC1M 6EZ.   (hq)
  020 7397 8122   fax 020 7397 8121
  email enquiries@saema.org   http://www.saema.org
  Sec: Stephen Kennefick
- ▲ Un-incorporated Society
- ○ *T; the manufacture, supply or hire of power operated systems to provide access to buildings
- ● Mtgs - Inf - LG
- < Nat Access & Scaffolding Confedn
- M 24 f

Specialist Anglers Alliance   (SAA)   2001
- ■ 41 Crofts Path, HEMEL HEMPSTEAD, Herts, HP3 8HB.   (hsp)
  01442 398022   fax 01442 398044
  email secretary@saauk.org   http://www.saauk.org
  Sec: Michael Heylin
- ▲ Un-incorporated Society
- ○ *G, *K, *S; to defend the angling rights of all members; to campaign for a cleaner water environment; to provide a unified body for all specialist anglers; to combat anti-angling propaganda
- ● Res - SG - Inf - LG - Representation on British Record Fish Committees
- < Anglers' Consvn Assn; Inst Fisheries Mgt; Nat Fedn Anglers
- M 650 i, 4 f, 14 org, UK / 15 i, o'seas
- ¶ New Specialist Angler - 2; ftm, £2.50 nm.
  NL - 2; ftm only.

Specialist Cheesemakers' Association   (SCA)   1989
- ■ 17 Clerkenwell Green, LONDON, EC1R 0DP.   (hq)
  020 7253 2114   fax 020 7608 1645
  email info@provtrade.co.uk
  http://www.specialistcheesemakers.co.uk
  Sec: Mrs Clare Cheney
- ▲ Company Limited by Guarantee
- ○ *T; to encourage excellence in cheesemaking, promote speciality cheeses & represent the interests of members to Government & the media
- ● Mtgs - Res - Exhib - Inf - VE - LG
- < Amer Cheese Soc; Ir Cheesemakers Assn; Stilton Cheesemakers Assn; Farmhouse Cheesemakers Assn
- M 235 f, UK / 20 f, o'seas
- ¶ SCA NL - 4; ftm only.
  Guide to the Finest Cheeses of Britain & Ireland; £5.95.

Specialist Engineering Contractors Group   (SEC group)   1992
- ■ 34 Palace Court, LONDON, W2 4JG.   (hq)
  020 7313 4919   fax 020 7727 9268
  email pmattison@hvca.org.uk
  Chief Exec: Prof Rudi Klein
- ▲ Un-incorporated Society
- ○ *N, *T; represents six trade associations (with a total membership of 8,000 companies) in the specialist engineering sector of the construction industry (including mechanical, electrical, plumbing, steel & lifts) to the government & other industry bodies
- M 6 associations:
  Association of Plumbing & Heating Contractors
  British Constructional Steelwork Association
  Electrical Contractors Association
  Electrical Contractors Association of Scotland
     (this trades as SELECT)
  Heating & Ventilating Contractors Association
  Lift & Escalator Industry Association
- ¶ Guides on contractual & legal matters (these can be obtained from HVCA Publications on 01768 860405).

Speedway Control Board   (SCB)   1940
- NR ACU House, Wood St, RUGBY, Warks, CV21 2YX.
  01788 565603   fax 01788 552308
  email office.scb@lineone.net
- ▲ Company Limited by Guarantee
- ○ *S; governing body of speedway motorcycle racing in GB
- ● ET
- < Fédn Intle Motocyclisme (FIM); RAC; Auto-Cycle U (ACU)
- M i & clubs

Spinal Injuries Association   (SIA)   1974
- NR SIA House, 2 Trueman Place, Oldbrook, MILTON KEYNES, MK6 2HH.   (hq)
  0845 678 6633   fax 01908 608492
  email sia@spinal.co.uk   http://www.spinal.co.uk
  Chief Exec: Paul Smith
- ▲ Company Limited by Guarantee
- ○ *W; the national charity for spinal cord injured people & their families; controlled & run by people who are themselves paralysed, its aim is to enable spinal cord injured people to control their lives & achieve their goals
- Gp Helpline service; Publications
- ● Conf - Inf - Lib - LG
  Helpline: 0800 980 0501
- < Brit Coun of Disabled People; Dial UK; ADAIP; RADAR; NCVO
- M 6,000 i, 500 org, UK / 400 i, o'seas
- ¶ Forward (NL) - 6.   AR.
  Moving Forward: a guide to living with spinal cord injury.
  Other publications available.

Spinal Injuries Scotland   (SIS)   1960
- NR Festival Business Centre, 150 Brand St, GLASGOW, G51 1DH.   (hq)
  0141-314 0056; 0141-314 0057 (helpline)
  Exec Officer: John O'Neill
- ▲ Company Limited by Guarantee; Registered Charity
- ○ *K, *W; to help back to an active life in the community those who have suffered spinal cord damage through birth, injury or disease
- ● Inf - telephone counselling helpline
- M 570 i
- ¶ Newsline - 4; ftm.

Spiral Staircase Manufacturers Association
- NR c/o Crescent of Cambridge Ltd, 46 Edison Rd, ST IVES, Cambs, PE27 3LG.   (hsb)
  01480 301522
  Sec: Richard Butler
- ○ *T; for manufacturers of spiral stairs in steel, wood, concrete & other materials

Spiritualist Association of Great Britain   (SAGB)   1872
- NR 33 Belgrave Sq, LONDON, SW1X 8QB.   (hq)
  020 7235 3351   fax 020 7245 9706
  http://www.spiritualistassociation.org.uk
  Pres & Co Sec: Mrs Selma Blair
- ▲ Company Limited by Guarantee; Registered Charity
- ○ *R; spiritualist healing; proof of survival after death
- ● Mtgs - Res
- M c 900 i, UK / c 200 i, o'seas
- ¶ Service - 3; ftm, £1 nm.

Spiritualists' National Union   (SNU)   1890
- NR Redwoods, Stansted Hall, STANSTED MOUNTFITCHET, Essex, CM24 8UD.   (hq)
  0845 458 0768
  Gen Sec: Charles S Coulston
- ▲ Company Limited by Guarantee; Registered Charity
- Br 15
- ○ *R; to promote the religion & religious philosophy of Spiritualism
- Gp Spiritualists' Lyceum Union (youth movement); The Arthur Findlay College (residential training school)
- ● Conf - Mtgs - ET - Exam - Res - SG - Inf - Lib
- M 2,200 i, 382 churches, UK / 80 i, 8 churches, o'seas
- ¶ Ybk & Diary.

SPLINTA
- ■ PO Box 398, STEVENAGE, Herts, SG1 9DR.
  07831 805455
  http://www.splintacampaign.co.uk
  Nick Salmon
- ○ *K; are against sellers' pack on house sales

Spode Society   1986

NR   c/o Spode Museum, Church St, STOKE-on-TRENT, Staffs,
       ST4 1BX.   (editor/b)
       01782 744011
▲   Un-incorporated Society
○   *G; to increase knowledge of the Spode/Copeland factory & its
       wares
●   Mtgs - Res - VE
M   c170 i, the Museum, UK / c20 i, o'seas
¶   Spode Society Review - 2; ftm only.

Spohr Society of Great Britain   1969

■   123 Mount View Rd, SHEFFIELD, S Yorks, S8 8PJ.   (hq)
       0114-258 5420   fax 0114-273 5454
       email chtutt@yahoo.co.uk
       Sec: C H Tutt
▲   Un-incorporated Society
○   *D; to promote the music of the German composer Louis Spohr
       (1784-1859) through recordings, broadcasts & live
       performances; to research into his life & music
●   Mtgs - Res - Inf - Loan of performing material - Promoting
       recordings
<   Intle Louis Spohr Gesellschaft (Germany)
M   44 i, UK / 26 i, o'seas
¶   Spohr Jnl - 1; ftm, £1.50 nm.   NL - 4; ftm, 40p each nm.

Spoken Word Publishing Association
       since 2004 **Audiobook Publishing Association**

Sport Horse Breeding of Great Britain   (SHB(GB))   1886

NR   96 High St, EDENBRIDGE, Kent, TN8 5AR.   (hq)
       01732 866277
       Sec: Miss C Burdock
▲   Registered Charity
○   *B; to support the horse industry by way of incentives for
       breeders, education, information & high standard grading
       schemes & shows
Gp   Council; C'ees: Show, Brood mare, Stallion
●   Conf - Mtgs - ET - Exhib - Comp - Stat - Inf - Lib
<   Wld Breeding Fedn for Sport Horses
M   3,000 i
¶   NL - 1.   Hbk - 1.   Sales List - 12.
       Show List - 1.   Show Secretaries List - 1.   Judges List - 1.
       Stallion List - 1.   Rulebook - 1.

Sports Coach UK

NR   114 Cardigan Rd, Headingley, LEEDS, W Yorks, LS6 3BJ.
       0113-274 4082   fax 0113-275 5019
       email coaching@sportscoachuk.org
       http://www.sportscoachuk.org
       Chief Exec: John Stevens
○   *S

Sports & Fitness Equipment Association   (SAFEA)   1990

■   Federation House, STONELEIGH PARK, Warks, CV8 2RF.   (hq)
       024 7641 4999   fax 024 7641 4990
       email safea@sportsandplay.com
       http://www.safea.co.uk
▲   Company Limited by Guarantee
○   *T; for companies engaged in the supply & installation of sports
       hall, games, fitness & gymnasium equipment (incl physical
       education in schools)
●   Conf - Mtgs - Exhib - Inf - Lib - LG
<   a group of the Fedn of Sports & Play Assns (FSPA)
M   20 f

Sports Industries Federation Ltd
       since 2006 **Federation of Sports & Play Associations**

Sports Journalists' Association of Great Britain   (SJA)   1948

NR   c/o Start2Finish Event Management, Unit 92 Capital Business
       Centre, 22 Carlton Rd, SOUTH CROYDON, Surrey,
       CR2 0BS.   (asa)
       020 8916 2234   fax 020 8916 2235
       http://www.sportsjournalists.org.uk
○   *P, *S; for journalists who specialise in sport
●   Conf - Mtgs - Educ - Inf - LG (through UK Sport & Sport
       England) - Careers advice - Promotion of annual Sports
       Journalists of the Year & Sportsman, Sportswoman & Sports
       Team of the Year Awards
<   Assn Intle de la Presse Sportive (AIPS); U Eur de la Presse
       Sportive (UEPS)
M   550 i
¶   Bulletin - 2;   NL - 3/4;   Hbk; all free.
×   2003 Sports Writers Association of Great Britain

**Sports Manufacturers & Retailers Trade Association   (SMART)
2006**

■   Federation House, STONELEIGH PARK, Warks, CV8 2RF.   (hq)
       024 7641 4999   fax 024 7641 4990
       email smart@sportsandplay.com
       http://www.sportsandplay.com
       Sec: Jane Montgomery
○   *T; to represent sports manufacturers & retailers in the UK
●   Mtgs - Inf - LG
<   a group of the Federation of Sports & Play Associations (FSPA)
M   30 i
×   2006 (merged):
       Bowls Group
       Cricket & Hockey Association
       Cue Sports Association
       Darts Association
       Fitness Products Association
       Independent Sports Retailers Association
       Racket Sports Association
       Sports Textiles & Footwear Association

Sports Massage Association   (SMA)   1999

NR   1 Woodville Terrace, LYTHAM, Lancs, FY8 5QB.   (hq)
       0870 005 2678   fax 0870 005 2679
       email info@thesma.org   http://www.thesma.org
○   *P; to establish & maintain the ethical, professional &
       educational standards of practitioners so as to give
       confidence to the general & sporting public, the medical
       profession & government agencies that practitioners are
       suitably trained
●   Conf - Mtgs - ET - Exam - Res
M   700 i, UK / 10 i, o'seas
¶   Sportex Dynamics - 4; ftm, £26 yr nm.

Sports & Play Construction Association   (SAPCA)   1997
- ■ Federation House, STONELEIGH PARK, Warks, CV8 2RF.   (hq)
  024 7641 6316   fax 024 7641 4773
  email info@sapca.org.uk   http://www.sapca.org.uk
  Chief Exec: Christopher Trickey
- ▲ Company Limited by Guarantee
- ○ *T; 'the recognised UK trade association for the sports facility construction industry'
- Gp Principal contractors (inc multi-sport, natural sportsturf, pitch, play surfaces, tennis court, track divisions)
  Surfacing contractors; Ancillary contractors; Manufacturers & suppliers; Professional services
- ● Conf - Mtgs - ET - Res - Exhib - SG - Stat - Expt - Inf - VE - LG
- < a group of the Sports Industries Federation
- > Brit Assn Landscape Inds (BALI); Brit Paralympic Assn (BPA); England & Wales Cricket Bd (ECB); Inst of Groundsmanship (IOG); Intl Assn for Sports & Leisure Facilities (IAKS); Intl Sports Engg Assn (ISEA); Intl Tennis Fedn (ITD); Lawn Tennis Assn (LTA); Nat Playing Fields Assn (NPFA); Nat Trainers Fedn NTF); Oxford Playing Fields Assn (OPFA); Quarry Products Assn (QPA); Recreation Mgrs Assn (RMA); Sports Coun of NI (SCNI); Sports Rurf Res Inst(STRI); UK Athletics (UKA); Waste Resources Action Programme (WRAP)
- M 170 f, 30 org, UK / 10 f, 4 org, o'seas
- × 2002-04 Sports & Play Contractors' Association

Sports Pony Studbook Society   (SPSS)
- NR Bernwode Stud, Sock Farm, Chilthorne Domer, YEOVIL, Somerset, BA22 8QZ.
  01935 840029
- ○ *B

Sports Textiles & Footwear Association
   since 2006 **Sports Manufacturers & Retailers Trade Association**

Sports Turf Research Institute   (STRI)   1929
- ■ St Ives Estate, BINGLEY, W Yorks, BD16 1AU.   (hq)
  01274 565131   fax 01274 561891
  email anne.wilson@stri.org.uk   http://www.stri.co.uk
  Head of External Affairs: Anne Wilson,
  Chief Exec: Dr Gordon McKillop
- ▲ Company Limited by Guarantee
- Br 13
- ○ *Q, *S; independent non-profit-making research & advisory service: sports field & golf course management & construction; research on sports turf surfaces
- Gp Golf course ecology & land management; Golf course architecture & design; Sports turf construction & irrigation
- ● Conf - ET - Res - Exhib - Inf - Lib - VE
- < Sports Coun; All sports governing bodies
- M 150 i, 200 f, 1,900 org, UK / 120 i, 15 f, 200 org, o'seas [above are subscribers not members]
- ¶ Jnl of Turfgrass & Sports Surface Science - 1; ftm, £28 nm.
  International Turfgrass Bulletin - 4; ftm, £55 yr nm.
  STRI Green Pages Trade Directory; online only.
  Various publications on turf related issues, available from their specialist online & mail order book service.

Sports Writers' Association of Great Britain
   since 2003 **Sports Journalists' Association of Great Britain**

Sportsmans Association of Great Britain & Northern Ireland (SAGBNI)   1996
- NR 2 Clockhouse Place, LONDON, SW15 2EL.   (hq)
  020 8789 1211   fax 020 8789 1211
  email sagbnia@btconnect.com
  http://www.sportsmansassociation.org.uk
  Gen Sec: M B Wells
- ▲ Un-incorporated Society
- ○ *K; 'to campaign against the ban on target pistol shooting & for freedom of choice & fair & effective firearms legislation'
- ● Res - Inf - LG
- < Brit Shooting Sports Coun
- M c 3,000 i, 14 f
- ¶ NL - 12; ftm only.

Spotted Horse & Pony Society   (SHAPS)   1992
- ■ Horseshoes, Kelvedon Rd, Tolleshunt d'Arcy, MALDON, Essex, CM9 8EL.   (hsp)
  01621 816106   fax 01621 816106
  Hon Sec: Miss A Southgate
- ▲ Un-incorporated Society
- ○ *B
- ● Exhib - Comp - Stat - Inf - PL - LG
- M c 100 i, 1 f, UK / 10 i, o'seas
- ¶ NL - 4; ftm only.

Spotted Pony Breed Society   1996
- NR Toll Bar Cottage, Butterley Park, RIPLEY, Derbys, DE5 3QW.
  (sp)
  01773 748502
  Mem Sec & Registrar: Mrs Angie Ward
- ▲ Company Limited by Guarantee
- ○ *B; registration of native British spotted ponies
- ● Mtgs - ET - Res - Exhib - Comp - SG - Inf
- < Brit Horse Soc
- M 150 i, 2 f, 2 org
- ¶ NL - 3; ftm, £9 yr nm.

Sprayed Concrete Association   (SCA)   1976
- ■ 99 West St, FARNHAM, Surrey, GU9 7EN.   (asa)
  01252 739153   fax 01252 739140
  email sca@associationhouse.org.uk
  http://www.sca.org.uk
  Sec: John G Fairley
- ○ *T; to promote & foster the use of sprayed concrete, otherwise known as 'gunite' or 'shotcrete'
- ● Conf - Mtgs - ET - Res - Exhib
- < Eur Fedn of Nat Assns of Specialist Contrs & Material Suppliers for the Construction Ind (EFNARC)
- M 40 f
- ¶ LM; free.   Technical Data Sheets; ftm, £1 each nm.
  An Introduction to Sprayed Concrete.
  EFNARC Specification for Sprayed Concrete; £10.
  Seminar Papers & other technical publications; list available.

Square Dance Callers Club of Great Britain   (SDCCGB)   1955
- ■ 2 Crossbridge Cottages, Thornborough Rd, Thornton, MILTON KEYNES, Bucks, MK17 0HE.   (hsp)
  01280 816940
  email graybo@freenet.co.uk
  Hon Sec: Susie Kelly
- ▲ Un-incorporated Society
- ○ *D; to promote & further American square & round dancing by the provision & instruction of callers & teachers
- ● Mtgs - ET - SG - Lib
- < Intl Assn of Square Dance Callers (CALLERLAB-USA)
- M 170 i, UK / 10 i, o'seas
- ¶ NL - 6; ftm.

Squash Rackets Association   (England Squash)   1929
■   National Squash Centre, Rowsley St, MANCHESTER,
       M11 3FF.   (hq)
       0161 231 4499   fax 0161 231 4231
       email enquiries@englandsquash.com
       http://www.englandsquash.com
       Chief Exec: Nick Rider
▲   Company Limited by Guarantee
○   *S; the governing body for squash in England
<   Wld Squash Fedn; Eur Squash Fedn
M   25,000 i, 1,000 clubs, UK / 10 i, o'seas

Squash Wales Ltd   2005
■   St Mellons Country Club, St Mellons, CARDIFF, Glam,
       CF3 2XR.   (hq)
       01633 682108   fax 01633 680998
       email squashwales@squashwales.co.uk
       http://www.squashwales.co.uk
       Finance & Office Mgr: Sue Evans
▲   Company Limited by Guarantee
○   *S; the governing body of squash in Wales
●   ET - Regulation
<   Wld Squash Fedn; Eur Squash Fedn; C'wealth Games Coun for
       Wales; Welsh Sports Assn
M   3,170 i, 122 clubs
¶   NL - 3/4.   Fixture List - 1.

St ...

       see **Saint ...**

Stable Lads Association   (SLA)   1975
■   74 High St, SWADLINCOTE, Derbys, DE11 8HS.   (hsb)
       01283 211522
       Nat Sec: W A J Adams
○   *U
●   ET - Inf - Empl - LG
¶   NL - 2; free.

Staff & Educational Development Association   (SEDA)
■   John Foster House, 36 Gordon Square, LONDON, WC1H 0PF.
       020 7380 6767   fax 020 7387 2655
       email office@seda.ac.uk   http://www.seda.ac.uk
○   *P; for staff & educational developers

**Staffordshire Archaeological & Historical Society   (SAHS)
1959**
NR   29 Boldmere Drive, Boldmere, SUTTON COLDFIELD,
       W Midlands, B73 5ES.   (hsp)
       0121-350 3497
       email sahs@britishlibrary.net   http://www.sahs.uk.net
       Hon Gen Sec: James Debney
▲   Registered Charity
Br   1
○   *L, *Q; the study, investigation, description & preservation of
       antiquities & historical records, particularly of Staffordshire
Gp   Sub-c'ees: Editorial, Survey & excavation
●   Mtgs - Res - SG - VE - Publishing results of research -
       Archaeological excavations - Standing historical buildings
       survey
<   Coun for Brit Archaeology
M   180 i, 70 org
¶   Annual Transactions - 1; ftm.

**Staffordshire & Birmingham Agricultural Society   (SBAS)
1800**
NR   County Showground, Weston Rd, STAFFORD, ST18 0BD.   (hq)
       01785 258060
       Chief Exec: R C Williams
▲   Company Limited by Guarantee; Registered Charity
○   *F; promotion of agriculture through the County Show & the
       National Primestock Show
●   Conf - Exhib - Comp
<   Birmingham Agricl Exhib Soc
M   1,500 i
¶   Showground News - 1;   AR; both ftm only.

Staffordshire Parish Registers Society   (SPRS)   1900
■   35 Middlefield Lane, HAGLEY, W Midlands, DY9 0PY.
       (chmn/p)
       01562 882210   fax 01562 882210
       email chair@sprs.org.uk   http://www.sprs.org.uk
       Chmn: Dr Peter D Bloore
▲   Registered Charity
○   *L; publication in printed form of Staffordshire parish registers,
       mainly to 1837
●   Mtgs (AGM) - Res - Transcription & printing of parish registers
M   280 i, 10 libraries, UK / 5 i, 5 libraries, o'seas
¶   Registers (up to 1837) - 2/3; prices vary.

Staffordshire Record Society   1879
■   c/o William Salt Library, Eastgate St, STAFFORD, ST16 2LZ.
       (hsb)
       Hon Sec: D A Johnson
▲   Registered Charity
○   *L; the editing & printing of original documents relating to the
       County of Stafford & the publication of articles relating to the
       history of the county
M   i, f & org
¶   Collections for a history of Staffordshire - irreg; ftm,
       prices vary nm.

Stage Management Association   (SMA)   1954
■   55 Farringdon Rd, LONDON, EC1M 3JB.   (hq)
       020 7242 9250   fax 020 7242 9303
       email admin@stagemanagementassociation.co.uk
       http://www.stagemanagementassociation.co.uk
       Chmn: Alan Wallace
▲   Company Limited by Guarantee
○   *P; to support & represent professional stage management in
       the UK
Gp   Professionally working stage managers (full members); Recent
       graduates (provisional members); Student members (on
       NCDT accredited courses); Non-professional associates
●   ET - Inf - VE
<   Stage Mgrs Assn (USA); Indep Theatre Coun
M   620 i
¶   Cue Line (NL) - 6; ftm only.
       SMA Guide to Props & Propping; £4.50 m, £7 nm.
       Freelist (LM available for work) - 12; free.
       Stage Management: a career guide, free.
       Stage Management Notes.   Notes for Company Managers.
       [prices available on website].
       A Stage Manager's Guide to...
          ... the West End Agreement;
          ... the Provincial Commercial Contract;
          ... the Subsidised Repertory Agreement;
          all £2 m, £3.50 nm.

Stainless Steel Wire Industry Association
       merged in May 2002 with the UK Steel Association to become the
       Engineering Employers Federation, which in 2003 became **EEF, the
       manufacturers' organisation**

Stair Society   1935
NR   14 Murrayfield Drive, EDINBURGH, EH12 6EB.   (hsb)
      0131-337 3465
      email stairsecretary@aol.com   http://www.stairsociety.org
      Sec: Thomas H Drysdale
▲   Un-incorporated Society
○   *L; to encourage the study & to advance the knowledge of the
      history of Scots law
●   Mtgs - Publication of original documents - Reprinting & editing
      of works of sufficient rarity or importance
M   291 i, 88 f & org, 12 students, UK / 15 i, 63 f & org, o'seas
¶   AR; free.

Stalin Society   1991
■   BM Box 2521, LONDON, WC1N 3XX.   (mail/address)
      020 8571 9723   fax 020 8571 9723
      http://www.stalinsociety.org.uk
      Chmn: Harpal Brar
○   *G, *L; research into the history of the USSR under Joseph
      Stalin (1879-1953) [Iosif Vissarionovich Dzhugashvili]
●   Mtgs - Res
M   [not stated]
¶   List of research presentations; on request.

**Standardbred and Trotting Horse Association of Great Britain &
Ireland   (STAGBI)**
■   Little Craig, LLANDEGLEY, Powys, LD1 5UD.
      01544 350246
○   *B

Statewatch
NR   PO Box 1516, LONDON, N16 0EW.   (hq)
      020 8802 1882
○   *K; a civil liberties group concerned with secrecy laws & the
      public's 'right to know'

Statistical & Social Inquiry Society of Ireland   (SSISI)   1847
IRL   Dept of Statistics & Actuarial Science, University College Dublin,
      Belfield, DUBLIN 4, Republic of Ireland.
      353 (1) 716 7155   fax 353 (1) 716 1186
      Sec: Shane Whelan
○   *L

Statisticians in the Pharmaceutical Industry   (PSI)   1977
NR   Resources for Associations, Association House, South Park Rd,
      MACCLESFIELD, Cheshire, SK11 6SH.   (regd/office)
      01625 267882   fax 01625 267879
      email admin@psiweb.org   http://www.psiweb.org
      Exec Sec: Laura Kennedy
▲   Company Limited by Guarantee
○   *P; to promote professional standards of statistics in the
      pharmaceutical industry
●   Conf - Mtgs - ET - SG - Stat
<   Eur Fedn of Statisticians in the Pharmaceutical Ind
M   834 i, 306 f, UK / 211 i, 148 f, o'seas
¶   Pharmaceutical Statistics (Jnl) - 4; free (electronic).
      Spin (NL) - 4;   LM - 1;   AR; all ftm only.

Statistics Users' Council
      since 2005 is the Statistics User Forum of the **Royal Statistical
      Society**

Statute Law Society   1968
NR   21 Goodwyns Vale, LONDON, N10 2HA.   (hsb)
      020 8883 1700
      Sec: Mary Block
▲   Registered Charity
○   *K, *L; to promote technical improvements in the form &
      manner in which legislation is expressed & published to
      make it more intelligible
●   Conf - Lectures
M   150 i & f
¶   The Statute Law Review - 4.

Steam Boat Association of Great Britain   (SBA)   1971
NR   Avoca Cottage, NITON, Isle of Wight, PO38 2BP.   (hsp)
      Hon Sec: Adrian Birtles
▲   Un-incorporated Society
○   *G, *L; to encourage steam boating & the building,
      development, preservation & restoration of steam boats &
      steam machinery
●   Mtgs - Exhib - VE - Cruising events throughout summer
<   Eur Steamboat Fedn
M   1163 i, UK & o'seas
¶   Funnel - 4.

Steam Plough Club   (SPC)   1966
■   Old Station House, Twyford, READING, Berks, RG10 9NA.
      (hsp)
      0118-934 0381
      http://www.steamploughclub.org.uk
      Hon Sec: John Billard
▲   Un-incorporated Society
○   *G; to encourage & expand interest in the use of steam plough
      cultivation by demonstration, discussion & archive research
●   Mtgs - ET - Res - Comp - SG - Stat - Inf - Lib - PL - VE
<   Nat Traction Engine Club; Fedn Brit Historic Vehicle Clubs
M   400 i
¶   Steam Plough Times - 4; ftm, £1 nm.

Steel Construction Institute   (SCI)   1986
NR   Silwood Park, ASCOT, Berks, SL5 7QN.   (hq)
      01344 623345
      Dir: G W Owens
▲   Company Limited by Guarantee
○   *L; to promote the proper & effective use of steel in
      construction, both offshore & onshore
Gp   Computing: Structural analysis, CAD/CAE technical information
      database; Multi-media, Internet site development
      Design development & advisory: Technical advice to industry,
      Offshore & onshore engineering;
      Education: organises courses on all aspects of steel design
●   Conf - ET - Res - Inf - Lib - VE
M   50 i, 800 f, UK / 30 i, 150 f, o'seas
¶   New Steel Construction - 6.   SCI News (NL) - 4.
      Ybk.   AR.
      Range of technical publications; £15-£50.

Steel Lintel Manufacturers' Association   (SLMA)   1978
■   Corus Strip Products, PO Box 10, NEWPORT, Monmouthshire,
      NP19 4XN.   (sb)
      01633 755113
      email info@slma.co.uk   http://www.slma.co.uk
      Sec: Dr Clive Challinor
○   *T; steel lintels used for construction applications
●   Mtgs
M   4 f

Steel Window Association   (SWA)   1967
NR   The Building Centre, 26 Store St, LONDON, WC1E 7BT.   (hq)
      020 7637 3571
▲   Un-incorporated Society
Br   1
○   *T; represents manufacturers of steel windows & associated
      products
●   Conf - Mtgs - ET - Res - Exhib - Inf - LG
M   25 f
¶   Specifier's Guide to Steel Windows;   Factsheets 1-8;
      LM; all free.

© CBD Research Ltd · Beckenham · BR3 5JS · Tel 020 8650 7745 · Fax 020 8650 0768 · E-mail cbd@cbdresearch.com · www.cbdresearch.com

Stephenson Locomotive Society (SLS) 1909
- ■ 25 Regency Close, CHIGWELL, Essex, IG7 5NY. (hsp)
  020 8501 1210
  email briangilliam@beeb.net
  Gen Sec: Brian F Gilliam
- Br 15
- ○ *G, *L; study of railways, particularly locomotives
- ● Mtgs - Lib - PL - VE
- < Heritage Rlys Assn
- M c 700 i & org
- ¶ SLS Jnl - 6; ftm.

STEPS: the Association for People with Lower Limb Abnormalities (STEPS) 1980
- NR Warrington Lane, LYMM, Cheshire, WA13 0SA. (hq)
  0871 717 0044   fax 0871 717 0045
  email info@steps-charity.org.uk
  http://www.steps-charity.org.uk
  Gen Sec: Sue Banton,   Principal Contact: Bev Ritson
- ▲ Registered Charity
- Br 25
- ○ *W; a charity which gives support, contact, help, advice & information to families with children with lower limb abnormalities (club foot, congenital dislocated hip (CDH), developmental dysplasia of the hip (DDH), lower limb deficiency)
- ● Conf - Inf - Register of families for contact
- < Contact-a-Family (GB)
- M 1,200 i, 10 org
- ¶ NL - 4; ftm.   AR; free.
  Handbooks for parents:
  CDH/DDH Splints.
  CDH/DDH Plasters.
  Lower Limb Deficiency.
  Talipes.

Stereoscopic Society (Stereo Society) 1893
- ■ 32 Orkney Close, HINCKLEY, Leics, LE10 0TA. (hsp)
  01455 635520
  http://www.stereoscopicsociety.org.uk
  Hon Sec: Neville Jackson
- ▲ Un-incorporated Society
- ○ *L; 3D photography, graphics & computer graphics; the advancement of stereo images
- Gp Transparencies; Prints; Computer
- ● Conf - Mtgs - Exhib - Comp - Lib - VE - Workshops - Auctions
- < Intl Stereoscopic U; Photographic Alliance of GB; Photographic Soc of America (Stereo Divn)
- M 527 i, UK / 81 i, o'seas
- ¶ Jnl of Stereo Imaging - 4; ftm, £2 each nm.

**** Sterilised Suture Manufacturers Association**
  Organisation lost: see Introduction paragraph 3

Steroid Aid Group (SAG) 1979
- ■ 21 Dunmow Rd, ANDOVER, Hants, SP10 2DR. (mail) address
  Coordinator: Mrs B Copestake
- ▲ Un-incorporated Society
- ○ *K; a self-help group for patients taking steroids; to campaign for more awareness of dangers of over-prescribing; to publicise side-effects
- ● Mtgs - Inf
- M 500 i, UK / 8 i, o'seas
- ¶ NL - 3; ftm.   Information leaflets.
  (subscription £5 yr).

Stewart Society 1899
- ■ 53 George St, EDINBURGH, EH2 2HT. (asa)
  0131-220 4512   fax 0131-220 4512
  email info@stewartsociety.org
  Chief Exec & Sec: Mrs M V Stark
- ▲ Registered Charity
- Br Australia, Canada, Europe, Far East, N Zealand, USA
- ○ *G, *L; research into the Stewart family & its history
- ● Res - Lib - VE
- M 320 i, UK / 391 i, o'seas
- ¶ The Stewarts (Jnl) - 1; ftm, £5 nm.   NL - 2; free.

Stickler Syndrome Support Group (SSSG) 1989
- ■ PO Box 371, WALTON-ON-THAMES, Surrey, KT12 2YS.
  (regd/office)
  01932 267635
  Chmn & Founder: Mrs Wendy Hughes
- ▲ Registered Charity
- ○ *W; to raise awareness of Stickler syndrome amongst the medical profession & the general public
- ● Conf - Inf
- M 400 families, 150 i (professionals), UK / 40 families, o'seas
- ¶ NL - 4;   AR - 1;   Information Booklets; all ftm.
  Stickler the Elusive Syndrome.   Ten Years On.

Stillbirth & Neonatal Death Society (SANDS) 1978
- NR 28 Portland Place, LONDON, W1B 1LY. (hq)
  020 7436 7940   fax 020 7436 3715
  email support@uk-sands.org   http://www.uk-sands.org
  Chmn: Susan Annis-Salter
- ▲ Company Limited by Guarantee; Registered Charity
- Br 150
- ○ *M, *W; to provide support for bereaved parents & their families when their baby dies at or soon after birth; the key elements of that support are: the National telephone helpline service, UK-wide network of local self-help groups run by & for bereaved parents, Information & publications for parents & healthcare professionals
- ● ET - Inf - LG - Helpline: 020 7436 5881
- M c 1,000 i
- ¶ NL - 3.   AR.   Support leaflets.
  Pregnancy Loss & the Death of a Baby (guidelines for professionals).
  Understanding Pregnancy Loss.   When a Baby Dies.
  Saying Goodbye to Your Baby.

Stilton Cheese Makers' Association (SCMA) 1936
- ■ PO Box 384a, SURBITON, Surrey, KT5 9YL. (asa)
  020 8255 1334   fax 020 8255 1335
  http://www.stiltoncheese.com
  Sec: Nigel White
- ▲ Un-incorporated Society
- Br USA
- ○ *T; to promote marketing of Stilton cheese - to protect the use of the 'Stilton' trade name & device
- ● Mtgs - ET - Res - Exhib - Stat - Expt - Inf - LG
- < Cheese Importers Assn of America; Dairy Ind Assn
- M 5 i, 6 f
- ¶ Recipe leaflets & information leaflets; free.

Stockport Chamber of Commerce & Industry
  is the Stockport office of the **Greater Manchester Chamber of Commerce**

Stoke-on-Trent Museum Archaeological Society   (SOTMAS) 1959
■ The Potteries Museum, Bethesda St, Hanley, STOKE-on-TRENT, Staffs, ST1 3DW.   (hq)
01782 232323
Hon Sec: Mrs R Helen Outram
▲ Un-incorporated Society
○ *Q; to promote & encourage research into the archaeology in N Staffordshire
● Mtgs - ET - Res - Inf - Lib - VE
< Coun Brit Archaeology; Coun for Indep Archaeology
M c 60 i, UK / 1 i, o'seas
¶ Staffordshire Archaeological Studies - irreg.
NL - 3; free.

Stone Federation Great Britain   (SFGB)   1974
NR Channel Business Centre, Ingles Manor, Castle Hill Ave, FOLKESTONE, Kent, CT20 2RD.   (hq)
01303 856123   fax 01303 221095
email enquiries@stone-federationgb.org.uk
http://www.stone-federationgb.org.uk
Dir: Jane Buxey
▲ Un-incorporated Society
○ *T; product information, technical guidance & advice on all aspects of specifying & working with natural stone in all its uses (quarry, design, fix, masonry, cleaning, restoring, landscape & internal)
Gp Stone cleaning & surface repair c'ee; Technical c'ee; Training group for natural stone industry
● Conf - Mtgs - ET - Res - Exhib - Comp - Inf - VE - LG - Courses & seminars (RIBA & CPD approved) on stone
> Brit Slate Assn; Heritage Bldg Contractors Gp; Standing Jt C'ee on Natural Stone
M 200+ f, UK / 5 f, o'seas
¶ Specifications Guide (Members Directory) - 1; ftm, price varies nm.
Codes of Practice on:
Kitchen Worktops/Countertops.   Cleaning.
Natural Stone Floors.   Restoration.
Technical Data Sheets.

Stone Roofing Association   1995
■ Ceunant, CAERNARFON, Gwynedd, LL55 4SA.   (hsb)
01286 650402   fax 0709 230 7784
email terry@slateroof.co.uk
http://www.stoneroof.org.uk
Chmn: Ted Hughes
▲ Un-incorporated Society
○ *T; to support the manufacturers of stone slates in the UK; to act as a point of reference for users & specifiers with the stone slate industry
● Mtgs - Inf
M 20 f

Stonehenge Society
is incorporated in the **Megalithic Society**

Storage Equipment Manufacturers' Association   (SEMA)   1970
■ McLaren Building (6th floor), 35 Dale End, BIRMINGHAM, B4 7LN.   (hq)
0121-200 2100   fax 0121-200 1306
email enquiry@sema.org.uk   http://www.sema.org.uk
Sec: David B Corns
▲ Company Limited by Guarantee
○ *T
Gp Technical
● Mtgs - ET - Exhib - Stat - Inf - Issuing codes of practice for the design, manufacture & use of storage equipment
< Brit Materials Handling Fedn; Fédn Européenne de la Manutention; METCOM
M 22 f
¶ Various codes of practice & guidelines on storage equipment - irreg; prices vary.

Storage & Handling Equipment Distributors' Association (SHEDA)   1978
■ Heathcote House, 136 Hagley Rd, Edgbaston, BIRMINGHAM, B16 9PN.   (hq)
0121-454 4141   fax 0121-454 4949
email sp@heathcote-coleman.co.uk
http://www.sheda.org.uk
Sec: Mrs Sharon J Parker
▲ Un-incorporated Society
○ *T; to support & protect the reputation, status & interests of storage equipment distributors
● Mtgs - ET - Exhib
< Storage Eqpt Mfrs Assn (SEMA)
M 60 f
¶ SHEDA News - 4; free.   LM; ftm.

Strategic Planning Society   1967
■ Buxton House, 7 Highbury Hill, LONDON, N5 1SU.   (hq)
0845 056 3663   fax 0845 751 8216
email enquiries@sps.org.uk   http://www.sps.org.uk
Managing Dir: Annette Quinn,   Chmn: Jon Vyse
▲ Registered Charity
○ *P; to foster & promote research, innovation & best practice in strategic thought & action
Gp Corporate strategy; Financial services; Innovation & corporate venturing; Knowledge economy; Public sector; Risk; SMEs; Technology, media &telecoms (TMT); Utilities; Voluntary sector
● Conf - Mtgs - ET - Res - Inf
< Eur Strategic Planning Fedn (ESPLAF)
M 1,300 i, 50 f, UK / 200 i, 20 f, o'seas
¶ Long Range Planning (Jnl) - 6;   Strategy - 4; both ftm only.
Email NL - 12; free.

Strathspey Railway Association Ltd   (SRA)   1972
NR Spey Lodge, Aviemore Station, Dalfaber Rd, AVIEMORE, Inverness-shire, PH21 1ET.   (hq)
▲ Company Limited by Guarantee
○ *G; to support the operation of the railway by provision of staff, maintenance of stock & restoration of relics
Gp Permanent way; Signalling; Locomotive engineering; Carriage & wagon; Civil engineering works; Publicity; Marketing
● Mtgs - ET - Res - Exhib - Inf - Lib - VE
M 730 i, 2 org, UK / 20 i, o'seas
¶ The Strathspey Express - 2; ftm.

Stratospheric Ozone Review Group
no longer in existence

Straw Bale Building Association   (SBBA (WISE))   1998
■ c/o Hollinroyd Farm, Butts Lane, TODMORDEN, Lancs, OL14 8RJ.   (hsp)
Contact: Chug Tugby (01442 825421)
Hon Sec: B Rowan
▲ Un-incorporated Society
○ *G; for people who build, live in or are interested in buildings made of straw bales
Gp Intl straw bale building; Research & testing; Volunteer opportunities
● Conf - ET - Res - Inf - Lib - PL - VE - Networking
< Global Straw Bale Network; Eur Straw Bale Network
M 45 i, 5 f, UK / 7 i, o'seas
¶ The Last Straw (Jnl) - 4;   Baling Out (NL) - 4.

Street Sled Sports Racers   (SSSprint)   1995
NR 33a Canal St, OXFORD, OX2 6BQ.   (chmn/b)
01865 311179   fax 01865 426007
email dingboston@oxfordstuntfactory.com
http://www.streetluge.co.uk
Chmn: David Boston
▲ Un-incorporated Society
○ *S; the regulation, safety, promotion & supply of all facets of street luging & land luging
● Mtgs - ET - Res - Comp - Inf - LG
M i
¶ NL - 8/10.

Strict Baptist Historical Society (SBHS) 1960
- 33 Addison Rd, CATERHAM-on-the-HILL, Surrey, CR3 5LU. (hsp)
  01883 341909
  email thesecretary@sbhs.org.uk
  http://www.strictbaptisthistory.org.uk
  Hon Sec: Pauline Johns
- ▲ Registered Charity
- ○ *L; all matters of Particular Baptist & Strict Baptist history
- ● Mtgs - Inf - Lib
- M 110 i, 1 org, UK / 2 i, o'seas
- ¶ Bulletin - 1; ftm, £1 nm.   NL - 1; free.

Stroke Association   1899
- § Stroke House, 240 City Rd, LONDON, EC1Y 8JJ.   (hq)
  020 7566 0300   fax 020 7490 2686
  email stroke@stroke.org.uk   http://www.stroke.org.uk
  Chief Exec: Miss Margaret Goose
  A registered charity offering practical help, emotional support & information to people who have had strokes & to their families. It funds research into all aspects of stroke. It works to prevent strokes by informing the public of the risk factors

Structural Precast Association
  a product association of the **British Precast Concrete Federation**

Structural Waterproofing Group
  is a group of the **British Wood Preserving & Damp-proofing Association**

Student Radio Association
  is a group of the **Radio Academy**

Sub-Aqua Association (SAA) 1976
- NR Space Solutions Business Centre, Sefton Lane, Maghull, LIVERPOOL, L31 8BX.   (hq)
  0151-287 1001   fax 0151-287 1026
  email admin@saa.org.uk   http://www.saa.org.uk
  Contact: Irene Sartorius
- ▲ Registered Charity
- Br 350
- ○ *S
- Gp Boat handling; Chartwork & navigation; Marine life identification; Nautical archaeology
- ● Conf - Mtgs - ET - Exam - Res - Exhib - Inf
- < R Yachting Assn; Marine Conservation Soc; Nautical Archaeol Soc
- M 6,000 i
- ¶ Scuba World - 12.
  Introduction to SAA - on enrolment; free.

Subsea UK   2003
- NR The Innovation Centre, Aberdeen Offshore Technology Park, Bridge of Don, ABERDEEN, AB23 8GX.   (hq)
  01224 355355
  http://www.subseauk.com
  Chief Exec: David Pridden
- ○ *T
- × 2003 Scottish Subsea Technology Group (merged assets on closing)

Subsidence Repair Techniques & Engineered Foundation Solutions
  see **ASUCplus - Subsidence Repair Techniques & Engineered Foundation Solutions**

Subterranea Britannica (SUB.BRIT) 1974
- c/o CNHSS Ltd, 96a Brighton Rd, S CROYDON, Surrey, CR2 6AD.   (hq)
  020 8681 6293
  http://www.subbrit.org.uk
  Chmn: Paul W Sowan
- ○ *L; to study the history & archaeology of disused spaces, made & used by people, of any period in a safe & lawful manner. Cold War structures, underground or not, & associated aboveground structures are also studied
- Gp Cold War Research Group
- ● Conf - Mtgs - Res - SG - Inf - VE
- < Coun Brit Archaeology; Nat Assn Mining History Socs
- M 819 i, 22 org, UK & o'seas
- ¶ Bulletin Subterranea Britannica - irreg;
  Subterranea - 2/3; both ftm only.

Sudden Death Support Association (SDSA) 1994
- Eldon House, The Street, Eversley, HOOK, Hants, RG27 0PJ. (hq)
  0118 988 8996   fax 0118 988 8996
  Sec: Mrs Sarah Firth
- ▲ Registered Charity
- ○ *W; to help anyone who has suffered a bereavement through sudden death
- ● Mtgs - Befriending service

Suffolk Agricultural Association (SAA) 1831
- NR Trinity Park, Felixstowe Rd, IPSWICH, Suffolk, IP3 8UH.   (hq)
  01473 707110
  Exec Dir: C P Bushby
- ▲ Registered Charity
- ○ *F; to improve agriculture (incl forestry, horticulture & allied industries); to develop & improve agricultural instruments & machinery
- ● Conf - Mtgs - Exhib
- M c 3,500 i
- ¶ Suffolk Scene - 3; free.

Suffolk Chamber of Commerce, Industry & Shipping Incorporated   1884
- NR Felaw Maltings, South Kiln, 42 Felaw St, IPSWICH, Suffolk, IP1 2DE.   (hq)
  01473 680600   fax 01473 603888
  email info@suffolkchamber.co.uk
  http://www.suffolknetwork.co.uk
  Chief Exec: John Dugmore
- ▲ Company Limited by Guarantee
- ○ *C
- Gp International Trade; Transport; Business Library; Training; Home & economic affairs; Ipswich Port; Ipswich Chamber
- ● Conf - Mtgs - ET - Exhib - Expt - Inf - Lib
- < Brit Chams Comm
- M 1,360 f
- ¶ Suffolk Business Magazine - 12.
  SI Trader - 12.   Economic Survey - 4.
  Suffolk Business Directory - 1.

Suffolk Horse Society   1877
- The Market Hill, WOODBRIDGE, Suffolk, IP12 4LU.   (hq)
  01394 380643   fax 01394 610058
  email sec@suffolkhorsesociety.org.uk
  http://www.suffolkhorsesociety.org.uk
  Chmn: Martin Goymour
- ▲ Company Limited by Guarantee; Registered Charity
- ○ *B
- ● Stat - Inf - Maintenance of stud book
- M 900 i
- ¶ Suffolk Horse Magazine - 3; ftm, £3.50 nm.

Suffolk Institute of Archaeology & History (SIA) 1848

- ■ Roots, Church Lane, Playford, IPSWICH, Suffolk, IP6 9DS. (hsp)
  01473 624556
  Hon Sec: B J Seward
- ▲ Registered Charity
- ○ *L; the study of the archaeology & history of Suffolk
- Gp Archaeological field gp
- ● Mtgs - ET - Res - Exhib - Inf - Lib - VE
- < Coun Brit Archaeology
- M 790 i, 61 org, UK / 8 i, 20 org, o'seas
- ¶ Proceedings - 1; NL - 2; both ftm.

Suffolk Record Society (SRS) 1958

- ■ Suffolk Record Office, 77 Raingate St, BURY ST EDMUNDS, Suffolk, IP33 2AR. (hsb)
  01284 352350 fax 01284 352355
  Hon Sec: R G Thomas
- ○ *L; publication of documents relating to Suffolk & its people in all periods
- M i & org
- ¶ Annual Volume; ftm.

Suffolk Sheep Society 1886

- NR The Sheep Centre, Blackmore Park Rd, MALVERN, Worcs, WR13 6PH. (hq)
  01684 893366
  Sec: Miss Penny Lawrence
- ○ *B
- M i, f, org

Sugar Association of London (SAOL) 1882

- ■ 15-18 Lime St (4th floor), LONDON, EC3M 7AQ. (hq)
  020 7626 1745 fax 020 7283 3831
  email moond@sugar-assoc.co.uk
  Sec: N Durham
- Br 2
- ○ *T; supervisors of raw sugar cargoes; provision of rules & contract conditions for the raw sugar trade
- Gp Supervisors of raw sugar cargoes; Arbitrators; Rules & contract conditions
- ● Mtgs - ET - Inf - Empl - LG
- M 40 f, UK / 60 f, o'seas
- ¶ Rules & Regulations; £35 m, £60 nm.

Sugar Traders Association of the UK (STAUK) 1952

- ■ c/o C Czarnikow Sugar Ltd, 24 Chiswell St, LONDON, EC1Y 4SG. (hsb)
  020 7972 6631 fax 020 7972 6699
  email sugartraders@sugartraders.co.uk
  http://www.sugartraders.co.uk
  Hon Sec: David Clark
- ▲ Un-incorporated Society
- ○ *T; to promote, support, develop, protect & maintain the trade in sugar
- ● Mtgs - LG
- < Assn Profl Orgs Sugar Tr EU (ASSUC)
- M 12 f, 5 org

Sunbed Association 1995

- ■ Chess House, 105 High St, CHESHAM, Bucks, HP5 1DE. (hq)
  01494 785941 fax 01494 786791
  Sec: Kathy Banks
- ▲ Company Limited by Guarantee
- ○ *T; interests of sunbed manufacturers, operators & hirers
- ● Mtgs - ET - Stat - Inf - LG - Printed merchandise
- < Eur Sunlight Assn
- M 1,000 f
- ¶ NL - 2; ftm only. LM - 12; free.

Sunday Shakespeare Society (SSS) 1874

- ■ 308 Copperfield, CHIGWELL, Essex, IG7 5JZ. (hsp)
  020 8501 2841
  Hon Sec: Susan E Taylor
- ▲ Un-incorporated Society
- ○ *A, *G; to encourage the study of Shakespeare's plays by dramatic readings by members on Sundays
- ● Mtgs
- M 41 i
- ¶ NL - 12; Programme - 1; both free.

** Sunderland Antiquarian Society

Organisation lost: see Introduction paragraph 3

Superintendents' Association of Northern Ireland (PSANI) 1972

- ■ PSNI College, Garnerville, Garnerville Rd, BELFAST, BT4 2NX. (hq)
  028 9092 2201 fax 028 9092 2169
  email mail@psani.org http://www.psani.org
  Hon Sec: Supt Guy Thomson
- ▲ Un-incorporated Society
- ○ *P; representing the interests of superintendents in the police service of Northern Ireland
- ● Conf - Mtgs - Empl - LG
- M 100 i

Superyacht UK
  a group of the **British Marine Federation**

Support Dogs

- NR 21 Jessops Riverside, Brightside Lane, SHEFFIELD, S Yorks, S9 2RX.
  0870 609 3476
  http://www.support-dogs.org.uk
- ▲ Registered Charity
- ○ *W; the only organisation worldwide that trains dogs to help disabled people with everyday tasks & also to recognise & predict an epileptic seizure

Support after Murder & Manslaughter
  see **SAMM National**

Support Society for Children of High Intelligence (CHI) 1993

- NR PO Box 21461, LONDON, N6 6WW. (hq)
  020 8347 8927
  Chmn: Clare Lorenz
- ▲ Company Limited by Guarantee; Registered Charity
- ○ *W; to support pupils whose intelligence falls into the top 5% with problems they may encounter at home or school
- Gp UK nationwide helplines of contact members
  Specialist members/advisers: educational psychologists, consultant paediatrician, teachers, dyslexia consultant
- ● ET - Res - SG - Inf - Lib - Classes for highly gifted children - Inner city teacher support
- M i & org
- ¶ CHI News - 3. CHI Hbk.
  Library list. AR.
  Growing Up - baby/childhood monitor.

Supporters of Nuclear Energy (SONE) 1998

- NR c/o BNES, 7 Great George St, LONDON, SW1P 3ZS. (hq)
  email sec@sone.org.uk http://www.sone.org.uk
  Sec: Sir Bernard Ingham
- ▲ Company Limited by Guarantee
- ○ *K; promotion of nuclear energy policy
- ● Conf - Mtgs - Inf - LG
- M 280 i
- ¶ NL - 12; free on website.

Supporting Adults affected by Adoption   (NORCAP)   1982
- ■ 112 Church Rd, WHEATLEY, Oxon, OX33 1LU.   (hq)
  01865 875000
  email enquiries@norcap.org   http://www.norcap.org.uk
- ▲ Registered Charity
- ○ *W; a support group for adult adopted people & both their
  adoptive & birth parents
- M i & org
- ✕ 2004-05 National Organisation for Counselling Adoptees &
  their Parents

**Surf Life Saving Association of Great Britain Ltd   (SLSAofGB)
1955**
- NR 19 Southernhay West (1st floor), EXETER, Devon, EX1 1PJ.   (hq)
  08700 753911   fax 01382 217898
  http://www.surflifesaving.org.uk
  Nat Sec: Kate Morgan
- ▲ Company Limited by Guarantee; Registered Charity
- ○ *K, *S; promotion of beach & surf safety; provision of
  community service by voluntary lifeguards on British beaches;
  promotion of surf life saving as a competitive sport
- Gp Commissions: Technical, Powercraft, Sport, Youth development
- ● Conf - Mtgs - ET - Exam - Comp - Stat - Inf - LG
- < Intl Life Saving
- M 4,000 i, 25 f, 75 org
- ¶ Swim & Save - 12.

Surface Engineering Association   (SEA)   1997
- ■ Federation House, 10 Vyse St, BIRMINGHAM, B18 6LT.   (hq)
  0121-237 1123   fax 0121-237 1124
  email info@sea.org.uk   http://www.sea.org.uk
  Chief Exec: David Elliott
- ▲ Company Limited by Guarantee
- ○ *T
- Gp British Surface Treatment Suppliers Association; Contract Heat
  Treatment Association; Metal Finishing Association (& its
  division the British Electroless Nickel Society); Paint & Powder
  Finishing Association; Wolfson Heat Treatment Centre
  Process technology; Organic coating equipment; Health, safety
  & environment
- ● Conf - Mtgs - ET - Res - Exhib - Comp - SG - Stat - Inf - VE - LG
- < Aluminium Finishing Assn (AFA); Contract Heat Treatment Assn
  (CHTA)
- M c 400 f
- ¶ SEA News - 4;   Watchword - 4; both ftm.

Surfers against Sewage   (SAS)
- ■ Unit 2, Wheal Kitty Workshops, ST AGNES, Cornwall,
  TR5 0RD.   (hq)
  01872 553001   fax 01872 552615
  email info@sas.org.uk   http://www.sas.org.uk
  Campaigns Dir: Richard Hardy
- ▲ Company Limited by Guarantee
- ○ *K; campaign for clear, safe recreational waters
- ● ET - Res - Campaigning - Fundraising (including selling
  merchandise)
- M c 9,000 i, 200 f, UK / 100 i, o'seas
- ¶ Pipeline (NL) - 4; ftm only.

Surgical Dressings Manufacturers' Association   (SDMA)   1936
- ■ 70 Egremont Rd, Milnrow, ROCHDALE, Lancs, OL16 4ES.
  (hsb)
  01706 641035   fax 01706 641035
  http://www.sdma.org.uk
  Sec: David Metcalfe
- ○ *T
- ● Mtgs - SG - Stat - Expt - Inf - Empl - Consideration of legislative
  measures - Discussions with government departments
- M 17 f

Surrey Archaeological Society   (SyAS)   1854
- ■ Castle Arch, GUILDFORD, Surrey, GU1 3SX.   (hq)
  01483 532454   fax 01483 532454
  email surreyarch@compuserve.com
  http://www.ourworld.compuserve.com/homepages/
  surreyarch
  Hon Sec: P E Youngsy Monk
- ▲ Company Limited by Guarantee; Registered Charity
- ○ *L; archaeology, history & antiquities of Surrey (including those
  parts now in Greater London)
- Gp Guildford; Historic landscape; Roman Studies; Surrey Industrial
  History Society; Plateau
- ● Conf - ET - Res - SG - Lib - PL - VE
- < Brit Assn Local History; Coun Brit Archaeology; Field Studies
  Coun
- M 787 i, 126 org, UK / 5 i, 38 org, o'seas
- ¶ Surrey Archaeological Collections - 1.
  Bulletin - 9.   AR.

Surrey Chambers of Commerce Ltd
- NR 48-54 Goldsworth Rd, WOKING, Surrey, GU21 6LE.   (hq)
  01483 726655   fax 01483 740217
  email info@surrey-chambers.co.uk
  http://www.surrey-chambers.co.uk
  Chief Exec: Louise Punter
- ▲ Company Limited by Guarantee
- Br 3
- ○ *C; representing chambers in Surrey
- Gp Regional offices: East, Guildford & Spelthorne
- ● Conf - Mtgs - ET - Res - Exhib - SG - Stat - Expt - Inf - Lib - LG
- < Brit Chams Comm
- M 3,300 f
- ¶ The Chamber - 6;   NL - 12; both ftm only.
  Members Directory - 1; ftm, £65 nm.

Surrey County Agricultural Society   (SCAS)   1829
- ■ 8 Birtley Courtyard, BRAMLEY, Surrey, GU5 0LA.   (hq)
  01483 890810   fax 01483 890820
  email scas@surreycountyshow.co.uk
  http://www.surreycountyshow.co.uk
  Chief Exec: Mrs Sonia Ashworth
- ▲ Company Limited by Guarantee; Registered Charity
- ○ *F, *H; to promote agriculture, farming, breeding, horticulture,
  conservation & environment
- Gp Farming; Horticulture; Agriculture; Breeding (animals)
- ● Comp - Mtgs - Exhib
- < ASAO
- M 379 i, 3 f, 1 school
- ¶ AR - 1; free.

Surrey Industrial History Society
  a group of the **Surrey Archaeological Society**

Surrey Record Society   (SRS)   1913
- ■ c/o Surrey History Centre, 130 Goldsworth Rd, WOKING,
  Surrey, GU21 6ND.   (hsb)
  01483 518754
  Hon Sec: Mrs M Vaughan-Lewis
- ▲ Registered Charity
- ○ *L; to publish records relating to areas within the ancient county
  of Surrey (including those parts now in Greater London)
- ● Publication
- < Brit Records Assn
- M 102 i, 72 org, UK / 4 i, 41 org, o'seas
- ¶ Record volumes; ftm, prices vary nm.   AR; ftm.

Surtees Society   (SS)   1834
NR   Dept of History, 43-45 North Bailey, DURHAM, DH1 3EX.
     (hsb)
     0191-334 1040   fax 0191-334 1041
     email surtees.society@dur.ac.uk
     http://www.surteessociety.org.uk
     Hon Sec: Dr Michael Stansfield
▲   Registered Charity
○   *L; publication of unedited historical manuscripts illustrative of
     the intellectual, moral, religious or social condition of the
     ancient Kingdom of Northumbria (those parts of England &
     Scotland between the Humber & Firth of Forth in the east &
     the Mersey & the Clyde to the west)
     Named after Robert Surtees 1779-1834, antiquary &
     topographer
●   Publication
M   225 i & org
¶   Annual Volume - 1; ftm (subscription £20), £40 nm.

Sussex Archaeological Society (The)   1846
■   Bull House, 92 High St, LEWES, E Sussex, BN7 1XH.   (hq)
     01273 486260
     Chief Exec: John Manley
▲   Company Limited by Guarantee; Registered Charity
Br 6
○   *L; to further interest in & knowledge of the history &
     archaeology of Sussex
Gp Sussex archaeology forum; Sussex history forum;
     Archaeological excavations
●   Conf - Mtgs - ET - Res - Exhib - SG - Inf - Lib - PL - VE - LG -
     Opens to the public society-owned museums, sites &
     properties
M   2,102 i, 123 org, UK / 12 i, 69 org, o'seas
¶   Sussex Past & Present - 3.
     Sussex Archaeological Collections - 1.

Sussex Cattle Society   1879
NR   Station Rd, ROBERTSBRIDGE, E Sussex, TN32 5DG.   (hq)
     01580 880105
     Sec: Miss S Kennedy
○   *B; Sussex & Sussex cross cattle
M   i
¶   NL - 4; ftm only.   Herd Book - 2 yrly.
     Breeders Directory - 1; free.

Sussex Chamber of Commerce & Enterprise   (SCCTE)   1945
NR   Greenacre Court, Station Rd, BURGESS HILL, W Sussex,
     RH15 9DS.   (hq)
     01444 259259   fax 01444 259190
     email information@sussexenterprise.co.uk
     http://www.sussexenterprise.co.uk
     Chief Exec: Mark Froud
▲   Company Limited by Guarantee
○   *C; as the Chamber of Commerce & Business Link for Sussex to
     help Sussex business prosper & develop
Gp International services; Important advice services; Employee
     development advice; Membership organisation
●   Conf - Mtgs - ET - Res - Exhib - Stat - Expt - Inf - LG
<   Brit Chams Comm
M   2,500 f
¶   Business Edge - 10.
     Business Directory - 1.
     Note: Trades as Sussex Enterprise.

Sussex Enterprise
     the trading name of **Sussex Chamber of Commerce, Training &
     Enterprise**

Sussex Industrial Archaeology Society   (SIAS)   1967
■   42 Falmer Avenue, Saltdean, BRIGHTON, E Sussex,
     BN2 8FG.   (hsp)
     01273 271330
     email ronald@martin42.fsnet.co.uk
     http://www.fastnet.co.uk/sias
     Gen Sec: R G Martin
▲   Registered Charity
○   *L; recording, repairing & preserving documentary & other
     recordings & sites of economic & industrial activity in Sussex
Gp Mills; Breweries & malthouses; Fuel power supplies; Ice houses;
     Railways; Limekilns
●   Conf - Mtgs - Res - Exhib - VE
<   Sussex Archaeol Soc; Assn for Indl Archaeology; S E Region
     Indl Archaeology Conf
M   340 i, 25 f, 10 org, UK / 1 i, o'seas
¶   Sussex Industrial History - 1; ftm, £4.25 nm.
     NL - 4; ftm, 50p nm.

Sussex Record Society   (SRS)   1901
■   Barbican House, High St, LEWES, E Sussex, BN7 1YE.   (hq)
     01273 405739
     Hon Sec: P M Wilkinson
▲   Registered Charity
○   *L; transcribing & publishing in book form documents relating
     to the County of Sussex
●   Publication
M   268 i, 47 org, UK / 11 i, 39 org, o'seas
¶   Sussex Record Society [volume. . .] - 1; ftm, prices vary nm.
     NL - 1;   LM - irreg;   AR - 1; all ftm.

**Sustain: the Alliance for Better Food & Farming   (SUSTAIN)
1999**
■   94 White Lion St, LONDON, N1 9PF.   (hq)
     020 7837 1228   fax 020 7837 1141
     email sustain@sustainweb.org
     http://www.sustainweb.org
     Coordinator: Jeanette Longfield
▲   Registered Charity
○   *F, *K, advocates food & agricultural policies & practices that
     enhance the health & welfare of people & animals, improve
     the working & living environment, promote equity & enrich
     society & culture
     Represents about 100 national public interest organisations
     working at international, national, regional & local level
Gp Food Poverty Network; London Food Link; Sustainable Food
     Chains; FSA; Children's Food Bill
●   Conf - ET - Res - Stat - Inf - LG
M   100 org
¶   Publication list available.

Sustainable Food Chains
     is a group of **Sustain: the Alliance for Better Food & Farming**

Sutton Business Federation
     since 2004 **Sutton Chamber**

Sutton Chamber   1936
NR   Quadrant House, The Quadrant, SUTTON, Surrey, SM5 4LE.
     (hq)
     020 8642 9661
     http://www.suttonchamber.biz
     Chmn: Paul Cawthorne
▲   Company Limited by Guarantee
○   *C; for the London Borough of Sutton
●   Mtgs - ET - Exhib - Inf
×   2004 Sutton Business Federation

Swale Chamber of Commerce
     a branch of **North Kent Chamber of Commerce**

Swaledale Sheep Breeders' Association   (SSBA)   1920
NR   The Shooting Lodge, Eggleston, BARNARD CASTLE,
　　Co Durham, DL12 0DP.   (sp)
　　01833 650516
　　Sec: John Stephenson
▲   Company Limited by Guarantee
○   *B
●   Mtgs - Inf
<   Nat Sheep Assn
M   1,356 i
¶   Flock Book - 1; ftm only.

Swaziland Society   1991
■   4 Sybil's Way, HOUGHTON CONQUEST, Beds, MK45 3AQ.
　　01234 742815
　　Sec: Vera Robbins
▲   Un-incorporated Society
○   *X; developing & strengthening educational, cultural, economic
　　& social ties between Britain & Swaziland; to foster friendship
　　& uderstanding between the peoples of the two countries
●   Mtgs - VE - Social gatherings - Financial assistance to
　　development projects in Swaziland
M   160 i, UK / 86 i, o'seas
¶   Focus on Swaziland - 3; ftm.
　　[subscription £18 (double), £12 (single).]

Swedenborg Society   1810
NR   20-21 Bloomsbury Way, LONDON, WC1A 2TH.   (hq)
　　020 7405 7986
　　Sec: Richard Lines
▲   Company Limited by Guarantee; Registered Charity
○   *A, *L; printing & publication of works of Emanuel Swedenborg
　　(1688-1772) the Swedish philosopher scientist & theologian
●   Mtgs - Inf - Lib
M   1,000 i
¶   AR; free.
　　Descriptive catalogue of publications.

Swedish Chamber of Commerce for the United Kingdom   1906
NR   5 Upper Montagu St, LONDON, W1G 0AZ.   (hq)
　　020 7224 8001
　　Dir: Christina Liljeström
○   *C; to promote trade between Great Britain & Sweden
●   Conf - Mtgs - Res - SG - Expt - Inf - Lib - VE
<   Intl Cham Comm (Sweden); British-Swedish Cham Comm
　　(Sweden)
M   40 i, 420 f, UK / 20 i, 40 f, o'seas
¶   LINK (Jnl) - 11;   AR - 1; both ftm.
　　Swedish-British Trade Directory (incl LM) - 1; ftm, £35 nm.

Swimming Pool & Allied Trades Association Ltd   (SPATA)   1961
■   SPATA House, 1a Junction Rd, ANDOVER, Hants, SP10 3QT.
　　(hq)
　　01264 356210   fax 01264 332628
　　email admin@spata.co.uk   http://www.spata.co.uk
　　Managing Dir: Allen Brobyn,   Pres: Bob Spring
▲   Company Limited by Guarantee
○   *T; interests of contractors & manufacturers of equipment &
　　accessories for swimming pools & spas
●   Conf - Mtgs - ET - Exhib - Inf - Lib
M   220 f, UK / 14 f, o'seas
¶   Various publications on standards for installations, water
　　treatment for swimming pools & spas.

Swimming Teachers' Association Ltd   (STA)   1932
NR   Anchor House, Birch St, WALSALL, W Midlands, WS2 8HZ.
　　(hq)
　　01922 645097   fax 01922 720628
　　email sta@sta.co.uk   http://www.sta.co.uk
▲   Company Limited by Guarantee; Registered Charity
Br   16; Australia, Hong Kong, Singapore, Taiwan
○   *E, *S; 'to save lives by the teaching of swimming, lifesaving &
　　survival techniques'
●   Conf - Mtgs - ET - Exam
<   Intl Fedn of Swimming Teachers Assns (IFSTA)
M   5,000 i
¶   Swim & Save - 6; ftm, £18 yr nm (UK) (£24 Europe).

Swindon Chamber of Commerce & Industry   (SCCI)   1894
■   24-26 Cricklade Rd, Gorse Hill, SWINDON, Wilts, SN2 8AA.
　　(hq)
　　01793 642225   fax 01793 521165
　　email info@swindonchamber.co.uk
　　http://www.swindonchamber.co.uk
　　Chief Exec: Dennis Grant
▲   Company Limited by Guarantee
○   *C
●   Conf - Mtgs - ET - Exhib - Expt - Inf - VE - LG
<   Brit Chams Comm; South West Chams Comm; Wiltshire Cham
　　Comm
M   700 f
¶   The Edge Magazine - 4;   Wiltshire Business - 12;
　　E-Zine Newsletter - 12; all ftm only.
　　Business West Annual Directory - 1; £50 m, £85 nm.

Swiss Railways Society   (SRS)   1980
NR   Alf-n-Alf Cottage, Kingsbury Episcopi, MARTOCK, Somerset,
　　TA12 6AZ.   (hsp)
▲   Un-incorporated Society
Br   Australia, N Zealand, USA
○   *G; to bring together those interested in the railways of
　　Switzerland, both prototype & model
●   Mtgs - Exhib - Inf - Lib
<   Schweizer Verband Eisenbahn Amateur (SVEA)
M   930 i, UK / 115 i, o'seas
¶   Swiss Express - 4; ftm only.

Synchronised Swimming Coaches Association
■   Harold Fern House, Derby Square, LOUGHBOROUGH, Leics,
　　LE11 5AL.   (hq)
　　01509 618746
　　email istc@swimming.org.uk
　　http://www.swimming.org.uk
　　Admin: Jane Nickerson
○   *P, *S
　　no further information supplied

Synthetic Fibre Rug & Mat Association   (SFRMA)   1965
■   Kingsway House, Wrotham Rd, Meopham, GRAVESEND, Kent,
　　DA13 0AU.   (hsp)
▲   Un-incorporated Society
○   *T
●   Conf - Mtgs - Stat - Lib
M   5 f
¶   NL - 4;   AR; both ftm only.
×   2003 Synthetic Fibre Rug Manufacturers Association

Systematics Association   1937
NR   CABI Bioscience, Bakeham Lane, EGHAM, Surrey, TW20 9TY.
　　(hsb)
　　01491 829080
　　Sec: Dr Zofia Lawrence
▲   Registered Charity
○   *L; for the study of systematics (the classification of organisms)
　　in relation to general biology & evolution
●   Conf - Mtgs - ET - Inf
<   Inst of Biology (London)
M   300 i, UK / 250 i, o'seas
¶   NL - 3/4; free.   Proceedings of Symposia - 3/4.

T E Lawrence Society (TELS) 1985
- ■ PO Box 728, OXFORD, OX2 6YP.   (mail)
  - email info@telsociety.org
  - http://www.telsociety.org address
  - Sec: Ian Heritage,   Chmn: Jeremy Wilson
- ▲ Registered Charity
- Br 3; Japan, Netherlands, USA
- ○ *A; to promote interest & research into the life & works of
  T E Lawrence (Lawrence of Arabia), 1888-1935
- ● Conf - Mtgs - Res - Exhib - Inf - Lib - VE
- M 348 i, UK / 235 i, o'seas
- ¶ Jnl - 2; ftm, £8 nm.   NL - 4; ftm only.
  [subscription £7]

Table Soccer Players Association (TSPA) 1954
- ■ 68 Gresham Drive, Chadwell Heath, ROMFORD, RM6 4TS.
  (sp)
  - 020 8270 1028
  - email jeff.jordan1@ntlworld.com
  - Sec: Jeff Jordan
- Br 7 (regional)
- ○ *S; to play & promote 'subbuteo' (a type of table soccer) at
  national & international level
- Gp Subbuteo Collectors Club
- ● Conf - Mtgs - Exhib - Comp - VE - TV & radio work
- M 32 i
- ¶ The Bulletin - 12; ftm, 50p issue nm.
  Playing Rules Official Book - 1; ftm, £1.20 nm.
  National B&W Premier League Fixture Book - 1;
  LM;   Hbk; all ftm only.

Table Tennis Association of Wales (TTAW) 1921
- NR 7 Hopkins Close, Thornbury, BRISTOL, BS35 2PX.   (hsp)
  - 01454 417491
  - Sec: John Fraser
- ○ *S
- Gp Sub-c'ees: Coaching, Veteran, Selection, Umpires,
  Management, Computer ranking
- M i & org

Table Tennis Scotland
  the trading name of the **Scottish Table Tennis Association**

**Talking Newspaper Association of the United Kingdom
(TNAUK) 1974**
- ■ National Recording Centre, HEATHFIELD, E Sussex,
  TN21 8DB.   (hq)
  - 01435 866102   fax 01435 865422
  - email info@tnauk.org.uk   http://www.tnauk.org.uk
  - Chief Exec: Tim McDonald
- ▲ Registered Charity
- ○ *M, *W; to provide 230 national newspapers & magazines on
  tape, e mail, CD-ROM & bulletin board service to blind,
  visually impaired & disabled people
- ● Inf
- M c 11,500 i

Tall Persons Club GB & Ireland (TPC) 1991
- ■ The Richmond Business Centre, 23-24 George St, RICHMOND,
  Surrey, TW9 1HY.   (hq)
  - 0700 082 5512
  - email admin@tallclub.co.uk   http://www.tallclub.co.uk
  - The Director
- ▲ Company Limited by Guarantee
- Br Links with clubs in Europe & USA
- ○ *K; to provide information for & to promote the interests of
  those who are taller than average; includes practical,
  medical, psychological & social aspects
- Gp Little Big Ones (for tall children & their parents)
- ● Mtgs - ET - Stat - Inf - VE
- < Links with Tall Clubs in Europe & USA
- M 1,000 i
- ¶ 6 FT+ - 4; ftm.
  Tall Suppliers Directory - 2; ftm, £35 nm.

Talybont Welsh Sheep Society 2002
- ■ c/o Montague Harris & Co, 16 Ship St, BRECON,
  Brecknockshire, LD3 9AD.   (hsb)
  - 01874 623200
  - Sec: John A Lewis
- < Nat Sheep Assn
- M c 40

Talyllyn Railway Preservation Society (TRPS) 1950
- ■ Wharf Station, TYWYN, Merioneth, LL36 9EY.   (hq)
  - 01654 710472   fax 01654 711755
  - email secretary@talyllyn.co.uk
  - http://www.talyllyn.co.uk
  - Hon Sec: John S Robinson
- ▲ Un-incorporated Society
- Br 8
- ○ *G; operation of the Talyllyn Railway as an example of a
  steam-operated narrow-gauge railway built in the 19th
  century
- ● Mtgs - ET - Exhib - VE - Practical work on railway by volunteers
- > Talyllyn Holdings Ltd; Talyllyn Rly Co; Narrow Gauge Rly
  Museum Trust
- M 3,700 i, UK / 110 i, o'seas
- ¶ Talyllyn News - 4; ftm.   AR.

Tamworth Breeders Club
- ■ Boundary House, Gainsborough Rd, Girton, NEWARK, Notts,
  NG23 7HX.
  - 01522 778757
  - http://www.tamworthbreedersclub.co.uk
- ○ *B; Tamworth pigs

Tank Storage Association (TSA) 1978
- ■ Black Dog Farm, Waverton, CHESTER, Cheshire, CH3 7PB.
  (dir/p)
  - 01244 335627   fax 01244 332198
  - email tsa@tankstorage.org.uk
  - http://www.tankstorage.org.uk
  - Dir: Dr K H M Bray
- ▲ Company Limited by Guarantee
- ○ *T; to represent companies operating in the UK whose main
  business is the storage of bulk liquids for third parties
- ● Mtgs - LG
- < Fedn of Eur Tank Storage Assns (FETSA)
- M 13 f

Tapestry Frame Manufacturers Association (TFMA) 1991
- NR 81 Park View, Colins Rd, LONDON, N5 2UD.
- ○ *T
- ● Mtgs
- M 10 f
- ¶ In the Frame (NL) - 1.

© CBD Research Ltd · Beckenham · BR3 5JS · Tel 020 8650 7745 · Fax 020 8650 0768 · E-mail cbd@cbdresearch.com · www.cbdresearch.com

Tattoo Club of Great Britain   1975
- ■ 389 Cowley Rd, OXFORD, OX4 2BS.   (hq)
  01865 715253   fax 01865 775610
  email tcgb@tattoo.co.uk   http://www.tattoo.co.uk
  Pres: Lionel Titchener
- ○ *G; for tattoo artists & enthusiasts interested in furthering
  greater understanding of tattoo art
- Gp TCGB Engineering is the manufacturing division of tattooing
  equipment supplied to trade worldwide
- ● Mtgs - Res - Exhib
- < Brit Tattoo Artists Fedn
- M 2,500 i, UK / 1,500 i, o'seas
- ¶ Tattoo International - 6.

Taunton Chamber of Commerce
- NR PO Box 421, TAUNTON, Somerset, TA1 4WB.   (hq)
  01823 353353   fax 01823 353353
  email info@taunton-chamber.co.uk
  http://www.taunton-chamber.co.uk
  Exec Officer: M Stewart
- ○ *C
- ● Mtgs - Exhib - Inf - VE - LG - Promotional services
- < Brit Chams Comm; Bristol Cham Comm & Initiative
- M c 200 f
- ¶ Business News (Jnl) - 12; ftm only.

Taxpayers Alliance
- NR 1 Warwick Row, LONDON, SW1E 5ER.
  0845 330 9554
  email info@taxpayersalliance.com
  http://www.taxpayersalliance.com
  Chief Exec: Matthew Elliott
- ○ *K

Tay-Sachs & Allied Diseases Association
- NR c/o Dr Sybil Simon, Ward 2 1st floor, Booth Hall Children's
  Hospital, Charlestown Rd, MANCHESTER, M9 7AA.
  0161-918 5094
  email sybilsimon@cmmc.nhs.uk
  Dir: Dr Sybil Simon
- ○ *W

Tea Buying Brokers Association of London   (TBBA)
- ■ c/o Writer & Writer Ltd, Unit 15 Rich Industrial Estate,
  Crimscott St, LONDON, SE1 5TE.   (hsb)
  020 7232 2080
  Sec: Brian W Writer
- ▲ Un-incorporated Society
- ○ *T; for purchasers of tea in the London tea auctions
- < UK Tea Assn
- M 11 f

Teachers' Union of Ireland
- IRL 73 Orwell Rd, Rathgar, DUBLIN 6, Republic of Ireland.
  353 (1) 492 2588   fax 353 (1) 492 2953
  email tui@tui.ie   http://www.tui.ie
  Gen Sec: James Dorney

Teenage Magazine Arbitration Panel   (TMAP)
- ■ 28 Kingsway, LONDON, WC2B 6JR.   (hq)
  020 7405 0819   fax 020 7404 4167
  email info1@ppa.co.uk   http://www.tmap.org.uk
  Secretariat: D Thomas
- ▲ Un-incorporated Society
- ○ *T; 'the magazine industry's self-regulatory body which ensures
  that the sexual content of teenage magazines is presented in
  a responsible & appropriate manner; TMAP is the final
  arbiter on the interpretation of the TMAP Guidelines, which
  cover sexual matter in teenage magazines...'
- ● Mtgs - Res - Inf - LG
- M 7 i
- ¶ Guidelines;   Research Report;   Complaints (flyer);
  AR; all free.

Teeswater Sheep Breeders' Association Ltd   (TSBA)   1949
- ■ Wodencroft, Cotherstone, BARNARD CASTLE, Co Durham,
  DL12 9UQ.   (hq)
  01833 650032
  Sec: Mrs M S Braithwaite
- ▲ Company Limited by Guarantee
- ○ *B; registration of pedigrees & promotion of Teeswater sheep
- ● Mtgs - Exhib - Recording lambs for the Flock Book
- M 80 i
- ¶ Flock Book - 1; ftm.

Telecare Services Association   (TSA)   1994
- NR 10 Railway St, CHATHAM, Kent, ME4 4JL.   (hq)
  01634 846209
  The Secretary
- ▲ Company Limited by Guarantee
- ○ *T; to set standards for providers; to improve the available
  hardware & software
- Gp Technical; Education; Training
- ● Conf - Mtgs - ET - Exhib - Stat - LG
- M 126 f
- ¶ NL - 8; ftm only.
- × 2005 Association of Social Alarms Providers

Telecommunications Heritage Group   (THG)   1987
- ■ PO Box 561, SOUTH CROYDON, Surrey, CR2 6YL.   (hsp)
  0870 321 2887   fax 0870 321 2889
  email membership@thg.org.uk   http://www.thg.org.uk
  Mem Sec: Alex Clark
- ▲ Un-incorporated Society
- ○ *L; to promote the study & preservation of telephone &
  telegraph apparatus & related literature
- ● Mtgs - ET - Res - Exhib - SG - Inf - Lib - VE
- M 450 i
- ¶ THG Jnl - 2;   THG News - 4; both ftm only.

Telecommunications Industry Association   (TIA)   1984
- NR Douglas House, 32-34 Simpson Rd, Fenny Stratford, Bletchley,
  MILTON KEYNES, Bucks, MK1 1BA.   (hq)
  01908 645000
  http://www.tia.org.uk
  Dir Gen: Alan P Cobb
- ▲ Company Limited by Guarantee
- ○ *T; for the telecommunications industry in GB; with particular
  focus on the voice, data networking, computer-
  telephony (CT), local area networking (LAN) & building
  structured cable sectors
- M c 300 f, 1 org

Telecommunications & Internet Federation   3
- IRL Confederation House, 84-86 Lower Baggot St, DUBLIN 2,
  Republic of Ireland.
  353 (1) 660 1011   fax 353 (1) 660 1717
  Dir: Tommy McCabe
- ○ *T
- < IBEC

**Telecommunications United Kingdom Fraud Forum Ltd
(TUFF)   2000**
- NR PO Box 28353, LONDON, SE20 7WJ.   (hq)
  020 8778 9864   fax 020 8659 9561
  email tuff@tuff.co.uk   http://www.tuff.co.uk
  Chief Exec: Jack Wraith
- ▲ Company Limited by Guarantee
- ○ *G, *T; to provide a forum for the exchange of information
  between telecom companies in respect to fraud & crime; to
  provide training for the telecom professional
- Gp Communications & operations; Training; Technical research &
  programs; Premium rate services
- ● Mtgs - ET - Exam - Res - SG - Inf - LG
- < Ir Telecommunications Fraud Forum
- M 150 i, 45 f, 5 org
- ¶ The Jnl - 2; ftm only.   In the Frame (NL) - 5; free.

Telecommunications Users' Association (Independent Association of Telecommunications Users' Ltd) (TUA) 1965
- ■ 57 London Rd, ENFIELD, Middx, EN2 6SW. (hq)
  0870 220 2071
  email tua@dial.pipex.com   http://www.tua.co.uk
  Chief Exec: Bill Mieran,   Sec: John Baylis
- ▲ Company Limited by Guarantee
- ○ *T; support & information for corporate companies in telecommunications
- Gp Research; Training; Consultancy; Workshops; Seminars; Publications; Members' helpline; Call management representation
- ● Conf - ET - Res - Exhib - Inf - LG
- M c 1,000 f
- ¶ In Focus - 4; ftm, £100 yr nm.
  Factline - 12; ftm, £250 yr nm.

Telephone Helplines Association (THA) 1996
- NR 9 Marshalsea Rd, LONDON, SE1 1EP. (hq)
  0845 120 3767
  Dir: Kathy Mulville
- ▲ Company Limited by Guarantee; Registered Charity
- Br 1
- ○ *K, *W; 'promotion & support for the provision of quality helpline services'
- ● Conf - Mtgs - ET - Res - LG - Provide range of benefits for members
- < Nat Coun Voluntary Orgs; NI Coun Voluntary Orgs; Scot Coun Voluntary Orgs; Wales Coun Voluntary Orgs
- M c 450 helplines
- ¶ Exchange - 3.   Telephone Helplines Directory - 1.
  Telephone Helplines 'Guides for Good Practice'.
  Quality Standard Workbook.

Television & Radio Industries Club (TRIC) 1931
- NR Drake House, 2 Duckling Lane, SAWBRIDGEWORTH, Herts, CM21 9QA. (hq)
  01279 721100
  email info@tric.org.uk
  Sec: George Stone
- ○ *P
  no further information supplied

Telework Association (TA) 1993
- NR Dodd Meadow, Wallingford Rd, KINGSBRIDGE, Devon, TQ7 1NF. (hq)
  024 7669 6986   fax 024 7669 6538
  email enquiries@telework.org.uk
  http://www.telework.org.uk
  Exec Dir: Alan Denbigh
- ▲ Company Limited by Guarantee
- ○ *G; the use of information technology (IT) & telecommunications for the development of local (particularly rural) economies, incl the use of shared facilities in local centres (telecottages); for telecottages (telecentres) & teleworkers (people who work from home)
- ● Conf - Res - Inf & advice line - Networking with mem
- M 2,000 i, 100 f, UK / 100 i, 20 f, o'seas
- ¶ Teleworker (Jnl) - 6; £34.50 yr.
  Teleworking Handbook - 1; £16.
  Note: The Telework Association is the trading name of the Telecottage Association
- ✕ 2002 Telework, Telecottage & Telecentre Association

Telework, Telecottage & Telecentre Association
  since 2002 **Telework Association**

Ten Sixty Six (1066) Enterprise   1993
- NR Summerfields Business Centre, Bohemia Rd, HASTINGS, E Sussex, TN34 1EX. (hq)
  01424 205511
  Mgr: Linda Williams
- ▲ Company Limited by Guarantee
- ○ *C
- ● Mtgs - ET - Inf - Business support services
- < Sussex Enterprise
- M 175 f
  Note: Ten Sixty Six Enterprise is the Hastings & St Leonards Chamber of Commerce

Tenant Farmers' Association Ltd   (TFA)   1981
- ■ 5 Brewery Court, Theale, READING, Berks, RG7 5AJ. (hq)
  0118-930 6130   fax 0118-930 3424
  email tfa@tenant-farmers.org.uk   http://www.tfa.org.uk
  Chief Exec: George Dunn
- ▲ Company Limited by Guarantee
- Br 9
- ○ *F
- Gp Listed land agents; Professional legal advice
- ● Conf - Mtgs - Exhib - Stat - Inf - VE - LG
- M c 4,000 i
- ¶ TFA News Sheet - 6;   Briefing Notes - 52;
  Information Sheets - irreg;   all ftm only.

Tenants & Residents Organisations of England   (TAROE)   1997
- ■ 41-42 Estate Buildings, Railway St, HUDDERSFIELD, W Yorks, HD1 1JY. (hsb)
  01484 223466   fax 01484 223478
  email gen@kftra.demon.co.uk   http://www.taroe.org
  Sec: Cora Carter
- ▲ Company Limited by Guarantee
- ○ *N; the representative body of tenants & residents groups, associations & federations in England relating to housing
- ● Conf - Mtgs - Inf - Lib - Support for tenants
- < Intl U of Tenants
- M 10 i, 90 org

Tennis & Rackets Association   (TandRA)   1907
- NR The Queen's Club, Palliser Rd, West Kensington, LONDON, W14 9EQ. (hq)
  020 7386 3447
  http://www.tennisandrackets.com
  Chief Exec & Sec: James D Wyatt,   Chmn: P G Mallinson
- ○ *S; to act as the national governing body in Great Britain in all matters connected with the games of real tennis & rackets
- Gp Rackets; 'Real' tennis

Tennis Scotland   1895
- ■ 177 Colinton Rd, EDINBURGH, EH14 1BZ. (hq)
  0131-444 1984   fax 0131-444 1973
  http://www.tennisscotland.org
  Chief Exec: James Campbell
- ▲ Registered Charity
- ○ *S; controlling body of the game in Scotland
- ● Mtgs - ET - Comp
- < Lawn Tennis Assn
- M 9 district org
- ¶ Scottish Tennis - 4/6; free.

Tennis Wales
- NR Welsh National Tennis Centre, Ocean Way, Ocean Park, CARDIFF, Glam, CF24 5HF. (hq)
  029 2046 3335
  email info@tenniswales.org.uk
  Exec Dir: Peter Hybart
- ○ *S; to promote & develop tennis in Wales
- ● Mtgs - ET - Exam - Comp - Coaching
- < Lawn Tennis Assn
- M 85 clubs

Tennyson Society   1960
■   Tennyson Research Centre, Central Library, Free School Lane, LINCOLN, LN2 1EZ.   (hsb)
01522 552862   fax 01522 552858
email linnet@lincolnshire.gov.uk
http://www.tennysonsociety.org.uk
Hon Sec: Miss K Jefferson
▲   Registered Charity
Br   USA
○   *A, *L; life & work of Alfred, Lord Tennyson
●   Conf - Mtgs - Exhib - Res - Inf - Lib - VE
<   City University, New York (Victorian C'ee)
M   150 i, 20 universities & academic bodies, UK / 200 i, 130 universities, o'seas
¶   Tennyson Research Bulletin - 1; ftm.   AR.
Monographs & Occasional Papers (2 series) - 1; ftm.
Tape recordings & gramophone records.

Tenpin Bowling Proprietors Association of Great Britain (TBPA)   1966
NR   Pen-y-Banc Farm, RHAYADER, Radnorshire, LD6 5NY.   (sp)
01597 810523   fax 01597 810870
email ghcpyb@zetnet.co.uk   http://www.gotenpin.co.uk
Gen Sec: Gordon H Caie
▲   Un-incorporated Society
○   *S, *T; to promote & develop tenpin bowling; to ensure that members accept international standards of the sport
●   Mtgs - Comp - PL - LG
M   35 f, 100 centres

Tenterden Railway Co Ltd
since 2004 **Kent & East Sussex Railway Co Ltd**

Tertiary Research Group   (TRG)   1969
NR   81 Crofton Lane, ORPINGTON, Kent, BR5 1HB.   (hsp)
01689 871565
Hon Sec: David Ward
○   *L; for those interested in geology, palaeontology, stratigraphy

Test Card Circle   (TTCC)   1989
■   20 Seymour Rd, STOURBRIDGE, W Midlands, DY9 8TB.   (sp)
01384 351033
Sec: Paul Sawtell
○   *G; researching & archiving non-needletime music (ie that NOT available to the public) specifically used on TV trade test transmissions; Researching & archiving slide/photographs & other visual material (test cards, captions etc) & engineering test films shown throughout trade test periods; study of musical & technical aspects relevant 1947-1983
●   Conf - Mtgs - Res - Comp - SG - Inf - Lib
M   200 i
¶   The Test Card Circle - 4; ftm only.

Teston Independent Society of Cricket Ball Makers
has closed

Textile Finishers' Association   (TFA)   1989
■   Merrydale House, Roysdale Way, BRADFORD, W Yorks, BD4 6SB.   (hq)
01274 683745   fax 01274 682293
email info@cbwt.co.uk
Sec: John Lambert
▲   Company Limited by Guarantee
○   *T
●   Mtgs - Inf - LG
<   BATC; Eur Textile Finishing Assn
M   30 f

Textile Institute International   1910
■   St James's Buildings (1st floor), Oxford St, MANCHESTER, M1 6FQ.   (Intl)
0161-237 1188   fax 0161-236 1991
email tiihq@textileinst.org.uk
http://www.textileinstitute.org hq
Hon Sec: David Wooliscroft
▲   Registered Charity
Br   2; 7 worldwide
○   *L, *P; for people involved in the textile, clothing & footwear industries worldwide
Gp   Design & product marketing; Finishing; Fibre Science; Industrial; Engineering & technical; Textiles; Knitting; Marketing; Narrow fabrics; Quality; Floorcoverings; Weaving; Yarn; Management & economics; Human resources; Young members
●   Conf - Mtgs - Res - Exhib - Comp - SG - Stat - Inf - Lib - VE - LG
M   1,601 i, 48 f UK / 1,495 i, 51 f, o'seas
¶   Journal of the Textile Institute - 6; £60 m, £99 nm.
Textile Progress - 4; c £30 m, £45 nm.
Textiles Magazine - 4; ftm, £45 nm.
TI News (NL) - 4;   Membership Directory - 1;
LM (web-based) - continuous;   AR; all ftm only.

Textile Recycling Association   (TRA)   1913
■   PO Box 965, MAIDSTONE, Kent, ME17 3WD.   (sp)
0845 600 8276   fax 0845 600 8276
email info@textile-recycling.org.uk
http://www.textile-recycling.org.uk
Nat Liaison Mgr: Alan Wheeler
○   *T; interests of persons trading in discarded textiles
Gp   Recyclatex (bonded textile recycling scheme)
●   Conf - Mtgs - Inf - LG
<   Bureau of Intl Recycling
M   45 f, UK / 4 f, o'seas
¶   Bulletins; m only.   LM;   AR; both free.
Recyclatex leaflet for local authorities.
Recyclatex booklet for schools.

Textile Services Association   (TSA)   1886
NR   7 Churchill Court, 58 Station Rd, NORTH HARROW, Middx, HA2 7SA.   (hq)
020 8863 7755
email tsa@tsa-uk.org
Chief Exec: Murray Simpson
▲   Company Limited by Guarantee
○   *T; for the drycleaning, laundry & textile rental industry
M   i & f

Textile Society: for the study of art, design & history   1981
■   8 Hillside, Denby Dale, HUDDERSFIELD, W Yorks, HD8 8QZ.   (hsp)
http://www.textilesociety.org.uk
Hon Sec: Katina Bill
▲   Registered Charity
○   *A; to unite scholars, designers, teachers, practitioners, artists, collectors & others who share an interest in the study of textile art, design & history
Gp   Collectors (advice on private collections)
●   Conf - Mtgs - SG - VE - Annual Antique Textile Fair
M   345 i, 64 universities & museums, UK / 25 i, o'seas
¶   Text (Jnl) - 1; ftm, £5 nm.   AR; ftm.

Thalidomide Society Ltd   1963
Coordinator: Vivien Kerr
▲   Company Limited by Guarantee; Registered Charity
○   *W; to provide support & information to thalidomide & similarly impaired people
●   Mtgs - Inf
M   300 i
¶   NL - 2; ftm, £10 nm.
Note: contact by telephone or email only.

Thames Boating Trades Association (TBTA) 1993
NR 51 New Rd, BOURNE END, Bucks, SL8 5BT. (hsp)
01628 524376
Hon Sec: P Wagstaff
▲ Un-incorporated Society
○ *T; to liaise with the British Marine Federation & with members; the area covered is from the source of the Thames to the Barrier (approx 15 miles from each bank)
● Mtgs - ET
M 182 i, 182 f
¶ Boatyards, Marinas & Services around the River Thames - 2 yrly; free.

Thames & Chilterns Vineyards' Association (T&CVA) 1988
NR c/o Brightwell Vineyard, Rush Court, WALLINGFORD, Oxon, OX10 8LJ. (hsp)
01491 836586
Chmn: Bob Nielsen
▲ Un-incorporated Society
○ *T; to promote public interest in & knowledge of the wines of the region; membership is open to people associated with the industry
Gp Commercial vineyards; Amateur growers
● Conf - Mtgs - ET - Exhib - Comp - SG - Inf - VE - LG - Wine Challenge (annual)
M c 100 i, 25 f
¶ NL - 4;   AR; both ftm only.

Thames Hire Cruiser Association
a group of the **British Marine Federation**

Thames Valley Chamber of Commerce & Industry (TVCCi) 1993
NR 467 Malton Ave, SLOUGH, Berks, SL1 3SB. (hq)
01753 870500
Chief Exec: Paul Briggs
▲ Company Limited by Guarantee
Br 8
○ *C
Gp Branch Chams Comm at: Aylesbury, Bracknell, Heathrow, High Wycombe, Newbury, Oxford, Reading, Wokingham
● Conf - Mtgs - ET - Exhib - Stat - Expt - Inf - Lib - LG
< Brit Chams Comm
M c 2,500 f
¶ Business Jnl - 6.   CCi News - 12. Directory - 1.

Thanet & East Kent Chamber Ltd
NR Kent Innovation Centre, BROADSTAIRS, Kent, CT10 2QQ.
01843 609289   fax 01843 609291
http://www.tekc.co.uk
Admin: Kay Tift
○ *C

The . . .
Except for 3 exceptions the word **The** has not been used to start any organisation's title; this controls the left-hand margin of the text & puts the emphasis on the first noun of the title.

Theosophical Society in England (TS) 1888
NR 50 Gloucester Place, LONDON, W1U 8EA. (hq)
020 7935 9261
Nat Pres: Colin Price
○ *L; to form a nucleus of the universal brotherhood of humanity without distinction of race, creed, sex, caste or colour; to encourage study of comparative religion, philosophy & science; investigation of unexplained laws of nature & the powers latent in man
M i
Note: is a section of the International Theosophical Society (1875), Adyar, Madras 20, India.

Thermal Insulation Contractors Association (TICA) 1957
NR TICA House, Allington Way, Yarm Road Business Park, DARLINGTON, Co Durham, DL1 4QB. (hq)
01325 466704   fax 01325 487691
email enquiries@tica-acad.co.uk
http://www.tica-acad.co.uk
Chief Exec: Ralph Bradley
▲ Company Limited by Guarantee
○ *T; for companies involved in industrial thermal insulation & asbestos removal
Gp ACAD - Asbestos control & abatement division; IETA - Insulation & environmental training agency
● Conf - Mtgs - ET - Inf - Empl - LG
< Wld Insulation & Acoustics Congress Org (WIACO); Fédn Eur des Syndicats d'Entreprises d'Isolation (FESI)
M 220 f, UK / 2 f, o'seas
¶ ACADdemy (asbestos removal) - 4; ftm, on application nm.
FESI - European Insulation Standards; on application.
Health & Safety Handbook for Operatives.
Man-made Mineral Fibre (1990 IOM Report).

Thermal Insulation Manufacturers & Suppliers Association (TIMSA) 1978
■ 99 West St, FARNHAM, Surrey, GU9 7EN. (asa)
01252 739154   fax 01252 739140
email info@associationhouse.org.uk
http://www.timsa.org.uk
Sec: J G Fairley
○ *T; to improve standards of thermal insulation contributing to energy conservation & fuel efficiency
Gp Building insulation; Technical; Publicity; Acoustics
● Mtgs - LG
< Thermal Insulation Contractors Assn
M 18 i, 4 i (associates)
¶ Insulation (Jnl) - 6.   Hbk & Directory - 3; free.

Thermal Spraying & Surface Engineering Association (TSSEA) 1984
NR 38 Lawford Lane, Bilton, RUGBY, Warks, CV22 7JP. (hq)
0870 760 5203   fax 0870 760 5206
email info@tssea.org   http://www.tssea.co.uk
Sec: Ivor H Hoff
▲ Company Limited by Guarantee
○ *T; to promote the use & development of thermal (metal) spraying techniques used 1: to provide corrosion resistant coatings to structural steelwork, 2: to confer specific surface properties (wear/corrosion resistance, thermal protection, restore size)
Gp Health & safety; Euro-international standards
● Conf - Mtgs - ET - Exhib - SG - Inf - LG
< Inst of Materials
M 10 i, 75 f, 2 org, UK / 10 f, 1 org, o'seas
¶ Coatings (NL) - 4; free.

Thermostatic Mixing Valves Association
as part of BEAMA Energy is a group of **BEAMA**

Thimble Society of London 1981
■ 1 Cathcart St, LONDON, NW5 3BL. (hq)
020 7419 9562
Sec: Bridget McConnel
○ *G; collection of antique sewing articles & thimbles
● Conf - Mtgs - Res - Inf
M 600 i, UK / 100 i, o'seas
¶ Magazine - 3.

© CBD Research Ltd · Beckenham · BR3 5JS · Tel 020 8650 7745 · Fax 020 8650 0768 · E-mail cbd@cbdresearch.com · www.cbdresearch.com

Thomas Hardy Society Ltd   1968
- ■ PO Box 1438, DORCHESTER, Dorset, DT1 1YH.
     (accom/address)
     01305 251501   fax 01305 251501
     email info@hardysociety.org.
     http://www.hardysociety.org
     Sec: Mike Nixon,   Chmn: Prof Michael Irwin
- ▲ Company Limited by Guarantee; Registered Charity
- ○ *A; promotion, study & appreciation of the works of Thomas
     Hardy
- ● Conf - Mtgs - Res
- M 800 i, UK / 400 i, o'seas; universities, UK & o'seas
- ¶ The Thomas Hardy Jnl - 3; ftm, £4 nm.

Thomas Lovell Beddoes Society   1994
- ■ 9 Amber Court, BELPER, Derbys, DE56 1HG.   (chmn/p)
     01773 828066   fax 01773 828066
     email john@beddoes.demon.co.uk
     http://www.beddoes.org + tlbeddoes.org
     Sec: Christine Hunkinson
- ▲ Registered Charity
- ○ *A; to promote interest in the life & work of the poet Thomas
     Lovell Beddoes (1803-1849)
- Gp the study of Maria Edgeworth
- ● Conf - Mtgs - Res - Exhib - VE
- < Alliance of Literary Societies
- > Walter Savage Landor Soc
- M 70 i, 5 f, UK / 10 i, o'seas
- ¶ NL - 1; ftm, £4.50 nm.

Thomas Merton Society of Great Britain & Ireland   (TMS-GBI)   1993
- NR 9 Springfield Rd, LEICESTER, LE2 3BB.   (hsp)
      http://www.thomasmertonsociety.org
      Sec: David White
- ▲ Un-incorporated Society
- ○ *A; to encourage the study of the life & works of Thomas
     Merton (1915-1968) poet, monk & prophet
- ● Conf - Mtgs - Res - Inf - Lib
- < Intl Thomas Merton Soc (USA)
- M 300 i
- ¶ The Merton Jnl - 2; ftm, £4 nm.
     Conference Papers - 2 yrly; £12.99 m.

Thoresby Society   1889
- NR 23 Clarendon Rd, LEEDS, W Yorks, LS2 9NZ.   (hq)
      0113-247 0704
      http://www.thoresby.org.uk
- ▲ Registered Charity
- ○ *L; history of Leeds & its neighbourhood
- ● Mtgs - Lib - VE - Publishing
- M 461 i, 54 libraries, UK / 6 i, 42 libraries, o'seas
- ¶ Annual Volume; ftm, price on application nm.

Thoroton Society of Nottinghamshire   1897
- ■ Little Dower House, Station Rd, BLEASBY, Notts, NG14 7FX.
     (hsp)
     01636 830284
     email bjcast@aol.com   http://www.thorotonsociety.org.uk
     Hon Sec: Barbara Cast
- ▲ Registered Charity
- ○ *L; to promote & foster study of the history, archaeology &
     antiquities of Nottinghamshire
- Gp Record; Archaeological
- ● Mtgs - Res - VE
- M c 500 i
- ¶ NL - 4;   Transactions - 1;   AR - 1; Record Series; all ftm.

Thoroughbred Breeders' Association   (TBA)   1917
- NR Stanstead House, The Avenue, NEWMARKET, Suffolk,
      CB8 9AA.   (hq)
      01638 661321
      Exec Dir: Gavin Pritchard-Gordon
      Chief Exec: Louise Kemble
- ▲ Registered Charity
- ○ *B; the science of maintaining the thoroughbred horse in Great
     Britain
- Gp Equine Fertility Unit; National Stud Staff Training Scheme
- ● Mtgs - ET - Res - Expt - Inf - Lib - VE - LG - Prizes & awards
- < Eur Breeders' Fund; a member of the Brit Horse Ind Confedn
- M 2,400 i, UK / 400 i, o'seas
- ¶ Pacemaker - 12.   Sires - 1.   Thoroughbred Breeder - 12.

Three Counties Agricultural Society   (TCAS)   1797
- ■ The Showground, MALVERN, Worcs, WR13 6NW.   (hq)
     01684 584900
- ▲ Company limited by Guarantee
- ○ *F, *H; promotion of agriculture & horticulture in the shires of
     Gloucester, Hereford & Worcester
- Gp C'ees: Livestock, Flower, Dog Show
- ● Conf - Mtgs - ET - Exhib - Comp - Shows
- M c 5,500 i & f
- ¶ Members' News;   AR; both ftm.

Three Counties Cider & Perry Association   (3CCPA)   1993
- ■ Gregg's Pit, Much Marcle, LEDBURY, Herefords, HR8 2NL.
     (hsp)
     01521 660687
     email hmwoodman@beer.com
     http://www.thethreecountiesciderandperryassociation.co.uk
     Hon Sec: Helen Woodman
- ▲ Un-incorporated Society
- ○ *T; for top quality cider & perry makers
- ● Mtgs - ET - Comp - VE
- < Nat Assn of Cider Makers (NACM)
- M c 80 i, f & org
- ¶ NL - 4;   Technical Bulletin - 1;   LM - 1; all ftm only.

THRIVE   1978
- NR Geoffrey Udall Centre, Trunkwell Park, Beech Hill, READING,
      RG7 2AT.   (hq)
      0118-988 5688   fax 0118-988 5677
      email info@thrive.org.uk   http://www.thrive.org.uk
      Chief Exec: Nicola Carruthers
- ▲ Company Limited by Guarantee; Registered Charity
- Br 4 gardens
- ○ *W; to promote the use of horticulture & gardening in therapy,
     rehabilitation, vocational training, leisure & employment for
     all disabled people (includes people with mental health
     problems, sensory, physical or learning disabilities)
- Gp Service for projects; Training service; Full-time volunteers;
     Garden advisory service; Advisory committee of blind
     gardeners
- ● ET - Exam - Res - Inf - Lib - PL
- < R Horticl Soc
- M 800 i, 40 org, UK / 120 i, o'seas
- ¶ Growth Point - 4; ftm, £10 nm.
     Come Gardening (braille & tape only) - 4; £5 m only.
     Leaflets; prices vary.

Thyroid Eye Disease Charitable Trust   (TEDct)   1990
NR   PO Box 2954, CALNE, Wilts, SN11 8WR.   (hq)
       0844 800 8133
       email ted@tedct.co.uk   http://www.tedct.co.uk
       Contact: Margaret Russell
▲   Registered Charity
Br   13 support groups
○   *M, *W; to provide information, care & support to those
       affected by the disease; to promote better awareness of the
       condition amongst the medical profession & the general
       public
Gp   Medical helpline of consultants
●   Conf - ET - Res - Inf
<   Thyroid Fedn Intl; Brit Thyroid Assn
M   c 700 i
¶   NL - 4; free.
✕   2003 (April) Thyroid Eye Disease Association

TIGA: the Independent Games Developers Association   (TIGA)
■   Brighton Business Centre, 95 Ditchling Rd, BRIGHTON,
       E Sussex, BN1 4ST.
       01273 605053
       Chief Exec: Fred Hasson
○   *T; for the computer games industry
M   97 i

Tile Association   (TTA)   2000
NR   83 Copers Cope Rd, BECKENHAM, Kent, BR3 1NR.   (hq)
       020 8663 0946   fax 020 8663 0949
       email info@tiles.org.uk   http://www.tiles.org.uk
       Exec Officer: Mrs Lesley Reid
▲   Company Limited by Guarantee
○   *T; to represent manufacturers, suppliers & tiling contractors in
       the UK wall & floor tile industry
Gp   Tile adhesive & accessory mfrs; Distributors, retailers & agents
       of wall & floor tiles; Tiling contractors
●   Conf - Mtgs - Exam - Inf - Empl - LG
<   Ceram-Unie; CET; EUF
M   430 f

**Tiles & Architectural Ceramics Society   (Tile Society)   (TACS)
1981**
■   Oakhurst, Cocknage Rd, Rough Close, STOKE-ON-TRENT,
       ST3 7NN.   (mail/address)
       01782 397996
       http://www.tilesoc.org.uk
       Sec: Kath Adams
▲   Registered Charity
○   *G, *L; the national society responsible for the study &
       protection of tile & architectural ceramics
●   Conf - Res - Exhib - SG - Inf - VE - Tile location index
M   c 420 i, f & org
¶   Jnl - 2;   Glazed Expressions - 2;   NL - 4;   all ftm,
       charged to nm.
       Tour Notes.   Tile Bibliography - up-dated.

Tilling Society
       wound up

Timber Arbitrators Association   (TAA)
NR   26-27 Oxendon St, LONDON, SW1Y 4EL.   (hq)
       020 7839 1891   fax 020 7930 0094
○   *P
<   a division of the Timber Trade Federation
M   11 i

Timber Brick Council
       merged in January 2002 with the Timber Frame Industry Association
       to form the **United Kingdom Timber Frame Association**

Timber Decking Association Ltd   (TDA)   1999
■   5 Flemming Court, CASTLEFORD, W Yorks, WF10 5HW.   (hq)
       01977 558147
       email info@tda.org.uk   http://www.tda.org.uk
       Dir: Steve Young
▲   Company Limited by Guarantee
○   *T; technical & advice organisation established to set standards
       for the quality of materials & installation good practice in the
       UK; operates 'Deckmark'- a quality assurance scheme for
       products & contractors involved in timber deck design &
       construction
Gp   Manufacturing; Preservatives & coating; Design installation;
       Forestry & sawmilling
●   ET - Stat - PL - LG - Promotion of standards
<   Wood Protection Assn
M   43 f, 3 org, UK / 3 f , o'seas
¶   The Timber Decking Manual; ftm, £32 nm.
       An Introduction to Creating Quality Decks; free.
       Parapet Design; ftm, £5 nm.
       Statutory Regulations; free.
       Decking - the essential guide for DIY; £5.99.

Timber Frame Industry Association
       merged in January 2002 with the Timber Brick Council to become the
       United Kingdom Timber Frame Association

Timber Growers Association Ltd
       2002 merged with the Association of Professional Foresters to form
       the **Association of Timber Growers & Forestry Professionals**

Timber Packaging & Pallet Confederation   (TIMCON)   1940
NR   840 Melton Rd, Thurmaston, LEICESTER, LE4 8BN.   (hq)
       0116-264 0579   fax 0116-264 0141
       email timcon@associationhq.org.uk
       http://www.timcon.org
       Exec Sec: Miss Sharon Hutchinson
▲   Company Limited by Guarantee
○   *T; to represent the timber packaging industry
●   Conf - Mtgs - ET - Exhib - Stat - Inf
<   Eur Fedn of Wooden Pallet & Packaging Mfrs (FEFPEB); Brit Nat
       C'ee for EPAL - Eur Pallet Assn)(BREPAL)
M   110 f, UK / 20 f, o'seas

Timber Research & Development Association
       the association still exists but all activities are carried out through
       TRADA Technology Ltd

Timber Trade Federation   (TTF)   1893
NR   26-27 Oxendon St, LONDON, SW1Y 4EL.   (hq)
       020 7839 1891   fax 020 7930 0094
       email ttf@ttf.co.uk   http://www.ttf.co.uk
○   *T; imported timber trade
Gp   Divisions: National softwood; Hardwood & panel products
M   c 500 f
✕   2002 (National Association for Softwood
              (National Hardwood Association
              (National Panel Products Association

Time Haiku   1994
■   Basho-an, 105 King's Head Hill, LONDON, E4 7JG.   (hsp)
       Sec: Erica Facey
○   *A; to promote haiku & haiku related forms (Japanese poetry &
       prose)
●   ET - SG - Inf
M   c 500 i, c 50 f, UK / c 500i, c 50 f, o'seas
¶   Time Haiku - 2; ftm.

© CBD Research Ltd · Beckenham · BR3 5JS · Tel 020 8650 7745 · Fax 020 8650 0768 · E-mail cbd@cbdresearch.com · www.cbdresearch.com

Timeshare Consumers Association   1997
- ■   Hodsock, WORKSOP, Notts, S81 0TF.   (hq)
      01909 591100   fax 01909 591338
      email info@timeshare.org.uk
      http://www.timeshare.org.uk
      Chmn: Sandy Grey
- ○   *G
      No further information supplied

Tissue Viability Society   1981
- NR   1 Lancaster Place, LONDON, WC2E 7HR.   (hq)
      020 7240 1353
      email tvs@dial.pipex.com   http://www.tvs.org.uk
- ▲   Registered Charity
- ○   *L, *M; promotion of good practice in the care & maintenance
      of the human skin, particularly with regard to pressure sores,
      leg ulcers & wound management
- ●   Conf - Mtgs - ET - Res - Exhib - SG - Inf
- M   1,200 i, 100 f, 110 libraries, UK / 50 i, 20 f, o'seas
- ¶   Jnl of Tissue Viability - 4; ftm.

Toastmasters of England   1971
- ■   12 Little Bornes, Dulwich, LONDON, SE21 8SE.   (pres/b)
      020 8670 5585
      http://www.ivorspencer.com
      Pres: Ivor Spencer
- ▲   Un-incorporated Society
- ○   *T; to organise & arrange authentic banquets with traditional
      ceremonies here & abroad; to act as promotional advisers to
      firms of repute; to engage only members of the Guild of
      International Professional Toastmasters for special
      engagements in the USA, Canada, Japan, New Zealand, &
      Australia
- ●   Conf - Mtgs - Expt - VE
- <   Gld Intl Profl Toastmasters
- M   20 i

Toastmasters of Great Britain   1970
- ■   12 Little Bornes, Dulwich, LONDON, SE21 8SE.   (hq)
      020 8670 5585
      http://www.ivorspencer.com
      Pres: Ivor Spencer
- ▲   Un-incorporated Society
- ○   *T; to act as advisers to firms of repute; to promote for them
      special traditional banquets with authentic ceremonies in
      Europe (incl Ireland).
      The only toastmasters engaged are from the Guild of
      International Professional Toastmasters
- ●   Conf - Mtgs - Expt - VE
- <   Gld Intl Profl Toastmasters
- M   20 i

Toastmasters for Royal Occasions   1970
- ■   12 Little Bornes, Dulwich, LONDON, SE21 8SE.   (pres/b)
      020 8670 5585
      http://www.ivorspencer.com
      Pres: Ivor Spencer
- ▲   Un-incorporated Society
- ○   *T; officiation as toastmasters in this country & abroad on Royal
      & State occasions
- ●   Conf - Mtgs - SG - Expt - VE
- <   Gld Intl Profl Toastmasters
- M   20 i

Tobacco Alliance   1984
- ■   12 Berghem Mews, Blythe Rd, LONDON, W14 0HN.   (hq)
      0800 008282
      http://www.tobaccoalliance.org.uk
      Nat Spokeswoman: Audrey Wales
- ○   *K; to raise awareness of the issue of tobacco smuggling & the
      detrimental effects this has on independent retailers
- ●   Conf - Mtgs - Res - VE - LG
- M   17,000 i

Tobacco Industry Employers' Association   (TIEA)
- ■   Astwick House, Croughton, BRACKLEY, Northants,
      NN13 5LL.   (hq)
      01869 811400   fax 01869 811311
      email tiea93@hotmail.com
      Mgr & Sec: John L Hadley
- ○   *T
- ●   Mtgs - ET - SG - Employee relations - Safety & health
- M   4 f

Tobacco Manufacturers' Association   (TMA)   1940
- ■   Burwood House (5th floor), 14-16 Caxton St, LONDON,
      SW1H 0ZB.   (hq)
      020 7544 0100   fax 020 7544 0117
      http://www.the-tma.org.uk
      Chief Exec: Tim Lord
- ▲   Un-incorporated Society
- ○   *T; for companies manufacturing tobacco products in the UK
- ●   Mtgs - Inf - LG
- <   Confedn of the Eur Community's Cigarette Mfrs (CECCM)
- M   5 f

Toc H   (TocH)   1915
- ■   Toc H Central Services, The Stable Block, The Firs, High St,
      WHITCHURCH, Bucks, HP22 4JU.   (hq)
      01296 642020 & 640011   fax 01296 640022
      email info@toch.org.uk   http://www.toch.org.uk
      Dir: Geoffrey Smith
- ▲   Registered Charity
- ○   *W; to break down barriers by challenging both individuals'
      preconceptions of others & the divisions which exist in society,
      with the aim of creating a more tolerant, more harmonious,
      less prejudiced society
- Gp   Friendship circles; Families & people under pressure scheme
- ●   Mtgs - Community projects
- M   3,032 i
- ¶   Point 3 - 5; £5 yr nm.   Annual Review; free.
      Annual Events Brochure; free.

Together: working for wellbeing   1879
- ■   Lincoln House (1st floor), 296-302 High Holborn, LONDON,
      WC1V 7JH.   (hq)
      020 7061 3400   fax 020 7061 3401
      email contactus@together-uk.org
      http://www.together-uk.org
      Chief Exec: Gil Hitchon
- ▲   Company Limited by Guarantee; Registered Charity
- ○   *W; provides high quality services in the community, hospitals &
      prisons for people with mental health needs & their carers
- M   c 150 i
- ¶   AR; free.
- ✕   2005 (July) Mental After Care Association

Token Corresponding Society   (TCS)   1972
- ■   7 Anson Way, BRIDGWATER, Somerset, TA6 3TB.   (sp)
      01278 450199
      email davidyoungco@yahoo.co.uk
      Editor: David Young
- ▲   Un-incorporated Society
- ○   *G; for all interested in British tokens, tickets, tallies & checks
- ●   Res
- M   180 i, UK / 12 i, o'seas
- ¶   Bulletin - 4; m only.

Tolkien Society (TS) 1969

- ■ 65 Wentworth Crescent, Ash Vale, ALDERSHOT, Hants, GU12 5LF. (h/mem/sp)
  fax 0870 052 5569
  email tolksoc@tolkiensociety.org
  http://www.tolkiensociety.org
  Mem Sec: Trevor Reynolds
- ▲ Registered Charity; Un-incorporated Society
- Br 23; Australia, Brazil, Canada, Germany, Italy, Malta, Mexico, Netherlands, Taiwan, USA
- ○ *A; to promote research into the life & works of J R R Tolkien
- Gp The Tolkien Collector (book collecting); Quettar (linguistics); Nigglings (fiction)
- ● Conf - Mtgs - Exhib - Lib - Archives
- < Alliance of Literary Socs
- M 613 i, 3 org, UK / 502 i, 18 org, o'seas
- ¶ Mallorn (Jnl) - 1;
  Anon Hen (NL) - 6; both ftm, £22 nm (UK).

Tool & High Speed Steel Suppliers Association (THSSSA) 1994

- ■ Wensleydale, DROITWICH, WR9 8PF. (sb/p)
  01905 778165
  email thsssa@btinternet.com
  Sec: William Powell
- ▲ Un-incorporated Society
- ○ *T; 'to promote & support the interest of its members in all matters affecting their business as suppliers of tool & high speed products, wheresoever their markets shall be'
- ● Mtgs - Stat - Inf - VE
- M 10 f

Tool & Trades History Society (TATHS) 1983

- NR Woodbine Cottage, Budleigh Hill, EAST BUDLEIGH, Devon, EX9 7DT. (hsp)
  email taths@aol.com http://www.taths.org.uk
  Mem Sec: Brigitte Graham
- ▲ Registered Charity
- ○ *G, *L; 'to further the knowledge & understanding of hand-tools & the trades & persons that used them'
- ● Conf - Mtgs - Exhib - Inf - Lib
- M 420 i, 29 org, UK / 73 i, 10 org, o'seas
- ¶ Tools & Trades (Jnl) - 1; ftm, £15 nm (+p&p). NL - 4; ftm.

Tools for Self Reliance (TFSR) 1979

- ■ Netley Marsh, SOUTHAMPTON, Hants, SO40 7GY. (hq)
  023 8086 9697
  Chief Exec: Janice Kidd
- ▲ Company Limited by Guarantee; Registered Charity
- Br 65
- ○ *K; volunteers refurbish & ship handtools & sewing machines to village development groups in some of the poorest communities in Africa
- ● Conf - Exhib - Collection of tools
- M 300 i, UK / 50 i, o'seas
- ¶ Forging Links - 3.   AR - 1.

Tornado & Storm Research Organisation (TORRO) 1974

- ■ 22 Wilmslow Crescent, Thelwall, WARRINGTON, Cheshire, WA4 2JE. (hsp)
  0781 307 5509
  email sam.hall@torro.org.uk http://www.torro.org.uk
  Hon Sec: Miss Samantha J A Hall
- ▲ Un-incorporated Society
- ○ *L, *Q; to research into severe weather in the UK; to document, archive & research severe weather events: Tornadoes & other whirlwinds; Severe thunderstorms & hail; Heavy rain, floods, snowstorms & blizzards; Ball lightning & other lightning incidents. To educate the general public but not limited to severe weather forecasts
- Gp Divisions: Ball lightning, Blizzards & heavy snowfalls, Coastal impacts, Hailstorm, Ligtning impacts, Tornado, Thunderstorm census, Weather disasters, Extreme rainfall, Flashfloods
- ● Conf - Mtgs - ET - Res - Stat - Inf - Lib - PL
- < Intl Jnl of Meteorology
- M c 400 worldwide
- ¶ International Jnl of Meteorology - 10; ftm, £38 nm.
  Convection - 2; Members' Hbk - 1; both ftm only.
  [subscription £39.50].

Tortoise Trust 1986

- ■ BM Tortoise, LONDON, WC1N 3XX. (asa)
  email tortoisetrust@aol.com http://www.tortoisetrust.org
- ○ *V; provides sanctuary & hospital facilities for tortoises; educational material relating to tortoise welfare & conservation; carries out conservation projects overseas
- M i, f & org
- ¶ Jnl - 4.   NL - 6.
  Guide to Tortoises & Turtles - 1.

Tory Reform Group (TRG) 1975

- NR 29 Tufton St, LONDON, SW1P 3QL. (hq)
  020 7222 4409
  email trg@trg.org.uk
  Dir: Clare Whelan
- ○ *K, *Z; to influence Conservative Party policy
- ● Conf - Mtgs - Res - Inf - LG
- M 'confidential'
- ¶ Reformer (Jnl) - 4.   Policy Papers - irreg.

Tourette Syndrome (UK) Association (TSA(UK)) 1980

- NR PO Box 26149, DUNFERMLINE, KY12 7YU. (hq)
  0845 458 1252 fax 0845 458 1252
  email enquiries@tsa.org.uk http://www.tsa.org.uk
  Chief Exec: Judith Kidd
- ▲ Company Limited by Guarantee; Registered Charity
- ○ *W; the relief of persons suffering from the neurological movement disorder Gilles de la Tourette syndrome; to provide support for their families; to promote & fund research
- ● Inf
- < TSA Inc (USA) & (Australia)
- M 1,830 i
- ¶ NL - 1;   Publications; £2.50 each.

Tourism for All UK

- ■ c/o Vitalise, Snap Road Industrial Estate, KENDAL, Cumbria, LA9 6NZ.
  0845 124 9973
  email info@tourismforall.org.uk
  http://www.tourismforall.org.uk
- ○ *K; accessible tourism
  no further information supplied

© CBD Research Ltd · Beckenham · BR3 5JS · Tel 020 8650 7745 · Fax 020 8650 0768 · E-mail cbd@cbdresearch.com · www.cbdresearch.com

Tourism Alliance   2001
- ■ Centre Point, 103 New Oxford St, LONDON, WC1A 1DU.
  (hq)
  020 7395 8246   fax 020 7395 8178
  email kurt.janson@tourismalliance.com
  http://www.tourismalliance.com
  Policy Dir: Kurt Janson
- ▲ Company Limited by Guarantee
- ○ *T; to work with & lobby government on all issues related to the growth of tourism & its contribution to the British economy
- ● Conf - Mtgs - LG
- M 46 org
- ¶ NL - 12;   AR - 1; both free.

Tourism Concern   1989
- NR Stapleton House, 277-281 Holloway Rd, LONDON, N7 8HN.   (hq)
  020 7133 3330   fax 020 7133 3331
  email info@tourismconcern.org.uk
  http://www.tourismconcern.org.uk
  Inf Officer: Francesca Leadlay
- ▲ Company Limited by Guarantee; Registered Charity
- ○ *G, *K; 'a UK-based organisation campaigning worldwide for just & sustainable tourism - tourism that is fairly traded'
- ● Conf - ET - Res - Exhib
- < Ecumenical Coalition on Third World Tourism (ECTWT); Third World European Network (TEN)
- M i
- ¶ Tourism in Focus - 4.   Being There.
  The Good Alternative Travel Guide.

Tourism Management Institute   (TMI)   1997
- ■ 18 Cuninghill Avenue, INVERURIE, Aberdeenshire, AB51 3TZ.   (hsp)
  01467 620769
  email secretary@tmi.org.uk   http://www.tmi.org.uk
  Hon Sec: Cathy Guthrie
- ▲ Company Limited by Guarantee
- ○ *P; 'the professional voice for tourism destination managers'
- Gp Panels: Education & training, Marketing, ICT
- ● Conf - ET - LG
- M 230 i, 14 f, UK / 3 i, o'seas
- ¶ The Tourism Manager (NL) - 3;   LM (website);
  TMI online (email NL) - 4; all m only.

Tourism Society Ltd   1977
- ■ 1-2 Queen Victoria Terrace, Sovereign Court, LONDON, E1W 3HA.   (hq)
  020 7488 2789   fax 020 7488 9148
  email admin@tourismsociety.org
  http://www.tourismsociety.org
  Chief Exec: Sue Finch
- ▲ Company Limited by Guarantee
- ○ *P; networking organisation for professionals working, or interested in, tourism
- Gp Association Tourism Teachers & Trainers (ATTT); Tourism Society Consultants' Group (TSCG)
- ● Conf - Mtgs - Comp - Expt - Journal production
- M 1,110 i, 2 f, UK / 100 i, o'seas
- ¶ Tourism - 4; ftm, £85 nm.
  Membership Executive - 1; free; £85 nm.

Tower Crane Interest Group
   a special interest group of the **Construction Plant-hire Association**

Town & Country Planning Association   (TCPA)   1899
- NR 17 Carlton House Terrace, LONDON, SW1Y 5AS.   (hq)
  020 7930 8903   fax 020 7930 3280
- ▲ Registered Charity
- ○ *K; to promote a national policy of land-use planning

Townswomen's Guilds   (TG)   1929
- NR Tomlinson House (1st floor), 329 Tyburn Rd, BIRMINGHAM, B24 8HJ.   (hq)
  0121-326 0400   fax 0121-326 1976
  email tghq@townswomen.org.uk
  http://www.townswomen.org.uk
  Nat Sec: Victoria Stubbs
- ▲ Registered Charity
- ○ *G, *K; a charitable organisation to educate women
- Gp Sports & creative leisure; Public affairs; National events
- ● Conf - Mtgs - ET - Exhib - Comp - Stat - Inf - Lib - VE
- M [not stated]
- ¶ Townswoman - 4.

Towpath Action Group   (TAG)   1988
- ■ 23 Hague Bar, NEW MILLS, Derbys, SK22 3AT.   (hsp)
  01663 742198
  email andyscreen@towpath.org.uk
  Sec: Andrew Screen
- ▲ Un-incorporated Society
- ○ *G, *K; campaign for improving access to & along canal towpaths
- ● Inf - Campaigning & pressure gp activities
- < Inland Waterways Assn; Parliamentary Waterways Gp
- M 150 i, 10 org
- ¶ NL - 4; £4 yr (£3 students, pensioners).

Toy Retailers Association   (TRA)   1950
- ■ Gainsborough Waterfront Enterprise Centre, Lea Rd, GAINSBOROUGH, Lincs, DN21 1LX.   (hq)
  0870 753 7437   fax 0870 706 0042
  email enquiries@toyretailersassociation.co.uk
  http://www.toyretailersassociation.co.uk
  Sec: Derek Markie
- ▲ Company Limited by Guarantee
- ○ *T
- ● Conf - Exhib - Inf - LG
- M f
- × 2004 British Association of Toy Retailers

Tracheo-Oesophageal Fistula Support   (TOFS)   1982
- ■ St George's Centre, 91 Victoria Rd, Netherfield, NOTTINGHAM, NG4 2NN.   (hq)
  0115-961 3092   fax 0115-961 3097
  email info@tofs.org.uk   http://www.tofs.org.uk
  Hon Sec: Duncan Jackson
- ▲ Registered Charity
- ○ *W; 'to offer support & information to the families & carers of babies born with tracheo-oesophageal fistula (TOF), oesophageal atresia (OA) & related conditions; the group enables families to benefit from the friendship of other parents who have experienced the particular stresses of caring for these children - as well as the joy when problems have been overcome'
- ● Conf - Res - Inf - Support
- M 1,016 i, 40 f, UK / 120 i, 13 f, o'seas
- ¶ Chew (NL) - 4;   AR; both free.
  The TOF Child;   We Just Want Our Daughter to Live (books); both £9.99 m, £14.99 nm.

TRADA Technology Ltd   (TRADA)   1995
- ■ Chiltern House, Stocking Lane, Hughenden Valley, HIGH WYCOMBE, Bucks, HP14 4ND.   (hq)
  01494 569600   fax 01494 565487
  email information@trada.co.uk
  Chief Exec: Andrew Abbott
- ▲ Company Limited by Guarantee
- ○ *Q; technical advice relating to the correct use of timber in construction
- ● Conf - ET - Res - Exhib - Inf - PL
- M i, f & org
- ¶ Ybk;   AR; both ftm.   Numerous technical publications.
  Note: carries out all the activities of the Timber Research & Development Association.

Trade Association Forum   (TAF)   1997
- ■ Centre Point, 103 New Oxford St, LONDON, WC1A 1DU. (hq)
  020 7395 8238   fax 020 7395 8178
  http://www.taforum.org
  Manager: Stuart Bean
- ○ *N; promotion of trade associations & best practice in the UK
- ● Conf - Mtgs - ET - Res - Comp - Inf - LG
- < CBI
- M 300 trade associations
- ¶ Managing Trade Associations by Mark Boleat; £25.

Trade Marks Patents & Designs Federation   (TMPDF)   1920
- ■ 63-66 Hatton Garden (5th floor), LONDON, EC1N 8LE.   (hq)
  020 7242 3923   fax 020 7242 3924
  email admin@tmpdf.org.uk
  Sec: Sheila Draper
- ▲ Company Limited by Guarantee
- ○ *T; to express the views of industry on intellectual property
  matters
- ● Mtgs - LG
- < UNICE; CBI
- M 50 f
- ¶ Trends & Events - 1; free.

Trade & Professional Publishers Association   1976
- IRL 31 Deansgrange Rd, BLACKROCK, Co Dublin, Republic of
  Ireland.
  353 (1) 289 3305   fax 353 (1) 289 6406
  Chmn: David Markey
- ○ *T

Trade Publishers Council
a group of the **Publishers Association**

Trade Union Badge Collectors Society   (TUBCS)   1979
- ■ 6 Leven Close, LINSLADE, Beds, LU7 2XS.   (hsp)
  email adge@hotmail.co.uk
  Sec: Adrian Heffernan
- ▲ Un-incorporated Society
- ○ *G; to collect old & new trade union badges
- Gp Pre trade union amalgamation badges; Foreign badges
- ● Res - Exhib - Inf - Lib
- M i

Trade Valuers Institute
since 2004 **Institute of Stock Auditors & Valuers**

Trades Union Congress   (TUC)   1868
- NR Congress House, 23-28 Great Russell St, LONDON,
  WC1B 3LS.   (hq)
  Gen Sec: Brendan Barber
- ○ *U

Trading Standards Institute   (TSI)   1892
- NR 1 Sylvan Court (1st floor), Sylvan Way, Southfields Business
  Park, BASILDON, Essex, SS15 6TH.   (hq)
  0870 872 9000   fax 0870 872 9025
  email institute@tsi.org.uk   http://www.tsi.org.uk
  Sec: Dallas Wilcox,   Hon Sec: Christopher Armstrong
- ▲ Company Limited by Guarantee
- ○ *L, *P; to offer expertise & unique services to the wider
  consumer affairs sector & to businesses in consumer markets
- Gp History pen circle (historical metrology)
- ● Conf - Mtgs - ET - Exam - Res - Exhib - Comp - SG - Stat - Inf -
  Lib - VE - LG
- M 2,700 i
- ¶ Trading Standards Today - 12.
  Trading Standards Appointments - 12.

Traditional Cosmology Society   (TCS)   1984
- ■ Celtic & Scottish Studies, University of Edinburgh,
  27 George Sq, EDINBURGH, EH8 9LD.   (h/pres/b)
  0131-650 4152   fax 0131-650 4163
  email e.lyle@ed.ac.uk   http://www.tradcos.co.uk
  Pres: Emily Lyle
- ▲ Registered Charity
- ○ *L; to explore myth, religion & cosmology across cultural &
  disciplinary boundaries; to increase our understanding of
  world views past & present
- ● Conf - Mtgs - Res
- M 106 i, UK / 56 i, o'seas
- ¶ Cosmos (Jnl) - 2; ftm, £25 yr nm.

Traditional Farmfresh Turkey Association   (TFTA)   1985
- ■ PO Box 2089, SEAFORD, E Sussex, BN25 2WG.   (admin/sp)
  01323 899802   fax 01323 899583
  Admin Sec: Mrs P R Jones
- ○ *T; marketing & promoting Christmas turkeys
- M 45 f

Traditional Housing Bureau
a product association of the **British Precast Concrete Federation**

**Traditional Music & Song Association of Scotland   (TMSA)
1999**
- NR 95-97 St Leonards Street, EDINBURGH, EH8 9QY.   (hq)
  0131-667 5587
  The National Organiser
- ▲ Company Limited by Guarantee; Registered Charity
- Br 9
- ○ *A; the promotion, presentation & preservation of Scotland's
  traditional music & song, through educational workshops,
  concerts, festivals; to act as the source of information on
  traditional music in Scotland

Traditional Youth Marching Bands Association   (TYMBA)
- NR 3 Raby Drive, Moreton, WIRRAL, Cheshire, CH46 0TJ.
  0151-678 6124
  http://www.tymba.org.uk
  Sec: Mrs Beryl Howells
- ○ *G

Traffic Management Contractors Association   (TCMA)   1898
- ■ Kingsleigh 129 Whitton Rd, HOUNSLOW, Middx, TW3 2EL.
  (hsp)
  01737 647960   fax 01737 656006
  http://www.tmca.org.uk
  Sec: P Crickmay.   Chmn: R Pearson
- ▲ Company Limited by Guarantee
- ○ *T; traffic management on high speed roads
- ● Conf - Mtgs - Exhib - LG
- M 12 f
- ¶ Notes for Guidance - irreg; ftm, £2 nm.

Trail Riders Fellowship   (TRF)   1970
- ■ PO Box 196, DERBY, DE1 9EY.   (hsp)
  01483 535644
  email trfmemsec@aol.com   http://www.trf.org.uk
  Hon Sec: P R Cody
- Br 44
- ○ *G, *K; 'a national, voluntary & non-competitive body formed
  by motorcyclists to preserve our heritage of green lanes &
  our right to use them'
- ● Mtgs - Res - Exhib - Inf - VE - LG
- < Brit Motorcycle Fedn (BMF); Land Access & Recreation
  Assn (LARA); Motorcycle Action Gp (MAG); Nat Motorcycle
  Coun (NMC)
- M 3,000 i
- ¶ Trail (Jnl) - 12;   TRF Hbk - 1; both ftm only.

© CBD Research Ltd · Beckenham · BR3 5JS · Tel 020 8650 7745 · Fax 020 8650 0768 · E-mail cbd@cbdresearch.com · www.cbdresearch.com

Train Collectors Society (TCS) 1978
■ PO Box 20340, LONDON, NW11 6ZE. (mem/sp)
   020 8209 1589   fax 020 8209 1589
   email tcsinformation@btinternet.com
   http://www.traincollectors.org.uk
   Mem Sec: James Day
▲ Un-incorporated Society
○ *G; collection & restoration of model trains of any make, any
   age, any gauge
● Mtgs - Exhib - Gatherings in Biggleswade, Sandy & Leicester
M 470 i, UK / 30 i, 2 org, o'seas
¶ TCS News - 4; £18 yr (£22 Europe)(£25 world) m only.
   Spares Directory (loose-leaf or CD) 2003; ftm.
   Archive CDs TCS News; £10 m, £20 nm.

Trakehner Breeders Fraternity (TBF) 1989
NR Lower Lidham Hill Farm, North Lane, GUESTLING, E Sussex,
   TN35 4LX. (hsp)
   01424 813830
   email sian@birman.co.uk
   http://www.trakehnerbreeders.com
   Sec: Siân Reade,   Chmn: D Clarke
▲ Company Limited by Guarantee
○ *B; registration & promotion of the Trakehner horse in the UK
● Mtgs - Inf - VE
< Trakehner Verband (Germany)
M 220 i
   Note: is in the process of rebranding to Trakehners UK.

Tralee Chamber of Commerce
IRL 20 Denny St, TRALEE, Co Kerry, Republic of Ireland.
   353 (66) 712 1472
   email tralcham@iol.ie
   Pres: Daithi O'Connor
○ *C

Tramway & Light Railway Society (TLRS) 1938
■ 47 Soulbury Rd, LEIGHTON BUZZARD, Beds, LU7 2RW. (hsp)
   01525 377215
   Hon Sec: G R Tribe
▲ Registered Charity
○ *G; for those interested in tramways & light railways; to retain
   historic tramway archives; to encourage tramway modelling
M i
¶ Tramfare - 6.

Tramway Museum Society (TMS) 1955
NR National Tramway Museum, Crich, MATLOCK, Derbys,
   DE4 5DP.
   01773 854321
   Hon Sec: I M Dougill
▲ Company Limited by Guarantee; Registered Charity
○ *G; preservation & demonstration of the tramcar for museum
   purposes (by mobile operation in a period setting) &
   associated historical research
● Exhib - Res - Inf - Museum
< Assn Indep Museums; Assn Brit Transport & Engg Museums;
   Transport Trust; Heart of England Tourist Bd
M c 1,800 i
¶ Jnl - 4;   Contact (NL) - 12;   AR; all ftm.
   Tramway Museum Guidebook.

Trans-Antarctic Association 1960
NR British Antarctic Survey, Madingley Rd, CAMBRIDGE,
   CB3 0ET. (hsb)
   01223 221400 (switchboard)
○ *L, *Q; furthering research in subjects relating to Antarctica
● Awarding grants
M 5 i (committee of management), UK / i, o'seas.

Transform Scotland
NR Lamb's House, Burgess St, Leith, EDINBURGH, EH6 6RD.
   0131-467 7714   fax 0131-554 8656
   email info@transformscotland.org.uk
   http://www.transformscotland.org.uk
   Dir: Colin Howden
○ *K; sustainable transport

Transfrigoroute UK Ltd (TUK) 1984
NR 39a Meneage St, HELSTON, Cornwall, TR13 8RB. (hq)
   01326 569657   fax 01326 563859
   email secretary@transfrigoroute.co.uk
   http://www.transfrigoroute.com
   Sec: Liam E W Olliff
▲ Company Limited by Guarantee
Br 24 o'seas
○ *T; promotes & coordinates the interests of operators & users of
   temperature-controlled transport
● Conf - Mtgs - Res - Stat - Expt - Inf - LG
< Transfrigoroute Intl
M c 120 f
¶ TUK Talk (NL).   Code of Conduct.

Translators Association 1958
■ 84 Drayton Gardens, LONDON, SW10 9SB. (hq)
   020 7373 6642
   email inf0@societyofauthors.org
   http://www.societyofauthors.org
   Sec: Dorothy Sym
○ *P, *U; a specialist unit of the Society of Authors, exclusively
   concerned with the interests & problems of writers who
   translate foreign literary, dramatic or technical work into
   English for publication or performance
● Mtgs - Inf
< Fédn Intle Traducteurs
M 400 i
¶ The Author - 4.   In Other Words - 2.

Transparency International (UK) (TI(UK)) 1993
NR Downstream Bldg (3rd floor), 1 London Bridge, LONDON,
   SE1 9BG. (hq)
   020 7785 6356   fax 020 7785 6355
   email info@transparency.org.uk
   http://www.transparency.org.uk
   Chmn: Laurence Cockcroft
▲ Company Limited by Guarantee
○ *K; a non-profitmaking, independent, non-governmental
   organisation dedicated to increasing government
   accountability & to curbing national & international
   corruption
● Conf - Mtgs - Res
< Transparency International (Berlin)
M c 150 i, c 25 f
¶ TI Q - 4. AR.
   (for publications see websites)

Transport Association (TA) 1955
NR Peter Acton Associates, Aqua House, 30-32 High St, EPSOM,
   Surrey, KT19 8AH. (sb)
   01372 846482
   Sec: Peter Acton
○ *T
● Conf - Mtgs
M c 60 f

Transport & General Workers' Union (TGWU)
NR 128 Theobald's Rd, LONDON, WC1X 8TN (hq)
   020 7611 2500
   Gen Sec: Tony Woodley
○ *U
✕ 2004 National Union of Lock & Metal Workers (merged)

Transport 2000 Ltd   1973
- ■ The Impact Centre, 12-18 Hoxton St, LONDON, N1 6NG. (hq)
  020 7613 0743   fax 020 7613 5280
- ▲ Company Limited by Guarantee
- ○ *K, *N; to develop sustainable transport policies reducing dependence on private cars & road-based transport modes; to campaign for their implementation

Transport Research & Information Network
  merged on 1 January 2004 with the **Association of Community Rail Partnerships**

Transport Salaried Staffs' Association   (TSSA)   1897
- NR 10 Melton St, LONDON, NW1 2EJ.   (hq)
  020 7387 2101
  Gen Sec: Gerry Doherty
- ○ *U; for clerical, supervisory, professional & technical employees of British & Irish railways, London Regional Transport, British Waterways Board & allied undertakings, hotels, docks & road haulage

Transport Statistics Users Group
- NR Strategy & Service Development, London Underground Ltd, TfL, Room 494 (4th floor), 55 Broadway, LONDON, SW1H 0BD.
  020 7027 8340   fax 020 7918 3158
  http://www.tsug.org.uk
  Contact: Nina Webster
  a group of the **Statistics Users' Council**

Transport Ticket Society   (TTS)   1945
- NR Oaktree Lodge, 221A Botley Rd, Burridge, SOUTHAMPTON, Hants, SO31 1BJ.   (hsp)
  Mem Sec: D Randell
- ▲ Un-incorporated Society
- ○ *G, *L; study of transport tickets & theory & practice of fare collection
- ● Mtgs - Res - Exhib - SG - Inf - Lib
- < Roads & Road Transport History Conference
- M i, f & org
- ¶ Jnl - 12; ftm only.   Various occasional papers.

Transport Trust   (TT)   1965
- ■ 202 Lambeth Rd, LONDON, SE1 7JW.   (hq)
  020 7928 6464   fax 020 7928 6565
  email hq@thetransporttrust.org.uk
  Dir Gen: Col Anthony Walker
- ▲ Registered Charity
- ○ *G; to facilitate the preservation of items of transport of historical & technical interest (road, rail, air & water) including books, papers, ephemera & photographs
- Gp Railways; Road transport; Air (civil & military); Inland waterways; Coastal waters
- ● Conf - Res - Inf - Lib - VE
- < Heritage Railways (AIRPS); Assn Brit Transport Museums; The Maritime Trust; Vintage Sports-Car Club (VSCC); The Shuttleworth Trust
- M 600 i, 20 f, 150 org
- ¶ The Transport Digest (Jnl) - 3; ftm, 'normally free' nm.

Transport-Watch   2004
- ■ 12 Redland Drive, NORTHAMPTON, NN2 8QE.   (hq)
  01604 847438   fax 01604 455074
  email enquiries@transport-watch.co.uk
  http://www.transport-watch.co.uk
  Dir: Paul F Withrington
- ▲ Company Limited by Guarantee
- ○ *Q; 'research & development reference transport policy, particularly road & rail'
- Gp Congestion charging; Rail; Rapid transit; Traffic management; Transport policy
- ● Res - Stat
- M 10 i, UK / 1 i, o'seas

Transport on Water Association   (TOW)   1975
- NR Basin South, Gate 14, Woolwich Manor Way, LONDON, E16 2QY.   (hq)
  020 7476 2424
  Hon Dir: L Faram
- ▲ Registered Charity
- ○ *K; to promote the use of river & canals for commercial traffic
- ● Inf - LG
- M 200 i, 21 f

Travel Retail Forum
  see **United Kingdom Travel Retail Forum**

Travel Trust Association Ltd   (TTA)   1993
- ■ Albion House (3rd floor), High St, WOKING, Surrey, GU21 1BE.   (hq)
  0870 889 0577   fax 01483 730746
  email steve.clark@traveltrust.co.uk
  http://www.traveltrust.co.uk
  Dir: Stephen Jeffrey Clark
- ▲ Company Limited by Guarantee
- ○ *T; 'for the travel industry & regulatory body, coupled with commercial negotiations with suppliers'
- Gp Travel agents; Tour organisers
- ● Conf - Mtgs - ET - Res - Exhib - Stat - Inf - VE - LG
- < Inst Travel & Tourism (ITT)
- M 460 f
- ¶ NL - 4;   Fax Publications - 52; both ftm.

Treacher Collins Family Support Group
- NR 114 Vincent Rd, NORWICH, Norfolk, NR1 4HH.
  01603 433736   fax 01603 433736
  http://www.treachercollins.net
  Sec: Sue Moore
- ○ *W

Trebuchet Society   1998
- ■ 23 Viewside Close, Corfe Mullen, WIMBORNE, Dorset, BH21 3ST.   (hsp)
  01202 690224
  email richardbarton@caving5.freeserve.co.uk
  Sec: Richard Barton
- ▲ Un-incorporated Society
- ○ *G; research into early weaponry; designing & building replica weaponry; experiments into the effectiveness of early weaponry
- Gp Field research; Workshop; Research into trebuchet science; Computer database
- ● Res - SG - Inf - PL - VE
- < Coalhouse Fort Project; Artillery Assn GB
- M 6 i, 2 org
- × 1998 Historical Artillery Corps

Tree Care Industry Association
  the UK branch of this association has closed; the administration has moved to the USA

Tree Council of Ireland   1985
- IRL Cabinteely House, The Park, Cabinteely, DUBLIN 18, Republic of Ireland.
  353 (1) 284 9211   fax 353 (1) 284 9197
  email trees@treecouncil.ie   http://www.treecouncil.ie
  Pres: Dorothy Hayden
- ○ *H

© CBD Research Ltd · Beckenham · BR3 5JS · Tel 020 8650 7745 · Fax 020 8650 0768 · E-mail cbd@cbdresearch.com · www.cbdresearch.com

Trekking & Riding Society of Scotland   (TRSS)   1992
■   Bruaich-na-h'Abhainne, Maragowan, KILLIN, Perthshire,
     FK21 8TN.   (hsp)
     01567 820909   fax 01567 820909
     email trss@btinternet.com
     http://www.ridinginscotland.com
     Chief Exec: Mrs Susan Howard
▲   Un-incorporated Society
○   *T; to encourage & assist in the development of all forms of
     equestrian tourism in Scotland; to set & maintain standards
     of excellence
●   Conf - Mtgs - ET - Exam - Res - Exhib - SG - Stat - Inf - LG
<   Brit Horse Soc (Scotland); Scot Equestrian Assn; Scot Tourism
     Forum
M   c 70 f
¶   Promotional brochure by Scottish Tourist Board.

Trevithick Society   1935
■   PO Box 62, CAMBORNE, Cornwall, TR14 7ZN.   (hsp)
     01209 716811
     Hon Sec: Geoff Smith-Grogan
▲   Registered Charity
Br 2
○   *G, *L; the study of the history of technology in Cornwall & the
     preservation of buildings, machinery & sites connected with
     mining, engineering, china clay workings, transport, & any
     other industry carried on elsewhere where there are Cornish
     connections
●   Mtgs - ET - Res - PL - Organisation of King Edward Mine Ltd,
     which is responsible for the last group of remaining mine
     buildings at Camborne which are Grade II* listed; these are
     installed with historic tin extraction & separation machines &
     other relevant artifacts
<   Assn Indl Archaeology (AIA); Nat Assn of Mining History Orgs
M   400 i, 4 f, UK / 20 i, o'seas
¶   Jnl - 1; ftm, £5 nm.   NL - 4; ftm, £1.50 nm.

Tricycle Association   (TA)   1928
■   54 Bassnage Rd, HALESOWEN, W Midlands, B63 4HQ.   (hsp)
     0121-550 3644
     email normfenn@hotmail.com
     http://www.tricycleassociation.org.uk
     Nat Sec: Norman Fenn
○   *G, *S; to provide social & competitive activities for members.
     Membership is open to all past & present riders of the
     tricycle; defined as a humanly propelled machine making
     three tracks when in motion
●   Mtgs - Exhib - Comp - VE
<   Cycling Time Trials; Road Records Assn
M   400 i, UK / 35 i, o'seas
¶   Gazette - 4; ftm only.

Trigeminal Neuralgia Association   (TNA)
NR PO Box 413, BROMLEY, Kent, BR2 9XS.
     020 8462 9122
     http://www.tna.org.uk
▲   Registered Charity
○   *W; to provide information & support to members; to raise
     awareness of TN (an extremely severe facial pain which
     tends to come & go without warning) amongst medical
     professionals and general public
M   c 400 i

Trollope Society   1987
■   Maritime House, Clapham Old Town, LONDON, SW4 0JW.
     (hq)
     020 7720 6789
     Chmn: Priscilla Hungerford,
     PA: Pelham Ravenscroft
▲   Registered Charity
○   *A; to produce the first complete, uniform, edition of the novels
     of Anthony Trollope; to serve as a forum for discussions
●   VE - Annual dinner - Lecture
M   1,200 i, UK / 500 i, USA
¶   Trollopiana Jnl - 4;   Mailing - 4; ftm.

Tropical Agriculture Association   (TAA)   1979
■   43 Mount Place, GUILDFORD, Surrey, GU2 5HU.   (hsp)
     01483 454725   fax 01483 454725
     email general-secretary@taa.org.uk
     http://www.taa.org.uk
     Gen Sec: Paul Tuley
▲   Registered Charity
Br Regions: Southwest, Scotland & Borders, London & South East,
     East Anglia
○   *F; the promotion, practice, education & research in tropical
     agriculture
●   Conf - Mtgs - ET - Inf - VE
M   1,150 i, 12 f, UK / 350 i, o'seas
¶   TAA(UK) NL - 4; ftm, £2 nm.

Tropical Forest Forum
NR c/o Royal Botanic Gardens, Kew, RICHMOND, Surrey,
     TW9 2AB.
     020 8332 5717
     Dir: Jane Thornback
○   *P; professional body for those engaged in tropical forest work
     of any kind
     also known as the UK Tropical Forest Forum

Tropical Growers' Association Ltd   (TGA Ltd)   1907
■   9 Dane Park, BISHOPS STORTFORD, Herts, CM23 2PR.   (hsp)
     01279 656863   fax 020 8892 4177
     email tga@airt.dircon.co.uk
     Chief Exec & Hon Sec: Philip D Gatland
▲   Company Limited by Guarantee
○   *T; interests of all concerned with the cultivation of rubber, palm
     oil & other tropical crops
Gp Trade & technical c'ee
●   Mtgs - SG - VE
<   Tun Abdul Razak Research Centre (TARRC); Intl Rubber Study
     Gp (IRSG); Asian & Pacific Coconut Community
>   Tropical Agriculture Assn (TAA); Malaysian Palm Oil Bd (MPOB)
M   32 i, 6 f, 3 org (TAA) UK / 7 i, 2 f, 2 org o'seas

Trussed Rafter Association
NR 31 Station Rd, Sutton cum Lound, RETFORD, Notts, DN22 8PZ.
     01777 869281
     Sec: Peter Grimsdale
○   *T
     no further information supplied

Trust for Training & Education in Building Maintenance
     **see Upkeep: the Trust for Training & Education in Building
     Maintenance**

TT Riders Association   (TTRA)   1907
■   Mountainview, Glen Maye, PEEL, Isle of Man, IM5 3BJ.   (hsp/b)
     01624 843695
     email frances@thorpiom.freeserve.co.uk
     http://www.ttra.co.uk
     Hon Sec & Treas: Frances Thorp
▲   Registered Charity
○   *S; 'the continuance of the Isle of Man TT races; the creation of
     a social & charitable association of all those who take part,
     have taken part & those who race no more'
Gp Isle of Man TT race riders; Sidecar passengers
●   Conf - Stat - Inf - Lib
<   Intl Historic Racing Org; Auto-Cycle U; Fédn Intle
     Motocyclisme; Manx Grand Prix Riders Assn; Amer Historic
     Motorcycle Racing Assn
M   1,270 i, UK / 411 i, o'seas
¶   NL - 2; ftm.

Tuberous Sclerosis Association   (TSA)   1977
NR   PO Box 12979, Burnt Green, BIRMINGHAM, B45 5AN.   (sb)
        0121-445 6970
        email support@tuberous-sclerosis.org
        http://www.tuberous-sclerosis.org
        Head of Support: Mrs Janet Medcalf
▲   Company Limited by Guarantee; Registered Charity
○   *W; to support & help sufferers & their families; to raise
        awareness of & to encourage research into the causes of the
        disease
●   Conf - ET - Res - Inf
<   Tuberous Sclerosis Intl (associations in 25 countries)
M   1,500 i, UK / 100 i, 25 org, o'seas
¶   Scan (NL) - 3;   Medical Brochure;   Factsheets; all free.
        Publications list available.

Tue Iron Manufacturers Association   (TIMA)   1994
■   81 Park View, Collins Rd, LONDON, N5 2UD.   (asa)
▲   Un-incorporated Society
○   *T; 'the tue iron is a nozzle attached to a bellows, used in a
        forge to fan flames to a high heat'
●   Mtgs - ET - Exhib
M   17 f
¶   Hot Air (NL) - 4.

Tug of War Association   (TOWA)   1958
NR   57 Lynton Rd, CHESHAM, Bucks, HP5 2BT.   (hsp)
        Hon Sec Gen: Peter Craft
○   *S; controlling body of the game of tug-of-war in Britain

Tunnel Lining Manufacturers Association
        a product association of the **British Precast Concrete Federation**

Turfgrass Growers Association Ltd   (TGA)   1995
■   133 Eastgate, LOUGH, Lincs, LN11 0QG.   (asa)
        01507 607722   fax 01507 600101
        email info@turfgrass.co.uk   http://www.turfgrass.co.uk
        Co Sec: Tim Mudge
▲   Company Limited by Guarantee
○   *T; turf growers for domestic & commercial use
Gp   Producers; Suppliers of goods & services
●   Conf - Mtgs - Exhib
M   60 f

Turkey Club UK   2000
NR   Colts Farmhouse, Whithorn, NEWTON STEWART, DG8 8HA.
        (hsb)
        01988 600763
        Hon Sec & Treas: Janice Houghton-Wallace
○   *B; to conserve & promote the standards breeds of turkey; to
        encourage & assist with advice anyone wishing to keep
        turkeys; to establish a higher profile for the turkey as an
        exhibition bird & utility species of poultry (provider of eggs &
        meat)
Gp   Breeders of the original standard breeds of turkey
●   ET - Exhib - Comp - Inf - VE
<   Poultry Club of GB
M   200 i
¶   NL - 4;   Ybk - 1; both ftm only.
        a turkey column in 'Fancy Fowl' - 12.

Turkish-British Chamber of Commerce & Industry
■   33 Bury St, LONDON, SW1Y 6AU.   (hq)
        020 7321 0999
○   *C
        No further information supplied

Turner Society   1975
NR   BCM Box Turner, LONDON, WC1N 3XX.   (mail)
        http://www.turnersociety.org.uk address
▲   Registered Charity
○   *A; to promote interest in the life, work & influence of the
        painter J M W Turner (1775-1851)
●   Mtgs - VE
M   c 500 i & org, UK / c 100 i & org, o'seas
¶   Turner Society News - 3; ftm only.

Turner Syndrome Support Society (UK)   (TSSS)   1979
■   12 Irving Quadrant, HARDGATE, Clydebank, G81 6AZ.   (hq)
        01389 380385   fax 01389 380384
        email turner.syndrome@tss.org.uk
        http://www.tss.org.uk
        Exec Officer: Arlene Smyth
▲   Registered Charity
○   *W; information & support for those who have Turner syndrome
        (genetic abnormality incl short stature & lack of ovarian
        function, it affects only females & is caused by complete, or
        partial deletion, of the X chromosome in some, or all cells, of
        the body) their families & health professionals involved in
        their care
●   Conf - Mtgs - ET - Res - Comp - Inf
M   750 i, 20 org, UK / 10 i, o'seas
¶   Turner Syndrome - lifelong guidance & support;
        Talking About Turner Syndrome (video);
            both minimum donation £5 (UK), £10 (o'seas).
        Talking About Turner Syndrome (booklet); minimum donation
            £1 (UK), £3 (o'seas).
        Information leaflets: publications list available.

Twentieth Century Society   1979
■   70 Cowcross St, LONDON, EC1M 6BP.   (hq)
        020 7250 3857   fax 020 7251 8985
        email administrator@c20society.org.uk
        Dir: Catherine Croft
▲   Registered Charity
○   *G; preservation of architecture (post 1914); to stimulate public
        interest in the subject
●   Conf - ET - Res - VE
M   1,600 i, 30 f, 20 org, UK / 20 org, o'seas
¶   Jnl - 1; £15 m.   NL - 3; ftm only.

TWI Ltd
        the trading name of the **Welding Institute**

Twins & Multiple Births Association   (TAMBA)   1978
NR   2 The Willows, Gardner Rd, GUILDFORD, Surrey, GU1 4PG.
        (hq)
        0870 770 3305   fax 0870 770 3303
        email enquiries@tamba.org.uk
        http://www.tamba.org.uk
        Dir: Helen Forbes
▲   Registered Charity
○   *W; to provide information & mutual support networks for
        families of twins, triplets & more, highlighting their unique
        needs to all involved in their care
Gp   Supertwins; Infertility; Bereavement; One parent families;
        Special needs; Support groups
●   Conf - Mtgs - ET - Res - SG - Inf - PL
<   Intl Soc for Twin Studies
M   6,000 families
¶   Twins, Triplets & More - 4; ftm, £2.50 nm.   AR.
        Specialist Support Group NLs - irreg.

© CBD Research Ltd · Beckenham · BR3 5JS · Tel 020 8650 7745 · Fax 020 8650 0768 · E-mail cbd@cbdresearch.com · www.cbdresearch.com

Tyre Industry Council   (TIC)   1989
■   21-25 St Anne's Court, LONDON, W1F 0BJ.   (hq)
        020 7734 6363   fax 020 7437 7966
        email tic@tyresafety.co.uk   http://www.tyresafety.co.uk
        Dir: Peter Taylor
▲   Un-incorporated Society
○   *T; improving tyre safety awareness
●   Mtgs - ET - Res - Stat - Inf - PL - LG
<   Brit Rubber Mfrs Assn; Imported Tyre Mfrs Assn
M   19 f, 2 org
        British Rubber Manufacturers Association
        Imported Tyre Manufacturers Association
¶   Annual Report - 1; free.

Tyre Wholesalers Group
        a group of the **National Tyre Distributors Association**

UK ...
see **United Kingdom ...**
[All organisations whose names begin with 'UK' or 'United Kingdom' are printed & filed as 'United Kingdom' to avoid the confusion of two separate sequences]

UK Spill Association   (UKSPILL)   2004
■   21-22 Britannia Chambers, Town Quay, SOUTHAMPTON, Hants, SO14 2AQ.   (hsb)
  023 8082 8913
  email info@ukspill.org.   http://www.ukspill.org
  Exec Dir: Roger M Mabbott
▲   Company Limited by Guarantee
○   *T; for the UK oil spill industry, spill contractors, equipment manufacturers & consulting companies
●   Conf - Mtgs - Exhib - EXpt - Inf - LG
<   Soc of Marine Inds
M   10 i, 43 f
×   2004 British Oil Spill Control Association

UK Sweet Spreads Association
is an association within the **Food Processers' Association**

UKinbound   1977
■   14 Leicester Place, LONDON, WC2H 7BZ.   (hq)
  020 7734 9569   fax 020 7287 3217
  http://www.ukinbound.org
  Chief Exec: Stephen Dowd
○   *T; representing tour operators & suppliers to Britain
●   Conf - Mtgs - ET - Exhib - Stat
M   250 f
¶   Hbk & LM - 1.
×   2004 (November) British Incoming Tour Operators Association

Ukulele Society of Great Britain
NR   43 Finstock Rd, LONDON, W10 6LU.   (sp)
  020 8960 0459
  Sec: Fred Pearson
▲   Un-incorporated Society
○   *D; for all interested in the playing of ukuleles & ukulele banjos
M   i
  No further information supplied.

Ulster Agricultural Organisation Society Ltd
  has closed

Ulster Angling Federation   (UAF)   1937
NR   6 Beech Green, Doagh, BALLYCLARE, Co Antrim, BT39 0QB.
  (asst/sp)
  028 9334 0884   fax 028 9334 0884
  email phyllis.glenn@lineone.net
  Assistant Sec: Phyllis Glenn,   Hon Sec: Allan Kilgore
  Devt Officer: Newell McCreight (028 9084 4636)
▲   Company Limited by Guarantee
○   *S; representative body for game angling in Northern Ireland; to conserve the aquatic environment; to prevent water pollution
●   Mtgs - ET - Inf - LG
<   N Atlantic Salmon Consvn Org; Salmon & Trout Assn; Countryside Alliance
M   10,000 i, 80 clubs
¶   The Ulster Angler - 1; ftm.

Ulster Apple Exporters Association
  see **Northern Ireland Fruit Growers' Association (inc Ulster Apple Exporters Association)**

Ulster Archaeological Society   (UAS)   1935
■   Dept of Archaeology & Ethnography, Ulster Museum, Botanic Gardens, BELFAST, BT9 5AB.   (mail/add)
  http://www.uarcsoc.org
  Hon Sec: K Pullin
▲   Registered Charity
○   *L; to further in every way the study of the past, particularly in Ulster
●   Mtgs - Lectures - Fieldtrips
M   c 300 i
¶   Ulster Jnl of Archaeology - 1; ftm, £15 nm.
  NL - 4; ftm only.

Ulster Architectural Heritage Society   (UAHS)   1967
■   66 Donegall Pass, BELFAST, BT7 1BU.   (hq)
  028 9055 0213   fax 028 9055 0214
  email info@uahs.co.uk   http://www.uahs.co.uk
  Chmn: Peter O Marlow,   Hon Sec: Séan Hagan
▲   Company Limited by Guarantee; Registered Charity
○   *A, *K, *L; to promote & encourage appreciation of good architecture of all periods (from prehistoric to the contemporary) in the nine counties of Ulster; to encourage the preservation & restoration of buildings of merit or importance; to increase the public awareness of the beauty, history & character of local neighbourhoods
●   Conf - Mtgs - ET - Res - SG - Inf - Lib - VE - LG
M   1,200 i
¶   Books, Monographs, Essays, Lists & Surveys; £2-£24. List of publications available.

Ulster Automobile Club Ltd   (UAC)   1925
■   29 Shore Rd, HOLYWOOD, Co Down, BT18 9HX.   (hq)
  028 9042 6262   fax 028 9042 1818
  email office@ulsterautomobileclub.co.uk
  http://www.ulsterautomobileclub.co.uk
  Hon Sec: Tom Allison
▲   Company Limited by Guarantee
○   *S; organisation promotion of motor sport events
Gp   Communications team (radio); Competitions c'ee (event organisation)
●   Comp - VE
<   Fédn Intle des Véhicules Anciens (FIVA); Motor Sports Assn - UK (MSA-UK); Assn of NI Car Clubs (ANICC)
M   250 i, UK / 30 i, o'seas
¶   Wheelspin - 2; ftm, on request, nm.

Ulster Chemists' Association   (UCA)   1901
■   73 University St, BELFAST, BT7 1HL.   (hq)
  028 9032 0787   fax 028 9031 3737
  http://www.uca.org.uk
  Sec: Adrienne Clugston
▲   Un-incorporated Society
○   *P, *T; for retail pharmacy in Northern Ireland
●   Conf - Mtgs - ET - Inf - Liaison with trade - Assistance to small businesses
<   Nat Pharmaceutical Assn
M   487 i
¶   NI Pharmacy in Focus - 12; ftm only.

Ulster Coarse Fishing Federation   (UCFF)   1975
■   29 Georgian Villas, OMAGH, Co Tyrone, BT79 0AT.   (hsp)
  028 8224 5363
  email victor.refausse@omagh.ac.uk
  Hon Sec: Victor Refausse
▲   Un-incorporated Society
○   *S; to promote & develop coarse angling in Northern Ireland
●   ET - Comp - LG
<   Nat Coarse Fishing Fedn of Ireland
M   500 i, 10 org
¶   Calendar of Events - 1; £2.50.

© CBD Research Ltd · Beckenham · BR3 5JS · Tel 020 8650 7745 · Fax 020 8650 0768 · E-mail cbd@cbdresearch.com · www.cbdresearch.com

Ulster Farmers Union   (UFU)   1918
- ■ 475 Antrim Rd, BELFAST, BT15 3DA.   (hq)
    028 9037 0222   fax 028 9037 1231
    email info@ufuhq.com   http://www.ufuhq.com
    Chief Exec: Clarke Black
- ▲ Un-incorporated Society
- Br 25
- ○ *F; to defend the rights & promote the interests of farmers
- ● Conf - Mtgs - ET - Res - SG - Stat - Inf - Lib - LG
- M 12,000 i
- ¶ Farming News - 5.

Ulster Federation of Rambling Clubs   (UFRC)   1980
- ■ 10 Strangford Ave, BELFAST, BT9 6PG.   (chmn/p)
    028 9266 6358
    email secretary@ufrc-online.co.uk
    http://www.ufrc-online.co.uk
    Hon Sec: Ronnie Carser
- ▲ Un-incorporated Society
- ○ *S; 'to encourage recreational walking, appreciation & respect for the countryside'
- ● Mtgs - ET - LG
- < Ramblers' Assn
- M 26 org

Ulster Folk Life Society   (UFLS)   1961
- NR c/o Ulster Folk & Transport Museum, Cultra, HOLYWOOD, Co Down, BT18 0EU.   (mail) address
    Hon Sec: Mrs Hilary Maginnis
- ▲ Registered Charity
- ○ *L; study of the folklife, customs & traditions of Ulster
- ● VE
- M c 100 i
- ¶ Ulster Folklife (Jnl) - 1.

Ulster Historical Foundation   (UHF)   1956
- NR Balmoral Buildings, 12 College Square East, BELFAST, BT1 6DD.   (hq)
    028 9033 2288   fax 028 9023 9885
    email enquiry@uhf.org.uk
    http://www.ancestryireland.com
    Exec Dir: Fintan Mullan,   Res Dir: Dr Brian Trainor
- ▲ Registered Charity
- ○ *Q; research & assistance to those of Ulster descent wishing to know more about their ancestors & homeland
- ● Conf - ET - Res - Exhib - Inf - VE
- < Fedn of Families Hist Socs; Family Hist Coun (Republic of Ireland); Brit Assn of Ir Studies
- M 400 i, UK / 800 i, o'seas
- ¶ Familia: Ulster Genealogical Review - 1; ftm, £5.95 m.
    Guild interest list - 1; ftm, £6.95 nm.

Ulster Launderers Association   (ULA)   1912
- NR Lilliput Laundry, Unit 8 Dunmurray Industrial Estate, The Cutts, BELFAST, BT17 9HU.   (hsb)
    028 9061 8555
    Hon Sec: Geoffrey Wood
- ○ *T; interests of commercial launderers & cleaners in N Ireland
- ● Mtgs - SG - LG
- M 6 f

Ulster-Scots Language Society   (USLS)   1992
- NR c/o 218 York St (2nd floor), BELFAST, BT15 1GY.   (hsb)
    028 9075 8985
    email usls@ulster-scots.com
    Sec: Fiona McDonald
- ▲ Registered Charity
- ○ *L; to record, promote & uphold the use of Ulster-Scots language in writing, education & speech; to promote Ulster-Scots cultural traditions
- ● Mtgs - ET - Res - Exhib - SG - Inf - LG
- < Ulster-Scots Heritage Coun
- M c 250 i, UK / c 50 i, o'seas
- ¶ Ullans (Jnl) - 1.

Ulster Society of Organists & Choirmasters   1918
- NR c/o St Anne's Cathedral, Donegall St, BELFAST, BT1 2HB.   (hsb)
    028 903 8332
    http://www.d-n-a.net/users/dnetzMNU/usoc
    Hon Sec: Philip Stopford
- ▲ Un-incorporated Society
- ○ *D; to promote the interests of church musicians
- ● Conf - Mtgs - ET - VE
- < Inc Assn Organists (UK)
- M 180 i
- ¶ NL - 12; m only.

Ulster Society for Prevention of Cruelty to Animals   (USPCA)   1836
- ■ PO Box 103, Belfast, BT6 8US.   (hq)
    028 9081 4242
    Chief Exec: Stephen Philpott
- ▲ Company Limited by Guarantee; Registered Charity
- ○ *K, *V; care & prevention of cruelty to animals through education & inspectorate vigilance
- Gp Inspectors; Kennel assistants; Education officer; Appeals organiser
- ● ET - VE - Shelters for homeless animals
- < Wld Soc Protection of Animals
- M 1,000 i
- ¶ NL - 3.   AR.

Ulster Society for the Protection of the Countryside   (USPC)   2537
- ■ 22 Donegall Rd, BELFAST, BT12 5JN.   (hq)
    028 9024 9006
    email uspcinfo@tiscali.co.uk
    Hon Sec: Ian Lamont
- ▲ Un-incorporated Society
- ○ *K, *N; to safeguard the beauty of Northern Ireland; to campaign for the protection of Northern Ireland's countryside
- Gp Access the Countryside
- ● Conf - Mtgs - Exhib - Inf - LG
- < NI Envt Link
- > Cyclists' Touring Club of NI; Ulster Fedn of Rambling Clubs; Youth Hostel Assn of NI
- M 240 i, 5 org
- ¶ The USPC Countryside Recorder (NL) - 2;   AR; both free.

Ulster Teachers' Union   (UTU)   1919
- ■ 94 Malone Rd, BELFAST, BT9 5HP.   (hq)
    028 9066 2216   fax 028 9066 3055
    email office@utu.edu   http://www.utu.edu
    Gen Sec: Ray Calvin
- ○ *P, *U
- ● Conf - Mtgs - ET
- < ICTU
- M 6,500 i
- ¶ UTU News - 4;   NL - 12;   AR; all free.

Ulster Women's Hockey Union   (UWHU)   1896
- ■ The Hockey Office, The House of Sport, Upper Malone Rd, BELFAST, BT9 5LA.
    028 9038 3818   fax 028 9068 2757
    email lorrainethompson@houseofsport.net
    http://www.hockeyulster.org   (hq)
    Hon Sec: Mrs Jennifer Patterson
- ▲ Un-incorporated Society
- ○ *S; governing body of the sport
- ● Administration of women's hockey
- < Ir Hockey Assn
- M 51 clubs

Undeb Badminton Cymru
    see **Welsh Badminton Union   (Undeb Badminton Cymru)**

Undeb Hoci Cymru
    see **Welsh Hockey Union (Undeb Hoci Cymru)**

UNIFI
2004 merged with **Amicus**

Union of Country Sports Workers   (UCSW)   1977
■   PO Box 129, BANBURY, Oxon, OX17 2HX.   (hsp)
01295 712719   fax 01295 712719
email office@ucsw.org   http://www.ucsw.org
Chmn: Kieron Moore,   Sec/Admin: Phillippa White
○   *U; to represent anyone employed in country sports, either
directly or indirectly, full-time or part-time
●   LG - Stands at country fairs, game fairs - Lobbying
M   4,500 i
¶   Livin' Country - 3; ftm, £2 nm.

Union of Democratic Mineworkers   (UDM)   1985
NR   Berry Hill Lane, MANSFIELD, Notts, NG18 4JU.   (hq)
01623 626094   fax 01623 642300
Nat Pres: N Greatrex,   Gen Sec: M L Stevens
○   *U; operating in the UK coal mining industry
M   i

Union of Senior Revenue Officials   (USRO)   1901
NR   2 Caxton St, LONDON, SW1H 0QH.   (hq)
020 7343 1111   fax 020 7343 1105
email usro@fda.org.uk   http://www.usro.org.uk
Pres: Stephen Bibby
○   *P, *U; for senior revenue officials in the Inland Revenue
●   Conf - Mtgs - Empl - LG
M   2,200 i
¶   USRO Update - 10;   Quarterly Record - 4; both ftm only.
✕   2002 Association of HM Inspectors of Taxes

Union of Shop, Distributive & Allied Workers   (USDAW)   1947
NR   188 Wilmslow Rd, MANCHESTER, M14 6LJ.   (hq)
0161-224 2804
Gen Sec: John Hannett
○   *U; interests of workers in shops & stores
M   c 341,000 i
¶   Arena (Jnl) - 6.

Union of Women Teachers
see **National Association Schoolmasters Union of Women
Teachers**

Unison   (UNISON)   1993
NR   1 Mabledon Place, LONDON, WC1H 9AJ.   (hq)
0845 355 0845
Gen Sec: Dave Prentis
○   *U
M   i

Unitarian Historical Society   (UHS)   1915
■   223 Upper Lisburn Rd, BELFAST, BT10 0LL.   (hq)
Sec: Rev David Steers
○   *L; study of history of Unitarian & kindred movements;
preservation of records & antiquities
M   i & libraries
¶   Transactions - 1.

United Chiropractic Association   (UCA)   2000
NR   14 Drovers Way, Woodlands, IVYBRIDGE, PL21 9XA.   (hq)
01364 654994   fax 01364 654994
email melissa@united-chiropractic.org
http://www.united-chiropractic.org
Contact: Melissa Sandford
○   *M, *P; to represent principle-centred chiropractic (wellness
based)
●   Conf - Mtgs - ET - Res
M   150 i, UK / 10 i, o'seas

United Counties Agricultural Society   1895
NR   The Showground, Nantyci, CARMARTHEN, SA33 5DR.   (hq)
01267 232141   fax 01267 221884
▲   Registered Charity
○   *F, *H; covers Cardiganshire, Carmarthenshire &
Pembrokeshire
●   Exhibitions & shows

United Grand Lodge of England
NR   Freemasons' Hall, 60 Great Queen St, LONDON,
WC2B 5AZ.   (hq)
020 7831 9811

**United Kingdom Acquired Brain Injury Forum   (UKABIF)
1998**
NR   c/o Royal Hospital for Neuro-Disability, West Hill, LONDON,
SW15 3SW.   (admin/b)
020 8780 4500 ext 5140   fax 020 8780 4569
email ukabif@rhn.org.uk   http://www.ukabif.org.uk
Sec: Sally Jenkinson
▲   Registered Charity
○   *K, *L; to promote understanding of aspects of acquired brain
injury; to provide information & expert input to policy makers,
service providers & general public
●   Conf - Res - LG
M   70 i, 70 fm only.
¶   NL - 2; ftm only.

United Kingdom Agricultural Supply Trade Association
2003 merged with the Fertiliser Manufacturers' Association to form
the **Agricultural Industries Confederation**

United Kingdom Alliance   (UKA)   1853
NR   176 Blackfriars Rd, LONDON, SE1 8ET.   (hsb)
0798 501 1029
email douglas.sinclair@ntlworld.com
Gen Sec: Douglas Sinclair
○   *K; advising on the dangers of alcohol & drug abuse
●   Conf - Comp - Seminars for senior school pupils in House of
Commons committee rooms
M   c 400 i
¶   AR; ftm, £2 nm.

United Kingdom Alliance of Dance Teachers   1902
■   Centenary House, 38-40 Station Rd, BLACKPOOL, FY4 1EU.
(hq)
01253 408828
Gen Sec: Graham Vernon
▲   Company Limited by Guarantee
○   *D; to further the development of dance & movement in all its
forms; to provide a syllabus & examination service
●   Conf - Mtgs - ET - Exam - Exhib - Comp - SG - Inf - LG
<   Brit Coun of Ballroom Dancing; Scot Official Bd Highland
Dancing; Brit Keep Fit Confedn; Stage Dance Coun; CCPR
M   i

**United Kingdom Aluminium Packaging Recycling Organisation
(Alupro)   1989**
NR   1 Brockhill Court, Brockhill Lane, REDDITCH, Worcs,
B97 6RB.   (hq)
01527 597757   fax 01527 594140
http://www.alupro.org.uk
○   *T; to promote recycling of aluminium foil & cans & provide an
infrastructure of 'cash for cans' recycling centre/buy-back
centres; to provide educational material to schools / charities
/ individuals that want to set up a recycling initiative
●   Conf - Mtgs - ET - Res - Comp - Stat - PL - Provision of
educational materials to schools, groups etc to set up a
recycling initiative
M   350 centres
¶   Campaign NL - 4; ftm, on application nm.
✕   2000-02 Aluminium Packaging Recycling Organisation

© CBD Research Ltd · Beckenham · BR3 5JS · Tel 020 8650 7745 · Fax 020 8650 0768 · E-mail cbd@cbdresearch.com · www.cbdresearch.com

United Kingdom Association of Cancer Registries
NR National Cancer Intelligence Centre, Office for National
      Statistics, 1 Drummond Gate, LONDON, SW1V 2QQ.   (asa)
      020 7533 5257
      Chmn: Prof D Forman

United Kingdom Association of Celebrity Assistants (UKACA)
2003
NR Hammer House (7th floor), 113-117 Wardour St, LONDON,
      W1F 0UN.
      email info@ukcelebrityassistants.org
○   *P

United Kingdom Association for European Law   1974
■   King's College, Strand, LONDON, WC2R 2LS.   (hq)
      020 7722 9746   fax 020 7722 9746
      email eva.evans@kcl.ac.uk   http://www.ukael.org
      Admin: Mrs Eva Evans,   Pres: Sir Christopher Bellamy
▲   Registered Charity
○   *P
●   Conf
<   Fédn Intle du Droit Européen (FIDE)
M   200 i, 20 f, UK / 35 i, o'seas
¶   Conference publications - irreg.

United Kingdom Association of the FIS
      since 2003 a sector of the **Agricultural Industries Confederation**

United Kingdom Association of Fish Meal Manufacturers
(AFMM) 1917
NR c/o United Fish Products Ltd, Greenwell Place, ABERDEEN,
      AB12 3AY.   (hq)
      01225 854444   fax 01225 854333
      email secretariat@iffo.org.uk
○   *T; the production & use of fish meal & fish oil in the UK
M   12 i, 4 f

United Kingdom Association of Fish Producer Organisations
(UKAFPO) 1988
NR c/o Bridlington Shellfish, Old Harbour Master's Office,
      BRIDLINGTON, N Yorks, YO15 2NR.   (hsb)
      01262 409908
      Sec: Sue Wilson
▲   Friendly Society
○   *N, *T; to promote & develop cooperation between & the
      interests of fish producer organisations, both in the UK &
      other parts of the EU
●   Mtgs - LG
M   9 f

United Kingdom Association of Frozen Food Producers
(UKAFFP) 1959
NR 6 Catherine St, LONDON, WC2B 5JJ.   (hq)
      020 7420 7180
▲   Un-incorporated Society
○   *T; represents the interests of frozen food manufacturers
      especially in the field of legislation
Gp C'ees: Fish; Shellfish; Meat; Vegetable; Bakery
●   Mtgs - LG
<   FAFPAS; AIPCEE; CLITRAVI; UEITP
M   f
¶   RFIC Guide to the Storage & Handling of Frozen Foods.

United Kingdom Association of Letting Agents (UKALA)
1997
■   59 Mile End Rd, COLCHESTER, Essex, CO4 5BU.   (hq)
      01206 853741   fax 01206 851616
      email ukala@sys3internet.net   http://www.ukala.org.uk
      Gen Sec: John Peartree
▲   Company Limited by Guarantee
Br 319
○   *T; for letting agents & managing agents
●   ET - Stat - LG
M   206 i, 206 f
¶   Letting Update (Jnl) - 4; ftm, £75 yr nm.

United Kingdom Association of Manufacturers of Bakers' Yeast
(UKAMBY) 1973
■   6 Catherine St, LONDON, WC2B 5JJ.   (hq)
      020 7836 2460   fax 020 7836 0580
      email bob.price@fdf.org.uk
      Sec: R D Price
▲   Un-incorporated Society
○   *T
●   Mtgs
<   Comité des Fabricants de Levure de Panification de
      l'U Eur (COFALEC); Food & Drink Fedn
M   3 f

United Kingdom Association of Preservation Trusts (APT)
1989
NR Alhambra House (9th floor), 27-31 Charing Cross Rd,
      LONDON, WC2H 0AU.   (hq)
      020 7930 1629
      Chmn: Colin Johns
      Co-ordinator: Louise Bailey
▲   Registered Charity
Br 9
○   *N; to encourage & assist building preservation trusts; to
      expand their capacity to preserve the built heritage
●   Conf - Mtgs - SG - Inf - LG
M   c 275 trusts
¶   NL - 2.   Guidance Notes - irreg.

United Kingdom Association of Professional Engineers
(UKAPE) 1969
NR Hayes Court, West Common Rd, HAYES, Kent, BR2 7AU.   (hq)
      020 8462 7755
Br 15
○   *U; interests of engineers holding management, executive,
      supervisory, design & research appointments
●   Conf - Mtgs - SG - Stat - Inf - Empl
M   6,000 i
¶   The Professional Engineer - 4; ftm.

United Kingdom Association of Proposal Management
Professionals (UKAPMP) 2001
NR 3 North Street Workshops, STOKE sub HANDON, Somerset,
      TA14 6QR.   (chiefexec/b)
      01935 825200
      CEO: Tony Birch
Br Netherlands, USA
○   *P; 'to advance the arts, sciences & technology of new business
      acquisition & to promote the professionalism of those
      engaged in those pursuits'
●   Conf - Mtgs - ET - Exam - Res - Exhib - Stat - Inf - LG
M   c 200 i, UK / c 1,600 i, o'seas
¶   Jnl - 2; ftm only.

United Kingdom Association of Suggestion Schemes
      see **Ideas UK - the UK Association of Suggestion Schemes**

United Kingdom Athletics Ltd   (UKA)   1991
NR   Athletics House, Central Boulevard, Blythe Valley Park,
　　SOLIHULL, B90 8AJ.   (hq)
　　0870 998 6800
　　Chief Exec: Niels de Vos
▲   Company Limited by Guarantee
Br   3
○   *S; governing body for track & field athletics
●   ET - Comp - Stat - LG
<   Intl Amat Athletic Fedn
M   c 1,600 clubs
¶   UK Rules for Competition Book - 1.

United Kingdom Bartenders Guild   (UKBG)   1933
■   Rose Bank, Blackness, LINLITHGOW, W Lothian, EH49 7NL.
　　(admin/p)
　　01506 834448   fax 01506 834373
　　Admin Officer: Jim Slavin
▲   Un-incorporated Society
Br   4; 1 o'seas
○   *P; interests of bartenders
●   Mtgs - ET - Exam - Exhib - Comp
<   Intl Bartenders' Assn
M   600 i, UK / 15 i, o'seas

United Kingdom Botswana Society   (UKBS)   1980
NR   29 Tournay Rd, LONDON, SW6 7UG.   (hsp)
　　020 7385 7031
　　Hon Sec: Mrs F Pearson,   Chmn: M R B Williams
▲   Un-incorporated Society
○   *X; to encourage & strengthen ties between Britain & Botswana
●   Mtgs
M   380 i, 10 f, UK / 5 i, o'seas
¶   NL - 4; ftm only.

United Kingdom Brain Tumour Society
　　since 2004 **Brain Tumour UK**

United Kingdom Bungee Club   1992
NR   Rockwood Cottages, 43 Barnsley Rd, Flockton, WAKEFIELD,
　　W Yorks, WF4 4DW.   (hq)
　　0700 028 6433
　　Dir: Jon Nicholls
Br   2
○   *G, *S; 'thrill-seeking, fun, overcoming your fears'; for all
　　interested in bungee jumping (filming, stunt jumpers &
　　riggers); the group does not accept people with high blood
　　pressure, heart or neurological conditions, dizziness /
　　epilepsy, pregnancy, asthma, or diabetes
<   CityPaintball.com
M   30,000 i

**United Kingdom Cartridge Remanufacturers Association
(UKCRA)   1994**
■   19b School Rd, SALE, Cheshire, M33 7XX.   (asa)
　　01706 525050   fax 01706 647440
　　email info@ukcra.com   http://www.ukcra.com
　　Sec: Laura Heywood
▲   Company Limited by Guarantee
○   *T; for remanufactures & component suppliers to the toner, &
　　inkjet industry; to provide laser printer users with proven high
　　quality products, that are cost effective & environmentally
　　friendly alternatives to imported toner cartridges
Gp   Laser toner cartridge re-manufacturers; Inkjet cartridge refillers
●   Mtgs
M   2,000 i, 40 f
　　Note: the registered title of this organisation is Recyclers Great
　　　Britain, but trades as UK Cartridge Remanufacturers
　　　Associaton
×   2003 United Kingdom Cartridge Recyclers Association

United Kingdom Cast Stone Association   (UKCSA)   1991
NR   15 Stonehill Court, The Arbours, NORTHAMPTON, Northants,
　　NN3 3RA.   (hq)
　　01604 405666
　　http://www.ukcsa.co.uk
　　Sec: Neil Sparrow
▲   Un-incorporated Society
○   *T; for manufacturers of cast stone construction materials
●   Mtgs - Res - Stat - Inf
<   US Cast Stone Inst (USCSI); Brit Cement Assn (BCA)
M   23 f, 14 f (associate)
¶   The Tablet (NL) - 4;   Specification for Cast Stone;   Specifier
　　& User Guide; all free.

United Kingdom Chasers & Riders Ltd   1999
NR   Offchurch Bury, Offchurch, LEAMINGTON SPA, Warks,
　　CV33 9AR.   (hq)
　　01926 450049
　　Sec: Claire Booth
▲   Company Limited by Guarantee
Br   2
○   *G; 'to help you enjoy your horse more by providing riding
　　which is as varied, safe & enjoyable as possible. We provide
　　a nationwide network of xc courses & equestrian centres
　　providing competitions, facilities & safe off road riding for all
　　members'
●   ET - Comp - Inf
M   30,000+ i, 50 farms & equestrian centres, 10 riding clubs
¶   UK Chasers Handbook - 1; ftm only.
　　NL & Competitions Calendar - 2; free.
　　Holidays with your Horse; free.

United Kingdom Cheese Guild   1989
§   PO Box 1525, GILLINGHAM, Dorset, SP8 4WA.   (hq)
　　01747 822290   fax 01747 822289
　　email linda.farrand1@btinternet.com
　　http://www.finefoodworld.co.uk
　　Chmn: Robert Farrand
　　Note: trains staff involved in cheese retailing to NVQ standard

**United Kingdom Chrysanthemum Growers' Association Ltd
(UKCGA)   1966**
■   30 Pern Drive, BOTLEY, Hants, SO30 2GW.   (hsp)
　　01489 786638   fax 01489 798827
　　Sec: Mrs Veronica Mason
▲   Un-incorporated Society
○   *H, *T; for commercial chrysanthemum growers; to further
　　research
●   Mtgs - SG
M   4 i, 12 f
¶   NL - irreg;   LM;   AR; all ftm.
×   2005 All Year Round Chrysanthemum Growers' Association

**United Kingdom Cleaning Products Industry Association
(UKCPI)**
■   Century House (1st Floor Suite), High St, TATTENHALL,
　　Cheshire, CH3 9RJ.   (hq)
　　01829 770055
　　Dir-Gen: Dr Andrew N Williams
▲   Un-incorporated Society
○   *T; interests of UK producers of cleaning, hygiene & surface
　　care products
Gp   Technical; Packaging; Legal; Industrial & institutional products
●   Mtgs - Stat - Inf - LG - Detergent Industry Information Bureau
<   Assn Intle de la Savonnerie, de la Détergence et des Produits
　　d'Entretien (AISE); Chemical Industries Assn (CIA)
M   c 45 f

United Kingdom Clinical Pharmacy Association   (UKCPA) 1981

■   Alpha House, Countesthorpe Rd, WIGSTON, Leics, LE18 4PJ. (hq)
      0116-277 6999   fax 0116-277 6272
      email admin@ukcpa.co   http://www.ukcpa.org
      Sec: Graeme Hall
▲   Un-incorporated Society
○   *M, *P; to foster the concepts & practice of pharmaceutical care for the benefit of patients & public
Gp   Cardiology; Critical care; Diabetes; Education & training; Emergency care; Infection management; Leadership development; Medicines management in primary care; Quality & risk management; Respiratory; Rheumatology; Surgery & theatres
●   Conf - ET - Res - Exhib - SG - LG
M   2,000 i, 23 f, 4 hospitals, UK / 60 i, 1 hospital, o'seas
¶   In Practice (NL) - 4; ftm only.   Practice Guides; £2.50.
      Symposia Abstract Booklet - 2; ftm, £7 nm.

United Kingdom Coloured Pencil Society

NR   White Meadows, Horton, DEVIZES, Wilts, SN10 3DB.   (sp)
      http://www.ukcps.co.uk
      Sec: Pat Heffer
○   *A

United Kingdom Computer Measurement Group   (UKCMG) 1981

■   Suite A1 Kebbell House, Carpenders Park, WATFORD, Herts, WD19 5BE.   (asa)
      020 8421 5330   fax 020 8421 5457
      email ukcmg@ukcmg.org.uk   http://www.ukcmg.org.uk
      Sec: Mike Ley
○   *P; for information technology professionals

United Kingdom Confederation of Hypnotherapy Organisations (UKCHO)   1998

■   302 Regent St (Suite 401), LONDON, W1B 6HH.   (hq)
      0800 952 0560 (freephone)
      http://www.ukcho.org.uk
      Co Sec: Peter Matthews
▲   Company Limited by Guarantee
○   *N, *P
<   Conf - Mtgs - ET - Res - LG
M   8 org
¶   NL - irreg.

United Kingdom Council for Psychotherapy   (UKCP)   1992

NR   Edward House (2nd floor), 2 Wakley St, LONDON, EC1V 7LT.   (hq)
      020 7014 9955   fax 020 7014 9977
      email info@psychotherapy.org.uk
      http://www.psychotherapy.org.uk
      CEO: Valerie Tufnell
▲   Registered Charity
○   *P; to promote & maintain the profession of psychotherapy
Gp   Analytical psychology; Behavioural & cognitive psychotherapy; Experiential constructivist therapies; Family / couple / sexual & systemic therapy; Humanistic & integrative psychotherapy; Therapy with children
●   Conf - Mtgs - ET - Inf - LG
<   Eur Assn for Psychotherapy; Brit Assn for Counselling
M   6,500 i, 80 f
¶   The Psychotherapist (NL) - 2; ftm only.
      National Register of Psychotherapists - 1.
      Directory of Member Organisations & Training Courses - 1.

United Kingdom Dairy Association

      since 2005 is UK-IDF, the UK National Committee of the International Dairy Federation

United Kingdom Dance & Drama Federation   (UKDDF)   1989

NR   18 Ashbourne Grove, Hanley, STOKE-on-TRENT, Staffs, ST1 5QW.
      01782 257820
      email info@ukddf.co.uk   http://www.ukddf.co.uk
      Pres: Gloria Harrison
▲   Un-incorporated Society
○   *D; an examination body offering a full dance & drama syllabus for qualified & professional teachers of dance
●   ET - Exam
<   Gld of Profl Teachers of Dancing; Hong Kong Jazz Soc
>   [all dance bodies & teacher orgs are able to join]
M   c 55 i
¶   NL - 4; m only.

United Kingdom Education & Research Networking Association (UKERNA)

NR   Atlas Centre, Chilton, DIDCOT, Oxon, OX11 0QS.   (hq)
      01235 822200
○   *P

United Kingdom Egg Producers Association Ltd   (UKEP)   1972

■   Kings House, Maunsel Rd, North Newton, BRIDGWATER, Somerset, TA7 0BP.
      01278 661280   fax 01278 661009
      email ukep@chicken-doctor.demon.co.uk
      http://www.laidinbritaineggs.co.uk
      Sec: David Spackman
▲   Company Limited by Guarantee
○   *T; for British egg producers
●   Stat - Inf - LG
M   90 i
¶   UKEP/LIB Hotwire - 12; ftm only.

United Kingdom Employee Assistance Professionals Association (UKEAPA)   1991

NR   3 Moors Close, Ducklington, WITNEY, Oxon, OX28 5HY.   (asa)
      0800 783 7616
      Sec: Jane Timms
○   *P; the advancement of education in the field of employee assistance programmes (EAPs); the encouragement of growth & development of EAPs in all workplaces
M   100 i, 50 f

United Kingdom Environmental Law Association   (UKELA)   1986

■   Honeycroft House, Pangbourne Rd, UPPER BASILDON, Berks, RG8 8LP.   (hsp/b)
      01491 671184   fax 01491 671631
      http://www.ukela.org
      Sec: Dr Christina B T Hill
▲   Company Limited by Guarantee; Registered Charity
○   *L, *P; to promote the enhancement & conservation of the environment; to advance the education of the public relating to the development, teaching, application & practice of law relating to the environment
Gp   Nature conservation; Europe; Planning & EA; Waste; Contaminated land; Insurance; Integrated pollution control; Practice & procedure; Emissions trading
●   Conf - Mtgs - ET - Res - SG - Inf
<   Eur Envtl Law Assn
¶   Environmental Law (Jnl) - 4; ftm only.   LM - 2 yrly.

United Kingdom Environmental Mutagen Society (UKEMS) 1977

NR School of Biological Sciences, University of Wales Swansea, Singleton Park, SWANSEA, Glam, SA2 8PP. (permanent/office)
email info@ukems.org
▲ Registered Charity
○ *L; the advancement of genetic toxicology by research, discussion & developing methodology
Gp Industrial genotoxicology; Molecular epidemiology
● Conf - Mtgs - ET - Res - LG
< Eur Envtl Mutagen Soc (affiliated to Intl Assn Envtl Mutagen Socs)
M 320 i, UK / 35 i, o'seas
¶ Mutagenesis (Jnl) - 6.
Various other books & reports.

United Kingdom Excellence Federation 1999

NR 32-34 Great Peter St, LONDON, SW1P 2QX. (hq)
020 7654 5004
Sec: Paul Brennan
▲ Company Limited By Guarantee
○ *N; comprises the Regional Excellence Organisations (REO) who promote business excellence in areas aligned to the Regional Development Agency boundaries
● ET - SG
< Brit Quality Foundation
M 11 orgs

United Kingdom Fashion Exports 1983

■ 5 Portland Place, LONDON, W1B 1PW. (hq)
020 7636 5577
http://www.ukfashionexports.com
Dir: Paul Alger
▲ Company Limited by Guarantee
○ *T; to promote UK exports of clothing & accessories
● Conf - Mtgs - ET - Exhib - Comp - Expt - Inf - Lib - Seminars
M c 750 f
¶ The Exporter - 12.
✕ 2003-04 British Knitting & Clothing Export Council

United Kingdom Federation of Jazz Bands (UKFJB) 1977

■ Wallsend Community Centre, Vine St, WALLSEND, Tyne & Wear, NE28 6JE. (hq)
0191-262 8536 fax 0191-262 8536
email m.paxton@ukjazzbands.com
http://www.ukjazzbands.com
Nat Sec & Chief Exec: Mrs Margaret Paxton
▲ Registered Charity
Br 5
○ *D; 'to advance the musical education of children throughout the UK by helping to train them in the playing of marching band instruments & by means of concerts & exhibitions at which such children may perform as bands to advance the aesthetic education of the public'
● Mtgs - ET - Exhib - Comp - VE - LG
M 6,940 i
¶ [on website only]

United Kingdom Flat Glass Manufacturers' Association (FGMA)

■ c/o Pilkington UK Ltd, Prescot Rd, ST HELENS, Merseyside, WA10 3TT. (sb)
01744 692914 fax 01744 692838
Sec Gen: Rick Wilberforce
▲ Un-incorporated Society
○ *T; promote interests of the UK flat glass mfrs
● LG
M 1 f
✕ 2003 Flat Glass Manufacturers' Association

United Kingdom Forest Products Association (UKFPA) 1996

NR Office 14 John Player Building, Stirling Enterprise Park, Springbank Rd, STIRLING, FK7 7RP. (hq)
01786 449029 fax 01786 473112
email dsulman@ukfpa.co.uk http://www.ukfpa.co.uk
Exec Dir & Sec: David J Sulman
▲ Company Limited by Guarantee
○ *T; to represent the British timber industry - harvesting companies, sawmillers, merchants & other processors of British home grown timber & forest products
Gp Harvesting & contracting; Wood supply; Health & safety; Training; Environmental; Technical & devt
● Mtgs - ET - Res - Exhib - SG - Inf - VE - LG
M 116 f
¶ LM; AR - 1.

United Kingdom Fortifications Club (UKFC) 1973

■ c/o 4 Mablethorpe Rd, Wymering, PORTSMOUTH, Hants, PO6 3LJ. (chmn/p)
023 9238 7794
email bob.hunt2@ntlworld.com http://www.ukfortsclub
Chmn: Peter D Cobb
▲ Un-incorporated Society
○ *G; to foster the interest & study of British built fortifications in the UK & overseas
Gp Ancient (pre-Roman); Roman/British; Dark Ages; Medieval; Tudor; Stuart; 18th century; 19th century (Victorian & earlier); 20th century & modern
● SG - Inf - Lib - LG - Archive
< Survey of Redundant Defences (SORD); Coun for Brit Archaeology
M 107 i, 3 org, UK / 12 i, 1 org, o'seas
¶ ALDIS (Jnl) - 2; ftm, £2.55 nm.

United Kingdom Forum for Environmental Industries 2000

NR c/o Gill Nowell, Envirolink Northwest, Spencer House, 91 Dewhurst Rd, Birchwood, WARRINGTON, Cheshire, WA3 7PG. (secretariat)
01925 813200 fax 01925 819031
email info@ukfei.org http://www.ukfei.org
Co-ordinator: Gill Nowell, Chmn: Jackie Seddon
▲ Company Limited by Guarantee
○ *T; an informal group acting as a conduit for the environmental sector between regions & nations of the UK & central government
Gp Sub-groups: Biomass, Exports, New markets for recyclates, Skills
● Mtgs - Expt - Inf - LG
M RDA's/DA's, Trade Associations, Enabling bodies

United Kingdom eInformation Group (UKeiG) 1978

■ The Old Chapel, Walden, West Burton, LEYBURN, N Yorks, DL8 4LE. (admin/hq)
01969 663749 fax 01969 663749
email info@ukeig.org.uk http://www.ukeig.org.uk
Hon Sec: Christine A Baker
▲ Registered Charity
○ *P; to encourage communication & the exchange of knowledge about electronic information
● Conf - Mtgs - ET
< is a Special Interest Group (SIG) of CILIP: Chart Inst of Library & Inf Profls
M 1,650 i, 105 f, UK / 50 i, o'seas
¶ eLucidate (Jnl) - 6; ftm only.
✕ 2004-05 UK Online User Group

United Kingdom Harp Association (UKHA) 1964

NR 46 Trinity Church Square, LONDON, SE1 4HT. (editor/p)
Editor: Alison Martin
○ *P, *T; for harpists, harp makers & repairers & harp enthusiasts, includes players of non-pedal harps (the clarsach), Paraguayan harp & metal strung harps
● Mtgs - Inf
M c 400 i, UK / c 100 i, o'seas
¶ Magazine - 4; £15 yr m. Directory - 2 yrly; ftm only.

© CBD Research Ltd · Beckenham · BR3 5JS · Tel 020 8650 7745 · Fax 020 8650 0768 · E-mail cbd@cbdresearch.com · www.cbdresearch.com

United Kingdom Homecare Association   (UKHCA)   1988
NR   42B Banstead Rd, CARSHALTON BEECHES, Surrey,
         SM5 3NW.   (hq)
         020 8288 1551   fax 020 8288 1550
         email lesley.rimmer@ukhca.co.uk
         http://www.ukhca.co.uk
         Chief Exec: Lesley Rimmer
▲   Company Limited by Guarantee
○   *N, *W; professional association to promote highest standards
         of domiciliary care
●   Conf - Mtgs - ET - Exhib - LG
<   Jt Advy Gp on Domiciliary Care; Nat Coun Voluntary Orgs
         (NCVO); Continuing Care Conference (CCC); Care Forum
         Wales; Indep Care Orgs Network (ICON)
M   1,400 f
¶   The Homecarer (NL) - 6; ftm.

United Kingdom Homeopathic Medical Association
         since 2001 **Homeopathic Medical Association**

United Kingdom Horse Shoers Union   (UKHSU)   2002
■   3 Roughdown Villas Road, HEMEL HEMPSTEAD, Herts,
         HP3 0AX.
         01442 248657
         Sec: Martin Humphrey
○   *U
         no further information supplied

United Kingdom Housekeepers Association   (UKHA)   1985
■   Flat 7, 14-15 Molyneux St, LONDON, W1H 5HQ.   (hsp)
         fax 020 7724 7378
         email lynn.yambao@virgin.net   http://www.ukha.co.uk
         Sec: Lynn K D Yambao
Br   4
○   *P
●   Conf - Mtgs - Exhib - VE
M   i

United Kingdom Industrial Space Committee   (UKISC)   1975
NR   UKISC Secretariat, PO Box 14, Wisbech, Cambs, PE13 1JZ.
         (hq)
         http://www.sbac.co.uk
         Sec Gen: Paul Flanagan
▲   Un-incorporated Society
○   *N, *T to increase space & space-related business, & the share
         of the market for member companies
Gp   Sub-c'ees: Telecommunications & navigation; Earth
         observation; Launchers; Research, technology & science
         Working groups: Parliamentary affairs; Galileo Sat-Nav; Other
         groups as required
●   Conf - Mtgs - Exhib - SG - Stat - Expt - LG - Representation to
         national & international bodies - Recommendation of
         members for appointment to official boards & committees
<   FEI - Fedn Electronics Ind; Soc Brit Aerospace Cos; Eurospace
M   40 i, 23 f, UK / 2 i, o'seas
¶   Brochure - 1;   Brochures & policy papers - irreg; all ftm.

United Kingdom Industrial Sugar Users' Group   (UKISUG)
■   20-22 Stukeley St, LONDON, WC2B 5LR.
         020 7430 0356   fax 020 7831 6014
         email info@uksugar.org.uk   http://www.ukisug.org.uk
         Sec: Richard Laming
○   *T; for industrial users of sugar
●   Mtgs
<   CIUS
M   f

United Kingdom Industrial Vision Association   (UKIVA)   1992
■   PO Box 25, ROYSTON, Herts, SG8 6TL.
         01763 261419   fax 01763 261961
         email info@ukiva.org   http://www.ukiva.org
         Admin: Don Braggins
▲   Company Limited by Guarantee
○   *T; to promote the use of vision technology by the
         manufacturing industry in Britain
M   40 f, UK / 3 f, o'seas
¶   NL - 2;   LM; both free.
         21 Financial Justifications for using Machine Vision.
         Guide to Machine Vision; free to qualifying applicants.

United Kingdom Institute for Conservation of Historic & Artistic Works
         in 2005 merged with the Care of Collections Forum, Institute of Paper
         Conservation, Photographic Materials Conservation Group to form
         the **Institute of Conservation**

**United Kingdom & Ireland Society of Cataract & Refractive
         Surgeons   (UKISCRS)**
NR   PO Box 598, STOCKTON-ON-TEES, Co Durham, TS20 1WY.
         (hq)
         01642 651208   fax 01642 651208
         email ukiscrs@onyxnet.co.uk   http://www.ukiscrs.org.uk
         The Secretary
▲   Company Limited by Guarantee
○   *P; promotion & dissemination of knowledge of cataract &
         refractive surgery to interested healthcare professionals
●   Conf - Mtgs - ET
<   Eur Soc of Cataract & Refractive Surgeons (ESCRS)
M   500 i
¶   Jnl of Cataract & Refractive Surgery - 12; ftm, priced nm.
         NL - 2; ftm only.

United Kingdom Irrigation Association   (UKIA)   1980
NR   The Old Vicarage, Main St, Torksey, LINCOLN, LN1 2EE.
         (regd/off)
         01427 717627
         Exec Sec: Melvyn Kay
▲   Company Limited by Guarantee
○   *F, *H
Gp   Agriculture; Horticulture; Mains water; Sports turf & amenity
●   Conf - Mtgs - ET - Inf - LG
M   250 i, UK / 50 i, o'seas
¶   Irrigation News (Jnl) - 2.
         Monographs (Conference Proceedings).

**United Kingdom Jute Goods Association Ltd (incorporating
         NASMAR)   (UKJGA)   1948**
NR   33 Haynes Park Court, Slewins Close, HORNCHURCH, Essex,
         RM11 2DE.   (hsp/b)
         01708 453000   fax 01708 453010
         Sec: P W Rosamond
○   *T; jute goods trade (new & secondhand)
●   Conf - Mtgs - Stat - Empl - LG
M   i

**United Kingdom Land & Hydrographic Survey Association
         (TSA)   1979**
NR   Meadlake Place, Thorpe Lea Rd, EGHAM, Surrey, TW20 8BF.
         (hq)
         01784 223760   fax 01784 223775
         email office@tsa-uk.org.uk   http://www.tsa-uk.org.uk
         Sec Gen: Tom Dougherty
○   *T
●   Mtgs - Inf
M   60 f
¶   NL;   Members Directory; both free.

United Kingdom Literacy Association   (UKLA)   1961
NR   Upton House, Baldock St, ROYSTON, Herts, SG8 5AY.   (hq)
　　　01763 241188   fax 01763 243785
　　　email admin@ukla.org   http://www.ukla.org
　　　Hon Sec: Lyn Overall
▲　Registered Charity
○　*E; for professionals interested in the teaching & learning of
　　　language, literacy & communication
●　Conf - ET - Res - Exhib - LG - Book awards
<　Intl Reading Assn
M　500 i, 100 f, 80 schools
¶　Journal of Research in Reading - 3;　Literacy - 3;
　　　Language & Literacy News - 3; all ftm.
✕　2002-03 United Kingdon Reading Association

United Kingdom Lubricants Association Ltd   (UKLA)   1968
■　Berkhamsted House, 121 High St, BERKHAMSTED, Herts,
　　　HP4 2DJ.   (hq)
　　　01442 230589   fax 01442 259232
　　　email enquiries@ukla.org.uk   http://www.ukla.org.uk
　　　Exec Dir: Rod G Parker
▲　Company Limited by Guarantee
Br　4
○　*T; for the UK lubricants industry
Gp　Metalworking Fluid Product Stewardship Gp
●　Conf - Mtgs - Stat - Inf - VE - LG
<　Indep U of the Eur Lubricants Ind (UEIL)
M　100 f, UK / 2 f, o'seas
¶　Lube (Jnl) - 6; free.
✕　2005 (1 January) British Lubricants Federation

United Kingdom Magnetics Society
NR　Grove Business Centre, Grove Technology Park, WANTAGE,
　　　Oxon, OX12 9FA.   (asa)
　　　01235 770652
　　　No further information supplied

United Kingdom Maize Millers' Association   1997
NR　21 Arlington St, LONDON, SW1A 1RN.   (hq)
　　　020 7493 2521
　　　Sec: Alex Waugh
▲　Un-incorporated Society
○　*T; for the UK maize milling industry
●　Mtgs - LG
<　Euromaiziers
M　4 f

United Kingdom Maritime Pilots' Association   (UKMPA)   1884
NR　Transport House, 128 Theobald's Rd, LONDON, WC1X 8TN.
　　　(hq)
　　　020 7611 2570   fax 020 7611 2757
　　　email ukmpa@tgwu.org.uk   http://www.ukmpa.org
　　　Sec: John A Pretswell
▲　Un-incorporated Society
○　*P; interests of maritime pilots of ports of Great Britain &
　　　Northern Ireland
<　Intl Maritime Pilots' Assn; Eur Maritime Pilots' Assn; Transport &
　　　Gen Workers U
M　500 i

United Kingdom Metering Forum
NR　Gemserv, Centurion House (7th Floor), 24 Monument St,
　　　LONDON, EC3R 8AJ.
　　　020 7090 1000
○　*T

United Kingdom Metric Association   (UKMA)   2000
■　34 Wroxham Gardens, LONDON, N11 2BA.   (hsp)
　　　0778 054 2950
　　　email secretary@metric.org.uk   http://www.ukma.org.uk
　　　Sec: Derek Pollard
▲　Un-incorporated Society
○　*K; a non-political organisation which supports the use of the
　　　international metric system (SI) for all official, trade, health,
　　　safety, educational, media, legal & contractual purposes in
　　　the UK. It believes that the universal adoption of the metric
　　　system is in the best interests of the British Public
Gp　Cookery; Education; PR; Retail; Transport
●　Conf - Res - SG - Inf - LG
<　US Metric Assn (USMA)
M　80 i, UK / 5 i, o'seas
¶　NL - 4;　AR - 1; both ftm only.
　　　Technical Reports; £6.25 m, £12.50 nm.
✕　2001 UK Metrication Association

United Kingdom Mineral Wool Association
　　see **EURISOL-UK Ltd (UK Mineral Wool Association)**

United Kingdom Newsletter & Electronic Publishers Association (UK NEPA)
■　Aaron House, 6 Bardolph Rd, RICHMOND-UPON-THAMES,
　　　Surrey, TW9 2LS.   (hq)
　　　020 8288 7415   fax 020 8288 7415
　　　email uk.nepa@btconnect.com
　　　http://www.newsletters.org
　　　Dir: Karen Hindle
▲　Un-incorporated Society
Br　USA
○　*T; for producers of specialised business information, both
　　　newsletters & online, based in the UK
●　Conf - Mtgs - ET - Inf
<　is the UK chapter of Newsletter & Electronic Publishers Assn
　　　(USA)
M　70+ f
¶　Electronic Bulletin - 6;　UK NEPA Directory - 1; both ftm only.

United Kingdom Noise Association   (UKNA)   2000
■　Broken Wharf House (2nd floor), 2 Broken Wharf, LONDON,
　　　EC4V 3DT.   (hq)
　　　020 7329 0774
　　　email ukna@tesco.net   http://www.ukna.org.uk
　　　Sec: Val Weedon
▲　Un-incorporated Society
○　*K; campaigns for action against noise
●　Conf - Mtgs - Res - Exhib - Inf - LG
M　200 i, 40,000 org

United Kingdom Offshore Operators Association Ltd (UKOOA)   1973
NR　232-242 Vauxhall Bridge Rd, LONDON, SW1V 1AU.   (hq)
　　　020 7802 2400
　　　email info@ukooa.co.uk
　　　Dir Gen: Malcolm Webb
▲　Company Limited by Guarantee
○　*T; the representative organisation for the UK offshore oil & gas
　　　industry; members are companies licensed by the
　　　government to explore for & produce oil & gas in UK waters
Gp　20+ c'ees & sub c'ees on various technical & policy issues
●　Conf - Mtgs - ET - Res - Exhib - LG
<　Intl Assn of Oil & Gas Producers; Confedn of Brit Inds
M　30 f
¶　Publications list available.
　　　Note: the correct (registered) title is UK Offshore Operators
　　　Association Ltd
　　　see note under UK. . .

United Kingdom Online User Group
　　has become **UK einformation Group**

© CBD Research Ltd · Beckenham · BR3 5JS · Tel 020 8650 7745 · Fax 020 8650 0768 · E-mail cbd@cbdresearch.com · www.cbdresearch.com

United Kingdom Onshore Operators Group   (UKOOG)   1986
NR   Shepherds, CRANBROOK, Kent, TN17 3EN.   (hq)
      01580 715100
▲   Company Limited by Guarantee
○   *T; for UK onshore oil & gas operators licensed under UK
      Landward   Licences (Petroleum Production Act 1934)

**United Kingdom Overseas Territories Association   (UKOTA)
1998**
NR   c/o Gibraltar London Office, Arundel Great Court, 178-179
      Strand, LONDON, WC2R 1EL.
      020 7836 0777   fax 020 7240 6612
▲   Un-incorporated Society
○   *N, *W; to provide a forum for discussion for residents of British
      overseas territories on issues of common interest in the
      relevant areas
●   Conf - Mtgs - Inf
M   9 territories

United Kingdom Paint Horse Association
NR   Olde Walnut Tree Farm, Pristow Green Lane, Tibenham,
      NORWICH, NR16 1PU.
      01379 674551
      http://www.ukpha.co.uk
○   *B

United Kingdom Paintball Sports Federation   (UKPSF)   1991
■   5 Waingap Crescent, Whitworth, ROCHDALE, Lancs,
      OL12 8PX.   (chiefexec/p)
      0845 130 4252
      Chief Exec: Steven Bull
▲   Un-incorporated Society
○   *S; to promote the sport of paintball (the firing of paint 'blobs')
Gp   Players' Council
●   Exhib - Comp - Inf - LG
M   850 i, 175 f, 2 org, UK / 50 i, 10 f, o'seas
¶   Paintball UK (NL) - 4.   Paintball Games in Woodlands.
      Millennium Site Guide - 1.
      Code of Practice.   Site Survey - 1.

United Kingdom Parking Enforcement Agency   (PEA)   2003
NR   PO Box 186, ASHTON-under-LYNE, OL6 6ZU.   (hq)
      0870 787 3951
      email general@parkforce.com
▲   Company Limited by Guarantee
○   *T; for wheel-clamping companies
●   Conf - Mtgs - Res - Exhib - LG
M   100 i, 20 f
¶   [Code of practice].

**United Kingdom Petroleum Industry Association   (UKPIA)
1978**
NR   9 Kingsway, LONDON, WC2B 6XF.   (hq)
      020 7240 0289
      Dir Gen: Chris Hunt
▲   Company Limited by Guarantee
○   *T; represents oil companies involved in the supply, refining &
      distribution of oil in the UK
●   SG - Stat - Inf - LG - Media & public information
M   8 f
      Note: the correct title of the Association is - UK Petroleum
      Industry Association
      see note under UK...

United Kingdom Polarity Therapy Association   (UKPTA)   1996
NR   Monomark House, 27 Old Gloucester St, LONDON,
      WC1N 3XX.   (mail)
      0700 705 2748
      email info@ukpta.org.uk
      http://www.ukpta.org.uk address
▲   Un-incorporated Society
○   *P; 'for those who practice & teach the therapeutic system
      called Polarity Therapy developed by Dr Randolph Stone; to
      promote this form of therapy - a true holistic approach to
      health & healing employing a person's own energy to heal at
      physical, mental & emotional levels'
M   i & schools

United Kingdom Polocrosse Association Ltd   (UKPA)   1986
■   Grove House Farm, Main Rd, Wharncliffe Side, SHEFFIELD,
      S35 0DQ.   (hsp)
      01226 765126   fax 01226 370105
      email nfo@polocrosse.org.uk
      http://www.polocrosse.org.uk
      Hon Sec: Susan Brookes
▲   Company Limited by Guarantee
○   *S; to control & administer the game of Polocrosse (a team
      game played on horseback)
●   Mtgs - ET - Comp - VE
<   Intl Polocrosse Coun; Brit Horse Soc
M   500 i
¶   NL - 4;   Magazine - 1;   Ybk - 1; all ftm.

**United Kingdom Practical Shooting Association   (UKPSA)
1977**
■   PO Box 4478, HARLOW, Essex, CM17 0RS.   (mail)
      07010 703845   fax 0870 765 7721
      http://www.ukpsa.co.uk add
      Sec: Alan B Phillips
▲   Registered Charity
○   *S; to administer the sport of practical shooting in the UK
●   Comp - LG
<   Intl Practical Shooting Confedn (IPSC); Brit Assn for Shooting &
      Conservation (BASC); Nat Rifle Assn (NRA)
M   [not stated]
¶   DVC - 1;   eDVC - 9; both ftm only.

United Kingdom Preserve Manufacturers' Association
      has become the UK Sweet Spreads Association & is one of the three
      associations within the **Food Processors' Association**

United Kingdom Public Health Association   (UKPHA)   1988
■   Lion Court (suites 3 & 4), 25 Procter St, LONDON,
      WC1V 6NY.   (hq)
      020 7269 7964   fax 020 7269 7969
      email info@ukpha.org.uk   http://www.ukpha.org.uk
      Chief Exec: Angela Mawle
▲   Company Limited by Guarantee; Registered Charity
○   *K, *P; to promote the public health; to combat health
      inequalities, promote sustainable development & challenge
      anti-health forces
●   Conf - Mtgs - Res - Exhib - SG - LG
M   1,000 i, 200 org, UK / 100 i, o'seas

United Kingdom Quality Ash Association (UKQAA) 1997
- ■ Regent House, Bath Avenue, WOLVERHAMPTON, W Midlands, WV1 4EG.
  01902 810087   fax 01902 810187
  email enquiries@ukqaa.org.uk
  http://www.ukqaa.org.uk
  Technical Dir: Dr Lindon Sear
- ▲ Un-incorporated Society
- ○ *T; to represent the interests of producers & users of fly ash from coal fired power stations, eg the construction industry - use of fly ash in concrete fill, grouting; road construction
- ● Conf - Mtgs - ET - Res - Exhib - Inf - Lib
- < Eur Ash Assn (ECOBA)
- M 17 f
- ¶ Datasheets;   Case Studies;   Best Practice Guides - all irreg; all free.

** United Kingdom Radio Society
Organisation lost: see Introduction paragraph 3

United Kingdom Rainwater Harvesting Association (UK-RHA) 2004
- ■ Business Centre, Rio Drive, Collingham, NEWARK, Notts, NG23 7NB.   (sb)
  01636 894900   fax 01636 894909
  email terrynash@ukrha.org   http://www.ukrha.org
  Co Sec: Terry Nash
- ▲ Company Limited by Guarantee
- ○ *T; to encourage harvesting of rainwater; to enable individuals, organisations & companies engaged in the industry to work in partnership
- ● Cpnf - Mtgs - Exhib - SG - Stat - LG
- M 17 f

United Kingdom Reading Association
since 2002-03 **United Kingdon Literacy Association**

United Kingdom Renderers' Association Ltd (UKRA) 1966
- NR St Martha's Lodge, One Tree Hill Rd, GUILDFORD, Surrey, GU4 8PJ.   (sb)
  01483 503701
  Dir Gen: Alan Lawrence
- ○ *T
- M f

United Kingdom Resilient Flooring Association (UKRFA)
- ■ c/o Bunkers, 7 The Drive, HOVE, E Sussex, BN3 3JS.   (asa)
  01273 329797
  Sec: R J M Crawt
- ○ *T; manufacturers of vinyl & linoleum
- ● Mtgs - Inf (on vinyl & linoleum only)
- M 9 f

United Kingdom Revenue Protection Association (UKRPA) 1997
- NR Gemserv, Centurion House (7th Floor), 24 Monument St, LONDON, EC3R 8AJ.   (hsb)
  020 7090 1000
  http://www.ukrpa.org.uk
- ▲ Un-incorporated Society
- ○ *T; for companies involved in investigating & dealing with theft of electricity &/or interference with meters
- Gp Publicity c'ee; Technical c'ee
- ● Conf - Mtgs - ET - Inf - LG
- < Intl Utilities Revenue Protection Assn (IURPA)
- M 16 f

United Kingdom Rocketry Association (UKRA) 1996
- NR PO Box 1561, SHEFFIELD, S Yorks, S11 7XA.   (mail)
  email enquiries@ukra.org.uk
  http://www.ukra.org.uk address
- ▲ Un-incorporated Society
- ○ *G; to promote amateur rocketry in the UK; to provide a link between groups & individuals interested in rocketry in the UK; to create a recognised safety code & certification & achievement programme
- ● Mtgs - ET - Exam - Exhib - LG - Annual flying events - Monthly club meetings
- < Brit Model Flying Assn (BMFA)
- M 200 i, 7 org
- ¶ UKRA Hbk - 1.   10.9.8 - 4.

United Kingdom Roundabout Appreciation Society (UKRAS) 2003
- ■ 1 Rowborough Close, Astwood Bank, REDDITCH, Worcs, B96 6DQ.
  01527 894088   fax 01527 522545
  email kevin@beresfordB96.freeserve.co.uk
  http://www.roundaboutsok.britain.com
  Sec/Pres: Kevin Beresford
- ▲ Un-incorporated Society
- ○ *G; to collect data & other information on traffic islands, roundabouts & all traffic gyratory systems
- ● Mtgs - VE
- M 30 i
- ¶ Roundabouts of GB Calendar [for 26 towns] - 1; £5 m, £8 nm.
  Roundabouts of Britain (book); £7.99.
  Roundabouts from the Air (book); £8.99.

United Kingdom Science Park Association (UKSPA) 1984
- ■ Chesterford Research Park, Little Chesterford, SAFFRON WALDEN, Essex, CB10 1XL.   (hq)
  01799 532050   fax 01799 532049
  email info@ukspa.org.uk   http://www.ukspa.org.uk
  Chief Exec: Anthony P Wright
- ▲ Company Limited by Guarantee
- ○ *L, *N; 'to assist in the planning, development, operation & management of science parks / technology parks & incubators linked to universities & other institutes of higher education; to stimulate the growth of technology & knowledge based firms through the transfer of technology'
- ● Conf - Mtgs - ET - Res - Stat - Inf - LG
- < Intl Assn of Science Parks (IASP); World Alliance for Innovation (WAINOVA); Assn of Universities Res & Indl Links (AUKUL)
- M 60,000 i, 2,600 f
- ¶ Innovation into Success (Jnl) - 4; ftm, £4.95 nm.
  Annual Directory of Science Parks; ftm (£25 2nd copy), £50 nm.
  Evaluation of the Past & Future Economic Contribution of the UK Science Park Movement; £35 m, £75 nm.
  Planning, Development & Operation of Science Parks; £20.
  Best Practice Guides - irreg; £20 each or £60 the set.

United Kingdom Security Shredding Association (UKSSA)
- NR c/o Bolton Bros Ltd, Bromford Rd, Gt Blakenham, IPSWICH, Suffolk, IP6 0SL.   (hsb)
  01473 830948   fax 01473 830056
  http://www.ukssa.org
  Hon Sec: Reuben Bolton
- ▲ Un-incorporated Society
- ○ *T; to promote security shredding & information data destruction services together with legal requirements at local & national levels
- ● Mtgs
- M 10 f

© CBD Research Ltd · Beckenham · BR3 5JS · Tel 020 8650 7745 · Fax 020 8650 0768 · E-mail cbd@cbdresearch.com · www.cbdresearch.com

United Kingdom Serials Group   (UKSG)   1978
NR   Hilltop, Heath End, NEWBURY, Berks, RG20 0AP.   (admin)
        01635 254292   fax 01635 253826
        email alison@uksg.org   http://www.uksg.org p
        Business Manager: Alison Whitehorn
○   *L, *P; 'to promote & assist discussion & research on serials &
        their management between all interested parties in the
        information industry'
●   Conf - Mtgs - ET - Res - Exhib - Stat - Inf
M   c 600 org
¶   Serials (online Jnl) - 3; £72+VAT m only.

United Kingdom Shareholders' Association Ltd   (UKSA)   1992
        Chmn: David Blundell
        Nat Sec: Toby Keynes (membership@uksa.org.uk)
▲   Company Limited by Guarantee
Br   6
○   *K, *W; to promote improved standards of corporate
        governance for the benefit of the UK economy including all
        shareholders; to represent the interests of private
        shareholders; to assist private shareholders exercise their
        responsibilities as joint owners of their companies
Gp   Company activities group
●   Mtgs - ET - Res - SG - VE - LG
<   Euroshareholders (Eur Shareholders Gp)
M   500 i, 10 org, UK / 10 i, o'seas
¶   UKSA Update (NL) - 6; ftm only.
        Numerous policy papers available on website.

United Kingdom Sibelius Society   1984
NR   51 Vernon Ave, LONDON, SW20 8BN.   (hsp)
        020 8715 7659
        Pres: Edward Clark
▲   Un-incorporated Society
○   *D; to explore & promulgate Sibelius' achievement in 20th
        century music
●   Conf - Mtgs - Concerts - Seminars
M   120 i, UK / 40 i, o'seas
¶   NL - 4; free.

United Kingdom Simulation Training & Action Group
        a group of the **Defence Manufacturers Association**

United Kingdom Skeptics   (UK Skeptics)   1988
NR   10 Crescent View, LOUGHTON, Essex, IG10 4PZ.   (hsp)
        http://www.skeptic.org.uk
        Contact: Mike Hutchinson
▲   Un-incorporated Society
○   *K, *L; a non-membership body providing a rational, scientific
        response to paranormal &/or pseudoscientific claims; to
        inculcate critical thinking & an understanding of science
Gp   Remote viewing; Crystal power; Crop circles; Anti-gravity;
        Perpetual motion; Hypnotic regression (past lives); Re-
        incarnation; Health fraud; Astrology; ESP; Creationism (anti-
        evolution theories); Spoon bending; Fire-walking
●   Conf - Res - Inf
¶   The Skeptic - 4; £15 yr.

**United Kingdom Society of Investment Professionals   (UKSIP)
1956**
■   90 Basinghall St (4th floor), LONDON, EC2V 5AY.   (hq)
        020 7796 3000   fax 020 7796 3333
        email uksipstaff@uksip.org.uk   http://www.uksip.org
        Chief Exec: John Rogers
▲   Company Limited by Guarantee
○   *P
●   Conf - Mtgs - Exam - SG - Inf - VE
<   CFA Inst
M   6,000 i
¶   Professional Investor - 10.   Report - 1; ftm.
        Headline Earnings Definition.

United Kingdom Society for Trenchless Technology   (UKSTT)
NR   38 Holly Walk, LEAMINGTON SPA, Warks, CV32 4LY.   (hq)
        01926 330935
▲   Company Limited by Guarantee; Registered Charity
○   *P; to advance the science & practice of trenchless technology
        for public benefit; to promote education, training, study &
        research in trenchless technology
●   Conf - Mtgs - ET - Exhib - Expt - Inf - LG
<   Intl Soc for Trenchless Technology
¶   UKSTT News (NL) - 6; ftm.

United Kingdom Software Metrics Association   (UKSMA)
■   c/o Rob Ratcliff, Project Support Office, Level 2 Steria,
        Gun Wharf, Dock Rd, CHATHAM, Kent, ME4 4TU.   (chmn)
        01634 825715
        email admin@uksma.co.uk   http://www.uksma.co.uk
        Chmn: Rob Ratcliff
▲   Company Limited by Guarantee
○   *P; for organisations & individuals involved in the development,
        promotion or use of software metrics
●   Conf - Mtgs - ET - Exam - Res - Exhib - SG - Inf - Lib
M   i, f
¶   NL - 4; ftm, £10 nm.

United Kingdom Spoon Collectors Club   (UKSCC)   1980
■   72 Edinburgh Rd, NEWMARKET, Suffolk, CB8 0QD.   (hsp)
        01638 665457
        email david.cross340@ntlworld.com
        Hon Sec: David S Cross
▲   Un-incorporated Society
Br   6; Australia, N Zealand, South Africa, USA
○   *G; for those interested in collecting spoons (souvenir or
        antique)
●   Mtgs - AGM (October)
M   200 i
¶   Club Magazine - 4; subscription varies (£12- £1).

**United Kingdom Sports Association for People with Learning
        Disability   (UKSAPLD)   1980**
NR   Leroy House (ground floor), 436 Essex Rd, LONDON,
        N1 3QP.   (hq)
        0870 770 2464   fax 0870 770 2466
        email office@uksapld.freeserve.co.uk
        Nat Dir: Tracey McCillen
▲   Company Limited by Guarantee; Registered Charity
○   *N; to co-ordinate, promote & develop sport & recreational
        opportunities for all people with learning disability in the UK
●   Conf - ET - Inf
<   Intl Sports Fedn for Persons with Intellectual Disabilities (INAS-
        FID); Brit Paralympic Assn (BPA)
¶   Information Bulletin - 4; £6 yr.

**United Kingdom Spring Manufacturers Association   (UKSMA)
        1948**
NR   Henry St, SHEFFIELD, S Yorks, S3 7EQ.   (hq)
        0114-276 0542   fax 0114-272 0554
        email uksma@uksma.org.uk   http://www.uksma.org.uk
        Managing Dir: Andrew Watkinson
▲   Company Limited by Guarantee
○   *T
●   Conf - Mtgs - ET - Res - Inf - Lib - VE
<   Eur Spring Fedn
M   c 100 f
¶   Directory of British Spring Manufacturers - 1; free.

United Kingdom Steel   1967
- ■ Broadway House, Tothill St, LONDON, SW1H 9NQ.   (hq)
  020 7222 7777   fax 020 7222 3531
  email enquiries@uksteel.org.uk
  http://www.uksteel.org.uk
  Dir: Ian Rodgers
- ○ *T; representation of UK steel producing & processing
  companies
- Gp Tubes product (incorporating members of the former British
  Welded Steel Tube Assn)
- ● Conf - Mtgs - Stat - Expt - Inf - LG - Provision of detailed
  information on steel specifications to specifiers & users of
  steel
- < is a division of Engineering Employers' Federation
- > Energy Intensive Users Gp; Brit Metallurgical Plant Constructors
  Assn
- M 30 f
- ¶ LM;   Annual Statistics; AR; all free.
  Steel specifications [book & On-line]
- × 2003 UK Steel Association

United Kingdom Tai Chi Association
the association has become Hine Tai Chi Schools (which teach
the Tai Chi method for combatting stress & for good health)
& is therefore outside the scope of this directory

United Kingdom Tea Association   (UKTA)   1953
- NR UKTA Secretariat, 6 Catherine St, LONDON, WC2B 5JJ.   (asa)
  020 7420 7113   fax 020 7836 0580
  http://www.tea.co.uk
  Sec: Geraldine Smith
- ▲ Un-incorporated Society
- ○ *T
- ● Mtgs - LG
- < Food & Drink Fedn (FDF)
- M 35 f

United Kingdom Textile Laboratory Forum   (UKTLF)   2001
- ■ 8 Wentworth Way, LEEDS, W Yorks, LS17 7TG.   (hsp)
  0113-225 2945
  email info@uktlf.com   http://www.uktlf.com
  Hon Sec: Alan Rose
- ▲ Un-incorporated Society
- ○ *N, *T; to provide a technical forum for UKAS-accredited textile
  laboratories; to provide a system of inter-laboratory
  comparisons; to provide a professional interface with other
  relevant organisations
- Gp Working gps: Fibre composition, Flammability, Uncertainty of
  measurement
- ● Mtgs - ET - Inter-laboratory correlations
- > UKAS; Soc of Dyers & Colourists; Assn of Suppliers to Brit
  Clothing Ind
- M 1 i, 20 f, 3 org, UK

United Kingdom Thalassaemia Society   (UKTS)   1976
- ■ 19 The Broadway, Southgate Circus, LONDON, N14 6PH.
  (hq)
  020 8882 0011
  Pres: M Michael,   Coordinator: Elaine Miller
- ▲ Registered Charity
- ○ *M,*W; to provide advice, information & counselling to sufferers
  & carriers of thalassaemia (a hereditary blood disorder)
- ● Conf - Mtgs - ET - Res - Inf
- < Thalassaemia Intl Fedn (TIF)
- M c 600 i, UK / c 130 i, o'seas
- ¶ News Review (NL) - 4.   AR.
  Various booklets & leaflets.

United Kingdom Timber Frame Association   2002
- NR e centre, Cooperage Way Business Village, ALLOA,
  Clackmannanshire, FK10 3LP.   (chmn/b)
  01259 272140
  Chief Exec: Bryan Woodley
- ○ *T
- × 2002 (Timber Brick Council
  (Timber Frame Industry Association

United Kingdom Trades Confederation Ltd   (UKTC)   1995
- NR Braintree House (1st floor), Braintree Rd, RUISLIP, Middx,
  HA4 0EJ.   (hq)
  020 8842 4442   fax 020 8842 2461
  email admin@uktc.org   http://www.uktc.org
  Managing Dir: Derek Vaughan
- ▲ Company Limited by Guarantee
- Br 3
- ○ *N, *T; 'to promote & protect members' interests while reducing
  costs'
- Gp Debt recovery; Merchant services
- < Allied Trs Confedn
- M 9,000 f
- ¶ UK News - 4; free.

**United Kingdom Transplant Co-ordinators Association
(UKTCA)   1983**
- NR PO Box 47, KINGSBRIDGE, Devon, TQ7 4WG.   (mail address)
  07071 223171
- ▲ Un-incorporated Society
- ○ *N, *P; to increase organ transplantation & donation within the
  UK & Eire; to manage & promote the aims & interests of the
  personnel employed as transplant co-ordinators within the
  National Health Service
- ● Conf - Mtgs - ET - Res - Exhib - SG - VE - LG
- < Brit Transplantation Soc; UK Transplant Support Services
  Authority
- M 100 i, UK / 5 i, o'seas
- ¶ NL - 3;   LM - irreg; both free.
  Leaflets on transplantation (liver, kidneys, heart, heart/lungs);
  ftm & the medical profession.

United Kingdom Travel Retail Forum   (UKTRF)   1988
- ■ LGM House, Mill Green Rd, HAYWARDS HEATH, W Sussex,
  RH16 1XL.   (hq)
  01444 474700   fax 01444 474701
  email info@uktrf.co.uk
  Sec Gen: Barry Goddard
- ▲ Company Limited by Guarantee
- ○ *T; to improve trading conditions for companies involved in the
  supply & sale of duty paid goods to international travellers
  within the EU; to protect all duty & tax free sales where these
  still exist
- ● Mtgs - Stat - Expt - LG
- < Eur Travel Retail Coun
- M 26 f

United Kingdom Tropical Forest Forum
see **Tropical Forest Forum**

**United Kingdom Twin to Twin Transfusion Syndrome
Association   (twin2twin)   1997**
- NR 42 Wentworth Crescent, Harlington, Hayes, Middx, UB3 1NN.
  020 8581 7359
  email correen@twin2twin.org   http://www.twin2twin.org
  Founder: Correen Jackson
- ○ *M, *W; the preservation & protection of the health of unborn
  babies with twin to twin transfusion syndrome
- ¶ Leaflets.

© CBD Research Ltd · Beckenham · BR3 5JS · Tel 020 8650 7745 · Fax 020 8650 0768 · E-mail cbd@cbdresearch.com · www.cbdresearch.com

United Kingdom Ultimate Association   1981
NR   LONDON, WC1X 3XX.   (mail/address)
      0870 760 7189
▲   Un-incorporated Society
○   *S; for the seven-a-side team sport of Ultimate (Frisbee) - a
      game played indoors & outdoors by men & women using a
      flying disc
●   Comp (tournaments)
<   Wld Flying Disc Fedn (WFDF)
M   2,000 i
¶   Ultimatum (NL) - 4; ftm.

United Kingdom Unicycle Federation   (UKUF)   1988
■   103 Broad St, BARRY, Vale of Glamorgan, CF62 7AH.   (hsp)
      01446 740520
      email russell@pick-n-mix.co.uk
      http://www.pick-n-mix.co.uk
      Hon Sec: Russell Wells
▲   Un-incorporated Society
○   *G, *S; to promote, teach & give information on unicycling; to
      put people in touch with unicyclists
Gp   Cycling; Circus skills; Unicycle hockey; Juggling; Entertainers
●   Inf
M   [not stated]

United Kingdom Vineyards Association   (UKVA)   1996
NR   PO Box 985, BRETTISHAM, Cambs, CB5 9WW.   (hq)
      01223 813812
      Gen Sec: Robert Beardsmore
▲   Company Limited by Guarantee
○   *T; to promote viticulture in the British Isles
●   Conf - Mtgs - ET - Exam - Exhib - Comp - SG - Inf - VE
<   Nat Farmers U; Wine & Spirit Assn of GB
M   c 400 i
¶   The Grape Press - 4; ftm only.   Vineyards open to Visitors.

United Kingdom Warehousing Association   (UKWA)   1944
■   Walter House, 418-422 Strand, LONDON, WC2R 0PT.   (hq)
      020 7836 5522 & 0449   fax 020 7379 6904
      email dg@ukwa.org.uk   http://www.ukwa.org.uk
      Dir-Gen: R J Williams
▲   Un-incorporated Society
○   *T; represents public warehouse keepers in the UK
Gp   Customs & tax warehousing; Operations & safety
●   Conf - Mtgs - ET - Inf - VE - LG
<   Intl Fedn of Warehousing Logistics Assns; Eur Warehousing &
      Logistics Confedn
M   628 f
¶   NL - 10; ftm.
      Directory of Members' Services - 2 yrly; ftm, £60 nm.
      UKWA Warehouse Manual; £35 m, £70 nm.
      Fire Precautions Guide to Risk Assessment; £10 m, £20 nm.

United Kingdom Weighing Federation   (UKWF)   1920
■   Brooke House, 4 The Lakes, Bedford Rd, NORTHAMPTON,
      NN4 7YD.   (asa)
      01604 622023   fax 01604 631252
      email ukwf@brookehouse.co.uk
      http://www.ukwf.org.uk
▲   Company Limited by Guarantee
○   *T; acts on regulatory matters of legal metrology at UK, EEC &
      international levels
●   Conf - Mtgs - Inf - LG
<   Eur Fedn Scale & Weighing Machine Mfrs & Repairers (CECIP)
M   100 f
¶   NL - 4; ftm.   LM - 1;   AR.

United Kingdom Windsurfing Association   (UKWA)   1976
NR   12 Beach Court, Old Fort Rd, SHOREHAM BEACH, W Sussex,
      BN43 5RG.   (hq)
      01273 454654
      Admin: Arabella Andrup
Br   4 regions
○   *S; organisation of regional & national windsurfing, racing,
      wave sailing, freestyle & speed sailing events
●   Mtgs - PL - Regional & national windsurfing events
<   Intl Windsurfing Assn (IWA); Royal Yachting Assn (RYA)
M   700+ i
¶   UK Windsurfing Magazine - 4; ftm, £2 nm.
      Membership Hbk - 1; ftm only.
×   2001 (British Windsurfing Association
          (United Kingdom Boardsailing Association

United Kingdom Youth   1911
NR   Kirby House (2nd floor), 20-24 Kirby St, LONDON,
      EC1N 8TS.   (hq)
      020 7242 4045   fax 020 7242 4125
      email info@ukyouth.org   http://www.ukyouth.org
      Chief Exec: John Bateman
▲   Registered Charity
Br   42
○   *Y; 'to support & develop high quality voluntary youth work &
      informal educational opportunities for & with young people
      through a range of projects, accredited learning
      programmes, events & publications'
●   Conf - ET - Inf - LG
<   Eur Confedn of Youth Clubs; Nat Coun of Voluntary Orgs; Nat
      Coun for Voluntary Youth Services
M   i in clubs
¶   Publications list available.
      Note: the correct name of this organisation is UK Youth;
      see also note under UK. . .

**United Nations Association of Great Britain & Northern Ireland
(UNA)   1945**
NR   3 Whitehall Court, LONDON, SW1A 2EL.   (hq)
      020 7930 2931
▲   Company Limited by Guarantee
○   *X; to promote the principles of the UN charter & the role of the
      UN in international affairs
●   Conf - Mtgs - SG
<   Wld Fedn of UN Assns
M   5,500 i, 70 org
¶   New World - 4; ftm, £1 each nm.

United Reformed Church History Society   (URCHS)   1972
■   c/o Westminster College, Madingley Rd, CAMBRIDGE,
      CB3 0AA.
      01223 741300   fax 01223 300765
      Hon Sec: Revd Elizabeth J Brown
▲   Registered Charity
○   *L, *Q, *R; research into the history of Congregational &
      Presbyterian churches
●   Annual lecture & meeting - Inf - Lib (Collection specialises in
      C17 - C19 Presbyterianism)
M   175 i, 5 churches, UK / 60 i, o'seas
¶   Jnl - 2; ftm.

United Road Transport Union   (URTU)   1890
NR   76 High Lane, Chorlton cum Hardy, MANCHESTER,
      M21 9EF.   (hq)
      0161-881 6245   fax 0161-861 0976
      Gen Sec: Robert F Monks
○   *U; specialists in the road haulage & distribution industry
M   18,500 i, UK / 200+ i, o'seas
¶   Wheels (Jnl) - 6; ftm, £1.95 nm.

United Saddlebred Association   (USA UK)   1995
- ■ Meriden House, School Lane, Kitts Green, BIRMINGHAM, B33 8PD.   (hsp)
  0121-784 8171
  Sec: Rosemary Jinks
- ▲ Un-incorporated Society
- ○ *B; to promote interest in & care of American Saddlebreds; to show their versatility in all spheres of equestrianism
- Gp 5-gaited; Saddle seat equitation
- ● Conf - Mtgs - ET - Res - Exhib - Comp - Stat - Expt - Inf - Lib - PL - VE
- < Amer Saddle Horse Assn; Brit Morgan Horse Soc; Brit Skewbald, Piebald Assn; Coloured Horse & Pony Soc
- M c 100 i
- ¶ NL - 3;   Ybk - 1; both ftm only.   LM;   AR.

Unity   1825
- NR Hillcrest House, Garth St, Hanley, STOKE-on-TRENT, Staffs, ST1 2AB.   (hq)
  01782 272755   fax 01782 284902
  Gen Sec: G Bagnall
- ○ *U
- M i
- ✕ 2006 Ceramic & Allied Trades Union

Universities Association for Continuing Education
   since 2004 **Universities Association for Lifelong Learning**

Universities Association for Lifelong Learning   (UALL)   1992
- ■ Renaissance House (2nd floor), 20 Princess Rd West, LEICESTER, LE1 6TP.   (hq)
  0116-285 9702   fax 0116-204 6988
  email admin@uall.ac.uk   http://www.uace.org.uk
  Admin: Lucy Bate
- ▲ Registered Charity
- ○ *P; to represent the continuing education community within higher education; to liaise with policy makers & policy making bodies
- ● Conf - Mtgs - ET - Res - Inf - LG
- M 8 i, 107 f, 1 org, UK / 15 f, o'seas
- ¶ Ybk & AR - 1; ftm.   LM - 3; free.
  Occasional Papers - 3/4; ftm, £3 nm.
  Working Papers - 1; ftm, £3 nm.
  Conference Proceedings - 1; ftm, £3 nm.
- ✕ 2004 Universities Association for Continuing Education

Universities & Colleges Employers' Association   (UCEA)   1994
- ■ Woburn House, 20 Tavistock Sq, LONDON, WC1H 9HU.   (hq)
  020 7383 2444   fax 020 7383 2666
  email enquiries@ucca.ac.uk   http://www.ucca.ac.uk
  Chief Exec Officer: Jocelyn Prudence
- ▲ Company Limited by Guarantee
- ○ *P; the employers association for universities & colleges in the UK; to provide a framework within which salaries, conditions of service employee relations can be discussed & advice & guidance sought
- ● Conf - Mtgs - ET - Stat - Empl - Seminars
- M 164 f

Universities & Colleges Information Systems Association (UCISA)
- NR University of Oxford, 13 Banbury Rd, OXFORD, OX2 6NN.
  01865 283425   fax 01865 283426
  http://www.ucisa.ac.uk

Universities Federation for Animal Welfare   (UFAW)   1926
- ■ The Old School, Brewhouse Hill, WHEATHAMPSTEAD, Herts, AL4 8AN.   (hq)
  01582 831818
  email ufaw@ufaw.org.uk   http://www.ufaw.org.uk/
  Chief Exec: Dr J K Kirkwood,
  Sec: Donald Davidson
- ▲ Company Limited by Guarantee
- ○ *V; to prevent cruelty & promote humane behaviour towards domestic & wild animals in the UK & abroad, so as to reduce or eliminate pain, fear, suffering, distress or lasting harm inflicted upon them by humans; to contribute to the store of scientific knowledge by funding & engaging in animal welfare research
- ● Conf - ET - Res - Inf - Lib - VE - LG
- M c 1,200 i & f
- ¶ Animal Welfare (Jnl) - 4.   NL - 1.   AR.
  Publications list available.

Universities Psychotherapy & Counselling Association
- NR PO Box 312, LEATHERHEAD, Surrey, KT22 2AX.
  01372 842255   fax 01372 842255
  email admin@upca.co.uk   http://www.upca.co.uk

Universities Scotland
- NR 53 Hanover St, EDINBURGH, EH2 2PJ.
  0131-226 1111   fax 0131-226 1100
  http://www.universities-scotland.ac.uk
  Dir: David Caldwell
- ○ *N; to represent, promote & campaign for the Scottish higher education sector
- M 21 org
- ¶ Books.

Universities UK   (UUK)   2000
- NR Woburn House, 20 Tavistock Sq, LONDON, WC1H 9HQ.   (hq)
  020 7419 4111   fax 020 7388 8649
  email info@universitiesuk.ac.uk
  http://www.universitiesuk.ac.uk
  Chief Exec: Diana Warwick
- ▲ Company Limited by Guarantee; Registered Charity
- Br 2
- ○ *N; to be the essential voice for the UK universities; to promote & support their work & provide services to members; to speak out for a thriving & diverse higher education sector which creates benefits for all
- Gp Strategy groups: Business & industry, Student experience, Finance & resources, Health, International, Leadership, management & governance, Long-term strategy, Research policy, Teaching quality & life-long learning
- ● Conf - Mtgs - Res - Stat - Inf - LG
- M 126 i
- ¶ [all publications are available as downloadable pdf files on website].

© CBD Research Ltd · Beckenham · BR3 5JS · Tel 020 8650 7745 · Fax 020 8650 0768 · E-mail cbd@cbdresearch.com · www.cbdresearch.com

University Association for Contemporary European Studies (UACES) 1968

■ School of Public Policy, University College London, 24-30 Tavistock Sq, LONDON, WC1H 9QU.   (hq)
020 7794 4975
http://www.uaces.org
Exec Dir: Sue Davis
▲ Registered Charity
○ *L; exchanges ideas on Europe; to provide a forum for debate & act as a clearing house for information about European issues; it is directly involved in promoting research & establishing teaching & research networks.
Members include academics (economists, political scientists, lawyers & historians) & practitioners & graduate students
Gp Graduate students of European studies
● Conf - Mtgs - SG - Workshops
M 800 i, 105 universities, UK / 30 i, 10 universities, o'seas
¶ Jnl of Common Market Studies (JCMS) - 5.   NL - 4.
Directory of European Expertise: research interests of UACES members - 3 yrly; £26 m, £96 nm.
Listing of Courses in European Studies in UK Universities; on-line.

University & College Lecturers' Union
see NATFHE - the University & College Lecturers' Union

University and College Union

The Association of University Teachers & NATFHE (the University & College Lecturers' Union) amalgamated on 1 June 2006 to form the University & College Union; a transitional year will exist until full operational unity is achieved in June 2007

Unlock - National Association of Ex-Offenders 1999

■ 35A High St, SNODLAND, Kent, ME6 5AG.
01634 247350   fax 01634 247351
email unlockprison@btconnect.com
http://www.unlockprison.org.uk
Chief Exec: Bobby Cummins
▲ Registered Charity
○ *K, *W; to improve facilities & opportunities for serving prisoners to prepare for release & to overcome social exclusion & discrimination hindering them from re-integration into society; to prevent offending & re-offending by young people especially at risk; to campaign for serving prisoner's right to vote
● ET - Res - Inf - LG

Upkeep: the Trust for Training & Education in Building Maintenance (Upkeep) 1979

■ The Building Centre, 26 Store St, LONDON, WC1E 7BT.   (hq)
020 7631 1677   fax 020 7631 1699
email info@upkeep.org.uk   http://www.upkeep.org.uk
Dir: Annette McGill
▲ Company Limited by Guarantee; Registered Charity
○ *E, *T; to promote good standards of repair, maintenance & improvement of buildings, particularly houses & flats
M org

Urdd Gobaith Cymru   (yr Urdd) 1922

NR Swyddfa'r Urdd, Ffordd Llanbadarn, ABERYSTWYTH, Ceredigion, SY23 1EY.   (hq)
01970 613102
Chief Exec: Efa Griffith Jones
▲ Company Limited by Guarantee; Registered Charity
Br 1,200
○ *Y; 'to foster Welsh Christian citizenship with the youth of Wales'
● Conf - Mtgs - ET - Exhib - Comp - SG - Lib - VE
M 53,000 i
¶ Bore Da - 10.   CIP - 10.   IAW - 10.   (all children's magazines).

Urostomy Association   (UA) 1971

■ Central Office, 18 Foxglove Avenue, UTTOXETER, Staffs, ST14 8UN.   (hq)
0870 770 7931   fax 0870 770 7932
email info.ua@classmail.co.uk   http://www.uagbi.org
Nat Sec: Mrs Hazel Pixley
▲ Registered Charity
Br 20
○ *W; to assist those who are about to undergo (or have undergone) surgery resulting in diversion or removal of the bladder; to provide information, help & advice
● Conf - Mtgs - ET - Res - Inf - LG
< Intl Ostomy Assn
M 2,400 i, UK / 200 i, o'seas
¶ Magazine - 3; ftm.

Uveitis Information Group   (UIG) 1998

■ South House, Sweening, VIDLIN, Shetland Isles, ZE2 9QE.   (hsp)
01806 577310
email info@uveitis.net   http://www.uveitis.net
Hon Sec: P Hibbert
▲ Registered Charity
○ *W; to provide information & support for sufferers of uveitis; to further understanding of the condition amongst health professionals & other organisations involved in sight related matters
● ET - Inf
M 350 i, UK / 100 i, o'seas
¶ NL - 3; ftm, £5 nm.

Vale of Glamorgan Agricultural Society   1772

■ Pancross Barn, Llancarfan, nr BARRY, Glam, CF62 3AJ.   (hsp)
01446 710099
email vale.show@btinternet.com
http://www.valeglamorganshow.co.uk
Hon Sec: Nicola Gibson
▲ Company Limited by Guarantee; Registered Charity
○ *F; to promote British agriculture & its related industries
Gp Craft fair; Horticulture; Kennel Club dog show; Rural crafts;
    Livestock; Tradestands; Food Hall
    Competitions: Home produce, Livestock
● Exhib - Comp - Inf
< R Horticl Soc; R Nat Rose Soc; Breed socs; Horse socs
M 500 i, 10 f
¶ Schedule - 1.   AR.   Catalogue - 1.

Valpak   1997

■ Stratford Business Park, Banbury Rd, STRATFORD-upon-AVON,
    Warks, CV37 7GW.   (hsb)
0845 068 2572   fax 0845 068 2532
email info@valpak.co.uk   http://www.valpak.co.uk
Chief Exec: Steve Gough
▲ Company Limited by Guarantee
○ *T; the nationwide compliance scheme for the packaging waste
    regulations
● LG
< Pro Europe
M c3,000 f
¶ Ybk; ftm only.

Vascular Surgical Society
a group of the **Association of Surgeons of Great Britain &
Ireland**

VAT Practitioners Group   (VPG)   1982

■ 28 Crown Walk, Apsley Mills, HEMEL HEMPSTEAD, Herts,
    HP3 9WS.   (nat admin/p)
01442 255611   fax 01442 258449
email pf50@dial.pipex.com   http://www.vpgweb.com
Nat Admin: Susan Holman
▲ Un-incorporated Society
○ *P; a discussion group on Value Added Tax which makes
    representation to HM Customs & Excise on VAT matters; also
    has interests in Insurance Premium Tax (IPT), Landfill Tax & Air
    Passenger Duty (APD)
● Conf - Mtgs
M 520 i
¶ Bulletin - 10; ftm only.

Vegan Society Ltd   1944

NR Donald Watson House, 7 Battle Rd, ST LEONARDS-on-SEA,
    E Sussex, TN37 7AA.   (hq)
01424 427393   fax 01424 717064
email info@vegansociety.com
http://www.vegansociety.com
Chief Exec: Janet Pender
▲ Registered Charity
○ *K; 'to promote ways of living free from animal products, for
    the benefit of people, animals & the environment'
● ET - Res - Inf
M c 5,000 i
¶ The Vegan Magazine - 4.
    The Animal-Free Shopper - 2 yrly.
    Vegan Passport.   Vegan Stories.
    Plant Based Nutrition & Health.

Vegetarian Society of Ireland   1978

IRL PO Box 3010, DUBLIN 4, Republic of Ireland.
353 (1) 873 0451
email vegsoc@ireland.com   http://www.vegetarian.ie
Hon Sec: Patricia Timoney
○ *K

Vegetarian Society (UK) Ltd   (VegSoc)   1969

■ Parkdale, Dunham Rd, ALTRINCHAM, Cheshire, WA14 4QG.
    (hq)
0161-925 2000   fax 0161-926 9182
email info@vegsoc.org   http://www.vegsoc.org
Chief Exec: Tina Fox
▲ Company Limited by Guarantee; Registered Charity
Br 150 local groups
○ *G, *K, *V; to promote knowledge of the vegetarian diet for the
    benefit of human health, animal welfare & the environment
Gp Cordon Vert Cookery School for professional & amateur chefs
● Conf - ET - Inf - Lib
< Intl Vegetarian U
M 16,500 i, UK / 500 i, o'seas
¶ The Vegetarian - 4; ftm, £2.95 nm.   AR - 1; ftm only.

Vehicle Builders' & Repairers' Association   (VBRA)   1914

■ Belmont House, 102 Finkle Lane, Gildersome, LEEDS, W Yorks,
    LS27 7TW.   (hq)
0113-253 8333   fax 0113-238 0496
email vbra@vbra.co.uk   http://www.vbra.co.uk
Chief Exec: Malcolm Tagg
▲ Company Limited by Guarantee
○ *T; to represent the motor repair & body building industry; to
    support members by providing advice, information & training
Gp National Repairers Council; National Manufacturers Council
● Conf - Mtgs - ET - Exhib - Inf - VE - Empl - LG
< Assn Intle des Réparateurs en Carrosserie (AIRC) (Brussels)
M 1,100 f, 1,000 i (subscribers to Body)
¶ Body (Jnl) - 10; ftm, £4 each nm.
    Voice (NL) - 4; ftm only.   AR; free.
    Directory for Commercial Vehicle Bodybuilding, Repairs & Tail
    Lift Repairs;
    Suppliers Directory;   both ftm, £9 nm.

Vehicle Restraint Manufacturers Association   (VRMA)   1997

■ Heathcote House, 136 Hagley Rd, Edgbaston, BIRMINGHAM,
    B16 9PN.   (hq)
0121-454 4141   fax 0121-454 4949
email sp@heathcote-coleman.co.uk
Sec: Mrs Sharon J Parker
▲ Un-incorporated Society
○ *T; to establish & maintain fundamental, technical &
    commercial principles within the industry
Gp Product gps: Safety fence, Parapet, Anchorages
● Mtgs
M 16 f
    2002-03 Parapet & Safety Fence Manufacturers Association

Vernacular Architecture Group   (VAG)   1954

■ Ashley, Willows Green, Great Leighs, CHELMSFORD, Essex,
    CM3 1QD.   (hsp)
01245 361408
http://www.vag.org.uk
Hon Sec: Mrs B A Watkin
▲ Registered Charity
○ *L; study of small traditional buildings in GB & abroad
● Conf - Res - Inf - Lib - VE
M 619 i, 18 org, UK / 48 i, o'seas
¶ Vernacular Architecture - 1; ftm, £11 nm.
    NL - 2; ftm only.   Bibliography - 5 yrly; ftm, £9.50 nm.

Vet's Tennis GB   1974
■   39 Molasses House, Plantation Wharf, LONDON,
     SW11 3TN.   (hsp)
     020 7223 4361   fax 020 7801 0401
     email vw@vlta.net   http://www.vlta.net
     Sec: Valerie Willoughby
▲   Un-incorporated Society
○   *S; to promote national individual & club team championships
     for veteran players
●   Promotion of veterans lawn tennis events
<   Lawn Tennis Assn
M   220 clubs
×   2004 Veterans' Lawn Tennis Association

Veteran-Cycle Club   (V-CC)   1955
NR 44 Springfield Rd, Moseley, BIRMINGHAM, W Midlands,
     B13 9NW.   (mem/sp)
     0121-778 3615
     Mem Officer: Ms Sue Thorne
▲   Un-incorporated Society
Br 21 regional sections
○   *G; to promote the riding & restoration of old bicycles; to study
     & exchange information about the history of cycles & cycling
Gp Marque enthusiasts for 82 makes of machine
●   Mtgs - Res - Exhib - Lib
<   Intl Veteran Cycle Assn; Transport Trust
M   c 2,500 i
¶   News & Views - 6;   The 'Boneshaker' - 3;   Ybk - 1;
     all ftm only.

Veteran Horse Society   (VHS)   2000
■   Hedre Fawr, St Dogmaels, CARDIGAN, N Pembrokeshire,
     SA43 3LZ.   (hq)
     0870 242 6653
     http://www.veteran-horse-society.co.uk
     Dir: Miss Julianne Aston
▲   Company Limited by Guarantee
○   *V; dedicated to the health, welfare & profile of the horse &
     pony over the age of 15
●   Conf - Mtgs - ET - Res - Exhib - Comp - SG - Stat - Expt - Inf -
     PL - VE - Empl - LG
<   Nat Equine Welfare Coun (NEWC); Brit Equestrian Tr Assn
     (BETA)
M   4,000 i, UK / 50 i, o'seas
¶   Voice of the Veteran - 4.

Veteran Speedway Riders Association   (VSRA)   1958
■   90 Ruskin Ave, Long Eaton, NOTTINGHAM, NG10 3HX.   (hsp)
     0115-973 6041   fax 0115-946 5005
     email vwhite@legend3333.worldonline.co.uk
     Sec & Treas: Vic White
Br Australia, New Zealand
○   *S; 'to help former colleagues to keep in touch, to stage
     frequent reunions & to enjoy the pleasures of reliving old
     times in convivial company'
●   Exhib - Lunches - Dinners - Golf tournaments
M   c 550 i, UK & o'seas
¶   Opposite Lock (NL) - 4; ftm only.

Veterans' Lawn Tennis Association of Great Britain
     since 2004 **Vets Tennis GB**

**Veterinary Association for Arbitration & Jurisprudence
(VAAJ)   1992**
NR The Beeches, Rickerby, CARLISLE, Cumbria, CA3 9AA.   (hsp)
     01228 521450
     Hon Sec: G D Cawley
▲   Un-incorporated Society
○   *P; to promote the study of all aspects of jurisprudence,
     arbitration & Alternative Dispute Resolution (ADR) within the
     veterinary profession; to assist with training for members
Gp [all specialities]
●   Conf - Mtgs - ET - Inf
<   Forensic Science Soc; Inst of Biology
M   90 i, UK / 10 i, o'seas
¶   Proceedings - 2; ftm, £25 nm.   NL - irreg; free.

Veterinary Cardiovascular Society
     a group of the **British Small Animal Veterinary Association**

Veterinary Deer Society
     a group of the **British Veterinary Association**

Veterinary History Society   1962
■   17 Anseres Place, WELLS, Somerset, BA5 2RT.   (hsp)
     01749 673558
     Hon Sec: Jean Mann
▲   Un-incorporated Society
○   *L, *V; promotion of interest in veterinary history in the UK
●   Mtgs - Inf - VE
M   100 i, 15 libraries, UK / 20 i, 15 libraries, o'seas
¶   Bulletin of Veterinary History - 2; ftm, £10 nm.

Veterinary Ireland   1888
IRL 13 The Courtyard, Kilcarbery Park, Nangor Rd, DUBLIN 22,
     Republic of Ireland.
     353 (1) 457 7976   fax 353 (1) 457 7998
     email vetireland@eircom.net
     http://www.veterinary-ireland.org
     Chief Exec: John Horan
○   *P, *V

Veterinary Public Health Association
     a group of the **British Veterinary Association**

Victim Support
     see **National Association of Victims Support Schemes**

Victim Support Scotland   (VSS)   1985
■   15-23 Hardwell Close, EDINBURGH, EH8 9RX.   (hq)
     0131-668 4486   fax 0131-662 5400
     email info@victimsupportsco.demon.co.uk
     http://www.victimsupport.org
     Chief Exec & Co Sec: David McKenna
▲   Company Limited by Guarantee
Br 32 affiliated services (Scotland)
○   *W; to offer practical help, emotional support & essential
     information to victims, witnesses & others affected by crime.
     The service is free & provided by trained volunteers through a
     network of community based victim & court based witness
     services
●   Conf - Mtgs - ET - Res - Inf
     Helpline: 0845 603 9213 (0900-1630 Mon-Fri); outside these
     hours call UK Victim Support on 0845 303 0900
¶   Voice [NL] - 4.   AR.
     Generic Information Pack; free.

**Victoria Cross & George Cross Association   (VC&GCAssn)
1956**
- ■ Horse Guards, Whitehall, LONDON, SW1A 2AX.   (hq)
  020 7930 3506   fax 020 7930 4303
  Sec: Mrs D Grahame
- ○ *G; to establish a central focus for all Victoria Cross & George
  Cross holders
- ● Conf - Inf
- M 6 i (VC), 18 i (GC), UK / 6 i (VC), 7 i (GC), o'seas
- ¶ Rules.

Victorian Military Society   (VMS)   1975
- ■ 3 Franks Rd, GUILDFORD, Surrey, GU2 9NT.   (hsp)
  01483 856080
  http://www.vms.org.uk
  Sec: Ralph Moore-Morris
- ▲ Un-incorporated Society
- ○ *L, *Q; to encourage & foster the study of military aspects of
  the Victorian era (nominally 1837-1901, the period has been
  extended to 1914 to include the campaigns of the earlier
  part of the 20th century; the principal interest is in the forces
  of the British Empire & its adversaries, but forces of other
  countries are not excluded
- Gp Special interest groups: Anglo-Boer Wars, Zulu Wars, Sudan
  Wars, Wargames, India & Burma, Re-enactment (the
  Diehards, based on the Middlesex Regiment of 1890)
- ● Mtgs - Res - Exhib - Comp - SG - Stat - Inf - VE - Recording of
  all memorials of the Anglo-Boer War of 1899-1902
- M c 900 i
- ¶ Soldiers of the Queen (Jnl) - 4;   Soldiers Small Book;
  both ftm only.

Victorian Society   1958
- ■ 1 Priory Gardens, LONDON, W4 1TT.   (hq)
  020 8994 1019   fax 020 8747 5899
  email admin@victorian-society.org.uk
  http://www.victorian-society.org.uk
  Dir: Dr Ian Dungavell
- ○ *A, *L; to preserve & protect the best buildings of the 19th
  century; to study the arts & history of the period
- M c 3,500 i

Video Performance Ltd   (VPL)   1984
- NR 1 Upper James St, LONDON, W1F 9DE.   (hq)
  020 7534 1400
- ○ *T; 'the licensing of the broadcasting, public performance &
  diffusion rights (cable & satellite) in music videograms
  (cinematograph films) in the UK, pursuant to the Copyright
  Act 1956 & the Cable & Broadcasting Act'

**View: Association for the Education & Welfare of the Visually
Handicapped   (VIEW)   1979**
- NR Greenbank, Firbank Rd, Royton, OLDHAM, Lancs, OL2 6TU.
  (chmn/p)
  0161-911 3110
  Chmn: Julie Sweeting,   Sec: Kay Wrench
- ▲ Registered Charity
- ○ *E, *W; to alleviate hardship caused by visual handicap
- ● Conf - Mtgs - ET - Exam - Res - SG - Inf - LG
- M 700 i
- ¶ British Jnl of Visual Impairment - 3; ftm.

Viewing Facilities Association (UK)   (VFA)   1995
- ■ Davey House (suite 14), 31 St Neots Rd, Eaton Ford, ST NEOTS,
  Cambs, PE19 7BA.
  01480 211288   fax 01480 211267
  email rosemolloy@btconnect.com
  http://www.vfa-uk.org
  Chmn: Liz Sykes
- ▲ Company Limited by Guarantee
- ○ *T; for viewing facilities, market research, qualitative research
- ● Conf - Inf
- < Market Res Soc; Assn for Qualitative Res
- M 41 f
- ¶ [on website]

Viking Society for Northern Research   1892
- NR c/o Dept of Scandinavian Studies, University College London,
  Gower St, LONDON, WC1E 6BT.   (hq)
  020 7679 7176   fax 020 7679 7750
  http://www.shef.ac.uk/viking-society
  Hon Sec: Prof M P Barnes
- ▲ Un-incorporated Society
- ○ *A, *Q; literature & antiquities of the Scandinavian north,
  including Iceland
- ● Conf - Mtgs - ET - Res - Lib
- M 296 i, 47 org, UK / 120 i, 152 org, o'seas
- ¶ The Saga Book; £20.   Text Series - irreg; prices vary.
  Dorothea Coke Memorial Lecture - irreg.

The Vikings   1972
- NR 2 Wheatley Rd, ILKLEY, W Yorks, LS29 8TS.   (hq)
  01943 817924   fax 01943 817924
  http://www.vikingsonline.org.uk/
  Soc Leader: Tony Sayer
- ▲ Company Limited by Guarantee; Registered Charity
- Br c 30; Holland, USA
- ○ *G; dark age re-enactment (primarily that of the Vikings) incl
  battles, homelife, crafts & skills
- Gp Film extras
- ● Mtgs - Res - Exhib - Inf - Re-enactment shows - Banquets
- < Nat Assn Re-enactment Socs
- M 750 i, UK / 20 i, o'seas
- ¶ Runestaff (Jnl) - 6/8; ftm, £1 nm.
  Flyer (Broadsheet) - 6/8; free.   Ybk; £4.

**Village Retail Services Association Educational Trust   (ViRSA)
1992**
- NR The Quadrangle, WOODSTOCK, Oxon, OX20 1LH.   (hq)
  01993 814377   fax 01993 810849
  email virsa@ruralnet.org.uk   http://www.virsa.org
  Dir: Donna Smith
- ▲ Registered Charity
- Br 12
- ○ *E, *K; assisting rural communities in England & Wales to
  maintain, improve or revive their retail services
- ● ET - Res - Stat - Inf - LG - Working with individuals, community
  groups & others on specific retailing problems in rural areas
- M c 200 subscribers
- ¶ Talking Shop (NL) - 4.   AR.
  Hbk (village shops & post offices - a guide to village
  investment).
  Information sheets (set of 19).

Vinegar Brewers' Federation   (VBF)   1929
- ■ Crescent House, 34 Eastbury Way, SWINDON, Wilts,
  SN25 2EN.   (hsb)
  01793 727387   fax 01793 726485
  email vinegarbrewers@aol.com
  Sec: Walter J Anzer
- ▲ Un-incorporated Society
- ○ *T
- ● Mtgs - LG
- < Permanent Intl Vinegar C'ee, Common Market (CPIV)
- M 5 f

Vintage Arms Association   (VAA)   1973
- NR 9 Watton Green, Watton, THETFORD, Norfolk, IP25 6RB.
  (hsp)
  http://www.vaa.org.uk
  Hon Sec: Terry Newell
- Br 6; Jersey
- ○ *G; to encourage the collection, study & use of all vintage
  firearms, whether muzzle-loading, breechloading, rifles,
  pistols, shotguns or airguns; defined as being any small arm
  in production by 1933
- ● Conf - Mtgs - Res
- < Nat Rifle Assn
- M i [not stated]
- ¶ The Primer - 6; ftm only.

Vintage Carriages Trust   (VCT)   1964
- ■ The Railway Station, Haworth, KEIGHLEY, W Yorks,
  BD22 8NJ.   (mail)
  01535 680425   fax 01535 610796
  email admin@vintagecarriagestrust.org
  http://www.vintagecarriagestrust.org add
  Ingrow Railway Station Yard, Halifax Rd, Ingrow, KEIGHLEY,
  W Yorks, BD21 5AX.   (location)
  Hon Sec: Michael W Cope
- ▲ Registered Charity
- ○ *G; the conservation & restoration of railway carriages & other
  railway artifacts, & the interpretation of these through
  museum display
- Gp Railway carriage restoration & preservation
- ● ET - Operating the Museum of Rail Travel at Ingrow
- < Fedn of Eur Rlys (FEDECRAIL); Heritage Rly Assn (HRA);
  Transport Trust (TT)
- M 580 i, UK / 4 i, o'seas
- ¶ NL - 4.   All Aboard; £3.50p.   AR - 1; free.
  All Aboard: your guide to the story of rail travel for the ordinary
  passenger.

Vintage & Classic Powercraft Association
has closed

Vintage & Classic Sailing Association
has closed

Vintage Glider Club of Great Britain   (VGC)   1973
- NR 6 Buckland Close, Hazel Grove, STOCKPORT, SK7 4NG.
  (hsp)
  0161-487 4522
  email austenwood@onetel.com
  http://www.vintagegliderclub.org.uk
  Hon Sec: Austen Wood,   Chmn: David Shrimpton
- Br Australia, Austria, Belgium, Czech Republic, Denmark, France,
  Germany, Holland, Hungary, New Zealand, Norway, Poland,
  Sweden, Switzerland, USA
- ○ *S; 'to preserve old gliders in flying condition, & to prevent their
  mass destruction, as has happened in the past; there is no
  museum for them as yet in the UK'
- ● Mtgs - Aeromodelling - Archive (plans, photographs, films/
  videos) - Holding national & international rallies
- < Oldtime Gliding Club Wasserkuppe
- M 450 i, UK / 450 i, o'seas
- ¶ VGC News - 3.

**Vintage Horticultural & Garden Machinery Club   (VHGMC)
1993**
- ■ Glenview, Fosseway, Midsomer Norton, RADSTOCK, Somerset,
  BA3 4BB.   (sp)
  email vhgmc@btinternet.com   http://www.btinternet.com/
  ~vhgmc/index.htm/vintage.htm
  Club Sec: C Moore
- ○ *G, *H; to collect, preserve, restore & use garden &
  horticultural machinery, including hand tools
- ● Displays at vintage rallies & garden shows - Information service
  to members only
- M 680 i
- ¶ The Cultivator (NL) - 5; ftm only.

Vintage Motor Cycle Club Ltd   (VMCC)   1946
- ■ Allen House, Wetmore Rd, BURTON-upon-TRENT, Staffs,
  DE14 1TR.   (hq)
  01283 540557   fax 01283 510547
  email hq@vmcc.net   http://www.vmcc.net
  Chief Exec: James Hewing
- ▲ Company Limited by Guarantee
- Br 75
- ○ *G; to preserve, restore & use both for competition & pleasure,
  motorcycles, combinations & tricycles: veteran (pre 1914),
  vintage (1915-1930), post-vintage (1931-1944), post-war
  (1945-1960), & post-1960 (1961- & +25 yrs old)
- Gp Racing; Grasstrack; Sprint
- ● Mtgs - Exhib - Inf - Lib - PL - Archives - Insurance scheme
- < Auto-Cycle U (ACU); Fedn of Brit Historic Vehicle
  Clubs (FBHVC); RAC
- M 13,400 i, UK / 500 i, o'seas
- ¶ The Vintage Motor Cycle - 12; ftm only.

Vintage Sports Car Club Ltd   (VSCC)   1934
- ■ The Old Post Office, West St, CHIPPING NORTON, Oxon,
  OX7 5EL.   (hq)
  01608 644777   fax 01608 644888
  email info@vscc.co.uk   http://www.vscc.co.uk
  Sec: Stuart Pringle
- ▲ Company Limited by Guarantee
- ○ *G, *S; for owners of historic racing cars: Edwardian (1905-
  1918), vintage (pre 1931), post-vintage thoroughbred (pre
  1941), & certain front engined cars (pre 1961)
- Gp Alfa Romeo; Delage; Frazer Nash; Light Car & Edwardian
- ● Conf - Mtgs - Res - Comp - Inf - Lib - VE
- < RAC Motor Sports Assn; Fédn Intle des Automobiles Anciennes
- M c 7,500 i, 14 f, UK / 500 i, o'seas
- ¶ Bulletin - 4;   NL - 12;   Ybk; all ftm only.

Vintage Wooden Boat Association
- NR 3 Kingsholme Close, EAST HAGBOURNE, Oxon, OX11 9LL.
  http://www.vwba.org
  Mem Sec: Andrew McMeekin
- ○ *G

Vintners' Federation of Ireland   (VFI)   1973
- IRL VFI House, Castleside Drive, Rathfarnham, DUBLIN 14,
  Republic of Ireland.
  353 (1) 492 3400   fax 353 (1) 492 3577
  email enquiries@vintners.ie   http://www.vfi.ie
  Chief Exec: Tadg O'Sullivan
- ○ *T
- M c 6,000 f

Viola da Gamba Society   (VdGS)   1948
- NR 56 Hunters Way, Dringhouses, YORK, YO24 1JJ.   (hsp)
  01904 706959   fax 01904 706959
  email admin@vdgs.demon.co.uk
  http://www.vdgs.demon.co.uk
  Admin: Mrs Caroline Wood
- ▲ Registered Charity
- ○ *D; to advance the study of viols, their music, their playing &
  their making
- ● Conf - Mtgs - Res - Exhib - Inf
- < Viola da Gamba Soc of America; Lute Soc (UK)
- M 460 i, libraries & universities
- ¶ Music - 1; ftm.   Care of Viol (booklet).
  LM - 1; ftm.   AR.

Violet Needham Society   (VNS)   1985
- ■ 19 Ashburnham Place, LONDON, SE10 8TZ.   (hsp)
  020 8692 4562
  email richardcheffins@aol.com
  http://www.violetneedhamsociety.org
  Hon Sec: Richard H A Cheffins
- ▲ Un-incorporated Society
- ○ *A; interest in the life & works of Violet Needham & other children's writers of the period (1940s & 50s) & in Ruritanian fiction in general
- ● Mtgs - Res - Lib - VE
- M 260 i, 3 org, UK / 27 i, 1 org, o'seas
- ¶ Souvenir (Jnl) - 3; ftm, £2.50 nm.   NL - 3; ftm only.

Virgil Society   1943
- NR c/o 8 Purley Oaks Rd, SANDERSTEAD, Surrey, CR2 0NP.   (hsp)
  Treas & Mem Sec: J Kilsby
- ▲ Registered Charity
- ○ *L; study & interpretation of Virgil as the symbol of the central educational tradition of Western Europe
- ● Mtgs
- M c 160 i
- ¶ Proceedings - irreg.   NL - 2.

Virginia Woolf Society of Great Britain   (VWSGB)   1998
- ■ 106 Gloucester Rd, KINGSTON upon THAMES, Surrey, KT1 3QN.   (chmn/p)
  020 8546 5712
  email stephen.barkway@virgin.net
  http://www.virginiawoolfsociety.co.uk
  Chmn: Stephen Barkway,   Sec: Lynne Newland
- ▲ Un-incorporated Society
- ○ *A; 'to present Virginia Woolf (1882-1941) in her true light as a great novelist, essayist, publisher & woman of letters'
- ● Conf - Inf - VE
- M 250 i, 6 org, UK / 150 i, 3 org, o'seas
- ¶ Virginia Woolf Bulletin - 3; ftm, £5 nm.
  Annual Birthday Lecture - 1; £4 (£5 o'seas).

ViRSA Rural Shops Alliance
    see **Rural Shops Alliance**

Virus Tested Stem Cutting Growers Association   (VTSC)
- ■ 1 St Fillans Grove, Aberdour, BURNTISLAND, Fife, KY3 0XG.
  01383 860695
  email wjrennie@freeola.com
  Hon Sec: William John Rennie
- ○ *T
- ● Conf - Mtgs - VE - LG
- M 15 i, 30 f

Vision Homes Association   (VHA)   1985
- ■ Quadrant West, 210-222 Hagley Road West, Oldbury, BIRMINGHAM, B68 0NP.   (hq)
  0121-434 4644   fax 0121-434 5655
  email gayle@visionhomes.org & ewa@visionhomes.org
  Chief Exec: Ewa Stefanowska
- ▲ Company Limited by Guarantee; Registered Charity
- Br 8
- ○ *W; to provide residential & other services for people who have impaired vision & other (often profound) disabilities
- ● Mtgs - ET
- M 180 i
- ¶ Report; free.

Visual Arts & Galleries Association   (VAGA)   1978
- NR The Old Village School, High St, Witcham, ELY, Cambs, CB6 2LQ.   (hq)
  01353 776356   fax 01353 775411
  email admin@vaga.co.uk   http://www.vaga.co.uk
  Dir: Hilary Gresty
- ○ *A, *P; to improve the status of the visual arts within contemporary culture
- ● Conf - Mtgs - Res - SG - Inf - LG
- M c 350 i, f & affiliates
- ¶ VAGA update - 6; free.

Visual Arts Scotland   1989
- NR 39 Morningside Park, EDINBURGH, EH10 5EZ.   (hq)
  0131-447 2149
  http://www.visualartsscotland.org
  Admin: Margaret Anderson
- ▲ Registered Charity
- ○ *A; to promote contemporary & applied arts
- ● Exhib - Inf
- M i
- ¶ NL - 4; free.   Exhibition Catalogue - 1.   AR; free.

Vitiligo Society   1985
- NR 125 Kennington Rd, LONDON, SE11 6SF.   (hq)
  020 7840 0855
  http://www.vitiligosociety.org.uk
  Mgr: Jennifer Viles
- ▲ Registered Charity
- Br 14
- ○ *W; to give support & advice to people with vitiligo (a skin condition in which patches of skin turn white, although neither painful nor infectious)
- ● Mtgs - Res - Inf
- M c 2,000 i
- ¶ Dispatches (NL) - 4.
  Vitiligo: understanding the loss of skin colour (Hbk).

Vitreous Enamel Association
    2003-04 was incorporated into the **Institute of Vitreous Enamellers**

Voice Care Network UK   (VCN)   1993
- ■ 25 The Square, KENILWORTH, Warks, CV8 1EF.   (hq)
  01926 864000   fax 01926 864000
  email info@voicecare.org.uk
  http://www.voicecare.org.uk
  Admin: Angela Brooks
- ▲ Registered Charity
- ○ *P; promotion & development of healthy & effective use of the voice for all professional voice users & in particular, for teachers
- ● Conf - ET - Res - SG - Stat - Inf - Practical workshops (group teaching & one-to-one teaching)
- < Assn Teachers Singing (AOTOS): Soc Teachers Speech & Drama
- > Brit Voice Assn
- M 250 i, UK / c 30 i, o'seas
- ¶ Voice Matters (NL) - 3; ftm.
  Keeping a Young Voice (leaflet).
  Booklets:
     More Care for Your Voice.
     Voice Warm-up Exercises.
     A Voice Care Guide for Call Centre Managers.

Voice of Chief Officers of Culture, Community & Leisure Services in Scotland (VOCAL) 1975
NR c/o Rod Stone, Aberdeenshire Council, Woodhill House, Westburn Rd, ABERDEEN, AB16 5GE.   (hsb)
01224 664653
Hon Sec: Rod Stone
▲ Un-incorporated Society
○ *P; to promote recreation & leisure services in Scotland; to act as a support agency & forum for senior leisure professionals
● Conf - Mtgs - ET - Res - Inf - LG
M 50 i
✕ 2002-04 Scottish Association of Directors of Leisure Services

Voice of the Listener & Viewer Ltd (VLV) 1983
NR 101 King's Drive, GRAVESEND, Kent, DA12 5BQ.   (hq)
01474 352835   fax 01474 351112
email info@vlv.org.uk   http://www.vlv.org.uk
Chmn: Mrs Jocelyn Hay
▲ Registered Charity; Un-incorporated Society
○ *K; 'an independent consumer body which represents the citizen & consumer interest in broadcasting & works to ensure high quality, diversity & independence in British broadcasting; to represent the interests of listeners & viewers on all broadcasting issues; to maintain the principle of public service in broadcasting'
Gp Special interest gps for children's & educational broadcasting
● Conf - Mtgs - Inf - Lib - VE - LG
Holds the archives of:
British Action for Children's Television [ceased 1995]
Broadcasting Research Unit [ceased 1991]
< Eur Alliance of Listeners' & Viewers' Assns (EURALVA); Nat Coun for Voluntary Orgs (NCVO)
M 2,000 i, 28 org, c 50 universities & colleges, UK / 30 i, o'seas
¶ VLV Bulletin - 4; ftm, £20 yr (UK), £25 yr (o'seas) nm.
Conference Proceedings Reports - 10-12.   AR.
Submissions to Official Consultations - irreg.
Other ad hoc publications.

Volleyball England
a short title for **English Volleyball Association**

Voluntary Action History Society (VAHS) 1991
NR Regents Wharf, 8 All Saints St, LONDON, N1 9RL.   (hsb)
020 7520 8900
Hon Sec: Justin D Smith
○ *G; to promote & study the history of philanthropy & voluntary organisations

Voluntary Euthanasia Society
since 2006 **Dignity in Dying**

Voluntary Euthanasia Society of Scotland   (EXIT)
NR 17 Hart St, EDINBURGH, EH1 3RN.
0131-556 4404
Dir: Chris Docker
○ *K

Voluntary Service Overseas (VSO) 1958
■ 317 Putney Bridge Rd, LONDON, SW15 2PN.   (hq)
020 8780 7200   fax 020 8780 7300
email enquiry@vso.org.uk   http://www.vso.org.uk
Chief Exec: Mark Goldring
▲ Registered Charity
Br 35 in Africa & Asia
○ *W; a voluntary charity dedicated to assisting development in the Third World by sending experienced, practical people on 2-year projects to share their skills in Africa, Asia, the Caribbean & the Pacific
● ET - International development
< [too many to list]
M supporters
✕ 2005 (April) BESO

Volunteer Development England
no longer exists

Voucher Association 1996
NR c/o Gabriella D'Acri, Sycamore House, 5 Sycamore St, LONDON, EC1Y 0SG.   (asa)
0870 241 6445
Chmn: Andrew Johnson
▲ Un-incorporated Society
○ *T; an information & reference point for voucher suppliers & their customers; to raise the profile & use of vouchers within the UK, promoting the industry to consumers, business & government
● Mtgs - ET - Res - Exhib - Stat - Inf - LG
< Brit Promotional Merchandise Assn (BPMA); Direct Marketing Assn (DMA); Inst of Sales Promotion (ISP)
M 27 f, 27 associate f

Vulval Pain Society (VPS) 1996
■ PO Box 7804, NOTTINGHAM, NG3 5ZQ.   (mail/address)
http://www.vulvalpainsociety.org
Jt Secs: David Nunns,   Diane Handy
▲ Un-incorporated Society
○ *W; to provide sufferers with an increase in understanding of their condition; to raise awareness of the condition as an important aspect of women's health
● Inf
M c 200 i
¶ NL - 4; ftm only.   Factsheets; free.

W T Stead Memorial Society
no longer active in the UK

W W Jacobs Appreciation Society   (WWJ)   1988
■ 3 Roman Rd, SOUTHWICK, W Sussex, BN42 4TP.   (hsp)
01273 596217
Hon Sec: A R James
Br 2
○ *A; develop interest in literary, dramatic & filmed works of the
author W W Jacobs (1863-1943)
Gp Biographical; Bibliographical; Theatre & film
● Res - Inf - Lib - PL
< Assn of Literary Socs
M 40 i, UK / 15 i, o'seas
¶ Field Guide (bibliography); £6.
Biography; £12.   Films Directory; £2.
Bibliography (a specialist detailed work); £15.

Wagner Society   1953
■ 16 Doran Drive, REDHILL, Surrey, RH1 6AX.   (h/mem/p)
email mm@misterman.freeserve.co.uk
http://www.wagnersociety.org
Mem Sec: Mrs Margaret Murphy
▲ Registered Charity
○ *D; the appreciation & study of Richard Wagner's life & music
● Mtgs - Res - Lib
M i
¶ Wagner News - 6; both ftm only.

Wagon Building & Repairing Association   (WBRA)   1991
NR Homelea - Westland Green, Little Hadham, WARE, Herts,
SG11 2AG.   (hsp)
01279 843487
email geoffrey.pratt@btconnect.com
Sec Gen: Geoffrey Pratt
○ *T; all aspects of manufacture & repair of freight rolling stock
M 10 f

Wakeboard UK   (WUK)   1996
■ Arden Croft, Forshaw Heath Lane, EARLSWOOD, Warks,
B94 5LD.   (hsp)
01564 700309   fax 01564 700309
email graham@wakeboard.co.uk
http://www.wakeboard.co.uk
Chmn: Graham Creedy
▲ Un-incorporated Society
○ *S; to promote & monitor the sport of wakeboarding
Gp Competitions; Training for coaches to NVQ standard
● ET - Comp - Free 'come & try it days'
< Intl Waterski Fedn; Brit Waterski Fedn
M 150 i, UK / 10 i, o'seas
¶ NL - 4.

Wales-Argentine Society
see **Cymdeithas Cymru-Ariannin (Wales Argentine Society)**

Wales Association of Community & Town Councils
in 2004 joined with the National Association of Local Councils in
Wales to form **One Voice Wales**

**Wales Council for Voluntary Action   (Cyngor Gweithredu
Gwirfoddol Cymru)   (WCVA)   1934**
■ Baltic House, Mount Stuart Square, CARDIFF BAY, Glam,
CF10 5FH.   (hq)
0870 607 1666   fax 029 2043 1701
email help@wcva.org.uk   http://www.wcva.org.uk
Chief Exec: Graham Benfield
▲ Company Limited by Guarantee; Registered Charity
Br 2
○ *W; the voice of the voluntary sector in Wales.   It represents
the interests of, & campaigns for, all voluntary organisations
● Conf - Mtgs - ET - Res - Exhib - Stat - Inf - Lib - LG
< NCVO (sister org)
M 20 i, 80 f, 1,700 org
¶ NL - 12.   Directory - 2/3 yrly.
Wales Funding Handbook - 1.
publications list available.

Wales Craft Council   (WCC)   1977
■ Henfaes Lane, WELSHPOOL, Powys, SY21 7BE.   (hq)
01938 555313   fax 01938 556237
email inf0@walescraftcouncil.co.uk
http://www.walescraftcouncil.co.uk
Chmn: Philomena Hearn
▲ Company Limited by Guarantee
○ *P, *T; for full-time professional craft, gift & textile producers in
Wales
Gp Direct sales; Trade sales
● Exhib
M c 150 f
¶ Bulletin - 12; ftm.

Wales Pre-school Playgroups Association   (Wales PPA)   1987
■ Ladywell House, NEWTOWN, Powys, SY16 1JB.   (hq)
01686 624573   fax 01686 610230
email info@walesppa.org   http://www.walesppa.org
Dir: Thomas A Memery
▲ Company Limited by Guarantee; Registered Charity
Br 14
○ *E; to enhance the development, care & education of pre-
school children in Wales by encouraging parents to
understand & provide for their needs, through high quality
pre-school groups
● Conf - Mtgs - ET - Res - Exhib - Comp - Stat - Inf - Lib - LG
M 1,200 org
¶ Small Talk - 6; £2.50 m, £3.50 nm.   AR; ftm, £5 nm.

Wales Trades Union Congress
NR Transport House, 1 Cathedral Rd, CARDIFF, Glam,
CF11 9SD.   (hq)
029 2034 7010
http://www.wtuc.org.uk
○ *U
M 500,000 i in 50 unions
No further information supplied

Wales Trekking & Riding Association
■ North Barn, Glanirfon, LLANWRTYD WELLS, Powys, LD5 4RR.
01591 610818
Sec: Mrs Christine Stokes
○ *G

Wall Tie Installers Federation   (WTIF)   1989
NR Heald House, Heald St, LIVERPOOL, L19 2LY.   (hq)
       0151-494 2503   fax 0151-494 2511
       email admin@wtif.org.uk   http://www.wtif.org.uk
       Gen Sec: Hugh Banks
▲ Company Limited by Guarantee
○ *T; replacement of wall tie installations
● Conf - Mtgs - ET - Exhib - Inf - Lib - PL
M 80 f
¶ WTIF News - 12; ftm.

Wallcovering Distributors Association   (WDA)
■ c/o William Robinson, Daleside Rd, NOTTINGHAM, NG2 4DH.
       0115-979 9790
       Pres: Stuart Thorne,   Hon Sec: William Robinson
○ *T; for British distributors of wallcoverings, fabrics & decorating
       products
M f

Wallcovering Manufacturers' Association of Great Britain Ltd
▲ Company Limited by Guarantee
       2005 merged with the **British Coatings Federation** as the
       Wallcoverings Sector Council

Wallpaper History Society   1986
■ c/o Victoria & Albert Museum, Cromwell Rd, LONDON,
       SW7 2RL.   (mail) address
       49 Glenpark Drive, Southport, Merseyside, PR9 9FA. (mem/sp)
       Hon Sec: Anna Chalcraft (020 8977 4978),
       Mem Sec: Duncan Burton (01704 225429)
▲ Un-incorporated Society
○ *L; to encourage research & provide information on all aspects
       of wallpaper production, consumption & design.
       Encompasses not only the history of wallpaper, but also
       topics relating to other kinds of wallcoverings & interior
       design generally
● Conf - SG - VE
M c 225 i, f & org
¶ Jnl - 2 yrly; ftm.

Walmsley Society   1985
■ April Cottage 1 Brand Rd, Hampden Park, EASTBOURNE,
       E Sussex, BN22 9PX.   (hsp)
       01323 506447
       email walmsley@mabarraclough.f9.co.uk
       http://www.haughshw.demon.co.uk/walmsoc.htm
       Hon Sec: Fred W Lane
▲ Un-incorporated Society
○ *A; to promote & encourage an appreciation of the literary &
       artistic heritage left to us by J Ulric Walmsley (1860-1954) &
       Leo Walmsley (1892-1966)
Gp Research/archives; Publicity; Biography planning
● Mtgs - Res - Inf - VE - Encouraging the reprinting of books by
       Leo Walmsley or concerning the Walmsleys
< Alliance Literary Socs
M 200 i, UK / 4 i, o'seas
¶ Jnl - 2; ftm, £3 nm.   NL - 4/5; ftm only.
       Books & booklets.

Walpole
■ 1 Southwark Bridge, LONDON, SE1 9HL.   (hq)
       020 7873 3803
       email emily.petch@thewalpole.co.uk
       http://www.thewalpole.co.uk
       Contact: Emily Petch
○ *T; an organisation of Britain's 100 famous luxury brands
M c 100 f
       no further information supplied

Walpole Society   1911
■ Dept of Prints & Drawings, The British Museum, LONDON,
       WC1B 3DG.   (mail/address)
       020 7323 8408
       email dkealey@supanet.com
       http://www.walpolesociety.org.uk
       Chmn: Simon Swyfen Jervis
▲ Registered Charity
○ *A; to collect & publish archival & other material relating to the
       history of the arts in Great Britain
● Res - Publications
M 295 i, 90 org, UK / 50 i, 130 org, o'seas
       [the org represent museums, libraries & universities]
¶ Walpole Society Volume - 1; m only (£35 i, £45 corporate)
       AR; ftm.

Walter de la Mare Society   1997
■ Flat 15 Trinity Court, Vicarage Rd, TWICKENHAM, Middx,
       TW2 5TY.   (hsp)
       020 8898 6563
       http://www.bluetree.co.uk/wdlmsociety
       Hon Sec & Treas: Julie de la Mare
○ *A; to honour the memory of novelist, poet & essayist Walter
       de la Mare (1873-1956); to promote the study & deepen the
       appreciation of his works
● Mtgs
M 65 i, UK / 10 i, o'seas
¶ Jnl - 1; ftm (£15 subn).

War Memorials Trust   (WMT)   1995
NR 4 Lower Belgrave St, LONDON, SW1W 0LA.   (hq)
       020 7259 0403   fax 020 7259 0296
       email info@warmemorials.org
       http://www.warmemorials.com
▲ Registered Charity
○ *K; to preserve (both in the UK & overseas) the memorials to
       those who gave their lives in the cause of freedom; to
       monitor their condition; to liaise with ecclesiastical
       authorities, regiments & other responsible bodies
Gp Maritime section; War memorial heritage hospitals
● Exhib - Comp - Inf
       Conservation: 020 7881 0862
< Engl Heritage; Cadw; Historic Scotland; Countryside Agency; R
       Brit Legion; Imperial War Museum
M 1,100 i, 100 f, 100 org, UK / 20 i, o'seas
¶ NL - 4.
× 2004 Friends of War Memorials

War Research Society
§ 27 Courtway Ave, Birmingham, B14 4PP.   (hq)
       0121-430 5348   fax 0121-436 7401
       http://www.battlefieldtours.co.uk
       a company organising guided tours of WW1 & WW2
       battlefields & war sites

War Widows Association of Great Britain   (WWA)   1971
■ c/o British Legion, 48 Pall Mall, LONDON, SW1Y 5JY.   (hq)
       0870 241 1305   fax 0870 241 1305
       email info@warwidowsassociation.org.uk
       http://www.warwidowsassociation.org.uk
       The Hon Secretary
▲ Registered Charity
○ *W; to care for the welfare of War Widows; to speak on their
       behalf with government ministers
● Inf
M 5,500 i
¶ Courage (NL) - 3; ftm, donations welcomed nm.

Warrington Chamber of Commerce & Industry   1876
NR   International Business Centre, Delta Crescent, Westbrook,
        WARRINGTON, Cheshire, WA5 7WQ.   (hq)
        01925 715150
        Chief Exec: Colin Daniels
▲   Company Limited by Guarantee
○   *C
●   Mtgs - ET - Res - Stat - Expt - Inf - Lib - LG
<   Brit Chams Comm; Assn Cheshire Chams Comm; NW Chams
        Comm
M   360 f, UK / 20 f, o'seas
¶   Insight - 12;   Alliance - 6; both ftm only.
        Members' Directory - 1; ftm.   AR; ftm.

Waste Watch   1987
NR   56-64 Leonard St, LONDON, EC2A 4JX.   (hq)
        020 7549 0300   fax 020 7549 0301
        email info@wastewatch.org.uk
        http://www.wastewatch.org.uk
▲   Company Limited by Guarantee; Registered Charity
○   *K; to promote & support action for waste reduction & recycling
        by working with community groups, voluntary organisations,
        local authorities & businesses - providing practical support
        for local action; to encourage government & industry to
        support recycling; it is partly funded by DEFRA's
        Environmental Action Fund
●   Inf - LG - Operates Wasteline: a telephone & postal
        information service on what can be re-cycled & where
M   i, f & org
¶   Practical guides & specialist reports; list available.

Water Colour Society of Ireland
IRL   c/o Hon Sec, 74 Grange Park, Raheny, DUBLIN 5, Republic of
        Ireland.
        353 (1) 848 0802
        Hon Sec: Pauline Doyle
○   *A

Water for Health Alliance
■   1 Queen Anne's Gate, LONDON, SW1H 9BT.
        http://www.water.org.uk/home/water-for-health
        no further information supplied

Water Jetting Association   1980
■   17 St Judith's Lane, Sawtry, HUNTINGDON, Cambs,
        PE28 5XE.   (hq)
        01487 834034
        Dir: Norman Allen
○   *T
M   120 f
¶   Pressure Points (Jnl) - 2.
        Codes of Practice for safe working.
        Medical notes.   Medical card.
        Training course manuals.

Water Management Society Ltd   (WM Soc)   1970
■   6 Sir Robert Peel Mill, Tolson's Enterprise Park, Fazeley,
        TAMWORTH, Staffs, B78 3QD.   (hsb)
        01827 289558   fax 01827 250408
        email wmsoc@btconnect.com
        http://www.wmsoc.org.uk
        Gen Sec: Mrs Sue Pipe
▲   Company Limited by Guarantee
○   *P; the safe & efficient use of water in industry & commerce
Gp   Technical c'ee
●   Conf - ET - LG
M   594 i, UK / 20 i, o'seas
¶   Waterline - 4; ftm, £75 nm.
        Site Log Book for Water Services; £30 m, £50 nm.
        Guide to Risk Assessment for Water Services; £50 m, £75 nm.

Water UK   1998
NR   1 Queen Anne's Gate, LONDON, SW1H 9BT.   (hq)
        020 7344 1844
        http://www.water.org.uk
        Chief Exec: Pamela Taylor
○   *N; for water services companies of England & Wales
M   f

Waterford Chamber of Commerce
IRL   2 George's St, WATERFORD, Republic of Ireland.
        353 (51) 872639
        email info@waterfordchamber.ie
        http://www.waterfordchamber.ie
        Chief Exec: Monica Leech
○   *C

waterskiscotland   1974
NR   Scottish National Water Ski Centre, Townhill Country Park,
        DUNFERMLINE, Fife, KY12 0HT.   (hq)
        01383 620123   fax 01383 620122
        email info@waterskiscotland.co.uk
        Nat Co-ordinator: Alan G Murray
▲   Company Limited by Guarantee
○   *S; to act as the national governing body promoting water
        skiing in Scotland
Gp   Tournament; Racing; Barefoot; Recreational; Kneeboard;
        Disabled; Wakeboarding; Schools; Youth; Corporate
●   Conf - Mtgs - ET - Exam - Exhib - Comp - Inf - LG
<   Intl Water Ski Fedn; Brit Water Ski Fedn
M   c250 i
¶   NL - 4;   Rule Books;   Codes of Practice;   AR; all free.

WaterVoice
        in 2005 became the Consumer Council for Water; see
        companion volume **Councils, Committees & Boards**

Waterway Recovery Group Ltd   (WRG)   1970
NR   PO Box 114, RICKMANSWORTH, Herts, WD3 1ZY.   (hq)
        01923 711114
        Chief Exec: Neil Edwards
▲   Registered Charity
○   *G, *N; co-ordinating body for voluntary labour on the inland
        waterways of Britain; is a non-membership subsidiary
        company of the Inland Waterways Association interested in
        the conservation & restoration of the inland waterways of
        Britain
●   Mtgs - ET - Inf - LG
M   1,850 i, 20 f, 100 org, UK / 30 i, o'seas
¶   Navvies - 6.   Canal Camps Brochure - 1.
        Other occasional publications.

Watford & West Herts Chamber of Commerce & Industry   1895
NR   The Business Centre, Colne Way, WATFORD, Herts,
        WD24 7AA.   (hq)
        01923 442442
        Sec: Lorraine Marshall
▲   Company Limited by Guarantee
○   *C
●   Mtgs - ET - Expt - Inf - VE - Export documentation service
M   c 450 f
¶   Newsletter - irreg; ftm only.   LM - 1; ftm.

© CBD Research Ltd · Beckenham · BR3 5JS · Tel 020 8650 7745 · Fax 020 8650 0768 · E-mail cbd@cbdresearch.com · www.cbdresearch.com

Way Foundation (WAY) 1997
■ PO Box 6767, BRACKLEY, Northants, NN13 6YW.
    (mail/address)
    0870 011 3450
    email info@wayfoundation.org.uk
    http://www.wayfoundation.org.uk
    Gen Sec: SArah Castagnetti
▲ Registered Charity
○ *W; a self-help group fro men & women who are 50, or under,
    at the time of losing their partner; to help them, rebuild their
    lives by helping each other
● Inf - Support network
M 1,100 i
¶ NL - 4.

Web-offset Newspaper Association (WONA) 1964
NR 74-77 Great Russell St, LONDON, WC1B 3DA.   (hq)
    020 7636 7014   fax 020 7631 5119
    email gary@cullumpublishing.org
    Sec: Gary Cullum
○ *T; to exchange technical information & experience of printing
    newspapers on web-offset presses
M f

Wedgwood Society of Great Britain 1954
NR PO Box 5921, BISHOP'S STORTFORD, Herts, CM22 7FP.
    (mail) address
    Hon Sec: Dr W A M Holdaway
○ *A; to advance study, knowledge & appreciation of Wedgwood
    ware
M i

Welding Institute (TWI Ltd) 1968
■ Granta Park, Great Abington, CAMBRIDGE, CB1 6AL.   (hq)
    01223 891162   fax 01223 892588
    email twi@twi.co.uk   http://www.twi.co.uk
    Chief Exec: Dr Bob John
▲ Company Limited by Guarantee
○ *L, *P, *Q; to carry out confidential contract work on all aspects
    of welding& materials joining for industrial member
    companies; to teach good practice in welding, joining & non-
    destructive testing
Gp 10 technical gps on specific aspects of joining
● Conf - Mtgs - ET - Exam - Res - Inf - Lib - PL - Giving
    qualifications to welding & joining personnel
< Intl Inst Welding; Eur Welding Fedn; Assn Indep Res &
    Technology Orgs
M 7,000 i, 3,500 f
¶ Connect - 6; free.   Bulletin - 6;   AR; both ftm only.
    Note: trades as TWI Ltd

Welding Manufacturers' Association
    as part of BEAMA Power Ltd is a group of **BEAMA**

Well Drillers' Association (WDA) 1985
NR 12 Alder Way, BROMSGROVE, Worcs, B60 1AJ.   (chmn/sp/b)
    01527 876706   fax 01527 876706
    http://www.welldrillers.org.uk
    Chmn & Sec: Malcolm Gamble
▲ Un-incorporated Society
○ *T; promote & support scientific research into drilling & the
    exploration & utilisation of water sources
● Mtgs - ET - Inf - LG
< Brit Drilling Assn
M 23 f
¶ LM; free.

Well Services Contractors Association   (WSCA)
NR Unit 12 Frederick Street Business Centre, Frederick St,
    ABERDEEN, AB24 5HY.
    01224 640660   fax 01224 640660
    email chris_strang@wsca.co.uk   http://www.wsca.co.uk
    Dir: Chris Strang
○ *T

Welsh Agricultural Organisation Society Ltd (WAOS) 1922
NR Gorseland, North Rd, ABERYSTWYTH, Ceredigion,
    SY23 2WB.   (hq)
    01970 636688   fax 01970 624049
    email waos@wfsagri.net
    Chief Exec: Don Thomas
○ *F; agricultural marketing & consultancy (incl horticulture)

Welsh Amateur Boxing Association (WABA) 1910
NR 2 Old School Cott, Marcross, LLANTWIT MAJOR, S Glam,
    CF61 1ZD.   (hsb/p)
    01446 794444
    Hon Gen Sec: D B Francis
▲ Registered Charity
○ *S; to promote amateur boxing in Wales
Gp Training; Commissions
● Conf - Mtgs - ET - Exam - Comp - Inf
M i
¶ AR.

**Welsh Amateur Gymnastics Association   (Welsh Gymnastics)
1901**
NR Cardiff Central Youth Club, Ocean Park, Ocean Way, CARDIFF,
    Glam, CF24 5HE.   (hq)
    029 2043 1240
    Gen Sec: Mrs Annette Brown
○ *S; governing body of gymnastics in Wales
Gp Women's artistic, Men's artistic, Rhythmic, General recreational,
    Sports acrobatics, Sports aerobics, Preschool, People with
    disabilities
● Mtgs - ET - Comp
< C'wealth Confedn; Brit Gymnastics
M i & clubs
¶ NL - 4.

**Welsh Amateur Music Federation   (Ffederasiwn Cerddoriaeth
Amatur Cymru) (WAMF/FfCAC) 1968**
■ Tŷ Cerdd-Music Centre Wales, Wales Millennium Centre,
    CARDIFF, CF10 5AL.   (hq)
    029 2063 5640   fax 029 2063 5641
    email wamf@tycerdd.org   http://www.tycerdd.org
    Chief Exec: Keith Griffin
▲ Registered Charity; Un-incorporated Society
○ *D, *N, Y; support for amateur music making organisations
    through advice, grants, workshops & courses
Gp National Youth Brass Band of Wales; National Youth Choir of
    Wales;
    National Youth Jazz Orchestra of Wales; National Youth Wind
    Orchestra of Wales; National Youth Synphonic Brass Wales
    Bands; Choirs; Folk; Musical theatre societies
● Conf - Mtgs - ET - Res - Comp - Stat - Inf - Lib - VE - LG - Youth
    activities, grants & guarantees for performance - Music
    promotion & support
M c 400 societies (representing 25,000 amateur performers)
¶ Annual Review of Activities; ftm, £1 nm.
    Various pamphlets etc.

Welsh Amateur Rowing Association   (WARA)
NR 4 Garrick Drive, Thornhill, CARDIFF, CF14 9BG.   (hsp)
    029 2075 3910
    http://www.wara.org.uk
    Sec: Sally Haines
▲ Un-incorporated Society
○ *S; to regulate & promote the sport of rowing for men &
    women in Wales, for recreation as well as for national &
    international competition
Gp Coastal rowing; Welsh Longboat Association
● Mtgs - ET - Exam - Comp - Liaison with Welsh Assembly & the
    Sports Council for Wales
M 1,200 i (Wales)
¶ [website only]

Welsh Amateur Swimming Association   (WASA)   1897
■   Wales National Pool, Sketty Lane, SWANSEA, SA2 8QG.   (hq)
   01792 513636   fax 01792 513637
   email secretary@welshasa.co.uk
   http://www.welshasa.co.uk
   Head of Admin: Mrs Julie Tyler
○   *S; the governing body for swimming in Wales
Gp Swimming; Diving; Water polo; Masters swimming
●   ET (national team training) - Comp
<   Amat Swimming Fedn GB (ASFGB)
M   10,000 i
¶   WASA Hbk - 1; £10 m.

Welsh Athletics   1897
NR Cardiff Athletics Stadium, Leckwith Rd, CARDIFF, Glam,
   CF11 8AZ.   (hq)
   0870 162 2530   fax 0870 162 2531
   http://www.welshathletics.org
   Dir of Athletics: Steve Brace,
   Hon Sec: Mrs Jan Evans-Nugent
○   *S; to promote & develop athletics in Wales
●   Mtgs - ET - Exam - Comp - Stat - Inf
<   Brit Athletics Fedn; Welsh Sports Assn
M   100 clubs
¶   NL - 2.   Ybk.   AR.
×   2005 Athletics Association of Wales

Welsh Badminton Union   (Undeb Badminton Cymru)
(WBU)   1928
NR Unit E4, South Point Industrial Estate, Foreshore Rd, CARDIFF,
   CF10 4SP.   (hq)
   029 2049 7225   fax 029 2049 7224
○   *S; governing body of sport for badminton
Gp Welsh Coaches Register; Welsh Umpires; Welsh Referees
●   Conf - Mtgs - ET - Exhib - Comp - Inf
<   Intl Badminton Fedn (IBF); Eur Badminton U (EBU)
M   i & clubs
¶   Badminton in Wales - 4.   Coaches NL - 6.

Welsh Black Cattle Society   (WBCS)   1904
■   13 Bangor St, CAERNARFON, Gwynedd, LL55 1AP.   (hq)
   01286 672391   fax 01286 672022
   http://www.welshblackcattlesociety.org
   Pres: Evan Tudor,   Chief Exec: Andrew James
▲   Registered Charity
Br 2; Australia, Canada, Germany, N Zealand
○   *B
●   Mtgs - Res - Exhib - Comp - Inf
M   884 i, UK / 17 i, o'seas
¶   Jnl - 1; £7.50.   NL - irreg.   Herd Book - 1; £35.

Welsh Bowling Association   (WBA)   1904
NR 6 Nordale Court, Fidlas Rd, CARDIFF, CF14 0NJ.   (hsp)
   029 2063 4995
   Hon Sec: Jim Ireland
▲   Un-incorporated Society
○   *S; to control & organise the men's flat green game of bowls in
   Wales
Gp Welsh Bowls Umpires Assn; Welsh Bowls Coaching Assn
●   Mtgs - Comp
<   Wld Bowls Bd; Brit Isles Bowling Coun
M   c 11,000 i
¶   WBA Official Ybk - 1.

Welsh Bowls Coaching Association
   a group of the **Welsh Bowling Association**

Welsh Bowls Umpires Association
   a group of the **Welsh Bowling Association**

Welsh Bridge Union   (WBU)   1933
NR 31 Deri Rd, CARDIFF, CF23 5AH.   (chiefexec/p)
   029 2025 5162
   email wbu@wbu.org.uk   http://www.wbu.org.uk
   Chief Exec: Linda Greenland
▲   Un-incorporated Society
○   *G; for players of Contract Bridge
●   Mtgs
<   Wld Bridge Fedn; Eur Bridge League
>   East, Mid, North & West Wales Bridge Assns
M   c 2,000 i
¶   Competition & Masterpoint Journal - 1; ftm, £5 nm.

Welsh Chess Union   (WCU)   1960
■   Rosemount, Vaughan Terrace, Penrhiwceiber, MOUNTAIN ASH,
   CF45 3TF.   (exec/dir)
   Exec Director: Leighton Williams
▲   Un-incorporated Society
○   *S; to foster the game of chess in Wales
●   Exam
<   Fédn Intle des Echecs (FIDE)
M   900 i
¶   NL - 4.   Ybk - 1; ftm.
   Pawns (junior NL) - 12; free to juniors.

Welsh Culinary Association   (WCA)   1994
■   c/o The Bungalow, Maes-y-Neuadd, TALSARNAU, Gwynedd,
   LL47 6YA.   (chmn/p)
   01766 780319   fax 01766 780211
   email info@welshculinaryassociation.com
   http://www.welshculinaryassociation.com
   Chmn: Peter Jackson,   Sec: Nick Davies
▲   Company Limited by Guarantee
○   *P; to represent & promote the chefs of Wales
●   Conf - Mtgs - ET - Res - Exhib - Comp - Expt
<   Wld Assn of Cooks Socs
M   320 i, Wales / 2 i, o'seas

Welsh Cycling Union Ltd   (WCU)   1972
NR Wales National Velodrome, Newport International Sports
   Village, NEWPORT, Monmouthshire, NP19 4PT.   (hq)
   01633 670540   fax 01633 670540
   email information@welshcyclingunion.com
   http://www.welshcyclingunion.com
   Admin Officer: Edith Clark
▲   Company Limited by Guarantee
○   *G, *S; the governing body for cycling in Wales & covers: road
   racing, track racing, mountain bike, BMX, cyclo cross & cycle
   speedway
●   Mtgs - ET - Comp - Inf - LG
<   Brit Cycling Fedn; Sports Coun Wales; U Cycliste Intle
M   950 i, 70 org

Welsh Federation of Housing Associations
NR Norbury House, Norbury Rd, Fairwater, CARDIFF, CF5 3AS.
   029 2030 3160   fax 029 2056 0668
   http://www.welshhousing.org.uk
○   *W

Welsh Folk Dance Society
   see **Cymdeithas Ddawns Werin Cymru   (Welsh Folk Dance**
   Society)

Welsh Folk Song Society   (CAGC)   1906
■   9 High St, CRICCIETH, Gwynedd, LL52 0BS.   (hsp)
   01766 522096
   http://www.canugwerin.org
   Hon Sec: Mrs Buddug Lloyd Roberts
▲   Registered Charity
○   *D; to collect, preserve, interpret & perform Welsh folk-songs;
   to foster an interest in folk literature & music in general
●   Conf - Res - Inf
M   250 i, 10 org, UK / 5 org, o'seas
¶   Canu Gwerin (Folk Song) (Jnl) - 1; £10 yr m.

© CBD Research Ltd · Beckenham · BR3 5JS · Tel 020 8650 7745 · Fax 020 8650 0768 · E-mail cbd@cbdresearch.com · www.cbdresearch.com

Welsh Golfing Union   (WGU)   1895
NR   Catsash, NEWPORT, Monmouthshire, NP18 1JQ.   (hq)
01633 430830
Sec: Richard Dixon
○   *S; the governing body for golf in Wales
●   Mtgs - ET - Res - Comp - SG - Stat - Inf - VE
<   Coun Nat Golf Unions; Eur Golf Assn
M   62,000 i, 159 affiliated clubs
¶   Ybk; free.   Information leaflets.

Welsh Halfbred Sheep Breeders Association Ltd   1955
NR   Brynteg, Pen-y-garnedd, Llanrhaeadr-ym-Mochnant,
OSWESTRY, Powys, SY10 0AW.   (hsp)
01691 860336
Sec: Mrs Gillian Napper
○   *B; marketing of the Welsh Halfbred sheep (the cross of a
Welsh Mountain ewe & a Border Leicester ram)
●   Exhib - Shows & five annual sales
<   Nat Sheep Assn
M   400 i
¶   Welsh Halfbred News - 2; ftm only.

Welsh Highland Railways Association   (WHR)   1964
■   Tremadog Rd, PORTHMADOG, Gwynedd, LL49 9DY.
(hq/regd)
01766 513402   fax 01766 513402
email info@whr.co.uk   http://www.whr.co.uk office
Chmn: James Hewett
▲   Company Limited by Guarantee; Registered Charity
○   *G; to recreate the Welsh Highland Railway of the 1920s &
1930s; to provide a quality education, interactive, visitor
attraction; to preserve & increase the skills involved in
running a railway
Gp   Locomotives - steam & diesel; Carriage & wagon; Civils;
Commercial; Museum; Telecommunications
●   Mtgs - ET - Exhib - Inf - PL - VE
<   Heritage Rly Assn; N Wales Tourism; Great Little Trains of Wales
M   800 i, UK / 150 i, o'seas
2006 (Welsh Highland Railway Ltd
(Welsh Highland Railway Society
(Welsh Highland Railway Heritage Group
¶   The Jnl - 3; ftm, £1.75 nm.   The Russell - irreg; free.

Welsh Hill Speckled Face Sheep Society   1968
NR   Nantypantmawr, LLANIDOES, Powys, SY18 6SY.   (asa)
01686 440279
Contact: R Griffiths
▲   Un-incorporated Society
○   *B
●   Mtgs - Comp
M   i [not stated]

Welsh Hockey Coaches Association
a group of **Welsh Hockey Union Ltd**

Welsh Hockey Umpires Association
a group of **Welsh Hockey Union Ltd**

Welsh Hockey Union Ltd   (Undeb Hoci Cymru)   (WHU)   1897
NR   Severn House, Station Terrace, Ely, CARDIFF, Glam,
CF5 4AA.   (hq)
029 2057 3940   fax 029 2057 3941
email info@welsh-hockey.co.uk
http://www.welsh-hockey.co.uk
Operating Manager: Chris Brewer
▲   Company Limited by Guarantee
○   *S; governing body for hockey in Wales
Gp   Welsh Hockey Coaches Assn; Welsh Hockey Umpires Assn
●   Mtgs - ET - Exam - Comp - Inf - VE - LG - Promotion of hockey
throughout Wales
<   Fédn Intle de Hockey; Eur Hockey Fedn
M   4,500 i, 115 clubs, 300 schools
¶   NL - 1;   Circulars - 4; both ftm.
Hbk - 1; ftm.

Welsh Hospitals & Health Services Association   (WHA Healthcare)   1948
■   60 Newport Rd, CARDIFF, Glam, CF24 1YG.   (hq)
029 2048 5461   fax 029 2048 8859
email mail@whahealthcare.co.uk
http://www.whahealthcare.co.uk
Chief Exec: Huw L Cooke
▲   Company Limited by Guarantee
○   *W; payment of cash benefits to members & their families in
respect of incidental & statutory expenses incurred in
obtaining NHS treatment as well as part refund of fees for
specialist consultations & physiotherapy
●   Conf - Mtgs
<   Brit Health Care Assn
M   46,500 i, 600 f
¶   AR & Accounts; free.

Welsh Hound Association   (WHA)   1921
NR   Althrey Lodge Cottage, Overton Rd, Bangor-is-y-Coed,
WREXHAM, LL13 0DA.   (hsp)
01978 780598
Sec: M J Medcalf
▲   Un-incorporated Society
○   *B; to improve & record the breeding of the Welsh hound
●   Inf
M   100 i
¶   Welsh Hound Stud Book - 3 yrly.

Welsh Indoor Bowls Association   (WIBA)   1934
■   50 Penyrheol Rd, Gorseinon, SWANSEA, Glam, SA4 4GA.
(hsp)
01792 538061   fax 01792 548221
Hon Sec: David Phillips
▲   Un-incorporated Society
Br   25 clubs
○   *S; to promote indoor bowls throughout Wales
<   Wld Indoor Bowls Assn; Brit Isles Indoor Bowls Coun
M   7,500 i, 25 clubs
¶   Hbk - 1; ftm, £1.50 nm.   AR; ftm only.

Welsh Jazz Society   1963
■   26 The Balcony, Castle Arcade, CARDIFF, Glam, CF10 1BY.
(hq)
029 2034 0591   fax 029 2066 5160
email welshjazz@btconnect.com
http://www.jazzwales.org.uk
Chief Exec: B J Hennessey
▲   Company Limited by Guarantee; Registered Charity
○   *D; promotion, learning & presentation of jazz music
●   Mtgs - ET - Inf - PL - Concert performances
<   Jazz Services Ltd
M   800 i, 8 org
¶   Jazz UK - 6; free.

Welsh Judo Association   (WJA)   1964
■   6 Ynys-y-Mond Rd, Alltwen, Neath, PORT TALBOT, Glam,
SA8 3BA.   (hsb)
01792 869460   fax 01792 869460
email welsh_judo@hotmail.com
http://www.welshjudo.com
Sec: J E Melen
▲   Company Limited by Guarantee
○   *S; promotion of judo
●   Mtgs - ET - Exam - Comp
<   Brit Judo Assn; C'wealth Judo Assn
M   2,200 i
¶   NL - 12; free.

Welsh Language Society
see **Cymdeithas yr Iaith Gymraeg (Welsh Language Society)**

Welsh Library Association
since 2002 is a division of **CILIP**

Welsh Local Government Association   1996

NR   Local Government House, Drake Walk, CARDIFF, Glam,
    CF10 4LG.   (hq)
    029 2046 8600
    Dir: Steve Thomas
○   *N; to promote local democracy & represent the interests of
    local government in Wales
●   Conf - Mtgs - Res - Inf - LG
<   Local Govt Assn
M   22 local authorities, 10 associates
¶   Occasional publications on matters of interest.

Welsh Mills Society   (Cymdeithas Melinau Cymru)   1984

NR   Y Felin, Tynygraig, YSTRAD MEURIG, Ceredigion, SY25 6AE.
    (hsp)
    Hon Sec: Mrs Hilary Malaws
○   *G, *L; to study, record, interpret & publicise the wind & water
    mills of Wales; to advise on their preservation & use; to
    encourage working millers
●   Conf - Mtgs - Res - Inf
M   c 250 i, 15 f & org
¶   Melin - 1.

Welsh Mines Society   (WMS)   1979

NR   20 Lutterburn St, Ugborough, IVYBRIDGE, Devon, PL21 0NG.
    (hsp)
    01752 896432
    http://www.welshmines.org
    Sec: Dr David Roe
○   *G; for those interested in all aspects of Welsh mines, especially
    the mineralogy, history & archaeology; preservation of sites
M   i

Welsh Mountain Sheep Society - Hill Flock Section   1950

NR   c/o WAOS, Gorseland, North Rd, ABERYSTWYTH, Ceredigion,
    SY23 2HE.   (hq)
    01970 636688
○   *B

Welsh Mountain Sheep Society - Registered Section   (WMSS)   1905

■   Ty'n-y-Mynydd Farm, Boduan, PWLLHELI, Gwynedd,
    LL53 8PZ.   (hsp)
    01758 721898
    email info@welsh-sheep.org
    http://www.welsh-sheep.org
    Sec: Mrs D Tyne
▲   Registered Charity
○   *B
●   Conf - Mtgs - Exhib - Comp - Inf - Production of a flock book
<   Nat Sheep Assn
M   60 i
¶   NL - 2.   Ybk - 1.   Sale Catalogue - 1.
✕   18 May 2005 Welsh Mountain Sheep Society - Pedigree section

Welsh Mule Sheep Breeders Association   1978

NR   c/o WAOS, Gorseland, North Rd, ABERYSTWYTH, Ceredigion,
    SY23 1DR.   (hq)
    01970 636688
○   *B

Welsh Music Guild   1954

NR   9 Brown St, Ferndale, RHONDDA, CF43 4SF.   (contact/p/b)
    Vice Chmn: John H Lewis
○   *D; to promote Welsh music in its composition, performance &
    the teaching of the same; emphasis on Welsh contemporary
    music & its composers
●   Conf - Mtgs - Exhib - Comp - Inf - Lib - LG
M   i
¶   Welsh Music (Jnl) - 3;   AR; both ftm.
✕   2003 Guild for the Promotion of Welsh Music

Welsh National Literature Promotion Agency
    see ACADEMI - Welsh National Literature Promotion Agency

Welsh Netball Association   (WNA)   1945

■   33-35 Cathedral Rd, CARDIFF, Glam, CF11 9HB.   (hq)
    029 2023 7048   fax 029 2022 6430
    email welshnetball@welshnetball.com
    http://www.welshnetball.co.uk
    Chief Exec: Susan J Holvey
▲   Company Limited by Guarantee
○   *S; to promote & develop the game of netball within Wales
●   Mtgs - ET - Comp
<   Intl Fedn Netball Assns (IFNA); Fedn Eur Netball Assns (FENA)
M   2,500 i, 500 schools & colleges
¶   Netball News (Jnl) - 2; ftm, £1 nm.

Welsh Pony & Cob Society   (WPCS)   1901

NR   6 Chalybeate St, ABERYSTWYTH, Ceredigion, SY23 1HP.   (hq)
    01970 617501
    Sec: Mrs G Sazeykoven
▲   Company Limited by Guarantee; Registered Charity
○   *B; registration of Welsh Ponies & Cobs & their part-breeds
●   Mtgs - ET - Exhib - Inf - Archive Museum
<   Brit Horse Soc; Nat Pony Soc
M   8,000 i
¶   Jnl - 1.   NL - 2.   Welsh Ponies & Cobs (magazine) - 4.
    Stud Book - 1.

Welsh Rugby Union Ltd   (WRU)   1881

■   Golate House (1st floor), 101 St Mary Street, CARDIFF, Glam,
    CF10 1GE.   (hq)
    0870 013 8600
    http://www.wru.co.uk
    Chief Exec: Steven M Lewis
▲   Company Limited by Guarantee
○   *S; governing body of Rugby Union football in Wales
●   Conf - Mtgs - ET - Comp - Inf - Lib - VE - Arranging
    international matches
<   Intl Rugby Football Bd (IRB)
>   Welsh Districts Rugby U; Welsh Schools Rugby U
M   240+ clubs
¶   WRU Hbk - 1; ftm, £5 nm.

Welsh Weight Training Association   (WWTA)   1985

■   13 Barquentine Place, Atlantic Pl, CARDIFF, Glam, CF10 4NJ.
    (hsp)
    029 2049 3919   fax 029 2049 3919
    Sec: Lorraine Gray
▲   Un-incorporated Society
Br   5
○   *S; to promote weight training; to improve & standardise
    coaching & instruction throughout Wales
●   Mtgs - ET - Exam (coaches)
<   Intl Coun for Health & Fitness
M   2,000 i
¶   Basic Coaches Manual.

Welshpool & Llanfair Light Railway Preservation Co Ltd   1960

NR   Llanfair Station, LLANFAIR CAEREINION, Powys, SY21 0SF.
    (hq)
    01938 810441
▲   Company Limited by Guarantee; Registered Charity
○   *G; preservation & operation of narrow-gauge railway, using
    British, African, Caribbean & Continental steam locomotives
    & rolling stock

Wensleydale Longwool Sheep Breeders' Association   1890

■   Coffin Walk, Sheep Dip Lane, PRINCETHORPE, Warks,
    CV23 7SP.
    01926 633439
    http://www.wensleydale-sheep.com
    Sec: Dr D L Clouder
▲   Company Limited by Guarantee
○   *B
●   Expt - Inf - Displays at agricultural shows & sheep events
M   200 i, UK / 9 i, o'seas
¶   Jnl - Every 2-3 years; ftm, £2 nm.
    Flock Book - 1; ftm only.

Wesley Historical Society   (WHS)   1893
- ■   34 Spiceland Rd, BIRMINGHAM, W Midlands, B31 1NJ.   (hsp)
  0121-475 4914
  email edgraham@tesco.net
  http://www.wesleyhistoricalsociety.org.uk
  Gen Sec: Dr E Dorothy Graham
- ▲   Registered Charity
- Br   Irish (North & Eire), New Zealand (both automomous)
- ○   *R; to assist corporate & individual study of all branches of
  Methodist history & literature
- ●   Conf - Res - Exhib - Inf - Lib
- M   800 i, 60 org
- ¶   Proceedings - 3; ftm.

Wessex Association of Chambers of Commerce   1994
- NR   Pentagon House, 52 Castle St, TROWBRIDGE, Wilts, BA14 8AU.
  01225 355553   fax 01225 355554
  email info@wessexchambers.org.uk
  http://www.wessexchambers.org.uk
- ○   *C

West Africa Business Association   (WABA)   1956
- NR   2 Vincent St, LONDON, SW1P 4LD.   (hq)
  020 7828 5544
  http://www.waba.co.uk
- ▲   Un-incorporated Society
- Br   Cote d'Ivoire, Ghana, Nigeria, Gambia, Senegal, Guinea,
  Sierra Leone, S Africa
- ○   *T; to represent & sustain overseas investment in the
  Anglophone & Francophone countries of West Africa
- ●   Conf - Mtgs - Res - Expt - VE - LG
- <   W African Enterprise Network; Business Coun Europe - Africa,
  Mediterranean; Brit African Business Assn
- M   c 200 i & f
- ¶   London NL - 12;   Country Reports - 12; both ftm only.

West African Shippers' Association
has closed

West Kent Chamber of Commerce & Industry   1858
- NR   West Kent Business Centre, 3-4 River Walk, TONBRIDGE, Kent,
  TN9 1DT.   (hq)
  01732 366653
  Chief Exec: Jackie Matthias
- ○   *C

West Wales Chamber of Commerce   (Siambr Fasnach Gorllewin Cymru)   1848
- NR   Creswell Buildings, 1 Burrows Place, SWANSEA, Glam,
  SA1 1SW.   (hq)
  01792 653297   fax 01792 648345
  email info@wwcc.co.uk
  Mgr: H L Harries
- ○   *C
- M   c 300 f
  No further information supplied

Westcliff-on-Sea Chamber of Commerce
is a branch office of the **Essex Chambers of Commerce**

Western Equestrian Society   (WES)   1985
- NR   20 Newlands Close, YATELEY, Hants, GU46 6HE.   (sp)
  01252 875896
  Chmn: D Lloyd
- ○   *S; to promote & stimulate interest & high standards in the style
  of Western (American) horsemanship

Western Front Association   (WFA)   1980
- ■   PO Box 1918, STOCKPORT, Cheshire, SK4 4WN.   (hq)
  0161-443 1918
  email westernfrontassociation.com
  Hon Sec: S Oram
- ▲   Registered Charity
- ○   *G; to educate the public in the history of the Great War with
  particular reference to the Western Front
- ●   Conf - Mtgs - ET - Comp
- M   6,500 i, UK / 1,000 i, o'seas
- ¶   Stand To - 3;   Bulletin - 3; both ftm only.

Western Horsemen's Association of Great Britain   (WHA)   1968
- NR   3 Poplar Close, HIGH CROSS, Herts, SG11 1AY.   (hsp)
  Hon Sec: Jacqui Williams
- ▲   Un-incorporated Society
- ○   *G; for all interested in the Western (American) way of riding
- ●   Conf - Mtgs - ET - Exam - Exhib - Comp - SG - Inf - Lib - PL -
  VE - Trail rides
- <   Brit Horse Soc
- M   c 250 i
- ¶   NL - 6.   LM - 1.   Introduction to the WHA.
  Information sheet of coming events.
  List of Establishments in UK offering Western Riding.
  Converting the English Horse to Western.

Western Isles Chamber of Commerce   1995
- NR   30 Francis St, STORNOWAY, Isle of Lewis, HS1 2ND.   (hq)
  y
  Contact: Nicola Jarvie
- ▲   Un-incorporated Society
- ○   *C
- ●   Mtgs - Inf - LG
- <   Aberdeen & Grampian Cham Comm
- M   c 100 i

Westminster Chamber of Commerce
see **London Chamber of Commerce & Industry (incorporating
the Westminster Chamber of Commerce)**

Westminster Property Owners Association   (WPOA)   1988
- NR   1 Warwick Row (7th floor), LONDON, SW1E 5ER.   (hq)
  020 7630 1782
- ▲   Un-incorporated Society
- ○   *T; interests of owners of property in the City of Westminster
- ●   Mtgs - LG
- <   Brit Property Fedn Ltd
- M   120 f
- ¶   AR & accounts - 1; free.

Westmorland County Agricultural Society   (WCAS)   1799
- ■   Lane Farm, Crooklands, MILNTHORPE, Cumbria, LA7 7NH.
  (hq)
  01539 567804   fax 01539 567011
  email manager@westmorland.org.uk
  http://www.westmorland-county-show.co.uk
  Chief Exec: Christine Knipe
- ▲   Company Limited by Guarantee; Registered Charity
- ○   *F, *H; to encourage & support agriculture, horticulture & rural
  crafts
- ●   Conf - Mtgs - ET - Exhib - SG - Inf
- <   Assn Show & Agricl Orgs; Nat Farmers U; R Agricl Soc
  England; Nat Sheep Assn
- M   1,019 i, 10 org
- ¶   Field & Fell NL - 4; ftm.   AR - 1; free.

Westmorland Damson Association
- NR   Greenside, Crosthwaite, KENDAL, Cumbria, LA8 8JL.
  Sec: Bill Clifford
- ○   *H

Wexford Chamber of Industry & Commerce
IRL The Ballast Office, Crescent Quay, WEXFORD, Republic of
    Ireland.
    353 (53) 912 2226   fax 353 (53) 912 4170
    email info@wexchamber.ie   http://www.wexchamber.ie
    Chief Exec: Emer Lovett
○ *C

Wey & Arun Canal Trust Ltd   (W&ACT)   1970
■ The Granary, Flitchfold Farm, Loxwood, BILLINGSHURST,
    W Sussex, RH14 0RH.   (hq/hsb)
    01403 752403   fax 01403 753991
    email office@weyandaron.co.uk
    Hon Sec: Julian Morgan
▲ Registered Charity
○ *G; to restore the derelict Wey & Arun canal in Surrey & W
    Sussex
● Mtgs - Working parties - Exhib - Inf - Fund raising - Talks -
    Sales stalls - Public boat trips
< Inland Waterways Assn; Civic Trust; Brit Trust for Conservation
    Volunteers; SE England Tourist Bd; Sussex (& Surrey) Wildlife
    Trust(s)
M 2,050 i, 30 f, UK / 18 i, o'seas
¶ Wey-South Bulletin - 4; ftm, (large sae nm).

WHA Healthcare
    see **Welsh Hospitals & Health Services Association**

Whale & Dolphin Conservation Society   (WDCS)   1987
NR Brookfield House, 38 St Paul St, CHIPPENHAM, Wilts,
    SN15 1LJ.   (hq)
    01249 449500
▲ Registered Charity
○ *K; to promote public awareness of the threats facing whales &
    dolphins throughout the world
M i
¶ Sonar (Jnl) - 2.   WDCS News (NL) - 2.
    Teachers Education Pack - 1.

Wheelpower   1972
■ Guttmann Rd, STOKE MANDEVILLE, Bucks, HP21 9PP.   (hq)
    01296 395995   fax 01296 424171
    email info@wheelpower.org.uk
    http://www.wheelpower.org.uk
    Chief Exec: Martin McElhatton
▲ Company Limited by Guarantee; Registered Charity
○ *S, *W; the national organisation for wheelchair sport in the
    UK; to provide, promote & develop opportunities for men,
    women & children with disabilities to participate in
    recreational & competitive wheelchair sport
Gp Sports associations throughout UK
● ET - Comp - Inf - Organises events at novice, junior, national &
    international level
M c 3,000 i, 1 f, 20 org
¶ NL - 3/4; free.

White Ensign Association Ltd   1958
NR HMS Belfast, Tooley ST, LONDON, SE1 2JH.   (hq)
    020 7407 8658   fax 020 7357 6298
    email office@whiteensign.co.uk
    http://www.whiteensign.co.uk
    Sec: Capt J A Rimington
▲ Company Limited by Guarantee; Registered Charity
○ *W; advisory service to serving & retired members of the Royal
    Navy & Royal Marines on employment, resettlement &
    financial matters
● ET - Inf
M 115 i, 32 f
¶ LM;   AR; both free.

White Face Dartmoor Sheep Breeders Association   1950
NR 13 West St, ASHBURTON, Devon, TQ13 7DT.   (hsb)
    01364 652304
    Hon Sec: Gordon T Chambers
▲ Un-Incorporated Society
○ *B
● Mtgs - Comp
< Nat Sheep Assn
M 40 i

White Faced Woodland Sheep Breeders Group   1986
NR 1 Tutta Bridge Cottages, Greta Bridge, BARNARD CASTLE,
    Durham, DL12 9SB.   (hsp)
    01833 627424
    Hon Sec: Rachel Godschalk
○ *B
● Workshops
M 50 i
¶ NL.
× 2000 White Faced Woodland Sheep Society

White Goods Association   (IMDA)   1995
IRL Confederation House, 84-86 Lower Baggot St, DUBLIN 2,
    Republic of Ireland.
○ *T
< IBEC

White Park Cattle Society   (WPCS)   1972
NR 77 High St, Great Barford, BEDFORD, MK44 3LF.   (hsp)
    Sec: Marie Handscombe
○ *B
M i

Whitebred Shorthorn Association Ltd   1962
■ High Green Hill, Kirkcambeck, BRAMPTON, Cumbria,
    CA8 2BL.   (hsp)
    01697 748228
    email info@whitebredshorthorn.com
    http://www.whitebredshorthorn.com
    Hon Sec: Mrs Rosie Mitchinson
▲ Registered Charity
○ *B
● Mtgs - Sales - Shows
< Nat Beef Assn
M 51 i
¶ Herd Book - 2; ftm, £10 nm.   AR.

**Wholesale Confectionery & Tobacco Alliance Ltd   (WCTA)
1987**
NR Hope Cottage, Stoneyfields, FARNHAM, Surrey, GU9 8DU.
    (hq)
    01252 727769   fax 01252 727779
    Chief Exec: John Bowden
▲ Company Limited by Guarantee
○ *T; for independent wholesalers
● Mtgs - Inf - LG
M 260 f
¶ Ybk.

Wholesale Markets Brokers' Association   (WMBA)   1994
NR Cable House, 54-62 New Broad St, LONDON, EC2M 1ST.
    (hq)
    020 7200 7000 ext 7553
    email wmba@wmba.org.uk   http://www.wmba.org.uk
    Contact: Michelle Caulfield
▲ Un-incorporated Society
○ *P; to represent broking companies listed by the Financial
    Services Authority whose primary purpose is to facilitate
    cooperation in areas of mutual interest & benefit to members
● Mtgs - ET - Exam - Comp - LG
M 9 f

Wicklow & District Chamber of Commerce
IRL Wicklow Enterprise Park, The Murrough, WICKLOW, Republic of
     Ireland.
     353 (404) 66610   fax 353 (404) 66607
     email info@wicklowchamber.ie
     http://www.wicklowchamber.ie
     Pres: Dirk van de Flier
○   *C

Wild Flower Society   (WFS)   1886
■   82A High St, SAWSTON, Cambs, CB2 4HJ.   (asa)
     01223 839804
     email wfs@grantais.demon.co.uk
     http://www.rbge.org.uk/data/wfsoc
     Gen Sec: Stephen Parker
▲   Registered Charity
○   *G, *L; increasing the understanding of field botany in the UK
●   Mtgs - Exhib - VE
M   900 i
¶   Wild Flower Society Magazine - 4; ftm only.

Wild Trout Trust   (WTT)   1997
NR   PO Box 120, WATERLOOVILLE, Hants, PO8 0WZ.
     023 9257 0985
     http://www.wildtrout.org
▲   Registered Charity
○   *K, *V; conservation of wild trout habitat & populations in the
     UK & Ireland
●   Conf
M   1,650 i, 5 org, UK / 55 i, o'seas
¶   Jnl - 1;   NL - 4; both ftm only.
✕   2001 Wild Trout Society

Wildlife and Countryside Link
■   89 Albert Embankment, LONDON, SE1 7TP.
     020 7820 8600   fax 020 7820 8620
     http://www.wcl.org.uk
○   *N; for voluntary environmental organisations
M   org
     no further information supplied

Wildlife Sound Recording Society   (WSRS)   1968
■   c/o British Library, 96 Euston Rd, LONDON, NW1 2DB.   (mail)
     020 7412 7402 add
▲   Un-incorporated Society
○   *L; to encourage the recording of wildlife sounds & further the
     appreciation of animal language
●   Mtgs - Comp
M   300 i, UK / 30 i, o'seas
¶   Wildlife Sound (Jnl) - 2;   NL - 3;   LM - 3 yrly;
     CD magazine of members' work - 4; all ftm.
     Introduction to Wildlife Sound Recording; £2.50.

**Wildlife Trust for Bedfordshire, Cambridgeshire,
  Northamptonshire & Peterborough   1990**
■   The Manor House, Broad St, Great Cambourne, CAMBRIDGE,
     CB3 6DH.   (hq)
     01954 713500   fax 01954 710051
     email enquiries@wildlifebcnp.org
     http://www.wildlifebcnp.org
     Dir: Nicholas Hammond
▲   Registered Charity
Br   4
○   *G, *L; to improve habitats & biodiversity throughout the area &
     to enhance people's enjoyment & understanding of wildlife
●   ET - Res - VE - LG
M   21,000 i, c 40 f
¶   Wildlife Action - 4; ftm only.

Wildlife Trust of South & West Wales   2002
■   The Nature Centre, Fountain Rd, Tondu, BRIDGEND, Glam,
     CF32 0EH.   (hq)
     01656 724100   fax 01656 726980
     email info@welshwildlife.org(09>wildlifetrust.org.uk/
     wtsww
     Chief Exec: Dr Madeleine Havard,   Chmn: Roger Turner
▲   Company Limited by Guarantee; Registered Charity
Br   2
○   *K; wildlife conservation across south & west Wales dealing with
     species & habitats
Gp   Local wildlife; Species (birds, marine)
●   Conf - Mtgs - ET - Res - Inf - VE - LG - Surveys (habitat &
     species)
<   R Soc Wildlife Trusts (RSWT)
M   17,500 i, 29 org
¶   Welsh Wildlife - 3;   Local NL - 3;   AR; all ftm only.
✕   2002 (Glamorgan Wildlife Trust
         (Wildlife Trust West Wales (merged April)

Wildlife Trust (West Wales)
     April 2002 merged with Glamorgan Wildlife Trust to become
     Wildlife Trust of South & West Wales

Wildlife Trusts
     a working title of the **Royal Society for Nature Conservation**

Wilfred Owen Association   1989
NR   c/o 17 Belmont, SHREWSBURY, Shropshire, SY1 1TE.
     (chmn/p)
     http://www.1914-18.co.uk/owen
     Chmn: Michael Grayer
▲   Registered Charity
○   *A; to commemorate & promote awareness of the life & work
     of Wilfred Owen, the First World War poet
●   Mtgs - Res - Exhib - Inf - VE
M   400 i
¶   Jnl - 1.   NL - 2.

Wilhelm Furtwängler Society UK   1967
■   6 Goodwin Court, Devonshire Rd, LONDON, SW19 2EQ.
     (chmn/p)
     Chmn: John Hunt
○   *D; liaison with record companies to obtain greater
     representation of Furtwängler's art on record; dissemination
     of news & matters relating to articles, books & records by &
     about Furtwängler as man & artist

Wilkie Collins Society   (WCS)   1981
■   3 Merton House, 36 Belsize Park, LONDON, NW3 4EA.
     (chmn/p)
     email apogee@apgee.co.uk
     http://www.wilkie-collins.info
     4 Ernest Gardens, LONDON, W4 3QU. (mem sec/p)
     email paul@paullewis.co.uk
     Chmn: Andrew Gasson,   Mem Sec: Paul Lewis
▲   Un-incorporated Society
Br   USA
○   *A, *G; to promote research into the life & works of Wilkie
     Collins (1824-89); to foster original, critical studies of his
     novels, plays, stories & essays
●   Mtgs
<   Alliance of Literary Socs
¶   Jnl - 1.   NL - 2/3.   Occasional Reprints.

William Barnes Society   1983
- ■ 58 Melstock Avenue, DORCHESTER, Dorset, DT1 2BQ. (chmn/p)
  01305 265358
  Chmn: Alfred W Barrett
- ○ *A; for those interested in the Rev William Barnes (1801-1886), the Dorset dialect poet
- ● Mtgs - VE
- M 200 i, UK / c 8 i, o'seas
- ¶ NL - 2/3; ftm only.

William Cobbett Society   1976
- ■ 10 Grenehurst Way, PETERSFIELD, Hants, GU31 4AZ.   (hsp)
  01730 262060
  email williamcobbett@fsmail.net
  Chmn: Mrs Molly Townsend
- ▲ Un-incorporated Society
- ○ *L; to make better known the life & writings of William Cobbett (1763-1835)
- ● Mtgs - Inf - Lib - VE - Annual Memorial Lecture
- < Alliance of Literary Socs; Historical Assn; Thomas Paine Soc
- M 120 i, 6 libraries
- ¶ Cobbett's New Register - 1; ftm, £2 nm.

William Herschel Society   1979
- ■ 19 New King St, BATH, BA1 2BL.   (hq)
  01225 446865
  email efring@lineone.net
  http://www.williamherschel.org.uk
  Chmn: Prof Francis Ring
- ▲ Registered Charity
- Br Germany, Japan
- ○ *L; for all interested in: the life & achievements of William Herschel, his family & immediate descendants; the history of science, astronomy & 18th century music; telescope making; links with modern space discovery
- ● Conf - Mtgs - Res - Inf - Public lectures on astronomy & space research
- < The Royal Soc; R Astronomical Soc
- M 185 i, UK / 20 i, o'seas
- ¶ The Speculum - 2; ftm, £7.50 yr nm (£10 yr o'seas).

William Morris Society   1955
- ■ Kelmscott House, 26 Upper Mall, LONDON, W6 9TA.   (hq)
  020 8741 3735   fax 020 8748 5207
  email william.morris@care4free.net
  http://www.morrissociety.org
  Hon Sec: Peter Faulkner
- ▲ Registered Charity
- ○ *A, *L; to promote the study of the life, work & influence of William Morris (1834-96) designer & poet; to make his life, work & ideas better known
- ● Mtgs - ET - Res - Exhib - Inf - Lib - VE
- M 2,000 i
- ¶ Jnl - 2.   NL - 4; both ftm only.

Williams Syndrome Foundation Ltd   (WSF)   1980
- NR 161 High St, TONBRIDGE, Kent, TN9 1BX.   (hq)
  01732 365152
  http://www.williams-syndrome.org.uk
  Chief Exec: John Nelson
- ▲ Company Limited by Guarantee
- ○ *W; to help parents & carers of children & adults who have Williams Syndrome (infantile hypercalcaemia - a rare non-hereditary genetic syndrome occurring at random); to stimulate interest, particularly among the medical profession
- Gp Families with affected children; Medical profession; Students; Care workers
- ● Conf - Mtgs - Res - Inf - Lib
- < Mencap; Genetic Interest Gp; Contact-a-Family
- M 900 i, UK / 100 i, o'seas
- ¶ NL - 2.   Video.
  Various Guideline publications.

Willing Workers on Organic Farms
since 2003 **World-Wide Opportunities on Organic Farms**

Willwriters' Association   (WA)   1987
- NR Harbro House, Crown Lane, DENBIGH, LL16 3SY.   (hq)
  0800 035 0604
  Sec: Carol Baird
- ▲ Un-incorporated Society
- Br 2
- ○ *P; to advance quality of willwriting industry; members will visit homes to write wills
- Gp Legal helpline (24 hr); Will registration & storage; Marketing services; Willwriting software & system
- ● Conf - ET - Exam - Comp - Inf - LG
- < Assn Lawyers & Legal Advisers
- M 650 i, 600 f, 8 org
- ¶ Codicil - 1.   Briefing - 4.
  The Freephone Directory of Legal Services - 1.
  The British Directory of Legal Services - 2.

Wiltshire Archaeological & Natural History Society   (WANHS)   1853
- ■ Wiltshire Heritage Museum, 41 Long St, DEVIZES, Wilts, SN10 1NS.   (hq)
  01380 727369   fax 01380 722150
  email wanhs@wiltshireheritage.org.uk
  http://www.wiltshireheritage.org.uk
  Sec: Mrs W Lansdown
- ▲ Company Limited by Guarantee; Registered Charity
- ○ *L; to promote, research & publish on the archaeology, art, history & natural history of Wiltshire for the public benefit
- Gp Archaeology field gp
- ● Mtgs - ET - Res - Exhib - SG - Inf - Lib - PL - VE - Maintenance of a museum & library displaying designated collections
- M 1,041 i, 83 org
- ¶ Wiltshire Archaeological & Natural History Magazine (Jnl) - 1; ftm, £15 nm.
  NL - 2.   AR.

Wiltshire Horn Sheep Society   1923
- ■ 11 Towcester Rd, Littleborough, TOWCESTER, Northants, NN12 8JA.   (hsp)
  01327 830739
  Contact: Hon Sec
- ○ *B
- ● Mtgs - Exhib - Comp - Expt
- < Nat Sheep Assn
- M 125 i, UK / 5 i, o'seas
- ¶ Flock Book - 1.

Wiltshire Record Society   (WRS)   1937
- ■ c/o Wiltshire & Swindon Record Office, Bythesea Rd, TROWBRIDGE, Wilts, BA14 8BS.   (hsb)
  01225 713136   fax 01225 713715
  Hon Sec: J N d'Arcy
- ▲ Registered Charity
- ○ *L; to promote publication of documentary sources of Wiltshire history
- ● AGM & Lecture
- M 150 i, 63 universities & public libraries, UK / 10 i, 75 org, o'seas
- ¶ Volume of edited documents - 1; £15 m, £20 nm.
  AR; ftm only.

Wine & Spirit Association of Ireland   1911
- IRL 33 Clarinda Park West, DÚN LAOGHAIRE, Co Dublin, Republic of Ireland.
  353 (1) 280 4666   fax 353 (1) 280 7566
  email info@wineboard.com
  Chmn: John Pearson
- ○ *T

© CBD Research Ltd · Beckenham · BR3 5JS · Tel 020 8650 7745 · Fax 020 8650 0768 · E-mail cbd@cbdresearch.com · www.cbdresearch.com

Wine & Spirit Trade Association   (WSTA)   1824
NR   International Wine & Spirit Centre, 39-45 Bermondsey St,
        LONDON, SE1 3XF.   (hq)
        020 7089 3877   fax 020 7089 3870
        email info@wsta.co.uk   http://www.wsta.co.uk
        Chief Exec: Jeremy Beadles
▲   Company Limited by Guarantee
○   *T; to represent the interests of shippers & distributors of wine &
        imported spirits in the UK
Gp   various specialist: Freight forwarders, Mailorder, UK wine
        growers, British Wine producers
●   Mtgs - SG - Stat - Inf - LG
<   Fédn Intle de Vin et Spiritueux (FIVS); Eur Fedn of Wine & Spirit
        Importers & Distributors (EFWSID)
M   c 300 f, UK & o'seas
¶   General Circular - 12.   AR.
        Checklists (the sole commercial guide to European wine & spirit
        legislation) - 1.
×   2005 Wine & Spirit Association

Wire Products Association   (WPA)   1953
NR   Riverside House, Bow Industrial Park, Carpenters Rd, LONDON,
        E15 2DZ.   (pres/b)
        020 8525 7100
        Pres: Richard Brundle
○   *T; wholesaling & marketing of agricultural wire products (incl
        chain-link fencing) & wire nails
Gp   Wire nails; Agricultural wire products
●   Conf - Mtgs

Wireless for the Bedridden Society Inc   1938
§   159A High St, HORNCHURCH, Essex, RM11 3YB.   (hq)
        0800 018 2137   fax 01708 620816
        http://www.w4b.org.uk
        Chief Exec: Barry Hobbs
        provision of radio & television facilities to housebound invalids
        & the aged who are unable to afford them for themselves

Wireless Messaging Association
        is now the European Mobile Messaging Association & is
        therefore outside the scope of this directory.

Wireless Preservation Society & National Wireless Museum
        has closed; artifacts have been passed to the Bodleian Library,
        Oxford

Wirral Chamber of Commerce & Industry   1911
NR   16 Grange Road West, Birkenhead, WIRRAL, Merseyside,
        CH41 4DA.   (hq)
        0151-647 8899
        Chief Exec: Ken Davies
▲   Company Limited by Guarantee
○   *C
Gp   Education link; Environment; Central traders; Finance
●   Conf - Mtgs - ET - Res - Exhib - Stat - Expt - Inf - VE - LG
M   f
¶   Newsletter - 12.   LM - 1.   Diary - 1.

Wolf Society of Great Britain
        since September 2005 **Wolves & Humans Foundation**

Wolverton & District Archaeological & Historical Society   1955
■   82 Clarence Rd, Stony Stratford, MILTON KEYNES, Bucks,
        MK11 1JD.   (hsp)
        01908 565481
        Hon Sec: Mrs Audrey Lambert
○   *L; archaeology & local history within the Milton Keynes area &
        adjoining villages of North Buckinghamshire & South
        Northamptonshire; preservation & recording of sites &
        buildings under threat of destruction
●   Mtgs - Exhib - Inf - Lib
<   Coun Brit Archaeology; Bucks Archaeol Soc; Northants
        Archaeol Soc
M   145 i
¶   NL - 6; ftm.

Wolves & Humans Foundation   (WAH)   2005
■   2 Blackrod Cottages, Compton Durville, SOUTH PETHERTON,
        Somerset, TA13 5EX.   (hsp)
        01460 242593
        email info@wolvesandhumans.org
        http://www.wolvesandhumans.org
        Sec: Richard Morley
▲   Registered Charity
○   *K; support & promotion of research & scientific study of wolves
        & other large carnivores; the education & training in methods
        of managing conflict between such animals & agriculture &
        other human interests
●   Conf - ET - Res - Exhib - Inf
M   200 i, UK / 20 i, o'seas
¶   Wolves & Humans NL - 4; ftm only (subscription £25).
×   2005 (September) Wolves Society of Great Britain

Women's Aid Federation (England) Ltd   (WAFE)   1986
NR   PO Box 391, BRISTOL, BS99 7WS.   (hq)
        0117-944 4411
        Dir: Nicola Harwin
▲   Company Limited by Guarantee; Registered Charity
Br   250
○   *N, *W; to coordinate & resource refuge groups for women &
        their children in need of temporary accommodation because
        of mental, physical or sexual abuse
●   ET - Res - Inf - LG - Public information work on domestic
        violence - Seminars - Networking
        Helpline: 0800 200 0247 (freephone 24-hr) the national
        domestic violence helpline run in partnership between
        Women's Aid & Refuge
<   Fedn Indep Advice Centres (FIAC)
¶   NL - 12; ftm only.   Publications list available.

Women's Cycle Racing Association
        a group of the **British Cycling Federation**

Women's Engineering Society   (WES)   1919
NR   Michael Faraday House, Six Hills Way, STEVENAGE, Herts,
        SG1 2AY.   (hq)
        01438 765506   fax 01438 765506
        email info@wes.org.uk   http://www.wes.org.uk
        Hon Sec: Dorothy Hatfield
▲   Company Limited by Guarantee; Registered Charity
○   *P; 'to promote the study, training & practice of engineering
        among women; to facilitate returners after career breaks,
        influence & educate the public & policy makers, & support &
        encourage women in a minority in their profession'
●   Conf - Mtgs - Inf - VE - LG - Mentoring - Speaking in schools
M   700 i, 20 f, 12 student groups, UK / 40 i, 1 f, o'seas
¶   The Woman Engineer - 4; ftm, £20 yr (UK), £25 yr (o'seas) nm.

Women's Environmental Network   (WEN)   1988

- ■ PO Box 30626, LONDON, E1 1TZ.   (hq)
    020 7481 9004   fax 020 7481 9144
    email info@wen.org.uk
    Co-ordinators: Liz Suitton, Helen Lynn
- ▲ Company Limited by Guarantee; Registered Charity
- Br 55 local gps
- ○ *K; to inform, educate & empower women who care about the environment
- ● ET - Res - Exhib - Inf
- M 3,500 i, 30 f, 160 org, UK / 50 i, 5 f, 10 org, o'seas
- ¶ NL - 4; ftm only.

Women's Farm & Garden Association   (WFGA)   1899

- NR 175 Gloucester St, CIRENCESTER, Glos, GL7 2DP.   (hq)
    01285 658339   fax 01285 642356
    email admin@wfga.fsbusiness.co.uk
    Chief Exec: Patricia McHugh
- ▲ Registered Charity
- ○ *F, *H; to unite all involved in agriculture & horticulture in the UK & overseas
- ● Conf - Mtgs - ET - Comp - VE - LG
- M 1,000 i
- ¶ Women Rule The Plot; £12.95.
    Role of Women in British Agriculture; £3.50.
    The Hidden Workforce: A Self-help Guide to Safeguards & Benefits; £2.

Women's Food & Farming Union   (WFU)   1979

- NR WFU National Office, STONELEIGH PARK, Warks, CV8 2LZ.
    (hq)
    024 7669 3171
    Pres: Ionwen Lewis
    Nat Sec: Sue Archer
- ▲ Un-incorporated Society
- Br 26
- ○ *F; to link the producer & the consumer by promoting demand for British farm produce; to encourage farmers & growers to practise better marketing; to ensure British produce is available & well marketed; to lobby against unfair competition
- Gp Crops; Dairy; Livestock
- ● Conf - Mtgs - ET - LG
- < Nat Coun Women GB
- M 800 i
- ¶ Update - 5; ftm only.   Annual Review - 1; free.

Women's Royal Voluntary Service   (WRVS)   1938

- NR Garden House, Milton Hill, Steventon, ABINGDON, Oxon, OX13 6AD.   (hq)
    01235 442900   fax 01235 861166
    email info@wrvs.org.uk   http://www.wrvs.org.uk
    Chief Exec: Mark Lever
- ▲ Company Limited by Guarantee; Registered Charity
- Br 'hundreds'
- ○ *W; voluntary welfare service to local communities in Britain, working alongside local authorities & hospital trusts; 'to help people maintain independence & dignity in their local communities, particularly later in life'
- ● Hospital services; Emergency services; Services for older people
- < NCVO
- M 95,000 i
- ¶ AR.

Wood Panel Industries Federation   (WPIF)   1996

- ■ 28 Market Place, GRANTHAM, Lincs, NG31 6LR.   (hq)
    01476 563707   fax 01476 579314
    email enquiries@wpif.org.uk   http://www.wpif.org.uk
    Dir Gen: Alastair F Kerr
- ▲ Company Limited by Guarantee
- ○ *T; technical standards & environmental data, developments & policy issues for industrial members only (does not include agents, distributors or merchants)
- Gp Product application; Research evaluation; Ecology
- ● Mtgs - Res - Inf - LG
- < Eur Confedn Woodworking Inds; Eur Fedn Assns Particleboard Mfrs; Nat Coun Bldg Material Producers
- M 18 f, 3 org

Wood Protection Association
    is a group of the **British Wood Preserving & Damp-proofing Association**

Woodcraft Folk   1925

- NR 13 Ritherdon Rd, LONDON, SW17 8QE.
    020 8672 6031
    http://www.woodcraft.org.uk

Wooden Spoon Society   1984

- NR 41 Frimley High St, FRIMLEY, Surrey, GU16 7HJ.   (hq)
    01276 410180   fax 01276 410181
    Chief Exec: Geoff Morris
- ▲ Company Limited by Guarantee; Registered Charity
- Br 36 regional c'ees
- ○ *W; 'to enhance the quality & prospect of life for children & young people in the UK who are presently disadvantaged either physically, mentally or socially'
- ● Social & sporting activities for fundraising purposes
- M c 10,000 i
- ¶ Spoonews - 2;   Stirring Times - 4; both ftm only.

Woodworkers, Builders & Miscellaneous Tools Association
    a group of the **Federation of British Hand Tool Manufacturers**

Woodworking Machinery Suppliers Association   (WMSA)   1983

- ■ The Counting House, Mill Road, Cromford, MATLOCK, Derbys, DE4 3RQ.
    01629 826998   fax 01629 826997
    email info@wmsa.org.uk   http://www.wmsa.org.uk
    Admin Coordinator: Claire Parkinson
- ○ *T
- ● Conf - Mtgs - Exhib
- M 90 f
- ¶ NL - 4; m only.
    Directory of Members & Buyers' Guide - 2 yrly; free.

Woolhope Naturalists' Field Club   1851

- ■ Chy an Whyloryon, Wigmore, LEOMINSTER, Herefords, HR6 9UD.   (hsp)
    01568 770356
    http://www.woolhopeclub.org.uk
    Hon Sec: J W Tonkin
- ▲ Registered Charity
- ○ *L; archaeology, natural history & allied subjects of Herefordshire & the area immediately adjacent
- Gp Archaeology; Natural history
- ● Mtgs - SG - Lib - VE
- M 550 i, 38 org, UK / 3 i, 6 org, o'seas
- ¶ Transactions - 1; m only.

© CBD Research Ltd · Beckenham · BR3 5JS · Tel 020 8650 7745 · Fax 020 8650 0768 · E-mail cbd@cbdresearch.com · www.cbdresearch.com

Worcestershire Archaeological Society   (WAS)   1860
- ■ 26 Albert Park Rd, MALVERN, Worcester, WR14 1HN.   (hsp)
  01684 565190
  http://www.communigate.co.uk/worcs/
  worcestershirearchaeoligicalsociety/index.ptml
  Exec Sec: Janet Dunleavey
- ▲ Registered Charity
- ○ *L; to promote study of archaeology & local history in the
  County of Worcestershire & the diocese of Worcester
- Gp Architectural study
- ● Mtgs - SG - Lib - VE
- M 150 i, c 60 org, UK / c 30 org, o'seas
- ¶ The Worcestershire Recorder - 2; ftm.
  Transactions - 2 yearly; £2 m, £25 nm.

Work Experience UK
  is a group of **English UK**

Work Foundation   1918
- NR Peter Runge House, 3 Carlton House Terrace, LONDON,
  SW1Y 5DG.   (hq)
  0870 165 6700
  http://www.theworkfoundation.com
  Chief Exec: Will Hutton
- ▲ Registered Charity
- ○ *K; 'to work with employees to improve the productivity &
  quality of working life in the UK'
- ● Res - Inf - Lib - LG
- M 400 i, 1,450 f, UK
- ✕ 2002 (April) Industrial Society

Workers' Educational Association   (WEA)   1903
- ■ Quick House, 65 Clifton St, LONDON, EC2A 4JE.   (hq)
  020 7426 3450   fax 020 7426 3451
  Gen Sec: Richard Bolsin
- ▲ Registered Charity
- Br 650
- ○ *E; as the largest voluntary provider of adult education in the
  UK the WEA has particular concern for the socially,
  economically & educationally disadvantaged; the voluntary &
  democratic traditions have created an approach that is
  unique in adult education
- M 5,000 i

Workers' Music Association   (WMA)   1936
- ■ 12 St Andrew's Sq, LONDON, W11 1RH.   (hsp)
  020 7243 0920
  http://www.btinternet.com/~steve.a.taylor/
  Hon Sec: Mavis Cook
- ▲ Company Limited by Guarantee
- ○ *D; 'to print, publish & sell (including for export) music & the
  literature of music, & to deal in musical instruments
  (including instruments for the reproduction of music); to
  produce & sell (including for export) recorded music & films;
  to encourage the composition & performance of music, with
  special regard to music which 1) expresses the ideals & aims
  of mankind towards the improved organisation of society,
  2) exerts an influence against the social injustices of our
  present society, 3) encourages & reflects the activities &
  aspirations of the labour & peace movements for a new
  society, & to this latter end to provide whatever services of
  education & performance for the labour & peace movements
  as may be determined by the AGM of the Association; &
  generally, by all means which may be determined by the
  Executive Committee from time to time, including grants of
  financial aid to any persons, corporations or associations
  whether by loan, subscription or donation, to carry out these
  objects'
- Gp Summer school c'ee; WMA singers
- ● Mtgs - ET - Lib - Annual summer school - Weekend musical
  events - Performances by WMA singers - Concerts
- < Birmingham Clarion Singers; Cardiff Red Choir
- M 200 i, 4 choirs, UK / 10 i, o'seas
- ¶ Bulletin - 6;   NL - irreg;   AR; all ftm.
  Peace Song Book.   Easter Rising in Song & Ballad.

Working Families   1985
- ■ 1 Berry St, LONDON, EC1V 0AA.   (hq)
  020 7253 7243
  Chief Exec: Sarah Jackson
- ▲ Company Limited by Guarantee; Registered Charity
- ○ *W; 'helping children, parents & employers by helping parents
  to balance their work commitments with their home
  responsibilities'
- ● Conf - ET - Comp - LG - Helplines
- M i & f
- ✕ 2004 (New Ways to Work
  (Parents at Work

Working Men's Club & Institute Union Ltd   (CIU)   1862
- ▥ 253-254 Upper St, LONDON, N1 1RY.   (hq)
  020 7226 0221   fax 020 7354 1847
  email information@wmciu.org   http://www.wmciu.org
  Gen Sec: Kevin Smyth
- Br 29
- ○ *W; 'an advisory & defensive organisation for non-profit
  making members' clubs'
- ● Conf - Mtgs - ET - Exam - Res - Exhib - Comp - SG - Stat - Inf -
  VE - Empl - LG - Provision of convalescent homes, recreation
  & sporting facilities
- < C'ee of Registered Clubs Assns; Workers Educational Assn;
  Ruskin College
- M 6,000,000 i, 2,903 clubs
- ¶ Club Jnl - 12; 60p each.   AR.

Working for Wellbeing
  see **Together: working for wellbeing**

World Pheasant Association UK   (WPA)   1975
- NR 7-9 Shaftesbury St, FORDINGBRIDGE, Hants, SP6 1JF.   (hq)
  01425 657129
  Admin: Pat Savage
- ▲ Registered Charity
- Br 12 o'seas
- ○ *K; to ensure the survival of the individual species of pheasant
  & related gamebirds which are threatened with extinction; the
  maintenance of viable populations of these groups of birds in
  natural habitat in their countries of origin
- Gp Pheasants; Grouse; Partridge, quail & francolin; Megapodes;
  Cracids
- ● Conf - Mtgs - Res - Inf - Lib
- < species survival commission of the Intl U for the Consvn of
  Nature (IUCN); Birdlife Intl
- M 650 i, UK / 1,200 i, o'seas
- ¶ WPA News - 3, with Annual Review.
  Publications list available.

World War Two Living History Association   (LHA)   1978
- NR 25 Olde Farm Drive, Darby Green, CAMBERLEY, Surrey,
  GU17 0DU.   (chmn/p)
- ▲ Company Limited by Guarantee
- ○ *G; to mount public displays of battle re-enactment & private
  'living history' re-enactments for members only
- M i

** World War Two Railway Study Group
  Organisation lost: see Introduction paragraph 3

World-Wide Opportunities on Organic Farms   (WWOOF) 1971

■ PO Box 2675, LEWES, E Sussex, BN7 1RB.   (co-ordinator/p)
01273 476286
http://www.wwoof.org.uk
Coordinator: Fran Whittle

▲ Company Limited by Guarantee

Br 24 countries o'seas

○ *F; in return for work on organic farms, gardens & smallholdings, volunteers are given meals & a place to sleep. Participants get first hand experience of organic farming & growing as well as the opportunity to get into the countryside. WWOOF operates on the Continent & there are similar organisations worldwide

● Conf - Practical work on farms

M 2,000 i, 5,000 i (independents), UK / i, o'seas

¶ WWOOF UK News - 6; ftm.
WWINDY News (NL) - 6; free, online only.
List of branches overseas with host names.

✕ 2003 Willing Workers on Organic Farms

Worldchoice   1978

NR Worldchoice House, Minerva Business Park, Lynch Wood, PETERBOROUGH, Cambs, PE2 6FT.   (hq)
01733 390900   fax 01733 396823
email cheal@worldchoice.co.uk
http://www.worldchoice.co.uk
Chmn: Colin Heal,   Co Sec: Duncan Pickering

▲ Company Limited by Guarantee

○ *T; independent travel agent consortia

● Conf - ET

M c 700 f

Worthing Chamber of Commerce & Industry   1938

NR 7 Richmond Rd, WORTHING, W Sussex, BN11 1PN.   (hq)
01903 203484

▲ Company Limited by Guarantee

○ *C

● Mtgs - Exhib - Inf - VE - LG - Corporate entertainment

< Sussex Enterprise

M c 300 f

¶ NL - 6.   Diary - 1.

✕ 2003 Worthing Chamber of Trade & Commerce Ltd

Wound Care Society   1987

■ PO Box 170, Hartford, HUNTINGDON, Cambs, PE29 1PL.   (hq)
01480 434401   fax 01480 434401
email wound.care.society@talk21.com
http://www.woundcaresociety.org
Admin: Mrs Hazel Morley

▲ Registered Charity

○ *M, *P; to promote & further the best practice in the prevention, treatment & management of wounds through the provision of educational resources

● Conf - ET - Exhib - SG - Inf

M 1,500 i, 37 f, 3 org, UK / 35 i, o'seas

¶ Wound Care Jnl - 4; ftm only.
Educational booklets; all £2 m, £2.50 nm:
Cavity Wounds.   Diabetic Foot.
Eczema - Aetiology & Management.
Equipment Selection.   Graduated Compression Hosiery.
Management of Exuding Wounds.   Pain & Wound Care.
Palliative Management of Fungating Malignant Wounds.
Wounds & Infection.
Educational booklets 4-hole punched:
Anatomy & Physiology Wound Healing & Wound Assessment.
Dressings Selection.
Principles of Leg Ulcer Management & Prevention.
Principles of Pressure Ulcer Management & Prevention.
Standardised Assessment Tools & the Management of Complex Wounds.
Silver in Wound Care & Management.
Pressure Ulcer Prevention Manual; £5.

Woven Wire Association

NR c/o Peter Mills, Soar Engineering Ltd, Beaumont Rd, BANBURY, Oxon, OX16 1SD.
Sec: Peter Mills

○ *T
no further information supplied

Writers' Guild of Great Britain   (WGGB)   1959

■ 15 Britannia St, LONDON, WC1X 9JN.   (hq)
020 7833 0777   fax 020 7833 4777
email admin@writersguild.org.uk
http://www.writersguild.org.uk
Gen Sec: Bernie Corbett

○ *P, *U; for professional writers in the spheres of film, television, radio, theatre & books, children's writing & new media

Gp Film & television; Radio; Theatre; Books; Children

● Mtgs - ET - Inf - Empl - LG - Legal & professional advice & representation of members over contracts, fees, rights & other issues connected with their work as writers

< Writers' Guilds: Australia, Canada, Ireland, New Zealand, USA; European Writers' Congress; TUC

M 2,000 i, 100 f, UK / 100 i, 10 f, o'seas

¶ UK Writer - 4; ftm, £25 yr nm.

Writers & Photographers unLimited   (WPU)   2003

■ PO Box 520 Bamber Bridge, PRESTON, Lancs, PR5 8LF.   (hsp)
01772 321243   fax 0870 137 8888
email info@wpu.org.uk   http://www.wpu.org.uk
Mgr: Terry Marsh

▲ Un-incorporated Society

○ *P; to promote the work of members

● Inf - PL

M 20 i

Writing Equipment Society   (WES)   1980

■ 33 Glanville Rd, HADLEIGH, Suffolk, IP7 5SQ.   (sp)
Sec: John Daniels

○ *G; for all interested in the collection, conservation & study of writing instruments & accessories - including pens, pencils, inkpots, quills, letter scales & information & ephemera connected with the subject

● Mtgs - SG - VE

M 400 i, 20 f, UK / 150 i, 10 f, 5 org, o'seas

¶ Jnl (incl LM) - 3;   LM; both ftm only.

Writing Instruments Association   (WIA)

NR 12 Corporation St, HIGH WYCOMBE, Bucks, HP13 6TQ.   (hq)
0845 450 1565
Chmn: Chris Reynolds

▲ Company Limited by Guarantee

○ *T

● Conf - Mtgs - SG - Stat

< Eur Writing Instruments Assn; is an affiliate of the British Office Supplies & Services Federation

M f

WW2 HMSO Paperbacks Society   1994

■ 3 Roman Rd, SOUTHWICK, W Sussex, BN42 4TP.   (hsp)
01273 596217
Hon Sec: A R James

○ *G; interest & research in World War Two publications by the Ministry of Information &/or HM Stationery Office

● Res - SG - Inf - Lib - PL

M 20 i, 1 f (HMSO), UK / 5 i, o'seas

¶ WW2 HMSO Paperbacks Collectors' Guide; £5.
Informing the People (HMSO) 1996; £10.

© CBD Research Ltd · Beckenham · BR3 5JS · Tel 020 8650 7745 · Fax 020 8650 0768 · E-mail cbd@cbdresearch.com · www.cbdresearch.com

Xenophon   1989
- ■   98 Cambridge Gardens, LONDON, W10 6HS.   (hsp)
     020 8968 1360
     email plnrm@rbkc.gov.uk
     Hon Sec: Regor J Nagrom   (020 8968 1360 (hsb))
- ▲   Un-incorporated Society
- ○   *G; the study for recreational & historical purposes of secret
     communication & its recovery
- ●   Res - Comp - SG - Inf - Lib
- M   20 i
- ¶   Crypt - 1; ftm, £5 nm.

Yacht Brokers, Designers & Surveyors Association (Holdings) Ltd
     the trading company for the **Association of Brokers & Yacht
     Agents** & the **Yacht Designers & Surveyors Association**

Yacht Charter Association Ltd
     in September 2005 merged with the Association of Bonded Sailing
     Companies & the National Federation of Sea Schools to form the
     Marine Leisure Association

Yacht Designers & Surveyors Association   (YDSA)   1912
- ■   The Glass Works, Penns Rd, PETERSFIELD, Hants, GU32 2EW,
     (hq)
     01730 710425   fax 01730 710423
     email info@ybdsa.co.uk   http://www.ybdsa.co.uk
     Co Sec: Jane Gentry
- ▲   Company Limited by Guarantee
- ○   *P; for yacht surveyors & designers
- ●   Conf - Mtgs - ET - Exam
- <   Trades (with the Association of Brokers & Yacht Agents) as the
     Yacht Brokers, Designers & Surveyors Association (Holdings)
     Ltd
- M   100 i, UK / 15 i, o'seas
- ¶   NL - 4; ftm only.

Yacht Harbour Association Ltd   (TYHA)   1963
- ■   12 Evegate Park Barn, Smeeth, ASHFORD, Kent, TN25 6SX.
     (hq)
     01303 814434
     http://www.yachtharbourassociation.com
     Sec: Sue Lambert,   Chief Exec: Sam J Bourne
- ▲   Company Limited by Guarantee
- ○   *T; for the development of international, coastal & inland
     boating facilities
- ●   Conf - Mtgs - VE
- <   Brit Marine Fedn
- M   290 f, UK / 20 f, o'seas
- ¶   Fore & Aft (NL) - 4.

Yachting Journalists' Association   (YJA)   1960
- NR   Booker's Yard - The Street, Walberton, ARUNDEL, W Sussex,
     BN18 0PF.   (hsb)
     01243 555561
- ▲   Un-incorporated Society
- ○   *P; to further the interest of yachting (sail & power); to provide
     support & assistance to journalists in the field
- ●   Mtgs - Inf - Organisation of annual awards - Yachtsman of the
     Year & Young Sailor of the Year
- M   270 i, UK / 28 i, o'seas
- ¶   Hbk (incl LM) - 1.

Yeovil Agricultural Society   (YAS)   1833
- NR   Barwick Park Lodge, Barwick, YEOVIL, Somerset, BA22 9TA.
     (hsp)
     01935 424785
     Hon Sec: Martin Wrixon
- ▲   Registered Charity
- ○   *F; interests of farming & assistance of students at colleges in
     Somerset & Dorset; applications in respect of education in
     farming methods
- ●   Showground for use by local groups: horse shows, trials &
     events
- M   40 i

YMCA England   (YMCA)   1844
- NR   640 Forest Rd, LONDON, E17 3DZ.   (hq)
     020 8520 5599
     Nat Sec: Angela Sarkis
- ▲   Registered Charity
- Br   150
- ○   *Y; to encourage the physical, mental & spiritual development
     of all young people (male & female) so that they make the
     most of their lives & play a worth-while role in their
     communities

YMCA Ireland
- IRL   Inishmore Industrial Pk, West Village, BALLINCOLLIG, Co Cork,
     Republic of Ireland.
     353 (21) 485 0015
     http://www.ymca-ireland.org
     Sec: Stephen Turner
- ○   *W, *Y

Ymgyrch Diogelu Cymru Wledig
     see **Campaign for the Protection of Rural Wales (Ymgyrch
     Diogelu Cymru Wledig)**

York & North Yorkshire Chamber of Commerce   1911
- NR   Arabesque House, Monks Cross Drive, Huntington, YORK,
     N Yorks, YO32 9WU.   (hq)
     01904 629513
     Chief Exec: Len Cruddas
- ○   *C
- ●   Stat - Expt - Inf
- M   i, f & org
- ¶   Business Update - 6; Business North - 6; both free.
     Directory - 1; ftm.

Yorkshire Agricultural Society   1837

■ Great Yorkshire Showground, HARROGATE, N Yorks,
   HG2 8PW.   (hq)
   01423 541000   fax 01423 541414
   email info@yas.co.uk   http://www.yas.co.uk
   Chief Exec: Nigel Pulling
▲ Registered Charity
○ *F, *H; aims to improve agricultural practices & understanding
   within Yorkshire, incl forestry, pisciculture, the breeding of
   livestock & rural crafts; to hold the largest agricultural show
   in the North
● Conf - Mtgs - ET - Res - Exhib - Comp - SG - VE - Annual show
M 9,500 i, 500 f
¶ NL - 3;   AR - 1; both ftm only.
   Great Yorkshire Show: Programme £3 / Catalogue £5.

Yorkshire Archaeological Society   (YAS)   1863

NR 23 Clarendon Rd, LEEDS, W Yorks, LS2 9NZ.   (hq)
   0113-245 7910
   Hon Gen Sec: M J Heron
▲ Company Limited by Guarantee, Registered Charity
○ *L; history & archaeology of Yorkshire
● Mtgs - Res
M i & org
¶ Yorkshire Archaeological Jnl - 1.

Yorkshire Dialect Society   (YDS)   1897

■ 51 Stepney Ave, SCARBOROUGH, N Yorks, YO12 5BW.   (hsp)
   01723 371296
   Hon Sec: Michael Park
▲ Un-incorporated Society
○ *L; study of Yorkshire speech & traditional life
● Mtgs - Res - Inf
M 450 i, UK / 90 i, o'seas
¶ Transactions - 1; ftm, £4 nm.
   Summer Bulletin - 1;   LM - 5 yrly; both ftm only.

Yorkshire Geological Society   (YGS)   1837

■ 19 Thorngate, BARNARD CASTLE, Co Durham, DL12 8QB.
   (sp)
   01833 638893
   email tjm4@tutor.open.ac.uk
   http://www.yorksgeolsoc.org.uk
   Gen Sec: Dr Trevor J Morse
▲ Registered Charity
○ *L; to promote & record the results of research in geology & its
   allied sciences, especially in Yorkshire & Northern England
● Conf - Mtgs - Exhib - Lib - VE
< Geologists' Assn
M 800 i, 80 f
¶ Proceedings - 2; £30 m.   Circular - 8; ftm only.

Yorkshire Philosophical Society   (YPS)   1822

NR The Lodge, Museum Gardens, YORK, YO1 7DR.   (hq)
   01904 656713   fax 01904 656713
   email info@yorkphilsoc.org.uk
   http://www.yorkphilsoc.org.uk
   Clerk: Miss Francis Chambers,   Hon Sec: William G Smith
▲ Registered Charity
○ *L; the study of natural science, archaeology & antiquities in the
   county
Gp York excavation; Woodland history
● Conf - ET - VE
< is the local branch of the British Association for the
   Advancement of Science
M 500 i, 10 org
¶ NL - 4;   AR; both free.

** young@now

   believed to have closed - we should appreciate confirmation.

Young Embroiderers Group
   a group of the **Embroiderers' Guild**

Young Explorers' Trust: the Association of Youth Exploration Societies   (YET)   1970

NR at the Royal Geographical Society, 1 Kensington Gore,
   LONDON, SW7 2AR.   (regd/address)
   Hon Sec: Ted Grey
▲ Company Limited by Guarantee; Registered Charity
○ *E; to increase opportunities for young people to take part in
   exploration, discovery & challenging adventure

Young Women's Christian Association
   see **YWCA (Young Women's Christian Association)**

Young Women's Christian Association of Ireland
   see **YWCA of Ireland (Young Women's Christian Association of Ireland)**

youngchoirs
   see **British Federation of Young Choirs**

Youth Access   1975

■ 1A Taylor's Yard, 67 Alderbrook Rd, LONDON, SW12 8AD.
   (hq)
   020 8772 9900   fax 020 8772 9746
   email admin@youthaccess.org.uk
   Dir: Barbara Rayment
▲ Registered Charity
○ *W, *Y; provision of a referrals line for young people, parents &
   carers, to obtain information of their most local advice,
   counselling & information services
● ET - Inf - Consultancy
< Young Minds; Nat Children's Bureau
M i & agencies

Youth Action Network   1995

NR Crest House, 7 Highfield Rd, BIRMINGHAM, B15 3ED.   (hq)
   0121-455 9732   fax 0121-455 9697
   email info@youth-action.org.uk
   http://www.youth-action.org.uk
   Chief Exec: Davina Goodchild
▲ Registered Charity
○ *Y; supports & develops a range of youth volunteering projects
   across England; provides training, information & guidance
   on recruiting, supporting & recognising the achievements of
   young volunteers; develops youth action projects led by
   young people & engages young people in decision making
● Conf - Mtgs - ET - Res - Inf - Lib - VE - LG - Development /
   start-up support for orgs - Promotion of youth action in the
   media
M 95 org
¶ Activate - 6.
   Reach Quality Framework - 1.
× 2002 (Jan) National Federation of Youth Action Agencies

Youth Action Northern Ireland   1945

§ Hampton, Glenmachan Park, BELFAST, BT4 2PJ.   (hq)
   028 9076 0067   fax 028 9076 8799
   email info@youthaction.org
   Dir: June Trimble
▲ Registered Charity
○ *Y; to support the social & economic inclusion of young people
   in communities; 'the development agency for young people
   in community'

Youth Camping Club
   a group of the **Camping & Caravanning Club**

© CBD Research Ltd · Beckenham · BR3 5JS · Tel 020 8650 7745 · Fax 020 8650 0768 · E-mail cbd@cbdresearch.com · www.cbdresearch.com

**Youth Hostel Association of Northern Ireland Ltd   (YHANI)
1931**
- ■ 22-32 Donegall Rd, BELFAST, BT12 5JN.   (hq)
   028 9032 4733   fax 028 9043 9699
   Gen Sec: Ken Canavan
- ▲ Company Limited by Guarantee; Registered Charity
- ○ *Y; to promote an appreciation of the countryside among
   young people through provision of hostel accommodation
- Gp Fell walking
- ● Conf - Mtgs - Exhib - Inf - VE
- < Intl Youth Hostel Fedn (IYHF)
- M 6,500 i
- ¶ AR; free.

Youth Hostels Association (England & Wales) Ltd   (YHA)   1930
- ■ Trevelyan House, Dimple Rd, MATLOCK, Derbys, DE4 3YH.
   (hq)
   01629 592600   fax 01629 592702
   email customerservices@yha.org.uk
   http://www.yha.org.uk
   Chief Exec: Roger Clarke
- ▲ Company Limited by Guarantee; Registered Charity
- Br 217
- ○ *Y; 'to help all, especially young people of limited means, to a
   greater knowledge, love & care of the countryside, &
   appreciation of the cultural values of towns & cities,
   particularly by providing youth hostels or other
   accommodation for them in their travels, & thus to improve
   their health, recreation & education'
- ● Exhib - VE - Accommodation provision
- < Intl Youth Hostelling Fedn (IYHF)
- M 247,000 i
- ¶ Triangle Magazine - 2;; ftm, £2 nm.   Escape To. . . - 1; free.
   Guidebook - 2 yrly; ftm, £3.99 nm.   AR; free.

Youth Scotland   1930
- NR Balfour House, 19 Bonnington Grove, EDINBURGH,
   EH6 4BL.   (hq)
   0131-554 2561
   Chief Exec: Carol Downie
- ▲ Company Limited by Guarantee; Registered Charity
- Br 14 area assns
- ○ *N, *Y; 'to support, develop & improve the range & quality of
   informal educational, social & leisure opportunities available
   to young people in Scotland'
- ● Conf - Mtgs - ET - Comp - Inf - Lib - LG
- < UK Youth; Youthlink; Scot Coun Voluntary Orgs (SCVO)
- M 53,000 i, 670 clubs & area assns
- ¶ Magnet (Jnl) - 4; free. Area Association Newsletter - 6; ftm.
   Safe & Sound - Building a Safer Youth Work Environment; £5
   (first copy ftm).

YWCA of Ireland
- IRL 64 Lower Baggot St, DUBLIN 2, Republic of Ireland.
   353 (1) 644 9536   fax 353 (1) 644 9537
   email ywca@indigo.ie
   Pres: Dot Little
- ○ *W, *Y

YWCA (Young Women's Christian Association)   (YWCA)   1855
- NR Clarendon House, 52 Cornmarket St, OXFORD, OX1 3EJ.
   (hq)
   01865 304200   fax 01865 204805
   Chief Exec: Gill Tishler
- ▲ Company Limited by Guarantee; Registered Charity
- Br 18
- ○ *W, *Y; is a force for change for women who are facing
   discrimination & inequalities of all kinds; to enable young
   women who are experiencing disadvantage to identify &
   realise their full potential; to influence public policy in order
   to achieve equality & social justice for young women
- ¶ Members' NL - 2; ftm only.   Annual Review - 1; free.

Z

Zebra Finch Society
   a member body of the **Society for the Protection of Aviculture**

Zionist Federation of Great Britain & Ireland   (ZF)   1899
- NR 741 High Rd, LONDON, N12 0BQ.   (hq)
   Exec Dir; Alan Iziz
- ○ *R; promotion of Zionism

Zipper Club
   see **British Cardiac Patients Association**

Zoo Federation
   see **British & Irish Association of Zoos & Aquariums**

Zoological Society of Ireland   1830
- IRL Phoenix Park, DUBLIN 8, Republic of Ireland.
   353 (1) 474 8900   fax 353 (1) 677 1660
   email info@dublinzoo.ie   http://www.dublinzoo.ie
   Hon Sec: Margaret Sinanan
- ○ *L, *V

Zoological Society of London   (ZSL)   1826
- NR Regent's Park, LONDON, NW1 4RY.   (hq)
   020 7722 3333
- ▲ Registered Charity
- ○ *L, *Q, *V; to promote worldwide conservation of animal
   species & their habitats by stimulating public awareness &
   concern
- M i
- ¶ Journal of Zoology - 12.   Zoological Record - 1.

Zwartbles Sheep Association   (ZSA)   1995
- ■ North Lee Farm, Hacche Lane, SOUTH MOLTON, Devon,
   EX36 3EH.   (hsp)
   01598 740248
   email back@northlee.com   http://www.zwartbles.co.uk
   Sec: Rebecca Evans
- ▲ Company Limited by Guarantee; Registered Charity
- ○ *B
- ● Conf - Mtgs - ET - VE
- < Netherlands Zwartbles Soc (NZS); Nat Sheep Assn
- M 270 i
- ¶ NL - 4;   Ybk; both free.

*Symbol of tradition
and progress*

*in directory and
database publishing*

We welcome your enquiries

Enquiry 1 —— Why CBD?

Answer: *The first edition of "Current British Directories" was compiled by George and Prue Henderson in 1952; it rapidly became known in the reference library world — at that time thirsty for any reliable guide to business information — as "CBD"; when we formed the company in 1961 there was no better name for it than "CBD Research Ltd".*

——

Since then the company has kept to the tradition of publishing only "seen and verified" information — 24 different titles in a total of 80 editions.

——

In 1966 the company was the only British founder member of the European Association of Directory Publishers; and it was a founder member in 1970 of the Association of British Directory Publishers (now the Data Publishers Association).

——

We <u>still</u> welcome your enquiries

CBD Research Ltd

15 Wickham Road, Beckenham, Kent, BR3 5JS
Tel: 020 8650 7745 **Fax:** 020 8650 0768
E-mail: cbd@cbdresearch.com

www.cbdresearch.com

ABBREVIATIONS INDEX

A

A&A	Art & Architecture
A-A	Arrhythmia Alliance
A-DS	Anglo-Danish Soc
AA	Advertising Assn
	Alcoholics Anonymous
	Arboricultural Assn
	Architectural Assn
	Arthritic Assn
	Astrological Assn
	Automobile Assn
AAA	AAA (Action against Allergy)
	Anglo-Albanian Assn
	Assn Authors' Agents
	Assn Average Adjusters
	Automotive Aftermarket Assn
	Ayrshire Agricl Assn
AAAC	Assn Air Ambulance Charities
AAAofE	Amat Athletic Assn
AAB	Assn Applied Biologists
AABA	Assn Accountancy & Business Affairs
AAC	Assn ATOL Companies
AAC UK	American Auto Club UK
AAD	Assn Amer Dancing
AAE	Assn Astronomy Educ
AAGBI	Assn Anaesthetists
AAH	Assn Art Historians
AAI	Assn Advertisers in Ireland Ltd
	Assn Alabaster Importers & Whlsrs
AAI&S	Assn Archaeol Illustrators & Surveyors
AAPA	Assn Authorised Public Accountants
AAS	Anglesey Antiquarian Soc & Field Club
	Applied Arts Scotland
AASDN	Architectural & Archaeol Soc Durham & Northumberland
AAT	Assn Accounting Technicians
ABA	Antiquarian Booksellers Assn
	Assn Biomedical Andrologists
	Assn Burial Authorities
	Assn Business Administration
ABAE	Amat Boxing Assn England
ABBA	Assn Business to Business Agencies
ABBC	Assn Brit Brewery Collectables
ABC	Assn Brickwork Contrs
	Assn Brit Climatologists
	Assn Brit Climbing Walls
	Assn Brit Counties
	Austro-Brit Cham
ABCB	Assn Brit Certification Bodies
ABCC	Assn Brit Correspondence Colls
ABCD	Assn Bldg Cleaning Direct Service Providers
	Assn Brit Choral Dirs
ABCIFER	Assn Brit Civilian Internees Far East
ABCM	Assn Bldg Component Mfrs
ABCP	Assn Brit Concert Promoters
ABCUL	Assn Brit Credit Us
ABD	Assn Brit Drivers
	Assn Broadcasting Doctors
ABDO	Assn Brit Dispensing Opticians
ABDS	Assn Brit Designer Silversmiths
ABE	Assn Bldg Engrs
	Assn Business Executives
ABHI	Assn Brit Healthcare Inds
ABI	Assn Brit Insurers
	Assn Brit Investigators
ABIA	Assn Brit Introduction Agencies
ABIM	Assn Bakery Ingredient Mfrs
ABIS	Assn Brit & Ir Showcaves
ABJM	Assn Brit Jazz Musicians
ABKC	Assn Brit Kart Clubs
ABLS	Assn Brit Language Schools

ABM	Assn Breastfeeding Mothers
ABMA	Assn Business Mgrs & Administrators
ABMEC	Assn Brit Mining Eqpt Cos
ABN	Assn Brit Neurologists
ABO	Assn Brit Orchestras
ABOI	Assn Brit Offshore Inds
ABP	Assn Business Psychologists
ABPC	Assn Brit Pewter Craftsmen
ABPCO	Assn Brit Profl Conf Organisers
ABPI	Assn Brit Pharmaceutical Ind
ABPN	Assn Brit Paediatric Nurses
ABPS	Assn Brit Philatelic Socs
ABPT	Assn Blind Piano Tuners
ABRS	Assn Brit Riding Schools
ABS	Amat Boxing Scotland
	Anglo-Belgian Soc
	Assn Brit Sailmakers
	Assn Business Schools
ABSE	Assn Boat Safety Examiners
ABSP	Assn Brit Scrabble Players
ABSTD	Assn Basic Science Teachers Dentistry
ABSW	Assn Brit Science Writers
ABTA	Assn Brit Travel Agents
ABTAPL	Assn Brit Theological... Libraries
ABTEM	Assn Brit Transport & Engg Museums
ABTO	Assn Brit Tennis Officials
ABTOF	Assn Brit Tour Operators France
ABTT	Assn Brit Theatre Technicians
ABWAK	Assn Brit Wild Animal Keepers
ABYA	Assn Brokers & Yacht Agents
AC	Alpine Club
	Archaeology Cymru
	Assn Coaching
ACA	Aircrew Assn
	Aircrewman's Assn
	Anglers Consvn Assn
	Assn Consultant Architects
	Assn Consulting Actuaries
	Assn Continence Advice
ACADEMI	ACADEMI
ACAI	Assn Consultant Approved Inspectors
ACAL	Assn Child Abuse Lawyers
ACALG	Assn Chief Archivists Local Govt
ACAMH	Assn Child & Adolescent Mental Health
ACAT	Assn Cognitive Analytic Therapy
ACAVA	Assn Cultural Advancement through Visual Art
ACB	Assn Clinical Biochemistry
ACBMC	Assn Community-based Maternity Care
ACCA	Assn Chart Certified Accountants
ACCE	Assn County Chief Executives
ACCEO	Assn Caravan & Camping Exempted Orgs
ACCI	Ayrshire Cham Comm & Ind
ACCM	Assn Computer Cable Mfrs
ACCS	Assn County Cricket Scorers
ACCU	Assn C & C++ Users
ACDM	Assn Clinical Data Mgt
ACE	Assn Circulation Executives
	Assn Confs & Events
	Assn Consultancy & Engg
	Assn Consvn Energy
ACEA	Assn Civil Enforcement Agencies
ACEG	Assn Careers Educ & Guidance
ACES	Assn Cannibals' Eqpt Suppliers
	Assn Chief Estates Surveyors... Local Govt
ACEVO	Assn Chief Executives Voluntary Orgs
ACF	Assn Charitable Foundations
ACFA	Army Cadet Force Assn
ACFM	Assn Cereal Food Mfrs
ACFO	ACFO Ltd
ACG	ACG Ltd (Arts Centre Gp)
	Anti Counterfeiting Gp
ACH	Academy Curative Hypnotherapists
ACI	Assn Copyright Investigators
ACID	Anti Copying Design

ACIE	Assn Charity Indep Examiners	AEC	Assn Exhibition Contrs
ACIFC	Assn Concrete Indl Flooring Contrs	AECB	Assn Envt Conscious Bldg
ACIS	Assn Contemporary Iberian Studies	AECI	Assn Electrical Contrs, Ireland
ACJ	Assn Contemporary Jewellery	AEF	Aviation Envt Fedn
ACLM	Assn Contact Lens Mfrs	AEGIS	Assn Educ & Guardianship Intl Students
ACM	Assn Coll Mgt	AEME	Assn Events Mgt Educ
ACMA	Air Cleaner Mfrs Assn	AEMES	AEMES
ACMC	Assn Cost Mgt Consultants	AEMT	Assn Electrical & Mechanical Trs
ACML	Anti Common Market League	AENA	All England Netball Assn
ACO	Assn Charity Officers	AEO	Assn Exhibition Organisers
ACOGB	Autograph Club	AEP	Assn Educl Psychologists
ACoRP	Assn Community Rail Partnerships		Assn Electricity Producers
ACostE	Assn Cost Engrs	AES	Agricl Economics Soc
ACP	Assn Child Psychotherapists		Amat Entomologists' Soc
	Assn Circus Proprietors		Audio Engg Soc
	Assn Clinical Pathologists	AESS	Assn Engl Singers & Speakers
	Assn Computer Profls	AEV	Assn Event Venues
ACPO	Assn Chief Police Officers	AEWM	Assn Educ Welfare Mgt
ACPO(S)	Assn Chief Police Officers (Scotland)	AF	Albinism Fellowship
ACPP	Assn Clinical Professors Paediatrics	AFA	Advocates for Animals
ACPU	Assd Chiropodists & Podiatrists U		Amat Football Alliance
ACRA	Assn Company Registration Agents	AFAA	Assn Families Adopted Abroad
ACRE	Action Communities Rural England	Afasic	AFASIC
ACRIB	Air Conditioning & Refrigeration Ind Bd	AFB	Assn Foreign Banks
ACS	Additional Curates Soc	AfC	Assn Charities
	Anglo Catalan Soc	AFC	Assn Fundraising Consultants
	Assn Charity Shops	AFCA	Assn Financial Controllers & Administrators
	Assn Convenience Stores	AFCMA	Aberdeen Fish Curers'…Assn
	Assn Cricket Statisticians & Historians	AFDEC	Assn Franchised Distbrs Electronic Components
ACSeS	Assn Coun Secretaries & Solicitors	AFHSW	Assn Family Hist Socs Wales
ACSS	Academy Social Sciences	AFLS	Assn French Language Studies
ACT	Aid Children with Tracheostomies	AFMM	UK Assn Fish Meal Mfrs
	Assn Canoe Trades	AFO	Assn Festival Organisers
	Assn Children Life-Threatening… Conditions	AFS	Assn Football Statisticians
	Assn Christian Teachers		Assn Friendly Socs
	Assn Corporate Treasurers	AFT	Assn Family Therapy
	Assn Cycle Traders	AGA	Asparagus Growers' Assn
ACTA	Animal Consultants & Trainers Assn	AGB	Assn Guernsey Banks
	Assn Cardiothoracic Anaesthetists	AGCAS	Assn Graduate Careers Advy Services
ACTC	Assn Classic Trials Clubs	AGCS	Assn Golf Club Secretaries
ACTCTC	Assn Charter Trustee Towns &… Couns	AGDS	Assn Garage Door Specialists
ACTH	Assn Cushing's Treatment & Help	AgeCare	R Surgical Aid Soc
ACTO	Assn Community TV Operators	AGI	Assn Geographic Inf
ACU	Assn C'wealth Universities	AGIF	Amusement & Gaming Ind Forum
	Auto-Cycle U	AGIP	Assn Gp & Individual Psychotherapy
ACU&S	Assn Cricket Umpires & Scorers	AGR	Assn Graduate Recruiters
ACVW	Assn Countryside Voluntary Wardens	AGRA	Assn Genealogists & Researchers in Archives
ACW	Gwartheg Hynafol Cymru	AGRC	Assn Gastroenterological Res Charities
ACWRT(UK)	American Civil War Round Table	AGS	Alpine Garden Soc
ADA	Antiquities Dealers Assn		Assn Geotechnical & Geoenvironmental Specialists
	Assn Drainage Authorities	AGSD(UK)	Assn Glycogen Storage Diseases
ADCAS	Assn Ductwork Contrs & Allied Services	AGT	Assn Gardens Trusts
ADCCAT	Assn Distributors, Coaters… Adhesive Tapes	AGW	Assn Golf Writers
ADCH	Assn Dogs & Cats Homes	AHC	Assn Healthcare Communicators
ADES	Assn Directors Educ Scotland	AHC (UK)	Assn Hist & Computing
ADF	Automotive Distribution Fedn	AHDA	Animal Health Distbrs Assn
ADFAM	ADFAM Nat	AHDS	Assn Headteachers & Deputies Scotland
ADH	Assn Dental Hospitals	AHEM	Brit Fluid Power Assn
ADI	Assn Dental Implantology	AHG	Assn Hist Glass
ADINJC	Approved Driving Instructors Nat Jt Coun	AHGTC	Ancient & Honourable Gld Town Criers
ADLS	Assn Dunkirk Little Ships	AHI	Assn Heritage Interpretation
ADM	Assn Domestic Mgt	AHIPP	Assn Home Inf Packs Providers
ADMG	Assn Deer Mgt Gps	AHIS	Assn Heads Indep Schools
ADMT UK	Assn Dance Movement Therapy	AHOEC	Assn Heads Outdoor Educ Centres
ADP	Assn Disabled Profls	AHP(B)	Assn Humanistic Psychology
ADSA	Automatic Door Suppliers Assn	AHPMA	Absorbent Hygiene Products Mfrs Assn
ADSET	ADSET	AHS	Antiquarian Horological Soc
ADsPH	Assn Directors Public Health	AHSS	Architectural Heritage Soc Scotland
ADSS	Assn Directors Social Services	AIA	Anglo-Israel Assn
ADSW	Assn Directors Social Work		Assn Indl Archaeology
Advice UK	Advice UK		Assn Intl Accountants
AEA	Academy Execs & Admins	AIAC	Assn Indep Advice Centres
	Agricl Engrs Assn	AIC	Agricl Inds Confedn
	Aluminium Extruders Assn	AICA	Assn Indep Care Advisers
	Assn Educ & Ageing		Assn Indep Construction Adjudicators
	Assn Electoral Administrators	AICC	Assn Indep Crop Consultants
	Assn Envtl Archaeology	AICES	Assn Intl Courier & Express Services
	Assn Erotic Artists	AICR	Assn Intl Cancer Res

© CBD Research Ltd · Beckenham · BR3 5JS · Tel 020 8650 7745 · Fax 020 8650 0768 · E-mail cbd@cbdresearch.com · www.cbdresearch.com

AICS	Assn Indep Computer Specialists
AIF	Assn Interchurch Families
AIFA	Assn Indep Financial Advisers
AIIC	Assn Indep Inventory Clerks
AILU	Assn Indl Laser Users
AIM	Assn Indep Museums
	Assn Indep Music
	Assn Intl Marketing
AIMH UK	Assn Infant Mental Health UK
AIMMI	Assn Institutional Multi-Manager Investing
AIMMS	Assn Indep Mgt & Maritime Services
AIMS	A1 Motor Stores
	Assn Improvements Maternity Services
	Assn Indep Meat Suppliers
AIM UK	Automatic Identification Mfrs & Suppliers Assn
AINA	Assn Inland Navigation Authorities
AIOA	Assn Indep Organ Advisers
AIR	Alliance Indep Retailers
AIRMIC	Assn Insurance & Risk Mgrs
AIRSO	Assn Indl Road Safety Officers
AIRTO	AIRTO
AIS	Anglo-Indonesian Soc
	Assn Insurance Surveyors
	Assn Interior Specialists
AISMA	Assn Indep Specialist Med Accountants
AISSG	Androgen Insensitivity Syndrome Support Gp
AITA	Adult Ind Trade Assn
	Artificial Insemination Equines Trade Assn
AITC	Assn Investment Trust Companies
AITO	Assn Indep Tour Operators
AITS	Assn Indep Tobacco Specialists
AITT	Assn Indl Truck Trainers
AIVC	Assn Inter-Varsity Clubs
AJA	Amat Jockeys Assn
	Anglo-Jewish Assn
AJEX	Assn Jewish Ex-Servicemen & Women
AJS	Anglo-Jordanian Soc
Al-Anon	Al-Anon Family Gps
ALA	Agricl Law Assn
	Agricl Lime Assn
	Auto Locksmiths Assn
ALACE	Assn Local Authority Chief Execs
ALAE	Assn Licensed Aircraft Engrs
ALARM	ALARM
	Assn Local Authority Risk Mgrs
ALBUM	Assn Local Bus Co Mgrs
ALC	Assn Lawyers Children
ALCD	Assn Law Costs Draftsmen
ALCI	Assn Landscape Contrs Ireland (NI)
ALCS	Assn Low Countries Studies
	Authors' Licensing & Collecting Soc
ALD	Assn Lighting Designers
ALEM	Assn Loading & Elevating Eqpt Mfrs
ALEP	Assn Leasehold Enfranchisement Practitioners
ALERT	Alert Euthanasia
ALFED	Aluminium Fedn
ALG	Assn London Government
ALGAO	Assn Local Govt Archaeol Officers
ALIP	Assn Leisure Ind Profls
ALK	Assn Lighthouse Keepers
ALL	Assn Language Learning
	Assn Latin Liturgy
	Astrological Lodge Lond
ALLEF UK	Assn Learning Languages En Famille
ALLMI	Assn Lorry Loader Mfrs & Importers
ALM	Assn Lloyd's Members
ALMR	Assn Licensed Mult Retailers
ALP	Assn Labour Providers
	Horticultural Trs Assn
ALPSP	Assn Learned & Profl Soc Pubrs
ALRC	Assn Land Rover Clubs
ALS	Alliance Literary Socs
	Assn Lipspeakers
ALT	Assn Law Teachers
	Assn Learning Technology
ALTO	ALTO [IRL]
ALTT	Assn Light Touch Therapists
Alupro	UK Aluminium Packaging Recycling Org

ALVA	Assn Leading Visitor Attractions
AMA	Accident Mgt Assn
	Amat Martial Assn
	Anthroposophical Med Assn
	Arts Marketing Assn
	Assn Mining Analysts
	Assn Model Agents
AMABO	Assn Med Advisers Brit Orchestras
AMCA	Amat Motor Cycle Assn
AMDEA	Assn Mfrs Domestic Appliances
AMDIS	Assn Marketing & Devt Indep Schools
AME	Assn Marriage Enrichment
AMEC	Assn Media Evaluation Cos
AMED	Assn Mgt Educ & Devt
AMEE	Assn Managerial Electrical Executives
AMEM	Assn Miniature Engine Mfrs
AMHSA	Automated Material Handling Systems Assn
AMI	Assn Meat Inspectors
AMII	Assn Med Insurance Intermediaries
AMIMB	Assn Members Indep Monitoring Bds
AMLBO	River Assn Freight & Transport
AMM	Assn Med Microbiologists
AMMA	Art Metalware Mfrs' Assn
AMO	Assn Meter Operators
AMONO	Assn Mainframe Operators & Network Administrators
AMPS	Assn Member-Directed Pension Schemes
	Assn Mfrs Power generating Systems
	Assn Mgt & Profl Staffs
	Assn Motion Picture Sound
AMRA	Automotive Mfrs' Racing Assn
AMRC	Assn Med Res Charities
AMRCO	Assn Motor Racing Circuit Owners
AMRSS	Assn Model Rly Socs Scotland
AMS	Academy Medical Sciences
	Academy Multi-Skills
	Agricl Manpower Soc
	Ancient Monuments Soc
	Antique Metalware Soc
	Assurance Med Soc
AMSPAR	Assn Med Secretaries...& Receptionists
AMTRA	Animal Medicines Training Regulatory Authority
AMU	Assn Master Upholsterers & Soft Furnishers
An Taisce	Nat Trust Ireland
ANAIS	Assn New Age Inds
ANBG	Assn Natural Burial Grounds
ANC	Assn Noise Consultants
ANDISP	Assn Nat Driver Improvement Scheme Providers
ANEC	Assn N E Couns
ANEW Ltd	Assd Nat Electrical Whlsrs
ANH	Alliance Natural Health
ANHSO	Ashmolean Natural Hist Soc Oxfordshire
ANIC	Assn NI Colleges
ANIELB	Assn NI Educ & Library Bds
ANLHS	Assn Northumberland Local Hist Socs
ANLP	Assn Neuro-Linguistic Programming
ANM	Assn Natural Medicine
ANMW	Assn Newspaper Magazine Whlsrs
ANPA	Assn Nat Park Authorities
ANRCW	Assn Nursing Religious
ANSA	Assn Nurses Substance Abuse
ANTC	Assn Nursery Training Colls
ANTOR	Assn Nat Tourist Office Representatives
ANTS	Anglo-Norman Text Soc
AOA	Airport Operators Assn
AoC	Assn Colleges
AODP	Assn Operating Dept Practitioners
AOHNP	AOHNP (UK)
AoI	Assn Illustrators
AOP	Assn Online Publishers
	Assn Optometrists
AOPA	Aircraft Owners & Pilots Assn
AOPA Ireland	Aircraft Owners & Pilots Assn [IRL]
AoR	Assn Reflexologists
AoT	Assn Tutors
AOTI	Assn Occupational Therapists Ireland
AOTOS	Assn Teachers Singing
AOVC	Assn Old Vehicle Clubs NI

APA	Advertising Producers Assn	ARKS	Assn Racing Kart Schools
	Army Parachute Assn	ARLA	Assn Residential Letting Agents
	Assn Police Authorities	ARLIS	ARLIS UK & Ireland
	Assn Practising Accountants	ARLT	Assn Latin Teaching
	Assn Profl Astrologers	ARM	Assn Radical Midwives
	Assn Public Analysts	ARMA	Arthritis & Musculoskeletal Alliance
	Assn Publishing Agencies		Assn Residential Managing Agents
	Audiobook Publishing Assn	ARMS	Assn Researchers in Medicine & Science
APACS	Assn Payment Clearing Services	ARNO	Assn R Navy Officers
APAGBI	Assn Paediatric Anaesthetists	ARNTRA	Arthritis & Rheumatism Natural Therapy Res Assn
APAP	Assn Profl Ambulance Personnel	AROS	Assn Registrars Scotland
APAS	Assn Public Analysts Scotland	ARP	Assn Relocation Agents
APBC	Assn Pet Behaviour Counsellors	ARPMA	Aluminium Rolled Products Mfrs Assn
APCC	Assn Private Crematoria & Cemeteries	ARR	Assn Radiation Res
APCIMS	Assn Private Client Investment Mgrs & Stockbrokers	ARS	Anaesthetic Res Soc
APCMH	Assn Pastoral Care Mental Health	ARTP	Assn Respiratory Technology & Physiology
APCO	Assn Pleasure Craft Operators		Assn Rly Training Providers
APDT	Assn Pet Dog Trainers	ARTSM	Assn Road Traffic Safety & Mgt
APE	Assn Physical Educ	ARVAC	Assn Res Voluntary & Community Sector
APEA	Assn Petroleum & Explosives Admin	AS	Acupuncture Soc
APEC	Action Pre-Eclampsia		Alzheimer's Soc
APG	Account Planning Gp		Avicultural Soc
APGI	Assn Profl Genealogists Ireland	ASA	Advice Services Alliance
APHA	Animal & Plant Health Assn [IRL]		Aluminium Stockholders Assn
	Assn Port Health Authorities		Amat Swimming Assn
APHC	Assn Plumbing & Heating Contrs		Ambulance Service Assn
API	Assn Play Inds		Assn Sealant Applicators
APIL	Assn Personal Injury Lawyers		Assn Social Anthropologists C'wealth
APL	Assn Pension Lawyers		Assn Subscription Agents & Intermediaries
	Horticultural Trs Assn	ASA.GB	American Saddlebred Assn
APM	Assn Palliative Medicine	ASAO	Assn Show & Agricl Orgs
	Assn Project Mgt	ASAUK	African Studies Assn
APMC	Assn Pioneer Motor Cyclists	ASBAH	Assn Spina Bifida & Hydrocephalus
APMI	Assn Printing Machinery Importers	ASBCI	ASBCI - Forum Clothing & Textiles
APMM	Assn Policy Market Makers	ASC	Assn Scotland's Colls
APMO	Assn Private Market Operators		Assn Security Consultants
APMT	Assn Profl Music Therapists		Assn Speakers Clubs
APNI	Assn Postnatal Illness	ASC/NAWCH	Action Sick Children
APNT	Assn Physical & Natural Therapists	ASCC	Assn Scot Community Couns
APP	Assn Psychoanalytic Psychotherapy NHS	ASCEL	Assn Senior Children's & Educ Librarians
APPC	Assn Profl Political Consultants	ASCHB	Assn Studies Consvn Historic Bldgs
APPCC	Assn Private Pet Cemeteries & Crematoria	ASCL	Assn School & College Leaders
APPSS	Assn Police & Public Security Suppliers	ASDC	Assn Separated & Divorced Catholics
APR	Assn Promoting Retreats	ASDMA	Architectural & Specialist Door Mfrs Assn
APRA	Anomalous Phenomena Research Agency	ASE	Assn Science Educ
APRO	Assn Private Rly Wagon Owners		Astronomical Soc Edinburgh
APROP	Action Proper Regulation Private Hospitals	ASEASUK	Assn S E Asian Studies UK
APRS	Assn Profl Recording Services	ASEN	Assn Study Ethnicity & Nationalism
APS	Assn Project Safety	ASET	Assn Sandwich Educ & Training
APS (UK)	Assn Punjab Studies (UK)	ASFAD	Assn Stainless Fastener Distbrs
APSA	Assn Profl Sales Agents (Sports & Leisure Inds)	ASFB	Assn Salmon Fishery Bds
	Assn Profls Services Adolescents	ASFCEW	Assn Sea Fisheries C'ees [E&W]
APSCEH	Assn Prof Staffs Colls Educ [IRL]	ASFI	Assn Suppliers Furniture Ind
APSE	Assn Public Service Excellence	ASFP	Assn Specialist Fire Protection
APSGB	Academy Pharmaceutical Sciences	ASG	Acne Support Gp
APT	Assn Psychological Therapies		Air Safety Gp
	UK Assn Presvn Trusts		Anorchidism Support Gp
APTG	Assn Profl Tourist Guides	ASGBI	Assn Surgeons
APV	Assn Profl Videomakers	ASGFM	Assn Stillwater Game Fishery Mgrs
AQCH	Assn Qualified Curative Hypnotherapists	ASGP	Assn Study German Politics
AQHA-UK	American Quarter Horse Assn	ASGRA	Assn Scot Genealogists & Researchers Archives
AQR	Assn Qualitative Res	ASH	Action Smoking & Health
ARA	Aircraft Res Assn	ASHTAV	Assn Small Historic Towns & Villages
	Amat Rowing Assn	ASI	Ambulance Service Inst
	Assn Roman Archaeology	ASIIP	Adlerian Soc
ARBA	Amat Rose Breeders Assn	ASIM	Assn Solicitors & Investment Mgrs
ARC	Alliance Religions & Consvn	ASinGB	Anthroposophical Soc
	Assn Real Change	ASiT	Assn Surgeons in Training
ARCA	Adult Residential Colls Assn	ASK	Assn Systematic Kinesiology
	ARCA	ASLEC	Assn Street Lighting Electrical Contrs
ARCH	Action Rights Children	aslib	Aslib
ARCISS	Assn Res Centres Social Sciences	ASLS	Assn Scot Literary Studies
ARCOS	Assn Rehabilitation Communication & Oral Skills	ASLTIP	Assn Speech & Language Therapists
ARCS	Assn Registration & Celebratory Services	ASM	Assn Supervisors Midwives
AREA	Assn Resettlement & Employment Advisors	ASMCF	Assn Study Modern & Contemporary France
AREF	Assn Real Estate Funds	ASMD	Assn Sewing Machine Distbrs
ARH	Alliance Registered Homeopaths	ASME	Assn Study Med Educ
ARHM	Assn Retirement Housing Mgrs	ASMI	Assn Study Modern Italy

© CBD Research Ltd · Beckenham · BR3 5JS · Tel 020 8650 7745 · Fax 020 8650 0768 · E-mail cbd@cbdresearch.com · www.cbdresearch.com

ASN	Assn Solicitor Notaries Greater London
ASO	Assn Study Obesity
ASP	Assn Service Providers
ASPE	Assn Study Primary Educ
ASPEC	Assn Studio & Production Eqpt Companies
ASPECT	Assn Profls Educ & Children's Trusts
ASPIRE	Assn Spinal Injury Res...
ASPROM	Assn Study & Presvn Roman Mosaics
ASPS	Assn Scot Philatelic Socs
	Assn Scot Police Superintendents
ASRA	Assn Student Residential Accommodation
ASS CPHO	Assn County Public Health Officers
ASSA	Assn Scot Schools Architecture
ASSAP	Assn Scientific Study Anomalous Phenomena
ASSC	Assn Scotland's Self-Caterers
ASSG	Assn Scot Shellfish Growers
AssHEP	Assn Hot Foil Printers
AST	Assn Stress Therapists
ASTA BEAB	ASTA BEAB Certification Services
ASTI	Assn Secondary Teachers, Ireland
ASTO	Assn Sea Training Orgs
ASTOS	Assn Specialist Techl Orgs Space
ASTRA	Assn Scotland Res Astronautics
ASUCplus	ASUCplus
ASVA	Assn Scot Visitor Attractions
ASYC	Assn Scot Yacht Charterers
ATA	Angling Trs Assn
ATA Assn	Air Transport Auxiliary Assn
ATAXIA	Ataxia UK
ATC	Aromatherapy Tr Coun
	Assn Therapeutic Communities
	Assn Translation Companies
ATCM	Assn Tank & Cistern Mfrs
	Assn Town Centre Mgt
ATCO	Assn Transport Co-ordinating Officers
ATCU	Assd Train Crew U
ATGFP	Assn Timber Growers & Forestry Profls
ATH	Assn Therapeutic Healers
ATL	Assn Teachers & Lecturers
	Assn Therapy Lecturers
ATLA	Assn Teachers Lipreading to Adults
ATLAS	Assn Technical Lighting & Access Specialists
ATM	Assn Teachers Mathematics
ATMA	Adhesive Tape Mfrs' Assn
ATOC	Assn Train Operating Companies
ATP	Assn Teaching Psychology
	Assn Therapeutic Philosophy
ATPH	Assn Transport Photographers & Historians
ATS	Ataxia-Telangiectasia Soc
ATSCO	Assn Technology Staffing Companies
ATSS	Assn Teaching Social Sciences
ATT	Assn Taxation Technicians
Attend	Attend
ATTP	Assn Thallophyte Treatment Plants
AUA	Assn University Administrators
AUKML	Assn UK Media Librarians
AUKOI	Assn UK Oil Indeps
AUKVA	Alliance UK Virtual Assistants
AUMPC	Assn Unpasteurised Milk Producers
AURA	Assn Users Res Agencies
AURIL	Assn University Res & Ind Links
AURPO	Assn University Radiation Protection Officers
AUT	Assn University Teachers
AVA	Automatic Vending Assn
AVID	Assn Visitors Immigration Detainees
AVLP	Assn Valuers Licensed Property
AvMA	Action Med Accidents
AVRO	Assn Vehicle Recovery Operators
AWD	Assn Welding Distbrs
AWEBB	Assn Whls Electrical Bulk Buyers
AWFF	Animal Welfare Filming Fedn
AWG	Art Workers Gld
AWHEM	Assn Wellhead Eqpt Mfrs
AXrEM	Assn X-ray Eqpt Mfrs
AYME	Assn Young People with ME
AYRS	Amat Yacht Res Soc

B

B MET A	Birmingham Metallurgical Assn
B&CCC	Brit & Colombian Cham Comm [Lond]
B-AS	Britain-Australia Soc
B-ICC	Brit-Israel Cham Comm
BA	Basketmaker's Assn
	Booksellers Assn
BA of E	Badminton Assn England
BAA	Brit Academy Audiology
	Brit Accounting Assn
	Brit Aggregates Assn
	Brit Archaeol Assn
	Brit Astronomical Assn
BAAC	Brit Assn Aviation Consultants
BAAF	Brit Assn Adoption & Fostering
BAAL	Brit Assn Applied Linguistics
BAAM	Brit Assn Anger Mgt
BAAP	Brit Assn Academic Phoneticians
	Brit Assn Audiological Physicians
BAAPS	Brit Assn Aesthetic Plastic Surgeons
BAAS	Brit Assn Amer Studies
BAASDC	Brit Assn Amer Square Dance Clubs
BAAT	Brit Assn Art Therapists
BABA	Brit African Business Assn
	Brit Air Boat Assn
	Brit Artist Blacksmiths Assn
BABC	Brit Amer Business Coun
BABCP	Brit Assn Behavioural... Psychotherapies
BABi	Brit Amer Business Inc
BABO	Brit Assn Balloon Operators
BABS	Brit Assn Barbershop Singers
BABTAC	Brit Assn Beauty Therapy & Cosmetology
BAC	Business Archives Coun
BAC+S	Brit Academy Composers & Songwriters
BACA	Baltic Air Charter Assn
	Brit Assn Clinical Anatomists
BACB	Brit Assn Communicators in Business
BAcC	Brit Acupuncture Coun
BACC	Brit Argentine Cham Comm
BACD	Brit Assn Conf Destinations
BACDA	Brit Assn Community Doctors in Audiology
BACEE	Brit Assn Cent & Eastn Europe
BACFI	Bar Assn Comm, Finance & Ind
BACG	Brit Assn Crystal Growth
BACM-TEAM	Brit Assn Colliery Mgt
BACP	Brit Assn Counselling & Psychotherapy
BACR	Brit Assn Cancer Res
BACS	Brit Assn Canadian Studies
	Brit Assn Chemical Specialities
	Brit Assn Chinese Studies
BACSA	Brit Assn Cemeteries S Asia
BACTA	Brit Amusement Catering Trs Assn
BAD	Brit Assn Dermatologists
BADA	Brit Antique Dealers Assn
	Brit Audio Dealers Assn
BADC	Brit Academy Dramatic Combat
BADCO	Ceretas
BADN	Brit Assn Dental Nurses
BADS	Brit Assn Day Surgery
BADT	Brit Assn Dental Therapists
BADth	Brit Assn Dramatherapists
BAeA	Brit Aerobatic Assn
BAeF	Brit Aerophilatelic Fedn
BAEM	Brit Assn Emergency Medicine
BAEPD	Brit Assn Eur Pharmaceutical Distbrs
BAES	Brit Assn Endocrine Surgeons
	Brit Aviation Enthusiasts Soc
BAF	Brit Abrasives Fedn
	Brit Aerobiology Fedn
BAFA	Brit Amer Football Assn
	Brit Arts Festivals Assn
BAFD	Brit Assn Fastener Distbrs
BAFE	Brit Approvals Fire Eqpt
BAFEP	Brit Assn Flower Essence Producers

BAFM	Brit Assn Forensic Medicine
	Brit Assn Friends Museums
BAFRA	Brit Antique Furniture Restorers Assn
BAFS	Brit Academy Forensic Sciences
BAFSA	Brit Automatic Fire Sprinkler Assn
BAFSAM	Brit Assn Feed Supplement & Additives Mfrs
BAFTA	Brit Academy Film & TV Arts
BAFTS	Brit Assn Fair Tr Shops
BAFUNCS	Brit Assn Former UN Civil Servants
BAGA	Brit Amat Gymnastics Assn
BAGB	Bingo Association
BAGCC	Brit Assn Golf Course Constructors
BAGCD	Brit Assn Green Crop Driers
BAGMA	Brit Agricl & Garden Machinery Assn
BAHA	Brit Activity Holiday Assn
	Brit Alliance Healing Assns
	Brit Assn Hospitality Accountants
BAHID	Brit Assn Human Identification
BAHM	Brit Assn Homoeopathic Mfrs
BAHNO	Brit Assn Head & Neck Oncologists
BAHREP	Brit Assn Hotel Representatives
BAHS	Brit Agricl Hist Soc
BAHSHE	Brit Assn Health Services in Higher Educ
BAHVS	Brit Assn Homoeopathic Veterinary Surgeons
BAILER	Brit Assn Inf & Library Educ & Res
BAIS	Brit Assn Ir Studies
BAJS	Brit Assn Japanese Studies
BAKS	Brit Assn Korean Studies
BALGPS	Bar Assn Local Govt & Public Service
BALH	Brit Assn Local Hist
BALI	Brit Assn Landscape Inds
BALID	Brit Assn Literacy in Devt
BALPA	Brit Air Line Pilots Assn
BALPPA	Brit Assn Leisure Parks, Piers & Attractions
BALR	Brit Assn Lung Research
BAMA	Brit Aerosol Mfrs Assn
BAMM	Brit Assn Med Mgrs
BAMS	Brit Art Medal Soc
BANA	Brit Acoustic Neuroma Assn
BANC	Brit Assn Nature Conservationists
BANS	Brit Assn Numismatic Socs
BANT	Brit Assn Nutritional Therapy
BAO-HNS	Brit Assn Otorhinolaryngologists
BAOMS	Brit Assn Oral & Maxillofacial Surgeons
BAOT/COT	Brit Assn Occupational Therapists
BAP	Brit Assn Psychopharmacology
	Brit Assn Psychotherapists
BAPAM	Brit Assn Performing Arts Medicine
BAPC	Brit Assn Print & Communication
	Brit Aviation Presvn Coun
BAPCO	Brit Assn Public Safety Communications Officers
BAPCR	Brit Assn Paintings Conservator-Restorers
BAPH	Brit Assn Paper Historians
BAPLA	Brit Assn Picture Libraries & Agencies
BAPM	Brit Assn Perinatal Medicine
BAPO	Brit Assn Prosthetists & Orthotists
BAPRAS	Brit Assn Plastic, Reconstructive & Aesthetic Surgeons
BApS	Brit Appaloosa Soc
BAPS	Brit Assn Paediatric Surgeons
	Brit Astrological & Psychic Soc
BAPSH	Brit Assn Purebred Spanish Horse
BAPT	Brit Assn Physical Training
	Brit Assn Play Therapists
	Brit Assn Psychological Type
BAPTO	Brit Assn Pool Table Operators
BAPW	Brit Assn Pharmaceutical Whlsrs
BAR	Brit Assn Removers
BARA	Brit Automation & Robot Assn
BARB	Brit Assn Rose Breeders
BARC	Brit Automobile Racing Club
BARD	Brit Assn Record Dealers
BAREMA	Barema
BARG	Berkshire Archaeology Res Gp
BARLA	Brit Amat Rugby League Assn
BARMA	Boiler & Radiator Mfrs Assn
BARQA	Brit Assn Res Quality Assurance
BARSC	Brit Assn Remote Sensing Companies

BAS	Brit Alpaca Soc
	Brit Ambulance Soc
	Brit Andrology Soc
	Brit Aphasiology Soc
	Brit Assn Steel Bands
	Brit Autogenic Soc
BASA	Black & Asian Studies Assn
	Brit Adhesives & Sealants Assn
	Brit Airgun Shooters' Assn
	Brit Assn Seed Analysts
BASBWE	Brit Assn Symphonic Bands & Wind Ensembles
BASC	Brit Assn Shooting & Consvn
	Brit Assn Skin Camouflage
BASCD	Brit Assn Study Community Dentistry
BASDA	Business Application Software Developers Assn
BASE	Brit Assn Service Elderly
	Brit Assn Supported Employment
BASEA	Brit Airport Services & Eqpt Assn
BASEES	Brit Assn Slavonic & E Eur Studies
BASEM	Brit Assn Sport & Exercise Medicine
BASES	Brit Assn Seating Eqpt Suppliers
	Brit Assn Sport & Exercise Sciences
BASH	Brit Assn Study Headache
BASHH	Brit Assn Sexual Health & HIV
BASI	Brit Assn Snowsport Instructors
BASICS	Brit Assn Immediate Care
BASMA	Boot & Shoe Mfrs Assn
BASO-ACS	BASO
BASPCAN	Brit Assn Study & Prevention Child Abuse
BASR	Brit Assn Study Religions
	Brit Soc Study Religions
BASRT	Brit Assn Sexual & Relationship Therapy
BASSAC	Brit Assn Settlements & Social Action Centres
BASW	Brit Assn Social Workers
BATA	Brit Air Transport Assn
BATB	Brit Assn Tissue Banking
BATC	Brit Apparel & Textile Confedn
BATD	Brit Assn Teachers Dancing
Bath & West	R Bath & W England Soc
BATOD	Brit Assn Teachers Deaf
BAUS	Brit Assn Urological Surgeons
BAVE	Bates Assn Vision Educ
BAW	Basketball Assn Wales
BAWE	Brit Assn Women Entrepreneurs
BB	Boys' Brigade
BBA	Better Brickwork Alliance
	Brit Bankers' Assn
	Brit Biomagnetic Assn
	Brit Bison Assn
	Brit Bobsleigh Assn
	Brit Bridalwear Assn
	Brit Buddhist Assn
	Brit Burn Assn
BBAA	Brit Business Angels Assn
BBAC	Brit Balloon & Airship Club
BBBCS	Brit Belgian Blue Cattle Soc
BBC	Brit Bird Coun
	Brit Bodyboarding Club
BBCC	Brit Bulgarian Cham Comm
BBCS	Brit Beermat Collectors' Soc
	Brit Big Cat Soc
BBCT	Bumblebee Conservation Trust
BBFS	Brit Bulgarian Friendship Soc
BBG	Brit Brands Gp
BBGA	Brit Business & Gen Aviation Assn
BBI	Brit Bottlers' Inst
BBKA	Brit Bee-Keepers' Assn
BBMA	Brit Battery Mfrs Assn
	Brit Bluegrass Music Assn
	Brit Brush Mfrs Assn
BBN	Blue Badge Network
BBO	Brit Ballet Org
BBPA	Brit Bedding & Pot Plant Assn
	Brit Body Piercing Assn
BBRS	Blair Bell Res Soc
BBS	Brit Biophysical Soc
	Brit Boomerang Soc
	Brit Brick Soc

© CBD Research Ltd · Beckenham · BR3 5JS · Tel 020 8650 7745 · Fax 020 8650 0768 · E-mail cbd@cbdresearch.com · www.cbdresearch.com

	Brit Bryological Soc		Brit Cardiovascular Soc
	Brit Button Soc		Brit Carillon Soc
	Brittle Bone Soc		Brit Cartographic Soc
BBSA	Brit Blind & Shutter Assn		Brit Classification Soc
BBTS	Brit Blood Transfusion Soc		Brit Computer Soc
BCA	Brit Cables Assn		Brit Crossbow Soc
	Brit Camelids Assn	BCSA	Brit Constructional Steelwork Assn
	Brit Casino Assn		Brit Cutlery & Silverware Assn
	Brit Caving Assn	BCSC	Brit Coun Shopping Centres
	Brit Cement Assn	BCSS	Brit Cactus & Succulent Soc
	Brit Cheerleading Assn		Brit Charollais Sheep Soc
	Brit Chiropractic Assn	BCT	Bat Consvn Trust
	Brit Confectioners Assn	bctc	Bournemouth Cham Tr & Comm
	Brit Costume Assn	BCTGA	Brit Christmas Tree Growers Assn
	Brit Crystallographic Assn	BCU	Brit Canoe U
bca	Business Centre Assn	BDA	Brick Devt Assn
BCAS	Brit Compressed Air Soc		Brit Deaf Assn
BCBA	Brit Marine Fedn		Brit Dental Assn
BCBC	Brit Cattle Breeders' Club		Brit Dietetic Assn
BCC	Badge Collectors Circle		Brit Doula Assn
	Boston Cham Comm & Ind		Brit Dragon Boat Racing Assn
	Brit Ceramic Confedn		Brit Drilling Assn
	Brit Cham Comm Luxembourg		Brit Dyslexia Assn
	Brit Chams Comm	BDAA	Biodynamic Agricl Assn
	Brit Cleaning Coun	BDF	Ballroom Dancers Fedn
	Brit Cryogenics Coun	BDFA	Batten Disease Family Assn
BCCA	Brit Cheque Cashers Assn		Brit Deer Farmers Assn
BCCB	Brit Cham Comm Belgium		Brit Dried Flowers Assn
BCCBL	Black Country Cham	BDGA	Brit Disc Golf Assn
BCCC	Brit Cham Comm China - Beijing	BDHA	Brit Dental Hygienists Assn
	Brit Chilean Cham Comm	BDMA	Brit Damage Mgt Assn
BCCCA	Biscuit, Cake, Chocolate... Assn	BDO	Brit Darts Org
BCCF	Brit Calcium Carbonates Fedn	BDOA	Brit Domesticated Ostrich Assn
BCCG	Brit Cham Comm Germany	BDPMA	Brit Dental Practice Mgrs Assn
BCCH	Brit Cham Comm Hungary	BDRS	Brit Double Reed Soc
BCCI	Barnsley Cham Comm & Ind	BDS	Brit Dam Soc
	Birmingham Cham Comm & Ind		Brit Deer Soc
	Brit Cham Comm Italy		Brit Display Soc
BCCIB	Brit Cham Comm & Ind Brazil		Brit Dragonfly Soc
BCCJ	Brit Cham Comm Japan		Brit Driving Soc
BCCL	Brit Cham Comm Latvia	BDSC	Brit Deaf Sports Coun
BCCM	Brit Cham Comm Morocco	BDTA	Brit Dental Tr Assn
BCCS	Brit Compact Collectors' Soc	BDWCA	Brit Decoy & Wildfowl Carvers Assn
	Brit Correspondence Chess Soc	BEA	Brit Egg Assn
BCCT	Brit Cham Comm Taipei		Brit Epilepsy Assn
	Brit Cham Comm Thailand	BEAMA	BEAMA
	Brit Cham Comm Turkey	BEAWec	Brit Energy Assn
BCDTA	Brit Chemical Distbrs... Assn	BECA	Brit Exhib Contrs' Assn
BCECA	Brit Chemical Engg Contrs Assn	BECTU	Broadcasting, Entertainment Cinematograph...U
BCF	Brit Coatings Fedn	BEDA	Bar Entertainment & Dance Assn
	Brit Cycling Fedn	BEEF	Buildings Energy Efficiency Fedn
	English Chess Federation	BEF	Brit Equestrian Fedn
BCFA	Brit Contract Furnishing Assn	BEGS	Brit & Eur Geranium Soc
BCG	Brit Chelonia Gp	BEHA	Baby Eqpt Hirers Assn
BCGA	Brit Compressed Gases Assn	BELMAS	Brit Educl Leadership, Mgt & Admin Soc
BCGBA	Brit Crown Green Bowling Assn	BEMA	Brit Engg Mfrs Assn
BCGTMA	Brit Ceramic Gift & Tableware Mfrs' Assn		Brit Essence Mfrs' Assn
BChA	Brit Chiropody & Podiatry Assn	BEMCA	BEAMA
BCHS	Brit Camargue Horse Soc	BEMSEE	Brit Motor Cycle Racing Club
BCI	Business Continuity Inst	BENERGY	BEAMA
BCIA	Brit Clothing Ind Assn	BENHS	Brit Entomological & Natural Hist Soc
BCIS	Building Cost Infm Service	BEOA	Brit Essential Oils Assn
BCLA	Brit Comparative Literature Assn	BEPA	Brit Edible Pulse Assn
	Brit Contact Lens Assn		Brit Egg Products Assn
BCMA	BEAMA	BERA	Brit Educl Res Assn
	Brit Colour Makers Assn	BERSA	Brit Elastic Rope Sports Assn
	Brit Complementary Medicine Assn	BES	Brit Ecological Soc
	Brit Country Music Assn		Brit Endodontic Soc
BCMPA	Brit Contract Mfrs & Packers Assn	BESA	Brit Earth Sheltering Assn
BCO	Brit Coun Offices		Brit Educl Suppliers Assn
	College Optometrists	BESCA	Heating & Ventilating Contrs Assn
BCofC	Bradford Cham Comm & Ind	BETA	Brit Educl Travel Assn
BCPA	Brit Cardiac Patients Assn		Brit Equestrian Tr Assn
BCPS	Brit Connemara Pony Soc	BExA	Brit Exporters Assn
BCRA	Brit Cave Res Assn	BFA	Bee Farmers Assn
BCRC	Brit Cave Rescue Coun		Brit Fedn Audio
BCS	Biblical Creation Soc		Brit Florist Assn
	Black Country Soc		Brit Flyball Assn

	Brit Footwear Assn	BHMA	Brit Herbal Medicine Assn
	Brit Franchise Assn		Brit Holistic Med Assn
	Brit Freediving Assn	BHPA	Brit Hang Gliding & Paragliding Assn
BFAWU	Bakers', Food & Allied Workers' U	BHPR	Brit Health Profls in Rheumatology
BFBB	Brit Fedn Brass Bands	BHPS	Brit Hedgehog Presvn Soc
BFBi	Brewing, Food & Beverage Ind Suppliers Assn	BHRC	Brit Harness Racing Club
BFC	Brit Falconers' Club	BHRS	Bedfordshire Histl Record Soc
	Brit Fire Consortium	BHS	Brit Haiku Soc
BFCMA	Brit Flue & Chimney Mfrs' Assn		Brit Herpetological Soc
BFFF	Brit Frozen Food Fedn		Brit Horn Soc
BFFS	Brit Fedn Film Socs		Brit Horse Soc
BFHS	Brit Fedn Histl Swordplay		Brit Hydrological Soc
BFI	Brit Film Inst		Brit Hypertension Soc
BFIDA	Brit Food Importers & Distrbrs Assn	BHSMA	Brit Hay & Straw Mchts' Assn
BFJA	Brit Fruit Juice Assn	BHSS	Brit Banking History Soc
BFM	BFM Ltd	BHTA	Brit Healthcare Trs Assn
BFMC	Brit Friction Materials Coun		Brit Herb Tr Assn
BFMS	Brit False Memory Soc	BIA	BioIndustry Assn
BFPA	Brit Fluid Power Assn	BIAC	Brit Inst Agricl Consultants
BFPDA	Brit Fluid Power Distrbrs Assn	BIALL	Brit & Ir Assn Law Librarians
BFPSA	Brit Fire Protection Systems Assn	BIAS	Bristol Indl Archaeol Soc
BFREPA	Brit Free Range Egg Producers Assn	BIASLIC	Britain & Ireland Assn Aquatic Science Libraries...
BFS	Brit Fantasy Soc	BIAZA	Brit & Ir Assn Zoos & Aquariums
	Brit Fertility Soc	BIBA	Brit Insurance Brokers' Assn
	Brit Flute Soc		Brit Isles Backgammon Assn
	Brit Fuchsia Soc	BIBBA	Bee Improvement & Bee Breeders Assn
BFSA	Brit Fire Services Assn	BIBC	Brit Isles Bowls Coun
BFSTD	Brit Fedn Sexually Transmitted Diseases	BIBTA	Brit Isles Baton Twirling Assn
BFTA	Brit Fur Tr Assn	BICA	Brit Indoor Cricket Assn
BFVEA	Brit Flower & Vibrational Essences Assn		Brit Infertility Counselling Assn
BFWG	Brit Fedn Women Graduates	BICS	Brit Inst Cleaning Science
BFWMSS	Badger Face Welsh Mountain Sheep Soc	BIDA	Brit Interior Design Assn
BGA	Brit Gear Assn	BIE	Brit Inst Embalmers
	Brit Geomembrane Assn	BIEE	Brit Inst Energy Economics
	Brit Geotechnical Assn	BIFA	Brit Intl Freight Assn
	Brit-German Assn	BIFCA	Brit Indl Furnace Construction Assn
	Brit Gliding Assn	BIFD	Brit Inst Funeral Directors
	Brit Glove Assn	BIFGA	Brit Indep Fruit Growers Assn
	Brit Go Assn	BIFM	Brit Inst Facilities Mgt
BGAS	Bristol & Gloucestershire Archaeol Soc	BIG	Brit Inst Graphologists
BGCS	Boys' & Girls' Clubs Scotland	BIGGA	Brit & Intl Golf Greenkeepers' Assn
BGIA	Brit Golf Ind Assn	BII	Brit Inst Innkeeping
BGJA	Brit-German Jurists' Assn	BIIBC	Brit Isles Indoor Bowls Coun
BGMA	Brit Generic Mfrs' Assn	BIICL	Brit Inst Intl & Comparative Law
BGS	Brit Geriatrics Soc	BIIS	Breast Implant Inf Soc
	Brit Gladiolus Soc	BILA	Brit Insurance Law Assn
	Brit Goat Soc	BILD	Brit Inst Learning Disabilities
	Brit Grassland Soc	BILETA	Brit & Ir Legal Educ Technology Assn
BGSS	Brit Gotland Sheep Soc	BIMA	Brit Interactive Media Assn
BGTW	Brit Gld Travel Writers	BIMM	Brit Inst Musculoskeletal Medicine
BH&HPA	Brit Holiday & Home Parks Assn	BIMTA	Brit Indep Motor Tr Assn
BHA	Brit Hamster Assn	BINST	BEAMA
	Brit Hawking Assn	BInstNDT	Brit Inst Non-Destructive Testing
	Brit Homoeopathic Assn	BIOA	Brit & Ir Ombudsman Assn
	Brit Horseball Assn	BIOG	Defence Mfrs Assn
	Brit Hospitality Assn	BIOS	Brit Inst Organ Studies
	Brit Humanist Assn		Brit & Ir Orthoptic Soc
	Brit Hydropower Assn	BIPA	Brit Internet Publishers Alliance
	Brit Hypnotherapy Assn	BIPDT	Brit Inst Profl Dog Trainers
BHAB	Brit Helicopter Advy Bd	BIPEA	Brit Indep Plastic Extruders Assn
BHBF	Brit Marine Fedn	BIPP	Brit Inst Profl Photography
BHBIA	Brit Healthcare Business Intelligence Assn	BIPS	Brit Inst Persian Studies
BHCA	Brit Health Care Assn	BIR	Brit Inst Radiology
BHCC	Brit Hellenic Cham Comm	BIS	Brit Interlingua Soc
BHCF	Brit Marine Fedn		Brit Interplanetary Soc
BHECTA	Brit Hardmetal & Engineers' Cutting Tool Assn		Brit Iris Soc
BHF	Brit Hardware Fedn		Brit Italian Soc
	Brit Horological Fedn	BISA	Brit Intl Studies Assn
BHG	Brit Hat Gld	BiSHA	Brit Inline Skater Hockey Assn
	Horticultural Trs Assn	BISL	Brit Inst Securities Laws
BHGS	Brit Histl Games Soc	BITA	Brit Indl Truck Assn
BHHMA	Brit Hardware & Housewares Mfrs Assn		Brit Interior Textiles Assn
BHHS	Brit Hosta & Hemerocallis Soc	BIVDA Ltd	Brit In Vitro Diagnostics Assn
BHI	Brit Horological Inst	BIVR	Brit Inst Verbatim Reporters
BHIVA	Brit HIV Assn	BJA	Boat Jumble Assn
BHKC	Brit Hand Knitting Confedn		Brit Jewellers Assn
BHL	Brit Housewives League		Brit Judo Assn
		BJGF	Brit Jewellery, Giftware & Finishing Fedn

BJPL	Brit Jigsaw Puzzle Library	BNEA	Brit Naval Eqpt Assn
BJS	Brit Jazz Soc	BNES	Brit Nuclear Energy Soc
BKA	Brit Kodály Academy	BNF	Brit Nutrition Foundation
	Brit Korfball Assn	BNFA	Brit Narrow Fabrics Assn
BKKPS	Brit Kune Kune Pig Soc	BNFMF	Brit Non-Ferrous Metals Fedn
BKPA	Brit Kidney Patient Assn	BNHS	Birmingham Natural Hist Soc
BKSTS	BKSTS		Brit Natural Hygiene Soc
BLA	Brit Learning Assn	BNMA	Brit Number Plate Mfrs Assn
	Brit Legal Assn	BNMAA	Brit Nat Martial Arts Assns
	Brit Lime Assn	BNMS	Brit Nuclear Medicine Soc
BLC	BLC, Leather Technology Centre	BNPA	Brit Neuropsychiatry Assn
BLCC	Belgian-Luxembourg Cham Comm GB	BNS	Brit Neuropathological Soc
BLCS	Brit Limousin Cattle Soc		Brit Numismatic Soc
BLDSA	Brit Long Distance Swimming Assn		Britain Nepal Soc
BLESMA	Brit Limbless Ex-Service Men's Assn	BNTA	Brit Numismatic Tr Assn
BLF	Brit Lace Fedn	BNTL	Brit Nat Temperance League
BLISS	BLISS	BNZTC	Brit New Zealand Tr Coun
BLMA	Brit Ladder Mfrs Assn	BOA	Brit Olympic Assn
BLMRA	Brit Lawn Mower Racing Assn		Brit Oncological Assn
BLPS	Brit Lop Pig Soc		Brit Orthopaedic Assn
BLS	Branch Line Soc		Brit Osteopathic Assn
	Brit Lichen Soc	BOBMA	Brit Oat & Barley Millers Assn
	Brit Llama Soc	BOC	Brit Orchid Coun
	Brit Lymphology Soc		Brit Ornithologists Club
BLSA	Brit Land Speedsail Assn	BODMA	Brit Oncology Data Mgrs Assn
BLSBA	Bluefaced Leicester Sheep Breeders Assn	BODY	Brit Organ Donor Soc
BMA	Bathroom Mfrs' Assn	BOF	Brit Orienteering Fedn
	Brit Med Assn		Brit Othello Fedn
BMAA	Brit Microlight Aircraft Assn	BOFSS	Brit Orthopaedic Foot Surgery Soc
BMAPA	Brit Marine Aggregate Producers' Assn	BOGA	Brit Orchid Growers Assn
BMAS	Brit Med Acupuncture Soc	BOHS	Brit Occupational Hygiene Soc
BMC	Brit Mountaineering Coun	BOOBA	Brit Olive Oil Buyer's Assn
BMEA	Brit Marine Eqpt Assn	BOPA	Brit Outdoor Profls Assn
	Brit Marine Fedn	BORDA	Brit Off-Road Driving Assn
BMF	Brit Marine Fedn		Brit Oriental Rug Dealers Assn
	Brit Motorcyclists Fedn	BOS	Brit Origami Soc
	Builders Mchts Fedn		Brit Orthodontic Soc
BMFA	Brit Marine Finfish Assn	BOSS	Brit Obesity Surgery Soc
	Brit Model Flying Assn	BOU	Brit Ornithologists U
BMG	Brit Assn Mountain Guides	BPA	Baby Products Assn
BMHA	Brit Malignant Hyperthermia Assn		Brit Packaging Assn
BMHF	Brit Materials Handling Fedn		Brit Parachute Assn
BMHS	Brit Miniature Horse Soc		Brit Paralympic Assn
	Brit Morgan Horse Soc		Brit Parking Assn
	Brit Music Hall Soc		Brit Pig Assn
BMI	Birmingham & Mid Inst		Brit Porphyria Assn
BML&BS	Brit Matchbox, Label & Booklet Soc		Brit Ports Assn
BMLA	Brit Maritime Law Assn		Brit Psychodrama Assn
	Brit Med Laser Assn	BPA(FMG)	Brit Pyrotechnists' Assn
BMLDA	Brit Manual Lymph Drainage Assn	BPC	Backpackers Club
BMLSS	Brit Marine Life Study Soc		Brit Peanut Coun
BMMC	Brit Motorsport Marshals Club		Brit Poultry Coun
BMPA	Brit Meat Processors Assn		Brit Psychoanalytic Coun
BMPCA	Brit Metallurgical Plant Constructors Assn	BPCA	Brit Pest Control Assn
BMRA	Brit Metals Recycling Assn	BPCC	Brit-Peruvian Cham Comm
BMS	Brit Magical Soc		Brit-Polish Cham Comm
	Brit Malaysian Soc		Brit-Polish Cham Comm [London]
	Brit Masonry Soc		Brit-Portuguese Cham Comm
	Brit Menopause Soc	BPCF	Brit Precast Concrete Fedn
	Brit Mexican Soc	BPEX	British Pig Executive
	Brit Microcirculation Soc	BPF	Brit Plastics Fedn
	Brit Moroccan Soc		Brit Polio Fellowship
	Brit Mule Soc		Brit Property Fedn
	Brit Museum Friends	BPFMA	Brit Plumbing Fittings Mfrs Assn
	Brit Music Soc	BPG	Brit Photodermatology Gp
	Brit Mycological Soc	BPGMA	Pressure Gauge & Dial Thermometer Assn
BMSS	Brit Model Soldier Soc	BPGS	Brit Pelargonium Geranium Soc
BMTA	Brit Measurement & Testing Assn		Brit Plant Gall Soc
BMUS	Brit Med Ultrasound Soc	BPHS	Brit Percheron Horse Soc
BMVA	Brit Machine Vision Assn...	BPI	Brit Phonographic Ind
BNA	Brit Naturalists Assn	BPIF	Brit Printing Inds Fedn
	Brit Naturopathic Assn	BPMA	Brit Promotional Merchandise Assn
	Brit Neuroscience Assn		Brit Pump Mfrs Assn
	Britain-Nigeria Assn	BPMTG	Brit Puppet & Model Theatre Gld
BNARA	Brit N Amer Res Assn	BPOWER	BEAMA
BNC	Berwickshire Naturalists Club	BPPA	Brit Precision Pilots Assn
BNCC	Britain-Nepal Cham Comm		Soc Wedding & Portrait Photographers
BNCS	Brit Nat Carnation Soc	BPRS	Brit Polarological Res Soc

BPS	Brit Palomino Soc	BSDA	Brit Sheep Dairying Assn
	Brit Pharmacological Soc		Brit Soft Drinks Assn
	Brit Postmark Soc	BSDB	Brit Soc Developmental Biology
	Brit Printing Soc	BSDH	Brit Soc Disability & Oral Health
	Brit Psychological Soc	BSDMFR	Brit Soc Dental & Maxillofacial Radiology
	Brit Pteridological Soc	BSDR	Brit Soc Dental Res
BPTA	Briar Pipe Tr Assn	BSECH	Brit Soc Experimental & Clinical Hypnosis
	Brit Polyolefin Textiles Assn	BSEM	Brit Soc Ecological Medicine
BPW UK Ltd	Business & Profl Women	BSES	BSES Expeditions
BQF	Brit Quality Foundation	BSF	Biosciences Fedn
BRA	Brit Records Assn		Brit Shogi Fedn
	Brit Reflexology Assn		Brit Soc Flavourists
	Brit Refrigeration Assn	BSFA	Brit Science Fiction Assn
BRADA	Brit Resorts & Destinations Assn	BSG	Brit Soc Gastroenterology
BrAPP	Brit Assn Pharmaceutical Physicians		Brit Soc Gerontology
BRBA	Brit Marine Fedn		Brit Stickmakers Gld
BRBMA	Ball & Roller Bearing Mfrs Assn		Brit Sugarcraft Gld
BRC	Brit Rabbit Coun	BSGA	Brit Sign & Graphics Assn
	Brit Retail Consortium	BSGB	Bead Soc
BRCA	Brit Radio Car Assn	BSGDS	Brit Soc Gen Dental Surgery
BRCS	Brit Red Cross Soc	BSGE	Brit Soc Gynaecological Endoscopy
BRGA	Brit Reed Growers Assn	BSH	Brit Soc Haematology
	Brit Rose Growers Assn		Brit Soc Hypnotherapists
BRIC	Brit Refractories & Indl Ceramics	BSHAA	Brit Soc Hearing Aid Audiologists
BRINDEX	Assn Brit Indep Oil Exploration Cos	BSHC&RHA	Brit Show Hack... & Riding Horse Assn
BRISC	Biological Recording Scotland	BSHG	Brit Soc Human Genetics
BRISMES	Brit Soc Middle Eastn Studies	BSHM	Brit Soc Hist Mathematics
Britpave	Britpave		Brit Soc Hist Medicine
BRMA	Brit Rubber Mfrs Assn	BSHP	Brit Soc Hist Pharmacy
BRMCA	Brit Ready Mixed Concrete Assn		Brit Soc Hist Philosophy
BROA	Brit Rig Owners Assn	BSHS	Brit Soc Hist Science
BRPS	Bluebell Rly Presvn Soc	BSI	Brit Soc Immunology
	Brit Retinitis Pigmentosa Soc		Brit Suzuki Inst
BRS	Bone Res Soc	BSIA	Brit Security Ind Assn
BRSA	Brit Rope Skipping Assn		Brit Starch Ind Assn
BRSCC	Brit Racing & Sports Car Club	BSIF	Brit Safety Ind Fedn
BRTMA	Brit Rootzone & Top Dressing Mfrs Assn	BSKF	Brit Shorinji Kempo Fedn
BRUFMA	Brit Rigid Urethane Foam Mfrs Assn	BSM	Brit Soc Miniaturists
BS	Beaumont Soc	BSMA	Building Socs Mems Assn
	Brit Marine Fedn	BSMDH	Brit Soc Med & Dental Hypnosis
	Budgerigar Soc	BSME	Brit Soc Magazine Editors
BS-AC	Brit Sub-Aqua Club	BSMFD	Brit Soc Mercury Free Dentistry
BSA	Boarding Schools Assn	BSMGP	Brit Soc Master Glass Painters
	Brit Sandwich Assn	BSMM	Brit Soc Med Mycology
	Brit Soc Aesthetics	BSMT	Brit Soc Music Therapy
	Brit Soc Audiology	BSNR	Brit Soc Neuroradiologists
	Brit Sociological Assn	BSOE	Brit Soc Enamellers
	Brit Stammering Assn	BSOM	Brit Soc Oral Medicine
	Brit Surfing Assn	BSOP	Brit Soc Oral & Maxillofacial Pathology
	Building Socs Assn	BSP	Brit Soc Parasitology
	Business Services Assn		Brit Soc Perfumers
	Business Software Alliance		Brit Soc Periodontology
BSAC	Brit Soc Antimicrobial Chemotherapy	BSPA	Brit Skewbald & Piebald Assn
BSACI	Brit Soc Allergy & Clinical Immunology		Brit Speedway Promoters Assn
BSAS	Brit Sausage Appreciation Soc	BSPB Ltd	Brit Soc Plant Breeders
	Brit Soc Animal Science	BSPOGA	Brit Soc Psychosomatic Obstetrics...
BSAVA	Brit Small Animal Veterinary Assn	BSPP	Brit Soc Plant Pathology
BSBA	Brit Marine Fedn	BSpPS	Brit Spotted Pony Soc
BSBI	Botanical Soc Brit Isles	BSPR	Brit Soc Proteome Res
BSBSPA	Brit Sugar Beet Seed Producers Assn	BSPS	Brit Show Pony Soc
BSC	Brit Comedy Soc		Brit Soc Philosophy Science
	Brit Soc Cinematographers		Brit Soc Population Studies
	Brit Soc Criminology	BSR	Brit Soc Rheology
BSCB	Brit Soc Cell Biology		Brit Soc Rheumatology
BSCC	Brit Shell Collectors Club	BSRA	Brit Soc Res Ageing
	Brit Soc Clinical Cytology		Brit Sound Recording Assn
	Brit Swedish Cham Comm Sweden	BSRD	Brit Soc Restorative Dentistry
	Brit-Swiss Cham Comm [Lond]	BSRIA	BSRIA
	Brit-Swiss Cham Comm [Switzerland]	BSRM	Brit Soc Rehabilitation Medicine
BSCD	Brit Ski Club Disabled	BSS	Botanical Soc Scotland
BSCDA	Brit Stock Car Drivers Assn		Brit Sleep Soc
BSCH	Brit Soc Clinical Hypnosis		Brit Standards Soc
BSCN	Brit Soc Clinical Neurophysiology		Brit Sundial Soc
BSCPIA	Brit Soluble Coffee Packers & Importers Assn	bssa	Brit Shops & Stores Assn
BSCRA	Brit Slot Car Racing Assn	BSSA	Brit Sjogren's Syndrome Assn
BSCS	Brit Simmental Cattle Soc		Brit Stainless Steel Assn
BSCW	Brit Soc Comedy Writers	BSSAA	Brit Snoring & Sleep Apnoea Assn
BSD	Brit Soc Dowsers	BSSC	Brit Shooting Sports Coun

© CBD Research Ltd · Beckenham · BR3 5JS · Tel 020 8650 7745 · Fax 020 8650 0768 · E-mail cbd@cbdresearch.com · www.cbdresearch.com

BSSG	Brit Soc Scientific Glassblowers
BSSH	Brit Soc Surgery Hand
BSSM	Brit Soc Sexual Medicine
	Brit Soc Strain Measurement
BSSO	Bristol Steamship Owners' Assn
	Brit Scooter Sport Org
BSSPD	Brit Soc Study Prosthetic Dentistry
BSSS	Brit Soc Soil Science
BSTP	Brit Soc Toxicological Pathologists
BSUK	BaseballSoftballUK
BTA	Brit Tinnitus Assn
	Brit Toilet Assn
	Brit Triathlon Assn
	Brit Trout Assn
	Brit Tugowners Assn
BTAA	Brit Travelgoods & Accessories Assn
BTAF	Brit Tattoo Artists Fedn
BTBA	Brit Tenpin Bowling Assn
BTC	BTC Testing Advisory Gp
BTCA	Brit Tennis Coaches Assn
BTCV	Brit Trust Consvn Volunteers
BTDA	Brit Theatre Dance Assn
BTG	Brit Toymakers Gld
BTHA	Brit Toy & Hobby Assn
	Brit Travel Health Assn
BTHG	Birmingham Transport Histl Gp
BTIA	Brit Toy Importers Assn
BTLIA	Brit Turf & Landscape Irrigation Assn
BTMA	Brit Textile Machinery Assn
	Brit Turned-Parts Mfrs Assn
BTO	Brit Trust Ornithology
BTOG	Brit Transport Officers Gld
BTRA	Brit Truck Racing Assn
BTS	Brit Tarantula Soc
	Brit Technion Soc
	Brit Temperance Soc
	Brit Titanic Soc
	Brit Toxicology Soc
	Brit Transplantation Soc
	Brit Trolleybus Soc
	Brit Trombone Soc
	Brit Tunnelling Soc
	Britain-Tanzania Soc
	Business Tourism Scotland
BTSA	Brit Tensional Strapping Assn
BTSS	Brit Texel Sheep Soc
BTTG	Brit Textile Technology Gp
BU	Baptist U
BUAV	Brit U Abolition Vivisection
BUFCA	Brit Urethane Foam Contrs Assn
BUFORA	Brit UFO Res Assn
BUFVC	Brit Universities Film & Video Coun
BUIRA	Brit Universities Indl Relations Assn
BUPMSA	Brit Used Printing Machinery Supplrs Assn
BURA	Brit Urban Regeneration Assn
BUSA	Brit Universities Sports Assn
BUUK	Bus Users UK
BVA	Brit Veterinary Assn
	Brit Video Assn
	Brit Voice Assn
BVAA	Brit Valve & Actuator Assn
BVC	Brit Vacuum Coun
BVCA	BVCA
BVCS	Brit Veterinary Camelid Soc
BVF	Brit Volleyball Fedn
BVHA	Brit Veterinary Hospitals Assn
BVMA	Brit Violin Making Assn
BVNA	Brit Veterinary Nursing Assn
BVRLA	Brit Vehicle Rental & Leasing Assn
BVS	Battery Vehicle Soc
BVSF	Brit Vehicle Salvage Fedn
BVWS	Brit Vintage Wireless Soc
BWA	Bonded Warehousekeepers' Assn
	Bridge Deck Waterproofing Assn
	Brit Waterbed Assn
	Brit Waterfowl Assn
	Brit Westerners Assn

	Brit Woodcarvers Assn
	Brit Wrestling Assn
BWAHDA	Brit Warm Air Hand Drier Assn
BWAS	Birmingham & Warwickshire Archaeol Soc
BWBA	Brit Wheelchair Bowls Assn
	Brit Wild Boar Assn
BWBS	Brit Warm-Blood Soc
BWCA	Brit Water Cooler Assn
BWCMG	Brit Watch & Clock Makers Gld
BWCS	Brit White Cattle Soc
BWDA2000	Brit Western Dance Assn
BWDMA	Brit Web Design Marketing Assn
BWEA	Brit Wind Energy Assn
BWF	Brit Walking Fedn
	Brit Woodworking Fedn
BWLA	Brit Weight Lifters Assn
BWMA	Brit Weights & Measures Assn
BWPA	Brit Women Pilots Assn
	Brit Wood Pulp Assn
BWPDA	Brit Wood Preserving & Damp-proofing Assn
BWRA	Brit Whippet Racing Assn
BWS	Brit Watercolour Soc
BWSF	Brit Water Ski Fedn
BWTA	Brit Wood Turners Assn
BWY	Brit Wheel Yoga
BYBA	Brit Youth Band Assn
BZA	Brit Zen Aiki Assn
	Brit Zeolite Assn
BZS	Britain-Zimbabwe Soc

C

CA	Classical Assn
	Composting Assn
	Consumers' Assn
	Croquet Assn
	Cruising Assn
CAA	Cathedral Architects Assn
	Cement Admixtures Assn
	Cinema Advertising Assn
	Concert Artistes' Association
CAAA	County Antrim Agricl Assn
CAABU	Coun Advancement Arab-Brit Understanding
CAAT	Campaign Arms Trade
CAAV	Central Assn Agricl Valuers
CAB	Coun Aluminium Bldg
CABFAA	Coach & Bus First Aid Assn
CAC	Campaign Censorship
CADAS	Coventry & District Archaeol Soc
CADD	Campaign Drinking & Driving
CAEF	Campaign Euro-federalism
CAGC	Welsh Folk Song Soc
CAH	Campaign Hysterectomy &…Operations on Women
CAI	Confedn Aerial Inds
CAJ	C'ee Admin Justice [NI]
CAMILK	Campaign Real Milk
CAMRA	Campaign Real Ale
CANI	Canoe Assn NI
CAPEL	Capel
CAPPA	Compulsory Annuity Purchase Protest Alliance
CAPS	Captive Animal Protection Soc
CAS	Caithness Agricl Soc
	Cambridge Antiquarian Soc
	Cheshire Agricl Soc
	Chester Archaeol Soc
	Citizens Advice Scotland
	Contemporary Art Soc
	Cornwall Archaeol Soc
CASE	Campaign Science & Engg UK
	Campaign State Educ
CASH	Campaign Stage Hypnosis
CASS GB	Clarinet & Saxophone Soc GB
CASW	Contemporary Art Soc Wales
CATRA	Cutlery & Allied Trs Res Assn

CAWS	County Armagh Wildlife Soc
CBA	Canal Boatbuilders Assn
	Coun Brit Archaeology
	Criminal Bar Assn [E&W]
CBBC	Caribbean-Brit Business Coun
	China-Britain Business Coun
CBC	Conservatoires UK
CBDG	Concrete Bridge Devt Gp
CBHS	Children's Books Hist Soc
	Cleveland Bay Horse Soc
CBI	Confedn Brit Ind
CBOA	Comml Boat Operators Assn
CBS(UK)	Caspian Breed Soc
CBSI	Confedn Brit Security Ind
CBSL	Carnival Band Secretaries League
CBWT	Confedn Brit Wool Textiles
CC	Construction Confedn
CCA	Chilled Ceilings Assn
	Company Chemists Assn
	Consumer Credit Assn
	Customer Contact Assn
CCAA	Children's Chronic Arthritis Assn
CCAB	Cámara Comercio Argentino Britanica
CCBN	Central Coun Brit Naturism
CCC	Cambridgeshire Chams Comm
	Club Cricket Conf
	Cumbria Cham Comm
CCCB	Cámara Comercio Colombo-Británica
CCCC	Canal Card Collectors Circle
	Clarice Cliff Collectors Club
CCCI	Cornwall Cham Comm & Ind
CCFA	Combined Cadet Force Assn
CCFGB	Chambre Comm Française GB
CCFRA	Campden & Chorleywood Food Res Assn
CCG	Comics Creators Gld
CCGB	Cartoonists' Club
CCI	Chambers Ireland
CCMAUK	Call Centre Mgt Assn
CCMM	Cornish Cham Mines & Minerals
CCRA	Clinical Contract Res Assn
CCS	Circular Chess Soc
	Commemorative Collectors Soc
	Computer Consvn Soc
	Confedn Construction Specialists
CCSA	Cathedral & Church Shops Assn
CCT	Chesterfield Canal Trust
CCTA	Consumer Credit Tr Assn
CCUA	Civil Court Users Assn
CDA	Central Dredging Assn
	Chemists Defence Assn
	Copper Devt Assn
	Country Doctors Assn
CDB	Coun Docked Breeds
CDdWC	Cymdeithas Ddawns Werin Cymru
CDET	Coun Dance Educ & Training
cdfa	Community Devt Finance Assn
CDNA	Community & District Nursing Assn
CDS	Conf Drama Schools
CDTA	Clinical Dental Technicians Assn
CE	Christian Endeavour U
CEA	Cinema Exhibitors Assn
	Combustion Engg Assn
	Construction Eqpt Assn
CECA	Civil Engg Contrs' Assn
CEDA	Catering Eqpt Distbrs Assn GB
CEDIA UK	Custom Electronic Design & Installation Assn
CEF	Construction Emplrs Fedn
CEFF	Confedn Engl Fly Fishers
CEI	Cycle Engrs' Inst
CEM	Christian Educ
	College Emergency Medicine
CENTA	Combined Edible Nut Tr Assn
CERAM	Brit Ceramic Res
CES	Christian Evidence Soc
CESA	Catering Eqpt Supplier's Assn
CFA	Chilled Food Assn
	Circus Friends Assn
	Construction Fixings Assn

	Contract Flooring Assn
	Craft Gld Chefs
CFBA	Canine & Feline Behaviour Assn
CFDG	Charity Finance Directors' Gp
CFDS	Campaign Dark Skies
CFHS	Catholic Family Hist Soc
CFI	Campaign Freedom Infm
	Campaign Industry
CFMA	Chair Frame Mfrs Assn
CFOA	Chief Fire Officers Assn
CFOI/CFI	Campaign Freedom Infm
CFTCC	Campaign Traditional Cathedral Choir
CGA	Country Gentlemen's Assn
CGF	Child Growth Foundation
CGGB	Ciné Glds GB
	Colour Gp
CGS	Contemporary Glass Soc
	Cottage Garden Soc
CGTBF	Craft Gld Traditional Bowyers & Fletchers
CHA	Children's Heart Assn
	Comml Horticl Assn
	Community Hospitals Assn
CHAPS(UK)	Coloured Horse & Pony Soc
CHCS	Chemical Hazards Communication Soc
CHE	Campaign Homosexual Equality
CHEM	Container Handling Eqpt Mfrs Assn
CHF	Crystal & Healing Fedn
CHI	Support Soc Children High Intelligence
CHME	Coun Hospitality Mgt Educ
CHO	Confedn Healing Orgs
CHPA	Combined Heat & Power Assn
CHS	Caernarvonshire Histl Soc
	Caspian Horse Soc
	Clarinet Heritage Soc
	Clydesdale Horse Soc
CHSA	Cleaning & Hygiene Suppliers' Assn
CIA	Chemical Inds Assn
CIArb	Chart Inst Arbitrators
CIAT	Chart Inst Architectural Technologists
CIB	Campaign Indep Britain
CIBSE	Chart Instn Bldg Services Engrs
CIC	Construction Ind Coun
CICA	Chemical & Indl Consultants' Assn
	Construction Ind Computing Assn
CIDDA	Cast Iron Drainage Devt Assn
CIEH	Chart Inst Envtl Health
CIF	Cork Ind Fedn
CIFE	Coun Indep Educ
CIFMA	Corpn Insurance, Financial & Mortgage Advisers
CiG	City Inf Gp
CIG	Conf Interpreters Gp
CII	Chart Insurance Inst
CIIG	Construction Ind Inf Gp
CILA	Chart Inst Loss Adjusters
CILIP	CILIP
CILT(UK)	Chart Inst Logistics & Transport UK
CIM	Chart Inst Marketing
CIMA	Cereal Ingredients Mfrs' Assn
	Chart Inst Mgt Accountants
CIOB	Chart Inst Bldg
CIoH	Chart Inst Housing
CIPA	Chart Inst Patent Attorneys
CIPD	Chart Inst Personnel & Devt
CIPFA	CIPFA
CIPR	Chart Inst Public Relations
CIPS	Chart Inst Purchasing & Supply
	Choice in Personal Safety
CIRIA	Construction Ind Res & Infm Assn
CITE	Construction Ind Trading Electronically
CIU	Working Men's Club & Inst U
CIWEM	Chart Instn Water & Envtl Management
CIWM	Chart Instn Wastes Mgt
CKS	Coble & Keelboat Soc
CL&CGB	Church Lads & Church Girls Brigade
CLA	Care Leavers Assn
	Country Land & Business Assn
CLAPA	Cleft Lip & Palate Assn
CLEANAIR	CLEANAIR

© CBD Research Ltd · Beckenham · BR3 5JS · Tel 020 8650 7745 · Fax 020 8650 0768 · E-mail cbd@cbdresearch.com · www.cbdresearch.com

CLHS	Cambridgeshire Local Hist Soc
Climb	Children Living Inherited Metabolic Diseases
CLING	Defence Mfrs Assn
CLOA	Chief Cultural & Leisure Officers Assn
CLÉ	CLÉ
CMA	Cardiomyopathy Assn
	Communications Mgt Assn
	Community Media Assn
	Complementary Med Assn
	Countryside Mgt Assn
CMAS Ltd	Coal Mchts Assn Scotland
CMF	Cast Metals Fedn
	Coal Mchts Fedn
CMI	Chart Mgt Inst
CML	Coun Mortgage Lenders
CMP	Coalition Medical Progress
CMPE	Contractors Mechanical Plant Engrs
CMS	Church Monuments Soc
	Cricket Memorabilia Soc
CMT	Commemoratives Museum Trust
CMYF	Charlotte M Yonge Fellowship
CNCS	Campaign Nat Community Service
CND	Campaign Nuclear Disarmament
CNHSS	Croydon Natural Hist & Scientific Soc
CNITA	Chart & Nautical Instrument Tr Assn
CNS	Cardiff Naturalists Soc
COA	Cathedral Organists Assn
COALPRO	Confedn UK Coal Producers
COBSEO	Confedn Brit Service & Ex-Service Orgs
CoDA	Co-Dependents Anonymous
CODE	Confedn Dental Emplrs
COF	Coach Operators Fedn
CofCS	Coun Cricket Socs
COG	Component Obsolescence Gp
COGasSafety	Carbon Monoxide & Gas Safety Soc
COGDEM	Coun Gas Detection & Envtl Monitoring
Cognition	Cognition
COMA	Coke Oven Mgrs Assn
COMBAR	Comml Bar Assn
COMPASS	Central Org Maritime Pastimes...
COMPETA	Computer & Peripherals Eqpt Tr Assn
ConfEd	Confedn Children's Services Mgrs
CONFOR	Confedn Forest Inds
Construct	Construct, Concrete Structures Gp
CORCA	C'ee Registered Clubs Assns
CORDA	Coronary Artery Disease Res Assn
CORE	Comment Reproductive Ethics
CORGI	Coun Registered Gas Installers
CORH	Coun Orgs Registering Homeopaths
COS	Cinema Organ Soc
COSCA	COSCA
COSLA	Convention Scot Local Authorities
COT	Mansfield & Dist Cham Tr & Comm
COTIS	Confedn Transcribed Inf Services
CP	Cats Protection
CPA	Charities Property Assn
	Chiropractic Patients' Assn
	City Property Assn
	Composites Processing Assn
	Concert Promoters Assn
	Construction Plant-hire Assn
	Construction Products Assn
	Consumer Protection Assn
	Cornish Pasty Assn
	Craft Potters Assn
	Credit Protection Assn
	Crop Protection Assn
	Inst Certified Public Accountants Ireland
CPAS	Car Park Appreciation Soc
CPBF	Campaign Press & Broadcasting Freedom
CPCC	Caithness Paperweight Collectors Club
CPDA	Clay Pipe Devt Assn
CPF	Campaign Philosophical Freedom
	Crystal Palace Foundation
CPI	Confedn Paper Inds
CPRE	Campaign Protect Rural England
CPRW	Campaign Protection Rural Wales

CPS	Cambridge Philosophical Soc
	Carnivorous Plant Soc
CPSA	Clay Pigeon Shooting Assn
CPT	Confedn Passenger Transport
CR/Ea/	Composting Assn Ireland
CRA	Caledonian Rly Assn
	Chemical Recycling Assn
	Concrete Repair Assn
	Creator's Rights Alliance
	Crime Reporters Assn
CRAE	Children's Rights Alliance England
CRC	Confedn Roofing Contrs
CRCA	Comml Radio Companies Assn
CRE	Campaign Real Educ
CReSTeD	Coun Registration Schools Teaching Dyslexic Pupils
CRM Soc	Charles Rennie Mackintosh Soc
CRNAF	Campaign Restoration Nat Anthem & Flag
CRS	Cambridgeshire Records Soc
	Catholic Record Soc
	Conflict Res Soc
CRSA	Cold Rolled Sections Assn
CRT	Cambridge Refrigeration Technology
CRTC	Clay Roof Tile Coun
CRUSE	Cruse - Bereavement Care
CSA	Channel Swimming Assn
	Choir Schools Assn
	Commissioning Specialists Assn
	Coun Scot Archaeology
	Credit Services Assn
	Cued Speech Assn
CSAR	Cambridge Soc Application Res
CSBS	Community Self Build Scotland
CSD	Chart Soc Designers
CSDF	Cold Storage & Distbn Fedn
CSEU	Confedn Shipbuilding & Engg Us
CSGBI	Conchological Soc
CSJ	Confraternity Saint James
CSMA	Cementitious Slag Makers Assn
CSO	Christian Social Order
CSP	Chart Soc Physiotherapy
CSRG	Children's Services Res Gp
CSS	Costume Soc Scotland
	County Surveyors Soc
CSSA	Cleaning & Support Services Assn
CSTA	Craniosacral Therapy Assn
CSV	Community Service Volunteers
CTA	Cinema Theatre Assn
	Comml Trailer Assn
	Community Transport Assn
CTAUK	Chinese Takeaway Assn (UK)
CTC	Coach Tourism Coun
	Cyclists Touring Club
CTF	Coffee Tr Fedn
CTHCM	Confedn Tourism, Hotel & Catering Mgt
CTMA	Brit Civil Engg Test Eqpt Mfrs Assn
CTPA	Cosmetic, Toiletry & Perfumery Assn
CTRG	Charities' Tax Reform Gp
CTT	Cycling Time Trials
CU	Casualties Union
	Catholic U
CURL	CURL
CVBC	Cámara Venezolana Británica Comercio
CWA	Careers Writers' Assn
	Crime Writers Assn
CWAAS	Cumberland & Westmorland Antiquarian... Soc
CWU	Communication Workers U
CWW	Circle Wine Writers
CYWU	Community & Youth Workers U

D

D&AD	D&AD
DA	Depression Alliance
	Design Assn
	Despatch Assn

DAAS	Dad's Army Appreciation Soc
DACS	Design & Artists Copyright Soc
DAHS	Derbyshire Agricl & Horticl Soc
DALES PS	Dales Pony Soc
DAS	Derbyshire Archaeol Soc
	Devon Archaeol Soc
	Dorchester Agricl Soc
DASA	Domestic Appliance Service Assn
DATA	Design & Technology Assn
DAW	Drama Assn Wales
DBA	Design Business Assn
	Dutch Barge Assn
DBC	Deaf Broadcasting Coun
DBS	Donkey Breed Soc
DCA	District Courts Assn
DCAA	Devon County Agricl Assn
DCAS	Durham County Agricl Soc
DCBS	Devon Cattle Breeders' Soc
DCCE	Doncaster Cham Comm
DCCI	Dorset Cham Comm & Ind
DCF	Digital Content Forum
DCLHS	Durham County Local Hist Soc
DCRS	Devon & Cornwall Record Soc
DCS	Diecasting Soc
DDA	Dispensing Doctors Assn
DDS	Dawn Duellists' Soc
DDSBA	Dorset Down Sheep Breeders Assn
DEA	Devt Educ Assn
DEBRA	Dystrophic Epidermolysis Bullosa Res Assn
DELTA	Deaf Educ Listening & Talking
DES	Drake Exploration Soc
DFI	Disability Fedn Ireland
DFSG	Duchenne Family Support Gp
DGGB	Directors Gld
DGNHAS	Dumfriesshire & Galloway Natural Hist… Soc
DGSS	Derbyshire Gritstone Sheepbreeders Soc
DHAPS	Dun Horse & Pony Soc
DHDS	Dolmetsch Hist Dance Soc
DHF	Door & Hardware Fedn
DHS	Design Hist Soc
DHSBA	Dorset Horn Poll Sheep Breeders Assn
DI	Dyslexia Inst
DIA	Design & Inds Assn
	Driving Instructors Assn
DIG Scotland	Disablement Income Gp Scotland
DLA	Dental Laboratories Assn
	Discrimination Law Assn
DMA	Defence Mfrs Assn
	Direct Marketing Assn (UK) Ltd
DMF	Disabled Motorists Fedn
DNH&AS	Dorset Natural Hist & Archaeol Soc
DPA	Dartmoor Presvn Assn
	Data Pubrs Assn
	Dental Practitioners Assn
DPAA	Draught Proofing Advy Assn
DPIS	Derby Porcelain Intl Soc
DPS	Dartmoor Pony Soc
DRS	Derbyshire Record Soc
DSA	Devt Studies Assn
	Direct Selling Assn
	Down's Syndrome Assn
	Drilling & Sawing Assn
DSABRO	District Surveyors Assn Ltd
DSBA	Dartmoor Sheep Breeders Assn
DSGB	Dozenal Soc
DSSA	Dental System Suppliers Assn
DSWA	Dry Stone Walling Assn
DTA	Devt Trusts Assn
DUCC	Danish-UK Cham Comm
DWT	Durham Wildlife Trust
DWTA	BEAMA

E

EAA	Eastern Africa Assn
	Electricity Arbitration Assn
EAB	Esperanto Assn Britain
EAG	Eur Atlantic Gp
EAGB	Executives Assn
EAHC	Essex Archaeol & Histl Congress
EAMA	Engg & Machinery Alliance
EAP	English Apples & Pears
EAS	Epilepsy Action Scotland
EASCO	English Assn Self Catering Operators
EAUK	Evangelical Alliance
EBA	Electric Boat Assn
	English Boccia Assn
	English Bowling Assn
EBBA	England Basketball
EBCC	Egyptian Brit Cham Comm
EBEA	Economics & Business Educ Assn
EBF	Equine Behaviour Forum
EBS	Edinburgh Bibliographical Soc
EBU	English Bridge U
ECA	Educl Centres Assn
	Electrical Contrs Assn
	English Clergy Assn
	English Curling Assn
	Eur Catering Assn (GB)
ECB CA	England & Wales Cricket Bd Coaches Assn
ECCA	English Community Care Assn
	English Cross Country Assn
ECCI	Essex Chams Comm
ECIA	Engg Construction Ind Assn
ECO	Environmental Communicators Org
ECSA	Estuarine & Coastal Sciences Assn
ECWS	English Civil War Soc
EDA	Eating Disorders Assn
	Electrical Distbrs Assn
	English Draughts Assn
EDC	Early Dance Circle
EDCC Ltd	Eastbourne & District Cham Comm
EDS	Ectodermal Dysplasia Soc
EEF	EEF
EEMUA	Engg Eqpt & Materials Users Assn
EES	Egypt Exploration Soc
EESA	Electrical & Engg Staff Assn
EETS	Early English Text Soc
EEZ	Defence Mfrs Assn
EFA	Employers Forum on Age
	Eton Fives Assn
EFDSS	English Folk Dance & Song Soc
EGAD	Defence Mfrs Assn
EGB	Endurance GB
EGBA	English Goat Breeders Assn
EGCS	English Guernsey Cattle Soc
EGS	English Goethe Soc
EGU	English Golf U
EHA	England Handball Assn
EHAS	E Herts Archaeol Soc
EHCCI	E Hampshire Cham Comm & Ind
EHS	Ecclesiastical Hist Soc
EHTF	English Historic Towns Forum
EI	Energy Inst
	Evaluation Intl
EIA	Electrical Insulation Assn
	Engg Inds Assn
	Environmental Investigation Agency
	Eur Inf Assn
	Events Ind Alliance
EIBA	English Indoor Bowling Assn
EIC	Energy Inds Coun
	Environmental Inds Commission
EIF	Environmental Inds Fedn
EIFI	Electrical Inds Fedn Ireland
EIG	Explosives Ind Gp
EIQA	Excellence Ireland Quality Assn

EIS	Educl Inst Scotland	FA	Families Anonymous
	Engg Integrity Soc		Football Assn
EISA	EIS Assn	FAA	Fife Agricl Assn
EJO Society	Elsie Jeanette Oxenham Appreciation Soc	FAB	Futon Assn
ELA	Employment Lawyers Assn	FACE(UK)	Fedn Assns Country Sports Europe
	English Lacrosse Assn	FacPharmMed	Fac Pharmaceutical Med
ELAFNS	E Lothian Antiquarian... Naturalists Soc	FACT	Falsely Accused Carers & Teachers
ELAM	BEAMA		Fedn Copyright Theft
ELAS	Education Law Assn	FAEI	Fedn Aerospace Enterprises Ireland
ELCCI	E Lancs Cham Comm	FAERO	Fedn Authorised Energy Rating Orgs
eLN	eLearning Network	FAGB	Fairground Assn
ELSPA	Entertainment & Leisure Software Pubrs Assn (UK)	FAI	Football Assn Ireland
ELWA	Eur Liquid Waterproofing Assn	FAIA	Food Additives & Ingredients Assn
EMAB	BEAMA	FARA	Fedn Active Retirement Assns [IRL]
EMCIA	EMC Ind Assn		Formula Air Racing Assn
EMGS	EM Gauge Soc	FARMA	Nat Farmers' Retail & Markets Assn
EMMSA	Envelope Makers' & Mfrg Stationers' Assn	FAS	Fedn Astronomical Socs
EMS	Edinburgh Mathematical Soc	FASET	Fall Arrest Safety Eqpt Training
ENABLE	ENABLE	FASNA	Foundation & Aided Schools Nat Assn
ENCAMS	ENCAMS	FASS	Fedn Aerospace Support Services
ENT.UK	Brit Assn Otorhinolaryngologists	FAST	Farnborough Air Sciences Trust
EO	Education Otherwise		Fedn Software Theft
EPA	English Pool Assn	FATE	Fedn Automatic Transmission Engrs
EPCS	English Playing-Card Soc	FATG	Fine Art Tr Gld
Ephsoc	Ephemera Soc	FB	Fac Bldg
EPNS	English Place-Name Soc	FBA	Fedn Bloodstock Agents
EPS	Emergency Planning Soc		Fedn Brit Artists
	Experimental Psychology Soc		Freshwater Biological Assn
EPSG	Epiphytic Plant Study Gp	FBAF	Fédn Britannique Alliances Françaises
EPSS	English Poetry & Song Soc	FBAS	Fedn Brit Aquatic Socs
EPTA	Electro-physiological Technologists Assn	FBCA	Fedn Brit Cremation Authorities
Equity	Brit Actors' Equity Assn	FBCCI	Franco-Brit Cham Comm & Ind
ERA	Evacuees Reunion Assn	FBCMA	Fibre Bonded Carpet Mfrs' Assn
ERC	Economic Res Coun	FBHTM	Fedn Brit Hand Tool Mfrs
ERoSH	ERoSH	FBHVC	Fedn Brit Hist Vehicle Clubs
ERRVA	Emergency Response & Rescue Vessels Assn	FBS	Fire Brigade Soc
ERS	Electoral Reform Soc	FBSC	Fedn Bldg Specialist Contrs
	Electric Rly Soc	FBU	Fire Brigades' U
ES	Ergonomics Soc	FBY Soc	Francis Brett Young Soc
ESA	Environmental Services Assn	FC&PMS	Fort Cumberland... Militaria Soc
ESAH	Essex Soc Archaeology & Hist	FCA	Fedn Commodity Assns
ESC	Snowsport England		Fencing Contrs Assn
ESG	Ekbom Support Gp		Forestry Contracting Assn
ESG0	Exhibition Study Gp	FCBG	Fedn Children's Book Gps
ESITO	Events Sector Ind Trg Org	FCC	Fedn Cocoa Commerce
ESMA	Equine Sports Massage Assn		Fedn Crafts & Comm
ESMG	Electric Steel Makers Gld	FCDE	Fedn Clothing Designers & Executives
ESRI	Economic & Social Res Inst [IRL]	FCDL	Fedn Community Devt Learning
ESSA	Emergency Social Services Assn	FCFCG	Fedn City Farms & Community Gardens
ESTA	Earth Science Teachers Assn	FCM	Friends Cathedral Music
	Energy Systems Tr Assn	FCMA	Fibre Cement Mfrs Assn
ESU	English Speaking U C'wealth	FCOT	Fellowship Cycling Old-Timers
ETA	ETA Services Ltd	FCPPA	Frozen & Chilled Potato Processors' Assn
ETAPS	Environmental & Technical Assn Paper Sack Ind	FCS	Fedn Chefs Scotland
ETCI	Electro-Technical Coun Ireland		Fedn Communication Services
ETHIC	Electric Trace Heating Ind Coun	FCSI (UK)	Foodservice Consultants Soc Intl (UK)
ETI	Ethical Trading Initiative	FDA	Assn First Division Civil Servants
ETTA	English Table Tennis Assn		Factors & Discounters Assn
ETwA	English Tiddlywinks Assn		Fellowship Depressives Anonymous
EURISOL-UK	EURISOL-UK		Film Distbrs' Assn
EVA	English Volleyball Assn	FDF	Food & Drink Fedn
	Exhibition Venues Assn	FDP	Friends Dymock Poets
EWBA	English Women's Bowling Assn	FDW	Friends Dr Watson
EWI	Expert Witness Inst	FEDC	Fedn Engg Design Cos
EWIBA	English Women's Indoor Bowling Assn	FEF	Forecourt Eqpt Fedn
EWP	English Wine Producers	FER	Fedn Engine Re-Mfrs
EWS	English Westerners Soc	FERA	Further Educ Res Assn
EWT	Essex Wildlife Trust	FeRFA	FeRFA
EXIT	Voluntary Euthanasia Soc Scotland	FESA	Foundry Eqpt & Supplies Assn
		FETA	Fedn Envtl Tr Assns
			Fire Extinguishing Trs Assn
		FEU	Fedn Entertainment Us
		FEW	Freemen England & Wales
		FFA	Family Farmers' Assn
			Farmers Action
			Flying Farmers Assn
		FFB	Food Britain Fast Track
		FfCAC	Welsh Amat Music Fedn

F

F of M	Friends Mendelssohn
F&PA	Flowers & Plants Assn

FFHS	Fedn Family Hist Socs
FFMA	Funeral Furnishing Mfrs Assn
FFPRHC	Fac Family Planning & Reproductive Healthcare
FFS	Farms for Schools
FFVMA	Fire Fighting Vehicles Mfrs Assn
FGC	Flat Glass Coun
FGMA	UK Flat Glass Mfrs Assn
FHA	Family Holiday Assn
FHAGBI	Friesian Horse Assn
FHBF Ltd	Freelance Hair & Beauty Fedn
FHS	Flintshire Histl Soc
	Friends Histl Soc
	Furniture Hist Soc
FHT	Fedn Holistic Therapists
FIA	Fibreoptic Ind Assn
	Fitness Ind Assn
FIBA	Brit FIB (Flying Inflatable Boat) Assn
FIBKA	Fedn Ir Beekeepers' Assns
FIC	Fire Ind Confedn
FID	Fedn Indep Detectorists
FIEC	Fellowship Indep Evangelical Churches
FIM	Fedn Indep Mines
FIPO	Fedn Indep Practitioner Orgs
FIRA	Furniture Ind Res Assn
FIRESA	Fire & Rescue Suppliers Assn
FIS	Fedn Ir Socs
FLA	Family Law Assn Scotland
	Finance & Leasing Assn
FLBA	Family Law Bar Assn
FLD	Friends Lake District
Fleet Data	Road Transport Fleet Data Soc
FLTA	Fork Lift Truck Assn
FLVA	Fedn Licensed Victuallers Assns
FMA	Facilities Mgt Assn
	Family Mediators' Assn
	Fan Mfrs' Assn
FMA UK	Fibromyalgia Assn
FMB	Fedn Master Builders
FMC	Fire Mark Circle
FMD	Friends Medieval Dublin [IRL]
FMG	Brit Pyrotechnists' Assn
FMI	Family Matters Inst
FMO	Fedn Mfrg Opticians
FMPS	Farm Machinery Presvn Soc
FMS	Family Mediation Scotland
FNF	Families Need Fathers
FNL	Friends Nat Libraries
FNSA	Fjord Horse Nat Stud Book Assn
FOA	Fire Officers Assn
	Futures & Options Assn
FOB	Fedn Bakers
	Friends Blue
FOBBS	Fedn Brit Bonsai Socs
FOBFO	Fedn Brit Fire Orgs
FoC	Friends Classics
FOCAL	FOCAL Intl
FODO	Fedn Ophthalmic & Dispensing Opticians
FOE	Friends Earth
FOM RCP	Fac Occupational Medicine
FoMRHI	Fellowship Makers… Histl Instruments
FoNSCA	Fedn Nat Self Catering Assns
FOPDAC	Fedn O'seas Property Developers… & Consultants
FOPS	Fair Organ Presvn Soc
FOREST	Freedom Org Right Enjoy Smoking Tobacco
FoRL	Friends Real Lancashire
FOSC	Fedn Sidecar Clubs
FOSFA	Fedn Oils, Seeds & Fats Assns
FOSSUK	Fedn Swiss Socs UK
FPA	Fire Protection Assn
	Flexible Packaging Assn
	Food Processors' Assn
	Foodservice Packaging Assn
	Foreign Press Assn Lond
	fpa
FPB	Forum Private Business
FPC	Fresh Produce Consortium
FPDC	Fedn Plastering & Drywall Contrs
FPFC	Fair Play for Children Assn

FPI	Friends Pianola Inst
FPM	Fellowship Postgraduate Medicine
FPRA	Fedn Private Residents' Assns
FPS	Fedn Petroleum Suppliers
	Fedn Piling Specialists
	Fell Pony Soc
FRA	Fell Runners Assn
	Flat Roofing Alliance
FRAME	Fund Replacement Animals Med Experiments
FRC	Pulp & Paper Fundamental Res Soc
FRG	Family Rights Gp
FRLTNI	Fedn Retail Licensed Tr NI
FRMS	Fedn Recorded Music Socs
FRONTIER	Soc Envtl Exploration
FRSL	Ffestiniog Railway Society Ltd
FSB	Fedn Small Businesses
FSBL	Friends St Bride Library
FSC	Fedn Stadium Communities
	Field Studies Coun
FSF	Football Supporters' Fedn
FSG	Fortress Study Gp
FSID	Foundation Study Infant Deaths
FSPA	Fedn Sports & Play Assns
FSPG	Fire Service Presvn Gp
FSR	Fedn Specialist Restaurants
FSS	Feng Shui Soc
FSSoc	Forensic Science Soc
FST	Fedn Scot Theatre
FTA	Fedn Tax Advisers
	Floatation Tank Assn
	Freight Transport Assn
FTCA	Fac Taxation Consultants & Advisers
FTI	Fedn Technological Inds
FTL	Free Trade League
FTO	Fedn Tour Operators
FUW	Farmers' U Wales
FWA	Family Welfare Assn
	Fleece Washers & Dyers Assn
FWAG	Farming & Wildlife Advy Gp
FWC	Fedn Window Cleaners
FWD	Fedn Whls Distbrs
FWWCP	Fedn Worker Writers & Community Pubrs

G

G&SS	Gilbert & Sullivan Soc
GA	Galvanizers Assn
	Geographical Assn
	Geologists' Assn
GADAR	Gld Antique Dealers & Restorers
GAFTA	Grain & Feed Tr Assn
GAG	Grandparents Action Group
GAI	Gld Architectural Ironmongers
GAPAN	Gld Air Pilots & Air Navigators
GARDENEX	GARDENEX
GAS	Glasgow Agricl Soc
	Glasgow Archaeol Soc
	Group Analytic Soc
GATCO	Gld Air Traffic Control Officers
GAUK	Gestalt Assn UK
GAvA	Gld Aviation Artists
GBB	Great Britain Basketball
GBC	Gld Builders & Contrs
GBCT	Gld Brit Camera Technicians
GBD	Gld Brit Découpeurs
GBDF	Great Britain Diving Fedn
GBFE	Gld Brit Film & TV Editors
GBPCC	Great Britain Postcard Club
GBRF	Great Britain Racquetball Fedn
GBS	Guillain Barré Syndrome Support Gp
GBTSF	Great Britain Target Shooting Fedn
GBWRA	GB Wheelchair Rugby Association
GCA	Garden Centre Assn
	Gasket Cutters' Assn

	Golf Consultants Assn
	Greeting Card Assn
GCB	Gld Church Braillists
GCCF	Governing Coun Cat Fancy
GCGB	Golf Club GB
GCH	Gld Curative Hypnotherapists
GCI	Global Commons Inst
GCL	Gld Cleaners & Launderers
GCM	Gld Church Musicians
GCMT	Gen Coun Massage Therapy
GCRN	Gen Coun & Register Naturopaths
GCT / GCL	Game Conservancy Trust
GCTSM	Dress & Textile Specialists
GDBA	Guide Dogs for Blind Assn
GE	Gld Enamellers
GEA	Garage Eqpt Assn
GEM	Gld Experienced Motorists
	Group Educ Museums
GEM-A	Gemmological Assn
GEMMA	Gilt-Edged Market Makers' Assn
GEMS	Gender Trust
GEO	Glosa Educ Org
GFA	Game Farmers Assn
GFFR	Gld Fine Food Retailers
GFS	George Formby Soc
GFTU	Gen Fedn Tr Us
GFW	Gld Food Writers
GGA	Good Gardeners' Assn
	Guernsey Growers Assn
GGF	Glass & Glazing Fedn
GHC/ACW	Gwartheg Hynafol Cymru
GHS	Garden Hist Soc
GIG	Genetic Interest Gp
GIMA	GIMA
GKCSoc	Chesterton Soc
GLASS	Green Lane Assn
GLDA	Garden & Landscape Designers Assn
GLIAS	Greater Lond Indl Archaeology Soc
GLM Ltd	Gld Letting & Mgt
GLTA	Glued Laminated Timber Assn
GLULAM/GLTA	Glued Laminated Timber Assn
GMA	Glasgow Mathematical Assn
GMC	Gld Master Craftsmen
GNAS	Grand Nat Archery Soc
GNR Society	Great Nthn Rly Soc
GNSRA	Great N Scotland Rly Assn
GODA	Gld Drama Adjudicators
GOONS	Gld One-Name Studies
GOSPBC	Gloucestershire Old Spot Pig Breeders' Club
GOT	Gld Taxidermists
GP	Gld Photographers
GPBT	Gld Profl Beauty Therapists
GPDA	Gypsum Products Devt Assn
GPEA	Gld Profl Estate Agents
GPP	Gld Pastoral Psychology
GPTD	Gld Profl Teachers Dancing
GPV	Gld Profl Videographers
GRCA	Intl Glassfibre Reinforced Concrete Assn
GRS	German Rly Soc
GSA	Girls' Schools Assn
GSIA	Gloucestershire Soc Indl Archaeology
GSPS	Goon Show Preservation Soc
GTA	Gun Tr Assn
GTMA	Gauge & Tool Makers Assn
GTMC	Gld Travel Mgt Cos
GTOA	Group Travel Organisers Assn
GVA	Gin & Vodka Assn
	Gulf Veterans Assn
GVCAC	Girls' Venture Corps Air Cadets
GWG	Garden Writers Gld
GWS	Great Wstn Soc
GWT	Gwent Wildlife Trust

H

HA	Heritage Afloat
	Histl Assn
	Historic Artillery
	Honey Assn
	Humanities Assn
HAA	Historic Aircraft Assn
HACSG	Hyperactive Children's Support Gp
HAMPRA	Health & Med Public Relations Assn
HART	Horticultural Assn Retail Traders
HAS	Hawick Archaeol Soc
	Headteachers Assn Scotland
	History Anaesthesia Soc
HBA	Herring Buyers Assn
	Home Business Alliance
HBAA	Hotel Booking Agents Assn
HBEF	Health & Beauty Emplrs Fedn
HBF	Home Builders Fedn
HBS	Havergal Brian Soc
	Henry Bradshaw Soc
HBSA	Hairdressing & Beauty Suppliers Assn
	Histl Breechloading Smallarms Assn
HBWMA	Home Beer & Wine Mfrs Assn
HCA	History Curriculum Assn
	Holiday Centres Assn
	Hospital Caterers Assn
HCAUK	Handcycling Assn
HCC	Historic Caravan Club
HCCI	Hitchin Cham Comm & Ind
HCGB	Hovercraft Club
HCIMA	Hotel & Catering Intl Mgt Assn
HCKA	Historic Canoe & Kayak Assn
HCS	Highland Cattle Soc
HCSA	Hospital Consultants & Specialists Assn
HCVS	Historic Comml Vehicle Soc
HDA	Huntington's Disease Assn
HDRA	Henry Doubleday Res Assn
	Home Decoration Retailers' Assn
HDS	Histl Diving Soc
HDSBA	Hampshire Down Sheep Breeders Assn
HEA	Horticultural Exhibitors Assn
HEADWAY	HEADWAY
HEAS	Home Educ Advy Service
HEFF	Heart of England Fine Foods
HELOA	Higher Educ Liaison Officers' Assn
HEMSA	Highway Electrical Mfrs & Supprs Assn
HES(UK)	History Educ Soc
HEVAC	Heating, Ventilating & Air Conditioning Mfrs' Assn
HFC	Hampshire Field Club & Archaeol Soc
HFMA	Health Food Mfrs Assn
	Healthcare Financial Mgt Assn
HGA	Human Genetics Alert
HGS	Harness Goat Soc
	Hurdy-Gurdy Soc
HGWS	H G Wells Soc
HHA	Historic Houses Assn
HIPPO	Help Intl Plant Protein Org
HIPS(97)	Nat Support Gp Victims Failed Home Income Plans
HISHA	Highlands & Islands Sheep Health Assn
HITA	Hamper Ind Tr Assn
HLCC	Home Laundering Consultative Coun
HLRA	Handbag Liners & Repairers Assn
HMA	Homeopathic Med Assn
	Hop Mchts Assn
HMCA	Hospital & Med Care Assn
	Public Contrs Assn
HMRS	Histl Model Rly Soc
HMS	Histl Metallurgy Soc
HMSA	Hose Mfrs' & Suppliers Assn
	Hypermobility Syndrome Assn
HMT	Hovercraft Museum Trust
HOBA	Heating Oil Buyers Assn
HOT	Hawk & Owl Trust

HPA	Handley Page Assn
	Heat Pump Assn
	Hurlingham Polo Assn
HPS	Hardy Plant Soc
	Highland Pony Soc
HRA	Heritage Rly Assn
	Horse Rangers Assn
HRAS	Harry Roy Appreciation Soc
HRFBS	Hill Radnor Flock Book Soc
HRGB	Handbell Ringers
HRIA	Horticulture Res Intl Assn
HRS	Human Rights Soc
HSA	Horseracing Sponsors Assn
	Hospital Saving Assn
	Humane Slaughter Assn
HSA(NI)	Hospital Scientists Assn
HSBA	Herdwick Sheep Breeders Assn
HSGB	Haflinger Soc
HSLC	Historic Soc Lancashire & Cheshire
HSS	Humanist Soc Scotland
HSSA	Health & Safety Sign Assn
HTA	Heavy Transport Assn
	Horticultural Trs Assn
	Hound Trailing Assn
HTFS	Heat Transfer & Fluid Flow Service
HUNC	Halon Users Nat Consortium
HVA-SPHERE	Herpes Virus Assn
HVCA	Heating & Ventilating Contrs Assn
HWPA	Horserace Writers & Photographers Assn
HWS	Henry Williamson Soc

I

ia	ia
IAAT	Intl Assn Animal Therapists
IAATI	Intl Assn Auto Theft Investigators
IABA	Ir Amat Boxing Assn
IAC	Inst Amat Cinematographers
IACP	Ir Assn Counselling & Psychotherapy
IAEA	Inst Automotive Engr Assessors
IAgrE	Instn Agricl Engrs
IAgSA	Inst Agricl Secretaries & Administrators
IAI	Inst Archeologists Ireland
IAIEC	Ir Assn Intl Express Carriers
IAL	Inst Art & Law
IAM	Inst Administrative Mgt
	Inst Advanced Motorists
	Inst Assn Mgt
IAO	Inc Assn Organists
IAP	Instn Analysts & Programmers
IAPF	Ir Assn Pension Funds
IAPI	Inst Advertising Practitioners Ireland
IAPS	Inc Assn Preparatory Schools
IAS	Indl Agents Soc
IAT	Inst Animal Technology
	Inst Asphalt Technology
IATI	Inst Accounting Technicians Ireland
IAVI	Ir Auctioneers & Valuers Inst
IBA	Inst Business Admin
	Inst Business Advisers
	Ir Bowling Assn
IBAS	Indep Banking Advy Service
IBAT	Inst Bookbinding & Allied Trs
IBC	Inst Barristers' Clerks
IBD	Inst Brewing & Distilling
IBDA	Indep Battery Distbrs Assn
IBE	Inst Business Ethics
IBEC	Ir Business & Emplrs Confedn
IBIA	Ir BioIndustry Assn
IBIS	Imaginative Book Illustration Soc
IBL	Indep Business League
IBM	Inst Builders Mchts
IBMS	Inst Biomedical Science
IBS	Inst Broadcast Sound
IBSS	Intl Bond & Share Soc

ICA	Ice Cream Alliance
	Inst Consumer Affairs
	Inst Contemporary Arts
	Ir Countrywomen's Assn
ICAEW	Inst Chart Accountants England & Wales
ICAF	Inst Communications Arbitration & Forensics
ICAS	Inst Chart Accountants Scotland
ICATA	Ir Clothing & Textiles Alliance
ICB	Inst Certified Book-Keepers
ICCL	Ir Coun Civil Liberties
ICCM	Inst Cemetery & Crematorium Mgt
ICCT	Islington Cham Comm & Tr
ICDA	Ir Cosmetics, Detergents... Prods Assn
ICDDS	Inst Civil Defence & Disaster Studies
ICE	Instn Civil Engrs
ICEA	Inst Cost & Executive Accountants
	Intl Consulting Economists Assn
ICES	Instn Civil Engg Surveyors
ICF	Inst Chart Foresters
ICFM	Inst Car Fleet Mgt
ICG	Inst Career Guidance
ICHAC	Indep Children's Homes Association
ICHAWI	Inst Consvn Historic &... Works Ireland
ICHCA	ICHCA Intl
IChemE	Instn Chemical Engrs
ICM	Inst Comml Mgt
	Inst Complementary Medicine
	Inst Conflict Mgt
	Inst Construction Mgt
	Inst Credit Mgt
ICM-BRCP	Brit Register Complementary Practitioners
ICMA	Ir Chemical Marketers Assn
ICME	Inst Cast Metal Engrs
ICMSA	Ir Creamery Milk Suppliers Assn
ICNA	Infection Control Nurses Assn
ICOM	ICOM Energy Assn
ICON	Indep Consultants Consortium
ICorr	Inst Corrosion
ICOS	Ir Co-op Org Soc
ICR	Inst Clinical Res
ICRA	Internet Content Rating Assn
ICS	Inst Chart Shipbrokers
	Inst Customer Service
	Intensive Care Soc
ICSA	ICSA [IRL]
	Inst Chart Secretaries & Administrators
ICSc	Inst Consumer Sciences
ICT	ICT Ireland
	Inst Concrete Technology
ICTU	Ir Congress Tr Us
ICW	Inst Clayworkers
	Inst Clerks Works
IDA	Ir Dental Assn
IDAS	Implanted Defibrillator Assn Scotland
IDE	Inst Demolition Engrs
IDFA	Infant & Dietetic Foods Assn
IDGTE	Instn Diesel & Gas Turbine Engrs
IDHEE	Inst Domestic Heating... Engrs
IDHS(GB)	Ir Draught Horse Soc
IDI	Ir Dairy Inds Assn
IDM	Inst Direct Marketing
IDMA	Ir Direct Marketing Assn
IEA	Inst Economic Affairs
	Ir Exporters Assn
IEAM	Inst Entertainment & Arts Mgt
IED	Instn Economic Devt
	Instn Engg Designers
IEEM	Inst Ecology & Envtl Mgt
IEMA	Inst Envtl Mgt & Assessment
IEnvSc	Instn Envtl Sciences
IER	Inst Employment Rights
IESIS	Instn Engrs & Shipbuilders Scotland
IET	Instn Engg & Technology
IExpE	Inst Explosives Engrs
IF	Inst Fundraising
IFA	Indep Motor Tr Factors Assn
	Inst Field Archaeologists

© CBD Research Ltd · Beckenham · BR3 5JS · Tel 020 8650 7745 · Fax 020 8650 0768 · E-mail cbd@cbdresearch.com · www.cbdresearch.com

	Inst Financial Accountants		Petfood Mfrs Assn Ireland
	Ir Football Assn		White Goods Assn [IRL]
IFBB	Indep Family Brewers	IMechE	Instn Mechanical Engrs
iFE	Instn Fire Engrs	IMF	Inst Metal Finishing
IFLSA	Brit Marine Fedn	IMHS	Indian Military Histl Soc
IFM	Inst Fisheries Mgt	IMI	Inst Med Illustrators
IFMA	Inst Football Mgrs & Admin		Inst Motor Ind
IFON	Indep Fedn Nursing Scotland		Ir Mgt Inst
IFP	Inst Financial Planning	IMIS	Inst Mgt Inf Systems
IFPA	Ir Family Planning Assn	IMIT	Inst Musical Instrument Technology
IFRA	Indep Footwear Retailers Assn	IMLA	Intermediary Mortgage Lenders Assn
ifs	Inst Financial Services		Ir Maritime Law Assn
IFS	Inst Fiscal Studies	IMMM	Inst Materials, Minerals & Mining
IFSA	Instock Footwear Suppliers Assn	IMO	Ir Med Org
	Intumescent Fire Seals Assn	IMPACT	Ir Municipal, Public & Civil TU
IFST	Inst Food Science & Technology	IMPT	Inst Maxillofacial Prosthetists...
IFUT	Ir Fedn University Teachers	IMRG	Interactive Media Retail Group
IGA	IGA-UK	IMS	Inst Mgt Services
	Inst Gp Analysis		Inst Mgt Specialists
IGAP	Indep Gp Analytical Psychologists	IMW	Inst Masters Wine
IGC	Inst Guidance Counsellors [IRL]	IMWoodT	Inst Machine Woodworking Technology
IGD	Inst Grocery Distbn	INA	Ir Naturist Assn
IGEM	Instn Gas Engrs & Mgrs	INCA	INCA [IRL]
IGPA	Intl Gen Produce Assn	INCONTACT	Incontact
IGRS	Ir Genealogical Res Soc	Incpen	Ind Coun Packaging & Envt
IGS	Ir Georgian Soc	INFACT	Ir Nat Fedn against Copyright Theft
IHBC	Inst Historic Bldg Consvn	INHO	Ir Nursing Homes Org
IHEEM	Inst Healthcare Engg & Estate Mgt	INO	Ir Nurses Org
IHFR	Health Food Inst	InstDSc	Inst Decontamination Services
IHGS	Inst Heraldic & Genealogical Studies	InstMC	Inst Measurement & Control
IHI	Inst Home Inspectors	InstP	Inst Piping
	Ir Hospitality Inst	INTO	Ir Nat Teachers Org
IHIE	Inst Highway Inc Engrs	INucE	Instn Nuclear Engrs
IHM	Inst Health Care Mgt	IoA	Inst Acoustics
IHPA(BGB)	Ice Hockey Players Assn	IOB	Inst Biology
IHPE	Inst Health Promotion & Educ	IOC	Inst Carpenters
IHRIM(UK)	Inst Health Record & Inf Mgt		Inst Copywriting [?CBRI
IHS	Inst Home Safety	IOCS	Inst Construction Specialists
IHSGB	Icelandic Horse Soc	IoD	Inst Directors
IHT	Instn Highways & Transportation	IoE	Inst Export
IHUK	Ice Hockey UK	IOFGA	Ir Organic Farmers & Growers Assn
II	Inst Inventors	IOG	Inst Groundsmanship
IIA-UK	Inst Internal Auditors UK & Ireland	IOH	Inst Horticulture
IIB	Inst Indep Business	IOJ	Chart Inst Journalists
IICM	Ir Inst Credit Mgt	IoL	Chart Inst Linguists
IIE	Inst Indl Engrs [IRL]	IOL	Inst Outdoor Learning
IIF	Ir Insurance Fedn	IOM	Inst Operations Mgt
IILP	Inst Intl Licensing Practitioners	IOMNHAS	Isle of Man Natural Hist...Soc
IIPMM	Ir Inst Purchasing & Materials Mgt	ION	Inst Optimum Nutrition
IIS	Ir Instn Surveyors	IoP	Inst Physics
IIT	Inst Indirect Taxation	IoR	Inst Refrigeration
IKA	Ir Kidney Assn		Inst Roofing
ILA	Insolvency Lawyers Assn	IOSF	Intl Otter Survival Fund
	Intl Law Assn	IOSH	Instn Occupational Safety & Health
ILAM	Inst Leisure & Amenity Mgt	IoTA	Inst Transport Administration
	Inst Leisure & Amenity Mgt (Ireland)	IOV	Inst Videography
ILCA	Inst Legal Cashiers & Administrators	IPA	Indep Pilots Assn
ILCU	Ir League Credit Us		Indl Packaging Assn
ILE	Instn Lighting Engrs		Insolvency Practitioners Assn
ILEX	Inst Legal Executives		Inst Practitioners Advertising
ILI	Ir Landscape Inst		Inst Public Administration [IRL]
ILM	Inst Leadership & Mgt		Involvement & Participation Assn
ILPA	Immigration Law Practitioners Assn	IPD	Inst Profl Designers
ILS	Indl Locomotive Soc	IPEM	Inst Physics & Engg in Medicine
	Inst Legal Secretaries & PAs	IPF	Intl Pen Friends
ILSGB	Intl Language [IDO] Soc		Investment Property Forum
ILT	Inst Paralegal Training		Ir Printing Fedn
ILTSA	Inst Licensed Tr Stock Auditors	IPFMA	Ir Property & Facility Mgmt Assn
IMA	Indep Midwives Assn	IPG	Indep Pubrs Gld
	Inst Mathematics & Applications		Inst Profl Goldsmiths
	Investment Mgt Assn	IPHA	Ir Pharmaceutical Healthcare Assn
IManf	Inst Manufacturing	IPHE	Inst Plumbing & Heating Engg
IMarEST	Inst Marine Engg, Science & Technology	IPI	Inst Patentees & Inventors
IMBM	Inst Maintenance & Bldg Mgt		Inst Profl Investigators
IMCA	Intl Marine Contrs Assn	IPIA	Indep Print Inds Assn
IMCI	Inst Mgt Consultants Ireland	IPLA	Inst Public Loss Assessors
IMDA	Ir Med Devices Assn	IPMA	Inflatable Play Mfrs Assn
	Margarine Mfrs Assn Ireland	IPPM	Inst Payroll & Pensions Mgt

IPROW	Inst Public Rights Way Officers
IPS	Inc Phonographic Soc
	Inst Profl Sport
	Instn Planning Supervisors
IPSA	Ir ProShare Assn
IPSM	Inst Public Sector Mgt
IPW	Inst Profl Willwriters
IPWFI	Incorporation Plastic Window Fabricators & Installers
IQ	Inst Quarrying
IQA	Inst Quality Assurance
IQPS	Inst Qualified Profl Secretaries
IRATA	Indl Rope Access Tr Assn
IRC	Indep Retailers Confedn
IRE	Inst Refractories Engrs
IRFU	Ir Rugby Football U
IRM	Inst Risk Mgt
IRMA	Ir Recorded Music Assn
IRPM	Inst Residential Property Mgt
IRR	Inst Race Relations
IRRV	Inst Revenues, Rating & Valuation
IRS	Indl Rly Soc
	Investor Relations Soc
IRSE	Instn Rly Signal Engrs
IRSO	Inst Road Safety Officers
IRTA	Ir Real Tennis Assn
IRTS	Ir Radio Transmitters Soc
ISA	Indep Schools Assn
	Ir Soc Autism
ISAA	Ir Ship Agents' Assn
ISBA	Inc Soc Brit Advertisers
	Indep Schools Bursars Assn
ISBE	Inst Small Business & Entrepreneurship
ISC	Indep Schools Coun
ISCA	Indep Safety Consultants Assn
ISCE	Inst Sound & Communications Engrs
ISCIS	Indep Schools Coun Inf Service
ISecM	Inst Security Mgt
ISIA	Ir Security Ind Assn
ISKB	Imperial Soc Knights Bachelor
ISM	Inc Soc Musicians
	Inst Spiritualist Mediums
ISMA (UK)	Intl Stress Management Assn (UK)
ISME	Inst Sheet Metal Engg
	Ir Small & Medium Enterprises Assn
ISMM	Inst Sales & Marketing Mgt
ISOB	Inc Soc Organ Builders
ISOM	Ir Soc Occupational Medicine
ISP	Inst Sales Promotion
ISPA	Internet Service Providers Assn
ISPAL	Inst Sports, Parks & Leisure
ISPCA	Ir Soc Prevention Cruelty Animals
ISPCC	Ir Soc Prevention Cruelty Children
ISPE	Inst Swimming Pool Engrs
ISRM	Inst Sport & Recreation Mgt
ISRN	Inc Soc Registered Naturopaths
ISS	Inn Sign Soc
IST	Inst Science Technology
	Inst Spring Technology
ISTA	Intl Steel Tr Assn
ISTC	Inst Scientific & Technical Communicators
	Inst Swimming Teachers & Coaches
ISTD	Imperial Soc Teachers Dancing
	Intl Soc Typographic Designers
ISTR	Inst Safety Technology & Res
IStructE	Instn Structural Engrs
IT	Inst Trichologists
ITA	Indl Tyre Assn
	Inst Transactional Analysis
ITAI	Inst Traffic Accident Investigators
ITBA	Ir Thoroughbred Breeders Assn
ITC	Indep Theatre Coun
ITGA	Ir Timber Growers Assn
ITI	Inst Translation & Interpreting
ITIC	Ir Tourist Ind Confedn
ITM	Inst Transport Mgt
	Inst Travel Mgt

ITMA	Imported Tyre Mfrs Assn
	Inst Tr Mark Attorneys
ITOL	Inst Training & Occupational Learning
ITPAC	Imported Tobacco Products Advy Coun
ITSSAR	Indep Training Standards Scheme & Register
ITT	Inst Travel & Tourism
IUA	Ir Universities Assn
IVA	Inst Assessors & Internal Verifiers
IVE	Inst Vitreous Enamellers
IVEA	Ir Vocational Educ Assn
IVM	Inst Value Mgt
IVR	Inst Vehicle Recovery
IWA	Indep Warranty Assn
	Inland Waterways Assn
	Inst Welsh Affairs
IWBA	Ir Women's Bowling Assn
IWO	Inst Welfare
	IWO
IWPPA	Indep Waste Paper Processors Assn
IWPS	Inland Waterways Protection Soc
IWSc	Inst Wood Science
IYHA	Ir Youth Hostels Assn

J

JABPPAC	Jt Animal By Products... C'ee
JABS	Justice Awareness & Basic Support
JACT	Jt Assn Classical Teachers
JAGB	Jockeys Assn
JAPTA	Jazz Piano Teachers Assn
JBAS	Jussi Björling Appreciation Soc
JBS	Josephine Butler Soc
JCCI	Japanese Cham Comm & Ind UK
JCS	Jersey Cattle Soc
	Justices' Clerks' Soc
JDA	Jewellery Distbrs Assn
JFU	Jersey Farmers' U
JHS	James Hilton Soc
	John Hampden Soc
JHSE	Jewish Histl Soc England
JIMA	John Innes Mfrs Assn
JPR	Inst Jewish Policy Res
JSL	Johnson Soc Lond
JSS	Jacob Sheep Soc

K

KAS	Kent Archaeol Soc
KBSA	Kitchen Bathroom Bedroom Specialists Assn
KC	Kennel Club
KCAS	Kent County Agricl Soc
KCoC	Kingston Cham Comm
KEBS	Kmoch Eur Bands Soc
KES	Karg-Elert Archive
KF	Kinesiology Fedn
KFA	Keep Fit Assn
KIF	Knitting Inds Fedn
KSA	Klinefelter's Syndrome Assn
KSGB	Kite Soc
KSMA	Keats-Shelley Memorial Assn
KWVRPS	Keighley & Worth Valley Rly Presvn Soc

L

LA	Lighting Assn
LAA	Lancashire Authors' Assn
	Livestock Auctioneers Assn
	London Anglers Assn
LABBS	Ladies' Assn Brit Barbershop Singers
LACA	Local Authority Caterers' Assn
LACS	League Cruel Sports

© CBD Research Ltd · Beckenham · BR3 5JS · Tel 020 8650 7745 · Fax 020 8650 0768 · E-mail cbd@cbdresearch.com · www.cbdresearch.com

LAGB	Linguistics Assn
LAHS	Leicestershire Archaeol & Histl Soc
LAMAS	London & Middlesex Archaeol Soc
LAPADA	Assn Art & Antique Dealers
LARA	Motoring Orgs' Land Access & Recreation Assn
LARIA	Local Authorities Res & Intelligence Assn
LARSOA	Local Authority Road Safety Officers' Assn
LAS	London Appreciation Soc
LAS Ltd	Leicestershire Agricl Soc
LASA	Laboratory Animal Science Assn
LASMA	Ladder Systems Mfrs Assn
LASSA	Licensed Animal Slaughterers. . . Assn
LBBA	Brit Marine Fedn
	Brit Marine Fedn
LBES	Lifeboat Enthusiasts' Soc
LBMA	London Bullion Mkt Assn
LBSG	Letter Box Study Gp
LBSGB	Lusitano Breed Soc
LC	Lutheran Coun
LCA	Lead Contrs Assn
	London Cornish Assn
LCAS	Lancashire & Cheshire Antiquarian Soc
LCC	Legalise Cannabis Campaign
	London Cycling Campaign
LCCI	Liverpool Cham Comm & Ind
	London Cham Comm & Ind
LCF	Law Centres Fedn
	Librarians' Christian Fellowship
LCGB	Locomotive Club
LCRS	Record Soc Lancashire & Cheshire
LCTC	Loyal Company Town Criers
LDCA	Land Drainage Contrs Assn
LDOS	Lord's Day Observance Soc
LDS	Lakeland Dialect Soc
LDSA	London Dist Surveyors Assn
LDWA	Long Distance Walkers Assn
LEA	Leasehold Enfranchisement Assn
LECT	League Exchange C'wealth Teachers
LEEA	Lifting Eqpt Engrs Assn
LEIA	Lift & Escalator Ind Assn
LES	Licensing Executives Soc
LFCMA	Liquid Food Carton Mfrs' Assn
LFI	Let's Face It
LFMA	London Fish Mchts (Billingsgate) Ltd
LGA	Leek Growers' Assn
	Local Govt Assn
LGU	Ladies' Golf U
LHA	Left-Handers Assn
	World War Two Living Hist Assn
LHC	Left Handers Club
LI	Landscape Inst
LIBA	London Investment Banking Assn
Liberty	Liberty
LIF	Lighting Ind Fedn
LIFE	Life
Lifesavers	R Life Saving Soc
LIRMA	Intl Underwriting Assn Lond
LIS	List & Index Soc
LISE	Librarians of Insts & Schools of Educ
LIT & PHIL	Manchester Literary & Philosophical Soc
LITRG	Low Incomes Tax Reform Gp
LJA	London Jute Assn
LLSBA	Leicester Longwool Sheep Breeders Assn
LMA	League Mgrs Assn
	Lloyd's Market Assn
	Loan Market Assn
	London Mayors Assn
LMBBS	Laurence-Moon-Bardet-Biedl Soc
LMCA	LMCA
LMCPA	London Motor Cab Proprietors' Assn
LMMA	London Money Market Assn
LMS	Latin Mass Soc
	London Mathematical Soc
	London Medieval Soc
LNHS	London Natural Hist Soc
LOFA	Leisure & Outdoor Furniture Assn
LOOK	LOOK
LPA	Leather Producers' Assn

LPC	League Profl Craftsmen
LPGA	L P Gas Assn
LPOC	Listed Property Owners Club
LPRS	Lancashire Parish Register Soc
LRBA	London Rice Brokers Assn
LRCS	Lincoln Red Cattle Soc
LRG	Landscape Res Gp
LRS	Lincoln Record Soc
LRTA	Light Rail Transit Assn
LSA	Lead Sheet Assn
	Leisure Studies Assn
	Lowe Syndrome Assn
LSBA	Lonk Sheep Breeders Assn
LSDS	London Swing Dance Soc
LSN	Lymphoedema Support Network
LSRA	Lead Smelters & Refiners Assn
LSSA	Legal Software Suppliers Assn
	London Subterranean Survey Assn
LTA	Lawn Tennis Assn
	Livestock Traders Assn
LTDA	Licensed Taxi Drivers' Assn
LTG	Little Theatre Gld
LTS	London Topographical Soc
LTWA	Lawn Tennis Writers Assn
LURS	London Underground Rly Soc
LWA	London Welsh Assn
LYRPS	Lancashire & Yorkshire Rly Presvn Soc
LYRS	Lancashire & Yorkshire Rly Soc

M

M Her S	Military Heraldry Soc
MA	Mathematical Assn
	Miscarriage Assn
	Museums Assn
MAA	Manufacturers' Agents' Assn
	Medical Artists Assn
MAARA	Midlands Asthma & Allergy Res Assn
MAC	Mastic Asphalt Coun
MACDATA	Materials Components Developing & Testing Assn
MACS	Micro & Anophthalmic Children's Soc
MADEC	Martial Arts Devt Commission
MAEA	Medical Ethics Alliance
MAFVA	Miniature Armoured Fighting Vehicles Assn
MAG(UK)	Motorcycle Action Gp
MAGB	Maltsters Assn
Malsoc	Malacological Soc Lond
MAMA	Meet-a-Mum Assn
MAMSA	Managing & Marketing Sales Assn
MARCH	Nat Assn Mental After-Care in. . . Homes
MARQUES	MARQUES
MAS	Merioneth Agricl Soc
MASS	Motor Accident Solicitors Soc
MATCH	Mothers Apart Children
MAUK	Mast Action UK
	Mining Assn
MBA	Mountain Bothies Assn
MBAUK	Marine Biological Assn
MBF	Multiple Births Foundation
MBSGB	Musical Box Soc
MCA	Mail Consolidators Assn
	Management Consultancies Assn
	Master Carvers' Assn
	Master Craftsmen's Assn
	McTimoney Chiropractic Assn
MCCA	Minor Counties Cricket Assn
MCCC	Midlands Club Cricket Conf
MCCE	Macclesfield Cham Comm
MCGB	Master Chefs GB
MCI	Mountaineering Coun Ireland
MCIA	Motor Cycle Ind Assn
MCofS	Mountaineering Coun Scotland
MCRMA	Metal Cladding & Roofing Manufacturers Association Ltd
MCS	Marine Consvn Soc

MCU	Modern Churchpeople's U
MDA	MDA Europe
	Mobile Data Assn
MDAS	Malt Distillers Assn Scotland
MDDUS	Medical & Dental Defence U Scotland
MDF	MDF
MDHA	Masters Deerhounds Assn
MDS	Macular Disease Soc
MDSG	Myotonic Dystrophy Support Gp
MDU	Medical Defence U
MEA	Medical Equestrian Assn
	Middle East Assn
	Myalgic Encephalopathy Assn
MEC	Music Educ Coun
MEDACT	Medical Action Global Security
MEDATS	Medieval Dress & Textile Soc
MEEMA	Marine Engine & Eqpt Mfrs Assn
MEG	Museum Ethnographers Gp
MENCAP	MENCAP
MERG	Model Electronic Rly Gp
MES	Minerals Engg Soc
MESF	Mobile Electronics & Security Fedn
METCOM	Mechanical & Metal Trs Confedn
MF	Morris Fedn
MFHA	Masters Foxhounds Assn
MGA	Maize Growers Assn
	Mushroom Growers Assn
	Myasthenia Gravis Assn
MGAGB	Mounted Games Assn
MGMA	Metal Gutter Mfrs Assn
MHA	Manila Hemp Assn
MHEA	Materials Handling Engrs Assn
MHNA	Mental Health Nurses Assn
MHRA	Modern Humanities Res Assn
MHS	Military Histl Soc
MIA	Maritime Inf Assn
	Meetings Ind Assn
	Mortar Ind Assn
	Motorsport Ind Assn
	Music Inds Assn
MICAF	Mobile Ind Crime Action Forum
MIG	Defence Mfrs Assn
MIHS	Merseyside Indl Heritage Soc
MILMA	Miners' & Indl Lamp Mfrs' Assn
MIND	Mind
MINSOC	Mineralogical Soc
MIPAA	Motor Industry Public Affairs Assn Ltd
MIRA	MIRA Ltd
MIRAD	MIRAD
MIRO	Mineral Ind Res Org
MJA	Medical Journalists Assn
MKKM	Assn Men Kent & Kentish Men
MLA	Master Locksmiths Assn
MLAGB	Muzzle Loaders Assn
MLSBG	Manx Loaghtan Sheep Breeders Gp
MMA	Microtome Mfrs Assn
	Music Masters' & Mistresses' Assn
MMDA	Miniature Mediterranean Donkey Assn
MMMA	Metalforming Machinery Makers Assn
	Milking Machine Mfrs' Assn
MMS	Manchester Med Soc
MNFU	Manx Nat Farmers U
MNLPS	Merchant Navy Locomotive Presvn Soc
MODUS	Manufacturers Domestic Unvented Systems
MOMENTUM	Momentum - Northern Ireland ICT Fedn
Mont Soc	Montessori Soc
MOOS	Mechanical Organ Owners Soc
MOS	Men of the Stones
MOSA	Medical Officers Schools Assn
MOTA	Mail Order Trs Assn
MPA	Major Projects Assn
	Master Photographers Assn
	Music Pubrs' Assn
MPAGB	Modern Pentathlon Assn
MPBA	Modular & Portable Bldg Assn
MPG	Museum Profls Gp
	Music Producers Gld
MPGA	Metropolitan Public Gardens Assn

MPMA	Metal Packaging Mfrs Assn
MPS	Medical Protection Soc
	Soc Mucopolysaccharide Diseases
MRC	Model Rly Club
MRI	Meuse Rhine Issel Cattle Soc
MRQSA	Market Res Quality Standards Assn
MRS	Market Res Soc
	Medical Res Soc
MS	Media Soc
MS Society	Multiple Sclerosis Soc
MSA	Margarine & Spreads Assn
	Modern Studies Assn
	Motor Schools Assn
	MultiService Assn
MSAUK	Motor Sports Assn
MSBA	Masham Sheep Breeders Assn
MSGB	Manorial Soc
MSHS	Medical Sciences Histl Soc
MSRG	Medieval Settlement Res Gp
MSSC	Marine Soc & Sea Cadets
MTA	Manufacturing Technologies Assn
	Marine Trs Assn
	Microwave Technologies Assn
MU	Mothers' U
	Musicians' U
MUA	Machinery Users Assn
	Mail Users' Assn
MVDA	Motor Vehicle Dismantlers Assn
MVRA Ltd	MVRA Ltd
MVT	Military Vehicle Trust
MVWGS	Multi Vintage Wine Growers Soc
MWF	Medical Women's Fedn
MWSA	Mixed Wood-chip Suppliers Assn
MYA	Model Yachting Assn
MYCCI	Mid Yorkshire Cham Comm & Ind

N

N.A.G.	Nat Assn Goldsmiths
N.A.P.P.	Nat Assn Patient Participation
NA	Napoleonic Assn
NAA	Nat Arenas Assn
NAAC	Nat Assn Agricl Contrs
Naace	Naace
NAADAC	Nat Assn Alcohol & Drug Abuse Counsellors
NAAIDT	Nat Assn Advisers. . . Design & Technology
NAAMI	Nat Assn Advanced Motorcycle Instructors
NAAONB	Nat Assn Areas Outstanding Natural Beauty
NAAOSEN	Nat Assn Advy Officers Special Educational Needs
NAAPS	Nat Assn Adult Placement Services
NAAS	Nerine & Amaryllid Soc
NAB	Nat Assn Bookmakers Ltd
NABAS	NABAS
NABBA	Nat Amat Bodybuilders Assn
NABBC	Nat Assn Brass Band Conductors
NABCO	Nat Assn Bldg Co-ops [IRL]
NABD	Nat Assn Bikers Disability
NABIC	Nat Assn Bank & Insurance Customers
NABIM	Inc Nat Assn Brit & Ir Millers
NABMA	Nat Assn Brit Market Authorities
NABO	Nat Assn Boat Owners
NAC	Nat Assn Choirs
NACAB	Citizens Advice Bureaux
NACB	Nat Assn Catering Butchers
NACC	Nat Assn Colitis & Crohn's Disease
NACCC	Nat Assn Child Contact Centres
NACE	Nat Assn Able Children in Educ
	Nat Assn Chimney Engrs
NACFB	Nat Assn Comml Finance Brokers
NACHP	Nat Assn Counsellors, Hypnotherapists. . .
NACM	Nat Assn Cider Makers
NACMO	Nat Assn Cigarette Machine Operators
NACO	Nat Assn Cooperative Officials
NACOA	Nat Assn Children Alcoholics [NON mem
NACP	Nat Assn Complaints Personnel. . .

© CBD Research Ltd · Beckenham · BR3 5JS · Tel 020 8650 7745 · Fax 020 8650 0768 · E-mail cbd@cbdresearch.com · www.cbdresearch.com

NACS	Nat Assn Chimney Sweeps
NACSA	Nat Assn Child Support Action
NACT	Nat Assn Clinical Tutors
NACVS	Nat Assn Voluntary & Community Action
NACYP	Nat Assn Clubs Young People
NAD	Nat Assn Deaf People [IRL]
NADA	Nat Acupuncture Detoxification Assn
NADD	Nat Assn Deputising Doctors
NADFAS	Nat Assn Decorative & Fine Arts Socs
NADHAT	Nat Assn Dentistry Health Authorities...
NADP	Nat Assn Deafened People
NAEA	Nat Assn Estate Agents
NAEE	Nat Assn Envtl Educ
NAEGA	Nat Assn Educl Guidance Adults
NAESC	Nat Assn Educ Sick Children
NAFAC	Nat Assn Fisheries & Angling Consultatives
NAFAS	Nat Assn Flower Arrangement Socs
NAFB&AE	Nat Assn Farriers...
NAFD	Nat Assn Funeral Directors
NAFLIC	Nat Assn Leisure Ind Certification
NAFO	Nat Assn Fire Officers
NAFSO	Nat Assn Field Studies Officers
NAG	Nat Acquisitions Gp
NAGALRO	NAGALRO
NAGC	Nat Assn Gifted Children
NAGS	Nat Assn NFU Gp Secretaries
NAHBO	Nat Assn Hospital Broadcasting Orgs
NAHEMI	Nat Assn Higher Educ Moving Image
NAHFO	Nat Assn Hospital Fire Officers
NAHG	Nat Assn Homeopathic Gps
NAHPS	Nat Assn Hospital Play Staff
NAHS	Nat Assn Health Stores
NAHT	Nat Assn Head Teachers
NAIPS	Nat Assn Investigators & Process Servers
NAKMAS	Nat Assn Karate & Martial Arts Schools
NALA	Nat Assn Language Advisers
NALC	Nat Assn Ladies Circles
	Nat Assn Laryngectomee Clubs
	Nat Assn Local Couns
NALD	Nat Assn Literature Devt
NALGAO	Nat Assn Local Govt Arts Officers
NALI	Nat Assn Launderette Ind
NALOO	Nat Assn Licensed Opencast Operators
NALP	Nat Assn Licensed Paralegals
NAMA	Nat Assn Mathematics Advisers
NAMB	Nat Assn Master Bakers
NAME	Nat Assn Microwave Engrs
	Nat Assn Music Educators
NAMEM	Nat Assn Med Educ Mgt
NAMHI	Nat Assn Mentally H'capped Ireland
NAMHO	Nat Assn Mining Hist Orgs
NAMIR	Nat Assn Musical Instrument Repairers
NAMLC	Nat Assn Master Letter Carvers
NAMM	Nat Assn Memorial Masons
NANS	Nat Assn Nappy Services
NAO	Nat Accordion Org
NAOMI	Nat Assn Ovulation Method Instructors
NAOPV	Nat Assn Official Prison Visitors
NAPA	Nat Acrylic Painters' Assn
	Nat Assn Press Agencies
	Nat Assn Providers Activities Older People
	Neutral Alcohol Producers Assn
NAPAC	Nat Assn People Abused Childhood
Napaeo	Napaeo
NAPAS	Nat Assn Private Ambulance Services
NAPBH	Nat Assn Probation & Bail Hostels
NAPC	Nat Assn Primary Care
NAPCE	Nat Assn Pastoral Care Educ
	Nat Assn Primary Care Educators
NAPE	Nat Assn Primary Educ
NAPF	Nat Assn Pension Funds
NAPFP	Nat Assn Pre-Paid Funeral Plans
NAPGC	Nat Assn Public Golf Courses
NAPHR	Nat Assn Park Home Residents
NAPLIB	Nat Assn Aerial Photographic Libraries
NAPM	Nat Assn Paper Mchts
NAPO	Nat Assn Probation Officers

NAPS	Nat Assn Premenstrual Syndrome
	Nat Auricula & Primula Soc (Mid & West)
NAPT	Nat Assn Percussion Teachers
NARA	Non-Administrative Receivers Assn
NARES	Nat Assn Re-enactment Socs
NARM	Nat Assn Rooflight Mfrs
NARPD	Nat Assn Relief Paget's Disease
NARPO	Nat Assn Retired Police Officers
NARTM	Nat Assn Road Transport Museums
NAS	Nat Arabidopsis Soc
	Nat Assn Shopfitters
	Nat Autistic Soc
	Nautical Archaeology Soc
	Noise Abatement Soc
NASAA	Nat Assn Supporting Artistes Agents
NASC	Nat Access & Scaffolding Confedn
NASCH	Nat Assn Swimming Clubs H'capped
NASCR	Nat Assn Specialist Computer Retailers
NASD	Nat Assn Staff Devt in Post 16 Sector
NASDU	Nat Assn Security Dog Users
nasen	nasen
NASGP	Nat Assn Sessional GP's
NASH	Nat Assn Support Victims Stalking & Harassment
NASMAH	Nat Assn Screen Make-up Artists & Hairdressers
NASO	Nat Adult School Org
NASP	Nat Assn Sole Practitioners
NASPCS	Nat Advy Service Parents Children with a Stoma
NASPM	Brit Potato Trs Assn
NASS	Nat Ankylosing Spondylitis Soc
	Nat Assn Small Schools
	Nat Assn Steel Stockholders
NASUWT	Nat Assn Schoolmasters U Women Teachers
NASWE	Nat Assn Social Workers Educ
NAT	Nat Assn Toastmasters
NATD	Nat Assn Teachers Dancing
	Nat Assn Teaching Drama
	Nat Assn Tripe Dressers
NATE	Nat Assn Teaching Engl
	Nat Assn Therapeutic Educ
NATECLA	Nat Assn Teaching Engl &...Community Languages
NATFHE	NATFHE
NATN	Assn Perioperative Practice
NATO	Nat Assn Tenants Orgs [IRL]
NatSCA	Natural Sciences Collections Assn
NATT	Nat Assn Teachers Travellers
NATTA	Network Alternative Technology &... Assessment
NAVA	Nat Assn Valuers & Auctioneers
NAVS	Nat Anti-Vivisection Soc
NAVSM	Nat Assn Voluntary Service Mgrs
NAW	Nat Assn Widows
NAWB(A)	Nat Assn Wine & Beer Makers
NAWC	Nat Assn Women's Clubs
NAWE	Nat Assn Writers in Educ
NAWG	Nat Assn Writers' Gps
NAWH	Action Sick Children
NAWO	Nat Alliance Women's Orgs
NAWP	Nat Assn Women Pharmacists
NAYCEO	Nat Assn Youth & Community Educ Officers
NAYD	Nat Assn Youth Drama [IRL]
NAYJ	Nat Assn Youth Justice
NAYO	Nat Assn Youth Orchestras
NAYT	Nat Assn Youth Theatres
NBA	Nat Beef Assn
NBF	Nat Bed Fedn
NBGA	Nat Bingo Game Assn
NBS	Nat Begonia Soc
NBTA	Nat Baton Twirling Assn
NBTVA	Narrow Bandwidth TV Assn
NCA	Nat Campaign Arts
	Nat Cancer Alliance
	Nat Care Assn
	Nat Coun Aviculture
	Nat Courier Assn
NCASS	Nationwide Caterers Assn
NCC	Nat Caravan Coun
	Nat Cavy Club
NCCA	Nat Carpet Cleaners Assn

NCCPG	Nat Coun Consvn Plants & Gardens	NGH	Nat Gp Homeworking
NCDS	Nat Coun Divorced & Separated	NGLIS	Network Govt Library & Inf Specialists
NCF	Nat Consumer Fedn	NGO	Nat Gamekeepers Org
	Nat Cooperage Fedn	NGRC	Nat Greyhound Racing Club
NCFS	Nat Campaign Firework Safety	NGRS	Narrow Gauge Rly Soc
NCH	Nat Coun Hypnotherapy &... Register	NGS	Nat Gardens Scheme Charitable Trust
NCIUA	Nat Cochlear Implant Users Assn		Nat Gerbil Soc
NCLS	New Canterbury Literary Soc	NGSA	Nat Grammar Schools Assn
NCMA	Nat Childminding Assn	NGVA	Natural Gas Vehicle Assn
NCMD	Nat Coun Metal Detecting	NH	Nat Heritage
NCNE	Nat Campaign Nursery Educ	NHA	Nat Hop Assn
NCP	Nat Coun Psychotherapists	NHBS	Nat Horse Brass Soc
NCPTA	Nat Confedn Parent-Teacher Assns	NHCCI	N Hampshire Cham Comm & Ind
NCS	Nat Chinchilla Soc	NHCRA	Naval Histl Collectors & Res Assn
	Nat Chrysanthemum Soc	NHF	Nat Hairdressers Fedn
NCT	Nat Childbirth Trust	NHIC	Nat Home Improvement Coun
NCU	Northern Cricket U Ireland	NHL	Nat Harmonica League
NCWA	Nat Children's Wear Assn	NHLS	Nat Hedgelaying Soc
NCWJ	Nat Campaign Water Justice	NHSC	Nat Historic Ships
ND	Nat Drama		NHS Confedn
NDCCI	N Devon Cham Comm & Ind	NHSN	Natural Hist Soc Northumbria
NDCS	Nat Deaf Children's Soc	NHSTA	NHS Trusts Assn
NDFA	Nat Drama Festivals Assn	NI	Nautical Inst
NDFTA	Nat Dried Fruit Tr Assn	NIA	Nat Insulation Assn
NDNA	Nat Day Nurseries Assn		Nuclear Ind Assn
NDS	Nat Dahlia Soc	NIAB	NIAB
NDTA	Nat Dance Teachers Assn	NIABC	Boys' & Girls' Clubs NI
NDWA	Nat Dog Wardens Assn	NIACE	Nat Inst Adult Continuing Educ (E&W)
NEA	Nat Energy Action	NIACRO	NI Assn Care & Resettlement Offenders
	Nat Exhibitors Assn	NIACTA	NI Amusement Caterer's Tr Assn
NEAC	Nat Entertainment Agents Coun	NIAF	NI Athletic Fedn
NEHS	N England Horticl Soc	NIAS	NI Archery Soc
NEIMME	N England Inst Mining & Mechanical Engrs	NIASP	NI Assn Study Psychoanalysis
NEMA	Nat Early Music Assn	NIBA	NI Bankers Assn
NEMAL	Nat Egg Marketing Assn	NIBG	NI Bat Gp
NEMSA	N England Mule Sheep Assn	NICCI	NI Cham Comm & Ind
NEODA	Nat Edible Oil Distbrs Assn	NICF	Nat Inst Carpet & Floorlayers
NES	Nat Eczema Soc		NI Cycling Fedn
	Nat Endometriosis Soc	NICSA	NI Countryside Staff Assn
NFA	Nat Fedn Anglers	NICVA	NI Coun Voluntary Action
	Nat Fillings Assn	NIDS	NI Deer Soc
	Nat Fireplace Assn	NIF	Nat Inf Forum
	Non-Ferrous Alliance	NIFA	Network Indep Forensic Accountants
NFAS	Nat Field Archery Soc	NIFGA	NI Fruit Growers Assn
NFBA	Nat Fedn Bridleway Assns	NIFHA	NI Fedn Housing Assns
NFBG	Nat Fedn Badger Gps	NIGTA	NI Grain Tr Assn
NFBR	Nat Fedn Biological Recording	NILGA	NI Local Govt Assn
NFBUK	Nat Fedn Blind	NIMBA	NI Master Butchers Assn
NFCF	Nat Fedn Cemetery Friends	NIMEA	NI Meat Exporters Assn
NFDC	Nat Fedn Demolition Contrs	NIMH	Nat Inst Med Herbalists
NFEA	Nat Fedn Enterprise Agencies	NIMMA	NI Mixed Marriage Assn
NFEC	Nat Forum Engg Centres	NIMPA	NI Master Plumbers Assn
NFER	Nat Foundation Educl Res E&W	NINA	Netball NI
NFF	Nat Fedn Fishmongers	NIPBA	NI Potato Breeders Assn
NFFF	Nat Fedn Fish Friers	NIPSA	NI Public Service Alliance
NFFO	Nat Fedn Fishermen's Orgs	NISA	Nat Ice Skating Assn
NFG	Nat Fedn Glaziers		NI Shows Assn
NFIWFM	Nat Fedn Inland Whls Fish Mchts		NISA Today's Holdings Ltd
NFM	Nat Family Mediation	NISO	Nat Ir Safety Org
NFPB&CS	New Forest Pony ... & Cattle Soc	NITTA	NI Timber Tr Assn
NFPTA	Natural Family Planning Teachers Assn	NIVA	NI Volleyball Assn
NFRC	Nat Fedn Roofing Contrs	NIWAF	NI Women's Aid Fedn
NFRL	Nat Fedn Residential Landlords	NJF	Nat Jumblers Fedn
NFRS	Nat Fancy Rat Soc	NJUG	Nat Jt Utilities Gp
NFS	Nat Fedn Shopmobility	NKA	Nat Karting Assn
NFSA	Nat Fedn Sea Anglers	NLA	Nat Landlords' Assn
NFSH	Nat Fedn Spiritual Healers		Nat Literacy Assn
NFSP	Nat Fedn Sub-Postmasters	NLB	Nat Library Blind
NFTMMS	Nat Fedn Terrazzo Marble & Mosaic Specialists	NLHA	Nottinghamshire Local Hist Assn
NFU	Nat Farmers U	NMC	Nat Motorcycle Coun
NFUS	NFU Scotland		Nat Mouse Club
NFWI	Nat Fedn Women's Insts	NMES	Northern Mill Engine Soc
NFWS	Nat Ferret Welfare Soc	NMI	Nat Microelectronics Inst
	Nat Fox Welfare Soc	NMRS	Northern Mine Res Soc
NFYFC	Nat Fedn Young Farmers Clubs (E&W)	NMTF	Nat Market Traders Fedn
ngb2b	Newport & Gwent Cham Comm, Enterprise & Ind		Nat Metal Trs Fedn
NGCAA	Nat Golf Clubs Advy Assn	NNAC	Nat Network Assessment Cntres
NGDA	Nat Game Dealers Assn	NNI	Nat Newspapers Ireland

NNS	Neonatal Soc
NO PANIC	Nat Org Phobias, Anxiety. . .Inf & Care
NO2ID	NO2ID
NOA	Nat Outsourcing Assn
NOAH	Nat Office Animal Health
NODA	Nat Operatic & Dramatic Assn
NOEA	Nat Outdoor Events Assn
NOF	Northern Offshore Fedn
NORCAP	Supporting Adults affected by Adoption
NOS	Nat Osteoporosis Soc
NOTA	Nat Org Treatment of Abusers
NPA	Nat Pawnbrokers Assn
	Nat Pharmacy Assn
	Nat Pig Assn
	Nat Pigeon Assn
	Nat Portage Assn
	Nat Portraiture Assn
	New Producers Alliance
	Newspaper Pubrs Assn
NPC	Nat Packaging Coun
	Nat Pensioners' Convention
NPFA	Nat Playing Fields Assn
NPHA	Nat Private Hire Assn
NPS	Nat Philatelic Soc
	Nat Phobics Soc
	Nat Piers Soc
	Nat Pony Soc
	Northumbrian Pipers Soc
NPTA	Nat Pest Technicians Assn
NQA	Nat Quoits Assn
NRA	Nat Renderers Assn
	Nat Rifle Assn
	Nat Rounders Assn
NRAC	Nat Register Access Consultants
NRAS	Nat Rheumatoid Arthritis Soc
NRHA	Nat Roller Hockey Assn
NRHP	Nat Register Hypnotherapists & Psychotherapists
NRPT	Nat Register Personal Trainers
NRS	Navy Records Soc
	Norfolk Record Soc
NS	Nat Soc Painters, Sculptors & Printmakers
NSA	Nat Sawmilling Assn
	Nat Sewerage Assn
	Nat Sheep Assn
	Nat Sprint Assn
	Nuclear Stock Assn
NSALG	Nat Soc Allotment & Leisure Gardeners
NSBA	Nat School Band Assn
NSCA	Nat Soc Clean Air. . .
	Natural Sausage Casings Assn
NSCC	Nat Specialist Contrs Coun
NSCCI	N Staffs Cham Comm & Ind
NSE	Nat Soc Epilepsy
NSEAD	Nat Soc Educ in Art & Design
NSI	Nat Security Inspectorate
NSMT	Nat Soc Master Thatchers
NSPCC	Nat Soc Prevention Cruelty to Children
NSPH	Nat Soc Profl Hypnotherapists
NSPKU	Nat Soc Phenylketonuria
NSPP	Nat Soc Promotion Punctuality
NSPS	Nat Sweet Pea Soc
NSRA	Nat Small-Bore Rifle Assn
	Nat Soc Res Allergy
NSS	Nat Secular Soc
NTA	Nat Taxi Assn
	Nat Trolleybus Assn
NTDA	Nat Tyre Distbrs Assn
NTF	Nat Trainers Fedn
NTS	Nat Trust Scotland
NTTA	Nat Trailer & Towing Assn
NUJ	Nat U Journalists
NUM	Nat U Mineworkers
NUMA	Needleloom Underlay Mfrs' Assn
NUMAST	Nat U Marine. . . Transport Officers
NURA	Nat U Residents' Assns
NUS	Nat U Students UK
NUT	Nat U Teachers
NVS	Nat Vegetable Soc

NVTEC	Nat Vintage Tractor & Engine Club
NWA	NWA
NWABA	N W Area Bd Assn
NWLCC	N & Wstn Lancs Cham Comm & Ind
NWMRCA	N Wstn Model Rly Clubs Assn
NWR	Nat Women's Register
NWT	Norfolk Wildlife Trust
NWTEC	Nat Wool Textile Expt Corpn
NWTTA	N W Timber Tr Assn
NYCI	Nat Youth Coun Ireland
NYMR	N York Moors Hist Rly Trust

O

OA	Officers' Assn
	Overeaters Anonymous
OAA	Obstetric Anaesthetists Assn
	Outdoor Advertising Assn
OAHS	Oxfordshire Architectural & Hist Soc
OATA	Ornamental Aquatic Tr Assn
OBCofGB	Old Bottle Club
OCA	Offshore Contrs' Assn
OCCA	Oil & Colour Chemists Assn
OCS	Oriental Ceramic Soc
ODA	Offa's Dyke Assn
ODS	Owner Drivers Soc
ODSBA	Oxford Down Sheep Breeders Assn
OEDA	Occupational & Envtl Diseases Assn
OEMSA	Optical Eqpt Mfrs & Suppliers Assn
OES	Offshore Engg Soc
OEUK	Optra Exhibitions UK
OFF	Organic Food Fedn
OFIMA	Optical Frame Importers' & Mfrs' Assn
OFTEC	Oil Firing Technical Assn Petroleum Ind
OILC	Offshore Ind Liaison C'ee
OLMADA	Ophthalmic Lens Mfrs' & Distrbrs' Assn
OLS	Ocean Liner Soc
OMRS	Orders & Medals Res Soc
OPA	Occupational Pensioners Alliance
OPFCA	Ornamental Pool Fountain Constructors Assn
OPFS	One Parent Families Scotland
OPKA	Original Pearly King's & Queen's Assn
OPMA	Overseas Press & Media Assn
OPSCS	Observers Pocket Series Collectors' Soc
OPSIS	Nat Assn Educ, Training. . . Blind. . . People
OPTIC (UK)	Ophthalmological Prods Tr & Ind Conf
ORA	Oil Recycling Assn
ORS	Oxfordshire Record Soc
ORSoc	Operational Res Soc
OS	Omnibus Soc
	Ordnance Soc
OSB	Oxford Sandy & Black Pig Soc
OSCA	Onsite Communications Assn
	Osteopathic Sports Care Assn
OSGB	Orchid Soc
OSMA	On Site Massage Assn
OSME	Ornithological Soc Middle East
OTA	Offenders Tag Assn
	Orthodontic Technicians Assn
OUAS	Oxford University Archaeol Soc
OVW	One Voice Wales
OWC	Order Woodcraft Chivalry
OWG	Outdoor Writers' Gld
OWS	Oscar Wilde Soc

P

P&SEHCC&I	Portsmouth & S E Hampshire Cham Comm. . .
PA	Politics Assn
	Protestant Alliance
	Publishers Assn

PAA	Paper Agents Assn
	Profl Anglers Assn
	Psoriatic Arthropathy Alliance
PAAT	Profl Assn Alexander Teachers
PACE	PACE: Profl Assn Catering Educ
PACT	Prison Advice & Care Trust
	Producers Alliance Cinema & TV
PADS	People & Dogs Soc
PAGB	Photographic Alliance
	Proprietary Assn
PAMRA	Performing Artists' Media Rights Assn
PANN	Profl Assn Nursery Nurses
PAPA	Pizza, Pasta & Italian Food Assn
PARN	Profl Assns Res Network
PAS	Pembrokeshire Agricl Soc
	Percussive Arts Soc
	Perthshire Agricl Soc
PASMA	Prefabricated Access Suppliers' & Mfrs' Assn
PAT	Profl Assn Teachers
PAtT	Profls Allied Teaching
PBA	Profl Bodyguard Assn
PBFA	Provincial Booksellers Fairs Assn
PBIF	Plastics & Board Inds Fedn
PBS	Prayer Book Soc
PcA	Permaculture Assn
PCA	Profl Charter Assn
	Profl Computing Assn
	Profl Cricketers' Assn
	Public Contrs Assn
PCAM	Soc Producers & Composers Applied Music
PCC	Perthshire Cham Comm
PCCGB	Photographic Collectors Club
PCCI	Plymouth Cham Comm & Ind
PCDS	Primary Care Dermatology Soc
PCFA	Profl Coarse Fisheries Assn
PCFRE	Profl Coun Religious Educ
PCG	Profl Contrs Gp
PCGB	Poultry Club
PCL	Publicity Club Lond
PCS	Penguin Collectors' Soc
	Property Consultants Soc
	Public & Comml Services U
PDA	Pump Distbrs Assn
PDMHS	Peak District Mines Hist Soc
PDPA	Profl Darts Players Assn
PDS	Parkinson's Disease Soc
PDSG	Pick's Disease Support Gp
PEA	UK Parking Enforcement Agency
PEC	Plain Engl Campaign
PELS	Locomotive 6201
PERTEXA	Performance Textiles Assn
PESGB	Petroleum Exploration Soc
PETMA	Portable Electric Tool Mfrs Assn
PETS	Pre Eclampsia Soc
PF	Packaging Fedn
	Pagan Fedn
PFA	Popular Flying Assn
	Power Fastenings Assn
	Profl Footballers Assn
PFMA	Pet Food Mfrs Assn
PFNI	Police Fedn NI
PFPF	Passive Fire Protection Fedn
PFRA	Public Fundraising Regulatory Assn
PFS	Palmerston Forts Soc
	Personal Finance Soc
PFSS	Pet Fostering Service Scotland
PGA	Prison Governors Assn
	Profl Golfers Assn
PGG	Profl Gardeners' Gld
PGRO	Processors & Growers Res Org
PGS	Percy Grainger Soc
PHA	Pullet Hatcheries Assn
	Pulmonary Hypertension Assn
PHC	Pet Health Coun
PHS	Pembrokeshire Histl Soc
PhS	Philosophical Soc England
PHS	Plastics Histl Soc
	Police Hist Soc
	Postal Hist Soc
	Printing Histl Soc
PHSA	Provincial Hospital Services Assn
PHSI	Presbyterian Hist Soc Ireland
PiA	Primary Immunodeficiency Assn
PIBA	Personal Injuries Bar Assn
PIC	Photo Imaging Coun
PICA GB	Police Insignia Collectors Assn
PiF	Patient Inf Forum
PIFA	Packaging & Indl Films Assn
PIG	Pipeline Inds Gld
PIMA	PEP & ISA Mgrs Assn
PIPA	Pharmaceutical Inf & Pharmacovigilance Assn
PISUKI	Pacific Islands Soc
PITA	Paper Ind Technical Assn
PJA	Pipe Jacking Assn
PLA	Pre-School Learning Alliance
	Private Libraries Assn
PLASA	Profl Lighting & Sound Assn
PLS	Philip Larkin Soc
	Publishers Licensing Soc
PMA	Personal Mgrs Assn
	Probation Mgrs Assn
PMATA	Paper Makers' Allied Trs Assn
PMC	Printmakers Coun
PMI	Pensions Mgt Inst
PMMDA	Polymer Machinery Mfrs & Distbrs Assn
PMMMA	Pattern, Model, & Mould Mfrs Assn
PMMS	Plainsong & Mediæval Music Soc
PMPA	Public Mgt & Policy Assn
PMSA	Public Monuments & Sculpture Assn
PNFS	Peak & Nthn Footpaths Soc
POA	Pinball Owners Assn
	Prison Officers' Assn
Poll Club	Poll Holstein Breeders Club
Ponies(UK)	Ponies Assn
Pony Club	Pony Club
POVC	Post Office Vehicle Club
PPA	Periodical Pubrs Assn
	Play Providers Assn
	Pool Promoters Assn
	Potato Processors Assn
PPAi	Periodical Pubrs Assn - Interactive
PPG	Player Piano Gp
PPI	Phonographic Performance (Ireland)
PPL	Phonographic Performance
PPLA	Profl Photographic Laboratories Assn
PPMA	Processing & Packaging Machinery Assn
	Public Sector People Mgrs' Assn
PPORA	Point-to-Point Owners & Riders Assn
PPSA	Pigging Products & Services Assn
PPU	Peace Pledge U
PPUG	Profl Plant Users Gp
PRA	Paint Res Assn
	Picture Res Assn
	Premium Rate Assn
	Profl Rugby Players Assn
	Psychiatric Rehabilitation Assn
PRCA	PRCA Ireland
	Public Relations Consultants Assn
Premsoc	Premenstrual Soc
PRESSBOF	Press Standards Bd Finance
PRFA	Pop & Rock Fans' Assn
PRFSS	Peterborough R Foxhound Show Soc
PRII	Public Relations Inst Ireland
ProfBTM	Profl Business & Technical Mgt
PRS	Pre-Raphaelite Soc
	Protestant Reformation Soc
PS	Poetry Soc
PSA	Personal Safety Assn
	Political Studies Assn
	Production Services Assn
	Profl Speakers Assn
	Prostate Cancer Support Assn
PSA/PSARA	Passenger Shipping Assn
PSANI	Superintendents' Assn NI
PSARA	Passenger Shipping Assn
PSGB	Primate Soc

© CBD Research Ltd · Beckenham · BR3 5JS · Tel 020 8650 7745 · Fax 020 8650 0768 · E-mail cbd@cbdresearch.com · www.cbdresearch.com

PSI	Statisticians Pharmaceutical Ind
PSMA	Pressure Sensitive Mfrs Assn
PSnet	Public Services Network
PSNI	Pharmaceutical Soc NI
PSNS	Perthshire Soc Natural Science
PSPA	Photoluminescent Safety Products Assn
PSPS	Paddle Steamer Presvn Soc
PSS	Partially Sighted Soc
PTA	Pianoforte Tuners' Assn
	Post-tensioning Assn
	Postcard Traders' Assn
PTF	Provision Tr Fedn
PTS	Pali Text Soc
	Philatelic Traders Soc
	Protestant Truth Soc
PUMPA	Purine Metabolic Patients Assn
PVGA	Processed Vegetable Growers Assn
PWF	Private Wagon Fedn
PWI	Permanent Way Instn
PWSA (UK)	Prader-Willi Syndrome Assn

Q

Q butchers	Gld Q Butchers
QBC	Quality Brit Celery Assn
QCA	Quoted Companies Alliance
QES	Queen's Engl Soc
QG	Quality Gld
QMA	Quality Methods Assn
QMC	Quekett Microscopical Club
QMS	Quality Meat Scotland
QNI	Queen's Nursing Inst
QPA	Quarry Products Assn
Quakers	Religious Society of Friends (Quakers)
QuiTE	Assn Promotion Quality TESOL Educ

R

R&A	R & Ancient Golf Club
R&CHS	Rly & Canal Histl Soc
R&D	Res & Devt Soc
R3	Assn Business Recovery Profls
RA	R Academy Arts
	Radionic Association Ltd
	Ramblers' Assn
	Retreat Assn
	Rice Assn
RABDF	R Assn Brit Dairy Farmers
RAD	R Academy Dance
	R Assn Deaf People
RADA	R Academy Dramatic Art
RADAR	R Assn Disability & Rehabilitation
Radius	Religious Drama Soc
RAeC Trust	R Aero Club Trust
RAeS	R Aeronautical Soc
RAFA	R Air Forces Assn
RAFHS	R Air Force Histl Soc
RAFT	River Assn Freight & Transport
RAGB	Restaurant Assn
RAI	R Anthropological Inst
	R Archaeol Inst
RAM	R Academy Music
RAS	R Asiatic Soc
	R Astronomical Soc
RASC	R Agricl Soc C'wealth
RASE	R Agricl Soc England
RATD	Register Apparel & Textile Designers
RBA	Refined Bitumen Assn
	Retail Book, Stationery... Employees Assn
	Retail Bridalwear Assn
RBCC	Russo-Brit Cham Comm
RBLS	R Brit Legion Scotland
RBOA	Residential Boat Owners Assn

RBS	R Botanical & Horticl Soc Manch
	R Brit Soc Sculptors
RBSA	R Birmingham Soc Artists
RBST	Rare Breeds Survival Trust
RCA	R Cambrian Academy Art
	Racecourse Assn
	Rural Crafts Assn
RCAA	R Cornwall Agricl Assn
RCCC	R Caledonian Curling Club
RCCGB	Roller Coaster Club
RCGP	R Coll Gen Practitioners
RCHM	Register Chinese Herbal Medicine
RCHS	R Caledonian Horticl Soc
RCM	R Coll Midwives
RCN	R Coll Nursing
RCO	R Coll Organists
RCOG	R Coll Obstetricians & Gynaecologists
RCP	R Coll Physicians Lond
RCPath	R Coll Pathologists
RCPCH	R Coll Paediatrics & Child Health
RCPSGlasg	R Coll Physicians & Surgeons Glasgow
RCPsych	R Coll Psychiatrists
RCS	R Choral Soc
	R Coll Surgeons England
RCSEd	R Coll Surgeons Edinburgh
RCSI	R Coll Surgeons Ireland
RCSLT	R Coll Speech & Language Therapists
RCTA	Retail Confectioners & Tobacconists Assn
RCTS	Rly Correspondence & Travel Soc
RCVS	R Coll Veterinary Surgeons
RDS	R Dublin Soc
	Res Defence Soc
	Rly Devt Soc
RE	R Soc Painter-Printmakers
Re-Solv	Re-Solv - Soc Prevention Solvent... Abuse
REA	Renewable Energy Assn
	Rhea & Emu Assn
REACH	REACH - Assn Children with Hand or Arm Deficiency
REAL	Road Emulsion Assn
REC	Recruitment & Employment Confedn
RedR - IHE	RedR - Engrs Disaster Relief
Regia	Regia Anglorum
REHIS	R Envtl Health Inst Scotland
REMA	BEAMA
	Retroreflective Eqpt Mfrs Assn
REntSoc	R Entomological Soc Lond
RES	R Economic Soc
Rethink	Rethink
RETRA	Radio, Electrical & TV Retailers' Assn
RFA	Rugby Fives Assn
RFBS	Ryeland Flock Book Soc
RFG	Rail Freight Gp
RFL	Rugby Football League
RFPG	R Fac Procurators in Glasgow
RFS	R Forestry Soc England, Wales & NI
	Robert Farnon Soc
RFSBA	Rough Fell Sheep Breeders Assn
RFU	Rugby Football U
RGA	Remote Gambling Assn
	Restricted Growth Assn
RGDATA	RGDATA [IRL]
RGI	R Glasgow Inst Fine Arts
RGS-IBG	R Geographical Soc
RHA	Road Haulage Assn
RHASS	R Highland & Agricl Soc Scotland
RHET	R Highland Educ Trust
RHistS	R Histl Soc
RHS	R Horticl Soc
	R Humane Soc
	Rider Haggard Soc
RHSI	R Horticl Soc Ireland
RI	R Instn GB
RIA	R Ir Academy
	Rly Ind Assn
	Roofing Ind Alliance
RIAC	R Ir Automobile Club
RIAI	R Inst Architects Ireland

RIAM	R Ir Academy Music
RIAS	R Incorporation Architects Scotland
RIBA	R Inst Brit Architects
RIC	R Instn Cornwall
RICA	Rail Ind Contrs Assn
RICS	R Instn Chart Surveyors
RIDBA	Rural & Indl Design & Bldg Assn
RIG	Remote Imaging Group
RIIA	R Inst Intl Affairs
RIN	R Inst Navigation
RINA	R Instn Naval Architects
RIPH	R Inst Public Health
RIPTA	Register Indep Profl Turfgrass Agronomists
RISW	R Instn S Wales
RIWAS	R Isle of Wight Agrl Soc
RJA&HS	R Jersey Agricl & Horticl Soc
RLAS	R Lancashire Agricl Soc
RLS	Road Locomotive Soc
RLS Club	Robert Louis Stevenson Club
RMA	R Musical Assn
	Recreation Mgrs' Assn
	Retread Mfrs Assn
RMCU	R Martyr Church U
RMetSoc	R Meteorological Soc
RMI	Retail Motor Ind Fedn
RMS	R Medical Soc
	R Microscopical Soc
	R Soc Miniature Painters …
	Records Mgt Soc
RMT	Rail, Maritime & Transport U
RNA	R Naval Assn
	Romantic Novelists Assn
RNAA	R Norfolk Agricl Assn
RNAI	Regional Newspapers Assn Ireland
RNAS	R Nthn Agricl Soc
RNBWS	R Naval Bird Watching Soc
RNES	R Navy Enthusiasts' Soc
RNHA	Registered Nursing Home Assn
RNIB	R Nat Inst Blind
RNID	RNID
RNLI	R Nat Lifeboat Instn
RNRS	R Nat Rose Soc
RNS	R Numismatic Soc
ROA	Racehorse Owners Assn
ROOM	ROOM
ROSECARPE	N England Rose, Carnation… Horticl Soc
ROSL	R Over-Seas League
RoSPA	R Soc Prevention Accidents
ROW	Rights of Women
Royal Manx	R Manx Agricl Soc
RPA	Rationalist Assn
RPAS	Restaurant Property Advisors Soc
RPRA	R Pigeon Racing Assn
RPS	R Philharmonic Soc
	R Photographic Soc
	Rare Poultry Soc
RPSG	R Philosophical Soc Glasgow
RPSGB	R Pharmaceutical Soc
RPSI	Rly Presvn Soc Ireland
RPSL	R Philatelic Soc Lond
RRA	Road Records Assn
	Road Roller Assn
RRC	Road Runners Club
RRRA	Road Rescue Recovery Assn
RSA	R Scot Academy Art & Architecture
	R Soc … Arts
	Refined Sugar Assn
	Regional Studies Assn
	Rett Syndrome Assn
	Rly Study Assn
	Rural Shops Alliance
RSAC(MS)	RSAC Motor Sport
RSAI	R Soc Antiquaries Ireland
RSAMD	R Scot Academy Music & Drama
RSC	R Soc Chemistry
RSCDS	R Scot Country Dance Soc
RSCM	R School Church Music
RSCTA	Rough & Smooth Collie Training Assn

RSDA	Road Surface Dressing Assn
RSE	R Soc Edinburgh
RSFS	R Scot Forestry Soc
RSGB	Radio Soc GB
RSGS	R Scot Geographical Soc
RSL	R Soc Literature
RSM	R Soc Medicine
	R Soc Musicians
RSMA	Road Safety Markings Assn
RSMG	Rubber Stamp Mfrs' Gld
RSPB	R Soc Protection Birds
RSPBA	R Scot Pipe Band Assn
RSPCA	R Soc Prevention Cruelty Animals
RSPSoc	Remote Sensing & Photogrammetry Soc
RSS	R Statistical Soc
	Ronald Stevenson Soc
RSSA	R Scot Soc Arts (Science & Technology)
RSSS	R S Surtees Soc
RSTM&H	R Soc Tropical Medicine & Hygiene
RSUA	R Soc Ulster Architects
RSW	R Scot Soc Painters in Water Colours
RSWT	R Soc Wildlife Trusts
RTA	Rural Theology Assn
RTA Ltd	Racehorse Transporters Assn
RTBI	Nat Assn Round Tables
RTCS	Round Tower Churches Soc
RTPI	R Town Planning Inst
RTS	R Television Soc
	River Thames Soc
RUAS	R Ulster Agricl Soc
RUF	Refractory Users Fedn
RUI	Resource Use Inst
RUKBA	R UK Beneficent Assn
RURAL	Soc Responsible Use Resources Agriculture & Land
RUSI	R Utd Services Inst Defence… Studies
RVA	Residential Ventilation Assn
	Returned Volunteer Action
RWA	Rabbit Welfare Assn
	Race Walking Assn
RWAS	R Welsh Agricl Soc
RWS	R Watercolour Soc
RYA	R Yachting Assn
RYAS	R Yachting Assn Scotland
RZSS	R Zoological Soc Scotland

S

S of F Ltd	Soc Floristry
S&TA	Salmon & Trout Assn
S2C2	Scot Soc Contamination Control
SA	Scot Athletics
SAA	Scot Aeromodellers Assn
	Scot Archery Assn
	Scot Assessors' Assn
	Soc Archer-Antiquaries
	Soc Artists' Agents
	Specialist Anglers Alliance
	Sub-Aqua Assn
	Suffolk Agricl Assn
SAAA	Scot Agricl Arbiters Assn
SAAD	Soc Advancement Anaesthesia Dentistry
SABRITA	Brit Cham Business Sthn Africa
SACGB	Shark Angling Club
SACRO	SACRO
SACS	Scot Assn Country Sports
SACU	Scot Auto-Cycle U
	Soc Anglo-Chinese Understanding
SADA	SAD Assn
SAE-UK	Soc Automotive Engrs
SAEMA	Specialist Access Engg & Maintenance Assn
SAFA	Scot Amat Football Assn
SAFEA	Sports & Fitness Eqpt Assn
SAFed	Safety Assessment Fedn
SAG	Steroid Aid Gp

© CBD Research Ltd · Beckenham · BR3 5JS · Tel 020 8650 7745 · Fax 020 8650 0768 · E-mail cbd@cbdresearch.com · www.cbdresearch.com

SAGB	Schizophrenia Assn		Specialist Cheesemakers' Assn
	Silk Assn		Sprayed Concrete Assn
	Skibob Assn	SCAG	Gld Stunt & Action Coordinators
	Spiritualist Assn	SCALA	Soc Chief Architects Local Auths
SAGBNI	Sportsman's Assn	SCAS	Soc Companion Animal Studies
SAGGA	Scout & Guide Graduate Assn		Surrey County Agricl Soc
SAGT	Scot Assn Geography Teachers	SCATA	Soc Computing & Technology Anaesthesia
SAH	Soc Automotive Historians	SCB	Speedway Control Bd
SAHAAS	Saint Albans & Hertfordshire Architectural. . . Soc	SCC	Sea Cadet Corps
SAHGB	Soc Architectural Historians		Soc Cheese Connoisseurs
SAHR	Soc Army Histl Res	SCCI	Sheffield Cham Comm & Ind
SAHS	Shropshire Archaeol & Histl Soc		Solihull Cham Comm & Ind
	Staffordshire Archaeol. . .Soc		Swindon Cham Comm & Ind
SAI	Soc Architectural Illustration	SCCTE	Sussex Cham Comm, Training & Enterprise
SAIF	Soc Allied & Indep Funeral Directors	SCDA	Scot Community Drama Assn
SALC	Scot Assn Law Centres	SCDI	Scot Coun Devt & Ind
SALSC	Scot Assn Local Sports Couns	SCEME	Soc Local Govt Electrical. . .Engrs
SAM	Scot Assn Metals	SCF	Scot Crofting Foundation
SAMA	Scot Amat Music Assn	SCGB	Satellite & Cable Broadcasters' Gp
SAMB	Scot Assn Master Bakers		Ski Club
SAMH	Scot Assn Mental Health	SCHA	Scot Catholic Histl Assn
SAMS	Scot Assn Marine Science	SCHC	Soc Coat Hook Collectors
SAMSA	Silica & Moulding Sands Assn	SCHHA	Southern Counties Heavy Horse Assn
SAMW	Scot Assn Meat Whlsrs	SCHS	Scot Church Hist Soc
SAN	Sonic Arts Network	SCHVPT	Southern Counties Historic Vehicle Presvn Trust
SANA	Scot Anglers Nat Assn	SCI	Soc Chemical Ind
SANDS	Stillbirth & Neonatal Death Soc		Steel Construction Inst
SANE	SANE	SCL	Soc Chief Librarians England & Wales
SANHS	Somerset Archaeol & Natural Hist Soc		Soc Construction Law
SANT	Soc Antiquaries Newcastle upon Tyne	SCMA	Scot Childminding Assn
SAOL	Sugar Assn Lond		Stilton Cheese Makers Assn
SAOS	Scot Agricl Org Soc	SCNP	Scot Coun Nat Parks
SAP	Soc Applied Philosophy	SCO	Scot C'ee Optometrists
SAPCA	Sports & Play Construction Assn	SCOD	Scot Coun Deafness
SAPCT	Scot Assn Painting Craft Teachers	SCoFF	Southern Counties Folk Fedn
SAPERE	Sapere	Scolag	Scot Legal Action Gp
SAPT	Scot Assn Public Transport	ScotSAC	Scot Sub Aqua Club
SARA	Scot Amat Rowing Assn	ScottishSPCA	Scot Soc Prevention Cruelty Animals
SARS	Soc Academic & Res Surgery	ScotWays	Scot Rights Way & Access Soc
SAS	Surfers against Sewage	SCP	Soc Clinical Psychiatrists
SASA	Scot Swimming	SCPA	Scot Cashmere Producers Assn
SASH	Scot Assn Spiritual Healers	SCPC	Soc Crisp Packet Collectors
SASLI	Scot Assn Sign Language Interpreters	SCQS	Soc Construction & Quantity Surveyors Public Sector
SASS	Sir Arthur Sullivan Soc	SCRA	Scot Countryside Rangers Assn
SATIPS	Soc Assistants Teaching Preparatory Schools	SCREAMS	Soc Campaigning Removal Exasperating Automated Switchboards
SAUK	Scoliosis Assn	SCRSS	Soc Cooperation Russian Soviet Studies
SAVE	Save Britain's Heritage	SCS	Soc Chart Surveyors [IRL]
SAVM	Scot Assn Volunteer Mgt		Soc Co-operative Studies
SAYFC	Scot Assn Young Farmers Clubs		Soc Cosmetic Scientists
SBA	Sailing Barge Assn	SCSH	Scot Coun Single Homeless
	Scot Basketball Assn	SCST	Soc Cardiological Science & Technology
	Scot Beekeepers' Assn	SCT	Soc County Treasurers [E&W]
	Scot Bowling Assn	SCTA	Scot Clay Target Assn
	Soc Botanical Artists		Scot Corn Tr Assn
	Steam Boat Assn	SCTE	Soc Cable Telecommunication Engrs
SBAC	Soc Brit Aerospace Cos	SCTS	Soc Cardiothoracic Surgery
SBAS	Staffordshire & Birmingham Agricl Soc	SCVO	Scot Coun Voluntary Orgs
SBBA	Scot Brass Band Assn	SDA	Scot Darts Assn
SBBA (WISE)	Straw Bale Bldg Assn		Scurry Driving Assn
SBC	Scot Business Community	SDC	Soc Designer Craftsmen
SBCA	Scot Bldg Contrs Assn		Soc Dyers & Colourists
SBE	Soc Business Economists	SDCC	S Devon Cham Tr & Comm
SBGI	Soc Brit Gas Inds	SDCCGB	Square Dance Callers Club
SBHS	Strict Baptist Histl Soc	SDEA	Shop & Display Eqpt Assn
SBNS	Soc Brit Neurological Surgeons	SDF	Scot Decorators Fedn
SBP	Soc Business Practitioners	SDHBS	S Devon Herd Book Soc
SBPR	Soc Back Pain Res	SDMA	Surgical Dressings Mfrs Assn
SBS	Songbird Survival	SDNS	Scot Daily Newspaper Soc
SBTD	Soc Brit Theatre Designers	SDR	Soc Dance Res
SBU	Scot Badminton U	SDS	S Downs Soc
SBVA	Socialist Business Values Assn		Scot Disability Sport
SBWWI	Soc Brit Water & Wastewater Inds	SDSA	Sudden Death Support Assn
SC	Scot Cycling	SDT	Soc Dairy Technology
SCA	Scot Canoe Assn	SDTA	Scot Dance Teachers Alliance
	Scot Croquet Assn		
	Smoke Control Assn		
	Social Care Assn		

SEA	Scot Esperanto Assn
	Soc Equestrian Artists
	Surface Engg Assn
SEAL	Soc Economic Analysis
	Soc Effective Affective Learning
SEAMA	Small Electrical Appliance Marketing Assn
SEAS	S England Agricl Soc
SEB	Soc Experimental Biology
SEBDA	Sebda
SEC	Soc Educ Consultants
SEC group	Specialist Engg Contrs Gp
SECCI	Scot Emplrs Coun Clay Inds
SECED	Soc Earthquake & Civil Engg Dynamics
SEDA	Scot Ecological Design Assn
	Staff & Educl Devt Assn
SEE	Soc Envtl Engrs
SEMA	Storage Eqpt Mfrs Assn
SEMPRE	Soc Educ Music & Psychology Res
SEO	Soc Event Organisers
SERA	Scot Educl Res Assn
	Socialist Envt & Resources Assn
SES	Scientific Exploration Soc
SEW	Soc Expert Witnesses
SFA	Scot Football Assn
	Small Farms Assn
	Solid Fuel Assn
SFAA	Scot Field Archery Assn
Sfam	Soc Applied Microbiology
SFC	Sexual Freedom Coalition
SFCCI	Southampton & Fareham Cham Comm & Ind
SFDF	Scot Food & Drink Fedn
SfEP	Soc Editors & Proofreaders
SFF	Scot Fishermen's Fedn
SFGB	Stone Fedn
SFHA	Scot Fedn Housing Assns
SFL	Scot Football League
SFLA	Resolution
SFMA	Scot Flour Millers Assn
SFMTA	Scot Fedn Meat Traders Assns
SFRMA	Synthetic Fibre Rug & Mat Assn
SFS	Soc French Studies
SfS	Soc Storytelling
SFSA	Scot Fedn Sea Anglers
	Scot Field Studies Assn
SFTA	Scot Food Tr Assn
SFTAH	Autism Indep UK
SG	Siege Gp
SGA	Scot Gamekeepers' Assn
	Scot Games Assn
	Scot Gymnastics Assn
SGCC	Soc Greeting Card Collectors
SGD	Soc Garden Designers
SGF	Scot Grocers' Fedn
SGFA	Soc Graphic Fine Art
SGM	Soc Gen Microbiology
SGPP	Soc Garlic Growers, Processors & Packers
SGR	Scientists Global Responsibility
SGT	Soc Glass Technology
SGTS	Scot Gaelic Texts Soc
SGU	Scot Gliding U
	Scot Golf U
SGWDA	Sliding Glass Window Distrbrs Assn
SHA	Soc Heraldic Arts
	Socialist Health Assn
SHAC	Soc Hist Alchemy & Chemistry
SHAPA	Solids Handling & Processing Assn
SHAPS	Spotted Horse & Pony Soc
SHB(GB)	Sport Horse Breeding
SHBA	Scotch Half Bred Assn
SHCG	Social Hist Curators Gp
SHEDA	Storage & Handling Eqpt Distbrs Assn
SHEPS	Soc Health Educ & ... Specialists
SHIP	Safe Home Income Plans
SHLM	Soc Hospital Linen Service & Laundry Mgrs
SHMIS	Soc Headmasters & Headmistresses Indep Schools
SHOC	Sheltered / Retirement Housing Owners' Confed
SHPF	Scot Hang Gliding & Paragliding Fedn

SHS	Scot Hist Soc
	Shire Horse Soc
	Social Hist Soc
SHU	Scot Hockey U
	Scot Homing U
SI	Soc Indexers
SIA	Spinal Injuries Assn
	Suffolk Inst Archaeology & Hist
SIAA	Scot Indep Advocacy Alliance
SIAS	Sussex Indl Archaeol Soc
SIBA	Scot Indoor Bowling Assn
	Soc Indep Brewers
SIESO	SIESO
SIF	Soc Individual Freedom
SIFA	SIFA
SIFD	Soc Intl Folk Dancing
SIGB	Snowsport Inds
SIH	Soc Italic Handwriting
SIHS	Scot Indl Heritage Soc
SILA	Sarcoidosis & Intestitial Lung Assn
SIMI	Soc Ir Motor Ind
SIRP	Soc Indep Roundabout Proprietors
SIS	Scientific Instrument Soc
	Spinal Injuries Scotland
SISA	Scot Ice Skating Assn
SIT	Soc Intl Treasurers
SIWA	Scot Inland Waterways Assn
SJA	School Journey Assn
	Sports Journalists' Assn GB
SJH	Soc Jewellery Hist [>SJH002
SJJA	Scot Ju-Jitsu Assn
SK	Sealed Knot
SK-S	Sheila Kaye-Smith Soc
SKC	Scot Kennel Club
SKCM	Soc King Charles Martyr
SKLR	Sittingbourne & Kemsley Light Rly
SLA	School Library Assn
	Stable Lads Assn
SLAD	Soc Lond Art Dealers
SLANOPE	Scot Local Authority Network Physical Educ
SLAS	Scot Law Agents Soc
SLCC	Soc Local Coun Clerks
SLD	Scot Language Dictionaries
SLEAT	Soc Laundry Engrs & Allied Trs
SLGA	Scot Ladies' Golfing Assn
SLHA	Soc Lincolnshire Hist & Archaeology
SLHS	Scot Labour Hist Soc
SLm	Soc Limners
SLMA	Steel Lintel Mfrs Assn
SLMG	Shetland Livestock Marketing Gp
SLS	Scots Language Soc
	Soc Landscape Studies
	Soc Legal Scholars
	Stephenson Locomotive Soc
SLSA	Socio-Legal Studies Assn
SLSAofGB	Surf Life Saving Assn
SLTA	Scot Licensed Tr Assn
SLTC	Soc Leather Technologists & Chemists
SLV	Licensed Trade Charity
SMA	Salt Mfrs Assn
	Schools Music Assn
	Soc Medieval Archaeology
	Soc Museum Archaeologists
	Sports Massage Assn
	Stage Mgt Assn
SMAE	SMAE Fellowship
SMART	Sports Mfrs & Retailers Tr Assn
SMDSA	Sanitary Med Disposal Services Assn
SMEE	Soc Model & Experimental Engrs
SMH&VTS	Scot Music Hall & Variety Theatre Soc
SMHS	Scot Military Histl Soc
SMMT	Soc Motor Mfrs & Traders
SMR	Soc Medicines Res
SMRC	Scot Motor Racing Club
SMS	Soc Model Shipwrights
SMTA	Scot Motor Tr Assn
	Sewing Machine Tr Assn
SMTO	Scot Massage Therapists Org

© CBD Research Ltd · Beckenham · BR3 5JS · Tel 020 8650 7745 · Fax 020 8650 0768 · E-mail cbd@cbdresearch.com · www.cbdresearch.com

SMWBA	Scot Master Wrights & Builders Assn	SPNM	Soc Promotion New Music
SMWS	Scotch Malt Whisky Soc	SPOA	Scot Plant Owners Assn
SNACMA	Snack, Nut & Crisp Mfrs Assn	SPPA	Scot Pre-School Play Assn
SNAD	Soc Numismatic Artists & Designers	SPR	Inc Soc Psychical Res
SNFWB	Scot Nat Fedn Welfare Blind		Soc Property Researchers
SNG	Scot Neuroscience Gp	SPRA	Single Ply Roofing Assn
SNIPEF	Scot & NI Plumbing Emplrs' Fedn	SPRS	Staffordshire Parish Registers Soc
SNN	Soc Nursery Nursing	SPS	Soc Portrait Sculptors
SNPA	Scot Newspaper Publishers Assn	SPSBS	Shetland Pony Stud Book Soc
SNR	Soc Nautical Res	SPSL	Scot Piping Soc Lond
SNSBI	Soc Name Studies Britain & Ireland	SPSS	Sports Pony Studbook Soc
SNSC	Snowsport Scotland	SPTW	Soc Promoting Training Women
SNU	Spiritualists Nat U	SPUC	Soc Protection Unborn Children
SOA	Scot Optoelectronics Assn	SPWA	Scot Pure Water Assn
	Scot Orienteering Assn	SQS	Scot Quality Salmon
	Soc Ancients	SRA	Scot Records Assn
SoA	Soc Authors		Scot Rifle Assn
SOAPA	Scot Pensions Assn		Shooters' Rights Assn
SOB	Soc Bookbinders		Social Res Assn
SoBS	Save our Bldg Socs		Strathspey Rly Assn
SOC	Scot Ornithologists Club	SRGC	Scot Rock Garden Club
	Soc Olympic Collectors	SRHE	Soc Res Higher Educ
SOCITM	Soc Inf Technology Mgt	SRHSB	Soc Res Hydrocephalus & Spina Bifida
SOCSA	Specialised Organic Chemicals Sector Assn	SRIP	Soc Reproductive & Infant Psychology
SoF	Sea Faith Network (UK)	SRP	Soc Radiological Protection
SOFAA	Soc Fine Art Auctioneers & Valuers		Soc Recorder Players
SOFHT	Soc Food Hygiene Technology	SRPBA	Scot Rural Property & Business Assn
SoG	Soc Genealogists	SRPS	Scot Rly Presvn Soc
SOL	Soc Ley Hunters	SRS	Scot Record Soc
SOLACE	Soc Local Authority Chief Execs & Senior Mgrs		Scot Reformation Soc
SOLCAP	Soc Leisure Consultants & Pubrs		Shakespeare Reading Soc
Solo NFSC	Nat Fedn Solo Clubs		Soc Renaissance Studies
SOM	Soc Metaphysicians		Suffolk Record Soc
	Soc Occupational Medicine		Surrey Record Soc
SOMW	Soc Medical Writers		Sussex Record Soc
SONE	Supporters Nuclear Energy		Swiss Rlys Soc
SOP	Save our Parsonages	SRU	Scot Rugby U
SOPA	Scot Organic Prodrs Assn	SS	Surtees Soc (Northumbria)
SOPO	Soc Procurement Officers Local Govt	SSA	Scot Security Assn
SoR	Soc Radiographers		Scot Sports Assn
SOS	Scot Otolaryngological Soc		Seasoning & Spice Assn
SOSS	Soc Schoolmasters & Schoolmistresses		Shipbuilders & Shiprepairers Assn
SOTMAS	Stoke-on-Trent Museum Archaeol Soc		Side Saddle Assn
SOTS	Soc Old Testament Study		Soc Scot Artists
SOVA	SOVA		Soc Study Addiction Alcohol. . .
SP-NS	Scot Place-Name Soc	SSAFA	Soldiers, Sailors & Airmen's Families Assn
SPA	Scot Pétanque Assn	SSAISB	Soc Study Artificial Intelligence & Simulation
	Scot Pipers Assn		Behaviour
	Scot Pubrs Assn	SSAM	Soc Sales & Marketing
	Sheet Plant Assn	SSAS	Soc S Asian Studies
	Soc Parliamentary Agents	SSAUK	Self Storage Assn
	Soc Popular Astronomy	SSBA	Scot School Bd Assn
	Soc Profl Accountants		Scot Spina Bifida Assn
	Soc Protection Aviculture		Shropshire Sheep Breeders Assn
	Soya Protein Assn		Swaledale Sheep Breeders Assn
SPA(UK)Ltd	Screen Printing Assn	SSBR	Soc Sailing Barge Res
SPAB	Soc Protection Ancient Bldgs	SSC	Scot Ski Club
SpaBA	Spa Business Assn		Silver Spoon Club
SPATA	Swimming Pool & Allied Trs Assn	SSCA	Scot Ship Chandlers Assn
SPBS	Scot Prayer Book Soc	SSCC	Scot Sporting Car Club
	Soc Promotion Byzantine Studies	SSCR	Scot Soc Crop Res
SPBW	Soc Presvn Beers Wood	SSCSoc	Soc Solicitors Supreme Courts Scotland
SPC	Soc Pension Consultants	SSEG	Scot Solar Energy Gp
	Steam Plough Club	SSF	Scot Schoolsport Fedn
SPCK	Soc Promoting Christian Knowledge		Scot Surfing Fedn
SPE	Soc Profl Engrs	SSHA	Soc Sexual Health Advisers
SPEF	Scot Print Emplrs Fedn	SSHB	Soc Study Human Biology
SPES	S Place Ethical Soc	SSHM	Scot Soc Hist Medicine
SPF	Scot Pharmaceutical Fedn		Soc Social Hist Medicine
	Scot Police Fedn	SSI	Sculptors' Soc Ireland
SPFA	Scot Pelagic Fishermen's Assn		Soc Scribes & Illuminators
SPHERE	Herpes Virus Assn	SSISI	Statistical & Social Inquiry Soc Ireland
SPI	Soc Publishers Ireland	SSLA	Scot Support Learning Assn
SPIN	Soc Public Inf Networks	SSLH	Soc Study Labour Hist
SPL	Scot Poetry Library	SSM	Soc Social Medicine
SPM	Soc Pharmaceutical Medicine	SSNS	Scot Soc Nthn Studies
SPMA	Scot Modern Pentathlon Assn	SSNTA	Scot Seed & Nursery Tr Assn
	Soc Post-Medieval Archaeology	SSR	Scot Soc Rehabilitation

SSS	Ship Stamp Soc	TAG	Arthrogryposis Gp
	Simplified Spelling Soc		Local Govt Technical Advisers Gp
	Sunday Shakespeare Soc		Towpath Action Gp
SSSA	Scot Salmon Smokers Assn	TALES	Assn Library Eqpt Suppliers
SSSG	Stickler Syndrome Support Gp	TAMBA	Twins & Mult Births Assn
SSSprint	Street Sled Sports Racers	TandRA	Tennis & Rackets Assn
SSSS	Soc Study Subterranean Survival	TAROE	Tenants & Residents Orgs England
SSTA	Scot Secondary Teachers' Assn	TARS	Arthur Ransome Soc
STA	Soc Technical Analysts	TAS	Aviation Soc
	Solar Tr Assn	TATHS	Tool & Trs Hist Soc
	Source Testing Assn	TBA	Thoroughbred Breeders' Assn
	Swimming Teachers Assn	TBBA	Tea Buying Brokers Assn Lond
StAAA	Saint Andrew's Ambulance Assn	TBF	Trakehner Breeders Fraternity
STAG	Single Travellers Action Gp	TBPA	Tenpin Bowling Proprietors Assn
STAGBI	Standardbred & Trotting Horse Assn	TBTA	Thames Boating Trs Assn
STAT	Soc Teachers Alexander Technique	TCAS	Three Counties Agricl Soc
STAUK	Sugar Traders Assn	TCF	Compassionate Friends
STEMPRA	Science, Technology, Engg. . . Public Relations Assn	TCMA	Traffic Mgt Contrs Assn
STEP	Soc Trust & Estate Practitioners	TCPA	Town & Country Planning Assn
STEPS	STEPS. . .	TCS	Token Corresponding Soc
Stereo Society	Stereoscopic Soc		Traditional Cosmology Soc
STGA	Scot Tourist Guides Assn		Train Collectors Soc
STLD	Soc TV Lighting Directors	TDA	Timber Decking Assn
STOWA	Scot Tug-of-War Assn	TDS	Dystonia Soc
STP	Soc Turnaround Professionals	TEAM	Eur Atlantic Movement
STR	Soc Theatre Res	TEDct	Thyroid Eye Disease Charitable Trust
STRI	Sports Turf Res Inst	TEGAS	Electric Guitar Appreciation Soc
STS	Scot Text Soc	TEHVA	BEAMA
STSD	Soc Teachers Speech & Drama	TELS	T E Lawrence Soc
STSG	Scot Transport Studies Gp	TESA	Event Services Assn
STTA	Scot Table Tennis Assn	TFA	Freedom Assn
	Scot Timber Tr Assn		Tenant Farmers' Assn
STUC	Scot Trs U Congress		Textile Finishers Assn
SUB.BRIT	Subterranea Britannica	TFIC	Fedn Image Consultants
SUSTAIN	Sustain	TFMA	Tapestry Frame Mfrs Assn
SUT	Soc Underwater Technology Ltd	TFSR	Tools Self Reliance
SVA	Scot Volleyball Assn	TFTA	Traditional Farmfresh Turkey Assn
SWA	Scot Whls Assn	TG	Townswomen's Glds
	Scotch Whisky Assn	TGA	Brit Tomato Growers Assn
	Small Woods Assn		Turfgrass Growers Assn
	Soc Women Artists	TGA Ltd	Tropical Growers' Assn
	Steel Window Assn	TGWU	Transport & Gen Workers' U
SWCPA	S W Coast Path Assn	THA	Telephone Helplines Assn
SWE	Soc Wood Engravers	THCA	Brit Marine Fedn
SWF	Scot Women's Football	The BA	Brit Assn Advancement Science
SWFPA	Scot White Fish Producers Assn	The GA	Giftware Assn
SWHIHR	Soc W Highland & Island Histl Res	The Hallé	Hallé Concerts Soc
SWHP	Soc Welfare Horses & Ponies	The RA	Referees' Assn
SWIBA	Scot Women's Indoor Bowling Assn	THG	Telecommunications Heritage Gp
SWLG	Scot Wild Land Gp	THSSSA	Tool & High Speed Steel Suppliers Assn
SWMA	Scot Wirework Mfrs Assn	TI(UK)	Transparency Intl (UK)
SWMAS	Shropshire & W Midlands Agricl Soc	TIA	Telecommunications Ind Assn
SWPP/BPPA	Soc Wedding & Portrait Photographers	TIC	Tyre Ind Coun
SWRI	Scot Women's Rural Insts	TICA	Thermal Insulation Contrs Assn
SWT	Scot Wildlife Trust	TIEA	Tobacco Ind Emplrs Assn
SWWAPS	Second Wld War Aircraft Presvn Soc	TIGA	TIGA
SyAS	Surrey Archaeol Soc	TIMA	Tue Iron Mfrs Assn
SYHA	Scot Youth Hostels Assn	TIMCON	Timber Packaging & Pallet Confedn
		TIMSA	Thermal Insulation Mfrs & Suppliers Assn
		TLRS	Tramway & Light Rly Soc
		TMA	Tobacco Mfrs' Assn
		TMAP	Teenage Magazine Arbitration Panel
		TMI	Movers Inst
			Tourism Mgt Inst
		TMPDF	Trade Marks Patents & Designs Fedn
		TMS	Tramway Museum Soc

T&CVA	Thames & Chiltern Vineyards Assn	TMS-GBI	Thomas Merton Soc
TA	Telework Assn	TMSA	Traditional Music & Song Assn Scotland
	Transport Assn	TMVA	BEAMA
	Tricycle Assn	TNA	Trigeminal Neuralgia Assn
TAA	Timber Arbitrators Assn	TNAUK	Talking Newspaper Assn
	Tropical Agriculture Assn	TocH	Toc H
TABMAC	All Brit Martial Arts Coun	TOFFS	Over Fifties Assn
TAC	Aeroplane Collection	TOFS	Tracheo-Oesophageal Fistula Support
TACMA	BEAMA	TORRO	Tornado & Storm Res Org
TACS	Tiles & Architectural Ceramics Soc	TOW	Transport Water Assn
TACT	Assn Corporate Trustees	TOWA	Tug of War Assn
TAF	Trade Assn Forum	TPC	Tall Persons Club

© CBD Research Ltd · Beckenham · BR3 5JS · Tel 020 8650 7745 · Fax 020 8650 0768 · E-mail cbd@cbdresearch.com · www.cbdresearch.com

TPG	Portman Gp
TRA	Reiki Assn
	Textile Recycling Assn
	Toy Retailers Assn
TRADA	TRADA Technology
TREOIR	Nat Fedn Services Unmarried Parents...[IRL]
TRF	Trail Riders Fellowship
TRG	Tertiary Res Gp
	Tory Reform Gp
TRIC	TV & Radio Inds Club
TRPS	Talyllyn Rly Presvn Soc
TRSS	Trekking & Riding Soc Scotland
TS	Theosophical Soc England
	Tolkien Soc
TSA	Tank Storage Assn
	Telecare Services Assn
	Textile Services Assn
	Tuberous Sclerosis Assn
	UK Land & Hydrographic Survey Assn
TSA(UK)	Tourette Syndrome (UK) Assn
TSBA	Teeswater Sheep Breeders Assn
TSI	Trading Standards Inst
TSPA	Table Soccer Players Assn
TSSA	Transport Salaried Staffs Assn
TSSEA	Thermal Spraying & Surface Engg Assn
TSSS	Turner Syndrome Support Soc
TT	Transport Trust
TTA	Tile Assn
	Travel Trust Assn
TTAW	Table Tennis Assn Wales
TTCC	Test Card Circle
TTF	Timber Tr Fedn
TTRA	TT Riders Assn
TTS	Transport Ticket Soc
TUA	Telecommunications Users Assn
TUBCS	Trade U Badge Collectors Soc
TUC	Trades U Congress
TUFF	Telecommunications UK Fraud Forum
TUK	Transfrigoroute UK
TVCCi	Thames Valley Cham Comm & Ind
TWI Ltd	Welding Inst
twin2twin	UK Twin to Twin Transfusion Syndrome Assn
TYHA	Yacht Harbour Assn
TYMBA	Traditional Youth Marching Bands Assn

U

UA	Urostomy Assn
UAC	Ulster Automobile Club
UACES	University Assn Contemporary Eur Studies
UAF	Ulster Angling Fedn
UAHS	Ulster Architectural Heritage Soc
UALL	Universities Assn Lifelong Learning
UAS	Ulster Archaeol Soc
UCA	Ulster Chemists Assn
	Utd Chiropractic Assn
UCEA	Universities & Colls Emplrs' Assn
UCFF	Ulster Coarse Fishing Fedn
UCISA	Universities & Colleges Inf Systems Assn
UCSW	U Country Sports Workers
UDM	U Democratic Mineworkers
UFAW	Universities Fedn Animal Welfare
UFLS	Ulster Folk Life Soc
UFRC	Ulster Fedn Rambling Clubs
UFU	Ulster Farmers U
UHF	Ulster Histl Foundation
UHS	Unitarian Hist Soc
UIG	Uveitis Inf Gp
UK NEPA	UK Newsletter & Electronic Pubrs Assn
UK Skeptics	UK Skeptics
UK-ISES	Solar Energy Soc
UK-RHA	UK Rainwater Harvesting Assn
UKA	UK Alliance
	UK Athletics
UKABIF	UK Acquired Brain Injury Forum

UKACA	UK Assn Celebrity Assistants
UKAFFP	UK Assn Frozen Food Producers
UKAFPO	UK Assn Fish Producer Orgs
UKALA	UK Assn Letting Agents
UKAMBY	UK Assn Mfrs Bakers Yeast
UKAN	Narcolepsy Assn
UKAPE	UK Assn Profl Engrs
UKAPMP	UK Assn Proposal Mgt Profls
UKBG	UK Bartenders Gld
UKBS	UK Botswana Soc
UKCGA	UK Chrysanthemum Growers' Assn
UKCHO	UK Confedn Hypnotherapy Orgs
UKCMG	UK Computer Measurement Gp
UKCP	UK Coun Psychotherapy
UKCPA	UK Clinical Pharmacy Assn
UKCPI	UK Cleaning Products Ind Assn
UKCRA	UK Cartridge Remanufacturers Assn
UKCSA	UK Cast Stone Assn
UKDDF	UK Dance Drama Fedn
UKEAPA	UK Employee Assistance Profls Assn
UKeiG	UK eInf Gp
UKELA	UK Envtl Law Assn
UKEMS	UK Envtl Mutagen Soc
UKEP	UK Egg Producers Assn
UKERNA	UK Educ & Res Networking Assn
UKFC	UK Fortifications Club
UKFJB	UK Fedn Jazz Bands
UKFPA	UK Forest Products Assn
UKHA	UK Harp Assn
	UK Housekeepers Assn
UKHCA	UK Homecare Assn
UKHSU	UK Horse Shoers U
UKIA	UK Irrigation Assn
UKISC	UK Indl Space C'ee
UKISCRS	UK & I Soc Cataract & Refractive Surgeons
UKISUG	UK Indl Sugar Users' Gp
UKIVA	UK Indl Vision Assn
UKJGA	UK Jute Goods Assn
UKLA	UK Literacy Assn
	UK Lubricants Assn
UKMA	UK Metric Assn
UKMPA	UK Maritime Pilots' Assn
UKNA	UK Noise Assn
UKOOA	UK Offshore Operators Assn
UKOOG	UK Onshore Operators Gp
UKOTA	UK O'seas Territories Assn
UKOWLA	One World Linking Assn
UKPA	UK Polocrosse Assn
UKPHA	UK Public Health Assn
UKPIA	UK Petroleum Ind Assn
UKPSA	UK Practical Shooting Assn
UKPSF	UK Paintball Sports Fedn
UKPTA	UK Polarity Therapy Assn
UKQAA	UK Quality Ash Assn
UKRA	UK Renderers Assn
	UK Rocketry Assn
UKRAS	UK Roundabout Appreciation Soc
UKRFA	UK Resilient Flooring Mfrs' Assn
UKRPA	UK Revenue Protection Assn
UKSA	UK Shareholders' Assn
UKSAPLD	UK Sports Assn People Learning Disability
UKSCC	UK Spoon Collectors Club
UKSG	UK Serials Gp
UKSIP	UK Soc Investment Profls
UKSMA	UK Software Metrics Assn
	UK Spring Mfrs Assn
UKSPA	UK Science Park Assn
UKSPILL	UK Spill Assn
UKSSA	UK Security Shredding Assn
UKSTAG	Defence Mfrs Assn
UKSTT	UK Soc Trenchless Technology
UKTA	UK Tea Assn
UKTC	UK Trs Confedn
UKTCA	UK Transplant Co-ordinators Assn
UKTLF	UK Textile Laboratory Forum
UKTRF	UK Travel Retail Forum
UKTS	UK Thalassaemia Soc
UKUF	UK Unicycle Fedn

UKVA	UK Vineyards Assn
UKWA	UK Warehousing Assn
	UK Windsurfing Assn
UKWF	UK Weighing Fedn
ULA	Ulster Launderers Assn
UNA	Utd Nations Assn GB & NI
UNISON	Unison
Upkeep	Upkeep
URCHS	Utd Reformed Church Hist Soc
URTU	Utd Road Transport U
USA UK	Utd Saddlebred Assn
USDAW	U Shop, Distributive & Allied Workers
USLS	Ulster-Scots Language Soc
USPC	Ulster Soc Protection Countryside
USPCA	Ulster Soc Prevention Cruelty Animals
USRO	U Senior Revenue Officials
UTU	Ulster Teachers U
UUK	Universities UK
UWHU	Ulster Women's Hockey U

V

V-CC	Veteran-Cycle Club
VAA	Vintage Arms Assn
VAAJ	Veterinary Assn Arbitration & Jurisprudence
VAG	Vernacular Architecture Gp
VAGA	Visual Arts & Galleries Assn
VAHS	Voluntary Action Hist Soc
VBF	Vinegar Brewers Fedn
VBRA	Vehicle Builders & Repairers Assn
VC&GCAssn	Victoria Cross & George Cross Assn
VCN	Voice Care Network
VCT	Vintage Carriages Trust
VdGS	Viola da Gamba Soc
VegSoc	Vegetarian Soc
VFA	Viewing Facilities Assn (UK)
VFI	Vintners Fedn Ireland
VGC	Vintage Glider Club
VHA	Vision Homes Assn
VHGMC	Vintage Horticl & Garden Machinery Club
VHS	Veteran Horse Soc
VIEW	View
ViRSA	Village Retail Services Assn...
VLV	Voice Listener & Viewer
VMCC	Vintage Motor Cycle Club
VMS	Victorian Military Soc
VNS	Violet Needham Soc
VOCAL	Voice Chief Offrs Culture... Scotland
VPG	VAT Practitioners Gp
VPL	Video Performance Ltd
VPS	Vulval Pain Soc
VRMA	Vehicle Restraint Mfrs Assn
VSCC	Vintage Sports Car Club
VSO	Voluntary Service Overseas
VSRA	Veteran Speedway Riders Assn
VSS	Victim Support Scotland
VTSC	Virus Tested Stem Cutting Growers Assn
VWSGB	Virginia Woolf Soc GB

W

W&ACT	Wey & Arun Canal Trust
WA	Willwriters' Assn
WABA	W Africa Business Assn
	Welsh Amat Boxing Assn
WAFE	Women's Aid Fedn (England)
WAH	Wolves & Humans Foundation
Wales PPA	Wales Pre-school Playgroups Assn
WAMF/FfCAC	Welsh Amat Music Fedn
WANHS	Wiltshire Archaeol & Natural Hist Soc
WAOS	Welsh Agricl Org Soc
WARA	Welsh Amat Rowing Assn
WAS	Worcestershire Archaeol Soc

WASA	Welsh Amat Swimming Assn
WAY	Way Foundation
WBA	Welsh Bowling Assn
WBCS	Welsh Black Cattle Soc
WBRA	Wagon Bldg & Repairing Assn
WBU	Welsh Badminton U
	Welsh Bridge U
WCA	Welsh Culinary Assn
WCAS	Westmorland County Agricl Soc
WCC	Wales Craft Coun
WCS	Wilkie Collins Soc
WCTA	Whls Confectionery & Tobacco Alliance
WCU	Welsh Chess U
	Welsh Cycling U
WCVA	Wales Coun Voluntary Action
WDA	Wallcovering Distbrs Assn
	Well Drillers' Assn
WDCS	Whale & Dolphin Consvn Soc
WEA	Workers' Educl Assn
WEN	Women's Envtl Network
WES	Western Equestrian Soc
	Women's Engg Soc
	Writing Eqpt Soc
WFA	Western Front Assn
WFDS	Cymdeithas Ddawns Werin Cymru
WFGA	Women's Farm & Garden Assn
WFS	Wild Flower Soc
WFU	Women's Food & Farming U
WGGB	Writers' Gld
WGU	Welsh Golfing U
WHA	Welsh Hound Assn
	Western Horsemen's Assn
WHR	Welsh Highland Rlys Assn
WHS	Wesley Histl Soc
WHU	Welsh Hockey U
WI	Fedn Women's Insts NI
WIA	Writing Instruments Assn
WIBA	Welsh Indoor Bowls Assn
WJA	Welsh Judo Assn
WM Soc	Water Mgt Soc
WMA	BEAMA
	Workers' Music Assn
WMBA	Whls Markets Brokers' Assn
WMS	Welsh Mines Soc
WMSA	Woodworking Machinery Suppliers Assn
WMSS	Welsh Mountain Sheep Society - Registered Section
WMT	War Memorials Trust
WNA	Welsh Netball Assn
WONA	Web-offset Newspaper Assn
WPA	Wire Products Assn
	World Pheasant Assn UK
WPCS	Welsh Pony & Cob Soc
	White Park Cattle Soc
WPIF	Wood Panel Inds Fedn
WPOA	Westminster Property Owners Assn
WPU	Writers & Photographers unLimited
WRG	Waterway Recovery Gp
WRS	Wiltshire Record Soc
WRU	Welsh Rugby U
WRVS	Women's R Voluntary Service
WSCA	Well Services Contrs Assn
WSF	Williams Syndrome Foundation
WSRS	Wildlife Sound Recording Soc
WSSociety	Soc Writers Her Majesty's Signet
WSTA	Wine & Spirit Trade Assn
WTIF	Wall Tie Installers Fedn
WTT	Wild Trout Trust
WUK	Wakeboard UK
WWA	War Widows Assn
WWJ	W W Jacobs Appreciation Soc
WWOOF	World-Wide Opportunities on Organic Farms
WWTA	Welsh Weight Training Assn

© CBD Research Ltd · Beckenham · BR3 5JS · Tel 020 8650 7745 · Fax 020 8650 0768 · E-mail cbd@cbdresearch.com · www.cbdresearch.com

Y

YAS	Yeovil Agricl Soc
	Yorkshire Archaeol Soc
YDCW	Campaign Protection Rural Wales
YDS	Yorkshire Dialect Soc
YDSA	Yacht Designers & Surveyors Assn
YET	Young Explorers' Trust
YGS	Yorkshire Geological Soc

YHA	Youth Hostels Assn (England & Wales)
YHANI	Youth Hostel Assn NI
YJA	Yachting Journalists' Assn
YMCA	YMCA England
youngchoirs	Brit Fedn Young Choirs
YPS	Yorkshire Philosophical Soc
YWCA	YWCA (Young Women's Christian Association)
ZF	Zionist Fedn
ZSA	Zwartbles Sheep Assn
ZSL	Zoological Soc London

**Symbol of tradition
and progress**

**in directory and
database publishing**

We welcome your enquiries

Enquiry 1 — Why CBD?

Answer: *The first edition of "Current British Directories" was compiled by George and Prue Henderson in 1952; it rapidly became known in the reference library world — at that time thirsty for any reliable guide to business information — as "CBD"; when we formed the company in 1961 there was no better name for it than "CBD Research Ltd".*

—

Since then the company has kept to the tradition of publishing only "seen and verified" information — 24 different titles in a total of 80 editions.

—

In 1966 the company was the only British founder member of the European Association of Directory Publishers; and it was a founder member in 1970 of the Association of British Directory Publishers (now the Data Publishers Association).

—

*We **still** welcome your enquiries*

CBD Research Ltd

15 Wickham Road, Beckenham, Kent, BR3 5JS

Tel: 020 8650 7745 **Fax:** 020 8650 0768

E-mail: cbd@cbdresearch.com

www.cbdresearch.com

PUBLICATIONS INDEX

Annual Expatriate Cost of Living Survey - Brit Cham Comm Thailand
Annual Gazette - Brit Women Pilots Assn
Annual Local Authority Road Maintenance Survey - Asphalt Ind Alliance
Annual Proceedings - Dorothy L Sayers Soc
Annual Survey of Business Finance - Finance & Leasing Assn
Annual Survey of Scottish Export Sales - Scot Coun Devt & Ind
Annual Transactions - Staffordshire Archaeol & Histl Soc
Anomaly - Assn Scientific Study Anomalous Phenomena
Anon Hen - Tolkien Soc
Anthropological Index Online - R Anthropological Inst
Anthropology Today - R Anthropological Inst
Anthroposophical Medical NL - Anthroposophical Med Assn
Antiquarian Horology - Antiquarian Horological Soc
Antiquaries Jnl - Soc Antiquaries London
The Antiquary - Chester Archaeol Soc
Antisemitism in the World Today - Inst Jewish Policy Res
Anxiety - SANE
Application & Measurement of Protective Coatings - Concrete Repair Assn
Applied Ergonomics - Ergonomics Soc
Applied Physics - Inst Physics
Arab Horse Society News - Arab Horse Soc
Arabian Type & Standard - Arab Horse Soc
Arbitration - Chart Inst Arbitrators
Archaeologia Aeliana - Soc Antiquaries Newcastle upon Tyne
Archaeologia Cambrensis - Cambrian Archaeol Assn
Archaeologia Cantiana - Kent Archaeol Soc
Archaeological Jnl - R Archaeol Inst
Archaeological Monographs - Dorset Natural History & Archaeol Soc
The Archaeologist - Inst Field Archaeologists
Archaeology Underwater, the NAS guide to principles & practice - Nautical Archaeology Soc
The Archbishop's Town: the making of mediaeval Croydon - Croydon Natural History & Scientific Soc
Archery Bulletin - NI Archery Soc
Archery UK - Grand Nat Archery Soc
Architectural Heritage Jnl - Architectural Heritage Soc Scotland
Architectural History - Soc Architectural Historians
Architectural Ironmongery Jnl - Gld Architectural Ironmongers
Architectural Technology - Chart Inst Architectural Technologists
Architectural Technology Careers Hbk - Chart Inst Architectural Technologists
Architecture Periodicals Index - R Inst Brit Architects
Archive Zones - FOCAL Intl Ltd
Archives & the User - Brit Records Assn
Archives Jnl - Brit Records Assn
Archives of Disease in Children - R Coll Paediatrics & Child Health
Archives of Natural History - Soc Hist Natural Hist
Area Association Newsletter - Youth Scotland
Arena - Assn Electoral Admins
Arena - U Shop, Distributive & Allied Workers
The Ark - Rare Breeds Survival Trust
Ark File - R Zoological Soc Scotland
Art & Architecture Jnl - Art & Architecture
Art Antiquity & Law - Inst Art & Law
The Art Book - Assn Art Historians
Art Business Today - Fine Art Tr Gld
The Art Directors Book - D&AD
Art History - Assn Art Historians
Art Libraries Jnl - ARLIS UK & Ireland
Art Quarterly - Nat Art Collections Fund
Art Treasures & War - Inst Art & Law
Arthritis News - Arthritis Care
Artisan - Gld Fine Food Retailers
Scot Assn Painting Craft Teachers
Artist Blacksmith - Brit Artist Blacksmiths Assn
Artists' Guide to Selling Work - Fine Art Tr Gld
Arts Care - Nat Campaign Arts
Arts News - Nat Campaign Arts
As We See It - Dyslexia Inst
Asbestos Facts - Occupational & Envtl Diseases Assn
ASGARD - Assn Scotland Res Astronautics
Aspects of Applied Biology - Assn Applied Biologists
Asphalt Now - Asphalt Ind Alliance

Asphalt Professional - Inst Asphalt Technology
Aspirations! - Assn Spinal Injury Res, Rehabilitation & Reintegration
Association Executive - Inst Assn Mgt
Asthma News - Asthma UK
Astrocalendar - Fedn Astronomical Socs
Astrological Jnl - Astrological Assn
Astrology - Astrological Lodge London
Astrology & Medicine - Astrological Assn
Astronomy & Geophysics - R Astronomical Soc
At the Sign of... - Inn Sign Soc
The Ataxia - Ataxia UK
ATLA Jnl - Fund Replacement Animals Med Experiments
Atlantic Daily Bulletin - Brit Titanic Soc
Atlantic Seabirds - Seabird Gp
Atlas of Enamel Defects - Inst Vitreous Enamellers
Atomic, Molecular & Optical Physics - Inst Physics
AUCC - Brit Assn Counselling & Psychotherapy
Audiens - Brit Assn Community Doctors Audiology
Audit - R Soc Promotion Health
The Author - Soc Authors
Translators Assn
The Authority of Case Law - Scot Rights of Way & Access Soc
Autism News - Autism Indep UK
AUTlook - Assn University Teachers
Autocad Symbol Library - Catering Eqpt Supplier's Assn
Automobile Abstracts - MIRA Ltd
Automotive Business News - MIRA Ltd
Automotive History Review - Soc Automotive Historians
Automotive Recycling & Disposal UK - Motor Vehicle Dismantlers Assn
Autumn Bulletin - Delphinium Soc
The Avicultural Magazine - Avicultural Soc
Aware - Scot Motor Neurone Disease Assn
Axis, the Jnl of Housing, Planning & Regeneration - ROOM, Nat Coun Housing & Planning
Ayrshire Dairyman - Ayrshire Cattle Soc
Ayrshire Jnl - Ayrshire Cattle Soc

B

Baby Watch - Meningitis Research Foundation
Back Chat - Chiropractic Patients' Assn
Backpack - Backpackers Club
Baconiana - Francis Bacon Soc Inc
The Badger - Badge Collectors Circle
Badminton in Wales - Welsh Badminton U
Badminton Magazine - Badminton Assn England
Balance - Diabetes UK
A Balanced View: Practical Tips for a Healthy Diet - Arthritic Assn
Baling Out - Straw Bale Building Assn
Balloonies - NABAS (the Balloon Assn)
Bamboo Wireless - Assn Brit Civilian Internees Far East Region
Bandersnatch - Lewis Carroll Soc
Bank of Scotland Learn to Swim (Adult & Child Syllabus) - Scot Swimming
Bank of Scotland Learn to Swim Syllabus - Scot Swimming
Bank Survey - Forum Private Business
Bankruptcy Explained - Bankruptcy Assn
Baptist Quarterly - Baptist Historical Soc
Baptist Times - Baptist U
Baptist Union Directory - Baptist U
Barge Buyers' Hbk - Dutch Barge Assn
Barristers in Local Government - Bar Assn Local Govt & Public Service
Base Thoughts - Antique Metalware Soc
Baseball & Softball Bulletins - BaseballSoftball UK
Basic Letterpress for Beginners - Brit Printing Soc
Basking Shark & Whale Report - Basking Shark Soc
Bat Monitoring Post - Bat Conservation Trust
Bat News - Bat Conservation Trust
Battery Vehicle Review - Battery Vehicle Soc
Battle of Britain Remembered - Battle of Britain Histl Soc
Be My Parent Newspaper - Brit Assn Adoption & Fostering
Be Sure - Hamper Ind Tr Assn

© CBD Research Ltd · Beckenham · BR3 5JS · Tel 020 8650 7745 · Fax 020 8650 0768 · E-mail cbd@cbdresearch.com · www.cbdresearch.com

The Beat - Brit Cham Comm Shanghai

Beating Arthritis & Beating Osteoporosis - Arthritis & Rheumatism Natural Therapy Res Assn

Beaumont Magazine - Beaumont Soc

Beautyguild Bulletin - Gld Profl Beauty Therapists Ltd

Beaver - Fac Building

The Beckford Jnl - Beckford Soc

Bee Improvement - Bee Improvement & Bee Breeders Assn

Beef Farmer - Nat Beef Assn

Beeline - Economics & Business Educ Assn

Beermat - Brit Beermat Collectors' Soc

Behaviour & Information Technology - Ergonomics Soc

Behavioural & Cognitive Psychotherapy - Brit Assn Behavioural & Cognitive Psychotherapies

Behavioural Problems in Huntington's Disease - Scot Huntington's Assn

Behind the Painted Smile - Meet-a-Mum Assn

Being There - Tourism Concern

Belted Galloway News - Belted Galloway Cattle Soc

Ben's Story: an introduction to child contact centres - Nat Assn Child Contact Centres

Best Practice - Inst Assessors & Internal Verifiers

Best Practices Jnl - Nat Fedn Enterprise Agencies

The Betjemanian - Betjeman Soc

Between the Flags - Point-to-Point Owners & Riders Assn

Beyond the Horizon - Brit Coun Shopping Centres

BH Magazine - Brit Hellenic Cham Comm

Bibafax - Brit Isles Backgammon Assn

Bifalink - Brit Intl Freight Assn

Bifocals without Tears - Assn Brit Dispensing Opticians

The Big Youth Theatre Manual - Nat Assn Youth Theatres

biiBUSINESS - Brit Inst Innkeeping

Biochemical Jnl - Biochemical Soc

Biographical Portraits Vol IV - Japan Soc

Biological Jnl - Linnean Soc London

Biological Reviews - Cambridge Philosophical Soc

Biologist - Inst Biology

Biomedical Scientist - Inst Biomedical Science

The Bioneer - Brit Assn Flower Essence Producers

Biotechnology & Applied Biochemistry - Biochemical Soc

Bird Study - Brit Trust Ornithology

Bird Table - Brit Trust Ornithology

Birds - R Soc Protection Birds

Birmingham & Solihull Business Guide & Directory - Solihull Cham Comm & Ind

Birmingham & West Midlands Chamber Directory - Solihull Cham Comm & Ind

Bison Hbk - Brit Bison Assn

Black & White Photography - Gld Master Craftsmen

Black Powder - Muzzle Loaders Assn

The Blackcountryman - Black Country Soc

Blake Jnl - Blake Soc at St James's

Blasmusik Bulletin - Kmoch European Bands Soc

Blastpipe - Scot Rly Presvn Soc

BLESMAG - Brit Limbless Ex-Service Men's Assn

Blinds & Shutters - Brit Blind & Shutter Assn

Blink - Assn Optometrists

Blithe Spirit - Brit Haiku Soc

Blonde - Brit Blonde Soc

Blood Royal, Queen's Golden Jubilee - Manorial Soc

Blowout - Offshore Ind Liaison C'ee

Blue Book - London Appreciation Soc

Blue Flag - Dutch Barge Assn

Blue Pages - Soc Brit Theatre Designers

Blue Print Magazine - Emergency Planning Soc

Bluebell News - Bluebell Rly Presvn Soc

BMI Bulletin - Building Cost Infm Service

BMI Price Book - Building Cost Infm Service

Boat Jumble Fixtures List - Boat Jumble Assn

Body - Vehicle Builders' & Repairers' Assn

The 'Boneshaker' - Veteran-Cycle Club

Book of Rules & Regulations - Fedn Commodity Assns

Bookbinder - Soc Bookbinders

The Bookplate Jnl - Bookplate Soc

Bookselling Essentials - Booksellers Assn

Bootprint - Outdoor Writers' Gld

Borate Glasses, Crystals & Melts - Soc Glass Technology

Bore Da - Urdd Gobaith Cymru (yr Urdd)

Bosc D'Antic on Glassmaking - Soc Glass Technology

Botanical Jnl - Linnean Soc London

Botanical Jnl of Scotland - Botanical Soc Scotland

The Bottle Street Gazette - Margery Allingham Soc

The Bottom Line - Production Mgrs Assn

Bound to Fail - Anti Common Market League

The Boutonneur - Buttonhook Soc

Bowls for the Beginner - Scot Bowling Assn

Bowls International - Scot Indoor Bowling Assn

BPI Statistical Hbk - Brit Phonographic Ind

B-Plus - Breast Implant Inf Soc

Bradleya - Brit Cactus & Succulent Soc

Branch Line News - Branch Line Soc

Branch Secretaries Circular - Nat Fedn Sub-Postmasters

Brand Book - English Westerners Soc

Brandwagon - Horseracing Sponsors Assn

Brazil Business Brief - Brazilian Cham Comm GB

Breaking Old Ground - a guide to contaminated land - Brit Urban Regeneration Assn

Breathe Easy - Fedn Bakers

Breeds Record Supplement - Kennel Club

The Brewer & Distiller - Inst Brewing & Distilling

Brewing & Distilling Directory - Inst Brewing & Distilling

Brick Bulletin - Brick Devt Assn Ltd

The Brief - Brit Cham Comm Thailand

Brit Naturism Magazine - Cent Coun Brit Naturism

Brit Oz Bulletin - Britain-Australia Soc

Britain - Anti Common Market League

Britain & Europe - Manorial Soc

Britain & Overseas - Economic Res Coun

Britain Brasil - Brit Cham Comm & Ind Brazil

Britain-Zimbabwe Review - Britain-Zimbabwe Soc

Britaly - Brit Cham Comm Italy, Inc

Britannia - Soc Promotion Roman Studies

British & Irish Archaeological Bibliography - Coun Brit Archaeology

British Actuarial Jnl - Fac Actuaries Scotland
Inst Actuaries

British American Business, the UK Hbk - Brit-American Business Inc

British Archaeology - Coun Brit Archaeology

British Bottle Review - Old Bottle Club

British Bulletin of Publications on Latin America, Spain & Portugal - Hispanic & Luso-Brazilian Coun

British Business in China Directory - Brit Cham Comm Shanghai

British Business Presence in Spain - Spanish Cham Comm GB

British Camelids Hbk - Brit Camelids Assn

British Cinematographer Magazine - Brit Soc Cinematographers Ltd

British Companies with Commercial Interests in Spain - Spanish Cham Comm GB

British Crematoria in Public Profile - Cremation Soc

British Dental Jnl - Brit Dental Assn

British Dental Nurses' Jnl - Brit Assn Dental Nurses

British Educational Research Jnl - Brit Educl Res Assn

British Envoys in Japan - Japan Soc

British Equestrian Directory - Brit Equestrian Tr Assn

British Farmer & Grower - Nat Farmers U

British-German Review - Brit-German Assn

British Go Jnl - Brit Go Assn

British Herbal Compendium - Brit Herbal Medicine Assn

The British Herbal Pharmacopoeia - Brit Herbal Medicine Assn

The British Homing World - R Pigeon Racing Assn

British Horse - Brit Horse Soc

British Hosta & Hemerocallis Society Bulletin - Brit Hosta & Hemerocallis Soc

British Jnl of Aesthetics - Brit Soc Aesthetics

British Jnl of Audiology - Brit Soc Audiology

British Jnl of Biomedical Science - Inst Biomedical Science

British Jnl of Canadian Studies - Brit Assn Canadian Studies

British Jnl of Clinical & Social Psychiatry - Soc Clinical Psychiatrists

British Jnl of Clinical Pharmacology - Brit Pharmacological Soc

British Jnl of Clinical Psychology - Brit Psychological Soc

British Jnl of Dermatology - Brit Assn Dermatologists

British Jnl of Developmental Psychology - Brit Psychological Soc

British Jnl of Educational Psychology - Brit Psychological Soc

British Jnl of Haematology - Brit Soc Haematology

British Jnl of Health Psychology - Brit Psychological Soc
British Jnl for the History of Philosophy - Brit Soc Hist Philosophy
British Jnl for the History of Science - Brit Soc Hist Science
British Jnl of Infection Control - Infection Control Nurses Assn
British Jnl of Learning Disabilities - Brit Inst Learning Disabilities
British Jnl of Mathematical & Statistical Psychology - Brit Psychological Soc
British Jnl of Middle Eastern Studies - Brit Soc Middle Eastern Studies
British Jnl of Music Therapy - Brit Soc Music Therapy
British Jnl of Nutrition - Nutrition Soc
British Jnl of Obstetrics & Gynaecology - R Coll Obstetricians & Gynaecologists
British Jnl of Occupational Therapy - Brit Assn Occupational Therapists Ltd
British Jnl of Oral & Maxillofacial Surgery - Brit Assn Oral & Maxillofacial Surgeons
British Jnl of Orthodontics - Brit Orthodontic Soc
British Jnl of Pharmacology - Brit Pharmacological Soc
British Jnl for the Philosophy of Science - Brit Soc Philosophy Science
British Jnl of Podiatry - Soc Chiropodists & Podiatrists
British Jnl of Psychiatry - R Coll Psychiatrists
The British Jnl of Psychodrama & Sociodrama - Brit Psychodrama Assn
British Jnl of Psychology - Brit Psychological Soc
British Jnl of Radiology - Brit Inst Radiology
British Jnl of Social Work - Brit Assn Social Workers
British Jnl for Special Education - nasen
British Jnl of Sports Medicine - Brit Assn Sport & Exercise Medicine
British Jnl of Visual Impairment - View
British Judo - Brit Judo Assn
British Latvian Trade - Brit Cham Comm Latvia
British Medical Jnl - Brit Med Assn
British Military Serials - Road Transport Fleet Data Soc
British Mining Memoirs - Northern Mine Res Soc
British Mining Monograph - Northern Mine Res Soc
British Museum Magazine - Brit Museum Friends
British National Formulary for Children - R Coll Paediatrics & Child Health
British Naturalist - Brit Naturalists' Assn
British Naturopathic Jnl - Brit Naturopathic Assn
British Numismatic Jnl - Brit Numismatic Soc
British Origami - Brit Origami Soc
British Orthopaedic News - Brit Orthopaedic Assn
British Orthoptic Jnl - Brit & Ir Orthoptic Soc
British Parent Companies with Swiss Subsidiaries - Brit-Swiss Cham Comm [Switzerland]
British Racing News - Brit Racing & Sports Car Club
British Railway Brakevans & Ballast Ploughs - Histl Model Rly Soc
British Railway Track - Permanent Way Instn
British Railways Mark 1 Coaches - Histl Model Rly Soc
British Rowing Almanack - Amateur Rowing Assn Ltd
The British Sugarcraft News - British Sugarcraft News
British Tennis - Lawn Tennis Assn
British Water Ski & Wakeboard - Brit Water Ski Fedn Ltd
The British Weightlifter - Brit Weight Lifters Assn
The Britsoft Book - Entertainment & Leisure Software Pubrs Assn
Broadsheet - Modern Pentathlon Assn
The Broker - Brit Insurance Brokers' Assn
Brunel's Cornish Viaducts - Histl Model Rly Soc
British-German Review - Brit-German Assn
The Buddhist Directory - Buddhist Soc
The Budgerigar - Budgerigar Soc
The Bugle - Soc Producers & Composers Applied Music
The Bugle Call Rag - Harry Roy Appreciation Soc
Building & Repairing Dry Stone Walls - Dry Stone Walling Assn
Building Engineer - Assn Bldg Engrs
Building for a Future - Assn Envt Conscious Bldg
Building on Success - Biosciences Fedn
Building Services Engineering Research & Technology - Chart Instn Bldg Services Engrs
Building Services Jnl - Chart Instn Bldg Services Engrs
Bulletin Board - Sound Sense
Bulletin of Legal Developments - Brit Inst Intl & Comparative Law
Bulletin of Veterinary History - Veterinary Hist Soc
Bulletin Subterranea Britannica - Subterranea Britannica

The Bulwark - Scot Reformation Soc
Burney Jnl - Burney Soc
Burney Letter - Burney Soc
Burning Issues - Freedom Org Right Enjoy Smoking Tobacco
Burns Chronicle - Robert Burns World Fedn
The Bursar's Review - Indep Schools' Bursars Assn
Bus Fare - Brit Trolleybus Soc
Busfare - Nat Playbus Assn
The Business - Dundee & Tayside Cham Comm & Ind
The Business - Nat Caravan Coun Ltd
Business Adviser - Inst Business Advisers
Business Bulletin - Aberdeen & Grampian Cham Comm (Inc)
Business Chat - N Kent Cham Comm
Business Comment - Edinburgh Cham Comm
Business Comment - Leith Cham Comm
The Business Connections - NI Cham Comm & Ind
The Business Economist - Soc Business Economists
Business Edge - Sussex Cham Comm & Enterprise
Business Executives - Assn Business Executives
Business Info Beyond the Lens - Assn Photographers Ltd
Business Intelligence - Hull & Humber Cham Comm, Ind & Shipping
Business Jnl - Thames Valley Cham Comm & Ind
Business Link - Brit Cham Comm Morocco
Business Magazine - Norfolk Cham Comm & Ind
Business Management Manual - Registered Nursing Home Assn Ltd
Business Matters - Lancaster Dist Cham Comm
Business Networking - Cumbria Cham Comm
Business Networking Magazine - Quality Gld
Business News - Brit Assn Landscape Inds
        Portsmouth & SE Hants Cham Comm & Ind
        Taunton Cham Comm
        York & N Yorks Cham Comm
Business Plus - Bradford Cham Comm & Ind
        Essex Chams Comm
The Business Practitioner - Soc Business Practitioners
Business South - Croydon Cham Comm & Ind
Business Standards - BSI
Business Survey - Scot Chams Comm
Business Technology Outsourcer - Nat Outsourcing Assn
Business to Business Flyer - Sefton Cham Comm & Ind Ltd
Business Travel Jnl - Advantage
Business Update - York & N Yorks Cham Comm
Business West Annual Directory - Swindon Cham Comm & Ind
But - What do you do in the Winter? - Concert Artistes' Assn
Butterflies of Gower - Gower Soc
Butterfly - Butterfly Consvn
Button Lines - Brit Button Soc
Buyers' Guide & Directory - Pigging Products & Services Assn
Buyers' Guide to Chillers - Polymer Machinery Mfrs' & Distbrs' Assn
Buyers' Guide to Dryers - Polymer Machinery Mfrs' & Distbrs' Assn
Buyers' Guide to Granulators - Polymer Machinery Mfrs' & Distbrs' Assn
Buyers' Guide to Robots - Polymer Machinery Mfrs' & Distbrs' Assn
Buyers' Guide to Temperature Control - Polymer Machinery Mfrs' & Distbrs' Assn

C

C Vu - Assn C & C++ Users
CA Magazine - Inst Chart Accountants Scotland
Cabletalk - SELECT
Cactus World - Brit Cactus & Succulent Soc
Café Culture Magazine - Café Soc
Cahiers - Assn French Language Studies
Caledonian Gardener - R Caledonian Horticl Soc
The Call Boy - Brit Music Hall Soc
Camden series - R Histl Soc
The Camelids Chronicle - Brit Camelids Assn
Campaign - Campaign Nuclear Disarmament
Camping & Caravanning Magazine - Camping & Caravanning Club Ltd
Can Makers Report - Can Makers

© CBD Research Ltd · Beckenham · BR3 5JS · Tel 020 8650 7745 · Fax 020 8650 0768 · E-mail cbd@cbdresearch.com · www.cbdresearch.com

Canal Camps Brochure - Waterway Recovery Gp
CannieSpell - Scot Language Dictionaries
Canoe Focus - Brit Canoe U
Canoeing Hbk - Brit Canoe U
Canu Gwerin - Welsh Folk Song Soc
Car Buyer's Guide - ETA Services Ltd
Caravanning Europe - Caravan Club Ltd
Care - Leukaemia CARE
Care Assistant Training Manual - Registered Nursing Home Assn Ltd
Care on the Road - R Soc Prevention Accidents
The Care & Storage of Photographs: recommendations for good practice - Nat Assn Aerial Photographic Libraries
Care of Viol - Viola da Gamba Soc
Career Prospects for Research Workers in the Biological & Medical Sciences - Assn Researchers Medicine & Science
Career Secretary - Inst Qualified Profl Secretaries Ltd
Careers Education & Guidance - Assn Careers Educ & Guidance
Careers for Barristers in Local Government - Bar Assn Local Govt & Public Service
Careers Guidance Today - Inst Career Guidance Ltd
Careers Software News - ADSET
Carefree Camping & Caravanning Guide to Europe - Camping & Caravanning Club Ltd
The Carer - Carers UK
Caribbean Airline News - Caribbean-Brit Business Coun
Caribbean Briefing - Caribbean-Brit Business Coun
Caring for Staff - Ceretas
Caring for the Nation's Health - Brit Health Care Assn
The Carrollian - Lewis Carroll Soc
The Cartographic Jnl - Brit Cartographic Soc
Cartographiti - Brit Cartographic Soc
Cartophilic Notes & News - Cartophilic Soc
Cascade - Action Sick Children
The Case for Customer Magazines - Assn Publishing Agencies
The Case against Hysterectomy - Campaign against Hysterectomy & Unnecessary Operations on Women
Case Studies - Assn Publishing Agencies
Casebook - Medical Protection Soc Ltd
Casemate - Fortress Study Gp
Caspian - Caspian Horse Soc
Casualty Simulation - Casualties U
The Cat - Cats Protection
Catalogue of British Suppliers - Energy Inds Coun
Catalysts & Catalysed Reactions - R Soc Chemistry
Catchword - Assn Teachers Lipreading Adults
Catena - Catenian Assn
Cathodic Protection of Reinforced Concrete - Corrosion Protection Assn
Catholic Ancestor - Catholic Family History Soc
Catholic Archives - Catholic Archives Soc
Catholic Medical Quarterly - Gld Catholic Doctors
Catnap - Narcolepsy Assn
CAUGers - Assn C & C++ Users
Cave & Karst Science - Brit Cave Res Assn
Cavies - Nat Cavy Club
Cavity Wounds - Wound Care Soc
CBI - Fitness Ind Assn
CCi News - Thames Valley Cham Comm & Ind
CDH/DDH Plasters - STEPS: Assn People with Lower Limb Abnormalities
CDH/DDH Splints - STEPS: Assn People with Lower Limb Abnormalities
Cecidology - Brit Plant Gall Soc
Cemetery & Churchyard Regulations - Assn Burial Authorities Ltd
Census - Automatic Vending Assn
Centre Circle - Inst Football Mgt & Admin
League Mgrs Assn
A Century of Archaeology in East Herts - E Herts Archaeol Soc
Ceramic Review - Craft Potters' Assn
Ceramics & Glass: a basic technology - Soc Glass Technology
Ceredigion - Cymdeithas Hanes Ceredigion Histl Soc
Certificate of Vesting - Confedn Construction Specialists
Ceska Muzika - Kmoch European Bands Soc
CF Talk - Cystic Fibrosis Trust
CF Today - Cystic Fibrosis Trust
Chacom - N & Wstn Lancs Cham Comm & Ind
Chairman's Update - Assn Private Pet Cemeteries & Crematoria

The Challenge for Parliament: Making Government - Hansard Soc Parliamentary Govt
Challenging OCD - OCD Action
The Chamber - Surrey Chams Comm Ltd
Chamber Chat - Newport & Gwent Cham Comm & Ind
Chamber Link - Doncaster Cham Comm
Chamber Matters - Rotherham Cham Comm
Chamber of Commerce News - Southampton & Fareham Cham Comm & Ind
Chamber Voice - N Hampshire Cham Comm & Ind
Chamberlink - Solihull Cham Comm & Ind
Changing the Future - Community Foundation Network
Changing with the Times - Scot Disability Sport
Chanter - Bagpipe Soc
Charolais News - Brit Charolais Cattle Soc Ltd
Chartered Architect - R Incorporation Architects Scotland
The Chartered Forester - Inst Chart Foresters
Chartered Secretary - Inst Chart Secretaries & Administrators
Chat - Children's Chronic Arthritis Assn
Deaf Educ Listening & Talking
Chat 2 - Children's Chronic Arthritis Assn
Chat for Teachers - Children's Chronic Arthritis Assn
Chatham House NL - R Inst Intl Affairs
Check It - Nat Specialist Contrs Coun
Checklists (the sole commercial guide to European wine & spirit legislation) - Wine & Spirit Assn
Checkout - Brit Coun Shopping Centres
Cheerleader - Brit Cheerleading Assn
Chemical Communications - R Soc Chemistry
The Chemical Engineer - Instn Chemical Engrs
Chemical Engineering Research & Design - Instn Chemical Engrs
Chemical Hazards in Industry - R Soc Chemistry
Chemical Society Reviews - R Soc Chemistry
Chemical World - R Soc Chemistry
Chemistry & Industry - Soc Chemical Ind
Cherryburn Times - Bewick Soc
Cherub Bulletin - R Coll Paediatrics & Child Health
Chess Moves - English Chess Fedn
Chester Zoo Life - N England Zoological Soc
Chew - Tracheo-Oesophageal Fistula Support
CHI Hbk - Support Soc Children High Intelligence
CHI News - Support Soc Children High Intelligence
Child & Adolescent Mental Health - Assn Child & Adolescent Mental Health
Child Abuse Review - Brit Assn Study & Prevention Child Abuse & Neglect
Childminding - Scot Childminding Assn
Children & Pets - Soc Companion Animal Studies
Children in Prison - Howard League Penal Reform
Chile News - Brit Chilean Cham Comm
Chimney Jnl - Nat Assn Chimney Sweeps
China in Focus - Soc Anglo-Chinese Understanding
China-Britain Trade Review - China-Britain Business Coun
Chipping In - English Golf U
The Chiropody Review - Inst Chiropodists & Podiatrists
Chivalry - Imperial Soc Knights Bachelor
Choice in Welfare - Inst Economic Affairs
Choir Schools Today - Choir Schools Assn
Choosing a Boarding School: a guide for parents - Boarding Schools Assn
Choreography As Work - Dance UK Ltd
Chowkidar - Brit Assn Cemeteries S Asia
Christian Librarian - Librarians' Christian Fellowship
Chromatography Abstracts - Chromatographic Soc
R Soc Chemistry
Chronicle - Regia Anglorum
Church & King - Soc King Charles Martyr
Church Monuments - Church Monuments Soc
Church Music Quarterly - R School Church Music
Churches Hbk - Fellowship Indep Evangelical Churches
CICA Bulletin - Construction Ind Computing Assn
Cider - Nat Assn Cider Makers
The Cigarette Packet - Cigarette Packet Collectors' Club
Cinema & Video Industry Audience Research - Cinema Advertising Assn Ltd
Cinema Technology - BKSTS
CIP - Urdd Gobaith Cymru (yr Urdd)

The Circler - Nat Assn Ladies' Circles Great Britain & Ireland
Circuit - Girls' Venture Corps Air Cadets
Circuit Chatter - Brit Radio Car Assn
Circulation - Brit Hydrological Soc
Circus News - Circus Soc
Cirplan - Soc Cirplanologists
City & County - Northumberland & Newcastle Soc
Civil Engineering Surveyor - Instn Civil Engg Surveyors
Clamavi - Regia Anglorum
Clan - Nat Assn Laryngectomee Clubs
Clapanews - Cleft Lip & Palate Assn
Clarinet & Saxophone - Clarinet & Saxophone Soc
Classical Quarterly - Classical Assn
Classical Review - Classical Assn
Classification of Adhesion of Vitreous Enamel to Steel - Inst Vitreous Enamellers
Clearing Blocked Crushers - Quarry Products Assn
The Clematis - Brit Clematis Soc
The Clerk - Soc Local Coun Clerks
Climate News - Assn Brit Climatologists
Climb - Children Living Inherited Metabolic Diseases
Clinical & Experimental Allergy - Brit Soc Allergy & Clinical Immunology
Clinical & Experimental Immunology - Brit Soc Immunology
Clinical Anatomy - Brit Assn Clinical Anatomists
Clinical Medicine - R Coll Physicians London
Clinical Oncology - R Coll Radiologists
Clinical Radiology - R Coll Radiologists
Clinical Rehabilitation - Brit Soc Rehabilitation Medicine
Clinical Research Focus - Inst Clinical Res
Clinical Science - Biochemical Soc
Medical Res Soc
Close-Up - Mid Yorks Cham Comm & Ind Ltd
Clothes to Suit - Scoliosis Assn (UK)
Club Jnl - Working Men's Club & Inst U Ltd
Club News - Camera Club
CMA News - Amicus - CMA Section
CND Today - Campaign Nuclear Disarmament
Coaches - Welsh Badminton U
Coachline - Brit Tennis Coaches Assn
Coat of Arms - Heraldry Soc
Coates Herd Book - Beef Shorthorn Cattle Soc
Coates Herd Book: Dairy Beef - Shorthorn Soc
Coatings - Thermal Spraying & Surface Engg Assn
Cobbett's New Register - William Cobbett Soc
Coblegram - Coble & Keelboat Soc
The Cobweb - Kentish Cobnuts Assn
Code of Caring - People & Dogs Soc
Code of Practice for Safe Use of Lifting Equipment - Lifting Eqpt Engrs Assn
Code of Practice for Safeguarding Machinery - Quarry Products Assn
Code of Practice for Solar Industry - Solar Tr Assn
Code of Practice for the better organisation of Traction Engine rallies, incorporating the Rally Authorisation Scheme - Nat Traction Engine Trust
Code of Practice for Traction Engines & Similar Vehicles - Nat Traction Engine Trust
Coin Hoards - R Numismatic Soc
The Coleridge Bulletin - Friends Coleridge
Collections News - MDA Europe
College News - R Coll Ophthalmologists
Colombian Correspondent - Brit & Colombian Cham Comm
Colour Index International - Soc Dyers & Colourists
Coloured Sheep News - Brit Coloured Sheep Breeders Assn
Come Gardening - THRIVE
Come Into Horticulture - Inst Horticulture
Comfort Engineering - Inst Domestic Heating & Envtl Engrs
Commentary on the Unidroit Convention - Inst Art & Law
Commercial Update - Newspaper Soc
The Commercials Book - D&AD
The Commission Agent - Manufacturers' Agents' Assn
Commissioning Engineers Compendium - Commissioning Specialists Assn
Commissioning Social Research: a good practice guide - Social Res Assn
Common Fisheries Policy - End or Mend? - Campaign Independent Britain

Commonwealth Universities Ybk - Assn Commonwealth Universities
Communicate - Assn Therapy Lecturers
Communicate - Assn Translation Cos
Communicating Quality (professional standards) - R Coll Speech & Language Therapists
Communication - Nat Autistic Soc
Communications Engineer - Instn Engg & Technology
Communicator - Inst Scientific & Technical Communicators
Communicators - Brit Assn Communicators in Business Ltd
Communiqué - Medical Action Global Security
Community - Nat Fedn Community Orgs
Community Dental Health - Brit Assn Study Community Dentistry
Community Extra - Nat Fedn Community Orgs
Community Foundations & Community Needs Assessment - Community Foundation Network
Community Transport - Community Transport Assn UK
Compact Scottish National Dictionary - Scot Language Dictionaries
Comparative & Physiological Psychology - Experimental Psychology Soc
Comparative Criticism - Brit Comparative Literature Assn
Compendium of Buttonhooks - Buttonhook Soc
Compendium of Data Sheets IOC Animal Medicines - Nat Office Animal Health
Competition & Masterpoint Jnl - Welsh Bridge U
Complete Corpus of Kempe Glass in the UK - Kempe Soc
Complete Guide to Avebury - Megalithic Soc
Complete Guide to Starting & Running a Bookshop - Booksellers Assn
The Complete Music for Solo Piano - Havergal Brian Soc
Composting News - Composting Assn
Compressed Air Condensate - Brit Compresed Air Soc
Computer Resurrection - Computer Conservation Soc
Computers & Law - Soc Computers & Law
Computers in Genealogy - Soc Genealogists
Computing & Control - Instn Engg & Technology
Concise English / Scots Dictionary - Scot Language Dictionaries
Concord - English Speaking U C'wealth
Concrete - Concrete Soc
Concrete Bridges - Concrete Bridge Devt Gp
Concrete Current Awareness - Brit Cement Assn
Concrete Cutter - Drilling & Sawing Assn
Concrete Engineers International Jnl - Concrete Soc
Concrete Quarterly - Brit Cement Assn
Concrete Substructures for Bridge - Concrete Bridge Devt Gp
Condensed Matter - Inst Physics
The Conductor - Nat Assn Brass Band Conductors
The Conduit - Cambridge Antiquarian Soc
Conference & Exhibition Fact Finder - Assn Confs & Events
Conference NL - Family Rights Gp
Congress Proceedings - R Envtl Health Inst Scotland
Connect - Brit Learning Assn
LMCA
Welding Inst
The Conradian - Joseph Conrad Soc (UK)
Conservation Holidays - Brit Trust Consvn Volunteers
Conservation Issues & The Maintenance of Cereal - Nat Soc Master Thatchers
Conserver - Brit Trust Consvn Volunteers
Conserving Lakeland - Friends Lake District
Consolidation or Change? A second survey of Family Based Respite Care Services in the UK - Shared Care Network
Construction & Law Review - Instn Civil Engg Surveyors
Construction History Jnl - Construction History Soc
Construction Industry Forecasts - Construction Products Assn
Construction Information Quarterly - Chart Inst Bldg
Construction Manager - Chart Inst Bldg
Construction Markets Trends - Construction Products Assn
Construction Products Briefing - Construction Products Assn
Construction Products Trade Survey - Construction Products Assn
Construction Trends Survey - Construction Confedn
Consumer Credit - Consumer Credit Tr Assn
Consumer Guides - Fedn Master Builders
Consumer Policy Review - Consumers' Assn
Consumer Sciences Today - Inst Consumer Sciences
Contact - Brit Chiropractic Assn
Brit-Polish Cham Comm

© CBD Research Ltd · Beckenham · BR3 5JS · Tel 020 8650 7745 · Fax 020 8650 0768 · E-mail cbd@cbdresearch.com · www.cbdresearch.com

Chart Inst Bldg
Guernsey Cham Comm
Inst Traffic Accident Investigators
Lutheran Coun
Tramway Museum Soc

Contact Point - Brit Assn Dental Therapists

Contacto - Brit Interlingua Soc

Contemporary Hypnosis - Brit Soc Experimental & Clinical Hypnosis

Context - Inst Historic Bldg Consvn

Continence - Assn Continence Advice

Continuity - Business Continuity Inst

Contract - Public Services Network

Contract Catering Survey - Brit Hospitality Assn

The Contract Flooring Jnl - Contract Flooring Assn Ltd

Contracting Bulletin - Nat Assn Agricultural Contrs

Control - Inst Operations Mgt

The Controversy of John Hampden's Death - John Hampden Soc

Convection - Tornado & Storm Research Org

Converting the English Horse to Western - Western Horsemen's Assn

Conway Memorial Lecture - S Place Ethical Soc

Cooperative Official - Nat Assn Cooperative Officials

Co-operatives - Co-operatives UK Ltd

Co-operatives UK Briefing - Co-operatives UK Ltd

The Copy Book - D&AD

Cornish Worldwide - London Cornish Assn

Correlation - Astrological Assn

Correspondence Chess - Brit Correspondence Chess Soc

Corrosion Management - Inst Corrosion

Corrosion Science - Inst Corrosion

Cosmos - Traditional Cosmology Soc

Cosmos & Culture - Astrological Assn

The Cost Engineer - Assn Cost Engrs Ltd

Cost Indices - Assn Cost Engrs Ltd

Costings of Agricultural Operations - Cent Assn Agricl Valuers

Costume - Costume Soc

The Cottage Gardener - Cottage Garden Soc

Council Vehicle News - Road Transport Fleet Data Soc

The Councillor - Nat Assn Councillors

The Councillors' Hbk - NI Local Govt Assn

Counselling & Psychotherapy Research - Brit Assn Counselling & Psychotherapy

Counselling at Work - Brit Assn Counselling & Psychotherapy

Counselling in Scotland - COSCA

Count Me In - Inst Stock Auditors & Valuers

Counterfoil - Brit Banking History Soc

The Counties - Assn Brit Counties

Country Landowner - Country Land & Business Assn

Country Sports - Countryside Alliance

Country-Side - Brit Naturalists' Assn

Countryside Building - Rural & Indl Design & Building Assn

County History - Ceredigion Historical Soc

Courage - War Widows Assn

Courier - Registered Nursing Home Assn Ltd

A Course for all Seasons: a guide to golf course management - R & Ancient Golf Club

The Court Historian - Soc Court Studies

Coverage & Frequency Guide - Cinema Advertising Assn Ltd

CPD Spotlight - Profl Assns Res Network

CPRE Voice - Campaign Protect Rural England

The Creation Manifesto - Biblical Creation Soc

Credit Management - Inst Credit Mgt

Credit Union News - Assn Brit Credit Us

The Creel - Friends Alan Rawsthorne

The Cricket Statistician - Assn Cricket Statisticians & Historians

The Crier - Ancient & Honourable Gld Town Criers

The Crofter - Scot Crofting Foundation

Crofter Forestry Experiences - Scot Crofting Foundation

Crofter Forestry Hbk - Scot Crofting Foundation

Cromwelliana - Cromwell Assn

The Croquet Gazette - Croquet Assn

Crossed Grain Magazine - Coeliac UK

Crossfire - American Civil War Round Table (UK)

Crossways - Assn Low Countries Studies

Crossword - Crossword Club

The Crown - Monarchist League

Croydon Church Townscape - Croydon Natural History & Scientific Soc

Cruising Construction Regulations - Hovercraft Club

Crypt - Xenophon

Crystallography News - Brit Crystallographic Assn

Crystals & Healing for Everyone - Crystal Healing Fedn

CrystEngComm - R Soc Chemistry

CTE - Soc Cable Telecommunication Engrs

The Cuckoo - Chesterfield Canal Trust Ltd

Cue Line - Stage Mgt Assn

Cultural & Socal History - Social Hist Soc

The Culverin - Siege Group

Current Awareness Service - Brit Inst Learning Disabilities

Current Folklore - Folklore Soc

Curriculum Framework for Operating Department Practice - Assn Operating Department Practitioners

Cushy - Assn Cushing's Treatment & Help

The Custodian (for Gamekeepers) - Brit Assn Shooting & Consvn

Customer First - Inst Customer Service

Cutting Edge - Brit Olympic Assn

Cuttings - Brit Lawn Mower Racing Assn

Cyclamen Jnl - Cyclamen Soc

Cycle Magazine - Cyclists' Touring Club

Czech Music - Dvořák Soc Czech & Slovak Music

D

Dad's Army Companion - Dad's Army Appreciation Soc

Dairy Farming Event Showguide - R Assn Brit Dairy Farmers

Dalton Transactions - R Soc Chemistry

Dams & Reservoirs - Brit Dam Soc

Dance - Imperial Soc Teachers Dancing

Dance Gazette - R Academy Dance

Dance Matters - Nat Dance Teachers Assn

Dance Research Jnl - Soc Dance Res

Dance Teaching Essentials - Dance UK Ltd

The Dancer - Brit Ballet Organization Ltd

Danceworld - Brit Theatre Dance Assn

Dartmoor Matters - Dartmoor Presvn Assn

Dartmoor Pony Soc - Dartmoor Diary

DATA Jnl - Design & Technology Assn

DATA News - Design & Technology Assn

Data Protection Act 1998: guidelines for social research - Social Res Assn

The David Jones Jnl - David Jones Soc

Davy's Devon Herd Book - Devon Cattle Breeders' Soc

Ddawns - Cymdeithas Ddawns Werin Cymru

Deadline - Assn UK Media Librarians

Deafness & Education - Brit Assn Teachers Deaf

The Declaration - Assn Indep Inventory Clerks

Dedicated - Inst Legal Secretaries & PAs

Deer - Brit Deer Soc

Deer Farming - Brit Deer Farmers Assn

Deer News - Brit Deer Farmers Assn

The Delphinium Garden - Delphinium Soc

Delphiniums - Delphinium Soc

Dementia - Ceretas

Dementia in Scotland - Alzheimer Scotland

The Democrat - Campaign against Euro-federalism

Democratic Broadsheet - Campaign against Euro-federalism

Demolition & Dismantling Jnl - Nat Fedn Demolition Contrs

Demolition Papers - Inst Demolition Engrs

Dental Care for People in Homes - Relatives & Residents Assn

Dental Historian Jnl - Lindsay Soc Hist Dentistry

Dental Implant Summaries - Assn Dental Implantology

Dental Laboratory - Dental Laboratories Assn

The Dental Trader - Brit Dental Trade Assn

Dentistry Opportunities - Confedn Dental Emplrs

Depression - SANE

Derbyshire Archaeological Jnl - Derbyshire Archaeol Soc

Derbyshire Miscellany - Derbyshire Archaeol Soc

Descriptions of Plant Viruses - Assn Applied Biologists

Design - Inst Scientific & Technical Communicators

The Designer - Chart Soc Desingers

The Designer Craftsman - Soc Designer Craftsmen

Designing Magazine - Design & Technology Assn
Desirable Criteria for Pain Mangaement Programmes - Brit Pain Soc
Despatches Magazine - Despatch Assn
Deutsch: Lehren und Lernen - Assn Language Learning
The Deva Pentice - Freemen & Glds City Chester
Development Action - Returned Volunteer Action
Development Education - Devt Educ Assn
Devon Archaeology - Devon Archaeol Soc
The Dexter Bulletin - Dexter Cattle Soc
Diabetes Update - Diabetes UK
Diabetic Foot - Wound Care Soc
Diabetic Medicine - Diabetes UK
Diagnostic Engineering - Instn Diagnostic Engrs
Dialogue - Inst Gp Analysis
Dictionary of Fire Technology - Instn Fire Engrs
Dictionary of International Marketing - Assn Intl Marketing
Dictionary of Scottish Building - Scot Language Dictionaries
Diecasting World - Inst Cast Metal Engrs
Dietetics Today - Brit Dietetic Assn
Diffusion - Sonic Arts Network
Digest - Brit Cattle Breeders' Club
The Digest - Brit Cham Comm Thailand
Digest - Restaurant Assn
Dine Out - Restaurant Assn
DinoMite - Dinosaur Soc
Dir of Markets in England, Wales & Scotland - Livestock Auctioneers Assn
Dir Youth & Student Orchestras - Nat Assn Youth Orchestras
Direct - Directors Gld
Direct News - Assn Public Service Excellence
Direct Selling, Consumer Goods in the UK - Direct Selling Assn
Direct Selling: from door to door to network marketing - Direct Selling Assn
Directory for Commercial Vehicle Bodybuilding, Repairs & Tail Lift Repairs - Vehicle Builders' & Repairers' Assn
Directory for Specifiers & Buyers - Brit Constructional Steelwork Assn Ltd
Directory of Accredited Behavioural / Cognitive & REBT Psychotherapists - Brit Assn Behavioural & Cognitive Psychotherapies
Directory of Acquisitions Librarians - Nat Acquisitions Gp
Directory of Approved Contractors - Arboricultural Assn
Directory of Book Publishers - Booksellers Assn
Directory of Booksellers - Booksellers Assn
Directory of Brass Bands - Brit Fedn Brass Bands
Directory of British Crematoria - Cremation Soc
Directory of British Spring Manufacturers - UK Spring Mfrs Assn
Directory of Business Administration Terms - Assn Business Admin
Directory of Collectors Interests - Cricket Memorabilia Soc
Directory of Contracting Officers - Assn Directors Social Services
Directory of Drama Adjudicators - Gld Drama Adjudicators
Directory of European Expertise: research interests of UACES members - University Assn Contemporary Eur Studies
Directory of Friendly Golf Clubs - Golf Club
Directory of Guidance Provision for Adults in the UK - ADSET
Directory of Insolvency Permit Holders - Inst Chart Accountants Scotland
Directory of Library & Information Facilities - Britain & Ireland Assn Aquatic Science Libraries & Information Centres
Directory of Ombudsmen - Brit & Ir Ombudsmen Assn
Directory of Pet Crematoria - Cremation Soc
Directory of Police & Public Security Suppliers - Assn Police & Public Security Suppliers
Directory of Practices - Chart Inst Architectural Technologists
Directory of Publishing in Scotland - Scot Publishing Assn
Directory of Pure Arabian Studs in GB & Ireland - Arab Horse Soc
Directory of Registered Consultants - Arboricultural Assn
Directory of Restoration - Quarry Products Assn
Directory of Storytellers - Soc Storytelling
Directory of Veterinary Practices - R Coll Veterinary Surgeons
Disability Now - Scope
Disability Rights Bulletin - Disability Alliance
Disability Rights Hbk - Disability Alliance
The Disabled Motorist - Mobilise Org
Discrimination Law Briefings - Discrimination Law Assn

Dispatches - Vitiligo Soc
Dispensing Optics - Assn Brit Dispensing Opticians
Distilleries to Visit Guide - Scotch Whisky Assn
Distillery Map - Scotch Whisky Assn
The Distributor - Jewellery Distbrs' Assn
Distributors' List - Music Publishers' Assn
DLA Directory - Dental Laboratories Assn
DLS Bulletin - Dorothy L Sayers Soc
DMA Annual Review - Defence Mfrs Assn
Dodo - E F Benson Soc
Dog Warden News - Nat Dog Wardens Assn
Doing Business in Brazil - Brit Cham Comm & Ind Brazil
Doing Business in Spain - Spanish Cham Comm GB
The Dolls' House Magazine - Gld Master Craftsmen
Domestic & commercial spas - Inst Swimming Pool Engrs Ltd
Domestic Sprinkler Systems - Brit Automatic Fire Sprinkler Assn
Don't Panic - Nat Phobics Soc
Dorset Series - Dorset Natural History & Archaeol Soc
Double Reed News - Brit Double Reed Soc
The Double Tressure - Heraldry Soc Scotland
Doula News - Brit Doula Assn
Dowsing Today - Brit Soc Dowsers
The Dozenal Jnl - Dozenal Soc
Dragon Line NL - Brit Dragon Boat Racing Assn
Dragonfly News - Brit Dragonfly Soc
The Drake Broadside - Drake Exploration Soc
Drama - Nat Drama
Drama NL - R Scot Academy Music & Drama
Drama Research - Nat Drama
Dressings Selection - Wound Care Soc
Driving after Amputation - Brit Limbless Ex-Service Men's Assn
Driving Instructor - Driving Instructors Assn
Driving Magazine - Driving Instructors Assn
Duchenne News - Duchenne Family Support Gp
The Dun Thing - Dun Horse & Pony Soc
The Dun Thing Update - Dun Horse & Pony Soc
Durable Post Tensioned Bridges - Concrete Bridge Devt Gp
Durbar - Indian Military Histl Soc
Durham Archaeological Jnl - Architectural & Archaeol Soc Durham & Northumberland
Durham Biographies - Durham County Local Hist Soc
Durham City and its MPs - Durham County Local Hist Soc
The Durham Crown Lordships - Durham County Local Hist Soc
Durham Wildlife - Durham Wildlife Trust
Dutch Crossing: a jnl of Low Countries studies - Assn Low Countries Studies
DVC - UK Practical Shooting Assn
Dymock Poets & Friends - Friends Dymock Poets
Dyslexia - Home Educ Advy Service

E

EAB Update - Esperanto Assn Britain
Early 19th Century Glassmaking in Austria & Germany - Soc Glass Technology
Early Education - Brit Assn Early Childhood Educ
Early Music Performer - Nat Early Music Assn
Early Settlement Rebate - Finance & Leasing Assn
Earth Matters - Friends Earth
The East Africa NL - Eastern Africa Assn
East Midlands Business Directory - Nottinghamshire Cham Comm & Ind
Easter Rising in Song & Ballad - Workers' Music Assn
Ecclesiology Today - Ecclesiological Soc
The Eckhart Review - Eckhart Soc
Ecobrief - Envtl Inds Fedn Ltd
Economic Affairs - Inst Economic Affairs
Economic Development - Instn Economic Devt
Economic History Review - Economic Hist Soc
The Economic Jnl - R Economic Soc
Ecos: a review of conservation - Brit Assn Nature Conservationists
Eczema - Aetiology & Management - Wound Care Soc
The Edge - Swindon Cham Comm & Ind
EDS (English Dance & Song) - English Folk Dance & Song Soc
Education & Training Courses in Horticulture - Inst Horticulture

© CBD Research Ltd · Beckenham · BR3 5JS · Tel 020 8650 7745 · Fax 020 8650 0768 · E-mail cbd@cbdresearch.com · www.cbdresearch.com

Education 3-13 - Assn Study Primary Educ
Education in Chemistry - R Soc Chemistry
Education Libraries Jnl - Librarians Insts & Schools Educ
Education Management & Administration - Brit Educl
   Leadership, Mgt & Admin Soc
Education Review - Nat U Teachers
Education in Science - Assn Science Educ
The Education Social Worker - Nat Assn Social Workers Educ
Education Today - Coll Teachers
Educational Gerontology - Assn Educ & Ageing
Educational Neometaphysical Lessons - Soc Metaphysicians Ltd
Educational Psychology in Practice - Assn Educl Psychologists
Educational Therapy & Therapeutic Teaching - Caspari
   Foundation Educl Therapy & Therapeutic Teaching
eDVC - UK Practical Shooting Assn
Effective Business in Taiwan - Brit Cham Comm Taipei
EFNARC Specification for Sprayed Concrete - Sprayed Concrete
   Assn
The Egg Crafter - Egg Crafters Gld
Egyptian Archaeology - Egypt Exploration Soc
Egyptian-British Trade - Egyptian Brit Cham Comm
The EIC Guide to the UK Environmental Industry - Envtl Inds
   Cmsn Ltd
EIS News - Engg Integrity Soc
El Hornero - Brit Uruguayan Soc
ELATEST - Nat Assn Literature Devt
Elder Abuse - Ceretas
Elections in the Age of the Internet: Lessons from the US -
   Hansard Soc Parliamentary Govt
Electric Boat News - Electric Boat Assn
The Electric Railway - Electric Rly Soc
Electrical Contractor - Electrical Contrs' Assn
Electronic Bulletin - UK Newsletter & Electronic Publishers Assn
Electronic Public Information - Soc Public Infm Networks
Electronic Scots School Dictionary - Scot Language Dictionaries
Electronic Systems & Software - Instn Engg & Technology
The Elgar Jnl - Elgar Soc
The Elgar News - Elgar Soc
eLucidate - UK eInformation Gp
The Embalmer - Brit Inst Embalmers
Embroidery - Embroiderers' Gld
Emergency Medicine Jnl - Brit Assn Emergency Medicine
E-Motion - Assn Dance Movement Therapy
Emotional & Behavioural Difficulties - Sebda
Endocrine Related Cancer - Soc Endocrinology
The Endocrinologist - Soc Endocrinology
Energy Action - Nat Energy Action
Energy World - Energy Inst
engage review - engage
engagements - engage
Engineering in Emergencies: a practical guide - RedR - Engrs
   Disaster Relief
Engineering Integrity - Engg Integrity Soc
Engineering Management - Instn Engg & Technology
Engineering & Technology - Instn Engg & Technology
The Engineering Designer - Instn Engg Designers
Engineers' & Architects' Guide to Hot Dip Galvanizing -
   Galvanizers Assn
England's Standard - R Soc St George
English 4-11 - English Assn
English Bridge - English Bridge U
English Draughts Jnl - English Draughts Assn
English in Education - Nat Assn Teaching English
English Golf - English Golf U
The English & Media Magazine - Nat Assn Teaching English
English in the UK - English UK
Enthusing the Next Generation - Biosciences Fedn
Environmental Archaeology: Jnl of Human Palaeoecology -
   Assn Envtl Archaeology
The Environmental Careers Hbk - Instn Envtl Sciences
Environmental Education - Nat Assn Envtl Educ
Environmental Health Scotland - R Envtl Health Inst Scotland
Environmental Law - UK Envtl Law Assn
Environmental Microbiology - Soc Applied Microbiology
The Environmental Scientist - Instn Envtl Sciences
Environments for All - Brit Trust Consvn Volunteers
The Ephemerist - Ephemera Soc
Epilepsy News - Epilepsy Action Scotland

Epilepsy Review - Nat Soc Epilepsy
Epilepsy Today - Brit Epilepsy Assn
Epiphytes - Epiphytic Plant Study Gp
Equestrian Trade News - Brit Equestrian Tr Assn
Equine Behaviour - Equine Behaviour Forum
Equipment Selection - Wound Care Soc
Equity Jnl - Brit Actors' Equity Assn
Ergonomics in Design - Ergonomics Soc
Ergonomics NL - Ergonomics Soc
The Ergonomist - Ergonomics Soc
ERS News - Electoral Reform Soc Ltd
ESBA Post - Badminton Assn England
Escape to... - Youth Hostels Assn
ESG 2004 - Soc Glass Technology
Esperanto en Skotlando - Scot Esperanto Assn
Essays & Studies - English Assn
Essays in Biochemistry - Biochemical Soc
Essence - Brit Flower & Vibrational Essences Assn
The Essential Guide to Aqueous Coating of Paper & Board -
   Paper Ind Technical Assn
Essex Archaeology & History - Essex Soc Archaeology & History
Essex Archaeology & History News - Essex Soc Archaeology &
   History
Essex Chambers Directory - Essex Chams Comm
Essex Jnl - Essex Archaeol & Histl Congress
Essex Wildlife - Essex Wildlife Trust Ltd
The Estate Agent - Nat Assn Estate Agents
An Estate Agent's Guide to the Property Misdescriptions Act -
   Nat Assn Estate Agents
ESU NL - English Speaking U C'wealth
Ethical Record - S Place Ethical Soc
Ethics & Wisdom in Medicine - Medical Ethics Alliance
ETS News - Envtl Inds Cmsn Ltd
EU News - Biosciences Fedn
Eureka - Kingston Cham Comm
Eurolink - Forum Private Business
European Eating Disorders Review - Eating Disorders Assn
European Jnl of Disorders of Communication - R Coll Speech &
   Language Therapists
European Jnl of Herbal Medicine - Nat Inst Med Herbalists Ltd
European Jnl of Information Systems - Operational Res Soc
European Jnl of Pediatric Surgery - Soc Res Hydrocephalus &
   Spina Bifida
European Jnl of Phycology - Brit Phycological Soc
European Jnl of Prosthodontics & Restorative Dentistry - Brit
   Soc Restorative Dentistry
European Jnl of Soil Science - Brit Soc Soil Science
European Jnl of Surgical Oncology - BASO
European Marketing Tips & Terms for the Single Market -
   Assn Intl Marketing
European Morgan Horse Magazine - Brit Morgan Horse Soc
European Race Bulletin - Inst Race Relations
European Racquetball NL - GB Racquetball Fedn
European Rail News - Rly Enthusiasts Soc
European-Atlantic Jnl - Eur Atlantic Gp
Europos Lietuvis - Lithuanian Assn
The Evacuee - Evacuees Reunion Assn
Evaluation of the Past & Future Contribution of the UK
   Science Park Movement - UK Science Park Assn
Event Organiser - Event Services Assn
Event Organisers Update - Soc Event Organisers
Evolution of Permanent Way - Permanent Way Instn
Examinations - Home Educ Advy Service
Excalibur - R Navy Enthusiasts' Soc
Excel - Assn Domestic Mgt
Exchange - Nat Eczema Soc
         Telephone Helplines Assn
Exchange List - Private Libraries Assn
Executive Accountant - Inst Cost & Executive Accountants
Exhibition Standard - Assn Event Venues
            Assn Exhibition Contrs
            Assn Exhibition Organisers
            Events Ind Alliance
Experimental Physiology - Physiological Soc
The Expert - Academy Experts
Explaining Vending - Automatic Vending Assn
Explosives Engineering - Inst Explosives Engrs
Export Opportunities Alerting Service - Defence Mfrs Assn

The Exporter - UK Fashion Exports
Exporting World - Inst Export
Extra Cover - Club Cricket Conf
Eye - R Coll Ophthalmologists
Eyes & Ears - Automotive Distbn Fedn
E-Zine - Swindon Cham Comm & Ind

F

FAB - Fanderson
Fabian Review - Fabian Soc
Face Facts - Brit Compact Collectors Soc
Face Forward - Acne Support Gp
FACTion - Falsely Accused Carers & Teachers
Factline - Telecommunications Users' Assn
Facts about the Arts - Nat Campaign Arts
Faileas - FÉisean nan GÈidheal
Fair Wear & Tear Guides - Brit Vehicle Rental & Leasing Assn
Fairy Tales - Fairy Ring
Faith & Heritage - Prayer Book Soc
Faith & Worship - Prayer Book Soc
Falconer - Brit Falconers' Club
Familia: Ulster Genealogical Review - Ulster Histl Foundation
Family Based Short-term Care: the future challenges - Shared Care Network
Family Bulletin - Family Educ Trust
Family History - Inst Heraldic & Genealogical Studies
Family History News & Digest - Fedn Family History Socs
Family Magazine - Fibromyalgia Assn UK
Family Matters - Family Rights Gp
Faraday Discussions - R Soc Chemistry
Farming News - Ulster Farmers U
Fast News - Farnborough Air Sciences Trust
Fasti of the General Assembly of the Presbyterian Church in Ireland 1840-1910 - Presbyterian Historical Soc Ireland
Faunus - Friends Arthur Machen
FCEM News Intl - Brit Assn Women Entrepreneurs
Feathered World - Nat Pigeon Assn
Federation Digest - Scot Fedn Housing Assns
Federation Focus - Scot Fedn Housing Assns
Federation Jnl - Gen Fedn Trade Us
Federation News - Fedn Community Devt Learning
Federation News - Gen Fedn Trade Us
Fedtalk tape - Nat Fedn Blind
Feedback - Confedn Aerial Inds
The Fell Runner - Fell Runners Assn
Fellowship News - Fellowship Cycling Old-Timers
Feng Shui News - Feng Shui Soc
Fern Gazette - Brit Pteridological Soc
FESI - European Insulation Standards - Thermal Insulation Conts Assn
Ffestiniog Railway Magazine - Ffestiniog Rly Soc Ltd
Fidelity - Nat Coun Psychotherapists
Field & Fell - Westmorland County Agricl Soc
Field Guide - W W Jacobs Appreciation Soc
Field Studies Magazine - Field Studies Coun
The Fifth Fuel - Assn Consvn Energy
Fight Back (physiotherapy video + DVD) - Nat Ankylosing Spondylitis Soc
The Fight Director - Brit Academy Dramatic Combat
Film & Video Maker - Inst Amat Cinematographers
Films Directory - W W Jacobs Appreciation Soc
Financial Controller - Assn Financial Controllers & Administrators
Financial Planner - Inst Financial Planning
Financial World - Inst Financial Services
Fine Food Digest (UK), - Gld Fine Food Retailers
Fingerprint Whorld - Fingerprint Soc
The Finial - Silver Spoon Club
Fire & Thatch - Nat Soc Master Thatchers
Fire Cover - Fire Brigade Soc
Fire Engineers Jnl - Instn Fire Engrs
Fire Prevention - Fire Protection Assn
Fire Protection for Structural Steel in Buildings - Assn Specialist Fire Protection
Fire Protection Ybk - Fire Protection Assn

Fire Technology - Calculations - Instn Fire Engrs
Fire Technology - Chemistry Combustion - Instn Fire Engrs
First - Local Govt Assn
First Five - Scot Pre-School Play Assn
First Voice - Fedn Small Businesses
Fish - Inst Fisheries Mgt
Fish Friers Review - Nat Fedn Fish Friers
Fish Trader - Nat Assn Range Mfrs
Fishing Boats - Forty Plus Fishing Boat Assn
Five Foot Three - Rly Presvn Soc Ireland
Fixture Book - Scot Football League
Flagmaster - Flag Inst
Flareoff - Offshore Ind Liaison C'ee
Fleet Excellence - Inst Car Fleet Mgt
Fleet Operator - ACFO Ltd
Flipside - Instn Engg & Technology
Floristry News - Brit Florist Assn
The Flow - Credit Protection Assn plc
The Flower Arranger - Nat Assn Flower Arrangement Socs
Flueways - Nat Assn Chimney Engrs
Flyball Record - Brit Flyball Assn
The Flydresser - Flydressers Gld
Flyer - Vikings
The Flying Scot - Scot Hang Gliding & Paragliding Fedn
The Flywheel - Northern Mill Engine Soc
Focal Point - Soc Floristry Ltd
Focus - Assn Personal Injury Lawyers
        Nystagmus Network
Focus Magazine - Brit Orienteering Fedn
        Inst Videography
        Self Storage Assn
Focus on Fives - Brit Assn Adoption & Fostering
Focus on Haflingers - Haflinger Soc
Focus on Italy - Brit Cham Comm Italy, Inc
Focus on Swaziland - Swaziland Soc
Folk Life: a jnl of ethnological studies - Soc Folk Life Studies
Folk Music Jnl - English Folk Dance & Song Soc
Folklore - Folklore Soc
Follies - Folly Fellowship
FoMRHI Quarterly - Fellowship Makers & Researchers Historical Instruments
Food & Bioproducts Processing - Instn Chemical Engrs
Food & Drinks Directory of the UK - Coeliac UK
Food Hygiene - Ceretas
Food Science & Technology - Inst Food Science & Technology
Food Service Standards at Ward Level: good practice guide - Hospital Caterers Assn
Food Trader - Nat Fedn Meat & Food Traders
Food Worker - Bakers', Food & Allied Workers' U
The Football Referee - Referees' Assn
Footnotes - Brit Chiropody & Podiatry Assn
Footprint - Brit Walking Fedn
Footprints - Brit Reflexology Assn
Fore & Aft - Yacht Harbour Assn
Forecourt - Retail Motor Ind Fedn
Forestry - Inst Chart Foresters
Forge - Nat Assn Farriers, Blacksmiths & Agricultural Engrs
Forging Links - Tools Self Reliance
Form of Direct Contract - Nat Fedn Demolition Contrs
The Formation Sign - Military Heraldry Soc
The Formulary - Friends Dr Watson
Fort - Fortress Study Gp
Forty Years On - Assn Past Rotarians
Forum View - Investment Property Forum
Forward - Spinal Injuries Assn
Foster Care - Fostering Network
Foundry Trade Jnl - (Foundry Equipment & Supplies Assn Ltd
        (Inst Cast Metal Engrs
Foundry Ybk & Castings Buyers Guide - Inst Cast Metal Engrs
Four Seasons News - S England Agricl Soc
FPA Jnl - Electrical & Engg Staff Assn
Frame News - Fund Replacement Animals Med Experiments
Framework - Leukaemia CARE
Franchise Link - Brit Franchise Assn
Franchisee Guide - Brit Franchise Assn
Franchisor Guide - Brit Franchise Assn
The Franco-British Trade Directory - Chambre Comm Française de Grande-Bretagne

Francophonie - Assn Language Learning
Free Life - Libertarian Alliance
Free Press - Campaign Press & Broadcasting Freedom
Freedom Today - Freedom Assn
The Freeman - Gld Freemen City London
Freeway - Brit Nat Temperance League
Freight - Freight Transport Assn
Freight Services Directory - Brit Intl Freight Assn
French Studies - Soc French Studies
Freshwater Forum - Freshwater Biological Assn
Friday Morning at BHTA - Brit Healthcare Trades Assn
Friends of Frame - Fund Replacement Animals Med Experiments
Fritillary - Ashmolean Natural Hist Soc Oxfordshire
From Netley to Maiwand - Friends Dr Watson
From Palace to Washhouse: A study of the Old palace, Croydon, from 1887 - Croydon Natural History & Scientific Soc
From Rome to Maastricht - Campaign Indep Britain
Frontline - Chart Soc Physiotherapy
Front-Line - Inst Career Guidance Ltd
The Fulcrum - Craniosacral Therapy Assn
Full Orchestra - Nat Assn Youth Orchestras
Funeral Director - Nat Assn Funeral Dirs
Funerals without God - Brit Humanist Assn
Funnel - Steam Boat Assn
Fur & Feather (inc Rabbits) - Brit Rabbit Coun
Furniture & Cabinetmaking - Gld Master Craftsmen
Furniture History - Furniture History Soc
Future & the Inventor - Inst Patentees & Inventors

G

G K Quarterly - Chesterton Soc
GA Magazine - Geologists' Assn
Gala Sales List - Brit Camelids Assn
The Gallipolian - Gallipoli Assn
Game Farming NL - Game Farmers Assn
Garage Watch NL - Garage Watch
The Garden - R Horticl Soc
Garden Design Jnl - Soc Garden Designers
Garden History - Garden History Soc
Gardening in Homes - Relatives & Residents Assn
Gardening Which? - Consumers' Assn
Gardens & Gardening Retailer - Alliance Indep Retailers
Gardens Open Directory - Alpine Garden Soc
Gas Business - Soc Brit Gas Inds
Gas Installer Magazine - Coun Registered Gas Installers
Gatelodge - Prison Officers' Assn
Gauchers News - Gauchers Assn
Gavel - Nat Assn Valuers & Auctioneers
Gazeteers of Industrial Archaeology - Derbyshire Archaeol Soc
Gazette - CILIP
Gem & Jewellery News - Gemmological Assn
Gems & Jewellery - Soc Jewellery Hist
Genealogists' Magazine - Soc Genealogists
General Circular - Wine & Spirit Assn
General Dental Practitioner - Dental Practitioners Assn
General Requirements for certification of personnel engaged in industrial rope access methods - Indl Rope Access Tr Assn
Generations Review - Brit Soc Gerontology
Genes & Development - Genetics Soc
Geochemical Transactions - R Soc Chemistry
Geography - Geographical Assn
GeogScot - R Scot Geographical Soc
Geophysical Jnl International - R Astronomical Soc
George Borrow Bulletin - George Borrow Soc
George Eliot Review - George Eliot Fellowship
German History - German History Soc
German Politics - Assn Study German Politics
Get Cruisewise - Passenger Shipping Assn
Get It Sussed - Meningitis Research Foundation
Getting better all the time: delivering & receiving quality services - Shared Care Network
Getting the best out of a School Board - Scot School Bd Assn
Gifted & Talented - Nat Assn Gifted Children
Gilbert & Sullivan News - Gilbert & Sullivan Soc

Giving Shares & Securities: information pack for financial advisers - Community Foundation Network
Glass Network - Contemporary Glass Soc
Glass Technology - Soc Glass Technology
Glaucus - Brit Marine Life Study Soc
Glazed Expressions - Tiles & Architectural Ceramics Soc
Glazing Manual - Glass & Glazing Fedn
The Gleam - Sheila Kaye-Smith Soc
Global Youth Work - Devt Educ Assn
Globe Trotter - Brit Gld Travel Writers
Glossary of Printing Terms - Brit Printing Soc
Glove Usage Guidelines - Infection Control Nurses Assn
GN News - Great Nthn Rly Soc
Gnomon - Assn Astronomy Educ
Go Outdoors Bulletin - Go Outdoors
Going Green - ETA Services Ltd
The Gold Decor Directory - Home Decoration Retailers' Assn
Gold Top News - Quality Milk Producers Ltd
Golf Club Management - Assn Golf Club Secretaries
Gongoozler - Canal Card Collectors Circle
The Good Alternative Travel Guide - Tourism Concern
Good Beer Guide - Campaign Real Ale Ltd
Good Beer Guide to Germany - Campaign Real Ale Ltd
Good Bottled Beer Guide - Campaign Real Ale Ltd
Good Cheese Magazine - Gld Fine Food Retailers
Good Cider Guide - Campaign Real Ale Ltd
Good Motoring Magazine - Gld Experienced Motorists
Good Piers Guide - Nat Piers Soc
Good Practice in Boarding Schools: a resource handbook for all those working in boarding - Boarding Schools Assn
Gower Walks - Gower Soc
Gower Way - Gower Soc
Graduated Compression Hosiery - Wound Care Soc
Grandparent Times - Grandparents' Assn
The Grape Press - UK Vineyards Assn
The Grapevine - Care Leavers Assn
Graphic Archaeology - Assn Archaeol Illustrators & Surveyors
The Graphics book - D&AD
The Graphologist - Brit Inst Graphologists
Grass & Forage Science - Brit Grassland Soc
Grass Farmer - Brit Grassland Soc
GRCA News - Intl Glassfibre Reinforced Concrete Assn
Great North Review - Great N Scotland Rly Assn
Great Western Echo - Great Wstn Soc
Greece & Rome - Classical Assn
Green Chemistry - R Soc Chemistry
Green Lanes - Green Lane Assn
Greenkeeper International - Brit & Intl Golf Greenkeepers' Assn
Greensheet - Military Vehicle Trust
The Gregynog Papers - Inst Welsh Affairs
The Grieg Companion - Grieg Soc
The Groundsman - Inst Groundsmanship
Groundswell - Brit Surfing Assn
The Grower - Assn Scot Shellfish Growers
The Growing Heap - Community Composting Network
Growing Places - Fedn City Farms & Community Gardens
Growing Up - baby / childhood monitor - Support Soc Children High Intelligence
Growth Point - THRIVE
GSQ - GS1
Guernsey Breeders NL - English Guernsey Cattle Soc
Guidance for the Design, Construction & Maintenance of Petrol Filling Stations - Assn Petroleum & Explosives Admin
Guidance on Alcohol & Drug Misuse in the Workplace - Fac Occupational Medicine
Guidance on Ethics for Occupational Physicians - Fac Occupational Medicine
The Guide to Accredited Independent Boarding Schools in the UK - Boarding Schools Assn
A Guide to Anaerobic Digestion - Composting Assn
Guide to Artificial Arms - REACH
Guide to Best Practice for the Installation of Pipe Jacks & Microtunnels - Pipe Jacking Assn
Guide to Best Practice in Sport & Regeneration - Brit Urban Regeneration Assn
Guide to British Piers - Nat Piers Soc
Guide to Business Schools - Assn MBAs
Guide to Car Fleet Management - Inst Car Fleet Mgt

Guide to Careers in Outdoor Learning - Inst Outdoor Learning
Guide to Carnivorous Plants - Carnivorous Plant Soc
Guide to Charter - Marine Leisure Assn
Guide to Commissioning - Inst Healthcare Engg & Estate Mgt
Guide to Community Composting - Community Composting Network
Guide to Contractor Detailing of Reinforcement in Concrete - Construct: Concrete Structures Gp
A Guide to Customer Publishing - Assn Publishing Agencies
Guide to Daywork Rates - Bldg Cost Infm Service
Guide to Doing Business in the UK - Spanish Cham Comm GB
A Guide to European Funding - Community Foundation Network
Guide to Funerals & Bereavement - Assn Burial Authorities Ltd
A Guide to Giving - Assn Charitable Foundations
Guide to Gower - Gower Soc
Guide to History of Science Courses in Britain - Brit Soc Hist Science
A Guide to In-Vessel Composting - Composting Assn
Guide to Literacy Resources - Nat Literacy Assn
Guide to Machine Vision - UK Indl Vision Assn
Guide to Making Model Hovercraft - Hovercraft Club
A Guide to Marketing in Europe - Assn Intl Marketing
A Guide to Play Therapy - Brit Assn Play Therapists
Guide Post - Gld Registered Tourist Guides
A Guide to Private Equity - BVCA (British Venture Capital Assn)
Guide to Professional Conduct - R Coll Veterinary Surgeons
Guide to Quality Chinchilla - Nat Chinchilla Club
A Guide to RADAR - R Assn Disability & Rehabilitation
Guide to Reach - Brit Adhesives & Sealants Assn
Guide to Scottish Industrial Heritage - Scot Indl Heritage Soc
Guide to Shiatsu - Shiatsu Soc
Guide to the Development of Children's Palliative Care Services - Assn Children Life-Threatening or Terminal Conditions...
Guide to the Law on Rights of Way in Scotland - Scot Rights of Way & Access Soc
Guide to Tortoises & Turtles - Tortoise Trust
Guide to Traditional Herbal Medicines - Brit Herbal Medicine Assn
Guidebook to Goddards - Lutyens Trust
Guidelines - Heritage Rly Assn
Guidelines - Scot Tourist Guides Assn
Guidelines for Essence Production - Brit Assn Flower Essence Producers
Guidelines for Hand Hygiene - Infection Control Nurses Assn
Guidelines on the use of rope access methods for industrial purposes - Indl Rope Access Tr Assn
Guiding - Girlguiding UK
Guild Letting Companion - Gld Letting & Mgt
Guildhall - Freemen & Glds City Chester
Gut - Brit Soc Gastroenterology
Gut Reaction - IBS Network
GWR Iron Minks - Histl Model Rly Soc
Gymnast Magazine - Brit Amat Gymnastics Assn

H

Hackney Stud Book - Hackney Horse Soc
Haemophilia Quarterly - Haemophilia Soc
The Haggard Jnl - Rider Haggard Soc
Haggardiana (ephemera folder) - Rider Haggard Soc
Hampshire Studies - Hampshire Field Club & Archaeol Soc
Hand Chain Blocks & Lever Hoists in the Offshore Environment - Lifting Eqpt Engrs Assn
Handling Service Users' Finances & Valuables - Ceretas
Hardware Today - Brit Hardware Fedn
The Hardy Plant - Hardy Plant Soc
Harmonica World - Nat Harmonica League
Harmony Express - Brit Assn Barbershop Singers
Havergal Brian on Music, Vol 1: British Music - Havergal Brian Soc
Havergal Brian's Gothic Symphony - two studies - Havergal Brian Soc
Hazard Analysis & Critical Control Point for Composting - Composting Assn

Hazards in the Office - R Soc Chemistry
Hbk for Fire Engineers - Instn Fire Engrs
Head to Head - Assn Headteachers & Deputies Scotland
Heading for the Scottish Hills - Mountaineering Coun Scotland
Headline Earnings Definition - UK Soc Investment Profls
Headline News - Nat Hairdressers' Fedn
Headlines - Newspaper Soc
Headway News - HEADWAY - Brain Injury Assn
Healing Today - Nat Fedn Spiritual Healers
Health & Homeopathy - Brit Homoeopathic Assn
Health & Safety at Composting Sites - Composting Assn
Health & Safety Europe - Brit Safety Ind Fedn
Health Club Management - Fitness Ind Assn
Health Estate Jnl - Inst Healthcare Engg & Estate Mgt
Health Which? - Consumers' Assn
Health Writer - Gld Health Writers
Healthcare Counselling & Psychotherapy Jnl - Brit Assn Counselling & Psychotherapy
Healthcare Finance - Healthcare Financial Mgt Assn
Health-Care Focus - Assn Brit Health Care Inds
Heart Beat - Children's Heart Assn
Heart Children - Heart Line Assn
Heat losses from indoor & outdoor pools - Inst Swimming Pool Engrs Ltd
Heat pumps - Inst Swimming Pool Engrs Ltd
Heavy Talk - Heavy Transport Assn
Hebe News - Hebe Soc
Hedgelaying Explained - Nat Hedgelaying Soc
Hedgeline - Hedgeline
Help & Advice - Inst Consumer Affairs
The Heraldic Craftsman - Soc Heraldic Arts
Heraldry Gazette - Heraldry Soc
Herbal Thymes - Nat Inst Med Herbalists Ltd
Herbnews - Brit Herb Tr Assn
Herbs - Herb Soc
Here's Health - Arthritis & Rheumatism Natural Therapy Res Assn
Heredity - Genetics Soc
Hertfordshire Archaeology - E Herts Archaeol Soc
                                 Saint Albans & Hertfordshire Architectural & Archaeol Soc
Heyday Magazine - Heyday
The Hidden Workforce: A Self-help Guide to Safeguards & Benefits - Women's Farm & Garden Assn
The High Sheriff - Shrievalty Assn
Highland Breeders Jnl - Highland Cattle Soc
Highland Railway Jnl - Highland Rly Soc
Hints to Businessmen: Turkey - Brit Cham Comm Turkey
Hippo News - Help Intl Plant Protein Org
HIPS (97) - Nat Support Gp Victims Failed Home Income Plans
The Historian - Histl Assn
Historic Caravan Scene - Historic Caravan Club
Historic Commercial News - Historic Comml Vehicle Soc
Historic House - Historic Houses Assn
Historical Dance - Dolmetsch Historical Dance Soc
Historical Diving Times - Histl Diving Soc
Historical Metallurgy - Histl Metallurgy Soc Ltd
History - Histl Assn
History of Education - History Educ Soc (UK)
History of Education Researcher - History Educ Soc (UK)
History of Printing Ink - Brit Printing Soc
History of the League - Fitness League
History of the Society 1845-1995 - Saint Albans & Hertfordshire Architectural & Archaeol Soc
Hitting the Seam - England & Wales Cricket Bd Coaches Assn
HIV Medicine - Brit HIV Assn
HLM: Howard League Magazine - Howard League Penal Reform
HMRS Jnl - Histl Model Rly Soc
HMRS News - Histl Model Rly Soc
Hobart Paperbacks - Inst Economic Affairs
Hobart Papers - Inst Economic Affairs
Hockey Scotland - Scot Hockey U
Holiday Which? - Consumers' Assn
A Home Afloat - Residential Boat Owners Assn
Home Decor & Furnishings - Home Decoration Retailers' Assn
Home Education Hbk - Home Educ Advy Service
Home Education Overseas - Home Educ Advy Service
The Homecarer - UK Homecare Assn
Homeopathy International - Homeopathic Med Assn

© CBD Research Ltd · Beckenham · BR3 5JS · Tel 020 8650 7745 · Fax 020 8650 0768 · E-mail cbd@cbdresearch.com · www.cbdresearch.com

Homeowners' Manual - Nat Care Assn

Homoeopathy for Today & the Future - Nat Assn Homoeopathic Gps

Homoeopathy Jnl - Fac Homeopathy

Hoosta Ga'an On? - Lakeland Dialect Soc

Horizons Magazine - Inst Outdoor Learning

The Horn - Brit Horn Soc

Horological Jnl - Brit Horological Fedn
Brit Horological Inst

The Horticulturist - Inst Horticulture

Hospital & Community Friend - Attend

Hospital Caterer - Hospital Caterers Assn

Hospital Caterer Ybk - Hospital Caterers Assn

Hospital Pharmacist - R Pharmaceutical Soc

Hospitality - Hotel & Catering Intl Mgt Assn

Hospitality Matters - Brit Hospitality Assn

Hospitality Ybk - Hotel & Catering Intl Mgt Assn

Hot & Cold - Assn Plumbing & Heating Contrs

Hot Dip Galvanizing - Galvanizers Assn

Hot Foil Printing - Assn Hot Foil Printers

Hot Rolled Asphalt Production Laying & Compaction - Inst Asphalt Technology

The Hotelier - Alliance Indep Retailers

House Builder Magazine - Home Builders Fedn

Housing - Chart Inst Housing

Housing Today - Nat Housing Fedn

Housman Jnl - Housman Soc

Housman's Places - Housman Soc

Hovercraft Construction Guide - Hovercraft Club

Hovercraft Museum NL - Hovercraft Museum Trust

How Can I Keep from Singing - Brit KodÈly Academy

How did it start? - Instn Fire Engrs

How to be an Advanced Motorcyclist - Inst Advanced Motorists Ltd

How to be an Advanced Motorist - Inst Advanced Motorists Ltd

How to Grow Roses - R Nat Rose Soc

How to Profit from Contracting Out - Cleaning & Support Services Assn

How's That! - Assn Cricket Umpires & Scorers

HQtoo! - Haemophilia Soc

Hrnes - Engliscan Gesíþas

Human Experimental Psychology - Experimental Psychology Soc

Human Fertility - Brit Fertility Soc

Human Genetics NL - Human Genetics Alert

Humanism Scotland - Humanist Soc Scotland

Humanities Now - Humanities Assn

Humanities Too - Humanities Assn

Huntington's Disease: What's it all about? A guide for young people - Scot Huntington's Assn

Hygeia - R Soc Promotion Health

Hygiene Good Practice Guide - Hospital Caterers Assn

The Hygienist - Brit Natural Hygiene Soc

Hypnotherapy Jnl - Assn Qualified Curative Hypnotherapists

I

I Sang In My Chain, Essays & Poems in Tribute to Dylan Thomas - Dylan Thomas Soc

IAW - Urdd Gobaith Cymru

Ibis (Jnl) - Brit Ornithologists' U

Ice Cream - Ice Cream Alliance

Ice Hockey Annual - Ice Hockey UK

Ice Link - Nat Ice Skating Assn

ICME Register of Members - Inst Automotive Engr Assessors

ICT in State Schools - Brit Educl Suppliers Assn

idea - Evangelical Alliance UK

Illustrated Guide to Fiction - Rider Haggard Soc

Illustrated Guide to Non-Fiction - Rider Haggard Soc

Image - Assn Photographers Ltd

Image Technology - BKSTS

Imaging - Brit Inst Radiology

Imaging & Oncology - Soc Radiographers

Imaging Science Jnl - R Photographic Soc

IMIS Jnl - Inst Mgt Infm Systems

Immunology - Brit Soc Immunology

Immunology News - Brit Soc Immunology

Impact - Career Development Gp

Impact - Inst Traffic Accident Investigators

Impact of Digital / Non-Impact Printing on Industry - Screen Printing Assn

Implications of the Human Rights Act 1998 for Local Govenment - Bar Assn Local Govt & Public Service

In Brief - Assn Qualitative Res

In Business - Chester, Ellesmere Port & N Wales Cham Comm

In the Field - Berkshire Archaeology Res Gp

In Flight Magazine - Brit Disc Golf Assn

In Focus - Assn Brit Health Care Inds
Telecommunications Users' Assn

In the Frame - Telecommunications UK Fraud Forum Ltd

In a Nutshell - Kentish Cobnuts Assn
Percy Grainger Soc

In Other Words - Translators Assn

In Practice - Brit Veterinary Assn
Inst Ecology & Envtl Mgt
UK Clinical Pharmacy Assn

In the Steps of the Patriot - John Hampden Soc

In There Somewhere - Dry Stone Walling Assn

In This Sad Web of Life - John Polidori Literary Soc

In Touch - Brit Chiropractic Assn

In Touch - Marfan Assn

In Touch - Netherlands-Brit Cham Comm

In Touch - On Site Massage Asn

In Touch - Scot Soc Autism

inbusiness - Inverness Cham Comm

Independence - Campaign Indep Britain

The Independent - Assn Cycle Traders

Independent - Brit Textile Technology Gp

Independent Business Today - Inst Indep Business

Independent Examiner - Assn Charity Indep Examiners

Independent Hostel Guide - Mountaineering Coun Scotland

The Independent Monitor - Assn Members Indep Monitoring Bds

The Independent Retailer - Alliance Indep Retailers

Independent Schools Ybk - Inc Assn Preparatory Schools

Index - Commissioning Specialists Assn

Index to ISPA News & Small Printer - Brit Printing Soc

The Indexer - Soc Indexers

Indexers Available - Soc Indexers

Indicator - Scot Coun Devt & Ind

Indirect Tax Voice - Inst Indirect Taxation

The Individual - Soc Individual Freedom

Industrial Archaeology News - Assn Indl Archaeology

Industrial Archaeology Review - Assn Indl Archaeology

The Industrial Laser User - Assn Indl Laser Users

The Industrial Locomotive - Indl Locomotive Soc

Industrial Railway Record - Indl Rly Soc

Industrial Textiles - Performance Textiles Assn

Industry Link - Nuclear Ind Assn

Industry Update - Brit Cement Assn

Infection Control Supplement - Infection Control Nurses Assn

Info - Chambre de Comm Française de Grande-Bretagne

In-Focus - Fedn Mfrg Opticians

Infofact - Scot Motor Neurone Disease Assn

Informant - Assn Registrars Scotland

Information Professional - Instn Engg & Technology

Informed - Investor Relations Soc

The Informer - Gasket Cutters' Assn

Infrastructure - Histl Model Rly Soc

Ingenia - R Academy Engg

Inland Racing Competition Regulation - Hovercraft Club

Inland Waterways Guide - Inland Waterways Assn

Inner Wheel - Assn Inner Wheel Clubs

Innes Review - Scot Catholic Histl Assn

Innovation in Print - Indep Print Inds Assn

Innovation into Success - UK Science Park Assn

Innovations in Information - Nat Infm Forum

Innovations in Primary Health Care Nursing - Community & District Nursing Assn

InRoads - Inst Road Safety Officers Ltd

Inscape - Brit Assn Art Therapists

Inside Track - Brit Olympic Assn
Green Alliance Trust

The Insider - Crohn's in Childhood Res Assn

Insight - Construction Ind Trading Electronically

Insight - Leukaemia CARE
Insight - Primary Immunodeficiency Assn
Insight - Warrington Cham Comm & Ind
Insight (non-destructive testing & condition monitoring) - Brit Inst Non-Destructive Testing
In-Situ Concrete Frames - Construct: Concrete Structures Gp
Insolvency Intelligence - Insolvency Lawyers Assn
Inspire - Assn Respiratory Technology & Physiology
Installation Guide - Brit Compressed Air Soc
The Installer - Nat Insulation Assn
Insulation - Thermal Insulation Mfrs & Supplrs Assn
Insurance Facts, Figures & Trends - Assn Brit Insurers
Insurance Trends - Assn Brit Insurers
Insurance Ybk - Assn Brit Insurers
Integral Bridges - Concrete Bridge Devt Gp
Intentions - Oscar Wilde Soc
Interact - Soc Advancement Games & Simulations in Educ & Tranining
Interaction - Action ME
Interchange News - NHS Confedn
Interchurch Families - Assn Interchurch Families
Intercom - Aircrew Assn
Interface - Inst Measurement & Control
Interfaces - Forensic Science Soc
Interior Insight - Assn Interior Specialists
Interiors Focus - Assn Interior Specialists
Internal Auditing & Business Risk - Inst Internal Auditors
International - Nat Acrylic Painters Assn
International & Comparative Law Quarterly - Brit Inst Intl & Comparative Law
International Affairs - R Inst Intl Affairs
International Directory - Nat Assn Estate Agents
International Endodontic Jnl - Brit Endodontic Soc
International Exchange - Motor Neurone Disease Assn
International Gas Engineering & Management - Instn Gas Engrs & Mgrs
The International Graphologist - IGA-UK
International Guidelines on the use of rope access methods for industrial purposes - Indl Rope Access Tr Assn
International Jnl of Art & Design Education - Nat Soc Educ Art & Design
International Jnl of Climatology - R Meteorological Soc
International Jnl of Cosmetic Science - Soc Cosmetic Scientists
International Jnl of Dairy Technology - Soc Dairy Technology
International Jnl of Food Science & Technology - Inst Food Science & Technology
International Jnl of Iberian Studies - Assn Contemporary Iberian Studies
International Jnl of Injury Control & Safety Promotion - Ergonomics Soc
International Jnl of Market Research - Market Res Soc
International Jnl of Meteorology - Tornado & Storm Research Org
International Jnl of Nautical Archaeology - Nautical Archaeology Soc
International Jnl of Obstetric Anaesthesia - Obstetric Anaesthetists Assn
International Jnl of Paediatric Dentistry - Brit Soc Paediatric Dentistry
International Jnl of Pharmaceutical Medicine - Soc Pharmaceutical Medicine
International Jnl of Pharmacy Practice - R Pharmaceutical Soc
International Jnl of Project Management - Assn Project Mgt
International Jnl of Psychoanalysis - Brit Psychoanalytical Soc Inst Psychoanalysis
International Jnl of Punjab Studies - Assn Punjab Studies (UK)
International Jnl of Remote Sensing - Remote Sensing & Photogrammetry Soc
International Jnl of Systematic & Evolutionary Microbiology - Soc Gen Microbiology
International Manual - Freight Transport Assn
International Manual - Nat Assn Estate Agents
International Marketing News - Assn Intl Marketing
International Simulation & Gaming Research Ybk - Soc Advancement Games & Simulations in Educ & Tranining
The International Therapist - Fedn Holistic Therapists
International Turfgrass Bulletin - Sports Turf Res Inst
The Internet in the UK Election - Hansard Soc Parliamentary Govt
The Intrepid Repairer - Nat Assn Musical Instrument Repairers

Introduction to Cochlear Implants - Nat Assn Deafened People
An Introduction to Commercial & Business Transfer Agency - Nat Assn Estate Agents
Introduction to Martial Arts - Nat Assn Karate & Martial Arts Schools
An Introduction to Pipe Jacking & Microtunnelling Design - Pipe Jacking Assn
An Introduction to Pipeline Pigging - Pigging Products & Services Assn
An Introduction to Sprayed Concrete - Sprayed Concrete Assn
Introduction to Volunteering Overseas - Returned Volunteer Action
Introduction to Wildlife Sound Recording - Wildlife Sound Recording Soc
Investigate - Assn Brit Investigators
Invoice - Inst Certified Book-Keepers
Involving Relatives & Friends: a good practice guide for homes for people - Relatives & Residents Assn
IPA Newsfile - Inst Practitioners Advertising
Iran - Brit Inst Persian Studies
Iris Ybk - Brit Iris Soc
Irish Studies Review - Brit Assn Ir Studies
Irrigation News - UK Irrigation Assn
Is it anything you ate? - Nat Soc Res Allergy
ISDF - Assn C & C++ Users
Island Business - Isle of Wight Cham Comm & Ind
Isle of Wight Birds - Isle of Wight Natural History & Archaeol Soc
Islington Business Newspaper - Islington Cham Comm & Tr Ltd
Issues in Environmental Science & Technology - R Soc Chemistry
IT Skills Trend Report Summary - Inst Mgt Infm Systems
IT Trends Ybk - Soc Inf Technology Mgt

J

Jacob Jnl - Jacob Sheep Soc Ltd
The Jacobite - Seventeen Fortyfive / 1745 Assn
Jade - Gld Erotic Artists
Janus - Assn Graduate Recruiters
Japan Experiences - Japan Soc
Japan Forum - Brit Assn Japanese Studies
Jazz UK - Welsh Jazz Soc
Jem - English Goat Breeders Assn
Jersey at Home - R Jersey Agricl & Hortl Soc
Jettison the Jargon - Grandparents' Assn
The Jeweller - Nat Assn Goldsmiths
Jewellery Studies - Soc Jewellery Hist
JICS - Intensive Care Soc
Jigsaw - Scot Soc Autism
The Jnl of Adolescence - Assn Profls Services Adolescents
Jnl of Adventure Education & Outdoor Learning - Inst Outdoor Learning
Jnl of Agricultural Economics - Agricl Economics Soc
Jnl of Agricultural Manpower - Agricl Manpower Soc
Jnl of American Studies - Brit Assn American Studies
Jnl of Analytical Atomic Spectrometry - R Soc Chemistry
Jnl of Anatomy - Anatomical Soc
Jnl of Animal Technology & Welfare - Inst Animal Technology
Jnl of Antimicrobial Chemotherapy - Brit Soc Antimicrobial Chemotherapy
Jnl of Applied Microbiology - Soc Applied Microbiology
Jnl of Applied Research in Intellectual Disabilities - Brit Inst Learning Disabilities
Jnl of Arts Marketing - Arts Marketing Assn
Jnl of Audiovisual Media in Medicine - Inst Med Illustrators
Jnl of Biological Education - Inst Biology
Jnl of Bone & Joint Surgery - Brit Orthopaedic Assn
Jnl of Bryology - Brit Bryological Soc
Jnl of Cataract & Refractive Surgery - UK & Ireland Soc Cataract & Refractive Surgeons
Jnl of Chemical Technology & Biotechnology - Soc Chemical Ind
Jnl of Child Health Care - Assn Brit Paediatric Nurses
Jnl of Child Psychology & Psychiatry - Assn Child & Adolescent Mental Health
Jnl of Classic Teaching - Jt Assn Classical Teachers

© CBD Research Ltd · Beckenham · BR3 5JS · Tel 020 8650 7745 · Fax 020 8650 0768 · E-mail cbd@cbdresearch.com · www.cbdresearch.com

The Jnl of Clinical Periodontology - Brit Soc Periodontology
Jnl of Common Market Studies - University Assn Contemporary Eur Studies
Jnl of Conchology - Conchological Soc
Jnl of Dental Research - Brit Soc Dental Res
Jnl of Design History - Design Hist Soc
Jnl for Drama in Education - Nat Assn Teaching Drama
Jnl of Education & Christian Belief - Assn Christian Teachers
Jnl of Egyptian Archaeology - Egypt Exploration Soc
Jnl of Electro-physiology & Technology - Electro-physiological Technologists' Assn
Jnl of Endocrinology - Soc Endocrinology
Jnl of Environmental Monitoring - R Soc Chemistry
Jnl of Experimental Botany - Soc Experimental Biology
Jnl of Family Planning & Reproductive Healthcare - Fac Family Planning & Reproductive Healthcare
Jnl of Family Therapy - Assn Family Therapy
Jnl of French Language Studies - Assn French Language Studies
Jnl of Further & Higher Education - NATFHE
Jnl of Gemmology - Gemmological Assn
Jnl of General Virology - Soc Gen Microbiology
Jnl of Hand Surgery - Brit Soc Surgery Hand
Jnl of Hellenic Studies - Soc Promotion Hellenic Studies
Jnl of Human Nutrition & Dietetics - Brit Dietetic Assn
Jnl of Infection - Brit Infection Soc
Jnl of Infertility Counselling - Brit Infertility Counselling Assn
Jnl of Interactive Marketing - Inst Direct Marketing
Jnl of International Development - Devt Studies Assn
Jnl of International Marketing - Assn Intl Marketing
Jnl of International Marketing & Marketing Research - Indl Marketing Assn
The Jnl of Latin Teaching - Assn Latin Teaching
Jnl of Linguistics - Linguistics Assn
Jnl of Materials Chemistry - R Soc Chemistry
Jnl of Medical Microbiology - Soc Gen Microbiology
Jnl into Melody - Robert Farnon Soc
Jnl of Microscopy - R Microscopical Soc
Jnl of Modern Italy - Assn Study Modern Italy
Jnl of Molecular Endocrinology - Soc Endocrinology
Jnl of Molluscan Studies - Malacological Soc London
Jnl of Museum Ethnography - Museum Ethnographers Gp
Jnl of Natural Medicine - Intl Register Consultant Herbalists & Homoeopaths
Jnl of Occupational & Organisational Psychology - Brit Psychological Soc
Jnl of Offshore Technology - Inst Marine Engg, Science & Technology
Jnl of One-Day Surgery - Brit Assn Day Surgery
Jnl of One-Name Studies - Gld of One-Name Studies
Jnl of Orthopaedic Medicine - Brit Inst Musculoskeletal Medicine
Jnl of Orthopaedic Medicine - Soc Orthopaedic Medicine Ltd
Jnl of Paediatric Surgery - Brit Assn Paediatric Surgeons
Jnl of Pathology - Pathological Soc
Jnl of Perioperative Practice - Assn Perioperative Pratice
Jnl of Pharmacy & Pharmacology + Pharmacy & Pharmacology Communities - R Pharmaceutical Soc
Jnl of Physics - Inst Physics
Jnl of Physiology - Physiological Soc
Jnl of Plastic, Reconstructive & Aesthetic Surgery - Brit Assn Plastic Surgeons
Jnl for Play Therapy - Brit Assn Play Therapists
Jnl of Psychopharmacology - Brit Assn Psychopharmacology
Jnl of Reproductive & Infant Psychology - Soc Reproductive & Infant Psychology
Jnl of Research in Reading - UK Literacy Assn
Jnl of Roman Studies - Soc Promotion Roman Studies
Jnl of the Science of Food & Agriculture - Soc Chemical Ind
Jnl of Sexual Aggression - Nat Org Treatment of Abusers
Jnl of Small Animal Practice - Brit Small Animal Veterinary Assn
Jnl of Sports Sciences - Ergonomics Soc
The Jnl of Stained Glass - Brit Soc Master Glass Painters
Jnl of Stereo Imaging - Stereoscopic Soc
Jnl of Tissue Viability - Tissue Viability Soc
Jnl of Turfgrass & Sports Surface Science - Sports Turf Res Inst
Jnl of Ultrasound - Brit Med Ultrasound Soc
The Jnl for Weavers, Spinners & Dyers - Assn Glds Weavers, Spinners & Dyers
Jnl of Zoology - Zoological Soc London

The John Buchan Jnl - John Buchan Soc
John Dalton Bibliography - Manchester Literary & Philosophical Soc
John Hampden & His Times - John Hampden Soc
John Hampden of Buckinghamshire: the people's hero - John Hampden Soc
John Polidori - creator of the literary vampire - John Polidori Literary Soc
Joint Code of Practice for Sprinklers in Schools - Brit Automatic Fire Sprinkler Assn
Joint Report - Children's Chronic Arthritis Assn
Jordaniana - Anglo-Jordanian Soc
A Journey through Infertility (video) - Infertility Network UK
Judges Guide - Nat Vegetable Soc
Judo News - Judo Scotland
Justice Bulletin - Nat Campaign Water Justice
The Justices' Clerk Jnl - Justices' Clerks' Soc

K

Keeping a Young Voice - Voice Care Network UK
Kennel Club Stud Book - Kennel Club
Kennel Gazette - Kennel Club
Kent - Assn Men Kent & Kentish Men
Kent Record Series & Monograph Series - Kent Archaeol Soc
Kent View - Kent County Agricl Soc
The Key - Prison Governors' Assn
The Key Frame - Fair Organ Presvn Soc
Key Issues in District Nursing - Community & District Nursing Assn
Keynote - Inst Food Science & Technology
The Keys of Peter - Christian Social Order
Keyways - Master Locksmiths' Assn
Kidney Life - Nat Kidney Fedn
King Pole - Circus Friends Assn
King's Army NL - English Civil War Soc
The Kipling Jnl - Kipling Soc
The Kiteflier - Kite Soc
Knitstats - Knitting Inds Fedn
Knitting - Gld Master Craftsmen
Knowing the Score 2 - Assn Brit Orchestras
Korfball - Brit Korfball Assn

L

La Brita Esperantisto - Esperanto Assn Britain
Lab on a Chip - R Soc Chemistry
Lablink - Profl Photographic Laboratories Assn
Laboratory Animals - Laboratory Animal Science Assn
Laboratory Hazards Bulletin - R Soc Chemistry
Labour & the House of Lords - Manorial Soc
Labour History Review - Soc Study Labour History
Lace - Lace Gld
Lacemaking - Lace Soc
Lady Golfer's Handbook - Ladies' Golf U
Lakeland Gems - Lakeland Dialect Soc
Lakeland Treasury - Lakeland Dialect Soc
Lallans - Scots Language Soc
Lamp - Assn Lighthouse Keepers
Lancashire Business View - E Lancs Cham Comm
The Lancastrian - Friends Real Lancashire
Land Registration Act - Manorial Soc
Land Registration Bill - Manorial Soc
Land Sailor - Brit Fedn Sand & Land Yacht Clubs
Landowning in Scotland - Scot Rural Property & Business Assn
Landscape Design - Landscape Inst
Landscape History - Soc Landscape Studies
Landscape News - Brit Assn Landscape Inds
Landscape Research Extra - Landscape Res Gp
Landscape Research Jnl - Landscape Res Gp
Landwards - Instn Agricl Engrs
Language & Literacy News - UK Literacy Assn

Language Issues - Nat Assn Teaching English &...Community Languages
Language Learning Jnl - Assn Language Learning
Language World - Assn Language Learning
The Lantern - Brit Housewives League
LAPADA Views - Assn Art & Antique Dealers Ltd
Lasers in Medical Science - Brit Med Laser Assn
The Last Straw - Straw Bale Building Assn
The Last Word - Assn Brit Scrabble Players
Latin CD - Assn Latin Liturgy
Laudate - Gld Church Musicians
Launderette & Cleaning World - Nat Assn Launderette Ind Ltd
The Laurel & Hardy Magazine - Laurel & Hardy Appreciation Soc
The Law Teacher - Assn Law Teachers
Layman's Guide to Osteochondritis - Perthes Assn
Leaders-digest.com - Evangelical Alliance UK
Learned Publishing - Assn Learned & Profl Soc Publishers
Learning & Development: an introduction to childcare in an early years setting - Scot Pre-School Play Assn
Learning Blitz - Brit Learning Assn
Learning Disability Bulletin - Brit Inst Learning Disabilities
Learning from Experience - Brit Urban Regeneration Assn
Learning to Live - Campaign for Learning
The Learning Spiral - Soc Effective Affective Learning
Leather Technologists Pocket Book - Soc Leather Technologists & Chemists Ltd
The Lecturer - NATFHE
The Left-Hander - Left Handers Club
Legal & Criminological Psychotherapy - Brit Psychological Soc
Legal Abacus - Inst Legal Cashiers & Administrators
Legal Aid Solicitors List (NI) - Law Soc NI
Legal Executive Jnl - Inst Legal Executives
Legal Information Management - Brit & Ir Assn Law Librarians
Legal Member Directory - Brit Assn Adoption & Fostering
Legal Studies - Soc Legal Scholars
Legionnaires Disease - Inst Plumbing & Heating Engg
The Legion - R Brit Legion
Leisure Management - Fitness Ind Assn
Leisure Manager - Inst Leisure & Amenity Mgt
Leisure News & Jobs - Inst Leisure & Amenity Mgt
Leisure Opportunities - Fitness Ind Assn
Let's Square Dance - Brit Assn American Square Dance Clubs
Letters in Applied Microbiology - Soc Applied Microbiology
Letting Update - UK Assn Letting Agents
Lewis Carroll Review - Lewis Carroll Soc
Liberation - Liberation
Liberty - Liberty
The Library - Bibliographical Soc
The Licensed Conveyancer - Soc Licensed Conveyancers
The Lichenologist - Brit Lichen Soc
Life News - Life
The Lifeboat - R Nat Lifeboat Instn
Lifeline - Brit Red Cross Soc
Lifeline - Overeaters Anonymous
Lifesavers Magazine - R Life Saving Soc
Lifespan - Brit Soc Res Ageing
Lifting Engineers Handbook - Lifting Eqpt Engrs Assn
Lifting Equipment - Lifting Eqpt Engrs Assn
Lifting the Veil of Silence on Emotional Problems after Childbirth - Meet-a-Mum Assn
Light Aviation - Aircraft Owners & Pilots Assn
Light Hovercraft - Hovercraft Club
Lightbox - Brit Assn Picture Libraries & Agencies
Lighting & Sound America - Profl Lighting & Sound Assn
Lighting & Sound International - Profl Lighting & Sound Assn
Lighting Jnl - Instn Lighting Engrs
Lighting News - Lighting Assn
Lighting Research & Technology - Chart Instn Bldg Services Engrs
Lime Stabilisation Manual - Quarry Products Assn
Lingua e Vita - Brit Interlingua Soc
The Linguist - Chart Inst Linguists
Link - Assn Spina Bifida & Hydrocephalus
The Link - Scot Envt Link
LINK - Swedish Cham Comm UK
Link Magazine - Nat Assn Writers' Gps
The Linnean - Linnean Soc London
List of A1 Bulls - Longhorn Cattle Soc
List of Agency Members - Brit Assn Adoption & Fostering

List of Establishments in UK Offering Western Riding - Western Horsemen's Assn
The List of French Investments in the UK - Chambre Comm Française de Grande-Bretagne
List of Schools run by AMI Trained Teachers - Montessori Soc
Listed Heritage - Listed Property Owners Club
Listing of Courses in European Studies in UK Universities - University Assn Contemporary Eur Studies
Listing of Dials in UK - Brit Sundial Soc
Lists of pre 1855 Monumental Inscriptions - Scot Genealogy Soc
Literacy - UK Literacy Assn
Literacy & ICT: cutting edge practice in the primary school - Nat Literacy Assn
Little People - Miniature Mediterranean Donkey Assn
Liturgical Studies - Alcuin Club
Livin' Country - U Country Sports Workers
Living Afloat - Residential Boat Owners Assn
Living Earth - Soil Assn Ltd
Living with Ankylosing Spondylitis - Nat Ankylosing Spondylitis Soc
Lobby - Campaign Nuclear Disarmament
Local Area Analysis & Portfolio Construction - Soc Property Researchers
Local Council Review - Nat Assn Local Couns
The Local Historian - Brit Assn Local Hist
Local History News - Brit Assn Local Hist
Local News - Gwent Wildlife Trust
Locomotives - Histl Model Rly Soc
Locomotives of the Hull & Barnsley Railway - Histl Model Rly Soc
The Locomotives of the Stockton & Darlington Railway - Histl Model Rly Soc
The Log - Brit Air Line Pilots Assn
The Log - Soc Model Shipwrights
The Log Book - Ship Stamp Soc
Logistics & Transport - Chart Inst Logistics & Transport
Logopedics, Phoniatrics & Vocology - Brit Voice Assn
London Bird Report - London Natural Hist Soc
London Business Matters - London Cham Comm & Ind
London Cyclist - London Cycling Campaign
London Guide's Guide - Gld Registered Tourist Guides
The London Naturalist - London Natural Hist Soc
London NL - W Africa Business Assn
The London Philatelist - R Philatelic Soc London
The London Practice - Friends Dr Watson
London Topographical Record - London Topographical Soc
London Welshman - London Welsh Soc
London's Industrial Archaeology - Greater London Indl Archaeology Soc
Long Distance Walkers Hbk - Long Distance Walkers Assn
Long Range Planning - Strategic Planning Soc
Look Before You Leap - Dance UK Ltd
Look North - Scot C'ee Optometrists
Looking After Your Grandchildren - Grandparents' Assn
Looking Ahead - Bluefaced Leicester Sheep Breeders Assn
Lottery Magazine - Lotteries Coun
Lower Limb Deficiency - STEPS: Assn People with Lower Limb Abnormalities
Lube - UK Lubricants Assn
The Luing Jnl - Luing Cattle Soc
Luing News - Luing Cattle Soc
Luso News - Lusitano Breed Soc
The Lute - Lute Soc
Lute News - Lute Soc
Lynes - Lithuanian Assn
The Mace-Bearer - Gld Macebearers

M

Machenalia - Friends Arthur Machen
Machine Knitting News - Gld Master Craftsmen
Machinery Update - Processing & Packaging Machinery Assn
The Magic Circular - Magic Circle
The Magistrate - Magistrates' Assn
Magnet - Youth Scotland

© CBD Research Ltd · Beckenham · BR3 5JS · Tel 020 8650 7745 · Fax 020 8650 0768 · E-mail cbd@cbdresearch.com · www.cbdresearch.com

Mailing - Trollope Soc
Mailshot - Inst Barristers' Clerks
The Maiwand Dispatch No 1 - Friends Dr Watson
The Maiwand Luncheon Monograph - Friends Dr Watson
Maize Grower - Maize Growers Assn
Make a Sundial - Brit Sundial Soc
Make Space! design for theatre & alternative spaces - Soc Brit Theatre Designers
Making Sense of Health Improvement Programmes - Nat Assn Primary Care
Making the Best of Amputation - Brit Limbless Ex-Service Men's Assn
Mallorn - Tolkien Soc
Mammal News - Mammal Soc
Mammal Review - Mammal Soc
Mammalaction News - Mammal Soc
Management in Education - Brit Educl Leadership, Mgt & Admin Soc
Management of Exuding Wounds - Wound Care Soc
The Management Specialist - Inst Mgt Specialists
Manager: the British Jnl of Administrative Management - Inst Administrative Mgt
Managing Absence - Ceretas
Managing Trade Associations - Trade Association Forum
Manchester Memoirs - Manchester Literary & Philosophical Soc
Manic Depression - SANE
Man-made Mineral Fibre - Thermal Insulation Contrs Assn
Manpower News - HR Soc Ltd
Manual of Actuarial Practice - Inst Actuaries
The Manual of the Mace - Gld Macebearers
Manual of Operating Standards - Retread Mfrs Assn
Manual of Sealant Practice - Brit Adhesives & Sealants Assn
Manufacturing - Inst Mfrg
Manufacturing Engineer - Instn Engg & Technology
Manufacturing Management - Inst Mfrg
Maplines - Brit Cartographic Soc
Maps & Surveys - Brit Cartographic Soc
MARCH Mental Health Circular - Nat Assn Mental After-Care in Residential Care Homes
Marine Conservation - Marine Consvn Soc
Marine Engineers Review - Inst Marine Engg, Science & Technology
The Mariners Mirror - Soc Nautical Res
Maritime IT & Electronics - Inst Marine Engg, Science & Technology
Market Leader - Marketing Soc
the marketer - Chart Inst Marketing
Marketing Newz - Sleep Coun
The Marquetarian - Marquetry Soc
Martial Arts Code of Safety - Nat Assn Karate & Martial Arts Schools
Masonry International - Brit Masonry Soc
Mass Spectrometry Bulletin - R Soc Chemistry
Master List of Cinemas - Cinema Advertising Assn Ltd
Masterbuilder - Fedn Master Builders
Masterchefs - Master Chefs
Mastersinger - Assn Brit Choral Directors
Masthead - Greenwich, Bexley & Lewisham Cham Comm
Match Label News - Brit Matchbox, Label & Booklet Soc
Mathematical & General Physics - Inst Physics
Mathematical Medicine & Biology - Inst Mathematics & Applications
Mathematical Proceedings - Cambridge Philosophical Soc
Mathematics Teaching - Assn Teachers Mathematics
Mathematics Today - Inst Mathematics & Applications
Matrix - Brit Science Fiction Assn
May Catholics choose Cremation? - Cremation Soc
Mayoral Dir - London Mayors Assn
McClintock Lecture Series - SACRO
McKenzie - Families Need Fathers
Measurement & Control - Inst Measurement & Control
Meat Hygienist - Assn Meat Inspectors
The Medal - Brit Art Medal Soc
Medical Companion - Myasthenia Gravis Assn
Medical Member Directory - Brit Assn Adoption & Fostering
Medical Methods of Treatment - SANE
Medical Microbiologists - Assn Med Microbiologists
Medical Practitioners' Financial Hbk - Assn Inep Specialist Med Accountants

Medical Science History - Medical Sciences Histl Soc
Medication - Ceretas
Medication for Narcolepsy - Narcolepsy Assn
Medicine & War - Medical Action Global Security
Medicine, Science & the Law - Brit Academy Forensic Sciences
Medieval Archaeology - Soc Medieval Archaeology
Meeting Houses in Britain - Friends Histl Soc
Melin - Welsh Mills Soc
Membership Executive - Tourism Soc Ltd
Memorandum Book - Scot Law Agents Soc
Memory Lane - Al Bowlly Circle
Mental Health Matters - NI Assn Mental Health
Mental Health Nursing - Mental Health Nurses Assn
The Mercia Bioscope - Mercia Cinema Soc
Mercury - Brit Astrological & Psychic Soc
Merkur - German Rly Soc
The Merton Jnl - Thomas Merton Soc
The Message - Nat Pensioners' Convention
Meteorological Applications - R Meteorological Soc
Methods in Organic Synthesis - R Soc Chemistry
Microbiology - Soc Gen Microbiology
Microbiology Today - Soc Gen Microbiology
Microlight Flying - Brit Microlight Aircraft Assn
Micromath - Assn Teachers Mathematics
Microscope - Meningitis Research Foundation
The Middle Way - Buddhist Soc
The Midlands & Eastern Instructor - Motor Schools Assn
Midwifery Matters - Assn Radical Midwives
Milestones & Waymakers - Milestone Soc
Milk Digest - R Assn Brit Dairy Farmers
Millennium Book - Manorial Soc
Millennium Site Guide - UK Paintball Sports Fedn
The Miner - Nat U Mineworkers
Minerva: Jnl of Swansea History - R Instn S Wales
Mining Heritage Guide - Nat Assn Mining History Orgs
Mining History - Peak District Mines Histl Soc
Miro News - Mineral Ind Res Org
Missing the Grade: Education for Children in Prison - Howard League Penal Reform
The Missing Link - Brit Sausage Appreciation Soc
Mitteilungsblatt - Anglo-German Family Hist Soc
Mixed Marriage in Ireland: A companion to those involved, or about to be involved, in a mixed marriage - NI Mixed Marriage Assn
Mixed Moss - Arthur Ransome Soc Ltd
MJA News - Medical Journalists Assn
Mobile News - Mobile Electronics & Security Fedn
Modelling Historic Architecture - Histl Model Rly Soc
Modern & Contemporary France - Assn Study Modern & Contemporary France
Modern Believing - Modern Churchpeople's U
Modern Language Review - Modern Humanities Res Assn
Modern Management - Inst Leadership & Mgt
MODUS - Design & Technology Assn
Molecular Plant Pathology - Brit Soc Plant Pathology
Mollusc World - Conchological Soc
Monarchy - Monarchist League
Money Laundering Guidelines - Brit Cheque Cashers Assn
Money Minder - Nat Assn Bank & Insurance Customers
Monitoring & Evaluation - Assn Charitable Foundations
Monitoring Report on Theatre Directors - Directors Gld
Montage - Picture Res Assn
Montessori Direction - Montessori Soc
The Montessori Review - Montessori Soc
Monthly Magazine - Assn Hot Foil Printers
Monthly Notices - R Astronomical Soc
Monthly Rice Circular - London Rice Brokers' Assn
Moors Line - N Yorks Moors Historical Rly Trust
More Care for Your Voice - Voice Care Network UK
Mosaic - Assn Study & Presvn Roman Mosaics
Most - Modern Studies Assn
Motor Caravanner - Motor Caravanners' Club Ltd
Motor Factor - Automotive Aftermarket Assn Group Auto-Union
Motor Industry Magazine - Inst Motor Ind
Motor Retailer - Retail Motor Ind Fedn
Motorcycle Rider - Brit Motorcyclists' Fedn
Motorcycling GB - Auto-Cycle U

Movement & Dance - Laban Gld Movement & Dance
Moving Forward: a guide to living with spinal cord injury - Spinal Injuries Assn
Moving News - Movers Inst
MQR - Minerals Engg Soc
MRS News - Market Res Soc
MS Matters - Multiple Sclerosis Soc
The Mule - Brit Mule Soc
Mule News - N England Mule Sheep Assn
Multiples - Soc Wood Engravers
The Museum Archaeologist - Soc Museum Archaeologists
Museum briefings - Museums Assn
Museum News - Nat Heritage
Museum Practice - Museums Assn
Museums Jnl - Museums Assn
Museums Ybk (a directory of museums & galleries of the British Isles) - Museums Assn
Mushroom Jnl - Mushroom Growers' Assn
Music - Viola da Gamba Soc
The Music Box - Musical Box Soc
Music Copyright Matters - Music Publishers' Assn
Music Jnl - Inc Soc Musicians
Musician - Musicians' U
Mustelid Meanderings - Nat Ferret Welfare Soc
Mutagenesis - UK Envtl Mutagen Soc
n:gauge - Nat Assn Goldsmiths

N

Narcolepsy: a layman's guide - Narcolepsy Assn
Narcolepsy: care & treatment - Narcolepsy Assn
National & Specialists Society bk - Assn Brit Philatelic Socs
National B&W Premier League Fixture Book - Table Soccer Players Assn
National Guide's Guide - Gld Registered Tourist Guides
National Meeting Book of Abstracts - Brit Neuroscience Assn
The National Plant Collections Directory - Nat Coun Consvn Plants & Gardens
National Register of Consultants - Brit Astrological & Psychic Soc
National Register of Psychotherapists - UK Coun Psychotherapy
National Swimming Award Pack - Scot Swimming
National Tobacconists Trade Exhibition Catalogue - Assn Indep Tobacco Specialists
Nations & Nationalism - Assn Study Ethnicity & Nationalism
Natterjack - Brit Herpetological Soc
Natterjack News - Landlife
Natural Medicine - Assn Natural Medicine
Natural Products Reports - R Soc Chemistry
Natural Products Updates - R Soc Chemistry
Natural World - R Soc Wildlife Trusts
Nautical Archaeology NL - Nautical Archaeology Soc
Naval Architect - R Instn Naval Architects
Navvies - Waterway Recovery Gp
Navy News - Sea Cadet Assn
The Nelson Dispatch - Nelson Soc
Neometaphysical Digest - Soc Metaphysicians Ltd
Netball Magazine - All England Netball Assn Ltd
Netball News - Welsh Netball Assn
Network - Assn Project Mgt
Network - Brit Sociological Assn
Network - Healthcare People Mgt Assn
Network for Regions - Motorcycle Action Gp
Network London - Brit-American Business Inc
Network New York - Brit-American Business Inc
Network Nottinghamshire - Nottinghamshire Cham Comm & Ind
Networker - Devt Trusts Assn
Networking - Brit Dental Practice Mgrs Assn
Neuropathology & Applied Neurobiology - Brit Neuropathological Soc
New Approach to Latin for the Mass - Assn Latin Liturgy
New Arrivals - Brit Humanist Assn
New Books in Folklore - Folklore Soc
New Comparison - Brit Comparative Literature Assn
New Crystal Palace Matters - Crystal Palace Foundation
New Direction - Herefordshire & Worcestershire Cham Comm

New Disease Reports - Brit Soc Plant Pathology
New Generation - Nat Childbirth Trust
New Ground - Socialist Environment & Resources Assn
New Humanist - Rationalist Assn
The New Idler - Johnson Soc London
New Jnl of Chemistry - R Soc Chemistry
New Latin-English Sunday Missal - Assn Latin Liturgy
New Pesticide Outlook - R Soc Chemistry
New Producer - New Producers Alliance
The New Rambler - Johnson Soc London
New Sjogren's Hbk - Brit Sjogren's Syndrome Assn
New Specialist Angler - Specialist Anglers Alliance
New Steel Construction - Brit Constructional Steelwork Assn Ltd / Steel Construction Inst
New Technical Guide (incl Roofing, Flooring, Paving, Tanking) - Mastic Asphalt Coun
New Tracks to the Cities - Permanent Way Instn
New View Magazine - Anthroposophical Soc
New Vision - Assn Separated & Divorced Catholics
New Welsh Review - ACADEMI
New Woodworking - Gld Master Craftsmen
New World - Utd Nations Assn
New Writing Scotland - Assn Scot Literary Studies
Newborn News - BLISS - Nat Charity Newborn
The Newman - Newman Assn
News & Ideas - Scout & Guide Graduate Assn
News Direct - Nat Baton Twirling Assn
News in Brief - Data Publishers' Assn
News Link - Brit Inst Non-Destructive Testing
News Magazine - Brit Limousin Cattle Soc Ltd
News On-line - Chart Instn Wastes Mgt
News Review - Brit Show Pony Soc
newsbrief - mediawatch-uk
Newsbriefing Magazine - Brit Assn Art Therapists
newsCASt - Citizens Advice Scotland
NI Master Butchers - NI Master Butchers Assn
NI Pharmacy in Focus - Ulster Chemists' Assn
The Nibbler - Nat Gerbil Soc
Niche Commercial - Nat Assn Comml Finance Brokers
No Pound: No Independence - Anti Common Market League
NOMINA - Soc Name Studies
The Nonconformist Experience in Croydon - Croydon Natural History & Scientific Soc
Norfolk & Norwich Clocks & Clockmakers - Antiquarian Horological Soc
Norfolk Archaeology - Norfolk & Norwich Archaeol Soc
Norgrass - N Scotland Grassland Soc
North Eastern Record - Histl Model Rly Soc
North West Notes - N Wstn Model Rly Clubs Assn
North Wind - George MacDonald Soc
Northamptonshire Past & Present - Northamptonshire Record Soc
Northern Bulletin - Green Lane Assn
The Northern Instructor - Motor Schools Assn
Northern Studies - Scot Soc Nthn Studies
North-West Geography - Manchester Geographical Soc
The Notary - Notaries' Soc
Notes & Records - Royal Soc
Notes for Company Managers - Stage Mgt Assn
Notice Board - Assn Chief Execs Voluntary Orgs
Noticeboard - HEADWAY - Brain Injury Assn
Nottinghamshire Business Directory - Nottinghamshire Cham Comm & Ind
Nottinghamshire Historian - Nottinghamshire Local Hist Assn
November News - Bluefaced Leicester Sheep Breeders Assn
The Nuclear Engineer - Instn Nuclear Engrs
Nuclear & Particle Physics - Inst Physics
Nuclear Medicine Communications - Brit Nuclear Medicine Soc
The Numismatic Chronicle - R Numismatic Soc
Nurse Prescribing - Community & District Nursing Assn
Nursery News - Nat Day Nurseries Assn
The Nursery Nursing Jnl - Soc Nursery Nursing
Nursing Care - Community & District Nursing Assn
Nursing Home News - Registered Nursing Home Assn Ltd
Nursing Management Manual - Registered Nursing Home Assn Ltd
Nursing Scotland - Indep Fedn Nursing Scotland
Nursing Standard - R Coll Nursing

Nutrition & Health - McCarrison Soc
Nutwood - Followers Rupert
The Nymphs & the Government - Friends St Bride Printing Library

O

Obsessions - SANE
The Obstetetrician & Gynaecologist - R Coll Obstetricians & Gynaecologists
Occupational Medicine Jnl - Soc Occupational Medicine
Occupational Safety & Health - R Soc Prevention Accidents
Occupational Therapy News - Brit Assn Occupational Therapists Ltd
Ocean Challenge - Challenger Soc Marine Science
Oculus - Partially Sighted Soc
Off Air - Radio Academy
Off The Run - Fire Service Presvn Gp
Official Methods of Analysis - Soc Leather Technologists & Chemists Ltd
Official Procurement Guide - Health Care Supplies Assn
Officiating News - Assn Brit Tennis Officials
Offshore Marine Technology - R Instn Naval Architects
OH Today - AOHNP
Oil on the Rails - Histl Model Rly Soc
Old Fell Side - Lakeland Dialect Soc
Omnibus - Jt Assn Classical Teachers
The Omnibus Magazine - Omnibus Soc
On Air - Nat Assn Hospital Broadcasting Orgs
On Display - Fair Organ Presvn Soc
On the Massage Scene - Scot Massage Therapists Org
On the Road - Assn Brit Drivers
On Track Magazine - Fitness Ind Assn
One & All - Nat Adult School Org
One in Seven - RNID
Onward - Inland Waterways Protection Soc
Onze Taal - Assn Language Learning
Open Hand Magazine - Deaf Blind UK
Open House - Nat Assn Bikers Disability
Open Space - Commons, Open Spaces & Footpaths Preservation Soc
Ophthalmic & Physiological Optics - Coll Optometrists
Opportunities - Brit-Peruvian Cham Comm
Opportunity - Milton Keynes & North Buckinghamshire Cham Comm
Opposite Lock - Veteran Speedway Riders Assn
Opticians in Business - Fedn Ophthalmic & Dispensing Opticians
Optics - Assn Brit Dispensing Opticians
Optics at a Glance - Fedn Ophthalmic & Dispensing Opticians
Optimum Nutrition - Inst Optimum Nutrition
Optonews - Scot Optoelectronics Assn
OR Insight - Operational Res Soc
Oracle - Inst Sheet Metal Engg
Oral History - Oral History Soc
Orbit - Domestic Appliance Service Assn
Orchid Cultivation Booklet - Orchid Soc
Orders & Medals - Orders & Medals Research Soc
Orff Times - Orff Soc (UK)
Organic & Biomolecular Chemistry - R Soc Chemistry
Organic Farming - Soil Assn Ltd
Organic Life - Gld Master Craftsmen
Organisation & People Jnl - Assn Mgt Educ & Devt
Organists' Review - Inc Assn Organists
Originals - Soc Artists' Agents
Origins - Biblical Creation Soc
Ornithological Bulletin - London Natural Hist Soc
Orts - George MacDonald Soc
Osteopathy Today - Brit Osteopathic Assn
Osteoporosis News - Nat Osteoporosis Soc
Osteoporosis Review - Nat Osteoporosis Soc
The Ostomy Book - ia: Ileostomy & Internal Pouch Support Gp
OT (Optometry Today / Optics Today) - Assn Optometrists
Otter News - Intl Otter Survival Fund
Our Common Land - Commons, Open Spaces & Footpaths Presvn Soc
Out on a Limb - Brit Limbless Ex-Service Men's Assn

Outdoor Photography - Gld Master Craftsmen
Outdoor Sourcebook - Inst Outdoor Learning
Outlaw - Arthur Ransome Soc Ltd
Outlook - Brit Chemical Distbrs & Traders Assn
Outlook - Fedn Sidecar Clubs
The Outrigger - Pacific Islands Soc
Overload - Assn C & C++ Users
Overseas - R Over-Seas League
Owner Magazine - Racehorse Owners Assn Ltd
The Oxford Down - One Hundred Years of Breeding - Oxford Down Sheep Breeders Assn
Oxoniensia - Oxfordshire Architectural & Histl Soc
Ozone - Inst Swimming Pool Engrs Ltd

P

PA2 - Brit Pharmacological Soc
Pacemaker - Thoroughbred Breeders' Assn
Paddle Wheels - Paddle Steamer Preservation Soc
Paddles Past - Historic Canoe & Kayak Assn
Pagan Dawn - Pagan Fedn
Pain & Wound Care - Wound Care Soc
Paint - SAA (Soc All Artists)
Paintball Games in Woodlands - UK Paintball Sports Fedn
Paintball UK - UK Paintball Sports Fedn
Palaeontology - Palaeontological Assn
Palliative Care for Young People 13-24 - Assn Children Life-Threatening or Terminal Conditions. . .
Palliative Management of Fungating Malignant Wounds - Wound Care Soc
Pallidula - Brit Shell Collectors Club
Palomino - Brit Palomino Soc
Pan - Brit Flute Soc
Panpodium - Brit Assn Steel Bands
Paper & Converting Machinery News - Picon Ltd
Paper Technology - Paper Ind Technical Assn
The Paralegal - Nat Assn Licensed Paralegals
Parallel Vision - Brit & Ir Orthoptic Soc
Paranormal Review Magazine - Inc Soc Psychical Res
Parent / Patient Hbk - Assn Glycogen Storage Disease
Parents & Schools - Campaign State Educ
Parking News - Brit Parking Assn
Parliament, the City & Financial Regulation - Hansard Soc Parliamentary Govt
Parliamentary NL - Green Alliance Trust
Parson & Parish - English Clergy Assn
A Part Work Encyclopaedia - Buttonhook Soc
Partners in Progress - Brit Cham Comm Thailand
PAST - Prehistoric Soc
Pastoral Care in Education - Nat Assn Pastoral Care Educ
The Patriot - John Hampden Soc
Patternmaking News - Pattern, Model, & Mould Mfrs Assn
Patterns of Prejudice - Inst Jewish Policy Res
Pawnbrokers Guide - Nat Pawnbrokers Assn
Pawns - Welsh Chess U
Pawprints - People & Dogs Soc
Pay Advice - Inst Payroll & Pensions Mgt
Payroll Managers Magazine - Payroll Alliance
Peace Song Book - Workers' Music Assn
Peewit! - Malcolm Saville Soc
Pelargonium News - Brit Pelargonium Ybk
Pencil Point - Obstetric Anaesthetists Assn
Pendulum - MDF - the Bipolar Org
The Penguin Collector - Penguin Collectors' Soc
Pension credit for beginners - Nat Pensioners' Convention
Pension Lawyer - Assn Pension Lawyers
Pensioner's Voice - Nat Fedn Retirement Pensions Assns
People & Places - Intl Pen Friends
A People Business - Direct Selling Assn
People Management - Chart Inst Personnel & Devt
Per Annum - Assn Chief Estates Surveyors & Property Mgrs in Local Government
Pera Abstracts - PERA
Percussive Notes - Percussive Arts Soc
Peregrine - Hawk & Owl Trust

Performance Bond - Confedn Construction Specialists
Permaculture Works - Permaculture Assn
The Permanent Way Institution - the first 100 years, 1884-1984 - Permanent Way Instn
Permission to Speak, Sir! - Dad's Army Appreciation Soc
Personal & Professional Boundaries - Ceretas
Personal Experiences - Narcolepsy Assn
Personal Injuries Hbk - Personal Injuries Bar Assn
Personal Safety - Ceretas
Perspective - R Soc Ulster Architects
Perspectives - Assn University Admins
　　　Myalgic Encephalopathy Assn
Pest Management Science - Soc Chemical Ind
Petroleum Review - Energy Inst
Pharmaceutical Jnl - R Pharmaceutical Soc
The Pharmaceutical Historian - Brit Soc Hist Pharmacy
Pharmaceutical Statistics - Statisticians Pharmaceutical Ind
Pharos International - Cremation Soc
Philosophy - R Inst Philosophy
Phobias - SANE
Phoenix - Assn Graduate Careers Advisory Services
Photochemical & Photobiological Sciences - R Soc Chemistry
The Photogrammetric Record - Remote Sensing & Photogrammetry Soc
The Photographer - Brit Inst Profl Photography
Photographica World - Photographic Collectors Club
PhotoNews - Assn Transport Photographers & Historians
PhysChemComm - R Soc Chemistry
Physical Chemistry Chemical Physics - R Soc Chemistry
Physical Education & Sports Pedagogy - Assn Physical Educ
Physical Education Matters - Assn Physical Educ
A Physician's Guide to the Management of Huntington's Disease - (Huntington's Disease Assn
　　　(Scot Huntington's Assn
Physics & Chemistry of Glasses - Soc Glass Technology
Physiotherapy - Chart Soc Physiotherapy
Physiotherapy (cassette) - Nat Ankylosing Spondylitis Soc
Picture House - Cinema Theatre Assn
The Picture Restorer - Brit Assn Paintings Conservator-Restorers
Piers - Nat Piers Soc
Pig Industry - Brit Pig Assn
Pigging Industry News - Pigging Products & Services Assn
Pimatters - PEP & ISA Mgrs' Assn
Pinball Player - Pinball Owners' Assn
Pine Cone - Order of Woodcraft Chivalry
Pint in Hand - Soc Presvn Beers Wood
Pioneers & Pathfinders - Assn Past Rotarians
The Pipe Band - R Scot Pipe Band Assn
Pipe Joint Guide - Brit Compresed Air Soc
Pipeline - Surfers against Sewage
Pipeline Industry Dir - Pipeline Inds Gld
Piping the News - Inc Assn Organists
The Piping Times - Coll Piping
Pitkin Guide to George Eliot - George Eliot Fellowship
The Place Names of [county] - English Place-Name Soc
Placement Vacancy Circular - Placements Ind Network
Plain English - Plain English Campaign 1979
Plainsong & Medieval Music - Plainsong & Mediæval Music Soc
The Planetarium of Giovanni de Dondi - Antiquarian Horological Soc
Plangon - Doll Club
Planning for Memorials - Assn Burial Authorities Ltd
Planning for Memorials after Cremation - Assn Burial Authorities Ltd
Planning, Development & Operation of Science Parks - UK Science Park Assn
Plant Based Nutrition & Health - Vegan Soc Ltd
Plant Biotechnology - Soc Experimental Biology
The Plant Engineer - Soc Operations Engrs
Plant Heritage - Nat Coun Consvn Plants & Gardens
The Plant Jnl - Soc Experimental Biology
Plant Pathology - Brit Soc Plant Pathology
Planting & Managing Amenity Woodlands - Arboricultural Assn
Plantlife - Plantlife Intl
Plastiquarian - Plastics Histl Soc
The Platform - Fairground Soc
Play Matters - Nat Assn Toy & Leisure Libraries
Playaction - Fair Play for Children Assn

Playaction Guides - Fair Play for Children Assn
Playing a Part: a study of the impact of youth theatre on the personal, social & political development of young people - Nat Assn Youth Theatres
Playing Rules Official Book - Table Soccer Players Assn
The Players Club - Profl Footballers Assn
The Players Jnl - Profl Footballers Assn
Plu Glosa Nota - Glosa Education Org
Plumb Heat - Scot & NI Plumbing Emplrs' Fedn
Plumbheat - NI Master Plumbers' Assn
Plumbing - Inst Plumbing & Heating Engg
Plumbing Engineering Services Design Guide - Inst Plumbing & Heating Engg
Plus News - Nat Fedn Eighteen Plus Gps
Pocket Book - Rugby Fives Assn
Pocket Scots Dictionary - Scot Language Dictionaries
Podiatry Now - Soc Chiropodists & Podiatrists
The Poetry News - Poetry Soc
The Poetry Review - Poetry Soc
Point 3 - Toc H
Pointer - Scot Coun Devt & Ind
Poisoning in Veterinary Practice - Nat Office Animal Health
Police - Police Fedn England & Wales
Police Beat - Police Fedn NI
Pollution Hbk - Nat Soc Clean Air & Envtl Protection
Polymer International - Soc Chemical Ind
Pony Express - Mounted Games Assn
Popular Astronomy - Soc Popular Astronomy
Popular Flying - Popular Flying Assn
Port Health - Assn Port Health Authorities
Port Health Lookout - Assn Port Health Authorities
Portage Post - Nat Portage Assn
Portfolio - Monumental Brass Soc
Postal Auction - Photographic Collectors Club
Postal History - Postal History Soc
Postbag - Nat Assn Music Educators
Postcard World - GB Postcard Club
Postgraduate Medical Jnl - Fellowship Postgraduate Medicine
Post-Medieval Archaeology - Soc Post-Medieval Archaeology
Potters - Craft Potters' Assn
Power Engineer - (Instn Diesel & Gas Turbine
　　　(Instn Engg & Technology
The Powys Jnl - Powys Soc
The Powys NL - Powys Soc
Practical Greenkeeping - R & Ancient Golf Club
A Practical Guide to Safe School Trips Booklet - Scot School Bd Assn
Practical Ophthalmic Lenses - Assn Brit Dispensing Opticians
Practice (Jnl) - Brit Assn Social Workers
Practice Guides - UK Clinical Pharmacy Assn
Practice Resource Manual - Brit Small Animal Veterinary Assn
Practice Safety Video/DVD - Nat Karting Assn
A Practitioner's Guide to Residential Letting & Property Management - Nat Assn Estate Agents
Precedents for Consent Orders - Resolution
Pregnancy Loss & the Death of a Baby - Stillbirth & Neonatal Death Soc
Prep School - Soc Assistants Teaching in Preparatory Schools Ltd
Prep School Magazine - Inc Assn Preparatory Schools
Pressure Points - Water Jetting Assn
Pressure Ulcer Prevention Manual - Wound Care Soc
Preview - R Caledonian Horticl Soc
A Price not worth Paying - Campaign Indep Britain
Primary Geographer - Geographical Assn
Primary History - Histl Assn
Primary Science Review - Assn Science Educ
Primate Eye - Primate Soc
Primed - Assn Brit Health Care Inds
The Primer - Vintage Arms Assn
Principles of Fire Investigation - Instn Fire Engrs
Principles of Leg Ulcer Management & Prevention - Wound Care Soc
Principles of Ophthalmic Lenses - Assn Brit Dispensing Opticians
Principles of Pressure Ulcer Management & Prevention - Wound Care Soc
Prism - Brit Fantasy Soc
Private Care Clarion - Brit Fedn Care Home Proprietors
Private Hire & Taxi Monthly - Nat Private Hire Assn

Private Hire News - London Private Hire Car Assn Ltd
The Private Library - Private Libraries Assn
Private Owner Wagons from the Ince Waggon & Ironworks Co - Histl Model Rly Soc
Pro Wholesaler - Fedn Wholesale Distbrs
Probation Jnl - Nat Assn Probation Officers
Process Safety & Environmental Protection - Instn Chemical Engrs
Proclaim - Assn Past Rotarians
ProContractor - Nat Assn Agricultural Contrs
The Product Book - D&AD
Production Jnl - Newspaper Soc
Professional Business & Technical Management - Profl Business & Tech Mgt
The Professional Engineer - Soc Profl Engrs
                               UK Assn Profl Engrs
The Professional Gardener - Profl Gardeners' Gld
Professional Imagemaker - Soc Wedding & Portrait Photographers
Professional Investor - UK Soc Investment Profls
Professional Manager - Chart Mgt Inst
Professional Pest Controller - Brit Pest Control Assn
The Professional Remover - Nat Gld Removers & Storers
Professional Social Work - Brit Assn Social Workers
Professionalism in Practice - Profl Assn Nursery Nurses
                               Profl Assn Teachers
                               Profls Allied to Teaching
Profile - Chart Inst Public Relations
                      Profl Golfers' Assn
Progress - Nat Home Improvement Coun
Progressive Greetings - Greeting Card Assn
Project Magazine - Assn Project Mgt
Pro-Life Times - Soc Protection Unborn Children
Promotions Buyer - Brit Promotional Merchandise Assn
Property Care Magazine - Brit Wood Preserving & Damp-proofing Assn
Property Care NL - Brit Wood Preserving & Damp-proofing Assn
Property Indices Report - Soc Property Researchers
The Property Magazine - Gld Profl Estate Agents
Pro-rat-a - Nat Fancy Rat Soc
Prosper - Black Country Cham
Protestant Truth - Protestant Truth Soc
Pruning Kentish Cobnuts - Kentish Cobnuts Assn
Psi Report - Scot Soc Psychical Res
Psoriasis - Psoriasis Assn
Psoriatic Care Fact File - Psoriatic Arthropathy Alliance
Psychiatric Bulletin - R Coll Psychiatrists
Psychiatry for the Millennium - Soc Clinical Psychiatrists
Psychoanalytic Psychotherapy - Assn Psychoanalytic Psychotherapy in the NHS
The Psychologist - Brit Psychological Soc
Psychology & Psychotherapy - Brit Psychological Soc
Psychology of Music - Soc Education, Music & Psychology Res
Psychology Teaching - Assn Teaching Psychology
The Psychotherapist - UK Coun Psychotherapy
PTA - Nat Confedn Parent-Teacher Assns
Pteridologist - Brit Pteridological Soc
Public Address - Inst Sound & Communications Engrs
Public Sculpture of Britain - Public Monuments & Sculpture Assn
Public Security - Assn Police & Public Security Suppliers
Public Service Magazine - Assn First Division Civil Servants
Public Utilities Bulletin - Road Transport Fleet Data Soc
Publication - Fedn Petroleum Suppliers
Pugwash NL - Brit Pugwash Gp
Pull! - Clay Pigeon Shooting Assn Ltd
Puppet Master - Brit Puppet & Model Theatre Gld
Pura Raza Español - Brit Assn Purebred Spanish Horse

Q

Q Review - Assn Private Client Investment Mgrs & Stockbrokers
Quaker Monthly - Religious Soc Friends (Quakers)
Quaker News - Religious Soc Friends (Quakers)
Quaker Projects - Religious Soc Friends (Quakers)
Quality Guild Directory - Quality Gld
Quality in Agency - Brit Assn Service Elderly

Quality Standard Workbook - Telephone Helplines Assn
Quality World - Inst Quality Assurance
Quarry Management - Inst Quarrying
Quarrying in Depth - recycling - Quarry Products Assn
Quarterly - Assn Disabled Profls
The Quarterly - Brit Assn Paper Historians
Quarterly Account - Inst Money Advisers
Quarterly Economic Survey - Brit Chams Comm
                            Nottinghamshire Cham Comm & Ind
Quarterly Jnl - Soc Expert Witnesses
Quarterly Jnl of Experimental Psychology - Experimental Psychology Soc
Quarterly Jnl of Forestry - R Forestry Soc
Quarterly Magazine - Inst Bookbinding & Allied Trades
Quarterly Record - U Senior Revenue Officials
Quarterly Review - Dinosaur Soc
Quarterly Survey of Private Businesses - Forum Private Business
Quasar Magazine - Brit Assn Res Quality Assurance
Quekett Jnl Microscopy - Quekett Microscopical Club
Quest - Queen's English Soc
A Quick Guide to Guillain Barré Syndrome - Guillain Barrée Syndrome Support Gp
The Quickprinter - Brit Assn Print & Communication
Quiet - Brit Tinnitus Assn
Quillers Today - Quilling Gld
Quilling Wise - Quilling Gld
The Quilter - Quilters' Gld
Quo Vadis? - Land's End - John O'Groats Assn

R

R A Magazine - R Academy Arts
Rabbiting On - Rabbit Welfare Assn
Race & Class - Inst Race Relations
Race & Political Recruitment - Hansard Soc Parliamentary Govt
Race Against Time - Meningitis Research Foundation
Race Walking Record - Race Walking Assn
Racing Construction Regulation - Hovercraft Club
The Rack-onteur - American Saddlebred Assn
Radcom - Radio Soc
Radical Statistics - Radical Statistics Gp
Radiography - Soc Radiographers
Radius - Religious Drama Soc
Rail Freight Group News - Rail Freight Gp
Railwatch - Rly Development Soc
The Railway Observer - Rly Correspondence & Travel Soc
Random Round - Percy Grainger Soc
The Ranger - Brit Free Range Egg Producers Assn
Ranger - Countryside Management Assn
Rapport - Assn Neuro-Linguistic Programming (UK) Ltd Community & Youth Workers U
Raptor Round up - Scot Ornithologists' Club
RATEL - Assn Brit Wild Animal Keepers
The Ravilious Notebook - Friends St Bride Printing Library
RDA News - Riding Disabled Assn
Reach Quality Framework - Youth Action Network
Reaching Out - Guillain Barré Syndrome Support Gp
Reaction - Nat Soc Res Allergy
Ready Mixed Concrete in Bridge Constructures - Concrete Bridge Devt Gp
Real Lives - Albinism Fellowship
Real Power - Brit Wind Energy Assn
Really Easy - English Bridge U
A Reasonable Faith: introducing the Sea of Faith Network - Sea Faith Network (UK)
Rebuilding Cost Guides for Houses & Flats - Building Cost Infm Service
Recommendations for Clinical Practice - Fac Family Planning & Reproductive Healthcare
Recommended Pracice for Troughed Belt Conveyors - Materials Handling Engrs Assn
The Record - Lancashire Authors' Assn
Record Book for the Recording of Explosives kept in Quarries' Blasting Sites - Quarry Products Assn

Record Book for the Recording of Explosives kept in Quarries' Explosives Stores - Quarry Products Assn
Recorder News - Biological Recording Scotland
Recording News - Brit Sound Recording Assn
Records of Buckinghamshire - Architectural & Archaeol Soc County Buckinghamshire
Records of Huntingdon - Huntingdonshire Local History Soc
Recovery - Assn Business Recovery Profls
Brit Damage Mgt Assn
Recovery Operator - Retail Motor Ind Fedn
Recovery Operator Magazine - Assn Vehicle Recovery Operators Ltd
Recruitment Matters - Recruitment & Employment Confedn
Recusant History - Catholic Record Soc
Red Herrings - Crime Writers Assn
Reference Manual for Construction Plant - Instn Civil Engg Surveyors
Referendum - Forum Private Business
Reflections - Nat Drama
Reflexions - Assn Reflexologists
Reformer - Tory Reform Gp
Refractories Engineer - Inst Refractories Engrs
Regatta Magazine - Amateur Rowing Assn Ltd
Regional Studies - Regional Studies Assn
Register of Certificated Wallers/Dykers - Dry Stone Walling Assn
Register of Homeopaths - Soc Homeopaths
Register of Musicians in Education - Inc Soc Musicians
Register of Patent Agents - Chart Inst Patent Attorneys
Register of Performers & Composers - Inc Soc Musicians
Register of Professional Private Music Teachers - Inc Soc Musicians
Register of Schools that Help Dyslexic Children - Coun Registration Schools Teaching Dyslexic Pupils
Register of Stage Designers - Soc Brit Theatre Designers
Register of Swimming Sessions for Disabled People - Nat Assn Swimming Clubs H'capped
Rehab Directory - Assn Personal Injury Lawyers
Reiki Magazine International - Reiki Assn
Reinforced Concrete: History, Properties & Durability - Corrosion Protection Assn
Relative Values... The Best Interests of the Child - Grandparents' Assn
Relative Values... Missing out on Contact? - Grandparents' Assn
Religion 2 Liberty - Inst Economic Affairs
The Remarkable James Livingstone - R Instn S Wales
Removals & Storage - Brit Assn Removers
Renaissance Studies - Soc Renaissance Studies
Renew - Network Alternative Technology &... Assessment
Renewables, Past, Present & Future - Network Alternative Technology &... Assessment
Replacing the State? - Assn Chief Execs Voluntary Orgs
Report of Investment Activity - BVCA (British Venture Capital Assn)
Reporter - Brit Inst Organ Studies
The Reporter - Soc Legal Scholars
Representation: jnl of democracy & electoral systems - Electoral Reform Soc Ltd
Res Medica - R Medical Soc
Research - Market Res Soc
Research Buyers Guide - Market Res Soc
Research in Post-Compulsory Education - Further Educ Res Assn
Research Intelligence - Brit Educl Res Assn
Research Results - Scot Tourism Forum
Residence Order Allowance Survey - Grandparents' Assn
Residential Renting - Nat Fedn Residential Landlords
Resin Flooring Industry Hbk - FeRFA: Resin Flooring Assn
Resource - Profl Coun Religious Educ
Restart - Assn Classic Trials Clubs Ltd
Resurgam - Fedn Brit Cremation Auths
Retail News - Scot Grocers' Fedn
Retail Outlook - Scot Grocers' Fedn
Retail Review - Brit Shops & Stores Assn
Retail Sales Garment Cleaning - Gld Cleaners & Launderers
The Retreader - Retread Mfrs Assn
Retreats - Assn Promoting Retreats
Retreats - Retreat Assn
Retrospection - Nat Assn Re-enactment Socs
Reverberations - Handbell Ringers

Review of Building Prices - Building Cost Infm Service
The Review of Economic Studies - Soc Economic Analysis
Review of International Studies - Brit Intl Studies Assn
The Review of the PRS - Pre-Raphaelite Soc
Revolutions - Motor Cycle Ind Assn Ltd
Rheology Abstracts - Brit Soc Rheology
Rheumatic Review - Arthritic Assn
Rheumatology - Brit Soc Rheumatology
The Ricardian - Richard III Soc
The Ricardian Bulletin - Richard III Soc
Richard III & Council of the North - Soc Friends King Richard III
Richard III & York - Soc Friends King Richard III
The Rifleman - Nat Small-Bore Rifle Assn
Rights - illustrators guide to professional practice - Assn Illustrators
Ring Directory - Morris Ring
Ringing Migration - Brit Trust Ornithology
Risk Management Round-up - Confedn Brit Security Ind
The River Wandle: Distribution of Its Flora - Croydon Natural History & Scientific Soc
Rivista - Brit Italian Soc
RLS Club News - Robert Louis Stevenson Club
RNBWS Bulletin - R Naval Bird Watching Soc
Road Haulage Manual - Road Haulage Assn
Roadway - Road Haulage Assn
The Rock Garden - Scot Rock Garden Club
Role of Women in British Agriculture - Women's Farm & Garden Assn
Rolling - Road Roller Assn
Rolling Stock - Histl Model Rly Soc
Romany Magazine - Romany Soc
Roofing Trades Jnl - Confedn Roofing Contrs
The Rose - R Nat Rose Soc
The Rotorhead - Brit Helicopter Advisory Bd Ltd
Roundhead Assn NL - English Civil War Soc
Round-Up - Brit Westerners Assn
Route Notes N to S, S to N - Offa's Dyke Assn
Route to a Succssful Concrete Repair - Concrete Repair Assn
The Router - Gld Master Craftsmen
Rowing Action - Scot Amateur Rowing Assn
Royal Highland Review - R Highland & Agricl Soc
Royal Highland Show Catalogue - R Highland & Agricl Soc
Royal Highland Show Guide - R Highland & Agricl Soc
Royal Martyr Annual - R Martyr Church U
Royal Stuart Papers - R Stuart Soc & Royalist League
Royal Stuart Review - R Stuart Soc & Royalist League
RSA NL - Fire Sprinkler Assn
Runestaff - Vikings
RURAL Briefing - Soc Responsible Use Resources in Agriculture & on the Land
Rural History Today - Brit Agricultural History Soc
Rural Review - R Lancs Agricl Soc
Rural Theology - Rural Theology Assn
Rural Wales / Cymru Wledig - Campaign Protection Rural Wales
The Ruskin Gazette - Ruskin Soc London
The Russell - Welsh Highland Rlys Assn
Russian Chemical Reviews - R Soc Chemistry
Russistika - Assn Language Learning

S

SACROsanct - SACRO
SACS Magazine - Scot Assn Country Sports
Safe & Sound - Youth Scotland
Safe Hygiene Practice - Ceretas
Safe School Travel Booklet - Scot School Bd Assn
Safety & Health Practitioner - Instn Occupational Safety & Health
Safety Education - R Soc Prevention Accidents
Safety Express - R Soc Prevention Accidents
Safety in Electrical Testing - Radio, Electrical & Television Retailers' Assn Ltd
Sage Race Relations Abstracts - Inst Race Relations
Saint John Life - Saint John Ambulance
Salaries & Benefits Survey - Nottinghamshire Cham Comm & Ind
Salers Jnl - Salers Cattle Soc

© CBD Research Ltd · Beckenham · BR3 5JS · Tel 020 8650 7745 · Fax 020 8650 0768 · E-mail cbd@cbdresearch.com · www.cbdresearch.com

Sampling Bituminous Materials - Inst Asphalt Technology
Samuri NL - Scot Ju-Jitsu Assn
Sandgrouse - Ornithological Soc
Sandwich & Snack News - Brit Sandwich Assn
SANE News - SANE
**SAVE Britain's Heritage 1975-2005: thirty years of
   campaigning -** Save Britain's Heritage
Saying Goodbye to Your Baby - Stillbirth & Neonatal Death Soc
SB Training Booklets - Scot School Bd Assn
Schizophrenia - SANE
The School Librarian - School Library Assn
School is Not Compulsory - Education Otherwise
School Science Review - Assn Science Educ
Schools News - Devt Educ Assn
Schumacher Briefings - Doctor E F Schumacher Soc
Schumacher NL - Doctor E F Schumacher Soc
Science & Justice - Forensic Science Soc
Science & Public Affairs - Brit Assn Advancement Science
   Royal Soc
Science Policy Priorities - Biosciences Fedn
Science Policy Report - Biosciences Fedn
Science Review - R Soc Prevention Cruelty to Animals
Science Technology - Inst Science Technology
SCOLAG - Scot Legal Action Gp
Scoliosis Hbk - Scoliosis Assn (UK)
Score - Scot Orienteering Assn
Scot Poetry Index - Scot Poetry Library
Scotch at a Glance - Scotch Whisky Assn
Scotch Whisky: matured to be enjoyed responsibly - Scotch
   Whisky Assn
Scotch Whisky: questions & answers - Scotch Whisky Assn
Scotlit - Assn Scot Literary Studies
Scotnotes - Assn Scot Literary Studies
Scots Bowler - Scot Indoor Bowling Assn
Scots Thesaurus - Scot Language Dictionaries
Scottish Archaeological Jnl - Glasgow Archaeol Soc
Scottish Archives - Scot Records Assn
Scottish Badminton - Scot Badminton U
Scottish Basketball - Scot Basketball Assn
The Scottish Beekeeper - Scot Beekeepers' Assn
Scottish Bird News - Scot Ornithologists' Club
Scottish Bird Report - Scot Ornithologists' Club
Scottish Birds - Scot Ornithologists' Club
Scottish Bylines - Headteachers' Assn Scotland
Scottish Chambers of Commerce Directory - Glasgow Cham
   Comm
Scottish Chess - Chess Scotland
Scottish Citizen - Citizens Advice Scotland
Scottish Clubs' Huts - Mountaineering Coun Scotland
Scottish Country Dancer - R Scot Country Dance Soc
Scottish Diver Magazine - Scot Sub Aqua Club
Scottish Educational Jnl - Educational Inst Scotland
Scottish Esperanto Bulletin - Scot Esperanto Assn
Scottish Farming Leader Update - NFU Scotland
Scottish Football Review Book - Scot Football League
Scottish Forestry - R Scot Forestry Soc
Scottish Gamekeeper - Scot Gamekeepers' Assn
The Scottish Genealogist - Scot Genealogy Soc
Scottish Geographical Jnl - R Scot Geographical Soc
Scottish Golfer - Scot Golf U
Scottish Headlines - Headteachers' Assn Scotland
Scottish Hill Tracks - Scot Rights of Way & Access Soc
Scottish Home & Country - Scot Women's Rural Insts
Scottish Jujitsu - Scot Ju-Jitsu Assn
Scottish Labour History - Scot Labour History Soc
Scottish Language - Assn Scot Literary Studies
The Scottish Law Gazette - Scot Law Agents Soc
Scottish Legion News - R Brit Legion Scotland
Scottish Licensee - Scot Licensed Trade Assn
Scottish National Directory - Aberdeen & Grampian Cham Comm
   (Inc)
Scottish NL - Scot Prayer Book Soc
Scottish Paddler - Scot Canoe Assn
Scottish Philately - Assn Scot Philatelic Socs
Scottish Skate Update - Scot Ice Skating Assn
Scottish Snowsport Hbk - Snowsport Scotland
Scottish Studies Review - Assn Scot Literary Studies
Scottish Transport Review - Scot Transport Studies Gp

Scottish Wildlife - Scot Wildlife Trust Ltd
Scouting - Scout Assn
Scrabble News - Scrabble Clubs
Scramble - Battle of Britain Histl Soc
Scramble - Scot Countryside Rangers Assn
Scribble - Scot Countryside Rangers Assn
The Scribe - Soc Scribes & Illuminators
The Scrichowl - Seventeenth Century Life & Times
The Scroll - Loyal Co Town Criers
Scuba World - Sub-Aqua Assn
The Sculpture Jnl - Public Monuments & Sculpture Assn
Sea Lines - Ocean Liner Soc
Sea Swallow - R Naval Bird Watching Soc
The Seafarer - Marine Soc & Sea Cadets
Sebda News - Sebda
Secondary Teacher - Scot Secondary Teachers' Assn
Secretary's Page - Scot Rock Garden Club
Securities & Investment Review - Securities & Investment Inst
Security Direct - Brit Security Ind Assn
Security Monitor - R Utd Services Inst Defence Studies
Seen & Heard - NAGALRO
Sefton Business Directory - Sefton Cham Comm & Ind Ltd
Self & Society - Assn Humanistic Psychology
Seminar Proceedings - Nat Fedn Bridleway Assns
**Serial Holdings of the UK Marine & Freshwater Sciences
   Libraries -** Britain & Ireland Assn Aquatic Science Libraries & Inf
   Centres
Serials - UK Serials Gp
Service - Spiritualist Assn
Sesame - Scientific Exploration Soc Ltd
The Sessional GP - Nat Assn Sessional GPs
Sex Reassignment Surgery - Gender Trust
Sexual & Relationship Therapy - Brit Assn Sexual & Relationship
   Therapy
The Shadow - Fedn Stadium Communities
Sharing the Future - Brit Humanist Assn
The Shavian - Shaw Soc
Sheep Dairy News - Brit Sheep Dairying Assn
Sheetlines - Charles Close Soc Study Ordnance Survey Maps
Sherborn Facsimiles - Soc Hist Natural Hist
Sherlock Holmes Jnl - Sherlock Holmes Soc London
The Shetland Breed - Shetland Sheep Soc
Shetland Pony Stud Book - Shetland Pony Stud Book Soc
Shiatsu in the NHS - Shiatsu Soc
Shifting Ground (video) - Quarry Products Assn
Ship & Boat Intl - R Instn Naval Architects
Ship Repair & Conversion Technology - R Instn Naval Architects
The Shipbroker - Inst Chart Shipbrokers
Shona's Story - Scoliosis Assn (UK)
Shooting & Conservation - Brit Assn Shooting & Consvn
Shopping at Home - Direct Selling Assn
Shoptalk - Shop & Display Equipment Assn
Shorewatch - Brit Marine Life Study Soc
Shortcuts - Gld Brit Découpeurs
Shorthorn Jnl - Beef Shorthorn Cattle Soc
   Shorthorn Soc
The Shot - Brit Wheelchair Bowls Assn
Showground News - Staffordshire & Birmingham Agricl Soc
Shropshire Business Matters - Shropshire Chamber of Commerce
Shroptalk - Shropshire Sheep Breeders Assn & Flock Book Soc
Shuttle Plus - Sewing Machine Tr Assn
SI Trader - Suffolk Cham Comm, Ind & Shipping Inc
Side View - Macular Disease Soc
Sidelights - Soc Indexers
Sidelights on Sayers - Dorothy L Sayers Soc
Sidelines - Heritage Rly Assn
Sign Matters - Brit Deaf Assn
Signals - Arthur Ransome Soc Ltd
Signet NL - Soc Writers to Her Majesty's Signet
Significant Ship - R Instn Naval Architects
Significant Small Craft - R Instn Naval Architects
Signpost - Eating Disorders Assn
   Peak & Nthn Footpaths Soc
Signs Jnl - Brit Sign & Graphics Assn Ltd
Signs of the Times - Modern Churchpeople's U
Silver in Wound Care & Management - Wound Care Soc
Simple Guide to CGs - Nat Assn Primary Care

A Simplified Guide to the Estate Agents Act 1979 & its Orders & Regulations - Nat Assn Estate Agents
Sires - Thoroughbred Breeders' Assn
Sisyphus - Assn Circulation Executives
Site Supplement - Caravan Club Ltd
Site Survey - UK Paintball Sports Fedn
Sites Directory & Map - Caravan Club Ltd
Sjogren's Today - Brit Sjogren's Syndrome Assn
Skater Hockey News - Brit Inline Skater Hockey Assn
The Skeptic - UK Skeptics
Skin 'n' Bones Connection - Psoriatic Arthropathy Alliance
Skydive, the British Mag - Brit Parachute Assn
Skypointer - Indep Pilots Assn
Skywings - Brit Hang Gliding & Paragliding Assn
Slip Knot - Knitting & Crochet Gld
Slot Car Racing News - Brit Slot Car Racing Assn
SMAE Jnl - SMAE Fellowship
Small Business Issues - Inst Small Business & Entrepreneurship
Small Firms Survey - Brit Chams Comm
Small Printer - Brit Printing Soc
Small Printing - Brit Printing Soc
Small Talk - Wales Pre-school Playgroups Assn
Small Woods Information Pack - Small Woods Assn
Smallwoods - Small Woods Assn
Snippets - Deaf Blind UK
Snowsport News - Snowsport Scotland
Snuff Bottle Review - Snuff Bottle Soc
So You Have Sarcoidosis! - Sarcoidosis & Interstitial Lung Assn
Social Caring - Social Care Assn
Social History of Medicine - Soc Social History Medicine
Social Inventions Annual Book - Inst Social Inventions
Social Science Teacher - Assn Teaching Social Sciences
Socialism & Health - Socialist Health Assn
Socio-LegalNL - Socio-Legal Studies Assn
Sociology - Brit Sociological Assn
Soil Use & Management - Brit Soc Soil Science
Solar Energy - Solar Tr Assn
Solar Energy Jnl - Solar Energy Soc
Soldier I Wish You Well - Housman Soc
Soldiers of the Queen - Victorian Military Soc
Soldiers Small Book - Victorian Military Soc
Solicitors of the Supreme Court of Northern Ireland - Law Soc NI
Sonar - Whale & Dolphin Consvn Soc
Songbird Survival - Songbird Survival
SORP Made Simple - Assn Charitable Foundations
A Sound Ear - Assn Brit Orchestras
Sound Track Audio Magazine - Brit Sound Recording Assn
Sounding Board - Sound Sense
Soundings - Hydrographic Soc
Inst Musical Instrument Technology
Residential Boat Owners Assn
South Asian Studies - Soc South Asian Studies
South Cheshire Business - S Cheshire Cham Comm & Ind
South Wales Business Directory - Newport & Gwent Cham Comm & Ind
South West Coast Path Guide - S W Coast Path Assn
South Western Circular - S Wstn Circle
Southdown Flock Book - Southdown Sheep Soc
Southdown Sheep - Southdown Sheep Soc
Southdown Year Book - Southdown Sheep Soc
Southern Bulletin - Green Lane Assn
Southern Express - Merchant Navy Locomotive Presvn Soc Ltd
The Southern Instructor - Motor Schools Assn
Souvenir - Violet Needham Soc
Spacereport - Assn Scotland Res Astronautics
Spanish Business Presence in the UK - Spanish Cham Comm GB
Spares Directory - Train Collectors Soc
Speak to the World - Brit Cham Comm Italy, Inc
Speak Up - Speakability
The Speaker - Assn Speakers Clubs
Speaking Out - Brit Stammering Assn
Spec Finish - Fedn Plastering & Drywall Contrs
Special - nasen
Special Education Needs - Home Educ Advy Service
Specification for Cast Stone - UK Cast Stone Assn
Specifier's Guide to Steel Windows - Steel Window Assn

Spectrum - Brit Security Ind Assn
Brit Wheel Yoga
The Speculum - William Herschel Soc
Speech & Drama - Soc Teachers Speech & Drama
Speleology - Brit Cave Res Assn
Brit Caving Assn
Spin Bulletin - Soc Public Inf Networks
Spohr Jnl - Spohr Soc
Spoonews - Wooden Spoon Soc
The Sport & Exercise Scientist - Brit Assn Sport & Exercise Sciences
Sportex Dynamics - Sports Massage Assn
Sports Therapy - Soc Sports Therapists
Sportslife - Fedn Sports & Play Assns
Spot Press - Gloucestershire Old Spot Pig Breeders' Club
Spotlight - HR Soc Ltd
The Sprat - Friends Alan Rawsthorne
Sprinkler Facts - Brit Automatic Fire Sprinkler Assn
Sprinkler Systems: The Facts - Brit Automatic Fire Sprinkler Assn
Sprinklers for Safety - Brit Automatic Fire Sprinkler Assn
Sprouts - R Highland Educ Trust
Staff Support, Supervision & Appraisal - Ceretas
Staffordshire Archaeological Studies - Stoke-on-Trent Museum Archaeol Soc
Stage Management Notes - Stage Mgt Assn
Stage Management: a career guide - Stage Mgt Assn
Stage Screen & Radio - Broadcasting Entertainment Cinematograph & Theatre U
Stagedoor - Scot Music Hall & Variety Theatre Soc
A Stage Manager's Guide to the Subsidised Repertory Agreement - Stage Mgt Assn
A Stage Manager's Guide to the West End Agreement - Stage Mgt Assn
A Stage Manager's Guide tot the Provisional Commercial Contract - Stage Mgt Assn
Stain Removal Guide - Gld Cleaners & Launderers
Stained Glass - Brit Soc Master Glass Painters
Stainless Steel Industry - Brit Stainless Steel Assn
The Stamp Lover - Nat Philatelic Soc
Stand To - Western Front Assn
The Standard - Assn Scotland's Self-Caterers
Standard Issue - Road Safety Markings Assn
Standard Method of Measurement - Concrete Repair Assn
Standardised Assessment Tools & the Management of Complex Wounds - Wound Care Soc
Standardised Protocol for the Sampling & Enumeration of Airborne Microorganisms at Composting Facilities - Composting Assn
Standards & Practices - Inst Decontamination Services
Standards News - Profl Lighting & Sound Assn
Standards of Environmental Cleanliness in Hospitals - Assn Domestic Mgt
Stanspec 2006 - Road Safety Markings Assn
Star & Furrow - Biodynamic Agricl Assn
Startline - Brit Automobile Racing Club
Stat News - Soc Teachers Alexander Technique
State Librarian - Network Govt Library & Inf Specialists
State of the Region Fact Card - Assn North East Couns
State of the Region Profile Report - Assn North East Couns
The Statute Law Review - Statute Law Soc
Staying Alive - R Soc Prevention Accidents
Steam Plough Times - Steam Plough Club
Steam Users Group NL - Combustion Engg Assn
Steaming - Nat Traction Engine Trust
Steel Construction News - Brit Constructional Steelwork Assn Ltd
Step Forward - Limbless Assn
The Stewarts - Stewart Soc
Stickler the Elusive Syndrome - Stickler Syndrome Support Group
The Stickmaker - Brit Stickmakers Gld
Still Improving Sport - Osteopathic Sports Care Assn
Stirring Times - Wooden Spoon Soc
The Stock Auditor - Inst Licensed Tr Stock Auditors
The Story of the Knights Bachelor - Imperial Soc Knights Bachelor
Storylines Magazine - Soc Storytelling
Straight Talk - Alcohol Concern
Strain - Brit Soc Strain Measurement
Strands - Braid Soc
Strategic Plan - SACRO
Strategy - Strategic Planning Soc

© CBD Research Ltd · Beckenham · BR3 5JS · Tel 020 8650 7745 · Fax 020 8650 0768 · E-mail cbd@cbdresearch.com · www.cbdresearch.com

The Strathspey Express - Strathspey Rly Assn Ltd
Street Biker - Motorcycle Action Gp
STRI Green Pages Trade Directory - Sports Turf Res Inst
Strider - Long Distance Walkers Assn
Strip maps of Offa's Dyke Path - Offa's Dyke Assn
The Structural Engineer - Instn Structural Engrs
Student & Graduate Magazine - Instn Engg & Technology
Studies in Anglesey History - Anglesey Antiquarian Soc & Field
   Club
Studies in Ethnicity & Nationalism [SEN] - Assn Study Ethnicity &
   Nationalism
The Subpostmaster - Nat Fedn Sub-Postmasters
Subterranea - Subterranea Britannica
Success with Houseplants - Saintpaulia & Houseplant Soc
Suffolk Business Directory - Suffolk Cham Comm, Industry &
   Shipping Inc
Suffolk Business Magazine - Suffolk Cham Comm, Industry &
   Shipping Inc
Suffolk Scene - Suffolk Agricultural Assn
Suggestion Schemes: the management tool of the 90's - Ideas
   UK
Suicide & Self Harm Prevention - Howard League Penal Reform
Summons - Medical & Dental Defence U Scotland
Sundial Makers - Brit Sundial Soc
The Supplement - Nat Pharmacy Assn
Suppliers Directory - Vehicle Builders' & Repairers' Assn
Support for Learning - nasen
The Supporter - Cleaning & Support Services Assn
Surface Coatings International - Oil & Colour Chemists' Assn
Surrey Archaeological Collections - Surrey Archaeol Soc
Survey of Contract Researchers - Assn Researchers Medicine &
   Science
Survey of MBA Salaries & Careers - Assn MBAs
Survey of Post-doctoral Researchers - Assn Researchers Medicine
   & Science
Survey of Salaries & Benefits - Soc Property Researchers
Survive - illustrators guide to a professional career - Assn
   Illustrators
Susannah Blamire - Lakeland Dialect Soc
Sussex Archaeological Collections - Sussex Archaeol Soc
Sussex Industrial History - Sussex Industrial Archaeology Soc
Sussex Past & Present - Sussex Archaeol Soc
Swedish-British Trade Directory - Swedish Cham Comm
Swim & Save - Surf Life Saving Assn
                  Swimming Teachers' Assn
Swimming for People with Disabilities - Halliwick Assn
   Swimming Therapy
Swimming Pool Industry Directory & Specifier (SPidas) - Inst
   Swimming Pool Engrs Ltd
Swimming Times - Inst Swimming Teachers & Coaches Ltd
Swiss Chimes Jnl - Brown Swiss Cattle Soc
Swiss Express - Swiss Rlys Soc
Swiss Review - Fedn Swiss Socs
Symposia Abstract Booklet - UK Clinical Pharmacy Assn
Symptoms - Meningitis Research Foundation
Synergy - Soc Radiographers

T

Table Tennis News - English Table Tennis Assn
The Tablet - UK Cast Stone Assn
TACAN - Aircrewman's Assn
Tackling Multiple Disadvantage - Community Foundation
   Network
TACT Review - Assn Corporate Trustees
Tag Talk - Arthrogryposis Gp
Tailboard - Photographic Collectors Club
Tak Teut - Heraldry Soc Scotland
Takedown - Brit Wrestling Assn
Taking Stock Book - Inst Licensed Tr Stock Auditors
Tales of Northwick - Nystagmus Network
Tales of Uruguay - Brit Uruguayan Soc
Taliesin - ACADEMI
Talipes - STEPS: Assn People with Lower Limb Abnormalities
Talk - Nat Deaf Children's Soc

Talkback - Nat Backpain Assn
talkBACK - Scot Spina Bifida Assn
Talking about Turner Syndrome - Turner Syndrome Support Soc
Talking Politics - Politics Assn
Talking Sense - Sense
Talking Treatments - SANE
Talkshop Catalogue - Soc Storytelling
Tall Suppliers Directory - Tall Persons Club
Tally Sheet - English Westerners Soc
Talyllyn News - Talyllyn Rly Presvn Soc
Tankette - Miniature Armoured Fighting Vehicles Assn
Tanzanian Affairs - Britain-Tanzania Soc
Tattoo International - Brit Tattoo Artists Fedn
                          Tattoo Club
Tax Adviser - Assn Taxation Technicians
Tax Adviser - Chart Inst Taxation
Tax Advisers Practice Hbk - Assn Taxation Technicians
The Teacher - Nat U Teachers
Teaching Business & Economics - Economics & Business Educ
   Assn
Teaching Earth Sciences - Earth Science Teachers Assn
Teaching History - Histl Assn
Teaching Mathematics & its Applications - Inst Mathematics & its
   Applications
Teaching Today - Nat Assn Schoolmasters U Women Teachers
Technic - Assn Operating Department Practitioners
Technical Bulletin - Brit Gear Assn
Technical Literature Survey - Brit Gear Assn
Technical Notes - agronomy / ruminant - Maize Growers Assn
Technical Vocational Training Programme - Inst
   Decontamination Services
The Telegraph - Nat U Marine, Aviation & Shipping Transport
   Officers
Telephone Helplines 'Guides for Good Practice' - Telephone
   Helplines Assn
Telephone Helplines Directory - Telephone Helplines Assn
Television Lighting - Soc Television Lighting Directors
Teleworker - Telework Assn
Teleworking - Telework Assn
Tempo - Gld Profl Teachers Dancing
Ten 26 - Nat Fedn Young Farmers' Clubs (England & Wales)
Tenanted Farm Survey - Cent Assn Agricl Valuers
Tennyson Research Bulletin - Tennyson Soc
Tenterden Terrier - Kent & East Sussex Rly Co Ltd
Tern - Norfolk Wildlife Trust
The Terrier - Assn Chief Estates Surveyors & Property Mgrs Local
   Govt
The Test Card Circle - Test Card Circle
Testament - Soc Will Writers & Estate Planning Practitioners
Tests of Agrochemicals & Cultivars - Assn Applied Biologists
Testudo - Brit Chelonia Gp
Texel Bulletin - Brit Texel Sheep Soc
Text - Textile Soc
Textile Progress - Textile Inst Intl
Textiles for Launderers & Drycleaners - Gld Cleaners &
   Launderers
Textiles Magazine - Textile Inst Intl
TGM a coherent dozenal metrology - Dozenal Soc
Thames Guardian - River Thames Soc
The Thatcher's Standard - Nat Soc Master Thatchers
Theatre Notebook - Soc Theatre Res
Theoretical Issues in Ergonomics - Ergonomics Soc
Therapeutic Communities Jnl - Assn Therapeutic Communities
Therapy Today - Brit Assn Counselling & Psychotherapy
There is an Alternative - Campaign Indep Britain
Third Force News & Inform - Scot Coun Voluntary Orgs
This Week - Proprietary Assn
The Thomas Hardy Jnl - Thomas Hardy Soc Ltd
Thoroughbred Breeder - Thoroughbred Breeders' Assn
Those of Us Who Loved Her: the men in George Eliot's life -
   George Eliot Fellowship
Three Bromsgrove Poets - Housman Soc
Thumbprint - Motor Neurone Disease Assn
TI Q - Transparency Intl (UK)
Tile Bibliography - Tiles & Architectural Ceramics Soc
Timber Grower - Assn Timber Growers & Forestry Profls
Time + Space, design for performers 1995-1999 - Soc Brit
   Theatre Designers

Time and Tide: Sea of Faith beyond the Millennium - Sea Faith Network
Tobacco Index - Assn Indep Tobacco Specialists
Toccata - Leopold Stokowski Soc
Today's Technician - Nat Pest Technicians Assn
The TOF Child - Tracheo-Oesophageal Fistula Support
Toffs - Over Fifties Assn
Together - Fellowship Indep Evangelical Churches
Tom Smith's Cricket Umpiring & Scoring - Assn Cricket Umpires & Scorers
Tools & Trades - Tool & Trades Hist Soc
Top Gear - Scot Sporting Car Club
Top Marks - Road Safety Markings Assn
Topsail - Soc Sailing Barge Res
Torch Bearer - Soc Olympic Collectors
Torpedo - Brit Marine Life Study Soc
Tot Watch - Meningitis Research Foundation
Touch - Reiki Assn
Touchstone - R Soc Architects Wales
Tourism - Tourism Soc Ltd
Tourism in Focus - Tourism Concern
Tourism Manager - Tourism Management Institute
Towards Community Care - Assn Directors Social Services
Towards Equality - Fawcett Soc
Townswoman - Townswomen's Glds
The Toymaker - Brit Toymakers Gld
Trackside - Brit Motorsport Marshals' Club
Traction Engine Register - Southern Counties Historic Vehicle Preservation Trust
Trade Directory - Brit Cham Comm Italy, Inc
Trade Fairs & Exhibitions - Brit Cham Comm Turkey
Trade Jnl - Brit Cham Comm Turkey
Trade Leads - Engg Inds Assn
Trade Mission Hbk - Brit Chams Comm
Trade Suppliers Directory - Brit Equestrian Tr Assn
Trade Talk - Assn Suppliers Furniture Ind
Tradewinds - Portuguese Cham
Trading Standards Appointments - Trading Standards Inst
Trading Standards Today - Trading Standards Inst
Trail Magazine - Trail Riders Fellowship
Train Times - Assn Community Rail Partnerships
Training & Education - Brit Inst Profl Dog Trainers
Training for the Caring Business - Assn Directors Social Services
Training, Charter & Holiday Yearbook - Marine Leisure Assn
Tramfare - Tramway & Light Rly Soc
Tramway Museum Guidebook - Tramway Museum Soc
Tramways & Urban Transit - Light Rail Transit Assn
Transforming Learning - Soc Effective Affective Learning
Transfusion Medicine - Brit Blood Transfusion Soc
Transit Magazine - Astrological Assn
Transmit - Gld Air Traffic Control Officers
The Transport Digest - Transport Trust
Transport Engineer - Soc Operations Engrs
Transport Jnl - Inst Transport Mgt
Transport Management - Inst Transport Admin
Transport Retort - Transport 2000 Ltd
Transportation Professional - Inst Highway Inc Engrs
Instn Highways & Transportation
The Travel Business - Gld Travel & Tourism
Travelwise - Brit Travel Health Assn
The Treasurer - Assn Corporate Treasurers
The Treasurers Hbk - Assn Corporate Treasurers
Treating Arthritis Naturally - Arthritic Assn
Treatment of Phenylketonuria - Nat Soc Phenylketonuria
Trees & Bats - Arboricultural Assn
Trends & Events - Trade Marks Patents & Designs Fedn
Trends & Statistics - Brit Hospitality Assn
TRF Hbk - Trail Riders Fellowship
Triangle - Youth Hostels Assn
Triathlon / Duathlon Hbk - Brit Triathlon Assn
The Trichologists - Inst Trichologists (Inc)
Trinews - Brit Triathlon Assn
Trolleybus - Brit Trolleybus Soc
Trolleybus Magazine - Nat Trolleybus Assn
Trollopiana Jnl - Trollope Soc
The Trombonist - Brit Trombone Soc
Trouble Shooting Guide - Assn Illustrators
True Blue - Friends Blue

The True Line - Caledonian Rly Assn
Trust & Foundation News - Assn Charitable Foundations
TUK Talk - Transfrigoroute UK
Turrner Syndrome - lifelong guidance & support - Turner Syndrome Support Soc
Tutors Directory - FÉisean nan GÈidheal
Tuttitalia - Assn Language Learning
Twins, Triplets & More - Twins & Multiple Births Assn
A Twist of Fate - Scoliosis Assn (UK)
Tyne & Tweed - Assn Northumberland Local History Socs
Typefounders London A-Z - Friends St Bride Printing Library
Typographic - Intl Soc Typographic Designers

U

UK Advertising Admissions Monitor - Cinema Advertising Assn Ltd
UK Allergy Clinic Database - Brit Soc Allergy & Clinical Immunology
UK Corrosion (conference papers) - Inst Corrosion
UK Excellence - Brit Quality Foundation
The UK Exhibition Facts - Exhibition Venues Assn
UK News - UK Trs Confedn Ltd
UK Railway Suppliers Directory - Rly Ind Assn
UK Schools Survey on Budget & Resource Provision - Brit Educl Suppliers Assn
UK Surface Coatings Hbk - Oil & Colour Chemists' Assn
UK Windsurfing Magazine - UK Windsurfing Assn
UK Writer - Writers' Gld
Ullans - Ulster-Scots Language Soc
The Ulster Angler - Ulster Angling Fedn
Ulster Countrywoman - Fedn Women's Insts NI
Ulster Folklife - Ulster Folk Life Soc
Ulster Jnl of Archaeology - Ulster Archaeological Soc
Ultimatum - UK Ultimate Assn
The Ultimate Cleavage: a complete practical guide to cosmetic breast enlargement surgery - Breast Implant Inf Soc
Uncensored - Campaign against Censorship
Under Five - Pre-School Learning Alliance
Underground News - London Underground Rly Soc
Understanding Nystagmus - Nystagmus Network
Understanding Pregnancy Loss - Stillbirth & Neonatal Death Soc
Underwater Technology - Soc Underwater Technology Ltd
Union News - Electrical & Engg Staff Assn
University Chemistry Education - R Soc Chemistry
Unkind to Unicorns - Housman Soc
Up & Under Updates - Australian Business
Update - CILIP
Update - Women's Food & Farming U
Update your Road Markings - Road Safety Markings Assn
Upholsterer & Soft Furnisher - Assn Master Upholsterers & Soft Furnishers Ltd

Chair Frame Mfrs' Assn
Uplift - Fork Lift Truck Assn
Urban Regeneration - Brit Urban Regeneration Assn
The Use of English - English Assn
Using a Pawnbroker - Nat Pawnbrokers Assn

V

Vacancy Bulletin (Portico) - Inst Career Guidance Ltd
Vacuum Technology, Applications & Ion Physics - Brit Vacuum Coun
VAGA update - Visual Arts & Galleries Assn
Value - Inst Value Mgt
Vaporising - Nat Vintage Tractor & Engine Club
Varieties for Thatching - Nat Soc Master Thatchers
Vector - Brit Science Fiction Assn
The Vegan Magazine - Vegan Soc Ltd
Vegan Passport - Vegan Soc Ltd
Vegan Stories - Vegan Soc Ltd
The Vegetarian - Vegetarian Soc (UK) Ltd
Vehicle Operator Lists - Road Transport Fleet Data Soc

Vehicle Salvage Professional - Brit Vehicle Salvage Fedn
Vehicle Technology - Soc Automotive Engrs
Vellum - George Formby Soc
VENDinform - Automatic Vending Assn
Vending Quality Standards - Automatic Vending Assn
Vernacular Architecture - Vernacular Architecture Gp
Vernacular Gower - Gower Soc
Veterinary Nursing Jnl - Brit Veterinary Nursing Assn
The Veterinary Record - Brit Veterinary Assn
Vida Hispánica - Assn Language Learning
Videoprofessional - Assn Profl Videomakers
Vienna Music - Johann Strauss Soc
The View - Girls' Brigade England & Wales
　　　　Inst Construction Mgt
　　　　Nat Fedn Blind
Viewpoint - Soc Architectural Illustration Ltd
Vineyards open to Visitors - UK Vineyards Assn
The Vintage Motor Cycle - Vintage Motor Cycle Club Ltd
Virginia Woolf Bulletin - Virginia Woolf Soc
Vision Education News - Bates Assn Vision Educ
Vitiligo: understanding the loss of skin colour - Vitiligo Soc
The Vitreous Enameller - Inst Vitreous Enamellers
VLV Bulletin - Voice Listener & Viewer Ltd
Voice - Assn Teachers Singing
　　　　Communication Workers U
　　　　Vehicle Builders' & Repairers' Assn
　　　　Victim Support Scotland
The Voice - NWA - assn housing & support mgrs
　　　　Ornamental Aquatic Trade Assn
A Voice for All Time - Assn Latin Liturgy
Voice Box - Ladies' Assn Brit Barbershop Singers
A Voice Care Guide for Call Centre Managers - Voice Care
　　Network UK
Voice of the Quarrying Industry - Quarry Products Assn
Voice of the Veteran - Veteran Horse Soc
Voice Warm-up Exercises - Voice Care Network UK
Vouchers at a Glance - Fedn Ophthalmic & Dispensing Opticians
Vox Humana - Mechanical Organ Owners Soc

W

Wagner News - Wagner Soc
Wales Funding Hbk - Wales Coun Voluntary Action
Walk - Living Streets
Waller & Dyker - Dry Stone Walling Assn
Wallpaper - Max Wall Soc
Wanderer - Historic Caravan Club
The War Correspondent - Crimean War Res Soc
Warship Technology - R Instn Naval Architects
Wastes Management - Chart Instn Wastes Mgt
Watchword - R Soc Wildlife Trusts
Watchword - Surface Engg Assn
Water & Environment Manager - Chart Instn Water & Envtl Mgt
Water treatment for pool operators - Inst Swimming Pool Engrs
　　Ltd
Waterline - Water Mgt Soc Ltd
The Waterloo Jnl - Assn Friends Waterloo C'ee
Waterways - Inland Waterways Assn
Watsonia - Botanical Soc Brit Isles
Watson's Wanderings - Friends Dr Watson
Watson's Wanderings Again - Friends Dr Watson
Watson's Weapons - Friends Dr Watson
The Way Ahead - Disabled Motorists Fedn
Way of Life - Gld Health
Waymark - Inst Public Rights Way Officers
WDCS News - Whale & Dolphin Consvn Soc
We Just Want Our Daughter to Live - Tracheo-Oesophageal
　　Fistula Support
Weather - R Meteorological Soc
A Wee Ray of Hope - Cystitis & Overactive Bladder Foundation
Welcome to the Camelid Family - Brit Camelids Assn
Welfare World - Inst Welfare
Wellards NHS Hbk - NHS Confedn
The Wellsian - H G Wells Soc
Welsh Business - Cardiff Cham Comm, Trade & Ind

Welsh Ceramics In Context - R Instn S Wales
Welsh Farmer - Farmers' U Wales
Welsh Halfbred News - Welsh Halfbred Sheep Breeders Assn Ltd
Welsh Hound Stud Book - Welsh Hound Assn
Welsh Music - Welsh Music Gld
Welsh Ponies & Cobs - Welsh Pony & Cob Soc
Welsh Wildlife - Wildlife Trust S & W Wales
West Highland Notes & Queries - Soc W Highland & Island
　　Historical Res
A Westerly Wanderer - Housman Soc
The Western Dancer Magazine - Brit Western Dance Assn
Wey-South Bulletin - Wey & Arun Canal Trust Ltd
What is CTPA? - Cosmetic, Toiletry & Perfumery Assn Ltd
What is Play Therapy? - Brit Assn Play Therapists
What to Wear - Brit Equestrian Tr Assn
What's In A Quarry (video) - Quarry Products Assn
What's Bottling - Assn Brit Brewery Collectables
What's Brewing - Campaign Real Ale Ltd
What's New in UK Aerospace - Soc Brit Aerospace Cos Ltd
Wheatsheaf - Kempe Soc
Wheel & Palette - Gld Rly Artists
Wheels - Brit Trolleybus Soc
　　　　Utd Road Transport U
Wheelspin - Ulster Automobile Club Ltd
When a Baby Dies - Stillbirth & Neonatal Death Soc
When a Pet Dies - Soc Companion Animal Studies
Where to Begin in Aphasia Research - Brit Aphasiology Soc
Where to Buy Directory - Brit Chemical Distbrs & Traders Assn
Which? - Consumers' Assn
Whitehall Papers - R Utd Services Inst Defence Studies
Who Cares Wins: the Buildings at Risk Register - Save Britain's
　　Heritage
Who Minds - Nat Childminding Assn
Who's Who Directory - Brit Assn Landscape Inds
Whole Life Costing - concrete bridges - Concrete Bridge Devt Gp
**Who's Who of Vice-Chancellors, Presidents & Rectors of
　　Commonwealth Universities -** Assn Commonwealth
　　Universities
Whose Job is it Anyway? - Road Safety Markings Assn
Why Rich People Give - Assn Charitable Foundations
WI Life - Nat Fedn Women's Insts
Wild Land News - Scot Wild Land Gp
The Wildean - Oscar Wilde Soc
Wildlife Action - Wildlife Trust Beds, Cambs, Northants &
　　Peterborough
Wildlife Sound - Wildlife Sound Recording Soc
William Bradshaw - a Leicestershire railway photographer -
　　Histl Model Rly Soc
Wiltshire Archaeological & Natural History Magazine -
　　Wiltshire Archaeol & Natural Hist Soc
Wiltshire Business - Swindon Cham Comm & Ind
Wind & Watermill - Soc Protection Ancient Bldgs
Window Talk - Fedn Window Cleaners
Winds - Brit Assn Symphonic Bands & Wind Ensembles
Windscreen - Military Vehicle Trust
Winged Words - Aviation Soc
Winking World - English Tiddlywinks Assn
Winning Edge - Inst Sales & Marketing Mgt
With Our Complements - Complementary Medical Assn
Within Reach - REACH
Wiþowinde - Engliscan Gesíþas
Wolves & Humans NL - Wolves & Humans Foundation
The Woman Engineer - Women's Engg Soc
Women Rule the Plot - Women's Farm & Garden Assn
Wood Protection NL - Brit Wood Preserving & Damp-proofing Assn
Woodcarver Gazette - Brit Woodcarvers Assn
Woodcarving - Gld Master Craftsmen
Woodland Initiatives Register - Small Woods Assn
Woods & Jack - English Indoor Bowling Assn
Woodturning - Gld Master Craftsmen
Woodworking Technology - Inst Machine Woodworking
　　Technology Ltd
Wooster Sauce - P G Wodehouse Soc (UK)
Worcestershire Recorder - Worcestershire Archaeol Soc
Wordsley - Black Country Soc
Work & Stress - Ergonomics Soc
Work, Employment & Society - Brit Sociological Assn

The Work of Subscription Agents - Assn Subscription Agents & Intermediaries
The Workbook - Embroiderers' Gld
Working in Schools - Indep Theatre Coun
Working Rule Agreement - Nat Fedn Demolition Contrs
Working Safely - Nat Care Assn
Working with your School Board Hbk for Headteachers - Scot School Bd Assn
World Bowls - Scot Indoor Bowling Assn
A World of Colour - Coloured Horse & Pony Soc
The World of Emissions - Garage Eqpt Assn
The World Today - R Inst Intl Affairs
Worldlywise - Devt Educ Assn
Worldwide Directory on Defence & Security Prime Contractors - Defence Mfrs Assn
Worldwide NL - Anthroposophical Med Assn
Wound Care Jnl - Wound Care Soc
Wounds & Infection - Wound Care Soc
WPA News - World Pheasant Assn UK
The Writ - Law Soc NI
The Writer - Soc Med Writers
Writing in Education - Nat Assn Writers Educ
WWINDY News - World-Wide Opportunities on Organic Farms

Y

Y Mag - Fedn Museums & Art Galleries in Wales

Yarak Jnl - Brit Hawking Assn
The Yardstick - Brit Weights & Measures Assn
Year's Work in Critical & Cultural Theory - English Assn
Year's Work in English Studies - English Assn
Yellow Book - Nat Gardens Scheme Charitable Trust
Yoga the World Over - Brit Wheel Yoga
Young Batworker - Bat Conservation Trust
Young Lacemaker - Lace Gld
Young Triathletes File - Brit Triathlon Assn
Your Big Sites Book - Camping & Caravanning Club Ltd
Your Body Your Risk - Dance UK Ltd
Your Business - Ayrshire Cham Comm & Ind
Your Child in an Immobilising Plaster: a few hints - Perthes Assn
Your Place in the Country - Camping & Caravanning Club Ltd
Youth Justice - Nat Assn Youth Justice
Youth Orchestra Tours Guide - Nat Assn Youth Orchestras

Z

Zipper News - Brit Cardiac Patients Assn
Zone Press - England Basketball
Zoological Jnl - Linnean Soc London
Zoological Record - Zoological Soc London

SUBJECT INDEX

Chambers of commerce & industry are included under the heading 'Chambers of commerce' and subdivided into general, local and overseas trade.

County agricultural societies are brought together under the heading 'Agriculture: county societies' and are listed in county order.

County archaeological societies are brought together under the heading 'Archaeology: county societies' and are listed in county order.

County record societies are brought together under the heading 'Records: historical - county societies' and are listed in county order.

Associations concerned with the teaching, technology, equipment & supplies and similar aspects of an activity are generally listed under the activity heading.

In general, headings relate to substantive groups rather than qualifying factors; thus the Society for Experimental Biology is listed under 'Biology'.

Unverified and lost associations are not indexed.

A

Abaca > Hemp
Abattoirs
    Assn Indep Meat Suppliers
    Licensed Animal Slaughterers. . . Assn
    Nat Assn Brit Market Authorities
Abercrombie (Lascelles)
    Friends Dymock Poets
Abnormal loads
    Heavy Transport Assn
    > + Road: haulage
Abortion
    Abortion Rights
    Soc Protection Unborn Children
Abrasives
    Brit Abrasives Fedn
Abuse (sexual)
    Nat Org Treatment of Abusers
    > + Sex & sexual law reform
Academics > + Universties
Accelerated learning
    Soc Effective Affective Learning
Access consultants
    Nat Register Access Consultants
Access covers
    Fabricated Access Cover Tr Assn
Access flooring
    Assn Interior Specialists
    > + Floors
Access scaffolding > Scaffolding
Accidents
    Accident Mgt Assn
    Brit Assn Emergency Medicine
    Brit Assn Immediate Care
    College Emergency Medicine
    Inst Home Safety
    Inst Traffic Accident Investigators
    Medical Equestrian Assn
    R Soc Prevention Accidents
    > + Safety
Accidents: victims
    Action Med Accidents
    Campaign Drinking & Driving
    Motor Accident Solicitors Soc
    Personal Injuries Bar Assn
    RoadPeace
Accommodation > Hotels & restaurants; Self catering; Students
Accordions & fiddles
    Nat Accordion Org
    Nat Assn Accordion & Fiddle Clubs
Accountancy
    Assn Accounting Technicians
    Assn Authorised Public Accountants
    Assn Chart Certified Accountants
    Assn Corporate Treasurers
    Assn Financial Controllers & Administrators
    Assn Indep Specialist Med Accountants
    Assn Intl Accountants
    Assn Practising Accountants
    Brit Accounting Assn
    Brit Assn Hospitality Accountants
    Chart Inst Mgt Accountants
    CIPFA

    District Auditors Soc
    Healthcare Financial Mgt Assn
    Insolvency Practitioners Assn
    Inst Accounting Technicians Ireland
    Inst Certified Public Accountants Ireland
    Inst Chart Accountants England & Wales
    Inst Chart Accountants Ireland
    Inst Chart Accountants Scotland
    Inst Cost & Executive Accountants
    Inst Financial Accountants
    Inst Inc Public Accountants [IRL]
    Inst Internal Auditors UK & Ireland
    Network Indep Forensic Accountants
    Soc Intl Treasurers
    Soc Law Accountants Scotland
    Soc Profl Accountants
    > + Bookkeeping; Cost engineering & control;   Insolvency
Acne
    Acne Support Gp
Acoustic music
    Assn Festival Organisers
    FolkArts England
Acoustic neuromas
    Brit Acoustic Neuroma Assn
Acoustics
    Assn Noise Consultants
    Heating, Ventilating & Air Conditioning Mfrs' Assn
    Inst Acoustics
    Inst Sound & Communications Engrs
    > + Hearing
Acquired immune deficiency syndrome > Genito-urinary medicine
Acrobatics > Gymnastics
Acrylic (painting in)
    Brit Soc Painters (in Oil, Pastels & Acrylic)
    Nat Acrylic Painters' Assn
    > + Art & artists
Activity holidays > Holiday camps & centres
Actors & actresses
    Brit Actors' Equity Assn
    Nat Assn Supporting Artistes Agents
    Soc Stars
    > + Theatre
Actuarial practice
    Assn Consulting Actuaries
    Fac Actuaries Scotland
    Inst Actuaries
    > + Insurance
Acupuncture
    Acupuncture Soc
    Brit Acupuncture Coun
    Brit Biomagnetic Assn
    Brit Med Acupuncture Soc
    Nat Acupuncture Detoxification Assn
    > + Complementary medicine
Addiction
    ADFAM Nat
    Families Anonymous
    Nat Acupuncture Detoxification Assn
    Nat Assn Alcohol & Drug Abuse Counsellors
    Sexaholics Anonymous
    Soc Study Addiction Alcohol. . .
    > + Alcoholism
Additives
    Food Additives & Ingredients Assn
Adhesive tape
    Adhesive Tape Mfrs' Assn

Assn Distributors, Coaters... Adhesive Tapes
Pressure Sensitive Mfrs Assn

Adhesives
Brit Adhesives & Sealants Assn
Contract Flooring Assn

Adler (Alfred)
Adlerian Soc

Admiralty chart agents
Chart & Nautical Instrument Tr Assn

Adolescents > Youth headings

Adoption
Adoption UK
Assn Families Adopted Abroad
Brit Assn Adoption & Fostering
Scot Adoption Assn
Supporting Adults affected by Adoption

Adrenoleukodystrophy
Adrenoleukodystrophy Family Support Trust

Adult education
Adult Educ Officers' Assn [IRL]
Adult Residential Colls Assn
Assn Profl Staffs Colls Educ [IRL]
Assn Sandwich Educ & Training
Assn Scotland's Colls
Brit Learning Assn
Educl Centres Assn
Inst Continuing Profl Devt
Nat Adult School Org
Nat Assn Educl Guidance Adults
Nat Assn Staff Devt in Post 16 Sector
Nat Inst Adult Continuing Educ (E&W)
NATFHE
Universities Assn Lifelong Learning
Workers' Educl Assn

Adult industry
Adult Ind Trade Assn

Adventure playgrounds > Playgrounds & playgroups

Advertising
Account Planning Gp
Advertising Assn
Assn Advertisers in Ireland Ltd
Assn Business to Business Agencies
D&AD
Inc Soc Brit Advertisers
Inst Advertising Practitioners Ireland
Inst Practitioners Advertising
Ir Direct Marketing Assn
Mobile Marketing Assn
Overseas Press & Media Assn
Publicity Club Ireland
Publicity Club Lond

Advertising: gifts > Incentive marketing

Advertising: music
Soc Producers & Composers Applied Music

Advertising: outdoor
Outdoor Advertising Assn
Outdoor Advertising Coun
Outdoor Media Assn [IRL]

Advertising: television & screen
Advertising Producers Assn
Cinema Advertising Assn

Advice centres & bureaux
Advice Services Alliance
Advice UK
Assn Indep Advice Centres
Citizens Advice Bureaux
Citizens Advice Scotland

Advocacy
Scot Indep Advocacy Alliance

Advocates > Law: Scotland

Aerial navigation > Navigation

Aerial phenomena > Unidentified flying objects

Aerial survey & photography
Brit Assn Remote Sensing Companies
Gld Brit Camera Technicians
Nat Assn Aerial Photographic Libraries
> + Landscape; Photography

Aerials: radio, telephone & television
Confedn Aerial Inds
Mast Action UK

Aerobatics
Brit Aerobatic Assn

Aerobiology
Brit Aerobiology Fedn
Midlands Asthma & Allergy Res Assn

Aerodromes > Aviation

Aerodynamics
Aircraft Res Assn
> + Aviation

Aeromodelling > Models: hobby

Aeronautical engineering > Aviation

Aerosols
Aerosol Soc
Brit Aerosol Mfrs Assn

Aerospace industry > Aviation

Aesthetic surgery > Plastic surgery

Aesthetics
Brit Soc Aesthetics

Aethelflaed, Lady of Mercia (c870-918)
Aethelflaed

Afghanistan
Middle East Assn

Africa
African Studies Assn
Black & Asian Studies Assn
Brit African Business Assn
Brit Cham Business Sthn Africa
One World Linking Assn
R African Soc

After dinner speakers > + Speakers

Age discrimination > Employment

Ageing > Geriatrics & ageing

Agents > under specific headings

Aggregates
Brit Aggregates Assn
Brit Marine Aggregate Producers' Assn
Quarry Products Assn

Agriculture
Agricl Inds Confedn
Agricl Manpower Soc
Agricl Science Assn [IRL]
Assn Show & Agricl Orgs
Biodynamic Agricl Assn
Brit Assn Seed Analysts
Brit Inst Agricl Consultants
Farming & Wildlife Advy Gp
Nat Assn Agricl Contrs
NI Shows Assn
Permaculture Assn
Principals' Profl Coun
R Agricl Soc C'wealth
R Agricl Soc England
R Highland & Agricl Soc Scotland
R Highland Educ Trust
R Welsh Agricl Soc
Scot Seed & Nursery Tr Assn
Soc Applied Microbiology
Soc Chemical Ind
Soc Responsible Use Resources Agriculture & Land
Soil Assn
Sustain
Tropical Agriculture Assn
Women's Farm & Garden Assn
Women's Food & Farming U
> + Farmers' organisations; Horticulture; Organic growing &
farming

Agriculture: buildings
Brit Constructional Steelwork Assn
Rural & Indl Design & Bldg Assn

Agriculture: chemicals
Animal & Plant Health Assn [IRL]
Assn Applied Biologists
Assn Public Analysts
Assn Public Analysts Scotland
Crop Protection Assn
Instn Agricl Engrs
Soc Chemical Ind
> + Fertilisers; Pest control

Agriculture: cooperatives
Scot Agricl Org Soc
Welsh Agricl Org Soc

Agriculture: county societies
Anglesey Agricl Soc
Antrim > County Antrim Agricl Assn
Ayrshire Agricl Assn
Bedfordshire > E England Agricl Soc
Berwickshire Agricl Assn
Birmingham > Staffordshire & Birmingham Agricl Soc
Border U Agricl Soc
Brecknockshire Agricl Soc
Bucks County Agricl Assn
Caithness Agricl Soc
Cambridgeshire > E England Agricl Soc

© CBD Research Ltd · Beckenham · BR3 5JS · Tel 020 8650 7745 · Fax 020 8650 0768 · E-mail cbd@cbdresearch.com · www.cbdresearch.com

Cardiganshire > Utd Counties Agricl Soc
Carmarthenshire > Utd Counties Agricl Soc
Cheshire Agricl Soc
Cleveland Agricl & Hortl Soc
Cornwall > R Cornwall Agricl Assn
County Antrim Agricl Assn
Cumberland Agricl Soc
Denbighshire & Flintshire Agricl Soc
Derbyshire Agricl & Horticl Soc
Devon County Agricl Assn
Dorchester Agricl Soc
Dorset > Dorchester Agricl Soc
Dorset > Yeovil Agricl Soc
Driffield Agricl Soc
Dublin > R Dublin Soc
Durham County Agricl Soc
E England Agricl Soc
Essex Agricl Soc
Fife Agricl Assn
Flintshire > Denbighshire & Flintshire Agricl Soc
Glamorgan > Vale Glamorgan Agricl Soc
Glasgow Agricl Soc
Gloucestershire > Three Counties Agricl Soc
Gwent > Monmouthshire Show Soc
Gwynedd > Merioneth Agricl Soc
Herefordshire > Three Counties Agricl Soc
Hertfordshire Agricl Soc
Isle of Man > R Manx Agricl Soc
Isle of Wight > R Isle of Wight Agricl Soc
Jersey > R Jersey Agricl & Horticl Soc
Kent County Agricl Soc
Lancashire > R Lancashire Agricl Soc
Leicestershire Agricl Soc
Lincolnshire Agricl Soc
Merioneth Agricl Soc
Monmouthshire Show Soc
N Somerset Agricl Soc
New Forest Agricl Show Soc
Newark & Nottinghamshire Agricl Soc
Norfolk > R Norfolk Agricl Assn
Northamptonshire > E England Agricl Soc
Nottinghamshire > Newark & Nottinghamshire Agricl Soc
Pembrokeshire Agricl Soc
Pembrokeshire > Utd Counties Agricl Soc
Perthshire Agricl Soc
R Bath & W England Soc
R Cornwall Agricl Assn
R Dublin Soc
R Guernsey Agricl & Horticl Soc
R Isle of Wight Agrl Soc
R Jersey Agricl & Horticl Soc
R Lancashire Agricl Soc
R Manx Agricl Soc
R Norfolk Agricl Assn
R Nthn Agricl Soc
R Ulster Agricl Soc
Rutland Agricl Soc
S England Agricl Soc
Scotland > R Nthn Agricl Soc
Shetland Livestock Marketing Gp
Shropshire & W Midlands Agricl Soc
Somerset > N Somerset Agricl Soc
Somerset > R Bath & W England Soc
Somerset > Yeovil Agricl Soc
Staffordshire & Birmingham Agricl Soc
Suffolk Agricl Assn
Surrey County Agricl Soc
Sussex > S England Agricl Soc
Three Counties Agricl Soc
Ulster > R Ulster Agricl Soc
Utd Counties Agricl Soc
Vale Glamorgan Agricl Soc
W Midlands > Shropshire & W Midlands Agricl Soc
Westmorland County Agricl Soc
Worcestershire > Three Counties Agricl Soc
Yeovil Agricl Soc
Yorkshire Agricl Soc
Yorkshire > Driffield Agricultural Soc
Agriculture: economics
    Agricl Economics Soc
Agriculture: education
    Assn Agricl & Horticl Colls [IRL]
    Napaeo
Agriculture: history
    Brit Agricl Hist Soc
Agriculture: irrigation > Irrigation

Agriculture: journalism
    Gld Agricl Journalists
Agriculture: law
    Agricl Law Assn
Agriculture: machinery
    Agricl Engrs Assn
    Brit Agricl & Garden Machinery Assn
    Farm Tractor & Machinery Tr Assn [IRL]
    Instn Agricl Engrs
    Soc Automotive Engrs
Agriculture: machinery - history
    Farm Machinery Presvn Soc
    Nat Vintage Tractor & Engine Club
    Southern Counties Historic Vehicle Presvn Trust
    Steam Plough Club
Agriculture: merchants
Agriculture: secretaries
    Inst Agricl Secretaries & Administrators
    Nat Assn NFU Gp Secretaries
Agriculture: valuation
    Central Assn Agricl Valuers
    Scot Agricl Arbiters Assn
Agrochemicals > Agriculture: chemicals
Agronomy
    Assn Indep Crop Consultants
AIDS (disease) > Genito-urinary medicine
Aikido > Martial arts
Air: ambulances > Ambulance services
Air: boats & inflatables
    Brit Air Boat Assn
    Brit FIB (Flying Inflatable Boat) Assn
    > + Boats & boating
Air: cargo > Aviation: freight
Air: charter industry > Travel & tourism
Air: conditioning & ventilating
    Air Cleaner Mfrs Assn
    Air Conditioning & Refrigeration Ind Bd
    Brit Refrigeration Assn
    BSRIA
    Chart Instn Bldg Services Engrs
    Chilled Ceilings Assn
    Commissioning Specialists Assn
    Fan Mfrs' Assn
    Fedn Envtl Tr Assns
    Heating, Ventilating & Air Conditioning Mfrs' Assn
    Heating & Ventilating Contrs Assn
    Hose Mfrs' & Suppliers Assn
    Residential Ventilation Assn
    Smoke Control Assn
    > + Heating
Air: courier services
    Assn Intl Courier & Express Services
Air: extraction > Dust control; Fans; Fumes & fume extraction
Air: guns & weapons > Arms & armour; Guns & ammunition; Shooting
Air: mail > Philately & postal history
Air: pilots, officers & crew > Aviation: pilots, officers & crew
Air: pollution
    CLEANAIR
    Nat Soc Clean Air. . .
    > + Air: conditioning & ventilating;   Pollution & pollution control
Air: sport
    R Aero Club Records Racing & Rally Assn
    R Aero Club UK
Air: surveying > Aerial survey & photography
Air: traffic control > Aviation: safety, control & training
Air: transport > Aviation
Aircraft > Aviation
Aircraft: historic > Aviation: history
Aircraft maintenance > + Aviation headings
Aircraft models > Models: hobby
Aircraft noise > Noise
Aircrete
Aircrew > + Aviation: pilots & officers
Airfields noise > Noise
Airports > Aviation
Airports: services & equipment
    Assn Port Health Authorities
    Brit Airport Services & Eqpt Assn
Air-sea rescue
    Goldfish Club
Airships > Balloons & airships
Alarms > Security
Albania
    Anglo-Albanian Assn
Albinism
    Albinism Fellowship

Alchemy
        Soc Hist Alchemy & Chemistry
Alcohol
        Neutral Alcohol Producers Assn
        > + Drink & beverage industry
Alcoholism
        Al-Anon Family Gps
        Alcohol Concern
        Alcoholics Anonymous
        Co-Dependents Anonymous
        Medical Coun Alcohol
        Nat Assn Alcohol & Drug Abuse Counsellors
        Portman Gp
        Soc Study Addiction Alcohol. . .
        UK Alliance
        > + Addiction
ALD disease > Adrenoleukodystrophy
Aldington (Richard)
        New Canterbury Literary Soc
Ale > Brewing; Real ale
Alexander technique
        Profl Assn Alexander Teachers
        Soc Teachers Alexander Technique
Algae
        Brit Phycological Soc
Alice in Wonderland
        Daresbury Lewis Carroll Soc
        Lewis Carroll Soc
Alkan (Charles Henri Valentin Morhange)
        Alkan Soc
All terrain vehicles
Allergy
        AAA (Action against Allergy)
        Allergy UK
        Anaphylaxis Campaign
        Androgen Insensitivity Syndrome Support Gp
        Brit Aerobiology Fedn
        Brit Inst Allergy & Envtl Therapy
        Brit Soc Allergy & Clinical Immunology
        Brit Soc Ecological Medicine
        Brit Soc Immunology
        Food & Chemical Allergy Assn
        Hyperactive Children's Support Gp
        Latex Allergy Support Gp
        Midlands Asthma & Allergy Res Assn
        Nat Soc Res Allergy
        > + Immunology
Allingham (Margery)
        Margery Allingham Soc
Allotments
        Nat Soc Allotment & Leisure Gardeners
        > + Gardens & gardening
Alloy(s) > Metal;   Steel: special & alloy
Almshouses
        Nat Assn Almshouses
Alopecia
        Hairline Intl
Alpacas > Camelids
Alpine gardening
        Alpine Garden Soc
        > + Rock gardens
Alpine guiding
        Brit Assn Mountain Guides
Alternative medicine > Complementary medicine; specific forms
Alternative technology > specific form of energy/technology
Altimeters
        Challenger Soc Marine Science
Aluminium
        Aluminium Alloy Mfrg & Recycling Assn
        Aluminium Extruders Assn
        Aluminium Fedn
        Aluminium Finishing Assn
        Aluminium Primary Producers Assn
        Aluminium Rolled Products Mfrs Assn
        Aluminium Stockholders Assn
        Coun Aluminium Bldg
        Inst Metal Finishing
        UK Aluminium Packaging Recycling Org
Aluminium: foil
        Assn Hot Foil Printers
        Flexible Packaging Assn
        > + Packaging
Aluminium: powder
        Aluminium Powder & Paste Assn
Aluminium: towers
        Prefabricated Access Suppliers' & Mfrs' Assn

Alzheimer's disease
        Alzheimer Scotland
        Alzheimer's Soc
Amaryllid
        Nerine & Amaryllid Soc
Amateur activities > specific activity
Ambulance services
        Ambulance Service Assn
        Ambulance Service Inst
        Assn Air Ambulance Charities
        Assn Profl Ambulance Personnel
        Brit Ambulance Assn
        Nat Assn Private Ambulance Services
        > + First aid & immediate care
Ambulances: collection & restoration
        Brit Ambulance Soc
        > + Motor vehicles: historic
Amenity management > Leisure, recreation & amenity management
America > Latin America; USA
American Civil War
        American Civil War Round Table
American football
        Brit Amer Football Assn
American 'West'
        Brit Western Dance Assn
        Brit Westerners Assn
        English Westerners Soc
        Western Equestrian Soc
        Western Horsemen's Assn
Ammunition > Guns & ammunition
Amnesia
Amphibians > Herpetology
Amputation > Limbless persons
Amusements & coin operated machines
        Amusement & Gaming Ind Forum
        Brit Amusement Catering Trs Assn
        Brit Assn Leisure Parks, Piers & Attractions
        > + Automatic vending
Amyotrophic lateral sclerosis > Motor neurone disease
Anaerobics
        Soc Anaerobic Microbiology
Anaesthesia
        Anaesthetic Res Soc
        Assn Anaesthetists
        Assn Cardiothoracic Anaesthetists
        Assn Dental Anaesthetists
        Assn Paediatric Anaesthetists
        Barema
        History Anaesthesia Soc
        Obstetric Anaesthetists Assn
        R Coll Anaesthetists
        Soc Advancement Anaesthesia Dentistry
        Soc Computing & Technology Anaesthesia
Analysts (computer) > Computers: professionals
Analysts (technical)
        Soc Technical Analysts
        > + Investment
Analytical chemistry
        Assn Public Analysts
        Assn Public Analysts Scotland
        Chromatographic Soc
        R Soc Chemistry
Anaphylaxsis > Allergy
Anatomy
        Anatomical Soc
        Brit Assn Clinical Anatomists
Anchorages (motor vehicle)
        Vehicle Restraint Mfrs Assn
Ancient monuments > Historic buildings
Anderson (Gerry)
        Fanderson. . .
Androgen insensitivity > Endocrinology
Andrology
        Brit Andrology Soc
        Brit Soc Psychosomatic Obstetrics. . .
Angels
        Fairy Ring
Anger management > Conflict & anger management
Angling > Fishing (sport);   Fishing tackle
Anglo-Saxon era
        Engliscan Gesíþas
        Ranulf Higden Soc
        Regia Anglorum
Angora wool
        Brit Angora Goat Soc
        Brit Goat Soc

© CBD Research Ltd · Beckenham · BR3 5JS · Tel 020 8650 7745 · Fax 020 8650 0768 · E-mail cbd@cbdresearch.com · www.cbdresearch.com

Animal by-products
  Brit Soc Animal Science
  Jt Animal By Products... C'ee
  Natural Sausage Casings Assn
  > + Rendering
Animal feed
  Brit Assn Feed Supplement & Additives Mfrs
  Brit Assn Green Crop Driers
  Brit Equestrian Tr Assn
  Grain & Feed Tr Assn
  Ir Grain & Feed Assn
  N Scotland Grassland Soc
  Nat Assn Agricl Contrs
  Nat Renderers Assn
  > + Pets & pet trade
Animals
  Brit Veterinary Assn
  Primate Soc
  R Inst Navigation
  Rare Breeds Survival Trust
  Soc Companion Animal Studies
  > + Conservation; Nature conservation;   Zoology & zoos; &
  specific animals
Animals: in entertainment
  Animal Consultants & Trainers Assn
Animals: language
  Wildlife Sound Recording Soc
Animals: slaughtering > Abattoirs
Animals: training
  Assn Pet Behaviour Counsellors
Animals: transportation
  Humane Slaughter Assn
  Racehorse Transporters Assn
Animals: welfare
  Advocates for Animals
  Animal Concern
  Animal Welfare Filming Fedn
  Cats Protection
  Humane Slaughter Assn
  Intl Assn Animal Therapists
  Ir Soc Prevention Cruelty Animals
  Nutrition Soc
  R Soc Prevention Cruelty Animals
  Scot Soc Prevention Cruelty Animals
  Ulster Soc Prevention Cruelty Animals
  Universities Fedn Animal Welfare
  > + Pets & pet trade; Veterinary headings; Vivisection; specific
  animal/trade
Ankylosing spondylitis
  Nat Ankylosing Spondylitis Soc
Annuities (compulsory)
  Compulsory Annuity Purchase Protest Alliance
Anodising
  Aluminium Finishing Assn
Anophthalmia
  Micro & Anophthalmic Children's Soc
Anorchidism
  Anorchidism Support Gp
Anorexia & bulimia nervosa > Eating disorders
Antarctic > Polar research
Anthropology
  Assn Social Anthropologists C'wealth
  Primate Soc
  R Anthropological Inst
Anthroposophy
  Anthroposophical Med Assn
  Anthroposophical Soc
Anti > object opposed
Antiques
  Assn Art & Antique Dealers
  Brit Antique Dealers Assn
  Brit Antique Furniture Restorers Assn
  Gld Antique Dealers & Restorers
  Meyrick Soc
  R Instn Chart Surveyors
Antiques: shippers & packers
  Assn Art & Antique Dealers
Antiquities
  Antiquities Dealers Assn
  Assn Study & Presvn Roman Mosaics
  Soc Antiquaries Scotland
  > + Archaeology; History
Anxiety attacks > Panic & anxiety attacks
Aphasia
  AFASIC
  Brit Aphasiology Soc
  > + Speech

Apiculture > Bees & beekeeping
Apnoea > Snoring & apnoea
Apostrophe (the)
  Apostrophe Protection Soc
Apparel > Clothing
Apparitions > Paranormal & psychical research
Appearance (personal)
  Fedn Image Consultants
Appetite loss > Eating disorders
Apples
  English Apples & Pears
Applied... > basic discipline
Appliqué
  Quilters' Gld
Appraisers (property)
  Inst Auctioneers & Appraisers Scotland
Aquaculture > Fish: farming
Aquaria
  Brit Marine Life Study Soc
  > + Fish: tropical & ornamental
Aquatic science > Marine: biology & biochemistry
Aquatic trade > Fish: tropical & ornamental
Arab states & peoples
  Coun Advancement Arab-Brit Understanding
  Middle East Assn
  Saudi Brit Soc
Arachnology > Spiders
Arachnophobia > Phobias
Arbitration
  Chart Inst Arbitrators
  Electricity Arbitration Assn
  Veterinary Assn Arbitration & Jurisprudence
Arboriculture > Forestry; Trees
Arc welding > Welding
Archaeology
  Archaeology Abroad
  Archaeology Cymru
  Assn Archaeol Illustrators & Surveyors
  Assn Envtl Archaeology
  Assn Local Govt Archaeol Officers
  Brit Academy
  Brit Archaeol Assn
  Brit Assn Local Hist
  Coun Indep Archaeology
  Egypt Exploration Soc
  Histl Metallurgy Soc
  Inst Field Archaeologists
  Medieval Settlement Res Gp
  Oriental Ceramic Soc
  Prehistoric Soc
  R Archaeol Inst
  Remote Sensing & Photogrammetry Soc
  Soc Landscape Studies
  Soc Medieval Archaeology
  Soc Museum Archaeologists
  Soc Post-Medieval Archaeology
Archaeology: country societies
  Cambrian Archaeol Assn
  Coun Brit Archaeology
  Coun Scot Archaeology
  Inst Archeologists Ireland
  R Instn S Wales
  R Ir Academy
  R Soc Antiquaries Ireland
  Soc Antiquaries Scotland
  Wales > Cambrian Archaeol Assn
Archaeology: county societies
  Abertay Histl Soc
  Anglesey Antiquarian Soc & Field Club
  Architectural & Archaeol Soc County Bucks
  Ashmolean Natural Hist Soc Oxfordshire
  Assn Northumberland Local Hist Socs
  Berkshire Archaeol Soc
  Berkshire Archaeology Res Gp
  Berwickshire Naturalists Club
  Birmingham & Warwickshire Archaeol Soc
  Bristol & Gloucestershire Archaeol Soc
  Buckinghamshire > Architectural & Archaeol Soc County Bucks
  Buckinghamshire > Wolverton & Dist Archaeol & Histl Soc
  Caernarvonshire Histl Soc
  Cambridge Antiquarian Soc
  Cambridgeshire Local Hist Soc
  Cheshire > Historic Soc Lancashire & Cheshire
  Cheshire > Lancashire & Cheshire Antiquarian Soc
  Chester Archaeol Soc
  Cornwall Archaeol Soc
  Cornwall > R Instn Cornwall

Coventry & District Archaeol Soc
Croydon Natural Hist & Scientific Soc
Cumberland & Westmorland Antiquarian. . . Soc
Cymdeithas Hanes Ceredigion Histl Soc
Cymdeithas Hanes Sir Ddinbych
Denbighshire > Cymdeithas Hanes Sir Ddinbych
Derbyshire Archaeol Soc
Derbyshire > Hunter Archaeol Soc
Derbyshire Record Soc
Devon Archaeol Soc
Dorset Natural Hist & Archaeol Soc
Dublin > Friends Medieval Dublin [IRL]
Dumfriesshire & Galloway Natural Hist. . . Soc
Durham > Architectural & Archaeol Soc of Durham &
Northumberland
Durham County Local Hist Soc
Durham > Soc Antiquaries Newcastle upon Tyne
E Herts Archaeol Soc
E Lothian Antiquarian. . . Naturalists Soc
Essex Archaeol & Histl Congress
Essex Soc Archaeology & Hist
Flintshire Histl Soc
Friends Medieval Dublin [IRL]
Galloway > Dumfries & Galloway Natural Hist. . . Soc
Glamorgan Hist Soc
Glasgow Archaeol Soc
Gloucestershire > Bristol & Gloucestershire Archaeol Soc
Guernsey > Société Guernesiaise
Hampshire Field Club & Archaeol Soc
Hawick Archaeol Soc
Hertfordshire > E Herts Archaeol Soc
Hertfordshire > St Albans & Hertfordshire Architectural. . . Soc
Historic Soc Lancashire & Cheshire
Hunter Archaeol Soc
Huntingdonshire Local Hist Soc
Isle of Anglesey > Anglesey Antiquarian Soc
Isle of Man Natural Hist. . .Soc
Isle of Wight Natural Hist & Archaeol Soc
Jersey > Société Jersiaise
Kent Archaeol Soc
Kent > Croydon Natural Hist & Scientific Soc
Lancashire & Cheshire Antiquarian Soc
Lancashire > Cumberland & Westmorland Antiquarian & Archaeol
Soc
Lancashire > Historic Soc Lancashire & Cheshire
Leicestershire Archaeol & Histl Soc
Lincolnshire > Soc Lincolnshire Hist & Archaeol
London & Middlesex Archaeol Soc
London Topographical Soc
Lothian > E Lothian Antiquarian &. . .Naturalists Soc
Middlesex > London & Middlesex Archaeol Soc
Norfolk & Norwich Archaeol Soc
Northamptonshire Natural History Soc
Northamptonshire > Wolverton & Dist Archaeol & Histl Soc
Northumberland > Architectural & Archaeol Soc Durham &
Northumberland
Northumberland > Assn Northumberland Local Hist Socs
Northumberland > Berwickshire Naturalists' Club
Northumberland > Soc Antiquaries Newcastle upon Tyne
Nottinghamshire Local Hist Assn
Nottinghamshire > Thoroton Soc Nottinghamshire
Oxford University Archaeol Soc
Oxfordshire Architectural & Hist Soc
Oxfordshire > Ashmolean Natural Hist Soc
Pembrokeshire Histl Soc
Perthshire Soc Natural Science
Powys > Radnorshire Soc
R Instn Cornwall
Radnorshire Soc
Roxburghshire > Hawick Archaeol Soc
Saint Albans & Hertfordshire Architectural. . . Soc
Shropshire Archaeol & Histl Soc
Soc Antiquaries Lond
Soc Antiquaries Newcastle upon Tyne
Soc Lincolnshire Hist & Archaeology
Société Guernesiaise
Société Jersiaise
Somerset Archaeol & Natural Hist Soc
Staffordshire Archaeol. . .Soc
Staffordshire > Stoke on Trent Museum Archaeol Soc
Stoke-on-Trent Museum Archaeol Soc
Suffolk Inst Archaeology & Hist
Surrey Archaeol Soc
Surrey > Croydon Natural Hist Scientific Soc
Sussex Archaeol Soc
Tayside > Abertay Histl Soc
Thoresby Soc

Thoroton Soc Nottinghamshire
Ulster Archaeol Soc
W Midlands > Birmingham & Warwickshire Archaeol Soc
Warwickshire > Birmingham & Warwickshire Archaeol Soc
Warwickshire > Coventry & District Archaeol Soc
Westmorland > Cumberland & Westmorland Antiquarian & Archaeol
Soc
Wiltshire Archaeol & Natural Hist Soc
Wolverton & Dist Archaeol & Histl Soc
Worcestershire Archaeol Soc
Yorkshire Archaeol Soc
Yorkshire > Hunter Archaeol Soc
Yorkshire Philosophical Soc
Yorkshire > Thoresby Soc

Archaeology: industrial
Arkwright Soc
Assn Indl Archaeology
Brewery Hist Soc
Bristol Indl Archaeol Soc
Gloucestershire Soc Indl Archaeology
Greater Lond Indl Archaeology Soc
Indl Locomotive Soc
Merseyside Indl Heritage Soc
Peak District Mines Hist Soc
Scot Indl Heritage Soc
Subterranea Britannica
Sussex Indl Archaeol Soc
Tool & Trs Hist Soc
Trevithick Soc
> + specific field of interest

Archaeology: nautical
Nautical Archaeology Soc
Sub-Aqua Assn

Archery
Craft Gld Traditional Bowyers & Fletchers
Grand Nat Archery Soc
Nat Field Archery Soc
NI Archery Soc
Plantagenet Medieval Archery. . . Soc
Scot Archery Assn
Scot Field Archery Assn
Soc Archer-Antiquaries

Architecture
ACG Ltd (Arts Centre Gp)
Architectural Assn
Art & Architecture
Assn Bldg Engrs
Assn Consultant Architects
Assn Scot Schools Architecture
Brit Earth Sheltering Assn
Chart Inst Architectural Technologists
Inst Profl Designers
Property Consultants Soc
Pugin Gld
R Incorporation Architects Scotland
R Inst Architects Ireland
R Inst Brit Architects
R Soc Architects Wales
R Soc Ulster Architects
Soc Chief Architects Local Auths

Architecture: history & preservation
Alexander Thomson Soc
Architectural & Archaeol Soc County Bucks
Architectural & Archaeol Soc Durham & Northumberland
Architectural Heritage Soc Scotland
Assn Art Historians
Campaign Protection Rural Wales
Cathedral Architects Assn
Charles Rennie Mackintosh Soc
Georgian Gp
Ir Georgian Soc
Men of the Stones
Nat Trust
Nat Trust Ireland
Nat Trust Scotland
Pugin Soc
R Archaeol Inst
Regency Soc Brighton & Hove
Saint Albans & Hertfordshire Architectural. . . Soc
Save Britain's Heritage
Soc Architectural Historians
Twentieth Century Soc
UK Assn Presvn Trusts
Ulster Architectural Heritage Soc
Vernacular Architecture Gp
Victorian Soc
> + Archaeology; Church: buildings

© CBD Research Ltd · Beckenham · BR3 5JS · Tel 020 8650 7745 · Fax 020 8650 0768 · E-mail cbd@cbdresearch.com · www.cbdresearch.com

Architecture: illustration
      Soc Architectural Illustration
Architecture: metalcraft
      Gld Architectural Ironmongers
      Inst Architectural Ironmongers
Architecture: naval > Shipbuilding & ship repairing
Architecture: religious > Church: buildings
Archives
      Assn Chief Archivists Local Govt
      Assn Genealogists & Researchers in Archives
      Brit Assn Friends Museums
      Business Archives Coun
      Catholic Archives Soc
      Soc Archivists
      > + Records: historical
Archives: conservation
      Ir Soc Archives
Arenas
      Nat Arenas Assn
Argentina
      Anglo-Argentine Soc
      Cámara Comercio Argentino Britanica
      Cymdeithas Cymru-Ariannin
Arithmetic
      Dozenal Soc
      > + Mathematics
Arkwright (Sir Richard)
      Arkwright Soc
Armed forces & veterans: welfare
      Gulf Veterans Assn
      Soldiers, Sailors & Airmen's Families Assn
      > + Ex-service organisations
Armorial bearings > Heraldry
Armoured fighting vehicles (miniature)
      Miniature Armoured Fighting Vehicles Assn
      > + Military vehicles
Arms & armour
      Arms & Armour Soc
      Histl Breechloading Smallarms Assn
      Historic Artillery
      Meyrick Soc
      Muzzle Loaders Assn
      Ordnance Soc
      Palmerston Forts Soc
      Trebuchet Soc
      Vintage Arms Assn
      > + Defence equipment; Shooting
Arms trade & control
      Campaign Arms Trade
Arm wrestling
      Brit Arm Wrestling Fedn
Army
      Victorian Military Soc
      > + Armed forces & veterans: welfare;   Cadets; Military history
Aromatherapy
      Aromatherapy & Allied Practitioners Assn
      Aromatherapy Tr Coun
      Assn Therapy Lecturers
      Scot Massage Therapists Org
Aromatic compounds > Fragrances & aromatic compounds
Arrhythmia
      Arrhythmia Alliance
      > + Cardiology
Arrows (for archery) > Archery
Art & artists
      ACG Ltd (Arts Centre Gp)
      Art & Architecture
      Art Workers Gld
      Arts & Business
      Arts Marketing Assn
      Assn Cultural Advancement through Visual Art
      Brit Soc Miniaturists
      Brit Soc Painters (in Oil, Pastels & Acrylic)
      Contemporary Art Soc
      Contemporary Art Soc Wales
      Fedn Brit Artists
      Fine Art Tr Gld
      Gld Aviation Artists
      Gld Rly Artists
      Hilliard Soc Miniaturists
      Inst Contemporary Arts
      Medical Artists Assn
      Nat Acrylic Painters' Assn
      Nat Campaign Arts
      Nat Portraiture Assn
      Nat Soc Painters, Sculptors & Printmakers
      Nature in Art Trust

Pre-Raphaelite Soc
Public Monuments & Sculpture Assn
R Academy Arts
R Birmingham Soc Artists
R Cambrian Academy Art
R Glasgow Inst Fine Arts
R Philosophical Soc Glasgow
R Scot Academy Art & Architecture
R Soc . . . Arts
R Soc Miniature Painters . . .
R Watercolour Soc
SAA
Soc Artists' Agents
Soc Botanical Artists
Soc Equestrian Artists
Soc Graphic Fine Art
Soc Heraldic Arts
Soc Scot Artists
Soc Women Artists
UK Coloured Pencil Soc
Visual Arts Scotland
      > + Artist by name; specific form of art
Art: applied
      Applied Arts Scotland
Art: appreciation
      Brit Soc Aesthetics
      engage
      Oriental Ceramic Soc
Art: auctioneers > Art: trade
Art: conservation
      ArtWatch UK
      Brit Assn Paintings Conservator-Restorers
      Fine Art Tr Gld
      Inst Consvn
      Inst Consvn Historic &. . . Works Ireland
      Ir Profl Conservators' & Restorers' Assn
      Nat Assn Decorative & Fine Arts Socs
      Soc Decorative Art Curators
      > + Historic buildings; Picture restoring
Art: education
      Manchester Literary & Philosophical Soc
      Nat Assn Local Govt Arts Officers
      Nat Soc Educ in Art & Design
Art: festivals > Festivals: art, drama & music
Art: galleries
      Assn Leading Visitor Attractions
      Brit Assn Friends Museums
      Contemporary Art Soc
      Contemporary Art Soc Wales
      Fedn Museums & Art Galleries Wales
      Fine Art Tr Gld
      Museums Assn
      Nat Art Collections Fund
      Nat Heritage
      Visual Arts & Galleries Assn
      > + Museums
Art: history
      Assn Art Historians
      Brit Academy
      Walpole Soc
Art: law &
      Inst Art & Law
Art: libraries
      ARLIS UK & Ireland
Art: management > Leisure, recreation & amenity management
Art: shippers & packers
      Assn Art & Antique Dealers
Art: therapy
      Brit Assn Art Therapists
Art: trade
      Assn Art & Antique Dealers
      Brit Art Market Fedn
      Fine Art Tr Gld
      Inst Auctioneers & Appraisers Scotland
      Soc Fine Art Auctioneers & Valuers
      Soc Lond Art Dealers
Arthritis & rheumatism
      Arthritic Assn
      Arthritis Care
      Arthritis & Musculoskeletal Alliance
      Arthritis & Rheumatism Natural Therapy Res Assn
      Behçet's Syndrome Soc
      Brit Coalition Heritable Disorders Connective Tissue
      Brit Health Profls in Rheumatology
      Brit Soc Rheumatology
      Children's Chronic Arthritis Assn

Nat Ankylosing Spondylitis Soc
Nat Rheumatoid Arthritis Soc
Primary Care Rheumatology Soc
Psoriasis Assn
Psoriatic Arthropathy Alliance
Arthrogryposis
Arthrogryposis Gp
Article numbering
Automatic Identification Mfrs & Suppliers Assn
GS1 Ireland
GS1 (UK)
Artificial intelligence
Soc Study Artificial Intelligence & Simulation Behaviour
Artificial limbs > Prosthetics
Artillery > Arms & armour
Artists > Art & artists
Asbestos
ARCA
Indep Safety Consultants Assn
Occupational & Envtl Diseases Assn
Thermal Insulation Contrs Assn
Ash
UK Quality Ash Assn
Asia
Assn Punjab Studies (UK)
Assn S E Asian Studies UK
Black & Asian Studies Assn
One World Linking Assn
Oriental Ceramic Soc
R Asiatic Soc
R Soc Asian Affairs
Soc S Asian Studies
Asia: languages
Assn Language Learning
Asparagus
Asparagus Growers' Assn
> + Vegetables: growing
Asphalt & coated macadam
Asphalt Ind Alliance
Inst Asphalt Technology
Mastic Asphalt Coun
Quarry Products Assn
> + Bitumen
Asset sales services
Nat Assn Valuers & Auctioneers
Association football > Football (Association)
Associations
Profl Assns Res Network
Associations: secretaries
Inst Assn Mgt
Assurance > Insurance
Asthma
Asthma Soc Ireland
Asthma UK
Brit Aerobiology Fedn
Midlands Asthma & Allergy Res Assn
> + Allergy
Astrology
Assn Profl Astrologers
Astrological Assn
Astrological Lodge Lond
Brit Assn Vedic Astrology
Brit Astrological & Psychic Soc
Fac Astrological Studies
UK Skeptics
Astronautics > Space research & exploration
Astronomy
Assn Astronomy Educ
Assn Scotland Res Astronautics
Astronomical Soc Edinburgh
Brit Astronomical Assn
Campaign Dark Skies
Fedn Astronomical Socs
Ir Astronomical Soc
R Astronomical Soc
R Inst Navigation
Soc Popular Astronomy
Asylum seekers
Assn Visitors Immigration Detainees
Ataxia
Ataxia-Telangiectasia Soc
Ataxia UK
Athletic clothing > Clothing
Athletics
Amat Athletic Assn
Brit Triathlon Assn
NI Athletic Fedn

Scot Athletics
Scot Games Assn
UK Athletics
Welsh Athletics
> + Sports
Atomic > Nuclear energy
Attention deficiency
Nat Acupuncture Detoxification Assn
Au pairs > Nannies & au pairs
Auctioneering
Inst Auctioneers & Appraisers Scotland
Inst Profl Auctioneers & Valuers [IRL]
Ir Auctioneers & Valuers Inst
Nat Assn Valuers & Auctioneers
Property Consultants Soc
Soc Fine Art Auctioneers & Valuers
Audio engineering > Sound recording & reproduction
Audio tape > Sound recording & reproduction
Audio visual: aids & equipment
Audio Visual Fedn [IRL]
Brit Universities Film & Video Coun
Deaf Broadcasting Coun
> + Sound recording & reproduction
Audio visual: libraries
FOCAL Intl
Audiobooks
Audiobook Publishing Assn
Audiology > Hearing
Auditing > Accountancy
Auriculas
Nat Auricula & Primula Soc (Mid & West)
Nat Auricula & Primula Soc (Nthn)
Nat Auricula & Primula Soc (Sthn)
Austen (Jane)
Jane Austen Soc
Australia
Australian Business
Britain-Australia Soc
Austria
Anglo-Austrian Soc
Austro-Brit Cham
German Rly Soc
Authors > Writing & writers; individual by name
Authors' agents
Assn Authors' Agents
> + Writing & writers
Autism
Autism Indep UK
Hyperactive Children's Support Gp
Ir Soc Autism
Nat Autistic Soc
Scot Soc Autism
> + Children: handicapped
Auto theft > Motor vehicles: theft (of/from)
Autograph collecting
Autograph Club
Autojumbles
Nat Jumblers Fedn
Automata > Musical boxes
Automatic identification
Automatic Identification Mfrs & Suppliers Assn
> + Article numbering
Automatic gates
Fencing Contrs Assn
Automatic metering > Meters & metering
Automatic vending
Automatic Vending Assn
Nat Assn Cigarette Machine Operators
> + Amusements & coin operated machines
Automation
Assn Instrumentation, Control, Automation. . .
Brit Automation & Robot Assn
> + Computers; Control engineering; Production engineering
Automobile > Car headings; Motor headings
Automotive engineers > Motor industry
Auxiliary languages > Languages: auxiliary
Avebury
Megalithic Soc
Average adjusters
Assn Average Adjusters
Aviation
Air Britain (Historians)
Air League
Air Transport Auxiliary Assn
Aircraft Res Assn
Airport Operators Assn
Assn ATOL Companies

© CBD Research Ltd · Beckenham · BR3 5JS · Tel 020 8650 7745 · Fax 020 8650 0768 · E-mail cbd@cbdresearch.com · www.cbdresearch.com

Assn Licensed Aircraft Engrs
Aviation Envt Fedn
Aviation Soc
Baltic Air Charter Assn
Brit Air Transport Assn
Brit Assn Aviation Consultants
Brit Business & Gen Aviation Assn
Britpave
Defence Mfrs Assn
Fedn Aerospace Enterprises Ireland
Instn Mechanical Engrs
R Aero Club Trust
R Aeronautical Soc
Soc Automotive Engrs
Soc Brit Aerospace Cos
> + Air: sport; Gliding & soaring; Helicopters
Aviation: aircraft maintenance
Fedn Aerospace Support Services
Aviation: airships > Balloons & airships
Aviation: art
Gld Aviation Artists
Aviation: freight
Brit Intl Freight Assn
> + Freight transport
Aviation: history
Aeroplane Collection
Air Britain (Historians)
Assn Transport Photographers & Historians
Brit Aviation Enthusiasts Soc
Brit Aviation Presvn Coun
Brooklands Soc
Farnborough Air Sciences Trust
Handley Page Assn
Historic Aircraft Assn
R Aeronautical Soc
Rly & Canal Histl Soc
Second Wld War Aircraft Presvn Soc
Aviation: medicine
R Aeronautical Soc
Aviation: pilots, officers & crew
Aircraft Owners & Pilots Assn
Aircraft Owners & Pilots Assn [IRL]
Aircrew Assn
Brit Air Line Pilots Assn
Brit Precision Pilots Assn
Brit Women Pilots Assn
Flying Farmers Assn
Gld Air Pilots & Air Navigators
Indep Pilots Assn
Ir Airline Pilots Assn
Nat U Marine... Transport Officers
Aviation: safety, control & training
Air Safety Gp
Aircraft Owners & Pilots Assn
Gld Air Pilots & Air Navigators
Gld Air Traffic Control Officers
Aviation: sport
Brit Aerobatic Assn
Brit Microlight Aircraft Assn
Formula Air Racing Assn
Popular Flying Assn
Aviculture > Birds
Ayurvedic medicine
Ayurvedic Med Assn

B

Babies > Cot deaths; Maternity; Obstetrics & gynaecology; Paediatrics
Baby goods > Nursery & baby products
Baby life-support systems
BLISS
Bacalao
Assn Brit Salted Fish Curers...
Bach remedies
Crystal & Healing Fedn
Back pain > Chiropractic; Spine & spinal injuries
Backgammon
Brit Isles Backgammon Assn
Backpacking
Backpackers Club
Long Distance Walkers Assn
Bacon
Provision Tr Fedn
> + Pigs

Bacon (Francis) Baron Verulam
Francis Bacon Soc
Bacteriology > Microbiology
Badgers
Nat Fedn Badger Gps
Badges & insignia
Badge Collectors Circle
Brit Badge Collectors Assn
Police Insignia Collectors Assn
Scot Military Histl Soc
Trade U Badge Collectors Soc
> + Numismatics
Badminton
Badminton Assn England
Scot Badminton U
Welsh Badminton U
Bagpipes > Pipe bands & music
Bailiffs
Assn Brit Investigators
Assn Civil Enforcement Agencies
Enforcement Services Assn
Baking
Assn Bakery Ingredient Mfrs
Bakers', Food & Allied Workers' U
Biscuit, Cake, Chocolate... Assn
Brit Confectioners Assn
Fedn Bakers
Nat Assn Master Bakers
Scot Assn Master Bakers
UK Assn Frozen Food Producers
UK Assn Mfrs Bakers Yeast
Ball clay
Kaolin & Ball Clay Assn
> + Clay & clay products
Ball milling
Inst Vitreous Enamellers
Ball & roller bearings
Ball & Roller Bearing Mfrs Assn
Ballet
Brit Ballet Org
Imperial Soc Teachers Dancing
R Academy Dance
> + Dancing
Balloons & airships
Airship Assn
Brit Assn Balloon Operators
Brit Balloon & Airship Club
> + Inflatable toys & structures
Balloons (decorated/toy)
NABAS
Ballroom dancing > Dancing
Baltic countries > individual country
Bamboo
Brit Bamboo Soc
Bands > Brass & silver bands; Dance bands; Pipe bands & music; Steel bands
Banjos > Ukuleles & banjos
Bank customers > Banking: customers & users
Banking
Assn Foreign Banks
Assn Guernsey Banks
Assn Payment Clearing Services
Brit Bankers' Assn
Chart Inst Bankers Scotland
Futures & Options Assn
Indep Banking Advy Service
Inst Bankers Ireland
Ir Bankers Fedn
Loan Market Assn
London Investment Banking Assn
NI Bankers Assn
Banking: customers & users
Campaign Community Banking Services
Nat Assn Bank & Insurance Customers
Banking: history
Brit Banking History Soc
Bankruptcy
Assn Business Recovery Profls
Bankruptcy Assn
Inst Money Advisers
Banners > Flags, banners & bunting
Bantock (Sir Granville) 1868-1946
Baptist church
Baptist Histl Soc
Baptist U
Strict Baptist Histl Soc
The Bar > Law

Barbecues
>> Leisure & Outdoor Furniture Assn
Barbershop singing
>> Brit Assn Barbershop Singers
>> Ladies' Assn Brit Barbershop Singers
Barbirolli (Sir John)
>> Barbirolli Soc
Barcodes > Article numbering
Barges
>> Dutch Barge Assn
>> River Assn Freight & Transport
>> Sailing Barge Assn
>> Soc Sailing Barge Res
Barley
>> Brit Oat & Barley Millers Assn
Barn engines
>> Farm Machinery Presvn Soc
>> + Agriculture: machinery & engineering
Barnes (William)
>> William Barnes Soc
Barons > Manors
Barrels > Cooperage
Barriers (safety)
>> Retroreflective Eqpt Mfrs Assn
>> + Stairs: gates & barriers
Barristers > Law
Bars (management & staff)
>> UK Bartenders Gld
Baseball
>> BaseballSoftballUK
Basements
>> ASUCplus
Basketball
>> Basketball Assn Wales
>> Brit Basketball Fedn
>> England Basketball
>> Great Britain Basketball
>> Ir Basketball Assn
>> Scot Basketball Assn
Baskets
>> Basketmaker's Assn
Bassoons (musical instruments)
>> Brit Double Reed Soc
Bathing water quality
>> Marine Consvn Soc
Baths & bathrooms
>> Bathroom Mfrs' Assn
>> Kitchen Bathroom Bedroom Specialists Assn
Baths: public
>> Inst Sport & Recreation Mgt
Baton twirling
>> Brit Isles Baton Twirling Assn
>> Nat Baton Twirling Assn
Bats
>> Bat Consvn Trust
>> NI Bat Gp
Batten disease
>> Batten Disease Family Assn
Battered wives > Domestic violence
Batteries
>> Brit Battery Mfrs Assn
>> Indep Battery Distbrs Assn
>> Oil Recycling Assn
Battery vehicles > Electric: transport
Battle of Britain > World War II
Battlefields
>> Battlefields Trust
Battles (re-enactment) > Fights (historic/re-enactment); specific period of interest
Beads
>> Bead Soc
Beagling
>> Ir Masters Beagles Assn
Beam engines
>> Trevithick Soc
Beams (concrete)
>> Brit Precast Concrete Fedn
>> + Concrete & concrete products
Bearings
>> Ball & Roller Bearing Mfrs Assn
Bears ('teddies') > Rupert Bear
Beauty specialists/treatment
>> Assn Therapy Lecturers
>> Brit Assn Beauty Therapy & Cosmetology
>> Freelance Hair & Beauty Fedn
>> Gld Profl Beauty Therapists
>> Hairdressing & Beauty Suppliers Assn

Health & Beauty Emplrs Fedn
>> + Cosmetology & cosmetic surgery; Electrolysis
Beckford (William)
>> Beckford Soc
Beddoes (Thomas Lovell)
>> Thomas Lovell Beddoes Soc
Bedrooms (fitted)
>> Kitchen Bathroom Bedroom Specialists Assn
Beds & bedding
>> Brit Waterbed Assn
>> Futon Assn
>> Nat Bed Fedn
>> Sleep Coun
Bedsores
>> Tissue Viability Soc
Beef > Cattle headings; Meat
Beekeeping > Bees & beekeeping
Beer > Brewing
Beer: bottles, cans, labels & mats
>> Assn Brit Brewery Collectables
>> Brit Beermat Collectors' Soc
>> Labologists Soc
Bees & beekeeping
>> Assn Beekeeping Appliance Mfrs
>> Bee Farmers Assn
>> Bee Improvement & Bee Breeders Assn
>> Brit Bee-Keepers' Assn
>> Bumblebee Conservation Trust
>> Fedn Ir Beekeepers' Assns
>> Scot Beekeepers' Assn
Beet sugar > Sugar headings
Beetles
>> Brit Entomological & Natural Hist Soc
>> + Water beetles
Begonias
>> Nat Begonia Soc
Behaviour simulation
>> Soc Study Artificial Intelligence & Simulation Behaviour
Behaviour studies
>> Brit Assn Behavioural... Psychotherapies
Behçet's syndrome
>> Behçet's Syndrome Soc
Belgium
>> Anglo-Belgian Soc
>> Assn Low Countries Studies
>> Belgian-Luxembourg Cham Comm GB
>> Brit Cham Comm Belgium
Bell (Adrian)
>> Adrian Bell Soc
Bellringing
>> Brit Carillon Soc
>> Central Coun Church Bell Ringers
>> Handbell Ringers
Bennett ([Enoch] Arnold)
>> Arnold Bennett Soc
Benson (Edward Frederic)
>> E F Benson Soc
Bereavement
>> Campaign Drinking & Driving
>> Compassionate Friends
>> Cruse - Bereavement Care
>> SAMM Nat
>> Sudden Death Support Assn
>> Way Foundation
>> + specific cause of bereavement
Berlioz (Hector)
>> Berlioz Soc
Bespoke tailoring > Tailoring
Betjeman (Sir John)
>> Betjeman Soc
Betting > Bookmaking; Casinos; Gaming
Beverage industry > Drink & beverage industry; & specific beverages
Bewick (Thomas)
>> Bewick Soc
Bible
>> Biblical Creation Soc
>> Soc Old Testament Study
>> Soc Promoting Christian Knowledge
Bibliography
>> Bibliographical Soc
>> Cambridge Bibliographical Soc
>> Edinburgh Bibliographical Soc
>> Soc Hist Natural Hist
>> + Book(s)
Bicross > Cycling
Bicycles > Cycles & motorcycles

© CBD Research Ltd · Beckenham · BR3 5JS · Tel 020 8650 7745 · Fax 020 8650 0768 · E-mail cbd@cbdresearch.com · www.cbdresearch.com

Bill broking
    London Money Market Assn
Billiards & snooker > Cue sports
Bingo
    Bingo Association
    Nat Bingo Game Assn
Biochemistry & biotechnology
    Assn Clinical Biochemistry
    Assn Clinical Biochemists Ireland
    Biochemical Soc
    BioIndustry Assn
    Brit In Vitro Diagnostics Assn
    Brit Soc Proteome Res
    Brit Soc Toxicological Pathologists
    Genetics Soc
    Ir BioIndustry Assn
    Pharmaceutical & Healthcare Sciences Soc
    Soc Chemical Ind
Biocides
    Brit Assn Chemical Specialities
Bioenergy
    Renewable Energy Assn
    Soc Metaphysicians
Biological engineering
    Soc Applied Microbiology
Biology
    Assn Applied Biologists
    Biological Recording Scotland
    Biosciences Fedn
    Brit Soc Developmental Biology
    Freshwater Biological Assn
    Inst Biology
    Institiúid Bitheolaíochta Eireann
    Natural Sciences Collections Assn
    Scot Freshwater Gp
    Soc Experimental Biology
    Soc Study Human Biology
    Systematics Assn
    > + Botany; Cell biology; Marine: biology & biochemistry; Plants
Biomagnetics
    Brit Biomagnetic Assn
Biomass > Bioenergy; Forestry
Biophysics
    Brit Biophysical Soc
Biotechnology > Biochemistry & biotechnology
Birds
    Avicultural Soc
    Brit Assn Shooting & Consvn
    Brit Bird Coun
    Brit Ornithologists Club
    Brit Ornithologists U
    Brit Trust Ornithology
    Nat Coun Aviculture
    Ornithological Soc Middle East
    R Inst Navigation
    R Naval Bird Watching Soc
    R Soc Protection Birds
    Scot Ornithologists Club
    Scot Soc Protection Wild Birds
    Seabird Gp
    Soc Protection Aviculture
    Songbird Survival
    > + Natural history
Birds of prey > Hawks & hawking
Birth & birth control > Family planning; Maternity; Obstetrics & gynaecology
Birthmarks & disfigurement
    Birthmark Support Gp
    Brit Assn Skin Camouflage
    Let's Face It
    > + Children: handicapped
Births > Population registration
Biscuits
    Biscuit, Cake, Chocolate... Assn
    Cereal Ingredients Mfrs' Assn
Bison
    Brit Bison Assn
Bitumen
    Refined Bitumen Assn
    Road Emulsion Assn
    > + Asphalt & coated macadam
Björling (Jussi)
    Jussi Björling Appreciation Soc
Blacksmiths & farriers
    Brit Artist Blacksmiths Assn
Bladder disease > Urology
Bladder problems > Incontinence

Blake (William)
    Blake Soc St James's
Blasting contractors
    Inst Explosives Engrs
Bleach
    Brit Assn Chemical Specialities
Bleeding disorders
    Haemophilia Soc
Blind & partially sighted
    Bates Assn Vision Educ
    Behçet's Syndrome Soc
    Brit Computer Assn Blind
    Brit Retinitis Pigmentosa Soc
    Community
    Confedn Transcribed Inf Services
    Deaf Blind UK
    Gld Church Braillists
    Guide Dogs for Blind Assn
    LOOK
    Macular Disease Soc
    Nat Assn Educ, Training... Blind... People
    Nat Fedn Blind
    Nat Library Blind
    Nystagmus Network
    Partially Sighted Soc
    R Nat Inst Blind
    Saint Dunstan's
    Scot Nat Fedn Welfare Blind
    Seeing Dogs Alliance
    Talking Newspaper Assn
    View
    Vision Homes Assn
Blinds > Windows: blinds & shutters
Blood > Haematology; Haemophilia
Blood pressure
    Blood Pressure Assn
Bloodstock > Horse(s) headings
Blues > Jazz & Blues
Blyton (Enid)
    Enid Blyton Soc
Boar (wild)
    Brit Wild Boar Assn
    > + Pigs
Board > Paper & paper products
Board: building > Building board & timber
Board: games > Wargaming; name of specific game
Board: sailing > Surfing, board & speed sailing
Boarding kennels
    Pet Care Trust
Boarding schools
    Assn Boarding School Survivors
    Boarding Schools Assn
    Girls' Schools Assn
    > + Independent & public schools
Boats & boating
    Assn Boat Safety Examiners
    Assn Scot Yacht Charterers
    Boat Jumble Assn
    Brit Air Boat Assn
    Brit Dragon Boat Racing Assn
    Brit FIB (Flying Inflatable Boat) Assn
    Brit Marine Fedn
    Brit Marine Fedn Scotland
    Cruising Assn
    Electric Boat Assn
    Marine Leisure Assn
    Nat Assn Boat Owners
    Nat Community Boats Assn
    Profl Boatmans Assn
    Thames Boating Trs Assn
    Vintage Wooden Boat Assn
    > + Sailing; Ship; Steam engines, boats & machinery; Yachts
Bob skeleton
    Brit Bob Skeleton Assn
Bobbins & bobbin-lace > Lace: handmade
Bobsleighing > Toboggan & luge racing/riding
Boccia
    English Boccia Assn
Body piercing
    Brit Body Piercing Assn
Bodyboarding
    Brit Bodyboarding Club
    > + Surfing, board & speed sailing
Bodybuilding
    Nat Amat Bodybuilders Assn
    > + Fitness

Bodyguards
          Profl Bodyguard Assn
Boilers & waterheaters
          Boiler & Radiator Mfrs Assn
          ICOM Energy Assn
          Manufacturers Domestic Unvented Systems
          > + Heating
Boilers & boilersetting
          Refractory Users Fedn
Bolts & nuts > Fasteners & turned parts
Bond collecting > Scripophily
Bonded warehouses
          Bonded Warehousekeepers' Assn
Bone
          Bone Res Soc
          Brittle Bone Soc
          Nat Ankylosing Spondylitis Soc
          Nat Assn Relief Paget's Disease
          Nat Osteoporosis Soc
          > + Orthopaedics
Bonsai
          Fedn Brit Bonsai Socs
          Japan Soc
Book: collecting
          Observers Pocket Series Collectors' Soc
          Penguin Collectors' Soc
          Private Libraries Assn
Book: match cover collecting > Matchbox labels
Bookbinding & print finishing
          Brit Printing Inds Fedn
          Inst Bookbinding & Allied Trs
          Soc Bookbinders
Bookkeeping
          Inst Certified Book-Keepers
          Inst Financial Accountants
          Payroll Alliance
          > + Accountancy; Computers; Data processing
Bookmaking
          Assn Brit Bookmakers
          Nat Assn Bookmakers Ltd

Bookplates
          Bookplate Soc

Books
          Booktrust
          Brit Printing Inds Fedn
          > + Libraries/librarians; Printing; Publishing
Books: secondhand
          Antiquarian Booksellers Assn
          Provincial Booksellers Fairs Assn
Bookselling
          Booksellers Assn
          Brit Educl Suppliers Assn
          Retail Book, Stationery. . . Employees Assn
Boomerangs
          Brit Boomerang Soc
Boots & shoes > Footwear headings
Boring > Drilling
Boroughs > Local government
Borrow (George Henry)
          George Borrow Soc
Botany
          Botanical Soc Brit Isles
          Botanical Soc Scotland
          Linnean Soc Lond
          Ray Soc
          Soc Botanical Artists
          Soc Experimental Biology
          Wild Flower Soc
          > + Horticulture; Nature conservation; Plants
Bothies > Mountain bothies
Botswana
          UK Botswana Soc
Bottle collecting
          Assn Brit Brewery Collectables
          Old Bottle Club
          Snuff Bottle Soc
Bottle feeding (babies)
          Baby Milk Action
Bottled water
          Brit Soft Drinks Assn
          Brit Water Cooler Assn
          > + Soft drinks;   Water: treatment & supply
Bottling
          Brewing, Food & Beverage Ind Suppliers Assn
          Brit Bottlers' Inst

Boughton (Rutland)
          Rutland Boughton Music Trust
Boules
          Brit Pétanque Fedn
Bouncy castles > Inflatable toys & structures
Boundary hedges > Hedges & hedge-laying
Bowel disease > Colitis/colostomy
Bowel (irritable)
          IBS Network
Bowling
          Brit Crown Green Bowling Assn
          Brit Isles Bowls Coun
          Brit Isles Indoor Bowls Coun
          Brit Tenpin Bowling Assn
          Brit Wheelchair Bowls Assn
          English Bowling Assn
          English Indoor Bowling Assn
          English Women's Bowling Assn
          English Women's Indoor Bowling Assn
          Ir Bowling Assn
          Ir Women's Bowling Assn
          Scot Bowling Assn
          Scot Indoor Bowling Assn
          Scot Women's Bowling Assn
          Scot Women's Indoor Bowling Assn
          Sports Mfrs & Retailers Tr Assn
          Tenpin Bowling Proprietors Assn
          Welsh Bowling Assn
          Welsh Indoor Bowls Assn
Bowlly (Al)
          Al Bowlly Circle
Bows (for archery) > Archery
Bows (for string instruments)
          Brit Violin Making Assn
          > + Archery
Boxes
          Brit Packaging Assn
          Metal Packaging Mfrs Assn
          > + Packaging
Boxing
          Amat Boxing Assn England
          Amat Boxing Scotland
          Ir Amat Boxing Assn
          Welsh Amat Boxing Assn
Boys clubs > Youth organisations
Bradburne (John)
          John Bradburne Memorial Soc
Bradshaw (Henry)
          Henry Bradshaw Soc
Braids
          Braid Soc
Braille
          Gld Church Braillists
          Nat Library Blind
          R Nat Inst Blind
Brain injury & research
          Brain Tumour UK
          > Children: handicapped; Head, neck & brain injury & disease
Brake linings
          Brit Friction Materials Coun
Branded products
          Anti Counterfeiting Gp
          Brit Brands Gp
          Walpole
Brass
          Cast Metals Fedn
          Copper Devt Assn
Brass & silver bands
          Brit Assn Symphonic Bands & Wind Ensembles
          Brit Fedn Brass Bands
          Brit Youth Band Assn
          Carnival Band Secretaries League
          Drum Corps UK
          Kmoch Eur Bands Soc
          Nat Assn Brass Band Conductors
          Nat School Band Assn
          Scot Brass Band Assn
          Traditional Youth Marching Bands Assn
          UK Fedn Jazz Bands
          Welsh Amat Music Fedn
          > + individual instrument
Brasses & church monuments
          Church Monuments Soc
          Monumental Brass Soc
Brassicas
          Brassica Growers Assn

Scot Soc Crop Res
> + Vegetables: growing
Brazil
Anglo-Brazilian Soc
Brazilian Cham Comm GB
Brit Cham Comm & Ind Brazil
Hispanic & Luso-Brazilian Coun
Brazing & soldering
Welding Inst
Breakfast cereals
Assn Cereal Food Mfrs
Breast feeding
Assn Breastfeeding Mothers
Breast implants
Breast Implant Inf Soc
Breed societies > type of animal bred
Brewery collectables
Assn Brit Brewery Collectables
Brewing
Brewery Hist Soc
Brewing, Food & Beverage Ind Suppliers Assn
Brit Beer & Pub Assn
Brit Gld Beer Writers
Campaign Real Ale
Craft Brewing Assn
Home Beer & Wine Mfrs Assn
Indep Family Brewers
Inst Brewing & Distilling
Ir Brewers Assn
Labologists Soc
Maltsters Assn
Nat Assn Wine & Beer Makers
Scot Beer & Pub Assn
Soc Indep Brewers
Soc Presvn Beers Wood
Brian (William Havergal)
Havergal Brian Soc
Bribery > Corruption
Bricklayers
Gld Bricklayers
Bricks
Assn Brickwork Contrs
Better Brickwork Alliance
Brick Devt Assn
Brit Archaeol Assn
Brit Brick Soc
Brit Ceramic Confedn
Brit Ceramic Res
Brit Refractories & Indl Ceramics
Nat Brickmakers Fedn
> + Clay & clay products; Refractories
Brides & bridalwear > Wedding headings
Bridge (card game)
English Bridge U
Ir Bridge Union
Welsh Bridge U
Bridges > Civil engineering; Road: construction
Bridges: concrete
Concrete Bridge Devt Gp
Bridleways
Nat Fedn Bridleway Assns
> + Footpaths & rights of way
Bright's disease
Doctor Richard Bright Soc
British independence
Anti Common Market League
Brit Housewives League
Campaign Indep Britain
British Telecom staff
Communication Workers U
Broadcasting
Assn Community TV Operators
Assn Service Providers
Assn UK Media Librarians
Deaf Broadcasting Coun
IBI
Inst Broadcast Sound
Nat U Journalists
Radio Academy
Voice Listener & Viewer
> + Radio; Television
Brokers > specific subject
Brontë family
Brontë Soc
Bronze
Cast Metals Fedn
Copper Devt Assn

Brooke (Rupert)
Friends Dymock Poets
Browning (Robert & Elizabeth Barrett)
Browning Soc
Brushes
Brit Brush Mfrs Assn
Coir Assn
Bryology
Brit Bryological Soc

Buchan (John) Lord Tweedsmuir
John Buchan Soc
Buddhism
Brit Buddhist Assn
Brit Zen Aiki Assn
Buddhist Soc
Pali Text Soc
Budgerigars
Budgerigar Soc
Budo > Martial arts
Builders' materials & supplies > Building materials & supplies
Builders & plumbers merchants
Builders Mchts Fedn
Inst Builders Mchts
Building
Assn Bldg Engrs
Assn Envt Conscious Bldg
Brit Masonry Soc
BSRIA
Building Cost Infm Service
Buildings Energy Efficiency Fedn
Chart Inst Architectural Technologists
Chart Inst Bldg
Chart Instn Bldg Services Engrs
Community Self Build Scotland
Confedn Construction Specialists
Construction Confedn
Construction Emplrs Fedn
District Surveyors Assn Ltd
Fac Bldg
Fedn Bldg Specialist Contrs
Fedn Master Builders
Gld Builders & Contrs
Home Builders Fedn
Homes for Scotland
Inst Clerks Works
Inst Maintenance & Bldg Mgt
London Dist Surveyors Assn
Materials Components Developing & Testing Assn
Nat Specialist Contrs Coun
Property Consultants Soc
Scot Bldg
Scot Bldg Contrs Assn
Scot Master Wrights & Builders Assn
> + Construction industries
Building board & timber
N W Area Bd Assn
> + Insulation
Building materials & supplies
Assn Bldg Component Mfrs
Brit Hardware Fedn
Brit Precast Concrete Fedn
Building Materials Fedn [IRL]
Construction Products Assn
Coun Aluminium Bldg
Ir Hardware & Bldg Materials Assn
Straw Bale Bldg Assn
Wall Tie Installers Fedn
> + specific items
Building societies
Building Socs Assn
Building Socs Mems Assn
Ir Mortgage Coun
Save our Bldg Socs
Building: survey & inspection > Surveying
Buildings: cleaning & maintenance
Cleaning & Support Services Assn
Buildings: conservation
Folly Fellowship
Inst Historic Bldg Consvn
Nat Register Property Presvn Specialists
Scot Stone Liaison Gp
Stone Fedn
UK Assn Presvn Trusts
Upkeep
Vernacular Architecture Gp

Victorian Soc
> + Historic buildings
Buildings: earth sheltered
Brit Earth Sheltering Assn
Buildings: historic & listed > Historic buildings
Buildings: insulation > Insulation
Buildings: literary connections > Historic buildings
Buildings: open to the public > Historic buildings
Bulbs
Brit Flower Bulbs Assn
> + Flowers, flower arrangement & floristry
Bulgaria
Brit Bulgarian Friendship Soc
Bulimia nervosa > Eating disorders
Bulk solids > Materials: management/handling
Bulk storage
Solids Handling & Processing Assn
Tank Storage Assn
Bullion dealing
Brit Jewellers Assn
London Bullion Mkt Assn
Bungee jumping
Brit Elastic Rope Sports Assn
UK Bungee Club
Bunting > Flags, banners & bunting
Burghs > Local government
Burglary
Assn Burglary Insurance Surveyors [>AIS011 (04)
Assn Insurance Surveyors
> + Security
Burial & cremation
Assn Burial Authorities
Assn Natural Burial Grounds
Assn Private Crematoria & Cemeteries
Brit Inst Embalmers
Brit Inst Funeral Directors
Cremation Soc
Fedn Brit Cremation Authorities
Funeral Furnishing Mfrs Assn
Inst Cemetery & Crematorium Mgt
Nat Assn Funeral Directors
Nat Assn Pre-Paid Funeral Plans
Soc Allied & Indep Funeral Directors
> + Cemeteries & churchyards
Burney (Fanny)
Burney Soc
Burns
Brit Burn Assn
Burns (Robert)
Robert Burns World Fedn
Bursars
Indep Schools Bursars Assn
Nat Bursars Assn
> + Independent & public schools
Bus & coach operators
Assn Local Bus Co Mgrs
Coach Operators Fedn
Coach Tourism Coun
Confedn Passenger Transport
Gld Brit Coach Operators
Routemaster Operators & Owners Assn
> + Passenger transport
Business
Alliance Business Consultants
Alliance Indep Retailers
Brit Business Angels Assn
Business Archives Coun
Business Continuity Inst
Business Mgt Assn
Business Services Assn
Confedn Trs & Comm
EIS Assn
Executives Assn
Fedn Crafts & Comm
Fedn Small Businesses
Forum Private Business
Indep Business League
Inst Business Admin
Inst Business Advisers
Inst Business Analysts & Consultants [IRL]
Inst Business Ethics
Inst Directors
Inst Family Business (UK)
Inst Indep Business
Inst Small Business & Entrepreneurship
Ir Small & Medium Enterprises Assn
Nat Fedn Enterprise Agencies

Quality Gld
Quoted Companies Alliance
R Soc . . . Arts
Small Firms Assn [IRL]
Soc Business Practitioners
UK Excellence Fedn
UK Trs Confedn
> + Employers
Business: administration > Management
Business: advisers > Management
Business: aircraft
Brit Business & Gen Aviation Assn
> + Aviation
Business: archives > Archives
Business: awards
Brit Business Awards Assn
Business: centres
Business Centre Assn
Business: communications systems > Radio: mobile;   Telecommunications
Business: counselling > Management
Business: economists
Soc Business Economists
Business: education
Assn Business Mgrs & Administrators
Assn Business Schools
Economics & Business Educ Assn
> + Commerce
Business: equipment > Office equipment & systems
Business: graduates > Commerce
Business: law > Law: industrial
Business: property agents
Brit Coun Offices
Indl Agents Soc
Business: sponsorship
Arts & Business
Scot Business Community
Business: systems > Office equipment & systems
Business: travel > Travel & tourism
Business: valuation
Soc Share & Business Valuers
Butchers
Gld Q Butchers
Nat Fedn Meat & Food Traders
> + Meat
Butlers
Gld Intl Butler Administrators. . .
Gld Intl Profl Toastmasters
Butter > Dairying
Buttercups (ranunculaceae)
Ranunculaceae Soc
Butterflies & moths
Butterfly Consvn
> + Entomology
Buttonhook
Buttonhook Soc
Buttons
Assn Button Merchants
Brit Button Soc
Buying > Purchasing & supply
Byron (George Gordon, Lord)
Byron Soc
Byzantium
Soc Promotion Byzantine Studies

C

Cable & satellite communications
Confedn Aerial Inds
Nat Jt Utilities Gp
Satellite & Cable Broadcasters' Gp
Soc Cable Telecommunication Engrs
Soc Public Inf Networks
Telecommunications Ind Assn
> + Telecommunications
Cables > Electric: cable & conduit
Cabs > Taxis & minicabs
Cacti & succulents
Brit Cactus & Succulent Soc
Cadets
Army Cadet Force Assn
Combined Cadet Force Assn
Cage birds > Birds; specific species

 © CBD Research Ltd · Beckenham · BR3 5JS · Tel 020 8650 7745 · Fax 020 8650 0768 · E-mail cbd@cbdresearch.com · www.cbdresearch.com

Cakes
    Biscuit, Cake, Chocolate. . . Assn
    Food Processors' Assn
Calcium carbonates
    Brit Calcium Carbonates Fedn
    > + Lime & limestone
Caldecott (Randolph)
    Randolph Caldecott Soc
Calibration > Measurement
Call centres
    Call Centre Mgt Assn
    Customer Contact Assn
Calligraphy > Handwriting
Camelids
    Brit Alpaca Soc
    Brit Camelids Assn
    Brit Llama Soc
    Brit Veterinary Camelid Soc
Camera technicians & crews
    Brit Soc Cinematographers
    Gld Brit Camera Technicians
    Gld TV Cameramen
    > + Film
Cameras (use of) > Photograph headings
Companology > Bellringing
Camping
    Backpackers Club
    Brit Holiday & Home Parks Assn
    Camping & Caravanning Club
    Order Woodcraft Chivalry
    Phoenix Camping Club
Camping equipment
    Go Outdoors
    Performance Textiles Assn
Canada
    Brit Assn Canadian Studies
    Brit Canadian Cham Tr & Comm
    Brit N Amer Res Assn
    Canada-UK Cham Comm
Canals > Inland waterways
Cancer
    Assn Intl Cancer Res
    Brain Tumour UK
    Brit Assn Cancer Res
    Brit Photodermatology Gp
    Ir Cancer Soc
    Nat Assn Relief Paget's Disease
    Nat Cancer Alliance
    Neuroblastoma Soc
    New Approaches to Cancer
    Oesophageal Patients Assn
    Ovacome
    Prostate Cancer Support Assn
    UK Assn Cancer Registries
    > + Oncology
Candida
    Nat Candida Soc
Candles
    Brit Candlemakers Fedn
Canes (walking)
    Brit Stickmakers Gld
Cannabis
    Legalise Cannabis Campaign
Canned foods > Cans & canning
Canoes & canoeing
    Assn Canoe Trades
    Backpackers Club
    Brit Canoe U
    Canoe Assn NI
    Historic Canoe & Kayak Assn
    Scot Canoe Assn
Cans & canning
    Brit Bottlers' Inst
    Brit Coatings Fedn
    Can Makers
    Provision Tr Fedn
    > + Food: packaging; specific commodity canned
Canvas & canvas goods
    Performance Textiles Assn
Capacitors
    BEAMA
Car > entries below & Motor headings
Car hire > Motor vehicle hire; Taxis & minicabs
Car parks
    Car Park Appreciation Soc
    > + Parking
Car radios/audio systems > Radio: mobile

Car security
    Auto Locksmiths Assn
Caravans & caravanning
    Assn Caravan & Camping Exempted Orgs
    Brit Holiday & Home Parks Assn
    Camping & Caravanning Club
    Caravan Club
    Historic Caravan Club
    Motor Caravanners Club
    Nat Caravan Coun
    Phoenix Camping Club
    > + Motor vehicles: historic
Carbon monoxide
    Brit Polarological Res Soc
    Carbon Monoxide & Gas Safety Soc
    Coun Gas Detection & Envtl Monitoring
Card collecting (cigarette & trade)
    Cartophilic Soc
Cardiology
    Arrhythmia Alliance
    Assn Cardiothoracic Anaesthetists
    Brit Cardiovascular Soc
    Brit Polarological Res Soc
    Cardiomyopathy Assn
    Children's Heart Assn
    Coronary Artery Disease Res Assn
    Heart Line Assn
    Heart UK
    Marfan Assn UK
    Soc Cardiological Science & Technology
    Soc Cardiothoracic Surgery
    Stroke Assn
Cardiology: patients
    Brit Cardiac Patients Assn
    Implanted Defibrillator Assn Scotland
Care & carers
    Assn Indep Care Advisers
    Carers Assn [IRL]
    Carers UK
    Ceretas
    Disablement Income Gp Scotland
    Nat Care Assn
    Relatives & Residents Assn
    Shared Care Network
    UK Homecare Assn
    Youth Access
    > + Geriatrics & ageing; Old peoples organisations;
    Residential: homes
Care homes > Residential: homes
Care labelling
    Home Laundering Consultative Coun
Careers
    Assn Careers Educ & Guidance
    Assn Graduate Careers Advy Services
    Careers Writers' Assn
    Inst Career Guidance
Carers
    Crossroads
    > Care & carers
Cargo: handling > Freight transport; Transport
Cargo: health inspection
    Assn Port Health Authorities
Caribbean > West Indies & the Caribbean
Carillons
    Brit Carillon Soc
    > + Bellringing
Carlyle (Thomas & Jane)
    Carlyle Soc
Carnations
    Brit Nat Carnation Soc
    N England Rose, Carnation. . . Horticl Soc
Carnivals & carnival goods
    Nat Carnival Gld
Carnivorous plants
    Carnivorous Plant Soc
Carp fishing
    Carp Soc
Carpentry & joinery > Woodworking
Carpets
    Brit Textile Technology Gp
    Carpet Foundation
    Contract Flooring Assn
    Fibre Bonded Carpet Mfrs' Assn
    Nat Carpet Cleaners Assn
    Nat Inst Carpet & Floorlayers
    > + Floors: floorcoverings

Carroll (Lewis)
> Daresbury Lewis Carroll Soc
> Lewis Carroll Soc

Carrots

Cars > Car; Motor

Cartography
> Brit Cartographic Soc
> Charles Close Soc
> R Inst Navigation

Cartonboard > Paper & paper products

Cartons
> Liquid Food Carton Mfrs' Assn
> > + Packaging; Paper & paper products

Cartoons
> Cartoonists' Club

Cartophily > Card collecting (cigarette & trade)

Cartridges (laser)
> UK Cartridge Remanufacturers Assn

Cases > Optical industry; Packaging; Travel goods & accessories

Cash & carry
> Fedn Whls Distbrs

Cash: security handling
> Brit Security Ind Assn

Cashew nuts
> Combined Edible Nut Tr Assn

Cashmere
> Brit Goat Soc
> Scot Cashmere Producers Assn

Casings > Sausage & food casings

Casinos
> Brit Casino Assn
> Casino Operators' Assn

Cassettes > Sound recording & reproduction; Video

Cast stone
> UK Cast Stone Assn
> > + Stone

Casting (metal) > Metal: casting

Castles > Fortresses & forts; Historic buildings; Inflatable toys & structures

Casualty simulation
> Casualties Union

Catalonia & Catalan language
> Anglo Catalan Soc

Cataracts (eyes)
> UK & I Soc Cataract & Refractive Surgeons

Catering
> Brit Hospitality Assn
> Confedn Tourism, Hotel & Catering Mgt
> Eur Catering Assn (GB)
> Foodservice Consultants Soc Intl (UK)
> Hospital Caterers Assn
> Hotel & Catering Intl Mgt Assn
> Ir Hospitality Inst
> Local Authority Caterers' Assn
> Nat Assn Catering Butchers
> Nat Assn Master Bakers
> NI Amusement Caterer's Tr Assn
> PACE: Profl Assn Catering Educ

Catering: equipment
> Catering Eqpt Distbrs Assn GB
> Catering Eqpt Supplier's Assn
> Nat Assn Range Mfrs

Catering: outdoor
> Nat Outdoor Events Assn
> Nationwide Caterers Assn

Cathedral & church shops
> Cathedral & Church Shops Assn

Cathedral & church music
> Assn Latin Liturgy
> Cathedral Organists Assn
> Fac Church Music
> Friends Cathedral Music
> Gld Church Musicians
> Hymn Soc
> R School Church Music
> Ulster Soc Organists & Choirmasters
> > + Organs, organists & organ music

Cathodic protection
> Corrosion Prevention Assn

Catholic > Roman Catholic

Cats
> Assn Dogs & Cats Homes
> Brit Big Cat Soc
> Cats Protection
> Governing Coun Cat Fancy

Catteries
> Pet Care Trust

Cattle breed societies
> Aberdeen-Angus Cattle Soc
> Aubrac Cattle Soc
> Ayrshire Cattle Soc
> Beef Shorthorn Cattle Soc
> Belted Galloway Cattle Soc
> Black Simmental Soc
> Blue Albion Cattle Soc
> Brit Bazadais Cattle Soc
> Brit Belgian Blue Cattle Soc
> Brit Blonde Soc
> Brit Charolais Cattle Soc
> Brit Gelbvieh Cattle Soc
> Brit Kerry Cattle Soc
> Brit Limousin Cattle Soc
> Brit Parthenais Cattle Soc
> Brit Piemontese Cattle Soc
> Brit Simmental Cattle Soc
> Brit White Cattle Soc
> Brown Swiss Cattle Soc
> Chillingham Wild Cattle Assn
> Devon Cattle Breeders' Soc
> Dexter Cattle Soc
> English Guernsey Cattle Soc
> Galloway Cattle Soc
> Gloucester Cattle Soc
> Gwartheg Hynafol Cymru
> Hereford Cattle Soc
> Highland Cattle Soc
> Holstein UK
> Ir Hereford Breed Soc
> Ir Moiled Cattle Soc
> Jersey Cattle Soc
> Lincoln Red Cattle Soc
> Longhorn Cattle Soc
> Luing Cattle Soc
> Maine-Anjou Cattle Soc
> Marchigiana Cattle Soc
> Meuse Rhine Issel Cattle Soc
> Murray Grey Beef Cattle Soc
> Poll Holstein Breeders Club
> Red Poll Cattle Soc
> S Devon Herd Book Soc
> Salers Cattle Soc
> Scot Hereford Breeders Assn
> Shetland Cattle Herd Book Soc
> Shorthorn Soc
> Sussex Cattle Soc
> Welsh Black Cattle Soc
> White Park Cattle Soc
> Whitebred Shorthorn Assn

Cattle food > Animal feed

Cattle & livestock
> Assn Show & Agricl Orgs
> Brit Cattle Breeders' Club
> Brit Soc Animal Science
> ICSA [IRL]
> Livestock Auctioneers Assn
> Livestock Traders Assn
> Nat Assn Agricl Contrs
> Nat Beef Assn
> Nat Cattle Assn - Dairy
> New Forest Pony . . . & Cattle Soc
> > + specific animals

Cattle markets > Markets: street & cattle

Cattle troughs
> Metropolitan Drinking Fountain &. . . Assn

Caves & caving
> Assn Brit & Ir Showcaves
> Brit Cave Res Assn
> Brit Cave Rescue Coun
> Brit Caving Assn

Cavies (guinea pigs)
> Nat Cavy Club

Cavity insulation > Insulation

Cecidology
> Brit Plant Gall Soc

Ceilings
> Assn Interior Specialists
> Chilled Ceilings Assn
> Fedn Plastering & Drywall Contrs

Celebrity assistants
> UK Assn Celebrity Assistants

Celery
> Quality Brit Celery Assn
> > + Vegetables: growing

© CBD Research Ltd · Beckenham · BR3 5JS · Tel 020 8650 7745 · Fax 020 8650 0768 · E-mail cbd@cbdresearch.com · www.cbdresearch.com

Cell biology
> Brit Soc Cell Biology
> Brit Soc Clinical Cytology
> Brit Soc Immunology
> Comment Reproductive Ethics
> R Microscopical Soc
> Soc Gen Microbiology

Cement & cement products
> Brit Cement Assn
> Cement Admixtures Assn
> Fibre Cement Mfrs Assn
> Instn Civil Engrs
> + Concrete & concrete products

Cemeteries & churchyards
> Assn Burial Authorities
> Assn Private Pet Cemeteries & Crematoria
> Brit Assn Cemeteries S Asia
> Metropolitan Public Gardens Assn
> Nat Fedn Cemetery Friends
> + Burial & cremation

Censorship
> Campaign Censorship
> mediawatch-uk
> Nat Secular Soc

Census > Population: registration
Central heating > Heating
Ceramic sanitaryware > Sanitaryware
Ceramics
> Brit Ceramic Confedn
> Brit Ceramic Gift & Tableware Mfrs' Assn
> Brit Ceramic Res
> Brit Refractories & Indl Ceramics
> Clarice Cliff Collectors Club
> Craft Potters Assn
> Derby Porcelain Intl Soc
> Oriental Ceramic Soc
> R Birmingham Soc Artists
> Scot Potters' Assn
> Soc Women Artists
> Tiles & Architectural Ceramics Soc
> Unity
> + Clay & clay products; Pottery; Refractories; specific products

Ceramics & pottery collecting > specific type collected
Cereals
> Assn Cereal Food Mfrs
> Campden & Chorleywood Food Res Assn
> Scot Soc Crop Res
> + Grain

Cerebral palsy
> Scope [England & Wales]
> Soc Stars

Certification bodies
> Assn Brit Certification Bodies
> + Quality assurance & control

Chain-link fencing
> Wire Products Assn
> + Fencing (enclosure)

Chains & chain testing
> Lifting Eqpt Engrs Assn
> + Lifting & loading equipment

Chairmanship (meetings)
> Assn Speakers Clubs

Chairs
> Basketmaker's Assn
> Chair Frame Mfrs Assn
> + Furniture

Chalet sites > Caravans & caravanning
Chalk > Lime & limestone
Chamber music > Music
Chambers of commerce: general
> Brit Chams Comm
> Chambers Ireland
> Intl Cham Comm UK
> Lanarkshire Cham Comm
> N E Cham Comm, Tr & Ind
> NI Cham Comm & Ind
> Scot Chams Comm

Chambers of commerce: local
> Aberdeen & Grampian Cham Comm
> Altrincham & Sale Cham Comm
> Ayrshire Cham Comm & Ind
> Ballymena Borough Cham Comm & Ind
> Banbury & District Cham Comm
> Barking & Dagenham Cham Comm
> Barnsley Cham Comm & Ind
> Bath Cham Comm
> Bedfordshire > (The) Chamber [Luton]

Bexley > Greenwich, Bexley & Lewisham Cham Comm
Birmingham Cham Comm & Ind
Black Country Cham
Boston Cham Comm & Ind
Bournemouth Cham Tr & Comm
Bradford Cham Comm & Ind
Bristol Cham Comm & Ind
Buckinghamshire > Milton Keynes & N Bucks Cham Comm
Burton & Dist Cham Comm Ind
Bury St Edmunds Cham Comm & Ind
Cairngorms Cham Comm
Caithness & Sutherland Cham Comm
Cambridgeshire Chams Comm
Cardiff Cham Comm, Tr & Ind
Chamber Comm & Mfrs Greenock
Chamber Comm N W
Chamber (The) [Luton]
Channel Cham Comm
Chelmsford > Essex Chams Comm
Cheshire > S Cheshire Cham Comm & Ind
Chester, Ellesmere Port & N Wales Cham Comm
Chichester Cham Comm & Ind
Cork Cham Comm [IRL]
Cornwall Cham Comm & Ind
Coventry & Warwickshire Cham Comm
Croydon Cham Comm & Ind
Cumbria Cham Comm
Dagenham > Barking & Dagenham Cham Comm
Derbyshire Cham & Business Link
Devon > N Devon Cham Comm & Ind
Devon > S Devon Cham Tr & Comm
Doncaster Cham Comm
Dorset Cham Comm & Ind
Drogheda Cham Comm [IRL]
Dublin Cham Comm [IRL]
Dumfries & Galloway Cham Comm
Dundalk Cham Comm [IRL]
Dundee & Tayside Cham Comm & Ind
E Hampshire Cham Comm & Ind
E Lancs Cham Comm
Eastbourne & District Cham Comm
Edinburgh Cham Comm
Ellesmere Port > Chester, Ellesmere Port & N Wales Cham Comm
Essex Chams Comm
Exeter Cham Comm
Exmouth Cham Tr & Comm
Fareham > Southampton & Fareham Cham Comm...
Fife Cham Comm & Ind
Galloway > Dumfries & Galloway Cham Comm
Galway Cham Comm [IRL]
Glasgow Cham Comm
Gloucestershire Cham Comm & Ind
Grampian > Aberdeen & Grampian Cham Comm
Grantham Cham Comm
Greater Manchester Cham Comm
Greenock > Cham Comm & Mfrs Greenock
Greenwich, Bexley & Lewisham Cham Comm
Guernsey Cham Comm
Gwent > Newport & Gwent Cham Comm & Ind
Hampshire > E Hants Cham Comm & Ind
Hampshire > N Hampshire Cham Comm
Hampshire > Portsmouth & SE Hampshire Cham Comm...
Harrow > NW Lond Cham Comm
Hastings > Ten Sixty Six Enterprise
Herefordshire & Worcestershire Cham Comm
Hertfordshire Cham Comm & Ind
Hertfordshire > Watford & W Herts Cham Comm & Ind
Hitchin Cham Comm & Ind
Hull & Humber Cham Comm...
Inverness Cham Comm
Iona > Mull & Iona Cham Comm
Isle of Man Cham Comm
Isle of Wight Cham Commerce, Tourism & Ind
Islington Cham Comm & Tr
Jersey Cham Comm & Ind Inc
Kent Invicta Cham Comm
Kent > W Kent Cham Comm & Ind
Kingston Cham Comm
Knowsley Cham Ind & Comm
Lancashire > E Lancs Cham Comm
Lancashire > N & Wstn Lancashire Cham Comm & Ind
Lancaster Dist Cham Comm
Leeds Cham Comm & Ind
Leicestershire Cham Comm
Leith Cham Comm
Lewisham > Greenwich, Bexley & Lewisham Cham Comm
Limerick Cham Comm [IRL]

Lincolnshire Cham Comm & Ind
Lisburn Cham Comm
Liverpool Cham Comm & Ind
London Cham Comm & Ind
London > N W Lond Cham Comm
Londonderry Cham Comm
Luton > (The) Chamber
Macclesfield Cham Comm
Maidenhead & Dist Cham Comm
Mansfield & Dist Cham Tr & Comm
Merton Cham Comm
Mid Yorkshire Cham Comm & Ind
Milton Keynes & N Bucks Cham Comm
Mull & Iona Cham Comm
N Devon Cham Comm & Ind
N Hampshire Cham Comm & Ind
N Kent Cham Comm
N London Cham Comm
N Staffs Cham Comm & Ind
N W Lond Cham Comm
N & Wstn Lancs Cham Comm & Ind
Newcastle > N E Cham Comm, Tr & Ind
Newport & Gwent Cham Comm, Enterprise & Ind
Norfolk Cham Comm & Ind
Northamptonshire Cham Comm...
Norwich > Norfolk & Waveney Cham Comm
Nottinghamshire Cham Comm & Ind
Orkney Cham Comm
Pembrokeshire Cham Comm
Perthshire Cham Comm
Peterborough > Cambridgeshire Chams Comm
Plymouth Cham Comm & Ind
Portsmouth & S E Hampshire Cham Comm...
Redbridge Cham Comm & Tr
Renfrewshire Cham Comm
Richmond Cham Comm
Rotherham Cham Comm
S Cheshire Cham Comm & Ind
S Devon Cham Tr & Comm
S Gloucestershire Cham Comm
Saint Albans District Cham Comm
Saint Helens Cham
Saint Leonards > Ten Sixty Six Enterprise
Sale > Altrincham & Sale Cham Comm
Salisbury & Dist Cham Comm & Ind
Sefton Cham Comm & Ind
Sevenoaks & District Cham Comm
Sheffield Cham Comm & Ind
Shropshire Chamber of Commerce & Enterprise
Solihull Cham Comm & Ind
Southampton & Fareham Cham Comm & Ind
Southport > Sefton Cham Comm & Ind
Southwark Cham Comm
Staffordshire > N Staffordshire Cham Comm & Ind
Staffordshire > Southern Staffordshire Cham Comm & Ind
Sthn Staffordshire Cham Comm & Ind
Suffolk Cham Comm & Ind
Surrey Chams Comm
Sussex Cham Comm, Training & Enterprise
Sutton Cham
Swale > N Kent Cham Comm
Swansea > W Wales Cham Comm
Swindon Cham Comm & Ind
Taunton Cham Comm
Tayside > Dundee & Tayside Cham Comm & Ind
Ten Sixty Six (1066) Enterprise
Thames Valley Cham Comm & Ind
Thanet & E Kent Cham
Tralee Cham Comm [IRL]
W Kent Cham Comm & Ind
W Wales Cham Comm
Wales > Chester, Ellesmere Port & N Wales Cham Comm
Warrington Cham Comm & Ind
Warwickshire > Coventry & Warwickshire Cham Comm & Ind
Waterford Cham Comm [IRL]
Watford & W Herts Cham Comm & Ind
Wessex Assn Chams Comm
Westcliff-on-Sea > Essex Chams Comm
Western Isles Cham Comm
Westminster > London Cham Comm & Ind
Wexford Cham Comm [IRL]
Wicklow & District Cham Comm [IRL]
Wirral Cham Comm & Ind
Worcester > Herefordshire & Worcestershire Cham Comm...
Worthing Cham Comm & Ind
York & N Yorkshire Cham Comm
Yorkshire > Mid Yorkshire Cham Comm & Ind

Chambers of commerce: overseas trade
Africa > Brit Chams Business Sthn Africa
Arab Brit Cham Comm
Argentine > Brit Argentine Cham Comm
Argentine > Cámara Comercio Argentino Britanica
Australian Business
Austro-Brit Cham
Belgium > Brit Cham Comm Belgium
Brazil > Brit Cham Comm Brazil
Brazilian Cham Comm GB
Brit Amer Business Coun
Brit Amer Business Inc
Brit Argentine Cham Comm
Brit Bulgarian Cham Comm
Brit Canadian Cham Tr & Comm
Brit Cham Business Sthn Africa
Brit Cham Comm Belgium
Brit Cham Comm China - Beijing
Brit Cham Comm Czech Republic
Brit Cham Comm Germany
Brit Cham Comm Hong Kong
Brit Cham Comm Hungary
Brit Cham Comm & Ind Brazil
Brit Cham Comm Italy
Brit Cham Comm Japan
Brit Cham Comm Korea
Brit Cham Comm Latvia
Brit Cham Comm Luxembourg
Brit Cham Comm Morocco
Brit Cham Comm Shanghai
Brit Cham Comm Singapore
Brit Cham Comm Slovak Republic
Brit Cham Comm Spain
Brit Cham Comm Taipei
Brit Cham Comm Thailand
Brit Cham Comm Turkey
Brit Chilean Cham Comm
Brit & Colombian Cham Comm [Lond]
Brit Hellenic Cham Comm
Brit-Israel Cham Comm
Brit New Zealand Tr Coun
Brit-Peruvian Cham Comm
Brit-Polish Cham Comm
Brit-Polish Cham Comm [London]
Brit-Portuguese Cham Comm
Brit Swedish Cham Comm Sweden
Brit-Swiss Cham Comm [Lond]
Brit-Swiss Cham Comm [Switzerland]
Britain-Nepal Cham Comm
Britain Nigeria Business Coun
Bulgaria > Brit Bulgarian Cham Comm
Cámara Chileno-Britanica Comercio
Cámara Comercio Argentino Britanica
Cámara Comercio Británica [Mexico]
Cámara Comercio Colombo-Británica
Cámara Comercio Uruguayo-Británica
Cámara Venezolana Británica Comercio
Canada > Brit Canadian Cham Tr & Comm
Canada-UK Cham Comm
Chambre Comm Française GB
Chile > Cámara Chileno-Britanica Comercio
Chile > Cámara Chileno-Britanica Comercio
China > Brit Cham Comm China - Beijing
China > Brit Cham Comm Shangai
Colombia > Brit & Colombian Cham Comm
Colombia > Cámara Comercio Colombo Británica
Czech Republic > Brit Cham Comm Czech Republic
Danish-UK Cham Comm
Egyptian Brit Cham Comm
Finnish-British Cham Comm
France > Chambre Comm Française GB
Franco-Brit Cham Comm & Ind
German-Brit Cham Ind & Comm
Germany > Brit Cham Comm Germany
Greece > Brit Hellenic Cham Comm
Hong Kong > Brit Cham Comm Hong Kong
Hungary > Brit Cham Comm Hungary
Israel > Brit-Israel Cham Comm
Italian Cham Comm Ind UK
Italy > Brit Cham Comm Italy
Japan > Brit Cham Comm in Japan
Japanese Cham Comm & Ind UK
Korea > Brit Cham Comm Korea
Latvia > Brit Cham Comm Latvia
Luxembourg > Belgian-Luxembourg Cham Comm in GB
Luxembourg > Brit Cham Comm Luxembourg
Mexico > Cámara Comercio Británica AC [Mexico]

Morocco > Brit Cham Comm Morocco
Nepal > Britain-Nepal Cham Comm
Netherlands-Brit Cham Comm
New Zealand > Australian Business
New Zealand > Brit New Zealand Tr Coun
Nigeria > Britain-Nigeria Assn
Nigeria > Britain-Nigeria Business Coun
Norwegian-Brit Cham Comm
Poland > Brit-Polish Cham Comm
Portugal > Brit-Portuguese Cham Comm
Portuguese Cham
Russia > Russo-Brit Cham Comm
Russo-Brit Cham Comm
S Africa > Brit Cham Business Sthn Africa
Singapore > Brit Cham Comm Singapore
Slovak Republic > Brit Cham Comm Slovak Republic
Spain > Brit Cham Comm Spain
Spanish Cham Comm GB
Sweden > Brit-Swedish Cham Comm Sweden
Swedish Cham Comm UK
Switzerland > Brit-Swiss Cham Comm [Lond]
Switzerland > Brit Swiss Cham Comm [Switzerland]
Taiwan > Brit Cham Comm Taipei
Thailand > Brit Cham Comm Thailand
Turkey > Brit Cham Comm Turkey
Turkish-Brit Cham Comm & Ind
Uruguay > Cámara de Comercio Uruguayo-Británica
Venezuela > Cámara Venezolana-Británica Comercio

Champagne
    Champagne Agent's Assn
    > + Wines & spirits: trade
Chandlers > Ships: stores & supplies
Channel Islands > individual island
Channel swimming (& crossing)
    Channel Crossing Assn
    Channel Swimming Assn
Channels (concrete) > Culverts & channels
Chapels > Church headings
Charcoal
    Forestry Contracting Assn
Charcot-Marie-Tooth disease
    CMT UK
Charcuterie
    Charcuterie Gld
Charities
    Assn Charitable Foundations
    Assn Charities
    Assn Charity Indep Examiners
    Assn Charity Officers
    Assn Charity Shops
    Assn Gastroenterological Res Charities
    Assn Med Res Charities
    Charities Property Assn
    Charities' Tax Reform Gp
    Charity Christmas Card Coun
    Charity Finance Directors' Gp
    Charity Law Assn
    Inst Fundraising
    Public Fundraising Regulatory Assn
Charities: guidance & lists
    Family Welfare Assn
    > + Introduction paragraph 6
Charles I King of England
    R Martyr Church U
    Sealed Knot
    Soc King Charles Martyr
Charts (nautical)
    Chart & Nautical Instrument Tr Assn
Charter operators > Travel & tourism
Charter trustee towns
    Assn Charter Trustee Towns &... Couns
Chauffeurs
    Brit Chauffeurs Gld
    London Private Hire Car Assn
Cheerleading
    Brit Cheerleading Assn
Cheese
    Brit Goat Soc
    Brit Sheep Dairying Assn
    Gld Fine Food Retailers
    Provision Tr Fedn
    Specialist Cheesemakers' Assn
    Stilton Cheese Makers Assn
    UK Cheese Gld
Chefs
    Brit Culinary Fedn
    Fedn Chefs Scotland

    Master Chefs GB
    Welsh Culinary Assn
    > + Catering
Chelonia
    Brit Chelonia Gp
    Nat Tortoise Club
    Tortoise Trust
    > + Herpetology
Chemical allergy > Allergy
Chemical engineering
    Brit Chemical Engg Contrs Assn
    Instn Chemical Engrs
    Soc Chemical Ind
Chemical hazards
    Brit Occupational Hygiene Soc
    Chemical Hazards Communication Soc
Chemical industry & trade
    Brit Chemical Distbrs... Assn
    BTC Testing Advisory Gp
    Chemical & Indl Consultants' Assn
    Chemical Inds Assn
    Ir Chemical Marketers Assn
    PharmaChemical Ireland
    Specialised Organic Chemicals Sector Assn
Chemical specialities
    Brit Assn Chemical Specialities
Chemical waste
    Chemical Recycling Assn
    > + Reclamation & recycling
Chemicals: packaging
    Indl Packaging Assn
Chemistry
    Institiúd Ceimice na h'Eireann [IRL]
    R Instn GB
    R Pharmaceutical Soc
    R Soc Chemistry
    Resource Use Inst
    > + specific applications
Chemistry: history
    Soc Hist Alchemy & Chemistry
Chemists & druggists > Pharmaceuticals
Chemotherapy > Pharmacology & chemotherapy
Cheques
    Brit Banking History Soc
    Brit Cheque Cashers Assn
    > + Banking
Chess
    Brit Correspondence Chess Soc
    Chess Scotland
    Circular Chess Soc
    English Chess Federation
    Welsh Chess U
Chest diseases > Thoracic diseases
Chesterton (Gilbert Keith)
    Chesterton Soc
Chickens > Poultry
Child abuse
    Assn Child Abuse Lawyers
    Brit Assn Study & Prevention Child Abuse
    Falsely Accused Carers & Teachers
    Nat Assn People Abused Childhood
    > + Children: welfare
Child contact centres
    Nat Assn Child Contact Centres
Child Support Agency
    Nat Assn Child Support Action
Childbirth > Maternity; Midwifery; Obstetrics & gynaecology
Childless > Fertility
Childminding (home/workplace)
    Nat Childminding Assn
    NI Childminding Assn
    Scot Childminding Assn
    > + Children: welfare;   Fostering & foster parents
Children: books
    Children's Books Hist Soc
    Fedn Children's Book Gps
    George MacDonald Soc
    Violet Needham Soc
    > + Bookselling; individual authors
Children: clothing > Clothing
Children: cot deaths > Cot deaths
Children: death by accident/violence
    Compassionate Friends
    RoadPeace
Children: gifted
    Nat Assn Able Children in Educ

Nat Assn Gifted Children
Support Soc Children High Intelligence
Children: handicapped
AFASIC
Assn Spina Bifida & Hydrocephalus
Assn Wheelchair Children
Brit Assn Teachers Deaf
Children's Heart Assn
Deaf Educ Listening & Talking
Foresight
MENCAP
nasen
Nat Assn Toy & Leisure Libraries
Nat Portage Assn
REACH - Assn Children with Hand or Arm Deficiency
Scope [England & Wales]
Sebda
Sense
Shaftesbury Soc
Soc Stars
STEPS. . .
Wooden Spoon Soc
> + specific types of handicap
Children: health > Paediatrics
Children: in hospital
Action Sick Children
Children Hospital Ireland
Nat Assn Educ Sick Children
Nat Assn Hospital Play Staff
Children: psychology
Assn Child & Adoloescent Mental Health
Assn Child Psychotherapists
Assn Infant Mental Health UK
Soc Reproductive & Infant Psychology
Children: & the theatre > Theatre: young people
Children: welfare
4children
Assn Children Life-Threatening. . . Conditions
Assn Families Adopted Abroad
Assn Shared Parenting
Brit Assn Study & Prevention Child Abuse
Children 1st
Children Law UK
Children Living Inherited Metabolic Diseases
Children's Rights Alliance England
Children Scotland
Children's Services Res Gp
Families Need Fathers
Family Rights Gp
Foundation Study Infant Deaths
Heart Line Assn
Indep Children's Homes Association
Ir Soc Prevention Cruelty Children
LOOK
Nat Assn Child Contact Centres
Nat Assn Child Support Action
Nat Care Assn
Nat Deaf Children's Soc
Nat Soc Prevention Cruelty to Children
One Parent Families Scotland
Parents Oral Contraception Children
Rett Syndrome Assn
> + Fostering & foster parents; Social: service;   Welfare:
administration
Chile
Anglo-Chilean Soc
Brit Chilean Cham Comm
Chilled beams & ceilings
Chilled Ceilings Assn
Chilled food > Food: frozen & chilled
Chimneys
Assn Technical Lighting & Access Specialists
Brit Flue & Chimney Mfrs' Assn
Nat Assn Chimney Engrs
Nat Assn Chimney Sweeps
Refractory Users Fedn
China (ceramic) > Ceramics; Pottery
China (country)
Brit Assn Chinese Studies
Brit Cham Comm China - Beijing
Brit Cham Comm Shanghai
China-Britain Business Coun
China Soc
Soc Anglo-Chinese Understanding
China clay (Kaolin)
Cornish Cham Mines & Minerals

Kaolin & Ball Clay Assn
Trevithick Soc
Chinchillas
Nat Chinchilla Soc
Chinese medicine
Acupuncture Soc
Register Chinese Herbal Medicine
> + Complementary medicine
Chipboard > Building board & timber
Chippendale (Thomas)
Chippendale Soc
Chips & crisps > Potatoes: products
Chiropody & podiatry
Alliance Private. . .Chiropody & Podiatry Practitioners
Assd Chiropodists & Podiatrists U
Brit Chiropody & Podiatry Assn
Inst Chiropodists & Podiatrists
Ir Chiropodists/Podiatrists Org
SMAE Fellowship
Soc Chiropodists & Podiatrists
Chiropractic
Brit Chiropractic Assn
Chiropractic Patients' Assn
McTimoney Chiropractic Assn
Scot Chiropractic Assn
Utd Chiropractic Assn
Chivalry
Heraldry Soc
Chocolate > Cocoa & chocolate; Confectionery
Choirs & choral music
Assn Brit Choral Dirs
Assn Ir Choirs
Brit Fedn Young Choirs
Campaign Traditional Cathedral Choir
Choir Schools Assn
Friends Cathedral Music
Making Music
Nat Assn Choirs
R Choral Soc
R Coll Organists
R School Church Music
Sing for Pleasure
Ulster Soc Organists & Choirmasters
Welsh Amat Music Fedn
> + Cathedral & church music
Cholesterol
Heart UK
> + Cardiology
Chopin (Frédéric)

Choreography
Dance UK
R Academy Dance
Christian activities
ACG Ltd (Arts Centre Gp)
Assn Denominational Histl Socs Cognate Libs
Christian Endeavour U
Christian Evidence Soc
Christian Social Order
Crusaders
Librarians' Christian Fellowship
Urdd Gobaith Cymru
> + Missionary organisations; Welfare organisations
Christian education
Assn Christian Teachers
Christian Educ
Nat Soc (CofE) Promoting Religious Educ
Profl Coun Religious Educ
Christmas cards
Charity Christmas Card Coun
Christmas hampers
Hamper Ind Tr Assn
Christmas trees
Brit Christmas Tree Growers Assn
> + Trees
Chromatography
Chromatographic Soc
Chrysanthemums
Nat Chrysanthemum Soc
UK Chrysanthemum Growers' Assn
> + Flowers, flower arrangement & floristry
Church: bells > Bellringing
Church: brasses & monuments > Brasses & church monuments
Church: buildings
Brit Assn Friends Museums
Capel
Cathedral Architects Assn

     © CBD Research Ltd · Beckenham · BR3 5JS · Tel 020 8650 7745 · Fax 020 8650 0768 · E-mail cbd@cbdresearch.com · www.cbdresearch.com

Chapels Soc
Ecclesiological Soc
Friends Friendless Churches
Pugin Gld
Round Tower Churches Soc
Save our Parsonages
Soc Friends St George's. . . [Windsor]
> + Historic buildings
Church: editors
Assn Church Editors
Church: of England
English Clergy Assn
Modern Churchpeople's U
Protestant Reformation Soc
Church: of England liturgy > Liturgy
Church: history & records
Canterbury & York Soc
Catholic Record Soc
Church England Record Soc
Ecclesiastical Hist Soc
Soc Archivists
> + Parish registers; individual churches
Church: monuments > Brasses & church monuments
Church: music > Cathedral & church music; Choirs & choral music; Liturgy
Church: of Scotland history
Scot Church Hist Soc
Church: services > Liturgy
Church: shops > Cathedral & church shops
Churchyards > Cemeteries & churchyards
Cider & perry
Craft Brewing Assn
Nat Assn Cider Makers
Three Counties Cider & Perry Assn
CIDP > Guillain-Barré Syndrome
Cigars & cigarettes
Imported Tobacco Products Advy Coun
Nat Assn Cigarette Machine Operators
> + Tobacco
Cigars & cigarettes: accessories
Cartophilic Soc
Cigarette Packet Collectors Club
Ciné equipment > Audio visual aids & equipment; Photographic industry & trade
Cinema > Film
Cinema buildings
Cinema Theatre Assn
Mercia Cinema Soc
Cinema organs
Cinema Organ Soc
> + Organs, organists & organ music
Circles (in crops & corn)
Megalithic Soc
UK Skeptics
Circuit plans
Soc Cirplanologists
Circuits > Printed circuits
Circuses & circus artistes
Assn Circus Proprietors
Captive Animal Protection Soc
Circus Friends Assn
Circus Soc
Cisterns, drums & tanks
Assn Tank & Cistern Mfrs
Brit Coatings Fedn
Indl Packaging Assn
Citizens' Advice Bureaux > Advice centres & bureaux
City farms
Fedn City Farms & Community Gardens
Civil aviation > Aviation
Civil defence & industrial emergencies
Emergency Planning Soc
Inst Civil Defence & Disaster Studies
SIESO
Civil engineering
Bridge Deck Waterproofing Assn
Brit Civil Engg Test Eqpt Mfrs Assn
Brit Constructional Steelwork Assn
Civil Engg Contrs' Assn
Confedn Construction Specialists
Construction Confedn
Construction Emplrs Fedn
Instn Civil Engg Surveyors
Instn Civil Engrs
Materials Components Developing & Testing Assn
Pipe Jacking Assn
> + Construction industries
Civil liberties > Individual freedom

Civil Service
Assn First Division Civil Servants
Assn Higher Civil & Public Servants [IRL]
Bar Assn Local Govt & Public Service
NI Public Service Alliance
Prospect
Public & Comml Services U
U Senior Revenue Officials
> + Public administration
Civil War (English)
Cromwell Assn
English Civil War Soc
John Hampden Soc
Sealed Knot
Siege Gp
Cladding
Brit Precast Concrete Fedn
Insulated Render & Cladding Assn
Metal Cladding & Roofing Manufacturers Association Ltd
> + Building materials & supplies
Clairvoyance
Brit Astrological & Psychic Soc
> + Paranormal & psychical research
Clare (John) 1793-1864
John Clare Soc
Clarinets & saxophones
Clarinet Heritage Soc
Clarinet & Saxophone Soc GB
Classic vehicles > Motor vehicles: historic
Classical studies
Assn Latin Teaching
Brit Academy
Classical Assn
Jt Assn Classical Teachers
Soc Promotion Hellenic Studies
Soc Promotion Roman Studies
Virgil Soc
Classification
Brit Classification Soc
Clay & clay products
Brit Ceramic Confedn
Brit Masonry Soc
Clay Pipe Devt Assn
Clay Roof Tile Coun
Kaolin & Ball Clay Assn
Mineralogical Soc
Resource Use Inst
Scot Emplrs Coun Clay Inds
> + Bricks; Pottery; Tiles (floor & wall)
Clay target (pigeon) shooting
Clay Pigeon Shooting Assn
Scot Clay Target Assn
> + Shooting
Clean air > Air: pollution
Cleaning & cleaning science
Assn Bldg Cleaning Direct Service Providers
Assn Domestic Mgt
Brit Cleaning Coun
Brit Inst Cleaning Science
Ir Contract Cleaning Assn
Cleaning equipment
Assn Domestic Mgt
BEAMA
Cleaning & Hygiene Suppliers' Assn
UK Cleaning Products Ind Assn
> + Soap & detergents
Cleaning & dyeing
Assn Glds Weavers, Spinners & Dyers
Gld Cleaners & Launderers
Nat Assn Launderette Ind
Soc Laundry Engrs & Allied Trs
Textile Services Assn
Ulster Launderers Assn
Cleansing > Street cleaning
Clearing services (banking)
Assn Payment Clearing Services
Cleft lip & palate
Cleft Lip & Palate Assn
Clematis
Brit Clematis Soc
Clergy
English Clergy Assn
> + Church: of England; other individual churches
Clerks of local councils > Local government: officers
Clerks of works
Inst Clerks Works

Cliff (Clarice)
  Clarice Cliff Collectors Club
Climate > Environment; Meteorology
Climbing
  Alpine Club
  Assn Heads Outdoor Educ Centres
  Brit Assn Mountain Guides
  Brit Mountaineering Coun
  Mountaineering Coun Ireland
  Mountaineering Coun Scotland
Clinical biochemistry
  Assn Clinical Biochemistry
  Assn Clinical Biochemists Ireland
  > + Biochemistry & biotechnology
Clinical data management
  Assn Clinical Data Mgt
  Brit In Vitro Diagnostics Assn
Clinical immunology > Allergy
Clinical pathology
  Assn Clinical Pathologists
Clinical pharmacy > Pharmacy
Clinical trials
  Brit Assn Res Quality Assurance
  Clinical Contract Res Assn
  Fac Pharmaceutical Med
  Inst Clinical Res
Clocks > Horology
Close (Sir Charles Frederick Arden-)
  Charles Close Soc
Closed-circuit television > Television: closed circuit
Closures (cork, metal, plastic)
  Cork Ind Fedn
  Metal Packaging Mfrs Assn
Clothing
  ASBCI - Forum Clothing & Textiles
  Brit Apparel & Textile Confedn
  Brit Clothing Ind Assn
  Fedn Clothing Designers & Executives
  Ir Clothing & Textiles Alliance
  Nat Children's Wear Assn
  Register Apparel & Textile Designers
  Textile Inst Intl
  UK Fashion Exports
  > + Fashion; Protective clothing/equipment; specific items of
  clothing
Clowns > Circuses & circus artistes
Clubs
  Assn Inter-Varsity Clubs
  Assn London Clubs
  C'ee Registered Clubs Assns
  Working Men's Club & Inst U
  > + specific activities or interests
Clutch facings
  Brit Friction Materials Coun
CMV > Cytomegalovirus
Coaches > Bus & coach operators;   Passenger transport
Coaches: sports
  Sports Coach UK
  > + individual sports
Coal: mining
  Confedn UK Coal Producers
  Fedn Indep Mines
  Minerals Engg Soc
  N England Inst Mining & Mechanical Engrs
  Nat U Mineworkers
  U Democratic Mineworkers
Coal: trade
  Coal Mchts Assn Scotland
  Coal Mchts Fedn
  > + Solid fuel
Coarse fishing > Fishing (sport)
Coastal waters > Estuaries; Water
Coastal look-out stations
  Nat Coastwatch Instn
Coated abrasives > Abrasives
Coated macadam > Asphalt & coated macadam
Coatings
  Brit Coatings Fedn
  Brit Textile Technology Gp
  Brit Urethane Foam Contrs Assn
  Eur Liquid Waterproofing Assn
  Paint Res Assn
  Sprayed Concrete Assn
  Thermal Spraying & Surface Engg Assn
Cobbett (William)
  William Cobbett Soc

Cobles & keelboats
  Coble & Keelboat Soc
  > + Ships: history & preservation
Cobnuts
  Kentish Cobnut Assn
Cobs > Horses & ponies
Cochlea implants
  Brit Academy Audiology
  Nat Cochlear Implant Users Assn
Cocktails
  UK Bartenders Gld
Cocoa & chocolate
  Biscuit, Cake, Chocolate... Assn
  Chocolate Soc
  Fedn Cocoa Commerce
Coconut matting
  Coir Assn
Codes of practice: standardisation
  BSI
Coeliac disease
  Coeliac Soc Ireland
  Coeliac UK
Coffee
  Brit Coffee Assn
  Brit Soluble Coffee Packers & Importers Assn
  Café Soc
  Coffee Tr Fedn
Coffins
  Funeral Furnishing Mfrs Assn
  > + Burial & cremation
Coin operated machines > Amusements & coin operated machines; Automatic
  vending
Coins & medals > Numismatics
Coir
  Coir Assn
Coke
  Coke Oven Mgrs Assn
  > + Solid fuel
Cold rolled metal
  Cold Rolled Sections Assn
  > + Metal: working
Cold sores > Herpes
Cold storage > Refrigeration; Temperature controlled storage
Cold War
  Subterranea Britannica
Coleridge (Samuel Taylor)
  Friends Coleridge
Colitis/colostomy
  Crohn's Disease Childhood Res Assn
  ia
  Nat Advy Service Parents Children with a Stoma
  Nat Assn Colitis & Crohn's Disease
Collars & ties
  Brit Clothing Ind Assn
  Master Craftsmen's Assn
Collecting hobbies > Object(s) collected
Collection agencies > Credit: reporting
Colleges > Adult education; Education; Technical education; Universities
Collieries > Coal: mining
Collins ([William] Wilkie)
  Wilkie Collins Soc
Coloboma
  Micro & Anophthalmic Children's Soc
Colombia
  Anglo-Colombian Soc
  Brit & Colombian Cham Comm [Lond]
  Cámara Comercio Colombo-Británica
Colostomy > Colitis/colostomy
Colour
  Brit Colour Makers Assn
  Colour Gp
  Oil & Colour Chemists Assn
  Soc Dyers & Colourists
  > + Paint
Colour: problem > Race relations
Colposcopy
  Brit Assn Sexual Health & HIV
Voluntary service > Charities; Community service: voluntary; Social: service;
  Welfare headings
Combat (dramatic) > Fights (historic/re-enactment)
Combustion engineering
  Combustion Engg Assn
  ICOM Energy Assn
Comedy & comedy writers
  Brit Comedy Soc
  Brit Soc Comedy Writers

© CBD Research Ltd · Beckenham · BR3 5JS · Tel 020 8650 7745 · Fax 020 8650 0768 · E-mail cbd@cbdresearch.com · www.cbdresearch.com

Comics
    Comics Creators Gld
Commemorative items & souvenirs
    Commemorative Collectors Soc
    Commemoratives Museum Trust
Commerce
    Assn Graduate Recruiters
    Assn MBAs
    Brit Chams Comm
    Fedn Crafts & Comm
    R Soc . . . Arts
    R Soc Edinburgh
    > + Chambers of commerce
Commercial management > Management
Commercial property agents
    Indl Agents Soc
    > + Estate agents
Commercial travellers > Sales management & representation
Commercial vehicles
    Historic Comml Vehicle Soc
    Nat Assn Road Transport Museums
    > + Motor headings
Commissioning (construction industry)
    Commissioning Specialists Assn
Commodities
    Fedn Commodity Assns
    Futures & Options Assn
    Intl Gen Produce Assn
    > + names of specific commodities
Common Market > European Union
Common Prayer
    Alcuin Club
    Prayer Book Soc
Commons & open spaces > Open spaces; Parks & gardens
Commonwealth affairs
    Brit Inst Intl & Comparative Law
    English Speaking U C'wealth
    R Over-Seas League
Commonwealth (1649-1688)
    Cromwell Assn
Communication services
    ALTO [IRL]
    Communications Mgt Assn
    Fedn Communication Services
    ICT Ireland
    Momentum - Northern Ireland ICT Fedn
    Onsite Communications Assn
    > + Cable & satellite communications
Communications
    Brit Assn Communicators in Business
    Inst Sound & Communications Engrs
    Publicity Club Lond
    > + form of communication
Communications: fraud
    Telecommunications UK Fraud Forum
Community: care
    Nat Care Assn
Community: development
    Community Devt Finance Assn
    Devt Trusts Assn
    Devt Trusts Assn Scot
    Scot Business Community
Community: drama > Theatre
Community: education
    Fedn Community Devt Learning
    Nat Assn Youth & Community Educ Officers
Community: medicine > Medical officers; Public health
Community: music
    Sound Sense
Community: organisations
    Assn Community Rail Partnerships
    Assn Scot Community Couns
    Campaign Community Banking Services
    Community Foundation Network
    Community Transport Assn
    Fedn City Farms & Community Gardens
    Nat Fedn Community Orgs
Community: resources (mobile) > Mobile community resources
Community: service (voluntary)
    Assn Res Voluntary & Community Sector
    Brit Red Cross Soc
    Campaign Nat Community Service
    Community Service Volunteers
    Nat Assn Round Tables
    Returned Volunteer Action
    Scot Assn Volunteer Mgt
    Scot Coun Voluntary Orgs

    Toc H
    Voluntary Service Overseas
    Women's R Voluntary Service
    > + Welfare headings
Commuters > Passenger transport
Companies: independent > Business
Companies: quoted/London Stock Exchange
    Quoted Companies Alliance
Company: directors
    Inst Directors
    Inst Directors Ireland
    > + Management
Company: registration agents
    Assn Company Registration Agents
Company: secretaries
    Inst Business Admin
    Inst Chart Secretaries & Administrators
    > + Secretaries & administrators
Comparative law > Law: comparative
Compasses & compass adjusting
    Chart & Nautical Instrument Tr Assn
Compères
    Gld Profl Toastmasters
    > + Toastmasters & masters of ceremonies
Complementary medicine
    Assn Light Touch Therapists
    Assn Stress Therapists
    Brit Complementary Medicine Assn
    Brit Register Complementary Practitioners
    Complementary Med Assn
    Confedn Healing Orgs
    Fedn Holistic Therapists
    Inst Complementary Medicine
    On Site Massage Assn
    SMAE Fellowship
    UK Polarity Therapy Assn
    > + specific forms eg Osteopathy
Composing > Music: composing & individual by name
Composites
    Composites Processing Assn
Composts & composting
    Community Composting Network
    Composting Assn
    Composting Assn Ireland
    Growing Media Assn
    John Innes Mfrs Assn
Comprehensive education
    Campaign State Educ
    > + Education
Compressed air
    Brit Compressed Air Soc
Compressed gases
    Brit Compressed Gases Assn
Compulsive/obsessive disorders > Obsessive/compulsive disorders
Computer & video games
    Brit Assn Record Dealers
    Entertainment & Leisure Software Pubrs Assn (UK)
    TIGA
Computers
    Brit Computer Assn Blind
    Brit Computer Soc
    Computer & Peripherals Eqpt Tr Assn
    Intellect, the Information Technology, Telecommunications & Electronics
    Ir Computer Soc
    Nat Assn Specialist Computer Retailers
    Profl Computing Assn
    > + Software headings
Computers: application
    Assn Hist & Computing
    Assn Survey Computing
    Construction Ind Computing Assn
    Dental System Suppliers Assn
    eLearning Network
    INCA [IRL]
    Instn Engg & Technology
    Nat Outsourcing Assn
Computers: chips
    Fedn Technological Inds
Computers: in education
    Naace
Computers: historic
    Computer Consvn Soc
Computers: professionals
    Assn C & C++ Users
    Assn Certified IT Profls
    Assn Computer Engrs & Technicians

Assn Computer Profls
Assn Indep Computer Specialists
Inst IT Training
Instn Analysts & Programmers
Soc Computers & Law
Computers: supplies for
Indep Print Inds Assn
Legal Software Suppliers Assn
UK Cartridge Remanufacturers Assn
Concentrates > Animal feed
Concerts
Assn Brit Concert Promoters
Concert Artistes' Association
Concert Promoters Assn
Hallé Concerts Soc
Nat Arenas Assn
Nat Early Music Assn
> + Music; Orchestras
Conchology
Brit Shell Collectors Club
Conchological Soc
Malacological Soc Lond
Concrete & concrete products
Assn Concrete Indl Flooring Contrs
Brit Cement Assn
Brit Masonry Soc
Brit Precast Concrete Fedn
Britpave
Concrete Bridge Devt Gp
Concrete Mfrs Assn Ireland
Concrete Repair Assn
Concrete Soc
Construct, Concrete Structures Gp
Corrosion Prevention Assn
Inst Concrete Technology
Instn Civil Engrs
Intl Glassfibre Reinforced Concrete Assn
Ir Concrete Fedn
Ir Concrete Soc
Post-tensioning Assn
Sprayed Concrete Assn
UK Quality Ash Assn
Concrete cutting
Drilling & Sawing Assn
Concrete pumping
Construction Plant-hire Assn
Conductors: music > individual by name
Cones & cylinders (road)
Retroreflective Eqpt Mfrs Assn
> + Road: lighting, markings & traffic signs
Confectionery
Biscuit, Cake, Chocolate... Assn
Nat Assn Master Bakers
Retail Confectioners & Tobacconists Assn
Whls Confectionery & Tobacco Alliance
> + Baking
Conferences & conventions
Assn Brit Profl Conf Organisers
Assn Confs & Events
Brit Assn Conf Destinations
Events Sector Ind Trg Org
Meetings Ind Assn
Soc Event Organisers
> + Exhibitions
Confinements (childbirth) > Maternity
Conflict & anger management
Brit Assn Anger Mgt
Conflict Res Soc
Inst Conflict Mgt
Personal Safety Assn
Congenital defects
Foresight
STEPS...
> + Birthmarks & disfigurement;   Children: Handicapped
Congestion charging
Transport-Watch
Congregational church
Congregational U Ireland
Utd Reformed Church Hist Soc
Conifers
Brit Christmas Tree Growers Assn
Horticultural Trs Assn
> + Trees
Conjuring & magic
Brit Magical Soc
Magic Circle

Connective tissue disorders
Brit Coalition Heritable Disorders Connective Tissue
Conrad (Joseph) 1857-1924
Joseph Conrad Soc
Conservation
Alliance Religions & Consvn
Assn Envt Conscious Bldg
Assn Protection Rural Scotland
Brit Assn Shooting & Consvn
Brit Trust Consvn Volunteers
Campaign Protect Rural England
Countryside Mgt Assn
English Historic Towns Forum
Environmental Investigation Agency
Farming & Wildlife Advy Gp
Friends Earth
Inst Consvn
Nat Trust
Nat Trust Ireland
Nat Trust Scotland
Scot Field Studies Assn
Scot Wild Land Gp
Selborne Soc
Soc Envtl Exploration
> + specific subjects eg Architecture; Natural history
Conservation: area organisations
Black Country Soc
Campaign Protection Rural Wales
Dartmoor Presvn Assn
Gower Soc
NI Countryside Staff Assn
Northumberland & Newcastle Soc
S Downs Soc
Ulster Soc Protection Countryside
> + Nature conservation: local reserves
Conservative politics
Tory Reform Gp
Conservatories
Glass & Glazing Fedn
Conservators (art) > Art: conservation
Constitutional reform
Charter 88
Construction equipment
Brit Compressed Air Soc
Construction Eqpt Assn
Construction Fixings Assn
Construction Plant-hire Assn
Construction Products Assn
Contractors Mechanical Plant Engrs
Scot Plant Owners Assn
Soc Chemical Ind
> + Materials: management/handling; specific items of equipment
Construction history
Construction Hist Soc
Construction industries
Assn Indep Construction Adjudicators
Assn Project Safety
Brit Civil Engg Test Eqpt Mfrs Assn
Brit Constructional Steelwork Assn
Builders' Conf
Building Cost Infm Service
Chart Inst Architectural Technologists
Commissioning Specialists Assn
Confedn Construction Specialists
Construction Confedn
Construction Ind Computing Assn
Construction Ind Coun
Construction Ind Fedn [IRL]
Construction Ind Inf Gp
Construction Ind Res & Infm Assn
Construction Ind Trading Electronically
Inst Construction Mgt
Inst Construction Specialists
Instn Civil Engg Surveyors
Instn Planning Supervisors
Major Projects Assn
Specialist Engg Contrs Gp
Steel Construction Inst
> + Building
Construction law & control > Law: construction
Construction materials > Building materials & supplies
Construction surveying
Soc Construction & Quantity Surveyors Public Sector
Constructional steelwork > Construction industries; Steel
Consultants > field of consultancy
Consumer affairs & protection
Assn Public Analysts

Cotton
    Brit Cotton Growing Assn
    > + Textile headings
Council tax
    IsItFair
    Scot Assessors' Assn
Councillors > Local government
Counselling
    Brit Assn Counselling & Psychotherapy
    COSCA
    Counselling
    Inst Guidance Counsellors [IRL]
    Ir Assn Counselling & Psychotherapy
    Nat Assn Counsellors, Hypnotherapists...
    Nat Coun Hypnotherapy &... Register
    Nat Coun Psychotherapists
    Psychiatric Rehabilitation Assn
    Universities Psychotherapy & Counselling Assn
    > + field of counselling
Counterfeiting
    Anti Counterfeiting Gp
Counties (British)
    Assn Brit Counties
Country dancing & music > Folk dance & song
Countryside preservation > Conservation; Nature conservation
County agricultural societies > Agriculture: county societies
County archaeological societies > Archaeology: county societies
County councils > Local government
County history > Archaeology;   Records: historical
Courier services
    Despatch Assn
    Inst Couriers
    Nat Courier Assn
Courtesy
    Campaign Courtesy
Courts of law > Law headings; Magistrates & magistrates courts
Courts (royal)
    Soc Court Studies
    > + Monarchy
Covenanters (Scottish)
    Scot Covenanter Memorials Assn
Cowboys > American 'West'
Cracids > Game & game birds
Cradles & suspended platforms
    Construction Plant-hire Assn
    Indl Rope Access Tr Assn
    Nat Access & Scaffolding Confedn
    Specialist Access Engg & Maintenance Assn
Crafts & craftsmanship
    Art Workers Gld
    Brit Toymakers Gld
    Gld Master Craftsmen
    League Profl Craftsmen
    Nat Assn Advisers... Design & Technology
    Rural Crafts Assn
    Soc Designer Craftsmen
    Wales Craft Coun
    > + individual crafts
Cranes
    Construction Plant-hire Assn
    Heavy Transport Assn
    > + Lifting & loading equipment
Cranio- > Head entries
Craniosacral therapy
    Craniosacral Therapy Assn
Cream > Dairying
The Creation
    Biblical Creation Soc
Credit & magnetic strip cards
    Automatic Identification Mfrs & Suppliers Assn
    > + Banking
Credit hire: vehicles
    Nat Assn Credit Hire Operators
Credit: reporting
    Civil Court Users Assn
    Consumer Credit Tr Assn
    Credit Services Assn
    Soc Messengers-at-Arms & Sheriff-Officers
Credit: trade
    Brit Cheque Cashers Assn
    Consumer Credit Assn
    Credit Protection Assn
    Finance & Leasing Assn
    Inst Credit Mgt
    Ir Finance Houses Assn
    Ir Inst Credit Mgt

Credit: unions
    Ace Credit U Services
    Assn Brit Credit Us
    Ir League Credit Us
Cremation & crematoria > Burial & cremation
Creutzfeldt-Jakob disease
    Alzheimer's Soc
Cricket
    Assn County Cricket Scorers
    Assn Cricket Statisticians & Historians
    Assn Cricket Umpires & Scorers
    Brit Indoor Cricket Assn
    Club Cricket Conf
    Coun Cricket Socs
    Cricket Memorabilia Soc
    Cricket Scotland
    Cricket Soc
    England & Wales Cricket Bd Coaches Assn
    Midlands Club Cricket Conf
    Minor Counties Cricket Assn
    Northern Cricket U Ireland
    Profl Cricketers' Assn
Cricket equipment
    Sports Mfrs & Retailers Tr Assn
    Sports & Play Construction Assn
Criers > Town criers
Crime protection & prevention
    Confedn Brit Security Ind
    Crime Concern
    Intl Assn Auto Theft Investigators
    Nat Assn Victims Support Schemes
    Victim Support Scotland
Crime writers
    Crime Writers Assn
Crimea War
    Crimean War Res Soc
Criminal law
    Criminal Bar Assn [E&W]
    Criminal Law Solicitors' Assn
    > + Law
Criminology
    Brit Soc Criminology
    Howard League for Penal Reform
Crisps > Potatoes: products
Critical incident de-briefing
    Nat Coun Psychotherapists
    > + Counselling
Criticism
    Critics' Circle
Crochet
    Knitting & Crochet Gld
    Lace Soc
Crocuses
    Brit Iris Soc
Crofters
    Scot Crofting Foundation
Crohn's disease > Colitis/colostomy
Cromwell (Oliver)
    Cromwell Assn
Crop: circles > Circles (in crops & corn)
Crop: consultants
    Assn Indep Crop Consultants
Crop: drying
    Brit Assn Green Crop Driers
    Instn Agricl Engrs
Crop: research
    NIAB
    > + Agriculture; Seeds
Crop: spraying & protection
    Nat Assn Agricl Contrs
Croquet
    Croquet Assn
    Scot Croquet Assn
Cross country running > Athletics; Running
Crossbow shooting
    Brit Crossbow Soc
    Grand Nat Archery Soc
    > + Archery
Crosswords
    Crossword Club
Crown green bowling > Bowling
Cruise lines (shipping)
    Passenger Shipping Assn
Cruising > Boats & boating; Yachting
Crustacea > Shellfish

© CBD Research Ltd · Beckenham · BR3 5JS · Tel 020 8650 7745 · Fax 020 8650 0768 · E-mail cbd@cbdresearch.com · www.cbdresearch.com

Cryogenics
>> Brit Cryogenics Coun
>> Heat Transfer & Fluid Flow Service
Cryptography
>> Xenophon
Crystal healing
>> Crystal & Healing Fedn
Crystal Palace
>> Crystal Palace Foundation
Crystallography
>> Brit Assn Crystal Growth
>> Brit Crystallographic Assn
>> Mineralogical Soc
Cue sports
>> Sports Mfrs & Retailers Tr Assn
Cued speech
>> Cued Speech Assn
>> > + Speech
Culverts & channels
>> Brit Precast Concrete Fedn
Curates (Church of England)
>> Additional Curates Soc
Curling
>> English Curling Assn
>> R Caledonian Curling Club
Curwen (John)
>> Curwen Inst
Cushing's Syndrome
>> Assn Cushing's Treatment & Help
Customer care
>> Inst Customer Service
Cutlery
>> Brit Cutlery & Silverware Assn
>> Cutlery & Allied Trs Res Assn
>> Silver Spoon Club
Cutters & reamers
>> Brit Hardmetal & Engineers' Cutting Tool Assn
Cutting tools > Tools
Cyclamen
>> Cyclamen Soc
Cycles & motorcycles
>> Assn Cycle Traders
>> Bicycle Assn
>> Cycle Engrs' Inst
>> Motor Cycle Ind Assn
>> Nat Motorcycle Coun
>> Retail Motor Ind Fedn
>> UK Unicycle Fedn
>> Veteran-Cycle Club
>> > + Motor cycling & scooter riding
Cyclical vomiting syndrome
>> Cyclical Vomiting Syndrome Assn
Cycling
>> Brit Cycling Fedn
>> Cycling Time Trials
>> Cyclists Touring Club
>> Fellowship Cycling Old-Timers
>> London Cycling Campaign
>> NI Cycling Fedn
>> Road Records Assn
>> Scot Cycling
>> Tricycle Assn
>> Welsh Cycling U
Cyclo-Cross > Cycling
Cylinders (gas)
>> Brit Compressed Gases Assn
Cystic fibrosis
>> Cystic Fibrosis Trust
Cystitis
>> Cystitis & Overactive Bladder Foundation
Cytology > Cell biology
Cytomegalovirus
>> Congenital CMV Assn
Czech Republic
>> Brit Cham Comm Czech Republic
>> Dvořák Soc Czech & Slovak Music
>> Kmoch Eur Bands Soc

D

Dad's Army (TV programme)
>> Dad's Army Appreciation Soc
Daffodils
>> Daffodil Soc

Dahlias
>> Nat Dahlia Soc
Dairy cattle > Cattle headings
Dairying
>> Assn Unpasteurised Milk Producers
>> Brit Friesland Sheep Soc
>> Brit Goat Soc
>> Brit Sheep Dairying Assn
>> Campaign Real Milk
>> Dairy Executives Assn [IRL]
>> Dairy UK
>> Ir Creamery Milk Suppliers Assn
>> Ir Dairy Inds Assn
>> Milking Machine Mfrs' Assn
>> Quality Milk Producers
>> R Assn Brit Dairy Farmers
>> Soc Dairy Technology
Damage management
>> Brit Damage Mgt Assn
Dampcourses & dampproofing
>> Brit Wood Preserving & Damp-proofing Assn
>> Inst Specialist Surveyors & Engrs
Dams & reservoirs
>> Brit Dam Soc
>> > + Water: treatment & supply
Damsons
>> Westmorland Damson Assn
Dance bands
>> Harry Roy Appreciation Soc
Dance notation > Choreography
Dancing
>> ACG Ltd (Arts Centre Gp)
>> Assn Amer Dancing
>> Assn Dance Movement Therapy
>> Ballroom Dancers Fedn
>> Brit Assn Teachers Dancing
>> Brit Ballet Org
>> Brit Theatre Dance Assn
>> Coun Dance Educ & Training
>> Dance UK
>> Dancesport Scotland
>> Dolmetsch Hist Dance Soc
>> Early Dance Circle
>> Gld Profl Teachers Dancing
>> Imperial Soc Teachers Dancing
>> Inst Contemporary Arts
>> Laban Gld Movement & Dance
>> London Swing Dance Soc
>> Nat Assn Teachers Dancing
>> Nat Campaign Arts
>> Nat Dance Teachers Assn
>> Old Time Dance Soc
>> R Academy Dance
>> Scot Dance Teachers Alliance
>> Soc Dance Res
>> UK Alliance Dance Teachers
>> UK Dance Drama Fedn
>> > + Ballet; Choreography; Folk dance & song
Dark skies
>> Campaign Dark Skies
Dartmoor
>> Dartmoor Presvn Assn
Darts
>> Brit Darts Org
>> Profl Darts Players Assn
>> Scot Darts Assn
Data capture
>> Automatic Identification Mfrs & Suppliers Assn
Data processing
>> Assn Clinical Data Mgt
>> Brit Oncology Data Mgrs Assn
>> Inst Mgt Inf Systems
>> Records Mgt Soc
>> > + Computers; Information: services & technology
Data protection
>> Fedn Software Theft
Day surgery
>> Brit Assn Day Surgery
>> > + Surgery
De-icing
>> Salt Mfrs Assn
Deafness
>> Assn Lipspeakers
>> Assn Teachers Lipreading to Adults
>> Brit Assn Teachers Deaf
>> Brit Deaf Assn
>> Brit Deaf Sports Coun

Deaf Blind UK
Deaf Educ Listening & Talking
Hearing Concern
Ir Deaf Soc / Nat Assn Deaf
Nat Assn Deaf People [IRL]
Nat Assn Deafened People
Nat Cochlear Implant Users Assn
Nat Deaf Children's Soc
R Assn Deaf People
RNID
Scot Assn Sign Language Interpreters
Scot Coun Deafness
Sense
> + Hearing; Speech
Death & bodily-death > Bereavement; Burial & cremation; Paranormal &
psychical research; Population registration
Debt
Bankruptcy Assn
Civil Court Users Assn
Credit Services Assn
Inst Money Advisers
Non-Administrative Receivers Assn
Debt collection > Credit: reporting
Decking (timber)
Timber Decking Assn
Decontamination
Inst Decontamination Services
Decorating > Painting & decorating
Decorations (medals) > Numismatics
Decorative arts
Nat Assn Decorative & Fine Arts Socs
> + Art headings
Decorative lighting > Lighting
Découpage
Gld Brit Découpeurs
Deer
Assn Deer Mgt Gps
Brit Deer Farmers Assn
Brit Deer Soc
Brit Veterinary Assn
Game Conservancy Trust
NI Deer Soc
Deerhounds
Masters Deerhounds Assn
> + Hunts & hunting
Defence
Brit Intl Studies Assn
Confedn Brit Security Ind
R Utd Services Inst Defence... Studies
> + Civil defence & industrial emergencies; Fortresses & forts
Defence equipment
Defence Mfrs Assn
Intellect, the Information Technology, Telecommunications &
Electronics
Defibrillators
Implanted Defibrillator Assn Scotland
Delinquency > Criminology
Delius (Frederick)
Delius Soc
Delphiniums
Delphinium Soc
Dementia
Alzheimer Scotland
Alzheimer's Soc
Pick's Disease Support Gp
> + Mental health
Demolition & dismantling
Brit Metals Recycling Assn
Inst Demolition Engrs
Inst Explosives Engrs
Nat Fedn Demolition Contrs
Denmark
Anglo-Danish Soc
Danish-UK Cham Comm
Dental hospitals
Assn Dental Hospitals
Dental hypnosis > Medical & dental hypnosis
Dental practice management
Brit Dental Practice Mgrs Assn
Dental radiology
Brit Soc Dental & Maxillofacial Radiology
Dentistry
Assn Dental Anaesthetists
Assn Dental Implantology
Assn Ir Dental Ind
Brit Assn Dental Nurses
Brit Assn Dental Therapists

Brit Assn Prosthetists & Orthotists
Brit Assn Study Community Dentistry
Brit Assn Teachers Conservative Dentistry
Brit Dental Assn
Brit Dental Hygienists Assn
Brit Dental Tr Assn
Brit Endodontic Soc
Brit Homoeopathic Dental Assn
Brit Orthodontic Soc
Brit Soc Dental Res
Brit Soc Disability & Oral Health
Brit Soc Gen Dental Surgery
Brit Soc Mercury Free Dentistry
Brit Soc Paediatric Dentistry
Brit Soc Periodontology
Brit Soc Restorative Dentistry
Brit Soc Study Prosthetic Dentistry
Clinical Dental Technicians Assn
Confedn Dental Emplrs
Craniofacial Soc
Dental Laboratories Assn
Dental Practitioners Assn
Dental System Suppliers Assn
Fac Dental Surgery
Fac Gen Dental Practitioners (UK)
Ir Dental Assn
Lindsay Soc Hist Dentistry
Nat Assn Dentistry Health Authorities...
Nat Assn Med Educ Mgt
Orthodontic Technicians Assn
R Coll Physicians & Surgeons Glasgow
R Coll Surgeons Edinburgh
Soc Advancement Anaesthesia Dentistry
Dentists: legal protection
Confedn Dental Emplrs
Medical & Dental Defence U Scotland
Medical Protection Soc
Department stores > Retail trade
Dependent territories (British) > Overseas territories (British)
Depression
Depression Alliance
Fellowship Depressives Anonymous
MDF
SANE
Dermatitis herpetiformis
Coeliac UK
Dermatology
Brit Assn Dermatologists
Brit Photodermatology Gp
Primary Care Dermatology Soc
Design
Anti Copying Design
Art Workers Gld
Assn Art Historians
Chart Soc Designers
D&AD
Design Assn
Design Business Assn
Design Hist Soc
Design & Technology Assn
Inst Designers Ireland
Inst Profl Designers
Instn Engg Designers
Nat Assn Advisers... Design & Technology
Nat Soc Educ in Art & Design
R Soc ... Arts
Register Apparel & Textile Designers
Scot Ecological Design Assn
Design: industrial > Industrial design
Design registration > Patents & trade marks
Despatch industry > Courier services
Desserts
Food Processors' Assn
Detection dogs
Nat Assn Security Dog Users
Detectives > Investigators
Detergents > Soap & detergents
Developing countries > Development education & studies; Overseas
development
Development education & studies
Devt Educ Assn
Devt Studies Assn
> + Education
Development trusts
Devt Trusts Assn
Devt Trusts Assn Scot
Developmental biology > Biology

© CBD Research Ltd · Beckenham · BR3 5JS · Tel 020 8650 7745 · Fax 020 8650 0768 · E-mail cbd@cbdresearch.com · www.cbdresearch.com

de Vere (Edward) Earl of Oxford
    De Vere Soc
Devon
    S W Coast Path Assn
Diabetes
    Diabetes Fedn Ireland
    Diabetes UK
Diagnostic engineering
    Instn Diagnostic Engrs
Dialects
    Lakeland Dialect Soc
    Lancashire Authors' Assn
    Yorkshire Dialect Soc
    > + English language & literature
Dialysis
    Brit Kidney Patient Assn
    Brit Transplantation Soc
Diamond drilling
    Drilling & Sawing Assn
Diamonds > Industrial diamonds; Gemstones; Jewellery
Dickens (Charles John Huffam)
    Dickens Fellowship
Diecasting
    Diecasting Soc
Diesel engines & fuel
    Heating Oil Buyers Assn
    Instn Diesel & Gas Turbine Engrs
Dietary supplements
    Coun Responsible Nutrition
Dietetics
    Brit Dietetic Assn
    Infant & Dietetic Foods Assn
    > + Nutrition
Digestive disorders
    Assn Gastroenterological Res Charities
Digital print
    Brit Printing Inds Fedn
Dinosaurs
    Dinosaur Soc
Diplomatic Service
    Diplomatic Service Families Assn
Diptera
    Dipterists Forum
Direct mail advertising > Advertising; Direct selling
Direct selling
    Direct Marketing Assn (UK) Ltd
    Direct Selling Assn
    Ir Direct Marketing Assn
    Publicity Club Lond
    > + Mail order trade
Directors (company)
    Inst Directors
    Inst Directors Ireland
    > + Management
Directory publishing
    Data Pubrs Assn
    > + Publishing
Disabled: road users
    Blue Badge Network
    Disabled Motorists Fedn
    Mobilise Org
    Nat Assn Bikers Disability
Disablement
    Assn Disabled Profls
    Brit Assn Supported Employment
    Brit Inst Learning Disabilities
    Brit Soc Rehabilitation Medicine
    Disability Alliance
    Disability Fedn Ireland
    Disablement Income Gp Scotland
    Employers Forum on Disability
    Ir Wheelchair Assn
    Limbless Assn
    MENCAP
    Nat Fedn Shopmobility
    Nat Inf Forum
    Nat Network Assessment Cntres
    R Assn Disability & Rehabilitation
    Riding Disabled Assn
    Scot Soc Rehabilitation
    Shaftesbury Soc
    Vision Homes Assn
    > + specific area of disability
Disarmament
    Campaign Nuclear Disarmament
    Medical Action Global Security
    Scientists Global Responsibility

Disasters & disaster relief
    RedR - Engrs Disaster Relief
    Tornado & Storm Res Org
    > + Civil defence & industrial emergencies;   Fire & flood damage restoration;   Welfare: organisations
Disc golf (flying discs)
    Brit Disc Golf Assn
    > + Ultimate
Discotheque equipment
    Profl Lighting & Sound Assn
Discount market
    Factors & Discounters Assn
    London Money Market Assn
Discrimination
    Discrimination Law Assn
    > + Race relations
Discs (music) > Sound recording & reproduction
Disease > Infection control & study;   Occupational health & hygiene
Disfigurement > Birthmarks & disfigurement;   Skin camouflage
Disinfectants
    Brit Assn Chemical Specialities
    > + Sterilising
Dismantling (waste trades) > Demolition & dismantling
Dispensing doctors
    Country Doctors Assn
    Dispensing Doctors Assn
Dispensing opticians > Optical practice
Display
    Brit Display Soc
    Shop & Display Eqpt Assn
Disposables
    Absorbent Hygiene Products Mfrs Assn
    Foodservice Packaging Assn
Distilling
    Inst Brewing & Distilling
    Maltsters Assn
Distribution
    Chart Inst Logistics & Transport UK
    Cold Storage & Distbn Fedn
    Freight Transport Assn
    Ir Assn Distributive Trs
    U Shop, Distributive & Allied Workers
    UK Warehousing Assn
    Utd Road Transport U
    > + Materials: management/handling; Retail trade; specific trade
District councils > Local government
District heating
    Combined Heat & Power Assn
    > + Heating
District nursing > Nursing

Diving (professional & scientific)
    Histl Diving Soc
    Intl Marine Contrs Assn
    Nautical Archaeology Soc
    Soc Underwater Technology Ltd
    > + Ocean industries
Diving (sport) > Swimming & diving
Divining > Dowsing
Divorced & separated people > Singles, divorced & separated
DIY > Do-it-yourself
Docked breeds
    Coun Docked Breeds
    > + Dogs
Docks > Ports
Doctors > Medical practice
Documents: historical > Records: historical
Documents: confidential disposal
    Brit Security Ind Assn
    UK Security Shredding Assn
Dodgson (Charles Lutwidge)
    Daresbury Lewis Carroll Soc
    Lewis Carroll Soc
Dogs
    Assn Dogs & Cats Homes
    Assn Lurcher Clubs
    Brit Flyball Assn
    Brit Whippet Racing Assn
    Coun Docked Breeds
    Dogs Trust
    Kennel Club
    Nat Assn Regd Petsitters
    Nat Assn Security Dog Users
    Nat Dog Wardens Assn
    Scot Kennel Club
    > + Hounds

Dogs: groomers
 Pet Care Trust
Dogs: training
 Assn Pet Behaviour Counsellors
 Assn Pet Dog Trainers
 Brit Inst Profl Dog Trainers
 People & Dogs Soc
 Rough & Smooth Collie Training Assn
 Support Dogs
 > + Pets & pet trade
Do-it-yourself
 Brit Hardware Fedn
Dolls & dolls' houses
 Doll Club GB
 > + Toys
Dolphins
 Whale & Dolphin Consvn Soc
Domestic appliances
 Assn Mfrs Domestic Appliances
 Domestic Appliance Service Assn
 White Goods Assn [IRL]
 > + Electrical industry & engineering
Domestic engineering > specific subjects, eg Heating
Domestic fowl > Poultry
Domestic heating > Heating
Domestic management
 Assn Domestic Mgt
Domestic science > Home economics
Domestic ventilation
 Residential Ventilation Assn
Domestic violence
 NI Women's Aid Fedn
 Women's Aid Fedn (England)
 > + Crime & crime prevention
Domiciliary care
 Nat Care Assn
 UK Homecare Assn
Donations (public)
 Donor Watch
Donizetti (Gaetano)
 Donizetti Soc
Donkeys
 Donkey Breed Soc
 Miniature Mediterranean Donkey Assn
Doors
 Architectural & Specialist Door Mfrs Assn
 Assn Garage Door Specialists
 Assn Interior Specialists
 Automatic Door Suppliers Assn
 Brit Woodworking Fedn
 Door & Hardware Fedn

Double glazing
 Glass & Glazing Fedn
 > + Insulation; Windows
Down's syndrome
 Down's Syndrome Assn
 Down's Syndrome Scotland
 > + Children: handicapped
Dowsing
 Assn Scientific Study Anomalous Phenomena
 Brit Soc Dowsers
Dragon boats
 Brit Dragon Boat Racing Assn
Dragonflies
 Brit Dragonfly Soc
Drainage
 Cast Iron Drainage Devt Assn
 Clay Pipe Devt Assn
 Land Drainage Contrs Assn
 > + Concrete & concrete products; Pipes; Water
Drake (Sir Francis)
 Drake Exploration Soc
Drama > Theatre
Drama festivals > Festivals: art, drama & music
Dramatists
 Ir Playwrights & Screenwriters Gld
 Soc Authors
 > + Writing & writers
Dramatherapy
 Brit Assn Dramatherapists
Draught proofing > Insulation
Draughts (board game)
 English Draughts Assn
Drawing > Art & artists
Drawing offices
 Fedn Engg Design Cos

Dredging
 Central Dredging Assn
 Fedn Dredging Contrs
Dress > Costume history, design & conservation; Fashion
Dressage > Horses & ponies
Dried flowers
 Brit Dried Flowers Assn
 > + Flowers, flower arrangement & floristry
Dried fruit
 Nat Dried Fruit Tr Assn
Drilling
 Brit Drilling Assn
 Brit Rig Owners Assn
 Drilling & Sawing Assn
 Well Drillers' Assn
Drink & beverage industry
 Beverage Coun Ireland
 Beverage Services Assn
 Brewing, Food & Beverage Ind Suppliers Assn
 Brit Soft Drinks Assn
 Campden & Chorleywood Food Res Assn
 Can Makers
 Drinks Ind Gp Ireland
 Food & Drink Fedn
 Food & Drink Ind Ireland
 Nat Fruit Wine, Mead & Liqueur Producers Assn
 Processing & Packaging Machinery Assn
 Scot Food & Drink Fedn
 > + Bottling
Drinking & driving
 Campaign Drinking & Driving
Drinking (compulsive) > Alcoholism
Drinking fountains
 Metropolitan Drinking Fountain &... Assn
Drinking straws & vessels
 Foodservice Packaging Assn
Drinkwater (John)
 Friends Dymock Poets
Drip mats > Beer: bottles, cans labels & mats
Driving (off-road)
 Brit Off-Road Driving Assn
 Motoring Orgs' Land Access & Recreation Assn
Driving tuition
 ADI Fedn
 Approved Driving Instructors Nat Jt Coun
 Assn Indl Road Safety Officers
 Assn Nat Driver Improvement Scheme Providers
 Driving Instructors Assn
 Inst Advanced Motorists
 Motor Schools Assn
 Nat Assn Advanced Motorcycle Instructors
Dromedary camels > Camelids
Drug addiction > Addiction
Drugs > Pharmaceuticals; Pharmacology & chemotherapy
Drugs: detection
 Nat Assn Security Dog Users
Druids
 Pagan Fedn
Drums (containers) > Cisterns, drums & tanks
Drums (musical instruments)
 Corps Drums Soc
 > Brass & silver bands
Dry cleaning > Cleaning & dyeing
Dry stone walling
 Dry Stone Walling Assn
Dry waste > + Waste disposal
Drylining
Dryrot
 Inst Specialist Surveyors & Engrs
 > + Dampcourses & dampproofing
Drywalling
 Fedn Plastering & Drywall Contrs
Dublin
 Friends Medieval Dublin [IRL]
 R Dublin Soc
Duchenne muscular dystrophy
 Duchenne Family Support Gp
Ducks
 Brit Poultry Coun
 Brit Waterfowl Assn
 > + Poultry
Ducks (decoy)
 Brit Decoy & Wildfowl Carvers Assn
Ducting
 Heating & Ventilating Contrs Assn
Duelling
 Dawn Duellists' Soc

Dumbness > Speech
Dunkirk
    Assn Dunkirk Little Ships
Duodecimal system
    Dozenal Soc
Durum flour
    Brit Durum Assn
Dust control
    Fan Mfrs' Assn
    Solids Handling & Processing Assn
    > + Air: conditioning & ventilating
Dutch > Netherlands: language & literature
Duty-free trade
    UK Travel Retail Forum
Dwarfism > Growth
Dyeing > Cleaning & dyeing
Dyeing & finishing
    Confedn Brit Wool Textiles
    Soc Dyers & Colourists
    Textile Finishers Assn
Dyestuffs
    Brit Chemical Distbrs... Assn
Dyking
    Dry Stone Walling Assn
Dymock poets
    Friends Dymock Poets
Dyslexia
    Brit Dyslexia Assn
    Coun Registration Schools Teaching Dyslexic Pupils
    Dyslexia Assn Ireland
    Dyslexia Inst
    Dyslexia Scotland
    Nat Network Assessment Cntres
    > + Children: handicapped
Dysmenorrhea
    Premenstrual Soc
Dysphasia
    Speakability
    > + Speech
Dysplasia (ectodermal)
    Ectodermal Dysplasia Soc
Dyspraxia
    Dyspraxia Foundation
Dystonia
    Dystonia Soc
Dystrophy > Muscular dystrophy; Myotonic dystrophy

Dzhugashvili (Iosif Vissarionovich) > Stalin (Joseph)

E

Earth sciences, structure & resources
    Dinosaur Soc
    Earth Science Teachers Assn
    Geological Soc
    Mineralogical Soc
    Remote Sensing & Photogrammetry Soc
    Soc Underwater Technology Ltd
    UK Indl Space C'ee
    Yorkshire Geological Soc
    > + Geology
Earth sheltered buildings
    Brit Earth Sheltering Assn
Earthenware > Ceramics; Clay & clay products; Pottery
Earthquake engineering
    Instn Civil Engrs
    Soc Earthquake & Civil Engg Dynamics
East/Eastern Africa
    Brit Assn Cent & Eastn Europe
    Eastern Africa Assn
Eastern Europe
    Brit Assn Cent & Eastn Europe
    > + individual countries
Eating disorders
    Eating Disorders Assn
    Overeaters Anonymous
    > + Obesity
EC > European Union
Ecclesiastical > Church headings; individual religions
Eckhart (Johannes)
    Eckhart Soc
Ecology
    Brit Ecological Soc

Inst Ecology & Envtl Mgt
    > + Conservation; Environment
Economic development
    Instn Economic Devt
Economic history
    Economic Hist Soc
    Economic & Social Hist Soc Ireland
Economics
    Agricl Economics Soc
    Brit Academy
    David Hume Inst
    Economic Res Coun
    Economic & Social Res Inst [IRL]
    Economics & Business Educ Assn
    Inst Economic Affairs
    Inst Fiscal Studies
    Intl Consulting Economists Assn
    R Economic Soc
    Resource Use Inst
    Scot Economic Soc
    Soc Business Economists
    Soc Economic Analysis
Ectodermal dysplasia
    Ectodermal Dysplasia Soc
Ectopic pregnancy > Miscarriage
Ecuador
    Anglo-Ecuadorian Soc
Eczema
    Nat Eczema Soc
Edgings (concrete) > Concrete & concrete products
Edible nuts > Nuts (edible)
Edible oils & fats
    Fedn Oils, Seeds & Fats Assns
    Nat Edible Oil Distbrs Assn
    Seed Crushers & Oil Processors Assn
    Soc Chemical Ind
    UK Assn Fish Meal Mfrs
    > + individual fats; Rendering
Edinburgh
    Cockburn Assn
Editing & editors
    Assn Church Editors
    Assn Freelance Editors, Proofreaders & Indexers [IRL]
    Brit Soc Magazine Editors
    Picture Res Assn
    Soc Editors
    Soc Editors & Proofreaders
    > + Publishing
Education
    Assn Colleges
    Assn Community & Comprehensive Schools [IRL]
    Assn NI Colleges
    Assn Study Primary Educ
    Assn Tutors
    Brit Assn Early Childhood Educ
    Brit Educl Leadership, Mgt & Admin Soc
    Brit Educl Res Assn
    Campaign Learning
    Campaign Real Educ
    Caspari Foundation for Educl Therapy...
    Children's Services Res Gp
    Coun Indep Educ
    Further Educ Res Assn
    Group Educ Museums
    Ir Vocational Educ Assn
    Modern Studies Assn
    Montessori Soc
    nasen
    Nat Assn Envtl Educ
    Nat Assn Primary Educ
    Nat Assn Therapeutic Educ
    Nat Forum Engg Centres
    Nat Foundation Educl Res E&W
    Sapere
    Scot Educl Res Assn
    Scot School Bd Assn
    Scot Support Learning Assn
    Soc Res Higher Educ
    Staff & Educl Devt Assn
    > + Adult education; Independent & public schools; Teachers; specific subjects
Education: computers in
    Naace
Education: equipment & supplies
    ADSET
    Brit Educl Suppliers Assn

Education: games & simulation
    Soc Advancement Games & Simulations Educ & Training
Education: guardians
    Assn Educ & Guardianship Intl Students
Education: guidance
    Nat Assn Educl Guidance Adults
Education: history
    History Educ Soc
Education: home based
    Education Otherwise
    Home Educ Advy Service
    Nat Assn Educ Sick Children
    Nat Portage Assn
    Schoolhouse Home Educ Assn
Education: occupational > Occupational training & education
Education: outdoor
    Assn Heads Outdoor Educ Centres
    Inst Outdoor Learning
Education: specialists
    Assn Coll Mgt
    Assn Directors Educ Scotland
    Assn Educ Welfare Mgt
    Assn Educl Psychologists
    Assn NI Educ & Library Bds
    Assn Profls Educ & Children's Trusts
    Assn University Administrators
    College Teachers
    Confedn Children's Services Mgrs
    Coun Hospitality Mgt Educ
    Higher Educ Liaison Officers' Assn
    History Curriculum Assn
    Inst Educl Assessors
    Inst Health Promotion & Educ
    Librarians of Insts & Schools of Educ
    Nat Assn Mathematics Advisers
    Nat Assn Youth & Community Educ Officers
    Nat Governors' Assn
    NATFHE
    Soc Educ Consultants
Education: technology
    Assn Learning Technology
    Brit Educl Suppliers Assn
    Brit Learning Assn
EEC > European Union
Effluents > Sewers, sewage & effluents
Egg decoration
    Egg Crafters Gld
Eggs & egg products
    Brit Egg Assn
    Brit Egg Products Assn
    Brit Free Range Egg Producers Assn
    Nat Egg Marketing Assn
    UK Egg Producers Assn
Egypt
    AEMES
    Egypt Exploration Soc
    Egyptian Brit Cham Comm
Ekbom syndrome
    Ekbom Support Gp
Elastic fabrics
    Brit Narrow Fabrics Assn
Elastic rope sports
    Brit Elastic Rope Sports Assn
Elderly persons > Geriatrics & ageing; Old people's organisations
Elections & electoral legislation
    Assn Electoral Administrators
    Charter 88
    Electoral Reform Soc
    Scot Assessors' Assn
    Unlock
Electoral reform > Elections & electoral legislation
Electric: cable & conduit
    ASTA BEAB Certification Services
    Brit Cables Assn
Electric: fencing
    Fencing Contrs Assn
Electric: heating > Heating
Electric: lighting > Lighting
Electric: motors
    BEAMA
Electric: tools
    Portable Electric Tool Mfrs Assn
Electric: transport
    Battery Vehicle Soc
    Electric Boat Assn
    Electric Rly Soc

Electrical goods trade
    Assd Nat Electrical Whlsrs
    Assn Electrical & Mechanical Trs
    Assn Whls Electrical Bulk Buyers
    Electrical Distbrs Assn
    Electrical & Electronic Retailers Assn Ireland
    Small Electrical Appliance Marketing Assn
Electrical industry & engineering
    Amicus
    Assn Electrical Contrs, Ireland
    Assn Managerial Electrical Executives
    Assn Mfrs Domestic Appliances
    ASTA BEAB Certification Services
    BEAMA
    Chart Instn Bldg Services Engrs
    Electric Trace Heating Ind Coun
    Electrical Contrs Assn
    Electrical & Engg Staff Assn
    Electrical Inds Fedn Ireland
    EMC Ind Assn
    Instn Mechanical Engrs
    SELECT
Electricity
    Assn Coal Mine Methane Operators
    Assn Electricity Producers
    Assn Mfrs Power generating Systems
    BEAMA
    Electricity Arbitration Assn
    Energy Inds Coun
    Energy Networks Assn
    Energy Retail Assn
    Nat Jt Utilities Gp
    UK Revenue Protection Assn
    > + Solar technology
Electricity meters > Meters & metering
Electro-ceramics
    Brit Refractories & Indl Ceramics
    > + Ceramics
Electrochemistry
    R Soc Chemistry
    Soc Chemical Ind
Electrodiagnostic medicine
    Brit Soc Clinical Neurophysiology
Electroencephalography
    Brit Soc Clinical Neurophysiology
    Electro-physiological Technologists Assn
Electroheat
    BEAMA
Electrohydraulic control
    Brit Fluid Power Assn
Electro-imaging
    Soc Metaphysicians
Electroluminescence
    Keygraphica
Electrolysis
    Brit Inst & Assn Electrolysis
    > + Beauty specialists/treatment
Electromagnetics
    EMC Ind Assn
Electronic: components (obsolescence)
    Component Obsolescence Gp
Electronic: data/information interchange
    Construction Ind Trading Electronically
    Soc Public Inf Networks
Electronic: industry & engineering
    Assn Franchised Distbrs Electronic Components
    Assn Instrumentation, Control, Automation. . .
    BEAMA
    Electro-Technical Coun Ireland
    EMC Ind Assn
    Instn Engg & Technology
    Intellect, the Information Technology, Telecommunications &
    Electronics
    > + Computers; Data processing; Optoelectronics; Radio
Electronic: organs > Organs, organists & organ music
Electronic: surveillance > Security
Electronic: trade & commerce
    Consumer Electronics Distbrs Assn [IRL]
    GS1 (UK)
    Radio, Electrical & TV Retailers' Assn
Electronic: traffic control
    ITS UK
    > + Traffic: control
Electro-optics > Optoelectronics
Electrophoresis
    Brit Soc Proteome Res
    > + Biochemistry & biotechnology

© CBD Research Ltd · Beckenham · BR3 5JS · Tel 020 8650 7745 · Fax 020 8650 0768 · E-mail cbd@cbdresearch.com · www.cbdresearch.com

Electrophysiology
> Scot Neuroscience Gp
Electroplating
> Surface Engg Assn
Electro-static equipment
Elgar (Sir Edward)
> Elgar Soc
Elia
> Charles Lamb Soc
Eliot (George) [Mary Ann Evans]
> George Eliot Fellowship
Embalming
> Brit Inst Embalmers
Embroidery
> Embroiderers' Gld
Embryo research
> Brit Soc Developmental Biology
Emergency planning > Civil defence & industrial emergencies
Emigration > Immigration & emigration
Emission monitoring
> BTC Testing Advisory Gp
> Source Testing Assn
Employee assistance programmes
> UK Employee Assistance Profls Assn
Employee involvement > Industrial involvement & participation
Employers
> Confedn Brit Ind
> Employers Forum on Disability
> Ir Business & Emplrs Confedn
> > + specific industry
Employment
> Brit Assn Supported Employment
> Employers Forum on Age
> HR Soc
> Over Fifties Assn
> Recruitment Soc
> > + Careers
Employment agents & consultants
> Assn Graduate Recruiters
> Assn Resettlement & Employment Advisors
> Assn Technology Staffing Companies
> Recruitment & Employment Confedn
Emus
> Rhea & Emu Assn
> > + Ostrich farming
Enamel: vitreous > Vitreous enamel
Enamelling
> Brit Soc Enamellers
> Gld Enamellers
Encephalitis
> Action ME
> Encephalitis Soc
> > + Myalgic encephalitis/encephalopathy
Endocrinology
> Androgen Insensitivity Syndrome Support Gp
> Brit Assn Endocrine Surgeons
> Soc Endocrinology
Endodontics > Dentistry
Endometriosis
> Nat Endometriosis Soc
Endoscopy
> Brit Soc Gastroenterology
> Brit Soc Gynaecological Endoscopy
Endowment policies (secondhand)
> Assn Policy Market Makers
> > + Insurance
Energy
> Assn Consvn Energy
> Brit Assn Colliery Mgt
> Brit Energy Assn
> Brit Hydropower Assn
> Brit Inst Energy Economics
> Buildings Energy Efficiency Fedn
> Combined Heat & Power Assn
> Energy Inds Coun
> Energy Inst
> Energy Networks Assn
> Energy Systems Tr Assn
> Fedn Authorised Energy Rating Orgs
> Inst Domestic Heating. . . Engrs
> Instn Civil Engrs
> Instn Engg & Technology
> Ir Hydro Power Assn
> Nat Energy Action
> Renewable Energy Assn
> Resource Use Inst
> > + Renewable energy; specific form of energy

Enforcement agents
> Assn Civil Enforcement Agencies
> Enforcement Services Assn
Engineering
> Amicus
> Assn Brit Transport & Engg Museums
> Assn Consultancy & Engg
> Assn Consulting Engrs Ireland
> Assn Indep Mgt & Maritime Services
> Brit Assn Advancement Science
> Brit Engg Mfrs Assn
> EEF
> Engg Inds Assn
> Engg Integrity Soc
> INCA [IRL]
> Inst Indl Engrs [IRL]
> Inst Materials, Minerals & Mining
> Instn Civil Engrs
> Instn Diagnostic Engrs
> Instn Engg Designers
> Instn Engg & Technology
> Instn Engrs Ireland
> Instn Engrs & Shipbuilders Scotland
> Intellect, the Information Technology, Telecommunications & Electronics
> Prospect
> R Academy Engg
> Royal Soc (The)
> Science, Engg & Mfrg Technologies Alliance
> Science, Technology, Engg. . . Public Relations Assn
> Scot Engg
> Soc Operations Engrs
> Soc Profl Engrs
> UK Assn Profl Engrs
> Women's Engg Soc
> > + other branches of engineering
Engineering: bricks > Bricks
Engineering: education
> Brit Educl Suppliers Assn
> Nat Forum Engg Centres
Engineering: equipment & materials
> Engg Eqpt & Materials Users Assn
Engineering: history
> Newcomen Soc
> Stephenson Locomotive Soc
> Trevithick Soc
Engineering: plant > Plant: industrial
Engineers' tools > Tools
Engines > specific type of engine
England
> Campaign English Parliament
> Campaign Protect Rural England
> R Soc St George
English language & literature
> Aethelflaed
> Anglo-Norman Text Soc
> Assn Brit Language Schools
> Assn Promotion Quality TESOL Educ
> Early English Text Soc
> Engliscan Gesíþas
> English Assn
> English Poetry & Song Soc
> English UK
> Modern Humanities Res Assn
> Nat Assn Teaching Engl
> Nat Assn Teaching Engl &. . .Community Languages
> Plain Engl Campaign
> Queen's Engl Soc
> R Soc Literature
> Ranulf Higden Soc
> Simplified Spelling Soc
> > + individual writers by name
Engravers
> MultiService Assn
> R Soc Painter-Printmakers
> Soc Wood Engravers
> > + Art & artists
Enterprise agencies
> Nat Fedn Enterprise Agencies
Entertainment
> Agents Assn
> Brit Magical Soc
> Broadcasting, Entertainment Cinematograph. . .U
> Concert Artistes' Association
> Fedn Entertainment Us
> Inst Entertainment & Arts Mgt
> Nat Arenas Assn

Nat Entertainment Agents Coun
Personal Mgrs Assn
Production Services Assn
> + Leisure, recreation & amenity management;   specific forms of entertainment

Entertainment: equipment
Profl Lighting & Sound Assn

Entomology
Amat Entomologists' Soc
Assn Applied Biologists
Birmingham Natural Hist Soc
Brit Entomological & Natural Hist Soc
Buglife
R Entomological Soc Lond
> + Nature conservation

Envelopes
Envelope Makers' & Mfrg Stationers' Assn

Environment
Assn Brit Certification Bodies
Assn Envtl Archaeology
Assn Heritage Interpretation
Brit Urban Regeneration Assn
Doctor E F Schumacher Soc
Environmental Communicators Org
Environmental Inds Commission
Environmental Inds Fedn
Environmental Investigation Agency
ETA Services Ltd
Friends Earth
Global Commons Inst
Green Alliance Trust
Inst Ecology & Envtl Mgt
Inst Envtl Mgt & Assessment
Landscape Res Gp
Nat Assn Envtl Educ
Nat Register Access Consultants
Nat Soc Clean Air...
Regional Studies Assn
Scot Envt Link
Soc Chemical Ind
Soc Envtl Exploration
Soc Responsible Use Resources Agriculture & Land
Socialist Envt & Resources Assn
UK Envtl Law Assn
UK Forum Envtl Inds
Valpak
Wildlife Countryside Link
Women's Envtl Network
> + Conservation; Pollution & pollution control

Environment: engineering/health
Assn Public Analysts
Assn Public Analysts Scotland
Brit Soc Ecological Medicine
Chart Inst Envtl Health
ENCAMS
Environmental Health Officers Assn [IRL]
Inst Domestic Heating... Engrs
Instn Envtl Sciences
R Envtl Health Inst Scotland
SIESO
Soc Envtl Engrs
UK Envtl Mutagen Soc

Environmental illness > Occupational health & hygiene

Environmental services
Environmental Services Assn

Enzootic abortion of ewes
Highlands & Islands Sheep Health Assn

Ephemera
Brit Matchbox, Label & Booklet Soc
English Playing-Card Soc
Ephemera Soc

Epidermolysis bullosa
Dystrophic Epidermolysis Bullosa Res Assn

Epigraphy
Brit Epigraphy Soc

Epilepsy
Brainwave
Brit Epilepsy Assn
Epilepsy Action Scotland
Nat Soc Epilepsy

Epiphytes
Epiphytic Plant Study Gp
> + Plants

Equal opportunities
Nat Alliance Women's Orgs
Over Fifties Assn

Parity
> + Employment

Equestrian trade
Brit Equestrian Tr Assn
> + Horse headings

Equipment > Leasing; Mining: equipment; Office equipment & systems

Equity finance
BVCA
EIS Assn

Equity release plans
Safe Home Income Plans

Ergonomics
Ergonomics Soc

Eritrea
Middle East Assn

Erotic art
Assn Erotic Artists
Gld Erotic Artists

Escalators
Lift & Escalator Ind Assn

Esperanto
Esperanto Assn Britain
Scot Esperanto Assn

Essences
Brit Assn Flower Essence Producers
Brit Essence Mfrs' Assn

Essential oils
Aromatherapy Tr Coun
Brit Essential Oils Assn
Brit Soc Perfumers
Intl Gen Produce Assn

Estate agents
Assn Residential Letting Agents
Gld Letting & Mgt
Gld Profl Estate Agents
Inst Auctioneers & Appraisers Scotland
Nat Assn Estate Agents
Property Consultants Soc
UK Assn Letting Agents
> + Property & land owners

Estate management
Country Land & Business Assn
Inst Clerks Works
Inst Healthcare Engg & Estate Mgt
Inst Maintenance & Bldg Mgt
Manorial Soc

Estate & trust planning > Trusts, trusteeship & estate planning

Estuaries
Estuarine & Coastal Sciences Assn

Ethics
Comment Reproductive Ethics
S Place Ethical Soc

Ethiopia
Middle East Assn

Ethnic studies
Assn Study Ethnicity & Nationalism

Ethnography
Museum Ethnographers Gp
R Anthropological Inst

Eton Fives
Eton Fives Assn

Eugenics
Galton Inst

Eurhythmics
Dalcroze Soc
Laban Gld Movement & Dance

Europe
Brit Assn Cent & Eastn Europe
Brit Assn Slavonic & E Eur Studies
Eur Atlantic Gp
Eur Atlantic Movement
Eur Inf Assn
Eur Movement
University Assn Contemporary Eur Studies

European Union
Anti Common Market League
Atlantic Coun
Brit Inst Intl & Comparative Law
Campaign Euro-federalism
Campaign Indep Britain
Democracy Movement

Euthanasia
Alert Euthanasia
Care not Killing Alliance
Dignity in Dying
Human Rights Soc
Medical Ethics Alliance

Soc Protection Unborn Children
Voluntary Euthanasia Soc Scotland
Evacuees (WWII)
Evacuees Reunion Assn
Evangelism
Evangelical Alliance
Fellowship Indep Evangelical Churches
> + Christian activities
Evens (Rev G Bramwell)
Romany Soc
Events > Corporate hospitality; Exhibitions; Shows & events
Excavation & land clearance
Inst Explosives Engrs
Exchanges: international
Assn Learning Languages En Famille
Exchequer records
Pipe Roll Soc
Exhibitions
Assn Brit Profl Conf Organisers
Assn Event Venues
Assn Exhibition Contrs
Assn Exhibition Organisers
Brit Exhib Contrs' Assn
Events Ind Alliance
Events Sector Ind Trg Org
Exhibition Study Gp
Exhibition Venues Assn
Nat Exhibitors Assn
Soc Event Organisers
> + Conferences & conventions
Exhumation
Inst Cemetery & Crematorium Mgt
> + Burial & cremation

Experts & expert witness
Academy Experts
Assn Consulting Scientists
Expert Witness Inst
Soc Expert Witnesses
Exploration
BSES Expeditions
Scientific Exploration Soc
Young Explorers' Trust
Exploration: history
Hakluyt Soc
Explosives
Assn Petroleum & Explosives Admin
Brit Cave Res Assn
Explosives Ind Gp
Inst Demolition Engrs
Inst Explosives Engrs
Nat Assn Security Dog Users
Explosives: detection
Nat Assn Security Dog Users
Export & import
Brit Exporters Assn
China-Britain Business Coun
Free Trade League
Inst Export
Inst Intl Tr [IRL]
Ir Exporters Assn
> + Chambers of commerce: overseas trade
Export packers
Brit Intl Freight Assn
> + specific trade
Ex-service organisations
Assn Jewish Ex-Servicemen & Women
Assn Resettlement & Employment Advisors
Brit Limbless Ex-Service Men's Assn
Confedn Brit Service & Ex-Service Orgs
Not Forgotten Assn
Officers' Assn
R Brit Legion
R Brit Legion Scotland
R Naval Assn
Extra sensory perception > Paranormal & psychical research
Eyes > Blind & partially sighted; Ophthalmology; specific diseases
Eyewear > Optical industry

F

Fabric care
Home Laundering Consultative Coun
Fabrics > Textile: industry & trade

Fabry disease
Soc Mucopolysaccharide Diseases
Facial disfigurement > Birthmarks & disfigurement
Facilities management
Brit Inst Facilities Mgt
Chart Inst Bldg
Facilities Mgt Assn
Ir Property & Facility Mgmt Assn
R Instn Chart Surveyors
> + Offices (serviced)
Factoring (banking & finance)
Factors & Discounters Assn
Nat Assn Comml Finance Brokers
Factors: motor > Motor factors
Fair trade
Brit Assn Fair Tr Shops
Fairgrounds & equipment
Fair Organ Presvn Soc
Fairground Assn
Fairground Soc
Mechanical Organ Owners Soc
Roller Coaster Club
Showmen's Gld
Soc Indep Roundabout Proprietors
Fairs
Nat Assn Brit Market Authorities
Fairy rings & fairies
Fairy Ring
Faith healing > Spiritual healing
Falconry > Hawks & hawking
Falkland Islands
Falkland Islands Assn
Falklands Consvn
Falkner (John Meade)
John Meade Falkner Soc
Fall arrest equipment
Fall Arrest Safety Eqpt Training
False memory
Brit False Memory Soc
Falsework
Nat Access & Scaffolding Confedn
Familial hypercholesterolaemia > + Cardiology
Family history > Genealogy
Family law
Assn Family Therapy
Children Law UK
Family Law Assn Scotland
Family Law Bar Assn
Family Mediators' Assn
Family Rights Gp
NAGALRO
Nat Family Mediation
Resolution
Family planning
Fac Family Planning & Reproductive Healthcare
Fertility Care Scotland
fpa
Ir Family Planning Assn
Nat Assn Nurses Contraception & Sexual Health
Nat Assn Ovulation Method Instructors
Natural Family Planning Teachers Assn
Parents Oral Contraception Children
Family therapy
Assn Family Therapy
Family Matters Inst
Family welfare > Welfare organisations
Fan clubs > subject of interest
Fancy dress
Brit Costume Assn
> + Costume history, design & conservation
Fancy goods > Giftware
Fans
Fan Mfrs' Assn
Heating, Ventilating & Air Conditioning Mfrs' Assn
> + Air: conditioning & ventilating; Heating
Fantasy
Brit Fantasy Soc
Fare collection
Transport Ticket Soc
Farm animals > Animals; specific animals
Farm buildings
Instn Agricl Engrs
Rural & Indl Design & Bldg Assn
Farm machinery > Agriculture: machinery
Farm shops & food
Nat Farmers' Retail & Markets Assn
Women's Food & Farming U

Farmers' organisations
    Comml Farmers Gp
    Family Farmers' Assn
    Farmers Action
    Farmers Club
    Farmers' U Wales
    Farms for Schools
    Flying Farmers Assn
    Ir Farmers Assn
    Jersey Farmers' U
    Manx Nat Farmers U
    Nat Assn NFU Gp Secretaries
    Nat Farmers' Retail & Markets Assn
    Nat Farmers U
    Nat Fedn Young Farmers Clubs (E&W)
    NFU Scotland
    Scot Assn Young Farmers Clubs
    Small Farms Assn
    Tenant Farmers' Assn
    Ulster Farmers U
Farming
    GreenSpace
    > Agriculture; Dairying; Organic growing & farming
Farnon (Robert)
    Robert Farnon Soc
Farriers
    Nat Assn Farriers. . .
    UK Horse Shoers U
    > Blacksmiths & farriers
Fashion
    Assn Model Agents
    Assn Photographers
    Brit Clothing Ind Assn
    Costume Soc
    > + Clothing; Costume history, design & conservation
Fasteners & turned parts
    Assn Stainless Fastener Distbrs
    Brit Assn Fastener Distbrs
    Brit Turned-Parts Mfrs Assn
    Confedn Brit Metalforming
    Power Fastenings Assn

Fatigue
    Action ME
    Assn Young People with ME
    Myalgic Encephalopathy Assn
    > Materials: technology & testing
Fats, edible & processing > Edible oils & fats; Rendering; individual fats
Fauna > Animals; Nature conservation; specific animals
Feed (animal) > Animal feed
Feet
    Brit Orthopaedic Foot Surgery Soc
    > Chiropody & podiatry; Footwear; Orthopaedics
Fell running
    Fell Runners Assn
    > + Running
Fell walking > Walking
Fellmongers > Hides & skins
Felt
    Nat Fillings Assn
    Needleloom Underlay Mfrs' Assn
Felt & flat roofing > Roofing
Fencing (enclosure)
    Fencing Contrs Assn
    Wire Products Assn
Fencing (sport)
    Brit Fedn Histl Swordplay
    Brit Fencing Assn
    Scot Fencing
Feng shui
    Feng Shui Soc
Ferns
    Brit Pteridological Soc
Ferrets
    Nat Ferret Welfare Soc
Ferries
    Passenger Shipping Assn
    > + Shipping
Fertilisers
Fertility
    Assn Biomedical Andrologists
    Brit Andrology Soc
    Brit Fertility Soc
    Brit Infertility Counselling Assn
    Brit Soc Psychosomatic Obstetrics. . .
    Daisy Network Premature Menopause Support Gp

    Infertility Network UK
    Soc Reproduction & Fertility
Festivals: art, drama & music
    Assn Festival Organisers
    Brit Arts Festivals Assn
    Brit & Intl Fedn Festivals Music, Drama & Speech
    Gld Drama Adjudicators
    Nat Drama Festivals Assn
Fibre building board > Building board & timber
Fibre drums > Cisterns, drums & tanks
Fibre cement
    Fibre Cement Mfrs Assn
Fibre optics
    Fibreoptic Ind Assn
Fibreboard > Packaging
Fibromyalgia
    Fibromyalgia Assn
Fiddles > Accordions & fiddles
Field archery
    Nat Field Archery Soc
    Scot Field Archery Assn
Field sports
    Countryside Alliance
    Countryside Ireland
    Fedn Assns Country Sports Europe
    Scot Assn Country Sports
    > + individual sport
Field study > Natural history; other subjects of field study
Fights (historic/re-enactment)
    English Civil War Soc
    Historic Artillery
    Knights R England
    Napoleonic Assn
    Nat Assn Re-enactment Socs
    Plantagenet Medieval Archery. . . Soc
    Regia Anglorum
    Sealed Knot
    Siege Gp
    Victorian Military Soc
    World War Two Living Hist Assn
    > + Stunts & stunt coordination
Fights (stage/film)
    Brit Academy Dramatic Combat
    > + Stunts & stunt coordination
Filing systems > Office equipment & systems
Filling stations
    Assn Petroleum & Explosives Admin
    Garage Watch Ltd
Fillings (furniture)
    Nat Fillings Assn
Film
    access CINEMA [IRL]
    ACG Ltd (Arts Centre Gp)
    Brit Academy Film & TV Arts
    Brit Fedn Film Socs
    Brit Film Inst
    FOCAL Intl
    Inst Amat Cinematographers
    Inst Contemporary Arts
    Ir Film Inst
    Mercia Cinema Soc
    Nat Assn Higher Educ Moving Image
    Test Card Circle
    > + Photography
Film: advertising > Advertising: television & screen
Film: educational > Audio-visual aids & equipment
Film: festivals > Festivals: art, drama & music
Film: production & distribution
    Advertising Producers Assn
    Animal Welfare Filming Fedn
    Assn Studio & Production Eqpt Companies
    BKSTS
    Brit Soc Cinematographers
    Broadcasting, Entertainment Cinematograph. . .U
    Ciné Glds GB
    Cinema Exhibitors Assn
    Directors Gld
    Film Distbrs' Assn
    Gld Brit Camera Technicians
    Gld Brit Film & TV Editors
    New Producers Alliance
    Producers Alliance Cinema & TV
    Production Mgrs Assn
    Screen Producers Ireland
    > + specialists concerned; Radio & TV; Video

© CBD Research Ltd · Beckenham · BR3 5JS · Tel 020 8650 7745 · Fax 020 8650 0768 · E-mail cbd@cbdresearch.com · www.cbdresearch.com

Film: special effects
        Inst Explosives Engrs
        > + Stunts & stunt coordination
Film: stunts > Stunts & stunt coordination
Filters
        Heating, Ventilating & Air Conditioning Mfrs' Assn
Filtration
        Filtration Soc
Finance/Financial services
        Community Devt Finance Assn
        Inst Financial Services
        > + Accountancy; Banking; Investment; Management accountancy
Finance: brokers & agents
        Corpn Insurance, Financial & Mortgage Advisers
        Finance Ind Standards Assn
        London Investment Banking Assn
        Nat Assn Comml Finance Brokers
        Whls Markets Brokers' Assn
Finance: hire purchase > Credit: trade;   Credit: unions
Finance: planning
        Inst Financial Planning
Financial officers & controllers > Accountancy
Fine arts > Art headings
Fingerprinting
        Fingerprint Soc
Finishes/finishing > Coatings;   Metal: finishing;   Paint
Finland
        Finnish-British Cham Comm
Fire & flood damage restoration
        Brit Damage Mgt Assn
        Nat Carpet Cleaners Assn
Fire loss adjusters
        Chart Inst Loss Adjusters
Fire marks
        Fire Mark Circle
Fire protection & prevention
        Architectural & Specialist Door Mfrs Assn
        Assn Bldg Engrs
        Assn Brit Fire Trs
        Assn Brit Insurers
        Assn Specialist Fire Protection
        Brit Approvals Fire Eqpt
        Brit Automatic Fire Sprinkler Assn
        Brit Fire Consortium
        Brit Fire Protection Systems Assn
        Brit Textile Technology Gp
        Brit Urethane Foam Contrs Assn
        Brit Wood Preserving & Damp-proofing Assn
        Fedn Brit Fire Orgs
        Fire Extinguishing Trs Assn
        Fire Fighting Vehicles Mfrs Assn
        Fire Ind Confedn
        Fire Officers Assn
        Fire Protection Assn
        Fire Sprinkler Assn
        Glass & Glazing Fedn
        Halon Users Nat Consortium
        Indep Fire Engg & Distrbrs Assn
        Instn Fire Engrs
        Intumescent Fire Seals Assn
        Passive Fire Protection Fedn
        Soc Chemical Ind
Fire protection & prevention: equipment
        Fire & Rescue Suppliers Assn
Fire protection & prevention: history
        Fire Brigade Soc
        Fire Mark Circle
        Fire Service Presvn Gp
Fire protection & prevention: personnel
        Brit Fire Services Assn
        Chief Fire Officers Assn
        Chief Fire Officers Assn Ireland
        Fire Brigades' U
        Nat Assn Fire Officers
        Nat Assn Hospital Fire Officers
Firearms > Arms & armour; Guns & ammunition; Shooting
Firebricks > Refractories
Fireproofing > Fire Protection & prevention
Fires & fireplaces
        Nat Fireplace Assn
Fireworks
        Brit Pyrotechnists' Assn
        Explosives Ind Gp
        Inst Explosives Engrs
        Nat Campaign Firework Safety
Firms > Business

First aid & immediate care
        Brit Assn Immediate Care
        Brit Red Cross Soc
        Casualties Union
        Coach & Bus First Aid Assn
        Grand Priory. . . Hospital. . . St John
        Ir Red Cross Soc
        Medical Equestrian Assn
        Order of Malta [IRL]
        Saint Andrew's Ambulance Assn
        Saint John Ambulance Assn
Fiscal studies
        Inst Fiscal Studies
        > + Taxation
Fish: biology > Ichthyology
Fish: curing
        Aberdeen Fish Curers'. . .Assn
        Assn Brit Salted Fish Curers. . .
Fish: farming
        Brit Marine Finfish Assn
        Brit Trout Assn
        > + Salmon & trout
Fish: frying
        Nat Assn Range Mfrs
        Nat Fedn Fish Friers
Fish: meal & fish oil
        UK Assn Fish Meal Mfrs
Fish: trade
        Fedn Brit Port Whls Fish Mchts Assns
        Herring Buyers Assn
        Ir Fish Processors & Exporters Assn
        Ir Fish Producers Org
        London Fish Mchts (Billingsgate) Ltd
        Nat Fedn Fishermen's Orgs
        Nat Fedn Fishmongers
        Nat Fedn Inland Whls Fish Mchts
        Scot Seafood Processors Fedn
        Seafood Scotland
        Seafood Shetland
        UK Assn Fish Producer Orgs
Fish: tropical & ornamental
        Fedn Brit Aquatic Socs
        Ornamental Aquatic Tr Assn
Fishing
        Assn Salmon Fishery Bds
        Assn Sea Fisheries C'ees [E&W]
        Britain & Ireland Assn Aquatic Science Libraries. . .
        Coracle Soc
        Fishermen's Assn
        Inst Fisheries Mgt
        Ir Fishermen's Org
        Marineco
        Profl Coarse Fisheries Assn
        Scot Fishermen's Fedn
        Scot Fishermen's Org
        Scot Pelagic Fishermen's Assn
        Scot White Fish Producers Assn
Fishing (sport)
        Anglers Consvn Assn
        Angling Trs Assn
        Assn Stillwater Game Fishery Mgrs
        Carp Soc
        Confedn Engl Fly Fishers
        Countryside Alliance
        Ir Fedn Sea Anglers
        London Anglers Assn
        Nat Assn Fisheries & Angling Consultatives
        Nat Fedn Anglers
        Nat Fedn Sea Anglers
        Profl Anglers Assn
        Salmon & Trout Assn
        Scot Anglers Nat Assn
        Scot Assn Country Sports
        Scot Fedn Sea Anglers
        Shark Angling Club
        Specialist Anglers Alliance
        Ulster Angling Fedn
        Ulster Coarse Fishing Fedn
Fishing tackle
        Angling Trs Assn
Fishing vessels > Ships: history & preservation
Fitness
        Body Control Pilates Assn
        Fitness Ind Assn
        Fitness League
        Fitness NI
        Keep Fit Assn

Medau Soc
Nat Amat Bodybuilders Assn
Nat Register Personal Trainers
Profl Assn Alexander Teachers
Soc Teachers Alexander Technique
> + Health headings

Fitness equipment
Fitness Ind Assn
Sports & Fitness Eqpt Assn
Sports Mfrs & Retailers Tr Assn

Fives > Eton Fives; Rugby Fives

Fixing systems
Construction Fixings Assn

Flags, banners & bunting
Brit Sign & Graphics Assn
Campaign Restoration Nat Anthem & Flag
Flag Inst
Heraldry Soc
Performance Textiles Assn

Flat glass > Glass & glazing

Flat green bowling > Bowling

Flat roofing > Roofing

Flats: maintenance/management
Upkeep

Flavourings
Brit Essence Mfrs' Assn
Brit Soc Flavourists

Fleet Air Arm

Fleet car operators & management
ACFO Ltd
Inst Car Fleet Mgt
> + Motor headings

Flexible hoses
Hose Mfrs' & Suppliers Assn

Flexible packaging > Packaging;   Plastics: film

Flight safety > Aviation: safety, control & training

Flight simulation
R Aeronautical Soc

Floatation
Floatation Tank Assn

Flock & felt > Felt

Flood damage restoration > Fire & flood damage restoration

Flood protection
Assn Drainage Authorities
Flood Protection Assn

Flood research
Tornado & Storm Res Org

Floors
Assn Concrete Indl Flooring Contrs
Brit Precast Concrete Fedn
FeRFA
Nat Inst Carpet & Floorlayers

Floors: floorcoverings
Carpet Foundation
Contract Flooring Assn
Nat Inst Carpet & Floorlayers
UK Resilient Flooring Mfrs' Assn
> + Carpets

Floors: tiles & quarries > Tiles (floor & wall)

Floristry > Flowers, flower arrangement & floristry

Flour
Inc Nat Assn Brit & Ir Millers
Scot Flour Millers Assn

Flowers, flower arrangement & floristry
Brit Dried Flowers Assn
Brit Florist Assn
Flower Import Tr Assn
Flowers & Plants Assn
Fresh Produce Consortium
INTERFLORA
Nat Assn Flower Arrangement Socs
Pressed Flower Gld
Soc Floristry
> + Horticulture; specific varieties of flowers

Flower remedies
Brit Assn Flower Essence Producers
Brit Flower & Vibrational Essences Assn
Crystal & Healing Fedn

Flues > Chimneys

Fluid mechanics > Hydraulics & hydromechanics

Fluoridation
Brit Fluoridation Soc
Scot Pure Water Assn

Flute playing
Brit Flute Soc

Fly ash > Ash

Flyball
Brit Flyball Assn

Fly-dressing
Flydressers Gld

Flying > Air: sport; Aviation

Flying discs (sport) > Disc golf (flying discs); Ultimate

Foam (plastic) > Plastics: foam

Foil: aluminium > Aluminium: foil

Folk dance & song
Assn Festival Organisers
Brit Bluegrass Music Assn
Brit Country Music Assn
Brit Western Dance Assn
Cymdeithas Ddawns Werin Cymru
Elsie Jeanette Oxenham Appreciation Soc
English Folk Dance & Song Soc
Folk Music Soc Ireland
FolkArts England
Musicians' U
Order Woodcraft Chivalry
R Scot Country Dance Soc
Soc Intl Folk Dancing
Southern Counties Folk Fedn
Welsh Amat Music Fedn
Welsh Folk Song Soc
> + Highland dancing

Folk life & lore
Cornish Language Coun
Dracula Soc
Folklore Ireland Soc
Folklore Soc
Lakeland Dialect Soc
Soc Folk Life Studies
Traditional Cosmology Soc
Ulster Folk Life Soc

Follies
Folly Fellowship
> + Historic buildings

Food
Bakers', Food & Allied Workers' U
Brewing, Food & Beverage Ind Suppliers Assn
Brit Nutrition Foundation
Campden & Chorleywood Food Res Assn
Food Devt Assn
Food & Drink Fedn
Gld Food Writers
Henry Doubleday Res Assn
Inst Food Science & Technology
Inst Food Science & Technology Ireland
Instn Agricl Engrs
Maltsters Assn
McCarrison Soc
Soc Chemical Ind
Soc Food Hygiene Technology
Sustain
> + Health food; Organic growing & farming

Food: additives
Assn Public Analysts
Assn Public Analysts Scotland
Food Additives & Ingredients Assn
> + Animal feed

Food: allergy > Allergy

Food: casings > Sausage & food casings

Food: farm > Farm shops & food

Food: frozen & chilled
Chilled Food Assn
Cold Storage & Distbn Fedn
Provision Tr Fedn
UK Assn Frozen Food Producers

Food: hampers
Hamper Ind Tr Assn

Food: packaging
Brit Bottlers' Inst
Campden & Chorleywood Food Res Assn
Foodservice Packaging Assn
Indl Packaging Assn
Liquid Food Carton Mfrs' Assn
Metal Packaging Mfrs Assn
Processing & Packaging Machinery Assn

Food: processing
Food Processors' Assn
Instn Chemical Engrs
Instn Chemical Engrs

Food: safety
Assn Port Health Authorities
Brit Pest Control Assn

© CBD Research Ltd · Beckenham · BR3 5JS · Tel 020 8650 7745 · Fax 020 8650 0768 · E-mail cbd@cbdresearch.com · www.cbdresearch.com

R Envtl Health Inst Scotland
Soc Applied Microbiology
Food: speciality & fine foods
    Cornish Pasty Assn
    Gld Fine Food Retailers
    Heart of England Fine Foods
    Melton Mowbray Pork Pie Assn
    Provision Tr Fedn
    Rural Crafts Assn
Food: trade
    Brit Food Importers & Distrbrs Assn
    Brit Frozen Food Fedn
    Campden & Chorleywood Food Res Assn
    Food Britain Fast Track
    Food & Drink Ind Ireland
    Ir Assn Distributive Trs
    Nat Fedn Meat & Food Traders
    Organic Food Fedn
    Scot Food & Drink Fedn
    Scot Food Tr Assn
    > + Grocery & provision trade; Health food; Takeaway & fast food
Food: transport > Road: haulage; Temperature controlled transport
Foodservice
    Foodservice Consultants Soc Intl (UK)
    Foodservice Packaging Assn
Foosball
    Brit Foosball Assn
Foot > Footwear; Orthopaedics
Football (American) > American football
Football (Association)
    Amat Football Alliance
    Assn Football Statisticians
    Football Assn
    Football Assn Ireland
    Football Assn Wales
    Football League
    Football Supporters' Fedn
    Football Writers Assn
    Inst Football Mgrs & Admin
    Ir Football Assn
    League Mgrs Assn
    Profl Footballers Assn
    Referees' Assn
    Scot Amat Football Assn
    Scot Football Assn
    Scot Football League
    Scot Women's Football
Football (Rugby)
    Brit Amat Rugby League Assn
    Ir Rugby Football U
    Profl Rugby Players Assn
    Rugby Football League
    Rugby Football U
    Rugby Memorabilia Soc
    Scot Rugby U
    Welsh Rugby U
Football (table)
    Brit Foosball Assn
    Table Soccer Players Assn
Football pools
    Pool Promoters Assn
Footpaths & rights of way
    Commons, Open Spaces... Presvn Soc
    Green Lane Assn
    Inst Public Rights Way Officers
    Motoring Orgs' Land Access & Recreation Assn
    Offa's Dyke Assn
    Peak & Nthn Footpaths Soc
    Ramblers' Assn
    S Downs Soc
    S W Coast Path Assn
    Scot Rights Way & Access Soc
    Towpath Action Gp
    Trail Riders Fellowship
    > + Conservation; Open spaces
Footwear: industry
    Boot & Shoe Mfrs Assn
    Brit Equestrian Tr Assn
    Brit Footwear Assn
    Community
    Master Craftsmen's Assn
    Textile Inst Intl
Footwear: repairs
    Cutting Edge
    MultiService Assn
Footwear: trade
    Indep Footwear Retailers Assn

Instock Footwear Suppliers Assn
Soc Shoe Fitters
Forage > Animal feed; Grass & grassland
Forces > Armed forces & veterans: welfare;   Army; Royal Navy
Forensic accountancy
    Network Indep Forensic Accountants
    > + Accountancy
Forensic science
    Assn Consulting Scientists
    Brit Academy Forensic Sciences
    Brit Assn Forensic Medicine
    Brit Assn Human Identification
    Fingerprint Soc
    Forensic Science Soc
    R Coll Psychiatrists
    > + Medicine & the law
Forestry
    Assn Timber Growers & Forestry Profls
    Brit Inst Agricl Consultants
    Confedn Forest Inds
    Forestry Contracting Assn
    Horticultural Trs Assn
    Inst Chart Foresters
    Instn Agricl Engrs
    Ir Timber Growers Assn
    Permaculture Assn
    R Forestry Soc England, Wales & NI
    R Highland & Agricl Soc Scotland
    R Scot Forestry Soc
    R Welsh Agricl Soc
    S England Agricl Soc
    Soc Ir Foresters
    Tropical Agriculture Assn
    Tropical Forest Forum
    UK Forest Products Assn
    > + Timber
Forestry: machinery
    Agricl Engrs Assn
Forging > Metal: forming
Fork-lift trucks
    Assn Indl Truck Trainers
    Brit Indl Truck Assn
    Fork Lift Truck Assn
    Indep Training Standards Scheme & Register
    > + Lifting & loading equipment
Formby (George)
    George Formby Soc
Fortresses & forts
    Fort Cumberland... Militaria Soc
    Fortress Study Gp
    Palmerston Forts Soc
    Subterranea Britannica
    UK Fortifications Club
Forwarding > Aviation; Shipping & forwarding
Fossils > Palaeontology
Fostering & foster parents
    Brit Assn Adoption & Fostering
    Fostering Network
Foundations (buildings)
    ASUCplus
    Fedn Piling Specialists
    Ground Forum
    > + Building
Foundries
    Foundry Eqpt & Supplies Assn
    Inst Cast Metal Engrs
    Nat Metal Trs Fedn
Fountains
Four by fours [4-wheel drive vehicles]
    Alliance Urban 4x4s
Fowl > Poultry
Foxes
    Nat Fox Welfare Soc
Foxhounds
    Masters Foxhounds Assn
    Peterborough R Foxhound Show Soc
    > + Hunts & hunting
Fragile X syndrome
    Fragile X Soc
Fragrances & aromatic compounds
    Brit Fragrance Assn
    Intl Gen Produce Assn
Frames > Concrete & concrete products; Picture framers
France
    Assn Brit Tour Operators France
    Assn Study Modern & Contemporary France
    Fédn Britannique Alliances Françaises

Franco-Brit Cham Comm & Ind
Franco-British Soc
Franco-Scottish Soc Scotland
Napoleonic Soc
France: language & literature
Anglo-Norman Text Soc
Assn French Language Studies
Fédn Britannique Alliances Françaises
Soc French Studies
Franchising
Assn Franchised Distbrs Electronic Components
Brit Franchise Assn
Ir Franchise Assn
Fraud & victims of fraud
Free Churches > individual Churches
Free trade
Free Trade League
Freedom of the individual > Individual freedom
Freemasonry
Grand Lodge Antient. . . Masons Scotland
Utd Grand Lodge England
Freemen
Freemen England & Wales
Freemen & Glds City Chester
Gld Freemen City Lond
Freestyle dancing > Dancing
Freeze drinks
Freezing (& chilled) food > Food: frozen & chilled; Refrigeration
Freight transport
Brit Intl Freight Assn
Chart Inst Logistics & Transport UK
Freight Transport Assn
ICHCA Intl
Ir Intl Freight Assn
Rail Freight Gp
> + Road: haulage;   Transport
French > France: language & literature
Freshwater biology > Biology
Friction
Brit Friction Materials Coun
Instn Mechanical Engrs
Friedreich's Ataxia
Ataxia UK
Friendly societies
Assn Friendly Socs
Friends (Quakers)
Friends Histl Soc
Religious Society of Friends (Quakers)
Frisbees > Disc golf (flying discs); Ultimate (sport)
Frogs
Frost (Robert)
Friends Dymock Poets
Frozen food > Food: frozen & chilled; Refrigeration
Fruit: growing
Brit Indep Fruit Growers Assn
English Apples & Pears
Ir Comml Horticl Assn
NI Fruit Growers Assn
Nuclear Stock Assn
Scot Soc Crop Res
Fruit: juice
Brit Fruit Juice Assn
Brit Soft Drinks Assn
Fruit: machines > Amusements & coin operated machines
Fruit: preserving
Fruit: trade
Fresh Produce Consortium
Nat Dried Fruit Tr Assn
Frying media
Nat Edible Oil Distbrs Assn
Fuchsias
Brit Fuchsia Soc
Fuel
Chemical Recycling Assn
Heating Oil Buyers Assn
> + specific fuels
Fuel ash > Ash
Fumes & fume extraction
Fan Mfrs' Assn
> + Air: pollution; Air: conditioning & ventilation
Fundraisers
Assn Arts Fundraisers
Assn Fundraising Consultants
Inst Fundraising
Funerals > Burial & cremation
Fungi > Mycology

Fur
Brit Fur Tr Assn
Furnace technology & construction
Brit Glass Mfrs' Confedn
Brit Indl Furnace Construction Assn
Inst Refractories Engrs
Refractory Users Fedn
Furnishing fabrics
Brit Interior Textiles Assn
Furniture
Assn Suppliers Furniture Ind
BFM Ltd
Brit Antique Furniture Restorers Assn
Brit Educl Suppliers Assn
Furniture Ind Res Assn
Leisure & Outdoor Furniture Assn
Furniture: contract > Contract services
Furniture: history
Chippendale Soc
Furniture Hist Soc
Furniture: warehousing & removal
Brit Assn Removers
Movers Inst
Nat Gld Removers & Storers
Further education > Adult education; Education; Technical education;
Universities
Furtwängler (Wilhelm)
Wilhelm Furtwängler Soc
Futons
Futon Assn
> + Beds & bedding
Futures & options
Futures & Options Assn

G

Gaelic language & culture
Cheshaght Ghailckagh (Yn)
Comunn Clàrsaich
Comunn Gaidhealach
Fèisean Gàidheal
Gaelic Athletic Assn
R Celtic Soc
Scot Gaelic Texts Soc
> + Scotland: language & literature
Galliformes
World Pheasant Assn UK
> + Game & game birds
Gallipoli
Gallipoli Assn
Galls (plants)
Brit Plant Gall Soc
Galvanising
Galvanizers Assn

Game & game birds
Brit Assn Shooting & Consvn
Game Conservancy Trust
Game Farmers Assn
Nat Game Dealers Assn
Nat Gamekeepers Org
Scot Gamekeepers' Assn
World Pheasant Assn UK
Games > Athletics; Highland games; Sports; individual sports & games
Games: equipment > Sports: equipment
Gaming
Amusement & Gaming Ind Forum
Casino Operators' Assn
Remote Gambling Assn
> + Casinos
Garages (equipment & waste)
Assn Garage Door Specialists
Automotive Aftermarket Assn
Forecourt Eqpt Fedn
Garage Eqpt Assn
Oil Recycling Assn
Retail Motor Ind Fedn
> + Filling stations; Motor trade
Garden centres & shops
Garden Centre Assn
Horticultural Assn Retail Traders
Garden furniture > Horticulture: machinery & supplies; Outdoor furniture

© CBD Research Ltd · Beckenham · BR3 5JS · Tel 020 8650 7745 · Fax 020 8650 0768 · E-mail cbd@cbdresearch.com · www.cbdresearch.com

Garden machinery
        Brit Hardware Fedn
        > Horticulture & garden: machinery
Gardens & gardening
        Assn Gardens Trusts
        Assn Leading Visitor Attractions
        Brit Assn Landscape Inds
        Cottage Garden Soc
        Fedn City Farms & Community Gardens
        Garden Hist Soc
        Garden & Landscape Designers Assn
        Good Gardeners' Assn
        Houses, Castles & Gardens Ireland
        Japanese Garden Soc
        Museum Garden Hist
        Nat Coun Consvn Plants & Gardens
        Nat Gardens Scheme Charitable Trust
        Nat Soc Allotment & Leisure Gardeners
        Profl Gardeners' Gld
        Soc Garden Designers
        > + Horticulture; Parks & gardens
Gardens & gardening: for disabled
        Gardening Disabled Trust & Garden Club
        THRIVE
Gardens & gardening: writers
        Garden Writers Gld

Gas
        Brit Compressed Gases Assn
        Carbon Monoxide & Gas Safety Soc
        Coun Registered Gas Installers
        Energy Inds Coun
        Gas Forum
        ICOM Energy Assn
        Instn Gas Engrs & Mgrs
        Nat Jt Utilities Gp
        Offshore Contrs' Assn
        Soc Brit Gas Inds
        UK Offshore Operators Assn
        UK Onshore Operators Gp
        > + Ocean industries
Gas appliances > Domestic appliances; Gas detection
Gas chromatography
        Chromatographic Soc
Gas detection
        Coun Gas Detection & Envtl Monitoring
Gas engines & turbines
        Instn Diesel & Gas Turbine Engrs
        Natural Gas Vehicle Assn
Gaskell (Mrs Elizabeth Cleghorn)
        Gaskell Soc
Gaskets
        Gasket Cutters' Assn
Gastroenterology
        Assn Gastroenterological Res Charities
        Brit Soc Gastroenterology
Gates > Automatic gates;   Stairs: gates & barriers
Gaucher's disease
        Gaucher's Assn
Gauges
        Gauge & Tool Makers Assn
        Pressure Gauge & Dial Thermometer Assn
        > + Control engineering
Gay organisations > Homosexuality
Gears
        Brit Gear Assn
Geese
        Brit Poultry Coun
        Brit Waterfowl Assn
        > + Poultry
Gemstones
        Brit Jewellers Assn
        Gemmological Assn
Gender dysphoria > Transsexuality & transvestism
Genealogy
        Anglo-German Family Hist Soc
        Assn Family Hist Socs Wales
        Assn Genealogists & Researchers in Archives
        Assn Profl Genealogists Ireland
        Assn Scot Genealogists & Researchers Archives
        Catholic Family Hist Soc
        Fedn Family Hist Socs
        Harleian Soc
        Heraldry Soc
        Inst Heraldic & Genealogical Studies
        Ir Family Hist Soc
        Ir Genealogical Res Soc

        Scot Genealogy Soc
        Soc Genealogists
        Ulster Histl Foundation
        > + Heraldry
General practitioners > Hospitals; Medical practice
Generators (electrical power)
        Assn Coal Mine Methane Operators
        Assn Mfrs Power generating Systems
        > + Electricity
Generic medicines
        Brit Generic Mfrs' Assn
        > + Pharmaceuticals
Genetics
        BioIndustry Assn
        Brit Livestock Genetics Consortium Ltd
        Brit Soc Human Genetics
        Genetic Interest Gp
        Genetics Soc
        Human Genetics Alert
        Soc Gen Microbiology
Genito-urinary medicine
        Brit Assn Sexual Health & HIV
        Brit Fedn Sexually Transmitted Diseases
        Brit HIV Assn
        Soc Sexual Health Advisers
Genomics > Genetics
Geography
        Assn Geographic Inf
        Geographical Assn
        Geographical Soc Ireland
        Manchester Geographical Soc
        R Geographical Soc
        R Scot Geographical Soc
        Scot Assn Geography Teachers
        Systematics Assn
Geology
        Earth Science Teachers Assn
        Edinburgh Geological Soc
        Geological Soc
        Geologists' Assn
        Inst Geologists Ireland
        Ir Assn Economic Geology
        Ir Geological Assn
        Mineral Ind Res Org
        Remote Sensing & Photogrammetry Soc
        Tertiary Res Gp
        Yorkshire Geological Soc
        > + Earth sciences, structure & resources; Palaeontology
Geomembranes
        Brit Geomembrane Assn
Geomorphology
        Geological Soc
        Geological Soc
        > + Geography
Geophysics
        R Astronomical Soc
George Cross
        Victoria Cross & George Cross Assn
Geospatial engineering
        Instn Civil Engg Surveyors
Geotechnics
        Assn Geotechnical & Geoenvironmental Specialists
        Brit Geotechnical Assn
        Ground Forum
        Soc Underwater Technology Ltd
Geraniums & pelargoniums
        Brit & Eur Geranium Soc
        Brit Pelargonium Geranium Soc
        Hardy Plant Soc
Gerbils
        Nat Gerbil Soc
Geriatrics & ageing
        Assn Educ & Ageing
        Brit Assn Service Elderly
        Brit Geriatrics Soc
        Brit Soc Gerontology
        Brit Soc Res Ageing
        Relatives & Residents Assn
        > + Old people's organisations
German > Germany: language & literature
German measles (Rubella)
        Sense
Germany
        Anglo-German Family Hist Soc
        Assn Study German Politics
        Brit Cham Comm Germany
        Brit-German Assn

German-Brit Cham Ind & Comm
German Hist Soc
German Rly Soc
Germany: language & literature
    Assn Language Learning
Germany: law
    Brit-German Jurists' Assn
Gestalt Therapy
    Gestalt Assn UK
Ghosts
    Assn Scientific Study Anomalous Phenomena
    > + Paranormal & psychical research
Gibson (Wilfred)
    Friends Dymock Poets
Gifted children > Children: gifted
Gifts (public) > Donations (public)
Giftware
    Brit Ceramic Confedn
    Brit Ceramic Gift & Tableware Mfrs' Assn
    Brit Jewellery, Giftware & Finishing Fedn
    Giftware Assn
    Wales Craft Coun
Gilbert (Sir William Schwenk)
    Gilbert & Sullivan Soc
Gilding
    Brit Antique Furniture Restorers Assn
Gin & vodka
    Gin & Vodka Assn
    > + Wines & spirits: trade
Gipsies > Gypsies & travelling people
Girls organisations > Youth organisation headings
Gladiolus
    Brit Gladiolus Soc
Glamour items > Cosmetic items (collecting)
Glass & glazing
    Brit Glass Mfrs' Confedn
    Flat Glass Coun
    Glass & Glazing Fedn
    Nat Fedn Glaziers
    Soc Glass Technology
    UK Flat Glass Mfrs Assn
Glass blowing
    Brit Soc Scientific Glassblowers
    Contemporary Glass Soc
Glass engraving
    Contemporary Glass Soc
    Gld Glass Engravers
Glass painting
    Brit Soc Master Glass Painters
    Glass & Glazing Fedn
    Kempe Soc
Glassfibre
    Intl Glassfibre Reinforced Concrete Assn
Glasshouse crops > Horticulture
Glasshouses & conservatories
    Glass & Glazing Fedn
Glassware
    Assn Hist Glass
    Contemporary Glass Soc
    Glass Circle
Glassware: scientific
    Brit Soc Scientific Glassblowers
    > + Laboratory equipment & technology
Glazing > Glass & glazing
Gliding & soaring
    Brit Gliding Assn
    Scot Gliding U
    Vintage Glider Club
    > + Hang gliding
Global warming
    Global Commons Inst
    > + Environment
Glosa
    Glosa Educ Org
Gloves
    Brit Glove Assn
Glucose
    Brit Starch Ind Assn
Glue sniffing > Solvent abuse
Glulam (glued laminated timber)
    Glued Laminated Timber Assn
Glycogen storage disease
    Assn Glycogen Storage Diseases
Gnomonics > Sundials
Go
    Brit Go Assn

Goats
    Brit Angora Goat Soc
    Brit Goat Soc
    Brit Veterinary Assn
    English Goat Breeders Assn
    Golden Guernsey Goat Soc
    Harness Goat Soc
    Pygmy Goat Club
    Scot Cashmere Producers Assn
Goethe (Johann Wolfgang von)
    English Goethe Soc
Gold (dealing in) > Bullion dealing
Gold panning
    Brit Goldpanning Assn
Goldsmiths & silversmiths
    Assn Brit Designer Silversmiths
    Brit Cutlery & Silverware Assn
    Brit Jewellery, Giftware & Finishing Fedn
    Company Goldsmiths Dublin
    Inst Profl Goldsmiths
    Nat Assn Goldsmiths
Golf
    Assn Golf Club Secretaries
    Assn Golf Writers
    English Golf U
    Golf Club GB
    Golf Consultants Assn
    Golfing U Ireland
    Ir Ladies Golf U
    Ladies' Golf U
    Nat Golf Clubs Advy Assn
    Profl Golfers Assn
    R & Ancient Golf Club
    Scot Golf U
    Scot Ladies' Golfing Assn
    Welsh Golfing U
Golf courses
    Brit Assn Golf Course Constructors
    Brit & Intl Golf Greenkeepers' Assn
    Nat Assn Public Golf Courses
    Sports Turf Res Inst
    > + Sportsgrounds & synthetic surfaces
Golf equipment
    Brit Golf Ind Assn
Goon Show
    Goon Show Preservation Soc
Gooseberries
    Gooseberry Soc
Gothic literature > Horror literature
Gout
    Purine Metabolic Patients Assn
Government > Parliamentary government
Government: accountability
    Transparency Intl (UK)
Graduates in business > Commerce
Graffiti
    Anti-Graffiti Assn
Graham (Winston)
Grain
    Grain & Feed Tr Assn
    Ir Grain & Feed Assn
    NI Grain Tr Assn
    Scot Corn Tr Assn
    > + Agriculture: merchants;   Flour
Grainger (Percy Aldridge)
    Percy Grainger Soc
Grammar schools
    Nat Grammar Schools Assn
    > + Education;   Independent & public schools
Gramophones > Sound recording & reproduction
Grandparents
    Grandparents Action Group
    Grandparents Assn
    > + Parents
Grapes > Wines & viticulture
Graphic arts & design
    Chart Soc Designers
    > + Industrial graphics; Printing headings
Graphology & graphoanalysis
    Brit Astrological & Psychic Soc
    Brit Inst Graphologists
    Brit Soc Graphoanalysts
    IGA-UK
Grass & grassland
    Brit Grassland Soc
    Ir Grassland Assn

N Scotland Grassland Soc
> + Seeds; Sportsgrounds & synthetic surfaces; Turf
Grasses (dried)
Brit Dried Flowers Assn
Gravel > Sand & gravel
Gravy
Food Processors' Assn
Grease > Lubricants
Greece
Anglo-Hellenic League
Brit Hellenic Cham Comm
Greek Inst
Soc Promotion Hellenic Studies
> + Classical studies
Green lanes/roads > Footpaths & rights of way
Greenhouses > Glasshouses & conservatories
Greeting cards
Greeting Card Assn
Greyhounds
Brit Veterinary Assn
Nat Greyhound Racing Club
Grieg (Edvard Hagerup)
Grieg Soc
Grills & security shutters
Brit Blind & Shutter Assn
> + Doors; Windows: blinds & shutters
Grinding & milling machinery
Solids Handling & Processing Assn
Grit > Aggregates
Grocery & provision trade
Assn Convenience Stores
Fedn Whls Distbrs
Inst Grocery Distbn
Provision Tr Fedn
RGDATA [IRL]
Scot Food Tr Assn
Scot Grocers' Fedn
Scot Whls Assn
> + Food
Grooms & grooming
Pet Care Trust
Grottoes
Folly Fellowship
Groundnuts
Fedn Oils, Seeds & Fats Assns
Groundsmen
Inst Groundsmanship
> + Sportsgrounds & synthetic surfaces
Group analysis
Group Analytic Soc
Inst Gp Analysis
Grouse > Game & game birds
Grouts & grouting
UK Quality Ash Assn
Growth
Child Growth Foundation
Prader-Willi Syndrome Assn
Restricted Growth Assn
Tall Persons Club
Turner Syndrome Support Soc
Guanacos > Camelids
Guard & patrol services
Brit Security Ind Assn
Guardians (educational) > Education: guardians
Guernsey (Channel Islands)
Guernsey Cham Comm
Guernsey Growers Assn
Société Guernesiaise
Guide dogs
Guide Dogs for Blind Assn
Seeing Dogs Alliance
Guide lecturers > Travel & tourism: guides
Guides (girls) > Youth organisation headings
Guillain Barré syndrome
Guillain Barré Syndrome Support Gp
Guinea pigs > Cavies
Gulf War veterans
Gulf Veterans Assn
Gums > Resins & gums
Gunite > Concrete & concrete products
Guns & ammunition
Gun Tr Assn
Histl Breechloading Smallarms Assn
Ordnance Soc
> + Shooting
Guttering
Metal Gutter Mfrs Assn

Gymnasium: equipment
Sports & Fitness Eqpt Assn
Gymnastics
Brit Amat Gymnastics Assn
Scot Gymnastics Assn
Welsh Amat Gymnastic Assn
> + Physical education
Gynaecology > Maternity; Obstetrics & gynaecology
Gypsies & travelling people
Nat Assn Teachers Travellers
Gypsum
Gypsum Products Devt Assn

H

Hackney carriages
Nat Taxi Assn
Hacks > Horse(s) headings
Haematology
Blood Pressure Assn
Brit Blood Transfusion Soc
Brit Hypertension Soc
Brit Microcirculation Soc
Brit Soc Haematology
Haemochromatosis Soc
Haemophilia
Haemophilia Soc
Haggard (Sir (Henry) Rider
Rider Haggard Soc
Haiku
Brit Haiku Soc
Time Haiku
Hailstorms
Tornado & Storm Res Org
Hair (curled)
Nat Fillings Assn
Hair & scalp treatment
Hairline Intl
Inst Trichologists
Hairdressing
Freelance Hair & Beauty Fedn
Hairdressing & Beauty Suppliers Assn
Inc Gld Hairdressers
Nat Assn Screen Make-up Artists & Hairdressers
Nat Hairdressers Fedn
Halibut
Brit Marine Finfish Assn
> + Fish headings
Halon
Halon Users Nat Consortium
Ham > Bacon
Hammer-throwing
Hammer Circle
Hampden (John) 1594-1693
John Hampden Soc
Hamper products
Hamper Ind Tr Assn
Hamsters
Brit Hamster Assn
Hand driers (warm air)
Brit Warm Air Hand Drier Assn
Hand knitting > Knitting & knitting wool/yarns
Hand tools > Tools
Handbags
Brit Travelgoods & Accessories Assn
> + Leathergoods
Handball
England Handball Assn
Gaelic Athletic Assn
Handbell ringing
Handbell Ringers
> + Bellringing
Handcycling
Handcycling Assn
Handicapped persons > Children: handicapped;   Disablement
Handicraft > Crafts & craftsmanship
Handley Page (Sir Frederick)
Handley Page Assn
Handling > Materials: management/handling
Hands
Brit Soc Surgery Hand
Handwriting
Calligraphy & Lettering Arts Soc
IGA-UK

Soc Italic Handwriting
Soc Limners
Soc Scribes & Illuminators
> + Graphology & graphoanalysis
Hang gliding
Brit Hang Gliding & Paragliding Assn
Scot Hang Gliding & Paragliding Fedn
> + Gliding & soaring
Harassment
Nat Assn Support Victims Stalking & Harassment
Harbours > Ports; Yachting
Hardboard > Building board & timber
Hardmetal > Metal
Hardware & housewares
Brit Hardware Fedn
Brit Hardware & Housewares Mfrs Assn
Consumer Electronics Distbrs Assn [IRL]
Cutlery & Allied Trs Res Assn
Door & Hardware Fedn
Ir Hardware & Bldg Materials Assn
> + Building materials & supplies
Hardwoods
Timber Tr Fedn
> + Timber
Hardy (Thomas)
Dorset Natural Hist & Archaeol Soc
Thomas Hardy Soc
Hares
Assn Masters Harriers & Beagles
Game Conservancy Trust
Harmonicas
Nat Harmonica League
Harness racing
Brit Harness Racing Club
Harps & harpists
Comunn Clàrsaich
UK Harp Assn
Hat pins
Hat Pin Soc
Hatcheries
Pullet Hatcheries Assn
Hats
Brit Hat Gld
Haulage > Freight transport; Road: haulage
Hauntings > Paranormal & psychical research
Hawks & hawking
Brit Falconers' Club
Brit Hawking Assn
Hawk & Owl Trust
Scot Assn Country Sports
> + Birds
Hay & straw
Brit Hay & Straw Mchts' Assn
Straw Bale Bldg Assn
Haydn (Franz Joseph)
Haydn Soc
Hayfever > Allergy
Hazards > Home: safety; Road: safety & control; Safety
Head, neck & brain injury & disease
Brit Assn Otorhinolaryngologists
Brit Neuropathological Soc
Brit Neuroscience Assn
Brit Soc Oral & Maxillofacial Pathology
Craniofacial Soc
Headlines
HEADWAY
UK Acquired Brain Injury Forum
Headaches > Migraine & headaches
Heads of schools
Assn Heads Indep Schools
Assn Headteachers & Deputies Scotland
Assn School & College Leaders
Foundation & Aided Schools Nat Assn
Girls' Schools Assn
Headmasters & Headmistresses Conf
Headteachers Assn Scotland
Nat Assn Head Teachers
Soc Headmasters & Headmistresses Indep Schools
> + Teachers
Headwear
Brit Hat Gld
> + Protective clothing/equipment
Healing
Assn Therapeutic Healers
Brit Alliance Healing Assns
Brit Soc Dowsers

Confedn Healing Orgs
> + Complementary medicine; Medicine headings
Health
Alliance Health Profls
Alliance Natural Health
Brit Assn Sport & Exercise Sciences
Gld Health Writers
Health & Beauty Emplrs Fedn
Inst Health Promotion & Educ
Ir Health Services Mgt Inst
McCarrison Soc
R Soc Promotion Health
Soc Health Educ & ... Specialists
UK Public Health Assn
> + other aspects of health
Health administration
Assn Healthcare Communicators
Inst Health Care Mgt
> + National Health Service
Health care
Brit Healthcare Business Intelligence Assn
Care not Killing Alliance
Fedn Healthcare Science
HL7 UK Ltd
Nat Assn Primary Care
Health care: equipment & supplies
Assn Brit Healthcare Inds
Brit Assn Pharmaceutical Whlsrs
Brit Healthcare Trs Assn
Health Care Supplies Assn
Pharmaceutical & Healthcare Sciences Soc
Health & fitness > Fitness
Health food
Consumers Health Choice
Health Food Inst
Health Food Mfrs Assn
Nat Assn Health Stores
> + Food
Health records
Inst Health Record & Inf Mgt
Health resorts > Spas
Health & safety
Health & Safety Sign Assn
Indep Safety Consultants Assn
> + subject concerned eg Health
Hearing
Brit Academy Audiology
Brit Assn Audiological Physicians
Brit Assn Community Doctors in Audiology
Brit Soc Audiology
Brit Soc Hearing Aid Audiologists
Brit Tinnitus Assn
> + Deafness
Heart disease > Cardiology
Heat treatment
Inst Materials, Minerals & Mining
Surface Engg Assn
Heat pumps
Heat Pump Assn
Heaths & heathers
Heather Soc
Horticultural Trs Assn
Heating
Assn Plumbing & Heating Contrs
BEAMA
BSRIA
Chart Instn Bldg Services Engrs
Combined Heat & Power Assn
Commissioning Specialists Assn
Fedn Heating Spare Stockists
Heat Pump Assn
Heat Transfer & Fluid Flow Service
Heating, Ventilating & Air Conditioning Mfrs' Assn
Heating & Ventilating Contrs Assn
Hose Mfrs' & Suppliers Assn
ICOM Energy Assn
Inst Domestic Heating... Engrs
Inst Plumbing & Heating Engg
Manufacturers Domestic Unvented Systems
Oil Firing Technical Assn Petroleum Ind
Scot & NI Plumbing Emplrs' Fedn
Soc Brit Gas Inds
> + Air: conditioning & ventilating

Hebe
Hebe Soc

Hedgehogs
>> Brit Hedgehog Presvn Soc
Hedges & hedge-laying
>> Hedgeline
>> Nat Hedgelaying Soc
Helicopters
>> Brit Helicopter Advy Bd
>> R Aeronautical Soc
>> > + Aerial photography; Aviation
Hellenic studies > Classical studies
Helplines
>> Telephone Helplines Assn
>> > + specific area of interest
Hemerocallis > Hostas & Hemerocallis
Hemp
>> Manila Hemp Assn
Hens > Poultry
Henty (George Alfred)
>> Henty Soc
Heraldry
>> Harleian Soc
>> Heraldry Soc
>> Heraldry Soc Scotland
>> Inst Heraldic & Genealogical Studies
>> Soc Heraldic Arts
>> > + Genealogy
Herbicides > Agriculture: chemicals
Herbs & herbal medicine
>> Brit Herb Tr Assn
>> Brit Herbal Medicine Assn
>> Consumers Health Choice
>> Herb Soc
>> Herb Trust
>> Intl Gen Produce Assn
>> Intl Register Consultant Herbalists & Homoeopaths
>> Nat Inst Med Herbalists
>> Register Chinese Herbal Medicine
Herpes
>> Congenital CMV Assn
>> Herpes Virus Assn
Herpetology
>> Brit Herpetological Soc
Herring
>> Herring Buyers Assn
>> Scot Pelagic Fishermen's Assn
>> > + Fish headings; Fishing
Herschel (Sir [Frederick] William)
>> William Herschel Soc
Hides & skins > Leather
Hi-fi > Radio & TV trade; Sound recording & reproduction
Higden (Ranulf/Ralph)
>> Ranulf Higden Soc
Higher education > Education; Technical education
Highland dancing
>> Brit Assn Teachers Dancing
>> R Scot Country Dance Soc
>> Scot Dance Teachers Alliance
>> UK Alliance Dance Teachers
>> > + Dancing
Highland games
>> Scot Games Assn
Highway > Road headings
Hill farming
>> Blackface Sheep Breeders Assn
>> > + Agriculture
Hill running > Running
Hill walking > Walking
Hillclimbs (motorcycling)
>> Nat Hillclimb Assn
>> > + Motor cycling & scooter riding
Hilton (James) 1900-1954
>> James Hilton Soc
Hip (diseases of)
>> Perthes Assn
>> STEPS...
Hire purchase > Credit trade
Hispanists > Portugal; Spain
Historic aircraft > Aviation: history
Historic buildings
>> Ancient Monuments Soc
>> Assn Local Govt Archaeol Officers
>> Assn Studies Consvn Historic Bldgs
>> Brit Assn Friends Museums
>> Campaign Protection Rural Wales
>> Charles Rennie Mackintosh Soc
>> English Historic Towns Forum
>> Historic Houses Assn

Houses, Castles & Gardens Ireland
Inst Consvn Historic &... Works Ireland
Inst Historic Bldg Consvn
Listed Property Owners Club
Medieval Settlement Res Gp
Nat Assn Field Studies Officers
Nat Trust
Nat Trust Ireland
Nat Trust Scotland
Save Britain's Heritage
Soc Antiquaries Lond
Soc Protection Ancient Bldgs
UK Assn Presvn Trusts
Vernacular Architecture Gp
> + Archaeology: county societies;   Architecture;   Church:
buildings;   Conservation: area organisations
Historic vehicles > Motor vehicles: historic
Historical documents & records > Archives; Record agents;   Records: historical
History
Aethelflaed
Assn Hist & Computing
Brit Academy
Histl Assn
History Curriculum Assn
London Medieval Soc
Oral Hist Soc
R Histl Soc
Soc Genealogists
Social Hist Curators Gp
Social Hist Soc
> + Archaeology; other headings with 'history' as a sub-heading
HIV positive > Genito-urinary medicine
Hobbies
Brit Toy & Hobby Assn
> + object of interest
Hobbits
Tolkien Soc
Hockey
England Hockey
Ir Hockey Assn
Scot Hockey U
Sports Mfrs & Retailers Tr Assn
Ulster Women's Hockey U
Welsh Hockey U
> + Skating: board, inline & roller
Hodgkin's disease
Lymphoma Assn
Hoists
Construction Plant-hire Assn
Materials Handling Engrs Assn
Holiday camps & centres
Assn Heads Outdoor Educ Centres
Brit Activity Holiday Assn
Holiday Centres Assn
Scot Envtl & Outdoor Educ Centres Assn
Holiday property owners > Self catering
Holiday resorts
Brit Resorts & Destinations Assn
Tourism Mgt Inst
Holiday timesharing > Timeshare industry
Holidays > Travel & tourism
Holistic medicine
Assn Reflexologists
Brit Holistic Med Assn
Holistic Healers Assn
Inst Holistic Therapies
> + Complementary medicine
Holistic therapy
Fedn Holistic Therapists
Holland > Netherlands
Hollyhocks
Hollyhock Soc
Holmes (Sherlock)
Friends Dr Watson
Sherlock Holmes Soc Lond
Holography
R Photographic Soc
Home: confinements > Maternity
Home: decoration
Home Decoration Retailers' Assn
Nat Home Improvement Coun
> + Paint; Wallcoverings & wallpaper
Home: economics
Inst Consumer Sciences
Home: equity release schemes
Nat Support Gp Victims Failed Home Income Plans
Safe Home Income Plans

Home: information packs
> Assn Home Inf Packs Providers
> SPLINTA
Home: laundering
> Home Laundering Consultative Coun
> > + Laundering
Home: safety
> Inst Home Safety
Home: shopping
> Mail Order Trs Assn
> > + Mail order trade
Home: working from
> Home Business Alliance
> Nat Gp Homeworking
> Telework Assn
Homeless
> Homeless Link
> Scot Coun Single Homeless
> Shelter
Homes > Housing; Nursing homes; Social service
Homeworkers > Home: working from
Homing pigeons > Pigeons
Homoeopathy
> Brit Assn Homoeopathic Mfrs
> Brit Assn Homoeopathic Veterinary Surgeons
> Brit Homoeopathic Assn
> Brit Homoeopathic Dental Assn
> Coun Orgs Registering Homeopaths
> Fac Homeopathy
> Homeopathic Med Assn
> Intl Register Consultant Herbalists & Homoeopaths
> Nat Assn Homeopathic Gps
> Soc Homeopaths
Homosexuality
> Campaign Homosexual Equality
Honey
> Honey Assn
Hong Kong
> Brit Cham Comm Hong Kong
> Hong Kong Assn
Hopkins (Gerard Manley)
> Hopkins Soc
Hoppers > Silos & hoppers
Hops
> Brewery Hist Soc
> Hop Mchts Assn
> Nat Hop Assn
Horace [Quintus Horatius Flaccus]
> Horatian Soc
Hormone study & related diseases > Endocrinology
Hormone replacement therapy (HRT)
> Brit Menopause Soc
Horns (musical instruments)
> Brit Horn Soc
Horology
> Antiquarian Horological Soc
> Brit Horological Fedn
> Brit Horological Inst
> Brit Jewellers Assn
> Brit Jewellery, Giftware & Finishing Fedn
> Brit Sundial Soc
> Brit Watch & Clock Makers Gld
> MultiService Assn
> Nat Assn Goldsmiths
Horror literature
> Brit Fantasy Soc
> Dracula Soc
> John Polidori Literary Soc
Horse: brasses
> Nat Horse Brass Soc
Horse: loggers
> Forestry Contracting Assn
Horse: racing
> Amat Jockeys Assn
> Brit Harness Racing Club
> Fedn Bloodstock Agents
> Horserace Writers & Photographers Assn
> Horseracing Sponsors Assn
> Ir Thoroughbred Breeders Assn
> Jockeys Assn
> Nat Trainers Fedn
> Permit Trainers Assn
> Point-to-Point Owners & Riders Assn
> Racecourse Assn
> Racehorse Owners Assn
> Racehorse Transporters Assn

Horse: riding & driving
> Assn Brit Riding Schools
> Brit Driving Soc
> Brit Equestrian Fedn
> Brit Horse Soc
> Brit Show Hack... & Riding Horse Assn
> Brit Show Pony Soc
> London Harness Horse Parade Soc
> Medical Equestrian Assn
> Mounted Games Assn
> Nat Fedn Bridleway Assns
> Pleasure Horse Soc
> Point-to-Point Owners & Riders Assn
> Riding Disabled Assn
> Scot Assn Country Sports
> Scurry Driving Assn
> Side Saddle Assn
> Standardbred & Trotting Horse Assn
> Trekking & Riding Soc Scotland
> UK Chasers & Riders Ltd
> Welsh Trekking & Riding Assn
> > + American 'West'
Horseball
> Brit Horseball Assn
Horseboxes & trailers
> Org Horsebox & Trailer Owners
Horses & ponies
> Brit Equestrian Fedn
> Brit Equestrian Tr Assn
> Brit Horse Soc
> Endurance GB
> Equestrian Fedn Ireland
> Equine Behaviour Forum
> Equine Shiatsu Assn
> Equine Sports Massage Assn
> Nat Pony Soc
> Ponies Assn
> Pony Club
> Soc Welfare Horses & Ponies
> Thoroughbred Breeders' Assn
> Veteran Horse Soc
> > + Cattle & livestock; Pony trekking
Horses & ponies: breed societies
> American Quarter Horse Assn
> American Saddlebred Assn
> Arab Horse Soc
> Brit Appaloosa Soc
> Brit Assn Purebred Spanish Horse
> Brit Camargue Horse Soc
> Brit Connemara Pony Soc
> Brit Hanoverian Horse Soc
> Brit Miniature Horse Soc
> Brit Morgan Horse Soc
> Brit Palomino Soc
> Brit Percheron Horse Soc
> Brit Skewbald & Piebald Assn
> Brit Spotted Pony Soc
> Brit Warm-Blood Soc
> Caspian Breed Soc
> Caspian Horse Soc
> Cleveland Bay Horse Soc
> Clydesdale Horse Soc
> Coloured Horse & Pony Soc
> Connemara Pony Breeders Soc [IRL]
> Dales Pony Soc
> Dartmoor Pony Soc
> Donkey Breed Soc
> Dun Horse & Pony Soc
> Eriskay Pony Soc
> Exmoor Pony Soc
> Fell Pony Soc
> Fjord Horse Nat Stud Book Assn
> Friesian Horse Assn
> Glasgow Agricl Soc
> Gypsy Cob Soc
> Hackney Horse Soc
> Haflinger Soc
> Highland Pony Soc
> Icelandic Horse Soc
> Ir Draught Horse Soc
> Lipizzaner Nat Stud Book Assn GB
> Lipizzaner Soc
> Lusitano Breed Soc
> Morgan Horse Assn
> New Forest Pony... & Cattle Soc
> Scot Icelandic Horse Assn
> Shetland Pony Stud Book Soc

© CBD Research Ltd · Beckenham · BR3 5JS · Tel 020 8650 7745 · Fax 020 8650 0768 · E-mail cbd@cbdresearch.com · www.cbdresearch.com

Shire Horse Soc
Southern Counties Heavy Horse Assn
Sport Horse Breeding
Spotted Horse & Pony Soc
Spotted Pony Breed Soc
Suffolk Horse Soc
Trakehner Breeders Fraternity
UK Paint Horse Assn
Utd Saddlebred Assn
Welsh Pony & Cob Soc
Horses & ponies: grooms
Horticulture
Brit Bedding & Pot Plant Assn
Brit Dried Flowers Assn
Brit Inst Agricl Consultants
Comml Horticl Assn
Flowers & Plants Assn
Garden Centre Assn
Guernsey Growers Assn
Horticultural Exhibitors Assn
Horticultural Trs Assn
Horticulture Res Intl Assn
Inst Horticulture
Ir Comml Horticl Assn
N England Horticl Soc
N England Rose, Carnation... Horticl Soc
Nat Coun Consvn Plants & Gardens
Nat Farmers U
Nuclear Stock Assn
R Botanical & Horticl Soc Manch
R Caledonian Horticl Soc
R Guernsey Agricl & Horticl Soc
R Horticl Soc
R Horticl Soc Ireland
R Welsh Agricl Soc
S England Agricl Soc
Scot Seed & Nursery Tr Assn
Shropshire & W Midlands Agricl Soc
Soc Botanical Artists
UK Irrigation Assn
Westmorland County Agricl Soc
Women's Farm & Garden Assn
> + Agriculture: county societies; Gardens & gardening; Landscape
Horticulture: disabled > Gardens & gardening: for disabled
Horticulture: education
Assn Agricl & Horticl Colls [IRL]
Napaeo
Principals' Profl Coun
Horticulture & garden: machinery
Agricl Engrs Assn
Brit Agricl & Garden Machinery Assn
Brit Hardware Fedn
Farm Machinery Presvn Soc
Farm Tractor & Machinery Tr Assn [IRL]
Fedn Brit Hand Tool Mfrs
GARDENEX
GIMA
Horticultural Assn Retail Traders
John Innes Mfrs Assn
Vintage Horticl & Garden Machinery Club
> + Agriculture: machinery
Hoses (flexible)
Hose Mfrs' & Suppliers Assn
Hosiery
Knitting Inds Fedn
Hospices
Assn Children's Hospices
Human Rights Soc
Hospitality
Brit Hospitality Assn
Coun Hospitality Mgt Educ
Foodservice Consultants Soc Intl (UK)
PACE: Profl Assn Catering Educ
> + Catering, Corporate hospitality; Hotels & restaurants; Shows & events
Hospitals
Assn Dental Hospitals
Attend
Community Hospitals Assn
Hospitals: administrative staff
Brit Assn Med Mgrs
Hospital Caterers Assn
Inst Decontamination Services
Nat Assn Hospital Fire Officers
Soc Hospital Linen Service & Laundry Mgrs
UK Housekeepers Assn
> + National Health Service

Hospitals: broadcasting
Nat Assn Hospital Broadcasting Orgs
Hospitals: contributory schemes
Brit Health Care Assn
Hospital & Med Care Assn
Hospital Saving Assn
Provincial Hospital Services Assn
Welsh Hospitals & Health Services Assn
Hospitals: decontamination & cleaning
Assn Domestic Mgt
Inst Decontamination Services
Hospitals: engineering & equipment
Inst Healthcare Engg & Estate Mgt
Hospitals: medical staff
Assn Operating Dept Practitioners
Brit Assn Emergency Medicine
College Emergency Medicine
Hospital Consultants & Specialists Assn
Hospital Scientists Assn
Ir Hospital Consultants Assn
Hospitals: nursing staff > Nursing
Hospitals: patients > Patients
Hospitals: private
Action Proper Regulation Private Hospitals
Hospitals: veterinary
Brit Veterinary Hospitals Assn
Hostas & hemerocallis
Brit Hosta & Hemerocallis Soc
Hardy Plant Soc
Hostels (bail) > Probation service
Hot air balloons > Balloons & airships
Hot water storage & supply > Heating
Hotel accountants
Brit Assn Hospitality Accountants
Hotels & restaurants
Brit Assn Hotel Representatives
Brit Hospitality Assn
Confedn Tourism, Hotel & Catering Mgt
Fedn Specialist Restaurants
Hotel Booking Agents Assn
Hotel & Catering Intl Mgt Assn
Ir Hospitality Inst
Ir Hotels Fedn
NI Hotels Fedn
Restaurant Assn
Restaurant Property Advisors Soc
Restaurants Assn Ireland
Single Travellers Action Gp
Hound trailing
Hound Trailing Assn
Hounds
Masters Deerhounds Assn
Masters Foxhounds Assn
Peterborough R Foxhound Show Soc
Welsh Hound Assn
> + Hunts & hunting
House building > Building
House maintenance
Upkeep
House plants > Indoor & houseplants; Horticulture; individual plant
Household distribution
Direct Marketing Assn (UK) Ltd
Household textiles > Textile headings
Housekeepers
UK Housekeepers Assn
Houses open to the public > Historic buildings
Housewares > Hardware & housewares
Housewives
Nat Women's Register
> + Women's organisations
Housing
Chart Inst Housing
Housing Inst Ireland
Nat Assn Bldg Co-ops [IRL]
Nat Housing Fedn
NI Fedn Housing Assns
R Envtl Health Inst Scotland
ROOM
Scot Fedn Housing Assns
Welsh Fedn Housing Assns
> + Building societies; Tenants & residents
Housman (A E) & family
Housman Soc
Hovercraft
Hovercraft Club
Hovercraft Museum Trust

Howells (Herbert) 1892-1983
    Herbert Howells Soc
Huguenots
    Huguenot Soc
Human identification
    Brit Assn Human Identification
Human relationships
    Soc Companion Animal Studies
Human rights > Individual freedom
Humanism
    Brit Humanist Assn
    Humanist Assn Ireland
    Humanist Soc Scotland
    Nat Secular Soc
    Rationalist Assn
    S Place Ethical Soc
Humanities
    Humanities Assn
Humidity control
    Heating, Ventilating & Air Conditioning Mfrs' Assn
    > + Air: conditioning & ventilating
Hungary
    Brit Cham Comm Hungary
Huntington's disease
    Huntington's Disease Assn
    Scot Huntington's Assn
Hunts & hunting
    Assn Masters Harriers & Beagles
    Countryside Alliance
    Hunting Assn Ireland
    Ir Coun against Blood Sports
    > + Hounds
Hurdy-gurdy
    Hurdy-Gurdy Soc
Hurling (sport)
    Gaelic Athletic Assn
Hydraulics & hydromechanics
    Brit Fluid Power Assn
    Brit Fluid Power Distbrs Assn
Hydrocephalus > Spina bifida & hydrocephalus
Hydrology > Water
Hydromechanics > Hydraulics & hydromechanics
Hydropower > Renewable energy
Hydrotherapy
Hygiene > Cleaning; Health; Natural health & therapeutics; Occupational
    health & hygiene; Public health
Hymns
    Hymn Soc
Hyper active children
    Fragile X Soc
    Hyperactive Children's Support Gp
    > + Children: welfare
Hypercalcaemia
    Williams Syndrome Foundation
Hyperlipidaemia
Hypermobility Syndrome
    Hypermobility Syndrome Assn
Hypertension
    Brit Hypertension Soc
Hyperthermia
    Brit Malignant Hyperthermia Assn
Hypertrophic cardiomyopathy
    Cardiomyopathy Assn
Hypnosis & hypnotherapy
    Academy Curative Hypnotherapists
    Assn Qualified Curative Hypnotherapists
    Assn Therapeutic Philosophy
    Brit Hypnotherapy Assn
    Brit Soc Clinical Hypnosis
    Brit Soc Experimental & Clinical Hypnosis
    Brit Soc Hypnotherapists
    Brit Soc Med & Dental Hypnosis
    Campaign Stage Hypnosis
    Gld Curative Hypnotherapists
    Nat Assn Counsellors, Hypnotherapists. . .
    Nat Coun Hypnotherapy &. . . Register
    Nat Register Hypnotherapists & Psychotherapists
    Nat Soc Profl Hypnotherapists
    UK Confedn Hypnotherapy Orgs
Hypnotic regression
    Assn Scientific Study Anomalous Phenomena
    UK Skeptics
Hysterectomy
    Campaign Hysterectomy &. . .Operations on Women
    Hysterectomy Assn

I

Iberia > Portugal; Spain
IBS > Irritable bowel disease
Ice climbing > Climbing
Ice cream
    Ice Cream Alliance
Ice hockey
    Ice Hockey Players Assn
    Ice Hockey UK
Ice skating
    Nat Ice Skating Assn
    Scot Ice Skating Assn
Icehouses
    Sussex Indl Archaeol Soc
Ichthyology
Identity cards
    NO2ID
Ido
    Intl Language [IDO] Soc
Ileostomy
    Assn Coloproctology
    ia
    Nat Advy Service Parents Children with a Stoma
Illiteracy > Reading
Illuminated signs > Road lighting, markings & traffic signs;   Signs
Illumination > Lighting
Illuminators
    Soc Scribes & Illuminators
Illustration
    Assn Illustrators
    Comics Creators Gld
    Imaginative Book Illustration Soc
    Inst Med Illustrators
    Outdoor Writers' Gld
    Picture Res Assn
    Randolph Caldecott Soc
    Soc Architectural Illustration
    Soc Artists' Agents
    > + Art & artists
Image development (personal)
    Fedn Image Consultants
Imaging/image analysis
    Brit Assn Picture Libraries & Agencies
    Brit Machine Vision Assn. . .
    Photo Imaging Coun
    Profl Photographic Laboratories Assn
    R Photographic Soc
    Sira
    UK Indl Vision Assn
Immediate care > First aid & immediate care
Immigration & emigration
    Assn Visitors Immigration Detainees
    Immigration Law Practitioners Assn
Immunology
    Brit Soc Allergy & Clinical Immunology
    Brit Soc Immunology
    Brit Transplantation Soc
    Primary Immunodeficiency Assn
    > + Allergy
Impact absorbing surfaces
    Assn Play Inds
Imperial weights & measures
    Brit Weights & Measures Assn
    > + Measurement
Implants (medical)
    Breast Implant Inf Soc
    Pharmaceutical & Healthcare Sciences Soc
    Pharmaceutical & Healthcare Sciences Soc
    UK & I Soc Cataract & Refractive Surgeons
Import > Export & import
Impotence > Sexual dysfunction
Incentive marketing
    Brit Promotional Merchandise Assn
    Promota UK Ltd
Income tax > Taxation
Incontinence
    Absorbent Hygiene Products Mfrs Assn
    Assn Continence Advice
    Incontact
    Nat Advy Service Parents Children with a Stoma
Independent companies > Business
Independent further education > Education
Independent & public schools
    Assn Governing Bodies Indep Schools

Assn Heads Indep Schools
Assn Marketing & Devt Indep Schools
Girls' Schools Assn
Headmasters & Headmistresses Conf
Inc Assn Preparatory Schools
Indep Schools Assn
Indep Schools Bursars Assn
Indep Schools Coun
Soc Headmasters & Headmistresses Indep Schools
Indexing
Assn Freelance Editors, Proofreaders & Indexers [IRL]
Soc Indexers
India & Indian people
Soc S Asian Studies
India: armed forces history
Indian Military Histl Soc
Indirect taxation > Taxation
Individual freedom
C'ee Admin Justice [NI]
Campaign Philosophical Freedom
Choice in Personal Safety
Freedom Assn
Freedom Org Right Enjoy Smoking Tobacco
Ir Coun Civil Liberties
Libertarian Alliance
Liberty
Nat Secular Soc
NO2ID
Soc Individual Freedom
Statewatch
Indonesia
Anglo-Indonesian Soc
Indoor bowling > Bowling
Indoor & houseplants
Brit Bedding & Pot Plant Assn
Flowers & Plants Assn
Garden Centre Assn
Saintpaulia & Houseplant Soc
> + Horticulture; individual plants
Industrial agents
Indl Agents Soc
Industrial archaeology > Archaeology: industrial
Industrial biology > Biology
Industrial catering > Catering
Industrial cleaning > Cleaning equipment
Industrial containers > specific type of container, or material used in their
manufacture
Industrial copyright > Copyright;   Patents & trade marks
Industrial design
Chart Soc Designers
Design & Inds Assn
Fac R Designers Ind
Fedn Engg Design Cos
Intellectual Property Lawyers Assn
> + Design
Industrial diamonds
Brit Abrasives Fedn
Industrial editors
Brit Assn Communicators in Business
> + Technical writing & publishing
Industrial education > Occupational training & education
Industrial emergencies > Civil defence & industrial emergencies
Industrial fasteners > Fasteners & turned parts
Industrial finishing > Coatings; Metal: finishing
Industrial graphics
Keygraphica
> + Printing headings
Industrial involvement & participation
Involvement & Participation Assn
Scot Coun Devt & Ind
Industrial law > Law: industrial
Industrial leather > Leather
Industrial management > Management
Industrial marketing > Marketing
Industrial participation > Industrial involvement & participation
Industrial plant > Plant: industrial
Industrial pollution > Pollution & pollution control
Industrial property > Copyright; Patents & trade marks
Industrial relations
Brit Universities Indl Relations Assn
Ethical Trading Initiative
Inst Employment Rights
Ir Assn Indl Relations
Industrial research
AIRTO
Cambridge Soc Application Res
Major Projects Assn

Res & Devt Soc
> + specific industries
Industrial safety > Safety
Industrial security > Security
Industrial trucks
Assn Indl Truck Trainers
Industrial training & education > Occupational training & education
Industrial vision
UK Indl Vision Assn
Industrialised building components
Assn Bldg Component Mfrs
> + Building materials & supplies
Industry
Assn University Res & Ind Links
Campaign Industry
Confedn Brit Ind
Ir Business & Emplrs Confedn
R Soc Edinburgh
Infant food
Cereal Ingredients Mfrs' Assn
Infant & Dietetic Foods Assn
Infants > Children: welfare;   Cot deaths
Infection control & study
Brit Infection Soc
Infection Control Nurses Assn
John Snow Soc
Soc Applied Microbiology
Infertility > Fertility
Inflatable toys & structures
Assn Play Inds
Brit Toy & Hobby Assn
Inflatable Play Mfrs Assn
> + Air: boats & inflatables
Information: destruction > Documents: confidential disposal
Information: freedom of
Campaign Freedom Infm
Campaign Press & Broadcasting Freedom
Information: management > Data processing; Information services &
technology
Information: services & technology
ADSET
Aslib
Assn Geographic Inf
Brit Assn Inf & Library Educ & Res
Business Services Assn
CILIP
City Inf Gp
Communications Mgt Assn
Construction Ind Inf Gp
Eur Inf Assn
ICT Ireland
Inst Mgt Inf Systems
Inst Scientific & Technical Communicators
Instn Engg & Technology
Intellect, the Information Technology, Telecommunications &
Electronics
Momentum - Northern Ireland ICT Fedn
Network Govt Library & Inf Specialists
SELECT
Soc Inf Technology Mgt
Soc Public Inf Networks
UK Computer Measurement Gp
Universities & Colleges Inf Systems Assn
> + Data processing
Infra-red heating > Electroheat
Injections
Pharmaceutical & Healthcare Sciences Soc
Inkpots > Writing equipment & accessories
Inland waterways
Assn Inland Navigation Authorities
Assn Pleasure Craft Operators
Canal Boatbuilders Assn
Canal Card Collectors Circle
Chesterfield Canal Trust
Comml Boat Operators Assn
Inland Waterways Assn
Inland Waterways Assn Ireland
Inland Waterways Protection Soc
Nat Assn Boat Owners
Rly & Canal Histl Soc
Scot Inland Waterways Assn
Towpath Action Gp
Transport 2000 Ltd
Transport Water Assn
Waterway Recovery Gp
Wey & Arun Canal Trust
> + Rivers

Inline skating & rollerblading > Skating: board, inline & roller
Innes (John)
　　　　John Innes Mfrs Assn
　　　　> + Composts & composting
Innovation > Invention & innovation
Inns of Court > Law
Inns & innkeeping
　　　　Brit Inst Innkeeping
　　　　Inn Sign Soc
　　　　> + Wines & spirits: trade
Insects > Entomology
Insignia > Badges & insignia; Numismatics
Insolvency
　　　　Assn Business Recovery Profls
　　　　Insolvency Lawyers Assn
　　　　Insolvency Practitioners Assn
　　　　> + Accountancy
Instrumentation & control > Control engineering; Measurement
Instruments: musical > Musical instruments
Insulation
　　　　Brit Rigid Urethane Foam Mfrs Assn
　　　　Brit Urethane Foam Contrs Assn
　　　　Chart Instn Bldg Services Engrs
　　　　Draught Proofing Advy Assn
　　　　EURISOL-UK
　　　　Insulated Render & Cladding Assn
　　　　Nat Insulation Assn
　　　　Thermal Insulation Contrs Assn
　　　　Thermal Insulation Mfrs & Suppliers Assn
　　　　> + Building; Heating
Insulation board > Building board & timber
Insulation: electrical
　　　　Electrical Insulation Assn
Insurance
　　　　Assn Average Adjusters
　　　　Assn Brit Insurers
　　　　Assn Consulting Actuaries
　　　　Assn Lloyd's Members
　　　　Assn Policy Market Makers
　　　　Brit Insurance Law Assn
　　　　Chart Insurance Inst
　　　　Fac Actuaries Scotland
　　　　Indep Warranty Assn
　　　　Inst Risk Mgt
　　　　Insurance Inst Ireland
　　　　Intl Underwriting Assn Lond
　　　　Ir Insurance Fedn
　　　　Lloyd's Market Assn
　　　　Personal Finance Soc
　　　　Salvage Assn

　　　　Corpn Insurance, Financial & Mortgage Advisers
　　　　Inst Insurance Brokers
Insurance: business interruption
Insurance: companies staff
　　　　Assn Insurance & Risk Mgrs
Insurance: customers
　　　　Nat Assn Bank & Insurance Customers
　　　　Nat Support Gp Victims Failed Home Income Plans
Insurance: history
　　　　Fire Mark Circle
Insurance: medicine
　　　　Assn Med Insurance Intermediaries
　　　　Assurance Med Soc
Insurance: private health > Hospitals: contributory schemes
Intellectual property rights
　　　　Authors' Licensing & Collecting Soc
　　　　Licensing Executives Soc
　　　　MARQUES
Intelligence
　　　　Nat Assn Gifted Children
　　　　Support Soc Children High Intelligence
Intensive care
　　　　Intensive Care Soc
Interactive learning
　　　　Soc Advancement Games & Simulations Educ & Training
Interactive publishing
　　　　Assn Online Publishers
　　　　Periodical Pubrs Assn - Interactive
Interchurch families
　　　　Assn Interchurch Families
　　　　NI Mixed Marriage Assn
　　　　> + Welfare: organisations
Interior decoration & design
　　　　Assn Interior Specialists
　　　　Brit Assn Landscape Inds
　　　　Brit Interior Design Assn

　　　　Chart Soc Designers
　　　　Inst Profl Designers
　　　　Kitchen Bathroom Bedroom Specialists Assn
　　　　Wallpaper Hist Soc
Interlingua
　　　　Brit Interlingua Soc
Intermediate bulk containers
　　　　Indl Packaging Assn
Internal auditors
　　　　Inst Internal Auditors UK & Ireland
　　　　> + Accountancy
Internal combustion engines > Motor industry
International affairs
　　　　Brit Pugwash Gp
　　　　R Inst Intl Affairs
International friendship > individual countries
International law > Law: international
International mail consolidators > Postal services
International studies
　　　　Brit Intl Studies Assn
Internet
　　　　Brit Internet Publishers Alliance
　　　　Internet Content Rating Assn
　　　　Internet Service Providers Assn
　　　　Ir Internet Assn
　　　　Online Content UK
　　　　ScotlandIS
　　　　Soc Public Inf Networks
　　　　Telecommunications & Internet Fedn [IRL]
　　　　UK eInf Gp
　　　　> + Electronic: data/information interchange
Internment
　　　　Assn Brit Civilian Internees Far East
Interplanetary travel > Space research & exploration
Interpreters > Translation & interpretation
Intestinal disorders > specific illness
Intranet
　　　　Soc Public Inf Networks
　　　　> + Electronic: data/information interchange
Introduction agencies & marriage bureaux
　　　　Assn Brit Introduction Agencies
Intruder alarms
　　　　Nat Security Inspectorate
　　　　> + Security
Invention & innovation
　　　　Inst Intl Licensing Practitioners
　　　　Inst Inventors
　　　　Inst Patentees & Inventors
　　　　R Scot Soc Arts (Science & Technology)
Inventories
　　　　Assn Indep Inventory Clerks
　　　　> + Production control; Stocktaking/auditing
Investigators
　　　　Assn Brit Investigators
　　　　Inst Profl Investigators
　　　　Nat Assn Investigators & Process Servers
Investment
　　　　Assn Consulting Actuaries
　　　　Assn Corporate Trustees
　　　　Assn Indep Financial Advisers
　　　　Assn Institutional Multi-Manager Investing
　　　　Assn Investment Trust Companies
　　　　Assn Mining Analysts
　　　　Assn Private Client Investment Mgrs & Stockbrokers
　　　　Assn Real Estate Funds
　　　　Assn Solicitors & Investment Mgrs
　　　　Brit Insurance Brokers' Assn
　　　　BVCA
　　　　Financial Services Ireland
　　　　Futures & Options Assn
　　　　Gilt-Edged Market Makers' Assn
　　　　Gld Shareholders
　　　　Indep Valuers Assn
　　　　Investment Mgt Assn
　　　　Investment Property Forum
　　　　Investor Relations Soc
　　　　Ir Assn Investment Mgrs
　　　　London Investment Banking Assn
　　　　London Money Market Assn
　　　　PEP & ISA Mgrs Assn
　　　　Securities & Investment Inst
　　　　Soc Technical Analysts
　　　　UK Soc Investment Profls
　　　　> + Trusts, trusteeship & estate planning
Investment casting > Metal: casting
In Vitro diagnostics
　　　　Brit In Vitro Diagnostics Assn

Invoice factors > Factoring (banking & finance)
Iran
    Brit Inst Persian Studies
    Iran Soc
    Middle East Assn
Ireland
    Fedn Ir Socs
    Inst Public Administration [IRL]
    Ir Assn Cultural, Economic & Social Relations
Ireland: history, language & literature
    Brit Assn Ir Studies
    Economic & Social Hist Soc Ireland
    Friends Nat Collections Ireland
    Ir Texts Soc
    R Ir Academy
    R Soc Antiquaries Ireland
Irises
    Brit Iris Soc
Irish > Ireland
Iron
    Cast Metals Fedn
    Community
    Inst Materials, Minerals & Mining
    > + Steel
Iron & steel scrap > Metal: scrap
Iron & steel stockholders
    Nat Assn Steel Stockholders
Ironfoundries > Foundries
Ironmongery
    Brit Hardware Fedn
    Gld Architectural Ironmongers
    Inst Architectural Ironmongers
    > + Hardware & housewares
Irrigation
    Brit Turf & Landscape Irrigation Assn
    UK Irrigation Assn
    > + Water
Irritable bowel disease
    IBS Network
Israel
    Anglo-Israel Assn
    Brit-Israel Cham Comm
    > + Jewish organisations
Italian > Italy: language & literature
Italic hand > Handwriting
Italy
    Assn Study Modern Italy
    Brit Cham Comm Italy
    Brit Italian Soc
    Italian Cham Comm Ind UK
    Pizza, Pasta & Italian Food Assn
Italy: language & literature
    Assn Language Learning

J

Jacobites
    R Stuart Soc
    Seventeen Fortyfive Assn
Jacobs (W[illiam] W[ymark]
    W W Jacobs Appreciation Soc
Jams
    Food Processors' Assn
Japan
    Brit Assn Japanese Studies
    Brit Cham Comm Japan
    Japan Soc
    Japanese Cham Comm & Ind UK
Japan: literature
    Brit Haiku Soc
    Time Haiku
Japanning > Lacquer & japanning
Jazz & Blues
    Assn Brit Jazz Musicians
    Brit Jazz Soc
    Jazz Piano Teachers Assn
    Musicians' U
    Welsh Amat Music Fedn
    Welsh Jazz Soc
Jefferies (Richard)
    Richard Jefferies Soc
Jellies
    Food Processors' Assn

Jerome (Jerome K)
    Jerome K Jerome Soc
Jersey (Channel Islands)
    R Jersey Agricl & Horticl Soc
    Société Jersiaise
Jetting (fluids)
    Water Jetting Assn
Jewellery
    Assn Contemporary Jewellery
    Bead Soc
    Brit Jewellers Assn
    Brit Jewellery, Giftware & Finishing Fedn
    Fedn Jewellery Mfrs Ireland
    Gld Enamellers
    Inst Profl Goldsmiths
    Jewellery Distbrs Assn
    Nat Assn Goldsmiths
    Soc Jewellery Hist [>SJH002
Jewish history & lore
    Chapels Soc
    Jewish Histl Soc England
Jewish organisations
    Anglo-Jewish Assn
    Assn Jewish Ex-Servicemen & Women
    Fedn Synagogues
    Inst Jewish Policy Res
    Zionist Fedn
Jigsaws
    Brit Jigsaw Puzzle Library
Jirds
    Nat Gerbil Soc
Jiu jitsu > Martial arts
Jockeys > Horse: racing
John O'Groats
    Land's End - John O'Groats Assn
Johnson (Dr Samuel)
    Johnson Soc
    Johnson Soc Lond
Joinery > Woodworking
Jones (David Michael)
    David Jones Soc
Jordan
    Anglo-Jordanian Soc
Journalism
    Assn Brit Science Writers
    Assn Regional City Editors
    Brit Assn Journalists
    Chart Inst Journalists
    Crime Reporters Assn
    Foreign Press Assn Lond
    Gld Food Writers
    Gld Motoring Writers
    Media Soc
    Medical Journalists Assn
    Nat Assn Press Agencies
    Nat U Journalists
    Sports Journalists' Assn GB
    Yachting Journalists' Assn
    > + Media; Newspapers; Writing & writers
Jousting
    Knights R England
Ju jitsu > Martial arts
Judo > Martial arts
Jurisprudence > Law
Justices clerks > Magistrates & magistrates courts
Jute
    London Jute Assn
    UK Jute Goods Assn

Juvenile > Children headings; Family Law
Kaolin > China clay
Karate > Martial arts
Karg-Elert (Sigfrid)
    Karg-Elert Archive
Karting
    Assn Brit Kart Clubs
    Assn Racing Kart Schools
    Motor Sports Assn
    Nat Karting Assn
Kayaks
    Assn Canoe Trades
    Historic Canoe & Kayak Assn
Kaye-Smith (Sheila)
    Sheila Kaye-Smith Soc
Keats (John)
    Keats-Shelley Memorial Assn
Keelboats > Cobles & keelboats

Keep fit > Fitness
Kegs > Cisterns, drums & tanks
Kempe (Charles)
        Kempe Soc
Kempe (Margery)
        Margery Kempe Soc
Kempe (Rudolf)
        Rudolf Kempe Soc
Kendo > Martial arts
Kennels
        Pet Care Trust
Kent
        Assn Men Kent & Kentish Men
Kerbs > Paving & kerbs
Kerosene
        Heating Oil Buyers Assn
Keypads
        Keygraphica
Keys
        MultiService Assn
        > + Locks & latches
Kick boxing > Martial arts
Kidney structure & disease > Nephrology
Kilvert (Francis)
        Kilvert Soc
Kinesiology
        Assn Light Touch Therapists
        Assn Systematic Kinesiology
        Kinesiology Fedn
        > + Complementary medicine
Kings > under individual's name
Kipling ([Joseph] Rudyard)
        Kipling Soc
Kippers > Herring
Kitchen furniture & equipment
        Brit Woodworking Fedn
        Catering Eqpt Distbrs Assn GB
        Cutlery & Allied Trs Res Assn
        Kitchen Bathroom Bedroom Specialists Assn
Kite bugging
        Brit Fedn Sand & Land Yacht Clubs
Kite flying
        Kite Soc
Kite surfing > Surfing, board & speed sailing
Klinefelter's syndrome
        Klinefelter's Syndrome Assn
Knacker industry
        Licensed Animal Slaughterers... Assn
Knights bachelor
        Imperial Soc Knights Bachelor
Knitting & knitting wool/yarns
        Brit Hand Knitting Confedn
        Community
        Knitting & Crochet Gld
        > + Wool & wool products
Knitwear
        Knitting Inds Fedn
        UK Fashion Exports
Knots (tying)
        Intl Gld Knot Tyers
Kodály (Zoltán)
        Brit Kodály Academy
Korea
        Brit Assn Korean Studies
        Brit Cham Comm Korea
Korfball
        Brit Korfball Assn
Kosova
        Anglo-Albanian Assn

K

Kung fu > Martial arts

L

Labels: collecting
        Brit Matchbox, Label & Booklet Soc
        Labologists Soc
Labels: self adhesive & roll
        Brit Printing Inds Fedn

Labels: woven
        Brit Narrow Fabrics Assn
Laboratory animals
        Fund Replacement Animals Med Experiments
        Inst Animal Technology
        Laboratory Animal Science Assn
        Res Defence Soc
        > + Animals: welfare
Laboratory equipment & technology
        Assn Instrumentation, Control, Automation...
        Brit Assn Res Quality Assurance
        Inst Biomedical Science
        Inst Science Technology
        UK Textile Laboratory Forum
Labour politics
        Inst Employment Rights
        Scot Labour Hist Soc
        Soc Study Labour Hist
Labour (provision of)
        Assn Labour Providers
Labour relations > Industrial relations
Lace: handmade
        Lace Gld
        Lace Soc
Lace & net
        Brit Lace Fedn
Lacquer & japanning
        Brit Antique Furniture Restorers Assn
Lacrosse
        English Lacrosse Assn
Ladders
        Brit Ladder Mfrs Assn
        Ladder Systems Mfrs Assn
Ladies circles
        Nat Assn Ladies Circles
        > + also Women's organisations
Legacies (public) > Donations (public)
Lake District
        Friends Lake District
Lamas > Camelids
Lamb (Charles)
        Charles Lamb Soc
Lamb(s) > Meat; Sheep

Lancashire
        Friends Real Lancashire
Land: access & rights of way > Footpaths & rights of way
Land-based education
        Napaeo
Land: contaminated
        Assn Geotechnical & Geoenvironmental Specialists
Land: drainage
        Land Drainage Contrs Assn
        > + Plastics: pipes; Pipes; Water
Land: owners > Estate management; Property & land owners
Land: survey > Earth sciences, structure & resources;   Surveying
Land: usage > Conservation; Town & country planning
Land: valuation > Valuation
Land: yachting
        Brit Fedn Sand & Land Yacht Clubs
Landlords > Property & land owners
Landor (Walter Savage)
Land's End
        Land's End - John O'Groats Assn
Landscape
        Assn Landscape Contrs Ireland (NI)
        Brit Assn Landscape Inds
        Brit Turf & Landscape Irrigation Assn
        Garden & Landscape Designers Assn
        Horticultural Trs Assn
        Inst Groundsmanship
        Inst Profl Designers
        Ir Landscape Inst
        Landscape Inst
        Landscape Res Gp
        Permaculture Assn
        Profl Plant Users Gp
        Scot Seed & Nursery Tr Assn
        Soc Landscape Studies
        Soc Ley Hunters
        > + Earth sciences, structure & resources
Languages
        Assn Brit Language Schools
        Assn Language Learning
        Assn Learning Languages En Famille
        Brit Academy
        Brit Assn Academic Phoneticians

© CBD Research Ltd · Beckenham · BR3 5JS · Tel 020 8650 7745 · Fax 020 8650 0768 · E-mail cbd@cbdresearch.com · www.cbdresearch.com

Brit Assn Applied Linguistics
Chart Inst Linguists
Cheshaght Ghailckagh (Yn)
Linguistics Assn
Modern Humanities Res Assn
Nat Assn Language Advisers
Philological Soc
R Coll Speech & Language Therapists
UK Literacy Assn
Ulster-Scots Language Soc
> + Dialects; individual country

Languages: auxiliary
Brit Interlingua Soc
Esperanto Assn Britain
Glosa Educ Org
Intl Language [IDO] Soc
Scot Esperanto Assn

Larkin (Philip)
Philip Larkin Soc

Laryngology/Laryngectomy > Otolaryngology

Laser printers
UK Cartridge Remanufacturers Assn
> + Printing machinery & supplies

Lasers
Assn Indl Laser Users
Brit Med Laser Assn
Ophthalmological Prods Tr & Ind Conf

Latches > Locks & latches

Latex allergy
Latex Allergy Support Gp
> + Allergy

Latin > Classical studies

Latin America
Hispanic & Luso-Brazilian Coun
Latin Amer Assn
One World Linking Assn

Latin American dancing > Dancing

Latin Mass > Liturgy

Latvia
Brit Cham Comm Latvia

Lauder (Sir Harry)
Scot Music Hall & Variety Theatre Soc

Laundering
Gld Cleaners & Launderers
Nat Assn Launderette Ind
Nat Assn Nappy Services
Soc Laundry Engrs & Allied Trs
Textile Services Assn
Ulster Launderers Assn

Laurel & Hardy
Laurel & Hardy Appreciation Soc

Laurence-Moon-Bardet-Biedl disease
Laurence-Moon-Bardet-Biedl Soc

Law
Assn Lawyers & Legal Advisers
Assn Personal Injury Lawyers
Bar Assn Comm, Finance & Ind
Bar Assn Local Govt & Public Service
Brit Legal Assn
Comml Bar Assn
Criminal Bar Assn [E&W]
Family Law Bar Assn
Law Soc
Magistrates Assn
Medico-Legal Soc
Nat Assn Sole Practitioners
SIFA
Soc Advanced Legal Studies
Socio-Legal Studies Assn
> + headings below; Forensic science

Law: Ireland
Brit & Ir Assn Law Librarians
Honorable Soc King's Inns [IRL]]
Law Soc Ireland

Law: Northern Ireland
C'ee Admin Justice [NI]
Law Soc NI

Law: Scotland
Fac Advocates
Law Soc Scotland
Procurators Fiscal Soc
R Fac Procurators in Glasgow
Scot Indep Advocacy Alliance
Scot Law Agents Soc
Scot Legal Action Gp
Soc Solicitors Supreme Courts Scotland
Soc Writers Her Majesty's Signet

Law: art
Inst Art & Law
Law: centres
Law Centres Fedn
Scot Assn Law Centres
Law: charity
Charity Law Assn
Law: children
Assn Lawyers Children
Nat Assn Youth Justice
Law: clerks
Inst Barristers' Clerks
Justices' Clerks' Soc
Law: comparative
Brit Inst Intl & Comparative Law
Law: construction
Assn Consultant Approved Inspectors
Instn Planning Supervisors
Soc Construction Law
Law: costs
Assn Law Costs Draftsmen
Law: court officers
District Courts Assn
Law: education
Assn Law Teachers
Brit & Ir Legal Educ Technology Assn
Education Law Assn
Soc Legal Scholars
Law: employment
Employment Lawyers Assn
Law: environment
UK Envtl Law Assn
Law: European
Brit-German Jurists' Assn
UK Assn Eur Law
> + Law: international
Law: expert witness > Experts & expert witness
Law: family > Family law
Law: history
Selden Soc
Stair Soc
Law: immigration
Immigration Law Practitioners Assn
Law: industrial
Bar Assn Comm, Finance & Ind
Indl Law Soc
Law: insolvency
Insolvency Lawyers Assn
Law: insurance
Brit Insurance Law Assn
Law: international
Brit Inst Intl & Comparative Law
Intl Law Assn
Law: libraries
Brit & Ir Assn Law Librarians
Law: maritime
Brit Maritime Law Assn
Ir Maritime Law Assn
Law: motor accidents
Motor Accident Solicitors Soc
Law: paralegal
Inst Legal Executives
Inst Paralegal Training
Nat Assn Licensed Paralegals
Law: pension
Assn Pension Lawyers
Law: reform
Abortion Rights
Assn Law Teachers
> + specific aspects
Law: secretaries
Inst Legal Secretaries & PAs
Inst Paralegal Training
> + Law: paralegal
Law: Statute
Statute Law Soc
Lawn bowling > Bowling
Lawn mowers
Brit Lawn Mower Racing Assn
Old Lawn Mower Club
> + Horticulture & garden: machinery
Lawn tennis > Tennis
Lawrence (David Herbert)
D H Lawrence Soc
Lawrence (Thomas Edward)['of Arabia']
T E Lawrence Soc
Lawyers > Law; Legal advisers

Laying on of hands > Spiritual healing
Lead
    Lead Contrs Assn
    Lead Sheet Assn
    Lead Smelters & Refiners Assn
Learned society publishing
    Assn Learned & Profl Soc Pubrs
Learning
    Soc Effective Affective Learning
    > + Education
Learning disability
    Assn Real Change
    Brit Dyslexia Assn
    Brit Inst Learning Disabilities
    Caspari Foundation for Educl Therapy...
    Nat Assn Toy & Leisure Libraries
    Scot Support Learning Assn
    > + Children: handicapped
Learning resources > Education: technology
Leasing
    Assn Leasehold Enfranchisement Practitioners
    Finance & Leasing Assn
    Leasehold Enfranchisement Assn
Leather
    BLC, Leather Technology Centre
    Leather Producers' Assn
Leather chemistry
    Soc Leather Technologists & Chemists
Leathergoods
    Brit Travelgoods & Accessories Assn
    Soc Master Saddlers
Lebanon
    Brit Lebanese Assn
Lecturers
    Assn Teachers & Lecturers
    NATFHE
    > + Adult education; Teachers
Leeks
    Leek Growers' Assn
    Nat Pot Leek Soc
    > + Vegetable: growing
Left-handed people
    Left-Handers Assn
    Left Handers Club
Legacies (public) > Donations (public)
Legal > Law; & headings below
Legal advisers
    Assn Lawyers & Legal Advisers
    Scot Indep Advocacy Alliance
Legal cashiers
    Inst Legal Cashiers & Administrators
Legal secretaries > Law: secretaries
Legal studies > Law
Legionnaire's disease
    Inst Plumbing & Heating Engg
Leisure parks
    Assn Leading Visitor Attractions
    Brit Assn Leisure Parks, Piers & Attractions
    > + Amusements
Leisure, recreation & amenity management
    Assn Heritage Interpretation
    Assn Profl Sales Agents (Sports & Leisure Inds)
    Chief Cultural & Leisure Officers Assn
    Fitness Ind Assn
    Inst Entertainment & Arts Mgt
    Inst Leisure & Amenity Mgt
    Inst Leisure & Amenity Mgt (Ireland)
    Leisure Studies Assn
    Nat Assn Agricl Contrs
    Nat Assn Leisure Ind Certification
    Recreation Mgrs' Assn
    Scot Countryside Rangers Assn
    Soc Leisure Consultants & Pubrs
    Voice Chief Offrs Culture... Scotland
Leisure software > Software: leisure
Lending rights > Copyright
Lenses > Optical industry
Lepidoptera > Entomology
Lesch-Nyhan syndrome
    Purine Metabolic Patients Assn
Letter boxes
    Letter Box Study Gp
Letter carving > Stone masons & sculptors;   Wood carving
Letter files
    Letter File Mfrs Assn
    > + Office equipment & systems
Letter scales > Scales & weighing machines;   Writing equipment & accessories

Letting agents
    Assn Residential Letting Agents
    UK Assn Letting Agents
Lettuces
    Brit Leafy Salad Assn
    > + Vegetables: growing
Leukaemia
    Leukaemia Care
Leylandii hedges
    Hedgeline
Leylines
    Assn Scientific Study Anomalous Phenomena
    Soc Ley Hunters
Liberty > Individual freedom
Libraries/librarians
    ARLIS UK & Ireland
    Aslib
    Assn Brit Theological... Libraries
    Assn Denominational Histl Socs Cognate Libs
    Assn Indep Libraries
    Assn NI Educ & Library Bds
    Assn Senior Children's & Educ Librarians
    Assn UK Media Librarians
    Brit Assn Friends Museums
    Brit & Ir Assn Law Librarians
    Britain & Ireland Assn Aquatic Science Libraries...
    Career Devt Gp
    CILIP
    CURL
    Friends Nat Libraries
    Librarians of Insts & Schools of Educ
    Library Assn Ireland
    Library Campaign
    London Library
    Nat Acquisitions Gp
    Nat Assn Aerial Photographic Libraries
    Network Govt Library & Inf Specialists
    Private Libraries Assn
    School Library Assn
    Soc Chief Librarians England & Wales
    Voice Chief Offrs Culture... Scotland
    > + Picture libraries
Library schools
    Brit Assn Inf & Library Educ & Res
Library suppliers
    Assn Library Eqpt Suppliers
Libya
    Soc Libyan Studies
Licensed property (valuation)
    Assn Valuers Licensed Property
    Restaurant Property Advisors Soc
Licensed trade > Bars (management & staff); Wines & spirits: trade
Licensing laws
    Campaign Real Ale
Licensing (product) > Product licensing
Lichen
    Brit Lichen Soc
Life assurance > Insurance
Life saving
    Brit Long Distance Swimming Assn
    R Humane Soc
    R Life Saving Soc
    R Nat Lifeboat Instn
    Soc Protection Life Fire
    Surf Life Saving Assn
    Swimming Teachers Assn
    > + Safety
Lifeboats
    Lifeboat Enthusiasts' Soc
    R Nat Lifeboat Instn
Lifting & loading equipment
    Assn Loading & Elevating Eqpt Mfrs
    Assn Lorry Loader Mfrs & Importers
    Automated Material Handling Systems Assn
    Lifting Eqpt Engrs Assn
    Solids Handling & Processing Assn
    > + Construction equipment; Fork-lift trucks; Materials: management/handling
Lifts
    Chart Instn Bldg Services Engrs
    Lift & Escalator Ind Assn
Light alloys & metals > Metal headings
Light music > Music
Light railways > Railways: light;   Tramways & trams
Lighter-than-air craft > Balloons & airships
Lighterage
    River Assn Freight & Transport

© CBD Research Ltd · Beckenham · BR3 5JS · Tel 020 8650 7745 · Fax 020 8650 0768 · E-mail cbd@cbdresearch.com · www.cbdresearch.com

Lighthouses & lightships
>> Assn Lighthouse Keepers
Lighting
>> Assn Interior Specialists
>> Chart Instn Bldg Services Engrs
>> Instn Lighting Engrs
>> Lighting Assn
>> Lighting Ind Fedn
>> + Road: lighting, markings & traffic signs
Lightning
>> Tornado & Storm Res Org
Lightning conductors
>> Assn Technical Lighting & Access Specialists
Limbless persons
>> Limbless Assn
>> + Disablement
Lime & limestone
>> Agricl Lime Assn
>> Brit Calcium Carbonates Fedn
>> Brit Lime Assn
>> Ground Limestone Producers Assn [IRL]
>> Quarry Products Assn
Limekilns
>> Sussex Indl Archaeol Soc
Limousines
>> Nat Limousine Assn
Line dancing
>> Brit Western Dance Assn
>> + Dancing
Linen
>> Ir Linen Gld
>> + Textile headings
Liners (ships) > Ships: history & preservation
Linesmen > Referees
Linguistics > Languages
Linguists > Translation & interpretation
Linoleum
>> Contract Flooring Assn
>> UK Resilient Flooring Mfrs' Assn
Lintels
>> Steel Lintel Mfrs Assn
>> + Doors; Windows
Lipreading & lipspeaking
>> Assn Lipspeakers
>> Assn Teachers Lipreading to Adults
>> + Deafness
Liquefied petroleum gas
>> L P Gas Assn
Liqueurs > Wines & spirits: trade
Liquid roofing > Roofing
Liquidators
>> Insolvency Practitioners Assn
>> + Insolvency
Liquids: packaging
>> Liquid Food Carton Mfrs' Assn
Liquids: storage/warehousing
>> Tank Storage Assn
>> + Cisterns, drums & tanks
List broking
>> Direct Marketing Assn (UK) Ltd
>> + Advertising
Listed property
>> Listed Property Owners Club
>> + Historic buildings
Literacy
>> Brit Assn Literacy in Devt
>> Nat Literacy Assn
>> UK Literacy Assn
>> + Reading
Literary agents > Authors' agents
Literary rights > Copyright
Literary societies > individual writer; [Country]: language & literature
Literature
>> Alliance Literary Socs
>> Brit Academy
>> Brit Comparative Literature Assn
>> Manchester Literary & Philosophical Soc
>> Nat Assn Literature Devt
>> + English language & literature; & individual countries
Lithuania
>> Lithuanian Assn
Litigation > Law
Litigation: support
>> Network Indep Forensic Accountants
Liturgy
>> Alcuin Club
>> Ecclesiological Soc

Henry Bradshaw Soc
Latin Mass Soc
Prayer Book Soc
Scot Prayer Book Soc
Liver disease
>> Brit Soc Gastroenterology
Liverworts
>> Brit Bryological Soc
Livestock > Cattle & livestock; Poultry; Sheep
Living history
>> Engliscan Gesíþas
>> Regia Anglorum
>> Seventeenth Century Life & Times
>> Vikings (The)
>> + Fights (historic/re-enactment)
Living wills
>> Alert Euthanasia
Llamas > Camelids
Load conveyors > Lifting & loading equipment
Load restraint
>> Performance Textiles Assn
Loading equipment > Lifting & loading equipment
Local government
>> Action Communities Rural England
>> Assn Charter Trustee Towns &... Couns
>> Assn London Government
>> Assn Municipal Authorities Ireland
>> Assn N E Couns
>> Convention Scot Local Authorities
>> Gen Coun County Couns [IRL]
>> Local Authorities Res & Intelligence Assn
>> Local Govt Assn
>> Local Govt Reform Soc
>> Nat Assn Councillors
>> Nat Assn Local Couns
>> NI Local Govt Assn
>> One Voice Wales
>> Welsh Local Govt Assn
Local government: officers
>> Assn Chief Estates Surveyors... Local Govt
>> Assn Coun Secretaries & Solicitors
>> Assn County Chief Executives
>> Assn Local Authority Chief Execs
>> Assn Local Govt Archaeol Officers
>> Assn Local Govt Communications
>> Assn Town Clerks Ireland
>> Assn Transport Co-ordinating Officers
>> Bar Assn Local Govt & Public Service
>> Chief Cultural & Leisure Officers Assn
>> CIPFA
>> County Educ Officers Two Tier Authorities
>> District Surveyors Assn Ltd
>> Inst Leisure & Amenity Mgt
>> Inst Maintenance & Bldg Mgt
>> Inst Public Sector Mgt
>> Instn Economic Devt
>> Ir Assn Corporate Treasurers
>> Local Authority Caterers' Assn
>> Local Authority Road Safety Officers' Assn
>> Local Govt Technical Advisers Gp
>> Planning Officers Soc
>> Public Mgt & Policy Assn
>> Public Sector People Mgrs' Assn
>> Public Services Network
>> Soc Construction & Quantity Surveyors Public Sector
>> Soc County Treasurers [E&W]
>> Soc District Coun Treasurers
>> Soc Local Authority Chief Execs & Senior Mgrs
>> Soc Local Coun Clerks
>> Soc Local Govt Electrical...Engrs
>> Soc Procurement Officers Local Govt
Local government: services
>> ALARM
>> Assn Public Service Excellence
Local government: vehicles
>> Road Transport Fleet Data Soc
Local history & topography
>> Assn Local Hist Tutors
>> Brit Assn Local Hist
>> Scot Local History Forum
>> + Archaeology: county societies; Records: historical
Locks & latches
>> Assn Burglary Insurance Surveyors [>AIS011 (04)
>> Assn Insurance Surveyors
>> Auto Locksmiths Assn
>> Brit Locksmiths Assn

Master Locksmiths Assn
> + Security
Locomotives > Railway headings
Locomotives: road
Road Locomotive Soc
Logistics > Materials: management/handling
London
London Appreciation Soc
London & Middlesex Archaeol Soc
London Natural Hist Soc
London Soc
London Subterranean Survey Assn
London Topographical Soc
London boroughs > Local government
Long-bow archery > Archery
Long range planning > Strategic planning
Longevity > Geriatrics & ageing
Lords-of-the-Manor > Manors
Lorry loaders
Assn Lorry Loader Mfrs & Importers
> + Lifting & loading equipment
Loss assessment
Chart Inst Loss Adjusters
Inst Public Loss Assessors
Lost wax casting > Metal: casting
Lotteries
Lotteries Coun
Lovespoon carving
Brit Woodcarvers Assn
Low Countries
Assn Low Countries Studies
> + Belgium; Netherlands
Low temperatures > Cryogenics
Lowe syndrome
Lowe Syndrome Assn
Lower limb deficiency
STEPS. . .
> + Disablement
Lubricants
Oil Recycling Assn
UK Lubricants Assn
Luge racing > Toboggan & luge racing/riding
Luggage & travel goods > Travel goods & accessories
Lumber > Timber
Lung(s), disease & research > Thoracic diseases
Lupus
Lupus UK
Lutes & lute playing
Lute Soc
Lutheran Church
Lutheran Coun
Lutyens (Sir Edwin)
Lutyens Trust
Luxembourg
Belgian-Luxembourg Cham Comm GB
Brit Cham Comm Luxembourg
Lymphoedema & lymphology
Brit Lymphology Soc
Brit Manual Lymph Drainage Assn
Lymphoedema Support Network
Lymphoma Assn

M

Macadam > Asphalt & coated macadam
MacDonald (George)
George MacDonald Soc
Macebearers
Gld Macebearers
Macedonia
Macedonian Soc GB
Machen (Arthur)
Friends Arthur Machen
Machine tools
Brit Hardmetal & Engineers' Cutting Tool Assn
Engg & Machinery Alliance
Gauge & Tool Makers Assn
Manufacturing Technologies Assn
Machine vision
Brit Machine Vision Assn. . .
UK Indl Vision Assn
Machinery
Machinery Users Assn

Woodworking Machinery Suppliers Assn
> + specific types of machinery
Machinery: safety
Safety Assessment Fedn
Mackerel
Herring Buyers Assn
Scot Pelagic Fishermen's Assn
> + Fish headings; Fishing
Mackintosh (Charles Rennie)
Charles Rennie Mackintosh Soc
Macular disease
Macular Disease Soc
> + Blind & partially sighted
Madagascar
Anglo-Malagasy Soc
Magazines > Newspapers & periodicals: distribution; Periodicals
Magic > Conjuring & magic
Magic lanterns
Magic Lantern Soc
Magistrates & magistrates courts
Justices' Clerks' Soc
Magistrates Assn
Magna Carta
Magna Carta Soc
Magnetic strip cards > Credit & magnetic strip cards
Magnetism
UK Magnetics Soc
Mail > Postal services
Mail order trade
Mail Order Trs Assn
> + Advertising; Direct selling
Maintenance > Buildings: cleaning & maintenance;   Plant: industrial
Maintenance products
Brit Assn Chemical Specialities
Maize & maize starch
Brit Starch Ind Assn
Maize Growers Assn
UK Maize Millers' Assn
Majorettes
Brit Isles Baton Twirling Assn
Nat Baton Twirling Assn
Make-up (stage & screen)
Nat Assn Screen Make-up Artists & Hairdressers
> + Beauty specialists/treatment
Malacology > Conchology
Maladjusted children > Children: handicapped
Malaysia
Brit Malaysian Soc
Malt & malt products
Malt Distillers Assn Scotland
Maltsters Assn
> + Whisky
Mammals
Mammal Soc
Marine Consvn Soc
> + Nature conservation
Mammography
Brit Machine Vision Assn. . .
Management
Academy Execs & Admins
Assn Business Administration
Assn Business Executives
Assn Business Schools
Assn Indep Mgt & Maritime Services
Assn Mgt Educ & Devt
Brit Educl Leadership, Mgt & Admin Soc
Business Mgt Assn
Chart Mgt Inst
Ergonomics Soc
Inst Administrative Mgt
Inst Business Admin
Inst Business Advisers
Inst Comml Mgt
Inst Mgt Services
Inst Mgt Specialists
Inst Value Mgt
Ir Mgt Inst
Profl Business & Technical Mgt
Quality Methods Assn
Strategic Planning Soc
> + Project management
Management accountancy
Chart Inst Mgt Accountants
Management consultancy
Indep Consultants Consortium
Inst Mgt Consultants Ireland

© CBD Research Ltd · Beckenham · BR3 5JS · Tel 020 8650 7745 · Fax 020 8650 0768 · E-mail cbd@cbdresearch.com · www.cbdresearch.com

Management Consultancies Assn
>+ Employment agents & consultants
Manhole covers
Fabricated Access Cover Tr Assn
Manic depression > Depression
Manila hemp > Hemp
Manipulative medicine > specific type eg Osteopathy

Manors
Curia Baronis
Manorial Soc
Manpower > Employment
Manslaughter > Murder & manslaughter
Manufacturers/manufacturing
Brit Assn Res Quality Assurance
Brit Contract Mfrs & Packers Assn
Confedn Brit Ind
Ind Res & Devt Gp [IRL]
Inst Manufacturing
PERA
Rapid Prototyping & Mfrg Assn
Science, Engg & Mfrg Technologies Alliance
>+ specific industries
Manufacturers' agents
Manufacturers' Agents' Assn
Manx language
Cheshaght Ghailckagh (Yn)
Manx language
Maps > Cartography
Marble
Nat Fedn Terrazzo Marble & Mosaic Specialists
Mare, de la (Walter)
Walter de la Mare Soc
Marfan syndrome
Marfan Assn UK
Margarine
Margarine Mfrs Assn Ireland
Margarine & Spreads Assn
Marinas
Yacht Harbour Assn
>+ Yachting
Marine: aggregates
Brit Marine Aggregate Producers' Assn
>+ Aggregates
Marine: biology & biochemistry
Brit Marine Life Study Soc
Britain & Ireland Assn Aquatic Science Libraries. . .
Challenger Soc Marine Science
Linnean Soc Lond
Marine Biological Assn
Marine Consvn Soc
Scot Assn Marine Science
Scot Sub Aqua Club
Sub-Aqua Assn
>+ Oceanography
Marine: catering > Catering
Marine: contractors
Intl Marine Contrs Assn
>+ Ocean industries
Marine: education
Central Org Maritime Pastimes. . .
Marine Inst [IRL]
Marine Soc & Sea Cadets
Marine: energy > Renewable energy
Marine: engineering & equipment
Assn Indep Mgt & Maritime Services
Brit Marine Eqpt Assn
Brit Naval Eqpt Assn
Inst Marine Engg, Science & Technology
Instn Civil Engrs
Marine Engine & Eqpt Mfrs Assn
R Instn Naval Architects
Soc Automotive Engrs
Soc Consulting Marine Engrs & Ship Surveyors
Soc Maritime Inds
>+ Shipbuilding & ship repairing; Underwater engineering &
research
Marine: information
Britain & Ireland Assn Aquatic Science Libraries. . .
Maritime Inf Assn
>+ Nautical history
Marine: trading > Ships stores & supplies
Mariners
Nautical Inst
>+ Merchant Navy
Marital studies > Family headings
Maritime law > Law: maritime

Marker posts
Retroreflective Eqpt Mfrs Assn
>+ Road markings, lighting & traffic signs
Market gardening > Fruit: trade;   Horticulture
Marketing
Arts Marketing Assn
Assn Intl Marketing
Assn Users Res Agencies
Chart Inst Marketing
Direct Marketing Assn (UK) Ltd
Inst Direct Marketing
Inst Sales Promotion
Ir Direct Marketing Assn
Market Res Soc
Marketing Communication Consultants Assn
Marketing Inst [IRL]
Marketing Soc
Marketing Soc [IRL]
Profl Services Marketing Gp
Publicity Club Lond
Soc Sales & Marketing
>+ Incentive marketing; Sales management & representation
Marketing: researchers & interviewers
Assn Qualitative Res
Market Res Quality Standards Assn
Viewing Facilities Assn (UK)
Markets: street, cattle & farmers'
Assn Private Market Operators
Fedn Street Traders Us
Humane Slaughter Assn
Livestock Auctioneers Assn
Nat Assn Brit Market Authorities
Nat Farmers' Retail & Markets Assn
Nat Market Traders Fedn
Marlowe (Christopher)
Marlowe Soc
Marmalades
Food Processors' Assn
Marquees > Tents & marquees
Marquetry
Marquetry Soc
Marriage bureaux > Introduction agencies & marriage bureaux
Marriage guidance
Assn Marriage Enrichment
Marriages > Population registration
Martial arts
All Brit Martial Arts Coun
Amat Martial Assn
Brit Fedn Histl Swordplay
Brit Judo Assn
Brit Nat Martial Arts Assns
Brit Shorinji Kempo Fedn
Brit Zen Aiki Assn
Judo Scotland
Martial Arts Devt Commission
Nat Assn Karate & Martial Arts Schools
Scot Ju-Jitsu Assn
Soc Martial Arts
Welsh Judo Assn
Mary, Queen of Scots
Marie Stuart Soc
Masefield (John)
John Masefield Soc
Masonry > Stone
Massage
Gen Coun Massage Therapy
On Site Massage Assn
Scot Massage Therapists Org
Sports Massage Assn
Massenet (Jules)
Massenet Soc
Masters of ceremonies > Toastmasters & masters of ceremonies
Mastic asphalt > Asphalt & coated macadam
Masts (radio/telephone) > Aerials: radio, telephone & television
Matchbox labels
Brit Matchbox, Label & Booklet Soc
Materials (fabrics) > type of material
Materials: control > Stock & materials control
Materials: management/handling
Automated Material Handling Systems Assn
Brit Intl Freight Assn
Brit Materials Handling Fedn
Chart Inst Logistics & Transport Ireland
Chart Inst Logistics & Transport UK
Container Handling Eqpt Mfrs Assn
Materials Handling Engrs Assn
Solids Handling & Processing Assn

Storage & Handling Eqpt Distbrs Assn
UK Warehousing Assn
> + Freight transport
Materials: recycling > Reclamation & recycling
Materials: technology & testing
Brit Civil Engg Test Eqpt Mfrs Assn
Brit Inst Non-Destructive Testing
Brit Measurement & Testing Assn
Brit Soc Strain Measurement
BTC Testing Advisory Gp
Engg Integrity Soc
Inst Materials, Minerals & Mining
Lifting Eqpt Engrs Assn
Materials Components Developing & Testing Assn
R Microscopical Soc
Soc Dyers & Colourists
Welding Inst
Maternity
Action Pre-Eclampsia
Assn Community-based Maternity Care
Assn Improvements Maternity Services
Assn Postnatal Illness
Assn Radical Midwives
Assn Supervisors Midwives
BLISS
Brit Doula Assn
Life
Meet-a-Mum Assn
Nat Childbirth Trust
Neonatal Soc
Stillbirth & Neonatal Death Soc
> + Midwifery; Obstetrics & gynaecology
Mathematics
Assn Teachers Mathematics
Brit Soc Hist Mathematics
Dozenal Soc
Edinburgh Mathematical Soc
Glasgow Mathematical Assn
Inst Mathematics & Applications
London Mathematical Soc
MatheMagic
Mathematical Assn
Nat Assn Mathematics Advisers
Mats & matting
Coir Assn
Maxillofacial disease
Craniofacial Soc
> + Oral medicine
Mayors
London Mayors Assn
ME (disease) > Myalgic encephalomyelitis
Mead
Nat Fruit Wine, Mead & Liqueur Producers Assn
Meals on wheels
Measurement
Assn Instrumentation, Control, Automation. . .
Brit Measurement & Testing Assn
Brit Weights & Measures Assn
Evaluation Intl
Inst Measurement & Control
Trading Standards Inst
UK Metric Assn
> + Scales & weighing machines
Meat
Assn Indep Meat Suppliers
Assn Meat Inspectors
Brit Meat Processors Assn
Charcuterie Gld
Gld Q Butchers
Meat Industry Ireland
Nat Assn Catering Butchers
Nat Fedn Meat & Food Traders
NI Master Butchers Assn
NI Meat Exporters Assn
Provision Tr Fedn
Quality Meat Scotland
Scot Assn Meat Whlsrs
Scot Fedn Meat Traders Assns
UK Assn Frozen Food Producers
> + Bacon; Poultry
Meat substitutes
Soya Protein Assn
Mechanical components: obsolescence
Component Obsolescence Gp
Mechanical engineering
Instn Engg & Technology
Instn Mechanical Engrs

Mechanical & Metal Trs Confedn
N England Inst Mining & Mechanical Engrs
> + Engineering
Mechanical handling > Materials: management/handling
Mechatronics
Medals > Numismatics
Media
ACG Ltd (Arts Centre Gp)
Assn Media Evaluation Cos
Assn UK Media Librarians
Brit Assn Communicators in Business
Brit Interactive Media Assn
Community Media Assn
Creator's Rights Alliance
Directors Gld
Fedn Entertainment Us
MeCCSA with AMPE
Media Res Gp
Media Soc
Online Content UK
Publicity Club Lond
> + Newspapers & periodicals;   Radio; Television; Multimedia
Mediæval history
Colloquium Medieval & Renaissance Studies
Soc Ancients
> + Records: historical
Medical accidents
Action Med Accidents
Medical accountants
Assn Indep Specialist Med Accountants
Medical apparatus & appliances > Health care: equipment & supplies;
Sterilising; Surgical equipment
Medical broadcasts
Assn Broadcasting Doctors
Medical conditions: long-term
LMCA
Medical & dental hypnosis
Brit Assn Med Hypnosis
Brit Soc Med & Dental Hypnosis
> + Hypnosis & hypnotherapy
Medical education
Assn Study Med Educ
Nat Assn Clinical Tutors
Nat Assn Primary Care Educators
Medical herbalists > Herbs & herbal medicine
Medical illustration
Inst Med Illustrators
Medical Artists Assn
R Photographic Soc
Medical insurance > Hospitals: contributory schemes;   Medical practitioners'
legal defence
Medical journalism > Medical writing/journalism
Medical laboratory technology > Medical technology
Medical officers
Assn Directors Public Health
Medical Officers Schools Assn
Soc Occupational Medicine
Medical physics
Inst Physics & Engg in Medicine
Medical practice
Balint Soc
Brit Assn Med Mgrs
Country Doctors Assn
Fedn Indep Practitioner Orgs
Gld Catholic Doctors
Medical Ethics Alliance
Medical Women's Fedn
Nat Assn Deputising Doctors
Nat Assn Med Educ Mgt
Nat Assn Patient Participation
Nat Assn Sessional GP's
NHS Consultants' Assn
R Coll Gen Practitioners
Small Practices Assn
> + Medicine
Medical practice: administration
Assn Med Secretaries. . .& Receptionists
NHS Alliance
NHS Confedn
Medical practitioners' legal defence
Medical Defence U
Medical & Dental Defence U Scotland
Medical Protection Soc
Medical records
Inst Health Record & Inf Mgt
Medical research
Academy Medical Sciences

Anaesthetic Res Soc
Assn Researchers in Medicine & Science
Coalition Medical Progress
Inst Clinical Res
Medical Res Soc
Patients' Voice Med Advance
> + Medicine
Medical secretaries
Assn Med Secretaries. . .& Receptionists
Medical technology
Assn Brit Healthcare Inds
Inst Biomedical Science
Inst Physics & Engg in Medicine
Ir Med Devices Assn
Medical Sciences Histl Soc
> + individual science
Medical waste
Sanitary Med Disposal Services Assn
Medical writing/journalism
Assn Brit Science Writers
Medical Journalists Assn
Soc Medical Writers
Medicinal preparations > Pharmaceuticals
Medicine
Anthroposophical Med Assn
Assn Med Res Charities
Assn Palliative Medicine
Brit Holistic Med Assn
Brit Med Assn
Brit Med Ultrasound Soc
Brit Nuclear Medicine Soc
Brit Soc Rehabilitation Medicine
Fac Pharmaceutical Med
Fellowship Postgraduate Medicine
Harveian Soc Lond
Hunterian Soc
Intensive Care Soc
Ir Coll Gen Practitioners
Ir Med Org
Manchester Med Soc
Medical Soc Lond
Medical Women's Fedn
R Academy Medicine Ireland
R Coll Physicians Edinburgh
R Coll Physicians Ireland
R Coll Physicians Lond
R Coll Physicians & Surgeons Glasgow
R Medical Soc
R Soc Medicine
R Soc Tropical Medicine & Hygiene
Royal Soc (The)
Soc Social Medicine
Medicine: alternative > Complementary medicine; & specific forms
Medicine: herbal > Herbs & herbal medicine
Medicine: history
Brit Soc Hist Medicine
Medical Sciences Histl Soc
Scot Soc Hist Medicine
Soc Social Hist Medicine
Medicine & the law
Medico-Legal Soc
> + Forensic science
Medicine & religion
Assn Nursing Religious
Gld Catholic Doctors
Gld Health
Gld Pastoral Psychology
Medical Ethics Alliance
Medicine & sport > Sports medicine & therapy

London Medieval Soc
Medieval Settlement Res Gp
Ranulf Higden Soc
Meetings (conduct of)
Assn Speakers Clubs
Megaliths
Megalithic Soc
Megapodes > Game & game birds
Membrane switches
Keygraphica
> + Electrical industry & engineering
Membranes (intelligent)
Intelligent Membrane Tr Assn
Memorials
Church Monuments Soc
Nat Assn Memorial Masons

Public Monuments & Sculpture Assn
> + Stone masons & sculptors
Memory
Brit False Memory Soc
Mendelssohn-Bartholdy (Felix)
Friends Mendelssohn
Ménière's disease
Ménière's Soc
Meningitis
Meningitis Assn Scotland
Meningitis Res Foundation
Menopause (the)
Brit Menopause Soc
Brit Soc Psychosomatic Obstetrics. . .
Daisy Network Premature Menopause Support Gp
Menswear
> + Clothing; Tailoring
Mental health
Assn Child & Adoloescent Mental Health
Assn Infant Mental Health UK
Assn Pastoral Care Mental Health
Assn Therapeutic Communities
ENABLE
Fragile X Soc
MENCAP
Mental Health Ireland
Mental Health Nurses Assn
Mind
Nat Assn Mental After-Care in. . . Homes
Nat Assn Mentally H'capped Ireland
Nat Network Assessment Cntres
Nat Phobics Soc
NI Assn Mental Health
Psychiatric Rehabilitation Assn
Rethink
Scot Assn Mental Health
Together
> + Psychiatry; specific forms of mental illness
Mentoring: business
Inst Business Advisers
Merchant Navy
Nat U Marine. . . Transport Officers
Rail, Maritime & Transport U
> + Shipping
Mercury in dentistry
Brit Soc Mercury Free Dentistry
Merry-go-rounds > Fairgrounds & equipment
Merton (Thomas)
Thomas Merton Soc
Messengers-at-Arms
Soc Messengers-at-Arms & Sheriff-Officers
Metabolic disorders
Children Living Inherited Metabolic Diseases
Metal
Aluminium Alloy Mfrg & Recycling Assn
Brit Hardmetal & Engineers' Cutting Tool Assn
Community
Inst Materials, Minerals & Mining
Mechanical & Metal Trs Confedn
Minor Metals Tr Assn
Nat Metal Trs Fedn
Non-Ferrous Alliance
Scot Assn Metals
Metal: abrasives > Abrasives
Metal: boxes
Metal Packaging Mfrs Assn
Metal: casting
Cast Metals Fedn
Inst Cast Metal Engrs
Metal: detecting
Fedn Indep Detectorists
Nat Coun Metal Detecting
Metal: finishing
Aluminium Finishing Assn
Brit Jewellery, Giftware & Finishing Fedn
Inst Metal Finishing
Inst Vitreous Enamellers
Surface Engg Assn
Metal: forming
Confedn Brit Metalforming
Metalforming Machinery Makers Assn
Metal: mining > Mining
Metal: non-ferrous
Aluminium Stockholders Assn
Brit Non-Ferrous Metals Fedn
Metal: powder > Powder metallurgy

Metal: scrap
> Aluminium Alloy Mfrg & Recycling Assn
> Brit Metals Recycling Assn
> > + Reclamation & recycling
Metal: sheet
> Inst Sheet Metal Engg
Metal: sintering > Powder metallurgy
Metal: spraying
> Thermal Spraying & Surface Engg Assn
Metal: working
> Art Metalware Mfrs' Assn
> Brit Antique Furniture Restorers Assn
> Brit Artist Blacksmiths Assn
> Brit Metallurgical Plant Constructors Assn
> Cold Rolled Sections Assn
> Metalforming Machinery Makers Assn
> UK Lubricants Assn
Metallurgy
> Birmingham Metallurgical Assn
> Histl Metallurgy Soc
> Inst Materials, Minerals & Mining
> Mineral Ind Res Org
> Minerals Engg Soc
Metals: precious > Gemstones; Goldsmiths & Silversmiths; Jewellery
Metalware (antique)
> Antique Metalware Soc
Metamorphic technique
> Metamorphic Assn
Metaphysics
> Soc Metaphysicians
Meteorology
> Assn Brit Climatologists
> R Meteorological Soc
> Remote Imaging Group
> Tornado & Storm Res Org
Meters & metering
> Assn Meter Operators
> BEAMA
> Nat Campaign Water Justice
> Soc Brit Gas Inds
> Soc Brit Water & Wastewater Inds
> UK Metering Forum
> UK Revenue Protection Assn
Methane
> Assn Coal Mine Methane Operators
> UK Onshore Operators Gp
Methodist Church
> Soc Cirplanologists
> Wesley Histl Soc
Metrology
> Dozenal Soc
> Gauge & Tool Makers Assn
> Trading Standards Inst
> UK Metric Assn
> UK Weighing Fedn
> > + Measurement
Mexico
> Brit Mexican Soc
> Cámara Comercio Británica [Mexico]
Mice
> Nat Mouse Club
Microbiology
> Assn Applied Biologists
> Assn Med Microbiologists
> Brit Occupational Hygiene Soc
> Brit Soc Antimicrobial Chemotherapy
> Pathological Soc
> Soc Anaerobic Microbiology
> Soc Applied Microbiology
> Soc Gen Microbiology
Microcirculation > Haematology
Microelectronics
> Nat Microelectronics Inst
Microlight aircraft
> Brit Microlight Aircraft Assn
Microphthalmia
> Micro & Anophthalmic Children's Soc
Microscopy
> Quekett Microscopical Club
> R Microscopical Soc
Microwave ovens
> Microwave Technologies Assn
> Nat Assn Microwave Engrs
Middle East
> AEMES
> Brit Soc Middle Eastn Studies
> Middle East Assn

Midwifery
> Assn Radical Midwives
> Assn Supervisors Midwives
> Indep Midwives Assn
> R Coll Midwives
> > + Maternity; Obstetrics & gynaecology
Migraine & headaches
> Brit Assn Study Headache
> Migraine Action Assn
Milestones
> Milestone Soc
Military bands > Brass & silver bands
Military history
> Army Records Soc
> Brit Cartographic Soc
> Brit Model Soldier Soc
> Corps Drums Soc
> Military Heraldry Soc
> Military Histl Soc
> Patton Histl Soc
> R Utd Services Inst Defence... Studies
> Scot Military Histl Soc
> Soc Ancients
> Soc Army Histl Res
> Victorian Military Soc
> Western Front Assn
> > + Fortresses & forts
Military vehicles
> Military Vehicle Trust
> Miniature Armoured Fighting Vehicles Assn
> > + Motor vehicles: historic
Milk (incl milk products) > Dairying
Milk cartons
> Liquid Food Carton Mfrs' Assn
> > + Packaging
Milking machines
> Milking Machine Mfrs' Assn
Millinery > Headwear
Milling > Grinding & milling machinery; & product milled
Mills & mill engines
> Northern Mill Engine Soc
> Soc Protection Ancient Bldgs
> > + Steam engines, boats & machinery

Mineral insulating fibres > Insulation
Mineral water
> Spa Business Assn
> > + Bottled water; Soft drinks
Minerals
> Brit Aggregates Assn
> Gemmological Assn
> Mineral Ind Res Org
> Mineralogical Soc
> R Instn Chart Surveyors
> > + Geology
Miniature painting
> Brit Soc Miniaturists
> Hilliard Soc Miniaturists
> R Soc Miniature Painters ...
> Soc Limners
> > + Art & artists
Minicabs > Taxis & minicabs
Mining
> Assn Mining Analysts
> Brit Aggregates Assn
> Brit Assn Colliery Mgt
> Cornish Cham Mines & Minerals
> Ir Assn Economic Geology
> Ir Mining & Exploration Gp
> Ir Mining & Quarrying Soc
> Mineral Ind Res Org
> Minerals Engg Soc
> Mining Assn
> N England Inst Mining & Mechanical Engrs
> Nat Assn Licensed Opencast Operators
> > + Coal mining
Mining: equipment
> Assn Brit Mining Eqpt Cos
> Miners' & Indl Lamp Mfrs' Assn
Mining: history
> Nat Assn Mining Hist Orgs
> Northern Mine Res Soc
> Peak District Mines Hist Soc
> Subterranea Britannica
> Trevithick Soc
> Welsh Mines Soc

© CBD Research Ltd · Beckenham · BR3 5JS · Tel 020 8650 7745 · Fax 020 8650 0768 · E-mail cbd@cbdresearch.com · www.cbdresearch.com

Mire research
> Brit Ecological Soc
Mirrors
> Glass & Glazing Fedn
Miscarriage
> Foresight
> Miscarriage Assn
> > + Maternity
Missionary organisations
> Soc Promoting Christian Knowledge
Mobile catering > Catering: outdoor
Mobile communications > Communication services; Mobile phones; Paging (radio); Radio: mobile
Mobile community resources
> Nat Playbus Assn
Mobile data
> Mobile Data Assn
Mobile homes
> Nat Assn Park Home Residents
> > + Caravans & caravanning
Mobile phones
> Fedn Technological Inds
> Ir Cellular Industry Assn
> Mast Action UK
> Mobile Electronics & Security Fedn
> Mobile Ind Crime Action Forum
> Mobile Marketing Assn
> Mobile Operators Assn
Mobile radio > Radio: mobile
Mobility aids
> Brit Healthcare Trs Assn
> Seeing Dogs Alliance
> > + Blind & partially sighted; Disabled: road users; Health care: equipment & supplies
Model making
> Soc Architectural Illustration
> Soc Model & Experimental Engrs
> > + Models: hobby
Model theatre > Theatre: model
Models: fashion > Fashion
Models: hobby
> Brit Model Flying Assn
> Brit Model Soldier Soc
> Brit Radio Car Assn
> Brit Slot Car Racing Assn
> EM Gauge Soc
> Histl Model Rly Soc
> Miniature Armoured Fighting Vehicles Assn
> Model Electronic Rly Gp
> Model Rly Club
> Model Yachting Assn
> N Wstn Model Rly Clubs Assn
> Scot Aeromodellers Assn
> Soc Model Shipwrights
> Train Collectors Soc
Modern dancing > Dancing
Modern languages > Languages; & specific countries
Modular & portable buildings
> Modular & Portable Bldg Assn
Molluscs > Conchology; Shellfish
Monarchy
> Monarchist League
> R Stuart Soc
> > + Courts (royal)
Money transmission
> Assn Payment Clearing Services
Monumental masonry > Stone masons & sculptors
Monuments > Brasses; Historic buildings; Memorials
Moon type
> Nat Library Blind
Moore (John) conservationist
> John Moore Soc
Moorland
> Moorland Assn
Morocco
> Brit Cham Comm Morocco
> Brit Moroccan Soc
Morris dancing
> Morris Fedn
> Morris Ring
> > + Folk dance & song
Morris (William)
> William Morris Soc
Mortar
> Agricl Lime Assn
> Brit Lime Assn

Brit Masonry Soc
> Mortar Ind Assn
Mortgages
> Assn Mortgage Borrowers
> Corpn Insurance, Financial & Mortgage Advisers
> Coun Mortgage Lenders
> Indep Banking Advy Service
> Intermediary Mortgage Lenders Assn
> Ir Mortgage Coun
> Nat Assn Comml Finance Brokers
> Safe Home Income Plans
Mosaics
> Assn Study & Presvn Roman Mosaics
> Nat Fedn Terrazzo Marble & Mosaic Specialists
Mosses > Bryology
Mothers > Maternity; Obstetrics & gynaecology; Women's organisations
Moths > Butterflies & moths; Entomology
Motor > entries below & Car headings
Motor boats > Boats & boating
Motor cycles > Cycles & motorcycles
Motor cycles: historic > Motor vehicles: historic
Motor cycling & scooter riding
> Amat Motor Cycle Assn
> Assn Pioneer Motor Cyclists
> Assn Speedway Referees
> Auto-Cycle U
> Brit Motor Cycle Racing Club
> Brit Motorcyclists Fedn
> Brit Scooter Sport Org
> Brit Speedway Promoters Assn
> Fedn Sidecar Clubs
> Inst Advanced Motorists
> Motorcycle Action Gp
> Nat Assn Advanced Motorcycle Instructors
> Nat Assn Bikers Disability
> Nat Hillclimb Assn
> Nat Sprint Assn
> Scot Auto-Cycle U
> Speedway Control Bd
> Trail Riders Fellowship
> TT Riders Assn
> Veteran Speedway Riders Assn
> Vintage Motor Cycle Club
Motor(s): electric > Electric motors
Motor engines: reconditioning
> Fedn Engine Re-Mfrs
Motor factors
> Automotive Aftermarket Assn
> Automotive Distribution Fedn
> Group Auto U
> Indep Motor Tr Factors Assn
Motor industry
> Automotive Mfrs' Racing Assn
> BTC Testing Advisory Gp
> Fedn Automatic Transmission Engrs
> Fire Fighting Vehicles Mfrs Assn
> Inst Automotive Engr Assessors
> Inst Motor Ind
> Instn Mechanical Engrs
> MIRA Ltd
> Motor Industry Public Affairs Assn Ltd
> Motor Vehicle Dismantlers Assn
> MVRA Ltd
> Soc Automotive Engrs
> Soc Ir Motor Ind
> Soc Motor Mfrs & Traders
> Vehicle Builders & Repairers Assn
> > + Electric: transport
Motor insurance > Insurance
Motor neurone disease
> Motor Neurone Disease Assn
> Scot Motor Neurone Disease Assn
Motor sport
> Assn Motor Racing Circuit Owners
> Automotive Mfrs' Racing Assn
> Brit Automobile Racing Club
> Brit Motorsport Marshals Club
> Brit Off-Road Driving Assn
> Brit Racing & Sports Car Club
> Brit Stock Car Drivers Assn
> Brit Truck Racing Assn
> Brooklands Soc
> Motor Sports Assn
> Motoring Orgs' Land Access & Recreation Assn
> Motorsport Ind Assn
> RSAC Motor Sport
> Scot Motor Racing Club

Scot Sporting Car Club
Ulster Automobile Club
Motor trade
    A1 Motor Stores
    Automotive Aftermarket Assn
    Automotive Distribution Fedn
    Brit Indep Motor Tr Assn
    Nat Jumblers Fedn
    Retail Motor Ind Fedn
    Scot Motor Tr Assn
    > + Garages & garage equipment
Motor vehicles: American
Motor vehicles: customised
    Nat Street Rod Assn
Motor vehicles: electronic equipment
    Mobile Electronics & Security Fedn
Motor vehicles: fleet management
    Inst Car Fleet Mgt
Motor vehicles: hire
    Accident Mgt Assn
    Brit Vehicle Rental & Leasing Assn
    Car Rental Coun Ireland
    London Private Hire Car Assn
    Nat Limousine Assn
    Nat Private Hire Assn
Motor vehicles: historic
    Assn Classic Trials Clubs
    Assn Land Rover Clubs
    Assn Old Vehicle Clubs NI
    Brit Ambulance Soc
    Brooklands Soc
    Classic Rally Assn
    Farm Machinery Presvn Soc
    Fedn Brit Hist Vehicle Clubs
    Fire Service Presvn Gp
    Historic Comml Vehicle Soc
    Military Vehicle Trust
    Nat Assn Road Transport Museums
    Nat Jumblers Fedn
    Nat Traction Engine Trust
    Nat Trolleybus Assn
    Nat Vintage Tractor & Engine Club
    Post Office Vehicle Club
    Road Locomotive Soc
    Road Roller Assn
    Road Transport Fleet Data Soc
    Roads & Road Transport Hist Assn
    Soc Automotive Historians
    Southern Counties Historic Vehicle Presvn Trust
    Steam Plough Club
    Transport Trust
    Vintage Motor Cycle Club
    Vintage Sports Car Club
Motor vehicles: number plates
    Brit Number Plate Mfrs Assn
Motor vehicles: recovery
    Assn Vehicle Recovery Operators
    Inst Vehicle Recovery
    Retail Motor Ind Fedn
    Road Rescue Recovery Assn
Motor vehicles: salvage
    Brit Vehicle Salvage Fedn
Motor vehicles: taxation
    Alliance Urban 4x4s
Motor vehicles: theft (of/from)
    Intl Assn Auto Theft Investigators
Motoring journalism
    Gld Motoring Writers
Motoring organisations
    Assn Brit Drivers
    Automobile Assn
    Blue Badge Network
    Disabled Motorists Fedn
    Gld Experienced Motorists
    Inst Advanced Motorists
    Mobilise Org
    R Ir Automobile Club
Motoring schools > Driving tuition
Moulding sand
    Silica & Moulding Sands Assn
Moulding (rotational)
Moulds > Patternmaking
Mountain bothies
    Mountain Bothies Assn
Mountaineering > Climbing
Mounted games/activities > Horse: riding & driving
Movable walls > Partitioning

Mowers > Lawn mowers
Mucopolysaccharidosis
    Soc Mucopolysaccharide Diseases
Muggeridge (Malcolm)
    Malcolm Muggeridge Soc
Mules
    Brit Mule Soc
Multimedia
    Soc Public Inf Networks
Multiple births > Twins & multiple births
Multiple sclerosis
    Multiple Sclerosis Nat Therapy Centres
    Multiple Sclerosis Soc
    Multiple Sclerosis Soc Ireland
Multiple shops > Retail trade
Mumming > Folk dance & song
Municipal > Local government
Munro (Neil)
    Neil Munro Soc
Murder & manslaughter
    SAMM Nat
    > + Children: death by accident/violence
Murray (Keith)
    Keith Murray Collectors Club
Muscular Dystrophy
    Duchenne Family Support Gp
    Muscular Dystrophy Campaign
    Muscular Dystrophy Ireland
Musculoskeletal medicine
    Arthritis & Musculoskeletal Alliance
    Brit Inst Musculoskeletal Medicine
    Soc Orthopaedic Medicine
    > + Arthritis & rheumatism
Museums
    Assn Brit Transport & Engg Museums
    Assn Indep Museums
    Assn Leading Visitor Attractions
    Brit Assn Friends Museums
    Brit Museum Friends
    Fedn Museums & Art Galleries Wales
    Gld Taxidermists
    Group Educ Museums
    Heritage Rly Assn
    Ir Museums Assn
    MDA Europe
    Museum Profls Gp
    Museums Assn
    Nat Art Collections Fund
    Nat Assn Road Transport Museums
    Nat Heritage
    Soc Museum Archaeologists
    Social Hist Curators Gp
Mushrooms
    Mushroom Growers Assn
Music
    Assn Indep Music
    Brit Fedn Brass Bands
    Brit Music Soc
    Campaign Freedom Piped Music
    Dvořák Soc Czech & Slovak Music
    Fedn Recorded Music Socs
    Inst Contemporary Arts
    Ir Recorded Music Assn
    Light Music Soc
    Making Music
    Music Inds Assn
    Nat Assn Brass Band Conductors
    Nat Early Music Assn
    Plainsong & Mediæval Music Soc
    Pop & Rock Fans' Assn
    Production Services Assn
    R Musical Assn
    R Philharmonic Soc
    R Scot Academy Music & Drama
    Robert Farnon Soc
    Scot Amat Music Assn
    Soc Music Analysis
    Soc Producers & Composers Applied Music
    Soc Promotion New Music
    Sonic Arts Network
    Sound Sense
    Test Card Circle
    Viola da Gamba Soc
    Welsh Amat Music Fedn
    Welsh Music Gld
    Workers' Music Assn
    > + Choirs & choral music; Church music; Orchestras

© CBD Research Ltd · Beckenham · BR3 5JS · Tel 020 8650 7745 · Fax 020 8650 0768 · E-mail cbd@cbdresearch.com · www.cbdresearch.com

Music: composers & conductors
    Percy Grainger Soc
    Sir Arthur Sullivan Soc
    > + individual by name
Music: composing
    Brit Academy Composers & Songwriters
    Brit Music Rights
Music: copyright > Copyright
Music: festivals > Festivals: art, drama & music
Music: hall
    Brit Music Hall Soc
    Scot Music Hall & Variety Theatre Soc
Music: psychology
    Soc Educ Music & Psychology Res
Music: recording > Sound recording & reproduction
Music: sheet
    Music Pubrs' Assn
Music: teaching
    Brit Kodály Academy
    Brit Suzuki Inst
    Conservatoires UK
    Curwen Inst
    Fedn Music Services
    Inc Soc Musicians
    Jazz Piano Teachers Assn
    Music Educ Coun
    Music Masters' & Mistresses' Assn
    Nat Assn Music Educators
    Nat Assn Percussion Teachers
    Percussive Arts Soc
    R Academy Music
    R Ir Academy Music
    Schools Music Assn
    UK Fedn Jazz Bands
Music: therapy
    Assn Profl Music Therapists
    Brit Soc Music Therapy
Musical boxes
    Musical Box Soc
Musical instruments
    Brit Assn Symphonic Bands & Wind Ensembles
    Electric Guitar Appreciation Soc
    Fair Organ Presvn Soc
    Fellowship Makers. . . Histl Instruments
    Galpin Soc
    Hurdy-Gurdy Soc
    Inst Musical Instrument Technology
    Music Inds Assn
    Nat Assn Musical Instrument Repairers
    Nat Early Music Assn
    Scot Musical Instrument Retailers Assn
    > + specific instruments
Musicians
    Brit Music Rights
    Gld Musicians & Singers
    Inc Soc Musicians
    Musicians' U
    R Soc Musicians
Mussels > Shellfish
Mutton
    Mutton Renaissance Campaign
Muzak
    Campaign Freedom Piped Music
Myalgic encephalitis/encephalopathy
    Action ME
    Assn Young People with ME
    Myalgic Encephalopathy Assn
Myasthenia
    Myasthenia Gravis Assn
Mycology
    Birmingham Natural Hist Soc
    Brit Mycological Soc
    Brit Soc Antimicrobial Chemotherapy
    Brit Soc Med Mycology
Myositis
    Myositis Support Gp
Myotonic dystrophy
    Myotonic Dystrophy Support Gp
Myths & legends
    Traditional Cosmology Soc
    > + Folk life & lore

N

Naevus > Birthmarks & disfigurement
Nails
    Wire Products Assn
    > + Wire & wire products
Name plates
    Keygraphica
Names
    English Place-Name Soc
    Gld One-Name Studies
    Soc Name Studies Britain & Ireland
Nannies & au pairs
    Profl Assn Nursery Nurses
Napoleon I, II & III
    Assn Friends Waterloo C'ee
    Napoleonic Assn
    Napoleonic Soc
Nappies
    Absorbent Hygiene Products Mfrs Assn
    Nat Assn Nappy Services
Narcissus
    Daffodil Soc
Narcolepsy
    Narcolepsy Assn
Narrow fabrics
    Braid Soc
    Brit Narrow Fabrics Assn

National Health Service
    Health Care Supplies Assn
    Healthcare Financial Mgt Assn
    Healthcare People Mgt Assn
    Inst Health Care Mgt
    Nat Assn Healthcare Security
    Nat Assn Primary Care
    Nat Assn Voluntary Service Mgrs
    NHS Confedn
    NHS Support Fedn
    NHS Trusts Assn
    Socialist Health Assn
National Health Service: complaints
    Nat Assn Complaints Personnel. . .
National Parks
    Assn Nat Park Authorities
    Scot Coun Nat Parks
    > + Parks & gardens
National vocational qualifications
    Inst Assessors & Internal Verifiers
Nationalism
    Assn Study Ethnicity & Nationalism
Natural energy > Renewable energy; Solar technology
Natural gas
    Natural Gas Vehicle Assn
Natural health & therapeutics
    Alliance Natural Health
    Arthritis & Rheumatism Natural Therapy Res Assn
    Assn Natural Medicine
    Assn Systematic Kinesiology
    Brit Natural Hygiene Soc
    Consumers Health Choice
    Radionic Association Ltd
    > + Complementary medicine
Natural history
    Brit Entomological & Natural Hist Soc
    Brit Naturalists Assn
    Field Studies Coun
    Linnean Soc Lond
    Nat Assn Field Studies Officers
    Northamptonshire Natural History Soc
    Ray Soc
    Scot Field Studies Assn
    Soc Hist Natural Hist
    Wiltshire Archaeol & Natural Hist Soc
    > + Archaeology: county societies;   Conservation: area organisations
Nature conservation
    Assn Natural Burial Grounds
    Brit Assn Nature Conservationists
    Butterfly Consvn
    Countryside Alliance
    Farming & Wildlife Advy Gp
    Landlife
    Marine Consvn Soc
    Nat Assn Areas Outstanding Natural Beauty

Nat Coun Consvn Plants & Gardens
Nat Fedn Biological Recording
R Soc Wildlife Trusts
Scot Envt Link
Scot Wildlife Trust
Small Farms Assn
> + Conservation
Nature conservation: local reserves
Armagh > County Armagh Wildlife Soc
Ashmolean Natural Hist Soc Oxfordshire
Bedfordshire > Wildlife Trust Bedfordshire, Cambridgeshir...
Birmingham Natural Hist Soc
Cambridgeshire > Wildlife Trust Bedfordshire, Cambridgeshir...
County Armagh Wildlife Soc
Croydon Natural Hist & Scientific Soc
Durham Wildlife Trust
Essex Wildlife Trust
Falklands Consvn
Glasgow Natural Hist Soc
Gwent Wildlife Trust
Herefordshire > Woolhope Naturalists' Field Club
Isle of Wight Natural Hist & Archaeol Soc
London Natural Hist Soc
Natural Hist Soc Northumbria
Norfolk Wildlife Trust
Northamptonshire > Wildlife Trust Bedfordshire, Cambridgeshir...
Northumbria > Natural Hist Soc Northumbria
Peterborough > Wildlife Trust Bedfordshire, Cambridgeshir...
Wildlife Trust Bedfordshire, Cambridgeshire...
Wildlife Trust (S & W Wales)
Woolhope Naturalists' Field Club
Naturism
Central Coun Brit Naturism
Ir Naturist Assn
Naturopathy
Brit Naturopathic Assn
Gen Coun & Register Naturopaths
Inc Soc Registered Naturopaths
> + Natural health & therapeutics
Nautical archaeology > Archaeology: nautical
Nautical history
Hakluyt Soc
Mary Rose Soc
Naval Histl Collectors & Res Assn
Navy Records Soc
Soc Nautical Res
Nautical instruments
Chart & Nautical Instrument Tr Assn
Nautical training > Marine: education; Sailing
Naval archaeology > Archaeology: nautical
Naval architecture & equipment > Marine: engineering & equipment;
Shipbuilding & ship repairing
Naval history > Nautical history
Navigation
Assn Lighthouse Keepers
Gld Air Pilots & Air Navigators
Mobile Electronics & Security Fedn
Nautical Inst
R Inst Navigation
Sub-Aqua Assn
Navy > Royal Navy

Neck injury & disease > Head, neck & brain injury & disease
Needham (Violet)
Violet Needham Soc
Neighbourhood watch
Nelson (Admiral, Lord Horatio)
Nelson Soc
R Navy Enthusiasts' Soc
Nematology
Assn Applied Biologists
Neonatal death > Maternity
Nepal
Britain-Nepal Cham Comm
Britain Nepal Soc
Nephrology
Brit Kidney Patient Assn
Doctor Richard Bright Soc
Ir Kidney Assn
Nat Kidney Fedn
Purine Metabolic Patients Assn
Renal Assn
Nerine
Nerine & Amaryllid Soc
Nesbit (Edith)
Edith Nesbit Soc
Net > Lace & net

Netball
All England Netball Assn
Netball NI
Netball Scotland
Welsh Netball Assn
Netherlands
Anglo-Netherlands Soc
Assn Low Countries Studies
Netherlands-Brit Cham Comm
Netherlands: language & literature
Assn Language Learning
Netsuke carving
Brit Woodcarvers Assn
Netting > Lace & net; Wire & wire products
Networking
Intellect, the Information Technology, Telecommunications &
Electronics
Nat Outsourcing Assn
Telecommunications Ind Assn
UK Educ & Res Networking Assn
Neuralgia
Trigeminal Neuralgia Assn
Neuroblastoma
Neuroblastoma Soc
> + Cancer
Neurofibromatosis
Neurofibromatosis Assn
Neurology
Assn Brit Neurologists
Assn Neuro-Linguistic Programming
Batten Disease Family Assn
Brit Neuropsychiatry Assn
Brit Neuropsychological Soc
Brit Soc Neuroradiologists
Guillain Barré Syndrome Support Gp
Neurological Alliance
Soc Brit Neurological Surgeons
Neuropathology
Brit Neuropathological Soc
Neurophysiology
Brit Soc Clinical Neurophysiology
Electro-physiological Technologists Assn
Neuroscience
Brit Neuropsychiatry Assn
Brit Neuroscience Assn
Physiological Soc
Scot Neuroscience Gp
Neurosurgery
Soc Brit Neurological Surgeons
Neutral alcohol
Neutral Alcohol Producers Assn
New Zealand
Australian Business
Brit New Zealand Tr Coun
Hebe Soc
Newsagents > Newspapers & periodicals: distribution
Newsletters
UK Newsletter & Electronic Pubrs Assn
> + Periodicals
Newspapers
Assn Circulation Executives
Assn Regional City Editors
Assn UK Media Librarians
Brit Business Awards Assn
Foreign Press Assn Lond
Nat Newspapers Ireland
Newspaper Conf
Newspaper Pubrs Assn
Newspaper Soc
Press Standards Bd Finance
Regional Newspapers Assn Ireland
Scot Daily Newspaper Soc
Scot Newspaper Publishers Assn
Soc Editors
Talking Newspaper Assn
Web-offset Newspaper Assn
Newspapers & periodicals: distribution
Assn Newspaper Magazine Whlsrs
Assn Subscription Agents & Intermediaries
Ir Retail Newsagents Assn
Nat Fedn Retail Newsagents
Nickel
Surface Engg Assn
Nigeria
Britain-Nigeria Assn
Britain Nigeria Business Coun

© CBD Research Ltd · Beckenham · BR3 5JS · Tel 020 8650 7745 · Fax 020 8650 0768 · E-mail cbd@cbdresearch.com · www.cbdresearch.com

Noise
> Assn Noise Consultants
> Aviation Envt Fedn
> Campaign Freedom Piped Music
> Engg Integrity Soc
> Fencing Contrs Assn
> Heating, Ventilating & Air Conditioning Mfrs' Assn
> Inst Acoustics
> Materials Components Developing & Testing Assn
> Nat Soc Clean Air...
> Noise Abatement Soc
> UK Envtl Law Assn
> UK Noise Assn
> > + Insulation
Non-destructive testing > Materials: technology & testing
Non-ferrous metal > Metal
Non-wovens
> Brit Textile Technology Gp
> > + Textile headings
Norman-French texts
> Anglo-Norman Text Soc
> > + English language & literature
North America > USA; Canada
Norway
> Anglo-Norse Soc
> Norwegian-Brit Cham Comm
Notaries public
> Assn Solicitor Notaries Greater London
> Notaries Soc [E&W]
Novelists > under individual name
Nuclear disarmament > Disarmament
Nuclear energy
> Brit Nuclear Energy Soc
> Instn Civil Engrs
> Instn Nuclear Engrs
> Nuclear Ind Assn
> Supporters Nuclear Energy
Nudism > Naturism
Number plates
> Brit Number Plate Mfrs Assn
> MIRAD
> > + Motor headings
Numeracy > Literacy & numeracy
Numerical analysis
> Inst Mathematics & Applications
Numismatics
> Brit Art Medal Soc
> Brit Assn Numismatic Socs
> Brit Numismatic Soc
> Brit Numismatic Tr Assn
> Orders & Medals Res Soc
> R Numismatic Soc
> Scot Military Histl Soc
> Soc Numismatic Artists & Designers
> Token Corresponding Soc
> Victoria Cross & George Cross Assn
Nurseries & nursery schools
> Brit Assn Early Childhood Educ
> Nat Campaign Nursery Educ
> Nat Children's Nurseries Assn [IRL]
> Nat Day Nurseries Assn
> Pre-School Learning Alliance
Nursery & baby products
> Baby Eqpt Hirers Assn
> Baby Products Assn
Nursery stock > Horticulture
Nursing
> AOHNP (UK)
> Assn Brit Paediatric Nurses
> Assn Nursery Training Colls
> Assn Nurses Substance Abuse
> Assn Nursing Religious
> Assn Perioperative Practice
> Brit Assn Dental Nurses
> Brit Red Cross Soc
> Community & District Nursing Assn
> Indep Fedn Nursing Scotland
> Ir Nurses Org
> Mental Health Nurses Assn
> Nat Care Assn
> Pharmaceutical & Healthcare Sciences Soc
> Profl Assn Nursery Nurses
> Queen's Nursing Inst
> R Coll Nursing
> Soc Nursery Nursing
> > + Veterinary medicine

Nursing homes
> English Community Care Assn
> Ir Nursing Homes Org
> Registered Nursing Home Assn
Nutrition
> Brit Assn Nutritional Therapy
> Brit Dietetic Assn
> Brit Housewives League
> Brit Nutrition Foundation
> Brit Soc Ecological Medicine
> Coun Responsible Nutrition
> Health Food Inst
> Inst Optimum Nutrition
> McCarrison Soc
> Nutrition Soc
> > + Food
Nuts & bolts > Fasteners & turned parts
Nuts (allergy to)
> Anaphylaxis Campaign
> > + Allergy
Nuts (edible)
> Combined Edible Nut Tr Assn
> Fedn Oils, Seeds & Fats Assns
> Kentish Cobnut Assn
> Snack, Nut & Crisp Mfrs Assn
NVQs > National vocational qualifications
Nystagmus
> Nystagmus Network

Oatmeal
> Brit Oat & Barley Millers Assn
Obesity
> Assn Study Obesity
> Brit Obesity Surgery Patient Assn
> Brit Obesity Surgery Soc
> Prader-Willi Syndrome Assn
> > + Eating disorders
Oboes (musical instruments)
> Brit Double Reed Soc
Observer's Pocket Series
> Observers Pocket Series Collectors' Soc
Obsessive/compulsive disorders
> Nat Acupuncture Detoxification Assn
> Nat Phobics Soc
> OCD Action
> Tourette Syndrome (UK) Assn
> > + Mental health
Obsolescence (electronic & mechanical)
> Component Obsolescence Gp
Obstetrics & gynaecology
> Blair Bell Res Soc
> Brit Assn Perinatal Medicine
> Brit Soc Gynaecological Endoscopy
> Brit Soc Psychosomatic Obstetrics...
> Fac Family Planning & Reproductive Healthcare
> Obstetric Anaesthetists Assn
> R Coll Obstetricians & Gynaecologists
> > + Maternity; Midwifery
Occupational health & hygiene
> AOHNP (UK)
> Assn Med Advisers Brit Orchestras
> Brit Occupational Hygiene Soc
> Fac Occupational Medicine
> Inst Safety Technology & Res
> Instn Occupational Safety & Health
> Ir Soc Occupational Medicine
> Occupational & Envtl Diseases Assn
> Soc Chemical Ind
> Soc Occupational Medicine
Occupational safety > Safety
Occupational therapy
> Assn Occupational Therapists Ireland
> Brit Assn Occupational Therapists
Occupational training & education
> Assn Learning Providers
> Inst Training & Occupational Learning
> Ir Inst Training & Devt
> > + Education
Ocean energy > Renewable energy
Ocean industries
> Assn Brit Indep Oil Exploration Cos
> Assn Brit Offshore Inds

Assn Wellhead Eqpt Mfrs
Brit Rig Owners Assn
Emergency Response & Rescue Vessels Assn
Energy Inds Coun
Inst Marine Engg, Science & Technology
Intl Marine Contrs Assn
Ir Offshore Operators Assn
Northern Offshore Fedn
Offshore Contrs' Assn
Offshore Engg Soc
Offshore Ind Liaison C'ee
UK Offshore Operators Assn
Well Services Contrs Assn

Oceanography
Britain & Ireland Assn Aquatic Science Libraries...
Challenger Soc Marine Science
Hydrographic Soc UK
R Meteorological Soc
Remote Sensing & Photogrammetry Soc
Scot Assn Marine Science
> + Earth sciences, structure & resources

Odontology > Dentistry; Teeth
Oesophageal conditions > Tracheostomy
Offa's Dyke
Offa's Dyke Assn
Offenders > Prisoners: welfare & rehabilitation
Office equipment & systems
Brit Assn Removers
Brit Inst Facilities Mgt
Brit Office Supplies & Services Fedn
Finance & Leasing Assn
Indep Print Inds Assn
Intellect, the Information Technology, Telecommunications & Electronics
Office Products & Stationery Assn
Records Mgt Soc
Storage Eqpt Mfrs Assn
> + Computers

Office management
Brit Inst Facilities Mgt
Facilities Mgt Assn
Inst Administrative Mgt

Offices (serviced)
Brit Coun Offices
Business Centre Assn

Off-licences > Wines & spirits: trade
Off-road driving > Driving (off-road); Motor sport
Offshore engineering > Ocean industries
Off-street parking > Parking
Oil > Petroleum; & entries below
Oil burners & appliances
ICOM Energy Assn
Oil Firing Technical Assn Petroleum Ind
> + Boilers & waterheaters

Oil painting
Brit Soc Painters (in Oil, Pastels & Acrylic)
> + Art & artists

Oil spills > Spill control
Oils: edible > Edible oils & fats
Oils: essential > Essential oils
Oils: hydrocarbon > Petroleum
Oils: lubricating
UK Lubricants Assn
Oils: packaging
Indl Packaging Assn
Oils: recovery/waste
Oil Recycling Assn
Oils: users/consumers
Heating Oil Buyers Assn
Oilseed
Fedn Oils, Seeds & Fats Assns
Seed Crushers & Oil Processors Assn
Old people's organisations
Contact the Elderly
Heyday
Nat Assn Almshouses
Nat Assn Providers Activities Older People
Nat Fedn Retirement Pensions Assns
Nat Inf Forum
Nat Pensioners' Convention
R Surgical Aid Soc
Relatives & Residents Assn
> + Retirement

Old Testament > Bible
Olympic games
Brit Olympic Assn

Modern Pentathlon Assn
Soc Olympic Collectors
Oman
Anglo-Omani Soc
Ombudsman
Brit & Ir Ombudsman Assn
Oncology
BASO
Brain Tumour UK
Brit Acoustic Neuroma Assn
Brit Assn Head & Neck Oncologists
Brit Oncological Assn
Brit Oncology Data Mgrs Assn
> + Cancer
One parent families > Singles, divorced & separated
Onions
Brit Onion Producers' Assn
Online retailers
Interactive Media Retail Group
Online users & publishers
Assn Online Publishers
Periodical Pubrs Assn - Interactive
UK eInf Gp
Onshore engineering
UK Onshore Operators Gp
Open learning
Brit Learning Assn
> + Education
Open spaces
Commons, Open Spaces... Presvn Soc
> + Conservation; Footpaths & rights of way; Parks & gardens
Opencast mining > Mining; Coal mining
Opera
Nat Operatic & Dramatic Assn
> + name of composer or singer
Operational research
Inst Operations Mgt
Operational Res Soc
Ophthalmic opticians > Optical practice
Ophthalmology
Ophthalmological Prods Tr & Ind Conf
R Coll Ophthalmologists
UK & I Soc Cataract & Refractive Surgeons
Opinion polls
Market Res Soc
Optical character recognition
Automatic Identification Mfrs & Suppliers Assn
Optical industry
Fedn Mfrg Opticians
Ophthalmic Lens Mfrs' & Distrbrs' Assn
Optical Eqpt Mfrs & Suppliers Assn
Optical Frame Importers' & Mfrs' Assn
Optra Exhibitions UK
Optical practice
Assn Brit Dispensing Opticians
Assn Optometrists
Assn Optometrists Ireland
College Optometrists
Fedn Ophthalmic & Dispensing Opticians
Scot C'ee Optometrists
Options > Futures & options
Optoelectronics
Photonics Cluster
Scot Optoelectronics Assn
Oral medicine
Brit Assn Oral & Maxillofacial Surgeons
Brit Dental Hygienists Assn
Brit Soc Dental Res
Brit Soc Disability & Oral Health
Brit Soc Oral & Maxillofacial Pathology
Brit Soc Oral Medicine
Inst Maxillofacial Prosthetists...
> + Dentistry
Orchestras
Assn Brit Orchestras
Assn Med Advisers Brit Orchestras
Hallé Concerts Soc
Making Music
Nat Assn Youth Orchestras
R Philharmonic Soc
Welsh Amat Music Fedn
> + Music
Orchids
Brit Orchid Coun
Brit Orchid Growers Assn
Orchid Soc

© CBD Research Ltd · Beckenham · BR3 5JS · Tel 020 8650 7745 · Fax 020 8650 0768 · E-mail cbd@cbdresearch.com · www.cbdresearch.com

Orders (insignia) > Badges & insignia; Numismatics
Ordnance > Arms & armour
Ordnance Survey
        Charles Close Soc
Orff (Carl)
        Orff Soc
Organ donors
        Brit Organ Donor Soc
        NI Transplant Assn
        > + Transplant surgery
Organic chemicals > Chemical industry & trade
Organic growing & farming
        Biodynamic Agricl Assn
        Henry Doubleday Res Assn
        Ir Organic Farmers & Growers Assn
        Organic Food Fedn
        Scot Organic Prodrs Assn
        Soil Assn
        World-Wide Opportunities on Organic Farms
Organisation & methods > Management
Organs, organists & organ music
        Assn Indep Organ Advisers
        Brit Inst Organ Studies
        Cathedral Organists Assn
        Cinema Organ Soc
        Fair Organ Presvn Soc
        Friends Cathedral Music
        Inc Assn Organists
        Inc Soc Organ Builders
        Inst Brit Organ Bldg
        Karg-Elert Archive
        Mechanical Organ Owners Soc
        Organ Club
        Player Piano Gp
        R Coll Organists
        Ulster Soc Organists & Choirmasters
        > + Musical instruments
Oriental carpets & rugs
        Brit Oriental Rug Dealers Assn
        > + Carpets
Orienteering
        Brit Orienteering Fedn
        Scot Orienteering Assn
Origami
        Brit Origami Soc
Ornamental fish > Fish: tropical & ornamental
Ornithology > Birds; Nature conservation
Orthodontics > Dentistry
Orthopaedics
        Brit Coalition Heritable Disorders Connective Tissue
        Brit Orthopaedic Assn
        Soc Orthopaedic Medicine
Orthoptics
        Brit & Ir Orthoptic Soc
        > + Ophthalmology
Osteopathy
        Brit Osteopathic Assn
        Osteopathic Sports Care Assn
Osteoporosis > Bone
Ostrich farming
        Brit Domesticated Ostrich Assn
        > + Emus; Rheas
Othello (board game)
        Brit Othello Fedn
Otolaryngology
        Brit Assn Otorhinolaryngologists
        Brit Voice Assn
        Nat Assn Laryngectomee Clubs
        Scot Otolaryngological Soc
Otters
        Intl Otter Survival Fund
Outdoor advertising > Advertising: outdoor
Outdoor catering > Catering: outdoor
Outdoor centres > Holiday camps & centres
Outdoor education > Education: outdoor
Outdoor events > specific type of event
Outdoor furniture
        Leisure & Outdoor Furniture Assn
        > + Furniture
Outdoor professionals
        Brit Outdoor Profls Assn
Outsourcing (business technology)
        Nat Outsourcing Assn
Ovens
        Microwave Technologies Assn
        > + Domestic appliances
Overalls & workwear > Protective clothing/equipment

Overeating > Eating disorders; Obesity
Overseas development
        Devt Studies Assn
        Voluntary Service Overseas
Overseas property
        Fedn O'seas Property Developers... & Consultants
        > + Property & land owners
Overseas territories (British)
        UK O'seas Territories Assn
Ovulation
        Nat Assn Ovulation Method Instructors
Owen (Wilfred) 1893-1918
        Wilfred Owen Assn
Owls
        Hawk & Owl Trust
Oxenham (Elsie Jeanette)
        Elsie Jeanette Oxenham Appreciation Soc

Oysters > Shellfish

P

Pacific Islands
        Pacific Islands Soc
Packaging
        Brit Aerosol Mfrs Assn
        Brit Bottlers' Inst
        Brit Brands Gp
        Brit Packaging Assn
        Brit Plastics Fedn
        Brit Printing Inds Fedn
        Flexible Packaging Assn
        Ind Coun Packaging & Envt
        Indl Packaging Assn
        Ir Corrugated Packaging Assn
        Liquid Food Carton Mfrs' Assn
        Metal Packaging Mfrs Assn
        Nat Packaging Coun
        Packaging Fedn
        Packaging & Indl Films Assn
        Paper Agents Assn
        Pira Intl
        Processing & Packaging Machinery Assn
        Sheet Plant Assn
        Timber Packaging & Pallet Confedn
        Valpak
Packers & shippers for various trades
        Brit Contract Mfrs & Packers Assn
        > + trade concerned
Packing & packing cases > Packaging
Paddle steamers
        Paddle Steamer Presvn Soc
Paediatrics
        Assn Brit Paediatric Nurses
        Assn Clinical Professors Paediatrics
        Assn Paediatric Anaesthetists
        Brit Assn Paediatric Surgeons
        Brit Soc Gastroenterology
        Children's Chronic Arthritis Assn
        Neonatal Soc
        R Coll Paediatrics & Child Health
        > + Children headings
Paeonies
        Hardy Plant Soc
Paganism
        Pagan Fedn
Paget Gorman Signed Speech
        Paget Gorman Soc
        > + Sign language
Pagets disease
        Nat Assn Relief Paget's Disease
Paging (radio)
        Fedn Communication Services
        Onsite Communications Assn
Pain
        Brit Pain Soc
        Brit Soc Hypnotherapists
        Human Rights Soc
        > + Anaesthesia
Paint
        Brit Coatings Fedn
        Home Decoration Retailers' Assn
        Oil & Colour Chemists Assn

Paint Res Assn
Surface Engg Assn
Paintball
UK Paintball Sports Fedn
Painters > Art & artists
Painting & decorating
Painting & Decorating Assn
Scot Assn Painting Craft Teachers
Scot Decorators Fedn
Pakistan
Soc S Asian Studies
Palaeontology
Dinosaur Soc
Palaeontographical Soc
Palaeontological Assn
Systematics Assn
Tertiary Res Gp
Palate > Cleft lip & palate
Pallets
Timber Packaging & Pallet Confedn
> + Materials: management/handling; Packaging
Palliative care
Assn Palliative Medicine
Care not Killing Alliance
> + Medicine & related headings
Palmistry
Brit Astrological & Psychic Soc
Palm oil
Tropical Growers' Assn
Pancreas
Pancreatic Soc
Panels (wood)
Timber Tr Fedn
Panic & anxiety attacks
Nat Org Phobias, Anxiety. . .Inf & Care
Nat Phobics Soc
Paper & paper products
Brit Assn Paper Historians
Brit Packaging Assn
Confedn Paper Inds
Environmental & Technical Assn Paper Sack Ind
Foodservice Packaging Assn
Indep Print Inds Assn
Inst Paper, Printing & Publishing Intl
Nat Assn Paper Mchts
Paper Agents Assn
Paper Ind Technical Assn
Pira Intl
Pressure Sensitive Mfrs Assn
Pulp & Paper Fundamental Res Soc
Paper: conservation
Inst Consvn
Paper: folding > Origami
Paper: making equipment
Paper Makers' Allied Trs Assn
Picon Ltd
Paper: recovered & waste
Confedn Paper Inds
Indep Waste Paper Processors Assn
Pulp & Paper Fundamental Res Soc
Paperback collecting
WW2 HMSO Paperbacks Soc
> + Book: collecting
Paperweights
Caithness Paperweight Collectors Club
Paperweight Collectors Circle
Parachuting
Army Parachute Assn
Brit Freediving Assn
Brit Hang Gliding & Paragliding Assn
Brit Parachute Assn
Scot Hang Gliding & Paragliding Fedn
Parakarting
Brit Fedn Sand & Land Yacht Clubs
Parakarting
Brit Land Speedsail Assn
Paramedics > First aid & immediate care
Paranormal & psychical research
Assn Scientific Study Anomalous Phenomena
Brit Astrological & Psychic Soc
Brit UFO Res Assn
Inc Soc Psychical Res
Scot Soc Psychical Res
Soc Metaphysicians
UK Skeptics
Parapet fences
Vehicle Restraint Mfrs Assn

Paraplegia > Disablement; Spine & spinal injury;   Sports: disabled & handicapped
Parasitology
Brit Soc Parasitology
Parent-teacher associations
Nat Confedn Parent-Teacher Assns
Parents
Assn Shared Parenting
Brit False Memory Soc
Compassionate Friends
Families Need Fathers
Galton Inst
Gingerbread
Grandparents Assn
Mothers Apart Children
Nat Assn Child Contact Centres
Nat Fedn Services Unmarried Parents. . .[IRL]
Working Families
> + Adoption;   Fostering & foster parents;   Singles, divorced & separated
Parish registers
Harleian Soc
Lancashire Parish Register Soc
Staffordshire Parish Registers Soc
> + Records: historical;   Church: history & records
Park homes
Nat Assn Park Home Residents
Nat Caravan Coun
Parking
Brit Parking Assn
UK Parking Enforcement Agency
Parkinson's disease
Brit Geriatrics Soc
Parkinson's Disease Soc
Parks & gardens
Inst Leisure & Amenity Mgt
Metropolitan Public Gardens Assn
> + National Parks; Sportsgrounds & synthetic surfaces
Parliamentary agents
Soc Parliamentary Agents
Parliamentary government
Campaign English Parliament
Charter 88
Hansard Soc Parliamentary Govt
> + Government: accountability
Parrots
Parrot Soc
> + Birds
Parsnips
Parsonages
Save our Parsonages
> + Church: buildings
Partially sighted > Blind & partially sighted
Partitioning
Assn Interior Specialists
Fedn Plastering & Drywall Contrs
Partridges > Game & game birds
Passenger conveyors
Lift & Escalator Ind Assn
Passenger transport
Assn Commuter Transport
Assn Transport Co-ordinating Officers
Assn Transport Photographers & Historians
Bus Users UK
Coach Tourism Coun
Confedn Passenger Transport
Gld Brit Coach Operators
Ocean Liner Soc
Omnibus Soc
River Assn Freight & Transport
Routemaster Operators & Owners Assn
Scot Assn Public Transport
> + specific types of transport
Pasta
Pizza, Pasta & Italian Food Assn
Pastels (art)
Brit Soc Painters (in Oil, Pastels & Acrylic)
> + Art & artists
Pastoral care
Assn Pastoral Care Mental Health
Patchwork & quilting
Quilters' Gld
Patent glazing > Glass & glazing
Patents & trade marks
Assn Lawyers & Legal Advisers
Chart Inst Patent Attorneys
Inst Intl Licensing Practitioners

© CBD Research Ltd · Beckenham · BR3 5JS · Tel 020 8650 7745 · Fax 020 8650 0768 · E-mail cbd@cbdresearch.com · www.cbdresearch.com

Inst Patentees & Inventors
Inst Tr Mark Attorneys
Intellectual Property Lawyers Assn
Licensing Executives Soc
MARQUES
Trade Marks Patents & Designs Fedn
> + Copyright
Pathology
Assn Clinical Pathologists
Brit In Vitro Diagnostics Assn
Brit Soc Toxicological Pathologists
Pathological Soc
R Coll Pathologists
Pathology (of plants)
Brit Soc Plant Pathology
> + Plants
Patients
Action Sick Children
Nat Assn Patient Participation
Nat Cancer Alliance
Patient Inf Forum
Patients Assn
> + Medicine
Patio doors > Glass & glazing; Windows
Pattern recognition
Brit Machine Vision Assn. . .
> + Article numbering
Pattern sensing
Remote Sensing & Photogrammetry Soc
Patternmaking
Gauge & Tool Makers Assn
Pattern, Model, & Mould Mfrs Assn
Patton (General George S)
Patton Histl Soc
Paving & kerbs
Brit Precast Concrete Fedn
Pawnbroking
Nat Pawnbrokers Assn
Pay-to-play > Amusements & coin operated machines
Payroll staff
Inst Payroll & Pensions Mgt
Payroll Alliance
Peace
Brit Pugwash Gp
Medical Action Global Security
Peace Pledge U
Peal ringing
Central Coun Church Bell Ringers
Peanuts
Anaphylaxis Campaign
Brit Peanut Coun
Pearls
Brit Jewellers Assn
Pearly kings & queens
Original Pearly King's & Queen's Assn
Pears
English Apples & Pears
> + Fruit: growing
Peas
Processors & Growers Res Org
Peat
Growing Media Assn
Ir Peatland Consvn Coun
Pedestrians' safety
Living Streets
> + Road: safety & control
Peel (Sir Robert)
Peel Soc
Pelagic fish > Fish headings; Fishing
Pelargoniums > Geraniums & pelargoniums
Pen friends
Intl Pen Friends
Penal reform
Howard League for Penal Reform
Offenders Tag Assn
Unlock
Penguin books (collecting)
Penguin Collectors' Soc
Pens & pencils > Writing equipment & accessories
Pensions
Assn Consulting Actuaries
Assn Institutional Multi-Manager Investing
Assn Member-Directed Pension Schemes
Assn Pension Lawyers
Compulsory Annuity Purchase Protest Alliance
Inst Payroll & Pensions Mgt
Ir Assn Pension Funds

Ir Inst Pensions Mgrs
Nat Assn Pension Funds
Nat Fedn Retirement Pensions Assns
Nat Pensioners' Convention
Occupational Pensioners Alliance
Parity
Pensions Mgt Inst
Scot Pensions Assn
Soc Pension Consultants
Pentathlon
Modern Pentathlon Assn
Scot Modern Pentathlon Assn
Percussion (playing)
Nat Assn Percussion Teachers
Percussive Arts Soc
Performing animals > Animals: welfare;   Circuses & circus artistes
Performing arts medicine
Brit Assn Performing Arts Medicine
Performing right > Copyright
Perfumery
Brit Fragrance Assn
Brit Soc Perfumers
Cosmetic, Toiletry & Perfumery Assn
Inc Gld Hairdressers
Perfusion
Soc Clinical Perfusion Scientists
Perinatal medicine
Brit Assn Perinatal Medicine
Periodicals
Assn Circulation Executives
Assn Online Publishers
Assn Publishing Agencies
Brit Printing Inds Fedn
Brit Soc Magazine Editors
Periodical Pubrs Assn
Periodical Pubrs Assn - Interactive
Press Standards Bd Finance
Teenage Magazine Arbitration Panel
UK Newsletter & Electronic Pubrs Assn
UK Serials Gp
> + Newspapers & periodicals: distribution
Periodontology > Dentistry
Permaculture
Permaculture Assn
Perry > Cider & perry
Persia > Iran
Personal: assistants & secretaries > Secretaries & administrators
Personal: injury
Assn Personal Injury Lawyers
Personal Injuries Bar Assn
Personal: rights > Individual freedom
Personal: safety > Guard & patrol services; Protective equipment (personal);
Safety
Personal: trainers
Nat Register Personal Trainers
Personnel management
Chart Inst Personnel & Devt
Work Foundation
> + Management
Personnel services > Employment agents & consultants
Perthes disease
Perthes Assn
Peru
Anglo-Peruvian Soc
Brit-Peruvian Cham Comm
Pest control & pesticides
Brit Pest Control Assn
Nat Pest Technicians Assn
Soc Chemical Ind
> + Agriculture: chemicals
Pet > Pets & pet trade
Petrochemicals > Petroleum
Petrol pumps
Forecourt Eqpt Fedn
Petroleum
Assn Brit Indep Oil Exploration Cos
Assn Petroleum & Explosives Admin
Assn UK Oil Indeps
BTC Testing Advisory Gp
Energy Inds Coun
Energy Inst
Fedn Petroleum Suppliers
Geological Soc
Hydrographic Soc UK
Offshore Contrs' Assn
Petroleum Exploration Soc
Retail Motor Ind Fedn

UK Offshore Operators Assn
UK Onshore Operators Gp
UK Petroleum Ind Assn
Petroleum gas
L P Gas Assn
Petrology
Ir Assn Economic Geology
Mineralogical Soc
Pets & pet trade
Assn Pet Behaviour Counsellors
Brit Hardware Fedn
Nat Assn Regd Petsitters
Pet Care Trust
Pet Food Mfrs Assn
Pet Fostering Service Scotland
Pet Health Coun
Petfood Mfrs Assn Ireland
Soc Companion Animal Studies
> + Animal headings; individual animal
Pets: burial & cremation
Assn Private Pet Cemeteries & Crematoria
Cremation Soc
Pewter
Assn Brit Pewter Craftsmen
Pewter Soc
Pharmaceuticals
Academy Pharmaceutical Sciences
Assn Brit Pharmaceutical Ind
Assn Clinical Data Mgt
BioIndustry Assn
Brit Assn Eur Pharmaceutical Distbrs
Brit Assn Pharmaceutical Physicians
Brit Assn Pharmaceutical Whlsrs
Brit Generic Mfrs' Assn
Clinical Contract Res Assn
Company Chemists Assn
Fac Pharmaceutical Med
Inst Clinical Res
Ir Pharmaceutical Healthcare Assn
Ir Pharmaceutical U
Pharmaceutical & Healthcare Sciences Soc
Pharmaceutical Inf & Pharmacovigilance Assn
Pharmaceutical Soc Ireland
Pharmaceutical Soc NI
PharmaChemical Ireland
Proprietary Assn
Soc Chemical Ind
Soc Medicines Res
Soc Pharmaceutical Medicine
Statisticians Pharmaceutical Ind
Ulster Chemists Assn
Pharmacology & chemotherapy
Brit Assn Psychopharmacology
Brit Pharmacological Soc
Brit Soc Antimicrobial Chemotherapy
Brit Toxicology Soc
Pharmacy
Assn Pharmacy Technicians
Chemists Defence Assn
Nat Assn Women Pharmacists
Nat Pharmacy Assn
R Pharmaceutical Soc
Scot Pharmaceutical Fedn
UK Clinical Pharmacy Assn
Pharmacy: history
Brit Soc Hist Pharmacy
Pheasants
World Pheasant Assn UK
> + Game & gamebirds
Phenolic composites
Composites Processing Assn
Phenomena > Paranormal & psychical research;   specific type of phenomena
Phenylketonuria
Nat Soc Phenylketonuria
Philanthropy: history
Voluntary Action Hist Soc
Philately & postal history
Assn Brit Philatelic Socs
Assn Scot Philatelic Socs
Brit Aerophilatelic Fedn
Brit Postmark Soc
Letter Box Study Gp
Nat Philatelic Soc
Philatelic Traders Soc
Postal Hist Soc
R Philatelic Soc Lond

Ship Stamp Soc
Soc Olympic Collectors
Philology
Philological Soc
> + Dialects; Languages
Philosophy
Anthroposophical Soc
Aristotelian Soc
Assn Brit Theological. . . Libraries
Assn Therapeutic Philosophy
Brit Soc Hist Philosophy
Brit Soc Philosophy Science
Philosophical Soc England
R Inst Philosophy
R Philosophical Soc Glasgow
Soc Applied Philosophy
Soc Existential Analysis
Phobias
Brit Soc Hypnotherapists
Brit Tarantula Soc
Nat Org Phobias, Anxiety. . .Inf & Care
Nat Phobics Soc
Phonetics
Brit Assn Academic Phoneticians
Brit Voice Assn
> + Speech
Phonography > Shorthand writing;   Sound recording & reproduction
Photogrammetry
Instn Civil Engg Surveyors
Remote Sensing & Photogrammetry Soc
Photographic agencies
Brit Assn Picture Libraries & Agencies
Nat Assn Press Agencies
Photographic industry & trade
Photo Imaging Coun
Profl Photographic Laboratories Assn
Photographic waste
Photo Imaging Coun
Photography
Assn Photographers
Assn Transport Photographers & Historians
Brit Cave Res Assn
Brit Inst Profl Photography
Camera Club
Gld Photographers
Inst Consvn
Inst Med Illustrators
Ir Profl Photographers Assn
Master Photographers Assn
Nat Assn Aerial Photographic Libraries
Photographic Alliance
Photographic Collectors Club
R Photographic Soc
Scot Sub Aqua Club
Soc Wedding & Portrait Photographers
Stereoscopic Soc
Writers & Photographers unLimited
> + Film
Photoluminescent products
Photoluminescent Safety Products Assn
Photonics
Photonics Cluster
Scot Optoelectronics Assn
Photovoltaics
Renewable Energy Assn
Phycology
Brit Phycological Soc
Physical disability > Disablement
Physical education
Assn Physical Educ
Scot Local Authority Network Physical Educ
Sports & Fitness Eqpt Assn
Physical fitness > Fitness
Physical fitness: Equipment
Physically handicapped > Children: handicapped; Disablement
Physicians > Medical practice; Medicine
Physics
Inst Physics
Inst Physics & Engg in Medicine
Physiology
Physiological Soc
Soc Orthopaedic Medicine
Physiotherapy
Chart Soc Physiotherapy
Ir Soc Chart Physiotherapists
SMAE Fellowship

© CBD Research Ltd · Beckenham · BR3 5JS · Tel 020 8650 7745 · Fax 020 8650 0768 · E-mail cbd@cbdresearch.com · www.cbdresearch.com

Pianolas & pianola rolls
        Friends Pianola Inst
Pianos & piano playing
        Assn Blind Piano Tuners
        Jazz Piano Teachers Assn
        Pianoforte Tuners' Assn
        Player Piano Gp
Pick-your-own > Farm shops & food
Pickles & sauces
        Food Processors' Assn
Pick's disease
        Pick's Disease Support Gp
Picts
        Pictish Arts Soc
Picture dealers > Art: trade
Picture framers
        Fine Art Tr Gld
Picture libraries
        Brit Assn Picture Libraries & Agencies
        Nat Assn Aerial Photographic Libraries
Picture researching
        Picture Res Assn
Picture restoring
        Brit Assn Paintings Conservator-Restorers
        Fine Art Tr Gld
        > + Art: conservation
Piercing > Body piercing
Piers
        Brit Assn Leisure Parks, Piers & Attractions
        Nat Piers Soc
Pigeons
        Confedn Long Distance Racing Pigeon Us
        Nat Pigeon Assn
        R Pigeon Racing Assn
        Scot Homing U
Pigging (pipeline)
        Pigging Products & Services Assn
Pigment
        Brit Colour Makers Assn
Pigs
        Brit Kune Kune Pig Soc
        Brit Lop Pig Soc
        Brit Pig Assn
        Brit Saddleback Pig Breeders Club
        Brit Veterinary Assn
        Brit Wild Boar Assn
        Gloucestershire Old Spot Pig Breeders' Club
        Livestock Auctioneers Assn
        Nat Pig Assn
        Oxford Sandy & Black Pig Soc
        Tamworth Breeders Club
        > + Bacon; Cattle & livestock; Pigging (pipelines)
Pilates
        Body Control Pilates Assn
Pilchard
        Herring Buyers Assn
        > + Fish; Fishing
Pilgrims
        Confraternity Saint James
Piling
        Fedn Piling Specialists
Pillow-lace > Lace (handmade)
Pilots > Aviation: pilots, officers & crew;   Sea pilots
Pinball
        Pinball Owners Assn
        > + Amusements & coin operated machines
Pipe bands & music
        Bagpipe Soc
        College Piping
        Edinburgh Highland Reel & Strathspey Soc
        Inst Piping
        Northumbrian Pipers Soc
        Piobaireachd Soc
        Pipers' Gld
        R Scot Pipe Band Assn
        Scot Pipers Assn
        Scot Piping Soc Lond
        Traditional Music & Song Assn Scotland
Pipe organs
        Cinema Organ Soc
        Inst Brit Organ Bldg
        > + Organs, organists & organ music
Pipejacking
        Pipe Jacking Assn
Pipelines
        Land Drainage Contrs Assn
        Pigging Products & Services Assn

Pipeline Inds Gld
        Rly & Canal Histl Soc
        Soc Brit Water & Wastewater Inds
Pipes
        Brit Ceramic Confedn
        Brit Plumbing Fittings Mfrs Assn
        Brit Precast Concrete Fedn
        Clay Pipe Devt Assn
        Scot Emplrs Coun Clay Inds
        Soc Brit Water & Wastewater Inds
        > + Plastics: pipes;   Steel: tubes
Pipes: tobacco
        Briar Pipe Tr Assn
        > + Tobacco
Piracy (copyrighted goods) > Copyright
Pistol shooting
        Nat Rifle Assn
        > + Shooting
Pizzas
        Pizza, Pasta & Italian Food Assn
Place-names
        English Place-Name Soc
        Scot Place-Name Soc
        > + Names
Placement services (adult)
        Nat Assn Adult Placement Services
        > + Social: service
Plainsong
        Plainsong & Mediæval Music Soc
Planetary sciences
        R Astronomical Soc
        > + Astronomy
Planning > Town & country planning
Plant: construction > Construction equipment
Plant: industrial
        Brit Ceramic Confedn
        Brit Metallurgical Plant Constructors Assn
        Engg Construction Ind Assn
        Instn Diagnostic Engrs
        Safety Assessment Fedn
        Soc Operations Engrs
Plants
        Assn Applied Biologists
        Assn Indep Crop Consultants
        Brit Assn Rose Breeders
        Brit Bedding & Pot Plant Assn
        Brit Mycological Soc
        Brit Soc Plant Breeders
        Brit Soc Plant Pathology
        Epiphytic Plant Study Gp
        Hardy Plant Soc
        Linnean Soc Lond
        Nat Coun Consvn Plants & Gardens
        Plantlife Intl
        Profl Plant Users Gp
        Scot Soc Crop Res
        > + Flowers, flower arrangement & floristry; specific plants
Plants: galls
        Brit Plant Gall Soc
Plaques
        Brit Sign & Graphics Assn
        > + Signs
Plaster & plastering
        Fedn Plastering & Drywall Contrs
        Gypsum Products Devt Assn
Plastic surgery
        Brit Assn Aesthetic Plastic Surgeons
        Brit Assn Plastic, Reconstructive & Aesthetic Surgeons
        > + Surgery
Plastics
        Brit Indep Plastic Extruders Assn
        Brit Laminate Fabricators Assn
        Brit Plastics Fedn
        Composites Processing Assn
        NI Polymer Assn
        Plastics & Board Inds Fedn
        Plastics Histl Soc
        Plastics Ireland
        Rapra Technology Ltd
Plastics: cladding > Cladding
Plastics: drums > Cisterns, drums & tanks
Plastics: film
        Flexible Packaging Assn
        Packaging & Indl Films Assn
        Picon Ltd

Plastics: foam
>> Brit Rigid Urethane Foam Mfrs Assn
>> Brit Urethane Foam Contrs Assn
Plastics: machinery
>> Polymer Machinery Mfrs & Distbrs Assn
Plastics: pipes
>> Brit Plastics Fedn
>> Soc Brit Water & Wastewater Inds
Platforms > Cradles & suspended platforms
Play centres
>> Play Providers Assn
Play equipment
>> Assn Play Inds
>> Sports Mfrs & Retailers Tr Assn
>> > + Sports headings
Play therapy
>> Brit Assn Play Therapists
Playbuses
>> Nat Playbus Assn
Playgrounds & playgroups
>> Fair Play for Children Assn
>> Nat Assn Hospital Play Staff
>> Nat Campaign Nursery Educ
>> Nat Playing Fields Assn
>> Pre-School Learning Alliance
>> Scot Pre-School Play Assn
>> Wales Pre-school Playgroups Assn
Playing cards & games
>> English Playing-Card Soc
Playing fields > Sportsgrounds & synthetic surfaces
Plays > Dramatists; Theatre; Writing & writers
Pleasurecraft
>> Assn Pleasure Craft Operators
>> > + Boats & boating; Yachting
Ploughing
>> Soc Ploughmen
>> Southern Counties Heavy Horse Assn
Plumbers' merchants > Builders' & plumbers' merchants
Plumbing
>> Assn Plumbing & Heating Contrs
>> Brit Plumbing Fittings Mfrs Assn
>> Inst Plumbing & Heating Engg
>> Manufacturers Domestic Unvented Systems
>> NI Master Plumbers Assn
>> Scot & NI Plumbing Emplrs' Fedn
Pneumatics
>> Brit Compressed Air Soc
>> Brit Fluid Power Assn
>> Brit Fluid Power Distbrs Assn
>> Solids Handling & Processing Assn
>> > + Hydraulics & hydromechanics
Podiatry > Chiropody & podiatry
Poetry
>> English Poetry & Song Soc
>> Friends Dymock Poets
>> Poetry Soc
>> Scot Poetry Library
>> > + individual by name
Poisons > Toxicology
Poland
>> Anglo-Polish Soc
>> Brit-Polish Cham Comm
>> Brit-Polish Cham Comm [London]
>> Polish Soc
Polar research
>> Trans-Antarctic Assn
Polarity therapy
>> UK Polarity Therapy Assn
Polarography & polarology
>> Brit Polarological Res Soc
>> R Soc Chemistry
Police
>> Assn Chief Police Officers
>> Assn Chief Police Officers (Scotland)
>> Assn Police Authorities
>> Assn Police & Public Security Suppliers
>> Assn Scot Police Superintendents
>> Nat Assn Retired Police Officers
>> Police Fedn England & Wales
>> Police Fedn NI
>> Police Superintendents' Assn England & Wales
>> Scot Police Fedn
>> Superintendents' Assn NI
>> > + Security
Police: history
>> Peel Soc

Police Hist Soc
Police Insignia Collectors Assn
Policy research
>> David Hume Inst
Polidori (John William)
>> John Polidori Literary Soc
Poliomyelytis
>> Brit Polio Fellowship
Polishes
>> Brit Assn Chemical Specialities
Politeness
>> Campaign Courtesy
Political correctness
>> Campaign Political Correctness
Political consultants
>> Assn Profl Political Consultants
Political economy > Economics
Political parties > [Party] politics
Political studies & reform
>> Charter 88
>> Political Studies Assn
>> Politics Assn
Pollen
>> Brit Aerobiology Fedn
>> > + Allergy
Pollution & pollution control
>> Anglers Consvn Assn
>> Assn Commuter Transport
>> Environmental Inds Commission
>> Marine Biological Assn
>> Marine Consvn Soc
>> Source Testing Assn
>> Surfers against Sewage
>> UK Spill Assn
>> > + Air: pollution
Polo
>> Hurlingham Polo Assn
Polocrosse
>> UK Polocrosse Assn
Polyester fibre
>> Nat Fillings Assn
Polyethylene foam > Plastics: foam
Polymers
>> NI Polymer Assn
>> Plastics Histl Soc
>> Polymer Machinery Mfrs & Distbrs Assn
>> Rapra Technology Ltd
Polyolefin & polypropylene textiles
>> Brit Polyolefin Textiles Assn
>> > + Textile: industry & trade
Polytechnics > Adult education; Education; Technical education
Ponies > Horse headings
Pony trekking
>> Trekking & Riding Soc Scotland
Pool
>> Brit Assn Pool Table Operators
>> English Pool Assn
>> > + Cue sports
Pools > Football pools;   Swimming pools
Pop & rock music
>> Pop & Rock Fans' Assn
Population: registration
>> Assn Registrars Scotland
>> Assn Registration & Celebratory Services
Population: study of
>> Brit Soc Population Studies
Porcelain > Ceramics; Pottery
Pork butchery > Meat
Pork pies
>> Melton Mowbray Pork Pie Assn
Porphyria
>> Brit Porphyria Assn
Portable buildings > Modular & portable buildings
Portable engines
>> Road Locomotive Soc
Portable lamps (industrial)
>> Miners' & Indl Lamp Mfrs' Assn
Portage
>> Nat Portage Assn
Portland Cement
>> Brit Cement Assn
>> > + Cement & cement products
Portraits > Art & artists; Weddings: photography
Ports
>> Assn Indep Mgt & Maritime Services
>> Brit Ports Assn
>> Soc Sailing Barge Res

© CBD Research Ltd · Beckenham · BR3 5JS · Tel 020 8650 7745 · Fax 020 8650 0768 · E-mail cbd@cbdresearch.com · www.cbdresearch.com

Ports: health
    Assn Port Health Authorities
Portugal
    Anglo-Portuguese Soc
    Assn Contemporary Iberian Studies
    Brit-Portuguese Cham Comm
    Hispanic & Luso-Brazilian Coun
    Portuguese Cham
Portugal: language & literature
    Assn Language Learning
Post Office staff
    Amicus - CMA Section
    Communication Workers U
    > + Sub-postmasters
Post Office (GPO & BT) vehicles
    Post Office Vehicle Club
Postal history > Philately & postal history
Postal services
    Mail Consolidators Assn
    Mail Users' Assn
Postcards
    Canal Card Collectors Circle
    Great Britain Postcard Club
    Postcard Traders' Assn
Poster advertising > Advertising: outdoor
Postgraduate medical education
    Nat Assn Clinical Tutors
Postmarks > Philately & postal history
Post-natal depression
    Assn Postnatal Illness
    Meet-a-Mum Assn
Post-tensioning
    Concrete Bridge Devt Gp
    Post-tensioning Assn
Post-viral infection
    Action ME
    Assn Young People with ME
    Myalgic Encephalopathy Assn
Pot holing > Caves & caving
Pot plants > Horticulture; Indoor & houseplants; individual plants
Potatoes
    Brit Potato Trs Assn
    Fresh Produce Consortium
    NI Potato Breeders Assn
    NI Potato Marketing Assn
    Scot Soc Crop Res
    > + Vegetables: trade
Potatoes: products
    Frozen & Chilled Potato Processors' Assn
    Potato Processors Assn
    Snack, Nut & Crisp Mfrs Assn
Potter (Beatrix)
    Beatrix Potter Soc
Pottery
    Brit Ceramic Gift & Tableware Mfrs' Assn
    Brit Ceramic Res
    Scot Potters' Assn
    > + Ceramics
Pottery & ceramics collecting
    Clarice Cliff Collectors Club
    Friends Blue
    Old Bottle Club
    Spode Soc
    Wedgwood Soc
    > + specific type collected
Pottery: sanitary > Sanitaryware
Potting composts > Composts & composting
Poultry
    Assn Meat Inspectors
    Brit Poultry Coun
    Brit Veterinary Assn
    Domestic Fowl Trust
    Henkeepers' Assn
    NI Poultry Fedn
    Poultry Club
    Pullet Hatcheries Assn
    Pullet Rearers Assn
    Rare Poultry Soc
    Traditional Farmfresh Turkey Assn
    > + Game & game birds; Meat
The Pound
    Democracy Movement
Powder coatings
    Brit Coatings Fedn
    Surface Engg Assn
Powder compacts (collecting)
    Brit Compact Collectors' Soc

Powder handling
    Solids Handling & Processing Assn
Powder metallurgy
    Inst Materials, Minerals & Mining
Power > specific type of power
Power boating & powercraft
    R Yachting Assn
Power generation > Electricity
Power presses
    Metalforming Machinery Makers Assn
Power station contractors
    Brit Constructional Steelwork Assn
Power tools > Tools
Power track systems
    BEAMA
Powered access
    Assn Loading & Elevating Eqpt Mfrs
    Construction Plant-hire Assn
    Specialist Access Engg & Maintenance Assn
Powys (John Cooper) & family
    Powys Soc
Prader-Willi syndrome
    Prader-Willi Syndrome Assn
Prams & pushchairs > Nursery & baby products
Prayer book(s) > Common Prayer; Liturgy
Precast concrete > Concrete & concrete products
Precious metals & stones > Gemstones; Goldsmiths & silversmiths; Jewellery
Precision casting > Metal: casting
Pre-conceptual care > Family planning; Maternity
Pre-eclampsia
    Action Pre-Eclampsia
    Pre Eclampsia Soc
Prefabricated buildings > Modular & portable buildings
Pregnancy > Family planning; Maternity; Obstetrics & gynaecology
Prehistory
    Megalithic Soc
    Prehistoric Soc
    R Anthropological Inst
Premature ageing > Geriatrics & ageing
Premenstrual syndrome
    Nat Assn Premenstrual Syndrome
    Premenstrual Soc
Premium promotions > Incentive marketing
Preparatory schools
    Inc Assn Preparatory Schools
    Soc Assistants Teaching Preparatory Schools
    > + Independent & public schools
Pre-Raphaelites
    Pre-Raphaelite Soc
Presbyterian church: history
    Presbyterian Hist Soc Ireland
    Scot Covenanter Memorials Assn
    Utd Reformed Church Hist Soc
Pre-school playgroups > Playgrounds & playgroups
Preservation > Conservation; object preserved
Preserves
    Food Processors' Assn
Press > Information: freedom of; Journalism; Media; Newspapers; Periodicals
Press agencies
    Nat Assn Press Agencies
Pressure gauges > Gauges
Pressure sensitive products
    Brit Printing Inds Fedn
    Pressure Sensitive Mfrs Assn
Pressure sores
    Tissue Viability Soc
Priestley (John Boynton)
    J B Priestley Soc
Primary care > Health care
Primary education > Education
Primulas
    Nat Auricula & Primula Soc (Mid & West)
    Nat Auricula & Primula Soc (Nthn)
    Nat Auricula & Primula Soc (Sthn)
Print finishing > Bookbinding & print finishing
Printed circuits & wiring boards
    Inst Metal Finishing
Printing
    Assn Hot Foil Printers
    Brit Printing Inds Fedn
    Brit Printing Soc
    D&AD
    Friends St Bride Library
    Indep Print Inds Assn
    Inst Paper, Printing & Publishing Intl
    Intl Soc Typographic Designers
    Ir Master Printers Assn

Ir Printing Fedn
Pira Intl
Printing Histl Soc
Printmakers Coun
R Birmingham Soc Artists
Scot Print Emplrs Fedn
Printing machinery & supplies
Assn Printing Machinery Importers
Brit Coatings Fedn
Brit Used Printing Machinery Supplrs Assn
Oil & Colour Chemists Assn
Picon Ltd
UK Cartridge Remanufacturers Assn
Prints
R Scot Academy Art & Architecture
R Soc Painter-Printmakers
Soc Graphic Fine Art
Prison service
Prison Governors Assn
Prison Officers' Assn
Prisoners: of war
Assn Brit Civilian Internees Far East
Prisoners: welfare & rehabilitation
Assn Members Indep Monitoring Bds
Assn Visitors Immigration Detainees
Howard League for Penal Reform
NACRO
Nat Assn Official Prison Visitors
NI Assn Care & Resettlement Offenders
Prisoners Abroad
SACRO
SOVA
Unlock
> + Penal reform
Prisoners: wives & families
Action Prisoners' Families
Prison Advice & Care Trust
Private business > Business
Private hire
Nat Private Hire Assn
> + Motor vehicles: hire; Taxis & minicabs
Private medicine > Hospitals: contributory schemes
Private schools > Independent & public schools
Private secretaries > Secretaries & administrators
Probation service
Nat Assn Probation & Bail Hostels
Nat Assn Probation Officers
Probation Bds' Assn
Probation Mgrs Assn
SOVA
Process control > Control engineering
Process engineering
Energy Inds Coun
Instn Chemical Engrs
Instn Mechanical Engrs
Processing & Packaging Machinery Assn
Soc Chemical Ind
Solids Handling & Processing Assn
Process servers
Assn Brit Investigators
Nat Assn Investigators & Process Servers
Proctology
Assn Coloproctology
Procurators-Fiscal
Procurators Fiscal Soc
R Fac Procurators in Glasgow
> + Law: Scotland
Produce packaging & processing
Fresh Produce Consortium
Product licensing
Inst Intl Licensing Practitioners
Licensing Executives Soc
Production control
Inst Operations Mgt
Production engineering
Engg & Machinery Alliance
PERA
> + Automation
Products: counterfeiting
Anti Counterfeiting Gp
Programme producers > Film: production & distribution; Television: production
Project management
Assn Project Mgt
Major Projects Assn
Promotion merchandise > Incentive marketing

Proofreading
Assn Freelance Editors, Proofreaders & Indexers [IRL]
Soc Editors & Proofreaders
Property & land owners
Brit Property Fedn
City Property Assn
Country Land & Business Assn
Fedn O'seas Property Developers... & Consultants
Nat Fedn Residential Landlords
Nat Landlords' Assn
Residential Landlords Assn
Scot Assn Landlords
Scot Rural Property & Business Assn
Westminster Property Owners Assn
> + Estate management
Property: investment
Investment Property Forum
Property: maintenance/management
Assn Residential Letting Agents
Assn Residential Managing Agents
Inst Residential Property Mgt
UK Assn Letting Agents
> + Buildings: cleaning & maintenance
Property: market research
Soc Property Researchers
Property: marking (security)
Brit Security Ind Assn
Property: unit trusts
Assn Real Estate Funds
Proportional representation > Elections & electoral administration
Proprietary medicines
Proprietary Assn
> + Pharmaceuticals
Prostate disease
Prostate Cancer Support Assn
Prosthetics
Brit Assn Prosthetists & Orthotists
Brit Soc Study Prosthetic Dentistry
Inst Maxillofacial Prosthetists...
Let's Face It
REACH - Assn Children with Hand or Arm Deficiency
Prostitution
Josephine Butler Soc
Protective clothing/equipment
Brit Clothing Ind Assn
Brit Footwear Assn
Defence Mfrs Assn
Personal Safety Mfrs Assn
Photoluminescent Safety Products Assn
Retroreflective Eqpt Mfrs Assn
Protectorate (1649-1688) > Commonwealth (1649-1688);   Fights (historic/re-enactment)
Protein (vegetable) > Vegetables: protein
Proteomics
Brit Soc Proteome Res
Protestants
Protestant Alliance
Protestant Reformation Soc
Protestant Truth Soc
Scot Reformation Soc
Provision trade > Grocery & provision trade
Psoriasis
Psoriasis Assn
Psoriatic Arthropathy Alliance
Psychiatry
Assn Therapeutic Communities
Brit Neuropsychiatry Assn
Mental Health Nurses Assn
R Coll Psychiatrists
Soc Clinical Psychiatrists
Psychical research > Paranormal & psychical research
Psychoanalysis
Assn Jungian Analysts
Balint Soc
Brit Psychoanalytical Soc
Inst Psychoanalysis
NI Assn Study Psychoanalysis
> + Group analysis
Psychology
Adlerian Soc
Assn Business Psychologists
Assn Educl Psychologists
Assn Humanistic Psychology
Assn Profls Services Adolescents
Assn Teaching Psychology
Brit Assn Psychological Type
Brit Inst Graphologists

© CBD Research Ltd · Beckenham · BR3 5JS · Tel 020 8650 7745 · Fax 020 8650 0768 · E-mail cbd@cbdresearch.com · www.cbdresearch.com

Brit Neuropsychological Soc
Brit Psychological Soc
Brit Soc Psychosomatic Obstetrics...
Experimental Psychology Soc
Gld Pastoral Psychology
Indep Gp Analytical Psychologists
Nat Assn Therapeutic Educ
Psychological Soc Ireland
Soc Existential Analysis
Soc Reproductive & Infant Psychology
Psychopharmacology
Brit Assn Psychopharmacology
Psychotherapy
Assn Child Psychotherapists
Assn Gp & Individual Psychotherapy
Assn Indep Psychotherapists
Assn Psychoanalytic Psychotherapy NHS
Assn Psychological Therapies
Assn Therapeutic Philosophy
Brit Assn Behavioural... Psychotherapies
Brit Assn Counselling & Psychotherapy
Brit Assn Psychotherapists
Brit Autogenic Soc
Brit Hypnotherapy Assn
Brit Psychoanalytic Coun
Brit Psychodrama Assn
Brit Psychological Soc
Gestalt Assn UK
Gld Psychotherapists
Group Analytic Soc
Inst Gp Analysis
Inst Transactional Analysis
Nat Assn Counsellors, Hypnotherapists...
Nat Coun Psychotherapists
Nat Register Hypnotherapists & Psychotherapists
UK Coun Psychotherapy
Universities Psychotherapy & Counselling Assn
Pteridology > Ferns
Public access > Footpaths & rights of way; Open spaces
Public administration
Inst Public Administration [IRL]
> + Civil Service; Local government
Public analysts
Assn Public Analysts
Assn Public Analysts Scotland
Public auditing > Accountancy
Public conveniences
Brit Toilet Assn
Public gardens > Parks & gardens
Public health
Assn County Public Health Officers
Assn Directors Public Health
Assn Port Health Authorities
Chart Inst Envtl Health
Chart Instn Water & Envtl Management
Community & District Nursing Assn
Fac Public Health
HealthWatch
Ir Soc Public Health Medicine
R Inst Public Health
Scot Soc Contamination Control
> + Health
Public houses
Brit Beer & Pub Assn
Campaign Real Ale
Public lavatories
Brit Toilet Assn
Public lighting > Lighting
Public relations
Assn Local Govt Communications
Chart Inst Marketing
Chart Inst Public Relations
Health & Med Public Relations Assn
PRCA Ireland
Public Relations Consultants Assn
Public Relations Inst Ireland
Science, Technology, Engg... Public Relations Assn
Public schools > Independent & public schools
Public sector officials > Local government headings
Public speaking > Speakers
Public transport > Passenger transport
Public utilities > individual utility
Publicity > Advertising
Publishing
Assn Learned & Profl Soc Pubrs
Assn Publishing Agencies
Chart & Nautical Instrument Tr Assn

CLÉ
Data Pubrs Assn
Digital Content Forum
Indep Pubrs Gld
Inst Paper, Printing & Publishing Intl
Ir Educl Pubrs Assn
Periodical Pubrs Assn
Personal Mgrs Assn
Pira Intl
Publishers Assn
Publishers Licensing Soc
Scot Pubrs Assn
Soc Leisure Consultants & Pubrs
Soc Publishers Ireland
Trade & Profl Pubrs Assn [IRL]
> + Books; & other aspects of publishing
Pubs > Public houses
Pugin (Augustus Welby)
Pugin Soc
Pullets > Poultry
Pulmonaria
Hardy Plant Soc
Pulmonary hypertension
Pulmonary Hypertension Assn
> + Thoracic diseases
Pulp > Paper headings; Wood pulp
Pulses: edible
Brit Edible Pulse Assn
Grain & Feed Tr Assn
Pumps & pumping
Brit Pump Mfrs Assn
Fire Fighting Vehicles Mfrs Assn
Pump Distbrs Assn
Punch & Judy
Punch & Judy Coll Professors
Punctuation
Apostrophe Protection Soc
Punjab studies
Assn Punjab Studies (UK)
Puppetry
Brit Puppet & Model Theatre Gld
> + Theatre: young people
Purchasing & supply
Chart Inst Purchasing & Supply
GS1 (UK)
Ir Inst Purchasing & Materials Mgt
Soc Procurement Officers Local Govt
Purine metabolic disorders
Purine Metabolic Patients Assn
Push chairs > Nursery & baby products
PVC
Brit Plastics Fedn
Plastics & Board Inds Fedn
> + Plastics headings
Pyrotechnics > Fireworks
Pétanque
Brit Pétanque Fedn
Scot Pétanque Assn

Q

Quadricycling
Assn Pioneer Motor Cyclists
> + Cycles & motorcycles
Quail > Game & game birds
Quakers > Friends (Quakers)
Quality assurance & control
Assn Brit Certification Bodies
Brit Approvals Fire Eqpt
Brit Assn Res Quality Assurance
Brit Civil Engg Test Eqpt Mfrs Assn
Brit Quality Foundation
BSI
Excellence Ireland Quality Assn
Inst Quality Assurance
Market Res Quality Standards Assn
Mechanical & Metal Trs Confedn
UK Excellence Fedn
> + Materials: technology & testing
Quantity surveying
Instn Civil Engg Surveyors
Soc Construction & Quantity Surveyors Public Sector
Quarries & quarrying
Brit Aggregates Assn

Inst Explosives Engrs
Inst Quarrying
Ir Mining & Quarrying Soc
Minerals Engg Soc
Quarry Products Assn
Subterranea Britannica
> + specific stone quarried
Quarry tiles > Tiles (floor & wall)
Quickprinters & copyshops
Brit Assn Print & Communication
Quilling
Quilling Gld
Quills (pens) > Writing equipment & accessories
Quilting
Quilt Assn
Quilters' Gld
Quoits (game)
Nat Quoits Assn

R

Rabbits
Brit Rabbit Coun
Rabbit Welfare Assn
Race relations
Assn Jewish Ex-Servicemen & Women
Discrimination Law Assn
Inst Race Relations
Racecourses
Assn Ir Racecourses
Racecourse Assn
Rachmaninov (Sergei)
Rachmaninoff Soc
Racing > Horse racing; Motor sport
Rackets: equipment
Sports Mfrs & Retailers Tr Assn
Rackets (squash)
English Racketball
Great Britain Racquetball Fedn
Scot Squash
Squash Rackets Assn
Squash Wales
> + Tennis
Racking
Storage Eqpt Mfrs Assn
> + Storage equipment
Radiation > Radiology/radiation
Radiators
Boiler & Radiator Mfrs Assn
Radiesthesia > Radionics & radiesthesia
Radio
Assn Service Providers
Comml Radio Companies Assn
Community Media Assn
Intellect, the Information Technology, Telecommunications &
Electronics
Radio Academy
TV & Radio Inds Club
Voice Listener & Viewer
> + Aerials: radio & television;   Telecommunications
Radio: amateur
Ir Radio Transmitters Soc
Radio Soc GB
Radio: for blind & bedridden
Wireless Bedridden Soc
Radio: control
Brit Radio Car Assn
> + Models: hobby
Radio: community
Community Media Assn
Radio: engineering & industry > Electronic: industry & engineering
Radio: mobile
Fedn Communication Services
Mobile Electronics & Security Fedn
> + Radio: amateur
Radio: officers
Nat U Marine... Transport Officers
Radio: paging > Paging (radio)
Radio & TV: actors & actresses > Actors & actresses; Theatre
Radio & TV: censorship
mediawatch-uk
Radio & TV: medical broadcasts
Assn Broadcasting Doctors

Radio & TV: history
Brit Vintage Wireless Soc
Radio & TV: relay > Cable & satellite communications
Radio & TV: rental
Radio, Electrical & TV Retailers' Assn
Radio & TV: script writing
Soc Authors
Writers' Gld
Radio & TV: trade
Brit Audio Dealers Assn
Confedn Aerial Inds
Radio, Electrical & TV Retailers' Assn
Radiography > Radiology/radiation
Radiology/radiation
Assn Radiation Res
Assn University Radiation Protection Officers
Brit Inst Radiology
Brit Occupational Hygiene Soc
Brit Soc Dental & Maxillofacial Radiology
Brit Soc Neuroradiologists
R Coll Radiologists
Soc Radiographers
Soc Radiological Protection
Radionics & radiesthesia
Brit Soc Dowsers
Radionic Association Ltd
Radiotherapy > Radiology/radiation
Rafters
Trussed Rafter Assn
> + Roofing
Rafting
Brit Canoe U
Railways: development > Railways: promotion & development
Railways: engineering
Britpave
Instn Mechanical Engrs
Railways: equipment & rolling stock
Assn Private Rly Wagon Owners
Private Wagon Fedn
Rly Ind Assn
Wagon Bldg & Repairing Assn
Railways: history & preservation
Assn Transport Photographers & Historians
Branch Line Soc
Fedn Rly Clubs
German Rly Soc
Gld Rly Artists
Heritage Rly Assn
Histl Model Rly Soc
Indl Locomotive Soc
Indl Rly Soc
Locomotive Club
Merchant Navy Locomotive Presvn Soc
Narrow Gauge Rly Soc
Nat Assn Rly Clubs
Rly & Canal Histl Soc
Rly Correspondence & Travel Soc
Rly Enthusiasts Soc
Rly Presvn Soc Ireland
Scot Rly Presvn Soc
Swiss Rlys Soc
Transport 2000 Ltd
Transport Trust
Vintage Carriages Trust
> + Models: hobby
Railways: history & preservation - local
Bluebell Rly Presvn Soc
Caledonian Rly Assn
Cambrian Railways Soc
Ffestiniog Railway Society Ltd
Great N Scotland Rly Assn
Great Nthn Rly Soc
Great Wstn Soc
Highland Rly Soc
Keighley & Worth Valley Rly Presvn Soc
Kent & E Sussex Rly Co
Lancashire & Yorkshire Rly Presvn Soc
Lancashire & Yorkshire Rly Soc
Locomotive 6201
London Underground Rly Soc
N York Moors Hist Rly Trust
S Wstn Circle
Sittingbourne & Kemsley Light Rly
Stephenson Locomotive Soc
Strathspey Rly Assn
Sussex Indl Archaeol Soc
Talyllyn Rly Presvn Soc

Welsh Highland Rlys Assn
Welshpool & Llanfair Light Rly Presvn Co
Railways: light
Heritage Rly Assn
Light Rail Transit Assn
Tramway & Light Rly Soc
> + Tramways & trams
Railways: model
Assn Model Rly Socs Scotland
EM Gauge Soc
Model Electronic Rly Gp
N Wstn Model Rly Clubs Assn
Train Collectors Soc
Railways: operating
Assn Rly Training Providers
Assn Train Operating Companies
Rly Forum
Rly Study Assn
Railways: promotion & development
Assn Community Rail Partnerships
Electric Rly Soc
Locomotive & Carriage Instn
Permanent Way Instn
Rail Freight Gp
Rly Devt Soc
Transport-Watch
Railways: signalling
Instn Rly Signal Engrs
Railways: workers
Assd Train Crew U
Rail, Maritime & Transport U
Transport Salaried Staffs Assn
Rainwater
UK Rainwater Harvesting Assn
> + Water: treatment & supply
Rambling
Long Distance Walkers Assn
Ramblers' Assn
Ulster Fedn Rambling Clubs
Rangers & wardens
Assn Countryside Voluntary Wardens
Countryside Mgt Assn
Scot Countryside Rangers Assn
Ranges (cooking) > Catering: equipment
Ransome (Arthur Mitchell)
Arthur Ransome Soc
Rare breeds
Rare Breeds Survival Trust
> + Cattle; Sheep etc
Rating
Assn Chief Estates Surveyors. . . Local Govt
Inst Revenues, Rating & Valuation
Rating Surveyors Assn
Scot Assessors' Assn

Raw sugar > Sugar
Rawsthorne (Alan)
Friends Alan Rawsthorne
Raynaud's disease
Raynaud's & Scleroderma Assn
Razors > Shaving equipment & razors
Reading
Brit Dyslexia Assn
Dyslexia Inst
nasen
Nat Literacy Assn
Reading Assn Ireland
UK Literacy Assn
Ready-mixed concrete
Brit Ready Mixed Concrete Assn
Quarry Products Assn
> + Concrete & concrete products
Real ale
Campaign Real Ale
Soc Presvn Beers Wood
> + Brewing
Real estate > Estate headings; Property headings
Real tennis > Tennis
Receivers
Insolvency Practitioners Assn
Non-Administrative Receivers Assn
Receptionists (medical)
Assn Med Secretaries. . .& Receptionists
Reclamation & recycling
Aluminium Alloy Mfrg & Recycling Assn
Brit Metals Recycling Assn
Brit Vehicle Salvage Fedn

Can Makers
Chart Instn Wastes Mgt
Confedn Paper Inds
Environmental Services Assn
Inst Demolition Engrs
Oil Recycling Assn
Textile Recycling Assn
UK Aluminium Packaging Recycling Org
UK Cartridge Remanufacturers Assn
Waste Watch
> + Metal: scrap; & other waste trades
Record agents
Assn Genealogists & Researchers in Archives
Recorders (musical instruments)
Soc Recorder Players
Recording studios
Assn Profl Recording Services
Records: historical
Brit Record Soc
Brit Records Assn
Business Archives Coun
Catholic Record Soc
Ephemera Soc
Friends Nat Libraries
Hakluyt Soc
Harleian Soc
List & Index Soc
Manorial Soc
Navy Records Soc
Pipe Roll Soc
Scot Record Soc
Scot Records Assn
> + Archives; Parish registers
Records: historical - county societies
Bedfordshire Histl Record Soc
Caernarvonshire Histl Soc
Cambridgeshire Records Soc
Cheshire > Chetham Soc
Cheshire > Record Soc Lancashire & Cheshire
Chetham Soc
Cornwall > Devon & Cornwall Record Soc
Derbyshire Record Soc
Devon & Cornwall Record Soc
Dugdale Soc (Warwickshire)
Durham > Soc Antiquaries Newcastle upon Tyne
Hertfordshire > St Albans & Hertfordshire Architectural. . . Soc
Lancashire > Chetham Soc
Lancashire > Record Soc Lancashire & Cheshire
Lincoln Record Soc
London Record Soc
Norfolk Record Soc
Northamptonshire Record Soc
Northumberland > Soc Antiquaries Newcastle upon Tyne
Northumbria > Surtees Soc
Oxfordshire Record Soc
Record Soc Lancashire & Cheshire
Saint Albans & Hertfordshire Architectural. . . Soc
Soc Antiquaries Newcastle upon Tyne
Somerset Record Soc
Staffordshire Record Soc
Suffolk Record Soc
Surrey Record Soc
Surtees Soc (Northumbria)
Sussex Record Soc
Warwickshire > Dugdale Soc
Wiltshire Record Soc
Records: historical (conservation)
Assn Local Govt Archaeol Officers
> Archives: conservation
Records management
Records Mgt Soc
Records: musical > Copyright;   Sound recording & reproduction
Recovery & recycling > Reclamation & recycling
Recreation > Leisure, recreation & amenity management
Recruitment services > Employment agents & consultants
Recycling trades > Reclamation & recycling
Reeds & sedges
Brit Reed Growers Assn
Re-enactment of battles, fights etc > Fights (historic/re-enactment)
Referees
Referees' Assn
Referenda
Referenda Soc
Reflexology
Assn Light Touch Therapists
Assn Reflexologists
Assn Therapy Lecturers

Brit Reflexology Assn
Scot Massage Therapists Org
Reformed Church (Scottish)
Scot Reformation Soc
Refractive surgery
UK & I Soc Cataract & Refractive Surgeons
Refractories
Brit Ceramic Confedn
Brit Ceramic Res
Brit Refractories & Indl Ceramics
Inst Refractories Engrs
Refractory Users Fedn
Refreshment vending
Automatic Vending Assn
Refrigerated transport > Temperature controlled transport
Refrigeration
Air Conditioning & Refrigeration Ind Bd
Brit Refrigeration Assn
Halon Users Nat Consortium
Heat Transfer & Fluid Flow Service
Inst Refrigeration
Ir Cold Storage Fedn
> + Cryogenics; Temperature controlled storage
Refugees
Assn Visitors Immigration Detainees
Immigration Law Practitioners Assn
Nat Inf Forum
Refuse disposal > Waste disposal
Refuse incineration
Combined Heat & Power Assn
Registered designs > Copyright; Industrial design; Patents & trade marks
Registration of births etc > Population: registration
Regression > Hypnotic regression
Rehabilitation
Brit Soc Rehabilitation Medicine
English Community Care Assn
R Assn Disability & Rehabilitation
Scot Soc Rehabilitation
> + Disablement
Reiki healing
Assn Light Touch Therapists
Reiki Assn
Re-incarnation
UK Skeptics
Reinforcement
Intl Glassfibre Reinforced Concrete Assn
UK Steel
Reinsurance > Insurance
Relaxation
Brit Autogenic Soc
Floatation Tank Assn
Relay services > Radio;   Cable & satellite communications
Religion
Assn Brit Theological. . . Libraries
Assn Denominational Histl Socs Cognate Libs
Brit Assn Study Religions
Brit Soc Study Religions
Eckhart Soc
Pagan Fedn
Rural Theology Assn
Sea Faith Network (UK)
Traditional Cosmology Soc
Religion & medicine > Medicine & religion
Religious drama
Religious Drama Soc
Religious education > Christian education; & individual religions
Relocation agents & consultants
Assn Relocation Agents
Remedial education > Education
Remote imaging/sensing
Brit Assn Remote Sensing Companies
R Meteorological Soc
Remote Imaging Group
Remote Sensing & Photogrammetry Soc
Sira
Removers > Furniture: warehousing & removal
Renaissance
Colloquium Medieval & Renaissance Studies
Soc Renaissance Studies
Renal structure & disease > Nephrology
Rendering
Nat Renderers Assn
UK Renderers Assn
> + Animal by-products
Renewable energy
Brit Wind Energy Assn
Network Alternative Technology &. . . Assessment

Renewable Energy Assn
Scot Renewables Forum
Solar Energy Soc
> + specific types of energy
Rented accommodation
Nat Fedn Residential Landlords

Rents > + Property & land owners;   Tenants & residents
Repertory theatres > Theatre
Repetitive strain injury
Brit Assn Performing Arts Medicine
> + Occupational health & hygiene
Reporters > Journalism
Reproductive ethics
Comment Reproductive Ethics
Reptiles > Herpetology
Rescue equipment
Rescue organisations
Fire & Rescue Suppliers Assn
> First aid & immediate care;   Welfare organisations; & field of rescue
Research > subject of research
Reservoirs > Dams & reservoirs
Residential: boats
Residential Boat Owners Assn
Residential: colleges
Adult Residential Colls Assn
> + Adult education
Residential: homes
Assn Indep Care Advisers
English Community Care Assn
Inst Home Inspectors
Relatives & Residents Assn
> + Nursing homes
Residential: property > Property: maintenance/management
Residential: settlements
Brit Assn Settlements & Social Action Centres
Residential: social work > Social: service
Residents > Tenants & residents
Resins & gums
FeRFA
Resorts > Holiday resorts
Respiratory equipment
Assn Respiratory Technology & Physiology
Barema
Rest homes > Residential homes
Restaurants > Hotels & restaurants
Restaurants: engineering > Catering: equipment
Restless legs
Ekbom Support Gp
Restorative dentistry > Dentistry
Restorers/restoration > object(s) restored
Restricted growth > Growth
Resuscitation techniques > Life saving
Retail trade
Alliance Indep Retailers
Assn Private Market Operators
Brit Assn Fair Tr Shops
Brit Retail Consortium
Brit Shops & Stores Assn
Consumer Credit Assn
Indep Retailers Confedn
Inst Grocery Distbn
RGDATA [IRL]
Scot Retail Consortium
U Shop, Distributive & Allied Workers
UK Travel Retail Forum
Village Retail Services Assn. . .
> + specific trades
Retina (diseases of)
Brit Retinitis Pigmentosa Soc
Retirement
Fedn Active Retirement Assns [IRL]
Heyday
Life Academy
Nat Fedn Retirement Pensions Assns
Retirement homes & sheltered housing
Assn Retirement Housing Mgrs
ERoSH
NWA
Sheltered / Retirement Housing Owners' Confed
> + Nursing homes
Retreats (religious)
Assn Promoting Retreats
Retreat Assn
Retroreflective equipment
Retroreflective Eqpt Mfrs Assn

© CBD Research Ltd · Beckenham · BR3 5JS · Tel 020 8650 7745 · Fax 020 8650 0768 · E-mail cbd@cbdresearch.com · www.cbdresearch.com

Rett syndrome
     Rett Syndrome Assn
Revenue protection (electricity)
     UK Revenue Protection Assn
Rheas
     Rhea & Emu Assn
     > + Ostrich farming
Rheology
     Brit Soc Rheology
Rheumatism > Arthritis & rheumatism
Rhinology > Otolaryngology
Ribbon
     Brit Narrow Fabrics Assn
Rice
     Grain & Feed Tr Assn
     London Rice Brokers Assn
     Rice Assn
Richard III King of England
     Richard III Soc
     Soc Friends King Richard III
Riding > Horse: riding & driving
Rifle shooting
     Nat Rifle Assn
     Nat Small-Bore Rifle Assn
     Scot Rifle Assn
     Scot Target Shooting Fedn
     > + Shooting
Rights of the individual > Individual freedom
Rights of way > Footpaths & rights of way
Rigs (drilling)
     Brit Rig Owners Assn
Risk assessment
     SIESO
Risk management
     ALARM
     Assn Risk Mgt
     Inst Risk Mgt
     > + Insurance
Rivers
     Anglers Consvn Assn
     Assn Rivers Trusts
     Estuarine & Coastal Sciences Assn
     > + Inland waterways;   Water
Rivets > Fasteners & turned parts
Road: accidents > Accidents; Road: safety & control
Road: construction
     Britpave
     County Surveyors Soc
     Inst Highway Inc Engrs
     Instn Civil Engrs
     Instn Highways & Transportation
     Road Block
Road: construction materials
     Brit Precast Concrete Fedn
     Refined Bitumen Assn
     Road Emulsion Assn
     Road Surface Dressing Assn
     UK Quality Ash Assn
Road: control > Road: safety & control
Road: haulage
     Freight Transport Assn
     Heavy Transport Assn
     Ir Road Haulage Assn
     Road Haulage Assn
     Soc Operations Engrs
     Transport Assn
     Utd Road Transport U
     > + Transport
Road: lighting, markings & traffic signs
     Assn Road Traffic Safety & Mgt
     Assn Street Lighting Electrical Contrs
     Highway Electrical Mfrs & Supprs Assn
     Photoluminescent Safety Products Assn
     Retroreflective Eqpt Mfrs Assn
     Road Safety Markings Assn
     > + Signs
Road: locomotives
     Road Locomotive Soc
     > + Steam engines, boats & machinery
Road: rollers > Steam engines, boats & machinery
Road: safety & control
     Assn Indl Road Safety Officers
     Campaign Drinking & Driving
     Inst Road Safety Officers
     Inst Traffic Accident Investigators
     ITS UK
     Local Authority Road Safety Officers' Assn

R Soc Prevention Accidents
     RoadPeace
     Safe Speed
     Traffic Mgt Contrs Assn
     Vehicle Restraint Mfrs Assn
     > + Motoring organisations; Safety
Road: signs > Road: lighting, markings & traffic signs;   Signs
Road: sweeping > Street cleaning
Road: transport > Road: haulage
Robotics
     Brit Automation & Robot Assn
     Materials Handling Engrs Assn
     Soc Underwater Technology Ltd
Rock climbing > Climbing
Rock gardens
     Alpine Garden Soc
     Hardy Plant Soc
     Scot Rock Garden Club
Rock mechanics > Soil & rock mechanics
Rock > Pop & rock music
Rocketry
     Assn Scotland Res Astronautics
     UK Rocketry Assn
Roller bearings > Ball & roller bearings
Roller coasters
     Roller Coaster Club
     > + Fairgrounds & equipment
Roller hockey
     Nat Roller Hockey Assn
     > Skating: board, inline & roller
Rollerblading > Skating: board, inline & roller
Roman archaeology & antiquities
     Assn Roman Archaeology
     Assn Study & Presvn Roman Mosaics
     Soc Promotion Roman Studies
     > + Archaeology
Roman Catholic Church
     Assn Separated & Divorced Catholics
     Catenian Assn
     Catholic Archives Soc
     Catholic Family Hist Soc
     Catholic Record Soc
     Catholic U
     Chapels Soc
     Gld Catholic Doctors
     Latin Mass Soc
     Newman Assn
     Scot Catholic Histl Assn
     > + Liturgy
Roman Empire
     Soc Promotion Roman Studies
     > + Classical studies
Romance
     Romantic Novelists Assn
Romanies > Gypsies & travelling people
Romany of the BBC
     Romany Soc
Roofing
     Brit Precast Concrete Fedn
     Confedn Roofing Contrs
     Copper Devt Assn
     Eur Liquid Waterproofing Assn
     Flat Roofing Alliance
     Inst Roofing
     Metal Cladding & Roofing Manufacturers Association Ltd
     Nat Fedn Roofing Contrs
     Roofing Ind Alliance
     Single Ply Roofing Assn
     Stone Roofing Assn
Rooflights
     Nat Assn Rooflight Mfrs
     > + Windows
Rootzone materials
     Brit Rootzone & Top Dressing Mfrs Assn
     > + Composts & composting
Ropes > Cordage, ropes & twine
Ropework
     Intl Gld Knot Tyers
Rosacea
     Acne Support Gp
Roses
     Amat Rose Breeders Assn
     Brit Assn Rose Breeders
     Brit Rose Growers Assn
     N England Rose, Carnation. . . Horticl Soc
     R Nat Rose Soc

Rotary
> Assn Inner Wheel Clubs
> Assn Past Rotarians

Rotating electrical machines
> BEAMA

Rotorcraft > Helicopters

Round tables
> Nat Assn Round Tables

Roundabouts (fairground) > Fairgrounds & equipment

Roundabouts (traffic)
> UK Roundabout Appreciation Soc
> > + Road markings, lighting & traffic signs

Rounders
> Gaelic Athletic Assn
> Nat Rounders Assn

Roundheads > Cromwell (Oliver);   Fights (historic/re-enactment)

Route guidance
> ITS UK
> > + Road: safety & control

Routemaster buses
> Routemaster Operators & Owners Assn

Rowing
> Amat Rowing Assn
> Scot Amat Rowing Assn
> Welsh Amat Rowing Assn

Roy (Harry)
> Harry Roy Appreciation Soc

Royal Air Force
> R Air Force Histl Soc
> R Air Forces Assn
> Soldiers, Sailors & Airmen's Families Assn
> > + Armed forces & veterans: welfare

Royal Marines
> White Ensign Assn

Royal Navy
> Assn R Navy Officers
> Navy Records Soc
> R Naval Assn
> R Navy Enthusiasts' Soc
> White Ensign Assn
> > + Armed forces & veterans: welfare

Royal warrant holders
> R Warrant Holders Assn

RSI > Repetitive strain injury

Rubber
> Brit Plastics Fedn
> Brit Rubber Mfrs Assn
> Rapra Technology Ltd
> Tropical Growers' Assn

Rubber stamps
> Rubber Stamp Mfrs' Gld

Rubella > German measles

Rugby Fives
> Rugby Fives Assn

Rugby football > Football: Rugby

Rugs > Carpets; Oriental carpets & rugs

Running
> English Cross Country Assn
> Fell Runners Assn
> Road Runners Club
> > + Athletics

Rupert Bear
> Followers of Rupert

Rural interests
> Country Land & Business Assn
> Scot Rural Property & Business Assn
> Westmorland County Agricl Soc
> > + Conservation; Environment;   Local government

Rural life: history > Agriculture: history

Ruritanian fiction
> Violet Needham Soc

Ruskin (John)
> Ruskin Soc
> Ruskin Soc Lond

Rusks
> Cereal Ingredients Mfrs' Assn

Russia & associated states
> Brit Assn Slavonic & E Eur Studies
> Russo-Brit Cham Comm
> Scotland-Russia Forum
> Soc Cooperation Russian Soviet Studies

Russia: language & literature
> Assn Language Learning
> Brit Assn Slavonic & E Eur Studies
> Pushkin Club

S

Sacks
> Environmental & Technical Assn Paper Sack Ind

SAD (seasonal affective disorder)
> SAD Assn

Saddlery
> Brit Equestrian Tr Assn
> Soc Master Saddlers
> > + Leathergoods

Safes
> Brit Security Ind Assn

Safety
> Brit Safety Ind Fedn
> Crime Concern
> Health & Safety Sign Assn
> Indep Safety Consultants Assn
> Inst Safety Technology & Res
> Instn Occupational Safety & Health
> Nat Ir Safety Org
> Retroreflective Eqpt Mfrs Assn
> Safety & Reliability Soc
> Scot Hazards Campaign Gp
> SELECT
> > + Home: safety;   Road safety & control

Safety: assessment
> Assn Boat Safety Examiners
> Safety Assessment Fedn

Safety: barriers & fences
> Fencing Contrs Assn
> Vehicle Restraint Mfrs Assn

Safety: lamps
> Miners' & Indl Lamp Mfrs' Assn
> > + Mining: equipment

Safety: personal
> Choice in Personal Safety
> Fall Arrest Safety Eqpt Training
> Personal Safety Assn
> Personal Safety Mfrs Assn

Safety: rigging/nets
> Fall Arrest Safety Eqpt Training

Sailing
> Assn Sea Training Orgs
> Ir Sailing Assn
> Old Gaffers Assn
> > + Boats & boating;   Ships: history & preservation;   Yachting

Sailmaking
> Assn Brit Sailmakers
> Brit Marine Fedn
> Performance Textiles Assn

Sailors > Merchant Navy; Royal Navy

Sailors' welfare
> Soldiers, Sailors & Airmen's Families Assn
> > + Ex-service organisations

Sailplanes > Gliding & soaring

St James of Compostela
> Confraternity Saint James

Saintpaulia
> Saintpaulia & Houseplant Soc

Salads
> Brit Leafy Salad Assn
> > + Vegetable(s) headings

Sales agents (general)
> Brit Intl Freight Assn

Sales management & representation
> Inst Sales & Marketing Mgt
> Inst Sales Promotion
> Managing & Marketing Sales Assn
> Sales Inst Ireland
> Soc Sales & Marketing
> > + Marketing

Salmon & trout
> Assn Salmon Fishery Bds
> Brit Trout Assn
> Salmon & Trout Assn
> Scot Anglers Nat Assn
> Scot Quality Salmon
> Scot Salmon Smokers Assn
> Wild Trout Trust
> > + Fish: farming

Salt
> Salt Mfrs Assn

Salted fish
> Assn Brit Salted Fish Curers...

Salvage > Reclamation & recycling; Towage & salvage

© CBD Research Ltd · Beckenham · BR3 5JS · Tel 020 8650 7745 · Fax 020 8650 0768 · E-mail cbd@cbdresearch.com · www.cbdresearch.com

Salvage (underwater) > Underwater engineering & research
Salvage corps
    Brit Fire Services Assn
Sand & gravel
    Quarry Products Assn
Sand yachting
    Brit Fedn Sand & Land Yacht Clubs
Sandwiches & sandwich bars
    Brit Sandwich Assn
    Nationwide Caterers Assn
Sanitary protection
    Absorbent Hygiene Products Mfrs Assn
Sanitaryware
    Brit Ceramic Confedn
Sarcoidosis
    Sarcoidosis & Intestitial Lung Assn
    > + Thoracic diseases
Satellite communications > Cable & satellite communications
Satellite navigation
    UK Indl Space C'ee
    > + Navigation
Sauces > Pickles & sauces
Saunas
    Health & Beauty Emplrs Fedn
Sausage & food casings
    Natural Sausage Casings Assn
Sausages
    Brit Sausage Appreciation Soc
    Gld Q Butchers
    > + Meat
Saville (Malcolm)
    Malcolm Saville Soc
Savoy Operas
    Gilbert & Sullivan Soc
Sawmilling > Timber
Saxophones > Clarinets & saxophones
Sayers (Dorothy L[eigh]))
    Dorothy L Sayers Soc
Scaffolding
    Nat Access & Scaffolding Confedn
    Prefabricated Access Suppliers' & Mfrs' Assn
Scales & weighing machines
    Solids Handling & Processing Assn
    UK Weighing Fedn
    > + Measurement
Scallops > Shellfish
Scandinavia: literature & antiquities
    Regia Anglorum
    Scot Soc Nthn Studies
    Viking Soc Nthn Res
Scanning
    UK Indl Vision Assn
Scepticism
    UK Skeptics
Schizophrenia
    SANE
    Schizophrenia Assn
    Schizophrenia Ireland
School bands
    Nat School Band Assn
School governors
    Foundation & Aided Schools Nat Assn
School secretaries & administrators
    Nat Bursars Assn
    > + Secretaries & personal assistants
School teachers > Teachers
Schools
    Nat Assn Small Schools
    > + Education; Teachers; & individual type of school
Schools: hygiene
    Medical Officers Schools Assn
Schools: independent
    Indep Schools Coun Inf Service
Schools: inspection
    Assn Profls Educ & Children's Trusts
Schools: meals service
    Local Authority Caterers' Assn
Schubert (Franz Peter))
    Schubert Soc
Schumacher (Dr E F)
    Doctor E F Schumacher Soc
Science
    Assn Basic Science Teachers Dentistry
    Assn Brit Science Writers
    Assn Mgt & Profl Staffs
    Assn Researchers in Medicine & Science
    Assn Science Educ

    Brit Assn Advancement Science
    Brit Soc Philosophy Science
    Cambridge Philosophical Soc
    Campaign Science & Engg UK
    Manchester Literary & Philosophical Soc
    R Instn GB
    R Ir Academy
    R Scot Soc Arts (Science & Technology)
    R Soc Chemistry
    R Soc Edinburgh
    Royal Soc (The)
    Science, Engg & Mfrg Technologies Alliance
    Science, Technology, Engg... Public Relations Assn
    Scientists Global Responsibility
    UK Skeptics
    > + specific disciplines
Science fiction
    Brit Fantasy Soc
    Brit Science Fiction Assn
Science: history
    Brit Soc Hist Science
    Natural Sciences Collections Assn
Science parks
    UK Science Park Assn
Science: technology > Laboratory equipment & technology
Scientific film > Film
Scientific instruments
    Scientific Instrument Soc
    > + Glassware: scientific
Scientists > Science; specific disciplines
Scleroderma
    Raynaud's & Scleroderma Assn
    Scleroderma Soc
Sclerosis
    Multiple Sclerosis Soc
    Multiple Sclerosis Soc Ireland
    Tuberous Sclerosis Assn
Scoliosis
    Scoliosis Assn
Scooter riding > Motor cycling & scooter riding
Scorpions
    Brit Arachnological Soc
    Brit Tarantula Soc
Scotland
    Assn Protection Rural Scotland
    Assn Scot Visitor Attractions
    Saint Andrew Soc
    Saltire Soc
    Scot Envt Link
    Scot Wild Land Gp
Scotland: archaeology
    Soc Antiquaries Scotland
    > + Archaeology: county societies
Scotland: history
    Pictish Arts Soc
    R Celtic Soc
    Scot Catholic Histl Assn
    Scot Hist Soc
    Scot Record Soc
    Seventeen Fortyfive Assn
    Soc W Highland & Island Histl Res
Scotland: language & literature
    Assn Scot Literary Studies
    Robert Burns World Fedn
    Scot Language Dictionaries
    Scot Poetry Library
    Scot Text Soc
    Scots Language Soc
    Ulster-Scots Language Soc
    > + Gaelic language & culture
Scotland: law history
    Stair Soc
Scotland: music
    R Celtic Soc
    Robert Burns World Fedn
    Traditional Music & Song Assn Scotland
    > + Pipe bands & music
Scott (Sir Walter)
    Edinburgh Sir Walter Scott Club
Scouts > Youth organisations
Scrabble
    Assn Brit Scrabble Players
    Scrabble Clubs (UK)
Scrap > Materials: management/handling; Reclamation & recycling
Screen (film & television) > Film; Television headings
Screen printing
    Screen Printing Assn

Screens > Advertising: television & screen; Film; Partitioning; Sieves & screens
Screws & rivets > Fasteners & turned parts
Scribes
    Soc Scribes & Illuminators
Scripophily
    Intl Bond & Share Soc
Scriptwriting
    Brit Soc Comedy Writers
    > + Writing & writers
Scuba diving
    Scot Sub Aqua Club
    > + Water: sports
Sculpture
    Brit Art Medal Soc
    Nat Soc Painters, Sculptors & Printmakers
    Public Monuments & Sculpture Assn
    R Birmingham Soc Artists
    R Brit Soc Sculptors
    R Cambrian Academy Art
    R Scot Academy Art & Architecture
    Sculptors' Soc Ireland
    Soc Portrait Sculptors
    Soc Women Artists
    > + Stone masons & sculptors
Sea > Marine; Nautical; Sailing etc
Sea angling
    Assn Sea Fisheries C'ees [E&W]
    Nat Fedn Sea Anglers
    Scot Fedn Sea Anglers
    > + Fishing (sport)
Sea pilots
    Europilots - the Association of Licensed Deep Sea Pilots
    Nautical Inst
    UK Maritime Pilots' Assn
    > + Navigation
Sea pollution > Pollution & pollution control
Sea-bed exploration > Ocean industries
Seabirds > Birds
Seafood > Fish headings; individual type of fish
Sealants & sealing
    Assn Sealant Applicators
    Brit Adhesives & Sealants Assn
    Brit Fluid Power Assn
    Brit Textile Technology Gp
    Extruded Sealants Assn
    Gasket Cutters' Assn
Seamanship > Marine training; Sailing
Seamen > Merchant Navy; Royal Navy
Seaside piers > Piers
Seasonal affective disorder
    SAD Assn
Seasonings > Spices & seasonings
Seat belts
    Baby Products Assn
Seating (audience/sports)
    Brit Assn Seating Eqpt Suppliers
Seaweed > Algae
Secondary metal > Metal: scrap
Secondary schools
    Headteachers Assn Scotland
Secondary teachers > Teachers
Secret passages
    Subterranea Britannica
Secret writing
    Xenophon
Secretaries & administrators
    Alliance UK Virtual Assistants
    Assn Coun Secretaries & Solicitors
    Assn Med Secretaries...& Receptionists
    Gld Intl Butler Administrators...
    Inst Agricl Secretaries & Administrators
    Inst Assn Mgt
    Inst Legal Secretaries & PAs
    Inst Paralegal Training
    Inst Qualified Profl Secretaries
    Nat Assn NFU Gp Secretaries
    Nat Bursars Assn
Secularism
    Campaign Philosophical Freedom
    Nat Secular Soc
    > + Humanism
Securities > Investment; Stock & share dealing
Security
    Assn Burglary Insurance Surveyors [>AIS011 (04)
    Assn Insurance Surveyors
    Assn Police & Public Security Suppliers
    Assn Security Consultants

    Brit Blind & Shutter Assn
    Brit Security Ind Assn
    Confedn Aerial Inds
    Confedn Brit Security Ind
    Electrical Contrs Assn
    Fedn Employed Door Supervisors & Security
    Fencing Contrs Assn
    Inst Security Mgt
    Ir Security Ind Assn
    Mobile Electronics & Security Fedn
    Nat Assn Healthcare Security
    Nat Assn Security Dog Users
    Nat Security Inspectorate
    Scot Security Assn
    Security Inst Ireland
    Telecare Services Assn
    > + Police
Security: shredding > Documents: confidential disposal
Sedges > Reeds & sedges
Sedimentology
    Geological Soc
Seed crushing > Oilseed; Seeds
Seed potatoes > Potatoes
Seeds
    Biodynamic Agricl Assn
    Brit Assn Seed Analysts
    Ir Seed Tr Assn
    Nat Assn Agricl Contrs
    NIAB
    Scot Seed & Nursery Tr Assn
Self adhesive labels > Labels: self adhesive & roll
Self building
    Community Self Build Scotland
Self catering
    Assn Scotland's Self-Caterers
    Brit Holiday & Home Parks Assn
    English Assn Self Catering Operators
    Fedn Nat Self Catering Assns
    > + Caravans & caravanning; Travel & tourism etc
Self employment
    Fedn Small Businesses
    > + Business
Self harm
    Purine Metabolic Patients Assn
Self healing
    Metamorphic Assn
Selling > Direct selling; Sales management & representation
Semi conductors > Electronics: industry & engineering
Sensing > Remote imaging/sensing
Separated & divorced people > Singles, divorced & separated
Separation techniques
    Chromatographic Soc
Sequence dancing > Dancing
Serials > Periodicals
Servicemen's welfare > Armed forces & veterans: welfare;   Ex-service
    organisations
Services (local government)
    Assn Public Service Excellence
Settlements > Archaeology; Residential: settlements; Welfare: organisations
Sewers, sewage & effluents
    Chart Instn Water & Envtl Management
    Nat Sewerage Assn
    Soc Brit Water & Wastewater Inds
Sewing articles (collecting) > Thimbles
Sewing machines
    Assn Sewing Machine Distbrs
    Sewing Machine Tr Assn
    Tools Self Reliance
Sex equality > Women: equal rights
Sex & sexual law reform
    Brit Assn Sexual & Relationship Therapy
    Campaign Homosexual Equality
    Josephine Butler Soc
    Sexaholics Anonymous
    Sexual Freedom Coalition
Sexual dysfunction
    Brit Soc Sexual Medicine
    Sexual Dysfunction Assn
Sexually transmitted disease > Genito-urinary medicine
Shaft sinking > Tunnelling & shaft sinking
Shakespeare (William)
    De Vere Soc
    Shakespeare Reading Soc
    Sunday Shakespeare Soc
Share certificates (collecting) > Scripophily
Shareholders
    English Assn Amer Bond & Shareholders

© CBD Research Ltd · Beckenham · BR3 5JS · Tel 020 8650 7745 · Fax 020 8650 0768 · E-mail cbd@cbdresearch.com · www.cbdresearch.com

UK Shareholders' Assn
> + Investment; Stock & share dealing
Sharks
Basking Shark Soc
Shark Angling Club
Shaving equipment & razors
Cutlery & Allied Trs Res Assn
Shaw (George Bernard)
Shaw Soc
Shaw (Thomas Edward) > Lawrence (Thomas Edward)['of Arabia']
Sheep
Brit Veterinary Assn
Highlands & Islands Sheep Health Assn
ICSA [IRL]
Livestock Auctioneers Assn
Nat Sheep Assn
Sheep: breed societies
Badger Face Welsh Mountain Sheep Soc
Balwen Welsh Mountain Sheep Soc
Beltex Sheep Soc
Black Welsh Mountain Sheep Breeders Assn
Blackface Sheep Breeders Assn
Bluefaced Leicester Sheep Breeders Assn
Brecknock Hill Cheviot Sheep Soc
Brit Berrichon du Cher Sheep Soc
Brit Bleu du Maine Sheep Soc
Brit Charollais Sheep Soc
Brit Coloured Sheep Breeders Assn
Brit Friesland Sheep Soc
Brit Gotland Sheep Soc
Brit Icelandic Sheep Breeders Gp
Brit Île de France Sheep Soc
Brit Rouge de l'Ouest Sheep Soc
Brit Texel Sheep Soc
Brit Vendeen Sheep Soc
Cambridge Sheep Soc
Castlemilk Moorit Sheep Soc
Charmoise Hill Sheep Soc
Cheviot Sheep Soc
Clun Forest Sheep Breeders Soc
Cotswold Sheep Soc
Cymdeithas Defaid Llanwenog Sheep Soc
Dalesbred Sheep Breeders Assn
Dartmoor Sheep Breeders Assn
Derbyshire Gritstone Sheepbreeders Soc
Devon Closewool Sheepbreeders Soc
Devon & Cornwall Longwool Flock Book Assn
Dorset Down Sheep Breeders Assn
Dorset Horn Poll Sheep Breeders Assn
Eppynt Hill & Beulah Speckled Face Sheep Soc
Exmoor Horn Sheep Breeders Soc
Hampshire Down Sheep Breeders Assn
Hebridean Sheep Soc
Herdwick Sheep Breeders Assn
Hill Radnor Flock Book Soc
Jacob Sheep Soc
Kerry Hill Flock Book Soc
Leicester Longwool Sheep Breeders Assn
Lincoln Longwool Sheep Breeders Assn
Lleyn Sheep Soc
Lonk Sheep Breeders Assn
Manx Loaghtan Sheep Breeders Gp
Masham Sheep Breeders Assn
N Country Cheviot Sheep Soc
N England Mule Sheep Assn
Oxford Down Sheep Breeders Assn
Romney Sheep Breeders' Soc
Rough Fell Sheep Breeders Assn
Roussin Sheep Soc
Ryeland Flock Book Soc
Scotch Half Bred Assn
Scotch Mule Assn
Shetland Cheviot Marketing Soc
Shetland Flock Book Soc
Shetland Sheep Soc
Shropshire Sheep Breeders Assn
Soc Border Leicester Sheep Breeders
Southdown Sheep Soc
Suffolk Sheep Soc
Swaledale Sheep Breeders Assn
Talybont Welsh Sheep Soc
Teeswater Sheep Breeders Assn
Welsh Halfbred Sheep Breeders Assn
Welsh Hill Speckled Face Sheep Soc
Welsh Mountain Sheep Soc - Hill Flock
Welsh Mountain Sheep Society - Registered Section
Welsh Mule Sheep Breeders Assn

Wensleydale Longwool Sheep Breeders' Assn
White Face Dartmoor Sheep Breeders Assn
White Faced Woodland Sheep Breeders Gp
Wiltshire Horn Sheep Soc
Zwartbles Sheep Assn
> + Cattle & livestock
Sheep: dairying
Brit Milksheep Soc
Brit Sheep Dairying Assn
Sheet metal > Metal: sheet
Sheet music > Music
Shelley (Percy Bysshe)
Keats-Shelley Memorial Assn
Shellfish
Assn Scot Shellfish Growers
Seafood Shetland
Shellfish Assn
UK Assn Frozen Food Producers
Shells > Conchology
Sheltered housing > Retirement homes & sheltered housing
Shelving & racking > Storage equipment
Shepherds' crooks
Brit Stickmakers Gld
Sheriffs & sheriff-officers
Shrievalty Assn
Soc Messengers-at-Arms & Sheriff-Officers
Shiatsu
Equine Shiatsu Assn
Shiatsu Soc
> + Complementary medicine
Shingles
Herpes Virus Assn
Shinty (sport)
Camanachd Assn
Shipbroking
Inst Chart Shipbrokers
Ir Ship Agents' Assn
Shipbuilding & ship repairing
Amat Yacht Res Soc
Assn Indep Mgt & Maritime Services
Brit Marine Fedn
Confedn Shipbuilding & Engg Us
Instn Engrs & Shipbuilders Scotland
R Instn Naval Architects
Shipbuilders & Shiprepairers Assn
Steam Boat Assn
Thames Boating Trs Assn
> + Marine: engineering
Shippers & packers for specific trades > trade concerned
Shipping
Assn Port Health Authorities
Bristol Steamship Owners' Assn
Cambridge Refrigeration Technology
Chamber Shipping
Freight Transport Assn
Grain & Feed Tr Assn
Ir Cham Shipping
Ir Marine Fedn
London Shipowners' & River Users' Soc
Shipping & forwarding
Brit Intl Freight Assn
Ir Intl Freight Assn
> + Freight transport
Ships: history & preservation
Brit Titanic Soc
Coble & Keelboat Soc
Forty Plus (40+) Fishing Boat Assn
Heritage Afloat
Maritime Trust
Mary Rose Soc
Nat Historic Ships
Ocean Liner Soc
Soc Sailing Barge Res
Ships: stores & supplies
Marine Trs Assn
Scot Ship Chandlers Assn
Ships: survey
Salvage Assn
Soc Consulting Marine Engrs & Ship Surveyors
Shipwrecks > Ships: history & preservation
Shirts
Brit Clothing Ind Assn
Master Craftsmen's Assn
Shoehorns
Buttonhook Soc
Shoes > Footwear

Shooting
> Brit Airgun Shooters' Assn
> Brit Assn Shooting & Consvn
> Brit Shooting Sports Coun
> Countryside Alliance
> Great Britain Target Shooting Fedn
> Scot Assn Country Sports
> Shooters' Rights Assn
> Sportsman's Assn
> UK Practical Shooting Assn
> Vintage Arms Assn
> + Arms & armour; Rifle shooting

Shopfitting
> Glass & Glazing Fedn
> Inst Shopfitters
> Nat Assn Shopfitters
> Shop & Display Eqpt Assn

Shopmobility
> Nat Fedn Shopmobility

Shopping abroad

Shopping centres
> Brit Coun Shopping Centres

Shopping from home > Home: shopping

Shops & stores > Retail trade

Shoring technology
> Construction Plant-hire Assn

Shorinji kempo > Martial arts

Short-circuit testing
> ASTA BEAB Certification Services

Shorthand writing
> Brit Inst Verbatim Reporters
> Inc Phonographic Soc

Show jumping
> Brit Equestrian Fedn
> + Horse headings

Showmen (fairground)
> Showmen's Gld
> Soc Indep Roundabout Proprietors
> + Fairgrounds & equipment

Shows & events
> Assn Event Venues
> Assn Profl Videomakers
> Event Services Assn
> Events Sector Ind Trg Org
> Horticultural Exhibitors Assn
> Nat Outdoor Events Assn
> Soc Event Organisers
> + Corporate hospitality; Agriculture: county societies

Shredders (scrap)
> Brit Metals Recycling Assn

Shredding (security) > Documents: confidential disposal

Shutters > Windows: blinds & shutters

Sibelius (Jean)
> UK Sibelius Soc

Sickle cell anaemia
> Sickle Cell Soc

Side saddle riding
> Side Saddle Assn

Sidecars
> Fedn Sidecar Clubs
> + Motor cycling & scooter riding

Sieves & screens
> Solids Handling & Processing Assn

Sight > Blind & partially sighted; specific disease

Sigillology > Badges & insignia

Sign language
> Brit Deaf Assn
> Paget Gorman Soc
> Scot Assn Sign Language Interpreters
> + Deafness

Signs
> Brit Sign & Graphics Assn
> Health & Safety Sign Assn
> + Road: lighting, markings & traffic signs

Silhouettes
> Silhouette Collectors Club
> Soc Limners

Silica
> Quarry Products Assn
> Silica & Moulding Sands Assn

Silk
> Brit Throwsters Assn
> Silk Assn

Silos & hoppers
> Solids Handling & Processing Assn

Silver bands > Brass & silver bands

Silver (dealing in) > Bullion dealing

Silversmiths > Goldsmiths & silversmiths

Simultaneous translation
> Conf Interpreters Gp

Singapore
> Brit Cham Comm Singapore

Singing
> Assn Engl Singers & Speakers
> Assn Teachers Singing
> Brit Voice Assn
> Gld Musicians & Singers
> Sing for Pleasure
> + Choirs & choral music

Single transferable vote > Elections & electoral legislation

Singles, divorced & separated
> Assn Separated & Divorced Catholics
> Assn Shared Parenting
> Families Need Fathers
> Family Mediation Scotland
> Gingerbread
> Nat Coun Divorced & Separated
> Nat Fedn Solo Clubs
> One Parent Families Scotland
> Phoenix Camping Club
> Single Travellers Action Gp
> + Widows & widowers

Site investigation > Surveying

Sixth form colleges
> Assn Colleges
> Coun Indep Educ

Sjogren's syndrome
> Brit Sjogren's Syndrome Assn

Skateboarding > Skating: board, inline & roller

Skater hockey > Skating: board, inline & roller

Skating: ice > Ice skating

Skating: board, inline & roller
> Brit Inline Skater Hockey Assn
> Fedn Artistic Roller Skating

Skibob
> Skibob Assn

Skiing > Snowsports; Water sports

Skin camouflage
> Brit Assn Skin Camouflage
> + Birthmarks & disfigurement

Skin disease > Dermatology; individual diseases

Skin diving > Water: sports

Skins > Leather

Skipping
> Brit Rope Skipping Assn

Sky (visibility of)
> Campaign Dark Skies

Skylights > Rooflights

Slag: cementitious
> Cementitious Slag Makers Assn

Slate(s)
> Stone Fedn
> Stone Roofing Assn

Slaughtering > Abattoirs

Slavonic languages & culture
> Brit Assn Slavonic & E Eur Studies

Sleep
> Brit Sleep Soc
> Brit Snoring & Sleep Apnoea Assn
> Brit Waterbed Assn
> Narcolepsy Assn
> Sleep Apnoea Trust Assn

Sleepers (concrete)
> Brit Precast Concrete Fedn
> + Railways: engineering

Sliding doors
> Assn Interior Specialists
> + Doors

Slimming > Eating disorders; Obesity

Slot cars
> Brit Slot Car Racing Assn

Slot machines (vintage)
> Soc Indep Roundabout Proprietors

Slovak Republic
> Brit Cham Comm Slovak Republic

Slovakia: music
> Dvořák Soc Czech & Slovak Music

Small arms > Arms & armour; Shooting

Small business > Business; Self employment

Small claims
> Chart Inst Arbitrators

Small woods > Woodlands

Smoke & smoke control
> Air Cleaner Mfrs Assn

Intumescent Fire Seals Assn
Smoke Control Assn
> + Air: conditioning & ventilating;   Air: pollution
Smoking
Action Smoking & Health
Briar Pipe Tr Assn
Brit Temperance Soc
Freedom Org Right Enjoy Smoking Tobacco
Smoking: of food > type of food smoked
Snacks
Snack, Nut & Crisp Mfrs Assn
Snakes > Herpetology
Snooker equipment > Cue sports
Snoring & apnoea
Brit Snoring & Sleep Apnoea Assn
Snow (John)
John Snow Soc
Snowboarding > Snowsports
Snowsports
Alpine Club
Backpackers Club
BASP UK Ltd
Brit Assn Mountain Guides
Brit Assn Snowsport Instructors
Brit Ski Club Disabled
Mountaineering Coun Scotland
Scot Ski Club
Ski Club
Skibob Assn
Snowsport England
Snowsport GB
Snowsport Inds
Snowsport Scotland

Soap & detergents
Ir Cosmetics, Detergents... Prods Assn
Nat Renderers Assn
UK Cleaning Products Ind Assn
Soaring > Gliding & soaring
Social: history > History
Social: inventions
Inst Social Inventions
Social: reform
Social: sciences/research
Academy Social Sciences
Assn Res Centres Social Sciences
Assn Teaching Social Sciences
Brit Sociological Assn
Inst Social Inventions
Market Res Soc
Modern Studies Assn
Social Res Assn
Socio-Legal Studies Assn
Sociological Assn Ireland
Statistical & Social Inquiry Soc Ireland
Social: service
Assn Directors Social Services
Assn Directors Social Work
Assn Educ Welfare Mgt
Brit Assn Social Workers
Ceretas
Emergency Social Services Assn
Inst Welfare
Ir Assn Social Workers
NAGALRO
Nat Assn Adult Placement Services
Nat Assn Social Workers Educ
Nat Fedn Community Orgs
Social Care Assn
> + Community service: voluntary;   Welfare: administration
Social service: area organisations
NI Coun Voluntary Action
Wales Coun Voluntary Action
Socialism
Fabian Soc
Socialist Health Assn
Sociology > Social: sciences/research
Soft drinks
Beverage Coun Ireland
Brit Soft Drinks Assn
Soft furnishings
Assn Master Upholsterers & Soft Furnishers
Nat Carpet Cleaners Assn
> + Carpets; Upholstery
Soft tissue > Tissue paper
Softball
BaseballSoftballUK

Software
Component Obsolescence Gp
Intellect, the Information Technology, Telecommunications &
Electronics
Ir Software Assn
ScotlandIS
> + Computers
Software: development
Business Application Software Developers Assn
HL7 UK Ltd
UK Software Metrics Assn
Software: leisure
Entertainment & Leisure Software Pubrs Assn (UK)
Software: protection
Business Software Alliance
Fedn Software Theft
Softwoods
Timber Tr Fedn
> + Timber
Soil
Brit Soc Soil Science
Growing Media Assn
Instn Agricl Engrs
Soil Assn
Soil & rock mechanics
Brit Geotechnical Assn
Instn Civil Engrs
Solar technology
Glass & Glazing Fedn
Network Alternative Technology &... Assessment
R Astronomical Soc
Renewable Energy Assn
Scot Solar Energy Gp
Solar Energy Soc
Solar Tr Assn
> + Renewable energy
Soldering > Brazing & soldering
Soldiers' welfare > Armed forces & veterans: welfare
Sol-fa > Tonic Sol-fa
Solicitors > Law
Solicitors: matrimonial law > Family law
Solid fuel
ICOM Energy Assn
Solid Fuel Assn
> + Coal headings
Solid waste
Chart Instn Wastes Mgt
Solids in bulk > Materials: management/handling
Solo musicians
Inc Soc Musicians
> + performer by name
Soluble coffee > Coffee
Solvent abuse
R Coll Psychiatrists
Re-Solv - Soc Prevention Solvent... Abuse
Solvents
Brit Coatings Fedn
Chemical Recycling Assn
Soc Chemical Ind
> + Cleaning equipment

Songbirds > Birds
Songs & songwriting
Brit Academy Composers & Songwriters
English Poetry & Song Soc
Sound > Acoustics; Insulation; Noise
Sound recording & reproduction
Assn Motion Picture Sound
Assn Profl Recording Services
Audio Engg Soc
Brit Assn Record Dealers
Brit Fedn Audio
Brit Phonographic Ind
Brit Sound Recording Assn
Confedn Transcribed Inf Services
Fedn Recorded Music Socs
Friends Pianola Inst
Inst Broadcast Sound
Inst Sound & Communications Engrs
Ir Recorded Music Assn
Music Producers Gld
Profl Lighting & Sound Assn
> + Video
Soups
Food Processors' Assn
South Downs
S Downs Soc

Southern Africa
>> Brit Cham Business Sthn Africa
Souvenirs > Commemorative items & souvenirs
Soviet Union > Russia & associated states
Soya
>> Soya Protein Assn
Space: research & exploration
>> Assn Scotland Res Astronautics
>> Assn Specialist Techl Orgs Space
>> Brit Interplanetary Soc
>> R Aeronautical Soc
>> Soc Brit Aerospace Cos
>> UK Indl Space C'ee
Space: visitors from > Unidentified flying objects
Spain
>> Anglo-Spanish Soc
>> Assn Contemporary Iberian Studies
>> Brit Cham Comm Spain
>> Hispanic & Luso-Brazilian Coun
Spain: language & literature
>> Assn Language Learning
Spas
>> Inst Swimming Pool Engrs
>> Spa Business Assn
>> Swimming Pool & Allied Trs Assn
Spastics > Cerebral palsy
Speakers
>> Assn Engl Singers & Speakers
>> Assn Speakers Clubs
>> Profl Speakers Assn
Special education > Education
Spectacles > Optical industry
Spectator seating
>> Brit Assn Seating Eqpt Suppliers
Speech
>> AFASIC
>> Assn Engl Singers & Speakers
>> Assn Lipspeakers
>> Assn Rehabilitation Communication & Oral Skills
>> Assn Speech & Language Therapists
>> Brit Aphasiology Soc
>> Brit Assn Academic Phoneticians
>> Brit Dyslexia Assn
>> Brit Stammering Assn
>> Brit Voice Assn
>> Craniofacial Soc
>> Cued Speech Assn
>> R Assn Deaf People
>> R Coll Speech & Language Therapists
>> Soc Teachers Speech & Drama
>> Speakability
>> Voice Care Network
>> + Deafness
Speedsailing > Surfing, board & speed sailing
Speedway > Motor cycling & scooter riding
Speleology > Caves & caving
Spelling reform
>> Simplified Spelling Soc
Spices & seasoning
>> Intl Gen Produce Assn
>> Seasoning & Spice Assn
>> + Flavourings
Spiders
>> Brit Arachnological Soc
>> Brit Tarantula Soc
Spill control
>> UK Spill Assn
Spina bifida & hydrocephalus
>> Assn Spina Bifida & Hydrocephalus
>> Ir Assn Spina Bifida & Hydrocephalus
>> Scot Spina Bifida Assn
>> Soc Res Hydrocephalus & Spina Bifida
Spine & spinal injury
>> Assn Light Touch Therapists
>> Assn Spinal Injury Res...
>> Nat Ankylosing Spondylitis Soc
>> National Backpain Association   (BackCare)
>> Scoliosis Assn
>> Soc Back Pain Res
>> Spinal Injuries Assn
>> Spinal Injuries Scotland
Spinning: hand
>> Assn Glds Weavers, Spinners & Dyers
Spirits > Wine headings
Spiritual healing
>> Brit Alliance Healing Assns
>> Nat Fedn Spiritual Healers

Scot Assn Spiritual Healers
>> + Healing
Spiritualism
>> Inst Spiritualist Mediums
>> Spiritualist Assn
>> Spiritualists Nat U
Spode china
>> Spode Soc
Spohr (Louis)
>> Spohr Soc
Spoken word > Audiobooks
Spondylitis > Ankylosing spondylitis
Spoonbending
>> UK Skeptics
Spoons > Cutlery
Spoons: collecting
>> Silver Spoon Club
>> UK Spoon Collectors Club
Sporting guns & rifles > Shooting
Sports
>> Brit Assn Sport & Exercise Sciences
>> Brit Olympic Assn
>> Brit Outdoor Profls Assn
>> Brit Universities Sports Assn
>> Inst Profl Sport
>> Recreation Mgrs' Assn
>> Scot Assn Local Sports Couns
>> Scot Schoolsport Fedn
>> Scot Sports Assn
>> Sports Journalists' Assn GB
>> + individual sport
Sports: country
>> Countryside Alliance
>> U Country Sports Workers
>> + individual sport
Sports: disabled & handicapped
>> Brit Deaf Sports Coun
>> Brit Paralympic Assn
>> Brit Ski Club Disabled
>> Nat Assn Swimming Clubs H'capped
>> Scot Disability Sport
>> UK Sports Assn People Learning Disability
>> Wheelpower
Sports: equipment
>> Sports & Fitness Eqpt Assn
Sports: history
>> Brit Soc Sports Hist
Sports: law
>> Brit Assn Sport & Law
Sports: medicine & therapy
>> Assn Therapy Lecturers
>> Brit Assn Sport & Exercise Medicine
>> Osteopathic Sports Care Assn
>> Scot Massage Therapists Org
>> SMAE Fellowship
>> Soc Sports Therapists
>> Sports Massage Assn
Sports: stadia
>> Fedn Stadium Communities
Sports: trade
>> Assn Play Inds
>> Assn Profl Sales Agents (Sports & Leisure Inds)
>> Fedn Sports & Play Assns
>> Sports Mfrs & Retailers Tr Assn
Sportsgrounds & synthetic surfaces
>> Brit Rootzone & Top Dressing Mfrs Assn
>> Land Drainage Contrs Assn
>> Nat Assn Agricl Contrs
>> Nat Playing Fields Assn
>> Sports & Play Construction Assn
>> Sports Turf Res Inst
>> UK Irrigation Assn
>> + Playgrounds & playgroups
Sportshall equipment
>> Sports & Fitness Eqpt Assn
Sportswear
>> Fedn Sports & Play Assns
>> + Clothing
Sprats
>> Herring Buyers Assn
>> + Fish; Fishing
Sprayed concrete > Concrete & concrete products
Spreads & spreadable products
>> Food Processors' Assn
>> Margarine & Spreads Assn

Springs
>> Inst Spring Technology
>> UK Spring Mfrs Assn
Sprinklers: automatic
>> Brit Automatic Fire Sprinkler Assn
>> Fire Sprinkler Assn
>> > + Fire protection & prevention
Sprouts > Brassicas
Square dancing
>> Brit Assn Amer Square Dance Clubs
>> Square Dance Callers Club
Squash rackets > Rackets (squash)
Stable staff
>> Stable Lads Assn
>> > + Horse: racing
Stadia (sports)
>> Fedn Stadium Communities
Staff recruitment > Employment agents & consultants
Staffordshire Blue
>> Friends Blue
Stage > Theatre
Staged fights > Fights (historic re-enactment)
Staging / Gantries > + Construction equipment
Stained glass > Glass painting
Stainless steel > Steel: special & alloy
Stairs
>> Spiral Staircase Mfrs Assn
Stairs: gates & barriers
>> Baby Products Assn
Stalin (Joseph)
>> Stalin Soc
Stalking & harassment
>> Nat Assn Support Victims Stalking & Harassment
Stammering
>> Brit Stammering Assn
>> > + Speech
Stamp collecting > Philately & postal history
Standardisation
>> Brit Standards Soc
>> BSI
>> Inst Quality Assurance
Standby ships
>> Emergency Response & Rescue Vessels Assn
>> > + Ocean industries
Starch
>> Brit Starch Ind Assn
State education > Comprehensive education
Static (electric) > Electro-static equipment
Stationery
>> Brit Office Supplies & Services Fedn
>> Brit Printing Inds Fedn
>> Envelope Makers' & Mfrg Stationers' Assn
>> Office Products & Stationery Assn
Statistics
>> Brit Classification Soc
>> Nat Assn Mathematics Advisers
>> R Statistical Soc
>> Radical Statistics Gp
>> Statistical & Social Inquiry Soc Ireland
>> Statisticians Pharmaceutical Ind
Statute law
>> Statute Law Soc
>> > + Law headings
Statutory auditors
>> Assn Authorised Public Accountants
Steam engines, boats & machinery
>> Nat Traction Engine Trust
>> Northern Mill Engine Soc
>> Paddle Steamer Presvn Soc
>> Road Locomotive Soc
>> Road Roller Assn
>> Soc Indep Roundabout Proprietors
>> Southern Counties Historic Vehicle Presvn Trust
>> Steam Boat Assn
>> Steam Plough Club
>> Transport Trust
>> Trevithick Soc
>> > + Archaeology: industrial;   Fairgrounds & equipment; Railways;
>> Shipbuilding & ship repairing
Steel
>> Brit Stainless Steel Assn
>> Cast Metals Fedn
>> Community
>> Electric Steel Makers Gld
>> Intl Steel Tr Assn
>> Nat Assn Steel Stockholders
>> Steel Construction Inst

>> Tool & High Speed Steel Suppliers Assn
>> UK Steel
>> > + Iron
Steel: bands
>> Brit Assn Steel Bands
Steel: drums > Cisterns, drums & tanks
Steel: foundries > Foundries
Steel: special & alloy
>> Aluminium Stockholders Assn
>> Assn Stainless Fastener Distbrs
Steel: stockholders > Iron & steel stockholders
Steel: tubes
>> Nat Assn Steel Stockholders
Steel: wire > Wire & wire products
Steeplejacks
>> Assn Technical Lighting & Access Specialists
Steiner (Rudolf)
>> Anthroposophical Soc
>> Biodynamic Agricl Assn
Stereoscopy
>> Stereoscopic Soc
Sterilisation > Family planning
Sterilising
>> Inst Decontamination Services
Steroids
>> Steroid Aid Gp
Stevenson (Robert Louis)
>> Robert Louis Stevenson Club
Stevenson (Ronald)
>> Ronald Stevenson Soc
Stewart family
>> Stewart Soc
Stickler syndrome
>> Stickler Syndrome Support Gp
Stickmaking
>> Brit Stickmakers Gld
>> Brit Woodcarvers Assn
Stillbirth > Maternity; Obstetrics & gynaecology
Stock (animals) > Cattle & livestock
Stock & materials control
>> Chart Inst Logistics & Transport UK
>> Ir Inst Purchasing & Materials Mgt
>> > + Materials management/handling
Stock & share dealing
>> Assn Foreign Banks
>> Assn Private Client Investment Mgrs & Stockbrokers
>> Brit Inst Securities Laws
>> Fac Actuaries Scotland
>> Gilt-Edged Market Makers' Assn
>> London Investment Banking Assn
>> London Stock Exchange
>> Securities & Investment Inst
>> > + Investment
Stockings > Hosiery
Stocktaking/auditing
>> Inst Licensed Tr Stock Auditors
>> Inst Stock Auditors & Valuers
Stokowski (Leopold)
>> Leopold Stokowski Soc
Stoma > Colitis/colostomy; Ileostomy; Urology
Stone
>> Cornish Cham Mines & Minerals
>> Men of the Stones
>> Scot Stone Liaison Gp
>> Stone Fedn
>> Stone Roofing Assn
>> UK Cast Stone Assn
>> > + Quarries & quarrying; specific types of stone
Stone masons & sculptors
>> Brit Masonry Soc
>> Master Carvers' Assn
>> Nat Assn Master Letter Carvers
>> Nat Assn Memorial Masons
Stonehenge
>> Megalithic Soc
Stones (precious) > Gemstones
Storage
>> Movers Inst
>> Nat Gld Removers & Storers
>> Self Storage Assn
Storage equipment
>> Storage Eqpt Mfrs Assn
>> Storage & Handling Eqpt Distbrs Assn
>> > + Materials: management/handling
Store cards
>> Finance & Leasing Assn
Stores: control > Stock & materials control

Stores: department > Retail trade
Storm research > Tornadoes & storm research
Storytelling
  Soc Storytelling
Stoves > Catering equipment; Domestic appliances; Fires & fireplaces
Strain injury > Repetitive strain injury; Sports: medicine & therapy
Strain measurement
  Brit Soc Strain Measurement
  Instn Mechanical Engrs
  > + Materials: technology & testing
Strapping
  Brit Tensional Strapping Assn
Strategic planning
  County Surveyors Soc
  Strategic Planning Soc
Stratigraphy
  Tertiary Res Gp
Strauss (Johann) & family
  Johann Strauss Soc
Strauss (Richard)
  Richard Strauss Soc
Straw > Hay & straw
Straw: crafts
  Gld Straw Craftsmen
Street cleaning
  Chart Instn Wastes Mgt
Street furniture > Road: lighting, markings & traffic signs
Street lighting > Road: lighting, markings & traffic signs
Street luge
  Street Sled Sports Racers
Street markets > Markets: street & cattle
Street organs > Organs & organists
Stress (physical & mental)
  Assn Stress Therapists
  Brit Assn Anger Mgt
  Brit Autogenic Soc
  Floatation Tank Assn
  Intl Stress Management Assn (UK)
  Nat Acupuncture Detoxification Assn
  Nat Coun Hypnotherapy &... Register
  Nat Coun Psychotherapists
String instruments > Musical instruments; & individual instruments
stripper/bar dancers???
  Bar Entertainment & Dance Assn
Strokes
  Stroke Assn
Structural engineering
  Instn Structural Engrs
  > + Construction industries
Structural steel > Construction industries; Steel
Structural waterproofing
  Brit Structural Waterproofing Assn
Stuart, House of
  R Stuart Soc
Students
  Assn Educ & Guardianship Intl Students
  Assn Student Residential Accommodation
  Brit Assn Health Services in Higher Educ
  Brit Educl Travel Assn
  Nat Assn Mgrs Student Services
  Nat Network Assessment Cntres
  Nat U Students UK
  > + Youth organisations
Stunts & stunt coordination
  Gld Stunt & Action Coordinators
  UK Bungee Club
  > + Fights (historic/re-enactment)
Stuttering > Stammering
Sub-aqua > Underwater; Water: sports
Sub-contractors > Building
Sub-postmasters
  Nat Fedn Sub-Postmasters
Sub-sea > Underwater headings
Subbuteo
  Table Soccer Players Assn
Submersibles
  Soc Underwater Technology Ltd
Subsidence > Foundations (buildings)
Succulents > Cacti & succulents
Sudden infant death syndrome > Cot deaths
Sugar
  Refined Sugar Assn
  Sugar Assn Lond
  Sugar Traders Assn
  UK Indl Sugar Users' Gp
Sugar beet seed
  Brit Sugar Beet Seed Producers Assn

Sugarcraft
  Brit Sugarcraft Gld
Suggestion schemes
  Ideas UK
Suggestopedia
  Soc Effective Affective Learning
Suicide
  Alert Euthanasia
  Care not Killing Alliance
  Compassionate Friends
  Samaritans
Suitcases > Travel goods & accessories
Sullivan (Sir Arthur Seymour)
  Gilbert & Sullivan Soc
  Sir Arthur Sullivan Soc
Sulphuric acid
  Chemical Inds Assn
Sunbeds
  Sunbed Assn
Sunblinds > Windows: blinds & shutters
Sunday observance
  Lord's Day Observance Soc
Sundials
  Brit Sundial Soc
Supermarkets
  Inst Grocery Distbn
  NISA Today's Holdings Ltd
  > + Grocery & provision trade
Supervisory management
  Inst Leadership & Mgt
Supply > Purchasing & supply
Support vessels
  Chamber Shipping
Surface coatings > Coatings
Surfactants
  Brit Assn Chemical Specialities
  Soc Chemical Ind
Surfing, board & speed sailing
  Brit Bodyboarding Club
  Brit Kite Surfing Assn
  Brit Land Speedsail Assn
  Brit Surfing Assn
  R Yachting Assn
  Scot Surfing Fedn
  UK Windsurfing Assn
Surgery
  Assn Surgeons
  Assn Surgeons in Training
  Brit Assn Day Surgery
  Brit Assn Emergency Medicine
  Brit Assn Endocrine Surgeons
  Brit Assn Plastic, Reconstructive & Aesthetic Surgeons
  Brit Soc Surgery Hand
  College Emergency Medicine
  Medical Soc Lond
  R Coll Physicians & Surgeons Glasgow
  R Coll Surgeons Edinburgh
  R Coll Surgeons England
  R Coll Surgeons Ireland
  Soc Academic & Res Surgery
  > + specific branches
Surgical equipment
  Assn Brit Healthcare Inds
  Brit Healthcare Trs Assn
  Cutlery & Allied Trs Res Assn
  Surgical Dressings Mfrs Assn
Surgical technology
  Brit Assn Prosthetists & Orthotists
Surtees (Robert Smith)
  R S Surtees Soc
Surveying
  Assn Bldg Engrs
  Assn Consultant Approved Inspectors
  Assn Geotechnical & Geoenvironmental Specialists
  Brit Cartographic Soc
  Chart Inst Bldg
  Chief Bldg Surveyors Soc
  District Surveyors Assn Ltd
  Ground Forum
  Hydrographic Soc UK
  Inst Specialist Surveyors & Engrs
  Instn Civil Engg Surveyors
  Ir Instn Surveyors
  London Dist Surveyors Assn
  Property Consultants Soc
  R Instn Chart Surveyors
  Rating Surveyors Assn

Soc Chart Surveyors [IRL]
            UK Land & Hydrographic Survey Assn
Suspended access equipment & cradles > Cradles & suspended platforms
Suspended ceilings > Ceilings
Sussex Downs
            S Downs Soc
Sutures > Surgical equipment
Suzuki (Dr Shinicki)
            Brit Suzuki Inst
Swaziland
            Swaziland Soc
Sweden
            Anglo-Swedish Soc
            Brit Swedish Cham Comm Sweden
            Swedish Cham Comm UK
Swedenborg (Emanuel)
            Swedenborg Soc
Sweet peas
            N England Rose, Carnation. . . Horticl Soc
            Nat Sweet Pea Soc
Sweets > Confectionery
Swimming & diving
            Amat Swimming Assn
            Amat Swimming Fedn
            Brit Long Distance Swimming Assn
            Great Britain Diving Fedn
            Halliwick Assn Swimming Therapy
            Inst Swimming Teachers & Coaches
            Nat Assn Swimming Clubs H'capped
            Scot Swimming
            Swimming Teachers Assn
            Synchronised Swimming Coaches Assn
            Welsh Amat Swimming Assn
            > + Water: sports
Swimming pools
            Inst Sport & Recreation Mgt
            Inst Swimming Pool Engrs
            Swimming Pool & Allied Trs Assn
Swing dance
            London Swing Dance Soc
            > + Dancing
Switchgear (electrical)
            BEAMA
Switzerland
            Brit-Swiss Cham Comm [Lond]
            Brit-Swiss Cham Comm [Switzerland]
            Fedn Swiss Socs UK
Swordplay > Fencing (sport)
Synagogues
            Fedn Synagogues
            > + Jewish organisations
Synchronised swimming
            Amat Swimming Assn
            Synchronised Swimming Coaches Assn
            > + Swimming & diving
Synthetic surfaces > Sportsgrounds & synthetic surfaces
Systematics
            Systematics Assn

T

Table football
            Brit Foosball Assn
            Table Soccer Players Assn
Table tennis
            English Table Tennis Assn
            Scot Table Tennis Assn
            Table Tennis Assn Wales
Table wines > Wines
Tableware
            Brit Ceramic Confedn
            > + Cutlery; Glass; Pottery
Taekwondo > Martial arts
Tai Chi > Martial arts
Tailoring
            Brit Clothing Ind Assn
            Master Craftsmen's Assn
Taiwan
            Brit Cham Comm Taipei
Takeaway & fast food
            Chinese Takeaway Assn (UK)
            Nationwide Caterers Assn

Talipes (club foot)
            STEPS. . .
            > + Children: handicapped
Tall people
            Tall Persons Club
            > + Growth
Tangsoodo > Martial arts
Tank storage
            Tank Storage Assn
            > + Cisterns, drums & tanks
Tankers
            Inst Chart Shipbrokers
Tanning > Leather headings; Sunbeds
Tanzania
            Britain-Tanzania Soc
Tape recording > Sound recording & reproduction
Tarantulas
            Brit Tarantula Soc
Target archery > Archery
Target shooting > Pistol shooting; Rifle shooting
Tarot
            Brit Astrological & Psychic Soc
Tarpaulins
            Performance Textiles Assn
Tatting
            Lace Soc
            Ring of Tatters
Tattooing
            Brit Tattoo Artists Fedn
            Tattoo Club
Taxation
            Assn Corporate Trustees
            Assn Taxation Technicians
            Charities' Tax Reform Gp
            Chart Inst Taxation
            EIS Assn
            Fac Taxation Consultants & Advisers
            Inst Fiscal Studies
            Inst Indirect Taxation
            Ir Taxation Inst
            IsItFair
            Low Incomes Tax Reform Gp
            Profl Contrs Gp
            Taxpayers Alliance
            U Senior Revenue Officials
            VAT Practitioners Gp
Taxidermy
            Gld Taxidermists
Taxis & minicabs
            Ir Taxi Drivers' Fedn
            Licensed Taxi Drivers' Assn
            London Motor Cab Proprietors' Assn
            London Private Hire Car Assn
            Nat Private Hire Assn
            Nat Taxi Assn
            Owner Drivers Soc
            Soc Profl Licensed Taxi Drivers
            > + Motor vehicles: hire
Tay-Sachs disease
            Tay-Sachs & Allied Diseases Assn
Tea
            Tea Buying Brokers Assn Lond
            UK Tea Assn
Teachers
            Assn Christian Teachers
            Assn Promotion Quality TESOL Educ
            Assn Secondary Teachers, Ireland
            Assn Teachers & Lecturers
            Assn University Teachers
            Educl Inst Scotland
            Ir Fedn University Teachers
            Ir Nat Teachers Org
            League Exchange C'wealth Teachers
            Nat Assn Schoolmasters U Women Teachers
            Nat Assn Staff Devt in Post 16 Sector
            Nat Assn Teachers Travellers
            Nat U Teachers
            Profl Assn Teachers
            Scot Secondary Teachers' Assn
            Soc Assistants Teaching Preparatory Schools
            Soc Schoolmasters & Schoolmistresses
            Teachers' U Ireland
            Ulster Teachers U
            > + Education; for teachers of specific subjects see subject taught
Teaching support staff
            Profls Allied Teaching

Technical drawing
     Assn Illustrators
Technical education
     Assn Colleges
     Design & Technology Assn
     Nat Assn Advisers. . . Design & Technology
     Principals' Profl Coun
Technical information > Information: services & technology
Technical terminology
     BSI
Technical writing & publishing
     Assn Brit Science Writers
     Inst Scientific & Technical Communicators
The Technion, Israel
     Brit Technion Soc
Technology parks > Science parks
Technology transfer
     Inst Intl Licensing Practitioners
     Licensing Executives Soc
     PERA
     UK Science Park Assn
Tectonics
     Geological Soc
Teeth
     Bone Res Soc
     > + Dentistry
Tegestology
     Brit Beermat Collectors' Soc
Telecommunications
     ALTO [IRL]
     Assn Cost Mgt Consultants
     Communication Workers U
     Communications Mgt Assn
     CONNECT
     Customer Contact Assn
     Fedn Communication Services
     Intellect, the Information Technology, Telecommunications &
     Electronics
     Nat Jt Utilities Gp
     Premium Rate Assn
     SELECT
     Soc Cable Telecommunication Engrs
     Telecommunications Ind Assn
     Telecommunications & Internet Fedn [IRL]
     Telecommunications Users Assn
     UK Indl Space C'ee
     > + Electronic: industry & engineering
Telecommunications: history
     Telecommunications Heritage Gp
Telecottages
     Telework Assn
Telepathy > Paranormal & psychical research
Telephone cables > Electric: cable & conduit
Telephones > Mobile phones; Telecommunications
Teletext & videotex
     Soc Public Inf Networks
Television
     Animal Welfare Filming Fedn
     Assn Community TV Operators
     Assn Studio & Production Eqpt Companies
     BKSTS
     Brit Academy Film & TV Arts
     Brit Film Inst
     Broadcasting, Entertainment Cinematograph. . .U
     Directors Gld
     Gld TV Cameramen
     Narrow Bandwidth TV Assn
     R Television Soc
     Soc TV Lighting Directors
     TV & Radio Inds Club
     Voice Listener & Viewer
     > + Audio visual aids & equipment
Television: advertising > Advertising: television & screen
Television: cable > Cable & satellite communications
Television: closed circuit
     Brit Security Ind Assn
     Fibreoptic Ind Assn
     Nat Security Inspectorate
Television: engineering > Electronic: industry & engineering
Television: history
     Brit Vintage Wireless Soc
Television: manufacturing > Electronic: industry & engineering
Television: production
     Gld Brit Film & TV Editors
     Producers Alliance Cinema & TV
     Production Mgrs Assn
Television: relay > Cable & satellite communications

Television: rental > Radio & TV: rental
Television: trade > Radio & TV: trade
Teleworkers
     Telework Assn
Temperance
     Brit Nat Temperance League
     Brit Temperance Soc
     UK Alliance
Temperature controlled storage
     Assn Meat Inspectors
     Brit Refrigeration Assn
     Cold Storage & Distbn Fedn
     Nat Assn Brit Market Authorities
     UK Warehousing Assn
Temperature controlled transport
     Cambridge Refrigeration Technology
     Transfrigoroute UK
Tenants & residents
     Chart Inst Housing
     Fedn Private Residents' Assns
     Nat Assn Tenants Orgs [IRL]
     Nat U Residents' Assns
     Tenant Farmers' Assn
     Tenants & Residents Orgs England
     > + Property & land owners
Tennis
     Assn Brit Tennis Officials
     Brit Tennis Coaches Assn
     Ir Real Tennis Assn
     Lawn Tennis Assn
     Lawn Tennis Writers Assn
     Tennis & Rackets Assn
     Tennis Scotland
     Tennis Wales
     Vets' Tennis Assn
Tennis: courts & equipment
     Sports & Play Construction Assn
Tennyson (Alfred, Lord)
     Tennyson Soc
Tenpin bowling > Bowling
Tensional strapping > Strapping
Tents & marquees
     Performance Textiles Assn
Terminals (ports) > Ports
Terrapins > Chelonia
Terrazzo-mosaic
     Nat Fedn Terrazzo Marble & Mosaic Specialists
Tertiary colleges > Adult education
Tertiary era geology
     Tertiary Res Gp
     > + Geology
Test cards (TV)
     Test Card Circle
Test pilots
     R Aeronautical Soc
     > + Aviation: pilots, officers & crew

Testing laboratories
     Assn Consulting Scientists
     > + Materials: technology & testing
Testing methods
     AIRTO
Testing (non-destructive) > Materials: technology & testing
Textile: conservation > Costume history, design & conservation
Textile: design
     Chart Soc Designers
     Register Apparel & Textile Designers
     Textile Inst Intl
     Textile Soc
Textile: industry & trade
     ACG Ltd (Arts Centre Gp)
     ASBCI - Forum Clothing & Textiles
     Brit Apparel & Textile Confedn
     Brit Interior Textiles Assn
     Brit Narrow Fabrics Assn
     Brit Polyolefin Textiles Assn
     Brit Textile Machinery Assn
     Brit Textile Technology Gp
     Brit Throwsters Assn
     Confedn Brit Wool Textiles
     Ir Clothing & Textiles Alliance
     Textile Finishers Assn
     Textile Inst Intl
     UK Textile Laboratory Forum
     Wales Craft Coun
     Wallcovering Distbrs Assn
     > + specific textiles

© CBD Research Ltd · Beckenham · BR3 5JS · Tel 020 8650 7745 · Fax 020 8650 0768 · E-mail cbd@cbdresearch.com · www.cbdresearch.com

Textile: rental
>>>>Textile Services Assn
Textured coatings > Concrete & concrete products
Thai boxing > Martial arts
Thailand
>>>>Anglo-Thai Soc
>>>>Brit Cham Comm Thailand
Thalassaemia
>>>>UK Thalassaemia Soc
Thalidomide
>>>>Thalidomide Soc
Thames
>>>>River Thames Soc
>>>>Thames Boating Trs Assn
Thatching & thatched roofs
>>>>Nat Soc Master Thatchers
Theatre
>>>>Assn Brit Theatre Technicians
>>>>Broadcasting, Entertainment Cinematograph. . .U
>>>>Conf Drama Schools
>>>>Directors Gld
>>>>Drama Assn Wales
>>>>Drama League Ireland
>>>>Fedn Scot Theatre
>>>>Gld Drama Adjudicators
>>>>Gld Profl Teachers Dancing
>>>>Indep Theatre Coun
>>>>Inst Contemporary Arts
>>>>Little Theatre Gld
>>>>Nat Assn Teaching Drama
>>>>Nat Drama
>>>>Nat Operatic & Dramatic Assn
>>>>Player-Playwrights
>>>>R Academy Dramatic Art
>>>>R Scot Academy Music & Drama
>>>>Religious Drama Soc
>>>>Scot Community Drama Assn
>>>>Soc Brit Theatre Designers
>>>>Soc Teachers Speech & Drama
>>>>Soc Theatre Consultants
>>>>Stage Mgt Assn
>>>>UK Dance Drama Fedn
>>>>Writers' Gld
>>>>> + Entertainment;   Music: hall
Theatre: history
>>>>Cinema Theatre Assn
>>>>Malone Soc
>>>>Soc Theatre Res
Theatre: lighting
>>>>Assn Lighting Designers
>>>>Profl Lighting & Sound Assn
Theatre: model
>>>>Brit Puppet & Model Theatre Gld
Theatre: young people
>>>>Nat Assn Youth Drama [IRL]
>>>>Nat Assn Youth Theatres
>>>>Nat Drama
>>>>Scot Community Drama Assn
Theology > Religion
Theosophy
>>>>Theosophical Soc England
Therapeutic communities
>>>>Assn Therapeutic Communities
>>>>> + Mental health
Therapeutic education
>>>>Nat Assn Therapeutic Educ
>>>>> + Education headings
Therapy
>>>>Assn Physical & Natural Therapists
>>>>Assn Rational Emotive Behaviour Therapy
>>>>Assn Therapy Lecturers
>>>>> + individual forms of therapy
Thermal insulation > Insulation
Thermal spraying
>>>>Thermal Spraying & Surface Engg Assn
>>>>> + Coatings
Thermal waters
>>>>Spa Business Assn
Thermoplastics > Plastics
Thermometers
>>>>Pressure Gauge & Dial Thermometer Assn
Thimbles
>>>>Thimble Soc Lond
Thirkell (Angela)
>>>>Angela Thirkell Soc
Thomas (Dylan Marlais)
>>>>Dylan Thomas Soc

Thomas ([Philip] Edward)
>>>>Edward Thomas Fellowship
>>>>Friends Dymock Poets
Thomson (Alexander)
>>>>Alexander Thomson Soc
Thoracic diseases
>>>>Brit Assn Lung Research
>>>>Pulmonary Hypertension Assn
>>>>Sarcoidosis & Intestitial Lung Assn
>>>>Soc Cardiothoracic Surgery
>>>>Stroke Assn
Throwsters
>>>>Brit Throwsters Assn
Throwsticks
>>>>Brit Boomerang Soc
Thunderstorms
>>>>Tornado & Storm Res Org
Thyroid disease
>>>>Thyroid Eye Disease Charitable Trust
Tickets
>>>>Omnibus Soc
>>>>Token Corresponding Soc
>>>>Transport Ticket Soc
Tidal modelling
Tiddlywinks
>>>>English Tiddlywinks Assn
Ties > Collars & ties
Tights > Hosiery
Tiles (floor & wall)
>>>>Cork Ind Fedn
>>>>Nat Fedn Terrazzo Marble & Mosaic Specialists
>>>>Tile Assn
>>>>Tiles & Architectural Ceramics Soc
Tiling > Roofing
Timber
>>>>Assn Timber Growers & Forestry Profls
>>>>Glued Laminated Timber Assn
>>>>N W Timber Tr Assn
>>>>Nat Sawmilling Assn
>>>>NI Timber Tr Assn
>>>>Scot Timber Tr Assn
>>>>Timber Arbitrators Assn
>>>>Timber Decking Assn
>>>>Timber Tr Fedn
>>>>TRADA Technology
>>>>UK Forest Products Assn
>>>>> + Forestry; Wood
Timber buildings
>>>>Modular & Portable Bldg Assn
>>>>TRADA Technology
>>>>UK Timber Frame Assn
Timber containers > Packaging
Timber decking
>>>>Timber Decking Assn
Timber preserving
>>>>Brit Wood Preserving & Damp-proofing Assn
Timber roofing > Roofing
Time recording > Horology
Timeshare industry
>>>>Timeshare Consumers Assn
>>>>> + Property & landowners
Tin boxes > Metal: boxes
Tin cans > Cans & canning
Tin mining > Mining
Tin plate
Tinnitus
>>>>Brit Tinnitus Assn
Tipping vehicles
Tissue banking
>>>>Brit Assn Tissue Banking
Tissue paper
>>>>Confedn Paper Inds
>>>>> + Paper & paper products
Tissue viability
>>>>Tissue Viability Soc
Titanic (the RMS)
>>>>Brit Titanic Soc
Toastmasters & masters of ceremonies
>>>>Brit Profl Toastmasters Authority
>>>>Gld Intl Profl Toastmasters
>>>>Gld Profl Toastmasters
>>>>Nat Assn Toastmasters
>>>>Toastmasters England
>>>>Toastmasters GB
>>>>Toastmasters Royal Occasions
Tobacco
>>>>Air Cleaner Mfrs Assn

Assn Indep Tobacco Specialists
Cigarette Packet Collectors Club
Imported Tobacco Products Advy Coun
Retail Confectioners & Tobacconists Assn
Tobacco Alliance
Tobacco Ind Emplrs Assn
Tobacco Mfrs' Assn
Whls Confectionery & Tobacco Alliance
> + Cigars & cigarettes;   Pipes: tobacco   Smoking

Toboggan & luge racing/riding
Brit Bob Skeleton Assn
Brit Bobsleigh Assn
Great Britain Luge Assn
Street Sled Sports Racers

Toiletries
Cosmetic, Toiletry & Perfumery Assn

Toilets (public)
Brit Toilet Assn

Tokens
Token Corresponding Soc

Tolkien (J R R)
Tolkien Soc

Tomatoes
Brit Tomato Growers Assn
> + Vegetable: growing

Tonic Sol-fa
Brit Kodály Academy
Curwen Inst
> + Music: teaching

Tools
Brit Compressed Air Soc
Brit Hardmetal & Engineers' Cutting Tool Assn
Brit Hardware Fedn
Cutlery & Allied Trs Res Assn
Fedn Brit Hand Tool Mfrs
Gauge & Tool Makers Assn
Portable Electric Tool Mfrs Assn
Power Fastenings Assn
Tool & High Speed Steel Suppliers Assn
Tools Self Reliance
> + specific tool

Tools: historic
Museum Garden Hist
Tool & Trs Hist Soc
Vintage Horticl & Garden Machinery Club

Top dressing materials
Brit Rootzone & Top Dressing Mfrs Assn

Tornadoes & storm research
Tornado & Storm Res Org

Tortoises > Chelonia

Tourette syndrome
Tourette Syndrome (UK) Assn

Tourism > Travel & tourism

Tourist guides
Assn Profl Tourist Guides

Towage & salvage
Brit Tugowners Assn

Towbars
Nat Trailer & Towing Assn

Tower cranes > Cranes

Tower fabricators
Brit Constructional Steelwork Assn
Prefabricated Access Suppliers' & Mfrs' Assn

Town & country planning
Assn Project Safety
Assn Small Historic Towns & Villages
Assn Town Centre Mgt
English Historic Towns Forum
Ir Planning Inst
Outdoor Advertising Coun
Planning Officers Soc
R Town Planning Inst
Regional Studies Assn
ROOM
Town & Country Planning Assn

Town criers
Ancient & Honourable Gld Town Criers
Loyal Company Town Criers

Townswomen
Townswomen's Glds

Towpaths > Footpaths & rights of way

Tow-ropes > Cordage, rope & twine

Toxicology
Brit Soc Toxicological Pathologists
Brit Toxicology Soc
Fund Replacement Animals Med Experiments
Soc Medicines Res

Soc Pharmaceutical Medicine
UK Envtl Mutagen Soc

Toxophily > Archery

Toys
Brit Toy & Hobby Assn
Brit Toy Importers Assn
Brit Toymakers Gld
Doll Club GB
Nat Assn Toy & Leisure Libraries
Toy Retailers Assn

Trace heating
Electric Trace Heating Ind Coun

Tracheostomy
Aid Children with Tracheostomies
Tracheo-Oesophageal Fistula Support

Track events > Athletics

Tracking (cars)
Mobile Electronics & Security Fedn

Tracks (sports) > Sportsgrounds & synthetic surfaces

Traction engines > Steam engines, boats & machinery;   Fairgrounds & equipment

Tractors > Agriculture: machinery

Trade > Commerce; Export & import; individual trades

Trade associations
Inst Assn Mgt
Trade Assn Forum

Trade marks & names > Patents & trade marks

Trade unions
Amicus
Communication Workers U
Fedn Entertainment Us
Gen Fedn Tr Us
Ir Conf Profl & Service Assns
Ir Congress Tr Us
Ir Municipal, Public & Civil TU
Rail, Maritime & Transport U
Scot Trs U Congress
SIPTU [IRL]
Trades U Congress
Transport & Gen Workers' U
Unison
Wales Tr U Congress

Trading standards
Soc Chief Officers Trading Standards Scotland
Trading Standards Inst
> + Consumer affairs & protection

Traffic: accidents > Accidents; Road safety & control

Traffic: control
ITS UK
Traffic Mgt Contrs Assn
> + Road safety & control; Transport

Traffic: gyratory systems
UK Roundabout Appreciation Soc
> + Road: markings, lighting & traffic signs

Traffic: signs > Road: lighting, markings & traffic signs; Signs

Trail riding
Trail Riders Fellowship

Trailers: motor vehicle
Comml Trailer Assn
Nat Trailer & Towing Assn
Org Horsebox & Trailer Owners

Training (industrial) > Occupational training & education

Trains > Railways

Trampolining > Gymnastics

Tramways & trams
Light Rail Transit Assn
Omnibus Soc
Rly & Canal Histl Soc
Tramway & Light Rly Soc
Tramway Museum Soc
> + Railways: light

Tranquilisers
Nat Org Phobias, Anxiety. . .Inf & Care

Transactional analysis
Inst Transactional Analysis

Transformers > Electrical industry & engineering

Transfusion science
Brit Blood Transfusion Soc
> + Haematology

Transit shed operators
Brit Intl Freight Assn

Translation & interpretation
Assn Police & Court Interpreters
Assn Translation Companies
Chart Inst Linguists
Conf Interpreters Gp
Inst Translation & Interpreting

© CBD Research Ltd · Beckenham · BR3 5JS · Tel 020 8650 7745 · Fax 020 8650 0768 · E-mail cbd@cbdresearch.com · www.cbdresearch.com

Ir Translators & Interpreters Assn
Translators Assn
> + Languages
Transmission towers > Tower fabricators
Transplant surgery
Brit Transplantation Soc
UK Transplant Co-ordinators Assn
> + Organ donors
Transport
Assn Brit Transport & Engg Museums
Brit Intl Freight Assn
Brit Transport Officers Gld
Chart Inst Logistics & Transport Ireland
Chart Inst Logistics & Transport UK
Community Transport Assn
ETA Services Ltd
Freight Transport Assn
Hovercraft Museum Trust
Inst Highway Inc Engrs
Inst Transport Administration
Inst Transport Mgt
Instn Civil Engrs
Instn Engg & Technology
Instn Highways & Transportation
Ir Assn Intl Express Carriers
Rail, Maritime & Transport U
Road Transport Fleet Data Soc
Scot Transport Studies Gp
Transform Scotland
Transport & Gen Workers' U
Transport 2000 Ltd
Transport Salaried Staffs Assn
Transport Ticket Soc
Transport-Watch
> + individual forms of transport
Transport: (of animals) > Animals: transportation
Transport: history
Birmingham Transport Histl Gp
Rly & Canal Histl Soc
Roads & Road Transport Hist Assn
Transport Trust
> + specific forms of transport
Transport: security
Brit Security Ind Assn
> + Security
Transsexuality & transvestism
Beaumont Soc
Gender Trust
Travel & tourism
Advantage
Assn Brit Tour Operators France
Assn Brit Travel Agents
Assn Indep Tour Operators
Assn Leading Visitor Attractions
Assn Leisure Ind Profls
Assn Nat Tourist Office Representatives
Assn Scot Visitor Attractions
Baltic Air Charter Assn
Brit Gld Travel Writers
Brit Resorts & Destinations Assn
Business Tourism Scotland
Confedn Tourism, Hotel & Catering Mgt
Eventia
Fedn Tour Operators
Gld Travel Mgt Cos
Gld Travel & Tourism
Group Travel Organisers Assn
Inst Travel Mgt
Inst Travel & Tourism
Ir Tourist Ind Confedn
Ir Travel Agents Assn
Outdoor Writers' Gld
Scot Tourism Forum
Soc Incentive & Travel Executives
Tourism for All
Tourism Alliance
Tourism Concern
Tourism Mgt Inst
Tourism Soc
Travel Trust Assn
UKinbound
Worldchoice
> + individual modes of travel
Travel & tourism: educational
Brit Educl Travel Assn

Travel & tourism: guides
Gld Registered Tourist Guides
Scot Tourist Guides Assn
Travel & tourism: health
Brit Travel Health Assn
Travel goods & accessories
Brit Travelgoods & Accessories Assn
Travelling people > Gypsies & travelling people
Treacher Collins
Treacher Collins Family Support Gp
Treasurers > Accountancy;   Local government: officers
Trees
Ancient Tree Forum
Arboricultural Assn
Brit Christmas Tree Growers Assn
Horticultural Trs Assn
Scot Soc Crop Res
Tree Coun Ireland
> + Forestry
Trenchless technology
Soc Brit Water & Wastewater Inds
UK Soc Trenchless Technology
Triathlon
Brit Triathlon Assn
Tribology > Friction
Trichology
Inst Trichologists
> + Hairdressing
Trichotillomania
Hairline Intl
Tricycling
Assn Pioneer Motor Cyclists
Tricycle Assn
> + Cycles & motorcycles
Tridentine Mass
Latin Mass Soc
Trigeminal neuralgia > Neuralgia
Tripedressing
Nat Assn Tripe Dressers
Trolleybuses
Brit Trolleybus Soc
Nat Trolleybus Assn
Omnibus Soc
Trollope (Anthony)
Trollope Soc
Trombones
Brit Trombone Soc

Tropical crops
Tropical Growers' Assn
Tropical environment
Soc Envtl Exploration
Tropical fish > Fish: tropical & ornamental
Tropical medicine
R Soc Tropical Medicine & Hygiene
> + Medicine
Troughed belt conveyors
Materials Handling Engrs Assn
Trout > Salmon & trout
Trucks > Fork-lift trucks; Lifting & loading equipment
Trucks: racing
Brit Truck Racing Assn
Trusts, trusteeship & estate planning
Assn Corporate Trustees
Assn Member-Directed Pension Schemes
Insolvency Practitioners Assn
Soc Trust & Estate Practitioners
Soc Will Writers & Estate Planning Practitioners
> + Investment; Pensions
TT racing
TT Riders Assn
> + Motor cycling & scooter riding
Tuberculosis > Thoracic diseases
Tuberous sclerosis > Sclerosis
Tubes > Pipes
Tug of war
Scot Tug-of-War Assn
Tug of War Assn
Tugs
Brit Tugowners Assn
Tumours & tumerous diseases > Oncology
Tunnel lining
Brit Precast Concrete Fedn
Tunnelling & shaft sinking
Brit Tunnelling Soc
Ground Forum
Inst Explosives Engrs

Pipe Jacking Assn
Subterranea Britannica
Turbines > Gas engines & turbines;   Renewable energy
Turf
Agricl Engrs Assn
Brit Turf & Landscape Irrigation Assn
Land Drainage Contrs Assn
Register Indep Profl Turfgrass Agronomists
Turfgrass Growers Assn
> + Grass & grassland; Sportsgrounds & synthetic surfaces
Turkey
Anglo-Turkish Soc
Brit Cham Comm Turkey
Middle East Assn
Turkeys (birds)
Brit Poultry Coun
Traditional Farmfresh Turkey Assn
Turkey Club
> + Poultry
Turnaround specialists
Assn Business Recovery Profls
Soc Turnaround Professionals
Turned parts > Fasteners & turned
Turner (Joseph Mallord William)
Indep Turner SocIndep   Turner Soc
Turner Soc
Turner syndrome
Turner Syndrome Support Soc
Turning > Woodworking
Turtles > Chelonia
Tutors
Assn Local Hist Tutors
Assn Tutors
Tweed > Wool & wool products
Twine > Cordage, ropes & twine
Twins & multiple births
Multiple Births Foundation
Twins & Mult Births Assn
UK Twin to Twin Transfusion Syndrome Assn
Typography > Printing
Tyres
Brit Rubber Mfrs Assn
Imported Tyre Mfrs Assn
Indep Tyre Distbrs Network
Indl Tyre Assn
Ir Tyre Ind Assn
Nat Tyre Distbrs Assn
Retread Mfrs Assn
Tyre Ind Coun

U

UFOs > Unidentified flying objects
Ukuleles & banjos
Ukulele Soc
Ulcers
Tissue Viability Soc
Ulster-Scots language
Ulster-Scots Language Soc
Ultimate (sport)
UK Ultimate Assn
Ultrasound
Brit Med Ultrasound Soc
Umbrellas
Umpires > Cricket
Underfelt > Felt
Underfloor heating > Heating
Underground (the London)
London Underground Rly Soc
> + Railways: history & preservation
Underground machinery > Mining: equipment
Underground structures
Subterranea Britannica
Underlay (carpet)
Needleloom Underlay Mfrs' Assn
Underpinning
ASUCplus
> Foundations (buildings)
Underwater engineering & research
Histl Diving Soc
Inst Explosives Engrs
Inst Marine Engg, Science & Technology
Nautical Archaeology Soc
Soc Underwater Technology Ltd

Subsea UK
> + Marine: biology & biochemistry; Ocean industries
Underwater photography
Gld Brit Camera Technicians
> + Photography
Underwater sports > Water: sports; individual sport
Underwriting > Insurance
Unicycles
UK Unicycle Fedn
> + Cycles & motor cycles
Unidentified flying objects
Anomalous Phenomena Research Agency
Assn Scientific Study Anomalous Phenomena
Brit UFO Res Assn
Uniforms & protective clothing > Protective clothing/equipment
Unions > Trade unions
Unit trusts > Investment
Unitarian Church
Unitarian Hist Soc
United Nations
Brit Assn Former UN Civil Servants
Utd Nations Assn GB & NI
United Reformed Church
Utd Reformed Church Hist Soc
> + Congregational Church; Presbyterian Church
United States > USA
Universities
Assn C'wealth Universities
Assn University Administrators
Assn University Res & Ind Links
Assn University Teachers
Brit Universities Sports Assn
Ir Universities Assn
Universities & Colls Emplrs' Assn
Universities Scotland
Universities UK
University students > Students
Unpasteurised milk
Assn Unpasteurised Milk Producers
Campaign Real Milk
> + Dairying
Unvented heating systems
Manufacturers Domestic Unvented Systems
Upholstery
Assn Master Upholsterers & Soft Furnishers
Nat Carpet Cleaners Assn
Nat Fillings Assn
Urban studies > Environment
Urethane foam > Plastics: foam
Urology
Assn Continence Advice
Brit Assn Urological Surgeons
Cystitis & Overactive Bladder Foundation
Nat Advy Service Parents Children with a Stoma
Urostomy Assn
> + Genito-urinary medicine
Uruguay
Brit Uruguayan Soc
Cámara Comercio Uruguayo-Británica
USA
Brit Assn Amer Studies
Brit N Amer Res Assn
English Speaking U C'wealth
Pilgrims (The)
USSR
Stalin Soc
> + Russia & associated states; Slavonic languages & culture
Uveitis
Uveitis Inf Gp

V

Vaccination
Assn Brit Pharmaceutical Ind
Justice Awareness & Basic Support
Vacuum technology
Brit Compressed Air Soc
Brit Vacuum Coun
Solids Handling & Processing Assn
Valuation
Assn Art & Antique Dealers
Assn Chief Estates Surveyors... Local Govt
Assn Valuers Licensed Property
Central Assn Agricl Valuers

© CBD Research Ltd · Beckenham · BR3 5JS · Tel 020 8650 7745 · Fax 020 8650 0768 · E-mail cbd@cbdresearch.com · www.cbdresearch.com

Indep Valuers Assn
Inst Profl Auctioneers & Valuers [IRL]
Inst Revenues, Rating & Valuation
Inst Stock Auditors & Valuers
Ir Auctioneers & Valuers Inst
Nat Assn Valuers & Auctioneers
Property Consultants Soc
Scot Assessors' Assn
Soc Fine Art Auctioneers & Valuers
Soc Share & Business Valuers
> + Rating
Value management
Inst Value Mgt
Valves & actuators
BEAMA
Brit Valve & Actuator Assn
Solids Handling & Processing Assn
> + Electronic: industry & engineering
Vampires > Horror literature
Variety theatre > Music: hall
VAT (value added tax)
VAT Practitioners Gp
> + Taxation
Veganism > Vegetarianism & veganism
Vegetables: growing
Horticulture Res Intl Assn
Ir Comml Horticl Assn
Nat Vegetable Soc
Processed Vegetable Growers Assn
Processors & Growers Res Org
> + individual vegetable
Vegetables: oils > Edible oils & fats
Vegetables: preservation
UK Assn Frozen Food Producers
Vegetables: protein
Help Intl Plant Protein Org
Soya Protein Assn
Vegetables: trade
Fresh Produce Consortium
Vegetarianism & veganism
Vegan Soc
Vegetarian Soc
Vegetarian Soc Ireland
Vehicles > All terrain vehicles; Electric transport; Military vehicles; Motor
Vehicle number plates > Number plates
Vending machines > Automatic vending
Venereal disease > Genito-urinary medicine
Venezuela
Anglo-Venezuelan Soc
Cámara Venezolana Británica Comercio
Venison
Assn Deer Mgt Gps
Brit Deer Farmers Assn
> + Deer; Meat
Ventilating > Air: conditioning & ventilating
Venture capital
BVCA
Venues > Arenas; Corporate hospitality
Verbatim reporting
Brit Inst Verbatim Reporters
> + Shorthand writing
Verse > Poetry
Veteran cars > Motor vehicles: historic
Veteran horses & ponies
Veteran Horse Soc
Veterans > Ex-service organisations
Veterinary medicine
Animal Health Distbrs Assn
Animal Medicines Training Regulatory Authority
Animal & Plant Health Assn [IRL]
Brit Veterinary Hospitals Assn
Equine Shiatsu Assn
Equine Sports Massage Assn
Nat Office Animal Health
> + specific animal
Veterinary science
Brit Assn Homoeopathic Veterinary Surgeons
Brit Small Animal Veterinary Assn
Brit Soc Immunology
Brit Veterinary Assn
Brit Veterinary Nursing Assn
R Coll Veterinary Surgeons
Veterinary Assn Arbitration & Jurisprudence
Veterinary Hist Soc
Veterinary Ireland
Veterinary tranquiliser dart recovery
Fedn Indep Detectorists

Vexillology > Flags, banners & bunting
Vibration
Assn Noise Consultants
Engg Integrity Soc
Heating, Ventilating & Air Conditioning Mfrs' Assn
Materials Components Developing & Testing Assn
Vibration healing
Brit Flower & Vibrational Essences Assn
Crystal & Healing Fedn
Victims of accidents > Accidents: victims
Victims of crime > Crime & crime prevention; Domestic violence
Victoria Cross
Victoria Cross & George Cross Assn
Victuallers > Meat;   Wines & spirits: trade
Vicuñas > Camelids
Video
Advertising Producers Assn
Assn Motion Picture Sound
Assn Profl Videomakers
Brit Interactive Media Assn
Brit Sound Recording Assn
Brit Universities Film & Video Coun
Brit Video Assn
Deaf Broadcasting Coun
Gld Profl Videographers
Inst Videography
Nat Assn Higher Educ Moving Image
Production Mgrs Assn
Video Performance Ltd
> + Film;   Sound recording & reproduction;   Television
Video games
Brit Academy Film & TV Arts
> Computer & video games
Videograms > Audio visual aids & equipment;   Video
Videotex > Teletext & videotex
Viewing facilities
Viewing Facilities Assn (UK)
Vikings > Scandinavia: literature & antiquities
Villages: deserted
Medieval Settlement Res Gp
Villages: shops
Rural Shops Alliance
Village Retail Services Assn...
Vinegar
Vinegar Brewers Fedn
Vintage vehicles > Motor vehicles: historic
Vintners > Wines & spirits: trade
Vinyl flooring
Contract Flooring Assn
UK Resilient Flooring Mfrs' Assn
Violins & violas
Brit Violin Making Assn
Viola da Gamba Soc
> + Musical instruments
Violence (work-related)
Inst Conflict Mgt
Virgil
Virgil Soc

Virology > Microbiology
Virus tested stock
Nuclear Stock Assn
Virus Tested Stem Cutting Growers Assn
Vision > Blind & partially sighted; Ophthalmology; Orthoptics
Vision technology > Machine vision
Visual aids > Audio visual aids & equipment
Visual planning > Office equipment & systems
Visually impaired > Blind & partially sighted
Vitamins
Coun Responsible Nutrition
Viticulture > Wines & viticulture
Vitiligo
Vitiligo Soc
Vitreous enamel
Inst Vitreous Enamellers
Vivisection
Advocates for Animals
Animal Concern
Brit U Abolition Vivisection
Fund Replacement Animals Med Experiments
Ir Anti-Vivisection Soc
Nat Anti-Vivisection Soc
Res Defence Soc
Vocational guidance > Careers
Vodka > Gin & vodka;   Wines & spirits: trade

Voice
        Voice Care Network
        > + Speech
Voice recognition
        Automatic Identification Mfrs & Suppliers Assn
Volcanoes
        Geological Soc
        > + Earth sciences, structure & resources; Geology
Volleyball
        Brit Volleyball Fedn
        English Volleyball Assn
        NI Volleyball Assn
        Scot Volleyball Assn
Voluntary organisations/service
        Assn Chief Officers Scot Voluntary Orgs
        > + Charities; Community service: voluntary; Social: service;
        Welfare headings
Voluntary service: history
        Voluntary Action Hist Soc
Voucher system
        Voucher Assn
Vulval disease & pain
        Brit Soc Study Vulval Diseases
        Vulval Pain Soc

W

Wagner ([Wilhelm] Richard)
        Wagner Soc
Wakeboarding
        Wakeboard UK
Wales
        Campaign Protection Rural Wales
        Inst Welsh Affairs
        Welsh Local Govt Assn
Wales: archaeology, language & culture
        ACADEMI
        Cambrian Archaeol Assn
        Capel
        Cardiff Naturalists Soc
        Cymdeithas Ddawns Werin Cymru
        Cymdeithas Iaith Gymraeg
        Honourable Soc Cymmrodorion
        London Welsh Assn
        R Instn S Wales
        Welsh Folk Song Soc
        Welsh Music Gld
        > + Archaeology: county societies
Walking
        Brit Mountaineering Coun
        Brit Walking Fedn
        Long Distance Walkers Assn
        Mountaineering Coun Ireland
        Mountaineering Coun Scotland
        Race Walking Assn
Walking sticks
        Brit Stickmakers Gld
        Brit Woodcarvers Assn
Wall (Max[well George Lorimer])
        Max Wall Soc
Wall ties
        Wall Tie Installers Fedn
Wall tiles > Tiles (floor & wall)
Wallcoverings & wallpaper
        Home Decoration Retailers' Assn
        Wallcovering Distbrs Assn
        Wallpaper Hist Soc
Walling
        Dry Stone Walling Assn
Walls: insulation
        Insulated Render & Cladding Assn
        > + Insulation
Walls: movable > Partitioning
Walmsley (Leo) & (Ulric)
        Walmsley Soc
Walnuts
        Combined Edible Nut Tr Assn
War(s) > under name of War
War memorials
        War Memorials Trust
Wardens > Rangers & wardens
Warehousing
        Bonded Warehousekeepers' Assn

Chart Inst Logistics & Transport UK
        UK Warehousing Assn
Wargaming
        Brit Histl Games Soc
        Soc Ancients
        Victorian Military Soc
        > + Fights (historic/re-enactment);   Models: hobby
Warlock (Peter)
        Peter Warlock Soc
Warm air hand driers
        Brit Warm Air Hand Drier Assn
Warne (F) publishers
        Observers Pocket Series Collectors' Soc
Warranty against work under guarantee
        Indep Warranty Assn
Warships > Marine: engineering & equipment
Washing instruction & labelling
        Home Laundering Consultative Coun
Waste disposal
        Chart Instn Wastes Mgt
        Chemical Recycling Assn
        County Surveyors Soc
        Environmental Inds Commission
        Environmental Services Assn
        Nat Assn Waste Disposal Officers
        Oil Recycling Assn
        R Envtl Health Inst Scotland
        R Instn Chart Surveyors
        Valpak
        > + Water: treatment & supply
Waste disposal: dry wste
        Container Handling Eqpt Mfrs Assn
        Indl Packaging Assn
Waste disposal: medical
        Sanitary Med Disposal Services Assn
Waste disposal: photographic
        Photo Imaging Coun
Waste trades > Reclamation & recycling; specific type of waste
Watches > Horology
Water
        Assn Drainage Authorities
        Brit Cave Res Assn
        Brit Hydrological Soc
        Brit Hydropower Assn
        Estuarine & Coastal Sciences Assn
        Hydrographic Soc UK
        Land Drainage Contrs Assn
        Soc Chemical Ind
        UK Land & Hydrographic Survey Assn
        UK Rainwater Harvesting Assn
        Water Health Alliance
        > + Hydraulics & hydromechanics; Water treatment & supply
Water: divining
        Brit Soc Dowsers
Water: jetting
        Water Jetting Assn
Water: mills > Wind & water mills
Water: sports
        Amat Swimming Assn
        Amat Swimming Fedn
        Brit Sub-Aqua Club
        Brit Water Ski Fedn
        Fedn Water Fitness Profls
        Scot Sub Aqua Club
        Sub-Aqua Assn
        waterskiscotland
        Welsh Amat Swimming Assn
Water: treatment & supply
        Assn Public Analysts
        Assn Public Analysts Scotland
        Brit Assn Chemical Specialities
        Brit Polarological Res Soc
        Brit Water
        Chart Instn Water & Envtl Management
        Instn Civil Engrs
        IWO
        Nat Campaign Water Justice
        Nat Jt Utilities Gp
        Nat Pure Water Assn
        Scot Pure Water Assn
        Soc Brit Water & Wastewater Inds
        UK Irrigation Assn
        Water Mgt Soc
        Water UK
        Well Drillers' Assn
        > + Bottled water

© CBD Research Ltd · Beckenham · BR3 5JS · Tel 020 8650 7745 · Fax 020 8650 0768 · E-mail cbd@cbdresearch.com · www.cbdresearch.com

Waterbeds
    Brit Waterbed Assn
    > + Beds & bedding
Waterbeetles > + Beetles
Watercolour painting
    Brit Watercolour Soc
    R Scot Soc Painters in Water Colours
    R Watercolour Soc
    Water Colour Soc Ireland
    > + Art & artists
Waterfowl
    Brit Waterfowl Assn
Waterheaters > Boilers & waterheaters
Waterloo (Battle of)
    Assn Friends Waterloo C'ee
Waterproofing (membranes)
    Intelligent Membrane Tr Assn
Waterproofing (structural)
    Brit Structural Waterproofing Assn
    Eur Liquid Waterproofing Assn
Waterways: inland > Inland waterways
Watson (Dr John)
    Friends Dr Watson
    Sherlock Holmes Soc Lond
    > + Holmes (Sherlock)
Wave energy > Renewable energy
Wealth management > Investment; Securities
Weapons
    Brit Pugwash Gp
    Defence Mfrs Assn
    > + Arms & armour; Defence equipment; Guns & ammunition
Weather > Meteorology
Weaving
    Assn Glds Weavers, Spinners & Dyers
    Confedn Brit Wool Textiles
Webb (Mary Gladys)
    Mary Webb Soc
Webbing
    Brit Narrow Fabrics Assn
Websites
    Brit Web Design Marketing Assn
    Inst Profl Designers
Weddings
    Brit Bridalwear Assn
    Gld Profl Wedding Services
    Retail Bridalwear Assn
Weddings: photography
    Assn Profl Videomakers
    Gld Photographers
    Master Photographers Assn
    Soc Wedding & Portrait Photographers
Weed control
    Assn Applied Biologists
Weighing machines > Scales & weighing machines
Weight control (personal) > Obesity
Weight lifting & training
    Brit Weight Lifters Assn
    Welsh Weight Training Assn
Weights & measures > Consumer affairs & protection; Measurement; Trading standards
Welding
    Assn Welding Distbrs
    BEAMA
    Plastics & Board Inds Fedn
    Welding Inst
Welfare: administration
    Inst Welfare
    Nat Assn Voluntary & Community Action
    Nat Assn Voluntary Service Mgrs
    > + Social: services
Welfare: organisations
    Assn Chief Executives Voluntary Orgs
    Brit Assn Settlements & Social Action Centres
    Brit Red Cross Soc
    Care Leavers Assn
    Family Educ Trust
    Family Mediation Scotland
    Family Welfare Assn
    Grand Priory. . . Hospital. . . St John
    Ir Red Cross Soc
    Nat Assn Pastoral Care Educ
    Nat Family Mediation
    R UK Beneficent Assn
    Saint John Ambulance Assn
    Salvation Army
    Shared Care Network
    SOVA

Women's R Voluntary Service
Youth Access
    > + Community service; objects of welfare
Well drilling & equipment
    Assn Wellhead Eqpt Mfrs
    UK Onshore Operators Gp
    Well Drillers' Assn
    Well Services Contrs Assn
Wellington (Arthur Wellesley) Duke of
    Assn Friends Waterloo C'ee
Wells (Herbert George ['HG'])
    H G Wells Soc
Welsh > Wales: archaeology, language & culture
Wesley (John & Charles)
    Wesley Histl Soc
West Africa
    W Africa Business Assn
West Indies & the Caribbean
    Black & Asian Studies Assn
    Caribbean-Brit Business Coun
    One World Linking Assn
Western Front
    Western Front Assn
    > + Military history
Wet-garden plants
    Brit Hosta & Hemerocallis Soc
Whales
    Whale & Dolphin Consvn Soc
Wharves
    River Assn Freight & Transport
Wheel clamping
    UK Parking Enforcement Agency
Wheelchairs
    Ir Wheelchair Assn
    > + Health care: equipment & supplies
Whippets
    Brit Whippet Racing Assn
    Nat Whippet Assn
Whisky
    Malt Distillers Assn Scotland
    Scotch Malt Whisky Soc
    Scotch Whisky Assn
    > + Wines
White goods > Domestic appliances
White Star Line
    Brit Titanic Soc
Whole milk > Unpasteurised milk
Wholesale markets > Finance: brokers & agents
Wholesale trade > specific trade
Widows & widowers
    Cruse - Bereavement Care
    Nat Assn Widows
    Nat Coun Divorced & Separated
    Nat Fedn Solo Clubs
    War Widows Assn
    Way Foundation
    > + Singles, divorced & separated; Women's organisations
Wigs
    Hairdressing & Beauty Suppliers Assn
    Inc Gld Hairdressers
    > + Hairdressing
Wild animals
    Assn Brit Wild Animal Keepers
    Brit Big Cat Soc
    Captive Animal Protection Soc
    Universities Fedn Animal Welfare
    > + Zoology & zoos; specific animal
Wild flowers
    Landlife
Wilde (Oscar Fingall O'Flahertie Wills)
    Oscar Wilde Soc
Wildfowl
    Brit Assn Shooting & Consvn
    Brit Decoy & Wildfowl Carvers Assn
    Brit Waterfowl Assn
    > + Birds
Wildlife: art
    Nature in Art Trust
    > + Art & artists
Wildlife: recording
    Nat Fedn Biological Recording
    Wildlife Sound Recording Soc
    > + Nature conservation

Williams (Charles)
    Charles Williams Soc

Williamson (Henry)
    Henry Williamson Soc
Williams syndrome
    Williams Syndrome Foundation
Williamson (Henry)
Wills
    Alert Euthanasia
    Assn Lawyers & Legal Advisers
    Brit Records Assn
    Inst Profl Willwriters
    Soc Will Writers & Estate Planning Practitioners
    Willwriters' Assn
Wind instruments > Brass & silver bands; Musical instruments
Wind energy > Renewable energy
Wind tunnel testing
    Aircraft Res Assn
Wind & water mills
    Soc Protection Ancient Bldgs
    Sussex Indl Archaeol Soc
    Welsh Mills Soc
Windows
    Brit Plastics Fedn
    Brit Woodworking Fedn
    Incorporation Plastic Window Fabricators & Installers
    Materials Components Developing & Testing Assn
    Nat Assn Rooflight Mfrs
    Plastics Window Fedn
    Steel Window Assn
    > + Glass & glazing
Windows: blinds & shutters
    Brit Blind & Shutter Assn
    Door & Hardware Fedn
Windows: cleaning
    Fedn Window Cleaners
Windsurfing > Surfing, board & speed sailing

Wines & spirits: trade
    Assn Convenience Stores
    Assn Licensed Mult Retailers
    Bonded Warehousekeepers' Assn
    Fedn Licensed Victuallers Assns
    Fedn Retail Licensed Tr NI
    Gin & Vodka Assn
    Inst Masters Wine
    Licensed Trade Charity
    Licensed Vintners' Assn [IRL]
    Nat Fruit Wine, Mead & Liqueur Producers Assn
    Nat Off-Licence Assn [IRL]
    Scot Grocers' Fedn
    Scot Licensed Tr Assn
    Scotch Whisky Assn
    Vintners Fedn Ireland
    Wine & Spirit Assn Ireland
    Wine & Spirit Trade Assn
Wines & viticulture
    Assn Wine Educators
    Circle Wine Writers
    English Wine Producers
    Home Beer & Wine Mfrs Assn
    Thames & Chiltern Vineyards Assn
    UK Vineyards Assn
Wire & wire products
    Scot Wirework Mfrs Assn
    Wire Products Assn
    Woven Wire Assn
Wireless: for blind & bedridden > Radio: for blind & bedridden
Wireless: history
    Brit Vintage Wireless Soc
Wireless: mobile phone marketing
    Ir Cellular Industry Assn
    Mobile Marketing Assn
Witchcraft
    Pagan Fedn
Witness (expert) > Experts & expert witness
Wodehouse (Sir P[elham] G[renville])
    P G Wodehouse Soc
Wolves
    Wolves & Humans Foundation
Women: employment
    Brit Assn Women Entrepreneurs
    Business & Profl Women
    Soc Promoting Training Women
    Working Families
    > + special occupations
Women: equal rights
    Fawcett Soc
    Rights of Women

Women's organisations
    Brit Fedn Women Graduates
    Brit Housewives League
    Brit Women Pilots Assn
    Fedn Women's Insts NI
    Ir Countrywomen's Assn
    Ir Fedn Women's Clubs
    Mothers Apart Children
    Nat Alliance Women's Orgs
    Nat Assn Ladies Circles
    Nat Assn Women's Clubs
    Nat Fedn Women's Insts
    Nat Women's Register
    NI Women's Aid Fedn
    Scot Women's Rural Insts
    Townswomen's Glds
    Women's Aid Fedn (England)
    YWCA (Young Women's Christian Association)
Women's wear > Clothing; Fashion
Wood
    Inst Wood Science
    UK Forest Products Assn
    > + Timber
Wood burning stoves
    Nat Fireplace Assn
Wood carving
    Brit Decoy & Wildfowl Carvers Assn
    Brit Woodcarvers Assn
    Chippendale Soc
    Master Carvers' Assn
Wood floors > Floors
Wood panels
    Wood Panel Inds Fedn
    > + Building board & timber
Wood preservation & care
    Brit Coatings Fedn
    Brit Wood Preserving & Damp-proofing Assn
    Timber Decking Assn
Wood pulp
    Brit Wood Pulp Assn
Woodforde (James)
    Parson Woodforde Soc
Woodlands
    Assn Timber Growers & Forestry Profls
    Small Woods Assn
    > + Forestry
Woodworking
    Brit Wood Turners Assn
    Brit Woodworking Fedn
    Inst Carpenters
    Inst Machine Woodworking Technology
    Register Profl Turners
    Soc Wood Engravers
    Woodworking Machinery Suppliers Assn
Woodworm
    Inst Specialist Surveyors & Engrs
Wool & wool products
    Brit Hand Knitting Confedn
    Brit Textile Technology Gp
    Cloth Merchants Assn
    Confedn Brit Wool Textiles
    Nat Wool Textile Expt Corpn
    Welsh Mills Soc
    > + Sheep: breed societies
Woolf (Virginia)
    Virginia Woolf Soc GB
Word blindness > Dyslexia
Work-related violence
    Inst Conflict Mgt
Work sciences & study > Management
Worker participation > Industrial involvement & participation
Working dogs
    Brit Inst Profl Dog Trainers
    > + Dogs
Works management > Management
Workspaces (managed)
    Business Centre Assn
Workwear > Protective equipment (personal)
World War II
    Battle Britain Histl Soc
    World War Two Living Hist Assn
    WW2 HMSO Paperbacks Soc
Wounds
    Wound Care Soc
Woven labels
    Brit Narrow Fabrics Assn

© CBD Research Ltd · Beckenham · BR3 5JS · Tel 020 8650 7745 · Fax 020 8650 0768 · E-mail cbd@cbdresearch.com · www.cbdresearch.com

Wrestling
    Brit Arm Wrestling Fedn
    Brit Wrestling Assn
Writers' agents > Authors' agents
Writers to the Signet > Law: Scotland
Writing equipment & accessories
    Writing Eqpt Soc
    Writing Instruments Assn
Writing paper
    Paper Agents Assn
    > + Paper & paper products
Writing & writers
    Alliance Literary Socs
    Assn Golf Writers
    Brit Soc Comedy Writers
    Fedn Worker Writers & Community Pubrs
    Gld Health Writers
    Ir Writers' U
    Keats-Shelley Memorial Assn
    Lancashire Authors' Assn
    Nat Assn Writers in Educ
    Nat Assn Writers' Gps
    Outdoor Writers' Gld
    Romantic Novelists Assn
    Soc Authors
    Soc Authors Scotland
    Writers' Gld
    Writers & Photographers unLimited
    > + Journalism; & individual subjects
Writing & writers: authors > under individual author's name

Wurlitzers > Cinema organs

X

X-ray equipment
    Assn X-ray Eqpt Mfrs

Y

Yachting
    Assn Brokers & Yacht Agents
    Brit Fedn Sand & Land Yacht Clubs
    Cruising Assn
    R Yachting Assn
    R Yachting Assn Scotland
    Yacht Harbour Assn
    Yachting Journalists' Assn
Yachts: building & designing
    Amat Yacht Res Soc
    Brit Marine Fedn
    Model Yachting Assn
    Yacht Designers & Surveyors Assn
Yachts: chartering
    Assn Scot Yacht Charterers
    Marine Leisure Assn
    Profl Charter Assn
Yarns
    Brit Throwsters Assn
    Coir Assn
    > + Textile headings;   Wool & wool products
Yeast
    UK Assn Mfrs Bakers Yeast
Yoga
    Brit Wheel Yoga
Yoghurt
    Provision Tr Fedn
    > + Dairying
Yonge (Charlotte Mary)
    Charlotte M Yonge Fellowship
Yoseikan > Martial arts
Young farmers clubs > Farmers organisations

Young (Francis Brett)
    Francis Brett Young Soc
Youth employment > Careers
Youth hostels
    Ir Youth Hostels Assn
    Scot Youth Hostels Assn
    Youth Hostel Assn NI
    Youth Hostels Assn (England & Wales)
Youth organisations
    Boys' & Girls' Clubs NI
    Boys' & Girls' Clubs Scotland
    Brit Nat Temperance League
    Central Org Maritime Pastimes...
    Church Lads & Church Girls Brigade
    Horse Rangers Assn
    Marine Soc & Sea Cadets
    Nansen Highland
    Nat Assn Clubs Young People
    Nat Assn Youth Orchestras
    Nat Fedn Eighteen Plus Gps
    Nat Youth Coun Ireland
    Scot Assn Young Farmers Clubs
    Scout Assn
    Scout & Guide Graduate Assn
    Sea Cadet Corps
    UK Youth
    Urdd Gobaith Cymru
    Woodcraft Folk
    YMCA England
    Young Explorers' Trust
    Youth Access
    Youth Action Network
    Youth Action NI
    Youth Scotland
Youth organisations: boys & young men
    Boys' Brigade
    Scouting Ireland
    YMCA Ireland
Youth organisations: girls & young women
    Girlguiding UK
    Girls' Brigade
    Girls' Venture Corps Air Cadets
    Ir Girl Guides
    YWCA Ireland
Youth psychiatry
    Assn Profls Services Adolescents
Youth work
    Community & Youth Workers U
    Nat Assn Youth & Community Educ Officers
    Nat Assn Youth Justice
    Nat Youth Fedn [IRL]

Z

Zen Buddhism > Buddhism
Zeolites
    Brit Zeolite Assn
Zimbabwe
    Britain-Zimbabwe Soc
Zinc
    Cast Metals Fedn
Zinc coatings
    Galvanizers Assn
Zionism > Jewish organisations
Zoology & zoos
    Assn Brit Wild Animal Keepers
    Brit Herpetological Soc
    Brit & Ir Assn Zoos & Aquariums
    Captive Animal Protection Soc
    Linnean Soc Lond
    N England Zoological Soc
    Natural Sciences Collections Assn
    R Zoological Soc Scotland
    Ray Soc
    Zoological Soc Ireland
    Zoological Soc London

Directory of BRITISH ASSOCIATIONS

*All entries in this Directory are **FREE** - you incur no financial obligation by completing & returning this form*

1. **Name of organisation** (as stated in Articles, Constitution or Rules):

2. **Abbreviation** by which the organisation is generally known:

3. **Year of formation:**

4. **Telephone:**

5. **Postal address**, including postcode:

6. **Fax:**

7. **Email:**

8. **Website:**

9. Is the above address that of:

Permanent headquarters with its own staff ☐   Honorary secretary's private house ☐

A firm of secretaries, accountants or solicitors ☐   Honorary secretary's business office ☐

Other:

10. **Name** of Secretary / Honorary Secretary / Chief Executive – please state office held:

11. **Branches** in the UK – give number only: Branches overseas – give countries only:

12. **Objects / Sphere of interest** – please state concisely the purpose of your organisation & its field of interest – this information is required for the subject index, therefore please explain any technical terms used:

13. **Specialist groups** or sections – please list fully:

14. **Subject index** – please suggest any specific subjects under which your organisation should be indexed:

15. **Affiliations:** to international & other organisations – please give names in **FULL**:

Affiliations: bodies affiliated to yours:

16. **Membership** – give present number in each category:

	Individual persons	Companies / Firms	Other organisations (clubs, societies etc.)
UK			
Overseas			

Please complete overleaf ▷

17. Activities:

- ☐ Conferences
- ☐ Regular Meetings
- ☐ Education & / or training
- ☐ Examinations
- ☐ Research
- ☐ Exhibitions

Other activities

- ☐ Competitions
- ☐ Study Groups
- ☐ Statistics
- ☐ Export promotion
- ☐ Information service
- ☐ Library

- ☐ Picture Library
- ☐ Visits & / or excursions
- ☐ Negotiations of pay / employment
- ☐ Liaison with government

---

18. **Publications:** Please give details (Journal, Newsletter, List of Members, Yearbook, Annual Report etc).
Please supply specimen copies and, if possible put us on your mailing list, thank you.
Please give member's price if not included in subscription

Title	Frequency	Price (members)	Price (non-members)

19. Changes of name, or amalgamations, during the last 5 years – please give names and dates:

---

20. **Moving or changing name?** if likely in the next 2 years please tick here ☐ and send new details when known.
We answer 100's of enquiries a year about associations that have moved. **PLEASE** tell us when you do.

---

21. Are you also secretary of any other international / national organisation? Please give full title(s):

---

22. Is your organisation:

a Company limited by guarantee ☐   a Registered Charity ☐   an Un-incorporated Society ☐

---

23. Your name and office held (in CAPITALS please):

If you wish to receive details of the Directory of British Associations when it is published please tick ☐

The editors' decision over the content, or exclusion, of any entry is final. | 18

CBD Research Ltd   15 Wickham Road, Beckenham, Kent BR3 5JS, UK.   Tel: 020 8650 7745   Fax: 020 8650 0768
Established 1961   cbd@cbdresearch.com   www.cbdresearch.com

MEMBERS OF: Data Publishers Association   Independent Publishers Guild

ABBREVIATIONS: 1 – IN MAIN ALPHABETICAL DIRECTORY

Validity indicators:

■	entry based on questionnaire, or other document, returned by organisation
NR	No reply received for this edition
IRL	Irish entry - see introduction 3(b)
§	Organisation outside normal scope of DBA but included for convenience of users
**	Organisation unverified or lost

Address:

asa	official secretariat		hsp	honorary secretary's private address
hq	organisation's permanent headquarters		sb/p	secretary's business or private address
hsb	honorary secretary's business address		regd off	registered office

Name of secretary or chief executive, with designation of office held:

Chmn	Chairman	Sec	Secretary	Org Sec	Organising Secretary
Dir	Director	Gen Sec	General Secretary	Pres	President
Exec	Executive	Hon Sec	Honorary Secretary	Hon Treas	Honorary Treasurer
Mgr	Manager	Mem Sec	Membership Secretary	PRO	Public Relations Officer

▲ Type of constitution

Br Branches

○ Type of organisation & sphere of interest: indicated by one or more of the following letters, with an amplification or explanation only where necessary; if an organisation's interests are obvious from its name, only the starred letter is given

*A	Art & Literature		*N	Co-ordinating bodies
*B	Breed Societies		*P	Professional
*C	Chambers of Commerce Industry or Trade		*Q	Research Organisations
			*R	Religious Organisations
*D	Dance, Music & Theatre		*S	Sports
*E	Educational		*T	Trade
*F	Farming & Agriculture		*U	Trade Unions
*G	General Interest & Hobbies		*V	Veterinary & Animal Welfare
*H	Horticultural		*W	Welfare Organisations
*K	Campaigns & Pressure Groups		*X	International Friendship
*L	Learned, Scientific & Technical Socs		*Y	Youth Organisations
*M	Medical Interest		*Z	Political Organisations

Gp(s) Groups

● Activities:

Comp	Competitions		LG	Liaison with Government
Conf	Conference(s)		Lib	Library
Empl	Negotiations of pay & conditions of employment		Mtgs	Regular Meetings
ET	Education &/or training for professional or other qualifications		PL	Picture Library
Exam	Examinations for professional or other qualifications		Res	Scientific or other systematic research
Exhib	Exhibitions & Shows		SG	Study Groups
Expt	Export promotion		Stat	Collection of Statistics
Inf	Information service available		VE	Visits & Excursions

< Affiliations to international & other organisations
> Bodies affiliated to the organisation

M Membership Data

i=individuals   f=firms   org=organisations

¶ Publications

AR	Annual Report		m	members
ftm	free to members		NL	Newsletter
hbk	Handbook		nm	non-members
Jnl	Journal		Ybk	Year book
LM	List of members		yr	per annum

X Former name or names of organisation if changed during past five years (preceded by date of change, if known)